The Broadview Anthology of

BRITISH LITERATURE

Concise Edition

Volume A
Second Edition

The Broadview Anthology of British Literature: Concise Edition

The Medieval Period
The Renaissance and the Early Seventeenth Century
The Restoration and the Eighteenth Century

The Broadview Anthology of

BRITISH LITERATURE

Concise Edition

Volume A
Second Edition

GENERAL EDITORS

Joseph Black, University of Massachusetts
Leonard Conolly, Trent University
Kate Flint, University of Southern California
Isobel Grundy, University of Alberta
Don LePan, Broadview Press
Roy Liuzza, University of Tennessee
Jerome J. McGann, University of Virginia
Anne Lake Prescott, Barnard College, Columbia University
Barry V. Qualls, Rutgers University
Claire Waters, University of Virginia

broadview press

LIBRARY AND ARCHIVES CANADA CATALOGUING IN PUBLICATION

The Broadview anthology of British literature / general editors, Joseph Black ... [et al]. — Concise ed., 2nd ed.

Includes bibliographical references and index.
ISBN 978-1-55481-048-2 (v. A.)

1. English literature. I. Black, Joseph, 1962– II. Title: British Literature.

PR1109.B773   2011   820.8   C2011-902318-0

BROADVIEW PRESS is an independent, international publishing house, incorporated in 1985.

We welcome comments and suggestions regarding any aspect of our publications—please feel free to contact us at the addresses below or at broadview@broadviewpress.com.

North America	UK, Ireland, Central Asia, Middle East, Africa, India, and Southeast Asia	Australia and New Zealand
PO Box 1243		NewSouth Books
Peterborough, Ontario	European Group	c/o TL Distribution
Canada K9J 7H5	3 Henrietta St.	15-23 Helles Avenue
	London WC2E 8LU, UK	Moorebank, NSW, Australia 2170
2215 Kenmore Ave.	TEL: 44 (0) 1767 604972	TEL: (02) 8778 9999
Buffalo, NY, USA 14207	FAX: 44 (0) 1767 601640	FAX: (02) 8778 9944
TEL: (705) 743-8990	eurospan@turpin-distribution.com	orders@tldistribution.com.au
FAX: (705) 743-8353		
customerservice@broadviewpress.com		

www. broadviewpress.com

Broadview Press acknowledges the financial support of the Government of Canada through the Canada Book Publishing Fund for our publishing activities.

Cover design by Lisa Brawn

PRINTED IN CANADA

CONTRIBUTING EDITORS AND WRITERS

MANAGING EDITOR	Don LePan
DEVELOPMENTAL EDITOR	Jennifer McCue
GENERAL ACADEMIC AND TEXTUAL EDITORS	Laura Buzzard, Laura Cardiff, Colleen Franklin, Morgan Rooney
DESIGN COORDINATOR	Kathryn Brownsey

CONTRIBUTING EDITORS

Katherine O. Acheson
Suzy Anger
Melissa Bachynski
Robert Barrett
Sandra Bell
Emily Bernhard Jackson
Joseph Black
Robert Boenig
Benjamin Bruch
Laura Buzzard
Michael Calabrese
Laura Cardiff
Lisa Celovsky
Noel Chevalier
Mita Choudhury
Youngjin Chung
Thomas J. Collins
Leonard Conolly
Darryl Domingo
Dianne Dugaw
Rose Eckert-Jantzie
Warren Edminster
Garrett Epp
Michael Faletra
Christina Fitzgerald

Adrienne Fitzpatrick
Stephen Glosecki
Amanda Goldrick-Jones
Isobel Grundy
Douglas Hayes
Heather Hill-Vasquez
John Holmes
Diane Jakacki
Eleanor Johnson
Susan Kattwinkel
Michael Keefer
Amy King
David Klausner
Scott Kleinman
Gary Kuchar
Don LePan
Roy Liuzza
Marie Loughlin
D.L. Macdonald
Hugh Magennis
Anne McWhir
Tobias Menely
Britt Mize
Meghan Nieman
David Oakleaf

Maureen Okun
Virginia Philipson
Jude Polsky
Anne Lake Prescott
Joyce Rappaport
Herbert Rosengarten
Jason Rudy
Janice Schroeder
John T. Sebastian
Emily Steiner
David Swain
Carol Symes
Andrew Taylor
Peggy Thompson
Jane Tolmie
Yevgeniya Traps
Martine van Elk
Fred Waage
Craig Walker
Claire Waters
David Watt
William Weaver
Vivienne Westbrook
Adrienne Williams Boyarin
James Winny

CONTRIBUTING WRITERS

Laura Cardiff
Jude Polsky
Victoria Abboud
Jane Beal
Jennifer Beauvais
Rachel Bennett
Emily Bernhard Jackson
Rebecca Blasco
Julie Brennan
Andrew Bretz
Laura Buzzard
Emily Cargan
Darryl Domingo

Adrienne Eastwood
Wendy Eberle-Sinatra
Peter Enman
Joanne Findon
Jane Grove
Camille Isaacs
Erik Isford
Stephanie King
Gabrielle L'Archeveque
Don LePan
Anna Lepine
John McIntyre
Carrie Nartkler

Byron Nelson
Robin Norris
Kenna Olsen
Kendra O'Neal Smith
Laura Pellerine
Virginia Philipson
Jason Rudy
Anne Salo
Janice Schroeder
Carrie Shanafelt
Nicole Shukin
James Soderholm
Anne Sorbie

Martha Stoddard Holmes
Jenna Stook
Candace Taylor

Yevgeniya Traps
David van Belle
Shari Watling

Matthew Williams
Bj Wray
Nicole Zylstra

LAYOUT AND TYPESETTING

Kathryn Brownsey   Susan Chamberlain

ILLUSTRATION FORMATTING AND ASSISTANCE

Cheryl Baldwin   Lisa Brawn   Eileen Eckert

PRODUCTION COORDINATORS

Barbara Conolly
Chris Griffin

Leonard Conolly
Tara Lowes

Judith Earnshaw
Tara Trueman

PERMISSIONS COORDINATORS

Merilee Atos
Chris Griffin

Emily Cargan
Amy Nimegeer

Jennifer Elsayed

PROOFREADERS

Jennifer Bingham
Joe Davies
Lynn Fraser
Lynn Neufeld

Martin Boyne
Judith Earnshaw
Anne Hodgetts

Lucy Conolly
Rose Eckert-Jantzie
Amy Neufeld

EDITORIAL ADVISORS

Rachel Ablow, University at Buffalo, SUNY
Dabney Bankert, James Madison University
Stephen C. Behrendt, University of Nebraska
Sumangala Bhattacharya, Pitzer College
Rita Bode, Trent University
Susan Brown, University of Guelph
Catherine Burroughs, Wells College
Elizabeth Campbell, Oregon State University
William Christmas, San Francisco State
    University
Nancy Cirillo, University of Illinois, Chicago
Joanne Cordón, University of Connecticut
David Cowart, University of South Carolina
Alex Dick, University of British Columbia
Len Diepeveen, Dalhousie University
Daniel Fischlin, University of Guelph
Robert Forman, St. John's University
Mark Fulk, Buffalo State College, SUNY
Barbara Gates, University of Delaware
Dawn Goode, James Madison University
Chris Gordon-Craig, University of Alberta
Tassie Gwilliam, University of Miami
Stephen Guy-Bray, University of British
    Columbia

Elizabeth Hodgson, University of British Columbia
John Holmes, University of Reading
Romana Huk, University of Notre Dame
Michael Keefer, University of Guelph
Gordon Kipling, University of California,
    Los Angeles
Emily Kugler, University of California, SanDiego
Sarah Landreth, University of Ottawa
William Liston, Ball State University
Paula Loscocco, Lehman College
Peter Mallios, University of Maryland
Carl G. Martin, Norwich University
Rod Michell, Thompson Rivers University
Byron Nelson, West Virginia University
Michael North, University of California,
    Los Angeles
Lesley Peterson, University of North Alabama
John Pollock, San Jose State University
Jason Rudy, University of Maryland
Carol Senf, Georgia Tech
Ken Simpson, Thompson Rivers University
Sharon Smulders, Mount Royal College
Goran Stanivukovic, St. Mary's University
Julian Yates, University of Delaware

CONTENTS

THE MEDIEVAL PERIOD

THE RENAISSANCE AND THE EARLY SEVENTEENTH CENTURY

Twelfth Night (www.broadviewpress.com/babl) (Also available as a stand-alone volume)
King Lear (www.broadviewpress.com/babl) (Also available as a stand-alone volume)
IN CONTEXT: The Shakespearean Theater (www.broadviewpress.com/babl)
        The Swan Theatre

THE RESTORATION AND THE EIGHTEENTH CENTURY

PREFACE

CONCISE EDITION

Each of the two volumes of the Concise Edition of *The Broadview Anthology of British Literature* has now become more popular than any of the six volumes of the full anthology. More and more frequently we hear academics saying that they are reluctant to choose a full anthology—whether the Broadview, the Longman, or the Norton—for a British Literature survey course, but that they want a concise anthology that offers more than do competitors such as Norton's Major Authors edition or Longman's *Masters of British Literature*. The two-volume Concise Edition of *The Broadview Anthology* is certainly less comprehensive than the full six volumes of *The Broadview Anthology*—but it nevertheless offers tremendous breadth as well as real depth of coverage. That was true of the first edition of this volume, and we believe it to be even more the case with this second edition.

When we asked academics for advice as we began to prepare a second edition, we received a great many helpful suggestions. In many cases we have been able to adopt those suggestions; we have added *The Dream of the Rood* and *Sir Orfeo*; we have added more Elizabeth I, more Sidney, more Spenser, and more Donne, as well as more of Shakespeare's sonnets and more of *Paradise Lost*. We have added more Pope and more Dryden too, and expanded the excerpts from *Robinson Crusoe* and from Equiano's *Interesting Narrative*. And—in response to a number of requests—we have added more on the transatlantic currents of literature and culture.

Most academics we consulted were also of the view, however, that we should not make what was already a very wide-ranging and comprehensive "concise" edition any larger than it already was; the consensus was that any additions should be balanced by cuts. One way to decrease the size of an anthology is of course through excerpting—but excerpting is in many ways an unsatisfactory compromise, and for the most part we have

resisted any impulse to take that approach with greater frequency. Indeed, the excerpts from More's *Utopia* that appeared in the first edition of this volume have now been moved to the anthology's website. We should hasten to add for those who like to teach *Utopia*, however, that the full work is now available from Broadview as a stand-alone edition. As with our other stand-alone editions, it may readily be combined with one or more anthology volumes in a shrink-wrapped specially priced package. (In such cases there is often no additional cost whatsoever to the student; in others there may be a nominal additional charge.)

We have taken a similar approach with Shakespeare. In recognition of the fact that those who wish to teach a Shakespeare play will always be likely to prefer a selection *other* than the one or two choices provided in an anthology, we have decided for the new Concise Edition to include a very substantial selection of Shakespeare's sonnets within the core anthology, while making available excellent teaching editions of *King Lear*, *Twelfth Night*, and *As You Like It*—and before long, other plays too—in stand-alone volumes. Our hope is that by taking this approach we will be able to provide instructors with a Shakespeare play (or plays) that they would really like to teach, without taking up space in the anthology with plays that they have no interest in teaching.

That, then, is how we have tried to "square the circle" of including more material in the new edition without making it any larger; we hope you will like the result.

As with the first edition, we have been pleased that a substantial majority of those we consulted have shared our own feeling that it would be a shame to take an entirely "major authors" approach to a concise edition—to include *only* those authors and works already established as canonical. Obviously, the emphasis in any concise anthology will inevitably be more on the canonical than is the case with a more comprehensive anthology. But we have wanted to provide some alternatives for those instructors who prefer, even within the restricted compass of a two-term British literature survey, to teach one or two lesser-known works alongside a good selection of the "greatest hits." Readers will thus find in these pages John Wilmot and Aemelia Lanyer as well as William Shakespeare and Christopher Marlowe; Eliza Haywood and Anne Finch as well as Jonathan Swift and Alexander Pope; Augusta Webster and Algernon Charles Swinburne as well as Alfred, Lord Tennyson and Matthew Arnold; Katherine Mansfield as well as T.S. Eliot and Virginia Woolf.

Much as we have valued the wealth of advice we have received, we should also confess that in a few cases we have *not* followed the consensus that emerged from our editorial research. The initial research we conducted, for example, suggested very clearly that we should omit any selection of Hardy's prose fiction from the anthology. While we acknowledge the view that Hardy's fiction can only be taught adequately through a reading of his novels, we feel a strong case can be made that the outstanding qualities of his fiction may also be found in compressed form in some of his short stories—"The Son's Veto" being an outstanding example. And, had we relied only on the results of our editorial research, we would also not have included Carol Ann Duffy in the concise edition. That research, however, was conducted primarily among academics in North America; in this case, our departure from the course of action suggested by the research was driven by our sense that Duffy is increasingly acknowledged within Britain itself as a poet of central importance.

A particularly well-received feature in the full anthology has been the inclusion of a wealth of contextual materials. Inevitably, many of these have been dropped in the concise edition, but we have resisted any impulse to cut all the "contexts" to make way for the texts themselves; even within the confines of the shorter version of the anthology, we felt it important to offer a selection of materials to help illuminate some of the historical and cultural background.

The central principles of the full anthology are of course retained in this concise edition. The introductory materials and the annotations are unchanged, as are the supplementary materials.

A Fresh Approach

To those with some awareness of the abundance of fresh material and lively debate in the field of English Studies in recent generations, it may seem surprising that this abundance has not been more fully reflected in the number of available anthologies. Thirty-five years ago there were two comprehensive anthologies designed for courses surveying British Literature: *The Norton Anthology of English Literature* and one alternative. In the years before the 2006 publication of *The Broadview Anthology* there were still two choices available—the *Norton* and one alternative. Over that time span *The Longman Anthology of British Literature* had replaced *The Oxford Anthology of English Literature* in the role of "alternative," but there had been no expansion in range of available choices to match the expansion of content and of approach that had come to characterize the discipline itself. The number of available handbooks and guides to writing had multiplied steadily (to the point where there are literally hundreds of available choices), while the number of comprehensive anthologies of British literature had remained at two.

For those of us who have worked on *The Broadview Anthology of British Literature*, it is not difficult to understand why. The very expansion of the discipline makes the task of assembling and editing an anthology that fully and vibrantly reflects the ways in which the British literary tradition is studied and taught an extraordinarily daunting one. The sheer amount of work involved is enormous, but so too is the amount of expertise that needs to be called on. With that background very much in mind, we charted a new course when it came to the preparation of *The Broadview Anthology of British Literature*. Rather than dividing up the work among a relatively small number of academics, and asking each of them to handle on their own the work of choosing, annotating, and preparing introductions to texts in their own areas of specialization, we involved a large number of contributors in the process (as the pages following the title page to this volume attest), and encouraged a high degree of collaboration at every level. First and foremost were (and are) the distinguished academics who serve as our General Editors for the project, but in all there were literally hundreds of people involved at various stages in researching, drafting headnotes or annotations, reviewing material, editing material, and finally carrying out the work of designing and typesetting the texts and other materials. That approach allowed us to draw on a diverse range of talent, and to prepare a large anthology with unusual speed. It also facilitated the maintenance of a high degree of consistency. Material was reviewed and revised in-house at Broadview, by outside editors (chief among them Colleen Franklin, an academic with a wide-ranging background and also a superb copy editor), by a variety of academics with an extraordinarily diverse range of backgrounds and academic specialities, and by our team of General Editors for the project as a whole. The aim was not only to ensure accuracy but also to make sure that the same standards were applied throughout the anthology to matters such as extent and coverage in author introductions, level of annotation, tone of writing, and student accessibility.

We have followed those same principles in the preparation of this second edition. Our General Editors have throughout taken the lead in the process of making selections. Along the way we have been guided by several core principles. We have endeavored to provide a selection that is broadly representative, while also being mindful of the importance of choosing texts that have the capacity to engage readers' interest today. Where inexpensive editions of works are available in our series of paperback Broadview Editions, we have often decided to omit them here, on the grounds that those wishing to teach one or more such works may easily order them in a combination package with the anthology; on these grounds we have decided against including *Frankenstein*, *Pride and Prejudice*, or *Heart of Darkness*. (However, we have included selections from *The Last Man* to represent Shelley and the first four chapters of *Pride and Prejudice* to represent Austen.)

Any discussion of what is distinctive about *The Broadview Anthology of British Literature* must focus above all on the contents. In every section of the anthology there is material that is distinctive and fresh— including not only selections by lesser-known writers but also less familiar selections from canonical writers. The anthology takes a fresh approach also to a great many canonical texts. Perhaps most notably, the Medi-

eval section of the anthology includes not only Roy Liuzza's translation of *Beowulf* (widely acclaimed as the most engaging and reliable translation available), but also new translations by Liuzza of many other works of Old English poetry and prose. Also included in the Medieval section is a new translation by Claire Waters of Marie de France's *Lanval*.

In a number of these cases the distinctive form of the anthology facilitates the presentation of content in an engaging and practical fashion. Notably, the adoption of a two-column format allows for some translations (the Waters translation of Marie de France's *Lanval*, the James Winny translation of *Sir Gawain and the Green Knight*) to be presented in parallel column format alongside the original texts, enabling readers to experience something of the flavor of the original while providing convenient access to an accessible translation. Similarly, passages from four translations of the Bible are laid out parallel to one another for ready comparison.

The large trim size and two-column format also allow for greater flexibility in the presentation of visual materials. Throughout we have aimed to make this an anthology that is fully alive to the connections between literary and visual culture, from the discussion of the CHI-RHO page of the Lindisfarne Gospels in the Medieval section of the anthology (and the accompanying color illustration) to the inclusion in the twentieth-century section of several skits from "Monty Python's Flying Circus" that may be discussed in connection with film or television versions. Along the way appear several full-page illustrations from the Ellesmere manuscript of Chaucer's *Canterbury Tales* and illustrations to a wide variety of other works, such as *Robinson Crusoe* and *Gulliver's Travels*.

CONTEXTUAL MATERIALS

Visual materials are also an important part of the background materials that form a significant component of the anthology. These materials are presented in two ways. Several "Contexts" sections on particular topics or themes appear in each volume of the anthology. Presented independent of any particular text or author, these include broadly based groupings of material on such topics as "Religion and Spiritual Life," "Print Culture, Stage Culture," "The New Art of Photography," "The Abolition of Slavery," "Work and Poverty in Victorian England," and "The Place of Women in Society." The groups of "In Context" materials each relate to a particular text or author. They range from the genealogical tables provided as a supplement to *Beowulf*; to materials on "The Eighteenth-Century Sexual Imagination" (presented in conjunction with Haywood's *Fantomina*); to the Easter 1916 Proclamation of the Irish Republic and rebellion leader Padraic Pearse's statement, which accompany W.B. Yeats's "Easter 1916." For the most part these contextual materials are, as the word suggests, included with a view to setting texts in their broader literary, historical, and cultural contexts; in some cases, however, the materials included in "Contexts" sections are themselves literary works of a high order. The autobiographical account by Eliza M. of nineteenth-century life in Cape Town, for example (included in the section in Volume 5 on "Race and Empire"), is as remarkable for its literary qualities as it is for the light it sheds on the realities of colonial life. In the inclusion of texts such as these, as well as in other ways, the anthology aims to encourage readers to explore the boundaries of the literary and the non-literary, and the issue of what constitutes a "literary text."

WOMEN'S PLACE

A central element of the broadening of the canon of British literature in recent generations has of course been a great increase in the attention paid to texts by women writers. As one might expect from a publisher that has played an important role in making neglected works by women writers widely available, this anthology reflects the broadening of the canon quantitatively, by including a substantially larger number of women writers than have earlier anthologies of British literature. But it also reflects this broadening in other ways. In many anthologies of literature (anthologies of British literature, to be sure, but also anthologies of literature of a variety of other sorts) women writers are set somewhat apart, referenced in introductions and headnotes only in relation to issues of gender, and treated as important only for the fact of their being women writers. *The Broadview Anthology* strenuously resists such segregation; while women writers are of course discussed in relation

to gender issues, their texts are also presented and discussed alongside those by men in a wide variety of other contexts, including seventeenth-century religious and political controversies, the abolitionist movement, and World War I pacifism. Texts by women writers are front and center in the discussion of the development of realism in nineteenth-century fiction.

"BRITISH," "ENGLISH," "IRISH," "SCOTTISH," "WELSH," "OTHER"

The broadening of English Studies, in conjunction with the expansion and subsequent contraction of British power and influence around the world, has considerably complicated the issue of exactly how inclusive anthologies should be. In several respects this anthology (like its two main competitors) is significantly more inclusive than its title suggests, including a number of non-British writers whose works connect in important ways with the traditions of British literature. We have endeavored first of all to portray the fluid and multilingual reality of the medieval period through the inclusion not only of works in Old and Middle English but also, where other cultures interacted with the nascent "English" language and "British" culture, works in Latin, in French, and in Welsh. In later periods the word "British" becomes deeply problematic in different respects, but on balance we have preferred it to the only obvious alternative, "English." There are several objections to the latter in this context. Perhaps most obviously, "English" excludes authors or texts not only from Ireland but also from Scotland and from Wales, both of which retain to this day cultures quite distinct from that of the English. "English literature," of course, may also be taken to mean "literature written in English," but since the anthology does not cover *all* literature written in English (most obviously in excluding American literature), the ambiguity would not in this case be helpful.

The inclusion of Irish writers presents a related but even more tangled set of issues. Through most of the seventeenth, eighteenth, and nineteenth centuries almost the whole of Ireland was under British control—but for the most part unwillingly. In the last of the six periods covered by the anthology, Ireland was partitioned, with Northern Ireland becoming a part of the United Kingdom and the Republic of Ireland declared independent of Britain on 6 December 1921. Less than two months earlier, James Joyce had completed *Ulysses*, which was first published as a complete work the following year (in Paris, not in Britain). It would be obviously absurd to regard Joyce as a British writer up to just before the publication of *Ulysses* and an Irish writer thereafter. And arguably he and other Irish writers should never be regarded as British, whatever the politics of the day. If on no other grounds than their overwhelming influence on and connection to the body of literature written in the British Isles, however, we have included Irish writers—among them Swift, Wilde, Shaw, Beckett, and Heaney as well as Joyce—in this anthology. We have also endeavored to give a real sense in the six period introductions of the anthology, in the headnotes to individual authors, and in the annotations to the texts themselves, of the ways in which the histories and the cultures of England, Ireland, Scotland, and Wales, much as they interact with one another, are also distinct.

Also included in this anthology are texts by writers from areas that are far removed geographically from the British Isles but that are or have been British possessions. Writers such as Olaudah Equiano and Mary Prince are included, as they spent all or most of their lives living in what were then British colonial possessions. Writers who came of age in an independent United States, on the other hand, are not included, unless (like T.S. Eliot) they subsequently put down roots in Britain and became important British literary figures. Substantial grey areas, of course, surround such issues. One might well argue, for example, that Henry James merits inclusion in an anthology of British literature, or that W.H. Auden is more an American poet than a British one. But the chosen subject matter of James's work has traditionally been considered to mark him as having remained an American writer, despite having spent almost two-thirds of his life in England. And Auden so clearly made a mark in Britain before crossing the Atlantic that it would seem odd to exclude him from these pages on the grounds of his having lived the greater part of his adult life in America. One of our competitors includes Sylvia Plath in their anthology of British literature; Plath lived in England for only five of her thirty years, though, and her poetry is generally agreed to have more in common with the traditions of Lowell, Merwin, and Sexton than with the currents of British poetry in the 1950s and '60s.

As a broad principle, we have been open to the inclusion of twentieth- and twenty-first-century work in English not only by writers from the British Isles but also by writers from British possessions overseas, and by writers from countries that were once British possessions and have remained a part of the British Commonwealth. In such cases, we have often chosen selections that relate in one way or another to the tradition of British literature and the British colonial legacy. For example, the Chinua Achebe story in the anthology concerns the divide between British colonial culture and traditional Nigerian culture.

THE HISTORY OF LANGUAGE, AND OF PRINT CULTURE

Among the liveliest discussions at meetings of our General Editors were those concerning the issue of whether or not to bring spelling and punctuation into accord with present-day practice. We finally decided that, in the interests of making the anthology accessible to the introductory student, we should *in most cases* bring spelling and punctuation in line with present-day practice. An important exception has been made for works in which modernizing spelling and punctuation would alter the meaning or the aural and metrical qualities. In practice this means that works before the late sixteenth century tend to be presented either in their original form or in translation, whereas later texts tend to have spelling and punctuation modernized. But where spelling and punctuation choices in later texts are known (or believed on reliable authority) to represent conscious choice on the part of the author rather than simply the common practice of the time, we have in those cases, too, made an exception and retained the original spelling and punctuation. (Among these are texts by Edmund Spenser, William Cowper, Samuel Taylor Coleridge, William Blake, Emily Brontë, and Bernard Shaw.)

Beyond this, we all agreed that we should provide for readers a real sense of the development of the language and of print culture. To that end we have included in each volume examples of texts in their original form—in some cases through the use of pages shown in facsimile, in others by providing short passages in which spelling and punctuation have not been modernized. A list of these appears near the beginning of each volume of the anthology.

We have also included a section of the history of the language as part of the introduction to each period. And throughout the anthology we include materials—visual as well as textual—relating to the history of print culture.

A DYNAMIC AND FLEXIBLE ANTHOLOGY

We at Broadview recognize that, although time constraints, make the concise anthology a practical and economical text choice for many instructors, some may nevertheless want to teach a number of non-canonical works—not all of which may be included in our concise edition. For this reason, we offer those instructors the possibility of choosing some additional texts that are included in the full, six-volume *Broadview Anthology of British Literature* but not in the concise edition. Simply visit our website, peruse the full anthology's table of contents, and provide the publisher with a list of desired selections; Broadview will then make available to students through their university bookstore a custom-made coursepack with precisely those materials included.

The two volumes of the anthology may be shrink-wrapped together at a special price, and each volume may also be combined in a special-price shrink-wrapped package with one or more of the over 300 volumes in the Broadview Editions series.

THE BROADVIEW LIST

One of the reasons we were able to bring a project of this sort to fruition in such a relatively short time is that we have been able to draw on the resources of the full Broadview list: the many titles in the Broadview Editions series, and also the considerable range of other Broadview anthologies. As the contributors' pages and the permissions acknowledgments pages indicate, a number of Broadview authors have acted as contributing editors to this volume, providing material from other volumes that has been adapted to suit the needs of the present anthology; we gratefully acknowledge their contribution.

As it has turned out, the number of cases where we have been able to draw on the resources of the Broadview list in the full sense, using in these pages texts and annotations in very much the same form in which they appear elsewhere, has been relatively small; whether because of an issue such as the level of textual modernization or one of style of annotation, we have more often than not ended up deciding that the requirements of this anthology were such that we could not use material from another Broadview source as-is. But even in these cases we often owe a debt of gratitude to the many academics who have edited outstanding editions and anthologies for Broadview. For even where we have not drawn directly from them, we have often been inspired by them—inspired to think of a wider range of texts as possibilities than we might otherwise have done, inspired to think of contextual materials in places where we might otherwise not have looked, inspired by the freshness of approach that so many of these titles exemplify.

EDITORIAL PROCEDURES AND CONVENTIONS

APPARATUS: The in-house set of editorial guidelines for *The Broadview Anthology of British Literature* now runs to over 40 pages, covering everything from conventions for the spacing of marginal notes, to the use of small caps for the abbreviations CE and BCE, to the approach we have adopted to references in author headnotes to name changes. Perhaps the most important core principle in the introductions to the various volumes, in the headnotes for each author, in the introductions to "Contexts" sections, and in annotations throughout the anthology, is to endeavor to provide a sufficient amount of information to enable students to read and interpret these texts, without making evaluative judgments or imposing particular interpretations. In practice that is all a good deal more challenging than it sounds; it is often extremely difficult to describe why a particular author is considered to be important without using language that verges on the interpretive or the evaluative. But it is a fine line that we have all agreed is worth trying to walk;

we hope that readers will find that the anthology achieves an appropriate balance.

ANNOTATION: It is also often difficult to make judgments as to where it is appropriate to provide an explanatory annotation for a word or phrase. Our policy has been to annotate where we feel that most first- or second-year students are likely to have difficulty understanding the denotative meaning. (We have made it a practice not to provide notes discussing connotative meanings.) But in practice the vocabularies and levels of verbal facility of first- and second-year students may vary enormously, both from institution to institution and within any given college or university class. On the whole, we provide somewhat more annotation than our competitors, and somewhat less interpretation. Again, we hope that readers will find that the anthology has struck an appropriate balance.

THE ETHICS AND POLITICS OF ANNOTATION: On one issue regarding annotation we have felt that principles are involved that go beyond the pedagogical. Most anthologies of British literature allow many words or phrases of a racist, sexist, anti-Semitic, or homophobic nature either to pass entirely without comment, or to be glossed with apologist comments that leave the impression that such comments were excusable in the past, and may even be unobjectionable in the present. Where derogatory comments about Jewish people and money-lending are concerned, for example, anthologies often leave the impression that money-lending was a pretty unsavory practice that Jewish people entered by choice; it has been all too rare to provide readers with any sense of the degree to which English society consistently discriminated against Jews, expelling them entirely for several centuries, requiring them to wear physical marks identifying their Jewish status, prohibiting them from entering most professions, and so on. *The Broadview Anthology* endeavors in such cases, first of all, not to allow such words and phrases to pass without comment; and second, to gloss without glossing over.

DATES: We make it a practice to include the date when a work was first made public, whether publication in print or, in the case of dramatic works, made public through the first performance of the play. Where that date is known to differ substantially from the date of composition, a note to this effect is included in parentheses. With medieval works, where there is no equivalent to the "publication" of later eras, where texts often vary greatly from one manuscript copy to another, and where knowledge as to date of original composition is usually imprecise, the date that appears at the end of each work is an estimate of the date of the work's origin in the written form included in the anthology. Earlier oral or written versions are of course in some cases real possibilities.

TEXTS: Where translations appear in this anthology, a note at the bottom of the first page indicates what translation is being used. Similar notes also address overall textual issues where choice of copy text is particularly significant. Reliable editions of all works are listed in the bibliographies for each period, which are included on *The Broadview Anthology of British Literature* website (http://www.broadviewpress.com/babl/) to facilitate ready revision. (In addition to information as to reliable editions, the bibliographies provide for each author and for each of the six periods a select list of important or useful historical and critical works.) Information on which editions have been drawn on in preparing texts for these pages is also included with the bibliographies. Copyright information for texts not in the public domain, however, is provided within the books in a section listing Permissions Acknowledgments.

INTRODUCTIONS: In addition to the introductory headnotes for each author included in the anthology, each "Contexts" section includes a substantial introduction, and each period includes an introduction to the period as a whole. These period introductions provide a sense not only of the broad sweep of literary developments in the period, but also of the historical, social, and political background, and of the cultural climate. Readers should be cautioned that, while there is inevitably some overlap between information presented here and information presented in the author headnotes, an effort has been made to avoid such repetition as much as possible; the general introduction to each period should thus be read in conjunction with the author headnotes. The general introductions aim not only to provide an overview of ways in which texts and authors included in these pages may connect with one another, but also to give readers a sense of connection with a range of other writers and texts of the period.

READING POETRY: For much of the glossary and for the "Reading Poetry" section that appears as part of the appendices to each volume, we have drawn on the superb material prepared by Herbert Rosengarten and Amanda Goldrick-Jones for *The Broadview Anthology of Poetry*; this section provides a concise but comprehensive introduction to the study of poetry. It includes discussions of diction, imagery, poetic figures, and various poetic forms, as well as offering an introduction to prosody.

MAPS: Also appearing within the books are maps especially prepared for this anthology, including, for each period, a map of Britain showing towns and features of relevance. Each volume also includes a map showing the counties of Britain and of Ireland, maps of both the London area and the inner city, and world maps indicating the locations of some of the significant places referenced in the anthology—and for the second volume, showing the extent of Britain's overseas territories.

GLOSSARY: Some other anthologies of British literature include both glossaries of terms and essays introducing students to various political and religious categories in British history. Similar information is included in *The Broadview Anthology of British Literature*, but we have adopted a more integrated approach, including political and religious terms along with literary ones in a convenient general glossary. While we recognize that "googling" for information of this sort is often the student's first resort (and we recognize too the value of searching the web for the wealth of background reference information available there), we also recognize that information culled from the Internet is often far from reliable; it is our intent, through this glossary, through our introductions and headnotes, and through the wealth of accessible annotation in the anthology, to provide as part of the anthology a reliable core of information in the most convenient and accessible form possible.

OTHER MATERIALS: A chart of monarchs and prime ministers is also provided within these pages. A range of other adjunct materials may be accessed through *The Broadview Anthology of British Literature* website. "Texts and Contexts" charts for each volume provide a convenient parallel reference guide to the dates of literary texts and historical developments. "British Money" provides a thumbnail sketch of the world of pounds, shillings, and pence, together with a handy guide to estimating the current equivalents of monetary values from earlier eras.

ACKNOWLEDGMENTS

The names of those on the Editorial Board that shaped this anthology appear on the title page, and those of the many who contributed directly to the writing, editing, and production of the project on the following two pages. Special acknowledgment should go to Jennifer McCue, who as Editorial Coordinator has been instrumental in tying together all the vast threads of this project and in making it a reality; to Laura Cardiff and Jude Polsky, who have carried larger loads than any others in drafting introductory materials and annotations, and who have done so with great skill and unfailing grace; to Kathryn Brownsey, who has been responsible for design and typesetting, and has continued to do a superb job and to maintain her good spirits even when faced with near-impossible demands; to Colleen Franklin, for the range of her scholarship as well as for her keen eye as our primary copy editor for the entire project; to Emily Cargan, Jennifer Elsayed and Amy Nimegeer who have together done superb work on the vast job of clearing permissions for the anthology; and to Michelle Lobkowicz and Anna Del Col, who have ably and enthusiastically taken the lead with marketing matters.

The academic members of the Advisory Editorial Board and all of us in-house at Broadview owe an enormous debt of gratitude to the hundreds of academics who have offered assistance at various stages of this project. In particular we would like to express our appreciation and our thanks to the following:

Rachel Ablow, University of Rochester
Katherine Acheson, University of Waterloo
Bryan Alexander, Middlebury College
Sharon Alker, Whitman College
James Allard, Brock University
Ella Allen, St. Thomas University
Rosemary Allen, Georgetown College
Laurel Amtower, San Diego State University
Robert Anderson, Oakland University
Christopher Armitage, University of North Carolina, Chapel Hill
Clinton Atchley, Henderson State University
Gerry Baillargeon, University of Victoria
John Baird, University of Toronto
William Baker, Northern Illinois University
Karen Bamford, Mount Allison University
John Batchelor, University of Newcastle
Lynn Batten, University of California, Los Angeles
Alexandra Bennett, Northern Illinois University
John Beynon, California State University, Fresno
Daniel Bivona, Arizona State University
Robert E. Bjork, Arizona State University

Scott Black, Villanova University
Rita Bode, Trent University
Robert Boenig, Texas A & M University
Rick Bowers, University of Alberta
Patricia Brace, Columbus State University
David Brewer, Ohio State University
William Brewer, Appalachian State University
Susan Brown, University of Guelph
Sylvia Brown, University of Alberta
Sheila Burgar, University of Victoria
Catherine Burroughs, Wells College
Rebecca Bushnell, University of Pennsylvania
Elizabeth Campbell, Oregon State University
Gregory Castle, Arizona State University
Cynthia Caywood, University of San Diego
Jane Chance, Rice University
Ranita Chatterjee, California State University, Northridge
William Christmas, San Francisco State University
Nancy Cirillo, University of Illinois, Chicago
Eric Clarke, University of Pittsburgh
Jeanne Clegg, University of Aquila, Italy

Thomas J. Collins, University of Western Ontario
Kevin Cope, Louisiana State University
David Cowart, University of South Carolina
Catherine Craft-Fairchild, University of St. Thomas
Carol Davison, University of Windsor
Alex Dick, University of British Columbia
Len Diepeveen, Dalhousie University
Mary Dockray-Miller, Lesley College
James Doelman, Brescia University College,
    University of Western Ontario
Frank Donoghue, Ohio State University
Chris Downs, Saint James School
Alfred Drake, Chapman University
Julie Early, University of Alabama, Huntsville
Siân Echard, University of British Columbia
Garrett Epp, University of Alberta
Joshua Eyler, Columbus State University
Ruth Feingold, St. Mary's College, Maryland
Dino Franco Felluga, Perdue University
Joanne Findon, Trent University
Daniel Fischlin, University of Guelph
Christina Fitzgerald, University of Toledo
Verlyn Flieger, University of Maryland
Robert Forman, St. John's University
Allyson Foster, Hunter College
Roberta Frank, Yale University
Jeff Franklin, University of Colorado, Denver
Maria Frawley, George Washington University
Mark Fulk, Buffalo State College
Andrew Galloway, Cornell University
Michael Gamer, University of Pennsylvania
Barbara Gates, University of Delaware
Jonathan C. Glance, Mercer University
Susan Patterson Glover, Laurentian University
Daniel Gonzalez, University of New Orleans
Jan Gorak, University of Denver
Chris Gordon-Craig, University of Alberta
Ann-Barbara Graff, Georgia Tech University
Mary Griffin, Kwantlen University College
Michael Griffin, formerly of Southern Illinois University
George C. Grinnell, University of British Columbia,
    Okanagan
Elisabeth Gruner, University of Richmond
Kevin Gustafson, University of Texas at Arlington
Stephen Guy-Bray, University of British Columbia
Ruth Haber, Worcester State College

Margaret Hadley, University of Calgary
Robert Hampson, Royal Holloway University of London
Carol Hanes, Howard College
Michael Hanly, Washington State University
Lila Harper, Central Washington State University
Joseph Harris, Harvard University
Anthony Harrison, North Carolina State University
Douglas Hayes, Lakehead University
Jennifer Hellwarth, Allegheny University
David Herman, Ohio State University
Peter Herman, San Diego State University
Kathy Hickock, Iowa State University
John Hill, US Naval Academy
Thomas Hill, Cornell University
Elizabeth Hodgson, University of British Columbia
Joseph Hornsby, University of Alabama
Scott Howard, University of Denver
Sylvia Hunt, Goergian College
Tara Hyland-Russell, St. Mary's College
Catherine Innes-Parker, University of Prince Edward
    Island
Jacqueline Jenkins, University of Calgary
John Johansen, University of Alberta
Gordon Johnston, Trent University
Richard Juang, Susquehanna University
Michael Keefer, University of Guelph
Sarah Keefer, Trent University
Lloyd Kermode, California State University,
    Long Beach
Brandon Kershner, University of Florida
Jon Kertzer, University of Calgary
Helen Killoran, Ohio University
Gordon Kipling, University of California, Los Angeles
Anne Klinck, University of New Brunswick
Elizabeth Kraft, University of Georgia
Mary Kramer, University of Massachusetts, Lowell
Marilyn Lantz, East Mississippi Community College
Kate Lawson, University of Waterloo
Linda Leeds, Bellevue Community College
Mary Elizabeth Leighton, University of Victoria
Eric Lindstrom, University of Vermont
William Liston, Ball State University
Sharon Locy, Loyola Marymount University
Peter Mallios, University of Maryland
Arnold Markley, Penn State University
Louis Markos, Houston Baptist University

Pamela McCallum, University of Calgary
Patricia McCormack, Itawamba Community College
Kristen McDermott, Central Michigan University
John McGowan, University of North Carolina
Brian McHale, Ohio State University
Jim McKeown, McLennan Community College
Thomas McLean, University of Otago, New Zealand
Jodie Medd, Carleton University
Rod Michell, Thompson Rivers University
David Miller, Mississippi College
Kitty Millett, San Francisco State University
Britt Mize, Texas A&M University
Richard Moll, University of Western Ontario
Amy L. Montz, Texas A&M University
Monique Morgan, McGill University
John Morillo, North Carolina State University
Lucy Morrison, Salisbury University
Lorri Nandrea, University of Wisconsin-Steven's Point
Byron Nelson, West Virginia University
Carolyn Nelson, West Virginia University
Claudia Nelson, Southwest Texas State University
Holly Faith Nelson, Trinity Western University
John Niles, University of Wisconsin, Madison
Michael North, University of California, Los Angeles
Mary Anne Nunn, Central Connecticut State University
David Oakleaf, University of Calgary
Tamara O'Callaghan, Northern Kentucky University
Karen Odden, Assistant Editor for *Victorian Literature and Culture* (formerly of University of Wisconsin, Milwaukee)
Erika Olbricht, Pepperdine University
Patrick O'Malley, Georgetown University
Patricia O'Neill, Hamilton College
Delilah Orr, Fort Lewis College
John Pagano, Barnard College
Kirsten Parkinson, Hiram College
Diana Patterson, Mount Royal College
Cynthia Patton, Emporia State University
Russell Perkin, St. Mary's University
Marjorie G. Perloff, Stanford University
Jim Persoon, Grand Valley State University
John Peters, University of North Texas
Todd Pettigrew, Cape Breton University
Alexander Pettit, University of North Texas
Jennifer Phegley, The University of Missouri, Kansas City

John Pollock, San Jose State University
Mary Poovey, New York University
Gautam Premnath, University of Massachusetts, Boston
Regina Psaki, University of Oregon
Katherine Quinsey, University of Windsor
Geoff Rector, University of Ottawa
Margaret Reeves, Atkinson College, York University
Cedric Reverand, University of Wyoming
Gerry Richman, Suffolk University
John Rickard, Bucknell University
Michelle Risdon, Lake Tahoe Community College
David Robinson, University of Arizona
Solveig C. Robinson, Pacific Lutheran University
Laura Rotunno, Pennsylvania State University, Altoona
Brian Rourke, New Mexico State University
Nicholas Ruddick, University of Regina
Jason Rudy, University of Maryland
Donelle Ruwe, Northern Arizona University
Michelle Sauer, Minot State University
SueAnn Schatz, Lock Haven University of Pennsylvania
Dan Schierenbeck, Central Missouri State University
Norbert Schürer, California State University, Long Beach
Debora B. Schwartz, California Polytechnic University
Janelle A. Schwartz, Loyola University
John T. Sebastian, Loyola University
David Seed, University of Liverpool
Carol Senf, Georgia Tech University
Lynn Shakinovsky, Wilfred Laurier University
John Sider, Westmont College
Judith Slagle, East Tennessee State University
Johanna Smith, University of Texas at Arlington
Sharon Smulders, Mount Royal College
Malinda Snow, Georgia State University
Goran Stanivukovic, St. Mary's University
Thomas Steffler, Carleton University
Richard Stein, University of Oregon
Eric Sterling, Auburn University Montgomery
James Stokes, University of Wisconsin, Stevens Point
Mary-Ann Stouck, Simon Fraser University
Nathaniel Strout, Hamilton College
Brad Sullivan, Western New England College
Lisa Surridge, University of Victoria
Joyce A. Sutphen, Gustavus Adolphus College
Beth Sutton-Ramspeck, Ohio State University
Nanora Sweet, University of Missouri, St. Louis

Dana Symons, Simon Fraser University
Andrew Taylor, University of Ottawa
Elizabeth Teare, University of Dayton
Doug Thorpe, University of Saskatchewan
Jane Toswell, University of Western Ontario
Herbert Tucker, University of Virginia
John Tucker, University of Victoria
Mark Turner, King's College, University of London
Eleanor Ty, Wilfrid Laurier University
Deborah Tyler-Bennett, Loughborough University
Kirsten Uszkalo, University of Alberta
Lisa Vargo, University of Saskatchewan
Gina Luria Walker, The New School, New York City
Kim Walker, Victoria University of Wellington
Miriam Wallace, New College of Florida
Hayden Ward, West Virginia State University
David Watt, University of Manitoba

Ruth Wehlau, Queen's University
Lynn Wells, University of Regina
Dan White, University of Toronto at Mississauga
Patricia Whiting, Carleton University
Thomas Willard, University of Arizona
Tara Williams, Oregon State University
Chris Willis, Birkbeck University of London
Lisa Wilson, SUNY College at Potsdam
Ed Wiltse, Nazareth College
Anne Windholz, Augustana College
Susan Wolfson, Princeton University
Kenneth Womack, Pennsylvania State University
Carolyn Woodward, University of New Mexico
Julia Wright, Wilfrid Laurier University
Julian Yates, University of Delaware
Arlene Young, University of Manitoba
Lisa Zeitz, University of Western Ontario

The Medieval Period

How are the boundaries of literary traditions to be defined? Of necessity we fall back on terms of convenience such as "British literature" and "English literature" for the titles of books or of academic courses, but it is essential from the outset to appreciate how problematic these may be. In any collection of this kind, decisions must be made about what does and does not "fit," about lines of influence between works, and about defining the boundaries of a literary tradition. Medieval literature written in England, for instance, was by no means entirely, nor indeed mostly, written in English; works in Latin, Anglo-Norman French, Middle Welsh, and Old Irish all survive alongside works in the languages now known to us as Old and Middle English. Many of these non-English texts had a profound influence on the literary tradition in English; to the extent that we have had to omit such works here, we have created gaps in the story this anthology tries to tell.

Our designation of this literature as "British" raises a terminological difficulty that is almost as old as the Middle Ages itself. "British" and "English" are by no means interchangeable terms in the medieval period, and the uses of these terms as labels for a language and literary tradition have always been entwined with political realities and national identities. Broadly speaking, the word "British" derives from the Roman name for early Celtic settlers in what we now call the British Isles; "English" refers to the Germanic invaders and settlers who began arriving in the fifth century, pushed the Celtic inhabitants to the west and the north (now Wales and Scotland), and eventually ruled the central part of the island. For many centuries, the English defined themselves by their difference from the British, and *vice versa*. At the same time, those who attempted to claim legitimate rulership of England made strategic use of the "British" tradition, perhaps most obviously in the ongoing traditions surrounding King Arthur, whose origins lie deep in British legendary history. But the intercultural appropriation between "British" and "English" has often worked both ways and continues to do so: the Anglo-Irish poet Seamus Heaney laces his modern translation of *Beowulf*, a decidedly "English" poem, with idiosyncratic Ulsterisms and Celtic turns of phrase.

Finally, the very word "literature" (deriving from the Latin *litterae*, "letters") implies an existence in writing, but a great deal of what remains in written form from the Middle Ages had a prior existence as, or owes enormous debts to, oral forms. Most of what we now read as medieval British literature, from romances to lyrics to sermons, was written to be heard, not read. Texts of vernacular works in the Middle Ages are by no means as solidly fixed—as "textual"—as works of modern literature, or of medieval works in Latin, for that matter; the circumstances of their creation and reception often tend to be performative and communal, not silent and solitary like a modern student reading this book. Modern literary culture tends to regard the written text, fixed and inert, as the primary or "real" form of a literary work; for some medieval works, especially those from the earlier Middle Ages, the written text seems to be almost an afterthought, little more than an aid to the memory of the reader/performer who recreates the "real" work by voicing the text out loud.

The concept of an anthology—a collection that gathers the authoritative examples of a cultural tradition—would have been very familiar to medieval readers, who made extensive use of such collections. Medieval manuscripts that contain multiple works may be anything from carefully planned volumes presented to a patron, to somewhat haphazard gatherings of texts, to collections composed by an individual for his or her own use; our current knowledge of medieval literary culture could rightly be said to rest on medieval anthologies. Thus a reader who first encounters these texts in an anthologized form will encounter them in a format not so unlike their original manuscript context. The single-text "monograph"—one work between two covers—is by no means the most common mode of transmission for medieval texts, and the effort to determine the relationships between texts in medieval manuscripts, the intentions of the creators of such compilations, and their effect upon readers is one of the most interesting and important areas of contemporary medieval literary studies.

The drawing of artificial lines, whether geographical or temporal, is a profound limitation on one's understanding of the history of Western literature. At the same time, we cannot simply ignore the geographical facts—which are historical and political facts as well, insofar as the unity of the island of Britain was imagined and achieved—or the differences between one age and another, although the borders (both of historical periods and of kingdoms) may always be contested. This collection likewise relies on distinctions—sometimes arbitrary, sometimes necessary, some obvious and some obscure—to provide shape and contour, form and structure. In English literary history one of the most obvious divisions lies between the literature of the Anglo-Saxons—the English before the Norman Conquest (1066)—and that of the English after the Conquest. Within these two broadly drawn periods further divisions can be made: early Old English literature, as far as we can reconstruct it, differs markedly from literature after the reign of Alfred the Great (d. 899), who sought to begin a program of vernacular literacy and bestowed a certain royal authority on English as a quasi-official written language.

After the Conquest, although English manuscripts were produced and read in somewhat reduced numbers, Norman French was the language of courtly culture in England. In the absence of schools and pedagogical traditions, English began to manifest the changes that characterize "Middle" English. After this period of "early" Middle English—roughly from the century after the Conquest until the beginning of the fourteenth century—English began to take its place alongside the culturally more prestigious Latin (the language of the church) and French (the language of the court, of law, and of administration); authors increasingly chose to write literary texts in English for aristocratic readers. The fifteenth century saw a gradual redevelopment of a written "standard" English, and an outpouring of literary works (particularly of a devotional nature) that fostered and responded to rising literacy rates. With the advent of printing in the later fifteenth century, books became ever more widely available and the language increasingly standardized; in the sixteenth century, with the wider spread of printing in England, the standard became more and more fixed, even as the language was rapidly changing again, into what linguists call early Modern English.

HISTORY, NARRATIVE, CULTURE

Even a set of very broad periodizations like these raises questions about the relation between historical events and literary developments and that between culture and the imagination. Can we understand these literary works better by learning more about their historical context? Or can these works of the imagination shed light on that context and help us fill in its blank spaces? Which partner in the inseparable pairing of text and context will serve as the solid ground from which we can survey the other? Has the human imagination changed so much that we only have access to it historically, and not immediately? On the other hand, what can we really *know* about the past, except what is said about it?

These questions vexed the minds of many medieval authors as well. Most modern scholars, like their medieval predecessors such as Isidore of Seville (a Spanish bishop who lived c. 560–636), are careful to note that history is not simply "what happened" in the past, but the *stories we tell* about what happened in the past. Events, objects, even stories, do not speak for themselves; they have to be arranged and explained, looked at and looked into, and gradually placed in a context constructed from our interpretations of other objects, events, and stories. In this sense, no matter how great our respect for objectivity or how carefully balanced our analysis may be, our study of the past says as much about us as it does about the past we try to study. And texts help us understand their context as much as contexts help us understand texts.

In his poem *Ars Poetica* the modern author Archibald MacLeish insisted that "a poem should not mean / But be," but readers of literature from the distant past cannot indulge in the soothing luxury of that misconception. A rock can simply "be"; the remains of a stone wall, however, must "mean" something—they mark a boundary, claim a space, indicate a settlement. A rough diamond lying underground might "be"; but when it has been mined, cut, polished, weighed, set, valued, bought, and worn as jewelry, it is no longer "palpable and mute / as a globed fruit"; it has entered the noisy world of meaning. Similarly, a poem like *Beowulf* or *Sir Gawain and the Green Knight* does not simply exist as a self-evident story; like any work of the human imagination, it responds to and acts on the world in which it was created. Objects and events—the Sutton Hoo ship burial, Durham Cathedral, the Magna Carta, the Black Death of the fourteenth century—positively hum with meaning and intention and human consequences; they are inextricably caught in the web of signification and interpretation. Nothing goes without saying. Even a thing of astonishing beauty that we may enjoy simply for the aesthetic pleasure it gives us is not a self-contained object; it had a function in the society that made it, and part of its meaning—even the meaning of its beauty—lies in that function, which might range from the deepest of spiritual blessings to the purest gaudy display of its owner's ability to possess and appreciate expensive objects. To ignore the cultures that surrounded, created, and consumed these objects—whether they are artifacts in a museum or texts in a book—would be a fundamental mistake.

The famous CHI-RHO page of the early eighth-century Lindisfarne Gospels (London, British Library, MS Cotton Nero D.iv, a color illustration of which appears elsewhere in this volume), offers one example of the kinds of context we might consider when looking at a medieval artifact. We may begin by admiring its beauty, enjoying its exotic strangeness or Celtic "alterity," and marveling at the skill of its creators (whose names, as it happens, are recorded in the manuscript). Such an image could have a number of different effects on its viewers: it might impress those who can't read with the beauty and value of God's Word; it might attest to the devotion of the artists who made such a complex design, as well as their sophistication and expertise as craftsmen; it might display a religious house's capability for such "conspicuous consumption" in the service of God. As we consider it more closely, we may find ourselves puzzled by the presence of a Greek monogram in a Latin text decorated in a distinctively "Insular" style in Northumbria c. 700. At least three

cultures are on display here. The page insists on the intersection of English, Irish, and Latin cultures—as intricately woven together as the knotty patterns of its own design. Looking more closely, we can see an English interlinear gloss to the Latin text, written in much smaller script, added some 200 years later. Its presence creates yet another layer of meaning and raises further questions. Who would write in such a rich and beautiful book? Is the gloss a necessary addition, suggesting that the Latin text was not sufficiently accessible to those using the book? What might its presence tell us about the status of Latin as a learned language, or a sacred one, in medieval England? The questions arising from this single page of a manuscript remind us that it is not simply a work of remarkable beauty, but a complex artifact of cultural history.

Saint Luke, Lindisfarne Gospels. This page and a decorative "carpet page" precede the text of the gospel itself.

First text page, Gospel of Saint Luke, Lindisfarne Gospels. The text reads as follows: "Quoniam quidem multi conati sunt ordinare narrationem," "Since many have undertaken to put in narrative order …"

Note: A reproduction of the CHI-RHO page from the Lindisfarne Gospels appears in the section of color illustrations.

The CHI-RHO page embodies, in a particularly striking way, the reciprocal relationship of text and context; while it has much to tell us about the world of its creators, what we know about their world must also be brought to bear on our understanding of the manuscript. To take another example, the poem *Beowulf* has been used to explain other texts (or objects, in the case of the early East Saxon ship-burial at Sutton Hoo; the poem was introduced as evidence in the inquest that determined the ownership and disposition of the priceless objects unearthed from that site in 1939); conversely, other texts and objects can be brought to bear on the obscurities of the text of *Beowulf* and used as explanatory tools. And of course the poem has a place in a series of cultural moments—the unknown moment of its creation, the moment of its transcription into the manuscript in which it survives, the moment of its rediscovery and publication, the modern moment in which it is studied today. Each of these contributes, in some way, to the "meaning" of *Beowulf*, and however tempting it may be to give priority to the more distant (and hence less familiar) contexts, no one of these cultural moments, strictly speaking, has a greater claim on the poem than another. We may wish to regard material objects as somehow more "real" than stories, but from the distant perspective from which we observe them now, they are not: these bright objects on a blank background are as mute and as meaningful, as mysterious and as communicative, as the anonymous stories surviving in single manuscripts by unknown hands.

So the questions we might ask as we approach these texts involve less what they "are" than what they "do," what they might mean not only to their imagined original audience(s) but to us, and how that meaning might change as our knowledge develops. What draws us to these old tales? What do we derive from them? Can we understand them in anything like their original form, with our inevitably modern minds? To what extent can we negotiate the difference between the present and the past? This is a constant problem, a challenge for any reader of early literature. A reader of a contemporary novel is seldom aware of the complex web of cultural assumptions that sustains the narrative; these assumptions are transparent and automatic. For readers of early literature the assumptions are solid, opaque, at times impenetrable—but this awareness of the alterity of the reader to the text is, we think, a very healthy thing. It is always good to be reminded that meanings are not simply "there" in the text, waiting for the reader to stumble over them; they are kindled by the friction between the reader, the story, and the world they both inhabit. Medieval texts force this awareness upon us, but it serves us well as readers of any literary work.

The cultures of the Middle Ages are as varied as they are numerous, and diverse as well in the ways in which they interacted with one another. Moreover, the medieval period was one of continual change. Such change tended to occur at a slower pace than it does in our own time, but the medieval era saw vast and violent upheavals, and great cultural and social developments. From long habit, however, we refer to the millennium following the collapse of the Roman Empire in the fifth century CE as one period: the Middle Ages (or, using the Latinized form of the same phrase, the medieval period). At the end of this long expanse of time falls what we still sometimes call the Renaissance (or "rebirth"). This term reflects Renaissance writers' and thinkers' view of their own time. Many modern historians and literary scholars see the Renaissance of the fourteenth to sixteenth centuries as representing the final flowering of medieval culture rather than a dramatic break with the past; where historians *in* the Renaissance saw difference and division, historians *of* the period tend to see continuity and development.

Even so, many readers coming to the study of medieval literature or culture for the first time will be struck by a sense of strangeness in much of what they encounter. They will enter worlds in which nature is malevolent, not benign; in which Christ fights as a warrior; in which the walls of an ancient city are said to have been broken by fate; in which it is possible to have one's head sliced off and carry it around before putting it back on; in which doubtful legal claims may be decided by the judgment of God through trial by ordeal or by battle; in which water may be thought to flow upward; and in which the middle of a literary text can be said to be inherently better from a moral point of view than the beginning or the end. Much as this overview aims to convey, and offer a context for, the complexity and sophistication that often characterize medieval texts, it will also recognize that it is difficult—and perhaps even undesirable—for modern readers to lose entirely their sense of strangeness and even wonder in experiencing the products of medieval literature and medieval culture.

Just as the literature of the Middle Ages may seem unusual to us, many modern readers may be surprised by the marginal political status of England and the English language in the Middle Ages. Britain was geographically on the edge of the world, and at the periphery of the political life of the continent; England was for many centuries the object rather than the subject of imperial ambitions. The status of English varied considerably from one century to another, but it was never at any time the dominant global force it is today. The ways in which an extraordinarily diverse cultural and linguistic mix began, over the course of the Middle Ages, to produce the works discussed here—as well as, ultimately, the language of this book—will be a major theme of these pages.

ENGLAND BEFORE THE NORMAN CONQUEST

ROMAN AND CELTIC BRITAIN

We know little or nothing of the inhabitants of Britain before 500 BCE, when groups of people that we now call the Celts began to migrate from continental Europe to Britain and Ireland. We have come to think of these peoples as a unified group in large part because the artistic and literary heritage of Celtic culture that has come down to us displays considerable unity in the characteristics of its narratives, in the bold decorative style of its visual arts, and in the close ties among Celtic languages. But the Celts, who had spread throughout much of Europe in the centuries before they began to inhabit Britain, were very much a loose grouping of societies, often at odds with one another, with no overarching administrative authority or social coherence.

The Romans invaded and conquered Celtic Britain in the first century CE. Britain lay at the edge of the Roman Empire; the Romans never managed to conquer Ireland or what is now Scotland, then largely inhabited by a Celtic or possibly pre-Celtic people of particularly fierce reputation known as the Picts. (In the early second century CE the Romans constructed the rampart known as Hadrian's Wall across the island as a defense against them.) Throughout most of what is now England and Wales, however, the Romans were successful in establishing administrative structures that made *Britannia* a province of the Roman Empire. Though far from the heart of the Empire, Britain was clearly a rich and valuable province, and much of the population, at least in the center of the island, was thoroughly Romanized. It is now thought that the island was densely populated; it enjoyed a thriving money economy and commerce, with a number of large urban centers including a settlement on the banks of the Thames River named *Londinium*, a network of roads, large villas in the Roman style, heated baths, water and sewage service in some areas, and sturdy traditions of Roman administration, education, and literacy. When Christianity spread throughout the Roman empire, it spread in Britain as well—Christian mosaics have been discovered on the site of a large fourth-century villa, and in 314 three British bishops attended a council in Arles, France. In the early years of the fifth century Saint Patrick, a Roman Briton, traveled through Ireland as a missionary bishop, spearheading the conversion of that island. In many respects Britain in the fourth century had a prosperity it would not see again until the fourteenth century.

Roman Britain was highly fortified and well defended from its hostile neighbors, but at the turn of the fifth century the Roman legions stationed in Britain were withdrawn for deployment in the heart of the Empire, in part to defend Rome from the various barbarian tribes pouring across its eastern frontiers. Soon afterwards, the Scots and the Picts began to encroach upon the territories of the Romanized British. It is unclear who ruled the island during these years or how it was defended; the Britons were left to their own devices, and tradition portrays them as hapless and virtually helpless. The traditional story, told among other places in the writing of a sixth-century Briton named Gildas, tells how the Britons turned to the Germanic peoples of continental Europe for assistance. The Angles, Saxons, and Jutes, Germanic tribes who occupied the coastal areas of what is now northwestern Germany and Denmark, were quite willing to work as soldiers for hire, but once they had established themselves in Britain as allies of the Britons, they began to demand land of their own, seized power from their employers, slaughtered and dispossessed them, and soon established themselves in the eastern parts of the island.

Contemporary archaeological evidence suggests, however, that the Germanic migrations actually took place in numerous waves from the later fourth century on. Relations between these Germanic invaders, who were probably not numerous, and the British are hard to reconstruct, but it appears that British culture was

eventually supplanted not simply because the British were driven out. Many of them intermingled with their Germanic conquerors and adopted the dress, language, and culture of their new ruling class so that whatever their cultural heritage, they became, to later archaeologists and historians, indistinguishable from the Germanic Angles and Saxons. When the Romans had ruled, the Britons were Romanized; when the Saxons ruled, they were Saxonized. There are few words of British origin in Old English, the language of the Germanic invaders, and it is certainly significant that the Old English word *wealh* means both "slave" and "Welshman."

Whatever the reasons for its erosion, by around 600 CE a distinctively British culture was largely confined to Wales and Cornwall. On the continent a parallel series of events occurred, with groups of Franks pushing the Celtic peoples of Gaul to the geographical margin of Brittany. Although they had been marginalized geographically and politically, however, the Celtic peoples continued to exert a powerful shaping influence on what would become English literature. Their influence persisted even after the Norman Conquest, in the retelling of Irish and Welsh legends, in the survival of the genre of story known as the "Breton lay," and in the fragmentary memories of British kings and warlords who led a temporarily successful resistance against the Saxon invaders—stories that formed the kernel of truth at the heart of the legends of King Arthur, arguably the great political myth of the Middle Ages.

Migration and Conversion

The culture of the Angles, Saxons, and Jutes was quite different from that of the Romanized Britons. Though there is some evidence for continuing populations in Roman cities, the Germanic migrants were largely rural rather than urban, and built primarily in wood rather than stone—most of the great buildings of the Romans fell into ruin or were plundered for building materials. Society was apparently organized, at least during the migration period, around a male leader and warrior band rather than the hearth and family, or the city or state. If the characterization of the first-century CE Roman historian Tacitus is to be believed, the continental Germanic tribes were a notably warlike culture: "they are not so easily persuaded to plow the earth and to wait for the year's produce as they are to challenge an enemy and earn the honor of wounds," Tacitus comments. "They actually think it tame and stupid to acquire by the sweat of toil what they might win by their blood." Certainly later centuries regarded the Germanic tribes as particularly fierce. The Angles and Saxons had a writing system—runic carvings—but no culture of literacy in which it might be put to more than the simplest uses. Their economy was based on barter and gift-exchange, not money. Perhaps most importantly, the Angles and Saxons were pagan, worshiping a pantheon of northern gods such as Woden and Thor, and as they came to dominate Britain the influence of Christianity moved (with the Britons themselves) to the margins.

But Christianity did not disappear as Britain became England (from *engla-land*, the land of the Angles). When Augustine (now known as Augustine of Canterbury, not to be confused with the more famous Augustine, bishop of Hippo in north Africa) was sent by Pope Gregory the Great on a mission to convert the English in 597, he met with extraordinary early success, in part no doubt because Christianity already had a strong presence in Britain. King Æthelberht of Kent, for example, who was Augustine's first notable convert, was married to a Frankish Christian named Bertha. The expansion of English power over the west and southwest of the island undoubtedly brought many British Christians under English rule. Apart from any question of spiritual benefit, conversion to Christianity offered the appeal of new political alliances with other Christian kings, and the considerable power of Latin literacy, law, science, philosophy, and education. Nonetheless conversion was a significant cultural change, and the momentum of conversion wavered back and forth for a century or so, with large areas of resistance and a good deal of backsliding; Christianized England was not everywhere peaceful and prosperous or even thoroughly converted. By the beginning of the eighth century, however, the English were Christian enough to send missionaries such as St. Boniface to preach the gospel to the pagan Saxons in Germany.

Alongside the Franks, the native British Christians, and the Roman missionaries, the Irish were busy in this period establishing monasteries in northern England. St. Columba founded the important monastery of Iona in Scotland in the mid-sixth century. This early insular monastic culture produced the extraordinary flourishing of Christian decorative art that finds its greatest expression in the Book of Kells. Tensions between the churches of the Roman mission and the idiosyncratic and relatively independent Irish churches were often high, but many of the most enduring Christian documents from the first centuries following the conversion of Britain, even those made in Northumbrian monasteries after the official rejection of the "Irish" model of Christianity at the Synod of Whitby (664), are manuscripts in the Celtic tradition.

One of the most remarkable of these is the Lindisfarne Gospels, mentioned above, dating from around 700. (A full-page illustration appears in the color pages in this volume.) Like the Book of Kells, this manuscript of the gospels is remarkable for the profusion and richness of its detailed illustrations; the motifs of intertwined lions of different colors, the zoomorphic shapes, and the sheer density of intricate detail of these gospel manuscripts make them central documents in the history of both Christian and Celtic art. It would be misleading to mention the visually impressive Lindisfarne Gospels, however, without placing it in context with other manuscripts such as the Codex Amiatinus, a massive (75-pound) copy of the Bible now in Florence. This manuscript, though visually more sedate than the Lindisfarne Gospels, contains a biblical text so closely similar to the original Latin translation of St. Jerome (known as the Vulgate Bible) that today it forms the basis for the scholarly reconstruction of Jerome's text. The Codex Amiatinus was made at the same time as the Lindisfarne Gospels, in the monastery of Wearmouth-Jarrow in the kingdom of Northumbria. While the Lindisfarne Gospels are a strong testimony to the Irish influence on Christian culture in England, the Codex Amiatinus is a powerful statement of Northumbrian monasticism's aspirations to pure *romanitas* as opposed to the provincial practices of

Page from the Gospel of St. Mark, Book of Kells (ninth century). The page size of the original is 9 ½ inches by 12 ½ inches. Like many early Insular manuscripts, the provenance of this book is uncertain. The monastery at Kells in County Meath, Ireland, was established by monks from the large monastery at Iona, off the coast of Scotland, at the time of the Viking invasions early in the ninth century. Among the many hypotheses as to the book's origin are theories that the monks brought the book with them from Iona in its present (unfinished) state; that some work was done at Iona, some at Kells; and even that the book originated at Lindisfarne in the north-east of England. This uncertainty indicates the high degree of interaction among the monasteries of Ireland, Scotland, and northern England during this period.

the Irish and British. Between the shifting forces of these various traditions—the ideals of Roman orthodoxy, the influence of the Irish monasteries, the political pull of the Frankish world, and the remnants, however tattered, of the native British church—England became a Christian nation.

When the Northumbrian historian Bede wrote his *Ecclesiastical History of the English People* around 725, in fact, religion was the only unity the English had; political unity had to grow out of this unity of religious practice. Near the beginning of his history, Bede lists the various languages of Britain: "At the present time [i.e., the early 700s], there are five languages in Britain, English, British, Irish, Pictish, and Latin, just as the divine law is written in five books, each in its own way devoted to seeking out and setting forth one and the same knowledge of sublime truth and true sublimity. The Latin tongue, through the study of the Scriptures, has become common to all the rest." By "English" Bede refers to what we now call Old English; by "British" he means the Celtic language of the Britons, ancestor of modern Welsh. The fact that Bede counts Latin, the learned language of religion and science, among the languages of Britain, however, suggests that he is not speaking of cultures or ethnic divisions in the modern sense. His point is not so much anthropological as it is spiritual—Britain was the fortunate recipient of the unifying force of Latin Christianity—but it does remind us of the linguistic, cultural, and intellectual diversity to be found in Anglo-Saxon England.

The story that Bede recounts of the period from 597 to 700 is in some respects parallel to the story of Britain under Roman rule. As it had been under the Romans, the island became an outpost at the edge of an empire—in this case, however, an empire founded on religion rather than on secular power. Just as Roman administrators in Britain had reported to their superiors in Rome, so too the archbishops of Canterbury and of York (the two pre-eminent centers of Christianity in Britain, as ordained by Pope Gregory the Great) derived their authority from the pope in Rome; the Roman church had inherited many of the bureaucratic systems, and some of the universalizing aspirations, of the Roman Empire, and the Pope assumed the role and name of *pontifex maximus* (from which he retains the

modern title "Pontiff"), the priestly aspect of imperial power. England's was, to be sure, a missionary church, not always willing or able to follow the Roman church in all respects; the English church developed in a relationship, with varying degrees of tension and accommodation, between Christian conversion and secular Germanic culture, and from an early date the English church displayed distinctively local features. As a purely practical matter, too, communication was an enormous challenge in an era when a courier traveling across Europe on horseback could typically cover little more than thirty miles (fifty kilometers) per day. To send a message from London to Rome and receive a reply could thus be expected to take the better part of two months. And yet many people made the journey, and were expected to make it—the roads between England and Rome were familiar to bishops, pilgrims, penitents, monks, messengers, and merchants. Within Britain, too, transportation and communication—and thus any form of centralized control—were made problematic by purely logistical considerations.

It was also in accordance with the church's own inclinations to make some effort to preserve traditional culture and customs, reinvesting existing practices with a Christian meaning. Bede's *Ecclesiastical History* preserves a letter written by Pope Gregory to the Abbot Mellitus in 601, as the latter was going to join Augustine's mission in Britain; Gregory instructs him to tell Augustine that

the temples of the idols in that nation ought not to be destroyed; but let the idols that are in them be destroyed; let holy water be made and sprinkled in the said temples, let altars be erected, and relics placed. For if those temples are well built, it is requisite that they be converted from the worship of devils to the service of the true God; that the nation, seeing that their temples are not destroyed, may remove error from their hearts, and knowing and adoring the true God, may the more familiarly resort to the places to which they have been accustomed. And because they have been used to slaughter many oxen in the sacrifices to devils, some solemnity must be exchanged for them on this account, as that on the day of the dedication, or the nativities of the holy martyrs, whose relics are there deposited, they may build themselves huts of the boughs of trees, about those churches which have been turned to that use from temples, and celebrate the solemnity with religious feasting, and no more offer beasts to the Devil, but kill cattle to the praise of God in their eating, and return thanks to the Giver of all things for their sustenance; to the end that, whilst some gratifications are outwardly permitted them, they may the more easily consent to the inward consolations of the grace of God.

Gregory may not be entirely clear on the precise nature of English paganism—he seems to imagine England to be like Rome, with temples and priesthoods—but his strategy permits many sorts of accommodations of Christian practice to English culture, and *vice versa*. Doubtless this hastened the process of conversion; Bede himself, writing barely a century after the beginning of the Roman mission to England, does not seem to regard lingering paganism among the English as a contemporary problem worth mentioning. The old pagan gods of the north were abandoned along with pagan temples and rituals—though remnants of their importance persisted, as they do today in our days of the week: *Wednesday* is "Woden's day," *Thursday* is "Thor's Day," and so on. But the Anglo-Saxons managed to adopt the civilization offered by Christianity and at the same time adapt it to their own Germanic heritage. From the perspective of literary history, this policy of "cleansing the temples" fostered an amazing interpenetration of Germanic and Christian ideas; each is rethought and revised in terms of the other, and it is impossible as well as inappropriate to separate "Christian" from "pagan" elements in the literature of the Anglo-Saxons. A longing for the heavenly home could be expressed in the tones of traditional elegy, Christ could be portrayed as a mighty warrior and his crucifixion as a heroic battle, and the pagan past could be depicted with regretful admiration and poignant sadness in a long poem like *Beowulf*.

Throughout this period monasteries were the most important outposts of Christian culture in England. The institutions of monasticism had their roots in the ascetic tradition of early Christianity, the belief that one could serve God best by living apart from the world in a state of constant prayer and self-denial. A monastery, as the concept developed in the third and fourth centuries CE, was a place where ascetically minded Christians could live together, supporting one another in prayer and penitential practice while mitigating some of the harsher aspects of the solitary life. As monastic communities grew, various rules were devised, some no more than collections of observations and advice. In the sixth century the *Rule* of St. Benedict outlined a clear and codified plan for the communal life, a plan that is still followed today in monastic communities around the world. The Benedictine rule—which, however rigorous it might seem to a modern reader, was meant to curb some of the ascetic extremes seen in Benedict's own time—was the foundation on which the great monastic establishments were built, where work, communal prayer, and study comprised the *Opus Dei* or "work of God," and which spread what Jean Leclercq has called "the love of learning and the desire for God" throughout early medieval Europe.

Many different rules and monastic orders developed throughout the Middle Ages; their practices differed from one order to another and one house to the next, but the general principles were constant. Monks were not usually ordained as priests and had no pastoral responsibilities to minister to a congregation (though monasteries often did, especially in the early Middle Ages, provide pastoral care in areas without an established system of parishes). Monks were obliged to give up worldly wealth, their position in society, and their connections with family and friends so as to live in a community of individuals devoted to the same goals; at the same time, however, abbots were often from the same families as the secular rulers, and became powerful rulers and possessors of great wealth. Monastic communities always observed, at least in theory, a strict separation of the sexes, but the monastic life was open to women as much as to men; the English practice in the century before Bede was to have double monastic houses of monks and nuns, in almost all cases headed by an abbess such as the famous and noble Hild of Whitby. The monasteries, as the most important locus for intellectual activity and for the preservation and creation of cultural artifacts, became essential to the continuance of Latin culture, the practices of literacy, and the texts both of the church fathers and of classical authors, which were copied and read even as they were sometimes regarded with suspicion. Monastic culture flourished so vigorously in the north of England that one scholar has described Northumbria in the generations around 700 as a "veritable monastic Riviera."

INVASION AND UNIFICATION

This came to a dramatic end in the 790s with the first wave of invasions by the various Scandinavian peoples known to history as "Vikings," and organized monastic life in England seems to have fallen into a state of more or less complete disrepair in the course of the ninth century. (It would be restored in the later tenth century by the reformers Oswald, Dunstan, and Æthelwold; by this time, however, the centers of monastic culture were in Canterbury, Winchester, and Glastonbury rather than the far north, which was thoroughly Danish and in some places re-paganized.) Among the first targets of Viking attack were the holy island of Lindisfarne, which fell in 793, and Bede's monastery at Jarrow, which was destroyed in 794; the raids would continue on and off for two centuries. The Vikings were in many ways an extraordinary group of peoples. Whereas previous invaders such as the Angles, Saxons, and Jutes traveled relatively short distances, the Vikings constructed longships that proved capable of crossing the Atlantic; the remains of a Viking settlement at L'Anse aux Meadows in Newfoundland, dating from about 1000, are evidence that they traveled even to the New World. They established settlements in Iceland and Greenland, and settled in Ireland, Scotland, and Normandy as well as in England (the territory of Normandy takes its name from the "northmen"). The popular image of the Vikings is one of raiders who would arrive, plunder, and return to their homeland; in fact, Viking raids were followed in most areas by invasion and settlement, and gradually Viking groups were absorbed into local populations. For most of the tenth century Viking raids ceased; the former raiders had become farmers, and had begun to intermarry with Anglo-Saxons in a process of cultural and linguistic assimilation that continued through the eleventh century.

The Viking presence contributed significantly to the unification of the Anglo-Saxon kingdoms and the first

The ruins at Lindisfarne.

stirrings of what might be called, for lack of a better term, national feeling, both in Scotland and in England. The centers of political power shifted southward, to Mercia in the eighth century and Wessex in the ninth; smaller kingdoms formed alliances and larger ones expanded their rule, until most of England was united under King Alfred the Great of Wessex, who reigned from 871 to 899. Alfred was able to raise a substantial army and stop the Vikings militarily; while the Vikings maintained control over the north and northeast of England, Alfred and his successors controlled most of the remainder of the country.

With peace secured, Alfred began promoting education and literary culture. What is of incalculable importance for the history of English literature is that he proposed to encourage the translation of Latin works into English and the cultivation of vernacular literacy. Alfred surrounded himself with a learned circle of advisors after the manner of the Frankish emperor Charlemagne (d. 814), and was himself literate in Latin—he translated several works from Latin, including Boethius's *Consolation of Philosophy*, though probably with a great deal of assistance from his advisors. He sets out the reasoning behind his policy of English translation in the preface to his translation of Gregory the Great's *Pastoral Care*—and it is significant that he announces his program of education and translation in a book on how to rule and govern:

I recalled how the law was first composed in the Hebrew language, and thereafter, when the Greeks learned it, they translated it all into their own language, and all other books as well. And so too the Romans, after they had mastered them, translated them all through myriad interpreters into their own language…. Therefore it seemed better to me … that we too should turn certain books which are the most necessary for all men to know into a language that we can all understand.

Alfred's educational program was designed primarily to help him govern, but one of its legacies is the relatively large quantity of literary, historical, legal, spiritual, and political writing in English (about 30,000 lines of poetry and about ten times as much prose) that has survived, almost all of it in manuscripts from the tenth and eleventh centuries. Under Alfred the *Anglo-Saxon Chronicle* was probably begun; to this year-by-year historical record we owe a great deal of our knowledge of the period.

The authority of even the most capable and ambitious rulers in the early Middle Ages was seldom able to survive long after their deaths. More often than not family feuding would undo much of what had been accomplished, as happened when fighting among Charlemagne's three sons led to the tripartite division of the Carolingian empire. Alfred had rather better luck with his descendants, who were able to consolidate his accomplishments and even extend them somewhat; his descendant Edgar (r. 959–75) commanded the allegiance of all of the most important English lords, had ties to the most important families on the continent, and had in his control all senior church appointments. Under the weaker leadership of the next generation, however, in particular Æthelred II (r. 978–1016), and in the face of a renewed series of Viking attacks (dramatically depicted in the poetic *Battle of Maldon*, written some time after the actual battle in 991), the allegiance of the great lords and landholders to the king loosened, and the shameful decline of the English nobility described in the *Anglo-Saxon Chronicle* culminated in the Danish King Cnut (r. 1016–35) taking the English throne.

The end of the tenth century was by no means entirely a period of decline, however; it was also a time of such literary figures as the homilist and grammarian Ælfric, the archbishop Wulfstan, and the scholar Byrhtferth of Ramsey; during these years a number of *deluxe* decorated manuscripts were produced, and important works such as the *Rule* of St. Benedict and the Gospels were translated into English. It is a tribute to the strength of Alfred's reforms that much of the administrative, military, and church structures he had put into place survived the conquest of England by a Danish king—as, indeed, they would in part survive the conquest fifty years later by the Normans. That these conquests did not cause more destruction than they did must also be attributed in part to the fact that these invading cultures were far from alien to English culture. In the centuries between the early Viking invasions and the reign of Cnut, Christianity had reached Scandinavia; whereas the early Vikings had raided and destroyed monasteries, Cnut was a Christian who continued to support the monasteries much as Alfred and his descendants had done. Similarly, while the Vikings had conquered Normandy in the early tenth century, by the time the Normans invaded Britain in 1066, the Viking culture of Normandy had largely been assimilated to that of Christian France.

England after the Norman Conquest

The Normans and Feudalism

The Norman Conquest of England in 1066 was the next in the long series of invasions and migrations—Celts, Romans, Angles, Saxons, Jutes, and Vikings—that have shaped English culture. That it has held a special place as a focal point in English history is no doubt partly due to its timing, almost exactly at the point where many scholars see larger forces creating a dividing line between the early and the later Middle Ages. French language and culture never threatened to extinguish the existing Anglo-Saxon culture and English language, although they did exert enormous and lasting influence on them. The contrast with the Anglo-Saxon migrations is striking: these effectively and permanently imposed an English culture on Britain, while conquest by the Normans never permanently imposed French

hIC EXEVNT:CABAIII   DENAVIBVS ⁓ ET hIC:MILITES: FE

From the Bayeux Tapestry (late eleventh century). This object is actually an embroidered banner, around 20 inches high and 230 feet long, rather than a woven tapestry. It was probably created by English embroiderers, who were particularly skilled in this kind of work. This section of the tapestry shows the Norman ships landing at Pevensy, Sussex, 28 September; several ships have already landed on the beach, and horses are being unloaded from another ship that has just arrived. The text of the tapestry at this point (translated from the Latin) reads as follows: Here the horses are getting out of the ships. And here the soldiers [hurry to Hastings to seize supplies].

culture on England. But the Norman invasion helped to change Britain in fundamental ways—most obviously in language, but also in social and economic structure.

For all its far-reaching consequences, the invasion itself was a relatively modest affair. When Harold was crowned as king following the death of King Edward, the succession was disputed by William, Duke of Normandy, who settled the matter militarily; with a force probably numbering no more than 8,000, he crossed the Channel and soon defeated and killed Harold in a day-long battle just outside Hastings. His victory brought England under the rule of a French-speaking king with substantial territorial claims in France, a situation that would persist for roughly the next three hundred years. Despite this obvious shift, and despite the triumphant narrative of the Bayeux Tapestry (probably made within a generation of the battle for a Norman patron), the effects of the Conquest, particularly as it was viewed at close range rather than years later, apparently did not always loom so large. In this connection it is interesting to compare the five different accounts in different manuscripts of the *Anglo-Saxon Chronicle* that have come down to us. At one extreme is the remarkably brief account of a scribe writing at Winchester in the manuscript known as the

Parker MS: "In this year King Edward died and Earl Harold succeeded to the kingdom, and held it forty weeks and one day; and in this year William came and conquered England. And in this year Christ Church was built and a comet appeared on 18 April." By contrast, a scribe writing a generation or more later in Peterborough presents a much fuller account of how Harold was forced to fight a Norse invader in the north of the country before meeting William at Hastings, and conveys more of the immediate effects of William's conquest. Yet even here one has the sense that the death of a local abbot is regarded as being of almost as much importance as the Norman invasion:

And King Harold was informed [of the victory of a Norse king near the town of York], and he came with a very great force of English men and met him at Stamford Bridge, and killed him and Earl Tostig and valiantly overcame all the invaders. Meanwhile Count William landed at Hastings on Michaelmas Day, and Harold came from the north and fought with him before all of the army had come and there he fell and his two brothers Gyrth and Leofwine; and William conquered this country, and came to Westminster, and Archbishop Aldred consecrated him king, and people paid taxes to him, and gave him hostages and afterwards bought their land. And Leofric, Abbot of Peterborough, was at that campaign and fell ill there, and came home and died soon after, on the Eve of All Saints. God have mercy on his soul. In his day there was every happiness and every good at Peterborough, and he was beloved by everyone, so that the King gave to Saint Peter and him the Abbacy of Burton and that of Coventry which Earl Leofric, who was his uncle, had built, and that of Crowland and that of Thorne. And he did much for the benefit of the monastery of Peterborough with gold and silver and vestments and land, more indeed than any before or after him.

Significant here is the mention of people paying taxes to William and "buying" their lands. William exacted tribute from the conquered both in the immediate aftermath of his invasion and on an ongoing basis, keeping as much as a fifth of English lands for himself and dividing much of the rest among members of his family and the barons who had supported him, who in turn maintained their own followers. While neither the lords nor the peasants of Anglo-Saxon England had held legal title to their land in quite the way that we conceive of it today, they had in practice exercised rights over that land similar to those that we would describe as the rights of ownership. Under the Normans, by contrast, nobles held the land that they occupied not on any permanent basis but as part of a system of exchange. The king granted land to a nobleman as a *fief*; in return for the right to its use the nobleman was obliged to perform services for the king, including making payments at various times and providing armed knights whenever the king might demand them. The nobleman, in his turn, would grant land—again, as a fief—to a knight, who in return would owe to the nobleman military service and other dues. The knight would typically retain a substantial portion of this land, and then divide the rest among the peasantry. There were obligations in the other direction, as well: knights were obliged to provide protection for the peasantry, nobles for the knights, and the king for the nobles. The relationship at each level was, in theory at least, entirely voluntary and often publicly proclaimed, with the

"vassal" (or holder of the fief) kneeling and promising homage and fealty to his lord, and a kiss between the two then sealing their mutual obligation.

The institution of this new system was marked in a unique way by William through the compilation of the Domesday Book (so-called in reference to the "Day of Judgment" at the end of the world), an extraordinary survey on a county-by-county basis of all the lands held by the king and by his vassals, recording all the obligations of the landholders. Without the sort of commitment to record-keeping and enforcement that the Domesday Book represented (a commitment made possible, it must be said, by the underlying social order inherited from the Anglo-Saxons), the Normans might not have succeeded to such a great degree in imposing a new network of obligation on the conquered people. It must be noted, however, that the Domesday Book was seldom used to settle disputes or clarify ownership—the two functions for which, one might suppose, such a comprehensive census would be undertaken—in the first century of its existence. The eleventh-century ability to make records outpaced the development of a system in which to exploit them, and it would take some time before the mechanisms of government could make efficient use of such burdensome archives of documents. It has been argued that the Domesday Book, for all the impressive bureaucracy that brought it about, reflects a mistaken idea of the nature of written obligations: William may have imagined that the island of Britain could be granted to him by a written charter, like any other piece of land, and that recording the disposition of property and population would somehow fix them permanently in that state. But even if Domesday was more symbolic than useful, the imposition of feudal obligations was fairly thorough in England; the Anglo-Saxon nobles were quickly assimilated, dispossessed, or killed, leaving William in effective control of England. The Norman conquests of Wales and Scotland, however, were much slower and more piecemeal, and the Anglo-Norman kings never exercised very much control over Ireland.

The late eleventh century in England saw the arrival of the Jews as well as the French invaders. Christian disdain for moneylending—although there were certainly Christian usurers—and the exclusion of Jews from some other professions meant that Jews tended to become strongly associated with, and very important in, the financial workings of the kingdom. In the twelfth and thirteenth centuries, until their expulsion in 1290, they served at times as a financial last resort for the king; their relatively unprotected status as non-Christians made them vulnerable to much more severe forms of taxation and the abrogation of debts incurred by Christians but never repaid. Another important development of the later eleventh century, which would become much more central to civic life in the late Middle Ages, was the rise of guilds—initially merchant guilds that exercised a monopoly over the trade in a particular area, but later craft guilds that established regulations allowing them to control who could practice a given craft and that offered social and financial support to their members, as well as regulating the quality of production. While guilds and confraternities of some description, often purely religious in orientation, had existed since perhaps the seventh century, they became increasingly important in the course of the twelfth and thirteenth centuries, particularly in England, and their rise coincided with the growth of urban centers and of new forms of religious devotion.

HENRY II AND AN INTERNATIONAL CULTURE

If William was the key figure in establishing Norman and feudal rule in England, his great-grandson Henry II (r. 1154–89) was the key figure in its preservation and extension through the later Middle Ages. Henry's coming to the throne in 1154 brought to an end almost twenty years of civil war under the disputed kingship of Stephen, in the course of which barons and church leaders had taken advantage of the collapse of royal authority to expand local powers. Many of them began to encroach on land claimed by the Crown, and to build private castles to protect their domains. Henry put a stop to these practices, taking back the lands, tearing down the castles, and reorganizing royal authority in a fashion that was increasingly supported by standardized records and documents. Central authority over legal matters, which had previously been largely restricted to capital cases, was now extended to legal matters of all

sorts; the first legal textbook was composed in Henry's reign. The expansion of the Crown's legal control came in part at the expense of the church, and provoked one of the most famous incidents of Henry's reign, his clash with Thomas Becket (1118–70), Archbishop of Canterbury, who wanted the clergy to retain their right to be tried in church courts independent of the secular legal system. The Archbishop was subsequently murdered, allegedly on the orders of Henry, an event that exercised a tremendous hold on the contemporary imagination. As John of Salisbury tells the story (in the earliest surviving account of the murder, written in 1171), Becket was standing before the altar when the knights who had come in pursuit of him arrived and told him that it was his time to die. John writes:

> Steadfast in speech as in spirit, he replied: "I am prepared to die for my God, to preserve justice and my church's liberty. But if you seek my head, I forbid you on behalf of God almighty and on pain of anathema to do any hurt to any other man, monk, clerk or layman, of high or low degree…. I embrace death readily, so long as peace and liberty for the church follow from the shedding of my blood." … He spoke, and saw that the assassins had drawn their swords; and bowed his head like one in prayer. His last words were "To God and St. Mary and the saints who protect and defend this church, and to the blessed Denis, I commend myself and the church's cause." … A son's affection forbids me to describe each blow the savage assassins struck, spurning all fear of God, forgetful of all fealty and any human feeling. They defiled the cathedral and the holy season with a bishop's blood and with slaughter.

It remains unclear whether or not Henry ordered Becket's murder. What is clear is that the outcry was so great that Henry was forced to perform public penance—and to accept that the church would, to some extent, remain outside the realm of royal authority. Becket's martyrdom created the Canterbury shrine that was the destination of Chaucer's pilgrims, among many others.

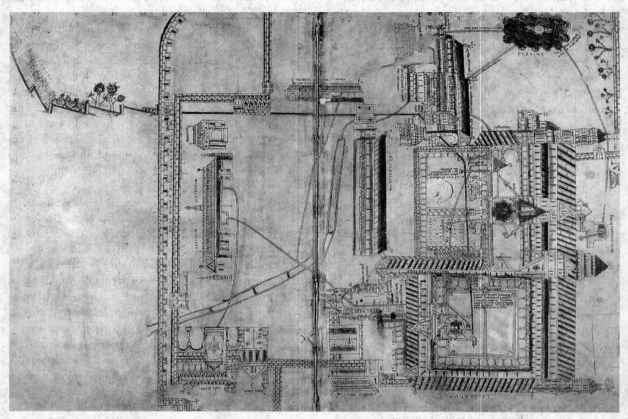

Plan for Canterbury Cathedral, c. 1160. Canterbury Cathedral, the seat of the Archbishop of Canterbury, head of the English Church, is a kind of time capsule of Christianity in Britain since Anglo-Saxon times. The earliest church known to have stood on this site was that of St. Augustine of Canterbury, who arrived as a missionary in 597 CE; traces of this building are believed to lie beneath the current structure. An Anglo-Saxon church was built over that of Augustine in the ninth or tenth century; it was destroyed by fire in 1067 and rebuilt by the Normans shortly afterward, and this construction still forms the basic fabric of the existing church, although it was modified and decorated further in the succeeding centuries. The plan shows the extensive monastic buildings as well as the cathedral itself. The lines shown connecting the buildings represent the plumbing system. At the top left the vineyard and orchard are indicated. The murder of St. Thomas Becket, then Archbishop, in the Cathedral's altar, made Canterbury a major pilgrimage shrine.

Durham Cathedral, begun in 1093, is regarded as one of the finest examples of Norman architecture in Europe; this style, a form of the Romanesque, is characterized by round arches (as here, along the sides of the nave) and vast but relatively spare interiors. Durham also displays some features (such as the pointed vaulting) that came to characterize the Gothic style of many later cathedrals.

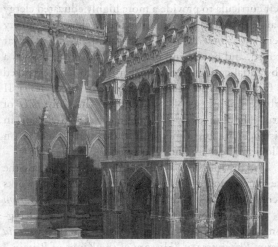

Lincoln Cathedral, Galilee Porch. Begun in 1072 and substantially rebuilt in the late twelfth and early thirteenth

centuries, Lincoln Cathedral shows some of the classic features of both Romanesque and Gothic architecture. The Gothic Galilee Porch dates from c. 1230.

Salisbury Cathedral (thirteenth century). With a spire of 404 feet, this was until the 1960s the tallest building in England. It is a classic example of the high Gothic style, with its pointed arches, flying buttresses to support a higher vault, and greater intricacy of design, including decorative features such as exterior sculpture and stained glass windows.

If Henry's extension of the power of the English throne throughout the realm was unprecedented—though not, as the example of Becket suggests, entirely unopposed—so too was his extension of that power beyond the British Isles. Like previous Anglo-Norman monarchs, Henry controlled much of what is now northern France as well as England. With his marriage to Eleanor of Aquitaine in 1152 he had acquired control of much of southern France; he also exerted control over most of Scotland and Wales, and in 1171 he invaded and took control of Ireland, where he quickly imposed the same feudal structures and judicial system on the Irish people as he had on the English. Despite England's political control over Ireland—which itself was of varying strength over the next centuries—there was relatively little cultural assimilation, and the English nobles ruling in Ireland formed to a large extent a self-contained enclave. Like Scotland and Wales, with which it formed intermittent alliances, Ireland throughout this period pursued its own political strategies in the British Isles and on the continent. And despite the efforts of Henry and the kings who followed him, the English presence in France was far less enduring than its presence in Ireland. By 1453, at the close of the Hundred Years' War between France and England, the port town of Calais was the only remnant of English control over France.

Henry II and Eleanor of Aquitaine sailing across the English Channel. Detail of illustration from Matthew Paris, *Historia Major* (c. 1240). The king and queen made the crossing many times as they traveled between their French and English kingdoms.

The period around the Norman Conquest also coincided with important developments in learned culture. England had produced outstanding scholars at various points in the early Middle Ages—among them Bede, the Latin poet Aldhelm, Ælfric, Byrhtferth, and most famously Alcuin of York, a monk who became master of Charlemagne's palace school—and in the eleventh century was home to the illustrious Anselm of Bec (1033–1109), one of the founders of scholastic thought, whose career demonstrates the international culture of the church and the schools, both of which used Latin, an international language. Born in Italy, Anselm became abbot of a monastery in Normandy and was eventually appointed Archbishop of Canterbury—the leading church position in England. His development of the ontological argument for the existence of God in his *Why God Became Man* (starting from the premise that God is that than which nothing greater can be conceived) is a good example of scholastic ways of thinking, proceeding on the basis of deductive logic to new theological conclusions. While there were outstanding individual thinkers at this time, however, the universities were still in their infancy; in most of Europe, schools had existed for the most part only in association with cathedrals or monasteries and their chief purpose was to provide training for clerics. In the wake of monastic and ecclesiastical reform in the tenth and eleventh centuries, these schools began to expand their curricula to provide a more highly educated clergy at all levels. Already by the end of the eleventh century there was some form of instruction taking place at Oxford, and by the end of the twelfth century it was a substantial enough center of learning to have attracted its first foreign student and to benefit when Henry II forbade English scholars to study at the University of Paris. The University of Bologna was also already in existence at this time, and these three were soon followed by others across Europe.

The British Isles in the twelfth century also saw the rise of new modes of historical writing, including works such as William of Malmesbury's *Gesta Regum Anglorum* or "Deeds of the English Kings," Henry of Huntingdon's *Chronicle*, and Geoffrey of Monmouth's *Historia Regum Britanniae* or "History of the Kings of Britain." These writers' approach to history emphasized, as their titles suggest, the deeds of kings and the rise and fall of nations; in this they departed from predecessors more interested in depicting the Christian framework of history. The period also illustrates the political uses of literature. While Henry II—unlike, for example, King Alfred—is not particularly remembered for his own literary activities, numerous works in Anglo-Norman are associated with him as a patron or dedicatee, and his desire to solidify and extend his claims on both French and English lands was one of the things that made him an important figure for literary history. Henry and his descendants are known as the Angevin (or Plantagenet) kings, a reference to Henry's father, Geoffrey "Planta-genet" of Anjou, and this designation accurately repre-sents their ongoing political and cultural interest in France. Henry's reign saw the production and wide dissemination of numerous literary and historical works that proved foundational for British literature, especially the development of the Arthurian legend.

Geoffrey of Monmouth's *History*, completed around 1139, offers an account of the history of the realm going back to its mythical Trojan founder, Brutus (from whom the name Britain supposedly derived), and provided the foundation for the Arthurian stories of the later Middle Ages. Henry II, the descendant of Normans who, like the mythical British under Arthur, had battled the Saxons for control of Britain, was only the first in a long line of kings to find this legend, with its potential to offer an authoritative and legitimizing history, an appealing subject; Arthur's imperial ambi-tions, as told in this version of the tale, also offered a supposed historical precedent for English claims to rule on the continent.[1] Geoffrey's *History* was popular throughout Europe, and in the British Isles alone was translated into Middle Welsh, Anglo-Norman, and Middle English. The Anglo-Norman version *Brut*, by the poet Wace, was dedicated to Henry's queen, Eleanor of Aquitaine, a further suggestion of the story's royal allure. Later in the century, French authors—most notably Chrétien de Troyes (c. 1150–90)—inserted into the legendary history of Arthur episodes that focused on the individual achievements of knights and on romantic (sometimes adulterous) love, creating a considerably greater role for female characters. Their works took their name from the language in which they were written, *roman* (French, from which we derive the modern literary term *romance* as well as the name for the *romance* languages), as opposed to Latin, a choice that reflected the growing audience for vernacular poetry in the European courts.

A form closely related to the romance, and also written in the vernacular, was the Breton lay, a short narrative with, usually, a significant element of the marvelous and a central emphasis on a romantic relationship rather than large-scale political or military events. The lays' emphasis on the supernatural, which is often attributed to their origin in the Celtic culture of Brittany, is reminiscent at times of the early twelfth-century prose tales of the *Mabinogi* from medieval Wales—which, however, also show notable chivalric and courtly features. By far the most famous medieval lays are those by an Anglo-Norman author who calls herself simply "Marie" and who apparently wrote in England in Henry's time; her twelve short tales—two of which are set in the world of Arthurian legend—offer particularly careful attention to women's roles in the conflicts of loyalty that often characterize romance narratives, and are among the relatively few medieval works by a named female author. The Marie who wrote the lays is usually identified with the "Marie de France" who composed a collection of fables and an account of a knight's visionary journey to purgatory. Romance and the lays took some time to make their way into English; Layamon translated Wace's *Brut* into English around the turn of the thirteenth century, but most Middle English romances date from the late thirteenth and fourteenth centuries, probably reflecting the linguistic tendencies of their primary audience, the French-speaking nobility, before the fourteenth century.

As had happened centuries earlier in the wake of Alfred's rule, royal authority was scaled back under Henry's successors, who included two of his sons: first Richard I (the Lionheart), who ruled from 1189 to 1199, and then John, who ruled until 1216. In order to raise money in his struggle against Philip II of France for

---

[1] Although the Normans may have liked to associate themselves with the British side in the Arthurian legends, Welsh poets of the time, whose culture was the more direct descendant of the early British, cast the Normans in the role of the despised English.

territory on the continent, John imposed extraordinary taxes on English barons and other nobles; the barons rebelled and forced the king to sign a document setting out the rights and obligations both of the nobles and of the king himself, and making explicit that the king was not to contravene these customary arrangements without consulting the barons. The document also reaffirmed the freedom of the English church, particularly the freedom from royal interference in the election of bishops or other officeholders. Under this "great charter" or Magna Carta, the power of the king was for the first time limited by the terms of a written document.

THE THIRTEENTH CENTURY

The year 1215 was momentous in medieval Europe. In addition to the signing of Magna Carta—whose ultimately far-reaching effects were at the time felt only in England—this year witnessed the Fourth Lateran Council, a major gathering of church leaders under the guidance of the energetic Pope Innocent III. Lateran IV represented an extraordinarily wide-ranging attempt to unify Christian practice and raise standards of Christian observance. The canons of the Council covered almost all aspects of Christian life, and their effects on both religious practice and religious instruction resounded through the rest of the Middle Ages. Christians from now on were required to confess their sins formally and receive Communion at least once a year, and the sacrament of the altar was officially declared to involve transubstantiation, meaning that the body and blood of Christ were actually present in, rather than merely represented by, the bread and wine consecrated at the Mass (a doctrine that became a matter of serious dispute, however, in later medieval England). A new network of regulation was put into place to govern marriages, with secret marriages prohibited and marriage itself declared a sacrament.

Associated with the increased emphasis on the importance of priests administering sacraments to the faithful were increased efforts to ensure that members of the clergy were educated and competent; one of the canons involved the maintenance of cathedral schools free to clerics. Bishops were required to preach in their dioceses or ensure that there were others who could do

so in their stead, and clergy were forcefully reminded of the requirement of clerical celibacy. Individual Christians, for their part, were expected to be able to recite a small number of prayers, but there was no thought of encouraging widespread education of a sort that would enable the populace to read the word of God on their own. On the contrary, it was considered important to keep the Bible at a remove from the common people so that it could be safely interpreted to them through church intermediaries. The controversy that later developed over this issue would extend over several centuries and become a crucial concern for the Lollard or Wycliffite sect in fourteenth- and fifteenth-century England, as well as a central distinguishing point between the Roman Catholic Church and the various Protestant faiths in the Reformation.

As this suggests, the reforms of the Fourth Lateran Council aimed to strengthen the Christian community, but with a new emphasis on differentiating, excluding, and penalizing unorthodox believers and non-Christians. The canons include extensive commentary on the need to control and excommunicate heretics; they require Jews and "Saracens" (Muslims) to wear distinctive clothing lest they be mistaken for Christians; they prohibit Jews from holding public office; and they make provisions to encourage crusading against Muslim control of the Holy Land. The English joined whole-heartedly in the Crusades and the restrictions placed on Jews. There had already been massacres of Jews, particularly at York, by the late twelfth century; expulsions from various cities by the local lords became widespread as early as the 1230s; and in 1290 Edward I expelled all Jews from England. It is not surprising, in view of this, that anti-Jewish miracle stories became popular across Europe during this period; Chaucer's *Prioress's Tale* is a later example of this genre. Heresy remained a concern throughout Europe, although in this period the persecutions were more severe in France and other parts of the continent than in England.

The Fourth Lateran Council was in part a response to increased lay devotion and interest in religion, which offered a challenge to the sometimes inadequate pastoral care provided by the clergy. In the early thirteenth century, for example, the records of the Bishop of Winchester show numerous priests being forced to declare that they will learn the Creed, the Ten Commandments, the Seven Deadly Sins, and various other basic Christian doctrines within the space of a year, or pay a fine of forty shillings, a far from unusual instance which suggests that their preparation was not all that could have been wished. We may note, however, that some of the greatest works of Middle English religious literature survive in a closely related group of texts from around this same time: the *Ancrene Riwle* (Rule for Anchoresses) and the saints' lives and other spiritual-guidance texts that accompany it in the manuscripts testify to the presence of learned and committed religious men and women in early thirteenth-century England.

The new religious movements that arose in the course of the twelfth and thirteenth centuries—movements often instigated by the laity—were in some cases accepted by the church, though others were declared heretical; the growth in such movements was so great that the Council decreed that no new religious orders could be instituted after 1215, a decree that was largely observed. Among the new groups, the most significant, particularly for literary history, were the fraternal orders or friars (terms that derive from the Latin and French words for "brother"): the Augustinian hermits, Carmelites, and, especially, Dominicans and Franciscans. Like the monks of the early church, the members of these new movements embraced poverty and learning. Unlike previous monks of any era, however, they devoted themselves to carrying religion directly to the people, rather than living an enclosed life; their aim was to pursue the "vita apostolica," the way of life of the Apostles. Founded in the first part of the thirteenth century, they spread with great rapidity, and had a substantial presence in the British Isles by around 1250.

The friars' considerable success and speedy growth derived in no small part from their practice of preaching and establishing foundations in urban centers. The tremendous growth in the European economy from the eleventh century onward had fostered the development of ever-larger towns and cities. Urban growth in turn made possible an increasing specialization of labor that is reflected in the rise of craft guilds and, in another sense, in the friars themselves. The religious and civic cultures that each represented were deeply entwined.

Guilds, which by this time were at the center of civic life, had patron saints and made religious fellowship a central part of their collective identities; their later sponsorship of the great cycle plays of the fourteenth to sixteenth centuries was a natural outgrowth of this melding. And although St. Francis, the founder of the Franciscans, had entirely rejected his merchant background upon his conversion, the preachers of his order and others found the towns, with their concentrated populations and alleged moral turpitude, an ideal place for their work.

Builders at work. Detail of illustration to Matthew Paris, *Historia Major* (c. 1240). Matthew Paris, a monk at the famous Benedictine Abbey of St. Alban's, near London, took over the chronicle kept by his abbey in 1235 and continued it until his death in 1259. He is one of the liveliest sources for all kinds of information on the mid-thirteenth century, and was among those who commented (with some disapproval) on the spread of the friars and, among other things, their extensive building projects as their orders grew ever larger.

In the British Isles as elsewhere, the friars proved popular and controversial in almost equal measure; a fierce critique of them by the Irish bishop Richard FitzRalph (c. 1299–1360) survives in over seventy manuscripts from every part of Europe, and the friars' influence at the University of Paris in the mid-thirteenth century so infuriated the other clerics there that the pope had to intervene. Their preaching was widely admired, however, perhaps especially by lay audiences, and while they quickly became part of the church and university hierarchies, they also claimed a particular affinity for pastoral work. Their mission thus promoted the translation and dissemination of religious teaching among the laity, and their energy in this activity made their writings an important influence on the development of literature in the vernacular languages of Europe, including England. Their emergence and quick expansion both coincided with and furthered the rise of lay involvement in religious life, whether this took the form of pilgrimage, spiritual reading or writing, attendance at sermons and church services, or devotion to saints' cults, particularly that of the Virgin Mary. Nor were the friars the only force for increased religious education; English churchmen were particularly active in their response to the canons of the Fourth Lateran Council, and many works of spiritual instruction for the clergy or the laity, in Latin, Anglo-Norman, or English, attempted to disseminate the basic tenets of the faith. The *Speculum Confessionis* usually attributed to the learned Robert Grosseteste (c. 1170–1253), Bishop of Lincoln, is one example of the new works that responded to the requirement of yearly confession; another is the Anglo-Norman *Manuel des Pechiez* (c. 1270), the source for Robert Mannyng's *Handlyng Synne* (1303), which aimed to give laypeople the knowledge they needed to live in accordance with Christian teaching. Just as the influence of the French aristocracy after the Norman Conquest brought French language and literature into the realm of English literary history, so the broader emphasis on basic Christian instruction in the thirteenth century and beyond made Latin works and church teachings increasingly available to vernacular audiences.

The growing lay participation in religion is reflected in the growth of certain characteristic literary genres.

The *exemplum*, or illustrative short story, most famously characteristic of medieval sermons, often provided a narrative argument for avoiding particular sins or emulating certain virtues; the closely related form of the *miraculum*, or miracle story, aimed to impress the reader or hearer with a sense of wonder. In the later Middle Ages *exempla* and other short narratives were often especially associated with the preaching of the friars; such stories were thought to be appealing to laypeople, who might need help with the fine points of doctrine and would find narrative more accessible. These tales were sometimes criticized for being more entertaining than instructive, and indeed are not always very different from the genres of fable or fabliau—the latter being a "funny short story in verse," often dealing with sexual or economic deception and valuing cleverness over morality. Popular in French, fabliaux are essentially non-existent in (written) English until Chaucer, whose *Miller's*, *Reeve's*, and *Shipman's Tales*, among others, are based on this genre.

Saints' lives, another widely popular literary form, are also one of the oldest genres in English literature; the Old English *Martyrology* of the ninth century is a particularly comprehensive example, but some of the earliest texts in Middle English are the lives of three virgin martyrs (Juliana, Katherine, and Margaret), all dating from the early thirteenth century. Intriguingly, lives of women martyrs of the early church were extremely popular in late-medieval England; Chaucer's *Second Nun's Tale*, which recounts the life of St. Cecilia, is another well-known (later) example. As with the Bible, even texts that do not center on the life or deeds of a saint may invoke the saints or briefly recount their miracles; they were part of the common knowledge of the time, and widely represented in art. Saints were regarded as protectors and intercessors, and the retelling of their lives was part of the effort to promote their cults and gain their assistance; their stories could provide points of contact with the sacred, particularly since they came from many walks of life.

The growing attention to pastoral care further stimulated the need for clerical education, and the worldly duties of the clergy—from the care of souls (including the writing of sermons) to administration of lands or finances—made studies in logic, rhetoric, and other subjects beyond theology or canon law an important part of their training. At the same time, contact with Arab scholars made both Arabic learning and the writings of classical philosophers—Aristotle most influential among them—newly available in western Europe. The need to assimilate these traditions and bring them into accord with Christian teaching fostered the development of the scholastic method, or scholasticism, which gathered the evidence of various authorities and worked to synthesize it, usually by means of a debate form, into a single coherent authority. The structure of university study was quite different from its modern descendant, though not unrecognizably so. A student would first study the seven liberal arts, around which higher education was organized throughout the later Middle Ages: grammar, rhetoric, and logic (or dialectic), collectively known as the trivium, and arithmetic, music, astronomy, and geometry, called the quadrivium. Students who wished to continue could pursue further studies in theology, medicine, or law— roughly the equivalent of modern graduate schools.

Despite the intellectual flowering of the eleventh to thirteenth centuries, education remained in essence a luxury for most of the population. Not only laborers, but many of the nobility and even some of the clergy never learned to read, although the widespread practice of reading or reciting aloud—both secular and religious works—and of course the experience of hearing sermons meant that those who could not read were not cut off from literate culture. Our own inevitable focus on the written sources that survive should not blind us to the ways in which those who could not themselves read or write still had considerable access to the great narratives and images of their culture.

THE ENGLISH MONARCHY

The religious and cultural energy of the thirteenth century in England was not particularly reflected in its monarchs; the period's important political developments tended to arise, as we have seen in the case of John and Magna Carta, from limitations on the king's power rather than, as with William the Conqueror or Henry II, his exercise of that power. The reign of John's son Henry III (1216–72) was long but not particularly

successful; he came to the throne as a child and by the end of his reign his son held effective power. Under his rule the monarchy lost ground to both external and internal forces. The French dauphin Louis controlled the southern part of England upon Henry's accession, but was expelled in 1217; later in the century, however, Henry had to sell most of his French possessions to pay war debts, and the English barons continually challenged the king's authority, culminating in his effective deposition in 1264–65 by the forces led by the baron Simon de Montfort, who as regent convened a kind of proto-Parliament. Simon's death in 1265 at the hands of Henry's troops made him a martyr to many of the English, and both praise-poems and laments in his honor survive from the period. The most significant legacy of the barons' increased power was the consolidation of the principle of the king's limited rulership and the idea that the people of the realm (primarily the nobility) should take some part in its governance. The losses of French territory had contributed to a growing tendency for the ruling inhabitants of England to regard themselves as *English* (rather than Norman, Angevin, French, and so on); the broader participation in government in the course of the century may have solidified this tendency. By the early fourteenth century, language could be seen as a unifying force in the nation: "both the learned and unlearned man who were born in England can understand English," asserts one commentator of the period.

Henry's son Edward I, a much more successful ruler than his father, managed to mend the relationship between monarchy and people, in part by strengthening administrative structures related to law (Chancery), finances (the Exchequer), and governance (the Council); in this he built on the legacy of Henry II and the achievements of the baronial challenge, and the meetings of his Council were the first to bear the name of Parliaments. He also conquered Wales, which never fully regained its independence, although resistance to English rule continued. Like other English monarchs, however, he was unable to gain much control over Ireland, and despite diplomatic and military attempts, he never managed to conquer Scotland, which remained officially independent of England until the eighteenth century. A significant outcome of the ongoing English-

Scots conflict was the growth of a sense of national identity among the Scots at least as marked as that among the English; we see this in the declaration of Arbroath (1320), sent to the pope by the nobles of Scotland as a group, in which they declared that they were speaking for "the community of the realm" and that "for so long as one hundred men remain alive, we shall never under any conditions submit to the domination of the English." Edward's attempts to subdue Scotland demonstrated once more the political usefulness of legendary history: in putting forward the English claim on Scottish territory, he made reference to the historical assertions of Layamon's *Brut*, the Middle-English translation of the legends gathered in Geoffrey of Monmouth's *History of the Kings of Britain*.

The strong, if sometimes brutal, kingship of Edward I contrasts sharply with the troubled rule of his son Edward II (r. 1307–27), who was frequently at odds with his nobles and eventually was deposed by his French queen, Isabella, and her lover, Roger Mortimer, an English baron. Edward was succeeded by his son Edward III (r. 1327–77), whose long reign provided a certain stability but involved considerable losses for England. Edward III forcefully reasserted his claims to French territory through his French mother, and began the long-lasting conflict that came to be known as the Hundred Years' War (1337–1453). This conflict displayed the ongoing contradictoriness of medieval English attitudes toward France: Edward's embrace of a French-derived chivalric culture and claim to the French throne tended to link the nobility of both countries, who exchanged hostages and diplomatic missions, while at the same time the battles provided a focus for anti-French sentiment (which went back to the Norman Conquest) and for renewed claims for English as a valued national language. This was not, of course, a sudden development; already in the thirteenth century a writer could assert that "common men know no French, among a hundred scarcely one," and similar claims become increasingly common in the fourteenth century. Despite considerable early success in the war, meanwhile, England's French holdings dwindled almost to nothing by the time of Edward III's death, and his continuing demand for funds to pursue his military projects put considerable strain on the economy, already weakened by the northern European famine of 1315–18.

Even more significant than the famine was the great plague of 1348–49, the "Black Death," which had a lasting impact on the demography, the economy, and ultimately the culture of Britain and of Europe more generally. It is believed that roughly one-third of western Europe's population died in the plague, though not evenly across all areas; the population of London is estimated to have fallen by almost half, from perhaps 70,000 to about 40,000. In the wake of the plague, there was—not surprisingly—a severe labor shortage; this facilitated a certain amount of social mobility as people were able to take higher-paying work, and the countryside suffered further depopulation as laborers left for the towns. Some employers competed for scarce labor by improving wages or conditions of labor, but the Statute of Laborers of 1351 officially restricted both wages and labor mobility; it became a cause of long-standing friction between the working population of England and its large landholders. Some of that tension found violent expression early in the reign of Edward's successor, his grandson Richard II (r. 1377–99), who inherited the throne at the age of only ten. (His father, the Black Prince, had died in 1376.) Severe taxation and limits on wages imposed in the wake of the Black Death caused considerable distress among the general populace, and helped to spark the Rising of 1381 (at which time the kingdom was still under the regency of John of Gaunt, Richard's uncle), in which groups from all over the country challenged the legislative and fiscal policies of the nobility, although they declared their allegiance to King Richard. While this uprising was easily quelled, it was a tremendous shock to the political and cultural establishment and foreshadowed the struggles for legitimacy that continued throughout the early fifteenth century; it also left behind an unusually rich record of non-nobles' views on the political economy of their day. The general unrest, exacerbated by Richard's autocratic style and struggles with his nobles for control of the country, made the last quarter of the fourteenth century a politically fragile time in England. The king's preference for his own favorites over other, more powerful lords led these "Lords Appellant," as they called themselves, to challenge his authority. Eventually, they succeeded in severely circumscribing his power—and, in 1388, in executing several of his closest advisors. A major source of the conflict between these lords and the king was Richard's desire to make peace with France; the king did eventually succeed in instituting a truce in 1396 through his marriage to the French princess Isabella (his beloved first wife, Anne of Bohemia, had died in 1394). In his later years he regained much of his control, in part through the help of his uncle John of Gaunt, but became increasingly despotic and took harsh revenge on the lords who had threatened his power. The contest culminated in the usurpation of the throne in 1399 by the Lancastrian Henry Bolingbroke (Henry IV), who had earlier been banished from the kingdom; Henry took advantage of Richard's absence in Ireland, where he was continuing his fruitless efforts to bring it under English control. Richard was later murdered in prison, echoing the fate of his deposed great-grandfather, Edward II.

CULTURAL EXPRESSION IN THE FOURTEENTH CENTURY

Richard's rulership may not have been a great success, but he is known, like Henry II, for his deep interest in artistic and cultural production and for the extraordinary literary output that took place during his reign—output that was, unlike that of Henry's reign, as likely to be in English as in French. The writers of the period, some of the best-known figures of medieval English literature, include John Gower, Geoffrey Chaucer, the *Gawain*-poet, and William Langland; because they all thrived under Richard II they are sometimes referred to as the "Ricardian poets." Despite their contemporaneity, however, their writings by no means reflect a unified literary culture. There are certainly overlaps and, in the case of Chaucer and Gower, even mutual references between some of their works, but the main thing they have in common apart from historical era is that they all wrote in English. As this overview has tried to suggest, this in itself is a striking fact; only at the end of the fourteenth century do we begin to see the major works of later-medieval English literature participating, often deliberately, in the project of making English a literary language considered worthy of taking its place alongside Latin and the illustrious continental vernaculars, particularly French and Italian, and of being accorded a position of renewed prominence and respect in its native country after a perceived period of neglect. At the same time, these authors were anything but removed from non-English influences. Gower composed works in Latin and French as well as English; Chaucer translated French and Italian works, and borrowings from continental and Latin traditions shape all his poetry; Langland's *Piers Plowman* contains numerous lines in Latin and is strongly influenced by monastic Latin literary forms, while in its use of personification allegory it echoes a popular pan-European mode (also seen in the hugely influential French *Romance of the Rose*); in *Sir Gawain and the Green Knight*, the legendary history of Arthur is blended with borrowings from Celtic sources and Christian chivalric culture.

This brings us to an important point about medieval writers—one that applies to almost all of them, but that is usefully demonstrated by the Ricardian poets: they did not regard originality in the modern sense as an essential component of a literary work's value. While a medieval poet or preacher or chronicler certainly aimed to tell their story or convey their message in the best possible way, he or she would willingly draw on, combine, borrow from, translate, and rewrite the work of previous authors or storytellers. (The same could, of course, be said of Shakespeare.) Indeed, a link to authoritative sources—which could be written or oral—is often a crucial component of a medieval composition's own claims to authority. The increasing availability of Latin works, through preaching or written translation into the vernacular, or French ones, through performance or translation into English, along with Welsh, Breton, and Irish story material and works in other continental vernaculars, thus provided a rich trove from which Middle English authors constructed their writings.

The tendency of the "big four" Ricardian poets to attract so much attention can overshadow their debts to, and continuity with, the century that preceded them. *Sir Gawain* is part of a substantial tradition of Middle English romance—Arthurian and other—that includes *Sir Orfeo*, *Sir Launfal*, and the *Alliterative* and *Stanzaic Morte Arthure*, among many others. These vary in form but show the tendency of romance, too, to draw on a wide range of traditions for its subject matter. The lay *Sir Orfeo*, for example, reworks the story of Orpheus and Eurydice into a form with both Celtic and chivalric aspects: the classical underworld of Hades becomes a fairy land ruled by a powerful lord. The *Alliterative* and the *Stanzaic Morte Arthure*, meanwhile, each recount the fall of Arthur's kingdom, but with very different emphases—the *Alliterative Morte* sees imperial ambition and family treachery as essential elements, while the *Stanzaic* focuses on the adulterous love of Lancelot and Guinevere and the clash of blood brotherhood with the fraternal ties of the Round Table. Chaucer mocks traditional romance forms in his parodic *Tale of Sir Thopas* from *The Canterbury Tales*, and was all too aware of the challenges posed to idealized chivalry by the military realities of the fourteenth century. But as a member of the royal court, he could appreciate the virtues of what has rightly been called "the principal secular literature of entertainment" of the later Middle Ages and the appeal to an idealized past or a magic-laden landscape, the conflicts of loyalties or contests for love that characterize many romances and help to structure works as otherwise diverse as the *Franklin's*, *Wife of Bath's*, *Knight's*, and *Merchant's Tales*.

Religious belief and practice are another crucial context for much late fourteenth-century writing. Early in the century, the poet and canon Robert Mannyng (fl. 1288–1338) translated a handbook on basic Christian teachings from Anglo-Norman to English, titling it *Handlyng Synne* (1303) and illustrating it lavishly with *exempla*. There was a growing audience for such spiritual "self-help" works in the English vernacular, and it has been suggested that *Handlyng Synne* also influenced many later works, including Gower's *Confessio Amantis*, Chaucer's *The Canterbury Tales*, and Langland's *Piers Plowman*. Whether or not Mannyng's work formed part of their background, the authors were all able to draw on extensive knowledge of biblical material and Christian history, as well as on the wealth of exemplary narratives that characterized many works designed for religious instruction in the vernacular.

The late fourteenth century also sees the first records of the biblical drama of late-medieval England. Though little is certain regarding the origins of such drama, we do know that in the late fourteenth century substantial groups of plays presenting biblical subject matter began to be performed in several English towns, often in conjunction with festival days of late spring or summer such as Whitsun ("White Sunday"), or Pentecost (the seventh Sunday after Easter), and the Feast of Corpus Christi (a celebration of the Eucharist, held eleven days later); such plays continued to be performed until their suppression in the late sixteenth century. We know too that the presentation of the plays (which have variously been termed "miracle plays," "mystery plays," and "cycle plays"—designations that are all problematic in one way or another as blanket terms) varied. The texts that survive from the northern towns of York and Chester consist of more-or-less unified sequences of short plays—often called "pageants," like the wagons in which they were performed—that present the full sweep of biblical history. The sequence of plays from Coventry is in some respects similar, but includes only New Testament material. Two much more disparate manuscript collections of plays also exist; these are known as "the N-Town plays" and "the Towneley plays." No firm evidence suggests that either group of plays was ever performed as a sequence—or, indeed, that there was ever any intention to perform the collected plays as a sequence. The N-Town collection contains what was once a separate play on the childhood of Mary as well as a two-part Passion play. The Towneley collection is of particular interest for a small group of remarkable plays traditionally ascribed to the "Wakefield Master." (Three of these plays contain textual allusions to the area of Wakefield.)

Individual biblical plays, particularly in the northern sequences, were generally produced by particular craft guilds, representing a large outlay of time and money; in addition to providing religious instruction and entertainment, the plays reflected and emphasized the guilds' central importance to civic life at this time, as well as the growth of lay power in the governance of many towns. But production of biblical drama was not restricted to annual guild-sponsored performances in towns; some plays were produced by local parishes and some plays were performed in the halls of great houses, often by troupes of traveling players.

The scope of late-medieval English drama is similarly diverse. The body of surviving religious drama deriving from some other areas, such as East Anglia, includes not only biblical plays but also a large number of plays depicting the lives of saints or the performance of miracles. Passion plays and Christmas plays were also frequently performed in the late-medieval period, as were interludes (typically short comic sketches, intended for performance at court); mummings (dumb shows with masked performers); folk plays (featuring music and dance as well as dialogue, typically depicting the death and revival of a legendary hero); and Robin Hood plays.

A fifteenth- and sixteenth-century form that has attracted particular interest is the genre conventionally referred to as the "morality play." Plays in this genre (such as *Mankind* and *The Castle of Perseverance*) depict in allegorical form the struggles of a universal human figure; vices and virtues are personified as characters and participate fully in the action of the play. Morality plays were clearly intended to encourage devout individuals to consider their own moral position and to maintain a keen awareness of the state of their souls. But morality plays could also offer a broad range of entertainment—as the humor and energy of *Mankind* amply demonstrate.

The continuing growth of lay participation in spiritual matters that we see reflected in a work such as *Handlyng Synne* or in the biblical dramas became, in other contexts, one of the most contentious issues in fourteenth- and fifteenth-century England. The critiques of the clergy, and particularly of monks and friars, that had accompanied ecclesiastical reform movements from the tenth century onward were strongly endorsed in the works of the Oxford theologian John Wyclif (c. 1324–84). In the course of a long and influential writing career, he attacked the church for its enormous wealth and criticized clerics for their moral failings, questioned the doctrine of transubstantiation, and moved toward a view that all laypeople should have direct access to the Bible and could communicate directly with God, needing no priestly intermediation (although he was in many cases sympathetic to parish priests). His views, some of which were declared heretical by the Archbishop of Canterbury's council in 1382, were nonetheless widely shared, including by some of the nobility at Richard II's court. Wyclif provided much of the intellectual foundation for the

English sect known as Wycliffites or Lollards, and had an enormous influence on the religious, literary, and political culture of late-medieval England. Many of the issues that aroused his wrath are addressed also in Langland's *Piers Plowman*, a text highly critical of clerical and ecclesiastical shortcomings (though unlike the writings of Wyclif and his followers it was not generally regarded as heretical).

Yet another aspect of fourteenth-century spirituality is evident in the *Showings* of the anchoress Julian of Norwich, one of the most important visionary texts of the Middle Ages. Julian's theologically complex and deeply learned account of her experience forms part of both a long tradition of women's visionary literature in medieval Europe (going back at least to the twelfth-century German abbess Hildegard of Bingen) and a flowering of vernacular religious writing in late fourteenth-century England that also includes authors such as Richard Rolle and Walter Hilton. To set Julian's image of the created world as a hazelnut in the palm of God's hand alongside *Sir Gawain and the Green Knight*'s richly detailed hunting scenes or the mysterious John Mandeville's accounts of satyrs, the phoenix, and the exotic kingdoms of the East is to be reminded of the enormous diversity of the literature of late-medieval England. As we noted at the beginning of this introduction, moreover, medieval manuscripts would in many cases have kept this diversity immediately present to readers, recording texts of very different genres alongside one another: saints' lives with confessional manuals, fabliaux with satirical poetry, romances with recipes. Such compilations are reflected in miniature, as it were, by "compilation poems" like *The Canterbury Tales*, which place stories from varied genres and traditions within a unifying frame, or *Piers Plowman*, which blends social critique, personification allegory, and anti-clerical satire into a visionary autobiography.

FIFTEENTH-CENTURY TRANSITIONS

Writers in fifteenth-century England were deeply aware of the rich and authoritative literary tradition that immediately preceded them, drawing on and praising the works of their predecessors even as they devised a distinctive tradition of their own. In political and religious terms as well, the fifteenth century was not immune to the turmoil of the late fourteenth, beginning with a crisis of royal authority as the "usurper" Henry IV tried to solidify his claims to the throne and to contain a major nationalist rebellion in Wales led by Owain Glyndwr (Owen Glendower). Religious legitimacy was also at issue, as ongoing Wycliffite (or Lollard) challenges to current church practices caused aggressive responses on the part of the ecclesiastical and secular hierarchies—most notably the royal decree *De heretico comburendo* of 1401, ordering that recalcitrants be burnt at the stake as heretics (the first institution of such punishment in England), and the famous *Constitutions* (1407–09) of Thomas Arundel, Archbishop of Canterbury, which declared that the making or owning of Bibles in English was forbidden and set strict limits on acceptable religious composition in the vernacular. William Thorpe's testimony during his trial for heresy before Archbishop Arundel (an excerpt from which appears in the website component of the anthology) demonstrates the depth of commitment and the high level of religious understanding that the Lollards brought to this struggle, which both sides regarded as a matter of eternal life and death as well as immediate political importance. The religious and political threats came together in the short-lived rebellion led by Sir John Oldcastle in 1413, in which he and other Londoners tried to depose the new King Henry V; the fact that Oldcastle had at this time already been convicted of heresy (as a Lollard) solidified the link many secular and church lords made between religious and worldly sedition. While Henry V's military success in France—most famously at the battle of Agincourt in 1415—and his strength as a ruler eased some of the strain, anxiety about the monarchy's legitimacy and about composition in the vernacular are evident in much of the literary production of the century.

One of the modes in which these anxieties were expressed was an outpouring of carefully orthodox religious literature in English, often in forms such as saints' lives, visionary narratives, or meditations on the life of the Virgin or on Christ's Passion. The great religious foundations of Henry V, Sheen Charterhouse and Syon Abbey, were important centers for both the dissemination of fourteenth-century writings and the creation of new works (many of which were translations from Latin or French); when Henry VI came to the throne after his father's early death, his own devout tendencies reinforced the link between the Lancastrian court and monastic spirituality. Religious devotion was far from limited to the elite, however; probably the most famous English text of the first half of the fifteenth century is the *Book of Margery Kempe*, composed by a laywoman as an account of her spiritual experiences, visions, pilgrimages, and trials for heresy. Margery's frequent conversations with divine and saintly personages show her to be simultaneously extraordinary in and typical of her time; fifteenth-century devotion, particularly in the vernacular, often emphasized emotional connection to and a sense of familiarity with the figures of salvation history.

The intense spirituality of figures such as Margery Kempe contrasts sharply in tone with many of the historical events of the later part of the century. The civil war between the Lancastrian and Yorkist factions—known to us as the Wars of the Roses from the two groups' emblems—pitted descendants of Edward III against one another as claimants to the throne. Begun under the weak kingship of Henry VI, who was deposed by the Yorkist faction in 1460, returned briefly to the throne in 1470, and was executed in 1471, the struggle went on until 1485 when Henry Tudor, a Lancastrian descendant (on his mother's side) of Edward III, defeated Richard III of the house of York and united the warring houses by marrying Elizabeth, daughter of the Yorkist king, Edward IV (r. 1461–70, 1471–83). Henry's direct descent, on his father's side, from the twelfth-century Welsh prince Rhys made his rulership the apparent fulfillment of longstanding Welsh prophecies that a Briton would rule England once more.

The chaos and disillusionment that attended the period of civil war echo through the *Morte Darthur* of Thomas Malory, who drew on Middle English and French works to create his massive cycle of Arthurian romances. This text, a kind of summation of the Arthurian obsessions of late-medieval England, became one of the first printed books in England when William Caxton published it in 1485. In his preface, Caxton—who gave Malory's work the title by which we know it—described the *Morte Darthur* as recounting "noble chivalry, courtesy, humanity, friendliness, hardiness, love, friendship, cowardice, murder, hate, virtue and sin," a catalogue whose ending echoes the often dark tone of Malory's work. The *Morte Darthur* seems to reflect and perhaps comment upon the decline of the chivalric world that Malory, a knight who apparently fought on both sides in the Wars of the Roses, would have known well, and its account of the competing loyalties that eventually destroy Arthur and his kingdom would surely have resonated with contemporary events.

The printing of Malory's work by Caxton was only one small piece of the latter's enormous output. Between about 1475 and his death in 1491, he published almost a hundred different works, many of them his own translations; the most famous of the latter is his *Golden Legend*, an English version of a monumentally influential thirteenth-century Latin compendium of saints' lives. He is probably best known, however, for his awareness of and influence on the canon of British literature; works by Chaucer, Lydgate, and Gower were among his most important productions, with Malory joining them not long after. His attention to the ever-growing market for vernacular literature and his admiration for the great authors of the past made his professional life one of the great shaping forces on the development of the British tradition, as well as, of course, the instrument of England's entry into the world of printed books.

Table of contents and woodcut illustration from *The Game and Play of Chesse*, printed by William Caxton (2nd edition, 1481).

Caxton's (numerous) early readers included members of the Paston family, a wealthy Norfolk clan. Their extensive surviving letters, which range in date from 1422 to 1529, deal not with legendary heroism or magical encounters, but with the minutiae of everyday life: bills, quarrels with neighbors, marriages, deaths, and political gossip. Like the Tudor dynasty, the civic dramas and the early print culture of England carry us forward into the sixteenth century, and offer a glimpse of the kinds of everyday events and concerns that formed the original contexts for all the works discussed here.

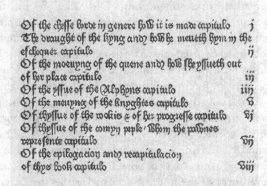

Advertisement issued by William Caxton (c. 1477).

Language and Prosody

Old English poetry differs in important ways from later English poetry. Whereas a modern poem can be written in any of a number of forms—sonnets, blank verse, ballad meter, free verse, and so on—all surviving Old English poetry is written in essentially the same meter and form. Lines in modern English metrical poetry are built out of a fixed number of feet, each of which has (in principle) the same sequence of stressed and unstressed syllables; in Old English poetry, apart from a small number of extended or hypermetric lines appearing irregularly throughout the corpus of surviving verse and a handful of isolated "half-lines" that may or may not be errors, every line consists of two half-lines, each containing (usually) two stressed syllables and a varying number of unstressed syllables. The two half-lines are linked by alliteration between one or both stressed syllables in the first half-line and the first stressed syllable of the second half-line. Alliteration and stress held together the lines of an Old English poem, as meter and rhyme hold together the lines of a Shakespearean sonnet; they were not decorative, as they are in modern poetry, but necessary structural elements.

The opening lines of the poem *Beowulf* illustrate this poetic structure:

Hwæt: We gardena   in geardagum
þeodcyninga   þrym gefrunon,
hu ða æþelingas   ellen fremedon!
Oft Scyld Scefing   sceaþena þreatum
monegum mægþum   meodosetla ofteah,
egsode eorl,   syððan ærest wearð
feasceaft funden.   He þæs frofre gebad,
weox under wolcnum,   weorðmyndum þah,
oð þæt him æghwylc   þara ymbsittendra
ofer hronrade   hyran scolde,
gomban gyldan.   Þæt wæs god cyning.
Ðæm eafera wæs   æfter cenned
geong in geardum,   þone God sende
folce to frofre.   Fyrenðearfe ongeat
þæt hie ær drugon   aldorlease
lange hwile.   Him þæs Liffrea,
wuldres wealdend,   woroldare forgeaf.
Beowulf wæs breme,   blæd wide sprang,
Scyldes eafera   Scedelandum in.
Swa sceal geong guma   gode gewyrcean,
fromum feohgiftum   on fæder bearme,
þæt hine on ylde   eft gewunigen
wilgesiþas,   þonne wig cume,
leode gelæsten.   Lofdædum sceal
in mægþa gehwære   man geþeon.

Most of this passage (to *fæder*, line 21) is on fol. 129r of the *Beowulf* manuscript. Old English script is relatively easy to read, though some letter forms are different from those of modern printed English (especially the round *d*, the open *g*, the long *f*, *r*, and *s*, the short *t*, the p-shaped *w* called *wynn*, and the *ae* ligature called *aesc* or "ash") and some letters have not survived (the crossed *d* called *eth* (ð) and the long *p*-shaped letter called *thorn* (þ), both of which represent the sound spelled *th* in Modern English). As with other surviving Old English poems, the scribe does not put each line of verse on its own line but writes straight across the page. Abbreviations in this text are rare, consisting mostly of a line over a final vowel to indicate that it is followed by the consonant *m* or *n* (e.g., *monegū* for the adjective *monegum*, "many," in line 5). Punctuation is much lighter than in Modern English, and the divisions between what modern linguists recognize as words is not always clear, so that the scribe combines a preposition with the word that follows it, and divides the two parts of a compound word to write *in geardagum* in line 1, or combines two short words to write *hu ða* in line 3.

Though many thousands of words have changed their shape, disappeared, or been added to the lexicon over the past millennium, Old English is still recognizably the ancestor of Modern English. The most common words have changed hardly at all: pronouns such as *we*, *he*, *him*, and *that* (though it is spelled *þæt* in Old English); prepositions such as *in*, *under*, and *over* (spelled *ofer*, but pronounced just like Modern English *over*); and adverbs such as *hu* (how) and *oft*. Many other words are either the same as Modern English words though spelled differently (*god* "good," *wæs* "was") or related to surviving words: *gearda-gum* is recognizable as "yore-days" (i.e., "days of yore"); *wolcnum*, an inflected plural form of the noun *wolcn*, survives as the archaic word "welkin" and still means "the heavens"; *funden* is the past participle of *findan*, which is the modern word "find"; *hyran* is the ancestor of modern "hear," though it means "obey" as well as "hear" in Old English. Some other words, however, especially those in the aristocratic or poetic register, vanished from the language soon after the arrival of the Normans—examples here include *æþelingas* "noblemen," *ellen* "brave (deeds)," *þrym* "glory," and *frofre* "consolation."

Other important differences between Old and Modern English are found in word order and inflection. A literal translation of these lines into Modern English clearly reveals this (words in parentheses are grammatical particles required in Modern English but expressed by inflectional endings in Old English):

What! We (of the) spear-Danes   in yore-days
of people's-kings   glory heard
how those noblemen   brave-deeds did!
Often Scyld Son-of-Sheaf   (of) enemies (from) troops
(from) many tribes   mead-benches took away
terrified (the) noblemen,   after first (he) was
penniless found.   He (for) that comfort awaited,
grew under (the) skies,   (in) honors prospered,
until (to) him each   (of those) surrounding-sitters
over (the) whale's-riding-place   to obey had to,
tribute pay.   That was (a) good king.
(To) that (one) (a) son was   afterwards born
young in (the) yards,   whom God sent
(the) people to comfort.   Severe-need (he) perceived
that they before endured   lord-less
(a) long while.   (To) him (for) that (the) Life-lord,
(of) glory (the) wielder,   world-honor gave.
Beowulf was famous,   fame widely sprang,
(of) Scyld (the) son   Scandinavian-lands in.
So shall (a) young man   good make-happen
(with) pious gifts   from (his) father's coffers,
so that him in old-age   afterwards might support
willing-companions,   when war (should) come,
the people (might) support. (With) praise-deeds shall
in tribes each one   (a) man prosper.

If we compare this literal rendering to the translation below, we can see that Old English tended to place verbs after direct objects and at the ends of clauses, while Modern English requires a fairly strict subject-verb-object order:

Listen!
We have heard of the glory in bygone days
of the folk-kings of the spear-Danes,
how those noble lords did lofty deeds.
Often Scyld Scefing seized the mead-benches
from many tribes, troops of enemies,
struck fear into earls. Though he first was
found a waif, he awaited solace for that—
he grew under heaven and prospered in honor
until every one of the encircling nations
over the whale's-riding had to obey him,
grant him tribute. That was a good king!
A boy was later born to him,
young in the courts, whom God sent
as a solace to the people—He saw their need,
the dire distress they had endured, lordless,
for such a long time. The Lord of Life,
Wielder of Glory, gave him worldly honor;
Beowulf, the son of Scyld, was renowned,
his fame spread far and wide in Scandinavian lands.
Thus should a young man bring about good
with pious gifts from his father's possessions,
so that later in life loyal comrades
will stand beside him when war comes,
the people will support him—with praiseworthy deeds
a man will prosper among any people.

Old English, then, expresses most grammatical relationships by inflection, while Modern English requires grammatical particles such as prepositions and definite articles. Sentence elements could be multiplied without explicit connections such as "and" or "or": *gardena* and *þeodcyninga* in lines 1–2 are both plural possessives modifying *þrym*, and the whole phrase means something like "the glory of the spear-Danes (who were) the kings of the people"; *sceaþena þreatum* and *monegum mægþum* in lines 4–5 are both plural datives modifying the verb *ofteah*, so the phrase means "took away from troops of enemies (who were) from many tribes." The sentence beginning *He þæs frofre* on line 7 has three verbs, *gebad*, *weox*, and *þah*; it can be translated "He awaited consolation for that (as he) grew under the heavens (and) prospered in honors"—even though the three verbs are in one sense a temporal series (first he waited, then he grew, and finally he prospered), they are (more importantly) three variations of one idea (the consolation, the growing, and the prospering are all the same thing). As this example suggests, Old English poetry can be considerably more compressed than a modern translation, and its unlinked chains of multiple statements often require the reader's time and consideration to unfold their full meaning.

The borrowings of French words into the English vocabulary are many, and generally seem to have been culturally motivated; thus, English borrows words for government (*peace, justice, court, judge, sentence*—though *gallows* is an English word) and culture (*noble, dame, gentle, honor, courtesy, polite, manners*). One effect of all this borrowing is that English has a great flexibility in its synonyms; we can express things in several different ways using words from different origins: we can *ask* or *question* someone, and get an *answer* or a *response*, which may make us *glad* or *pleased*, or it may make us *mad* or *angry*, and lead to a *fight* or *dispute* (or even an *altercation*). Often the English and French words for the same thing have come to differ in meaning: it has long been observed, for example, that animals used for meat are called by their English names when they are in the field—*cow, calf, pig, sheep, deer*—and by their French names on the table—*beef, veal, pork, mutton, venison*. This linguistic development reflects the social situation of post-Conquest England, in which the lower-class English raised the animals and the upper-class French ate them; it may also have something to do with the superiority of French over English cooking, which was recognized even a thousand years ago.

Alongside this generous borrowing of vocabulary and literary forms, one of the most important changes in Middle English was the wearing-away of the complex inflectional system of Old English, which had already begun to disappear by the end of the tenth century in some dialects, and the concomitant fixing of word order into something more like its modern form. Another was the representation of many different regional dialects in written Middle English; Old English had regional varieties, but by far the majority of surviving manuscripts are written in some approximation of the standard West Saxon of the late tenth century. In the absence of a strong educational system teaching a standard for English spelling, regional dialects were much more fully represented in written Middle English. The differences between Old and Middle English can be seen in the following three passages, each translating the opening verses of Psalm 23. The first is from the Old English "Paris Psalter" of the ninth century. The second is from the Wycliffite translation of the Bible in the later fourteenth century. The third shows the same verses from the modern Douay-Rheims Bible, also translated from the Latin Vulgate:

> Drihten me ræt, ne byð me nanes godes wan, and he me geset on swyðe good feohland. And fedde me be wætera staðum, and min mod gehwyrfde of unrotnesse on gefean. He me gelædde ofer þa wegas rihtwisnesse, for his naman.

> The Lord gouerneth me, and no thing schal faile to me; in the place of pasture there he hath set me. He nurschide me on the watir of refreischyng; he conuertide my soule. He ledde me forth on the pathis of rigtfulnesse; for his name.

> The LORD ruleth me; and I shall want nothing. He hath set me in a place of pasture: he hath brought me up, on the water of refreshment. He hath converted my soul. He hath led me on the paths of justice, for his own name's sake.

Even in these few lines the differences between Old and Middle English are notable: considerable developments in vocabulary (*Drihten > Lord, ræt > gouerneth, feohland > the place of pasture, mod > soule, gehwyrfde > conuertide, wegas > pathis*), changes in word order (*Drihten me ræt > The Lord gouerneth me, he me geset > he hath set me, min mod gehwyrfde > he conuertide my soule*), and the erosion of inflectional endings (*be wætera staðum > on the watir of refreischyng, for his naman > for his name*) all indicate the movement of English toward its present state. The Middle English passage is nearly identical to the early Modern English of the Douay-Rheims version. To understand something of the dialect diversity in written Middle English, however, one should compare the Wycliffite version to the same passage in two other

Middle English texts, the *West Midlands Psalter* and the Yorkshire version of Richard Rolle, both written around the middle of the fourteenth century:

> (*West Midlands Psalter*) Our Lord gouerneþ me, and noþyng shal defailen to me; in þe stede of pasture he sett me þer. He norissed me vp water of fyllyng; he turned my soule fram þe fende. He lad me vp þe bistiges of rigtfulnes for his name.

> (*Richard Rolle Psalter*) Lord gouerns me and naþyng sall me want; in sted of pasture þare he me sett. On þe watere of rehetynge forþ he me broght; my saule he turnyd. He led me on þe stretis of rightwisnes; for his name.

By the end of the thirteenth century English began to appear once again as a language of official documents and public occasions. In 1337 a lawyer addressed the Parliament in English for the first time, as a chronicle says, "so that he might be better understood by all"; in 1362 Parliament ordered all lawsuits to be conducted in English. There is some indication that at the beginning of the fourteenth century the nobility had to be taught French—the language still held prestige, but it was by no means the native tongue of those born on English soil. Not surprisingly, it is in the same period, the fourteenth century, that English literary output becomes significant again. But the language that emerged had been strongly altered by two centuries of "underground" existence and the shaping pressure from the dominant French language and literary culture. It is thought that the use of alliterative verse in the Old English style may have persisted through the twelfth and thirteenth centuries, though evidence of this is scarce and ambiguous. In the fourteenth century alliterative verse reappears in written form throughout much of England, and is used for subjects as varied as Arthurian legendary history (the *Alliterative Morte Arthure*), Christian dream vision (*Pearl*), and satiric commentary (Langland's *Piers Plowman*), among others. Rhymed, metrical, non-alliterative poetry such as that of Chaucer and Gower was largely inspired by French traditions.

The literary flowering of the second half of the fourteenth century was by no means restricted to one region. Chaucer wrote in the dialect of London and the east Midlands which, more than any other, is the ancestor of Modern English; the author of *Sir Gawain and the Green Knight*, on the other hand, wrote in a dialect of the northwest Midlands. As Chaucer himself put it, there was great "diversitee in English and in writing of our tonge." With the coming of the printing press in the fifteenth century, the printed language began to take on more and more common characteristics, though it would be not until the late eighteenth and early nineteenth centuries that grammar, spelling, and punctuation were standardized.

In reading Old and Middle English (in whatever dialect) it is important to be aware of the major ways in which the language differs from our own. For any historical period of English the reconstruction of pronunciation is only approximate, but a careful study of sound changes, spelling, cognate languages, and word histories allows scholars to make highly educated guesses about the way Old and Middle English sounded. Old English used some letters not found in the Latin alphabet, including *thorn* (þ), *eth* (ð), and *yogh* (ȝ); the first two survived into Middle English, where þ gradually came to be written much like the letter *y* (giving rise to the common misreading of "ye" for "the" in faux-antique signs like "ye olde shoppe"). Some Old English consonant clusters were pronounced in unusual ways; *sc* was pronounced like *sh* and *cg* like *dg*, so that Old English *scip* and *ecg* sounded much like their modern descendants *ship* and *edge*. The consonants *c* and *g* were pronounced differently depending on their position in a word; the Old English words *gold* and *camb* were pronounced much as in Modern English *gold* and *comb*, but *geat* was pronounced with a *y* as if it were roughly *yat*, and *ciric* was pronounced with *ch* sounds as in its modern descendant *church*.

One way in which Old and Middle English are dramatically different from Modern English is in sounding all consonants, including those in combinations such as *kn*, *gn*, *lk*, and *wr* that have become largely or entirely silent in Modern English. The word "knight," for example, is pronounced something like "k-ni*cht*" (with the *i* short). Final unstressed *e* in words is always sounded in Old English, and sounded far more frequently in Middle English than is the case in Modern English—though during the late-medieval period the sounding of the final *e* was beginning to die out, and scholars continue to dispute how frequently the final *e* should be sounded in Chaucerian English. Vowels are pronounced roughly as in French or Spanish—the Modern English values are the result of a "Great Vowel Shift" that began in the fifteenth century. The long *a* in words such as "made," for example, was pronounced like the *a* in "father"; the long *e* in words such as "sweete" was sounded like the *a* in "mate"; the long *i* (or *y*) in words such as "lif" and "myn" was pronounced in the same way we sound the *i* in "machine"; the long *o* in words such as "do" and "spoon" was sounded as we pronounce the *o* in "note"; and the long *u* (or *ou* or *ow*) in words such as "flowr" was sounded as we would pronounce the *oo* in "boot."

While Middle English is far less inflected than Old English, meaning that fewer grammatical differences are signaled in the form of words, matters are, as noted above, complicated by dialect. Third person singular formations of verbs, for example, tend to end in -*s* or -*ys* in northern dialects, and in -*th* or -*ith* (later -*eth*) in southern dialects. "She has" is thus a form deriving from northern Middle English dialects, and "she hath" from southern English forms (cf. Richard Rolle's "Lord gouerns me" where the Wycliffite version has "The Lord gouerneth me"). When the sheep thief Mak in *The*

Second Shepherds' Play pretends to be from southern England he says "ich be" instead of "I am" as northerners then (and all English speakers nowadays) would say. Word order in Middle English is often substantially different from modern practice, with the verb often coming later in the sentence than is our custom in statements, but coming at the beginning of the sentence in questions, as is the practice in many Romance languages. Many Middle English words are of course unfamiliar to the modern reader, but there are also many "false friends"—words that look identical or very similar to Modern English words but carry significantly different denotations. *Lewd*, which in Old English means "secular, not relating to the clergy," evolved in Middle English to mean "unlearned," but without any suggestion of a sexual character. *Sely*, though the ancestor of the modern "silly," can mean "poor," "miserable," or "innocent" as well as "strange" or "foolish." Even at the level of a single word, one might say, we can see the peculiar and provocative mixture of strangeness and familiarity, the haunting family resemblances and the disconcerting dissonances, that make the study of medieval literary culture so compelling and rewarding. We hope that in this collection of works you will come to know its powerful appeal.

History of the Language
and of Print and Manuscript Culture

In an effort to provide for readers a direct sense of the development of the language and of print culture, examples of texts in their original form have been provided in each volume. A list of these within the present volume appears below.

(An overview of developments in the history of language during this period appears on pages 29–33.)

The Dream of the Rood, lines 1–21 of the Vercelli Book: p. 61.

Beowulf, lines 1–21: p. 64.

Lindisfarne Gospels, pages from the Gospel of St. Luke: p. 3, 4; CHI-RHO, color insert.

Book of Kells, opening page from the Gospel of St. Matthew: front cover; page from the Gospel of St. Mark: p. 8.

"Sumer is icumen in," Harley Manuscript 978: p. 128.

Sir Orfeo, lines 417–34: p. 154–56.

Sir Gawayn and the Grene Knyght, illustrations from the original manuscript: p. 228.

The Game and Play of Chesse, printed by William Caxton, Table of Contents and illustration: p. 29.

Chaucer, *The Canterbury Tales*, pages from the Ellesmere Manuscript: p. 230, 235, 252–53, 286, 299, (and color insert) 320–21, 333–34.

Decorative pages, various gospels: p. 382–84.

Lambeth Bible, illuminated page showing the Virgin Mary: p. 387.

The Wakefield Master, *The Second Shepherds' Play*, opening page: p. 417.

Everyman, title page (www.broadviewpress.com/babl)

Malory, *Morte Darthur*: passage in original spelling and punctuation: p. 453–54; illustrations from William Caxton's 1498 edition: p. 464.

BEDE
c. 673 – 735

Bede "the Venerable," the most learned writer of the Anglo-Saxon period, was born in North-umbria around 673. At the age of seven he entered the twin monastery of Wearmouth-Jarrow and remained there, except for a few short excursions, until his death. Under the Abbot Ceolfrith, Bede received a thorough education in grammar, rhetoric, mathematics, music, natural science and the study of Scripture; he was ordained a deacon at 19 and a priest at 30. In a brief autobiographical note appended to his *Ecclesiastical History* he describes himself in this manner: "Amid the observance of the discipline of the Rule [of St. Benedict] and the daily task of singing in the church, it has always been my delight to learn or to teach or to write." Over the course of his life Bede produced a body of writing that remains impressive for its clarity, intelligence, range and devotion. His works, which survive in hundreds of manuscripts, were deeply influential and widely copied throughout the Middle Ages. Apart from a brief and enigmatic Old English poem and a lost translation of the Gospel of John he is said to have composed on his deathbed, all Bede's works were written in Latin, then the international language of scholarship and of the Church.

The founder of Jarrow monastery, Benedict Biscop, had traveled extensively and assembled an impressive library; during Bede's lifetime this remote outpost on the northeastern coast of England—founded about the year Bede was born, and scarcely 50 years after the rulers of Northumbria had converted to Christianity—was perhaps the most learned monastic center in all of Europe. Bede's writings include numerous works of Scriptural commentary, many homilies, works on meter and orthography, lives of several saints, books of poetry and hymns, and several treatises on cosmology and timekeeping. He was deeply interested in time and its measurement, a matter of some urgency in his lifetime because the Irish and Roman churches had different methods for calculating the date of Easter. In some years the two churches celebrated the feast on different days, which to Bede was a shocking sign of disunity. In his works promoting the Roman method of reckoning Easter he also helped establish the foundations of medieval astronomy and chronology; Bede is primarily responsible for popularizing the western "BC" and "AD" system of reckoning dates using the *anno domini* or "year of (the birth of) our Lord" as the dividing principle.

It is Bede's historical works, however, that are best known today. His *Historia Ecclesiastica Gentis Anglorum* (*Ecclesiastical History of the English People*), completed in 731, is an extensive history of England which takes as its theme the conversion of the Anglo-Saxon invaders who had displaced the native Britons. The *Ecclesiastical History* imagines an "English" people united not so much by culture or language or geography as by faith, the Roman Christianity brought to the island by Augustine of Canterbury and other missionaries sent by Pope Gregory the Great in 597. This work still provides the foundation for much of our knowledge of England in the fourth, fifth, and sixth centuries. Bede's talent as a historian was his ability to take multiple sources—documents, other histories, local oral traditions and legends—and weave them together into a coherent narrative. Though Bede was not fully a historian in the modern sense, his approach is far less foreign to the modern historical sensibility than that of most medieval chroniclers; unlike many writers of the time, for example, he makes frequent reference to the sources for the material he is recounting. In Bede's narrative, written very much from the Northumbrian point of view, the English are gradually and inevitably brought into the happy embrace of the Roman church, triumphing against the bitterness and treachery of the native Britons, the well-meaning but deluded zeal of the Irish missionaries, and the temporizing and backsliding of one pagan king after another. It is a tribute to Bede's great literary talent that in many ways the story he constructs from whatever meager evidence was available to him is still regarded as a fundamentally accurate account.

The following selections give some of the flavor of Bede's work: a geographical prologue describing the island of Britain; a lively narrative of the coming of the Angles and Saxons derived largely from the early sixth-century Briton Gildas's *De excidio Britonum* ("On The Ruin of Britain"), a passionate work of moral exhortation written from a stridently anti-English perspective; a detailed psychological portrait of the Northumbrian king Edwin's slow movement towards conversion; and an account of two remarkable figures from the monastery of Whitby, the abbess Hild and the lay brother Cædmon. Cædmon's story is far more widely read today. According to Bede, Cædmon receives a miraculous talent for poetic composition and becomes a great composer of religious verse; Cædmon's *Hymn* (which Bede records in Latin, not English) is sometimes treated as the first English Christian poetic work. Bede's account of the life and miracles of the abbess Hild, however, plays a role of equal importance in his larger history; it is included here to suggest that the paired lives of a learned aristocratic woman and an illiterate peasant can tell us a great deal about the boundaries of Bede's narrative and the kinds of material it excludes, about the relationship between history and hagiography, and about the ways in which the cultural roles prescribed by one's gender and class affect the shape of one's spiritual journey.

⌘ ⌘ ⌘

from *Ecclesiastical History of the English People*[1]

1. A DESCRIPTION OF THE ISLAND OF BRITAIN AND ITS INHABITANTS (I.1)

Britain, an island in the ocean, formerly called Albion, is situated in the northwest, opposite the coasts of Germany, France, and Spain, which form the greatest part of Europe, though at a considerable distance from them. It extends 800 miles to the north and is 200 miles broad, except where several promontories extend further in breadth, which makes the circuit of its coastline 3600 miles. To the south lies Belgic Gaul, from which the closest port for travelers is the city of *Rutubi Portus*, corrupted by the English into "Reptacestir."[2] The distance from there across the sea to *Gessoriacum*,[3] the closest point in the land of the Morini, is fifty miles, or as some writers say, 450 *stadia*. Behind the island, where it opens upon the boundless ocean, are the Orkney Islands.

Britain is rich in grain and trees, and is well adapted for feeding cattle and beasts of burden. It also produces vines in some places, and has plenty of land and waterfowls of various kinds; it is remarkable also for its rivers, abounding in fish, particularly salmon and eels, and plentiful springs. Seals and dolphins are frequently taken, and even whales; besides many sorts of shellfish

---

[1] *Ecclesiastical History of the English People*   The standard edition of the *Historia Ecclesiastica*, with a modern English translation, is Bertram Colgrave and R.A.B. Mynors, eds., *Bede's Ecclesiastical History of the English People* (Oxford, 1969). This translation, by R.M. Liuzza, relies heavily on that work, as well as the earlier work of L. Stevens (London: J.M. Dent; New York: E.P. Dutton, 1910) and J.M. Wallace-Hadrill's *Bede's Ecclesiastical History of the English People: A Historical Commentary* (Oxford: Clarendon Press, 1991).

[2] *Reptacestir*   Richborough.

[3] *Gessoriacum*   Boulogne.

such as mussels, in which are often found excellent pearls of all colors, red, purple, violet, and green, but mostly white. There is also a great abundance of cockles, from which a scarlet dye is made, a most beautiful color which never fades from the heat of the sun nor exposure to the rain; but the older it is, the more beautiful it becomes. Britain has salt springs and hot springs, and from them flow rivers which furnish hot baths, suitable for all ages and sexes, arranged for each separately. For water, as St. Basil says,[1] receives the quality of heat when it passes through certain metals, so that it becomes not only hot but scalding. Britain has also many veins of metals, copper, iron, lead, and silver; it produces much excellent jet, which is black and sparkling, burns in fire, and when heated drives away serpents; when it is warmed by rubbing it attracts whatever is applied to it, like amber. The island was once famous for its twenty-eight noble cities, besides innumerable castles which were all strongly secured with walls, towers, gates, and locks.

Because Britain lies almost under the North Pole, the nights are light in summer, so that at midnight it is difficult for those who are watching to tell whether the evening twilight still lingers, or the dawn of morning is coming, since the sun at night returns to the east through the northern regions without passing far below the horizon. For this reason the summer days are extremely long; on the other hand the winter nights are also of great length, namely eighteen hours, for the sun then withdraws into the regions of Africa. In summer too the nights are extraordinarily short, as are the days in winter, each containing only six equinoctial hours,[2] while in Armenia, Macedonia, Italy, and other countries in the same latitude, the longest day or night extends to fifteen hours, and the shortest to nine.

At the present time, there are five languages in Britain, the English, British,[3] Irish, Pictish, and Latin,
just as the divine law is written in five books, each in its own way devoted to seeking out and setting forth one and the same knowledge of sublime truth and true sublimity. The Latin tongue, through the study of the Scriptures, has become common to all the rest. At first this island had no other inhabitants than the Britons, from whom it derived its name, and who, coming over into Britain, so it is said, from Armorica,[4] took possession of the southern parts of it. When they had made themselves masters of the greatest part of the island, beginning from the south, it is said that the Pictish race from Scythia,[5] putting to sea in a few long ships, were driven by the winds beyond the shores of Britain and arrived on the northern coast of Ireland. There they found the Irish race and asked to be allowed to settle among them, but their request was refused. Ireland is the largest island next to Britain, and lies to the west of it; but though it is shorter than Britain to the north, yet it runs out far beyond it to the south, opposite to the northern parts of Spain, though a wide sea lies between them. The Picts came to this island, as has been said, by sea and asked that a place be granted them where they might settle. The Irish answered that the island could not hold them both; but they said, "We can give you some good advice as to what to do. We know of another island not far from ours, to the east, which we often see in the distance on a clear day. If you will go there, you can make settlements; but if anyone should oppose you, you shall have our help." And so the Picts, sailing over into Britain, began to occupy the northern parts of the island, because the Britons had seized the southern parts. Now the Picts had no wives, so they asked the Irish for some; they consented to give them women only on condition that, when any difficulty should arise, they should choose a king from the female line rather than the male; this custom, as is well known, has been observed among the Picts to this day. In the course of time Britain received a third nation in addition to the Britons and the Picts, namely the Irish, who came from Ireland under their leader Reuda,

---

[1] *St. Basil says*   In his *Hexaemeron*, a treatise on the six days of creation.

[2] *equinoctial hours*   As Bede explains in his *De temporum ratione* (*The Reckoning of Time*), these hours are those which divide the day evenly into twenty-four parts (i.e., like a modern day); "common" hours divide day and night into twelve hours each of uneven length, so that summer hours are long during the day and short at night, and winter hours are just the reverse.

[3] *British*   I.e., Welsh.

---

[4] *Armorica*   Area along the northwest coast of France somewhat larger than modern Brittany.

[5] *Scythia*   Irish tradition reports that the Picts come from Thrace; Bede may be following this here, or using "Scythia" to mean the farthest northern regions of the world, Ultima Thule.

Ornamental belt buckle (early 7th century CE) from the Sutton Hoo burial site. Twentieth century excavations at Sutton Hoo in southeast England uncovered a remarkable collection of artifacts from an Anglo-Saxon ship-burial. In addition to this buckle, 40 other gold objects were discovered in the burial mound, together with human remains, the bones of horses, weaponry, silverware, and the remains of large open ships.

CHI-RHO page from the Lindisfarne Gospels (c. 698 CE). See the introduction for a discussion of this page.

Nave, Durham Cathedral (1093–1133). One of the largest and most imposing of English cathedrals, Durham was built by Norman bishops over a remarkably short period. A shrine for Saint Cuthbert, it also houses the bones of the Venerable Bede.

"The Parable of the Sower" (detail), stained glass, Canterbury Cathedral (early 13th century). The extensive use of stained glass in church architecture began in the twelfth century; when Abbot Suger of Saint-Denis in France rebuilt sections of his church c. 1135. He commissioned stained glass windows, the light from which he believed would assist worshipers to raise themselves to "the purity of heaven."

Map of Britain (c. 1250), drawn by Matthew Paris for his history of England, *Historia Major*. As well as counties and major towns, Matthew identifies features such as Hadrian's Wall, noting that it "once divided the English and the Picts."

"Annunciation to the Shepherds," stained glass (later 14th century), Victoria and Albert Museum.

"Virgin and Child," stained glass (14th century), Eaton Bishop Church, Herefordshire.

"Sir James Berners," stained glass (later 14th century), St. Mary's Church, West Horseley, Surrey. This knight, who was beheaded in 1388, is shown here wearing armor typical of the period.

Opening page of the Prologue to *The Wife of Bath's Tale*, Ellesmere manuscript. (Reprinted by permission of *The Huntington Library, San Marino, California*. EL 26 C9 f. 72r.)

and won lands from the Picts either by fair means or by force of arms. They still possess these lands. They are to this day called *Dalreudini* after their commander—in their language, *Dal* signifies a part.

Ireland far surpasses Britain in breadth and in wholesomeness and serenity of climate, for the snow rarely lies there above three days. No man makes hay in the summer for winter use, or builds stables for his beasts of burden. No reptiles are found there, and no snake can live there; for although serpents have often been carried to Ireland from Britain, as soon as the ship comes near the shore and the scent of the air reaches them, they die. In fact almost everything in the island is good against poison. We have seen how, for example, when people have been bitten by serpents, the leaves of manuscripts from Ireland were scraped, and the scrapings put in water and given to them to drink. These scrapings immediately expelled the spreading poison, and eased the swelling. The island abounds in milk and honey, nor is there any lack of vines, fish, or fowl; and it is noted for deer and goats. It is properly the native land of the Irish; they migrated from there, as has been said, and formed the third nation in Britain in addition to the Britons and the Picts. There is a very wide arm of the sea, which originally divided the nation of the Picts from the Britons; it runs from the west very far into the land, where, to this day, stands the strong city of the Britons, called Alcluith.[1] The Irish settled on the north side of this bay and made their home there.

2. THE COMING OF THE ENGLISH TO BRITAIN

[After the Goths attack Rome in 410, the Roman legions in Britain withdraw, leaving the British defenseless, "utterly ignorant of the arts of war." They are immediately attacked by the Irish from the west and the Picts from the north. Bede's source for this section is the British historian Gildas, whose *De excidio Britonum* ("On the Ruin of Britain") is a stern and prophetic work upbraiding the British for their sins and lamenting the punishments they suffered at the hands of the Saxon invaders. Bede's allegiances are different, of course, but the harsh tone of Gildas's polemic, and his assertion that the

coming of the English was ordained by God, is put to good use in Bede's excoriation of the British (Bede's deep dislike of the British arose, ostensibly at least, from their refusal to convert their conquerors to Christianity).]

In the year of our Lord 423, Theodosius the younger became emperor after Honorius, the forty-fifth from Augustus, and governed the Roman empire twenty-six years. In the eighth year of his reign Palladius was sent by Celestinus, the Roman pontiff, to the Irish who believed in Christ, to be their first bishop.[2] In the twenty-third year of his reign Aetius, a man of high rank and a patrician, held his third consulship with Symmachus. The wretched remnants of the Britons sent him a letter which began: "To Aetius, thrice Consul, the groans of the Britons." In the course of the letter they expressed their sorrows: "The barbarians drive us to the sea; the sea drives us back to the barbarians: between them we face two sorts of death—we are either slaughtered or drowned." Yet all this could not procure any assistance from him, because he was engaged in a deadly war with Blædla and Attila, kings of the Huns. And even though Blædla had been murdered the year before this by the treachery of his brother Attila, nevertheless Attila himself remained so dangerous an enemy to the state that he devastated almost all of Europe, attacking and destroying cities and castles. At the same time there was a famine in Constantinople, which was followed shortly afterwards by the plague, and a great part of the walls of that city fell to the ground, along with fifty-seven towers. Many cities also fell into ruins, and the famine and pestilential stench which filled the air destroyed thousands of men and cattle.

Meanwhile this famine afflicted the Britons more and more, leaving a lasting memory of its malice to posterity. It forced many of them to submit themselves to their predatory enemies; others still held out, trusting in divine assistance when none was to be had from men. These continually made raids from the mountains, caves, and forests, and at last they began to inflict severe

[1] *Alcluith* Dumbarton.

[2] *Palladius was sent … bishop* Nothing much is known of Palladius beyond what Bede reports; Bede never mentions St. Patrick, who is generally remembered as the "Apostle to the Irish."

losses on the enemy who had been plundering their land for so many years. The shameless Irish robbers then returned home, intending to come back before long; the Picts, from that time on, remained quiet in the farthest part of the island, though they did not cease to plunder and harass the Britons from time to time.

When the ravages of the enemy finally ceased, there was such an abundance of grain in the island as had never been known before. With abundance came an increase in luxury, which was immediately followed by every sort of crime; in particular, cruelty and hatred of truth and love of falsehood increased so much that if anyone among them happened to be milder than the rest and somewhat inclined to truth, all the rest heaped hatred and missiles upon him, as if he had been the enemy of Britain. Not only were laymen guilty of these things, but even our Lord's own flock and their pastors too; they cast off the light yoke of Christ[1] and thrust their necks under the burden of drunkenness, hatred, argument, strife, envy, and other crimes of this sort. In the meantime a severe plague suddenly fell upon that corrupt generation, and soon destroyed so many of them that there were scarcely enough people left alive to bury the dead: yet those who survived could not be awakened from the spiritual death which their sins had brought upon them, either by the death of their friends or by the fear of their own death. For this reason, a still more severe retribution soon afterwards fell upon this sinful nation for their horrible wickedness. They consulted as to what should be done, and where they should seek help to prevent or repel the very frequent attacks of the northern nations, and they all agreed with their King Vortigern[2] that they should call the Saxons to their aid from across the sea. As events clearly showed, this was ordained by the will of our Lord Himself so that evil might fall upon them for their wicked deeds.

In the year of our Lord 449 Marcian became emperor with Valentinian, the forty-sixth emperor from Augustus, and ruled for seven years. At this time the nation of the Angles or Saxons, being invited by Vortigern, came to Britain in three long ships; they were granted a place to settle in the eastern part of the island so that they might appear to be fighting for their country, but their real intention was to enslave it. Accordingly they first fought against the enemy who attacked from the north, and won the victory. When this became known at home in their own country, and also the fertility of the country and the cowardice of the Britons, a much larger fleet was quickly sent over with a greater number of men; this, added to the troop already there, made an invincible army. The newcomers received a grant of land from the Britons, on condition that they wage war against their enemies for the peace and safety of the country, and the Britons agreed to pay them.

Those who came over were from three powerful tribes in Germany—the Saxons, Angles, and Jutes. From the Jutes are descended the people of Kent and of the Isle of Wight, and that part of the kingdom of the West Saxons just opposite the Isle of Wight, which is still today called the nation of the Jutes. From the country of the Saxons, that is, the region which is now known as Old Saxony, came the East Saxons, the South Saxons, and the West Saxons. From the country of the Angles—that is, the region between the provinces of the Jutes and the Saxons which is called *Angulus*, and which is said to remain deserted from that day to this—came the East Angles, the Middle Angles, the Mercians, and all the Northumbrian race (that is, those people that dwell north of the river Humber), and the other Anglian tribes.[3] Their first commanders are said to have been two brothers, Hengest and Horsa. Horsa was afterwards killed in battle by the Britons, and was buried in the eastern part of Kent, where there is still a monument bearing his name. They were the sons of Wihtgils, son of Witta, son of Woden, from whose stock the royal

---

[1] *Not only ... of Christ* See Matthew 11.29.

[2] *King Vortigern* Bede expands on his source Gildas here to supply the name of the king Vortigern (which means "chief lord"—Gildas calls him only *superbus tyrannus*, which basically means the same thing) and the names of the Saxons Hengest and Horsa (both names mean "horse"). Vortigern later has a prominent (though ignominious) role in the Arthurian legends as shaped by Geoffrey of Monmouth's *History of the Kings of Britain*.

[3] *Anglian tribes* Or "English people." In the title of his work, and in its text as well, Bede refers to all the invading tribes as the *gens Anglorum* or "English people."

families of many kingdoms claim their descent.[1]

In a short time hordes of these peoples flooded into the island, and their numbers increased so much that they became a terror to the natives who had invited them. Then suddenly they joined forces with the Picts, whom they had by this time driven far away by the force of their arms, and began to turn their weapons against their allies. First they made them supply a greater quantity of food; then, seeking an occasion to quarrel, they insisted that unless more plentiful supplies were brought to them, they would break the alliance and ravage the whole island. Nor were they slow in carrying out their threats—to make a long story short, the fire kindled by the hands of these pagans executed God's just revenge on the nation for its crimes, not unlike the fire once kindled by the Chaldeans which consumed the walls and city of Jerusalem.[2] Likewise here in Britain the just Judge ordained that the fire of these brutal conquerors should ravage all the neighboring cities and countryside from the east to the western sea, without opposition, until it covered almost every part of the doomed island. Public and private buildings fell into ruins; priests were everywhere slain before the altars; the prelates and people alike were destroyed with fire and sword regardless of their rank; and there was no one left to bury those who had died in such a cruel slaughter. Some of the miserable remnant were captured in the mountains and butchered in heaps; others, exhausted by hunger, came forward and submitted themselves to the enemy, ready to accept perpetual slavery for the sake of food, if only they were not killed on the spot. Some fled sorrowfully beyond the sea, while others remained in their own land and led a miserable life among the forests, crags, and mountains, always expecting every moment to be their last.

When the victorious army had destroyed and dispersed the native peoples, and returned home to their own settlements,[3] the Britons slowly began to gather strength and courage. They emerged from their hiding places and unanimously prayed for divine assistance that they might not be utterly destroyed. Their leader at that time was Ambrosius Aurelius,[4] a modest man who was, by chance, the sole member of the Roman nation to survive the storm in which his parents, who were of a royal and famous family, had perished. Under his leadership the Britons regained their strength, challenged their victors to battle and, by the help of God, won the victory. From that time on, sometimes the natives, and sometimes their enemies, prevailed, until the year of the siege of Mount Badon, when the Britons made no small slaughter of their enemies, about forty-four years after their arrival in England. But more of this hereafter.

3. THE LIFE AND CONVERSION OF EDWIN, KING OF NORTHUMBRIA; THE FAITH OF THE EAST ANGLES

[The conversion of Edwin is in many ways the central event in Bede's long history—it sets England firmly on the road to Christianity and represents the crowning achievement of the mission of Augustine of Canterbury, sent by Pope Gregory the Great to convert the island. Bede probably relied on local knowledge and memories for his story; he therefore has to explain why Edwin's conversion is significantly delayed and accomplished with much foot-dragging.

According to Bede's account, Edwin secured his kingship in Northumbria with the help of Rædwald, the king of East Anglia, in 616; later he married Æthelburh, daughter of the Christian king Æthelberht of Kent, in 625. One of the conditions of the marriage was that he put no obstacles in the way of Christian worship in his kingdom, and promise to consider becoming a Christian himself. Æthelburh arrives in Northumbria accompanied by the bishop Paulinus; though Paulinus works diligently to convert Edwin, he is unsuccessful for a long time.

---

[1] *They were the ... their descent*   Bede is apparently not troubled by the fact that Woden is a Germanic god, suggesting that by his day active worship of Woden was not widespread. In medieval historical writing, the various classical and Germanic gods (when they are not written off as demons masquerading to lead men astray) are usually explained as ancient heroes whose exploits and stature were inflated over time until they were worshipped as gods.

[2] *not unlike ... Jerusalem*   See 2 Kings 25.8–10.

[3] *settlements*   I.e., in Britain, not Germany.

[4] *Ambrosius Aurelius*   Bede's information comes from Gildas; no earlier or more reliable source is known for Ambrosius Aurelius, later transformed into King Arthur. The battle of Mount Badon, if it occurred at all, probably took place around 500 CE.

When Edwin survives an assassination attempt by the West Saxons on the same day he celebrates the birth of his daughter (whom he allows to be baptized), he promises to convert if God will grant him victory over his enemies. After his campaign against the West Saxons is successful, however, he delays fulfilling his promise for a long time, despite the instruction of Paulinus, the prayers of his wife, and the entreaties of the Pope (Boniface) himself.

Bede's account of Edwin's conversion is sometimes caught between its contradictory impulses towards hagiography (in which conversion is described as a personal journey to faith, punctuated by miracles) and political history (in which conversion is seen as an act of royal policy). But it is marked by a lively sense of scene and character, and vividly conveys the fragile and sometimes dangerous nature of early Anglo-Saxon kingship, the power of the "heroic" code as an ideal of behavior, and the complex implications of conversion; Bede's report (or invention) of the council at which Edwin hears the opinions of his advisors—the unnamed philosophical nobleman, the opportunistic high priest Coifi—is a classic scene, a Christian writer's lyrical, almost elegiac imagination of the pagan heart.]

Such was the letter that Pope Boniface wrote for the salvation of King Edwin and his nation. But a heavenly vision, which God in His mercy had once chosen to reveal to Edwin when he was in exile at the court of Rædwald, king of the Angles, was of greater use in urging him to understand and embrace the counsels of salvation. Paulinus saw how difficult it was for the king's proud mind to bow to the humility of the way of salvation and accept the mystery of the life-giving cross, but at the same time he continued to use both exhortation with men and prayer to God for his and his subjects' salvation. At length, as we may suppose, he was shown in spirit the nature of the vision that had once been revealed to the king. Nor did he lose any time in warning the king to fulfill the vow he had made when he saw the vision, which he had promised to undertake if he should be delivered from the trouble he was in at that time, and ascend to the throne.

His vision was this: when his predecessor Æthelfrith was persecuting him, he wandered secretly for many years through several places and kingdoms, and at last came to Rædwald, asking him for protection against the plots of his powerful persecutor. Rædwald gladly received him, and promised to do what he asked. But when Æthelfrith learned that he had been seen in that kingdom, and had been hospitably entertained by the king and his retainers, he sent messengers to offer Rædwald a great sum of money to kill Edwin. But this had no effect; he sent a second and a third time, offering more and more each time, and threatening to make war on him if he refused. Rædwald, either terrified by his threats or corrupted by his bribes, yielded to his request and promised either to kill Edwin or to give him up to the messengers. A trusty friend of Edwin's found this out, and went into his chamber when he was going to bed, for it was the first hour of the night. He called him outside, told him what the king had promised to do with him, adding, "If you are willing, I will take you from this kingdom right now, and lead you to a place where neither Rædwald nor Æthelfrith will ever find you." Edwin answered, "I thank you for your goodwill, but I cannot do what you suggest, lest I be the first to break the compact I have made with this great king; he has done me no wrong, nor shown me any enmity. If I must die, let it rather be by his hand than by that of some meaner person. For where should I now fly, when I have for so many years been a vagabond through all the kingdoms of Britain, trying to escape the snares of my enemies?" His friend went away, and Edwin remained alone outside; sitting with a heavy heart in front of the palace, he began to be overwhelmed with many thoughts, not knowing what to do or which way to turn.

He remained a long time in silent anguish, brooding over his misfortunes, when suddenly in the dead of night he saw a man approach him whose face and dress were equally strange. He was more than a little frightened at this unexpected sight. The stranger came close, saluted him, and asked why he sat there alone and melancholy on a stone at that time, when everyone else was resting, and fast asleep. Edwin asked in reply what concern it was to him whether he spent the night indoors or out. The stranger replied, "Do not think that I am unaware of the cause of your grief, your sleeplessness, and your sitting alone outside. For I know who you are, and why you grieve, and the evils which you fear will fall upon you. But tell me, what reward would you give the man who would free you from this anguish, and persuade Rædwald neither to harm you himself, nor to give you up to be murdered by your enemies?" Edwin replied that he would give that person all that he was able in return for such a favor. The other continued, "What if he also assured you that you will overcome your enemies, and be a king who surpasses in power not only all your ancestors, but also all who have reigned before you over the English?" Edwin, encouraged by these questions, did not hesitate to promise that he would make a suitable return to anyone who should offer him such great benefits. Then the man said, "If the one who truly foretold so many good things could also give you better and more useful advice for your life and salvation than any of your ancestors or kindred ever heard of, would you consent to obey him, and to follow his saving counsel?" Edwin did not hesitate to promise that he would follow in every detail the directions of the one who could rescue him from so many troubles and raise him to the throne. At this answer the man who was speaking to him laid his hand on his head saying, "When this sign shall come to you, remember this conversation that has passed between us, and do not hesitate to fulfill what you have now promised." Having uttered these words, it is said that he immediately disappeared, so that the king might realize that it was not a man but a spirit that had appeared to him.

The young prince sat there alone for a time, rejoicing in the consolation he had received but deeply troubled and anxiously wondering who it was that had talked to him in that way, or where he had come from. Meanwhile the friend mentioned earlier returned, greeted him pleasantly and said, "Rise, go inside, and let yourself sleep without fear! The king has changed his mind and intends to do you no harm but rather to keep the promise he made you; when he secretly revealed to the queen the plan I told you before, she talked him out of it, warning that was unworthy of so great a king to sell his good friend for gold when he was in such distress, and to sacrifice his own honor, more precious than any ornament, for the love of money." In short, the king did as he had said, and not only refused to betray the banished man to his enemy's messengers, but helped Edwin to recover his kingdom. As soon as the messengers had returned home, he raised a mighty army to overthrow Æthelfrith. Rædwald did not give him time to gather all his forces; he attacked him with a much larger army and killed him on the borders of the kingdom of Mercia, on the east bank of the river Idle. In this battle Rædwald's son Regenhere was killed. And thus Edwin, in accordance with the vision he had received, not only escaped the snares of the king his enemy, but after his death succeeded him on the throne.

King Edwin hesitated to accept the word of God preached by Paulinus, and for some time, as we have said, used to sit alone for several hours at a time, earnestly debating within himself what he ought to do and what religion he should follow. One day the man of God[1] came to him, laid his right hand on the king's head, and asked him if he recognized this sign. The king, trembling, was about to fall down at his feet but Paulinus raised him up and said in a voice that seemed familiar, "Behold, with God's help you have escaped the hands of the enemies you feared; behold, you have obtained by His gift the kingdom you desired; take heed not to delay what you promised to do—receive the faith and keep the commandments of Him who rescued you from earthly adversity and has raised you to the honor of an earthly kingdom. If, from this time forward, you are willing to follow his will, which is made known to you through me, He will not only deliver you from the everlasting torments of the wicked, but also make you a partaker with Him of His eternal kingdom in heaven."

When the king heard these words, he answered that he was both willing and bound to accept the faith which Paulinus taught, but that he would confer about it with his chief men and counselors so that, if they agreed with him, they might all together be cleansed in Christ, the Fountain of Life. Paulinus agreed, and the king did as he said: holding a meeting with his council of wise men, he asked each one in turn what he thought of this new doctrine, and the new worship of God that had been proclaimed.

Coifi, chief of his own priests, immediately answered, "Consider, O king, this new doctrine that is

---

[1] *man of God* I.e., Paulinus.

being preached to us. For I say to you truly that as far as I can tell, the religion we have practiced until now has no virtue in it. None of your people has devoted himself more diligently to the worship of our gods than I, and yet there are many who receive greater favors and greater honor from you than I do, and are more prosperous in all their undertakings. If the gods had any power they would have helped me more readily, since I have been more careful to serve them. It follows, therefore, that if on examination those new doctrines which are now preached to us are found to be better and more effective, we should accept them immediately and without delay."

Another of the king's chief men agreed with his words and his advice, and then added: "This is how the present life of man, O king, seems to me in comparison with that time which is unknown to us: as if you are sitting in your feasting-hall with your ealdormen and thanes[1] in wintertime, with a good fire burning in the middle of the hall and all inside is warm, while outside the winter storms of rain and snow are raging; and a sparrow flies swiftly through the hall, entering in at one door and quickly flying out at another. While he is within the winter storms cannot touch him; but after the briefest moment of calm he immediately vanishes out of your sight, out of the winter and back into it again. So this life of man appears just for a moment—of what went before, or what is to follow, we know nothing at all. If this new doctrine contains anything more certain, it seems right that we should follow it." The other elders and counselors spoke in the same way, by divine inspiration.

Coifi added that he wanted to listen more attentively to what Paulinus had to say about the God he preached. The king ordered Paulinus to speak and Coifi, hearing his words, cried out, "I have long realized that our religion is worthless—the the more diligently I sought the truth in our worship, the less I found it. But now I freely confess that such truth shines forth clearly in this preaching, which can bestow on us the gift of life, salvation, and eternal happiness. Therefore I advise, O king, that we instantly abandon and set fire to those temples and altars which we have consecrated without reaping any benefit from them." What more is there to say? The king publicly accepted the gospel which

Paulinus preached, renouncing idolatry, and confessed his faith in Christ; and when he asked the high priest who should be the first to profane the altars and temples of their idols, together with the enclosures around them, Coifi answered, "I will; for who can more properly than myself destroy those things which I once worshipped in ignorance, through the wisdom which has been given me by the true God, and set an example for others?" And immediately, casting aside his former superstitions, he asked the king to furnish him with arms and a stallion, and mounting it he set out to destroy the idols. Now the high priest was not allowed to carry arms or to ride on any horse but a mare; but with a sword girded about him and a spear in his hand, he mounted the king's stallion and set off for the idols.[2] The common people, seeing this, thought he was mad; but wasting no time, as soon as he drew near the temple he profaned it by casting into it the spear which he held, and rejoicing in the knowledge of the worship of the true God, he ordered his companions to destroy and set fire to the temple and all its enclosures. This place where the idols once stood is still shown, a short distance east of York beyond the river Derwent. Today it is called Goodmanham, the place where the high priest, by the inspiration of the true God, profaned and destroyed the altars which he had himself consecrated.

So King Edwin and all the nobles of his nation, and a large number of the common people, received the faith and regeneration by holy baptism in the eleventh year of his reign, that is in the year of our Lord 627, and about 180 years after the coming of the English into Britain. He was baptized at York on Easter day, the 12th of April, in the church of St. Peter the Apostle which he himself had built of timber, while he was a catechumen[3] and receiving instruction in order to receive baptism. In the same city he established an episcopal see for his instructor and bishop Paulinus. As soon as he was baptized he began, under the direction of Paulinus, to build a larger and more noble church of stone in the same place, in the midst of which the chapel which he

---

[1]   *ealdormen and thanes*   Noblemen.

[2]   *Now the high priest … idols*   Bede is our only authority for this custom, or for the existence of "high priests" in Anglo-Saxon pagan religion.

[3]   *catechumen*   Person preparing to be baptized into the Catholic faith.

had built first would be enclosed. The foundations were laid and he began to build the church square, surrounding the former chapel, but before the walls were raised to their proper height, the king was cruelly slain[1] and the work was left to his successor Oswald. Paulinus continued to preach the word of the Lord in the kingdom for six years, that is, until the end of the king's reign, with his consent and favor, and all who were predestined for eternal life believed and were baptized. Among these were Osfrid and Eadfrid, King Edwin's sons, who were born to him while he was in exile; their mother was Cwenburh, daughter of Ceorl, king of the Mercians.

Other children of his by Queen Æthelburh were baptized later, namely Æthelhun and a daughter Æthelthryth and a second son Uscfrea; the first two were snatched from this life while still in their white garments,[2] and buried in the church at York. Yffi, son of Osfrith, was also baptized, and many more nobles and members of the royal family. It is said that the fervor of the faith and the longing for the washing of salvation was so great among the Northumbrians that once when Paulinus came to the king and queen in their royal palace called *Ad gefrin*,[3] he spent thirty-six days there fully occupied in catechising and baptizing, and during these days, from morning till night, he did nothing but instruct the people who came from every village and region in Christ's saving word. When they were instructed, he washed them with the water of absolution in the river Glen, which is nearby. This palace was abandoned by the kings who followed Edwin and another built instead, at the place called *Mælmin*.[4]

All this happened in the kingdom of Bernicia; but in the kingdom of Deira also, where Paulinus used to stay frequently with the king, he baptized in the river Swale, which runs by the village of Catterick, for in the earliest days of the church there they could not build chapels or baptistries. But in *Campodonum*,[5] where there was also a royal dwelling, he built a church which afterwards was burned down, together with all the buildings, by the pagans who killed King Edwin. In its place later kings built a dwelling for themselves in the region called *Loidis*.[6] The altar, which was made of stone, escaped the fire and is still preserved in the monastery of the most reverend abbot and priest Thrythwulf, which is in the forest of Elmet.

Edwin was so devoted to the true worship that he also persuaded Eorpwald, son of Rædwald and king of the East Saxons, to abandon his idolatrous superstitions and, with his whole kingdom, to accept the Christian faith and sacraments. Indeed his father Rædwald had long before been initiated into the mysteries of the Christian faith in Kent, but in vain; for on his return home, he was seduced by his wife and by certain perverse teachers, and turned back from the sincerity of the faith, so that his last state was worse than his first.[7] Like the ancient Samaritans, he seemed at the same time to serve Christ and the gods whom he had previously served, and in the same temple he had one altar for Christian sacrifice and another small one to offer victims to devils. Ealdwulf, ruler of that kingdom up to our own time, testified that the temple had stood until his time, and that he had seen it when he was a boy. King Rædwald, noble by birth but ignoble in his actions, was the son of Tytil, whose father was Wuffa, from whom the kings of the East Angles are called Wuffings.[8]

Eorpwald, not long after he had embraced the Christian faith, was killed by a heathen called Ricberht;

---

[1] *The king was cruelly slain*   In battle against Cædwalla, king of the Britons, and Penda, King of the Mercians.

[2] *white garments*   I.e., still wearing the white robe given to those who are newly baptized and worn every day for the first week after the sacrament.

[3] *Ad gefrin*   Present-day Yeavering, Northumberland. Archaeologists have excavated the site of Edwin's hall, an impressive complex of large buildings and outdoor spaces on the site of a Neolithic hill fort.

[4] *Mælmin*   Near present-day Millfield, Northumberland.

[5] *Campodonum*   Roman site near Dewsbury, Yorkshire.

[6] *Loidis*   Leeds.

[7] *so that his … his first*   See Luke 11.26.

[8] *King Rædwald … Wuffings*   Bede's account of Rædwald's incomplete conversion and excessive ecumenism contrasts sharply with that of Edwin's deep, thoughtful and fervent faith; moreover, since he is a Northumbrian, Bede's center of gravity is in the north, not least because his sources of information were probably richer. But the treacherous and backsliding East Saxons should not be underrated: Rædwald is widely thought to be the king honored by the elaborate and richly decorated ship-burial at Sutton Hoo, and the *Wuffings* may or may not be the same as the Swedish *Wylfings* mentioned in *Beowulf*.

and afterwards the kingdom remained in error for three years, until Eorpwald's brother Sigeberht came to the throne. Sigeberht was a devout Christian and a learned man; he was in exile during his brother's life and went to live in Gaul, where he was admitted to the sacraments of the Christian faith. As soon as he came to the throne he made it his business to see that the whole kingdom shared his faith. His efforts were strongly supported by Bishop Felix. The bishop had been born and ordained in Burgundy; when he came to Archbishop Honorius and expressed his desires, the archbishop sent him to preach the word of life to this nation of the Angles. Nor were his wishes in vain, for the devoted sower reaped an abundant harvest of believers in this spiritual field— indeed, as his name signified,[1] he delivered all of that kingdom from longstanding evil and unhappiness, brought it to the faith and to the works of righteousness, and gave it the gift of everlasting felicity. He received the see of his bishopric in the city of *Dommoc*,[2] and when he had ruled as bishop over the kingdom for seventeen years, he ended his days there in peace.

Paulinus also preached the word to the kingdom of Lindsey, the first land on the south bank of the river Humber, bordering on the sea. He first converted the prefect of the city of Lincoln, whose name was Blæcca, and his whole family. In this city he also built a stone church of beautiful workmanship; its roof has now either fallen through age or been thrown down by enemies, but the walls are still standing, and every year some miraculous cures are wrought in that place for the benefit of those who seek them in faith. When Justus departed to Christ, in his place Paulinus consecrated Honorius as bishop in that church, as we will later tell in its proper place.

An abbot and priest of the monastery of Partney, a most truthful man whose name was Deda, told me this about the faith of this kingdom: an old man had told him that he himself had been baptized at noon by Bishop Paulinus, in the presence of King Edwin, with a great number of people, in the river Trent, near the city which in English is called *Tiowulfingacæstir*.[3] He also

used to describe the appearance of Paulinus: he was tall, a little stooping, with black hair, a thin face, a slender and aquiline nose, and an aspect both venerable and majestic. In his ministry he also had with him a deacon named James, a man of zeal and great reputation in Christ's Church, who survived right up to our days.

It is reported that there was such perfect peace in Britain, wherever the dominion of King Edwin extended, that, as the proverb still says, a woman with a new-born child could walk throughout the island from sea to sea without receiving any harm. The king cared so much for the good of his nation that in various places where he had noticed clear springs near the highways, he had stakes set up with bronze drinking-cups hanging from them, for the convenience of travelers. No one dared to touch them for any other purpose than the one they were designed for, because they feared the king and loved him dearly. His dignity was so great throughout his realm that not only were banners carried before him in battle, but even in time of peace, when he rode about his cities, estates, or regions with his thegns, a standard-bearer always used to go before him, and when he walked along the roads, there used to be carried before him the type of standard which the Romans call a *tufa* and the English a *thuf*.

4. ABBESS HILD OF WHITBY; THE MIRACULOUS POET CÆDMON

In the year of our Lord 680 Hild, the most devout servant of Christ, abbess of the monastery that is called Whitby,[4] departed on the 17th of November after having performed many heavenly works on earth, to receive the rewards of the heavenly life, at the age of sixty-six. She spent her first thirty-three years living most nobly in the secular habit, and more nobly dedicated the remaining half to our Lord in the monastic life. She was of noble birth, being the daughter of Hereric, nephew to King Edwin; in Edwin's company she received the faith and mysteries of Christ at the preaching of Paulinus of blessed memory, the first bishop of the Northumbrians, and she preserved her

---

[1] *as his name signified*   Felix means "fortunate" or "happy" in Latin.

[2] *Dommoc*   Dunwich.

[3] *Tiowulfingacæstir*   Littleborough.

[4] *Whitby*   Bede uses the Old English name "Streaneshalch."

faith undefiled until she was rewarded with the sight of Him in heaven.

Resolving to give up the secular habit and serve Him alone, she withdrew to the kingdom of the East Angles, for she was related to the king there; she intended to pass over from there into Gaul, leaving her native land and all that she had to live as a stranger for our Lord's sake in the monastery of Chelles, so that she might more easily reach her eternal home in heaven. Her sister Hereswith, mother of Ealdwulf, king of the East Angles, was at that time living in the same monastery under the discipline of the monastic Rule, waiting for her heavenly crown. Inspired by her example, Hild continued a whole year in the kingdom of the East Angles with the intention of going abroad; Bishop Aidan called her home, however, and gave her enough land to support herself on the north side of the river Wear, where she lived in the monastic life for a year, with a small group of companions.

After this she was made abbess in the monastery called *Heruteu*,[1] which had been founded not long before by Heiu, a devoted handmaid of Christ, who is said to have been the first woman in the kingdom of Northumbria to take the habit and vows of a nun, having been ordained by Bishop Aidan. But soon after she had founded that monastery, Heiu went away to the town of *Calcaria*, which the English call *Kælcacæstir*,[2] and there made her dwelling. Hild, the handmaid of Christ, was appointed to rule over that monastery, and immediately began to establish a rule of life there in all things, as she had been taught by many learned men; for Bishop Aidan and other devout men who knew her visited her frequently, instructed her diligently, and loved her dearly for her innate wisdom and devotion to the service of God.

When she had ruled over this monastery for some years, wholly intent upon establishing a rule of life there, it happened that she also undertook either to found or to reform a monastery in the place called *Streaneshalch*,[3] which she carried out with great industry. She established the same rule in this monastery as in the other, and she taught there the strict observance of justice, piety, chastity, and other virtues, above all peace and charity. After the example of the primitive church, no one there was rich, and no one was poor, for all things were common to all, and none had any private property. Her wisdom was so great that not only ordinary people, but even kings and princes sometimes asked for and received her advice; she obliged those who were under her direction to devote so much time to the study of the Holy Scriptures, and to exercise themselves so much in works of justice, that there might be no difficulty in finding many there who were fit for ecclesiastical duties, that is for the service of the altar.

In fact we have seen five men from that monastery become bishops, all of them men of singular merit and sanctity: Bosa, Ætla, Oftfor, John, and Wilfrid. The first of them, as we related elsewhere, was consecrated bishop of York; of the second, it may be observed that he was appointed bishop of Dorchester. Of the two last we shall later relate that John was consecrated bishop of Hexham and Wilfrid, bishop of York; of Oftfor we will here note that after he applied himself to the reading and observance of the Scriptures in both of Hild's monasteries, being anxious to attain to greater perfection, he went to Kent to join Archbishop Theodore, of blessed memory. After he had spent more time in sacred studies there, he resolved to go to Rome, which in those days was considered to be an act of great merit. After his return to Britain, he went to the province of the Hwicce, where King Osric then ruled, and remained there a long time, preaching the word of faith and setting an example of holy life to all who saw and heard him. At that time Bosel, the bishop of that kingdom, suffered such weakness of body that he could not carry out his episcopal duties; so Oftfor was appointed bishop in his place by universal consent, and was consecrated at King Æthelred's command by Bishop Wilfrid, of blessed memory, who was at that time bishop of the Middle Angles because Archbishop Theodore was dead, and no other bishop had been ordained in his place. Before Bosel, a most learned and industrious man of excellent ability named Tatfrid had been chosen bishop there, also from Hild's monastery, but he had been snatched away by an untimely death before his consecration.

---

[1] *Heruteu* Hartlepool.

[2] *Kælcacæstir* Uncertain; possibly Tadcaster.

[3] *Streaneshalch* Site in northeastern Yorkshire (now Whitby) where the Abbess Hilda founded a double monastery.

All who knew Abbess Hild, the handmaid of Christ, called her Mother because of her outstanding piety and grace. She was not only an example of holy life to those who lived in her monastery, but provided an opportunity for repentance and salvation to many who lived far away who heard the happy news of her diligence and virtue. This was bound to happen so that the dream which her mother Breguswith had during Hild's infancy should be fulfilled. When her husband Hereric lived in exile under the British king Cerdic, where he was later poisoned, Breguswith dreamed that she was looking for him most carefully, and could find no sign of him anywhere; but suddenly, after having tried with all her might to find him, she found a most precious necklace under her garment, and as she was gazing at it very attentively, it cast such a blaze of light that it spread throughout all Britain. This dream came true in her daughter Hild, whose life was a bright example, not only to herself, but to many who desired to live well.

After she had governed this monastery many years, it pleased Him who has made such merciful provision for our salvation to subject her holy soul to the trial of a long sickness so that, like the apostle, her strength might be made perfect in weakness.

She was struck by a fever and fell into a violent heat, and for six years was afflicted continually; during all which time she never failed to give thanks to her Maker or to instruct the flock entrusted to her care both in public and in private. From her own experience she admonished everyone to serve the Lord dutifully in health and always to return thanks to Him in adversity or bodily illness. In the seventh year of her illness, she began to suffer internally and approached her last day. Around cock-crow, having received the viaticum of Holy Communion,[1] she called together the handmaids of Christ who were in the monastery, and admonished them to preserve the Gospel peace among themselves and towards all others; and as she was exhorting them she joyfully saw death approaching or, to use the words of our Lord, she passed from death into life.

That same night it pleased Almighty God by a vision to reveal her death in another monastery at some distance from hers called Hackness, which she had built that same year. In that monastery was a nun called Begu, who for thirty years or more had dedicated her virginity to God and served Him in the monastic life. While she was in the dormitory of the sisters, she suddenly heard in the air the familiar sound of the bell which used to awaken the sisters and call them to prayers when any one of them had been taken out of this world. Opening her eyes, she seemed to see the top of the house open, and a strong light pour in from above; looking intently at that light, she saw the soul of the handmaid of the Lord borne into heaven in the midst of that light, attended by angels. Then awaking and seeing the other sisters lying around her, she realized that what she had seen was either a dream or a vision; greatly frightened, she rose immediately and ran to a maiden named Frigyth, who was then presiding over the monastery in place of the abbess. With many tears and sighs, Begu told her that the Abbess Hild, mother of them all, had departed this life, and that she had seen her ascend with a great light, and with angels conducting her, into eternal bliss and the company of the inhabitants of heaven. When Frigyth heard this, she awoke all the sisters, and called them to the church; she ordered them to pray and sing psalms for Hild's soul, which they did for the rest of the night. At break of day, the brothers came from the place she had died with news of her death. They answered that they already knew it, and when they told how and when they had heard it, it was found that her death had been revealed to them in a vision in the very same hour that the brothers said she had died. Thus it was happily ordained by Heaven that when some watched her departure out of this world, others watched her entrance into the eternal life of the spirit. These monasteries are about thirteen miles distant from each other.

It is also reported that her death was made known in a vision the same night to one of the holy maidens who loved her most passionately, in the same monastery where this servant of God died. She saw Hild's soul ascend to heaven in the company of angels; and she declared this, the very same hour it happened, to those servants of Christ who were with her, and awakened them to pray for her soul, even before the rest of the congregation had heard of her death, for it was only

---

[1] *viaticum … Communion* Communion received by someone who is possibly near death.

made known to the whole monastery the next morning. This same nun was at that time with some other servants of Christ in the remotest part of the monastery, where the women who had recently entered the monastery used to spend their time of probation until they were instructed in the Rule and admitted to the society of the community.

In Hild's monastery was a certain brother specially marked by the grace of God, who used to make pious and religious verses, so that whatever he learned from the holy Scriptures through interpreters, he soon afterwards turned into poetry of great sweetness and humility, in English, which was his native language. By his verses the minds of many were often inspired to despise the world and to long for the heavenly life. After him other Englishmen tried to compose religious poems, but none could ever compare with him, for he did not learn the art of poetry from men or through a man,[1] but received the gift of song freely by divine grace. For this reason he never could compose any trivial or foolish poem, but only those which were concerned with devotion and were fitting for his pious tongue to utter.

He had lived in the secular life until he was well advanced in years, and had never learned any verses; therefore sometimes at feasts, when it was agreed for the sake of entertainment that all present should take a turn singing, when he saw the harp coming towards him, he would rise up from the table in the middle of the feast, go out, and return home. On one occasion when he did this, he left the house of feasting and went to the stable, where it was his turn to take care of the animals that night. In due time he stretched out to rest; a person appeared to him in his sleep, saluted him by name, and said, "Cædmon, sing me something." Cædmon answered, "I cannot sing; that is why I left the feast and came here, because I could not sing." The man who was talking to him replied, "Nevertheless, you must sing to me."

"What shall I sing?" he asked. "Sing about the beginning of created things," he replied. At that, Cædmon immediately began to sing verses which he had never heard before in praise of God, whose general sense is this: "We ought now to praise the Maker of the heavenly kingdom, the power of the Creator and his counsel, the deeds of the Father of glory and how He, since He is the eternal God, was the author of all marvels and first, as almighty Guardian of the human race, created heaven as a roof for the sons of men, and then the earth."[2] This is the sense but not the actual order of the words he sang in his sleep, for poetry, no matter how well composed, cannot be literally translated from one language into another without losing much of its beauty and dignity. Awaking from his sleep, Cædmon remembered all that he had sung in his dream, and soon added more verses in the same manner, praising God in a worthy style.

In the morning he went to the steward, his master, and told him of the gift he had received; the steward led him to the abbess, who ordered him, in the presence of many learned men, to recount his dream and repeat his poem, so that they might all decide what it was and where it had come from. It was clear to all of them he had received a gift of heavenly grace from our Lord. Then they explained to him a passage of sacred history or doctrine, and ordered him, if he could, to turn it into verse. He undertook this task and went away; when he returned the next morning he repeated it to them, composed in excellent verse. At this the abbess, recognizing the grace of God in this man, instructed him to renounce the secular habit and take up the monastic life; when this was done she joined him to the rest of the brethren in her monastery and ordered that he should be taught the whole course of sacred history. He learned all that he could by listening, and turned it over in his mind like a clean beast chewing the cud,[3] turned it into the most harmonious verse, and recited it so sweetly that his teachers became in turn his audience. He sang of the creation of the world, the origin of the human race, and all the history of Genesis; and made many verses on the departure of the children of Israel from Egypt, and their entry into the Promised Land,

---

[1] *from men or through a man*   See Galatians 1.1.

[2] *We ought now ... the earth*   See below for Cædmon's *Hymn* in Old English. Bede gives only this paraphrase; in two manuscripts of Bede's Latin *Historia* a poem in the Northumbrian dialect of Old English is added in the margins. When Bede's work was translated into Old English at the end of the ninth century, the translators substituted a version of this poem for Bede's paraphrase, and omitted the disclaimer that follows it.

[3] *He learned ... the cud*   See Leviticus 11.3; Deuteronomy 14.6.

and many other stories from the holy Scriptures; of the Incarnation, Passion, and Resurrection of our Lord, and of His Ascension into heaven, of the coming of the Holy Spirit and the teaching of the apostles, also of the terror of future judgment, the horror of the pains of hell, and the joys of the kingdom of heaven, and many more songs about the divine mercies and judgments by which he tried to turn all men away from the love of vice and to inspire in them the love and practice of good works. He was a very devout man, humbly submissive to the discipline of the monastic rule, but full of zeal against those who behaved otherwise; for this reason his life had a lovely ending.

When the hour of his departure drew near, for fourteen days he was afflicted with a bodily weakness which seemed to prepare the way, yet mild enough that he could talk and walk the whole time. Nearby was the house to which the sick and dying were carried. As evening fell on the night he was going to depart this life, he asked his attendant[1] to prepare a place for him there so he could take his rest. The attendant wondered why he should desire that, because there seemed to be no sign of his dying soon, but did what he had asked. They went there and were talking pleasantly and joyfully with the people who were already in the house; when it was past midnight he asked them whether they had the Eucharist there. They answered, "What need do you have of the Eucharist? You are not likely to die, since you talk so merrily with us, just as though you were in perfect health." "Nevertheless," he said, "bring me the Eucharist." When he had taken it into his hand he asked whether they were all in charity with him, without any complaint or quarrel. They answered that they were all in perfect charity, and free from anger; and likewise asked him whether he felt the same towards them. He answered at once, "My sons, I am in charity with all the servants of God." Then strengthening himself with the heavenly viaticum, he prepared for his entrance into the next life; he asked how near it was to the time when the brothers had to awaken to sing their nightly praise of our Lord. They answered, "It is not far off." He said, "Good; let us wait until then," and signing himself with the sign of the holy cross, he laid his head on the pillow and fell into a slumber, and so ended his life quietly. Thus it came to pass that, just as he had served God with a simple and pure mind and quiet devotion, so now he departed into His presence and left the world by a quiet death, and his tongue, which had composed so many holy words in praise of the Creator, uttered its last words while he was in the act of signing himself with the cross, and commending his spirit into God's hands; and from what has been said, it seems he had foreknowledge of his death.

5. CÆDMON'S HYMN IN OLD AND MODERN ENGLISH

Nu sculon herian   heofonrices weard,
Metodes meahta   ond his modgeþanc,
weorc wuldorfæder,   swa he wundra gehwæs,
ece Drihten,   or astealde.
He ærest scop   ielda bearnum
heofon to hrofe,   halig Scieppend;
þa middangeard   manncynnes weard,
ece Drihten,   æfter teode,
firum foldan   Frea ælmihtig.

Now (we) ought to praise Heaven-kingdom's guardian,
the Maker's might and his mind's thoughts,
the work of the glory-father, as he of each of wonders,
eternal Lord, established a beginning.[2]
He first shaped for men's sons
Heaven as a roof, the holy Creator;
then middle-earth mankind's guardian,
eternal Lord, afterwards prepared
the earth for men, the Lord almighty.
—C. 731

---

[1] *his attendant* Older monks were attended by young novices who took care of them.

[2] *Lord … beginning* I.e., He established the beginning of every wonder.

EXETER BOOK ELEGIES

Most of the Old English poetry that has survived is contained in only four manuscripts. The richest and most diverse of these is Exeter Cathedral Library MS 3501, a large anthology of secular and religious poems. The Exeter Book was given to the Cathedral library by the bishop Leofric some time before 1072 CE (and has remained there ever since), but it was written probably a century earlier, somewhere in the south of England. Because some pages have been lost from the manuscript, we cannot say how many poems it originally contained, and we do not know the impulse behind its compilation. But the Exeter Book is a fascinating miscellany, ranging from serious religious poetry on the Advent and Ascension of Christ, to verse lives of St. Guthlac and Juliana, to a translation of a Latin poem on the Phoenix, to a collection of almost 100 verse riddles which are sometimes comical or obscene. The poems are probably by many different authors; a poet named Cynewulf encoded his own name (in runes) in two poems, *Juliana* and *Christ II*, but all others are anonymous and untitled.

The Exeter Book includes a group of short philosophical poems, differing in style and outlook but similar in tone, which have come to be known as "elegies": among these are *The Wanderer*, *The Seafarer*, *The Wife's Lament*, *The Ruin*, *Wulf and Eadwacer*, and *The Husband's Message*. The label "elegy" here is potentially misleading. In Greek and Latin literature the term refers to a particular metrical form, and since the sixteenth century the word has been used in English literature to describe a poem of lament or mourning (the most famous English elegies include Milton's *Lycidas*, Shelley's *Adonais*, and Tennyson's *In Memoriam*). But the term "elegy" is sometimes used more loosely to describe any serious meditative poem, and it is in this sense that these Old English poems should be considered elegies. The poems share certain themes and concerns—the passage of time and the transience of earthly things, the pain of exile and separation, the ache of absence and longing—as well as certain images and scenes such as ruined or abandoned buildings, desolate landscapes, storms at sea, darkness, night and the chill of winter. These themes, and the traditional language in which they are presented, are also found in other Old English poems; certain passages of *Beowulf* may be called elegiac, and the contemplation of earthly instability sometimes seems to pervade Old English literature. The tone and language of elegy may have roots deep in the traditions of Germanic poetry, but it is also influenced by late classical works such as Boethius's *Consolation of Philosophy*; the recognition that the "world under the heavens" is a place of tragic impermanence would probably be regarded as equally good Christian doctrine and pagan wisdom. Both *The Wanderer* and *The Ruin* also appear to borrow from the Latin convention of posing "ubi sunt?" questions—in literal translation, "Where are they" or "Where are these things?"

Most of the Old English elegies are monologues spoken by an unidentified character whose situation is unclear but who seems to be cut off from human society and the comforts of home and friendship. But even though they share the poetic language of exile and longing, each poem has its own shape and purpose, and each makes its own statement about the problems and possibilities of earthly life. *The Wanderer* is initially concerned with a wandering warrior who has lost his Lord; the focus of the second half of the poem opens up to lament the passing of a whole way of life, the heroic world of the warrior's hall. *The Wife's Lament* (one of only two poems in the Exeter Book to be written from a woman's point of view) is a poem of intense personal longing for an absent husband or lover. *The Seafarer*, like *The Wanderer*, divides into two parts. The opening lines of the poem consist of a first-person narrative describing the hardships of going to sea, and contrasting them with the comforts of staying at home on land; around line 65 the poem shifts from a narrative to a spiritual meditation that is at times explicitly and even aggressively homiletic and Christian. *The Ruin* describes the remains of an ancient city—most probably an ancient Roman city in Britain, such as Bath, which had been abandoned centuries before the writing of this poem. The poem is detached and dispassionate about the scene it describes, and—in contrast to *The Seafarer*—whatever moral judgments it makes are implicit and indirect.

Each of the four poems presented below has some structural and interpretive difficulties. *The Wanderer* is a dramatic monologue with a prologue and epilogue, but the beginnings and endings of speeches are not indicated in the manuscript and can only be guessed at. *The Seafarer* switches tone so radically that many readers (including Ezra Pound, who translated the poem) have simply rejected the second, more homiletic half. *The Wife's Lament* is obscure more by virtue of its language than its structure—a number of the poem's key terms are ambivalent or uncertain. And the pages of the Exeter Book containing *The Ruin* have been so damaged that the poem is itself a ruin, crumbling into incoherence. The poems develop philosophical arguments and present evidence and conclusions, but Old English poetic language is not necessarily congenial to the demands of precise reasoning; sentence boundaries and relationships between clauses are often uncertain. And yet despite these interpretive problems, the Exeter Book "elegies" are among the most moving and powerful poems in Old English; their vision of life as both infinitely precious and inevitably transitory still strikes a responsive chord in the hearts of many readers.

⌘ ⌘ ⌘

The Wanderer [1]

Always the one alone longs for mercy,
the Maker's mildness, though, troubled in mind,
across the ocean-ways he has long been forced
to stir with his hands the frost-cold sea,
5 and walk in exile's paths. *Wyrd* [2] is fully fixed!

Thus spoke the Wanderer, mindful of troubles,
of cruel slaughters and the fall of dear kinsmen: [3]
"Often alone, every first light of dawn,
I have lamented my sorrows. There is no one living
10 to whom I would dare to reveal clearly
my heart's thoughts. I know it is true

that it is in the lordly nature of a nobleman
to closely bind his spirit's coffer,
hold his treasure-hoard, whatever he may think.
15 The weary mind cannot withstand *wyrd*,
the troubled heart can offer no help,
and so those eager for fame often bind fast
in their breast-coffers a sorrowing soul,
just as I have had to take my own heart—
20 often wretched, cut off from my homeland,
far from dear kinsmen—and bind it in fetters,
ever since long ago I hid my gold-giving friend
in the darkness of earth, and went wretched,
winter-sad, over the ice-locked waves,
25 sought, hall-sick, a treasure-giver,
wherever I might find, far or near,
someone in a meadhall who knew of my people,
or who'd want to comfort me, friendless,
accustom me to joy. He who has come to know
30 how cruel a companion is sorrow
to one who has few dear protectors, will understand
     this:
the path of exile claims him, not patterned gold,
a winter-bound spirit, not the wealth of earth.
He remembers hall-holders and treasure-taking,
35 how in his youth his gold-giving lord
accustomed him to the feast—that joy has all faded.

---

[1] *The Wanderer* The present text has been translated for *The Broadview Anthology of British Literature* by R.M. Liuzza.

[2] *Wyrd* A powerful but not quite personified force; the closest parallel in modern English is "Fate." It is related to the verb "weorthan," meaning roughly "to occur." Its meanings range from a neutral "event" to a prescribed "destiny" to a personified "Fate"; it is useful to think of "wyrd" as "what happens," usually in a negative sense.

[3] *Thus spoke ... kinsmen* The manuscript in which the poem survives does not have quotation marks, or clear indications of where speeches begin and end in this poem; we are not sure whether lines 1–5 are spoken by the same character who speaks the following lines, or whether they are the narrator's opinion on the general situation of the Wanderer.

And so he who has long been forced to forgo
his dear lord's beloved words of counsel will understand:
when sorrow and sleep both together
40 often bind up the wretched exile,
it seems in his mind that he clasps and kisses
his lord of men, and on his knee lays
hands and head, as he sometimes long ago
in earlier days enjoyed the gift-throne.[1]
45 But when the friendless man awakens again
and sees before him the fallow waves,
seabirds bathing, spreading their feathers,
frost falling and snow, mingled with hail,
then the heart's wounds are that much heavier,
50 longing for his loved one. Sorrow is renewed
when the memory of kinsmen flies through the mind;
he greets them with great joy, greedily surveys
hall-companions—they always swim away;
the floating spirits bring too few
55 well-known voices. Cares are renewed
for one who must send, over and over,
a weary heart across the binding of the waves.[2]

    And so I cannot imagine for all this world
why my spirit should not grow dark
60 when I think through all this life of men,
how they suddenly gave up the hall-floor,
mighty young retainers. Thus this middle-earth
droops and decays every single day;
and so a man cannot become wise, before he has
    weathered
65 his share of winters in this world. A wise man
    must be patient,
neither too hot-hearted nor too hasty with words,
nor too weak in war nor too unwise in thoughts,
neither fretting nor fawning nor greedy for wealth,
never eager for boasting before he truly understands;
70 a man must wait, when he makes a boast,
until the brave spirit understands truly
whither the thoughts of his heart will turn.

    The wise man must realize how ghastly it will be
when all the wealth of this world stands waste,

75 as now here and there throughout this middle-earth
walls stand blasted by wind,
beaten by frost, the buildings crumbling.
The wine halls topple, their rulers lie
deprived of all joys; the proud old troops
80 all fell by the wall. War carried off some,
sent them on the way, one a bird carried off
over the high seas, one the gray wolf
shared with death—and one a sad-faced man
covered in an earthen grave. The Creator
85 of men thus wrecked this enclosure,
until the old works of giants[3] stood empty,
without the sounds of their former citizens.

    He who deeply considers, with wise thoughts,
this foundation and this dark life,
90 old in spirit, often remembers
so many ancient slaughters, and says these words:
'Where has the horse gone? where is the rider? where
    is the giver of gold?
Where are the seats of the feast? where are the joys
    of the hall?
O the bright cup! O the brave warrior!
95 O the glory of princes! How the time passed away,
slipped into nightfall as if it had never been!'
There still stands in the path of the dear warriors
a wall wondrously high, with serpentine stains.
A storm of spears took away the warriors,
100 bloodthirsty weapons, *wyrd* the mighty,
and storms batter these stone walls,
frost falling binds up the earth,
the howl of winter, when blackness comes,
night's shadow looms, sends down from the north
105 harsh hailstones in hatred of men.
All is toilsome in the earthly kingdom,
the working of *wyrd* changes the world under heaven.
Here wealth is fleeting, here friends are fleeting,
here man is fleeting, here woman is fleeting,
110 all the framework of this earth will stand empty."
    So said the wise one in his mind, sitting apart
        in meditation.

---

[1] *it seems ... gift-throne* The description seems to be of some sort of ceremony of loyalty, charged with intense regret and longing.

[2] *Cares are ... waves* The grammar and reference of this intense, almost hallucinatory scene are not entirely clear; the translation reflects one commonly proposed reading.

[3] *works of giants* Ruined buildings are called "the work of giants" (*enta geweorc*) in several places in Old English literature.

He is good who keeps his word,[1] and the man who
    never too quickly
shows the anger in his breast, unless he already
    knows the remedy
115 a noble man can bravely bring about. It will be
    well for one who seeks mercy,
consolation from the Father in heaven, where for
    us all stability stands.

      —C. 975

The Seafarer [2]

I sing a true song of myself,
  tell of my journeys, how in days of toil
I've often suffered troubled times,
hard heartache, come to know
5 on the keel of a ship many of care's dwellings,
terrible tossing of the waves, where the anxious
night-watch often held me at the ship's stem
when it knocks against the cliffs. Pinched with cold
were my feet, bound by frost
10 in cold fetters, while cares seethed
hot around my heart, hunger tore from within
my sea-weary mind. That man does not know,
he whose lot is fairest on land,
how I, wretched with care, dwelt all winter
15 on the ice-cold sea in the paths of exile,
deprived of dear kinsmen,
hung with icicles of frost while hail flew in showers.
I heard nothing there but the noise of the sea,
the ice-cold waves; the wild swan's song
20 sometimes served as my music, the gannet's call
and the curlew's[3] cry for the laughter of men,
the seagull's singing for mead-drink.
Storms beat the stone cliffs where the tern answered
    them,
icy-feathered; often the eagle screamed,
25 dewy-feathered—no sheltering family

could bring consolation to my desolate soul.
  And so[4] he who has tasted life's joy in towns,
suffered few sad journeys, scarcely believes,
proud and puffed up with wine, what I, weary,
30 have often had to endure in my seafaring.
The night-shadow darkened; snow came from the
    north,
frost bound the ground, hail fell on earth,
coldest of grains. And so[5] they compel me now,
my heart-thoughts, to try for myself
35 the high seas, the tossing salt streams;
my heart's desire urges my spirit
time and again to travel, so that I might seek
far from here a foreign land.
  And so no man on earth is so proud in spirit,
40 nor so gifted in grace or so keen in youth,
nor so bold in deeds, nor so beloved of his lord,
that he never has sorrow over his seafaring,
when he sees what the Lord might have in store for
    him.
He has no thought of the harp or the taking of rings,
45 nor the pleasures of woman or joy in the world,
nor anything else but the tumbling waves—
he always has longing who hastens to sea.
The groves take blossom, the cities grow fair,
the fields brighten, the world rushes on;
50 all these urge the eager-hearted
spirit to travel, when one has a mind
to journey far over the flood-ways.
Even the cuckoo urges with its sad voice,
summer's guardian announces sorrow

---

1 *who keeps his word* Or "keeps faith." These last lines offer an answer to the Wanderer's unresolved melancholia—the wisdom of self-control and the hope of Christian salvation.

2 *The Seafarer* The present text has been translated for *The Broadview Anthology of British Literature* by R.M. Liuzza.

3 *gannet ... curlew* Seabirds.

4 *And so* The repeated connecting word "forthon" is notoriously difficult in this poem—it points forwards and/or backwards, meaning either "therefore" or "thus" or "because." In a poem in which a logical progression is by no means clear or easy to follow this is a significant source of ambiguity. Rendering it with the vague "and so," preserves some of the interpretive difficulty found in the original.

5 *And so* The disjunction between what has come before and what come after this line is so great that it has been proposed that a second speaker is introduced here (there are no quotation marks in Old English that might clarify this ambiguity). Though this "two-speaker" theory is no longer widely accepted, it reflects the difficulty many critics have reconciling the conflicting attitudes presented in the poem—sea voyage as terrible suffering, sea voyage as longed-for escape, sea-voyage as metaphor for spiritual pilgrimage, or even for life itself.

55 bitter in the breast-hoard. He does not know,
the man blessed with ease, what those endure
who walk most widely in the paths of exile.
     And so now my thought flies out from my breast,
my spirit moves with the sea-flood,
60 roams widely over the whale's home,
to the corners of the earth, and comes back to me
greedy and hungry; the lone flier cries out,
incites my heart irresistibly to the whale's path
over the open sea—because hotter to me
65 are the joys of the Lord than this dead life,
loaned, on land.[1] I will never believe
that earthly goods will endure forever.
Always, for everyone, one of three things
hangs in the balance before its due time:
70 illness or age or attack by the sword
wrests life away from one doomed to die.
And so for every man the praise of posterity,
those coming after, is the best eulogy—
that before he must be on his way, he act
75 bravely on earth against the enemies' malice,
do bold deeds to beat the devil,
so the sons of men will salute him afterwards,
and his praise thereafter live with the angels
forever and ever, in the joy of eternal life,
80 delight among heaven's host. The days are lost,
and all the pomp of this earthly kingdom;
there are now neither kings nor emperors
nor gold-givers as there once were,
when they did the greatest glorious deeds
85 and lived in most lordly fame.
All this noble host is fallen, their happiness lost,
the weaker ones remain and rule the world,
get what they can with toil. Joy is laid low,
the earth's nobility grows old and withers,
90 just like every man throughout middle-earth.
Old age overtakes him, his face grows pale,
the graybeard grieves; he knows his old friends,

offspring of princes, have been given up to the earth.
When life fails him, his fleshly cloak will neither
95 taste the sweet nor touch the sore,
nor move a hand nor think with his mind.
Though a brother may wish to strew his brother's
grave with gold, bury him among the dead
with myriad treasures to take with him,
100 that gold will be useless before the terror of God
for the soul that is full of sin,
the gold he had hidden while he lived here on earth.
     Great is the terror of God, the earth trembles
          before it;
He established the sturdy foundations,
105 the earth's solid surface and the high heavens.
Foolish is he who dreads not the Lord; death will
          find him unprepared.
Blessed is he who lives humbly; that mercy comes
          to him from heaven,
the Maker strengthens his spirit, for he believes in
          His might.
A man must steer a strong mind and keep it stable,
110 steadfast in its promises, pure in its ways;
every man must hold in moderation
his love for a friend and his hatred for a foe,
though he may wish him full of fire …
     … or his friend consumed
115 on a funeral pyre.[2] Fate is greater,
the Maker mightier than any man's thoughts.
     Let us consider where we should have our home,
and then think how we may come there,
and let us also strive to reach that place
120 of eternal blessedness,
where life is found in the love of the Lord,
hope in Heaven. Thanks be to the Holy One
that He has so honored us, Ruler of Glory,
Eternal Lord, throughout all time. Amen.[3]
—c. 975

---

[1] *And so ... on land* At this point the sea-voyage is revealed to be a journey of spiritual discovery. The hermit-monks of Ireland had a particular penchant for taking to small boats and trusting in God for their safety. Some reached Iceland, some are rumored to have reached the Americas; many others, no doubt, found rest at the bottom of the sea.

---

[2] *full of fire … funeral pyre* Something is missing from the manuscript here; the translation is conjectural and makes as little sense as the original.

[3] *Let us consider … Amen* The tone of these last lines, different in many respects from the rest of the poem, seems to place the poem finally in a homiletic setting—the exhortation of a preacher rather than the confession of a weathered mariner.

The Wife's Lament [1]

I make this song of myself, deeply sorrowing,
my own life's journey. I am able to tell
all the hardships I've suffered since I grew up,
but new or old, never worse than now—
5   ever I suffer the torment of my exile.

    First my lord left his people
over the tumbling waves; I worried at dawn
where on earth my leader of men might be.
When I set out myself in my sorrow,
10   a friendless exile, to find his retainers,
that man's kinsmen began to think
in secret that they would separate us,
so we would live far apart in the world,
most miserably, and longing seized me.

15   My lord commanded me to live here;[2]
I had few loved ones or loyal friends
in this country, which causes me grief.
Then I found that my most fitting man
was unfortunate, filled with grief,
20   concealing his mind, plotting murder
with a smiling face. So often we swore
that only death could ever divide us,
nothing else—all that is changed now;
it is now as if it had never been,
25   our friendship. Far and near, I must
endure the hatred of my dearest one.

    They forced me to live in a forest grove,
under an oak tree in an earthen cave.[3]
This earth-hall is old, and I ache with longing;
30   the dales are dark, the hills too high,
harsh hedges overhung with briars,
a home without joy. Here my lord's leaving
often fiercely seized me. There are friends on earth,
lovers living who lie in their bed,
35   while I walk alone in the first light of dawn
under the oak-tree and through this earth-cave,
where I must sit the summer-long day;

there I can weep for all my exiles,
my many troubles; and so I can never
40   escape from the cares of my sorrowful mind,
nor all the longings that seize me in this life.

    May the young man always be sad-minded
with hard heart-thoughts, yet let him have
a smiling face along with his heartache,
45   a crowd of constant sorrows. Let to himself
all his worldly joys belong! let him be outlawed
in a far distant land, so my friend sits
under stone cliffs chilled by storms,
weary-minded, surrounded by water
50   in a sad dreary hall! My beloved will suffer
the cares of a sorrowful mind; he will remember
too often a happier home. Woe to the one
who must wait with longing for a loved one.[4]
—C. 975

The Ruin [5]

Wondrous is this foundation—the fates have broken
and shattered this city; the work of giants
    crumbles.
The roofs are ruined, the towers toppled,
frost in the mortar has broken the gate,
5   torn and worn and shorn by the storm,
eaten through with age. The earth's grasp
holds the builders, rotten, forgotten,
the hard grip of the ground, until a hundred
generations of men are gone. This wall, rust-stained
10   and covered with moss, has seen one kingdom after
    another,
stood in the storm, steep and tall, then tumbled.
The foundation remains, felled by the weather,
it fell … .[6]

---

[1]   *The Wife's Lament*   The present text bas been translated for *The Broadview Anthology of British Literature* by R.M. Liuzza.

[2]   *My lord … to live here*   Or, "take up a dwelling in a grove" or "live in a (pagan) shrine." The precise meaning of the line, like the general meaning of the poem, is a matter of dispute and conjecture.

[3]   *earthen cave*   Or "an earthen grave" or barrow.

[4]   *May the young man … loved one*   These difficult lines have been read as a particular reflection, imagining the mental state of her distant beloved, or as a general reflection on the double-faced nature of the world; here, following the reading of some critics, they are taken as a kind of curse.

[5]   *The Ruin*   The present text has been translated for *The Broadview Anthology of British Literature* by R.M. Liuzza.

[6]   *it fell … .*   Several lines are lost here; the translation tries to make sense of a few surviving words.

grimly ground up ….

15 …… cleverly created ….

…… a crust of mud surrounded …

….. put together a swift

and subtle system of rings; one of great wisdom

wondrously bound the braces together with wires.

20   Bright were the buildings, with many bath-houses,

high noble gables and a great noise of armies,

many a meadhall filled with men's joys,

until mighty fate made an end to all that.

The slain fell on all sides, plague-days came,

25 and death destroyed all the brave swordsmen;

the seats of their idols became empty wasteland,

the city crumbled, its re-builders collapsed

beside their shrines. So now these courts are empty,

and the rich vaults of the vermilion[1] roofs

30 shed their tiles. The ruins toppled to the ground,

broken into rubble, where once many a man

glad-minded, gold-bright, bedecked in splendor,

proud, full of wine, shone in his war-gear,

gazed on treasure, on silver, on sparkling gems,

35 on wealth, on possessions, on the precious stone,[2]

on this bright capital of a broad kingdom.

    Stone buildings stood, the wide-flowing stream

threw off its heat; a wall held it all

in its bright bosom where the baths were,

40 hot in its core, a great convenience.

They let them gush forth …..

the hot streams over the great stones,

under…

until the circular pool …. hot …

45 ….. where the baths were.

Then ….

….. that is a noble thing,

how …. the city ….[3]

—c. 975

---

[1] *vermilion* Shade of red.

[2] *precious stone* The singular form here is unexpected, but may be nothing more than a collective noun.

[3] *the city* …. The poem, appropriately, trails off into decay.

The Dream of the Rood

The devotional and visionary poem known as *The Dream of the Rood* survives in a manuscript called the Vercelli Book; the manuscript was written in the southeast of England in the later tenth century but was left in the northern Italian town of Vercelli (an important stop on the pilgrimage route from England to Rome) by the end of the eleventh century. The Vercelli Book contains twenty-three prose homilies and six poems; as with most Old English literature, its origins, authorship, and audience are not known.

Although the Vercelli book was copied in the tenth century, *The Dream of the Rood* may be considerably older. Several lines from the poem are carved in runic characters on a large stone monument known as the Ruthwell Cross, found in a small church in Dumfriesshire (on the western border of England and Scotland). The Cross, which has been dated to the early eighth century, is elaborately carved with scenes from the Gospels and lives of the saints, antiphons in Latin, and decorative scroll-work; if the runic inscriptions were part of the original monument (and not a later addition), then portions of *The Dream of the Rood* are among the earliest written Old English poems.

The Ruthwell Cross.

The Dream of the Rood tells the story of the Crucifixion of Christ from the point of view of the Cross, which appears to the narrator in a dream and recounts its experiences. Christ is presented as a heroic warrior, eagerly leaping on the Cross to do battle with Death; the Cross is a loyal retainer who is painfully and paradoxically forced to participate in his lord's execution. The narrator who witnesses all then shares his vision, describes the virtues of devotion to the Cross, and looks forward to the time when the righteous, protected by the Cross, will be taken up into the banquet-halls of heaven. The blending of Christian themes and heroic conventions is a striking example of how the Anglo-Saxons vigorously re-imagined Christianity even as they embraced it. *The Dream of the Rood* interweaves biblical, liturgical, and devotional material with the language of heroic poetry and elegy, and something of the ambiguity and wordplay of the *Riddles*; its complex structure of echoes, allusions, repetitions, and verbal parallels makes it one of the most carefully constructed poems in Old English.

⌘ ⌘ ⌘

The Dream of the Rood [1]

Listen! I will speak of the sweetest dream,
    what came to me in the middle of the night,
when speech-bearers slept in their rest.

It seemed that I saw a most wondrous tree
5 raised on high, circled round with light,
    the brightest of beams. All that beacon was
        covered in gold; gems stood
    fair at the earth's corners, and five there were
    up on the cross-beam. All the angels of the lord
        looked on,

---

[1] *The Dream of the Rood*   Translated by R.M. Liuzza for *The Broadview Anthology of British Literature*.

fair through all eternity;[1] that was no felon's gallows,

10 but holy spirits beheld him there,

men over the earth and all this glorious creation.

　　Wondrous was the victory-tree, and I was fouled

　　　　by sins,

wounded with guilt; I saw the tree of glory

honored in garments, shining with joys,

15 bedecked with gold; gems had

covered worthily the creator's tree.

And yet beneath that gold I began to see

an ancient wretched struggle, for it first began

to bleed on the right side. I was all beset with sorrows,

20 fearful for that fair vision; I saw that eager beacon

change garments and colors—now it was drenched,

stained with blood, now bedecked with treasure.

　　And yet, lying there a long while,

I beheld in sorrow the savior's tree,

25 until I heard it utter a sound;

that best of woods began to speak words:

"It was so long ago—I remember it still—

that I was felled from the forest's edge,

ripped up from my roots. Strong enemies seized me

　　there,

30 made me their spectacle, made me bear their criminals;

they bore me on their shoulders and then set me on a

　　hill,

enemies enough fixed me fast. Then I saw the lord of

　　mankind

hasten eagerly when he wanted to ascend onto me.

There I dared not bow down or break,

35 against the lord's word, when I saw

the ends of the earth tremble. Easily I might

have felled all those enemies, and yet I stood fast.

Then the young hero made ready—that was God

　　almighty—

strong and resolute; he ascended on the high gallows,

40 brave in the sight of many, when he wanted to

　　ransom mankind.

I trembled when he embraced me, but I dared not

　　bow to the ground,

or fall to the earth's corners—I had to stand fast.

I was reared as a cross: I raised up the mighty king,

the lord of heaven; I dared not lie down.

45 They drove dark nails through me; the scars are

　　still visible,

open wounds of hate; I dared not harm any of them.

They mocked us both together; I was all drenched

　　with blood

flowing from that man's side after he had sent

　　forth his spirit.

　　Much have I endured on that hill

50 of hostile fates: I saw the God of hosts

cruelly stretched out. Darkness had covered

with its clouds the ruler's corpse,

that shining radiance. Shadows spread

grey under the clouds; all creation wept,

55 mourned the king's fall: Christ on the cross.

And yet from afar men came hastening

to that noble one; I watched it all.

I was all beset with sorrow, yet I sank into their hands,

humbly, eagerly. There they took almighty God,

60 lifted him from his heavy torment; the warriors then

　　left me

standing drenched in blood, all shot through with arrows.

They laid him down, bone-weary, and stood by

　　his body's head;

they watched the lord of heaven there, who

　　rested a while,

weary from his mighty battle. They began to build a

　　tomb for him

65 in the sight of his slayer; they carved it from bright stone,

and set within the lord of victories. They began to

　　sing a dirge for him,

wretched at evening, when they wished to travel hence,

weary, from the glorious lord—he rested there

　　with little company.[2]

And as we stood there, weeping, a long while

70 fixed in our station, the song ascended

from those warriors. The corpse grew cold,

the fair life-house. Then they began to fell us

all to the earth—a terrible fate!

They dug for us a deep pit, yet the lord's thanes,

75 friends found me there …

---

[1] *All the … eternity* These lines are difficult and much debated; another possible translation is "All creation, eternally fair / beheld the Lord's angel there," the Lord's angel presumably being the Cross itself, God's messenger to earth.

---

[2] *with little company* I.e., utterly alone.

adorned me with gold and silver.[1]
    Now you can hear, my dear hero,
that I have endured the work of evil-doers,
harsh sorrows. Now the time has come
80 that far and wide they honor me,
men over the earth and all this glorious creation,
and pray to this sign. On me the son of God
suffered for a time; and so, glorious now
I rise up under the heavens, and am able to heal
85 each of those who is in awe of me.
Once I was made into the worst of torments,
most hateful to all people, before I opened
the true way of life for speech-bearers.
Lo! the King of glory, guardian of heaven's kingdom
90 honored me over all the trees of the forest,
just as he has also, almighty God, honored
his mother, Mary herself,
above all womankind for the sake of all men.
    Now I bid you, my beloved hero,
95 that you reveal this vision to men,
tell them in words that it is the tree of glory
on which almighty God suffered
for mankind's many sins
and Adam's ancient deeds.
100 Death he tasted there, yet the Lord rose again
with his great might to help mankind.
He ascended into heaven. He will come again
to this middle-earth to seek mankind,
on doomsday, almighty God,
105 the lord himself and his angels with him,
and he will judge—he has the power of judgment—
each one of them as they have earned
beforehand here in this loaned life.
No one there may be unafraid
110 at the words which the ruler will speak:
he will ask before the multitude where the man
    might be
who for the lord's name would taste
bitter death, as he did earlier on that tree.
But they will tremble then, and little think
115 what they might even begin to say to Christ.
But no one there need be very afraid

who has borne in his breast the best of beacons;
but through the cross shall seek the kingdom
every soul from this earthly way,
120 whoever thinks to rest with the ruler."
    Then I prayed to the tree with a happy heart,
eagerly, there where I was alone
with little company. My spirit longed to start
the journey forth; it has felt
125 so much of longing. It is now my life's hope
that I may seek the tree of victory
alone, more often than all men,
and honor it well. I wish for that
with all my heart, and my hope of protection is
130 fixed on the cross. I have few wealthy friends
on earth; they all have gone forth,
fled from worldly joys and sought the king of glory;
they live now in heaven with the high father,
and dwell in glory, and each day I look forward
135 to the time when the cross of the lord,
on which I have looked while here on this earth,
will fetch me from this loaned life,
and bring me where there is great bliss,
joy in heaven, where the lord's host
140 is seated at the feast, with ceaseless bliss;
and then set me where I may afterwards
dwell in glory, share joy
fully with the saints. May the lord be my friend,
he who here on earth once suffered
145 on the hanging-tree for human sin;
he ransomed us and gave us life,
a heavenly home. Hope was renewed
with cheer and bliss for those who were burning there.[2]
The son was successful in that journey,
150 mighty and victorious, when he came with a multitude,
a great host of souls, into God's kingdom,
the one ruler almighty, the angels rejoicing
and all the saints already in heaven
dwelling in glory, when almighty God,
155 their ruler, returned to his rightful home.
—10TH CENTURY

---

1 *silver* There is no gap in the manuscript here, but something is obviously missing—the story of the Finding of the True Cross, told (among other places) in the Old English poem *Elene*. The Cross is buried, hidden, forgotten, then recovered by Helen, mother of the emperor Constantine; its authenticity is established and it becomes an object of veneration and sign of victory.

2 A well-known Christian tradition known as the "Harrowing of Hell" tells how Jesus, after His death on the Cross, descended into Hell and broke open its gates, releasing the souls of those unjustly imprisoned by Satan since the creation of human beings. Jesus conveyed them to Heaven, then returned to earth for His resurrection.

Lines 1-21 of the Vercelli Book.

Beowulf

Only one copy of the poem that modern editors call *Beowulf* has survived, and it probably survived only by accident. A manuscript containing *Beowulf* and a small collection of other texts—a poetic treatment of the Old Testament story of Judith, a prose life of St. Christopher, and two treatises of fantastical geography known as *The Wonders of the East* and *Alexander's Letter to Aristotle*—was copied by two scribes, probably in the decade after 1000, in a monastic center somewhere in the south of England; it lay disregarded for centuries, narrowly escaped destruction by fire in 1731, and is now preserved in the British Library under the shelfmark Cotton Vitellius A.xv.

Beowulf is the longest surviving poem in Old English, consisting of 3,182 extant lines of alliterative verse divided into forty-four sections. Its language is allusive and embellished and its narrative digressive and complex, but its relatively straightforward plot follows the outlines of a folktale: a young hero who fights in isolation from friends and family engages in fabulous battles against monstrous foes, faces three challenges in ascending order of difficulty, and in the end wins glory and fame. The fabulous outlines of the story equally recall the deep undertones of myth: the mighty Beowulf may be a distant cousin of Thor, and his death may contain a hint of Ragnarok, the northern apocalypse.

But whatever its underlying structural patterns, *Beowulf* is neither myth nor folktale; its stories of dragon-slaying and night-battles are set against a complex background of legendary history. The action of the poem unfolds in a recognizable version of Scandinavia: Hrothgar's hall Heorot has been plausibly placed in the village of Lejre on the Danish island of Zealand; Beowulf's tribe of Geats may be the historical Gautar of Southern Sweden; and a number of the poem's characters (Heremod, Hrothgar, Ingeld, and Hygelac) are mentioned in other sources as if they were figures of history rather than fable. Moreover, *Beowulf* is an intensely political poem; the poet seems as intrigued by Danish diplomacy and the bitter feud between the Geats and Swedes as he is by the hero's monster-slaying. Kingdoms and successions, alliances and truces, loyalties and the tragically transient stability of heroic society are the poem's somber subtext, a theme traced less in the clashes of the battlefield than in the patterns of marriage and kin, in stories remembered and retold, in allusion and digression and pointed foreshadowing.

Despite the poem's historical interests, we cannot read *Beowulf* with any modern expectation of historical accuracy. Like many medieval works, *Beowulf* is frustratingly ambivalent—not quite mythical enough to be read apart from the history it purports to contain, nor historical enough to furnish clear evidence for the past it poetically recreates. The action of the poem is set in a somewhat vague heroic *geardagum* ("bygone days"), an age not meant to be counted on a calendar, nor its kingdoms and tribes marked on a map. Nor, undoubtedly, were the monstrous races of Grendels and dragons so clearly distinct in the poet's mind from the real dangers of the real world just beyond the margins of the known. While medieval authors certainly made distinctions between *historia* and *fabula*, the boundaries between these terms are not nearly as impermeable as those of our modern categories "history" and "fable."

Both the ultimate and the immediate origins of *Beowulf* are unknown. Most scholars assume that the single surviving manuscript, written around 1000–20, is a copy of an earlier text, and probably the last in a long chain of copies. But it may be impossible to determine when that chain of texts began, or what cultural and literary milieu gave birth to the poem; proposed dates have ranged from 700 to 1000, and most years in between. The poem seems to arise from a world in which such stories were common, and it presupposes our own position in this world. The poem begins with the assumption that we are hearing a well-known story, or a least a story from a familiar milieu: "We have heard of the glory … of the folk-kings of the spear-Danes," the poet asserts, and the way he tosses out cryptic allusions throughout the poem suggests that his audience was already familiar with songs and stories of other kings and heroes. But at what time in the history of the Anglo-Saxons did such a world exist? And can we trust the narrator as a faithful reporter of this world, or should we view him as a vivid creator of the illusion of antiquity?

The question of the origin of *Beowulf* is not just philological pedantry: the poem will yield very different meanings if it is imagined to have been produced in the time of Bede (c. 725, just a generation or two after the conversion of the English) or of Alfred (c. 880, a time of nation-building and political centralization) or of Ælfric (c. 1000, after half a century of monastic reform and a decade which saw the demoralizing collapse of national security). The earlier we think the poem to be, the more potentially authentic its historical material; the later we imagine it, the more openly fictional and nostalgic it seems. Moreover, the more closely we try to assign a date and place of origin to the poem, the more closely we read it as a text, the intention of a single author or a reflection of a particular ideology, rather than a product of a poetic art whose composition may have been oral and communal and whose traditional roots are beyond discovery.

Most critics agree that the heroic action of the poem is thoroughly accommodated to a world in which the truths of Christianity are accepted without question; they disagree, often sharply, on the meaning and purpose of that accommodation. Some scholars have argued that *Beowulf* is a type of Christ, because he gives his life for his people; others have read the poem as a condemnation of pagan pride, greed and violence. These two extreme positions capture the poem's deliberate ambivalence: *Beowulf* is a secular Christian poem about pagans which avoids the easy alternatives of automatic condemnation or enthusiastic anachronism. The person responsible for putting *Beowulf* in its final form was certainly a Christian: the technology of writing in the Anglo-Saxon period was almost entirely a monopoly of the church. The manuscript in which *Beowulf* survives contains a saint's legend and a versified Bible story, and the poet indicates a clear familiarity with the Bible and expects the same from his audience. Though the paganism of *Beowulf*'s world is downplayed, however, it is not denied; his age is connected to that of the audience but separated by the gulf of conversion and the seas of migration.

More recent work, rather than trying to define a single source for the poem's complex and peculiar texture (whether that source is pure Germanic paganism or orthodox Augustinian Christianity), recognizes that *Beowulf*, like the culture of the Anglo-Saxons themselves, reflects a variety of interdependent and competing influences and attitudes, even a certain tension inherent in the combination of biblical, patristic, secular Latin, and popular Germanic material. The search for a single unified "audience" of *Beowulf*, and with it a sense of a single meaning, has given way to a recognition that there were many readers in Anglo-Saxon England, often with competing and conflicting interests.

⌘⌘⌘

Beowulf, lines 1–21
(British Library, Ms Cotton Vitellius A.xv, fol. 129r).

Beowulf [1]

PROLOGUE

Listen!
We have heard of the glory in bygone days
of the folk-kings of the spear-Danes,[2]
how those noble lords did lofty deeds.

Often Scyld Scefing[3] seized the mead-benches
5   from many tribes, troops of enemies,
struck fear into earls. Though he first was
found a waif, he awaited solace for that—
he grew under heaven and prospered in honor
until every one of the encircling nations
10   over the whale's-riding[4] had to obey him,
grant him tribute. That was a good king!
A boy was later born to him,
young in the courts, whom God sent
as a solace to the people—He saw their need,
15   the dire distress they had endured, lordless,
for such a long time. The Lord of Life,
Wielder of Glory, gave him worldly honor;
Beowulf,[5] the son of Scyld, was renowned,
his fame spread wide in Scandinavian lands.
20   Thus should a young man bring about good
with pious gifts from his father's possessions,
so that later in life loyal comrades
will stand beside him when war comes,
the people will support him—with praiseworthy deeds
25   a man will prosper among any people.

Scyld passed away at his appointed hour,
the mighty lord went into the Lord's keeping;
they bore him down to the brimming sea,

his dear comrades, as he himself had commanded
30   while the friend of the Scyldings[6] wielded speech—
that dear land-ruler had long held power.
In the harbor stood a ring-prowed ship,
icy, outbound, a nobleman's vessel;
there they laid down their dear lord,
35   dispenser of rings, in the bosom of the ship,
glorious, by the mast. There were many treasures
loaded there, adornments from distant lands;
I have never heard of a more lovely ship
bedecked with battle-weapons and war-gear,
40   blades and byrnies;[7] in its bosom lay
many treasures, which were to travel
far with him into the keeping of the flood.
With no fewer gifts did they furnish him there,
the wealth of nations, than those did who
45   at his beginning first sent him forth
alone over the waves while still a small child.[8]
Then they set a golden ensign
high over his head, and let the waves have him,
gave him to the Deep with grieving spirits,
50   mournful in mind. Men do not know
how to say truly—not trusted counselors,
nor heroes under the heavens—who received that cargo.

I

Then Beowulf Scylding, beloved king,
was famous in the strongholds of his folk
55   for a long while—his father having passed away,
a lord from earth—until after him arose
the great Healfdene, who held the glorious Scyldings
all his life, ancient and fierce in battle.
Four children, all counted up,
60   were born to that bold leader of hosts:
Heorogar, Hrothgar, and Halga the Good,
I heard that …[9] was Onela's queen,

---

[1] *Beowulf* This translation is by R.M. Liuzza, from the edition published by Broadview Press.

[2] *spear-Danes* The Danes are described by many different epithets in the poem.

[3] *Scyld Scefing* The name means "Shield, Son of Sheaf" (i.e., of grain). The mysterious origins of Scyld, who seems to arrive providentially from nowhere and is returned to the sea after his death, have occasioned much critical speculation.

[4] *whale's-riding* A condensed descriptive image of the sea—the riding-place of whales. Elsewhere the sea is the "gannet's bath" and the "swan's riding."

[5] *Beowulf* Not the monster-slaying hero of the title, but an early Danish king. Many scholars argue that the original name was *Beow*.

[6] *Scyldings* The Danes, "sons of Scyld."

[7] *byrnie* Coat of ring-mail.

[8] *With no fewer … small child* Scyld was found destitute—this statement is an example of *litotes*, or ironic understatement, not uncommon in Anglo-Saxon poetry.

[9] A name is missing from the manuscript here; it has been conjectured from parallel sources that is should be Yrse, or Ursula. The Swedish ("Scylfing") king Onela appears later in the story, causing much distress to Beowulf's nation.

dear bedfellow of the Battle-Scylfing.

65 Then success in war was given to Hrothgar,
honor in battle, so that his beloved kinsmen
eagerly served him, until the young soldiers grew
into a mighty troop of men. It came to his mind
that he should order a hall-building,
have men make a great mead-house
70 which the sons of men should remember forever,[1]
and there inside he would share everything
with young and old that God had given him,
except for the common land and the lives of men.
Then the work, as I've heard, was widely proclaimed
75 to many nations throughout this middle-earth,
to come adorn the folk-stead. It came to pass
swiftly among men, and it was soon ready,
the greatest of halls; he gave it the name "Heorot,"[2]
he who ruled widely with his words.
80 He remembered his boast; he gave out rings,
treasure at table. The hall towered
high and horn-gabled—it awaited hostile fires,
the surges of war; the time was not yet near
that the sword-hate of sworn in-laws
85 should arise after ruthless violence.[3]

A bold demon who waited in darkness
wretchedly suffered all the while,
for every day he heard the joyful din
loud in the hall, with the harp's sound,
90 the clear song of the scop.[4] He said
who was able to tell of the origin of men
that the Almighty created the earth,
a bright and shining plain, by seas embraced,
and set, triumphantly, the sun and moon
95 to light their beams for those who dwell on land,
adorned the distant corners of the world
with leaves and branches, and made life also,
all manner of creatures that live and move.

— Thus this lordly people lived in joy,
100 blessedly, until one began
to work his foul crimes—a fiend from Hell.
This grim spirit was called Grendel,
mighty stalker of the marches, who held
the moors and fens; this miserable man
105 lived for a time in the land of giants,
after the Creator had condemned him
among Cain's race—when he killed Abel[5]
the eternal Lord avenged that death.
No joy in that feud—the Maker forced him
110 far from mankind for his foul crime.
From thence arose all misbegotten things,
trolls and elves and the living dead,
and also the giants who strove against God
for a long while—He gave them their reward for that.

2

115 When night descended he went to seek out
the high house, to see how the Ring-Danes
had bedded down after their beer-drinking.
He found therein a troop of nobles
asleep after the feast; they knew no sorrow
120 or human misery. The unholy creature,
grim and ravenous, was ready at once,
ruthless and cruel, and took from their rest
thirty thanes;[6] thence he went
rejoicing in his booty, back to his home,
125 to seek out his abode with his fill of slaughter.
When in the dim twilight just before dawn
Grendel's warfare was made known to men,
then lamentation was lifted up after the feasting,
a great mourning-sound. Unhappy sat
130 the mighty lord, long-good nobleman,
suffered greatly, grieved for his thanes,
once they beheld that hostile one's tracks,
the accursed spirit; that strife was too strong,
loathsome and long.
                    It was not longer
135 than the next night until he committed
a greater murder, mourned not at all
for his feuds and sins—he was too fixed in them.

---

[1] *a great ... forever* Or "a greater meadhall / than the sons of men had ever heard of." The reading adopted here is that of Mitchell and Robinson.

[2] *Heorot* "Hart." An object recovered from the burial-mound at Sutton Hoo, perhaps a royal insignia, is surmounted by the image of a hart.

[3] *it awaited ... violence* The hall Heorot is apparently fated to be destroyed in a battle between Hrothgar and his son-in-law Ingeld the Heathobard, a conflict predicted by Beowulf at 2024–69. The battle itself happens outside the action of the poem.

[4] *scop* Poet-singer.

[5] *Cain ... Abel* See Genesis 4.1–16.

[6] *thanes* Companions of a king.

Then it was easy to find a thane
who sought his rest elsewhere, farther away,
140　a bed in the outbuildings,[1] when was pointed out—
truly announced with clear tokens—
that hall-thane's hate; he kept himself afterwards
farther and safer, who escaped the fiend.
So he ruled, and strove against right,
145　one against all, until empty stood
the best of houses. And so for a great while—
for twelve long winters the lord of the Scyldings
suffered his grief, every sort of woe,
great sorrow, for to the sons of men
150　it became known, and carried abroad
in sad tales, that Grendel strove
long with Hrothgar, bore his hatred,
sins and feuds, for many seasons,
perpetual conflict; he wanted no peace
155　with any man of the Danish army,
nor ceased his deadly hatred, nor settled with money,
nor did any of the counselors need to expect
bright compensation from the killer's hands,[2]
for the great ravager relentlessly stalked,
160　a dark death-shadow, lurked and struck
old and young alike, in perpetual night
held the misty moors. Men do not know
whither such whispering demons wander about.

　　　Thus the foe of mankind, fearsome and solitary,
165　often committed his many crimes,
cruel humiliations; he occupied Heorot,
the jewel-adorned hall, in the dark nights—
he saw no need to salute the throne,
he scorned the treasures; he did not know their love.[3]
170　That was deep misery to the lord of the Danes,
a breaking of spirit. Many a strong man sat

in secret counsel, considered advice,
what would be best for the brave at heart
to save themselves from the sudden attacks.
175　At times they offered honor to idols
at pagan temples, prayed aloud
that the soul-slayer[4] might offer assistance
in the country's distress. Such was their custom,
the hope of heathens—they remembered Hell
180　in their minds, they did not know the Maker,
the Judge of deeds, they did not know the Lord God,
or even how to praise the heavenly Protector,
Wielder of glory. Woe unto him
who must thrust his soul through wicked force
185　in the fire's embrace, expect no comfort,
no way to change at all! It shall be well for him
who can seek the Lord after his deathday
and find security in the Father's embrace.

3

With the sorrows of that time the son of Healfdene[5]
190　seethed constantly; nor could the wise hero
turn aside his woe—too great was the strife,
long and loathsome, which befell that nation,
violent, grim, cruel, greatest of night-evils.
　　　Then from his home the thane of Hygelac,[6]
195　a good man among the Geats, heard of Grendel's deeds—
he was of mankind the strongest of might
in those days of this life,
noble and mighty. He commanded to be made
a good wave-crosser, said that that war-king
200　he would seek out over the swan's-riding,
the renowned prince, when he was in need of men.
Wise men did not dissuade him at all
from that journey, though he was dear to them;
they encouraged his bold spirit, inspected the omens.
205　From the Geatish nation that good man
had chosen the boldest champions, the best
he could find; one of fifteen,
he sought the sea-wood. A wise sailor
showed the way to the edge of the shore.
210　The time came—the craft was on the waves,

---

[1] *outbuildings* Hrothgar's hall is apparently surrounded by smaller buildings, including the women's quarters (see lines 662–5, 920–4). Under normal circumstances the men sleep together in the hall, ready for battle (1239–50).

[2] *bright compensation* Germanic and Anglo-Saxon law allowed that a murderer could make peace with the family of his victim by paying compensation, or *wergild*. The amount of compensation varied with the rank of the victim.

[3] *Thus the foe … love* This is a much-disputed passage; this reading follows a suggestion made by Fred C. Robinson in "Why is Grendel's Not Greeting the *gifstol a wræc micel?*" and repeated in Mitchell and Robinson's *Beowulf*.

[4] *soul-slayer* The Devil.

[5] *son of Healfdene* I.e., Hrothgar.

[6] *thane of Hygelac* I.e., Beowulf.

moored under the cliffs. Eager men
climbed on the prow—the currents eddied,
sea against sand—the soldiers bore
into the bosom of the ship their bright gear,
215 fine polished armor; the men pushed off
on their wished-for journey in that wooden vessel.
Over the billowing waves, urged by the wind,
the foamy-necked floater flew like a bird,
until in due time on the second day
220 the curved-prowed vessel had come so far
that the seafarers sighted land,
shining shore-cliffs, steep mountains,
wide headlands—then the waves were crossed,
the journey at an end. Thence up quickly
225 the people of the Weders[1] climbed onto the plain,
moored their ship, shook out their mail-shirts,
their battle-garments; they thanked God
that the sea-paths had been smooth for them.
        When from the wall the Scyldings' watchman,
230 whose duty it was to watch the sea-cliffs,
saw them bear down the gangplank bright shields,
ready battle-gear, he was bursting with curiosity
in his mind to know who these men were.
This thane of Hrothgar rode his horse
235 down to the shore, and shook mightily
his strong spear, and spoke a challenge:
"What are you, warriors in armor, wearing
coats of mail, who have come thus sailing
over the sea-road in a tall ship,
240 hither over the waves? Long have I been
the coast-warden, and kept sea-watch
so that no enemies with fleets and armies
should ever attack the land of the Danes.
Never more openly have there ever come
245 shield-bearers here, nor have you heard
any word of leave from our warriors
or consent of kinsmen. I have never seen
a greater earl on earth than that one among you,
a man in war-gear; that is no mere courtier,
250 honored only in weapons—unless his looks belie him,
his noble appearance! Now I must know
your lineage, lest you go hence
as false spies, travel further
into Danish territory. Now, you sea-travelers

255 from a far-off land, listen to my
simple thought—the sooner the better,
you must make clear from whence you have come."

4

        The eldest one answered him,
leader of the troop, unlocked his word-hoard:
260 "We are men of the Geatish nation
and Hygelac's hearth-companions.
My father was well-known among men,
a noble commander named Ecgtheow;
he saw many winters before he passed away,
265 ancient, from the court; nearly everyone
throughout the world remembers him well.
With a friendly heart have we come
seeking your lord, the son of Healfdene,
guardian of his people; be of good counsel to us!
270 We have a great mission to that famous man,
ruler of the Danes; nor should any of it be
hidden, I think. You know, if things are
as we have truly heard tell,
that among the Scyldings some sort of enemy,
275 hidden evildoer, in the dark nights
manifests his terrible and mysterious violence,
shame and slaughter. With a generous spirit
I can counsel Hrothgar, advise him how,
wise old king, he may overcome this fiend—
280 if a change should ever come for him,
a remedy for the evil of his afflictions,
and his seething cares turn cooler;
or forever afterwards a time of anguish
he shall suffer, his sad necessity, while there stands
285 in its high place the best of houses."
        The watchman spoke, as he sat on his horse,
a fearless officer: "A sharp shield-warrior
must be a judge of both things,
words and deeds, if he would think well.
290 I understand that to the Scylding lord
you are a friendly force. Go forth, and bear
weapons and armor—I shall guide your way;
and I will command my young companions
to guard honorably against all enemies
295 your ship, newly-tarred, upon the sand,
to watch it until the curved-necked wood
bears hence across the ocean-streams

---

[1] *Weders* I.e., Geats.

a beloved man to the borders of the Weders—
and such of these good men as will be granted
300 that they survive the storm of battle."
They set off—their vessel stood still,
the roomy ship rested in its riggings,
fast at anchor. Boar-figures shone
over gold-plated cheek-guards,[1]
305 gleaming, fire-hardened; they guarded the lives
of the grim battle-minded. The men hastened,
marched together, until they could make out
the timbered hall, splendid and gold-adorned—
the most famous building among men
310 under the heavens—where the high king waited;
its light shone over many lands.
Their brave guide showed them the bright court
of the mighty ones, so that they might go
straight to it; that fine soldier
315 wheeled his horse and spoke these words:
"Time for me to go. The almighty Father
guard you in his grace,
safe in your journeys! I must to the sea,
and hold my watch against hostile hordes."

5

320   The road was stone-paved, the path led
the men together. Their mail coats shone
hard, hand-linked, bright rings of iron
rang out on their gear, when right to the hall
they went trooping in their terrible armor.
325 Sea-weary, they set their broad shields,
wondrously-hard boards, against the building's wall;
they sat on a bench—their byrnies rang out,
their soldiers' war-gear; their spears stood,
the gear of the seamen all together,
330 a gray forest of ash. That iron troop
was worthy of its weapons.
                Then a proud warrior[2]

asked those soldiers about their ancestry:
"From whence do you carry those covered shields,
gray coats of mail and grim helmets,
335 this troop of spears? I am herald and servant
to Hrothgar; never have I seen
so many foreign men so fearless and bold.
For your pride, I expect, not for exile,
and for greatness of heart you have sought out Hrothgar."
340 The courageous one answered him,
proud prince of the Weders, spoke words
hardy in his helmet: "We are Hygelac's
board-companions—Beowulf is my name.
I wish to explain my errand
345 to the son of Healfdene, famous prince,
your lord, if he will allow us,
in his goodness, to greet him."
Wulfgar spoke—a prince of the Wendels,
his noble character was known to many,
350 his valor and wisdom: "I will convey
to the friend of the Danes, lord of the Scyldings,
giver of rings, what you have requested,
tell the famous prince of your travels,
and then quickly announce to you the answer
355 which that good man sees fit to give me."
    He hastily returned to where Hrothgar sat
old and gray-haired, with his band of earls;
he boldly went, stood by the shoulder
of the Danish king—he knew the noble custom.
360 Wulfgar spoke to his friend and lord:
"There have arrived here over the sea's expanse,
come from afar, men of the Geats;
the oldest among them, the fighting men
call Beowulf. They have requested
365 that they, my lord, might be allowed
to exchange words with you—do not refuse them
your reply, gracious Hrothgar!
In their war-trappings they seem worthy
of noble esteem; notable indeed is that chief
370 who has shown these soldiers the way hither."

6

    Hrothgar spoke, protector of the Scyldings:
"I knew him when he was nothing but a boy—
his old father was called Ecgtheow,

---

[1] *Boar-figures ... cheek-guards* The boar was a sacred animal in
Germanic mythology; in his *Germania* the Roman historian Tacitus
mentions warriors wearing boar-images into battle (ch. 45). Images
of boars may have been placed on helmets to protect the wearer from
the "bite" of a sword, which was often quasi-personified as a serpent.
Archaeologists have unearthed several Anglo-Saxon helmets with
various kinds of boar-images on them.

[2] *proud warrior* I.e., Wulfgar.

to whom Hrethel the Geat[1] gave in marriage
375 his only daughter; now his daring son
has come here, sought a loyal friend.
Seafarers, in truth, have said to me,
those who brought to the Geats gifts and money
as thanks, that he has thirty
380 men's strength, strong in battle,
in his handgrip. Holy God
in His grace has guided him to us,
to the West-Danes, as I would hope,
against Grendel's terror. To this good man
385 I shall offer treasures for his true daring.
Be hasty now, bid them enter
to see this troop of kinsmen all assembled;
and tell them in your words that they are welcome
to the Danish people."
390   He announced from within:[2]
"My conquering lord commands me to tell you,
ruler of the East-Danes, that he knows your ancestry,
and you are to him, hardy spirits,
welcome hither from across the rolling waves.
395 Now you may go in your war-gear
under your helmets to see Hrothgar,
but let your battle-shields and deadly spears
await here the result of your words."
    The mighty one arose, and many a man with him,
400 powerful thanes; a few waited there,
guarded their battle-dress as the bold man bid them.
They hastened together as the man led them,
under Heorot's roof; [the warrior went][3]
hardy in his helmet, until he stood on the hearth.
405 Beowulf spoke—his byrnie gleamed on him,
war-net sewn by the skill of a smith—:
"Be well, Hrothgar! I am Hygelac's kinsman
and young retainer; in my youth I have done
many a glorious deed. This business with Grendel
410 was made known to me on my native soil;
seafarers say that this building stands,

most excellent of halls, idle and useless
to every man, after evening's light
is hidden under heaven's gleaming dome.
415 Then my own people advised me,
the best warriors and the wisest men,
that I should, lord Hrothgar, seek you out,
because they knew the might of my strength;
they themselves had seen me, bloodstained from battle,
420 come from the fight, when I captured five,
slew a tribe of giants, and on the salt waves
fought sea-monsters by night, survived that tight spot,
avenged the Weders' affliction—they asked for trouble!—
and crushed those grim foes; and now with Grendel,
425 that monstrous beast, I shall by myself have
a word or two with that giant. From you now I wish,
ruler of the Bright-Danes, to request,
protector of the Scyldings, a single favor,
that you not refuse me, having come this far,
430 protector of warriors, noble friend to his people—
that I might alone, O my own band of earls
and this hardy troop, cleanse Heorot.
I have also heard that this evil beast
in his wildness does not care for weapons,
435 so I too will scorn—so that Hygelac,
my liege-lord, may be glad of me—
to bear a sword or a broad shield,
a yellow battle-board, but with my grip
I shall grapple with the fiend and fight for life,
440 foe against foe. Let him put his faith
in the Lord's judgment, whom death takes!
I expect that he will, if he is allowed to win,
eat unafraid the folk of the Geats
in that war-hall, as he has often done,
445 the host of the Hrethmen.[4] You'll have no need
to cover my head—he will have done so,
gory, bloodstained, if death bears me away;
he will take his kill, think to taste me,
will dine alone without remorse,
450 stain his lair in the moor; no need to linger
in sorrow over disposing of my body!
Send on to Hygelac, if battle should take me,
the best battledress, which my breast wears,
finest of garments; it is Hrethel's heirloom,

---

1 *Hrethel the Geat* Father of Hygelac and grandfather of Beowulf.

2 *people … within* There is no gap in the manuscript, but the two halves of the line do not alliterate, and something is probably missing from the text at this point. Most editors add two half-lines with the sense "Then Wulfgar went to the door."

3 *[the warrior went]* A half-line is missing; the translation follows the most innocuous conjecture.

---

4 *Hrethmen* I.e., Geats.

455 the work of Weland.[1] *Wyrd* always goes as it must!"[2]

7

Hrothgar spoke, protector of the Scyldings:
"For past favors, my friend Beowulf,
and for old deeds, you have sought us out.
460 Your father struck up the greatest of feuds,
when he killed Heatholaf by his own hand
among the Wylfings. When the Weder tribe
would not harbor him for fear of war,
thence he sought the South-Dane people
over the billowing seas, the Honor-Scyldings;
465 then I first ruled the Danish folk
and held in my youth this grand kingdom,
city of treasure and heroes—then Heorogar
was dead, my older brother unliving,
Healfdene's firstborn—he was better than I!
470 Later I settled that feud with fee-money;
I sent to the Wylfings over the crest of the waves
ancient treasures; he swore oaths to me.[3]
It is a sorrow to my very soul to say
to any man what Grendel has done to me—
475 humiliated Heorot with his hateful thoughts,
his sudden attacks. My hall-troop,
my warriors, are decimated; *wyrd* has swept them away
into Grendel's terror. God might easily
put an end to the deeds of this mad enemy!
480 Often men have boasted, drunk with beer,
officers over their cups of ale,
that they would abide in the beerhall
Grendel's attack with a rush of sword-terror.
Then in the morning this meadhall,
485 lordly dwelling, was drenched with blood,
when daylight gleamed, the benches gory,

the hall spattered and befouled; I had fewer
dear warriors when death took them away.
Now sit down at my feast, drink mead in my hall,[4]
490 men's reward of victory, as your mood urges."
Then a bench was cleared in the beerhall
for the men of the Geats all together;
the strong-minded men went to sit down,
proud in their strength. A thane did his service,
495 bore in his hands the gold-bright ale-cup,
poured the clear sweet drink. The scop sang
brightly in Heorot—there was the joy of heroes,
no small gathering of Danes and Geats.

8

Unferth[5] spoke, son of Ecglaf,
500 who sat at the feet of the Scylding lord,
unbound his battle-runes[6]—Beowulf's journey,
that brave seafarer, sorely vexed him,
for he did not wish that any other man
on this middle-earth should care for glory
505 under the heavens, more than he himself:
"Are you the Beowulf who strove with Breca
in a swimming contest on the open sea,
where in your pride you tried the waves
and for a foolish boast risked your life
510 in the deep water? No man, whether
friend or foe, could dissuade you two
from that sad venture, when you swam in the sea;
there you seized in your arms the ocean-streams,
measured the sea-ways, flailed your hands
515 and glided over the waves—the water roiled,
wintry surges. In the keeping of the water
you toiled for seven nights, and he outswam you,
and had more strength. Then in the morning
the swells bore him to the Heathoream shore;
520 from thence he sought his own sweet land,
beloved by his people, the land of the Brondings,
the fair fortress, where he had his folk,

---

[1] *Weland*   Legendary blacksmith of the Norse gods. The antiquity of weapons and armor added to their value.

[2] *Wyrd*   The Old English word for "fate" is sometimes quasi-personified, though apparently not to the extent that the goddess *Fortuna* was in Roman poetic mythology. The word survives, via Shakespeare's *Macbeth*, as the Modern English word "weird."

[3] *I sent … me*   Hrothgar pays the *wergild* for the man Ecgtheow killed, and Ecgtheow swears an oath of loyalty and support. It is this oath, passed on to the next generation, that Beowulf is fulfilling (at least this is Hrothgar's public sentiment; his thoughts in the privacy of his council are somewhat different).

[4] *Now sit … hall*   The meaning of this line in Old English is disputed.

[5] *Unferth*   Unferth's name, which may be significant, means either "un-peace" or "un-reason." In the manuscript it is always spelled "Hunferth," though it alliterates with a vowel. His position at Hrothgar's feet appears to be one of honor.

[6] *unbound his battle-runes*   Or "unleashed his hostile secret thoughts." *Run* in Old English often means "secret."

his castle and treasure. He truly fulfilled,
the son of Beanstan, his boast against you.

525 So I expect a worse outcome from you—
though you may have survived the storm of battle,
some grim combats—if for Grendel you dare
to lie in wait the whole night long."

Beowulf spoke, son of Ecgtheow:

530 "What a great deal, Unferth my friend,
drunk with beer, you have said about Breca,
told his adventures! I will tell the truth—
I had greater strength on the sea,
more ordeals on the waves than any other man.

535 When we were just boys we two agreed
and boasted—we were both still
in our youth—that out on the great ocean
we would risk our lives, and we did just that.
We had bare swords, when we swam in the sea,

540 hard in our hands; we thought to protect
ourselves from whales. Not for anything
could he swim far from me on the sea-waves,
more swiftly on the water, nor would I go from him.
We two were together on the sea

545 for five nights, until the flood drove us apart,
surging waves, coldest of weathers,
darkening night, and a northern wind,
knife-sharp, pushed against us. The seas were choppy;
the fishes of the sea were stirred up by it.

550 There my coat of armor offered help,
hard, hand-locked, against those hostile ones,
my woven battle-dress lay on my breast
adorned with gold. Down to the ocean floor
a grisly foe dragged me, gripped me fast

555 in his grim grasp, yet it was given to me
to stab that monster with the point of my sword,
my war-blade; the storm of battle took away
that mighty sea-beast, through my own hand.

9

"Time and again those terrible enemies

560 sorely threatened me. I served them well
with my dear sword, as they deserved.
They got no joy from their gluttony,
those wicked maneaters, when they tasted me,
sat down to their feast on the ocean floor—

565 but in the morning, wounded by my blade,

they were washed ashore by the ocean waves,
dazed by sword-blows, and since that day
they never hindered the passage of any
sea-voyager. Light shone from the east,

570 God's bright beacon; the waves grew calm,
so that I could see the sea-cliffs,
the windswept capes. *Wyrd* often spares
an undoomed man, when his courage endures!
And so it came about that I was able to kill

575 nine of these sea-monsters. I have never heard
of a harder night-battle under heaven's vault,
nor a more wretched man on the water's stream;
yet I escaped alive from the clutches of my enemies,
weary from my journey. Then the sea washed me up,

580 the currents of the flood, in the land of the Finns,
the welling waters. I have never heard a word
about any such contest concerning you,
such sword-panic. In the play of battle
Breca has never—nor you either—

585 done a deed so bold and daring
with his decorated blade—I would never boast of it!—
though you became your brothers' killer,
your next of kin; for that you needs must suffer
punishment in Hell, no matter how clever you are.[1]

590 I will say it truly, son of Ecglaf,
that never would Grendel have worked such terror,
that gruesome beast, against your lord,
or shames in Heorot, if your courage and spirit
were as fierce as you yourself fancy they are;

595 but he has found that he need fear no feud,
no storm of swords from the Victory-Scyldings,
no resistance at all from your nation;
he takes his toll, spares no one
in the Danish nation, but indulges himself,

600 hacks and butchers and expects no battle
from the Spear-Danes. But I will show him
soon enough the strength and courage
of the Geats in war. Afterwards, let him who will

---

1 *though you became ... you are* Unferth's fratricide brings the general theme of kin-slaying, represented by Grendel's descent from Cain, inside Hrothgar's hall. In reality—at least in the reality of the heroic world depicted in poetry—it may not have been unthinkable for kinsmen to find themselves on opposite sides of a battle; loyalty to one's lord was supposed to outweigh the claims of blood-relation. The word "Hell" is not in the manuscript, but it is attested by one of the early transcriptions. Some scholars read *healle*, i.e., "hall."

go bravely to mead, when the morning light
605 of a new day, the sun clothed in glory
shines from the south on the sons of men!"
        Then the giver of treasure was greatly pleased,
gray-haired and battle-bold; the Bright-Danes' chief
had faith in his helper; that shepherd of his folk
610 recognized Beowulf's firm resolution.
There was man's laughter, lovely sounds
and winsome words. Wealhtheow went forth,
Hrothgar's queen, mindful of customs;
adorned with gold, she greeted the men in the hall,
615 then that courteous wife offered the full cup
first to the guardian of the East-Danes' kingdom,
bid him be merry at his beer-drinking,
beloved by his people; with pleasure he received
the feast and cup, victorious king.
620 The lady of the Helmings then went about
to young and old, gave each his portion
of the precious cup, until the moment came
when the ring-adorned queen, of excellent heart,
bore the mead-cup to Beowulf;
625 she greeted the Geatish prince, thanked God
with wise words that her wish had come to pass,
that she could rely on any earl for relief
from those crimes. He took the cup,
the fierce warrior, from Wealhtheow,
630 and then eager for battle he made his announcement.
Beowulf spoke, son of Ecgtheow:
"I resolved when I set out over the waves,
sat down in my ship with my troop of soldiers,
that I would entirely fulfill the wishes
635 of your people, or fall slain,
fast in the grip of my foe. I shall perform
a deed of manly courage, or in this meadhall
I will await the end of my days!"
These words well pleased that woman,
640 the boasting of the Geat; she went, the gold-adorned
and courteous folk-queen, to sit beside her lord.
        Then, as before, there in that hall were
strong words spoken, the people happy,
the sounds of a victorious nation, until shortly
645 the son of Healfdene wished to seek
his evening rest; he knew that the wretched beast
had been planning to do battle in the high building
from the time they could first see the sunrise

until night fell darkening over all,
650 and creatures of shadow came creeping about
pale under the clouds. The company arose.
One warrior greeted another there,
Hrothgar to Beowulf, and wished him luck,
gave him control of the wine-hall in these words:
655 "I have never entrusted to any man,
ever since I could hold and hoist a shield,
the great hall of the Danes—except to you now.
Have it and hold it, protect this best of houses,
be mindful of glory, show your mighty valor,
660 watch for your enemies! You will have all you desire,
if you emerge from this brave undertaking alive."

10

        Then Hrothgar and his troop of heroes,
protector of the Scyldings, departed from the hall;
the war-chief wished to seek Wealhtheow,
665 his queen's bedchamber. The glorious king[1]
had set against Grendel a hall-guardian
— as men had heard said—who did special service
for the king of the Danes, kept a giant-watch.
Surely the Geatish prince greatly trusted
670 his mighty strength, the Maker's favor,
when he took off his iron byrnie,
undid his helmet, and gave his decorated iron,
best of swords, to his servant
and bid him hold his battle-gear.
675 The good man, Beowulf the Geat,
spoke a few boasting words before he lay down:
"I consider myself no poorer in strength
and battle-deeds than Grendel does himself;
and so I will not kill him with a sword,
680 put an end to his life, though I easily might;
he knows no arts of war, no way to strike back,
hack at my shield-boss, though he be brave
in his wicked deeds; but tonight we two will
forgo our swords, if he dare to seek out
685 a war without weapons—and then let the wise Lord
grant the judgment of glory, the holy God,
to whichever hand seems proper to Him."
        He lay down, battle-brave; the bolster took
the earl's cheek, and around him many

---

[1] *The glorious king* Or "King of Glory," i.e., God?

690 a bold seafarer sank to his hall-rest.
None of them thought that he should thence
ever again seek his own dear homeland,
his tribe or the town in which he was raised,
for they had heard it said that savage death
695 had swept away far too many of the Danish folk
in that wine-hall. But the Lord gave them
a web of victory, the people of the Weders,
comfort and support, so that they completely,
through one man's craft, overcame their enemy,
700 by his own might. It is a well-known truth
that mighty God has ruled mankind
always and forever.
                    In the dark night he came
creeping, the shadow-goer. The bowmen slept
who were to hold that horned hall—
705 all but one. It was well-known to men
that the demon foe could not drag them under
the dark shadows if the Maker did not wish it;
but he, wakeful, keeping watch for his enemy,
awaited, enraged, the outcome of battle.

II

710 Then from the moor, in a blanket of mist,
Grendel came stalking—he bore God's anger;
the evil marauder meant to ensnare
some of human-kind in that high hall.
Under the clouds he came until he clearly knew
715 he was near the wine-hall, men's golden house,
finely adorned. It was not the first time
he had sought out the home of Hrothgar,
but never in his life, early or late,
did he find harder luck or a hardier hall-thane.
720 To the hall came that warrior on his journey,
bereft of joys. The door burst open,
fast in its forged bands, when his fingers touched it;
bloody-minded, swollen with rage, he swung open
the hall's mouth, and immediately afterwards
725 the fiend strode across the paved floor,
went angrily; in his eyes stood
a light not fair, glowing like fire.
He saw in the hall many a soldier,
a peaceful troop sleeping all together,
730 a large company of thanes—and he laughed inside;
he meant to divide, before day came,

this loathsome creature, the life of each
man from his body, when there befell him
the hope of a feast. But it was not his fate
735 to taste any more of the race of mankind
after that night. The kinsman of Hygelac,
mighty one, beheld how that maneater
planned to proceed with his sudden assault.
Not that the monster[1] meant to delay—
740 he seized at once at his first pass
a sleeping man, slit him open suddenly,
bit into his joints, drank the blood from his veins,
gobbled his flesh in gobbets, and soon
had completely devoured that dead man,
745 feet and fingertips. He stepped further,
and took in his hands the strong-hearted
man in his bed; the monster reached out
towards him with his hands—he quickly grabbed him
with evil intent, and sat up against his arm.
750 As soon as that shepherd of sins discovered
that he had never met on middle-earth,
in any region of the world, another man
with a greater handgrip, in his heart he was
afraid for his life, but none the sooner could he flee.
755 His mind was eager to escape to the darkness,
seek out a host of devils—his habit there
was nothing like he had ever met before.
The good kinsman of Hygelac remembered then
his evening speech, and stood upright
760 and seized him fast. His fingers burst;
the giant turned outward, the earl stepped inward.
The notorious one meant—if he might—
to turn away further and flee, away
to his lair in the fen; he knew his fingers
765 were held in a hostile grip. That was an unhappy journey
that the harm-doer took to Heorot!
The great hall resounded; to the Danes it seemed,
the city's inhabitants, and every brave earl,
like a wild ale-sharing.[2] Both were angry,

---

[1] *monster* The OE word *æglæca*, which literally means "awesome one" or "terror," is elsewhere applied to the dragon-slaying Sigemund (line 892, where it is translated "fierce creature") and to Beowulf himself. Its translation here is admittedly tendentious. The word appears elsewhere, variously translated, in lines 159, 433, 732, 556, etc.

[2] *wild ale-sharing* The general sense of the OE word *ealuscerwen* is "panic" or "terror," but its precise meaning (probably "a dispensing of ale") is unclear; did the Danes think a wild party was going on? Or

770 fierce house-wardens—the hall echoed.
It was a great wonder that the wine-hall
withstood their fighting and did not fall to the ground,
that fair building—but it was fastened
inside and out with iron bands,
775 forged with skill. From the floor there flew
many a mead-bench, as men have told me,
gold-adorned, where those grim foes fought.
The Scylding elders had never expected
that any man, by any ordinary means,
780 could break it apart, beautiful, bone-adorned,
or destroy it with guile, unless the embrace of fire
might swallow it in flames. The noise swelled
new and stark—among the North-Danes was
horrible terror, in each of them
785 who heard through the wall the wailing cry—
God's adversary shrieked a grisly song
of horror, defeated, the captive of Hell
bewailed his pain. He pinned him fast,
he who among men was the strongest of might
790 in those days of this life.

12

That protector of earls would not for anything
let that murderous visitor escape alive—
he did not consider his days on earth
of any use at all. Many an earl
795 in Beowulf's troop drew his old blade,
longed to protect the life of his liege-lord,
the famous captain, however they could.
But they did not know as they entered the fight,
those stern-minded men of battle,
800 and thought to strike from all sides
and seek his soul, that no sword,
not the best iron anywhere in the world,
could even touch that evil sinner,
for he had worked a curse on weapons,
805 every sort of blade. His separation from the world
in those days of this life
would have to be miserable, and that alien spirit
would travel far into the keeping of fiends.
Then he discovered, who had done before

810 so much harm to the race of mankind,
so many crimes—he was marked by God—
that his body could bear it no longer,
but the courageous kinsman of Hygelac
had him in hand—hateful to each
815 was the life of the other. The loathsome creature felt
great bodily pain; a gaping wound opened
in his shoulder-joint, his sinews sprang apart,
his joints burst asunder. Beowulf was given
glory in battle—Grendel was forced
820 to flee, mortally wounded, into the fen-slopes,
seek a sorry abode; he knew quite surely
that the end of his life had arrived,
the sum of his days. The will of the Danes
was entirely fulfilled in that bloody onslaught!
825 He who had come from afar had cleansed,
wise and stout-hearted, the hall of Hrothgar,
warded off attack. He rejoiced in his night-work,
his great courage. That man of the Geats
had fulfilled his boast to the East-Danes,
830 and entirely remedied all their distress,
the insidious sorrows they had suffered
and had to endure from sad necessity,
no small affliction. It was a clear sign,
when the battle-brave one laid down the hand,
835 arm and shoulder—there all together
was Grendel's claw—under the curved roof.

13

Then in the morning was many a warrior,
as I have heard, around that gift-hall,
leaders of the folk came from far and near
840 throughout the wide land to see that wonder,
the loathsome one's tracks. His parting from life
hardly seemed sad to any man
who examined the trail of that inglorious one,
how he went on his weary way,
845 defeated by force, to a pool of sea-monsters,
doomed, put to flight, and left a fatal trail.
The water was welling with blood there—
the terrible swirling waves, all mingled together
with hot gore, heaved with the blood of battle,
850 concealed that doomed one when, deprived of joys,
he laid down his life in his lair in the fen,
his heathen soul—and Hell took him.

were they dismayed by the loss of their mead-hall? Or does OE *ealu*
mean "luck"?

Then the old retainers returned from there,
and many a youth on the joyful journey,
855 bravely rode their horses back from the mere,
men on their steeds. There they celebrated
Beowulf's glory: it was often said
that south or north, between the two seas,[1]
across the wide world, there was none
860 better under the sky's expanse
among shield-warriors, nor more worthy to rule—
though they found no fault with their own friendly lord,
gracious Hrothgar, but said he was a good king.
At times the proud warriors let their horses prance,
865 their fallow mares fare in a contest,
wherever the footpaths seemed fair to them,
the way tried and true. At times the king's thane,
full of grand stories, mindful of songs,
who remembered much, a great many
870 of the old tales, found other words
truly bound together; he began again
to recite with skill the adventure of Beowulf,
adeptly tell an apt tale,
and weave his words. He said nearly all
875 that he had heard said of Sigemund's
stirring deeds,[2] many strange things,
the Volsung's strife, his distant voyages
obscure, unknown to all the sons of men,
his feuds and crimes—except for Fitela,
880 when of such things he wished to speak to him,
uncle to nephew[3]—for always they were,

in every combat, companions at need;
a great many of the race of giants
they slaughtered with their swords. For Sigemund
885 no small fame grew after his final day,
after that hardened soldier, prince's son,
had killed a dragon, keeper of a hoard;
alone, he dared to go under gray stones,
a bold deed—nor was Fitela by his side;
890 yet so it befell him that his sword pierced
the wondrous serpent, stood fixed in the wall,
the manly iron; the dragon met his death.
That fierce creature had gone forth in courage
so that he could possess that store of rings
895 and use them at his will; the son of Wæls
loaded his sea-boat, bore the bright treasure
to the ship's hold. The serpent melted in its own heat.

He was the most famous of exiles, far and wide,
among all people, protector of warriors,
900 for his noble deeds—he had prospered for them—
since the struggles of Heremod had ceased,
his might and valor. Among the Eotens[4]
he was betrayed into his enemies' hands,
quickly dispatched. The surging of cares
905 had crippled him too long; he became a deadly burden
to his own people, to all noblemen;
for many a wise man had mourned
in earlier times over his headstrong ways
who had looked to him for relief from affliction,
910 hoped that that prince's son would prosper,
receive his father's rank, rule his people,
hoard and fortress, a kingdom of heroes,
the Scylding homeland. The kinsman of Hygelac
became to all of the race of mankind
915 a more pleasant friend; sin possessed him.[5]

Sometimes, competing, the fallow paths
they measured on horseback. When morning's light
raced on and hastened away, many a retainer,
stout-hearted, went to see the high hall
920 to see the strange wonder; the king himself,
guard of the treasure-hoard, strode glorious
from the woman's chambers with a great entourage,

---

[1] *between the two seas* A conventional expression like Modern English "coast to coast"; probably it originally referred to the North and Baltic seas.

[2] *He said ... deeds* Beowulf is praised indirectly, by being compared first to Sigemund, another famous monster-slayer (a different version of whose story is told in the Old Norse *Volsungasaga* and the Middle High German *Nibelungenlied*; there the dragon-slaying is attributed to Sigemund's son Siegfried), and then contrasted to Heremod, an earlier king of the Danes who descended into tyranny (it is sometimes assumed that the disastrous ending of Heremod's reign is the cause of the Danes' lordlessness and distress mentioned at the beginning of the poem). The implication is that Beowulf's deeds place him in the ranks of other exemplary figures. The method of narration is allusive and indirect, as though the audience were expected to know the details of the story and appreciate an elliptical reference to them.

[3] *uncle to nephew* Fitela is actually Sigemund's son by his own sister—either the poet is being discreet, or his version of the story differs from the Norse.

---

[4] *Eotens* Perhaps "Jutes." The word literally means "giants" and may be a tribal name, or an epithet, or may in fact refer to an actual race of giants.

[5] *sin possessed him* I.e., Heremod.

a chosen retinue, and his royal queen with him
measured the meadhall-path with a troop of maidens.

14

925   Hrothgar spoke—he went to the hall,
stood on the steps, beheld the steep roof
plated with gold, and Grendel's hand:
"For this sight let us swiftly offer thanks
to the Almighty! Much have I endured
930 of dire grief from Grendel, but God may always
work, Shepherd of glory, wonder upon wonder.
It was not long ago that I did not expect
ever in my life to experience relief
from any of my woes, when, stained with blood,
935 this best of houses stood dripping, gory,
a widespread woe to all wise men
who did not expect that they might ever
defend the people's fortress from its foes,
devils and demons. Now a retainer has done
940 the very deed, through the might of God,
which we all could not contrive to do
with all our cleverness. Lo, that woman could say,
whosoever has borne such a son
into the race of men, if she still lives,
945 that the God of Old was good to her
in childbearing. Now I will cherish you,
Beowulf, best of men, like a son
in my heart; hold well henceforth
your new kinship. You shall have no lack
950 of the worldly goods which I can bestow.
Often have I offered rewards for less,
honored with gifts a humbler man,
weaker in battle. Now by yourself
you have done such deeds that your fame will endure
955 always and forever—may the Almighty
reward you with good, as He has already done!"
    Beowulf spoke, son of Ecgtheow:
"Freely and gladly have we fought this fight,
done this deed of courage, daringly faced
960 this unknown power. I would much prefer
that you might have seen the foe himself
decked in his finery,[1] fallen and exhausted!

With a hard grip I hoped to bind him
quickly and keenly on the killing floor,
965 so that for my handgrasp he would have to
lie squirming for life, unless he might slip away;
I could not—the Creator did not wish it—
hinder his going, no matter how hard I held
that deadly enemy; too overwhelming was
970 that fiend's flight. Yet he forfeited his hand,
his arm and shoulder, to save his life,
to guard his tracks—though he got thereby,
pathetic creature, little comfort;
the loathsome destroyer will live no longer,
975 rotten with sin, but pain has seized him,
grabbed him tightly in its fierce grip,
its baleful bonds—and there he shall abide,
guilty of his crimes, the greater judgment,
how the shining Maker wishes to sentence him."
980   Then the son of Ecglaf[2] was more silent
in boasting words about his battle-works
after the noblemen, through the earl's skill,
looked on the hand over the high roof,
the enemy's fingers; at the end of each nail
985 was a sharp tip, most like steel,
heathen talons, the terrible spikes
of that awful warrior; each of them agreed
that not even the hardest of ancient and honorable
irons could touch him, or injure at all
990 the bloody battle-paw of that baleful creature.

15

    Then it was quickly commanded that Heorot
be adorned by hands inside; many there,
men and women, prepared that wine-hall,
the guest-house. Gold-dyed tapestries
995 shone on the walls, many wonderful sights
to any man who might look on them.
That shining building was nearly shattered
inside, entirely, fast in its iron bands,
its hinges sprung; the roof alone survived
1000 unharmed, when that horrible creature,
stained with foul deeds, turned in his flight,
despairing of life. Death is not an easy
thing to escape—try it who will—

---

[1] *in his finery* Literally "in his adornments," a peculiar phrase since Grendel is notoriously not armed and unadorned. Perhaps Beowulf means "covered in a garment of blood"?

[2] *son of Ecglaf* I.e., Unferth.

but compelled by necessity all must come
1005 to that place set aside for soul-bearers,
children of men, dwellers on earth,
where the body, fast on its bed of death,
sleeps after the feast.
                        Then was the set time
that the son of Healfdene went to the hall;
1010 the king himself wished to share in the feast.
I have never heard of a greater host
who bore themselves better before their treasure-giver.
Those men in their glory moved to their benches,
rejoiced in the feast; fairly those kinsmen
1015 took many a full mead-cup,
stouthearted in the high hall,
Hrothgar and Hrothulf. Heorot within was
filled with friends—no false treacheries
did the people of the Scyldings plot at that time.[1]
1020 He gave to Beowulf the blade of Healfdene,[2]
a golden war-standard as a reward for victory,
the bright banner, a helmet and byrnie,
a great treasure-sword—many saw them
borne before that man. Beowulf received
1025 the full cup in the hall, he felt no shame
at that gift-giving before his bowmen;
never have I heard tell of four treasures
given more graciously, gold-adorned,
from one man to another on the ale-benches.
1030 On the crown of the helmet as a head-protector
a ridge, wound with wire, stood without,
so that the file-sharp swords might not terribly
harm him, shower-hard, when shield-fighters
had to go against hostile forces.
1035 The protector of earls ordered eight horses
with ornamented bridles led into the building,
in under the eaves; on one sat

a saddle, skillfully tooled, set with gemstones;
that was the warseat of the high-king
1040 when the son of Healfdene sought to perform
his swordplay—the widely-known warrior
never failed at the front, when the slain fell about him.
And the lord of the Ingwines[3] gave ownership
of both of them to Beowulf,
1045 the horses and weapons, bid him use them well.
So manfully did the mighty prince,
hoard-guard of warriors, reward the storm of battle
with such steeds and treasures that none who will speak
the truth rightfully could ever reproach them.

16

1050   Then the lord of earls, to each of those
on the meadbenches who had made with Beowulf
a sea-journey, gave jeweled treasures,
antique heirlooms, and then ordered
that gold be paid for the man whom Grendel
1055 had wickedly slain—he would have done more,
if wise God and one man's courage
had not prevented that fate. The Maker ruled all
of the race of mankind, as He still does.
Therefore understanding is always best,
1060 spiritual foresight—he must face much,
both love and hate, who long here
endures this world in these days of strife.
    Noise and music mingled together
before the leader of Healfdene's forces,
1065 the harp was touched, tales often told,
when Hrothgar's scop was set to recite
among the mead-tables his hall-entertainment
about the sons of Finn, surprised in ambush,
when the hero of the Half-Danes, Hnæf the Scylding
1070 had to fall in a Frisian slaughter.[4]

---

[1] Implicit in this statement is the idea that, at some later time, the people of the Scyldings did plot false treacheries; from other sources it is possible to infer that after the death of Hrothgar, his nephew Hrothulf ruled rather than Hrethric, Hrothgar's son. Many scholars assume that the story of some sort of treacherous usurpation was known to the audience; this gives a special urgency to much of what happens in these scenes of feasting, especially the speeches of Wealhtheow.

[2] *He gave ... Healfdene* The translation follows the reading of Mitchell and Robinson, and see Bruce Mitchell, "Beowulf, line 1020b: *brand* or *bearn*?" The manuscript is usually emended to mean "The son of Healfdene gave to Beowulf."

[3] *Ingwines* I.e., Danes.

[4] *the sons of Finn ... Frisian slaughter* The story is obscure; the survival of a fragment of another poem ("The Fight at Finnsburg") telling the same story helps clarify the action somewhat. Hnæf, prince of the Danes, is visiting his sister Hildeburh at the home of her husband Finn, king of the Frisians. While there, the Danish party is treacherously attacked (perhaps by a Jutish contingent among Finn's troops, unless the "Jutes" and Frisians are one and the same people); after five days of fighting Hnæf lies dead, along with many casualties on either side. Hnæf's retainer Hengest is left to lead the remnant of Danish survivors.

Hildeburh, indeed, had no need to praise
the good faith of the Jutes.[1] Guiltless, she was
deprived of her dear ones in that shieldplay,
her sons and brothers—sent forth to their fate,
1075 dispatched by spears; she was a sad lady!
Not without cause did she mourn fate's decrees,
the daughter of Hoc, after daybreak came
and she could see the slaughter of her kin
under the very skies where once she held
1080 the greatest worldly joys. War took away
all of the thanes of Finn, except a few,
so that he could not continue at all
a fight with Hengest on the battlefield,
nor could that woeful remnant drive away
1085 the prince's thane—so they offered them terms:[2]
they would clear out another hall for them,
a house and high-seat, of which they should have
half the control with the sons of the Jutes,
and Folcwalda's son,[3] with feasting and gifts,
1090 should honor the Danes each and every day,
gladden the troops of Hengest with gold rings
and ancient treasures, ornamented gold,
just as often as he would encourage
the hosts of the Frisians in the beerhall.
1095 They swore their pledges then on either side,
a firm compact of peace. With unfeigned zeal
Finn swore his oaths to Hengest, pledged that he,
with the consent of his counselors, would
support with honor those sad survivors,
1100 and that none should break their pact in word or deed,
nor through malice should ever make mention,
though they should serve their ring-giver's slayer,
without a lord, as they were led by need—
and if, provoking, any Frisian spoke
1105 reminding them of all their murderous hate,
then with the sword's edge they should settle it.
The oath[4] was made ready, and ancient gold

was brought from the hoard; the Battle-Scyldings'
best fighting-man was ready for the fire.
1110 It was easy to see upon that pyre
the bloodstained battle-shirt, the gilded swine,
iron-hard boar-images, the noblemen
with fatal wounds—so many felled by war!
Then Hildeburh commanded at Hnæf's pyre
1115 that her own son be consigned to the flames
to be burnt, flesh and bone, placed on the pyre
at his uncle's shoulder; the lady sang
a sad lament. The warrior ascended;
to the clouds coiled the mighty funeral fire,
1120 and roared before their mound; their heads melted,
their gashes burst open and spurted blood,
the deadly body-bites. The flame devoured,
most greedy spirit, those whom war destroyed
of both peoples—their glory departed.

17

1125 The warriors left to seek their native lands,
bereft of friends, to behold Frisia,
their homes and high fortresses. Hengest still
stayed there with Finn that slaughter-stained winter,
unwilling, desolate. He dreamt of home,
1130 though on the frozen sea he could not[5] steer
his ring-prowed ship—the ocean raged with storms,
strove with the wind, and winter locked the waves
in icy bonds, until there came another
year to the courtyard—as it yet does,
1135 always observing its seasons and times,
bright glorious weather. Gone was the winter,
and fair the bosom of earth; the exile burned
to take leave of that court, yet more he thought
of stern vengeance than of sea-voyages,
1140 how he might arrange a hostile meeting,
remind the Jutish sons of his iron sword.
So he did not refuse the world's custom
when the son of Hunlaf[6] placed a glinting sword,

---

[1] *Jutes* I.e., Frisians.

[2] *them terms* The referent of this pronoun in not entirely clear—who offers what to whom? The terms of the truce are unthinkable—no hero could honorably follow the killer of his lord. In the following line "they" refers to the Frisians, "them" to the Danes.

[3] *Folcwalda's son* I.e., Finn.

[4] *oath* Some editors emend to *ad*, "pyre."

[5] *not* OE *ne* "not" is not in the manuscript; most editors and translators add it to make better sense of the passage and of Hengest's character.

[6] *the son of Hunlaf* It is not clear who this is: perhaps Guthlaf or Oslaf (mentioned a few lines later), perhaps not; apparently some retainers remained with Hengest in Finn's hall, nursing their resentment throughout the winter. Some scholars take the OE word

the best of battle-flames, upon his lap;
1145 its edge was not unknown among the Jutes.
And so, in turn, to the bold-minded Finn
befell cruel sword-evil in his own home,
when Guthlaf and Oslaf spoke of their grief,
the fierce attack after their sea voyage,
1150 and cursed their wretched lot—the restless heart
could not restrain itself. The hall was stained
with the lifeblood of foes, and Finn was slain,
the king among his host; the queen was seized.
The Scylding bowmen carried to their ships
1155 all the house property of that earth-king,
whatever they could find in Finn's homestead,
brooches and bright gems. On their sea journey
they bore that noble queen back to the Danes
and led her to her people.
                              The lay was sung,
1160 the entertainer's song. Glad sounds rose again,
the bench-noise glittered, cupbearers gave
wine from wondrous vessels. Wealhtheow came forth
in her golden crown to where the good two
sat, nephew and uncle; their peace was still whole then,
1165 each true to the other. Likewise Unferth, spokesman,[1]
sat at the foot of the Scylding lord; everyone trusted
    his spirit,
that he had great courage, though to his kinsmen he
    had not been
merciful in sword-play. Then the lady of the Scyldings
    spoke:
    "Take this cup, my noble courteous lord,
1170 giver of treasure! Be truly joyful,
gold-friend of men, and speak to the Geats
in mild words, as a man should do!
Be gracious to the Geats, mindful of the gifts
which you now have from near and far.
1175 I have been told that you would take this warrior
for your son. Heorot is cleansed,
the bright ring-hall—use your many rewards
while you can, and leave to your kinsmen
the folk and kingdom, when you must go forth

1180 to face the Maker's decree. I know that my own
dear gracious Hrothulf will hold in honors
these youths, if you should give up the world
before him, friend of the Scyldings;
I expect that he would wish to repay
1185 both our sons kindly, if he recalls all
the pleasures and honors that we have shown him,
in our kindness, since he was a child."
She turned to the bench where her boys sat,
Hrethric and Hrothmund, and the hero's son,
1190 all the youths together; the good man,
Beowulf the Geat, sat between the brothers.

18

    The flagon was borne to him, a friendly greeting
conveyed with words, and wound gold
offered with good will, two armlets,
1195 garments and rings, and the greatest neck-collar
ever heard of anywhere on earth.
Under heaven I have not heard tell of a better
hoard-treasure of heroes, since Hama carried off
to the bright city the Brosinga necklace,[2]
1200 the gem and its treasures; he fled the treachery
of Eormanric, chose eternal counsel.
    Hygelac the Geat on his last journey
had that neck-ring,[3] nephew of Swerting,
when under the banner he defended his booty,
1205 the spoils of slaughter. Fate struck him down
when in his pride he went looking for woe,
a feud with the Frisians. He wore that finery,
those precious stones, over the cup of the sea,
that powerful lord, and collapsed under his shield.
1210 Into Frankish hands came the life of that king,
his breast-garments, and the great collar too;
a lesser warrior looted the corpses
mown down in battle; Geatish men

---

hunlafing as the name of a sword.

[1] *spokesman* The Old English word *thyle* has been variously interpreted, from "court jester" to "official speechmaker." The present translation grants Unferth a measure of dignity and position to which, perhaps, he is not entitled.

[2] *Brosinga necklace* The Brosinga necklace had apparently been worn by the Norse goddess Freya. Nothing much is known of Hama, who apparently stole the necklace from Eormanric, famous king of the Goths. The "bright city" and "eternal counsel" may refer to his retreat into a monastery and Christianity (a story told in the Old Norse *Thidrekssaga*), though this is not entirely certain.

[3] *Hygelac ... neck-ring* The first of several mentions of Hygelac's ill-fated raid against the Frisians. Later we are told that Beowulf gives the necklace to Hygd, Hygelac's wife; she apparently let him borrow it when he went on his piratical raid.

held that killing field.

                    The hall swallowed the noise.

1215 Wealhtheow stood before the company and spoke:
"Beowulf, beloved warrior, wear this neck-ring
in good health, and enjoy this war-garment,
treasure of a people, and prosper well,
be bold and clever, and to these boys be
1220 mild in counsel—I will remember you for that.
You have made it so that men will praise you
far and near, forever and ever,
as wide as the seas, home of the winds,
surround the shores of earth. Be while you live
1225 blessed, o nobleman! I wish you well
with these bright treasures. Be to my sons
kind in your deeds, keeping them in joys!
Here each earl is true to the other,
mild in his heart, loyal to his liege-lord,
1230 the thanes united, the nation alert;
the troop, having drunk at my table, will do as I bid."

    She went to her seat. The best of feasts it was—
the men drank wine, and did not know *wyrd*,
the cruel fate which would come to pass
1235 for many an earl once evening came,
and Hrothgar departed to his own dwelling,
the mighty one to his rest. Countless men
guarded that hall, as they often had before.
They cleared away bench-planks, spread cushions
1240 and bedding on the floor. One of those beer-drinkers
lay down to his rest fated, ripe for death.
They set at their heads their round battle-shields,
bright boards; there on the bench was
easily seen over the noblemen
1245 the high battle-helmet, the ringed byrnie,
the mighty wooden spear. It was their custom
to be always ready, armed for battle,
at home or in the field, every one of them,
on whatever occasion their overlord
1250 had need of them; that was a good troop.

19

    They sank into sleep—one paid sorely
for his evening rest, as had often happened
when Grendel guarded that gold-hall,
committed his wrongs until he came to his end,
1255 died for his sins. It was clearly seen,

obvious to all men, that an avenger still
lived on after that enemy for a long time
after that grim battle—Grendel's mother,
monster-woman, remembered her misery,
1260 she who dwelt in those dreadful waters,
the cold streams, ever since Cain
killed with his blade his only brother,
his father's kin; he fled bloodstained,
marked for murder, left the joys of men,
1265 dwelled in the wasteland. From him awoke
many a fateful spirit—Grendel among them,
hateful accursed foe, who found at Heorot
a wakeful warrior waiting for battle.
There the great beast began to seize him,
1270 but he remembered his mighty strength,
the ample gifts which God had given him,
and trusted the Almighty for mercy,
favor and support; thus he overcame the fiend,
subdued the hellish spirit. He went away wretched,
1275 deprived of joy, to find his place of death,
mankind's foe. But his mother still
greedy, grim-minded, wanted to go
on her sorrowful journey to avenge her son's death.

    She reached Heorot, where the Ring-Danes
1280 slept throughout the building; sudden turnabout
came to men, when Grendel's mother
broke into the hall. The horror was less
by as much as a maiden's strength,
a woman's warfare, is less than an armed man's
1285 when a bloodstained blade, its edges strong,
hammer-forged sword, slices through
the boar-image on a helmet opposite.[1]
Then in the hall was the hard edge drawn,
swords over seats, many a broad shield
1290 raised in hands—none remembered his helmet
or broad mail-shirt when that terror seized them.
She came in haste and meant to hurry out,
save her life, when she was surprised there,
but she had quickly seized, fast in her clutches,
1295 one nobleman when she went to the fens.
He was the dearest of heroes to Hrothgar
among his comrades between the two seas,
mighty shield-warrior, whom she snatched from his rest,

---

[1] *The horror … opposite* In fact Grendel's mother is a much more
dangerous opponent for Beowulf; the point of these lines is not clear.

a glorious thane. Beowulf was not there,
but another place had been appointed
for the famous Geat after the treasure-giving.
Heorot was in an uproar—she took the famous hand,
covered in gore; care was renewed,
come again to the dwellings. That was no good exchange,
that those on both sides should have to bargain
with the lives of friends.
                              Then the wise old king,
gray-bearded warrior, was grieved at heart
when he learned that he no longer lived—
the dearest of men, his chief thane, was dead.
Quickly Beowulf was fetched to the chambers,
victory-blessed man. Just before dawn
that noble champion came with his companions,
went with his men to where the old king waited
wondering whether the Almighty would ever
work a change after his tidings of woe.
Across the floor walked the worthy warrior
with his small troop—the hall-wood resounded—
and with his words he addressed the wise one,
lord of the Ingwines, asked him whether
the night had been agreeable, after his urgent summons.

20

Hrothgar spoke, protector of the Scyldings:
"Ask not of joys! Sorrow is renewed
for the Danish people. Æschere is dead,
elder brother of Yrmenlaf,
my confidant and my counselor,
my shoulder-companion in every conflict
when we defended our heads when the footsoldiers
      clashed
and struck boar-helmets. As a nobleman should be,
always excellent, so Æschere was!
In Heorot he was slain by the hand
of a restless death-spirit; I do not know
where that ghoul went, gloating with its carcass,
rejoicing in its feast. She avenged that feud
in which you killed Grendel yesterday evening
in your violent way with a crushing vice-grip,
for he had diminished and destroyed my people
for far too long. He fell in battle,
it cost him his life, and now has come another

mighty evil marauder who means to avenge
her kin, and too far has carried out her revenge,
as it may seem to many a thane
whose spirit groans for his treasure-giver,
a hard heart's distress—now that hand lies dead
which was wont to give you all good things.
    I have heard countrymen and hall-counselors
among my people report this:
they have seen two such creatures,
great march-stalkers holding the moors,
alien spirits. The second of them,
as far as they could discern most clearly,
had the shape of a woman; the other, misshapen,
marched the exile's path in the form of a man,
except that he was larger than any other;
in bygone days he was called 'Grendel'
by the local folk. They knew no father,
whether before him had been begotten
any more mysterious spirits. That murky land
they hold, wolf-haunted slopes, windy headlands,
awful fenpaths, where the upland torrents
plunge downward under the dark crags,
the flood underground. It is not far hence
—measured in miles—that the mere stands;
over it hangs a grove hoar-frosted,
a firm-rooted wood looming over the water.
Every night one can see there an awesome wonder,
fire on the water. There lives none so wise
or bold that he can fathom its abyss.
Though the heath-stepper beset by hounds,
the strong-horned hart, might seek the forest,
pursued from afar, he will sooner lose
his life on the shore than save his head
and go in the lake—it is no good place!
The clashing waves climb up from there
dark to the clouds, when the wind drives
the violent storms, until the sky itself droops,
the heavens groan. Now once again all help
depends on you alone. You do not yet know
this fearful place, where you might find
the sinful creature—seek it if you dare!
I will reward you with ancient riches
for that feud, as I did before,
with twisted gold, if you return alive."

21

Beowulf spoke, son of Ecgtheow:
"Sorrow not, wise one! It is always better
1385 to avenge one's friend than to mourn overmuch.
Each of us shall abide the end
of this world's life; let him who can
bring about fame before death—that is best
for the unliving man after he is gone.
1390 Arise, kingdom's guard, let us quickly go
and inspect the path of Grendel's kin.
I promise you this: he[1] will find no protection—
not in the belly of the earth nor the bottom of the sea,
nor the mountain groves—let him go where he will!
1395 For today, you must endure patiently
all your woes, as I expect you will."
The old man leapt up, thanked the Lord,
the mighty God, for that man's speech.
     Then for Hrothgar a horse was bridled
1400 with plaited mane. The wise prince
rode in full array; footsoldiers marched
with shields at the ready. The tracks were seen
far and wide on the forest paths,
a trail through the woods, where she went forth
1405 over the murky moor, bore the young man's
lifeless body, the best of all those
who had held watch over Hrothgar's home.
The son of nobles crossed over
the steep stone cliffs, the constricted climb,
1410 a narrow solitary path, a course unknown,
the towering headlands, home of sea-monsters.
He went before with just a few
wise men to see the way,
until suddenly he saw mountain-trees,
1415 stunted and leaning over gray stone,
a joyless wood; the water went under,
turbid and dreary. To all the Danes,
the men of the Scyldings, many a thane,
it was a sore pain at heart to suffer,
1420 a grief to every earl, when on the seacliff
they came upon the head of Æschere.
The flood boiled with blood—the folk gazed on—
and hot gore. At times a horn sang

its eager war-song. The footsoldiers sat down.
1425 They saw in the water many kinds of serpents,
strange sea-creatures testing the currents,
and on the sloping shores lay such monsters
as often attend in early morning
a sorrowful journey on the sail-road,
1430 dragons and wild beasts. They rushed away
bitter, enraged; they heard the bright noise,
the sound of the battle-horn. A Geatish bowman
cut short the life of one of those swimmers
with a bow and arrow, so that in his body stood
1435 the hard war-shaft; he was a slower swimmer
on the waves, when death took him away.
At once in the water he was assailed
with the barbed hooks of boar-pikes,
violently attacked and dragged ashore,
1440 the strange wave-roamer; the men inspected
this grisly visitor.
               Beowulf geared up
in his warrior's clothing, cared not for his life.
The broad war-shirt, woven by hand,
cunningly made, had to test the mere—
1445 it knew well how to protect his bone-house
so that a battle-grip might not hurt his breast
nor an angry malicious clutch touch his life.
The shining helmet protected his head,
set to stir up the sea's depths,
1450 seek that troubled water, decorated with treasure,
encircled with a splendid band, as a weapon-smith
in days of old had crafted it with wonders,
set boar-images, so that afterwards
no blade or battle-sword might ever bite it.
1455 Not the smallest of powerful supports was that
which Hrothgar's spokesman lent him at need;
that hilted sword was named Hrunting,
unique among ancient treasures—
its edge was iron, etched with poison-stripes,
1460 hardened with the blood of war; it had never failed
any man who grasped it in his hands in battle,
who dared to undertake a dreadful journey
into the very home of the foe—it was not the first time
that it had to perform a work of high courage.
1465 Truly, the son of Ecglaf, crafty in strength,
did not remember what he had said before,
drunk with wine, when he lent that weapon

---

[1] *he* I.e., Grendel's mother. The hero does not note carefully
enough the gender of Grendel's mother, or else the pronoun *he* refers
to OE *magan* "kinsman," a masculine noun.

to a better swordsman; he himself did not dare
to risk his life under the rushing waves,

1470 perform a lordly act; for that he lost honor,
his fame for courage. Not so with the other,
when he had geared himself up for battle.

22

Beowulf spoke, son of Ecgtheow:
"Consider now, famous kinsman of Healfdene,

1475 wise prince, now that I am eager to depart,
gold-friend to men, what we spoke of before:
if ever in your service I should
lose my life, that you would always be
in a father's place to me when I have passed away.

1480 Be a protector to my band of men,
my boon-companions, if battle should take me,
and send on to Hygelac, beloved Hrothgar,
the gifts of treasure which you have given me.
The lord of the Geats will understand by that gold,

1485 the son of Hrethel will see by that treasure,
that I found a ring-giver who was good
in ancient customs and, while I could, enjoyed it.
And let Unferth have that ancient heirloom,
that well-known man have my wave-patterned sword,

1490 hard-edged, splendid; with Hrunting I shall
win honor and fame, or death will take me!"
After these words the Weder-Geat man
hastened boldly, by no means wished to
stay for an answer; the surging sea received

1495 the brave soldier. It was the space of a day[1]
before he could perceive the bottom.
Right away she who held that expanse of water,
bloodthirsty and fierce, for a hundred half-years,
grim and greedy, perceived that some man

1500 was exploring from above that alien land.
She snatched at him, seized the warrior
in her savage clutches, but none the sooner
injured his sound body—the ring-mail encircled him,
so that she could not pierce that war-dress,

1505 the locked coat of mail, with her hostile claws.
Then that she-wolf of the sea swam to the bottom,
and bore the prince of rings into her abode,
so that he might not—no matter how strong—

wield his weapons, but so many wonders

1510 set upon him in the water, many a sea-beast
with battle-tusks tearing at his war-shirt,
monsters pursuing him.[2]
                    Then the earl perceived
that he was in some sort of battle-hall
where no water could harm him in any way,

1515 and, for the hall's roof, he could not be reached
by the flood's sudden rush—he saw a fire-light,
a glowing blaze shining brightly.
Then the worthy man saw that water-witch,
a great mere-wife; he gave a mighty blow

1520 with his battle-sword—he did not temper that stroke—
so that the ring-etched blade rang out on her head
a greedy battle-song. The guest discovered then
that the battle-flame would not bite,
or wound her fatally—but the edge failed

1525 the man in his need; it had endured many
hand-to-hand meetings, often sheared through helmets,
fated war-garments. It was the first time
that the fame of that precious treasure had fallen.
Again he was stalwart, not slow of zeal,

1530 mindful of glory, that kinsman of Hygelac—
the angry challenger threw away that etched blade,
wrapped and ornamented, so that it lay on the earth,
strong, steel-edged. He trusted his strength,
the might of his handgrip—as a man should do

1535 if by his warfare he thinks to win
long-lasting praise: he cares nothing for his life.
The man of the War-Geats grabbed by the shoulder
Grendel's mother—he had no regret for that feud;
battle-hardened, enraged, he swung her around,

1540 his deadly foe, so she fell to the ground.
Quickly she gave him requital for that
with a grim grasp, and grappled him to her—
weary, he stumbled, strongest of warriors,
of foot-soldiers, and took a fall.

1545 She set upon her hall-guest and drew her knife,
broad, bright-edged; she would avenge her boy,
her only offspring. On his shoulders lay
the linked corselet; it defended his life,
prevented the entrance of point and blade.

1550 There the son of Ecgtheow would have ended his life

---

1   *It was the space of a day* Or "it was daylight."

2   *pursuing him* Or "attacked their adversary." The Old English
word *æglæcan* may refer here to Beowulf or to the sea-monsters.

under the wide ground, the Geatish champion,
had not his armored shirt offered him help,
the hard battle-net, and holy God
brought about war-victory—the wise Lord,
1555 Ruler of the heavens, decided it rightly,
easily, once he stood up again.

23

He saw among the armor a victorious blade,
ancient giant-sword strong in its edges,
an honor in battle; it was the best of weapons,
1560 except that it was greater than any other man
might even bear into the play of battle,
good, adorned, the work of giants.[1]
The Scyldings' champion seized its linked hilt,
fierce and ferocious, drew the ring-marked sword
1565 despairing of his life, struck in fury
so that it caught her hard in the neck,
broke her bone-rings; the blade cut through
the doomed flesh—she fell to the floor,
the sword was bloody, the soldier rejoiced.
1570   The flames gleamed, a light glowed within
even as from heaven clearly shines
the firmament's candle. He looked around the chamber,
passed by the wall, hefted the weapon
hard by its hilt, that thane of Hygelac,
1575 angry and resolute—nor was the edge useless
to that warrior, but he quickly wished
to pay back Grendel for the many battle-storms
which he had wrought on the West-Danes
much more often than on one occasion,
1580 when Hrothgar's hall-companions
he slew in their beds, devoured sleeping
fifteen men of the Danish folk,
and made off with as many more,
a loathsome booty. He paid him back for that,
1585 the fierce champion, for on a couch he saw
Grendel lying lifeless,
battle-weary from the wound he received
in the combat at Heorot. His corpse burst open
when he was dealt a blow after death,
1590 a hard sword-stroke, and his head chopped off.

Soon the wise men saw it,
those who kept watch on the water with Hrothgar—
all turbid were the waves, and troubled,
the sea stained with blood. The graybearded
1595 elders spoke together about the good one,
said they did not expect that nobleman
would return, triumphant, to seek
the mighty prince; to many it seemed
that the sea-wolf had destroyed him.
1600 The ninth hour came; the noble Scyldings
abandoned the headland, and home went
the gold-friend of men. The guests[2] sat
sick at heart, and stared into the mere;
they wished, but did not hope, that they would
1605 see their lord himself.
                    Then the sword began,
that blade, to waste away into battle-icicles
from the war-blood; it was a great wonder
that it melted entirely, just like ice
when the Father loosens the frost's fetters,
1610 unwraps the water's bonds—He wields power
over times and seasons; that is the true Maker.
The man of the Geats took no more precious treasures
from that place—though he saw many there—
than the head, and the hilt as well,
1615 bright with gems; the blade had melted,
the ornamented sword burned up; so hot was the blood
of the poisonous alien spirit who died in there.
Soon he was swimming who had survived in battle
the downfall of his enemies, dove up through the water;
1620 the sea-currents were entirely cleansed,
the spacious regions, when that alien spirit
gave up life-days and this loaned world.
    The defender of seafarers came to land,
swam stout-hearted; he rejoiced in his sea-booty,
1625 the great burden which he brought with him.
That splendid troop of thanes went towards him,
thanked God, rejoiced in their prince,
that they might see him safe and sound.
Then from that bold man helmet and byrnie
1630 were quickly unstrapped. Under the clouds
the mere stewed, stained with gore.
They went forth, followed the trail,
rejoicing in their hearts; they marched along the road,

---

[1] *the work of giants* Old, highly-praised weapons are often called
"the work of giants"—whether this reference is meant to connect the
sword to the giants "who fought against God" is not clear.

[2] *guests* I.e., the Geats who had come to Heorot with Beowulf.

the familiar path; proud as kings
1635   they carried the head from the sea-cliff
with great trouble, even for two pairs
of stout-hearted men; four of them had to
bear, with some strain, on a battle-pole
Grendel's head to the gold-hall,
1640   until presently fourteen proud
and battle-hardy Geats came to the hall,
warriors marching; the lord of those men,
mighty in the throng, trod the meadhall-plain.
Then the ruler of thanes entered there,
1645   daring in actions, honored in fame,
battle-brave hero, to greet Hrothgar.
Then, where men were drinking, they dragged by its hair
Grendel's head across the hall-floor,
a grisly spectacle for the men and the queen.
1650   Everyone stared at that amazing sight.

24

Beowulf spoke, son of Ecgtheow:
"Look! son of Healfdene, prince of the Scyldings,
we have brought you gladly these gifts from the sea
which you gaze on here, a token of glory.
1655   Not easily did I escape with my life
that undersea battle, did my brave deed
with difficulty—indeed, the battle would have been
over at once, if God had not guarded me.
Nor could I achieve anything at that battle
1660   with Hrunting, though that weapon is good;
but the Ruler of Men granted to me
that I might see on the wall a gigantic old sword,
hanging glittering—He has always guided
the friendless one—so I drew that weapon.
1665   In that conflict, when I had the chance, I slew
the shepherds of that house. Then that battle-sword
burned up with its ornaments, as the blood shot out,
hottest battle-sweat. I have brought the hilt
back from the enemy; I avenged the old deeds,
1670   the slaughter of Danes, as seemed only right.
Now you have my word that you may in Heorot
sleep without care with your company of men,
and every thane, young and old,
in your nation; you need fear nothing,
1675   prince of the Scyldings, from that side,
no deadly manslaughters, as you did before."

Then the golden hilt was placed in the hand
of the gray-haired war-chief, wise old leader,
that old work of giants; it came to the keeping
1680   of the Danish lord after the fall of demons,
a work of wonder-smiths; and when that evil-hearted man,
God's adversary, gave up the world,
guilty of murders—and his mother too—
it passed to the possession of the best
1685   of world-kings between the two seas,
of all those that dealt out treasures in Danish lands.
    Hrothgar spoke—he studied the hilt
of the old heirloom, where was written[1] the origin
of ancient strife, when the flood slew,
1690   rushing seas, the race of giants—
they suffered awfully. That was a people alien
to the eternal Lord; a last reward
the Ruler gave them through the raging waters.
Also, on the sword-guard of bright gold
1695   was rightly marked in rune-letters,
set down and said for whom that sword,
best of irons, had first been made,
with scrollery and serpentine patterns. Then spoke
the wise son of Healfdene—all fell silent:
1700   "One may, indeed, say, if he acts in truth
and right for the people, remembers all,
old guardian of his homeland, that this earl was
born a better man! My friend Beowulf,
your glory is exalted throughout the world,
1705   over every people; you hold it all with patient care,
and temper strength with wisdom. To you I shall fulfill
our friendship, as we have said. You shall become a comfort
everlasting to your own people,
and a help to heroes.
               Not so was Heremod
1710   to the sons of Ecgwala,[2] the Honor-Scyldings;[3]
he grew not for their delight, but for their destruction
and the murder of Danish men.
Enraged, he cut down his table-companions,
comrades-in-arms, until he turned away alone
1715   from the pleasures of men, that famous prince;
though mighty God exalted him in the joys

---

1   *written* Or "carved." It is not clear whether the scene is visual or textual, depicted or written in (presumably runic) characters.

2   *Ecgwala* A king of Danes.

3   *Honor-Scyldings* I.e., Danes.

of strength and force, advanced him far
over all men, yet in his heart he nursed
a blood-ravenous breast-hoard. No rings did he give
1720 to the Danes for their honor; he endured, joyless,
to suffer the pains of that strife,
a long-lasting harm to his people. Learn from him,
understand virtue! For your sake I have told this,
in the wisdom of my winters.
                           It is a wonder to say
1725 how mighty God in His great spirit
allots wisdom, land and lordship
to mankind; He has control of everything.
At times He permits the thoughts of a man
in a mighty race to move in delights,
1730 gives him to hold in his homeland
the sweet joys of earth, a stronghold of men,
grants him such power over his portion of the world,
a great kingdom, that he himself cannot
imagine an end to it, in his folly.
1735 He dwells in plenty; in no way plague him
illness or old age, nor do evil thoughts
darken his spirit, nor any strife
or sword-hate shows itself, but all the world
turns to his will; he knows nothing worse.

25

1740   "At last his portion of pride within him
grows and flourishes, while the guardian sleeps,
the soul's shepherd—that sleep is too sound,
bound with cares, the slayer too close
who, sinful and wicked, shoots from his bow.[1]
1745 Then he is struck in his heart, under his helmet
with a bitter dart—he knows no defense—
the strange, dark demands of evil spirits.
What he has long held seems too little;
angry and greedy, he gives no golden rings
1750 for vaunting boasts, and his final destiny
he neglects and forgets, since God, Ruler of glories,
has given him a portion of honors.
In the end it finally comes about
that the loaned life-dwelling starts to decay
1755 and falls, fated to die; another follows him

who doles out his riches without regret,
the earl's ancient treasure; he heeds no terror.
Defend yourself from wickedness, dear Beowulf,
best of men, and choose the better,
1760 eternal counsel; care not for pride,
great champion! The glory of your might
is but a little while; soon it will be
that sickness or the sword will shatter your strength,
or the grip of fire, or the surging flood,
1765 or the cut of a sword, or the flight of a spear,
or terrible old age—or the light of your eyes
will fail and flicker out; in one fell swoop
death, o warrior, will overwhelm you.
    "Thus, a hundred half-years I held the Ring-Danes
1770 under the skies, and kept them safe from war
from many tribes throughout this middle-earth,
from spears and swords, so that I considered none
under the expanse of heaven my enemy.
Look! Turnabout came in my own homeland,
1775 grief after gladness, when Grendel became
my invader, ancient adversary;
for that persecution I bore perpetually
the greatest heart-cares. Thanks be to the Creator,
eternal Lord, that I have lived long enough
1780 to see that head, stained with blood,
with my own eyes, after all this strife!
Go to your seat, enjoy the feast,
honored in battle; between us shall be shared
a great many treasures, when morning comes."
1785   Glad-hearted, the Geat went at once
to take his seat, as the wise one told him.
Then again as before, a feast was prepared
for the brave ones who occupied the hall
on this new occasion. The dark helm of night
1790 overshadowed the troop. The soldiers arose;
the gray-haired ruler was ready for bed,
the aged Scylding. Immeasurably well
did rest please the Geat, proud shield-warrior;
at once a chamberlain led him forth,
1795 weary from his adventure, come from afar,
he who attended to all the needs
of that thane, for courtesy, as in those days
all battle-voyagers used to have.
    The great-hearted one rested; the hall towered
1800 vaulted and gold-adorned; the guest slept within

---

[1] *At last ... bow* The slayer is sin or vice; the soul's guardian is
reason, conscience or prudence.

until the black[1] raven, blithe-hearted, announced
the joy of heaven. Then light came hurrying
[bright over shadows;] the soldiers hastened,
the noblemen were eager to travel
1805   back to their people; the bold-spirited visitor
wished to seek his far-off ship.

The hardy one ordered Hrunting to be borne
to the son of Ecglaf,[2] bid him take his sword,
lordly iron; he thanked him for the loan,
1810   and said that he regarded it as a good war-friend,
skillful in battle, and the sword's edges
he did not disparage; he was a noble man.
And when the warriors were eager for their way,
equipped in their war-gear, the nobleman went,
1815   the Danes' honor, to the high seat where the other was:
the hero, brave in battle, saluted Hrothgar.

26

Beowulf spoke, son of Ecgtheow:
"Now we seafarers, come from afar,
wish to say that we desire
1820   to seek Hygelac. Here we were honorably
entertained with delights; you have treated us well.
If ever on earth I can do any thing
to earn more of your affection,
than the battle-deeds I have done already,
1825   ruler of men, I will be ready at once.
If ever I hear over the sea's expanse
that your neighbors threaten you with terror
as your enemies used to do,
I will bring you a thousand thanes,
1830   heroes to help you. I have faith in Hygelac—
the lord of the Geats, though he be young,
shepherd of his people, will support me
with words and deeds, that I might honor you well
and bring to your side a forest of spears,
1835   the support of my might, whenever you need men.
If ever Hrethric decides, son of a prince,
to come to the Geatish court, he will find
many friends there; far-off lands

are better sought by one who is himself good."
1840   Hrothgar spoke in answer to him:
"The wise Lord has sent those words
into your heart; I have never heard
a shrewder speech from such a young man.
You are strong in might and sound in mind,
1845   prudent in speech! I expect it is likely
that if it should ever happen that the spear
or the horrors of war take Hrethel's son,[3]
or sickness or sword strike the shepherd of his people,
your lord, and you still live,
1850   that the sea-Geats could not select
a better choice anywhere for king,
hoard-guard of heroes, if you will hold
the realm of your kinsmen. Your character pleases me
better and better, beloved Beowulf.
1855   You have brought it about that between our peoples,
the Geatish nation and the spear-Danes,
there shall be peace, and strife shall rest,
the malicious deeds that they endured before,
as long as I shall rule this wide realm,
1860   and treasures together; many shall greet
another with gifts across the gannet's bath;[4]
the ring-necked ship shall bring over the sea
tribute and tokens of love. I know these nations
will be made fast against friend and foe,
1865   blameless in everything, in the old way."

The protector of heroes, kinsman of Healfdene,
gave him twelve great treasures in the hall;
bid him seek his own dear people in safety
with those gifts, and quickly come again.
1870   Then the good king, of noble kin, kissed
that best of thanes and embraced his neck,
the Scylding prince; tears were shed
by that gray-haired man. He was of two minds—
but in his old wisdom knew it was more likely
1875   that never again would they see one another,
brave in their meeting-place. The man was so dear to him
that he could not hold back the flood in his breast,
but in his heart, fast in the bonds of his thought,
a deep-felt longing for the dear man
1880   burned in his blood. Beowulf from thence,
gold-proud warrior, trod the grassy lawn,

---

[1] *black* Either OE *blac* "shining" or *blæc* "black"; the translation
prefers the irony of the image of the black raven, not otherwise
known as a harbinger of joy, announcing the surprising good news
of a dawn without slaughter.

[2] *Son of Ecglaf* I.e., Unferth.

[3] *Hrethel's son* I.e., Hygelac.

[4] *gannet's bath* I.e., the sea.

exulting in treasure; the sea-goer awaited
its lord and owner, where it rode at anchor.
As they were going, the gift of Hrothgar
1885 was often praised; that king was peerless,
blameless in everything, until old age took from him
—it has injured so many—the joy of his strength.

27

Those men of high courage then came to the sea,
that troop of young retainers, bore their ring-mail,
1890 locked shirts of armor. The coast-guard observed
the return of those earls, as he had once before;
he did not greet those guests with insults
on the clifftop, but he rode towards them,
said that the warriors in their shining armor
1895 would be welcome in their ships to the people of the
            Weders.
The sea-curved prow, the ring-necked ship,
as it lay on the sand was laden with war-gear,
with horses and treasures; the mast towered high
over Hrothgar's hoard-gifts.
1900 To the ship's guardian he[1] gave a sword,
bound with gold, so that on the mead-benches
he was afterwards more honored by that heirloom,
that old treasure. Onward they went, the ship
sliced through deep water, gave up the Danish coast.
1905 The sail by the mast was rigged fast with ropes,
a great sea-cloth; the timbers creaked,
the wind over the sea did not hinder at all
the wave-floater on its way; the sea-goer sped on,
floated foamy-necked, forth upon the waves,
1910 the bound prow over the briny streams,
until they could make out the cliffs of Geatland,
familiar capes; the keel drove forward
thrust by the wind, and came to rest on land.
Right away the harbor-guard was ready at the shore,
1915 who for a long time had gazed far
over the currents, eager for the beloved men;
he moored the broad-beamed ship on the beach
fast with anchor-ropes, lest the force of the waves
should drive away the handsome wooden vessel.
1920 He bade that the nobleman's wealth be borne ashore,
armor and plated gold; they had not far to go

----

1 *he* I.e., Beowulf.

----

to seek their dispenser of treasure,
Hygelac son of Hrethel, where he dwelt at home
with his companions, near the sea-wall.
1925   The building was splendid, the king quite bold,
high in his hall, Hygd[2] very young,
wise, well-mannered, though few winters
had the daughter of Hæreth passed within
the palace walls—yet not poor for that,
1930 nor stingy of gifts to the Geatish people,
of great treasures. She considered Thryth's pride,[3]
famous folk-queen, and her terrible crimes;
no man so bold among her own retainers
dared to approach her, except as her prince,[4]
1935 or dared to look into her eyes by day;
for he knew that deadly bonds, braided by hand,
were waiting for him—first the hand-grip,
and quickly after a blade appointed,
so that a patterned sword had to settle things,
1940 proclaim the execution. That is no queenly custom
for a lady to perform—no matter how lovely—
that a peace-weaver[5] should deprive of life
a friendly man after a pretended affront.
The kinsman of Hemming[6] put a halt to that:
1945 then ale-drinkers told another tale,
said she caused less calamity to the people,
less malicious evil, after she was
given gold-adorned to the young champion,
fair to that nobleman, when to Offa's floor
1950 she sought a journey over the fallow sea
at her father's wish, where she afterwards

----

2 *Hygd* Hygelac's queen.

3 *Thryth's pride* These lines are difficult. Some editions and translations read the name as "Modthryth"; the reading adopted here smoothes out a transition that is otherwise abrupt even by the standards of this poem. This "digression" on the character of a queen, with some elements of a folktale, is the counterpoint to the story of Heremod in earlier sections.

4 *her prince* I.e., as her husband or her father.

5 *peace-weaver* This epithet reflects the common practice, whose sometimes-tragic consequences are explored at length elsewhere in the poem, of settling intertribal feuds with a marriage between the daughter of one lord and the son of another.

6 *kinsman of Hemming* Offa I, fourth-century king of the continental Angles, not Offa II, the eighth-century king of Mercia. The elaborate praise offered to Offa I has been taken to suggest that the poem may have been written or circulated in the court of Offa II, but there is otherwise no evidence for this.

on the throne, famous for good things,
used well her life while she had it,
held high love with that chief of heroes,
1955   of all mankind, as men have told me,
the best between the two seas
of all the races of men; therefore Offa,
in gifts and battle, spear-bold man,
was widely honored, and held in wisdom
1960   his own homeland. From him arose Eomer
as a help to heroes, kinsman of Hemming,
grandson of Garmund, skilled in violence.

28

The hardy man[1] with his hand-picked troop
went across the sand, trod the sea-plain,
1965   the wide shore. The world's candle shone,
hastening from the south. They had survived their journey,
went boldly to where they knew
the protector of earls, slayer of Ongentheow,[2]
good young battle-king, gave out rings
1970   in his fortress. To Hygelac
the arrival of Beowulf was quickly reported,
that to the enclosures his battle-companion,
protector of warriors, came walking alive
back to his court, safe from his battle-play.
1975   Quickly, as the powerful one commanded,
the hall was cleared out inside for the foot-guests.
He sat down with him, who had survived the fight,
kinsmen together, after he greeted
his friend and liege-lord with a formal speech,
1980   with courteous words and cups of mead.
The daughter of Hæreth[3] passed through the hall,
cared for the people, bore the cup
to the hand of the hero.[4] Hygelac began
to question his companion courteously
1985   in the high hall—curiosity pressed him
to know how the sea-Geats' adventures were:
"How did you fare, beloved Beowulf,

in your journey, when you suddenly resolved
to seek a far-off strife over the salt sea,
1990   a battle in Heorot? Did you better at all
the well-known woe of Hrothgar,
the famous prince? For that I seethed
with heart-care and distress, mistrusted the adventure
of my beloved man; long I implored
1995   that you not seek that slaughter-spirit at all,
let the south-Danes themselves make
war against Grendel. I say thanks to God
that I might see you again safe and sound."
Beowulf spoke, son of Ecgtheow:
2000   "It is no mystery to many men,
my lord Hygelac—the great meeting,
what a time of great struggle Grendel and I
had in that place where he made so many
sorrows for the victory-Scyldings,
2005   life-long misery—I avenged them all,
so that none of Grendel's tribe needs to boast
anywhere on earth of that uproar at dawn,
whoever lives longest of that loathsome kind,
enveloped in foul evil. First I came there
2010   to the ring-hall to greet Hrothgar;
quickly the famous kinsman of Healfdene,
once he knew of my intentions,
assigned me a seat with his own sons.
That troop was in delight; never in my life
2015   have I seen among hall-sitters, under heaven's vault,
a more joyous feast. At times the famous queen,
bond of peace to nations, passed through the hall,
urged on her young sons; often she gave
twisted rings before she took her seat.
2020   At times before the hall-thanes the daughter of Hrothgar
bore the ale-cup to the earls in the back—
Freawaru, I heard the men in the hall
call her, when the studded treasure-cup
was passed among them. She is promised,
2025   young, gold-adorned, to the gracious son of Froda;[5]
the ruler of the Scyldings has arranged this,
the kingdom's shepherd, and approves the counsel
that he should settle his share of feud and slaughter

---

[1]   *The hardy man*   I.e., Beowulf.

[2]   *slayer of Ongentheow*   Hygelac. The death of the Swedish king
Ongentheow (at the hands of Wulf and Eofor, retainers of Hygelac)
is told below, section 40.

[3]   *daughter of Hæreth*   I.e., Hygd.

[4]   *to the hand of the hero*   The manuscript reads "to the hands of
heathens," which makes sense, but is usually emended.

---

[5]   *the gracious son of Froda*   Ingeld, prince of the Heathobards. His
attack on the Danes, alluded to earlier in the poem (80–5), was
apparently unsuccessful; another Old English poem, *Widsith*, reports
that "Hrothulf and Hrothgar … humbled Ingeld's battle-array."

with this young woman. But seldom anywhere
2030 after the death of a prince does the deadly spear rest
for even a brief while, though the bride be good!

"It may, perhaps, displease the Heathobards' prince,
and every retainer among his tribe,
when across the floor, following that woman, goes
2035 a noble son of the Danes, received with honors;
on him glitters an ancestral heirloom,
hard, ring-adorned, once a Heathobard treasure
as long as they were able to wield their weapons.

29

"And then in that deadly shield-play they undid
2040 their beloved comrades and their own lives.
Then an old spear-bearer[1] speaks over his beer,
who sees that ring-hilt and remembers all
the spear-deaths of men—his spirit is grim—
begins, sad-minded, to test the mettle
2045 of a young thane with his innermost thoughts,
to awaken war, and says these words:

'Can you, my friend, recognize that sword,
which your father bore into battle
in his final adventure beneath the helmet,
2050 that dear iron, when the Danes struck him,
ruled the field of slaughter after the rout of heroes,
when Withergyld[2] fell—those valiant Scyldings?
Now here some son or other of his slayer
walks across this floor, struts in his finery,
2055 brags of the murder and bears that treasure
which ought, by right, to belong to you.'

He urges and reminds him on every occasion
with cruel words, until the time comes
that Freawaru's thane, for his father's deeds,
2060 sleeps, bloodstained from the bite of a sword,
forfeits his life; from there the other
escapes alive, for he knows the land well.
Then on both sides the sworn oaths of earls
will be broken, once bitter violent hate
2065 wells up in Ingeld, and his wife-love

grows cooler after his surging cares.
Thus I expect that the Heathobards' part
in the Danish alliance is not without deceit,
nor their friendship fast.

I will speak further
2070 concerning Grendel, so that you might certainly know,
giver of treasure, how it turned out,
the heroic wrestling-match. When heaven's gem
slipped under the ground, the angry spirit came,
horrible, evening-grim, sought us out
2075 where, unharmed, we guarded the hall.
The attack came first against Hondscio[3] there,
deadly to that doomed man—he fell first,
a girded champion; Grendel was
that famous young retainer's devourer,
2080 gobbled up the body of that beloved man.
None the sooner did that slayer, blood in his teeth,
mindful of misery, mean to leave
that gold-hall empty-handed,
but in his mighty strength he tested me,
2085 grabbed with a ready hand. A glove[4] hung
huge, grotesque, fast with cunning clasps;
it was all embroidered with evil skill,
with the devil's craft and dragons' skins.
Inside there, though I was innocent,
2090 that proud evil-doer wanted to put me,
one of many; but it was not to be,
once I angrily stood upright.

30[5]

"It is too long to tell how I handed back payment
to the people's enemy for all his evils—
2095 there, my prince, I did honor to your people
with my actions. He escaped away,
enjoyed his life a little while longer;
yet behind him, guarding his path, was his right

---

[1] *an old spear-bearer*   Of the Heathobards, outraged by the presence of his former enemies, the Danes. In heroic poetry when a warrior falls, his killer is often awarded his armor; the sword is a vivid reminder of the fate of its former owner and the duty of revenge which is passed on to the next generation.

[2] *Withergyld*   Apparently a famous Heathobard warrior.

[3] *Hondscio*   We finally learn the name of the retainer killed in section 11. The name, as in modern German (Handschuh), means "glove."

[4] *glove*   It is not clear what this is; apparently a pouch of some kind. It is characteristic of a troll in Norse legend. In any case it does not figure in the narrator's own description of Grendel's attack, and is but one of several discrepancies between the two tellings of the story.

[5] *30*   The placement of this section is conjectural; the sectional divisions of the manuscript are confused at this point.

hand in Heorot, and wretched, he went hence,
2100 sad at heart, and sank to the sea-floor.
　　　　For that bloody onslaught the friend of the Scyldings
repaid me greatly with plated gold,
many treasures, when morning came,
and we had gathered together to the feast again.
2105 There was song and joy; the aged Scylding,[1]
widely learned, told of far-off times;
at times the brave warrior touched the song-wood,
delight of the harp, at times made lays
both true and sad, at times strange stories
2110 he recounted rightly. That great-hearted king,
gray-bearded old warrior wrapped in his years,
at times began to speak of his youth again,
his battle-strength; his heart surged within him
when, old in winters, he remembered so much.
2115 And so there inside we took our ease
all day long, until night descended
again upon men. There, quickly ready
with revenge for her griefs, Grendel's mother
journeyed sorrowful; death took her son,
2120 the war-hate of the Weders. That monstrous woman
avenged her son, killed a soldier
boldly at once—there the life of Æschere,
wise old counselor, came to its end.
And when morning came the men of the Danes
2125 were not able to burn his body, death-weary,
with flames, nor place him on a funeral pyre,
beloved man; she bore away his corpse
in her evil embrace under the upland streams.
That, to Hrothgar, was the most wrenching distress
2130 of all those that had befallen that folk-leader.
Then the prince—by your life—implored me,
his mind wracked, that in the roaring waves
I should do a noble deed, put my life in danger,
perform glorious things—he promised me reward.
2135 In the waves I found, as is widely known,
a grim, horrible guardian of the abyss.
There, for a while, we fought hand-to-hand;
the sea foamed with blood, and I severed the head
of Grendel's mother with a mighty sword

2140 in that [battle-]hall;[2] I barely managed
to get away with my life—I wasn't doomed yet—
and the protector of earls once again gave me
many treasures, that kinsman of Healfdene.

31

　　"So that nation's king followed good customs;
2145 in no wise have I lost those rewards,
the prize for my strength, but the son of Healfdene
offered me treasures at my own choice,
which I wish to bring to you, o war-king,
to show good will. Still all my joys
2150 are fixed on you alone; I have few
close kinsmen, my Hygelac, except for you."
　　He ordered to be borne in the boar standard,
the helmet towering in battle, the gray byrnie,
the decorated sword, and told this story:
2155 "Hrothgar gave me this battle-gear,
wise prince, and commanded particularly
that first I should tell you the story of his gift—
he said that Heorogar the king[3] first had it,
lord of the Scyldings, for a long while;
2160 none the sooner would he give to his own son,
the valiant Heoroward—loyal though he was—
that breast-armor. Use all well!"
Then, as I've heard, four swift horses,
fallow as apples, well-matched, followed
2165 that war-gear; he gave him as a gift
the horses and harness—as kinsman should behave,
never knitting a net of malice for another
with secret plots, preparing death
for his hand-picked comrades. Hygelac's nephew
2170 was loyal to him, hardy in the fight,
and each man to the other mindful of benefits.—
I heard that he gave the necklace to Hygd,
the wondrous ornamented treasure which Wealhtheow
　　had given him,
to that lord's daughter, along with three horses
2175 graceful and saddle-bright; her breast was adorned
the more graciously after that ring-giving.
　　So the son of Ecgtheow showed himself brave,

---

[1] *the aged Scylding* It is not clear whether this is Hrothgar or not,
or how many storytellers and singers are at this banquet.

[2] *[battle-]hall* A word is missing; other editors and translators
supply different words, such as *grund* or "earth."

[3] *Heorogar the king* Eldest brother of Hrothgar.

renowned for battles and noble deeds,
pursued honor, by no means slew, drunken,
2180 his hearth-companions; he had no savage heart,
but the great gift which God had given him,
the greatest might of all mankind, he held,
brave in battle. He had been long despised,
as the sons of the Geats considered him no good,
2185 nor did the lord of the Weders wish to bestow
many good things upon him on the meadbenches,
for they assumed that he was slothful,
a cowardly nobleman. Reversal came
to the glorious man for all his griefs.
2190   The protector of earls, battle-proud king,
ordered the heirloom of Hrethel[1] brought in,
adorned with gold; among the Geats there was
no finer treasure in the form of a sword.
He laid the sword in Beowulf's lap,
2195 and gave him seven thousand hides[2] of land,
a hall and a princely throne. Both of them held
inherited land in that nation, a home
and native rights, but the wider rule
was reserved to the one who was higher in rank.
2200   Then it came to pass amid the crash of battle
in later days, after Hygelac lay dead,
and for Heardred[3] the swords of battle held
deadly slaughter under the shield-wall,
when the Battle-Scylfings sought him out,
2205 those hardy soldiers, and savagely struck down
the nephew of Hereric[4] in his victorious nation—
then came the broad kingdom
into Beowulf's hands; he held it well
for fifty winters—he was then a wise king,
2210 old guardian of his homeland—until
in the dark nights a dragon began his reign,
who guarded his hoard in the high heaths
and the steep stone barrows; the path below
lay unknown to men. Some sort of man
2215 went inside there, found his way to

the heathen hoard—his hand ...[5]
inlaid with jewels. He[6] got no profit there,
though he had been trapped in his sleep
by a thief's trickery: the whole nation knew,
2220 and all the people around them, that he was enraged.

32

Not for his own sake did he who sorely harmed him
break into that worm-hoard,[7] or by his own will,
but in sad desperation some sort of [slave][8]
of a warrior's son fled the savage lash,
2225 the servitude of a house, and slipped in there,
a man beset by sins. Soon he gazed around
and felt the terror from that evil spirit;
yet ...
          ...made...
2230   ... when the terror seized him
he snatched a jeweled cup.[9]
                              There were many such
antique riches in that earth-hall,
for in ancient days an unknown man
had thought to hide them carefully there,
2235 the rich legacy of a noble race,
precious treasures. In earlier times
death had seized them all, and he who still survived
alone from that nation's army lingered there,
a mournful sentry, expected the same,
2240 that he might enjoy those ancient treasures
for just a little while. A waiting barrow
stood in an open field near the ocean waves,
new on the cape, safe with crafty narrow entrances;
he bore within the noble wealth,
2245 the plated gold, that guardian of rings,
a share worthy of a hoard, and spoke few words:
     "Hold now, o thou earth, for heroes cannot,

---

[1] *Hrethel* Father of Hygelac.

[2] *hides* Units of land, originally the amount of land which could support a peasant and his family; its actual size varied from one region to another. Seven thousand hides is by any measure a very generous area.

[3] *Heardred* Son of Hygelac.

[4] *nephew of Hereric* I.e., Heardred.

[5] The manuscript is damaged here and some text is unreadable. Among many conjectural restorations one thing is clear—a cup is taken from the dragon's hoard.

[6] *He* The thief; "he" in the following line refers to the dragon. These lines are nearly illegible and other readings have been proposed.

[7] *worm-hoard* Dragon's treasure.

[8] *[slave]* The word is illegible in the manuscript; the translation follows most editions.

[9] *yet ... cup* The manuscript is unreadable at this point.

the wealth of men—lo, from you long ago
those good ones first obtained it! Death in war
2250 and awful deadly harm have swept away
all of my people who have passed from life,
and left the joyful hall. Now have I none
to bear the sword or burnish the bright cup,
the precious vessel—all that host has fled.
2255 Now must the hardened helm of hammered gold
be stripped of all its trim; the stewards sleep
who should have tended to this battle-mask.
So too this warrior's coat, which waited once
the bite of iron over the crack of boards,
2260 molders like its owner. The coat of mail
cannot travel widely with the war-chief,
beside the heroes. Harp-joy have I none,
no happy song; nor does the well-schooled hawk
soar high throughout the hall, nor the swift horse
2265 stamp in the courtyards. Savage butchery
has sent forth many of the race of men!"

　　So, grieving, he mourned his sorrow,
alone after all. Unhappy sped
both days and nights, until the flood of death
2270 broke upon his heart. An old beast of the dawn
found that shining hoard standing open—
he who, burning, seeks the barrows,
a fierce and naked dragon, who flies by night
in a pillar of fire; people on earth
2275 fear him greatly. It is his nature to find
a hoard in the earth, where, ancient and proud,
he guards heathen gold, though it does him no good.[1]

　　Three hundred winters that threat to the people
held in the ground his great treasury,
2280 wondrously powerful, until one man
made him boil with fury; he[2] bore to his liege-lord
the plated cup, begged for peace
from his lord. Then the hoard was looted,
the hoard of rings fewer, a favor was granted
2285 the forlorn man; for the first time
his lord looked on that ancient work of men.

　　When the dragon stirred, strife was renewed;
he slithered along the stones, stark-hearted he found
his enemy's footprint—he had stepped too far

2290 in his stealthy skill, too close to the serpent's head.
Thus can an undoomed man easily survive
wrack and ruin, if he holds to the Ruler's
grace and protection![3] The hoard-guardian
searched along the ground, greedy to find
2295 the man who had sorely harmed him while he slept;
hot, half-mad, he kept circling his cave
all around the outside, but no one was there
in that wilderness to welcome his warfare
and the business of battle. Soon he returned to his barrow,
2300 sought his treasure; he soon discovered
that some man had disturbed his gold,
his great wealth. The hoard-guardian waited
impatiently until evening came;
the barrow's shepherd was swollen with rage,
2305 the loathsome foe would repay with fire
his precious drinking-cup. Then day was departed
to the delight of that worm; he did not linger
on the barrow wall, but took off burning
in a burst of flames. The beginning was terror
2310 to the people on land, and to their ring-giving lord
the ending soon would be sore indeed.

33

　　Then that strange visitor began to spew flames
and burn the bright courts; his burning gleams
struck horror in men. That hostile flier
2315 would leave nothing alive.
The worm's warfare was widely seen,
his ferocious hostility, near and far,
how the destroyer hated and harmed
the Geatish people, then hastened to his hoard,
2320 his dark and hidden hall, before the break of day.
He had surrounded the people of that region with fire,
flames and cinders; he took shelter in his barrow,
his walls and warfare—but that trust failed him.

　　To Beowulf the news was quickly brought
2325 of that horror—that his own home,
best of buildings, had burned in waves of fire,
the gift-throne of the Geats. To the good man that was
painful in spirit, greatest of sorrows;
the wise one believed he had bitterly offended
2330 the Ruler of all, the eternal Lord,

---

[1] *It is ... good* The association of dragons and hoarded treasure is ancient and proverbial.

[2] *he* I.e., the thief.

[3] *Thus can ... protection* This is the narrator's version of Beowulf's comment at lines 572–73.

against the old law; his breast within groaned
with dark thoughts—that was not his custom.
The fire-dragon had found the stronghold of that folk,
that fortress, and had razed it with flames
2335 entirely and from without; for that the war-king,
prince of the Weders, devised revenge.
Then the lord of men bade them make,
protector of warriors, a wondrous war-shield,
all covered with iron; he understood well
2340 that wood from the forest would not help him,
linden against flames. The long-good nobleman
had to endure the end of his loaned days,
this world's life—and so did the worm,
though he had held for so long his hoarded wealth.
2345   Then that prince of rings scorned to seek out
the far-flung flier with his full force of men,
a large army; he did not dread that attack,
nor did he worry much about the dragon's warfare,
his strength or valor, because he had survived
2350 many battles, barely escaping alive
in the crash of war, after he had cleansed,
triumphant hero, the hall of Hrothgar,
and at battle crushed Grendel and his kin,
that loathsome race.
It was not the least
2355 of hand-to-hand combats when Hygelac was slain,
when the king of the Geats, in the chaos of battle,
the lord of his people, in the land of the Frisians,
the son of Hrethel, died sword-drunk,
beaten by blades. Beowulf escaped from there
2360 through his own strength, took a long swim;
he had in his arms the battle-armor
of thirty men, when he climbed to the cliffs.
By no means did the Hetware[1] need to exult
in that fight, when they marched on foot to him,
2365 bore their linden shields; few came back
from that brave soldier to seek their homes.
The son of Ecgtheow crossed the vast sea,
wretched, solitary, returned to his people,
where Hygd offered him the hoard and kingdom,
2370 rings and royal throne; she did not trust
that her son could hold the ancestral seat
against foreign hosts, now that Hygelac was dead.
But despite their misery, by no means

could they prevail upon that prince at all
2375 that he should become lord over Heardred,
or choose to rule the kingdom.
Yet he upheld him[2] in the folk with friendly counsel,
good will and honors, until he was older,
and ruled the Weder-Geats.
Wretched exiles,
2380 the sons of Ohthere,[3] sought him out across the seas;
they had rebelled against the Scylfings' ruler,[4]
the best of all the sea-kings
who dispensed treasure in the Swedish lands,
a famous king. That cost him[5] his life:
2385 for his hospitality he took a mortal hurt
with the stroke of a sword, that son of Hygelac;
and the son of Ongentheow afterwards went
to seek out his home, once Heardred lay dead,
and let Beowulf hold the high throne
2390 and rule the Geats—that was a good king.

34

In later days he[6] did not forget
that prince's fall, and befriended Eadgils
the wretched exile; across the open sea
he gave support to the son of Ohthere
2395 with warriors and weapons. He[7] wreaked his revenge
with cold sad journeys, and took the king's life.
And so the son of Ecgtheow had survived
every struggle, every terrible onslaught,
with brave deeds, until that one day
2400 when he had to take his stand against the serpent.

---

[1] *Hetware* A Frankish tribe apparently on the side of the Frisians.

[2] *upheld him* Beowulf upheld Heardred, as champion and in effect a kind of regent.

[3] *sons of Ohthere* I.e., Eanmund and Eadgils.

[4] *Scylfing's ruler* Onela, son of Ongentheow. Ohthere had succeeded his father Ongentheow, but after his death his brother Onela apparently seized the throne and drove the two young men Eanmund and Eadgils into exile. They take refuge at the Geatish court, for which Heardred is attacked and killed by Onela. Later Eanmund is killed by Weohstan (see section 36 below) but Eadgils, with the help of Beowulf, becomes king (section 34).

[5] *him* I.e., Heardred.

[6] *he* I.e., Beowulf, whose revenge for the death of his lord Heardred takes a curiously indirect form—he supports Eadgils' return to Sweden, where Onela is killed.

[7] *He* I.e., Eadgils.

Grim and enraged, the lord of the Geats
took a dozen men[1] to seek out the dragon;
he had found out by then how the feud arose,
the baleful violence; the precious vessel
2405 had come to him through the thief's hands.
He was the thirteenth man among that troop,
who had brought about the beginning of that strife,
a sad-minded captive—wretched and despised
he led the way to that plain. He went against his will
2410 to where he alone knew the earth-hall stood,
an underground cave near the crashing waves,
the surging sea; inside it was full
of gems and metal bands. A monstrous guardian,
eager for combat, kept his gold treasures
2415 ancient under the ground; getting them
was no easy bargain for any man.
　　　　The battle-hardened king sat down on the cape,
then wished good health to his hearth-companions,
the gold-friend of the Geats. His heart was grieving,
2420 restless and ripe for death—the doom was
　　　　immeasurably near
that was coming to meet that old man,
seek his soul's treasure, split asunder
his life and his body; not for long was
the spirit of that noble king enclosed in its flesh.
2425 　　　　Beowulf spoke, the son of Ecgtheow:
"In my youth I survived many storms of battle,
times of strife—I still remember them all.
I was seven years old when the prince of treasures,
friend to his people, took me from my father;[2]
2430 Hrethel the king held me and kept me,
gave me gems and feasts, remembered our kinship.
I was no more hated to him while he lived
—a man in his stronghold—than any of his sons,
Herebeald and Hæthcyn and my own Hygelac.
2435 For the eldest,[3] undeservedly,
a death-bed was made by the deeds of a kinsman,
after Hæthcyn with his horn bow
struck down his own dear lord with an arrow—
he missed his mark and murdered his kinsman,

2440 one brother to the other with a bloody shaft.
That was a fight beyond settling, a sinful crime,
shattering the heart; yet it had to be
that a nobleman lost his life unavenged.
　　　　"So it is sad for an old man
2445 to live to see his young son
ride on the gallows[4]—then let him recount a story,
a sorry song, when his son hangs
of comfort only to the ravens, and he cannot,
though old and wise, offer him any help.
2450 Each and every morning calls to mind
his son's passing away; he will not care
to wait for any other heir or offspring
in his fortress, when the first one has
tasted evil deeds and fell death.
2455 He looks sorrowfully on his son's dwelling,
the deserted wine-hall, the windswept home,
bereft of joy—the riders sleep,
heroes in their graves; there is no harp-music,
no laughter in the court, as there had been long before.

35

2460 "He takes to his couch and keens a lament
all alone for his lost one; all too vast to him
seem the fields and townships.
　　　　　　　　　　So the protector of the Weders[5]
bore surging in his breast heartfelt sorrows
for Herebeald. He could not in any way
2465 make amends for the feud with his murderer,
but neither could he hate that warrior
for his hostile deeds, though he was not dear to him.
Then with the sorrow which befell him too sorely,
he gave up man's joys, chose God's light;[6]
2470 he left to his children his land and strongholds
—as a blessed man does—when he departed this life.

---

[1] *a dozen men* Literally "one of twelve"—Beowulf, Wiglaf, and ten others. The thief who leads the way is the thirteenth man.

[2] *took me ... father* Beowulf was brought up as a noble foster-child in the royal court.

[3] *eldest* I.e., Herebeald.

[4] *So it is ... gallows* It is usually suggested that this is a kind of epic simile, comparing Hrethel's grief over his son's death—a death beyond the scope of vengeance—to the grief of a criminal's father, who cannot claim compensation for the execution of his son. Mitchell and Robinson suggest that this is rather a reference to a pagan practice, part of the cult of Odin (also known as "Woden"), in which the body of a man who did not die in battle was ritually hanged on a gallows. If this interpretation is correct, the "old man" is Hrethel himself.

[5] *the protector of ... Weders* I.e., Hrethel.

[6] *God's light* I.e., he died.

Then there was strife between Swedes and Geats,[1]
a quarrel in common across the wide water,
hard hostility after Hrethel died,
2475 until the sons of Ongentheow[2]
were bold and warlike, wanted no peace
over the sea, but around the Hill of Sorrows[3]
they carried out a terrible and devious campaign.
My friends and kinsmen got revenge for those
2480 feuds and evils[4]—as it is said—
although one of them paid for it with his own life,
a hard bargain; that battle was fatal
for Hæthcyn, king of the Geats.
Then, I've heard, the next morning, one kinsman
2485 avenged the other with the sword's edge,[5]
when Ongentheow attacked Eofor;
his battle-helm slipped, the old Scylfing
staggered, corpse-pale; Eofor's hand recalled
his fill of feuds, and did not withhold the fatal blow.

"I have paid in battle for the precious treasures
he[6] gave me, as was granted to me,
with a gleaming sword; he gave me land,
a joyous home. He had no need
to have to go seeking among the Gifthas
2495 or the Spear-Danes or the Swedes
for a worse warrior, or buy one with his wealth;
always on foot I would go before him,
alone in the front line—and all my life
I will wage war, while this sword endures,
2500 which before and since has served me well,
since I slew Dæghrefn, champion of the Hugas,[7]
with my bare hands in front of the whole army.
He could not carry off to the Frisian king

that battle-armor and that breast-adornment,[8]
2505 but there in the field the standard-bearer fell,
a nobleman in his strength; no blade was his slayer,
but my warlike grip broke his beating heart,
cracked his bone-house. Now the blade's edge,
hand and hard sword, shall fight for the hoard."
2510 Beowulf spoke, said boasting words
for the very last time: "I have survived
many battles in my youth; I will yet
seek out, an old folk-guardian, a feud
and do a glorious deed, if only that evildoer
2515 will come out to me from his earth-hall."
Then for the last time he saluted
each of the soldiers, his own dear comrades,
brave in their helmets: "I would not bear a sword
or weapon to this serpent, if I knew any other way
2520 I could grapple with this great beast[9]
after my boast, as I once did with Grendel;
but I expect the heat of battle-flames there,
steam and venom; therefore shield and byrnie
will I have on me. From the hoard's warden
2525 I will not flee a single foot, but for us
it shall be at the wall as *wyrd* decrees,
the Ruler of every man. My mind is firm—
I will forgo boasting against this flying foe.
Wait on the barrow, protected in your byrnies,
2530 men in war-gear, to see which of the two of us
after the bloody onslaught can better
bear his wounds. It is not your way,
nor proper for any man except me alone,
that he should match his strength against this monster,
2535 do heroic deeds. With daring I shall
get that gold—or grim death
and fatal battle will bear away your lord!"
Then that brave challenger stood up by his shield,
stern under his helmet, bore his battle-shirt
2540 under the stone-cliffs, trusted the strength
of a single man—such is not the coward's way.
He saw then by the wall—he who had survived
a great many conflicts, good in manly virtues,
the crash of battles when footsoldiers clashed—
2545 stone arches standing, and a stream

---

[1] *strife … Geats* This refers to a time a generation before the conflicts of Heardred, Eanmund and Eadgils; the Swedish-Geatish feud is longstanding.

[2] *sons of Ongentheow* I.e., Ohthere and Onela.

[3] *Hill of Sorrows* A hill in Geatland, in OE *Hreosnabeorh*.

[4] *My friends … evils* The scene of this revenge is apparently Sweden, in a place called "Ravenswood"; this battle is described again in sections 40 and 41.

[5] *one kinsman … sword's edge* Hygelac avenged the death of Hæthcyn on his slayer Ongentheow—not directly but through his man Eofor.

[6] *he* I.e., Hygelac.

[7] *Hugas* Frankish tribes allied to the Frisians; the battle in question may be the same as Hygelac's fatal raid.

---

[8] *breast-adornment* Possibly the same as the necklace described in 1195–1214.

[9] *great beast* The OE word *æglæcan* is here used of the dragon.

shooting forth from the barrow; its surge
was hot with deadly flames, and near the hoard
he could not survive for very long
unburnt, for the dragon's flaming breath.
2550 Enraged, the ruler of the Weder-Geats
let a word burst forth from his breast,
shouted starkly; the sound entered
and resounded battle-clear under the gray stone.
Hate was stirred up—the hoard-warden recognized
2555 the voice of a man; there was no more time
to sue for peace. First there issued
the steam of that great creature out of the stone,
hot battle-sweat; the earth bellowed.
The warrior in the barrow turned his shield-board
2560 against the grisly stranger, lord of the Geats,
when the writhing beast's heart was roused
to seek combat. The good war-king
had drawn his sword, its edges undulled,
an ancient heirloom; each of the two
2565 hostile ones was horrified by the other.
He stood stouthearted behind his steep shield,
that friend and commander, when the worm coiled itself
swiftly together—he waited in his war-gear.
Then coiled, burning, slithering he came,
2570 rushing to his fate. The shield defended well
the life and limb of the famous lord
for less time than he might have liked;
there on that day for the first time
he faced the outcome,[1] and *wyrd* did not
2575 grant victory in battle. The lord of the Geats
raised his hand, struck that mottled horror
with his ancient sword, so that that edge failed
bright against the bony scales, bit less strongly
than the king of that nation needed it to do,
2580 hard-pressed in battle. Then the barrow-warden
was more savage after that battle-stroke,
and spit out gruesome fire; wide sprang
the battle-flames. The gold-friend of the Geats
did not boast of his glorious victories; his bare sword
2585 failed at need, as it should never have done,
that ancient good iron. It was no easy journey
for the famous son of Ecgtheow to agree
to give up his ground in that place;

he was forced, against his will, to find
2590 a place of rest elsewhere—just as every one of us
must give up these loaned days.
                          It was not long
until those two great creatures[2] came together again.
The hoard-guard took heart, his breast swelled with breath
once again; he[3] suffered anguish,
2595 trapped by flames, he who had once ruled his folk.
His comrades, hand-chosen, sons of noblemen,
did not take their stand in a troop around him,
with warlike valor—they fled to the woods
and saved their lives. The spirit rose up in sorrow
2600 in the heart of one of them; nothing can overrule
kinship at all, in one who thinks well.

36

He was called Wiglaf, Weohstan's son,
a worthy shield-warrior, a prince of the Scylfings,[4]
kinsman of Ælfhere. He saw his liege-lord
2605 suffer heat under his war-helmet;
he recalled the honors he had received from him,
the wealthy homestead of the Waegmundings,
every folk-right that his father had possessed;
he could not hold back—his hand seized
2610 the pale linden shield, and he drew his old sword.
It was known among men as the heirloom of Eanmund,
son of Ohthere; that friendless exile
was slain in battle with the edge of a sword
by Weohstan, who brought to his kinsman
2615 the burnished helmet, the ringed byrnie,
the old giant-work sword; Onela gave to him
the war-equipment of his young kinsman,
the shining armor—he never spoke of a feud,
though he had slain his brother's son.[5]

---

[2] *creatures* OE *æglæcan* again, here referring to Beowulf and the dragon together.

[3] *he* I.e., Beowulf.

[4] *a prince of the Scylfings* Wiglaf's nationality is in question—he is both a Swede and a Wægmunding (like Beowulf; see lines 2813–14). His father fought on the Swedish side in their feuds with the Geats. Tribal allegiance is more fluid than modern nationality.

[5] *he never ... brother's son* Onela never spoke of a feud, though Weohstan had killed Onela's brother's son, for he wished him dead. As elsewhere in the poem, a sword is the reminder of both victory and vengeance.

---

[1] *for the first time ... outcome* Or "if he could have controlled the outcome for the first time."

2620 He[1] kept that war-gear for a great many years,
the blade and byrnie, until his boy could
perform brave deeds like his father before him;
he gave him among the Geats that battle-gear,
every piece of it, when, old, he departed this life
2625 and went forth. That was the first time
that the young warrior had to weather
the storm of battle beside his noble lord.
His courage did not melt, nor did his kinsman's legacy
weaken in war; the worm discovered that,
2630 when they began to meet together.
 Wiglaf spoke, said to his companions
many true words—he was mournful at heart—
"I remember the time that we took mead together,
when we made promises to our prince
2635 in the beer-hall—he gave us these rings—
that we would pay him back for this battle-gear,
these helmets and hard swords, if such a need
as this ever befell him. For this he chose us from the army
for this adventure by his own will,
2640 thought us worthy of glory, and gave me these treasures—
for this he considered us good spear-warriors,
proud helmet-wearers, even though our prince,
shepherd of his people, intended to perform
this act of courage all alone,
2645 because he has gained the most glory among men,
reckless heroic deeds. Now the day has come
that our noble lord has need of the support
of good warriors; let us go to it,
help our warlord, despite the heat,
2650 grim fire-terror. God knows for my part
that I would much prefer that the flames should enfold
my body alongside my gold-giving lord.
It seems wrong to me that we should bear shields
back to our land, unless we first might
2655 finish off this foe, defend the life
of the prince of the Weders. I know full well
that he does not deserve to suffer
this torment all alone among the Geatish troop,
or fall in the struggle; now sword and helmet,
2660 byrnie and battle-dress, shall be ours together!"
 He hurried through the deadly fumes, bore his
   helmet
to the aid of his lord, spoke little:

"Dear Beowulf, do all well,
as in your youth you said you would,
2665 that you would never let in your whole life
your fame decline; now firm in deeds,
single-minded nobleman, with all your strength
you must protect your life—I will support you."
After these words the worm came angrily,
2670 terrible vicious creature, a second time,
scorched with surging flames, seeking out his enemies,
the hated men. The hot flames rolled in waves,
burned the shield to its rim; the byrnie was not
of any use to the young soldier,
2675 but he showed his courage under his kinsman's shield,
the young warrior, when his own was
charred to cinders. Still the battle-king
remembered his glory, and with his mighty strength
swung his warblade with savage force,
2680 so that it stuck in the skull. Nægling shattered—
the sword of Beowulf weakened at battle,
ancient and gray. It was not granted to him
that iron-edged weapons might ever
help him in battle; his hand was too strong,
2685 he who, I am told, overtaxed every blade
with his mighty blows, when he bore to battle
a wound-hardened[2] weapon—it was no help to him at all.
 Then that threat to the people for a third time,
fierce fire-dragon, remembering his feud,
2690 rushed on the brave man, hot and bloodthirsty,
when he saw the chance, seized him by the neck
in his bitter jaws; he was bloodied
by his mortal wounds—blood gushed in waves.

37

Then, I have heard, in his king's hour of need
2695 the earl[3] beside him showed his bravery,
the noble skill which was his nature.
He did not heed that head when he helped his kinsman;
that brave man's hand was burned, so that
he struck that savage foe a little lower down,
2700 the soldier in armor, so that his sword plunged in
bejeweled and bloody, so that the fire began
to subside afterwards. The king himself

---

[1] *He* I.e., Weohstan.

[2] *wound-hardened* Or "wondrously hard"; the OE text is unclear.

[3] *earl* I.e., Wiglaf.

still had his wits, drew the war-dagger,
bitter and battle-sharp, that he wore in his byrnie;
2705 the protector of the Weders carved through the
    worm's midsection.
They felled their foe—their force took his life—
and they both together had brought him down,
the two noble kinsmen; a thane at need,
as a man should be! But that, for the prince, was
2710 his last work of victory, by his own will,
of worldly adventures.
               When the wound
which the earth-dragon had worked on him
began to burn and swell, he soon realized
that in his breast, with an evil force,
2715 a poison welled; then the nobleman went,
still wise in thought, so that he sat
on a seat by the wall. On that work of giants he gazed,
saw how stone arches and sturdy pillars
held up the inside of that ancient earth-hall.
2720 Then with his hands the thane, immeasurably good,
bathed with water his beloved lord,
the great prince, spattered with gore,
sated with battle, and unstrapped his helmet.
Beowulf spoke—despite his wound,
2725 that deadly cut; he knew clearly
that his allotted life had run out,
and his joys in the earth; all gone
was his portion of days, death immeasurably near:
    "Now I should wish to give my war-gear
2730 to my son, if there had been such,
flesh of my flesh, if fate had granted me
any heir. I held this people
fifty winters; there was no folk-king,
not any of the neighboring tribes,
2735 who dared to face me with hostile forces
or threaten fear. The decrees of fate
I awaited on earth, held well what was mine;
I sought no intrigues, nor swore many
false or wrongful oaths. For all that I may
2740 have joy, though sick with mortal wounds,
because the Ruler of men need not reproach me
with the murder of kinsmen, when my life
quits my body. Now go quickly
to look at the hoard under the hoary stone,
2745 dear Wiglaf, now that the worm lies dead,
sleeps with his wounds, stripped of his treasure.

Hurry, so I might witness that ancient wealth,
those golden goods, might eagerly gaze on
the bright precious gems, and I might more gently,
2750 for that great wealth, give up my
life and lordship, which I have held so long."

38

    Then swiftly, I have heard, the son of Weohstan
after these words obeyed his lord,
sick with wounds, wore his ring-net,
2755 the woven battle-shirt, under the barrow's roof.
As he went by the seat he saw there, triumphant,
the brave young warrior, many bright jewels,
glittering gold scattered on the ground,
wonders on the walls, and the lair of that worm,
2760 the old dawn-flier—flagons standing,
ancient serving-vessels without a steward,
their trappings all moldered; there was many a helmet
old and rusty, a number of arm-bands
with twisted ornaments.—Treasure may easily,
2765 gold in the ground, give the slip
to any one of us: let him hide it who will![1]—
Likewise he saw an ensign, all golden,
hanging high over the hoard, greatest hand-work,
linked together with skill; light gleamed from it
2770 so that he could see the cave's floor,
survey those strange artifacts. There was no sign
of the serpent there—a sword had finished him off.
Then the hoard in that barrow, as I've heard, was looted,
ancient work of giants, by one man alone;
2775 he piled in his arms cups and plates,
whatever he wanted; he took the ensign too,
brightest of beacons. His aged lord's blade
—its edge was iron— had earlier harmed
the one who was protector of those treasures
2780 for such a long time, who bore his fiery terror
flaming before the hoard, seething fiercely
in the darkest night, until he died a bloody death.
    The messenger rushed out, eager to return,
burdened with treasures; he was burning to know
2785 whether, stout-hearted, he would find still alive

---

[1] *give the slip ... who will* Or "can get the better of any man—heed [these words] who will!" The OE is uncertain; the translation follows Mitchell and Robinson.

the prince of the Weders, weakened by wounds,
in the place where he had left him on that plain.
Then with the treasures he found the famous prince,
his own lord, his life at an end,
2790 all bloody; he began once more
to sprinkle water on him, until the point of a word
escaped from his breast.
Old, full of grief, he looked on the gold:
        "For all these treasures, I offer thanks
2795 with these words to the eternal Lord,
King of Glory, for what I gaze upon here,
that I was able to acquire such wealth
for my people before my death-day.
Now that I have sold my old lifespan
2800 for this hoard of treasures, they will attend[1]
to the needs of the people; I can stay no longer.
The brave in battle will bid a tomb be built
shining over my pyre on the cliffs by the sea;
it will be as a monument to my people
2805 and tower high on Whale's Head,
so that seafarers afterwards shall call it
'Beowulf's Barrow,' when their broad ships
drive from afar over the darkness of the flood."
        The boldminded nobleman took from his neck
2810 a golden circlet, and gave it to the thane,
the young spear-carrier, and the gold-covered helmet,
ring and byrnie, bid him use them well:
"You are the last survivor of our lineage,
the Wægmundings; fate has swept away
2815 all of my kinsmen, earls in their courage,
to their final destiny; I must follow them."
That was the last word of the old warrior,
his final thought before he chose the fire,
the hot surging flames—from his breast flew
2820 his soul to seek the judgment of the righteous.[2]

---

[1] *they will attend* Usually translated "you [Wiglaf] will attend …";
the OE verb may be indicative or imperative, but it is unambigu-
ously plural, and the imperative plural is not used elsewhere in the
poem to address a single person.

[2] *the judgment of the righteous* Literally "the *dom* (fame) of the
truth-fast," an ambiguous pronouncement. It is not clear whether
this means that Beowulf's soul will receive the sort of judgment that
a righteous soul ought to receive (and so go to Heaven), or that it
will be judged by those "fast in truth" (and so go to Hell as an
unbaptized pagan).

39

        Then it came to pass with piercing sorrow
that the young warrior had to watch
his most precious lord fare so pitifully,
his life at an end. Likewise his slayer lay dead,
2825 the awesome earth-dragon deprived of his life,
overcome by force. The coiled serpent
could no longer rule his hoard of rings—
edges of iron did away with him,
the hard, battle-scarred shards of the smithy,
2830 so that the wide-flier, stilled by his wounds,
toppled to the ground near his treasure-house.
No more soaring about in the skies
at midnight, preening in his precious treasures,
showing his face—he fell to earth
2835 through that war-commander's handiwork.
Indeed, few men on earth, no matter how strong,
could succeed at that, as I have heard tell,
though he were daring in every deed,
could rush against the reek of that venomous foe,
2840 or rifle through that ring-hall with his hands,
if he should find a waking warden
waiting in that barrow. Beowulf's share
of that royal treasure was repaid by his death—
each of them had journeyed to the end
2845 of this loaned life.
                    It was not long before
the men late for battle left the woods,
ten of those weak traitors all together
who had not dared to hoist their spears
when their lord of men needed them most;
2850 now shamefaced, they carried their shields
and battledress to where the old man lay dead,
to stare at Wiglaf. He sat exhausted,
a foot-soldier at his lord's shoulder,
tried to rouse him with water—but it was no use.
2855 He could not, no matter how much he wanted,
keep the life in the body of his captain,
nor change any bit of the Ruler's decree;
the judgment of God would guide the deeds
of every man, as it still does today.
2860 Then it was easy to get a grim answer
from that youth to those who gave up courage.
Wiglaf spoke, son of Weohstan,
looked, sad-hearted, on those unloved:

"He can say—o yes—who would speak the truth
2865 that the liege-lord who gave you those gifts of treasures,
      the military gear that you stand in there,
      when on the ale-benches he often handed out
      helmets and byrnies to the hall-sitters,
      a lord to his followers, whatever he could find
2870 finest anywhere, far or near—
      that all that battle-dress he absolutely
      and entirely threw away, when war beset him.
      Our nation's king had no need to boast
      of his comrades-in-arms! But the Ruler of victories
2875 allowed that he, alone with his blade,
      might avenge himself when he needed your valor.
      Only a little life-protection could I offer
      him in battle, but began nevertheless
      to support my kinsman beyond my own strength;
2880 ever the worse was the deadly enemy
      when I struck with my sword, a fire less severe
      surging from his head. Too few supporters
      thronged around our prince in his great peril.
      Now the getting of treasure, the giving of swords,
2885 and all the happy joys of your homeland
      shall end for your race; empty-handed
      will go every man among your tribe,
      deprived of his land-rights, when noblemen learn
      far and wide of your flight,
2890 your inglorious deed. Death is better
      for any earl than a life of dishonor!"

40

      He bade that the battle-work be announced to
            the camp
      up by the cliff's edge, where that troop of earls,
      shield-bearers, sat sad-minded
2895 all the long morning, expecting either
      the final day of their dear lord
      or his homecoming. He who rode up to the cape
      was not at all silent with his new tidings,
      but he spoke truly in the hearing of all:
2900 "Now is the joy-giver of the Geatish people,
      the lord of the Weders, laid on his deathbed,
      holding a place of slaughter by the serpent's deeds;
      beside him lies his life-enemy,
      sick with knife-slashes; he could not with his sword

2905 make in the monstrous beast
      any kind of wound. Wiglaf sits,
      Weohstan's offspring, over Beowulf,
      one earl over the other, now dead;
      he holds with desperate heart the watch
2910 over friend and foe.
                          Now this folk may expect
      a time of trouble, when this is manifest
      to the Franks and Frisians, and the fall of our king
      becomes widespread news. The strife was begun
      hard with the Hugas, after Hygelac came
2915 travelling with his ships to the shores of Frisia,
      where the Hetware attacked him in war,
      advanced with valor and a vaster force,
      so that the warrior in his byrnie had to bow down,
      and fell amid the infantry; not at all did that lord
2920 give treasure to his troops. Ever after that
      the Merovingians have not shown mercy to us.
      "Nor do I expect any peace or truce
      from the Swedish nation, but it has been well-known
      that Ongentheow ended the life
2925 of Hæthcyn, son of Hrethel, in Ravenswood,
      when in their arrogant pride the Geatish people
      first sought out the Battle-Scylfings.
      Immediately the ancient father of Ohthere,
      old and terrifying, returned the attack—
2930 the old warrior cut down the sea-captain,[1]
      rescued his wife, bereft of her gold,
      Onela's mother and Ohthere's;
      and then hunted down his deadly enemies
      until they escaped, with some difficulty,
2935 bereft of their lord, into Ravenswood.
      With his standing army he besieged those sword-leavings,
      weary, wounded; he kept threatening woe
      to that wretched troop the whole night through—
      in the morning, he said, with the edge of his sword
2940 he would gut them, and leave some on the gallows-tree
      as sport for birds. But for those sad-hearted men
      solace came along with the sunrise,
      after they heard Hygelac's horn and trumpet
      sounding the charge, when the good man came
2945 following the trail of that people's troop.

---

[1] *old warrior ... sea-captain*   Ongentheow killed Hæthcyn. Hygelac
is not present at this battle, but arrives later.

41

"The bloody swath of the Swedes and Geats,
the slaughter of men, was easily seen,
how the folk had stirred up feud between them.
That good man[1] then departed, old, desperate,
2950 with a small band of kinsmen, sought his stronghold,
the earl Ongentheow turned farther away;
he had heard of proud Hygelac's prowess in battle,
his war-skill; he did not trust the resistance
he might muster against the seafarers' might
2955 to defend from the wave-borne warriors his treasure,
his women and children; he ran away from there,
old, into his fortress. Then the pursuit was offered
to the Swedish people, the standard of Hygelac
overran the place of refuge,
2960 after the Hrethlings thronged the enclosure.
There with the edge of a sword was Ongentheow,
old graybeard, brought to bay,
so that the king of that nation had to yield
to Eofor's will. Angrily he struck;
2965 Wulf the son of Wonred lashed at him with his weapon,
so that with his blow the blood sprang in streams
from under his hair. Yet the ancient Scylfing
was undaunted, and dealt back quickly
a worse exchange for that savage stroke,
2970 once the ruler of that people turned around.
The ready son of Wonred could not
give a stroke in return to the old soldier,
for he had cut through the helmet right on his head
so that he collapsed, covered in blood,
2975 fell to the ground—he was not yet fated to die,
but he recovered, though the cut hurt him.
The hardy thane of Hygelac[2] then let
his broad blade, as his brother lay there,
his ancient giant-made sword, shatter that gigantic helmet
2980 over the shield-wall; then the king stumbled,
shepherd of his people, mortally stricken.
      There were many there who bandaged his[3]
            kinsman,
quickly raised him up, when a way was clear for them,
so that they had control of that killing field.

2985 Then one warrior plundered another,[4]
took from Ongentheow the iron byrnie,
his hard hilted sword and his helmet too,
and carried the old man's armor to Hygelac.
He[5] took that war-gear and promised him gifts
2990 among his people—and he kept that promise;
the king of the Geats repaid that carnage,
the offspring of Hrethel, when he made it home,
gave to Eofor and Wulf extravagant treasures,
gave them each lands and locked rings,
2995 worth a hundred thousand. Not a man in this world
            could
reproach those rewards, since they had won them
            with their deeds;
and to Eofor he gave his only daughter,
the pride of his home, as a pledge of his friendship.
      "That is the feud and the fierce enmity,
3000 savage hatred among men, that I expect now,
when the Swedish people seek us out
after they have learned that our lord
has perished, who had once protected
his hoard and kingdom against all hostility,
3005 after the fall of heroes, the valiant Scyldings,[6]
worked for the people's good, and what is more,
performed noble deeds. Now we must hurry
and look upon our people's king,
and go with him who gave us rings
3010 on the way to the pyre. No small part
of the hoard shall burn with that brave man,
but countless gold treasures, grimly purchased,
and rings, here at last with his own life
paid for; then the flames shall devour,
3015 the fire enfold—let no warrior wear
treasures for remembrance, nor no fair maiden
have a ring-ornament around her neck,
but sad in mind, stripped of gold, she must
walk a foreign path, not once but often,
3020 now that leader of our troop has laid aside laughter,

---

[1] *good man* I.e., Ongentheow.

[2] *thane of Hygelac* I.e., Eofor, Wulf's brother.

[3] *his* I.e., Eofor's.

[4] *one ... another* Eofor plundered Ongentheow.

[5] *He* I.e., Hygelac.

[6] *Scyldings* The manuscript reading ("Scyldings" is a further object of "protected") is often emended to *Scylfingas*, i.e., Swedes, or *scildwigan*, "shield-warriors"; the present reading is that of Mitchell and Robinson. As it stands in the manuscript the Geatish herald is referring to Beowulf's earlier adventures against Grendel and his mother.

his mirth and joy. Thus many a cold morning
shall the spear be grasped in frozen fingers,
hefted by hands, nor shall the sound of the harp
rouse the warriors, but the dark raven,
3025　greedy for carrion, shall speak a great deal,
ask the eagle how he fared at his feast
when he plundered corpses with the wolf."[1]

　　Thus that brave speaker was speaking
a most unlovely truth; he did not lie much
3030　in words or facts. The troop of warriors arose;
they went, unhappy, to the Cape of Eagles,
with welling tears to look at that wonder.
There on the sand they found the soulless body
of the one who gave them rings in earlier times
3035　laid out to rest; the last day
had come for the good man, when the war-king,
prince of the Weders, died a wondrous death.
But first they saw an even stranger creature,
a loathsome serpent lying on the plain
3040　directly across from him; grim with his colors
the fire-dragon was, and scorched with his flames.
He was fifty feet long, lying there
stretched out; once he had joy in the air
in the dark night, and then down he would go
3045　to seek his den, but now he was fast in death;
he had come to the end of his cave-dwelling.
Cups and vessels stood beside him,
plates lay there and precious swords,
eaten through with rust, as if in the bosom of the earth
3050　they had lain for a thousand winters;
all that inheritance was deeply enchanted,
the gold of the ancients was gripped in a spell
so that no man in the world would be able to touch
that ring-hall, unless God himself,
3055　the true King of Victories, Protector of men,
granted to whomever He wished to open the hoard,
to whatever person seemed proper to Him.[2]

Then it was plain that the journey did not profit
the one[3] who had wrongfully hidden under a wall
3060　that great treasure. The guardian had slain
that one and few others;[4] then that feud was
swiftly avenged. It is a wonder to say
where a valiant earl should meet the end
of his span of life, when he may no longer
3065　dwell in the meadhall, a man with his kinsmen.
So it was with Beowulf, when he sought the barrow's
　　guardian
and a hostile fight; even he did not know
how his parting from life should come to pass,
since until doomsday mighty princes had deeply
3070　pronounced, when they placed it there,
that the man who plundered that place would be
harried by hostile demons, fast in hellish bonds,
grievously tortured, guilty of sins,
unless the Owner's grace had earlier
3075　more readily favored the one eager for gold.[5]
　　Wiglaf spoke, son of Weohstan:
"Often many earls must suffer misery
through the will of one man, as we have now seen.
We could not persuade our dear prince,
3080　shepherd of a kingdom, with any counsel,
that he should not greet that gold-guardian,
let him lie there where he long had been,
inhabit the dwellings until the end of the world:
he held to his high destiny. The hoard is opened,
3085　grimly gotten; that fate was too great
which impelled the king of our people thither.
I was in there, and looked over it all,
the hall's ornaments, when a way was open to me;
by no means gently was a journey allowed
3090　in under that earth-wall. In eager haste I seized
in my hands a great mighty burden

---

[1]　the dark raven … the wolf   The eagle, wolf, and raven, the "beasts of battle," are a recurring motif in Old English poetry.

[2]　unless God himself … proper to Him   The power of the pagan spell can be overruled by the will of the true God.

---

[3]　the one   I.e., the dragon.

[4]　that one and few others   Or "that one of a few," i.e., "a unique man" or "a man of rare greatness."

[5]　favored the one eager for gold   The OE text is corrupt and the precise meaning of this passage is not certain; the present translation tries to incorporate several suggested interpretations. The general sense seems to be clear enough—the gold was cursed, and only God's special grace would enable anyone to remove it. What this implies about Beowulf's failure, and his moral status, is less clear.

of hoard-treasure, and bore it out hither
to my king. He was still conscious then,
thoughtful and alert; he spoke of many things,
3095 an old man in his sorrow, and ordered that I greet you;
he asked that you build a great high barrow
for your prince's deeds, in the place of his pyre,
mighty and glorious, since he was of men
the most worthy warrior throughout the wide world,
3100 while he could enjoy the wealth of a hall.
Let us now make haste for one more time
to see and seek out that store of cunning gems,
the wonder under the wall; I will direct you
so that you can inspect them up close,
3105 abundant rings and broad gold. Let the bier be ready,
quickly prepared, when we come out,
then let us bear our beloved lord,
that dear man, to where he must long
rest in the keeping of the Ruler."
3110   Then the son of Weohstan, brave battle-warrior,
let it be made known to many heroes
and householders that they should bring from afar
the wood for the pyre to that good one,[1]
the leader of his folk: "Now the flames must devour,
3115 the black blaze rise over the ruler of warriors,
who often awaited the showers of iron
when the storm of arrows hurled from bow-strings
shot over the wall, the shafts did their duty
swift on feather-wings, sent on the arrow-heads."
3120   Lo, then the wise son of Weohstan
summoned from that host some of the best
of the king's thanes, seven altogether;
he went, one of eight, under that evil roof;
one of the brave warriors bore in his hands
3125 a flaming torch, and went before them.
It was not chosen by lots who should loot that hoard,[2]
once the men saw it sitting in the hall,
every part of it unprotected,
lying there wasting; there was little lament
3130 that they should have to hurry out with
the precious treasures. They also pushed the dragon,
the worm, over the cliff-wall, let the waves take him,
the flood embrace the guard of that finery;

then the twisted gold, an uncountable treasure,
3135 was loaded in a wagon, and the noble one was carried,
the gray-haired warrior, to the Cape of Whales.

43

    The people of the Geats then prepared for him
a splendid pyre upon the earth,
hung with battle-shields and helmets
3140 and bright byrnies, as he had bidden;
there in the middle they laid the mighty prince,
the heroes lamenting their dear lord.
Then the warriors kindled there on the cliff
the greatest of funeral pyres; dark over the flames
3145 the woodsmoke rose, the roaring fire
mingled with weeping—the wind lay still—
until it had broken that bone-house
hot at the heart. With heavy spirits
they mourned their despair, the death of their lord;
3150 and a sorrowful song sang the Geatish woman,[3]
with hair bound up, for Beowulf the king,
with sad cares, earnestly said
that she dreaded the hard days ahead,
the times of slaughter, the host's terror,
3155 harm and captivity. Heaven swallowed the smoke.
    Then the Weder people wrought for him
a barrow on the headland; it was high and broad,
visible from afar to sea-voyagers,
and in ten days they built the beacon
3160 of that battle-brave one; the ashes of the flames
they enclosed with a wall, as worthily
as the most clever of men could devise it.
In the barrow they placed rings and bright jewels,
all the trappings that those reckless men
3165 had seized from the hoard before,
let the earth hold the treasures of earls,
gold in the ground, where it yet remains,
just as useless to men as it was before.
Then round the mound rode the battle-brave men,
3170 offspring of noblemen, twelve in all;
they wished to voice their cares and mourn their king,

---

[1] *that good one* I.e., the dead Beowulf.

[2] *It was not chosen ... hoard* I.e., everybody had a share; there was
enough for all.

[3] *Geatish woman* The manuscript is damaged throughout this
section and the readings in this passage are conjectural; it is not clear
who the "Geatish woman" is, though her advanced age is indicated
by her bound-up hair. Typically, in Germanic poetry, it is women
(and poets) who mourn.

utter sad songs and speak of that man;
they praised his lordship and his proud deeds,
judged well his prowess. As it is proper

3175   that one should praise his lord with words,
should love him in his heart when the fatal hour comes,
when he must from his body be led forth,

so the men of the Geats lamented
the fall of their prince, those hearth-companions;

3180   they said that he was of all the kings of the world
the mildest of men and the most gentle,
the kindest to his folk and the most eager for fame.

In Context

Background Material

Glossary of Proper Names

Abel	slain by his brother **Cain**; the story is told in Genesis 4.1–16
Ælfhere	kinsman of **Wiglaf**
Æschere	a prominent Dane, advisor to **Hrothgar**; slain by Grendel's mother
Battle-Scyldings	see **Scyldings**
Battle-Scylfings	see **Scylfings**
Beanstan	father of **Breca**
Beowulf	(prologue) Danish king, son of **Scyld**
Breca	engaged in a youthful swimming contest with Beowulf
Bright-Danes	see **Danes**
Brondings	the people of **Breca**
Brosinga	makers of the magical necklace of Freya in Norse myth, to which a necklace in the story is compared
Cain	slayer of **Abel** in Genesis 4.1–16; father of the race of monsters
Dæghrefn	a warrior of the **Hugas** slain by Beowulf in hand-to-hand combat during Hygelac's ill-fated raid on **Frisia**
Danes	**Hrothgar**'s people; the **Scyldings**; also called Bright-, Half-, Ring-, Spear-, East-, West-, North-, and South-Danes
Eadgils	son of **Ohthere**, brother of **Eanmund**
Eanmund	son of **Ohthere**, brother of **Eadgils**; slain by **Weohstan**
East-Danes	see **Danes**
Ecglaf	father of **Unferth**
Ecgtheow	father of Beowulf
Ecgwala	a Danish king; the "sons of Ecgwala" are the **Danes**
Eofor	a warrior of the **Geats**; brother of **Wulf**; slayer of **Ongentheow**
Eomer	son of **Offa**
Eormanric	king of the Ostrogoths
Eotens	unclear: perhaps the **Jutes**, perhaps the **Frisians**, perhaps "giants" (the literal meaning of the word) as a nickname for one group or the other
Finn	king of the **Frisians**, husband of **Hildeburh**; killed by **Hengest**
Finns	the people of Finland; the Lapps
Fitela	legendary companion, nephew (and son) of **Sigemund**
Folcwalda	father of **Finn**
Franks	a Germanic tribe; see **Hetware, Hugas, Merovingians**

Freawaru	daughter of **Hrothgar**, betrothed to **Ingeld**
Frisians	a Germanic tribe; **Finn**'s people
Froda	chief of the **Heathobards**, father of **Ingeld**
Garmund	father of **Offa**
Geats	**Hygelac**'s people and Beowulf's; a Germanic tribe; also called War-Geats, Hrethmen, Hrethlings, Weders
Gifthas	an East-Germanic tribe
Grendel	descendent of **Cain**; monstrous marauder of the **Danes**
Guthlaf	a Danish warrior, companion of **Hengest**
Hæreth	father of **Hygd**
Hæthcyn	Geatish prince, second son of **Hrethel**
Half-Danes	see **Danes**
Halga	Danish prince, younger brother of **Hrothgar**
Hama	legendary Goth; stole **Brosinga** necklace
Healfdene	king of the **Danes**, father of **Hrothgar**
Heardred	king of the **Geats**, son of **Hygelac**
Heathobards	**Ingeld**'s people; a Germanic tribe
Heatholaf	a **Wylfing** slain by **Ecgtheow**
Heathoream	a Scandinavian tribe; Norwegians, more or less
Helmings	the family of **Wealhtheow**
Hemming	kinsman of **Offa** and **Eomer**
Hengest	leader of the **Danes**; killed **Finn** in **Frisia**
Heorogar	Dane, eldest brother of **Hrothgar**
Heorot	the great hall of **Hrothgar**
Heoroweard	Dane; son of **Heorogar**
Herebeald	Geatish prince, eldest son of **Hrethel**; killed by his brother **Hæthcyn**
Heremod	king of the **Danes** in the poem's distant past, before the **Scylding** dynasty
Hereric	brother of **Hygd**, uncle of **Heardred**
Hetware	a Frankish tribe, allied with the **Frisians**; fought against **Hygelac**
Hildeburh	sister of the Danish **Hnæf**, wife of the Frisian **Finn**
Hnæf	chief of the **Half-Danes**, brother of **Hildeburh**; killed by **Finn**
Hoc	Dane, father of **Hildeburh** and **Hnæf**
Hondscio	Geatish warrior, comrade of Beowulf; slain by **Grendel**
Honor-Scyldings	see **Scyldings**
Hrethel	king of the **Geats**, father of **Hygelac**, grandfather of Beowulf
Hrethlings	sons of **Hrethel**, i.e., the **Geats**
Hrethmen	the **Geats**
Hrethric	Dane, son of **Hrothgar**
Hrothgar	aged king of the **Danes** beset by **Grendel**; helped by Beowulf
Hrothmund	Dane, son of **Hrothgar**
Hrothulf	Dane, son of **Halga**, nephew of **Hrothgar**; not to be trusted
Hrunting	the sword of **Unferth**
Hugas	the **Franks**, allies of the **Frisians**
Hunlaf	father of one of the warriors in **Hengest**'s troop
Hygd	queen of the **Geats**, wife of **Hygelac**, daughter of **Hæreth**
Hygelac	king of the **Geats**, uncle of Beowulf
Ingeld	prince of the **Heathobards**, son of **Froda**, betrothed to **Freawaru**; after the events narrated in the poem he burns down the great hall of **Heorot**

Ingwines	the "friends of Ing": the **Danes**
Jutes	allies of the **Frisians**; see **Eotens**
Merovingians	the Franks
Nægling	Beowulf's sword
North-Danes	see **Danes**
Offa	king of the Angles, husband of **Thryth**
Ohthere	Swede, son of **Ongentheow**
Onela	Swede, son of **Ongentheow**; usurped throne
Ongentheow	Swedish king; killed by **Wulf** and **Eofor**
Oslaf	a Danish warrior, companion of **Hengest**
Ring-Danes	see **Danes**
Scyld Scefing	legendary founder of the Danish royal family
Scyldings	the Danes; also called Battle-, Honor-, Victory-Scyldings
Scylfings	the Swedes
Sigemund	legendary Germanic hero, son of **Wæls**
South-Danes	see **Danes**
Spear-Danes	see **Danes**
Swerting	uncle of **Hygelac**
Thryth	(often construed as **Modthryth**) wife of **Offa**
Unferth	Danish spokesman ("thyle") and courtier of **Hrothgar**
Victory-Scyldings	see **Scyldings**
Volsung	another name for **Sigemund**, son of **Wæls**
Wægmundings	the family of **Weohstan**, **Wiglaf**, and Beowulf
Wæls	father of **Sigemund**
War-Geats	see **Geats**
Wealhtheow	Danish queen, wife of **Hrothgar**
Weders	the **Geats**
Weland	legendary Germanic smith
Wendels	a Germanic tribe; perhaps the Vandals, perhaps not
Weohstan	father of **Wiglaf**; killed **Eanmund**
West-Danes	see **Danes**
Wiglaf	son of **Weohstan**, young retainer of Beowulf
Withergyld	a dead **Heathobard**
Wonred	a **Geat**, father of **Wulf** and **Eofor**
Wulf	a warrior of the **Geats**, brother of **Eofor**; assisted in killing **Ongentheow**
Wulfgar	a warrior of the **Danes**; herald at the court of **Hrothgar**
Wylfings	a Germanic tribe of which **Heatholaf** was a member, until **Ecgtheow** killed him
Yrmenlaf	a Dane, younger brother of **Æschere**

Genealogies

1. The Danes (Scyldings)

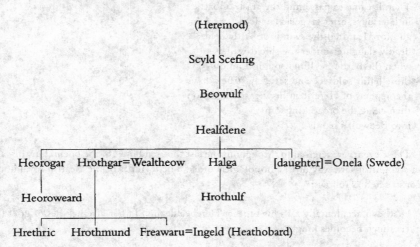

(Heremod)

Scyld Scefing

Beowulf

Healfdene

Heorogar   Hrothgar=Wealtheow   Halga   [daughter]=Onela (Swede)

Heoroweard   Hrothulf

Hrethric   Hrothmund   Freawaru=Ingeld (Heathobard)

2. The Geats

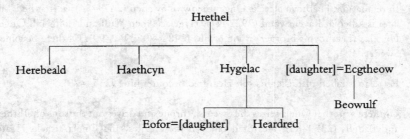

Hrethel

Herebeald   Haethcyn   Hygelac   [daughter]=Ecgtheow

Beowulf

Eofor=[daughter]   Heardred

3. The Swedes (Scylfings)

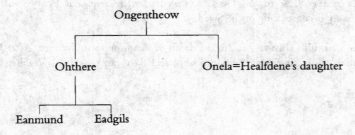

Ongentheow

Ohthere   Onela=Healfdene's daughter

Eanmund   Eadgils

The Geatish-Swedish Wars

When the story of Beowulf's fight with the dragon begins, the narrator leaps over fifty years in one brief passage. It is a tumultuous condensation of a complex chain of events (2200–08):

> Then it came to pass amid the crash of battle
> in later days, after Hygelac lay dead,
> and for Heardred the swords of battle held
> deadly slaughter under the shield-wall,
> when the Battle-Scylfings sought him out,
> those hardy soldiers, and savagely struck down
> the nephew of Hereric in his victorious nation—
> then came the broad kingdom
> into Beowulf's hands …

These events are referred to throughout the last thousand lines of the poem, but they are not told in a straightforward way or in chronological order. The fortunes of the Geatish royal house may be reconstructed as follows:

1. Hæthcyn accidentally kills his brother Herebeald; their father Hrethel dies of grief (2432–71). Hæthcyn becomes king.

2. After the death of Hrethel, Ohthere and Onela, the sons of the Swedish king Ongentheow, attack the Geats (2472–78).

3. In retaliation, Hæthcyn attacks Ongentheow in Sweden (2479–84); at first he is successful, but later is killed at Ravenswood (2922–41). Hygelac's men Wulf and Eofor kill Ongentheow, and Hygelac (Hæthcyn's brother) is victorious (2484–89, 2942–99). Ohthere becomes king of the Swedes.

4. Hygelac is killed in Frisia; his son Heardred becomes king (2354–78).

5. Ohthere's brother Onela seizes the Swedish throne and drives out the sons of Ohthere, Eanmund and Eadgils (2379–84). Heardred takes in these exiles, and Onela attacks Heardred for this hospitality and kills him. Onela allows Beowulf to rule the Geats (2385–90).

6. Around this time Weohstan, father of Wiglaf, kills Eanmund on behalf of Onela (2611–19).

7. Eadgils escapes later to kill Onela in Sweden, with help sent by Beowulf (2391–96); he presumably becomes king of the Swedes.

8. During Beowulf's fifty-year reign, the death of Eanmund is unavenged. After Beowulf's death, Eanmund's brother Eadgils will probably seek vengeance against Wiglaf, son of Weohstan (2999–3005).

Marie de France
c. 1155 – 1215

Although she is widely credited with being the earliest female poet in France, and was arguably the leading female writer of the Middle Ages, little is known about Marie de France; no surviving documents refer to her life outside of her literary activity. What has come down to us are three works, which vary widely in genre: the *Lais* (c. 1155–70), a collection of short romance narratives; the *Ysopet* or *Fables* (c. 1167–89), a collection commonly accepted as the earliest translation of Aesop into French; and the less-studied *Espurgatoire de Saint Patrice* (*Legend of the Purgatory of Saint Patrick*, c. 1189), a didactic tale in which Patrick, an Irish knight, makes a spiritual journey through Purgatory.

Her name is known from the self-identification she makes in each of her texts; this occurs most forcefully and descriptively in the epilogue of the *Ysopet*:

> I shall name myself so that it will be remembered;
> Marie is my name, I am of France.
> It may be that many clerks
> will take my labor on themselves.
> I don't want any of them to claim it.

"France" itself is a slippery designation here, since it had multiple possible meanings in this period; it may be intended to convey that she was from Continental Europe instead of England, for instance, or from northern France instead of the southern Languedoc. The Norman dialect in which her works are composed suggests that Marie was native to Normandy, and lived during the latter part of the 12th century. The "King Henry" to whom she dedicates her *Lais* is usually identified as Henry II, the Angevin French king of England from 1154–89, and Marie is thought to have been a member of his court, which spoke the form of Norman dialect in which her works come down to us. It has sometimes been suggested that she was Henry's illegitimate sister Marie, who became Abbess of Shaftesbury around 1181, and who died in 1216, but without any other corroborating documents, such theories are no more than intriguing speculation. It seems very likely, however, that she was attached to the court of Henry II and his wife, Eleanor of Aquitaine, and was of noble birth; her works reveal a level of education and culture that would not usually have been available to a layperson of lower rank during this time. It is clear that she was educated in Latin, as well as French, and perhaps even in the Breton language, since she claims to have translated her *Lais* from that tongue.

The *Lais* of Marie de France are brief narratives written in octosyllabic rhyming couplets, which was the conventional literary vehicle for French romance during this time. This collection is made up of twelve stories, each prefaced by a short prologue in which Marie reveals that she is translating into French for the first time a number of "Breton *lais*." The *lais* were Celtic tales of romance that often involved elements of the fantastic. The compressed space of the form requires Marie to handle her material with considerable finesse and she recounts her tales with an economy of words and a tight narrative control that lend the romances a down-to-earth precision without sacrificing meaning or nuance.

Many of the *lais* have a strongly female focus, and in this regard offer a certain contrast to the romances of Marie's contemporaries. The works of male romancers, while treating the subject of love, often emphasized the tension between love and chivalric pursuits, and the need to balance the two in order to fulfill both personal needs and social responsibilities. Marie is largely uninterested in such concerns, and focuses instead on the personal desires of her characters, especially those of her female characters. Her *lais* often depict intensely intimate love relationships set against a backdrop of a threatening society in which unfulfilling marriages, the arbitrary dictates of court life, and oppressive social practices hold sway.

    Lanval is drawn from the larger literary universe of Arthurian legend. It recounts the tale of a knight whose inherent worth is unrecognized by the Arthurian court, and who is able to escape this uncaring and arbitrary society through the love of an otherworldly fairy figure.

⌘ ⌘ ⌘

Lanval[1]

L'aventure d'un autre lai,	I shall tell you the adventure
cum ele avient, vus cunterai.	of another lay, just as it happened.
Fait fu d'un mut gentil vassal;	It was made about a very noble vassal;
en bretans l'apelent Lanval.	in Breton they call him Lanval.
A Kardoel surjurnot li reis	The king was staying at Cardoel—
Artur, li pruz e li curteis,	Arthur, the valiant and courteous—
pur les Escoz e pur les Pis,	on account of the Scots and Picts
que destrui[ei]ent le païs;	who were ravaging the country:
en la tere de Loengre entroënt	they came into the land of Logres[2]
e mut suvent la damagoënt.	and repeatedly caused destruction there.
A la Pentecuste en esté	At Pentecost, in the summer,
i aveit li reis sujurné.	the king had taken up residence there.
Asez i duna riches duns	He gave many rich gifts
e as cuntes e as baruns.	both to counts and to noblemen.
A ceus de la table runde—	To the members of the Round Table—
n'ot tant de teus en tut le munde—	they had no equal in all the world—
femmes e tere departi	he shared out wives and land
par tut, fors un ki l'ot servi:	among all except one who had served him:
ceo fu Lanval, ne l'en sovient,	that was Lanval, whom he did not remember,
ne nul de[s] soens bien ne li tient.	nor did any of his men favor him.
Pur sa valur, pur sa largesce,	For his valor, his generosity,
pur sa beauté, pur sa prüesce	his beauty, his prowess,
l'envioënt tut li plusur;	most people envied him;
tel li mustra semblant d'amur,	many a one pretended to love him
se al chevaler mesavenist,	who wouldn't have complained for a moment
ja une feiz ne l'en pleinsist.	if something bad had befallen the knight.
Fiz a rei fu de haut parage,	He was a king's son, of high lineage,
mes luin ert de sun heritage.	but he was far from his heritage.
De la meisné le rei fu.	He was part of the king's household.
Tut sun aveir ad despendu,	He had spent all his wealth,

Line numbers: 5, 10, 15, 20, 25, 30

---

[1] *Lanval* The translation is by Claire Waters, for *The Broadview Anthology of British Literature.*

[2] *Logres* The Celtic word for England.

kar li reis rien ne li dona
ne Lanval rien ne li demanda.
Ore est Lanval mut entrepris,
mut est dolent e mut pensis.
35 Seignurs, ne vus esmerveillez:
hume estrange descunseillez
mut est dolent en autre tere,
quant il ne seit u sucurs quere.
Le chevaler dunt jeo vus di,
40 que tant aveit le rei servi,
un jur munta sur sun destrer,
si s'est alez esbaneer.
Fors de la vilë est eissuz,
tut sul est en un pre venuz;
45 sur une ewe curaunt descent—
mes sis cheval tremble forment.
Il le descengle, si s'en vait;
en mi le pre vuiltrer le lait.
Le pan de sun mantel plia
50 desuz sun chief puis le cucha.
Mut est pensis pur sa mesaise;
il ne veit chose ke li plaise.
La u il gist en teu maniere,
garda aval lez la riviere,
55 [si] vit venir deus dameiseles;
unc n'en ot veü[es] plus beles.
Vestues ierent richement,
lacie[es] mut estreitement
en deus blians de purpre bis;
60 mut par aveient bel le vis.
L'eisnee portout un[s] bacins,
doré furent, bien faiz e fins;
le veir vus en dirai sans faile.
L'autre portout une tuaile.
65 Eles s'en sunt alees dreit
la u li chevaler giseit.
Lanval, que mut fu enseigniez,
cuntre eles s'en levad en piez.
Celes l'unt primes salué,
70 lur message li unt cunté:
"Sire Lanval, ma dameisele,
que tant est pruz e sage e bele,
ele nus enveit pur vus;
kar i venez ensemble od nus!
75 Sauvement vus i cundurums:

for the king gave him nothing,
nor did Lanval ask him for anything.
Now Lanval is very unhappy,
very sorrowful and anxious.
Lords, do not wonder:
a foreign man without support
is very sorrowful in another land
when he does not know where to seek help.
The knight of whom I'm telling you,
who had served the king so well,
got on his horse one day
and went off to enjoy himself.
He went out of the town
and came, all alone, to a meadow;
he got down beside running water—
but his horse trembled terribly.
He unsaddled it and went off;
he let it roll around in the middle of the meadow.
He folded the end of his mantle
and lay down with it under his head.
He is very worried by his difficult situation;
he sees nothing that pleases him.
As he lay there like this,
he looked down toward the bank
and saw two maidens coming;
he had never seen any more beautiful.
They were richly dressed
and very tightly laced
in tunics of dark purple;
they had exceedingly lovely faces.
The elder was carrying basins
of gold, fine and well made;
I shall tell you the truth without fail.
The other carried a towel.
They went right along
to where the knight was lying.
Lanval, who was very well bred,
got to his feet to meet them.
They greeted him first
and told him their message:
"Sir Lanval, my lady,
who is most noble, wise, and beautiful,
sent us for you;
now come along with us!
We will convey you safely to her.

	veez, pres est li paveilluns!"	Look, the pavilion is right here!"
	Le chevalers od eles vait;	The knight goes with them;
	de sun cheval ne tient nul plait,	he takes no heed of his horse,
	que devant li pe[ssei]t al pre.	who was off grazing in the meadow.
80	Treskë al tref l'unt amené,	They led him up to the tent,
	que mut fu beaus e bien asis.	which was very beautiful and well situated.
	La reïne Semiramis,	Not Queen Semiramis,
	quant ele ot unkes plus aveir	when she was at her richest
	e plus pussaunce e plus saveir,	and most powerful and wisest,
85	ne l'emperere Octovïen	nor the emperor Octavian
	n'esligasent le destre pan.	could have bought the right flap.
	Un aigle d'or ot desus mis;	A golden eagle was set on top of it;
	de cel ne sai dire le pris,	I can't tell its value,
	ne des cordes ne des peissuns	nor of the cords or the stakes
90	que del tref tienent les giruns;	that held the sides of the tent;
	suz ciel n'ad rei ki[s] esligast	no king under heaven could buy them
	pur nul aver k'il i donast.	for any wealth he might offer.
	Dedenz cel tref fu la pucele:	Inside the tent was the maiden:
	flur de lis [e] rose nuvele,	her beauty surpassed
95	quant ele pert al tens d'esté,	the lily and the new rose
	trespassot ele de beauté.	when they bloom in summer.
	Ele jut sur un lit mut bel—	She lay on a very beautiful bed—
	li drap valeient un chastel—	the sheets were worth a castle—
	en sa chemise senglement.	in nothing but her shift.
100	Mut ot le cors bien fait e gent.	Her body was very elegant and comely.
	Un cher mantel de blanc hermine,	She had thrown on for warmth
	covert de purpre alexandrine,	a costly mantle of white ermine,
	ot pur le chaut sur li geté.	lined with alexandrine silk.
	Tut ot descovert le costé,	Her side was entirely uncovered,
105	le vis, le col e la peitrine;	her face, her neck, and her breast;
	plus ert blanche que flur d'espine.	she was whiter than hawthorn blossom.
	Le chevaler avant ala,	The knight went forward,
	e la pucele l'apela;	and the maiden called to him;
	il s'est devant le lit asis.	he sat down in front of the bed.
110	"Lanval," fet ele, "beus amis,	"Lanval," she said, "handsome friend,
	pur vus vienc jeo fors de ma tere;	for you I have come out of my own land;
	de luinz vus sui venu[e] quere.	I have come from afar to look for you.
	Se vus estes pruz e curteis,	If you are valiant and courteous,
	emperere ne quens ne reis	no emperor, count, or king
115	n'ot unkes tant joie ne bien;	ever had such joy or good fortune;
	kar jo vus aim sur tute rien."	for I love you more than anything."
	Il l'esgarda, si la vit bele;	He looked at her, and saw she was beautiful;
	amurs le puint de l'estencele,	love stung him with a spark
	que sun quor alume e esprent.	that lit and inflamed his heart.
120	Il li respunt avenantment.	He responded fittingly.

"Bele," fet il, "si vus pleiseit	"Beautiful one," he said, "if it pleased you
e cele joie me aveneit	that such joy should come to me
que vus me vousissez amer,	as to have you consent to love me,
ja [ne savrïez] rien commander	you could never command anything
125 que jeo ne face a mien poeir,	that I would not do to the best of my power,
turt a folie u a saveir.	be it folly or wisdom.
Jeo frai voz comandemenz;	I will do what you command;
pur vus guerpirai tutes genz.	for you I will give up everyone.
Jamés ne queor de vus partir:	I never wish to part from you:
130 ceo est la rien que plus desir."	this is what I most desire."
Quant la meschine l' oï parler,	When the maiden heard him speak,
celui que tant la peot amer,	he who could love her so well,
s'amur e sun cors li otreie.	she granted him her love and her body.
Ore est Lanval en dreite veie!	Now Lanval is on the right path!
135 Un dun li ad duné aprés:	She gave him still one more gift:
ja cele rien ne vudra mes	he will never again want anything
që il nen ait a sun talent;	without having as much of it as he likes;
doinst e despende largement,	let him give and spend generously,
ele li troverat asez.	she will provide him with enough.
140 Mut est Lanval bien herbergez:[1]	Lanval is very well situated:
cum plus despendra richement,	the more richly he spends,
plus averat or e argent.	the more gold and silver he will have.
"Ami," fet ele, "ore vus chasti,	"Friend," she said, "now I warn you,
si vus comant e si vus pri,	I command and beg you,
145 ne vus descoverez a nul humme!	tell no one about this!
De ceo vus dirai ja la summe:	I will tell you the whole truth:
a tuz jurs m'avrïez perdue,	you would lose me forever
se ceste amur esteit seüe;	if this love should be known;
jamés ne me purriez veeir	you could never see me again
150 ne de mun cors seisine aveir."	or have possession of my body."
Il li respunt que bien tendra	He replies that he will certainly hold to
ceo que ele li comaundera.	what she commands.
Delez li s'est al lit cuchiez:	He lay down beside her on the bed:
ore est Lanval bien herbergez.	now Lanval is well lodged.
155 Ensemble od li la relevee	All afternoon he stayed with her
demurat tresque a l[a] vespree,	until the evening,
e plus i fust, së il poïst	and he would have stayed longer, if he could
e s'amie lui cunsentist.	and his beloved had consented.
"Amis," fet ele, "levez sus!	"Friend," she said, "get up!
160 Vus n'i poëz demurer plus.	You can't stay here any more.
Alez vus en, jeo remeindrai;	You go on, I will remain—
mes un[e] chose vus dirai:	but one thing I will tell you:
quant vus vodrez od mei parler,	when you want to talk with me,

---

1 *Mut ... herbergez*   Other manuscripts have here, "mut est Lanval bien *assenez*" (Lanval is very well provided for) and some editors prefer this reading, since the line as it stands is repeated below at l. 154.

ja ne saverez cel liu penser,	there is no place you can think of
165 u nuls puïst aver sa amie	where one could have his beloved
sanz reproece, sanz vileinie,	without reproach or villainy
que jeo ne vus seie en present	that I will not be with you at once
a fere tut vostre talent;	to do all your will;
nul humme fors vus ne me verra	no man but you will see me
170 ne ma parole nen orra."	or hear my words."
Quant il l'oï, mut en fu liez;	When he heard this, he was delighted;
il la baisa, puis s'est dresciez.	he kissed her, then got up.
Celes quë al tref l'amenerent	The maidens who had brought him to the tent
de riches dras le cunreerent;	covered him with rich clothes;
175 quant il fu vestu de nuvel,	when he was newly dressed,
suz ciel nen ot plus bel dancel.	there was no handsomer young man under heaven.
N'esteit mie fous ne vileins.	He was not at all foolish or base.
L'ewe li donent a ses meins	They gave him water for his hands
e la tuaille a [es]suier;	and the towel to dry them;
180 puis li portent a manger.	then they brought him to the table.
Od s'amie prist le super:	He took supper with his beloved:
ne feseit mie a refuser.	he by no means refused.
Mut fu servi curteisement,	He was served very courteously,
e il a grant joie le prent.	and accepted it with great joy.
185 Un entremés i ot plener,	There was an excellent extra dish
que mut pleiseit al chevalier:	that greatly pleased the knight,
kar s'amie baisout sovent	for he often kissed his lady
e acolot estreitement.	and embraced her closely.
Quant del manger furent levé,	When they had gotten up from the table,
190 sun cheval li unt amené.	they brought him his horse.
Bien li unt la sele mise;	They have put its saddle on well;
mut ad trové riche servise.	it has been richly looked after.
Il prent cungé, si est muntez;	He took his leave and mounted;
vers la cité s'en est alez.	he went toward the city.
195 Suvent esgarde ariere sei.	Several times he looks back.
Mut est Lanval en grant esfrei;	Lanval is greatly troubled;
de s'aventure vait pensaunt	he goes along thinking about his adventure
e en sun curage d[o]taunt.	and worrying to himself.
Esbaïz est, ne seit que creir,	He is astonished, he doesn't know what to think,
200 il ne la quide mie a veir.	he doesn't believe he will see her again.
Il est a sun ostel venuz;	He arrives at his lodging;
ses hummes treve bien vestuz.	he finds his men handsomely dressed.
Icele nuit bon estel tient;	That night he keeps a rich table,
mes nul ne sot dunt ceo li vient.	but no one knew where he got this from.
205 N'ot en la vile chevalier	There was no knight in the town
ki de surjur ait grant mestier,	who greatly needed sustenance

	quë il ne face a lui venir	whom Lanval does not have brought to him
	e richement e bien servir.	and well and richly served.
	Lanval donout les riches duns,	Lanval gave rich gifts,
210	Lanval aquitout les prisuns,	Lanval ransomed prisoners,
	Lanval vesteit les jugleürs,	Lanval clothed minstrels,
	Lanval feseit les granz honurs:	Lanval did great honor:
	n'i ot estrange ne privé	there was no stranger or dear friend
	a ki Lanval nen ust doné.	to whom Lanval did not give.
215	Mut ot Lanval joie e deduit:	Lanval had great joy and pleasure:
	u seit par jur u seit par nuit,	he can see his beloved often,
	s'amie peot veer sovent,	whether by day or by night;
	tut est a sun comandement.	she is entirely at his command.
	Ceo m'est avis, memes l'an,	That same year, as I understand,
220	aprés la feste seint Johan,	after the feast of St. John,
	d'ici qu'a trente chevalier	as many as thirty knights
	si erent alé esbanïer	were going out to enjoy themselves
	en un vergier desuz la tur	in a garden below the tower
	u la reïne ert a surjur.	where the queen was staying.
225	Ensemble od eus [esteit] Walwains	Gawain was with them
	e sis cusins, li beaus Ywains.	and his cousin, the handsome Yvain.
	E dist Walwains, li francs, li pruz,	Gawain, the noble, the valiant,
	que tant se fist amer de tuz:	who made himself so beloved by everyone, said,
	"Par Deu, seignurs, nus feimes mal	"By God, my lords, we have done wrong
230	de nostre cumpainun Lanval,	not to have brought along with us
	que tant est larges e curteis,	our companion Lanval,
	e sis peres est riches reis,	who is so generous and courteous,
	que od nus ne l'avum amené."	and whose father is a rich king."
	Atant se sunt ariere turné;	They turned back at once;
235	a sun ostel rev[u]nt ariere,	they go back to his lodging
	Lanval ameinent par preere.	and persuade Lanval to accompany them.
	A une fenestre entaillie	The queen was leaning
	s'esteit la reïne apuïe[e];	on a window ledge;
	treis dames ot ensemble od li.	she had three ladies along with her.
240	La maisné [le rei] choisi;	She saw the king's household;
	Lanval choisi e esgarda.	she saw Lanval and noticed him.
	Une des dames apela;	She called one of her ladies;
	par li manda ses dameiseles,	she got her to send for her maidens,
	les plus quointes [e] les plus beles:	the most elegant and lovely:
245	od li si irrunt esbanïer	they will go to enjoy themselves with her
	la u cil sunt al vergier.	there where the men are in the orchard.
	Trente en menat od li e plus;	She took thirty or more of them with her;
	par les degrez descendent jus.	they go down by the stairs.
	Les chevalers encuntre vunt,	The knights, who are delighted to see them,
250	que pur eles grant joïe unt.	go to meet them.
	Il les unt prises par les mains;	They took the ladies by the hand;

	cil [parlemenz] ni ert pas vilains.	the conversation was not unrefined.
	Lanval s'en vait a une part,	Lanval wanders off by himself,
	mut luin des autres. Ceo li est tart	quite far from the others. It seems long to him
255	que s'amie puïst tenir,	until he might have his beloved,
	baiser, acoler e sentir;	kiss, embrace, and touch her;
	l'autrui joie prise petit,	he values little another's joy
	si il n'ad le suen delit.	if he does not have what pleases him.
	Quant la reïne sul le veit,	When the queen sees him alone,
260	al chevaler en va tut dreit;	she goes right to the knight;
	lunc lui s'asist, si l'apela,	she sat by him and spoke to him,
	tut sun curage li mustra:	she showed him all her feelings:
	"Lanval, mut vus ai honuré	"Lanval, I have honored you greatly
	e mut cheri e mut amé.	and loved you and held you very dear.
265	tute m'amur poëz aveir;	You can have all my love;
	kar me dites vostre voleir!	tell me your desire!
	Ma drüerie vus otrei;	I am willing to be your lover;
	mut devez estre lié de mei."	you should be delighted with me."
	"Dame," fet il, "lessez m'ester!	"Lady," he said, "let me be!
270	Jeo n'ai cure de vus amer.	I have no interest in loving you.
	Lungement ai servi le rei;	For a long time I have served the king;
	ne li voil pas mentir ma fei.	I don't want to betray my faith to him.
	Ja pur vus ne pur vostre amur	Never for you or for your love
	ne mesfrai a mun seignur."	shall I wrong my lord."
275	La reïne s'en curuça;	The queen became furious at this;
	irie[e] fu, si mesparla.	in her anger, she spoke wrongly.
	"Lanval," fet ele, "bien le quit,	"Lanval," she said, "it's quite clear to me
	vuz n'amez gueres cel delit.	you have no interest in that pleasure.
	Asez le m'ad humme dit sovent	People have often told me
280	que des femmez n'avez talent.	that you're not interested in women.
	Vallez avez bien afeitiez,	You have shapely young men
	ensemble od eus vus deduiez.	and take your pleasure with them.
	Vileins cüarz, mauveis failliz,	Base coward, infamous wretch,
	mut est mi sires maubailliz	my lord is very badly repaid
285	que pres de lui vus ad suffert;	for allowing you to remain in his presence;
	mun escïent que Deus en pert!"	I believe that he will lose God by it!"
	Quant il l'oï, mut fu dolent;	When he heard this, he was very distressed;
	del respundre ne fu pas lent.	he was not slow to respond.
	Teu chose dist par maltalent	Out of anger he said something
290	dunt il se repenti sovent.	that he would often regret.
	"Dame," dist il, "de cel mestier	"Lady," he said, "I know nothing
	ne me sai jeo nïent aidier;	about that line of work;
	mes jo aim, [e] si sui amis	but I love, and am loved by,
	cele ke deit aver le pris	one who should be valued more highly
295	sur tutes celes que jeo sai.	than all the women I know.
	E une chose vus dirai,	And I'll tell you one thing,

bien le sachez a descovert:
une de celes ke la sert,
tute la plus povre meschine,
300 vaut meuz de vus, dame reïne,
de cors, de vis e de beauté,
d'enseignement e de bunté."
La reïne s'en par[t] atant,
en sa chambrë en vait plurant.
305 Mut fu dolente e curuciee
de ceo k'il [l']out [si] avilee.
En sun lit malade cucha;
jamés, ceo dit, ne levera,
si li reis ne l'en feseit dreit
310 de ceo dunt ele se plein[d]reit.

    Li reis fu del bois repeiriez;
mut out le jur esté haitiez.
As chambres la reïne entra.
Quant ele le vit, si se clamma;
315 as piez li chiet, merci crie,
e dit que Lanval l'ad hunie.
De drüerie la requist;
pur ceo que ele l'en escundist,
mut [la] laidi e avila.
320 De tele amie se vanta,
que tant iert cuinte e noble e fiere
que meuz valut sa chamberere,
la plus povre que [la] serveit,
que la reïne ne feseit.
325 Li reis s'en curuçat forment;
juré en ad sun serement:
si il ne s'en peot en curt defendre,
il le ferat arder u pendre.
Fors de la chambre eissi li reis,
330 de ses baruns apelat treis;
il les enveit pur Lanval,
quë asez ad dolur e mal.
A sun [o]stel fu revenuz;
il s'est[eit] bien aparceüz
335 qu'il aveit perdue s'amie:
descovert ot la drüerie.
En une chambre fu tut suls,
pensis esteit e anguissus;
s'amie apele mut sovent,
340 mes ceo ne li valut neent.
Il se pleigneit e suspirot,

know it well and openly:
any one of her servants,
even the poorest maid,
is worth more than you, lady queen,
in body, face, and beauty,
in manners and goodness."
The queen leaves at once
and goes into her chamber, crying.
She was very upset and angry
that he had insulted her in this way.
She took to her bed, sick;
never, she said, would she get up
if the king did not do the right thing
about the complaint she would make to him.

    The king returned from the woods;
he had had a very pleasant day.
He went into the queen's rooms.
When she saw him, she made her appeal;
she falls at his feet and asks for mercy
and says that Lanval has shamed her.
He asked her to be his lover;
because she refused him,
he insulted her greatly and said ugly things.
He boasted of such a beloved,
one who was so elegant, noble, and proud,
that her chambermaid,
the poorest girl who served her,
was worth more than the queen.
The king got extremely angry;
he swore an oath that
if Lanval cannot defend himself in court,
he will have him burnt or hanged.
The king went out of the chamber
and called three of his nobles;
he sends them for Lanval,
who has sorrow and trouble enough.
He had gone back to his lodging;
it was quite evident to him
that he had lost his beloved:
he had revealed their love.
He went into a chamber by himself,
anxious and distraught;
he calls on his beloved over and over,
and it does him no good at all.
He lamented and sighed,

	d'ures en autres se pasmot;	he fainted repeatedly;
	puis li crie cent feiz merci	then a hundred times he begs her to have pity
	que ele par[ol]t a sun ami.	and appear to her beloved.
345	Sun quor e sa buche maudit;	He cursed his heart and his mouth;
	ceo est merveille k'il ne s'ocit.	it's a wonder he does not kill himself.
	Il ne seit tant crïer ne braire	He cannot cry out or wail
	ne debatre ne sei detraire	or reproach or torment himself
	que ele en veulle merci aveir	enough to make her take pity on him,
350	sul tant que la puisse veeir.	even enough that he might see her.
	Oi las, cument se cuntendra?	Alas, what will he do?
	Cil ke li reis ci enveia,	Those the king sent there
	il sunt venu, si li unt dit	arrived, and said to him
	que a la curt voise sanz respit:	that he must go to the court without delay:
355	li reis l'aveit par eus mandé,	the king had sent the order through them,
	la reïne l'out encusé.	the queen had accused him.
	Lanval i vait od sun grant doel;	Lanval goes there in his great sorrow;
	il l'eüssent ocis [sun] veoil.	they could have killed him for all he cared.
	Il est devant le rei venu;	He came before the king;
360	mut fu dolent, taisanz e mu,	he was very sorrowful, silent and unspeaking,
	de grant dolur mustre semblant.	showing the appearance of great sorrow.
	Li reis li dit par maltalant,	The king says to him angrily,
	"Vassal, vus me avez mut mesfait!	"Vassal, you have done me a great wrong!
	Trop començastes vilein plait	You began too base a suit
365	de mei hunir e aviler	to shame and revile me
	e la reïne lendengier.	and insult the queen.
	Vanté vus estes de folie:	You boasted foolishly:
	trop par est noble vostre amie,	your beloved is far too exalted
	quant plus est bele sa meschine	when her maid is more beautiful
370	e plus vaillante que la reïne."	and worthy than the queen."
	Lanval defent la deshonur	Lanval denies the dishonor
	e la hunte de sun seignur	and shame of his lord
	de mot en mot, si cum il dist,	word by word, just as he said it,
	que la reïne ne requist;	for he had not requested the queen's love;
375	mes de ceo dunt il ot parlé	but he acknowledged the truth
	reconut il la verité,	of what he had said
	de l'amur dunt il se vanta:	concerning the love about which he boasted:
	dolent en est, perdue l'a.	he is sorrowful, for he has lost her.
	De ceo lur dit qu'il en ferat	Concerning this he says that he will do
380	quanque la curt esgarderat.	whatever the court judges best.
	Li reis fu mut vers li irez;	The king was quite furious with him;
	tuz ses hummes ad enveiez	he sent for all his men
	pur dire dreit que il en deit faire,	to say rightly what he must do,
	que hum ne li puis[se] a mal retraire.	so that no one would speak ill of it.
385	Cil unt sun commandement fait,	They did what he ordered,
	u eus seit bel, u eus seit lait.	whether they liked it or not.

Comunement i sunt alé
e unt jugé e esgardé
que Lanval deit aveir un jur;
390   mes plegges truisse a sun seignur
qu'il atendra sun jugement
e revendra en sun present:
si serat la curt esforcie[e],
kar n'i ot dunc fors la maisne[e].

395   Al rei revienent li barun,
si li mustrent la reisun.
Li reis ad plegges demandé.
Lanval fu sul e esgaré;
n'i aveit parent në ami.
400   Walwain i vait, ki l'a plevi,
e tuit si cumpainun aprés.
Li reis lur dit: "E jol vus les
sur quanke vus tenez de mei,
teres e fieus, chescun par sei."
405   Quant plevi fu, dunc n'[i] ot el;

alez s'en est a sun ostel.
Li chevaler l'unt conveé;
mut l'unt blasmé e chastïé
k'il ne face si grant dolur,
410   e maudïent si fol'amur.
Chescun jur l'aloënt veer,
pur ceo k'il voleient saveir
u il beüst, u il mangast;
mut dotouent k'il s'afolast.

415   Al jur que cil orent numé
li barun furent asemblé.
Li reis e la reïne i fu,
e li plegge unt Lanval rendu.
Mut furent tuz pur li dolent:
420   jeo quid k'il en i ot teus cent
ki feïssent tut lur poeir
pur lui sanz pleit delivre aveir;
il iert retté a mut grant tort.
Li reis demande le recort
425   sulunc le cleim e les respuns;
ore est trestut sur les baruns.
Il sunt al jugement alé,
mut sunt pensifz e esgaré

They all went off together
and judged and decided
that Lanval should have his day in court;
but he must provide guarantees for his lord
    that he will await his judgment
and return to his presence:
a larger court will be gathered,
for now there was no one there but the
      household.

The nobles return to the king
and explain to him their judgment.
The king demanded guarantees.
Lanval was alone and in great distress;
he had no family or friends.
Gawain goes to act as a guarantor for Lanval,
and all his companions after him.
The king says to them: "I commend him to you
on the basis of whatever you may hold of me,
lands and fiefs, each one for himself."
Once the pledge was made, there was
      nothing more to do;
Lanval went off to his lodging.
The knights went along with him;
they greatly rebuked and counseled him
not to be in such sorrow,
and they cursed such mad love.
Every day they went to see him,
for they wanted to know
if he was drinking, if he was eating;
    they greatly feared that he would do himself
      harm.

    On the day that they had named
the nobles gathered.
The king and queen were there,
and the guarantors brought Lanval.
Everyone was very sad for him:
I believe that there were some hundred there
who would have done anything in their power
to free him without a trial;
he was very wrongly accused.
The king demands the verdict
according to the charges and the defense;
now it is entirely up to the nobles.
They went to sit in judgment,
very anxious and dismayed

del franc humme d'autre païs
430   quë entre eus ert si entrepris.
Encumbrer le veulent plusur
pur la volenté sun seignur.
Ceo dist li quoens de Cornwaille:
"Ja endreit [nus] n'i avera faille;
435   kar ki que en plurt e ki que en chant,
le dreit estuet aler avant.
Li reis parla vers sun vassal,
que jeo vus oi numer Lanval;
de felunie le retta
440   e d'un mesfait l'acheisuna,

d'un'amur dunt il se vanta,
e ma dame s'en curuça.
Nuls ne l'apele fors le rei;
par cele fei ke jeo vus dei,
445   ki bien en veut dire le veir,
ja n'i deüst respuns aveir,
si pur ceo nun que a sun seignur
deit [hum] par tut fairë honur.[1]
Un serement l'engagera,
450   e li reis le nus pardura.

E s'il peot aver sun guarant
e s'amie venist avant
e ceo fust veir k'il en deïst,
dunt la reïne se marist,
455   de ceo avera il bien merci,
quant pur vilté nel dist de li.
E s'il ne peot garant aveir,
ceo li devum faire saveir:
tut sun servise perde del rei,
460   e sil deit cungeer de sei."
Al chevaler unt enveé,
si li unt dit e nuntïé
que s'amie face venir
pur lui tencer e garentir.
465   Il lur dit qu'il ne poeit:
ja pur li sucurs nen avereit.
Cil s'en rev[un]t as jugeürs,
ki n'i atendent nul sucurs.
Li reis les hastot durement

over the noble man from another country
who was in such trouble among them.
Many want to find him guilty
according to their lord's wishes.
The count of Cornwall said,
"We must not fall short,
for whoever may weep or sing,
the law must take precedence.
The king has spoken against his vassal,
whom I hear you call Lanval;
he accused him of a crime
and brought charges of wrongdoing against
    him,
concerning a love of which he boasted,
which made my lady angry.
No one accuses him but the king;
by the faith I owe you,
whoever wants to speak the truth,
there would not even be a case
except that to the name of his lord
a man should do honor in everything.
Lanval can affirm this by oath,
and the king will turn him over to us for
    judgment.
And if he can have his guarantor—
if his lady should come forward
and what he said about her,
which made the queen angry, was true—
then he will certainly receive mercy,
since he did not say it out of baseness.
And if he cannot produce proof,
we must make him understand this:
he loses all his service to the king
and must take his leave of him."
They sent to the knight,
and they told him and announced
that he should make his beloved come
to defend and bear witness for him.
He told them that he could not:
he would never get help from her.
They go back to the judges,
who expect no help from that quarter.
The king urged them fiercely

---

[1]   *d'un'amur ... honur* Lines 441–49 appear in a different order in the manuscript: 443–48, 442, 441. This emendation is made by most editors.

470	pur la reïne kis atent.
	Quant il deveient departir,
	deus puceles virent venir
	sur deus beaus palefreiz amblanz.
	Mut par esteient avenanz;
475	de cendal purpre sunt vestues
	tut senglement a lur char nues.
	Cil les esgardou volenters.
	Walwain, od li treis chevalers,
	vait a Lanval, si li cunta;
480	les deus puceles li mustra.
	Mut fu haitié, forment li prie
	qu'il li deïst si ceo ert [s]'amie.
	Il lur ad dit ne seit ki sunt
	ne dunt vienent ne u eles vunt.
485	Celes sunt alees avant
	tut a cheval; par tel semblant
	descendirent devant le deis,
	la u seeit Artur li reis.
	Eles furent de grant beuté,
490	si unt curteisement parlé:
	"Reis, fai tes chambers delivrer
	e de pa[il]es encurtiner,
	u ma dame puïst descendre
	si ensemble od vus veut ostel prendre."
495	Il lur otria mut volenters,
	si appela deus chevalers:
	as chambres les menerent sus.
	A cele feiz ne distrent plus.
	Li reis demande a ses baruns
500	le jugement e les respuns
	e dit que mut l'unt curucié
	de ceo que tant l'unt delaié.
	"Sire," funt il, "nus departimes
	pur les dames que nus veïmes;
505	[nus n'i avum] nul esgart fait.
	Or recumencerum le plait."
	Dunc assemblerent tut pensif;
	asez i ot noise e estrif.
	Quant il ierent en cel esfrei,
510	deus puceles de gent cunrei—
	vestues de deus pa[il]es freis,
	chevauchent deus muls espanneis—

for the sake of the queen who was waiting.

    Just as they were about to make their ruling,
they saw two maidens coming
on two beautiful brisk palfreys.
They were extremely lovely;
they were dressed in purple taffeta
down to their bare skin.
Everyone gazed at them eagerly.
Gawain, and three knights with him,
went to Lanval and told him;
he showed him the two maidens.
He was very happy, and begged him
to say whether this was his beloved.
Lanval tells them that he does not know who
        they are
or where they come from or where they are
        going.

The maidens went along
on their horses; in this fashion
they got down in front of the dais
where King Arthur was sitting.
They were very beautiful
and spoke courteously:
"King, make your chambers ready
and spread out silks
where my lady can step
if she wants to take lodging with you."
He very willingly granted this to them,
and called two knights:
they led them up to the chambers.
At that time they said no more.

    The king asks his nobles
for the judgment and the verdict
and says that they have made him very angry
by delaying for so long.
"Sire," they say, "we broke off our discussion
on account of the ladies that we saw;
we have not made a decision.
Now we will resume the trial."
Then they gathered, quite concerned;
there was a great deal of noise and debate.
While they were in this disarray,
they saw coming down the road
two maidens of noble bearing,
dressed in cool silks,

	virent venir la rue aval.
	Grant joie en eurent li vassal;
515	entre eus dïent que ore est gariz
	Lanval li pruz e li hardiz.
	Yweins i est a lui alez,
	ses cumpainuns i ad menez.
	"Sire," fet il, "rehaitiez vus!
520	Pur amur Deu, parlez od nus!
	Ici vienent deus dameiseles
	mut acemees e mut beles:
	ceo est vostre amie vereiment!"
	Lanval respunt hastivement
525	e dit qu'il pas nes avuot
	ne il nes cunut ne nes amot.
	Atant furent celes venues,
	devant le rei sunt descendues.
	Mut les loërent li plusur
530	de cors, de vis e de colur;
	n'i ad cele meuz ne vausist
	que unkes la reïne ne fist.
	L'aisnee fu curteise e sage,
	avenantment dist sun message:
535	"Reis, kar nus fai chambres baillier
	a oés ma dame herbergier;
	ele vient ici a tei parler."
	Il les cumandë a mener
	od les autres quë ainceis viendrent.
540	Unkes des muls nul plai[t] ne tindrent.
	Quant il fu d'eles deliverez,
	puis ad tuz ses baruns mandez
	que le jugement seit renduz:
	trop ad le jur esté tenuz.
545	La reïne s'en curuceit,
	que si lunges les atendeit.
	Ja departissent a itant,
	quant par la vile vient errant
	tut a cheval une pucele:
550	en tut le secle n'ot plus bele.
	Un blanc palefrei chevachot,
	que bel e süef la portot.
	Mut ot bien fet e col e teste:
	suz ciel nen ot plus bele beste.
555	Riche atur ot al palefrei:
	suz ciel nen ad quens ne rei
	ki tut [le] p[e]üst eslegier

riding two Spanish mules.
The vassals were delighted by this;
they say to each other that now Lanval,
the bold and strong, is cured.
Yvain went to him,
taking his companions with him.
"Sir," he said, "rejoice!
For the love of God, speak to us!
Here come two maidens,
very elegant and beautiful:
surely it is your beloved!"
Lanval answers hastily
and says that he neither claimed them
nor knew them nor loved them.
Just then the maidens arrived
and dismounted before the king.
Many people greatly praised
their bodies, faces and coloring;
both of them were certainly worth
more than the queen ever was.
The elder was courteous and wise;
she spoke her message becomingly:
"King, make ready rooms for us
to receive my lady;
she is coming here to speak to you."
He orders that they be taken
to the others who had arrived previously.
They need not worry about the mules.
When he had sent them off,
he ordered all his nobles
that the judgment be given:
too much of the day had been taken up.
The queen was getting angry
that she was kept waiting so long by them.
They were about to take a decision,
when through the town comes
a maiden riding on a horse:
there was no lady in the world more beautiful.
She was riding a white palfrey,
which carried her well and gently.
It had a well-shaped neck and head:
there was no more beautiful animal under heaven.
The palfrey was richly harnessed:
no count or king under heaven
could have afforded it all

	sanz tere vendre u engagier.	without selling or mortgaging land.
	Ele iert vestue en itel guise:	She was dressed in this manner:
560	de chainsil blanc e de chemise,	in a shift of white linen,
	que tuz les costez li pareient,	which let both her sides be seen,
	que de deus parz laciez esteient.	as it was laced on either side.
	Le cors ot gent, basse la hanche,	She had a lovely body, a long waist,
	le col plus blanc que neif sur branche,	a neck whiter than snow on a branch,
565	les oilz ot vairs e blanc le vis,	grey-green eyes and white skin,
	bele buche, neis bien asis,	a beautiful mouth, a well-formed nose,
	les surcilz bruns e bel le frunt	dark eyebrows and a lovely forehead
	e le chef cresp e aukes blunt;	and curling golden hair;
	fil d'or ne gette tel luur	no golden thread casts such a gleam
570	cum sun chevel cuntre le jur.	as did her hair in the sun.
	Sis manteus fu de purpre bis;	Her mantle was dark purple;
	les pans en ot entur li mis.	she had wrapped its ends around her.
	Un espervier sur sun poin tient,	She holds a falcon on her fist,
	e un leverer aprés lui vient.	and a greyhound runs behind her.
575	Il n'ot al burc petit ne grant	There was no one in the town, great or small,
	ne li veillard ne li enfant	not the old men or the children,
	que ne l'alassent esgarder.	who did not go to look at her.
	Si cum il la veent errer,	As they saw her pass,
	de sa beauté n'iert mie gas.	there was no joking about her beauty.
580	Ele veneit meins que le pas.	She came along quite slowly.
	Li jugeür, que la veeient,	The judges, who saw her,
	a [grant] merveille le teneient;	considered it a great marvel;
	il n'ot un sul ki l'esgardast	there was not one who looked at her
	de dreite joie ne s'eschaufast.	who did not grow warm with sheer joy.
585	Cil ki le chevaler amoënt	Those who loved the knight
	a lui veneient, si li cuntouent	came to him, and told him
	de la pucele ki veneit,	of the maiden who was coming,
	si Deu plest, que le delivereit:	who, if it pleased God, would set him free:
	"Sire cumpain, ci en vient une,	"Sir companion, here comes one
590	mes ele n'est pas fave ne brune;	who is not tawny nor dark;
	ceo'st la plus bele del mund,	she is the loveliest in the world,
	de tutes celes kë i sunt."	of all the women who live."
	Lanval l'oï, sun chief dresça;	Lanval heard this, he lifted his head;
	bien la cunut, si suspira.	he knew her well, and sighed.
595	Li sanc li est munté al vis;	The blood rose to his face;
	de parler fu aukes hastifs.	he was very quick to speak.
	"Par fei," fet il, "ceo est m'amie!	"In faith," he said, "it is my beloved!
	Or m'en est gueres ki m'ocie,	Now I care little who may kill me,
	si ele n'ad merci de mei;	if she does not take pity on me;
600	kar gariz sui, quant jeo la vei."	for I am cured when I see her."
	La damë entra al palais;	The lady entered the palace;
	unc si bele n'i vient mais.	such a beauty had never come there.

	Devant le rei est descendue	She dismounted before the king
	si que de tuz iert bien [veüe].	so that she was quite visible to all.
605	Sun mantel ad laissié ch[e]eir,	She let her mantle fall
	que meuz la puïssent veer.	so that they could see her better.
	Li reis, que mut fu enseigniez,	The king, who was very well-bred,
	il s'est encuntre lui dresciez,	got up to meet her,
	e tuit li autre l'enurerent,	and all the others honored her
610	de li servir se presenterent.	and offered themselves to serve her.
	Quant il l'orent bien esgardee	When they had looked at her well
	e sa beauté forment loëe,	and greatly praised her beauty,
	ele parla en teu mesure,	she spoke in this way,
	kar de demurer nen ot cure:	for she did not wish to delay:
615	"Reis, jeo ai amé un tuen vassal:	"King, I have fallen in love with one of your vassals:
	veez le ici, ceo est Lanval!	you see him here, it is Lanval!
	Acheisuné fu en ta curt.	He was accused in your court.
	Ne vuil mie que a mal li turt	I do not wish it to be held against him,
	de ceo qu'il dist; ceo sachez tu	concerning what he said; you should know
620	que la reïne ad tort eü:	that the queen was wrong:
	unc nul jur ne la requist.	he never asked for her love.
	De la vantance kë il fist,	And concerning the boast he made,
	si par me peot estre aquitez,	if he can be acquitted by me,
	par voz baruns seit deliverez!"	let your nobles set him free!"
625	Ceo qu'il jugerunt par dreit	The king grants that it should be so,
	li reis otrie ke issi seit.	that they should judge rightly.
	N'i ad un sul que n'ait jugié	There was not one who did not judge
	que Lanval ad tut desrainié.	that Lanval was completely exonerated.
	Deliverez est par lur esgart,	He is freed by their judgment,
630	e la pucele s'en depart.	and the maiden takes her leave.
	Ne la peot li reis retenir;	The king cannot detain her;
	asez gent ot a li servir.	she had enough people to serve her.
	Fors de la sale aveient mis	Outside the hall was set
	un grant perrun de marbre bis,	a great block of dark marble,
635	u li pesant humme muntoënt,	where heavy men mounted,
	que de la curt le rei [aloënt]:	who were leaving the king's court:
	Lanval esteit munté desus.	Lanval got up on it.
	Quant la pucele ist fors a l'us,	When the maiden came through the gate,
	sur le palefrei, detriers li,	with one leap Lanval
640	de plain eslais Lanval sailli.	jumped on the palfrey, behind her.
	Od li s'en vait en Avalun,	With her he went to Avalon,
	ceo nus recuntent li Bretun,	so the Bretons tell us,
	en un isle que mut est beaus;	to a very beautiful island;
	la fu ravi li dameiseaus.	the young man was carried off there.
645	Nul hum n'en oï plus parler,	No one ever heard another word of him,
	ne jeo n'en sai avant cunter.	and I can tell no more.

MIDDLE ENGLISH LYRICS

The Middle English poems in this section are for the most part difficult to date with any precision. In some cases they draw on relatively sophisticated lyric traditions from continental sources, but very largely they seem to be rooted in popular traditions that were probably already old when the earliest surviving copies of these poems were made. Like most short medieval poems that have survived, they are anonymous. From the familiarity with medieval Latin exhibited in some of the poems and their survival in manuscripts containing Latin alongside English (and French) texts, we may infer that many were read and quite possibly written by clerics—though even in these cases the authors may well have been adapting existing popular materials. Such poems have by convention been referred to for centuries as "medieval lyrics," though the term has been thought by some to be both anachronistic (the earliest appearance of the word "lyric" in English is in 1581) and somewhat misleading; in tone and subject matter many of these poems have little in common with the poems we have become accustomed to think of as "lyrical."

The majority of medieval lyrics that have survived deal with religious subjects, the most common being devotion to Jesus or the Virgin Mary (or both), often with a focus on Christ's Passion as it is linked to the theme of salvation and sacrifice, or Mary's roles as intercessor and suffering mother ("Stond well, moder, under Rode"). Other religious lyrics contemplate Adam's fall and the transitory nature of life ("Farewell this world, I take my leve forever"), or the importance of constancy in faith. A number of religious lyrics draw on the conventions of secular literature, employing the topoi of so-called courtly love. Such is the case, for example, in "I sing of a maiden," in which Christ appears as a lover-knight and Mary is depicted as an unblemished maiden who chooses Christ as her son in the way that a secular poem might depict a lady bestowing her favor on a lover.

Modern readers may find a more immediate appeal in the lyrics that deal with secular themes. Earthly love is a frequent subject of these poems, sometimes dwelling on the perceived virtue and attractiveness of the beloved ("Betwene Mersh and Averil"), sometimes employing lewd word play ("I have a gentil cock"), and often taking the form of a lover's lament or complaint about a beloved's absence ("My lefe is faren in a lond"). Satires against women (such as "Of all creatures women be best") are common; most authorities think it probable that these medieval lyrics were all (or almost all) written by men, even those written in a woman's voice (such as "I lovede a child of this cuntree").

The range of emotion and expression in the lyrics is remarkably wide. Some poems are light-hearted celebrations of the pleasures of the ale-house ("Bring us in good ale") or the simple joy of experiencing nature's abundance ("Sumer is icumen in"). There is a refreshing directness (and sometimes a refreshing crudity) to many of these poems. Yet even those lyrics that clearly aim at comic entertainment can employ sophisticated poetic devices, such as internal rhyme, wordplay and allegory. Some lyrics (such as "Foweles in the frith") are ambiguous and perhaps ambivalent in their content, capable of both secular and religious readings.

We do not know how many of these poems were set to music, but the practice was apparently common; several manuscripts have come down to us that provide music to accompany their lyrics.

⌘ ⌘ ⌘

Harley Manuscript 978, now in the British Museum, is a miscellany dating from the second half of the thirteenth century; it was compiled and transcribed by monks at Reading Abbey. The page shown here provides the music as well as the English words to "Sumer is icumen in," which remains perhaps the best known of all medieval lyrics. Between the lines alternative words in Latin (focused on the "celicus agricola," or heavenly farmer) are provided by the monks.

Sumer is icumen in

S umer° is icumen° in   *summer / has come*
  Sing, cuccu, nu.[1] Sing, cuccu.
Sing, cuccu. Sing, cuccu, nu.

Sumer is icumen in—
5 Lhude° sing, cuccu.   *loudly*
Groweth sed° and bloweth° med°   *seed / blooms / meadow*
And springth the wude° nu[2]—   *wood*
Sing, cuccu.

Awe° bleteth after lomb,   *ewe*
10 Lhouth after calve cu,[3]
Bulluc sterteth, bucke verteth,
Murie° sing,[4] cuccu.   *merry*
Cuccu, cuccu,
Well singes thu,° cuccu—   *thou*
15 Ne swik thu naver nu![5]
    —EARLIER 13TH CENTURY

Foweles in the frith

F oweles° in the frith,°   *birds / wood*
  The fisses° in the flod,°   *fishes / river, stream*
And I mon waxe wod:[6]
Much sorw I walk with
5 For beste of bon and blod.[7]
    —LATER 13TH CENTURY

Betwene Mersh and Averil

B etwene Mersh° and Averil,°   *March / April*
  When spray beginneth to springe,[8]
The lutel° fowl hath hire will   *little*
On hire lud to singe.[9]
5 Ich libbe° in love-longinge   *I live*
For semlokest° of alle thinge—   *the most fair, seemly*
He° may me blisse bringe;   *she*
Ich am in hire baundoun.°   *power, control*

An hendy hap ich habbe ihent![10]
10 Ichot° from Hevene it is me sent.   *I know*
From alle wimmen my love is lent,
And light on Alisoun.[11]

On hue hire hair is fair enough,
Hire browe browne, hire eye blake;
15 With lossum chere he° on me logh,[12]   *she*
With middle small and well imake.°   *fashioned*
Bote° he me wolle° to hire take,   *unless / will*
For to ben hire owen make,[13]
Longe to liven ichulle° forsake,   *I shall*
20 And feye fallen adoun.[14]

Nightes when I wende° and wake—   *twist, turn*
Forthy mine wonges waxeth won[15]—
Levedy,° all for thine sake,   *lady*
Longinge is ilent me on.[16]
25 In world nis non so witer mon

---

1 *cuccu, nu* Cuckoo, now.

2 *Groweth sed ... wude nu* Seed grows and meadow blooms, and the wood now brings forth growth.

3 *Lhouth ... cu* The cow lows after the calf.

4 *Bulluc ... sing* The bullock starts, the buck breaks wind, sing merrily!

5 *Well singes ... naver nu* You sing well, cuckoo—now never cease!

6 *mon ... wod* Must go mad.

7 *For ... blod* For beast of bone and blood.

---

8 *When ... springe* When twigs/shoots begin to grow.

9 *The lutel ... singe* The little bird has her wish to sing in her language.

10 *An hendy ... ihent* I have received a fair fortune!

11 *From alle ... on Alisoun* My love is taken from all women, and falls upon Alisoun.

12 *With lossum ... logh* With beautiful face she laughed at me.

13 *For to ... make* To be her own lover/companion.

14 *Longe ... adoun* I shall not live long, and fated to die, fall down.

15 *Forthy ... won* Therefore my cheeks grow pale.

16 *Longinge ... on* Longing has fallen on me.

That all hire bounte tell con:[1]
Hire swire is whittore then the swon,[2]
And fairest may in toun.[3]

Ich am for wowing° all forwake,°   *wooing / exhausted*
30 Wery so water in wore,[4]
Lest eny reve me my make,
Ich habbe iyirned yore.[5]
Betere is tholien while sore
Then mournen evermore.[6]
35 Geynest° under gore,[7]   *fairest*
Herkne to my roun!°   *song, cry*
—LATER 13TH CENTURY–EARLY 14TH CENTURY

Stond well, moder, under Rode

"Stond well, moder,° under Rode.°   *mother / rood, cross*
Behold thy sone with glade mode°—   *mind, heart*
Blithe° moder might thou be."   *joyful*
"Sone, how shulde I blithe stonde?
5 I se thine fet,° I se thine honde,°   *feet / hands*
Nailed to the harde Tree."

"Moder, do wey° thy wepinge.   *away*
I thole° deth for monkinde—   *suffer*
For my gult° thole I non."   *sin*
10 "Sone, I fele the dedestounde:°   *hour of death*
The swerd is at mine herte grounde,
That me bihet Simeon."[8]

"Moder, thou rewe all of thy bern:[9]
Thou woshe° away the blody tern°—   *wash / tears*
15 It doth me worse then my ded."°   *death*
"Sone, how may I teres werne?[10]
I se the blody stremes erne°   *run*
From thine herte to my fet."

"Moder, now I may thee seye,°   *say*
20 Betere is that ich one deye[11]
Then all monkunde° to helle go."   *mankind*
"Sone, I se thy body beswungen,°   *hung*
Fet and honden thourhout stongen°—   *pierced*
No wonder thah me be wo."[12]

25 "Moder, now I shall thee telle,
Yef I ne deye thou gost to helle:[13]
I thole ded for thine sake."
"Sone, thou art so meke and minde,[14]
Ne wit me naht, it is my kinde[15]
30 That I for thee this sorewe make."

"Moder, mercy, let me deye!
For Adam out of helle beye,°   *to redeem*
And his kun that is forlore."[16]
"Sone, what shall me to rede?[17]
35 My peine pineth me to dede.[18]
Lat° me deye thee before."   *let*

"Moder, now thou might well leren°   *learn*
Whet sorewe haveth that children beren,[19]
Whet sorewe it is with childe gon."

---

[1] *In world ... con* In the world there is no man so wise that he could tell all her virtue.

[2] *Her swire ... swon* Her neck is whiter than the swan.

[3] *And ... in toun* And she is the fairest maiden in town.

[4] *Ich am ... in wore* I am all wearied from wooing, as weary as water on the shore.

[5] *Lest ... yore* Lest any deprive me of my beloved, whom I have yearned for for so long.

[6] *Betere ... evermore* It is better to suffer miserably for a while than to mourn forever.

[7] *Geynest under gore* Loveliest under clothing (a common expression meaning "most beautiful").

[8] *The swerd ... Simeon* The sword that Simeon promised me has pierced the bottom of my heart. See Luke 2.25–35.

[9] *rewe ... bern* Have pity on your child.

[10] *how ... werne* How may I deny my tears?

[11] *Betere ... deye* It is better that I alone die.

[12] *No wonder ... wo* No wonder though I grieve.

[13] *Yef ... helle* If I do not die you will go to hell.

[14] *meke and minde* Gentle and thoughtful.

[15] *Ne wit ... kinde* Do not blame me, it is my nature.

[16] *kun ... forlore* Kin that is lost.

[17] *what shall ... rede* What shall I do?

[18] *peine ... dede* Pain tortures me to death.

[19] *sorewe ... beren* Sorrow they have who bear children.

40   "Sorewe, iwis,° I con thee telle!   *indeed, truly*
      Bote it be the pine of helle,
      More sorewe wot° I non."   *know*

      "Moder, rew of moder care,[1]
      For now thou wost of moder fare,[2]
45   Thou thou be clene maiden-mon."[3]
      "Sone, help at alle nede
      Alle tho that to me grede,°   *cry out*
      Maiden, wif and fol wimmon."°   *prostitutes*

      "Moder, may I no lengore° dwelle.   *longer*
50   The time is come I shall to helle.
      The thridde° day I rise upon."   *third*
      "Sone, I will with thee founden.°   *go*
      I deye, iwis, for° thine wounden,°   *of / wounds*
      So soreweful ded nes never non."[4]

55   When he ros tho° fell hire sorewe,   *then*
      Hire blisse sprong the thridde morewe:° *morrow, morning*
      Blithe moder were thou tho.
      Levedy, for that ilke blisse,[5]
      Besech thy sone of sunnes lisse—[6]
60   Thou be oure sheld ayein oure fo.[7]

      Blessed be thou, full of blisse,
      Let us never Hevene misse,
      Thourh thy swete sones might.
      Louerd,° for that ilke blod   *Lord*
65   That thou sheddest on the Rod,
      Thou bring us into Hevene light.
      Amen.
      —LATER 13TH CENTURY–EARLY 14TH CENTURY

---

[1] *rew … care* Pity a mother's care.

[2] *wost … fare* Know of motherhood.

[3] *clene maiden-mon* Pure virgin.

[4] *So soreweful … non* There was never such a sorrowful death.

[5] *Levedy … blisse* Lady, for that same joy.

[6] *of sunnes lisse* Relief of sins.

[7] *ayein oure fo* Against our foe.

I lovede a child of this cuntree

   Were it undo that is ido,
   I wolde bewar.[8]

I lovede a child of this cuntree,°   *country*
   And so I wende° he had do me;[9]   *thought*
5 Now myself the sothe° I see,   *truth*
   That he is far.°   *far away, remote*

   He seide to me he wolde be true,
   And change me for non other new;
   Now I sikke° and am pale of hue,   *sigh*
10 For he is far.

   He said his sawes° he wolde fulfille: *promises*
   Therfore I let him have all his wille;
   Now I sikke and mourn stille,[10]
   For he is far.
   —C. 14TH CENTURY

I have a gentil cock

I have a gentil° cock,   *noble*
   Croweth° me day: *who crows*
   He doth° me risen erly   *makes*
   My matins° for to say.   *morning prayers*

   I have a gentil cock,
   Comen he is of gret:°   *great or noble family*
   His comb° is of° red coral,   *crest / like*
   His tail is of jet.

   I have a gentil cock,
10 Comen he is of kinde:
   His comb is of red coral,
   His tail is of inde.°   *indigo*

---

[8] *Were it … bewar* If whatever done could be undone, I would be careful (possibly a refrain to be repeated following each stanza).

[9] *I lovede … do me* I loved a young man of this country, and so I believed he also loved me.

[10] *stille* Continually.

His legges ben of asor,[1]
So gentle and so smale;
15 His spores° arn of silver whit   *spurs*
Into the wortewale.[2]

His eynen° arn of cristal,   *eyes*
Loken° all in aumber:°   *set / amber*
And every night he percheth him
20 In mine ladye's chaumber.
—EARLIER 15TH CENTURY

I sing of a maiden

I sing of a maiden
    That is makeles:°   *matchless, unique*
King of alle kinges
To here sone she ches.[3]

5 He cam also° stille°   *as / quietly, gently*
Ther his moder was,
As dew in Aprille
That falleth on the grass.

He cam also stille
10 To his moderes bowr,°   *chamber*
As dew in Aprille
That falleth on the flowr.

He cam also stille
Ther his moder lay,
15 As dew in Aprille
That falleth on the spray.

Moder and maiden
Was never non but she:[4]
Well may swich° a lady   *such*
20 Godes moder be.
—EARLIER 15TH CENTURY

Adam lay ibounden

Adam lay ibounden,°   *bound*
    Bounden in a bond:
Foure thousand winter
Thought he not too long.
5 And all was for an apple,
An apple that he tok,
As clerkes° finden   *scholars*
Wreten in here° book.   *their*

Ne hadde the apple take ben,[5]
10 The apple taken ben,
Ne hadde never our Lady
A ben Hevene Quen.[6]
Blissed be the time
That apple take was!
15 Therfore we moun° singen,   *may*
"Deo gracias!"[7]
—EARLIER 15TH CENTURY

Farewell this world, I take my leve forever

Farewell this world, I take my leve forever,
    I am arrestid° to appere affore°   *at rest, waiting / before*
        Godis face.
O mercyfull God, Thow knowest that I had lever°   *rather*
Than all this worldis good to haue an owre° space *hour*
5 For to make aseth° for my gret trespace.   *amends*
My harte, alas, is brokyn for that sorow.
Som be this day that shall not be tomorow.

This world, I see, is but a chery fayre,[8]
All thyngis passith and so moste I algate.°   *inevitably*
10 This day I satt full royally in a chayre
Tyll sotyll° deth knokkid at my gate   *subtle*
And vnavised° he said to me, "Chekmate!"   *unexpected*
Loo,° how sodynly he maketh a devorce°   *look / separation*

---

[1] *ben of asor*   Are like azure.

[2] *Into the wortewale*   Up to the root (of the cock's spur).

[3] *To here ... ches*   She chose for her son.

[4] *Moder ... but she*   Never was any but she both mother and
maiden.

[5] *Ne hadde ... ben*   Had the apple never been taken.

[6] *A ben ... Quene*   Been Queen of Heaven.

[7] *"Deo gracias!"*   I.e., *Deo gratias*. Latin: Thanks be to God!

[8] *is but ... fayre*   Is only a cherry festival (i.e., is passing or transient,
like the time of cherry harvest).

And wormes to fede° here he hath layde my
　　corse.°　　　　　　　　　　　　　　　　　*feed / corpse*

15　Speke softe, ye folkis,° for I am layde a° slepe.　　*folks / to*
　　I haue my dreme,° in triste is myche　　　　　*dream, vision*
　　　　treason.[1]
　　From dethis° hold fayn° wold I make a lepe　*death's / glad*
　　But my wisdom ys torned into feble° reason:　　*weak*
　　I see this worldis joye lastith but a season.
20　Wold God I had remembrid this beforne!
　　I say no more but beware of an horne.°　　　*summons (?)*

　　This febyll world, so false and so vnstable,
　　Promoteth his lovers but for a lytill while,
　　But at last he geveth them a bable°　　　　　*bauble, toy*
25　Whan his payntid trowth° is torned into
　　　　gile.°　　　　　　　　　　*painted truth / deceit*
　　Experyence cawsith° me the trowth to
　　　　compile,°　　　　　　　　　　*causes / gather*
　　Thynkyng this: to° late, alas, that I began;　　*too*
　　For foly and hope disseyveth° many a man.　*tricks, deceives*

　　Farewell my frendis, the tide° abidith°　　　*time / waits for*
　　　　no man;
30　I moste departe hens° and so shall ye,　　　*hence*
　　But in this passage° the beste songe that I can　*journey*
　　Is Requiem Eternam.[2] I pray God grant it me.
　　Whan I haue endid all myn adversite°　　　　*adversity*
　　Graunte me in paradise to haue a mancyon,°　*mansion*
35　That shede his blode for my redempcion.
　　Beati mortui qui in Domino moriuntur.
　　Humiliatus sum vermis.[3]

　　—15TH CENTURY

Bring us in good ale

Bring us in good ale, and bring us in good ale,
　　Fore our blessed Lady sak,° bring us in　　　*sake*
　　good ale.

Bring us in no browne bred, fore that is mad of brane;[4]
Nor bring us in no whit bred, fore therin is no game:
5　But bring us in good ale.

Bring us in no befe, for ther is many bones;
But bring us in good ale, for that goth downe at
　　ones,°　　　　　　　　　　　　　　　　　　*once*
And bring us in good ale.

Bring us in no bacon, for that is passing fat;
10　But bring us in good ale, and give us inought°　*enough*
　　of that,
And bring us in good ale.

Bring us in no mutton, for that is ofte lene;[5]
Nor bring us in no tripes, for they be seldom clene:
But bring us in good ale.

15　Bring us in no egges, for ther ar many shelles;
But bring us in good ale, and give us nothing elles,°　*else*
And bring us in good ale.

Bring us in no butter, for therin ar many heres;°　*hairs*
Nor bring us in no pigges flesh, for that will mak
　　us bores:°　　　　　　　　　　　　　　　　*boars*
20　But bring us in good ale.

Bring us in no podinges, for therin is all gotes blod;[6]
Nor bring us in no venison, for that is not for our good:
But bring us in good ale.

Bring us in no capon's° flesh, for that is ofte
　　der;°　　　　　　　　　　　　　　*fowl's / dear, costly*
25　Nor bring us in no dokes° flesh for they slobber in
　　the mer:°　　　　　　　　　　　　　　*ducks' / pond*
But bring us in good ale.
—LATER 15TH CENTURY

---

[1]　*in triste … treason*　Proverbial: "in trust is much treason," i.e., confidence is often deceived.

[2]　*Requiem Eternam*　Latin: Eternal rest (a requiem is a mass sung for the dead).

[3]　*Beati … vermis*　Latin: Blessed are the dead who die in the Lord. I am humbled by (or with) worms.

---

[4]　*mad of brane*　Made of bran.

[5]　*ofte lene*　Often lean.

[6]　*gotes blod*　I.e., goat's blood puddings.

Of all creatures women be best

Of all creatures women be best,
Cuius contrarium verum est.[1]

In every place ye may well see
That women be trewe° as tirtill° on tree,   *true / turtledove*
5   Not liberal° in langage but ever in secree,[2]   *licentious*
And gret joye amonge them is for to be.

The stedfastnes of women will never be don,
So gentil,° so curtes,° they be everichon,[3]   *noble / courteous*
Meke° as a lambe, still° as a stone,   *meek / quiet*
10   Croked° nor crabbed° find ye none.   *perverse / twisted*

Men be more cumbers° a thousandfold,   *troublesome*
And I mervail° how they dare be so bold   *marvel*
Against women for to hold,
Seeing them so pascient,° softe and cold.   *patient*

15   For tell a woman all your counsaile
And she can kepe it wonderly well:
She had lever° go quik° to hell   *rather/ alive*
Than to her neighbour she wold it tell.

Now say well by women or elles° be still,   *else*
20   For they never displesed man by ther will:

To be angry or wroth they can no skill,[4]
For I dare say they think non° ill.   *no*

Trow ye that women list to smater,[5]
Or against ther husbondes for to clater?°   *make noise*
25   Nay! they had lever fast, bred and water,
Then for to dele° in suche a matter.   *deal, act*

To the tavern they will not go,
Nor to the alehous never the mo,°   *more*
For, God wot,° ther hartes wold be wo°   *knows / sorry*
30   To spende ther husbondes money so.
—LATER 15TH CENTURY

My lefe is faren in a lond [6]

My lefe is faren in a lond—
Alas! why is she so?
And I am so sore bound
I may nat com her to.
5   She hath my hert in hold,°   *imprisoned*
Where-ever she ride or go,
With trew love a thousandfold.
—LATER 15TH CENTURY

---

[1] *Cuius … est*   Latin: The opposite of this is true.
[2] *in secree*   In secret, i.e., discreet.
[3] *they be everichon*   Is each one.

[4] *can no skill*   Are completely unable.
[5] *Trow ye … smater*   Do you believe that women enjoy chattering?
[6] *My lefe … lond*   My love has gone away (to another land). This lyric is referred to in Chaucer's *Nun's Priest's Tale* (1.112).

THE CRISES OF THE FOURTEENTH CENTURY
CONTEXTS

Britain in the fourteenth century suffered an unprecedented series of crises and catastrophes. The first of these was the great famine of 1315-18. Whereas we tend to think of famine as resulting from drought, the famine of the early fourteenth century was the result of too much water rather than too little. In Britain, as in the rest of Europe, a pattern of extraordinarily wet weather was repeated for several years; as the chronicle account below details, rot was followed by hunger, pestilence, and universal hardship.

The next great upheaval was the series of conflicts that eventually became known as the Hundred Years' War. Since the time of Henry II in the early thirteenth century, the English had held considerable territory in what is now France, and English kings continued to nurture ambitions of increasing their power on the other side of the English Channel. The French nobles' refusal to recognize Edward III's claim to the French throne acted as a spark to ignite conflict, and hostilities broke out in 1337 and would not truly end until 1453. With the help of the new technology of the longbow English forces at first enjoyed great success—most notably at the battles of Crécy (1346) and Poitiers (1356) under the leadership of Edward the Black Prince. Under the leadership of Henry V they inflicted a massive defeat upon the French armies at Agincourt (1415), but with the death of Henry V in 1422 and the extraordinary rise to military glory of the sixteen-year-old peasant Jeanne D'Arc (who is credited with leading the French to victory at Orléans in 1429) the tide of the conflict turned. By 1450 the English had abandoned almost all their possessions on the Continent, and the map of France had come to resemble closely its present-day shape. France had been left exhausted and impoverished by the struggle, but the events of the previous century helped to nurture a national myth that before long carried the French nation to new prosperity. The war gave rise to a national mythology in England too; the fact that the British had lost a vast expanse of territory was largely forgotten, while the famous victories of the Black Prince and of Henry V provided an ongoing source of nourishment for national pride.

The upheaval caused by the plague known as the Black Death that swept across Europe in the 1340s turned out to be just as long-lasting as that of the Hundred Years' War—and even more severe in its effects. The Black Death (so named for the color of the sores it brought with it) probably originated in China in 1320. Initially its spread was gradual, but once it reached the Crimean port of Calla in 1346 it began to spread much more rapidly; by the end of 1347 it was devastating much of continental Europe, and in the summer of 1348 it reached Britain. In many areas of Europe close to half the population succumbed; in some areas the figure exceeded seventy percent. The toll in Britain is believed to be in the range of a third of the people dead; not until a century later did the population begin to recover substantially. As the documents below indicate, the effects of such a vast and sudden demographic event were wide-ranging. One of the most significant was a persistent shortage of labor, which in turn contributed to scarcities and price increases. The almost universal response from the authorities was to attempt to impose wage and price controls, with mixed results; the aftershocks of the plague continued to ripple through the economic system, contributing significantly to the destabilizing and eventual disappearance of the feudal order.

Both the Hundred Years' War and the Black Death were underlying causes for another great fourteenth-century upheaval—the Uprising of 1381, sometimes called the Peasants' Revolt (though many non-peasants were involved). The shortage of labor caused by the Black Death—and the attempts of the authorities to suppress it, most notably Edward III's 1351 Statute of Laborers—had created a climate of restlessness among the peasantry. Thirty years on, when Parliament responded to the mounting costs of the wars with France by imposing a new tax on all adults (termed a "poll tax"), the action sparked the first widespread rebellion of commoners in English history. Though the revolt was suppressed, in its wake the peasantry were emboldened in dealing with their lords; feudal relationships of outright servitude began to die out, replaced by lease-hold arrangements under the terms of which peasants paid rent for the land they farmed.

⌘ ⌘ ⌘

The Great Famine

The chronicle excerpt below is of interest for its comments about such matters as price controls and relations between the Scots and the English as well as for its description of the effects of the famine.

from Anonymous (the "Monk of Malmesbury"), *Life of Edward the Second* (fourteenth century)

In this parliament [of February–March, 1315], because merchants going about the country selling victuals charged excessively, the earls and barons, looking to the welfare of the state, appointed a remedy for this malady; they ordained a fixed price for oxen, pigs and sheep, for fowls, chickens, and pigeons, and for other common foods. ... These matters were published throughout the land, and publicly proclaimed in shire courts and boroughs. ...

By certain portents the hand of God appears to be raised against us. For in the past year there was such plentiful rain that men could scarcely harvest the corn or bring it safely to the barn. In the present year worse has happened. For the floods of rain have rotted almost all the seed, so that the prophecy of Isaiah might seem now to be fulfilled; for he says that "ten acres of vineyard shall yield one little measure and thirty bushels of seed shall yield three bushels":[1] and in many places the hay lay so long under water that it could neither be mown nor gathered. Sheep generally died and other animals were killed in a sudden plague. It is greatly to be feared that if the Lord finds us incorrigible after these visitations, he will destroy at once both men and beasts; and I firmly believe that unless the English Church had

interceded for us, we should have perished long ago. ...

After the feast of Easter [in 1316] the dearth of corn[2] was much increased. Such a scarcity has not been seen in our time in England, nor heard of for a hundred years. For a measure of wheat sold in London and the neighboring places for forty pence, and in other less thickly populated parts of the country thirty pence was a common price. Indeed during this time of scarcity a great famine appeared, and after the famine came a severe pestilence, of which many thousands died in many places. I have even heard it said by some, that in Northumbria dogs and horses and other unclean things were eaten. For there, on account of the frequent raids of the Scots, work is more irksome, as the accursed Scots despoil the people daily of their food. Alas, poor England! You who once helped other lands from your abundance, now poor and needy are forced to beg. Fruitful land is turned into a salt-marsh; the inclemency of the weather destroys the fatness of the land; corn is sown and tares[3] are brought forth. All this comes from the wickedness of the inhabitants. Spare, O Lord, spare thy people! For we are a scorn and a derision to them who are around us. Yet those who are wise in astrology say that these storms in the heavens have happened naturally; for Saturn, cold and heedless, brings rough weather that is useless to the seed; in the ascendant now for three years he has completed his course, and mild Jupiter duly succeeds him. Under Jupiter these floods of rain will cease, the valleys will grow rich in corn, and the fields will be filled with abundance. For the Lord shall give that which is good and our land shall yield her increase. ...

---

[1] *ten acres ... bushels* Cf. Isaiah 5.10.

[2] *corn* Grain.

[3] *tares* Weeds.

[In 1318] the dearth that had so long plagued us ceased, and England became fruitful with a manifold abundance of good things. A measure of wheat, which the year before was sold for forty pence, was now freely offered to the buyer for sixpence. …

The Hundred Years' War

The *Chronicle* of Jean Froissart of Valenciennes is among the most valuable historical records we possess of the course of fourteenth-century history. Froissart (c. 1337–c. 1404) was in direct contact with many of the nobility on both sides of the conflict between France and England. His *Chronicle* appeared in four volumes between 1370 and 1400, and survives in over one hundred manuscript copies. The excerpt below describes the battle fought at Crécy in 1346, beginning with a French lord's unsuccessful attempt to give the French King, Philip VI, good tactical advice.

The second excerpt below may perhaps be regarded as an early equivalent of a newspaper; it is from a letter sent by Edward the Black Prince to the people of London, recounting the story of the English victory at Poitiers (1356).

from Jean Froissart, *Chronicle* (late fourteenth century)

The lord Moyne said [to the king of France], "Sir, I will speak, since it pleases you to order me, but with the assistance of my companions. We have advanced far enough to reconnoitre your enemies. Know, then, that they are drawn up in three battalions and are awaiting you. I would advise, for my part (submitting, however, to better counsel), that you halt your army here and quarter them for the night; for before the rear shall come up and the army be properly drawn out, it will be very late. Your men will be tired and in disorder, while they will find your enemies fresh and properly arrayed. On the morrow, you may draw up your army more at your ease and may reconnoitre at leisure on what part it will be most advantageous to begin the attack; for, be assured, they will wait for you."

The king commanded that it should be so done; and the two marshals rode, one towards the front, and the other to the rear, crying out, "Halt banners, in the name of God and St. Denis." Those that were in the front halted; but those behind said they would not halt until they were as far forward as the front. When the front perceived the rear pushing on, they pushed forward; and neither the king nor the marshals could stop them, but they marched on without any order until they came in sight of their enemies. As soon as the foremost rank saw them, they fell back at once in great disorder, which alarmed those in the rear, who thought they had been fighting. There was then space and room enough for them to have passed forward, had they been willing to do so. Some did so, but others remained behind.

All the roads between Abbeville and Crécy were covered with common people, who, when they had come within three leagues of their enemies, drew their swords, crying out, "Kill, kill"; and with them were many great lords who were eager to make show of their courage. There is no man, unless he had been present, who can imagine, or describe truly, the confusion of that day, especially the bad management and disorder of the French, whose troops were beyond number.

The English, who were drawn up in three divisions and seated on the ground, on seeing their enemies advance, arose boldly and fell into their ranks. That of the Prince was the first to do so, whose archers were formed in the manner of a portcullis, or harrow, and the men-at-arms in the rear.[1] The earls of Northampton and Arundel, who commanded the second division, had posted themselves in good order on his wing to assist and succor the Prince, if necessary.

You must know that these kings, dukes, earls, barons, and lords of France did not advance in any regular order, but one after the other, or in any way most pleasing to themselves. As soon as the King of France came in sight of the English his blood began to boil, and he cried out to his marshals, "Order the

---

[1] *archers were formed … in the rear* A portcullis (a kind of gate) and a harrow (a farming implement) both have prongs or teeth; in this formation, lines of bowmen would probably have advanced like the arms of a V ahead of the main troops. Lines of bowmen were roughly "vertical" in relation to the "horizontal" line of men-at-arms.

Genoese[1] forward, and begin the battle, in the name of God and St. Denis." There were about fifteen thousand Genoese cross-bowmen; but they were quite fatigued, having marched on foot that day six leagues, completely armed, and with their cross-bows. They told the constable that they were not in a fit condition to do any great things that day in battle. The Earl of Alençon, hearing this, said, "This is what one gets by employing such scoundrels, who fail when there is any need for them."

During this time a heavy rain fell, accompanied by thunder and a very terrible eclipse of the sun; and before this rain a great flight of crows hovered in the air over all those battalions, making a loud noise. Shortly afterwards it cleared up and the sun shone very brightly; but the Frenchmen had it in their faces, and the English at their backs.

When the Genoese were somewhat in order they approached the English and set up a loud shout in order to frighten them; but the latter remained quite still and did not seem to hear it. They then set up a second shout and advanced a little forward; but the English did not move. They hooted a third time, advancing with their cross-bows presented, and began to shoot. The English archers then advanced one step forward and shot their arrows with such force and quickness that it seemed as if it snowed.

When the Genoese felt these arrows, which pierced their arms, heads, and through their armor, some of them cut the strings of their cross-bows, others flung them on the ground, and all turned about and retreated, quite discomfited. The French had a large body of men-at-arms on horseback, richly dressed, to support the Genoese. The King of France, seeing them fall back, cried out, "Kill me those scoundrels; for they stop up our road, without any reason." You would then have seen the above-mentioned men-at-arms lay about them, killing all that they could of these runaways.

The English continued shooting as vigorously and quickly as before. Some of their arrows fell among the horsemen, who were sumptuously equipped, and, killing and wounding many, made them caper and fall among the Genoese, so that they were in such confusion they could never rally again. In the English army there were some Cornish- and Welshmen on foot who had armed themselves with large knives. These, advancing through the ranks of the men-at-arms and archers, who made way for them, came upon the French when they were in this danger and, falling upon earls, barons, knights and squires, slew many, at which the king of England was afterwards much exasperated.[2]

From a fifteenth-century manuscript of Froissart's *Chronicle*, "The Battle of Crécy."

From a fifteenth-century manuscript of Froissart's *Chronicle*, "The Battle of Poitiers."

---

[1]   *Genoese*   The Genoese (from Genoa, in Italy) are here fighting for the French as mercenaries; hence the comment of the Earl of Alençon, below.

[2]   *slew many … much exasperated*   It would have been typical at this time to capture aristocratic enemy fighters and return them for ransom, rather than killing them.

Late after vespers,[1] the King of France had not more about him than sixty men, every one included. Sir John of Hainault, who was of the number, had once remounted the king; for the latter's horse had been killed under him by an arrow. He said to the king, "Sir, retreat while you have an opportunity, and do not expose yourself so needlessly. If you have lost this battle, another time you will be the conqueror." After he had said this, he took the bridle of the king's horse and led him off by force; for he had before entreated him to retire.

The king rode on until he came to the castle of La Broyes, where he found the gates shut, for it was very dark. The king ordered the governor of it to be summoned. He came upon the battlements and asked who it was that called at such an hour. The king answered, "Open, open, governor; it is the fortune of France." The governor, hearing the king's voice, immediately descended, opened the gate, and let down the bridge. The king and his company entered the castle; but he had with him only five barons—Sir John Hainault, the lord Charles of Montmorency, the lord of Beaujeu, the lord of Aubigny, and the lord of Montfort. The king would not bury himself in such a place as that, but, having taken some refreshments, set out again with his attendants about midnight, and rode on, under the direction of guides who were well acquainted with the country, until, about daybreak, he came to Amiens, where he halted.

This Saturday the English never quitted their ranks in pursuit of anyone, but remained on the field, guarding their positions and defending themselves against all who attacked them. The battle was ended at the hour of vespers. When, on this Saturday night, the English heard no more hooting or shouting, nor any more crying out to particular lords, or their banners, they looked upon the field as their own and their enemies as beaten.

They made great fires and lighted torches because of the darkness of the night. King Edward [III] then came down from his post, who all that day had not put on his helmet, and, with his whole battalion, advanced to the prince of Wales [Edward the "Black Prince"], whom he embraced in his arms and kissed, and said, "Sweet son, God give you good preference. You are my son, for most loyally have you acquitted yourself this day. You are worthy to be a sovereign." The prince bowed down very low and humbled himself, giving all honor to the king his father.

The English, during the night, made frequent thanksgivings to the Lord for the happy outcome of the day, and without rioting; for the King had forbidden all riot or noise.

from Prince Edward, Letter to the People of London (1356)

Very dear and very much beloved: As concerning news in the parts where we are, know that since the time when we informed our most dread lord and father, the King [Edward III], that it was our purpose to ride forth against the enemies in the parts of France, we took our road through the country of Périgueux and of Limousin, and straight on towards Bourges in Vienne, where we expected to have found the [French] king's son, the count of Poitiers. …[2]

And then our people pursued them as far as Chauvigny, full three leagues further; for which reason we were obliged that day to take up our quarters as near to that place as we could, that we might collect our men. And on the morrow we took our road straight towards the king, and sent out our scouts, who found him with his army; set himself[3] in battle array at one league from Poitiers, in the fields; and we went as near to him as we could take up our post, we ourselves on foot and in battle array, and ready to fight with him.

Where came the said Cardinal [Talleyrand], requesting very earnestly for a little respite, that so there might parley together certain persons of either side, and so attempt to bring about an understanding and good peace; the which he undertook that he would bring about to a good end. Whereupon we took counsel, and granted him his request; upon which there were ordered

---

[1] *vespers* The hour for evening service in monastic practice; probably around 6:00 in the evening. This is one of the "canonical hours" used for telling time in monasteries.

[2] *the King's son … Poitiers* I.e., the French king, who at this time was Jean II, son of Philip VI; his son, the Dauphin, was later to become Charles V.

[3] *set himself* I.e., the French king.

certain persons of the one side and the other to treat upon this matter; which treating was of no effect. And then the said Cardinal wished to obtain a truce, by way of putting off the battle at his pleasure; to which truce we would not assent. And the French asked that certain knights on the one side and the other should take equal shares, so that the battle might not in any manner fail: and in such manner was that day delayed; and the battalions on the one side and the other remained all night, each one in its place, and until the morrow, about half prime;[1] and as to some troops that were between the said main armies, neither would give any advantage in commencing the attack upon the other. And for default of victuals, as well as for other reasons, it was agreed that we should take our way, flanking them, in such manner that if they wished for battle or to draw towards us, in a place that was not very much to our disadvantage, we should be the first; and so forthwith it was done. Whereupon battle was joined, on [September 19,] the eve of the day before St. Matthew; and, God be praised for it, the enemy was discomfited, and the King was taken, and his son; and a great number of other great people were both taken and slain; as our very dear bachelor Messire Neele Lorraine, our chamberlain, the bearer hereof, who has very full knowledge thereon, will know how to inform and show you more fully, as we are not able to write to you. To him you should give full faith and credence; and may our Lord have you in his keeping. Given under our privy seal, at Bordeaux, the 22nd day of October.

The Black Death

The excerpted letter below by Ralph of Shrewsbury, Bishop of Bath and a distinguished scholar as well as an administrator, was sent to several of his subordinates just after the plague had begun. The second excerpt, from the *Chronicle* of Henry Knighton, provides a much more wide-ranging sense of the devastation wrought by the Black Death.

from Ralph of Shrewsbury, Letter (17 August 1348)

… Since the disaster of such a pestilence has come from the eastern parts to a neighboring kingdom, it is greatly to be feared, and being greatly to be feared, it is to be prayed devoutly and without ceasing that such a pestilence not extend its poisonous growth to the inhabitants of this kingdom, and torment and consume them.

Therefore, to each and all of you we mandate, with firm enjoining, that in your churches you publicly announce this present mandate in the vulgar tongue[2] at opportune times, and that in the bowels of Jesus Christ you exhort your subordinates—regular, secular, parishioners, and others—or have them exhorted by others, to appear before the Face of the Lord in confession, with psalms and other works of charity.

Remember the destruction that was deservedly pronounced by prophetic utterance on those who, doing penance, were mercifully freed from the destruction threatened by the judgment of God. …

from Henry Knighton, *Chronicle* (1378–96)

In that year and the following year there was a universal mortality of men throughout the world. It began first in India, then in Tarsus, then it reached the Saracens and finally the Christians and Jews. …

On a single day 1,312 people died in Avignon, according to a calculation made in the pope's presence. On another day more than 400 died. 358 of the Dominicans in Provence died during Lent. At Montpellier only seven friars survived out of 140. At Magdalen seven survived out of 160, which is quite enough. From 140 Minorites [i.e., Franciscans] at Marseilles not one remained to carry the news to the rest. … At the same time the plague raged in England. It began in the autumn in various places and after racing across the country it ended at the same time in the following year.

… Then the most lamentable plague penetrated the coast through Southampton and came to Bristol, and virtually the whole town was wiped out. It was as if sudden death had marked them down beforehand, for few lay sick for more than two or three days, or even for

---

[1] *half prime* About 9:30 in the morning. Like vespers, prime is part of the monastic way of measuring time, the "canonical hours."

[2] *vulgar tongue* I.e., the vernacular (the language of the land) rather than Latin.

half a day. Cruel death took just two days to burst out all over a town. At Leicester, in the little parish of St. Leonard, more than 380 died; in the parish of Holy Cross more than 400; in the parish of St. Margaret 700; and a great multitude in every parish. The Bishop of Lincoln sent word through the whole diocese, giving general power to every priest (among the regular as well as the secular clergy) to hear confession and grant absolution with full and complete authority except only in cases of debt.[1] In such cases the penitent, if it lay within his power, ought to make satisfaction while he lived, but certainly others should do it from his goods after his death. Similarly the Pope granted plenary remission of all sins to those at the point of death, the absolution to be for one time only, and the right to each person to choose his confessor as he wished.[2] This concession was to last until the following Easter.

In the same year there was a great murrain[3] of sheep throughout the realm, so much so that in one place more than 5,000 sheep died in a single pasture, and their bodies were so corrupt that no animal or bird would touch them. And because of the fear of death everything fetched a low price. For there were very few people who cared for riches, or indeed for anything else. A man could have a horse previously valued at 40s. for half a mark, a good fat ox for 4s., a cow for 12d., a bullock for 6d., a fat sheep for 4d., a ewe for 3d., a lamb for 2d., a large pig for 5d., a stone of wool for 9d. And sheep and cattle roamed unchecked through the fields and through the standing corn, and there was no one to chase them and round them up. For want of watching animals died in uncountable numbers in the fields and in bye-ways and hedges throughout the whole country;

for there was so great a shortage of servants and laborers that there was no one who knew what needed to be done. There was no memory of so inexorable and fierce a mortality since the time of Vortigern, King of the Britons, in whose time, as Bede testifies in his *De gestis Anglorum*,[4] there were not enough living to bury the dead. In the following autumn it was not possible to hire a reaper for less than 8d. and his food, or a mower for 12d. with his food.[5] For which reason many crops rotted unharvested in the fields; but in the year of the pestilence, as mentioned above, there was so great an abundance of all types of grain that no one cared.

The Scots, hearing of the cruel plague of the English, declared that it had befallen them through the revenging hand of God, and they took to swearing "by the foul death of England"—or so the common report resounded in the ears of the English. And thus the Scots, believing that the English were overwhelmed by the terrible vengeance of God, gathered in the forest of Selkirk with the intention of invading the whole realm of England. The fierce mortality came upon them, and the sudden cruelty of a monstrous death winnowed the Scots. Within a short space of time around 5,000 died, and the rest, weak and strong alike, decided to retreat to their own country. But the English, following, surprised them and killed many of them. …

After the aforesaid pestilence many buildings of all sizes in every city fell into total ruin for want of inhabitants. Likewise, many villages and hamlets were deserted, with no house remaining in them, because everyone who had lived there was dead, and indeed many of these villages were never inhabited again. In the following winter there was such a lack of workers in all areas of activity that it was thought that there had hardly ever been such a shortage before; for a man's farm animals and other livestock wandered about without a shepherd and all his possessions were left unguarded. And as a result all essentials were so expensive that something which had previously cost 1d. was now worth

---

[1] *among the regular … cases of debt* "Regular" clergy are those bound by a rule of communal life (i.e., most commonly, monks), who ordinarily would not have the "care of souls," that is, the duty of hearing confession or other interactions with lay people. That was the job of the "secular" clergy, the clergy who lived and worked in the outside world, such as parish priests or bishops.

[2] *the right … as he wished* Like the call for regular clergy to take on the care of souls, the concessions on remission (i.e., forgiveness) of sins and on the right to choose a confessor reflect the church's anxiety about the salvation of the faithful in a time of crisis. Ordinarily one would have been expected to confess to one's parish priest.

[3] *murrain* Infectious disease of livestock.

---

[4] *Bede … Anglorum* *De Gestis Anglorum* (*On the Deeds of the English*) by Venerable Bede (673–735), English scholar.

[5] *In the following autumn … with his food* Before the Black Death, laborers were typically hired for 2 or 3 pence per day, so these wages represent a roughly four-fold increase. (The abbreviation "d." is of the Latin *denarius*, or penny.)

4d. or 5d. Confronted by this shortage of workers and the scarcity of goods the great men of the realm, and the lesser landowners who had tenants, remitted part of the rent so that their tenants did not leave. Some remitted half the rent, some more and some less; some remitted it for two years, some for three and some for one—whatever they could agree with their tenants. Likewise those whose tenants held by the year, by the performance of labor services (as is customary in the case of serfs), found that they had to release and remit such works, and either pardon rents completely or levy them on easier terms, otherwise houses would be irretrievably ruined and land left uncultivated. And all victuals and other necessities were extremely dear.

Fourteenth-century manuscript: plague victims.

The Uprising of 1381

The following excerpts from a 1350 set of London wage and price regulations and from the Statute of Laborers imposed the following year by King Edward III provide some sense of the economic background for the Uprising of 1381 (or the "Peasants' Revolt"). As the Statute of 1363 demonstrates, regulations continued to tighten thereafter in an attempt to maintain traditional social distinctions between ranks, which were threatened by the economic upheaval that followed the plague. The passage by Froissart recounts a sermon by one of the leading figures of the rebellion, John Ball, and the letter that follows was

allegedly written by Ball as a coded message to those sympathetic to the uprising. The extended passage from the *Chronicle* of Henry Knighton, a canon of St. Mary's Abbey in the city of Leicester, provides a vivid account of the climax of the rebellion.

from Regulations, London (1350)

To amend and redress the damages and grievances which the good folks of the city, rich and poor, have suffered and received within the past year, by reason of masons, carpenters, plasterers, tilers, and all manner of laborers, who take immeasurably more than they have been wont to take, by assent of Walter Turk, mayor, the aldermen, and all the commonalty of the city, the points under-written are ordained, to be held and firmly observed for ever; that is to say:

In the first place, that the masons, between the Feasts of Easter and St. Michael,[1] shall take no more by the working-day than 6d., without victuals or drink; and from the Feast of St. Michael to Easter, for the working-day, 5d. And upon Feast Days, when they do not work, they shall take nothing. And for the making or mending of their implements they shall take nothing.

Also, that the carpenters shall take, for the same time, in the same manner.

Also, that the plasterers shall take the same as the masons and carpenters take.

Also, that the tilers shall take for the working-day, from the Feast of Easter to St. Michael 5 ½ d., and from the Feast of St. Michael 4 ½ d.

Also, that the laborers shall take in the first half year 3 ½ d., and in the other half 3d. …

Also, that the tailors shall take for making a gown, garnished with fine cloth and silk, 18d.

Also, for a man's gown, garnished with linen thread and with buckram, 14d.

Also, for a coat and hood, 10d.

Also, for a long gown for a woman, garnished with fine cloth or with silk, 2s. 6d.

Also, for a pair of sleeves, to change, 4d.

Also, that the porters of the city shall not take more for their labor than they used to take in olden time, on

---

[1] *St. Michael* The Feast of St. Michael the Archangel is held on 29 September.

pain of imprisonment.

Also, that no vintner shall be so daring as to sell the gallon of wine of Vernaccia for more than 2s., and wine of Crete, wine of the River, Piement, and Clare, and Malveisin, at 16d. …

Also, that a pair of spurs shall be sold for 6d., and a better pair for 8d., and the best at 10d. or 12d., at the very highest.

Also, that a pair of gloves of sheepskin shall be sold for one penny, and a better pair at 1 ½ d., and a pair at 2d., so going on to the very highest.

Also, that the shearmen shall not take more than they were wont to take; that is to say, for a short cloth 12d., and for a long cloth 2s.; and for a cloth of striped serge, for getting rid of the stripes, and shearing the same, 2s.

Also, that the farriers[1] shall not take more than they were wont to take before the time of the pestilence, on pain of imprisonment and heavy ransom; that is to say, for a horse-shoe of six nails 1½ 2d., and for a horse-shoe of eight nails 2d.; and for taking off a horse-shoe of six nails or of eight, one halfpenny; and for the shoe of a courser 2 ½ d., and the shoe of a charger 3d.; and for taking off the shoe of a courser or charger, one penny.

Also, if any workman or laborer will not work or labor as is above ordained, let him be taken and kept in prison until he shall have found good surety, and have been sworn to do that which is so ordained. And if anyone shall absent himself, or go out of the city, because he does not wish to work and labor, as is before mentioned, and afterwards by chance be found within the city, let him have imprisonment for a quarter of the year, and forfeit his chattels which he has in the city, and then let him find surety, and make oath, as is before stated. And if he will not do this, let him forswear the city for ever.

from Statute of Laborers (1351)

Because a great part of the people and especially of the workers and servants has now died in the pestilence, some, seeing the needs of the masters and the scarcity of servants, are not willing to serve unless they receive excessive wages, and others, rather than gain their living through labor, prefer to beg in idleness. We, considering the grave inconveniences which might come from such a shortage, especially of ploughmen and such laborers, have held deliberation and discussion concerning this with the prelates and nobles and other learned men sitting by us, by whose consenting counsel we have seen fit to ordain that every man and woman of our kingdom of England, of whatever condition, whether serf or free, who is able bodied and below the age of 60 years, not living from trade or carrying on a definite craft, or having private means of living or private land to cultivate, and not serving another—if such a person is sought after to serve in a suitable service appropriate to that person's status, that person shall be bound to serve whomever has seen fit so to offer such employment, and shall take only the wages, liveries, reward or salary usually given in that place in the twentieth year of our reign in England, or the usual year of the five or six preceding ones. This is provided so that in thus retaining their service, lords are preferred before others by their serfs or land tenants, so that such lords nevertheless thus retain as many as shall be necessary, but not more. And if any man or woman, being thus sought after for service, will not do this, the fact being proven by two faithful men before the sheriffs or the bailiffs of our Lord the King, or the constables of the town where this happens to be done, immediately through them, or some one of them, that person shall be taken and sent to the next jail, and remain there in strict custody until offering security for serving in the aforesaid form. And if a reaper or mower, or other worker or servant, of whatever standing or condition, who is retained in the service of anyone, departs from the said service before the end of the agreed term without permission or reasonable cause, that person shall undergo the penalty of imprisonment, and let no one, under the same penalty, presume to receive or retain such a person for service. Let no one, moreover, pay or permit to be paid to anyone more wages, livery, reward or salary than was customary, as has been said.

… Likewise saddlers, skinners, tawyers,[2] cordwainers,[3] tailors, smiths, carpenters, masons, tilers, shipwrights, carters and all other artisans and laborers

---

[1] *farriers* Smiths who shoe horses.

[2] *tawyers* Producers of white leather.

[3] *cordwainers* Shoemakers.

shall not take for their labor and handiwork more than what, in the places where they happen to labor, was customarily paid to such persons in the said twentieth year and in the other usual years preceding, as has been said. And anyone who takes more shall be committed to the nearest jail in the aforesaid manner.

Likewise, let butchers, fishmongers, innkeepers, brewers, bakers, those dealing in foodstuffs and all other vendors of any victuals, be bound to sell such victuals for a reasonable price, having regard for the price at which such victuals are sold in the adjoining places, so that such vendors may have moderate gains, and not excessive ones, according as the distance of the places from which such victuals are carried may seem reasonably to require. And if anyone sells such victuals in another manner, and is convicted of it in the aforesaid way, that person shall pay double what was received to the injured party, or in default of the injured party, to another who shall be willing to prosecute in this behalf. ...

And because many sturdy beggars refuse to labor so long as they can live from begging alms, giving themselves up to idleness and sin and, at times, to robbery and other crimes, let no one, under the aforesaid pain of imprisonment, presume, under color of piety or alms, to give anything to those who can very well work, or to cherish them in their sloth, so that thus they may be compelled to work for the necessities of life.

from Statute (1363)

... Item. Regarding the outrageous and excessive apparel of diverse people, violating their estate and degree, to the great destruction and impoverishment of the whole land, it is ordained that grooms (both servants of lords and those employed in crafts) shall be served meat or fish once a day, and the remaining occasions shall be served milk, butter, and cheese, and other such food, according to their estate. They shall have clothes for their wear worth no more than two marks, and they shall wear no cloth of higher price which they have bought themselves or gotten in some other way. Nor shall they wear anything of silver, embroidered items, nor items of silk, nor anything pertaining to those things. Their wives, daughters, and children shall be of

the same condition in their clothing and apparel, and they shall wear no veils worth more than 12 pence a veil.

Item. Artisans and yeomen[1] shall not take or wear cloth for their clothing or stockings of a higher price than 40 shillings for the whole cloth, by way of purchase or by any other means. Nor may they take or wear silk, silver, or jeweled cloth, nor shall they take or wear silver or gold belts, knives, clasps, rings, garters, or brooches, ribbons, chains, or any manner of silk apparel which is embroidered or decorated. And their wives, daughters and children are to be of the same condition in their dress and apparel. And they are to wear no veils made of silk, but only of yarn made within the kingdom, nor are they to wear any manner of fur or of budge,[2] but only of lamb, rabbit, cat, or fox. ...

Item. Knights who have land or rent valued up to 200 marks a year shall take and wear clothes of cloth valued at 6 marks for the whole cloth, and nothing of more expensive cloth. And they shall not wear cloth of gold or mantles or gowns furred with pure miniver[3] or ermine, or any apparel embroidered with jewels or anything else. Their wives, daughters, and children will be of the same condition. And they shall not wear ermine facings or lettice[4] or any jeweled apparel, except on their heads. All knights and ladies, however, who have land or rent of more than 400 marks a year, up to the sum of 1,000 marks, shall wear what they like, except ermine and lettice, and apparel with jewels and pearls, unless on their heads.

Item. Clergy who have any rank in a church, cathedral, college, or schools, or a cleric of the King who has an estate that requires fur, will wear and use it according to the constitution of the same. All other clergy who have 200 marks from land a year will wear and do as knights who receive the same rent. Other clergy with the same rent will wear what the esquires who have 100 pounds in rent wear. All of them, both clergy and knights, may wear fur in winter, and in the same manner will wear linure[5] in summer.

---

[1] *yeomen* Freeholders; those who farm their own land.

[2] *budge* Lamb's wool fur.

[3] *miniver* Ermine when taken in its white winter coat.

[4] *lettice* White-gray fur.

[5] *linure* Fine linen.

Item. Carters, ploughmen, ploughdrivers, cowherds, shepherds, swineherds, and all other keepers of animals, wheat threshers and all manner of people of the estate of a groom occupied in husbandry, and all other people who do not have 40 shillings' worth of goods or chattels will not take or wear any kind of cloth but blanket, and russet worth 12 pence, and shall wear belts of linen according to their estate. And domestic servants shall come to eat and drink in the manner pertaining to them, and not excessively. And it is ordained that if anyone wears or does contrary to the above, that person will forfeit to the King all the apparel thus worn against this ordinance.

Item. In order to maintain this ordinance and keep it in all points without exception, it is ordained that all makers of cloth within the realm, both men and women, shall confirm that they make their cloth according to the price set by this ordinance. And all the clothmakers shall buy and sell their varieties of cloth according to the same price, so that a great supply of such cloths will be made and put up for sale in every city, borough, and merchant town and elsewhere in the realm, so that no lack of supply of such cloths shall cause the violation of this ordinance. And to that end the said clothmakers will be constrained in any way that shall seem best to the King and his council. And this ordinance on new apparel shall take effect at the next Candlemas.[1]

from Jean Froissart, *Chronicle* (late fourteenth century), Account of a Sermon by John Ball

There was a foolish priest in the county of Kent called John Ball, who, for his foolish words, had been three times in the Archbishop of Canterbury's prison; for this priest used oftentimes, on the Sundays after Mass, when the people were going out of the minster,[2] to go into the cloister[3] and preach, and made the people to assemble about him, and would say thus, "Ah, ye good people, things are not going well in England, nor shall they do so till everything be common, and till there be no villeins[4] nor gentlemen, but we be all united together, and the lords be no greater masters than we be. What have we deserved, or why should we be kept thus in serfdom? We be all come from one father and one mother, Adam and Eve; whereby can they say or show that they be greater lords than we be, except that they cause us to earn and labor for what they spend? They are clothed in velvet and camlet furred with gris,[5] and we be vestured with poor cloth; they have their wines, spices, and good bread, and we have the drawing out of the chaff and drink water; they dwell in fair houses and we have the pain and travail, rain and wind in the fields; and by what cometh of our labors they keep and maintain their estates: we be called their bondmen, and unless we readily do them service, we be beaten; and we have no sovereign to whom we may complain, nor that will hear us and do us right. Let us go to the King—he is young—and show him what serfage we be in, and show him how we will have it otherwise, or else we will provide us with some remedy, either by fairness or otherwise."[6] Thus John Ball said on Sundays, when the people issued out of the churches in the villages; wherefore many of the lowly people loved him, and said how he said truth; and so they would murmur one with another in the fields and in the ways as they went together, affirming how John Ball spoke the truth.

---

[1] *Candlemas* The Feast of the Purification of the Virgin Mary, celebrated on 2 February.

[2] *minster* Cathedral church.

[3] *cloister* Here, covered walkway connecting buildings of the Cathedral.

[4] *villeins* Peasants subject to lords or attached to manors.

[5] *camlet furred with gris* Fabric imported from the East and trimmed with gray fur.

[6] *the King … fairness or otherwise* The young King mentioned here is Richard II, who had come to the throne at the age of only ten years old, after the death of his grandfather, Edward III, in 1377; for the first three years of his kingship the kingdom was actually ruled by a council of nobles. This problematic royal transition contributed to the general uncertainties and tensions in England.

John Ball, Letter to the Common People of Essex, 1381[1]

Johan Schep[2] sometime[3] Seynte Marie's priest of York[4] and now of Colchester, greeteth wel Johan Nameless, and Johan the Millere, and Johon Cartere, and biddeth them that they be ware of gyle in borough,[5] and stondeth togidre in God's name, and biddeth Peres Ploughman[6] go to his werk, and chastise wel Hobbe the Robbere,[7] and taketh with you Johan Trewman, and alle his felowes, and no mo,[8] and look schappe you to one head,[9] and no mo.

Johan the Millere hath ygrounde smal,°   *ground finely*
    smal, smal;
The Kyng's Sone of Hevene schal paye for al.
Be ware or° ye be woe;   *before*
Knoweth your freend fro your foe;
Haveth ynow and seith 'Hoo';[10]
And do wel and bettre,[11] and fleeth sinne,
And seeketh peace, and hold you therinne;

And so biddeth Johan Trewman and alle his felowes.

---

[1] *John Ball's Letter … 1381* Text has been modernized for *The Broadview Anthology* from *Fourteenth Century Verse and Prose*, ed. Kenneth Sisam (Oxford: Clarendon, 1970).

[2] *Johan Schep* Alias for John Ball; priests were often referred to as shepherds. The various Johns named in this letter are probably allegorical aliases for figures involved in the revolt.

[3] *sometime* Formerly.

[4] *Seynte Marie's priest of York* Priest of Saint Mary's Church in New York.

[5] *gyle in borough* Trickery in town.

[6] *Peres Ploughman* This is a reference to William Langland's poem *Piers Plowman*, which contains sharp criticism of abuses by both ecclesiastical and secular powers.

[7] *Hobbe the Robbere* This figure appears in *Piers Plowman*, Passus 5.1.463; "Hobbe" is a nickname for Robert.

[8] *mo* More.

[9] *look schappe you to one head* Be sure that you follow one head, i.e., one leader.

[10] *Haveth … 'Hoo'* I.e., have what you need and say, "Enough."

[11] *do wel and bettre* Dowel and Dobet (Do-Well and Do-Better) are characters in *Piers Plowman*.

from Henry Knighton, *Chronicle* (1378–96)

In the year 1381, the second of the reign of King Richard II, during the month of May … that impious band began to assemble from Kent, from Surrey, and from many other surrounding places. Apprentices also, leaving their masters, rushed to join these. And so they gathered on Blackheath, where, forgetting themselves in their multitude, and neither contented with their former cause nor appeased by smaller crimes, they unmercifully planned greater and worse evils and determined not to desist from their wicked undertaking until they should have entirely extirpated the nobles and great men of the kingdom.

So at first they directed their course of iniquity to a certain town of the Archbishop of Canterbury called Maidstone, in which there was a jail of the said Archbishop, and in the said jail was a certain John Ball, a chaplain who was considered among the laity to be a very famous preacher; many times in the past he had foolishly spread abroad the word of God, by mixing tares with wheat, too pleasing to the laity and extremely dangerous to the liberty of ecclesiastical law and order, execrably introducing into the Church of Christ many errors among the clergy and laymen. For this reason he had been tried as a clerk and convicted in accordance with the law, being seized and assigned to this same jail for his permanent abiding place. On [June 12,] the Wednesday before the Feast of the Consecration, they came into Surrey to the jail of the King at Marshalsea, where they broke the jail without delay, forcing all imprisoned there to come with them to help them; and whomsoever they met, whether pilgrims or others of whatever condition, they forced to go with them.

On [June 14,] the Friday following the Feast of the Consecration, they came over the bridge to London; here no one resisted them, although, as was said, the citizens of London knew of their advance a long time before; and so they directed their way to the Tower where the King was surrounded by a great throng of knights, esquires, and others. It was said that there were in the Tower about one hundred and fifty knights together with one hundred and eighty others. …

John Leg and a certain John, a Minorite, a man active in warlike deeds, skilled in natural sciences, an intimate friend of Lord John, duke of Lancaster, hastened with three others to the Tower for refuge, intending to hide themselves under the wings of the King. The people had determined to kill the Archbishop and the others above mentioned with him; for this reason they came to this place, and afterwards they fulfilled their vows. The King, however, desired to free the Archbishop and his friends from the jaws of the wolves, so he sent to the people a command to assemble outside the city, at a place called Mile End, in order to speak with the King and to treat with him concerning their designs. The soldiers who were to go forward, consumed with folly, lost heart, and gave up, on the way, their boldness of purpose. Nor did they dare to advance but, unfortunately, struck as they were by fear, like women, kept themselves within the Tower.

But the King advanced to the assigned place, while many of the wicked mob kept following him. . . . More, however, remained where they were. When the others had come to the King they complained that they had been seriously oppressed by many hardships and that their condition of servitude was unbearable, and that they neither could nor would endure it longer. The King, for the sake of peace, and on account of the violence of the times, yielding to their petition, granted to them a charter with the great seal, to the effect that all men in the kingdom of England should be free and of free condition, and should remain both for themselves and their heirs free from all kinds of servitude and villeinage forever. This charter was rejected and decided to be null and void by the King and the great men of the kingdom in the Parliament held at Westminster in the same year, after the Feast of St. Michael.

While these things were going on, behold those degenerate sons, who still remained, summoned their father the Archbishop with his above-mentioned friends without any force or attack, without sword or arrow, or any other form of compulsion, but only with force of threats and excited outcries, inviting those men to death. But they did not cry out against it for themselves, nor resist, but, as sheep before the shearers, going forth barefooted with uncovered heads, ungirt, they offered themselves freely to an undeserved death, just as if they had deserved this punishment for some murder or theft. And so, alas! before the King returned, seven were killed at Tower Hill, two of them lights of the kingdom, the worthy with the unworthy. John Leg and his three associates were the cause of this irreparable loss. Their heads were fastened on spears and sticks in order that they might be told from the rest. . . .

Whatever representatives of the law they found or whatever men served the kingdom in a judicial capacity, these they slew without delay.

On the following day, which was Saturday, they gathered in Smithfield, where there came to them in the morning the King, who although only a youth in years yet was in wisdom already well versed. Their leader, whose real name was Wat Tyler, approached him; already they were calling him by the other name of Jack Straw. He kept close to the King, addressing him for the rest. He carried in his hand an unsheathed weapon which they call a dagger, and, as if in childish play, kept tossing it from one hand to the other in order that he might seize the opportunity, if the King should refuse his requests, to strike the King suddenly (as was commonly believed); and from this thing the greatest fear arose among those about the King as to what might be the outcome.

They begged from the King that all the warrens, well waters, park, and wood, should be common to all, so that a poor man as well as a rich should be able freely to hunt animals everywhere in the kingdom—in the streams, in the fish ponds, in the woods, and in the forest; and that he might be free to chase the hare in the fields, and that he might do these things and others like them without objection. When the King hesitated about granting this concession Jack Straw came nearer, and, speaking threatening words, seized with his hand the bridle of the horse of the King very daringly. When John de Walworth, a citizen of London, saw this, thinking that death threatened the King, he seized a sword and pierced Jack Straw in the neck. Seeing this, another soldier, by name Radulf Standyche, pierced his side with another sword. He sank back, slowly letting go with his hands and feet, and then died. A great cry and much mourning arose: "Our leader is slain." When this dead man had been meanly dragged along by the hands and feet into the church of St. Bartholomew, which was near by, many withdrew from the band, and, vanishing, betook themselves to flight, to the number it is believed of ten thousand. . . .

After these things had happened and quiet had been restored, the time came when the King caused the offenders to be punished. So Lord Robert Tresillian, one of the judges, was sent by order of the King to inquire into the uprisings against the peace and to punish the guilty. Wherever he came he spared no one, but caused great slaughter. …

For whoever was accused before him in this said cause, whether justly or as a matter of spite, he immediately passed upon him the sentence of death. He ordered some to be beheaded, others to be hanged, still others to be dragged through the city and hanged in four different parts thereof; others to be disemboweled, and the entrails to be burned before them while they were still alive, and afterwards to be decapitated, quartered, and hanged in four parts of the city according to the greatness of the crime and its desert. John Ball was captured at Coventry and led to St. Albans, where, by order of the King, he was drawn and hanged, then quartered, and his quarters sent to four different places.

From a fifteenth-century manuscript of Froissart's *Chronicle*, "The Death of Wat Tyler."

SIR ORFEO

c. 1325

The Breton *lai* is a poetic form that evolved in England and France during the twelfth century. Originally composed in Anglo-Norman, these relatively brief poems ostensibly originated in the oral legends of Brittany. The Breton *lais* generally retain the themes of longer chivalric poems—tales of adventure and noble love often colored by the supernatural—but their overall structure is much more concise and they are notable for the ways in which they often call attention to their own supposed origins in Breton stories. It is possible that the recitation of the tales was accompanied by music—the *lai* proper—and that (as in *Sir Orfeo*) the narrative originally served as something like a frame for a musical performance.

Eventually, English writers began to produce these works in their own language; *Sir Orfeo* is considered by many critics to be one of the best examples of the Breton *lai* in any language. As with many medieval English poems, the author of *Sir Orfeo* is unknown; the poem shows some signs of having been translated from a French original. The poem exists in three separate manuscripts, the earliest of which dates from the second quarter of the fourteenth century, the other two from the fifteenth century.

Sir Orfeo consists of a mixture of classical, romance, and Celtic elements. Its plot structure and main characters mirror those of the Greek myth of Orpheus and Eurydice, familiar to the Middle Ages particularly through versions in Ovid and Virgil. But the setting has been "domesticated" (the ancient city of Thrace is identified with Winchester) and many of the story's most distinctive plot elements have been altered to align it with romance rather than with classical myth. Whereas in the classical version Orpheus attempts to rescue Eurydice from Hades, the land of the dead, in this English version Sir Orfeo's task is to rescue Heurodis from the land of the fairies. The queen is not dead but merely "taken"; the king's descent into the wilderness precedes rather than follows his attempted rescue of the queen. Most strikingly, while the classical versions end in tragedy and loss—as he leads Eurydice from Hades, Orpheus glances back at her and thereby loses her forever—*Sir Orfeo* ends in reunion, recuperation, and recovery. The couple are reunited, the king regains his kingdom, and all live happily ever after. We cannot say with any certainty whether the author knowingly replaced the tragic ending of the classical version with this happier one, or why he did so, or whether readers of the story would have recognized or appreciated such a striking reversal. But these puzzling uncertainties about sources and form do not detract from the skill of the storytelling, in which even the most familiar plot devices are presented with precision, grace, and admirable narrative economy.

The poem was influential not only in its time (Chaucer's *Franklin's Tale* and *Wife of Bath's Tale* drew on some of the story material of *Sir Orfeo*) but also in the twentieth century; J.R.R. Tolkien studied the poem extensively and may well have been influenced by it in writing some portions of *The Lord of the Rings*.

⌘⌘

Sir Orfeo [1]

We redeth oft and findeth y-write,°   *written*
  And this clerkes° wele it wite,°   *scholars / know*
Layes that ben in harping°   *are in song*
Ben y-founde of ferli thing:°   *composed about marvelous things*
5 Sum bethe of wer° and sum of wo,°   *some are of war / grief*
And sum of joie° and mirthe also,   *gaiety*
And sum of trecherie and of gile,°   *deceit (or, trickery)*
Of old aventours° that fel while;°   *adventures / happened once*
And sum of bourdes° and ribaudy,°   *jokes / ribaldry*
10 And mani ther beth of fairy. [2]
Of al thinges that men seth,°   *relate*
Mest o° love, forsothe,° they beth.   *most of / in truth*
In Breteyne this° layes were wrought,°   *Brittany these / made*
First y-founde° and forth y-brought,°   *composed / produced*
15 Of aventours that fel bi dayes,°   *happened in olden times*
Wherof Bretouns maked her° layes.   *their*
When kinges might our y-here°   *anywhere hear*
Of ani mervailes° that ther were,   *marvels*
Thai token° an harp in gle° and game   *took / minstrelsy*
20 And maked a lay and gaf° it name.   *gave*
Now of this aventours that weren y-falle°   *have happened*
Y° can tel sum, ac° nought alle.   *I / but*
Ac herkneth,° lordinges that ben trewe,   *but listen*
Ichil° you telle of "Sir Orfewe."   *I will*
25 Orfeo mest° of ani thing   *most*
Lovede the gle° of harping. [3]   *glee or music*
Siker° was everi gode° harpour   *sure / good*
Of him to have miche° honour.   *much*
Himself he lerned forto° harp,   *he taught himself to*
30 And leyd° theron his wittes scharp;   *applied*
He lerned so ther nothing° was   *in no way*
A better harpour in no plas.°   *anywhere*
In al the warld was no man bore°   *born*
That ones° Orfeo sat before—   *once*
35 And° he might° of his harping here—   *if / could*

Bot he schuld thenche° that he were   *think*
In on° of the joies of Paradis,   *one*
Swiche melody in his harping is.
  Orfeo was a king,
40 In Inglond an heighe° lording,   *high*
A stalworth man and hardi bo;°   *brave as well*
Large° and curteys [4] he was also.   *generous*
His fader was comen° of King Pluto,   *descended from*
And his moder of King Juno, [5]
45 That sum time° were as godes   *who once*
    yhold°   *considered to be gods*
For aventours that thai dede° and told.   *did*
This king sojournd° in Traciens,   *dwelled*
That was a cité of noble defens—°   *fortifications*
For Winchester was cleped° tho°   *called / then*
50 Traciens, [6] withouten no.°   *denial*
  The king hadde a quen of priis°   *queen of excellence*
That was y-cleped° Dame Heurodis,   *called*
The fairest levedi, for the nones,°   *lady indeed*
That might gon on° bodi and bones,   *walk about in*
55 Ful of love and godenisse—°   *goodness*
Ac no man may telle hir fairnise.°   *beauty*

  Bifel° so in the comessing° of   *it happened / beginning*
  May
When miri° and hot is the day,   *merry (pleasant)*
And oway° beth winter schours,   *away*
60 And everi feld° is ful of flours,   *field*
And blosme breme° on everi bough   *blossoms bright*
Over al wexeth° miri anought,°   *everywhere grow / enough*
  This ich° quen, Dame Heurodis   *same*
Tok to° maidens of priis,   *two*
65 And went in an undrentide°   *late morning*
To play° bi an orchardside,   *enjoy themselves*
To se the floures sprede and spring
And to here the foules° sing.   *birds*
Thai sett hem° doun al thre   *sat themselves*

---

[1] *Sir Orfeo* For this anthology the text used is that prepared by Anne Laskaya and Eve Salisbury for their edition (published by Medieval Institute Publications, Kalamazoo).

[2] *fairy* The word "fairy" here and elsewhere in the poem means "land of the fays" or the "fays" themselves. The word "fay" comes from Old French "fée" derived from the Latin "fata," "the Fates."

[3] *Orfeo ... harping* Orfeo's name had a long tradition of being associated with music, art, and the power of eloquence; his name had been understood to mean "beautiful voice."

[4] *curteys* In medieval texts this word carries much greater weight than today's "courteous" or "polite"; it connotes courtly, elite, valuable, and cultured behavior as well as generosity.

[5] *King Pluto ... King Juno* Pluto was, according to classical myth, god of the underworld. Juno was a goddess, the wife of Jupiter, not a king.

[6] *This king ... Traciens* Because the poet has set the poem in England, classical and medieval places are conflated; hence, Winchester, the old capital, becomes Thrace.

70   Under a fair ympe-tre,° *grafted tree*
      And wel sone° this fair quene *very quickly*
      Fel on slepe° opon the grene. *asleep*
      The maidens durst° hir nought awake, *dared*
      Bot lete hir ligge° and rest take. *let her lie*
75   So sche slepe til after none,° *noon*
      That undertide° was al y-done.°[1] *until midday / past*
      Ac, as sone as sche gan° awake, *began (to)*
      Sche crid, and lothli bere gan make;° *terrible outcry made*
      Sche froted° hir honden° and hir fete, *rubbed / hands*
80   And crached hir visage°—it bled
          wete—° *scratched her face / profusely*
      Hir riche robe hye al to-rett° *she tore all to pieces*
      And was reveyd° out of hir wit. *driven*
      The two maidens hir biside
      No durst with hir no leng° abide, *longer*
85   Bot ourn° to the palays ful right° *ran / immediately*
      And told bothe squier and knight
      That her° quen awede wold,° *their / was going mad*
      And bad° hem go and hir at-hold.° *bade / seize*
      Knightes urn° and levedis also, *ran*
90   Damisels sexti and mo.° *numbering sixty and more*
      In the orchard to the quen hye come,° *they came*
      And her up in her armes nome,° *their arms took*
      And brought hir to bed atte last,
      And held hir there fine fast.° *very securely*
95   Ac ever she held in o° cri *persisted in one*
      And wold° up and owy.° *wished (to go) / away*
      When Orfeo herd° that tiding *heard*
      Never him nas wers for
          nothing.° *had he been as grieved by anything*
      He come with knightes tene° *ten*
100   To chaumber, right bifor the quene,
      And bi-held,° and seyd with grete pité,° *beheld her / sorrow*
      "O lef liif,° what is te,° *dear life / with you*
      That° ever yete° hast ben so stille° *who / yet / calm*
      And° now gredest wonder schille?° *but / cries strangely shrilly*
105   Thy bodi, that was so white y-core,° *exquisitely*
      With thine nailes is all to-tore.° *torn to pieces*
      Allas! thy rode,° that was so red, *face*
      Is al wan, as° thou were ded *pale as (if)*
      And also thine fingres smale° *slender*
110   Beth al blodi and al pale.
      Allas! thy lovesum eyyen to° *lovely two eyes*

      Loketh so° man doth on his fo!° *as / foe*
      A, dame, ich biseche,° merci! *I beg you*
      Lete ben° al this reweful° cri, *let be / pitiful*
115   And tel me what the is,° and
          hou,° *what's bothering you / how*
      And what thing may the help now."
      Tho° lay sche stille atte last *then*
      And gan to wepe swithe fast,° *very hard*
      And seyd thus the King to:
120   "Allas, mi lord, Sir Orfeo!
      Sethen° we first togider were, *since*
      Ones wroth never we
          nere;° *we were never once angry with each other*
      Bot ever ich have yloved the
      As mi liif and so thou me;
125   Ac now we mot delen ato;° *must separate*
      Do thi best, for y mot° go." *I must*
      "Allas!" quath he, "forlorn icham!° *I am utterly lost*
      Whider wiltow° go, and to wham?° *where will you / whom*
      Whider thou gost, ichil° with the, *I will go*
130   And whider y go, thou schalt with me."[2]
      "Nay, nay, Sir, that nought nis!° *cannot be*
      Ichil the telle al hou° it is: *all how*
      As ich lay this undertide
      And slepe under our orchardside,
135   Ther come to me to fair knightes,
      Wele y-armed al to rightes,° *quite properly*
      And bad me comen an heighing° *in haste*
      And speke with her lord the king.
      And ich answerd at° wordes bold, *with*
140   Y durst nought, no y nold.° *dared not, nor did I want to*
      Thai priked oyain as thai might drive;[3]
      Tho° com her king, also blive,° *then / as quickly*
      With an hundred knightes and mo,
      And damisels an hundred also,
145   Al on snowe-white stedes;
      As white as milke were her wedes.°[4] *their garments*
      Y no seighe° never yete bifore *saw*

---

[1] *So sche slepe … al y-done* Midday, or noon, was considered a perilous time in both folktales and Christian literature.

[2] *Whider … with me* Cf. Ruth 1.16: "Wither thou goest I will go, and where thou lodgest I will lodge." Although Ruth speaks these words not to her husband but to her mother-in-law, Naomi, the lines were frequently associated with marriage.

[3] *Thai … drive* They rode back again as fast as they could.

[4] *Al … her wedes* The white horse and the white clothes worn by those who escort or meet the protagonists at the boundary of the Otherworld are common in romance and dream vision literature.

So fair creatours y-core.
The king hadde a croun on hed;
150 It nas of silver, no of gold red,
Ac it was of a precious ston—
As bright as the sonne it schon.
And as son as he to me cam,
Wold ich, nold ich, he me
nam,°   *whether I wished or not he took me*
155 And made me with him ride
Opon a palfray° bi his side;   *horse*
And brought me to his palays,
Wele atird° in ich ways,°   *adorned / every way*
And schewed me castels and tours,°   *towers*
160 Rivers, forestes, frith with flours,°   *woods with flowers*
And his riche stedes ichon.°   *gorgeous steeds each one*
And sethen° me brought oyain hom°*afterwards / back home*
Into our owhen° orchard,   *own*
And said to me thus afterward,
165 "Loke, dame, tomorwe thatow° be   *that you*
Right here under this ympe-tre,
And than thou schalt with ous° go   *us*
And live with ous evermo.
And yif thou makest ous y-let,°   *a hindrance for us*
170 Whar° thou be, thou worst y-fet,°   *wherever / will be fetched*
And totore° thine limes° al   *torn apart / limbs*
That nothing help the no schal;
And thei thou best so totorn,°   *though (even if) you are so torn*
Yete thou worst with ous y-born."°   *will be carried with us*

175   When King Orfeo herd this cas,°   *matter*
"O we!"° quath he, "Allas, allas!   *woe*
Lever me were to lete° mi liif   *I'd rather lose*
Than thus to lese° the quen, mi wiif!"   *lose*
He asked conseyl at ich man,°   *advice from each person*
180 Ac no man him help no can.
Amorwe° the undertide is come   *the next day*
And Orfeo hath his armes y-nome,°   *taken*
And wele ten hundred knightes with him,
Ich y-armed, stout° and grim;°   *strong / fierce*
185 And with the quen wenten he
Right unto that ympe-tre.

Thai made scheltrom[1] in ich a side
And sayd thai wold there abide
And dye° ther everichon,°   *die / everyone*
190 Er° the quen schuld fram° hem gon.   *before / from*
Ac yete amiddes hem ful right° *yet amidst them straightaway*
The quen was oway y-twight,°   *snatched*
With fairi° forth y-nome.°   *enchantment / taken*
Men wist never° wher sche was bicome.° *never knew / gone*
195 Tho° was ther criing, wepe and wo!   *then*
The king into his chaumber is go,°   *went*
And oft swoned° opon the ston,° *swooned / stone (i.e., floor)*
And made swiche diol° and swiche mon° *such lament / moan*
That neighe° his liif was y-spent—.°   *almost / ended*
200 Ther was non amendement.°   *no remedy (for it)*
He cleped° togider his barouns,   *called*
Erls, lordes of renouns,
And when thai al y-comen were,
"Lordinges," he said, "bifor you here
205 Ich ordainy° min heighe steward[2]   *I ordain*
To wite° mi kingdom afterward;°   *rule / henceforth*
In mi stede° ben he schal   *place*
To kepe mi londes overal.
For now ichave° mi quen y-lore,°   *I have / lost*
210 The fairest levedi that ever was bore,
Never eft y nil no woman
se.°   *never again will I see another woman*
Into wildernes ichil te°   *I will go*
And live ther evermore
With wilde bestes in holtes hore;°   *woods grey*
215 And when ye understond that y be spent,°   *dead*
Make you than a parlement,
And chese° you a newe king.   *choose*
Now doth° your best with al mi thing."°   *do / affairs*

    Tho was ther wepeing in the halle
220 And grete cri among hem alle;
Unnethe° might old or yong°   *hardly / young*
For wepeing speke a word with tong.
Thai kneled adoun al y-fere°   *together*

---

[1] *scheltrom* From the OE "scyld-truma," a tribal battle formation in which warriors used their shields to create a wall of defense.

[2] *steward* High court official from the nobility.

And praid° him, yif his wille were,   *prayed*
That he no schuld nought fram hem go.
"Do way!"° quath he, "It schal be so!"   *enough!*
Al his kingdom he forsoke;
Bot° a sclavin° on him he toke.[1]   *only / pilgrim's mantle*
He no hadde kirtel no hode,°   *had neither tunic nor hood*
Schert,° ne no nother gode,°   *shirt / goods*
Bot his harp he tok algate°   *at any rate*
And dede him barfot° out atte gate;   *passed barefoot*
No man most° with him go.   *might*
O way! What ther was wepe and wo,
When he that hadde ben king with croun
Went so poverlich out of
    toun!°   *in such poverty out of his town*
Thurth° wode and over heth°   *through / heath*
Into the wildernes he geth.°   *goes*
Nothing he fint° that him° is ays,°   *finds / for him / comfort*
Bot ever he liveth in gret malais.°   *distress*
He that hadde y-werd the fowe and
    griis,°   *worn the variegated and grey fur*
And on bed the purper biis,°   *purple linen*
Now on hard hethe he lith,°   *lies*
With leves and gresse he him writh.°   *covers himself*
He that hadde had castels and tours,
River, forest, frith with flours,
Now, thei it comenci° to snewe° and
    frese,°   *although it begins / snow / freeze*
This king mot° make his bed in mese.°   *must / moss*
He that had y-had knightes of priis
Bifor him kneland,° and levedis,   *kneeling*
Now seth he nothing that him liketh,
Bot wilde wormes° bi him striketh.°   *snakes / glide*
He that had y-had plenté
Of mete and drink, of ich deynté,°   *delicacy*
Now may he al day digge° and wrote°   *dig / grub*
Er he finde his fille of rote.°   *roots*
In somer he liveth bi wild frut,°   *fruit*
And berien bot gode lite;°   *berries of little worth*
In winter may he nothing finde
Bot rote, grases, and the rinde.°   *bark*

Al his bodi was oway dwine°   *away dwindled*
For missays,° and al to-chine.°   *hardship / chapped*
Lord! who may telle the sore°   *sorrow*
This king sufferd ten yere and more?
His here° of his berd,° blac and rowe,°   *hair / beard / rough*
To his girdel-stede° was growe.   *waist*
His harp, whereon was al his gle,°   *pleasure*
He hidde in an holwe° tre;   *hollow*
And when the weder° was clere and bright,   *weather*
He toke his harp to him wel right
And harped° at his owhen wille.°   *played / own desire*
Into alle the wode the soun gan
    schille,°   *sound began to resound*
That alle the wilde bestes that ther beth
For joie abouten him thai teth,°   *gathered*
And alle the foules° that ther were   *birds*
Come and sete° on ich a brere°   *sat / every briar*
To here his harping a-fine—
So miche° melody was therin;   *much*
And when he his harping lete wold,°   *would leave off*
No best° bi him abide nold.°[2]   *beast / would remain*
    He might se him bisides,°   *nearby*
Oft in hot undertides,
The king o fairy with his rout°   *company*
Com to hunt him al about
With dim cri and bloweing,°   *blowing (of horns)*
And houndes also with him berking;°   *barking*
Ac no best thai no nome,°   *but they took no beast (game)*
No never he nist whider they
    bicome.°   *nor did he ever know where they went*
And other while° he might him se   *at other times*
As a gret ost° bi him te,°   *army / went*
Wele atourned,° ten hundred knightes,   *equipped*
Ich y-armed to his rightes,°   *all properly armed*
Of cuntenaunce° stout and fers,   *appearance*
With mani desplaid° baners,   *unfurled*
And ich his swerd y-drawe hold—
Ac never he nist whider° thai
    wold.°   *knew not whither / went*
And otherwile he seighe° other thing: *saw*
Knightes and levedis com daunceing

---

[1] *Al his kingdom … he toke* Among scholars, considerable disagreement surrounds Orfeo's exile. It has been seen as an act of despair, atonement, or spiritual retreat, as part of a process of initiation for Orfeo, as an expression of the great love (or too great a love) Orfeo has for Heurodis.

---

[2] *He toke his harp … abide nold* The tradition of harping as a way of "taming" the animals has roots in pre-Christian material as well as in the classical myth of Orpheus and in the Biblical story of David.

	In queynt° atire, gisely,°	*elegant / skilfully*
300	Queynt pas° and softly;	*graceful steps*
	Tabours and trunpes yede° hem bi,	*drums and trumpets went*
	And al maner menstraci.°	*sorts of minstrelsy*

	And on a day° he seighe him biside	*on a certain day*
	Sexti° levedis on hors ride,	*sixty*
305	Gentil and jolif as brid on ris;°	*lively as a bird on bough*
	Nought o man amonges hem ther nis;°	*not a single man was with them*
	And ich a faucoun on hond bere,°	*each a falcon on her hand bore*
	And riden on haukin bi o° rivere.	*a-hawking by a*
	Of game thai founde wel gode haunt—°	*great plenty*
310	Maulardes,° hayroun,° and cormeraunt;°	*mallards / heron / cormorant*
	The foules of the water ariseth,	
	The faucouns hem wele deviseth;°	*marked*
	Ich faucoun his pray slough—°	*prey killed*
	That seigh Orfeo, and lough:°	*laughed*
315	"Parfay!"° quath he, "ther is fair game;	*by my faith*
	Thider ichil,° bi Godes name;	*I'll go*
	Ich was y-won swiche werk to se!"[1]	
	He aros, and thider gan te.°	*began to approach*
	To a levedi he was y-come,	
320	Biheld, and hath wele undernome,°	*perceived*
	And seth bi al thing that it is	
	His owhen quen, Dam Heurodis.	
	Yern° he biheld hir, and sche him eke,°	*eagerly / also*
	Ac noither° to other a word no speke;	*neither*
325	For messais° that sche on him seighe,	*sadness*
	That° had ben so riche and so heighe;	*who*
	The teres fel out of her eighe.°	*eye*
	The other levedis this y-seighe	
	And maked hir oway to ride—	
330	Sche most with him no lenger abide.	
	"Allas!" quath he, "now me is wo!"	
	Whi nil° deth now me slo?°	*will not / slay*
	Allas, wreche, that y no might	
	Dye now after this sight!	
335	Allas! to long last° mi liif,	*too long lasts*
	When y no dar nought with mi wiif,	
	No hye° to me, o° word speke.	*nor she / one*
	Allas! Whi nil min hert breke!	

	Parfay!" quath he, "tide wat bitide,°	*come what may*
340	Whiderso this° levedis ride,	*wherever these*
	The selve° way ichil streche—°	*same / hasten*
	Of liif no° deth me no reche."°	*nor / I do not care*
	His sclavain he dede on also spac°	*pilgrim's gown he put on quickly*
	And henge his harp opon his bac,	
345	And had wel gode wil to gon—°	*great desire to go*
	He no spard° noither stub° no ston.	*avoided / stump*
	In at a roche° the levedis rideth,	*Into a rock*
	And he after, and nought abideth.	
	When he was in the roche y-go,°	*gone*
350	Wele thre mile other mo,	
	He com into a fair cuntray°	*country*
	As bright so sonne on somers° day,	*as sun on summer's*
	Smothe and plain° and al grene—	*smooth and level*
	Hille no dale nas ther non y-sene.°	*was not to be seen*
355	Amidde the lond a castel he sighe,	
	Riche and real° and wonder heighe.°	*royal / wondrously high*
	Al the utmast wal°	*all of the outermost wall*
	Was clere and schine° as cristal;	*bright*
	An hundred tours ther were about,	
360	Degiselich and bataild stout.[2]	
	The butras° com out of the diche°	*buttresses / moat*
	Of rede gold y-arched riche.	
	The vousour° was avowed° al	*vaulting / adorned*
	Of ich maner divers aumal.°	*with every kind of enamel*
365	Within ther wer wide wones,°	*spacious dwellings*
	Al of precious stones;	
	The werst piler on to biholde	
	Was al of burnist° gold.	*burnished*
	Al that lond was ever° light,	*always*
370	For when it schuld be therk° and night,	*dark*
	The riche stones light gonne°	*stone's light shone*
	As bright as doth at none° the sonne.	*noon*
	No man may telle, no thenche° in thought,	*nor think*
	The riche° werk that ther was wrought.°	*exquisite / made (done)*
375	Bi al thing him think° that it is	*it seems to him*
	The proude court of Paradis.	
	In this castel the levedis alight;°	*dismounted*
	He wold in after, yif° he might.	*wished to enter if*
	Orfeo knokketh atte gate;	
380	The porter was redi therate	
	And asked what he wold hav y-do.°	*wanted (to do)*

---

[1] *Ich … se!* I was accustomed to seeing such sport!

[2] *Degiselich and bataild stout* Wonderful with strong battlements.

"Parfay!" quath he, "icham° a minstrel, lo!   *I am*
To solas° thi lord with mi gle,°   *entertain / minstrelsy*
Yif his swete wille be."
385   The porter undede° the gate anon   *undid*
And lete him into the castel gon.

       Than he gan bihold about al,°   *look all around*
And seighe liggeand° within the wal   *remaining, living*
Of folk that were thider y-brought
390   And thought dede, and nare
          nought.°   *believed to be dead, but were not*
Sum stode° withouten hade,°   *stood / head*
And sum non armes nade,°   *had no arms*
And sum thurth° the bodi hadde wounde,   *through*
And sum lay wode,° y-bounde,   *mad*
395   And sum armed on hors sete,°   *sat*
And sum astrangled as thai ete;°   *they ate*
And sum were in water adreynt,°   *drowned*
And sum with fire al forschreynt.°   *shriveled*
Wives ther lay on childe bedde,
400   Sum ded and sum awedde,°   *driven mad*
And wonder fele° ther lay bisides   *wondrous many*
Right as° thai slepe her° undertides;   *just as / their*
Eche was thus in this warld y-nome,°   *taken*
With fairi thider y-come.°   *enchantment brought there*
405   Ther he seighe his owhen wiif,
Dame Heurodis, his lef liif,°   *dear life*
Slepe under an ympe-tre—
Bi her clothes he knewe that it was he.°   *she*
       And when he hadde bihold this mervails
          alle,°   *all these marvels*
410   He went into the kinges halle.
Than seighe he ther a semly° sight,   *fair*
A tabernacle blisseful° and bright,   *canopy beautiful*
Therin her maister king sete
And her quen, fair and swete.
415   Her crounes, her clothes schine so bright
That unnethe° bihold he him might.   *scarcely*
When he hadde biholden al that thing,
He kneled adoun bifor the king:
"O lord," he seyd, "yif it thi wille were,
420   Mi menstraci thou schust y-here."°   *should hear*
The king answered, "What man artow,°   *are you*
That art hider y-comen now?
Ich, no non° that is with me,   *neither I, nor no one*

No sent never after the.°   *you*
425   Sethen° that ich here regni° gan,   *since / reign*
Y no fond never so folehardi° man   *foolhardy*
That hider to ous durst wende°   *to us dared come*
Bot that ic him wald ofsende."[1]
"Lord," quath he, "trowe° ful wel,   *believe*
430   Y nam bot a pover menstrel;
And, sir, it is the maner of ous
To seche mani° a lordes hous—   *seek many*
Thei° we nought welcom no be,   *although (even if)*
Yete we mot proferi° forth our gle."   *must offer*

435   Bifor the king he sat adoun
And tok his harp so miri° of soun,°   *merry / sound*
And trempeth° his harp, as he wele
          can,°   *tunes / knows well how to do*
And blisseful notes he ther gan,°   *began*
That al that in the palays were
440   Com to him forto here,°   *to listen*
And liggeth° adoun to his fete—   *lie*
Hem thenketh° his melody so swete.   *they think*
The king herkneth° and sitt ful stille;°   *listens / sits quietly*
To here his° gle he° hath gode
          wille.   *his (Orfeo's) / he (the king)*
445   Gode bourde° he hadde of his gle;°   *great pleasure / songs*
The riche quen also hadde he.°   *she*
When he hadde stint° his harping,   *stopped*
Than seyd to him the king,
"Menstrel, me liketh° wel thi gle.   *pleases me*
450   Now aske of me what it be,°   *whatever you wish*
Largelich° ichil the pay;   *generously*
Now speke, and tow might asay."°   *if you wish to find out*
"Sir," he seyd, "ich bseche the°   *beseech you*
Thatow° woldest give me   *that you*
455   That ich° levedi, bright on ble,°   *same / of complexion*
That slepeth under the ympe-tre."
"Nay!" quath the king, "that nought
          nere!°   *that could never be*
A sori° couple of you it were,   *ill-matched*
For thou art lene, rowe° and blac,   *lean, rough*
460   And sche is lovesum,° withouten lac;°   *beautiful / blemish*
A lothlich° thing it were, forthi,°   *loathly / therefore*
To sen° hir in thi compayni."   *see*
"O sir!" he seyd, "gentil king,

----
[1] *Bot that … ofsende* Unless I wished him summoned.

Yete were it a wele fouler thing°   *much more disgraceful*
465 To here a lesing of° thi mouthe!   *hear a lie from*
So, sir, as ye seyd nouthe,°   *just now*
What ich wold aski,° have y
 schold,°   *wished to ask for / I should*
And nedes° thou most thi word hold."   *by necessity*
The king seyd, "Sethen it is so,
470 Take hir bi the hond and go;
Of° hir ichil thatow be
 blithe."°   *with / I wish that you be happy*
He kneled adoun and thonked him swithe.°   *quickly*
His wiif he tok bi the hond,°   *hand*
And dede° him swithe out of that lond,°   *went / land*
475 And went him out of that thede—°   *country*
Right as he come, the way he yede.°   *went*
So long he hath the way y-nome°   *taken*
To Winchester he is y-come,
That was his owhen cité;
480 Ac no man knewe that it was he.
No forther° than the tounes ende   *further*
For knoweleche no durst he wende,[1]
Bot with a begger, y-bilt ful
 narwe,°   *whose house was very small*
Ther he tok his herbarwe°   *lodging*
485 To him and to° his owhen wiif   *for himself and for*
As a minstrel of pover liif,
And asked tidinges of that lond,
And who the kingdom held in hond.
The pover begger in his cote°   *cottage*
490 Told him everich a grot:°   *every scrap*
Hou her quen was stole owy,°   *away*
Ten yer gon,° with fairy,°   *ago / by magic*
And hou her king en° exile yede,°   *into / went*
But no man nist° in wiche thede;°   *no one knew / country*
495 And how the steward the lond gan hold,
And other mani thinges him told.

 Amorwe, oyain nonetide,°   *the next day, towards noon*
He maked his wiif ther abide;°   *stay there*
The beggers clothes he borwed anon
500 And heng his harp his rigge° opon,   *back*
And went him into that cité
That men might him bihold and se.

Erls and barouns bold,
Buriays° and levedis him gun bihold.   *burgesses (citizens)*
505 "Lo!" thai seyd, "swiche a man!
Hou long the here° hongeth him opan!°   *hair / upon*
Lo! Hou his berd hongeth to his kne!
He is y-clongen also° a tre!"   *gnarled like*
And, as he yede in the strete,
510 With his steward he gan mete,
And loude he° sett on him° a
 crie: *he (Orfeo) / him (the steward)*
"Sir steward!" he seyd, "merci!
Icham° an harpour of hethenisse;°   *I am / from heathendom*
Help me now in this destresse!"
515 The steward seyd, "Com with me, come;
Of that ichave,° thou schalt have some.   *what I have*
Everich gode harpour is welcom me to
For mi lordes love, Sir Orfeo."
 In the castel the steward sat atte mete,°   *table*
520 And mani lording was bi him sete;
Ther were trompours° and tabourers,°   *trumpeters / drummers*
Harpours fele,° and crouders—[2]   *many*
Miche melody thai maked alle.
And Orfeo sat stille in the halle
525 And herkneth; when thai ben al stille,
He toke his harp and tempred schille;°   *tuned it loudly*
The blissefulest° notes he harped there   *most beautiful*
That ever ani man y-herd with ere—
Ich man liked wele his gle.
530 The steward biheld and gan y-se,°   *began to perceive*
And knewe the harp als blive.°   *at once*
"Menstrel!" he seyd, "so mot thou
 thrive,°   *if you wish to thrive*
Where hadestow° this harp, and hou?°   *did you get / how*
Y pray that thou me telle now."
535 "Lord," quath he, "in uncouthe° thede   *unknown*
Thurth a wildernes as y yede,
Ther y founde in a dale
With lyouns a man totorn smale,°   *torn in small pieces*
And wolves him frete° with teth so scharp.   *had devoured*
540 Bi him y fond this ich° harp;   *same*

---

1 *For knoweleche … wende* He did not dare go lest he be recognized.

2 *crouders* "Croud-players." The word probably derives from the Welsh "crwth," a Celtic string instrument which was played with a bow and plucked with the fingers. However, the *MED* refers to this line in *Sir Orfeo* and interprets the word as "one who plays the crowd."

Wele ten yere it is y-go."
"O!" quath the steward, "now me is wo!
That was mi lord, Sir Orfeo!
Allas, wreche, what schal y do,
545 That have swiche a lord y-lore?°   *lost*
A, way° that ich was y-bore!   *O, woe*
That him° was so hard grace
    y-yarked,°   *to him / bitter fortune allotted*
And so vile deth y-marked!"°   *(a) death was ordained*
Adoun he fel aswon° to grounde;   *in a faint*
550 His barouns him tok up in that stounde°   *moment*
And telleth him how it° geth—   *it (the world)*
"It is no bot of mannes
    deth!"   *there is no remedy for man's death!*
  King Orfeo knewe wele bi than
His steward was a trewe man
555 And loved him as he aught to do,
And stont up, and seyt thus, "Lo,
Steward, herkne now this thing:
Yif ich were Orfeo the king,
And hadde y-suffred ful yore°   *very long ago*
560 In wildernisse miche sore,°   *much sorrow*
And hadde ywon mi quen o-wy
Out of the lond of fairy,
And hadde y-brought the levedi hende°   *gracious*
Right here to the tounes ende,
565 And with a begger her in y-nome,°   *had placed her*
And were mi-self hider y-come
Poverlich to the, thus stille,
For to asay° thi gode wille,   *test*
And ich founde the thus trewe,
570 Thou no schust it never rewe.°   *should never regret it*
Sikerlich,° for love or ay,°   *surely / fear*
Thou schust° be king after mi day;   *should*
And yif° thou of mi deth hadest ben
    blithe,°   *but if / happy*

Thou schust have voided, also
    swithe."°   *been banished immediately*
575   Tho all tho that therin
That it was[1] King Orfeo underyete,
And the steward him wele knewe—
Over and over the bord he threwe,°   *overturned the table*
And fel adoun to his° fet;   *his (Sir Orfeo)*
580 So dede everich lord that ther sete,
And all thai seyd at o criing:°   *in one cry*
"Ye beth our lord, sir, and our king!"
Glad thai were of his live;°   *life*
To chaumber thai ladde him als belive°   *led him immediately*
585 And bathed him and schaved his berd,
And tired° him as a king apert;°   *clothed / openly*
And sethen,° with gret processioun,   *afterwards*
Thai brought the quen into the toun
With al maner menstraci—
590 Lord! ther was grete melody!
For joie thai wepe with her eighe
That hem so sounde y-comen seighe.
Now King Orfeo newe coround° is,   *newly crowned*
And his quen, Dame Heurodis,
595 And lived long afterward,
And sethen° was king the steward.   *and after that*
Harpours in Bretaine after than
Herd hou this mervaile bigan,
And made herof° a lay of gode
    likeing,°   *made of it / great delight*
600 And nempned° it after the king.   *named*
That lay "Orfeo" is y-hote;°   *called*
Gode is the lay, swete is the note.
Thus com Sir Orfeo out of his care:°   *sorrow*
God graunt ous alle wele to fare! Amen!

Explicit.°   *the end*
—C. 1325

---

1 *Tho all tho … That it was*   Then all those recognized that it was.

ther clothes he knewe for that he ·
When he hadde biþold þis mirical alle
e went in to þe kinges halle ·
an seye he þer a semly sizt ·
a taber nacle blisseful & brizt ·
er in her maister king sete ·
her quen fair & swete ·
er crounes her clothes schine so brizt ·
at vnneþe biþold he hem mizt ·
hen he hadde biþolden al þat þing ·
e kneled adoun bifor þe king ·
lord he seyd zif it þi wille were ·
mi menstraci zou schust y here ·
e king answerd what man artow ·
at art hider y comen now ·
ch no non þat is wiþ me ·
o sent neuer after þe ·
eþen þat ich here regni gan ·
no fond neuer so fole hardi man ·
at hider to ous durst wende ·
ot þat ich him wald of sende ·
ord quaþ he trowe ful wel ·
nam bot a pouer menstrel ·
sir it is þe maner of ous ·
o seche mani a lordes hous ·
ei we nouzt welcom no be ·
ete we mot proferi forþ our gle

The Auchinleck Manuscript (National Library of Scotland, Advocates' MS. 19.2.1), fol. 302r, the last 26 lines of the first column (lines 408–34).

SIR GAWAIN AND THE GREEN KNIGHT

Little is known about *Sir Gawain and the Green Knight* apart from what the poem itself tells us. Its author is anonymous. The work is preserved in a single manuscript copy that was originally bound up with three other poems, *Pearl*, *Cleanness*, and *Patience*, which are generally regarded as having the same author. Like *Sir Gawain and the Green Knight* they are written in alliterative verse. The collection is known to have belonged to a private library in Yorkshire during the late sixteenth and early seventeenth centuries. It came to light in the nineteenth century, and *Sir Gawain and the Green Knight* was edited and printed for the first time in 1839. By the middle of the twentieth century the great interest and imaginative power of the poem had been generally acknowledged, and had attracted an increasing number of scholarly studies and commentaries.

The poem is written in a regional dialect characteristic of northwestern England at the time of its probable composition during the last quarter of the fourteenth century. That would mean that the *Gawain*-poet was a contemporary of Chaucer, who died in 1400; but even a brief comparison of their work shows how widely they were separated linguistically and culturally.

In the northern country reflected in the wintry landscapes of *Sir Gawain and the Green Knight*, an older literary language seems to have persisted, relatively unmarked by French, a language which the poet associates with the elaborately courtly manners displayed by Gawain and his hostess. In Chaucer a reader may gain the impression that the English and French components of his language have formed a comfortable liaison, so much so that he uses both indifferently and without reserving either for particular tasks. *Sir Gawain and the Green Knight* creates a different impression: that the two elements have not yet reached an accommodation, and that the poet and his audience are sufficiently alive to the nuances of words still novel and alien to their regional culture that French words tend to be used for distinctive purposes.

The poem is composed in a unique stanza form, made up of a varying number of long alliterative lines followed by a "bob and wheel": five short lines rhyming *ababa*, of which the first consists of only two syllables. The number of stressed alliterative words in each long line also varies, the norm being three.

Evidently it suits the poet's purposes to present himself as a simple popular entertainer whose occasional comments to his audience—"I schal telle yow how thay wroght"—and explanatory remarks about incidents in the story—"Wyt ye wel, hit watz worth wele ful hoge"—create an impression of the close relationship that a storyteller must maintain with his listeners. In oral narration such remarks would arise spontaneously, but here they are contrived as part of a deliberate purpose. It is not difficult to understand why the poet should have adopted the manner of an oral tale in a written work. Alliterative poetry is addressed to the ear, not to the eye, and its effects are not fully realized unless what Chaucer called the "rum-ram-ruf" of its pounding consonants is heard. Until displaced by rhyming verse it was also the established form of English poetry, and it seems evident from *Sir Gawain and the Green Knight* that its author felt a strong attachment to native tradition and culture. That may explain why he adopted the persona of a popular storyteller in addressing his audience, when the tale itself—particularly the three episodes in Gawain's bedchamber—prove him unusually cultivated and well acquainted with the literature of courtly manners and ideals.

Sir Gawain and the Green Knight represents the close fusion of three separate stories which may have been individually familiar to the poet's audience, but which have not survived in any similar combination in England or any other country. The first is the legend of the beheading game, which provides the opening and closing episodes of the poet's story. The second is the "exchange of winnings" proposed by Gawain's host in the central episodes of his adventure, which overlaps with the third motif, the sexual testing of Gawain. Combining these three elements into a single romance was not in itself a remarkable feat. The poet's achievement lies in having amalgamated them in such a way that while they appear unrelated, the outcome of one is determined by Gawain's behavior in the quite separate circumstances of the other.

In *Sir Gawain and the Green Knight* the story takes substantially the same form as in *Fled Bricrend* (see *Contexts* below), but with many changes of detail. The giant is no longer terrifying and ugly but physically attractive, splendidly dressed, and mounted on a horse which like himself is emerald green. He makes his challenge on New Year's Day and requires his opponent to stand the return blow a year and a day later at the Green Chapel, which must be found without directions. Gawain is chosen as the court's representative, promises to meet the Green Knight as stipulated, and decapitates him. The victim picks up his head, leaps into his saddle, and after reminding Gawain of his undertaking gallops away. At the Green Chapel a year later Gawain stands three swings from the Green Knight's axe. The first two are checked just short of his neck, and the third gashes the flesh as punishment for Gawain's dishonesty in a matter which has no evident connection with the beheading game. In this and other respects *Sir Gawain and the Green Knight* is a much more elaborate and ingenious reworking of the legend, but its dependence upon that primitive story is obvious. There are reasons for supposing that the major changes in the *Gawain*-poet's version of the tale—the challenger's color, the midwinter setting, and the year's interval between blows, for instance—were of his own devising, for these are not inconsequential details but parts of the imaginative purpose that integrates the whole poem.

None of the analogues of the temptation theme used by the poet are very closely related to his story of Gawain's attempted seduction, and no source of the motif has been found in legend. In the Welsh *Mabinogi* Pwyll spends a year at the court of Arawn in his friend's likeness, sleeping beside the queen but respecting her chastity; but while his self-restraint is tested no attempt is made to seduce him. The story is one of many legends which require the hero or heroine to undergo a trial of patience, forbearance or self-denial, usually in preparation for some task that demands special powers. The French romance of *Le Chevalier à l'Épée* is distantly related to this theme, and one of several works which seem to have contributed to the *Gawain*-poet's version of the temptation story.

The James Winny translation of the poem which appears below has been widely praised for its sensitivity to nuances of meaning; given the facing-text presentation, the translator has not felt it necessary to imitate the alliterative qualities of the Middle English verse, and has thus been able to convey the sense of the original as clearly as possible for the modern reader.

⌘⌘⌘

Sir Gawayn and the Grene Knyght

FITT 1

Sithen the sege and the assaut watz sesed at Troye,
The borgh brittened and brent to brondez and askez,
The tulk that the trammes of tresoun ther wroght
Watz tried for his tricherie, the trewest on erthe.

Sir Gawain and the Green Knight[1]

PART 1

When the siege and the assault were ended at Troy,
The city laid waste and burnt into ashes,
The man who had plotted the treacherous scheme
Was tried for the wickedest trickery ever.

---

[1] *Sir Gawain and the Green Knight*   The translation is that of James Winny.

5 Hit watz Ennias the athel and his highe kynde[1]
   That sithen depreced provinces, and patrounes bicome
   Welneghe of al the wele in the west iles.
   Fro riche Romulus to Rome ricchis hym swythe;
   With gret bobbaunce that burghe he biges upon fyrst,
10 And nevenes hit his aune nome, as hit now hat;
   Tirius to Tuskan and teldes bigynnes,
   Langaberde in Lumbardie lyftes up homes,
   And fer over the French flod Felix Brutus
   On mony bonkkes ful brode Bretayn he settez
15   with wynne;
       Where werre and wrake and wonder
       Bi sythez hatz wont therinne,
       And oft both blysse and blunder
       Ful skete hatz skyfted synne.

20 Ande quen this Bretayn watz bigged bi this burn rych,
   Bolde bredden therinne, baret that lofden,
   In mony turned tyme tene that wroghten.
   Mo ferlyes on this folde han fallen here oft
   Then in any other that I wot, syn that ilk tyme.
25 Bot of alle that here bult, of Bretaygne kynges,
   Ay watz Arthur the hendest, as I haf herde telle.
   Forthi an aunter in erde I attle to schawe,
   That a selly in syght summe men hit holden,
   And an outtrage awenture of Arthurez wonderez.
30 If ye wyl lysten this laye bot on little quile
   I schal telle hit as-tit, as I in toun herde,[2]
         with tonge,[3]
       As hit is stad and stoken[4]
       In stori stif and stronge,
35   With lel letteres loken,
       In londe so hatz ben longe.

   This kyng lay at Camylot upon Krystmasse
   With mony luflych lorde, ledez of the best,
   Rekenly of the Rounde Table alle tho rich brether,
40 With rych revel oryght and rechles merthes.

5 It was princely Aeneas and his noble kin
   Who then subdued kingdoms, and came to be lords
   Of almost all the riches of the western isles.
   Afterwards noble Romulus hastens to Rome;
   With great pride he gives that city its beginnings,
10 And calls it by his own name, which it still has.
   Tirius goes to Tuscany and sets up houses,
   Langobard in Lombardy establishes homes,
   And far over the French sea Felix Brutus
   On many broad hillsides settles Britain
15   with delight;
       Where war and grief and wonder
       Have visited by turns,
       And often joy and turmoil
       Have alternated since.

20 And when Britain had been founded by this noble lord,
   Valiant men bred there, who thrived on battle.
   In many an age bygone they brought about trouble.
   More wondrous events have occurred in this country
   Than in any other I know of, since that same time.
25 But of all those whose dwelt there, of the British kings
   Arthur was always judged noblest, as I have heard tell.
   And so an actual adventure I mean to relate
   Which some men consider a marvelous event,
   And a prodigious happening among tales about Arthur.
30 If you will listen to this story just a little while
   I will tell it at once, as I heard it told
         in court.
       As it is written down
       In story brave and strong,
35   Made fast in truthful words,
       That had endured long.

   The king spent that Christmas at Camelot
   With many gracious lords, men of great worth,
   Noble brothers-in-arms worthy of the Round Table,
40 With rich revelry and carefree amusement, as was right.

---

[1] *Ennias the athel*   Here *athel* is used as a title appropriate to a prince (Aeneas), but at 2065 the word is applied to Gawain's guide.

[2] *as I in toun herde*   It seems unlikely that the poet had either read or heard this particular tale recited. Although the beheading game figures in an Irish legend and the test of chastity has many analogues, no other surviving story combines them in a single narrative. But originality was not expected of medieval storytellers.

---

[3] *with tonge*   Compare *wyth syght*, 197 and 226, and *meled with his muthe*, 447, for similar constructions.

[4] *stad and stoken*   Set down and fixed.

Ther tournayed tulkes by tymez ful mony,
Justed ful jolilé thise gentyle knightes,
Sythen kayred to the court caroles to make.
For ther the fest watz ilyche ful fiften dayes,
45 With alle the mete and the mirthe that men couthe avyse;
Such glaume and gle glorious to here,
Dere dyn upon day, daunsyng on nyghtes,
Al watz hap upon heghe in hallez and chambrez
With lordez and ladies, as levest him thoght.
50 With all the wel of the worlde thay woned ther samen,
The most kyd knyghtez under Krystes selven,
And the lovelokkest ladies that ever lif haden,
And he the comlokest kyng that the court haldes;
For al watz this fayre folk in her first age,[1]
55   on sille,
          The hapnest under heven,
          Kyng hyghest mon of wylle;
          Hit were now gret nye to neven
          So hardy a here on hille.

60 Wyle Nwe Yer watz so yep that hit watz nwe cummen,
That day doubble on the dece watz the douth served.
Fro the kyng watz cummen with knyghtes into the halle,
The chauntré of the chapel cheved to an ende,
Loude crye watz ther kest of clerkez and other,
65 Nowel[2] nayted onewe, nevened ful ofte;
And sythen riche forth runnen to reche hondeselle,
Yeghed yeres-giftes on high, yelde hem bi hond,[3]
Debated busyly aboute tho giftes;
Ladies laghed ful loude, thogh thay lost haden,
70 And he that wan watz not wrothe, that may ye wel trawe.[4]
Alle this mirthe thay maden to the mete tyme;
When thay had waschen worthyly thay wenten to sete,
The best burne ay abof,[5] as hit best semed,
Whene Guenore, ful gay, graythed in the myddes,
75 Dressed on the dere des, dubbed al aboute,
Smal sendal bisides, a selure hir over
Of tryed tolouse, of tars tapites innoghe,

There knights fought in tournament again and again,
Jousting most gallantly, these valiant men,
Then rode to the court for dancing and song.
For there the festival lasted the whole fifteen days
45 With all the feasting and merry-making that could be devised:
Such sounds of revelry splendid to hear,
Days full of uproar, dancing at night.
Everywhere joy resounded in chambers and halls
Among lords and ladies, whatever pleased them most.
50 With all of life's best they spent that time together,
The most famous warriors in Christendom,
And the loveliest ladies who ever drew breath,
And he the finest king who rules the court.
For these fair people were then in the flower of youth
55   in the hall.
          Luckiest under heaven,
          King of loftiest mind;
          Hard it would be
          Bolder men to find.

60 When New Year was so fresh that it had hardly begun,
Double helpings of food were served on the dais that day.
By the time the king with his knights entered the hall
When the service in the chapel came to an end,
Loud cries were uttered by the clergy and others,
65 "Nowel" repeated again, constantly spoken;
And then the nobles hurried to hand out New Year's gifts,
Cried their wares noisily, gave them by hand,
And argued excitedly over those gifts.
Ladies laughed out loud, even though they had lost,
70 And the winner was not angry, you may be sure.
All this merry-making went on until feasting time.
When they had washed as was fit they took their places,
The noblest knight in a higher seat, as seemed proper;
Queen Guenevere gaily dressed and placed in the middle,
75 Seated on the upper level, adorned all about;
Fine silk surrounding her, a canopy overhead
Of costly French fabric, silk carpets underfoot

---

1 *in her first age* In their youth.

2 *Nowel* I.e., Noël, a Christmas greeting.

3 *And sythen … hond* Some have suggested that *hondeselle* are given to servants and *yeres-giftes* to equals. But Arthur is said figuratively to have received a *hanselle* at 491.

4 *Ladies … trawe* The lines refer to some kind of Christmas game, perhaps involving guesses and paying a forfeit of kisses when the guess is wrong.

5 *The best burne ay abof* Members of the court are seated according to social degree, at the *hyghe table*, 107, or at *sidbordez*, 115. The reference to *lordes and ladis that longed to the Table*, 2515, suggests that the poet saw the Round Table as a social institution.

That were enbrawded and beten wyth the best gemmes
That myght be preved of prys[1] wyth penyes to bye,
80   in daye.[2]
    The comlokest to discrye
    Ther glent with yghen gray,[3]
    A semloker that ever he syghe
    Soth moght no mon say.

85 Bot Arthure wolde not ete til al were served,
He watz so joly of his joyfnes, and sumquat childgered:
His lif liked hym lyght, he lovied the lasse
Auther to longe lye or to longe sitte,
So bisied him his yonge blod and his brayn wylde.
90 And also an other maner meved him eke
That he thurgh nobelay had nomen, he wolde never ete
Upon such a dere day er hym devised were
Of sum aventurus thyng an uncouthe tale,
Of sum mayn mervayle, that he myght trawe,
95 Of alderes, of armes, of other aventurus,
Other sum segg hym bisoght of sum siker knyght
To joyne wyth hym in justyng, in jopardé to lay
Lede, lif for lyf, leve uchon other,
As fortune wolde fulsun hom, the fayrer to have.
100 This watz the kynges countenaunce where he in court were,
At uch farande fest among his fre meny
     in halle.
    Therfore of face so fere
    He stightlez stif in stalle,
105   Ful yep in that Nw Yere
    Much mirthe he mas withalle.

Thus ther stondes in stale the stif kyng hisselven,
Talkkande bifore the hyghe table of trifles ful hende.
There gode Gawan[4] watz graythed Gwenore bisyde,
110 And Agravain à la dure mayn on that other syde sittes,
Bothe the kynges sistersunes and ful siker knightes;
Bischop Bawdewyn abof biginez the table,
And Ywan, Uryn son, ette with hymselven.
Thise were dight on the des and derworthly served,
115 And sithen mony siker segge at the sidbordez.

That were embroidered and studded with the finest gems
That money could buy at the highest price
80   anywhere.
    The loveliest to see
    Glanced round with eyes blue-grey;
    That he had seen a fairer one
    Truly could no man say.

85 But Arthur would not eat until everyone was served,
He was so lively in his youth, and a little boyish.
He hankered after an active life, and cared very little
To spend time either lying or sitting,
His young blood and restless mind stirred him so much.
90 And another habit influenced him too,
Which he had made a point of honor: he would never eat
On such a special day until he had been told
A curious tale about some perilous thing,
Of some great wonder that he could believe,
95 Of princes, of battles, or other marvels;
Or some knight begged him for a trustworthy foe
To oppose him in jousting, in hazard to set
His life against his opponent's, each letting the other,
As luck would assist him, gain the upper hand.
100 This was the king's custom when he was in court,
At each splendid feast with his noble company
     in hall.
    Therefore with proud face
    He stands there, masterful,
105   Valiant in that New Year,
    Joking with them all.

So there the bold king himself keeps on his feet,
Chatting before the high table of charming trifles.
There good Gawain was seated beside Guenevere,
110 And Agravain à la Dure Main on the other side;
Both the king's nephews and outstanding knights.
Bishop Baldwin heads the table in the highest seat,
And Ywain, son of Urien, dined as his partner.
These knights were set on a dais and sumptuously served,
115 And after them many a true man at the side tables.

[1] *preved of prys* Proved of value.

[2] *in daye* Literally, ever.

[3] *yghen gray* Virtually obligatory in medieval heroines.

[4] *gode Gawan* So characterized throughout the story, even after his disgrace. The spelling of the hero's name varies considerably. He is *Gawan* consistently throughout Part 1. Later the poet or his scribe prefers the form *Gawayn* or *Gawayne*, which is used throughout Part 4. For alliterative purposes he is occasionally referred to as *Wawan, Wawen, Wowayn,* or *Wowen.* Less frequently he is *Gavan* or *Gavayn.*

Then the first cors come with crakkyng of trumpes,
Wyth mony baner ful bryght that therbi henged;
Nwe nakryn noyse with the noble pipes,
Wylde werbles and wyght wakned lote,
120 That mony hert ful highe hef at her towches.
Dayntés dryven therwyth of ful dere metes,
Foysoun of the fresche, and on so fele disches
That pine to fynde the place the peple biforne
For to sette the sylveren that sere sewes halden
125   on clothe.
          Iche lede as he loved hymselve
          Ther laght withouten lothe;
          Ay two had disches twelve,
          Good ber and bryght wyn bothe.

130 Now wyl I of hor servise say yow no more,
For uch wyghe may wel wit no wont that ther were.
An other noyse ful newe neghed bilive
That the lude myght haf leve liflode to cache;[1]
For unethe watz the noyce not a whyle sesed,
135 And the fyrst cource in the court kyndely served,
Ther hales in at the halle dor an aghlich mayster,
On the most[2] on the molde on mesure hyghe;
Fro the swyre to the swange so sware and so thik,
And his lyndes and his lymes so longe and so grete,
140 Half etayn in erde I hope that he were,
Bot mon most I algate mynn hym to bene,
And that the myriest in his muckel that myght ride;
For of his bak and his brest al were his bodi sturne,
Both his wombe and his wast were worthily smale,
145 And alle his fetures folyande, in forme that he hade,
          ful clene;
          For wonder of his hwe men hade,
          Set in his semblaunt sene;
          He ferde as freke were fade,
150   And overal enker-grene.

And al grathed in grene this gome and his wedes:
A strayte cote ful streght, that stek on his sides,
A meré mantile abof, mensked withinne
With pelure pured apert, the pane ful clene
155 With blythe blaunner ful bryght, and his hode bothe,
That watz laght fro his lokkez and layde on his schulderes;

Then the first course was brought in with trumpets blaring,
Many colorful banners hanging from them.
The novel sound of kettledrums with the splendid pipes
Waked echoes with shrill and tremulous notes,
120 That many hearts leapt at the outburst of music.
At the same time servings of such exquisite food,
Abundance of fresh meat, in so many dishes
That space could hardly be found in front of the guests
To set down the silverware holding various stews
125   on the board.
          Each man who loved himself
          Took ungrudged, pair by pair,
          From a dozen tasty dishes,
          And drank good wine or beer.

130 Now I will say nothing more about how they were served,
For everyone can guess that no shortage was there.
Another noise, quite different, quickly drew near,
So that the king might have leave to swallow some food.
For hardly had the music stopped for a moment,
135 And the first course been properly served to the court,
When there bursts in at the hall door a terrible figure,
In his stature the very tallest on earth.
From the waist to the neck so thick-set and square,
And his loins and his limbs so massive and long,
140 In truth half a giant I believe he was,
But anyway of all men I judge him the largest,
And the most attractive of his size who could sit on a horse.
For while in back and chest his body was forbidding,
Both his belly and waist were becomingly trim,
145 And every part of his body equally elegant
          in shape.
          His hue astounded them,
          Set in his looks so keen;
          For boldly he rode in,
150   Completely emerald green.

And all arrayed in green this man and his clothes:
A straight close-fitting coat that clung to his body,
A pleasant mantle over that, adorned within
With plain trimmed fur, the facing made bright
155 With gay shining ermine, and his hood of the same
Thrown back from his hair and laid over his shoulders.

---

[1] *haf leve liflode to cache* Arthur will not eat until he has *sen a selly*, 475, which is about to arrive.

[2] *On the most* Not "one of the biggest" but "the very biggest."

Heme wel-haled hose of that same,
That spenet on his sparlyr, and clene spures under
Of bryght golde, upon silk bordes barred ful ryche,
160 And scholes under schankes[1] there the schalk rides;
And all his vesture verayly watz clene verdure,
Bothe the barres of his belt and other blythe stones,
That were richely rayled in his aray clene
Aboutte hymself and his sadel, upon silk werkez.
165 That were to tor for to telle of tryfles[2] the halve
That were enbrauded abof, wyth bryddes and flyghes,
With gay gaudi of grene, the gold ay inmyddes.
The pendauntes of his payttrure, the proude cropure,
His molaynes, and alle the metail anamayld was thenne,
170 The steropes that he stod on stayned of the same,
And his arsounz al after and his athel skyrtes,
That ever glemered and glent al of grene stones;
The fole that he ferkkes on fyn of that ilke,
        sertayn.
175   A grene hors gret and thikke,
        A stede ful stif to strayne,
        In brawden brydel quik;
        To the gome he watz ful gayn.

Wel gay watz this gome gered in grene,
180 And the here of his hed of his hors swete.
Fayre fannand fax umbefoldes his schulderes;
A much berd as a busk over his brest henges,
That wyth his highlich here that of his hed reches
Watz evesed al umbetorne abof his elbowes,
185 That half his armes ther-under were halched in the wyse
Of a kyngez capados[3] that closes his swyre;
The mane of that mayn hors much to hit lyke,
Wel cresped and cemmed, wyth knottes ful mony
Folden in with a fildore aboute the fayre grene,
190 Ay a herle of the here, an other of golde;
The tayl and his toppyng twynnen of a sute,
And bounden bothe wyth a bande of a bryght grene,
Dubbed wyth ful dere stonez, as the dok lasted,
Sythen thrawen wyth a thwong a thwarle knot alofte,
195 Ther mony bellez ful bryght of brende golde rungen.
Such a fole upon folde, ne freke that hym rydes,

Neat tightly-drawn stockings colored to match
Clinging to his calf, and shining spurs below
Of bright gold, over embroidered and richly striped silk;
160 And without shoes on his feet there the man rides.
And truly all his clothing was brilliant green,
Both the bars on his belt and other gay gems
That were lavishly set in his shining array
Round himself and his saddle, on embroidered silk.
165 It would be hard to describe even half the fine work
That was embroidered upon it, the butterflies and birds,
With lovely beadwork of green, always centered upon gold.
The pendants on the breast-trappings, the splendid crupper,
The bosses on the bit, and all the metal enameled.
170 The stirrups he stood in were colored the same,
And his saddlebow behind him and his splendid skirts
That constantly glittered and shone, all of green gems;
The horse that he rides entirely of that color,
        in truth.
175   A green horse huge and strong,
        A proud steed to restrain,
        Spirited under bridle,
        But obedient to the man.

Most attractive was this man attired in green,
180 With the hair of his head matching his horse.
Fine outspreading locks cover his shoulders;
A great beard hangs down over his chest like a bush,
That like the splendid hair that falls from his head
Was clipped all around above his elbows,
185 So that his upper arms were hidden, in the fashion
Of a royal capados that covers the neck.
That great horse's mane was treated much the same,
Well curled and combed, with numerous knots
Plaited with gold thread around the fine green,
190 Always a strand of his hair with another of gold.
His tail and his forelock were braided to match,
Both tied with a ribbon of brilliant green,
Studded with costly gems to the end of the tail,
Then tightly bound with a thong to an intricate knot
195 Where many bright bells of burnished gold rang.
No such horse upon earth, nor such a rider indeed,

---

[1]   *scholes under schankes*   Meaning that he was not wearing the steel shoes belonging to a suit of armor; see 574. The Green Knight's feet are covered by the *wel-haled hose* of 157.

[2]   *tryfles*   Decorative emblems, such as are embroidered on Gawain's silk uryson, 611–12, and on the old lady's headdress, 960.

[3]   *capados*   Hood.

Watz never sene in that sale wyth syght er that tyme,
  with yghe.
   He loked as layt so lyght,
200   So sayd al that hym syghe;
   Hit semed as no mon myght
   Under his dynttez dryghe.

Whether hade he no helme ne no hawbergh[1] nauther,
Ne no pysan ne no plate that pented to armes,
205 Ne no schafte ne no schelde to schwve ne to smyte,
Bot in his on honde he hade a holyn bobbe,
That is grattest in grene when grevez ar bare,
And an ax in his other, a hoge and unmete,
A spetos sparthe to expoun in spelle, quoso myght.
210 The lenkthe of an elnyerde the large hede hade,
The grayn al of grene stele and of golde hewen,
The bit burnyst bryght, with a brod egge
As wel schapen to schere as scharp rasores,
The stele of a stif staf the sturne hit bi grypte,
215 That watz wounden wyth yrn to the wandez ende,
And al bigraven with grene in gracios werkes;
A lace lapped aboute, that louked at the hede,
And so after the halme halched ful ofte,
Wyth tryed tasselez therto tacched innoghe
220 On botounz of the bryght grene brayden ful ryche.
This hathel heldez hym in and the halle entres,
Drivande to the heghe dece, dut he no wothe,
Haylsed he never one, bot heghe he over loked.
The fyrst word that he warp, "Where is," he sayd,
225 "The governour of this gyng? Gladly I wolde
Se that segg in syght, and with hymself speke
   raysoun."[2]
   To knyghtez he kest his yghe,
   And reled hym up and doun;
230   He stemmed, and con studie
   Quo walt ther most renoun.

Ther watz lokyng on lenthe the lude to beholde,
For uch mon had mervayle quat hit mene myght

Had any man in that hall before thought to see
  with his eyes.
   His glance was lightning swift,
200   All said who saw him there;
   It seemed that no one could
   His massive blows endure.

Yet he had no helmet nor hauberk either,
No neck-armour or plate belonging to arms,
205 No spear and no shield to push or to strike;
But in one hand he carried a holly-branch
That is brilliantly green when forests are bare,
And an axe in the other, monstrously huge;
A cruel battle-axe to tell of in words, if one could.
210 The great head was as broad as a measuring-rod,
The spike made entirely of green and gold steel,
Its blade brightly burnished, with a long cutting-edge
As well fashioned to shear as the keenest razor.
The grim man gripped the handle, a powerful staff,
215 That was wound with iron to the end of the haft
And all engraved in green with craftsmanly work.
It had a thong wrapped about it, fastened to the head,
And then looped round the handle several times,
With many splendid tassels attached to it
220 With buttons of bright green, richly embroidered.
This giant bursts in and rides through the hall,
Approaching the high dais, disdainful of peril,
Greeting none, but haughtily looking over their heads.
The first words he spoke, "Where is," he demanded,
225 "The governor of this crowd? Glad should I be
To clap eyes on the man, and exchange with him
  a few words."
   He looked down at the knights,
   As he rode up and down,
230   Then paused, waiting to see
   Who had the most renown.

For long there was only staring at the man,
For everyone marveled what it could mean

---

[1] *hawbergh* I.e., hauberk, coat of chain mail.

[2] *raysoun* Words, implicit in *speke* but evidently idiomatic.

That a hathel and a horse myght such a hwe lach
235 As growe gren as the gres and grener hit semed,
Then grene aumayl on golde glowande bryghter.
Al studied that ther stod, and stalked hym nerre
With al the wonder of the worlde what he worche schulde.
For fele sellyez had thay sen, bot such never are;
240 Forthi for fantoun and fayryye the folk there hit demed.
Therfore to answare watz arghe mony athel freke,
And al stouned at his steven and stonstil seten
In a swogh sylence thurgh the sale riche;
As al were slypped upon slepe so slaked hor lotez
245   in hyghe;
   I deme hit not al for doute,
   Bot sum for cortaysye,
   Bot let hym that al schulde loute
   Cast unto that wyghe.

250 Thenne Arthour bifore the high dece that aventure byholdez,
And rekenly hym reverenced, for rad was he never,
And sayde, "Wyghe, welcum iwys to this place,
The hede of this ostel Arthour I hat;
Lyght luflych adoun and lenge, I the praye,
255 And quat-so thy wylle is we schal wyt after."
"Nay, as help me," quoth the hathel, "he that on hygh syttes,
To wone any quyle in this won hit watz not myn ernde;
Bot for the los of the, lede, is lyft up so hyghe,
And thy burgh and thy burnes best ar holden,
260 Stifest under stel-gere on stedes to ryde,
The wyghtest and the worthyest of the worldes kynde,
Preve for to playe wyth in other pure laykez,
And here is kydde cortaysye, as I haf herd carp,
And that hatz wayned me hider, iwyis, at this tyme.
265 Ye may be seker bi this braunch that I bere here
That I passe as in pes, and no plyght seche;
For had I founded in fere in feghtyng wyse,
I have a hauberghe at home and a helme bothe,
A schelde and a scharp spere, schinande bryghte,
270 Ande other weppenes to welde, I wene wel, als;
Bot for I wolde no were, my wedez ar softer.
Bot if thou be so bold as alle burnez tellen,
Thou wyl grant me godly the gomen that I ask
      bi ryght."
275   Arthour con onsware,
   And sayd, "Sir cortays knyght,

That a knight and a horse might take such a color
235 And become green as grass, and greener it seemed
Than green enamel shining brightly on gold.
All those standing there gazed, and warily crept closer,
Bursting with wonder to see what he would do;
For many marvels they had known, but such a one never;
240 So the folk there judged it phantasm or magic.
For this reason many noble knights feared to answer:
And stunned by his words they sat there stock-still,
While dead silence spread throughout the rich hall
As though everyone fell asleep, so was their talk stilled
245   at a word.
   Not just for fear, I think,
   But some for courtesy;
   Letting him whom all revere
   To that man reply.

250 Then Arthur confronts that wonder before the high table,
And saluted him politely, for afraid was he never,
And said, "Sir, welcome indeed to this place;
I am master of this house, my name is Arthur.
Be pleased to dismount and spend some time here, I beg,
255 And what you have come for we shall learn later."
"No, by heaven," said the knight, "and him who sits there,
To spend time in this house was not the cause of my coming,
But because your name, sir, is so highly regarded,
And your city and your warriors reputed the best,
260 Dauntless in armor and on horseback afield,
The most valiant and excellent of all living men,
Courageous as players in other noble sports,
And here courtesy is displayed, as I have heard tell,
And that has brought me here, truly, on this day.
265 You may be assured by this branch that I carry
That I approach you in peace, seeking no battle.
For had I traveled in fighting dress, in warlike manner,
I have a hauberk at home and a helmet too,
A shield and a keen spear, shining bright,
270 And other weapons to brandish, I assure you, as well;
But since I look for no combat I am not dressed for battle.
But if you are as courageous as everyone says,
You will graciously grant me the game that I ask for
      by right."
275   In answer Arthur said,
   "If you seek, courteous knight,

If thou crave batayl bare,[1]
Here faylez thou not to fyght."

280 "Nay, frayst I no fyght, in fayth I the telle,
Hit arn aboute on this bench bot berdlez chylder.
If I were hasped in armes on a heghe stede,
Here is no mon me to mach, for myghtez so wayke.
Forthy I crave in this court a Crystemas gomen,[2]
For hit is Yol and Nwe Yer, and here ar yep mony.
285 If any so hardy in this hous holdez hymselven,
Be so bolde in his blod, brayn in hys hede,[3]
That dar stifly strike a strok for an other,
I schal gif hym of my gyft thys giserne ryche,
This ax, that is hevé innogh, to hondele as hym lykes,
290 And I schal bide the fyrst bur as bare as I sitte.[4]
If any freke be so felle to fonde that I telle,
Lepe lyghtly me to, and lach this weppen,
I quit-clayme hit for ever, kepe hit as his awen,
And I schal stonde hym a strok, stif on this flet,
295 Ellez thou wyl dight me the dom to dele hym an other
                    barlay;[5]
        And yet gif hym respite
        A twelmonyth and a day;
        Now hyghe, and let se tite
300   Dar any herinne oght say."

If he hem stouned upon fyrst, stiller were thanne
Alle the heredmen in halle, the hyghe and the lowe.
The renk on his rouncé hym ruched in his sadel,
And runischly his red yghen he reled aboute,
305 Bende his bresed browez, blycande grene,
Wayved his berde for to wayte quo-so wolde ryse.
When non wolde kepe hym with carp he coghed ful hyghe,
Ande rimed hym ful richely, and ryght hym to speke:
"What, is this Arthures hous?" quoth the hathel thenne,
310 "That al the rous rennes of thurgh ryalmes so mony?
Where is now your sourquydrye and your conquestes,
Your gryndellayk and your greme, and your grete wordes?

A combat without armor,
You will not lack a fight."

280 "No, I seek no battle, I assure you truly;
Those about me in this hall are but beardless children.
If I were locked in my armor on a great horse,
No one here could match me with their feeble powers.
Therefore I ask of the court a Christmas game,
For it is Yule and New Year, and here are brave men in plenty.
285 If anyone in this hall thinks himself bold enough,
So doughty in body and reckless in mind
As to strike a blow fearlessly and take one in return,
I shall give him this marvelous battle-axe as a gift,
This ponderous axe, to use as he pleases;
290 And I shall stand the first blow, unarmed as I am.
If anyone is fierce enough to take up my challenge,
Run to me quickly and seize this weapon,
I renounce all claim to it, let him keep it as his own,
And I shall stand his blow unflinching on this floor,
295 Provided you assign me the right to deal such a one
                    in return;
        And yet grant him respite
        A twelvemonth and a day.
        Now hurry, and let's see
300   What any here dare say."

If he petrified them at first, even stiller were then
All the courtiers in that place, the great and the small.
The man on the horse turned himself in his saddle,
Ferociously rolling his red eyes about,
305 Bunched up his eyebrows, bristling with green,
Swung his beard this way and that to see whoever would rise.
When no one would answer he cried out aloud,
Drew himself up grandly and started to speak.
"What, is this Arthur's house?" said the man then,
310 "That everyone talks of in so many kingdoms?
Where are now your arrogance and your victories,
Your fierceness and wrath and your great speeches?

---

[1] *batayl bare* Either "without armor" (compare 290) or—as
suggested by *thre bare mote*, 1141—"in single combat."

[2] *a Crystemas gomen* In earlier times the midwinter festival
included many games and sports now forgotten. Many of them
involved mock-violence, of which traces remained in Blind Man's
Buff, played by striking a blindfolded victim and inviting him to
guess who had struck him. Others exposed a victim to ridicule by
playing a trick on him.

[3] *brayn* Crazy, reckless; usually *braynwod*, as at 1461.

[4] *as bare as I sitte* Without the protection of armor.

[5] *barlay* An obscure term, possibly meaning "by law," or here, "by
agreement."

Now is the revel and the renoun of the Rounde Table
Overwalt wyth a worde of on wyghes speche,
315 For al dares for drede withoute dynt schewed!"
Wyth this he laghes so loude that the lorde greved;
The blod schot for scham into his schyre face
        and lere;
    He wex as wroth as wynde,
320   So did alle that ther were.
    The kyng as kene bi kynde
    Then stod that stif mon nere,

And sayde, "Hathel, by heven, thy askyng is nys,
And as thou foly hatz frayst, fynde the behoves.
325 I know no gome that is gast of thy grete wordes,
Gif me now thy geserne, upon Godez halve,
And I schal baythen thy bone that thou boden habbes."
Lyghtly lepez he him to, and laght at his honde,
Then feersly that other freke upon fote lyghtis.
330 Now hatz Arthure his axe, and the halme grypez,
And sturnely sturez hit aboute, that stryke wyth hit thoght.
The stif mon hym bifore stod upon hyght,
Herre then ani in the hous by the hede and more.
With sturne schere ther he stod he stroked his berde,
335 And wyth a countenaunce dryghe he drogh doun his cote,
No more mate ne dismayd for hys mayn dintez[1]
Then any burne upon bench hade broght hym to drynk
        of wyne.
    Gawan, that sate bi the quene,
340   To the kyng he can enclyne:
    "I beseche now with sayez sene
    This melly mot be myne."[2]

"Wolde ye, worthilych lorde," quoth Wawan to the kyng,
"Bid me boghe fro this benche, and stonde by yow there,
345 That I wythoute vylanye mygth voyde this table,
And that my legge lady lyked not ille,[3]
I wolde com to your counseyl bifore your cort riche.
For me think hit not semly, as hit is soth knawen,
Ther such an askyng is hevened so hyghe in your sale,
350 Thagh ye yourself be talenttyf, to take hit to yourselven,
Whil mony so bolde yow aboute upon bench sytten
That under heven I hope non hagherer of wylle,
Ne better bodyes on bent ther baret is rered.

Now the revelry and repute of the Round Table
Are overthrown with a word from one man's mouth,
315 For you all cower in fear before a blow has been struck!"
Then he laughs so uproariously that the king took offense;
The blood rushed into his fair face and cheek
        for shame.
    Arthur grew red with rage,
320   As all the others did.
    The king, by nature bold,
    Approached that man and said,

"Sir, by heaven, what you demand is absurd,
And since you have asked for folly, that you deserve.
325 No man known to me fears your boastful words;
Hand over your battle-axe, in God's name,
And I shall grant the wish that you have requested."
He quickly goes to him and took the axe from his hand.
Then proudly the other dismounts and stands there.
330 Now Arthur has the axe, grips it by the shaft,
And grimly swings it about, as preparing to strike.
Towering before him stood the bold man,
Taller than anyone in the court by more than a head.
Standing there grim-faced he stroked his beard,
335 And with an unmoved expression then pulled down his coat,
No more daunted or dismayed by those powerful strokes
Than if any knight in the hall had brought him a measure
        of wine.
    Seated by Guenevere
340   Then bowed the good Gawain:
    "I beg you in plain words
    To let this task be mine."

Said Gawain to the king, "If you would, noble lord,
Bid me rise from my seat and stand at your side,
345 If without discourtesy I might leave the table,
And that my liege lady were not displeased,
I would offer you counsel before your royal court.
For it seems to me unfitting, if the truth be admitted,
When so arrogant a request is put forward in hall,
350 Even if you are desirous, to undertake it yourself
While so many brave men sit about you in their places
Who, I think, are unrivalled in temper of mind,
And without equal as warriors on field of battle.

---

[1] *for hys mayn dintez*   Because of Arthur's great practice blows.

[2] *This melly mot be myne*   Let this be my combat.

[3] *that my legge lady lyked not ille*   That the Queen (beside whom Gawain is sitting) would not be offended if I left her side.

I am the wakkest, I wot, and of wyt feblest,
355 And lest lur of my lyf, quo laytes the sothe:
Bot for as much as ye are myn em I am only to prayse,
No bounté bot your blod I in my bodé knowe;
And sythen this note is so nys that noght hit yow falles,
And I have frayned hit at yow fyrst, foldez hit to me;
360 And if I carp not comlyly, let alle this cort rych
        bout blame."
    Ryche togeder con roun,
    And sythen thay redden alle same,
    To ryd the kyng wyth croun
365   And gif Gawan the game.

Then comaunded the kyng the knyght for to ryse;
And he ful radly upros, and ruchched hym fayre,
Kneled doun bifore the kyng, and cachez that weppen;
And he luflyly hit hym laft, and lyfte up his honde
370 And gef hym Goddez blessyng, and gladly hym biddes
That his hert and his honde schulde hardi be bothe.
"Kepe the, cosyn," quoth the kyng, "that thou on kyrf sette,
And if thou redez hym ryght, redly I trowe
That thou schal byden the bur[1] that he schal bede after."
375 Gawan gotz to the gome with giserne in honde,
And he baldly hym bydez, he bayst never the helder.
Then carppez to Sir Gawan the knyght in the grene,
"Refourme we oure forwardes, er we fyrre passe.
Fyrst I ethe the, hathel, how that thou hattes
380 That thou me telle truly, as I tryst may."
"In god fayth," quoth the goode knyght, "Gawan I hatte,
That bede the this buffet, quat-so bifallez after,
And at this tyme twelmonyth take at the an other
Wyth what weppen so thou wylt, and wyth no wygh ellez
385   on lyve."
    That other onswarez agayn,
    "Sir Gawan, so mot I thryve,
    As I am ferly fayn
    This dint that thou schal dryve.

390 "Bigog," quoth the grene knyght, "Sir Gawan, me lykes
That I schal fange at thy fust that I haf frayst here.[2]
And thou hatz redily rehersed, bi resoun ful trwe,
Clanly al the covenaunt that I the kynge asked,
Saf that thou schal siker me, segge, bi thi trawthe,

I am the weakest of them, I know, and the dullest-minded,
355 So my death would be least loss, if truth should be told;
Only because you are my uncle am I to be praised,
No virtue I know in myself but your blood;
And since this affair is so foolish and unfitting for you,
And I have asked you for it first, it should fall to me.
360 And if my request is improper, let not this royal court
        bear the blame."
    Nobles whispered together
    And agreed on their advice,
    That Arthur should withdraw
365   And Gawain take his place.

Then the king commanded Gawain to stand up,
And he did so promptly, and moved forward with grace,
Kneeled down before the king and laid hold of the weapon;
And Arthur gave it up graciously, and lifting his hand
370 Gave Gawain God's blessing, and cheerfully bids
That he bring a strong heart and firm hand to the task.
"Take care, nephew," said the king, "that you strike one blow,
And if you deal it aright, truly I believe
You will wait a long time for his stroke in return."
375 Gawain approaches the man with battle-axe in hand,
And he waits for him boldly, with no sign of alarm.
Then the knight in the green addresses Gawain,
"Let us repeat our agreement before going further.
First I entreat you, sir, that what is your name
380 You shall tell me truly, that I may believe you."
"In good faith," said that virtuous knight, "I am called Gawain,
Who deals you this blow, whatever happens after,
On this day next year to accept another from you
With what weapon you choose, and from no other person
385   on earth."
    The other man replied,
    "Sir Gawain, as I live,
    I am extremely glad
    This blow is yours to give.

390 By God," said the Green Knight, "Sir Gawain, I am pleased
That I shall get from your hands what I have asked for here.
And you have fully repeated, in exact terms,
Without omission the whole covenant I put to the king;
Except that you shall assure me, sir, on your word,

---

[1] *thou schal byden the bur* You'll be kept waiting for his blow.

[2] *"Bigog," … here* The Green Knight does not explain why he is especially pleased that Gawain accepts the challenge.

395   That thou schal seche me thiself, where-so thou hopes
       I may be funde upon folde, and foch the such wages
       As thou deles me to-day bifore this douthe ryche."
       "Where schulde I wale the?" quoth Gawan, "Where is thy
           place?
       I wot never where thou wonyes, bi hym that me wroght,
400   Ne I know not the, knyght, thy cort ne thi name.
       Bot teche me truly therto, and telle me how thou hattes,
       And I schal ware alle my wyt to wynne me theder,
       And that I swere the for sothe, and by my seker traweth."
       "That is innogh in Nwe Yer,[1] hit nedes no more,"
405   Quoth the gome in the grene to Gawan the hende;
       "Yif I the telle trwly quen I the tape have,
       And thou me smothely hatz smyten, smartly I the teche
       Of my hous and my home and myn owen nome,
       Then may thou frayst my fare and forwardez holde;
410   And if I spende no speche, thenne spedez thou the better,
       For thou may leng in thy londe and layt no fyrre—
           bot slokes!
         Ta now thy grymme tole to the,
         And lat se how thou cnokez."
415   "Gladly, sir, for sothe,"
         Quoth Gawan: his ax he strokes.

       The grene knyght upon grounde graythely hym dresses,
       A littel lut with the hed, the lere he discoverez,
       His longe lovelych lokkez he layd over his croun,
420   Let the naked nec to the note schewe.
       Gawan gripped to his ax and gederes hit on hyght,
       The kay fot on the folde he before sette,
       Let hit doun lyghtly lyght on the naked,
       That the scharp of the schalk schyndered the bones,
425   And schrank thurgh the schyire grece, and schade hit in twynne,
       That the bit of the broun[2] stel bot on the grounde.
       The fayre hede fro the halce hit to the erthe,
       That fele hit foyned wyth hir fete, there hit forth roled;
       The blod brayed from the body, that blykked on the grene;
430   And nawther faltered ne fel the freke never the helder,
       Bot stythly he start forth upon styf schonkes,
       And runyschly he raght out, there as renkkez stoden,
       Laght to his lufly hed, and lyft hit up sone;
       And sythen bowez to his blonk, the brydel he cachchez,

395   That you will seek me yourself, wherever you think
       I may be found upon earth, to accept such payment
       As you deal me today before this noble gathering."
       "Where shall I find you?" said Gawain, "Where is your
           dwelling?
       I have no idea where you live, by him who made me;
400   Nor do I know you, sir, your court nor your name.
       Just tell me truly these things, and what you are called,
       And I shall use all my wits to get myself there,
       And that I swear to you honestly, by my pledged word."
       "That is enough for the moment, it needs nothing more,"
405   Said the man in green to the courteous Gawain,
       "If I answer you truly after taking the blow,
       And you have dextrously struck me, I will tell you at once
       Of my house and my home and my proper name,
       Then you can pay me a visit and keep your pledged word;
410   And if I say nothing, then you will fare better,
       For you may stay in your country and seek no further—
           but enough!
         Take up your fearsome weapon
         And let's see how you smite."
415   Said Gawain, "Gladly, indeed,"
         Whetting the metal bit.

       The Green Knight readily takes up his position,
       Bowed his head a little, uncovering the flesh,
       His long lovely hair he swept over his head,
420   In readiness letting the naked neck show.
       Gawain grasped the axe and lifts it up high,
       Setting his left foot before him on the ground,
       Brought it down swiftly on the bare flesh
       So that the bright blade slashed through the man's spine
425   And cut through the white flesh, severing it in two,
       So that the shining steel blade bit into the floor.
       The handsome head flew from the neck to the ground,
       And many courtiers kicked at it as it rolled past.
       Blood spurted from the trunk, gleamed on the green dress,
430   Yet the man neither staggered nor fell a whit for all that,
       But sprang forward vigorously on powerful legs,
       And fiercely reached out where knights were standing,
       Grabbed at his fine head and snatched it up quickly,
       And then strides to his horse, seizes the bridle,

---

[1] *innogh in Nwe Yer* Literally, "enough for this New Year's Day";
meaning that Gawain need say nothing more, as the Green Knight
goes on to say.

[2] *broun* Burnished.

435 Steppez into stelbawe and strydez alofte,
And his hede by the here in his honde haldez.
And as sadly the segge hym in his sadel sette
As non unhap had hym ayled, thagh hedlez he were
          in stedde.
440   He brayde his bulk aboute,
        That ugly bodi that bledde;
        Moni on of hym had doute
        Bi that his resounz were redde.

For the hede in his honde he haldez up even,
445 Toward the derrest on the dece he dressez the face,
And hit lyfte up the yghe-lyddez and loked ful brode,
And meled thus much with his muthe, as ye may now
          here:
"Loke, Gawan, thou be graythe to go as thou hettez,
And layte as lelly til thou me, lude, fynde,
450 As thou hatz hette in this halle, herande thise knyghtes;
To the grene chapel thou chose, I charge the, to fotte
Such a dunt as thou hatz dalt, disserved thou habbez
To be yederly yolden on Nw Yeres morn.
The knyght of the grene chapel men knowen me mony,
455 Forthi me for to fynde if thou fraystez, faylez thou never.
Therfore com, other recreaunt be calde thou behoves."
With a runisch rout the raynez he tornez,
Halled out at the hal dor, his hed in his hande,
That the fyr of the flynt flaghe fro fole hoves.
460 To quat kyth he becom knwe non there,
Never more then thay wyste from quethen he watz wonnen.
        What thenne?
        The kyng and Gawan thare
        At that grene thay laghe and grenne;
465   Yet breved watz hit ful bare
        A mervayl among tho menne.

Thagh Arther the hende kyng at hert hade wonder,
He let no semblaunt be sene, bot sayde ful hyghe
To the comlych quene wyth cortays speche,
470 "Dere dame, to-day demay yow never;
Wel bycommes such craft[1] upon Cristmasse,
Laykyng of enterludez, to laghe and to syng,
Among thise kynde caroles of knyghtez and ladyez.
Never the lece to my mete I may me wel dres,

435 Puts foot into stirrup and swings into his seat,
His other hand clutching his head by the hair;
And the man seated himself on horseback as firmly
As if he had suffered no injury, though headless he sat
          in his place.
440   He turned his body round,
        That gruesome trunk that bled;
        Many were struck by fear
        When all his words were said.

For he holds up the head in his hand, truly,
445 Turns its face towards the noblest on the dais,
And it lifted its eyelids and glared with wide eyes,
And the mouth uttered these words, which you shall now
          hear:
"See, Gawain, that you carry out your promise exactly,
And search for me truly, sir, until I am found,
450 As you have sworn in this hall in the hearing of these knights.
Make your way to the Green Chapel, I charge you, to get
Such a blow as you have dealt, rightfully given,
To be readily returned on New Year's Day.
As the Knight of the Green Chapel I am widely known,
455 So if you make search to find me you cannot possibly fail.
Therefore come, or merit the name of craven coward."
With a fierce jerk of the reins he turns his horse
And hurtled out of the hall door, his head in his hand,
So fast that flint-fire sparked from the hoofs.
460 What land he returned to no one there knew,
Any more than they guessed where he had come from.
        What then?
        Seeing that green man go,
        The king and Gawain grin;
465   Yet they both agreed
        They had a wonder seen.

Although inwardly Arthur was deeply astonished,
He let no sign of this appear, but loudly remarked
To the beautiful queen with courteous speech,
470 "Dear lady, let nothing distress you today.
Such strange goings-on are fitting at Christmas,
Putting on interludes, laughing and singing,
Mixed with courtly dances of ladies and knights.
None the less, I can certainly go to my food,

---

[1] *such craft* Display of skill. Arthur speaks as though the beheading had been a conjuring trick.

475 For I haf sen a selly, I may not forsake."
He glent upon Sir Gawen, and gaynly he sayde,
"Now sir, heng up thyn ax,[1] that hatz innogh hewen."
And hit watz don abof the dece on doser to henge,
Ther alle men for mervayl myght on hit loke,
480 And bi trwe tytel therof to telle the wonder.
Thenne thay bowed to a borde thise burnes togeder,
The kyng and the gode knyght, and kene men hem served
Of alle dayntyez double, as derrest myght falle;
Wyth alle maner of mete and mynstralcie bothe,
485 Wyth wele walt thay that day, til worthed an ende
in londe.
Now thenk wel, Sir Gawan,
For wothe that thou ne wonde
This aventure for to frayn
490 That thou hatz tan on honde.

FITT 2

This hanselle hatz Arthur of aventurus on fyrst
In yonge yer, for he yerned yelpyng to here.
Thagh hym wordez were wane[2] when thay to sete wenten,
Now ar thay stoken of sturne werk, stafful her hond.
495 Gawan watz glad to begynne those gomnez in halle,
Bot thagh the ende be hevy haf ye no wonder;
For thagh men ben mery quen thay han mayn drynk,
A yere yernes ful yerne, and yeldez never lyke,
The forme to the fynisment foldez ful selden.
500 Forthi this Yol overyede, and the yere after,
And uche sesoun serlepes sued after other:
After Crystenmasse com the crabbed lentoun
That fraystez flesch wyth the fysche and fode more symple;
Bot thenne the weder of the worlde wyth wynter hit threpez,[3]
505 Colde clengez adoun,[4] cloudez upliften,
Schyre schedez the rayn in schowrez ful warme,
Fallez upon fayre flat, flowrez there schewen,
Bothe groundez and the grevez grene ar her wedez,
Bryddez busken to bylde, and bremlych syngen

---

475 For I have witnessed a marvel, I cannot deny."
He glanced at Sir Gawain, and aptly he said,
"Now sir, hang your axe up, for it has severed enough."
And it was hung above the dais, on a piece of tapestry,
Where everyone might gaze on it as a wonder,
480 And the living proof of this marvelous tale.
Then these two men together walked to a table,
The king and the good knight, and were dutifully served
With delicious double helpings befitting their rank.
With every kind of food and minstrelsy
485 They spent that day joyfully, until daylight ended
on earth.
Now take good care, Gawain,
Lest fear hold you back
From leaving on the quest
490 You have sworn to undertake.

PART 2

This wonder has Arthur as his first New Year's gift
When the year was newborn, for he loved hearing challenges.
Though words were wanting when they sat down at table,
Now a grim task confronts them, their hands are cram-full.
495 Gawain was glad enough to begin those games in the hall,
But if the outcome prove troublesome don't be surprised;
For though men are light-hearted when they have strong drink,
A year passes swiftly, never bringing the same;
Beginning and ending seldom take the same form.
500 And so that Yule went by, and the year ensuing,
Each season in turn following the other.
After Christmas came mean-spirited Lent,
That tries the body with fish and plainer nourishment;
But then the weather on earth battles with winter,
505 The cold shrinks downwards, clouds rise higher,
And shed sparkling rain in warming showers,
Falling on smiling plains where flowers unfold.
Both open fields and woodlands put on green dress;
Birds hasten to build, and rapturously sing

---

1 *heng up thyn ax* Arthur *gaynly* or aptly quotes a proverbial saying, meaning "end your strife."

2 *wordez were wane* Because the Green Knight had taken their breath away.

3 *wyth wynter hit threpez* The seasons do not simply follow each other quietly but fight for succession: see 525, where autumn wind *wrastelez with the sunne*.

4 *Colde clengez adoun* Winter is driven down into the earth, waiting to emerge again.

510 For solace of the softe somer that sues therafter
        bi bonk;
    And blossumez bolne to blowe
    Bi rawez rych and ronk,
    Then notez noble innoghe
515   Ar herde in wod so wlonk.

    After the sesoun of somer wyth the soft wyndez,
    Quen Zeferus[1] syflez hymself on sedez and erbez,
    Wela wynne is the wort that waxes theroute,
    When the donkande dewe dropez of the levez,
520 To bide a blysful blusch of the bryght sunne.
    Bot then hyghes hervest, and hardenes hym sone,
    Warnez hym for the wynter to wax ful rype.
    He dryves wyth droght the dust for to ryse
    Fro the face of the folde to flyghe ful hyghe;
525 Wrothe wynde of the welkyn wrastelez with the sunne,
    The levez lancen fro the lynde and lyghten on the grounde,
    And al grayes the gres that grene watz ere.
    Thenne al rypez and rotez that ros upon fyrst,
    And thus yirnez the yere in yisterdayez mony,
530 And wynter wyndez agayn, as the worlde askez,
        no fage;
    Til Meghelmas[2] mone
    Watz cumen wyth wynter wage;
    Then thenkkez Gawan ful sone
535   Of his anious vyage.

    Yet quyl Al-hal-day[3] with Arther he lenges;
    And he made a fare on that fest for the frekez sake,
    With much revel and ryche of the Rounde Table.
    Knyghtez ful cortays and comlych ladies
540 Al for luf of that lede in longynge thay were,
    Bot never the lece ne the later thay nevened bot merthe;
    Mony joylez for that jentyle japez ther maden.
    And aftter mete with mournyng he melez to his eme,
    And spekez of his passage, and pertly he sayde,
545 "Now, lege lorde of my lyf, leve I yow ask;
    Ye knowe the cost of this cace, kepe I no more
    To telle yow tenez therof, never bot trifel;
    Bot I am boun to the bur barely to-morne
    To sech the gome of the grene, as God wyl me wysse."
550 Then the best of the burgh bowed togeder,

For joy of gentle summer that follows next
        on the slopes.
    And flowers bud and blossom
    In hedgerows rich with growth,
    And many splendid songs
515   From woodlands echo forth.

    Then comes the summer season with gentle winds,
    When Zephirus blows softly on seeding grasses and plants,
    Beautiful is the growth that springs from the seed,
    When the moistening dew drips from the leaves
520 To await a joyful gleam of the bright sun.
    But then autumn comes quickly and urges it on,
    Warns it to ripen before winter's approach.
    Dry winds of autumn force the dust to fly
    From the face of the earth high into the air;
525 Fierce winds of heaven wrestle with the sun,
    Leaves are torn from the trees and fall to the ground,
    And all withered is the grass that was green before.
    Then all ripens and rots that had sprung up at first,
    And in so many yesterdays the year wears away,
530 And winter comes round again, as custom requires,
        in truth;
    Until the Michaelmas moon
    Brought hint of winter's frost;
    And into Gawain's mind
535   Come thoughts of his grim quest.

    Yet until All Saints' Day he lingers in court,
    And Arthur made a feast on that day to honor the knight,
    With much splendid revelry at the Round Table.
    The most courteous of knights and beautiful ladies
540 Grieved out of love for that noble man,
    But no less readily for that spoke as if unconcerned.
    Many troubled for that nobleman made joking remarks.
    And after the feast sorrowfully he addressed his uncle,
    Raised the matter of his quest, and openly said,
545 "Liege lord of my being, I must ask for your leave;
    You know the terms of this matter, and I have no wish
    To bother you with them, saving one small point;
    But tomorrow without fail I set out for the blow,
    To seek this man in green, as God will direct me."
550 Then the noblest in the court gathered together,

---

[1] *Zeferus*   God of the West Wind.

[2] *Meghelmas*   I.e., Michaelmas, the feast of St. Michael, celebrated on 29 September.

[3] *Al-hal-day*   I.e., All Hallows' Day, or All Saints' Day, celebrated 1 November.

Aywan and Errik, and other ful mony,
Sir Doddinaval de Savage, the duc of Clarence,
Launcelot and Lyonel, and Lucan the gode,
Sir Boos and Sir Bydver, big men bothe,
555 And mony other menskful, with Mador de la Port.
Alle this compayny of court com the kyng nerre
For to counseyl the knyght, with care at her hert.
There watz much derve doel driven in the sale
That so worthé as Wawan schulde wende on that ernde,
560 To dryve a delful dynt, and dele no more
          wyth bronde.
     The knyght mad ay god chere,
     And sayde, "Quat schuld I wonde?
     Of destinés derf and dere
565   What may mon do bot fonde?"

He dowellez ther al that day, and dressez on the morn,
Askez erly hys armez, and alle were thay broght.
Fyrst a tulé tapit tyght over the flet,
And miche watz the gild gere that glent theralofte.
570 The stif mon steppez theron, and the stel hondelez,
Dubbed in a dublet of a dere tars,
And sythen a crafty capados, closed aloft,
That wyth a bryght blaunner was bounden withinne.
Thenne set thay the sabatounz upon the segge fotez,
575 His legez lapped in stel with luflych greves,
With polaynez piched therto, policed ful clene,
Aboute his knez knaged wyth knotez of golde;
Queme quyssewes then, that coyntlych closed
His thik thrawen thyghez, with thwonges to tachched;
580 And sythen the brawden bryné of bryght stel ryngez
Umbeweved that wygh upon wlonk stuffe,
And wel bornyst brace upon his bothe armes,
With gode cowters and gay, and glovez of plate,
And alle the godlych gere that hym gayn schulde
585   that tyde;
     Wyth ryche cote-armure
     His gold sporez spend with pryde,
     Gurde wyth a bront ful sure
     With silk sayn umbe his syde.

590 When he watz hasped in armes, his harnays watz ryche:
The lest lachet other loupe lemed of golde.
So harnayst as he watz he herknez his masse,
Offred and honoured at the heghe auter.
Sythen he come to the kyng and to his cort-ferez,

Ywain and Eric, and many others,
Sir Dodinal le Sauvage, the duke of Clarence,
Lancelot and Lionel, and Lucan the good,
Sir Bors and Sir Bedevere, both powerful men,
555 And several other worthy knights, including Mador de la Port.
This group of courtiers approached the king,
To give advice to Gawain with troubled hearts.
Much deep sorrowing was heard in the hall
That one as noble as Gawain should go on that quest,
560 To stand a terrible blow, and never more brandish
          his sword.
     Keeping an unchanged face,
     "What should I fear?" he said;
     "For whether kind or harsh
565   A man's fate must be tried."

He stays there all that day, and makes ready the next,
Calls early for his accouterment, and all was brought in.
First a crimson carpet was stretched over the floor,
A heap of gilded armor gleaming brightly piled there.
570 The brave knight steps on it and examines his armour,
Dressed in a costly doublet of silk
Under a well-made capados, fastened at the top
And trimmed with white ermine on the inside.
Then they fitted metal shoes upon the knight's feet,
575 Clasped his legs in steel with elegant greaves
With knee-pieces attached to them, highly polished
And fastened to his knees with knots of gold.
Next fine cuisses that neatly enclosed
His thick muscular thighs, with thongs attached,
580 And then the linked mail-shirt made of bright steel rings
Covered that man and his beautiful clothes:
Well burnished braces on both his arms,
With fine elbow-pieces and gloves of steel plate,
And all the splendid equipment that would benefit him
585   at that time;
     With costly coat-armor,
     His gold spurs worn with pride,
     Girt with a trusty sword,
     A silk belt round him tied.

590 All locked in his armor his gear looked noble:
The smallest fastening or loop was gleaming with gold.
In armor as he was, he went to hear mass
Offered and celebrated at the high altar.
Then he comes to the king and his fellows at court,

595	Lachez lufly his leve at lordez and ladyez;	Graciously takes his leave of lords and ladies;
	And thay him kyst and conveyed, bikende hym to Kryst.	And they kissed and escorted him, commending him to Christ.
	Bi that watz Gryngolet grayth, and gurde with a sadel	By then Gringolet was ready, fitted with a saddle
	That glemed ful gayly with mony golde frenges,	That splendidly shone with many gold fringes,
	Ayquere naylet ful nwe, for that note ryched;	Newly studded all over for that special purpose;
600	The brydel barred aboute, with bryght golde bounden,	The bridle striped all along, and trimmed with bright gold;
	The apparayl of the payttrure and of the proude skyrtez,	The adornment of the trapping and the fine saddle-skirts,
	The cropore and the covertor, acorded wyth the arsounez;	The crupper and the horse-cloth matched the saddle-bows,
	And al watz rayled on red ryche golde naylez,	All covered with gold studs on a background of red,
	That al glytered and glent as glem of the sunne.	So that the whole glittered and shone like the sun.
605	Thenne hentes he the helme, and hastily hit kysses,	Then Gawain seizes his helmet and kisses it quickly,
	That watz stapled stifly, and stoffed wythinne.	That was strongly stapled and padded inside.
	Hit watz hyghe on his hede, hasped bihynde,	It stood high on his head, fastened at the back
	Wyth a lyghtly urysoun over the aventayle,	With a shining silk band over the mailed neck-guard,
	Enbrawden and bounden wyth the best gemmez	Embroidered and studded with the finest gems
610	On brode sylkyn borde, and bryddez on semez,	On a broad border of silk with birds covering the seams—
	As papjayez paynted pervyng bitwene,	Popinjays depicted between periwinkles,
	Tortors and trulofez entayled so thyk	Turtledoves and true-love flowers embroidered so thick
	As many burde theraboute had ben seven wynter	As if many women had worked on it seven years
	in toune.	in town.
615	The cercle watz more o prys	A circlet still more precious
	That umbeclypped hys croun,	Was ringed about his head,
	Of diamauntez a devys	Made with perfect diamonds
	That bothe were bryght and broun.[1]	Of every brilliant shade.
	Then thay schewed hym the schelde, that was of schyr goulez,	Then they brought out the shield of shining gules,
620	Wyth the pentangel depaynt of pure gold hwez.	With the pentangle painted on it in pure gold.
	He braydez hit by the bauderyk, aboute the hals kestes,	He swings it over his baldric, throws it round his neck,
	That bisemed the segge semlyly fayre.	Where it suited the knight extremely well.
	And quy the pentangel apendez to that prynce noble	And why the pentangle should befit that noble prince
	I am in tent yow to telle, thof tary hyt me schulde:	I intend to explain, even should that delay me.
625	Hit is a syngne that Salomon set sumquyle	It is a symbol that Solomon designed long ago
	In bytoknyng of trawthe, bi tytle that hit habbez,	As an emblem of fidelity, and justly so;
	For hit is a figure that haldez fyve poyntez,	For it is a figure consisting of five points,
	And uche lyne umbelappez and loukez in other,	Where each line overlaps and locks into another,
	And ayquere hit is endelez; and Englych hit callen	And the whole design is continuous, and in England is called
630	Overal, as I here, the endeles knot.[2]	Everywhere, I am told, the endless knot.
	Forthy hit acordez to this knyght and to his cler armez,	Therefore it suits this knight and his shining arms,
	For ay faythful in fyve and sere fyve sythez	For always faithful in five ways, and five times in each case,
	Gawan watz for gode knawen, and as golde pured,	Gawain was reputed as virtuous, like refined gold,
	Voyded of uche vylany, wyth vertuez ennourned	Devoid of all vice, and with all courtly virtues
635	in mote;	adorned.

---

[1] *bryght and broun* Clear and colored.

[2] *the endeles knot* No other use of this phrase is known. Like the poet's claim to have heard the story recited, and his closing of refer-

---

ence to its place in *the best boke of romaunce*, l. 2521, the remark should probably be regarded as poetic license. The line does not alliterate.

Forthy the pentangel nwe
He ber in schelde and cote,
As tulk of tale most trwe
And gentylest knyght of lote.

640 Fyrst he watz funden fautlez in his fyve wyttez,
And eft fayled never the freke in his fyve fyngres,
And alle his afyaunce upon folde watz in the fyve woundez
That Cryst caght on the croys, as the crede tellez;
And quere-so-ever thys mon in melly watz stad,
645 His thro thoght watz in that, thurgh alle other thyngez,
That alle his forsnes he feng at the fyve joyez
That the hende heven-quene had of hir chylde;
At this cause the knyght comlyche hade
In the inore half of his schelde hir image depaynted,
650 That quen he bluschede therto his belde never payred.
The fyft fyve that I fynde that the frek used
Watz fraunchyse and felaghschyp forbe al thyng,
His clannes and his cortaysye croked were never,
And pité,[1] that passez alle poyntez: thyse pure fyve
655 Were harder happed on that hathel then on any other.
Now alle these fyve sythez, for sothe, were fetled on this
    knyght,
And uchone halched in other, that non ende hade,
And fyched upon fyve poyntez, that fayld never,
Ne samned never in no syde, ne sundred nouther,
660 Withouten ende at any noke I oquere fynde,
Whereever the gomen bygan, or glod to an ende.
Therfore on his schene schelde schapen watz the knot
Ryally wyth red golde upon rede gowlez,
That is the pure pentaungel wyth the peple called
665   with lore.
        Now graythed is Gawan gay,
        And laght his launce ryght thore,
        And gef them alle goud day,
        He wende for evermore.

670 He sperres the sted with the spurez and sprong on his way,
So stif that the ston-fyr stroke out therafter.
Al that sey that semly syked in hert,
And sayde sothly[2] al same segges til other,
Carande for that comly, "Bi Kryst, hit is scathe
675 That thou leude, schal be lost, that art of lyf noble!

So this new-painted sign
He bore on shield and coat,
As man most true of speech
And fairest-spoken knight.

640 First he was judged perfect in his five senses,
And next his five fingers never lost their dexterity;
And all his earthly faith was in the five wounds
That Christ suffered on the cross, as the creed declares.
And wherever this man found himself in battle
645 His fixed thought was that, above all other things,
All his fortitude should come from the five joys
That the mild Queen of Heaven found in her child.
For this reason the gracious knight had
Her image depicted on the inside of his shield,
650 So that when he glanced at it his heart never quailed.
The fifth group of five the man respected, I hear,
Was generosity and love of fellow-men above all;
His purity and courtesy were never lacking,
And surpassing the others, compassion: these noble five
655 Were more deeply implanted in that man than any other.
Now truly, all these five groups were embodied in that
    knight,
Each one linked to the others in an endless design,
Based upon five points that was never unfinished,
Not uniting in one line nor separating either;
660 Without ending anywhere at any point that I find,
No matter where the line began or ran to an end.
Therefore the knot was fashioned on his bright shield
Royally with red gold upon red gules,
That is called the true pentangle by learned people
665   who know.
        Now Gawain, lance in hand,
        Is ready to depart;
        He bade them all farewell,
        Not to return, he thought.

670 He set spurs to his horse and sprang on his way
So vigorously that sparks flew up from the stones.
All who watched that fair knight leave sighed from the heart,
And together whispered one to another,
Distressed for that handsome one, "What a pity indeed
675 That your life must be squandered, noble as you are!

---

[1] *pité* Cannot readily be translated in one word, as it means both pity and piety.

[2] *sothly* A dialect term meaning "quietly."

To fynde hys fere upon folde, in fayth, is not ethe.
Warloker to haf wroght had more wyt bene,
And haf dyght yonder dere a duk to have worthed;
A lowande leder of ledez in londe hym wel semez,
680 And so had better haf ben then britned to noght,
Hadet wyth an alvisch mon, for angardez pryde.
Who knew ever any kyng such counsel to take
As knyghtez in cavelaciounz on Crystmasse gomnez!"
Wel much watz the warme water that waltered of yghen,
685 When that semly syre soght fro tho wonez
        thad daye.
    He made non abode,
    Bot wyghtly went hys way;
    Mony wylsum way he rode,
690   The bok as I herde say.

Now ridez this renk thurgh the ryalme of Logres,[1]
Sir Gawan, on Godez halve, thagh hym no gomen thoght.
Oft leudlez and alone he lengez on nyghtez
Ther he fonde noght hym byfore the fare that he lyked.
695 Hade he no fere bot his fole by frythez and dounez,
Ne no gome bot God bi gate wyth to carp,
Til that he neghed ful neghe into the Northe Walez.
Alle the iles of Anglesay on lyft half he haldez,
And farez over the fordez by the forlondez,
700 Over at the Holy Hede, til he hade eft bonk
In the wyldrenesse of Wyrale; wonde ther bot lyte
That auther God other gome wyth goud hert lovied.
And ay he frayned as he ferde, at frekez that he met,
If thay hade herde any karp of a knyght grene,
705 In any grounde theraboute, of the grene chapel;
And al nykked hym wyth nay, that never in her lyve
Thay seye never no segge that watz of suche hwez
        of grene.
    The knyght tok gates straunge
710   In mony a bonk unbene,
    His cher ful oft con chaunge
    That chapel er he myght sene.

Mony klyf he overclambe in contrayez straunge,
Fer floten fro his frendez fremedly he rydez.
715 At uche warthe other water ther the wyghe passed
He fonde a foo hym byfore, bot ferly hit were,
And that so foule and so felle that feght hym byhode.
So mony mervayl bi mount ther the mon fyndez,

To find his equal on earth is not easy, in faith.
To have acted more cautiously would have been much wiser,
And have appointed that dear man to become a duke:
To be a brilliant leader of men, as he is well suited,
680 And would better have been so than battered to nothing,
Beheaded by an ogrish man out of excessive pride.
Whoever knew a king to take such foolish advice
As knights offer in arguments about Christmas games?"
A great deal of warm water trickled from eyes
685 When that elegant lord set out from the city
        that day.
    He did not linger there,
    But swiftly went his way;
    Taking perplexing roads
690   As I have heard books say.

Now rides this knight through the realm of England,
Sir Gawain, in God's name, though he found it no pleasure.
Often friendless and alone he passes his nights,
Finding before him no food that he liked.
695 He had no fellow but his horse by forest and hill,
And no one but God to talk to on the way,
Until he came very close to the north part of Wales.
All the islands of Anglesey he keeps on his left,
And crosses over the fords at the headlands,
700 There at the Holyhead, and came ashore again
In the wilderness of Wirral. There few people lived
Whom either God or good-hearted men could love.
And always as he rode he asked those whom he met
If they had heard anyone speak of a green knight
705 Or of a green chapel in any place round about;
And they all answered him no, that never in their lives
Had they ever seen a man who had such color
        of green.
    Strange roads the knight pursued
710   Through many a dreary space,
    Turning from side to side
    To find the meeting-place.

Many fells he climbed over in territory strange,
Far distant from his friends like an alien he rides.
715 At every ford or river where the knight crossed
He found an enemy facing him, unless he was in luck,
And so ugly and fierce that he was forced to give fight.
So many wonders befell him in the hills,

---

[1] *Logres* Celtic name for England.

Hit were to tore for to telle of the tenthe dole.
720 Sumwhyle wyth wormez he werrez, and with wolves als,
Sumwhyle wyth wodwos that woned in the knarrez,
Bothe wyth bullez and berez, and borez otherquyle,
And etaynez that hym anelede of the heghe felle;
Nade he ben dughty and dryghe, and Dryghtyn had served,
725 Douteles he hade ben ded and dreped ful ofte.
For werre wrathed hym not so much that wynter nas wors,
When the colde cler water fro the cloudez schadde,
And fres er hit falle myght to the fale erthe.
Ner slayn wyth the slete he sleped in his yrnes
730 Mo nyghtez then innoghe in naked rokkez,
Ther as claterande fro the crest the colde borne rennez,
And henged heghe over his hede in hard iisse-ikkles.
Thus in peryl and payne and plytes ful harde
Bi contray caryez this knyght, tyl Krystmasse even,
735   al one;
        The knyght wel that tyde
        To Mary made his mone,
        That ho hym red to ryde
        And wysse hym to sum wone.

740 Bi a mounte on the morne meryly he rydes
Into a forest ful dep, that ferly watz wylde;
Highe hillez on uche a halve, and holtwodez under
Of hore okez ful hoge a hundreth togeder;
The hasel and the haghthorne were harled al samen,
745 With roghe raged mosse rayled aywhere,
With mony bryddez unblythe upon bare twyges,
That pitosly ther piped for pyne of the colde.
The gome upon Gryngolet glydez hem under,
Thurgh mony misy and myre, mon al hym one,
750 Carande for his costes, lest he ne kever schulde
To se the servyse of that syre, that on that self nyght
Of a burde watz borne, our baret to quelle;
And therfore sykyng he sayde, "I beseche the, lorde,
And Mary, that is myldest moder so dere,
755 Of sum herber ther heghly I myght here masse,
And thy matynez[1] to-morne, mekely I ask,
And therto prestly I pray my pater[2] and ave[3]
        and crede."[4]

It would be tedious to recount the least part of them.
720 Sometimes he fights dragons, and wolves as well,
Sometimes with wild men who dwelt among the crags;
Both with bulls and with bears, and at other times boars,
And ogres who chased him across the high fells.
Had he not been valiant and resolute, trusting in God,
725 He would surely have died or been killed many times.
For fighting troubled him less than the rigorous winter,
When cold clear water fell from the clouds
And froze before it could reach the faded earth.
Half dead with the cold Gawain slept in his armor
730 More nights than enough among the bare rocks,
Where splashing from the hilltops the freezing stream runs,
And hung over his head in hard icicles.
Thus in danger, hardship and continual pain
This knight rides across the land until Christmas Eve
735   alone.
        Earnestly Gawain then
        Prayed Mary that she send
        Him guidance to some place
        Where he might lodging find.

740 Over a hill in the morning in splendor he rides
Into a dense forest, wondrously wild;
High slopes on each side and woods at their base
Of massive grey oaks, hundreds growing together;
Hazel and hawthorn were densely entangled,
745 Thickly festooned with coarse shaggy moss,
Where many miserable birds on the bare branches
Wretchedly piped for torment of the cold.
The knight on Gringolet hurries under the trees,
Through many a morass and swamp, a solitary figure,
750 Troubled about his plight, lest he should be unable
To attend mass for that lord who on that same night
Was born of a maiden, our suffering to end;
And therefore sighing he prayed, "I beg of you, Lord,
And Mary, who is gentlest mother so dear,
755 For some lodging where I might devoutly hear mass
And your matins tomorrow, humbly I ask;
And to this end promptly repeat my Pater and Ave
        and Creed."

---

[1] *matynez* I.e., matins, morning prayer, but here a church service specifically devoted to Mary as the mother of Jesus Christ ("matins of the blessed Virgin Mary").

[2] *pater* Latin: father; i.e., "The Lord's Prayer" ("Our Father, who art in Heaven … ").

[3] *ave* Latin: hail; i.e., "Ave Maria" ("Hail Mary").

[4] *crede* Latin: I believe ("The Creed").

He rode in his prayere,
760   And cryed for his mysdede,
He sayned hym in sythes sere,[1]
And sayde, "Cros Kryst me spede!"

Nade he sayned hymself, segge, bot thrye,
Er he watz war in the wod of a wone in a mote,
765   Abof a launde, on a lawe, loken under boghez
Of mony borelych bole aboute bi the diches:
A castle the comlokest that ever knyght aghte,
Pyched on a prayere, a park al aboute,
With a pyked palays pyned ful thik,
770   That umbeteye mony tre mo then two myle.
That holde on that on syde the hathel avysed
As hit schemered and schon[2] thurgh the schyre okez;
Thenne hatz he hendly of his helme, and heghly he thonkez
Jesus and sayn Gilyan,[3] that gentyle ar bothe,
775   That cortaysly had hym kydde, and his cry herkened.
"Now bone hostel,"[4] cothe the burne, "I beseche yow yette!"
Thenne gerdez he to Gryngolet with the gilt helez,
And he ful chauncely hatz chosen to the chef gate,
That broght bremly the burne to the bryge ende
780   in haste.
        The bryge watz breme upbrayde,
        The gatez were stoken faste,
        The wallez were wel arayed
        Hit dut no wyndez blaste.

785   The burne bode on blonk, that on bonk hoved
Of the depe double dich that drof to the place;
The walle wod in the water wonderly depe,
And eft a ful huge heght hit haled upon lofte
Of harde hewen ston up to the tablez,
790   Enbaned under the abataylment in the best lawe;
And sythen garytez ful gaye gered bitwene,
Wyth mony luflych loupe that louked ful clene:
A better barbican that burne bluschéd upon never.
And innermore he behelde that halle ful hyghe,
795   Towres telded bytwene, trochet ful thik,
Fayre fylyolez that fyghed, and ferlyly long,

Bewailing his misdeeds,
760   And praying as he rode,
He often crossed himself
Crying, "Prosper me, Christ's cross!"

Hardly had he crossed himself, that man, three times,
Before he caught sight through the trees of a moated building
765   Standing over a field, on a mound, surrounded by boughs
Of many a massive tree-trunk enclosing the moat:
The most splendid castle ever owned by a knight,
Set on a meadow, a park all around,
Closely guarded by a spiked palisade
770   That encircled many trees for more than two miles.
That side of the castle Sir Gawain surveyed
As it shimmered and shone through the fine oaks;
Then graciously takes off his helmet, and devoutly thanks
Jesus and St. Julian, who kindly are both,
775   Who had treated him courteously, and listened to his prayer.
"Now good lodging," said the man, "I beg you to grant!"
Then he urged Gringolet forward with his gilt spurs,
And by good chance happened upon the main path
That led the knight directly to the end of the drawbridge
780   with speed.
        The bridge was drawn up tight,
        The gates were bolted fast,
        The walls were strongly built,
        They feared no tempest's blast.

785   The knight sat on his horse, pausing on the slope
Of the deep double ditch that surrounded the place.
The wall stood in the water incredibly deep,
And then soared up above an astonishing height,
Made of squared stone up to the cornice,
790   With coursings under battlements in the latest style.
At intervals splendid watch-towers were placed,
With many neat loop-holes that could be tightly shut:
Better outworks of a castle the knight had never seen.
Further inside he noticed a lofty hall
795   With towers set at intervals, richly ornate,
Splendid pinnacles fitted into them, wonderfully tall,

---

[1]   *in sythes sere*   Every time he prayed.

[2]   *hit schemered and schon*   See also *that blenked ful quyte*, 799.

[3]   *sayn Gilyan*   I.e., St. Julian, patron saint of hospitality.

[4]   *bone hostel*   "Good lodging," a traditional invocation to St. Julian.

With corvon coprounez craftyly sleghe.[1]
Chalkwhyt chymnees ther ches he innoghe[2]
Upon bastel rovez, that blenked ful quyte;
800 So mony pynakle paynted watz poudred ayquere,
Among the castel carnelez clambred so thik
That pared out of papure[3] purely hit semed.
The fre freke on the fole hit fayre innoghe thoght,
If he myght kever to com the cloyster wythinne,
805 To herber in that hostel whyl halyday lested,
            avinant.
        He calde, and son ther com
        A porter pure plesaunt,
        On the wal his ernde he nome,
810   And haylsed the knyght erraunt.

"Gode sir," quoth Gawan, "woldez thou go myn ernde,
To the hegh lorde of this hous, herber to crave?"
"Ye, Peter,"[4] quoth the porter, "and purely I trowee
That ye be, wyghe, welcum to wone quyle yow lykez."
815 Then yede the wyghe yerne and com agayn swythe,
And folke frely hym wyth, to fonge the knyght.
Thay let doun the grete draght and derely out yeden,
And kneled doun on her knes upon the colde erthe
To welcum this ilk wygh as worthy hom thoght;
820 Thay yolden hym the brode gate, yarked up wyde,
And he hem raysed rekenly, and rod over the brygge.
Sere segges hym sesed by sadel, quel he lyght,
And sythen stabled his stede stif men innoghe.
Knyghtez and swyerez comen doun thenne
825 For to bryng this buurne wyth blys into halle;
Quen he hef up his helme, ther hyghed innoghe
For to hent it at his honde, the hende to serven;
His bronde and his blasoun both thay token.
Then haylsed he ful hendly tho hathelez uchone,
830 And many proud mon ther presed that prynce to honour.
Alle hasped in his hegh wede to halle thay hym wonnen,

Topped by carved crocketing, skillfully worked.
Chalk-white chimneys he saw there without number
On the roofs of the towers, that brilliantly shone.
800 So many painted pinnacles were scattered everywhere,
Thickly clustered among the castle's embrasures,
That, truly, the building seemed cut out of paper.
To the noble on the horse it was an attractive thought
That he might gain entrance into the castle,
805 To lodge in that building during the festival days
            at his ease.
        A cheerful porter came
        In answer to his shout,
        Who stationed on the wall
810   Greeted the questing knight.

"Good sir," said Gawain, "will you carry my message
To the master of this house, to ask for lodging?"
"Yes, by St. Peter," said the porter, "and I truly believe
That you are welcome, sir, to stay as long as you please."
815 Then the man went speedily and quickly returned,
Bringing others with him, to welcome the knight.
They lowered the great drawbridge and graciously came out,
Kneeling down on their knees upon the cold ground
To welcome this knight in the way they thought fit.
820 They gave him passage through the broad gate, set open wide,
And he courteously bade them rise, and rode over the bridge.
Several men held his saddle while he dismounted,
And then strong men in plenty stabled his horse.
Knights and squires came down then
825 To escort this man joyfully into the hall.
When Gawain took off his helmet, several jumped forward
To receive it from his hand, serving that prince.
His sword and his shield they took from him both.
Then he greeted politely every one of these knights,
830 And many proud men pressed forward to honor that noble.
Still dressed in his armor they brought him into hall,

---

[1] *craftyly sleghe* The castle architecture abounds with crafts-manship. *Sleghe*, meaning skillful, intricate, subtle, is a term of some significance in the poem. Gawain's fellow-guests hope to see *sleghtez of thewez*, 916, skillful displays of good manners; and after creeping into his bedchamber the lady calls him *a sleper unslyghe*, 1209 or unwary, a related term. On being told that he cannot be killed *for slyght upon erthe*, 1854, while wearing the belt, Gawain tells himself that such a *sleght were noble*, 1858. Here the word shades off towards modern "sleight," with overtones of trickery or deceit appropriate to

the story. But many passages of the poem illustrate the poet's fondness for the elaborate craftsmanship or *wylyde werke* that is evident in his own writing, particularly in the *entrelacement* of Part 3.

[2] *ches he innoghe* He saw enough of them, meaning there were very many.

[3] *papure* Paper, a word newly introduced into English, perhaps by the poet.

[4] *Peter* I.e., St. Peter, one of Christ's twelve apostles and, tradi-tionally, the gate-keeper of Heaven.

Ther fayre fyre upon flet fersly brenned.
Thenne the lorde of the lede loutez fro his chambre
For to mete wyth menske the mon on the flor;
835 He sayde, "Ye ar welcum to welde as yow lykez
That here is: al is yowre awen, to have at yowre wylle
        and welde."
      "Graunt mercy," quoth Gawayn,
      "Ther Kryst hit yow foryelde."
840   As frekez that semed fayn
        Ayther other in armez con felde.

Gawan glynte on the gome that godly hym gret,
And thught hit a bolde burne that the burgh aghte;
A hoge hathel for the nonez, and of hyghe eldee;
845 Brode, bryght, watz his berde, and al bever-hwed,
Sturne, stif on the stryththe on stalworth schonkez,
Felle face as the fyre, and fre of hys speche,
And wel hym semed, for sothe, as the segge thught,
To lede a lortschyp in lee of leudez ful gode.
850 The lorde hym charred to a chambre, and chefly cumaundez
To delyver hym a leude, hym lowly to serve;
And there were boun at his bode burnez innoghe,
That broght hym to a bryght boure, ther beddyng was
        noble,
Of cortynes of clere sylk wyth cler golde hemmez,
855 And covertorez ful curious with comlych panez
Of bryght blaunner above, enbrawded bisydez,
Rudelez rennande on ropez, red golde ryngez,
Tapitez tyght to the wowe of tuly and tars,
And under fete, on the flet, of folyande sute.
860 Ther he watz dispoyled, wyth speches of myerthe,
The burne of his bruny and of his bryght wedez.
Ryche robes ful rad renkkez hym broghten,
For to charge and to chaunge, and chose of the best.
Sone as he on hent, and happed therinne,
865 That sete on hym semly wyth saylande skyrtez,
The ver by his visage verayly hit semed
Welnegh to uche hathel, alle on hwes
Lowande and lufly alle his lymmez under,
That a comloker knyght never Kryst made,
870   hem thoght.
      Whethen in worlde he were,
      Hit semed as he moght

Where a blazing fire was fiercely burning.
Then the lord of that company comes down from his chamber,
To show his respect by meeting Gawain there.
835 He said, "You are welcome to do as you please
With everything here: all is yours, to have and command
        as you wish."
      Said Gawain, "Thanks indeed,
      Christ repay your noblesse."
840   Like men overjoyed
        Each hugged the other close.

Gawain studied the man who greeted him courteously,
And thought him a bold one who governed the castle,
A great-sized knight indeed, in the prime of life;
845 Broad and glossy was his beard, all reddish-brown,
Stern-faced, standing firmly on powerful legs;
With a face fierce as fire, and noble in speech,
Who truly seemed capable, it appeared to Gawain,
Of being master of a castle with outstanding knights.
850 The lord led him to a chamber and quickly orders
A man to be assigned to him, humbly to serve;
And several attendants stood ready at his command
Who took him to a fine bedroom with marvelous
        bedding:
Curtains of pure silk with shining gold borders,
855 And elaborate coverlets with splendid facing
Of bright ermine on top, embroidered all around;
Curtains on golden rings, running on cords,
Walls covered with hangings from Tharsia and Toulouse
And underfoot on the floor of a matching kind.
860 There he was stripped, with joking remarks,
That knight, of his mail-shirt and his fine clothes.
Men hurried to bring him costly robes
To choose from the best of them, change and put on.
As soon as he took one and dressed himself in it,
865 Which suited him well with its flowing skirts,
Almost everyone truly supposed from his looks
That spring had arrived in all its colors;
His limbs so shining and attractive under his clothes
That a handsomer knight God never made,
870   it seemed.
      Wherever he came from,
      He must be, so they thought,

Be prynce withouten pere
In felde ther felle men foght.

A prince unparalleled
In field where warriors fought.

875 A cheyer¹ byfore the chemné, ther charcole brenned,
Watz grathed for Sir Gawan graythely with clothez,
Whyssynes upon queldepoyntes that koynt wer bothe;
And thenne a meré mantyle watz on that mon cast
Of a broun bleeaunt, enbrauded ful ryche
880 And fayre furred wythinne with fellez of the best,
Alle of ermyn in erde, his hode of the same;
And he sette in that settel semlych ryche,
And achaufed hym chefly, and thenne his cher mended.
Sone watz telded up a tabil on trestez ful fayre,
885 Clad wyth a clene clothe that cler quyt schewed,
Sanap, and salure, and sylverin sponez.
The wyghe wesche at his wylle and went to his mete:
Seggez hym served semly innoghe,
Wyth sere sewes and sete, sesounde of the best,
890 Double-felde, as hit fallez, and fele kyn fischez,²
Summe baken in bred, summe brad on the gledez,
Summe sothen, summe in sewe savered with spyces,
And ay sawes so sleghe that the segge lyked.
The freke calde hit a fest ful frely and ofte
895 Ful hendely, quen alle the hatheles rehayted hym at onez,
        as hende,
    "This penaunce now ye take,
    And eft hit schal amende."
    That mon much merthe con make,
900 For wyn in his hed that wende.

875 A chair before the fireplace where charcoal glowed
Was made ready with coverings for Gawain at once:
Cushions set on quilted spreads, both skilfully made,
And then a handsome robe was thrown over the man
Made of rich brown material, with embroidery rich,
880 And well fur-lined inside with the very best pelts,
All of ermine in fact, with a matching hood.
Becomingly rich in attire he sat in that chair,
Quickly warmed himself, and then his expression softened.
Soon a table was deftly set up on trestles,
885 Spread with a fine tablecloth, brilliantly white,
With overcloth and salt-cellar, and silver spoons.
When he was ready Gawain washed and sat down to his meal.
Men served him with every mark of respect,
With many excellent dishes, wonderfully seasoned,
890 In double portions, as is fitting, and all kinds of fish:
Some baked in pastry, some grilled over coals,
Some boiled, some in stews flavored with spices,
Always with subtle sauces that the knight found tasty.
Many times he graciously called it a feast,
895 Courteously when the knights all urged him together,
        as polite,
    "Accept this penance now,
    Soon you'll be better fed."
    Gawain grew full of mirth
900 As wine went to his head.

Thenne watz spyed and spured upon spare wyse
Bi prevé poyntez of that prynce, put to hymselven,
That he biknew cortaysly of the court that he were
That athel Arthure the hende haldez hym one,
905 That is the ryche ryal kyng of the Rounde Table,
And hit watz Wawen hymself that in that won syttez,
Comen to that Krystmasse, as case hym then lymped.
When the lorde hade lerned that he the leude hade,
Loude laghed he therat, so lef hit hym thoght,

Then he was tactfully questioned and asked
By discreet enquiry addressed to that prince,
So that he must politely admit he belonged to the court
Which noble Arthur, that gracious man, rules alone,
905 Who is the great and royal king of the Round Table;
And that it was Gawain himself who was sitting there,
Having arrived there at Christmas, as his fortune chanced.
When the lord of the castle heard who was his guest,
He laughed loudly at the news, so deeply was he pleased;

---

¹ *A cheyer*   Chairs were relatively rare, and to be given one was a mark of respect. The usual form of seat is indicated by the Green Knight's reference to knights *aboute on this bench*, 280, and by Gawain's request for permission to *boghe fro this benche*, 344.

² *fele kyn fischez*   Many kinds of fish. Because Christmas Eve is a fast-day, no red meat is served. The meal is jokingly referred to as penance, 897, and Gawain is promised something better on the next day, 898.

910 And alle the men in that mote maden much joye
To apere in his presense prestly that tyme,
That alle prys and prowes and pured thewes[1]
Apendes to hys persoun, and praysed is ever;
Byfore alle men upon molde his mensk is the most.
915 Uch segge ful softly sayde to his fere:
"Now schal we semlych se sleghtez of thewez
And the teccheles termes of talkyng noble,
Wich spede is in speche unspurd may we lerne,[2]
Syn we haf fonged that fyne fader of nurture.
920 God hatz geven us his grace godly for sothe,
That such a gest as Gawan grauntez us to have,
When burnez blythe of his burthe schal sitte
        and synge.
    In menyng of manerez mere
925   This burne now schal us bryng,
    I hope that may hym here
    Schal lerne of luf-talkyng."

Bi that the diner watz done and the dere up
Hit watz negh at the niyght neghed the tyme.
930 Chaplaynez to the chapeles chosen the gate,
Rungen ful rychely, ryght as thay schulden,
To the hersum evensong of the hyge tyde.
The lorde loutes therto, and the lady als,
Into a cumly closet coyntly ho entrez.
935 Gawan glydez ful gay and gos theder sone;
The lorde laches hym by the lappe and ledez hym to sytte,
And couthly hym knowez and callez hym his nome,
And sayde he watz the welcomest wyghe of the worlde;
And he hym thonkked throly, and ayther halched other,
940 And seten soberly samen the servise quyle.
Thenne lyst the lady to loke on the knyght,
Thenne com ho of hir closet with mony cler burdez.
Ho watz the fayrest in felle,[3] of flesche and of lyre,
And of compas and colour and costes, of all other,
945 And wener then Wenore, as the wyght thoght.
Ho ches thurgh the chaunsel to cheryche that hende:
An other lady hir lad bi the lyft honde,
That watz alder then ho, an auncian hit semed,
And heghly honowred with hathelez aboute.

910 And all the men in the castle were overjoyed
To make the acquaintance quickly then
Of the man to whom all excellence and valor belongs,
Whose refined manners are everywhere praised,
And whose fame exceeds any other person's on earth.
915 Each knight whispered to his companion,
"Now we shall enjoy seeing displays of good manners,
And the irreproachable terms of noble speech;
The art of conversation we can learn unasked,
Since we have taken in the source of good breeding.
920 Truly, God has been gracious to us indeed,
In allowing us to receive such a guest as Gawain,
Whose birth men will happily sit down and celebrate
        in song.
    In knowledge of fine manners
925   This man has expertise;
    I think that those who hear him
    Will learn what love-talk is."

When dinner was finished and Gawain had risen,
The time had drawn on almost to night:
930 Chaplains made their way to the castle chapels,
Rang their bells loudly, just as they should,
For devout evensong on that holy occasion.
The lord makes his way there, and his lady too,
Who gracefully enters a finely carved pew.
935 Gawain hastens there, smartly dressed, and quickly arrives;
The lord takes him by the sleeve and leads him to a seat,
And greets him familiarly, calling him by his name,
And said he was the welcomest guest in the world.
Gawain thanked him heartily, and the two men embraced,
940 And sat gravely together while the service lasted.
Then the lady wished to set eyes on the knight
And left her pew with many fair women.
She was the loveliest on earth in complexion and features,
In figure, in coloring and behavior above all others,
945 And more beautiful than Guenevere, it seemed to the knight.
She came through the chancel to greet him courteously,
Another lady leading her by the left hand,
Who was older than she, an aged one it seemed,
And respectfully treated by the assembled knights.

---

[1] *alle prys and prowes and pured thewes* Great excellence, military valor, and refined manners.

[2] *Wich spede is in speche unspurd may we lerne* We may learn without asking what success in conversation consists of.

[3] *the fayrest in felle* Literally, the most beautiful in skin.

950 Bot unlyke on to loke tho ladyes were,
For if the yonge watz yep, yolwe watz that other;
Riche red on that on rayled ayquere,
Rugh ronkled chekez that other on rolled;
Kerchofes of that on, wyth mony cler perlez,
955 Hir brest and hir bryght throte bare displayed,
Schon schyrer then snawe that schedez on hillez;
That other wyth a gorger watz gered over the swyre,
Chymbled over hir blake chyn with chalkquyte vayles,
Hir frount folden in sylk, enfoubled ayquere,
960 Toreted and treleted with tryfles aboute,
That noght watz bare of that burde bot the blake browes,
The tweyne yghen and the nase, the naked lyppez,
And those were soure to se and sellyly blered;
A mensk lady on molde mon may hire calle,
965   for Gode!
        Hir body watz schort and thik,
        Hir buttokez balgh and brode,
        More lykkerwys on to lyk
        Watz that scho hade on lode.

970 When Gawayn glent on that gay, that graciously loked,
Wyth leve laght of the lorde he lent hem agaynes;
The alder he haylses, heldande ful lowe,
The loveloker he lappez a lyttel in armez,
He kysses hir comlyly, and knyghtly he melez.
975 Thay kallen hym of aquoyntaunce, and he hit quyk askez
To be hir servaunt sothly, if hemself lyked.
Thay tan hym bytwene hem, wyth talkyng hym leden
To chambre, to chemné, and chefly thay asken
Spycez,[1] that unsparely men speded hom to bryng,
980 And the wynnelych wyne therwith uche tyme.
The lorde luflych aloft lepez ful ofte,
Mynned merthe to be made upon mony sythez,
Hent heghly of his hode, and on a spere henged,
And wayned hom to wynne the worchip therof,
985 That most myrthe myght meve that Crystenmasse whyle:[2]
"And I schal fonde, bi my fayth, to fylter wyth the best
Er me wont the wede, with help of my frendez."
Thus wyth laghande lotez the lorde hit tayt makez,
For to glade Sir Gawayn with gomnez in halle
990   that nyght,

950 But very different in looks were those two ladies,
For where the young one was fresh, the other was withered;
Every part of that one was rosily aglow:
On that other, rough wrinkled cheeks hung in folds.
Many bright pearls adorned the kerchiefs of one,
955 Whose breast and white throat, uncovered and bare,
Shone more dazzling than snow new-fallen on hills;
The other wore a gorget over her neck,
Her swarthy chin wrapped in chalkwhite veils,
Her forehead enfolded in silk, muffled up everywhere,
960 With embroidered hems and lattice-work of tiny stitching,
So that nothing was exposed of her but her black brows,
Her two eyes and her nose, her naked lips,
Which were repulsive to see and shockingly bleared.
A noble lady indeed you might call her,
965   by God!
        With body squat and thick,
        And buttocks bulging broad,
        More delectable in looks
        Was the lady whom she led.

970 Gawain glanced at that beauty, who favored him with a look,
And taking leave of the lord he walked towards them.
The older one he salutes with a deep bow,
And takes the lovelier one briefly into his arms,
Kisses her respectfully and courteously speaks.
975 They ask to make his acquaintance, and he quickly begs
Truly to be their servant, if that would please them.
They place him between them and lead him, still chatting,
To a private room, to the fireplace, and immediately call
For spiced cakes, which men hurried to bring them unstinted,
980 Together with marvelous wine each time they asked.
The lord jumps up politely on several occasions,
Repeatedly urging his guests to make merry;
Graciously pulled off his hood and hung it on a spear,
And encouraged them to gain honor by winning it,
985 So that the Christmas season would abound with mirth.
"And I shall try, on my word, to compete with the best,
Before I lose my hood, with the help of my friends."
Thus with laughing words the lord makes merry,
To keep Sir Gawain amused with games in hall
990   that night,

---

[1] *Spycez* Spiced cakes, still a Christmas tradition. Cloves, ginger, and cinnamon were available.

[2] *Hent heghly … Crystenmasse whyle* Another Christmas game, evidently a jumping contest, typically boisterous in character.

Til that hit watz tyme
The lord comaundet lyght;
Sir Gawen his leve con nyme
And to his bed hym dight.

995 On the morne, as uch mon mynez that tyme
That Dryghtyn for oure destyné to deye watz borne,
Wele waxez in uche a won in world for his sake;
So did hit there on that day thurgh dayntés mony.
Bothe at mes and at mele messes ful quaynt[1]
1000 Derf men upon dece drest of the best.
The olde auncian wyf heghest ho syttez,
The lorde lufly her by lent, as I trowe;
Gawan and the gay burde togeder thay seten,
Even inmyddez, as the messe metely come,
1005 And sythen thurgh al the sale as hem best semed.
Bi uche grome at his degré graythely watz served,
Ther watz mete, ther watz myrthe, ther watz much joye,
That for to telle therof hit me tene were,
And to poynte hit yet I pyned me paraventure.
1010 Bot yet I wot that Wawen and the wale burde
Such comfort of her compaynye caghten togeder
Thurgh her dere dalyaunce of her derne wordez,
Wyth clene cortays carp closed fro fylthe,
That hor play watz passande uche prynce gomen,
1015   in vayres.
          Trumpes and nakerys,
          Much pypyng ther repayres;
          Uche mon tented hys,[2]
          And thay two tented thayres.

1020 Much dut watz ther dryven that day and that other,
And the thryd as thro thronge in therafter;
The joye of sayn Jonez day[3] watz gentyle to here,
And watz the last of the layk, leudez ther thoghten.
Ther wer gestes to go upon the gray morne,
1025 Forthy wonderly thay woke, and the wyn dronken,
Daunsed ful dreghly wyth dere carolez.
At the last, when hit watz late, thay lachen her leve,
Uchon to wende on his way that watz wyghe straunge.[4]

Until it was so late
That lights were ordered in;
Then taking courteous leave
To chamber went Gawain.

995 On the next day, when everyone remembers the time
When God who died for our salvation was born,
Joy spreads through every dwelling on earth for his sake.
So did it there on that day, through numerous pleasures;
Both light meals and great dishes cunningly prepared
1000 And of exquisite quality bold men served on the dais.
The ancient lady sits in the place of honor,
The lord politely taking his place by her, I believe.
Gawain and the lovely lady were seated together,
Right in the middle of the table, where food duly came,
1005 And was then served throughout the hall in proper sequence.
By the time each man had been served according to rank,
Such food and such merriment, so much enjoyment were there
That to tell you about it would give me much trouble,
Especially if I tried to describe it in detail.
1010 Yet I know that Gawain and his beautiful partner
Found such enjoyment in each other's company,
Through a playful exchange of private remarks,
And well-mannered small-talk, unsullied by sin,
That their pleasure surpassed every princely amusement,
1015   for sure.
          Trumpets, kettledrums
          And piping roused all ears.
          Each man fulfilled his wishes,
          And those two followed theirs.

1020 Great joy filled that day and the one following,
And a third as delightful came pressing after;
The revelry on St. John's Day was glorious to hear,
And was the end of the festivities, the people supposed.
The guests were to leave early next morning,
1025 And so they reveled all night, drinking the wine
And ceaselessly dancing and caroling songs.
At last, when it was late, they take their leave,
Each one who was a guest there to go on his way.

---

[1] *messes ful quaynt* Finely prepared meals, set out (*drest*) on the high table. Elsewhere *koynt*, 877 is a variant spelling, again indicating skillfully made things.

[2] *Uche mon tented hys* Each man attended to his own needs or pleasures.

[3] *sayn Jonez day* 27 December, but three days later it is New Year's Eve—a day too early. Some editors have suggested a line may be missing here.

[4] *wyghe straunge* Stranger or visitor to the castle.

Gawan gef hym god day, the godmon hym lachchez,
1030 Ledes hym to his awen chambre, the chemné bysyde,
And there he drawez hym on dryghe, and derely hym thonkkez
Of the wynne worschip that he hym wayved hade,
As to honour his hous on that hygh tyde,
And enbelyse his burgh with his bele chere.[1]
1035 "Iwysse, sir, quyl I leve, me worthez the better
That Gawayn hatz ben my gest at Goddez awen fest."
"Grant merci, sir," quoth Gawayn, "in god fayth hit is yowrez,
Al the honour is your awen—the heghe kyng yow yelde!
And I am wyghe at your wylle to worch youre hest,
1040 As I am halden therto, in hyghe and in lowe,
          bi right."
     The lorde fast can hym payne
     To holde lenger the knyght;
     To hym answarez Gawayn
1045 Bi non way that he myght.[2]

Then frayned the freke ful fayre at himselven
Quat derve dede had hym dryven at that dere tyme
So kenly fro the kyngez kourt to kayre al his one,
Er the halidayez holly were halet[3] out of toun.
1050 "For sothe, sir," quoth the segge, "ye sayn bot the trawthe,
A heghe ernde and a hasty me hade fro tho wonez,
For I am sumned myselfe to sech to a place,
I ne wot in the worlde whederwarde to wende hit to fynde.
I nolde bot if I hit negh myght on Nw Yeres morne
1055 For alle the londe inwyth Logres, so me oure lorde help!
Forthy, sir, this enquest I require yow here,
That ye telle me with trawthe if ever ye tale herde
Of the grene chapel, quere hit on grounde stondez,
And of the knyght that hit kepes, of colour of grene.
1060 Ther watz stabled bi statut a steven us bitwene
To mete that mon at that mere, yif I myght last;
And of that ilk Nw Yere bot neked now wontez,
And I wolde loke on that lede, if God me let wolde,
Gladloker, bi Goddez sun, then any god welde!
1065 Forthi, iwysse, bi yowre wylle, wende me bihoves,
Naf I now to busy bot bare thre dayez,
And me als fayn to falle feye as fayly of myyn ernde."
Thenne laghande quoth the lorde, "Now leng the byhoves,

Gawain bids goodbye to his host, who takes hold of him,
1030 Leads him to his own room, beside the fire,
And there he detains him, thanks him profusely
For the wonderful kindness that Gawain had shown
By honoring his house at that festive time,
And by gracing the castle with his charming presence.
1035 "Indeed, sir, as long as I live I shall be the better
Because Gawain was my guest at God's own feast."
"All my thanks, sir," said Gawain, "in truth it is yours,
All the honor falls to you, and may the high king repay you!
And I am at your commandment to act on your bidding,
1040 As I am duty bound to in everything, large or small,
          by right."
     The lord tried strenuously
     To lengthen Gawain's stay,
     But Gawain answered him
1045 That he could not delay.

Then the lord politely enquired of the knight
What pressing need had forced him at that festive time
So urgently from the royal court to travel all alone,
Before the holy days there had completely passed.
1050 "Indeed, sir," said the knight, "you are right to wonder;
A task important and pressing drove me into the wild,
For I am summoned in person to seek out a place
With no idea whatever where it might be found.
I would not fail to reach it on New Year's morning
1055 For all the land in England, so help me our Lord!
Therefore, sir, this request I make of you now,
That you truthfully tell me if you ever heard talk
Of a Green Chapel, wherever it stands upon earth,
And of a knight who maintains it, who is colored green.
1060 A verbal agreement was settled between us
To meet that man at that place, should I be alive,
And before that New Year little time now remains;
And I would face that man, if God would allow me,
More gladly, by God's son, than come by great wealth!
1065 With your permission, therefore, I must indeed leave:
I have now for my business only three short days,
And would rather be struck dead than fail in my quest."
Then the lord said, laughing, "Now you must stay,

---

[1] *enbelyse … bele chere* Bertilak (Gawain's host) makes an uncharacteristic sortie into courtly French terms.

[2] *Bi non way that he myght* He could not by any means.

[3] *Er the halidayez holly were halet* Before the holidays were completely over. A curious remark. Gawain reaches the castle, Hautdesert, after a long journey (*towen fro ferre*, 1093) as the festivities are reaching their height, having left Camelot long before the holiday season began.

For I schal teche yow to that terme bi the tymes ende,
1070 The grene chapayle upon grounde greve yow no more;
Bot ye schal be in yowre bed, burne, at thyn ese,
Quyle forth dayez, and ferk on the fyrst of the yere,
And cum to that merk at mydmorn, to make quat yow likez
    in spenne.
1075   Dowellez whyle New Yeres daye,
  And rys, and raykez thenne,
  Mon schal yow sette in waye,
  Hit is not two myle henne."

Thenne watz Gawan ful glad, and gomenly he laghed:
1080 "Now I thonk yow thryvandely thurgh alle other thynge,
Now acheved is my chaunce, I schal at your wylle
Dowelle, and ellez do quat ye demen."
Thenne sesed hym the syre and set hym bysyde,
Let the ladiez be fette to lyke hem the better.
1085 Ther watz seme solace by hemself stille;
The lorde let for luf lotez so myry
As wygh that wolde of his wyte, ne wyst quat he myght.
Thenne he carped to the knyght, criande loude,
"Ye han demed to do the dede that I bidde;
1090 Wyl ye halde this hes here at thys onez?"
"Ye, sir, for sothe," sayd the segge trwe,
"Whyl I byde in yowre borghe, be bayn to yowre hest."
"For ye haf travayled," quoth the tulk, "towen fro ferre,
And sythen waked me wyth, ye arn not wel waryst
1095 Nauther of sostnaunce ne of slepe, sothly I knowe;
Ye schal lenge in your lofte, and lyghe in your ese
To-morn quyle the messequyle, and to mete wende
When ye wyl, wyth my wyf, that wyth yow schal sitte
And comfort yow with compayny, til I to cort torne;
1100   ye lende,
  And I schal erly ryse,
  On huntyng wyl I wende."
  Gavayn grantez alle thyse,
  Hym heldande, as the hende.

1105 "Yet firre," quoth the freke, "a forwarde we make:
Quat-so-ever I wynne in the wod hit worthez to yourez,
And quat chek so ye acheve[1] chaunge me therfore.
Swete, swap we so, sware with trawthe,

For I shall direct you to your meeting at the year's end.
1070 Let the whereabouts of the Green Chapel worry you no more;
For you shall lie in your bed, sir, taking your ease
Until late in the day, and leave on the first of the year,
And reach that place at midday, to do whatever pleases you
    there.
1075   Stay till the year's end,
  And leave on New Year's Day;
  We'll put you on the path,
  It's not two miles away."

Then Gawain was overjoyed, and merrily laughed:
1080 "Now I thank you heartily for this, above everything else,
Now my quest is accomplished, I shall at your wish
Remain here, and do whatever else you think fit."
Then the host seized him, set Gawain by his side,
And bid the ladies be fetched to increase their delight.
1085 They had great pleasure by themselves in private;
In his excitement the lord uttered such merry words
Like a man out of his mind, not knowing what he did.
Then he said to the knight exuberantly,
"You have agreed to carry out whatever deed I ask;
1090 Will you keep this promise now, at this very instant?"
"Yes, sir, assuredly," said the true knight,
"While I am under your roof, I obey your bidding."
"You have wearied yourself," said the man, "traveling from far,
And then reveled all night with me: you have not recovered
1095 Either your lost sleep or your nourishment, I am sure.
You shall stay in your bed and lie at your ease
Tomorrow until mass-time, and then go to dine
When you like, with my wife, who will sit at your side
And be your charming companion until I come home.
1100   You stay;
  And I shall rise at dawn
  And hunting will I go."
  All this Gawain grants,
  With a well-mannered bow.

1105 "Yet further," said the man, "let us make an agreement:
Whatever I catch in the wood shall become yours,
And whatever mishap comes your way give me in exchange.
Dear sir, let us swap so, swear me that truly,

---

[1] *quat chek so ye acheve* Whatever fortune you win. The remark is
equivocal. *Chek* also has the sense of misfortune—see 1857 and
2195.

Quether, leude, so lymp, lere other better."[1]
1110 "Bi God," quoth Gawayn the gode, "I grant thertylle,
And that yow lyst for to layke, lef hit me thynkes."
"Who bryngez uus this beverage, this bargayn is maked":
So sayde the lorde of that lede; thay laghed uchone,
Thay dronken and dalyeden and dalten untyghtel,
1115 Thise lordez and ladyez, quyle that hem lyked;
And sythen with Frenkysch fare[2] and fele fayre lotez
Thay stoden and stemed and stylly speken,
Kysten ful comlyly and kaghten her leve.
With mony leude ful lyght and lemande torches
1120 Uche burne to his bed watz broght at the laste,
      ful softe.
     To bed yet er thay yede,
     Recorded covenauntez ofte;
     The olde lorde of that leude
1125 Cowthe wel halde layk alofte.

FITT 3

Ful erly bifore the day the folk uprysen,
Gestes that go wolde hor gromez thay calden,
And thay busken up bilyve blonkkez to sadel,
Tyffen her takles, trussen her males,
1130 Richen hem the rychest, to ryde alle arayde,
Lepen up lightly, lachen her brydeles,
Uche wyghe on his way ther hym wel lyked.
The leve lorde of the londe watz not the last
Arayed for the rydyng, with renkkes ful mony;
1135 Ete a sop hastyly, when he hade herde masse,
With bugle to bent-felde he buskez bylyve.
By that any daylyght lemed upon erthe
He with his hatheles on hyghe horsses weren.
Thenne thise cacheres that couthe cowpled hor houndez,
1140 Unclosed the kenel dore and calde hem theroute,
Blwe bygly in buglez thre bare mote;[3]
Braches bayed therfore and breme noyse maked;
And thay chastysed and charred on chasyng that went,

Whatever falls to our lot, worthless or better."
1110 "By God," said the good Gawain, "I agree to that,
And your love of amusement pleases me much."
"If someone brings us drink, it will be an agreement,"
Said the lord of that company: everyone laughed.
They drank wine and joked and frivolously chatted
1115 For as long as it pleased them, these lords and ladies;
And then with exquisite manners and many gracious words
They stood at a pause, conversing quietly,
Kissed each other affectionately and then took their leave.
With many brisk servingmen and gleaming torches
1120 Each man was at last escorted to a bed
      downy soft.
     Yet first, and many times
     Again the terms were sworn;
     The master of those folk
1125 Knew how to foster fun.

PART 3

Early before daybreak the household arose;
Guests who were leaving called for their grooms,
And they hurried quickly to saddle horses,
Make equipment ready and pack their bags.
1130 The noblest prepare themselves to ride finely dressed,
Leap nimbly into saddle, seize their bridles,
Each man taking the path that attracted him most.
The well-loved lord of the region was not the last
Prepared for riding, with a great many knights;
1135 Snatched a hasty breakfast after hearing mass,
And makes ready for the hunting-field with bugles blowing.
By the time the first glimmers of daylight appeared
He and his knights were mounted on horse.
Then experienced huntsmen coupled the hounds,
1140 Unlocked the kennel door and ordered them out,
Loudly blowing three long notes on their horns.
Hounds bayed at the sound and made a fierce noise;
And those who went straying were whipped in and turned back,

---

[1] *Quether, leude, so lymp, lere other better* Whichever man wins
something worthless or better. The literal sense of *lymp* is "falls to
his lot."

[2] *Frenkysch fare* Refined manners, modeled on courtly French
behavior.

[3] *thre bare mote* Three single notes on the horn, ordering the
release of the hounds.

A hundreth of hunteres, as I haf herde telle,
1145   of the best.
    To trystors vewters yod,[1]
    Couples huntes of kest;
    Ther ros for blastez gode
    Gret rurd in that forest.

1150 At the fyrst quethe of the quest quaked the wylde;
    Der drof in the dale, doted for drede,
    Highed to the hyghe, bot heterly thay were
    Restayed with the stablye, that stoutly ascryed.
    Thay let the herttez haf the gate, with the hyghe hedes,
1155 The breme bukkez also with hor brode paumez;
    For the fre lorde hade defende in fermysoun tyme
    That ther schulde no mon meve to the male dere.
    The hindez were halden in with hay! and war!
    The does dryven with gret dyn to the depe sladez.
1160 Ther myght mon se, as thay slypte, slenting of arwes—
    At uche wende under wande wapped a flone—
    That bigly bote on the broun with ful brode hedez.
    What! thay brayen and bleden, bi bonkkez thay deyen,
    And ay rachches in a res radly hem folwes,
1165 Hunterez wyth hyghe horne hasted hem after
    Wyth such a crakkande kry as klyffes haden brusten.
    What wylde so atwaped wyghes that schotten
    Watz al toraced and rent at the resayt,
    Bi thay were tened at the hyghe and taysed to the wattres;
1170 The ledez were so lerned at the lowe trysteres,
    And the grehoundez so grete, that geten hem bylyve
    And hem tofylched, as fast as frekez myght loke,
            ther-ryght.
        The lorde for blys abloy
1175   Ful ofte con launce and lyght,
        And drof that day wyth joy
        Thus to the derk nyght.

    Thus laykez this lorde by lynde-wodez evez,
    And Gawayn the god mon in gay bed lygez,
1180 Lurkkez[2] quyl the daylyght lemed on the wowes,
    Under covertour ful clere, cortyned aboute;
    And as in slomeryng he slode, sleghly he herde
    A littel dyn at his dor, and dernly upon;
    And he hevez up his hed out of the clothes,

By a hundred hunters, as I have been told,
1145   of the best.
    With keepers at their posts
    Huntsmen uncoupled hounds;
    Great clamor in the woods
    From mighty horn-blasts sounds.

1150 At the first sound of the hunt the wild creatures trembled;
    Deer fled from the valley, frantic with fear,
    And rushed to the high ground, but were fiercely turned back
    By the line of beaters, who yelled at them savagely.
    They let the stags with their tall antlers pass,
1155 And the wonderful bucks with their broad horns;
    For the noble lord had forbidden in the close season
    Anyone to interfere with the male deer.
    The hinds were held back with shouts of hay! and war!
    The does driven with great noise into the deep valleys.
1160 There you might see, as they ran, arrows flying—
    At every turn in the wood a shaft whistled through the air—
    Deeply piercing the hide with their wide heads.
    What! they cry out and bleed, on the slopes they are slaughtered,
    And always swiftly pursued by the rushing hounds;
1165 Hunters with screaming horns gallop behind
    With such an ear-splitting noise as if cliffs had collapsed.
    Those beasts that escaped the men shooting at them
    Were all pulled down and killed at the receiving points,
    As they were driven from the high ground down to the streams.
1170 The men at the lower stations were so skilful,
    And the greyhounds so large, that they seized them quickly
    And tore them down as fast as men could number,
            right there.
        On horseback and on foot
1175   The lord, filled with delight,
        Spent all that day in bliss
        Until the fall of night.

    Thus this nobleman sports along the edges of woods,
    And the good man Gawain lies in his fine bed,
1180 Lying snug while the daylight gleamed on the walls,
    Under a splendid coverlet, shut in by curtains.
    And as he lazily dozed, he heard slily made
    A little noise at his door and it stealthily open;
    And he raised up his head from the bedclothes,

---

[1] *To trystors vewters yod* Keepers of hounds went to their hunting-stations.

[2] *Lurkkez* Lay snug; but the term has pejorative overtones that are heard again at 1195.

1185 A corner of the cortyn he caght up a lyttel,
And waytez warly thiderwarde quat hit be myght.
Hit watz the ladi, loflyest to beholde,
That drow the dor after hir ful dernly and stylle,
And bowed towarde the bed; and the burne schamed,[1]
1190 And layde hym doun lystyly and let as he slepte;
And ho stepped stilly and stel to his bedde,
Kest up the cortyn and creped withinne,
And set hir ful softly on the bed-syde,
And lenged there selly longe to loke quen he wakened.
1195 The lede lay lurked a ful longe quyle,
Compast in his concience to quat that cace myght
Meve other mount—to mervayle hym thoght,
Bot yet he sayde in hymself, "More semly hit were
To aspye wyth my spelle in space quat ho wolde."
1200 Then he wakenede, and wroth, and to hir warde torned,
And unlouked his yghe-lyddez, and let as hym wondered,
And sayned hym, as bi his saghe the saver to worthe,
              with hande.
        Wyth chynne and cheke ful swete,
1205   Both quit and red in blande,
        Ful lufly con ho lete
        Wyth lyppez smal laghande.

"God moroun, Sir Gawayn," sayde that gay lady,
"Ye ar a sleper unslyghe, that mon may slyde hider;
1210 Now ar ye tan as-tyt![2] Bot true uus may schape,
I schal bynde yow in your bedde, that be ye trayst."
Al laghande the lady lanced tho bourdez.
"Goud moroun, gay," quoth Gawayn the blythe,
"Me schal worthe at your wille, and that me wel lykez,[3]
1215 For I yelde me yederly, and yeghe after grace,
And that is the best, be my dome, for me byhovez nede":
And thus he bourded agayn with mony a blythe laghter.
"Bot wolde ye, lady lovely, then leve me grante,
And deprece your prysoun, and pray hym to ryse,
1220 I wolde bowe of this bed, and busk me better;
I schulde kever the more comfort to karp yow wyth."
"Nay, for sothe, beau sire," sayde that swete,

1185 Lifted a corner of the curtain a little,
And takes a glimpse warily to see what it could be.
It was the lady, looking her loveliest,
Who shut the door after her carefully, not making a sound,
And came towards the bed. The knight felt confused,
1190 And lay down again cautiously, pretending to sleep;
And she approached silently, stealing to his bed,
Lifted the bed-curtain and crept within,
And seating herself softly on the bedside,
Waited there strangely long to see when he would wake.
1195 The knight shammed sleep for a very long while,
Wondering what the matter could be leading to
Or portend. It seemed an astonishing thing,
Yet he told himself, "It would be more fitting
To discover straightway by talking just what she wants."
1200 Then he wakened and stretched and turned towards her,
Opened his eyes and pretended surprise,
And crossed himself as if protecting himself by prayer
              and this sign.
        With lovely chin and cheek
1205   Of blended color both,
        Charmingly she spoke
        From her small laughing mouth.

"Good morning, Sir Gawain," said that fair lady,
"You are an unwary sleeper, that one can steal in here:
1210 Now you are caught in a moment! Unless we agree on a truce,
I shall imprison you in your bed, be certain of that!"
Laughing merrily the lady uttered this jest.
"Good morning, dear lady," said Gawain gaily,
"You shall do with me as you wish, and that pleases me much,
1215 For I surrender at once, and beg for your mercy,
And that is best, in my judgment, for I simply must."
Thus he joked in return with a burst of laughter.
"But if, lovely lady, you would grant me leave
And release your captive, and ask him to rise,
1220 I would get out of this bed and put on proper dress,
And then take more pleasure in talking with you."
"No, indeed not, good sir," said that sweet one,

---

[1] *and the burne schamed* And the knight was embarrassed.

[2] *Now ar ye tan as-tyt!* Now are you captured in a moment! There may be a suggestion here of another traditional game, played by women on Hock Monday, the week after Easter. It consisted of seizing and binding men, who were released after paying a small sum of money.

[3] *that me wel lykez* That pleases me very much.

"Ye schal not rise of your bedde, I rych yow better,
I schal happe yow here that other half als,
1225 And sythen karp wyth my knyght that I kaght have;
For I wene wel, iwysse, Sir Wowen ye are,
That alle the worlde worchipez quere-so ye ride;
Your honour, your hendelayk is hendely praysed
With lordez, wyth ladyes, with alle that lyf bere.
1230 And now ye are here, iwysse, and we bot oure one;
My lorde and his ledez ar on lenthe faren,
Other burnez in her bedde, and my burdez als,
The dor drawen and dit with a derf haspe;
And sythen I have in this hous hym that al lykez,
1235 I schal ware my whyle wel, quyl hit lastez,
        with tale.
    Ye ar welcum to my cors,[1]
    Yowre awen won to wale,
    Me behovez of fyne force
1240   Your servaunt be, and schale."

"In god fayth," quoth Gawayn, "gayn hit me thynkkez,
Thagh I be not now he that ye of speken;
To reche to such reverence as ye reherce here
I am wyghe unworthy, I wot wel myselven.
1245 Bi God, I were glad, and yow god thoght,
At saghe other at servyce that I sette myght
To the plesaunce of your prys[2]—hit were a pure joye."
"In god fayth, Sir Gawayn," quoth the gay lady,
"The prys and the prowes that plesez al other,
1250 If I hit lakked other set at lyght, hit were little daynté;
Bot hit ar ladyes innoghe that lever were nowthe
Haf the, hende, in hor holde, as I the habbe here,
To daly with derely your daynté wordez,
Kever hem comfort and colen her carez,
1255 Then much of the garysoun other gold that thay haven.
Bot I louve that ilk lorde that the lyfte haldez
I have hit holly in my honde that al desyres,
        thurghe grace."
    Scho made hym so gret chere,
1260   That watz so fayr of face,
    The knyght with speches skere
    Answered to uche a case.

"You shall not leave your bed, I intend something better.
I shall tuck you in here on both sides of the bed,
1225 And then chat with my knight whom I have captured.
For I know well, in truth, that you are Sir Gawain,
Whom everyone reveres wherever you go;
Your good name and courtesy are honorably praised
By lords and by ladies and all folk alive.
1230 And now indeed you are here, and we two quite alone,
My husband and his men have gone far away,
Other servants are in bed, and my women too,
The door shut and locked with a powerful hasp;
And since I have under my roof the man everyone loves,
1235 I shall spend my time well, while it lasts,
        with talk.
    You are welcome to me indeed,
    Take whatever you want;
    Circumstances force me
1240   To be your true servant."

"Truly," replied Gawain, "I am greatly honored,
Though I am not in fact such a man as you speak of.
To deserve such respect as you have just described
I am completely unworthy, I know very well.
1245 I should be happy indeed, if you thought it proper,
That I might devote myself by words or by deed
To giving you pleasure: it would be a great joy."
"In all truth, Sir Gawain," replied the beautiful lady,
"If the excellence and gallantry everyone admires
1250 I were to slight or disparage, that would hardly be courteous;
But a great many ladies would much rather now
Hold you, sir, in their power as I have you here,
To spend time amusingly with your charming talk,
Delighting themselves and forgetting their cares,
1255 Than much of the treasure or wealth they possess.
But I praise that same lord who holds up the heavens,
I have completely in my grasp the man everyone longs for,
        through God's grace."
    Radiant with loveliness
1260   Great favor she conferred;
    The knight with virtuous speech
    Answered her every word.

---

[1] *Ye are welcum to my cors* A suggestive ambiguity that cannot be translated. *My cors* may mean "me," just as "your honor" or "your worship" mean "you." But the literal sense of the phrase, "my body," is present.

[2] *To the plesaunce of your prys* To pleasing you, or to carrying out your wishes, *your prys* meaning your noble self.

"Madame," quoth the myry mon, "Mary yow yelde,
For I haf founden, in god fayth, yowre fraunchis nobele,
1265 And other ful much of other folk fongen bi hor dedez,
Bot the daynté that thay delen, for my disert nys even,
Hit is the worchyp of yourself, that noght bot wel connez."
"Bi Mary," quod the menskful, "me thynk hit an other;
For were I worth al the wone of wymmen alyve,
1270 And al the wele of the worlde were in my honde,
And I schulde chepen and chose to cheve me a lorde,
For the costes that I haf knowen upon the, knyght, here,
Of bewté and debonerté and blythe semblaunt,
And that I haf er herkkened and halde hit here trwee,
1275 Ther schulde no freke upon folde bifore yow be chosen."
"Iwysse, worthy," quoth the wyghe, "ye haf waled wel
        better,[1]
Bot I am proude of the prys that ye put on me,
And soberly your servaunt, my soverayn I holde yow,
And yowre knyght I becom, and Kryst yow foryelde."
1280 Thus thay meled of muchquat til mydmorn paste,
And ay the lady let lyk as hym loved mych.
The freke ferde with defence, and feted ful fayre;
Thagh ho were burde bryghtest the burne in mynde hade,[2]
The lasse luf in his lode for lur that he soght
1285   bout hone—
        The dunte that schulde hym deve,
        And nedez hit most be done.
        The lady thenn spek of leve,
        He granted hir ful sone.

1290 Thenne ho gef hym god day, and wyth a glent laghed,
And as ho stod, ho stonyed hym wyth ful stor wordez:
"Now he that spedez uche spech this disport yelde yow!
Bot that ye be Gawan, hit gotz in mynde."
"Querfore?" quoth the freke, and freschly he askez,
1295 Ferde lest he hade fayled in fourme of his castes;
Bot the burde hym blessed, and "Bi this skyl" sayde:
"So god as Gawayn gaynly is halden,
And cortaysye is closed so clene in hymselven,
Couth not lightly haf lenged so long wyth a lady,
1300 Bot he had craved a cosse, bi his courtayse,

"Lady," said the man pleasantly, "may Mary repay you,
For I have truly made proof of your great generosity,
1265 And many other folk win credit for their deeds;
But the respect shown to me is not at all my deserving:
That honor is due to yourself, who know nothing but good."
"By Mary," said the noble lady, "to me it seems very different;
For if I were the worthiest of all women alive,
1270 And held all the riches of the earth in my hand,
And could bargain and pick a lord for myself,
For the virtues I have seen in you, sir knight, here,
Of good looks and courtesy and charming manner—
All that I have previously heard and now know to be true—
1275 No man on earth would be picked before you."
"Indeed, noble lady," said the man, "you have chosen
        much better,
But I am proud of the esteem that you hold me in,
And in all gravity your servant, my sovereign I consider you,
And declare myself your knight, and may Christ reward you."
1280 So they chatted of this and that until late morning,
And always the lady behaved as if loving him much.
The knight reacted cautiously, in the most courteous of ways,
Though she was the loveliest woman he could remember:
He felt small interest in love because of the ordeal he must face
1285   very soon—
        To stand a crushing blow,
        In helpless sufferance.
        Of leaving then she spoke,
        The knight agreed at once.

1290 Then she bade him goodbye, glanced at him and laughed,
And as she stood astonished him with a forceful rebuke:
"May he who prospers each speech repay you this pleasure!
But that you should be Gawain I very much doubt."
"But why?" said the knight, quick with his question,
1295 Fearing he had committed some breach of good manners;
But the lady said "Bless you" and replied, "For this cause:
So good a knight as Gawain is rightly reputed,
In whom courtesy is so completely embodied,
Could not easily have spent so much time with a lady
1300 Without begging a kiss, to comply with politeness,

---

[1] *ye haf waled wel better* You have made a much better choice;
reminding the lady that she has a husband.

[2] *Thagh ho were burde bryghtest the burne in mynde hade* The
frightening prospect facing Gawain (*the lur that he soght*, 1284) does

not allow him to become distracted by the lady's beauty, though her
loveliness surpasses anything he can remember. The manuscript
reading of this line, *Thagh I were burde bryghtest the burde in mynde
hade,* is usually amended as shown.

Bi sum towch of summe tryfle at sum talez ende."
Then quoth Wowen, "Iwysse, worthe as yow lykez;
I schal kysse at your comaundement, as a knyght fallez,
And fire, lest he displese yow, so plede hit no more."
1305 Ho comes nerre with that and cachez hym in armez,
Loutez luflych adoun and the leude kysses.
Thay comly bykennen to Kryst ayther other;
Ho dos hir forth at the dore withouten dyn more;
And he ryches hym to ryse and rapes hym sone,
1310 Clepes to his chamberlayn, choses his wede,
Bowez forth, quen he watz boun, blythely to masse;
And thenne he meved to his mete that menskly hym keped,
And made myry al day, til the mone rysed,
                    with game.
1315   Watz never freke fayrer fonge
            Bitwene two so dyngne dame,
            The alder and the yonge;
            Much solace set thay same.

And ay the lorde of the londe is lent on his gamnez,
1320 To hunt in holtez and hethe at hyndez barayne;
Such a sowme he ther slowe bi that the sunne heldet,
Of dos and of other dere, to deme were wonder.
Thenne fersly thay flokked in folk at the laste,
And quykly of the quelled dere a querré thay maked.
1325 The best bowed therto with burnez innoghe,
Gedered the grattest of gres that ther were,
And didden hem derely undo as the dede askez;
Serched hem at the asay summe that ther were,
Two fyngeres thay fonde of the fowlest of alle.
1330 Sythen thay slyt the slot, sesed the erber,
Schaved wyth a scharp knyf, and the schyre knitten;
Sythen rytte thay the four lymmes, and rent of the hyde,
Then brek thay the balé, the bowelez out token
Lystily for laucyng the lere of the knot;
1335 Thay gryped to the gargulun, and graythely departed
The wesaunt fro the wynt-hole, and walt out the guttez;
Then scher thay out the schulderez with her scharp knyvez,
Haled hem by a lyttel hole to have hole sydes.
Sithen britned thay the brest and brayden hit in twynne,
1340 And eft at the gargulun bigynez on thenne,
Ryvez hit up radly ryght to the byght,
Voydez out the avanters, and verayly therafter
Alle the rymez by the rybbez radly thay lance;
So ryde thay of by resoun bi the rygge bonez,

By some hint or suggestion at the end of a remark."
Then Gawain said, "Indeed, let it be as you wish;
I will kiss at your bidding, as befits a knight,
And do more, rather than displease you, so urge it no further."
1305 With that she approaches him and takes him in her arms,
Stoops graciously over him and kisses the knight.
They politely commend each other to Christ's keeping:
She goes out of the room without one word more.
And he prepares to get up as quickly as he can,
1310 Calls for his chamberlain, selects his clothes,
Makes his way, when he was ready, contentedly to mass;
And then went to his meal that worthily awaited him,
And made merry all day until the moon rose
                    with games.
1315   Never knight was entertained
            By such a worthy pair,
            One old, the other young;
            Much pleasure did they share.

And still the lord of that land is absorbed his sport,
1320 Chasing through woodland and heath after barren hinds.
What a number he killed by the time the day ended
Of does and other deer would be hard to imagine.
Then proudly the hunters flocked together at the end,
And quickly made a quarry of the slaughtered deer.
1325 The noblest pressed forward with many attendants,
Gathered together the fattest of the deer,
And neatly dismembered them as ritual requires.
Some of those who examined them at the assay
Found two inches of flesh in the leanest of them.
1330 Then they slit the base of the throat, took hold of the gullet,
Scraped it with a sharp knife and knotted it shut;
Next they cut off the four legs and ripped off the hide,
Then broke open the belly and took out the entrails
Carefully to avoid loosening the ligature of the knot.
1335 They took hold of the throat, and quickly separated
The gullet from the windpipe, and threw out the guts.
Then they cut round the shoulders with their keen knives,
Drawing them through an aperture to keep the sides whole.
Next they cut open the breast and split it in two,
1340 And then one of them turns again to the throat
And swiftly lays open the body right to the fork,
Throws out the neck-offal, and expertly then
Quickly severs all the membranes on the ribs.
So correctly they cut off all the offal on the spine

1345 Evenden to the haunche, that henged al samen,
     And heven it up al hole, and hwen hit of there,
     And that thay neme for the noumbles bi nome, as I trowe,
          bi kynde;
       Bi the byght al of the thyghes
1350   The lappez thay lance bihynde;
       To hewe hit in two thay hyghes,
       Bi the bakbon to unbynde.

     Bothe the hede and the hals thay hwen of thenne,
     And sythen sunder thay the sydez swyft fro the chyne,
1355 And the corbeles fee[1] thay kest in a greve;
     Thenn thurled they ayther thik side thurgh bi the rybbe,
     And henged thenne ayther bi hoghes of the fourchez,
     Uche freke for his fee, as fallez for to have.
     Upon a felle of the fayre best fede thay thayr houndes
1360 Wyth the lyver and the lyghtez, the lether of the paunchez,
     And bred bathed in blod blende theramongez.
     Baldely thay blw prys,[2] bayed thayr rachchez,
     Sythen fonge thay her flesche, folden to home,
     Strakande ful stoutly mony stif motez.
1365 Bi that the daylyght watz done the douthe watz al wonen
     Into the comly castel, ther the knyght bidez
          ful stille,
       Wyth blys and bryght fyr bette.
       The lorde is comen thertylle;
1370   When Gawayn wyth hym mette
       Ther watz bot wele at wylle.

     Thenne comaunded the lorde in that sale to samen alle the
          meny,
     Bothe the ladyes on lowe to lyght with her burdes
     Bifore alle the folk on the flette, frekez he beddez
1375 Verayly his venysoun to fech hym byforne,
     And al godly in gomen Gawayn he called,
     Techez hym to the tayles[3] of ful tayt bestes,
     Schewez hym the schyree grece schorne upon rybbes.
     "How payez yow this play? Haf I prys wonnen?
1380 Have I thryvandely thonk thurgh my craft served?"
     "Ye, iwysse," quoth that other wyghe, "here is wayth fayrest
     That I sey this seven yere in sesoun of wynter."
     "And al I gif yow, Gawayn," quoth the gome thenne,

1345 Right down to the haunches, in one unbroken piece,
     And lifted it up whole, and cut it off there;
     And to that they give the name of numbles, I believe,
          as is right.
       Then where the hind legs fork
1350   At the back they cut the skin;
       Then hacked the carcass in two,
       Swiftly along the spine.

     Both the head and the neck they cut off next,
     And then rapidly separate the sides from the chine;
1355 And the raven's fee in a thicket they threw.
     Then they pierced both thick sides through the ribs,
     Hanging each of them by the hocks of their legs,
     For each man's payment, as his proper reward.
     They put food for their hounds on a fine beast's skin—
1360 The liver and lights, the lining of the stomach,
     And bread soaked in blood, mixed up together.
     Noisily they blew capture, their hounds barking,
     Then shouldering their venison they started for home,
     Vigorously sounding many loud single notes.
1365 By the time daylight failed they had ridden back
     To the splendid castle, where the knight waits
          undisturbed,
       With joy and bright fire warm.
       Then into hall the lord
1370   Came, and the two men met
       In joyfullest accord.

     Then the lord commanded the household to assemble in
          hall,
     And both ladies to come downstairs with their maids.
     In front of the gathering he orders his men
1375 To lay out his venison truly before him;
     And with playful courtesy he called Gawain to him,
     Reckons up the tally of well-grown beasts,
     Points out the splendid flesh cut from the ribs.
     "Does this game please you? Have I won your praise?
1380 Do I deserve hearty thanks for my hunting skill?"
     "Yes indeed," said the other, "this is the finest venison
     That I have seen for many years in the winter season."
     "And I give it all to you, Gawain," said the man then,

---

[1] *the corbeles fee* A piece of gristle thrown to the birds as part of the ritual.

[2] *blw prys* A blast on the horn when the quarry is taken.

[3] *the tayles* Left on the carcasses to facilitate the tally, or count.

"For by acorde of covenaunt ye crave hit as your awen."

1385 "This is soth," quoth the segge, "I say yow that ilke:
That I haf worthyly wonnen this wonez wythinne,
Iwysse with as god wylle hit worthez to yourez."
He hasppez his fayre hals his armez wythinne,
And kysses hym as comlyly as he couthe awyse:

1390 "Tas yow there my chevicaunce, I cheved no more;
I wowche hit saf fynly, thagh feler hit were."
"Hit is god," quoth the godmon, "grant mercy therfore.
Hit may be such hit is the better, and ye me breve wolde
Where ye wan this ilk wele bi wytte of yorselven."

1395 "That watz not forward," quoth he, "frayst me no more.
For ye haf tan that yow tydez, trawe non other
          ye mowe."
        Thay laghed, and made hem blythe
        Wyth lotez that were to lowe;

1400   To soper thay yede as-swythe,
        Wyth daynités nwe innowe.

And sythen by the chymné in chamber thay seten,
Wyghez the walle wyn weghed to hem oft,
And efte in her bourdyng thay baythen in the morn

1405 To fylle the same forwardez that thay byfore maden:
Wat chaunce so bytydez hor chevysaunce to chaunge,
What nwez so thay nome, at naght quen thay metten.
Thay acorded of the covenauntez byfore the court alle;
The beverage watz broght forth in bourde at that tyme,

1410 Thenne thay lovelych leghten leve at the last,
Uche burne to his bedde busked bylyve.
Bi that the coke hade crowen and cakled bot thryse[1]
The lorde watz lopen of his bedde, the leudez uchone;
So that the mete and the masse watz metely delyvered,

1415 The douthe dressed to the wod er any day sprenged,
          to chace;
        Hegh with hunte and hornez
        Thurgh playnez thay passe in space,
        Uncoupled among tho thornez

1420   Rachez that ran on race.

Sone thay calle of a quest in a ker syde,
The hunt rehayted the houndez that hit fyrst mynged,
Wylde wordez hym warp wyth a wrast noyce;
The howndez that hit herde hastid thider swythe,

"For by the terms of our compact you may claim it as yours."

1385 "That is true," said the knight, "and I say the same to you:
What I have honorably won inside this castle,
With as much good will truly shall be yours."
He takes the other's strong neck in his arms,
And kisses him as pleasantly as he could devise.

1390 "Take here my winnings, I obtained nothing else;
I bestow it on you freely, and would do so were it more."
"It is excellent," said the lord, "many thanks indeed.
It could be even better if you would inform me
Where you won this same prize by your cleverness."

1395 "That was not in our agreement," said he, "ask nothing else;
For you have had what is due to you, expect to receive
          nothing more."
        They laughed and joked awhile
        In speech deserving praise;

1400   Then quickly went to sup
        On new delicacies.

Afterwards they sat by the fire in the lord's chamber,
And servants many times brought in marvelous wine;
And once again in their jesting they agreed the next day

1405 To observe the same covenant as they had made before:
Whatever fortune befell them, to exchange what they won,
Whatever new things they were, at night when they met.
They renewed the agreement before the whole court—
The pledge-drink was brought in with jokes at that time—

1410 Then they graciously took leave of each other at last,
Every man hastening quickly to bed.
By the time cock-crow had sounded three times
The lord had leapt out of bed and each of his men,
So that breakfast and mass were duly done,

1415 And long before daybreak they were all on their way
          to the chase.
        Through fields they canter soon,
        Loud with hunting-horns;
        Headlong the hounds run

1420   Uncoupled among the thorns.

Soon they give tongue at the edge of a marsh;
The huntsman urged on the hounds that found the scent first,
Shouting at them wildly in a loud voice.
The hounds who heard him raced there in haste

---

[1] *crowen ... bot thryse* Cocks supposedly crowed at midnight, 3
a.m., and 6 a.m.

1425 And fellen as fast to the fuyt, fourty at ones;
Thenne such a glaver ande glam of gedered rachchez
Ros that the rocherez rungen aboute;
Hunterez hem hardened with horne and wyth muthe.
Then al in a semblé sweyed togeder
1430 Bitwene a flosche in that fryth and a foo cragge;
In a knot bi a clyffe, at the kerre syde,
Ther as the rogh rocher unrydely was fallen,
Thay ferden to the fyndyng, and frekez hem after;
Thay umbekesten the knarre and the knot bothe,
1435 Wyghez, whyl thay wysten wel wythinne hem it were,
The best that ther breved watz wyth the blodhoundez.
Thenne thay beten on the buskez, and bede hym upryse,
And he unsoundyly out soght seggez overthwert;
On the sellokest swyn swenged out there,
1440 Long sythen fro the sounder that sighed for olde,
For he watz borelych and brode, bor alther-grattest,
Ful grymme quen he gronyed; thenne greved mony,
For thre at the fyrst thrast he thryght to the erthe,
And sparred forth good sped boute spyt more.
1445 Thise other halowed hyghe! ful hyghe, and hay! hay!
     cryed,
Haden hornez to mouthe, heterly rechated;
Mony watz the myry mouthe of men and of houndez
That buskkez after this bor with bost and wyth noyse
          to quelle.
1450   Ful ofte he bydez the baye,
     And maymez the mute inn melle;
     He hurtez of the houndez, and thay
     Ful yomerly yaule and yelle.

Schalkez to shote at hym schowen to thenne,
1455 Haled to hym of her arewez, hitten hym oft;
Bot the poyntez payred at the pyth that pyght in his scheldez,
And the barbez of his browe bite non wolde;
Thagh the schaven schafte schyndered in pieces,
The hede hypped agayn were-so-ever hit hitte.
1460 Bot quen the dyntez hym dered of her dryghe strokez,
Then, braynwod for bate, on burnez he rasez,
Hurtz hem ful heterly ther he forth hyghez,
And mony arghed therat, and on lyte droghen.
Bot the lorde on a lyght horse launces hym after,
1465 As burne bolde upon bent his bugle he blowez,
He rechated, and rode thurgh ronez ful thyk,
Suande this wylde swyn til the sunne schafted.

1425 And rushed towards the trail, forty of them together.
Then such a deafening babel from gathered hounds rose
That the rocky bank echoed from end to end.
Huntsmen encouraged them with horn-blasts and shouts;
And then all in a throng they rushed together
1430 Between a pool in that thicket and a towering crag.
On a wooded knoll near a cliff at the edge of the marsh
Where fallen rocks were untidily scattered,
They ran to the dislodging, with men at their heels.
The hunters surrounded both the crag and the knoll
1435 Until they were certain that inside their circle
Was the beast which had made the bloodhounds give tongue.
Then they beat on the bushes and called him to come out;
And he broke cover ferociously through a line of men.
An incredible wild boar charged out there,
1440 Which long since had left the herd through his age,
For he was massive and broad, greatest of all boars,
Terrible when he snorted. Then many were dismayed,
For three men in one rush he threw on their backs,
And made away fast without doing more harm.
1445 The others shouted "hi!" and "hay, hay!" at the tops of
     their voices,
Put horns to mouth and loudly sounded recall.
Many hunters and hounds joyfully gave tongue,
Hurrying after this boar with outcry and clamor
          to kill.
1450   Often he stands at bay,
     And maims the circling pack,
     Wounding many hounds
     That piteously yelp and bark.

Men press forward to shoot at him then,
1455 Loosed their arrows at him, hit him many times;
But those that struck his shoulders were foiled by their toughness,
And none of them could pierce through the bristles on his brow.
Although the polished shaft shivered into pieces,
The head rebounded away wherever it struck.
1460 But when the hits hurt him with their constant blows,
Frenzied with fighting he turns headlong on the men,
And injures them savagely when he charges out,
So that many grew fearful and drew back further.
But the lord on a lively horse races after him,
1465 Like a valiant hunter, blowing his horn.
He urged the hounds on, and through dense thickets rode
Following this wild boar until the sun went down.

This day wyth this ilk dede thay dryven on this wyse,
Whyle oure luflych lede lys in his bedde,
1470 Gawayn graythely at home, in gerez ful ryche
        of hewe.
      The lady noght forgate
      Com to hym to salue;
      Ful erly ho watz hym ate[1]
1475   His mode for to remwe.

Ho commes to the cortyn, and at the knyght totes.
Sir Wawen her welcumed worthy on fyrst,
And ho hym yeldez agayn ful yerne of hir wordez,
Settez hir softly by his syde, and swythely ho laghez,
1480 And wyth a luflych loke ho layde hym thyse wordez:
"Sir, yif ye be Wawen, wonder me thynkkez,
Wyghe that is so wel wrast alway to god,
And connez not of compaynye[2] the costez undertake;
And if mon kennes yow hom to knowe, ye kest hom of
        our mynde;
1485 Thou hatz foryeten yederly that yisterday I taght te
Bi alder-trest token of talk that I cowthe."
"What is that?" quoth the wyghe, "Iwysse I wot never;
If hit be sothe that ye breve, the blame is myn awen."
"Yet I kende yow of kyssyng," quoth the clere thenne,
1490 "Quere-so countenaunce is couthe[3] quikly to clayme;
That bicumes uche a knyght that cortaysy uses."
"Do way," quoth that derf mon, "my dere, that speche;
For that durst I not do, lest I devayed[4] were.
If I were werned, I were wrang, iwysse, yif I profered."
1495 "Ma fay,"[5] quoth the meré wyf, "ye may not be werned,
Ye ar stif innoghe to constrayne wyth strenkthe, yif yow lykez,
Yif any were so vilanous that yow devaye wolde."
"Ye, be God," quoth Gawayn, "good is your speche;
Bot threte is unthryvande in thede ther I lende,
1500 And uche gift that is geven not with goud wylle.
I am at your comaundement, to kysse quen yow lykez,
Ye may lach quen yow lyst, and leve quen yow thynkkez,
        in space."
      The lady loutez adoun
1505   And comlyly kysses his face;

So they spent the day in this manner, in this wild chase,
While our gracious knight lies in his bed:
1470 Gawain, happily at home amid bright-colored bedding
        so rich.
      Nor did the lady fail
      To wish her guest good day;
      Early she was there
1475   His mood to mollify.

She comes to the curtain and peeps in at the knight.
Sir Gawain welcomes her politely at once,
And she returns his greeting with eager speech,
Seats herself gently at his side and quickly laughs,
1480 And with a charming glance at him uttered these words:
"Sir, if you are Gawain, it astonishes me
That a man always so strongly inclined to good,
Cannot grasp the rules of polite behavior,
And if someone instructs him, lets them drop out of
        mind.
1485 You have quickly forgotten what I taught you yesterday,
By the very truest lesson I could put into words."
"What was that?" said the knight, "Indeed, I don't know at all.
If what you say is true, the blame is all mine."
"Yet I told you about kissing," the fair lady replied,
1490 "To act quickly wherever a glance of favor is seen;
That befits every knight who practises courtesy."
"Dear lady, enough of such talk," said that brave man,
"For I dare not do that, lest I were refused.
If repulsed, I should be at fault for having presumed."
1495 "Ma foi," said the gay lady, "you could not be refused;
You are strong enough to force your will if you wish,
If any woman were so ill-mannered as to reject you."
"Yes, indeed," said Gawain, "what you say is quite true;
But in my country force is considered ignoble,
1500 And so is each gift that is not freely given.
I am at your disposal, to kiss when it pleases you,
You may take one when you like, and stop as seems good,
        in a while."
      She bends down over him
1505   And gives the knight a kiss;

---

[1] *watz hym ate* At him in one of two senses or both: in his bedchamber, and bothering him.

[2] *compaynye* Critics have suggested that the term may have amorous connotations.

[3] *Quere-so countenaunce is couthe* Wherever looks of favor are shown.

[4] *devayed* Denied, refused: a neologism from Old French, repeated by the lady at 1497.

[5] *"Ma fay"* I.e., *ma foi*, French: "by my faith," as asseveration.

Much speche thay ther expoun
Of druryes greme and grace.

"I woled wyt at yow, wyghe," that worthy then sayde,
"And yow wrathed not therwyth, what were the skylle
1510 That so yong and so yepe as ye at this tyme,
So cortayse, so knyghtly, as ye ar knowen oute—
And of alle chevalry to chose, the chef thyng alosed
Is the lel layk of luf, the letture of armes;
For to telle of this tevelyng of this trwe knyghtez,
1515 Hit is the tytelet token and tyxt of her werkkez;
How ledes for her lel lufe hor lyvez han auntered,
Endured for her drury dulful stoundez,
And after wenged with her walour and voyded her care,
And broght blysse into boure¹ with bountees hor awen—
1520 And ye ar knyght comlokest kyd of your elde,
Your worde and your worchip walkez ayquere,
And I haf seten by yourself here sere twyes,
Yet herde I never of your hed helde no wordez
That ever longed to luf, lasse ne more;
1525 And ye, that are so cortays and coynt of your hetes,²
Oghe to a yonke thynk yern to schewe
And teche sum tokenez of trweluf craftes.
Why, ar ye lewed, that alle the los weldez?
Other elles ye demen me to dille your dalyaunce to herken?
1530   For schame!
   I com hider sengel, and sitte
   To lerne at yow sum game;
   Dos, techez me of your wytte
   Whil my lorde is fro hame."

1535 "In goud faythe," quoth Gawayn, "God yow foryelde!
Gret is the gode gle, and gomen to me huge,
That so worthy as ye wolde wynne hidere,
And pyne yow with so pouer a man, as play wyth your
        knyght
With anyskynnez countenaunce, hit keverez me ese;
1540 Bot to take the torvayle to myself to trwluf expoun,
And towche the temez of tyxt and talez of armez
To yow that, I wot wel, weldez more slyght
Of that art, bi the half, or a hundreth of seche
As I am, other ever schal, in erde ther I leve,
1545 Hit were a folé felefolde, my fre, by my trawthe.

For long they then discuss
Love's misery and bliss.

"I would learn from you, sir," said that gentle lady,
"If the question was not irksome, what the reason was
1510 That someone as young and valiant as yourself,
So courteous and chivalrous as you are known far and wide—
And of all the aspects of chivalry, the thing most praised
Is the true practice of love, knighthood's very lore;
For to speak of the endeavors of true knights,
1515 The written heading and text of their deeds is that:
How knights have ventured their lives for true love,
Suffered for their love-longings dismal times,
And later taken revenge on their misery through valor,
Bringing joy to their ladies through their personal merits—
1520 And you are the outstanding knight of your time,
Your fame and your honor are known everywhere,
And I have sat by you here on two separate occasions
Yet never heard from your mouth a solitary word
Referring to love, of any kind at all.
1525 And you, who make such courteous and elegant vows,
Should be eager to instruct a youthful creature,
And teach her some elements of skill in true love.
What, are you ignorant, who enjoy such great fame?
Or do you think me too silly to take in courtly chat?
1530   For shame!
   I come here alone, and sit
   To learn your special play;
   Show me your expertise
   While my husband is away."

1535 "In good faith," said Gawain, "may God reward you!
It gives me great gladness and pleases me hugely
That one as noble as yourself should make your way here,
And trouble yourself with a nobody, trifling with your
        knight
With any kind of favor: it gives me delight.
1540 But to take the task on myself of explaining true love,
And treat the matter of romance and chivalric tales
To you whom—I know well—have more expertise
In that subject by half than a hundred such men
As myself ever can, however long I may live,
1545 Would be absolute folly, noble lady, on my word.

---

¹ *into boure* Into the lady's bower.

² *coynt of your hetes* Gracious in your promises of knightly service.

I wolde yowre wylnyng worche at my myght,
As I am hyghly bihalden, and evermore wylle
Be servaunt to yourselven, so save me Dryghtyn!"
Thus hym frayned that fre, and fondet hym ofte,
1550 For to haf wonnen hym to woghe,[1] what-so scho thoght ellez;
Bot he defended hym so fayr that no faut semed,
Ne non evel on nawther halve, nawther thay wysten
      bot blysse.
    Thay laghed and layked long;
1555   At the last scho con hym kysse,
    Hir leve fayre con scho fonge,
    And went hir waye, iwysse.

Then ruthes hym the renk and ryses to the masse,
And sithen hor diner watz dyght and derely served.
1560 The lede with the ladyez layked alle day,
Bot the lorde over the londez launced ful ofte,
Swez his uncely swyn, that swyngez bi the bonkkez
And bote the best of his braches the bakkez in sunder
Ther he bode in his bay, tel bawemen hit breken,
1565 And madee hym mawgref his hed[2] for to mwe utter,
So felle flonez ther flete when the folk gedered.
Bot yet the styffest to start bi stoundez he made,
Til at the last he watz so mat he myght no more renne,
Bot in the hast that he myght he to a hole wynnez
1570 Of a rasse bi a rokk ther rennez the boerne.
He gete the bonk at his bak, bigynez to scrape,[3]
The frothe femed at his mouth unfayre bi the wykez,
Whettez his whyte tuschez; with hym then irked
Alle the burnez so bolde that hym by stoden
1575 To nye hym on-ferum, bot neghe hym non durst
      for wothe;
    He hade hurt so mony byforne
    That al thught thenne ful lothe
    Be more wyth his tusches torne
1580   That breme watz and braynwode bothe.

Til the knyght com hymself, kachande his blonk,
Sygh hym byde at the bay, his burnez bysyde;
He lyghtes luflych adoun, levez his corsour,
Braydez out a bryght bront and bigly forth strydez,
1585 Foundez fast thurgh the forth ther he felle bydez.

I will carry out your desires with all my power,
As I am in all duty bound, and always will be
The servant of your wishes, may God preserve me!"
Thus that lady made trial of him, tempting him many times
1550 To have led him into mischief, whatever her purpose;
But he defended himself so skillfully that no fault appeared,
Nor evil on either side, nor anything did they feel
      but delight.
    They laughed and bantered long;
1555   Then she kissed her guest;
    Charmingly took her leave,
    And went her way at last.

Then Gawain rouses himself and dresses for mass,
And afterwards dinner was cooked and splendidly served.
1560 The knight diverted himself with the ladies all day,
But the lord raced ceaselessly over the countryside,
After his menacing boar, that scurries over the hills,
And bit the backs of his bravest hounds asunder
Where he stood at bay, until archers broke it,
1565 And forced him unwillingly to move into the open;
So thickly the arrows flew when the hunters gathered.
But yet he made the bravest of them flinch at times,
Until at last he was so tired that he could run no more,
And as fast as he can he makes his way to a hole
1570 By a rocky ledge overlooking the stream.
He gets the river-bank at his back, begins to scrape—
The froth foamed hideously at the corners of his mouth—
And whets his white tusks. Then it grew irksome
For all the bold men who surrounded him trying
1575 To wound him from afar, but for the danger none dared
      to get close;
    So many had been hurt
    That no one wished to risk
    To be more savaged by
1580   A maddened boar's tusk.

Until the lord himself came, spurring his horse,
Saw the boar standing at bay, ringed by his men;
He nimbly dismounts, leaving his courser,
Unsheathes a bright sword and mightily strides,
1585 Hastens quickly through the stream towards the waiting boar.

---

[1] *to haf wonnen hym to woghe*   It is uncertain whether *woghe* means "wrong" or "woo."

[2] *mawgref his hed*   In spite of himself.

[3] *bigynez to scrape*   Angrily scrapes (the earth with his feet).

The wylde watz war of the wyghe with weppen in honde,
Hef heghly the here, so hetterly he fnast
That fele ferde for the freke, lest felle hym the worre.
The swyn settez hym out on the segge even,
1590 That the burne and the bor were both upon hepez
In the wyghtest of the water: the worre hade that other,
For the mon merkkez hym wel, as thay mette fyrst,
Set sadly the scharp in the slot even,
Hit hym up to the hult, that the hert schyndered,
1595 And he yarrande hym yelde, and yedoun the water
          ful tyt.
      A hundreth houndez hym hent,
      That bremely con hym bite,
      Burnez him broght to bent,
1600   And doggez to dethe endite.

There watz blawyng of prys in many breme horne,
Heghe halowing on highe with hathelez that myght;
Brachetes bayed that best, as bidden the maysterez
Of that chargeaunt chace that were chef huntes.
1605 Thenne a wyghe that watz wys upon wodcraftez
To unlace this bor lufly bigynnez.
Fyrst he hewes of his hed and on highe settez,
And sythen rendez him al roghe bi the rygge after,
Braydez out the boweles, brennez hom on glede,
1610 With bred blent therwith his braches rewardez.
Sythen he britnez out the brawen in bryght brode cheldez,
And hatz out the hastlettez, as hightly bisemez;
And yet hem halchez al hole the halvez togeder,
And sythen on a stif stange stoutly hem henges.
1615 Now with this ilk swyn thay swengen to home;
The bores hed watz borne bifore the burnes selven
That him forferde in the forthe thurgh forse of his honde
          so stronge.
      Til he seye Sir Gawayne
1620   In halle hym thoght ful longe;
      He calde, and he com gayn
      His feez ther for to fonge.

The lorde ful lowde with lote and laghter myry,
When he seye Sir Gawayn, with solace he spekez;
1625 The goude ladyez were geten, and gedered the
          meyny,
He schewez hem the scheldez, and schapes hem the tale
Of the largesse and the lenthe, the lithernez alse

The beast saw the man with his weapon in hand,
Raised his bristles erect, and so fiercely snorted
That many feared for the man, lest he got the worst of it.
The boar charged out, straight at the man,
1590 So that he and the beast were both in a heap
Where the water was swiftest. The other had the worse;
For the man takes aim carefully as the two met,
And thrust the sword firmly straight into his throat,
Drove it up to the hilt, so that the heart burst open,
1595 And squalling he gave up, and was swept through the water
          downstream.
      Seized by a hundred hounds
      Fierce and sharp of tooth,
      Men dragged him to the bank,
1600   And dogs do him to death.

There was sounding of capture from many brave horns,
Proud shouting by knights as loud as they could,
Hounds bayed at that beast, as bidden by the masters
Who were the chief huntsmen of that wearisome chase.
1605 Then a man who was expert in hunting practice
Skilfully begins to dismember this boar.
First he cuts off the head and sets it on high,
And then roughly opens him along the spine,
Throws out the entrails, grills them over embers,
1610 And rewards his hounds with them, mixed with bread.
Next he cuts out the boar's-meat in broad glistening slabs,
And takes out the innards, as properly follows;
Yet he fastens the two sides together unbroken,
And then proudly hangs them on a strong pole.
1615 Now with this very boar they gallop towards home;
Carrying the boar's head before the same man
Who had killed it in the stream by force of his own
          strong hand.
      Until he saw Gawain
1620   It seemed a tedious time,
      He gladly came when called,
      His due reward to claim.

The lord, noisy with speech and merry laughter,
Joyfully exclaims at the sight of Sir Gawain.
1625 The good ladies were brought down and the household
          assembled;
He shows them the sides of meat, and gives an account
Of the boar's huge size and the ferocity

Of the were of the wylde swyn in wod ther he fled.

That other knyght ful comly comended his dedez,

1630 And praysed hit as a gret prys that he proved hade,

For suche a brawne of a best, the bolde burne sayde,

Ne such sydes of a swyn segh he never are.

Thenne hondeled thay the hoge hed, the hende mon hit praysed,

And let lodly therat the lorde for to here.

1635 "Now, Gawayn," quoth the godmon, "this gomen is your awen

By fyn forwarde and faste, faythely ye knowe."

"Hit is sothe," quoth the segge, "and as siker trwe

Alle my get I schal yow gif agayn, bi my trawthe."

He hent the hathel aboute the halse, and hendely hym kysses,

1640 And eftersones of the same he served hym there.

"Now ar we even," quoth the hathel, "in this eventide,

Of alle the covenauntes that we knyt, sythen I com hider, bi lawe."

The lorde sayde, "Bi saynt Gile,

1645 Ye ar the best that I knowe!

Ye ben ryche in a whyle,

Such chaffer and ye drowe."[1]

Thenne thay teldet tablez trestes alofte,

Kesten clothez upon; clere lyght thenne

1650 Wakned by wowes, waxen torches;

Segges sette and served in sale al aboute;

Much glam and gle glent up therinne

Aboute the fyre upon flet, and on fele wyse

At the soper and after, mony athel songez,

1655 As coundutes of Krystmasse and carolez newe,

With al the manerly merthe that mon may of telle.

And ever oure luflych knyght the lady bisyde,

Such semblaunt to that segge semly ho made

Wyth stille stollen countenaunce, that stalworth to plese,

1660 That al forwondered watz the wyghe, and wroth with hymselven,

Bot he nolde not for his nurture nurne hir agaynez,

Bot dalt with hir al in daynté, how-se-ever the dede turned towrast.

Quen thay hade played in halle

1665 As longe as hor wylle hom last,

Of the fight with the beast in the wood where he fled.

The other knight warmly commended his deeds,

1630 And praised his action as proof of his excellence,

For such boar's-meat, the brave knight declared,

And such sides of wild boar he had never seen before.

Then they picked up the huge head, the polite man praised it

And pretended to feel horror, to honor the lord.

1635 "Now, Gawain," said his host, "this quarry is all yours,

By fully ratified covenant, as you well know."

"That is so," said the knight, "and just as truly indeed

I shall give you all I gained in return, by my pledged word."

He grasped the lord round the neck and graciously kisses him,

1640 And then a second time treated him in the same way.

"Now we are quit," said Gawain, "at the end of the day,

Of all the agreements we have made since I came here, in due form."

The lord said, "By St. Giles,

1645 You're the best man I know!

You'll be a rich one soon

If you keep on trading so."

Then tables were set up on top of trestles,

And tablecloths spread on them: bright light then

1650 Glittered on the walls from waxen torches.

Attendants laid table and served throughout hall.

A great noise of merry-making and joking arose

Round the fire in the center; and of many kinds,

At supper and afterwards, noble songs were sung,

1655 Such as Christmas carols and the newest dances,

With all the fitting amusement that could be thought;

Our courteous knight sitting with the lady throughout.

Such a loving demeanor she displayed to that man,

Through furtive looks of affection to give him delight,

1660 That he was utterly astonished and angry inside;

But he could not in courtesy rebuff her advances,

But treated her politely, even though his actions might be misconstrued.

When the revelry in hall

1665 Had lasted long enough,

---

1 *Such chaffer and ye drowe* If you carry on such a trade (since on the second day Gawain has doubled his takings). Bertilak makes another joking allusion to marketing at the third exchange: see ll. 1938–39.

To chambre he con hym calle,
And to the chemné thay past.

Ande ther thay dronken, and dalten, and demed eft nwe
To norne on the same note on Nwe Yerez even;
1670 Bot the knyght craved leve to kayre on the morn,
For hit watz neghe at the terme that he to schulde.
The lorde hym letted of that, to lenge hym resteyed,
And sayde, "As I am trwe segge, I siker my trawthe
Thou schal cheve to the grene chapel thy charres to make,
1675 Leude, on Nw Yeres lyght, longe bifore pryme.[1]
Forthy thow lye in thy loft and lach thyn ese,
And I schal hunt in this holt, and halde the towchez,[2]
Chaunge wyth the chevisaunce, bi that I charre hider;
For I haf fraysted the twys, and faythful I fynde the.
1680 Now 'thrid tyme throwe best' thenk on the morne,
Make we mery quyl we may and mynne upon joye,
For the lur may lach when-so mon lykez."
This watz graythely graunted, and Gawayn is lenged,
Blithe broght watz hym drynk, and thay to bedde yeden
1685   with light.
      Sir Gawayn lis and slepes
      Ful stille and softe al night;
      The lorde that his craftez kepes,[3]
      Ful erly he watz dight.

1690 After messe a morsel he and his men token;
Miry watz the mornyng, his mounture he askes.
Alle the hatheles that on horse schulde helden hym after
Were boun busked on hor blonkkez bifore the halle gatez.
Ferly fayre watz the folde, for the forst clenged;
1695 In red rudede upon rak rises the sunne,
And ful clere castez the clowdes of the welkyn.
Hunteres unhardeled bi a holt syde,
Rocheres roungen bi rys for rurde of her hornes;
Summe fel in the fute ther the fox bade,
1700 Traylez ofte a traveres[4] bi traunt of her wyles;
A kenet kryes therof, a hunt on hym calles;
His felawes fallen hym to, that fnasted ful thike,
Runnen forth in a rabel in his ryght fare,

To the fireside in his room
The lord took Gawain off.

And there they drank and chatted, and spoke once again
To repeat the arrangement on New Year's Eve;
1670 But the knight begged leave to depart the next day,
For it was near time for the appointment that he had to keep.
The lord held him back, begging him to remain,
And said, "As I am an honest man, I give you my word
That you shall reach the Green Chapel to settle your affairs,
1675 Dear sir, on New Year's Day, well before nine.
Therefore lie in your bed enjoying your ease,
And I shall hunt in the woods, and keep the compact,
Exchange winnings with you when I return here;
For I have tested you twice, and find you trustworthy.
1680 Now tomorrow remember, 'Best throw third time';
Let us make merry while we can and think only of joy,
For misery can be found whenever a man wants it."
This was readily agreed, and Gawain is stayed;
Drink was gladly brought to him, and with torches they went
1685   to their beds.
      Sir Gawain lies and sleeps
      All night taking his rest;
      While eager for his sport
      By dawn the lord was dressed.

1690 After mass he and his men snatched a mouthful of food:
The morning was cheerful, he calls for his horse.
All the knights who would ride after him on horses
Were ready arrayed in the saddle outside the hall doors.
The countryside looked splendid, gripped by the frost;
1695 The sun rises fiery through drifting clouds,
And then dazzling bright drives the rack from the sky.
At the edge of a wood hunters unleashed the hounds;
Among the trees rocks resounded with the noise of their horns.
Some picked up the scent where a fox was lurking,
1700 Search back and forwards in their cunning practice.
A small hound gives tongue, the huntsman calls to him,
His fellows rally around, panting loudly,
And dash forward in a rabble right on the fox's track.

---

[1] *Thou schal cheve … bifore pryme* Prime begins either at 6 a.m. or at sunrise. At 1073 Bertilak promises that Gawain will *cum to that merk at mydmorn*, meaning at 9 a.m. In fact the sun rises when he is on the way to the Green Chapel, 2085–86. In northwest England midwinter sunrise would not occur before 8 a.m. Two hours earlier it would be completely dark.

[2] *halde the towchez* Keep the terms of the agreement.

[3] *that his craftez kepes* Who attends to his pursuits.

[4] *Traylez ofte a traveres* Track the scent by working back and forth across the line.

And he fyskez hem byfore; thay founden hym sone,
1705 And quen thay seghe hym with syght thay sued hym fast,
Wreghande hym ful weterly with a wroth noyse;
And he trantes and tornayeez thurgh mony tene greve,
Havilounez, and herkenez bi hegges ful ofte.
At the last bi a littel dich he lepez over a spenne,
1710 Stelez out ful stilly bi a strothe rande,
Went half wylt of the wode[1] with wylez fro the houndes;
Thenne watz he went, er he wyst, to a wale tryster,
Ther thre thro at a thrich thrat hym at ones,
        al graye.
1715   He blenched agayn bilyve,
        And stifly start on-stray,[2]
        With alle the wo on lyve
        To the wod he went away.

Thenne watz hit list upon lif to lythen the houndez,
1720 When alle the mute hade hym met, menged togeder:
Such a sorwe at that syght thay sette on his hede
As alle the clamberande clyffes hade clatered on hepes;
Here he watz halawed, when hathelez hym metten,
Loude he watz yayned with yarande speche;
1725 Ther he watz threted and ofte thef called,
And ay the titleres at his tayl, that tary he ne myght.
Ofte he watz runnen at, when he out rayked,
And ofte reled in agayn, so Reniarde[3] watz wylé.
And ye, he lad hem bi lagmon,[4] the lorde and his meyny,
1730 On this maner bi the mountes quyle myd-over-under,[5]
Whyle the hende knyght at hom holsumly slepes
Withinne the comly cortynes, on the colde morne.
Bot the lady for luf let not to slepe,
Ne the purpose to payre that pyght in hir hert,
1735 Bot ros hir up radly, rayked hir theder,
In a mery mantyle, mete to the erthe,
That watz furred ful fyne with fellez wel pured;
No hwez[6] goud on hir hede bot the hagher stones
Trased aboute hir tressour by twenty in clusteres;
1740 Hir thryven face and hir throte throwen al naked,

---

[1] *Went haf wylt of the wode*   Thought to have escaped out of the wood.

[2] *on-stray*   In a different direction.

[3] *Reniarde*   Renard was the crafty fox hero of a series of old French poems.

[4] *he lad hem bi lagmon*   The critic Norman Davis explains *lagmon* as "the last man in a line of reapers," who would advance diagonally across a field; hence "strung out."

He scampers ahead of them, they soon found his trail,
1705 And when they caught sight of him followed fast,
Abusing him furiously with an angry noise.
He twists and dodges through many a dense copse,
Often doubling back and listening at the hedges.
At last he jumps over a fence by a little ditch,
1710 Creeps stealthily by the edge of a bush-covered marsh,
Thinking to escape from the wood and the hounds by his wiles.
Then he came, before he knew it, to a well-placed station,
Where three fierce greyhounds flew at him at once
        in a rush.
1715   Undaunted changing course
        He quickly swerved away,
        Pursued into the woods
        With hideous outcry.

Then it was joy upon earth to hear the hounds giving tongue
1720 When all the pack had come upon him, mingled together:
Such a cursing at that sight they called down on his head
As if all the clustering cliffs had crashed down in a mass.
Here he was yelled at when hunters happened upon him,
Loudly he was greeted with chiding speech;
1725 There he was reviled and often called thief,
And always the hounds at his tail, that he could not pause.
Many times he was run at when he made for the open,
And many times doubled back, so cunning was Reynard.
And yes! strung out he led them, the lord and his followers,
1730 Across the hills in this manner until mid-afternoon,
While the knight in the castle takes his health-giving sleep
Behind splendid bed-curtains on the cold morn.
But out of love the lady did not let herself sleep,
Nor the purpose to weaken that was fixed in her heart;
1735 But rose from her bed quickly and hastened there
In a charming mantle reaching to the ground,
That was richly lined with well-trimmed furs:
No modest coif on her head, but skillfully cut gems
Arranged about her hair-fret in clusters of twenty;
1740 Her lovely face and throat displayed uncovered,

---

[5] *quyle myd-over-under*   Variously explained as mid-morning, midday, or afternoon. When the fox is killed it is *niegh nyght* (1922).

[6] *hwez*   So the manuscript; some critics prefer *hwef*. The sense of the passage is that the lady is not wearing the headdress of a married woman.

Hir brest bare bifore, and bihinde eke.
Ho comez withinne the chambre dore, and closes hit hir after,
Wayvez up a wyndow, and on the wyghe callez,
And radly thus rehayted hym with hir riche wordes,
1745   with chere:
     "A, mon, how may thou slepe,
     This morning is so clere?"
     He watz in drowping depe,
     Bot thenne he con hir here.

1750 In dregh droupyng of dreme draveled that noble,[1]
As mon that watz in mornyng of mony thro thoghtes,
How that destiné schulde that day dele hym his wyrde
At the grene chapel, when he the gome metes,
And bihoves his buffet abide withoute debate more;
1755 Bot quen that comly com he kevered his wyttes,
Swenges out of the swevenes, and swarez with hast.
The lady luflych com laghande swete,
Felle over his fayre face, and fetly hym kyssed;
He welcumez hir worthily with a wale chere.
1760 He sey hir so glorious and gayly atyred,
So fautles of hir fetures and of so fyne hewes,
Wight wallande joye warmed his hert.
With smothe smylyng and smolt thay smeten into merthe,
That al watz blis and bonchef that breke hem bitwene,
1765   and wynne.
     Thay lanced wordes gode,
     Much wele then watz therinne;
     Gret perile bitwene hem stod,
     Nif Maré of hir knyght mynne.

1770 Fo that prynces of pris depressed hym so thikke,
Nurned hym so neghe the thred, that nede hym bihoved
Other lach ther hir luf other lodly refuse.
He cared for his cortaysye, lest crathayn he were,
And more for his meschef yif he schulde make synne,
1775 And be traytor to that tolke that that telde aght.
"God schylde," quoth the schalk, "that schal not befalle!"
With luf-laghyng a lyt he layd hym bysyde
Alle the spechez of specialté that sprange of her mouthe.
Quoth that burde to the burne, "Blame ye disserve
1780 Yif ye luf not that lyf that ye lye nexte,

Her breast was exposed, and her shoulders bare.
She enters the chamber and shuts the door after her,
Throws open a window and calls to the knight,
Rebuking him at once with merry words
1745   in play:
     "Ah, sir, how can you sleep?
     The morning is so clear!"
     Deep in his drowsiness
     Her voice broke in his ear.

1750 In the stupor of a dream that nobleman muttered,
Like a man overburdened with troublesome thoughts;
How destiny would deal him his fate on the day
When he meets the man at the Green Chapel,
And must stand the return blow without any more talk:
1755 But when that lovely one spoke he recovered his wits,
Broke out of his dreaming and hastily replied.
The gracious lady approached him, laughing sweetly,
Bent over his handsome face and daintily kissed him.
He welcomes her politely with charming demeanor;
1760 Seeing her so radiant and attractively dressed,
Every part of her so perfect, and in color so fine,
Hot passionate feeling welled up in his heart.
Smiling gently and courteously they made playful speech,
So that all that passed between them was happiness, joy
1765   and delight.
     Gracious words they spoke,
     And pleasure reached its height.
     Great peril threatened, should
     Mary not mind her knight.

1770 For that noble lady so constantly pressed,
Pushed him so close to the verge, that either he must
Take her love there and then or churlishly reject it.
He felt concerned for good manners, lest he behaved like a boor,
And still more lest he shame himself by an act of sin,
1775 And treacherously betray the lord of the castle.
"God forbid!" said the knight, "That shall not come about!"
With affectionate laughter he put to one side
All the loving inducements that fell from her mouth.
Said that lady to the knight, "You deserve rebuke
1780 If you feel no love for the person you are lying beside,

---

[1] *In dregh droupyng of dreme draveled that noble* A literal translation
—"In a heavy troubled sleep that nobleman muttered"—misses the
grinding effect of the alliterated words.

Bifore alle the wyghez in the worlde wounded in hert,
Bot if ye haf a lemman, a lever, that yow lykez better,
And folden fayth to that fre, festned so harde
That yow lausen ne lyst—and that I leve nouthe;
1785   And that ye telle me that now trwly I pray yow,
For alle the lufez upon lyve layne not the sothe
          for gile."
          The knyght sayde, "Be sayn Jon,"
          And smethely con he smyle,
1790   "In fayth I welde right non,
          Ne non wil welde the quile."

"That is a worde," quoth that wyght, "that worst is of alle,
Bot I am swared for sothe, that sore me thinkkez.
Kysse me now comly, and I schal cach hethen,
1795   I may bot mourne upon molde, as may that much lovyes."
Sykande ho sweghe doun and semly hym kyssed,
And sithen ho severes hym fro, and says as ho stondes,
"Now, dere, at this departyng do me this ese,
Gif me sumquat of thy gifte, thi glove if hit were,
1800   That I may mynne on the, mon, my mournyng to lassen."
"Now iwysse," quoth that wyghe, "I wolde I hade here
The levest thing for thy luf that I in londe welde,
For ye haf deserved, for sothe, sellyly ofte
More rewarde bi resoun then I reche myght;
1805   Bot to dele yow for drurye that dawed bot neked,
Hit is not your honour to haf at this tyme
A glove for a garysoun of Gawaynez giftez;
And I am here an erande in erdez uncouthe,
And have no men wyth no males with menskful thingez;
1810   That mislykez me, ladé, for luf at this tyme,
Iche tolke mon do as he is tan, tas to non ille
          ne pine."
          "Nay, hende of hyghe honours,"
          Quoth that lufsum under lyne,
1815   "Thagh I hade noght of yourez,
          Yet schulde ye have of myne."

Ho raght hym a riche rynk of red golde werkez,
With a starande ston stondande alofte
That bere blusshande bemez as the bryght sunne—
1820   Wyt ye wel, hit watz worth wele ful hoge.
Bot the renk hit renayed, and redyly he sayde,
"I wil no giftez, for God, my gay, at this tyme;
I haf none yow to norne, ne noght wyl I take."

More than anyone on earth wounded in her heart;
Unless you have a mistress, someone you prefer,
And have plighted troth with that lady, so strongly tied
That you wish not to break it—which now I believe;
1785   And I beg you now to confess that honestly:
For all the loves in the world hide not the truth
          in guile."
          The knight said, "By St. John,"
          And gave a pleasant smile,
1790   "In truth I have no one,
          Nor seek one for this while."

"That remark," said the lady, "is the worst you could make,
But I am answered indeed, and painfully, I feel.
Kiss me now lovingly, and I will hasten from here,
1795   I must spend my life grieving, as a woman deeply in love."
Sighing she stooped down and kissed him sweetly,
And then moves away from him and says, standing there,
"Now, dear sir, do me this kindness at parting,
Give me something as a present, for instance your glove,
1800   That I may remember you by, to lessen my sorrow."
"Now truly," said that man, "I wish I had here
The dearest thing in the world I possess for your love,
For you have truly deserved, wonderfully often,
More recompense by right than I could repay.
1805   But to give you as love-token something worth little
Would do you no honor, or to have at this time
A glove for a keepsake, as Gawain's gift.
I am here on a mission in unknown country,
And have no servants with bags full of precious things;
1810   That grieves me, lady, for your sake at this time,
But each man must do as conditions allow; take no offense
          or pain."
          "No, most honored sir,"
          Then said that lady free,
1815   "Though I get no gift from you,
          You shall have one from me."

She held out a precious ring of finely worked gold
With a sparkling jewel standing up high,
Its facets flashing as bright as the sun:
1820   Take my word, it was worth an enormous sum.
But the knight would not accept it, and straightaway said,
"I want no gifts, I swear, dear lady, at this time;
I have nothing to offer you, and nothing will I take."

Ho bede hit hym ful bysily, and he hir bode wernes,
1825 And swere swyfte by his sothe that he hit sese nolde,
And ho soré that he forsoke, and sayde therafter,
"If ye renay my rynk, to ryche for hit semez,
Ye wolde not so hyghly halden be to me,
I schal gif yow my girdel, that gaynes yow lasse."
1830 Ho lacht a lace lyghtly that leke umbe hir sydez,
Knit upon hir kyrtel under the clere mantyle;
Gered hit watz with grene sylke and with golde schaped,
Noght bot arounde brayden,[1] beten with fyngrez;
And that ho bede to the burne, and blythely bisoght,
1835 Thagh hit unworthi were, that he hit take wolde.
And he nay that he nolde neghe in no wyse
Nauther golde ne garysoun, er God hym grace sende
To acheve to the chaunce that he hade chosen there.
"And therfore, I pray yow, displese yow noght,
1840 And lettez be your bisinesse, for I baythe hit yow never
      to graunte.
    I am derely to yow biholde
    Bicause of your sembelaunt,
    And ever in hot and colde
1845   To be your trwe servaunt."

"Now forsake ye this silke," sayde the burde thenne,
"For hit is symple in hitself? and so wel hit semez.
Lo, so hit is littel, and lasse hit is worthy;
But who-so knew the costes that knit ar therinne,
1850 He wolde hit prayse at more prys, paraventure.
For quat gome so is gorde with this grene lace,
While he hit hade hemely halched aboute,
Ther is no hathel under heven tohewe hym that myght,
For he myght not be slayn for slyght upon erthe."
1855 Then kest the knyght, and hit come to his hert
Hit were a juel for the jopardé that hym jugged were:
When he acheved to the chapel his chek for to fech,
Myght he haf slypped to be unslayn, the sleght were noble.
Thenne he thulged with hir threpe and tholed hir to speke,
1860 And ho bere on hym the belt and bede hit hym swythe—
And he granted and hym gafe with a goud wylle—
And bisoght hym, for hir sake, discever hit never,
Bot to lelly layne fro hir lorde; the leude hym acordez
That never wyghe schulde hit wyt, iwysse, bot thay twayne
1865   for noghte.

She pressed him insistently, and he declines her request,
1825 Swearing quickly on his word that he would never touch it,
And she was grieved that he refused it, and said to him then,
"If you reject my ring because you think it too precious,
And wish not to be so deeply indebted to me,
I shall give you my girdle, that profits you less."
1830 Quickly she unbuckled a belt clipped round her waist,
Fastened over her kirtle beneath the fine mantle;
It was woven of green silk and trimmed with gold,
Embroidered at the edges and decorated by hand;
And this she offered to the knight, and sweetly implored him
1835 That despite its slight value he would accept it.
And he declared absolutely that he would never agree
To take either gold or keepsake before God gave him grace
To finish the task he had undertaken.
"And therefore I beg you, do not be displeased,
1840 And cease your insisting, for I shall never be brought
      to consent.
    I am deeply in your debt
    Because of your kind favor,
    And will through thick and thin
1845   Remain your servant ever."

"Now, do you refuse this belt," the lady said then,
"Because it is worth little? and so truly it appears.
See, it is indeed a trifle, and its worth even less;
But anyone who knew the power woven into it
1850 Would put a much higher price on it, perhaps.
For whoever is buckled into this green belt,
As long as it is tightly fastened about him
There is no man on earth who can strike him down,
For he cannot be killed by any trick in the world."
1855 Then the knight reflected, and it flashed into his mind
This would be a godsend for the hazard he must face
When he reached the chapel to receive his deserts;
Could he escape being killed, the trick would be splendid.
Then he suffered her pleading and allowed her to speak,
1860 And she pressed the belt on him, offering it at once—
And he consented and gave way with good grace—
And she begged him for her sake never to reveal it,
But loyally hide it from her husband. Gawain gives his word
That no one should ever know of it, not for anything,
1865   but themselves.

---

[1] *Noght bot arounde brayden* No part of which was not embroidered at the edges.

He thonkked hir oft ful swythe,
Ful thro with hert and thoght.
Bi that on thrynne sythe
Ho hatz kyst the knyght so toght.

1870 Thenne lachchez ho hir leve, and levez hym there,
For more myrthe of that mon moght ho not gete,
When ho watz gon, Sir Gawayn gerez hym sone,
Rises and riches him in araye noble,
Lays up the luf-lace the lady hym raghte,
1875 Hid hit ful holdely, ther he hit eft fonde.
Sythen chevely to the chapel choses he the waye,
Prevély aproched to a prest, and prayed hym there
That he wolde lyste his lyf [1] and lern hym better
How his sawle schulde be saved when he schuld seye hethen.
1880 There he schrof hym schyrly and schewed his mysdedez,
Of the more and the mynne, and merci besechez,
And of absolucioun he on the segge calles;
And he asoyled hym surely and sette hym so clene
As domezday schulde haf ben dight on the morn.
1885 And sythen he mace hym as mery among the fre ladyes,
With comelych caroles and alle kynnes joye,
As never he did bot that daye, to the derk nyght,
        with blys.
    Uche mon hade daynté thare
1890   Of hym, and sayde, "Iwysse,
    Thus mery he watz never are,
    Syn he com hider, er this."

Now hym lenge in that lee, ther luf hym bityde!
Yet is the lorde on the launde ledande his gomnes.
1895 He hatz forfaren this fox that he folwed longe;
As he sprent over a spenne to spye the schrewe,
Ther as he herd the howndes that hasted hym swythe,
Renaud com richchande thurgh a roghe greve,
And alle the rabel in a res ryght at his helez.
1900 The wyghe watz war of the wylde, and warly abides,
And braydez out the bryght bronde, and at the best castez.
And he schunt for the scharp, and schulde haf
        arered;

He gave her heartfelt thanks
With earnest mind and sense;
By then she has three times
Kissed that valiant prince.

1870 Then she takes her departure, leaving him there,
For more pleasure from that man was not to be had.
When she had gone, Gawain quickly makes himself ready,
Gets up and dresses himself in splendid array,
Puts away the love-token the lady gave him,
1875 Hid it carefully where he could find it again.
Then quickly to the chapel he makes his way,
Approached a priest privately, and besought him there
To hear his confession and instruct him more clearly
How his soul could be saved when he leaves this world.
1880 There he confessed himself honestly and admitted his sins,
Both the great and the small, and forgiveness begs,
And calls on the priest for absolution.
And the priest absolved him completely, and made him as clean
As if the Judgment were appointed for the next day.
1885 And then Gawain makes merry with the noble ladies,
With charming dance-songs and gaiety of all kinds,
As he never did before that day, until darkness fell,
        with joy.
    Each man had courtesy
1890   From him, and said, "Sure,
    So merry since he came
    He never was before."

Let him stay in that shelter, and love come his way!
But still the lord is afield, enjoying his sport.
1895 He has headed off the fox that he pursued so long;
As he leapt over a hedge to look for the villain,
Where he heard the hounds barking as they chased him fast,
Reynard came running through a rough thicket
With the pack howling behind him, right at his heels.
1900 The man caught sight of the fox, and warily waits,
Unsheathes his bright sword and slashes at the beast;
And he swerved away from the blade and would have
        turned back.

---

[1] *lyste his lyf*   Hear his confession. Much ink has been spilt over the passage. If Gawain tells the priest about his love-token he would be obliged to return it; if he does not reveal the liaison he cannot be *schrof schyrly* or given absolution.

A rach rapes hym to, ryght er he myght,
And ryght bifore the hors fete thay fel on hym alle,
1905 And woried me this wyly[1] wyth a wroth noyse.
The lorde lyghtez bilyve, and lachez hym sone,
Rased hym ful radly out of the rach mouthes,
Haldez heghe over his hede, halowez faste,
And ther bayen aboute hym mony brath houndez.
1910 Huntes hyghed hem theder with hornez ful mony,
Ay rechatande aryght til thay the renk seyen.
Bi that watz comen his compeyny noble
Alle that ever ber bugle blowed at ones,
And alle thise other halowed that had no hornes;
1915 Hit watz the myriest mute that ever men herde,
The rich rurd that ther watz raysed for Renaude saule
          with lote.
       Hor houndez thay ther rewarde,
       Her hedez thay fawne and frote,
1920   And sythen thay tan Reynarde
       And tyrven of his cote.

And thenne thay helden to home, for hit watz niegh nyght,
Strakande ful stoutly in hor store hornez.
The lorde is lyght at last at hys lef home,
1925 Fyndez fire upon flet, the freke ther-byside,
Sir Gawayn the gode, that glad watz withalle,
Among the ladies for luf he ladde much joye.
He were a bleaunt of blwe that bradde to the erthe,
His surkot semed hym wel that softe watz forred,
1930 And his hode of that ilke henged on his schulder,
Blande al of blaunner were bothe al aboute.
He metez me this godmon inmyddez the flore,
And al with gomen he hym gret, and goudly he sayde,
"I schal fylle upon fyrst oure forwardez nouthe,
1935 That we spedly han spoken, ther spared watz no drynk."
Then acoles he the knyght and kysses hym thryes,
As saverly and sadly as he hem sette couthe.
"Bi Kryst," quoth that other knyght, "ye cach much sele
In chevisaunce of this chaffer, yif ye hade goud chepez."[2]

A hound rushed at him before he could turn,
And right at the horse's feet the pack fell on him all,
1905 Tearing at the wily one with an enraged noise.
The lord swiftly dismounts, grabs the fox at once,
Lifted it quickly out of the hounds' mouths,
Holds it high over his head, halloos loudly,
And many fierce hounds surround him there, baying.
1910 Hunters hurried towards him with many horns blowing,
Sounding rally in proper fashion until they saw the lord.
When his noble company was all assembled,
Everyone carrying a bugle blew it at once,
And the others, without horns, raised a great shout.
1915 It was the most glorious baying that man ever heard,
The noble clamor set up there for Reynard's soul
          with din.
       Hunters reward their hounds,
       Heads they rub and pat;
1920   And then they took Reynard
       And stripped him of his coat.

And then they set off for home, for it was nearly night,
Stridently sounding their mighty horns.
At last the lord dismounts at his well-loved home,
1925 Finds a fire burning in hall, the knight waiting beside,
Sir Gawain the good, completely content,
Taking great pleasure from the ladies' affection.
He wore a blue mantle of rich stuff reaching the ground;
His softly furred surcoat suited him well,
1930 And his hood of the same stuff hung on his shoulder,
Both trimmed with ermine along the edges.
He meets his host in the middle of the hall,
Laughingly greeted him, and courteously said,
"Now I shall first carry out the terms of our covenant,
1935 Which we readily agreed on when wine was not spared."
Then he embraces the lord and gives him three kisses,
With as much relish and gravity as he could contrive.
"By God," said that other knight, "you had much luck
In winning this merchandise, if the price was right."

---

[1] *woried me this wyly* Tore at the fox. The ethic dative *me* is colloquial. Other examples occur at 2014 and 2144.

[2] *yif ye hade goud chepez* If you struck a good bargain.

1940 "Ye, of the chepe no charg," quoth chefly that other,
"As is pertly payed the porchaz that I aghte."
"Mary," quoth that other man, "myn is bihynde,
For I haf hunted al this day, and noght haf I geten
Bot this foule fox felle—the fende haf the godez!
1945 And that is ful pore for to pay for suche prys thinges
As ye haf thryght me here thro, suche thre cosses
      so gode."
        "Inogh," quoth Sir Gawayn,
        "I thonk yow, bi the rode";[1]
1950   And how the fox watz slayn
        He tolde hym as thay stode.

With merthe and mynstralsye, wyth metez at hor wylle,
Thay maden as mery as any men moghten
With laghyng of ladies, with lotez of bordez.
1955 Gawayn and the godemon so glad were thay bothe
Bot if the douthe had doted, other dronken ben other.[2]
Both the mon and the meyny maden mony japez
Til the sesoun watz seghen that thay sever moste;
Burnez to hor bedde behoved at the laste.
1960 Thenne lowly his leve at the lorde fyrst
Fochchez this fre mon, and fayre he hym thonkkez:
"Of such a selly sojorne as I haf hade here,
Your honour at this hyghe fest, the hyghe kyng yow yelde!
I gef yow me for on of yourez, if yowreself lykez,
1965 For I mot nedes, as ye wot, meve to-morne,
And ye me take sum tolke to teche, as ye hyght,
The gate to the grene chapel,[3] as God wyl me suffer
To dele on Nw Yerez day the dome of my wyrdes."[4]
"In god faythe," quoth the godmon, "wyth a goud wylle
1970 Al that ever I yow hyght halde schal I redé."
Ther asyngnes he a servaunt to sette hym in the waye,
And coundue hym by the downez, that he no drechch had,
For to ferk thurgh the fryth[5] and fare at the gaynest
      bi greve.

1940 "Oh, never mind the price," replied the other quickly,
"So long as the goods I got have been honestly paid."
"Marry," said the other man, "mine don't compare,
For I have hunted all day, and yet have caught nothing
But this stinking fox pelt—the devil take the goods!
1945 And that is a meager return for such precious things
As you have warmly pressed on me, three such kisses
      so good."
        "Enough," said Gawain,
        "I thank you, by the Rood";
1950   And how the fox was killed
        He heard as there they stood.

With mirth and minstrelsy, and all the food they would wish,
They made as much merriment as any men could
With laughter of ladies and jesting remarks.
1955 Both Gawain and the lord were ravished with joy
As if the company had gone crazy or taken much drink.
Both the lord and his retainers played many tricks
Until the time came round when they must separate:
Folk to their beds must betake them at last.
1960 Then humbly this noble knight first takes leave
Of the lord, and graciously gives him thanks:
"For such a wonderful stay as I have had here,
Honored by you at this holy feast, may God repay you!
I offer myself as your servant, if you agree,
1965 For I am compelled, as you know, to leave tomorrow,
If you will assign someone to show me, as you promised,
The road to the Green Chapel, as God will allow me,
To get what fate ordains for me on New Year's Day."
"In good faith," said the lord, "very willingly,
1970 Everything I ever promised you I shall readily give."
There he appoints a servant to put Gawain on the road
And guide him over the fells, so that he would not be delayed,
To ride through the woods and take the shortest path
      in the trees.

---

[1] *bi the rode* I.e., by the Cross (on which Christ was crucified).

[2] *Gawayn … other* The syntax of these two lines seems erratic. Instead of following *so glad* with a comparison "as if" the poet continues *Bot if*, meaning unless. The intended sense of the passage seems to be, "They could only have been more deliriously happy if the whole company had gone crazy or got drunk."

[3] *I gef yow … grene chapel* Gawain politely offers to become Bertilak's servant (*on of yourez*) if he will give him a man (*take sum tolke*) to guide him to the Green Chapel.

[4] *the dome of my wyrdes* The judgment of my fate.

[5] *to ferk thurgh the fryth* To ride through the wood, as Gawain does at 2084. *Bi greve* refers to it again.

1975	The lorde Gawayn con thonk,
	Such worchip he wolde hym weve.
	Then at tho ladyez wlonk
	The knyght hatz tan his leve.
	With care and wyth kyssyng he carppez hem tille,
1980	And fele thryvande thonkkez he thrat hom to have,
	And thay yelden hym agayn yeply that ilk.
	Thay bikende hym to Kryst with ful colde sykyngez.
	Sythen fro the meyny he menskly departes;
	Uche mon that he mette, he made hem a thonke
1985	For his servyse and his solace and his sere pyne,
	That thay wyth busynes had ben aboute hym to serve;
	And uche segge as soré to sever with hym there
	As thay hade wonde worthyly with that wlonk ever.
	Then with ledes and lyght he watz ladde to his chambre,
1990	And blythely broght to his bedde to be at his rest.
	Yif he ne slepe soundyly say ne dar I,
	For he hade muche on the morn to mynne, yif he wolde,
	in thoght.
	Let hym lyghe there stille,
1995	He hatz nere that he soght;
	And ye wyl a whyle be stylle[1]
	I schal telle yow how thay wroght.

FITT 4

	Now neghez the Nw Yere, and the nyght passez,
	The day dryvez to the derk, as Dryghtyn biddez;
2000	Bot wylde wederez of the worlde wakned theroute,
	Clowdes kesten kenly the colde to the erthe,
	Wyth nyghe innoghe of the northe the naked to tene.
	The snawe snitered ful snart, that snayped the wylde;
	The werbelande wynde wapped fro the hyghe,
2005	And drof uche dale ful of dryftes ful grete.
	The leude lystened ful wel that ley in his bedde,
	Thagh he lowkez his liddez, ful lyttel he slepes;
	Bi uch kok that crue he knwe wel the steven.
	Deliverly he dressed up, er the day sprenged,
2010	For there watz lyght of a laumpe that lemed in his chambre;
	He called to his chamberlayn, that cofly hym swared,

1975	Gawain thanked the lord,
	Paying him great respect;
	Then from those noble ladies
	Took leave, as was correct.
	With tears and with kisses he addresses them both,
1980	And begged them to accept many profuse thanks,
	And they immediately returned the same words to him.
	They commended him to Christ with many deep sighs.
	Then from the household he takes courteous leave;
	To each man whom he met he expressed his thanks
1985	For his service and kindness and the personal pains
	They had taken in busying themselves for his sake;
	And each man was as sorry to part from him there
	As if they had honorably lived with that nobleman ever.
	Then with attendants and torches he was led to his room,
1990	And cheerfully brought to his bed and his rest.
	Whether or not he slept soundly I dare not say,
	For he had much about the next day to turn over, if he wished,
	in his mind.
	Let him lie there undisturbed,
1995	He is close to what he sought;
	Be quiet a short while,
	And I'll tell how things turned out.

PART 4

	Now the New Year approaches and the night wears away,
	The dawn presses against the darkness, as the Creator bids,
2000	But rough weather blows up in the country outside,
	Clouds empty their bitter cold contents on the earth,
	With enough malice from the north to torment the ill-clad.
	Snow pelted down spitefully, stinging the wild creatures;
	The wind shrilly whistled down from the fells,
2005	Choking the valleys with enormous drifts.
	The knight lay in bed listening intently,
	Although his eyelids are shut very little he sleeps;
	Each cock-crow reminded him of his undertaking.
	He got up quickly before the day dawned,
2010	For there was light from a lamp burning in his room;
	He called to his chamberlain, who answered him promptly,

---

[1] *stille … stylle* Literary convention of the time allowed homonyms to be used as rhyme-words different in sense; here "without moving," 1994, and "without noise," 1996.

And bede hym bryng hym his bruny and his blonk sadel;
That other ferkez hym up and fechez hym his wedez,
And graythez me Sir Gawayn upon a grett wyse.
2015 Fyrst he clad hym in his clothez the colde for to were,
And sythen his other harnays, that holdely watz keped,
Bothe his paunce and his platez, piked ful clene,
The ryngez rokked of the roust of his riche bruny;
And al watz fresch as upon fyrst, and he watz fayn thenne
2020   to thonk.
        He hade upon uche pece,
        Wypped ful wel and wlonk;
        The gayest unto Grece
        The burne bede bryng his blonk.

2025 Whyle the wlonkest wedes he warp on hymselven—
His cote wyth the conysaunce of the clere werkez
Ennurned upon velvet, vertuus stonez
Aboute beten and bounden, enbrauded semez,
And fayre furred withinne wyth fayre pelures—
2030 Yet laft he not the lace, the ladiez gifte,
That forgat not Gawayn for gode of hymselven.
Bi he hade belted the bronde upon his balghe haunchez,
Thenn dressed he his drurye double hym aboute,
Swythe swethled umbe his swange swetely that knyght
2035 The gordel of the grene silk, that gay wel bisemed,
Upon that ryol red clothe that ryche watz to schewe.
Bot wered not this ilk wyghe for wele this gordel,
For pryde of the pendauntez, thagh polyst thay were,
And thagh the glyterande golde glent upon endez,
2040 Bot for to saven hymself, when suffer hym byhoved,
To byde bale withoute dabate of bronde hym to were
        other knyffe.
        Bi that the bolde mon boun
        Wynnez theroute bilyve,
2045   Alle the meyny of renoun
        He thonkkez ofte ful ryve.

Thenne watz Gryngolet graythe, that gret watz and huge,
And hade ben sojourned saverly and in a siker wyse,
Hym lyst prik for poynt, that proude hors thenne.
2050 The wyghe wynnez hym to and wytez on his lyre,
And sayde soberly hymself and by his soth swerez:
"Here is a meyny in this mote that on menske thenkkez,
The mon hem maynteines, joy mot thay have;
The leve lady on lyve luf hir bityde;

Bade him bring his mail-shirt and saddle his horse.
The man leaps out of bed and fetches him his clothes,
And gets Gawain ready in splendid attire.
2015 First he puts clothing on him to keep out the cold,
And then the rest of his gear, that had been well looked after,
His body-armor and his plate, all polished clean,
The rings of his fine mail-shirt rocked free of rust;
Everything unstained as at first, for which he gladly
2020   gave thanks.
        Wearing each metal piece
        Rubbed clean of stain and spot,
        The best-dressed man on earth
        Ordered his horse be brought.

2025 While he dressed himself in his noblest clothes—
His coat with its finely embroidered badge
Set upon velvet, with stones of magical power
Inlaid and clasped round it, with embroidered seams,
And richly lined on the inside with beautiful furs—
2030 He did not leave out the belt, the lady's present:
For his own good Gawain did not forget that.
When he had buckled his sword on his curving hips,
That noble knight bound his love-token twice
Closely wrapped round his middle, with delight;
2035 The girdle of green silk, whose color went well
Against that splendid red surcoat that showed so fine.
But the knight did not wear the belt for its costliness,
Or for pride in its pendants, however they shone,
Or because its edges gleamed with glittering gold,
2040 But to safeguard himself when he had to submit,
To await death without sword to defend himself
        or blade.
        When he was fully dressed
        The knight hurries outside,
2045   And pays that noble household
        His debt of gratitude.

Then Gringolet was ready, that great horse and huge,
Who had been stabled securely, keeping him safe;
In such fine condition that he was eager to gallop.
2050 The knight walks up to him and examines his coat,
And said gravely to himself, swearing by his true word,
"There is a company in the castle that keeps courtesy in mind;
And a lord who supports them, may he have joy,
And may the dear lady be loved all her life!

2055 Yif thay for charyté cherysen a gest,	2055 If out of kindliness they cherish a guest
And halden honour in her honde, the hathel hem yelde	And dispense hospitality, may the noble lord
That haldez the heven upon hyghe, and also yow alle!	Who holds up heaven repay them, and reward you all!
And yif I myght lyf upon londe lede any quyle,	And were I to live any long time on earth
I schuld rech yow sum rewarde redyly, if I myght."	I would gladly recompense you, if I could."
2060 Thenn steppez he into stirop and strydez alofte;	2060 Then he sets foot in stirrup and vaults on to his horse;
His schalk schewed hym his schelde, on schulder he hit laght,	His servant gave him his shield, he slung it on his shoulder,
Gordez to Gryngolet with his gilt helez,	Strikes spurs into Gringolet with his gilt heels,
And he startez on the ston, stod he no lenger	And he leaps forward on the paving, he waited no longer
to praunce.	to prance.
2065 His hathel on hors watz thenne,	2065 His man was mounted then,
That bere his spere and launce.	Carrying his spear and lance.
"This kastel to Kryst I kenne":	"I commend this house to God,
He gef hit ay god chaunce.[1]	May it never meet mischance."
The brygge watz brayed doun, and the brode gatez	The drawbridge was lowered, and the broad gates
2070 Unbarred and born open upon bothe halve.	2070 Unbarred and pushed open upon both sides.
The burne blessed hym bilyve, and the brede passed—	The knight blessed himself quickly and rode over the planks,
Prayses the porter bifore the prynce kneled,	Praises the porter who knelt before him
Gef hym God and goud day, that Gawayn he save—	Commending Gawain to God, that he should the knight save,
And went on his way with his wyghe one,	And went on his way with his single guide,
2075 That schulde teche hym to tourne to that tene place	2075 Who would show him the way to that perilous place
Ther the ruful race he schulde resayve.	Where he must submit to a fearful stroke.
Thay bowen bi bonkkez ther boghez ar bare,	They struggled up hillsides where branches are bare,
Thay clomben bi clyffez ther clengez the colde.	They climbed up past rock-faces gripped by the cold.
The heven watz uphalt, bot ugly ther-under;	The clouds were high up, but murky beneath them,
2080 Mist muged on the mor, malt on the mountez,	2080 Mist shrouded the moors, melted on the hills.
Uche hille hade a hatte, a myst-hakel huge.	Each summit wore a hat, a huge cloak of mist.
Brokez byled and breke bi bonkkez about,	Streams foamed and splashed down the slopes around them,
Schyre schaterande on schorez ther thay doun showved.	Breaking white against the banks as they rushed downhill.
Wela wylle watz the way ther thay bi wod schulden,	Very wandering was the way they must take to the wood,
2085 Til hit watz sone sesoun that the sunne ryses	2085 Until soon it was time for sunrise at that point
that tyde.	of the year.
Thay were on a hille ful hyghe,	They were high up in the hills,
The quyte snaw lay bisyde;	By snow surrounded then;
The burne that rod hym by	The servant at his side
2090 Bede his mayster abide.	2090 Bade Gawain draw rein.
"For I haf wonnen yow hider, wyghe, at this tyme,	"For I have guided you here, sir, on this day,
And now nar ye not fer fro that note place	And now you are not far from that notorious place
That ye han spied and spuryed so specially after;	That you have searched and enquired for so specially.
Bot I schal say yow for sothe, sythen I yow knowe,	But I shall tell you truly—since I know who you are,

---

[1]   *He gef hit ay god chaunce*   Either Gawain wishes the castle lasting good fortune or, continuing his prayer in the previous line, hopes that Christ will do so, *He gef* then meaning "May he give."

<table>
<tr>
<td>

2095 And ye are a lede upon lyve that I wel lovy,
Wolde ye worch bi my wytte, ye worthed the better.
The place that ye prece to ful perelous is halden;
Ther wonez a wyghe in that waste, the worst upon erthe,
For he is stiffe and sturne, and to strike lovies,
2100 And more he is then any mon upon myddelerde,
And his body bigger then the best fowre
That ar in Arthurez hous, Hestor, other other.
He chevez that chaunce at the chapel grene,
Ther passes non bi that place so proude in his armes
2105 That he ne dyngez hym to dethe with dynt of his honde;
For he is a mon methles, and mercy non uses,
For be hit chorle other chaplayn that bi the chapel rydes,
Monk other masseprest, other any mon elles,
Hym thynk as queme hym to quelle as quyk go hymselven.
2110 Forthy I say the, as sothe as ye in sadel sitte,
Com ye there, ye be kylled, I may the knyght rede;[1]
Trawe ye me that trwely, thagh ye had twenty lyves
        to spende.
        He hatz wonyd here ful yore,
2115   On bent much baret bende,
        Agayn his dyntez sore
        Ye may not yow defende.

"Forthy, goude Sir Gawayn, let the gome one,
And gotz away sum other gate, upon Goddez halve!
2120 Cayrez bi sum other kyth, ther Kryst mot yow spede,
And I schal hygh me hom agayn, and hete yow fyrre
That I schal swere bi God and alle his gode halwez,
As help me God and the halydam, and othez innoghe,
That I schal lelly yow layne,[2] and lance never tale
2125 That ever ye fondet to fle for freke that I wyst."
"Grant merci," quoth Gawayn, and gruchyng he sayde,
"Wel worth the, wyghe, that woldez my gode,
And that lelly me layne I leve wel thou woldez.
Bot helde thou hit never so holde, and I here passed,
2130 Founded for ferde for to fle, in fourme that thou tellez,
I were a knyght kowarde, I myght not be excused.
Bot I wyl to the chapel, for chaunce that may falle,
And talk wyth that ilk tulk the tale that me lyste,

</td>
<td>

2095 And you are a man whom I love dearly—
If you would follow my advice, it would be better for you.
The place you are going to is extremely dangerous;
There lives a man in that wilderness, the worst in the world,
For he is powerful and grim, and loves dealing blows,
2100 And is bigger than any other man upon earth:
His body is mightier than the four strongest men
In Arthur's household, Hector or any other.
He so brings it about at the Green Chapel
That no one passes that place, however valiant in arms,
2105 Who is not battered to death by force of his hand;
For he is a pitiless man who never shows mercy.
For whether peasant or churchman passes his chapel,
Monk or mass-priest, or whatever man else,
To him killing seems as pleasant as enjoying his own life.
2110 Therefore I tell you, as sure as you sit in your saddle,
If you go there you'll be killed, I warn you, sir knight,
Believe that for certain, though you had twenty lives
        to lose.
        He has dwelt there long,
2115   And brought about much strife;
        Against his brutal blows
        Nothing can save your life.

"Therefore, good Sir Gawain, let the man be,
And for God's sake get away from here by some other road!
2120 Ride through some other country, where Christ be your help,
And I will make my way home again, and further I vow
That I shall swear by God and all his virtuous saints—
As help me God and the holy thing, and many more oaths—
That I shall keep your secret truly, and never reveal
2125 That ever you took flight from a man that I knew."
"Many thanks," replied Gawain, and grudgingly he spoke,
"Good luck to you, man, who wishes my good,
And that you would loyally keep my secret I truly believe.
But however closely you kept it, if I avoided this place,
2130 Took to my heels in fright, in the way you propose,
I should be a cowardly knight, and could not be excused.
But I will go to the chapel, whatever may chance,
And discuss with that man whatever matter I please,

</td>
</tr>
</table>

---

[1] *I may the knyght rede*   I can tell you, knight. The original text does not include the first personal pronoun.

[2] *I schal lelly yow layne*   The guide repeats Gawain's promise to the lady at 1863.

Worthe hit wele other wo, as the wyrde lykez
            hit hafe.
        Thaghe he be a sturn knape
        To stightel, and stad with stave,
        Ful wel con Dryghtyn schape
        His servauntez for to save."

2140 "Mary!" quoth that other man, "now thou so much spellez
That thou wylt thyn awen nye nyme to thyselven,
And the lyste lese thy lyf, the lette I ne kepe.
Haf here thi helme on thy hede, thi spere in thi honde,
And ryde me doun this ilke rake bi yon rokke syde,
2145 Til thou be broght to the bothem of the brem valay;
Thenne loke a littel on the launde, on thy lyfte honde,
And thou schal se in that slade the self chapel,
And the borelych burne on bent that hit kepez.
Now farez wel, on Godez half, Gawayn the noble!
2150 For alle the golde upon grounde I nolde go wyth the,
Ne bere the felaghschip thurgh this fryth on fote fyrre."
Bi that the wyghe in the wod wendez his brydel,
Hit the hors with the helez as harde as he myght,
Lepez hym over the launde, and levez the knyght there
2155   al one.
        "Bi Goddez self," quoth Gawayn,
        "I wyl nauther grete ne grone;
        To Goddez wylle I am ful bayn,
        And to hym I haf me tone."

2160 Thenne gyrdez he to Gryngolet, and gederez the rake,
Schowvez in bi a schore at a schawe syde,
Ridez thurgh the roghe bonk ryght to the dale;
And thenne he wayted hym aboute, and wylde hit hym thoght,
And seye no syngne of resette bisydez nowhere,
2165 Bot hyghe bonkkez and brent upon bothe halve,
And rughe knokled knarrez with knorned stonez;
The skwez of the scowtes skayned hym thoght.
Thenne he hoved, and wythhylde his hors at that tyde,
And ofte chaunged his cher the chapel to seche:
2170 He seye non suche in no syde, and selly hym
            thoght,
Save, a lyttle on a launde, a lawe as hit were;
A balgh berw bi a bonke the brymme bysyde,
Bi a forgh of a flode that ferked thare;
The borne blubred therinne as hit boyled hade.
2175 The knyght kachez his caple and com to the lawe,

Whether good or ill come of it, as destiny
            decides.
        Though an opponent grim
        To deal with, club in hand,
        His faithful servants God
        Knows well how to defend."

2140 "Marry!" said the other man, "since your words make it clear
That you will deliberately bring harm on yourself,
And lose your life by your own wish, I won't hinder you.
Put your helmet on your head, take your spear in your hand,
And ride down this track beside the rock over there
2145 Until it brings you to the bottom of the wild valley;
Then look to your left, some way off in the glade,
And you will see in that dale the chapel itself,
And the giant of a man who inhabits the place.
Now in God's name, noble Gawain, farewell!
2150 For all the wealth in the world I would not go with you,
Nor keep you company through this wood one further step."
With that the man at his side tugs at his bridle,
Struck his horse with his heels as hard as he could,
Gallops over the hillside and leaves the knight there
2155   alone.
        Said Gawain, "By God himself,
        I shall not moan or cry;
        My life is in his hands,
        His will I shall obey."

2160 Then he sets spurs to Gringolet and picks up the path,
Makes his way down a slope at the edge of a wood,
Rides down the rugged hillside right to the valley,
And then looked about him, and it seemed a wild place,
And saw no sign of a building anywhere near,
2165 But high and steep hillsides upon both sides,
And rough rocky crags of jagged stones:
The clouds grazing the jutting rocks, as it seemed.
Then he halted, and checked his horse for a while,
Often turning his face to look for the chapel.
2170 He saw nothing of the kind anywhere, which he thought
            strange,
Except a way off in a glade, something like a mound;
A rounded hillock on the bank of a stream,
Near the bed of a torrent that tumbled there;
The water foamed in its course as though it had boiled.
2175 The knight urges his horse and comes to the mound,

Lightez doun luflyly, and at a lynde tachez
The rayne and his riche with a roghe braunche.
Thenne he bowez to the berwe, aboute hit he walkez,
Debatande with hymself quat hit be myght.
2180 Hit hade a hole on the ende and on ayther syde,
And overgrowen with gresse in glodes aywhere,
And al watz holw inwith, nobot an olde cave,[1]
Or a crevisse of an olde cragge, he couthe hit noght deme
      with spelle.
2185   "We, lorde!" quoth the gentyle knyght,
    "Whether this be the grene chapelle?
    Here myght aboute mydnyght
    The dele his matynnes telle!

 "Now iwysse," quoth Wowayn, "wysty is here;
2190 This oritore is ugly, with erbez overgrowen;
Wel bisemez the wyghe wruxled in grene
Dele here his devocioun on the develez wyse.
Now I fele hit is the fende, in my fyve wyttez,
That hatz stoken me this steven to strye me here.
2195 This is a chapel of meschaunce, that chekke hit bytyde!
Hit is the corsedest kyrk that ever I com inne!"
With hegh helme on his hede, his launce in his honde,
He romez up to the roffe of the rogh wonez.
Thene herde he of that hyghe hil, in a harde roche
2200 Biyonde the broke, in a bonk, a wonder breme noyse:
Quat! hit clatered in the clyff, as hit cleve schulde,
As one upon a gryndelston hade grounden a sythe.
What! hit wharred and whette, as water at a mulne;
What! hit rusched and ronge, rawthe to here.
2205 Thenne "Bi Godde," quoth Gawayn, "that gere, as I trowe,
Is rryched at the reverence me, renk, to mete
      bi rote.[2]
    Let God worche! 'We loo'
    Hit helppez me not a mote.
2210   My lif thagh I forgoo,
    Drede dotz me no lote."

Thenne the knyght con calle ful hyghe,
"Who stightlez in this sted me steven to holde?

Alights nimbly, and makes fast to a tree
The reins and his noble steed with a rough branch.
Then he goes to the mound and walks around it,
Wondering to himself what it could be.
2180 It had a hole at the end and on either side,
And was covered all over with patches of grass,
And was all hollow inside; nothing but an old cave,
Or a fissure in an old rock: what to call it he hardly
      could tell.
2185   "Good lord!" said the noble knight,
    "Can the Green Chapel be this place?
    Here probably at midnight
    The devil his matins says!

"Now truly," said Gawain, "this is a desolate place;
2190 This chapel looks evil, with grass overgrown;
Here fittingly might the man dressed in green
Perform his devotions, in devilish ways.
Now all my senses tell me that the devil himself
Has forced this agreement on me, to destroy me here!
2195 This is a chapel of disaster, may ill-luck befall it!
It is the most damnable church I was ever inside."
With tall helmet on head, his lance in his hand,
He climbs to the top of that primitive dwelling.
Then he heard up the hillside, from behind a great rock,
2200 On the slope across the stream, a deafening noise:
What! it echoed in the cliffs, as though they would split,
As if someone with a grindstone were sharpening a scythe.
What! it whirred and sang, like water at a mill;
What! it rasped and it rang, terrible to hear.
2205 Then said Gawain, "By God, these doings, I suppose,
Are a welcoming ceremony, arranged in my honor
      as a knight.
    God's will be done: 'Alas'
    Helps me no whit here.
2210   Although my life be lost,
    Noise cannot make me fear."

Then the knight shouted at the top of his voice,
"Who is master of this place, to keep tryst with me?

---

[1] *nobot an olde cave* An unlikely guess. The hollow mound half-covered with grass, with *a hole on the ende and on ayther syde*, has the characteristic form of a prehistoric burial chamber.

[2] *Is ryched … bi rote* Is intended in honor of me, in order to meet a knight with due ceremony; or, if *renk* means a field of combat or a dueling-place, the noise is intended to mark (*mete*) it out ceremoniously.

For now is gode Gawayn goande ryght here.[1]
2215 If any wyghe oght wyl, wynne hider fast,
Other now other never, his nedez to spede."
"Abyde," quoth on on the bonke aboven his hede,
"And thou schal haf al in hast that I the hyght ones."
Yet he rusched on that rurde rapely a throwe,
2220 And wyth quettyng awharf, er he wolde lyght;
And sythen he keverez bi a cragge, and comez of a hole,
Whyrlande out of a wro wyth a felle weppen,
A denez ax nwe dyght, the dynt with to yelde,
With a borelych bytte bende bi the halme,
2225 Fyled in a fylor, fowre foot large—
Hit watz no lasse bi the lace that lemed ful bryght—[2]
And the gome in the grene gered as fyrst,
Bothe the lyre and the leggez, lokkez and berde,
Save that fayre on his fote he foundez on erthe,
2230 Sette the stele to the stone, and stalked bysyde.
When he wan to the watter, ther he wade nolde,
He hypped over on hys ax, and orpedly strydez,
Bremly brothe on a bent that brode watz aboute,
　　on snawe.
2235 　　Sir Gawayn the knyght con mete,
　　He ne lutte hym nothyng lowe;
　　That other sayde, "Now, sir swete,
　　Of steven mon may the trowe.

"Gawayn," quoth that grene gome, "God the mot loke!
2240 Iwysse thou art welcom, wyghe, to my place,
And thou hatz tymed thi travayl as truee mon schulde,
And thou knowez the covenauntez kest uus bytwene:
At this tyme twelmonyth thou toke that the falled,
And I schulde at this Nwe Yere yeply the quyte.
2245 And we ar in this valay verayly oure one;
Here are no renkes us to rydde, rele as uus lykez.
Haf thy helme of thy hede, and haf here thy pay.
Busk no more debate then I the bede thenne
When thou wypped of my hede at a wap one."
2250 "Nay, bi God," quoth Gawayn, "that me gost lante,

For now is good Gawain waiting right here.
2215 If anyone wants something, let him hurry here fast,
Either now or never, to settle his affairs."
"Wait," said someone on the hillside above,
"And you shall quickly have all that I promised you once."
Yet he kept making that whirring noise for a while,
2220 And turned back to his whetting before he would come down;
And then makes his way among the rocks, bursting out of a hole,
Whirling out of a nook with a fearsome weapon—
A Danish axe newly made—for dealing the blow,
With a massive blade curving back on the shaft,
2225 Honed with a whetstone, four feet across—
No less than that, despite the gleaming green girdle—
And the man in the green, dressed as at first,
Both his flesh and his legs, hair and beard,
Except that grandly on foot he stalked on the earth,
2230 Set the handle to the ground and walked beside it.
When he came to the stream he refused to wade:
He hopped over on his axe and forcefully strides,
Fiercely grim on a clearing that stretched wide about,
　　under snow.
2235 　　Sir Gawain met the knight,
　　Made him a frosty bow;
　　The other said, "Good sir,
　　A man may trust your vow.

"Gawain," said that green man, "may God protect you!
2240 You are indeed welcome, sir, to my place;
You have timed your journey as a true man should,
And you know the agreement settled between us:
A twelvemonth ago you took what fell to your lot,
And I was to repay you promptly at this New Year.
2245 And we are in this valley truly by ourselves,
With no knights to separate us, so we can fight as we please.
Take your helmet off your head, and here get your pay.
Make no more argument than I offered you then,
When you slashed off my head with a single stroke."
2250 "No, by God," said Gawain, "who gave me a soul,

---

[1] *goande ryght here* Walking right here, with a suggestion of being ready to leave immediately if no one answers.

[2] *Hit watz no lasse bi that lace that lemed ful bryght* Commentators disagree about which lace the poet is referring to. The axe used by Gawain has *a lace lapped aboute, that louked at the hede*, 217 as part of its decoration. But the axe which the Green Knight has just finished sharpening is a different weapon, newly made and not apparently decorated. The other lace is the green girdle or *luf-lace*;

see 1830, *a lace … that leke umbe hir sydez*, and 2030, *the lace, the ladiez gifte*. The belt is so designated at least eight times between 1830 and 2505, while lace in the first sense is not clearly mentioned again after 217. The more likely reading of the line is that the axe seemed enormous to Gawain, despite the assurance of the green belt, whose *glyterande golde* decoration explains *lemed ful bryght*.

I schal gruch the no grwe for grem that fallez.
Bot styghtel the upon on strok, and I schal stonde stylle
And warp the no wernyng to worch as the lykez,
     nowhare."[1]
2255   He lened with the nek, and lutte,
    And schewed that schyre al bare,
    And lette as he noght dutte;
    For drede he wolde not dare.

Then the gome in the grene graythed hym swythe,
2260 Gederez up hys grymme tole Gawayn to smyte;
With alle the bur in his body he ber hit on lofte,
Munt as maghtyly as marre hym he wolde;
Hade hym dryven adoun as dregh as he atled,
Ther hade ben ded of his dynt that doghty watz ever.[2]
2265 Bot Gawayn on that giserne glyfte hym bysyde,
As hit com glydande adoun on glode hym to schende,
And schranke a lytel with the schulderes for the scharp yrne.
That other schalk wyth a schunt the schene wythhaldez,
And thenne repreved he the prynce with many prowde wordez:
2270 "Thou art not Gawayn," quoth the gome, "that is so goud
    halden,
That never arghed for no here by hylle ne be vale,
And now thou fles for ferde er thou fele harmez!
Such cowardise of that knyght cowthe I never here.
Nawther fyked I ne flaghe, freke, quen thou myntest,
2275 Ne kest no cavelacioun in kyngez hous Arthor.
My hede flagh to my fote, and yet flagh I never;
And thou, er any harme hent, arghez in hert.
Wherfore the better burne me burde be called
    therfore."
2280   Quoth Gawayn, "I schunt onez,
    And so wyl I no more;
    Bot thagh my hede falle on the stonez,
    I con not hit restore.

"But busk, burne, bi thi fayth, and bryng me to the poynt.
2285 Dele to me my destiné, and do hit out of honde,[3]
For I schal stonde the a strok, and start no more
Til thy ax have me hitte: haf here my trawthe."
"Haf at the thenne!" quoth that other, and hevez hit alofte,
And waytez as wrothely as he wode were.

---

[1] *nowhare* Anywhere you like. Gawain is only concerned that the Green Knight shall restrict himself to one stroke (l. 2253).

[2] *that doghty watz ever* The man who was always brave.

I shall bear you no grudge at all, whatever hurt comes about.
Just limit yourself to one blow, and I will stand still
And not resist whatever it pleases you to do
    at all."
2255   He bent his neck and bowed,
    Showing the flesh all bare,
    And seeming unafraid;
    He would not shrink in fear.

Then the man dressed in green quickly got ready,
2260 Raised his terrible axe to give Gawain the blow;
With all the strength in his body he heaved it in the air,
Swung it as fiercely as if meaning to mangle him.
Had he brought the axe down as forcibly as he acted,
That courageous knight would have been killed by the blow;
2265 But Gawain glanced sideways at that battle-axe
As it came sweeping down to destroy him there,
And hunched his shoulders a little to resist the sharp blade.
The other man checked the bright steel with a jerk,
And then rebuked the prince with arrogant words:
2270 "You're not Gawain," said the man, "who is reputed so
    good,
Who never quailed from an army, on valley or on hill,
And now flinches for fear before he feels any hurt!
I never heard of such cowardice shown by that knight.
I neither flinched nor fled, sir, when you aimed one at me,
2275 Nor raised any objections in King Arthur's house.
My head fell to the floor, yet I gave no ground;
But you, though not wounded, are trembling at heart,
So I deserve to be reckoned the better man
    for that."
2280   Gawain said, "I flinched once,
    But won't twice hunch my neck,
    Though if my head should fall
    I cannot put it back.

"But hurry up, man, by your faith, and come to the point.
2285 Deal out my fate to me, and do it out of hand,
For I shall let you strike a blow, and not move again
Until your axe has hit me, take my true word."
"Have at you then!" said the other, and raises it up,
Contorting his face as though he were enraged.

---

[3] *out of honde* I.e., out of hand: at once. The first recorded use of the phrase.

2290	He myntez at hym maghtyly, bot not the mon rynez,
	Withhelde heterly his honde er hit hurt myght.
	Gawayn graythely hit bydez, and glent with no membre,
	Bot stode stylle as the ston, other a stubbe auther
	That ratheled is in roché grounde with rotez a hundreth.
2295	Then muryly efte con he mele, the mon in the grene,
	"So, now thou hatz thi hert holle, hitte me bihovs.
	Halde the now the hyghe hode that Arthur the raght,
	And kepe thy kanel at this kest, yif hit kever may."
	Gawayn ful gryndelly with greme thenne sayde:
2300	"Wy! thresch on, thou thro mon, thou thretez to longe;
	I hope that thi hert arghe wyth thyn awen selven."
	"For sothe," quoth that other freke, "so felly thou spekez,
	I wyl no lenger on lyte lette thin ernde[1]
	right nowe."
2305	Thenne tas he hym strythe to stryke,
	And frounsez bothe lyppe and browe,
	No mervayle thagh hym myslyke
	That hoped of no rescowe.
	He lyftes lyghtly his lome, and let hit doun fayre
2310	With the barbe of the bitte bi the bare nek;
	Thagh he homered heterly, hurt hym no more
	Bot snyrt hym on that on syde, that severed the hyde.
	The scharp schrank to the flesche thurgh the schyre grece,
	That the schene blod over his schulderes schot to the erthe;
2315	And quen the burne sey the blode blenk on the snawe,
	He sprit forth a spenne-fote[2] more then a spere lenthe,
	Hent heterly his helme, and his hed cast,
	Schot with his schulderes his fayre schelde under,
	Braydez out a bryght sworde, and bremly he spekez—
2320	Never syn that he watz burne borne of his moder
	Watz he never in this worlde wyghe half so blythe—
	"Blynne, burne, of thy bur, bede me no mo!
	I haf a stroke in this sted withoute stryf hent,
	And if thow rechez me any mo, I redyly schal quyte,
2325	And yelde yederly agayn—and therto ye tryst—
	and foo.
	Bot on stroke here me fallez—
	The covenaunt ryght schop so,
	Fermed in Arthurez hallez—
2330	And therfore, hende, now hoo!"

2290	He swings the axe at him savagely, without harming the man,
	Checked his blow suddenly before it could inflict hurt.
	Gawain awaits it submissively, not moving a limb,
	But stood as still as a stone, or the stump of a tree
	Anchored in rocky ground by hundreds of roots.
2295	Then the man in green spoke mockingly again,
	"So, now you have found courage it is time for the blow.
	Now may the order of knighthood given you by Arthur
	Preserve you and your neck this time, if it has power!"
	Then Gawain replied angrily, mortified deeply,
2300	"Why, strike away, you fierce man, you waste time in threats;
	I think you have frightened yourself with your words."
	"Indeed," said that other man, "you speak so aggressively
	That I will no longer delay or hinder your business
	at all."
2305	He takes his stance to strike,
	Puckering mouth and brow;
	No wonder if Gawain feels
	No hope of rescue now.
	He swiftly raises his weapon, and brings it down straight
2310	With the cutting edge of the blade over Gawain's bare neck;
	Although he struck fiercely, he hurt him no more
	Than to slash the back of his neck, laying open the skin.
	The blade cut into the body through the fair flesh
	So that bright blood shot over his shoulders to the ground.
2315	And when the knight saw his blood spatter the snow
	He leapt forward with both feet more than a spear's length,
	Snatched up his helmet and crammed it on his head,
	Jerked his shoulders to bring his splendid shield down,
	Drew out a gleaming sword and fiercely he speaks—
2320	Never since that man was born of his mother
	Had he ever in the world felt half so relieved—
	"Hold your attack, sir, don't try it again!
	I have passively taken a blow in this place,
	And if you offer me another I shall repay it promptly
2325	And return it at once—be certain of that—
	with force.
	One single blow is due;
	The contract is my proof,
	Witnessed in Arthur's hall;
2330	And therefore, sir, enough!"

---

[1] *I wyl no lenger on lyte lette thin ernde*   Literally: I will no longer in delay hinder your mission.

[2] *spenne-fote*   With feet together.

The hathel heldet hym fro, and on his ax rested,
Sette the schaft upon schore, and to the scharp lened,
And loked to the leude that on the launde yede,
How that doghty, dredles, dervely ther stondez
2335 Armed, ful aghles: in hert hit hym lykez.
Thenn he melez muryly wyth a much steven,
And with a rynkande rurde he to the renk sayde:
"Bolde burne, on this bent be not so gryndel.
No mon here unmanerly the mysboden habbez,
2340 Ne kyd bot as covenaunde at kyngez kort schaped.
I hyght the a strok and thou hit hatz, halde the wel payed;
I relece the of the remnaunt of ryghtes alle other.
Iif I deliver had bene, a boffet paraunter
I couthe wrotheloker haf waret, to the haf wroght anger.
2345 Fyrst I mansed the muryly with a mynt one,
And rove the wyth no rofe-sore, with ryght I the profered
For the forwarde that we fest in the fyrst nyght,[1]
And thou trystyly the trawthe and trwly me haldez,
Al the gayne thow me gef, as god mon schulde.
2350 That other munt for the morne, mon, I the profered,
Thou kyssedes my clere wyf—the cosses me raghtez.
For bothe two here I the bede bot two bare myntes
        boute scathe.[2]
    Trwe mon trwe restore,
2355   Thenne thar mon drede no wathe.
    At the thrid thou fayled thore,
    And therfore that tappe ta the.

"For hit is my wede that thou werez, that ilke woven girdel,
Myn owen wyf hit the weved, I wot wel for sothe.
2360 Now know I wel thy cosses, and thy costes als,
And the wowyng of my wyf: I wroght it myselven.
I sende hir to asay the, and sothly me thynkkez
On the fautlest freke that ever on fote yede;
As perle bi the quite pese is of prys more,
2365 So is Gawayn, in god fayth, bi other gay knyghtez.
Bot here yow lakked a lyttel, sir, and lewté yow wonted;
Bot that watz for no wylyde werke,[3] ne wowyng nauther,
Bot for ye lufed your lyf; the lasse I yow blame."
That other stif mon in study[4] stod a gret whyle,
2370 So agreved for greme he gryed withinne;
Alle the blod of his brest blende in his face,

The knight kept his distance, and rested on his axe,
Set the shaft on the ground and leaned on the blade,
Contemplating the man before him in the glade;
Seeing how valiant, fearlessly bold he stood there
2335 Armed and undaunted, he admired him much.
Then he spoke to him pleasantly in a loud voice,
And said to the knight in a resounding tone,
"Brave sir, don't act so wrathfully in this place.
No one has discourteously mistreated you here,
2340 Or acted contrary to the covenant sworn at the king's court.
I promised you a blow and you have it; think yourself well paid;
I free you from the rest of all other obligations.
Had I been more dextrous, maybe I could
Have dealt you a more spiteful blow, to have roused your anger.
2345 First I threatened you playfully with a pretence,
And avoided giving you a gash, doing so rightly
Because of the agreement we made on the first night,
When you faithfully and truly kept your pledged word,
Gave me all your winnings, as an honest man should.
2350 That other feint, sir, I gave you for the next day,
When you kissed my lovely wife and gave me those kisses.
For both occasions I aimed at you two mere mock blows
        without harm.
    True man must pay back truly,
2355   Then he need nothing fear;
    You failed me the third time
    And took that blow therefore.

"For it is my belt you are wearing, that same woven girdle,
My own wife gave it to you, I know well in truth.
2360 I know all about your kisses, and your courteous manners,
And my wife's wooing of you: I arranged it myself.
I sent her to test you, and to me truly you seem
One of the most perfect men who ever walked on the earth.
As pearls are more valuable than the white peas,
2365 So is Gawain, in all truth, before other fair knights.
Only here you fell short a little, sir, and lacked fidelity,
But that was not for fine craftsmanship, nor wooing either,
But because you wanted to live: so I blame you the less."
That other brave man stood speechless a long while,
2370 So mortified and crushed that he inwardly squirmed;
All the blood in his body burned in his face,

---

[1] *fyrst nyght*   The night before the first hunt.

[2] *boute scathe*   Without injury, unscathed.

[3] *wylyde werke*   Intricate workmanship (of the belt).

[4] *in study*   Lost in thought, speechless.

That al he schranke for schome that the schalk talked.
The forme worde upon folde that the freke meled:
"Corsed worth cowarddyse and covetyse bothe!
2375 In yow is vylany and vyse that vertue disstryez."
Thenne he kaght to the knot, and the kest lawsez,
Brayde brothely the belt to the burne selven:
"Lo, ther the falssyng, foule mot hit falle!
For care of thy knokke cowardyse me taght
2380 To acorde me with covetyse, my kynde to forsake,
That is larges and lewté that longez to knyghtez.
Now am I fawty and falce, and ferde haf ben ever
Of trecherye and untrawthe: bothe bityde sorwe
        and care!
2385   I biknowe yow, knyght, here stylle,
        Al fawty is my fare;
        Letez me overtake your wylle
        And efte I schal be ware."

The loghe that other leude and luflyly sayde,
2390 "I halde hit hardily hole, the harme that I hade.[1]
Thou art confessed so clene, beknowen of thy mysses,
And hatz the penaunce apert of the poynt of myn egge,
I halde the polysed of that plyght, and pured as clene
As thou hadez never forfeted sythen thou watz fyrst borne;
2395 And I gif the, sir, the gurdel that is golde-hemmed;
For hit is grene as my goune, Sir Gawayn, ye maye
Thenk upon this ilke threpe, ther thou forth thryngez
Among prynces of prys, and this a pure token
Of the chaunce of the grene chapel at chevalrous
        knyghtez.
2400 And ye schal in this Nwe Yer agayn to my wonez,
And we schyn revel the remnaunt of this ryche fest
        ful bene."
        Ther lathed hym fast the lorde
        And sayde, "Wyth my wyf, I wene,
2405   We schal yow wel acorde,
        That watz your enmy kene."

"Nay, for sothe," quoth the segge, and sesed hys helme,
And hatz hit of hendely, and the hathel thonkkez,
"I haf sojorned sadly; sele yow bytyde
2410 And he yelde hit yow yare that yarkkez al menskes!
And comaundez me to that cortays, your comlych fere,
Bothe that on and that other, myn honoured ladyez,

So that he winced with shame at what the man said.
The first words that the knight uttered there
Were, "A curse upon cowardice and coveteousness!
2375 You breed boorishness and vice that ruin virtue."
Then he took hold of the knot and looses the buckle,
Flung the belt violently towards that man:
"There it is, the false thing, may the devil take it!
For fear of your blow taught me cowardice,
2380 To give way to covetousness, be false to my nature,
The generosity and fidelity expected of knights.
Now I am false and unworthy, and have always dreaded
Treachery and deceit: may misfortune and grief
        befall both!
2385   Sir, humbly I confess
        My good name is marred.
        Let me regain your trust,
        Next time I'll be on guard."

Then the other man laughed, and graciously said,
2390 "The wrong you did me I consider wiped out.
You have so cleanly confessed yourself, admitted your fault,
And done honest penance on the edge of my blade.
I declare you absolved of that offence, and washed as clean
As if you had never transgressed since the day you were born.
2395 And I make you a gift, sir, of my gold-bordered belt;
Since it is green like my gown, Sir Gawain, you may
Remember this meeting in the world where you mingle
With princes of rank: it will be a true token
Of the exploit of the Green Chapel among chivalrous
        knights.
2400 And you shall come back to my castle at this New Year,
And we will see out the revelry of this high feast
        with joy."
        He pressed him earnestly
        And said, "We shall, I know,
2405   Reconcile you with my wife,
        Who was your cunning foe."

"No, indeed," said the knight, and seizing his helmet
Takes it off politely and gives the lord thanks;
"I have stayed long enough: good fortune attend you,
2410 And may he who gives all honors soon send you reward!
And commend me to that gracious one, your lovely wife,
Both the one and the other of those honorable ladies

---

[1] *the harme that I hade*   I.e., being cheated of his winnings.

That thus hor knyght wyth hor kest han koyntly bigyled.
Bot hit is no ferly thagh a fole madde,

2415 And thurgh wyles of wymmen be wonen to sorwe,
For so watz Adam in erde with one bygyled,
And Salamon with fele sere, and Samson eftsonez—
Dalyda dalt hym hys wyrde—and Davyth therafter
Watz blended with Barsabe, that much bale tholed.[1]

2420 Now these were wrathed wyth her wyles, hit were a wynne huge
To luf hom wel and leve hem not, a leude that couthe.
For thes wer forne the freest, that folwed alle the sele
Exellently of alle thyse other, under hevenryche
          that mused;

2425   And alle thay were biwyled
          With wymmen that thay used.
          Thagh I be now bigyled
          Me think me burde be excused.

"Bot your gordel," quoth Gawayn, "God yow foryelde!

2430 That wyl I welde wyth goud wylle, not for the wynne golde,
Ne the saynt, ne the sylk, ne for syde pendaundes,
For wele ne for worchyp, ne for the wlonk werkkez,
Bot in syngne of my surfet I schal se hit ofte,
When I ride in renoun, remorde to myselven

2435 The faut and the fayntyse of the flesche crabbed,
How tender hit is to entyse teches of fylthe;
And thus, quen pryde schal me pryk for prowes of armes,
The loke to this luf-lace schal lethe my hert.
Bot on I wolde yow pray, displeses yow never:

2440 Syn ye be lorde of the yonder londe her I haf lent inne
Wyth yow wyth worschyp—the wyghe hit yow yelde
That uphaldez the heven and on hygh sittez—
How norne ye yowre ryght nome, and thenne no more?"
"That schal I telle the trwly," quoth that other thenne,

2445 "Bertilak de Hautdesert I hat in this londe.
Thurgh myght of Morgne la Faye, that in my hous lenges,
And koyntyse of clergye, bi craftes wel lerned,
The maystrés of Merlyn mony hatz taken—
For ho hatz dalt drwry ful dere sumtyme

2450 With that conable klerk, that knowes alle your knyghtez
          at hame.
          Morgne the goddes
          Therfore hit is hir name:
          Weldez non so hyghe hawtesse

2455   That ho ne con make ful tame—

Who have so cleverly deluded their knight with their game.
But it is no wonder if a fool acts insanely

2415 And is brought to grief through womanly wiles;
For so was Adam beguiled by one, here on earth,
Solomon by several women, and Samson was another—
Delilah was cause of his fate—and afterwards David
Was deluded by Bathsheba, and suffered much grief.

2420 Since these were ruined by their wiles, it would be a great gain
To love women and not trust them, if a man knew how.
For these were the noblest of old, whom fortune favored
Above all others on earth, or who dwelt
          under heaven.

2425   Beguiled were they all
          By women they thought kind.
          Since I too have been tricked
          Then I should pardon find.

"But for your belt," said Gawain, "God repay you for that!

2430 I accept it gratefully, not for its wonderful gold,
Nor for the girdle itself nor its silk, nor its long pendants,
Nor its value nor the honor it confers, nor its fine workmanship,
But I shall look at it often as a sign of my failing,
And when I ride in triumph, recall with remorse

2435 The corruption and frailty of the perverse flesh,
How quick it is to pick up blotches of sin.
And so, when pride in my knightly valor stirs me,
A glance at this girdle will humble my heart.
Just one thing I would ask, if it would not offend you,

2440 Since you are the lord of the country that I have dwelt in,
Honorably treated in your house—may he reward you
Who holds up the heavens and sits upon high!—
What do you call yourself rightly, and then no more demands?"
"I will tell you that truthfully," replied that other man,

2445 "Bertilak of Hautdesert I am called in this land.
Through the power of Morgan le Fay, who lives under my roof,
And her skill in learning, well taught in magic arts,
She has acquired many of Merlin's occult powers—
For she had love-dealings at an earlier time

2450 With that accomplished scholar, as all your knights know
          at home.
          Morgan the goddess
          Therefore is her name;
          No one, however haughty

2455   Or proud she cannot tame.

---

1 *For so watz Adam ... tholed* Famous stories of female betrayal from the Old Testament.

"Ho wayned me upon this wyse to your wynne halle
For to assay the surquidré, yif hit soth were
That rennes of the grete renoun of the Rounde Table.
Ho wayned me this wonder your wyttez to reve,
2460 For to have greved Gaynour and gart hir to dyghe
With glopnyng of that ilke gome that gostlych speked
With his hede in his honde bifore the hyghe table.
That is ho that is at home, the auncian lady;
Ho is even thyn aunt, Arthurez half-suster,
2465 The duches doghter of Tyntagelle, that dere Uter after
Hade Arthur upon, that athel is nowthe.
Therfore I ethe the, hathel, to com to thyn aunt,
Make myry in my hous; my meny the lovies,
And I wol the as wel, wyghe, bi my faythe,
2470 As any gome under God for thy grete trauthe."
And he nikked hym naye, he nolde bi no wayes.
Thay acolen and kyssen and kennen ayther other
To the prynce of paradise, and parten ryght there
          on coolde;
2475   Gawayn on blonk ful bene
        To the kyngez burgh buskez bolde,
        And the knyght in the enker-grene
        Whiderwarde-so-ever he wolde.

Wylde wayez in the worlde Wowen now rydez
2480 On Gryngolet, that the grace hade geten of his lyve;
Ofte he herbered in house and ofte al theroute,
And mony aventure in vale, and venquyst ofte,
That I ne tyght at this tyme in tale to remene.
The hurt watz hole that he hade hent in his nek,
2485 And the blykkande belt he bere theraboute
Abelef as a bauderyk bounden by his syde,
Loken under his lyfte arme, the lace, with a knot,
In tokenyng he watz tane in tech of a faute.
And thus he commes to the court, knyght al in sounde.
2490 Ther wakned wele in that wone when wyst the grete
That gode Gawayn watz commen; gayn hit hym thoght.
The kyng kysses the knyght, and the whene alce,
And sythen mony syker knyght that soght hym to haylce,
Of his fare that hym frayned; and ferlyly he telles,
2495 Biknowez alle the costes of care that he hade,
The chaunce of the chapel, the chere of the knyght,
The luf of the ladi, the lace at the last.
The nirt in the neck he naked hem schewed

"She sent me in this shape to your splendid hall
To make trial of your pride, and to judge the truth
Of the great reputation attached to the Round Table.
She sent me to drive you demented with this marvel,
2460 To have terrified Guenevere and caused her to die
With horror at that figure who spoke like a specter
With his head in his hand before the high table.
That is she who is in my castle, the very old lady,
Who is actually your aunt, Arthur's half-sister,
2465 The duchess of Tintagel's daughter, whom noble Uther
Afterwards begot Arthur upon, who now is king.
So I entreat you, good sir, to visit your aunt
And make merry in my house: my servants all love you,
And so will I too, sir, on my honor,
2470 As much as any man on earth for your great truth."
But Gawain told him no, not for any persuasion.
They embrace and kiss, and commend each other
To the prince of paradise, and separate there
          in the cold;
2475   On his great horse Gawain
        To the king's court quickly goes,
        And the knight in emerald green
        Went wheresoever he chose.

Over wild country Gawain now makes his way
2480 On Gringolet, after his life had been mercifully spared.
Sometimes he lodged in a house and often out of doors,
And was vanquisher often in many encounters
Which at this time I do not intend to relate.
The injury he had received in his neck was healed,
2485 And over it he wore the gleaming belt
Across his body like a baldric, fastened at his side,
And this girdle tied under his left arm with a knot,
To signify he had been dishonored by a slip.
And so safe and sound he arrives at the court.
2490 Joy spread through the castle when the nobles learnt
That good Gawain had returned: they thought it a wonder.
The king kisses the knight, and the queen too,
And then many true knights who came to embrace him,
Asking how he had fared; he tells a marvelous story,
2495 Describes all the hardships he had endured,
What happened at the chapel, the Green Knight's behavior,
The lady's wooing, and finally the belt.
He showed them the scar on his bare neck

That he laght for his unleuté at the leudes hondes
2500   for blame.
    He tened quen he schulde telle,
    He groned for gref and grame;
    The blod in his face con melle,
    When he hit schulde schewe, for schame.

2505 "Lo, lorde," quoth the leude, and the lace hondeled,
"This is the bende of this blame I bere in my nek,
This is the lathe and the losse that I laght have
Of cowardise and covetyse that I haf caght thare,
This is the token of untrawthe that I am tane inne,
2510 And I mot nedez hit were wyle I may last;
For mon may hyden his harme, bot unhap ne may hit,
For ther hit onez is tachched twynne wil hit never."
The kyng comfortez the knyght, and alle the court als
Laghen loude therat, and luflyly acorden
2515 That lordes and ladis that longed to the Table,
Uche burne of the brotherhede, a bauderyk schulde have,
A bende abelef hym aboute of a bryght grene,
And that, for sake of that segge, in swete to were.
For that watz acorded the renoun of the Rounde Table,
2520 And he honoured that hit hade evermore after,
As hit is breved in the best boke of romaunce.
Thus in Arthurus day this aunter bitidde,
The Brutus bokez therof beres wyttenesse;
Sythen Brutus, the bolde burne, bowed hider fyrst,
2525 After the segge and the asaute watz sesed at Troye,[1]
      iwysse,
    Mony aunterez here-biforne
    Haf fallen suche er this.
    Now that bere the croun of thorne
2530   He bryng uus to his blysse! AMEN.

HONY SOYT QUI MAL PENCE.[2]

That he received for his dishonesty at the lord's hands
2500   in rebuke.
    Tormented by his tale
    He groaned for grief and hurt;
    The blood burned in his face
    When he showed the shameful cut.

2505 "See, my lord," said the man, and held up the girdle,
"This belt caused the scar that I bear on my neck;
This is the injury and damage that I have suffered
For the cowardice and covetousness that seized me there;
This is the token of the dishonesty I was caught committing,
2510 And now I must wear it as long as I live.
For a man may hide his misdeed, but never erase it,
For where once it takes root the stain can never be lifted."
The king consoles the knight, and the whole court
Laughs loudly about it, and courteously agrees
2515 That lords and ladies who belong to the Table,
Each member of the brotherhood, should wear such a belt,
A baldric of bright green crosswise on the body,
Similar to Sir Gawain's and worn for his sake:
And that became part of the renown of the Round Table,
2520 And whoever afterwards wore it was always honored,
As is set down in the most reputable books of romance.
So in the time of Arthur this adventure happened,
And the chronicles of Britain bear witness to it;
After the brave hero Brutus first arrived here,
2525 When the siege and the assault were ended at Troy,
      indeed.
    Many exploits before now
    Have happened much like this.
    Now may the thorn-crowned God
2530   Bring us to his bliss! AMEN.

HONI SOIT QUI MAL Y PENSE.

---

[1] *After the segge and the asaute watz sesed at Troye*   The last long line
of the poem repeats the first one, as though bringing the story full
circle after its hundred and one stanzas.

[2] *Hony Soyt Qui Mal Pence*   Old French: evil be to him who evil
thinks, the motto embroidered on the blue velvet garter worn by
Knights of the Garter, the highest order of English knighthood
bestowed by the sovereign. According to Froissart, the order was
instituted about 1344. The poet's use of the motto has not been
accounted for.

IN CONTEXT

Fled Bricrend

The earliest known example of the beheading-game legend appears in the Irish story *Fled Bricrend*, written down about the year 1100 but probably a good deal older. It tells how a terrifying ogre enters the hall where several heroes are gathered, carrying a huge club in one hand and an enormous axe in the other. He explains that he is searching for a man who will deal with him fairly, and that the reputation of the Ulaid has brought him there in the hope of finding one. The terms of fair play that he proposes are that he will cut off the head of one of the heroes, who on the following night will decapitate him. This arrangement is not accepted, and the ogre agrees to reverse the conditions by standing a blow forthwith and returning on the next day to give one in return. One of the heroes accepts the challenge and cuts off the ogre's head, filling the hall with blood; but the ogre rises, picks up his head and the axe, and leaves the hall, still bleeding profusely. When he returns on the following night his opponent shirks his undertaking to stand the return blow. Two further heroes take up the challenge with the same result, but when the ogre returns on the fourth night contemptuous of the false and cowardly Ulaid, Cú Chulaind (Cuchulainn) is present. He too decapitates the ogre and smashes the head for good measure. On the next night Cú Chulaind places his neck on the block to receive the return blow, and is mocked by the ogre because his neck does not cover the enormous block. Cú Chulaind rebukes the ogre for tormenting him, and insists on being despatched at once. The ogre raises the huge axe and brings it down on Cú Chulaind's neck with the blade uppermost. After praising Cú Chulaind's courage and fidelity the ogre vanishes. In a shorter version of the story he swings the axe at Cú Chulaind three times, each time with the blade reversed.

from *Fled Bricrend/Bricriu's Feast*

O nce, when the Ulaid were at Emuin Machae, tired after the fair and the games, Conchubur and Fergus and the other Ulaid chieftains returned from the playing field to sit in Conchubur's Cráebrúad. Lóegure and Conall and Cú Chulaind were not there that evening, but the best of the other warriors of Ulaid were. As night drew on, they saw a huge, ugly churl coming towards them in the house, and it seemed to them that there was not in all Ulaid a warrior half as tall. His appearance was frightful and terrifying: a hide against his skin, and a dun cloak round him, and a great bushy tree overhead where a winter shed for thirty calves could fit. Each of his two yellow eyes was the size of an ox-cauldron; each finger was as thick as a normal man's wrist. The tree trunk in his left hand would have been a burden for twenty yoked oxen; the axe in his right hand, whence had gone three fifties of glowing metal pieces, had a handle that would have been a burden for a team of oxen, yet it was sharp enough to cut hairs against the wind.

He came in this guise and stood beneath the forked beam at one end of the fire. "Do you find the house so narrow," said Dubthach Dóeltenga, "that there is no place to stand but under the forked beam? You may wish to contest the position of house candlebearer, but you are more likely to burn the house than to illuminate the company inside." "Although that is my gift," the churl replied, "perhaps you will grant that, despite my height, the entire household may be lit without the house's being burnt. But that is not my primary gift, and I have others. That which I have come to seek I have not found in Ériu or the Alps or Europe or Africa or Asia or Greece or Scythia or Inis Orc or the Pillars of Hercules or Tor mBregoind or Inis Gaid. Nowhere have I found a man to keep my bargain. Since you Ulaid surpass the hosts of every land in anger and prowess and weaponry, in rank and pride and dignity, in honor and generosity and excellence, let one of you keep faith with me in the matter over which I have come."

"It is not right," said Fergus, "to dishonor a province because of one man's failure to keep his word—perhaps death is no nearer to him than it is to you." "It is not I who shirk death," replied the churl. "Then let us hear your proposal," said Fergus. "Only if I am allowed fair play," said the churl. "It is right to allow him that," said Senchae son of Ailill, "for it would be no fair play if a great host broke faith with a completely unknown individual. Besides, it would seem to us that if you are to find the man you seek, you will find him here." "I exempt Conchubur, for he is the king, and I exempt Fergus, for he is of equal rank," said the churl. "Whoever else may dare, let him come that I may cut off his head tonight, he mine tomorrow."

"After those two," said Dubthach, "there is certainly no warrior here worthy of that." "Indeed, there is," said Muinremur son of Gerrgend, and he sprang into the center of the house. Now, Muinremur had the strength of one hundred warriors, and each arm had the strength of one hundred. "Bend down, churl," he said, "that I may cut off your head tonight—you may cut off mine tomorrow night." "I could make that bargain anywhere," said the churl. "Let us rather make the bargain I proposed: I will cut off your head tonight, and you will avenge that by cutting off my head tomorrow night." "I swear by what my people swear by," said Dubthach Dóeltenga, "such a death would not be pleasant if the man you killed tonight clung to you tomorrow. But you alone have the power to be killed one night and to avenge it the next." "Then whatever conditions you propose I will fulfil, surprising as you may find that," said the churl, whereupon he made Muinremur pledge to keep his part of the bargain the following night.

With that, Muinremur took the churl's axe, whose two edges were seven feet apart. The churl stretched his neck out on the block, and Muinremur so swung the axe that it stuck in the block underneath; the head rolled to the foot of the forked beam, and the house was filled with blood. At once, the churl rose, gathered his head and his block and his axe and clutched them to his chest, and left the house, blood streaming from the neck and filling the Cráebrúad on every side. The household were horrorstruck by the wondrousness of the event they had witnessed. "I swear by what my people swear by," said Dubthach Dóeltenga, "if that churl returns tomorrow after having been killed tonight, not a man in Ulaid will be left alive."

The following night, the churl returned, but Muinremur avoided him. The churl complained, saying "Indeed, it is not fair of Muinremur to break his part of the bargain." Lóegure Búadach, however, was present that night, and when the churl continued, "Who of the warriors who contest the champion's portion of Ulaid will fulfil this bargain with me tonight? Where is Lóegure Búadach?", Lóegure said, "Here I am!" The churl pledged Lóegure as he had pledged Muinremur, but Lóegure, like Muinremur, failed to appear the following night. The churl then pledged Conall Cernach, and he too failed to appear and keep his pledge.

When he arrived on the fourth night, the churl was seething with rage. All the women of Ulaid had gathered there that night to see the marvel that had come to the Cráebrúad, and Cú Chulaind had come as well. The churl began to reproach them, then, saying, "Men of Ulaid, your skill and courage are no more. Your warriors covet the champion's portion, yet they are unable to contest it. Where is that pitiful stripling you call Cú Chulaind? Would his word be better than that of his companions?" "I want no bargain with you," said Cú Chulaind. "No doubt you fear death, wretched fly," said the churl. At that, Cú Chulaind sprang towards the churl and dealt him such a blow with the axe that his head was sent to the rafters of the Cráebrúad, and the entire house shook. Cú

Chulaind then struck the head with the axe once more, so that he shattered it into fragments. The churl rose nonetheless.

The following day, the Ulaid watched Cú Chulaind to see if he would avoid the churl the way his companions had done; they saw that he was waiting for the churl, and they grew very dejected. It seemed to them proper to begin his death dirge, for they feared greatly that he would live only until the churl appeared. Cú Chulaind, ashamed, said to Conchubur, "By my shield and by my sword, I will not go until I have fulfilled my pledge to the churl—since I am to die, I will die with honor."

Towards the end of the day, they saw the churl approaching them. "Where is Cú Chulaind?" he asked. "Indeed, I am here," said Cú Chulaind. "You speak low, tonight, wretch, for you fear death greatly," said the churl. "Yet for all that, you have not avoided me." Cú Chulaind rose and stretched his neck out on the block, but its size was such that his neck reached only halfway across. "Stretch out your neck, you wretch," said the churl. "You torment me," said Cú Chulaind. "Kill me quickly. I did not torment you last night. Indeed, I swear, if you torment me now, I will make myself as long as a heron above you." "I cannot dispatch you, not with the length of the block and the shortness of your neck," said the churl.

Cú Chulaind stretched himself, then, until a warrior's foot would fit between each rib, and he stretched his neck until it reached the other side of the block. The churl raised his axe so that it reached the rafters of the house. What with the creaking of the old hide that he wore and the swish of his axe as he raised it with the strength of his two arms, the sound he made was like that of a rustling forest on a windy night. The churl brought the axe down, then, upon Cú Chulaind's neck—with the blade turned up. All the chieftains of Ulaid saw this.

"Rise, Cú Chulaind!" the churl then said. "Of all the warriors in Ulaid and Ériu, whatever their merit, none is your equal for courage and skill and honor. You are the supreme warrior of Ériu, and the champion's portion is yours, without contest; moreover, your wife will henceforth enter the drinking house before all the other women of Ulaid. Whoever might dispute this judgment, I swear by what my people swear by, his life will not be long." After that, the churl vanished. It was Cú Rui son of Dáre, who in that guise had come to fulfil the promise he had made to Cú Chulaind.

Illustrations from the Original Manuscript

In the manuscript in which *Sir Gawain and the Green Knight* appears the text is accompanied by four illustrations. Two of these are reproduced below. The first, which appears before the text in the original manuscript, brings together two scenes from the poem in a single illustration. Gawain is shown both taking the axe from King Arthur (who appears with the Queen on his left), and holding the axe (having just decapitated the Green Knight); the Green Knight is shown on horseback, holding his head.

In the second illustration reproduced here, the lady of the castle is shown visiting Gawain. (The two lines appearing above the illustration were written in a hand other than that of the manuscript scribe, and are not connected to the poem.)

The two illustrations not reproduced here are somewhat indistinct in the manuscript; they portray Gawain at the Green Chapel with the Green Knight above, axe in hand, and Gawain kneeling in front of Arthur and Guenevere.

The Thorn and the Yogh

The "original" text of *Sir Gawain and the Green Knight* as provided above substitutes modern English letters for two letters in Middle English that have now died out. One of these, the letter þ ("thorn"), was sounded very much as we sound the letters "th" today. The other, ȝ ("yogh"), various represented sounds that we represent with "gh," "y," and "z." Following is the first part of the poem with Middle English letters.

Siþþen þe sege and þe assaut watz sesed at Troye,
Þe borȝ brittened and brent to brondeȝ and askez,
Þe tulk þat þe trammes of tresoun þer wroȝt
Watz tried for his tricherie, þe trewest on erþe:
Hit watz Ennias þe athel, and his highe kynde,
Þat siþþen depreced prouinces, and patrounes bicome
Welneȝe of al þe wele in þe west iles.
Fro riche Romulus to Rome ricchis hym swyþe,
With gret bobbaunce þat burȝe he biges vpon fyrst,
And neuenes hit his aune nome, as hit now hat;
Tirius to Tuskan and teldes bigynnes,
Langaberde in Lumbardie lyftes vp homes,
And fer ouer þe French flod Felix Brutus
On mony bonkkes ful brode Bretayn he settez wyth wynne,
Where werre and wrake and wonder
Bi syþez hatz wont þerinne,
And oft boþe blysse and blunder
Ful skete hatz skyfted synne.

GEOFFREY CHAUCER
c. 1343 — 1400

Little is known about the private life of the greatest English author of the Middle Ages, but because Geoffrey Chaucer spent most years of his adult life in service to the Crown and the government, medieval records tell us much about his working life. These records, in which Chaucer's name is mentioned some 500 times, document decades of work for various royal households—as a page, a controller of customs, and a justice of the peace, among other positions. What they fail to provide are any details about Chaucer's education, literary life, or personal life.

As the author of the exquisite *Troilus and Criseyde* and of a variety of shorter poems and prose works, Chaucer would be regarded among the most important medieval English writers. But it is *The Canterbury Tales* that has secured his place as one of the greatest English authors of any era. From the time of its first appearance in the late fourteenth century, this linked series of stories has remained one of the most popular works of literature of the Middle Ages. The *Tales* were, in fact, among the first works ever printed in England, after William Caxton introduced the printing press to the country in 1474, some two decades after Gutenberg's invention of moveable type. In his Preface to *Fables Ancient and Modern* (1700), John Dryden called Chaucer the "father of English poetry," not only for his great influence upon future generations, but also for the fact that he was one of the first poets to compose his works in English, rather than French, Latin, or Anglo-Norman. Indeed, like Dante before him, Chaucer used the everyday language of the common people and proved its poetic capacity.

Chaucer was born at a time that saw the beginnings of a breakdown in strict divisions between the aristocracy, the Church, and the commoners. Although he was not born into the noble class, he was able to transcend the restrictions of the old social order and to procure a variety of high positions. Chaucer was born to Agnes Copton and John Chaucer just a few years before the beginning of the Hundred Years' War between France and England; his childhood also saw the outbreak of bubonic plague in England (which eventually killed between thirty and forty per cent of the population). Both of his parents held court positions at various times, but his father was primarily a prosperous wine merchant in London. With his knowledge of Latin, French, and Italian, the young Chaucer was likely educated in a good London grammar school; later he may have attended university. Court documents show that in his early teens he held a position as page in the household of the Countess of Ulster and Prince Lionel, son of the ruling monarch, Edward III.

In 1359 Chaucer took part in the war in France and was captured and ransomed to the king, who procured his release in 1360. Speculation has it that during this period on the continent Chaucer began his literary career, translating from the French the popular and influential allegorical poem *Le Roman de la Rose* (*The Romance of the Rose*), written by Guillaume de Lorris and Jean de Meun. In 1366 Chaucer married Philippa Roet, a lady-in-waiting to the queen. The couple had at least two children; Chaucer addressed *A Treatise on Astrolabe* (1391) to "little Lewis," and another son, Thomas, was eventually knighted.

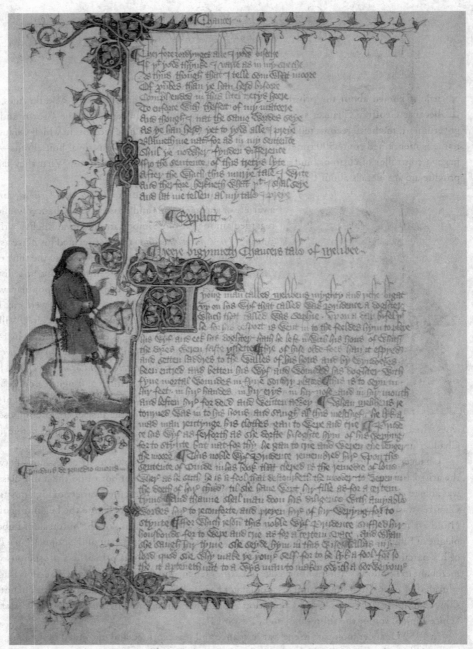

The first page of Chaucer's *Tale of Melibee*, from the Ellesmere manuscript of *The Canterbury Tales*. The figure on horseback is generally taken to be a representation of Chaucer. The actual size of pages in the Ellesmere manuscript is approximately 15¾ x 11⅛". (Rerprinted by permission of *The Huntington Library, San Marino, California*. EL 26 C9 f.153v.)

Over the course of the next twenty years, Chaucer continued his work for the royal household, serving in the army in France under John of Gaunt and in 1372 traveling on a diplomatic mission to Italy, where he probably acquired his knowledge of the works of Dante, Petrarch, and Boccaccio. *The Book of the Duchess* (1368), written when he was about twenty-five, is already an accomplished work. After his trip to Italy, however, Chaucer's writing began to show a new level of maturity and innovative technique, as well as a vast knowledge of both classical and contemporary literature and the various languages associated with these writings. *The House of Fame* (c. 1377) owes a debt to Dante, *The Parliament of Fowls* (1380) to Boccaccio and Cicero, and *Troilus and Criseyde* (c. 1385) again to Boccaccio; it is a reworking of Boccaccio's *Il Filostrato*.

Troilus, a long romantic poem recounting the fateful love of the Trojan Prince Troilus for Criseyde, has often been considered the most perfectly realized of all Chaucer's works. Although it exhibits less range than *The Canterbury Tales*, its elegant and supple verse, sustained narrative accomplishment, and depth of characterization are unsurpassed in medieval poetry in English.

In his next (and unfinished) work, *The Legend of Good Women*, written as a series of tales, Chaucer parodies his own authorial persona, taking himself to task for the writing of Criseyde's betrayal of Troilus by telling the stories of famous women who were themselves deceived by men.

Although the beginning of the 1380s were difficult times for Chaucer and for the country (he was accused of abduction or rape by a young woman named Cecilia Chaumpaigne, and 1381 saw the uprising against the poll tax), he seemed to regain inspiration in the latter part of the decade, at the same time as he held some important positions in the court. He became Controller of Customs and Justice of the Peace, and in 1386 was elected Member of Parliament for Kent; in 1389 Chaucer was appointed Clerk of the King's Works, a vital and challenging position in which he oversaw repairs and maintenance of government buildings. During these years he began work on *The Canterbury Tales*, generally considered his masterpiece. Rather than adapting old legends or reworking ancient stories of heroes, as was the norm, Chaucer told the stories of a gallery of English characters, from knight to clerk, parson to cook, nobility and commoners alike. Frequently hilarious, sometimes bawdy, and often revealing, *The Canterbury Tales* claims to be a series of stories told by a group of pilgrims on their way from London to Canterbury to visit the shrine of the martyr St. Thomas Becket. Similar framing devices had been used by other writers of the Middle Ages, but Chaucer's inclusion of such a wide range of classes and types of people, as well as his tonal range and his melding of diverse styles, were without precedent in English.

Although the work as it stands includes 24 tales and runs to over 17,000 lines, *The Canterbury Tales* was far from complete at the end of Chaucer's life. *The General Prologue*, in which the narrator introduces some thirty pilgrims, suggests that Chaucer intended to write more than 100 tales, with each narrator telling two tales on the journey to Canterbury and two on the way back. Chaucer must have known that such a plan was entirely unrealistic, however. Perhaps he allowed it to stand in the *General Prologue*, which he probably revised on several occasions, to indicate that *The Canterbury Tales* was a work that could never be finished. The narratives we do have are fleshed out by linking passages recounting exchanges among the pilgrims. Although these characters are fictional, the text provides a wealth of insight into the customs and practices of the time. Many of the pilgrims are medieval "types," but by varying narrative style with each speaker, Chaucer breathes imaginative life into the characters as individuals and into their world as a whole.

Chaucer's moral stance in *The Canterbury Tales* has been the subject of much discussion. The *Retraction* that follows *The Parson's Tale* disavows on moral grounds not only the *Tales*, but virtually all his more secular writings. Is this "Geoffrey Chaucer" merely another imaginary personage, or did the aging author truly repent of all "worldly vanitees"? At so great a remove as we are from medieval sensibilities, it is impossible to be sure. It can be said, however, that through most of *The Canterbury Tales* the author refrains from moralizing or casting judgment. The whole notion of a religious pilgrimage is frequently undermined by the actions of the characters, many of whom show themselves to be more interested in carnal than spiritual quests. Other characters, such as the Pardoner, may seem at first to be of high moral character, but deliberately or unwittingly expose their own compromised morality as they tell their stories. More broadly, there is an ongoing and unresolved tension in the tales between the spiritual and the worldly. This tension operates not only within many of the individual tales but also in the work as a whole, with the elevated tone of *The Knight's Tale*, for example, standing in marked contrast to the bawdiness of *The Miller's Tale*, the irreverence of the Wife of Bath's fantasy, or the elaborate pretense of artlessness in the fable recounted by the Nun's Priest. There is tension as well between the social classes represented among the pilgrims, between different religious views, between the sexes, and over the extent to which the traditions and conventions of the past should still be respected and adhered to. *The Canterbury Tales* is of all the classics of English literature one of the most entertaining and also one of the most open: open-minded in its underlying sensibilities, and open to an extraordinary range of interpretation.

The final year of Chaucer's life saw great upheaval in England's monarchy. In 1399, Richard II, who had supported Chaucer, was overthrown by Henry Bolingbroke (Henry IV), the oldest son of Richard's uncle, John of Gaunt, Duke of Lancaster, who had also been one of Chaucer's patrons. It may have been due to his gifts as a poet that Chaucer managed to retain the favor of the new regime, which was anxious for respectability. Chaucer wrote his final poem, "Complaint to His Purse," as a plea to King Henry to pay income owing from Richard II's reign; while the king did promise payment, Chaucer never collected the money. He died in October of 1400 and was buried in the south transept of Westminster Abbey. A century and a half later a monument to Chaucer was erected on the spot; thus began the tradition of the abbey's "Poets' Corner."

⌘ ⌘ ⌘

To Rosemounde
A Balade

Madame, ye ben of al beaute shryne°   *shrine*
As fer as cercled° is the   *rounded*
  mapamounde,°[1]   *map of the world*
For as the cristal glorious ye shyne,
And lyke ruby ben your chekes rounde.
5 Therwith ye ben so mery and so jocounde° *pleasant, joyful*
That at a revel° whan that I see you daunce,   *festival*
It is an oynement° unto my wounde,   *ointment*
Thogh ye to me ne do no daliaunce.[2]

For thogh I wepe of teres ful a tyne,°   *barrel*
10 Yet may that wo myn herte nat confounde;°   *destroy*
Your semy° voys that ye so smal out   *small, high*
  twyne°   *twist out*
Maketh my thoght in joy and blis habounde.° *abound, be full of*
So curtaysly I go with love bounde
That to myself I sey in my penaunce,
15 "Suffyseth me to love you, Rosemounde,
Thogh ye to me ne do no daliaunce."[3]

Nas never pyk walwed° in galauntyne[4]   *immersed*
As I in love am walwed and ywounde,°   *wound*

---

[1] *ye ben of al ... mapamounde* You are the shrine of all beauty throughout the world.

[2] *Thogh ... daliaunce* Even though you give me no encouragement.

[3] *daliaunce* Sociable interaction, or more explicitly amorous or sexual exchange.

[4] *Nas ... galauntyne* No pike was ever steeped in galantine sauce.

20 For which ful ofte I of myself devyne° *discover, understand*
That I am trewe Tristam[1] the secounde.
My love may not refreyde° nor   *grow cold*
   affounde,°   *founder, grow numb*
I brenne° ay in an amorous plesaunce.°   *burn / desire*
Do what you lyst,° I wyl your thral be founde,[2]   *wish*
Thogh ye to me ne do no daliaunce.

tregentil————————//————————chaucer[3]
—c. 1477

The Canterbury Tales

It is some indication of its popularity that *The Canterbury Tales* survives in so many manuscripts: fifty-five complete or nearly complete collections and a further twenty-eight manuscripts that contain one or more tales. Of these manuscripts, two of the earliest, the Hengwrt, now in the National Library in Wales, and the Ellesmere, now in the Huntington Library in Pasadena, California, have provided the basis for most editions. The two manuscripts were copied by the same scribe, Adam Pynkhurst, in the first few years after Chaucer's death in 1400, or just possibly in the last year or two of Chaucer's life. The differences between the two manuscripts raise one of the great puzzles in Chaucerian scholarship: how close Chaucer came to finishing *The Canterbury Tales*. Ellesmere, generally agreed to be slightly later, presents the tales in an order that many modern readers have found to make strong artistic sense; Ellesmere also contains material—most notably the *Canon's Yeoman's Tale*, an account of a fraudulent alchemical workshop—that is missing from Hengwrt. On the other hand, many individual lines in Ellesmere contain small errors or are missing words. Why Pynkhurst, having managed to get an accurate (although incomplete) text from which to copy when he was writing the Hengwrt manuscript, should then have failed to do so when writing

Ellesmere remains unclear. This edition reproduces the text of the Ellesmere manuscript, preserving its spellings and modifying only its word division and punctuation. Where the text of the Ellesmere is clearly deficient or does not make sense, the editors have drawn on Hengwrt. In each case, these alterations are noted.

The Ellesmere manuscript includes a considerable number of marginal notes, or glosses. In the tales included in this anthology, these glosses are particularly numerous in *The Wife of Bath's Tale* and in *The Franklin's Tale*. Who first composed these glosses is still an open question, although there are strong grounds for believing that Chaucer himself composed quite a few of them. In these pages the texts of a number of the more interesting marginal glosses have been included in the notes at the bottom of the page.

The Ellesmere manuscript is large, its pages measuring roughly 15 by 11 inches, and elegantly decorated. It is the kind of luxury volume that might have been commissioned by an aristocrat, a prosperous London merchant, or a senior civil servant of the early fifteenth century. Various personal inscriptions in the manuscript indicate that it once belonged to John de Vere, who became the twelfth earl of Oxford in 1417, and whose guardians (possibly the book's first owners) were Thomas Beaufort, Duke of Exeter (one of the sons of John of Gaunt) and Henry IV's third son, John, Duke of Bedford, a great book collector.

The General Prologue

Chaucer's account of meeting a group of twenty-nine pilgrims at the Tabard Inn in Southwark, on the south bank of the Thames, has such an air of verisimilitude that it was once read as an account of an actual pilgrimage, with much attention devoted to determining just when it took place (1387 being the most favored date), how many days it took the pilgrims to get to Canterbury, and who the pilgrims were in real life. In fact, *The Canterbury Tales* draws on a tradition of medieval estates satire, poems that describe members of the three estates (those who pray, i.e., monks and nuns; those who fight, i.e., knights; and those who work, i.e., peasants) in terms of their characteristic vices. Many of Chaucer's most memorable and vivid characters, including his Friar and the Wife of Bath, are drawn from satirical figures found in such works as *Le Roman de la Rose* (*The Romance of the Rose*), in which a lover's quest for his lady

---

[1] *Tristam* Tristan, lover of Isolde, often presented as the ideal lover in medieval romance.

[2] *I ... founde* I will remain your servant.

[3] *tregentil ... chaucer* Although the words appear joined (or separated) by a line or flourish in the manuscript, the status of *tregentil* is uncertain. It may be an epithet (French: very gentle) or a proper name.

(the rose) serves as an occasion for broad social commentary. Chaucer knew the work well, having translated it from French, and also knew the major example of English estates satire, William Langland's *Piers Plowman*, which Langland composed and then repeatedly reworked in the 1370s and 1380s.

Chaucer includes a Knight and a Plowman among his pilgrims, but for the most part they are drawn from the middle ranks of society, including prosperous members of the clergy, or first estate, such as the Friar, the Monk, and the Prioress, and those of the third estate who no longer fitted among the peasantry, such as the five prosperous Guildsmen, the Wife of Bath, the Merchant, the Physician, the Sergeant of Law, and the Manciple. Energetic and often clever, or at least sophisticated, the pilgrims are all professionally successful and—with a few exceptions—they thrive in the vibrant money economy of the later fourteenth century. To describe these people, Chaucer employs an affable and naively enthusiastic narrator, who mingles easily with them, admiring and even echoing their speeches, all apparently uncritically. As George Lyman Kittredge has observed, however, Chaucer was a professional tax collector and "a naïf collector of Customs would be a paradoxical monster." The poet and his narrator must not be confused.

The framing device of the pilgrimage allows Chaucer to explore the social tensions and moral debates of his day more freely than would otherwise be possible, transposing all conflict into an apparently innocent tale-telling competition. The question of who will tell the tale that offers the "best sentence and moost solaas" (line 798), i.e., the best moral meaning and the most enjoyment, is a standing invitation to probe beneath the surface and ask what the meaning of each tale really is. The pilgrimage frame also allows Chaucer to experiment with almost every major literary genre of his day and to assemble an encyclopedic compilation of ancient wisdom, history, and moral lessons. The learned aspect of this compilation is reinforced in the Ellesmere manuscript by the large number of marginal glosses, which identify the source for quotations and draw attention to particularly sententious passages.

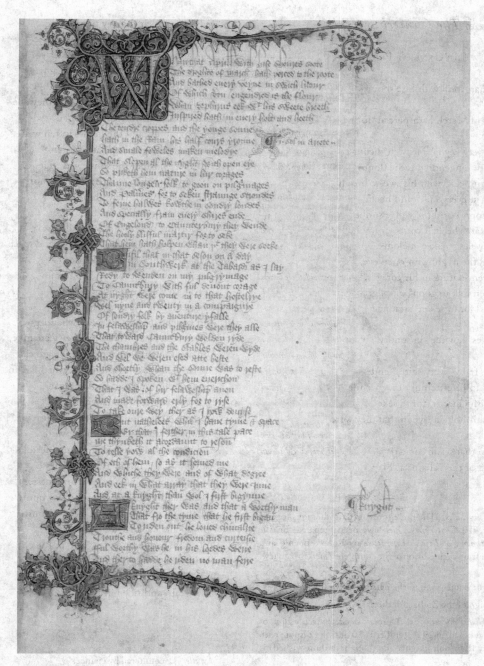

Opening page of *The General Prologue*, Ellesmere manuscript. (Reprinted by permission of *The Huntington Library, San Marino, California*. EL 26 C9 f. 1r.)

from *The Canterbury Tales*[1]

THE GENERAL PROLOGUE

Whan that Aprill with hise shoures° soote°   *showers / sweet*
The droghte° of March hath perced° to the
   roote   *drought / pierced*
And bathed every veyne° in swich° licour°   *vein / such / liquid*
Of which vertu° engendred is the flour,°   *power / flower*
5 Whan Zephirus[2] eek° with his sweete breeth   *also*
Inspired hath in every holt° and heeth°   *wood / heath*
The tendre croppes and the yonge sonne
Hath in the Ram[3] his half cours yronne°   *run*
And smale foweles° maken melodye   *birds*
10 That slepen al the nyght with open eye,
So priketh° hem nature in hir corages,°   *excites / their hearts*
Thanne longen folk to goon° on pilgrimages   *go*
And palmeres° for to seken° straunge
   strondes°   *pilgrims / seek / shores*
To ferne halwes° kowthe° in sondry
   londes.   *far-off shrines / known*
15 And specially, fram° every shires° ende   *from / shire's*
Of Engelond to Caunterbury they wende,°   *travel*
The hooly blisful martir[4] for to seke
That hem° hath holpen° whan that they were
   seeke.°   *them / helped / sick*
Bifil° that in that seson° on a day   *it happened / season*
20 In Southwerk[5] at the Tabard[6] as I lay

Redy to wenden° on my pilgrymage   *travel*
To Caunterbury with ful devout corage,°   *heart*
At nyght were come into that hostelrye°   *inn*
Wel nyne° and twenty in a compaignye   *nine*
25 Of sondry° folk by aventure yfalle[7]   *various*
In felaweshipe, and pilgrimes were they alle
That toward Caunterbury wolden° ryde.   *would*
The chambres° and the stables weren wyde,°   *bedrooms / wide*
And wel we weren esed° atte beste.   *fed*
30 And shortly, whan the sonne was to reste,
So hadde I spoken with hem° everichon°   *them / everyone*
That I was of hir° felaweshipe anon°   *their / soon*
And made forward° erly° for to ryse   *a pact / early*
To take oure wey ther as I yow devyse.°   *as I will tell you*
35 But nathelees,° whil I have tyme and space   *nevertheless*
Er that I ferther° in this tale pace,°   *further / go*
Me thynketh it° acordaunt° to resoun   *it seems to me / according*
To telle yow al the condicioun°   *i.e., character and estate*
Of ech of hem,° so as it semed me,   *each of them*
40 And whiche they were and of what degree°   *rank*
And eek° in what array° that they were inne,   *also / clothing*
And at a knyght than wol I first bigynne.
A Knyght ther was and that a worthy man,
That fro the tyme that he first bigan
45 To riden out, he loved chivalrie,
Trouthe and honour, fredom and curteisie.[8]
Ful worthy was he in his lordes werre°   *war*
And therto hadde he riden no man ferre°   *further*
As wel in Cristendom as in hethenesse°   *pagan lands*
50 And evere honoured for his worthynesse.
At Alisaundre he was whan it was wonne.
Ful ofte tyme he hadde the bord bigonne[9]
Aboven alle nacions in Pruce.
In Lettow hadde he reysed° and in Ruce,   *raided*
55 No Cristen man so ofte of his degree.
In Gernade at the seege eek° hadde he be   *also*
Of Algezir, and riden in Belmarye.

---

[1] *The Canterbury Tales* The present text of introductions to, and quotations for *The Canterbury Tales* have been prepared for *The Broadview Anthology of British Literature* by Robert Boenig and Andrew Taylor from their edition of the complete *Tales* (Broadview, 2008).

[2] *Zephirus* The name given to the personified west wind.

[3] *Ram* The sign of the Zodiac for the early spring.

[4] *The hooly blisful martir* St. Thomas Becket, Archbishop of Canterbury, was killed on 29 December 1170 during a dispute with his King, Henry II, by four knights who thought the king wished his death.

[5] *Southwerk* Southwark is the region, now officially part of London but not so during Chaucer's time, on the southern bank of the Thames, directly across from the old city of London.

[6] *Tabard* This is the name of Harry Bailly's inn. A "tabard" was a type of tunic often worn over chain-mail armor.

[7] *yfalle* Encountered by chance.

[8] *Trouthe ... curteisie* Keeping one's word, preserving one's reputation or honor, generosity, and courtesy or courtly manners are central values in the code of chivalry.

[9] *hadde the bord bigonne* Sat at the first table—an honor in victory banquets.

At Lyeys was he and at Satalye

Whan they were wonne and in the Grete See.

60 At many a noble armee° hadde he be.   *army*

At mortal batailles hadde he been fiftene

And foughten for oure feith° at Tramyssene   *faith*

In lystes° thries—and ay slayn his foo.   *jousting arenas*

This ilke° worthy knyght hadde been also   *same*

65 Somtyme with the lord of Palatye

Agayn another hethen° in Turkye,[1]   *heathen*

And everemoore he hadde a sovereyn° prys.° *sovereign / reputation*

And though that he were worthy,° he was wys,° *brave / prudent*

And of his port° as meeke as is a mayde.   *behavior*

70 He nevere yet no vileynye ne sayde

In al his lyf unto no maner wight.[2]

He was a verray,° parfit,° gentil° knyght.   *true / perfect / noble*

But for to tellen yow of his array,°   *appearance*

His hors° weren goode, but he was nat gay.° *horses / gaudy*

75 Of fustian° he wered a gypon°   *rough cloth / tunic*

Al bismotered° with his habergeon,°   *soiled / mail coat*

For he was late ycome° from his viage°   *arrived / voyage*

And wente for to doon° his pilgrymage.   *do*

    With hym ther was his sone, a yong Squier,[3]

80 A lovyere° and a lusty° bacheler   *lover / vigorous*

With lokkes crulle° as they were leyd in presse. *curled locks*

Of twenty yeer of age he was, I gesse.°   *guess*

Of his stature he was of evene lengthe°   *moderate height*

And wonderly delyvere° and of greet strengthe.   *quick*

85 And he hadde been somtyme in chyvachie° *calvary expedition*

In Flaundres, in Artoys, and Pycardie[4]

And born hym weel as of so litel space°   *in so short a time*

In hope to stonden° in his lady grace.°   *stand / lady's favor*

Embrouded° was he as it were a meede,° *embroidered / meadow*

90 Al ful of fresshe floures whyte and reede.°   *white and red*

Syngynge he was or floytynge° al the day.   *playing the flute*

He was as fressh as is the monthe of May.

Short was his gowne with sleves longe and wyde.

Wel koude he sitte on hors and faire ryde.

95 He koude songes make and wel endite,°   *compose verse*

Juste and eek daunce and weel putreye° and write.   *draw*

So hoote° he lovede, that by nyghtertale°   *hotly / nighttime*

He slepte namoore° than dooth a nyghtyngale.   *no more*

Curteis he was, lowely,° and servysable°   *humble / helpful*

100 And carf° biforn his fader at the table.   *carved (meat)*

    A Yeman[5] hadde he and servantz namo°   *no more*

At that tyme for hym liste° ride so,   *desired*

And he was clad in cote° and hood of grene.   *coat*

A sheef of pecok arwes° bright and kene° *peacock arrows / sharp*

105 Under his belt he bar ful thriftily.°   *very carefully*

Wel koude he dresse his takel° yemanly.   *equipment*

His arwes drouped° noght with fetheres° lowe, *drooped / feathers*

And in his hand he baar° a myghty bowe.   *bore*

A not heed° hadde he, with a broun visage.° *curly head / face*

110 Of wodecraft wel koude° he al the usage.°   *knew / customs*

Upon his arm he baar° a gay bracer,°   *bore / leather bracelet*

And by his syde a swerd° and a bokeler°   *sword / small shield*

And on that oother syde a gay° daggere   *bright*

Harneised wel° and sharpe as point of spere;   *well-sheathed*

115 A cristophere° on his brest of silver

    sheene.°   *St. Christopher medal / bright*

An horn he bar;° the bawdryk° was of grene. *bore / shoulder-belt*

A forster° was he, soothly° as I gesse.°   *forester / truly / guess*

---

[1] *Alisaundre … Turkye* The locations of the Knight's battles are as follows: Alexandria in Egypt (1365), Prussia, Lithuania, Russia (the scenes of much fighting against hold-out pagans in the last decades of the fourteenth century), Grenada (in Spain) whose city Algezir was captured in 1344, Banu Merin (in North Africa), Ayash (Lyeys in Syria, captured in 1367), Antalya (Satalye, in modern Turkey, captured in 1361), Tlemcen (in modern Algeria), Balat (Palatye, in modern Turkey, involved in campaigning in both the 1340s and 1365), and Turkey. The places not identified with a specific date of battle saw protracted hostilities between Christians and non-Christians during the period in question. The "great sea" is the Mediterranean. It would, of course, have been impossible for a knight to have taken part in all these campaigns.

[2] *In … wight* He was never rude to anyone. Middle English often uses double or even triple negatives to intensify each other rather than to cancel each other out.

[3] *yong Squier* A squire would serve a knight, especially by helping to arm him, and would fight with him in battle. In some cases, as here, squires were young men training to be knights, but squires could also be older men, such as Chaucer.

[4] *In … Pycardie* These places in Flanders saw military action in 1383, as the English troops fought for Pope Urban VI against his rival, Anti-Pope Clement VII. The campaign, led by the war-loving Bishop of Norwich, was a great disaster for the English.

[5] *A Yeman* Yeoman, a small landholder or tenant farmer, often prosperous enough to serve as an infantryman or archer in a knight's retinue.

Ther was also a Nonne,° a Prioresse,[1]   *nun*
That of hir smylyng was ful° symple and coy.°   *very / modest*
120 Hire gretteste ooth was but "By Seint Loy!"[2]
And she was cleped° Madame Eglentyne.[3]   *called*
Ful weel she soong° the service dyvyne,[4]   *sung*
Entuned°in hir nose ful semely.°   *intoned / seemly*
And Frenssh she spak ful faire and fetisly°   *elegantly*
125 After the scole° of Stratford atte Bowe:[5]   *school*
For Frenssh of Parys was to hire unknowe.°   *unknown*
At mete° wel ytaught° was she withalle.   *dinner / taught*
She leet° no morsel from hir lippes falle,   *let*
Ne wette hir fyngres in hir sauce depe.
130 Wel koude she carie a morsel and wel kepe,°   *take care*
That no drope ne fille upon hire brist.°   *breast*
In curteisie° was set ful muchel° hir list.°   *courtesy / much / pleasure*
Hir over-lippe° wyped° she so clene,°   *upper lip / wiped / clean*
That in hir coppe° ther was no ferthyng°
sene   *cup / coin-sized spot*
135 Of grece° whan she dronken hadde hir draughte.°   *grease / draft*
Ful semely after hir mete° she raughte.°   *food / reached*
And sikerly° she was of greet desport°   *surely / geniality*
And ful plesaunt and amyable° of port°   *amiable / disposition*
And peyned° hire to counterfete cheere°   *took pains / manners*
140 Of court and to been estatlich° of manere   *stately*

And to ben holden° digne° of reverence.   *held / worthy*
But for to speken° of hire conscience,°   *speak / conscience*
She was so charitable and so pitous,°   *compassionate*
She wolde wepe° if that she saugh° a mous°   *weep / saw / mouse*
145 Kaught in a trappe if it were deed° or bledde.°   *dead / bleeding*
Of smale houndes hadde she that she fedde
With rosted flessh or milk and wastel breed.[6]
But soore wepte she if any of hem were deed°   *dead*
Or if men smoot it with a yerde° smerte.°   *yardstick / smartly*
150 And al was conscience and tendre herte.°   *tender heart*
Ful semyly hir wympul[7] pynched was;
Hir nose tretys,° hir eyen° greye as glas,   *shapely / eyes*
Hir mouth ful smal, and therto softe and reed.°   *red*
But sikerly, she hadde a fair forheed.
155 It was almoost a spanne brood,° I
trowe,°   *a hand's span across / believe*
For hardily° she was nat undergrowe.°   *certainly / not undergrown*
Full fetys° was hir cloke, as I was war.°   *elegant / aware*
Of smal coral aboute hire arm she bar
A peire° of bedes, gauded° al with grene,[8]   *pair / divided*
160 And theron heng a brooch of gold ful sheene,°   *very shiny*
On which ther was first write° a crowned "A"   *written*
And after, "Amor vincit omnia."[9]
Another Nonne with hire hadde she
That was hir chapeleyne,° and Preestes° thre.   *chaplain / priests*
165 A Monk ther was, a fair for the maistrie,°   *i.e., better than all*
An outridere[10] that lovede venerie,°   *hunting*
A manly man, to been an abbot able.
Ful many a deyntee° hors hadde he in stable.   *fine*
And whan he rood, men myghte his brydel heere°   *hear*
170 Gynglen° in a whistlynge wynd als cleere°   *jingling / as clear*

---

[1] *Prioresse* A prioress is either the second-in-command of an abbey, a large convent governed by an abbess, or is in charge of a priory, a smaller convent.

[2] *Seint Loy* St. Eligius, a seventh-century Bishop of Noyon in France. He is patron saint of both goldsmiths and blacksmiths.

[3] *Eglentyne* Eglantine, also known as sweet briar, is an early species of rose. It is known for its sweet, apple-like smell (which even the leaves emit if crushed) and five-petaled coral flowers, which appear once a year, in spring. Eglantine was not a common name in the Middle Ages.

[4] *service dyvyne* Divine service; the phrase refers to the Office (or Canonical Hours)—the round of services dominated by psalm-singing that monks and nuns perform on a daily basis. The names of the individual services are Matins, Lauds, Prime, Terce, Sext, None, Vespers, and Compline.

[5] *Stratford atte Bowe* Stratford-at-Bow is in Middlesex, just to the west of London. Chaucer's point, elaborated in the next line, is that the Prioress does not speak French properly but with a provincial accent. The Benedictine Priory of St. Leonard's was at Stratford-at-Bow and in Chaucer's day it had nine nuns, one of them named Argentine. The similarity of the names is suggestive, but Argentine was not the prioress there.

[6] *wastel breed* White bread (which, in the Middle Ages, was a delicacy reserved for the nobility).

[7] *wympul* Cloth folded cover the neck sides of the head, leaving only the face exposed. It was worn by both nuns and lay women.

[8] *A ... grene* She carries a set of coral rosary beads, a chain of prayer-beads. These are divided at intervals by green beads. The green beads indicated the end of the "decade," one set of prayers, and the beginning of the next.

[9] *Amor vincit omnia* Latin: love conquers all.

[10] *An outridere* An outrider was a monk whose job was to leave the cloister (which, as Chaucer makes clear below, was not the ideal thing for a monk to do) to take care of his monastery's business in the world at large. One of the common accusations made against monks was that they loved the secular world more than the cloister.

And eek as loude as dooth the chapel belle

Theras° this lord was kepere of the celle.[1] *since*

The Reule° of Seint Maure or of Seint Beneit,[2] *rule*

Bycause that it was old and somdel streit,° *somewhat restrictive*

175 This ilke monk leet olde thynges pace° *pass*

And heeld after the newe world the space.° *course*

He yaf nat° of that text a pulled° hen *gave not / plucked*

That seith that hunters beth nat hooly° men, *not holy*

Ne that° a monk whan he is recchelees° *nor when / reckless*

180 Is likned til° a fissh that is waterlees. *likened to*

This is to seyn,° a monk out of his cloystre.° *say / cloister*

But thilke° text heeld he nat worth an oystre. *that same*

And I seyde his opinioun was good.

What° sholde he studie and make hymselven
wood° *why / crazy*

185 Upon a book in cloystre° alwey to poure° *cloister / poor*

Or swynken° with his handes and laboure° *work / labor*

As Austyn[3] bit?° How shal the world be served? *commanded*

Lat Austyn have his owene swynk° to hym reserved! *work*

Therfore he was a prikasour aright.° *hard rider*

190 Grehoundes he hadde as swift as fowel° in flight. *bird*

Of prikyng° and of huntyng for the hare *riding*

Was al his lust.° For no cost wolde he spare. *pleasure*

I seigh his sleves° ypurfiled° at the hond° *sleeves / lined / hand*

With grys°—and that the fyneste° of a
lond.° *expensive gray fur / finest / the land*

195 And for to festne° his hood under his chyn° *fasten / chin*

He hadde of gold ywroght° a ful° curious pyn:° *made / very / pin*

A love knotte in the gretter° ende ther was. *bigger*

His heed was balled,[4] that shoon as any glas,

And eek his face as it hadde been enoynt.° *anointed*

200 He was a lord ful fat and in good poynt,[5]

Hise eyen° stepe° and rollynge in his heed, *eyes / bright*

That stemed as a forneys° of a leed, *furnace*

His bootes souple,° his hors in greet estaat.° *supple / in best shape*

Now certeinly he was a fair prelaat.° *prelate*

205 He nas nat° pale as a forpyned goost.° *was not / distressed ghost*

A fat swan loved he best of any roost.° *roast*

His palfrey[6] was as broun as is a berye.° *berry*

A Frere° ther was, a wantowne° and a
merye,° *friar / pleasure-seeking / merry*

A lymytour,[7] a ful solempne° man. *distinguished*

210 In alle the ordres foure[8] is noon° that kan° *no one / knows*

So muchel° of daliaunce° and fair langage. *much / flirtation*

He hadde maad° ful many a mariage *made*

Of yonge wommen at his owene cost.

Unto his ordre he was a noble post!° *pillar*

215 And wel biloved and famulier was he

With frankeleyns° ever al in his contree *franklins (gentry)*

And with worthy wommen of the toun,

For he hadde power of confessioun,

As seyde hymself, moore than a curat,° *curate (local priest)*

220 For of his ordre he was licenciat.° *licensed*

Ful swetely° herde he confessioun, *sweetly*

And plesaunt was his absolucioun.

He was an esy° man to yeve° penaunce, *easy / give*

Theras° he wiste° to have a good
pitaunce.° *where / thought / donation*

225 For unto a povre° ordre for to yive° *poor / give*

Is signe that a man is wel yshryve.° *confessed*

For if he yaf,° he dorste° make avaunt,° *gave / dared / assert*

---

[1] *celle* Priory or outlying house governed by the central monastery.

[2] *Seint Maure ... Seint Beneit* Monks. St. Benedict, a sixth-century Italian monk and abbot, compiled the famous Rule that goes by his name. It became normative for most of Western monasticism. St. Maurus, by legend one of his monks, was credited with bringing his Rule to France.

[3] *Austyn* "Austin" is the typical Middle English abbreviation for Augustine, the great Doctor of the Church and Bishop of Hippo in Northern Africa (354–430 CE). He was famous for his theological writings, particularly *The City of God* and *The Confessions*, the latter his spiritual autobiography. He is also credited with writing the Rule (followed by Augustinian canons and monks) to which this passage alludes.

[4] *His heed was balled* Monks shaved the crowns of their heads in a haircut known as a tonsure.

[5] *in good poynt* Idiomatic: in good condition.

[6] *palfrey* Everyday horse, as opposed to a destrier (war-horse) or a plowhorse.

[7] *lymytour* Friar licensed to preach, minister, and hear confessions in a specified, limited area.

[8] *In ... foure* There were four main orders of friars in the later Middle Ages—the Franciscans, the Dominicans, the Carmelites, and the Augustinians. Like monks, the friars took vows of poverty, chastity, and obedience, but they were supposed to go out in the world and preach to the laity, whereas monks were supposed to live apart from the world and devote themselves to prayer.

He wiste that a man was repentaunt.[1]
For many a man so hard is of his herte,
230   He may nat wepe° althogh hym soore
        smerte.°   *weep / sorely hurts*
Therfore instede of wepynge° and preyeres,°   *weeping / prayers*
Men moote yeve° silver to the povre freres!   *should give*
His typet[2] was ay farsed° ful of knyves   *stuffed*
And pynnes° for to yeven yonge
        wyves.°   *pins / give to young women*
235   And, certeinly, he hadde a murye note;°   *merry melody*
Wel koude he synge and pleyen on a rote.°   *play on a lyre*
Of yeddynges° he baar outrely° the
        pris.°   *songs / completely / prize*
His nekke° whit° was as the flour-de-lys.°   *neck / white / lily*
Therto he strong was as a champion.
240   He knew the tavernes wel° in al the toun   *well*
And everich hostiler and
        tappestere°   *each innkeeper and barmaid*
Bet° than a lazar° or a beggestere.°   *better / leper / female beggar*
For unto swich° a worthy man as he   *such*
Acorded nat as by his facultee[3]
245   To have with sike lazars aqueyntaunce.°   *sick lepers acquaintance*
It is nat honeste,° It may nat avaunce,°   *respectable / advance (one)*
For to deelen° with no swich poraille°   *deal / poor folk*
But al with riche° and selleres of vitaille.°   *rich / sellers of food*
And overal theras profit sholde arise,
250   Curteis he was and lowely° of servyse.   *humble*
Ther nas no° man nowher so vertuous;   *was not*
He was the beste beggere in his hous.°[4]   *convent*
For thogh a wydwe° hadde noght a sho,°   *widow / not a shoe*
So plesaunt was his "In principio,"[5]

255   Yet wolde he have a ferthyng° er he wente.   *farthing (coin)*
His purchas° was wel bettre than his rente,°   *income / expenses*
And rage° he koude as it were right a whelp.°   *cavort / dog*
In love-dayes ther koude he muchel° help,   *could he (offer) much*
For ther he was nat lyk a cloystrer°   *monk*
260   With a thredbare cope° as is a povre scoler,°   *cloak / poor student*
But he was lyk a maister or a pope.
Of double worstede° was his semycope°   *thick cloth / short-cloak*
That rounded as a belle out of the presse.°   *mold*
Somwhat he lipsed° for his wantownesse°   *lisped / affectation*
265   To make his Englissh sweete upon his tonge.
And in his harpyng, whan that he hadde songe,
Hise eyen° twynkled in his heed aryght°   *eyes / aright*
As doon° the sterres° in the frosty nyght.   *do / stars*
This worthy lymytour° was cleped Huberd.   *limiter*
270   A Marchant was ther with a forked berd;°   *beard*
In motlee° and hye° on horse he sat,   *multi-colored cloth / high*
Upon his heed a Flaundryssh° bevere° hat,   *Flemish / beaver*
His bootes clasped faire and fetisly.
Hise resons° he spak ful solempnely,   *opinions*
275   Sownynge° alwey th'encrees° of his
        wynnyng.°   *concerning / increase / profit*
He wolde° the see° were kept for anythyng   *wished / sea*
Bitwixe° Middelburgh and Orewelle.[6]   *between*
Wel koude he in eschaunge° sheeldes selle.[7]   *exchange*
This worthy man ful wel his wit bisette;°   *employed*
280   Ther wiste no wight that he was in dette,[8]
So estatly° was he of his governaunce,°   *dignified / management*
With his bargaynes and with his
        chevyssaunce.°   *commerce for interest*
Forsothe,° he was a worthy man withalle.°   *truly / for all that*
But sooth to seyn, I noot how men hym calle.[9]

---

[1] *For ... repentaunt* For if a man gave money then he (the Friar) knew that man was repentant. The Friar is imposing a light penance in exchange for a donation to his order.

[2] *typet* Long ornamental piece of cloth worn either as a kind of scarf or as part of a hood or as sleeves. It provided a convenient place to put small objects.

[3] *For ... facultee* It was not appropriate according to his profession.

[4] The Hengwrt manuscript at this point includes the following two lines, usually numbered 252b and 252c: "And yaf a certeyn ferme for the graunt / Noon of his bretheren cam ther in his haunt" (And he paid a certain annual amount for the rights [to beg] / so that none of his brother friars came into his territory).

[5] *In principio* Latin: "in the beginning was the Word," the opening line of the Gospel of John.

---

[6] *Middelburgh and Orewelle* These two ports were in the Netherlands and in England respectively. There was much trade in the late Middle Ages between the two countries, particularly in textiles.

[7] *sheeldes selle* A shield, or *écu*, was a French coin. This kind of trade between national currencies was regarded with suspicion. It was often illegal and could be used as a way of surreptitiously charging interest on a loan (which the Church condemned as usury).

[8] *Ther ... dette* The syntax is ambiguous. Either "No one knew that he was in debt" (implying he was) or "No one knew him to be in debt" (implying he was not) or, since merchants were normally in debt, "No one knew how much he was in debt."

[9] *sooth ... calle* To tell the truth, I don't know what he was called.

285 A Clerk[1] ther was of Oxenford° also — *Oxford*
That unto logyk hadde longe ygo,° — *who had [committed himself] to*
And leene° was his hors as is a rake. — *lean*
And he nas nat right° fat, I undertake,° — *was not very / declare*
But looked holwe° and therto sobrely.° — *hollow / soberly*
290 Ful thredbare was his overeste courtepy,° — *overcoat*
For he hadde geten hym yet no benefice[2]
Ne was so worldly for to have office.
For hym was levere° have at his beddes
     heed° — *would rather / bed's head*
Twenty bookes clad° in blak or reed° — *bound / red*
295 Of Aristotle and his philosophie
Than robes riche or fithele° or gay sautrie.° — *fiddle / psaltery*
But al be that he was a philosophre,
Yet hadde he but litel gold in cofre.°[3] — *little gold in a chest*
But al that he myghte of his freendes° hente,° — *friends / obtain*
300 On bookes and on lernynge° he it spente — *learning*
And bisily° gan for the soules preye° — *busily / prayed*
Of hem° that yaf° hym wherwith to
     scoleye.° — *them / gave / the means to study*
Of studie took he moost cure° and moost heede. — *care*
Noght o° word spak he moore than was neede, — *one*
305 And that was seyd in forme° and reverence — *formally*
And short and quyk and ful of hy sentence.° — *meaning*
Sownynge in° moral vertu was his speche, — *tending towards*
And gladly wolde he lerne and gladly teche.

A Sergeant of the Lawe[4] war° and wys° — *shrewd / wise*
310 That often hadde been at the Parvys[5]
Ther was also, ful riche of excellence.
Discreet he was and of greet reverence.
He semed swich, his wordes weren so wise.
Justice° he was ful often in assise° — *judge / court*
315 By patente and by pleyn commissioun,[6]
For his science° and for his heigh renoun.° — *knowledge / renown*
Of fees and robes hadde he many oon;° — *many a one*
So greet a purchasour[7] was nowher noon.° — *nowhere at all*
Al was fee symple[8] to hym in effect.
320 His purchasyng myghte nat been infect.° — *invalidated*
Nowher so bisy° a man as he ther nas,° — *busy / was not*
And yet he semed bisier° than he was. — *seemed busier*
In termes° hadde he caas° and doomes
     alle° — *files / cases / judgments*
That from the tyme° of Kyng William[9] were
     yfalle.° — *time / given*
325 Therto he koude endite° and make a thyng.° — *write / brief*
Ther koude no wight° pynchen° at his
     writyng. — *nobody / quibble*
And every statut koude he pleyn by rote.° — *recite by heart*
He rood but hoomly° in a medlee° cote, — *simply / multi-colored*
Girt with a ceint° of silk with barres° smale. — *belt / ornaments*
330 Of his arraye tell I no lenger tale.

---

[1] *Clerk* The term clerk can mean student or professor, priest or priest's assistant, or learned man or philosopher, depending on the context. University students were supposed to be preparing for the priesthood. Some became priests, which required a vow of celibacy, and could then win promotion in the ranks of the Church. Others only took minor orders (which meant they could marry), and either remained at university or, in many cases, became members of the growing royal, baronial, and civic administration. Chaucer's Clerk, who is studying advanced logic, is roughly the equivalent of a graduate student or junior professor.

[2] *benefice* Position as a priest or clergyman. In the Middle Ages there had developed a much-criticized custom of granting the income from some benefices to people who would apportion a small amount of the income to a poorer clergyman to do the work and then live off the rest. This practice made some bishops with multiple benefices very wealthy, and it became a means of supporting a well-connected scholar at one of the universities.

[3] *But ... cofre* Chaucer is punning on the word philosopher, which can also mean alchemist. The search for the Philosopher's Stone, thought to be the key to turning metal to gold, was a particular study of alchemists.

[4] *Sergeant of the Lawe* In late fourteenth-century England, a Sergeant of Law was not simply a lawyer; he was one of about twenty or so lawyers who functioned as legal advisors to the king and served as judges.

[5] *Parvys* Shortened form of "Paradise," a name given to the porch in front of large churches. Here the reference is to the porch of Saint Paul's Cathedral in London, where lawyers would meet with their clients, the lawyer's office being unknown to late-fourteenth-century England.

[6] *By ... commissioun* Letters patent were royal letters of appointment that were open, i.e., public, documents that anyone was allowed to read. The full commission gives the Sergeant the right to hear all legal cases in the Court of Assizes, circuit courts that would move from county to county.

[7] *purchasour* I.e., purchaser, someone who acquired feudal property by money rather than feudal service.

[8] *fee symple* Ownership without feudal obligations.

[9] *Kyng William* William the Conqueror, who ruled England from 1066 to 1087. His reign marked a turning point in English governance.

A Frankeleyn[1] was in his compaignye.
Whit° was his heed° as is a dayesye.°   *white | head | daisy*
Of his complexioun he was sangwyn;[2]
Wel loved he by the morwe a sope in wyn.[3]

335   To lyven° in delit° was evere his wone,°   *live | delight | custom*
For he was Epicurus[4] owene sone°   *son*
That heeld opinioun that pleyn delit°   *full delight*
Was verray° felicitee parfit.°   *true | perfect happiness*
An housholdere and that a greet was he;

340   Seint Julian[5] was he in his contree.
His breed,° his ale was always after oon;[6]   *bread*
A bettre envyned man° was nevere noon.   *man stocked with wine*
Withoute bake mete° was nevere his hous   *baked food*
Of fissh and flessh, and that so plentevous°   *plentiful*

345   It snewed° in his hous of mete and drynke,   *snowed*
Of alle deyntees° that men koude thynke.   *delicacies*
After the sondry° sesons° of the yeer   *various | seasons*
So chaunged he his mete° and his soper.°   *food | meals*
Ful° many a fat partrich° hadde he in   *very | partridge*
muwe°   *coop*

350   And many a breem° and many a luce° in   *bream | pike*
stuwe.°   *pond*
Wo° was his cook but if° his sauce were   *woe | unless*
Poynaunt° and sharpe° and redy al his   *pungent | spicy*
geere.°   *utensils*

His table dormant[7] in his halle alway
Stood redy covered al the longe day.
355   At sessiouns° ther was he lord and sire;   *court sessions*
Ful ofte tyme he was Knyght of the Shire.[8]
An anlaas° and a gipser° al of silk   *dagger | pouch*
Heeng° at his girdel whit° as morne°
milk.   *hung | white | morning*
A shirreve° hadde he been and countour.°   *sheriff | tax-collector*
360   Was nowher swich a worthy vavasour.°   *feudal land holder*
An Haberdasshere[9] and a Carpenter,
A Webbe,° a Dyere, and a Tapycer,°   *weaver | tapestry-maker*
And they were clothed alle in o° lyveree[10]   *one*
Of a solempne and a greet fraternitee.[11]
365   Ful fressh and newe hir geere° apiked° was.   *equipment | polished*
Hir knyves were chaped° noght° with bras°   *mounted | not | brass*
But al with silver, wroght ful clene° and weel   *made very elegantly*
Hire girdles° and hir pouches everydeel.°   *belts | every bit*
Wel semed° ech of hem a fair burgeys°   *seemed | citizen*
370   To sitten in a yeldehalle° on a deys.°   *guildhall | raised platform*
Everich° for the wisdom that he kan°   *everyone | knew*

---

[7] *His table dormant* Always standing. Most medieval tables on which meals were set were trestle tables, i.e., a long board placed on top of what we would call saw-horses. After the meal was over, the table would normally be taken down. Not so the Franklin's.

[8] *Knyght of the Shire* Official designation for people chosen to represent their region in Parliament. Chaucer himself, while he was never knighted and only held the rank of squire, served as Knight of the Shire for Kent in 1386, the year before the fictitious pilgrimage to Canterbury takes place. The Franklin has also presided at the sessions of the Justices of the Peace (line 355) and served as Sheriff, the chief royal officer in a county who was responsible for collecting its taxes, and as the county auditor, who assisted the Sheriff.

[9] *Haberdasshere* Seller of ribbons, buttons, hats, gloves, and small articles of clothing.

[10] *lyveree* Uniform. Members of craft or religious guilds, as well as retainers of various lords, wore liveries. At this time the wearing of liveries encouraged factionalism and attendant violence, and there were some legal attempts to curb abuses.

[11] *fraternitee* Trade guilds or religious guilds. The trade guilds regulated who was allowed to follow a given trade in a given town, and the religious guilds functioned as mutual aid societies, burying their dead and helping members who were sick or had fallen into poverty. These guildsmen, though identified by their trades, are members of a religious guild, since trade guilds admitted only members of a single trade.

---

[1] *Frankeleyn* From the word franc or free, a wealthy independent landowner and a member of the minor gentry.

[2] *Of … sangwyn* The Franklin's physiological makeup is dominated by blood, one of the four humors, which makes him red-faced and cheerful.

[3] *Wel … wyn* He greatly loved in the morning bread soaked in wine. Such was the preferred breakfast for those wealthy enough to afford wine, which had to be imported from Gascony, the sole remaining territory England retained in what we now call France.

[4] *Epicurus* The Greek philosopher Epicurus (341–270 BCE) maintained that the pursuit of pleasure was the natural state of humankind.

[5] *Seint Julian* St. Julian, the patron saint of hospitality in the Middle Ages. Julian set up a way-station for travelers in penance for unwittingly killing his parents, who had unknowingly lodged in his house while journeying.

[6] *after oon* Consistent, i.e., consistently good.

Was shaply° for to been an alderman.[1]   *suitable*
For catel° hadde they ynogh° and rente,°*belongings | enough | rent*
And eek hir wyves° wolde it wel assente°   *wives | agree*
375 And elles° certeyn were they to blame.   *otherwise*
It is ful fair to been ycleped° "Madame"   *called*
And goon to vigilies[2] al bifore
And have a mantel roialliche ybore.°   *cloak royally carried*
       A Cook° they hadde with hem° for the
            nones°   *cook | them | occasion*
380 To boille° the chiknes° with the
            marybones°   *boil | chickens | marrowbones*
And poudre-marchant tart and galyngale.[3]
Wel koude he knowe a draughte of Londoun ale.
He koude rooste and sethe° and boille° and frye, *simmer | boil*
Maken mortreux° and wel bake a pye.   *stews*
385 But greet harm° was it as it thoughte me°   *pity | seemed to me*
That on his shyne° a mormal° hadde he.   *shin | ulcer*
For blankmanger[4] that made he with the beste.
       A Shipman was ther wonynge° fer by
            weste.°   *living | far in the west*
For aught I woot,° he was of Dertemouthe.[5]   *all I know*
390 He rood° upon a rouncy° as he kouthe°   *rode | nag | could*
In a gowne of faldyng° to the knee.   *woollen cloth*
A daggere hangynge on a laas° hadde he   *lace*
About his nekke under his arm adoun.°   *downwards*
The hoote° somer hadde maad° his hewe°   *hot | made | color*
       al broun,
395 And certeinly he was a good felawe.
Ful many a draughte° of wyn° had he
            drawe°   *draft | wine | drawn*

Fro Burdeuxward whil that the chapman° sleepe.[6]   *merchant*
Of nyce° conscience took he no keepe.°   *scrupulous | notice*
If that he faught° and hadde the hyer
            hond,°   *if he fought | upper hand*
400 By water he sente hem hoom° to every lond.[7]   *home*
But of his craft° to rekene° wel his tydes,° *ability | reckon | tides*
His stremes° and his daungers° hym
            bisides,°   *currents | dangers | all around him*
His herberwe° and his moone,° his
            lodemenage,°   *harborage | moon | piloting*
Ther nas noon swich° from Hull to
            Cartage.[8]   *was not such a one*
405 Hardy he was and wys to undertake;°   *wise in his endeavors*
With many a tempest hadde his berd° been
            shake.°   *beard | shaken*
He knew alle the havenes° as they were   *havens*
Fro Gootlond to the Cape of Fynystere[9]
And every cryke° in Britaigne° and in
            Spayne.°   *inlet | Brittany | Spain*
410 His barge ycleped was the Maudelayne.
       With us ther was a Doctour of Physik.[10]
In al this world ne was ther noon hym
            lik°   *there was no one like him*
To speke of phisik° and of surgerye,   *medicine*
For he was grounded in astronomye.[11]
415 He kepte° his pacient a ful greet deel   *watched over*

---

[1] *alderman* In late medieval England, as in some cities today, the board of aldermen governs under the mayor. The five guildsmen have prospered, rising from artisans to masters. They are successful businessmen who run their own shop or shops, participate in civic government, and aspire, with their wives, to the status of the lesser gentry.

[2] *vigilies* Church services held the night before an important holy day. The aldermen and their wives would lead the procession, with their cloaks carried by a servant.

[3] *And ... galyngale* And tart ground spice and aromatic roots (such as ginger).

[4] *blankmanger* Stew of milk, rice, almonds, and chicken or fish.

[5] *Dertemouthe* I.e., Dartmouth, a port on the English Channel in the southwest of England, near Plymouth.

[6] *Ful ... sleepe* Sailing home from Bordeaux with a cargo of wine, the Shipman would secretly steal some while the wine merchant (chapman) was asleep.

[7] *By ... lond* I.e., he threw his defeated opponents overboard.

[8] *Hull to Cartage* Hull is a port in northern England; Cartage is either Carthage on the Mediterranean coast of North Africa or Cartagena in Spain.

[9] *Fro ... Fynystere* Gotland is an island in the Baltic Sea off the coast of southern Sweden; Cape Finisterre is the point of land that juts out into the Atlantic Ocean in northwest Spain.

[10] *Doctour of Physik* Physician. The term "doctor" means "teacher," as everyone in the Middle Ages knew, so the type of doctor who taught medicine and sometimes practiced it needed to be distinguished from other types of doctors, who taught academic subjects in the universities.

[11] *For ... astronomye* In the Middle Ages, physicians often based their schedules of treatment on astrological tables.

In houres by his magyk natureel.[1]
Wel koude he fortunen the ascendent°   *calculate a planet's position*
Of hise ymages[2] for his pacient.
He knew the cause of everich° maladye,   *every*
420 Were it of hoot or coold or moyste or drye,[3]
And where they engendred and of what humour.
He was a verray, parfit praktisour:°   *practitioner*
The cause yknowe° and of his harm the roote,°   *known | root*
Anon he yaf° the sike man his boote.°   *gave | remedy*
425 Ful redy hadde he hise apothecaries°   *pharmacists*
To sende hym drogges° and his letuaries,°   *drugs | syrups*
For ech° of hem° made oother for to wynne.°   *each | them | profit*
Hir° frendshipe nas nat newe° to
      bigynne.°   *their | recently | begun*
Wel knew he the olde Esculapius[4]
430 And Deyscorides and eek Rufus,
Olde Ypocras, Haly, and Galyen,

Serapion, Razis, and Avycen,
Averrois, Damascien, and Constantyn,
Bernard and Gatesden and Gilbertyn.
435 Of his diete° mesurable° was he,   *diet | moderate*
For it was of no superfluitee°   *excess*
But of greet norissyng° and digestible.   *nourishment*
His studie was but litel on the Bible.[5]
In sangwyn° and in pers° he clad was al,   *red | blue*
440 Lyned with taffata and with sendal.[6]
And yet he was but esy of dispence.°   *moderate in spending*
He kepte that he wan° in pestilence.°[7]   *what he earned | plague*
For gold in phisik° is a cordial.°   *medicine | heart-medicine*
Therfore he lovede gold in special.°   *especially*
445   A good Wif was ther of biside Bathe,[8]
But she was somdel deef,° and that was
      scathe.°   *somewhat deaf | a shame*
Of clooth makyng she hadde swich an haunt,°   *skill*
She passed hem of Ypres and of Gaunt.[9]
In al the parisshe° wif ne was ther noon   *parish*
450 That to the offrynge°[10] bifore hire sholde goon.   *offering*
And if ther dide, certeyn so wrooth° was she,   *angry*
That she was out of alle charitee.
Hir coverchiefs° ful fyne were of ground°—   *kerchiefs | texture*
I dorste swere° they weyeden° ten pound—   *dare swear | weighed*
455 That on a Sonday weren upon hir heed.
Hir hosen weren of fyn° scarlet reed,°   *fine | red*
Ful streite yteyd° and shoes ful moyste° and
      newe.   *tightly laced | supple*

---

[1] *In ... natureel* Hours are the times in the day when the various planetary influences were pronounced, when the Physician watched over (kepte) his patient. Natural magic is opposed to black magic, which involves contact with malicious spirits.

[2] *Of hise ymages* The practice of astrologically-based medicine involved the use of images of the planets as talismans.

[3] *He ... drye* Medieval medicine was also based on a theory, traceable back to Greek physicians such as the ones Chaucer mentions below, of the balance of the four bodily humors (blood, phlegm, black bile, and yellow bile) and their qualities of hot, cold, moist, and dry mentioned in this line.

[4] *Wel ... Esculapius* Aesculapius was a mythological demi-god, son to Apollo. Dioscorides, Rufus of Ephesus, Hippocrates (associated with the Hippocratic Oath physicians still swear), and Galen were famous Greek physicians. Galen (129–199) was particularly influential, since he set out the theory of four humors which was the basis of medieval medicine. "Haly" is probably the Persian physician Ali Ben el-Abbas (d. 994). Rhazes (d. c. 930) was an Arab astronomer and physician. Avicenna, or Ibn Sina (980–1037), and Averroes (1126–98) were Islamic philosophers and physicians. John of Damascus was a Syrian physician of the ninth century. Constantine the African came from Carthage, converted to Christianity, became a Benedictine monk, and taught at Salerno in Italy in the eleventh century. His work on aphrodisiacs earns him the title the "cursed monk" in *The Merchant's Tale*, line 1810. Islamic science was widely influential in the Middle Ages; it first brought Greek thought to the Latin West. The last three authorities are British. Bernard Gordon was a Scottish physician who taught at Montpellier in the fourteenth century. John Gaddesden (d. c. 1349) taught at Oxford and served as court doctor to Edward II. Gilbert was an English physician in the thirteenth century and the author of a major medical treatise.

[5] *His ... Bible* In the Middle Ages physicians were often thought to be religious skeptics, partly because of their knowledge of classical astronomy.

[6] *Lyned ... sendal* Taffeta and sendal are types of silk cloth; silk, imported from Asia, was a mark of status and wealth.

[7] *He ... pestilence* Possibly a reference to the Black Death, which killed at least a third of the population of England between 1348 and 1349, although there were later outbreaks of plague in 1362, 1369, and 1376.

[8] *Bathe* I.e., Bath, a town in southwest England near Bristol. It is famous for its hot springs (hence its name) and Roman ruins. The parish of St. Michael's, just north of Bath, was famous for its weavers.

[9] *Ypres ... Gaunt* Cities in Flanders (now north-western Belgium) known for cloth trading. There were also skilled weavers from these cities working in England.

[10] *offrynge* In eucharistic services, gifts are brought to the altar during the Offering, or Offertory.

Boold° was hir face and fair and reed of hewe.°   *bold | color*

She was a worthy womman al hir lyve.

460 Housbondes at chirche dore° she hadde fyve,°[1] *church door | five*

Withouten° oother compaignye in youthe.   *apart from*

But therof nedeth nat to speke as nowthe.°   *for now*

And thries° hadde she been at Jerusalem.[2]   *three times*

She hadde passed many a straunge strem.°   *foreign water*

465 At Rome she hadde been and at Boloigne,

In Galice at Seint Jame and at Coloigne.

She koude muchel of wandrynge by the weye.[3]

Gat-tothed was she, soothly for to seye.[4]

Upon an amblere° esily° she sat,   *saddle-horse | easily*

470 Ywympled[5] wel, and on hir heed° an hat   *head*

As brood° as is a bokeler or a targe,°   *broad | shields*

A foot mantel° aboute hir hipes large   *outer skirt*

And on hir feet a paire of spores° sharpe.   *spurs*

In felaweshipe wel koude she laughe and carpe.°   *joke*

475 Of remedies of love she knew perchaunce,°   *as it happened*

For she koude° of that art the olde daunce.   *knew*

    A good man was ther of religioun

And was a povre Persoun° of a toun,   *poor parson*

But riche he was of hooly thoght° and werk.° *holy thought | work*

480 He was also a lerned man, a clerk,

That Cristes° gospel trewely wolde preche.°   *Christ's | preach*

Hise parisshens° devoutly wolde he teche.   *parishioners*

Benygne° he was and wonder diligent   *benign*

And in adversitee ful pacient,

485 And swich° he was preved° ofte sithes.° *such | proven | many times*

Ful looth° were hym to cursen° for hise

    tithes,[6]   *reluctant | excommunicate*

But rather wolde he yeven° out of doute°   *give | without doubt*

Unto his povre parisshens aboute

Of his offryng and eek of his substaunce.

490 He koude in litel thyng have suffisaunce.[7]

Wyd° was his parisshe and houses fer asonder, *wide | far apart*

But he ne lefte° nat for reyn° ne thonder *did not neglect | rain*

In siknesse nor in meschief° to visite   *trouble*

The ferreste° in his parisshe muche and

    lite,°   *farthest | of greater or lesser (rank)*

495 Upon his feet and in his hand a staf.°   *staff*

This noble ensample° to his sheepe he yaf,   *example*

That firste he wroghte° and afterward that he taughte. *acted*

Out of the gospel he tho° wordes caughte,°   *those | took*

And this figure° he added eek therto,°   *figure of speech | to it*

500 "That if gold ruste, what shal iren° do?"   *iron*

For if a preest be foul on whom we truste,

No wonder is a lewed man° to ruste,   *layman*

And shame it is if a preest take keepe°—   *heed*

A shiten° shepherde and a clene°

    sheepe.   *soiled with excrement | clean*

505 Wel oghte° a preest ensample for to yeve   *ought*

By his clennesse how that his sheepe sholde lyve.

He sette nat° his benefice to hyre   *did not offer*

And leet° his sheepe encombred° in the myre° *left | stuck | mud*

And ran to Londoun unto Seint Poules[8]

510 To seken hym° a chauntrie° for soules *seek for himself | chantry*

Or with a bretherhed° to been withholde,°[9]   *guild | hired*

But dwelleth at hoom and kepeth wel his

    folde°   *sheepfold (i.e., flock)*

---

[1] *Housbondes ... fyve* Marriage vows were exchanged on the church steps and were followed by a Mass inside the church.

[2] *And ... Jerusalem* Jerusalem was the greatest of all pilgrimages. From England, a trip there and back could take a couple of years. The other pilgrimages mentioned below are Rome, where the Apostles Peter and Paul were buried; Boulogne-sur-mer in France, famous for its miraculous image of the Blessed Virgin; Compostella in Galicia, where the relics of St. James were venerated; and Cologne, where the relics of the Three Kings (or Three Magi) were kept.

[3] *She ... weye* She knew much about wandering along the road.

[4] *Gat-tothed ... seye* According to medieval physiognomy, a gap between the teeth was a sign that a woman was bold, lecherous, faithless, and suspicious.

[5] *Ywympled* Wearing a wimple.

[6] *tithes* Periodic assessments made to determine one tenth of a person's goods, harvest, and animals, which would then be claimed by the Church. Parish priests could excommunicate parishioners who would not pay them.

[7] *He ... suffisaunce* He was able to have enough in little things.

[8] *Seint Poules* St. Paul's Cathedral in London. The custom Chaucer refers to is related to the issue of benefices. A chantry is an endowed position, usually at large churches and cathedrals, in which a priest sings masses for the soul of the person who left money for the endowment. It involved very little work, unlike the Parson's toil described in his section of the General Prologue.

[9] *Or ... withholde* The brotherhood here is a guild. Guilds hired priests to serve as their chaplains.

So that the wolf ne made° it nat

    myscarie.°   *would not make / come to grief*

He was a shepherde and noght° a mercenarie,° *not / mercenary*

515 And though he hooly were and vertuous,

He was nat to synful men despitous,°   *scornful*

Ne of his speche daungerous° ne digne,° *proud / haughty*

But in his techyng discreet and benygne,°   *kind*

To drawen folk to hevene by fairnesse,

520 By good ensample. This was his bisynesse.

But it were any persone obstinat,[1]

Whatso° he were of heigh or lough estat,° *whether / low class*

Hym wolde he snybben° sharply for the

    nonys.°   *rebuke / occasion*

A bettre preest I trowe° that nowher noon ys. *believe*

525 He waiteth after° no pompe and reverence, *expected*

Ne maked° hym a spiced° conscience. *affected / overly fastidious*

But Cristes loore° and hise apostles twelve *teaching*

He taughte, but first he folwed it hymselve.

    With hym ther was a Plowman, was° his brother, *(who) was*

530 That hadde ylad° of dong ful many a fother.° *hauled / cartload*

A trewe swynkere° and a good was he,   *true worker*

Lyvynge in pees and parfit charitee.

God loved he best with al his hoole herte

At alle tymes, thogh he gamed or smerte,[2]

535 And thanne° his neighebore right° as hymselve. *then / just*

He wolde thresshe° and therto dyke° and

    delve°   *thresh / dig / shovel*

For Cristes sake for every povre wight° *poor person*

Withouten hire° if it lay in his myght.   *pay*

Hise tithes payde he ful faire and wel,

540 Bothe of his propre swynk° and his catel.° *own work / possessions*

In a tabard° he rood upon a mere.°   *over-shirt / mare*

    Ther was also a Reve° and a Millere,   *reeve*

A Somnour°[3] and a Pardoner[4] also,   *summoner*

A Maunciple°[5] and myself. Ther were namo.° *manciple / no more*

545 The Millere was a stout carl° for the nones. *sturdy fellow*

Ful byg he was of brawn and eek of bones.

That proved wel,° for overal ther° he

    cam°   *was clear / everywhere / came*

At wrastlynge° he wolde have alwey the ram.[6] *wrestling*

He was short-sholdred,° brood,° a thikke

    knarre.°   *stocky / broad / thick fellow*

550 Ther was no dore that he ne wolde heve of harre[7]

Or breke it at a rennyng° with his heed. *by running at it*

His berd as any sowe° or fox was reed,   *sow*

And therto brood as though it were a spade.

Upon the cope° right of his nose he hade   *ridge*

555 A werte° and theron stood a toft of herys,° *wart / tuft of hairs*

Reed as the brustles° of a sowes erys.° *bristles / sow's ears*

Hise nosethirles° blake were and wyde.° *nostrils / wide*

A swerd and a bokeler bar° he by his syde.   *bore*

His mouth as greet was as a greet forneys.° *furnace*

560 He was a janglere° and a goliardeys,[8]   *joker*

And that was moost of synne° and harlotries.° *sin / obscenities*

Wel koude he stelen° corn° and tollen

    thries,°   *steal / grain / take his toll (percentage) thrice*

And yet he hadde a thombe° of gold,

    pardee.°   *thumb / by God*

A whit cote° and a blew° hood wered° he. *white coat / blue / wore*

565 A baggepipe wel koude he blowe and sowne,° *sound*

And therwithal he broghte us out of towne.

    A gentil° Maunciple was ther of a temple *gracious*

Of which achatours° myghte take exemple   *buyers*

For to be wise in byynge° of vitaille.° *buying / food*

570 For wheither that he payde or took by taille,° *credit*

Algate he wayted so in his achaat

That he was ay biforn and in good staat.[9]

---

[1] *But ... obstinat* But if anyone were obstinate.

[2] *At ... smerte* At all times, whether he gamed (i.e., did pleasant things) or hurt.

[3] *A Somnour* Deliverer of legal summonses to either secular or ecclesiastical courts, although more often the latter. The ecclesiastical courts were run by the Church and had jurisdiction over all clerics but also over any lay person charged with a moral offense such as adultery or fornication.

[4] *Pardoner* Seller of indulgences, which were writs authorized by the Church to raise money for charitable causes. Indulgences usually promised reduction of time in penance and, after death, in Purgatory.

[5] *Maunciple* Servant at one of the Inns of Court, the legal brotherhoods in London. The Inns of Court were also called temples.

[6] *ram* Typical prize for victors at trade fairs.

[7] *Ther ... harre* There was not a door that he would not heave off its hinges.

[8] *goliardeys* The reference is to Goliards, wandering scholars in the eleventh and twelfth centuries who were known for their rowdy life.

[9] *Algate ... staat* He was always so watchful in his purchasing (achaat) / That he always came out ahead (biforn) and did well.

Now is nat that of God a ful faire grace

That swich a lewed° mannes wit shal pace°   *unlearned | surpass*

575   The wisdom of an heepe° of lerned men?   *heap*

Of maistres hadde he mo° than thries ten°   *more | three times ten*

That weren° of lawe° expert and curious,°   *were | law | skilled*

Of whiche ther weren a duszeyne° in that hous   *dozen*

Worthy to been stywardes° of rente and lond   *stewards*

580   Of any lord that is in Engelond,

To maken hym lyve by his propre good°   *own means*

In honour dettelees°—but if he were wood—   *without debt*

Or lyve as scarsly° as hym list desire,°   *frugally | as he wanted*

And able for to helpen al a shire°   *an entire county*

585   In any caas° that myghte falle or happe,°   *situation | happen*

And yet this Manciple sette hir aller cappe.°   *cheated them all*

The Reve was a sclendre,° colerik° man.[1]   *slender | angry*

His berd was shave° as ny° as ever he kan,   *shaven | closely*

His heer° was by his erys° ful round yshorn.°   *hair | ears | cut*

590   His tope was dokked° lyk a preest biforn.[2]   *clipped*

Ful longe were his legges and ful lene°—   *lean*

Ylyk° a staf° ther was no calf ysene.°   *like | staff | seen*

Wel koude he kepe a gerner° and a bynne;°   *granary | bin*

Ther was noon auditour koude of hym

wynne.°   *get the better of*

595   Wel wiste° he by the droghte° and by the

reyn°   *knew | drought | rain*

The yeldynge° of his seed and of his greyn.°   *yield | grain*

His lordes sheepe, his neet,° his dayerye,°   *cattle | dairy cows*

His swyn,° his hors, his stoor,° and his

pultrye°   *swine | livestock | poultry*

Was hoolly° in this Reves governyng,   *wholly*

600   And by his covenant° yaf the rekenyng°   *contract | reckoning*

Syn° that his lord was twenty yeer of age.   *since*

Ther koude no man brynge hym in arrerage.°   *arrears*

Ther nas baillif ne hierde nor oother hyne,

That he ne knew his sleighte and his covyne.[3]

605   They were adrad° of hym as of the deeth.°[4]   *afraid | death*

His wonyng° was ful faire upon an heeth;°   *dwelling | heath*

With grene trees shadwed was his place.

He koude bettre than his lord purchace.°   *buy land*

Full riche he was, astored pryvely.°   *privately stocked*

610   His lord wel koude he plesen subtilly,°   *please subtly*

To yeve and lene° hym of his owene good°   *loan | goods*

And have a thank and yet a gowne and hood.[5]

In youthe he hadde lerned° a good myster:°   *learned | craft*

He was a wel good wrighte,° a carpenter.   *craftsman*

615   This Reve sat upon a ful good stot°   *farm horse*

That was al pomely° grey and highte° Scot.   *dappled | named*

A long surcote° of pers upon he hade,   *overcoat*

And by his syde he baar a rusty blade.

Of Northfolk° was this Reve of which I telle,   *Norfolk*

620   Biside a toun men clepen Baldeswelle.[6]

Tukked° he was as is a frere° aboute,[7]   *belted | friar*

And ever he rood the hyndreste° of oure route.°   *last | company*

A Somonour was ther with us in that place

That hadde a fyr reed,° cherubynnes° face,[8]   *fire red | cherub-like*

625   For saucefleem° he was with eyen narwe.°   *blotchy | narrow eyes*

As hoot he was and lecherous as a sparwe,°[9]   *sparrow*

With scaled browes blake and piled berd.[10]

Of his visage° children were aferd.°   *face | afraid*

---

[1] *The … man* A reeve was someone, often originally a peasant, who served as a supervisor on a lord's estate. Among other things, reeves collected the portion of the harvest due to the lords and made sure peasants performed their customary labor for the lords. They were much resented. Chaucer's Reeve is dominated by choler, or yellow bile, which makes him suspicious and irritable.

[2] *His … biforn* The top of his head was cut short in the front like a priest's haircut. This would have been an unfashionable cut for a layman, and suitable to a man who was poor, or miserly, or austere.

[3] *Ther nas … covyne* There was not a bailiff (foreman), herdsman, or other worker whose tricks and deception he did not know.

[4] *adrad … deeth* Death in general, or possibly the plague.

[5] *His lord … hood* This reeve cheats his lord by storing away the lord's goods as his own and then using them to provide loans to the lord, receiving payment and thanks. Payment in the Middle Ages was most often in tangible goods, like the clothing mentioned here, rather than in money.

[6] *Baldeswelle* I.e., Bawdeswell, a town in the northern part of Norfolk, the northernmost county in East Anglia on the east coast of England.

[7] *Tukked … aboute* Franciscan friars wore habits tied about the waist with ropes.

[8] *That … face* Cherubim, the second highest order of angels, were bright red. See Ezekiel 1.13.

[9] *sparwe* Since sparrows travel in flocks, they had a reputation in the Middle Ages for being lecherous, similar to the more modern reputation of rabbits.

[10] *With … berd* The Summoner's eyebrows have a disease called the scall, and his beard has been losing tufts of hair.

Ther nas quyksilver, lytarge, ne brymstoon,
630 Boras, cerice, ne oille of Tartre noon,[1]
Ne oynement° that wolde clense° and
         byte°   *ointment / cleanse / bite*
That hym myghte helpen of the whelkes° white   *blemishes*
Nor of the knobbes sittynge° on his chekes.°   *sitting / cheeks*
Wel loved he garleek, oynons, and eek lekes°   *leeks*
635 And for to drynken strong wyn reed as blood.
Thanne wolde he speke and crie° as he were wood.   *yell*
And whan that he wel dronken hadde the wyn,
Thanne wolde he speke no word but Latyn.
A fewe termes hadde he, two or thre,
640 That he had lerned out of som decree.°   *legal document*
No wonder is, he herde it al the day,
And eek ye knowen wel how that a jay°   *chattering bird*
Kan clepen "Watte"° as wel as kan the Pope.   *Walter*
But whoso koude in oother thyng him grope,°   *examine*
645 Thanne hadde he spent al his philosophie.
Ay° "Questio quid iuris!"[2] wold he crie.   *always*
He was a gentil harlot and a kynde;°   *noble and kindly scoundrel*
A bettre felawe° sholde men noght° fynde.   *fellow / not*
He wolde suffre for a quart of wyn
650 A good felawe to have his concubyn°   *mistress*
A twelf monthe° and excuse hym atte fulle.°   *a year / fully*
Ful prively° a fynch° eek koude he pulle.[3]   *secretly / finch*
And if he foond° owher° a good felawe,   *found / anywhere*
He wolde techen° hym to have noon awe°   *teach / no respect*
655 In swich caas of the Ercedekenes curs—[4]
But if°a mannes°soule were in his purs.°   *unless / man's / purse*
For in his purs he sholde ypunysshed be:°   *be punished*
Purs is the Ercedekenes Helle, seyde he.
But wel I woot° he lyed° right in dede.°   *know / lied / indeed*
660 Of cursyng° oghte ech gilty man him drede;   *excommunication*

For curs wol slee° right as° assoillyng°   *kill / just as / absolution*
         savith.
And also war° him of a "Significavit"![5]   *beware*
In daunger° hadde he at his owene gise°   *power / pleasure*
The yonge girles[6] of the diocise°   *diocese*
665 And knew hir conseil° and was al hir reed.[7]   *their secrets*
A gerland° hadde he set upon his heed   *garland*
As greet as it were for an ale stake.[8]
A bokeleer hadde he, maad° hym of a cake.° *made / loaf of bread*
 With hym ther was a gentil° Pardoner   *noble*
670 Of Rouncivale,[9] his freend and his compeer,°   *companion*
That streight° was comen fro the court of Rome.   *straight*
Ful loude he soong "Com Hider, Love, to Me;"[10]
This Somonour bar to hym a stif burdoun.[11]
Was nevere trompe° of half so greet a soun!   *trumpet*
675 This Pardoner hadde heer as yelow as wex,°   *wax*
But smothe it heeng as dooth a strike° of flex.°   *bunch / flax*
By ounces° henge hise lokkes that he hadde,   *strands*
And therwith he hise shuldres°
         overspradde,°   *shoulders / spread over*
But thynne° it lay by colpons° oon° and oon. *thin / strands / one*
680 But hood for jolitee° wered° he noon,   *fun / wore*
For it was trussed° up in his walet.°   *packed / bag*
Hym thoughte° he rood al of the newe
         jet.°   *it seemed to him / fashion*

---

[1] *Ther … noon* The unsuccessful remedies are mercury (sometimes known as quicksilver), lead monoxide (lytarge), sulfur (sometimes known as brimstone), borax, white lead (cerice), and cream of tartar.

[2] *Questio quid iuris* Latin: Question: what point of the law? The expression was often used in the ecclesiastical courts.

[3] *Ful … pulle* Obscene expression that meant, literally, "to pluck a bird."

[4] *In … curs* In such a case of the excommunication (curse) of the archdeacon. An archdeacon was the ecclesiastical official in charge of the ecclesiastical court of a diocese.

---

[5] *Significavit* Latin: it signified. It is the first word in a writ authorizing the civil court to imprison someone who had been excommunicated.

[6] *yonge girles* In Middle English, girls can mean young people of both sexes, but here it may just mean young women.

[7] *was al hir reed* Was all their advice. Idiomatic: the Summoner was in their confidence.

[8] *ale stake* Ale-sign; a long pole that stuck out into the street and showed that ale was being sold on the premises.

[9] *Of Rouncivale* The Pardoner belongs to the Hospital of the Blessed Mary of Roncesvalles in London, a dependent house of the larger one at Roncesvalles, the mountain pass between Spain and France which many pilgrims used when they traveled to St. James of Compostela. Hospitals in the Middle Ages were not purely medical facilities; they also served as inns and poor houses.

[10] *Com Hider, Love, to Me* This song, "Come Here, Love, to Me," does not survive.

[11] *This … burdoun* The Summoner accompanied him with a strong bass. In medieval carols, each sung verse was separated by a burden, a kind of refrain. Carols originally had many subjects, not just the joys of Christmas.

Dischevelee° save° his cappe° he rood° al
    bare.   *with his hair loose | except | cap | rode*
Swiche glarynge° eyen hadde he as an hare.[1]   *bulging*
685 A vernycle[2] hadde he sowed° upon his cappe;   *sewn*
His walet° biforn° hym in his lappe,°   *wallet | before | lap*
Bretful° of pardoun, comen from Rome al hoot.   *brimful*
A voys° he hadde as smal° as hath a
    goot.°   *voice | high-pitched | goat*
No berd hadde he, ne never sholde° have: *would*
690 As smothe° it was as° it were late yshave.°   *smooth | as if | shaven*
I trowe° he were a geldyng° or a mare.[3]   *believe | gelding*
But of his craft fro° Berwyk into Ware[4]   *from*
Ne was ther swich° another pardoner.   *there was not such*
For in his male° he hadde a pilwe beer,°   *bag | pillow-case*
695 Which that he seyde was oure Lady veyl;°[5]   *Virgin Mary's veil*
He seyde he hadde a gobet° of the seyl°   *piece | sail*
That Seint Peter hadde when that he wente
Upon the see til Jhesu Crist hym hente.°[6]   *grabbed him*
He hadde a croys° of latoun° ful of stones,   *cross | brass*
700 And in a glas° he hadde pigges bones.   *glass*
But with thise relikes whan that he fond
A povre person dwellynge upon lond,
Upon a day he gat hym° moore moneye   *got himself*
Than that the person gat in monthes tweye.
705 And thus with feyned° flaterye and japes°   *pretended | jokes*
He made the person and the peple his apes.°   *dupes*
But trewely, to tellen atte laste,
He was in chirche a noble ecclesiaste.°   *churchman*

---

[1] *hare* According to medieval lore, hares were hermaphroditic, becoming both male and female in order to reproduce. Bulging eyes were thought to be a sign of lust and folly.

[2] *vernycle* Badge depicting St. Veronica's veil, a relic at Rome. St. Veronica wiped Jesus's face with her veil as he carried the cross, and by miracle his image was imprinted upon it. Pilgrims collected such badges.

[3] *I ... mare* I believe he was either a gelding (a castrated horse) or a mare.

[4] *Berwyk into Ware* Berwick is in the extreme north of England near the border with Scotland; Ware is near London.

[5] *For ... veyl* Chaucer's point is that the Pardoner sells fraudulent relics (sacred objects associated with Jesus or the saints).

[6] *That ... hente* The reference is to Peter's unsuccessful attempt to imitate Christ by walking on the water. Christ had to rescue him. See Matthew 14.22–33.

Wel koude he rede a lessoun° or a
    storie.°   *lesson | story (from the Bible)*
710 But alderbest° he song° an offertorie,[7]   *best of all | sang*
For wel he wiste whan that song was songe
He moste preche° and wel affile° his
    tonge°   *must preach | sharpen | tongue*
To wynne° silver as he ful wel koude.   *acquire*
Therfore he song the murierly° and loude.   *more merrily*
715 Now have I toold yow shortly° in a clause   *briefly*
Th'estaat,° th'array,° the nombre, and eek the
    cause   *social position | appearance*
Why that assembled was this compaignye
In Southwerk at this gentil hostelry
That highte the Tabard, faste by the Belle.[8]
720 But now is tyme to yow° for to telle   *you*
How that we baren° us that ilke nyght   *behaved*
Whan we were in that hostelrie alyght,°   *arrived*
And after wol I tell of oure viage
And al the remenaunt of oure pilgrimage.
725 But first I pray yow of youre curteisye
That ye n'arette it nat my vileynye,[9]
Thogh that I pleynly° speke in this mateere   *plainly*
To telle yow hir wordes and hir cheere,°   *comportment*
Ne thogh I speke hir wordes proprely.°   *exactly*
730 For this ye knowen also wel as I:
Whoso° shal telle a tale after a man,   *whoever*
He moot° reherce as ny° as ever he kan   *should | closely*
Everich a word° if it be in his charge,   *every word*
Al° speke he never so rudeliche° or
    large,°   *although | crudely | freely*
735 Or ellis° he moot° telle his tale untrewe,   *else | must*
Or feyne thyng,° or fynde wordes newe.   *falsify something*
He may nat spare althogh he were his brother;
He moot as wel seye o word as another.

---

[7] *offertorie* The Offertory was chanted when the congregation was bringing gifts to the altar.

[8] *Belle* Previous editors have capitalized this word, guessing that it was the name of another inn—there were several called the Bell in that area — or perhaps a house of prostitution. Perhaps the word should not be capitalized, as it may imply a notable bell in the neighborhood.

[9] *That ... vileynye* That you not attribute it to my lack of manners. Vileynye does not mean villainy in the modern sense. A villein was originally an inhabitant of a rural village; thus the word signifies the state of being rustic rather than civilized.

Crist spak hymself ful brode° in Hooly
    Writ,°   *freely | Holy Scripture*
740 And wel ye woot no vileynye is it.
Eek Plato seith, whoso kan hym rede,
The wordes moote be cosyn° to the dede.°[1]   *cousin | deed*
Also I prey yow to foryeve° it me   *forgive*
Al° have I nat set folk in hir degree°   *although | according to rank*
745 Heere in this tale as that they sholde stonde.
My wit° is short, ye may wel understonde.   *intelligence*
    Greet chiere° made oure Hoost us everichon,°   *cheer | everyone*
And to the soper sette he us anon.
He served us with vitaille at the beste;
750 Strong was the wyn, and wel to drynke us leste.°   *it pleased us*
A semely° man oure Hoost was withalle   *suitable*
For to been a marchal° in an halle.[2]   *marshal*
A large man he was, with eyen stepe.°   *bright*
A fairer burgeys° was ther noon in Chepe,[3]   *citizen*
755 Boold of his speche and wys and wel ytaught,°   *learned*
And of manhod hym lakked° right naught.°   *lacked | nothing*
Eek therto° he was right a myrie man,   *in addition*
And after soper pleyen° he bigan°   *play | began*
And spak of myrthe amonges othere thynges
760 Whan that we hadde maad oure rekenynges[4]
And seyde thus, "Now lordynges, trewely,
Ye been° to me right welcome hertely.°   *are | heartily*
For by my trouthe, if that I shal nat lye,
I saugh nat this yeer so myrie a compaignye
765 Atones° in this herberwe° as is now.   *at once | inn*
Fayn° wolde I doon yow myrthe, wiste I°
    how.   *gladly | if I knew*
And of a myrthe I am right now bythoght°   *in mind*
To doon yow ese,° and it shal coste noght.°   *do you ease | nothing*
    Ye goon to Caunterbury: God yow
    speede!°   *God bring you success!*
770 The blissful martir quite° yow youre meede!°   *pay | reward*

And wel I woot as ye goon by the weye,
Ye shapen yow° to talen° and to pleye.°   *intend | tell tales | play*
For trewely,° confort° ne myrthe is noon   *truly | comfort*
To ride by the weye doumb as the stoon.[5]
775 And therfore wol I maken yow disport,°   *entertainment*
As I seyde erst,° and doon yow som
    confort.°   *first | bring you some comfort*
And if yow liketh° alle by oon assent°   *pleases you | unanimously*
For to stonden at° my juggement°   *abide by | judgment*
And for to werken° as I shal yow seye,   *proceed*
780 Tomorwe, whan ye riden by the weye,
Now by my fader soule° that is deed,°   *father's soul | dead*
But if ye be myrie, I wol yeve yow myn heed!
Hoold up youre hondes withouten moore speche."
    Oure conseil° was nat° longe for to seche.°   *counsel | not | seek*
785 Us thoughte° it was noght worth to make it wys,[6]   *we thought*
And graunted hym withouten moore avys°   *more debate*
And bad° hym seye his voirdit° as hym
    leste.°   *asked | verdict | as he wanted*
"Lordynges," quod he, "now herkneth for the beste,
But taak it nought, I prey° yow, in desdeyn.°   *beg | disdain*
790 This is the poynt, to speken short and pleyn,
That ech of yow to shorte° with oure weye   *shorten*
In this viage shal telle tales tweye°   *two*
To Caunterburyward,° I mene° it so,   *towards Canterbury | mean*
And homward he shal tellen othere two
795 Of aventures that whilom° han bifalle.°   *once | have happened*
And which of yow that bereth hym° best of
    alle,   *conducts himself*
That is to seyn, that telleth in this caas°   *occasion*
Tales of best sentence° and moost solaas,°   *meaning | enjoyment*
Shal have a soper at oure aller cost°   *at all our cost*
800 Heere in this place, sittynge by this post,
Whan that we come agayn fro Caunterbury.
As for to make yow the moore mury,°   *merry*
I wol myself goodly° with yow ryde,   *gladly*
Right at myn owene cost, and be youre gyde.
805 And whoso wole my juggement withseye°   *resist*
Shal paye al that we spenden by the weye.°   *along the way*
And if ye vouchesauf° that it be so,   *grant*
Tel me anon withouten wordes mo,

---

[1] *Eek ... dede* The reference is to Plato's *Timaeus*, the only one of his dialogues available in translation to the Latin West in the Middle Ages. The quotation is found in section 29. The passage is also discussed by Boethius in his *Consolation of Philosophy* (3, prose 12), a work that Chaucer had translated and drew upon frequently.

[2] *For ... halle* A marshal is a steward or chief butler; a hall is a manor house or town house of a lord.

[3] *Chepe* Cheapside was the merchants' district in London.

[4] *Whan ... rekenynges* When we had paid our bills.

[5] *For ... stoon* For truly there is neither comfort nor mirth in riding along as silent as a stone.

[6] *to make it wys* Idiomatic: to make a big deal of it.

And I wol erly° shape me° therfore."° *early | get ready | for it*

810 This thyng was graunted and oure othes° swore° *oaths | sworn*

With ful glad herte, and preyden° hym also *asked*

That he wolde vouchesauf for to do so

And that he wolde been oure governour

And of oure tales juge° and reportour° *judge | referee*

815 And sette a soper at a certeyn pris° *price*

And we wol reuled been at his devys° *wish*

In heigh and lough.° And thus by oon° assent *all matters | one*

We been acorded° to his juggement, *agreed*

And therupon the wyn was fet° anon.° *fetched | immediately*

820 We dronken and to reste wente echon° *each one*

Withouten any lenger taryynge.° *longer delaying*

Amorwe,° whan that day gan° for to

sprynge,° *the next day | began | dawn*

Up roos° oure Hoost and was oure aller cok° *rose | rooster for us all*

And gadrede° us togidre° all in a flok.° *gathered | together | flock*

825 And forth we ridden,° a litel moore than

paas,° *rode | a horse's walking pace*

Unto the Wateryng of Seint Thomas.[1]

And there oure Hoost bigan his hors areste° *rein in*

And seyde, "Lordynges, herkneth if yow leste!° *please*

Ye woot youre foreward° and it yow recorde;° *contract | recall*

830 If evensong° and morwesong° accorde,[2] *Evensong | Matins*

Lat se° now who shal telle the firste tale. *let us see*

As evere mote° I drynke wyn or ale, *might*

Whoso be rebel to my juggement

Shal paye for al that by the wey is spent.

835 Now draweth cut er that we ferrer twynne;[3]

He which that hath the shorteste shal bigynne.

Sire Knyght," quod he, "my mayster and my lord,

Now draweth cut,° for that is myn accord.° *a straw | decision*

Cometh neer," quod he, "my lady Prioresse,

840 And ye, sire Clerk, lat be youre shamefastnesse,° *shyness*

Ne studieth noght.° Ley° hond° to every

man." *stop studying | lay | hand*

Anon to drawen every wight° bigan, *person*

And shortly for to tellen as it was,

Were it by aventure or sort or cas,[4]

845 The sothe° is this: the cut° fil° to the knyght, *truth | straw | fell*

Of which ful blithe° and glad was every wyght. *very happy*

And telle he moste his tale as was resoun,° *reasonable*

By foreward° and by composicioun,° *agreement | arrangement*

As ye han herd. What nedeth wordes mo?

850 And whan this goode man saugh° that it was so, *saw*

As he that wys was and obedient

To kepe his foreward by his free assent,

He seyde, "Syn° I shal bigynne the game, *since*

What, welcome be the cut, a Goddes° name! *in God's*

855 Now lat us ryde and herkneth what I seye."

And with that word we ryden forth oure weye.

And he bigan with right a myrie cheere° *cheerful expression*

His tale anon, and seyde in this manere.[5]

---

[1] *Wateryng of Seint Thomas* The Watering of St. Thomas was the name given to a brook just outside London on the way to Canterbury.

[2] *If … accorde* I.e., if you still say in the morning what you said last evening.

[3] *Now … twynne* "Now draw a straw before we depart further."

[4] *Were … cas* Adventure, sort, and case mean roughly the same thing: chance.

[5] *His … manere* Hengwrt and some other manuscripts read "and seyde as ye may heere," not "and seyde in this manere," a suggestion that *The Canterbury Tales* were to be read aloud as well as silently.

The Knight's Tale

The Knight has the highest social status of the pilgrims and it is appropriate that he should initiate the tale-telling and do so with a work that reflects the interests of his class, a philosophical romance. As befits the teller, the poem is stately in tone and pace and filled with lengthy descriptions of aristocratic rituals, including the great final tournament and the funeral of one of the two lovers. It offers a fantasy of idealized aristocratic love, set in a world of violence to which the love sometimes contributes. In so doing it also raises questions of free will and astrological determinism, inviting us to ask whether a providential order can be reconciled with the violence and disorder of earthly life.

Chaucer originally composed *The Knight's Tale* as a separate work, probably during the 1380s. His source was Boccaccio's story of Theseus, the *Teseida* (written c. 1340), a work of nearly 10,000 lines, in twelve books, and written in Italian to provide a vernacular rival to Virgil's Latin epic, the *Aeneid*. The 2350 lines of *The Knight's Tale* make it Chaucer's longest single poem after *Troilus and Criseyde*, although it is only a quarter of the length of Boccaccio's *Teseida*.

The Knight's central subject is the love of two young nobles, Palamon and Arcite, for the beautiful Emelye, which follows the conventions of *amour courtois* or courtly love, a refined love that is inspired by the sight of the beloved and is violent in its intensity, demanding absolute devotion and years of painful service. Palamon and Arcite fall in love with Emelye while gazing from their prison window and without exchanging a word with her, their passion remains as intense as ever seven years later. The literature of courtly love often takes a legalistic turn, inviting readers or listeners to join in a debate on a formal question, known as a *demande d'amour*; in this case, the question is whether the lover who can see his lady but do nothing to win her is in a worse position than the lover who can struggle to win her but can never see her.

Chaucer, or his Knight, complicates the basic love story by repeated references to cosmic forces. The three earthly lovers are in the character of pagan gods of love, war, and chastity, whose conflict is ultimately resolved by Saturn, the oldest of the gods and a source of destruction. Chaucer takes the sub-plot of the pagan gods from Boccaccio, but he greatly expands the descriptions of the grim effects of Mars and Saturn on human life, evoking the wars, rebellions, plagues, and devastation of his own day. One might describe this world as a thoroughfare of woe, as Theseus's father Egeus does (line 1987). Alternatively, one could look beyond it to a higher order, as Theseus does, in an evocation of cosmic harmony that draws on one of Chaucer's most important sources, the *Consolation of Philosophy* of the late Roman philosopher Boethius. For Theseus, the principle that maintains this order is either Jupiter, chief of the pagan gods, or the First Mover of Aristotelian philosophy (l. 2127), but Chaucer's readers would have understood this principle in Christian terms. In many respects, Theseus speaks for the Knight's values, but whether the tale always confirms them is more questionable.

Detail, opening page of *The Knight's Tale*, Ellesmere manuscript.
(Reprinted by permission of *The Huntington Library, San Marino, California*. EL 26 C9 f. 10r.)

Opening page of *The Knight's Tale*, Ellesmere manuscript. (Reprinted by permission of *The Huntington Library, San Marino, California*. EL 26 C9 f. 10r.)

THE KNIGHT'S TALE

Iamque domos patrias, Scithice post aspera gentis
Prelia, laurigero[1]

HEERE BIGYNNETH THE KNYGHTES TALE

Whilom,° as olde stories tellen us, — *once*
    Ther was a duc° that highte° Theseus. — *duke / was named*
Of Atthenes° he was lord and governour, — *Athens*
And in his tyme swich° a conquerour — *such*
5   That gretter° was ther noon° under the sonne. — *greater / none*
Ful many a riche contree hadde he wonne,° — *won*
What with his wysdom and his chivalrie.° — *knightly prowess*
He conquered al the regne of Femenye[2]
That whilom was ycleped° Scithia[3] — *called*
10 And wedded the queene Ypolita° — *Hippolita*
And broghte hire hoom° with hym in° his contree — *home / to*
With muchel° glorie and greet
    solempnytee,° — *much / great ceremony*
And eek° hir faire suster° Emelye.° — *also / sister / Emily*
And thus with victorie and with melodye
15 Lete° I this noble duc to Atthenes ryde — *let*
And al his hoost° in armes hym bisyde.° — *host / beside him*
  And certes,° if it nere to long to
    heere,° — *certainly / were not too long to hear*
I wolde° yow have toold fully the manere° — *would / manner*
How wonnen° was the regne of Femenye — *won*
20 By Theseus and by his chivalrye° — *knights*
And of the grete bataille° for the
    nones° — *great battle / on that occasion*
Bitwixen° Atthenes and Amazones — *between*
And how asseged° was Ypolita, — *besieged*

The faire, hardy queene of Scithia,
25 And of the feste° that was at hir weddynge — *feast*
And of the tempest at hir hoomcomynge.° — *homecoming*
But al that thyng I moot° as now
    forbere.° — *must / for the moment resist (telling)*
I have, God woot,° a large feeld to ere,° — *God knows / plow*
And wayke° been° the oxen in my plough. — *weak / are*
30 The remenant of the tale is long ynough:° — *enough*
I wol nat letten° eek noon° of this route.°— *hinder / none / company*
Lat° every felawe° telle his tale aboute!° — *let / fellow / in turn*
And lat se° now, who shal the soper wynne? — *let us see*
And ther° I lefte I wol ayeyn° bigynne. — *where / again*
35   This duc of whom I make mencioun,
Whan he was come almoost unto the toun
In al his wele° and in his mooste pride,° — *prosperity / great pride*
He was war° as he caste his eye aside — *aware*
Where that ther° kneled° in the weye° — *there / kneeled / road*
40 A compaignye of ladyes tweye and tweye,° — *two by two*
Ech after oother clad in clothes blake.
But swich a cry and swich a wo° they make, — *woe*
That in this world nys° creature lyvynge — *is no*
That herde° swich another waymentynge.° — *heard / sorrowing*
45 And of this cry they nolde° nevere stenten° — *would not / cease*
Til they the reynes of his brydel henten.° — *grasped*
    "What folk been° ye, that at myn homcomynge — *are*
Perturben° so my feste with criynge?" — *disturb*
Quod° Theseus. "Have ye so greet envye° — *said / envy*
50 Of myn honour that thus compleyne and crye?
Or who hath yow mysboden° or offended? — *harmed*
And telleth me if it may been amended
And why that ye been clothed thus in blak."
    The eldeste lady of hem alle spak,
55 Whan she hadde swowned° with a deedly°
    cheere° — *fainted / deathly / face*
That it was routhe° for to seen and heere, — *pity*
And seyde, "Lord to whom fortune hath yeven° — *given*
Victorie and as a conquerour to lyven,° — *live*
Nat greveth us° youre glorie and youre
    honour, — *we are not grieved by*
60 But we biseken° mercy and socour!° — *ask / help*
Have mercy on oure wo° and oure distresse! — *woe*
Som drope of pitee thurgh° thy gentillesse° — *through / nobility*
Upon us wrecched wommen lat thou falle.
For certes,° lord, ther is noon of us alle — *certainly*
65 That she ne hath been a duchesse or a queene.
Now be we caytyves,° as it is wel seene, — *miserable people*

---

[1] *Iamque ... laurigero* Latin: And now Theseus, [drawing near] his native land in a chariot covered with laurels, after fierce battle with the Scythians [is heralded by glad applause and the shouts of the people to the heavens and the merry trumpet celebrating the end of the war]. This passage occurs at the end of Latin poet Statius's epic poem about the Theban War, *The Thebaid*, which was one of Chaucer's sources for *The Knight's Tale*. This passage describes the triumphant return of Theseus at the very end of the poem.

[2] *Femenye* Land of the Amazons, a race of female warriors.

[3] *Scithia* Scythia was an ancient country of nomads who inhabited the Caucasus region and was believed to be the homeland of the Amazons.

Thanked be Fortune and hire false wheel,[1]
That noon estaat assureth to be weel!° *assures no estate prospers*
And certes, lord, to abyden° youre presence, *await*
70 Heere in the temple of the goddesse
    Clemence° *clemency (mercy)*
We han° been waitynge al this
    fourtenyght.° *have | two-week period*
Now help us, lord, sith° it is in thy myght! *since*
    "I, wrecche° which that wepe° and crie thus, *wretched one | weep*
Was whilom wyf to Kyng Cappaneus[2]
75 That starf° at Thebes, cursed be that day! *died*
And alle we that been in this array° *condition*
And maken al this lamentacioun,
We losten alle oure housbondes at that toun
Whil° that the seege° theraboute lay. *while | siege*
80 And yet now the olde Creon,[3] weylaway,° *alas*
That lord is now of Thebes the citee,
Fulfild of ire° and of iniquitee,° *filled with anger | wickedness*
He for despit° and for his tirannye *spite*
To do the dede bodyes vileynye° *disgrace*
85 Of alle oure lordes whiche that been slawe,° *killed*
He hath alle the bodyes on an heepe°
    ydrawe° *heap | gathered together*
And wol nat suffren hem by noon
    assent° *permit them on any terms*
Neither to been yburyed° nor ybrent,° *buried | burned*
But maketh houndes° ete° hem in despit!"° *dogs | eat | spite*
90   And with that word, withouten° moore respit, *delay*
They fillen gruf° and criden° pitously, *fell groveling | cried*
"Have on us wrecched wommen som mercy,
And lat oure sorwe synken° in thyn herte!" *sink*
    This gentil° duc doun from his courser°
    sterte° *noble | horse | jumped*
95 With herte pitous° whan he herde hem speke. *pitying*
Hym thoughte that his herte wolde breke
Whan he saugh° hem so pitous and so maat,° *saw | downcast*
That whilom weren of so greet estaat.

And in his armes he hem alle up hente° *took*
100 And hem conforteth in ful good entente° *with good will*
And swoor his ooth as he was trewe knyght
He wolde doon so ferforthly° his myght *completely*
Upon the tiraunt° Creon, hem to wreke,° *tyrant | avenge*
That al the peple of Grece sholde speke
105 How Creon was of Theseus yserved° *dealt with*
As he that hadde his deeth ful wel deserved.
And right anoon° withouten moore abood,° *immediately | delay*
His baner° he desplayeth and forth rood° *banner | rode*
To Thebesward° and al his hoost° biside. *towards Thebes | army*
110 No neer° Atthenes° wolde he go ne° ride *nearer | Athens | nor*
Ne take his ese° fully half a day, *rest*
But onward on his wey that nyght he lay
And sente anon Ypolita the queene
And Emelye hir yonge suster sheene° *bright*
115 Unto the toun of Atthenes to dwelle.
And forth he rit;° ther is namoore to telle *rode*
    The rede° statue of Mars with spere° and
    targe° *red | spear | shield*
So shyneth in his white baner large
That alle the feeldes glyteren° up and doun, *glitter*
120 And by his baner born° is his penoun° *carried | pennant*
Of gold ful riche, in which ther was ybete° *embroidered*
The Mynotaur[4] which that he slough° in Crete. *killed*
Thus rit this duc. Thus rit this conquerour,
And in his hoost of chivalrie the flour,° *flower*
125 Til that he cam to Thebes and alighte° *dismounted*
Faire in a feeld theras° he thoughte fighte. *where*
But shortly for to speken of this thyng,
With Creon, which° that was of Thebes kyng, *who*
He faught and slough hym manly as a knyght
130 In pleyn bataille,° and putte the folk to flyght. *open battle*
And by assaut° he wan° the citee after *assault | captured*
And rente adoun° bothe wall and sparre° and
    rafter. *pulled down | beam*
And to the ladyes he restored agayn
The bones of hir housbondes that weren slayn

---

[1] *Fortune ... wheel* The Wheel of Fortune appears in Boethius's *Consolation of Philosophy*, a work Chaucer translated into English. The goddess Fortune turns her Wheel, and those on the top, in prosperity, fall to the bottom, and misery.

[2] *Kyng Cappaneus* King Cappaneus was one of seven leaders who attacked and besieged Thebes.

[3] *Creon* Creon was the king of Thebes and brother of Jocasta, mother of Oedipus.

[4] *The Mynotaur* An earlier deed of Theseus's is his killing of the Minotaur, a half-bull, half-human monster, who was kept in the labyrinth on the island of Crete and there given Athenian youths to devour for food. The Cretan King Minos's daughter, Ariadne, helped Theseus in this feat by giving him a ball of thread to roll out behind him so he could find his way out of the labyrinth once his deed was done.

135 To doon obsequies° as was tho the
    gyse.°   *funeral rites | then the custom*
But it were al to longe for to devyse°   *narrate*
The grete clamour and the waymentynge°   *lamentation*
That the ladyes made at the brennynge°   *cremation*
Of the bodies and the grete° honour   *great*
140 That Theseus the noble conquerour
Dooth to the ladyes whan they from hym wente;
But shortly for to telle is myn entente.
    Whan that this worthy duc, this Theseus
Hath Creon slayn and wonne Thebes thus,
145 Stille° in that feeld he took al nyght his reste   *quietly*
And dide with al the contree as hym leste.°   *desired*
    To ransake in the taas° of the bodyes dede   *pile*
Hem for to strepe° of harneys° and of
    wede°   *strip | armor | clothes*
The pilours° diden bisynesse and cure[1]   *scavengers*
150 After the bataille and disconfiture.°   *defeat*
And so bifel that in the taas they founde,
Thrugh girt° with many a grevous, blody wounde,   *pierced*
Two yonge knyghtes liggynge° by and by,°   *lying | side by side*
Bothe in oon armes wroght ful richely,[2]
155 Of whiche two, Arcita highte° that oon   *was named*
And that oother knyght highte Palamon.
Nat fully quyke° ne fully dede they were,   *alive*
But by hir cote-armures° and by hir gere°   *coat of arms | equipment*
The heraudes° knewe hem best in special°   *heralds | particularly*
160 As they that weren of the blood roial°   *were | royal*
Of Thebes, and of sustren° two yborn.°   *sisters | born*
Out of the taas the pilours han hem torn°   *had pulled them*
And han hem caried softe° unto the tente   *softly*
Of Theseus. And ful soone he hem sente
165 To Atthenes to dwellen in prisoun
Perpetuelly. He nolde° no raunsoun.[3]   *would take*
And whan this worthy duc hath thus ydon,
He took his hoost and hoom he rood anon

With laurer° crowned as a conquerour.   *laurel*
170 And ther he lyveth in joye and in honour
Terme of lyve.° What nedeth wordes
    mo?°   *for the rest of his life | more*
And in a tour° in angwissh° and in wo   *tower | anguish*
This Palamon and his felawe° Arcite   *companion*
For everemoore; ther° may no gold hem
    quite.°   *where | buy them back*
175   This passeth yeer by yeer and day by day,
Til it fil° ones° in a morwe° of May   *happened | once | morning*
That Emelye, that fairer was to sene°   *see*
Than is the lylie° upon his stalke grene   *lily*
And fressher than the May with floures newe—
180 For with the rose colour stroof° hire hewe;   *competed*
I noot° which was the fyner° of hem two!—   *know not | finer*
Er it were day, as was hir wone° to do,   *custom*
She was arisen and al redy dight,°   *dressed*
For May wol have no slogardrie° anyght!°   *laziness | at night*
185 The sesoun° priketh° every gentil herte°   *season | incites | heart*
And maketh hym out of his slep to sterte
And seith, "Arys and do thyn observaunce!"°   *pay your respects*
This maked Emelye have remembraunce
To doon honour to May and for to ryse.
190 Yclothed was she fressh for to devyse.
Hir yelow heer° was broyded° in a tresse°   *hair | braided | plait*
Bihynde hir bak, a yerde° long, I gesse.   *yard*
And in the gardyn at the sonne upriste°   *sunrise*
She walketh up and doun, and as hire liste
195 She gadereth° floures, party° white and rede,   *gathers | mingled*
To make a subtil° gerland for hire hede.   *intricate*
And as an aungel hevenysshly° she soong.   *heavenly*
The grete tour that was so thikke and stroong
Which of the castel was the chief dongeoun,[4]
200 Theras° the knyghtes weren in prisoun,   *where*
Of whiche I tolde yow and tellen shal,
Was evene joynaunt° to the gardyn wal   *next to*
Theras this Emelye hadde hir pleyynge.°   *enjoyment*
Bright was the sonne and cleer that morwenynge.
205 And this Palamoun, this woful prisoner,
As was his wone° by leve° of his gayler°   *custom | leave | jailor*
Was risen and romed° in a chambre an heigh°   *roamed | on high*

---

[1] *diden … cure* Worked hard.

[2] *Bothe … richely* Both in one coat of arms fashioned very richly. As members of the same family, Palamon and Arcite have the same heraldic markings on a light cloth jacket worn over their armor.

[3] *He … raunsoun* In the fourteenth century, the custom was to try to capture enemy soldiers in battle rather than kill them, for ransoming was profitable. Although the tale is ostensibly set in classical antiquity, the descriptions of warfare and the social customs are based on those of Chaucer's own day.

---

[4] *dongeoun* In the Middle Ages, a tower, often part of a castle. Dungeons were sometimes indeed used as prisons, as is the case here, but they had other functions as well, both domestic and military. The word here does not imply a miserable place of imprisonment.

In which he al the noble citee seigh°   *saw*
And eek the gardyn ful of braunches grene
210 Theras this fresshe Emelye the shene°   *bright*
Was in hir walk and romed up and doun.
This sorweful prisoner, this Palamoun
Goth in the chambre romynge° to and fro,   *roaming*
And to hymself compleynynge of his wo
215 That he was born. Ful ofte he seyde, "Allas!"
And so bifel by aventure° or cas°   *chance | accident*
That thurgh a wyndow thikke of many a
barre°   *thickly set with bars*
Of iren° greet° and square as any sparre,°   *iron | great | beam*
He caste his eye upon Emelya.
220 And therwithal° he bleynte° and cride, "A!" *with that | went pale*
As though he stongen° were unto the herte.   *stung*
And with that cry Arcite anon up sterte
And seyde, "Cosyn° myn, what eyleth° thee   *cousin | ails*
That art so pale and deedly° on to see?   *deathly*
225 Why cridestow?° Who hath thee doon offence?   *did you cry*
For Goddes love, taak° al° in pacience   *take | all*
Oure prisoun, for it may noon oother be!°   *may not be otherwise*
Fortune hath yeven° us this adversitee.   *given*
Som wikke° aspect or disposicioun   *wicked*
230 Of Saturne by som constellacioun
Hath yeven us this, although we hadde it sworn.
So stood the hevene whan that we were born.[1]
We moste endure! This is the short and playn!"°   *simple (truth)*
      This Palamon answerde and seyde agayn,
235 "Cosyn, forsothe° of this opinioun   *in truth*
Thow hast a veyn° ymaginacioun!°   *foolish | misconception*
This prison caused me nat for to crye.
But I was hurt right now thurghout myn eye
Into myn herte, that wol my bane° be!   *death-blow*
240 The fairnesse of that lady that I see
Yond° in the gardyn romen to and fro   *yonder*
Is cause of al my crying and my wo.
I noot where° she be woman or goddesse,   *whether*
But Venus[2] is it, soothly° as I gesse!"   *truly*
245 And therwithal on knees doun° he fil   *down*

And seyde, "Venus, if it be thy wil,
Yow in this gardyn thus to transfigure°   *change shape*
Bifore me, sorweful wrecche° creature,   *wretched*
Out of this prisoun helpe that we may scapen!°   *escape*
250 And if so be my destynee be shapen°   *predetermined*
By eterne° word to dyen in prisoun,   *eternal*
Of oure lynage° have som compassioun   *lineage*
That is so lowe ybroght by tirannye!"
And with that word Arcite gan espye°   *to see*
255 Wheras° this lady romed to and fro,   *where*
And with that sighte hir beautee hurte hym so
That if that Palamon was wounded soore,
Arcite is hurt as muche as he or moore.
And with a sigh he seyde pitously,
260 "The fresshe beautee sleeth me sodeynly
Of hire that rometh in the yonder place,
And but° I have hir mercy and hir grace,   *unless*
That I may seen hire atte leeste° weye,   *at least*
I nam° but deed! Ther is namoore° to seye." *am not | no more*
265   This Palamon, whan he tho° wordes herde,   *those*
Dispitously° he looked and answerde,   *angrily*
"Wheither seistow° this in ernest or in pley?"° *do you say | jest*
      "Nay," quod Arcite, "in ernest, by my fey!°   *faith*
God helpe me so, me list ful yvele pleye!"[3]
270   This Palamon gan knytte° his browes tweye.   *knit*
"It nere,"° quod he, "to thee no greet honour   *were not*
For to be fals ne for to be traitour
To me that am thy cosyn and thy brother,
Ysworn° ful depe, and ech of° us til oother,   *sworn | each to*
275 That nevere, for to dyen in the peyne,[4]
Til that deeth departe shal us tweyne,
Neither of us in love to hyndre° oother   *hinder*
Ne in noon oother cas, my leeve° brother,   *beloved*
But that thou sholdest trewely forthren° me   *help*
280 In every cas as I shal forthren thee.
This was thyn ooth and myn also, certeyn,
I woot° right wel, thou darst it nat withseyn.°   *know | deny*
Thus artow° of my conseil° out of
doute,°   *are you | counsel | doubtless*
And now thow woldest falsly been aboute°   *set about*
285 To love my lady, whom I love and serve
And evere shal, til that myn herte sterve.°   *dies*

---

[1] *So ... born* Some evil aspect or alignment of Saturn with some
other constellation has given us this fate, which we must endure
although we had sworn to do otherwise. The stars were arranged that
way when we were born. (Saturn was the Roman god of time and old
age.)

[2] *Venus* Roman goddess of love, reproduction, and peace.

[3] *me ... pleye* I desire to play very little.

[4] *That ... peyne* Even if we were to die by torture.

Nay, certes, false Arcite, thow shalt nat so.
I loved hire first, and tolde thee my wo
As to my conseil° and to my brother sworn   *my counsellor*
290 To forthre° me, as I have toold biforn,°   *help | before*
For which thou art ybounden° as a knyght   *obligated*
To helpen me if it lay in thy might,
Or elles artow fals, I dar wel seyn."
   This Arcite ful proudly spak ageyn.
295 "Thow shalt," quod he, "be rather fals than I.
And thou art fals, I telle thee outrely,°   *completely*
For paramour° I loved hire first er thow.°   *as a lover | you*
What wiltow seyn? Thou wistest nat yet
      now°   *did not yet know just now*
Wheither she be a womman or goddesse!
300 Thyn is affeccioun° of hoolynesse,°   *feeling | religious devotion*
And myn is love, as to a creature,°   *human being*
For which I tolde thee myn aventure
As to my cosyn and my brother sworn.
I pose° that thow lovedest hire biforn: *suppose*
305 Wostow nat wel the olde clerkes sawe[1]
That 'Who shal yeve° a lovere any lawe?'   *give*
Love is a gretter° lawe, by my pan,°   *greater | skull*
Than may be yeve° of any erthely man.   *given*
And therfore positif lawe[2] and swich decree
310 Is broken alday,° for love in ech degree.°   *daily | social rank*
A man moot nedes love, maugree his heed.°   *despite his intentions*
He may nat flee it thogh he sholde be deed,°   *dead*
Al be she° mayde° or wydwe° or elles°
      wyf.   *even if she is | maiden | widow | else*
And eek, it is nat likly al thy lyf
315 To stonden in hir grace;° namoore° shal I.   *favor | no more*
For wel thou woost° thyselven° verraily°   *know | yourself | truly*
That thou and I be dampned° to prisoun   *condemned*
Perpetuelly. Us gayneth no raunsoun.°   *no ransom will free us*
We stryven° as dide the houndes for the boon;°   *quarrel | bone*
320 They foughte al day, and yet hir° part was noon: *their*
Ther cam a kyte° whil they weren so wrothe°   *buzzard | angry*
And baar awey° the boon bitwixe hem bothe.   *carried away*
And therfore at the kynges court, my brother,
Ech man for hymself! Ther is noon oother!
325 Love if thee list, for I love and ay° shal.   *always*

And soothly,° leeve brother, this is al.   *truly*
Heere in this prisoun moote we endure°   *must we remain*
And everich° of us take his aventure!"   *each*
   Greet was the strif and long bitwix hem tweye,
330 If that I hadde leyser° for to seye.   *leisure*
But to th'effect:° It happed on a day,   *result*
To telle it yow as shortly as I may,
A worthy duc that highte Perotheus,
That felawe° was to Duc Theseus   *companion*
335 Syn° thilke° day that they were children lite,° *since | the same | little*
Was come to Atthenes his felawe to visite
And for to pley, as he was won° to do.   *accustomed*
For in this world he loved no man so,
And he loved hym als° tendrely agayn.   *as*
340 So wel they lovede, as olde bookes sayn,
That whan that oon was deed, soothly to telle,
His felawe wente and soughte hym doun in Helle![3]
But of that storie, list me nat° to write.   *I do not desire*
Duc Perotheus loved wel Arcite
345 And hadde hym knowe at Thebes yeer by yere.
And finally at requeste and preyere
Of Perotheus, withouten any raunsoun,
Duc Thesuus hym leet out of prisoun
Frely° to goon wher that hym liste overal   *freely*
350 In swich a gyse° as I you tellen shal.   *such a manner*
   This was the forward,° pleynly for
      t'endite,°   *agreement | to write it plainly*
Bitwixen Theseus and hym Arcite:
That if so were that Arcite were yfounde°   *found*
Evere in his lif by day or nyght or stounde°   *hour*
355 In any contree of this Theseus
And he were caught, it was acorded° thus: *agreed*
That with a swerd he sholde lese° his heed.°   *lose | head*
Ther nas noon oother remedie ne reed,°   *counsel*
But taketh his leve° and homward he him spedde.   *leave*
360 Lat hym bewar! His nekke lith to wedde!°   *lies as a pledge*
   How greet a sorwe suffreth now Arcite!

[1] *Wostow ... sawe* Do you not know well the old scholar's saying.
[2] *positif lawe* Positive law is that written into the statute books, as opposed to natural law, which is self-evident from God's creation.
[3] *His ... Helle* The classical legend is that Theseus accompanied Pirithous (Chaucer's Perotheus) to the Underworld in his unsuccessful attempt to rescue Proserpina, who had been abducted by Pluto, king of that region. Both men eventually returned alive, although Theseus was imprisoned and rescued by Hercules. The suggestion that Theseus went down to rescue Pirithous because he had died probably comes from the long thirteenth-century medieval allegory *The Romance of the Rose*, which Chaucer translated from French.

The deeth he feeleth thurgh his herte smyte!°   *strike*
He wepeth, wayleth, crieth pitously.
To sleen hymself he waiteth prively.°   *secretly*
365 He seyde, "Allas that day" that he "was born!¹
Now is my prisoun worse than biforn!
Now is me shape° eternally to dwelle   *ordained*
Nat in my Purgatorie but in Helle!
Allas, that evere knew I Perotheus,
370 For elles hadde I dwelled with Theseus
Yfetered° in his prisoun everemo!   *chained*
Thanne hadde I been in blisse and nat in wo!
Oonly the sighte of hire whom that I serve,
Though that I nevere hir grace may deserve,
375 Wolde han suffised right ynough for me!
O deere cosyn Palamon," quod he,
"Thyn is the victorie of this aventure.
Ful blissfully in prisoun maistow dure.°   *may you remain*
In prisoun? certes nay,° but in Paradys!   *no*
380 Wel hath Fortune yturned thee the dys°   *dice*
That hast the sighte of hire, and I th'absence.
For possible is, syn° thou hast hire presence   *since*
And art a knyght, a worthy and an able,
That som cas,° syn Fortune is chaungeable,   *(by) some event*
385 Thow maist to thy desir somtyme atteyne.°   *attain*
But I that am exiled and bareyne°   *lacking*
Of alle grace and in so greet dispeir
That ther nys° erthe, water, fir, ne eir,°   *is not / nor air*
Ne creature that of hem maked is
390 That may me heele° or doon confort° in
    this,   *heal / bring comfort*
Wel oughte I sterve in wanhope° and distresse!   *despair*
Farwel my lif,° my lust,° and my gladnesse!   *life / desire*
    "Allas, why pleynen° folk so in commune° *complain / commonly*
On° purveiaunce° of God or of Fortune   *against / foresight*
395 That yeveth hem° ful ofte in many a gyse°   *gives them / way*
Wel bettre than they kan hemself devyse?
Som man desireth for to han richesse
That cause is of his moerdre° or greet siknesse,   *murder*
And som man wolde out of his prisoun fayn°   *gladly (get)*
400 That in his hous is of his meynee° slayn.   *his retinue*

Infinite harmes been in this mateere.°   *matter*
We witen nat° what we preyen heere;°   *know not / pray for*
We faren° as he that dronke is as a mous.°   *behave / mouse*
A dronke man woot wel that he hath an hous,
405 But he noot° which the righte wey is
    thider,°   *does not know / there*
And to a dronke man the wey is slider.°   *slippery*
And certes in this world so faren° we: *fare*
We seken faste° after felicitee,°   *determinedly / happiness*
But we goon wrong ful often, trewely.
410 Thus may we seyn° alle and namely° I,   *see / especially*
That wende° and hadde a greet opinioun   *expected*
That if I myghte escapen from prisoun,
Thanne hadde I been in joye and parfit heele°   *well-being*
That now I am exiled fro my wele,°   *happiness*
415 Syn° that I may nat seen you, Emelye!   *since*
I nam° but deed! Ther nys no remedye!"   *am not*
    Upon that oother syde° Palamon,   *side*
Whan that he wiste Arcite was agon,°   *gone*
Swich sorwe° he maketh that the grete tour   *sorrow*
420 Resouned° of his youlyng° and clamour.   *resounded / yowling*
The pure fettres° on his shynes°
    grete°   *very chains / shins / swollen*
Weren of his bittre salte teeres wete.°   *wet*
"Allas," quod he, "Arcita, cosyn myn!
Of al oure strif,° God woot, the fruyt° is thyn!   *strife / fruit*
425 Thow walkest now in Thebes at thy large,°   *freely*
And of my wo thow yevest° litel° charge!   *give / little*
Thou mayst, syn° thou hast wisdom and
    manhede,°   *since / manhood*
Assemblen alle the folk of oure kynrede°   *kindred*
And make a werre so sharpe on this citee
430 That by som aventure or som tretee°   *treaty*
Thow mayst have hire° to lady and to wyf   *her*
For whom that I moste nedes lese° my lyf.   *lose*
For as by wey of possibilitee,
Sith thou art at thy large of prisoun free
435 And art a lord, greet is thyn avauntage
Moore than is myn that sterve here in a cage.
For I moot° wepe and wayle whil I lyve   *must*
With al the wo that prison may me yeve°   *give*
And eek with peyne that love me yeveth also
440 That doubleth al my torment and my wo!"
Therwith the fyr° of jalousie up sterte   *fire*
Withinne his brest and hente° him by the herte   *grabbed*
So woodly° that he lyk was to biholde   *madly*

---

¹ *Allas ... born* Many editions prefer the reading, found in several other manuscripts, "Allas the day that I was born." The Ellesmere variant (which we have preserved, although it may indeed be an error) would originally have been less awkward, since the quotation marks are a modern addition.

The boxtree[1] or the asshen° dede and colde.   *ashes*

445   Thanne seyde he, "O crueel goddes that governe
This world with byndyng° of youre word eterne   *binding*
And writen in the table of atthamaunt°   *adamant (diamond)*
Youre parlement and youre eterne graunt,°   *eternal decree*
What is mankynde moore unto you holde°   *indebted*
450   Than is the sheepe that ronketh° in the folde?   *huddles*
For slayn is man right as another beest
And dwelleth eek in prison and arreest°   *arrest*
And hath siknesse and greet adversitee
And ofte tymes giltlees,° pardee!°   *guiltless | by God*
455   What governance is in this prescience
That gildees tormenteth innocence?[2]
And yet encresseth° this al my penaunce,   *increases*
That man is bounden to his observaunce
For Goddes sake to letten of° his wille,   *restrain*
460   Theras° a beest may al his lust fulfille.   *whereas*
And whan a beest is deed, he hath no peyne,
But after his deeth man moot wepe and pleyne,
Though in this world he have care and wo;
Withouten doute it may stonden so!
465   The answere of this lete° I to dyvynys,°   *leave | religious scholars*
But wel I woot that in this world greet pyne ys.
Allas, I se° a serpent or a theef°   *see | thief*
That many a trewe man hath doon mescheef
Goon at his large° and where hym list may turne.   *go freely*
470   But I moot been in prisoun thurgh Saturne
And eek thurgh Juno,[3] jalous° and eek wood,°   *jealous | crazy*
That hath destroyed wel ny° al the blood   *very nearly*
Of Thebes with hise° waste° walles wyde,   *its | wasted*
And Venus sleeth me on that oother syde
475   For jalousie and fere° of hym Arcite."   *fear*
Now wol I stynte° of Palamon a lite°   *stop (speaking) | little*
And lete hym in his prisoun stille° dwelle   *quietly*
And of Arcita forth I wol yow telle.

The sonne passeth, and the nyghtes longe

Encressen doublewise° the peynes stronge   *double*
480   Bothe of the lovere and the prisoner.
I noot° which hath the wofuller°
mester.°   *do not know | sadder | profession*
For shortly for to seyn,° this Palamoun   *say*
Perpetuelly is dampned° to prisoun   *condemned*
485   In cheynes and in fettres to been deed,°   *to die*
And Arcite is exiled upon his heed°   *upon pain of losing his head*
Forever mo as out of that contree,
Ne nevere mo he shal his lady see.
Yow loveres, axe° I now this questioun: *ask*
490   Who hath the worse, Arcite or Palamoun?
That oon may seen his lady day by day,
But in prison he moot dwelle alway.
That oother wher hym list may ride or go,
But seen his lady shal he nevere mo.[4]
495   Now demeth° as you list, ye that kan,   *judge*
For I wol telle forth as I bigan.

EXPLICIT PRIMA PARS

SEQUITUR PARS SECUNDA[5]

Whan that Arcite to Thebes comen was,
Ful ofte a day he swelte° and seyde, "Allas,"   *fainted*
For seen his lady shal he nevere mo.
500   And shortly to concluden° al his wo,   *summarize*
So muche sorwe hadde nevere creature
That is or shal° whil° that the world may
dure.°   *shall be | while | endure*
His slepe, his mete,° his drynke is hym biraft°   *food | taken away*
That lene° he wexeth° and drye as is a shaft.° *lean | grows | arrow*
505   Hise eyen holwe° and grisly° to biholde,   *hollow | grim*
His hewe° falow° and pale as asshen colde, *complexion | yellow*
And solitarie he was and evere allone
And waillynge al the nyght, makynge his mone.°   *moan*
And if he herde song or instrument,
510   Thanne wolde he wepe. He myghte nat be stent.°   *stopped*
So feble eek were hise spiritz and so lowe
And chaunged so that no man koude knowe

---

[1]   *The boxtree* The box tree is known for its light yellow wood.
Palamon is as pale as ashes.

[2]   *What ... innocence* What governing principle is in this foresight
that torments innocent people who are guiltless?

[3]   *Juno* In Roman mythology, Juno, wife of Jupiter (king of the
gods), was the goddess of the hearth and of domesticity, and was
frequently jealous of Jupiter's love affairs. Juno hated Thebes
because of Jupiter's love affairs with the Theban women Semele,
mother of Bacchus, and Alcmena, mother of Hercules.

[4]   *But ... mo* This is a typical *demande d'amour* (French: question
of love) that sets forth a problem in the aristocratic code of love for
courtiers to debate.

[5]   *Explicit ... Secunda* Latin: Here ends the first part. The second
part follows.

His speche nor his voys,° though men it herde,   *voice*
And in his geere° for al the world he ferde°   *manner / fared*
515 Nat oonly lik the loveris maladye
Of hereos[1] but rather lyk manye°   *mania*
Engendred of humour malencolik[2]
Biforn his owene celle fantastik.[3]
And shortly, turned was al up so doun°   *upside-down*
520 Bothe habit and eek disposicioun
Of hym this woful lovere daun Arcite.°   *Sir Arcite*
    What sholde I al day of his wo endite?°   *write*
Whan he endured hadde a yeer or two
This crueel torment and this peyne and wo
525 At Thebes in his countree, as I seyde,
Upon a nyght in sleepe as he hym leyde,°   *lay*
Hym thoughte° how that the wynged god Mercurie[4]   *it seemed*
Biforn hym stood and bad° hym to be murie.°   *commanded / merry*
His slepy yerde° in hond he bar°
    uprighte;   *sleep-producing staff / bore*
530 An hat he werede° upon hise heris° brighte.   *wore / hairs*
Arrayed was this god, as I took keepe,°   *noticed*
As he was whan that Argus[5] took his sleepe,
And seyde hym thus: "To Atthenes shaltou
    wende.°   *shall you go*
Ther is thee shapen° of thy wo an ende."   *for you ordained*
535 And with that word Arcite wook° and sterte.°   *woke / got up*
"Now trewely, hou° soore° that me
    smerte,"°   *however / sore / it may injure*
Quod he, "to Atthenes right now wol I fare.°   *travel*
Ne for the drede of deeth shal I nat spare°   *avoid*
To se my lady that I love and serve.
540 In hire presence I recche nat° to sterve!"   *care not*
    And with that word he caughte° a greet mirour°   *seized / mirror*

And saugh° that chaunged was al his colour   *saw*
And saugh his visage° al in another kynde.°   *face / nature*
And right anon it ran hym in his mynde
545 That sith his face was so disfigured
Of maladye, the which he hadde endured,
He myghte wel, if that he bar hym lowe,°   *acted humbly*
Lyve in Atthenes everemoore unknowe
And seen his lady wel ny day by day.°   *nearly every day*
550 And right anon he chaunged his array°   *dress*
And cladde hym as a povre° laborer.   *poor*
And al allone save only a squier
That knew his privetee° and al his cas,°   *secret / case*
Which was disguised povrely as he was,
555 To Atthenes is he goon the nexte way,°   *shortest way*
And to the court he wente upon a day,
And at the gate he profreth° his servyse   *offered*
To drugge° and drawe° what so men wol
    devyse.°   *drudge / draw (water) / demand*
And shortly of this matere for to seyn,
560 He fil in office° with a chamberleyn°   *was employed / chamberlain*
The which that dwellynge was with Emelye,
For he was wys° and koude soone espye°   *wise / see*
Of every servaunt which that serveth here.°   *her*
Wel koude he hewen° wode and water bere,°   *cut / carry*
565 For he was yong and myghty for the nones.°   *occasion*
And therto he was long° and big of bones   *tall*
To doon that° any wight° kan hym devyse.   *whatever / person*
A yeer or two he was in this servyse,
Page° of the chambre° of Emelye the
    brighte,   *young servant / chamber*
570 And Philostrate[6] he seyde that he highte.°   *was named*
But half so wel biloved a man as he
Ne was ther nevere in court of his degree.
He was so gentil° of condicioun   *noble*
That thurghout al the court was his renoun.°   *renown*
575 They seyden that it were a charitee°   *would be an act of charity*
That Theseus wolde enhauncen his degree°   *promote him*
And putten hym in worshipful servyse°   *honorable service*
Theras° he myghte his vertu excercise.°   *where / demonstrate*
And thus withinne a while his name is spronge°   *spread about*
580 Bothe of hise dedes and his goode tonge,°   *elegant speech*
That Theseus hath taken hym so neer°   *close (to himself)*

---

[1] *hereos* Hereos or amor hereos was the name given for the "disease" of love.

[2] *humour malencolik* Melancholic humor is one of the four humors of the body according to classical and medieval medicinal theory. The other humors are the choleric, phlegmatic, and sanguine. Melancholic humor, of course, makes one sad—hence our word "melancholy."

[3] *celle fantastik* The portion of the brain where the imagination resided. The other two cells were those of memory and reason.

[4] *Mercurie* Roman messenger of the gods.

[5] *Argus* In Roman mythology, Argus had a hundred eyes and bore watch over Io, whom Jupiter loved. Mercury put him to sleep with his staff and then killed him.

---

[6] *Philostrate* Greek: one knocked down by love.

That of his chambre[1] he made hym a squier
And gaf° hym gold to mayntene° his
   degree.°   *gave / maintain / rank*
And eek men broghte hym out of his contree
585 From yeer to yeer ful pryvely° his rente.[2]   *privately*
But honestly and slyly° he it spente,   *discreetly*
That no man wondred how that he it hadde.
And thre yeer° in this wise° his lif he ladde° *years / way / led*
And bar hym° so, in pees° and eek in
   werre,°   *conducted himself / peace / war*
590 Ther was no man that Theseus hath derre.° *held more dear*
And in this blisse lete I now Arcite
And speke I wole of Palamon a lite.°   *little*
   In derknesse and horrible and strong prisoun
Thise seven yeer hath seten Palamoun
595 Forpyned,° what for wo and for distresse.   *tormented*
Who feeleth double soor° and hevynesse° *soreness / heaviness*
But Palamon that love destreyneth° so,   *afflicts*
That wood° out of his wit he goth° for wo? *crazy / goes*
And eek therto he is a prisoner
600 Perpetuelly, noght oonly for a yer.
   Who koude ryme° in Englyssh proprely   *rhyme*
His martirdom? Forsothe, it am nat I!
Therfore I passe as lightly° as I may.   *quickly*
   It fel that in the seventhe yer in May,
605 The thridde° nyght, as olde bookes seyn   *third*
That al this storie tellen moore pleyn,°   *plainly*
Were it° by aventure or destynee,   *whether it were*
As whan a thyng is shapen° it shal be,   *ordained*
That soone after the mydnyght Palamoun
610 By helpyng of a freend° brak° his prisoun *friend / escaped*
And fleeth° the citee faste as he may go.   *flees*
For he hadde yeve° his gayler° drynke so, *given / jailor*
Of a clarree° maad° of a certeyn wyn *spiced drink / made*
Of nercotikes° and opie° of Thebes fyn° *narcotics / opium / fine*
615 That al that nyght thogh that men wolde him shake,

This gayler sleepe; he myghte nat awake!
And thus he fleeth as faste as evere he may.
The nyght was short and faste by the day° *it was almost day*
That nedes cost° he moot° hymselven hyde, *necessarily / must*
620 And til° a grove faste therbisyde°   *to / nearby*
With dredeful° foot thanne stalketh°
   Palamon.   *fearful / walks quietly*
For shortly, this was his opinion
That in that grove he wolde hym hyde al day,
And in the nyght thanne wolde he take his way
625 To Thebesward,° his freendes for to preye° *towards Thebes / ask*
On Theseus to helpe hym to werreye.°   *make war*
And shortly outher° he wolde lese° his lif *either / lose*
Or wynnen° Emelye unto his wyf.   *win*
This is th'effect and his entente pleyn.°   *plain intent*
630 Now wol I turne to Arcite ageyn,°   *again*
That litel wiste how ny° that was his care,   *near*
Til that Fortune had broght him in the snare.
   The bisy larke, messager of day,
Salueth° in hir song the morwe gray,   *salutes*
635 And firy Phebus[3] riseth up so brighte
That al the orient° laugheth of the lighte   *east*
And with hise stremes° dryeth° in the
   greves°   *beams / dries / branches*
The silver dropes hangynge on the leves.°   *leaves*
And Arcita that is in the court roial
640 With Theseus, his squier principal,
Is risen and looketh on the myrie° day.   *merry*
And for to doon his observaunce to May,[4]
Remembrynge on the poynt° of his desir,   *point*
He on a courser° startlynge° as the fir° *war-horse / prancing / fire*
645 Is riden into the feeldes° hym to pleye.   *fields*
Out of the court were it a myle° or tweye,   *mile*
And to the grove of which that I yow tolde
By aventure his wey he gan to holde
To maken hym a gerland of the greves,°   *branches*
650 Were it of wodebynde° or hawethorn
   leves.°   *woodbine / hawthorn leaves*
And loude he song ayeyn the sonne shene,° *in the bright sunshine*
"May, with alle thy floures and thy grene,°   *green*
Welcome be thou, faire, fresshe May,

---

1 *That of his chambre* Medieval English kings relied heavily on knights of their chamber for administrative duties of government. Originally servants who performed various domestic functions, these people had honorific titles implying these duties but took on the duties of governmental administration instead.

2 *From … rente* The rent here referred to is not something Arcite must pay but what is owed to him. Medieval lords possessed land and were owed various rents and services from those whom they allowed use it. A high lord like Arcite would have had much income from such sources.

3 *Phebus* Name for Apollo, god of the sun.

4 *And … May* The custom was for courtly people to rise early in mornings in May and roam about in the countryside to enjoy the good weather that had recently returned.

In hope that I som grene° gete may."   *something green*
And from his courser° with a lusty
    herte°   *war-horse | spirited heart*
Into a grove ful hastily he sterte,
And in a path he rometh° up and doun   *roams*
Theras° by aventure this Palamoun   *where*
Was in a bussh that no man myghte hym se,°   *see*
For soore aferd of his deeth thanne was he.
Nothyng ne knew he° that it was Arcite.   *he did not know*
God woot, he wolde have trowed° it ful lite!°   *believed | very little*
But sooth is seyd, so sithen° many yeres,°   *after | years*
That "Feeld hath eyen and the wode° hath eres."°   *wood | ears*
It is ful fair a man to bere hym evene,
For al day meeteth men at unset stevene.[1]
Ful litel woot Arcite of his felawe
That was so ny to herknen° al his sawe,°   *listen to | speech*
For in the bussh he sitteth now ful stille.

    Whan that Arcite hadde romed all his fille
And songen al the roundel[2] lustily,
Into a studie° he fil° al sodeynly,   *meditative mood | fell*
As doon thise loveres in hir queynte° geres.°   *curious | customs*
Now in the crope,° now doun in the breres,°   *tree-top | briars*
Now up, now doun as boket° in a welle.   *bucket*
Right as the Friday, soothly°for to telle,   *truly*
Now it shyneth, now it reyneth° faste: *rains*
Right so kan geery° Venus overcaste   *fickle*
The hertes of hir folk. Right as hir day[3]
Is gereful,° right so chaungeth she array.   *fickle*
Selde° is the Friday al the wowke
    ylike.°   *seldom | like the rest of the week*
    Whan that Arcite had songe,° he gan to sike°   *sung | sigh*
And sette hym doun withouten any moore.
"Allas," quod he, "that day that I was bore!
How longe, Juno, thurgh thy crueltee
Woltow werreyen° Thebes the citee?   *make war on*

Allas, ybroght° is to confusioun   *brought*
The blood roial of Cadme and Amphioun[4]—
Of Cadmus which that was the firste man
That Thebes bulte,° or first the toun bigan,   *built*
And of the citee first was crouned kyng.
Of his lynage am I and his ofspryng
By verray ligne° as of the stok° roial,   *true lineage | stock*
And now I am so caytyf° and so thral,°   *captive | enslaved*
That he that is my mortal enemy
I serve hym as his squier povrely.°   *poorly*
And yet dooth Juno me wel moore° shame,   *much more*
For I dar noght biknowe° myn owene name!   *reveal*
But theras I was wont to highte Arcite,
Now highte I Philostrate, noght worth a myte!°   *small coin*
Allas, thou felle° Mars,[5] allas, Juno!   *cruel*
Thus hath youre ire° oure kynrede° al
    fordo,°   *anger | kindred | destroyed*
Save oonly me and wrecched Palamoun
That Theseus martireth° in prisoun.   *martyrs*
And over al this to sleen me outrely,°   *completely*
Love hath his firy dart so brennyngly°   *burningly*
Ystiked° thurgh my trewe,° careful° herte,   *stuck | true | sorrowful*
That shapen° was my deeth° erst than my
    sherte.[6]   *ordained | death | shirt*
Ye sleen me with youre eyen, Emelye!
Ye been the cause wherfore that I dye!
Of al the remenant of myn oother care,
Ne sette I nat° the montance° of a tare,°   *I do not set | value | weed*
So that I koude doon aught to youre plesaunce."
And with that word he fil doun in a traunce
A longe tyme, and after he up sterte.

    This Palamoun that thoughte that thurgh his herte
He felte a coold swerd sodeynliche° glyde,   *suddenly*
For ire° he quook.° No lenger wolde he
    byde.°   *anger | shook | wait*
And whan that he had herd Arcites tale,
As he were wood,° with face deed° and pale,   *crazy | dead*
He stirte hym up out of the buskes° thikke°   *bushes | thick*
And seide, "Arcite, false traytour wikke,°   *wicked*
Now artow° hent° that lovest my lady so,   *are you | caught*

---

[1] *It ... stevene* It is very desirable for a man to behave with restraint, for every day people meet at an unexpected time.

[2] *roundel* Type of popular song in both France and England in the fourteenth century. It was characterized by repeated phrases of both music and words.

[3] *Right as hir day* The days of the week were originally devoted to the various gods and goddesses, as our names for them still attest (Saturn's day—Saturday; Thor's day—Thursday). Venus's day was Friday (*Veneris dies*) in the Romance languages; the Germanic goddess most resembling Venus was named Freya.

[4] *Cadme and Amphioun* Earlier kings of Thebes.

[5] *Mars* Roman god of war.

[6] *That ... sherte* The reference here is probably to the *first* shirt made for Arcite when he was a baby.

For whom that I have al this peyne and wo!

725 And art my blood° and to my conseil°   *of my blood | counsel*
        sworn,

As I ful ofte have seyd thee heer biforn,

And hast byjaped° heere Duc Theseus   *tricked*

And falsly chaunged hast thy name thus—

I wol be deed or elles thou shalt dye!

730 Thou shalt nat love my lady Emelye!

But I wol love hire oonly and namo,°   *no more*

For I am Palamon, thy mortal foo!°   *foe*

And though that I no wepene have in this place,

But out of prison am astert° by grace,   *escaped*

735 I drede noght° that outher° thow shalt dye   *fear not | either*

Or thow ne shalt nat loven Emelye.

Chees° which thou wolt,° or thou shalt nat   *choose | wish*
        asterte!”

    This Arcite, with ful despitous° herte,   *scornful*

Whan he hym knew° and hadde his tale herd,   *recognized*

740 As fiers as leoun pulled out his swerd

And seyd thus: “By God that sit above,

Nere it° that thou art sik° and wood for love,   *were it not | sick*

And eek that thow no wepne° hast in this place,   *weapon*

Thou sholdest nevere out of this grove pace°   *escape*

745 That thou ne sholdest dyen of° myn hond!   *by*

For I defye° the seurete° and the bond   *defy | promise*

Which that thou seist that I have maad° to thee.   *made*

What, verray fool, thynk wel that love is free,

And I wol love hire maugree° al thy myght!   *despite*

750 But for as muche thou art a worthy knyght

And wilnest to darreyne hire by bataille,[1]

Have heer° my trouthe:° tomorwe I wol nat faille,   *here | vow*

Withoute wityng° of any oother wight,°   *the knowledge | person*

That heere I wol be founden as a knyght,

755 And bryngen harneys° right ynough° for thee,   *armor | enough*

And chese the best and leve the worste for me.

And mete° and drynke this nyght wol I brynge   *food*

Ynough for thee and clothes for thy beddynge.

And if so be that thou my lady wynne°   *win*

760 And sle° me in this wode ther I am inne,°   *kill | in*

Thow mayst wel have thy lady as for me!”

    This Palamon answerde, “I graunte it thee!”

And thus they been departed til amorwe,°   *the next day*

Whan ech of hem had leyd his feith° to   *word | as a pledge*
        borwe.°

765 O Cupide,[2] out of all charitee!

O regne,° that wolt no felawe° have with thee!   *reign | equal*

Ful sooth is seyd that love ne lordshipe

Wol noght, hir thankes, have no felaweshipe.[3]

Wel fynden that Arcite and Palamoun!

770 Arcite is riden anon unto the toun,

And on the morwe er it were dayes light

Ful prively two harneys° hath he dight,°   *suits of armor | prepared*

Bothe suffisaunt° and mete° to   *sufficient | fitting | decide*
        darreyne°

The bataille in the feeld bitwix hem tweyne.

775 And on his hors allone as he was born

He carieth al the harneys hym biforn.

And in the grove at tyme and place yset,°   *appointed*

This Arcite and this Palamon ben° met.   *are*

To chaungen gan the colour in hir° face,   *their*

780 Right as the hunters in the regne of
        Trace°   *(Greek) kingdom of Thrace*

That stondeth at the gappe° with a spere,°   *gap | spear*

Whan hunted is the leoun and the bere°   *bear*

And hereth hym come russhyng in the greves°   *brush*

And breketh bothe bowes and the leves

785 And thynketh, “Heere cometh my mortal enemy!

Withoute faille, he moot be deed or I!

For outher I moot sleen hym at the gappe

Or he moot sleen me if that me myshappe”°—   *I am unlucky*

So ferden° they in chaungyng of hir hewe   *fared*

790 As fer as everich of hem oother knewe.°   *knew the other*

    Ther nas no° good day ne no saluyng,°   *was neither | saluting*

But streight° withouten word or
        rehersyng°   *immediately | conversation*

Everich of hem heelpe for to armen oother°   *to arm the other*

As freenly° as he were his owene brother.   *friendly*

795 And after that with sharpe speres stronge

They foynen° ech at oother wonder° longe.   *thrust | wonderfully*

Thou myghtest wene° that this Palamoun   *expect*

In his fightyng were a wood leoun,

And as a crueel tigre was Arcite.

800 As wilde bores gonne° they to smyte,   *began*

---

[1] *And ... bataille* And wish to vindicate your right to her by battle.

[2] *Cupide* Cupid, son of Venus, is the Roman god of love.

[3] *Ful ... felaweshipe* Truly it is said that neither love nor lordship will willingly have company.

That frothen whit as foom for ire wood.[1]
Up to the anclee° foghte they in hir blood,   ankle
And in this wise I lete hem fightyng dwelle°   still fighting
And forth I wole of Theseus yow telle.

805   The destinee, ministre° general   agent
That executeth in the world over al
The purveiaunce° that God hath seyn° biforn,   foresight / seen
So strong it is that though the world had sworn
The contrarie of a thyng by ye or nay,
810   Yet somtyme it shal fallen° on a day   happen
That falleth nat eft° withinne a thousand yeere.   not again
For certeinly oure appetites heere,
Be it of werre or pees° or hate or love,   war or peace
Al is this reuled° by the sighte above.   ruled
815   This mene° I now by myghty Theseus,   mean
That for to hunten is so desirus,°   eager
And namely at the grete hert° in May,   deer
That in his bed ther daweth° hym no day   dawns
That he nys clad° and redy° for to ryde   is not clothed / ready
820   With hunte and horn and houndes hym bisyde,
For in his huntyng hath he swich delit
That it is al his joye and appetit°   desire
To been hymself the grete hertes bane.°   slayer
For after Mars he serveth now Dyane.[2]
825   Cleer was the day, as I have toold er this,
And Theseus with alle joye and blis
With his Ypolita the faire queene
And Emelye clothed al in grene
On huntyng° be they riden° roially.   a-hunting / are they riding
830   And to the grove that stood ful faste by°   very nearby
In which ther was an hert, as men hym tolde,
Duc Theseus the streighte wey° hath holde.°   road / has held
And to the launde° he rideth hym ful right,°   clearing / directly
For thider° was the hert wont° have his flight, there / accustomed
835   And over a brook and so forth in his weye,
This duc wol han a cours° at hym or tweye   chase
With houndes swiche as hym list comaunde.°   to command
    And whan this duc was come unto the launde
Under the sonne he looketh. And anon
840   He was war° of Arcite and Palamon,   aware
That foughten breme° as it were bores° two.   boldly / boars

The brighte swerdes wenten to and fro
So hidously that with the leeste strook°   stroke
It semed as it wolde fille° an ook!°   fell / oak
845   But what they were, nothyng he ne woot.[3]
This duc his courser with his spores° smoot,°   spurs / struck
And at a stert° he was bitwix hem two   in an instant
And pulled out a swerd and cride, "Hoo!°   whoa!
Namoore, upon peyne of lesynge° of youre heed!   losing
850   By myghty Mars, he shal anon be deed
That smyteth any strook° that I may seen.   stroke
But telleth me what mystiers men ye been[4]
That been so hardy° for to fighten here   bold
Withouten juge° or oother officere   judge (referee)
855   As it were in a lystes° roially."   jousting ground
    This Palamon answerde hastily
And seyde, "Sire, what nedeth wordes mo?
We have the deeth disserved bothe two.[5]
Two woful wrecches been we, two caytyves°   wretches
860   That been encombred of° oure owene lyves.   burdened by
And as thou art a rightful lord and juge,
Ne yeve° us neither mercy ne refuge.   do not give
But sle° me first, for Seinte Charitee,[6]   slay
But sle my felawe eek as wel as me.
865   Or sle hym first! For though thow knowest it lite,°   little
This is thy mortal foo.° This is Arcite   foe
That fro thy lond is banysshed on his heed,[7]
For which he hath deserved to be deed.
For this is he that cam unto thy gate
870   And seyde that he highte Philostrate.
Thus hath he japed° thee ful many a yer,   fooled
And thou hast maked hym thy chief squire,
And this is he that loveth Emelye.

_____

[3] _But ... woot_ He did not know anything about who they were.

[4] _But ... been_ But tell me what occupation you follow, i.e., what kind of men you are. Mystiers is cognate with mystery, which in the Middle Ages meant a trade or occupation and gave the name to the religious plays the trade guilds put on in various cities—mystery plays.

[5] _We ... two_ They deserve death because of the terms of their conditional sentence: Palamon must stay in prison or die, while Arcite must remain in exile or die.

[6] _Seinte Charitee_ Holy Charity. Charity is the old word for God's love.

[7] _banysshed on his heed_ Banished with the consequence of losing his head should he return without pardon.

_____

[1] _That ... wood_ That froth (at the mouth), white as foam, with raging anger.

[2] _Dyane_ Roman goddess of the hunt.

For sith the day is come that I shal dye,
875 I make pleynly° my confessioun   *fully*
That I am thilke° woful Palamoun   *the same*
That hath thy prisoun broken° wikkedly.   *escaped*
I am thy mortal foo, and it am I
That loveth so hoote° Emelye the brighte,   *hotly*
880 That I wol dye,° present in hir sighte.   *die*
Wherfore I axe° deeth and my juwise.°   *ask / sentence*
But sle my felawe in the same wise,
For bothe han we deserved to be slayn!"
    This worthy duc answerde anon agayn
885 And seyde, "This is a short conclusioun!°   *quick decision*
Youre owene mouth by youre confessioun
Hath dampned° yow, and I wol it recorde.   *damned*
It nedeth noght to pyne yow with the corde:[1]
Ye shal be deed, by myghty Mars the rede!"°   *red*
890   The queene anon for verray wommanhede°   *womanhood*
Gan for to wepe and so dide Emelye
And alle the ladyes in the compaignye.
Greet pitee was it as it thoughte hem alle,°   *it seemed to them*
That evere swich a chaunce° sholde falle.°   *event / happen*
895 For gentil men they were, of greet estaat,
And no thyng but for love was this debaat,°   *quarrel*
And saugh hir blody woundes wyde and soore
And alle crieden° bothe lasse and
        moore,°   *cried / the lesser and the greater*
"Have mercy, lord, upon us wommen alle!"
900 And on hir bare knees adoun they falle
And wolde have kist° his feet theras° he stood, *kissed / where*
Til at the laste aslaked° was his mood.   *calmed*
For pitee renneth° soone in gentil herte.   *runs*
And though he first for ire quook° and sterte,   *shook*
905 He hath considered shortly° in a clause   *briefly*
The trespas° of hem bothe and eek the cause.   *crime*
And although that his ire hir gilt° accused,   *their guilt*
Yet in his resoun° he hem bothe excused   *reason*
As thus: he thoghte wel that every man
910 Wol° helpe hymself in love if that he kan°   *will*
And eek delivere hymself out of prisoun.
And eek his herte hadde compassioun
Of wommen, for they wepen evere in oon.°   *in unity*
And in his gentil herte he thoughte anon
915 And softe unto hymself he seyde, "Fy°   *shame*

Upon a lord that wol have no mercy
But been a leoun bothe in word and dede
To hem that been in repentaunce and drede,
As wel as to a proud, despitous° man   *scornful*
920 That wol mayntene that he first bigan.
That lord hath litel of discrecioun
That in swich cas kan° no divisioun   *knows*
But weyeth° pride and humblesse after oon."° *weighs / equally*
And shortly, whan his ire is thus agoon,°   *gone*
925 He gan to looken up with eyen lighte
And spak thise same wordes al on highte:°   *aloud*
"The god of love, a, *benedicite*,°[2]   *bless you*
How myghty and how greet a lord is he!
Ayeyns° his myght ther gayneth° none
        obstacles!   *against / prevails*
930 He may be cleped° a god for hise myracles.   *called*
For he kan maken at his owene gyse°   *in his own way*
Of everich herte as that hym list divyse.° *as he wishes to arrange*
Lo heere this Arcite and this Palamon,
That quitly° weren out of my prisoun   *freely*
935 And myghte han lyved in Thebes roially,
And witen° I am hir mortal enemy   *know*
And that hir deth lith° in my myght also,   *lies*
And yet hath love maugree hir° eyen two[3]   *despite their*
Broght hem hyder° bothe for to dye.   *here*
940 Now looketh: is nat that an heigh° folye?   *great*
Who may been a fool but if he love?°   *unless he who loves*
Bihoold, for Goddes sake that sit above:
Se how they blede! Be they noght wel arrayed?°   *decorated*
Thus hath hir lord, the god of love, ypayed°   *paid*
945 Hir wages and hir fees for hir servyse!
And yet they wenen for to been ful
        wyse°   *consider (themselves) very wise*
That serven love, for aught that may
        bifalle.°   *anything that may happen*
But this is yet the beste gam° of alle,   *game*
That she for whom they han° this jolitee°   *have / amusement*
950 Kan° hem therfore as muche thank as me.   *owes*
She woot namoore° of al this hoote°
        fare,°   *knows no more / rash / business*

---

1 *It ... corde*   There is no need to torture you with a rope (i.e., with
a rope twisted about the prisoner's head).

2 *benedicite*   Latin: bless you.

3 *maugree ... two*   Despite anything they could do.

By God, than woot a cokkow° of an hare.[1]   *cuckoo*
But al moot been assayed,° hoot and coold!   *tried*
A man moot been a fool or yong or oold.[2]

955 I woot it by myself ful yore agon,°   *very long ago*
For in my tyme a servant[3] was I oon,
And therfore syn° I knowe of loves peyne   *since*
And woot hou soore° it kan a man
    distreyne,°   *how painfully / afflict*
As he that hath been caught ofte in his laas,°   *trap*
960 I yow° foryeve° al hoolly° this trespass   *you / forgive / completely*
At requeste of the queene that kneleth heere
And eek of Emelye, my suster deere.°   *dear sister(-in-law)*
And ye shul bothe anon unto me swere
That nevere mo ye shal my contree° dere,°   *country / harm*
965 Ne make werre° upon me nyght ne day   *war*
But been my freendes in al that ye may.
I yow foryeve this trespas every deel."°   *completely*
And they hym sworen his axyng° faire and weel   *asking*
And hym of lordshipe° and of mercy
    preyde,°   *his protection as lord*
970 And he hem graunteth grace,° and thus he seyde: *his favor*
    "To speke of roial lynage and richesse,
Though that she were a queene or a princesse,
Ech of you bothe is worthy, doutelees,
To wedden whan tyme is, but nathelees—
975 I speke as for my suster Emelye,
For whom ye have this strif° and jalousye.   *strife*
Ye woot yourself she may nat wedden two
Atones,° though ye fighten everemo.   *at once*
That oon of you, al be hym looth or lief,° *whether he likes it or not*
980 He moot pipen in an yvy leef.°[4]   *pipe in an ivy leaf*
This is to seyn, she may nat now han bothe,
Al be° ye never so jalouse ne so wrothe.   *although*
And forthy° I yow putte in this degree,°   *therefore / situation*
That ech of yow shal have his destynee
985 As hym is shape,° and herkneth in what wyse;°   *ordained / way*
Lo heere° youre ende of that I shal devyse.   *here is*

"My wyl° is this for plat° conclusioun,   *will / plain*
Withouten any repplicacioun:°   *reply*
If that you liketh, take it for the beste,
990 That everich° of you shal goon where hym leste   *each*
Frely° withouten raunson or daunger,   *freely*
And this day fifty wykes fer ne ner[5]
Everich of you shal brynge an hundred knyghtes
Armed for lystes° up at alle rightes,°[6]   *arena / points*
995 Al redy° to darreyne° hire by bataille.   *ready / decide*
And this bihote° I yow withouten faille°   *promise / fail*
Upon my trouthe and as I am a knyght:
That wheither of yow bothe that hath myght,
This is to seyn, that wheither he or thow
1000 May with his hundred as I spak° of now   *spoke*
Sleen his contrarie° or out of lystes dryve,   *opponent*
Thanne shal I yeve° Emelya to wyve   *give*
To whom that Fortune yeveth so fair a grace.
The lystes shal I maken in this place,
1005 And God so wisly° on my soule rewe,°   *wisely / have mercy*
As I shal evene° juge been and trewe.   *fair*
Ye shul noon oother ende° with me maken,   *resolution*
That oon of yow ne shal be deed or taken.°   *captured*
And if yow thynketh this is weel ysayd,°   *well said*
1010 Seyeth youre avys° and holdeth you apayd.° *opinion / satisfied*
This is youre ende and youre conclusioun."
    Who looketh lightly now but Palamoun?
Who spryngeth up for joye but Arcite?
Who kouthe° telle or who kouthe endite°   *could / write*
1015 The joye that is maked in the place
Whan Theseus hath doon so fair a grace?°   *behaved so graciously*
But doun on knees wente every maner wight° *manner of person*
And thonken hym with al hir herte and myght,
And namely the Thebans often sithe.°   *many times*
1020 And thus with good hope and with herte blithe°   *happy*
They taken hir leve and homward gonne° they ride   *began*
To Thebes with hise° olde walles wyde.   *its*

EXPLICIT SECUNDA PARS

---

[1] *of an hare* Many editors prefer the reading "or a hare," which is found in many manuscripts, but "less than a cuckoo knows about a hare" also makes sense.

[2] *A … oold* A man must be a fool, either when he is young or when he is old.

[3] *For … servant* I.e., a servant of Cupid.

[4] *pipen in an yvy leef* I.e., make an attempt at an impossible task.

---

[5] *fifty … ner* Fifty weeks from this day, neither more nor less.

[6] *Armed … rightes* Lists were the spaces fenced off for a medieval tournament, in which knights fought in two groups, and for individual jousts. The description of the lists set up by Theseus in the lines below, however, is based on accounts of Roman arenas, like the Coliseum in Rome.

SEQUITUR PARS TERTIA[1]

	I trowe° men wolde deme° it necligence	*believe / judge*
	If I foryete° to tellen the dispence°	*forget / expense*
1025	Of Theseus that gooth so bisily	
	To maken up the lystes° roially	*arena*
	That swich a noble theatre° as it was,	*amphitheater*
	I dar wel seyn in this world ther nas.°	*was not*
	The circuit a myle was aboute,	
1030	Walled of stoon° and dyched° al withoute.	*stone / ditched*
	Round was the shape, in manere of compas,	
	Ful of degrees, the heighte of sixty pas,°	*spaces*
	That whan a man was set on o° degree,	*one*
	He lette nat° his felawe for to see.	*hindered not*
1035	Estward ther stood a gate of marbul whit,°	*white marble*
	Westward right swich another in the opposit.	
	And shortly to concluden, swich a place	
	Was noon in erthe° as in so litel space,	*earth*
	For in the lond ther was no crafty° man	*skillful*
1040	That geometrie or ars metrik° kan,°	*arithmetic / knew*
	Ne portreitour,° ne kervere° of ymages°	*portrait-painter / carver / statues*
	That Theseus ne yaf° mete° and wages	*did not give / food*
	The theatre for to maken and devyse.	
	And for to doon his ryte° and sacrifise	*ceremonies*
1045	He estward hath upon the gate above	
	In worshipe of Venus, goddesse of love,	
	Doon make° an auter° and an oratorie,°	*had made / altar / chapel*
	And on the westward in memorie	
	Of Mars, he maked hath right swich° another,	*just such*
1050	That coste largely of gold a fother.[2]	
	And northward in a touret° on the wal	*turret*
	Of alabastre° whit and reed° coral	*alabaster / red*
	An oratorie riche for to see	
	In worshipe of Dyane of chastitee	
1055	Hath Theseus doon wrought in noble wyse.°	*manner*
	But yet hadde I foryeten° to devyse°	*forgotten / describe*
	The noble kervyng° and the portraitures,°	*carving / portraits*
	The shape, the contenaunce, and the figures	
	That weren in thise oratories thre.	
1060	First, in the temple of Venus maystow se°	*you may see*

	Wroght on the wal ful pitous° to biholde	*pitiful*
	The broken slepes° and the sikes° colde,	*sleeps / sighs*
	The sacred teeris° and the waymentynge,°	*tears / lamentation*
	The firy strokes and the desirynge	
1065	That loves servantz° in this lyf enduren,	*love's servants*
	The othes° that hir covenantz assuren,°	*oaths / assure*
	Plesaunce° and Hope, Desir, Foolhardynesse,	*pleasure*
	Beautee and Youthe, Bauderie,° Richesse,	*bawdiness*
	Charmes and Force, Lesynges,° Flaterye,	*lies*
1070	Despense,° Bisyness,° and Jalousye,	*spending / anxiety*
	That wered° of yelewe° gooldes° a gerland	*wore / yellow / marigolds*
	And a cokkow° sittynge on hir hand.	*cuckoo*
	Festes,° instrumentz, caroles,[3] daunces,	*feasts*
	Lust,° and array,° and all the circumstaunces	*pleasure / dress*
1075	Of love, whiche that I rekned° have and rekne shal,	*reckoned*
	By ordre weren peynted on the wal,	
	And mo than I kan make of mencioun.°	*make mention*
	For soothly, al the Mount of Citheroun[4]	
	Ther° Venus hath hir principal dwellynge,	*where*
1080	Was shewed on the wal in portreyynge°	*painting*
	With al the gardyn and the lustynesse.	
	Nat was forgeyten the porter Ydelnesse	
	Ne Narcius[5] the faire of yore agon,°	*days of old*
	And yet the folye of Kyng Salomon,[6]	
1085	And eek the grete strengthe of Ercules,°	*Hercules*
	Th'enchauntementz of Medea and Circes,[7]	
	Ne of Turnus[8] with the hardy fiers corage,	
	The riche Cresus,[9] kaytyf° in servage.°	*captive / servitude*

---

[3] *caroles* Dances performed to the accompaniment of singing.

[4] *Mount of Citheroun* In Roman mythology, Venus rose from the sea fully-formed at the island of Cythera. In a number of medieval texts, including *The Knight's Tale,* Mount Cithaeron is confused with this island.

[5] *Narcius* Narcissus fell in love with his own image when he saw it in a pool. See Ovid's *Metamorphoses.*

[6] *folye of Kyng Salomon* King Solomon, famously the wisest of men, fell into folly under the influence of the many wives and concubines in his harem.

[7] *Medea and Circes* In Greek mythology, Medea and Circe were sorceresses. They were in love with Jason and Odysseus respectively.

[8] *Turnus* In the later books of Virgil's *Aeneid,* Turnus is Aeneas's main antagonist and his rival for the hand of Lavinia in marriage.

[9] *The riche Cresus* In Roman mythology, Croesus, King of Lydia, was fabulously rich but died a wretched death, captured by Cyrus.

---

[1] *Explicit … Tertia* Latin: Here ends the second part. The third part follows.

[2] *That … fother* That cost many a cart-load of gold.

Thus may ye seen that wysdom ne richesse,
1090 Beautee ne sleighte,° strengthe, hardynesse   *trickery*
Ne may° with Venus holde
    champartie.°   *may not / equal partnership*
For as hir list,° the world than° may she
    gye.°   *she desires / then / rule*
Lo, alle thise folk so caught were in hir las,°   *snare*
Til they for wo ful ofte seyde, "Allas!"
1095 Suffiseth° heere ensamples° oon or two,   *it is enough / examples*
And though I koude rekene a thousand mo.

    The statue of Venus glorious for to se
Was naked, fletynge° in the large see,°   *floating / sea*
And fro° the navele doun al covered was   *from*
1100 With wawes° grene and brighte as any glas.   *waves*
A citole[1] in hir right hand hadde she,
And on hir heed, ful semely° for to se,   *very beautiful*
A rose gerland fressh and wel smellynge;°   *sweet smelling*
Above hir heed hir dowves° flikerynge.°   *doves / fluttering*
1105 Biforn hire stood hir sone Cupido.
Upon his shuldres wynges hadde he two,
And blynd° he was as it was often seene.   *blind*
A bowe he bar° and arwes° brighte and
    kene.°   *carried / arrows / sharp*
    Why sholde I noght° as wel eek telle yow al   *not*
1110 The portreiture that was upon the wal
Withinne the temple of myghty Mars the rede?
Al peynted was the wal in lengthe and brede°   *breadth*
Lyk to the estres° of the grisly place   *interior*
That highte° the grete temple of Mars in
    Trace°   *was called / Thrace*
1115 In thilke° colde, frosty regioun   *the same*
Theras° Mars hath his sovereyn° mansioun.[2]   *where / chief*
    First on the wal was peynted a forest
In which ther dwelleth neither man ne best,
With knotty, knarry,° bareyne° trees olde,   *gnarled / barren*
1120 Of stubbes° sharpe and hidouse° to biholde,   *stumps / hideous*
In which ther ran a rumbel° and a   *rumble / rush of wind*
    swough°
As though a storm sholde bresten° every bough.   *break*

---

[1] *A citole* Musical instrument that had a fingerboard and was plucked with a plectrum. It was a distant descendant of the classical lyre.

[2] *mansioun* A "mansion" of a god/planet was, in astrological terms, its appropriate region in the sky, but here the reference is to Mars's greatest temple, in Thracia in northern Greece.

And dounward from an hille under a bente,°   *slope*
Ther stood the temple of Mars Armypotente,°   *powerful in arms*
1125 Wroght al of burned° steel of which the
    entree°   *polished / entrance*
Was long and streit° and gastly for to see.   *narrow*
And therout cam a rage° and swich a veze,°   *roar of wind / blast*
That it made al the gate for to rese.°   *shake*
The northren lyght in at the dores° shoon,   *doors*
1130 For wyndowe on the wal ne was ther noon
Thurgh which men myghten any light discerne.
The dore was al of adamant eterne,°   *eternal*
Yclenched° overthwart° and
    endelong°   *supported / crosswise / lengthwise*
With iren tough, and for to make it strong
1135 Every pyler° the temple to sustene   *pillar*
Was tonne-greet° of iren° bright and shene.   *big as a barrel / iron*
    Ther saugh I first the dirke ymaginyng°   *dark plotting*
Of Felonye° and the compassyng,°   *crime / scheming*
The crueel Ire, reed° as any gleede,°   *red / ember*
1140 The pykepurs° and the pale Drede,°   *pick-pocket / dread*
The smylere° with the knyf° under the
    cloke,°   *smiler / knife / cloak*
The shepne° brennynge° with the blake smoke,   *stable / burning*
The tresoun of the mordrynge° in the bedde,°   *murdering / bed*
The open werre° with woundes al bibledde,°   *war / bleeding*
1145 Contek° with blody knyf and sharpe manace;°   *conflict / menace*
Al ful of chirkyng° was that sory° place.[3]   *groaning / sorry*
The sleere of hymself° yet saugh° I ther: *suicide / saw*
His herte blood hath bathed al his heer,°   *hair*
The nayl° ydryven° in the shode°
    anyght,°   *nail / driven / temple / at night*
1150 The colde deeth with mouth gapyng upright.
Amyddes° of the temple sat
    Meschaunce°   *in the middle / misfortune*
With disconfort° and sory contenaunce.   *distress*
Yet saugh I Woodnesse° laughynge in his rage,   *madness*
Armed Compleint,° Outhees,° and fiers
    Outrage.°   *grievance / outcry / violence*
1155 The careyne° in the busk° with throte
    ycorne,°   *corpse / forest / cut throat*
A thousand slayn and nat oon of qualm
    ystorve,°   *killed by plague*

---

[3] *The tresoun ... place* The images and statues on the walls of the temple of Mars show the planet's influence, which causes not only war but other sorts of violence and catastrophe.

The tiraunt° with the pray° by force yraft,°   *tyrant / prey / seized*
The toun° destroyed: ther was nothyng laft!   *town*
Yet saugh I brent° the shippes
    hoppesteres,°   *burned / dancing ships*
1160 The hunte° strangled with° the wilde
    beres,°   *hunter / killed by / bears*
The sowe° freten° the child right in the cradel,   *sow / eat*
The cook yscalded° for al his longe ladel.°   *scalded / ladle*
Noght was foryeten° by the infortune° of
    Marte:°   *forgotten / adverse influence / Mars*
The cartere,° overryden° with his carte.   *carter / run over by*
1165 Under the wheel ful lowe° he lay adoun.   *very low*
Ther were also of Martes divisioun°   *company*
The laborer and the bocher° and the smyth   *butcher*
That forgeth sharpe swerdes° on his styth.°[1]   *swords / anvil*
And al above depeynted° in a tour°   *painted / tower*
1170 Saugh I Conquest sittynge in greet honour
With the sharpe swerd over his heed
Hangynge by a soutil twynes threed.°   *thin twine's thread*
Depeynted° was the slaughtre° of Julius,   *painted / assassination*
Of grete Nero and of Antonius.[2]
1175 Al° be that thilke tyme they were
    unborn,°   *although / not yet born*
Yet was hir deth° depeynted ther biforn°   *death / painted before*
By manasynge° of Mars, right by figure.°   *menacing / by horoscope*
So was it shewed in that protreiture
As is depeynted in the certres[3] above
1180 Who shal be slayn or elles deed for love.
Suffiseth° oon ensample in stories olde;   *suffices*
I may nat rekene° hem alle, though I wolde.°   *count / wanted to*
  The statue of Mars upun a carte° stood   *upon a chariot*
Armed, and looked grym° as he were wood.°   *looking grim / crazy*
1185 And over his heed ther shynen° two figures   *shone*
Of sterres° that been cleped in
    scriptures,°   *stars / called in writings*
That oon Puella, that oother Rubeus.[4]
This god of armes was arrayed thus:

A wolf ther stood biforn° hym at his feet   *before*
1190 With eyen rede,° and of a man he eet.°   *red / ate*
With soutil pencel° was depeynted this storie   *brush*
In redoutynge° of Mars and of his glorie.°   *honor / glory*
  Now to the temple of Dyane the chaste
As shortly as I kan I wol me haste
1195 To telle yow al the descripsioun.
Depeynted been the walles up and doun
Of huntyng and of shamefast° chastitee.   *modest*
Ther saugh I how woful Calistopee,[5]
Whan that Diane agreved° was with here,°   *angry / her*
1200 Was turned from a womman til° a bere,°   *into / bear*
And after was she maad° the loode sterre.°   *made / pole-star*
Thus was it peynted. I kan° sey you no ferre.°   *can / further*
Hir sone[6] is eek a sterre, as men may see.
Ther saugh I Dane[7] yturned° til a tree—   *turned*
1205 I mene° nat the goddesse Diane,   *mean*
But Penneus doghter° which that highte°
    Dane.   *Penneus's daughter / named*
Ther saugh I Attheon[8] an hert° ymaked°   *deer / made*
For vengeaunce that he saugh Diane al naked.
I saugh how that hise houndes have hym caught
1210 And freeten° hym for that they knewe hym
    naught.°   *ate / did not know him*
Yet peynted a litel forthermoor°   *further away*
How Atthalante[9] hunted the wilde boor°   *boar*

---

[1]   *The laborer … styth*   These trades, which all use sharp tools, are under the protection of Mars.

[2]   *Depeynted … Antonius*   Julius Caesar, the Emperor Nero, and Marc Antony all met violent deaths.

[3]   *As … certres*   Depicted in the astrological certainties.

[4]   *Puella … Rubeus*   Patterned figures used in the method of predicting the future known as geomancy—a method of arranging dots into columns according to chance.

[5]   *Calistopee*   Callisto was a favorite companion of Diana. In order to sleep with Callisto, Jupiter disguised himself as Diana. Diana discovered the trick and forced Callisto from her company. Shortly after she left Diana, she found she was pregnant. She gave birth to a boy, Arcas. Juno, Jupiter's wife, jealously changed Callisto into a bear. When her son Arcas was about to kill her mistakenly in a hunt, Jupiter changed her into the constellation Ursa Major, the Great Bear.

[6]   *Hir sone*   Callisto's son is Arcas, whom Jupiter transformed into the constellation Ursa Minor, the Little Bear.

[7]   *Dane*   I.e., Daphne, who was chased by the god Apollo. At her request, the gods turned her into a laurel tree to protect her from him. See Ovid's *Metamorphoses*.

[8]   *Attheon*   I.e., Actaeon, who saw the naked Diana taking a bath. She changed him into a deer to punish him and he was killed by his own hunting dogs.

[9]   *Atthalante*   I.e., Atalanta, a maiden, a hunter who acquitted herself well in the Calydonian Boar Hunt.

And Meleagree[1] and many another mo,

For which Dyane wroghte hym° care and wo. *fashioned for him*

1215 Ther saugh I many another wonder° storie, *wonderful*

The whiche me list nat drawen to memorie.[2]

This goddesse on an hert ful wel hye seet,° *sat very high*

With smale houndes al aboute hir feet,

And undernethe hir feet she hadde a moone.° *moon*

1220 Wexynge° it was and sholde wanye° soone. *waxing / wane*

In gaude grene° hir statue clothed was, *yellow-green*

With bowe in honde and arwes in a cas.° *quiver*

Hir eyen caste she ful lowe adoun

Ther° Pluto[3] hath his derke regioun. *where*

1225 A womman travaillynge° was hire biforn, *in labor*

But for° hir child so longe was unborn *because*

Ful pitously, "Lucyna!"[4] gan she calle

And seyde, "Helpe! For thow mayst best° of

alle!" *may best (help)*

Wel koude he peynten lifly° that it wroghte;° *life-like / made*

1230 With many a floryn° he the hewes°

boghte.° *gold coin / colors / bought*

Now been the lystes maad° and Theseus *made*

That at his grete cost arrayed° thus *arranged*

The temples and the theatre every deel,° *part*

Whan it was doon, hym lyked wonder

weel.° *it pleased him very well*

1235 But stynte° I wole of Theseus a lite *stop speaking*

And speke of Palamon and of Arcite.

The day approcheth of hir retournynge

That everich sholde an hundred knyghtes brynge

The bataille to darreyne° as I yow tolde. *decide*

1240 And til Atthenes,° hir covenantz° for to

holde, *to Athens / agreement*

Hath everich of hem broght an hundred knyghtes

Wel armed for the werre at alle rightes.° *in all aspects*

And sikerly,° ther trowed° many a man *surely / believed*

That nevere sithen° that the world bigan, *never since*

1245 As for to speke of knyghthod° of hir hond, *deeds of knighthood*

As fer as God hath maked see or lond

Nas° of so fewe so noble a compaignye. *there was not*

For every wight° that lovede chivalrye *person*

And wolde his thankes° han a passant° name *gladly / surpassing*

1250 Hath preyd° that he myghte been of° *prayed / (part) of*

that game.

And wel was hym that therto chosen was,

For if ther fille° tomorwe swich a cas, *befell*

Ye knowen wel that every lusty knyght

That loveth paramours° and hath his myght, *as a lover*

1255 Were it in Engelond or elleswhere,

They wolde hir thankes° wilnen° to be there *gladly / wish*

To fighte for a lady, benedicitee.

It were a lusty° sighte for to see! *pleasant*

And right so ferden° they with Palamon. *did*

1260 With hym ther wenten knyghtes many on.° *one*

Som wol ben° armed in an haubergeon° *one would be / mail-coat*

And in bristplate° and in light gypon,° *breast-plate / over-garment*

And somme woln have a paire plates,[5]

And somme woln have a Pruce-sheeld° or a *Prussian shield*

targe.

1265 Somme woln ben armed on hir legges° weel° *legs / well*

And have an ax, and somme a mace[6] of steel.

There is no newe gyse° that it nas° old. *fashion / was not*

Armed were they as I have yow told,

Everych after his opinioun.

1270 Ther maistow seen comynge° with Palamoun *see coming*

Lygurge[7] hymself, the grete kyng of Trace.

Blak was his berd, and manly was his face.

The cercles of hise eyen in his heed,

They gloweden bitwixen yelow and reed,

1275 And lik a grifphon[8] looked he aboute,

With kempe heeris° on hise browes stoute,° *combed hairs / large*

Hise lymes° grete, his brawnes° harde and

stronge, *limbs/ muscles*

His shuldres brode,° hise armes rounde and

longe. *shoulders broad*

And as the gyse° was in his contree, *fashion*

1280 Ful hye upon a chaar° of gold stood he *chariot*

---

[1] *Meleagree* Meleager was awarded Atalanta after the hunt for the Calydonian boar, occasioning jealousy between him and his family.

[2] *The … memorie* Which I do not wish to call to memory.

[3] *Pluto* God of the Underworld, the realm of the dead.

[4] *Lucyna* Lucina is another name for Diana. One of Diana's attributes was the goddess of childbirth.

[5] *paire plates* Plate armor, as opposed to chain-mail armor.

[6] *mace* Here, a spiked metal club.

[7] *Lygurge* King of Sparta, in Greece, known for his austere militarism.

[8] *grifphon* Mythological beast with a lion's hindquarters and an eagle's torso and head.

With foure white boles° in the trays.°   bulls / harness
Instede of cote armure° over° his
　　harnays,°   coat of arms / on / armor
With nayles° yelewe and brighte as any gold,   nails
He hadde a beres skyn, col blak for old.°   coal-black with age
1285　His longe heer was kembd° bihynde his bak;   combed
As any ravenes fethere° it shoon° for blak.   raven's feather / shone
A wrethe° of gold, arm-greet,° of huge
　　wighte°   wreath / arm-thick / weight
Upon his heed, set ful of stones° brighte,   jewels
Of fyne rubyes° and of dyamauntz.°   rubies / diamonds
1290　Aboute his chaar ther wenten white alauntz,°   wolfhounds
Twenty and mo, as grete as any steer
To hunten at the leoun or the deer,
And folwed hym with mosel° faste ybounde,   muzzle
Colered° of gold and tourettes° fyled°
　　rounde.   collared / leash-rings / filed
1295　An hundred lordes hadde he in his route,
Armed ful wel with hertes stierne° and stoute.   stern
　　With Arcite in stories as men fynde
The grete Emetreus,[1] the kyng of Inde,°   India
Upon a steede bay,° trapped in steel,   bay horse
1300　Covered in clooth of gold dyapred[2] weel,
Cam ridynge lyk the god of armes, Mars.
His cotearmure° was of clooth of Tars,°   cloth tunic / Tartary
Couched° with perles white and rounde and grete.   decorated
His sadel° was of brend° gold newe ybete,[3]   saddle / burnished
1305　A mantel° upon his shulder hangynge   tunic
Bratful° of rubyes rede as fyr sparklynge;   full to the brim
His crispe heer° lyk rynges was yronne,°   curly hair / curled
And that was yelow and glytered as the sonne.
His nose was heigh, hise eyen bright citryn,°   lemon-colored
1310　Hise lippes rounde, his colour was sangwyn;°   red
A fewe frakenes° in his face yspreynd,°   freckles / sprinkled
Bitwixen yelow and somdel blak°
　　ymeynd;°   somewhat black / mixed

---

[1] *The grete Emetreus*　King Emetreus is not attested in classical mythology nor is he to be found in Chaucer's sources.

[2] *dyapred*　"Diapered" is a technical term drawn from the world of medieval manuscript illumination that indicates the diamond-shaped patterns used as the background for many paintings in medieval books. King Emetreus's horse wears a decorative cloth covered with this type of pattern.

[3] *newe ybete*　I.e., newly beaten. A goldsmith works goldplate jewelry into pleasing patterns by beating it with a small hammer.

And as a leoun he his lookyng caste;°   he looked about
Of fyve and twenty yeer his age I caste.°   guess
1315　His berd was wel bigonne for to sprynge.°   grow
His voys was as a trompe thondrynge.°   thundering trumpet
Upon his heed he wered° of laurer° grene   wore / laurel-leaves
A gerland fressh and lusty° for to sene.   pleasant
Upon his hand he bar° for his deduyt°   carried / pleasure
1320　An egle° tame as any lilye whyt.   eagle
An hundred lordes hadde he with hym there,
Al armed save hir heddes° in al hir gere,°except their heads / armor
Ful richely in alle maner thynges.
For trusteth wel that dukes, erles, kynges
1325　Were gadered° in this noble compaignye   gathered
For love and for encrees° of chivalrye.   increase
Aboute this kyng ther ran on every part
Ful many a tame leoun and leopard,
And in this wise thise lordes alle and some
1330　Been on the Sonday to the citee come
Aboute pryme, and in the toun alight.°   arrived
　　This Theseus, this duc, this worthy knyght,
Whan he had broght hem into his citee
And inned hem° everich in his
　　degree,°   lodged them / according to his rank
1335　He festeth° hem and dooth so greet labour   feasted
To esen° hem and doon hem al honour,°   refresh / every honor
That yet man weneth° that no maner wit   imagines
Of noon estaat ne koude amenden it.°   make it better
　　The mynstralcye,° the service at the feeste, musical performances
1340　The grete yiftes° to the meeste and
　　leeste,°   gifts / most and least (important)
The riche array° of Theseus paleys,   decoration
Ne who sat first ne last upon the deys,°   dais (high table)
What ladyes fairest been or best daunsynge,
Or which of hem kan dauncen best and synge,
1345　Ne who moost felyngly speketh of love,
What haukes° sitten on the perche above,   hawks
What houndes liggen° in the floor adoun,   lie
Of al this make I now no mencioun,
But al th'effect° that thynketh me° the
　　beste.[4]   only the general effect / seems to me
1350　Now cometh the point, and herkneth° if yow
　　leste.°   listen / wish

---

[4] *But ... beste*　Here Chaucer offers an example of *occupatio*, the rhetorical figure in which one lists at great length the things one is not going to describe, thus describing them.

The Sonday nyght er day bigan to sprynge,
Whan Palamon the larke herde synge,
Although it nere nat day by houres two,
Yet song the larke and Palamon also.
1355 With hooly herte and with an heigh corage°   *high spirit*
He roos° to wenden° on his pilgrymage   *rose / go*
Unto the blisful Citherea° benigne.°   *Venus / kind*
I mene Venus, honurable and digne.°   *worthy*
And in hir houre he walketh forth a pas°   *slowly*
1360 Unto the lystes ther hire temple was,
And doun he kneleth with ful humble cheere°   *expression*
And herte soor, and seyde in this manere:
    "Faireste of faire, O lady myn, Venus,
Doughter to Jove and spouse of Vulcanus,
1365 Thow gladere° of the mount of Citheron,   *one who delights*
For thilke° love thow haddest to° Adoon,[1]   *the same / for*
Have pitee of my bittre teeris smerte°   *bitter, painful tears*
And taak myn humble preyere at° thyn herte.   *to*
Allas, I ne have no langage° to telle   *words*
1370 Th'effectes ne° the tormentz of myn helle!°   *nor / my hell*
Myn herte may myne harmes° nat biwreye.°   *wrongs / reveal*
I am so confus, that I kan noght seye
But 'Mercy!' Lady bright, that knowest weele
My thought and seest what harmes that I feele,
1375 Considere al this and rewe° upon my soore,°   *have mercy / pain*
As wisly° as I shal for everemore,   *surely*
Emforth° my myght, thy trewe servant be,   *according to*
And holden werre° alwey with chastitee,   *be at war*
That make I myn avow,° so° ye me helpe.   *promise / if*
1380 I kepe noght° of armes for to yelpe,°   *do not care / boast*
Ne I ne axe° nat tomorwe to have victorie   *nor do I ask*
Ne renoun in this cas,° ne veyneglorie°   *event / pride*
Of pris° of armes blowen up and
    doun.°   *reputation / made widely known*
But I wolde have fully possessioun
1385 Of Emelye, and dye in thy servyse.
Fynd thow the manere hou° and in what
    wyse.°   *means how / way*
I recche nat but° it may bettre be   *do not care whether*
To have victorie of hem or they of me,
So that I have my lady in myne armes!
1390 For though so be that Mars is god of armes,
Youre vertu° is so greet in hevene above,   *power*

That if yow list, I shal wel have my love.
Thy temple wol I worshipe everemo,
And on thyn auter, where° I ride or go,   *wherever*
1395 I wol doon sacrifice and fires beete.°   *kindle fires (of sacrifice)*
And if ye wol nat so,° my lady sweete,   *you will not (do) so*
Thanne preye I thee tomorwe with a spere
That Arcita me thurgh the herte bere!°   *pierce*
Thanne rekke° I noght whan I have lost my lyf,   *care*
1400 Though that Arcita wynne hire to° his wyf.   *as*
This is th'effect and ende of my preyere.°   *prayer*
Yif° me my love, thow blisful lady deere."   *give*
    Whan the orison was doon° of Palamon,   *done*
His sacrifice he dide and that anon
1405 Ful pitously with alle circumstaunce,°   *ritual*
Al° telle I noght as now° his observaunce.   *although / for now*
But atte laste the statue of Venus shook
And made a signe wherby that he took
That his preyere accepted was that day.
1410 For thogh the signe shewed a delay,
Yet wiste he wel that graunted was his boone.°   *request*
And with glad herte he wente hym hoom ful soone.
    The thridde houre inequal[2] that Palamon
Bigan to Venus temple for to gon,°   *go*
1415 Up roos the sonne, and up roos Emelye,
And to the temple of Dyane gan hye.°   *went*
Hir maydens,° that she thider with hire
    ladde,°   *ladies-in-waiting / led*
Ful redily with hem the fyr° they
    hadde,.°   *fire (for sacrifice) / carried*
Th'encens,° the clothes, and the remenant al   *the incense*
1420 That to the sacrifice longen shal,°   *belongs*
The hornes° fulle of meeth,° as was the
    gyse;°   *drinking horns / mead / custom*
Ther lakked noght to doon hir sacrifise.
Smokynge° the temple ful of clothes
    faire,°   *incensing / beautiful cloth hangings*

---

[1] *Adoon* Adonis was a youth whom Venus loved. He was killed by a boar, and Venus transformed his blood into a flower.

[2] *houre inequal* In Chaucer's day there were two ways of dividing up time into hours. "Artificial" hours are those we use today, where both day and night are divided into twelve hours equal in amount. "Unequal" hours, the older system used in an age that did not have the clocks that made the artificial hours possible, was the division of the daylight time into twelve hours and the time of dark into twelve. The length of these hours would change according to the seasons. They were the same as the artificial hours only at the spring and autumn equinoxes. Each hour of the day was devoted to one of the gods/planets.

This Emelye, with herte debonaire,°   gentle
1425 Hir body wessh° with water of a welle.   washed
But hou° she dide hir ryte,° I dar nat telle,   how / rite
But° it be anythyng in general.   unless
And yet it were a game° to heeren al.   joy
To hym that meneth wel, it were no charge,°   burden
1430 But it is good a man been at his large.°   free (to speak)
Hir brighte heer was kembd, untressed° al;   unbraided
A coroune° of a grene ook° cerial[1]   crown / oak
Upon hir heed was set ful fair and meete.°   fitting
Two fyres on the auter gan she beete°   kindled
1435 And dide hir thynges° as men may biholde   performed her duties
In Stace° of Thebes and thise bookes olde.   Statius
Whan kyndled was the fyr, with pitous cheere
Unto Dyane she spak as ye may heere:
"O chaste goddesse of the wodes grene,
1440 To whom bothe hevene and erthe and see° is sene,°   sea / seen
Queene of the regne of Pluto derk° and lowe,   dark
Goddesse of maydens° that myn herte hast
knowe°   maidens / known
Ful many a yeer, and woost° what I desire,   knows
As keepe me fro thy vengeaunce and thyn ire,
1445 That Attheon aboughte° cruelly.   paid for
Chaste goddesse, wel wostow° that I   you know
Desire to ben a mayden al my lyf.
Ne nevere wol I be no love ne wyf!
I am, thow woost, yet of thy compaignye,
1450 A mayde, and love huntynge° and venerye°   hunting / the chase
And for to walken in the wodes wilde
And noght to ben a wyf and be with childe.
Noght° wol I knowe the compaignye of man.   by no means
Now helpe me, lady, sith ye may and kan,
1455 For tho° thre formes[2] that thou hast in thee,   those
And Palamon that hath swich love to me
And eek Arcite that loveth me so soore,
This grace I preye thee withoute
moore:°   without any more (words)
And sende love and pees° bitwixe hem two,   peace
1460 And fro me turne awey hir hertes so
That al hire hoote love and hir desir
And al hir bisy° torment and hir fir°   intense / fire

---

[1] cerial   Distinct species of oak, *quercus cerris*.

[2] thre formes   I.e., three attributes of Diana, goddess of the hunt, of the underworld, and of chastity.

Be queynt° or turned in another place.   quenched
And if so be thou wolt do° me no grace,°   grant / favor
1465 And if my destynee be shapen so
That I shal nedes° have oon of hem two,   necessarily
As sende me hym that moost° desireth me.   most
Bihoold, goddesse of clene° chastitee,   pure
The bittre teeris that on my chekes falle!
1470 Syn° thou art mayde and kepere° of us alle,   since / keeper
My maydenhede° thou kepe and wel
conserve,°   virginity / preserve
And whil I lyve, a mayde I wol thee serve."
The fires brenne upon the auter cleere°   bright
Whil Emelye was thus in hir preyere,
1475 But sodeynly she saugh a sighte queynte.°   curious
For right anon oon of the fyres queynte°   went out
And quyked agayn,° and after that anon   kindled again
That oother fyr was queynt° and al
agon.°   quenched / completely gone
And as it queynte, it made a whistlynge
1480 As doon thise wete° brondes° in hir brennynge,   wet / sticks
And at the brondes ende out ran anon
As it were blody dropes° many oon,°   bloody drops / many a one
For which so soore° agast° was Emelye,   sorely / appalled
That she was wel ny mad° and gan to crye,   almost crazy
1485 For she ne wiste° what it signyfied,   did not know
But oonly for the feere° thus hath she cried   fear
And weepe, that it was pitee for to heere,
And therwithal° Dyane gan appeere   with all of this
With bowe° in honde, right as an hunteresse,   bow
1490 And seyde, "Doghter, stynt° thyn hevynesse!°   stop / laments
Among the goddes hye,° it is affermed°   high / affirmed
And by eterne word writen and confermed:
Thou shalt ben wedded unto oon of tho°   those
That han for thee so muchel care and wo,
1495 But unto which of hem, I may nat telle.
Farwel, for I ne may no lenger dwelle.
The fires whiche that on myn auter brenne
Shulle° thee declaren, er that thou go henne,°   shall / away
Thyn aventure° of love as in this cas."   fortune
1500 And with that word, the arwes in the caas°   quiver
Of the goddesse clateren° faste and rynge,°   clatter / ring
And forth she wente and made a vanysshynge,°   vanished
For which this Emelye astoned° was   astonished
And seyde, "What amounteth this,° allas?   what does this mean
1505 I putte me in thy proteccioun,
Dyane, and in thy disposicioun."°   care

And hoom she goth anon the nexte weye.
This is th'effect. Ther is namoore to seye.
   The nexte houre of Mars folwynge this,
1510 Arcite unto the temple walked is
With alle the rytes of his payen wyse.°   *rites / pagan customs*
Of fierse Mars to doon his sacrifise
With pitous herte and heigh devocioun
Right thus to Mars he seyde his orisoun:
1515   "O stronge god that in the regnes° colde   *kingdoms*
Of Trace honoured art and lord yholde,°   *considered lord*
And hast in every regne and every lond
Of armes al the brydel in thyn hond,[1]
And hem fortunest° as thee lyst
      devyse,°   *give fortune to them / wish to arrange*
1520 Accepte of me my pitous° sacrifise.   *pious*
If so be that my youthe may deserve
And that my myght° be worthy for to serve   *strength*
Thy godhede,° that I may been oon of thyne,   *divinity*
Thanne preye I thee to rewe° upon my pyne.   *have pity*
1525 For thilke peyne and thilke hoote fir°   *the same hot fire*
In which thow whilom° brendest for desir   *once*
Whan that thow usedest° the beautee   *used*
Of faire, yonge, fresshe Venus fre°   *noble*
And haddest hire in armes at thy wille
1530 (Although thee ones° on a tyme mysfille°   *once / had a misfortune*
Whan Vulcanus hadde caught thee in his las°   *trap*
And foond thee liggynge° by his wyf, allas!)[2]—   *lying*
For thilke sorwe° that was in thyn herte,   *sorrow*
Have routhe as wel upon my peynes smerte!°   *smart*
1535 I am yong and unkonnynge,° as thow
      woost,°   *unknowing / know*
And, as I trowe,° with love offended° moost   *believe / injured*
That evere was any lyves° creature.   *living*
For she that dooth° me al this wo endure°   *does / enduring woe*
Ne reccheth° nevere wher° I synke° or
      fleete!°   *does not care / whether / sink / float*
1540 And wel I woot er° she me mercy heete,°   *before / promise*
I moot with strengthe wynne hire in the place.

---

[1] *Of armes … hond* Mars has complete control (has the bridle, or as might be said now, the reins) of all matters relating to arms.

[2] *Although … allas* Arcite refers here to the story of Vulcan's jealousy over the affair his wife, Venus, had with Mars. As the greatest of smiths, he fashioned an invisible net, which fell upon Mars and Venus when they were in bed together, trapping them for all the gods to see their shame.

And wel I woot withouten helpe or grace
Of thee ne may° my strengthe noght availle.°   *may not / succeed*
Thanne helpe me, lord, tomorwe in my bataille
1545 For thilke fyr that whilom brente° thee   *once burned*
As wel as° thilke fyr now brenneth me,   *just as*
And do° that I tomorwe have victorie.   *cause it*
Myn be the travaille° and thyn be the glorie!   *trouble*
Thy sovereyn temple wol I moost honouren
1550 Of any place, and alwey moost labouren
In thy plesaunce° and in thy craftes[3] stronge,   *pleasure*
And in thy temple I wol my baner honge.°   *hang*
And alle the armes of my compaignye,
And evere mo unto that day I dye
1555 Eterne fir I wol biforn thee fynde,°   *provide*
And eek to this avow° I wol me bynde: *promise*
My beerd, myn heer that hongeth° long adoun   *hangs*
That nevere yet ne felte offensioun°   *felt offense (was cut)*
Of rasour° nor of shere° I wol thee yeve°   *razor / scissors / give*
1560 And ben° thy trewe servant whil I lyve.   *be*
Now, lord, have routhe upon my sorwes soore.
Yif° me the victorie. I aske thee namoore."°   *give / no more*
   The preyere stynt° of Arcita the stronge.   *ends*
The rynges on the temple dore that honge,°   *hung*
1565 And eek the dores, clatereden° ful faste,   *clattered*
Of which Arcita somwhat hym agaste.°   *was somewhat afraid*
The fyres brenden upon the auter brighte,
That it gan al the temple for to lighte,
And sweete smel the ground anon up yaf.°   *immediately gave*
1570 And Arcita anon his hand up haf°   *raised*
And moore encens° into the fyr he caste°   *incense / threw*
With othere rytes° mo. And atte laste   *rites*
The statue of Mars bigan his hauberk° rynge,   *mail-coat*
And with that soun° he herde a
      murmurynge°   *sound / murmuring*
1575 Full lowe and dym,° and seyde thus: "Victorie,"   *low and dim*
For which he yaf° to Mars honour and glorie.   *gave*
And thus with joye and hope wel° to fare,   *well*
Arcite anon unto his in° is fare°   *inn / has gone*
As fayn° as fowel° is of the brighte sonne.   *happy / bird*
1580   And right anon swich strif° ther is bigonne   *strife*
For thilke grauntyng° in the hevene
      above   *this granting (of answers to prayers)*
Bitwixe Venus the goddesse of love

---

[3] *craftes* I.e., those that belong to war—wielding the sword and lance and horsemanship foremost among them.

And Mars the stierne° god armypotente,°   *stern / strong in arms*
That Juppiter was bisy it to stente,°   *stop*
1585 Til that the pale Saturnus the colde
That knew so manye of aventures olde
Foond° in his olde experience and art   *found*
That he ful soone hath plesed every part.°   *each side*
As sooth° is seyd, elde° hath greet avantage;   *truly / age*
1590 In elde is bothe wysdom and usage.°   *experience*
Men may the olde atrenne° and noght
       atrede.°   *outrun / not out-wit*
Saturne anon, to stynten strif and drede,°   *stop strife and fear*
Albeit that it is agayn° his kynde,°   *against / nature*
Of al this strif he gan remedie fynde.°   *found a remedy*
1595   "My deere doghter, Venus," quod Saturne,
"My cours° that hath so wyde° for to
       turne   *course (across the sky) / wide*
Hath moore power than woot any man.[1]
Myn is the drenchyng° in the see° so wan.°   *drowning / sea / pale*
Myn is the prison° in the derke cote.°   *imprisonment / dark cell*
1600 Myn is the stranglyng and hangyng by the throte,°   *throat*
The murmure° and the cherles
       rebellyng,°   *murmur / peasants' rebellion*
The groynynge° and the pryvee
       empoysonyng.°   *groaning / secret poisoning*
I do vengeance and pleyn correccioun°   *full punishment*
Whil I dwelle in signe of the leoun.[2]
1605 Myn is the ruyne° of the hye° halles,   *ruin / high*
The fallynge of the toures° and of the walles   *towers*
Upon the mynour° or the carpenter.[3]   *miner*
I slow° Sampsoun shakynge the piler.[4]   *killed*

---

[1] *My ... man* Saturn, in the Middle Ages the farthest known planet from the sun, was believed to have a cold and harmful influence. The following speech of Saturn enumerates disasters that he as god and planet (i.e., as an astrological influence) typically causes.

[2] *signe of the leoun* Saturn is most harmful when he is in the astrological house of Leo.

[3] *mynour or the carpenter* Here, military men who helped dig tunnels under besieged walls of towns and castles. The walls would be shored up with timber, and then, at the right time for an attack to start, the timbers would be set on fire, thus insuring the collapse of the walls. The disaster envisioned here is that which would occur if the miners and carpenters did not leave the tunnel in time before the walls collapsed.

[4] *I slow ... piler* Samson, blinded and enslaved by his enemies, pulled down the pillars supporting their temple, killing them and himself as well. See Judges 13–16.

And myne be the maladyes colde,[5]
1610 The derke tresons° and the castes° olde.   *treasons / plots*
My lookyng is the fader° of pestilence.   *father*
Now weepe namoore. I shal doon diligence°   *take care*
That Palamon, that is thyn owene knyght,
Shal have his lady as thou hast hym hight.°   *promised*
1615 Though Mars shal helpe his knyght, yet nathelees
Bitwixe yow ther moot be somtyme pees,°   *peace*
Al° be ye noght of o compleccioun,°   *although / one temperament*
That causeth al day swich divisioun.
I am thyn aiel,° redy at thy wille.   *your grandfather*
1620 Weepe now namoore. I wol thy lust fulfille."°   *satisfy your desire*
       Now wol I stynten° of the goddes above,   *stop speaking*
Of Mars and of Venus, goddesse of love,
And telle yow as pleynly as I kan
The grete effect° for which that I bygan.   *result*

EXPLICIT TERCIA PARS
SEQUITUR PARS QUARTA[6]

1625   Greet was the feeste in Atthenes that day,
And eek the lusty seson° of that May   *pleasant season*
Made every wight to been in swich plesaunce°   *enjoyment*
That al that Monday justen° they and daunce   *joust*
And spenten it in Venus heigh servyse.
1630 And by the cause° that they sholde ryse°   *because / had to rise*
Eerly for to seen the grete fight,
Unto hir reste wenten they at nyght,
And on the morwe whan that day gan sprynge,
Of hors° and harneys,° noyse and claterynge   *horse / equipment*
1635 Ther was in hostelryes° al aboute,   *inns*
And to the paleys° rood° ther many a route°   *palace / rode / crowd*
Of lordes upon steedes and palfreys.
Ther maystow seen divisynge of harneys°   *preparation of gear*
So unkouth° and so riche and wroght so weel   *unusual*
1640 Of goldsmythrye,° of browdynge,° and of
       steel,   *goldsmithery / embroidering*
The sheeldes brighte, testeres,° and
       trappures,°   *horses' headpieces / horse-armor*
Gold-hewen helmes, hauberkes,° cote-armures,   *mail-coats*
Lordes in parementz° on hir courseres,   *robes*

---

[5] *And ... colde* Diseases caused by a preponderance of the cold humor.

[6] *Explicit ... Quarta* Latin: Here ends the third part. The fourth part follows.

Knyghtes of retenue and eek squieres
1645 Nailynge the speres° and helmes
    bokelynge,° — *nailing spears / buckling helmets*
Giggynge of sheeldes° with layneres
    lacynge° — *setting straps / lacing straps*
(Thereas° nede° is, they weren nothyng
    ydel°), — *where / need / idle*
The fomy° steedes on the golden brydel° — *foamy / bridle*
Gnawynge,° and faste° the armurers°
    also — *gnawing / quickly / armorers*
1650 With fyle° and hamer prikynge° to and fro, — *file / galloping*
Yemen° on foote and communes° many oon — *yeomen / commoners*
With shorte staves thikke° as they may goon, — *densely*
Pypes, trompes,° nakerers,° clariounes,° — *trumpets / drums / bugles*
That in the bataille blowen° blody sounes,° — *blow / bloody sounds*
1655 The paleys ful of peples up and doun,
Heere thre, ther ten, holdynge° hir questioun, — *debating*
Dyvynynge of° thise Thebane knyghtes two. — *guessing about*
Somme seyden thus; somme seyde it shal be so;
Somme helden with° hym with the blake berd; — *sided with*
1660 Somme with the balled,° somme with the thikke
    herd;° — *bald / thick-haired*
Somme seyde he looked grymme° and he wolde
    fighte;° — *fierce / wanted to fight*
"He hath a sparth° of twenty pound of wighte!"° — *axe / weight*
Thus was the halle ful of divynynge
Longe after that the sonne gan to sprynge.
1665   The grete Theseus that of his sleepe awaked
With mynstralcie° and noyse that was maked — *music*
Heeld yet the chambre of his paleys riche
Til that the Thebane knyghtes, bothe yliche° — *equally*
Honured, were into the paleys fet.° — *fetched*
1670 Duc Theseus was at a wyndow set,
Arrayed right as he were a god in trone.° — *on (his) throne*
The peple preesseth thiderward° ful soone — *towards there*
Hym for to seen and doon heigh reverence
And eek to herkne his heste° and his
    sentence.° — *command / decision*
1675 An heraud° on a scaffold made an "Oo!"° — *herald / whoa!*
Til al the noyse of peple was ydo.° — *stopped*
And whan he saugh the noyse of peple al stille,
Tho° shewed he the myghty dukes wille. — *then*
  "The lord hath of his heigh discrecioun
1680 Considered that it were destruccioun
To gentil° blood to fighten in the gyse° — *noble / manner*
Of mortal bataille now in this emprise.° — *enterprise*

Wherfore to shapen° that they shal nat dye,° — *ensure / die*
He wolde his firste purpos modifye.
1685 No man therfore up° peyne of los of lyf — *upon*
No maner shot,° polax,° ne short knyf — *arrow / battle-axe*
Into the lystes sende ne thider brynge,° — *bring there*
Ne short swerd for to stoke° with poynt
    bitynge° — *stab / biting point*
Ne man ne drawe ne bere° by his syde. — *carry*
1690 Ne no man shal unto his felawe° ryde — *against his opponent*
But o° cours° with a sharpe ygrounde
    spere;° — *one / turn / sharpened spear*
Foyne, if hym list, on foote hymself to were.[1]
And he that is at meschief° shal be take° — *in trouble / taken*
And noght slayn,° but be broght unto the stake — *not killed*
1695 That shal ben ordeyned° on either syde, — *set up*
But thider he shal° by force and there abyde. — *shall (go)*
And if so be the chieftayn° be take° — *leader / taken*
On outher syde or elles sleen° his make,° — *killed / opponent leader*
No lenger shal the turneiynge° laste. — *tourneying*
1700 God spede you! Gooth forth and ley° on faste! — *lay*
With long swerd and with maces fighteth youre fille!
Gooth now youre wey! This is the lordes wille!"
  The voys° of peple touched the hevene,° — *voice / sky*
So loude cride they with murie stevene,° — *merry voice*
1705 "God save swich a lord that is so good!
He wilneth° no destruccion of blood!" — *wills*
Up goon the trompes and the melodye,
And to the lystes rit° the compaignye, — *rides*
By ordinance° thurghout the citee large, — *decree*
1710 Hanged with clooth of gold and nat° with
    sarge.° — *not / serge (plain cloth)*
  Ful lik a lord this noble duc gan ryde,
Thise two Thebans upon either syde.
And after rood the queene and Emelye,
And after that another compaignye
1715 Of oon and oother after hir degree.
And thus they passen thurghout the citee
And to the lystes come they by tyme.° — *in time*

---

[1] *Foyne … were* Let him parry, if he wishes, to protect himself when he is on foot. Knights who had been dismounted in a tournament would often continue to fight on foot. Although set in an arena and conducted under the eyes of the Roman gods, the tournament will follow the customs of Chaucer's own day.

It nas nat° of the day yet fully pryme[1]   *was not*
Whan set was Theseus ful riche and hye,
1720 Ypolita the queene, and Emelye,
And othere ladys in degrees aboute.
Unto the seetes° preesseth al the route.   *seats*
And westward thurgh the gates under Marte°   *Mars*
Arcite, and eek the hondred of his parte,°   *party*
1725 With baner reed is entred right anon.
And in that selve° moment Palamon   *same*
Is under Venus estward° in the place   *eastward*
With baner whyt and hardy chiere and face.
In al the world to seken° up and doun   *seek*
1730 So evene, withouten variacioun,
Ther nere° swiche compaignyes tweye!   *were not*
For ther was noon so wys that koude seye
That any hadde of oother° avauntage   *(the) other*
Of worthynesse ne of estaat ne age,
1735 So evene were chosen for to gesse.°   *guess*
And in two renges° faire they hem
dresse°   *ranks / arrange themselves*
Whan that hir names rad° were everichon,   *read*
That in hir nombre° gyle° were ther noon.   *number / trickery*
Tho° were the gates shet° and cried was loude: *then / shut*
1740 "Do now youre devoir,° yonge° knyghtes proude!"   *duty / young*
The heraudes lefte hir prikyng° up and doun.   *riding*
Now ryngen trompes loude and clarioun.°   *bugle*
Ther is namoore to seyn, but west and est
In goon the speres ful sadly° in arrest;°   *firmly / holder*
1745 In gooth the sharpe spore° into the syde.   *spur*
Ther seen men who kan° juste° and who kan
ryde.   *know how (to) / joust*
Ther shyveren° shaftes upon sheeldes thikke;   *shiver*
He feeleth thurgh the herte-spoon° the prikke.°   *breast / point*
Up spryngen speres twenty foot on highte,
1750 Out gooth the swerdes as the silver brighte;
The helmes they tohewen° and toshrede.°   *cut up / shred up*
Out brest° the blood with stierne stremes rede;   *bursts*
With myghty maces the bones they tobreste.°   *break up*
He thurgh the thikkeste of the throng° gan
threste.°   *crowd / thrust*
1755 Ther semblen° steedes stronge, and doun gooth al!   *stumble*
He rolleth under foot as dooth a bal.°   *ball*
He foyneth° on his feet with his tronchon,°   *parries / spear-shaft*

And he hym hurtleth° with his hors adoun.   *strikes*
He thurgh the body is hurt and sithen
ytake,°   *afterwards captured*
1760 Maugree his heed,° and broght unto the
stake;   *despite all he could do*
As forward° was, right there he moste abyde.   *the agreement*
Another lad° is on that oother syde.   *led*
And somtyme dooth hem° Theseus to reste,   *causes them*
Hem to fresshen° and drynken if hem
leste.°   *take refreshment / they wanted*
1765 Ful ofte° a day han thise Thebanes two   *very often*
Togydre ymet and wroght° his felawe wo.   *caused*
Unhorsed hath ech oother° of hem tweye.   *each other*
Ther nas no tygre in the vale of Galgopheye[2]
Whan that hir whelpe° is stole° whan it is lite   *cub / stolen*
1770 So crueel on the hunte as is Arcite
For jelous herte° upon this Palamoun,   *heart*
Ne in Belmarye[3] ther nys so fel leoun°   *is not so fierce a lion*
That hunted is or for his hunger wood
Ne of his praye° desireth so the blood   *prey*
1775 As Palamoun to sleen his foo Arcite.
The jelous strokes on hir helmes byte;°   *bite*
Out renneth blood on bothe hir sydes rede.
Somtyme an ende ther is of every dede,°   *deed*
For er the sonne unto the reste wente,
1780 The stronge Kyng Emetreus gan hente°   *captured*
This Palamon as he faught with Arcite
And made his swerd depe in his flessh to byte.
And by the force of twenty is he take°   *taken*
Unyolden° and ydrawe° unto the stake.   *not yielding / drawn*
1785 And in the rescus° of this Palamon   *rescue*
The stronge Kyng Lygurge is born adoun,°   *knocked down*
And Kyng Emetreus for al his strengthe
Is born° out of his sadel a swerdes lengthe,   *carried*
So hitte hym Palamoun er he were take.°   *taken*
1790 But al for noght.° He was broght to the stake;   *nothing*
His hardy herte myghte hym helpe naught.°   *by no means*
He moste abyde° whan that he was caught   *had to stay*
By force and eek by composicioun.°   *agreement*
Who sorweth now but woful Palamoun,
1795 That moot namoore goon agayn° to fighte?   *go again*

---

[2] *Galgopheye* I.e., Galgophia, a valley in Greece.

[3] *Belmarye* I.e., Benmarin, a region of Morocco. In the General Prologue, we find that the Knight has fought there.

And whan that Theseus hadde seyn° this sighte,   *seen*
Unto the folk that foghten° thus echon,°   *fought / each one*
He cryde, "Hoo!° Namoore! For it is doon!   *stop!*
I wol be trewe juge and no partie.°   *partisan*
1800 Arcite of Thebes shal have Emelie,
That by his fortune hath hire faire ywonne!"°   *won fairly*
Anon ther is a noyse of peple bigonne
For joye of this so loude and heighe withalle
It semed that the lystes sholde falle.
1805   What kan now faire Venus doon° above?   *do*
What seith she now? What dooth this queene of love
But wepeth so for wantynge° of hir wille   *lack*
Til that hir teeres in the lystes fille?
She seyde, "I am ashamed doutelees!"°   *doubtless*
1810 Saturnus seyde, "Doghter, hoold thy pees!
Mars hath his wille. His knyght hath al his bone.°   *request*
And by my heed, thow shalt been esed° soone!"   *be eased*
    The trompes with the loude mystralcie,°   *music*
The heraudes that ful loude yolle° and crie   *yell*
1815 Been° in hire wele° for joye of Daun° Arcite.   *be / prosperity / sir*
But herkneth me,° and stynteth° now a
    lite   *listen to me / keep quiet*
Which a myracle ther bifel anon.
    This fierse Arcite hath of his helm ydon,°   *removed*
And on a courser for to shewe his face
1820 He priketh endelong° the large place,   *from end to end of*
Lokynge upward upon Emelye.
And she agayn° hym caste a freendlich° eye[1]   *towards / friendly*
And was al his chiere as in his herte.
    Out of the ground a furie infernal sterte,°   *infernal fury arose*
1825 From Pluto sent at requeste of Saturne,
For which his hors for fere° gan to turne   *fear*
And leepe° aside and foundred° as he
    leepe.°   *leap / stumbled / leapt*
And er that Arcite may taken keepe,°   *care*
He pighte hym° on the pomel° of his
    heed,   *knocked himself / crown*
1830 That in the place he lay as he were deed.

His brest tobrosten° with his sadel bowe,   *broken up*
As blak he lay as any cole° or crowe,   *coal*
So was the blood yronnen° in his face.   *run*
Anon he was yborn° out of the place   *carried*
1835 With herte soor° to Theseus paleys.   *sore*
Tho° was he korven° out of his harneys°   *then / cut / armor*
And in a bed ybrought° ful faire and blyve,°   *brought / quickly*
For he was yet in memorie° and alyve°   *conscious / alive*
And alwey criynge° after Emelye.   *crying*
1840   Duc Theseus with al his compaignye
Is comen hoom to Atthenes his citee
With alle blisse and greet solempnitee.°   *ceremony*
Albeit° that this aventure° was
    falle,°   *although / mishap / had happened*
He nolde noght° disconforten° hem alle.   *would not / distress*
1845 Men seyde eek that Arcite shal nat dye.°   *not die*
He shal been heeled° of his maladye!   *be healed*
And of another thyng they weren as fayn,°   *glad*
That of hem alle was ther noon yslayn.°   *killed*
Al° were they soore yhurt and namely
    oon°   *although / especially one*
1850 That with a spere was thirled° his brest
    boon.°   *pierced / breast-bone*
To othere woundes and to broken armes
Somme hadden salves, and somme hadden charmes.[2]
Fermacies° of herbes and eek save°   *medicines / sage*
They dronken, for they wolde hir lymes
    have.°   *to save their limbs*
1855 For which this noble duc, as he wel kan,
Conforteth and honoureth every man
And made revel al the longe nyght
Unto the straunge° lordes, as was right,   *foreign*
Ne ther was holden no disconfitynge
1860 But as a justes or a tourneiynge.[3]
For soothly, ther was no disconfiture.°   *dishonor*
For fallyng nys nat° but an aventure,   *is nothing*
Ne to be lad by force unto the stake
Unyolden° and with twenty knyghtes take,   *unyielded*
1865 O° persone allone withouten mo,   *one*
And haryed° forth by arm, foot and too,°   *dragged / toe*

---

[1] *And ... eye* The following lines occur in most editions of *The Canterbury Tales* after this one: "For wommen, as to speken in comune, / Thei folwen alle the favour of Fortune." Ellesmere and Hengwrt both omit these lines. They are found in Oxford, Corpus Christi College MS 198. Dated c. 1410–20, this manuscript, like Ellesmere and Hengwrt, is a very early witness to the text of *The Canterbury Tales*.

[2] *Somme ... charmes* Some had salves and some had charms. Herbal medicine and medicinal magic were widely practiced in the Middle Ages.

[3] *Ne ... tourneiynge* Nor was it considered a defeat for anyone except of the kind appropriate to a joust or tournament.

And eek his steede dryven forth with staves,°   *spears*
With footmen, bothe yemen° and eek knaves,°   *yeomen / boys*
It nas arretted hym no vileynye.[1]

1870 Ther may no man clepen° it cowardye.°   *call / cowardice*
For which anon Duc Theseus leet crye°   *proclaimed*
To stynten alle rancour and envye,
The gree° as wel of o° syde as of oother,   *victory / one*
And eyther syde ylik° as ootheres brother,   *either side like*
1875 And yaf hem yiftes° after hir degree   *gave them gifts*
And fully heeld° a feeste dayes three   *held*
And convoyed° the kynges worthily   *accompanied*
Out of his toun a journee° largely.   *day's ride*
And hoom went every man the righte way.
1880 Ther was namoore but "Farewel! Have good day!"
Of this bataille I wol namoore endite
But speke of Palamoun and of Arcite.
   Swelleth° the brest of Arcite, and the soore°   *swells / sore*
Encreesseth at his herte moore and moore.
1885 The clothered° blood for any lechecraft°   *clotted / skill in medicine*
Corrupteth° and is in his bouk° ylaft,°   *corrupts / chest / left*
That neither veyne-blood ne ventusynge[2]
Ne drynke of herbes may ben° his helpynge.°   *be / helping*
The vertu expulsif[3] or animal
1890 Fro thilke vertu° cleped° natural[4]   *power / called*
Ne may the venym° voyden° ne expelle.   *poison / purge*
The pipes of his longes° gonne° to swelle,   *lungs / began*
And every lacerte° in his brest adoun°   *muscle / down*
Is shent° with venym° and corrupcioun.   *destroyed / poison*
1895 Hym gayneth° neither, for to gete° his lif,   *it helps him / preserve*
Vomyt° upward ne dounward laxatif.°   *vomit / laxative*
Al is tobrosten thilke regioun;
Nature hath now no dominacioun.
And certeinly ther° nature wol nat wirche,°   *where / work*
1900 Farewel phisik!° Go ber° the man to
   chirche!°   *medicine / carry / church*
This al and som:° that Arcita moot dye,   *this briefly (means)*

For which he sendeth after Emelye
And Palamon, that was his cosyn deere.°   *dear cousin*
Thanne° seyde he thus, as ye shal after heere: *then*
1905 "Naught° may the woful spirit in myn herte   *by no means*
Declare o° point of alle my sorwes smerte°   *one / painful sorrows*
To yow, my lady that I love moost,
But I biquethe the servyce of my goost°   *spirit*
To yow aboven every creature,
1910 Syn that my lyf may no lenger dure.°   *last*
Allas the wo! Allas the peynes stronge
That I for yow have suffred and so longe!
Allas the deeth! Allas, myn Emelye!
Allas, departynge of oure compaignye!
1915 Allas, myn hertes queene! Allas my wyf,[5]
Myn hertes lady, endere of my lyf!°   *one who ends my life*
What is this world? What asketh men to have?
Now with his love, now in his colde grave,
Allone, withouten any compaignye.
1920 Farewel, my sweete foo, myn Emelye!
And softe, taak° me in youre armes tweye   *take*
For love of God, and herkneth what I seye:
   I have heer with my cosyn Palamon
Had strif and rancour many a day agon°   *past*
1925 For love of yow and for my jalousye.
And Juppiter so wys° my soule gye°   *wise / guide*
To speken of a servaunt° properly   *a servant (of love)*
With alle circumstances trewely—
That is to seyn, trouthe, honour, knyghthede,°   *knighthood*
1930 Wysdom, humblesse,° estaat, and heigh
   kynrede,°   *humility / high kindred*
Fredom, and al that longeth° to that art—   *pertains*
So Juppiter have of my soule part
As in this world right now ne knowe I non°   *I know none*
So worthy to ben loved as Palamon,
1935 That serveth yow and wol doon° al his lyf.   *will do*
And if that evere ye shul ben a wyf,
Foryet nat° Palamon, the gentil man."   *forget not*
And with that word his speche faille gan,°   *speech began to fail*
And from his herte up to his brest was come
1940 The coold of deeth, that hadde hym overcome.
And yet moreover,° for in hise armes two   *and that is not all*

---

[1] *It ... vileynye* It was not attributed to him as any dishonor.

[2] *veyne-blood ne ventusynge* *Vein-blood* Blood-letting; *ventusing* Cupping. Two medieval medical procedures.

[3] *expulsif* The power of the body to expel unhealthy humors, medieval medicine's version of modern immune theory. "Animal" was a term applied to this power, which was supposed to reside in one's brain.

[4] *Fro ... natural* Natural power in medieval medicine was supposed to reside in the liver, and it too helped combat illness.

---

[5] *Allas ... wyf* Arcite may simply be thinking of Emily as the woman who is destined to be his wife, but in Boccaccio's *Teseida*, Chaucer's immediate source, Arcite actually marries Emily on his death-bed.

The vital strengthe° is lost and al ago.°   *power of life | gone*
Oonly the intellect withouten moore
That dwelled in his herte syk and soore,
1945 Gan faillen whan the herte felte deeth.[1]
Dusked° hise eyen two, and failled breeth.   *darkened*
But on his lady yet caste he his eye.
His laste word was "Mercy, Emelye!"
His spirit chaunged hous° and wente ther°   *its dwelling | where*
1950 As I can nevere;° I kan nat tellen wher.   *can never know*
Therfore I stynte. I nam no divinistre.°   *theologian*
Of soules fynde I nat in this registre,°   *list*
Ne me ne list° thilke opinions to telle   *I do not wish*
Of hem° though that they writen wher they
        dwelle.   *them (other writers)*
1955 Arcite is coold. Ther Mars his soule gye!°   *guide*
Now wol I speken forth of Emelye.
    Shrighte° Emelye, and howleth Palamon,   *shrieks*
And Theseus his suster took anon,
Swownynge,° and baar° hire fro the corps
        away.   *fainting | carried*
1960 What helpeth it to tarien forth° the day   *while away*
To tellen how she weepe bothe eve and morwe?°   *morning*
For in swich cas wommen have swich sorwe,
Whan that hir housbond is from hem ago,°   *gone*
That for the moore part they sorwen° so   *sorrow*
1965 Or ellis fallen in swich maladye
That at the laste certeinly they dye.
    Infinite been the sorwes and the teeres
Of olde folk and eek of tendre yeeres°   *(those of) tender years*
In al the toun for deeth of this Theban.
1970 For hym ther wepeth bothe child and man.
So greet a wepyng was ther noon, certayn,
Whan Ector[2] was ybroght al fressh yslayn°   *freshly killed*
To Troye. Allas, the pitee that was ther,
Cracchynge° of chekes, rentynge° eek of
        heer!°   *scratching | tearing | hair*
1975 "Why woldestow° be deed," thise wommen crye, *would you*
"And haddest gold ynough and Emelye?"
    No man myghte gladen° Theseus   *make glad*
Savynge° his olde fader° Egeus,   *except for | father*
That knew this worldes transmutacioun,°   *changing*

1980 As he hadde seyn° it up and doun—   *seen*
Joye after wo and wo after gladnesse—
And shewed hem ensamples° and liknesse.°   *examples | analogies*
"Right as ther dyed° nevere man," quod he,   *died*
"That he ne lyvede° in erthe° in som degree,   *did not live | earth*
1985 Right so ther lyvede never man," he seyde,
"In al this world that somtyme he ne deyde.°   *did not die*
This world nys° but a thurghfare°   *is nothing | thoroughfare*
        ful of wo,
And we been pilgrymes passynge to and fro.
Deeth is an ende of every worldes soore."°   *sorrow*
1990 And over al this yet seyde he muchel more
To this effect, ful wisely to enhorte°   *exhort*
The peple that they sholde hem reconforte.°   *comfort themselves*
    Duc Theseus with al his bisy cure°   *anxious care*
Cast° now wher that the sepulture°   *considered | grave*
1995 Of goode Arcite may best ymaked be
And eek moost honurable in his degree.°   *according to his rank*
And at the laste he took conclusioun
That theras° first Arcite and Palamoun   *where*
Hadden for love the bataille hem bitwene,°   *between them*
2000 That in that selve° grove swoote° and grene   *same | sweet*
Theras° he hadde hise amorouse desires,   *where*
His compleynte,° and for love hise hoote° fires, *lament | hot*
He wolde make a fyr in which the office°   *ceremony*
Funeral he myghte al accomplice,°   *accomplish*
2005 And leet comande° anon to hakke and hewe°   *ordered | cut*
The okes° olde and leye hem on a rewe°   *oaks | row*
In colpons° wel arrayed° forto brenne.   *piles | arranged*
Hise officers with swifte feet they renne°   *run*
And ryden anon at his comandement.°   *commandment*
2010 And after this Theseus hath ysent°   *has sent*
After a beere,° and it al overspradde   *bier*
With clooth of gold, the richeste that he hadde,
And of the same suyte° he cladde° Arcite.   *material | clothed*
Upon his hondes hadde he gloves white,
2015 Eek on his heed a coroune° of laurer° grene, *crown | laurel*
And in his hond a swerd ful bright and kene.°   *sharp*
He leyde hym, bare the visage,° on the beere,   *bare-faced*
Therwith° he weepe that pitee was to heere.   *thus*
And for the peple sholde seen hym alle,
2020 Whan it was day, he broghte hym to the halle,
That roreth° of the criyng and the soun.°   *roars | sound*
    Tho° cam° this woful Theban Palamoun   *then | came*

---

[1] *Oonly … deeth* Only when the heart felt death did the intellect begin to fail.

[2] *Ector* I.e., Hector, the greatest of Trojan warriors, killed by the Greek Achilles. See Homer's *Iliad*.

With flotery° berd° and rugged, asshy heeres,[1]   *fluttering / beard*

In clothes blake,° ydropped° al with teeres,   *black / wet*

2025 And passynge° othere of wepynge,° Emelye, *surpassing / weeping*

The rewefulleste° of al the compaignye.   *most pitiful*

Inasmuche as the servyce sholde be

The moore noble and riche in his degree,

Duc Theseus leet forth thre steedes brynge,[2]

2030 That trapped° were in steel al gliterynge°   *equipped / glittering*

And covered with the armes° of Daun Arcite.   *coat of arms*

Upon thise steedes grete and white

Ther sitten folk of whiche oon baar° his sheeld,   *carried*

Another his spere in his hondes heeld,

2035 The thridde baar with hym his bowe Turkeys°   *Turkish bow*

(Of brend gold was the caas° and eek the harneys),   *quiver*

And riden forth a paas° with sorweful cheere   *slowly*

Toward the grove, as ye shul after heere.

The nobleste of the Grekes that ther were

2040 Upon hir shuldres caryeden the beere

With slak° paas and eyen rede and wete   *slow*

Thurghout the citee by the maister strete,°   *main street*

That sprad°was al with blak, and wonder

hye°   *spread / wonderfully high*

Right of the same is the strete ywrye.[3]

2045 Upon the right hond wente olde Egeus,

And on that oother syde Duc Theseus

With vessel° in hir hand of gold ful fyn,°   *jar / fine*

Al ful of hony,° milk, and blood, and wyn,°   *honey / wine*

Eek Palamon with ful greet compaignye.

2050 And after that cam woful Emelye

With fyr in honde as was that tyme the gyse°   *custom*

To do the office of funeral servyse.

  Heigh labour and ful greet apparaillynge°   *preparation*

Was at the service and the fyr makynge,°   *making of the fire*

2055 That with his grene tope° the hevene raughte°[4]   *top / reached*

And twenty fadme° of brede° the armes

straughte°—   *fathoms / breadth / stretched*

This is to seyn, the bowes° weren so brode.°   *boughs / broad*

Of stree° first ther was leyd° ful many a lode.° *straw / laid / load*

But how the fyr was maked upon highte°   *high*

2060 Ne eek the names that the trees highte°—   *were called*

As ook, firre, birch, aspe, alder, holm, popeler,

Wylugh, elm, plane, assh, box, chasteyn, lynde, laurer,

Mapul, thorn, bech, hasel, ew, whippeltree—[5]

How they weren fild° shal nat be toold for me,   *cut down*

2065 Ne hou° the goddes ronnen up and doun,   *nor how*

Disherited° of hire habitacioun°   *disinherited / dwelling*

In whiche they woneden° in reste and pees—   *lived*

Nymphus,° fawnes, and amadrides°—[6] *nymphs / hamadryads*

Ne hou the beestes and the briddes° alle   *birds*

2070 Fledden° for fere whan the wode° was

falle,°   *fled / wood / cut down*

Ne how the ground agast was° of the light   *was frightened*

That was nat wont° to seen the sonne bright,   *accustomed*

Ne how the fyr was couched° first with stree°   *made / straw*

And thanne with drye stokkes cloven athre° *sticks cut in three*

2075 And thanne with grene wode and spicerye°   *spices*

And thanne with clooth of gold° and with

perrye°   *golden cloth / jewels*

And gerlandes hangynge with ful many a flour,

The mirre,° th'encens, withal so greet odour,   *myrrh / incense*

Ne how Arcite lay among al this,

2080 Ne what richesse aboute his body is,

Ne how that Emelye, as was the gyse,

Putte in the fyr of funeral servyse,

Ne how she swowned whan men made fyr,

Ne what she spak, ne what was hir desir,

2085 Ne what jeweles men in the fyre caste

Whan that the fyr was greet and brente faste,

---

[1] *With … heeres* To throw ashes on one's hair is an ancient form of mourning.

[2] *Duc Theseus … brynge* Duke Theseus commanded that three horses be brought out.

[3] *ywrye* Draped. The walls of the houses along the main street have been draped high with black cloth, a standard practice in the late Middle Ages for the funerals of great nobles.

[4] *That … raughte* The huge pile of trees, with its branches still green, reaches to the sky and is 120 feet (twenty fathoms) wide. Chaucer draws his description of the funeral from Boccaccio's *Teseida* (Book 11) and also probably from the Statius's *Thebaid*

(6.98–106), which in turn draws on Virgil's *Aeneid*. Unlike the warfare, courtship, and tournament in the *Knight's Tale*, the funeral rituals are those of classical antiquity and not of Chaucer's own day.

[5] *Ne … whippeltree* Catalogues of trees are a feature of several epic poems from ancient times. The trees here listed are oak, fir, birch, aspen, alder, holm-oak, poplar, willow, elm, plane, ash, boxtree, chestnut, linden, laurel, maple, thorn, beech, hazel, yew, and dogwood.

[6] *Disherited … amadrides* In Roman mythology, lesser gods and goddesses like those listed here lived in the woods and fields. Since the grove is cut down for the funeral, the gods and goddesses normally inhabiting it no longer have a home.

Ne how somme caste hir sheeld° and somme hir spere — *some threw in their shields*

And of hire vestimentz° whiche that they were° — *clothing | were wearing*

And coppes° fulle of wyn and milk and blood — *cups*

2090 Into the fyr that brente as it were wood,

Ne how the Grekes with an huge route

Thries° riden al the place about — *thrice*

Upon the left hand° with a loud shoutynge — *counter-clockwise*

And thries with hir speres claterynge,

2095 And thries how the ladyes gonne crye

And how that lad was homward Emelye,

Ne how Arcite is brent to asshen colde,

Ne how that lych-wake° was yholde° — *funeral wake | held*

Al thilke nyght, ne how the Grekes pleye

2100 The wake-pleyes,° ne kepe° I nat to seye — *funeral games | care*

What° wrastleth° best naked with oille enoynt,° — *who | wrestles | anointed*

Ne who that baar hym best in no disjoynt.° — *difficulty*

I wol nat tellen eek how that they goon

Hoom til Atthenes° whan the ple° is doon, — *to Athens | funeral game(s)*

2105 But shortly to the point thanne wol I wende° — *turn*

And maken of my longe tale an ende.

By processe° and by lengthe of certeyn yeres, — *in due course*

Al stynted is the moornynge° and the teres — *mourning*

Of Grekes by oon general assent.

2110 Thanne semed me° ther was a parlement° — *it seemed to me | parliament*

At Atthenes upon certein pointz° and caas,° — *points | cases*

Among the whiche pointz yspoken° was — *spoken*

To have with certein contrees° alliaunce° — *countries | alliance*

And have fully of Thebans obeisaunce,° — *obedience*

2115 For which this noble Theseus anon

Leet senden° after gentil Palamon, — *had sent*

Unwist of hym° what was the cause and why, — *unknown by him*

But in hise blake clothes sorwefully

He cam at his comandement in hye.° — *in haste*

2120 Tho° sente Theseus for Emelye — *then*

Whan they were set and hust° was al the place. — *quieted*

And Theseus abiden° hadde a space — *waited*

Er° any word cam fram his wise brest. — *before*

Hise eyen sette he theras was his lest,° — *where he wished*

2125 And with a sad visage he siked stille,° — *sighed quietly*

And after that right thus he seyde his wille:

"The Firste Moevere[1] of the cause above,

Whan he first made the faire cheyne° of love, — *chain*

Greet was th'effect and heigh was his entente.

2130 Wel wiste he why and what therof he ment.

For with that faire cheyne of love he bond° — *bound*

The fyr, the eyr, the water, and the lond[2]

In certeyn boundes, that they may nat flee.

That same prince and that same Moevere," quod he,

2135 Hath stablissed° in this wrecched° world adoun° — *established | wretched | below*

Certeyne dayes and duracioun° — *duration*

To al that is engendred° in this place, — *born*

Over the which day they may nat pace,° — *not go beyond*

Al mowe° they yet tho° dayes wel abregge.° — *although | those | shorten*

2140 Ther nedeth noght noon auctoritee allegge,[3]

For it is preeved° by experience. — *proven*

But that me list declaren° my sentence.° — *I wish to give | judgment*

Thanne may men by this ordre° wel discerne — *order*

That thilke Moevere stable is and eterne.

2145 Wel may men knowe, but it be° a fool, — *unless (the man) is*

That every part dirryveth° from his hool.° — *derives | its wholeness*

For Nature hath taken his bigynnyng° — *its beginning*

Of no partie° or of cantel° of a thyng, — *part | portion*

But of a thyng that parfit° is and stable, — *perfect*

2150 Descendynge° so til it be corrumpable.° — *descending | corruptible*

And therfore of his wise purveiaunce° — *foresight*

He hath so wel biset° his ordinaunce° — *well established | laws*

That speces° of thynges and progressiouns° — *species | natural processes*

Shullen enduren° by successiouns,° — *last | one after another*

2155 And nat eterne,° withouten any lye.° — *not (be) eternal | lie*

This maystow understonde and seen at eye.° — *see with your eye*

"Loo, the ook° that hath so long a norisshynge° — *oak | growing*

From tyme that it first bigynneth sprynge° — *begins to grow*

And hath so long a lif, as we may see,

---

[1] *The Firste Moevere* I.e., God. According to Aristotle, the First Mover is the principle that sets all other things into motion. The idea that love unites all the elements, each of which is linked to the others in a hierarchical order (the Great Chain of Being), goes back to Plato and is described in Boethius's *Consolation of Philosophy* (Book 2, meter 8), on which this passage is based.

[2] *The … lond* Four elements from which everything was thought to be made.

[3] *Ther … allegge* There is no need to cite authority.

2160 Yet at the laste wasted is the tree.
      "Considereth eek how that the harde stoon
      Under oure feet, on which we trede° and goon,°   tread / go
      Yet wasteth it° as it lyth by the weye.°   it wastes / lies along the road
      The brode ryver° somtyme wexeth dreye,°   broad river / grows dry
2165 The grete toures° se° we wane and
            wende;.°   towers / see / diminishing and changing
      Thanne may ye se that al this thyng hath ende.
      "Of man and womman seen we wel also
      That nedeth in oon of thise termes two,
      This is to seyn, in youthe or elles age,
2170 He moot be deed—the kyng as shal a page:
      Som in his bed, som in the depe see,
      Som in the large feeld, as men may see.
      Ther helpeth noght.° Al goth that ilke weye.   nothing can help
      Thanne may I seyn al this thyng moot deye.
2175   What maketh this° but Juppiter the kyng,[1]   who does this
      That is prince and cause of alle thyng,
      Convertynge al unto his propre welle,°   own source
      From which it is dirryved,° sooth° to telle?   derived / truth
      And heer agayns no creature on lyve
2180 Of no degree availleth for to stryve.[2]
      "Thanne° is it wysdom, as it thynketh me°   then / seems to me
      To maken vertu of necessitee
      And take it weel that we may nat eschue,°   avoid
      And namely that to us alle is due.
2185 And whoso gruccheth° ought, he dooth
            folye,°   whoever / complains at all / folly
      And rebel is to hym that al may gye.°   who may guide all (Jupiter)
      And certeinly a man hath moost honour
      To dyen° in his excellence and flour°   die / flower
      Whan he is siker° of his goode name: sure
2190 Thanne hath he doon° his freend ne hym° no
            shame.   done / nor himself
      And gladder oghte° his freend been of his deeth   ought
      Whan with honour up yolden° is his breeth   yielded up
      Than whan his name apalled° is for age,   faded
      For al forgeten is his vassellage.°   service in arms
2195 Thanne is it best as for a worthy fame
      To dyen whan that he is best of name.
      "The contrarie of al this is wilfulnesse.

Why grucchen° we? Why have we hevynesse° complain / sadness
That goode Arcite, of chivalrie flour,
2200 Departed is with duetee° and honour   duty
      Out of this foule prisoun of this lyf?
      Why grucchen heere his cosyn and his wyf
      Of his welfare, that loved hem so weel?
      Kan he hem thank? Nay, God woot, never a deel,°   not a bit
2205 That bothe his soule and eek hemself offende,°   harm
      And yet they mowe° hir lustes nat amend.   can
      What may I concluden of this longe serye,°   series of arguments
      But after wo I rede° us to be merye°   advise / merry
      And thanken Juppiter of al his grace?
2210 And er that we departen from this place,
      I rede we make of sorwes two
      O° parfit joye, lastynge everemo.   one
      And looketh now, wher° moost sorwe is
            herinne,°   where / in this matter
      Ther wol we first amenden° and bigynne.   amend
2215   "Suster," quod he, "this is my fulle assent,°   desire
      With al th'avys° heere° of my parlement,   advice / here
      That gentil Palamon, thyn owene° knyght,   your own
      That serveth yow with wille,° herte, and myght   (all his) will
      And evere hath doon syn that ye first hym knewe,
2220 That ye shul of youre grace upon hym rewe° have pity upon him
      And taken hym for housbonde and for lord.
      Lene° me youre hond, for this is oure accord.   give
      Lat se° now of youre wommanly pitee.   let (us) see
      He is a kynges brother sone, pardee,°   by God
2225 And though he were a povre bacheler,°   poor young knight
      Syn he hath served yow so many a yeer
      And had for yow so greet adversitee,
      It moste been° considered, leeveth me.°   must be / believe me
      For gentil mercy oghte to passen right."°   prevail over justice
2230   Thanne seyde he thus to Palamon ful right,°   forthrightly
      "I trowe ther nedeth litel sermonyng°   few words
      To make yow assente to this thyng.
      Com neer, and taak youre lady by the hond!"
      Bitwixen hem was maad° anon the bond   made
2235 That highte matrimoigne° or mariage,   matrimony
      By al the conseil° and the baronage,°   council / company of barons
      And thus with alle blisse and melodye
      Hath Palamon ywedded Emelye.
      And God that al this wyde world hath wroght°   made
2240 Sende hym his love that it deere aboght.° who purchased it dearly
      For now is Palamon in alle wele,°   good fortune
      Lyvynge in blisse, in richesse, and in heele,°   health

---

[1] *What ... kyng*   Theseus here identifies Jupiter, as the King of the
classical gods, with the First Mover.

[2] *And ... stryve*   And against this it is of no use for any living
creature, of whatever rank, to struggle.

And Emelye hym loveth so tendrely,
And he hire serveth so gentilly,°   *nobly*
2245   That nevere was ther no word hem bitwene
Of jalousie or any oother teene.°   *discord*

Thus endeth Palamon and Emelye.
And God save al this faire compaignye! Amen.

HEERE IS ENDED THE KNYGHTES TALE

The Miller's Prologue and Tale

When the Knight has finished his tale, much applauded by the "gentles," the Host turns to the pilgrim who, after the Prioress, ranks next in the social hierarchy: the Monk, a senior brother from a wealthy monastery. But the Miller, who has already placed himself at the head of the pilgrims to lead them out of town with his discordant bagpipes, has no respect for social hierarchy. He insists that he will "quyte" the Knight, that is, repay him or match him, and his tale does just that. With the insertion of *The Miller's Tale*, Chaucer breaks decisively from less dynamic frame narratives such as Boccaccio's *Decameron*, in which the stories are told by a homogeneous and harmonious group of aristocrats, and launches a social comedy in which the various tellers will contest each other's authority and values.

The Miller's Tale belongs to the medieval genre of the *fabliau,* a short tale of trickery often set among lower-class or bourgeois characters. These tales may have circulated orally, but they were also written down, and the written versions were enjoyed by aristocratic, not peasant, readers. Chaucer draws on two well-established *fabliau* plots. In the first, a young scholar cuckolds an old husband by making him believe that a second flood is coming; in the second, a young lover humiliates a rival by tricking him into a misdirected kiss. Chaucer may have drawn on a source that had already combined these two plots or may have combined them himself. Early critics, embarrassed by the tale's vulgarity, tended to regard it as a regrettable lapse and take Chaucer at his word when he apologizes in *The General Prologue* for his boorish lower-class characters, whom he designates as "churls" who insist on telling churlish stories. But Chaucer devoted all his powers of comic timing, sensual description, and social satire to expanding the basic story line into a comic masterpiece, in which the two plots come together when Nicholas calls for water.

The Miller tells his tale, a "legend or a life" (which would normally mean a saint's life) of the cuckolding of an old carpenter, in part to attack the Reeve, who is also a carpenter—and a professional rival, since reeves were expected to catch dishonest millers. The Miller's rivalry with the Knight, however, and his claim that he will "quyte" him, invite readers to observe how extensively his tale parallels that of the Knight. These parallels all serve to subvert the values of *The Knight's Tale*, calling into question its lengthy tribute to cosmic order, its chivalric dignity, and its depiction of refined love from afar. Whereas Palamon and Arcite are almost interchangeable, Nicholas, who is "hende" or handy in so many ways, is completely unlike the squeamish Absolon; and Alison, in complete contrast to the passive Emelye, is an energetic schemer, who participates gleefully in Absolon's humiliation.

Set in Oxford, *The Miller's Tale* gives a vivid sense of medieval student life and reveals the tensions between the more prosperous members of the peasantry and cunning clerics. Most unusually, the butt of the story, the old cuckolded husband, becomes a complex and often sympathetic character. John the carpenter is allowed to expand upon his philosophy of life, warning against prying into God's secrets, just as the Miller warns the Reeve not to pry into his wife's secrets. With the fast pace of burlesque or a modern situation comedy, *The Miller's Tale* is filled with vivid details of domestic life; it could not be more different from the Knight's, and its insistence that cleverness or proximity will triumph over high ideals is one of its many possible morals. The tale offers solace and *sentens*, but exactly what this *sentens* is remains the source of continual debate.

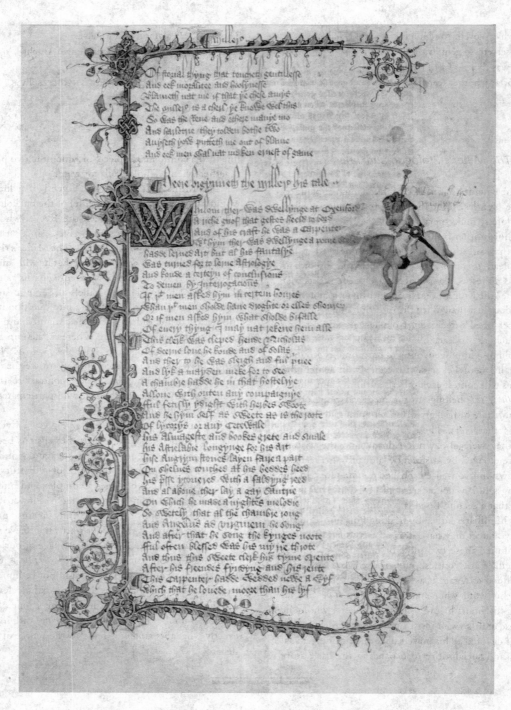

Opening page to *The Miller's Tale*, Ellesmere manuscript. (Reprinted by permission of *The Huntington Library, San Marino, California*. EL 26 C9 f. 34v.)

THE MILLER'S PROLOGUE

HERE FOLWEN THE WORDES BITWENE THE HOOST AND THE MILLERE

Whan that the Knyght hath thus his tale ytoold,°   *told*
   In al the route° ne was ther° yong
      ne° oold   *company / there was not / nor*
That he ne seyde° it was a noble storie   *did not say*
And worthy for to drawen to memorie,°   *learn by heart*
5 And namely° the gentils°
      everichon.°   *especially / gentlefolk / every one*
Oure Hoost lough° and swoor,° "So moot I
      gon,[1]   *laughed / swore*
This gooth aright!° Unbokeled° is the
      male.°   *goes well / unbuckled / purse*
Lat se,° now, who shal telle another tale?   *let's see*
For trewely, the game is wel bigonne.
10 Now telleth on, Sire Monk, if that ye konne,°   *if you can*
Somwhat to quite with° the knyghtes tale."   *match*
The Millere, that for dronken° was al pale   *being drunk*
So that unnethe° upon his hors he sat,   *scarcely*
He nolde° avalen° neither hood ne hat   *would not / take off*
15 Ne abyde° no man for his curteisie,°   *put up with / courtesy*
But in Pilates[2] voys° he gan° to crie   *voice / began*
And swoor, "By armes and by blood and bones,[3]
I kan° a noble tale for the nones°   *know / occasion*
With which I wol now quite° the Knyghtes tale!"   *match*
20 Oure Hoost saugh° that he was dronke of ale   *saw*
And seyde, "Abyd,° Robyn, my leeve° brother,   *wait / dear*
Som bettre man shal telle us first another.
Abyde, and lat° us werken° thriftily."°   *let / work / respectably*
    "By Goddes soule," quod° he, "that wol° nat I.   *said / will*
25 For I wol speke or elles° go my wey."°   *else / way*
Oure Hoost answerde, "Tel on a devele wey!°   *in the devil's name*
Thou art a fool! Thy wit is overcome!"
    "Now herkneth,"° quod the Millere, "alle and
      some.°   *listen / one and all*

But first I make a protestacioun°   *protest*
30 That I am dronke; I knowe it by my soun.°   *sound*
And therfore if that I mysspeke or seye,°   *say something wrong*
Wyte it° the ale of Southwerk, I preye.°   *blame it on / pray*
For I wol tell a legende and a lyf[4]
Bothe of a carpenter and of his wyf,
35 How that a clerk° hath set the wrightes cappe."[5]   *student*
    The Reve answerde and seyde, "Stynt thy
      clappe!°   *shut your mouth*
Lat be thy lewed,° dronken°
      harlotrye!°   *ignorant / drunken / bawdiness*
It is a synne° and eek° a greet° folye°   *sin / also / great / folly*
To apeyren° any man or hym° defame°   *harm / him / slander*
40 And eek to bryngen wyves in swich° fame.°   *such / dishonor*
Thou mayst ynogh° of othere thynges seyn."°   *enough / speak*
    This dronke° Millere spak° ful° soone
      agayn°   *drunken / spoke / very / again*
And seyde, "Leve brother Osewold,
Who hath no wyf, he is no cokewold.[6]
45 But I sey nat therfore that thou art oon.°   *one*
Ther been ful goode wyves many oon,°   *a one*
And evere a thousand goode ayeyns° oon badde.°   *against / bad*
That knowestow wel° thyself, but if° thou
      madde.°   *you know well / unless / are mad*
Why artow° angry with my tale now?   *are you*
50 I have a wyf, perdee,° as wel as thow,   *by God*
Yet nolde° I for the oxen in my plogh°   *would not / plow*
Take upon me moore than ynogh,°   *enough*
As demen° of myself that I were oon.°   *judge / one (i.e., a cuckold)*
I wol bileve° wel that I am noon.°   *believe / none*
55 An housbonde shal nat been inquisityf°   *inquisitive*
Of Goddes pryvetee° nor of his wyf.   *secrets*
So he may fynde° Goddes foyson° there,   *find / abundance*
Of the remenant nedeth nat enquere!"°   *he need not inquire*
    What sholde I moore seyn, but this Millere,
60 He nolde° his wordes for no man
      forbere,°   *would not / bear patiently*
But tolde his cherles° tale in his manere.°   *boor's / manner*
M'athynketh° that I shal reherce° it heere,   *I regret / repeat*

---

[1] *So ... gon* I.e., as I hope to live.

[2] *But in Pilates* I.e., Pontius Pilate, the Roman governor who condemned Jesus to be crucified. In medieval religious plays he was depicted as a loud, rampaging villain.

[3] *By ... bones* Swearing during the Middle Ages and Renaissance often involved taking oaths on various parts of God's body—here God's arms, blood, and bones.

[4] *legende and a lyf* Normally a "saint's life," or biography of a Christian saint.

[5] *set the wrightes cappe* Made a fool of the carpenter.

[6] *cokewold* I.e., cuckold: a husband whose wife has sex with another man.

And therfore every gentil° wight° I preye,°   *noble | person | pray*
For Goddes love demeth° nat° that I seye°   *judge | not | speak*
65 Of yvel entente,° but that I moot reherce°   *evil intent | repeat*
Hir° tales, all be they° bettre or werse,   *their | although they be*
Or elles° falsen° som of my mateere.°   *else | falsify | matter*
And therfore,° whoso° list° it nat
yheere,°   *whoever | wishes | not to hear*
Turne over the leef,° and chese° another tale.   *page | choose*
70 For he shal fynde° ynowe,° grete° and
smale,°   *find | enough | great | small*
Of storial° thyng that toucheth gentillesse°   *historical | nobility*
And eek moralitee° and hoolynesse.°   *morality | holiness*
Blameth nat me if that ye chese amys.°   *choose wrongly*
The millere is a cherl.° Ye knowe wel this.   *boor*
75 So was the Reve, and othere manye mo,°   *more*
And harlotrie° they tolden bothe two.   *bawdiness*
Avyseth yow;° putteth me out of blame,   *be advised*
And eek men shal nat maken ernest° of game.°   *seriousness | joke*

THE MILLER'S TALE

HEERE BIGYNNETH THE MILLERE HIS TALE

Whilom° ther was dwellynge° at
Oxenford°   *once | living | Oxford*
80 A riche gnof° that gestes° heeld to bord,[1]   *fellow | guests*
And of his craft° he was a carpenter.   *profession*
With hym ther was dwellynge a povre° scoler°   *poor | student*
Hadde lerned° art, but al his fantasye°   *learned | interest*
Was turned for to lerne astrologye,
85 And koude a certeyn of condusiouns[2]
To demen° by interrogaciouns°   *judge | questions*
If that men asked hym in certein houres[3]
Whan that men sholde have droghte° or elles
shoures,°   *drought | rain*
Or if men asked hym what sholde bifalle°   *happen*
90 Of every thyng—I may nat rekene° hem° all.   *count up | them*
This clerk was cleped° hende° Nicholas.   *named | handy*

---

[1] *heeld to bord* Rented out rooms.

[2] *koude a certeyn of conclusiouns* Knew some (astrological) calculations.

[3] *houres* I.e., astrological hours—times when certain planets
exerted a certain influence.

Of deerne° love he koude° and of solas,°   *secret | knew | pleasure*
And therto he was sleigh° and ful privee°   *sly | very secretive*
And lyk° a mayden meke° for to see.   *like | meek*
95 A chambre° hadde he in that hostelrye,°   *room | lodging*
Allone° withouten any compaignye.   *alone*
Ful fetisly° ydight° with herbes[4]
swoote,°   *fashionably | decorated | sweet*
And he hymself as swete as is the roote°   *root*
Of lycorys° or any cetewale.[5]   *licorice*
100 His *Almageste*[6] and bookes grete and smale,
His astrelabie[7] longynge for° his art,   *pertaining to*
Hise augrym stones[8] layen° faire apart°   *lay | somewhat away*
On shelves couched° at his beddes heed,°   *arranged | bed's head*
His presse° ycovered° with a faldyng°
reed,°   *cupboard | covered | cloth | red*
105 And al above ther lay a gay sautrie°[9]
On which he made a nyghtes° melodie°   *nightly | melody*
So swetely that al the chambre rong.°   *rang*
And *Angelus ad virginem*[10] he song,
And after that he song *The Kynges Noote*;[11]
110 Full often blessed was his myrie° throte!°   *merry | throat*
And thus this sweete clerk his tyme spente
After his freendes fyndyng[12] and his rente.°   *income*

---

[4] *ydight with herbes* Spread with dried and sweet smelling herbs.

[5] *cetewale* The spice zedoary, similar to ginger.

[6] *Almageste* I.e., *Almagest*, the basic textbook for medieval
astronomy. It was the work of Claudius Ptolemy (2nd century CE),
who gives his name to the Ptolemaic system, in which the sun
revolves around the earth. According to Ptolemy, the heavens
comprised nine concentric crystal spheres that revolved and on
which the planets and stars were affixed.

[7] *astrelabie* I.e., astrolabe, a scientific instrument used to measure
angles of heavenly bodies. Chaucer wrote *The Treatise on the
Astrolabe*, a prose work that is one of the first pieces of technical
writing in the English language.

[8] *augrym stones* I.e., Augrim stones; they were marked with
numbers and were used for making mathematical calculations.

[9] *sautrie* I.e., psaltery, a stringed musical instrument.

[10] *Angelus ad virginem* Latin: The Angel to the Virgin. The song,
an antiphon used in liturgical service, depicts the conversation
between the angel Gabriel and the Virgin Mary about the coming
birth of Jesus.

[11] *The Kynges Noote* This song has not survived.

[12] *After his freendes fyndyng* According to what his friends found to
give him.

This carpenter hadde wedded newe° a wyf   *newly married*
Which that he lovede moore than his lyf.
115 Of eighteteene yeer she was of age.
Jalous° he was and heeld hire narwe° in cage,[1]   *jealous / closely*
For she was yong and wylde and he was old,
And demed° hymself been° lik° a
        cokewold.°   *guessed / to be / likely / cuckold*
He knew nat Catoun,[2] for his wit° was
        rude,°   *intelligence / unformed*
120 That bad° man sholde wedde his
        simylitude.°   *who advised / equal*
Men sholde wedden after hire° estaat,°   *their / condition*
For youthe and elde° is often at debaat.°   *age / in dispute*
But sith° that he was fallen in the snare,°   *since / trap*
He moste endure as oother folk his care.°   *sorrow*
125   Fair was this yonge wyf and therwithal
As any wezele° hir body gent° and smal.   *weasel / delicate*
A ceynt° she werede° ybarred° al of silk,   *girdle / wore / striped*
A barmclooth° as whit° as morne° milk   *apron / white / morning*
Upon hir lendes,° ful of many a goore.°   *hips / pleat*
130 Whit° was hir smok° and broyden° al
        bifoore°   *white / undergarment / embroidered / in front*
And eek bihynde on hir coler° aboute   *collar*
Of col-blak° silk withinne and eek withoute.   *coal-black*
The tapes° of hir white voluper°   *ribbons / cap*
Were of the same suyte° of hir coler,   *pattern*
135 Hir filet° brood° of silk and set ful hye,°   *headband / broad / high*
And sikerly° she hadde a likerous° eye.   *certainly / flirtatious*
Ful smale ypulled° were hire browes° two,   *plucked / eyebrows*
And tho° were bent and blake° as any
        sloo.°   *they / black / sloeberry*
She was ful moore blisful° on to see   *much more pleasant*
140 Than is the newe perejonette tree,°   *pear tree*
And softer than the wolle° is of a wether.°   *wool / male sheep*
And by hir girdel° heeng a purs of
        lether°   *belt / hung a purse of leather*
Tasseled with grene° and perled° with
        latoun.°   *green / decorated / brass*
In al this world to seken° up and doun   *seek*

145 Ther nas° no man so wys° that koude
        thenche°   *was not / wise / imagine*
So gay a popelote° or swich a wenche.°   *doll / peasant girl*
Full brighter was the shynyng° of hir hewe°   *shining / complexion*
Than in the Tour° the noble° yforged°
        newe![3]   *tower / gold coin / forged*
But of hir song, it was as loude and yerne°   *eager*
150 As any swalwe° sittynge on a berne.°   *swallow / barn*
Therto she koude skippe° and make game°   *dance / play*
As any kyde° or calf folwynge his dame.°   *kid (young goat) / mother*
Hir mouth was sweete as bragot° or the
        meeth°   *ale / mead (fermented honey)*
Or hoord° of apples leyd° in hey° or
        heeth.°   *hoard / stored / hay / heather*
155 Wynsynge° she was as is a joly° colt,   *skittish / pretty*
Long as a mast and upright° as a bolt.°   *straight / arrow*
A brooch° she baar° upon hir loue
        coler°   *broach / wore / low collar*
As brood° as is the boos[4] of a bokeler.°   *broad / shield*
Hir shoes were laced on hir legges hye.°   *high*
160 She was a prymerole,° a piggesnye°   *primrose / pig's eye (flower)*
For any lord to leggen° in his bedde   *lay*
Or yet for any good yeman° to wedde.   *yeoman*
        Now sire° and eft° sire, so bifel° the cas   *sir / again / befell / event*
That on a day this hende° Nicholas   *handy*
165 Fil° with this yonge wyf to rage° and pleye   *fell / romp*
Whil that hir housbonde was at Oseneye,[5]
As clerkes been ful subtile° and ful queynte,°   *subtle / clever*
And prively° he caughte hire by the queynte°[6]   *secretly / genitals*
And seyde, "Ywis,° but if° ich° have my wille,   *indeed / unless / I*
170 For deerne° love of thee, lemman,° I
        spille,"°   *secret / sweetheart / die*
And heeld hire harde by the haunche bones°   *thighs*

---

[1] *in cage* In a cage; i.e., he guarded her carefully.

[2] *Catoun* I.e., Cato. The *Distichs*, a widely circulating collection of proverbs and wise sayings in verse couplets, often used for teaching Latin in schools, were ascribed in the Middle Ages to the Roman writer Dionysius Cato.

---

[3] *Than ... newe* Gold coins were forged in the Tower of London.

[4] *boos* I.e., boss, the center bulge of a shield, occasionally used to injure an enemy.

[5] *Oseneye* I.e., Oseney, a small town just to the west of Oxford (now part of the modern city) where there was an abbey.

[6] *queynte* A rhyme on two homonyms (such as *blue / blew* or *guest / guessed*), near homonyms (such as *seke / seke*, i.e., *seek* and *sick* in the General Prologue, lines 18–19) or on two different meanings of the same word, as here with *queynte*, was known as "rime riche" and was much valued by the French court poets of Chaucer's day. The modern term "rich rhyme" has a slightly narrower meaning and is confined to rhymes on homonyms.

And seyde, "Lemman,° love me al at
    ones°   *sweetheart | immediately*
Or I wol dyen,° also° God me save!"   *die | as*
And she sproong° as a colt dooth° in the
    trave,°   *sprang | does | stall*
175 And with hir heed she wryed° faste awey.   *twisted*
She seyde, "I wol nat kisse thee, by my fey!°   *faith*
Why, lat be, quod ich,°[1] lat be Nicholas,   *I say*
Or I wol crie 'Out, harrow, and allas!'[2]
Do wey° youre handes, for youre curteisye!"   *let go*
180   This Nicholas gan mercy for to crye
And spak so faire and profred° hire so faste   *urged*
That she hir love hym graunted atte last°   *at last*
And swoor hir ooth,° "By Seint Thomas of
    Kent,"°   *oath | St. Thomas à Becket*
That she wol° been at his comandement   *would*
185 Whan that she may hir leyser° wel espie.°   *leisure | see*
"Myn housbonde is so ful of jalousie
That but° ye wayte° wel and been privee,°   *unless | wait | secretive*
I woot° right wel I nam° but deed," quod she.   *know | am not*
"Ye moste been ful deerne° as in this cas."°   *secretive | business*
190   "Nay, therof care thee noght,"° quod Nicholas,   *have no care*
"A clerk hadde lutherly biset his whyle[3]
But if° he koude a carpenter bigyle."°   *unless | trick*
And thus they been accorded° and ysworn°   *agreed | sworn*
To wayte a tyme° as I have told biforn.°   *wait (for a time) | before*
195   Whan Nicholas had doon° thus everideel°   *done | every bit*
And thakked° hire aboute the lendes° weel,°   *patted | loins | well*
He kiste hire sweete and taketh his sawtrie°   *psaltery*
And pleyeth° faste and maketh melodie.   *plays*
    Thanne fil it° thus that to the paryssh chirche   *it happened*
200 Cristes owene werkes° for to wirche,°   *works | perform*
This goode wyf wente on an haliday.[4]
Hir forheed° shoon° as bright as any day,   *forehead | shone*
So was it wasshen° whan she leet° hir werk.°   *washed | left | work*

Now was ther of that chirche° a parissh clerk[5]   *church*
205 The which that was ycleped° Absolon.[6]   *called*
Crul° was his heer, and as the gold it shoon,   *curled*
And strouted° as a fanne° large and
    brode;°   *stretched out | fan | broad*
Ful streight and evene lay his joly shode.°   *parting of his hair*
His rode° was reed,° hise eyen greye as
    goos,°   *complexion | red | goose*
210 With Poules wyndow[7] corven° on his shoos.°   *carved | shoes*
In hoses° rede° he wente fetisly.°   *stockings | red | elegantly*
Yclad° he was ful smal° and proprely   *clothed | very tightly*
Al in a kirtel° of a lyght waget.°   *tunic | blue*
Ful faire and thikke° been the poyntes° set,   *thick | laces*
215 And therupon he hadde a gay surplys° *surplice (liturgical garment)*
As whit as is the blosme upon the rys.°   *twig*
A myrie° child° he was, so God me save.   *merry | young man*
Wel koude he laten blood° and clippe and shave[8]   *let blood*
And maken a chartre° of lond° or
    acquitaunce.°   *contract | land | quit-claim*
220 In twenty manere koude he trippe and daunce
After the scole° of Oxenford tho,°   *school | then*
And with his legges casten to and fro
And pleyen songes on a smal
    rubible.°   *rebec (bowed stringed instrument)*
Therto he song somtyme a loud quynyble,°   *falsetto*
225 And as wel koude he pleye on his
    giterne.°   *gittern (plucked stringed instrument)*
In al the toun° nas° brewhous ne taverne   *town | was not*
That he ne visited° with his solas°   *did not visit | comfort*
Ther any gaylard tappestere° was.   *merry bar-maid*
But sooth to seyn, he was somdeel
    squaymous°   *somewhat squeamish*

---

[1] *quod ich* Both Ellesmere and Hengwrt read "ich" here, yet modern editors emend to "she," under the assumption that Chaucer is here slipping in and out of direct discourse. The manuscript readings can be defended on the basis of her uttering these words: "Let me be, I said, let me be, Nicholas…!"

[2] *Out, harrow, and allas* Common cries of alarm to summon assistance.

[3] *lutherly biset his whyle* Wasted his time.

[4] *haliday* I.e., holy day; a saint's day or the day of a major religious celebration.

[5] *a parissh clerk* Absolon is an assistant to the parish priest. He is a member of the clergy and probably in minor orders and might, in due course, be ordained as a priest himself.

[6] *Absolon* The Biblical Absalom, son of King David, was famous for his beauty. Cf. 2 Samuel 14.25–26.

[7] *Poules wyndow* Fancy shoes were sometimes cut to produce a lattice pattern, which Chaucer compares to the stained glass rose window at St. Paul's Cathedral, London, which burned down in the disastrous fire in 1666.

[8] *clippe and shave* Medieval barbers not only worked on one's hair but also did minor surgery like letting blood. This procedure, which involved opening a vein and allowing blood to flow out, was considered important in keeping the body's four humors (one of which was blood) in balance, thus insuring good health.

230 Of fartyng, and of speche daungerous.°   *fastidious*
    This Absolon that jolif° was and gay   *jolly*
Gooth° with a sencer° on the haliday,[1]   *goes / incense censer*
Sensynge° the wyves° of the parisshe
    faste.°   *incensing / wives / diligently*
And many a lovely look on hem° he caste,   *them*
235 And namely° on this carpenteris wyf.   *especially*
To looke on hire hym thoughte a myrie lyf.
She was so propre and sweete and likerous,
I dar wel seyn if she hadde been a mous°   *mouse*
And he a cat, he wolde hire° hente° anon.   *her / grab*
240 This parissh clerk, this joly Absolon,
Hath in his herte swich a love longynge
That of no wyf took he noon offrynge.°   *no offering*
For curteisie, he seyde, he wolde noon.°   *wanted none*
    The moone, whan it was nyght, ful brighte shoon,
245 And Absolon his gyterne° hath ytake;°   *gittern / taken*
For paramours° he thoghte for to wake.°   *love's sake / stay awake*
And forth he gooth, jolif° and amorous,   *jolly*
Til he cam to the carpenteres hous
A litel after cokkes° hadde ycrowe°   *roosters / crowed*
250 And dressed° hym up by a
    shot-wyndowe°   *approached / hinged window*
That was upon the carpenteris wal.°   *wall*
He syngeth in his voys° gentil° and
    smal,°   *voice / refined / high-pitched*
"Now deere lady, if thy wille be,
I pray yow that ye wole thynke on me,"
255 Ful wel acordaunt° to his
    gyternynge.°   *in accord / playing of the gittern*
This carpenter awook and herde synge
And spak unto his wyf and seyde anon,
"What, Alison, herestow nat° Absolon   *don't you hear*
That chaunteth° thus under oure boures°
    wal?"   *who sings / bedroom's*
260 And she answerde hir housbonde therwithal,
"Yis, God woot,° John! I heere it every deel."   *God knows / every bit*
    This passeth forth. What wol ye bet than
    weel?°   *what more do you want?*
Fro day to day this joly Absolon
So woweth° hire that hym is wobigon.°   *woos / filled with woe*
265 He waketh al the nyght and al the day.

He kembeth° hise lokkes° brode and made hym
    gay.   *combs / hair*
He woweth hire by meenes° and brocage°   *go-betweens / agents*
And swoor he wolde been hir owene page.°   *young servant*
He syngeth brokkynge° as a nyghtyngale.   *twittering*
270 He sent hire pyment,° meeth,° and spiced ale   *spiced wine / mead*
And wafres° pipyng hoot° out of the
    gleede,°   *wafer cakes / hot / fire*
And for° she was of towne, he profreth meede.°   *because / money*
For som folk wol ben wonnen° for richesse,   *won*
And somme for strokes,° and somme for
    gentillesse.°   *force / nobility*
275 Somtyme to shewe his lightnesse° and maistrye°   *agility / ability*
He playeth Herodes[2] upon a scaffold° hye.°   *stage / high*
But what availleth hym as in this cas?
She loveth so this hende Nicholas
That Absolon may blowe the bukkes° horn.[3]   *buck's*
280 He ne hadde° for his labour but a scorn.   *did not have*
And thus she maketh Absolon hire ape,
And al his ernest° turneth til a jape.°   *seriousness / joke*
Ful sooth° is this proverbe, it is no lye,°   *true / lie*
Men seyn right thus: "Alwey the nye slye°   *near sly one*
285 Maketh the ferre° leeve° to be looth."°   *far / loved one / hated*
For though that Absolon be wood° or wrooth,°   *crazy / angry*
Bycause that he fer° was from hire sighte,   *far*
This nye Nicholas stood in his lighte.
    Now bere° thee wel, thou hende Nicholas,   *bear*
290 For Absolon may waille° and synge "Allas!"   *complain*
And so bifel it° on a Saterday   *it happened*
This carpenter was goon° til Osenay,°   *gone / to Oseney*
And hende Nicholas and Alisoun
Acorded° been to this conclusioun   *agreed*
295 That Nicholas shal shapen° hym a wyle°   *fabricate / scheme*
This sely,° jalous housbonde to bigyle,°   *simple / trick*
And if so be the game wente aright,
She sholde slepen° in his arm al nyght,   *sleep*
For this was his desir and hire° also.   *hers*
300 And right anon, withouten wordes mo,
This Nicholas no lenger wolde tarie,°   *delay*
But dooth ful softe° unto his chambre carie°   *quietly / carry*

---

[1] *Gooth … holiday*   It was and is the custom in liturgical churches to burn incense in a censer, a metal container which hung from a chain and was swung about by a cleric called a thurifer.

[2] *Herodes*   I.e., King Herod. Told of the birth of the Messiah, Herod ordered the slaughter of all male children born in Bethlehem, an event depicted in some religious plays.

[3] *blowe the bukkes horn*   The expression "blow the buck's horn" more or less means "go whistle."

Bothe mete° and drynke for a day or tweye°   *food | two*
And to hire housbonde bad hire for to seye,°   *asked her to say*
305 If that he axed° after Nicholas,   *asked*
She sholde seye she nyste° where he was;   *did not know*
Of al that day she saugh° hym nat° with eye.   *saw | not*
She trowed° that he was in maladye,°   *believed | sickness*
For° for° no cry hir mayde koude hym calle.   *because | with*
310 He nolde° answere for thyng° that myghte
     falle.°   *would not | anything | happen*
     This passeth forth al thilke° Saterday,   *that same*
That Nicholas stille° in his chambre lay   *quietly*
And eet° and sleepe° or dide what hym
     leste,°   *ate | slept | what he wanted*
Til Sonday that the sonne gooth to reste.
315 This sely carpenter hath greet merveyle°   *wondered greatly*
Of Nicholas or what thyng myghte hym eyle°   *ail (trouble)*
And seyde, "I am adrad,° by Seint Thomas,   *afraid*
It stondeth nat aright with Nicholas.
God shilde° that he deyde° sodeynly!   *forbid | died*
320 This world is now ful tikel,° sikerly.°   *uncertain | certainly*
I saugh today a cors° yborn° to chirche   *body | carried*
That now on Monday last I saugh hym wirche!°   *work*
     Go up," quod he unto his knave°
     anoon,°   *serving boy | immediately*
"Clepe° at his dore or knokke with a stoon.   *call*
325 Looke how it is and tel me boldely."
     This knave gooth hym up ful sturdily
And at the chambre dore whil that he stood,
He cride and knokked as that he were wood,
"What how! What do ye, maister Nicholay?
330 How may ye slepen al the longe day?"
     But al for noght. He herde nat a word.
An hole he foond ful lowe upon a bord°   *board*
Theras° the cat was wont° in for to
     crepe,°   *where | accustomed | creep*
And at that hole he looked in ful depe
335 Til at the laste he hadde of hym a sighte.
This Nicholas sat capyng evere uprighte°   *gaping upwards*
As he had kiked° on the newe moone.   *looked*
Adoun° he gooth and tolde his maister soone   *down*
In what array° he saugh that ilke° man.   *condition | same*
340 This carpenter to blessen[1] hym bigan°   *began*

And seyde, "Help us, Seinte Frydeswyde![2]
A man woot litel what hym shal bityde!°   *shall happen to him*
This man is falle° with his astromye°   *fallen | astronomy*
In som woodnesse° or in som agonye.°   *madness | fit*
345 I thoghte ay° wel how that it sholde be.   *I always thought*
Men sholde nat knowe of Goddes pryvetee.°   *secrets*
Yblessed° be alwey a lewed° man   *blessed | uneducated*
That noght but oonly° his Bileve[3] kan.°   *nothing other than | knows*
So ferde° another clerk with astromye:°   *it happened | astronomy*
350 He walked in the feeldes° for to prye°   *fields | pry (study foolishly)*
Upon the sterres,° what ther sholde bifalle,   *stars*
Til he was in a marleput[4] yfalle.°   *fallen*
He saugh nat that! But yet by Seint Thomas,
Me reweth° soore of hende Nicholas.   *I have pity*
355 He shal be rated of° his studiyng   *scolded for*
If that I may, by Jhesus hevene° kyng!   *Heaven's*
Get me a staf° that I may underspore,°   *staff | pry*
Whil that thou, Robyn, hevest of the dore.°   *heave off the door*
He shal out of his studiyng, as I gesse."°   *guess*
360 And to the chambre dore° he gan hym dresse.°   *door | approached*
His knave° was a strong carl° for the
     nones,°   *servant | fellow | occasion*
And by the haspe° he haaf it of°
     atones;°   *hinge | heaved it off | at once*
Into° the floor the dore° fil° anon.   *onto | door | fell*
This Nicholas sat ay° as stille as stoon°   *ever | stone*
365 And evere caped° upward into the eir.°   *gaped | air*
This carpenter wende° he were in despeir,   *believed*
And hente° hym by the sholdres° myghtily   *grabbed | shoulders*
And shook hym harde and cride spitously,°   *loudly*
"What Nicholay! What, how! What! Looke adoun!
370 Awake and thenk° on Cristes Passioun!   *think*
I crouche° thee from elves and fro
     wightes."°   *sign with the cross | evil creatures*
Therwith the nyght spel[5] seyde he anonrightes°   *right away*

---

[2] *Seinte Frydeswyde* The Anglo-Saxon St. Frideswide, a young noblewoman who was persecuted for her desire to be a nun, is the patron saint of the town of Oxford. She was abbess of a monastery that was on the site of the present Christ Church, Oxford.

[3] *Bileve* Carpenter John's "Believe" is his Creed—the Apostle's Creed, which, along with the Lord's Prayer, was to be memorized by every Christian.

[4] *marleput* I.e., marl-pit, a ditch on a farm for keeping marl, a type of soil rich in clay and used for fertilizing fields.

[5] *nyght spel* Spell or charm said at night to ward off evil spirits.

---

[1] *blessen* I.e., to bless oneself, to make the sign of the cross.

On foure halves° of the hous aboute · *four corners*
And on the threshfold° of the dore withoute. · *threshold*

375 "Jhesu Crist and Seint Benedight[1]
Blesse this hous from every wikked wight
For nyghtes nerye° the white Pater Noster:° · *save / Lord's Prayer*
Where wentestow,° Seint Petres soster?"[2]
    And atte laste this hende Nicholas

380 Gan for to sike° soore and seyde, "Allas! · *sigh*
Shal al this world be lost eftsoones° now?" · *immediately*
    This carpenter answerde, "What seystow?° · *do you say*
What! Thynk on God as we doon, men that swynke."[3]
    This Nicholas answerde, "Fecche° me drynke, · *get*

385 And after wol I speke in pryvetee
Of certeyn thyng that toucheth me and thee.
I wol telle it noon oother° man certeyn." · *(to) no other*
    This carpenter goth doun and comth ageyn° · *comes again*
And broghte of myghty ale a large quart.

390 And whan that ech of hem had dronke his part,
This Nicholas his dore faste shette° · *shut*
And doun the carpenter by hym he sette.
    He seyde, "John, myn hoost, lief° and deere, · *beloved*
Thou shalt upon thy trouthe swere me here

395 That to no wight thou shalt this conseil° wreye,° · *counsel / betray*
For it is Cristes conseil that I seye!
And if thou telle man, thou art forlore,° · *lost*
For this vengeaunce thou shalt han therfore:° · *for it*
That if thou wreye° me, thou shalt be wood." · *betray*

400 "Nay, Crist forbede it for his hooly blood!"
Quod tho this sely man, "I nam no labbe.° · *am no blabber*
Ne, though I seye, I am nat lief to gabbe.° · *accustomed to gab*
Sey what thou wolt, I shal it nevere telle
To child ne wyf, by hym that harwed helle!"[4]

---

405 "Now John," quod Nicholas, "I wol nat lye.
I have yfounde° in myn astrologye · *found*
As I have looked in the moone bright
That now a Monday next° at quarter nyght[5] · *next Monday*
Shal falle a reyn,° and that so wilde and wood · *rain*

410 That half so greet° was nevere Noees° Flood. · *great / Noah's*
This world," he seyde, "in lasse than an hour · *less*
Shal al be dreynt,° so hidous is the shour.° · *drowned / downpour*
Thus shal mankynde drenche° and lese hir lyf." · *drown*
    This carpenter answerde, "Allas, my wyf!

415 And shal she drenche? Allas, my Alisoun!"
For sorwe° of this he fil° almoost adoun · *sorrow / fell*
And seyde, "Is ther no remedie in this cas?"
    "Why, yis, for Gode," quod hende Nicholas.
"If thou wolt werken° after loore° and reed.° · *act / teaching / advice*

420 Thou mayst nat werken after thyn owene
    heed,° · *head (intelligence)*
For thus seith Salomon,[6] that was ful trewe:
'Werk° al by conseil and thou shalt nat rewe!'° · *do / regret*
And if thou werken wolt by good conseil,
I undertake withouten mast and seyl° · *sail*

425 Yet shal I saven hire° and thee and me. · *save her*
Hastou nat herd how saved was Noe° · *Noah*
Whan that oure Lord hadde warned hym biforn° · *before*
That al the world with water sholde be lorn?"° · *lost*
    "Yis," quod this carpenter, "ful yoore ago."° · *very long ago*

430   "Hastou nat herd," quod Nicholas, "also,
The sorwe of Noe with his felaweshipe
Er that he myghte brynge his wyf to shipe?[7]
Hym hadde be levere,° I dar° wel
    undertake,° · *he had rather / dare / affirm*
At thilke tyme° than alle hise wetheres
    blake° · *at that time / black sheep*

435 That she hadde had a shipe hirself° allone. · *to herself*
And therfore woostou° what is best to doone? · *do you know*

---

[1] *Seint Benedight* St. Benedict of Nursia was an early sixth-century abbot who wrote the famous Rule for monasteries.

[2] *For nyghtes … soster* These lines have never been satisfactorily explained and probably represent John's mangling of popular charms or invocations; *Where wentestow* Where did you go; *soster* Sister.

[3] *men that swynke* Men who labor. John is making the old distinction between the three estates here. The first estate comprises those who pray (the profession for which Nicholas is studying), the second, those who fight (the nobility), and the third, those who work and thus provide the food for all three estates.

[4] *harwed helle* The Harrowing of Hell (another subject of medieval religious drama) was the victorious entry Christ made into Hell between his death and resurrection to save the righteous souls held in limbo.

[5] *quarter nyght* One-fourth of the way through the night.

[6] *Salomon* Solomon, the ancient King of Israel, was known for his wisdom and was thought to be the author of several books of the Hebrew Bible. The reference here is to Ecclesiasticus 32.24. John makes a mistake here: Ecclesiasticus, part of the Greek Old Testament considered apocryphal by Protestants or deuterocanonical by Catholics, was written by Jesus ben Sirach, not Solomon, as Saint Augustine (among others) noted.

[7] *to shipe* On board. The difficulty Noah has in getting his wife aboard the Ark is depicted in medieval drama.

This asketh° haste, and of an hastif thyng°   *requires / urgent business*
Men may nat preche or maken tariyng.°   *delay*
   "Anon, go gete us faste into this in°   *house*
440 A knedyng trogh° or ellis a kymelyn°   *kneading pot / tub*
For ech° of us—but looke that they be large—   *each*
In whiche we mowe swymme° as in a barge,   *may float*
And han therinne vitaille suffissant°   *enough food*
But for a day. Fy on° the remenant!   *disregard*
445 The water shal aslake° and goon away   *ebb*
Aboute pryme° upon the nexte day.   *prime (an early hour of prayer)*
But Robyn may nat wite° of this, thy knave,°   *know / servant*
Ne eek thy mayde Gille I may nat save.
Axe nat° why, for though thou aske me,   *ask not*
450 I wol nat tellen Goddes pryvetee.°   *secrets*
Suffiseth thee, but if thy wittes madde,
To han as greet a grace as Noe hadde.[1]
Thy wyf shal I wel saven, out of doute.°   *doubtless*
Go now thy wey, and speed thee heer aboute.
455   "But whan thou hast for hire and thee and me
Ygeten° us thise knedyng tubbes thre,   *gotten*
Thanne shaltow hange hem° in the roof ful hye,   *hang them*
That° no man of oure purveiaunce° spye.   *so that / preparations*
And whan thou thus hast doon as I have seyd
460 And hast oure vitaille faire in hem yleyd,°   *laid*
And eek an ax to smyte the corde° atwo°   *rope / in two*
Whan that the water comth, that we may go,
And breke an hole anheigh° up on the gable   *on high*
Unto the gardynward° over the stable,   *towards the garden*
465 That we may frely passen forth oure way
Whan that the grete shour is goon away.
Thanne shal I swymme as myrie,° I undertake,°   *merrily / expect*
As dooth the white doke° after hire drake.°   *duck / male duck*
Thanne wol I clepe,° 'How, Alison! How, John!   *call*
470 Be myrie, for the flood wol passe anon!'
And thou wolt seyn, 'Hayl,° maister Nicholay,   *hail*
Good morwe! I se thee wel, for it is day.'
And thanne shul° we be lordes al oure lyf   *shall*
Of al the world, as Noe and his wyf.
475   "But of o° thyng I warne thee ful right:°   *one / directly*
Be wel avysed on that ilke nyght°   *that same night*
That we ben entred° into shippes bord   *entered*
That noon of us ne speke nat a word,

Ne clepe,° ne crie, but been in his preyere,   *call*
480 For it is Goddes owene heeste° deere.   *commandment*
    "Thy wyf and thou moote hange fer° atwynne,°   *far / apart*
For that bitwixe yow shal be no synne,°   *sin*
Namoore in lookyng than ther shal in deede.
This ordinance° is seyd. Go, God thee speede!   *commandment*
485 Tomorwe at nyght, whan folk ben alle aslepe,
Into oure knedyng tubbes wol we crepe,
And sitten there abidyng Goddes grace.
Go now thy wey. I have no lenger space°   *no more time*
To make of this no lenger sermonyng.°   *speech*
490 Men seyn thus: 'Sende the wise and sey nothing.'
Thou art so wys, it nedeth thee nat to preche.°   *preach*
Go save oure lyf, and that I the biseche."°   *implore*
    This sely carpenter goth forth his wey.
Ful ofte he seith "Allas!" and "Weylawey!"
495 And to his wyf he tolde his pryvetee.°   *secret*
And she was war° and knew it bet° than he   *aware / better*
What al this queynte cast° was for to seye.   *unusual scheme*
But nathelees she ferde as° she wolde deye,   *acted as if*
And seyde, "Allas! Go forth thy wey anon.
500 Help us to scape° or we been lost echon!°   *escape / everyone*
I am thy trewe, verray° wedded wyf.   *faithful*
Go, deere spouse, and help to save oure lyf!"
    Lo, which a greet° thyng is affeccioun!   *what a great*
Men may dyen° of ymaginacioun,°   *die / imagination*
505 So depe° may impressioun be take.°   *deep / taken*
This sely carpenter bigynneth quake.°   *to shake*
Hym thynketh verraily° that he may see   *it truly appears to him*
Noees° Flood come walwynge° as the see   *Noah's / surging*
To drenchen° Alisoun, his hony deere.   *drown*
510 He wepeth, weyleth, maketh sory cheere.°   *a sorry face*
He siketh with ful many a sory swogh.°   *groan*
He gooth and geteth hym a knedyng trogh,
And after that a tubbe and a kymelyn,
And pryvely he sente hem to his in°   *house*
515 And heng hem in the roof in pryvetee.
His owene hand made laddres thre
To clymben by the ronges and the stalkes°   *shafts*
Into the tubbes hangynge in the balkes,°   *beams*
And hem vitailleth,° bothe trogh and tubbe,   *provides food for*
520 With breed and chese and good ale in a jubbe,°   *jug*
Suffisynge right ynogh as for a day.
But er that he hadde maad al this array°   *these preparations*
He sente his knave and eek his wenche also
Upon his nede° to London for to go.   *need*

---

[1] *Suffiseth ... hadde* It is enough for you (i.e., you should be grateful), unless you are insane, to have as much favor as Noah had (by being warned of the Flood).

525	And on the Monday whan it drow to nyght,°	*approached night*
	He shette° his dore withoute candel lyght	*shut*
	And dresseth° alle thyng as it shal be.	*arranged*
	And shortly, up they clomben alle thre.	
	They sitten stille, wel a furlong way.[1]	
530	Now, "Pater Noster, clom!"° seyde Nicholay.	*be quiet*
	And "Clom," quod John. And "Clom," seyde Alisoun.	
	This carpenter seyde his devocioun,°	*prayers*
	And stille he sit and biddeth his preyere,°	*offers his prayers*
	Awaitynge on the reyn, if he it heere.	
535	The dede° sleepe, for wery° bisynesse,	*dead / weary*
	Fil° on this carpenter, right as I gesse,°	*fell / guess*
	About corfew° tyme[2] or litel moore.	*curfew*
	For travaille° of his goost° he groneth soore	*labor / spirit*
	And eft° he routeth,° for his heed°	
	myslay.°	*also / snores / head / lay wrong*
540	Doun of the laddre stalketh Nicholay,	
	And Alisoun ful softe adoun she spedde.°	*hastens*
	Withouten wordes mo they goon to bedde	
	Theras° the carpenter is wont to lye.	*where*
	Ther was the revel° and the melodye,	*fun*
545	And thus Alison and Nicholas	
	In bisynesse of myrthe and of solas	
	Til that the belle of laudes[3] gan to rynge	
	And freres° in the chauncel[4] gonne synge.°	*friars / began to sing*
	This parissh clerk, this amorous Absolon	
550	That is for love alwey so wobigon,°	*sorrowful*
	Upon the Monday was at Oseneye	
	With a compaignye hym to disporte and	
	pleye,°	*play and have fun*
	And axed upon cas° a cloistrer°	*asked by chance / monk*
	Ful prively° after John the carpenter.	*very secretly*
555	And he drough hym apart° out of the chirche	*drew him aside*
	And seyde, "I noot.° I saugh hym heere nat wirche	*don't know*
	Syn° Saterday.[5] I trowe° that he be went°	*since / believe / is gone*

	For tymber ther° oure abbot hath hym sent,	*timber where*
	For he is wont° for tymber for to go	*accustomed*
560	And dwellen° at the grange° a day or two.[6]	*stay / farm-house*
	Or elles he is at his hous, certeyn.	
	Where that he be, I kan nat soothly seyn."°	*truly say*
	This Absolon ful joly was and light	
	And thoghte, "Now is tyme wake° al nyght,	*to stay awake*
565	For sikirly,° I saugh hym nat stirynge°	*certainly / not stirring*
	Aboute his dore syn day bigan to sprynge.°	*dawn*
	"So moot I thryve,° I shall at cokkes crowe	*thrive*
	Ful pryvely knokke at his wyndowe	
	That stant ful lowe upon his boures wal.°	*bedroom's wall*
570	To Alison now wol I tellen al	
	My love-longynge, for yet I shal nat mysse	
	That at the leeste wey° I shal hire kisse;	*very least*
	Som maner° confort shal I have, parfay.°	*kind of / in faith*
	My mouth hath icched° al this longe day:	*itched*
575	That is a signe of kissyng atte leeste!	
	Al nyght me mette° eek I was at a feeste.°	*I dreamed / feast*
	Therfore I wol goon slepe an houre or tweye	
	And al the nyght thanne° wol I wake and pleye."	*then*
	Whan that the firste cok° hath crowe anon,	*rooster*
580	Up rist° this joly lovere Absolon	*rose*
	And hym arraieth° gay at poynt devys.[7]	*dresses*
	But first he cheweth greyn° of lycorys°	*a grain / licorice*
	To smellen sweete er he hadde kembd his heer.	
	Under his tonge° a trewe-love[8] he beer,°	*tongue / carried*
585	For therby wende° he to ben gracious.°	*expected / attractive*
	He rometh° to the carpenteres hous,	*roams*
	And stille he stant° under the	
	shot-wyndowe—°	*stands / hinged window*
	Unto his brist° it raughte,° it was so lowe—	*breast / reached*
	And softe he knokketh with a semy soun.°	*quiet sound*
590	"What do ye, honycomb, sweete Alisoun,	
	My faire bryd,° my sweete cynamone?°	*bird / cinnamon*
	Awaketh, lemman myn,° and speketh to me.	*my sweetheart*
	Wel litel° thynken ye upon my wo,	*very little*
	That for youre love I swete° ther° I go.	*sweat / where*
595	No wonder is thogh° that I swelte° and	
	swete;	*is it though / swelter*

---

[1] *They … way* For the time it takes to walk a furlong (about an eighth of a mile).

[2] *corfew tyme* Curfew, from the French for "cover your fire," announced the time when all fires had to be covered and houses were shut up for the night.

[3] *laudes* I.e., Lauds, the monastic hour of prayer that occurs very early in the morning, before dawn.

[4] *chauncel* Chancel, the area of a church or chapel near the altar.

[5] *I … Saterday* I do not know. I have not seen him work here since Saturday.

---

[6] *And … two* Abbeys usually had outlying estates, such as this one where John the carpenter is working.

[7] *at poynt devys* I.e., at point devise: perfectly.

[8] *a trewe-love* Four-leaved clover.

I moorne° as dooth° a lamb after the tete.°   *yearn / does / teat*
Ywis,° lemman,° I have swich love longynge   *indeed / sweetheart*
That lik a turtel° trewe is my moornynge.°   *turtle-dove / mourning*
I may nat ete namoore° than a mayde."   *anymore*
600   "Go fro the wyndow, Jakke fool,"° she sayde.   *Jack-fool*
"As help me God, it wol nat be 'com pa me.'°   *come kiss me*
I love another, and elles° I were to blame,   *else*
Wel bet° than thee, by Jhesu, Absolon.   *better*
Go forth thy wey, or I wol caste a ston,°   *throw a stone*
605   And lat me slepe, a twenty devel wey!"[1]
    "Allas," quod Absolon, "and weylawey,
That trewe love was evere so yvel biset!°   *ill bestowed*
Thanne kys me, syn° it may be no bet,°   *since / better*
For Jhesus love and for the love of me."
610   "Wiltow thanne go thy wey?" quod she.
    "Ye, certes, lemman," quod this Absolon.
    "Thanne make thee redy," quod she. "I come anon."
And unto Nicholas she seyde stille,°   *quietly*
"Now hust,° and thou shalt laughen al thy fille."   *shush*
615   This Absolon doun sette hym on his knees
And seyde, "I am lord at alle degrees,°   *in every way*
For after this I hope ther cometh moore.
Lemman, thy grace, and sweete bryd,° thyn oore!"°   *bird / favor*
    The wyndow she undoth° and that in haste.   *unlatched*
620   "Have do," quod she. "Com of and speed the faste,[2]
Lest that oure neighebores thee espie."°   *see you*
    This Absolon gan wype his mouth ful drie.
Dirk° was the nyght as pich° or as the cole,°   *dark / pitch / coal*
And at the wyndow out she pitte° hir hole.   *put*
625   And Absolon hym fil° no bet° ne wers,°   *fell / better / worse*
But with his mouth he kiste° hir naked ers°   *kissed / ass*
Ful savourly° er he was war° of this.   *with relish / aware*
Abak° he stirte° and thoughte it was
    amys,°   *backwards / jumped / wrong*
For wel he wiste a womman hath no berd.°   *beard*
630   He felte a thyng al rough and longe yherd°   *long-haired*
And seyde, "Fy! Allas! What have I do?"°   *done*
    "Tehee!" quod she, and clapte° the wyndow to,   *slammed*
And Absolon gooth forth a sory° pas.°   *sorry / step*
    "A berd,° a berd!" quod hende Nicholas.   *beard, trick*
635   "By Goddes corpus,° this goth° faire and weel!"   *body / goes*
    This sely° Absolon herde every deel°   *foolish / part*

And on his lippe° he gan for anger byte,°   *lip / began to bite*
And to hymself he seyde, "I shall thee quyte!"°   *repay*
    Who rubbeth now, who froteth° now his lippes   *wipes*
640   With dust, with sond, with straw, with clooth, with
    chippes°   *chips (of wood)*
But Absolon, that seith ful ofte, "Allas!
My soule bitake° I unto Sathanas°   *commit / Satan*
But me were levere° than al this toun," quod he,   *rather*
"Of this despit° awroken° for to be.   *insult / avenged*
645   Allas," quod he, "Allas, I ne hadde
    ybleynt!"°   *had not restrained (myself)*
His hoote love was coold and al yqueynt.°   *quenched*
For fro that tyme that he hadde kist hir ers,
Of paramours° he sette nat a kers,[3]   *lovemaking*
For he was heeled of his maladie.
650   Ful ofte paramours he gan deffie,°   *defied*
And weepe as dooth a child that is ybete.°   *beaten*
A softe paas° he wente over the strete°   *quiet step / street*
Until° a smyth° men cleped daun°
    Gerveys,   *unto / blacksmith / master*
That in his forge smythed plough° harneys.   *plow*
655   He sharpeth shaar° and kultour° bisily.   *plowshare / plow-blade*
This Absolon knokketh al esily°   *quietly*
And seyde, "Undo,° Gerveys, and that anon."   *open up*
    "What! Who artow?"° "I am heere Absolon."   *are you*
"What! Absolon, for Cristes sweete tree,°   *cross*
660   Why rise ye so rathe?° Ey,° benedicitee!   *early / ah*
What eyleth° yow? Som gay gerl,° God it
    woot,°   *ails / girl / knows*
Hath broght yow thus upon the viritoot.[4]
By Seinte Note,[5] ye woot wel what I mene."
    This Absolon ne roghte nat a bene°   *did not care a bean*
665   Of al his pley. No word agayn he yaf.°   *gave*
He hadde moore tow° on his distaf[6]   *flax*
Than Gerveys knew, and seyde, "Freend so deere,°   *kind*
That hoote° kultour° in the chymenee heere,   *hot / plow-blade*
As lene° it me. I have therwith to doone,°   *lend / do*
670   And I wol brynge it thee agayn ful soone."

---

[1]   *a twenty devel wey* For the sake of twenty devils.

[2]   *Com … faste* "Hurry up," she said, "make haste and be quick."

[3]   *sette nat a kers* Cared nothing. (A *kers* is a watercress.)

[4]   *upon the viritoot* Up and about.

[5]   *Seinte Note* I.e., St. Neot, a ninth-century monk from Glastonbury who became a hermit.

[6]   *distaf* I.e., distaff, a tool used in making thread to be spun into cloth.

Gerveys answerde, "Certes, were it gold
Or in a poke° nobles° alle untold,°   *bag / gold coins / unnumbered*
Thou sholdest have,° as I am trewe smyth.   *have (it)*
Ey, Cristes foo,° what wol ye do therwith?"   *foe*
675 "Therof," quod Absolon, "be as be may.
I shal wel telle it thee tomorwe day,"
And caughte the kultour by the colde stele.
Ful softe out at the dore he gan to stele°   *began to steal*
And wente unto the carpenteris wal.
680 He cogheth° first and knokketh therwithal   *coughs*
Upon the wyndowe right° as he dide er.   *just*
  This Alison answerde, "Who is ther
That knokketh so? I warante it a theef."
  "Why, nay," quod he, "God woot, my sweete leef,°   *loved one*
685 I am thyn Absolon, my deerelyng.°   *darling*
Of gold," quod he, "I have thee broght a ryng.
My mooder yaf° it me, so God me save.   *gave*
Ful fyn° it is and therto wel ygrave.°   *fine / engraved*
This wol I yeve° thee if thou me kisse."   *give*
690 This Nicholas was risen for to pisse
And thoughte he wolde amenden° al the jape: *make better*
He sholde kisse his ers er that he scape.°   *escape*
And up the wyndowe dide he hastily,
And out his ers he putteth pryvely
695 Over the buttok to the haunche bon.°   *thigh*
And therwith spak this clerk, this Absolon:
"Spek, sweete bryd,° I noot nat° where thou
    art."   *bird / do not know*
  This Nicholas anon leet fle° a fart   *let fly*
As greet as it had been a thonder dent,°   *thunder-clap*
700 That with the strook he was almoost yblent.°   *blinded*
And he was redy with his iren hoot,°   *hot iron*
And Nicholas amydde the ers° he
    smoot.°   *in the middle of the ass / struck*
  Of gooth° the skyn° an hande brede°
    about,   *off goes / skin / a hand-breadth*
The hoote kultour brende° so his toute,°   *burned / rear*
705 And for the smert° he wende° for to dye.°   *pain / expected / die*
As he were wood for wo, he gan to crye,
"Help, water, water, help, for Goddes herte!"
  This carpenter out of his slomber sterte°   *jumped*
And herde oon crien,° "Water!" as he were wood,   *heard one cry*
710 And thoughte, "Allas, now comth Nowelis Flood!"
He sit hym up withouten wordes mo,
And with his ax he smoot the corde atwo,

And doun gooth al! He foond neither to selle,
Ne breed ne ale, til he cam to the celle[1]
715 Upon the floor, and there aswowne° he lay.   *in a faint*
  Up stirte hire Alison and Nicholay,
And criden, "Out!" and "Harrow!" in the strete.
The neighebores, bothe smale and grete,°   *big*
In ronnen° for to gauren on° this man   *ran in / gape at*
720 That yet aswowne he lay, bothe pale and wan,
For with the fal° he brosten hadde° his arm.   *fall / had broken*
But stonde he moste unto his owene harm.[2]
For whan he spak, he was anon bore doun°   *shouted down*
With° hende Nicholas and Alisoun.   *by*
725 They tolden every man that he was wood.
He was agast° so of Nowelis Flood   *afraid*
Thurgh fantasie° that of his vanytee°   *fantasy / folly*
He hadde yboght° hym knedyng tubbes thre   *bought*
And hadde hem hanged in the rove° above,   *roof*
730 And that he preyde° hem for Goddes love   *asked*
To sitten in the roof par compaignye.°   *for company*
  The folk gan laughen at his fantasye.
Into the roof they kiken° and they cape°   *stare / gape*
And turned al his harm unto a jape.°   *joke*
735 For what° so that this carpenter answerde,   *whatever*
It was for noght.° No man his reson° herde.   *nothing / explanation*
With othes° grete he was so sworn adoun°   *oaths / shouted down*
That he was holde° wood in al the toun,   *considered*
For every clerk° anonright heeld° with oother;   *scholar / agreed*
740 They seyde, "The man was wood, my leeve° brother."   *dear*
And every wight gan laughen of this stryf.°   *strife*
Thus swyved° was this carpenteris wyf   *made love to*
For al his kepyng° and his jalousye,   *guarding*
And Absolon hath kist hir nether° eye,   *lower*
745 And Nicholas is scalded in the towte.°   *rear*
This tale is doon, and God save al the rowte!°   *company*

HEERE ENDETH THE MILLERE HIS TALE

---

[1] *Ne … celle* He did not find bread or ale to sell until he came to the bottom; i.e., he did not stop on his way down.

[2] *moste … harm* This idiomatic expression has been interpreted differently. John the Carpenter must endure (or put up with, or take responsibility for) his own injury, or he must stand up for himself even though it turned out badly.

The Wife of Bath's Prologue and Tale

With the opening words of her extremely long prologue, the Wife of Bath introduces one of her central themes, the conflict between the experience of life, which for the Wife means sexual experience foremost, and "auctoritee," the written commentary of learned men on religious, moral, and philosophical issues. These men, who included both the patristic writers (such as Saints Ambrose and Jerome) and classical philosophers, have little good to say about women, whom they repeatedly depict as deceitful, quarrelsome, and lecherous. Escape from this tradition, as the Wife herself indicates in her account of the debate between the man and the lion, is not easy. Just as all paintings of lions will always be painted by men, so in classical and medieval society almost all writing, especially writing that had official authority, was done by men. The Wife herself, in one of the tale's many layers of ventriloquism, places traditional criticisms of women in the mouths of her first three husbands, whom she accuses of abusing her with these repeated insults. The criticisms can also be found in her fifth husband's book, a compilation of misogynistic texts from Jerome and others, all counseling against marriage.

The great irony is that the Wife herself is drawn from this tradition. Her character is based in part on the Old Woman in *The Romance of the Rose*, a sexually experienced cynic who teaches young people the tricks of love, and both the Wife's history and the literary shape of her prologue and tale conform to many of the traditional misogynistic stereotypes found in her husband's book. The subtle layering of the text makes its final moral elusive. Readers continue to argue whether the Wife should be taken as a moral warning against unbridled carnality or admired for her independence, courage, and vitality. The glosses in the Ellesmere manuscript tend to support the first view, but the Wife herself has some telling comments to offer on men who write glosses.

The tale that the Wife finally tells is an Arthurian romance. It follows a well-established folk-tale plot in which a knight is given a year to answer a question or die and can only get the answer from an old and ugly woman who will not give it to him unless he promises either to marry her or, as in Chaucer's version, to give her whatever she wants, which later turns out to be marriage. In several versions, including *The Tale of Florent* in John Gower's *Confessio Amantis*, the question the knight must answer is what women most desire. Chaucer modifies the familiar story in a number of ways, so that the tale contributes to the argument the Wife has been making in her prologue. The knight in the Wife's version is not innocent—he is a rapist—and he objects to the marriage not just because the woman is old and ugly, but also because she is of low birth, an objection she counters in a long disquisition on the nature of true gentility. Even the knight's final choice, which in the other versions takes the form of "foul by day and fair by night" or the reverse, is subtly altered in keeping with the Wife's interests.

Detail, opening page of the Prologue to *The Wife of Bath's Tale*, Ellesmere manuscript; see color insert for full page. (Reprinted by permission of *The Huntington Library, San Marino, California*. EL 26 C9 f. 63r.)

THE WIFE OF BATH'S PROLOGUE

THE PROLOGUE OF THE WYVVES TALE OF BATHE

"Experience, though noon auctoritee
Were in this world, were right ynogh to me[1]
To speke° of wo° that is in mariage.   *speak | woe*
For lordynges,° sith° I twelve yeer was of age,   *lords | since*
5 Ythonked° be God that is eterne on lyve,° *thanked | eternally alive*
Housbondes at chirche dore° I have had fyve,° *church door | five*
For I so ofte have ywedded° bee,°[2]   *wedded | been*
And alle were worthy men in hir° degree.   *their*
But me was toold certeyn° nat longe
    agoon° is,   *certain | not long ago*
10 That sith that Crist ne wente° nevere but onis° *did not go | once*
To weddyng in the Cane° of Galilee,[3]   *Cana*
By the same ensample° thoughte me° *example | it seemed to me*
That I ne sholde° wedded be but ones.° *should not | once*
Herkne eek° which a sharpe word for the
    nones°   *listen also | for the occasion*
15 Biside° a welle Jhesus, God and man,   *beside*
Spak° in repreeve° of the Samaritan;[4]   *spoke | rebuke*
'Thou hast yhad° fyve housbondes,' quod° he, *have had | said*
'And that man the which that hath now thee° *who now has you*
Is noght thyn housbonde.' Thus seyde he certeyn.
20 What that he mente therby,° I kan nat
    seyn.°   *meant by this | cannot say*
But that I axe,° why that the fifthe man   *ask*
Was noon housbonde to the Samaritan?
How manye myghte she have in mariage?
Yet herde I nevere tellen° in myn age   *never heard told*
25 Upon this nombre° diffinicioun.°   *number | definition*
Men may devyne° and glosen° up and doun, *guess | gloss | down*
But wel I woot° expres° withoute lye,° *well I know | clearly | lie*

God bad° us forto wexe° and multiplye.°[6] *commanded | to increase*
That gentil° text kan° I understonde!   *noble | can*
30 Eek wel I woot, he seyde myn housbonde
Sholde lete fader and mooder° and take
    me.°[7]   *should leave father and mother*
But of no nombre° mencioun made
    he°   *number | did he make mention*
Of bigamye° or of octogamye.° *bigamy | marriage to eight spouses*
Why sholde men speke° of it vileynye?° *speak | as villainy*
35 "Lo heere° the wise kyng daun° Salamon: *consider | master*
I trowe° he hadde wyves mo° than oon.°[8] *believe | more | one*
As wolde God, it were leveful unto me[9]
To be refresshed° half so ofte° as he!   *refreshed | often*
Which yifte° of God hadde he for alle hise wyvys;° *gift | wives*
40 No man hath swich° that in this world alyve° is. *such | alive*
God woot,° this noble kyng, as to my
    wit,°   *knows | as far as I know*
The first nyght° had many a myrie° fit   *night | merry*
With ech° of hem,° so wel was hym° on
    lyve.°   *each | them | he was so lucky*
Yblessed be God that I have wedded five![10]
45 Welcome the sixte, whanevere he shal.° *whenever he shall arrive*
Forsothe,° I wol nat kepe me chaast in al° *in truth | entirely chaste*
Whan myn housbonde is fro° the world ygon.° *from | gone*
Som° Cristen° man shal wedde me
    anon,°   *some | Christian | immediately*
For thanne° th'apostle seith°[11] I am free *then | the apostle says*
50 To wedde, a Goddes half, where it liketh me.[12]

---

[6] *God bad … multiplye*   See Genesis 6.1.

[7] *myn housbonde … me*   See Genesis 2.24.

[8] *I … oon*   According to the Bible, King Solomon had seven hundred wives and three hundred concubines. See 1 Kings 11.33.

[9] *As wolde … me*   If only God would permit that it should be lawful for me.

[10] *Yblessed … five*   Some manuscripts contain the following six-line passage:

> "Of whiche I have pyked out the beste
> Bothe of here nether purs and of here cheste.
> Diverse scoles maken parfyt clerkes,
> And diverse practyk in many sondry werkes,
> Maken the workman parfit, sekirly;
> Of five husbandes scoleiyng am I."

John Manly and Edith Rickert suggest that these lines are "a late Chaucerian insertion," i.e., part of a late rough draft of the poem.

[11] *th'apostle seith*   I.e., St. Paul. See 1 Corinthians 7.25–38.

[12] *To wedde … me*   To wed, by God's permission, wherever I wish.

---

[1] *Experience … me*   Experience, even if there were no written authority in the world, would be quite enough for me. Authority, in this sense, refers to the writings of learned men, especially the patristic writers and ancient philosophers.

[2] *For … bee*   Many manuscripts have "If I so ofte myghte have ywedded be," i.e., if these multiple marriages were indeed lawful.

[3] *Cane of Galilee*   See John 2.1–11.

[4] *Samaritan*   See John 4.1–42.

[5] *glosen*   Crucial points in the Bible, and other religious, philosophical, or legal texts were explained in glosses (comments written in the margins or between the lines).

He seith to be wedded is no synne:°   *sin*

"Bet° is to be wedded than to brynne."°[1]   *better / burn*

What rekketh me,° thogh folk seye°

   vileynye°   *what do I care / say / villainy*

Of shrewed° Lameth[2] and of bigamye?°   *cursed / bigamy*

55 I woot wel° Abraham[3] was an hooly° man *know well / holy*

And Jacob eek, as ferforth as I kan,°   *as far as I know*

And ech of hem° hadde wyves mo than two   *them*

And many another man also.

Whanne° saugh° ye evere in manere° age *when / saw / any*

60 That hye° God defended° mariage   *high / forbade*

By expres° word? I pray yow, telleth me. *specific*

Or where comanded he virginitee?°   *virginity*

I woot as wel as ye,° it is no drede,[4] *know as well as you*

Whan th'apostel° speketh of maydenhede° *virginity*

65 He seyde that precept° therof° hadde he

   noon.°[5]   *commandment / about / none*

Men may conseille° a womman to been oon,° *counsel / single*

But conseillyng is nat comandement.

He putte it in oure owene juggement.° *left it to our own judgment*

For hadde° God comanded maydenhede, *had*

70 Thanne° hadde he dampned° weddyng with the

   dede.°   *then / condemned / in the act*

And certein,° if ther were no seed ysowe° *certainly / sown*

Virginitee, wherof thanne° sholde° it growe? *how then / should*

Poul° ne dorste nat° comanden atte

   leeste°   *St. Paul / dared not / command at least*

A thyng of which his maister° yaf° noon

   heeste.°   *master / gave / no command*

75 The dart[6] is set up of virginitee:

Cacche whoso may. Who renneth best, lat see![7]

"But this word is nat taken of every

   wight,°   *does not apply to everyone*

But theras God lust gyve it of his myght.[8]

I woot wel the apostel was a mayde.°   *virgin*

80 But nathelees,° thogh° that he wroot° and

   sayde   *nevertheless / though / wrote*

He wolde° that every wight° were swich° as

   he,   *wished / person / such*

Al nys but conseil° to virginitee.   *is not but advice*

And for to been° a wyf he yaf° me leve° *be / gave / leave*

Of indulgence,° so it is no repreve°   *by permission / reproach*

85 To wedde me if my make° dye,°   *mate / should die*

Withouten excepcioun° of bigamye.°   *objection / bigamy*

Al° were it good no womman for to touche, *although*

He mente° as in his bed or in his couche.° *meant / couch*

For peril is bothe fyr and tow t'assemble.[9]

90 Ye knowe what this ensample° may resemble. *example*

This is al and som,° that virginitee   *the whole matter*

Moore profiteth than weddyng in freletee;[10]

Freletee° clepe I° but if° that he and she *weakness / I call it / unless*

Wolde lede° al hir lyf° in chastitee.   *would lead / their life*

95 "I graunte° it wel; I have noon envie,° *grant / no envy*

Thogh maydenhede preferre bigamye.[11]

Hem liketh° to be clene,° body and

   goost.°   *they prefer / pure / spirit*

Of myn estaat° I nyl nat° make no

   boost.°   *my condition / will not / boast*

For wel ye knowe, a lord in his houshold,

100 He nath nat° every vessel al of gold.   *does not have*

Somme been of tree° and doon° hir° lord

   servyse.   *wood / do / their*

God clepeth° folk to hym in sondry wyse.° *calls / in different ways*

And everich hath° of God a propre

   yifte°—   *everyone has / particular gift*

Som this, som that, as hym liketh shifte.° *as he pleases to give*

105 "Virginitee is greet perfeccioun

And continence° eek with devocioun.° *chastity / religious devotion*

---

[1] *Bet … brynne* See 1 Corinthians 7.9.

[2] *Lameth* Lamech is the first to marry two wives. See Genesis 4.19.

[3] *Abraham* The patriarch Abraham, as recounted in the book of Genesis, was favored by God, yet he had more than one wife, as did his grandson Jacob.

[4] *it is no drede* Do not doubt it.

[5] *He … noon* Paul admits that he could find no justification for his view in the Old Testament. See 1 Corinthians 7.25.

[6] *dart* A spear was sometimes given as a prize for a race in England in the Middle Ages. Many editors prefer the reading "for virginity" (found in many other manuscripts), which makes virginity the competitor rather than the prize.

[7] *Cacche … see* Let whoever can catch it. Let us see who runs best.

[8] *But … myght* Except where God wishes, through his might, to impose this principle (of virginity).

[9] *fyr … t'assemble* To bring together fire and flax (flammable material of which wicks are made).

[10] *Moore … freletee* Remaining a virgin is better than marrying through weakness.

[11] *Thogh … bigamye* Though virginity be preferred to bigamy.

But Crist that of perfeccioun° is welle°   *perfection | well (source)*
Bad° nat every wight sholde go selle   *commanded*
Al that he hadde and gyve° it to the poore   *give*
110 And in swich wise folwe hym¹ and his foore.°   *steps*
He spak to hem that wolde lyve parfitly.°   *wished to live perfectly*
And, lordynges, by youre leve,° that am nat I!   *leave*
I wol bistowe° the flour° of myn age   *will bestow | flower*
In the actes and in fruyt° of mariage.   *fruit*
115   "Telle me also, to what conclusioun
Were membres ymaad° of generacioun?²   *made*
And for what profit° was a wight ywroght?°   *purpose | person made*
Trusteth° right wel, they were nat maad° for
noght.°   *believe me | not made | nothing*
Glose whoso wole and seye bothe up and doun,³
120 That they were maad for purgacioun°   *releasing*
Of uryne° and oure bothe thynges
smale,°   *urine | our two small things (sexual organs)*
And eek to knowe° a femele from a male,   *distinguish*
And for noon oother cause: sey° ye no?   *say*
The experience woot wel° it is   *experience (in general) knows well*
noght so.
125 So that the clerkes° be nat with me wrothe,°   *theologians | angry*
I sey yis,° that they beth maked° for
bothe!   *say yes | are made*
That is to seye, for office and for ese°   *pleasure*
Of engendrure,⁴ ther we nat God
displese.°   *where we do not displease God*
Why sholde men elles° in hir bookes sette°   *otherwise | set down*
130 That a man shal yelde to his wyf hire dette?⁵
Now, wherwith° sholde he make his
paiement°   *with what | payment*
If he ne used° his sely° instrument?   *did not use | innocent*
Thanne were they maad upon a creature
To purge uryne° and for engendrure.°   *release urine | conception*
135   "But I seye noght° that every wight is holde°   *not | obligated*

That hath swich harneys,° as I of tolde,   *such equipment*
To goon° and usen hem° in engendrure.   *go | them*
They shul° nat take of chastitee no cure.°   *shall | attention*
Crist was a mayde° and shapen° as a man,   *virgin | formed*
140 And many a seint sith° the world bigan,   *since*
Yet lyved they evere in parfit° chastitee.   *perfect*
I nyl nat envye° no virginitee.   *will not envy*
Lat hem° be breed° of pured whete°
seed,   *let them | bread | pure wheat*
And lat us wyves hoten° barly breed.   *be called*
145 And yet with barly breed, Mark⁶ telle kan,
Oure Lord refresshed° many a man.   *gave food to*
In swich estaat° as God hath cleped us°   *condition | has called us*
I wol persevere.° I nam nat precius.°   *remain | fastidious*
In wyfhode I wol use myn instrument°   *sexual organ*
150 As frely° as my makere hath it sent.   *freely*
If I be daungerous,° God yeve° me sorwe.   *stand-offish | give*
Myn housbonde shal it have bothe eve and morwe
Whan that hym list com forth and paye his dette.⁷
An housbonde I wol have, I nyl nat lette,°   *will not stop*
155 Which shal° be bothe my dettour° and my
thral°   *who shall | debtor | slave*
And have his tribulacioun° withal°   *tribulation | also*
Upon his flessh whil I am his wyf.
I have the power durynge° al my lyf   *during*
Upon his propre° body, and noght he.   *own*
160 Right thus the apostel⁸ tolde it unto me
And bad° oure housbondes for to love us
weel.°   *commanded | well*
Al this sentence me liketh every deel."⁹
   Up stirte° the Pardoner and that anon.°   *jumped | immediately*
"Now, Dame," quod he, "by God and by Seint John,
165 Ye been° a noble prechour° in this cas!°   *are | preacher | matter*
I was aboute to wedde a wyf, allas!
What sholde I bye it on my flessh so deere?¹⁰

---

¹ *swich wise* Such a manner; *folwe hym* Follow him.

² *membres ... of generacioun* Sexual organs.

³ *Glose ... doun* Let whoever wishes to do so offer an interpretation and say both up and down.

⁴ *Of engendrure* Of conception. The phrase "office and ease of engendrure" means for a purpose (that is, conceiving children) and for the pleasure of procreation.

⁵ *yelde ... dette* Having sex. I.e., both partners owed each other a certain sexual fulfillment, lest sexual frustration drive one of them to adultery. The line is a quotation from 1 Corinthians 7.3.

⁶ *And ... man* The reference here is to John 6.9 and the miracle of the loaves and fishes, not to a passage in the Gospel of Mark.

⁷ *Whan ... dette* When he wishes to come forth and pay his debt.

⁸ *the apostel* I.e., St. Paul, whose insights on marriage the Wife of Bath has been mentioning since she began to speak. In addition to the passage referred to above in note 5, Paul's other major pronouncement on marriage is in Ephesians 5.21–33.

⁹ *Al ... deel* All this lesson (of Scripture) pleases me, every part (of it).

¹⁰ *What ... deere* Why should I pay so dearly for it with my flesh.

Yet hadde I levere° wedde no wyf to yeere!"°   *rather | this year*
   "Abyde,"° quod she, "my tale is nat bigonne!   *wait*
170 Nay, thou shalt drynken° of another
   tonne°   *drink | cask (of wine)*
Er that I go, shal savoure wors° than ale!   *that shall taste worse*
And whan that I have toold forth my tale
Of tribulacioun that is in mariage,
Of which I am expert in al myn age°—   *throughout my life*
175 This to seyn,° myself have been the whippe°—   *say | whip*
Than maystow chese wheither° thou wolt
   sippe°   *choose whether | will sip*
Of that tonne that I shal abroche.°   *open*
Bewar of it er thou to ny° approche,°   *too near | approach*
For I shal telle ensamples° mo° than ten.   *examples | more*
180 Whoso that wol nat bewar by othere men,[1]
By hym shul othere men corrected be.
The same wordes writeth Protholomee.°   *Ptolemy*
Rede° it in his *Almageste* and take it there![2]   *read*
   "Dame, I wolde praye° if youre wyl° it were,"   *ask | will*
185 Seyde this Pardoner, "as ye bigan
Telle forth youre tale. Spareth° for no man,   *spare*
And teche us yonge men of youre praktike!"°   *practice*
   "Gladly, sires,° sith it may yow like.°   *sirs | it may please you*
But yet I praye to al this compaignye,
190 If that I speke after my fantasye,°   *fancy*
As taketh it nat agrief° that° I seye,   *take it not wrong | what*
For myn entente is but for to pleye.
   "Now sire, now wol I telle forth my tale.
As evere moote° I drynken wyn or ale,   *might*
195 I shal seye sooth° of tho housbondes that I hadde,   *say the truth*
As thre of hem were goode and two were badde.
The thre men were goode and riche and olde.
Unnethe° myghte they the statut° holde   *scarcely | regulation*
In which that they were bounden° unto me.[3]   *bound*
200 Ye woot wel what I meene° of this, pardee.°   *mean | by God*
As help me God, I laughe whan I thynke
How pitously anyght° I made hem swynke!°   *at night | work*
And by my fey,° I tolde of it no stoor.°   *faith | set no store by it*

They had me yeven° hir° gold and hir
   tresoor.°   *given | their | treasure*
205 Me neded nat do lenger diligence[4]
To wynne hir love or doon hem reverence.°   *honor them*
They loved me so wel, by God above,
That I ne tolde no deyntee of hir love.[5]
A wys° womman wol sette hire evere in
   oon°   *wise | will always determine*
210 To gete hire° love theras° she hath
   noon.°   *get herself | where | has none*
But sith I hadde hem° hoolly° in myn hond,   *them | wholly*
And sith they hadde me yeven° al hir lond,°   *given | all their land*
What sholde I taken heede° hem for to plese,°   *bother | please*
But if° it were for my profit and myn ese?°   *unless | pleasure*
215 I sette hem so a werk,° by my fey,°   *to work | faith*
That many a nyght they songen° 'Weilawey!'°   *sang | alas*
The bacon was nat fet° for hem, I trowe,°   *fetched | believe*
That som° men han° in Essex at Dunmowe.[6]   *some | have*
I governed hem so wel after my lawe,
220 That ech°of hem was ful blisful° and fawe°   *each | very happy | eager*
To brynge me gaye thynges° fro the fayre.°   *pretty things | fair*
They were ful glad whan I spak to hem faire,°   *nicely*
For, God it woot, I chidde hem spitously!°   *scolded them spitefully*
   "Now herkneth hou° I baar me° proprely,   *how | bore myself*
225 Ye wise wyves that kan understonde.
Thus shul ye speke and beren hem on honde.[7]
For half so boldely kan ther no man
Swere° and lye° as kan a womman.   *swear | lie*
I sey nat this by° wyves that been wyse,   *about*
230 But if° it be whan they hem
   mysavyse.°   *unless | give themselves bad advice*
A wys wyf, if that she kan hir good,°   *knows what is good for her*
Shal bere hym on hond the cow is wood[8]
And take witnesse of hir owene mayde°   *own maid*

---

[1] *Whoso … men* The one who will not be warned (by examples offered) by others.

[2] *Rede … there* The aphorism is not found in the *Almagest*, the great astrological treatise of Claudius Ptolemy (second century CE), but in the preface to one of the translations of his work.

[3] *In … me* I.e., the three old husbands could barely fulfill their obligation to pay the marriage debt.

[4] *Me … diligence* I did not need to make any more effort.

[5] *ne tolde … love* Did not put any value on their love.

[6] *The bacon … Dunmowe* In the village of Dunmow, it was the custom to award a side of bacon to a married couple if they did not quarrel for a year.

[7] *beren hem on honde* Either to deceive them or to accuse them falsely. The Wife does both to her husbands.

[8] *A wys … wood* A wise woman can convince her husband that a tale-telling cowbird (a kind of jackdaw) who tells him she has been unfaithful is mad and use her own maid as a witness.

Of hir° assent, but herkneth° how I
    sayde:°   *her / listen to / how I spoke*
235   "'Sire olde kaynard,° is this thyn array?°   *fool / your way of behaving*
Why is my neighebores wyf so gay?°   *well dressed*
She is honoured over al ther she gooth.°   *wherever she goes*
I sitte at hoom. I have no thrifty clooth.°   *appropriate clothing*
What dostow° at my neighebores hous?   *are you doing*
240   Is she so fair? Artow° so amorous?   *are you*
What rowne° ye with oure mayde,° benedicite? *whisper / maid*
Sire olde lecchour,° lat thy japes° be!   *sir old lecher / tricks*
And if I have a gossib° or a freend,°   *confidant / friend*
Withouten gilt,° thou chidest° as a feend!° *guilt / complain / fiend*
245   If that I walke or pleye unto his hous,
Thou comest hoom as dronken as a mous[1]
And prechest° on thy bench, with yvel
    preef!°   *preach / bad luck to you*
   "'Thou seist° to me it is a greet
    meschief°   *you say / great misfortune*
To wedde a povre° womman for costage.°   *poor / expense*
250   And if she be riche and of heigh parage,°   *lineage*
Thanne seistow° it is a tormentrie°   *you say / torment*
To suffren° hire pride and hire malencolie.   *endure*
And if she be fair, thou verray knave,[2]
Thou seyst that every holour° wol hire have: *lecher*
255   She may no while in chastitee abyde°   *remain*
That is assailled upon ech a syde.°   *every side*
   Thou seyst that som folk desiren us for richesse,
Somme for oure shape, somme for oure fairnesse
And som for she kan synge and daunce
260   And som for gentillesse° and som for
    daliaunce,°   *nobility / flirtation*
Som for hir handes and hir armes smale.°   *slender*
Thus goth al to the devel,° by thy tale!   *devil*
Thou seyst men may nat kepe° a castel wal,° *not hold / wall*
It may so longe assailled been overal!°   *everywhere*
265   "'And if that she be foul,° thou seist that she   *ugly*
Coveiteth every man that she may se.°   *see*
For as a spaynel° she wol on hym lepe,°   *spaniel / leap*
Til that she fynde som man hire to chepe.°   *to buy her*
Ne noon so grey goos gooth in the lake

270   As, seistow, wol been withoute make.[3]
And seyt it is an hard thyng for to welde,°   *control*
A thyng that no man wole his thankes helde.° *willingly hold*
   "'Thus seistow, lorel,° whan thow goost to bedde, *fool*
And that no wys man nedeth° for to wedde,   *needs*
275   Ne° no man that entendeth unto
    hevene.°   *nor / intends to go to heaven*
With wilde thonder dynt° and firy
    levene°   *thunder claps / fiery lightening*
Moote° thy welked nekke° be
    tobroke!°   *may / withered neck / broken*
   "'Thow seyst that droppyng° houses and eek smoke *dripping*
And chidyng° wyves maken men to flee   *nagging*
280   Out of hir owene houses. A, benedicitee,
What eyleth° swich an old man for to chide?   *ails*
   "'Thow seyst that we wyves wol oure vices hide
Til we be fast,° and thanne we wol hem shewe.° *secure / show*
Wel may that be a proverbe of a shrewe!°   *villain*
285   "'Thou seist that oxen, asses, hors,° and houndes, *horses*
They been assayd° at diverse stoundes;° *tried / different times*
Bacyns,° lavours° er that men hem bye,° *basins / bowls / buy them*
Spoones and stooles and al swich
    housbondrye,°   *household equipment*
And so been pottes,° clothes, and array.°   *pots / ornaments*
290   But folk of wyves maken noon assay°   *do not try them out*
Til they be wedded. Olde dotard° shrewe!   *foolish*
Thanne seistow we wol oure vices shewe.
   "'Thou seist also that it displeseth me
But if° that thou wolt preyse° my beautee *unless / will praise*
295   And but° thou poure° alwey upon my face   *unless / gaze*
And clepe° me "faire dame!" in every place,   *call*
And but thou make a feeste° on thilke° day *feast / the same*
That I was born, and make me fressh and gay,
And but thou do to my norice[4] honour
300   And to my chambrere° withinne my
    bour.°   *chambermaid / bedroom*
And to my fadres° folk and his allyes: *father's / relatives*
Thus seistow, olde barel° ful of lyes!°   *barrel / lies*
   "'And yet of oure apprentice Janekyn,

---

[1] *dronken as a mous* It is not clear why mice are thought to be drunk, but the expression was common in medieval England.

[2] *thou verray knave* You true villain.

[3] *Ne noon ... make* Proverbial: There is no goose in the lake, no matter how grey, who does not have a mate.

[4] *norice* Nurse. Wealthy medieval people were attended to in their childhood by wet nurses, who often became, for a time, surrogate mothers.

For his crispe heer° shynynge° as gold so
    fyn,°   *curly hair / shining / fine*

305 And for he squiereth° me bothe up and doun,   *escorts*

Yet hastow° caught a fals suspecioun.   *you have*

I wol° hym noght,° though thou were deed
    tomorwe!   *want / not*

    "'But tel me, why hydestow° with sorwe   *do you hide / sorrow*

The keyes of my cheste° awey fro me?   *chest (safety box)*

310 It is my good° as wel as thyn, pardee!°   *possession / by God*

What, wenestow to make an ydiot of oure dame?[1]

Now by that lord that called is Seint Jame,°   *Saint James*

Thou shalt nat bothe, thogh° thou were wood,°   *though / crazy*

Be maister° of my body and of my good!°   *master / possessions*

315 That oon thou shalt forgo, maugree thyne eyen![2]

What nedeth thee of me to enquere° or spyen?°   *inquire / spy*

I trowe thou woldest loke me in thy chiste![3]

Thou sholdest seye, "Wyf, go wher thee liste.[4]

Taak youre disport!° I wol leve° no
    talys.°   *enjoyment / believe / tales*

320 I knowe yow for a trewe wyf, Dame Alys!"

We love no man that taketh kepe or charge°   *takes heed or cares*

Wher that we goon. We wol ben at oure large.°   *free*

    "'Of alle men, blessed moot° he be,   *may*

The wise astrologien° Daun
    Protholome°   *astronomer / Master Ptolemy*

325 That seith this proverbe in his *Almageste*,

"Of alle men his wysdom is the hyeste°   *highest*

That rekketh nevere who hath the world in honde."[5]

By this proverbe thou shalt understonde:

Have thou ynogh, what thar thee recche or care[6]

330 How myrily° that othere folkes fare?°   *merrily / behave*

For certeyn, olde dotard,° by youre leve,°   *fool / leave*

Ye shul have queynte[7] right ynogh° at eve!°   *enough / at night*

He is to greet° a nygard° that wolde
    werne°   *too great / skinflint / refuse*

A man to lighte his candle at his lanterne.

335 He shal have never the lasse° light, pardee!   *less*

Have thou ynogh, thee thar nat pleyne thee.[8]

    "'Thou seyst also that if we make us gay

With clothyng and with precious array,°   *expensive adornment*

That it is peril of° oure chastitee.   *a danger to*

340 And yet with sorwe thou most° enforce
    thee°   *must / support yourself*

And seye thise wordes in the apostles name:[9]

"In habit° maad° with chastitee and shame   *clothing / made*

Ye wommen shul apparaille yow,"° quod he   *dress yourselves*

"And noght° in tressed heer° and gay
    perree,°   *not / braided hair / jewels*

345 As perles,° ne with gold ne clothes riche."   *pearls*

After thy text° ne after thy rubriche°   *quotation / rubric*

I wol nat wirche° as muchel as a gnat![10]   *work*

    "'Thou seydest this, that I was lyk° a cat.   *like*

For whoso wolde senge° a cattes skyn,   *singe*

350 Thanne wolde the cat wel dwellen in his in.°   *lodgings*

And if the cattes skyn be slyk° and gay,   *sleek*

She wol nat dwelle in house half a day,

But forth she wole° er any day be dawed°   *will go / dawned*

To shewe hir skyn and goon a caterwawed.[11]

355 This is to seye, if I be gay, sire shrewe,°   *sir villain*

I wol renne out my borel° for to shewe!   *cheap clothing*

    "'Sire olde fool, what eyleth° thee to spyen?°   *ails / spy*

---

[1] *What ... dame* What, do you expect to make an idiot of our lady? I.e., the Wife herself.

[2] *That ... eyen* You must give up one of them, despite your eyes! (I.e., despite anything you can do.)

[3] *I trowe ... chiste* I believe you would lock me in your chest. Medieval merchants used large locked chests to lock up their coins and their valuables.

[4] *Thou ... liste* You should say, "Wife, go wherever you want."

[5] *That ... honde* Who does not care who possesses the world.

[6] *Have ... care* If you have enough, why do you need to bother yourself or care.

[7] *queynte* Literally meaning elegant, clever, or pleasing thing, queynte is also a medieval euphemism for the female sexual organs.

[8] *Have ... thee* If you have enough, you do not need to complain for yourself.

[9] *the apostles name* St. Paul. The following quotation is from 1 Timothy 2.9.

[10] *After thy ... gnat* I will not follow (work after) your quotation or your text in the smallest way, or, any more than a gnat would. In medieval service books and books of devotion, rubrics (whose name comes from the red ink in which they were written) were directions about how to use the texts to which they referred either in communal worship or private devotion.

[11] *caterwawed* Caterwauling, the loud noise cats make while they are mating.

Thogh thou preye Argus[1] with hise hundred eyen
To be my wardecors,° as he kan° best.   *bodyguard / knows how*
360 In feith, he shal nat kepe me but me lest!°   *unless I want to be kept*
Yet koude I make his berd,° so moot I thee!²   *fool him*
    "'Thou seydest eek that ther been thynges thre,°   *three things*
The whiche thynges troublen° al this erthe   *trouble*
And that no wight may endure the ferthe.°   *fourth*
365 O leeve° sire shrewe! Jhesu° shorte° thy lyf!   *dear / Jesus / shorten*
Yet prechestow° and seyst an hateful wyf   *still you preach*
Yrekned is for° oon of thise
    meschances.°   *is counted as / misfortunes*
Been ther none othere resemblances
That ye may likne° youre parables to,   *liken*
370 But if a sely° wyf be oon of tho?°   *innocent / those*
    "'Thou liknest° wommenes love to helle,   *liken*
To bareyne° lond° ther° water may nat   *barren / land / where*
    dwelle.
Thou liknest it also to wilde fyr:
The moore° it brenneth,° the moore it hath   *more / burns*
    desir°   *desires*
375 To consumen° everythyng that brent wole be.   *consume*
Thou seyst, right as wormes° shendeth° a tree,   *grubs / harm*
Right so a wyf destroyeth hire housbond;
This knowe they that been to wyves bonde.'°   *bound*
    "Lordynges, right thus as ye have understonde
380 Baar I stifly myne olde housbondes on honde,
That thus they seyden in hir dronkenesse!³
And al was fals, but that I took witnesse
On Janekyn and on my nece° also.   *niece*
O Lord, the pyne° I dide hem° and the wo,   *pain / to them*
385 Ful giltlees,° by Goddes sweete pyne!°   *guiltless / pain*
For as an hors I koude byte and whyne.°   *whinny*
I koude pleyne° thogh° I were in the
    gilt,°   *complain / though / guilty*
Or elles oftentyme hadde I been spilt.°   *destroyed*
Whoso comth° first to mille,° first
    grynt.°   *whoever comes / mill / grinds*
390 I pleyned first, so was oure were° ystynt.°   *war / concluded*
They were ful glad to excuse hem° blyve°   *them / quickly*

Of thyng of which they nevere agilte hir lyve.⁴
Of wenches° wolde I beren hym on honde,°   *girls / accuse him*
Whan that for syk° unnethes° myghte he
    stonde.   *sickness / scarcely*
395 "Yet tikled° it his herte,° for that° he   *tickled / heart / because*
Wende° that I hadde of hym° so greet
    chiertee.°   *thought / for him / love*
I swoor° that al my walkynge° out by
    nyghte°   *swore / walking / night*
Was for t'espye° wenches that he dighte.°   *spy / had sex with*
Under that colour° hadde I many a myrthe,°   *pretense / mirth*
400 For al swich thyng was yeven° us in oure byrthe.°   *given / birth*
Deceite, wepyng, spynnyng° God hath yeve°   *spinning / given*
To wommen kyndely° whil that they may lyve.   *naturally*
And thus of o° thyng I avaunte° me: *one / boast*
Atte° ende, I hadde the bettre° in ech
    degree°   *at the / better / instance*
405 By sleighte,° or force, or by som maner
    thyng,°   *deceit / manner of thing*
As by continueel murmure° or
    grucchyng.°   *continual murmur / complaining*
Namely° abedde° hadden they
    meschaunce;°   *especially / in bed / misfortune*
Ther wolde I chide° and do hem no plesaunce.°   *nag / pleasure*
I wolde no lenger° in the bed abyde°   *longer / remain*
410 If that I felte his arm over my syde°   *side*
Til he had maad his raunsoun° unto me.   *paid his ransom*
Thanne wolde I suffre hym do his nycetee.°   *foolishness*
And therfore every man this tale I telle:
Wynne° whoso may, for al is for to selle.°   *win / for sale*
415 With empty hand men may none° haukes° lure;   *no / hawks*
For wynnyng° wolde I al his lust endure   *profit*
And make me a feyned° appetit.   *pretended*
And yet in bacon⁵ hadde I nevere delit.°   *delight*
That made me that evere I wolde hem chide,
420 For thogh the Pope hadde seten hem biside,°   *sat beside them*
I wolde nat spare hem at hir owene bord.°   *table*
For by my trouthe, I quitte hem,° word for word,   *requited them*
As° helpe me verray° God omnipotent!   *so / true*
Though I right now sholde make my testament,
425 I ne owe hem nat a word that it nys quit.°   *was not paid back*

---

¹ *Argus* Hundred-eyed creature of Greek mythology hired by Hera
to guard her husband Zeus's mistress Io. He was killed by Hermes.

² *so moot I thee* I.e., indeed, or by my word.

³ *Baar ... dronkenesse* I bore witness firmly to my old husbands
that they said this when they were drunk.

---

⁴ *Of ... lyve* Of a thing that they had never been guilty of in their
lives.

⁵ *bacon* Old meat preserved by salting; in other words, old men.

I broghte° it so aboute, by my wit,   *brought*
That they moste yeve it up° as for the beste   *had to give it up*
Or elles hadde we nevere been in reste.°   *at rest*
For thogh° he looked as a wood leoun,°   *although | crazy lion*
430   Yet sholde he faille of his conclusion.°   *intent*
       "Thanne wolde I seye, 'Goodlief, taak keepe
How mekely looketh Wilkyn oure sheepe! [1]
Com neer, my spouse. Lat me ba° thy cheke.   *kiss*
Ye sholde been al pacient and meke°   *meek*
435   And han° a sweete, spiced conscience,°   *have | delicate conscience*
Sith ye so preche° of Jobes pacience.°[2]   *preach | Job's patience*
Suffreth alwey,° syn ye so wel kan preche,   *endure always*
And but° ye do, certein we shal yow teche°   *unless | teach you*
That it is fair to have a wyf in pees.°   *peace*
440   Oon of us two moste bowen,° doutelees,°   *must bow | doubtless*
And sith a man is moore resonable
Than womman is, ye moste been suffrable.°   *you must be patient*
What eyleth yow,° to grucche° thus and
       grone?°   *ails you | complain | groan*
Is it for ye wolde have my queynte°
       allone?°   *female sexual organs | alone*
445   Wy,° taak it al! Lo, have it everydeel!°   *why | every bit*
Peter, I shrewe yow but ye love it weel! [3]
For if I wolde selle my bele chose,[4]
I koude walke as fressh as is a rose. [5]
But I wol kepe it for youre owene tooth.°   *own taste (pleasure)*
450   Ye be to blame, by God, I sey yow sooth!'°   *tell you the truth*
       "Swiche manere wordes hadde we on honde.[6]
Now wol I speken of my fourthe housbonde.
       "My fourthe housbonde was a revelour°—   *party-goer*
This is to seyn, he hadde a paramour°—   *lover*
455   And I was yong and ful of ragerye,°   *high spirits*
Stibourne° and strong and joly° as a
       pye.°   *stubborn | pretty | magpie*

Wel koude I daunce to an harpe smale°   *small harp*
And synge,° ywis,° as any nyghtyngale   *sing | indeed*
Whan I had dronke a draughte of sweete wyn.°   *wine*
460   Metellius,[7] the foule cherl, the swyn,°   *swine*
That with a staf° birafte° his wyf hir lyf   *club | stole from*
For° she drank wyn, thogh I hadde been his wyf,   *because*
He sholde nat han daunted me fro drynke![8]
And after wyn, on Venus[9] moste° I thynke.   *must*
465   For also siker° as cold engendreth hayl,°   *as sure | causes hail*
A likerous° mouth moste han° a likerous
       tayl.°   *lecherous | must have | tail*
In wommen vinolent is no defence.[10]
This knowen lecchours° by experience.   *lechers*
       "But, Lord Crist, whan that it remembreth
       me°   *when I remember*
470   Upon my yowthe° and on my jolitee,°   *youth | gaiety*
It tikleth° me aboute myn herte roote.°   *tickles | heart's root*
Unto this day it dooth myn herte boote°   *does my heart good*
That I have had my world as in my tyme.°   *time*
But age, allas, that al wole envenyme,°   *will poison all*
475   Hath me biraft° my beautee and my pith.° *stolen from me | strength*
Lat go! Farewel! The devel go therwith!°   *with it*
The flour is goon,° ther is namoore° to telle;   *gone | no more*
The bren° as I best kan now moste° I selle.   *bran | must*
But yet to be right myrie° wol I fonde.°   *merry | try*
480   Now wol I tellen of my fourthe housbonde.
       "I seye I hadde in herte° greet despit°   *heart | great anger*
That he of any oother° had delit.°   *any other (woman) | delight*
But he was quit,° by God and by Seint Joce![11]   *punished*
I made hym of the same wode° a croce.°   *wood | cross*
485   Nat of my body in no foul manere,°   *manner*
But certein I made folk swich cheere,°   *hospitality*
That in his owene grece° I made hym frye°   *own grease | fry*
For angre and for verray jalousie.°   *true jealousy*
By God, in erthe I was his purgatorie,°   *purgatory*

---

[1] *Thanne ... sheepe*   Then would I say, "Sweetheart, note well, how meekly Willie, our sheep (i.e., her husband) looks."

[2] *Jobes pacience*   God allowed Satan to attempt to shake Job's faith through a series of terrible misfortunes. See the Biblical Book of Job.

[3] *Peter ... weel*   By St. Peter!, I curse you unless you love it well, i.e., do you ever love it well.

[4] *bele chose*   French: beautiful thing, i.e. sexual organs.

[5] *I ... rose*   In other words, if I sold myself sexually, I could dress myself beautifully with the proceeds.

[6] *Swiche ... honde*   We were occupied by this kind of conversation.

[7] *Metellius*   See *Facta et dicta memorabilia* (*Memorable Facts and Deeds*), a collection of short stories for orators, written by Valerius Maximus (1st century CE).

[8] *He ... drynke*   He should not have prevented me from drink.

[9] *Venus*   Goddess of love.

[10] *In ... defence*   There is no defense in drunken women, i.e., they are defenseless.

[11] *Seint Joce*   St. Judoc or St. Joyce was a seventh-century prince in Brittany who gave up his succession to the throne to become a priest. He was also famous for going on a pilgrimage to Rome.

490 For which I hope his soule be in glorie.

For God it woot,° he sat ful ofte and song°   knows it / sang

Whan that his shoo° ful bitterly hym
    wrong.°   shoe / hurt him very bitterly

Ther was no wight save God and he that wiste°   who knew

In many wise° how soore° I hym twiste.°   ways / sorely / tormented

495 He deyde° whan I cam fro°
    Jerusalem   died / came from (a pilgrimage to)

And lith ygrave° under the roode beem,[1]   lies buried

Al° is his tombe° noght so curyus°   although / tomb / elaborate

As was the sepulcre of hym Daryus,°   Darius

Which that Appeles wroghte° subtilly.°[2]   made / subtly

500 It nys° but wast to burye hym preciously.°   is not / expensively

Lat hym° fare wel! God yeve° his soule reste.   may he / give

He is now in his grave and in his cheste.°   coffin

    "Now of my fifthe housbonde wol I telle.

God lete his soule nevere come in Helle!

505 And yet was he to me the mooste shrewe.

That feele I on my ribbes° al by rewe,°   ribs / in a row

And evere shal unto myn endyng day.

But in oure bed he was ful fressh and gay.

And therwithal so wel koude he me glose,°   flatter

510 Whan that he wolde han my bele chose,

That thogh he hadde me bet° on every bon,°   beaten / bone

He koude wynne agayn my love anon.

I trowe° I loved hym best for that he   believe

Was of his love daungerous° to me.   standoffish

515 We wommen han, if that I shal nat lye,

In this matere a queynte fantasye:°   odd whim

Wayte,° what° thyng we may nat lightly   know (that) / whatever
    have,

Therafter° wol we crie al day and crave!   after it

Forbede° us thyng,° and that desiren we;   forbid / something

520 Preesse on us faste, and thanne wol we fle.°   flee

With daunger oute we al oure chaffare;[3]

Greet prees° at market maketh deere
    ware,°   crowd / expensive goods

And to greet cheepe° is holde at litel
    prys.°   too much merchandise / little price

This knoweth every womman that is wys.

525 My fifthe housbonde, God his soule blesse,

Which that I took for love and no richesse,

He somtyme° was a clerk° of Oxenford°   once / student / Oxford

And hadde left scole° and wente at hom° to
    bord°   school / home / rent a room

With my gossib,° dwellynge in oure toun.   confidant

530 God have hir soule! Hir name was Alisoun.

She knew myn herte and eek my privetee°   secrets

Bet° than oure parisshe preest, as moot I
    thee!°   better / may I thrive

To hire biwreyed° I my conseil° al.   revealed / counsel

For hadde myn housbonde pissed on a wal°   wall

535 Or doon a thyng that sholde han cost his lyf,

To hire and to another worthy wyf

And to my nece,° which that I loved weel,   niece

I wolde han toold his conseil everydeel.°   every bit

And so I dide ful often, God it woot!°   God knows it

540 That made his face ful often reed and hoot°   hot

For verray° shame, and blamed hymself, for he   true

Had toold to me so greet a pryvetee.

    "And so bifel° that ones° in a Lente[4]—   it happened / once

So oftentymes I to my gossyb° wente,   confidant

545 For evere yet I loved to be gay

And for to walke in March, Averill, and May

Fro hous to hous to heere sondry talys°—   various tales

That Jankyn clerk and my gossyb Dame Alys

And I myself into the feeldes° wente.   fields

550 Myn housbonde was at Londoun al the Lente;

I hadde the bettre leyser° for to pleye   better opportunity

And for to se° and eek for to be seye°   see / seen

Of lusty folk. What wiste I wher my grace

Was shapen for to be or in what place?[5]

555 Therfore I made my visitaciouns°   visits

---

[1] *And ... beem* Her fourth husband was buried inside the local parish church under the cross-beam of the cross near the high altar, a place reserved for only the most influential members of a parish.

[2] *As was ... subtilly* The legendary tomb of Darius the Mede, fashioned by the Jewish sculptor Appeles, was famous for its beauty.

[3] *With ... chaffare* Either (where we are greeted) with scorn, we (put) out all our goods (i.e., are anxious to sell), or we (put) out all our goods with (a show of) scorn (i.e., as if we did not care if anyone buys them).

---

[4] *Lente* Period in the late winter and early spring when Christians prepare for Easter by fasting and doing penance.

[5] *What wiste ... place* How could I know where or in what place my good luck was destined to be? or possibly (to avoid the redundancy) how could I know whether I was destined to have good luck, or where?

To vigilies and to processiouns,[1]

To prechyng° eek and to thise pilgrimages,   *preaching*

To pleyes° of myracles and to mariages,   *plays*

And wered upon° my gaye scarlet gytes.°   *wore / robes*

560 Thise wormes, ne thise motthes,° ne thise mytes°   *moths / mites*

Upon my peril frete° hem never a deel,°   *eat / never a bit*

And wostow° why? For they were used weel.   *do you know*

   "Now wol I tellen forth what happed me.°   *happened to me*

I seye that in the feeldes walked we

565 Til trewely we hadde swich daliance,°   *flirtation*

This clerk and I, that of my purveiance°   *foresight*

I spak to hym and seyde° hym how that he,   *said to*

If I were wydwe,° sholde wedde me.   *widowed*

For certeinly I sey for no bobance,°   *pride*

570 Yet was I nevere withouten purveiance

Of mariage n'of° othere thynges eek.   *nor of*

I holde a mouses herte° nat worth a leek   *mouse's heart*

That hath but oon hole forto sterte° to,   *escape*

And if that faille,° thanne is al ydo.°[2]   *should fail / completely done for*

575   "I bar hym on honde° he hadde enchanted me;   *accused him*

My dame° taughte me that soutiltee.°   *mother / trick*

And eek I seyde I mette° of hym al nyght: *dreamed*

He wolde han slayn° me as I lay upright,°   *killed / on my back*

And al my bed was ful of verray blood.

580 But yet I hope that he shal do me good,

For blood bitokeneth° gold, as me was taught.[3]   *signifies*

And al was fals! I dremed of it right naught.°   *not at all*

But I folwed ay° my dammes

    loore,°   *followed ever / mother's teaching*

As wel of this as othere thynges° moore.°   *matters / more*

585   "But now sire, lat me se° what I shal seyn.   *see*

Aha! By God, I have my tale ageyn!°   *again*

   "Whan that my fourthe housbonde was on beere,°[4]   *bier*

I weepe algate° and made sory cheere,°   *continuously / face*

As wyves mooten,° for it is usage,°   *must / custom*

590 And with my coverchief° covered my visage.°   *kerchief / face*

But for that° I was purveyed of° a

    make,°   *because / provided with / mate*

I wepte but smal,° and that I undertake.°   *little / attest*

   "To chirche° was myn housbonde born

    amorwe,°   *church / in the morning*

With neighebores that for hym maden sorwe,°   *sorrow*

595 And Jankyn oure clerk was oon of tho.°   *one of those*

As help me God, whan that I saugh° hym go   *saw*

After the beere, me thoughte he hadde a paire

Of legges and of feet so clene° and faire,°   *neat / attractive*

That al myn herte I yaf° unto his hoold.°   *gave / possession*

600 He was, I trowe,° a twenty wynter oold,   *believe*

And I was fourty, if I shal seye sooth.°   *say the truth*

And yet I hadde alwey a coltes° tooth.   *colt's*

Gat-tothed I was, and that bicam me weel;[5]

I hadde the prente° of Seint Venus seel.[6]   *print*

605 As help me God, I was a lusty oon,

And faire and riche and yong and wel bigon.°   *established*

And trewely, as myne housbondes tolde me,

I hadde the beste 'quonyam'° myghte be.   *sexual organ*

For certes, I am al venerien[7]

610 In feelynge,° and myn herte is marcien.[8]   *feeling*

Venus me yaf° my lust, my likerousnesse,°   *gave / lecherousness*

And Mars yaf me my sturdy hardynesse.°   *courage*

Myn ascendent was Taur, and Mars therinne.[9]

Allas! Allas! That evere love was synne!°   *sin*

615 I folwed° ay° myn indinacioun°   *followed / ever / inclination*

By vertu° of my constellacioun,°   *influence / constellation*

---

[1] *To ... processiouns* To vigils and to processions. Vigils were church services held on the evening before the feast day of a saint. Ceremonial processions formed part of the service on the day itself.

[2] *I holde ... y do* The mouse who has only one hole to which it can escape appears in various proverbs as well as in the *Romance of the Rose* (line 13554), whose character La Vieille, the old woman who knows all about love, is one of the models for the Wife of Bath. Not worth a leek means worth nothing at all.

[3] *blood ... taught* Blood could serve as a token or symbol of gold, which was often described as red.

[4] *beere* Bier, i.e., in his coffin.

[5] *Gat-tothed ... weel* I was gap-toothed, and that suited me well. Women with gaps between their teeth were said to have lustful and licentious natures.

[6] *I hadde ... seel* I had the imprint of Venus's seal; in other words, Venus has given the Wife of Bath a birthmark, another supposed indication of a lascivious nature.

[7] *venerien* In astrology, one who is influenced by the planet Venus—i.e., prone to love.

[8] *marcien* In astrology, one who is influenced by the planet Mars—i.e., war-like.

[9] *Myn ... therinne* At the moment when the Wife was born the constellation of stars known as Taurus (the Bull) was coming over the horizon (ascendant) along with the planet Mars. It was believed that if a woman is born with Venus and Mars ascending together she will be unchaste.

That made me I koude noght withdrawe°   *withhold*
My chambre° of Venus from a good felawe.°   *organ / fellow*
Yet have I Martes° mark[1] upon my face—   *Mars's*
620 And also in another privee place.
For God so wys° be my savacioun,°   *wise / salvation*
I ne loved nevere° by no discrecioun   *never loved*
But evere folwed myn appetit,°   *appetite*
Al° were he short or long° or blak° or
      whit.°   *whether / tall / dark / fair*
625 I took no kepe,° so that he liked° me,   *did not care / pleased*
How poore he was ne eek of what degree.
   "What sholde I seye, but at the monthes ende,
This joly° clerk Jankyn that was so hende°   *pretty / handy*
Hath wedded me with greet solempnytee.°   *ceremony*
630 And to hym yaf° I al the lond and fee°   *gave / property*
That evere was me yeven° therbifoore.°   *given / before this*
But afterward repented me ful soore!°   *I regretted it sorely*
He nolde suffre nothyng of my list.[2]
By God, he smoot° me ones° on the lyst,°   *hit / once / ear*
635 For that° I rente° out of his book a leef,° *because / tore / page*
That of the strook° myn ere° wax° al
      deef.°   *blow / ear / grew / completely deaf*
Stibourne° I was as is a leonesse°   *stubborn / lioness*
And of my tonge° a verray°
      jangleresse.°   *tongue / true / ceaseless talker*
And walke I wolde as I had doon biforn°   *before*
640 From hous to hous, although he had it sworn.°   *forbidden*
For which he often tymes wolde preche°   *preach*
And me of olde Romayn geestes[3] teche°   *teach*
How he Symplicius Gallus lefte his wyf
And hire forsook for terme° of al his lyf,   *the rest*
645 Noght but for open heveded,[4] he hir say,
Lookynge out at his dore° upon a day.   *door*
   "Another Romayn tolde he me by name,
That, for° his wyf was at a someres game° *because / entertainment*
Withouten his wityng,° he forsook hire eke.   *knowledge*
650 And thanne wolde he upon his Bible seke°   *seek*

That ilke° proverbe of Ecclesiaste[5]   *same*
Where he comandeth and forbedeth faste°   *firmly*
Man shal nat suffre° his wyf go roule° aboute. *allow / wander*
Thanne wolde he seye right thus, withouten doute:
655 'Whoso that buyldeth his hous al of salwes[6]
And priketh° his blynde hors° over the
      falwes°   *spurs / blind horse / fields*
And suffreth his wyf to go seken halwes°   *shrines*
Is worthy to been° hanged on the galwes.'°[7]   *be / gallows*
But al for noght! I sette noght an hawe°   *hawthorn berry*
660 Of his proverbes n'of° his olde lawe,   *nor of*
Ne I wolde nat of hym° corrected be.   *by him*
I hate hym that my vices telleth me°   *tells me about*
And so doo mo,° God woot,° of us than I.   *do more / knows*
This made hym with me wood° al outrely:°   *crazy / entirely*
665 I nolde noght° forbere° hym in no cas.°   *would not / endure / case*
   "Now wol I seye° yow° sooth,° by Seint
      Thomas,[8]   *tell / you / the truth*
Why that I rente out of his book a leef,
For which he smoot me so that I was deef.
   "He hadde a book that gladly, nyght and day,
670 For his desport° he wolde rede° alway.   *fun / read*
He cleped° it *Valerie and Theofraste*,[9]   *called*
At which book he lough° alwey ful faste.°   *laughed / very much*
And eek ther was somtyme° a clerk° at Rome, *once / theologian*
A cardinal that highte° Seint Jerome,[10]   *was named*

---

[1] *Martes mark*   Red birthmark.

[2] *He ... list*   He would not allow anything I desired.

[3] *Romayn geestes*   Roman stories. Like the reference to Metellius above in line 460, the following are old misogynistic or anti-matrimonial stories dating back to ancient Rome.

[4] *Noght ... heveded*   Just because he saw her bare-headed.

[5] *That ... Ecclesiaste*   See Ecclesiasticus 25.34.

[6] *Whoso ... salwes*   Whoever builds his house of all willow branches

[7] *Whoso ... galwes*   Proverb.

[8] *Seint Thomas*   There are three possible candidates for this St. Thomas: Thomas the apostle, mentioned in the Gospels; St. Thomas Aquinas, the thirteenth-century theologian (though his second name was more often used than not); and St. Thomas Becket, whose shrine the Canterbury pilgrims are journeying to visit. Thomas the apostle was often referred to as "Thomas of India." Becket is the likely reference.

[9] *Valerie and Theofraste*   The Wife of Bath is actually referring to two separate works, often bound together into one volume in the Middle Ages—the *Dissuasio Valerii ad Rufinum* by the English scholar and courtier Walter Map (c. 1140–c. 1208) and the *Golden Book of Marriages* by Theophrastus, a supposed disciple of Aristotle. Both books were full of stories attacking women and discouraging men from marrying.

[10] *Seint Jerome*   Late fourth and early fifth centuries and was a theologian who wrote many influential works, including a translation of the Bible into Latin. *Against Jovinian*, which extolls virginity, is one of Chaucer's major sources for the "Wife of Bath's Prologue."

675   That made a book, *Agayn*° Jovinian,   *against*
     In which book eek ther was Tertulan,[1]
     Crisippus,[2] Trotula,[3] and Helowys[4]
     That was abbesse nat fer° fro Parys,   *not far*
     And eek the *Parables of Salomon*,[5]
680   Ovides° *Art*,[6] and bookes many on.°   *Ovid's / many (other) books*
     And alle thise were bounden in o° volume.   *one*
     And every nyght and day was his custume
     Whan he hadde leyser° and vacacioun°   *leisure / opportunity*
     From oother worldly occupacioun
685   To reden on this *Book of Wikked Wyves*.[7]
     He knew of hem mo legendes and lyves°   *biographies*
     Than been° of goode wyves in the Bible.   *there are*
     For, trusteth wel, it is an inpossible°   *impossibility*
     That any clerk wol speke good of wyves
690   But if° it be of hooly seintes lyves,   *unless*
     Ne of noon other womman never the mo.
     Who peynted the leoun,[8] tel me who?
     By God, if wommen hadde writen stories
     As clerkes han° withinne hire° oratories,°   *have / their / chapels*
695   They wolde han writen of men moore wikkednesse
     Than al the mark of Adam° may redresse.   *male sex (i.e., men)*
     The children of Mercurie and Venus[9]

     Been in hir wirkyng ful contrarius.[10]
     Mercurie loveth wysdam° and science,°   *wisdom / knowledge*
700   And Venus loveth ryot° and dispence.° *parties / squandering money*
     And for hire diverse disposicioun,°   *natures*
     Ech falleth in otheres exaltacioun,°   *exaltation*
     And thus, God woot, Mercurie is desolat
     In Pisces, wher Venus is exaltat,°   *exalted*
705   And Venus falleth ther° Mercurie is reysed.   *where*
     Therfore no womman of no clerk is preysed.
     The clerk, whan he is oold and may noght° do   *cannot*
     Of Venus werkes[11] worth his olde sho,°   *shoe*
     Thanne sit he doun and writ in his dotage[12]
710   That wommen kan nat kepe hir mariage.
     "But now to purpos° why I tolde thee   *the reason*
     That I was beten° for a book, pardee.°   *beaten / by God*
     Upon a nyght Jankyn, that was oure sire,°   *master*
     Redde on his book as he sat by the fire
715   Of Eva° first, that for hir wikkednesse   *Eve*
     Was al mankynde broght to wrecchednesse,
     For which Crist hymself was slayn,
     That boghte° us with his herte blood agayn.   *who bought*
     Lo, heere,° expres° of womman may ye fynde *here, specifically*
720   That womman was the los° of al mankynde.   *destruction*
     "Tho° redde he me how Sampson[13] loste hise
       heres:°   *then / hairs*
     Slepynge, his lemman° kitte° it with hir
       sheres,°   *lover / cut / scissors*
     Thurgh° which tresoun° loste he bothe hise
       eyen.   *through / betrayal*
     "Tho redde he me, if that I shal nat lyen,°   *lie*
725   Of Hercules and of his Dianyre,[14]
     That caused hym to sette hymself afyre.°   *on fire*
     Nothyng° forgat he the sorwe and wo   *not at all*

---

[1] *Tertulan* Early third-century theologian who wrote several treatises about the value of virginity.

[2] *Crisippus* Mentioned in Jerome's treatise, referred to in line 671, but none of his works survive.

[3] *Trotula* Female doctor who taught medicine at the University of Salerno in the eleventh century and wrote a treatise about gynecology.

[4] *Helowys* Tried to persuade her lover Abelard not to marry her, giving typical anti-matrimonial reasons. She eventually became the abbess of the Paraclete, a convent of nuns near Paris.

[5] *Parables of Solomon* Biblical Book of Proverbs.

[6] *Ovides Art* Ovid's *Art of Love* concludes with a long argument about why it is prudent to avoid love.

[7] *Book of Wikked Wyves* Title of the whole compendium volume mentioned above.

[8] *Who ... leoun* In medieval versions of the fable of Aesop, a man and a lion were having a dispute about who was the stronger. For proof, the man showed the lion a picture of a man killing a lion, and the lion then asked the man who painted the lion—implying the painting is biased. Then the lion ate the man.

[9] *The children ... Venus* I.e., scholars and lovers.

[10] *Been ... contrarius* In addition to influencing the body's humors (Cf. *General Prologue*, lines 413 ff.), the planets were thought to govern various parts of the body and various trades. Mercury was the planet of scholars and merchants, who, in their ways of doing things, are completely at odds with lovers.

[11] *Venus werkes* I.e., sex.

[12] *Thanne ... dotage* Then he sits down and writes in his old age.

[13] *Tho ... Sampson* See Judges 16.15–22.

[14] *Hercules ... Dianyre* Deianira was the wife of Hercules and inadvertently caused his death by giving him a shirt that she thought would keep him faithful. It was in fact poisoned and he had himself burned alive to escape the pain.

That Socrates hadde with hise wyves two,
How Xantippa[1] caste° pisse° upon his heed.°   *threw / urine / head*
730   This sely° man sat stille° as he were
     deed.°   *innocent / quietly / dead*
He wiped his heed. Namoore dorste° he seyn   *dared*
But, 'Er° that thonder stynte,° comth a
     reyn.°'   *before / stops / rain*
     "Of Phasipha, that was the queene of Crete,
For shrewednesse° hym thoughte the tale
     swete.°   *nastiness / sweet*
735   Fy! Spek namoore! It is a grisly thyng,
Of hire horrible lust and hir likyng![2]
     "Of Clitermystra,[3] for hire lecherye,
That falsly made hire housbonde for to dye,°   *die*
He redde it with ful good devocioun.
740   "He tolde me eek for what occasioun
Amphiorax at Thebes loste his lyf:[4]
Myn housbonde hadde a legende° of his wyf,   *story*
Eriphilem, that for an ouche° of gold   *brooch*
Hath prively° unto the Grekes told   *secretly*
745   Wher that hir housbonde hidde hym in a place,
For which he hadde at Thebes sory° grace.   *sorry*
     "Of Lyvia tolde he me and of Lucye.[5]
They bothe made° hir° housbondes for to dye—   *caused / their*
That oon for love, that oother was for hate.
750   Lyvia hir housbonde upon an even° late   *evening*
Empoysoned° hath, for that she was his fo;°   *poisoned / foe*
Lucia likerous° loved hire housbonde so,   *lustfully*

That, for he sholde alwey upon hire thynke,
She yaf° hym swich a manere° love drynke°   *gave / type of / potion*
755   That he was deed° er it were by the morwe.°   *dead / morning*
And thus algates° housbondes han sorwe.°   *always / have sorrow*
     "Thanne tolde he me how that oon Latumyus[6]
Compleyned unto his felawe° Arrius   *friend*
That in his gardyn growed swich a tree
760   On which he seyde how that hise wyves thre
Hanged hemself° for herte° despitus.°   *themselves / heart / cruel*
'O leeve° brother,' quod this Arrius,   *dear*
'Yif° me a plante° of thilke° blissed tree,   *give / seedling / that*
And in my gardyn planted it shal bee.'
765   "Of latter date of wyves hath he red,
That somme han slayn hir housbondes in hir bed
And lete hir lecchour dighte hire al the nyght[7]
Whan that the corps lay in the floor upright,
And somme han dryve° nayles° in hir brayn[8]   *driven / nails*
770   Whil that they slepte, and thus they han hem slayn;
Somme han hem yeve poysoun in hire drynke.[9]
He spak moore harm than herte may bithynke.°   *imagine*
And therwithal° he knew of mo proverbes   *with all this*
Than in this world ther growen gras or herbes.
775   'Bet° is,' quod he, 'thyn habitacioun°   *better / dwelling place*
Be with a leoun or a foul dragoun
Than with a womman usynge° for to chyde.   *accustomed*
Bet is,' quod he, 'hye° in the roof abyde   *high*
Than with an angry wyf doun in the hous,
780   They been° so wikked and contrarious;   *are*
They haten that hir housbondes loveth ay.'[10]
He seyde, 'A womman cast° hir shame away   *throws*
Whan she cast of° hir smok.° And forthermo,   *off / undergarment*
A fair womman, but° she be chaast° also,   *unless / chaste*
785   Is lyk a gold ryng in a sowes° nose.'   *pig's*
Who wolde leeve or who wolde suppose°   *believe*
The wo that in myn herte was and pyne?°   *pain*
     "And whan I saugh he wolde nevere fyne°   *finish*
To reden on this cursed book al nyght,

---

[1]   *Xantippa*   I.e., Xanthippe (late fifth c. BCE) famously shrewish wife of the philosopher Socrates (469–399 BCE).

[2]   *Phasipha … likyng*   In Greek mythology, Queen Pasiphae of Crete had sex with a bull and gave birth to the monster Minotaur; *likyng* Desire.

[3]   *Clitermystra*   I.e., Clytemnestra, who with her lover Aegisthus murdered her husband Agamemnon when he returned from the Trojan war.

[4]   *Amphiorax … lyf*   Amphiaraus hid so he would not have to fight in war, but his hiding place was betrayed by his wife Eriphyle, and he was killed in battle.

[5]   *Of … Lucye*   Livia was either Augustus's wife, who poisoned several prominent Romans (including her own husband) for political gain, or Livilla, Livia's granddaughter, who poisoned her husband at the instigation of her lover Sejanus. Lucilla poisoned her husband, the Roman philosopher Lucretius (c. 99–c.55 BCE), author of *On the Nature of Things*, with a love-potion intended to increase his desire for her.

[6]   *Thanne … Latumyus*   The incident related below is another misogynistic story from ancient Rome, for which Chaucer's source is probably Walter Map's *Dissuasio Valerii*.

[7]   *And … nyght*   And let her lover have sex with her all night.

[8]   *And … brayn*   See Judges 4.17–22.

[9]   *Somme … drynke*   Some have given them poison in their drink.

[10]   *They … ay*   They always hate what their husbands love.

790 Al sodeynly thre leves have I plyght°   plucked
Out of his book, right as he radde. And eke
I with my fest° so took° hym on the cheke,   fist / hit
That in oure fyr he fil° bakward adoun.   fell
And he up stirte° as dooth a wood leoun,   jumps
795 And with his fest he smoot me on the heed,
That in° the floor I lay as I were deed.   on
And whan he saugh how stille that I lay,
He was agast° and wolde han fled his way.°   afraid / away
Til atte laste out of my swogh° I breyde.°   faint / awoke
800 'O hastow° slayn me, false theef?' I seyde.   have you
'And for my land thus hastow mordred me!
Er° I be deed, yet wol I kisse thee.'   before
    "And neer he cam and kneled faire° adoun   pleasantly
And seyde, 'Deere suster° Alisoun,   sister
805 As help me God, I shal thee nevere smyte!
That I have doon, it is thyself to wyte.°   blame
Foryeve it me, and that I thee biseke!'°   beg
And yet eftsoones° I hitte hym on the cheke   once more
And seyde, 'Theef, thus muchel am I wreke.°   avenged
810 Now wol I dye. I may no lenger speke.'
But atte laste, with muchel care and wo,
We fille acorded° by usselven° two.   came to an agreement / ourselves
He yaf me al° the bridel° in myn hond   completely / bridle
To han the governance of hous and lond,
815 And of his tonge and his hond also,
And made hym brenne his book anon right tho.°   there
And whan that I hadde geten° unto me   gotten
By maistrie° al the soveraynetee,   mastery
And that he seyde, 'Myn owene trewe wyf,
820 Do as thee lust to terme of al thy lyf:[1]
Keepe thyn honour and keepe eek myn estaat.'—
After that day we hadden never debaat.°   disagreement
God helpe me so, I was to hym as kynde
As any wyf from Denmark unto Ynde°   India
825 And also trewe, and so was he to me.
I prey to God that sit in magestee,
So blesse his soule for his mercy deere.
Now wol I seye° my tale, if ye wol heere."   tell

BIHOLDE THE WORDES BITWENE THE SOMONOUR AND THE FRERE

The Frere° lough° whan he hadde herd al this.   friar / laughed
830 "Now dame," quod he, "so have I joye or blis,
This is a long preamble of a tale!"
And whan the Somonour herde the Frere gale,°   speak up
"Lo," quod the Somonour, "Goddes armes two![2]
A frere wol entremette hym evere mo![3]
835 Lo, goode men, a flye and eek a frere
Wol falle in every dyssh and mateere![4]
What spekestow° of preambulacioun?° what do you say / preambling
What! Amble or trotte° or pees° or go sit doun!   trot / pace
Thou lettest° oure disport° in this manere."   spoil / fun
840   "Ye, woltow so,° sire Somonour?" quod the
        Frere.   will you say so
"Now by my feith, I shal er that I go
Telle of a somonour swich a tale or two,
That alle the folk shal laughen in this place!"
    "Now elles,° Frere, I bishrewe° thy face!"   otherwise / curse
845 Quod this Somonour, "and I bishrewe me
But if° I telle tales two or thre   unless
Of freres er I come to Sidyngborne![5]
That I shal make thyn herte for to morne,°   mourn
For wel I woot thy pacience is gon."
850   Oure Hoost cride, "Pees,° and that anon!"   peace
And seyde, "Lat the womman telle hire tale.
Ye fare° as folk that dronken were of ale!   behave
Do, dame, telle forth youre tale, and that is best."
    "Alredy,° sire," quod she, "right as yow lest,°   ready / wish
855 If I have licence of this worthy Frere."
    "Yis, dame," quod he, "tel forth, and I wol heere."

HEERE ENDETH THE WYF OF BATHE HIR PROLOGE AND BIGYNNETH HIR TALE

[2] *Goddes armes two* God's two arms. This is an oath like those uniformly condemned by the Church.

[3] *A … mo* A friar will always put himself in the middle of things.

[4] *Wol … mateere* Will fall into every dish and matter.

[5] *Sidyngborne* I.e., Sittingbourne, a small town about forty miles from London on the road to Canterbury.

THE WIFE OF BATH'S TALE

In th'olde dayes of Kyng Arthour,
Of which that Britons speken greet honour,[1]
Al was this land fulfild of° fairye.[2]   *filled up with*
860　The Elf Queene with hir joly compaignye
Daunced ful ofte in many a grene mede.°   *meadow*
This was the olde opinion, as I rede°—   *read*
I speke of manye hundred yeres ago.
But now kan no man se none elves mo,°   *no more elves*
865　For now the grete charitee and prayeres
Of lymytours[3] and othere hooly° freres   *holy*
That serchen every lond and every streem,
As thikke as motes° in the sonne beem,   *dust particles*
Blessynge halles, chambres, kichenes, boures,°   *bedrooms*
870　Citees, burghes,° castels, hye toures,°   *fortified towns | towers*
Thropes,° bernes,° shipnes,°
　　dayeryes°—   *villages | barns | stables | dairies*
This maketh° that ther been° no fairyes.   *causes it | are*
For theras° wont° to walken was an elf,   *where | accustomed*
Ther walketh now the lymytour° hymself   *friar*
875　In undermeles° and in morwenynges,   *early afternoons | mornings*
And seyth his matyns° and his hooly
　　thynges°   *morning service | prayers*
As he gooth in his lymytacioun.°   *limited area*
Wommen may go saufly° up and doun: *safely*
In every bussh or under every tree
880　Ther is noon oother incubus[4] but he,
And he ne wol doon hem but dishonour.[5]
And so bifel° that this Kyng Arthour   *it happened*
Hadde in hous a lusty bachelor°   *young knight*
That on a day cam ridynge fro ryver,°   *from a river*
885　And happed that, allone° as he was born,   *lone*
He saugh a mayde° walkynge hym biforn,°   *maid | in front of him*
Of° which mayde anon, maugree° hir heed,°   *from | despite | will*
By verray° force birafte° hire maydenhed,   *true | stole*

For which oppressioun was swich clamour°   *outcry*
890　And swich pursute° unto the Kyng Arthour,   *appeal*
That dampned° was this knyght for to be
　　deed°   *condemned | dead*
By cours of lawe, and sholde han lost his heed—
Paraventure° swich was the statut tho°—   *by chance | then*
But that the queene and othere ladyes mo
895　So longe preyden° the kyng of grace,°   *requested | mercy*
Til he his lyf hym graunted in the place
And yaf hym to the queene al at hir wille
To chese° wheither she wolde hym save or spille.°   *choose | kill*
The queene thanketh the kyng with al hir myght
900　And after this thus spak she to the knyght
Whan that she saugh hir tyme upon a day:
"Thou standest yet," quod she, "in swich array°   *condition*
That of thy lyf yet hastow° no suretee.°   *have you | certainty*
I grante thee lyf if thou kanst tellen me
905　What thyng is it that wommen moost desiren.
Bewar and keepe thy nekke boon° from iren!°   *bone | iron*
And if thou kanst nat tellen it anon,
Yet shal I yeve thee leve for to gon°   *go*
A twelf month and a day to seche° and leere°   *seek | learn*
910　An answere suffisant° in this mateere.   *sufficient*
And suretee° wol I han er that thou pace°—   *guarantee | leave*
Thy body for to yelden° in this place."   *return*
Wo° was this knyght, and sorwefully he siketh,°   *sad | sighs*
But he may nat do al as hym liketh.°   *as he wishes*
915　And at the laste he chees° hym for to wende,°   *chooses | go*
And come agayn right at the yeres° ende   *year's*
With swich answere as God wolde hym purveye,°   *provide*
And taketh his leve and wendeth forth his weye.
He seketh every hous and every place
920　Whereas° he hopeth for to fynde grace   *where*
To lerne what thyng wommen loven moost,
But he ne koude arryven in no coost°   *region*
Wheras he myghte fynde in this mateere
Two creatures accordynge° in feere.°   *agreeing | together*
925　Somme seyde wommen loven best richesse;
Somme seyde honour, somme seyde jolynesse,°   *jollity*
Somme riche array.° Somme seyden lust
　　abedde°   *clothing | in bed*
And ofetyme to be wydwe° and wedde.°   *widowed | married*
Somme seyde that oure hertes been moost esed°   *refreshed*
930　Whan that we been° yflatered and yplesed.   *are*

---

[1]　*Kyng Arthour … honour* Legendary British king of roughly the fifth or sixth century CE, the subject of many medieval tales and romances.

[2]　*fairye* Supernatural beings known as elves or fairies.

[3]　*lymytours* Friars who were licensed to preach in a limited area in a parish or county.

[4]　*incubus* Devilish spirit who would appear to women in dreams and thereby impregnate them.

[5]　*ne … dishonour* Will do them nothing but dishonor.

He gooth ful ny the sothe, I wol nat lye!¹
A man shal wynne us best with flaterye
And with attendance° and with bisynesse°   *attention / diligence*
Been we° ylymed² bothe moore and lesse.   *we are*
935 And somme seyn that we loven best
For to be free and so do right° as us lest°   *just / wish*
And that no man repreve us° of oure vice   *complain to us*
But seye that we be wise and nothyng° nyce.°   *not / foolish*
For trewely, ther is noon° of us alle,   *none*
940 If any wight° wol clawe° us on the galle,°   *person / claw / a sore*
That we nel kike,° for he seith us sooth.   *will not kick*
Assay° and he shal fynde it that so dooth.   *try*
For be we never so vicious° withinne,°   *wicked / within*
We wol been holden° wise and clene   *wish to be considered*
    of synne.
945 And somme seyn that greet delit han we
For to been holden stable and eek secree,°   *discreet*
And in o° purpos stedefastly to dwelle,   *one*
And nat biwreye° thyng° that men us telle.   *betray / something*
But that tale is nat worth a rake-stele!°   *handle of a rake*
950 Pardee, we wommen konne nothyng hele.³
Witnesse on Myda.⁴ Wol ye heere the tale?
Ovyde, amonges othere thynges smale,
Seyde Myda hadde under his longe heres°   *hairs*
Growynge upon his heed two asses eres,
955 The which vice he hydde as he best myghte
Ful subtilly° from every mannes sighte,   *carefully*
That save his wyf, ther wiste of it namo.°   *no one else*
He loved hire moost and triste° hire also.   *trusted*
He preyde° hire that to no creature   *asked*
960 She sholde tellen of his disfigure.°   *disfigurement*
She swoor hym nay: for al this world to wynne°   *gain*
She nolde° do that vileynye or synne   *would not*
To make hir housbonde han so foul a name.
She nolde nat telle it for hir owene shame.
965 But nathelees, hir thoughte that she dyde,°   *would die*
That° she so longe sholde a conseil° hyde.   *if / secret*

Hir thoughte it swal so soore aboute hir herte
That nedely som word hire moste asterte.⁵
And sith she dorste° telle it to no man,   *dared*
970 Doun to a mareys° faste by° she ran;   *marsh / close by*
Til she cam there hir herte was afyre.°   *on fire*
And as a bitore⁶ bombleth° in the myre,°   *calls out / mud*
She leyde hir mouth unto the water doun.
"Biwreye me nat, thou water, with thy soun,"°   *sound*
975 Quod she. "To thee I telle it and namo:
Myn housbonde hath longe asses erys two!
Now is myn herte al hool.° Now is it oute!   *whole*
I myghte no lenger kepe it, out of doute."°   *without doubt*
Heere may ye se,° thogh we a tyme° abyde,   *see / for a time*
980 Yet out it moot!° We kan no conseil hyde.   *must (go)*
The remenant of the tale if ye wol heere,
Redeth Ovyde, and ther ye may it leere.°   *learn*
This knyght of which my tale is specially,
Whan that he saugh he myghte nat come therby,
985 This is to sey, what wommen love moost,
Withinne his brest ful sorweful was the goost.°   *spirit*
But hoom he gooth. He myghte nat sojourne.°   *delay*
The day was come that homward moste he tourne.
And in his wey it happed hym to ryde
990 In al this care under a forest syde
Wheras he saugh upon a daunce⁷ go
Of ladyes foure and twenty and yet mo,
Toward the which daunce he drow ful yerne°   *drew very eagerly*
In hope that som wysdom sholde he lerne.
995 But certeinly, er he cam fully there,
Vanysshed was this daunce he nyste° where.   *knew not*
No creature saugh he that bar lyf,°   *bore life*
Save on the grene° he saugh sittynge a wyf °—   *meadow / woman*
A fouler° wight ther may no man devyse.°   *uglier / imagine*
1000 Agayn° the knyght this olde wyf gan ryse°   *towards / rose up*
And seyde, "Sire Knyght, heer forth ne lith° no
    wey.°   *lies / road*
Tel me what that ye seken, by youre fey.°   *faith*

---

¹ *He ... lye* He gets very near the truth, I will not lie.

² *ylymed* Limed. Lime was used to catch birds.

³ *Pardee ... hele* By God, we women know nothing about how to keep a secret.

⁴ *Myda* I.e., Midas. See Ovid's *Metamorphoses*, Book 11 (although in Ovid's version it is the king's barber, not his wife, who whispers the secret).

⁵ *Hir thoughte ... asterte* It seemed to her that it became so sorely swollen around her heart, that by necessity some word had to burst out.

⁶ *bitore* I.e., bittern, a small heron.

⁷ *Wheras ... daunce* One way in which mortals were said to encounter elves was at night in the woods, where the elves performed a ritual dance.

Paraventure it may the bettre be;

1005 Thise olde folk kan° muchel° thyng," quod she.   *know / many*

"My leeve° mooder,"° quod this knyght certeyn,   *dear / mother*

"I nam but° deed but if° that I kan seyn   *am as good as / unless*

What thyng it is that wommen moost desire.

Koude ye me wisse, I wolde wel quite youre hire."[1]

"Plight° me thy trouthe° heere in myn hand,"   *pledge / word*
    quod she,

1010 "The nexte thyng that I require° thee,   *ask of*

Thou shalt it do if it lye in thy myght,

And I wol telle it yow° er it be nyght."   *to you*

"Have heer my trouthe," quod the knyght. "I grante."

"Thanne," quod she, "I dar° me wel avante°   *dare / boast*

1015 Thy lyf is sauf,° for I wol stonde therby.   *safe*

Upon my lyf, the queene wol seye as I.

Lat se° which is the proudeste of hem alle   *let's see*

That wereth on a coverchief° or a calle°   *kerchief / hairnet*

That dar seye nay of that I shal thee teche.°   *teach*

1020 Lat us go forth withouten lenger speche."

Tho° rowned° she a pistel° in his ere   *then / whispered / lesson*

And bad hym to be glad and have no fere.

Whan they be comen to the court, this knyght

Seyde he had holde° his day as he hadde hight°   *kept / promised*

1025 And redy was his answere, as he sayde.

Full many a noble wyf and many a mayde

And many a wydwe,° for that they been° wise,   *widow / are*

The queene hirself sittynge as justise,°   *sitting as a judge*

Assembled been° his answere for to heere,   *are*

1030 And afterward this knyght was bode°
    appeere.°   *commanded / to appear*

To every wight comanded was silence

And that the knyght sholde telle in audience°   *in their hearing*

What thyng that worldly wommen loven best.

This knyght ne stood nat° stille as doth a
    best,°   *did not stand / beast*

1035 But to his questioun anon answerde

With manly voys,° that al the court it herde.   *voice*

"My lige° lady, generally," quod he,   *liege*

"Wommen desiren to have sovereynetee   *to have sovereignty*

As wel over hir housbond as hir love

1040 And for to been in maistrie hym above.

This is youre mooste° desir, thogh ye me kille.   *greatest*

Dooth as yow list. I am at youre wille."

In al the court ne was ther° wyf ne mayde   *there was neither*

Ne wydwe that contraried that he sayde,

1045 But seyden he was worthy han° his lyf.   *to have*

And with that word up stirte° the olde wyf   *jumped*

Which that the knyght saugh sittynge in the grene.

"Mercy," quod she, "my sovereyn lady queene!

Er that youre court departe, do me right.

1050 I taughte this answere unto the knyght,

For which he plighte° me his trouthe° there,   *promised / word*

The firste thyng I wolde hym requere,

He wolde it do if it lay in his myght.

Bifore the court thanne preye° I thee, sire knyght,"   *ask*

1055 Quod she, "that thou me take unto thy wyf.

For wel thou woost° that I have kept thy lyf.   *know*

If I seye fals, sey nay, upon thy fey!"°   *faith*

This knyght answerde, "Allas and weylawey!°   *woe is me*

I woot° right wel that swich° was my
    biheste.°   *know / such / promise*

1060 For Goddes love, as chees° a newe requeste!   *choose*

Taak° al my good,° and lat° my body go!"   *take / possessions / let*

"Nay thanne,"° quod she, "I shrewe° us bothe two,   *then / curse*

For thogh that I be foul, oold, and poore,

I nolde° for al the metal ne for oore°   *would not / ore*

1065 That under erthe° is grave° or lith° above   *earth / buried / lies*

But if thy wyf I were and eek thy love."

"My love!" quod he. "Nay, my dampnacioun!°   *damnation*

Allas, that any of my nacioun°   *family*

Sholde evere so foule disparaged° be!"   *badly shamed*

1070 But al for noght! Th'end is this: that he

Constreyned° was. He nedes moste hire wedde,   *compelled*

And taketh his olde wyf and gooth to bedde.

Now wolden som men seye paraventure°   *perhaps*

That for my necligence I do no cure°   *care*

1075 To tellen yow the joye and al th'array°   *the arrangements*

That at the feeste was that ilke° day,   *same*

To which thyng shortly answere I shal.

I seye ther nas° no joye ne feeste at al.   *was no*

Ther nas° but hevynesse and muche sorwe.   *was nothing*

1080 For prively he wedded hire on a morwe,°   *morning*

And al day after hidde hym as an owle,

So wo was hym, his wyf looked so foule.

Greet was the wo the knyght hadde in his thoght

Whan he was with his wyf abedde ybroght.[2]

---

1   *Koude … hire* If you could inform me, I would pay you back well.

2   *Whan … ybroght* It was a custom for wedding guests to escort the bride and groom to their bedroom.

1085 He walweth,° and he turneth to and fro.	*writhes about*
His olde wyf lay smylynge° evere mo	*smiling*
And seyde, "O deere housbonde, benedicitee,°	*bless you*
Fareth° every knyght thus with his wyf as ye?	*behaves*
Is this the lawe of Kyng Arthures hous?	
1090 Is every knyght of his so dangerous?°	*standoffish*
I am youre owene love and youre wyf;	
I am she which that saved hath youre lyf.	
And certes, yet ne dide° I yow nevere unright:°	*did not / injustice*
Why fare ye thus with me this firste nyght?	
1095 Ye faren lyk a man had lost his wit.	
What is my gilt?° For Goddes love, tel it,	*guilt*
And it shal been amended if I may."	
"Amended!" quod this knyght. "Allas, nay! Nay!	
It wol nat been amended nevere mo.°	*forever more*
1100 Thou art so loothly° and so oold° also,	*ugly / old*
And therto comen of so lough° a kynde,°	*low / lineage*
That litel wonder is thogh° I walwe° and wynde.°	*though / writhe / twist about*
So wolde God myn herte wolde breste!"°	*burst*
"Is this," quod she, "the cause of youre unreste?"	
1105 "Ye, certeinly," quod he, "no wonder is!"	
"Now sire," quod she, "I koude amende al this	
If that me liste° er it were dayes thre,°	*I wished / three days*
So wel ye myghte bere yow unto me.[1]	
But for° ye speken of swich gentillesse	*because*
1110 As is descended out of old richesse,	
That therfore sholden ye be gentilmen,	
Swich arrogance is nat worth an hen!	
Looke who that is moost vertuous alway,	
Pryvee and apert and moost entendeth ay	
1115 To do the gentil dedes that he kan:[2]	
Taak hym for the grettest gentilman.	
Crist wole° we clayme° of hym oure gentillesse,	*desires that / claim*
Nat of oure eldres° for hire old richesse.	*ancestors*
For thogh they yeve us al hir heritage,	
1120 For which we clayme to been of heigh parage,°	*lineage*
Yet may they nat biquethe° for nothyng	*bequeath*
To noon° of us hir vertuous lyvyng°	*none / living*
That made hem° gentilmen ycalled be,	*them*

And bad us folwen hem in swich degree.	
1125 Wel kan the wise poete of Florence	
That highte Dant° speken in this sentence.°	*is named Dante / matter*
Lo, in swich maner rym° is Dantes tale:	*such a kind of rhyme*
'Ful selde up riseth by his branches smale	
Prowesse of man.[3] For God of his goodnesse	
1130 Wole° that of hym we clayme oure gentillesse.'	*wishes*
For of oure eldres may we nothyng clayme	
But temporel thyng° that man may hurte and mayme.°	*temporal things / maim*
Eek every wight woot this as wel as I.	
If gentillesse were planted natureelly°	*implanted by nature*
1135 Unto a certeyn lynage doun the lyne,°	*line (of generations)*
Pryvee nor apert thanne wolde they nevere fyne	
To doon of gentillesse the faire office.[4]	
They myghte do no vileynye or vice.	
Taak fyr° and ber° it in the derkeste hous	*fire / carry*
1140 Bitwix this and the mount of Kaukasous°	*Caucasus*
And lat men shette the dores and go thenne:°	*go away*
Yet wole the fyr as faire lye° and brenne°	*blaze / burn*
As twenty thousand men myghte it biholde.	
His° office natureel ay° wol it holde,	*its / ever*
1145 Up peril of my lyf, til that it dye.[5]	
Heere may ye se wel how that genterye	
Is nat annexed° to possessioun,	*linked*
Sith folk ne doon hir operacioun°	*do not behave*
Alwey as dooth the fyr, lo, in his kynde.°	*according to its nature*
1150 For God it woot, men may wel often fynde	
A lordes sone do shame and vileynye,	
And he that wole han° pris of° his gentrye,	*will have / esteem for*
For he was born of a gentil hous	
And hadde hise eldres noble and vertuous,	
1155 And nel hymselven° do no gentil dedis°	*will not himself / deeds*
Ne folwen his gentil aunestre that deed° is,	*dead*
He nys nat° gentil, be he duc° or erl,°	*is not / duke / earl*
For vileyns synful dedes make a cherl.°	*churl*
For gentillesse nys but° renomee°	*is not / renown*

---

[1] *So ... me* Provided that you might behave yourself well towards me.

[2] *Looke ... kan* Look for whoever is always most virtuous in private and in public and always strives to do the most noble deeds.

[3] *Ful ... man* The excellence of a man seldom extends to the further branches (of his family tree); i.e., the sons are seldom worthy of the father. Cf. Dante's *Convivio* 4 and *Purgatorio* 7.121.

[4] *Pryvee ... office* Then they would never stop doing the fair office of gentle deeds either in private or in public.

[5] *His ... dye* Upon my life, it will always perform its natural function (i.e., burn) until it dies.

1160 Of thyne auncestres for hire heigh bountee,° *their high goodness*
Which is a strange° thyng to thy persone. *separate*
Thy gentillesse cometh fro God allone.
Thanne comth oure verray gentillesse of grace;
It was nothyng biquethe us° with oure
place.° *bequeathed to us / social position*
1165 Thenketh how noble, as seith Valerius,
Was thilke° Tullius Hostillius,[1] *that*
That out of poverte roos° to heigh noblesse. *rose*
Reed Senek and redeth eek Boece:[2]
Ther shul ye seen expres° that no drede° is *specifically / doubt*
1170 That he is gentil that dooth gentil dedis.
And therfore, leeve housbonde, I thus conclude,
Al° were it that myne auncestres weren
rude,° *although / of low birth*
Yet may the hye° God—and so hope I— *high*
Grante me grace to lyven° vertuously. *live*
1175 Thanne am I gentil whan that I bigynne° *begin*
To lyven vertuously and weyve synne.° *avoid sin*
And theras° ye of poverte me repreeve,° *since / reproach*
The hye God on whom that we bileeve
In wilful° poverte chees° to lyve his lyf. *voluntary / chose*
1180 And certes, every man, mayden, or wyf
May understonde that Jesus Hevene kyng° *King of Heaven*
Ne wolde nat chesen° vicious lyvyng. *choose*
Glad° poverte is an honeste thyng, certeyn. *joyful*
This wole Senec and othere clerkes° seyn.° *writers / say*
1185 Whoso that halt hym payd of° his poverte, *satisfied with*
I holde° hym riche, al° hadde he nat a sherte. *consider / although*
He that coveiteth° is a povere wight, *covets*
For he wolde han that° is nat in his myght. *what*
But he that noght hath ne coveiteth have° *and does not covet*
1190 Is riche, although ye holde hym but a knave.
Verray poverte, it syngeth properly.
Juvenal[3] seith of poverte myrily,° *merrily*
'The povre man, whan he goth by the weye,° *along the road*
Bifore the theves he may synge and pleye.'
1195 Poverte is hateful good and, as I gesse,

A ful greet bryngere° out of bisynesse,° *very great bringer / busyness*
A greet amendere° eek of sapience° *improver / wisdom*
To hym that taketh it in pacience.° *patience*
Poverte is this, although it seme alenge:° *wretched*
1200 Possessioun that no wight wol chalenge.° *claim*
Poverte ful ofte, whan a man is lowe,
Maketh° his God and eek hymself to knowe. *causes*
Poverte a spectacle° is, as thynketh me, *lens*
Thurgh° which he may hise verray° freendes see. *through / true*
1205 And therfore sire, syn that I noght yow greve,° *do not grieve you*
Of my poverte namoore° ye me repreve. *no more*
Now sire, of elde° ye repreve me, *old age*
And certes, sire, thogh noon auctoritee
Were in no book, ye gentils° of honour *nobles*
1210 Seyn that men sholde an oold wight doon favour° *do honor*
And clepe° hym fader for youre gentillesse. *call*
And auctours° shal I fynden, as I gesse. *authorities*
Now ther° ye seye that I am foul and old: *where*
Than drede° you noght to been a cokewold.[4] *fear*
1215 For filthe and eelde, also moot I thee,° *might I thrive*
Been grete wardeyns upon° chastitee. *guardians of*
But nathelees, syn I knowe youre delit,° *delight*
I shal fulfille youre worldly appetit.
Chese now," quod she, "oon of thise thynges tweye:° *two*
1220 To han me foul and old til that I deye
And be to yow a trewe, humble wyf
And nevere yow displese° in al my lyf, *displease you*
Or elles° ye wol han me yong and fair *else*
And take youre aventure of the repair
1225 That shal be to youre hous bycause of me,
Or in som oother place, may wel be.[5]
Now chese yourselven wheither that yow
liketh."° *whichever pleases you*
This knyght avyseth° hym and sore siketh,° *considers / sorely sighs*
But atte laste he seyde in this manere:
1230 "My lady and my love and wyf so deere,
I put me in youre wise governance.
Cheseth youreself which may be moost plesance° *most pleasant*
And moost honour to yow and me also.
I do no fors° the wheither of the two, *I do not care*
1235 For as yow liketh, it suffiseth me."

---

[1] *Valerius … Hostillius* Tullius Hostillius started life as a peasant and rose to become king. The story is told by the Roman writer Valerius Maximus.
[2] *Senek* I.e., Seneca, Stoic philosopher (c. 5 BCE–65 CE); *Boece* I.e., Boethius. See his *Consolation of Philosophy*, book 3, prose 6 and metre 3.
[3] *Juvenal* Roman poet and satirist (55–127 CE).

[4] *cokewold* I.e., cuckold, a man whose wife has been unfaithful to him.
[5] *And … be* And take your chances of the visiting (i.e., by lovers) at your house, or perhaps in some other places, in order to see me.

"Thanne have I gete° of yow maistrie,"° quod   *gotten / mastery*
    she,
"Syn I may chese and governe as me lest?"°   *as I wish*
"Ye certes, wyf," quod he, "I holde it best."
"Kys me," quod she, "we be no lenger wrothe.°   *angry*
1240 For by my trouthe,° I wol be to yow bothe.   *truth*
This is to seyn, ye, bothe° fair and good.   *indeed both*
I prey to God that I moote sterven wood°   *die crazy*
But° I to yow be also good and trewe   *unless*
As evere was wyf, syn that the world was newe.
1245 And but° I be tomorn° as fair to seene   *unless / tomorrow*
As any lady, emperice,° or queene   *empress*
That is bitwixe the est and eke the west,
Dooth° with my lyf and deth right° as yow lest.°   *do / just / wish*
Cast up the curtyn. Looke how that it is."
1250 And whan the knyght saugh veraily al this,

That she so fair was and so yong therto,
For joye he hente° hire in hise armes two.   *held*
His herte° bathed in a bath of blisse.   *heart*
A thousand tyme arewe° he gan hire kisse.   *in a row*
1255 And she obeyed hym in everythyng
That myghte doon hym plesance or likyng.°   *enjoyment*
And thus they lyve unto hir lyves ende
In parfit° joye. And Jesu Crist us sende   *perfect*
Housbondes meeke, yonge, and fressh abedde°   *in bed*
1260 And grace to t'overbyde° hem that we wedde.   *control*
And eek I pray Jhesu shorte hir lyves°   *shorten their lives*
That nat wol be governed by hir wyves.
And olde and angry nygardes° of dispence,°   *skinflints / spending*
God sende hem soone verray pestilence!

HEERE ENDETH THE WYVES TALE OF BATHE

The Pardoner's Prologue and Tale

The Pardoner calls himself "a full vicious man," yet, paradoxically, his tale is one of the few that has a completely straightforward moral: covetousness is the root of all evil. The tale is actually a popular sermon of the kind that the Pardoner has given so often that he knows it by rote. A story of three men who go in search of death, *The Pardoner's Tale* has at its core an *exemplum*, a short and gripping story with a clear moral message. To this exemplum a preacher might add, as the Pardoner does, dramatic denunciations of the Seven Deadly Sins, supported by Biblical quotations, and calls for repentance. Medieval popular preachers were often excellent storytellers, but the level of detail in *The Pardoner's Tale* goes beyond the needs of any sermon. Like the Miller, the Pardoner is a churl, and their two tales share an interest in the concrete and seamy aspects of daily life, down to such matters as how people rented rooms or poisoned rats. Although the time period is not specified the Pardoner's story captures the brutal joys of the tavern and the grim atmosphere of England in a time of plague, with the death cart making the rounds to retrieve the bodies, as it would have done during the Black Death of 1348–49. The enigmatic old man who cannot die but knows where death is to be found further enriches the basic *exemplum*.

The Pardoner's greatest modification of a popular sermon, however, is to offer a full commentary on his own art, describing his motivation (simple covetousness) and the various tricks, including blackmail, which he uses to persuade his listeners to buy his spurious relics and pardons. By holding out false promises of salvation, the Pardoner is endangering the souls of others and his own. His character has fascinated readers, perhaps because it is so enigmatic. There has been much discussion of what drives the Pardoner to such extensive self-revelation and why, having just explained his methods to the pilgrims, he is so rash as to make a final sales pitch for his relics. In one much-discussed line in *The General Prologue*, "I trowe [I believe] he were a gelding [a castrated stallion] or a mare," the narrator indicates that he does not precisely know what to make of the Pardoner, while defining him as other than "masculine." Based on this line and other features of his depiction, some have seen the Pardoner as a tormented outsider, anxious to win group approval, others as a figure of spiritual sterility, corrupted by his own covetousness and in turn corrupting those who listen to him.

Opening page of *The Pardoner's Tale*, Ellesmere manuscript (detail). (Reprinted by permission of *The Huntington Library, San Marino, California*. EL 26 C9 f. 138r.)

Opening page of *The Pardoner's Tale*, Ellesmere manuscript. (Reprinted by permission of *The Huntington Library, San Marino, California*. EL 26 C9 f. 138r.)

THE INTRODUCTION TO THE PARDONER'S TALE

THE WORDES OF THE HOOST
TO THE PHISICIEN AND THE PARDONER

Oure Hoost gan to swere° as° he were
    wood.° *began to swear / as if / crazy*
"Harrow!" quod he. "By nayles and by blood!¹
This was a fals° cherl° and a fals justice.° *false / churl / judge*
As shameful deeth° as herte° may devyse° *death / heart / imagine*
5 Come to thise° false juges° and hire
    advocatz!° *these / judges / their lawyers*
Algate° this sely° mayde° is slayn,
    allas!² *but / innocent / maid / killed*
Allas, to deere° boughte she beautee! *too dearly*
Wherfore° I seye° al day as men may see, *therefore / say*
That yiftes° of Fortune and of nature *gifts*
10 Been° cause of deeth to many a creature. *are*
Of bothe yiftes that I speke of now
Men han ful ofte° moore for harm than
    prow.° *have very often / profit*
But trewely,° myn owene maister° deere,° *truly / master / dear*
This is a pitous° tale for to here.° *pitiful / hear*
15 But nathelees,° passe over.° Is no
    fors.° *nevertheless / let it pass / matter*
I pray to God so save thy gentil cors° *noble body*
And eek thyne urynals and thy jurdones,³
Thyn ypocras° and eek thy galiones° *hypocras / galians (medicines)*
And every boyste° ful of thy letuarie.° *box / medicine*
20 God blesse hem° and oure Lady, Seint Marie! *them*
So moot° I theen,° thou art a propre° man *might / thrive / fine*
And lyk° a prelat,° by Seint Ronyan!⁴ *like / prelate (high clergyman)*

Seyde I nat wel? I kan nat speke in terme,° *in the right jargon*
But wel I woot,° thou doost myn herte to
    erme,° *know / make my heart grieve*
25 That I almoost have caught a cardynacle.⁵
By corpus bones,° but° I have triacle⁶ *by God's bones / unless*
Or elles a draughte° of moyste° and corny°
    ale, *drink / moist / malty (strong)*
Or but I heere anon° a myrie° tale, *immediately / merry*
Myn herte is lost for pitee of this mayde.
30 Thou beel amy,° thou Pardoner," he sayde, *good friend*
"Telle us som myrthe or japes° right anon." *jokes*
    "It shal be doon!" quod he, "by Seint Ronyon!
But first," quod he, "heere at this ale-stake⁷
I wol bothe drynke and eten° of a cake."° *eat / bread*
35   And right anon the gentils° gonne° to crye, *gentle folk / began*
"Nay, lat hym telle us of no ribaudye!° *ribald story*
Telle us som moral thyng that we may leere° *learn*
Som wit,° and thanne wol we gladly here." *piece of wisdom*
    "I graunte, ywis,"° quod he. "But I moot
    thynke° *indeed / must think*
40 Upon som honeste thyng° whil that I drynke." *respectable subject*

THE PARDONER'S PROLOGUE

HEERE FOLWETH THE PROLOGE OF THE PARDONERS TALE

Radix malorum est Cupiditas. Ad Thimotheum 6.10⁸

"Lordynges,"° quod he, "in chirches° whan I
    preche,° *lords / churches / preach*

---

¹ *Harrow … blood Harrow* Help; *Nails and blood* By Christ's nails and by Christ's blood, i.e., alas. Medieval swearing often referred to parts of Christ's body.

² *Harow … alas* The tale told previously, by the Physician, involved an innocent young girl who agrees to let her father kill her in order to save her from the lewd desires of a corrupt judge.

³ *urynals* Vessels to hold urine; *jurdones* Jars. These were both part of the equipment medieval doctors used.

⁴ *Seint Ronyan* There were several medieval saints called St. Ronan—a seventh-century Scottish hermit, a Breton bishop who died in Cornwall, a Scottish bishop who helped settle a dispute about the date of Easter, and an early bishop of Caesarea, whose arm was kept as a relic at Canterbury Cathedral. Most editors state that it was the Scottish hermit to whom the Host refers here, but the last

Saint Ronan, given his association with Canterbury, seems the most likely reference, for the pilgrims are traveling to the place where his relic was kept. There may also be a pun on runnions (male sexual organs).

⁵ *cardynacle* The Host means heart attack, though he blunders for the proper word, which is cardiacle.

⁶ *triacle* Medicine or cordial, usually made primarily from molasses.

⁷ *ale-stake* Post set up outside a house when the people who lived there had brewed up some ale and were ready to sell it to those passing by.

⁸ *Radix … Cupiditas* Latin: The root of evils is cupidity. From 1 Timothy 6.10. Cupidity is often translated as avarice, or love of money, but, like the word covetousness, it can also refer to any excessive or sinful love of earthly things.

I peyne me to han° an hauteyn
   speche°   *take pains to have | dignified speech*
And rynge° it out as round° as gooth a
   belle,°   *ring | roundly | rings a bell*
For I kan° al by rote° that I telle.°   *know | by memory | say*
45 My theme[1] is alwey oon° and evere was: *always one*
   Radix malorum est cupiditas.
    First I pronounce° whennes° that I come,   *say | whence*
And thanne my bulles[2] shewe I alle and some.°   *one and all*
Oure lige lordes seel° on my
   patente,°   *liege lord's (i.e., the bishop's) seal | license*
50 That shewe I first, my body to warente,°   *protect*
That no man be so boold,° ne preest ne clerk,[3]   *bold*
Me to destourbe° of Cristes hooly werk.   *disturb*
And after that thanne° telle I forth my tales.   *then*
Bulles of popes and of cardynales,°   *cardinals*
55 Of patriarkes° and bisshopes° I shewe,   *patriarchs | bishops*
And in Latyn° I speke a wordes fewe   *Latin*
To saffron with[4] my predicacioun°   *preaching*
And for to stire hem° to devocioun.   *stir them*
Thanne shewe I forth my longe cristal stones,°   *glass cases*
60 Ycrammed° ful of cloutes° and of bones.   *crammed | rags*
Relikes been they, as wenen they echoon.°   *as everyone believes*
Thanne have I in latoun° a sholder boon°   *brass | shoulder bone*
Which that was of an hooly Jewes sheepe.°   *holy Jew's sheep*
"Goode men," I seye, "taak of my wordes keepe.°   *heed*
65 If that this boon be wasshe° in any welle,   *washed*
If cow or calf or sheepe or oxe swelle°   *swell*
That any worm° hath ete° or worm
   ystonge,°   *snake | has eaten | stung*
Taak water of that welle and wassh his tonge,
And it is hool° anon. And forthermoor,   *healthy*

70 Of pokkes° and of scabbe° and every soor°   *pocks | scab | sore*
Shal every sheepe be hool that of this welle
Drynketh a draughte. Taak kepe° eek° what I
   telle!   *take heed | also*
If that the goode man that the beestes° oweth°   *beasts | owns*
Wol every wyke° er° that the cok° hym
   croweth°   *week | before | rooster | crows*
75 Fastynge° drynke of this welle a draughte,   *while fasting*
As thilke° hooly Jew oure eldres° taughte,   *that | ancestors*
Hise beestes and his stoor° shal multiplie.   *possessions*
   And sire, also it heeleth° jalousie.   *heals*
For though a man be falle° in jalous rage,   *fallen*
80 Lat maken with this water his potage,°   *stew*
And nevere shal he moore his wyf mystriste,°   *mistrust*
Though he the soothe° of hir defaute°
   wiste,°   *truth | default | knew*
Al had she taken preestes two or thre.[5]
   Heere is a miteyn° eek that ye may se.   *mitten*
85 He that his hand wol putte in this mitayn,
He shal have multipliyng of his grayn°   *grain*
Whan he hath sowen, be it whete° or otes,°   *wheat | oats*
So that he offre pens or elles grotes.[6]
   Goode men and wommen, o° thyng warne I yow: *one*
90 If any wight° be in this chirche now   *person*
That hath doon° synne° horrible, that he   *committed | sin*
Dar nat for shame of it yshryven° be,   *confessed*
Or any womman, be she yong or old,
That hath ymaked° hir housbonde cokewold,[7]   *made*
95 Swich folk shal have no power ne no grace
To offren° to my relikes in this place.   *make an offering*
And whoso fyndeth hym out° of swich
   fame,°   *is not subject to | (ill-) repute*
They wol come up and offre on° Goddes name,   *in*
And I assoille hem° by the auctoritee°   *absolve them | authority*
100 Which that by bulle ygraunted was to me.
   By this gaude° have I wonne° yeer° by yeer   *trick | gained | year*
An hundred mark sith I was pardoner.[8]

---

1 *theme* "Text." Medieval sermons were usually organized around a short passage from the Bible.

2 *bulles* I.e., papal bulls (written documents which put official policy into effect). Pardoners had licenses from the Pope to raise money for charitable causes by selling indulgences (certificates that reduce the number of years the buyer must serve in Purgatory after death).

3 *ne preest ne clerk* The term clerk can refer to students, scholars, or assistants to priests (as in *The Miller's Tale*), so neither priest nor clerk means not a member of the clergy. The parish clergy often regarded wandering preachers as interlopers.

4 *To saffron with* To season with saffron, a very expensive yellow spice imported from the East.

5 *Al ... thre* Even if she had taken two or three priests as lovers.

6 *So ... grotes* Provided that he offers pennies or else groats (a coin worth fourpence).

7 *cokewold* I.e., cuckold, a man whose wife has committed adultery.

8 *An ... pardoner* A hundred marks equaled over £66, making the Pardoner a wealthy man. In comparison, in 1367 Chaucer was granted an annual pension of 20 marks.

I stonde lyk a clerk° in my pulpet,   *theologian*
And whan the lewed peple[1] is doun yset,°   *settled down*
105   I preche so as ye han herd bifoore°   *have heard before*
And telle an hundred false japes° moore.   *tricks*
Thanne peyne I me° to strecche° forth the
          nekke   *I take pains / stretch*
And est° and west upon the peple° I bekke°   *east / people / nod*
As dooth a dowve° sittynge on a berne.°   *sitting / barn*
110   Myne handes and my tonge goon so yerne°   *eagerly*
That it is joye to se° my bisynesse.°   *see / busyness*
Of avarice and of swich cursednesse°   *cursedness*
Ys° al my prechyng, for to make hem free°   *is / generous*
To yeven hir pens°—and namely unto me.   *give their pence*
115   For myn entente° is nat but for to wynne°   *intent / profit*
And nothyng° for correccioun° of synne.   *by no means / correction*
I rekke° nevere whan they been beryed,°   *care / buried*
Though that hir soules goon a blakeberyed![2]
For certes, many a predicacioun°   *sermon*
120   Comth ofte tyme of yvel entencioun°—   *evil intent*
Som for plesance° of folk and flaterye   *pleasure*
To been avaunced by ypocrisye°   *hypocrisy*
And som for veyneglorie° and som for hate.   *pride*
For whan I dar noon oother weyes° debate,   *in no other way*
125   Thanne wol I stynge° hym[3] with my tonge
          smerte°   *sting / sharp*
In prechyng, so that he shal nat asterte°   *escape*
To been defamed falsly if that he
Hath trespased° to my bretheren or to me.   *has done harm*
For though I telle noght° his propre° name,   *not / own*
130   Men shal wel knowe that it is the same
By signes and by othere circumstances.
Thus quyte° I folk that doon us displesances.°   *pay back / offenses*
Thus spitte I out my venym under hewe°   *guise*
Of hoolynesse, to semen° hooly and trewe.   *seem*
135   But shortly, myn entente I wol devyse:°   *describe*
I preche of nothyng but for coveityse.°   *covetousness*
Therfore my theme is yet and evere was

Radix malorum est cupiditas.
Thus kan I preche agayn° that same vice   *against*
140   Which that I use, and that is avarice.
But though myself be gilty in that synne,
Yet kan I maken oother folk to twynne°   *turn away*
From avarice and soore° to repente.   *sorely*
But that is nat my principal entente;°   *intent*
145   I preche nothyng but for coveitise.°   *covetousness*
Of this mateere it oghte ynogh suffise.°   *should be sufficient*
   Thanne telle I hem ensamples° many
          oon°   *examples / many a one*
Of olde stories longe tyme agoon,°   *ago*
For lewed peple° loven tales olde;   *laypeople*
150   Swiche thynges kan they wel reporte and holde.°   *remember*
What? Trowe ye,° the whiles I may preche   *do you believe*
And wynne° gold and silver for I teche,°   *gain / because I teach*
That I wol lyve in poverte wilfully?°   *willingly*
Nay, nay! I thoghte it nevere, trewely.
155   For I wol preche and begge in sondry landes;°   *different countries*
I wol nat do no labour with myne handes
Ne make baskettes and lyve therby,
Bycause I wol nat beggen ydelly.°   *beg in vain*
I wol noon of the apostles countrefete![4]
160   I wol have moneie,° wolle,° chese, and
          whete,°   *money / wool / wheat*
Al° were it yeven°of the povereste page°   *even if / given / poorest boy*
Or of the povereste wydwe° in a village,   *widow*
Al sholde hir children sterve° for famyne.   *die*
Nay, I wol drynke licour of the vyne
165   And have a joly wenche° in every toun.   *pretty girl*
But herkneth,° lordynges, in conclusioun: *listen*
Youre likyng° is that I shal telle a tale.   *pleasure*
Now have I dronke a draughte of corny ale,
By God, I hope I shal yow telle a thyng
170   That shal by resoun° been at youre liking.   *with reason*
For though myself be a ful° vicious man,   *very*
A moral tale yet I yow telle kan,
Which I am wont° to preche for to wynne.   *accustomed*
Now hoold youre pees!° My tale I wol bigynne.   *peace*

---

[1]   *lewed peple*   Uneducated, illiterate (in the medieval sense—i.e.,
unable to read Latin), or simple, but it can also refer to lay people in
general. It does not have the modern meaning of sexual offensive-
ness.

[2]   *a blakeberyed*   Go picking blackberries (i.e., wandering).

[3]   *hym*   I.e., any opponent. Pardoners were much criticized by the
parish clergy and by reformers.

---

[4]   *noon … countrefete*   In the Gospels and the Book of Acts the
apostles were enjoined to live in poverty so as to give surplus goods
to the poor.

THE PARDONER'S TALE

HEERE BIGYNNETH THE PARDONERS TALE

175 In Flaundres° whilom° was a
    compaignye°   *Flanders | once | company*
Of yonge folk that haunteden folye
As riot, hasard, stywes, and tavernes,[1]
Whereas° with harpes, lutes, and gyternes[2]   *where*
They daunce and pleyen° at dees° bothe day and   *play | dice*
    nyght
180 And eten also and drynken over hir myght,°   *capacity*
Thurgh which they doon the devel sacrifise°   *sacrifice to the devil*
Withinne that develes temple[3] in cursed wise°   *manner*
By superfluytee° abhomynable.   *excess*
Hir othes° been so grete and so dampnable°   *oaths | damnable*
185 That it is grisly° for to heere hem swere.   *horrible*
Oure blissed° Lordes body they to-tere°—   *blessed | tear apart*
Hem thoughte that Jewes rente hym noght ynough![4]
And ech of hem at otheres synne° lough.°   *sin | laughed*
And right anon thanne comen tombesteres°   *female acrobats*
190 Fetys° and smale° and yonge
    frutesteres,°   *elegant | slender | fruit-sellers*
Syngeres with harpes, baudes,° wafereres,°   *pimps | pastry-sellers*
Whiche been° the verray devels officeres   *who are*
To kyndle and blowe the fyr of lecherye
That is annexed unto° glotonye.°   *allied with | gluttony*
195 The Hooly Writ° take I to my witnesse   *Bible*
That luxurie° is in wyn° and dronkenesse.   *lust | wine*
    Lo how that dronken Looth[5] unkyndely°   *unnaturally*
Lay by hise doghtres° two unwityngly!°   *daughters | unknowingly*
So dronke he was, he nyste° what he
    wroghte.°   *did not know | did*

200 Herodes,[6] whoso wel the stories soghte,[7]
Whan he of wyn was replest° at his feeste,°   *most filled | feast*
Right at his owene table he yaf° his heeste°   *gave | command*
To sleen° the Baptist John ful giltelees.[8]   *kill*
Senec[9] seith a good word, doutelees.°   *doubtless*
205 He seith he kan no difference fynde
Bitwix° a man that is out of his mynde   *between*
And a man which that is dronkelewe,°   *often drunk*
But that woodnesse,° fallen° in a
    shrewe,°   *madness | occurring | villain*
Persevereth° lenger than dooth dronkenesse.   *lasts*
210 O glotonye, ful of cursednesse,
O cause first of oure confusioun,
O original of oure dampnacioun,[10]
Til Crist hadde boght° us with his blood agayn!   *redeemed*
Lo how deere,° shortly for to seyn,°   *expensively | say*
215 Aboght° was thilke° cursed vileynye!   *purchased | that*
Corrupt was al this world for glotonye.
    Adam oure fader and his wyf also
Fro° Paradys to labour and to wo°   *from | woe*
Were dryven° for that vice, it is no drede.°   *driven | doubt*
220 For whil that Adam fasted, as I rede,°   *read*
He was in Paradys, and whan that he
Eet° of the fruyt deffended° on the tree,   *ate | prohibited*
Anon he was outcast to wo and peyne.
O glotonye, on thee wel oghte us pleyne!°   *complain*
225 O, wiste a man how manye maladyes°   *diseases*
Folwen of excesse and of glotonyes,
He wolde been the moore mesurable°   *temperate*
Of his diete, sittynge at his table.
Allas, the shorte throte,° the tendre mouth   *throat*
230 Maketh that° est and west and north and south,   *causes*
In erthe, in eir, in water man to swynke°   *labor*
To gete a glotoun° deyntee° mete° and
    drynke.   *glutton | delicious | meat*

---

[1] *Of yonge … tavernes* Of young folk that gave themselves to foolish living, such as loud parties, gambling, brothels, and taverns.

[2] *gyternes* Like the harp and the lute, the medieval gittern was a plucked stringed instrument.

[3] *develes temple* I.e., a tavern.

[4] *Hem … ynough* They thought that Jews did not tear him apart enough. The oaths figuratively tore God's body apart, according to the moralists. In the Middle Ages, Jews were usually blamed for Christ's crucifixion.

[5] *Looth* I.e., Lot. The story of how Lot, while drunk, made his daughters pregnant is recounted in Genesis 19.30–38.

---

[6] *Herodes* I.e., Herod, King of the Jewish people (74–3 BCE).

[7] *whoso … soghte* As whoever consulted the stories carefully can confirm.

[8] *ful giltelees* Entirely guiltless. See Matthew 14.1–12.

[9] *Senec* I.e., Seneca, Roman playwright, orator, and philosopher (4 BCE–65 CE).

[10] *O cause … dampnacioun* A reference to the role of gluttony in causing Adam and Eve to eat the forbidden fruit of the Tree of Knowledge in the Garden of Eden. See Genesis 2–3.

Of this matiere, O Paul,[1] wel kanstow trete:° — *can you write*
"Mete unto wombe° and wombe eek unto mete: — *stomach*
235 Shal God destroyen bothe," as Paulus seith.[2]
Allas, a foul thyng is it, by my feith,
To seye this word, and fouler is the dede
Whan man so drynketh of the white and
     rede,° — *white and red wine*
That of his throte he maketh his pryvee,° — *latrine*
240 Thurgh thilke cursed superfluitee.° — *excess*
  The apostel[3] wepyng seith ful pitously,° — *pitifully*
"Ther walken manye of whiche yow told have I.° — *I have told you*
I seye it now wepyng with pitous voys:° — *pitiful voice*
Ther been° enemys of Cristes croys° — *are / cross*
245 Of whiche the ende is deeth.° Wombe is hir god."[4] — *death*
O wombe, o bely, o stynkyng cod,° — *stinking bag (stomach)*
Fulfilled of donge° and of corrupcioun, — *filled with dung*
At either ende of thee foul is the soun!° — *sound*
How greet labour and cost is thee to fynde.° — *provide for*
250 Thise cookes, how they stampe° and streyne° and
     grynde — *pound / strain*
And turnen substaunce into accident[5]
To fulfillen al thy likerous° talent!° — *lecherous / inclination*
Out of the harde bones knokke they
The mary,° for they caste° noght awey — *marrow / throw*
255 That may go thurgh the golet° softe and swoote.° — *throat / sweet*
Of spicerie° of leef and bark and roote — *spices*
Shal been his sauce ymaked,° by delit° — *made / through delight*
To make° hym yet a newer appetit. — *give*
But certes, he that haunteth° swiche delices° — *follows / delights*
260 Is deed whil that he lyveth in tho° vices.[6] — *those*
  A lecherous thyng is wyn, and dronkenesse

Is ful of stryvyng° and of wrecchednesse. — *quarreling*
O dronke man, disfigured is thy face!
Sour is thy breeth! Foul artow° to embrace! — *are you*
265 And thurgh thy dronke nose semeth the
     soun° — *the sound seems to come*
As though thou seydest ay° "Sampsoun, Sampsoun!" — *ever*
And yet, God woot,° Sampsoun drank nevere no
     wyn![7] — *God knows*
Thou fallest as it were a styked swyn.° — *stuck (i.e., speared) pig*
Thy tonge is lost and al thyn honeste cure.° — *care*
270 For dronkenesse is verray sepulture° — *tomb*
Of mannes wit and his discrecioun.
In whom that drynke hath dominacioun,
He kan no conseil° kepe, it is no drede.° — *counsel / doubt*
Now kepe yow fro the white and fro the rede
275 And namely fro the white wyn of Lepe[8]
That is to selle° in Fyssh Strete or in Chepe.[9] — *for sale*
This wyn of Spaigne° crepeth subtilly — *Spain*
In othere wynes growynge faste° by,[10] — *near*
Of which ther ryseth swich fumositee° — *such vapors*
280 That whan a man hath dronken draughtes thre° — *three*
And weneth° that he be at hoom° in Chepe, — *thinks / home*
He is in Spaigne, right at the toune of Lepe—
Nat at the Rochele ne at Burdeux toun—[11]
And thanne wol he seye, "Sampsoun, Sampsoun!"
285   But herkneth, lordes, o° word, I yow preye, — *one*
That alle the sovereyn actes, dar I seye,
Of victories in the Olde Testament
Thurgh verray° God that is omnipotent — *true*
Were doon in abstinence and in preyere.
290 Looketh the Bible, and ther ye may it leere.° — *learn*
  Looke, Attilla[12] the grete conquerour

---

[1] *Paul*   I.e., St. Paul.

[2] *Shal … seith*   See 1 Corinthians 6.13.

[3] *apostel*   I.e., apostle, here St. Paul.

[4] *Ther walken … god*   See Philippians 3.18–19.

[5] *And … accident*   This distinction between the basic food and the flavors the cooks give to it draws on Aristotle's distinction between substance (essential inner reality) and its superficial qualities (accidents). This line could be read as an allusion to contemporary philosophical debates between Nominalists and Realists or to contemporary theological controversies concerning the process through which the bread and wine of the Eucharist are transformed into the body and blood of Christ.

[6] *he that … vices*   Cf. 1 Timothy 5.6: "But she that lives in pleasure is dead while she lives."

[7] *And yet … wyn*   As recounted in Judges 13, in which it is written that Samson's mother did not drink wine during her pregnancy.

[8] *Lepe*   Town in Spain.

[9] *Fyssh … Chepe*   I.e., Fish Street and Cheapside, two market districts in London.

[10] *This wyn … by*   Expensive French wines, shipped through Bordeaux and La Rochelle, were often surreptitiously mixed with cheaper, but stronger, Spanish wines.

[11] *the Rochele … Burdeaux toun*   I.e., La Rochelle and Bordeaux.

[12] *Attilla*   I.e., Attila the Hun, a fifth-century nomadic chieftain who ravaged vast stretches of central Europe. According to medieval histories, such as those of Jordanes and Paul the Deacon, he died from drink on the night that he took a new bride.

Deyde° in his sleepe with shame and dishonour,   *died*
Bledynge° ay at his nose in dronkenesse.   *bleeding*
A capitayn° sholde lyve in sobrenesse.   *leader*
295 And over al this° avyseth yow° right wel   *above all / consider*
What was comaunded unto Lamwel.[1]
Nat Samuel[2] but Lamwel, seye I.
Redeth the Bible, and fynde it expresly°   *specifically*
Of wyn yevyng° to hem that han
justise.°   *giving wine / have legal power*
300 Namoore of this, for it may wel suffise.
And now I have spoken of glotonye,
Now wol I yow deffenden° hasardrye.°   *prohibit / gambling*
Hasard is verray mooder° of lesynges°   *mother / lying*
And of deceite and cursed forswerynges,°   *perjury*
305 Blasphemyng of Crist, manslaughtre, and
wast° also   *wasteful spending*
Of catel° and of tyme. And forthermo,   *goods*
It is repreeve° and contrarie of° honour   *reproach / to*
For to ben holde° a commune hasardour.°   *be considered / gambler*
And ever the hyer° he is of estaat°   *higher / condition*
310 The moore is he holden° desolaat.°   *regarded as / vile*
If that a prynce° useth hasardrye,°   *prince / frequently gambles*
In alle governaunce and policye
He is as by commune opinioun
Yholde° the lasse° in reputacioun.   *held / less*
315 Stilboun,[3] that was a wys embassadour,
Was sent to Cornythe° in ful greet honour   *Corinth*
Fro Lacidomye° to maken hire alliaunce,   *Sparta*
And whan he cam, hym happed par chaunce[4]
That alle the grretteste that were of that lond
320 Pleyynge atte hasard he hem fond,
For which, as soone as it myghte be,
He stal hym° hoom agayn to his contree   *stole away*
And seyde, "Ther wol I nat lese° my name!   *lose*
Ne I wol nat take on me so greet defame°   *dishonor*
325 Yow for to allie° unto none hasardours.   *ally*
Sendeth otherewise° embassadours.   *other*

For by my trouthe, me were levere dye°   *rather die*
Than I yow sholde to hasardours allye.
For ye that been so glorious in honours
330 Shul nat allyen yow with hasardours,
As by my wyl,° ne as by my tretee."°   *will / treaty*
This wise philosophre thus seyde hee.
Looke eek that to the kyng Demetrius,
The kyng of Parthes,° as the book seith° us,[5]   *Parthia / tells*
335 Sente him a paire of dees° of gold in scorn,   *dice*
For he hadde used hasard ther-biforn,°   *often gambled before this*
For which he heeld his glorie or his renoun
At no value or reputacioun.
Lordes may fynden oother maner pley°   *kinds of amusement*
340 Honeste ynough to dryve the day awey.
Now wol I speke of othes° false and grete   *oaths*
A word or two, as olde bookes trete.
Greet sweryng° is a thyng abhominable,   *swearing*
And fals sweryng° is yet moore reprevable.°   *perjury / disgraceful*
345 The heighe God forbad sweryng at al,[6]
Witnesse on Mathew, but in special°   *specially*
Of sweryng seith the hooly Jeremye,°   *Jeremiah*
"Thou shalt seye sooth thyne othes° and nat lye   *truly your oaths*
And swere in doom° and eek in rightwisnesse."[7]   *judgment*
350 But ydel sweryng is a cursednesse.
Bihoold and se that in the firste table°   *tablet (of Moses)*
Of heighe Goddes heestes° honorable   *commandments*
Hou that the seconde heeste of hym° is this   *them*
"Take nat my name in ydel or amys."[8]
355 Lo, rather° he forbedeth swich   *earlier (in the commandments)*
sweryng
Than homycide or any cursed thyng.
I seye that as by ordre thus it stondeth.°   *stands*

---

[1] *Lamwel* I.e., Lemuel, King of Massa, whose mother warns him not to drink wine. See Proverbs 31.4–5.

[2] *Samuel* I.e., the prophet Samuel. See 1 Samuel.

[3] *Stilboun* I.e., Chilon, an ambassador who is mentioned in John of Salisbury's *Polycraticus*, 1.5.

[4] *And … chaunce* And when he came, it happened to him by chance.

---

[5] *The kyng … us* King Demetrius of Parthia has not been securely identified, but John of Salisbury tells his story in the *Policraticus* immediately after that of Chilon.

[6] *The heighe … al* See Matthew 5.34.

[7] *Thou … rightwisnesse* See Jeremiah 4.2; *rightwisnesse* Righteousness.

[8] *Take … amys* See Deuteronomy 5.7–21. In the Middle Ages the first two commandments were normally grouped as one, making what is now considered the third commandment the second, as it is here. The tenth commandment was then broken into two to make up the difference; *amys* In vain.

This knowen that hise heestes understondeth,[1]
How that the seconde heeste° of God is
    that. — *second commandment*
360 And forther over,° I wol thee telle al plat° — *furthermore / plainly*
That vengeance shal nat parten° from his hous — *depart*
That of his othes° is to° outrageous. — *oaths / too*
"By Goddes precious herte!" and "By his nayles"° — *nails*
And "By the blood of Crist that is in Hayles,[2]
365 Sevene is my chaunce and thyn is cynk° and treye!°[3] — *five / three*
By Goddes armes, if thou falsly pleye,
This daggere shal thurghout thyn herte go!"° — *pierce*
This fruyt° cometh of the bicched bones two—[4] — *fruit*
Forsweryng,° ire,° falsnesse, homycide. — *perjury / anger*
370 Now for the love of Crist that for us dyde,
Lete° youre othes, bothe grete and smale. — *leave*
But sires, now wol I telle forth my tale.
    Thise riotours° thre of whiche I telle — *party-goers*
Longe erst er° prime° rong° of any belle — *before / early morning / rang*
375 Were set hem in a taverne to drynke.
And as they sat, they herde a belle clynke° — *ring*
Biforn° a cors° was° caried to his
    grave. — *before / corpse / that was being*
That oon of hem gan callen to his knave,° — *servant*
"Go bet,"° quod he, "and axe° redily° — *quickly / ask / eagerly*
380 What cors is this that passeth heer forby,
And looke that thou reporte his name weel."
    "Sire," quod this boy, "it nedeth never a deel.° — *it is not necessary*
It was me toold er ye cam heer two houres.[5]
He was, pardee,° an old felawe° of youres, — *by God / friend*
385 And sodeynly he was yslayn tonyght.
For dronke as he sat on his bench upright
Ther cam a privee theef° men clepeth° Deeth, — *secret thief / call*
That in this contree al the peple sleeth,
And with his spere he smoot° his herte atwo° — *cut / in two*

390 And wente his wey withouten wordes mo.
He hath a thousand slayn this pestilence.°[6] — *during this epidemic*
And maister, er ye come in his presence,
Me thynketh that it were necessarie
For to bewar of swich an adversarie.
395 Beth° redy for to meete hym everemoore.° — *be / always*
Thus taughte me my dame.° I sey namoore." — *mother*
"By seinte Marie," seyde this taverner,° — *tavern-keeper*
"The child seith sooth, for he hath slayn this yeer
Henne° over a mile withinne a greet° village — *from here / large*
400 Bothe man and womman, child and hyne° and
    page. — *hired hand*
I trowe° his habitacioun° be there. — *believe / dwelling*
To been avysed° greet wysdom it were, — *warned*
Er° that he dide° a man a dishonour."° — *lest / cause / harm*
    "Ye, Goddes armes," quod this riotour,
405 "Is it swich peril with hym for to meete?° — *encounter*
I shal hym seke by wey° and eek by strete,° — *road / street*
I make avow° to Goddes digne° bones. — *a vow / worthy*
Herkneth, felawes, we thre been al ones.° — *are three together*
Lat ech of us holde up his hand til oother,° — *to the other*
410 And ech of us bicomen° otheres brother, — *become*
And we wol sleen this false traytour, Deeth!
He shal be slayn, which that so manye sleeth,
By Goddes dignitee er it be nyght!"
    Togidres° han thise thre hir trouthes plight° — *together / promised*
415 To lyve and dyen ech of hem for oother
As though he were his owene yborn° brother. — *born*
And up they stirte° al dronken in this rage. — *jumped*
And forth they goon towardes that village
Of which the taverner hadde spoke biforn.
420 And many a grisly° ooth thanne han they sworn, — *horrible*
And Cristes blessed body they torente.° — *tear apart (with their oaths)*
Deeth shal be deed, if that they may hym hente!° — *catch him*
    Whan they han goon[7] nat fully half a mile

---

1 *This ... understondeth* Those who understand his commandments know this.

2 *Hayles* I.e., Hales Abbey in Gloucestershire, a monastery that
claimed to have some of Christ's blood as a relic.

3 *Sevene ... treye* The modern game of craps is a version of
medieval hazard, in which the player rolling the dice must call out
the numbers he hopes to get.

4 *bicched bones two* Two cursed bones; i.e., the dice, which were
made of bone in the Middle Ages.

5 *It ... houres* It was told to me two hours ago, before you came
here.

---

6 *Ther cam ... pestilence* The reference here is doubtless to plague,
the Black Death that spread from Italy across Europe, hit England
in 1348, and in the space of a year killed at least a third of the
population. There were further outbreaks in 1361–62, 1369, and
1375–76.

7 *han goon* Have gone. Chaucer frequently alternates between the
simple past (the rioters jumped up, the old man met with them) and
the present or the perfect forms (the rioters have gone rather than
had gone or went, which we would expect in modern English).

Right° as they wolde han troden over a stile,[1]   *just*

425   An oold man and a povre° with hem
     mette.°   *poor | encountered them*

This olde man ful mekely° hem grette°   *meekly | greeted*

And seyde thus: "Now, lordes, God yow see!"°   *watch over*

  The proudeste of thise riotours three

Answerde agayn, "What, carl,° with sory
     grace!°   *peasant | bad luck to you*

430   Why artow al forwrapped,° save thy face?   *wrapped up*

Why lyvestow° so longe in so greet age?"   *live you*

  This olde man gan looke in his visage°   *face*

And seyde thus: "For° I ne kan nat fynde   *because*

A man, though that I walked into Ynde,°   *India*

435   Neither in citee nor in no village,

That wolde chaunge his youthe for myn age.

And therfore moot I han myn age stille,

As longe tyme as it is Goddes wille.

Ne deeth, allas, ne wol nat han my lyf.

440   Thus walke I lyk a resteleez° kaityf,°   *restless | wretch*

And on the ground which is my moodres° gate   *mother's*

I knokke with my staf° bothe erly and late   *walking stick*

And seye, 'Leeve° Mooder, leet me in!   *dear*

Lo how I vanysshe°—flessh and blood and skyn!   *waste away*

445   Allas, whan shul my bones been at reste?

Mooder, with yow wolde I chaunge my cheste°   *money box*

That in my chambre° longe tyme hath be,°   *room | been*

Ye, for an heyre clowt° to wrappe me.'[2]   *hair-shirt*

But yet to me she wol nat do that grace,°   *favor*

450   For which ful pale and welked° is my face.   *withered*

  "But sires, to° yow it is no curteisye   *in*

To speken to an old man vileynye,°   *insults*

But° he trespasse° in word or elles in dede.   *unless | offend*

In Hooly Writ ye may yourself wel rede

455   'Agayns° an oold man hoor° upon his
     heed   *in the presence of | gray*

Ye sholde arise.'[3] Wherfore° I yeve° yow
     reed:°   *therefore | give | advice*

Ne dooth unto an oold man noon harm now,

Namoore than that ye wolde° men did to yow[4]   *desire*

In age—if that ye so longe abyde.°   *live long enough*

460   And God be with yow, where° ye go° or ryde.   *wherever | walk*

I moot go thider as° I have to go."   *thither where*

  "Nay, olde cherl, by God thou shalt nat so!"

Seyde this oother hasardour° anon.   *gambler*

"Thou partest nat° so lightly, by Seint John!   *do not get away*

465   Thou spak right now of thilke traytour Deeth,

That in this contree° alle oure freendes sleeth.   *country*

Have heer my trouthe:° as thou art his espye,°   *on my word | spy*

Telle where he is, or thou shalt it abye,°   *pay for it*

By God and by the hooly sacrement!°   *holy sacrament (the Eucharist)*

470   For soothly, thou art oon of his assent°   *plot*

To sleen us yonge folk, thou false theef!"

  "Now sires," quod he, "if that ye be so leef,°   *desirous*

To fynde Deeth, turne up this croked wey.°   *crooked way*

For in that grove I lafte hym, by my fey,°   *faith*

475   Under a tree, and there he wole abyde.°   *wait*

Noght for youre boost he wole him nothyng hyde.[5]

Se ye that ook?° Right there ye shal hym fynde.   *oak*

God save yow that boghte agayn° mankynde[6]   *redeemed*

And yow amende!"° Thus seyde this olde man.   *make you better*

480   And everich° of thise riotours ran   *each*

Til he cam to that tree, and ther they founde

Of floryns° fyne of gold ycoyned° rounde   *florins (coins) | coined*

Wel ny° an eighte busshels, as hem
     thoughte.°   *very nearly | it seemed to them*

No lenger thanne° after Deeth they soughte,   *then*

485   But ech of hem so glad was of that sighte,

For that the floryns been so faire and brighte,

That doun° they sette hem° by this precious
     hoord.°   *down | themselves | hoard*

The worste of hem, he spak the firste word.

  "Bretheren," quod he, "taak kepe° what I seye.   *pay attention to*

490   My wit is greet, though that I bourde° and pleye.   *joke*

This tresor hath Fortune unto us yeven°   *given*

In myrthe and joliftee° oure lyf to lyven.   *jollity*

And lightly° as it comth, so wol we spende.   *easily*

Ey, Goddes precious dignitee! Who wende°   *expected*

---

[1] *stile* Steps to get over a wall or fence.

[2] *Mooder ... me* People in the Middle Ages sometimes wore shirts made of hair, which irritated the body, expecting the pain to gain them spiritual benefit. Here the old man wishes be buried in such a shirt, exchanging it for the chest that holds his money.

[3] *Agayns ... arise* See Leviticus 19.3.

[4] *Namoore ... yow* Cf. the Golden Rule from Matthew 7:12: "So whatever you wish that men would do to you, do so to them."

[5] *Noght ... hyde* He will not hide himself in any way because of your boasting.

[6] *God ... mankynde* May God, who redeemed mankind (by sending his Son Jesus Christ to die on the Cross), save you.

495	Today that we sholde han so fair a grace?	
	But myghte this gold be caried fro this place	
	Hoom to myn hous, or elles unto yours—	
	For wel ye woot that al this gold is oures—	
	Thanne were we in heigh felicitee.°	*great happiness*
500	But trewely, by daye it may nat bee.°	*not be*
	Men wolde seyn that we were theves stronge°	*downright thieves*
	And for oure owene tresor doon us honge.°	*cause us to be hanged*
	This tresor moste ycaried be by nyghte	
	As wisely and as slyly as it myghte.	
505	Wherfore I rede° that cut° among us alle	*advise / lots*
	Be drawe° and lat se wher the cut wol falle,	*drawn*
	And he that hath the cut with herte blithe°	*happy*
	Shal renne to towne, and that ful swithe,°	*quickly*
	And brynge us breed and wyn ful prively.°	*secretly*
510	And two of us shul kepen subtilly°	*cleverly*
	This tresor wel. And if he wol nat tarie,°	*delay*
	Whan it is nyght we wol this tresor carie	
	By oon assent° whereas us thynketh best."	*in agreement*
	That oon of hem the cut° broghte in his fest°	*lots / fist*
515	And bad hem drawe and looke where it wol falle.	
	And it fil on the yongeste of hem alle,	
	And forth toward the toun he wente anon.	
	And also soone as that he was gon,	
	That oon spak thus unto that oother:	
520	"Thow knowest wel thou art my sworn brother;	
	Thy profit° wol I telle thee anon.	*your advantage*
	Thou woost wel that oure felawe is agon,	
	And heere is gold, and that ful greet plentee,°	*a great deal of it*
	That shal departed° been among us thre.	*divided*
525	But nathelees, if I kan shape it so,	
	That it departed were among us two,	
	Hadde I nat doon a freendes torn° to thee?"	*friend's turn*
	That oother answerde, "I noot hou° that	*do not know how*
	may be.	
	He woot how that the gold is with us tweye.°	*two*
530	What shal we doon? What shal we to hym seye?"	
	"Shal it be conseil?"° seyde the firste shrewe.°	*our plan / villain*
	"And I shal tellen in a wordes fewe	
	What we shal doon and bryngen it wel aboute."	
	"I graunte," quod that oother, "out of doute,°	*without doubt*
535	That by my trouthe I shal thee nat biwreye."°	*betray*
	"Now," quod the firste, "thou woost wel we be tweye,	
	And two of us shul strenger be than oon.	

	Looke whan that he is set, that right anoon	
	Arys° as though thou woldest with hym pleye,	*arise*
540	And I shal ryve° hym thurgh the sydes tweye°	*stab / two sides*
	Whil that thou strogelest° with hym as in game,°	*struggle / jest*
	And with thy daggere, looke thou do the same.	
	And thanne shal al this gold departed be,	
	My deere freend, bitwixen me and thee.	
545	Thanne may we bothe oure lustes° all fulfille	*pleasures*
	And pleye at dees° right at oure owene wille."	*dice*
	And thus acorded been° thise shrewes tweye	*are agreed*
	To sleen° the thridde, as ye han herd me seye.	*kill*
	This yongeste, which that wente unto the toun,	
550	Ful ofte in herte he rolleth up and doun	
	The beautee of thise floryns newe and brighte.	
	"O Lord," quod he, "if so were that I myghte	
	Have al this tresor to myself allone,	
	Ther is no man that lyveth under the trone°	*throne*
555	Of God that sholde lyve so murye° as I!"	*merry*
	And atte laste the feend° oure enemy	*devil*
	Putte in his thought that he sholde poyson beye°	*buy*
	With which he myghte sleen hise felawes tweye,	*kill*
	For why the feend foond hym in swich lyvynge	
560	That he hadde leve hym to sorwe brynge.[1]	
	For this was outrely° his fulle entente,	*utterly*
	To sleen hem bothe and nevere to repent.	
	And forth he gooth—no lenger wolde he tarie—	
	Into the toun unto a pothecarie°	*apothecary*
565	And preyde hym that he hym wolde selle	
	Som poysoun that he myghte hise rattes° quelle.°	*rats / kill*
	And eek ther was a polcat in his hawe,	
	That, as he seyde, hise capouns hadde yslawe.[2]	
	And fayn° he wolde wreke hym,° if he	*gladly / avenge himself*
	myghte,	
570	On vermyn that destroyed° hym by nyghte.	*harmed*
	The pothecarie answerde, "And thou shalt have	
	A thyng that, also° God my soule save,	*as*
	In al this world ther is no creature	
	That eten or dronken hath of this confiture°	*concoction*

---

[1] *For why ... brynge* Because the devil found him living in such a way (i.e., so sinfully) that he had permission (from God) to bring him to sorrow (i.e., damnation).

[2] *And eek ... yslawe* And also there was a polecat (a type of weasel) in his yard that, as he said, had killed his poultry.

575 Noght° but the montance° of a corn° of	
whete,	*nothing / size / grain*
That he ne shal his lif anon° forlete.°	*immediately / lose*
Ye, sterve° he shal, and that in lasse while°	*die / less time*
Than thou wolt goon a paas° nat but a mile,	*at a walking pace*
The poysoun is so strong and violent."	
580 This cursed man hath in his hond yhent°	*taken*
This poysoun in a box, and sith° he ran	*afterwards*
Into the nexte strete° unto a man	*street*
And borwed hym° large botels thre.	*borrowed from him*
And in the two his poyson poured he.	
585 The thridde he kepte clene for his owene drynke.	
For al the nyght he shoope° hym for to swynke°	*intended / labor*
In cariynge of the gold out of that place.	
And whan this riotour with sory grace°	*wretched misfortune*
Hadde filled with wyn hise grete botels thre,	
590 To hise felawes agayn repaireth he.	
What nedeth it to sermone° of it moore?	*talk*
For right so° as they hadde cast° his deeth	
bifoore,	*just as / determined*
Right so they han hym slayn, and that anon.	
And whan that this was doon, thus spak that oon:°	*the first*
595 "Now lat us sitte and drynke and make us merie,	
And afterward we wol his body berie."°	*bury*
And with that word it happed hym par cas°	*by chance*
To take the botel ther the poysoun was,	
And drank and yaf his felawe drynke also,	
600 For which anon they storven° bothe two.	*died*
But certes, I suppose that Avycen[1]	
Wroot° nevere in no *Canoun* ne in no *fen*°	*wrote / chapter*
Mo wonder° signes° of	
empoisonyng°	*more terrible / symptoms / poisoning*
Than hadde thise wrecches two er hir endyng.°	*before their death*
605 Thus ended been thise homycides° two	*murderers*
And eek the false empoysonere° also.	*poisoner*
O cursed synne of alle cursednesse,	
O traytours° homycide, o wikkednesse,	*traitorous*
O glotonye, luxurie,° and hasardrye,	*lust*
610 Looke which a seuretee° is it to yow alle	*guarantee*

Thou blasphemour of Crist with vileynye	
And othes grete° of usage° and of pride!	*great oaths / habit*
Allas, mankynde, how may it bitide°	*happen*
That to thy creatour, which that the wroghte°	*who made you*
615 And with his precious herte blood thee boghte,°	*redeemed*
Thou art so fals and so unkynde,° allas?	*unnatural*
Now goode men, God foryeve yow youre trespas	
And ware° yow fro the synne of avarice!	*guard*
Myn hooly pardoun may yow all warice,°	*save*
620 So° that ye offre nobles or sterlynges[2]	*provided*
Or elles silver broches, spoones, rynges.	
Boweth youre heed under this hooly bulle.°	*license*
Com up, ye wyves, offreth of youre wolle;°	*wool*
Youre names I entre heer in my rolle° anon.	*list*
625 Into the blisse of Hevene shul ye gon.	
I yow assoille° by myn heigh power,	*pardon*
As ye were born. And lo, sires, thus I preche.	
And Jesu Crist that is oure soules leche°	*soul's physician*
So graunte yow his pardoun to receyve.	
630 For that is best; I wol yow nat deceyve.	
"But sires, o° word forgat I in my tale.	*one*
I have relikes and pardoun in my male°	*pouch*
As faire as any man in Engelond,	
Whiche were me yeven° by the Popes hond.°	*given / hand*
635 If any of yow wole of devocioun°	*in devotion*
Offren and han myn absolucioun,	
Com forth anon, and kneleth heere adoun,	
And mekely° receyveth my pardoun.	*meekly*
Or elles taketh pardoun as ye wende,°	*go*
640 Al newe and fressh at every miles ende,	
So that ye offren alwey newe° and newe	*anew*
Nobles or pens,° whiche that be goode and trewe.[3]	*pence*
It is an honour to everich° that is heer	*everyone*
That ye mowe° have a suffisant° pardoneer	*may / capable*
645 T'assoille yow in contree° as ye ryde	*the country*
For aventures° whiche that may bityde.°	*accidents / befall*
Paraventure° ther may fallen oon or two	*perhaps*
Doun of his hors and breke his nekke atwo.°	*in two*
That I am in youre felaweshipe yfalle,°	*fallen into your company*
650 That may assoille yow bothe moore and	
lasse°	*greater and lesser (of rank)*

---

[1] *Avycen* I.e., Avicenna or Ibn Sina (980–1037 CE), a Persian philosopher who wrote, among other things, a treatise about medicine entitled *Liber Canonis Medicinae* (*The Book of the Canon of Medicine*). The word *Canon* in the next line refers to this book. It was divided into chapters called "fens," from the Arabic word for a part of a science.

---

[2] *nobles or sterlynges* Gold and silver coins respectively.

[3] *Nobles … trewe* Forgery and also the clipping of coins (i.e., shaving off some of the silver or gold from the edges) were major concerns in Chaucer's day.

Whan that the soule shal fro the body passe.
I rede° that oure Hoost heere shal bigynne,°   *advise | begin*
For he is moost envoluped in synne.
Com forth, sire Hoost, and offre first anon,
655 And thou shalt kisse my relikes everychon.
Ye, for a grote unbokele anon thy purs."[1]
      "Nay, nay," quod he, "thanne have I Cristes curs!°   *curse*
Lat be,"° quod he. "It shal nat be so, thee'ch!   *leave it be*
Thou woldest make me kisse thyn olde breech°   *pants*
660 And swere it were a relyk of a seint—
Though it were with thy fundement° depeint!°   *anus | stained*
But by the croys which that Seint Eleyne[2] fond,
I wolde I hadde thy coillons° in myn hond   *testicles*
Instide of relikes or of seintuarie!°   *reliquaries*
665 Lat kutte hem of!° I wol with thee hem
      carie.°   *let them be cut off | carry*

They shul be shryned° in an hogges
      toord!"°   *enshrined | hog's turd*
      This Pardoner answerde nat a word.
So wrooth° he was, no word ne wolde he seye.   *angry*
      "Now," quod oure Hoost, "I wol no lenger pleye°   *joke*
670 With thee ne with noon oother angry man!"
But right anon the worthy knyght bigan°   *began*
Whan that he saugh that al the peple lough,°   *laughed*
"Namoore of this! For it is right ynough!°   *quite enough*
Sire Pardoner, be glad and myrie of cheere.°   *merry of face*
675 And ye, sire Hoost, that been to me so deere,
I prey yow that ye kisse the Pardoner.
And Pardoner, I prey thee, drawe thee neer,
And as we diden,° lat us laughe and pleye!"   *did*
Anon they kiste and ryden forth hir weye.°   *their way*

HEERE IS ENDED THE PARDONERS TALE

---

[1] *Ye … purs* Yes, unbuckle your purse immediately for a groat
(fourpenny coin).

[2] *Seint Eleyne* I.e., St. Helena, the mother of the fourth-century
Roman emperor Constantine. Legend had it that she went to the
Holy Land and found there the cross on which Christ was crucified.

The Nun's Priest's Prologue and Tale

In the full *Canterbury Tales* this tale is preceded by *The Monk's Tale*, in which the Monk recites a long list of tragedies, which for him are simply stories of those who have fallen suddenly from great rank. This wearies the Knight, who interrupts him. When the Monk refuses to tell stories of hunting instead, the Host calls peremptorily upon the Nun's Priest. The Nun's Priest, who is not even described in the *General Prologue*, is at first almost a nonentity. By the end of his tale, however, he will have won whole-hearted admiration, at least from the rather undiscerning Host, whose response (also included here) is contained in a passage that does not appear in the Ellesmere Manuscript.

The tale offered by the Nun's Priest is a beast fable of the kind told by Aesop. It revolves around animals who are all too human in their follies, and it teaches a clear moral lesson: beware of flatterers. The Nun's Priest expands on this simple structure, beginning with a rich rhetorical evocation of the rooster Chauntecleer's crowing, which he contrasts to the austere life of the poor widow who owns him. The tale then moves into an elaborate debate on dream lore, in which the hen Pertelote speaks for the materialist for whom dreams are the result of indigestion, and Chauntecleer for those who see them as veiled prophecies. This debate alone takes up nearly half the lines in the tale. Throughout, the tale fluctuates between a world in which Chauntecleer and Pertelote are aristocratic lovers and a world in which they are just barnyard fowl. Much of the comedy lies in the elaborate rhetorical language, which is both celebrated and mocked. The Nun's Priest is clearly a master of this art, and it is typical of the tale's comic approach to the eloquence it proudly displays that he should invoke Geoffrey of Vinsauf and his basic textbook on rhetoric. This is a work that, while it is several steps up on Pertelote's only written authority, an elementary grammar drawn from the moral writings of Cato, is scarcely sophisticated. For all its comedy, the tale contains one of Chaucer's grimmest and most pointed historical references, to the rebels in 1381 who hunted down and murdered Flemish weavers.

The Nun's Priest ends by suggesting that the tale exists only for its moral, the fruit, and that we should discard the story, the chaff. All that is written, he tells us, is written for our doctrine, a line Chaucer repeats in his *Retraction*. But the Nun's Priest also tells us that his story is as true as that of Lancelot de Lake (line 445), that he speaks only in game (line 495), and that when he criticizes women his words are those of Chauntecleer (line 498). Filled with references to books and sayings, such as Chauntecleer's comment that "Mulier est hominis confusio" (Latin: Woman is man's confusion, line 397), that are misrepresented or otherwise untrustworthy, the tale does not allow such an easy distinction between literary art and moral content.

Opening page of *The Nun's Priest's Tale*, Ellesmere manuscript (detail).
(Reprinted by permission of *The Huntington Library, San Marino, California*. EL26C9F72r.)

Opening page of *The Nun's Priest's Tale*, Ellesmere manuscript. (Reprinted by permission of *The Huntington Library, San Marino, California*. EL26C9F72r.)

The Nun's Priest's Prologue

Heere Stynteth the Knyght the Monk of his Tale[1]

The Prologe of the Nonnes Preestes Tale

"Hoo,"° quod° the Knyght, "good sire, namoore° of this!   *whoa / said / no more*
That ye han seyd is right ynough, ywis,[2]
And muchel moore,° for litel hevynesse°   *much more / a little heaviness*
Is right ynough° to muche folk,° I gesse.   *enough / many people*
5 I seye° for me it is a greet disese,°   *say / great discomfort*
Whereas° men han been in greet welthe° and ese,°   *where / wealth / ease*
To heeren° of hire° sodeyn fal,° allas!   *hear / their / sudden fall*
And the contrarie° is joye and greet solas,°   *contrary / comfort*
As whan a man hath been in povre° estaat,°   *poor / condition*
10 And clymbeth° up, and wexeth° fortunate,   *climbs / grows*
And there abideth° in prosperitee.   *remains*
Swich° thyng is gladsom,° as it thynketh° me,   *such a / pleasant / seems to*
And of swich thyng were goodly for to telle."
    "Ye,"° quod oure Hoost, "by Seint Poules belle,[3]   *yes*
15 Ye seye right sooth.° This Monk, he clappeth lowed.°   *truth / chatters loudly*
He spak how Fortune covered with a clowde°   *cloud*
I noot° nevere what, and also of a tragedie   *know not*
Right now ye harde,° and, pardee,° no remedie°   *heard / by God / remedy*
It is for to biwaille° ne° compleyne°   *bewail / nor / lament*
20 That that° is doon,° and als° it is a peyne,°   *which / done / also / pain*
As ye han seyd, to heere of hevynesse.°   *sadness*
    "Sire Monk, namoore of this, so God yow blesse!
Youre tale anoyeth al this compaignye.
Swich talkyng is nat worth a boterflye!°   *butterfly*
25 For therinne is ther no desport° ne game.   *sport*

Wherfore,° sire Monk, daun° Piers by youre name,   *therefore / sir*
I pray yow hertely° telle us somwhat elles.°   *heartily / something else*
For sikerly,° nere° clynkyng° of youre belles   *surely / were not / clinking*
That on youre bridel° hange on every syde,   *bridle*
30 By Hevene Kyng° that° for us alle dyde,°   *the King of Heaven / who / died*
I sholde er° this han° fallen doun for sleepe,   *before / have*
Althogh the slough° had never been so deepe.   *mud*
Thanne hadde youre tale al be° toold in veyn.°   *been / vain*
For certeinly, as that thise clerkes seyn,°   *these scholars say*
35 Whereas° a man may have noon° audience,   *where / no*
Noght helpeth it° to tellen his sentence.°   *it is of no use / meaning*
And wel I woot, the substance is in me
If anythyng shal wel reported be.[4]
Sire, sey° somwhat of huntyng, I yow preye."   *tell us*
40 "Nay," quod this Monk, "I have no lust° to pleye.°   *desire / play*
Now lat° another telle as I have toold."   *let*
    Thanne spak oure Hoost with rude speche° and boold°   *rough speech / bold*
And seyde unto the Nonnes Preest° anon,°   *Nun's Priest / immediately*
"Com neer, thou Preest. Com hyder,° thou sire John![5]   *here*
45 Telle us swich thyng as may oure hertes glade.°   *gladden*
Be blithe,° though thou ryde upon a jade.°   *happy / bad horse*
What thogh° thyn hors be bothe foul and lene?°   *though / lean*
If he wol serve thee, rekke nat a bene!°   *do not care a bean*
Looke that thyn herte be murie° everemo."   *merry*
50 "Yis sire," quod he, "yis, Hoost, so moot I go.°   *as I may go*
But° I be myrie, ywis,° I wol be blamed."   *unless / indeed*
And right anon his tale he hath attamed,°   *has begun*
And thus he seyde unto us everichon,°   *everyone*
This sweete preest, this goodly man, sire John.

Explicit[6]

---

[1] *Heere … Tale* Here the Knight stops the Monk from telling his tale. The Monk's tragic tale recounted the fall of numerous people from greatness to wretchedness and misery.

[2] *That … ywis* What you have said is quite enough, indeed.

[3] *Seint Poules belle* I.e., the bell of St. Paul's Cathedral in London.

[4] *the substance … be* Either I have the stuff (substance) in me (i.e., the power) to understand if a story is well told, or possibly, if a story is well told, I know when I have grasped the substance of it.

[5] *thou sire John* The Host addresses the Nun's Priest with the familiar thou, not the polite you that he uses for the Knight, the Monk, or most of the other gentle folk.

[6] *Explicit* Latin: Here it ends.

THE NUN'S PRIEST'S TALE

HEERE BIGYNNETH THE NONNES PREESTES TALE OF THE COK AND HEN, CHAUNTECLEER AND PERTELOTE

55 A povre° wydwe° somdeel° stape° in
     age   *poor | widow | somewhat | advanced*
    Was whilom° dwellyng° in a narwe° cottage *once | living | small*
    Biside° a grene[1] stondynge° in a dale.   *beside | standing*
    This wydwe of which I telle yow my tale,
    Syn° thilke° day that she was last a wyf   *since | that*
60 In pacience ladde° a ful° symple lyf,   *led | very*
    For litel° was hir catel° and hir rente.°   *little | possessions | income*
    By housbondrie° of swich° as God
     hire° sente   *frugal use | such | her*
    She foond° hirself and eek° hir
     doghtren° two.   *provided for | also | daughters*
    Thre° large sowes hadde she and namo,°   *three | no more*
65 Thre keen,° and eek a sheepe that highte° *cows | was called*
     Malle.
    Ful sooty° was hir bour° and eek hir
     halle°   *dirty | bedroom | dining hall*
    In which she eet° ful many a sklendre meel.° *ate | meager meal*
    Of poynaunt° sauce hir neded never a deel;° *spicy | portion*
    No deyntee° morsel passed thurgh hir throte.° *dainty | throat*
70 Hir diete was accordant to hir cote.°   *in accord with her cottage*
    Repleccioun° ne made hire nevere sik.°   *gluttony | sick*
    Attempree° diete was al hir phisik,°   *temperate | medical remedy*
    And excercise and hertes suffisaunce.°   *heart's content*
    The goute lette hire nothyng for to daunce,[2]
75 N'apoplexie° shente° nat hir heed.°   *nor stroke | harmed | head*
    No wyn ne drank she, neither whit ne reed.
    Hir bord° was served moost with whit and blak— *table*
    Milk and broun breed, in which she foond no lak,[3]
    Seynd bacoun° and somtyme an ey° or
     tweye.°   *smoked bacon | egg | two*

80 For she was, as it were, a maner° deye.°   *kind of | dairy farmer*
    A yeerd° she hadde enclosed al aboute   *yard*
   With stikkes° and a drye dych[4] withoute,   *sticks*
   In which she hadde a cok° heet° Chauntecleer.[5] *rooster | named*
   In al the land of crowyng° nas° his peer.   *crowing | there was not*
85 His voys° was murier° than the murie
    orgon°   *voice | merrier | organ*
   On messedayes that in the chirche gon.[6]
   Wel sikerer° was his crowing in his logge° *reliable | lodging*
   Than is a clokke or an abbey orlogge.°   *monastery clock*
   By nature he crew° ech ascencioun°   *crowed | each ascension*
90 Of the equynoxial[7] in thilke° toun.   *that*
   For whan degrees fiftene weren ascended,
   Thanne crew he that it myghte nat been
    amended.°   *could not be improved*
   His coomb° was redder than the fyn° coral   *coxcomb | fine*
   And batailled° as it were a castel wal.[8]   *crenellated*
95 His byle° was blak, and as the jeet° it
    shoon.°   *bill | jet (gemstone) | shone*
   Lyk asure° were his legges and his toon,°   *azure | toes*
   Hise nayles° whitter than the lylye flour,° *nails | lily flower*
   And lyk the burned° gold was his colour.   *polished*
   This gentil° cok hadde in his governaunce° *noble | control*
100 Sevene hennes for to doon° al his plesaunce,° *do | pleasure*
   Whiche were hise sustres° and his paramours° *his sisters | lovers*
   And wonder lyk° to hym as of colours,   *marvelously similar*
   Of whiche the faireste hewed° on hir throte° *colored | her throat*
   Was cleped° faire damoysele° Pertelote.   *called | damsel*
105 Curteys° she was, discreet, and debonaire° *courteous | gracious*
   And compaignable,° and bar° hyrself so
    faire°   *friendly | behaved | well*

---

[1] *grene* I.e., green, a common area in a village used for pasturage or other agricultural pursuits that did not demand the plowing of the green into a field.

[2] *The goute ... daunce* The gout (a disease affecting the feet and brought on by over-eating or drinking) by no means hindered her from dancing.

[3] *in ... lak* Either defect or lack, so either: In which she found no fault, or of which she had no shortage.

[4] *drye dych* Contrasts with the moat of a castle.

[5] *Chauntecleer* From the French, "clear singer." Chauntecleer is the name of the rooster in *The Romance of Renard*, which tells the adventures of a wily fox and contains one of the best known medieval versions of the story told by the Nun's Priest.

[6] *On ... gon* That go (i.e., are played—the organ, an instrument of many pipes, was spoken of as plural) in Church on feast days.

[7] *By nature ... equynoxial* The sense of this passage is that Chauntecleer crows when each hourly point of the celestial equator rises past the horizon.

[8] *And ... wal* The crenellation on a castle's walls is the alternation of high, squared masonry with blank spaces. This would provide cover for the archers defending the castle against the arrows of the attackers.

Syn thilke day that she was seven nyght oold,°   *nights old*
That trewely, she hath the herte in hoold°   *holds the heart*
Of Chauntecleer, loken° in every lith.°   *locked / limb*
110 He loved hire so, that wel was hym therwith.
And swich a joye was it to here hem° synge,   *them*
Whan that the brighte sonne bigan to sprynge,°   *rise*
In sweete accord,° "My Lief Is Faren in Londe."[1]   *harmony*
For thilke tyme,° as I have understonde,   *at that time*
115 Beestes and briddes° koude speke and synge.   *birds*
    And so bifel° that in the dawenynge,°   *it happened / at dawn*
As Chauntecleer among hise wyves alle
Sat on his perche° that was in the halle,   *perch*
And next hym sat this faire Pertelote,
120 This Chauntecleer gan gronen° in his throte   *began to groan*
As man that in his dreem is drecched soore.°   *sorely disturbed*
And whan that Pertelote thus herde hym roore,°   *roar*
She was agast° and seyde, "O herte deere,   *afraid*
What eyleth° yow to grone in this manere?   *ails*
125 Ye been° a verray° slepere. Fy!° For shame!"   *are / good / fie*
    And he answerde and seyde thus: "Madame,
I pray yow that ye take it nat agrief.°   *amiss*
By God, me thoughte I was in swich meschief°   *such trouble*
Right now, that yet myn herte is soore afright.
130 Now God," quod he, "my swevene recche aright,[2]
And kepe my body out of foul prisoun!
Me mette° how that I romed up and doun   *I dreamed*
Withinne oure yeerd, wheereas° I saugh a beest   *where*
Was lyk an hound, and wolde han maad areest°   *grabbed hold*
135 Upon my body and han had me deed!°   *have had me dead*
His colour was bitwixe yelow and reed,°   *red*
And tipped was his tayl° and bothe hise eeris°   *tail / his ears*
With blak, unlyk° the remenant of hise heeris;°   *unlike / hairs*
His snowte° smal with glowynge eyen tweye.°   *nose / two*
140 Yet° of his look for feere° almoost I deye.   *still / fear*
This caused me my gronyng, doutelees."°   *doubtless*
    "Avoy!"° quod she. "Fy on yow, hertelees!°   *shame / coward*
Allas," quod she, "for by that God above,
Now han ye lost myn herte and al my love.
145 I kan nat love a coward, by my faith!

For certes,° whatso° any womman seith,   *certain / whatever*
We alle desiren, if it myghte bee,
To han housbondes hardy,° wise, and free,°   *brave / generous*
And secree° and no nygard° ne no fool,   *discreet / cheapskate*
150 Ne hym that is agast° of every tool,°   *afraid / weapon*
Ne noon avauntour,° by that God above.   *nor any braggart*
How dorste° ye seyn, for shame, unto youre love   *dare*
That anythyng myghte make yow aferd?°   *afraid*
Have ye no mannes herte,° and han a berd?°   *man's heart / beard*
155 Allas, and konne ye been agast of swevenys?°   *be afraid of dreams*
Nothyng, God woot,° but vanitee° in swevene
    is!   *knows / foolishness*
Swevenes engendren of° replecciouns°   *are caused by / overeating*
And ofte of fume° and of complecciouns[3]   *stomach-gas*
Whan humours been° to habundant° in a
    wight.°   *are / too abundant / person*
160 Certes, this dreem which ye han met° tonyght   *have dreamed*
Cometh of greet superfluytee°   *excess*
Of youre rede colera, pardee,[4]
Which causeth folk to dreden° in hir dremes   *fear*
Of arwes° and of fyr° with rede lemes,°   *arrows / fire / red flames*
165 Of grete beestes that they wol hem byte,°   *will bite them*
Of contek° and of whelpes° grete and lyte,°   *conflict / dogs / small*
Right° as the humour of malencolie[5]   *just*
Causeth ful many a man in sleepe to crie
For feere of blake beres° or boles° blake   *black bears / bulls*
170 Or elles blake develes wole hem take.
Of othere humours koude I telle also
That werken° many a man in sleepe ful wo,°   *cause / much woe*
But I wol passe° as lightly as I kan.   *pass over*
    "Lo Catoun,[6] which that was so wys° a man,   *wise*

---

1 *My ... Londe* My dear one has traveled into (a foreign) land. This is the title of a popular song, one version of which, from c. 1500, has survived in a manuscript at Trinity College, Cambridge.

2 *Now ... aright* "Now God," he said, "interpret my dream correctly."

---

3 *complecciouns* I.e., complexions, or temperaments. Medieval medical theory maintained that what we now call personality was a function of the balance in the body of the four bodily fluids known as humors. If these fluids were unbalanced, disease would result.

4 *Of ... pardee* Of your red choler, by God. Choler was one of the four bodily temperaments. It was formed by the combination of yellow bile (which was hot and dry) with blood (which was hot and moist).

5 *malencolie* I.e., melancholy, another of the four temperaments.

6 *Catoun* I.e., Dionysius Cato, a Roman politician who was believed in the Middle Ages to be the author of a widely-circulating collection of proverbs which was often used to teach basic Latin grammar.

175 Seyde he nat thus: 'Ne do no fors of dremes'?[1]
    "Now sire," quod she, "whan ye flee° fro the
        bemes,°   *fly down / beams*
    For Goddes love, as taak som laxatyf!°   *take some laxative*
    Up° peril of my soule and of my lyf,   *upon*
    I conseille° yow the beste—I wol nat lye°—   *counsel / lie*
180 That bothe of colere° and of malencolye   *choler*
    Ye purge yow,° and for ye shal nat
        tarie,°   *yourself / so you do not delay*
    Though in this toun is noon apothecarie,°   *no pharmacist*
    I shal myself to herbes° techen yow,   *about herbs*
    That shul been for youre heele° and for youre
        prow,°   *health / profit*
185 And in oure yeerd° tho° herbes shal I fynde,   *yard / those*
    The whiche han of hire propretee° by
        kynde°   *their property / nature*
    To purge yow bynethe and eek above.
    Foryet nat this, for Goddes owene love!
    Ye been ful coleryk of compleccioun.
190 Ware the sonne in his ascencioun
    Ne fynde yow nat repleet of humours hoote.[2]
    And if it do, I dar wel leye° a grote[3]   *bet*
    That ye shul° have a fevere terciane[4]   *shall*
    Or an agu° that may be youre bane.°   *ague (fever) / cause of death*
195 A day or two ye shul have digestyves°   *stomach medicines*
    Of wormes, er ye take youre laxatyves[5]
    Of lawriol,° centaure,° and fumetere,° *laurel / centaury / fumaria*
    Or elles of ellebor,° that groweth there;   *hellebore*
    Of katapuce° or of gaitrys beryis,°   *euphorbia / rhamus berries*
200 Of herbe yve,° growyng in oure yeerd ther mery
        is.°   *herb-ivy / where it is merry*

Pekke hem up right as they growe, and ete hem
    yn.°   *eat them up*
Be myrie, housbonde, for youre fader kyn!° *merry / father's kin*
Dredeth no dreem. I kan sey yow namoore."
    "Madame," quod he, "*graunt mercy*[6] of youre loore!° *advice*
205 But nathelees, as touchyng° daun
        Catoun,°   *pertaining to / Master Cato*
    That hath of° wysdom swich a greet renoun,°   *for / fame*
    Though that he bad° no dremes for to drede,   *commanded*
    By God, men may in olde bookes rede
    Of many a man moore of auctorite
210 Than evere Caton was, so moot I thee,°   *so might I thrive*
    That al° the revers° seyn of this sentence,   *completely / opposite*
    That han wel founden° by experience   *have found out well*
    That dremes been significaciouns°   *are signs*
    As wel of joye as of tribulaciouns°   *troubles*
215 That folk enduren in this lif present.
    Ther nedeth make of this noon argument.
    The verray preeve° sheweth it in dede.   *true proof / deed*
        "Oon of the gretteste auctour[7] that men rede
    Seith thus: that whilom° two felawes wente   *once*
220 On pilgrimage in a ful good entente,
    And happed so° they coomen in a toun,   *it so happened*
    Wheras ther was swich congregacioun°   *a gathering*
    Of peple, and eek so streit of
        herbergage,°   *such a shortage of lodging*
    That they ne founde as muche as o° cotage   *one*
225 In which they bothe myghte logged bee,
    Wherfore they mosten of necessitee
    As for that nyght departen compaignye.°   *part company*
    And ech of hem gooth to his hostelrye°   *lodging place*
    And took his loggyng as it wolde falle.°   *would happen*
230 That oon of hem was logged in a stalle°   *stall*
    Fer° in a yeerd, with oxen of the plough.   *far*
    That oother man was logged wel ynough,
    As was his aventure° or his fortune,   *chance*
    That us governeth alle as in commune.°   *in common*
235   "And so bifel that, longe er it were day,
    This man mette in his bed, theras° he lay,   *where*

---

[1] *Seyde ... dremes* Said he not this: "Do not pay attention to dreams"?

[2] *Ware ... hoote* Beware that the sun when it is climbing does not find you when you are (already) full of hot humors. The movements of the planets were thought to affect a patient's balance of humors.

[3] *grote* Coin equal to four pence.

[4] *fevere terciane* I.e., tertian fever. Medieval people classified the types of fevers they would contract by how frequently they recurred. This one would return every third day—meaning every other day, in which the first day is counted, as is the non-fever day and the recurring-fever day. The disease is possibly malaria.

[5] *laxatyves* The laxatives listed by the hen are all types of bitter herbs.

---

[6] *graunt mercy* From the French "grand merci" or "much thanks." Chauntecleer, as an aristocrat, employs French phrases.

[7] *Oon ... auctour* The Roman orator and writer (auctour) Cicero (106–43 BCE) tells the story in *On Divination*, and it is also found in the *Memorable Deeds and Sayings of Valerius Maximus* (see *The Wife of Bath's Prologue*, line 168).

How that his felawe gan upon hym calle°   *to call*
And seyde, 'Allas, for in an oxes stalle
This nyght I shal be mordred ther I lye!
240 Now helpe me, deere brother, or I dye.
In alle haste com to me,' he sayde.
This man out of his sleepe for feere abrayde,°   *woke up*
But whan that he was wakened of his sleepe,
He turned hym° and took of it no keepe.°   *turned over / notice*
245 Hym thoughte his dreem nas but a vanitee.°   *folly*
Thus twies in his slepyng dremed hee,
And atte thridde tyme yet his felawe
Cam as hym thoughte and seide, 'I am now slawe.°   *slain*
Bihoold my bloody woundes depe and wyde.
250 Arys° up erly in the morwe tyde,°   *arise / morning-time*
And at the west gate of the toun,' quod he,
'A carte ful of donge° ther shaltow° se°   *dung / shall you / see*
In which my body is hid ful prively.°   *secretly*
Do thilke carte arresten boldely.[1]
255 My gold caused my mordre, sooth to sayn,'°   *true to say*
And tolde hym every point how he was slayn
With a ful pitous face, pale of hewe.°   *color*
And truste wel, his dreem he foond ful trewe.
For on the morwe, as soone as it was day,
260 To his felawes in° he took the way,   *friend's inn*
And whan that he cam to this oxes stalle,
After his felawe he bigan to calle.
    "The hostiler° answerde hym anon   *innkeeper*
And seyde, 'Sire, youre felawe is agon.°   *gone*
265 As soone as day he wente out of the toun.'
    "This man gan fallen in suspecioun,°   *to be suspicious*
Remembrynge on hise dremes that he mette.°   *dreamed*
And forth he gooth—no lenger wolde he lette°—   *delay*
Unto the west gate of the toun and fond°   *found*
270 A dong-carte, as it were to donge lond°   *to manure a field*
That was arrayed in that same wise°   *way*
As ye han herd the dede man devyse.°   *describe*
And with an hardy herte he gan to crye,
'Vengeance and justice of this felonye!
275 My felawe mordred is this same nyght,
And in this carte heere he lith,° gapyng
    upright.°   *lies / facing upright*
I crye out on the ministres,'° quod he,   *magistrates*
'That sholden kepe° and reulen° this citee!   *care for / rule*

Harrow!° Allas! Heere lith my felawe slayn!'   *help*
280 What sholde I moore unto this tale sayn?
The peple out sterte° and caste the cart to grounde,   *jumped up*
And in the myddel of the dong they founde
The dede man that mordred was al newe.°   *recently*
    "O blisful° God that art so just and trewe,   *blessed*
285 Lo how that thou biwreyest° mordre alway!   *reveal*
Mordre wol out.° That se we day by day.   *will be found out*
Mordre is so wlatsom° and abhomynable°   *repulsive / abominable*
To God, that is so just and resonable,
That he ne wol nat suffre it heled° be,   *concealed*
290 Though it abyde a yeer or two or thre.
Mordre wol out! This my conclusioun.
And right anon, ministres of that toun
Han hent° the cartere, and so soore° hym
    pyned,°   *arrested / sorely / tortured*
And eek the hostiler so soore engyned,°   *tortured on a rack*
295 That they biknewe° hire wikkednesse anon   *confessed*
And were anhanged° by the nekke bon.°   *hanged / neck-bone*
    "Heere may men seen that dremes been to
        drede.°   *are to be feared*
And certes, in the same book I rede,
Right in the nexte chapitre after this—
300 I gabbe° nat, so have I joye or blis—   *babble*
Two men that wolde han° passed over see° *would have / the sea*
For certeyn cause into a fer contree,°   *distant country*
If that the wynd° ne hadde been contrarie,   *wind*
That made hem in a citee for to tarie°   *delay*
305 That stood ful myrie° upon an haven-syde.° *merrily / harbor-side*
But on a day agayn the eventyde,°   *towards evening*
The wynd gan chaunge and blew right as hem
    leste.°   *they wanted*
Jolif° and glad, they wente unto hir reste   *jolly*
And casten° hem ful erly for to saille.   *decided*
310 But herkneth: to that o man fil a greet mervaille.[2]
That oon of hem, in slepyng as he lay,
Hym mette° a wonder dreem agayn the
    day.°   *dreamed / toward daybreak*
Hym thoughte a man stood by his beddes syde
And hym comanded that he sholde abyde°   *wait*
315 And seyde hym thus: 'If thou tomorwe wende,°   *go*
Thow shalt be dreynt.° My tale is at an ende.'   *drowned*
He wook and tolde his felawe what he mette

---

[1] *Do ... boldely* Cause that cart to be seized boldly.

[2] *But ... mervaille* But listen! To one man there happened a great marvel.

And preyde hym his viage° to lette;°   *voyage / delay*
As for that day he preyde hym to byde.°   *wait*
320 His felawe, that lay by his beddes syde,
Gan for to laughe, and scorned hym ful faste.°   *very much*
'No dreem,' quod he, 'may so myn herte agaste°   *frighten*
That I wol lette for to do my thynges.°   *business*
I sette nat a straw by thy dremynges!°   *dreams*
325 For swevenes been but vanytees° and japes.°   *nonsense / tricks*
Men dreme al day of owles or of apes,
And of many a maze° therwithal.°   *delusion / with it all*
Men dreme of thyng that nevere was ne shal.°   *nor shall be*
But sith I see that thou wolt heere abyde,
330 And thus forslewthen° wilfully thy tyde,°   *waste / time*
God woot, it reweth me!° And have good day!'   *I regret it*
And thus he took his leve° and wente his way.   *leave*
But er that he hadde half his cours yseyled,°   *sailed*
Noot I nat° why, ne what myschaunce° it
    eyled,   *I know not / went wrong*
335 But casuelly° the shippes botme° rente,°   *by chance / bottom / split*
And shipe and man under the water wente
In sighte of othere shippes it bisyde°   *beside it*
That with hem seyled at the same tyde.°   *tide*
And therfore, faire Pertelote, so deere,
340 By swiche ensamples olde yet maistow leere°   *may you learn*
That no man sholde been to recchelees°   *too careless*
Of dremes. For I seye thee doutelees
That many a dreem ful soore is for to drede!
    Lo in the *Lyf of Seint Kenelm*[1] I rede,
345 That was Kenulphus sone,° the noble kyng   *Cenwulf's son*
Of Mertenrike,° how Kenelm mette° a thyng   *Mercia / dreamed*
A lite er° he was mordred on a day.   *little before*
His mordre in his avysioun° he say.°   *vision / saw*
His norice° hym expowned° every deel°   *nurse / explained / part*
350 His swevene, and bad hym for to kepe hym
    weel°   *protect himself*
For traisoun.° But he nas but° sevene   *from treason / was only*
    yeer oold,
And therfore litel tale hath he toold°   *paid little attention*
Of any dreem, so hooly° is his herte.   *holy*
By God, I hadde levere than my sherte

355 That ye hadde rad his Legende as have I,[2]
Dame Pertelote! I sey yow trewely,
Macrobeus, that writ the avisioun
In Affrike of the worthy Cipioun,[3]
Affermeth° dremes and seith that they   *affirms (the validity of)*
    been
360 Warnynge of thynges that men after seen.°   *see afterwards*
And forthermoore, I pray yow, looketh wel
In the Olde Testament of Daniel,
If he heeld° dremes any vanitee.°   *considered / folly*
Reed eek of Joseph,[4] and ther shul ye see
365 Wher dremes be somtyme—I sey nat alle°—   *not always*
Warnynge of thynges that shul after falle.°   *happen*
Looke of Egipte° the kyng daun Pharao,°   *Egypt / Lord Pharaoh*
His bakere and his butiller° also,   *butler*
Wher° they ne felte noon° effect in
    dremes.   *whether / did not feel any*
370 Whoso wol seken actes of sondry remes°   *various realms*
May rede of dremes many a wonder thyng.
Lo Cresus,[5] which that was of Lyde kyng,
Mette he nat° that he sat upon a tree,   *did he not dream*
Which signified he sholde anhanged° bee?   *hanged*
375 Lo heere Adromacha,° Ectores° wyf,   *Andromache / Hector's*

---

[2] *I hadde … I* I would rather that you had read this saint's life than that I had my shirt, or, as we might say, I'd give my shirt to have you read it.

[3] *In … Cipioun* The Roman writer Macrobius (c. 400 CE) wrote a commentary on the part of Cicero's *Republic* called "The Dream of Scipio." This book tells how Scipio Africanus Minor, a Roman consul, dreamed of meeting his famous ancestor, Scipio Africanus Major (so-called because he defeated Hannibal, the great general of Carthage, in North Africa) and urged him to pursue virtue for the sake of reward in a future life. Chauntecleer misinterprets his name, assuming the dream happened in Africa.

[4] *Daniel … Joseph* Both Daniel and Joseph were famous for their ability to interpret dreams. Daniel interpreted the dream of King Nebuchadnezzar to predict that the king would be banished for seven years (see Daniel 4). Joseph interpreted his own dream to predict that he would be lord over his brothers, interpreted the dreams of Pharaoh's butler and his baker to predict that the former would be restored to office but the latter hanged, and interpreted Pharaoh's dream to predict that Egypt would have seven years of good harvest followed by seven years of famine (see Genesis 37.5–11; 40.1–23; 41.1–32).

[5] *Cresus* The Monk had mentioned the dream of Croesus, the fabulously rich king of Lydia who was conquered by King Cyrus of Persia, in the previous tale.

---

[1] *Lyf … Kenelm* This is a saint's life, or hagiography, of Kenelm (Cenhelm), a seven-year-old Anglo-Saxon king of Mercia who was murdered at the command of his aunt.

That day that Ector sholde lese his lyf
She dremed on the same nyght biforn
How that the lyf of Ector sholde be lorn°   *lost*
If thilke day he wente into bataille.
380 She warned hym, but it myghte nat availle.° *could not help*
He wente for to fighte natheles,°   *nevertheless*
But he was slayn anon of Achilles.[1]
But thilke is al to° longe for to telle,   *too*
And eek it is ny° day. I may nat dwelle.° *near / not delay*
385 Shortly I seye, as for conclusioun,
That I shal han of this avisioun
Adversitee. And I seye forthermoor
That I ne telle of laxatyves no stoor!° *set no store in laxatives*
For they been venymes,° I woot° it weel. *venomous / know*
390 I hem diffye,° I love hem never a deel!° *reject them / not at all*
 "Now lat us speke of myrthe° and
  stynte° al this.   *mirth / be silent about*
Madame Pertelote, so have I blis,°   *happiness*
Of o° thyng God hath sent me large grace,° *one / great favor*
For whan I se the beautee of youre face—
395 Ye been so scarlet reed° aboute youre eyen— *red*
It maketh al my drede for to dyen.
For also siker° as *In principio*,[2]   *as certain*
Mulier est hominis confusio.[3]
Madame, the sentence° of this Latyn is, *meaning*
400 'Womman is mannes joye and al his blis.'
For whan I feele anyght° youre softe side— *at night*
Albeit that I may nat on yow ryde,°   *ride*
For that oure perche is maad° so narwe,° allas! *made / narrow*
I am so ful of joye and of solas
405 That I diffye° bothe swevene and dreem!"[4] *defy*

And with that word he fly° doun fro the beem,° *flew / beam*
For it was day, and eek hise hennes alle,° *did also all his hens*
And with a "chuk" he gan hem for to calle,
For he hadde founde a corn lay° in the yerd. *kernel that lay*
410 Real° he was. He was namoore aferd,   *regal*
And fethered Pertelote twenty tyme
And trad as ofte er it was pryme.[5]
He looketh as it were° a grym leoun,° *as if he were / fierce lion*
And on hise toos° he rometh° up and doun. *his toes / roams*
415 Hym deigned nat to sette his foot to grounde.
He chukketh° whan he hath a corn yfounde, *clucks*
And to hym rennen thanne° hise wyves alle. *run then*
Thus roial° as a prince is in an halle   *regal*
Leve° I this Chauntecleer in his pasture, *leave*
420 And after wol I telle his aventure.

 Whan that the monthe in which the world bigan,
That highte March, whan God first maked man,[6]
Was compleet, and passed were also,
Syn March bigan, thritty dayes and two,[7]
425 Bifel° that Chauntecleer in al his pryde, *it happened*
Hise sevene wyves walkynge by his syde,
Caste up hise eyen to the brighte sonne,
That in the signe of Taurus hadde yronne
Twenty degrees and oon° and somwhat *twenty-one degrees*
  moore,
430 And knew by kynde° and by noon oother
  loore°   *nature / teaching*
That it was pryme,° and crew with blisful
  stevene.°   *early morning / voice*
"The sonne," he seyde, "is clomben upon hevene
Fourty degrees and oon and moore, ywis.
Madame Pertelote, my worldes blis,
435 Herkneth thise blisful briddes,° how they synge, *birds*
And se the fresshe floures, how they sprynge.° *bloom*

---

[1] *Lo heere … Achilles* The narrative of the Trojan war recounted by Dares Phrygius (one of the standard versions of the story in the Middle Ages) includes the story of the dream of Hector's wife. Homer's *Iliad*, which was not well known in western Europe at the time, does not include the episode.

[2] *In principio* Latin: In the beginning; i.e., as certain as the Bible. These words begin both the book of Genesis and the Gospel of John.

[3] *Mulier … confusio* Latin: Woman is the confusion of man.

[4] *That … dreem* Chauntecleer appears to distinguish between two kinds of dreams here, but it is not clear what the difference is. Medieval dream theory distinguished between prophetic dreams and those that had no special significance, but the terms swevene and dreme (and also mette) cover both.

---

[5] *And fethered … pryme* He covered Pertelote with his feathers twenty times and copulated with her as often before it was the hour of prime (early morning).

[6] *That … man* According to various medieval authorities, including Saint Basil and the English monastic writer Bede, God created the world at the spring equinox.

[7] *Was compleet … two* The phrasing is ambiguous but the events seem to take place on May 3, when all of March and a further thirty-two days had passed. This date is in keeping with the position of the sun in the sky and the other astrological information. May 3 was considered an unlucky day and is also the day on which Palamon escapes from prison in *The Knight's Tale* (line 1462).

Ful is myn herte of revel° and solas." — *amusement*
But sodeynly hym fil° a sorweful cas,° — *befell / event*
For evere the latter ende of joye is wo.
440 God woot that worldly joye is soone ago!° — *gone*
And if a rethor° koude faire endite,° — *rhetorician / write well*
He in a cronycle saufly° myghte it write — *safely*
As for a sovereyn notabilitee.° — *very notable thing*
Now every wys man, lat hym herkne me.° — *listen to me*
445 This storie is also trewe, I undertake,° — *swear*
As is *The Book of Launcelot de Lake*,[1]
That wommen holde in ful greet reverence.
Now wol I come agayn to my sentence.° — *purpose*
 A colfox° ful of sly iniquitee,° — *coal-black fox / malice*
450 That in the grove hadde woned° yeeres three, — *lived*
By heigh ymaginacioun forncast,[2]
The same nyght thurghout° the hegges°
        brast° — *through / hedge / burst*
Into the yerd ther° Chauntecleer the faire — *where*
Was wont, and eek hise wyves, to repaire,° — *retire*
455 And in a bed of wortes° stille° he lay — *herbs / quietly*
Til it was passed undren° of the day, — *dawn*
Waitynge his tyme° on Chauntecleer to falle, — *opportunity*
As gladly doon thise homycides alle° — *all these murderers*
That in await liggen° to mordre men. — *lie in wait*
460 O false mordrour, lurkynge in thy den!
O newe Scariot,° newe Genylon!° — *(Judas) Iscariot / Ganelon*
False dissymulour,° o Greek Synon, — *liar*
That broghtest Troye al outrely° to sorwe!°[3] — *utterly*
O Chauntecleer, acursed be that morwe
465 That thou into that yerd flaugh° fro the bemes! — *flew*

Thou were ful wel ywarned by thy dremes
That thilke day was perilous to thee,
But what that God forwoot° moot nedes
        bee,° — *foreknows / necessarily be*
After° the opinioun of certein clerkis.° — *according to / scholars*
470 Witnesse on hym that any parfit clerk is,[4]
That in scole° is greet altercacioun° — *the universities / debate*
In this mateere, and greet disputisoun,
And hath been of an hundred thousand men.[5]
But I ne kan nat bulte it to the bren[6]
475 As kan the hooly doctour Augustyn,° — *holy scholar Augustine*
Or Boece, or the Bisshope Bradwardyn—[7]
Wheither that Goddes worthy forwityng° — *foreknowledge*
Streyneth° me nedely° to doon a thyng— — *constrains / necessarily*
"Nedely" clepe° I symple necessitee— — *call*
480 Or elles, if free choys be graunted me
To do that same thyng or do it noght,
Though God forwoot it er that it was wroght,° — *done*
Or if his wityng° streyneth° never a
        deel° — *knowing / constrains / not at all*
But by necessitee condicioneel.[8]

---

[1] *The Book ... Lake* This is the title of any one of a number of Arthurian romances that recount the adventures of Sir Lancelot, including his love affair with Guinevere, wife of King Arthur.

[2] *By ... forncast* Foreseen by exalted imagination. What this means is disputed. Many editors take it to refer to the mind or conception (ymaginacioun) of God, which foresees all events. Others take "ymaginacioun" as a reference, expressed in deliberately and ridiculously grandiose language, to Chauntecleer's dream, or as a reference to the plotting of the fox. In each case, the word "forncast" introduces the theme of predestination discussed in lines 468–696.

[3] *O newe ... sorwe* In the Gospel, Judas Iscariot betrayed Christ by identifying him to the Roman soldiers who came to arrest him; in *The Song of Roland*, Ganelon betrayed Roland with a plot that led to his death in the pass at Roncesvalles; and in *The Iliad*, Sinon betrayed Troy by suggesting the Greeks conceal themselves in a wooden horse to gain access to the city.

[4] *Witnesse ... is* As any fully qualified scholar can testify.

[5] *But what ... men* The question of how God's foreknowledge could be reconciled with human free will was always important in medieval theology, but the debate flared up in Chaucer's day. The radical theologian John Wycliffe (d. 1394), best known for initiating the translation of the Bible into English, argued that God's omniscience gave him absolute knowledge of who would be saved or damned. This meant for Wycliffe that there was no justification for the institutions of the earthly church or for penitential practices such as confession or pilgrimage.

[6] *But ... bren* But I cannot separate (the kernels) from the bran. That is, the Nun's Priest cannot sort out the issues in the debate about God's foreknowledge.

[7] *As kan ... Bradwardyn* The great patristic writer St. Augustine (d. 430 CE), the late Roman scholar Boethius (d. 524 CE), and Thomas Bradwardine, chancellor of Oxford and very briefly Archbishop of Canterbury (who died of the Black Death in 1349), all wrote about the concept of predestination. Although stressing God's omniscience, all three were thoroughly orthodox in their insistence that humans have free will.

[8] *necessitee condicioneel* Boethius distinguishes between simple necessity and conditional necessity in his *Consolation of Philosophy* 5, prose 6, and then draws on God's status outside time to resolve the theological dilemma. To use Boethius's example, that a man must die is a matter of simple necessity. But if you know someone is walking, while he must then necessarily be walking, the necessity is

485 I wol nat han to do of° swich mateere.   *have to do with*
     My tale is of a cok, as ye may heere,
     That took his conseil of his wyf with sorwe
     To walken in the yerd upon that morwe
     That he hadde met that dreem that I of tolde.
490 Wommennes conseils been ful ofte colde.°   *bad*
     Wommannes conseil broghte us first to wo
     And made Adam out of Paradys to go,
     Theras° he was ful myrie° and wel at ese.   *where / merry*
     But for I noot° to whom it myght displese,   *since I do not know*
495 If I conseil of wommen wolde blame,
     Passe over, for I seye it in my game.°   *in jest*
     Rede auctours° where they trete of swich mateere,   *authors*
     And what they seyn of wommen ye may heere.
     Thise been the cokkes wordes and nat myne!
500 I kan noon harm of no womman divyne!°   *imagine*
        Faire in the soond° to bathe hire myrily   *sand*
     Lith° Pertelote, and alle hire sustres by°   *lies / nearby*
     Agayn the sonne.° And Chauntecleer so free   *in the sunshine*
     Soong murier° than the mermayde in the   *sang more merrily*
         see—
505 For Phisiologus[1] seith sikerly°   *surely*
     How that they syngen wel and myrily—
     And so bifel that as he caste his eye
     Among the wortes° on a boterflye,   *herbs*
     He was war° of this fox that lay ful lowe.   *aware*
510 Nothyng ne liste hym thanne for to crowe,[2]
     But cride anon, "Cok! Cok!" and up he sterte
     As man that was affrayed in his herte.
     For natureelly a beest desireth flee

515 Fro his contrarie° if he may it see,   *enemy*
     Though he never erst hadde seyn it with his eye.
        This Chauntecleer, whan he gan hym espye,°   *spotted him*
     He wolde han fled, but that the fox anon
     Seyde, "Gentil sire, allas, wher wol ye gon?
     Be ye affrayed of me, that am youre freend?
520 Now certes, I were worse than a feend°   *fiend*
     If I to yow wolde° harm or vileynye!   *intended*
     I am nat come youre conseil for t'espye.°   *to spy on your council*
     But trewely, the cause of my comynge
     Was oonly for to herkne° how that ye synge.   *listen*
525 For trewely, ye have as myrie° a stevene°   *merry / voice*
     As any aungel that is in Hevene.
     Therwith ye han in musyk moore feelynge
     Than hadde Boece[3] or any that kan synge.
     My lord, youre fader, God his soule blesse,
530 And eek youre mooder of hire gentillesse
     Han in myn hous ybeen to my greet ese.
     And certes, sire, ful fayn° wolde I yow plese.   *very gladly*
     But for men speke of syngyng, I wol yow seye—
     So moote I brouke wel myne eyen tweye—[4]
535 Save yow,° herde I nevere man yet synge   *apart from yourself*
     As dide youre fader in the morwenynge.
     Certes, it was of herte° al that he song!   *from the heart*
     And for to make his voys the moore strong,
     He wolde so peyne hym° that with bothe hise eyen   *take pains*
540 He moste wynke°—so loude he wolde cryen—   *had to wink*
     And stonden on his tip-toon° therwithal,°   *tip-toes / in doing so*
     And strecche forth his nekke long and smal.°   *slender*
     And eek he was of swich discrecioun°   *discernment*
     That ther nas no man in no regioun
545 That hym in song or wisdom myghte passe.°   *surpass*
     I have wel rad° in *Daun Burnel the Asse*,[5]   *read*

---

only conditional; i.e., it depends on the condition of the man having decided to take a walk. From your perspective, he could have chosen not to do so. The issue here is whether God, in knowing in advance all future events and choices, necessarily removes free choice (for how can God be wrong?). The solution, proposed by Boethius, is this idea of conditional necessity: to know about an event is not necessarily to cause it. As he says, "God sees those future events which happen of free will as present events; so that these things when considered with reference to God's sight of them do happen necessarily as a result of the condition of divine knowledge; but when considered in themselves they do not lose the absolute freedom of their nature."

[1] *Phisiologus* The supposed author of a bestiary, a book explaining the allegorical significances of various animals. According to this work, mermaids use their sweet singing to lure sailors to their deaths.

[2] *Nothyng ... crowe* He did by no means want then to crow.

[3] *Boece* Boethius not only wrote *The Consolation of Philosophy*, which Chaucer translated, but also wrote the basic university textbook on music used in the Middle Ages.

[4] *So ... tweye* So may I enjoy the use of my eyes, a common expression meaning little more than "indeed," but it is ill suited to express musical appreciation.

[5] *Daun ... Asse* Title of a twelfth-century Latin satire by Nigel Wireker about a foolish donkey, Master Brunellus, who becomes a wandering scholar. The episode described below concerns a young man who was about to be ordained and to receive a benefice. The cock, whom he had injured in his youth, took its revenge by not crowing, causing the man to oversleep and miss his opportunity for a benefice.

Among hise vers,° how that ther was a cok, — *verses*
For that° a preestes sone yaf° hym a knok — *because | gave*
Upon his leg whil he was yong and nyce,° — *silly*
550 He made hym for to lese his benefice.
But certeyn, ther nys no° comparisoun — *is no*
Bitwixe the wisedom and discrecioun
Of youre fader and of his subtiltee.° — *cleverness*
Now syngeth, sire, for Seinte Charitee!° — *Holy Charity*
555 Lat se, konne ye youre fader countrefete?"° — *imitate*
　　This Chauntecleer hise wynges gan to bete° — *beat*
As man that koude his traysoun° nat espie,° — *betrayal | perceive*
So was he ravysshed with his flaterie.
Allas, ye lordes, many a fals flatour° — *false flatterer*
560 Is in youre courtes,° and many a losengeour° — *courts | spy*
That plesen yow wel moore, by my feith,
Than he that soothfastnesse° unto yow seith. — *truth*
Redeth Ecclesiaste[1] of° flaterye. — *on*
Beth war,° ye lordes, of hir trecherye! — *beware*
565 　　This Chauntecleer stood hye upon his toos,
Strecchynge his nekke, and heeld his eyen cloos° — *closed*
And gan to crowe loude for the nones.° — *occasion*
And Daun Russell the fox stirte up atones° — *jumped up at once*
And by the gargat° hente° Chauntecleer — *throat | grabbed*
570 And on his bak toward the wode hym beer,
For yet° ne was ther no man that hym sewed.° — *as yet | pursued*
　　O Destinee, that mayst nat been eschewed!° — *avoided*
Allas, that Chauntecleer fleigh fro the bemes!
Allas, his wyf ne roghte nat° of dremes! — *paid no attention*
575 And on a Friday fil al this meschaunce!
　　O Venus, that art goddesse of plesaunce,[2]
Syn that thy servant was this Chauntecleer,
And in thy servyce dide al his poweer° — *all he could*
Moore for delit than world to
　　multiplye,° — *to increase the world (procreate)*
580 Why woldestow suffre° hym on thy day to
　　dye?[3] — *would you allow*

O Gaufred,[4] deere maister soverayn,° — *sovereign teacher*
That whan thy worthy kyng Richard was slayn
With shot,° compleynedest° his deeth so soore, — *arrow | lamented*
Why ne hadde I now thy sentence° and thy
　　loore° — *meaning | learning*
585 The Friday for to chide as diden ye?
For on a Friday soothly° slayn was he. — *truly*
Thanne wolde I shewe yow how that I koude pleyne
For Chauntecleres drede and for his peyne!
Certes swich cry ne lamentacioun
590 Was nevere of ladyes maad° whan Ylioun° — *made | Ilion (Troy)*
Was wonne,° and Pirrus° with his streite
　　swerd,° — *conquered | Pyrrhus | drawn sword*
Whan he hadde hent° Kyng Priam by the berd° — *seized | beard*
And slayn hym, as seith us *Eneydos*,° — *Aeneid*
As maden alle the hennes in the clos° — *yard*
595 Whan they had seyn of Chauntecleer the sighte.
But sodeynly Dame Pertelote shrighte° — *shrieked*
Ful louder than dide Hasdrubales wyf
Whan that hir housbonde hadde lost his lyf
And that the Romayns hadde brend° Cartage.[5] — *burned*
600 She was so ful of torment and of rage
That wilfully into the fyr she sterte
And brende hirselven with a stedefast herte.
　　O woful hennes, right so criden ye
As, whan that Nero[6] brende the citee
605 Of Rome, cryden senatours wyves,
For that hir housbondes losten alle hir lyves.
Withouten gilt this Nero hath hem slayn.
Now turne I wole to my tale agayn.
　　This sely° wydwe and eek hir doghtres two — *innocent*
610 Herden thise hennes crie and maken wo,
And out at dores stirten they anon
And syen the fox toward the grove gon

---

[1] *Ecclesiaste* Ecclesiasticus 12.16 warns against deceptive enemies but does not specifically mention flattery. The reference might be a mistake for Ecclesiastes or for Proverbs, other books of the Bible that were, like Ecclesiasticus, attributed to King Solomon.

[2] *O ... plesaunce* In classical mythology, Venus is the goddess of love.

[3] *Why ... dye* According to medieval astrology, each of the planets had special influence on a given day of the week. Venus, who gives her name to Friday (*Veneris dies*) in Romance languages, controlled that day.

[4] *Gaufred* I.e., Geoffrey of Vinsauf, whose treatise *Poetria Nova*, a basic manual on how to write rhetorically elaborate poetry, is alluded to by Chaucer in the following lines. King Richard is Richard I, the Lion-hearted, who in 1199 was wounded on a Friday while besieging a castle and later died of his wound.

[5] *Hasdrubales ... Cartage* I.e., Hasdrubal (245–207 BCE), Carthaginian general, who died in battle at the Metaurus River in central Italy when he met the army of Caius Claudius Nero. Carthage was destroyed by Scipio Africanus in 146 BCE.

[6] *Nero* Nero (r. 54–68 CE), Emperor of Rome, who had his city burned while he stood by, according to Suetonius, playing the bagpipes. In the previous tale the Monk narrates this tragedy.

And bar upon his bak the cok away,
And cryden, "Out! Harrow!" and "Weylaway!°   *alas*
615 Ha! Ha! The fox!" And after hym they ran,
And eek with staves° many another man;   *clubs*
Ran Colle oure dogge, and Talbot and Gerland,[1]
And Malkyn with a dystaf° in hir hand.   *spinning staff*
Ran cow and calf and the verray hogges,
620 So fered° for berkyng of the dogges   *afraid*
And shoutyng of the men and wommen eek.
They ronne so hem thoughte hir herte breek;[2]
They yolleden° as feendes° doon in Helle.   *yelled / fiends*
The dokes° cryden as men wolde hem quelle,°   *ducks / kill them*
625 The gees° for feere flowen° over the trees,   *geese / flew*
Out of the hyve° cam the swarm of bees.   *hive*
So hydous° was the noyse,° a,   *hideous / noise / ah, bless us*
     benedicitee,°
Certes he Jakke Straw and his meynee°   *gang*
Ne made nevere shoutes half so shrille,
630 Whan that they wolden any Flemyng kille,[3]
As thilke day was maad upon the fox.
Of bras they broghten bemes and of box,
Of horn, of boon, in whiche they blewe and powped,[4]
And therwithal° they skriked° and they   *with this / shrieked*
     howped.°   *whooped*
635 It semed as that Hevene sholde falle.
     Now, goode men, I prey yow, herkneth alle.
Lo how Fortune turneth sodeynly
The hope and pryde of hir enemy.
This cok that lay upon the foxes bak,
640 In al his drede unto the fox he spak
And seyde, "Sire, if that I were as ye,
Yet wolde I seyn, as wys° God helpe me,   *wise*
'Turneth agayn, ye proude cherles° alle!   *churls*
A verray pestilence upon yow falle!°   *fall upon you*
645 Now I am come unto the wodes syde.°   *border*

Maugree youre heed,° the cok shal heere
     abyde.   *despite your efforts*
I wol hym ete,° in feith, and that anon!'"   *eat*
     The fox answerde, "In feith, it shal be don!"
And as he spak that word al sodeynly,
650 This cok brak° from his mouth delyverly°   *broke / quickly*
And heighe upon a tree he fleigh anon.
And whan the fox saugh that he was gon,
     "Allas!" quod he. "O Chauntecleer, allas!
I have to yow," quod he, "ydoon trespas,°   *done an insult*
655 In as muche as I maked yow aferd
Whan I yow hente° and broghte into this yerd.[5]   *seized*
But sire, I dide it of no wikke° entente.   *wicked*
Com doun, and I shal telle yow what I mente.
I shal seye sooth° to yow, God help me so!"   *tell the truth*
660   "Nay, thanne," quod he, "I shrewe° us bothe two! *curse*
And first I shrewe myself, bothe blood and bones,
If thou bigyle° me any ofter° than ones!°   *trick / more often / once*
Thou shalt namoore thurgh thy flaterye
Do me to synge and wynke with myn eye!
665 For he that wynketh whan he sholde see
Al wilfully,° God lat hym nevere thee!"°   *voluntarily / thrive*
     "Nay," quod the fox, "but God yeve° hym
        meschaunce°   *give / misfortune*
That is so undiscreet° of governaunce°   *indiscreet / behavior*
That jangleth° whan he sholde holde his pees!"°   *chatters / peace*
670   Lo, swich it is for to be recchelees°   *reckless*
And necligent° and truste on flaterye!   *negligent*
     But ye that holden° this tale a folye°   *consider / folly*
As of a fox or of a cok and hen,
Taketh the moralite,° goode men.   *moral*
675 For Seint Paul seith that al that writen is,
To oure doctrine° it is ywrite, ywis.[6]   *for our teaching*
Taketh the fruyt,° and lat the chaf be
     stille.°   *fruit / let the chaff alone*

---

1 *Colle … Talbot and Gerland* Names for dogs.

2 *They … breek* They ran so (fast) that they thought their hearts
would burst.

3 *Certes … kille* Jack Straw was the name of one of the leaders of
the Uprising of 1381; about thirty or forty Flemish merchants and
weavers were murdered in London during this period of violence and
rioting. This is one of the few contemporary events Chaucer
mentions directly in his writings.

4 *Of bras … powped* They brought trumpets (bemes) made of brass and
boxwood and of horn and of bone, on which they blew and puffed.

5 *into this yerd* This seems an obvious slip that should instead read
"out of this yerd," as this line does in some manuscripts. Derek
Pearsall, however, in the Variorum edition, defends "into" by
suggesting that the fox is still trying to deceive Chauntecleer and so
refers to the place they have come to as "this yerd" as if it were the
kind of safe enclosure the rooster were used to.

6 *For Seint … ywis* Cf. Romans 15.4. Chaucer cites the same line
in his "Retraction" and it is also paraphrased at the beginning of the
medieval translation and allegorical interpretation of Ovid's
Metamorphoses, the *Ovide Moralisé*.

Now, goode God, if that it be thy wille,
As seith my lord,[1] so make us alle goode men,
680 And brynge us to his heighe blisse. Amen!

HEERE IS ENDED THE NONNES PREESTES TALE

THE NUN'S PRIEST'S EPILOGUE[2]

"Sire Nonnes Preest," oure Hoost seide anoon,
"Iblissed° be thy breche° and every
      stoon!°   *blessed | buttocks | testicles*
This was a murie tale of Chauntecleer.
But by my trouthe, if thou were seculer°   *a lay man*

685 Thow woldest be a tredefoul[3] aright.
For if thou have corage° as thou hast myght,°   *spirit | power*
The were nede° of hennes, as I
      wene,°   *you would have need of | think*
Ya, moo° than sevene tymes seventeen!   *more*
Se which braunes° hath this gentil° preest,   *what muscle | fine*
690 So gret a nekke and swich a large breest.°   *chest*
He loketh as a sperhauke° with hise eyen.   *sparrowhawk*
Him nedeth nat his colour° for to dyghen°   *complexion | dye*
With brasile ne with greyn of Portingale.[4]
Now sire, faire falle yow° for your tale."   *may good befall you*
695 And after that he with ful murie chere
Seide unto another as ye shuln here.

Chaucer's *Retraction*

The *Retraction* is found in all complete manuscripts of *The Canterbury Tales*, including the Ellesmere. In it Chaucer revokes most of his poems, including his early elegy *The Book of the Duchess*; his dream vision *The House of Fame*, which deals with worldly reputation; his great love poem *Troilus and Criseyde; The Legend of Good Women*, in which Chaucer compensates for telling the story of Criseyde's betrayal by telling of numerous good women; and those of *The Canterbury Tales* "that sownen into synne" (that tend to promote sin). Chaucer takes credit only for his translation of Boethius and for works of obvious moral or devotional content. Many critics, troubled by Chaucer's disavowal of so many of his poems as "worldly vanitees," have seen ironies in the *Retraction*. It effectively provides a list of his life's work, it does not name which of *The Canterbury Tales* it is revoking, and it is found in manuscripts that contain all the tales, including the ones that would seem to "sownen into synne." As a confession of Chaucer's sins, however, the *Retraction* follows logically from *The Parson's Tale*, which is not a tale at all but a penitential treatise, calling for full confession and repentance. As a penitent should, Chaucer lists all his works that may be sinful, even those he cannot remember writing. The connection to *The Parson's Tale* may also explain the opening line, with its reference to those who read or hear this "lityl treatise," a description that can only rather awkwardly fit the entire *Canterbury Tales*. By this point, the tale-telling pilgrims have faded from the scene. If we accept the retraction as a sincere act of personal atonement, however, the crucial question becomes how far this act should affect our understanding of *The Canterbury Tales* as a whole.

---

[1] *my lord*   The Nun's Priest might be referring to the Archbishop of Canterbury, Christ, or, since he is attached to the nunnery at Stratford-at-Bow near London, his immediate ecclesiastical superior, the Bishop of London.

[2] *The ... Epilogue*   This epilogue is found in nine manuscripts but not in either Ellesmere or Hengwrt. It seems most likely that the epilogue is part of an earlier draft that Chaucer later abandoned, incorporating some of the lines into the Host's words to the Monk.

---

[3] *tredefoul*   Copulator with chickens, a rooster.

[4] *brasile ... Portingale*   Imported red dyes.

CHAUCER'S RETRACTION

HEERE TAKETH THE MAKERE OF THIS BOOK HIS LEVE

Now preye° I to hem alle° that herkne° this litel tretys° or rede,° that if ther be anythyng in it that liketh hem,° that therof° they thanken oure Lord Jhesu Crist, of whom procedeth al wit and al goodnesse. And if ther be anythyng that displese hem,° I preye° hem also that they arrette° it to the defaute° of myn unkonnynge° and nat to my wyl,° that wolde° ful fayn° have seyd bettre, if I hadde had konnynge.° For oure book seith, "Al that is writen is writen for oure doctrine."[1] And that is myn entente.° Wherfore I biseke° yow mekely° for the mercy of God that ye preye for me, that Crist have mercy on me and foryeve° me my giltes,° and namely° of my translacions and enditynges° of worldly vanitees,° the whiche I revoke in my retracciouns—as is *The Book of Troilus*, *The Book* also *of Fame*, *The Book of the Five and Twenty Ladies*, *The Book of the Duchesse*, *The Book of Seint Valentynes Day of the Parlement of Briddes*,° *The Tales of Caunterbury* (thilke° that sownen into synne°), *The Book of the Leoun*,[2] and many another book (if they were in my remembrance) and many a song and many a leccherous° lay—that Crist for his grete° mercy foryeve me the synne.

But of the translacioun of Boece, *De Consolacioun*[3] and othere bookes of legendes° of seintes and omelies° and moralitee and devocioun, that thanke I oure Lord Jhesu Crist and his blisful mooder° and alle the seintes of Hevene, bisekynge hem° that they from hennes° forth unto my lyves° ende sende me grace to biwayle° my giltes and to studie° to the salvacioun of my soule and graunte me grace of verray° penitence, confessioun, and satisfaccioun to doon° in this present lyf thurgh the benigne grace of hym that is Kyng of kynges and Preest over alle preestes, that boghte° us with the precious blood of his herte,° so that I may been oon° of hem at the Day of Doome° that shulle° be saved. *Qui cum patre, etc.*[4]

HEERE IS ENDED THE BOOK OF THE TALES OF CAUNTERBURY COMPILED BY GEFFREY CHAUCER, OF WHOS SOULE JHESU CRIST HAVE MERCY, AMEN.

pray / them all / listen to / treatise/ read [it]
pleases them / for it

them / ask / ascribe / default
my ignorance / will / would / very gladly
knowledge
my intent / ask / meekly
forgive / sins
especially / writings/ acts of folly

Parliament of Fowles / those
tend towards sin
lecherous
great

moral stories / homilies
mother
asking them / hence / life's / lament
take thought
true / do

redeemed / heart / one
Judgment Day / shall

---

[1] *Al ... doctrine* From 2 Timothy 3.16; *doctrine* Instruction.

[2] *The ... Leoun* This text, probably a translation of the *Dit de Leon* by the French court poet Guillaume de Machaut (c. 1300 –77), one of Chaucer's major early influences, does not survive.

[3] *De Consolacioun* This is *The Consolation of Philosophy*, the famous treatise of the late Roman scholar and statesman Boethius.

[4] *Qui ... etc.* The full liturgical phrase is *Qui cum Patre et spiritu sancto vivit et regnat Deus per omnia secula, Amen.* Latin: Who with the Father and the Holy Spirit lives and reigns, God forever and ever, Amen.

Julian of Norwich
c. 1342 – c. 1416

We know very little of Julian of Norwich, one of the great medieval English mystics. It is possible that she was trained as Benedictine nun, and some have speculated that she may have received some form of education at Carrow Priory, the school attached to the Cathedral in Norwich. Her lineage, name, and even the date of her death are unknown. Given what we do know of her, though, it seems likely that she would want her readers to focus on her meditations—her "shewings" and what they revealed about the nature of God—rather than her own life.

Our knowledge of Julian of Norwich's life and mystical experiences is derived from the records she allowed others to keep. At the age of 30 years, on 8 May 1373, Julian of Norwich lay critically ill, her mother at her side. Her curate, called to administer the last rites, held a crucifix aloft at the foot of her bed. With her sight beginning to fail, she felt a creeping numbness spread from her toes to her waist. As her field of vision narrowed and she fixed her eyes on the crucifix near her bed, Julian reports that she suddenly saw the figure of Jesus begin to bleed from his forehead in drops that reminded her of rain falling from the eaves of a house. For several hours, while those around her presumed she was near death, Julian continued to experience what she termed a "bodely sight"—a total of sixteen visions. Soon after her recovery, Julian wrote a short narrative of her visions (the Short Text), and 20 years later, a longer and more theologically complex version (the Long Text) that incorporated the fruits of her years of intense and studied meditation on her sixteen original showings.

At some point after her miraculous recovery, Julian became an anchoress at St. Julian's church in Norwich, a bustling and thriving town in the north of England. Being an anchoress required taking a vow of seclusion, which would have meant that she lived the majority of her years in a small room within the sides of the church. This would probably have afforded her a certain autonomy; anchorites and anchoresses did not answer to any ecclesiastical authority other than the bishop. The ritual for enclosure included a Mass with prayers for the dead; as an anchoress Julian was, in effect, choosing to "die" to the world so that she could devote herself to prayer and meditation. Most anchoritic strongholds were small, perhaps no more than 12 or 15 feet square, with three windows. Through hers, Julian could view the altar and the Sacrament and hear Mass. She would have spoken to her confessor or counseled those, like Margery Kempe, who came to talk to her through this window. Another small window would have allowed access to those who saw to her physical needs, and a third, quite possibly facing the street but covered with a translucent cloth, would have allowed in light.

Although there is evidence that Julian, in her role as an anchoress, served her community for many years as a spiritual director and may have enjoyed at least a modicum of public attention, her written works did not garner much interest outside of ecclesiastical circles for over two centuries; in fact, the first time her writings are mentioned at length after her death is in the 1650s, during the Puritan Revolution. The anti-Catholic and anti-mystical temper of the political times led those who were sympathetic to her theological views to transfer their copies of her *Revelations* to several monastic houses in France, where, for all intents and purposes, her writings remained buried until the 1800s. Early in the twentieth century the scholar Evelyn Underhill revived interest in Julian's writings, which began to be read again by lay, clerical, and academic readers. Over the last few decades, partly as the result of a growing interest in works by women, Julian's writings have become the focus of considerable critical attention. Along with her contemporaries Richard Rolle, Walter Hilton, and the anonymous author of the *Cloud of Unknowing*, Julian is now regarded as one of the great fourteenth-century English mystics.

Her writing is known for its innovative and sometimes startling theology: perhaps most strikingly, she says God is Mother as well as Father. Her meditations on her visions over the years persuaded her that God is not a vindictive God, prone to punish or rebuke, although she emphasized that she adhered to Church doctrine about sin and damnation, as about all other matters; for a woman writing in her time, it was essential to avoid the charge of heresy. Julian found herself unable to embrace the idea of eternal damnation, however, and perceived a God who saw His people through the eyes of love and through grace brought by Christ's death and resurrection. The strength of her unique vision, together with her ability to tap the deep potential for image and metaphor afforded by the Middle English of her time, make her texts a fascinating study of the intersection between affective piety and the flowering of the English language.

⌘⌘⌘

from *A Revelation of Love*[1]

CHAPTER 1—A PARTICULAR OF THE CHAPTERS

The First chapter—of the number of the revelations particularly.

This is a revelation of love that Jesus Christ, our endless bliss, made in sixteen showings or revelations particular; of the which the first is of His precious crowning with thorns; and therein was contained and specified the Trinity with the incarnation and unity betwixt God and man's soul, with many fair showings of endless wisdom and teaching of love, in which all the showings that follow be grounded and joined.

The second is the discolouring of His fair face in tokening of his dear-worthy[2] passion.

The third is that our Lord God almighty, all wisdom and all love, right as verily[3] as He hath made every thing that is, also verily He doth and worketh all thing that is done.

The fourth is the scourging[4] of His tender body with plenteous shedding of His blood.

The fifth is that the fiend[5] is overcome by the precious passion of Christ.

The sixth is the worshipful thanking of our Lord God in which He rewardeth his blessed servants in heaven.

The seventh is often times feeling of wele[6] and woe—the feeling of wele is gracious touching and lightening, with true sikerness[7] of endless joy; the feeling of woe is temptation by heaviness and irkehede[8] of our fleshly living—with ghostly understanding that we are kept also sekirly[9] in love, in woe as in wele, by the goodness of God.

The eighth is the last pains of Christ and His cruel dying.

The ninth is of the liking which is in the blissful Trinity of the hard passion of Christ after his rueful dying; in which joy and liking he will that we be solaced and mirth with him till when we come to the fullness in[10] heaven.

The tenth is our Lord Jesus showeth in love his blissful heart even cloven in two enjoined.

The eleventh is a high ghostly showing of his dear-worthy mother.

The twelfth is that our Lord is the most worthy being.

---

[1] *A Revelation of Love*   For the present text the edition of Marion Glasscoe has been used as a copy text. Spelling and punctuation have been substantially modernized for this anthology.

[2] *tokening* Signifying; *dear-worthy* Precious.

[3] *right as verily* Just as truly.

[4] *scourging* Whipping, beating.

[5] *the fiend* Satan.

[6] *wele* Well being.

[7] *sikerness* Certainty.

[8] *irkehede* Distastefulness.

[9] *sekirly* Certainly.

[10] *in* Of.

The thirteenth is that our Lord God will we[1] have great regard to all the deeds that he hath done in the great nobility of all things making, and of the excellence of man making, which is above all his works, and of the precious amends that he hath made for man's sin, turning all our blame into endless worship; where also our Lord saith: Behold and see; for by the same mighty wisdom and goodness I shall make wele all that is not wele and thou[2] shalt see it. And in this he will we keep us in the faith and truth of Holy Church, not willing to wit his privities[3] now, but as it longeth to us in this life.

The fourteenth is that our Lord is ground of our beseeching.[4] Herein were seen two fair properties: that one is rightful prayer, that other is sekir trust, which he will both be alike large; and thus our prayers liketh him and he of his goodness fullfilleth it.

The fifteenth, that we shall suddenly be taken from all our pain and from all our woe and of his goodness we shall come up above where we shall have our Lord Jesus to our mede[5] and be fulfilled of joy and bliss in Heaven.

The sixteenth is that the blissful Trinity our Maker, in Christ Jesus our Saviour, endlessly dwells in our soul, worshipfully ruling and giving all things, us mightily and wisely saving and keeping for love, and we shall not be overcome of[6] our enemy.

CHAPTER 2

The Second chapter—of the time of these revelations, and how she asked three petitions.

These revelations were showed to a simple creature that could no letter,[7] the year of our Lord 1373, the 8th day of May; which creature desired afore three gifts of God: the first was mind[8] of the passion, the second was bodily sickness in youth at thirty years of age, the third was to have of God's gift

three wounds. As in the first, methought I had some feeling in the passion of Christ but yet I desired more by the grace of God. Methought I would have been that time with Mary Magdalene and with other that were Christ's lovers,[9] and therefore I desired a bodily sight wherein I might have more knowledge of the bodily pains of our Saviour, and of the compassion of Our Lady and of all his true lovers that seen that time his pains, for I would be one of them and suffer with Him.[10] Other sight nor showing of God desired I never none[11] till the soul was departed from the body. The cause of this petition was that after the showing I should have the more true mind in the passion of Christ. The second came to my mind with contrition, freely desiring that sickness so hard as to death that I might, in that sickness, undertaken all my rites[12] of Holy Church, myself wening[13] that I should die, and that all creatures might suppose the same that saw me; for I would have no manner comfort of earthly life. In this sickness I desired to have all manner pains bodily and ghostly that I should have if I should die, with all the dreads and tempests of the fiend, except the outpassing of the soul. And this I meant for I would be purged by the mercy of God and after live more to the worship of God because of that sickness; and that for the more speed in my death, for I desired to be soon with my God. These two desires of the passion and the sickness I desired with a condition, saying thus: Lord, thou woteth[14] what I would—if it be Thy will that I have it; and if it be not Thy will, good Lord, be not displeased, for I will nought but as Thou wilt. For the third, by the grace of God and teaching of Holy Church, I conceived a mighty desire to receive three wounds in my life: that is to say the wound of very[15] contrition, the wound of kind compassion and the wound of wilful longing to God. And all this last petition I asked without any condition. These two desires foresaid passed from my mind, and the third dwelled with me continually.

---

[1] *will we* Wishes that we.

[2] *thou* In the Middle Ages, "thou" was the term of familiar address, and "you" was the term of formal address.

[3] *wit* Know; *privities* Private secrets.

[4] *beseeching* Prayers.

[5] *mede* Reward.

[6] *of* By.

[7] *could no letter* Could not read.

[8] *mind* Remembrance, recollection.

[9] *Christ's lovers* Those who loved Christ.

[10] *one of them* See John 19.25.

[11] *desired I never none* I never desired any. Middle English often uses a double negative.

[12] *rites* The Last Rites given to the dying.

[13] *wening* Thinking.

[14] *woteth* Know.

[15] *very* True.

CHAPTER 3

Of the sickness she obtained of God by petition—Third chapter.

And when I was thirty years old and half God sent me a bodily sickness in which I lay three days and three nights; and on the fourth night I took all my rites of Holy Church and wened not to have lived till day. And after this I lay for two days and two nights. And on the third night I wened often-times to have passed, and so wened they that were with me. And yet, I thought great sweeme[1] to die; but for nothing that was in earth that me liked to live for, for no pain that I was afraid of, for I trusted in God of his mercy; but it was to have lived that I might have loved God better and longer time, that I might have the more knowing and loving of God in bliss of heaven. For methought all the time that I had lived here, so little and so short in reward of that endless bliss, I thought nothing. Wherefore I thought: Good Lord, may my living no longer be to Thy worship! And I understood by my reason and by my feeling of my pains that I should die. And I assented fully with all, with all the will of my heart, to be at God's will.

Thus I dured[2] till day, and by then my body was dead from the middle downwards as to my feeling. Then was I stered[3] to be set upright, underset[4] with help, for to have more freedom of my heart to be at God's will, and thinking on God while my life would last. My curate[5] was sent for to be at my ending, and before he came I had set my eyen[6] and might not speak. He set the cross before my face and said: I have brought thee the image of thy Maker and Saviour. Look thereupon and comfort thee therewith. Methought I was well, for my eyen were set uprightward into heaven where I trusted to come by the mercy of God. But nevertheless I assented to set my eyen in the face of the crucifix if I might, and so I did, for methought I might longer endure to look even forth[7] than right up. After this my sight began to fail and it was all dark about me in the chamber as it had be night,

save in the image of the cross wherein I beheld a common light, and I wist[8] not how. All that was beside the cross was ugly to me as if it had been much occupied with the fiends.

After this the other part of my body[9] began to die so far forth that scarcely I had any feeling, with shortness of wind.[10] And then I went soothly to have passed.[11] And, in this, suddenly all my pain was taken from me and I was as whole, and namely in the other part of my body, as ever I was before. I marvelled at this sudden change for methought it was a privy working of God and not of kind.[12] And yet by the feeling of this ease I trusted never the more to live; nor the feeling of this ease was no full ease to me, for methought I had lever[13] to be delivered of this world.

Then came suddenly to my mind that I should desire the second wound, of Our Lord's gracious gift, that my body might be fulfilled with mind and feeling of his blessed passion; for I would that his pains were my pains with compassion, and afterward longing to God. But in this I desired never bodily sight nor showing of God, but compassion, as a kind soul might have with our Lord Jesus, that for love would become a deadly[14] man; and therefore I desired to suffer with Him. . . .

CHAPTER 5

How God is to us everything that is good, tenderly wrapping us; and all thing that is made, in regard to Almighty God, it is nothing; and how man hath no rest till he knoweth himself and all thing for the love of God—the Fifth chapter.

In this same time Our Lord showed to me a ghostly sight of his homely[15] loving. I saw that he is to us everything that is good and comfortable for us. He is our clothing that for love wrappeth us, halseth[16] us and all becloseth us for tender love,

---

[1] *sweeme* Regret, grief.

[2] *dured* Endured.

[3] *stered* Moved.

[4] *underset* Supported.

[5] *curate* Priest.

[6] *set my eyen* Fixed my eyes.

[7] *even forth* Parallel to the ground.

[8] *wist* Know.

[9] *other part … body* The upper part of her body.

[10] *wind* Breath.

[11] *went … passed* Truly believed I would die.

[12] *kind* Nature.

[13] *lever* Rather.

[14] *deadly* Mortal.

[15] *homely* Familiar.

[16] *halseth* Embraces.

that he may never leave us, being to us all things that are good, as to mine understanding. Also in this he showed a little thing, the quantity of a hazelnut in the palm of my hand; and it was as round as a ball. I looked thereupon with eye of my understanding and thought: What may this be? And it was generally answered thus: It is all that is made. I marvelled how it might last, for methought it might suddenly have fallen to nought for little. And I was answered in my understanding: It lasteth and ever shall, for God loveth it; and so all things hath their being by the love of God.

In this little thing I saw three properties: the first is that God made it, the second is that God loveth it, the third, that God keepeth it. But what is to me soothly the maker, the keeper, and the lover I cannot tell; for, till I am substantially united to him, I may never have full rest nor very bliss; that is to say, that I be so fastened to him that there be right nought that is made betwixt my God and me.

It needeth us[1] to have knowing of the littleness of creatures and to nought[2] all thing that is made for to love and have God that is unmade. For this is the cause why we be not all in ease of heart and soul: for we seek here rest in these things that is so little, wherein is no rest, and know not Our God that is almighty, all wise, all good; for he is the very rest. God will be known, and Him liketh that we rest in Him; for all that is beneath Him sufficeth not us; and this is the cause why that no soul is rested till it is noughted[3] of all things that is made. When he is wilfully noughted, for love to have Him that is all, then is he able to receive ghostly rest.

Also our Lord God showed that it is full great pleasance to Him that a silly[4] soul come to Him nakedly and plainly and homely. For this is the kind[5] yearning of the soul by the touching of the Holy Ghost, as by the understanding that I have in this showing: God, of Thy goodness, give me Thyself; for Thou art enough to me and I may nothing ask that is less that may be full worship to Thee. And if I ask anything that is less, ever me wanteth, but only in Thee I have all.

And these words are full lovesome to the soul and full near touch the will of God and His goodness; for His goodness comprehendeth all his creatures and all His blessed works, and overpasseth without end, for He is the endlessness. And He hath made us only to Himself and restored us by His blessed passion and keepeth us in His blessed love. And all this is of His goodness. ...

CHAPTER 7

How Our Lady, beholding the greatness of her Maker, thought herself least, and of the great drops of blood running from under the garland, and how the most joy to man is that God most high and mighty is holiest and most courteous[6]—Seventh chapter.

And to learn[7] us this, as to mine understanding, our Lord God showed Our Lady Saint Mary in the same time; that is to mean the high wisdom and truth she had in beholding of her Maker so great, so high, so mighty and so good. This greatness and this nobility of the beholding of God fulfilled her of reverend dread, and with this she saw herself so little and so low, so simple and so poor, in reward of[8] her Lord God, that this reverend dread fulfilled her of meekness. And thus, by this ground, she was fulfilled of grace and of all manner of virtues and overpasseth all creatures.

In all the time that he showed this that I have said now in ghostly sight, I saw the bodily sight lasting of the plenteous bleeding of the head. The great drops of blood fell down from under the garland like pellets seeming as it had come out of the veins; and in the coming out it were brown red, for the blood was full thick; and in the spreading abroad it were bright red; and when it come to the brows, then it vanished; notwithstanding the bleeding continued till many things were seen and understood. The fairness and the liveliness is like nothing but the same.

The plenteousness is like to the drops of water that fall on the eaves after a great shower of rain that fall so thick that no man may number them with bodily wit. And for the roundness, it were like to the scale of herring in the spreading on the forehead.[9]

---

[1] *It needeth us*   It is necessary for us, we must.

[2] *nought*   Despise.

[3] *noughted*   Freed.

[4] *silly*   Simple.

[5] *kind*   Natural.

[6] *most courteous*   The word "courtesy" had more connotations in the medieval period than it does today: it was suggestive of chivalry, goodness, moral virtue, and divine grace.

[7] *learn*   Teach.

[8] *in reward of*   By comparison to.

[9] *in the spreading... forehead*   As they spread over the forehead.

These three come to my mind in the time: pellets, for roundness, in the coming out of the blood; the scale of herring, in the spreading in the forehead, for roundness; the drops of eaves, for the plenteousness innumerable. This showing was quick and lively, and hideous and dreadful, sweet and lovely. And of all the sight it was most comfort to me that our God and Lord, that is so reverent and dreadful, is so homely and courteous. And this most fulfilled me with liking and sikerness of soul.

And to the understanding of this he showed this open example: it is the most worship that a solemn king or a great lord may do a poor servant if he will be homely with him, and namely if he shows it himself, of a full true meaning and with a glad cheer, both privately and openly. Then thinketh this poor creature thus: Ah! What might this noble lord do more worship and joy to show me, that am so simple, this marvellous homeliness? Soothly it is more joy and liking to me than he gave me great gifts and were himself strange[1] in manner. This bodily example was showed so high that man's heart might be ravished and almost forget himself for joy of this great homeliness.

Thus it fares by our Lord Jesus and by us; for soothly it is the most joy that may be, as to my sight, that He that is highest and mightiest, noblest and worthiest, is lowest and meekest, homeliest and most courteous. And truly and soothly this marvellous joy shall be shown us all when we see Him; and this will our Lord, that we believe and trust, joy and like, comfort us and solace us, as we may, with His grace and with His help, into the time that we see it verily;[2] for the most fullness of joy that we shall have, as to my sight, is the marvellous courtesy and homeliness of our Father that is our Maker, in our Lord Jesus Christ that is our brother and our Saviour. But this marvellous homeliness may no man wit in this time of life, but[3] he have it of special showing of our Lord, or of great plenty of grace inwardly given of the Holy Ghost. But faith and belief with[4] charity deserves the mede, and so it is had by grace; for in faith with hope and charity our life is grounded. The showing, made to whom that God will, plainly teaches the same, opened and declared with many privy points longing to our faith which be worshipful

to known. And when the showing, which is given in a time, is passed and hid, then the faith keeps it by grace of the Holy Ghost unto our life's end. And thus by the showing it is not other than the faith, not less nor more, as it may be seen by Our Lord's meaning in the same matter by then[5] it come to the end. . . .

Chapter 11

The third revelation etc., how God doth all things except sin, never changing his purpose without end, for he hath made all things in fullness of goodness—Eleventh chapter.

And after this I saw God in a point, that is to say, in mine understanding, by which sight I saw that He is in all things. I beheld with advisement,[6] seeing and knowing in sight with a soft dread, and thought: What is sin? for I saw truly that God doth all things be it never so little. And I saw truly that nothing is done by hap[7] nor by adventure, but all things be the foreseeing wisdom of God. If it be hap or adventure in the sight of man, our blindness and our unforesight[8] is the cause, for the things that are in the foreseeing wisdom of God been from without beginning, which rightfully and worshipfully and continually He leads to the best end as they come about, falling to us suddenly, ourselves unwitting;[9] and thus, by our blindness and our unforesight, we say these been haps and adventures; but to Our Lord God they be not so.

Wherefore me behooveth needs to grant[10] that all things that are done, are well done, for our Lord God doth all; for in this time the working of creatures was not showed, but of Our Lord God in the creature; for He is in the mid point of all things and all He doth, and I was sekir He does no sin. And here I saw soothly that sin is no deed,[11] for in all this was not sin showed. And I would no longer marvel in this, but beheld Our Lord, what He would show. And thus, as it might be for the time, the rightfulness of God's working was showed to the soul. Rightfulness has two fair properties: it is

---

[1] *strange* Distant.
[2] *verily* Truly.
[3] *but* Unless.
[4] *with* In.
[5] *by then* By the time.
[6] *beheld with advisement* Viewed the vision contemplatively.
[7] *hap* Chance.
[8] *unforesight* Lack of foresight.
[9] *unwitting* Unknowing.
[10] *wherefore me behooveth … grant* Thus I was compelled to admit.
[11] *no deed* Nothing.

right and it is full. And so are all the works of Our Lord God; and thereto needs neither the working of mercy nor grace, for it been all rightful, wherein fails not. And in another time He showed for the beholding of sin nakedly, as I shall say, where He uses working of mercy and grace.

And this vision was showed to mine understanding, for Our Lord will have the soul turned truly into the beholding of Him, and generally of all His works; for they are full good and all His doings be easy and sweet, and to great ease[1] bringing the soul that is turned from the beholding of the blind deeming[2] of man onto the faire sweet deeming of our Lord God; for a man beholds some deeds well done and some deeds evil, but Our Lord beholds them not so; for as all that has been in kind is of God's making, so are all things that are done in property of God's doing; for it is easy to understand that the best deed is well done; and so well as the best deed is done and the highest, so well is the least deed done; and all in property and in the order that Our Lord hath it ordained to from without beginning, for there is no doer but He.

I saw full sekirly that He changes never His purpose in no manner thing, nor never shall, without end; for there was nothing unknown to Him in His rightful ordinance from without beginning, and therefore all things was set in order, or[3] anything was made, as it should stand without end; and no manner thing shall fail of that point; for He made all things in fullness of goodness; and therefore the Blessed Trinity is ever full pleased in all His works. And all this showed he full blissfully, meaning thus: See I am God. See I am in all things. See I do all things. See I left never mine hands of mine works, nor never shall, without end. See I lead all things to the end I ordained it to from without beginning by the same might, wisdom and love that I made it. How should anything be amiss? Thus mightily, wisely and lovingly was the soul examined in this vision. Than saw I soothly that me behooved needs to assent[4] with great reverence, enjoying in God. . . .

---

[1] *ease* Rest.

[2] *deeming* Judgment.

[3] *or* Before.

[4] *me behooved … assent* I was compelled to agree.

CHAPTER 27—THE THIRTEENTH REVELATION

The thirteenth revelation is that Our Lord God will that we have great regard to all His deeds that He have[5] done in the great nobleness of all of all things making and of etc., how sin is not known by the pain—Twenty-Seventh chapter.

After this the Lord brought to my mind the longing that I had to Him before; and I saw that nothing letted[6] me but sin, and so I beheld generally in us all. And methought if sin had not been, we should all have been clean and like to our Lord as He made us; and thus, in my folly, before this time often I wondered why by the great foreseeing wisdom of God the beginning of sin[7] was not letted; for then, thought I, should have been well.

This stering[8] was mikel[9] to be forsaken, and nevertheless mourning and sorrow I made therefore without reason and discretion. But Jesus, that in this vision informed me of all that me needeth, answered by this word and said: Sin is behovely,[10] but all shall be well, and all shall be well, and all manner of thing shall be well. In this naked word sin our Lord brought to my mind generally all that is not good, and the shameful despite and the utter noughting[11] that He bare for us in this life, and His dying, and all His pains, and passions of all His creatures, ghostly and bodily—for we be all in part noughted,[12] and we shall be noughted following our master Jesus till we be full purged: that is to say, till we be fully purged of our deadly flesh and of all our inward affections which are not very good[13]—and the beholding of this, with all the pains that ever were or ever shall be. And with all these I understood the passion of Christ for most pain and over passing. And all this was showed in a touch and readily passed over into comfort. For our good Lord would not that the soul were afeared of this ugly sight.

---

[5] *have* Has. Medieval verb forms have been maintained wherever the sense seems clear.

[6] *letted* Hindered.

[7] *beginning of sin* See Romans 5.13.

[8] *stering* Impulse.

[9] *mikel* Much.

[10] *behovely* Necessary. See Matthew 18.7.

[11] *noughting* Belittling, disparagement.

[12] *noughted* Freed.

[13] *not very good* See Romans 6.12.

But I saw not sin; for I believe it hath no manner of substance nor party of[1] being, nor it might not be known but by the pain that it is cause of; and thus pain, it is something, as to my sight,[2] for a time, for it purgeth and maketh us to know ourselves and ask mercy; for the passion of Our Lord is comfort to us against all this, and so is His blessed will. And for the tender love that our good Lord hath to all that shall be saved He comforteth readily and sweetly, meaning thus: It is sooth that sin is cause of all this pain, but all shall be well, and all shall be well, and all manner thing shall be well.

These words were showed full tenderly, showing no manner of blame to me,[3] nor to none that shall be safe. Than were it a great unkindness to blame or wonder on God for my sin, sith[4] He blameth not me for sin.

And in these same words I saw a marvellous high privity[5] hid in God, which privity He shall openly make known to us in heaven; in which knowing we shall verily see the cause why He suffered sin to come; in which sight we shall endlessly joy in our Lord God.

CHAPTER 28

How the children of salvation shall be shaken in sorrows, but Christ enjoyeth with compassion; and a remedy against tribulation—Twenty-Eighth chapter.

Thus I saw how Christ hath compassion on us for the cause of sin. And right as I was before in the passion of Christ fulfilled with pain and compassion, so in this I was fulfilled a party with compassion of all my even[6] Christians; for that well, well beloved people that shall be saved: that is to say, God's servants, Holy Church, shall be shaken in sorrows and anguish and tribulation in this world as men shake a cloth in the wind. And as to this Our Lord answered in this manner:

A great thing shall I make hereof in heaven, of endless worships and everlasting joy. Yea, so far forth I saw that Our Lord enjoyeth of the tribulations of His servants with pity and compassion; to each person that He loveth to His bliss for to bring, He leaveth upon Him something that is no lack in His sight, whereby they are lowed[7] and despised in this world, scorned, and so outcast. And this He doth for to let[8] the harm that they should take of the pomp and the vainglory of this wretched life, and make their way ready to come to heaven in His bliss without end lasting; for He saith: I shall all[9] to—break you for your vain affections and your vicious pride; and after that I shall together gather you and make you mild and meek, clean and holy, by joining to me.[10]

And then I saw that each kind compassion that man hath on[11] His even Christian with charity, it is Christ in him. That same noughting that was showed in His passion, it was showed again here in this compassion wherein were two manner of understandings in Our Lord's meaning:[12] the one was the bliss that we are bought to, wherein He wills that we enjoy. That other is for comfort in our pain; for He will that we wit[13] that it shall all be turned to worship and profit by virtue of His passion, and that we wit that we suffer not alone but with Him, and see Him our ground, and that we see His pains and His noughting pass so for all that we may suffer, that it may not be full thought. And the beholding of this will save us from grouching and despair in the feeling of our pains; and if we see soothly that our sin deserveth it, yet His love excuseth us, and of His great courtesy He does away all our blame, and He holdeth us with ruth[14] and pity, as children innocent and unlothful.[15] ...

---

[1] *party of* Share in.

[2] *as to my sight* As far as I can see.

[3] *blame to me* See John 8.10–11.

[4] *sith* Since.

[5] *privity* Mystery.

[6] *even* Fellow. See I Peter 3.8.

[7] *lowed* Humbled.

[8] *let* Prevent.

[9] *I shall all* I shall do all.

[10] *I shall together ... me* See Matthew 23.37, 11.28–29, Ephesians 5.25–26.

[11] *on* For.

[12] *nothing that was ... meaning* Christ's love of humanity made Him see all the pains of the Passion as nothing, and such stoicism is achieved through two means.

[13] *wit* Know.

[14] *ruth* Compassion.

[15] *unlothful* Innocent.

CHAPTER 50

How the chosen soul was never dead in the sight of God, and of a marvel upon the same; and three things bolded her to ask of God the understanding of it— Fiftieth chapter.

And in this deadly life mercy and forgiveness is our way and evermore leadeth us to grace.[1] And by the tempest and the sorrow that we fall in on our part, we be often dead as to man's doom in earth, but in the sight of God the soul that shall be saved was never dead nor never shall. But yet here I wondered and marvelled with all the diligence of my soul, meaning[2] thus: Good Lord, I see Thee that Thou art very truth, and I know soothly that we sin grievously all day and be much blameworthy;[3] and I may neither leave the knowing of this sooth, nor I see not the showing to us no manner of blame. How may this be? For I knew by the common teaching of Holy Church and by mine own feeling that the blame of our sin continually hangeth upon us, from the first man[4] into the time that we come up into heaven. Then was this my marvel, that I saw our Lord God showing to us no more blame than if we were as clean as and holy as angels be in heaven.[5] And atwix[6] these two contraries my reason was greatly travailed[7] by my blindness, and could have no rest for dread that His blessed presence should pass from my sight and I to be left in unknowing how He beholdeth us in our sin. For either me behooved[8] to see in God that sin were all done away, or else me behooved to see in God how He seeth it, whereby I might truly know how it longeth to me to see sin and the manner of our blame.

My longing endured, Him continually beholding, and yet I could have no patience for great awe and perplexity, thinking: If I take it thus, that we be not sinners nor not blameworthy, it seemeth as I should err and fail of knowing of this sooth. And if it be so that we be sinners and blameworthy, good Lord, how may it then be that I cannot see this

soothness in Thee, which art my God, my Maker, in whom I desire to see all truths?

For three points make me hardy to ask it: the first is for it[9] is so low a thing, for if it were a high I should be adread;[10] the second is that it is so common, for if it were special and privy, also I should be adread; the third is that it needeth me to wit it, as me thinketh, if I shall live here, for knowing of good and evil, whereby I may by reason and grace the more depart them asunder, and love goodnesss and hate evil as Holy Church teacheth.

I cried inwardly with all my might, seeking unto God for help, meaning thus: Ah! Lord Jesus, King of bliss, how shall I be eased? Who that shall teach me and tell me that[11] me needeth to wit, if I may not at this time see it in Thee?

CHAPTER 51

The answer to the doubt afore by a marvellous example of a lord and a servant; and God will abide, for it was near twenty years after ere she fully understood this example; and how it is understood that Christ sitteth on the right hand of the Father—Fifty-First chapter.

And then our courteous Lord answered in showing full mystily[12] a wonderful example of a lord that hath a servant, and gave me sight to my understanding of both; which sight was showed double in the Lord, and the sight was showed double in the servant: than one party was showed ghostly in bodily likeness, and the other party was showed more ghostly without bodily likeness.[13] For the first thus: I saw two persons in bodily likeness, that is to say, a lord and a servant; and therewith God gave me ghostly understanding. The lord sitteth solemnly in rest and in peace, the servant standeth by, before his lord reverently, ready to do his lord's will. The lord looketh upon his servant full lovely and sweetly, and meekly he sendeth him to a certain place to do his will.[14] The servant, not only he goeth, but suddenly he starteth and runneth in

---

[1] *And in ... grace* See Psalm 118.132–33.

[2] *meaning* Saying.

[3] *Good Lord ... blameworthy* See Proverbs 24.16.

[4] *the first man* Adam.

[5] *I saw ... heaven* See Luke 20.35–36.

[6] *atwix* Between.

[7] *travailed* Tormented.

[8] *me behooved* It was incumbent upon me.

[9] *it* This question.

[10] *adread* Afraid.

[11] *that* That which.

[12] *mystily* Mistily, darkly.

[13] *ghostly in bodily ... ghostly without bodily* This refers to the spiritual sight versus bodily sight distinction that Julian sets up in the First Revelation.

[14] *do his will* See John 17.18.

great haste for love to don his lord's will. And anon he falleth in a slade[1] and taketh full great sore. And than he groaneth and moaneth and waileth and writheth, but he ne may risen[2] nor help himself by no manner way. And of all this the most mischief that I saw him in was failing of comfort; for he could not turn his face to look upon his loving lord, which was to him full near, in whom is full comfort;[3] but as a man that was feeble and unwise for the time, he intended to his feeling, and endured in woe, in which woe he suffered seven great pains. The first was the sore bruising he took in his falling, which was to him much pain. The second was the heaviness of his body. The third was feebleness following of these two. The fourth, that he was blinded in his reason and stonied[4] in his mind so far forth that almost he had forgotten his own love. The fifth was that he might not rise. The sixth was most marvellous to me, and that was that he lay alone. I looked all about and beheld, and far nor near, high nor low, I saw to him no help. The seventh was that the place which he lay on was a long, hard and grievous.

I marvelled how this servant might meekly suffer there all this woe. And I beheld with avisement to wit if I could perceive in him any default, or if the Lord should assign in him any blame, and soothly there was none seen; for only his good will and his great desire was cause of his falling; and he was as unlothful[5] and as good inwardly as when he stood afore his lord ready to do his will.

And right thus continually his loving lord full tenderly beholdeth him; and now with a double cheer:[6] one outward, full meekly and mildly with great ruth and pity, and this was of the first; another inward, more ghostly, and this was showed with a leading of my understanding into the lord, which I saw him highly enjoy, for the worshipful resting and nobleth[7] that he will and shall bring his servant to by his plenteous grace. And this was of that other showing. And now my understanding led again into the first, both keeping in mind.

Then saith this courteous lord in his meaning: Lo, lo, my loved servant. What harm and disease[8] he hath taken in my service for my love, yea, and for his good will! Is it not reason that I award him[9] his fright and his dread, his hurt and his maim and all his woe? And not only this, but falleth it not to me to given a gift that be better to him and more worshipful than his own whole should have been? And else methinketh I did him no grace.

And in this an inward ghostly showing of the Lord's meaning descended[10] into my soul, in which I saw that it behoveth needs to be, standing His great and His own worship, that His dear-worthy servant which he loved so much should be verily and blissfully rewarded without end above that he should have been if he had not fallen; yea, and so far forth that his falling and his woe that he hath taken thereby shall be turned into high and overpassing worship and endless bliss.

And at this point the showing of the example vanished, and our good Lord led forth mine understanding in sight and in showing of the revelation to the end. But notwithstanding all this forth-leading, the marvelling[11] of the example came never from me; for methought it was given me for an answer to my desire. And yet could I not taken therein full understanding to mine ease at that time. For in the servant that was showed for Adam, as I shall say, I saw many diverse properties that might by no manner or way be directed to single Adam.[12] And thus in that time I stood mikel in unknowing. For the full understanding of this marvellous example was not given me in that time; in which misty example three privities of the revelation be yet mikel hid, and notwithstanding this I saw and understood that every showing is full of privities. And therefore me behoveth now to tell three properties in which I am sumdele[13] eased.

The first is the beginning of teaching that I understood therein in the same time; the second is the inward learning that I have understood therein sithen;[14] the third all the whole

---

[1] *slade* Valley, dell.

[2] *ne may risen* Cannot rise.

[3] *full comfort* See 2 Corinthians 1.3.

[4] *stonied* Astonished, stunned.

[5] *unlothful* Innocent.

[6] *cheer* Countenance.

[7] *nobleth* Eminence, high standing.

[8] *disease* Distress.

[9] *award him* Remind him for.

[10] *descended* This is the only place where Julian speaks of a revelation as coming from above.

[11] *marvelling* Wonder.

[12] *to single Adam* I.e., to Adam alone.

[13] *sumdele* Somewhat.

[14] *sithen* Since.

revelation from the beginning to the end, that is to say, of this book, which our Lord God of his goodness bringeth oftentimes freely to the sight of mine understanding. And these three are so joined, as to my understanding, that I cannot, nor may, depart them. And by these three as one I have teaching whereby I owe to believe and trust in our Lord God, that of the same goodness that he showed it, and for the same end, right so of the same goodness and for the same end he shall declare it to us when it is His will.

For twenty years after the time of the showing, save three months, I had teaching inwardly, as I shall say: It longeth to thee to taken heed to all the properties and condition that were showed in the example though thou think that they been misty and indifferent to thy sight. I assented wilfully with great desire, seeing inwardly with avisement all the points and properties that were showed in the same time, as far forth as my wit and understanding would serve; beginning mine beholding at the lord and at the servant, and the manner of sitting of the lord, and the place that he sat on, and the colour of his clothing and the manner of shape, and his cheer without, and his nobleth and his goodness within; at the manner of standing of the servant and the place where and how, at his manner of clothing, the colour and the shape, at his outward having and at his inward goodness and his unlothfulness. The lord that sat solemnly in rest and in peace, I understand that he is God. The servant that stood before the lord, I understood that it was showed for Adam, that is to say, one man was showed that time, and his falling to make that thereby understand how God beholdeth a man and his falling; for in the sight of God all man is one man and one man is all man. This man was hurt in his might and made full feeble; and he was stonied in his understanding, for he turned from the beholding of his Lord. But his will was kept whole in God's sight; for his will I saw Our Lord commend and approve, but himself was letted and blinded of the knowing of this will. And this is to him great sorrow and grievous disease, for neither he sees clearly his loving lord, which is to him full meek and mild, nor he sees truly what himself is in the sight of his loving lord. And well I wot, when these two are wisely and truly seen, we shall getten rest and peace here in part, and the fullness of the bliss of heaven, by His plenteous grace.

And this was a beginning of teaching which I saw in the same time whereby I might come to knowing in what manner he beholdeth us in our sin. And then I saw that only

pains blameth and punisheth, and our courteous Lord comforteth and sorroweth; ever He is to the soul in glad cheer, loving and longing to bring us to His bliss.

The place that our Lord sat on was simple, on the earth barren and desert, alone in wilderness. His clothing was wide and syde,[1] and full seemly as falleth to a lord; the colour of his cloth was blue as azure, most sad[2] and fair. His cheer was merciful, the colour of his face was fair brown with fulsomely[3] features; his eyes were black, most fair and seemly, showing full of lovely pity; and within him an high ward,[4] long and broad, all full of endless heavens. And the lovely looking that he looked upon his servant continually, and namely in his falling, methought it might melt our hearts for love and brest[5] them in two for joy. The fair looking showed of a seemly medlur[6] which was marvellous to beholden: that one was ruth and pity, that other was joy and bliss. The joy and bliss passeth as far ruth and pity as heaven is above earth. The pity was earthly and the bliss was heavenly.

The ruth in the pity of the Father was of the falling of Adam, which is his most loved creature. The joy and the bliss was of his dear-worthy Son, which is even[7] with the Father. The merciful beholding of his lovely cheer fulfilled all earth and descended down with Adam into hell,[8] with which continuant pity Adam was kept from endless death. And this mercy and pity dwelleth with mankind until the time we come up into heaven. But man is blinded in this life, and therefore we may not see our Father, God, as He is. And what time that He of His goodness will show Him to man, He showeth Him homely[9] as man. Notwithstanding that, I saw verily we ought to know and believe that the Father is not man. But his sitting on the earth barren and desert is this to mean: he made man's soul to be his own city and his dwelling place, which is most pleasing to him of all his works; and what time that man was fallen into sorrow and pain he

---

[1]   *syde*   Ample.

[2]   *sad*   Deep or dark (blue).

[3]   *fulsomely*   Gracious.

[4]   *high ward*   Secure citadel, place of refuge. See 2 Kings 22.3, Psalm 58.17.

[5]   *brest*   Break.

[6]   *medlur*   Mixture.

[7]   *even*   Equal.

[8]   *into hell*   See Psalm 138.8–10.

[9]   *homely*   Familiarly.

was not all seemly to serven of that noble office; and therefore our kind Father would dight[1] him no other place but to sit upon the earth abiding mankind, which is meddled[2] with earth, till what time by His grace His dear-worthy Son had brought again His city into the noble fairness with His hard travail.[3]

The blueness of the clothing betokeneth his steadfastness. The brownness of his fair face with the seemly blackness of the eyen was most according to show his holy soberness. The largeness of his clothing, which were fair, flamand[4] about, betokeneth that he hath beclosed in him all heavens and all joy and bliss. And this was showed in a touch where I say mine understanding was led into the lord, in which I saw him highly enjoy for the worshipful restoring that he will and shall bring his servant to be his plenteous grace. And yet I marvelled, beholding the lord and the servant before said.

I saw the lord sit solemnly, and the servant standing reverently before his lord, in which servant is double understanding: one without, another within. Outward, he was clad simply as a labourer which were disposed to travail, and he stood full near the lord, not even for against[5] him, but in part aside, that on the left. His clothing was a white kirtle,[6] single, old and all defaced, dyed with sweat of his body, strait[7] fitting to him and short, as it were an handful beneath the knee, bare,[8] seeming as it should soon be worn up, ready to be ragged and rent. And in this I marvelled greatly, thinking: This is now an unseemly clothing for the servant that is so highly loved to stand afore so worshipful a lord. And inward, in him was showed a ground of love, which love he had to the lord was even like to the love that the lord had to him. The wisdom of the servant saw inwardly that there was one thing to do which should be to the worship of the lord. And the servant for love, having no reward to[9] himself nor to nothing that might fall of[10] him, hastily he started and ran at

the sending of his lord to do that thing which was his will and his worship. For it seemed be his outward clothing as he had been a continuant labourer of long time. And by the inward sight that I had, both in the lord and in the servant, it seemed that he was anew, that is to say, new beginning for to travail, which servant was never sent out before.

There was a treasure in the earth[11] which the lord loved. I marvelled and thought what it might be. And I was answered in mine understanding: It is a meat[12] which is lovesome and pleasant to the lord. For I saw the lord sit as a man, and I saw neither meat nor drink wherewith to serve him; this was one marvel. Another marvel was that this solemn lord had no servant but one, and him he sent out. I beheld, thinking what manner labour it might be that the servant should do. And then I understood that he should do the greatest labour and hardest travail, that is, he should be a gardener; delving and diking,[13] swinking[14] and sweating, and turn the earth upside down, and seek the deepness, and water the plants in time. And in this he should continue his travail and make sweet floods to run, and noble and plenteous fruits to spring, which he should bring before the lord and serve him therewith to his liking. And he should never turn again till he had dight this meat,[15] all ready as he knew that it liked the lord, and then he should take this meat with the drink, and bear it full worshipfully before the lord. And all this time the lord should sit on the same place abiding his servant whom he sent out.

And yet I marvelled from whence the servant came; for I saw in the lord that he hath within himself endless life and all manner of goodness, save that treasure that was in the earth and that was grounded in the lord in marvellous deepness of endless love—but it was not all to the worship till this servant had dight thus nobly it, and brought it before him, in himself present. And without the lord was nothing but wilderness. And I understood not all what this example meant, and therefore I marvelled whence the servant came.

In the servant is comprehended the second person in the Trinity; and in the servant is comprehended Adam, that is to say, all men. And therefore when I say the Son, it meaneth

---

[1] *dight* Prepare.

[2] *meddled* Mixed. See Genesis 2.7.

[3] *travail* Labor.

[4] *flamand* Flaming.

[5] *for against* In front of.

[6] *kirtle* Tunic.

[7] *strait* Close.

[8] *bare* Threadbare.

[9] *reward to* Regard for.

[10] *fall of* Happen to.

---

[11] *treasure in the earth* See Matthew 13.44.

[12] *meat* Food.

[13] *diking* Digging ditches.

[14] *swinking* Toiling.

[15] *dight this meat* Prepared this food.

the Godhead which is even with the Father, and when I say the servant, it meaneth Christ's manhood which is rightful Adam. By the nearness of the servant is understood the Son, and by the standing on the left side is understood Adam. The lord is the Father, God. The servant is the Son, Christ Jesus. The Holy Ghost is even love which is in them both. When Adam fell, God's Son fell; for the ruthful joining which was made in heaven, God's Son might not be separated from Adam, for by Adam I understand all man. Adam fell from life to death into the slade of this wretched world and after that into hell. God's Son fell with Adam into the slade of the maiden's womb, which was the fairest daughter of Adam, and therefore to excuse Adam from blame in heaven and in earth; and mightily he fetched him out of hell.[1] By the wisdom and goodness that was in the servant is understood God's Son. By the poor clothing as a labourer standing near the left side is understood the manhood and Adam, with all the mischief[2] and feebleness that followeth; for in all this our good lord showed his own Son and Adam but one man. The virtue and the goodness that we have is of Jesus Christ, the feebleness and the blindness that we have is of Adam; which two were showed in the servant.

And thus hath our good Lord Jesus taken upon Him all our blame; and therefore our Father may, nor will, no more blame assign to us than to his own dear-worthy Son, Christ. Thus was He the servant before His coming into the earth, standing ready before the Father in purpose till what time He would send him to do that worshipful deed by which mankind was brought again into heaven; that is to say, notwithstanding that He is God, even with the Father as against[3] the Godhead, but in His foreseeing purpose that He would be man to save man in fulfilling of his Father's will, so He stood afore his Father as a servant, wilfully taking upon Him all our charge. And then He start full readily at the Father's will, and anon he fell full low in the maiden's womb, having no reward to Himself nor to His hard pains.

The white kirtle is the flesh; the singleness is that there was right naught atwix[4] the Godhood and manhood; the straitness is poverty; the eld[5] is of Adam's wearing; the

defacing of sweat, of Adam's travail; the shortness showeth the servant's labour.

And thus I saw the Son standing, saying in His meaning: Lo, my dear Father, I stand before Thee in Adam's kirtle all ready to start and to run. I would be in the earth to do Thy worship when it is Thy will to send me. How long shall I desire? Full soothfastly wist the Son when it was the Father's will and how long He shall desire; that is to say, against the Godhead, for He is the wisdom of the Father. Wherefore this meaning was showed in understanding of the manhood of Christ; for all mankind that shall be saved by the sweet incarnation and blissful passion of Christ, all is the manhood of Christ; for he is the head and we be his members;[6] to which members the day and the time is unknown when every passing woe and sorrow shall have an end, and the everlasting joy and bliss shall be fulfilled; which day and time for to see all the company of heaven longeth. And all that shall be under heaven that shall come thither, their way is by longing and desire; which desire and longing was showed in the servant standing afore the Lord, or else thus, in the Son's standing before the Father in Adam's kirtle; for the languor and desire of all mankind that shall be saved appeared in Jesus; for Jesus is all that shall be saved and all that shall be saved is Jesus; and all of the charity of God, with obedience, meekness and patience, and virtues that longen[7] to us. Also in this marvellous example I have teaching with me, as it were the beginning of an ABC, whereby I may have some understanding of our Lord's meaning; for the privities of the revelation be hid therein, notwithstanding that all the showings are full of privities.

The sitting of the Father betokeneth His Godhead, that is to say, for showing of rest and peace; for in the Godhead may be no travail. And that he showed himself as lord betokeneth to our manhood. The standing of the servant betokeneth travail; on side and on the left betokeneth that he was not all worthy to stand even right before[8] the lord. His starting was the Godhead, and the running was the manhood; for the Godhead start from the Father into the maiden's womb, falling into the taking of our kind; and in this falling he took great sore; the sore that he took was our flesh in which he had feeling of deadly pains. By that he stood dreadfully before the lord, and not even right, betokeneth

---

[1]   *he fetched ... hell*   Here the text alludes to the Harrowing of Hell.

[2]   *mischief*   Misfortune.

[3]   *against*   Regards.

[4]   *right naught atwix*   Nothing at all between.

[5]   *eld*   Age.

[6]   *we be his members*   Cf. 1 Corinthians 12.12.

[7]   *longen*   Belong.

[8]   *even right before*   Directly in front of.

that his clothing was not honest to stand in even right before the Lord; nor that might not, nor should not, be his office while he was a labourer; nor also he might not sit in rest and peace with the Lord till he had won his peace rightfully with his hard travail; and by the left side, that the Father left His own Son wilfully in the manhood to suffer all man's pains without sparing of Him. By that his kirtle was in point to be ragged and rent is understood the rods and the scourges, the thorns and the nails, the drawing and the dragging, his tender flesh rending; as I saw in some part. The flesh was rent from the head-pan,[1] falling in pieces until the time the bleeding failed; and then it began to dry again, clinging to the bone. And by the wallowing and writhing, groaning and moaning is understood that he might never rise all mightily from the time that he was fallen into the maiden's womb till his body was slain and dead, he yielding the soul in the Father's hands with all mankind for whom he was sent.

And at this point He began first to show his might; for He went into hell, and when He was there He raised up the great right out of the deep deepness which rightfully was knit to Him in high heaven. The body was in the grave till Easter morrow, and from that time he lay never more. For then was rightfully ended the wallowing and the writhing, the groaning and the moaning; and our foul deadly flesh that God's Son took on him, which was Adam's old kirtle, strait, bare and short, then by Our Saviour was made fair now, white and bright and of endless cleanness, wide and syde, fairer and richer than was than the clothing which I saw on the Father; for that clothing was blue, and Christ's clothing is now of a fair, seemly medlur[2] which is so marvellous that I can it not discrien;[3] for it is all of very worships.

Now sitteth not the Lord on earth in wilderness, but He sitteth in his noblest seat which He made in heaven most to His liking. Now standeth not the Son before the Father as a servant dreadfully, unornly[4] clad, in part naked, but He standeth before the Father even right, richly clad in blissful largess, with a crown upon his head of precious riches; for it was showed that we be his crown, which crown is the Father's joy, the Son's worship, the Holy Ghost's liking, and endless marvellous bliss to all that be in heaven.

Now standeth not the Son before the Father on the left side as a labourer, but He sitteth on his Father's right hand in endless rest and peace. But it is not meant that the Son sitteth on the right hand, side by side, as one man sitteth by another in this life; for there is no such sitting, as to my sight, in the Trinity; but he sitteth on his Father's right hand, that is to say, in the highest nobleth of the Father's joys. Now is the spouse, God's Son, in peace with his loved wife, which is the fair maiden of endless joy. Now sitteth the Son, very God and man, in his city in rest and peace, which his Father hath adyte to[5] him of his endless purpose; and the Father in the Son, and the Holy Ghost in the Father and in the Son. . . .

CHAPTER 58

God was never displeased with His chosen wife; and of three properties in the Trinity; Fatherhead, Motherhead and Lordhead; and how our substance is in every person, but our sensuality is in Christ alone—Fifty-Eighth chapter.

God, the blessed Trinity which is everlasting being, right as He is endless from without beginning, right so it was in His purpose endless to make mankind; which fair kind first was dight to His own Son, the second person. And when He would, by full accord of all the Trinity, He made us all at once; and in our making He knit us and joined us to himself; by which joining we are kept as clean and as noble as we were made. By the virtue of that ilke[6] precious joining we love our Maker and liken him, praise Him and thank Him and endlessly enjoy in him. And this is the work which is wrought continually in every soul that shall be saved; which is the godly will beforesaid.

And thus in our making God almighty is our kindly Father; and God all wisdom is our kindly Mother, with the love and the goodness of the Holy Ghost; which is all one God, one Lord. And in the knitting and in the joining He is our very true spouse, and we His loved wife and His fair maiden, with which wife He is never displeased; for He saith: I love thee and thou lovest me, and our love shall never be departed on two.

I beheld the working of all the blessed Trinity, in which beholding I saw and understood these three properties: the property of the Fatherhead, the property of the Motherhead

---

[1] *head-pan* Forehead.

[2] *medlur* Mixture.

[3] *descrien* Describe.

[4] *unornly* Wretchedly.

[5] *adyte to* Prepared for.

[6] *ilke* Same.

and the property of the Lordship in one God. In our Father almighty we have our keeping and our bliss as our kindly substance, which is to us by our making without beginning; and in the second person, in wit and wisdom, we have our keeping as our sensuality, our restoring and our saving; for He is our Mother, Brother and Saviour. And in our good Lord the Holy Ghost we have our rewarding and our yielding for our living and our travail;[1] and endless overpassing all that we desire, in His marvellous courtesy, of His high plenteous grace. For all our life is in three. In the first we have our being and in the second we have our increasing and in the third we have our fulfilling. The first is kind;[2] the second is mercy; the third is grace.

For the first: I saw and understood that the high might of the Trinity is our Father, and the deep wisdom of the Trinity is our Mother, and the great love of the Trinity is our Lord; and all this have we in kind and in our substantial making. And furthermore, I saw that the second person, which is our Mother substantial, that same dear-worthy person is become our Mother sensual; for we are double of Gods making: that is to say, substantial and sensual. Our substance is the higher part, which we have in our Father, God Almighty; and the second person of the Trinity is our Mother in kind in our substantial making, in whom we are grounded and rooted, and He is our Mother in mercy in our sensuality taking. And thus our Mother is to us diverse manner working, in whom our parties are kept undeparted; for in our Mother, Christ, we profit and increase, and in mercy He reformeth us and restoreth, and, by the virtue of His passion and His death and uprising, joineth us to our substance. Thus worketh our Mother in mercy to all His children which are to Him buxom and obedient. And grace worketh with mercy, and namely in two properties as it was showed; which working longeth to the third person, the Holy Ghost. He worketh rewarding and giving; rewarding is a large giving of truth that the Lord doth to Him that hath travailed, and giving is a courtesy working which He doth freely of grace fulfil, and overpassing all that is deserved of creatures.

Thus in our Father, God Almighty, we have our being; and in our Mother of mercy we have our reforming and restoring, in whom our parties are joined and all made perfect man; and by yielding and giving in grace of the Holy Ghost we are fulfilled. And our substance is our Father, God Almighty, and our substance is our Mother, God all wisdom, and our substance is in our Lord the Holy Ghost, God all goodness; for our substance is whole in each person of the Trinity, which is one God. And our sensuality is only in the second person, Christ Jesus, in whom is the Father and the Holy Ghost; and in Him and by Him we are mightily taken out of hell and out of the wretchedness in earth, and worshipfully brought up into heaven and blissfully joined to our substance, increased in riches and nobleth, by all the virtue of Christ and by the grace and working of the Holy Ghost. ...

Chapter 60

How we be bought again[3] and forth-spread by mercy and grace of our sweet, kind and ever loving Mother Jesus, and of the properties of Motherhead; but Jesus is our very Mother, not feeding us with milk but with Himself, opening His side unto us and challenging all our love—Sixtieth chapter.

But now behoveth to say a little more of this forth-spreading, as I understand in the meaning of our Lord, how that we be bought again by the Motherhead of mercy and grace into our kindly stead[4] where that we were made by the Motherhead of kind love; which kind love it never leaveth us.

Our kind Mother, our gracious Mother, for He would all wholly become our Mother in all things, He took the ground of His work full low and full mildly in the maiden's womb. And that He showed in the first, where He brought that meek maid before the eye of mine understanding in the simple stature as she was when she conceived; that is to say, our high God is sovereign wisdom of all, in this low place He raised him and dight him full ready in our poor flesh, himself to do the service and the office of Motherhead in all things. The Mother's service is nearest, readiest and surest, for it is most of kind.[5] This office nor might, nor could, nor never none do to the full[6] but He alone. We wit that all our Mother's bearing is us to pain and to dying; and what is that but our very Mother Jesus? He, all love, beareth us to joy and to endless living; blessed may He be! Thus He sustaineth us within himself in love, and travailed into the full time that

---

[1]   *travail* Work.

[2]   *kind* Nature.

[3]   *bought again* Redeemed.

[4]   *kindly stead* Natural place

[5]   *kind* Nature.

[6]   *nor might ... full* None ever might, nor could, nor did fully.

He would suffer the sharpest thorns and the grievous pains that ever were or ever shall be, and died at the last. And when He had done, and so born us to bliss, yet might not all this make a seeth[1] to His marvellous love; and that showed He in these high over passing words of love: If I might suffer more, I would suffer more. He might no more die, but He would not stint[2] of working.

Wherefore Him behooveth to feed us, for the dearworthy love of Motherhead hath made Him debtor to us. The mother may give her child suck her milk, but our precious Mother Jesus, He may feed us with himself; and doth full courteously and full tenderly with the blessed sacrament that is precious food of very life. And with all the sweet Sacraments He sustaineth us full mercifully and graciously. And so meant He in this blessed word where that He said, I it am that Holy Church preacheth thee and teacheth thee. That is to say: All the health and life of sacraments, all the virtue and grace of my word, all the goodness that is ordained in Holy Church for thee, I it am.

The mother may lay the child tenderly to her breast, but our tender Mother Jesus, He may homely lead us into His blessed breast by His sweet open side,[3] and show therein part of the Godhead and the joys of heaven, with ghostly sekirnes[4] of endless bliss; and that showed in the giving the same understanding in this sweet word where He saith: Lo how I love thee, beholding into His side, enjoying.

This fair lovely word Mother, it is so sweet and so kind of the self that it may not verily be said of none but of Him, and to her that is very Mother of Him and of all. To the property of Motherhead longeth[5] kind love, wisdom and knowing, and it is good; for though it be so that our bodily forth-bringing be but little, low and simple in regard of our ghostly forth-bringing yet it is He that doth it in the creatures by whom that it is done. The kind, loving mother that wot and knoweth the need of her child, she keepeth it full tenderly as the kind and condition of motherhead will. And as it waxeth in age she changeth her working but not her love. And when it is waxen of more age, she suffered that it be chastised in breaking down of vices to make the child to receive virtues and graces. This working, with all that be fair and good, our Lord doth it in Him by whom it is done. Thus He is our Mother in kind by the working of grace in the lower part, for love of the higher part. And He will that we know it; for He will have all our love fastened to Him. And in this I saw that all our debt that we owe, by God's bidding, by Fatherhead and Motherhead, for God's Fatherhead and Motherhead is fulfilled in true loving of God; which blessed love Christ worketh in us. And this was showed in all, and namely in the high plenteous words where He saith: I it am that thou lovest....

Chapter 86

The good Lord showed this book should be otherwise performed than at the first writing; and for His working [we] will thus pray, Him thanking, trusting, and in Him enjoying; and how He made this showing because He will have it known, in which knowing He will give us grace to love him; for fifteen years after it was answered that the cause of all this showing was love, which Jesus grant us. Amen—Eighty-Sixth chapter.

This book is begun by God's gift and His grace, but it is not yet performed, as to my sight. For charity pray we all to God, with God's working, thanking, trusting, enjoying; for thus will our good Lord be prayed, as by the understanding that I took in all His own meaning, and in the sweet words where He saith full merrily: I am ground of thy beseeching. For truly I saw and understood in our Lord's meaning that He showed it for He will have it known more than it is, in which knowing He will give us grace to love Him and cleave to him; for He beheld His heavenly treasure with so great love on earth that He will give us more light and solace in heavenly joy in drawing of our hearts, for sorrow and darkness which we are in.

And from that time that it was showed I desired oftentimes to wit what was our Lord's meaning. And fifteen years after and more I was answered in ghostly understanding, saying thus: Wouldst thou wit thy Lord's meaning in this thing? Wit it well: love was His meaning. Who showed it thee? Love. What showed He thee? Love. Wherefore showed it he? For love. Hold thee therein and thou shalt wit and know more in the same; but thou shalt never know nor wit therein other thing without end.

---

[1] *make a seeth* Give satisfaction.

[2] *stint* Stop.

[3] *open side* Referring to the wound that Jesus received from a soldier's spear when he hung on the Cross. See John 19.34.

[4] *sekirnes* Certainly.

[5] *longeth* Belongeth, i.e., belongs.

Thus was I learned that love was our Lord's meaning. And I saw full sekirly in this and in all, that ere God made us He loved us; which love was never slaked, nor never shall. And in this love He hath done all His work; and in this love He hath made all things profitable to us; and in this love our life is everlasting. In our making we had beginning, but the love wherein He made us was in Him from without beginning; in which love we have our beginning. And all this shall be seen in God without end; which Jesus may grant us. Amen.

Thus endeth the revelation of love of the blessed Trinity showed by our Saviour Christ Jesus for our endless comfort and solace, and also to enjoy in Him in this passing journey of this life. Amen, Jesus, Amen.

I pray Almighty God that this book come not but to the hands of them that will be His faithful lovers, and to those that will submit them to the faith of Holy Church and obey the wholesome understanding and teaching of the men that be of virtuous life, sad[1] age and profound learning; for this revelation is high divinity and high wisdom, wherefore it may not dwell with him that is thrall to sin and to the devil. And beware thou take not one thing after thy affection and liking and leave another, for that is the condition of a heretic. But take everything with other and truly understand all is according to Holy Scripture and grounded in the same, and that Jesus, our very love, light and truth, shall show to all clean souls that with meekness ask perseverantly[2] this wisdom of Him. And thou, to whom this book shall come, thank highly and heartily our Saviour Christ Jesus that He made these showings and revelations for thee, and to thee, of His endless love, mercy and goodness, for thine and our safe guide and conduct to everlasting bliss; the which Jesus may grant us. Amen.

—LATE 14TH CENTURY

---

[1] *sad* Mature.

[2] *perseverantly* With perseverance.

MARGERY KEMPE
c. 1373 – 1439

Widely varying descriptions of Margery Kempe have been proposed in the past century—mystic, eccentric, feminist, lunatic, saint, fanatic, heretic, visionary—but for literary purposes, one point about her is central: hers is often considered the first extant autobiography written in English. Dictated to two different scribes, *The Book of Margery Kempe* describes the spiritual awakening and religious fervor of a medieval woman who could neither read nor write, but who had a wide and heartfelt knowledge of theology from listening to sermons and lectures. Modeling herself after various female saints (Bridget of Sweden and Katherine of Alexandria, for example), Kempe was herself on a self-described quest for sainthood; in her autobiography she describes the many obstacles that stood in her spiritual path, as well as her shrewd approaches to dealing with the impediments. Her willingness to challenge powerful men—including the Archbishop of York—and her determination to follow her calling at any cost make her story as fascinating as it is remarkable.

Margery Brunham Kempe's early life was typical of a prosperous woman of the fifteenth century. Her father was an important man in the affluent port town of Bishop's Lynn (now called King's Lynn) in Norfolk, England. John Brunham was five times mayor of the town, two times Member of Parliament, and he held various other estimable positions. At the age of 20 Margery married John Kempe, also of Bishop's Lynn; the couple had 14 children over the following 20 years. Kempe's autobiography begins with her marriage, although she mentions having committed some sin, possibly of a sexual nature, before the age of 20 and having felt deeply remorseful about it ever since; she seemed to feel that no amount of penance or atonement would redeem her. Following the difficult birth of her first child, Kempe, believing she was near death, called for a priest and attempted to confess her "crime." The priest's response was so unsympathetic and threatening that Kempe was not able to continue her confession, nor would she ever again mention her misdeed to anyone. She subsequently suffered what most modern readers would describe as a mental breakdown and experienced visions of the Devil and of Christ; she would endure many more travails before experiencing salvation.

At the age of 60, Kempe dictated an account of these travails and of the happiness she eventually found in God. Narrated in a colloquial and often non-chronological manner, her book describes her progress from a strong-willed wife who ran her own businesses to a strong-willed ascetic who renounced her family and her conjugal bed and set out on a series of pilgrimages. Kempe candidly describes the various ways in which she alienated both priests and laypeople wherever she went. Weeping and sobbing were not unusual occurrences in the medieval church, but Kempe's unrestrained crying and her obsessive discourse on religious topics annoyed many townsfolk and travelers and led some to believe that she was insane. More than once she was taken into custody as a heretic, only to use her wiles and her knowledge of Scripture to assuage (if not always win over) her accusers.

Although she had not lived with her husband for some years, when he suffered a bad accident Kempe rushed to his side and nursed him for several years until his death in 1431. While settled in Bishop's Lynn, she claimed to have performed a miracle that prevented the town from burning down, and her claim was widely believed. The last known mention of Kempe is in the town records of 1439, so she is presumed to have died around that time. These days Kempe is often studied alongside anchoress Julian of Norwich (in fact the two had once met when Kempe went to Julian to seek spiritual guidance), who also described mystical visions in her *Revelations of Divine Love*; Kempe's autobiography, however, affords greater insights into the lives of secular women and the lay spirituality of medieval England.

⌘⌘⌘

from *The Book of Margery Kempe*

THE PROEM

Here begins a short treatise, and a comforting one for sinful wretches, from which they can take great solace and comfort and understand the exalted and ineffable mercy of our sovereign Saviour Jesus Christ, whose name should be worshipped and exalted without end, who now in our time deigns to exercise His nobility and goodness upon us unworthy ones. All the works of our Savior serve as an example and instruction for us, and whatever grace He works in any creature is for our benefit, provided that a lack of charity does not hinder us.

And therefore, by leave of our merciful Lord Jesus Christ, for the exaltation of His Holy Name, Jesus, this little treatise will treat a small part of his wonderful works: how mercifully, how kindly, and how charitably He moved and stirred a sinful wretch[1] to love Him, a sinful wretch who for many years wished and intended, through the incitement of the Holy Spirit, to follow our Savior, and made great promises of fasting and many other acts of penance. And she was continually turned back from this in time of temptation, like a reed that bends with every wind and is never stable unless no wind blows, until the time when our merciful Lord Jesus Christ, taking pity and compassion on His handiwork and His creature, turned health into sickness, prosperity into adversity, honor into reproach, and love into hatred. With all these things turning upside down in this way, this creature, who for many years had gone astray and had always been unstable, was perfectly drawn and stirred to enter the way of noble righteousness, the righteous way that Christ our Savior exemplified in His own person. He trod it steadfastly and diligently prepared it.

Then this creature, whose way of life this treatise, through the mercy of Jesus, will partly show, was touched by the hand of our Lord with great bodily sickness, from which she lost her reason and her wits for a long time until our Lord restored her again by grace, as will be more clearly showed hereafter. Her worldly goods, which were plenteous and abundant at that time, shortly afterward became quite worthless and meager. Then pomp and pride were cast down and laid aside. Those who had honored her before reproached her most sharply; her kin and those who had been her friends were now her greatest enemies. Then she, considering this astonishing change, seeking help under the wings of her spiritual mother, Holy Church, went and submitted herself to her spiritual father, accusing herself of her misdeeds, and then did great bodily penance.

And in a short time our merciful Lord endowed this creature with plenteous tears of contrition, day by day, to such an extent that some men said she could weep at will, and slandered the work of God. She was so accustomed to being slandered and reproached, to being chided and rebuked by the world on account of the grace and virtue with which she was endowed through the strength of the Holy Spirit, that it was a kind of solace and comfort to her when she suffered any unhappiness for the love of God and for the grace that God worked in her. For the more slander and reproach that she suffered, the more she increased in grace and in devotion to holy meditation and deep contemplation and in the wonderful speech and conversation that our Lord spoke and provided in her soul, teaching her how she would be despised for love of Him, how she should have patience, putting all her trust, all her love, and all her affection in Him alone. She knew and understood many secret and hidden things that were going to happen afterward, by inspiration of the Holy Spirit. And often, while she was engaged in such holy speech and conversation, she would weep and sob so much that many people were greatly astonished, for they little

---

[1] *a sinful wretch* Kempe refers to herself in the third person throughout her text.

knew how much at home our Lord was in her soul. Nor could she herself ever tell the grace that she felt, it was so heavenly, so high above her reason and her bodily wits, and her body was so weak when grace was present in her that she could never express it in words as she felt it in her soul.

Then this creature was very much afraid of illusions and deceptions by her spiritual enemies. She went, at the bidding of the Holy Spirit, to many estimable learned men, both archbishops and bishops, teachers of divinity and scholars as well. She also spoke with many anchoresses[1] and showed them her way of life and the grace that the Holy Spirit, in His goodness, worked in her mind and in her soul, as well as her wits allowed her to express it. And all those to whom she showed her secrets said that she should greatly love our Lord for the grace that He showed her, and they counseled her to follow her movings and stirrings and trustingly believe they were from the Holy Spirit and not from an evil spirit.

Some of these worthy and estimable clerks accepted, on the peril of their souls and as they would answer to God for it, that this creature was inspired by the Holy Spirit, and asked her to have written and made for them a book of her experiences and her revelations. Some offered to write down her experiences with their own hands, and she would not by any means consent, for she was commanded in her soul not to write so soon. And so it was twenty years and more from the time when this creature had her first experiences and revelations before she had any of them written down. Afterward, when it pleased our Lord, He commanded and charged her that she should have her experiences and revelations and way of life written down so that His goodness might be known to all the world.

The creature had no writer who would fulfil her desire or give credence to her experiences until the time when a man living in Germany, who was an Englishman by birth and later was married in Germany and had both a wife and child there, having good knowledge of this creature and of her desire, moved, I trust, by the Holy Spirit, came to England with his wife and his belongings and lived with the aforementioned creature until he had written as much as she would tell him during the time they were together. And then he died. Then there was a priest for whom this creature had great affection, and so she conversed with him about this matter and brought him the book to read. The book was so badly written that he could do little with it, for it was neither good English nor German, and the letters were not shaped or formed as other letters are. Therefore the priest fully believed that no one would ever be able to read it, unless it were by special grace. Nevertheless, he promised her that if he could read it he would with good will copy it out and write it better.

Then there was such ill spoken of this creature and of her weeping that the priest, out of cowardice, did not dare speak with her often, and would not write as he had promised the aforementioned creature. And so he avoided and deferred the writing of this book well into the fourth year or more, despite the fact that the creature often asked him for it. At last he said to her that he could not read it, and so he would not do it. He would not, he said, put himself in danger from it. Then he advised her to go to a good man who had been well acquainted with the man who first wrote the book, on the supposition that he would be best able to read the book, for he had sometimes read letters in the other man's writing that were sent from overseas while he was in Germany. And so she went to that man, asking him to write this book down and never to let it be known as long as she lived, and granting him a large portion of goods for his labor. And this good man wrote about a page, and yet it was not much help, for he could not do much with it, the book was so badly presented and so poorly written.

Then the priest was troubled in his conscience, for he had promised her to write this book, if he could manage to read it, and had not done his part as well as he could have, and he asked this creature to get the book back if she were able. Then she got the book back and brought it to the priest with a glad face, asking him to do his best, and she would pray to God for him and get him grace to read and also to write it. The priest, trusting in her prayers, began to read this book, and it was much easier, it seemed to him, than it had been before. And so he read it over in this creature's presence, every word, with her sometimes helping him when there was any difficulty.

This book is not written in order, each thing after another as it was done, but just as the material came to the creature's mind when it was being written down, for it was so long before it was written that she had forgotten the time and the order in which things happened. And therefore she had nothing written down unless she knew for certain it was really true. When the priest first began to write this book, his eyes

---

[1] *anchoresses* Female religious ascetics who secluded themselves and devoted their lives to God.

failed him so that he could not see to form his letters, nor could he see to mend his pen. Everything else he could see well enough. He set a pair of spectacles on his nose, and then it was even worse than it had been before. He complained to the creature of his trouble. She said his enemy resented his good deed and would prevent him if he could, and she told him to do as well as God would give him grace to do, and not to stop. When he went back to his book, he could see as well, it seemed to him, as he had ever done before, by both daylight and candlelight. And for this reason, when he had written a quire,[1] he added a leaf to it, and then wrote this prologue to be clearer than the next one is, which was written before this one. *Anno domini*[2] 1436.

THE PREFACE

A short treatise of a creature living in great pomp and worldly pride, who then was drawn to our Lord by great poverty, sickness, shame, and great reproaches in many diverse countries and places, some of which tribulations will be depicted below, not in order as they happened but as the creature was able to recall them when it was written, for it was twenty years and more from the time when this creature had forsaken the world and eagerly devoted herself to our Lord before this book was written, even though this creature was greatly advised to have her tribulations and experiences written down, and a Carmelite friar[3] offered to write them willingly, if she would agree. And she was warned in her spirit that she should not write so soon. And many years afterward she was bidden in her spirit to write. And yet then it was first written by a man who wrote neither good English nor German, so it was unreadable except by special grace, for there was so much malicious talk and slander of this creature that few people would believe her. And so at last a priest was greatly moved to write this treatise, and he could not easily read it for four whole years. And then at the request of this creature and the urging of his own conscience he tried again to read it, and it was much easier than it had been previously. And so he began to write in the year of our Lord 1436, on

the day after Mary Magdalene's day,[4] according to the information of this creature.

from BOOK I

CHAPTER I

When this creature was twenty years old or a little more, she was married to a respected townsman and was pregnant within a short time, as nature would have it. And after she had conceived, she was afflicted with great fever until the child was born, and then, because of the labor she had in giving birth and the sickness that had gone before, she despaired of her life, believing she might not survive. And then she sent for her spiritual father, for she had something on her conscience that she had never told before that time, in all her life. For she was always prevented by her enemy, the devil, continually saying to her while she was in good health that she did not need confession but should do penance alone, by herself, and all would be forgiven, for God is merciful enough. And therefore this creature often did great penance by fasting on bread and water, and other charitable deeds with devout prayers, but she would not tell it in confession. And whenever she was sick or unwell, the devil said in her mind that she would be damned, for she was not absolved of that sin. Therefore, after the child was born, she, not trusting she would live, sent for her spiritual father, as was said before, with the full intention of being absolved for her entire life, as near as she could. And when she came to the point of saying the thing that she had concealed for so long, her confessor was a little too hasty, and began sharply to rebuke her before she had said everything she meant to, and so she would say no more for anything he could do.

And then, on account of the fear she had of damnation, on the one hand, and his sharp reproofs on the other hand, this creature went out of her mind and was terribly troubled and harassed by spirits for half a year, eight weeks and some days. And in this time she saw, as it seemed to her, devils opening their mouths, all aflame with burning flames of fire as though they would swallow her in, sometimes raging at her, sometimes threatening her, sometimes pulling her and dragging her, night and day, during this time. And also the devils cried out at her with great threats and told her to

---

[1] *quire* Four large sheets of paper folded to create eight sheets.

[2] *Anno domini* Latin: In the year of our Lord.

[3] *Carmelite friar* Monk of the religious order of Our Lady of Mount Carmel, founded in the twelfth century; Kempe refers here to Alan of Lynn.

[4] *Mary Magdalene's day* July 23rd.

forsake her Christianity, her faith, and deny her God, His mother, and all the saints in heaven, her good works and all good virtues, her father, her mother, and all her friends. And so she did. She slandered her husband, her friends and her own self; she spoke many reproving words and many harsh words; she knew no virtue or goodness; she desired all wickedness; just as the spirits tempted her to say and do, so she said and did. She would have destroyed herself many times at their instigation, and been damned with them in hell. And in demonstration of this, she bit her own hand so violently that it could be seen for the rest of her life afterward. And she tore the skin of her body above her heart with her nails pitilessly, for she had no other instrument, and she would have done worse except that she was bound and strongly restrained both day and night, so that she could not do what she wished.

And when she had been oppressed for a long time by these and many other temptations, so that no one thought she would escape or live, then at one point, as she lay alone and her keepers were away, our merciful Lord Jesus Christ, who is ever to be trusted, worshiped be His name, never forsaking His servant in time of need, appeared to His creature, who had forsaken Him, in the likeness of the loveliest, most beauteous, most pleasing man who could ever be seen with human eye, wearing a mantle of purple silk, sitting on her bedside, looking upon her with such a blessed face that she was strengthened in all her spirits, and He said to her these words: "Daughter, why have you forsaken me, and I never forsook you?"

And at once, as He said these words, she saw truly how the air opened, as bright as any light, and He rose up into the air, not hastily or quickly, but gently and easily so that she could see Him well in the air until it closed again.

And at once the creature was confirmed in her wits and her reason as well as she had ever been before, and asked her husband, as soon as he came to her, to give her the keys of the cellar so that she could get her food and drink as she had done before. Her maids and her keepers advised him not to give her any keys, for they said she would just give away whatever goods there were, for they believed she did not know what she was saying. Nevertheless, her husband, still having tenderness and compassion for her, commanded them to give her the keys. And she ate and drank as well as her bodily strength would allow her, and recognized her friends and her household and everyone else who came to see

how our Lord Jesus Christ had worked His grace in her, so blessed may He be who is always near in tribulation. When people think He is far from them, He is very near, by His grace. Then this creature did all the other tasks that fell to her wisely and soberly enough, but she did not truly know the ecstasy of our Lord.

CHAPTER 2

And when this creature had in this way, by grace, come to herself again, she thought she was indebted to God and that she would be His servant. Still, she would not leave the pride and pompous display that she had been accustomed to beforehand, either at her husband's or at anyone else's advice. And yet she knew full well that men said many bad things of her, for she wore ornaments of gold wire on her head and her hoods were fringed with tassels. Her cloaks were fringed as well and decorated with many colors between the fringes, so that they would be more striking to men's eyes and she herself would be more admired. And when her husband would tell her to leave her pride, she answered harshly and sharply and said that she came from such a worthy family that he could never have expected to marry her, for her father had once been mayor of the town N. and then was alderman of the noble Guild of the Trinity[1] in N., and therefore she would defend the honor of her kin whatever anyone said.

She was very envious of her neighbours if they were dressed as well as she was. All her desire was to be admired by people. She would not be warned by any chastisement nor be content with the goods God had given her, as her husband was, but always wanted more and more. And then, for pure greed and to support her pride, she began to be a brewer, and was one of the main brewers in the town of N. for three or four years until she lost a great deal of money, for she had no experience at it. For no matter how good her servants were, nor how knowledgeable about brewing, it would never ferment with them. For when the air was standing as nicely under the froth as anyone could see, suddenly the froth would fall down so that all the ale was lost, one brewing after another, so that her servants were ashamed and would not stay with her.

Then this creature thought of how God had punished

---

[1] *alderman ... Guild of the Trinity* Leader of an organization dedicated to the Holy Trinity that served as a social aid group; Kempe was inducted into the Guild in the 1440s.

her previously and she would not take the warning, and now again by the loss of her goods, and then she left it and did no more brewing. And then she asked her husband's pardon for not following his advice before, and she said that her pride and sin were the cause of all her punishment and that she would make good what she had done wrong, with good will. And yet she did not entirely leave the world, for now she thought of a new business. She had a horse-mill. She got two good horses and a man to grind people's corn and in this way she thought she would make her living. This plan did not last long, for a short while after, on the eve of Corpus Christi,[1] this marvel took place. The man was in good bodily health, and his two horses, which were strong and healthy, had pulled well in the mill before, but now he took one of these horses and put it in the mill as he had done before, and the horse would not pull at all in the mill, for anything the man might do. The man was upset and tried with all his wits to think how he could get the horse to pull. Now he led him by the head, now he beat him, now he coaxed him, and all to no avail, for he would rather go backward than forward. Then the man set a sharp pair of spurs on his heels and rode on the horse's back to make him pull, and still it was no better. When the man saw that it was not going to work, he put the horse back in the stable and gave him food, and he ate well and heartily. And then he took the other horse and put him in the mill, and just as his companion had done, so he did, for he would not pull for anything the man might do. And then the man gave up his position and would no longer stay with the aforesaid creature.

As soon as it was reported around the town of N. that no man or beast would work for the said creature, some said she was cursed; some said God took open vengeance on her; some said one thing and some said another. And some wise men, whose minds were more grounded in a love of our Lord, said it was the divine mercy of our Lord Jesus Christ that called and cried to her from the pride and vanity of the wretched world. And then this creature, seeing all the adversity coming on every side, thought it was the scourges of our Lord that were chastising her for her sin. Then she asked God's mercy and forsook her pride, her greed, and her desire for worldly honor, and did great bodily penance, and began to enter the way of everlasting life, as will be told hereafter.

CHAPTER 3

One night, as this creature lay in bed with her husband, she heard the sound of a melody as sweet and delectable, it seemed to her, as if she had been in Paradise. And at that she jumped out of bed and said, "Alas that ever I did sin; it is full merry in heaven."

This melody was so sweet that it surpassed, beyond comparison, all the melody that could ever be heard in this world, and caused this creature, when she heard any mirth or melody after that, to experience most plenteous and abundant tears of sincere devotion, and great sobbing and sighing after the bliss of heaven, without dreading the shame and spite of the wretched world. And after this spiritual ecstasy she always had in her mind the mirth and melody that were in heaven, so much so that she could not easily restrain herself from speaking of it. For, whenever she was in company, she would often say, "It is full merry in heaven."

And those who knew her previous behavior and now heard her speak so much of the bliss of heaven said to her, "Why do you talk in this way of the mirth that is in heaven? You do not know it, and you have not been there any more than we have," and they were angry with her because she would not hear any talk of worldly things as they did and as she had done before.

And after this time she never wished to have intercourse with her husband, for the debt of matrimony was so abominable to her that it seemed to her she would rather eat or drink slime, or the muck in the gutter, than to consent to any bodily intercourse, except out of obedience. And so she said to her husband, "I cannot deny you my body, but the love of my heart and my affection is drawn away from all earthly creatures and set only on God."

He would have his will, and she obeyed with great weeping and lamenting because she could not live chastely. And often this creature lived chastely, advised her husband to live chastely, and said that she knew well that they had often displeased God by their excessive love and the great enjoyment that they both had in sleeping together, and now it was right that they should, by the will and consent of both of them, both punish and chastise themselves deliberately by abstaining from their bodily lust. Her husband said it would be good to do so, but that he could not yet, and he would when God wished him to. And so he slept with her as he had done before, he would not restrain himself. And she continu-

---

ally prayed to God that she might live chastely, and three or four years later, when it pleased our Lord, her husband made a vow of chastity, as will be written hereafter by leave of Jesus.

And also, after this creature heard this heavenly melody, she did great bodily penance. She was confessed sometimes twice or three times in a day, and especially of that sin that she had so long concealed and hidden, as is written in the beginning of the book. She gave herself to great fasting and keeping vigils. She got up at two or three o'clock and went to church, and stayed there in her prayers until noontime and also all afternoon. And then she was slandered and reproached by many people because she lived so strict a life. Then she got a rough haircloth[1] from a kiln, of the kind that men use to dry malt on, and put it under her gown as craftily and secretly as she could, so that her husband would not notice it, and he did not, even though she lay by him every night in bed and wore the haircloth every day, and bore children during this time.

Then she spent three years being greatly troubled by temptations, which she bore as meekly as she could, thanking our Lord for all His gifts, and was as happy when she was reproached, scorned, or jeered at for love of our Lord, as she had been before at worldly honor—indeed, much happier. For she knew full well that she had sinned greatly against God and was worthy of more shame and sorrow than any man could do to her, and that being despised by the world was the right path to heaven, since Christ Himself chose that path. All His apostles, martyrs, confessors and virgins, and all who ever came to Heaven, passed along the path of tribulation, and she desired nothing so much as Heaven. Then she was glad in her conscience when she believed that she was entering the path that would lead her to the place that she most desired. And this creature had contrition and great remorse, with plenteous tears and many loud sobs for her sins and for her unkindness to her maker. She contemplated her unkindness since her childhood, which our Lord would many times bring to her mind. And then she, beholding her own wickedness, could only lament and weep and keep praying for mercy and forgiveness. Her weeping was so plenteous and so continual that many people thought that she could weep and stop weeping at will, and therefore many people said she was a false hypocrite and wept for show, for support and worldly good. And then a great many forsook

her who had loved her before, when she was in the world, and would not acknowledge her, and she continually thanked God for everything, desiring nothing but mercy and forgiveness of sin.

CHAPTER 4

The first two years when this creature was drawn to our Lord in this way, she had great rest in spirit with regard to temptations. She could easily endure fasting, it did not cause her suffering. She hated the joys of the world. She felt no rebellion in her flesh. She was so strong, it seemed to her, that she feared no devil in hell, for she did such great bodily penance. She thought that she loved God more than He loved her. She was struck with the deadly wound of vainglory and did not feel it, for she desired many times that the crucifix should free His hands from the Cross and embrace her as a sign of love. Our merciful Lord Jesus Christ, seeing this creature's presumption, sent her, as is written above, three years of great temptations, of which I propose to write about one of the hardest, as an example to those who come after that they should not trust in themselves or have joy in themselves as this creature had, for assuredly our spiritual enemy does not sleep, but very busily searches our characters and our dispositions, and wherever he finds us weakest, there, by our Lord's permission, he lays his snare, which no one can escape by his own power. And so he laid before this creature the snare of lechery, when she thought that all fleshly lust had been wholly quenched in her. And for a long time she was tempted with the sin of lechery, in spite of anything she could do. And yet she often went to confession, she wore the haircloth and did great bodily penance and wept many a bitter tear, and very often prayed to our Lord that he should preserve her and keep her so that she should not fall into temptation, for she thought she would rather be dead than consent to that. And all this time she had no desire to have intercourse with her husband, but found it very painful and horrible.

In the second year of her temptations it so happened that a man she loved well said to her on the eve of St. Margaret's Day, before evensong,[2] that come what may he would lie by her and have his bodily pleasure, and she would not withstand him, for if he could not have his will this time, he said,

---

[1] *haircloth* Coarse shirt made from animal hair and worn by penitents.

[2] *St. Margaret's Day* June 20th, feast of St. Margaret of Antioch, patron saint of pregnant women; *evensong* Vespers, or evening prayer.

he would have it another time, she had no choice. And he did it to test what she would do, but she thought he meant it entirely in earnest at that time, and said little in reply. So then they parted from one another and both went to hear evensong, for she attended St. Margaret's Church. This woman was so intent on the man's words that she could not hear evensong, or say her Lord's Prayer, or think any other good thought, but was more troubled than she had ever been before. The devil put it into her mind that God had forsaken her, and otherwise she would not have been so tempted. She believed the devil's persuasion and began to consent because she could not think any good thought. Therefore she believed that God had forsaken her. And when evensong was over, she went to the man and said that he should have his desire, as she thought he had wished, but he dissimulated[1] so that she did not know what he meant, and so they parted from one another for the night.

This creature was so troubled and vexed all that night that she had no idea what to do. She lay beside her husband, and having intercourse with him was so loathsome to her that she could not endure it, although it was lawful for her and at a lawful time[2] if she had wished. But she was continually thinking about the other man and about sinning with him, since he had spoken to her about it. At last she was overcome by the pressure of temptation and a lack of control, and consented in her mind, and went to the man to see if he would consent to her. And he said he would not do it for all the wealth in the world; he would rather be chopped up as small as meat for the cooking pot. She went away all ashamed and confused, seeing his stability and her own weakness. Then she thought of the grace God had given her before, how she had had two years of great rest in her soul, repentance for her sins with many bitter tears of compunction,[3] and a perfect will never to return to her sins, but to be dead rather than do so, it seemed to her. And now she saw how she had consented to do sin in her will. Then she fell half into despair. She thought she was in hell, she had such sorrow. She thought she was not worthy of any mercy because her consent was so willingly given, and not worthy to do him service because she was so false to him. Nevertheless she was

absolved[4] many times and often, and did whatever penance her confessor would order her to do, and was guided by the rules of the Church. God gave this creature that grace, blessed may He be, but He did not withdraw her temptation, but instead increased it, it seemed to her. And therefore she believed He had forsaken her and dared not trust in His mercy, but was oppressed by horrible temptations of lechery and despair for almost the whole rest of the year, except that our Lord, in His mercy, as she said herself, gave her almost every day two hours of compunction for her sins, with many bitter tears. And then she was troubled by the temptation to despair, as she had been before, and was as far from feeling grace as those who never felt it at all. And that she could not bear, and therefore she continually despaired. Except when she felt grace, her troubles were so overwhelming that she could hardly manage them, but continually mourned and lamented as though God had forsaken her. ...

CHAPTER 11

It happened one Friday, on Midsummer Eve in very hot weather, as this creature was coming from the direction of York, carrying a bottle of beer in her hand, and her husband with a cake tucked in his coat, that he asked his wife this question: "Margery, if a man came along with a sword and was going to cut off my head unless I had natural intercourse with you as I have done before, tell me the truth of your conscience—for you say you will not lie: would you allow my head to be cut off, or would you allow me to sleep with you again as I once did?"

"Alas, sir," she said, "why do you raise this matter, we having been chaste these eight weeks?"

"Because I want to know the truth of your heart."

And then she said with great sorrow, "Truly I would rather see you be killed than that we should go back to our uncleanness."

And he said to her, "You are no good wife."

And then she asked her husband why he had not slept with her for eight weeks before, since she lay beside him every night in his bed. And he said he was so afraid when he went to touch her that he dared do no more.

---

[1] *dissimulated* Pretended not to understand her.

[2] *at a lawful time* I.e., not during one of the many times when sex was prohibited—feast days, etc.

[3] *compunction* Remorse.

[4] *she was absolved* I.e., absolved of her sins through the sacrament of Confession.

"Now, good sir, amend yourself and ask God's mercy, for I told you nearly three years ago that you[1] would be killed, and here it is the third year, and still I hope I shall have my wish.[2] Good sir, I beg that you grant me what I ask, and I will pray that you may be saved through the mercy of our Lord Jesus Christ, and you will have greater reward in heaven than if you wore a hairshirt or a coat of mail. I beg you, allow me to make a vow of chastity by the hand of whatever bishop God wills."

"No," he said, "that I will not grant you, for now I can sleep with you without deadly sin, and then I could not do so."

Then she said again, "If it is the will of the Holy Spirit to fulfil what I have said, I pray God that you may consent to it; and if it is not the will of the Holy Ghost, I pray God you never consent."

Then they went on toward Bridlington in very hot weather, the aforesaid creature in a state of great sorrow and great fear for her chastity. And as they passed by a Cross, her husband sat himself down under the Cross, calling his wife to him and saying these words to her: "Margery, grant me my desire, and I shall grant you yours. My first desire is that we should continue to lie together in one bed as we have done before; the second that you shall pay my debts before you go to Jerusalem; and the third that you should eat and drink with me on a Friday as you used to do."

"Nay, sir," she said, "to break the Friday I will never grant you while I live."

"Well," he said, "then I shall sleep with you again."

She asked him to give her leave to make her prayers, and he granted it willingly. Then she kneeled down beside a Cross in the field and prayed in this manner, with a great abundance of tears: "Lord God, You know all things; You know what sorrow I have had to be chaste in my body for You these three years, and now I could have my will and I dare not for love of You. For if I were to break that custom of fasting that You commanded me to keep on Fridays, without meat or drink, I would now have my desire. But, blessed Lord, you know I will not go against Your will, and now my sorrow is great unless I find comfort in You. Now, blessed Jesus, make Your will known to me unworthy, that I may follow it and fulfil it with all my might."

And then our Lord Jesus Christ with great sweetness spoke to this creature, commanding her to go back to her husband and ask him to grant what she desired. "And he shall have what he desires. For, my most worthy daughter, this was the reason that I told you to fast, so that you should sooner obtain and get your desire, and it is granted you. I do not wish you to fast any longer, therefore I bid you in the name of Jesus, eat and drink as your husband does."

Then this creature thanked our Lord Jesus Christ for His grace and His goodness, and then rose up and went to her husband, saying to him, "Sir, if it please you, you shall grant me my desire, and you shall have your desire. Grant me that you shall not come into my bed, and I grant you to pay your debts before I go to Jerusalem. And put my body at God's disposal so that you never make any claims on me to ask me for any marriage debt after this day as long as you live, and I will eat and drink on Fridays at your bidding."

Then her husband said in reply, "May your body be as much at God's disposal as it has been at mine." This creature greatly thanked God, rejoicing that she had her desire, and asking her husband that they might say three Our Fathers in honor of the Trinity for the great grace that He had given them. And so they did, kneeling under a Cross, and then they ate and drank together in great gladness of spirit. This was on a Friday, on Midsummer Eve. Then they went on toward Bridlington and also to many other regions and spoke with God's servants, both hermits and recluses and many other lovers of our Lord, as well as many worthy clerks, doctors of divinity, and also scholars in many various places. And this creature showed to various of them her experiences and her contemplations, as she was commanded to do, to know if there were any deception in her experiences....

CHAPTER 50

When she got to York, she went to an anchoress who had loved her well before she went to Jerusalem to find out about her spiritual progress, and also wishing, for more spiritual conversation, to eat with the anchoress that day nothing but bread and water, for it was Our Lady's Eve.[3] And the anchoress would not receive her, for she had heard so much evil spoken of her. So she went off to other strangers and they made her very welcome for the love of our Lord.

One day, as she sat in a church in York, our Lord Jesus

---

1   *you*   I.e., your sexual desire.

2   *my wish*   To live chastely.

3   *Our Lady's Eve*   The eve of the Feast of St. Mary, i.e., 1 September.

Christ said in her soul, "Daughter, there is much tribulation coming to you."

She was somewhat dejected and upset at that, and therefore, sitting still, she did not answer. Then our blessed Lord said again, "What, daughter, are you unwilling to suffer more tribulation for love of Me? If you do not wish to suffer any more, I will take it away from you."

And then she said in reply, "Nay, good Lord, let me be at Your will and make me mighty and strong to suffer all that You will ever wish me to suffer, and grant me meekness and patience as well."

And so, from that time forward, knowing it was our Lord's will that she suffer more tribulation, she received it willingly when our Lord wished to send it, and thanked Him greatly for it, being truly glad and merry on any day when she suffered any misfortune. And over the course of time, she was not as merry nor as glad on a day when she suffered no tribulation as on a day when she did suffer tribulation.

Then, when she was in the aforementioned Minster[1] at York, a clerk came to her, saying, "Damsel, how long will you stay here?"

"Sir," she said, "I plan to stay for the next fourteen days."

And so she did. And in that time many good men and women asked to meet her and made her warmly welcome and were very glad to hear her conversation, marvelling greatly at the fruitfulness of her speech. And she also had many enemies who slandered, scorned and despised her, of whom one, a priest, came to her while she was in the said minster and, taking her by the collar of her gown, said, "You wolf, what is this cloth that you have on?"[2]

She stood still and would say nothing on her own behalf. Young men from the monastery who were going by said to the priest, "Sir, it is wool."

The priest was annoyed because she would not answer, and began to swear many great oaths. Then she spoke on God's behalf; she was not afraid. She said, "Sir, you should keep God's commandments and not swear so carelessly as you do."

The priest asked her who kept the commandments.

She said, "Sir, those who keep them."

Then he said, "Do you keep them?"

She said in reply, "Sir, it is my will to keep them, for I am bound to do so, and so are you and every man who will be saved at last."

When he had grumbled at her for some time, he went away secretly before she was aware of it, so that she did not know what became of him.

CHAPTER 52

There was a monk who was going to preach in York, who had heard much slander and much evil talk about the said creature. And when he was going to preach there was a great multitude of people there to hear him, and she was present with them. And so, when he was giving his sermon, he discussed many matters so openly that the people easily gathered that it was because of her, for which reason her friends who loved her well were very distressed and upset about it, and she was much happier, for she had something to test her patience and her charity, by which she hoped to please our Lord Jesus Christ. When the sermon was done, a doctor of divinity who loved her well, along with many others, also came to her and said, "Margery, how are things with you today?"

"Sir," she said, "very well, blessed be God. I have reason to be truly merry and glad in my soul if I can suffer anything for His love, for He suffered much more for me."

Soon after there came a man who loved her well with a good will, along with his wife and others, and led her seven miles from there to the Archbishop of York, and brought her into a handsome room, and a good clerk came in, saying to the good man who had brought her there, "Sir, why have you and your wife brought this woman here? She will sneak away from you, and cause you to be disgraced."

The good man said, "I dare well say that she will remain, and be here to answer for herself with a good will."

The next day she was brought into the Archbishop's chapel, and many of the Archbishop's household came in, scorning her, calling her "Lollard"[3] and "heretic," and they swore many a horrible oath that she would be burned. And she, through the strength of Jesus, said in reply to them, "Sirs, I fear you will be burned endlessly in hell unless you improve

---

[1] *Minster* Large church.

[2] *"You wolf ... have on."* See Matthew 7.15: "Beware of false prophets, which come to you in sheep's clothing, but inwardly they are ravening wolves."

[3] *Lollard* Follower of theologian John Wycliffe (1330–84), considered by some to be a heretic because of his severe criticisms of corruption in the institutional church and the failings of the clergy, as well as his views on certain church doctrines.

yourselves with regard to your swearing, for you do not keep God's commandments. I would not swear as you do for all the goods of this world."

Then they went away as if they were ashamed. She then, making a silent prayer, asked grace to behave herself that day in the way that would be most pleasing to God and profit to her own soul and a good example to her fellow Christians. Our Lord, answering her, said it would be just so. At last the said Archbishop came into the chapel with his clerks, and said sharply to her, "Why do you wear white? Are you a maiden?"[1]

She, kneeling on her knees before him, said, "No, sir, I am no maiden; I am a wife."

He commanded his people to fetch a pair of shackles and said she would be shackled, for she was a false heretic. And then she said, "I am no heretic, nor shall you prove me to be one."

The Archbishop went away and let her stand there alone. Then she prayed for a long while to our Lord God Almighty to help her and support her against all her enemies, spiritual and bodily, and her flesh trembled and shuddered terribly so that she wanted to put her hands under her clothing in order that it would not be seen.

Then the Archbishop came back into the chapel with many worthy clerks, among whom was the same doctor who had examined her before and the monk who had preached against her a little while before in York. Some of the people asked whether she was a Christian woman or a Jew; some said she was a good woman and some said not. Then the Archbishop took his seat, and her clerks also, each of them according to his rank, there being many people present. And in the time while the people were gathering together and the Archbishop taking his seat, the said creature stood to the back, making her prayers with deep devotion for help and succor against her enemies, for such a long time that she melted all into tears. And at last she cried out loudly as well, so that the Archbishop and his clerks and many people were astonished at her, for they had not heard such crying out before.

When her crying had passed she came before the Archbishop and fell on her knees, the Archbishop saying rudely to her, "Why do you weep like that, woman?"

She, answering, said, "Sir, you will wish some day that you had wept as hard as I."

And shortly, after the Archbishop had put to her the articles of our faith, which God gave her grace to answer well and truly and readily without any great thought so that he could not find fault with her, then he said to the clerks, "She knows her faith well enough. What shall I do with her?"

The clerks said, "We know well that she knows the articles of the faith, but we will not allow her to remain among us, for the people have great faith in her conversation, and perhaps she might lead some of them astray."

Then the Archbishop said to her, "I hear bad reports of you; I hear tell that you are a very wicked woman."

And she said back to him, "Sir, so I hear tell that you are a wicked man. And if you are as wicked as men say, you shall never get to heaven unless you mend your ways while you are here."

Then he said very rudely, "Why, you, what do people say about me?"

She answered, "Other people, sir, can tell you well enough."

Then a great clerk with a furred hood said, "Peace! You speak of yourself and let him be."

Then the Archbishop said to her, "Lay your hand on the book here in front of me and swear that you will leave my diocese as soon as you can."

"Nay, sir," she said, "I beg you, give me leave to go back to York to take leave of my friends."

Then he gave her leave for a day or two. She thought it was too short a time, so she said again, "Sir, I cannot leave this diocese so hastily, for I must stay and speak with good men before I go, and I must, sir, by your leave, go to Bridlington and speak with my confessor, who was the confessor of the good prior who is now canonized."

Then the Archbishop said to her, "You shall swear that you will not teach or scold the people in my diocese."

"Nay, sir, I will not swear," she said, "for I shall speak of God and rebuke those who swear great oaths wherever I go, until the time that the Pope and Holy Church have ordained that no one shall be so bold as to speak of God, for God Almighty does not forbid, sir, that we shall speak of Him. And moreover the Gospel mentions that when the woman had heard our Lord preach, she came before Him with a loud voice and said, 'Blessed be the womb that bore you and the breasts that gave you suck.' Then our Lord said in reply to her, 'Truly, so are they blessed who hear the word of God and

---

[1] *maiden* Virgin.

keep it."[1] And therefore, sir, it seems to me that the Gospel gives me leave to speak of God."

"Ah, sir," said the clerks, "here we truly think that she has a devil in her, for she speaks of the Gospel."[2]

At once a great clerk brought forth a book and for his part quoted St. Paul against her, that no woman should preach.[3] She, in response to this, said, "I do not preach, sir; I go into no pulpit. I use only conversation and good words, and that I will do as long as I live."

Then a doctor who had examined her previously said, "Sir, she told me the worst stories about priests that I ever heard."

The Bishop commanded her to tell that story.

"Sir, with all due respect, I spoke only of one priest by way of example, whom, as I have been told, God allowed to go astray in a wood, for the profit of his soul, until night came upon him. He, lacking in shelter, found a pleasant garden in which he rested that night, which had a lovely pear tree in the middle, all covered and adorned with flowers and blooms delightful to see, to which there came a big, rough bear, huge to behold, shaking the pear tree and knocking down the flowers. This dreadful beast greedily ate and devoured those fair flowers. And when he had eaten them, turning his tail end toward the priest, he excreted them out again from his hind parts.

"The priest, greatly disgusted at this loathsome sight, and struck with great doubt about its meaning, went on his way the next day melancholy and pensive, when it happened that it met with a handsome, aged man who looked like a palmer[4] or pilgrim, who asked the priest the cause of his melancholy. The priest, telling him what is written above, said he was struck by great fear and melancholy when he saw that loathsome beast defoul and devour such fair flowers and blooms and afterward excrete them from his backside so horribly in front of him, and that he did not understand what this could mean.

"Then the palmer, showing himself to be the messenger of God, explained it to him in this way: 'Priest, you yourself are the pear tree, partly flourishing and flowering by saying your service and administering the sacraments, though you do so undevoutly, for you pay little attention to how you say your matins[5] and your service, so long as you babble your way through it. Then you go to your Mass without devotion, and you have little contrition for your sin. You receive there the fruit of everlasting life, the Sacrament of the altar, in a most inappropriate state of mind. Then the whole day afterward you spend your time badly, devoting yourself to buying and selling, chopping and changing, as if you were a worldly man. You sit at your ale, giving yourself over to gluttony and excess, to bodily pleasure, through lechery and uncleanness. You break God's commandments by swearing, lying, slander, and backbiting and practicing other such sins. Thus through your misconduct you, like the loathsome bear, devour and destroy the flowers and blooms of virtuous living, to your endless damnation and the detriment of many people, unless you get the grace of repentance and amendment.'"

Then the Archbishop liked the story well and commended it, saying it was a good story. And the clerk who had examined her before in the absence of the Archbishop said, "Sir, this story strikes me to the heart."

The aforesaid creature said to the clerk, "Ah, honorable sir doctor, in the place where I mostly live there is a worthy clerk, a good preacher, who boldly speaks against the misconduct of the people and will flatter no one. He says many times in the pulpit, 'If any man dislikes my preaching, let him take note, for he is guilty.' And just so, sir," she said to the clerk, "is your experience with me, God forgive you."

The clerk did not know what to say to her. Afterward the same clerk came to her and asked her forgiveness for having been so much against her. He also asked her especially to pray for him.

And then soon after the Archbishop said, "Where can I find a man who will take this woman away from me?"

At once many young men jumped up, and every one of them said, "My lord, I will go with her."

The Archbishop answered, "You are too young; I will not have you." Then a good solid man of the Archbishop's household asked his lord what he would give him if he would take her. The Archbishop offered him five shillings and the

---

[1] *Blessed be the womb ... and keep it* From Luke 11.27–28.

[2] *she has a devil ... Gospel* Reading the Scriptures in English was one of the major points of debate in the Lollard conflict. The Catholic Church did not wish the Bible to be made available in the vernacular or for anyone other than the clergy to engage in Biblical interpretation. The Lollards took issue with the established Church on both counts.

[3] *St. Paul ... preach* See 1 Timothy 2.11–12.

[4] *palmer* Pilgrim to the Holy Land.

[5] *matins* Morning services.

man asked for a noble.[1] The Archbishop, answering, said, "I will not spend so much on her body." "Yes, good sir," said the aforesaid creature, "our Lord shall reward you well in return." Then the Archbishop said to the man, "See, here is five shillings, and take her quickly out of this region." She, kneeling down on her knees, asked his blessing. He, asking her to pray for him, blessed her and let her go. When she then went back to York she was welcomed by many people and worthy clerks, who rejoiced that our Lord had given her, who was unlearned, wit and wisdom to answer so many learned men without disgrace or blame, thanks be to God.

CHAPTER 53

Then the good man who was escorting her brought her out of town and then they went on to Bridlinton to her confessor, who was called Sleytham, and spoke with him and with many other good men who had entertained her previously and done much for her. Then she did not wish to stay but took her leave, to proceed on her journey. And then her confessor asked if she did not dare stay on account of the Archbishop of York, and she said, "No, indeed."

Then the good man gave her money, beseeching her to pray for him. And so she went on toward Hull. And there at one time, as they went in procession, a woman of high rank treated her with great contempt, and she said not a word. Many other people said she should be put in prison, and made great threats. And despite all their malice, a good man came and asked her to eat with him and made her very welcome. Then the malicious people who had scorned her before came to this man and told him not to be kind to her, for they believed that she was not a good woman. The next day in the morning her host led her out to the edge of town, for he did not dare entertain her any longer. And so she went to Hessle and wanted to cross the water at Humber.[2] Then she happened to find there two Dominican friars and two yeomen[3] of the Duke of Bedford. The friars told the yeomen who she was, and the yeomen arrested her as she was about to take her boat, and also arrested a man who was with her.

"For our lord the Duke of Bedford," they said, "has sent for you. And you are considered the greatest Lollard in this whole area and around London as well. And we have looked for you in many places, and we will have a hundred pounds for bringing you before our lord."

She said to them, "Sirs, I will willingly go with you where you want to take me."

Then they took her back to Hessle, and there people called her a Lollard, and women came running out of their houses with their distaffs,[4] crying out to the people, "Burn this false heretic."

And as she went on toward Beverley with the aforesaid yeomen and friars, they repeatedly met with people of that area who said, "Damsel, give up this life you are living, and go spin and card as other women do, and do not suffer so much shame and sorrow. We would not suffer so much for anything on earth."

Then she said to them, "I do not suffer as much sorrow as I wish to for our Lord's love, for I suffer only harsh words, and our merciful Lord Jesus Christ, worshipped be His name, suffered hard blows, bitter scourging, and at last shameful death for me and for all mankind, blessed may He be. And therefore what I suffer is truly nothing compared to what He suffered."

And so, as she went along with the aforesaid men, she said good things to them, until one of the Duke's men who had arrested her said, "I regret that I came upon you, for it seems to me that you say right good words."

Then she said to him, "Sir, do not regret or repent having come upon me. Do your lord's will, and I trust that all will be for the best, for I am very well pleased that you came upon me."

He said in reply, "Damsel, if ever you are a saint in heaven, pray for me."

She answered, saying to him in reply, "Sir, I hope you will be a saint yourself, and everyone that shall come to heaven."

So they went on until they came into Beverley, where the wife of one of the men who had arrested her lived. And they took her there and took her purse and her ring away from her. They prepared a pleasant room for her and a clean bed in it with the necessities, locking the door with the key and taking the key away with them. Then they took the man whom they had arrested with her, who was the Archbishop of York's man, and put him in prison. And soon after, that same day, word came that the Archbishop had come into the town where his man was in prison. The Archbishop was told

---

[1] *noble* English gold coin worth six shillings eightpence.

[2] *Humber* I.e., the River Humber.

[3] *yeomen* Attendants; men of high rank who serve a lord.

[4] *distaffs* Rods used for spinning wool.

of his man's imprisonment, and at once had them let him out. Then the man went angrily to the aforesaid creature, saying, "Alas that ever I knew you. I have been put in prison on your account."

She, comforting him, said, "Be meek and patient, and you will get a great reward in heaven for it."

So he went away from her. Then she stood looking out a window, saying many good words to those who wished to hear her, so that women wept hard and said with great sorrow in their hearts, "Alas, woman, why must you be burned?"

Then she asked the good woman of the house to give her something to drink, for she was ill with thirst. And the woman said her husband had taken the key away, and so she could not get to her nor give her anything to drink. And then the women got a ladder and put it up to the window and gave her a pint of wine in a pot and gave her some bread, beseeching her to put the pot and bread away secretly so that when the man of the house came he would not see it.

CHAPTER 54

The aforesaid creature, lying in her bed on the following night, heard with her bodily ears a loud voice calling, "Margery." At that voice she awoke, very frightened, and lying still in silence she made her prayers as devoutly as she could at the time. And soon our merciful Lord, who is present everywhere, comforting his unworthy servant, said to her, "Daughter, it is more pleasing to Me that you endure contempt and scorn, shame and reproof, wrongs and misfortunes than if your head were struck off three times a day, every day for seven years. And therefore, daughter, do not fear what any man may say to you; rather you have great reason to rejoice in My goodness and in the sorrows you have suffered for it, for when you come home to heaven, then every sorrow will turn to joy for you."

The next day she was brought into the chapterhouse of Beverley, and the Archbishop of York was there and many great clerks with him, priests, canons, and secular men. Then the Archbishop said to the aforesaid creature, "What, woman, have you come back? I would willingly be rid of you."

And then a priest brought her before him, and the Archbishop said, in the hearing of everyone present, "Sirs, I had this woman before me at Cawood, and there I and my clerks examined her in the faith and found no error in her. Furthermore, sirs, I have since that time spoken with good

men who consider her a righteous woman and a good woman. Nevertheless, I gave one of my men five shillings to lead her out of this area to keep the people quiet. And as they were going on their journey, they were taken and arrested, my man put in prison on her account, and her gold and silver taken away from her, as well as her prayer beads and her ring, and she is brought before me again. Is there anyone here who can say anything against her?"

Then other men said, "Here is a friar who knows many things against her."

The friar came forth and said that she led everyone astray from Holy Church, and uttered many bad things about her at that time. He also said that she would have been burnt at Lynn if his order, that is, the Dominicans, had not been there. "And sir, she says that she can weep and feel contrition when she wishes."

Then the two men who had arrested her came, saying like the friar that she was Cobham's[1] daughter and was sent to carry letters around the country. And they said she had not been to Jerusalem nor in the Holy Land nor on other pilgrimages,[2] when in truth she had been. They denied all truth and insisted on what was wrong, as many others had done before. When they had said enough for a great while and a long time, they held their peace.

Then the Archbishop said to her, "Woman, what do you say to this?"

She said, "My lord, with all due respect, every word they say is a lie."

Then the Archbishop said to the friar, "Friar, these are not heretical words; they are slanderous and erroneous words."

"My lord," said the friar, "she knows her faith well enough. Nevertheless, my lord of Bedford is angry with her, and he wishes to see her."

"Well, friar," said the Archbishop, "then you shall take her to him."

"Nay, sir," said the friar, "it is not for a friar to lead a woman around."

"And I do not wish," said the Archbishop, "for the Duke of Bedford to be angry with me on her account."

Then the Archbishop said to his men, "Keep watch on

---

[1] *Cobham* Sir John Oldcastle, Lord Cobham, one of the leaders of the Lollards in the early fifteenth century; he was executed as a heretic in 1417.

[2] *pilgrimages* Lollards did not condone pilgrimages.

the friar until I wish to see him again," and commanded another man to keep the aforesaid creature as well, until he wished to see her again another time at his pleasure. Then the aforesaid creature asked him by his lordship not to have her put among men, for she was a man's wife. And the Archbishop said, "No, you will not be harmed."

Then he who was entrusted with her took her by the hand and led her home to his house and asked her to sit with him at meat and drink, making her welcome. Soon afterwards many priests and other people came there to see her and speak with her, and many people felt great compassion that she was treated so badly.

Shortly afterward the Archbishop sent for her, and she came into his hall. His retinue was dining, and she was taken into his room and up to his bedside. Then she, obeying, thanked him for his gracious lordship that he had shown to her before.

"Yes, yes," said the Archbishop; "I am told worse of you than I ever was before."

She said, "My lord, if you would like to question me, I will tell the truth, and if I am found guilty, I will submit to your correction."

Then a Dominican who was a diocesan bishop[1] came forward and the Archbishop said to him, "Now, sir, say while she is present what you said to me when she was not present."

"Shall I really?" said the bishop.

"Yes," said the Archbishop.

Then the bishop said to the aforesaid creature, "Damsel, you were with Lady Westmoreland."

"When, sir?" she said.

"At Easter," said the suffragan.

She, not answering, said, "Well, sir?"

Then he said, "My lady herself was very pleased with you and liked your words, but you counselled Lady Greystoke to leave her husband, and she is a baron's wife and the daughter of Lady Westmoreland, and now you have said enough to be burnt for it." And so he spoke many harsh words in front of the Archbishop; it is not useful to repeat them.

At last she said to the Archbishop, "My lord, by your leave, I have not seen Lady Westmoreland for the past two years and more. Sir, she sent for me before I went to Jerusalem and, if you like, I will go to her again so she can attest that I never brought up any such matter."

"Nay," said those who stood about, "have her put in prison, and we will send a letter to the noble lady, and if what she says is true, let her go without any objection."[2]

And she said she was quite happy for it to be so. Then a great clerk who stood just beside the Archbishop, "Put her in prison for forty days and she will love God better all her life."

The Archbishop asked her what tale it was she had told Lady Westmoreland when she spoke with her.

She said, "I told her a good tale of a lady who was damned because she would not love her enemies and of a bailiff who was saved because he loved his enemies and forgave their trespasses against him, and yet he was considered a bad man."

The Archbishop said it was a good tale. Then his steward and many others said, crying out with a loud voice to the Archbishop, "Lord, we pray you, let her go away at this time, and if she should ever come back, we will burn her ourselves."

The Archbishop said, "I believe there was never a woman in England who was so much feared as she is and has been."

Then he said to the aforesaid creature, "I do not know what to do with you."

She said, "My lord, I pray you, let me have your letter and your seal to witness that I have defended myself against my enemies and nothing has been alleged against me, neither error nor heresy, that can be proved against me, thanked be our Lord, and have John, your man, take me back across the water."

And the Archbishop very kindly granted her all her desire, may our Lord reward him, and gave back her purse with her ring and prayer beads that the Duke of Bedford's men had taken from her before. The Archbishop was surprised that she had the means to travel around the country, and she said good men gave it to her asking her to pray for them.

Then she, kneeling down, received his blessing and took her leave in very good spirits, going out of his room. And the Archbishop's people asked her to pray for them, but the steward was angry because she laughed and was cheerful, and said to her, "Holy folk should not laugh."

She said, "Sir, I have great reason to laugh, for the more shame and contempt I suffer, the merrier I am in our Lord Jesus Christ."

---

[1] *diocesan bishop* Bishop suffragan: a bishop under the Archbishop's jurisdiction.

[2] *objection* I.e., resistance.

Then she went down into the hall and there stood the Dominican friar who had caused her all that trouble. And so she left the town with one of the Archbishop's men, carrying the letter that the Archbishop had granted her as a witness, and the man brought her to the River Humber, and there he took his leave of her, returning to his lord and taking the letter back with him, and so she was left alone without anyone she knew. All this misfortune came to her on a Friday,[1] thanked be God of all.

CHAPTER 55

When she had crossed the River Humber she was immediately arrested as a Lollard and taken toward prison. There happened to be a person who had seen her stand before the Archbishop of York, and he obtained permission for her to go where she wished and defended her against the bailiff and vouched for her that she was no Lollard. And so she escaped in the name of Jesus. Then she met a man from London and his wife. And she went along with them until she got to Lincoln, and there she suffered much scorn and many injurious words, answering back in God's cause at once so wisely and prudently that many people marveled at her cleverness.

There were lawyers who said to her, "We have gone to school for many years, and we are still not capable of answering as you do. Where do you get such cleverness?"

And she said, "From the Holy Spirit."

Then they asked, "Do you have the Holy Spirit?"

"Yea, sirs," she said, "no one can say a good word without the gift of the Holy Spirit, for our Lord Jesus Christ said to his disciples, 'Do not worry about what you will say, for it will not be your spirit that speaks in you, but the spirit of the Holy Ghost.'"[2] And thus our Lord gave her the grace to answer them, worshiped may He be.

Another time a great lord's men came to her and swore many great oaths, saying, "We have been told that you can tell us whether we shall be saved or damned."

She said, "Yes, indeed I can, for as long as you swear such horrible oaths and knowingly break the commandment of God as you do and will not give up your sin, I dare well say you will be damned. And if you will be contrite and confess your sin, willingly do penance and give it up while you can, with no intention of returning to it, I dare well say you will be saved."

"What, can you tell us nothing else but this?"

"Sirs," she said, "this is very good, it seems to me."

And then they went away from her.

After this she went on toward home again until she got to West Lynn. Once she was there, she sent to Bishop's Lynn for her husband, for Master Robert, her confessor, and for Master Alan, a doctor of divinity, and told them in part of her difficulties. And then she told them that she could not come home to Bishop's Lynn until she had gone to the Archbishop of Canterbury to get his letter and his seal. "For when I was called before the Archbishop of York," she said, "he would not believe what I said because I did not have a letter and seal from my lord of Canterbury. And so I promised him that I would not go to Bishop's Lynn until I had my lord's letter and the seal of Canterbury."

And then she took her leave of the aforesaid clerks, asking for their blessing, and went on with her husband to London. When she got there, she was provided with her letter at once by the Archbishop of Canterbury. And so she stayed in the city of London for a long time and was made very welcome by many worthy people.

Then she went toward Ely in order to get home to Lynn, and when she was three miles from Ely a man came riding after them at great speed and arrested her husband and her as well, intending to take them to prison. He cruelly rebuked and thoroughly insulted them, saying many chiding words. And at last she asked her husband to show him my lord of Canterbury's letter. When the man had read the letter, he spoke politely and kindly to them, saying, "Why didn't you show me your letter before?"

And so they left him and went on to Ely and from there home to Lynn, where she suffered much contempt, much reproach, many a slander, many a harsh word, and many a curse. And one time a reckless man, thinking little of his own shame, wilfully and on purpose threw a bowlful of water on her head as she came down the street. She, not at all bothered by it, said, "May God make you a good man," greatly thanking God for that, as she did for many other occasions. ...

—1436–38

---

[1] *on a Friday*   The day of Christ's Passion.

[2] *Do not worry ... Holy Ghost*   From Matthew 10.19–20.

Religious and Spiritual Life

CONTEXTS

Religion was so central to life in the Middle Ages that it is impossible in a section of this sort to do more than touch on a few important developments and themes.

Celtic culture forms a strong thread through the Christian culture of the early Middle Ages; several striking visual examples are included here. Among the most important developments in the transition from the Christianity of the Early to that of the High Middle Ages was a dramatic change in religious architecture; again, illustrations are provided below.

The prayers that Christians were expected to be able to recite and two excerpts from works of advice and instruction may give some sense of the reality of religious life for the laity. The Canons of the Fourth Lateran Council in 1215 were of enormous importance in regularizing Church practice throughout Western Europe; several of these are reproduced below.

Corruption within the Church was a recurring complaint—and a recurring reality—throughout the medieval period. During the fourteenth and early fifteenth centuries it was a particularly pressing concern both for reformist clerics such as John Wycliffe and the Lollards and for lay writers such as William Langland; in both cases relevant excerpts are included below.

The regularizing of Christian practice in the later Middle Ages was accompanied by the growth of exclusionist attitudes towards those who did not follow the designated path; as several of the readings at the end of this section illustrate, attitudes towards both heretics and Jews hardened significantly.

⌘ ⌘ ⌘

Celtic Christianity

Celtic art is characterized by formal intricacy and an extraordinarily high level of decorative skill. Its most famous expressions in a Christian context are in Gospels such as the Book of Kells and the Lindisfarne Gospels, but for centuries Celtic designs also featured prominently in a variety of forms of stone and metalwork.

Decorative page from the Book of Durrow (c. 670).

Carpet page from the Lindisfarne Gospels (8ᵗʰ century).

First text page, Gospel of Saint Luke, from the
Lindisfarne Gospels (8th century).

St. John from The Book of Kells (9th century).

Ardagh chalice (c. 700).
This extraordinarily elaborate chalice was
discovered in a hoard in a ring-fort in Limerick County in Ireland.

St. John, from The Macdurnan Gospels (9th century).

Pictish memorial stone (7th century?).
This stone stands at Glamis in Scotland;
accompanying the "Celtic cross" are a variety
of pictograms, the meaning of which is unknown.

Church and Cathedral

Greensted Church at Ongar, Essex (c. 850). Thought to be the oldest wooden church in the world, Greensted Church has walls formed of tree trunks split in two, erected curved-side outward.

The Norman Crypt, Canterbury Cathedral (12ᵗʰ c.). Round arches and heavy stone work are characteristic of Romanesque church architecture of the Norman Period.

Interior, Durham Cathedral (1093–1133). Durham is the most spare and imposing of the Norman cathedrals in England.

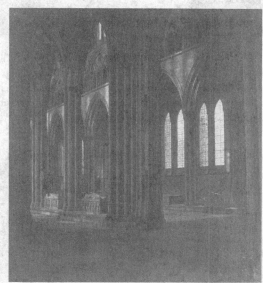

Roger Fenton, "Salisbury Cathedral" (1858). Salisbury Cathedral was built in the thirteenth century, with work beginning in 1220. The spire, which was completed near the end of the century, remains the tallest in England at 404 feet. Until the latter part of the nineteenth century it was one of the world's tallest structures. (From the late medieval period until the 1890s all but one of the world's tallest buildings were churches—the exception being the Pyramid of Cheops at Giza.)

Roger Fenton, *Cloisters, Westminster Abbey* (c. 1858). The cloisters date from the 13th and 14th centuries. Like Salisbury and York Minster, Westminster Abbey is built in the Gothic style, with pointed rather than rounded arches and extensive vaulting giving a stronger sense of verticality than in Romanesque architecture.

Roger Fenton, *York Minster, from the South East* (c. 1856). Built in the late thirteenth and fourteenth centuries, York Minster remains one of Britain's leading cathedrals.

Religion for All: The Apostles' Creed, the Pater Noster, and the Hail Mary

In the Middle Ages the Apostles' Creed was believed to have been jointly composed by the apostles, with each contributing one verse. Its origins are in fact unknown, though in its earliest forms the Creed almost certainly dates back to at least the fourth century. The following Latin text and English translation show the Creed divided into twelve constituent articles.

By the later medieval period all Christians were required to be able to recite the Apostles' Creed, the Pater Noster (or Lord's Prayer), and the Hail Mary in Latin rather than in the vernacular. The Pater Noster derives from two passages in the Gospels that were believed to contain Jesus's very words, Matthew 6.9–13 and Luke 11.2–4. The Pater Noster was ubiquitous throughout society, but few understood precisely what they were saying (the word "patter" derives from the sounds people made as they recited the Pater Noster quickly and without understanding); even among the clergy a working knowledge of Latin was far from universal.

The Hail Mary had come into wide use by the eleventh century, but it was not until the twelfth century that it became common for lay people to be required to be able to recite it.

The Apostle's Creed

Credo in Deum Patrem omnipotentem, Creatorem cæli et terræ.
Et in Jesum Christum, Fílium eius unicum, Dominum nostrum,
  qui conceptus est de Spiritu Sancto, natus ex Maria Virgine,
  passus sub Pontio Pilato, crucifixus, mortuus, et sepultus,
  descendit ad infernos, tertia die resurrexit a mortuis, ascendit ad cælos, sedet ad dexteram Dei Patris omnipotentis,
inde venturus est iudicare vivos et mortuos.
Credo in Spiritum Sanctum,
  sanctam Ecclesiam catholicam, sanctorum communionem,

remissionem peccatorum,
    carnis resurrectionem,
    vitam æternam. Amen.

I believe in God the Father Almighty,
    creator of heaven and earth,
    and in Jesus Christ, His only Son, our Lord;
    who was conceived by the Holy Spirit,
    born of the Virgin Mary,
    suffered under Pontius Pilate, was crucified, died,
        and was buried.
    He descended into hell; on the third day He arose
        again from the dead;
    He ascended into heaven and sits at the right hand
        of God the Father Almighty.
    From thence He shall come to judge the living and
        the dead.
I believe in the Holy Spirit,
    the Holy Catholic Church,
    the Communion of Saints,
    the forgiveness of sins,
    the resurrection of the body,
    and life everlasting. Amen.

The Pater Noster

Pater noster, qui es in caelis, sanctificetur nomen tuum. Adveniat regnum tuum. Fiat voluntas tua, sicut in caelo et in terra. Panem nostrum quotidianum da nobis hodie, et dimitte nobis debita nostra, sicut et nos dimittimus debitoribus nostris. Et ne nos inducas in tentationem: sed libera nos a malo. Amen.

Our Father, who art in heaven, hallowed be Thy name. Thy kingdom come. Thy will be done, on earth as it is in heaven. Give us this day our daily bread. And forgive us our trespasses, as we forgive those who trespass against us. And lead us not into temptation, but deliver us from evil. Amen.

[The following verse, which has never been part of the Roman Catholic Pater Noster, began to be added by various Protestant groups in the sixteenth century.]

For thine is the kingdom, the power and the glory, for ever and ever. Amen.

Illuminated page, Genesis-Job volume, Lambeth Bible (c. 1150).

This page illustrates the centrality of the Virgin Mary to medieval Christianity. During the Middle Ages the Latin words *virga* (stem) and *virgo* (virgin) were often assumed to be related. Here the illustration shows the stem of genealogy passing from Jesse through the Virgin Mary to Christ, with the four prophets (lower roundels), the four virtues of Mercy, Truth, Righteousness and Peace (middle roundels), and Moses with representatives of the Church Triumphant (upper roundels) looking on. In the corners are the four apostles.

The Hail Mary

Ave Maria, gratia plena, Dominus tecum, benedicta tu in mulieribus et benedictus fructus ventris tui.

Hail Mary, full of grace, the Lord is with thee, blessed art thou among women and blessed is the fruit of thy womb.

[The following verse began to be added during the fifteeth and sixteenth centuries.]

Sante Maria, Mater Dei, ora pro nobis peccatoribus, nunc et in hora mortis nostrae.

Holy Mary, Mother of God, pray for us sinners now and at the hour of our death.

from Robert Manning of Brunne, *Handlyng Synne* (early 14th century)

Robert Manning (c. 1264–c. 1340) was a Gilbertine monk at an abbey near Brunne (now Bourne) in Lincolnshire. Manning's poem *Handlying Synne*, written in English but very largely a translation of a similar work in French by William of Waddington, is an educational text designed to set out in everyday terms what is entailed in following the Ten Commandments, avoiding the Seven Deadly Sins, and so forth. Whereas most religious writing of the time was in Latin, Manning wrote in the vernacular for "lewd" men "that tales and rhyme will blithely hear" rather than for the educated minority who were literate in Latin. The extracts below set out specific examples of forbidden or morally questionable activities. Interestingly, miracle plays performed outside the church are included here on the list of proscribed activities—though depicting the birth and resurrection of Jesus within the church is "without danger."

… Of tournaments that are forbade
in holy church, as men do read,
of tournaments I shall prove therein,
seven points of deadly sin:
5 first is pride, as thou well know'st,
vanity, pomp, and many a boast;
of rich attire there is great flaunting,
spurring her horse with much vaunting.
Know you well this is envy
10 when one sees another do mastery,
some in words, some in deeds;

envy most of all him leads.
Ire and wrath cannot be late;
oft are tournaments made for hate.
15 If all knights loved each other well,
tournaments would never be held;
And of course they fall into slothfulness,
they love it more than God or Mass;
And truly, there can be no doubt,
20 they spend more gold thereabout—
that is, they give it all to folly—
than on any deed of mercy.
And yet be very careful lest
you forget Dame Covetousness,
25 for she shall be foolish, in all ways,
to win a horse and some harness.
And a man shall also do robbery,
or beguile his host where he shall stay.
Gluttony also is them among,
30 delicious meats do make him strong;
and gladly he drinks wine untold,
with gluttony to make him bold.
Also is there Dame Lechery;
from here comes all her mastery.
35 Many times, for women's sake,
knights these tournaments do make;
and when he goes to the tournament
she sends him some secret present,
and bids him do, if he loves her best,
40 all that he can at her behest,
for which he gets so much the worst,
that he may not sit upon his horse,
and that peradventure, in all his life,
shall he never after thrive.
45 Consider whether such tournaments
should more truly be called torments? …

It is forbidden him, in the decree,
miracle plays for to make or see,
for, miracles if thou begin,
50 it is a gathering, a site of sin.
He may in the church, through this reason,
portray the resurrection—
that is to say, how God rose,
God and man in strength and loss—
55 to make men hold to belief good,

that he rose with flesh and blood;
and he may play, without danger,
how God was born in the manger,
to make men to believe steadfastly
60 that he came to us through the Virgin Mary. …

A parson is slothful in holy church
who on his sheep will not work
how they should heed his own word
and please the church and their Lord.
65 The high Shepherd shall him blame,
for how he lets them go to shame.
If he should see in anything
that they have a lack of chastising,
unless he teach them and chastise so
70 that they from henceforth better do,
for them he shall, at God's assize,
be punished before the high Justice.
Also it behooves him to pray
that God, of grace, show him the way. …

75 Man or woman that has a child
that with bad manners grows too wild,
that will both mis-say and –do,
chastisement behooves them too;
But chastise them with all your might,
80 Otherwise you'll be in their plight.
Better were the child unborn
than lack chastising, and thus be forlorn.
Thus says the wise king Solomon
to men and women every one,
85 "If you want your children to be good,
give them the smart end of the rod;"
and teach them good manners each one;
but take care that you break no bone. …

Everywhere I see this custom:
90 that rich men have shrews for sons—
shrews in speech and in act—
Why? They hold no one in respect.
In his youth shall he mis-say
and scorn others by the way;
95 then says the father, "This child's story
doesn't hang together—sorry!"
And if he learns guilefulness,

false words and deceitful looks,
his father shouldn't acquit him then;
100 his sly wit will be his only friend.
If he injures foes in rages,
then says his father, "He shall be courageous,
he shall be hardy, and no man dread,
he begins early to be doughty in deed."
105 But right so shall it him befall
as it did with Eli's bad sons all. …

from William of Pagula, *Priest's Eye* (c. 1320)

William of Pagula was an English curate who wrote a work entitled *Oculis Sacerdotis* (*Priest's Eye*) between 1320 and 1323, intended for use as a handbook of instruction for parish priests–many of whom remained poorly educated. Both the full book and excerpts taken from it circulated widely; the following constituted a selection of twenty-one instructions taken from the larger work and issued independently in 1385.

1. A parish priest should recommend as many things to his parishioners on Sundays as seem useful to him for their instruction, and he should repeat them often so they will not slip from memory. First he should teach them the formula for baptizing infants in the absence of a priest if it becomes necessary. This is the vernacular version: *I crysten thee in the name of the fadyr and the sone and the holy ghost.* While saying this, sprinkle water over the child or immerse it in water three times or at the very least once. Anyone, whether cleric or lay person, may baptize a child in an emergency. Even the father of the child or its mother may do so without putting restrictions on their conjugal relations unless there is someone else present who knows how and wishes to do it. And if someone must baptize a child in an emergency using the above formula, he should speak the words distinctly and clearly only once, in no manner repeating the words of the rite or anything like them over the child. And if an infant baptized in this manner recovers, it should be taken to the church, and those who bring it should tell the priest that the child was baptized at home so that the priest will not baptize it again. But, excluding the immersion in water, he should perform the exorcism, the anointing, and the other customary actions that accompany baptism but were omitted. Let the priest teach his parishioners that they should baptize using only

water, no other liquids. Likewise let him warn men and women who are appointed the godparents of children at baptism that, except in an emergency they should not delay having their godchildren confirmed by a bishop. They should teach them or have them be taught the Lord's Prayer and the Creed, and admonish them when they reach adulthood or are capable of learning that they should guard their chastity, love justice, and practice charity.

The baptism of children born within eight days of Easter or Pentecost should be postponed for a week if it is convenient and they may be held back without danger, and then they should be baptized.

2. He should also warn them that anyone who has children who are not confirmed should make arrangements to have them confirmed by the time they are five years old if it is possible.

3. Also he should warn them that they should never put their children in bed with them in case through negligence they should roll over and smother them, which would be reckoned a case of homicide according to canon law. Nor should they thoughtlessly bind them in swaddling clothes or leave them alone by day or by night without someone watching them because of various dangers.

4. Also the priest should teach his parishioners that a spiritual kinship is established among godparents, god-children, and the parents of the godchildren. The same is true for sponsors at confirmation. Because of this kinship, marriage between any of these parties is prohibited. A spiritual kinship is established among ten people in baptism and the same number in confirmation.

5. He should also teach them that if a man and a woman shall have given their legitimate consent to contract a marriage by an exchange of words in the present tense, even though there has been no betrothal but only an oath, and even though, as is the custom, no carnal relations have occurred, still they have contracted a true marriage—so much so that if afterwards one of them should contract a second marriage and even have carnal relations with the new partner, they should be separated and that person should return to the first marriage. Also he should teach them that marriages should not be contracted except in the presence of

a priest and legitimate witnesses. Prior to the marriage ceremony banns should be solemnly published to the people in the church on three consecutive feast days. And any cleric or priest or other person who is present at a clandestine marriage shall be suspended from his office for three years.

6. Also he should warn them that boys and girls older than seven years should not lie together in the same bed because of the danger of fornication, nor should a brother share a bed with his sister because of the danger of incest.

7. Also he should publicly announce that any member of the faithful who has reached the age of discretion [i.e, fourteen] ought to confess all his sins to his own parish priest at least once a year and he should fulfill the penance imposed on him for his vices. During Eastertide he should receive the Body of Christ unless, with the counsel of his priest, for some reason he should abstain; otherwise while he is alive he should be barred from entering a church, and when he dies he should be without Christian burial. But if anyone does not wish to confess to his parish priest for a specific and well-founded reason, he should seek and obtain permission from his own priest to confess to another suitable priest.

8. Also he should teach them that pregnant women should be confessed beforehand so that they are prepared to receive the Eucharist if life-threatening danger should arise during their delivery, since it would seem improper for the priest to stay with them [hearing confession] during the course of their labor.

9. Also he should teach his parishioners that when the Host is elevated during the consecration of the Mass, they should genuflect if they can comfortably do so, and, adoring the Host, they should say in a low voice: "Hail salvation of the world, Word of the Father, true sacrifice, living flesh, fully God, truly man" or "Glory to you Lord who is born" or the Lord's Prayer or some other devout words. And they should also do this when they see the Body of Christ, preceded by lights and a ringing bell, carried to the sick.

10. Also he should warn his parishioners that they should faithfully pay their tithes on goods legitimately acquired. For faithfully paying tithes brings a fourfold reward: the first is an abundance of crops; the second is bodily health, according to

Augustine; the third is the remission of sins; the fourth is reward in the kingdom of heaven. But those who tithe badly are punished in four ways: first because they transgress a divine commandment. Second because once they had an abundance of all things when they tithed well, but now since they tithe badly they will be forced to tithe. Third, when tithes are poorly paid, God does not ward off locusts or other harmful things, nor does he dispel plagues or bring rain, except short-lived ones. Fourth, because of a lack of tithes, men justly collect taxes and tolls from the people since what Christ does not take, taxes will. Besides, those who do not pay their tithes are cursed by God. And merchants and artisans as much as carpenters, blacksmiths, weavers, alewives and other such people, and all other hired laborers and boon laborers all ought to be admonished to pay tithes from their earnings or else reach a settlement with the rector of their church.

11.   And the priest ought to announce to his people which days are feast days and which are days of fast.

12.   Also he should instruct his parishioners that they should not practice the magical arts, incantations, or sorcery, since these things have no power to cure either man or beast and besides are utterly worthless and unlawful. Moreover clerics who do these things shall be degraded and lay people shall be excommunicated.

13.   Also he should warn everyone not to lend money, grain, wine, oil or any other thing whatsoever by usury; namely by entering into a contract or having the intention to receive back more in repayment than he lent out. And if a cleric shall do this he shall be suspended from office; and a lay person shall be excommunicated until he makes restitution. To be sure, usury is forbidden in both the Old and the New Testaments.

14.   He should also warn his parishioners that they should not wait in order to sell their goods at a higher price, for they are obliged to repay what they have gained by this type of withholding. Likewise they should not sell their goods to travelers, pilgrims, and other wayfarers for a higher price than they charge to their neighbors or than they can receive at market.

15.   Let him also warn them that if anyone shall receive land or a dwelling as a pledge for a loan of money, after deducting his expenses, he should return the pledge; and if he receives more than that, it is to be reckoned as usury.

16.   Also he shall publicly announce three times yearly that all those men who wish to enjoy the privileges of the clergy shall be duly tonsured, displaying the crown of their head suitably shaved especially in the presence of their ordinaries and in churches and in congregations of the clergy.

17.   Also one day during Lent he should publicly preach the Creed, that is to say, the articles of faith.

18.   And he should admonish his parishioners that they should enter church humbly and devoutly and should behave reverently, peacefully, and devoutly while in it. And when they hear named the Name of Jesus they should genuflect at the very least in their hearts, or by bowing their head, or beating their breast.

19.   He should admonish them that no one should cause a disturbance, or a disagreement, or hold discussions, or useless and profane conversations in a church or its graveyard; nor should they provoke disputes or fights or anything else which could interrupt the divine services or dishonor the holiness of the place. Likewise business should not be conducted in the church or its graveyard and especially not fairs or markets, nor should courts, pleas, or secular judgments be held there. And dishonorable dances should not take place there, nor should improper songs be sung during the vigils of saints days or at other times, nor should there take place anything else by which the church or the graveyard could be dishonored.

20.   Also he should instruct them that neither a husband nor a wife should make an oath swearing to practice chastity, to fast, or to go on pilgrimage (except for a vow to go to the Holy Land) without the consent of the other. For a man and a wife are to be judged as equals in this regard.

21. He should also warn his parishioners that no one should harbor or defend in his home anyone who he knows has committed a known robbery.

from The Canons of the Fourth Lateran Council (1215)

> The following selections touch on the behavior of
> clerics, on confession, and on regulating the display and
> sale of the relics of saints. The final selection, Canon
> 68, is an illustration of the manner in which, as the
> canons of the Council acted to unify and strengthen the
> practices of Christians, equally they strengthened
> Christian hostility towards non-Christians.

Canon 14.   That the morals and general conduct of clerics
may be better reformed, let all strive to live chastely and
virtuously, particularly those in sacred orders, guarding
against every vice of desire, especially that on account of
which the anger of God came from heaven upon the children
of unbelief so that in the sight of Almighty God they may
perform their duties with a pure heart and chaste body. But
lest the facility to obtain pardon be an incentive to do wrong,
we decree that whoever shall be found to indulge in the vice
of incontinence, shall, in proportion to the gravity of his sin,
be punished in accordance with the canonical statutes, which
we command to be strictly and rigorously observed, so that he
whom divine fear does not restrain from evil, may at least be
withheld from sin by a temporal penalty. If therefore anyone
suspended for this reason shall presume to celebrate the divine
mysteries, let him not only be deprived of his ecclesiastical
benefices but for this twofold offense let him be forever
deposed. Prelates who dare support such in their iniquities,
especially in view of money or other temporal advantages,
shall be subject to a like punishment. But if those, who
according to the practice of their country [i.e., the Latin East]
have not renounced the conjugal bond, fall by the vice of
impurity, they are to be punished more severely, since they
can use matrimony lawfully.

Canon 15.   All clerics shall carefully abstain from drunkenness. Wherefore, let them accommodate the wine to
themselves, and themselves to the wine. Nor shall anyone be
encouraged to drink, for drunkenness banishes reason and
incites to lust. We decree, therefore, that that abuse be
absolutely abolished by which in some localities the drinkers
bind themselves in their manner to an equal portion of drink
and he in their judgment is the hero of the day who out-
drinks the others. Should anyone be culpable in this matter,
unless he heeds the warning of the superior and makes
suitable satisfaction, let him be suspended from his benefice

or office.

We forbid hunting and fowling to all clerics: wherefore,
let them not presume to keep dogs and birds for these
purposes.

Canon 21.   All the faithful of both sexes shall after they have
reached the age of discretion [then accepted to be fourteen]
faithfully confess all their sins at least once a year to their own
[parish] priest and perform to the best of their ability the
Penance imposed, receiving reverently at least at Easter the
sacrament of the Eucharist, unless perchance at the advice of
their own priest they may for a good reason abstain for a time
from its reception; otherwise they shall be [barred from
entering] the church during life and deprived of Christian
burial in death. Wherefore, let this salutary decree be published frequently in the churches, that no one may find in the
plea of ignorance a shadow of excuse. But if anyone for good
reason should wish to confess his sins to another priest, let
him first seek and obtain permission from his own priest,
since otherwise the other priest cannot absolve or bind him.

Let the priest be discreet and cautious, ... carefully
inquiring into the circumstances of the sinner and the sin,
from the nature of which he may understand what kind of
advice to give and what kind of remedy to apply, making use
of different means to heal the sick one. But let him exercise
the greatest precaution that he does not in any degree by
word, sign, or any other manner make known the sinner, but
should he need more prudent counsel, let him seek it cautiously without any mention of the person. He who dares to
reveal a sin confided to him in the tribunal of penance, we
decree that he be not only deposed from the priestly office
but also relegated to a monastery of strict observance to do
penance for the remainder of his life ...

Canon 62.   From the fact that some expose for sale and
exhibit promiscuously the relics of the saints, great injury is
sustained by the Christian religion. That this may not occur
hereafter, we ordain in the present decree that in the future
old relics may not be exhibited outside of a vessel or exposed
for sale. And let no one presume to venerate publicly new
ones unless they have been approved by the Roman pontiff.
In the future prelates shall not permit those who come to
their churches [for the sake of venerating relics] to be deceived
by worthless fabrications or false documents as has been done
in many places for the sake of gain. We forbid also that

seekers of alms, some of whom, misrepresenting themselves, preach certain abuses, be admitted, unless they exhibit genuine letters either of the Apostolic See or of the diocesan bishop, in which case they may not preach anything to the people but what is contained in those letters. We give herewith a form which the Apostolic See commonly uses in granting such letters, that the diocesan bishops may model their own upon it....

Canon 68.   In some provinces a difference of dress distinguishes the Jews and Saracens from the Christians, but in others confusion has developed to such a degree that no difference is discernible. Whence it happens sometimes through error that Christians mingle with the women of Jews and Saracens, and, on the other hand, Jews and Saracens mingle with those of the Christians. Therefore, that such religious commingling through error of this kind may not serve as a refuge for further excuse for excesses, we decree that such people of both sexes (that is, Jews and Saracens) in every Christian province and at all times be distinguished in public from other people by a difference in dress, since this was also enjoined on them by Moses. On the days of the Lamentations and on Passion Sunday they may not appear in public, because some of them, as we understand, on those days are not ashamed to show themselves more ornately attired and do not fear to amuse themselves at the expense of Christians, who in memory of the sacred passion go about attired in robes of mourning. That we most strictly forbid, lest they should presume in some measure to burst forth in contempt of the Redeemer. And, since we ought not be ashamed of him who blotted out our offenses, we command that the secular princes restrain presumptuous persons of this kind by condign punishment, lest they presume to blaspheme in some degree the one crucified for us.

Sin, Corruption, and Indulgence

from William Langland, *The Vision of Piers the Plowman* (B-text, c. 1377–81)

Langland's *Piers Plowman* is one of the major English literary texts of the fourteenth century— and also one of the most important historical documents in the overlapping histories of religious and secular developments during the period. The full poem is a long and in many ways a challenging and confusing text. It is framed as a Christian allegory, with characters such as Truth and Reason pronouncing on the ills of the world, and on the way to salvation. An important thread running through the poem is the attempt of an individual soul to seek out the stages that will lead to salvation; each of the various parts of the poem is called a "passus," or "step." The poem also includes powerful elements of social satire, in which many of the ways of the fourteenth-century world are harshly criticized. Chief among these are corrupt religious practices— perhaps most notably the practice of purchasing "indulgences" from the Church. (The principle of an indulgence was that a sacrifice of money, meant to help the Church with its financial obligations to the community, could ensure the forgiveness of the giver's sins.) Langland's text also includes wide-ranging criticisms of the greed and lack of charity that he saw as characterizing the behavior of the rich and privileged, nobles and clergy alike.

Langland did not advocate any revolutionary program to remedy society's ills and injustices; he intended to prick the consciences of the powerful to encourage them to mend their ways and carry out good works, but he did not intend to aid in any overthrow of their authority. Indeed, when it became clear that *Piers Plowman* was providing inspiration to the leaders of the uprising of 1381, Langland revised the poem in ways that made it less inflammatory.

Though Langland lived in London (he is believed to have held a modest position in the church), he eschewed the rhymed style of poetry that Chaucer and other Londoners had come to favor, preferring instead to write alliterative verse in a style reminiscent of that of Old English. (*Piers Plowman* is a key text in what scholars have come to refer to as the "alliterative revival" of the fourteenth century.) *Piers Plowman* has come down to us in many manuscripts, and exists in three versions, known as the A-, B-, and C- texts. The concise A-text and the considerably longer B-text are both more sharply critical of authority than is the C-text, which dates from after the 1381 rebellion (and in which Langland distances himself from the rebels' agenda).

Much as *Piers Plowman* is a central text of late medieval social protest, it is also a religious text and a spiritual allegory. The excerpts below give some sense both of the roots of social protest and of the degree to which what we would see as secular and religious elements are virtually inseparable in a text of this sort.

The first sixteen lines of the first Passus of the poem are provided below in the original as well as in a modernized version. As the selection from Passus 5 suggests, the poem has harsh advice for the common folk as well as for the well-to-do. But the prevailing note of criticism in the poem is of the sort seen in the excerpt below from Passus 7; these lines give some sense of the degree to which *Piers Plowman* takes in a broad sweep of the religious and social life of the fourteenth century.

from PASSUS 1

What this mountaigne bymeneth and the merke dale
And the feld ful of folk, I shal yow faire shewe.
A lovely lady of leere in lynnen yclothed
Cam doun from castel and called me faire,
5   And seide, "Sone, slepestow? Sestow this peple—

How bisie they ben aboute the maze?
The mooste partie of this peple that passeth on this
    erthe,
Have thei worship in this world, thei wilne no bettre;
Of oother hevene than here holde thei no tale."

10   I was afered of hire face, theigh she faire weere,
And seide, "Mercy, madame, what this to mene?"
    "The tour upon the toft," quod she, "Truthe is
        therinne,
And wolde that ye wroughte as his word techeth,
For he is fader of feith and formed yow alle
15   Bothe with fel and with face and yaf yow fyve wittes
For to worshipe hymn therwith while that ye ben here."

What this mountain means, and the dark dale
And the field full of folk[1] I fairly will show.
A lady, lovely of looks, in linen clothed,
Came down from a castle, and called me fairly
5   And said, "Son, are you sleeping? Do you see these
        people,
How busy they are, all thronging about?
Most of the people that pass their time on earth,

Have honor in this world, and they wish for no better
They don't care about any heaven but the one here
        on earth."

10   I was afraid of her face, though she was fair,
And I said, "Mercy, madam, what does this mean?"
    "The tower on the hill," she said, "Truth is therein

And he would like you to do as his word teaches;
For he is Father of Faith, who formed you all
15   Both with flesh and with face, and gave you five senses
To worship him with, while you are here."

---

1 The Prologue introduces the narrative as a dream vision, in which Piers recounts that he has seen a tower on a hilltop, and another in a valley, and a fair field full of folk between the two:
    A faire field full of folk found I there between,
    Of all manner of men, the mean and the rich …

PASSUS 5

The king and his knights to the church went
To hear matins of the day, and the Mass after.
Then waked I from my winking, and felt woeful
That I had not slept sounder, and so seen more.
5 But ere I had traveled a furlong, faintness so seized me
That I could not go further on foot, for lack of my
     sleep,
And I sat softly down, and said my belief,
And as I babbled on my beads,[1] they brought me asleep.
   And then saw I much more than I have already told,
10 For I saw the field full of folk that I before spoke of,
And how Reason got ready to preach to the realm,
And with a cross before the king commenced in this way
     to teach.
   He proved that these pestilences had to do purely
     with sin,
And the south-west wind on Saturday evening
15 Had plainly to do with pride, and for no point else.
Pear-trees and plum-trees were puffed to the earth
To show you people that you should do better.
Beeches and broad oaks were blown to the ground,
Their tails torn upwards, a dreadful sign
20 That at doomsday deadly sin shall be the sinners'
     undoing.
   Of this matter I may mumble at length
But I will say as I saw, God help me!
How plainly before the people Reason began to preach.
   He told Waster go work as best he could
25 And redeem himself for laziness with some sort of craft.
   And prayed that Pernele take off her costly array
And keep it in her box, in case she might need money
     later.
   Tom Stowe he taught to take two staves
And bring home Phyllis from women's punishment.
30   He warned Wat that his wife was to blame,
Saying that her hat was worth half a mark, but his hood
     cost not even a groat.
   And he bade Batt cut down a bough or even two
With which to beat Betty unless she would work.

---

[1] *beads* It is the practice of Roman Catholics to say their prayers to the Virgin Mary on a set of prayer beads called a rosary. The Apostles' Creed, or the "belief," as Piers says, is one of the prayers one recites when one says his or her rosary.

from PASSUS 7

Truth heard what was happening, and sent word to
   Piers
To take his team and to till the earth;
And Truth provided a pardon *a poena et a culpa*[2]
For him, and for his heirs, for evermore after.
5 And told him to stay at home, and plow up his fields,
And those that helped him to plow, to plant, or to sow,
Or any other work that might help Piers–
They too were granted pardon with Piers Plowman.
   Kings and knights that keep Holy Church
10 And rightfully in realms rule over the people
Have pardon to pass through purgatory lightly,
And to join patriarchs and prophets in paradise.
Bishops are most blessed, if they be as they should, …

Merchants had many years to the good,
15 But none were pardoned a *poena et a culpa* by the pope,
For they do not always observe the holy days, as the
     Holy Church teaches, …
Under his secret seal Truth sent them a letter
Saying they should buy boldly what they liked best,
And afterwards sell again, and save their profits
20 To use in helping *maisons Dieu*,[3] and in helping folk in
     misery;
In helping to repair rotten roads, where plainly needed;
And to build up bridges that were broken down;
In helping maidens to marry, or to become nuns;
In helping poor people and prisoners find their food;
25 And helping send scholars to school, or to some other
     craft;
In helping poor religious souls, and in lowering their
     rents …

Now has the Pope power to grant the people
Remission of penance, to pass directly into Heaven:
This is our belief, as lettered men teach us:
30 … I believe loyally (the Lord forbids anything else!)
That pardon, penance, and prayers cause people to be
     saved.

---

[2] *a poena et a culpa* Latin: from punishment and from guilt, i.e., absolving the holder of the pardon.

[3] *maisons Dieu* French: houses of God, i.e., hospitals, houses of charity, etc.

For souls that have sinned the seven deadly sins.
To trust to indulgences—truly I think
Is not so safe for the soul as it is to do well.
35   Therefore I advise all that are rich and
That trust of your treasure …
And especially you masters, mayors, and judges,
Who are held to be wise, and have the world's wealth
Available to purchase your pardons, and the Pope's
            bulls:[1]
40   At the dreadful Doom, when the dead shall arise
And you all will come before Christ, to have it reckoned
How you have led your life, and kept His laws,
And how you behaved day by day, the doom will declare
That however many pardons … of all the friars' orders
45   Promising two-fold indulgence—unless you have
Also good deeds to help you, I rate your patents
And pardons at one pea-pod's value!
Therefore I counsel Christians to cry to God for mercy,
And to Mary His mother to mediate for us,
50   That God grant us grace here, before that we depart,
That we may do such good works, while we are here
That after our death-day Do-well will declare
At the day of Doom that we did as he told us.

from Thomas Wimbleton, Sermon (c. 1388)

> The sermon from which the following passages are
> taken was preached by Thomas Wimbleton at Paul's
> Cross in London; it survives in over a dozen English
> (and two Latin) manuscripts.

… As I see, the first question that shall be purposed [to a
new curate or prelate] is this: how hast thou entered? Who
brought thee into this office? Truth other simony? God or
the devil? Grace or money? The flesh or the spirit?…

    And if we taken heed truly what abominations been
scattered in the church nowadays among priests, we
should well wit[2] that they all cometh nought into the fold
of Christ by Christ's clepynge[3] for the profit but by other
ways to get him worldly wealth; and this is cause of many

errors among the people…. When were [pride, envy,
wrath, and covetousness] so great as they are now, and so
of all other sins? …

The second question that every curate and prelate of holy
church shall answer to is this: how hast thou ruled, that is
to say the souls of the subjects and the goods of poor men?
Give now thine account. First, how hast thou governed
God's folk that was taken thee to keep? As a [shep]herd or
as a hired man that doth all for the love of his bodily hire?
As a father [or] as a wolf that eateth the sheep and keepeth
them nought? …

The third question that this first [curate or prelate] shall
answer to is this: how hast thou lived? What light of
holiness hast thou showed in thy living to the people? …
Reckon how thou hast lived. As a priest [or] as a lewd
man? As a man or as a beast? It is a wonder truly how the
life of priests is changed. They beith clothed as knights;
they speak as unhonestly as churls, [or] of winning as
merchants; they ride as princes; and all this that is thus
spent is of the goods of poor men and of Christ's heri-
tages.

Lollardy

One of the earliest movements in the direction of the
Reformation of Christianity was that of John Wycliffe
and the Lollards. Over a century before the upheavals
brought on by Martin Luther, Wycliffe spoke out
strongly against corruption and in favor of bringing all
Christians into more direct contact with the Word of
God. In Wycliffe's view the veneration of saints and
of relics, the drawing of a veil of mystery around the
Bible by refusing to authorize translations into the
vernacular, and the acceptance of vast levels of wealth
and privilege for members of the clergy were all of a
piece—and all deserved to be brought to an end.
Those who followed and extended Wycliffe's teachings came to be known as "Lollards"; their "heresies"
were ruthlessly stamped out in the fifteenth century.

from Account of the Heresy Trial of Margery Baxter

On April 1, 1429 Johanna Clifland, wife of William
Clifland, who lives in the parish of St. Mary the Less

---

[1] *Pope's bulls* Declarations by the Pope; specifically in this case,
declarations providing "indulgences," granting pardon for sins in
exchange for money.

[2] *wit* Know.

[3] *clepynge* Calling, bidding.

in Norwich, being cited, appeared in person before the reverend father and lord in Christ William, by the grace of God Bishop of Norwich [1426–36], holding court in his palace chapel. At the command of the bishop she placed her hand on God's Holy Gospels and swore that she would tell the truth about any and all questions asked of her that concerned matters of faith.

After swearing this oath, Johanna Clifland said that on the Friday [January 28] before the most recent feast of the Purification of the Blessed Mary, Margery Baxter, the wife of William Baxter the wright, recently living at Martham in the diocese of Norwich, was sitting and sewing near the fireplace with the witness in the witness's room. In the presence of the witness and her servants Johanna Grymell and Agnes Bethom, she told the witness and her servants that they should never swear oaths, saying in English: "Dame, beware of the bee, for every bee will sting; and therefore see that you swear neither by God nor by Our Lady nor by any other saint; and if you do the contrary the bee will sting your tongue and poison your soul."

Then the witness said Margery asked her what she did daily in church. The witness told her that as soon as she entered, after kneeling before the Cross it was her habit to say five Our Fathers in honor of the crucifix and the same number of Hail Marys in honor of Blessed Mary, the Mother of Christ. Then Margery scolded her and told the witness, "You act badly by kneeling like that and praying before images in these churches, because God has never been in such a church, and He never has gone forth from heaven nor will He ever. And He will not give or offer you any more merit for the genuflectings, and adorations, and prayers that you do in these churches than a lit candle hidden away under the cover of a baptismal font can give any light to people inside a church at nighttime." …

Next the witness said that the aforesaid Margery told her no child or infant born of Christian parents ought to be baptized in water according to the common custom since such a child had been sufficiently baptized in its mother's womb. So the image-worshipping and idolatry these false and accursed priests do when they dip babies in fonts in churches is done solely to wrench money from people in order to maintain these priests and their concubines.

Next the witness said Margery told her there that the consent of mutual love alone between a man and a woman sufficed to make the sacrament of marriage; no other exchange of words or ceremonies in a church were necessary.

Next she said Margery told her that no faithful man or woman was obliged to fast during Lent, Ember Days, Fridays, the vigils of saints, or other days indicated by the church; and that anyone could eat meat or any other kind of food during these times and on these days; and that on fast days it was better for someone to eat scraps of meat left over from Thursday than to go to the market and run up debts buying fish …

The witness also said Margery asked her and her servant Johanna to come secretly at night to Margery's house, and there they could hear her husband read the law of Christ to them, the law written in a book [i.e., the Bible] which her husband read to her at night; and she said her husband is an excellent teacher of Christianity.

Margery also said that she had spoken with Johanna West, a woman living near the churchyard of St. Mary-in-the-Marsh, about the law of Christ, and that Johanna is on the good road to salvation.

Furthermore, Margery said this to the witness: "Johanna, from your expression it looks like you plan to reveal what I've told you to the bishop." And the witness swore that she wished never to reveal her counsels in this regard unless Margery gave her cause to do so. Then Margery told her: "If you accuse me to the bishop, I'll do to you what I did to this Carmelite friar from Yarmouth who was the wisest friar in the land." The witness asked her what she had done to the friar. Margery answered that she had spoken with the friar, upbraiding him because he begged for his living, and telling him that it wasn't an act of charity to do good to someone or give him aid unless he himself wanted to take off his friar's habit and get behind a plow to work for a living, which would be more pleasing to God than following the way of life of some of these friars. Then the friar asked her whether she had anything else to tell him or teach him. So Margery, as the witness said, explained the Gospels to him in English. After that, the friar left Margery, so the witness said. Later this friar accused Margery of heresy. But Margery, hearing that the friar had denounced her, accused him of wanting to have sex with her, and since she would not give in to him, he accused her of heresy. Margery said this was the reason her husband wanted to kill the friar. Out of fear the friar shut up and left these parts in shame.

Margery also told the witness she had often made false confessions to the Dean of St. Mary-in-the-Fields so that he would think she led a good life. Because of this, he often gave Margery money. Then the witness asked her whether she had confessed all her sins to a priest. Margery told her she had never done harm to any priest, so she had never wanted to confess to a priest or be obedient to any priest, since a priest had no power to absolve anyone from sins; and in fact priests sinned more grievously every day than other people. Margery also said that every man and woman who shared Margery's opinion were good priests, and that the Holy Church exists only wherever all those people were who believed as she did. For that reason, Margery said she was obliged to confess only to God, not to any priest.

Next Margery told the witness that people honor the devils that fell from heaven with Lucifer who, when they fell to earth, entered into the statues standing in churches. They have dwelled in them since then and are still hiding in them, so that people who adore statues are committing idolatry.

Next the witness said Margery informed her that holy water and blessed bread were just trifles with no power, and that every church bell should be pulled down and destroyed, and that all those who set up bells in churches are excommunicated.

Margery also said that even if she were convicted of Lollardy, she shouldn't be burned because she, so the witness said, had and still has a charter of salvation in her womb.

Next Margery said she had won a judgment against the Lord Bishop of Norwich, and Henry Inglese, and the Lord Abbots associated with them.

Next the witness said she had sent Agnes Bethom, her servant, to Margery's house on the Saturday after last Ash Wednesday. Margery wasn't home but Agnes found a kitchen kettle on the fire, and boiling inside it were a piece of salt pork and oat flour—so Agnes reported to the witness.

[Margery confessed on 7 October, 1429. Her sentence included being flogged on four consecutive Sundays as she walked barefoot around her parish church.]

The Persecution of the Jews

The twelfth and thirteenth centuries were tumultuous and difficult times for Jews in Britain. Early Norman kings had encouraged the emigration of Jews from continental Europe, but in the latter part of the twelfth century attacks on Jews on the Continent by crusading Christians became common, and in Britain vicious propaganda against Jews (such as that found in Thomas of Monmouth's *Life and Miracles of St. William of Norwich*) began to be widely disseminated. Physical attacks on Jews (the most horrific of which was the massacre/mass suicide of approximately 150 Jews on 16 March, 1190, described below by Roger of Howden) became widespread in Britain in the late twelfth century. New taxes and restrictions (such as the 1194 Ordnances) began to be placed on Jews, and even more "favorable" developments (such as King John's Charter of 1201 confirming certain Jewish rights) were couched in such terms as to make clear that relations between Christians and Jews would remain entirely on an "us and them" footing. Restrictions became far more extreme with the Ordnances of Henry III, and in 1290 all Jews were expelled from the country by order of Edward I.

from Thomas of Monmouth, *The Life and Miracles of St. William of Norwich* (c. 1173)

When therefore [William] was flourishing in this blessed boyhood of his, and had attained to his eighth year [about 1140], he was entrusted to the skinners to be taught their craft. Gifted with a teachable disposition and bringing industry to bear upon it, in a short time he far surpassed lads of his own age in the craft aforesaid, and he equaled some who had been his teachers. So leaving the country, drawn by a divine urge he betook himself to the city and lodged with a very famous master of that craft, and some time passed away. He was seldom in the country, but was occupied in the city and sedulously gave himself to the practice of his craft, and thus reached his twelfth year.

Now, while he was staying in Norwich, the Jews who were settled there and required their cloaks or their robes or other garments (whether pledged to them, or their own property) to be repaired, preferred him before all other skinners. For [the Jews] esteemed him to be especially fit for their work, either because they had learnt that he was guileless and skillful, or, because attracted to him by their avarice, they thought they could bargain with him for a lower price, Or, as I rather believe, because by the ordering of divine Providence he had been predestined to martyrdom from the beginning of time, and gradually step by step was drawn on, and chosen to be made a mock of and to be put to death by the Jews, in scorn of the Lord's Passion. …

For I have learnt from certain Jews, who were afterwards converted to the Christian faith, how that at that time they had planned to do this very thing with some Christian, and in order to carry out their malignant purpose, at the beginning of Lent they had made choice of the boy William, being twelve years of age and a boy of unusual innocence. …

Then the boy, like an innocent lamb, was led to the slaughter. He was treated kindly by the Jews at first, and, ignorant of what was being prepared for him, he was kept till the morrow. But on the next day [Tuesday, 21 March], which in that year was the Passover for them, after the singing of the hymns appointed for the day in the synagogue, the chiefs of the Jews … suddenly seized hold of the boy William as he was having his dinner and in no fear of any treachery, and ill-treated him in various horrible ways. For while some of them held him behind, others opened his mouth and introduced an instrument of torture which is called a teazle [a wooden gag] and, fixing it by straps through both jaws to the back of his neck, they fastened it with a knot as tightly as it could be drawn.

After that, taking a short piece of rope of about the thickness of one's little finger and tying three knots in it at certain distances marked out, they bound round that innocent head with it from the forehead to the back, forcing the middle knot into his forehead and the two others into his temples, the two ends of the rope being most tightly stretched at the back of his head and fastened in a very tight knot. The ends of the rope were then passed round his neck and carried round his throat under his chin, and there they finished off this dreadful engine of torture in a fifth knot.

But not even yet could the cruelty of the torturers be satisfied without adding even more severe pains. Having shaved his head, they stabbed it with countless thorn points, and made the blood come horribly from the wounds they made. And so cruel were they and so eager to inflict pain that it was difficult to say whether they were more cruel or more ingenious in their tortures. For their skill in torturing kept up the strength of their cruelty and ministered arms thereto.

And thus, while these enemies of the Christian name were rioting in the spirit of malignity around the boy, some of those present adjudged him to be fixed to a Cross in mockery of the Lord's Passion, as though they would say: "even as we condemned the Christ to a shameful death, so let us also condemn the Christian, so that, uniting the lord and his servant in a like punishment, we may retort upon themselves the pain of that reproach which they impute to us."

Conspiring, therefore, to accomplish the crime of this great and detestable malice, they next laid their blood-stained hands upon the innocent victim, and having lifted him from the ground and fastened him upon the Cross, they vied with one another in their efforts to make an end of him.

And we, after enquiring into the matter very diligently, did both find the house, and discovered some most certain marks in it of what had been done there. …

As a proof of the truth and credibility of the matter we now adduce something which we have heard from the lips of Theobald, who was once a Jew, and afterwards a monk. He verily told us that in the ancient writings of his fathers it was written that the Jews, without the shedding of human blood, could neither obtain their freedom, nor could they ever return to their fatherland. Hence it was laid down by them in ancient times that every year they must sacrifice a Christian in some part of the world to the Most High God in scorn and contempt of Christ. …

from Roger Howden, *Chronicle* (1190)

In the same month of March [1190] … the Jews of the city of York, in number five hundred men, besides women and children, shut themselves up in the tower of York, with the consent of the sheriff, in consequence of their dread of the Christians; but when the sheriff and the constable sought to regain possession of it, the Jews refused to deliver it up. In consequence of this, the people of the said city, and the strangers who had come within the jurisdiction thereof, at the exhortation of the sheriff and the constable, with one consent made an attack upon the Jews.

After they had made assaults upon the tower day and night, the Jews offered the people a large sum of money to allow them to depart with their lives; but this the others refused to receive. Upon this, one skilled in their laws arose and said, "Men of Israel, listen to my advice. It is better that we should kill one another, than fall into the hands of the enemies of our law." Accordingly, all the Jews, both men and women, gave their assent to his advice, and each master of a family, beginning with the chief persons of his household, with a sharp knife first cut the throats of his wife and sons and daughters, and then of all his servants, and lastly his own. Some of them also threw their slain over the walls among the people; while others shut up their slain in the king's house and burned them, as well as the king's houses. Those who had slain the others were afterwards killed by the people. In the meantime, some of the Christians set fire to the Jews' houses, and plundered them; and thus all the Jews in the city of York were destroyed, and all acknowledgments of debts due to them were burnt.

from Ordinances of the Jews (1194)

All the debts, pledges, mortgages, lands, houses, rents, and possessions of the Jews shall be registered. The Jew who shall conceal any of these shall forfeit to the King his body and the thing concealed, and likewise all his possessions and chattels, neither shall it be lawful to the Jew to recover the thing concealed.

Likewise six or seven places shall be provided in which they shall make all their contracts, and there shall be appointed two lawyers that are Christians and two lawyers that are Jews, and two legal registrars, and before them and the clerks of William of the Church of St. Mary's and William of Chimilli, shall their contracts be made.

And charters shall be made of their contracts by way of indenture. And one part of the indenture shall remain with the Jew, sealed with the seal of him, to whom the money is lent, and the other part shall remain in the common chest: wherein there shall be three locks and keys, whereof the two Christians shall keep one key, and the two Jews another, and the clerks of William of the Church of St. Mary and of William of Chimilli shall keep the third. And moreover, there shall be three seals to it, and those who keep the seals shall put the seals thereto.

Moreover the clerks of the said William and William shall keep a roll of the transcripts of all the charters, and as the charters shall be altered so let the roll be likewise. For every charter there shall be threepence paid, one moiety thereof by the Jews and the other moiety by him to whom the money is lent; whereof the two writers shall have twopence and the keeper of the roll the third.

And from henceforth no contract shall be made with, nor payment, made to, the Jews, nor any alteration made in the charters, except before the said persons or the greater part of them, if all of them cannot be present. And the aforesaid two Christians shall have one roll of the debts or receipts of the payments which from henceforth are to be made to the Jews, and the two Jews one and the keeper of the roll one.

Moreover every Jew shall swear on his Roll, that all his debts and pledges and rents, and all his goods and his possessions, he shall cause to be enrolled, and that he shall conceal nothing as is aforesaid. And if he shall know that anyone shall conceal anything he shall secretly reveal it to the justices sent to them, and that they shall detect, and shew unto them all falsifiers or forgers of the charters and clippers of money, where or when they shall know them, and likewise all false charters.

from Charter of King John to the Jews (1201)

1. John, by the grace of God, &c. Know that we have granted to all the Jews of England and Normandy to have freely and honourably residence in our land, and to hold all that from us, which they held from King Henry, our father's grandfather, and all that now they reasonably hold in land and fees and mortgages and goods, and that they have all their liberties and customs just as they had them in the time of the aforesaid King Henry, our father's grandfather, better and more quietly and more honourably.

from Ordinances of Henry III (1253)

The king has provided and decreed ... that no Jew dwell in England unless he do the king service, and that as soon as a Jew shall be born, whether male or female, in some way he shall serve the king. And that there be no communities of the Jews in England save in those places wherein such communities were in the time of the lord King John, the king's father. And that in their synagogues the Jews, one and all, worship in subdued tones according to their rite, so that Christians hear it not. And that all Jews answer to the rector of the parish in which they dwell for all parochial dues belonging to their houses. And that no Christian nurse hereafter suckle or nourish the male child of any Jew, and that no Christian man or woman serve any Jew or Jewess, nor eat with them, nor dwell in their house. And that no Jew or Jewess eat or buy meat in Lent. And that no Jew disparage the Christian faith, nor publicly dispute touching the same. And that no Jew have secret intercourse with any Christian woman, nor any Christian man with a Jewess. And that every Jew wear on his breast a conspicuous badge. And that no Jew enter any church or any chapel save in passing through, nor stay therein to the dishonor of Christ. And that no Jew in any wise hinder another Jew willing to be converted to the Christian faith. And that no Jew be received in any town without the special licence of the king, save in those towns wherein Jews have been wont to dwell.

Illustration from *Flores Historianum* (14ᵗʰ century). Three Jews (all depicted with beards, as was customary) are attacked by a soldier.

And the justices appointed to the guardianship of the Jews are commanded to cause these provisions to be carried into effect and straitly kept on pain of forfeiture of the goods of the Jews aforesaid. Witness the king at Westminster on the 31st day of January. By the king and council.

Edward I's Order (1290)

Edward ... to the treasurer and barons of the exchequer, greeting. Whereas formerly in our Parliament at Westminster on the quinzaine of St. Michael in the third year of our reign, to the honor of God and the profit of the people of our realm, we ordained and decreed that no Jew thenceforth should lend anything at usury to any Christian on lands, rents or other things, but that they should live by their commerce and labor; and the same Jews, afterwards maliciously deliberating among themselves, contriving a worse sort of usury which they called courtesy, have depressed our people aforesaid on all sides under color thereof, the last offense doubling the first; whereby, for their crimes and to the honor of the Crucified, we have caused those Jews to go forth from our realm as traitors: we, wishing to swerve not from our former choice, but rather to follow it, do make totally null and void all manner of penalties and usuries and every sort thereof, which could be demanded by actions by reason of the Jewry from any Christians of our realm for any times whatsoever; wishing that nothing be in any wise demanded from the Christians aforesaid by reason of the debts aforesaid, save only the principal sums which they received from the Jews aforesaid; the amount of which debts we will that the Christians aforesaid verify before you by the oath of three good and lawful men by whom the truth of the matter may the better be known, and thereafter pay the same to us at terms convenient to them to be fixed by you. And therefore we command you that you cause our said grace so piously granted to be read in the aforesaid exchequer, and to be enrolled on the rolls of the same exchequer, and to be straitly kept, according to the form above noted. ...

THE WAKEFIELD MASTER
c. 1400 – 1450

Much is unclear about the identity of the "Wakefield Master" and about the group of plays ascribed to this individual. That group of plays is brought together in a manuscript that is believed to date from the mid sixteenth century. Nothing is sure about its origin, but by the seventeenth century it was in the library of a well-to-do Catholic family, the Towneleys of Towneley Hall near Burnley, Lancashire, from which the Towneley manuscript (now in the Huntington Library in San Marino, CA) takes its name. The manuscript includes thirty-two short plays based largely on biblical story material.

In the manuscript the plays appear in a sequence that approximates that of the Bible, beginning with a play depicting the story of the Creation. For that reason the Towneley Plays were long assumed to represent a cycle similar to that of the York and Chester cycles, in which a sequence of pageant plays was performed once every year, with performances beginning early in the day and running until dark, and with each play mounted under the auspices of one of the trade guilds of the town. Largely because the name "Wakefield" appears on the first page of two of the plays, the assumption took root that all thirty-two plays constituted a unified group that had been performed in that town, and the Towneley plays became widely referred to as the "Wakefield Cycle." As recent scholarship has emphasised, however, the thirty-two form a very disparate group. The plays have a variety of sometimes-incompatible staging requirements; several have been borrowed virtually intact from the York cycle of pageant plays; several exhibit inconsistencies suggesting that they were unlikely ever to have been performed as they now appear. It is thus now thought to be entirely possible that the manuscript collection simply represents a group of plays from various sources, assembled in quasi-chronological order. Some have speculated that the collection may have been brought together in one manuscript with a view more to reading than to performance (though marks in some plays suggest a performance history, it is not clear when these were added to the manuscript). It is now regarded as highly improbable that the thirty-two were all performed together as part of a unified cycle, in Wakefield or in any other town.

Within the Towneley Plays, however, are five plays with strong points of similarity: *Noah*, *The First Shepherds' Play*, *The Second Shepherds' Play*, *Herod the Great*, and *The Buffeting of Christ*. A sixth, *The Killing of Abel*, is sometimes also linked with these five, though it is not written in the same stanzaic form as the others. The two shepherds plays and *The Killing of Abel* (unlike other plays in the Towneley manuscript) contain textual allusions to the Wakefield area. The five maintain a strong metrical structure, presented in the manuscript in the form of nine-line stanzas, with a consistent a a a a b c c c b rhyming pattern throughout. The first four manuscript lines also contain rhyming half lines; in the light of this, recent scholarship is in agreement that an appropriate alternative to the way in which the lines are laid out in the manuscript is to read them as forming thirteen-line stanzas, rhymed a b a b a b a b c d d d c. These plays are also acknowledged to be distinguished by their lively characterization—and by the sheer skill of their composition. Since the nineteenth century they have generally been ascribed to a single author, now conventionally referred to as the "Wakefield Master." Here too, however, recent scholarship has challenged old assumptions. While the commonality of all five plays has not been questioned, we have no firm evidence as to authorship. The quotation marks placed around the name "Wakefield Master" are thus to be taken to indicate that the ascription of authorship is the product of convention rather than proven fact. All that can be said with confidence is that there seems clearly to have been a common force involved in the shaping of all five of these plays.

Whether through the medium of a single author or the shaping editorial hand of the compiler, the five plays demonstrate an extensive and sophisticated knowledge of the Bible. It is also possible that the author or editor had some knowledge of continental literature, as the structures suggest some influences from the French comic theater of the time. The plays are written in a northern dialect of Middle English.

The Second Shepherds' Play is the best known and most widely read of the English biblical pageant plays. As with all such plays, it seems to have been intended to make biblical stories interesting to a largely illiterate population. It is noteworthy, however, that the play contains a very significant amount of material that has no biblical source. The play interweaves a touching presentation of Christ's nativity (extrapolated from the biblical account) with a farcical plot involving the thief and trickster Mak. The story material that has been added has considerable entertainment value, but it also offers social commentary.

In *Herod the Great*, King Herod orders the slaughter of all male children in Bethlehem under two years of age in an attempt to kill the Christ child, whom he sees as a potential threat. In its dramatization of this Bible story, the play draws on several medieval literary traditions to portray Herod as an arch-villain. Taking a cue from the depiction of Herod in Matthew 2.16, medieval artists often portrayed Herod as a raving madman. (That this tendency was still alive in Shakespeare's time is evidenced by Hamlet's advice to the players to avoid a performance that "out-Herods Herod.") The play also portrays Herod as a Muslim, another medieval literary tradition; in medieval biblical plays, Herod and his cohorts were often costumed as Saracens. For the most part, however, the play makes no distinction between first-century Palestine and fifteenth-century England. Much as *The Second Shepherds' Play*, where characters anachronistically swear by Christ's cross and by Pontius Pilate before they know of the birth of Jesus, Herod here employs knights and receives the gift of medieval European lands.

⌘⌘⌘

The Second Shepherds' Play[1]

CHARACTERS:
First Shepherd
Second Shepherd
Third Shepherd
Mak
Gill
An Angel
Mary

(*Here begins their second.*)

[*A field near Bethlehem. Enter First Shepherd.*]

FIRST SHEPHERD.   Lord! what these weathers are cold!
　　And I am ill-happed;°　　　　　　　*poorly clothed*
I am near-hand dold,° so long have I napped;　*numb*

My legs they fold, my fingers are chapped;
It is not as I would, for I am all lapped°　　*wrapped*
　　In sorrow.
In storms and tempest,
Now in the east, now in the west,
Woe is him has never rest,
　　Mid-day nor morrow.

But we seely husbands[2] that walk on the moor,
In faith, we are near-hands out of the door;
No wonder, as it stands, if we be poor,
For the tilth of our lands lies fallow as the floor,[3]
　　As ye ken.°　　　　　　　　　　*know*
We are so hamed°　　　　　　　　*hamstrung*
For-taxed and ramed,[4]
We're made hand-tamed
　　With° these gentlery men.°　　*by / gentry*

---

[1] For the present text spelling and punctuation have been substantially modernized from the original Towneley text. The stage directions in Latin in the Towneley text are here translated into English and shown in parentheses. For clarity some other stage directions have been added; these appear in square brackets.

[2] *seely husbands* Poor farm workers.

[3] *the tilth ... floor* I.e., all of our land—the arable land (tilth) as much as the low–lying areas, is lying fallow; no crops are being grown there. During the fifteenth century many landowners were converting farmland to grazing land.

[4] *For-taxed and ramed* Overburdened and oppressed.

Thus they reave[1] us our rest, Our Lady them wary!°   *curse*
20   These men that are lord-fast,[2] they cause the plough tarry.
What men say is for the best, we find it contrary;
Thus are husbands° oppressed, in point to miscarry *farmers*
        In life.
Thus hold they us under,
25   Thus they bring us in blunder;°   *confusion*
It were great wonder,
        And° ever should we thrive.   *if*

For may he get a paint sleeve, or a brooch nowadays,
Woe is him that him grieve, or once again-says![3]
30   Dare no man him reprieve,° what mast'ry he
        makes;   *reprove*
And yet may no man lefe° one word that he says,   *believe*
        No letter.
He can make purveyance,[4]
With boast and bragance,
35   And all is through maintenance
        Of men that are greater. [5]

There shall come a swain, as proud as a po,°   *peacock*
He must borrow my wain,° my plough also;   *wagon*
Then I am full fain° to grant ere he go.   *delighted*
40   Thus live we in pain, anger, and woe,
        By night and day.
He must have if he longed,
If I should forgo it;[6]
I were better be hanged
45   Than once say him nay.

It does me good, as I walk thus by mine own,
Of this world for to talk in manner of moan.[7]

To my sheep will I stalk and hearken anon,
There abide on a balk,° or sit on a stone   *ridge*
50   Full soon.
For I trow,° pardie,[8]
True men if they be,   *trust*
We get more company
        Or° it be noon.   *before*

[*Enter Second Shepherd. He does not see the First Shepherd.*]

55   SECOND SHEPHERD.   Benste[9] and Dominus! what
        may this bemean?°   *indicate*
Why fares this world thus? Oft have we not seen,
Lord, these weathers are spiteous,° and the   *nasty*
        winds full keen;
And the frost so hideous they water mine eeyen,°   *eyes*
        No lie.
60   Now in dry, now in wet,
Now in snow, now in sleet,
When my shone° freeze to my feet   *shoes*
        It is not all easy.

But as far as I ken, or yet as I go,
65   We seely wed-men dre mekill woe;[10]
We have sorrow then and then, it falls° oft so.   *happens*
Seely Capel, our hen, both to and fro
        She cackles;
But begins she to croak,
70   To groan or to cluck,
Woe is him, our cock,
        For he is in the shackles.[11]

These men that are wed have not all their will;
When they are full hard stead,[12] they sigh full
        still;°   *continually*
75   God wayte° they are led full hard and full ill,   *knows*
In bower° nor in bed they say nought
        theretill,°   *bedroom / in reply*

---

1 *reave* Take away from.

2 *lord-fast* Attached to lords.

3 *For … again-says!* For, if anyone gets a painted sleeve or a brooch (i.e., wears livery) woe to the man who gives grief to or contradicts that person!

4 *purveyance* The requisition and purchase of provisions, specifically the right of the crown or of a lord to buy supplies for the household at a price set by a purveyor.

5 *through maintenance … greater* Through the support of those with greater power.

6 *He must … forgo it* If he has longed for a thing he must have it, even if I have to do without.

7 *in manner of moan* In a complaining way.

8 *pardie* By God (a corruption of the French "Pardieu").

9 *Benste* Bless us (a corruption of the Latin "Benedicte"); *Dominus* Latin: Lord.

10 *seely … woe* We poor married men suffer a great deal.

11 *Seely Capel … in shackles* The husband is in servitude to his wife, who is likened to a silly hen.

12 *full hard stead* Hard pressed, stricken by misfortune.

This tide.°   time
My part have I fun°—   found
I know my lesson:
80   Woe is him that is bun°   bound
            For he must abide.°   stay that way

But now late in our lives—a marvel to me,
That I think my heart rives° such wonders to see,   breaks
What that destiny drives, it should so be!—
85   Some men will have two wives, and some men three,
            In store.
Some are woe° that have any;   sad, woeful
But so far can I,[1]
Woe is him that has many,
90   For he feels sore.

[*To the audience.*]

But young men, of wooing, for God that you bought,[2]
Be well ware of wedding, and think in your thought:
"Had I wist"° is a thing that serves of nought;   known
Mekill still° mourning has wedding home   much steady
      brought,
95   And griefs,
With many a sharp shower,°   pang
For thou may catch in an hour
That shall sow° thou full sour°   grieve / bitterly
            As long as thou liffys.°   you live

100   For, as ever read I pistill, I have one to my fere[3]
As sharp as a thistle, as rough as a brier;
She is browed like a bristle, with a sour-loten°   looking
      cheer;
Had she once wet her whistle she could sing full clear
            Her pater-noster.[4]
105   She is as great as a whall,°   whale
She has a gallon of gall;
By him that died for us all,°   i.e., Jesus
            I would I had run to° I had lost her!   till

---

[1] *so far can I* This much I know.

[2] *you bought* Redeemed you.

[3] *as ever ... fere* As surely as I read the Epistle, I have one as my
companion.

[4] *pater-noster* Latin: Our Father; the Lord's Prayer.

FIRST SHEPHERD. God look over the row!°   audience
      Full deafly ye stand.
110 SECOND SHEPHERD. Yea, the devil in thy maw, so
      tarryand!°[5]   tarrying
   Saw thou anywhere of Daw?
FIRST SHEPHERD.   Yea, on a lea[6] land
   Heard I him blow;[7] he comes here at hand,
            Not far;
115 Stand still.
SECOND SHEPHERD. Why?
FIRST SHEPHERD. For he comes, hope I.
SECOND SHEPHERD. He will make° us both a lie   tell
            But if ° we beware.   unless

[*Enter Third Shepherd, a boy. He does not see the others.*]

120 THIRD SHEPHERD.   Christ's cross me speed, and Saint
      Nicholas!
   Thereof had I need, it is worse than it was.
   Whoso could, take heed, and let the world pass:
   It is ever in dread and brekill° as glass,   brittle
            And slithes.°   slides away
125 This world fared never so,
   With marvels more and more,
   Now in weal, now in woe,
            And all thing writhes.[8]

   Was never since Noah's flood such floods seen,
130 Winds and rains so rude, and storms so keen;
   Some stammered, some stood in doubt, as I
      ween;°   think
   Now God, turn all to good! I say as I mean.
            For ponder:
   These floods so they drown
135 Both in fields and in town,
   And bear all down,
            And that is a wonder.

[*He sees the others, but at first does not recognize them.*]

---

[5] *maw ... tarryand* Belly, for taking so long.

[6] *lea* Fallow, unploughed.

[7] *Heard ... blow* I heard him blow (his horn).

[8] *all thing writhes* Everything keeps turning.

We that walk in the nights, our cattle to keep,
We see sudden sights, when other men sleep.
140 Yet methink my heart lights—I see shrews° peep.   *villains*
Ye are two all-wights!° I will give my sheep   *monsters*
    A turn.
But full ill have I meant;
As I walk on this bent,°   *heath*
145 I may lightly repent
    My toes if I spurn.[1]
Ah, sir, God you save, and master mine!
A drink fain would I have, and somewhat to dine.

FIRST SHEPHERD.   Christ's curse, my knave, thou art a
    lither hind![2]
150 SECOND SHEPHERD.   What, the boy list° rave!   *likes to*

(*To the Third Shepherd.*)

    Abide unto sine;°   *later*
    We have made it.
Ill thrift° on thy pate!°[3]   *luck / head*

(*To the First Shepherd.*)

Though the shrew° came late,   *rascal*
155 Yet is he in state
    To dine, if he had it.[4]
THIRD SHEPHERD.   Such servants as I, that sweats and
    swinks,°   *labors, toils*
Eats our bread full dry, and that me forthinks;[5]
We are oft wet and weary when mastermen winks,°   *sleep*
160 Yet comes full lately° both dinners and drinks.   *very slowly*
    But naitly°   *thoroughly*
Both our dame and our sire,
When we have run in the mire,°   *muck*
They can nip at our hire,[6]

165   And pay us full lately.

But hear my truth, master: for the fare that ye make,
I shall do thereafter work as I take;[7]
I shall do a little, sir, emang ever lake;[8]
For yet lay my supper never on my stomach
170   In fields.[9]
Whereto should I threap?°   *complain*
With my staff can I leap,
And men say "light cheap
    Litherly foryields."[10]

175 FIRST SHEPHERD.   Thou were an ill lad—to ride on
    wowing
With a man that had but little of spending—
SECOND SHEPHERD.   Peace, boy, I bade; no more
    jangling,°   *chattering*
Or I shall make thee afraid, by the heaven's king,
    With thy gauds!°   *pranks*
180 Where are our sheep, boy? We scorn—
THIRD SHEPHERD.   Sir, this same day at morn
I left them in the corn,
    When they rang Lauds;[11]

They have pasture good—they cannot go wrong.
185 FIRST SHEPHERD.   That is right. By the rood,°   *cross*
    these nights are long!
Yet I would, ere we yode,° one gave us a song.   *went*
SECOND SHEPHERD.   So I thought as I stood, to mirth
    us among.[12]
THIRD SHEPHERD.   I grant.
FIRST SHEPHERD.   Let me sing the tenory.°   *tenor*
185 SECOND SHEPHERD.   And I the treble so high.
THIRD SHEPHERD.   Then the mean° falls to me; *middle part*
    Let's see how ye chant.

---

1   *But full ill … spurn*   The meaning here is obscure; the suggestion seems to be that a comical penance (of stubbing his toes) is to be imposed on the shepherd for having taken his fellow shepherds to be monsters.

2   *lither hind*   Wicked farm servant.

3   *Abide … pate*   Wait a while; we have had food already—bad luck to you.

4   *in state … had it*   Would like to eat, if he had food.

5   *me forthinks*   Upsets me.

6   *nip at our hire*   Reduce our wages.

7   *I shall do … take*   I will only work as well as I am being paid for it.

8   *emang ever lake*   Keep playing continually.

9   *For yet … fields*   For I have never had such a full stomach that it weighed me down in the fields.

10   *light cheap / Litherly foryields*   Proverbial saying: Low costs yield low returns, i.e., you get what you pay for.

11   *Lauds*   "Laud" was the first hour of the Church day, and it ended with the singing of a Psalm of praise (from the Latin for praise, *laus, laudem*).

12   *to mirth us among*   To have mirth among us.

(*Enter Mak, with a cloak thrown over his smock.*)

MAK.   Now, Lord, for thy names seven, that made
  both moon and stars,
  Well more than I can neven,[1] thy will, Lord, of me
   tharnys;[2]
190 I am all uneven,° that moves oft my harns;°   *upset / brains*
  Now would God I were in heaven, for there weep no
   bairns°   *children*
    So still!°   *incessantly*
FIRST SHEPHERD.   Who is that pipes so
  poor?°   *cries so wretchedly*
MAK.   Would God ye wist° how I foor!°   *knew / fared*
195 Lo, a man that walks on the moor,
   And has not all his will![3]

SECOND SHEPHERD.   Mak, where has thou gone? Tell
  us tidings.
THIRD SHEPHERD.   Is *he* come? Then each one take
  heed to his thing.[4]

(*Takes his cloak from him.*)

MAK.   What! *Ich*[5] be a yeoman, I tell you, of the king;
200 The self and the some,° sent from a great lording, *same*
   Und *sich*.°   *and such*
  Fie on you! Goeth hence!
  Out of my presence!
  I must have reverence.
205   Why, who be *Ich*?

FIRST SHEPHERD.   Why make ye it so quaint?° *affected*
  Mak, ye do wrong.
SECOND SHEPHERD.   But, Mak, play ye the saint? I
  trow that ye long.[6]

THIRD SHEPHERD.   I trow the shrew can paynt,[7] the
  devil might him hang!
MAK.   I shall make complaint, and make you all to
  thwang[8]
210   At a word.
  And tell even how ye doth.[9]
FIRST SHEPHERD.   But, Mak, is that truth?
  Now take out that southern tooth,[10]

    And set° in a turd!   *put*
215 SECOND SHEPHERD.   Mak, the devil in your eye! A
  stroke would I lean° you.   *give*
THIRD SHEPHERD.   Mak, know ye not me? By God, I
  could teen[11] you.

[*Mak now pretends to recognize the shepherds for the first time.*]

MAK.   God look you all three! Methought I had seen you.
  Ye are a fair company.
FIRST SHEPHERD.   Can ye now mene you?[12]
220 SECOND SHEPHERD.   Shrew, peep!° *look out!*
  Thus late as thou goes,
  What will men suppose?
  And thou has an ill noise
   Of stealing of sheep.[13]

225 MAK.   And I am true as steel, all men watt!° *know*
  But a sickness I feel, that holds me full hatt° *hot*
  My belly fares not well, it is out of estate.° *in poor shape*
THIRD SHEPHERD.   Seldom lies the devil dead by the
  gate.[14]
MAK. Therefore
230 Full sore am I and ill,
  If I stand stone still;

---

1 *neven*   Refer to, especially by name.

2 *of me tharnys*   Is unclear to me.

3 *Lo … will*   Look, I am just a man out walking, who does not
know what to do; or, does not have all he wants.

4 *Then … thing*   In that case everyone should look out for his
belongings.

5 *Ich*   The use of this word (together with "sich") suggests that
Mak is affecting a southern English dialect.

6 *play … long*   Are you pretending to be a saint? I believe that's
what you long to be.

7 *paynt*   Feign, deceive.

8 *thwang*   Be flogged.

9 *tell … doth*   I will even tell (the authorities) how you are acting.

10 *southern tooth*   Southern dialect.

11 *teen*   Vex, cause physical injury to.

12 *Can ye now mene you?*   Are you now able to recognize yourself
too?

13 *And thou … stealing of sheep*   And you have a bad reputation as a
sheep stealer.

14 *Seldom … gate*   Proverbial: When the devil seems to lie dead, it
is more likely that he is feigning.

I eat° not a needle   ate
    This month and more.

FIRST SHEPHERD.   How fares thy wife? By my hood,
    how fares sho?°   she
235 MAK.   Lies weltering,° by the rood, by the fire, lo!   sprawled
    And a house full of brood;° she drinks well, too;   children
    Ill speed other good that she will do!
        But so
    Eats as fast as she can,
240 And each year that comes to man,
    She brings forth a lakan°   baby
        And some years two.

    But were I now more gracious, and richer by far,
    I were° eaten out of house and of harbour;°   would be / home
245 Yet is she a foul douce,° if ye come near.   woman
    There is none that trows nor knows a worse
        Than ken I.
    Now will ye see what I proffer?
    To give all in my coffer
250 To-morn next to offer
        Her head-mass penny.[1]

SECOND SHEPHERD.   I know so forwaked[2] is none in
    this shire:
    I would sleep if I took less to my hire.[3]
THIRD SHEPHERD.   I am cold and naked, and would
    have a fire.
255 FIRST SHEPHERD.   I am weary, for-raked,°   exhausted
    and run in the mire.
        Wake thou!
SECOND SHEPHERD.   Nay, I will lie down-by,
    For I must sleep, truly.
THIRD SHEPHERD.   As good a man's son was I
260   As any of you.[4]

[Lies down.]

But, Mak, come hither! between shall thou lie down.

MAK.   Then might I lett you bedene of that ye would
    rowne;[5]
        No dread.
From my top to my toe
265 *Manus tuas commendo,*
Pontio Pilate! [6]
        Christ's cross me speed!

(*Then he rises, while the shepherds are asleep, and says:*)

Now were time for a man that lacks what he would,
To stalk privily then into a fold,°   sheepfold
270 And nimbly to work then, and be not too bold,
For he might aby the bargain, if it were told
        At the ending.[7]
Now is the time to reyll°   act quickly
But he needs good counsel
275 That fain would fare well,
        And has but little spending.[8]

[*Mak casts a spell on the sleeping shepherds.*]

But about you, a circle as round as a moon!
Till I have done that I will, till that it be noon,
That ye lie stone-still, to° that I have done.   till
280 And I shall say there-till of good words a fayne:°   few
    "On height,
Over your heads my hand I lift,
Out go your eyes, fordo° your sight!"   lose
But yet I must make better shift,°   arrangements
285   And° it be right.   if

[*Shepherds snore. Mak addresses the audience.*]

Lord, what they sleep hard! That may ye all hear.
Was I° never a shepherd, but now will I lere.°   I was / learn
If the flock be scared, yet shall I nip° near.   come

---

[1]   *head-mass penny*   Payment for her funeral mass.

[2]   *forwaked*   Tired from lack of sleep.

[3]   *I would … to my hire*   I would take less wages if I could sleep.

[4]   *As good … any of you*   I am just as good as you are (and therefore just as deserving of a rest).

[5]   *lett you … would rowne*   Hinder your whispering round me.

[6]   *Manus tuas commendo Pontio Pilate*   Latin: Into thy hands I commend (my spirit), Pontius Pilate. Mark misquotes Luke 23.46 ("Father, into thy hands I commend my spirit") and substitutes Pontius Pilate for God.

[7]   *he might … ending*   He (who is too bold) may pay a high price for it in the end.

[8]   *he needs … spending*   Someone who would like to fare better but has few resources needs to follow good advice.

How! Draw hitherward! Now mends our cheer
290   From sorrow.
A fat sheep, I dare say,
A good fleece, dare I lay.°   *wager*
Eft-whyte° when I may,   *repay*
        But this will I borrow.

[*Carries the sheep to the door of his house.*]

295 How, Gill, art thou in? Get us some light.
WIFE.   Who makes such din this time of the night?
I am set for to spin. I doubt that I might
Rise a penny to win; I shrew them on height!
        So fares
300 A huswiff that has been
To be raced thus between!¹
Here may no note° be seen   *benefit, profit*
        For such small chares.°   *chores*

MAK.   Good wife, open the hek!° Sees thou not   *door*
        what I bring?
305 WIFE.   I may let thee draw the sneck.° Ah, come in, *latch*
        my sweeting!
MAK.   Yea, thou there not reck of my long standing!²
WIFE.   By the naked neck art thou like for° to   *likely*
        hang!
MAK.   Do way!°   *stop that!*
I am worthy my meat,
310 For in a strait° can I get   *tight spot*
More than they that swink and sweat
        All the long day.

Thus it fell to my lot, Gill: I had such grace!³
WIFE.   It were a foul blot to be hanged for the case.
315 MAK.   I have scaped, Gillot, oft as hard a glace.° *blow*
WIFE.   But so long goes the pot to the water, men says,
        At last
Comes it home broken.
MAK.   Well know I the token,

---

¹ *I am set … between* I am all in a tizzy. I don't see how I can gain anything from this; I curse them mightily! This is how it goes for a housewife who has been interrupted like this!

² *Yea … standing* Yes, don't let it bother you how long I've been standing here!

³ *I had such grace* I was so blessed.

320 But let it never be spoken.
        But come and help fast.

I would he were flayn;° I list° well eat: *skinned / wish*
This twelvemonth was I not so fain of one sheep-
        meat.
WIFE.   Come they ere he be slain, and hear the sheep
        bleat—
325 MAK.   Then might I be ta'en: that were a cold sweat!
        Go spar°   *fasten*
The gate door.
WIFE.   Yes, Mak,
For and they come at thy back—
330 MAK.   Then might I buy, fro all the pack,
        The devil of the war!⁴

WIFE.   A good bowrde° have I spied, since thou   *trick*
        ken° none: *know*
Here shall we him hide too they be gone,
In my cradle abide. Let° me alone,   *leave*
335 And I shall lie beside in childbed and groan.
MAK.   Thou red°   *ready yourself*
And I shall say thou was lighted°   *delivered*
Of a knave°-child this night.   *male*
WIFE.   Now, well is me! Day bright
340   That ever I was bred!

This is a good guise and a far cast;°   *clever trick*
Yet a woman avyse° helps at the last!   *advice*
I wote never who spies; again, go thou fast!⁵
MAK.   But I come ere they rise, else blows a cold blast!
345   I will go sleep.

[*Mak returns to the Shepherds.*]

Yet sleeps all this meneye°   *group*
And I shall go stalk privily,°   *stealthily*
As it had never been I
        That carried their sheep.

[*He lies down among them. The shepherds begin to wake up.*]

---

⁴ *Then might … war* Then I might receive, from the pack of them, a hellishly bad experience.

⁵ *I wote never … fast* I don't know who may be looking; go back (to the shepherds) again quickly!

FIRST SHEPHERD.   *Resurrex a mortruis!*[1] Have hold my
350   hand!
Judas carnas dominus![2] I may not well stand.
My foot sleeps, by Jesus! and I water fastand.
I thought that we laid us full near England.[3]

SECOND SHEPHERD.   Ah, yea!
355   Lord, what, I have slept well!
As fresh as an eel,
As light I me feel
        As leaf on a tree.

THIRD SHEPHERD.   Benste be herein! So me quakes,
360   My heart is out of skin; what so it makes!
Who makes all this din? So my brows blakes
To the door will I win.[4] Hark, fellows, wake!
        We were four:
See ye anywhere of Mak now?

365   FIRST SHEPHERD.   We were up ere thou.
SECOND SHEPHERD.   Man, I give God a vow,
        That yede he nowhere.

THIRD SHEPHERD.   Methought he was lapt in a
        wolfskin.
FIRST SHEPHERD.   So are many happed now: namely,
        within.
370   THIRD SHEPHERD.   When we had long napped,
        methought with a gin°   *trap*
A fat sheep he trapped, but he made no din.
SECOND SHEPHERD.   Be still!°   *quiet*
Thy dream makes thee wood;°   *insane*
It is but phantom, by the rood.
375   FIRST SHEPHERD.   Now God turn all to good,
        If it be his will!

[*They turn to wake up Mak.*]

SECOND SHEPHERD.   Rise, Mak, for shame! Thou lies
        right long.
MAK.   Now Christ's holy name be us emang!°   *among*
What is this? For Saint James, I may not well go!

I trow I be the same. Ah, my neck has lain wrang°   *wrong*
380   Enough,
Mekill thank, since yester-even.°   *yesterday evening*
Now, by Saint Stephen,
I was flayed° by a sweven°   *scared / dream*
385   My heart out of slough.°   *skin*

I thought Gill began to croak, and travail° full sad,   *labor*
Well near at the first cock,° of a young lad   *cock-crow*
For to mend our flock. Then be I never glad;
I have tow on my rok[5] more than ever I had.
390   Ah, my head!
A house full of young tharms,°   *stomachs*
The devil knock out their harns!°   *brains*
Woe is him has many bairns,
        And so little bread!

395   I must go home, by your leave, to Gill, as I thought.
Pray you: look up my sleeve, that I steal nought:
I am loth you to grieve, or from you take aught.
[*Exits*]

THIRD SHEPHERD.   Go forth; ill might thou cheve.°   *fare*
        Now would I we sought,
            This morn,
400   That we had all our store.[6]
FIRST SHEPHERD.   But I will go before.
Let us meet.
SECOND SHEPHERD.   Where?
THIRD SHEPHERD.   At the crooked thorn.

[*They leave to check on their sheep. The scene shifts to Mak's
house.*]

405   MAK.   (*Knocking.*) Undo this door! Who is here? How
        long shall I stand?
WIFE.   Who makes such a bere?° Go walk in the   *noise*
        wanyand![7]
MAK.   Ah, Gill, what cheer? It is I, Mak, your
        husband.
WIFE.   Then may we see here the devil in a band.°   *noose*
        Sir Guile!

---

[1]   *Resurrex a mortruis*   Garbled Latin: He has risen from the dead!

[2]   *Judas carnas dominus*   Corrupted Latin: Judas, lord of the flesh!

[3]   *I water … England*   I have eaten so little that I thought we had
been lying down very close to England.

[4]   *So my brows … will I win*   My brows furrow (out of fear at the
commotion) and I will run away.

[5]   *tow on my rok*   Flax on my distaff (i.e., trouble).

[6]   *Now would I … store*   Now I would (think we should) check, this
morning, that we have all our belongings.

[7]   *wanyand*   Waning of the moon (an unlucky time).

Lo, he comes with a lote,°   *noise*
As° he were holden in° the throat.   *as if / held by*
I may not sit at my note°   *work*
    A hand-long° while.   *little*

410

MAK.   Will ye hear what fare she makes to get her a
    gloze?°   *an excuse*
And does nought but lakys,° and claws° her   *plays / scratches*
    toes.

415

WIFE.   Why, who wanders, who wakes, who comes,
    who goes?
Who brews, who bakes? What makes me thus hose?
    And then
It is sad to behold,
Now in hot, now in cold—
Full woeful is the household
    That wants° a woman!   *lacks*

420

But what end hast thou made with the herds,°   *herders*
    Mak?

MAK.   The last word that they said when I turned my
    back:
They would look that they had their sheep, all the pack.
I hope° they will not be well paid when they their   *expect*
    sheep lack,
    Per Die!°   *by God*
But howso the game goes,
It's me they will suppose,°   *suspect*
And make a foul noise,
    And cry out upon me.

425

430

But thou must do as thou hight.°   *promised*

WIFE.   I accord me theretill;
I shall swaddle him right in my cradle.
If it were a greater sleight,° yet could I help till.   *trick*
I will lie down straight; come hap me.

MAK.   I will.

WIFE.   Behind!
Come Coll and his marroo,°   *mate*
They will nip us full narroo.°   *pinch us hard*

MAK.   But I may cry out "Harroo!"°   *help*
    The sheep if they find.

435

440

WIFE. Hearken, aye, when they call: they will come anon.
Come and make ready all, and sing by thine own;
Sing "Lullay!" thou shall, for I must groan,

445

And cry out by the wall on Mary and John,
    Full sore.
Sing "Lullay" on fast
When thou hears at the last;
And but° I play a false cast,   *unless*
    Trust me no more.

450

[The shepherds meet in a field.]

THIRD SHEPHERD.   Ah, Coll, good morn! Why sleeps
    thou not?

FIRST SHEPHERD.   Alas, that ever was I born! We have
    a foul blot!
A fat wether° have we lorn.°   *sheep / lost*

THIRD SHEPHERD.   Marry, Gods forbott!° *God forbid!*

455

SECOND SHEPHERD.   Who should do us that scorn? That
    were a foul spot.

FIRST SHEPHERD.   Some shrew.°   *villain*
I have sought with my dogs
All Horbury Shrogs,[1]
And of fifteen hogs°   *young sheep*
    Found I but one ewe.

460

THIRD SHEPHERD.   Now trow me if ye will: by Saint
    Thomas of Kent,[2]
Either Mak or Gill was at that assent!°   *was involved!*

FIRST SHEPHERD.   Peace, man, be still! I saw when he
    went.
Thou slanders him ill; thou ought to repent
    Good speed.°   *speedily*

465

SECOND SHEPHERD.   Now as ever might I the°   *thrive*
If I should even here die,
I would say it were he
    That did that same deed.

470

THIRD SHEPHERD.   Go we thither, I rede,° and   *advise*
    run on our feet;
Shall I never eat bread, the sooth till I wit.[3]

FIRST SHEPHERD.   Nor drink in my head with him till I meet.

SECOND SHEPHERD.   I will rest in no stead° till   *place*
    that I him greet.
    My brother,

475

---

[1] *All Horbury Shrogs* All the hedges of Horbury (a town near
Wakefield).

[2] Thomas à Becket (1118?-1170), Archbishop of Canterbury.

[3] *the sooth till I wit* Until I know the truth.

One thing I hight:°   *promise*
Till I see him in sight
Shall I never sleep one night
        There I do another.[1]

[*They approach Mak's house. They hear Gill groaning and Mak
singing a lullaby.*]

480 THIRD SHEPHERD.   Will ye hear how they hack?[2] Our
        sire list croon.°   *likes to sing*
FIRST SHEPHERD.   Heard I never none crack so clear
        out of tune.
        Call on him.
SECOND SHEPHERD.   Mak! undo your door soon.
MAK.   Who is that spake, as it were noon,
485   On loft?°   *loudly*
        Who is that, I say?
THIRD SHEPHERD.   Good fellows, were it day!

[*Opening the door.*]

MAK.   As far as ye may,
            Good,° speak soft,   *good fellows*

490 Over a sick woman's head that is at malease;
I had liefer° be dead than she had any   *rather*
        disease.°   *discomfort, distress*
WIFE.   Go to another stead; I may not well
        quease.°   *breathe*
Each foot that ye tread goes through my nose,
        So hee!°   *loudly*
495 FIRST SHEPHERD.   Tell us, Mak, if ye may,
How fare ye, I say?
MAK.   But are ye in this town today?
        Now how fare ye?

Ye have run in the mire, and are wet yit?°   *yet*
500 I shall make you a fire, if ye will sit.
A nurse would I hire—think ye on it?
Well quit is my hire—my dream, this is it!—

[*Points to the cradle.*]

A season.[3]
I have bairns, if ye knew,
505 Well more than a few;
But we must drink as we brew,
        And that is but reason.°   *reasonable*

I would ye dined ere ye yode; methink that ye sweat.
SECOND SHEPHERD.   Nay, neither mends our mood,
        drink nor meat.
510 MAK.   Why, sir, ails you aught but good?[4]
THIRD SHEPHERD.   Yea, our sheep that we get
Are stolen as they yode; our loss is great.
MAK.   Sirs, drinks!
        Had I been there,
515 Some should have bought it° full sore.   *paid the price*
FIRST SHEPHERD.   Marry, some men trows°   *believe*
        that ye *were*,
            And that us forthinks.°   *displeases us*

SECOND SHEPHERD.   Mak, some men trows that it
        should be ye.
THIRD SHEPHERD.   Either ye or your spouse; so say we.
520 MAK.   Now, if ye have suspowse to° of Gill   *suspicion of*
        or of me,
Come and rip our house, and then may ye see
            Who had° her.   *took*
If I any sheep got,
Either cow or stot°—   *heifer*
525 And Gill, my wife, rose not
            Here since she laid her[5]—

As I am both true and lele,° to God here I pray,   *loyal*
That this be the first meal that I shall eat this day.
FIRST SHEPHERD.   Mak, as I have zeal, watch out, I say;
530 He learned timely to steal, that could not say nay.

[*They begin to search.*]

WIFE.   I swelt!°   *faint*

---

[1] *Shall I ... do another*   I will never sleep in the same place two
nights in succession.

[2] *hack*   To break a note, i.e., sing badly.

[3] *A nurse ... season*   I would like to hire a nursemaid—what do you
think of the idea? I've got what was coming to me—just what I had
dreamt of—another child every year.

[4] *Why, sir ... good?*   Sir, does something that is not good trouble
you?

[5] *And Gill ... laid her*   And my wife Gill has not gotten up since she
lay down here.

Out, thieves, from my wonys!°   *home*

Ye come to rob us, for the nonce.°   *on purpose*

MAK.   Hear ye not how she groans?

535   Your hearts should melt.

[*They approach the cradle.*]

WIFE.   Out, thieves, from my barn!° Nigh°   *child / approach*

him not there!

MAK.   Wist ye how she had farne,° your hearts   *labored*

would be sore.

Ye do wrong, I you warn, that thus comes before

To a woman that has farne[1]—but I say no more!

540 WIFE.   Ah, my middle!

I pray to God so mild,

If ever I you beguiled,

That I eat this child

          That lies in this cradle.

545 MAK.   Peace, woman, for God's pain, and cry not so:

Thou spills thy brain, and makes me full woe.

SECOND SHEPHERD.   I trow our sheep be slain. What

find ye two?

THIRD SHEPHERD.   All work we in vain; as well may we go.

          But hatters![2]

550 I can find no flesh,

Hard nor nesh,°   *soft*

Salt nor fresh,

          But° two bare platters …   *except*

[*Peers into cradle.*]

Whik° cattle like this, tame nor wild,   *live*

555 None, as I have bliss, as loud° as he smiled.°   *strongly / smelled*

WIFE.   No, so God give me bliss, and give me joy of my

child!

FIRST SHEPHERD.   We have marked amiss; I hold us

beguiled.

SECOND SHEPHERD.   Sir, done!

Sir, Our Lady him save!

560 Is your child a knave?°   *boy*

MAK.   Any lord might him have,

          This child, to° his son.   *as*

When he wakens, he kipps°—what joy to see.   *grips*

THIRD SHEPHERD.   In good time to his hips, and in seel![3]

565 But who was his gossips,° so soon ready?   *godparents*

MAK.   So fair fall their lips![4]

FIRST SHEPHERD.   (*Aside.*) Hark now, a lie.

MAK.   So God them thank,

Parkin, and Gibbon Waller, I say,

570 And gentle John Horne, in good fay—°   *faith*

He made all the garray°   *noise*

          With his great shank.°   *legs*

SECOND SHEPHERD.   Mak, friends will we be, for we

are all one.

MAK.   [*Aside.*] We! Now I hold for me, for

mends° get I none.   *amends*

575 [*To the Shepherds.*] Farewell all three! [*Aside again.*] All

glad were ye gone.

[*They leave the house.*]

THIRD SHEPHERD.   Fair words may there be, but love

is there none

          This year.

FIRST SHEPHERD.   Gave ye the child anything?

SECOND SHEPHERD.   I trow, not one farthing.

580 THIRD SHEPHERD.   Fast again will I fling—

          Abide ye me there.

[*Goes back into the house.*]

Mak, take it to no grief° if I come to thy bairn. *don't be upset*

MAK.   Nay, thou does me great reprefe,° and foul   *reproof*

has thou farn.°   *done*

THIRD SHEPHERD.   The child will it not grieve, that

little day-star.

585 Mak, with your leave, let me give your bairn

          But sixpence.

MAK.   Nay, do way: he sleeps.

THIRD SHEPHERD.   Methinks he peeps.

MAK.   When he wakens he weeps.

590   I pray you go hence.

[*First and Second Shepherds return.*]

---

1 *Ye do wrong … has farne* I warn you, you do wrong, coming like

this before a woman who has given birth.

2 *But hatters* An exclamation, "by God's clothing."

---

3 *In good time … in seel* Good fortune to him, and happiness!

4 *So fair … lips* Blessings on their lips.

THIRD SHEPHERD.   Give me leave him to kiss, and lift
    up the clout.°   *cloth*

[*Lifts the covering.*]

What the devil is this? He has a long snout!
FIRST SHEPHERD.   He is marked amiss.[1] We wait ill
    about.
SECOND SHEPHERD.   Ill-spun weft, I wis, ay comes
    foul out.[2]
595   Aye, so? [*Recognizes the sheep.*]
He is like to our sheep!
THIRD SHEPHERD.   How, Gib, may I peep?
FIRST SHEPHERD.   I trow, kind° will creep   *nature*
        Where it may not go.°   *walk (go in a forthright way)*

600 SECOND SHEPHERD.   This was a quaint gaud,° *cunning prank*
    and a far cast°—   *clever trick*
It was a high fraud!
THIRD SHEPHERD.   Yea, sirs, was't.
Let burn this bawd, and bind her fast. (*To Gill.*)
A false skawde° hangs at the last;   *scold*
605   So shall thou.
Will ye see how they swaddle
His four feet in the middle?
Saw I never in a cradle
        A horned lad ere now.

610 MAK.   Peace, bid I! What, let go your blare!
I am he that him got, and yond woman him bare.°*bore him*
FIRST SHEPHERD.   What devil shall ye hat° Mak? *be called*
    Lo, God, Mak's heir!
SECOND SHEPHERD.   Let be all that. Now God give
    him care,
    I sagh.°   *saw*
615 WIFE.   A pretty child is he,
As sits on a woman's knee;
A dilly-down[3] par Die,
        To make a man laugh.

---

[1] *marked amiss* Deformed, misshapen.

[2] *Ill-spun weft … foul out* Proverbial: I.e., the deformity of the parents comes out in the offspring.

[3] *dilly-down* Term of endearment.

THIRD SHEPHERD.   I know him by the ear-mark—that
    is a good token.
620 MAK.   I tell you, sirs, hark, his nose was broken.
Afterwards, he was forspoken.°   *bewitched*
FIRST SHEPHERD.   This is a false work—I would fain
    be wroken:°   *avenged*
        Get a weapon!
WIFE.   He was taken by with° elf,   *by*
625 I saw it myself;
When the clock struck twelve,
        Was he forshapen.°   *deformed*

SECOND SHEPHERD.   Ye two are well feft° same in a
    stead.°   *endowed / together*
FIRST SHEPHERD.   Since they maintain their theft, let's
    do them to dead.
630 MAK.   If I trespass eft,° gird° off my head! *again / cut*
With you will I be left.
FIRST SHEPHERD.   Sirs, do my rede:° *take my advice*
        For this trespass,
We will neither ban° nor flyte,°   *curse / quarrel*
635 Fight nor chite,°   *chide*
But have done as tight,°   *quickly*
        And cast him in canvas.

[*They toss Mak up and down in a sheet, and then leave his house.*]

FIRST SHEPHERD.   Lord, what! I am sore, in point for
    to brist;°   *burst*
In faith, I may no more; therefore will I rist.° *rest*
640 SECOND SHEPHERD.   As a sheep of seven score he
    weighed in my fist.
For to sleep anywhere, methink that I list.
THIRD SHEPHERD.   Now I pray you,
Lie down on this green.
FIRST SHEPHERD.   On these thieves yet I mene.° *think*
645 THIRD SHEPHERD.   Whereto should ye tene?° *be angry*
    Do as I say you.

[*The shepherds lie down.*]
(*An angel sings "Glory to God in the highest"; then let him say:*)

ANGEL.   Rise, herdmen kind, for now is he born
Who shall take from the fiend that which Adam had
    lorn:°   *lost*

That warlock to sheynd,° this night is he born.   destroy
650 God is made your friend now at this morn.
      He behests
At Bedlam° go see,   Bethlehem
There lies that free°   noble one
In a crib full poorly,
655   Betwixt two beasts.

FIRST SHEPHERD.   This was a quaint stevyn° that ever
    yet I heard.   voice
It is a marvel to nevyn,° thus to be scared.   report
SECOND SHEPHERD.   Of God's son of heaven, he
    spake upward.
All the wood on a leynn,° methought that he   lighting
    he gard°   made
660   Appear.[1]
THIRD SHEPHERD.   He spake of a bairn
In Bedlam, I you warn.°   tell
FIRST SHEPHERD.   That betokens yond star;
    Let us seek him there.

665 SECOND SHEPHERD.   Say, what was his song? Heard ye
    not how he cracked it,
Three breves° to a long?   short notes
THIRD SHEPHERD.   Yea, marry, he hacked° it.   sang
Was no crochet° wrong, nor nothing that lacked it.   note
FIRST SHEPHERD.   For to sing us among, right as he
    knacked it,[2]
670   I can.
SECOND SHEPHERD.   Let see how ye croon.
Can ye bark at the moon?
THIRD SHEPHERD.   Hold your tongues; have done!
FIRST SHEPHERD.   Hark after, then.

675 SECOND SHEPHERD.   To Bedlam he bade that we
    should gang;°   go
I am full fard° that we tarry too lang.°   afraid / long
THIRD SHEPHERD.   Be merry and not sad; of mirth is
    our sang.°   song
Everlasting glad to mede° may we fang°   reward / get
      Without noise.
680 FIRST SHEPHERD.   Hie we thither, forthy,
If we be wet and weary,

To that child and that lady:
      We have it not to lose.

SECOND SHEPHERD.   We find by the prophecy—let be
    your din!—
685 Of David and Isaiah, and more than I min°—   mind
They prophesied by clergy, that in a virgin
Should he light° and lie, to slokyn° our sin   alight / quench
    And slake it,
Our kind from woe;
690 For Isaiah said so:
Ecce virgo
    Concipiet[3] a child that is naked.

THIRD SHEPHERD.   Full glad may we be and
    abide° that day,   wait for
That Lovely One to see that all mights may.[4]
695 Lord, well were me for once and for ay,°   always
Might I kneel on my knee some word for to say
      To that child.
But the angel said:
In a crib was he laid,
700 He was poorly arrayed,
      Both mener° and mild.   poor

FIRST SHEPHERD.   Patriarchs that have been, and
    prophets beforn,°   before now
They desired to have seen this child that is born.
They are gone full clean;° that have they lorn.°   completely / lost
705 We shall see him, I ween, ere it be morn,
      To° a token.   as a
When I see him and feel,
Then wot I full well
It is true as steel
710   That prophets have spoken:

To so poor as we are that he would appear,
First find, and declare by his messenger.
SECOND SHEPHERD.   Go we now, let us fare; the place is us
    near.
THIRD SHEPHERD.   I am ready and yare°—go we in
    fere°   eager / together
715   To that bright.

---

[1] *methought ... Appear*   It seemed to me that he made the whole
wood light up in a flash.

[2] *knacked it*   Sang it in a lively or ornate manner.

[3] *Ecce virgo Concipiet*   Latin: Behold, a virgin shall conceive...
(Isaiah 7.14).

[4] *That Lovely One ... mights may*   To see that lovely one that is able
to do all things that can be done.

Lord, if thy wills be,
We are lewd°, all three;   *unlearned*
Thou grant us somekins° glee,   *some kind of*
  To comfort thy wight.°   *creature*

[*They enter the stable in Bethlehem.*]

720 FIRST SHEPHERD. Hail, comely and clean! hail, young
  child!
Hail, Maker, as I mean, of° a maiden so mild!   *born of*
Thou has waried,° I ween, the warlock so wild,[1]   *cursed*
The false guiler° of teyn° now goes he
  beguiled.   *deceiver / suffering*
   Lo, he merries![2]
725 Lo, he laughs, my sweeting!
A well-fare meeting!
I have holden my heting°—   *kept my promise*
  Have a bob° of cherries!   *bunch*

SECOND SHEPHERD. Hail, sovereign saviour, for thou
  has us sought!
730 Hail, freely foyde° and flower, that all thing   *noble child*
  has wrought!
Hail, full of favour, that made all of nought!
Hail! I kneel and I cower. A bird have I brought
  To my barn.
Hail, little tiny mop,°   *moppet*
735 Of our creed thou art crop!°   *harvest*
I would drink in thy cup,
  Little day-star!

THIRD SHEPHERD. Hail, darling dear, full of godhead!
I pray thee be near, when that I have need.
740 Hail! sweet is thy cheer! My heart would bleed

To see thee sit here in so poor weed,°   *clothes*
  With no pennies.
Hail! put forth thy dall,°   *hand*
I bring thee but a ball;
745 Have and play thee withall,
  And go to the tennis.

MARY. The Father of Heaven, God omnipotent,
That made all in seven, his son has he sent.
My name couth he neven,° and light ere he   *uttered*
  went.°[3]   *walked*
750 I conceived him full even, through might, as he meant;
  And now he is born.
He keep you from woe!
I shall pray him so;
Tell forth as ye go,
755   And mind on° this morn.   *remember*

FIRST SHEPHERD. Farewell, lady, so fair to behold,
With thy child on thy knee.
SECOND SHEPHERD.   But he lies full cold.
Lord, well is me! Now we go, thou behold.
760 THIRD SHEPHERD. Forsooth, already it seems to be told
  Full oft.
FIRST SHEPHERD. What grace we have fun!°   *found*
SECOND SHEPHERD. Come forth, now have we won.
THIRD SHEPHERD. To sing are we bun—°   *bound*
765   Let take on loft! [*They exit, singing.*]

(*Here ends the shepherds' pageant.*)
—C. 1400–1450

---

[1] *the warlock so wild* I.e., the devil.
[2] *Lo, he merries!* Look, he (Christ) is merry.

[3] *and light ere he went* And he could leap before he could walk.
The allusion is to the medieval idea of the Seven Leaps of Christ,
one of which was the Incarnation: Christ was thought of as having
miraculously "leapt" down from heaven into Mary's womb.

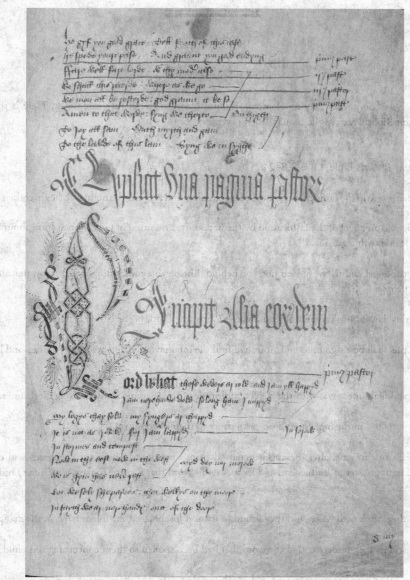

Opening page, *The Second Shepherds' Play*, Towneley Plays 1F.38. (Reprinted by permission of *The Huntington Library, San Marino, California*.)

―――――――

IN CONTEXT

Biblical Source Material

The Second Shepherds' Play supplements Biblical source material very extensively. Here is the relevant Biblical text, in the Douay-Rheims version.

from Douay-Rheims Bible, Luke 2.8–21

8   And there were in the same country shepherds watching, and keeping the night watches over their flock.

9   And behold an angel of the Lord stood by them, and the brightness of God shone round about them; and they feared with a great fear.

10   And the angel said to them: Fear not; for, behold, I bring you good tidings of great joy, that shall be to all the people:

11   For, this day, is born to you a Saviour, who is Christ the Lord, in the city of David.

12   And this shall be a sign unto you. You shall find the infant wrapped in swaddling clothes, and laid in a manger.

13   And suddenly there was with the angel a multitude of the heavenly army, praising God, and saying:

14   Glory to God in the highest; and on earth peace to men of good will.

15   And it came to pass, after the angels departed from them into heaven, the shepherds said one to another: Let us go over to Bethlehem, and let us see this word that is come to pass, which the Lord hath shewed to us.

16   And they came with haste; and they found Mary and Joseph, and the infant lying in the manger.

17   And seeing, they understood of the word that had been spoken to them concerning this child.

18   And all that heard, wondered; and at those things that were told them by the shepherds.

19   But Mary kept all these words, pondering them in her heart.

20   And the shepherds returned, glorifying and praising God, for all the things they had heard and seen, as it was told unto them.

21   And after eight days were accomplished, that the child should be circumcised, his name was called JESUS, which was called by the angel, before he was conceived in the womb.

Sir Thomas Malory

c. 1405– 1471

Thomas Malory's place in English literary history rests on one great work, his *Morte Darthur* (*The Death of Arthur*), the first major prose work of the English language. Malory's version is the basis for the Arthurian mythology that endures to the present day. Malory drew on various sources, both French and English, but crafted those sources to provide a full narrative of the life of Arthur and the Knights of the Round Table. Tennyson's *Idylls of the King* is perhaps the best known of the works inspired by *Morte Darthur*, but Malory's work has also strongly influenced the writings of Spenser, Milton, and Arnold, the paintings of Rossetti and Watts, and the music of Wagner.

The facts of Malory's life are few, his story a matter of conjecture and dispute, but the available information suggests that he led an extraordinary life. There were several individuals with the name Thomas Malory in the fifteenth century. The one who is most commonly, though by no means certainly, identified with the author of the *Morte Darthur* was born to John Malory and Philippa Chetwynd of Newbold Revell, Warwickshire, near the beginning of the fifteenth century. John Malory was a man of some distinction, having served as a sheriff, a Member of Parliament, and a Justice of the Peace in Warwickshire.

The records that survive, however, give John's son Thomas a rather dubious reputation. The political intrigues of the 1450s eventually led to the Wars of the Roses, the battle for the English throne that was carried on by the families of York and Lancaster, and Thomas Malory appears to have been a participant in the turmoil. Surviving records show that he was charged with significant crimes during the 1450s including extortion, theft, horse stealing, and rape. It is possible that Malory's political activities earned him some enemies who engaged in a slander campaign against him, or he may indeed have been responsible for the crimes for which he was charged. In 1451 a warrant was issued for Malory's arrest. He was imprisoned at Coleshill, Warwickshire, but escaped; in 1452 he was recaptured and put in jail in London, where he spent most of the next eight years awaiting trial.

By the mid-1450s the Wars of the Roses were in full force. Malory's loyalty seems to have wavered between the two warring houses, and his fortunes rose and fell on that basis. While in prison, Malory was pardoned by the Duke of York; the Lancastrian court, however, dismissed the pardon. When the Yorkists overthrew the Lancastrians, Malory was pardoned and released. He then fought against the Lancastrians in a number of key battles. Malory seems then to have changed sides in the dispute—in 1468 his name appeared on a list of men allied with the Lancastrians. He was arrested by the Yorkists for his support of the Lancastrians, and again imprisoned in London. During these last years of imprisonment, Malory wrote *Morte Darthur*, describing himself in the text as a "knight presoner."

Malory's primary source for the *Morte Darthur* was the French Arthurian Prose Cycle (1225–30), but he also borrowed from Geoffrey of Monmouth's *History of the Kings of Britain* (1136–39) and two anonymous English works of the later fourteenth century, the alliterative *Morte Arthure* and the stanzaic *Morte Arthur*. Some of the details of the narrative are purely Malory's own inventions, but he nevertheless takes care to ascribe each of his additions to "the Freynshe booke."

Morte Darthur is vast in its scale. Malory tells eight tales over 21 books with 507 chapters. Malory originally titled the work *The Book of King Arthur and his Noble Knights of the Round Table;* William Caxton, the printer who published the book in 1485, changed the title to *Morte Darthur*. Caxton also made a significant number of editorial changes, as was discovered in 1934, when a manuscript copy of Malory's work that was significantly at variance with Caxton's text came to light. It became clear that Caxton had brought together what had been eight separate romances into twenty-one books, making alterations so as to give the appearance of a more unified text. Caxton had also deleted the personal remarks with which Malory concluded each romance.

Within a year of the completion of *Morte Darthur*, the Lancastrians briefly returned to power, and Malory was once again released from prison. He died six months later and was buried in Greyfriars Church, in London.

⌘⌘⌘

from *Morte Darthur*

from BOOK I, CHAPTER 5[1]

So in the greatest church of London, whether it were Paul's[2] or not the French book[3] maketh no mention, all the estates[4] were long ere day[5] in the church for to pray. And when matins[6] and the first mass was done there was seen in the churchyard, against the high altar, a great stone four square,[7] like unto a marble stone, and in midst thereof was like an anvil of steel a foot on high, and therein stuck a fair sword naked[8] by the point, and letters there were written in gold about the sword that said thus: "WHOSO PULLETH OUT THIS SWORD OF THIS STONE AND ANVIL IS RIGHTWISE[9] KING BORN OF ALL ENGLAND." Then the people marvelled and told it to the Archbishop.

"I command," said the Archbishop, "that ye keep you within your church and pray unto God still; that no man touch the sword till the high mass be all done."

So when all masses were done all the lords went to behold the stone and the sword. And when they saw the scripture some essayed,[10] such as would have been king, but none might stir the sword nor move it.

"He is not here," said the Archbishop, "that shall achieve the sword, but doubt not God will make him known. But this is my counsel,"[11] said the Archbishop, "that we let purvey[12] ten knights, men of good fame,[13] and they to keep[14] this sword."

So it was ordained, and then there was made a cry[15] that every man should essay that would for to win the sword. And upon New Year's Day the barons let make a jousts and a tournament, that all knights that would joust or tourney there might play. And all this was ordained for to keep the lords together and the commons,[16] for the Archbishop trusted that God would make him known that should win the sword.

So upon New Year's Day, when the service was done, the barons rode unto the field, some to joust and some to tourney. And so it happed[17] that Sir Ector, that had great livelihood[18] about London, rode unto the jousts, and with him rode Sir Kay, his son, and young Arthur that was his nourished brother;[19] and Sir Kay was made knight at All Hallowmass[20] afore. So as they rode

---

[1] *Book I, Chapter 5*   The numbering of books and chapters employed here is that used in the Eugene Vinaver edition.

[2] *Paul's*   Church of St. Paul. This church stood on the site of the present-day St. Paul's Cathedral.

[3] *French book*   Unnamed French source from which Malory supposedly takes his material, actually a group of thirteenth-century Old French texts.

[4] *estates*   Clergy, nobility, and commoners.

[5] *long ere day*   Long before dawn.

[6] *matins*   Church service conducted at daybreak.

[7] *four square*   Having four equal sides.

[8] *naked*   Unsheathed.

[9] *Rightwise*   Rightfully.

[10] *essayed*   Tried.

[11] *counsel*   Advice.

[12] *let purvey*   Appoint.

[13] *fame*   Reputation.

[14] *keep*   Guard.

[15] *cry*   Request.

[16] *commons*   Commoners.

[17] *happed*   Happened.

[18] *livelihood*   Property from which income is derived.

[19] *nourished brother*   Foster brother.

[20] *All Hallowmass*   All Saint's Day, Christian holy day celebrated on 1 November.

to the jousts-ward[1] Sir Kay had lost[2] his sword, for he had left it at his father's lodging, and so he prayed[3] young Arthur for to ride for his sword.

"I will well," said Arthur, and rode fast after the sword.

And when he came home the lady and all were out to see the jousting. Then was Arthur wroth,[4] and said to himself, "I will ride to the churchyard and take the sword with me that sticketh in the stone, for my brother Sir Kay shall not be without a sword this day." So when he came to the churchyard Sir Arthur alight and tied his horse to the stile,[5] and so he went to the tent and found no knights there, for they were at the jousting. And so he handled the sword by the handles, and lightly and fiercely[6] pulled it out of the stone, and took his horse and rode his way until he came to his brother Sir Kay and delivered him the sword.

And as soon as Sir Kay saw the sword he wist[7] well it was the sword of the stone, and so he rode to his father Sir Ector and said,

"Sir, lo here is the sword of the stone, wherefore[8] I must be king of this land."

When Sir Ector beheld the sword he returned again and came to the church, and there they alight all three and went into the church, and anon[9] he made Sir Kay to swear upon a book[10] how he came to that sword.

"Sir," said Sir Kay, "by my brother Arthur, for he brought it to me."

"How got ye this sword?" said Sir Ector to Arthur.

"Sir, I will tell you. When I came home for my brother's sword I found nobody at home to deliver me his sword, and so I thought my brother Sir Kay should not be swordless, and so I came hither eagerly[11] and

pulled it out of the stone without any pain."[12]

"Found ye any knights about this sword?" said Sir Ector.

"Nay," said Arthur.

"Now," said Sir Ector to Arthur, "I understand ye must be king of this land."

"Wherefore[13] I?" said Arthur, "and for what cause?"

"Sir," said Ector, "for God will have it so, for there should never man have drawn out this sword but he that shall be rightwise king of this land. Now let me see whether ye can put the sword thereas[14] it was and pull it out again."

"That is no mastery,"[15] said Arthur, and so he put it in the stone. Therewithal[16] Sir Ector essayed to pull out the sword and failed.

"Now essay," said Sir Ector unto Sir Kay. And anon he pulled at the sword with all his might, but it would not be.

"Now shall ye essay," said Sir Ector to Arthur.

"I will well," said Arthur, and pulled it out easily.

And therewithal Sir Ector kneeled down to the earth and Sir Kay.

"Alas!" said Arthur, "my own dear father and brother, why kneel ye to me?"

"Nay, nay, my lord Arthur, it is not so. I was never your father nor of your blood, but I wot[17] well ye are of an higher blood than I weened[18] ye were." And then Sir Ector told him all, how he was betaken[19] him for to nourish him and by whose commandment, and by Merlin's deliverance.[20]

Then Arthur made great dole[21] when he understood that Sir Ector was not his father.

"Sir," said Ector unto Arthur, "will ye be my good and gracious lord when ye are king?"

---

[1] *jousts-ward* Toward the jousting-place.

[2] *lost* Realized he had forgotten.

[3] *prayed* Asked.

[4] *wroth* Angry.

[5] *stile* Turnstile entrance to the churchyard.

[6] *lightly and fiercely* Easily and boldly.

[7] *wist* Knew.

[8] *lo* Behold; *wherefore* For which reason.

[9] *anon* Immediately.

[10] *a book* I.e., a copy of the Bible.

[11] *hither eagerly* Here quickly.

[12] *pain* Difficulty.

[13] *Wherefore* Why.

[14] *thereas* Where.

[15] *mastery* Action requiring great skill.

[16] *Therewithal* That being done.

[17] *wot* Know.

[18] *weened* Understood, knew.

[19] *betaken* Entrusted to.

[20] *deliverance* Delivery.

[21] *dole* Sorrow.

"Else were I to blame," said Arthur, "for ye are the man in the world that I am most beholding[1] to, and my good lady and mother your wife that as well as her own hath fostered me and kept. And if ever it be God's will that I be king as ye say, ye shall desire of me what I may do, and I shall not fail you. God forbid I should fail you."

"Sir," said Sir Ector, "I will ask no more of you but that ye will make my son, your foster brother Sir Kay, seneschal[2] of all your lands."

"That shall be done," said Arthur, "and more, by the faith of my body, that never man shall have that office but he while he and I live."

Therewithal they went unto the Archbishop and told him how the sword was achieved and by whom. And on Twelfth-day[3] all the barons came thither[4] and to essay to take the sword who that would essay, but there afore them all there might none take it out but Arthur. Wherefore there were many lords wroth, and said it was great shame unto them all and the realm to be over-governed with a boy of no high blood born. And so they fell out[5] at that time, that[6] it was put off till Candlemas,[7] and then all the barons should meet there again; but always the ten knights were ordained to watch the sword day and night, and so they set a pavilion over the stone and the sword, and five always watched.

So at Candlemas many more great lords came hither for to have won the sword, but there might none prevail. And right as Arthur did at Christmas he did at Candlemas, and pulled out the sword easily, whereof the barons were sore aggrieved[8] and put it off in delay till the high feast of Easter. And as Arthur sped[9] afore so did he at Easter. Yet there were some of the great lords had indignation that Arthur should be king, and put it off in a delay till the feast of Pentecost.[10] Then the Archbishop of Canterbury, by Merlin's providence,[11] let purvey then of the best knights that they might get, and such knights as Uther Pendragon[12] loved best and most trusted in his days, and such knights were put about Arthur as Sir Baudwin of Britain, Sir Kaynes, Sir Ulfius, Sir Brastias; all these with many other were always about Arthur day and night till the feast of Pentecost.

And at the feast of Pentecost all manner of men essayed to pull at the sword that would essay, but none might prevail but Arthur, and he pulled it out afore all the lords and commons that were there. Wherefore all the commons cried at once,

"We will have Arthur unto[13] our king! We will put him no more in delay, for we all see that it is God's will that he shall be our king, and who that holdeth against[14] it we will slay him!"

And therewithal they kneeled at once, both rich and poor, and cried Arthur mercy[15] because they had delayed him so long. And Arthur forgave them, and took the sword between both his hands and offered it upon the altar where the Archbishop was, and so was he made knight of the best man that was there. . . .

---

1   *beholding*   Bound in duty.

2   *seneschal*   Steward, official overseeing the administration of a king's lands and court.

3   *Twelfth-day*   Twelfth day after Christmas, or the Feast of the Epiphany, celebrating the visit of the three wise men Jesus and their recognition of his divinity.

4   *thither*   There.

5   *fell out*   Quarreled.

6   *that*   So that.

7   *Candlemas*   Holy day commemorating the purification of the Virgin Mary after the birth of Jesus and the presentation of Christ at the Temple, celebrated on 2 February.

8   *aggrieved*   Distressed.

9   *sped*   Succeeded.

10   *Pentecost*   Christian celebration commemorating the descent of the Holy Spirit on the apostles, at which time they were given the gift of tongues, which would allow them to spread Christianity to other lands. The Feast of Pentecost is celebrated on the seventh Sunday after Easter.

11   *providence*   Arrangement.

12   *Uther Pendragon*   King of Britain before the action of the story and Arthur's true father.

13   *unto*   As.

14   *holdeth against*   Holds out against his acclamation.

15   *cried ... mercy*   Begged Arthur's forgiveness.

The Death of King Arthur
or The Most Piteous Tale of the
Morte Arthur Saunz Guerdon[1]

I

Slander and Strife

In May, when every heart flourisheth and burgeoneth (for as the season is lusty[2] to behold and comfortable,[3] so man and woman rejoiceth and gladdeth[4] of summer coming with his fresh flowers, for winter with his rough winds and blasts causeth lusty[5] men and women to cower and to sit by fires), so this season it befell in the month of May a great anger and unhap that stinted[6] not till the flower of chivalry of all the world was destroyed and slain.

And all was long upon two unhappy knights[7] which were named Sir Agravain and Sir Mordred,[8] that were brethren unto Sir Gawain.[9] For this Sir Agravain and Sir Mordred had ever a privy[10] hate unto the Queen, Dame Guinevere, and to Sir Lancelot;[11] and daily and nightly they ever watched upon Sir Lancelot.

So it misfortuned Sir Gawain and all his brethren[12] were in King Arthur's chamber, and then Sir Agravain said thus openly, and not in no counsel,[13] that many knights might hear:

"I marvel that we all be not ashamed both to see and to know how Sir Lancelot lies daily and nightly by the Queen. And all we know well that it is so, and it is shamefully suffered of us all[14] that we should suffer so noble a king as King Arthur is to be shamed."

Then spoke Sir Gawain and said,

"Brother, Sir Agravain, I pray you and charge you,[15] move no such matters no more[16] afore me, for wit[17] you well, I will not be of your counsel."[18]

"So God me help," said Sir Gaheris and Sir Gareth, "we will not be known of[19] your deeds."

"Then will I!" said Sir Mordred.

"I lieve[20] you well," said Sir Gawain, "for ever unto all unhappiness, sir, you will grant.[21] And I would[22] that ye left all this and made you not so busy, for I know," said Sir Gawain, "what will fall[23] of it."

"Fall whatsoever fall may,"[24] said Sir Agravain, "I will disclose it to the king!"

"Not by my counsel," said Sir Gawain, "for, an[25] there arise war and wrake[26] betwixt Sir Lancelot and us, wit you well, brother, there will many kings and great lords hold[27] with Sir Lancelot. Also, brother Sir Agravain," said Sir Gawain, "ye must remember how oftentimes Sir Lancelot has rescued the king and the queen; and the best of us all had been full cold to the heart-root[28] had not Sir Lancelot been better than we, and that has he proved himself full oft.[29] And as for my

---

[1] *Saunz Guerdon*   Old French: without reward.

[2] *lusty*   Here, joyful.

[3] *comfortable*   Pleasant.

[4] *gladdeth*   Are glad.

[5] *lusty*   Here, strong, healthy.

[6] *unhap that stinted*   Misfortune that ceased.

[7] *long upon ... knights*   Because of two ill-fated knights.

[8] *Sir Mordred*   Arthur's son from his accidental incestuous union with Morgause, his half-sister.

[9] *Sir Gawain*   Arthur's nephew and one of the chief knights of the Round Table.

[10] *privy*   Secret.

[11] *Dame Guinevere ... Lancelot*   The Queen has been in a love-affair with Lancelot, the foremost knight of Arthur's court, universally acclaimed for his prowess in battle.

[12] *brethren*   Gawain's brothers are Agravain, Gaheris, Gareth and Mordred.

[13] *not ... counsel*   Not in private.

[14] *it ... us all*   It is shameful to us that we should allow.

[15] *pray ... you*   Beg you and order you.

[16] *move ... more*   Suggest no such thing any more.

[17] *wit*   Know.

[18] *I ... counsel*   I will not go along with you.

[19] *not ... of*   We do not wish to be associated with your plans.

[20] *lieve*   Believe.

[21] *grant*   Go with, agree with.

[22] *would*   Wish.

[23] *fall*   Happen.

[24] *Fall ... may*   Whatever may happen.

[25] *an*   If.

[26] *wrake*   Strife.

[27] *hold*   Side.

[28] *full ... heart-root*   Dead.

[29] *full oft*   Often.

part," said Sir Gawain, "I will never be against Sir Lancelot for one day's deed, and that was when he rescued me from King Carados of the Dolorous Tower and slew him and saved my life. Also, brother Sir Agravain and Sir Mordred, in like wise[1] Sir Lancelot rescued both you and three score and two[2] from Sir Tarquin. And therefore, brother, methinks such noble deeds and kindness should be remembered."

"Do you as ye list,"[3] said Sir Agravain, "for I will lain[4] it no longer."

So with these words came in Sir Arthur.[5]

"Now, brother," said Sir Gawain, "stint[6] your strife."

"That will I not," said Sir Agravain and Sir Mordred.

"Well, will ye so?" said Sir Gawain. "Then God speed[7] you, for I will not bear of your tales, neither be of your counsel."[8]

"No more will I," said Sir Gaheris.

"Neither I," said Sir Gareth, "for I shall never say evil by that man that made me knight."

And therewithal they three departed, making great dole.[9]

"Alas!" said Sir Gawain and Sir Gareth, "now is this realm wholly destroyed and mischieved,[10] and the noble fellowship of the Round Table shall be disparbled."[11]

So they departed, and then King Arthur asked them what noise they made.[12]

"My lord," said Sir Agravain, "I shall tell you, for I may keep it no longer. Here is I and my brother Sir Mordred break[13] unto my brother Sir Gawain, Sir Gaheris and to Sir Gareth—for this is all, to make it short—how that we know all that Sir Lancelot holdeth your queen, and hath done long, and we be your sister's sons, we may suffer it no longer. And all we wote[14] that you should be above Sir Lancelot; and ye are the king that made him knight, and therefore we will prove it that he is a traitor to your person."

"If it be so," said the king, "wit you well, he is none other. But I would be loth[15] to begin such a thing but[16] I might have proofs of it, for Sir Lancelot is an hardy[17] knight, and all you know that he is the best knight among us all, and but if he be taken with[18] the deed he will fight with him that bringeth up the noise,[19] and I know no knight that is able to match him. Therefore, an it be sooth[20] as ye say, I would that he were taken with the deed."

For, as the French book saith, the king was full loath that such a noise[21] should be upon Sir Lancelot and his queen; for the king had a deeming[22] of it, but he would not hear thereof, for Sir Lancelot had done so much for him and for the queen so many times that wit you well the king loved him passingly well.

"My lord," said Sir Agravain, "ye shall ride to-morn an-hunting, and doubt ye not, Sir Lancelot will not go with you. And so when it draweth toward night ye may send the queen word that ye will lie out all that night, and so may ye send for your cooks. And then, upon pain of death, that night we shall take[23] him with the queen, and we shall bring him unto you, quick[24] or dead."

"I will well," said the king. "Then I counsel you to take with you sure[25] fellowship."

"Sir," said Sir Agravain, "my brother Sir Mordred and I will take with us twelve knights of the Round Table."

---

[1] *like wise* Similar fashion.

[2] *three ... two* Sixty-two.

[3] *list* Please.

[4] *lain* Hide.

[5] *Sir Arthur* I.e., King Arthur.

[6] *stint* Cease.

[7] *speed* Help.

[8] *neither ... counsel* Nor will I participate in your plans.

[9] *dole* Sorrow.

[10] *mischieved* Brought to ruin.

[11] *disparbled* Dispersed.

[12] *what noise they made* What had upset them, why they were upset.

[13] *break* Make known.

[14] *wote* Know.

[15] *loth* Reluctant.

[16] *but* Unless.

[17] *hardy* Strong.

[18] *but if ... with* Unless he be caught at.

[19] *bringeth up the noise* Presents the accusation.

[20] *sooth* True.

[21] *noise* Accusation.

[22] *deeming* Suspicion.

[23] *take* Catch.

[24] *quick* Alive.

[25] *sure* Trustworthy.

"Beware," said King Arthur, "for I warn you, ye shall find him wight."[1]

"Let us deal,"[2] said Sir Agravain and Sir Mordred.

So on the morn King Arthur rode an-hunting and sent word to the queen that he would be out all the night. Then Sir Agravain and Sir Mordred got to them twelve knights and hid themselves in a chamber in the castle of Carlisle. And these were their names: Sir Colgrevance, Sir Madore de la Porte, Sir Guingalen, Sir Meliot de Logres, Sir Petipace of Winchelsea, Sir Galeron of Galway, Sir Melion de la Mountayne, Sir Ascomore, Sir Gromorsom Eriore, Sir Cursessalain, Sir Florence, and Sir Lovell. So these twelve knights were with Sir Mordred and Sir Agravain, and all they were of Scotland, other else[3] of Sir Gawain's kin, other well-willers[4] to his brother.

So when the night came Sir Lancelot told Sir Bors how he would go that night and speak with the queen.

"Sir," said Sir Bors, "ye shall not go this night by my counsel."[5]

"Why?" said Sir Lancelot.

"Sir, for I dread me ever of Sir Agravain that[6] waits upon you daily to do you shame and us all. And never gave my heart against no going that ever ye went to the queen so much as now,[7] for I mistrust that the king is out this night from the queen because peradventure[8] he has lain some watch for you and the queen. Therefore I dread me sore of some treason."

"Have you no dread," said Sir Lancelot, "for I shall go and come again and make not tarrying."[9]

"Sir," said Sir Bors, "that me repents,[10] for I dread me sore that your going this night shall wrath[11] us all."

"Fair nephew," said Sir Lancelot, "I marvel me much why you say thus, since the queen has sent for me. And wit you well, I will not be so much a coward, but she shall understand I will see her good grace."

"God speed you well," said Sir Bors, "and send you sound and safe again!"

So Sir Lancelot departed and took his sword under his arm, and so he walked in his mantle,[12] that noble knight, and put himself in great jeopardy. And so he passed on till he came to the queen's chamber, and so lightly[13] he was had into the chamber. For, as the French book says, the queen and Sir Lancelot were together, and whether they were abed other at other manner of disports me list not thereof make no mention,[14] for love at that time was not as love is nowadays.

But thus as they were together there came Sir Agravain and Sir Mordred with twelve knights with them of the Round Table, and they said with great crying and scaring voice,

"Thou traitor, Sir Lancelot, now art thou taken!" And thus they cried with a loud voice, that all the court might hear it. And these fourteen knights all were armed at all points,[15] as they should fight in a battle.

"Alas!" said Queen Guinevere, "now are we mischieved both!"

"Madame," said Sir Lancelot, "is there here any armour within you that might cover my body withal?[16] And if there be any, give it me and I shall soon stint their malice, by the grace of God!"

"Now, truly," said the queen, "I have none armour, neither helm, shield, sword, neither spear, wherefore I dread me sore our long love is come to a mischievous end. For I hear by their noise there be many noble knights, and well I wot they be surely armed, and against them ye may make no resistance. Wherefore ye are likely to be slain, and then I shall be brent![17] For an ye might escape them," said the queen, "I would not

---

[1] *wight* Strong and courageous.

[2] *deal* Take action.

[3] *other else* Or else.

[4] *other well-willers* Or well-wishers.

[5] *counsel* Advice.

[6] *I … that* I fear always Sir Agravain, who.

[7] *And … now* Never before now did my heart warn me so much against your visiting the Queen.

[8] *peradventure* Perhaps.

[9] *make not tarrying* Not delay.

[10] *me repents* Distresses me.

[11] *wrath* Bring to disaster.

[12] *mantle* Cloak.

[13] *lightly* Quickly.

[14] *disports* Amusements; *me … mention* I do not wish to discuss.

[15] *armed … points* Fully armed.

[16] *withal* With.

[17] *brent* Burned at the stake.

doubt but that ye would rescue me in what danger that I ever stood in."

"Alas," said Sir Lancelot, "in all my life thus was I never bestrad[1] that I should be thus shamefully slain for lack of mine armour."

But ever Sir Agravain and Sir Mordred cried,

"Traitor knight, come out of the queen's chamber! For wit thou well thou art beset[2] so that thou shalt not escape."

"Ah, Jesu mercy!" said Sir Lancelot, "this shameful cry and noise I may not suffer, for better were death at once than thus to endure this pain."

Then he took the queen in his arms and kissed her and said, "Most noblest Christian queen, I beseech ye, as you have been ever my special good lady, and I at all times your poor knight and true unto my power and as I never failed you in right nor in wrong since the first day King Arthur made me knight, that you will pray for my soul if that I be slain. For well I am assured that Sir Bors, my nephew, and all the remnant of my kin, with Sir Lavain and Sir Urry, that they will not fail you to rescue you from the fire. And therefore, mine own lady, recomfort yourself,[3] whatsoever come of me, that ye go with Sir Bors, my nephew, and Sir Urry, and they all will do you all the pleasure that they may, and you shall live like a queen upon my lands."

"Nay, Sir Lancelot, nay!" said the queen. "Wit thou well that I will not live long after thy days. But an you be slain I will take my death as meekly as ever dead martyr take his death for Jesu Christ's sake."

"Well, madame," said Sir Lancelot, "sith[4] it is so that the day is come that our love must depart, wit you well I shall sell my life as dear as I may. And a thousandfold," said Sir Lancelot, "I am more heavier[5] for ye than for myself! And now I had liefer[6] than to be lord of all Christendom that I had sure armour upon me, that men might speak of my deeds or ever I were slain."[7]

"Truly," said the queen, "an it might please God, I would that they would take me and slay me and suffer you to escape."

"That shall never be," said Sir Lancelot, "God defend me from such a shame! But, Jesu Christ, be thou my shield and mine armour!"

And therewith Sir Lancelot wrapped his mantle about his arm well and surely; and by then they had gotten a great form[8] out of the hall, and therewith they all rushed at the door.

"Now, fair lords," said Sir Lancelot, "leave[9] your noise and your rushing, and I shall set open this door, and then may ye do with me what it liketh you."[10]

"Come off, then," said they all, "and do it, for it availeth thee not to strive against us all! And therefore let us into this chamber, and we shall save thy life until thou come to King Arthur."

Then Sir Lancelot unbarred the door, and with his left hand he held it open a little, that but one man might come in at once. And so there came striding a good knight, a much[11] man and a large, and his name was called Sir Colgrevance of Gore. And he with a sword struck at Sir Lancelot mightily, and so he put aside the stroke, and gave him such a buffet[12] upon the helmet that he fell grovelling[13] dead within the chamber door.

Then Sir Lancelot with great might drew the knight within the chamber door. And then Sir Lancelot, with help of the queen and her ladies, he was lightly armed in Colgrevance[14] armour. And ever stood Sir Agravain and Sir Mordred, crying,

"Traitor knight! Come forth out of the queen's chamber!"

"Sirs, leave your noise," said Sir Lancelot, "for wit you well, Sir Agravain, ye shall not prison me this night! And therefore, an ye do by my counsel, go ye all from this chamber door and make you no such crying and

---

[1] *bestrad* Attacked.

[2] *beset* Surrounded.

[3] *recomfort yourself* Take courage.

[4] *sith* Since.

[5] *more heavier* More sorrowful.

[6] *liefer* Rather.

[7] *or ... slain* Before I was killed.

[8] *form* Bench.

[9] *leave* Cease.

[10] *what ... you* What pleases you.

[11] *much* Big.

[12] *buffet* Stroke.

[13] *grovelling* Upon his belly.

[14] *Colgrevance* I.e., Colgrevance's.

such manner of sclander[1] as ye do. For I promise you by my knighthood, an ye will depart and make no more noise, I shall as to-morn appear afore you all and before the king, and then let it be seen which of you all, other else ye all,[2] that will depreve[3] me of treason. And there shall I answer you, as a knight should, that hither I came to the queen of no manner of *mal engin,*[4] and that will I prove and make it good upon you with my hands."

"Fie[5] upon thee, traitor," said Sir Agravain and Sir Mordred, "for we will have thee maugre thine head[6] and slay thee, an we list![7] For we let thee wit we have the choice of King Arthur to save thee other slay thee."

"Ah, sirs," said Sir Lancelot, "is there none other grace with you? Then keep[8] yourself!"

And then Sir Lancelot set all open the chamber door, and mightily and knightly he strode in among them. And anon at the first stroke he slew Sir Agravain, and anon after twelve of his fellows. Within a while he had laid them down cold to the earth, for there was none of the twelve knights might stand Sir Lancelot one buffet. And also he wounded Sir Mordred, and therewithal he fled with all his might. And then Sir Lancelot returned again unto the queen and said,

"Madame, now wit you well, all our true love is brought to an end, for now will King Arthur ever be my foe. And therefore, madame, an it like you[9] that I may have you with me, I shall save you from all manner adventurous[10] dangers."

"Sir, that is not best," said the queen, "meseems,[11] for now ye have done so much harm it will be best that ye hold you still[12] with this. And if ye see that as to-morn they will put me unto death then may ye rescue me as ye think best."

"I will well," said Sir Lancelot, "for have ye no doubt, while I am a man living I shall rescue you."

And then he kissed her, and either of them gave other a ring, and so the queen he left there and went until[13] his lodging.

When Sir Bors saw Sir Lancelot he was never so glad of his home-coming.

"Jesu mercy!" said Sir Lancelot, "why be ye all armed? What meaneth this?"

"Sir," said Sir Bors, "after ye were departed from us we all that been of your blood and your well-willers were so adretched[14] that some of us leapt out of our beds naked, and some in their dreams caught naked swords in their hands. And therefore," said Sir Bors, "we deemed there was some great strife on hand, and so we deemed that we were betrapped with some treason; and therefore we made us thus ready what need that ever ye were in."

"My fair nephew," said Sir Lancelot unto Sir Bors, "now shall ye wit all that this night I was more hard bestad than ever I was days of my life. And thanked be God, I am myself escaped their danger." And so he told them all how and in what manner, as ye have heard toforehand.[15] "And therefore, my fellows," said Sir Lancelot, "I pray ye all that you will be of heart good, and help me in what need that ever I stand, for now is war coming to us all."

"Sir," said Sir Bors, "all is welcome that God sendeth us, and we have taken much weal[16] with you and much worship,[17] we will take the woe[18] with you as we have taken the weal." And therefore they said, all the good knights, "Look you take no discomfort! For there is no band of knights under heaven but we shall be able to grieve[19] them as much as they may us, and therefore discomfort not yourself by no manner. And we shall gather together all that we love and that loves us, and

[1] *sclander* Slander.

[2] *other else ye all* Or else you all.

[3] *depreve* Accuse.

[4] *mal engin* Old French: ill intent.

[5] *Fie* Shame.

[6] *maugre … head* In spite of your head, i.e., despite all you can do.

[7] *an … list* If we wish.

[8] *keep* Defend.

[9] *an … you* If it pleases you.

[10] *adventurous* Here, accidental.

[11] *meseems* It seems to me.

[12] *hold … still* Be content.

[13] *until* Unto, i.e., to.

[14] *adretched* Troubled.

[15] *toforehand* Beforehand.

[16] *weal* Prosperity.

[17] *worship* Praise, honor.

[18] *woe* Misfortune.

[19] *grieve* Injure.

what that you will have done shall be done. And therefore let us take the woe and the joy together."

"Grantmercy,"[1] said Sir Lancelot, "of your good comfort, for in my great distress, fair nephew, ye comfort me greatly. But this, my fair nephew, I would that ye did in all haste that you may or it is far days past:[2] that ye will look in their lodging that been lodged nigh here about the king, which will hold with me and which will not. For now I would know which were my friends from my foes."

"Sir," said Sir Bors, "I shall do my pain,[3] and or it be seven of the clock I shall wit of such as ye have doubt for,[4] who that will hold with you."

Then Sir Bors called unto him Sir Lionel, Sir Ector de Maris, Sir Blamour de Ganis, Sir Bleoberis de Ganis, Sir Gahalantin, Sir Galyhodin, Sir Galihud, Sir Menaduke, Sir Villiers the Valiant, Sir Hebes le Renown, Sir Lavain, Sir Urry of Hungary, Sir Neroveous, Sir Plenorius (for these two were knights that Sir Lancelot won upon a bridge, and therefore they would never be against him), and Sir Garry le Fitz Lake, and Sir Selises of the Dolorous Tower, Sir Melias de Lisle, and Sir Bellengere le Beuse, that was Sir Alexander le Orphelin's son; because his mother was Alice la Belle Pellerine, and she was kin unto Sir Lancelot, he held with him. So came Sir Palomides and Sir Saphir, his brother; Sir Clegis, Sir Sadok, Sir Dinas and Sir Clarius of Cleremont.

So these two-and-twenty[5] knights drew them together, and by then they were armed and on horseback they promised Sir Lancelot to do what he would. Then there fell to[6] them, what of North Wales and of Cornwall, for Sir Lamorak's sake and for Sir Tristram's sake, to the number of a seven score[7] knights. Then spoke Sir Lancelot:

"Wit you well, I have been ever since I came to this court well-willed unto my lord Arthur and unto my lady Queen Guinevere unto my power.[8] And this night because my lady the queen sent for me to speak with her, I suppose it was made by[9] treason; howbeit I dare largely[10] excuse her person, notwithstanding I was there by a forecast nearhand slain but as[11] Jesu provided for me."

And then that noble knight Sir Lancelot told them how he was hard bestad in the queen's chamber, and how and in what manner he escaped from them.

"And therefore wit you well, my fair lords, I am sure there is but war unto me and to mine. And for cause I have slain this night Sir Agravain, Sir Gawain's brother, and at the least twelve of his fellows, and for this cause now am I sure of mortal war. For these knights were sent by King Arthur to betray me, and therefore the king will in this heat[12] and malice judge the queen unto brenning, and that may not I suffer that she should be brent for my sake. For an I may be heard and suffered and so taken,[13] I will fight for the queen, that she is a true lady[14] until her lord. But the king in his heat, I dread, will not take[15] me as I ought to be taken."

"My lord, Sir Lancelot," said Sir Bors, "by mine advice, ye shall take the woe with the weal, and take it in patience and thank God of it. And since it is fallen as it is, I counsel you to keep yourself, for an ye will yourself,[16] there is no fellowship of knights christened that shall do you wrong. And also I will counsel you, my lord, that my lady Queen Guinevere, an she be in any distress, insomuch as she is in pain for your sake, that ye knightly rescue her; for an you did any other wise all the world would speak you shame to the world's end. Insomuch as ye were taken with her, whether you did right other wrong, it is now your part to hold with the

---

1. *Grantmercy* Thank you.

2. *or ... past* Before too many days go by.

3. *I ... pain* I will strive to do so.

4. *ye ... for* You are uncertain of.

5. *two-and-twenty* As some editors have pointed out, this may be a scribal error; there are twenty-five knights in total.

6. *fell to* Joined with.

7. *seven score* One hundred and forty.

8. *unto ... power* As far as it was in my power.

9. *made by* Arranged by.

10. *largely* Wholly.

11. *by a forecast ... but as* By a pre-arrangement nearly slain had not.

12. *heat* Anger.

13. *so taken* Accepted (as Guinevere's protector).

14. *true lady* Faithful wife.

15. *take* Accept.

16. *an ye will yourself* I.e., as you must accept yourself ("if you will").

queen, that she be not slain and put to a mischievous death. For an she so die, the shame shall be evermore yours."

"Now Jesu defend me from shame," said Sir Lancelot, "and keep and save my lady the queen from villainy and shameful death, and that she never be destroyed in my default.[1] Wherefore, my fair lords, my kin and my friends," said Sir Lancelot, "what will ye do?"

And anon they said all with one voice, "We will do as ye will do."

"Then I put this case unto you," said Sir Lancelot, "that my lord King Arthur by evil counsel will to-morn in his heat put my lady the queen unto the fire, and there to be brent, then, I pray you, counsel me what is best for me to do." Then they said all at once with one voice,

"Sir, us thinks best that ye knightly rescue the queen. Insomuch as she shall be brent, it is for your sake; and it is to suppose, an ye might be handled,[2] ye should have the same death, other else a more shame-fuller death. And, sir, we say all that you have rescued her from her death many times for other men's quarrels; therefore us seems it is more your worship that you rescue the queen from this quarrel, insomuch that she has it for your sake."

Then Sir Lancelot stood still and said,

"My fair lords, wit you well I would be full loath that my lady the queen should die such a shameful death. But an it be so that ye will counsel me to rescue her, I must do much harm or I rescue her, and perad-venture I shall there destroy some of my best friends, and that should much repent me.[3] And peradventure there be some, an they could well bring it about or disobey my lord King Arthur, they would soon come to me, the which[4] I were loath to hurt. And if so be that I may win the queen away, where shall I keep her?"

"Sir, that shall be the least care of us all," said Sir Bors, "for how did the most noble knight Sir Tristram?[5]

By your good will, kept not he with him La Beale Isode[6] near three year in Joyous Gard,[7] the which was done by your althers advice?[8] And that same place is your own, and in like wise may ye do, an ye list, and take the queen knightly away with you, if so be that the king will judge her to be brent. And in Joyous Gard may ye keep her long enough until the heat be past of the king, and then it may fortune you to bring the queen again to the king with great worship, and peradventure you shall have then thank for your bringing home, whether other may happen to have maugre."[9]

"That is hard for to do," said Sir Lancelot, "for by Sir Tristram I may have a warning: for when by means of treatise[10] Sir Tristram brought again La Beale Isode unto King Mark from Joyous Gard, look ye now what fell on[11] the end, how shamefully that false traitor King Mark slew him as he sat harping afore his lady, La Beale Isode. With a grounden glaive[12] he thrust him in behind to the heart, which grieveth sore me," said Sir Lancelot, "to speak of his death, for all the world may not find such another knight."

"All this is truth," said Sir Bors, "but there is one thing shall courage[13] you and us all: you know well that King Arthur and King Mark were never like of condi-tions,[14] for there was never yet man that ever could prove King Arthur untrue of his promise."

But so, to make short tale, they were all conde-scended[15] that, for better other for worse, if so were that the queen were brought on that morn to the fire, shortly they all would rescue her. And so by the advice of Sir Lancelot they put them all in a bushment[16] in a wood as nigh Carlisle as they might, and there they abode[17] still to wit what the king would do.

---

[1] *in my default*   Because of my failure, because I am not there.

[2] *handled*   Captured.

[3] *that … me*   I.e., I would be sorry about that.

[4] *the which*   Whom.

[5] *how … Tristram*   What did the most noble knight Sir Tristram do?; *Tristram*   Knight who fell in love with Iseut, the wife of his uncle Mark. Malory recounts this episode in *The Book of Sir Tristram de Lyones*.

[6] *La Beale Isode*   The Beautiful Iseut, Tristram's lover.

[7] *Joyous Gard*   Lancelot's castle.

[8] *your … advice*   The advice of you all.

[9] *whether … maugre*   Even if some may dislike it.

[10] *treatise*   Negotiation.

[11] *fell on*   Happened in.

[12] *grounden glaive*   Sharpened spear or lance.

[13] *courage*   Encourage.

[14] *like of conditions*   Similar in disposition, character.

[15] *condescended*   In agreement.

[16] *bushment*   Ambush.

[17] *abode*   Waited.

Now turn we again, that when Sir Mordred was escaped from Sir Lancelot he got his horse and mounted upon him, and came to King Arthur sore wounded and all forbled,[1] and there he told the king all how it was, and how they were all slain save himself alone.

"Ah, Jesu, mercy! How may this be?" said the king. "Took ye him in the queen's chamber?"

"Yea, so God me help," said Sir Mordred, "there we found him unarmed, and anon he slew Sir Colgrevance and armed him in his armour."

And so he told the king from the beginning to the ending.

"Jesu mercy!" said the king, "he is a marvellous knight of prowess. And alas," said the king, "me sore repenteth that ever Sir Lancelot should be against me, for now I am sure the noble fellowship of the Round Table is broken for ever, for with him will many a noble knight hold. And now it is fallen so," said the king, "that I may not with my worship but[2] my queen must suffer death," and was sore amoved.[3]

So then there was made great ordinance in this ire,[4] and the queen must needs be judged[5] to the death. And the law was such in those days that whatsoever they were, of what estate or degree, if they were found guilty of treason there should be none other remedy but death, and other the menour[6] other the taking with the deed should be causer[7] of their hasty judgement. And right so was it ordained for Queen Guinevere: because Sir Mordred was escaped sore wounded, and the death of thirteen knights of the Round Table, these proofs and experiences caused King Arthur to command the queen to the fire, and there to be brent. Then spake Sir Gawain and said,

"My lord Arthur, I would counsel you not to be over-hasty, but that ye would put it in respite,[8] this judgement of my lady the queen, for many causes. One is this, though it were so that Sir Lancelot were found in the queen's chamber, yet it might be so that he came thither for none evil. For you know, my lord," said Sir Gawain, "that my lady the queen has oftentimes been greatly beholden[9] unto Sir Lancelot, more than to any other knight; for oftentimes he hath saved her life and done battle for her when all the court refused the queen. And peradventure she sent for him for goodness and for none evil, to reward him for his good deeds that he had done to her in times past. And peradventure my lady the queen sent for him to that intent that Sir Lancelot should come privily[10] to her, weening that it had be best in eschewing[11] and dreading of slander; for oftentimes we do many things that we ween for the best be, and yet peradventure it turns to the worst. For I dare say," said Sir Gawain, "my lady, your queen, is to you both good and true. And as for Sir Lancelot, I dare say he will make it good upon any knight living that will put upon him[12] villainy or shame, and in like wise he will make good for my lady the queen."

"That I believe well," said King Arthur, "but I will not that way work with Sir Lancelot,[13] for he trusteth[14] so much upon his hands and his might[15] that he doubteth[16] no man. And therefore for my queen he shall nevermore fight, for she shall have the law. And if I may get[17] Sir Lancelot, wit you well he shall have as shameful a death."

"Jesu defend me," said Sir Gawain, "that I never see it nor know it!"

"Why say you so?" said King Arthur. "For, pardy,[18] ye have no cause to love him! For this night last past he slew your brother, Sir Agravain, a full good knight, and almost he had slain your other brother, Sir Mordred, and also there he slew thirteen noble knights. And also remember you, Sir Gawain, he slew two sons of yours, Sir Florence and Sir Lovell."

---

[1]   *forbled*   Covered with blood.

[2]   *I may … but*   I may not keep my honor unless.

[3]   *amoved*   Moved to emotion.

[4]   *ordinance … ire*   Preparation in this wrath.

[5]   *must needs … judged*   Must be condemned.

[6]   *menour*   Manner, behavior.

[7]   *taking … causer*   Being caught in the act is the reason for.

[8]   *respite*   Delay.

[9]   *beholden*   Obligated, in debt.

[10]   *privily*   Privately.

[11]   *eschewing*   Avoiding.

[12]   *put … him*   Accuse him of.

[13]   *I … Lancelot*   I will not deal in that manner with Sir Lancelot.

[14]   *trusteth*   Has confidence in.

[15]   *might*   Strength.

[16]   *doubteth*   Fears.

[17]   *get*   Capture.

[18]   *pardy*   By God.

"My lord," said Sir Gawain, "of all this I have a knowledge, which of their deaths sore repents me. But insomuch as I gave them warning and told my brother and my sons afore-hand what would fall on the end, and insomuch as they would not do by my counsel, I will not meddle me thereof, nor revenge me nothing of their deaths; for I told them that there was no boot to strive[1] with Sir Lancelot. Howbeit I am sorry of the death of my brother and of my two sons, but they are the causers of their own death; and oftentimes I warned my brother Sir Agravain, and I told him of the perils the which be now fallen."

Then said King Arthur unto Sir Gawain,

"Make you ready, I pray you, in your best armour, with your brethren, Sir Gaheris and Sir Gareth, to bring my queen to the fire and there to have her judgement."

"Nay, my noble king," said Sir Gawain, "that will I never do, for wit you well I will never be in that place where so noble a queen as is my lady Dame Guinevere shall take such a shameful end. For wit you well," said Sir Gawain, "my heart will not serve me for to see her die, and it shall never be said that ever I was of your counsel[2] for her death."

"Then," said the king unto Sir Gawain, "suffer your brethren Sir Gaheris and Sir Gareth to be there."

"My lord," said Sir Gawain, "wit you well they will be loath to be there present, because of many adventures that is like to fall,[3] but they are young and full unable to say you nay."

Then spake Sir Gaheris and the good knight Sir Gareth unto King Arthur,

"Sir, you may well command us to be there, but wit you well it shall be sore against our will. But an we be there by your straight commandment, ye shall plainly hold us there excused: we will be there in peaceable wise, and bear none harness[4] of war upon us."

"In the name of God," said the king, "then make you ready, for she shall have soon her judgement."

"Alas," said Sir Gawain, "that ever I should endure to see this woeful day!"

So Sir Gawain turned him and wept heartily, and so he went into his chamber. And so the queen was led forth without Carlisle, and anon she was despoiled into her smock.[5] And then her ghostly father[6] was brought to her to be shriven[7] of her misdeeds. Then was there weeping and wailing and wringing of hands of many lords and ladies; but there were but few in comparison that would bear any armour for to strength[8] the death of the queen.

Then was there one that Sir Lancelot had sent unto that place, which went to espy what time the queen should go unto her death. And anon as he saw the queen despoiled into her smock and shriven, then he gave Sir Lancelot warning anon. Then was there but spurring and plucking up[9] of horse, and right so they came unto the fire. And who that stood against them, there were they slain; there might none withstand Sir Lancelot.

So all that bore arms and withstood them, there were they slain, full many a noble knight. For there was slain Sir Belias le Orgulous, Sir Segwarides, Sir Griflet, Sir Brandiles, Sir Aglovale, Sir Tor, Sir Gauter, Sir Gillimer, Sir Reynold, three brethren, and Sir Damas, Sir Priamus, Sir Kay l'Estrange, Sir Driant, Sir Lambegus, Sir Herminde, Sir Pertolip, Sir Perimones, two brethren which were called the Green Knight and the Red Knight.

And so in this rushing and hurling,[10] as Sir Lancelot thrang[11] here and there, it misfortuned him to slay Sir Gaheris and Sir Gareth, the noble knight, for they were unarmed and unawares. As the French book saith, Sir Lancelot smote[12] Sir Gareth upon the brain-pan, where-through that[13] they were slain in the field. Howbeit in very truth Sir Lancelot saw them not. And so were they found dead among the thickest of the press.[14]

---

[1] *no boot to strive*   No use in quarreling.

[2] *I … counsel*   I was in agreement with you.

[3] *adventures … fall*   Perils likely to happen.

[4] *harness*   Gear.

[5] *despoiled … smock*   Stripped to her undergarment.

[6] *ghostly father*   Confessor.

[7] *shriven*   Confessed and given absolution.

[8] *for … strength*   To assist in.

[9] *plucking up*   Spurring forward.

[10] *rushing and hurling*   Pushing and dashing violently.

[11] *thrang*   Thrust (his weapon) about.

[12] *smote*   Struck.

[13] *brain-pan … that*   Skull by means of which.

[14] *press*   Crowd.

Then Sir Lancelot, when he had thus done, and slain and put to flight all that would withstand him, then he rode straight unto Queen Guinevere and made cast a kirtle[1] and a gown upon her, and then he made her to be set behind him and prayed her to be of good cheer. Now wit you well the queen was glad that she was at that time escaped from the death, and then she thanked God and Sir Lancelot.

And so he rode his way with the queen, as the French book saith, unto Joyous Gard, and there he kept her as a noble knight should. And many great lords and many good knights were sent him, and many full noble knights drew unto him. When they heard that King Arthur and Sir Lancelot were at debate[2] many knights were glad, and many were sorry of their debate.

2

THE VENGEANCE OF SIR GAWAIN

Now turn we again unto King Arthur, that when it was told him how and in what manner the queen was taken away from the fire, and when he heard of the death of his noble knights, and in especial Sir Gaheris and Sir Gareth, then he swooned for very pure sorrow. And when he awoke of his swough, then he said,

"Alas, that ever I bore crown upon my head! For now have I lost the fairest fellowship of noble knights that ever held Christian king together. Alas, my good knights be slain and gone away from me, that now within this two days I have lost nigh forty knights, and also the noble fellowship of Sir Lancelot and his blood,[3] for now I may nevermore hold them together with my worship. Now, alas, that ever this war began!"

"Now, fair fellows," said the king, "I charge you that no man tell Sir Gawain of the death of his two brethren, for I am sure," said the king, "when he heareth tell that Sir Gareth is dead, he will go nigh out of his mind. Mercy Jesu," said the king, "why slew he Sir Gaheris and Sir Gareth? For I dare say, as for Sir Gareth, he loved Sir Lancelot of[4] all men earthly."

"That is truth," said some knights, "but they were slain in the hurling as Sir Lancelot thrang in the thickest of the press. And as they were unarmed he smote them and wist not whom that he smote, and so unhappily they were slain."

"Well," said Arthur, "the death of them will cause the greatest mortal war that ever was, for I am sure that when Sir Gawain knoweth thereof that Sir Gareth is slain, I shall never have rest[5] of him till I have destroyed Sir Lancelot's kin and himself both, other else he to destroy me. And therefore," said the king, "wit you well, my heart was never so heavy as it is now. And much more I am sorrier for my good knights' loss than for the loss of my fair queen; for queens I might have enough, but such a fellowship of good knights shall never be together in no company. And now I dare say," said King Arthur, "there was never Christian king that ever held such a fellowship together. And alas, that ever Sir Lancelot and I should be at debate! Ah, Agravain, Agravain!" said the king, "Jesu forgive it thy soul, for thine evil will that thou hadst and Sir Mordred, thy brother, unto Sir Lancelot has caused all this sorrow."

And ever among these complaints the king wept and swooned.

Then came there one to Sir Gawain and told him how the queen was led away with Sir Lancelot, and nigh a four-and-twenty knights slain.

"Ah, Jesu, save me my two brethren!" said Sir Gawain. "For full well wist I," said Sir Gawain, "that Sir Lancelot would rescue her, other else he would die in that field; and to say the truth he were not of worship but if he had rescued the queen, insomuch as she should have been brent for his sake. And as in that," said Sir Gawain, "he has done but knightly, and as I would have done myself an I had stood[6] in like case. But where are my brethren?" said Sir Gawain, "I marvel that I see not of them."

Then said that man, "Truly, Sir Gaheris and Sir Gareth be slain."

"Jesu defend!" said Sir Gawain, "For all this world I would not that they were slain, and in especial my good brother, Sir Gareth."

---

[1] *kirtle* Petticoat, under-skirt.

[2] *at debate* At odds.

[3] *blood* Kin.

[4] *of* Above.

[5] *rest* Peace.

[6] *stood* Been.

"Sir," said the man, "he is slain, and that is great pity."

"Who slew him?" said Sir Gawain.

"Sir Lancelot," said the man, "slew them both."

"That may I not believe," said Sir Gawain, "that ever he slew my good brother, Sir Gareth, for I dare say, my brother loved him better than me and all his brethren, and the king both. Also I dare say, an Sir Lancelot had desired my brother Sir Gareth with him, he would have been with him against the king and us all. And therefore I may never believe that Sir Lancelot slew my brethren."

"Verily,[1] sir," said the man, "it is noised that he slew him."

"Alas," said Sir Gawain, "now is my joy gone!"

And then he fell down and swooned, and long he lay there as he had been dead. And when he arose out of his swough he cried out sorrowfully, and said,

"Alas!"

And forthwith[2] he ran unto the king, crying and weeping, and said,

"Ah, mine uncle King Arthur! My good brother Sir Gareth is slain, and so is my brother Sir Gaheris, which were two noble knights."

Then the king wept and he both, and so they fell on-swooning. And when they were revived, then spake Sir Gawain and said,

"Sir, I will go and see my brother Sir Gareth."

"Sir, you may not see him," said the king, "for I caused him to be interred and Sir Gaheris both, for I well understood that you would make overmuch sorrow, and the sight of Sir Gareth should have caused your double sorrow."

"Alas, my lord," said Sir Gawain, "how slew he my brother, Sir Gareth? I pray you tell me."

"Truly," said the king, "I shall tell you as it hath been told me: Sir Lancelot slew him and Sir Gaheris both."

"Alas," said Sir Gawain, "they bore none arms against him, neither of them both."

"I wot not how it was," said the king, "but as it is said, Sir Lancelot slew them in the thick press, and knew them not. And therefore let us shape a remedy for to revenge their deaths."

"My king, my lord, and mine uncle," said Sir Gawain, "wit you well, now I shall make you a promise which I shall hold by my knighthood, that from this day forward I shall never fail[3] Sir Lancelot until that one of us have slain that other. And therefore I require you, my lord and king, dress you unto the war,[4] for wit you well, I will be revenged upon Sir Lancelot; and therefore, as ye will have my service and my love, now haste you thereto and assay[5] your friends. For I promise unto God," said Sir Gawain, "for the death of my brother, Sir Gareth, I shall seek Sir Lancelot throughout seven kings' realms, but I shall slay him, other else he shall slay me."

"Sir, you shall not need to seek him so far," said the king, "for as I hear say, Sir Lancelot will abide me and us all within the castle of Joyous Gard. And much people draweth unto him as I hear say."

"That may I right well believe," said Sir Gawain; "but, my lord," he said, "assay your friends and I will assay mine."

"It shall be done," said the king, "and as I suppose I shall be big enough to drive him out of the biggest[6] tower of his castle."

So then the king sent letters and writs throughout all England, both the length and the breadth, for to assummon all his knights. And so unto King Arthur drew many knights, dukes, and earls, that he had a great host, and when they were assembled the king informed them how Sir Lancelot had bereft him[7] his queen. Then the king and all his host made them ready to lay siege about Sir Lancelot where he lay within Joyous Gard.

And anon Sir Lancelot heard thereof and purveyed him of[8] many good knights; for with him held many knights, some for his own sake and some for the queen's sake. Thus they were on both parties well furnished and garnished[9] of all manner of things that longed unto[10] the war. But King Arthur's host was so great that Sir Lancelot's host would not abide him in the field. For he was

---

[1] *Verily* Truly.

[2] *forthwith* Immediately.

[3] *fail* Stop pursuing.

[4] *dress … war* Prepare for war.

[5] *assay* Appeal to.

[6] *big* Powerful; *biggest* Strongest.

[7] *bereft him* Robbed him of.

[8] *purveyed … of* Provided himself with.

[9] *garnished* Provided.

[10] *longed unto* Were required for.

full loath to do battle against the king; but Sir Lancelot drew him unto his strong castle with all manner of victual plenty, and as many noble men as he might suffice[1] within the town and the castle.

Then came King Arthur with Sir Gawain with a great host and laid siege all about Joyous Gard, both the town and the castle. And there they made strong war on both parties, but in no wise Sir Lancelot would ride out, nor go out of the castle, of long time; and neither he would not suffer none of his good knights to issue out, neither of the town neither of the castle, until fifteen weeks were past.

So it fell upon a day in harvest time that Sir Lancelot looked over the walls and spake on height[2] unto King Arthur and to Sir Gawain:

"My lords both, wit you well all this is in vain that ye make at this siege, for here win ye no worship, but maugre and dishonour. For an it list me to come myself out and my very good knights, I should full soon make an end of this war."

"Come forth," said King Arthur unto Sir Lancelot, "an thou darest, and I promise thee I shall meet thee in midst of this field."

"God defend me," said Sir Lancelot, "that ever I should encounter with the most noble king that made me knight."

"Now, fie upon thy fair language!"[3] said the king, "for wit thou well and trust it, I am thy mortal foe and ever will to my death-day; for thou hast slain my good knights and full noble men of my blood, that shall I never recover again. Also thou hast lain by my queen, and holden her many winters, and sithen, like a traitor, taken her away from me by force."

"My most noble lord and king," said Sir Lancelot, "ye may say what ye will, for ye wot well with yourself I will not strive. But thereas ye say that I have slain your good knights, I wot well that I have done so, and that me sore repenteth; but I was forced to do battle with them in saving of my life, other else I must have suffered them to have slain me. And as for my lady, Queen Guinevere, except your person of your highness and my lord Sir Gawain, there is no knight under heaven that dare make it good upon me that ever I was traitor unto your person. And where it please you to say that I have holden my lady, your queen, years and winters, unto that I shall ever make a large[4] answer, and prove it upon any knight that beareth the life, except your person and Sir Gawain, that my lady, Queen Guinevere, is as true a lady unto your person as is any lady living unto her lord, and that will I make good with my hands. Howbeit[5] it hath liked her good grace to have me in favour and cherish me more than any other knight; and unto my power again[6] I have deserved her love,[7] for oftentimes, my lord, you have consented that she should have been brent and destroyed in your heat, and then it fortuned[8] me to do battle for her; and or I departed from her adversary they confessed their untruth, and she full worshipfully excused.[9] And at such times, my lord Arthur," said Sir Lancelot, "you loved me and thanked me when I saved your queen from the fire, and then you promised me for ever to be my good lord. And now methinketh you reward me evil for my good service. And, my lord, meseemeth I had lost[10] a great part of my worship in my knighthood an I had suffered my lady, your queen, to have been brent, and insomuch as she should have been brent for my sake; for sithen I have done battles for your queen in other quarrels than in mine own quarrel, meseemeth now I had more right to do battle for her in her right quarrel. And therefore, my good and gracious lord," said Sir Lancelot, "take your queen unto your good grace, for she is both true and good."

"Fie on thee, false recreant[11] knight!" said Sir Gawain. "For I let thee wit: my lord, mine uncle King Arthur shall have his queen and thee both maugre thy visage,[12] and slay you both and save you, whether it

---

[1] *suffice* Provide for.

[2] *on height* Loudly.

[3] *fair language* Courteous speech.

[4] *large* Bold.

[5] *Howbeit* Nevertheless.

[6] *unto … again* To the best of my ability in return.

[7] *I … love* I have tried to deserve her love.

[8] *fortuned* Fell to.

[9] *worshipfully excused* Honorably acquitted.

[10] *meseemeth I had lost* It seems to me I would have lost.

[11] *recreant* Cowardly, villainous (a particularly insulting term).

[12] *maugre … visage* In spite of your face, i.e., in spite of all that you can do.

please him."[1]

"It may well be," said Sir Lancelot, "but wit thou well, my lord Sir Gawain, an me list to come out of this castle you should win me and the queen more harder[2] than ever you won a strong battle."

"Now, fie on thy proud words!" said Sir Gawain. "As for my lady the queen, wit thou well I will never say of her shame. But thou, false and recreant knight," said Sir Gawain, "what cause hadst thou to slay my good brother, Sir Gareth, that loved thee more than me and all my kin? And alas, thou madest him knight thine[3] own hands! Why slewest thou him that loved thee so well?"

"For to excuse me," said Sir Lancelot, "it boteneth me not,[4] but by Jesu, and by the faith that I owe unto the high Order of Knighthood, I would with as good a will have slain my nephew Sir Bors de Ganis at that time. And alas, that ever I was so unhappy," said Sir Lancelot, "that I had not seen Sir Gareth and Sir Gaheris!"

"Thou liest, recreant knight," said Sir Gawain, "thou slewest them in the despite of me![5] And therefore wit thou well, Sir Lancelot, I shall make war upon thee, and all the while that I may live be thine enemy!"

"That me repents," said Sir Lancelot, "for well I understand it boteneth me not to seek none accord-ment[6] while ye, Sir Gawain, are so mischievously set.[7] And if ye were not, I would not doubt to have the good grace of my lord King Arthur."

"I lieve well, false recreant knight, for thou hast many long days overlaid[8] me and us all, and destroyed many of our good knights."

"Sir, you say as it pleaseth you," said Sir Lancelot, "yet may it never be said on me[9] and openly proved that ever I by forecast of treason[10] slew no good knight as ye,

my lord Sir Gawain, have done;[11] and so did I never but in my defence, that I was driven thereto in saving of my life."

"Ah, thou false knight," said Sir Gawain, "that thou meanest by Sir Lamorak.[12] But wit thou well, I slew him!"

"Sir, you slew him not yourself," said Sir Lancelot, "for it had been overmuch for you, for he was one of the best knights christened of his age. And it was great pity of his death!"

"Well, well, Sir Lancelot," said Sir Gawain, "sithen thou enbraidest me[13] of Sir Lamorak, wit thou well, I shall never leave thee till I have thee at such avail[14] that thou shalt not escape my hands."

"I trust you well enough," said Sir Lancelot, "an ye may get me, I get but little mercy."

But the French book saith King Arthur would have taken his queen again and to have been accorded with Sir Lancelot, but Sir Gawain would not suffer him by no manner of mean.[15] And so Sir Gawain made many men to blow upon[16] Sir Lancelot, and so all at once they called him "false recreant knight." But when Sir Bors de Ganis, Sir Ector de Maris and Sir Lionel heard this outcry they called unto them Sir Palomides and Sir Lavain and Sir Urry with many more knights of their blood, and all they went unto Sir Lancelot and said thus:

"My lord, wit you well we have great scorn of the great rebukes[17] that we have heard Sir Gawain say unto you; wherefore we pray you, and charge you as you will have our service, keep us no longer within these walls, for we let you wit plainly we will ride into the field and do battle with them. For you fare as a man that were afeard, and for all your fair speech it will not avail you, for wit you well Sir Gawain will never suffer you to

---

[1] *whether ... him* Whichever might please him.

[2] *win ... harder* Get me and the queen at a greater price.

[3] *thine* With your.

[4] *For ... not* It is of no use for me to offer explanations.

[5] *in ... me* Purposefully to harm me.

[6] *accordment* Reconciliation.

[7] *mischievously set* Bent on destruction.

[8] *overlaid* Overpowered.

[9] *on me* About me.

[10] *forecast ... treason* Premeditated betrayal.

[11] *as ... done* In "The Tale of Sir Tristram de Lyones," Malory recounts how Gawain, Gaheris, Agravain and Mordred conspire to murder Sir Lamorak for sleeping with their mother, Morgause. Lamorak is conventionally considered Arthur's third best knight, after Lancelot and Tristram.

[12] *that ... Lamorak* You speak of Sir Lamorak.

[13] *sithen ... me* Throw in my face the matter.

[14] *avail* Disadvantage.

[15] *by ... mean* By no means.

[16] *blow upon* Discredit.

[17] *rebukes* Insults.

accord with King Arthur. And therefore fight for your life and right, an ye dare."

"Alas," said Sir Lancelot, "for to ride out of this castle and to do battle I am full loath."

Then Sir Lancelot spake on height unto King Arthur and Sir Gawain:

"My lord, I require you and beseech you, sithen that I am thus required and conjured[1] to ride into the field, that neither you, my lord King Arthur, neither you, Sir Gawain, come not into the field."

"What shall we do then?" said Sir Gawain. "Is not this the king's quarrel to fight with thee? And also it is my quarrel to fight with thee because of the death of my brother, Sir Gareth."

"Then must I needs unto battle,"[2] said Sir Lancelot. "Now wit you well, my lord Arthur and Sir Gawain, ye will repent it whensomever I do battle with you."

And so then they departed either from other; and then either party made them ready on the morn for to do battle, and great purveyance[3] was made on both sides. And Sir Gawain let purvey many knights for to wait upon Sir Lancelot, for to overset him and to slay him. And on the morn at underne[4] King Arthur was ready in the field with three great hosts.

And then Sir Lancelot's fellowship came out at the three gates in full good array;[5] and Sir Lionel came in the foremost battle, and Sir Lancelot came in the middle, and Sir Bors came out at the third gate. And thus they came in order and rule as full noble knights. And ever Sir Lancelot charged[6] all his knights in any wise[7] to save King Arthur and Sir Gawain.

Then came forth Sir Gawain from the king's host and proffered to joust. And Sir Lionel was a fierce knight, and lightly he encountered with him, and there Sir Gawain smote Sir Lionel throughout the body, that he dashed to the earth like as he had been dead. And then Sir Ector de Maris and other mo bare[8] him into the castle.

And anon there began a great stour,[9] and much people were slain; and ever Sir Lancelot did what he might to save the people on King Arthur's party. For Sir Bors and Sir Palomides and Sir Saphir overthrew many knights, for they were deadly knights, and Sir Blamour de Ganis and Sir Bleoberis, with Sir Bellengere le Beuse, these six knights did much harm. And ever was King Arthur about Sir Lancelot to have slain him, and ever Sir Lancelot suffered him and would not strike again. So Sir Bors encountered with King Arthur, and Sir Bors smote him; and so he alight and drew his sword, and said to Sir Lancelot,

"Sir, shall I make an end of this war?" (For he meant to have slain him.)

"Not so hardy,"[10] said Sir Lancelot, "upon pain of thy head, that thou touch him no more! For I will never see that most noble king that made me knight neither slain nor shamed."

And therewithal Sir Lancelot alight of his horse and took up the king and horsed him again, and said thus:

"My lord the king, for God's love, stint this strife, for ye get here no worship an I would do mine utterance.[11] But always I forbear[12] you and ye nor none of yours forbeareth not me. And therefore, my lord, I pray you remember what I have done in many places, and now am I evil rewarded."

So when King Arthur was on horseback he looked on Sir Lancelot; then the tears brast out of his eyen,[13] thinking of the great courtesy that was in Sir Lancelot more than in any other man. And therewith the king rode his way, and might no longer behold him, saying to himself, "Alas, alas, that ever yet this war began!"

And then either party of the battles withdrew them to repose them, and buried the dead, and searched[14] the wounded men, and laid to their wounds soft salves;[15] and thus they endured that night till on the morn. And on the morn by underne they made them ready to do

---

[1] *conjured* Begged.

[2] *Then … battle* Then it is necessary that I go into battle.

[3] *purveyance* Preparation.

[4] *underne* Ecclesiastical third hour of the day, i.e., early morning.

[5] *array* Military precision.

[6] *charged* Ordered.

[7] *in … wise* At any cost.

[8] *other mo bare* Many more bore.

[9] *stour* Battle.

[10] *Not … hardy* Not so fast!

[11] *utterance* Utmost.

[12] *forbear* Spare.

[13] *brast … eyen* Burst out of his eyes.

[14] *searched* Examined.

[15] *salves* Healing ointments.

battle, and then Sir Bors led the vaward.[1]

So upon the morn there came Sir Gawain, as brim[2] as any boar, with a great spear in his hand. And when Sir Bors saw him he thought to revenge his brother, Sir Lionel, of the despite Sir Gawain gave him the other day.

And so, as they that knew either other, fewtred[3] their spears, and with all their might of their horses and themselves so fiercely they met together and so felonously[4] that either bare other through, and so they fell both to the bare earth.

And then the battle joined, and there was much slaughter on both parties. Then Sir Lancelot rescued Sir Bors and sent him into the castle, but neither Sir Gawain neither Sir Bors died not of their wounds, for they were well holpen.[5]

Then Sir Lavain and Sir Urry prayed Sir Lancelot to do his pain[6] and fight as they do:

"For we see that ye forbear and spare, and that doth us much harm. And therefore we pray you spare not your enemies no more than they do you."

"Alas," said Sir Lancelot, "I have no heart to fight against my lord Arthur, for ever meseemeth I do not as me ought to do."

"My lord," said Sir Palomides, "though ye spare them never so much all this day they will never con you thank;[7] and if they may get you at avail ye are but a dead man."

So then Sir Lancelot understood that they said him truth. Then he strained himself more than he did toforehand, and because of his nephew, Sir Bors, was sore wounded he pained[8] himself the more. And so within a little while, by evensong[9] time, Sir Lancelot's party the better stood; for their horses went in blood past the fetlocks,[10] there were so many people slain.

And then for very[11] pity Sir Lancelot withheld his knights and suffered King Arthur's party to withdraw them inside. And so he withdrew his meiny[12] into the castle, and either parties buried the dead and put salve unto the wounded men. So when Sir Gawain was hurt, they on King Arthur's party were not so orgulous[13] as they were toforehand to do battle.

So of this war that was noised through all Christian realms, and so it came at the last by relation[14] unto the Pope. And then the Pope took a consideration of the great goodness of King Arthur and of the high prowess of Sir Lancelot, that was called the most noblest knight of the world. Wherefore the Pope called unto him a noble clerk that at that time was there present (the French book saith it was the Bishop of Rochester), and the Pope gave him bulls under lead,[15] and sent them unto the king, charging him upon pain of interdicting[16] of all England that he take his queen again and accord with Sir Lancelot.

So when this Bishop was come unto Carlisle he showed the king his bulls, and when the king understood them he wist not what to do: but full fain[17] he would have been accorded with Sir Lancelot, but Sir Gawain would not suffer him. But to have the queen, he thereto agreed; but in no wise he would suffer the king to accord with Sir Lancelot; but as for the queen, he consented. So the Bishop had of the king his great seal and his assurance, as he was a true and anointed king, that Sir Lancelot should go safe and come safe, and that the queen should not be said unto of[18] the king, neither of none other, for nothing done of time past. And of all these appointments[19] the Bishop brought with him sure

---

[1] *vaward* Vanguard, first troops.

[2] *brim* Fierce.

[3] *fewtred* Set firmly.

[4] *felonously* Cruelly.

[5] *holpen* Helped.

[6] *pain* Utmost.

[7] *never ... thank* No matter how much you spare them, they will never be able to thank you.

[8] *pained* Exerted.

[9] *evensong* Ecclesiastical office taking place just before dusk.

[10] *fetlocks* Tufts of hair above and behind horses' hooves.

[11] *very* True.

[12] *meiny* Retinue.

[13] *orgulous* Haughty.

[14] *relation* Report.

[15] *bulls under lead* Mandates sealed with lead.

[16] *charging... interdicting* Ordering him upon pain of excommunication.

[17] *fain* Gladly.

[18] *said ... of* Rebuked by.

[19] *appointments* Conditions.

writing[1] to show unto Sir Lancelot.

So when the Bishop was come to Joyous Gard, there he showed Sir Lancelot how he came from the Pope with writing unto King Arthur and unto him. And there he told him the perils, if he withheld the queen from the king.

"Sir, it was never in my thought," said Sir Lancelot, "to withhold the queen from my lord Arthur, but I keep her for this cause: insomuch as she should have be[2] brent for my sake, meseemed[3] it was my part to save her life and put her from that danger till better recover[4] might come. And now I thank God," said Sir Lancelot, "that the Pope hath made her peace. For God knoweth," said Sir Lancelot, "I will be a thousandfold more gladder to bring her again than ever I was of her taking away, with this I may be sure to come safe and go safe, and that the queen shall have her liberty as she had before, and never for nothing that hath be surmised afore this time that she never from this stand in no peril. For else," said Sir Lancelot, "I dare adventure me to keep her from an harder shour[5] than ever yet I had."

"Sir, it shall not need you," said the Bishop, "to dread thus much, for wit you well, the Pope must be obeyed, and it were not the Pope's worship neither my poor honesty[6] to know you distressed neither the queen, neither in peril neither shamed."

And then he showed Sir Lancelot all his writing, both from the Pope and King Arthur.

"This is sure enough," said Sir Lancelot, "for full well I dare trust my lord's own writing and his seal, for he was never shamed of[7] his promise. Therefore," said Sir Lancelot unto the Bishop, "ye shall ride unto the king afore and recommend me unto his good grace, and let him have knowledging that this same day eight days,[8] by the grace of God, I myself shall bring the queen unto him. And then say ye to my redoubted[9] king that I will say largely for the queen;[10] that I shall none except[11] for dread neither for fear but the king himself and my lord Sir Gawain, and that is for the king's love more than for himself."[12]

So the Bishop departed and came to the king to Carlisle, and told him all how Sir Lancelot answered him; so that made the tears fall out at the king's eyen. Then Sir Lancelot purveyed him an hundred knights, and all well clothed in green velvet, and their horses trapped[13] in the same to the heels, and every knight held a branch of olive in his hand in tokening of peace. And the queen had four-and-twenty gentlewomen following her in the same wise. And Sir Lancelot had twelve coursers[14] following him, and on every courser sat a young gentleman; and all they were arrayed in white velvet with sarpes of gold about their quarters,[15] and the horse trapped in the same wise down to the heels, with many ouches iset[16] with stones and pearls in gold, to the number of a thousand. And in the same wise was the queen arrayed, and Sir Lancelot in the same, of white cloth of gold tissue.[17]

And right so as you have heard, as the French book maketh mention, he rode with the queen from Joyous Gard to Carlisle. And so Sir Lancelot rode throughout Carlisle, and so into the castle, that all men might behold them. And there was many a weeping eyen. And then Sir Lancelot himself alight and voided[18] his horse, and took adown the queen, and so led her where King Arthur was in his seat; and Sir Gawain sat afore him, and many other great lords.

So when Sir Lancelot saw the king and Sir Gawain, then he led the queen by the arm, and then he kneeled down and the queen both. Wit you well, then was there many a bold knight with King Arthur that wept as

---

[1] *sure writing* Guarantees in writing.

[2] *be* Been.

[3] *meseemed* It seemed to me.

[4] *recover* Rescue.

[5] *I … shour* I would dare risk myself to protect her by fighting a harder battle.

[6] *were not … honesty* Would not be to the Pope's honor or my humble credit.

[7] *shamed of* Untrue to.

[8] *same … days* Eight days from today.

[9] *redoubted* Noble.

[10] *I … queen* I will speak wholly in defense of the queen.

[11] *none except* Except no one from my challenge to trial by combat.

[12] *himself* I.e., Gawain.

[13] *trapped* Adorned.

[14] *coursers* Powerful horses.

[15] *sarpes … quarters* Chains of gold around their thighs.

[16] *ouches iset* Jeweled ornaments set.

[17] *gold tissue* Gauzy cloth of gold.

[18] *voided* Dismounted.

tenderly as they had seen all their kin dead afore them! So the king sat still and said no word. And when Sir Lancelot saw his countenance he arose up and pulled up the queen with him, and thus he said full knightly:

"My most redoubted king, ye shall understand, by the Pope's commandment and yours, I have brought to you my lady the queen, as right requireth. And if there be any knight, of what degree that ever he be of, except your person, that will say or dare say but that she is true and clean to you, I here myself, Sir Lancelot du Lake, will make it good upon his body that she is a true lady unto you.

"But, sir, liars ye have listened,[1] and that hath caused great debate betwixt you and me. For time hath been, my lord Arthur, that ye were greatly pleased with me when I did battle for my lady, your queen; and full well you know, my most noble king, that she hath be put to great wrong or this time. And sithen it pleased you at many times that I should fight for her, therefore meseemeth, my good lord, I had more cause to rescue her from the fire when she should have been brent for my sake.

"For they that told you those tales were liars, and so it fell upon them: for by likelihood, had not the might of God been with me, I might never have endured with fourteen knights. And they were armed and afore purposed,[2] and I unarmed and not purposed;[3] for I was sent unto my lady, your queen, I wot not for what cause, but I was not so soon within the chamber door but anon Sir Agravain and Sir Mordred called me traitor and false recreant knight."

"By my faith, they called thee right!" said Sir Gawain.

"My lord, Sir Gawain," said Sir Lancelot, "in their quarrel they proved not themselves the best, neither in the right."

"Well, well, Sir Lancelot," said the king, "I have given you no cause to do to me as ye have done, for I have worshipped you and yours more than any other knights."

"My lord," said Sir Lancelot, "so ye be not displeased, ye shall understand that I and mine have done you oftentimes better service than any other knights

have done, in many diverse places; and where ye have been full hard bestad diverse times, I have rescued you from many dangers; and ever unto my power I was glad to please you and my lord Sir Gawain. In jousts and in tournaments and in battles set, both on horseback and on foot, I have often rescued you, and you, my lord Sir Gawain, and many mo of your knights in many diverse places.

"For now I will make avaunt,"[4] said Sir Lancelot: "I will that ye all wit that as yet I found never no manner of knight but that I was overhard for him an I had done mine utterance, God grant mercy! Howbeit I have been matched with good knights, as Sir Tristram and Sir Lamorak, but ever I had favour unto them and a deeming what they were.[5] And I take God to record, I never was wroth nor greatly heavy with[6] no good knight an I saw him busy and about to win worship; and glad I was ever when I found a good knight that might anything[7] endure me on horseback and on foot. Howbeit Sir Carados of the Dolorous Tower was a full noble knight and a passing strong man, and that wot ye, my lord Sir Gawain; for he might well be called a noble knight when he by fine force pulled you out of your saddle and bound you overthwart[8] afore him to his saddle-bow.[9] And there, my lord Sir Gawain, I rescued you and slew him afore your sight. Also I found your brother, Sir Gaheris, and Sir Tarquin leading him abounden[10] afore him; and there also I rescued your brother and slew Sir Tarquin and delivered three score and four[11] of my lord Arthur's knights out of his prison. And now I dare say," said Sir Lancelot, "I met never with so strong a knight nor so well-fighting as was Sir Carados and Sir Tarquin, for they and I fought to the uttermost. And therefore," said Sir Lancelot unto Sir Gawain, "meseemeth ye ought of right to remember this; for, an I might have your good will, I would trust to God for to have my lord

---

1 *liars ... listened* You have listened to liars.

2 *afore purposed* Had planned ahead of time.

3 *not purposed* Unprepared.

4 *I ... avaunt* I will make a boast..

5 *I had ... were* I went easy on them because I suspected who they were (i.e., friends he did not want to harm).

6 *greatly ... with* Too hard upon.

7 *anything* At all.

8 *overthwart* Lying across.

9 *saddle-bow* Front part of saddle.

10 *abounden* Bound up.

11 *delivered ... four* Rescued sixty-four.

Arthur's good grace."

"Sir, the king may do as he will," said Sir Gawain, "but wit thou well, Sir Lancelot, thou and I shall never be accorded while we live, for thou hast slain three of my brethren. And two of them thou slew traitorly and piteously,[1] for they bore none harness against thee, neither none would do."

"Sir, God would they had been armed," said Sir Lancelot, "for then had they been on life.[2] And wit ye well, Sir Gawain, as for Gareth, I loved no kinsman I had more than I loved him, and ever while I live," said Sir Lancelot, "I will bewail Sir Gareth his death, not all only for the great fear I have of you, but for many causes which causeth me to be sorrowful. One is that I made him knight; another is, I wot well he loved me above all other knights; and the third is, he was passing noble and true, courteous and gentle and well-conditioned.[3] The fourth is, I wist well, anon as I heard that Sir Gareth was dead, I knew well that I should never after have your love, my lord Sir Gawain, but everlasting war betwixt us. And also I wist well that you would cause my noble lord King Arthur forever to be my mortal foe. And as Jesu be my help, and by my knighthood, I slew never Sir Gareth neither his brother by my willing; but alas that ever they were unarmed that unhappy day!

"But this much I shall offer me to you," said Sir Lancelot, "if it may please the king's good grace and you, my lord Sir Gawain: I shall first begin at Sandwich, and there I shall go in my shirt, bare-foot; and at every ten miles' end I shall found and gar make[4] an house of religion, of what order that you will assign me, with an holy convent, to sing and read day and night in especial for Sir Gareth and Sir Gaheris. And this shall I perform from Sandwich until Carlisle; and every house shall have sufficient livelihood.[5] And this shall I perform while that I have any livelihood in Christendom, and there is none of all these religious places but they shall be performed, furnished and garnished with all things as an holy place ought to be. And this were fairer and more holier and more parfit[6] to their souls than ye, my most noble king, and you, Sir Gawain, to war upon me, for thereby shall you get none avail."[7]

Then all the knights and ladies that were there wept as they were mad, and the tears fell on King Arthur's cheeks.

"Sir Lancelot," said Sir Gawain, "I have right well heard thy language and thy great proffers. But wit thou well, let the king do as it pleaseth him, I will never forgive thee my brothers' death, and in especial the death of my brother Sir Gareth. And if mine uncle, King Arthur, will accord with thee, he shall lose my service, for wit thou well," said Sir Gawain, "thou art both false to the king and to me."

"Sir," said Sir Lancelot, "he beareth not the life that may make it good![8] An ye, Sir Gawain, will charge me with so high[9] a thing, ye must pardon me, for then needs must I answer you."

"Nay, nay," said Sir Gawain, "we are past that as at this time, and that causeth the Pope,[10] for he hath charged mine uncle the king that he shall take again his queen and to accord with thee, Sir Lancelot, as for this season, and therefore thou shalt go safe as thou came. But in this land thou shalt not abide past a fifteen-days, such summons[11] I give thee, for so the king and we were condescended and accorded ere thou came. And else," said Gawain, "wit thou well, thou should not a-comen here but if it were maugre thine head. And if it were not for the Pope's commandment," said Sir Gawain, "I should do battle with thee mine own hands, body for body, and prove it upon thee that thou hast been false unto mine uncle, King Arthur, and to me both; and that shall I prove on thy body, when thou art departed from hence, wheresomever that I find thee!"

Then Sir Lancelot sighed, and therewith the tears fell on his cheeks, and then said he thus:

"Most noblest Christian realm, whom I have loved above all other realms! And in thee I have gotten a great part of my worship, and now that I shall depart in this

---

[1] *piteously* Sadly.
[2] *on life* Alive.
[3] *well-conditioned* Of a pleasant disposition.
[4] *gar make* Order to be made.
[5] *livelihood* Endowment, possessions.
[6] *parfit* Perfect, right.
[7] *avail* Disadvantage.
[8] *he ... good* There is no one alive who can prove that.
[9] *charge ... high* Accuse me of so serious.
[10] *causeth ... Pope* Because of the Pope.
[11] *summons* Terms.

wise, truly me repents that ever I came in this realm, that I should be thus shamefully banished, undeserved and causeless. But fortune is so variant, and the wheel so mutable[1] that there is no constant abiding. And that may be proved by many chronicles, as of noble Hector of Troy[2] and Alexander,[3] the mighty conqueror, and many more other: when they were most in their royalty, they alight passing low.[4] And so fareth it by me," said Sir Lancelot, "for in this realm I had worship, and by me and mine all the whole Round Table hath been increased more in worship, by me and mine, than ever it was by any of you all.

"And therefore wit thou well, Sir Gawain, I may live upon lands as well as any knight that here is. And if ye, my most redoubted king, will come upon my lands with Sir Gawain to war upon me, I must endure you as well as I may. But as to you, Sir Gawain, if that ye come there, I pray you charge me not with treason neither felony, for an ye do, I must answer you."

"Do thou thy best," said Sir Gawain, "and therefore hie[5] thee fast that thou were gone! And wit thou well we shall soon come after, and break the strongest castle that thou hast, upon thy head!"

"It shall not need that," said Sir Lancelot, "for an I were as orgulous set[6] as ye are, wit you well I should meet you in midst of the field."

"Make thou no more language," said Sir Gawain, "but deliver the queen from thee, and pike thee lightly[7] out of this court!"

"Well," said Sir Lancelot, "an I had wist of this shortcoming,[8] I would 'a advised me[9] twice or that I had come here. For an the queen had been so dear unto me

as ye noise her, I durst have kept her from the fellowship of the best knights under heaven."

And then Sir Lancelot said unto Queen Guinevere, in hearing of the king and them all,

"Madam, now I must depart from you and this noble fellowship for ever. And sithen it is so, I beseech you to pray for me, and I shall pray for you. And tell ye me, an if ye be hard bestead by any false tongues, but lightly, my good lady, send me word; and if any knight's hands under the heaven may deliver you by battle, I shall deliver you."

And therewithal Sir Lancelot kissed the queen, and then he said all openly,

"Now let see whatsomever he be in this place that dare say the queen is not true unto my lord Arthur, let see who will speak an he dare speak."

And therewith he brought the queen to the king, and then Sir Lancelot took his leave and departed. And there was neither king, duke, earl, baron, nor knight, lady nor gentlewoman, but all they wept as people out of mind, except Sir Gawain. And when this noble knight Sir Lancelot took his horse to ride out of Carlisle, there was sobbing and weeping for pure dole of his departing.

And so he took his way to Joyous Gard, and then ever after he called it the "Dolorous Gard." And thus departed Sir Lancelot from the court forever.

And so when he came to Joyous Gard he called his fellowship unto him and asked them what they would do. Then they answered all wholly together with one voice, they would do as he would do.

"Then, my fair fellows," said Sir Lancelot, "I must depart out of this most noble realm. And now I shall depart, it grieveth me sore, for I shall depart with no worship; for a fleamed[10] man departeth never out of a realm with no worship.[11] And that is to me great heaviness,[12] for ever I fear after my days that men shall chronicle upon me that I was fleamed out of this land. And else, my fair lords, be ye sure, an I had not dread shame, my lady Queen Guinevere and I should never have departed."

---

[1] *fortune … mutable* Fortune so variable, and the Wheel of Fortune so changeable.

[2] *Hector of Troy* Heroic prince of Troy, killed by Achilles in Homer's *Iliad*.

[3] *Alexander* Famed conqueror (356–323 BCE) of Greece, Egypt, and Persia.

[4] *alight … low* Fell to the bottom. (Ever changeable, the Wheel of Fortune might raise up those who were low and cast down those who were at the top.)

[5] *hie* Hasten.

[6] *orgulous set* Proudly determined.

[7] *pike thee lightly* Quickly get yourself.

[8] *shortcoming* Unfortunate situation.

[9] *'a advised me* Have thought.

[10] *fleamed* Banished.

[11] *no worship* Any honor. Middle English often uses the double negative for additional emphasis.

[12] *heaviness* Sadness.

Then spake noble knights, as Sir Palomides and Sir Saphir, his brother, and Sir Bellengere le Beuse, and Sir Urry with Sir Lavain, with many other:

"Sir, an ye will so be disposed to abide in this land we will never fail you; and if ye list not abide in this land, there is none of the good knights that here be that will fail you, for many causes. One is, all we that be not of your blood shall never be welcome unto the court. And sithen it liked us to take a part with you in your distress in this realm, wit you well it shall like us as well to go in other countries with you, and there to to take such part as you do."

"My fair lords," said Sir Lancelot, "I well understand you, and as I can, I thank you. And you shall understand, such livelihood as I am born unto I shall depart with you in this manner of wise: that is for to say, I shall depart[1] all my livelihood and all my lands freely among you, and myself will have as little as any of you; for, have I sufficient that may long unto my person,[2] I will ask none other riches neither array. And I trust to God to maintain you[3] on my lands as well as ever you were maintained."

Then spake all the knights at once: "Have he shame that will leave you! For we all understand in this realm will be no quiet, but ever debate and strife now the fellowship of the Round Table is broken. For by the noble fellowship of the Round Table was King Arthur upborne, and by their noblesse[4] the king and all the realm was ever in quiet and rest. And a great part," they said all, "was because of your most noblesse, Sir Lancelot."

"Now, truly I thank you all of your good saying! Howbeit, I wot well that in me was not all the stability of this realm, but in that I might I did my dever.[5] And well I am sure I knew many rebellions in my days that by me and mine were peased;[6] and that I trow we all shall hear of in short space, and that me sore repenteth. For ever I dread me," said Sir Lancelot, "that Sir Mordred will make trouble, for he is passing envious, and applyeth him much to trouble."

And so they were accorded to depart with Sir Lancelot to his lands. And to make short this tale, they trussed, and paid[7] all that would ask them; and wholly an hundred knights departed with Sir Lancelot at once, and made their avows they would never leave him for weal ne[8] for woe.

And so they shipped at Cardiff, and sailed unto Benwick: some men call it Bayan[9] and some men call it Beaune, where the wine of Beaune is. But say the sooth, Sir Lancelot and his nephews was lord of all France and of all the lands that longed unto[10] France; he and his kindred rejoiced[11] it, all through Sir Lancelot's noble prowess.

And then he stuffed and furnished and garnished all his noble towns and castles. Then all the people of those lands came unto Sir Lancelot on foot and hands.[12] And so when he had 'stablished all those countries, he shortly called a parliament; and there he crowned Sir Lionel king of France, and Sir Bors he crowned him king of all King Claudas' lands, and Sir Ector de Maris, Sir Lancelot's younger brother, he crowned him king of Benwick and king of all Guienne, which was Sir Lancelot's own lands. And he made Sir Ector prince of them all.

And thus he departed his lands and advanced[13] all his noble knights. And first he advanced them of his blood, as Sir Blamour, he made him duke of Limousin in Guienne, and Sir Bleoberis, he made him duke of Poitiers. And Sir Gahalantin, he made him duke of Auvergne; and Sir Galyhodin, he made him duke of Saintonge; and Sir Galihud, he made him earl of Perigord; and Sir Menaduke, he made him earl of Rouergue; and Sir Villiers the Valiant, he made him earl of Bearn; and Sir Hebes le Renown, he made him earl of Comminges; and Sir Lavain, he made him earl of Armagnac; and Sir Urry, he made him earl of Astarac; and Sir Neroveous, he made him earl of Pardiac; and Sir Plenorius, he made him earl of Foix; and Sir Selises of

---

1   *depart*   Divide.

2   *for ... person*   For if I have what I need.

3   *maintain you*   Provide for you.

4   *noblesse*   Noble quality.

5   *in ... dever*   Insofar as I could, I did my duty.

6   *peased*   Reconciled.

7   *trussed ... paid*   Equipped themselves and hired.

8   *ne*   Nor.

9   *Bayan*   Bayonne.

10   *longed unto*   Belonged to.

11   *rejoiced*   Possessed.

12   *on ... hands*   Submissively.

13   *advanced*   Promoted in station.

the Dolorous Tower, he made him earl of Marsan; and Sir Melias de Lisle, he made him earl of Tursan; and Sir Bellengere le Beuse, he made him earl of the Landes; and Sir Palomides, he made him duke of Provence; and Sir Saphir, he made him duke of Languedoc. And Sir Clegis, he gave him the earldom of Agen; and Sir Sadok, he gave him the earldom of Sarlat; and Sir Dinas le Seneschal, he made him duke of Anjou; and Sir Clarrus, he made him duke of Normandy.

Thus Sir Lancelot rewarded his noble knights, and many more meseemeth it were too long to rehearse.

3
THE SIEGE OF BENWICK

So leave we Sir Lancelot in his lands and his noble knights with him, and return we again unto King Arthur and unto Sir Gawain that made a great host aready to the number of three-score thousand. And all thing was made ready for shipping to pass over the sea, to war upon Sir Lancelot and upon his lands. And so they shipped at Cardiff.

And there King Arthur made Sir Mordred chief ruler of all England, and also he put the queen under his governance: because Sir Mordred was King Arthur's son, he gave him rule of his land and of his wife.

And so the king passed the sea and landed upon Sir Lancelot's lands, and there he brent and wasted, through the vengeance of Sir Gawain, all that they might over-run. So when this word was come unto Sir Lancelot, that King Arthur and Sir Gawain were landed upon his lands and made full great destruction and waste, then spake Sir Bors and said,

"My lord Sir Lancelot, it is shame that we suffer them thus to ride over our lands. For wit you well, suffer ye them as long as ye will, they will do you no favour an they may handle[1] you."

Then said Sir Lionel that was ware[2] and wise, "My lord, Sir Lancelot, I will give you this counsel: let us keep our strong-walled towns until they have hunger and cold and blow on their nails; and then let us freshly[3] set upon them and shred them down as sheep in a fold,

that ever after aliaunts[4] may take ensample[5] how they land upon our lands!"[6]

Then spoke King Bagdemagus to Sir Lancelot and said, "Sir, your courtesy will shend[7] us all, and your courtesy hath waked all this sorrow; for an they thus override our lands, they shall by process bring us all to nought while we thus in holes us hide."

Then said Sir Galihud unto Sir Lancelot, "Sir, here been knights come of king's blood that will not long droop and dare[8] within these walls. Therefore give us leave, like as we been knights, to meet them in the field, and we shall slay them and so deal with them that they shall curse the time that ever they came into this country."

Then spake seven brethren of North Wales which were seven noble knights; for a man might seek seven kings' lands or he might find such seven knights. And these seven noble knights said all at once,

"Sir Lancelot, for Christ's sake, let us ride out with Sir Galihud, for we were never wont[9] to cower in castles neither in noble towns."

Then spake Sir Lancelot, that was master and governor of them all, and said, "My fair lords, wit you well I am full loath to ride out with my knights for shedding of Christian blood; and yet my lands I understand be full bare for to sustain any host awhile for the mighty wars that whilom[10] made King Claudas upon this country and upon my father, King Ban, and on mine uncle, King Bors. Howbeit we will at this time keep our strong walls. And I shall send a messenger unto my lord Arthur a treatise for to take, for better is peace than always war."

So Sir Lancelot sent forth a damsel with a dwarf with her, requiring King Arthur to leave his warring upon his lands. And so she start upon a palfrey,[11] and a dwarf ran by her side. And when she came to the

---

[1] *handle* Capture.

[2] *ware* Wary.

[3] *freshly* Quickly.

[4] *aliaunts* Foreigners.

[5] *ensample* Example.

[6] *how … lands* What will happen to them if they come upon our lands like this.

[7] *shend* Ruin.

[8] *droop and dare* Cower and be still.

[9] *wont* Accustomed.

[10] *whilom* Formerly, in the past.

[11] *palfrey* Saddled horse, regarded as a suitable mount for a woman.

pavilion of King Arthur, there she alight; and there met her a gentle knight, Sir Lucan the Butler, and said,

"Fair damsel, come you from Sir Lancelot du Lake?"

"Yea, sir," she said, "therefore came I hither to speak with my lord the king."

"Alas," said Sir Lucan, "my lord Arthur would accord with Sir Lancelot, but Sir Gawain will not suffer him." And then he said, "I pray to God, damsel, that ye may speed well,[1] for all we that been about the king would that Lancelot did best of any knight living."

And so with this Sir Lucan led the damsel to the king, where he sat with Sir Gawain, for to hear what she would say. So when she had told her tale the water ran out of the king's eyen. And all the lords were full glad for to advise the king to be accorded with Sir Lancelot, save all only Sir Gawain. And he said,

"My lord, mine uncle, what will ye do? Will ye now turn again, now ye are past this far upon your journey? All the world will speak of you villainy and shame."

"Now," said King Arthur, "wit you well, Sir Gawain, I will do as ye advise me; and yet meseemeth," said King Arthur, "his fair proffers were not good to be refused. But sithen I am come so far upon this journey, I will that ye give the damsel her answer, for I may not speak to her for pity: for her proffers been so large."

Then Sir Gawain said unto the damsel thus: "Say ye to Sir Lancelot that it is waste labour now to sue[2] to mine uncle. For tell him, an he would have made any labour for peace, he should have made it or this time, for tell him now it is too late. And say to him that I, Sir Gawain, so send him word, that I promise him by the faith that I owe to God and to knighthood, I shall never leave him till he has slain me or I him!"

So the damsel wept and departed, and so there was many a weeping eye. And then Sir Lucan brought the damsel to her palfrey; and so she came to Sir Lancelot, where he was among all his knights, and when Sir Lancelot had heard her answer, then the tears ran down by his cheeks. And then his noble knights came about him and said,

"Sir Lancelot, wherefore make ye such cheer? Now think what ye are, and what men we are, and let us, noble knights, match them in midst of the field."

"That may be lightly[3] done," said Sir Lancelot, "but I was never so loath to do battle. And therefore I pray you, sirs, as ye love me, be ruled at this time as I will have you. For I will always flee that noble king that made me knight; and when I may no further, I must needs defend me. And that will be more worship for me and us all than to compare with that noble king whom we have all served."

Then they held their language,[4] and as that night they took their rest. And upon the morning early, in the dawning of the day, as knights looked out, they saw the city of Benwick besieged round about, and gan fast to set up ladders. And they within kept them out of the town and beat them mightily from the walls. Then came forth Sir Gawain, well armed, upon a stiff[5] steed, and he came before the chief gate with his spear in his hand, crying:

"Where art thou, Sir Lancelot? Is there none of all your proud knights that dare break a spear with me?"

Then Sir Bors made him ready and came forth out of the town. And there Sir Gawain encountered with Sir Bors, and at that time he smote him down from his horse, and almost he had slain him. And so Sir Bors was rescued and borne into the town.

Then came forth Sir Lionel, brother to Sir Bors, and thought to revenge him, and either fewtred their spears and so ran together, and there they met spiteously,[6] but Sir Gawain had such a grace[7] that he smote Sir Lionel down and wounded him there passingly sore. And then Sir Lionel was rescued and borne into the town.

And thus Sir Gawain came every day, and failed not but that he smote down one knight or other. So thus they endured half a year, and much slaughter was of people on both parties.

Then it befell upon a day that Sir Gawain came afore the gates, armed at all pieces,[8] on a noble horse, with a great spear in his hand, and then he cried with a loud voice and said,

---

[1] *speed well* Succeed.

[2] *sue* Petition, ask.

[3] *lightly* Easily.

[4] *held … language* Remained quiet.

[5] *stiff* Sturdy.

[6] *spiteously* Violently.

[7] *grace* Good luck.

[8] *armed … pieces* Completely armed.

"Where art thou now, thou false traitor, Sir Lancelot? Why holdest thou thyself within holes and walls like a coward? Look out, thou false traitor knight, and here I shall revenge upon thy body the death of my three brethren!"

And all this language heard Sir Lancelot every deal.[1] Then his kin and his knights drew about him, and all they said at once unto Sir Lancelot,

"Sir, now must you defend you like a knight, either else ye be shamed for ever, for now ye be called upon[2] treason it is time for you to stir! For ye have slept over long and suffered overmuch."

"So God me help," said Sir Lancelot, "I am right heavy at Sir Gawain's words, for now he charges me with a great charge. And therefore I wot as well as ye I must needs defend me, either else to be recreant."

Then Sir Lancelot bade saddle his strongest horse and bade let fetch his arms and bring all to the tower of the gate. And then Sir Lancelot spake on high unto the king and said,

"My lord Arthur and noble king that made me knight! Wit you well I am right heavy for your sake that ye thus sue upon me.[3] And always I forbear you, for an I would be vengeable[4] I might have met you in midst the field or this time, and there to have made your boldest knights full tame. And now I have forborne you and suffered you half a year, and Sir Gawain, to do what you would do. And now I may no longer suffer to endure, but needs I must defend myself, insomuch as Sir Gawain hath becalled me of treason; which is greatly against my will that ever I should fight against any of your blood, but now I may not forsake it: for I am driven thereto as beast till a bay."[5]

Then Sir Gawain said unto Sir Lancelot,

"An thou darest do battle, leave thy babbling and come off, and let us ease our hearts!"

Then Sir Lancelot armed him and mounted upon his horse, and either of them got great spears in their hands. And so the host without stood still all apart, and the noble knights of the city came a great number, that when King Arthur saw the number of men and knights he marvelled and said to himself,

"Alas, that ever Sir Lancelot was against me! For now I see that he has forborne me."

And so the covenant was made, there should no man nigh them neither deal with them till the tone were dead other yolden.[6]

Then Sir Lancelot and Sir Gawain departed a great way in sunder,[7] and then they came together with all their horse[8] mights as fast as they might run, and either smote other in midst of their shields. But the knights were so strong and their spears so big that their horse might not endure their buffets, and so their horses fell to the earth. And then they avoided their horses and dressed their shields afore them; then they came together and gave many sad strokes on diverse places of their bodies, that the blood brast out on many sides.

Then had Sir Gawain such a grace and gift that an holy man had given him, that every day in the year, from undern till high noon, his might increased those three hours as much as thrice his strength. And that caused Sir Gawain to win great honour. And for his sake King Arthur made an ordinance that all manner of battles for any quarrels that should be done afore King Arthur should begin at undern; and all was done for Sir Gawain's love, that by likelihood if Sir Gawain were on the tone party, he should have the better in battle while his strength endured three hours. But there were that time but few knights living that knew this advantage that Sir Gawain had, but King Arthur all only.

So Sir Lancelot fought with Sir Gawain, and when Sir Lancelot felt his might evermore increase, Sir Lancelot wondered and dread him sore to be shamed; for, as the French book saith, he wende,[9] when he felt Sir Gawain's double his strength, that he had been a fiend and none earthly man. Wherefore Sir Lancelot traced and traversed,[10] and covered himself with his shield, and kept his might and his breath during three hours. And that while Sir Gawain gave him many sad brunts and many sad strokes, that all knights that beheld Sir Lance-

---

[1] *every deal* Every bit.

[2] *called upon* Accused of.

[3] *thus sue upon me* Pursue me in this way.

[4] *vengeable* Vengeful.

[5] *till ... bay* At bay.

[6] *till ... yolden* Until one were dead or had yielded.

[7] *in sunder* Apart.

[8] *horse* Horses'.

[9] *wende* Thought.

[10] *traversed* Dodged.

lot marvelled how he might endure him, but full little understood they that travail that Sir Lancelot had to endure him.

And then when it was past noon Sir Gawain's strength was gone and he had no more but his own might. When Sir Lancelot felt him so come down, then he stretched him up and strode near Sir Gawain and said thus:

"Now I feel ye have done your worst! And now, my lord Sir Gawain, I must do my part, for many a great and grievous strokes I have endured you this day with great pain."

And so Sir Lancelot doubled his strokes and gave Sir Gawain such a stroke upon the helmet that sideling[1] he fell down upon his one side. And Sir Lancelot withdrew him from him.

"Why withdrawest thou thee?" said Sir Gawain. "Turn again, false traitor knight, and slay me out! For an thou leave me thus, anon as I am whole I shall do battle with thee again."

"Sir," said Sir Lancelot, "I shall endure you, by God's grace! But wit thou well, Sir Gawain, I will never smite a felled knight."

And so Sir Lancelot departed and went unto the city. And Sir Gawain was borne unto King Arthur's pavilion, and anon leeches[2] were brought unto him of the best, and searched and salved him with soft ointments. And then Sir Lancelot said,

"Now have good day, my lord and king! For wit you well ye win no worship at these walls, for an I would my knights outbring, there should many a doughty[3] man die. And therefore, my lord Arthur, remember you of old kindness, and howsoever I fare, Jesu be your guide in all places."

"Now, alas," said the king, "that ever this unhappy war began! For ever Sir Lancelot forbeareth me in all places, and in like wise my kin, and that is seen well this day, what courtesy he showed my nephew, Sir Gawain."

Then King Arthur fell sick for sorrow of Sir Gawain, that he was so sore hurt, and because of the war betwixt him and Sir Lancelot. So after that they on King Arthur's party kept the siege with little war withoutforth,

and they withinforth kept their walls and defended them when need was.

Thus Sir Gawain lay sick and unsound three weeks in his tents with all manner of leechcraft[4] that might be had. And as soon as Sir Gawain might go and ride, he armed him at all points and bestrode a stiff courser and got a great spear in his hand, and so he came riding afore the chief gate of Benwick. And there he cried on high and said,

"Where art thou, Sir Lancelot? Come forth, thou false traitor knight and recreant, for I am here, Sir Gawain, that will prove this that I say upon thee!"

And all this language Sir Lancelot heard and said thus: "Sir Gawain, me repents of your foul saying, that ye will not cease your language. For ye wot well, Sir Gawain, I know your might and all that ye may do, and well ye wot, Sir Gawain, ye may not greatly hurt me."

"Come down, traitor knight," said he, "and make it good the contrary with thy hands! For it mishapped me the last battle to be hurt of thy hands, therefore, wit thou well, I am come this day to make amends, for I ween this day to lay thee as low as thou laidest me."

"Jesu defend me," said Sir Lancelot, "that ever I be so far in your danger[5] as ye have been in mine, for then my days were done. But, Gawain," said Lancelot, "ye shall not think that I shall tarry long, but sithen that ye unknightly call me thus of treason, ye shall have both your hands full of me!"

And then Sir Lancelot armed him at all points and mounted upon his horse and got a great spear in his hand and rode out at the gate. And both their hosts were assembled, of them without and within, and stood in array full manly, and both parties were charged to hold them still to see and behold the battle of these two noble knights.

And then they laid their spears in their rests and so came together as thunder. And Sir Gawain brake his spear in an hundred pieces to his hand, and Sir Lancelot smote him with a greater might that Sir Gawain's horse feet raised, and so the horse and he fell to the earth. Then Sir Gawain deliverly[6] devoided his horse and put his shield afore him, and eagerly drew his sword and

---

[1] *sideling* Sideways.

[2] *leeches* Physicians.

[3] *doughty* Brave.

[4] *leechcraft* Medical arts.

[5] *danger* Power.

[6] *deliverly* Quickly.

bade Sir Lancelot, "Alight, traitor knight!" and said, "If a mare's son hath failed me, wit thou well a king's son and a queen's son shall not fail thee!"

Then Sir Lancelot devoided his horse and dressed his shield afore him and drew his sword, and so came eagerly together and gave many sad strokes, that all men on both parties had wonder.

But when Sir Lancelot felt Sir Gawain's might so marvellously increase, he then withheld his courage and his wind,[1] and so he kept him under covert of his might and of his shield: he traced and traversed here and there to break Sir Gawain's strokes and his courage. And ever Sir Gawain enforced himself with all his might and power to destroy Sir Lancelot, for, as the French book saith, ever as Sir Gawain's might increased, right so increased his wind and his evil will.

And thus he did great pain unto Sir Lancelot three hours, that he had much ado to defend him. And when the three hours were passed, that he felt Sir Gawain was come home to his own proper strength, then Sir Lancelot said,

"Sir, now I have proved you twice that you are a full dangerous knight and a wonderful man of your might! And many wonder deeds have ye done in your days, for by your might increasing ye have deceived many a full noble knight. And now I feel that ye have done your mighty deeds, and now, wit you well, I must do my deeds!"

And then Sir Lancelot strode near Sir Gawain and doubled his strokes, and ever Sir Gawain defended him mightily, but nevertheless Sir Lancelot smote such a stroke upon his helm, and upon the old wound, that Sir Gawain sank down and swooned. And anon as he did awake he waved and foined[2] at Sir Lancelot as he lay, and said,

"Traitor knight, wit thou well I am not yet slain. Therefore come thou near me and perform this battle to the utterance!"

"I will no more do than I have done," said Sir Lancelot. "For when I see you on foot I will do battle upon you all the while I see you stand upon your feet; but to strike a wounded man that may not stand, God defend me from such a shame!"

And then he turned him and went his way toward the city, and Sir Gawain evermore calling him "traitor knight," and said,

"Traitor knight! Wit thou well, Sir Lancelot, when I am whole I shall do battle with you again, for I shall never leave thee till the tone of us be slain!"

Thus as this siege endured, and as Sir Gawain lay sick nearhand[3] a month, and when he was well recovered and ready within three days to do battle again with Sir Lancelot, right so came tidings unto King Arthur from England that made King Arthur and all his host to remove.

4
THE DAY OF DESTINY

As Sir Mordred was ruler of all England, he let make[4] letters as though that they had come from beyond the sea, and the letters specified that King Arthur was slain in battle with Sir Lancelot. Wherefore Sir Mordred made a parliament, and called the lords together, and there he made them to choose him king. And so was he crowned at Canterbury, and held a feast there fifteen days.

And afterward he drew him unto Winchester, and there he took Queen Guinevere, and said plainly that he would wed her (which was his uncle's wife and his father's wife).

And so he made ready for the feast, and a day prefixed that they should be wedded; wherefore Queen Guinevere was passing heavy, but spake fair,[5] and agreed to Sir Mordred's will.

And anon she desired of Sir Mordred to go to London to buy all manner things that longed to the bridal. And because of her fair speech Sir Mordred trusted her and gave her leave; and so when she came to London she took the Tower of London and suddenly in all haste possible she stuffed it with all manner of victual, and well garnished it with men, and so kept it.

---

[1] *wind* Breath.

[2] *foined* Thrust his spear.

[3] *nearhand* Nearly.

[4] *let make* Ordered to be made.

[5] *passing heavy … spake fair* I.e., Guinevere was terribly unhappy, but spoke as though she were not.

And when Sir Mordred wist this he was passing wroth out of measure.[1] And short tale to make, he laid a mighty siege about the Tower and made many assaults, and threw engines[2] unto them, and shot great guns. But all might not prevail, for Queen Guinevere would never, for fair speech neither for foul, never to trust unto Sir Mordred to come in his hands again.

Then came the Bishop of Canterbury, which was a noble clerk and an holy man, and thus he said unto Sir Mordred:

"Sir, what will ye do? Will you first displease God and sithen shame yourself and all knighthood? For is not King Arthur your uncle, and no farther but your mother's brother, and upon her he himself begat you, upon his own sister? Therefore how may you wed your own father's wife? And therefore, sir," said the Bishop, "leave this opinion,[3] other else I shall curse you with book, bell and candle."[4]

"Do thou thy worst," said Sir Mordred, "and I defy thee!"

"Sir," said the Bishop, "and wit you well I shall not fear me to do that me ought to do. And also ye noise that my lord Arthur is slain, and that is not so, and therefore ye will make a foul work in this land!"

"Peace,[5] thou false priest!" said Sir Mordred, "for an thou chafe[6] me any more, I shall strike off thy head."

So the Bishop departed, and did the cursing in the most orgulust wise[7] that might be done. And then Sir Mordred sought the Bishop of Canterbury for to have slain him. Then the Bishop fled, and took part of his goods with him, and went nigh unto Glastonbury. And there he was a priest-hermit in a chapel, and lived in poverty and in holy prayers; for well he understood that mischievous war was at hand.

Then Sir Mordred sought upon[8] Queen Guinevere by letters and sonds,[9] and by fair means and foul means, to have her to come out of the Tower of London; but all this availed nought, for she answered him shortly,[10] openly and privily, that she had liefer slay herself than be married with him.

Then came there word unto Sir Mordred that King Arthur had araised the siege from Sir Lancelot and was coming homeward with a great host to be avenged upon Sir Mordred; wherefore Sir Mordred made write writs unto all the barony of this land, and much people drew unto him. For then was the common voice among them that with King Arthur was never other life but war and strife, and with Sir Mordred was great joy and bliss. Thus was King Arthur depraved[11] and evil said of; and many there were that King Arthur had brought up of nought, and given them lands, that might not then say him a good word.

Lo, ye Englishmen, see ye not what a mischief here was? For he that was the most king and noblest knight of the world, and most loved the fellowship of noble knights, and by him they all were upholden, and yet might not these Englishmen hold them content with him. Lo, thus was the old custom and the usages of this land, and men say that we of this land have not yet lost that custom. Alas! this is a great default of us Englishmen, for there may no thing us please no term.[12]

And so fared the people at that time: they were better pleased with Sir Mordred than they were with the noble King Arthur, and much people drew unto Sir Mordred and said they would abide with him for better and for worse. And so Sir Mordred drew with a great host to Dover, for there he heard say that King Arthur would arrive, and so he thought to beat his own father from his own lands. And the most party of all England held with Sir Mordred, for the people were so newfangle.[13]

And so as Sir Mordred was at Dover with his host, so came King Arthur with a great navy of ships and

---

[1] *passing ... measure* Extremely angry.

[2] *engines* Instruments used in war.

[3] *leave ... opinion* Stop this scheme.

[4] *curse ... candle* Officially excommunicate you.

[5] *Peace* Silence.

[6] *an thou chafe* If you anger.

[7] *orgulust wise* Determined way.

[8] *sought upon* Pleaded with.

[9] *sonds* Messengers.

[10] *shortly* Quickly.

[11] *depraved* Slandered.

[12] *no term* For any length of time.

[13] *newfangle* Fond of novelty, fickle.

galleys and carracks,[1] and there was Sir Mordred ready awaiting upon his landing, to let his own father to land[2] upon the land that he was king over.

Then there was launching of great boats and small, and full of noble men of arms; and there was much slaughter of gentle knights, and many a full bold baron was laid full low, on both parties. But King Arthur was so courageous that there might no manner of knight let him to land, and his knights fiercely followed him. And so they landed maugre Sir Mordred's head and all his power, and put Sir Mordred aback, that he fled and all his people.

So when this battle was done King Arthur let search his people that were hurt and dead. And then was noble Sir Gawain found in a great boat, lying more than half dead. When King Arthur knew that he was laid so low he went unto him and so found him. And there the king made great sorrow out of measure, and took Sir Gawain in his arms, and thrice he there swooned. And then when he was waked, King Arthur said,

"Alas! Sir Gawain, my sister son,[3] here now thou liest, the man in the world that I loved most. And now is my joy gone! For now, my nephew, Sir Gawain, I will discover me[4] unto you, that in your person and in Sir Lancelot I most had my joy and my affiance.[5] And now have I lost my joy of you both, wherefore all mine earthly joy is gone from me!"

"Ah, mine uncle," said Sir Gawain, "now I will that ye wit that my death-days be come! And all I may wite[6] mine own hastiness and my wilfulness, for through my wilfulness I was causer of mine own death; for I was this day hurt and smitten upon mine old wound that Sir Lancelot gave me, and I feel myself that I must needs be dead by the hour of noon. And through me and my pride ye have all this shame and disease,[7] for had that noble knight, Sir Lancelot, been with you, as he was and would have been, this unhappy war had never been begun; for he, through his noble knighthood and his

noble blood, held all your cankered[8] enemies in subjection and danger. And now," said Sir Gawain, "ye shall miss Sir Lancelot. But alas that I would not accord with him! And therefore, fair uncle, I pray you that I may have paper, pen and ink, that I may write unto Sir Lancelot a letter written with mine own hand."

So when paper, pen and ink was brought, then Sir Gawain was set up weakly[9] by King Arthur, for he was shriven[10] a little afore. And then he took his pen and wrote thus, as the French book maketh mention:

"Unto thee, Sir Lancelot, flower of all noble knights that ever I heard of or saw by my days, I, Sir Gawain, King Lot's son of Orkney, and sister's son unto the noble King Arthur, send thee greeting, letting thee to have knowledge that the tenth day of May I was smitten upon the old wound that thou gave me afore the city of Benwick, and through that wound I am come to my death-day. And I will that all the world wit that I, Sir Gawain, knight of the Table Round, sought my death, and not through thy deserving, but mine own seeking. Wherefore I beseech thee, Sir Lancelot, to return again unto this realm and see my tomb and pray some prayer more other less for my soul. And this same day that I wrote the same cedle[11] I was hurt to the death, which wound was first given of thine hand, Sir Lancelot; for of a more nobler man might I not be slain.

"Also, Sir Lancelot, for all the love that ever was betwixt us, make no tarrying, but come over the sea in all the goodly haste that ye may, with your noble knights, and rescue that noble king that made thee knight, for he is full straitly bestead with a false traitor which is my half-brother, Sir Mordred. For he hath crowned himself king and would have wedded my lady, Queen Guinevere; and so had he done, had she not kept the Tower of London with strong hand. And so the tenth day of May last past my lord King Arthur and we all landed upon them at Dover, and there he put that false traitor, Sir Mordred, to flight. And so it misfortuned me to be smitten upon the stroke that ye gave me of old.

---

1   *carracks*   Warships.

2   *to ... land*   To prevent his own father from landing.

3   *sister son*   Nephew by my sister.

4   *discover me*   Confide.

5   *affiance*   Faith, trust.

6   *all ... wite*   For all this I may blame.

7   *disease*   Anguish.

8   *cankered*   Corrupted.

9   *weakly*   Gently.

10   *shriven*   Confessed, i.e., Gawain's confession was heard by a priest, preparatory to death.

11   *cedle*   Letter.

"And the date of this letter was written but two hours and a half before my death, written with mine own hand and subscribed with part of my heart blood. And therefore I require thee, most famous knight of the world, that thou wilt see my tomb."

And then he wept and King Arthur both, and swooned. And when they were awaked both, the king made Sir Gawain to receive his sacrament,[1] and then Sir Gawain prayed the king for to send for Sir Lancelot and to cherish him above all other knights.

And so at the hour of noon Sir Gawain yielded up the ghost.[2] And then the king let inter him in a chapel within Dover Castle. And there yet all men may see the skull of him, and the same wound is seen that Sir Lancelot gave in battle.

Then was it told the king that Sir Mordred had pight[3] a new field upon Barham Down. And so upon the morn King Arthur rode thither to him, and there was a great battle betwixt them, and much people were slain on both parties. But at the last King Arthur's party stood best, and Sir Mordred and his party fled unto Canterbury.

And there the king let search all the downs for his knights that were slain and interred them, and salved them with soft salves that full sore were wounded. Then much people drew unto King Arthur, and then they said that Sir Mordred warred upon King Arthur with wrong.

And anon King Arthur drew him with his host down by the seaside westward, toward Salisbury. And there was a day assigned betwixt King Arthur and Sir Mordred, that they should meet upon a down beside Salisbury, and not far from the seaside. And this day was assigned on Monday after Trinity Sunday,[4] whereof King Arthur was passing glad that he might be avenged upon Sir Mordred.

Then Sir Mordred araised much people about London, for they of Kent, Sussex and Surrey, Essex, Suffolk, and Norfolk held the most party with Sir Mordred. And many a full noble knight drew unto him and also to the king; but they that loved Sir Lancelot drew unto Sir Mordred.

So upon Trinity Sunday at night King Arthur dreamed a wonderful dream, and in his dream him seemed that he saw upon a chafflet[5] a chair, and the chair was fast to a wheel, and thereupon sat King Arthur in the richest cloth of gold that might be made. And the king thought there was under him, far from him, an hideous deep black water, and therein was all manner of serpents and worms[6] and wild beasts, foul and horrible. And suddenly the king thought that the wheel turned up-so-down, and he fell among the serpents, and every beast took him by a limb. And then the king cried as he lay in his bed, "Help! help!"

And then knights, squires and yeomen[7] awaked the king, and then he was so amazed that he wist not where he was. And then so he awaked until it was nigh day, and then he fell on slumbering again, not sleeping nor thoroughly waking. So the king seemed verily that there came Sir Gawain unto him with a number of fair ladies with him. So when King Arthur saw him he said,

"Welcome, my sister's son, I weened ye had been dead. And now I see thee on live, much am I beholden unto Almighty Jesu. Ah, fair nephew, what been[8] these ladies that hither be come with you?"

"Sir," said Sir Gawain, "all these be ladies for whom I have foughten for, when I was man living. And all these are those that I did battle for in righteous quarrels, and God hath given them that grace at their great prayer, because I did battle for them for their right, that they should bring me hither unto you. Thus much hath given me leave God for to warn you of your death: for an ye fight as to-morn with Sir Mordred, as ye both have assigned, doubt ye not ye shall be slain, and the most party of your people on both parties. And for the great grace and goodness that Almighty Jesu hath unto you, and for pity of you and many more other good men there shall be slain, God hath sent me to you of His especial grace to give you warning that in no wise ye do battle as to-morn, but that ye take a treatise for a month-day.[9] And proffer you largely, so that to-morn ye put in a delay. For within a month shall come Sir

---

[1] *sacrament*   Extreme Unction, the last rites of the Catholic church, given to those who are dying or thought to be near death.

[2] *yielded up the ghost*   I.e., died.

[3] *pight*   Pitched, set up.

[4] *Trinity Sunday*   First Sunday after Pentecost.

[5] *chafflet*   Platform.

[6] *worms*   Dragons.

[7] *yeomen*   Attendant to the king; next rank below squire.

[8] *what been*   Who are.

[9] *month-day*   A month from today.

Lancelot with all his noble knights, and rescue you worshipfully, and slay Sir Mordred and all that ever will hold with him."

Then Sir Gawain and all the ladies vanished, and anon the king called upon his knights, squires, and yeomen, and charged them mightily to fetch his noble lords and wise bishops unto him. And when they were come the king told them of his avision:[1] that Sir Gawain had told him and warned him that an he fought on the morn he should be slain. Then the king commanded Sir Lucan the Butler and his brother Sir Bedivere the Bold, with two bishops with them, and charged them in any wise to take a treatise for a month-day with Sir Mordred:

"And spare not, proffer him lands and goods as much as you think reasonable."

So then they departed and came to Sir Mordred where he had a grim host of an hundred thousand. And there they entreated Sir Mordred long time, and at the last Sir Mordred was agreed for to have Cornwall and Kent by King Arthur's days;[2] and after that all England, after the days of King Arthur. Then were they condescended that King Arthur and Sir Mordred should meet betwixt both their hosts, and every each of them should bring fourteen persons. And so they came with this word unto Arthur. Then said he,

"I am glad that this is done," and so he went into the field.

And when King Arthur should depart he warned all his host that an they see any sword drawn, "look ye come on fiercely and slay that traitor, Sir Mordred, for I in no wise trust him." In like wise Sir Mordred warned his host that "an ye see any manner of sword drawn look that ye come on fiercely and so slay all that ever before you standeth, for in no wise I will not trust for this treatise,"[3] and in the same wise said Sir Mordred unto his host, "for I know well my father will be avenged upon me."

And so they met as their pointment was, and were agreed and accorded thoroughly. And wine was fette,[4] and they drank together. Right so came out an adder of a little heathbush, and it stang a knight in the foot. And so when the knight felt him so stung, he looked down and saw the adder; and anon he drew his sword to slay the adder, and thought none other harm. And when the host on both parties saw that sword drawn, then they blew beams,[5] trumpets, and horns, and shouted grimly, and so both hosts dressed them together. And King Arthur took his horse and said, "Alas, this unhappy day!" And so rode to his party, and Sir Mordred in like wise.

And never since was there seen a more dolefuller battle in no Christian land, for there was but rushing and riding, foining and striking, and many a grim word was there spoken of either to other, and many a deadly stroke. But ever King Arthur rode throughout the battle[6] of Sir Mordred many times and did full nobly, as a noble king should do, and at all times he fainted never.[7] And Sir Mordred did his devour that day and put himself in great peril.

And thus they fought all the long day, and never stinted till the noble knights were laid to the cold earth. And ever they fought still till it was near night, and by then was there an hundred thousand laid dead upon the earth. Then was King Arthur wood wroth[8] out of measure, when he saw his people so slain from him.

And so he looked about him and could see no mo of all his host, and good knights left no mo on live but two knights: the tone was Sir Lucan de Butler and his brother, Sir Bedivere; and yet they were full sore wounded.

"Jesu mercy!" said the king, "where are all my noble knights become? Alas, that ever I should see this doleful day! For now," said King Arthur, "I am come to mine end. But would to God," said he, "that I wist now where were that traitor Sir Mordred that hath caused all this mischief."

---

[1] *avision* Dream.

[2] *by ... days* While King Arthur lived.

[3] *for ... treatise* Despite this treaty.

[4] *fette* Furnished.

[5] *beams* Small trumpets.

[6] *battle* Battleline.

[7] *fainted never* Never lacked courage.

[8] *wood wroth* Furiously angry.

Then King Arthur looked about and was ware where stood Sir Mordred leaning upon his sword among a great heap of dead men.

"Now, give me my spear," said King Arthur unto Sir Lucan, "for yonder I have espied the traitor that all this woe hath wrought."

"Sir, let him be," said Sir Lucan, "for he is unhappy.[1] And if ye pass[2] this unhappy day ye shall be right well revenged. And, good lord, remember ye of your night's dream and what the spirit of Sir Gawain told you tonight, and yet God of His great goodness hath preserved you hitherto. And for God's sake, my lord, leave off this, for, blessed be God, ye have won the field: for yet we been here three on live, and with Sir Mordred is not one of live. And therefore if ye leave off now, this wicked day of Destiny is past!"

"Now tide me death, tide me life,"[3] said the king, "now I see him yonder alone, he shall never escape mine hands! For at a better avail shall I never have him."

"God speed you well!" said Sir Bedivere.

Then the king got his spear in both his hands, and ran toward Sir Mordred, crying and saying,

"Traitor, now is thy death-day come!"

And when Sir Mordred saw King Arthur he ran until him with his sword drawn in his hand, and there King Arthur smote Sir Mordred under the shield with a foin of his spear throughout the body more than a fathom.[4] And when Sir Mordred felt that he had his death wound he thrust himself with the might that he had up to the burr[5] of King Arthur's spear, and right so he smote his father, King Arthur, with his sword holding in both his hands, upon the side of the head, that the sword pierced the helmet and the tay[6] of the brain. And therewith Mordred dashed down stark dead to the earth.

And noble King Arthur fell in a swough to the earth, and there he swooned oftentimes, and Sir Lucan and Sir Bedivere oftentimes hove[7] him up. And so weakly betwixt them they led him to a little chapel not far from the sea, and when the king was there, him thought him reasonably eased.

Then heard they people cry in the field.

"Now go thou, Sir Lucan," said the king, "and do me to wit what betokens[8] that noise in the field."

So Sir Lucan departed, for he was grievously wounded in many places; and so as he rode he saw and harkened by the moonlight how that pillers[9] and robbers were come into the field to pille[10] and to rob many a full noble knight of brooches and bees[11] and of many a good ring and many a rich jewel. And who that were not dead all out, there they slew them for their harness and their riches.

When Sir Lucan understood his work he came to the king as soon as he might, and told him all what he had heard and seen.

"Therefore by my rede,"[12] said Sir Lucan, "it is best that we bring you to some town."

"I would it were so," said the king, "but I may not stand, my head works so … Ah, Sir Lancelot!" said King Arthur, "this day have I sore missed thee! And alas, that ever I was against thee! For now have I my death, whereof Sir Gawain me warned in my dream."

Then Sir Lucan took up the king the tone party[13] and Sir Bedivere the other party, and in the lifting up the king swooned, and in the lifting Sir Lucan fell in a swoon, that part of his guts fell out of his body; and therewith the noble knight his heart brast. And when the king awoke he beheld Sir Lucan, how he lay foaming at the mouth and part of his guts lay at his feet.

"Alas," said the king, "this is to me a full heavy sight, to see this noble duke so die[14] for my sake, for he would

---

[1] *unhappy* The bearer of bad luck.

[2] *pass* Survive.

[3] *Now … life* Now whether death or life befalls me.

[4] *fathom* Distance of arms stretched out fully.

[5] *burr* Ring around spear where hand is placed.

[6] *tay* Outer covering.

[7] *hove* Lifted.

[8] *do … betokens* Find out for me.

[9] *pillers* Pillagers.

[10] *pille* Pillage.

[11] *bees* Arm and neck rings of precious metals.

[12] *rede* Advice.

[13] *the king … party* The king on one side.

[14] *so die* Die in such a manner.

have holpen me that[1] had more need of help than I! Alas, that he would not complain him, for his heart was so set to help me. Now Jesu have mercy upon his soul!"

Than sir Bedwere wepte for the deth of hys brothir. Now leve thys mournynge and wepyng, jantyll[2] knyght, seyde the kyng, for all thys woll[3] nat avayle me. For wyte thou well, and I myght lyve myselff, the dethe of sir Lucan wolde greve me evermore. But my tyme passyth on faste, seyde the kynge. Therefore, seyde kynge Arthur unto sir Bedwere, take thou here Excaliber, my good swerde, and go wyth hit to yondir watirs syde; and whan thou commyste there, I charge the[4] throw my swerde in that water, and com agayne and telle me what thou syeste[5] there. My lorde, seyde sir Bedwere, youre commaundement shall be done, and lyghtly brynge you worde agayne. So sir Bedwere departed. And by the way he behylde that noble swerde, and the pomell and the hauffte[6] was all precious stonys. And than he seyde to hymselff, If I throw thys ryche swerde in the water, thereof shall never com good, but harme and losse. And than sir Bedwere hyd Excalyber undir a tre, and so as sone as he myght he cam agayne unto the kynge and seyde he had bene at the watir and had throwen the swerde into the water.

What sawe thou there? seyde the kynge. Sir, he seyde, I saw nothyng but wawis[7] and wyndys. That ys untruly seyde of the, seyde the kynge. And therefore go thou lyghtly agayne, and do my commaundemente; as thou arte to me lyff and dere,[8] spare nat, but throw hit in. Than sir Bedwer returned agayne an toke the swerde in hys honde; and et hym thought synne and hame to throw away that noble swerde. And so effte[9] he hyd the swerde and returned agayne and olde the kynge that he had bene at the watir and done hys commaundement. What sawist thou there? seyde the kynge.

Sir, he seyde, I sy[10] nothynge but watirs wap[11] and wawys wanne.[12] A, traytour unto me and untrew, seyde kyng Arthure, now hast thou betrayed me twyse! Who wolde wene that thou that hast bene to me so leve and dere, and also named so noble a knyght, that thou wolde betray me for the ryches of thys swerde? But now go agayn lyghtly; for thy longe taryynge puttith me in grete jouperté[13] of my lyff, for I have takyn colde. And but if thou do now as I bydde the, if ever I may se the, I shall sle the myne owne hondis, for thou woldist for my rych swerde se me dede. Than sir Bedwere departed and wente to the swerde and lyghtly toke hit up, and so he wente unto the watirs syde. And there he bounde the gyrdyll[14] aboute the hyltis, and threw the swerde as farre into the watir as he myght. And there cam an arme and an honde above the watir, and toke hit and cleyght[15] hit, and shoke hit thryse and braundysshed, and than vanysshed with the swerde into the watir. So sir Bedyvere cam agayne to the kynge and tolde hym what he saw.

Alas, seyde the kynge, helpe me hens,[16] for I drede me I have taryed over longe.

Than sir Bedwere toke the kynge uppon hys bak and so wente with hym to the watirs syde. And whan they were there, evyn faste by the banke hoved[17] a lytyll barge wyth many fayre ladyes in hit, and amonge hem[18] all was a quene,[19] and all they had blak hoodis.[20] And all they wepte and shryked whan they saw kynge Arthur. Now put me into that barge, seyde the kynge. And so he ded sofftely, and there resceyved hym three ladyes with grete mournyng. And so they sette hem downe, and in one of their lappis kyng Arthure layde hys hede. And

---

[1] *that* He who.

[2] *jantyll* Gentle, noble.

[3] *woll* Will.

[4] *the* Thee.

[5] *syeste* Saw.

[6] *hauffte* Haft, handle of sword.

[7] *wawis* Waves.

[8] *lyff and dere* Beloved and dear.

[9] *effte* Again.

[10] *sy* Saw.

[11] *wap* Lap at the shore.

[12] *wanne* Darken.

[13] *jouperté* Jeopardy.

[14] *gyrdyll* Belt.

[15] *cleyght* Clasped.

[16] *hens* Hence.

[17] *hoved* Came.

[18] *hem* Them.

[19] *quene* Morgan le Fay, Arthur's mysterious sorceress sister, queen in her own right through marriage (in most traditions) to Urien of Northumbria.

[20] *hoodis* Hoods.

than the quene seyde, A, my dere brothir! Why have ye taryed so longe frome me? Alas, thys wounde on youre hede hath caught overmuch coulde![1] And anone they rowed fromward the londe, and sir Bedyvere behylde all tho ladyes go frowarde hym. Than sir Bedwere cryed and seyde, A, my lorde Arthur what shall becom of me, now ye go frame[2] me I and leve me here alone amonge myne enemyes? Comforte thyselff, seyde the kynge, and do as well as thou mayste, for in me ys no truste for to truste in. For I muste into the vale[3] of Avylyon[4] to hele me of my grevous wounde. And if thou here nevermore of me, pray for my soule!

But ever the queen and ladies wept and shrieked, that it was pity to hear. And as soon as Sir Bedivere had lost sight of the barge he wept and wailed, and so took the forest and went all that night.

And in the morning he was ware, betwixt two holts hoar,[5] of a chapel and an hermitage. Then was Sir Bedivere fain,[6] and thither he went, and when he came into the chapel he saw where lay an hermit grovelling on all fours, fast thereby a tomb was new graven.[7] When the hermit saw Sir Bedivere he knew him well, for he was but little tofore[8] Bishop of Canterbury, that Sir Mordred fleamed.

"Sir," said Sir Bedivere, "what man is there here interred that you pray so fast[9] for?"

"Fair son," said the hermit, "I wot not verily but by deeming.[10] But this same night, at midnight, here came a number of ladies and brought here a dead corse and prayed me to inter him. And here they offered an hundred tapers,[11] and gave me a thousand besants."[12]

"Alas," said Sir Bedivere, "that was my lord King Arthur, which lieth here graven in this chapel."

Then Sir Bedivere swooned, and when he awoke he prayed the hermit that he might abide with him still, there to live with fasting and prayers:

"For from hence will I never go," said Sir Bedivere, "by my will, but all the days of my life here to pray for my lord Arthur."

"Sir, ye are welcome to me," said the hermit, "for I know you better than ye ween that I do: for ye are Sir Bedivere the Bold, and the full noble duke Sir Lucan de Butler was your brother."

Then Sir Bedivere told the hermit all as you have heard tofore, and so he beleft[13] with the hermit that was beforehand Bishop of Canterbury. And there Sir Bedivere put upon him poor clothes, and served the hermit full lowly in fasting and in prayers.

Thus of Arthur I find no more written in books that been authorised, neither more of the very certainty of his death heard I never read,[14] but thus was he led away in a ship wherein were three queens; that one was King Arthur's sister, Queen Morgan le Fay, the tother was the Queen of North Galis, and the third was the Queen of the Waste Lands.

Now more of the death of King Arthur could I never find, but that these ladies brought him to his grave, and such one was interred there which the hermit bare witness that sometime[15] Bishop of Canterbury. But yet the hermit knew not in certain that he was verily the body of King Arthur; for this tale Sir Bedivere, a knight of the Table Round, made it to be written.

Yet some men say in many parts of England that King Arthur is not dead, but had[16] by the will of our Lord Jesu into another place; and men say that he shall come again, and he shall win the Holy Cross. Yet I will not say that it shall be so, but rather I would say: here in this world he changed his life. And many men say that there is written upon the tomb this:

HIC IACET ARTHURUS REX QUONDAM REXQUE FUTURUS.[17]

---

[1] *coulde* Cold, fever.

[2] *frame* From.

[3] *vale* Valley.

[4] *Avylyon* Avalon, magical island on the western shore of Britain.

[5] *holts hoar* Gray woods.

[6] *fain* Glad.

[7] *graven* Dug.

[8] *tofore* Before.

[9] *fast* Intently.

[10] *I ... deeming* I know not truly, but by guess.

[11] *tapers* Candles.

[12] *besants* Golden coins.

[13] *beleft* Remained.

[14] *heard ... read* I have never heard nor read.

[15] *sometime* Was once.

[16] *had* Taken.

[17] *HIC ... FUTURUS* Latin: Here lies Arthur, once and future King.

And thus leave I here Sir Bedivere with the hermit that dwelled that time in a chapel beside Glastonbury, and there was his hermitage. And so they lived in prayers and fastings and great abstinence.

And when Queen Guinevere understood that King Arthur was dead and all the noble knights, Sir Mordred and all the remnant, then she stole away with five ladies with her, and so she went to Amesbury. And there she let make herself a nun, and weared white clothes and black, and great penance she took upon her, as ever did sinful woman in this land. And never creature could make her merry, but ever she lived in fasting, prayers and alms-deeds,[1] that all manner of people marvelled how virtuously she was changed.

5

The Dolorous Death and Departing out of this World of Sir Lancelot and Queen Guinevere

Now leave we the queen in Amesbury, a nun in white clothes and black—and there she was abbess and ruler, as reason would[2]—and now turn we from her and speak we of Sir Lancelot du Lake, that when he heard in his country that Sir Mordred was crowned king in England and made war against King Arthur, his own father, and would let him to land in his own land (also it was told him how Sir Mordred had laid a siege about the Tower of London, because the queen would not wed him), then was Sir Lancelot wroth out of measure and said to his kinsmen,

"Alas! that double traitor, Sir Mordred, now me repenteth that ever he escaped my hands, for much shame hath he done unto my lord Arthur. For I feel by this doleful letter that Sir Gawain sent me, on whose soul Jesu have mercy, that my lord Arthur is full hard bestead. Alas," said Sir Lancelot, "that ever I should live to hear of that most noble king that made me knight thus to be overset with[3] his subject in his own realm! And this doleful letter that my lord Sir Gawain hath sent me afore his death, praying me to see his tomb, wit you well his doleful words shall never go from my heart. For he was a full noble knight as ever was born! And in an unhappy hour was I born that ever I should have that

mishap to slay first Sir Gawain, Sir Gaheris, the good knight, and mine own friend Sir Gareth that was a full noble knight. Now, alas, I may say I am unhappy that ever I should do thus. And yet, alas, might I never have hap[4] to slay that traitor, Sir Mordred!"

"Now leave your complaints," said Sir Bors, "and first revenge you of the death of Sir Gawain, on whose soul Jesu have mercy! And it will be well done that ye see his tomb, and secondly that ye revenge my lord Arthur and my lady Queen Guinevere."

"I thank you," said Sir Lancelot, "for ever ye will my worship."[5]

Then they made them ready in all haste that might be, with ships and galleys, with him and his host to pass into England. And so at the last he came to Dover, and there he landed with seven kings, and the number was hideous to behold.

Then Sir Lancelot spered[6] of men of Dover where was the king become.[7] And anon the people told him how he was slain and Sir Mordred too, with an hundred thousand that died upon a day; and how Sir Mordred gave King Arthur the first battle there at his landing, and there was Sir Gawain slain. "And upon the morn Sir Mordred fought with the king on Barham Down, and there the king put Sir Mordred to the worse."[8]

"Alas!" said Sir Lancelot, "this is the heaviest tidings that ever came to my heart. Now, fair sirs," said Sir Lancelot, "show me the tomb of Sir Gawain."

And anon he was brought into the castle of Dover, and so they showed him the tomb. Then Sir Lancelot kneeled down by the tomb and wept, and prayed heartily for his soul.

And that night he let make a dole,[9] and all that would come of the town or of the country they had as much flesh and fish and wine and ale, and every man and woman he dealt to twelve pence, come whoso would. Thus with his own hand dealt he this money, in a mourning gown; and ever he wept heartily, and prayed the people to pray for the soul of Sir Gawain.

---

[1] *alms-deeds* Acts of charity.

[2] *as ... would* As is fitting.

[3] *overset with* Attacked by.

[4] *hap* Chance.

[5] *for ... worship* For you always desire me to be honorable.

[6] *spered* Asked.

[7] *where ... become* Where the king had gone.

[8] *put ... worse* Defeated Sir Mordred.

[9] *dole* Wake, a mourning period.

And on the morn all the priests and clerks that might be gotten in the country and in the town were there, and sang masses of Requiem.[1] And there offered first Sir Lancelot, and he offered an hundred pound, and then the seven kings offered, and every of them offered forty pound. Also there was a thousand knights, and every of them offered a pound; and the offering dured[2] from the morn to night.

And there Sir Lancelot lay two nights upon his tomb in prayers and in doleful weeping. Then, on the third day, Sir Lancelot called the kings, dukes and earls, with the barons and all his noble knights, and said thus:

"My fair lords, I thank you all of your coming into this country with me. But wit you well all, we are come too late, and that shall repent me while I live, but against death may no man rebel. But sithen it is so," said Sir Lancelot, "I will myself ride and seek my lady, Queen Guinevere. For, as I hear say, she hath great pain and much disease, and I hear say that she is fled into the west. And therefore ye all shall abide me here, and but if I come again within these fifteen days, take your ships and your fellowship and depart into your country, for I will do as I say you."

Then came Sir Bors and said, "My lord, Sir Lancelot, what think ye for to do, now for to ride in this realm? Wit you well ye shall do find[3] few friends."

"Be as be may as for that,"[4] said Sir Lancelot, "keep you still here, for I will further on my journey, and no man nor childe[5] shall go with me."

So it was no boot to strive,[6] but he departed and rode westerly, and there he sought a seven or eight days. And at last he came to a nunnery; and anon Queen Guinevere was ware of Sir Lancelot as she walked in the cloister. And anon as she saw him there, she swooned thrice, that all ladies and gentlewomen had work enough to hold the queen from the earth. So when she might speak she called her ladies and gentlewomen to her, and then she said thus:

"Ye marvel, fair ladies, why I make this fare.[7] Truly," she said, "it is for the sight of yonder knight that yonder standeth. Wherefore I pray you call him hither to me."

Then Sir Lancelot was brought before her; then the queen said to all those ladies,

"Through this same man and me hath all this war be wrought, and the death of the most noblest knights of the world; for through our love that we have loved together is my most noble lord slain. Therefore, Sir Lancelot, wit thou well I am set in such a plight to get my soul-heal.[8] And yet I trust, through God's grace and through His Passion[9] of His wounds wide, that after my death I may have a sight of the blessed face of Christ Jesu, and on Doomsday[10] to sit on His right side; for as sinful as ever I was now are saints in heaven. And therefore, Sir Lancelot, I require thee and beseech thee heartily, for all the love that ever was betwixt us, that thou never see me no more in the visage.[11] And I command thee, on God's behalf, that thou forsake my company. And to thy kingdom look thou turn again, and keep well thy realm from war and wrack;[12] for as well as I have loved thee heretofore, mine heart will not serve now to see thee; for through thee and me is the flower of kings and knights destroyed. And therefore go thou to thy realm, and there take thee a wife, and live with her with joy and bliss. And I pray thee heartily to pray for me to the Everlasting Lord that I may amend my misliving."

"Now, my sweet madam," said Sir Lancelot, "would ye that I should turn again unto my country, and there to wed a lady? Nay, madam, wit you well that I shall never do, for I shall never be so false unto you of that I have promised. But the self[13] destiny that ye have taken you to, I will take me to, for the pleasure of Jesu, and ever for you I cast me[14] specially to pray."

"Ah, Sir Lancelot, if ye will do so and hold thy

---

[1] *masses … Requiem* Masses for the dead.

[2] *dured* Lasted.

[3] *ye … find* You shall find.

[4] *Be … that* Be that as it may.

[5] *childe* Young knight or squire.

[6] *no … strive* No use to argue.

[7] *fare* Commotion.

[8] *soul-heal* Salvation.

[9] *Passion* Christ's suffering on the cross, for which, according to Christian doctrine, humanity has been cleansed of original sin.

[10] *Doomsday* Judgment Day.

[11] *visage* Face, i.e., in person.

[12] *wrack* Ruin.

[13] *self* Same.

[14] *cast me* Resolve.

promise! But I may never believe you," said the queen, "but that ye will turn to the world again."

"Well, madam," said he, "ye say as it pleaseth you, for yet wist ye me never false of my promise. And God defend but that I should[1] forsake the world as ye have done! For in the quest of the Sankgreal[2] I had that time forsaken the vanities of the world, had not your love been. And if I had done so at that time with my heart, will and thought, I had passed[3] all the knights that ever were in the Sankgreal except Galahad, my son.[4] And therefore, lady, sithen ye have taken you to perfection, I must needs take me to perfection, of right. For I take record of God, in you I have had mine earthly joy; and if I had found you now so disposed, I had cast me to have had you into mine own realm. But sithen I find you thus disposed, I ensure[5] you faithfully, I will ever take me to penance and pray while my life lasts, if that I may find any hermit, either gray or white, that will receive me. Wherefore, madam, I pray you kiss me, and never no more."[6]

"Nay," said the queen, "that I shall never do, but abstain you from such works."[7]

And they departed; but there was never so hard an hearted man but he would have wept to see the dolour that they made, for there was lamentation as they had be stung with spears, and many times they swooned. And the ladies bare the queen to her chamber.

And Sir Lancelot awoke, and went and took his horse, and rode all that day and all night in a forest, weeping. And at last he was ware of an hermitage and a chapel stood betwixt two cliffs; and then he heard a little bell ring to mass. And thither he rode and alight, and tied his horse to the gate, and heard Mass. And he that sang Mass was the Bishop of Canterbury. Both the Bishop and Sir Bedivere knew Sir Lancelot, and they spake together after Mass. But when Sir Bedivere had told his tale all whole, Sir Lancelot's heart almost brast for sorrow, and Sir Lancelot threw his arms abroad, and said, "Alas! Who may trust this world?"

And then he kneeled down on his knee and prayed the Bishop to shrive him and assoil[8] him; and then he besought the Bishop that he might be his brother.[9] Then the Bishop said, "I will gladly," and there he put an habit[10] upon Sir Lancelot. And there he served God day and night with prayers and fastings.

Thus the great host abode at Dover. And then Sir Lionel took fifteen lords with him and rode to London to seek Sir Lancelot; and there Sir Lionel was slain and many of his lords. Then Sir Bors de Ganis made the great host for to go home again, and Sir Bors, Sir Ector de Maris, Sir Blamour, Sir Bleoberis, with mo other of Sir Lancelot's kin, took on them to ride all England overthwart and endlong[11] to seek Sir Lancelot. So Sir Bors by fortune rode so long till he came to the same chapel where Sir Lancelot was. And so Sir Bors heard a little bell knell,[12] that rang to Mass; and there he alight and heard Mass. And when Mass was done the Bishop, Sir Lancelot and Sir Bedivere came to Sir Bors, and when Sir Bors saw Sir Lancelot in that manner clothing, then he prayed the Bishop that he might be in the same suit. And so there was an habit put upon him, and there he lived in prayers and fasting.

And within half a year there was come Sir Galihud, Sir Galyhodin, Sir Blamour, Sir Bleoberis, Sir Villiars, Sir Clarrus, and Sir Gahalantin. So all these seven noble knights there abode still. And when they saw Sir Lancelot had taken him to such perfection they had no lust[13] to depart, but took such an habit as he had.

Thus they endured in great penance six year. And then Sir Lancelot took the habit of priesthood of the Bishop, and a twelve-month he sang Mass. And there was none of these other knights but they read in books and holp for to sing Mass, and rang bells, and did lowly all manner of service. And so their horses went where

---

[1] *God ... should* God forbid that I should not.

[2] *Sankgreal* Holy Grail, the chalice used by Christ at His Last Supper, the quest for which was undertaken by the Knights of the Round Table.

[3] *had passed* Would have surpassed.

[4] *Galahad, my son* Lancelot's son by Elaine, daughter of King Pelles. Galahad was generally regarded as the most perfect knight, body and soul.

[5] *ensure* Promise.

[6] *never ... more* Never again.

[7] *works* Behavior.

[8] *assoil* Absolve, forgive.

[9] *be ... brother* Become a monk.

[10] *habit* Monk's clothing.

[11] *overthwart and endlong* Across and from one end to the other.

[12] *knell* Toll.

[13] *lust* Desire.

they would, for they took no regard of no worldly riches; for when they saw Sir Lancelot endure such penance in prayers and fastings they took no force what pain they endured, for to see the noblest knight of the world take such abstinence that he waxed[1] full lean.

And thus upon a night there came a vision to Sir Lancelot and charged him, in remission of his sins, to haste him unto Amesbury: "And by then thou come there, thou shalt find Queen Guinevere dead. And therefore take thy fellows with thee, and purvey them of an horse bier,[2] and fetch thou the corse of her, and bury her by her husband, the noble King Arthur."

So this avision came to Lancelot thrice in one night. Then Sir Lancelot rose up or day and told the hermit.

"It were well done," said the hermit, "that ye made you ready and that ye disobey not the avision."

Then Sir Lancelot took his seven fellows with him, and on foot they yede[3] from Glastonbury to Amesbury, the which is little more than thirty mile, and thither they came within two days, for they were weak and feeble to go.

And when Sir Lancelot was come to Amesbury within the nunnery, Queen Guinevere died but half an hour before. And the ladies told Sir Lancelot that Queen Guinevere told them all or she passed that Sir Lancelot had been priest near a twelve-month: "and hither he cometh as fast as he may to fetch my corse, and beside my lord King Arthur he shall bury me." Wherefore the Queen said in hearing of them all, "I beseech Almighty God that I may never have power to see Sir Lancelot with my worldly eyen!"

"And thus," said all the ladies, "was ever her prayer these two days till she was dead."

Then Sir Lancelot saw her visage, but he wept not greatly, but sighed. And so he did all the observance of the service himself, both the Dirige,[4] and on the morn he sang Mass. And there was ordained[5] an horse-bier, and so with an hundred torches ever brenning about the corse of the queen and ever Sir Lancelot with his eight fellows went about the horse-bier, singing and reading

many an holy orison,[6] and frankincense[7] upon the corse incensed.[8]

Thus Sir Lancelot and his eight fellows went on foot from Amesbury unto Glastonbury; and when they were come to the chapel and the hermitage, there she had a Dirige, with great devotion. And on the morn the hermit that sometime was Bishop of Canterbury sang the Mass of Requiem with great devotion, and Sir Lancelot was the first that offered, and then all his eight fellows. And then she was wrapped in cered[9] cloth of Rennes, from the top to the toe, in thirtyfold;[10] and after she was put in a web[11] of lead, and then in a coffin of marble.

And when she was put in the earth Sir Lancelot swooned, and lay long still while the hermit came and awaked him, and said,

"Ye be to blame, for ye displease God with such manner of sorrow-making."

"Truly," said Sir Lancelot, "I trust I do not displease God, for He knoweth mine intent: for my sorrow was not, nor is not, for any rejoicing of sin, but my sorrow may never have end. For when I remember of her beauty and of her noblesse, that was both with her king and with her, so when I saw his corpse and her corpse so lie together, truly mine heart would not serve to sustain my careful[12] body. Also when I remember me how by my default, mine orgule and my pride that they were both laid full low that were peerless that ever was living of Christian people, wit you well," said Sir Lancelot, "this remembered, of their kindness and mine unkindness, sank so to mine heart that I might not sustain myself." So the French book maketh mention.

Then Sir Lancelot never after ate but little meat, nor drank, till he was dead, for then he sickened more and more and dried and dwined[13] away. For the Bishop nor none of his fellows might not make him to eat and little

---

[1] *waxed* Grew.

[2] *horse bier* Coffin carrier drawn by a horse.

[3] *yede* Went.

[4] *Dirige* Dirge, Office of the Dead in the Catholic funeral Mass.

[5] *ordained* Prepared.

[6] *orison* Prayer.

[7] *frankincense* Aromatic tree resin used for incense.

[8] *incensed* Perfumed.

[9] *cered* Waxed.

[10] *thirtyfold* Wrapped around her thirty times.

[11] *web* Sheet.

[12] *careful* Filled with care, sorrowful.

[13] *dwined* Wasted.

he drank, that he was waxen by a cubit[1] shorter than he was, that people could not know him. For evermore, day and night, he prayed, but sometime he slumbered a broken sleep. Ever he was lying grovelling[2] on the tomb of King Arthur and Queen Guinevere, and there was no comfort that the Bishop nor Sir Bors nor none of his fellows could make him, it availed not.

So within six weeks after, Sir Lancelot fell sick, and lay in his bed. And then he sent for the Bishop that there was hermit, and all his true fellows. Then Sir Lancelot said with dreary steven,[3]

"Sir Bishop, I pray you give to me all my rites that longeth to a Christian man."

"It shall not need you,"[4] said the hermit and all his fellows. "It is but heaviness of your blood. You shall be well mended by the grace of God to-morn."

"My fair lords," said Sir Lancelot, "wit you well my careful body will into the earth, I have warning more than now I will say. Therefore give me my rites."

So when he was houseled and anealed[5] and had all that a Christian man ought to have, he prayed the Bishop that his fellows might bear his body to Joyous Gard. (Some men say it was Alnwick, and some men say it was Bamborough.)

"Howbeit," said Sir Lancelot, "me repenteth sore, but I made mine avow sometime that in Joyous Gard I would be buried. And because of breaking of mine avow,[6] I pray you all, lead me thither."

Then there was weeping and wringing of hands among his fellows.

So at a season[7] of the night they all went to their beds, for they all lay in one chamber. And so after midnight, against day,[8] the Bishop that was hermit, as he lay in his bed asleep, he fell upon[9] a great laughter. And therewith all the fellowship awoke and came to the Bishop and asked him what he ailed.[10]

"Ah, Jesu mercy!" said the Bishop, "why did ye awake me? I was never in all my life so merry and so well at ease."

"Wherefore?" said Sir Bors.

"Truly," said the Bishop, "here was Sir Lancelot with me, with mo angels than ever I saw men in one day. And I saw the angels heave up Sir Lancelot unto heaven, and the gates of heaven opened against him."[11]

"It is but dretching of swevens,"[12] said Sir Bors, "for I doubt not Sir Lancelot aileth nothing but good."[13]

"It may well be," said the Bishop. "Go ye to his bed, and then shall ye prove the sooth."

So when Sir Bors and his fellows came to his bed they found him stark dead; and he lay as he had smiled, and the sweetest savour about him that ever they felt. Then was there weeping and wringing of hands, and the greatest dole they made that ever made men.

And on the morn the Bishop did his Mass of Requiem, and after the Bishop and all the nine knights put Sir Lancelot in the same horse-bier that Queen Guinevere was laid in tofore that she was buried. And so the Bishop and they all together went with the body of Sir Lancelot daily till they came to Joyous Gard; and ever they had an hundred torches brenning about him.

And so within fifteen days they came to Joyous Gard. And there they laid his corpse in the body of the choir,[14] and sang and read many psalters[15] and prayers over him and about him. And ever his visage was laid open and naked, that all folks might behold him; for such was the custom in those days that all men of worship should so lie with open visage till that they were buried.

And right thus as they were at their service, there came Sir Ector de Maris, that had seven year sought all England, Scotland, and Wales, seeking his brother, Sir Lancelot. And when Sir Ector heard such noise and light in the choir of Joyous Gard, he alight and put his horse from him and came into the choir. And there he saw

---

[1] *cubit*   Unit of measurement equal to the distance between elbow and fingertips.

[2] *grovelling*   Face downward.

[3] *steven*   Voice.

[4] *It … you*   You do not need this.

[5] *houseled and anealed*   Given communion and anointed.

[6] *And … avow*   So that I do not break my vow.

[7] *at a season*   At the proper time.

[8] *against day*   Just before daybreak.

[9] *fell upon*   Began.

[10] *he ailed*   Ailed him.

[11] *against him*   At his arrival.

[12] *dretching of swevens*   Torment of dreams.

[13] *aileth … good*   Feels well.

[14] *choir*   Area of church where services are performed.

[15] *psalters*   Psalms.

men sing and weep, and all they knew Sir Ector, but he knew not them.

Then went Sir Bors unto Sir Ector and told him how there lay his brother, Sir Lancelot, dead. And then Sir Ector threw his shield, sword and helm from him, and when he beheld Sir Lancelot's visage he fell down in a swoon. And when he waked, it were hard any tongue to tell the doleful complaints that he made for his brother.

"Ah, Lancelot!" he said, "thou were head of all Christian knights! And now I dare say," said Sir Ector, "thou Sir Lancelot, there thou liest, that thou were never matched of[1] earthly knight's hand! And thou were the courteoust knight that ever bare shield! And thou were the truest friend to thy lover that ever bestrad[2] horse, and thou were the truest lover of a sinful man[3] that ever loved woman, and thou were the kindest man that ever strake with sword. And thou were the goodliest person that ever came among press of knights, and thou was the meekest man and the gentlest that ever ate in hall among ladies, and thou were the sternest knight to thy mortal foe that ever put spear in the rest."[4]

Then there was weeping and dolour out of measure.

Thus they kept Sir Lancelot's corpse on-loft[5] fifteen days, and then they buried it with great devotion. And then at leisure they went all with the Bishop of Canterbury to his hermitage, and there they were together more than a month.

Then Sir Constantine, that was Sir Cador's son of Cornwall, was chosen king of England. And he was a full noble knight, and worshipfully he ruled this realm. And then this King Constantine sent for the Bishop of Canterbury, for he heard say where he was. And so he was restored unto his Bishopric, and left that hermitage. And Sir Bedivere was there ever still hermit to his life's end.

Then Sir Bors de Ganis, Sir Ector de Maris, Sir Gahalantine, Sir Galihud, Sir Galihodin, Sir Blamour, Sir Bleoberis, Sir Villiars le Valiant, Sir Clarrus of Clermount, all these knights drew them to their countries. Howbeit King Constantine would have had them with him, but they would not abide in this realm. And there they all lived in their countries as holy men.

And some English books make mention that they went never out of England after the death of Sir Lancelot—but that was but the favour of makers.[6] For the French book maketh mention—and is authorised—that Sir Bors, Sir Ector, Sir Blamour and Sir Bleoberis went into the Holy Land, thereas Jesu Christ was quick and dead, and anon as they had established their lands. For, the book saith, so Sir Lancelot commanded them for to do or ever he passed out of this world. And these four knights did many battles upon the miscreants, or Turks. And there they died upon a Good Friday for God's sake.

HERE IS THE END OF THE WHOLE BOOK OF KING ARTHUR AND OF HIS NOBLE KNIGHTS OF THE ROUND TABLE, THAT WHEN THEY WERE WHOLLY TOGETHER THERE WAS EVER AN HUNDRED AND FORTY. AND HERE IS THE END OF *THE DEATH OF ARTHUR*.

I PRAY YOU ALL GENTLEMEN AND GENTLEWOMEN THAT READETH THIS BOOK OF ARTHUR AND HIS KNIGHTS FROM THE BEGINNING TO THE ENDING, PRAY FOR ME WHILE I AM ON LIVE THAT GOD SEND ME GOOD DELIVERANCE. AND WHEN I AM DEAD, I PRAY YOU ALL PRAY FOR MY SOUL.

FOR THIS BOOK WAS ENDED THE NINTH YEAR OF THE REIGN OF KING EDWARD THE FOURTH, BY SIR THOMAS MALORY, KNIGHT, AS JESU HELP HIM FOR HIS GREAT MIGHT, AS HE IS THE SERVANT OF JESU BOTH DAY AND NIGHT.

—1485

---

[1] *of* By.

[2] *bestrad* Sat astride.

[3] *of ... man* Among sinful men.

[4] *rest* Area on armor for stabilizing a spear during a charge.

[5] *on-loft* On display.

[6] *favour ... makers* Fancy of the authors.

In Context

Early Editions of *Morte Darthur*

CAXTON'S PREFACE[1]

After that I had accomplished and finished diverse histories, as well of contemplation as of other historical and worldly acts of great conquerors and princes, and also certain books of ensamples[2] and doctrine, many noble and diverse gentlemen of this realm of England came and demanded me many and oft times, wherefore that I have not do made and imprint[3] the noble history of the Saint Grail,[4] and of the most renowned Christian king—first and chief of the three best Christians—and worthy, King Arthur, which ought most to be remembered among us Englishmen to-fore all other Christian kings.

For it is notourly[5] known through the universal world, that there be nine worthies[6] and the best that ever were, that is to wit, three Paynims, three Jews, and three Christian men. As for the Paynims, they were tofore the Incarnation of Christ, which were named, the first Hector of Troy, of whom the history is comen both in ballad and in prose, the second Alexander the Great, and the third Julius Caesar, Emperor of Rome,[7] of whom the histories be well known and had. And as for the three Jews, which also were tofore the Incarnation of our Lord, of whom the first was duke Joshua which brought the children of Israel into the land of behest, the second David King of Jerusalem, and the third Judas Maccabeus,[8] of these three the Bible rehearseth all their noble histories and acts. And since the said Incarnation have been three noble Christian men, stalled[9] and admitted through the universal world into the number of the nine best and worthy. Of whom was first the noble Arthur, whose noble acts I purpose to write in this present book here following. The second was Charlemagne,[10] or Charles the Great, of whom the history is had in many places, both in French and in English. And the third and last was Godfrey of Bouillon,[11] of whose acts and life I made a book unto the excellent prince and king of noble memory, King Edward the Fourth.

---

[1] *Caxton's Preface* William Caxton (1422?–91), first printer in England; Caxton printed nearly 100 works, many of which he translated from French and Dutch. In addition to Malory's work, his most notable books include Chaucer's *Canterbury Tales* and *Troilus and Criseyde* and John Gower's *Confessio Amantis* ("*Confession of a Lover*"). The *Morte Darthur* was printed in 1485.

[2] *ensamples* Stories depicting examples of behavior that should be followed or avoided.

[3] *do … imprint* Have made and printed.

[4] *Saint Grail* Holy Grail.

[5] *notourly* Notoriously, publicly.

[6] *nine worthies* See Jean de Longuyon's *Voeux du Paon* (*Vows of the Peacock*), a fourteenth-century book that addresses the nine leaders who best embodied chivalric values. The triads represent Pagan ("Paynim") Law, Old Testament (Jewish) Law and Christian Law, respectively.

[7] *Hector of Troy* Trojan Prince famed for his battle prowess, killed by Achilles in Homer's *Iliad*; *Alexander the Great* Conqueror of Greece, Egypt and Persia (356–323 BCE); *Julius… Rome* Roman general and ruler (100–44 BCE) who was murdered by political rivals.

[8] *Joshua* Successor to Moses as Israel's leader; *land of behest* Land belonging to Israel by right of God's promise; *David … Jerusalem* Biblical figure who defeated the giant Goliath and became King of Jerusalem; *Judas Maccabeus* Jewish military leader.

[9] *stalled* Installed.

[10] *Charlemagne* Charles I (768–814), King of the Franks and Emperor of much of Western Europe. His court became the center of a renaissance of art and culture.

[11] *Godfrey of Bouillon* One of the leaders of the First Crusade (1058–1100).

The said noble gentlemen instantly[1] required me to imprint the history of the said noble king and conqueror King Arthur, and of his knights, with the history of the Saint Grail, and of the death and ending of the said Arthur; affirming that I ought rather to imprint his acts and noble feats, than of Godfrey of Bouillon, or any of the other eight, considering that he was a man born within this realm, and king and emperor of the same, and that there be in French diverse and many noble volumes of his acts, and also of his knights.

To whom I answered that diverse men hold opinion that there was no such Arthur, and that all such books as been made of him be feigned and fables, because that some chronicles make of him no mention, nor remember him nothing,[2] nor of his knights.

Whereto they answered, and one in special said, that in him that should say or think that there was never such a king called Arthur might well be aretted[3] great folly and blindness. For he said that there were many evidences of the contrary. First ye may see his sepulchre in the monastery of Glastonbury. And also in *Polychronicon*,[4] in the fifth book the sixth chapter, and in the seventh book the twenty-third chapter, where his body was buried, and after found, and translated[5] into the said monastery. Ye shall see also in the history of Bochas, in his book *De Casu Principum*,[6] part of his noble acts, and also of his fall. Also Galfridus in his British book[7] recounteth his life: and in diverse places of England many remembrances be yet of him, and shall remain perpetually, and also of his knights. First in the Abbey of Westminster, at St. Edward's shrine, remaineth the print of his seal in red wax closed in beryl,[8] in which is written, Patricius Arthurus, Britannie, Gallie, Germanie, Dacie, Imperator.[9] Item[10] in the castle of Dover ye may see Gawaine's skull, and Cradok's mantle; at Winchester the Round Table; in other places Lancelot's sword and many other things. Then all these things considered, there can no man reasonably gainsay but there was a king of this land named Arthur. For in all places, Christian and heathen, he is reputed and taken for one of the nine worthy, and the first of the three Christian men. And also, he is more spoken of beyond the sea, more books made of his noble acts, than there be in England, as well in Dutch, Italian, Spanish, and Greek, as in French. And yet of record remain in witness of him in Wales, in the town of Camelot, the great stones and the marvellous works of iron lying under the ground, and royal vaults, which diverse now living have seen. Wherefore it is a marvel why he is no more renowned in his own country, save only it accordeth to the Word of God, which saith that no man is accepted for a prophet in his own country.

---

[1] *instantly* Pressingly.

[2] *remember … nothing* Record nothing of him.

[3] *aretted* Reckoned, considered.

[4] *Polychronicon* Long chronicle that strives to couple universal history with theology, written in Latin by Ranulf Higden (1299–1363) and translated into English by John Trevisa (in 1387), printed by Caxton in 1482.

[5] *translated* Transferred.

[6] *Bochas* Giovanni Boccaccio (1313–75), Italian writer, author of the *Decameron* and various other works; *De Casu Principum* Probably *De Casibus Virorum Illustrium* (*On the Downfalls of Famous Men*), a biographical work written by Boccaccio between 1357 and 1363 that recounts the stories of great men who fell from the heights of success and happiness.

[7] *Galfridus* Geoffrey of Monmouth (1100?–1155), early British chronicler; *British book* Geoffrey's *Historia Regum Britanniae* (*History of the Kings of Britain*), completed c. 1138, which begins in a legendary past and continues up to Cadwallader, the last "British" king.

[8] *beryl* Emerald.

[9] *Patricius … Imperator* Latin: Noble Arthur, Emperor of Britain, Gaul, Germany, and Dacia.

[10] *Item* Also.

Then all these things aforesaid alleged, I could not well deny but that there was such a noble king named Arthur, and reputed one of the nine worthy, and first and chief of the Christian men. And many noble volumes be made of him and of his noble knights in French, which I have seen and read beyond the sea, which be not had in our maternal tongue.[1] But in Welsh be many and also in French, and some in English but nowhere nigh all. Wherefore, such as have late[2] been drawn out[3] briefly into English I have after the simple conning[4] that God hath sent to me, under the favour and correction of all noble lords and gentlemen, enprised[5] to imprint a book of the noble histories of the said King Arthur, and of certain of his knights, after a copy unto me delivered, which copy Sir Thomas Malory did take out of certain books of French, and reduced[6] it into English.

And I, according to my copy, have done set it in imprint,[7] to the intent that noble men may see and learn the noble acts of chivalry, the gentle and virtuous deeds that some knights used in those days, by which they came to honour, and how they that were vicious were punished and oft put to shame and rebuke; humbly beseeching all noble lords and ladies, with all other estates of what estate or degree[8] they been of, that shall see and read in this said book and work, that they take the good and honest acts in their remembrance, and to follow the same. Wherein they shall find many joyous and pleasant histories, and noble and renowned acts of humanity, gentleness, and chivalry. For herein may be seen noble chivalry, courtesy, humanity, friendliness, hardiness, love, friendship, cowardice, murder, hate, virtue, and sin. Do after the good and leave the evil, and it shall bring you to good fame and renown.

And for to pass the time this book shall be pleasant to read in, but for to give faith and belief that all is true that is contained herein, ye be at your liberty; but all is written for our doctrine,[9] and for to beware that we fall not to vice nor sin, but to exercise and follow virtue, by which we may come and attain to good fame and renown in this life, and after this short and transitory life to come unto everlasting bliss in heaven; the which He grant us that reigneth in heaven, the blessed Trinity. Amen.

Then to proceed forth in this said book, which I direct unto all noble princes, lords and ladies, gentlemen or gentlewomen, that desire to read or hear read of the noble and joyous history of the great conqueror and excellent king, King Arthur, sometime king of this noble realm, then called Britain; I, William Caxton, simple person, present this book following, which I have enprised to imprint, and treateth of the noble acts, feats of arms of chivalry, prowess, hardiness, humanity, love, courtesy, and very gentleness, with many wonderful histories and adventures.

---

[1]   *maternal tongue*   Mother tongue, i.e., English vernacular.

[2]   *late*   Lately.

[3]   *drawn out*   Translated.

[4]   *conning*   Knowledge, understanding.

[5]   *enprised*   Undertaken.

[6]   *reduced*   Translated.

[7]   *done ... imprint*   Caused it to be printed.

[8]   *estate or degree*   Social class or position.

[9]   *doctrine*   Instruction. See Romans 15.4.

Illustrating *Morte Darthur*

The first edition of Malory's work, printed by William Caxton in 1485, was not illustrated; however, in the next edition (1498), Wynkyn de Worde added a number of woodcut illustrations. Two of these are reproduced below.

Balin unsheathing Excalibur (after Arthur and various of his knights have failed to do so).

The Battle of Salisbury Plain.

The Renaissance and the Early Seventeenth Century

The term "Renaissance" has turned out to be a good deal less stable than was once assumed. The word "Rinascenza" (Italian: "rebirth"), from which "Renaissance" derives, was coined by the Italian historian Giorgio Vasari in 1550 to refer to what Vasari saw as having taken place in Italy over the previous two centuries: a rebirth of the ideas and the aesthetic values associated with the classical cultures of ancient Greece and Rome, after a thousand-year-long era in which civilization had gone into eclipse. By the time of Vasari it had already become conventional to think of that thousand-year period as the "Middle Ages" (or, using the Latinized form of the same phrase, the "medieval period").[1] Subsequently the habit developed of seeing the Renaissance as being followed by another discrete era, the Reformation, a period characterized above all by the challenge presented by Protestantism to the authority of the Church of Rome.

Recent generations of scholarship have done much to destabilize this conceptual framework. Medievalists have located a variety of "renaissances" in, for example, the ninth and the twelfth centuries, and have thoroughly debunked the idea that the supposed "dark ages" were lacking intellectual or cultural life. Scholars have also distinguished among the later renaissances of the fourteenth through sixteenth centuries: a renaissance in Italy that began in the early fourteenth century (with the writings of Dante and Petrarch and the paintings of Giotto) and reached its full flowering in the late fifteenth and early sixteenth centuries (the age of Machiavelli, of Leonardo da Vinci, and of Michelangelo); a renaissance that occurred in northern Europe in the late fifteenth and early sixteenth centuries, especially in the Low Countries but also manifesting itself in France and in England (among the leading figures of this renais-

sance were the great Humanist thinkers Desiderius Erasmus and Sir Thomas More, and the painters Jan van Eyck and Hans Holbein); and a renaissance that occurred in England toward the end of the sixteenth century in the latter part of the reign of Elizabeth I (the age of Edmund Spenser, Sir Philip Sidney, and Christopher Marlowe as well as Shakespeare). Other scholars, though, have questioned whether or not England ever experienced anything that can properly be termed a "Renaissance."

At a minimum, then, the phenomena associated with "the Renaissance" extended over a considerable stretch of time and across much of Europe. But they were not isolated from one another, sharing a tendency to focus on human concerns in new ways (and, in the visual arts, to depict the human form in persuasively realistic if often idealized representations). Historically too, the various renaissances were connected by a variety of direct links, many of them stemming from royal initiatives. The French King Francis I (1494–1547) lent vibrant support to new ideas from Italy and brought to France such renowned Italian artists as Andrea del Sarto and Leonardo da Vinci. In England, Henry VII (1457–1509) and his mother, Margaret, encouraged the "new learning" and brought to England the great Dutch scholar Erasmus; promoted men such as Thomas More, the scholar John Colet and Bishop John Fisher, who championed better education and classical learning; patronized William Caxton (who in 1476 had set up the first printing press in England); and founded two colleges at Cambridge University.

It was on this foundation that Henry's son, Henry VIII, built his fully developed Renaissance court. The prevailing image of Henry VIII is that of the figure he became in the 1530s and '40s, adding pound upon pound as he accumulated wife after wife. The young Henry—trim and lively, a sporting monarch and a man of culture, the "golden boy" peer of Francis I of France and Charles V, the Holy Roman Emperor—is a very different figure. Under the young Henry an interna-

---

[1] The earliest recorded expression of the idea of a "Middle Age" between the classical world and the modern one appears in the writing of Flavio Biondo around 1439. Petrarch, writing in the 1330s, is thought to have been the first to characterize what we now term the medieval period as an age of darkness (one which he believed himself still inhabiting).

tional culture flourished in which leading continental humanist thinkers and great artists—the Dutch painter Hans Holbein most prominent among them—were persuaded to spend substantial amounts of time in England.

Artist unknown, *Henry VIII*, c. 1509.

Hans Holbein, *Henry VIII*, 1536.

This manifestation of English Renaissance culture in the early sixteenth century was followed near the end of the century by an extraordinary cultural flowering of a different character—the Elizabethan Renaissance. This Renaissance followed the Protestant Reformation, and in consequence took on a different religious coloring from that of the Christian humanism so central to the Italian Renaissance and the early Northern Renaissance, which took shape before Martin Luther launched the Protestant Reformation in 1517. The word "Renaissance" is commonly applied to sixteenth-century and early seventeenth-century English culture, but many historians and even literary historians now prefer to term the era between about 1600 and some time in the eighteenth century the "early modern period."

Regardless of terminology, the period between 1500 and 1660 in Britain[1] saw massive political, social, and religious change, change intimately connected to developments on the continent. The period begins and ends with a country exhausted by war: in 1500 memories of a long series of wars fought over the right of succession to the English throne (the "Wars of the Roses") were still fresh, and in 1660 the return of Charles II from exile marked the end of the republican Commonwealth established after civil wars that had brought tumult to England, Scotland, and Ireland. Over these 160 years the national church—the foundation of the country's devotional practices and beliefs—changed its entire orientation at least four times and was subject to constant debate and evolution. Centuries-old rites and traditions in the countryside, which still resonated strongly throughout society in the early sixteenth century, began to disappear and even to become objects of nostalgia. The world of maypoles and of Morris dancing, of hobbyhorses and bonfires, was bitterly opposed as "pagan" or "papist" by more radical reformers, and while such traditional pastimes were supported by the early Stuart monarchs, they were a thing of the past by the end of the period. Medieval ideals of chivalry were kept alive (or resurrected) largely for political and social purposes even as a developing moneyed economy was refashioning the world. A succession of monarchs established munificent (if

---

[1] "Britain" is here used as a term of convenience; strictly speaking, there was no "Britain" before 1603 when the accession of King James VI/I brought a de facto union of England and Scotland.

sometimes rough-hewn) court cultures, and a vibrant street life in London and other towns was a vital part of English culture. The English language, though still widely thought inferior to Latin, experienced exuberant growth. Scientific investigations of a recognizably "modern" sort were beginning to be carried out toward the end of the period, even as belief in demons, witches, and astrology increased, as did a more recondite belief in alchemy. For many years a woman reigned as monarch, and in literature a common conceit had it that male lovers were slaves to the females they adored; yet the actual status of women probably did not improve over this period. How did this jumble coalesce in literature? Let us begin by looking more closely at Renaissance humanism and at the Protestant Reformation.

HUMANISM

Nowadays the word *humanist* is often used to imply a "secular" opposition to religion in general and Christianity in particular. The opposite is the case with Renaissance humanism, particularly north of Italy. Humanists were distinguished from other scholars not by exclusive focus on human or secular texts, but rather by their focus on secular writings, particularly classical ones, *as well as* on religious texts and thought. Thus Erasmus produced books on Greco-Roman culture *and* editions of the New Testament in the original Greek and of works by patristic writers. In one key particular, humanism was in accord with Protestant thought: Erasmus and many other humanists supported making the Bible available in the vernacular. But—as attested by Thomas More's willingness to die rather than approve England's separation from the Roman Catholic Church—humanists tended to be more willing than Luther or, later, Calvin to remain connected to Roman Catholic tradition. (Erasmus, for example, favored reform within the Catholic Church but opposed a full Protestant Reformation.)

The recovery and reappraisal of works from classical Greece and Rome was central to Renaissance humanism —as it had been to medieval scholasticism centuries earlier. The recovery of texts by the scholastics, however,

had stressed applying classical learning to theological ends, emphasized Aristotle's works, and tended to treat classical writings as authoritative. For Renaissance humanists, classical writings were of interest for many purposes: the epic poems of Homer and Virgil and the erotic poems of Ovid were of as much interest as the writings of the philosophers. And many humanists felt little obligation to demonstrate that a seemingly new idea in fact accorded with ancient authority. Renaissance humanism was often prepared to break new ground, and to acknowledge breaking it.

Of the Greek philosophers, Plato, rather than Aristotle, came to the fore. Of particular importance was the Platonic concept of ideal forms—the notion that for every physical object, metaphysical concept, and ethical principle there is an ideal abstract form that in fact is more "real" than its manifestations in the actual or material world. It is not difficult to see how Platonic "ideas" could be harmonized with Christian ideals, and many humanist thinkers endeavored to do just that.[1] But Platonic philosophy also lent force to the sometime humanist impulse, particularly in Italy, to celebrate humanity itself, if not without reference to a Creator then with unprecedented emphasis on human potential and free will. A groundbreaking text here was the *Oration on the Dignity of Man* (1486) by the Florentine writer Pico della Mirandola. As Pico saw it,

> upon man, at the moment of his creation, God bestowed seeds pregnant with all possibilities, the germs of every form of life. Whichever of these a man shall cultivate, the same will mature and bear fruit in him. If vegetative, he will become a plant; if sensual, he will become brutish; if rational, he will reveal himself as a heavenly being; if intellectual, he will be an angel and the son of God.... Who then will not look with awe upon this our chameleon?

Northern humanists such as Erasmus and More were less optimistic about human nature, but nevertheless the contrast between Pico's confidence and the emphasis on the inherent sinfulness of man (and even more of woman) in both medieval Christianity and the theology of the French Protestant John Calvin (1509–64) could

---

[1] Some writers (e.g., Spenser and Rabelais) welcomed Platonism's vision of a world of ideas to which we can rise but also stressed God's descent to the world of flesh.

hardly be more marked. It is in the writings of the humanists that we see the possibility of imagining human society as a body independent of the workings of God. The supreme English example is More's *Utopia*, which imagines, although with a countering irony and ambivalence, the transformation of a culture through fundamentally different but entirely human-made social structures and practices.

Though scholars differ as to its extent and influence, most agree that Renaissance humanism helped transform sixteenth-century English literature. The poems of Thomas Wyatt, a member of Henry VIII's court who introduced the Petrarchan sonnet to English literature, show the impact of Renaissance humanism, as do prose works such as Sir Thomas Elyot's *The Book of the Governor* (1531) and Roger Ascham's *The Schoolmaster* (1570). Renaissance humanism is also generally agreed to have contributed to a new exuberance and a new richness in the English language, despite its occasional tendency toward philological pedantry and a sometimes uncomprehending prejudice against medieval scholastic philosophy. One contribution was the introduction of yet more tropes of classical rhetoric into English and an increased attention to English as a language worth study and further polish. According to Ascham, the study of Latin, "wisely brought into schools, truly taught, and constantly used," would "work a true choice [in] placing of words, a right ordering of sentences, and easy understanding of the tongue, a readiness to speak, a facility to write, a true judgement both of his own and other men's doings, what tongue soever he doth use." (Ascham is here practicing what he preaches, using several of the figures of classical rhetoric in the construction of his long and elaborately balanced sentence.)

Humanists such as Erasmus wrote primarily in Latin, but their rhetorical impulse and linguistic exuberance spilled over into the vernacular. Under the influence of Joachim Du Bellay, who had defended French in similar terms, Richard Mulcaster (Edmund Spenser's teacher) asked some pointed questions and gave impassioned answers:

> Is it not indeed a marvellous bondage, to become servants to one tongue for learning's sake the most of our time, with loss of most time, whereas we may have the very same treasure in our own tongue, with the gain of more time? Our own bearing the joyful title of our liberty and freedom, the Latin tongue remembering us of our thraldom and bondage? I love Rome, but London better; I favour Italy, but England more; I honour the Latin, but I worship the English.

Like much else about this period, the extent to which "Renaissance humanism" is a useful concept is subject to debate. Earlier notions of Renaissance humanism often assumed a top-down view of the period in which coherent intellectual movements were prime moving forces of socio-economic as well as political and cultural change. Recent scholars doubt that such movements in intellectual history are often quite so unified and coherent, believing that bottom-up change driven by socio-economic or religious forces may have at least as great an impact. Nevertheless, "Renaissance humanism" remains central to any discussion of the period.

SCIENTIFIC INQUIRY

Science and technology had not been dead in the Middle Ages, as witness developments in, for example, optics. It is the early modern period, however, that saw the start of what was later to be called, with a little exaggeration, "the scientific revolution." And yet the story of scientific development in early modern Europe is one of twists and paradox, not least because the Renaissance saw an increased, not a decreased, interest and belief in astrology, alchemy, and demonology. These fields of exploration are now called "pseudo-sciences," but the observations they entailed and the technology they encouraged, futile though the sciences themselves turned out to be, contributed to what we would call real science. Even the great Isaac Newton believed in the occult. Did Renaissance humanism play a part? Humanist fascination with ancient texts doubtless aided in the recovery or fresh understanding of scientific works by such classical authorities as Aristotle, Euclid, Hippocrates, and Galen (the latter two edited by Rabelais). Even more important was the increased use of Arabic numerals and that mathematically crucial concept, zero (realized in India and perfected by the Arabs).

Although he failed to understand the necessity of mathematics to his dreams of scientific progress, Sir Francis Bacon (1561–1626) was a key figure in formulating new approaches. As his essays demonstrate, Bacon's interests were wide. His *Novum Organum* (1620) was a plan to base scientific endeavor and an understanding of the cosmos more on objective observation and less on armchair theory or the consensus of the past. As Bacon put it, "man, custodian and interpreter of Nature, performs and understands so much as he has collected concerning the order of nature by observation or reason; nor do his powers or his knowledge extend farther." Among those who put into practice the inductive approach advocated by Bacon was William Harvey (1578–1657), an English physician who, through experiment and observation, determined how blood circulates in the human body. As Harvey observed in his *De Motu Cordis et Sanguinis*,[1] *On the Motions of the Heart and Blood* (1628):

> Almost all anatomists, physicians, and philosophers, up to the present time, have supposed with Galen that the object of the pulse was the same as that of respiration…. But as the structure and movements of the heart differ from those of the lungs, and the motions of the arteries from those of the chest, so seems it likely … that the pulsations and uses of the heart, likewise of the arteries, will differ in many respects from the heavings and uses of the chest and lungs.

What Harvey did for the human body, the astronomers Copernicus, Galileo, and Kepler did for the universe. Galileo provided further proof of the Copernican theory that the cosmos does not revolve around the earth, and Kepler showed that the earth's path is an ellipse (although he continued to believe that the planets make beautiful harmony and tried to work out the musical notation involved). As the poet John Donne put it in his *Anatomy of the World*, if with some exaggeration, the "new philosophy," by which he meant the new natural science, "calls all in doubt":

The sun is lost, and the earth, and no man's wit,
Can well direct him where to look for it.

The lines are often quoted, but in truth some welcomed the new astronomy: in the older system, the Earth was at the center of the universe, but that center was a dark, dirty, and unmusical place, unlike the fiery and harmonious planets and stars.

Much as discoveries such as those of Harvey and Galileo affected the intellectual constructs through which people viewed each other and the world, some things remained unchanged from the late-medieval to the Renaissance period. One of these, challenged but persistent, was the habit of thought according to which the macrocosm was made up of four elements—earth, water, air, and fire—and the microcosm of the individual human was made up of four "humors," each with a physical association. Thus a sanguine humor or temperament was associated with blood, a choleric or angry temperament was associated with one sort of bile, a melancholic temperament was associated with a different sort of bile, and a phlegmatic temperament was associated with water. (Melancholia, which often meant what we would call neurosis and which was often thought to be linked to high intelligence and creativity, came in for particular attention in the Jacobean era: Jacques in Shakespeare's *As You Like It* is a paradigm of the type. And, in a different genre, Robert Burton's *The Anatomy of Melancholy* [1621] is a full and entertaining treatise on the subject.) Ideally, all four humors would be balanced. The domination of one humor could be the subject of a medical diagnosis—or of literary satire. Ben Jonson in such plays as *Everyman in his Humour* and *Everyman out of his Humour* was the most notable among many Elizabethan and Jacobean writers to make the "humors" of human individuals the subject of comedy. Such ways of thinking persisted into the late seventeenth century. As so often with scientific or technological developments, there was a lag between a discovery and its general acceptance.

---

[1] Like Bacon and like almost all authors of scientific work until the late seventeenth and eighteenth centuries, Harvey wrote in Latin.

THE REFORMATION IN ENGLAND

The Protestant Reformation was in part about power: would the Roman Catholic Church retain power to act as an intermediary between Christians and God, power to define the nature of God, power to control all aspects of worship, power over the legitimacy of marriage and of children, and in many cases vast power over lands and financial resources, including the power to impose tithes and taxes? For centuries the Church of Rome had exerted supreme authority in all these areas.

The spark that set off the Reformation was a challenge put forward by Martin Luther on 31 October 1517 to the long-standing Church practice of selling "indulgences"—certificates granting absolution for sins. Luther saw the practice as a flagrant abuse of Church authority that discouraged people from confessing their sins in a spirit of true repentance. According to tradition, Luther nailed his *Ninety-Five Theses*—a substantial document in which he set out his arguments—to the door of the castle church in Wittenberg. Thanks to the new printing technology, the *Theses* were translated and distributed throughout Europe within two months, and within a year Luther was condemned by the Pope as a heretic.

Before long, the controversy set off by Luther had widened as much conceptually as it had geographically. Luther's protest broadened into a wide-ranging call for reforms in the Church, including the elimination of perceived abuses such as the sale of indulgences as well as a new emphasis on making the Word of God, the Bible—for Luther the one true authority—available directly to all in the vernacular, a new focus on faith alone as the key to salvation, and a denial that human beings have free will (only with grace, he said, and not from the exertion of will, can people choose the good). In 1529, the Diet (or Assembly) of Speyer passed a comprehensive condemnation of Luther and his followers, but a minority of delegates delivered a *Protestatio*—the origin of the term "Protestant" that has come to be applied to the various new churches that sprang up across Europe in opposition to the Church of Rome, and that assumed leading roles in Germany, Holland, and England.

In England, controversies over the use or abuse of power by the Catholic Church were substantially complicated by the fact that this power was exercised from afar, from Italy; even in the Middle Ages such power had been resented in England, and in the early sixteenth century an increased resentment against traditional doctrines and practices can be attributed in part to their origin in Rome (or so said Reformers, for Catholics claimed to have derived them from Scripture, from continued revelation, or from the broader consensus of Christendom). And once the Reformation in England was an established fact, national feeling sometimes played a significant role in fanning the flames of religious hatred. As early as the 1540s, some Protestants had advanced the claim that the Pope was the embodiment of Antichrist, and such sentiment grew when in 1580 Pope Pius V pronounced that assassinating Elizabeth I of England would not constitute a mortal sin. It should nevertheless be remembered, as a number of recent scholars have stressed, that of the large minority of English men and women who remained Catholic and did not move to the continent, most remained loyal to both their faith and their monarch.

In attempting to sort out the causes of the Reformation, what weight should we give to the issue that sparked Luther's rebellion—what many perceived as corruption in the Church, and in particular the sale of indulgences? It is now generally accepted that the degree of corruption in the late-medieval church was exaggerated both at the time and by most later historians; its true extent is still debated. We do know that in the late-medieval period many, including many loyal Catholics, accused the institutional Roman Catholic Church of abandoning its own ideals of concern for the poor, chastity for priests, and Gospel simplicity. Simony—the practice of buying and selling spiritual offices for spiritual benefits—was widespread, as other such abuses were said, not always unjustly, to be. But there were other questions being asked. Should the clergy act as intermediaries in interpreting the Bible for the laity? Or should everyone, even the humble, be allowed to read and interpret the Bible (perhaps even actively encouraged to do so)? Is administering the sacraments and presiding over other rites the most important function of the clergy? (And how many sacraments are there? Catholics said seven; Protestants said only two: baptism and holy communion.) Or is preaching and spreading the word of God the central obligation of a clergyman?

Is the sacrament of Confession (the confessing of one's sins to a priest) essential to salvation? Or should confession, no longer a sacrament, be between an individual and God? Is the substance, although not the appearance (the "accidents"), of bread and wine literally transformed during the sacrament of the Eucharist into the body and the blood of Christ by a process called "transubstantiation" that re-enacts Christ's sacrifice? Or are Lutherans right to say that God is "really" but not physically present in the bread and wine? Calvinists (and the Church of England) called the sacrament of the Eucharist a "sign"—connecting signifier to signified so as to make it more than a mere reminder—of God's spiritual presence and His connection to the believer. Not true, said some more radical Protestants, Communion is merely a memorial. Others, even more radical, thought it best to dispense with the ceremony altogether.

There were yet more questions. Are church hierarchies necessary to the carrying out of God's will? Or do they exist only for convenience? Is salvation dependent on good works performed, on sins not committed, and on remaining in communion with God? Or is it dependent purely on one's faith in God, a faith that may in turn be acquired only at God's pleasure? Might the salvation of "the elect" even be predestined by God? Is it a sign of appropriate respect to honor the Virgin Mary and the saints as well as the divinity through splendid displays of devotion? Or does that risk idolatry? (Protestants accused Catholics of actually worshiping saints and of elevating Mary beyond her due as the mother of Christ.) Or does a plain style honor God most fittingly? (In which case elaborate or colorful decoration in churches, let alone beautiful images venerated in themselves, are properly seen as further expressions of idolatry.) Should realism and discretion be exercised in any consideration of measures to "enforce purity" outside the Church? Or is it one's duty as a Christian to pursue purity through restrictions on irresponsible or pleasure-seeking behavior? May we (as King James I was to urge) enjoy a range of traditional practices that probably have pagan roots (maypoles, hobbyhorses, bonfires, bells, Christmas revelry) or must we, as many "Puritans" said, condemn such enjoyments as wicked, even devilish? Divergent answers to such questions separated Catholic from Protestant, and accompanied a number of divisions within Protestantism.

Thomas Wolsey, a butcher's son who became a cardinal of the Roman Catholic Church, and was for many years Lord Chancellor under Henry VIII. Wolsey was as controversial as he was powerful, and his legacy remains controversial today. Widely praised by some for his administrative abilities and his adroitness in foreign affairs, to others he exemplified the corruption of the Church and the dangers of mingling religious office with secular authority. Holding the highest religious position in the land, he was also the King's chief minister, shaping both domestic and foreign policy. He left a lasting legacy in building Hampton Court Palace and founding Cardinal College at Oxford University, but when Henry VIII petitioned the Pope for an annulment of his marriage, Wolsey became caught in the struggle between his two masters. Henry stripped him of his government offices and of most of his property. His servant George Cavendish reported that as he lay dying on his way to what would have doubtless been a trial and execution, he said "If I had served my God as diligently as I have done the King he would not have given me over in my gray hairs."

The Reformation came to England through circuitous means. The rejection by Henry VIII of papal supremacy *led* to a Protestant English Reformation but did not *constitute* a Protestant Reformation of the Church in England; only under Henry's son, Edward VI, was a more explicit Protestantism, both theological and institutional, established in England, and for reasons quite different from those that had motivated Henry. (Likewise, although some in the England of the 1520s and 1530s shared the varieties of Protestantism that were bringing sweeping change in parts of Europe, such beliefs were not yet widespread or powerful enough to establish the Reformation in England. Even when Elizabeth first began her reign it is possible that a majority of her subjects were still loyal to Rome.) Most immediately, Henry's break with Rome was caused by his desire to end his marriage to Catherine of Aragon and obtain a male heir by marrying Anne Boleyn. There is little doubt that he was in love with Anne, but almost certainly he would not have gone to such lengths to marry her had he not become convinced that Catherine would never give him a son.[1]

The key developments in the break from Rome are as follows. In 1533, after Henry had exerted intense pressure on the English clergy to support his course of action, the marriage of Henry and Catherine was annulled, his marriage to (a pregnant) Anne Boleyn was consecrated, and she became Queen. At that point Pope Clement VII, who had been trying diplomatically to placate Henry without doing any violence to Catholic doctrine (or offending Catherine's nephew, the Holy Roman Emperor), now excommunicated Henry: forbidden to receive Communion, Henry was thereby excluded from salvation. Henry's response was to pass an Act of Succession through Parliament, under which all adult males in England would have to swear that they supported the change in the King's marital arrangements. Henry also decreed that the Bible should be made available in English, and that church services should be in English rather than in Latin, a radical break with the practice of the Church of Rome. Later that year the English Church was formally made independent from Rome, and all adult males were additionally required to swear allegiance to the King in his new capacity as "Supreme Head of the Church in England." Among the few who refused so to swear were Sir Thomas More, author of *Utopia* and from 1528 to 1532 Henry's Lord Chancellor, and John Fisher, Bishop of Rochester. In 1535 both were convicted of treason for their refusals and executed. Both were canonized by the Catholic Church in 1935.

As so often with Henry, the personal was entangled with the political. In an effort to build support for the break with Rome, he gave preferment to Protestants who not long before had been labeled heretics. This move helped both to buttress his own authority and to undermine Catholic institutions, most significantly the monasteries, bastions of privilege and possessors of immense wealth. Protestants were fervent in their opposition to the monasteries. Whereas monks had originally been venerated as embodiments of the godly life, they had come to be widely suspected (sometimes rightly) of corrupt and immoral behavior; in some parts of the realm, moreover, they were widely unpopular as landlords despite the role of some monasteries and convents in providing basic schooling and medical aid. In 1535, two years after the break with Rome, Henry appointed commissioners to look into these allegations; as he had doubtless intended them to do, the commissioners confirmed the allegations of corruption, and beginning in 1536 Henry ordered the dissolution of

---

[1] The root of Henry VIII's break with Rome may be traced to the desire of Henry VII to improve his standing with the Spanish monarchy by marrying his son to Catherine of Aragon, daughter of Ferdinand and Isabella. Catherine was betrothed to Arthur, Henry's eldest son, in 1488; she was three years old and Arthur a year younger. The two were 15 and 14 respectively when the long-awaited wedding took place in 1501, but within six months Arthur fell sick and died. Henry VII obtained a papal dispensation allowing Catherine to marry Arthur's younger brother Henry; this second marriage for Catherine took place in 1509. She bore several children, but only her daughter Mary survived. Catherine was 42 years old in 1527 when Henry, despairing of her ability to give him a son, and with perhaps some degree of sincerity convinced that his lack of an heir was God's punishment for his living in sin with his deceased brother's wife, began to petition Pope Clement VII to grant him an annulment on the grounds that Catherine's marriage to his brother had made their own union unlawful. Catherine put up strenuous resistance to Henry's petition; she appealed to the Pope herself, insisting that she and Arthur had not consummated their marriage and had therefore never truly been husband and wife. Catherine's nephew was Charles V, the Holy Roman Emperor, whom the Pope had no wish to offend, and the matter was soon at a stale-mate— where it remained for six years, while Pope Clement continued to resist Henry's appeals.

monasteries throughout England and annexed the land to the Crown. He thus provided himself with a vast and ongoing source of additional revenue, as well as with the ability to extend his generosity more widely to friends and supporters. Through Thomas Cranmer (Archbishop of Canterbury and hence the Primate of the English Church), Henry also broke with Catholic tradition by arranging for the publication of the first English Bible authorized for public use, the 1539 "Great Bible" of Miles Coverdale. The "dissolution" of the monasteries typically entailed their physical destruction, often to provide stones for the Tudor great houses that the gentry and nobility were beginning to build. "Bare, ruined choirs, where late the sweet birds sang" became a common sight in sixteenth-century England.

Roger Fenton, *Riveaulx Abbey*. Riveaulx (located in East Yorkshire), once one of the greatest of English monasteries, had subsequently dwindled in importance, and housed fewer than two dozen monks at the time of the Dissolution. In 1538 the remaining monks were forced to leave, and the abbey and surrounding lands were granted to Thomas Manners, who destroyed many of the buildings but left the shell of the early thirteenth-century church standing.

John Speed, vignette of Nonsuch Palace from the map of Surrey in Speed's atlas of Britain, 1616. Nonsuch Palace, the greatest of Henry VIII's edifices and one of the most noted works of Tudor architecture, was begun in 1538, and completed in 1547. It later became a favorite residence of Elizabeth I.

Throughout his reign, Henry, who probably did not consider himself a "Protestant" in any profound or theological sense, attempted to steer a middle course between Protestant demands for further reform and residual Catholic tradition and theology. But for Henry, steering a middle way did not mean conciliation or consensus; it meant veering between censoring, imprisoning, and even executing greater numbers of one side or of the other. Even in the mid-1530s, as he was counting on Protestant support in building a campaign against the monasteries, Henry was also restricting licenses to preach and curtailing other forms of free religious expression that he thought extremist but which the Protestants demanded.

Wall-painting of the Last Judgment, Stratford Guild Chapel, early sixteenth century. This picture, in which Hell-mouth appears at lower right, is one of a series of wall paintings in the Chapel that were whitewashed over in the later sixteenth century to remove Catholic imagery. The paintings were discovered in 1804, and watercolor copies were published in 1807.

Scholars continue to debate both the manner in which the Reformation came to England and the speed with which it did. Was the Reformation pushed forward primarily by pressure from above—by administrators such as Cranmer? Or was it driven more by pressure from below by a population dissatisfied with the old Church? Was England already Protestant at heart when Mary Tudor began her reign? Or did the Reformation in England remain a work in progress until the 1570s? Just how large was the Catholic minority—and when did it become a minority? Over such issues there is little consensus, although the recent tendency has been to affirm the vitality of the Roman Catholic Church on the eve of Henry's reforms and the continued presence of large numbers of Catholics in officially Protestant England. In any case, the broad outlines of the narrative are clear. For most English people in the sixteenth and seventeenth centuries, matters of faith were intensely felt realities, not abstract theological questions—even if they could be those too. Although educated lay Christians had long practiced versions of piety that included reciting parts of the Bible, we can get some sense of the freshness and the fervency of the feelings aroused by the increased stress on Bible reading through the words of Queen Elizabeth herself:

> I walk many times into the pleasant fields of the Holy Scriptures, where I pluck up the goodly green herbs of sentences, eat them by reading, chew them up musing, and lay them up at length in the seat of memory ... so I may less perceive the bitterness of this miserable life.

It is not difficult to appreciate the aesthetic and cultural importance of religious issues in an age in which everyone was a church-goer (Elizabethan law required it, in part to determine who might be Catholic), in which crucifixes, rosaries, and so on—if now frowned upon by strict Protestants—had long figured in daily life as reminders of Christian doctrine, but in which the practice of reading the Bible had only recently become available to the population at large (if only by hearing it read out loud). The sixteenth and early seventeenth centuries were robustly secular, but they were also passionately religious. Cultures can be both, and it is important not to forget the strength of the religious

ferment that extended throughout this period—or the fact that for many of those involved in it, religious matters defined the age and set it off in bold relief from earlier times. Such was the vision of the Protestant reformer John Foxe, whose *Acts and Monuments* (popularly known as the *Book of Martyrs*) was one of the most influential and widely read books of the age. Far from seeing the Middle Ages as a lost Age of Faith, Foxe regarded the thousand years before the Reformation as the millennium of Satan's rule prophesied by the Biblical Book of Daniel.

WALES, SCOTLAND, IRELAND

Henry VIII was an international figure beyond his support of Renaissance humanism; he was also a colonizing monarch, if largely confining his efforts to what is now the United Kingdom and northeast France. A continual thread that runs through the history of the sixteenth and seventeenth centuries is England's conflict with constituent parts of the British Isles. English power reached an early peak around 1300, when the English were able to exert at least loose control over the greater part of Ireland as well as over Scotland and Wales. In all three areas the English faced continuing resistance, however. Scotland was able to re-establish its position as an independent kingdom; in Ireland, the English control diminished to a relatively small area surrounding Dublin known as "the Pale"; and in Wales, though the Normans had managed to install "English" settlers in many of the more fertile lowland areas, those in the mountainous regions remained very largely a traditional society that was effectively independent of English rule. When a Welshman, Henry VII, became King of England in 1485, however, administrative control of Wales from London began to harden. The process culminated under Henry VIII with the Acts of Union of 1536–43: the old Welsh areas of lordships were converted into shires on the English model, and the Welsh code of law was brought into conformity with its English counterpart. The traditional Welsh kinship system, under which equal inheritance among all male children was the norm, was replaced by a system of primogeniture, with land typically held on a freehold basis. Interestingly, though, the Welsh language does not seem to have been threatened during this period, despite English incursions into Welsh custom and culture.

Under Thomas Cromwell, Henry VIII's chief minister in the 1530s, the English attempted the same sort of "reforms" in Ireland that had been imposed in Wales—with much less success. Along with changes to traditional kinship systems, the English attempted to bring about the same religious changes in Ireland that were occurring in England: royal rather than papal supremacy over the Church, the Bible to be read in the vernacular, and the dissolution of the monasteries. These English efforts met with only sporadic success, and Henry did not push the point; it was not until the 1570s, when Elizabeth I's government found itself increasingly threatened by the aggressively expansionist Catholic regime of Philip II in Spain, that a more determined approach was taken toward "stubbornly" Catholic Ireland. Several revolts that had been actively

John Speed, *Wilde Irish Woman* and *Wilde Irish Man*, two of several decorative miniatures surrounding the map of England in Speed's 1616 atlas.

encouraged by Spain were suppressed, and England resumed its efforts to colonize Irish territories (particularly in the north) that had been abandoned in the early fourteenth century. Ireland continued to be a thorn in the side of the English government, however. In one notable episode, Elizabeth's favorite courtier, Robert Devereux, the Earl of Essex, pressed the Queen for permission to lead an army against an Irish rebellion in 1599 led by the Earl of Tyrone. As had many before him, Essex found Irish resistance stronger than he had expected, was forced to make peace with Tyrone (against the Queen's orders), and returned to London in disgrace. (When he responded to his banishment from court by attempting a coup against the Queen, she suppressed his revolt far more successfully than he had managed to suppress that of Tyrone: Essex was beheaded in 1601.)

The English poet Edmund Spenser spent most of the last twenty years of his life in Ireland, where he had gone in 1580 to take up a position as secretary and aide to the Lord Deputy of Ireland. *A View of the Present State of Ireland*, published posthumously as well as anonymously but generally attributed to Spenser, gives a sense of the brutal force to which the English often resorted in their efforts to break Irish resistance and colonize the land: relocation of entire communities to make way for English settlers, acts of wanton destruction aimed at intimidating the population, and even the destruction of crops were common. Things did not improve in the seventeenth century. When Irish forces revolted in the early 1640s against English brutality and the expropriation of the best land for newly arrived English colonists, a considerable number of English settlers were killed. In response, Oliver Cromwell led an army into Ireland that more than matched the killing spree of the rebels, who were completely defeated by 1650. The 1652 Act of Settlement decreed that expropriations be continued until two-thirds of all Ireland was owned by Englishmen, and that the majority of the Irish population be settled in a single county. These terms were never fully enacted, but enough was done to ensure that Irish resentment of and resistance to English colonial policies would continue far into the future.

In the fifteenth and early sixteenth centuries English and Scottish forces had fought a series of battles, perhaps the most important of which was the English victory at Flodden in 1513, a slaughter that put an end to an early Scottish Renaissance. Despite such defeats Scotland remained an independent kingdom. But as the sixteenth century went on, it was more and more a kingdom with significant internal divisions. Throughout these turbulent times, much of the Highlands of Scotland remained out of the fray: it was a world largely separate from the culture of Edinburgh, but unlike Edinburgh's, a traditional and far less literate clan-based culture. In the Lowland areas (most importantly, the east-west stretch of Lowland in which both Glasgow and Edinburgh are located), English had long been the preferred language, a market economy had taken root, and after 1560 John Knox and his Scottish Presbyterian reformers had assumed a dominant position in society. At this point, as a result of royal marriages, Scotland was technically a province of France; Mary Stuart, Queen of Scotland and Queen Consort of France, had assumed the throne in Scotland and was advancing a claim to be Queen of England too. (Mary resided in France, and—somewhat confusingly for the modern student—was represented in Scotland by her mother, Mary of Guise, who acted as regent.) With French troops entering Scotland it indeed seemed that the English throne might be under threat, but with the assistance of English soldiers and English financing, Knox and the Scots Protestant faction won the day; under the terms of the 1560 Treaty of Edinburgh, French troops left Scotland and Knox's Protestants were left in effective control. Mary, Queen of Scots was allowed to hold the throne in Scotland, but only on the condition that she renounce all claims to that of England. (Mary, a Catholic and cousin to Elizabeth I, in fact never renounced that claim, and remained a thorn in Elizabeth's side until England executed Mary for treason.)

When Mary's son came to the throne as James VI of Scotland, however, and particularly when he also assumed the English throne in 1603 as James I of England, Scotland came to be more and more at peace both within itself and with its southern neighbor. Under James the process that would culminate with the Act of Union of 1707 was very much underway.

Edward VI, Mary I, and Elizabeth I

Henry VIII was succeeded in 1547 by his 10-year-old son, Edward (the third of Henry's wives, Jane Seymour, had finally provided him with a male heir). The boy's uncle, Edward Seymour, Duke of Somerset, acted as Lord Protector. Though Edward's reign was short, it was not uneventful. Edward, his uncle, and other important figures of the time (such as Thomas Cranmer, the Archbishop of Canterbury) were more Protestant than Henry VIII had been, and more influenced by John Calvin. They accelerated the move away from Catholic practices and doctrines that had begun late in Henry's reign.

Edward died in 1553, however, and the move toward Protestantism was thrown into reverse with the accession to the throne of Mary I (not to be confused with the two Marys discussed above, Mary, Queen of Scots and Mary of Guise). Mary, daughter of Henry VIII by Catherine of Aragon, had remained a Roman Catholic and in 1554 married Philip of Spain (later to become Philip II). Among the many controversial measures Mary put into effect were the restoration of the Catholic Mass in Latin, the banning of the newly produced Book of Common Prayer, and the reaffirmation of the authority of the Pope over the Church of England. She earned the grim nickname "Bloody Mary" when she authorized the execution of various Protestant leaders, including Thomas Cranmer at Smithfield, from 1555 to 1558. In all, some 300 men and women were burned at the stake during Mary's reign.[1]

Yet the long-term effect of Mary's rule was to strengthen English Protestantism, and English nationalism as well. The image of the martyrs burnt at Smithfield was etched in the English consciousness through the accounts in John Foxe's *Book of Martyrs* as a lasting image of the evils of Catholic rule, and when in 1558 Mary managed to lose Calais, England's last remaining possession on the continent, in an ill-judged attempt to defend some of her husband's interests on the other side of the English Channel, the loss united

Detail of woodcut illustration showing Thomas Cranmer being burnt at the stake, from the 1563 edition of Foxe's *Book of Martyrs*.

the country against her. She died in November of that same year; as the Elizabethan historian Raphael Holinshed put it shortly thereafter, she had neither "the favor of God, nor the hearts of her subjects, nor the love of her husband." After 25 years of religious turmoil and violence the stage was set for the religious settlement of 1559 and for the long, stable, relatively consistent, and relatively tolerant Protestant reign of Elizabeth I. The stage was set as well for the English to feel an unprecedented sense of confidence and indeed arrogance as to their place in the world; this, said Foxe in his *Book of Martyrs*, was an "elect nation."

Elizabeth I and Gender

Perhaps the best known gender-related comment of the sixteenth and early seventeenth centuries is John Knox's 1557 outburst against "this monstrous regiment of women" ("regiment" here means rule). Knox, the Scottish Protestant leader, was at odds not only with Mary, Queen of Scots, and her regent, Mary of Guise (Mary's French mother), but also with Mary I, Queen of England: all of them Catholic, all of them opposed

---

[1] Appalling as this number is, numbers in some areas of continental Europe were far higher; somewhere in the neighborhood of 6,000 people accused of heresy were burned by Charles V in the Low Countries.

Artist unknown, *Henry VIII at the Opening of Parliament*, 1523. In this watercolor drawing the King is seated below the royal coat of arms, wearing his crown and holding the scepter, his feet resting on a cushion. To his right (i.e., to the left of the picture) are Archbishop Warham of Canterbury and Cardinal Wolsey. Before him two earls hold the cap of maintenance and the sword of state. Dukes wear coronets; other peers of the realm wear hats; to the left nine bishops (in red) and seventeen black abbots wear their miters.

Detail from *Londinum Feracissimi Angliae Regni Metropolis*, the bird's eye view of London in Georg Braun's atlas *Orbis Terrarum*, c. 1574. The view is believed to show London as it was c. 1558. An image of the full map appears on the facing page.

Map of London from *Orbis Terrarum*, c. 1574. (A detail is enlarged on the facing page.)

Artist unknown, untitled watercolor depicting food being served during a game of cards, early seventeenth century (Folger Shakespeare Library). A companion watercolor image is reproduced in the "Culture: A Portfolio" section elsewhere in this volume.

Artist unknown, *Queen Elizabeth I.*

Artist unknown, *William Cecil, Lord Burghley,*
c. 1585. Burghley was for many years Queen
Elizabeth's most trusted and powerful civil servant.

Artist unknown, *Lady Jane Dudley (née Grey)*, c. 1550.

Isaac Oliver, *Portrait of a Young Man*, c. 1590–95. This miniature portrait of an unidentified man is one of the most famous Renaissance paintings. The full length miniature, first developed by Oliver in the 1580s, allowed the artist to depict a background to the figure and to hint at narrative elements. Here, for example, we see the young man's melancholy expression, his one discarded glove, and his isolated position on a rock overlooking an unidentified garden background, where two figures are walking. Horace Walpole suggested in the eighteenth century that the young man depicted here could be statesman and poet Sir Philip Sidney; however, no evidence has been found to support this theory.

Attributed to David des Granges, *The Salsonstall Family*, 1630s. The painting anachronistically shows Sir Richard Salsonstall together with both his first wife (who died in childbirth) and his second wife (shown at right holding her child), as well as his two children.

Anthony Van Dyck, *Charles I on Horseback with Seigneur de St. Antoine*, 1633. De St. Antoine was the king's riding master. This portrait was widely admired in its time; one contemporary commented that, "if our eyes alone were to be believed they would boldly assert that the King himself is alive in the portrait."

Samuel Cooper, *Oliver Cromwell*, 1649. This, the earliest portrait of Cromwell known to exist, dates from the year in which Charles I was executed.

to most of the reforms for which Knox was pressing. (Ironically, Knox was one of the very few to advocate universal education for females as well as for males.) He found the Protestant regime of Elizabeth I, who came to the English throne the next year, considerably less monstrous, but his phrase has retained currency as a memorable expression of the almost universal feeling among men in the sixteenth and seventeenth centuries that it was far more appropriate for men to rule over women than for a woman to "reign and have empire above men" (in Knox's words). To the extent that a woman was perceived by men to have intelligence or good judgment in matters of state, men tended also to think of her as manly.

Elizabeth I was a figure who both exemplified conventional notions of gender and stood as the great exception. From the moment she came to the throne in 1558 she ruled with diplomacy, but also with sure-handed authority. Against a background of the violent upheavals of Mary's reign, of many Catholics continuing to hold positions of influence (including control of the House of Lords), of militant Protestants pressing to establish a "perfect school of Christ" throughout the land and controlling the House of Commons, and against threats from abroad (particularly from the powerful Catholic monarchy in Spain), Elizabeth dexterously negotiated a religious settlement that established a stable, relatively moderate Protestant state. She negotiated compromises with Parliament that resulted in a Supremacy Bill of 1559 that established her as "Supreme Governor" of the Church of England (not "Supreme Head," a more controversial title) and reintroduced the Book of Common Prayer. In 1563 she set out the Thirty-nine Articles, the theological foundation of the Church of England, further establishing religious uniformity. It was mandated that there were to be 9,000 parishes (in theory, enabling everyone in England to walk to church), and a hierarchy was maintained in the Church so that the world of faith continued to mirror the world of politics. The Church of England was established as a national church, and attendance was far from voluntary. By the standards of the time, however, Elizabeth was no extremist: while some "heretics" were executed, the relative religious calm of her reign is set in stark relief by comparison to the continent, where over

Portrait of Elizabeth I, from the manuscript miscellany of Thomas Trevelyon. Trevelyon's collection includes a record of important events of each year, decorative alphabets, and embroidery patterns, as well as a variety of other portraits.

the same period invasion, slaughter, and religious turmoil remained the norm.

It should not be imagined that the Elizabethan Settlement satisfied everyone. Many, often called "Recusants," felt varying degrees of loyalty to Rome, a loyalty that led some to flee to the continent and others to risk their lives by committing such crimes as hiding Catholic priests or encouraging the Catholic underground press. Many others, on the other hand, felt strongly that the new Church, with its retention of the old hierarchy of bishops and lower clergy, with a liturgy still closely modeled on that of the Catholic Mass, and with many other trappings of the old Church, had been insufficiently purged of Catholic elements. In such feelings were sown the seeds of Puritanism, the movement for greater "purity" of religion that would form one side of the religious debate that reached its zenith under Oliver Cromwell during the civil wars and led some to leave England for the Americas. Under Elizabeth, though, the tenor of such opposition was as yet one of resentment rather than revolution.

If diplomacy on Elizabeth's part was essential to reach a religious settlement, a willingness to exercise power ruthlessly was sometimes necessary to maintain it. As Elizabeth repeatedly demonstrated (perhaps most dramatically in her reluctant decision to sign the death warrant of her cousin, Mary, Queen of Scots, when evidence seemed to suggest that Mary had been involved in a Catholic plot against her), she was prepared to do whatever was necessary to remain in power and maintain the peace. And when war with Spain became inevitable, she marshaled sufficient financial and military resources to enable her commanders to stave off the threat. After some wavering, she sent troops to France to help Henri IV battle his Catholic enemies and other troops to help the Netherlands in their revolt against Spain.

Yet for all her sure-handedness in exercising power, Elizabeth contrived to remain throughout her reign an icon of female virtues—although of course stressing the virginal ideal, not the maternal, as Elizabeth never married or had children. In part this was possible through a sleight-of-hand accomplished by lawyers and other advisors who, exploiting the old concept of the "king's two bodies," theorized that the Queen embodied an immortal "body politic" that was without gender and without defect, together with a "body natural" that was entirely human in character. Yet despite some grumblings over her refusal to marry and some evidence of exasperation with her tendency to delay, Elizabeth was for the most part admired, even worshiped, as both a woman and a monarch. She built up around her a glittering court and a culture of courtesy, grace, performance, and display that fostered an extraordinarily productive cultural outpouring, and that glorified (if sometimes with subtle reservations) her own person as the center around which all else revolved. Elizabeth, Edmund Spenser explained in the letter to Sir Walter Ralegh that accompanied *The Faerie Queene*, was both Belphœbe, a beautiful maiden who represent-ed the Queen as a woman, and Gloriana, who represented the "most excellent and glorious person of our sovereign the queene and her kingdome in Faery

land." Elizabeth was thus both a woman and a queen, a *virgin* queen. Much as she had ample romantic and political opportunity to marry, and much as her advisors pressed her to remember the importance of producing an heir, Elizabeth must have realized that marriage would entail a loss of power, and a loss too of the special aura that had grown up around her. For most women in English society, marriage brought a loss of power: whereas a single woman could act as a legal entity in owning property or being a party to legal agreements, all such rights passed over on marriage to the husband. Elizabeth's situation as monarch was of course different, but even for her, marriage would have brought with it an expectation of submission to male authority.

Nor was it only marriage that would have brought a diminution of authority: for Elizabeth to have openly acknowledged her sexuality in any way other than the virginal would have badly damaged her mystique.

Why did "virgin" resonate so differently in the late sixteenth and early seventeenth centuries than it does today? Some have suggested that the bifurcation in many male minds of opinions concerning woman—a bifurcation that had taken strong hold in the late-medieval period—may have deepened in the sixteenth century. Certainly that was a dichotomy with wide-ranging roots, some of which may be found in Christian traditions of ambivalence toward sex. Along with the growth in the exaltation of the Virgin Mary in the late-medieval period had grown a widespread (albeit far from universal) habit of venerating woman only if in a "pure" or asexual state. Alongside that paradigm had grown its polar opposite, one in which womanhood was associated with temptation, impure sexuality, and fleshly sin. Too often perhaps, little lay in between. Yet the issue is resistant to easy explanation; the dangers of oversimplification in this area cannot be too strongly stressed. The Reformation in general led to an increased emphasis on the virtues of marriage, and Protestant England in particular vigorously privileged marriage. Throughout the period the Church accepted the reality of sexuality for most people (to offer only one example, a marriage could be annulled if a wife refused to have sexual relations with her husband); indeed, outright rejection of the flesh would have been heretical. That said, disgust with the flesh did certainly remain widespread—and some found it easy to project upon the female objects of their lust the disgust or anxiety that their culture had encouraged them to feel not so much about woman *per se*, but about sexual desire. Such misogynistic projections, all too common in other forms around the globe, remained a staple of English culture in the late sixteenth century (and are of course not dead yet). When poets thought of "false love" as Walter Ralegh did, for example, in terms of "a gilded hook that holds a poisoned bait," many found it hard to resist locating the source of the poison in women rather than in their male speakers.[1] Seventeenth-century male writers also not infrequently sexualized religious controversy by reading the religious other as problematically female; Ben Jonson parodies such rhetoric when he has his Puritan character, Tribulation, speak of standing up "against the menstruous cloth and rag of Rome," referring to the deep red vestments worn by the clergy in the Roman Catholic Church. And early seventeenth-century popular pamphlets such as Joseph Swetnam's *An Arraignment of Lewd, Idol, Froward, and Unconstant Women* (1615) excited considerable controversy over their attacks on women.

What did women think of all this? The literature of the period is overwhelmingly male-authored, but a few female voices found their way into print. Aemilia Lanyer (1569–1645), for example, one of the first women in England to publish her own poems (and to have obtained patronage in the way that was conventional for male poets), put forward in her *Salve Deus Rex Judaeorum* a bold and cogent denial that Eve was chiefly to blame for the Fall of Man: "Your fault being greater," she asked, "why should you disdain our being your equals, free from tyranny?" Swetnam was also answered directly by Rachel Speght and others, and even figured in a play devoted to his discomfiture. It is probably as unwise to read the texts in this "querelle des femmes" with utter seriousness (some are riotous and hyperbolic in the way of much Renaissance satire) as it would be to dismiss the reality of the issues and the subtle thought that the (often female) defenders of women writers put into their arguments.

English Noblewomen. Detail of an engraving c. 1582 by Flemish artist Georg Hoefnagel.

In sum, expressions of misogyny in Renaissance England were not always utterly serious and were countered by other voices, both male and female—but misogyny was nevertheless a daily reality. Women, even rich and well-born women, lived with what by modern standards were severe restrictions, legally and socially, on what they could do or be. That so many middle- and upper-class women did manage to write, to learn, to influence political, religious, and cultural life is both a testament to their determination and a reminder that social status was often just as important as gender in determining what a person could or could not do.[2]

Modern scholarship has extensively explored these issues; in recent years it has also recognized more fully the ways in which sexuality and gender are not entirely

---

[1] It should be noted, however, that in many such instances what may look like misogyny in the work of sophisticated poets may be tempered by irony and self-mockery.

[2] The restrictions imposed upon the poor, indeed, were more severe than were gender-based restrictions.

essential, but are mediated by the larger culture. For example, recent studies have explored the frequent sixteenth- and seventeenth-century assumption, derived from ancient medical theories, that women are the same as men but, so to speak, inside out and born without enough vital heat to "perfect" them into maleness. And scholars have explored a number of aspects of the history of sexual behavior during the period. It appears, for example, that although sodomy as such was illegal (and loosely defined), the laws against it were not rigorously enforced. Research suggests too that the early modern period was much less anxious than were the next several centuries about the auto-erotic. Thomas Nashe's notorious "Choice of Valentines"—also known as "Nashe's Dildo"—is an important literary example here. (Though Nashe's work was not published at the time, early modern curiosity about masturbation, particularly that by women, is also evident in other literature of the period, both in England and on the continent.)

HOMOEROTICISM AND TRANSGENDERING

Research of the past generation has also increased our appreciation of the ways in which same-sex desire is mediated by history and by culture, and our awareness of the complexity of the issues involved. In any historical or cultural context it is important to distinguish between homosexuality (the definition of which is likely to vary from era to era, even within the same culture), and a broader homoeroticism that might or might not entail physical desire or behavior—and that again is shaped by history and culture. In reading back into history it is far from easy for the modern reader always to draw such distinctions reliably.[1]

That said, one of the most striking developments of English literature of the early modern period is the widespread appearance of same-sex eroticism. Not surprisingly, given the transgressive nature of such love at the time, it does so in an often conflicted or

ambiguous fashion, frequently adopting as a model the conventions of male-female love. In Shakespeare's twentieth sonnet, for example—one of the sonnets that first indicates his speaker's love of another man as a central theme—the poet exploits some of the tropes of Petrarchan poetry in contrasting this love with that of "false" women:

A woman's face with Nature's own hand painted
Hast thou, the master-mistress of my passion;
A woman's gentle heart, but not acquainted
With shifting change, as is false women's fashion;
An eye more bright than theirs, less false in rolling.

The poem is perhaps the most famous expression of ambiguity in Shakespeare's sonnets, one that both admits and denies simultaneously. The lover imagines his beloved, the "master mistress of my passion" as once a woman, although less false than women are, but remade by Nature into a man. Since, says the speaker, Nature has "added one thing [i.e., a penis] to my purpose nothing" and "pricked him out" to be male, women can have the use of his body and the speaker can have his love. At first this seems like a denial that the love in question is homosexual or even homoerotic, but as recent critics have been quick to point out, the puns on "nothing" (slang for vagina) and "prick" (slang for a penis) make the denial look far less certain.

The nature of homoeroticism in literature was not always openly acknowledged by the writers of the time even when it was openly expressed. Of some of his clearly homoerotic sonnets, for example, Richard Barnfield offered utterly implausible denials of the clear sense of his verse, saying that he had merely been trying to write like Virgil. (Imitating the classics proved to be useful in giving homoerotic verse a good cover story, so to speak; by taking as his model Virgil's second eclogue, for instance, Marlowe could make his shepherd's invitation to "Come Live with Me" less certainly addressed to a female "nymph.") But the ground-breaking literary expressions are quite real. In this as in so many other respects Shakespeare and Marlowe (in this case along with Barnfield, a much lesser poet) were pioneers; in the 1590s they are the first literary figures we know of to write openly and unequivocally

[1] For example, the late fourteenth-century expressions of love by the famous theologian Anselm of Bec, while making no explicit sexual references, are as fervent when addressed to men as they are when addressed to women; these expressions of love may well have been written without sexual intent, but are likely to seem to modern readers as if they were highly charged with eroticism.

homoerotic literature.[1] Marlowe imagines Neptune making a pass at the naked young Leander as he swims the Hellespont in the poem *Hero and Leander*, and in his play *Edward II* depicts the King's alienation from his kingdom and his wife in direct consequence of being "love sick for this minion," Lord Gaveston. (In the end Edward is reduced to a despairing hope that he may have "some nook or corner left / To frolic with" his "dearest Gaveston.") Barnfield is more explicit, whatever his odd denials in his prefatory material, about the transgressive nature of the desires being expressed: "If it be sin to love a lovely lad / Oh then sin I."

We have only minimal evidence as to whether the homoerotic expressions of feeling by any of these poets extended beyond the literary. In the case of Shakespeare, at least, we know that such expressions did not preclude marriage and children. More generally, we know that "cross-over" activity of several sorts was characteristic of the age. When Marlowe's Gaveston paints an idyllic picture of the world he desires, for example, it is one featuring "men like satyrs grazing on the lawns" but also young men resembling women:

> Sometime a lovely boy in Diane's shape,
> With hair that guilds the water as it glides,
> Crownets of pearl about his naked arms,
> And in his sportful hands an olive tree,
> To hide those parts which men delight to see …

The place of female homoeroticism, let alone lesbianism, in sixteenth-century England is largely unclear. What we call "lesbianism" was certainly recognized in the early modern period, although the vocabulary differed from our own (a woman involved with another woman was more often called a "tribade" than "lesbian" or "Sapphic"). In general such love seems to have aroused much less anxiety than did male same-sex love. It did arouse curiosity, but there remained a good deal of ignorance as to the realities of same-sex love; it seems to have been a widespread assumption, for example, that same-sex love amongst women would inevitably entail such sex aids as dildos.

Despite some vague flirtations with the topic by Spenser (a woman falls in love with his armed female knight in Book III of *The Faerie Queene*, for example) and by Shakespeare (in whose plays the matter of gender and sexuality is complicated by the fact that boy actors took the roles of women, with effects that are not entirely clear from this historical distance), female-female eroticism is much less evident in the literature of the late sixteenth and early seventeenth centuries than is its male counterpart. One of the few extant literary expressions of such feeling is an elegy by John Donne, that perhaps takes as a model some French poems, in which Sappho expresses her homoerotic longing for her friend "Philaenis." Somewhat later in the seventeenth century, however, representations of such desire begin to appear in some profusion, particularly in the visual arts. In literature the most widely discussed seventeenth-century representations of such desire, more ambiguously expressed, appear in Katherine Philips's poems to her "dearest Lucasia." Philips writes that "there's a religion in our love"; it remains uncertain whether such love is homosexual, homoerotic, or the expression of intense female bonding, a celebration of friendship that may seem more sexual to a modern eye than it seemed at the time. (It is wise to remember that powerful declarations of friendship were less likely to be read as homoerotic in early modern times than they are now, whatever the actual psychodynamics involved.)

---

[1] The importance of this aspect of Shakespeare's writing has only relatively recently begun to be fully and openly acknowledged. The 1609 publication of the sonnets excited no comment that has come down to us. Though some eighteenth-century editions of Shakespeare included the sonnets, others omitted them on clearly homophobic grounds. George Stevens, for example, the editor of a multi-volume edition of Shakespeare's works published in 1793, declared that it was "impossible to read this fulsome panegyric, addressed to a male object, without an equal measure of disgust and indignation." In the nineteenth century some (such as Robert Browning) regarded Shakespeare as representing a pinnacle in the history of sonnet writing in English, but others were distressed. Henry Hallam, for example, found it "impossible not to wish that Shakespeare had never written" the sonnets. And as late as 1930 published comments continued to allude with discomfort to the poems' homoeroticism: as Herbert Thurston wrote in that year, "regretfully as we must say it, the sonnets in their plain and obvious meaning point to a plague spot." It is only relatively recently, then, that the homoeroticism of the sonnets has ceased to be regarded as a taint—and that the poems themselves have been accepted unequivocally and universally as central to the Shakespearian canon. Some in the general public, though, are still taken aback to discover that, for example, the sonnet "Let me not to the marriage of true minds admit impediment" does not refer to heterosexual marriage.

A common literary motif throughout the period is the assumption by a protagonist of a transgendered role. One of the male heroes of Sir Philip Sidney's *Arcadia*, for example, assumes a female disguise as an "Amazon" and is even identified as "she" for the greater part of that work. Shakespeare, too, imagines strong and resourceful female figures (played of course by boys) who at some point pretend to be men, such as Viola in *Twelfth Night*, Rosalind in *As You Like It*, Portia in *The Merchant of Venice*, and Helena in *All's Well That Ends Well*. Evidently such behavior existed occasionally in real life as well, although not so much among the well-born: Moll Cutpurse, the lead character of *The Roaring Girl*, a popular 1611 comedy by Thomas Dekker and Thomas Middleton, seems to have been modeled on Mary Frith, a woman notorious for (among other things) dressing as a man.

ECONOMY AND SOCIETY IN THE SIXTEENTH AND SEVENTEENTH CENTURIES

Economic life in Britain over this period was as paradoxical as it was two centuries later during what we now call the Industrial Revolution. Although there was nothing like the explosion of technology in the late eighteenth and nineteenth centuries, there were revolutionary changes in the economy and in industry—"industry" in the sense of how people worked, at what they worked, how much they worked, and what they received in exchange for their labor. The roots of these changes extend back into the fourteenth and fifteenth centuries. The Black Death in 1348–49 wiped out at least a third and perhaps as much as half of the population; the best guess is that the population of Britain did not recover to its pre-1348 levels until the seventeenth century. That catastrophic drop in population led to a surplus of grain (or, to be more precise, a surplus in grain-growing capacity) in the rural areas, and to a labor shortage in the towns as well as on the land. Inevitably, many young people were lured to the towns by the prospect of work in one or another of a variety of trades, and despite the best efforts of the

authorities, real wages for such work increased significantly through the later Middle Ages. Whereas in the mid-fourteenth century the economy of England had still been overwhelmingly agricultural, with most rents paid "in kind" (in the form of grain or other agricultural goods) rather than in money, by the end of the sixteenth century approximately half the English population relied entirely on money wages.

But if some were lured to the towns, others were driven there by a process usually referred to as "enclosure." Under the feudal system, those who worked the land did not own it. As large land holders decided that their fields could be put to use more profitably as grazing land for cattle or, especially, sheep, those lands that had typically been without hedges, fences, or other means of enclosure, and farmed on a largely communal basis by the peasantry, were enclosed, thereby depriving many of their livelihood.[1] John Rous, chaplain to the Earl of Warwick in the late fifteenth and early sixteenth centuries, described what happened in such circumstances with chilling concision: "all the inhabitants were expelled." To Rous, the plagues of former times were now being succeeded by a "plague of avarice," and he was far from alone in his outrage; indeed, enclosure was condemned by a chorus of voices in the fifteenth and early sixteenth centuries. When a character in More's *Utopia* says that nowadays sheep eat men, he captures in one comic and yet horrifying expression the full effect of enclosures. The pace of enclosures in fact slowed considerably in the first half of the sixteenth century (with the exception of a period following the dissolution of the monasteries and the distribution by Henry VIII of many of their lands to his allies among the gentry and nobility). But the growth in population now meant that there was often a surplus of labor in the towns. Real wages for the majority were in decline through most of the sixteenth century, reaching their nadir in the late sixteenth and early seventeenth centuries.

---

[1] Economic matters were of course the primary issues of concern here, but they were not the only ones: in 1514, for example, London apprentices protested the enclosure of open fields outside the city, which they had traditionally used for sports and games, by tearing up the newly planted hedges.

Claes Jansz Visscher, detail from a panoramic view of London (1616). "The Bear Garden" and "The Globe" are both identified on the south bank of the Thames.

The practice of enclosure was particularly common in the south of England; a large proportion of the wool from sheep raised on the enclosed pastureland was exported to Flanders and in particular to Antwerp, center of the cloth industry. By the early sixteenth century the English economy had become to a large degree based on the trade of raw materials—lead, iron, tin, and coal as well as wool and livestock. That pattern now began to change, with considerable growth, particularly in the textile industry. (Many weavers from Flanders had immigrated to England in pursuit of cheaper wool.) Many finished goods were still imported, but towns in both England and Scotland were diversifying and acquiring new economic capabilities. This tendency toward specialization and division of labor often involved entire towns as well as individuals. Thus Newcastle was known for coal production, Coventry and Norwich for textile production, Northampton for leather goods, Glasgow and Perth for various sorts of manufacturing, and Edinburgh for silverware and jewelery. By far the greatest diversification (and the greatest growth) occurred in London, which grew from a population of about 50,000 in 1500, to about 100,000 in 1570, to about 200,000 in 1600, and to 500,000 in 1650, becoming what was probably the largest city in the world.[1] Such growth was a mixed blessing. Despite the "bill of sewers" put forward under the auspices of Thomas More and passed by Parliament in 1531, sanitation could not keep up with population growth, and much of London had a foul smell most of the time. It also became a city largely blackened by soot; the introduction of chimneys in the mid-sixteenth century enabled households and businesses alike to switch from wood fires to coal—a more efficient heat source, but also more polluting.

By comparison, other urban centers, despite their growth, were tiny. In the late sixteenth century Norwich had a population of approximately 13,000; Edinburgh, Dublin, Bristol, and Newcastle each had approximately 10,000; and Glasgow, Exeter, York, Coventry, and Limerick all had about 5,000. The population of England as a whole seems to have risen from something over 2,000,000 in the early sixteenth century, to about 4,000,000 by 1600, to over 5,000,000 in the mid-seventeenth century. Over the same period, the population of Scotland rose from about 600,000 to perhaps 900,000 by 1600; that of Wales went from just under 250,000 to over 400,000; and that of Ireland from around 1,000,000 to around 1,500,000. In England the percentage of the population living in urban areas thus increased from something like 5 per cent in 1500 to between 10 and 15 per cent in the mid-seventeenth century.

This 1762 watercolor by Richard Greene, one of the earliest representations of the house in Stratford-Upon-Avon where Shakespeare was born, provides a clear image of the half-timbered style of sixteenth- and seventeenth-century urban architecture in England.

For city dwellers, even more than for rural folk, life was a perilous business. Roughly half of all those born did not reach adulthood. If one were lucky enough to get through one's teens, one might expect to live until "old age"—but "old age" was typically regarded as beginning at 50. Overall life expectancy with infant mortality taken into account was about 30. As a result of poor sanitation, mortality rates—particularly for infants—were higher in London. And so too was the risk of violence; though the level of violent crime has sometimes been exaggerated, its threat was a real presence, particularly during periods when the population had been swollen even more than usual by impoverished new arrivals, or when a larger than normal number of unemployed apprentices were roaming the streets.

---

[1] The populations of London and of England as a whole were of course still modest by modern standards, and it is unsurprising that so many of the leading figures of the day were acquainted with one another.

If a shift of people, of economic activity, and of wealth to the cities was one trend throughout the sixteenth and seventeenth centuries, a similar shift from the north to the south of England was another. The Wars of the Roses in the fifteenth century had drained the resources of a substantial proportion of the nobility of northern and western England, and the dissolution of the monasteries (which had been widely distributed throughout the realm) in the 1530s further depleted concentrations of wealth in the North and the Midlands. The southern concentration of the wool and textile industries then had the effect of increasing the shift of wealth from north to south. The merchant traders of Kingston upon Hull voiced a complaint of a sort common throughout the north when they blamed London for the decline of their own business:

> Item, by means of the said companies (the government whereof is ruled only in the city of London) all the whole trade of merchandise is in a manner brought to the city of London; whereby all the wealthy chapmen and the best clothiers are drawn to London, and other ports have in a manner no traffic, but falleth to a great decay, the smart where we feel in our port of Kingston upon Hull.

There was likewise a disparity between social and economic developments in England and those in Scotland, Wales, and Ireland. In the Lowlands of Scotland (and in particular the towns of Edinburgh, Glasgow, and Perth) the pattern of development was not dissimilar to that of southern England, but in the Scottish Highlands small-scale agriculture continued to be the dominant mode of production, and the families of the nobility were often consumed in blood feuds. In Ireland there was a similar dichotomy, with economic growth and diversification in towns such as Cork, Waterford, and Limerick as well as in Dublin (and in the Pale generally), while other areas remained virtually untouched by economic change.

Much as the lot of the dispossessed and of wage laborers was often desperately unhappy, the economic turmoil of the sixteenth and early seventeenth centuries also brought to many others a level of prosperity that by the mid-seventeenth century was unprecedented; per capita, Britain in 1650 was the wealthiest nation in the world. How to explain this extraordinary economic growth? Part of the answer, some have argued, is Protestantism. At the heart of Calvinist belief in predestination and the "community of the elect" lies a widely noted paradox: for all of Luther's and especially Calvin's emphasis on the inherent sinfulness of humanity, the doctrines of predestination and of salvation through faith alone can in practice encourage self-confidence and a focus on the pursuit of prosperity. Not surprisingly, most people preferred to see themselves as elect and, despite warnings of Calvin and others, to read prosperity as a sign of God's approval. As the sociologist Max Weber put it a century ago in his famous analysis of this effect, *The Protestant Ethic and the Spirit of Capitalism*, Calvinist theology "in practice means God helps those who help themselves." (To be sure, primarily Catholic lands such as France and Italy also witnessed an increased accumulation and manipulation of capital; one did not need to be a Calvinist to be a smart merchant or a canny investor.)

The impact of Protestantism—especially in its Calvinist and Puritan strains—on economic life was no less powerful as a result of being indirect in its operation. Protestant cultures often showed an aversion to "sloth," and while many did not share a "Puritan" disapproval of traditional sports, games, the theater, and other pastimes, the period saw a substantial reduction in leisure time. Though "vacations" in the modern sense were unknown, it had become customary by the end of the Middle Ages not only to observe Sunday as a day of rest but also to celebrate a very large number of religious holidays (many of them in honor of saints that Protestants rejected)—so much so that some economic historians have calculated that a third of the year's 365 days may for most people have been leisure time in the early sixteenth century. Such was not the case by the late seventeenth century.

A further indirect but powerful influence on economic life was the Protestant emphasis on literacy. The initial motivation here was religious; in this respect Luther and Calvin (and many later Protestants) followed the evangelical (if also humanist) hopes of scholars such as Erasmus, who had declared that he wished that "even the weakest woman should read the Gospel ... and I wish that [the books of the New Testament] were translated into all the languages so that they might be read and understood, not only by

Scots and Irishmen, but also by Turks and Saracens.... I long that the husbandman should sing portions to himself as he follows the plough, that the weaver should hum them to the tune of his shuttle." But the literacy that was useful to a clearer understanding of the faith was also useful at work—for women as well as for men. Erasmus's dream of the rural husbandman who could read did not become a reality in this period; most of the rural population in the sixteenth and early seventeenth centuries remained illiterate. But in the towns there was a steady increase in the percentage of the population that could read and write. Thomas More's estimate in the 1530s that half the population could do so was probably high, but by the mid-sixteenth century almost all the aristocracy and landed gentry were literate, and by the early seventeenth century it is likely that more than half the adult population in the towns could read and write, certainly including a high percentage of merchants, shopkeepers, and their wives, who would often assist with bookkeeping. (Significantly, it was through merchant subsidy that the first municipal libraries in England were started, early in the seventeenth century.)

Religious change may have helped to create a climate conducive to economic transformation, but on its own it could neither create nor maintain the actual engines of capitalism. The sixteenth and seventeenth centuries in England saw these engines—at once exhilarating and appalling in the ferocity of their operation—being forged. At the most fundamental level, capitalism is a series of means of transferring financial resources from those unable or unwilling to use it productively to those who can exploit such resources to create a financial return. Until well into the sixteenth century, the wealthy (like the monarch) tended to store whatever wealth they were not planning to spend in the form of gold in the Tower of London. An important exception was the large stock of gold and silver valuables in the possession of the monasteries. The dissolution of the monasteries in the 1530s—and the distribution of their wealth to various of the nobility and the gentry—substantially increased the available supply of gold and silver, and with it demand for goldsmiths and silversmiths to fashion or refashion precious metal into a variety of forms. Sometime in the early seventeenth century many goldsmiths began as a service to offer to keep supplies of gold in whatever form in their vaults. They soon realized that only a very small percentage of the amounts they were holding for safe keeping would be removed by the owners over the course of any given period; with that in mind they began to lend out the "unused" gold themselves (or, as time went by, use promissory notes in lieu of the gold itself). The precedent for this sort of activity had been set on the continent: the first public bank is thought to have been founded in Venice in 1587, and the Bank of Amsterdam was founded in 1609. The development of banking in England was accelerated by the actions of Charles I in the 1630s. Adamantly refusing to summon Parliament, Charles was thus unable to raise funds to carry on the activities of the government (or of warfare) through what was by then the usual means, by passage of an Act of Parliament. One means to which he resorted in his desperation was simply to appropriate for the Crown gold belonging to others that had been stored in the Tower of London. Not surprisingly, the practice of keeping one's gold in the Tower became much less common thereafter, and the amounts stored with the goldsmiths of London (and thus available to be loaned out) greatly increased. Though the Bank of England itself would not be founded until 1694, in practice something resembling modern banking had by then been present in England for close to a century. Ben Jonson's *Volpone* (1607), set in Venice but informed very largely by the economic realities of the time in England, gives some sense of the workings of the English economic world, or at least of how they could be satirically imagined, and of the importance of credit to their operation. Early in the play Volpone declares that he rejects the "common way" of earning a living:

> ... I use no trade, no venture;
> I ruin no earth with plowshares, Fat no beasts
> To feed the shambles [slaughterhouse]; have no
>   mills for iron,
> Oil, corn, or men, to grind them into powder;
> I blow no subtle glass, expose no ships
> To threat'nings of the furrow-faced sea;
> I turn no monies in the public bank,
> Nor usurer private....

That "usurer private" was a well-known practice in the early seventeenth century is evident from a variety of literary sources. In *The Warring Girl*, for example, Sir Davy Dapper is described as "damned a usurer as ever was among Jews: if he were sure his father's skin would yield him any money, he would, when he dies, flea it off, and sell it to cover drums for children at Bartholomew Fair." Almost always spoken of in derogatory terms, and almost always associated with Jews,[1] moneylending was nevertheless becoming a more and more common practice throughout Christian society—and was thereby facilitating the very substantial economic growth of the seventeenth century.

Economic transformation brought with it massive change to England's class structure, if not always in legal definition then in social reality (to be a gentleman with a right to bear a coat of arms was a legal matter, and only the Crown could create a nobleman no matter what a person's fortune or fame). Much as the physical mobility of the labor force was wrenching and economically unfulfilling for many, for a considerable number of others the turmoil opened possibilities for real if usually limited social mobility. A 1508 legal document gives something of the flavor of what was possible, describing one Thomas Spring of the town of Lavenham in Suffolk as "cloth worker alias yeoman alias gentleman alias merchant." Spring had been accepted into the gentry (with the rank of Esquire) by the time he died, and his son was knighted. Perhaps the fullest literary expression in the late sixteenth century of such aspirations is to be found in the prose fiction of Thomas Deloney. Unlike most of the prose fiction writers from early in the century, Deloney had the benefit neither of a privileged background nor a university education; he was a silk weaver from Norwich who became well known in the early 1590s as a writer of ballads. Between 1596 and 1600 he produced four short works of prose fiction, all of which

were extraordinarily popular. Deloney referred to aristocrats as "idle butterflies" and, whereas the norm for aspiring writers was to dedicate works to prominent members of the nobility in the hope of obtaining patronage from them, Deloney dedicated *Jack of Newbury* "to all famous cloth workers in England":

> Among all manual arts used in this land, none is more famous for desert or more beneficial to the commonwealth than is the most necessary art of clothing; and therefore as the benefit thereof is great, so are the professors of the same to be both loved and maintained.
>
> [… This] excellent commodity … half being and yet is the nourishing of many thousands of poor people. Wherefore to you, most worthy clothiers, do I dedicate this my rude work, which hath raised out of the dust of forgetfulness a most famous and worthy man, whose name was John Winchcomb, alias Jack of Newbury, of whose life and love I have briefly written, and in a plain and humble manner that it may be the better understood of those for whose sake I take pains to compile it. That is, for the well minded clothiers, that herein they may behold the great worship and credit which men of this trade have in former time come unto.

As the dedication suggests, Deloney challenges both literary convention and the significance of social class not by emphasizing the degree to which a wage worker is downtrodden, but by imagining the possibility that he may rise to become like Jack of Newbury who, although no gentleman born (or even a gentleman made), nevertheless "set continually 500 poor people at work to the great benefit of the commonwealth" through his success as a clothier, and who "had the choice of many wives—men's daughters of good credit and widows of great wealth." To his credit, Newbury chooses none of those but rather "one of his own servants,… knowing her careful in her business, faithful in her dealing and an excellent good housewife." It is telling from a number of angles that *Jack of Newbury* continued to be enormously popular throughout the seventeenth century.

---

[1] Both during the Middle Ages before the expulsion of the Jews under Edward I, and after Cromwell's decision to re-admit them to England, Jews were barred from seeking employment in most occupations (and from all professions considered respectable); one of the few trades a Jew could legally pursue was that of moneylender.

¶A briefe content of certaine clauses

of the Statutes of King Henrie the eyght, and Queene Marie,
with some moderation thereof, and other prouisions to be obserued,
according to her Maiesties Proclamation
aboue mentioned.

¶Mens apparell.

None shall weare in his apparell—

Sylke of the colour Purple, cloth of Golde, or Siluer Tissued, nor Furre of Sables. } Under the degree of an Earle.

Cloth of Golde, Siluer, or Tinsell Satten.
Sylke, Cloth, Canuas, or any stuffe in any apparell, that shalbe myxed or imbrodered with any Gold or Siluer. } Under the degree of a Baron.

Woollen clothe made out of the Realme, sauing in Cappes only.
Veluet { Crymson, Carnation, or Blewe.
Scarlet cloth.
Furres of { Blacke Jenets, or Luzernes.
Imbroderie, or Taylers worke, hauing Golde, or Siluer, or Pearle therin. Nor any Enamell, Muske, Ambergrece, Agate, or any other pretious Stone, in Chayne, Button, or Aglet. Nor any Dublet, Jerkin, or other apparel of any stuffe perfumed. } Under the degree of { A knight of the order, one of the priuie Counsel, or a Gentleman of the priuie Chamber.

Gownes, Clokes, Capes, or other vppermost garments } of Veluet.
Furres of Libardes.
Imbroderie, or Taylers woorke like to imbroderie, with Sylke, Bugle, or any other like thing.
Nor any Cappes, Hats, Hatbandes, Capbands, Garters, Bootehose, trymmed with } Golde or Syluer.
Or Sylke neather Stockes.
Shertes, Shertbardes { garnished, mixte, or wrought with Golde.
Ruffes made or wrought out of Englande, commonly called Cutworke. } Under the degree of { A Barons sonne, a knight, & Gentleman in ordinarie office, attending vpon her Maiesties person, or persons that are assessed in the last subsidy books at. CC. li. lands, or fees.

None shall weare—
Spurres,
Swordes,
Rapiers,
Skaynes,
Woodknyues, or Haungers.
Buckles of Gyrdles.
{ Damasked, vnder the degree of { A knight of the order. One of the priuie Counsell. A Gentleman of the priuie chamber.
Guylte, vnder the degree of a knight.
Syluered, vnder the degrees and persons before mentioned.

From a proclamation by Elizabeth I concerning apparel, 12 February 1580. For each rank separate restrictions on apparel are given, specifying who is allowed to wear particular colors or forms of decorative clothing ("furre of sables," material "imbroidered with any Gold or Silver," "Ruffes made or wrought out of England," etc.).

Much of the social fluidity and economic and social mobility that developed through the sixteenth and early seventeenth centuries came despite efforts by the government to control it. The 1563 statutes of artificers (i.e., concerning apprentices) declared the obligation of everyone to "toil" and declared as well the importance of "degree, priority, and place" as part of the natural order laid down by God. Through the second half of the sixteenth and the first half of the seventeenth centuries, however, it no longer seemed natural that dedication to work would act to support the existing system of "degree, priority, and place."

If the aspiring middle class threatened the old social order, so, too, did the increasing number of landless poor. In the face of the substantial increase in "vagrants and beggars" in the towns in the fifteenth and early sixteenth centuries, authorities began to license beggars and to accept some formal responsibility for the poorest members of society. The culmination of this process came in the 1590s, a decade of extraordinary literary achievement, one that saw some of Shakespeare's greatest plays and his sonnets, the plays and poetry of Marlowe, the early plays of Ben Jonson, much of the secular poetry of John Donne, Spenser's *The Faerie Queene*, and the printing of Philip Sidney's *Arcadia*, *Atrophic and Stella*, and *The Defense of Poesy*. It was also a decade in which the court of Elizabeth I reached its glittering zenith and in which England, fresh from its defeat of the Spanish Armada in 1588, experienced the early stages of its growth into a world power. Elizabeth herself was, wrote John Davies in 1596, "our glorious English court's divine image, / As it should be in this our Golden Age." But this decade was also one of the most economically depressed in English history, with poor harvests causing increased prices and further depressing already-low wages for many of the poor; by one calculation living costs in the late 1590s were in the range of five times as high as they had been at the start of the century, and real wages in 1597 less than a third of what they had been a century earlier. Nor were matters helped by the recurrent visitations of plague, by underemployment souring the temper of some university graduates, and by widespread anger among the well-to-do at Elizabeth's seemingly unfair allotment of economic monopolies. In 1598 the Poor Law Act set out provisions for collecting and distributing a "poor rate" to individual parishes so as to alleviate the worst of the suffering, but improvements in the lot of the poor were at best very gradual over the succeeding decades.

To a considerable degree poverty was structural, relating not only to the substantial degree of control exercised by the authorities over wages and prices, but also to the system of apprenticeship. Unlike modern apprentices, apprentices in the guild system as it had grown up through the later Middle Ages and the sixteenth century were not free to leave the work into which their parents had bound them (typically, by paying a fee of several pounds). They were obligated to serve a master for at least seven years and sometimes many more, in exchange for which they received training and very basic room and board, but no payment beyond that. In 1595 apprentices in London rebelled, with crowds taking large quantities of the food they could not afford to buy and destroying the Cheapside Pillories at which many of them had previously been punished for petty offenses.

From about 1600 onwards, however, the old apprenticeship system—and indeed the guild system generally—began to go into decline. The newer (and usually faster-growing) trades tended to be established outside the city boundaries and outside the control of the guilds; apprentices, who made up approximately 15 per cent of the London population in 1600, made up no more than 5 per cent of its much larger population a century later. Apprentices still made their presence felt through much of the seventeenth century (most notably in the turmoil of the 1640s), but by century's end were no longer a significant force; the age of wage labor for all, however young, was by then well underway.

The spread of forward-looking thought was both a cause and a consequence of the economic dynamism of the seventeenth century. Despite the persistence of old prejudices against moneylending and against Jews (witness Shakespeare's Shylock in *The Merchant of Venice* or Marlowe's more satirically imagined Barabas in *The Jew of Malta*), both the lending of money outright and the extension of credit increased fairly steadily through this period, thereby greatly facilitating the expansion of trade and of industry. This expansion of moneylending and credit, it should perhaps be noted, came almost entirely within mainstream Christian society. (Jews had been expelled from

England by Edward I in the late thirteenth century, but small numbers returned in the sixteenth and early seventeenth centuries, and in the mid-seventeenth century they were given official sanction to live in England, albeit without all of the rights and privileges enjoyed by Christians.) More and more, habits of thinking into the future were based on calculations of probability rather than on expressions of hope or fear or prophecy. An important indicator of this change was the development in the mid-sixteenth century of insurance. Not until the late seventeenth century, however, were future probabilities calculated for the purpose of insurance in anything like the way they are today; initially, insurance on ships and their cargos (the earliest form of insurance in England) would never be contemplated until a ship was already overdue. Premiums would then be set according to how long overdue the ship was, how dangerous the route was considered to be, and so on.

Although economic change together with higher levels of education and literacy encouraged the spread of rationalist thought, belief in magic and the supernatural barely diminished and in some areas increased (as evidenced, for example, by the proliferation in the seventeenth century of texts on alchemy and astrology). Rationalism and a reliance on supernatural explanations coexisted within most individual minds as well as within society at large. Elizabeth I turned to John Dee for astrological advice, and when the alchemist Cornelius Lannoy could not deliver on his promise to create gold, she made him suffer for his failure. The intellectually lively James I was the author of a treatise on witches (and responsible as well for executing considerable numbers of women alleged to be witches in Scotland). Most people still interpreted unusual occurrences in the heavens as does Gloucester in Shakespeare's *King Lear*: "these late eclipses in the sun and moon portend no good to us." Modern audiences may find it difficult to take seriously the predictions of the witches in Shakespeare's *Macbeth* or the doctor's faith in "demonstrations magical" in Marlowe's *Doctor Faustus*; the skepticism found in Jonson's *The Alchemist* and the disbelieving scoffs that enliven Reginald Scot's *Discoveries of Witchcraft* are more in line with modern sensibilities. But most late sixteenth- and early seventeenth-century people saw

such things differently. Indeed, the power to draw simultaneously on rationalist ways of connecting cause and effect *and* on traditional supernatural thought is one reason for the remarkable resonance of much Renaissance drama.

"The Round Earth's Imagined Corners"

Recent scholarship has done much to broaden and to destabilize older notions of Britain and her place in the world. Until the late twentieth century, most accounts of the Renaissance and seventeenth century in England were Anglocentric and, whatever the personal convictions of the historian, apt to ignore English Catholicism and to read the English Reformation as a narrative of obvious progress. Such a perspective, moreover, often accompanied a certain triumphalism in which English history—political, economic, or cultural—was a story of steady movement from one high point to another as the influence of various triumphs radiated outward from their London epicenter. It is now more often recognized that England was then—and as part of the United Kingdom is still—a historical and geographical point connected to a myriad of other points around the globe. At the beginning of the period covered by this chapter, England was a small, modestly significant nation on the edge of Europe; by its end, England was Great Britain and a significant world power. But scholars increasingly connect this rise to developments in other countries as much as to developments within Britain itself: in terms of religious, economic, political, and intellectual as well as literary and cultural history, changes in early modern Britain interacted with those in Italy, Holland, France, Germany, and Spain. In addition, Britain in this period began more significantly to interact with the world beyond Europe.

Throughout this period, the government regulated international trade and settlement with the same care as it regulated wages, prices, or religion. It was often only with the blessing or even sponsorship of the Crown that the great sea voyages of the late sixteenth and early seventeenth centuries could take place, whatever the disappointment on the part of some would-be colonizers with sometimes less than enthusiastic royal support for their overseas projects. Despite the moral qualms Elizabeth is reported to have expressed regarding John Hawkins's pioneering ventures in the slave trade beginning in the 1560s, she became an investor in his ventures. For the most part she supported Sir Walter Ralegh's famous voyages of exploration and sometimes of colonization to Virginia, the West Indies, and South America. She also supported the voyages of plunder carried out against the Spaniards by Sir Francis Drake and others and knighted Drake when he returned to England after voyaging around the world from 1577 to 1580. Unlike the Spanish, English adventurers did not manage to claim any colonies rich with gold. But their failure in this respect was surely a blessing in disguise: Spain's preoccupation with adding to its hoard of precious metals almost certainly contributed to the eventual stagnation of its economy and society.

In the seventeenth century, British arrangements for worldwide trade began to be formalized, largely through the creation of state-sanctioned monopolies. The East India Company was granted its charter in 1600, the Hudson's Bay Company in 1670, and the Royal African Company in 1672; these corporations were to play a vital role not only in establishing trade but also in colonizing India and most of the northwest of North America. Arguably, though, the voyage in this period with the greatest impact on world history was one launched in reaction to the religious policies of the Crown—that of the 102 Protestant sectaries (the "Pilgrims") who, despairing at their religious and political prospects in Jacobean England, left first for the religiously tolerant Netherlands and then, in 1620, set sail on the *Mayflower* for the New World, founding a colony at Plymouth, Massachusetts.

Given this developing engagement with the peoples of the New World, India, and Africa, what of attitudes toward race at this time? From passages such as the following exchange in Ben Jonson's comedy *Volpone* (1607), we may infer that black Africans were commonly regarded with as much derision as other groups against which there was strong prejudice:

CORVINO. Has he children?
MOSCA.   Bastards,
  Some dozen or more, that he begot on beggars,
  Gypsies, and Jews, and black-moors, when he was
    drunk.
  Knew you not that, sir? 'Tis the common fable.

Yet we have no evidence to suggest that there was discomfort with Shakespeare's portrayal of the "black-moor" Othello as a tragic hero. (In the eighteenth and nineteenth centuries there was a considerable reaction against any suggestion that such a hero could be black, but we have no record of such a response in the early seventeenth century.) We have noted that Elizabeth invested in John Hawkins's slaving voyages, but she also is said to have described such activity as "detestable" and prophesied it would prompt the "vengeance of Heaven" upon those who participated in it. The problem of determining early modern racial attitudes in Britain is further complicated by shifts in the meaning of the word "race" and the use of the word "black" to mean what we would call "brunette" or "dark." In any case, there was to many minds something of the exotic about almost any dark skin: Henry VIII, Elizabeth I, and James I all included a few African servants in their entourages, and a good portion of the nobility seems to have followed their lead in the late sixteenth century. There can be no question, though, that racial prejudice existed during this period even if evolving in its nature and assumptions. In some cases distinctions appear to have been made based on gradations of color. Some, for example, distinguished "black-moor" from the "white-moor," or drew a tripartite division of black-moor, tawny-moor, and white-moor. Others, however, seem to have used "moor" as synonymous with "black-moor" and, indeed, to have seen all dark skins in very much the same light. Even the native peoples of North America are sometimes described as "black creatures."

THE STUARTS AND THE CIVIL WARS

Elizabeth's decision to remain unmarried helped her negotiate delicate political and religious balances throughout her reign. But her lack of a direct heir meant that at her death in 1603 the crown passed to her distant cousin, James VI of Scotland, now also James I of England, son of the executed Mary, Queen of Scots. Elizabeth was the last of the Tudors, the royal family that had ruled England since 1485. James was a Stuart, the royal family that would rule through direct succession until the early eighteenth century, and whose descendants wear the English crown today. The accession of James united the crowns of England and Scotland. With Wales already annexed officially to England under Henry VIII, this union with Scotland was widely celebrated as the revival of the ancient, undivided island realm of Britain (though the country did not officially become "Great Britain" until 1707). The shift from England to Britain marked a new phase of the English Renaissance in the early seventeenth century. But this "British factor" also introduced a new set of political, religious, and social tensions that would in a few decades help tear the country apart in civil wars, wars that would eventually usher in the changed political and cultural world of the Restoration and eighteenth century.

James came to the English throne an experienced king: monarch of Scotland in name from the age of one, he had been educated for the role since childhood and had in his own right successfully ruled his fractious northern kingdom since the mid-1580s. His ascent to the throne was in consequence widely welcomed. While the later 1590s had been a period of astonishing cultural accomplishment in England, these years had also been marked by deep frustration with an aging queen increasingly reluctant to make decisions: most members of the English political class looked optimistically to James for a renewal of energy and action. James, however, would not always live up to these expectations. To begin with, any change in monarchs meant a change in the respective political fortunes of the ruling elite. One observer of the London court commented dryly that as soon as James was named King, would-be courtiers began to race north toward Edinburgh, "as if it were nothing else but first

come first served, or that preferment were a goal to be got by footmanship." Some members of the Elizabethan court would keep their positions: Robert Cecil, Secretary of State from 1596, continued to hold the same office under James. Some individuals (like Sir Francis Bacon) and families who had not thrived politically under Elizabeth found great success under James. Others saw their power decline or disappear into the hands of Scottish favorites who happily left their estates in impoverished Scotland and descended hungrily on London. James generously shared his good fortune. While the parsimonious Elizabeth had been served by 18 "gentlemen of the privy chamber," James provided for 48, and appointed as well 200 "gentlemen extraordinary." Many had little to offer the country except charm and beauty, good legs and skilled dancing—qualities that could take a courtier far in the Jacobean court. As funds started to dwindle, new money-making schemes flourished, with James in effect selling aristocratic titles (including a new one, the baronetcy) by the score, and knighthoods by the hundreds. The figure of the newly jumped-up knight or minor aristocrat soon appeared as a satirical target on the London stage.

Religious reformers—Presbyterians and Separatists, collectively known as "Puritans" despite their widely differing ideas about church government—were another disappointed constituency. The Scottish Reformation of 1560 had been a Presbyterian Reformation, producing a church government that, officially at least, did not recognize the authority of bishops. While the Scottish episcopate never quite disappeared, its existence from 1560 to about 1610 was always precarious. English Presbyterians consequently hoped that James, up to that point the monarch of a "reformed" national church, would move the Church of England in a more strongly Protestant direction. But when they petitioned James in 1604, he flatly rejected their request for a church with an egalitarian structure along the lines of the Presbyterian Kirk. "No bishop, no king," he replied, voicing the analogical thinking so characteristic of the period: a challenge to hierarchy in the religious sphere threatened the idea of political hierarchy. Within a few decades, he would be proved right: Scottish revolutionaries in the late 1630s and English revolutionaries in the 1640s both abolished episcopacy as soon as they had the power to do so, as a prelude to their attacks on the authority of the Crown.

James did agree to sponsor a new translation of the Bible, in a project that is probably one of the very few masterpieces ever produced by committee. The King James (or "Authorized") version of 1611 for the most part retained the language of Tyndale's version from the 1530s, but in terms of religious politics it represented an important step forward: it was the product of years of collective negotiation over controversial phrases. This translation would shape literary language for centuries to follow, and retain (with some revisions) its primacy

Bates.   R. Winter.   C. Wright.   J. Wright.   Percy.   Fawkes.   Catesby.   T. Winter.

Though the proportion of Catholics in early seventeenth-century Britain is thought to have been low, some Catholics still hoped for an overthrow of Protestant rule and a re-establishing of the Roman Catholic Church. In 1605 extremist Catholics, among them one Guy Fawkes, were reported to have been discovered to be plotting acts of terrorism; bombs, officials claimed, had been discovered beneath the House of Lords. Though James at first noted that not "all professing the Romish religion were guilty of the same," he soon made clear that he had no more tolerance for Catholic dissent than he did for the Puritan variety. Many priests suspected of Catholic leanings were stripped of their posts and/or imprisoned. As for Guy Fawkes, James authorized his torture (he confessed after two days on the rack) and his subsequent execution. To this day November 5, the anniversary of the discovery of the Gunpowder Plot, is celebrated with bonfires and merrymaking through much of England. Some scholars claim that evidence for this conspiracy was exaggerated, perhaps even planted, by officials who sought to fan the flames of anti-Catholic sentiment.

in the Church of England through to the second half of the twentieth century. But James did not succeed in mollifying the more extreme Puritans, and indeed had no intention of trying to do so. Within a few years, some Separatists (later called Independents or Congregationalists, in that they denied the legitimacy of any state church) left for the toleration of Amsterdam and Leiden, and in 1620 sailed to the New World to found their colony in Massachusetts. But on the whole the English church was less divided and contentious under James than under Elizabeth, and scholars refer to a broad "Calvinist consensus" in his reign. It was probably not until the 1630s that debates between "Anglican" and "Puritan" once again became a central component of national debates about the powers of church and state.

James's relationship with his House of Commons was complex, and scholars continue to disagree over how to characterize the politics of his reign. In principle, James was an absolutist, and his reign saw the popularization in England of theories of "divine right" monarchy. But in practice, James was a canny negotiator, and seemed to have good instincts for when to push his theoretical claims for absolute power and when to make concessions (as, for example, in his 1610 speech to Parliament asserting both that "kings are justly called gods" and that all kings "that are not tyrants" will bind themselves "within the limits of their laws"). Some scholars read this period as marking the beginnings of parliamentary and democratic rebellion that would lead to civil war; others argue that James was on the whole a politically successful monarch, and that the real political challenges developed in reaction to the far less flexible absolutism of his son, Charles I. Certainly, many members of Parliament and the population were exasperated by James's financial extravagances. But they were also exasperated by his refusal to incur the further expense of intervening in the religious wars that devastated Europe after 1618—a decision many saw as particularly irresponsible since James's own daughter, Elizabeth, was Queen of Bohemia and had been compelled to abandon her throne when Bohemia was invaded by a Catholic army. But whatever his motives, James, much like Elizabeth, managed largely to keep Britain out of wars during a period in which warfare consumed Europe. As far as

internal politics are concerned, James kept the affairs of his English and Scottish kingdoms quite separate: he had originally favored union between England and Scotland but came to accept that this would be impracticable. But he perhaps sowed the seeds of future trouble by his attempts to impose rule on Scotland from afar, and by encouraging mass emigration by English and particularly by Scots (later called the "Scots-Irish") to Ireland, where he authorized them to dispossess local inhabitants of their lands.

With the death of James and the accession of his son Charles I in 1625, cracks began to appear in the political and religious consensus that James had managed to maintain. Charles's court was far more refined than that of his father, and was artistically brilliant: Charles amassed one of the greatest art collections in Europe. But he lacked his father's willingness to compromise. What Charles looked for in his advisors and his people was primarily obedience, and he believed more firmly than his father in the divine right of kings. When Parliament challenged royal prerogatives with the "Petition of Right" (1628), a declaration of the "rights and liberties of the subject," Charles eventually assented—but within a year he in effect shut down Parliament and ruled without it for the next decade. Since Parliament traditionally voted the funds that supported the monarchy, throughout the 1630s Charles was compelled to rely on increasingly resented alternative means of raising money, such as legally dubious taxes. When he was forced by an invading Scottish army to recall Parliament in 1640, he found himself facing a body interested in little but confronting him with the grievances that had accumulated in the previous decade.

Religious reformers who remained discontented with the Elizabethan Settlement and James's "Calvinist consensus" were outraged—and radicalized—by changes in the Church under Charles and William Laud, named Archbishop of Canterbury in 1633. Many were suspicious (possibly legitimately) of Charles's own religious beliefs: his Queen, Henrietta Maria, was a French Catholic, and her personal priests were widely thought to have too much power in the court. While Laud was not looking to reimpose Catholicism on the Church of England, as his enemies maintained, he was very concerned to introduce a greater degree of ritual, ceremony, and uniformity in Church practice, and many people in England saw Laud's "High Church" innovations as at least Catholicizing. When John Milton writes that he had been prevented from entering the ministry because he was "church-outed by prelates," he was referring to the Laudian Church and its increased emphasis on obedience to hierarchy: to Milton and many others, bishops had become worldly, powerful prelates. Laud himself had been a member of the King's Privy Council since 1628, and many disapproved of this intermingling of religious and secular power.

In the summer of 1637, Charles I and Laud attempted to introduce a revised (Anglican) prayer book for use in Presbyterian Scotland. Many Scots, however, failed to see why an English desire for uniformity of worship meant that they were the ones who needed to change. The new liturgy consequently became a focus of discontent with decades of royal policy. Well-planned riots greeted readings of the new service, followed over the next two years by a chain of events often termed the Scottish Revolution. In 1638, Scots drafted the National Covenant, vowing to withstand innovations and maintain the Presbyterian cause. Charles raised an army to subdue the "Covenanters" by force, but a series of compromises and humiliations for the English culminated in the Scottish occupation of Newcastle in the summer of 1640. These "Bishops' Wars" of 1639–40, named for the perception that they were the result of Laud's Church policies, played a significant role in the buildup to the civil wars that followed.

Charles called Parliament back into session, but found himself compelled to make humiliating concessions: the Scots were not his only subjects with grievances. The King eventually agreed to hand over to Parliament the two men most closely identified with his political and religious policies: his chief advisor, Sir Thomas Wentworth, was tried and executed in 1641, and Archbishop William Laud was imprisoned in 1641 and executed four years later. A 1641 rebellion in Ireland, the third country Charles ruled, further weakened his position. The Irish who had been dispossessed in the wave of emigration begun under James rose against the Protestant usurpers, and killed considerable numbers (though not nearly as many as

people in England believed at the time). When Charles asked Parliament for funds to invade Ireland, they feared he in fact planned to form an alliance with Irish Catholics, invade England, and re-establish absolute rule. Mobs of apprentices (who began to be referred to derogatively as "roundheads" in reference to their shorn heads) began to demonstrate for the overthrow of episcopacy. Debates in 1641 over the "Grand Remonstrance," a Parliamentarian manifesto, hardened divisions between those loyal to Parliament and those loyal to the King, now beginning to be called "cavaliers" (originally a term for an armed horseman, but by this time a word with implications of roistering, swaggering gallantry). An attempt by Charles to arrest five members of Parliament in January 1642 backfired by uniting members of both parliamentary Houses, Lords and Commons, against the King. In the turmoil that followed, Charles fled to the north of England, Parliament began to raise its own army, and war officially broke out when Charles raised his standard at Nottingham in August 1642.

Anthony Van Dyck, *Charles I in Three Positions*, 1635–36. Van Dyck's painting was intended to provide an Italian sculptor with the visual information he needed to prepare a bust of the English king in absentia.

The causes of the civil wars of the 1640s continue to be one of the most heatedly debated subjects in British history. Scholars have argued that the wars were primarily about religion, and that the 1640s were a "puritan" revolution; many contemporaries certainly saw religion as a central issue in the conflict. Others see the wars as the inevitable outgrowth of political tensions between king and parliament, or of long-term social or economic factors such as a declining aristocracy or a rising middle class. Other historians point out that the conflict divided families (John Milton's younger brother, Christopher Milton, was a Royalist), a complication for broad social or economic theories. These historians have focused instead on shorter-term explanations, often the disastrous decisions made by Charles himself, or the sequence of events created by the inherent tensions of having one king ruling three quite different countries. Many scholars see some combination of ideological and circumstantial factors at work. The idea that a civil war might break out in their lifetimes, resulting in the execution of the monarch by his own subjects, would probably have been dismissed as ridiculous by most people in England even just a few years earlier. Yet somehow it happened, and over the next decade about 100,000 people died as a result of the war, with many more wounded, in a country with a population of about 5 million. When Milton describes the destruction and violence of even heavenly warfare in *Paradise Lost*, he expected that almost all his readers would have had their lives touched in some way by war.

The "first" civil war raged from 1642 to 1646, and ended with the defeat of the Royalist armies and left Parliament, dominated by Presbyterians, in charge. They were supported by the victorious New Model Army, formed in 1645, commanded by Sir Thomas Fairfax, and led in battle by a brilliant general named Oliver Cromwell. Many of the more radicalized members of the population resisted the rule of newly empowered Presbyterians, finding them to be as authoritarian as the Laudian bishops they had fought to overthrow. By 1647, the Army had managed to become the dominant power in the country, and the Army, Parliament, and King, each distrusting the other two, attempted to negotiate a political and religious settlement. More radical voices began to join the conversation, expressing ideas created by the intellectual hothouse of the previous half-decade, a period in which the most fundamental political and social certainties seemed suddenly open to debate. Groups such as the Levellers argued for universal manhood suffrage, a written constitution, freedom of worship, and equality before the law; soon enough groups such as the Diggers were arguing that property is theft. When the Leveller Colonel Thomas Rainsborough argued that "every man that is to live under a government ought first by his own consent to put himself under that government," he was articulating an idea that would have been almost unthinkable before 1640. The Levellers are widely regarded as founding voices in the development of modern democracy. But they were not allowed to speak for long: a Leveller mutiny in the Army was crushed by Cromwell, the captured king soon afterward escaped, and a "second" civil war (in effect, a series of Royalist uprisings) broke out in 1648, culminating with the recapture, trial, and execution of King Charles in January 1649 by a Parliament purged by the Army of all but its own supporters. In May 1649, England officially became a Commonwealth, though open hostilities only ended after Cromwell, now commander-in-chief, won bloody campaigns in Ireland (1649–50) and against Scottish Royalists (1650–51).

Oliver Cromwell was now the most powerful man in Britain and effectively ruler (though in theory the "Rump" Parliament held political control). But "the inglorious arts of peace" (as Andrew Marvell termed them) were not always his strength. Cromwell responded to widespread discontent with the Rump Parliament by forcibly dissolving it and replacing it with one nominated by religious congregations; this Parliament proving a failure, Cromwell gave himself the title of "Lord Protector" in late 1653 and over the next few years ruled increasingly by decree. Had he lived, Cromwell might have retained a strong grip on power for many years. While he can be described as a kind of benevolent despot, he was not a tyrant: he attempted to demilitarize the government, and he introduced a great degree of religious freedom, including the readmission of Jews to England. In 1657 he refused Parliament's offer to make him king, and he died in 1658. Oliver Cromwell continues to be an ambivalent figure in the British cultural imagination: he is both admired and condemned, and his character, his motives, and many of his actions remain surrounded by controversy.

Cromwell's regime could not survive without him:

his son Richard assumed power on his father's death, and proved unable to hold the nation together. A period of chaos was finally ended with the restoration of the monarchy in 1660. Charles II was proclaimed king by a new Parliament called by General George Monck, a man who had fought for Charles I in the first civil war, but for Cromwell in Ireland, and who was commander-in-chief of the Cromwellian army in Scotland. But Monck returned to his Royalist beginnings, and marched south from Scotland and took control in London. On May 25th Charles landed at Dover, and four days later he received a tumultuous welcome in the capital. The restored monarchy, however, was a very different thing from that which had operated under Charles I. Never again would Parliament be trifled with: Britain was now a parliamentary monarchy. For a brief period following the death of Charles II in 1685 there was again a crisis of power and religion, as Charles had died with no heir and his brother, the Catholic James II, came to the throne. Anti-Catholic sentiment, however, made it impossible for James to rule long, and the bloodless "Glorious Revolution" of 1688 forced James into exile and restored Protestant rule in the person of the Dutch Protestant William of Orange and his wife Mary (daughter of James II).

LITERARY GENRES

The course of British literature over the sixteenth and early seventeenth centuries is marked by the transformation of a number of literary genres, by the creation of others, and by massive changes in the relationships among authors, texts, and readers and audiences. This overview is intended to provide a broad outline of some of the more important changes, and some sense as well of the range of writing within the various genres.

LITERATURE IN PROSE AND THE DEVELOPMENT OF PRINT CULTURE

Arguably the development most important to the literature of this period occurred not in the sixteenth or seventeenth centuries but in the 1450s, with the invention of moveable type and of the printing press by the German craftsman and entrepreneur Johann Gutenberg. In 1476, William Caxton became the first to print books in England, and Caxton was instrumental in the publication of a number of important works of English literature (including Malory's *Morte Darthur*) using the new technology. But in the late fifteenth and early sixteenth centuries a great deal of writing in England retained an "un-English" character. The most important prose work in this period, Sir Thomas More's *Utopia* (1516), was first printed not in England but in Flanders (where More had lived and worked for some time the previous year), and was written not in English but in Latin. In this respect at least, *Utopia* was representative: in the late fifteenth and early sixteenth centuries the majority of books were published in Latin. Even in the late fifteenth century, however, publication in English was more common than is often supposed: of the 90 books printed by Caxton between 1477 and his death in 1491, 74 were in English. And by the second half of the sixteenth century, the movement away from Latin had become much stronger. The Latin edition of *Utopia* lost currency in England upon the publication of an English translation (by Ralph Robinson) in 1551. John Foxe published an early version of his *Book of Martyrs* in Latin in 1559; from 1563 onward editions were published only in English. The market for books in Latin diminished over the course of the seventeenth century, aided by the appearance of English translations of most of the important classical and continental texts. The lone category in which a majority of works continued to be written in Latin was that of scientific writing—ironically, as a result of their authors' belief that they would be more accessible to serious readers in centuries to come if they were written in Latin rather than in English.

More's *Utopia* resonates widely as an expression of the interests of its age. Its tone, at once playful and deeply serious, parallels that of the great work of the northern Renaissance in continental Europe, Erasmus's *In Praise of Folly*. More's focus on the fundamental nature of government follows on important work by writers of the Italian Renaissance (Niccolò Machiavelli most prominently), and foreshadows the considerable attention that would be paid to this issue in England in the later sixteenth and seventeenth centuries. In addition, More's investigation of society on the level of first principles, and his imaginative curiosity about the possibilities offered by a wider world, are deeply characteristic of the Renaissance. Finally, and not least of all, *Utopia* anticipates the great growth in prose fiction that occurred later in the century.

Utopia gave its name to a new genre defined by subject matter: works presenting an imagined world in such a way as to prompt reflection upon the inadequacies and absurdities of the present world. In this period, works wholly or largely "utopian" in character include Francis Bacon's *The New Atlantis* and Margaret Cavendish's *The Description of a New World, Called the Blazing World*. In Bacon's work, European travelers discover Bensalem, an idealized community devoted to scientific pursuits and to enlarging "the bounds of Human Empire" over the natural world. In Cavendish's alternative fantasy, nature is presented in a more unstable fashion: the protagonist discovers a "Blazing World" of extraordinary light, in which the laws of space and time do not apply—a world that evidently cannot be contained by "human empire" or indeed within any system of human thought. In later eras the utopian (and "dystopian") tradition of imagined worlds extends through works such as Jonathan Swift's *Gulliver's Travels* (1726), in which four separate worlds are imagined; to William Morris's late Victorian anti-capitalist utopia, *News from Nowhere* (1872); to twentieth-century works such as Aldous Huxley's *Brave New World* (1932) and George Orwell's *1984* (1949) that project the extension of some of the most disturbing social tendencies of their day into horrific imagined futures.

While utopian fiction is defined by its subject matter, the genre of prose fiction as a whole also came into its own in sixteenth-century British literature: a wide variety of prose fiction in English had appeared by the end of the century, aimed at the increasingly wide variety of audiences that the printing press had made possible. At one end of the spectrum are writers who consciously appealed to a popular audience—writers such as Thomas Deloney, whose commoner protagonists and dedication to "all famous cloth workers in England" have already been touched on. Another writer who appealed to a broad public in some of his work was

Thomas Nash, whose *The Unfortunate Traveler* is a work of prose fiction that has proven almost impossible to classify. At once an exuberant satire of the literary and court conventions of the time, it has also been variously termed a tragicomedy, a picaresque novel, a pioneering work of travel literature, and a celebration of violence. It is also a work alive with the possibilities and tensions of the new print culture. The tensions between the old court culture and a nascent culture of broad-based literacy emerge in the book's wordplay as well as its storyline: pages are related to printing as well as to princes as Jack Wilton, a humble page, bequeaths to the "pages of the court" certain "pages of his misfortune."

If the popular fiction of Deloney and Nash stands at one end of the spectrum of late sixteenth- and early seventeenth-century prose fiction, another is perhaps most clearly exemplified by John Lyly. Lyly had been a young man of fashion at university, and for a time his *Euphues* (1578) set a fashion too—a fashion that drew attention above all to highly refined and rhetorical prose style. Lyly sets the tone in his dedicatory epistle:

> How so ever the case standeth, I look for no praise for my labor, but pardon for my goodwill; it is the greatest reward that I dare ask, and the least that they can offer. I desire no more, I deserve no less. Should the style nothing delight the dainty ear of the curious sifter, yet will the matter recreate the mind of the courteous reader.

The same style of ornamented sentences, with clauses precisely balanced in supporting or antithetical relationships, is carried through the narrative itself as it tells the story of "a young gentleman of great patrimony, and of so comely a personage, that it was doubted whether he were more bound to nature for the lineaments of his person, or through fortune for the increase of his possessions." This expansive style, which came to be called "Euphuism" after Lyly's title, was for a time very popular, especially among the women at court, where it was reported in 1632 that in the 1590s "the beauty in court who could not parley Euphuism was as little regarded as she which now there speaks not French." Within a few years the style had come to be widely parodied, including by Shakespeare, as for example when Falstaff "elevates" his speech while pretending to be the King addressing Prince Hal in *Henry IV, Part 1*: "Harry, I do not only marvel where thou spendest thy time, but also how thy art accompanied, for though the chamomile, the more it is trodden on the faster it grows, yet youth, the more it is wasted, the sooner it wears."

What was satirized by Shakespeare (as well as by Nash, Ben Jonson, and others) was not the use of balance or antithesis *per se*, but rather their excessive and repetitive use, and the habit of using a great many words to say very little. Shakespeare, Nash, Jonson, and virtually every other late sixteenth- and early seventeenth-century writer of any significance also employed a great number of rhetorical figures, but aimed more for variety, concision, and pointedness than for abundance of expression. John Donne may command our attention with his colloquial directness of language in lines such as "For God's sake hold your tongue, and let me love," but his poems are filled with parallel structures ("My face in thine eye, thine in mine appears," "With wealth your state, your mind with arts improve") that embody the dichotomies and paradoxes of which he speaks. Ben Jonson may begin his play *The Alchemist* with a crude verbal slanging match in which one character says to another "I fart at thee," but in speeches throughout the play he also draws substantially on the Renaissance traditions of rhetorical figures ("Your fortunes may make me a man, As mine have preserved you a woman").

Like so many other sixteenth-century developments, the growth of prose fiction drew substantially on texts from ancient Greece and Rome, and from Renaissance Italy and France. Compilations of short fiction such as William Painter's *The Palace of Pleasure* (1566) and George Pettie's *A Petite Palace of Pettie His Pleasure* (1576) began to make translations and adaptations of French and Italian tales of romance and adventure much more widely available, and by the end of the century the genre of prose romance was becoming well established in English. Writers of prose romances often borrowed freely from earlier materials, and their works were in turn borrowed from freely, by dramatists and poets as well as by other writers of prose fiction. Thus, for example, Robert Greene's *Pando to* (1588), which drew on an Italian source, provided the story material for Shakespeare's comedy *The Winter's Tale*, and

Thomas Lodge's *Rosalinda* (1590), a prose fiction that drew on a Middle English romance called *Gamely* for its story material, provided Shakespeare with material for his comedy *As You Like It*. There was no shame attached to such borrowing: aesthetic value was located in the way in which one told or retold a tale and combined different elements of story material into a pleasing whole, not in whether one had thought up the stories oneself.

In the 1590s, Greene and Nash, together with George Peele and a few others, constituted a group known as the "university wits." Like Christopher Marlowe and Edmund Spenser, they had attended university on scholarships or with the financial assistance of others, and the three lived something of a precarious existence after leaving Oxford or Cambridge; these were among the earliest English writers to try to earn their living entirely through their writing. Such a goal was still impossible to achieve directly through payments made by printers or publishers; it remained necessary to seek the support of wealthy patrons. That such support was often anything but reliable is evidenced from the dedications to their works. Greene's 17 different books are dedicated to a total of 16 different patrons; Nash's dedication for the first edition of *The Unfortunate Traveler* to Henry Wriothesley, Earl of Southampton, is dropped in subsequent editions; and so on.

A very different writer of prose fiction was Sir Philip Sidney. Sidney's *Arcadia* (1590, 1593), an engaging and elegantly written pastoral prose romance, drew substantially on continental and classical models, and was instrumental in popularizing in England the genre of heroic Hellenistic prose romance—stories of romance and adventure set in imagined and "timeless" locales, featuring shepherds, damsels, and noblemen in disguise. The work remained immensely popular through the seventeenth century both in England (where it was issued in ten authorized printings) and abroad (where it was translated into French, German, and Dutch). Works inspired by Sidney's *Arcadia* include Lady Mary Worth's *The Countess of Montgomery's Urania* (1621), the first published work of fiction by an Englishwoman, which mixes pastoral narrative with pointed political commentary, and Anna Weems's sequel, *A Continuation of Sir Philip Sidney's*

Arcadia (1651), less of a hybrid than Worth's work, but like hers a romance narrative with some political overtones.

Sidney was a central figure not only in the development of prose romance: he was also a pioneer in the use of the sonnet sequence, and as the author of *The Defense of Poesies* (written 1583) he produced the first extended work of literary theory and criticism in English. Sidney's approach embraced both structural analysis from an aesthetic point of view and moral commentary—though that is to put his design very much in modern terms. In general, neither Sidney nor his contemporaries saw a clear boundary between the moral and the aesthetic: what was considered aesthetically good was considered so in large part for its perceived efficacy in conveying moral principles. The occasion for Sidney's *Defense* was a rambling and vituperative attack on the stage by Stephen Gossoon entitled *The School of Abuse* (1579), and Sidney's focus is very largely on the drama. In the next generation, his *Defense* was followed by a number of works focused on other genres, among them George Puttenham's *The Art of English Poesies* (1589), noteworthy in particular for its discussion of rhetorical figures, and Thomas Campion's *Observations in the Art of English Poesies* (1602), a groundbreaking work relating the prosody of classical Greece and Rome to that of English poetry.

Arguably the most important prose writings of the late sixteenth and early seventeenth centuries were religious non-fiction works; certainly these were far and away the most popular. Aside from the Bible itself (first made available in the complete English-language printed edition in 1535 by Miles Coverdale) and such masterpieces of liturgical prose as the Book of Common Prayer, the most popular book in England through most of the sixteenth century was the English translation of *The Golden Legend*, by the thirteenth-century Italian scholar Jacobs de Voyaging, a collection of narratives of the lives of Christian saints organized so as to be read in conjunction with the feast associated with each saint over the course of the year. In the first hundred years after the appearance of the printing press, more than 150 different editions of *The Golden Legend* appeared across Europe in various languages. William Caxton translated *The Golden Legend* himself and published it in 1483: "in likewise as gold is most

noble above all other metals," he declared in his foreword to the book, "in likewise is this legend Holden most noble above all other works."

In the wake of the Protestant Reformation, the most widely read book aside from the Bible seems to have been for many decades John Foxe's *Acts and Monuments*, first published in English in 1563. There are significant parallels between this work and *The Golden Legend*. Whereas the earlier work provided in convenient form the lives of saints of the Roman Catholic Church, many of whom attained cult-like status, Foxe's book performed the same function for Protestant religious figures, especially those martyred at the stake by Henry VIII or by Mary I. By the late sixteenth century these figures had also attained cult-like status, and Foxe's book was repeatedly issued in new editions, each time in an expanded form. In addition to these biographical texts, the genre of the sermon was, in the hands of a John Donne or a Lancelot Andrewes, the site of some of the finest prose of the Renaissance; even works of theology and religious controversy could enter what we now consider the "literary" realm when written by Anglican divines such as Richard Hooker or Jeremy Taylor, or by nonconforming radicals such as the pseudonymous satirist Martin Marprelate.

Throughout this period substantial increases in literacy were accompanied by increases in the number of households that possessed books. In 1560 roughly one in ten English households possessed at least one book; by 1640 this figure had risen to approximately 50 per cent of all households. Not surprisingly, such figures were higher in the late sixteenth and early seventeenth centuries in Protestant nations. In the late sixteenth century there was a higher percentage of households in Germany that possessed books than in any other part of Europe, but by 1640 that distinction belonged to England. If the printing press was one engine for the expansion of literacy, the expansion of formal education was another, and with the considerable increase in the number of schools over the course of the period came a demand for textbooks. Of these there were few, but one above all appears to have been almost universally studied—a Latin grammar text by William Lily (grandfather of John Lyly of *Euphues* fame). Indeed, it is possible that more copies were printed of this book than of any other during this period save the Bible.

Throughout this period there was also a growing readership for works that celebrated national accomplishment. Raphael Holinshed's *Chronicles of England, Scotland, and Ireland* (1587) drew on many sources to present a compilation of stories of early Britain, some based on fact, some purely legendary. Holinshed is best known nowadays as the source on which Shakespeare drew for his history plays; in these dramatized versions as well as more directly, the portrait Holinshed sketched of earlier eras exerted a wide influence. Similarly, William Camden's *Britannia* (1586), a "description of the most flourishing kingdoms, England, Scotland, and Ireland, and the islands adjoining," was immensely popular in its English translation, entitled simply *Britain* (1610). Like the "Britain" of many Englishmen, that of Camden was overwhelmingly southern English in character; Camden in fact had little to say about Wales, Scotland, or Ireland, and for the purposes of his county-by-county survey did not travel north of Hadrian's Wall. But such works helped to feed a growing sense among the English that England could be more or less equated with "the British Isles" or "Britain." Popular too was Richard Hakluyt's *Principal Navigations, Voyages and Discoveries of the English Nation* (1589), a unique compilation of more or less accurate accounts of true voyages of English explorers and merchants, combined with accounts based purely on myth and imagination. Nationality was the key criterion for inclusion: "I meddle in this work with the navigations only of our own nation," Hakluyt declares in his preface to the first edition. Ironically enough, "Hakluyt's Voyages," the work's popular title, retained a place in history not so much for the historical accounts it presented but rather for the inspiration it gave Englishmen to embark on the sorts of voyages Hakluyt had only imagined—and in the inspiration it gave Shakespeare for some of the stories in his plays. Furthermore, the kind of writing exemplified by Hakluyt's mariners and merchants, with their straightforward "plain" prose, sustained narratives, and detailed descriptions of the places and people they encountered, would (some scholars argue) eventually contribute as much to the development of the narrative style and strategy of the English novel as the classically inspired romances of Sidney and Lyly.

More's extraordinary vision of human government in *Utopia* was followed in the sixteenth century by a number of influential non-fiction works on the nature of government—works of political theory, we would call them today. A recurrent focus of such work was the relationship of a monarch and his or her subjects to God and to the body of law. Sir Thomas Elyot's *The Book of the Governor* (1531) saw a universe ordered by nature in hierarchical fashion:

> … undoubtedly the best governance is by one king or prince…. For who can deny that all thing in heaven and earth is governed by one God, by one perpetual order, by one Providence? One sun ruleth over the day, one moon over the night. And to descend down to the earth … the bees … hath among them one principal bee for their governor, who excelleth all other in greatness.

The Laws of Ecclesiastical Polity by Richard Hooker (1593–1614), which aimed in large part to justify the position of the monarch in England as head of the established Church, also appealed to nature, distinguishing between universal natural law ("nature herself teacheth laws and statutes to live by") and "positive" law (the written body of human law that varies from one jurisdiction to another). Hooker saw the position of monarch as consistent with natural law, but he also thought it highly desirable that the monarch should abide by "positive" law, rather than regarding himself as above the law: "where the king doth guide the state, and the law the king, that commonwealth is like a harp or melodious instrument."

The most important writer of non-fiction prose of the age was Francis Bacon, the writer renowned today both for introducing the essay form into English, and for the contribution he made to the development of research based on experimentation and inductive reasoning—popularly termed the "scientific method." Bacon wrote in both Latin and English. Ironically, the works by Bacon that continue to be widely read are the works in English that he considered less significant: his essays; his short work on the classification of knowledge, *The Advancement of Learning*; and his unfinished scientific utopian fantasy, *The New Atlantis*.

Of Truth.

I.

HAT *is Truth;* said jesting *Pilate;* And would not stay for an Answer. Certainly there be, that delight in Giddinesse; And count it a Bondage, to fix a Beleefe; Affecting Free-will in Thinking, as well as in Acting. And though the Sects of Philosophers of that Kinde be gone, yet there remaine certaine discoursing Wits, which are of the same veines, though there be not so much Bloud in them, as was in those of the Ancients. But it is not

B   onely

Page from the 1625 edition of Francis Bacon's *Essays*.

As the religious controversies of the age again became more heated during the Jacobean period and later Interregnum (the period "between kings," 1649–60), so too did the volume of political and religious writing increase. The collapse of censorship laws in the early 1640s led to the appearance of a vast volume of pamphlet literature that represented all points of view; much of this writing was addressed to a popular audience and remains readable for its interest as rhetorical prose as well for its historical influence.

Some of the most interesting of these texts are the work of political and religious radicals such as the Levellers, Diggers, Ranters, and later Quakers, in particular writers such as William Wally and Richard Overton. But the era also brought forth a number of more substantial works of prose non-fiction. On the Royalist side perhaps the most influential of these was *Eikon Basilica* ("The Image of the King") (1649), a self-justifying overview of key events of the war from the point of view of Charles I. Supposedly written by Charles himself, the treatise was almost certainly ghostwritten by the clergyman John Garden, and John Milton would call attention to his own anti-monarchical credentials by responding with *Eikonoklastes* (1649; his Greek title means "Image Breaker"). Of far greater influence over the course of succeeding centuries was Thomas Hobbes's *Leviathan* (1651), now recognized as a central document of political philosophy in the Western tradition. Hobbes wrote *Leviathan* while acting as secretary to a Royalist family, the Cavendishes, who were in exile in Paris during the Interregnum; unsurprisingly in the circumstances, his arguments provide support to the claims of a monarch wishing to exercise absolute sovereignty. But whereas monarchs such as Charles I (and sixteenth-century political theorists such as Elyot and Hooker) had claimed that such power stemmed directly from God, Hobbes saw it as the embodiment of a social contract, under the terms of which the people agree to submit themselves to the authority of a ruler in order to obtain the benefits of social order. By shifting the ground on which arguments for the unfettered authority of rulers were founded, Hobbes's great work in the end had the effect of undermining all claims to a right of absolute rule: if power was ultimately derived from the people, then why should not the people have an ongoing say in how that power was to be exercised, and by whom?

Many of the most important works of prose non-fiction by writers on the Royalist side were not overtly political documents—yet even non-political works were almost inevitably tinged with the controversies of the age. Thomas Browne's 1642–43 work *Religion Medici* ("The Religion of a Doctor") endeavored to present religion from a personal rather than a polemical point of view, adopting a tolerant and sympathetic attitude toward those of all religious backgrounds, while maintaining a strong attachment to the formal structures and rituals of the Church of England. Izaak Walton's most lasting work of prose non-fiction, *The Complete Angler* (1653), might seem on the face of it to be even further from political or religious advocacy than *Religion Medici*. But this treatise on the art of fishing carries with it a running subtext that celebrates the wise, peaceful, open-hearted, and contemplative values of Picador (Latin: the fisher), representing the values of the Church of England, in which each member of the clergy acts as a fisher of souls.

Perhaps the most remarkable of all writers of non-fiction prose in the mid-seventeenth century was Margaret Cavendish, Duchess of Newcastle (of the same family to whom Hobbes acted as secretary)—called "Mad Madge" by some dismissive contemporaries. Cavendish's works are as remarkable for their breadth as they are for originality and for their accomplished writing: her works include scientific and philosophical essays, utopian fantasy, poetry, numerous plays, a biography of her husband, William Cavendish, and *A True Relation of My Birth, Breeding and Life* (1656), one of the most original and important works of a genre still in its infancy during the seventeenth century—autobiography. For most of the Middle Ages the practice of writing autobiographically (with the exception of some writing in a confessional vein) seems to have virtually disappeared, as indeed did biographical writing, with the exception of the lives of saints or martyrs. It is an important indicator of the increased emphasis on the individual in the Renaissance that the writing of such works, as well as the practice of writing diaries, appears to have grown steadily through the seventeenth century. One important element that contributed to this new focus on interiority and the self was the Protestant insistence on documenting the internal, spiritual life. But as so often in the sixteenth and seventeenth centuries, the new practices were also justified by an appeal to classical models. Cavendish expressed the hope that "my readers will not think me vain for writing my life, since there have been many that have done the like, as Caesar, Ovid, and many more, both men and women, and I know no reason I may not do it as well as they." The confidence as well as the individualism of the age finds no fuller expression than it does in the writings of Margaret Cavendish.

Other members of the nobility on the Royalist side (notably Anne Fanshaw and Anne Halkett) followed Cavendish in writing autobiographically during the Interregnum. And such writing appears to have flourished to some extent too among the revolutionaries; perhaps the most notable examples on that side are the writings of Lucy Hutchinson, who, like Cavendish, balanced a memoir recounting the life of her husband with a separate account of her own life. Anna Trapnel, perhaps best known for her extraordinary religious prophecies, also left a remarkable autobiographical account "of her journey from London into Cornwall" during which she was arrested and interrogated on suspicion of witchcraft. Much non-fiction prose writing among those on the revolutionary side tended to address directly the religious and political issues of the time. James Harrington's *The Commonwealth of Oceana* (1656), for example, employs the structure of a utopian vision to address the pressing contemporary issue of how a republic may be founded so as to ensure the perpetuation of government that is both representative and fair.

The leading light of revolutionary writing is unquestionably John Milton, whose non-fiction prose includes not only a wide range of essays and tracts in defense of Parliamentary and Puritan causes, but also groundbreaking treatises in defense of divorce and, perhaps, most importantly, *Areopagitica* (1644), an extended argument for toleration and freedom of expression. It is difficult for those living in the present-day liberal democracies of the Western world to appreciate fully the degree to which societies such as that of sixteenth- and seventeenth-century Britain may operate without any reference to any presumed right of free speech—or, indeed, any reference to any human "rights" at all. Censorship of texts is almost symbiotic in Europe with the invention of the printing press. In England, Henry VIII required that all book publications be approved by the Privy Council, and Elizabeth I instituted a system under which books could not be published without the approval of either the Archbishop of Canterbury or the Bishop of London. The punishments for those who defied the rules were occasionally extreme: John Stubbs, for example, who had the temerity in 1579 to publish a work warning the Queen against marrying the brother of the King of

France, was punished by having one of his hands cut off. King James I banned the publication of pamphlets of news, and these early forms of the newspaper would not appear again until the 1640s. For much of the period a system of registration through the Stationers' Company was in essence a comprehensive system of censorship. Admittedly, enforcement of the rules governing printing had always been erratic, and there are not very many examples of actual censorship of books in this period; it has even been argued that many of the laws governing printing were not imposed upon printers but were in fact requested by them as a means of protecting their economic monopoly. But it was the idea of pre-publication licensing of books that was the particular focus of Milton's arguments in *Areopagitica*, and his arguments have been turned to again and again over the intervening centuries by those endeavoring to defend freedom of expression.

POETRY

A comparison with medieval poetry reveals the remarkable changes the Renaissance brought to poetic form in English verse. Late-medieval poets used many different verse forms, ranging from alliterative accentual patterns with anywhere from three to six beats in each line, to complex rhyming stanzaic patterns in lyric poems with a dance-like variety of accentual rhythms, to Chaucer's ten-syllable lines, sometimes more loosely organized around stress rather than a strict number of syllables. But strictly accentual-syllabic verse was rare in the medieval English period, whereas from the Renaissance to the early twentieth century it was the dominant poetic form in English.

The late fifteenth- and early sixteenth-century poetry of John Skelton still has one foot in the medieval period, at least as far as meter is concerned. Lines such as the following are written in accentual verse—that is to say, each contains a set number of accented syllables (in this case three), but has no set number of total syllables, and no regular arrangement of stressed and unstressed syllables:

Then will he rout;
Then sweetly together we lie,
As two pigs in a sty.

Detail from the frontispiece to Margaret Cavendish's *Philosophical and Physical Opinions* (1655). According to the poem accompanying the likeness of Cavendish, "studious she is and all alone ... Her library on which she looks, it is her head, her thoughts, her books ... Her own flames do her inspire."

Only a decade or so after Skelton was writing, other poets—most notably Sir Thomas Wyatt and his contemporary Henry Howard, Earl of Surrey—began to draw on classical and Italian forms of a quite different nature, forms that would dominate English poetry for the next four centuries. Wyatt and Surrey are most often given credit for introducing to English literature the sonnet form that Petrarch and others had established in Italy. Of broader importance was the tradition they established of writing in accentual-syllabic meters. Of these, iambic pentameter was the most frequent choice, whether in sonnets (such as Wyatt's "I find no peace, and all my war is done"), in unrhymed (or "blank") verse of the sort that Surrey was the first to write in English, or in other forms. Iambic tetrameter (i.e., having four "feet" or groups of stressed and unstressed syllables in every line, rather than five) was also common: for example, Surrey's "My friend, the things that do attain." Where Wyatt and Surrey led, others followed; the great outpouring of poetry in the 1580s and 1590s by Sidney, Spenser, Marlowe, Shakespeare, and the rest was entirely an outpouring of accentual-syllabic verse.

Accentual-syllabic meters were structured according to classical principles, with regular patternings of syllables forming poetic "feet," and a set number of feet in every line. But along the way the classical principles were transformed in one crucial respect. Unlike English, classical Greek and Latin are not characterized by large variations in the degree of stress placed on different syllables: there are no distinctions between accented (or stressed) syllables and unaccented (or unstressed) syllables. Distinctions between syllables for the purposes of their arrangement in poetic meter were in ancient times based on *duration* of sound—some syllables taking a shorter time to say, others a longer time—rather than on degrees of stress. In English, however, where the alternation of stressed and unstressed syllables is fundamental to the natural spoken rhythms of the language, the Greek framework and terminology came to be applied to alternations between stressed and unstressed (or "accented" and "unaccented") syllables rather than long or short syllables. Whereas the Greeks had used the term "iambic" to describe verse in which a syllable that took a short time to say was followed by a syllable that took a long time to say, English verse took an iamb to consist of an unstressed syllable followed by a stressed syllable. And so on for trochees (one long syllable followed by one short became one stressed syllable followed by one unstressed); dactyls (one long syllable followed by two short became one stressed syllable followed by two unstressed); anapests (two short followed by one long syllable became two unstressed followed by one stressed syllable); and spondees (two long syllables became two stressed syllables). Regular patterning of what the late sixteenth-century poet, musician, and poetic theorist Thomas Campion referred to as "the heaviness of the syllables" became the ruling principle of English poetic meter.

Borrowing from—and transforming—classical poetic models was a central feature of English poetry throughout the late sixteenth and early seventeenth centuries. From Spenser's *The Shepheardes Calendar* to Milton's "Lucida" and beyond, the pastoral poem, with its conventions of musical shepherds singing songs of love and of sorrow, was a poetic staple. Classical poetic models for satires, for wedding songs (as with Spenser's *Epithalamion*), for elegies, and for love poetry in lyric form were also widely imitated and adapted. And the two great long poems of the period—Spenser's *The Faerie Queene*, and Milton's *Paradise Lost*—so different in some respects, are alike in drawing substantially on classical models.

Just as romance narratives were an important sub-genre of late sixteenth-century prose, so too was verse romance important to the poetry of the late sixteenth century. The 1590s opened with the publication of the greatest of all verse romances in English, *The Faerie Queene*, which Spenser had begun in 1580. No other verse romance of the period attempted anything so ambitious, but a remarkable succession of shorter verse romances appeared over the course of a few years in the late 1580s and early 1590s: Marlowe's *Hero and Leander* (1598); Lodge's *Scylla's Metamorphosis* (1589); Daniel's *The Complaint of Rosamond* (1592); Shakespeare's *Venus and Adonis* (1593); and Drayton's *Endymion and Phoebe* (1595). These poems draw heavily on the mythological stories recounted by the Roman poet Ovid in his *Metamorphoses*, *Heroines*, and *Amours*, though in form and tone they all bear a decidedly Elizabethan stamp. They all bear the stamp of the court, as well: these were poems intended for the aristocracy and, indeed, for the monarch herself.

The Renaissance was an age of artifice ("artificial" was during this period used exclusively as a term of praise), and much of the poetry of the 1580s and 1590s is given to imagery that is extravagant in its inventiveness. Some of the extravagance is tongue-in-cheek, as is surely the case with Shakespeare's evident lampooning in his early comedy *Love's Labor's Lost* of the verbal excess of the character Holofernes, whose "gift" is "a foolish extravagant spirit, full of forms, figures, shapes, objects, ideas, apprehensions, motions, revolutions: these are begot in the ventricle of memory, nourished in the womb of *pia mater*, and delivered upon the mellowing of occasion." In his poetry of the

THE FAERIE QVEENE.

Difpofed into twelue books,

Fashioning

XII. Morall vertues.

LONDON

Printed for William Ponfonbie.

1590.

Title page of the first edition of *The Faerie Queene* (1590).

later 1590s and of the early seventeenth century, Shakespeare tamed his earlier tendency toward extravagant cleverness, though he never abandoned artifice. Much the same may be said of Ben Jonson, who advocated "plain language" and told poets to take care of their style in writing: "Be not winding, or wanton with far-fetched descriptions," he advised.

Many of the most important poets of the early seventeenth century, however, aspired to new heights of inventiveness. Chief among these was John Donne. Donne's early verse in particular often plays in elaborate fashion with extraordinary comparisons. It also twists and turns syntactically, mirroring in its form the surprising paradoxes or contradictions conveyed in the sense of the lines. These sorts of images, drawing extreme comparisons, have come to be known as "conceits." In some cases a conceit may be extended over several lines, or indeed a full poem. So, for example, Donne compares a tear to the globe, and his mistress's body to his "America," his "new-found land." The seventeenth-century poets who have been most often associated with these poetic tendencies—Donne and Abraham Cowley chief among them, with the devotional poets George Herbert, Richard Crashaw, and Henry Vaughan rather more loosely associated—have since the time of Samuel Johnson in the eighteenth century been referred to as "the metaphysical poets." Johnson's unfavorable assessment of such poetry has been rejected by most critics and scholars for the past century or more; T.S. Eliot, in particular, famously praised the metaphysical poets for uniting feeling and intellect in their verse. Yet Johnson captured something of the truth in his description of metaphysical poets as endeavoring "to be singular in their thoughts," and of the ideas produced through the intellectual gymnastics of many metaphysical poems as "often new, but seldom natural." Eventually Donne turned away from extravagance, abandoning much of the sensual content as well as the extreme conceits of his early verse as he turned to religion and to religious poetry, and Herbert made his efforts to suppress his own skills in rhetorical ornamentation a subject of his poetry:

> My thoughts began to burnish, sprout, and swell,
> Curling with metaphors a plain intention,
> Decking the sense, as if it were to sell.

Yet the audacity of the metaphysical poets has left a lasting mark on English literature: the ways of talking about religious faith and about love of God in the language of human physical love and vice versa; the ways of talking *to* God that Herbert developed; and the extremity of the conceits themselves have all found imitators as well as admirers in subsequent eras.

Lively debates have taken place over the past generation about whether or not the term "metaphysical poetry" in fact conveys something meaningful about a diverse body of work; it is often argued in particular that grouping Herbert with "the metaphysical" brings us no closer to what is unique and interesting about his poetry. So too has it been debated whether the term "cavalier poetry" as an umbrella term to identify a group of poets from later in the seventeenth century conveys much that is meaningful. Certainly there is a common tendency among poets such as Thomas Carew (pronounced "Carey"), Sir John Denham, Robert Herrick, Richard Lovelace, James Shirley, Sir John Suckling, and Edmund Waller toward smooth rhythms and mellifluous sounds. And they are inevitably associated with one another simply by having been on the Royalist side—though only some were given to infusing verse with a strong political or religious content. (The strongest poetic statement on a Royalist theme may well be Katherine Philips's "Upon the Double Murder of King Charles," in which she poses the following question: "He broke God's laws, and therefore he must die, / and what shall then become of thee and I?") The cavalier poets all tend to write frequently of the good life and of love—but there the similarities largely end. Interestingly, though, the love poetry of the cavalier poets—whether the highly charged eroticism of poets such as Carew and Suckling or the more chaste and chivalrous variety of Lovelace—is unequivocally heterosexual. The homoeroticism that infuses so much of the finest poetry of the 1590s, and that was a significant presence in the court of James I in the early seventeenth century, is nowhere evident in the verse of these later poets.

Few seventeenth-century poets, even the most courtly and cavalier, failed to produce at least some devotional poems. In literature as in life, the seventeenth century mixes devotional and secular responses to the world, inextricably intertwining the language of religion with the language of social life and politics. An increasingly important reference point in devotional poetry as the century wore on became the attitude one held toward prelapsarian existence—humankind before the Fall. Whereas Aemilia Lanier, writing in 1611, took the Fall as an occasion for weighing the relative merits of man and woman, Lovelace paints an idyllic version of love before the fall of Adam and Eve:

No serpent kiss poisoned the taste,
Each touch was naturally chaste,
And their mere sense a miracle.

Henry Vaughan, a Royalist who saw himself as a "son of George Herbert," took a more gloomy view, and one that partook only of a male perspective. For Vaughan, writing in 1650, it is impossible to conceive of the prelapsarian state in a tone other than that of melancholy: "He sighed for Eden, and would often say, / 'Ah! what bright days were those!'"

There are fewer Puritan or Parliamentary poets of note than there are Royalist ones, but among them are the two pre-eminent poets of the age: Andrew Marvell and John Milton. Milton, indeed, has often been regarded as towering above not only his contemporaries but also over all other English poets, with the sole exception of Shakespeare. Milton is the supremely paradoxical figure of English literature. He was a devout Christian who more or less abandoned institutionalized religion in favor of a "church of one"; he wrote what remains the great Christian epic poem in English, *Paradise Lost*—but gave Satan the leading role; he was a Puritan who eschewed plain style for Latinate inversions and epic grandeur. Milton managed to convey perhaps more fully than any other writer in English both prelapsarian innocence in the "heav'n on earth" of Eden and the "guilty shame, dishonest shame" of humans after their Fall.

Like Milton, Marvell supported the "Good Old Cause" of Cromwell and political Republicanism. To the extent that we can be sure about Marvell's thoughts on any subject, however, Marvell appears to have seen Cromwell more as the embodiment of a pure force of nature than as a representative of pure moral and religious values: his "An Oration Ode upon Cromwell's Return from Ireland" is among the most subtly balanced pieces of English political verse of any era. Even more than Milton, however, Marvell was a poet of the garden—a garden in which a sense of the Fall was never far away, but yet one of surpassing beauty and innocence. To the contemplation of such scenes

Marvell brought his own unique perspective; rather than focus on prelapsarian pleasure, Marvell imagined the supreme joys to be those of solitary contemplation of the beauties of nature:

> Two Paradises 'there in one
> To live in Paradise alone.

The Drama

The flowering of drama in England from the late 1580s to the 1620s is widely accepted as the greatest cultural achievement in the history of English literature. The list of important dramatists who flourished during this period includes not only Marlowe, Shakespeare, and Jonson but also Thomas Kyd, John Lyly, George Peele, John Webster, Cyril Tourneur, Francis Beaumont, John Fletcher, Thomas Middleton, John Ford, James Shirley, John Marston, Thomas Dekker, Thomas Heywood, and Philip Massinger. It is an outpouring the more remarkable for there being so few advance signs of its coming. In the middle years of the sixteenth century, the main forms of medieval drama were very much alive: audiences were still watching guild-sponsored biblical plays, allegorical dramas such as *Everyman*, and various kinds of (generally crude) secular comedy performed by traveling troupes of players or local inhabitants as part of feast-day celebrations. As the forces behind the Protestant Reformation gathered steam, however, a substantial body of opinion became convinced that neither the popular secular drama nor the often irreverent representations of religious material in the biblical plays were proper to be played at all: a key factor in the demise of the biblical plays is thought to have been hostility from those sympathetic to the Protestant Reformation.

As the biblical plays were dying out, the revival of classical literature ushered in by humanism helped give birth to new forms of English drama. The first phase in the introduction of these new models was the translation of classical plays, particularly Roman tragedies by Seneca and Roman comedies by Plautus and Terence. Of the two, it was Roman comedy that first had an impact in England, with English schools and colleges presenting comedies by Plautus or Terence to school audiences (or occasionally to aristocratic ones,

by invitation). The earliest known adaptation into English of one of these comedies is Nicholas Udall's *Ralph Roister Doister*, probably written by Udall during the years when he was the headmaster of Eton, 1534 to 1541. Such performances typically involved scenery painted on canvas stretched out behind the acting area, the canvas often painted so as to represent a street in perspective according to what was believed to be "the manner of the ancients." The play itself is lively, but adds little to its Roman model; it lacks any of the depth that characterizes so much of the drama of the late 1580s to the 1620s.

Of classical models for tragedy the most highly esteemed were the tragedies of Seneca; these began to be performed in Latin on the Italian stage very early in the sixteenth century, and by 1551 are known to have been performed in England at Trinity College, Cambridge. Seneca's tragedies began to be translated into English by Jasper Haywood in the late 1550s, and within 20 years all of Seneca's plays had been translated into English. Ironically, these plays had almost certainly not been acted out fully on the Roman stage: they are filled with set-piece speeches, and are believed by classical scholars to have been recited by a single actor. The Elizabethans, however, took Seneca's plays as a model for lively action, borrowing not only their five-act structure but also their preponderance of long set-piece speeches. Such borrowings were at first very much an upper-class phenomenon: English Senecan plays such as *Gorboduc*, *Jokester*, *Tancred*, and *Gismunda* were performed in the houses of the nobility or at the Inns of Court on special occasions. To Sir Philip Sidney, endeavoring to apply as a matter of literary theory the rules of classical drama to the English stage, Thomas Norton and Thomas Sackville's *Gorboduc* was particularly deserving of praise. Only the fact of its being "very defections in the circumstances"—in other words, of its not conforming closely enough to the classical ideal of the "unities," in which a play's action occurred in one setting and over a length of time not exceeding one day—prevented *Gorboduc* from being taken "as an exact model of all tragedies." To later ages, by contrast, it is almost unimaginable that *Gorboduc* could be a model for anything dramatic. Its long speeches seem static; extraordinary and violent actions are reported but never displayed before the audience;

and the play is never structured so as to arouse audience expectations.

How did the most dynamic and open period of theater in the history of the English stage develop so quickly out of such a static and restrictive background? A key moment in this extraordinary development was the decision by a London businessman, James Burbage, to build a playhouse northeast of London—outside the city limits, so as to be outside the regulatory authority of the city, but close enough to enable Londoners to attend performances. "The Theatre," as Burbage rather unimaginatively called the new playhouse, became a model for other theaters such as the Globe and the Swan, the latter two both constructed in Southwark, just across the Thames from London—again, outside the London city limits. Before this time such "professional" actors as there had been belonged to troupes that traveled from town to town, typically performing old plays again and again in different venues. The establishment of permanent theaters in the London area reflected the demographic shifts of the time—not only the rapid growth of population, but also its increasing concentration in and around London. But the presence of these playing spaces had a number of important effects. Perhaps most obviously, they suddenly created a steady and ongoing demand for new plays: if Londoners were to be enticed to the new playhouses, the theater companies could not simply keep playing nothing but old standards. And London audiences were the most literate and the most diverse of any in Britain; though the monarch never deigned to attend performances in such venues, audiences certainly included all other elements of the population. Apprentices and others of scant means would pay a penny to stand on the ground in front of and on both sides of the stage (the members of the audience Hamlet calls "groundlings"). Levels of seating, protected from the elements, rose around on all sides; a covered seat for a performance typically cost two pence. Or a performance could be observed from the privacy of a "lord's room" for sixpence. (In Renaissance London, as in London or New York today, the most expensive seats in the theater were sold for the equivalent of a day's wage for a common laborer.)

A theater soon grew up that differed substantially from both the performances of the traveling troupes and the academic theater that had been imitating Roman models. For this "theater in the round," little or no attempt was made to provide realistic sets or backdrops: most props were handheld. There was a good deal of rapid movement and rapid dialogue, and long set speeches became a rarity. Comic characters and comic scenes were introduced into tragedies (a practice strictly forbidden according to Sidney or the classical theorists). And plays began more and more to depict all strata of society, and to depict women as well as men in leading roles. (Throughout this period, it was considered unseemly for women to appear on the public stage, though they did perform in court masques. In public theaters in England, female roles were played by adolescent boy actors, a practice that provided for multiple opportunities for complex layering in storylines such as those of Shakespeare's *Twelfth Night* and *The Merchant of Venice* involving females pretending to be males.)

Playwrights, for their part, were paid a flat fee for their work, typically six pounds per play. Popular plays were performed again and again over many years, but the playwright would receive no additional income from these performances; the incentive for playwrights was thus to produce new work. And produce they did: the 37 plays that Shakespeare is known to have written over the course of approximately 25 years may seem extraordinary by modern standards, but it pales by comparison with the productivity of Thomas Heywood, now best known as the author of the domestic tragedy *A Woman Killed with Kindness* (1603) and of a defense of the theater, *An Apology for Actors* (1612). In an address to the reader prefacing *The English Traveler* (1633), Heywood refers to the "two hundred and twenty plays in which I have had either an entire hand or at least the main finger" (of these, only about 20 survive). In the press to complete more work, collaboration of the sort that Heywood alludes to was frequent. Shakespeare collaborated with other playwrights on at least two projects; Ben Jonson collaborated with Thomas Dekker; Dekker collaborated with Thomas Middleton; Francis Beaumont and John Fletcher usually wrote in collaboration with each other; Philip Massinger collaborated with Dekker and with Nathaniel Field; and so on. In its modes of composition as much as in other respects, then, the Elizabethan drama was fluid and dynamic.

It should not be supposed that classical models were altogether abandoned in this flurry of creative activity; far from it. Comedies of the late 1580s and early 1590s (such as Shakespeare's *The Comedy of Errors*) were in many ways closely modeled on the comedies of Plautus, and tragedies from the same period (such as Thomas Kyd's *The Spanish Tragedy*, Marlowe's *Tamburlaine*, and Shakespeare's *Titus Andronicus*) borrowed extensively from Senecan tragedy. But Shakespeare and other comic dramatists quickly left behind the more formulaic aspects of Plautine comedy. They changed the shape of Senecan tragedy, too; a certain amount of static speechifying was still featured, but now the violence that in Seneca was typically reported as having occurred offstage began to be performed before the eyes of the audience. Audiences remained rapt: *The Spanish Tragedy*, *Tamburlaine*, and *Titus Andronicus* were all enormously popular.

For ten years or more following the establishment of the first permanent theater outside London, most of the plays produced seem to have been fairly crude in their construction. (Since few plays from this period have survived, generalizations must be advanced with caution.) Certainly plays such as those by George Peele from the 1580s and early 1590s, the anonymous *Mucedorus* (c. 1590)—and for that matter *Tamburlaine* and *Titus Andronicus*—are loosely constructed on episodic principles, with nothing to facilitate any sense of awareness in the audience of a concatenation of events unfolding. But by the early 1590s, Marlowe and Shakespeare in particular had refined the craft of playwriting so as to create through their plotting an ongoing sense of the future action as well as of the present. When a character such as Richard III (in the opening scene of Shakespeare's *Richard III*) expresses his intentions to the audience ("Plots I have laid, inductions dangerous ..."), the speech itself is not dissimilar to the set-piece speeches in *Gorboduc*. But here the intentions of Richard III are woven into the plot so as to become a driving force behind the play—a play that was performed more frequently than any other on the Elizabethan and Jacobean stage.

The theaters "in the round" outside the city limits were not the only venues for drama in London during this period. Notably, the old monastery at Blackfriars in

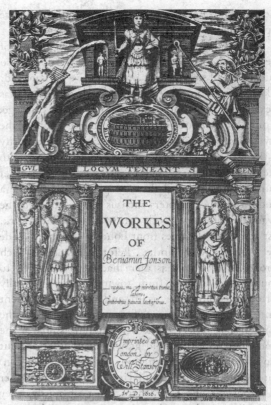

Title page, *The Workes of Benjamin Jonson* (1616). The publication in 1616 of Jonson's collected works is a landmark in the history of English drama as literature.

London had begun as early as the 1550s to be used as a venue for the production of plays, and by the early seventeenth century it was a leading London theater. As a former monastic area it enjoyed, through a legal loophole, the same immunity from regulation and taxation by the city of London that the theaters outside the city limits enjoyed. The Blackfriars stage, though, was indoors, not outdoors like the public theaters; the stage itself was not surrounded by members of the audience on three sides as were the stages in the other theaters; and the audiences themselves were less diverse: there were no groundlings in the audience at private theaters such as Blackfriars and the Royal Court.

Even when outside the jurisdiction of the city, dramatic performances in the Elizabethan and Jacobean age entailed considerable risk. When in 1605 James I

From the frontispiece to William Alabaster, *Roxana Tragedia* (1632). This is one of the earliest printed representations of an English dramatic performance.

was apprised of the satirical treatment accorded the Scottish court in a play by Ben Jonson, John Marston, and George Chapman (*Eastward Ho!*), he disbanded the company that had mounted the production—even though his wife, Queen Anne, was its patron. Because of the potentially transgressive content of many Elizabethan and Jacobean plays, few were given a local and contemporary setting; even if one wished to convey pointed messages about contemporary politics, it was safer to do so elliptically, by setting the action of a play in Italy and in a vaguely defined past rather than in London in the present.

The range of the drama in the early years of the seventeenth century is, if anything, even broader than that of the 1590s. This is the era of Shakespeare's great tragedies and of his dark comedies as well as his late romances; of many of Ben Jonson's finest comedies; of

a group of violent "revenge tragedies" by Webster and Tourneur; and of a group of "city comedies" concerning London society by Dekker, Middleton, and others. Overall, the tone of the Jacobean drama is darker than that of the Elizabethan stage—the satire more biting, the tragedy more bleak. This is also the era of the masque, a form of court drama that stands in marked contrast to that of "theater in the round." Masques were as much spectacle as drama. They were astonishingly expensive productions performed for the aristocracy by a mixture of professionals and members of the court itself; they typically drew on pastoral or mythological themes; they often involved interaction between performers and spectators; they usually featured elaborate costumes, painted scenery, special effects, and set-piece displays; and they always included a good deal of song, music, and dance.

As the seventeenth century wore on, the theater came more and more frequently under attack by Puritans. Since the late 1580s dramatists had walked a fine line, desiring always to give to those elements of the crowd that were entertained by displays of bawdiness and violence a good deal of what they were looking for, while still insisting that such displays fulfilled a didactic purpose. The description of the action of the domestic tragedy *Arden of Faversham* (c. 1585–90) gives something of the flavor:

> The lamentable and true tragedy of M. Arden of Faversham of Kent. Who was most wickedly murdered by the means of his disloyal and wanton wife.... Where-in is showed the great malice and dissimulation of a wicked woman, the unsatiable desire of filthy lust and the shameful end of all murderers.

Wickedness, in other words, is shown to be punished, but along the way a good deal of titillation for the audience is provided. The theaters managed to resist the criticisms from the Puritans for more than five decades. But when Charles I was forced from London and the Puritans took control at the onset of the civil war in 1642, the theaters were closed by city officials—at the time, probably for political as much as moral reasons (the first thing all authorities traditionally do in a time of revolution is close the sites where large groups of people can meet together). They remained closed for almost two decades, until the Restoration in 1660. The most remarkable era in the history of the English stage was at an end.

The English Language in the Sixteenth and Seventeenth Centuries

If the rediscovery of Greek and Latin literature was a central element of the Renaissance in England, the increased currency of the Greek and Latin languages—and of Latin especially—was central to the changes that occurred in the English language in this period. Of the thousands of new English words imported from Greek and Latin, many were words that named new concepts or things for which no English equivalent existed (from *area* and *equilibrium* to *vacuum*). Such words enlarged the expressive capacity of the English language in several directions, increasing the stock of scientific, mathematical, rhetorical, and philosophical terms, and more broadly increasing the capacity of the language to express abstract concepts. (The word "abstraction" itself is first recorded as having been used in 1547.) Many Latin words remained intact as they entered the English language, including *antenna*, *apparatus*, *cerebellum*, *militia*, and *tedium*. Others became reshaped, often losing their original suffixes, as with, for example, the Latin words *complexus* and *desperatus*. On the other hand, Latin prefixes (among the most common of which are *ob-*, from; *post-*, after; *pre-*, before; and *sub-*, under) tended more often than not to be retained without alteration. In some cases words with Latin roots that had originally entered the English language in an altered form from the French now had a form closer to the Latin original "restored" in English.

There were also extensive borrowings during this period from the French (e.g., *bayonet*, *muscle*), from the Italian (e.g., *argosy*, *squadron*), from the Spanish (e.g., *cargo*, *sherry*), and from the Dutch (e.g., *deck*, *dock*, and *yacht*). In these borrowings one can see something of the pattern of interaction between Britons and these other nationalities, with borrowings from the Spanish often concerned with warfare, and from the Dutch often concerned with commerce, the sea, and painting (e.g., *easel*, *sketch*, and *landscape*).

Among the educated classes there were always those who resisted or mocked aspects of this "invasion" of foreign words. Thomas Wilson, for example, lamented in his *Art of Rhetoric* (1553) the use of "inkhorn terms" that were regarded as signs of scholarly affectation. Ralph Lever, responding to the wholesale importation of Latin terms, suggested in 1573 that the existing resources of native English could be adapted in ways that would be preferable to the Latin terms—that *endsay*, for example, should be preferred to *conclusion*, *saywhat* should be preferred to *definition*, and so on. And Ben Jonson in his play *Poetaster* mocked the excessive use of real or presumptive foreign imports such as *defunct*, *fatuate*, *furibund*, *inflate*, *prorumpted* ("What a noise it made!" comments one character at the mention of this word), *strenuous*, *turgidious*, and *ventositous*. "O terrible windy words," laments one character. "A sign of a windy brain," agrees another. We may safely infer that such satire (like that by Shakespeare in *Love's Labours Lost*) had a recognizable referent in real life—that some did indeed use the new coinages in an affected or pompous fashion. But some of the resistance appears to have represented no more than the prejudice that seems inevitable in any age against linguistic change. Just as William Strunk and E.B. White fulminated in the 1950s against the new word *finalize*, unable to recognize how it might fulfill a useful linguistic function, so Jonson and the others made fun of words such as *defunct* and *strenuous* that have ended up taking a permanent (and permanently useful) place in the English language.

The fact that more new words appear in the works of Shakespeare than in those of any other writer from this period has prompted the unjustified assumption that Shakespeare "introduced" more new words to the English language than anyone else. That claim may well be true, but we can of course speak with certainty only of first written occurrences of words and phrases; it is in almost every case entirely possible that a word or phrase had been in common currency for some time before it appears in a piece of writing that has survived. At the very least, however, we may confidently say that Shakespeare was extraordinarily receptive to new coinages, and that his works played a role in helping to shape the changing language during this period. It is noteworthy that among the many words that first appear in English in Shakespeare there are not only a great many borrowings from Latin (e.g., *abstemious*, *arose, assignation*) but also a number of words formed by inventive re-combinations of English words, or through part of speech conversions (e.g., *gloomy, leapfrog, lonely*). In his place in the history of the language as in other respects, Shakespeare stands pre-eminent.

It is worth noting here that many phrases or expressions that we now think of as proverbial also originated in Shakespeare's works. The phrase "vanish into thin air," for example, is used on a daily basis, so much so that it is difficult to recapture a fresh sense of the aptness of the image. Other expressions that make their first appearance in Shakespeare include *come full circle, eaten out of house and home, has seen better days, the live-long day,* and *there's method in his madness.*

Though the printing press had been introduced in 1476, the regularization of spelling that one might have expected to follow as a natural consequence of the spread of printing began to happen only very slowly over the course of the sixteenth and seventeenth centuries. Certainly through to the early seventeenth century it remained common for writers to spell the same word in different ways in the same document, and even for individuals to spell their name in different ways at different times. Pronunciation also began to move toward a common standard as London became more and more dominant in English life, but these changes too, occurred slowly; there remained several distinct dialects of English in the mid-seventeenth century. The great vowel shift was virtually complete by the early sixteenth century, as was the change in habits of pronunciation of the final *e* in many English words; by the end of the fifteenth century that practice had almost entirely died out.

The Renaissance brought several changes in English grammar and syntax. In the sixteenth and seventeenth centuries the *–eth* third person singular verb ending (e.g., *followeth, thinketh*) began to die out, though some common contractions of these forms (e.g., *hath* for *haveth, doth* for *doeth*) persisted into the late seventeenth century. There were changes, too, in the formation of pronouns. In the third person plural, the forms *they / them / their* replaced the old *they / hem / hire* that we find in Chaucerian English. And the second person *you* replaced the old *ye* during this period. With second person pronouns, however, the situation is complicated by changes in usage involving the second person pronoun *thou* (and its object form *thee*). These forms were used when one was addressing another in a more familiar or less respectful fashion, whether because of the circumstances or because of the relative social standing of the individuals in conversation. (A child or an animal would also typically be addressed as *thou.*) In less familiar and more respectful contexts *you* would be used. (The distinction here resembles that still existing in languages such as French, in which one may choose when addressing an individual between the more familiar *tu* and the more formal *vous*, which also serves as the second person plural form.) The use of the familiar *thou* and *thee* began to die out early in the sixteenth century, and by the seventeenth century *you* was used almost universally as the second person pronoun in all circumstances.

Finally, there were significant changes during the sixteenth and early seventeenth centuries in the formation of negatives and interrogatives, and in the use of *do* as an auxiliary verb. Instead of saying *we went not* or asking *know you her?* it became common to say *we did not go* and to ask *do you know her?* The use of *do* as an auxiliary spread quickly, and indeed for much of the early modern period came to be used in ways that have since died out; in the sixteenth century the forms *I think* and *I do think* were used interchangeably where now (unless we wish to add emphasis) we would use only the former.

History of the Language and of Print Culture

In an effort to provide for readers a direct sense of the development of the language and of print culture, examples of texts in their original form (and of illustrations) have been provided in each volume. A list of these within the present volume, arranged chronologically, appears below.

Katherine Philips, "Friendship's Memory, To my Dearest Lucasia," poem in original spelling and punctuation, pp. 894–95.

John Milton, *Paradise Lost*, title page, 1674 edition, p. 919; *Paradise Lost*, passage in original spelling and punctuation, pp. 920–21.

William Tyndale
1494? – 1536

The English phrases that we now think of when we hear the term "Biblical language" are very largely the product of the work of one individual: William Tyndale. Tyndale met constant opposition from church and government officials throughout the course of his adult life. The work of translating the scriptures into the vernacular—English—was so dangerous that he went into hiding in continental Europe while trying to complete it. He was finally executed for his work, but within a few years of his death, his Bible was becoming widely read throughout England.

Tyndale was born in the mid-1490s, most likely in Stinchcombe, Gloucestershire, near the Welsh border. Not much is known about his early life and parentage. We do know that he attended Magdalen Hall, Oxford, was awarded a B.A. in 1512 and was incepted as M.A. in 1515, and was ordained a priest in London that same year. While at Oxford he was greatly influenced by the work of the Dutch philosopher Desiderius Erasmus —particularly by the venerable scholar's study of the *Septuagint*, the original Greek version of the books that Christians now refer to as the New Testament.

After graduation Tyndale returned to Gloucestershire, serving as household chaplain to Sir John and Lady Anne Walsh and as tutor to their children. During this period he began studying Erasmus's Greek New Testament and considered attempting his own English translation, which he hoped would enable local lay people to read the Scriptures for themselves. His translation of Erasmus's *Enchiridion militis Christiani* (*Manual of the Christian Knight*), which encourages the study the New Testament, helped gain the Walshs' support of his position. At this time Tyndale was also in demand as a preacher, but his sermons offended the local clergy, and he was brought before the Bishop's Chancellor on charges of heresy.

Tyndale left the area in 1523 and headed for London, hoping to find support for his translation work. He approached Bishop Cuthbert Tunstall, Erasmus's friend and Bishop of London, hoping he would serve as patron for the project. The Bishop not only refused his request, but became a vocal opponent of any plan to translate the Bible into the vernacular. Tyndale was forced to leave London in May 1524. With the sponsorship of Sir Humphrey Monmouth, a London merchant, he went to Germany, which at the time was more open to the ideas of the Protestant Reformation. He never returned to England.

The details of Tyndale's life in Germany are sketchy. His status as intellectual outlaw meant that he moved around considerably. He stayed in Hamburg for a while and then went to Wittenberg, where it is likely that he met with the famous Reformation leader Martin Luther. Eventually he settled in Cologne, where he set about having his translation of the *New Testament* published. Before it was finished, however, city magistrates caught wind of the project and ordered the printing house raided. Tyndale was able to escape with a portion of his printed New Testament, and this "Cologne Fragment" (which included most of the first Gospel, that of Matthew) circulated throughout England, accompanied by a prologue and marginal notes by Luther. Tyndale fled to Worms, a German town that had demonstrated more openness to the Reformation, where he was able to have the complete *New Testament* printed in 1526. The pocket-sized books (without Luther's preface or notes) were smuggled by boat into England and Scotland, where they circulated quickly. In January 1530, Tyndale completed a translation of the Pentateuch, the first five books of the Hebrew scriptures. Although he never managed to translate all of what Christians refer to as the Old Testament, his translation of the Pentateuch also became very widely read in England. Tyndale was the first to create an English language translation from Hebrew and Greek, the original languages in which the scriptures were written. Earlier English translations existed (created by Bede, John Wycliffe, and others), but they used the Vulgate, the church's official Latin translation, as their base text. But it is not only for removing this Latin "filter" that Tyndale is remembered. His elegant and powerful phrases were instrumental in establishing the Bible in English as both a literary and a religious text. And because his translation appeared at a time when it could be distributed widely through the use of the recently invented printing press, he had considerable influence in shaping the patterns of English speech. Tyndale introduced into the language phrases such as "the signs of the times," "fight the good fight," "the powers that be," and "a law unto themselves," which remain common currency today.

After his translations were in print, Tyndale turned to writing theological treatises and commentaries on the Bible. While his translations had angered the clergy, his treatises infuriated the government of England. In *The Practice of the Prelates* (1530) Tyndale harshly criticized King Henry VIII for divorcing his wife. The king responded by ordering Tyndale captured and returned to England. In 1534 Tyndale moved to Antwerp, then part of the Netherlands, thinking that there a new measure of openness to the Reformation would give him a greater measure of security. In 1535, however, he was betrayed by Henry Phillips, an English spy working in the Netherlands. He was arrested and held for 18 months in Vilvorde Castle prison near Brussels, where he was convicted of heresy. On 6 October 1536 he was scheduled to be burned at the stake, but as a mark of his distinction as a scholar, he was strangled to death and then his body was burnt.

Ironically, within a year of his death the English government approved Tyndale's translation. His Old Testament was completed by Miles Coverdale and was published with his New Testament in 1539; to avoid embarrassment, however, the English government did not allow Tyndale's name to appear. With Mary's accession to the throne in 1553, there was an abrupt change in policy, and Bibles in English were again banned. In the face of this censorship, a group of exiles in Geneva prepared a more scholarly translation, accompanied by substantial (and often tendentious) marginal notes. That version, known as the Geneva Bible, became widely available in England once Elizabeth I had replaced Mary as monarch. In response, Catholics in the Elizabethan era (many of them now in exile, as many Protestants had been under Mary) prepared a translation of their own, the Douay-Rheims version, also accompanied by interpretive notes. As the excerpts below demonstrate, other versions drew heavily on Tyndale's pioneering work of translation.

In 1611, a new authorized version of the Bible (now known as the King James Version) was released in England. The story of the creation of the authorized version is a complex and interesting one. It was a vast collaborative venture of considerable significance in English religious history. The result, however, was a text very much based on Tyndale's. For the books that Tyndale had translated, more than eighty percent of the text of the authorized version was taken word for word from his translation. Indeed, as the excerpts below illustrate, the phrasing (and the rhythm) of the King James version is typically closer to that of Tyndale than it is to any of the "intermediate" versions.

⌘ ⌘ ⌘

Tyndale's *English Bible*

GENESIS: CHAPTER 1

In the beginning God created heaven and earth. The earth was void and empty, and darkness was upon the deep, and the spirit of God moved upon the water.

Then God said: let there be light and there was light. And God saw the light that it was good: and divided the light from the darkness, and called the light day, and the darkness night: and so of the evening and morning was made the first day.

And God said: let there be a firmament between the waters, and let it divide the waters asunder. Then God made the firmament and parted the waters which were under the firmament, from the waters that were above the firmament: And it was so. And God called the firmament heaven. And so of the evening and morning was made the second day.

And God said, let the waters that are under heaven gather themselves unto one place, that the dry land may appear: And it came so to pass. And God called the dry land the earth and the gathering together of waters called he the sea. And God saw that it was good.

And God said: let the earth bring forth herb and grass that sow seed, and fruitful trees that bear fruit every one in his kind, having their seed in themselves upon the earth. And it came so to pass: and the earth brought forth herb and grass sowing seed every one in his kind and trees bearing fruit and having their seed in themselves every one in his kind. And God saw that it was good: and then of the evening and morning was made the third day.

King James *Bible*

GENESIS: CHAPTER 1

In the beginning God created the heaven and the earth. And the earth was without form, and void; and darkness *was* upon the face of the deep. And the spirit of God moved upon the face of the waters.

And God said, Let there be light: and there was light. And God saw the light, that *it was* good: and God divided the light from the darkness. And God called the light Day, and the darkness he called Night. And the evening and the morning were the first day.

And God said, Let there be a firmament in the midst of the waters, and let it divide the waters from the waters. And God made the firmament, and divided the waters which *were* under the firmament from the waters which *were* above the firmament: and it was so. And God called the firmament Heaven. And the evening and the morning were the second day.

And God said, Let the waters under the heaven be gathered together unto one place, and let the dry *land* appear: and it was so. And God called the dry *land* Earth; and the gathering together of the waters called he Seas: and God saw that it *was* good.

And God said, Let the earth bring forth grass, the herb yielding seed, *and* the fruit tree yielding fruit after his kind, whose seed *is* in itself, upon the earth: and it was so. And the earth brought forth grass, *and* herb yielding seed after his kind, and the tree yielding fruit, whose seed *was* in itself, after his kind: and God saw that it *was* good. And the evening and the morning were the third day.

Geneva Bible

GENESIS: CHAPTER 1

In the beginning God created the heaven and the earth. And the earth was without form and void, and darkness was upon the deep, and the Spirit of God moved upon the waters.

Then God said, Let there be light: and there was light. And God saw the light that it was good, and God separated the light from the darkness. And God called the light, Day, and the darkness, He called Night. So the evening and the morning were the first day.

Again God said, Let there be a firmament in the midst of the waters: and let it separate the waters from the waters. Then God made the firmament, and parted the waters, which were under the firmament, from the waters which were above the firmament: and it was so. And God called the firmament, Heaven. So the evening and the morning were the second day.

God said again, Let the waters under the heaven be gathered into one place, and let the dry land appear: and it was so. And God called the dry land, Earth, and He called the gathering together of the waters, Seas: and God saw that it was good.

Then God said, Let the earth bud forth the bud of the herb, that seedeth seed, the fruitful tree, which beareth fruit according to his kind, which may have his seed in itself upon the earth: and it was so. And the earth brought forth the bud of the herb, that seedeth seed according to his kind, also the tree that yieldeth fruit, which hath his seed in itself according to his kind: and God saw that it was good. So the evening and the morning were the third day.

Douay-Rheims Bible

GENESIS: CHAPTER 1

In the beginning God created heaven, and earth. And the earth was void and empty, and darkness was upon the face of the deep; and the spirit of God moved over the waters.

And God said: Be light made. And light was made. And God saw the light that it was good; and He divided the light from the darkness. And He called the light Day, and the darkness Night; and there was evening and morning one day.

And God said: Let there be a firmament made amidst the waters: and let it divide the waters from the waters. And God made a firmament, and divided the waters that were under the firmament, from those that were above the firmament, and it was so. And God called the firmament, Heaven; and the evening and morning were the second day.

God also said: Let the waters that are under the heaven, be gathered together into one place: and let the dry land appear. And it was so done. And God called the dry land, Earth; and the gathering together of the waters, He called Seas. And God saw that it was good.

And He said: let the earth bring forth the green herb, and such as may seed, and the fruit tree yielding fruit after its kind, which may have seed in itself upon the earth. And it was so done.

And the earth brought forth the green herb, and such as yieldeth seed according to its kind, and the tree that beareth fruit, having seed each one according to its kind. And God saw that it was good. And the evening and the morning were the third day.

Tyndale's *English Bible*

Then said God: let there be lights in the firmament of heaven to divide the day from the night, that they may be unto signs, seasons, days and years. And let them be lights in the firmament of heaven, to shine upon the earth. And so it was. And God made two great lights: A greater light to rule the day, and a less light to rule the night, and he made stars also. And God put them in the firmament of heaven to shine upon the earth, and to rule the day and the night, and to divide the light from darkness. And God saw that it was good: and so of the evening and morning was made the fourth day.

And God said, let the water bring forth creatures that move and have life, and fowls for to fly over the earth under the firmament of heaven. And God created great whales and all manner of creatures that live and move, which the waters brought forth in their kinds, and all manner of feathered fowls in their kinds. And God saw that it was good: and God blessed them saying: Grow and multiply and fill the waters of the seas, and let the fowls multiply upon the earth. And so of the evening and morning was made the fifth day.

And God said: let the earth bring forth living creatures in their kinds: cattle and worms and beasts of the earth in their kinds, and so it came to pass. And God made the beasts of the earth in their kinds and cattle in their kinds, and all manner worms of the earth in their kinds: and God saw that it was good.

And God said: let us make man in our similitude and after our likeness: that he may have rule over the fish of the sea, and over the fowls of the air, and over cattle, and over all the earth, and over all worms that creep on the earth. And God created man after His likeness, after the likeness of God created He Him: male and female created He them.

King James Bible

And God said, Let there be lights in the firmament of the heaven to divide the day from the night; and let them be for signs, and for seasons, and for days, and years. And let them be for lights in the firmament of the heaven to give light upon the earth: and it was so. And God made two great lights; the greater light to rule the day, and the lesser light to rule the night: *He made* the stars also. And God set them in the firmament of the heaven to give light upon the earth, and to rule over the day and over the night, and to divide the light from the darkness: and God saw that *it was* good. And the evening and the morning were the fourth day.

And God said, Let the waters bring forth abundantly the moving creature that hath life, and fowl *that* may fly above the earth in the open firmament of heaven. And God created great whales, and every living creature that moveth, which the waters brought forth abundantly, after their kind, and every winged fowl after his kind: and God saw that *it was* good. And God blessed them, saying, Be fruitful, and multiply, and fill the waters in the seas, and let fowl multiply in the earth. And the evening and the morning were the fifth day.

And God said, Let the earth bring forth the living creature after his kind, cattle, and creeping thing, and beast of the earth after his kind: and it was so. And God made the beast of the earth after his kind, and cattle after their kind, and every thing that creepeth upon the earth after his kind: and God saw that *it was* good.

And God said, Let us make man in our image, after our likeness: and let them have dominion over the fish of the sea, and over the fowl of the air, and over the cattle, and over all the earth, and over every creeping thing that creepeth upon the earth. So God created man in His own image, in the image of God created He him; male and female created He them.

Geneva Bible

And God said, Let there be lights in the firmament of the heaven, to separate the day from the night, and let them be for signs, and for seasons, and for days and years. And let them be for lights in the firmament of the heaven to give light upon the earth: and it was so. God then made two great lights: the greater light to rule the day, and the less light to rule the night: He made also the stars. And God set them in the firmament of the heaven, to shine upon the earth, And to rule in the day, and in the night, and to separate the light from the darkness: and God saw that it was good. So the evening and the morning were the fourth day.

Afterward God said, Let the waters bring forth in abundance every creeping thing that hath life: and let the fowl fly upon the earth in the open firmament of the heaven. Then God created the great whales, and every thing living and moving, which the waters brought forth in abundance, according to their kind, and every feathered fowl according to his kind: and God saw that it was good. Then God blessed them, saying, Bring forth fruit and multiply, and fill the waters in the seas, and let the fowl multiply in the earth. So the evening and the morning were the fifth day.

Moreover God said, Let the earth bring forth the living thing according to his kind, cattle, and that which creepeth, and the beast of the earth, according to his kind: and it was so. And God made the beast of the earth according to his kind, and the cattle according to his kind, and every creeping thing of the earth according to his kind: and God saw that it was good.

Furthermore God said, Let us make man in our image according to our likeness, and let them rule over the fish of the sea, and over the fowl of the heaven, and over the beasts, and over all the earth, and over every thing that creepeth and moveth on the earth. Thus God created the man in his image: in the image of God created He him: He created them male and female.

Douay-Rheims Bible

And God said: Let there be lights made in the firmament of heaven, to divide the day and the night, and let them be for signs, and for seasons, and for days and years: To shine in the firmament of heaven, and to give light upon the earth. And it was so done. And God made two great lights: a greater light to rule the day; and a lesser light to rule the night: and the stars. And He set them in the firmament of heaven to shine upon the earth. And to rule the day and the night, and to divide the light and the darkness. And God saw that it was good. And the evening and morning were the fourth day.

God also said: let the waters bring forth the creeping creature having life, and the fowl that may fly over the earth under the firmament of heaven. And God created the great whales, and every living and moving creature, which the waters brought forth, according to their kinds, and every winged fowl according to its kind. And God saw that it was good. And He blessed them, saying: Increase and multiply, and fill the waters of the sea: and let the birds be multiplied upon the earth. And the evening and morning were the fifth day.

And God said: Let the earth bring forth the living creature in its kind, cattle and creeping things, and beasts of the earth, according to their kinds. And it was so done. And God made the beasts of the earth according to their kinds, and cattle, and every thing that creepeth on the earth after its kind. And God saw that it was good.

And He said: Let us make man to our image and likeness: and let him have dominion over the fishes of the sea, and the fowls of the air, and the beasts, and the whole earth, and every creeping creature that moveth upon the earth. And God created man to His own image: to the image of God He created him: male and female He created them.

Tyndale's *English Bible*

And God blessed them, and God said unto them: Grow and multiply and fill the earth and subdue it, and have dominion over the fish of the sea, and over the fowls of the air, and over all the beasts that move on the earth.

And God said: see, I have given you all herbs that sow seed which are on all the earth, and all manner trees that have fruit in them and sow seed: to be meat for you and for all beasts of the earth, and unto all fowls of the air, and unto all that creepeth on the earth wherein is life, that they may have all manner herbs and grass for to eat, and even so it was. And God beheld all that he had made, and lo they were exceeding good: and so of the evening and morning was made the sixth day.

—1534

MATTHEW: CHAPTER 5

When He saw the people He went up into a mountain, and when He was set, His disciples came to him, and He opened His mouth, and taught them saying: Blessed are the poor in spirit: for theirs is the kingdom of heaven. Blessed are they that mourn: for they shall be comforted. Blessed are the meek: for they shall inherit the earth. Blessed are they which hunger and thirst for righteousness: for they shall be filled. Blessed are the merciful: for they shall obtain mercy. Blessed are the pure in heart: for they shall see God. Blessed are the peacemakers: for they shall be called the children of God. Blessed are they which suffer persecution for righteousness' sake: for theirs is the kingdom of heaven. Blessed are ye when men revile you, and persecute you, and shall falsely say all manner of evil sayings against you for my sake. Rejoice, and be glad, for great is your reward in heaven. For so persecuted they the Prophets which were before your days.

King James Bible

And God blessed them, and God said unto them, Be fruitful, and multiply, and replenish the earth, and subdue it: and have dominion over the fish of the sea, and over the fowl of the air, and over every living thing that moveth upon the earth.

And God said, Behold, I have given you every herb bearing seed, which *is* upon the face of all the earth, and every tree, in the which *is* the fruit of a tree yielding seed; to you it shall be for meat. And to every beast of the earth, and to every fowl of the air, and to every thing that creepeth upon the earth, wherein *there is* life, *I have given* every green herb for meat: and it was so. And God saw every thing that He had made, and, behold, *it was* very good. And the evening and the morning were the sixth day.

—1611

MATTHEW: CHAPTER 5

And seeing the multitudes, He went up into a mountain: and when He was set, His disciples came unto Him: and He opened His mouth, and taught them, saying, Blessed *are* the poor in spirit: for theirs is the kingdom of heaven. Blessed *are* they that mourn: for they shall be comforted. Blessed *are* the meek: for they shall inherit the earth. Blessed *are* they which do hunger and thirst after righteousness: for they shall be filled. Blessed *are* the merciful: for they shall obtain mercy. Blessed *are* the pure in heart: for they shall see God. Blessed *are* the peacemakers: for they shall be called the children of God. Blessed *are* they which are persecuted for righteousness' sake: for theirs is the kingdom of heaven. Blessed are ye, when *men* shall revile *you*, and persecute you, and shall say all manner of evil against you falsely, for my sake. Rejoice, and be exceeding glad: for great *is* your reward in heaven: for so persecuted they the prophets which were before you.

Geneva Bible

And God blessed them, and God said to them, Bring forth fruit and multiply, and fill the earth, and subdue it, and rule over the fish of the sea, and over the fowl of the heaven, and over every beast that moveth upon the earth.

And God said, Behold, I have given unto you every herb bearing seed, which is upon all the earth, and every tree, wherein is the fruit of a tree bearing seed: that shall be to you for meat. Likewise to every beast of the earth, and to every fowl of the heaven, and to every thing that moveth upon the earth, which hath life in itself, every green herb shall be for meat: and it was so. And God saw all that he had made, and lo, it was very good. So the evening and the morning were the sixth day.
—1599

MATTHEW: CHAPTER 5

And when He saw the multitude, He went up into a mountain: and when He was set, His disciples came to Him. And He opened His mouth and taught them, saying, Blessed *are* the poor in spirit, for theirs is the kingdom of heaven. Blessed *are* they that mourn: for they shall be comforted. Blessed *are* the meek: for they shall inherit the earth. Blessed *are* they which hunger and thirst for righteousness: for they shall be filled. Blessed *are* the merciful: for they shall obtain mercy. Blessed *are* the pure in heart: for they shall see God. Blessed *are* the peacemakers: for they shall be called the children of God. Blessed *are* they which suffer persecution for righteousness sake: for theirs is the kingdom of heaven. Blessed are ye when men revile you, and persecute *you*, and say all manner of evil against you for my sake, falsely. Rejoice and be glad, for great is your reward in heaven: for so persecuted they the Prophets which were before you.

Douay-Rheims Bible

And God blessed them, saying: Increase and multiply, and fill the earth, and subdue it, and rule over the fishes of the sea, and the fowls of the air, and all living creatures that move upon the earth.

And God said: Behold I have given you every herb bearing seed upon the earth, and all trees that have in themselves seed of their own kind, to be your meat: And to all beasts of the earth, and to every fowl of the air, and to all that move upon the earth, and wherein there is life, that they may have to feed upon. And it was so done. And God saw all the things that He had made, and they were very good. And the evening and morning were the sixth day.
—1609

MATTHEW: CHAPTER 5

And seeing the multitudes, He went up into a mountain, and when He was set down, His disciples came unto Him. And opening His mouth He taught them, saying: Blessed are the poor in spirit: for theirs is the kingdom of heaven. Blessed are the meek: for they shall possess the land. Blessed are they that mourn: for they shall be comforted. Blessed are they that hunger and thirst after justice: for they shall have their fill. Blessed are the merciful: for they shall obtain mercy. Blessed are the clean of heart: for they shall see God. Blessed are the peacemakers: for they shall be called the children of God. Blessed are they that suffer persecution for justice' sake: for theirs is the kingdom of heaven. Blessed are ye when they shall revile you, and persecute you, and speak all that is evil against you, untruly, for my sake: Be glad and rejoice, for your reward is very great in heaven. For so they persecuted the prophets that were before you.

Tyndale's *English Bible*

Ye are the salt of the earth: but and if the salt have lost her saltiness, what can be salted therewith? It is thenceforth good for nothing, but to be cast out, and to be trodden under foot of men. Ye are the light of the world. A city that is set on an hill, cannot be hid, neither do men light a candle and put it under a bushel, but on a candlestick, and it lighteth all that are in the house. Let your light so shine before men, that they may see your good works, and glorify your Father which is in heaven.

Think not that I am come to destroy the law, or the Prophets: no I am not come to destroy them, but to fulfil them. For truly I say unto you, till heaven and earth perish, one jot or one tittle[1] of the law shall not escape, till all be fulfilled.

Whosoever breaketh one of these least commandments, and teacheth men so, he shall be called the least in the kingdom of heaven. But whosoever observeth and teacheth, the same shall be called great in the kingdom of heaven.

For I say unto you, except your righteousness exceed the righteousness of the Scribes and Pharisees,[2] ye cannot enter into the kingdom of heaven.

Ye have heard how it was said unto them of the old time: Thou shalt not kill. For whosoever killeth, shall be in danger of judgment. But I say unto you, whosoever is angry with his brother, shall be in danger of judgment. Whosoever sayeth unto his brother Racha,[3] shall be in danger of a council. But whosoever sayeth thou fool, shall be in danger of hell fire.

King James Bible

Ye are the salt of the earth: but if the salt have lost his savor, wherewith shall it be salted? It is thenceforth good for nothing, but to be cast out, and to be trodden under foot of men. Ye are the light of the world. A city that is set on an hill cannot be hid. Neither do men light a candle, and put it under a bushel, but on a candlestick; and it giveth light unto all that are in the house. Let your light so shine before men, that they may see your good works, and glorify your Father which is in heaven.

Think not that I am come to destroy the law, or the prophets: I am not come to destroy, but to fulfil. For verily I say unto you, Till heaven and earth pass, one jot or one tittle shall in no wise pass from the law, till all be fulfilled.

Whosoever therefore shall break one of these least commandments, and shall teach men so, he shall be called the least in the kingdom of heaven: but whosoever shall do and teach *them*, the same shall be called great in the kingdom of heaven.

For I say unto you, That except your righteousness shall exceed *the righteousness* of the scribes and Pharisees, ye shall in no case enter into the kingdom of heaven.

Ye have heard that it was said by them of old time, Thou shalt not kill; and whosoever shall kill shall be in danger of the judgment: But I say unto you, That whosoever is angry with his brother without a cause shall be in danger of the judgment: and whosoever shall say to his brother, Raca, shall be in danger of the council: but whosoever shall say, Thou fool, shall be in danger of hell fire.

---

[1]   *one jot or one tittle*   Not a whit; from "jot": the smallest particle or least letter of an alphabet, and "tittle": tiny mark or dot used for punctuation, e.g., the dot on the letter *i*.

[2]   *Scribes*   Ancient interpreters of religious law; *Pharisees*   Members of an ancient orthodox Jewish sect.

[3]   *Racha*   Admonishment (sometimes spelled "Raca"), possibly meaning "fool" or "weakling."

Geneva Bible

Ye are the salt of the earth: but if the salt have lost his savor, wherewith shall it be salted? It is thenceforth good for nothing, but to be cast out, and to be trodden under foot of men. Ye are the light of the world. A city that is set on an hill, cannot be hid. Neither do men light a candle, and put it under a bushel, but on a candlestick, and it giveth light unto all that are in the house. Let your light so shine before men, that they may see your good works, and glorify your Father which is in heaven.

Think not that I am come to destroy the Law, or the Prophets. I am not come to destroy them, but to fulfil them. For truly I say unto you, Till heaven, and earth perish, one jot or one tittle of the Law shall not escape, till all things be fulfilled.

Whosoever therefore shall break one of these least commandments, and teach men so, he shall be called the least in the kingdom of heaven: but whosoever shall observe and teach *them*, the same shall be called great in the kingdom of heaven.

For I say unto you, except your righteousness exceed the *righteousness* of the Scribes and Pharisees, ye shall not enter into the kingdom of heaven.

Ye have heard that it was said unto them of the old time, Thou shalt not kill: for whosoever killeth, shall be culpable of judgment. But I say unto you, whosoever is angry with his brother unadvisedly, shall be culpable of judgment. And whosoever saith unto his brother, Raca, shall be worthy to be punished by the Council. And whosoever shall say, Fool, shall be worthy to be punished with hell fire.

Douay-Rheims Bible

You are the salt of the earth. But if the salt lose its savor, wherewith shall it be salted? It is good for nothing anymore but to be cast out, and to be trodden on by men. You are the light of the world. A city seated on a mountain cannot be hid. Neither do men light a candle and put it under a bushel, but upon a candlestick, that it may shine to all that are in the house. So let your light shine before men, that they may see your good works, and glorify your Father who is in heaven.

Do not think that I am come to destroy the law, or the prophets. I am not come to destroy, but to fulfil. For amen I say unto you, till heaven and earth pass, one jot, or one tittle shall not pass of the law, till all be fulfilled.

He therefore that shall break one of these least commandments, and shall so teach men, shall be called the least in the kingdom of heaven. But he that shall do and teach, he shall be called great in the kingdom of heaven.

For I tell you, that unless your justice abound more than that of the scribes and Pharisees, you shall not enter into the kingdom of heaven.

You have heard that it was said to them of old: Thou shalt not kill. And whosoever shall kill, shall be in danger of the judgment. But I say to you, that whosoever is angry with his brother, shall be in danger of the judgment. And whosoever shall say to his brother, Raca, shall be in danger of the council. And whosoever shall say, Thou fool, shall be in danger of hell fire.

Tyndale's *English Bible*

Therefore when thou offerest thy gift at the altar, and there rememberest that thy brother hath aught against thee: leave there thine offering before the altar, and go thy way first and be reconciled to thy brother, and then come and offer thy gift.

Agree with thine adversary quickly, while thou art in the way with him, lest that adversary deliver thee to the judge, and the judge deliver thee to the minister, and then thou be cast into prison. I say unto thee verily: thou shalt not come out thence till thou have paid the utmost farthing.[1]

Ye have heard how it was said to them of old time, Thou shalt not commit adultery. But I say unto you, that whosoever looketh on a wife, lusting after her, hath committed adultery with her already in his heart. . . .

Ye have heard how it is said, an eye for an eye: a tooth for a tooth. But I say to you, that ye resist not wrong. But whosoever give thee a blow on thy right cheek, turn to him the other. And if any man will sue thee at the law, and take away thy coat, let him have thy cloak also. And whosoever will compel thee to go a mile, go with him twain.[2] Give to him that asketh, and from him that would borrow turn not away.

Ye have heard how it is said: thou shalt love thine neighbour, and hate thine enemy. But I say unto you, love your enemies. Bless them that curse you. Do good to them that hate you. Pray for them which do you wrong and persecute you, that ye may be the children of your father that is in heaven: for he maketh his sun to arise on the evil, and on the good, and sendeth his rain on the just and unjust. For if ye love them, which love you: what reward shall ye have? Do not the Publicans[3] even so? And if ye be friendly to your brethren only: what singular thing do ye? Do not the Publicans likewise? Ye shall therefore be perfect, even as your Father which is in heaven, is perfect.

—1534

King James Bible

Therefore if thou bring thy gift to the altar, and there rememberest that thy brother hath aught against thee; Leave there thy gift before the altar, and go thy way; first be reconciled to thy brother, and then come and offer thy gift.

Agree with thine adversary quickly, whiles thou art in the way with him; lest at any time the adversary deliver thee to the judge, and the judge deliver thee to the officer, and thou be cast into prison. Verily I say unto thee, Thou shalt by no means come out thence, till thou hast paid the uttermost farthing.

Ye have heard that it was said by them of old time, Thou shalt not commit adultery: But I say unto you, That whosoever looketh on a woman to lust after her hath committed adultery with her already in his heart.

Ye have heard that it hath been said, An eye for an eye, and a tooth for a tooth: But I say unto you, That ye resist not evil: but whosoever shall smite thee on thy right cheek, turn to him the other also. And if any man will sue thee at the law, and take away thy coat, let him have thy cloak also. And whosoever shall compel thee to go a mile, go with him twain. Give to him that asketh thee, and from him that would borrow of thee turn not thou away.

Ye have heard that it hath been said, Thou shalt love thy neighbour, and hate thine enemy. But I say unto you, Love your enemies, bless them that curse you, do good to them that hate you, and pray for them which despitefully use you, and persecute you; That ye may be the children of your Father which is in heaven: for he maketh his sun to rise on the evil and on the good, and sendeth rain on the just and on the unjust. For if ye love them which love you, what reward have ye? do not even the publicans the same? And if ye salute your brethren only, what do ye more *than others*? do not even the publicans so? Be ye therefore perfect, even as your Father which is in heaven is perfect.

—1611

---

[1] *farthing* Coin of little value.
[2] *twain* Two.

[3] *publican* Tax-gatherer, a derogatory epithet.

Geneva Bible

If then thou bring thy gift to the altar, and there rememberest that thy brother hath aught against thee, Leave there thine offering before the altar, and go thy way: first be reconciled to thy brother, and then come and offer thy gift.

Agree with thine adversary quickly, while thou art in the way with him, lest thine adversary deliver thee to the judge, and the judge deliver thee to the sergeant, and thou be cast into prison. Verily I say unto thee, thou shalt not come out thence, till thou hast paid the utmost farthing.

Ye have heard that it was said to them of old time, Thou shalt not commit adultery. But I say unto you, that whosoever looketh on a woman to lust after her, hath committed adultery with her already in his heart....

Ye have heard that it hath been said, An eye for an eye, and a tooth for a tooth. But I say unto you, Resist not evil: but whosoever shall smite thee on thy right cheek, turn to him the other also. And if any man will sue thee at the law, and take away thy coat, let him have thy cloak also. And whosoever will compel thee *to go* a mile, go with him twain. Give to him that asketh, and from him that would borrow of thee, turn not away.

Ye have heard that it hath been said, Thou shalt love thy neighbour, and hate thine enemy. But I say unto you, Love your enemies: bless them that curse you: do good to them that hate you, and pray for them which hurt you, and persecute you, That ye may be the children of your father that is in heaven: for he maketh his sun to arise on the evil, and the good, and sendeth rain on the just, and unjust.

For if ye love them, which love you, what reward shall you have? Do not the Publicans even the same? And if ye be friendly to your brethren only, what singular thing do ye? do not even the Publicans likewise? Ye shall therefore be perfect, as your Father which is in heaven, is perfect.

—1599

Douay-Rheims Bible

If therefore thou offer thy gift at the altar, and there thou remember that thy brother hath anything against thee; Leave there thy offering before the altar, and go first to be reconciled to thy brother: and then coming thou shalt offer thy gift.

Be at agreement with thy adversary betimes, whilst thou art in the way with him: lest perhaps the adversary deliver thee to the judge, and the judge deliver thee to the officer, and thou be cast into prison. Amen I say to thee, thou shalt not go out from thence till thou repay the last farthing.

You have heard that it was said to them of old: Thou shalt not commit adultery. But I say to you, that whosoever shall look on a woman to lust after her, hath already committed adultery with her in his heart....

You have heard that it hath been said, An eye for an eye, and a tooth for a tooth. But I say to you not to resist evil: but if one strike thee on thy right cheek, turn to him also the other: And if a man will contend with thee in judgment, and take away thy coat, let go thy cloak also unto him. And whosoever will force thee one mile, go with him other two. Give to him that asketh of thee and from him that would borrow of thee turn not away.

You have heard that it hath been said, Thou shalt love thy neighbour, and hate thy enemy. But I say to you, Love your enemies: do good to them that hate you: and pray for them that persecute and calumniate[1] you: That you may be the children of your Father who is in heaven, who maketh his sun to rise upon the good, and bad, and raineth upon the just and the unjust. For if you love them that love you, what reward shall you have? do not even the publicans this? And if you salute your brethren only, what do you more? do not also the heathens this? Be you therefore perfect, as also your heavenly Father is perfect.

—1582

---

[1] *calumniate* Slander.

Title page, Authorized version of the Bible ["King James Version"], 1611.

Deathbed of Henry VIII, c. 1549. Henry is shown pointing towards his heir, the young Edward. Members of the Council of Regency (Edward Seymour, John Dudley, Thomas Cranmer, and John Russell), who together acted on the young King's behalf, are shown to the right of the picture. The Pope is shown at the bottom of the picture, with the new *Book of Common Prayer* pressing down on his neck.

Sir Thomas Wyatt
c. 1503 — 1542

During Thomas Wyatt's brief, 39-year lifespan, English men and women served two kings; three lord chancellors were executed; England waged war in four other lands (Scotland, Wales, Ireland, and France); and Henry VIII married five of his six wives, most of whom met sorry ends. Wyatt lived his entire adult life in service to the court, amidst the political intrigue and turmoil that accompanied the reign of King Henry VIII, and was twice imprisoned in the Tower of London. A few of his poems portray an idyllic life in the countryside away from the machinations of the king and his courtiers, yet they can carry a subtext about the ambient political disorder or the court's political dramas. One of his most famous poems, "Whoso list to hunt," based on a sonnet written by Petrarch (1304–74), is thought to express longing for Anne Boleyn, Henry's future second wife. Wyatt wrote in many poetic forms, but he is best known for the artistry of his satires and songs and, along with Henry Howard, Earl of Surrey (1517–47), for introducing the Italian sonnet to England.

Son of Anne Skinner and Sir Henry Wyatt, Thomas Wyatt was born in 1503 into wealth and status at Allington Castle in Kent, England. His later career as a statesman followed that of his father, as did his political trials and tribulations. Henry Wyatt had been imprisoned and tortured for over two years by the court of King Richard III for his loyalty to the Tudors. When Henry Tudor became King Henry VII, the elder Wyatt was made a Privy Councillor, and he was later knighted by Henry VIII.

Although it is not certain, it appears that Thomas Wyatt entered St. John's College, Cambridge at age twelve, and that he may have graduated by the age of sixteen. He was a man of many accomplishments, adept at music and poetry as well as politics, and he soon became a valued member of King Henry's court. After serving in various minor positions, Wyatt began his diplomatic career in 1526 with missions to France, Rome, and Venice, where, we may surmise, he acquired his knowledge of Italian sonnets. (At about this time Wyatt became estranged from his wife, Elizabeth Brooke, daughter of Lord Cobham, whom he had married at a young age.) He was knighted in 1536 but soon afterward had his first falling out with King Henry and was imprisoned in the Tower of London. Wyatt might have been under suspicion of having had an affair with Anne Boleyn when she was still unmarried; Henry VIII had divorced Catherine of Aragon for Boleyn and thereby provoked England's break with the Roman Catholic Church. Although Anne and five (almost certainly wrongly accused) lovers were all executed, Wyatt was released after a month.

Most of Wyatt's work to this point had been love poems, often containing themes of disappointment or unrequited love but rarely dark in tone. By contrast, poems written after his imprisonments can express bitterness.

Wyatt eventually regained both the king's favor and his diplomatic status. Unfortunately, though, he lost a great ally upon the fall and execution of the statesman Thomas Cromwell, in 1540, and in 1541 he was imprisoned again, this time on trumped-up charges of treason. Once again he was spared and was briefly in favor with the king. Wyatt succumbed to fever the next year, however, and died in Dorset in 1542.

Few of Wyatt's poems were printed in his lifetime, but many appeared in Richard Tottel's 1557 volume *Songes and Sonettes* (later to become known as *Tottel's Miscellany*); a third of the volume is made up of Wyatt's work. Some years later, the Elizabethan critic George Puttenham summarized Sir Thomas Wyatt's importance to the English literary tradition in terms that remain broadly accepted today: "[Wyatt and Surrey] travailed into Italie, and there tasted the sweet and stately measures and stile of the Italian Poesie as novices newly crept out of the schooles of Dante, Arioste and Petrarch. They greatly pollished our rude & homely maner of vulgar Poesie, from that it had been before, and for that cause may justly be said the first reformers of our English meetre and stile."

⌘⌘⌘

SONNETS[1]

10[2]

The long love that in my thought doth harbour
And in mine heart doth keep his residence
Into my face presseth with bold pretence
And therein campeth, spreading his banner.
5 She that me learneth° to love and suffer　　　　*teaches*
And will° that my trust and lust's negligence　　*wishes*
Be reined by reason, shame,° and reverence,　　*modesty*
With his hardiness° taketh displeasure.　　　　*daring*
Wherewithal unto the heart's forest he fleeth,
10 Leaving his enterprise with pain and cry,
And there him hideth and not appeareth.
What may I do when my master feareth,
But in the field with him to live and die?
For good is the life ending faithfully.

—1557

29[3]

The pillar perished is whereto I leant,
The strongest stay of mine unquiet mind;

The like of it no man again can find—
From east to west still seeking though he went—
5 To mine unhap,° for hap° away hath rent　*misfortune | chance*
Of all my joy the very bark and rind,
And I, alas, by chance am thus assigned
Dearly to mourn till death do it relent.°　　*abate*
But since that thus it is by destiny,
10 What can I more but have a woeful heart,
My pen in plaint,° my voice in woeful cry,　*complaint, lament*
My mind in woe, my body full of smart,°　　*pain*
And I myself, myself always to hate
Till dreadful death do cease my doleful state?

—1557

31

Farewell, Love, and all thy laws forever.
Thy baited hooks shall tangle me no more.
Senec[4] and Plato call me from thy lore
To perfect wealth my wit for to endeavour.[5]
5 In blind error when I did persevere,
Thy sharp repulse, that pricketh ay so sore,
Hath taught me to set in trifles no store
And 'scape forth, since liberty is lever.°　*dearer*
Therefore, farewell. Go trouble younger hearts
10 And in me claim no more authority.

---

[1] *Sonnets* For additional sonnets by Sir Thomas Wyatt, please refer to the Elizabethan Sonnet and Lyric section in this anthology.

[2] *10* This poem is an adaptation of sonnet 140 from Petrarch's *Rime sparse* (*Scattered Rhymes*), also translated by Wyatt's friend Henry Howard, Earl of Surrey.

[3] *29* An imitation of Petrarch's *Rime* 269. There has been some speculation that Wyatt here laments the execution of Thomas Cromwell, Wyatt's former patron.

[4] *Senec* Seneca, a Roman essayist and philosopher (c. 4 BCE—65 CE).

[5] *wealth* Well-being; *wit* Intellect; *endeavour* Exert.

With idle youth go use thy property,
And thereon spend thy many brittle darts.
For hitherto, though I have lost all my time,
Me lusteth° no longer rotten boughs to climb.   desire
—1557

EPIGRAMS

38

Alas, madam, for stealing of a kiss
Have I so much your mind there offended?
Have I then done so grievously amiss
That by no means it may be amended?
5 Then revenge you, and the next[1] way is this:
Another kiss shall have my life ended.
For to my mouth the first my heart did suck;
The next shall clean out of my breast it pluck.
—1557

48[2]

Vulcan[3] begat me; Minerva[4] me taught.
Nature my mother; craft nourished me year by year.[5]
Three bodies[6] are my food. My strength is in naught.[7]
Slaughter, wrath, waste, and noise are my children dear.
5 Guess, friend, what I am and how I am wrought:
Monster of sea or of land or of elsewhere?
Know me and use me, and I may thee defend
And, if I be thine enemy, I may thy life end.[8]
—1557

60

Tagus,[9] farewell, that westward with thy streams
Turns up the grains of gold already tried,°   refined
With spur and sail for I go seek the Thames,
Gainward° the sun that show'th her wealthy pride[10]   toward
5 And to the town which Brutus sought by dreams[11]
Like bended moon doth lend her lusty° side.   pleasant
My king, my country, alone for whom I live,
Of mighty love the wings for this me give.
—1557

BALLADS

80

They flee from me that sometime did me seek
With naked foot stalking° in my chamber.   treading softly
I have seen them gentle, tame, and meek
That now are wild and do not remember
5 That sometime they put themself in danger
To take bread at my hand; and now they range,
Busily seeking with a continual change.

Thanked be fortune it hath been otherwise
Twenty times better; but once in special,
10 In thin array after° a pleasant guise,°   in accordance with / style
When her loose gown from her shoulders did fall
And she me caught in her arms long and small,
Therewithal sweetly did me kiss
And softly said, "Dear heart, how like you this?"

15 It was no dream; I lay broad waking.°   wide awake
But all is turned, through my gentleness,
Into a strange fashion of forsaking.
And I have leave to go of her goodness,[12]
And she also to use newfangleness.°   inconstancy

---

1 *next* Nearest, most convenient.

2 *48* The first six lines of this riddle are a translation of a Latin riddle found in *Bombarda*, by Pandolfo Collinutio.

3 *Vulcan* The Roman god of fire and metal working.

4 *Minerva* The Roman goddess of war, as well as wisdom.

5 *Nature … year* I.e., the materials come from nature, but are formed through craft.

6 *Three bodies* The ingredients of gunpowder.

7 *is in naught* I.e., the "O" of the gun's mouth.

8 This riddle was titled "Description of a gun" when first published in *Tottel's Miscellany*.

---

9 *Tagus* River in Spain, where Wyatt spent several months as a diplomat. The Tagus is known for its gold colored sand.

10 *Gainward … pride* Unlike the Tagus, which flows westward, the Thames flows "against" the sun's path, or eastward.

11 *the town … dreams* London. According to Geoffrey of Monmouth, Brutus, a Trojan hero and descendant of Aeneas, was visited in a dream by the goddess Diana and told to sail to the cliffs of Albion, where he could build another Troy. When he landed, he proceeded inland and founded the city that became London.

12 *I have … goodness* I have her permission to go from her.

20 But since that I so kindly[1] am served,
I would fain° know what she hath deserved.   gladly
—1557

94

Blame not my lute, for he must sound
Of this or that as liketh° me.   pleases
For lack of wit the lute is bound
To give such tunes as pleaseth me.
5 Though my songs be somewhat strange,
And speaks such words as touch thy change,[2]
    Blame not my lute.

My lute, alas, doth not offend,
Though that perforce he must agree
10 To sound such tunes as I intend
To sing to them that heareth me.
Then though my songs be somewhat plain
And toucheth° some that use to feign,[3]   comments on
    Blame not my lute.

15 My lute and strings may not deny,
But as I strike they must obey;
Break not them then so wrongfully,
But wreak° thyself some wiser way.   avenge
And though the songs which I indite°   compose
20 Do quit° thy change with rightful spite,   requite
    Blame not my lute.

Spite asketh spite, and changing change,
And falsed faith must needs be known;
The faults so great, the case so strange
25 Of right it must abroad be blown.°   proclaimed
Then since that by thine own desert
My songs do tell how true thou art,
    Blame not my lute.

Blame but thyself, that hast misdone
30 And well deserved to have blame;
Change thou thy way so evil begun,
And then my lute shall sound that same.

But if till then my fingers play
By thy desert their wonted way,
35   Blame not my lute.

Farewell, unknown, for though thou break
My strings in spite with great disdain,
Yet have I found out for thy sake
Strings for to string my lute again.
40 And if perchance this foolish rhyme
Do make thee blush at any time,
    Blame not my lute.
—1557

Songs

109

My lute, awake! Perform the last
Labour that thou and I shall waste,
And end that I have now begun;
For when this song is sung and past,
5 My lute, be still for I have done.

As to be heard where ear is none,
As lead to grave in marble stone,[4]
My song may pierce her heart as soon.
Should we then sigh or sing or moan?
10 No, no, my lute, for I have done.

The rocks do not so cruelly
Repulse the waves continually
As she my suit and affection,
So that I am past remedy,
15 Whereby my lute and I have done.

Proud of the spoil that thou hast got
Of simple hearts thorough° Love's shot   through
By whom, unkind, thou hast them won,
Think not he hath his bow forgot,
20 Although my lute and I have done.

Vengeance shall fall on thy disdain
That makest but game on earnest pain.
Think not alone under the sun

---

[1] *kindly* Naturally, according to natural laws (i.e., that women are fickle). The word also ironically suggests the modern "with kindness." Tottel amends this to "unkindly," removing the irony.

[2] *change* Change of heart.

[3] *use to feign* Wont to dissemble.

[4] *As to … stone* When sound is heard where there are no ears to hear it, or when lead (the softest metal) is able to engrave on stone.

Unquit° to cause thy lovers plain,°   *unrequited | to lament*
25   Although my lute and I have done.

May chance[1] thee lie withered and old
The winter nights that are so cold,
Plaining in vain unto the moon.
Thy wishes then dare not be told.
30   Care then who list,° for I have done.   *likes*

And then may chance thee to repent
The time that thou hast lost and spent
To cause thy lovers sigh and swoon.
Then shalt thou know beauty but lent,
35   And wish and want as I have done.

Now cease, my lute. This is the last
Labour that thou and I shall waste,
And ended is that we begun.
Now is this song both sung and past.
40   My lute, be still, for I have done.
     —1557

123

V. Innocentia
Veritas Viat Fides
Circumdederunt me inimici mei[2]

Who list° his wealth° and ease retain,   *desires | well-being*
Himself let him unknown contain.°   *keep*
Press not too fast in at that gate
Where the return stands by disdain,[3]
5   For sure, *circa Regna tonat.*[4]

---

[1]   *May chance*   It may chance that.

[2]   *V. Innocentia … mei*   This is a rebus, a puzzle in which Wyatt has arranged words to suggest a phrase. Translated from Latin, the rebus reads:
     W[yatt] Innocence
     Truth Wyatt Faith
     My enemies surround me.
   It is believed that Wyatt wrote this poem in 1536, while he was imprisoned in the Bell Tower. In May of that year, Wyatt may have witnessed Anne Boleyn's execution from his cell.

[3]   *Where … disdain*   From which your forced exit will be disdained.

[4]   *circa Regna tonat*   Latin: [He] thunders around thrones. This line, referring to Jupiter, is taken from Seneca's *Phaedra*. The first two stanzas of Wyatt's poem are imitations of lines from that play.

The high mountains are blasted oft
When the low valley is mild and soft.
Fortune with Health° stands at debate.°   *well-being | odds*
The fall is grievous from aloft.
10   And sure, *circa Regna tonat.*

These bloody days have broken my heart.
My lust,° my youth did them depart,   *pleasure*
And blind desire of estate.°   *high status*
Who hastes to climb seeks to revert.°   *fall back down*
15   Of truth, *circa Regna tonat.*

The Bell Tower showed me such sight
That in my head sticks day and night.
There did I learn out of a grate,°   *barred window*
For all favour, glory, or might,[5]
20   That yet *circa Regna tonat.*

By proof, I say, there did I learn:
Wit helpeth not defence too yerne,°   *willingly*
Of innocency to plead or prate.[6]
Bear low,[7] therefore; give God the stern.°   *tiller*
25   For sure, *circa Regna tonat.*
     —1969 (written 1536)

EPISTOLARY SATIRES

149[8]

Mine own John Poyns,[9] since ye delight to know
The cause why that homeward I me draw
(And flee the press of courts, whereso they go,
Rather than to live thrall° under the awe   *enslaved*
5   Of lordly looks) wrapped within my cloak,
To will and lust° learning to set a law,   *pleasure*
It is not because I scorn or mock
The power of them to whom Fortune hath lent
Charge over us, of right to strike the stroke;

---

[5]   *For all … might*   Regardless of one's favor, glory, or might.

[6]   *Wit … prate*   Intellect does not help one to earn a defense, or to plead or prattle of one's innocence.

[7]   *Bear low*   Keep yourself in a humble position. Also a nautical term meaning "sail with the wind."

[8]   *149*   This poem is an imitation of *Satira 10* (1532), by Luigi Alamanni.

[9]   *John Poyns*   A fellow member of the court of Henry VIII and a friend of Wyatt's.

10 But true it is that I have always meant
      Less to esteem them than the common sort,
      Of outward things that judge in their intent[1]
Without regard what doth inward resort.°   *reside*
      I grant sometime that of glory the fire
15   Doth touch my heart; me list not to report
Blame by honour and honour to desire.[2]
      But how may I this honour now attain
      That cannot dye the colour black a liar?[3]
My Poyns, I cannot frame my tune to feign,
20   To cloak the truth for praise, without desert,[4]
      Of them that list all vice for to retain.
I cannot honour them that sets their part
      With Venus and Bacchus[5] all their life long,
      Nor hold my peace of them although I smart.
25 I cannot crouch nor kneel to do such wrong
      To worship them like God on earth alone
      That are like wolves these silly[6] lambs among.
I cannot with my words complain and moan
      And suffer naught, nor smart without complaint,
30   Nor turn the word that from my mouth is gone.
I cannot speak and look like a saint,
      Use wiles for wit° and make deceit a pleasure   *intellect*
      And call craft counsel, for profit still to paint.
I cannot wrest the law to fill the coffer,
35   With innocent blood to feed myself fat,
      And do most hurt where most help I offer.
I am not he that can allow° the state   *praise*
      Of high Caesar and damn Cato[7] to die,
      That with his death did 'scape out of the gate

40 From Caesar's hands, if Livy doth not lie,
      And would not live where liberty was lost,
      So did his heart the common wealth[8] apply.°   *serve*
I am not he such eloquence to boast
      To make the crow singing as the swan,
45   Nor call the lion of coward beasts the most,[9]
That cannot take a mouse as the cat can;
      And he that dieth for hunger of the gold,
      Call him Alexander,[10] and say that Pan
Passeth Apollo in music many fold;[11]
50   Praise Sir Thopas for a noble tale
      And scorn the story that the knight told;[12]
Praise him for counsel that is drunk of ale;
      Grin when he laugheth that beareth all the sway,[13]
      Frown when he frowneth and groan when he is pale,
55 On other's lust to hang both night and day.
      None of these points would ever frame° in me.   *fit, prosper*
      My wit is naught. I cannot learn the way.
And much the less of things that greater be,
      That asken help of colours of device
60   To join the mean with each extremity:
With the nearest virtue to cloak alway the vice
      And, as to purpose, likewise it shall fall,[14]
      To press the virtue,[15] that it may not rise.
As° drunkenness good fellowship to call;   *for example,*
65   The friendly foe with his double face
      Say he is gentle and courteous therewithal;
And say that Favel° hath a goodly grace   *flattery*

---

[1] *I have ... their intent*   I.e., I have always intended to esteem the great and powerful people less than do the common sort (of people), who form their opinions ("intent") based on external appearances.

[2] *me list ... desire*   I do wish to cast blame on honor, or attack honor, while at the same time desiring it.

[3] *cannot dye ... liar*   Cannot see black as anything but black.

[4] *without desert*   Without its being worthy or deserving.

[5] *Venus and Bacchus*   Goddess of love and god of drink, here representing lust and debauchery.

[6] *silly*   Simple, helpless, pitiable.

[7] *Cato*   Marcus Porcius Cato, the uncle of Brutus and an opponent of Caesar's who, after Caesar's victory, committed suicide rather than submit to his tyrannical authority. The story is recorded by the historian Titus Livius (Livy), mentioned on line 40.

[8] *common wealth*   Public welfare, the common good, or the state.

[9] *of coward beasts the most*   King of the (cowardly) beasts.

[10] *he that ... Alexander*   Alexander the Great conquered the known world. Wyatt says he will not call such a man "Alexander," a name that means "defender or protector of mankind."

[11] *Pan ... many fold*   Pan, half man, half goat, was the Greek god of shepherds and flocks. He played simple music on his "Pan's pipes," or "shepherd's pipes." Apollo was the great god of, among other things, poetry, music, and the sun.

[12] *Praise ... knight told*   In Chaucer's *Canterbury Tales*, Sir Thopas's tale is so ridiculous that the host asks him to stop before the end, while the knight's tale is considered by all to be the most noble.

[13] *beareth all the sway*   Holds all the power.

[14] *as to ... shall fall*   As shall likewise be opportune.

[15] *press the virtue*   Oppress virtue, condemn it as a vice.

In eloquence; and cruelty to name
Zeal of justice and change in time and place;[1]
70 And he that suffereth offence without blame,[2]
Call him pitiful,° and him true and plain   compassionate
That raileth reckless to every man's
shame;°   modesty, decency
Say he is rude that cannot lie and feign,
The lecher a lover, and tyranny

75 To be the right of a prince's reign.
I cannot, I! No, no, it will not be!
This is the cause that I could never yet
Hang on their sleeves that weigh, as thou mayst see,
A chip of chance° more than a pound of wit.   good fortune
80 This maketh me at home to hunt and to hawk
And in foul weather at my book to sit;
In frost and snow then with my bow to stalk.
No man doth mark whereso I ride or go;
In lusty° leas° in liberty I walk.   pleasant / pastures
85 And of these news I feel nor weal° nor woe,   happiness

Save that a clog[3] doth hang yet at my heel.
No force for that,[4] for it is ordered so
That I may leap both hedge and dike full well.
I am not now in France to judge the wine,
90 With savoury sauce the delicates to feel;°   smell and taste
Nor yet in Spain where one must him incline,
Rather than to be, outwardly to seem.
I meddle not with wits that be so fine.
Nor Flanders' cheer[5] letteth not my sight to deem[6]
95 Of black and white, nor taketh my wit away
With beastliness they, beasts,[7] do so esteem.
Nor I am not where Christ is given in prey
For money, poison, and treason at Rome—
A common practice used night and day.
100 But here I am in Kent and Christendom
Among the muses, where I read and rhyme,
Where if thou list,° my Poyns, for to come,   desire
Thou shalt be judge how I do spend my time.
—1557

In Context

Epistolary Advice

Below is a letter from Thomas Wyatt to his son, who had recently married (at age fifteen). The letter was sent from Paris on 15 April 1537. Although a personal letter that mentions Wyatt's failed marriage, this exhortation also draws on a long tradition of epistolary advice to the young; William Cecil and Walter Ralegh contributed to the genre and Shakespeare parodies its sententiousness in *Hamlet* when Polonius gives fatherly counsel to Laertes.

In as much as now you are come to some years of understanding, and that you should gather within yourself some frame of honesty, I thought that I should not lose my labor wholly if now I did

[1] *change in time and place*   I.e., the time and place in which the law was made differ from those of the crime.
[2] *suffereth ... blame*   Allows offences against those who are innocent.
[3] *clog*   Heavy block of wood, attached to impede motion.
[4] *No force for that*   No matter.
[5] *Flanders' cheer*   The Flemish were known for their love of drinking.
[6] *letteth not*   Prevents; *deems*   Distinguish.
[7] *beastliness*   Drunkenness; *beasts*   Drunks.

something advertise[1] to you to take the sure foundations and established opinions that leadeth to honesty. And here I call not "honesty" what men commonly call honesty, as reputation for riches, for authority, or some like thing, but that honesty that I dare well say your grandfather (whose soul God pardon) had rather left to me than all the lands he did leave me—that was wisdom, gentleness, soberness, desire to do good, friendliness to get the love of many, and truth[2] above all the rest. A great part to have all these things is to desire to have them: and although glory and honest name are not the very ends wherefore these things are to be followed, yet surely they must needs follow them, as light followeth fire, though it were kindled for warmth. Out of these things the chiefest and infallible ground is the dread and reverence of God, whereupon shall ensue the eschewing of the contraries of these said virtues—that is to say, ignorance, unkindness, rashness, desire of harm, unquiet enmity, hatred, many and crafty falsehood, the very root of all shame and dishonesty.

I say the only dread and reverence of God that seeth all things is the defense of the creeping in of all these mischiefs into you. As for my part, although I do not say there is no man that would his son better than I,[3] yet on my faith I had rather have you lifeless than subject to these vices. Think and imagine always that you are in [the] presence of some honest man that you know, as Sir John Russell, your father-in-law, your uncle, parson, or some other such, and you shall, if at any time you find a pleasure in naughty touches, remember what shame it were before these men to do naughtily. And sure this imagination shall cause you remember that the pleasure of a naughty deed is soon past, and that rebuke, shame, and the note[4] thereof shall remain ever. Then, if these things you take for vain imaginations, yet remember that it is certain and no imagination that you are always in the presence and sight of God: and though you see Him not, so much is the reverence the more to be had, for that He seeth and is not seen. Men punish with shame as [the] greatest punishment on earth, yea greater than death, but His punishment is first the withdrawing of His favour and grace, and in leaving His hand to rule the stern,[5] to let the ship run without guide to your own destruction, and suffereth[6] so the man that He forsaketh to run headlong, as subject to all mishaps, and at last with shameful end to everlasting shame and death. You may see continual examples both of one sort and th'other, and the better if you mark them well that yourself are come of.[7] And consider well your good grandfather what things that were in him, and his end; and they that knew him noted him thus: first and chiefly to have a great reverence of God and good opinion of Godly things, next that there was no man more pitiful,[8] no man more true of his word, no man faster to his friend, no man diligenter nor more circumspect, which thing both the kings his masters noted in him greatly. And if these things, and especially the grace of God that the fear of God always kept with him, had not been, the chances of this troublesome world that he was in had long ago overwhelmed him. This preserved him in prison from the hands of the tyrant[9] that could find in his heart to see him racked, from two years and more imprisonment in Scotland, in irons and stocks, from the danger of sudden changes and commotions diverse, until that well beloved of many, hated of none, in his fair age and good reputation, Godly and Christianly he went to Him that loved him for that he always had Him in reverence. And of myself

---

[1] *advertise* Advise, counsel, explain.

[2] *truth* Wyatt's word is "trough," which suggests both "truth" and "troth"—i.e., a trustworthy integrity.

[3] *that ... than I* That is, would wish better for his son.

[4] *rebuke ... note* Notice, reputation.

[5] *His ... stern* In withdrawing his hand from (the ship's) steering wheel, the tiller.

[6] *suffereth* Allows.

[7] *better ... of* If you observe well those from whom you derive—your family.

[8] *pitiful* Full of pity, merciful.

[9] *tyrant* Richard III.

I may be a mere example unto you of my folly and unthriftiness[1] that hath as I well deserved brought me into a thousand dangers and hazards, enmities, hatreds, imprisonments, despites[2] and indignations: but that God hath of His goodness chastised me and not cast me clean out of His favour, which thing I can impute to nothing but to the goodness of my good father, that I dare well say purchased with continual request of God His grace towards me more than I regarded or considered myself, and a little part to the small fear that I had of God in the most of my rage[3] and the little delight that I had in mischief. You therefore, if you be sure and have God in your sleeve, to call you to His grace at last, venture not hardily[4] by mine example upon naughty unthriftiness in trust of His goodness; and, besides the shame, I dare lay ten to one you shall perish in the adventure: for trust not that my wish or desire of God for you shall stand you in as much effect as I think my father's did for me: we are not all accepted of Him. Begin therefore betimes, make God and goodness your foundations. Make your examples of wise and honest me; shoot at the mark; be no mocker—mocks follow them that delight therein. He shall be sure of shame that feeleth no grief in other men's shames. Have your friends in a reverence and think unkindness to be the greatest offence, and least punished amongst men, but so much the more to be dreaded, for God is Justiser[5] upon that alone. Love well and agree with your wife, for where is noise and debate in the house, there is unquiet dwelling. And much more where it is in one bed. Frame well yourself to love, and rule well and honestly your wife as your fellow, and she shall love and reverence you as her head. Such as you are unto her, such shall she be unto you. Obey and reverence your father-in-law as you would me; and remember that long life followeth them that reverence their fathers and elders. And the blessing of God for good agreement between the wife and husband is fruit of many children, which I for the like thing do lack, and the fault is both in your mother and me, but chiefly in her.

Read oft this my letter and it shall be as though I had often written unto you. And think that I have herein printed a fatherly affection to you. If I may see that I have not lost my pain(s), mine shall be the contentation[6] and yours the profit. And upon condition that you follow my advertisement I send you God's blessing and mine, and as well to come to honesty as to increase of years.

At Paris the 15th of April, your loving father, Thomas Wyatt.

---

[1] *And ... unthriftiness*   Prodigality and imprudence.

[2] *despites*   Scorn.

[3] *rage*   Irrationality, madness.

[4] *hardily*   Boldly, incautiously.

[5] *Justiser*   Judge, justice-maker.

[6] *contentation*   Payment, satisfaction, contentment.

HENRY HOWARD, EARL OF SURREY

1517 – 1547

Like a number of other aristocrats, Henry Howard, Earl of Surrey, largely confined his literary writings to manuscript circulation among his friends and fellow members of Henry VIII's court; it was the posthumous appearance of his works in the printer Richard Tottel's *Miscellany* (1557) that won him widespread readership. His work is a landmark in the development of English literature, for he was among the first in England to import the Petrarchan sonnet, and, in his translation of Books II and IV of Virgil's *Aeneid*, the first to deploy blank verse. As a writer, Surrey was innovative; as a courtier, he was imprudent, and paid the price when the king had him beheaded.

Surrey was born in Hunsdon, Hertfordshire in 1517, eldest son of Lord Thomas Howard, third duke of Norfolk, and Lady Elizabeth Stafford. Surrey's ancestors on both sides of his family included royalty, and as a boy this talented member of one of England's greatest families spent some time at Windsor Castle with Henry VIII's illegitimate son, Henry Fitzroy, Duke of Richmond, and in 1524 was granted the title of earl. He received a sound humanist education and had early experience living abroad when his father served as Lord Lieutenant in Ireland. One of his cousins was Anne Boleyn, second of Henry VIII's six wives, who managed to prevent a proposed marriage between Surrey and the king's daughter, Mary Tudor. Instead, in 1533, Surrey married Lady Frances de Vere, the earl of Oxford's daughter, by whom he had five children. As an adult, Surrey served as a courtier and soldier; his travels in France on diplomatic or military ventures doubtless had an impact on his understanding of the Continental Renaissance in art and letters. Service to the King was a risky business during the King's later

years, however, for the King was increasingly suspicious and the court, especially after the Reformation, was split into competing factions. The balance had tipped against Surrey's family in 1536 when Henry VIII married Jane Seymour, his third wife, for the Seymours, who welcomed Henry's break with the Church of Rome, were bitter rivals of the Catholic Howards and took advantage of their new power (Surrey himself seems to have leaned toward Reform, although his exact views can be debated and perhaps shifted). Thanks to probably false accusations that he had sided with a rebellion against the King, the so-called Pilgrimage of Grace, Surrey was imprisoned between 1537 and 1539. His misfortune did not last, however, for Jane Seymour died shortly after giving birth. The King married Catherine Howard, another of Surrey's cousins, bringing the Howard family back into favor, at least until Catherine was found guilty of adultery and executed in early 1542. In 1541 the King named Surrey a Knight of the Garter, and for the next five years Surrey served the King in various English wars or administrative capacities.

During these years Surrey wrote verse (including love poems, elegies, satire, Biblical paraphrases, translated sections of Virgil's *Aeneid*, and a poignant meditation on Windsor Castle). During his lifetime he published only one poem, in praise of the deceased Sir Thomas Wyatt. Shakespeare and others would often adopt his sonnet structure, which instead of Petrarch's pattern—an octave followed by a sestet—most often has three quatrains (four lines usually rhyming alternately) and a couplet (a pair of lines). We call this the Shakespearean or English form, but it was Surrey who invented it. Even more important for the future of English literature is the blank verse that Surrey developed for his translations from Virgil, a flexible and harmonious meter that English writers such as Marlowe, Shakespeare, and Milton found the best equivalent for the dactylic hexameter of Latin epic.

In 1546, Surrey was involved in another political struggle. Henry VIII's health was bad, and the court was thinking about who might be regent for his little son, the future Edward VI. Surrey dared suggest openly that his father, the earl of Norfolk, would be Protector. Norfolk was next in the line of succession after Edward, and the Seymour family convinced the King that he was planning to depose the prince after Henry died and make himself king instead. Surrey was put on trial, the legal excuse being that he had treasonably placed the royal arms and insignia on his own coat of arms. He and his father were imprisoned in the Tower and there Surrey lost his head on 10 January 1547—the last person to be executed during Henry's reign. Norfolk was also condemned to die, but the death of Henry on January 28 voided the sentence at the last minute. Surrey is buried in Framlington, Suffolk.

⌘ ⌘ ⌘

Love, that Doth Reign and Live within My Thought [1]

Love, that doth reign and live within my thought,
And built his seat within my captive breast,
Clad in the arms wherein with me he fought,
Oft in my face he doth his banner rest.
5 But she that taught me love and suffer pain,
My doubtful hope and eke° my hot desire   *also*
With shamefast° look to shadow and refrain,   *modest*
Her smiling grace converteth straight to ire.
And coward Love, then, to the heart apace
10 Taketh his flight, where he doth lurk and plain,°   *complain*
His purpose lost, and dare not show his face.
For my lord's guilt thus faultless bide° I pain;   *endure*
Yet from my lord shall not my foot remove:
Sweet is the death that takes end by love.
—1557

Set Me Whereas the Sun Doth Parch the Green [2]

Set me whereas the sun doth parch the green,
Or where his beams may not dissolve the ice,
In temperate heat where he is felt and seen;
With proud people, in presence sad and wise;
5 Set me in base, or yet in high degree,
In the long night or in the shortest day,
In clear weather or where mists thickest be,
In lusty° youth or when my hairs be gray;   *vigorous*
Set me in earth, in heaven, or yet in hell,
10 In hill, in dale, or in the foaming flood;
Thrall° or at large, alive whereso I dwell,   *captive*
Sick or in health, in ill fame° or in good: *repute*
Yours will I be, and with that only thought
Comfort myself when that my hap° is nought.   *luck*
—1557

---

[1] *Love … Thought* This sonnet is a translation of Petrarch's *Rima* 140, which Surrey's friend Wyatt also translated.

[2] *Set … Green* Adaptation of Petrarch's *Rima* 145.

Alas! So All Things Now Do Hold Their Peace[1]

Alas! so all things now do hold their peace,
Heaven and earth disturbed in nothing.
The beasts, the air, the birds their song do cease;
The nightès chair[2] the stars about doth bring;
5   Calm is the sea, the waves work less and less:
So am not I, whom love, alas, doth wring,
Bringing before my face the great increase
Of my desires, whereat I weep and sing
In joy and woe, as in a doubtful ease.
10 For my sweet thoughts sometime do pleasure bring,
But by and by the cause of my disease°   uneasiness, distress
Gives me a pang that inwardly doth sting,
When that I think what grief it is again
To live and lack the thing should rid my pain.

So Cruel Prison How Could Betide[3]

So cruel prison how could betide, alas,
As proud Windsor, where I, in lust and joy,
With a king's son my childish years did pass
In greater feast than Priam's sons of Troy?[4]

5   Where each sweet place returns a taste full sour:
The large green courts, where we were wont to hove,°   linger
With eyes cast up unto the maidens' tower,
And easy sighs, such as folk draw in love.

The stately sales,[5] the ladies bright of hue,
10 The dances short, long tales of great delight,

With words and looks that tigers could but rue,[6]
Where each of us did plead the other's right.

The palm play,[7] where, despoiled° for the game,   stripped
With dazed eyes oft we by gleams of love
15 Have missed the ball and got sight of our dame,
To bait° her eyes, which kept the leads[8] above.   attract

The gravelled ground,° with sleeves tied   jousting ground
    on the helm,[9]
On foaming horse, with swords and friendly hearts,
With cheer° as though the one should overwhelm,
20 Where we have fought and chased oft with darts.°   javelins

With silver drops the meads yet spread for ruth,[10]
In active games of nimbleness and strength,
Where we did strain, trained by swarms of youth,
Our tender limbs that yet shot up in length.

25 The secret groves, which oft we made resound
Of pleasant plaint,° and of our ladies' praise,   lament
Recording soft what grace each one had found,
What hope of speed, what dread of long delays.

The wild forest, the clothed holts° with green;   wooded hills
30 With reins avaled, and swift ybreathed[11] horse,
With cry of hounds and merry blasts between,
Where we did chase the fearful hart° a force.[12]   male deer

The void[13] walls eke° that harboured us each night;   also
Wherewith, alas, revive within my breast

---

[6] *rue* Regard with compassion.

[7] *palm play* Game in which the ball was hit with the palms.

[8] *leads* Sheets of metal that covered the roofs of the courts. Spectators would watch the game from these.

[9] *helm* Helmet, to which jousters would tie a lady's sleeve (then a separate, ornamental covering) as a token of her favor.

[10] *With ... ruth* I.e., the meadows (meads) were still covered with dew; *ruth* Compassion.

[11] *avaled* Slackened; *swift ybreathed* Panting.

[12] *chase ... a force* Run down.

[13] *void* I.e., empty. In royal houses it was customary for all tapestries and wall-hangings to be taken down when the resident members of the court were not at home.

---

[1] *Alas ... Peace* Surrey's version of Petrarch's *Rima* 164.

[2] *nightès chair* The constellation Ursa Major.

[3] *So ... Betide* In 1537 Surrey was imprisoned in Windsor Castle for having struck a courtier and broken the peace in the king's domain. In this poem he remembers his earlier stay at the castle (1530–32) with Henry Fitzroy, Duke of Richmond and illegitimate son of Henry VIII. Richmond (who had married Surrey's sister in 1533) died in 1536.

[4] *Priam's ... Troy* Priam, the king of Troy at the time of the Trojan war, had fifty sons.

[5] *sales* Halls or spacious chambers (from the French "salle").

35   The sweet accord, such sleeps as yet delight,
     The pleasant dreams, the quiet bed of rest;

     The secret thoughts imparted with such trust,
     The wanton talk, the divers change of play,
40   The friendship sworn, each promise kept so just,
     Wherewith we past the winter night away.

     And with this thought the blood forsakes my face,
     The tears berain° my cheeks of deadly hue,   *rain upon*
     The which, as soon as sobbing sighs, alas,
     Upsupped° have, thus I my plaint renew: *swallowed*

45   "O place of bliss! renewer of my woes!
     Give me accompt,° where is my noble fere,°   *account/ companion*
     Whom in thy walls thou didst each night enclose,
     To other lief;° but unto me most dear?"   *precious*

     Each stone, alas, that doth my sorrow rue,
50   Returns thereto a hollow sound of plaint.
     Thus I alone, where all my freedom grew,
     In prison pine with bondage and restraint;

     And with remembrance of the greater grief,
     To banish the less, I find my chief relief.
     —1557

Wyatt Resteth Here

Wyatt resteth here, that quick° could never rest;   *alive*
     Whose heavenly gifts increased by disdain,°   *malice*
And virtue sank the deeper in his breast:
Such profit he by envy could obtain.

5   A head where wisdom mysteries° did frame,   *profound thoughts*
     Whose hammers beat still in that lively brain
     As on a stith,° where that some work of fame   *anvil*
     Was daily wrought to turn to Britain's gain.

     A visage stern and mild, where both did grow
10   Vice to contemn,° in virtue to rejoice;   *scorn*
     Amid great storms, whom grace assured so,
     To live upright and smile at fortune's choice.

     A hand that taught what might be said in rhyme;
     That reft° Chaucer the glory of his wit—   *robbed*
15   A mark the which (unperfected for time[1])
     Some may approach, but never none shall hit.

     A tongue that served in foreign realms his king;
     Whose courteous talk to virtue did inflame
     Each noble heart: a worthy guide to bring
20   Our English youth, by travail, unto fame.°   *good character*

     An eye whose judgment no affect° could blind,   *affection*
     Friends to allure and foes to reconcile;
     Whose piercing look did represent a mind
     With virtue fraught, reposed, void of guile.

25   A heart where dread yet never so impressed
     To hide the thought that might the truth advance;
     In neither fortune loft,° nor yet repressed,   *lifted*
     To swell in wealth or yield unto mischance.

     A valiant corps° where force and beauty met,   *body*
30   Happy—alas, too happy, but for foes;
     Lived and ran the race that nature set,
     Of manhood's shape, where she the mold did lose.

     But to the heavens that simple° soul is fled,   *free from guile*
     Which left with such as covet° Christ to know[2]   *desire*
35   Witness of faith that never shall be dead;
     Sent for our health, but not received so.

     Thus, for our guilt, this jewel have we lost;
     The earth his bones, the heavens possess his ghost.
     —1542

from *Certain Books of Virgil's Aeneis: Book 2*

The Greekës chieftains, all irked° with the war   *wearied*
     Wherein they wasted had so many years,
And oft repulsed by fatal destiny,
A huge horse made, high raised like a hill,

---

[1]   *for time*   For want of time.

[2]   *such as covet Christ to know*   I.e., Christians.

5   By the divine science of Minerva;[1]
Of cloven fir compacted were his ribs;
For their return a feigned sacrifice,
The fame whereof so wandered it at point.[2]
In the dark bulk they closed bodies of men,
10   Chosen by lot, and did enstuff[3] by stealth
The hollow womb with armed soldiers.
There stands in sight an isle hight° Tenedos,   *called*
Rich and of fame while Priam's[4] kingdom stood,
Now but a bay and road[5] unsure for ship.
15   Hither them secretly the Greeks withdrew,
Shrouding themselves under the desert shore;
And, weening° we they had been fled and gone,   *believing*
And with that wind had fet° the land of Greece,   *reached*
Troia discharged her long continued dole.°   *grief*
20   The gates cast up, we issued out to play,
The Greekish camp desirous to behold,
The places void, and the forsaken coasts.
Here Pyrrhus' band, there fierce Achilles', pight;[6]
Here rode their ships; there did their battles[7] join.
25   Astonnied,° some the scathful° gift beheld,   *astonished / harmful*
Behight° by vow unto the chaste Minerve,   *dedicated*
All wond'ring at the hugeness of the horse.
And first of all Timœtes gan° advise   *did*
Within the walls to lead and draw the same,

30   And place it eke° amid the palace court—   *moreover*
Whether of guile, or Troia's fate it would.[8]
Capys, with some of judgment more discreet,
Willed° it to drown, or underset with flame   *desired*
The suspect present of the Greeks' deceit,
35   Or bore and gauge the hollow caves uncouth:°   *unknown*
So diverse ran the giddy people's mind.
Lo! foremost of a rout° that followed him,   *company*
Kindled° Laöcoön[9] hasted from the tower,   *inflamed*
Crying far off, "O wretched citizens!
40   What so great kind of frenzy fretteth° you?   *consumes*
Deem ye the Greeks, our enemies, to be gone?
Or any Greekish gifts can you suppose
Devoid of guile? Is so Ulysses[10] known?
Either the Greeks are in this timber hid,
45   Or this an engine° is to annoy our walls,   *instrument of war*
To view our towers, and overwhelm our town.
Here lurks some craft. Good Trojans! give no trust
Unto this horse, for, whatsoever it be,
I dread the Greeks, yea[11] when they offer gifts."

—1557

---

[1] *Minerva* Goddess of wisdom, invention, the arts, and war.

[2] *the fame … point* I.e., the story (of the supposed sacrifice) travelled ("wandered it") conveniently ("at point").

[3] *enstuff* Fill, garrison.

[4] *Priam* King of Troy.

[5] *road* Sheltered area of water, close to shore, where boats can anchor.

[6] *Pyrrhus* Achilles's son. He became the new leader of the Myrmidons, Achilles's followers; *band* troop; *Achilles* Greatest Greek warrior; *pight* Were pitched.

[7] *battles* Bodies of troops in battle array.

[8] *Whether … would* I.e., either this idea was a result of Timœtes's treachery, or it was merely Troy's fate that the horse would enter the walls of Troy.

[9] *Laöcoön* A Trojan priest.

[10] *Ulysses* Odysseus, the king of Ithaca and the hero of Homer's *Odyssey*. Odysseus was the warrior who suggested the construction of the horse.

[11] *yea* Especially, even more.

The Elizabethan Sonnet and Lyric

Developed first in thirteenth-century Italy and wildly popular in Renaissance Europe, the sonnet (or "little song") became one of the most enduring forms of English verse. A lyric poem in fourteen lines, usually with ten or twelve syllables to a line, the standard sonnet follows one of several rhyme schemes. The most important are the Italian or "Petrarchan," the English (often referred to as the "Shakespearean," although it was Henry Howard, Earl of Surrey, who first developed it), and the Spenserian. The Petrarchan form, introduced by the Italian writer Francesco Petrarch in the fourteenth century, has two parts: first comes the "octave" of eight lines, which usually sets forth some situation, argument, narrative, analogy, comment, wish, or other thought. This is followed by the "sestet," six lines that often perform a volta, or turn, that gives some resolution, further elaboration, counter-argument, or other contrast to the octave. The rhyme scheme ordinarily is *abba abba cde cde*, although variations for the sestet (such as *cdc dcd or cde cde*) are acceptable.

The English poets Thomas Wyatt and Henry Howard, Earl of Surrey first introduced the sonnet into English, translating some of Petrarch's sonnets in the 1520s and 1530s and, in the case of Surrey, writing a few more in the Petrarchan manner. They were not published until 1557, but they circulated in manuscript. By the 1580s the popularity of the sonnet on the Continent led to its revival in England, and the posthumous publication in 1591 of Sir Philip Sidney's *Astrophil and Stella* started a fashion for the form and for the sonnet sequence that blazed for a few years with extraordinary intensity.

Shakespeare's sonnets (some of which certainly, and many others probably, were written in the 1590s although Shakespeare may well have revised them before they were published, well after the fashion was over, in 1609) typically have four parts: three "quatrains" (a set of four lines) each rhyming *abab cdcd efef* and then a couplet rhyming *gg*. The quatrains may trace the development of an idea, state the same notion several times, or describe a situation from several angles—the possibilities of this flexible form are nearly endless. The couplet may be a logical conclusion, a further thought, or even a dramatic denial of what has come before.

Edmund Spenser's *Amoretti* (1595) have yet another scheme, a sort of compromise between the Petrarchan and the Shakespearean, interlocking its quatrains with the rhyme scheme *abab bcbc cdcd* concluding with a couplet *ee*. Substantial selections from the sonnets by Wyatt, Surrey, Sidney, Shakespeare, and Spenser appear elsewhere in this volume, thus the sonnets in this section are designed to provide further insight into the origins and range of the form; the lyrics by Gascoigne and by an anonymous poet are meant to extend the reader's sense of how the short Elizabethan lyric could handle some of the themes—age, absence—found in the sonnets.

⌘ ⌘ ⌘

The Continental Background

Francesco Petrarch (1304–1374)

The influence of Petrarch's sonnet sequence, about his unfulfilled love for Laura, was immense, and provided European love poets with a way to shape the erotic experience in terms of frustration, self-scrutiny, self-division, praise, and longing and to express this through elaborate metaphor, paradox, and an intense focus on detail. Whether the object of imitation, revision, or satire, Petrarch's approach to love long remained the discourse against which and through which poets defined themselves when writing on love.

from *Rime Sparse*

134

Pace non trovo et non ò da far guerra,
e temo et spero, et ardo et son un ghiaccio,
et volo sopra 'l cielo et giacco in terra,
et nulla stringo et tutto 'l mondo abbraccio.

5 Tal m'à in pregion, che non m'apre né serra,
né per suo mi riten né sciolglie il laccio,
et non m'ancide Amore et non mi sferra,
né mi vuol vivo, né mi trae d'impaccio.

Veggio senza occhi, et non ò lingua et grido,
10 et bramo di perir, et cheggio aita,
et ò in odio me stesso et amo altrui.

Pascomi di dolor, piangendo rido,
egualmente mi spiace morte et vita.
In questo stato son, Donna, per vui.
—WRITTEN MID-14TH CENTURY

134

I find no peace and all my war is done,
I fear and hope, I burn and freeze like ice;
  I fly above the wind yet can I not arise;
  And naught I have and all the world I season° *seize upon*
5 That[1] looseth nor locketh holdeth me in prison
  And holdeth me not, yet can I 'scape no wise,
  Nor letteth me live nor die at my device.° *own choice*
  And yet of death it giveth none occasion.
Without eyen° I see and without tongue I
        plain;° *eyes / complain*
10 I desire to perish, and yet I ask health;
  I love another, and thus I hate myself;
I feed me in sorrow and laugh in all my pain;
  Likewise displeaseth me both death and life:
  And my delight[2] is causer of this strife.
—c. 1520s (TRANS. SIR THOMAS WYATT)

140

Amor, che nel penser mio vive et regna
e 'l suo seggio maggior nel mio cor tene,
talor armato ne la fronte vene;
ivi si loca et ivi pon sua insegna.

5 Quella ch' amare et sofferir ne 'nsegna
e vol che 'l gran desio, l'accesa spene
ragion, vergogna, et reverenza affrene,
di nostro ardir fra se stessa si sdegna.

Onde Amor paventoso fugge al core,
10 Lasciando ogni sua impresa, et piange et trema;
ivi s'asonde et non appar più fore.

Che poss' io far, temendo il mio signore,
se non star seco infin a l'ora estrema?
ché bel fin fa chi ben amando more.
—WRITTEN MID-14TH CENTEURY

140

Love, that doth reign and live within my thought
And built his seat° within my captive breast, *dwelling*
Clad in the arms wherein with me he fought
Oft in my face he doth his banner rest.
5 But she that taught me love and suffer pain,
My doubtful hope and eke° my hot desire *also*
With shamefast° look to shadow° and *modest / conceal*
        refrain,° *hold back*
Her smiling grace converteth straight to ire.
And coward Love then to the heart apace
10 Taketh his flight, where he doth lurk and plain;° *complain*
His purpose lost, and dare not show his face.
For my lord's guilt thus faultless bide I pain,
  Yet from my lord[3] shall not my foot remove:
  Sweet is the death that taketh end by love.
—c. 1530s (TRANS. HENRY HOWARD, EARL OF SURREY)

189

Passa la nave mia colma d'oblio
per aspro mare a mezza notte il verno

189

My galley chargèd with forgetfulness
Through sharp seas in winter nights doth pass

---

[1] *That* Which (i.e., Love).

[2] *my delight* His paradoxical pleasure in loving but also the lady—Laura, in Petrarch's poem.

[3] *lord* I.e., Love—the speaker's feudal lord.

enfra Scilla et Caribdi, et al governo
siede 'l signore anzi 'l nimico mio;
5   à ciascun remo un penser pronto et rio
che la tempesta e 'l fin par ch' abbi a scherno;
la vela rompe un vento umido eterno
di sospir, di speranze et di desio;
pioggia di lagrimar, nebbia di sdegni
10 bagna et rallenta la già stanche sarte
che son d'error con ignoranzia attorto.
Celansi i duo mei dolci usati segni,
morta fra l'onde è la ragion et l'arte
tal ch' i' 'ncomincio a desperar del porto.
—WRITTEN MID-14TH CENTURY

190

Una candida cerva sopra l'erba
verde m'apparve con duo corna d'oro,
fra due riviere all'ombra d'un alloro,
levando 'l sole a la stagione acerba.
5   Era sua vista sì dolce superba
ch' i' lasciai per seguirla ogni lavoro,
come l'avaro che 'n cercar tesoro
con diletto l'affanno disacerba.
"Nessun mi tocchi," al bel collo d'intorno
10 scritto avea di diamanti et di topazi.
"Libera farmi al mio Cesare parve."
Et era 'l sol già vòlto al mezzo giorno,
gli occhi miei stanchi di mirar, non sazi,
quand' io caddi ne l'acqua et ella sparve.
—WRITTEN MID-14TH CENTURY

'Tween rock and rock;[1] and eke° mine enemy, alas,   *also*
That is my lord,[2] steereth with cruelness;
And every oar a thought in readiness,
5   As though that death were light° in such a case.   *easy*
An endless wind doth tear the sail apace
Of forcèd sighs and trusty fearfulness.
A rain of tears, a cloud of dark disdain,
10 Hath done the wearied cords°   *ship's rigging*
great hinderance,
Wreathèd with error and eke with ignorance
The stars be hid that led me to this pain;
Drownèd is reason that should me consort,°   *accompany*
And I remain despairing of the port.
—C. 1520S (TRANS. SIR THOMAS WYATT)

190

Whoso list° to hunt, I know where is a   *wishes*
hind,°   *female deer*
But as for me, alas, I may° no more: *can*
The vain travail° hath wearied me so sore   *effort*
I am of them that farthest come behind.
5   Yet may I by no means my wearied mind
Draw from the deer: but, as she fleeth afore,
Fainting I follow. I leave off therefore,
Since in a net I seek to hold the wind.
Who list her hunt, I put him out of doubt,
As well as I may spend his time in vain.
10 And, graven with diamonds in letters plain,
There is written her fair neck round about:
"Noli me tangere,[3] for Caesar's I am,
And wild for to hold, although I seem tame."
—C. 1520S (ADAPTED BY SIR THOMAS WYATT)

---

[1] *'Tween rock and rock* Petrarch specifies Scylla and Charybdis, the dangerous monster who lived on a rock and the whirlpool on either side of a narrow channel through which Ulysses must sail in Homer's *Odyssey*.

[2] *lord* I.e., Cupid, Love.

[3] *Noli me tangere* "Do not touch me," words said by Christ after the Resurrection. Early commentators on Petrarch often read this as signifying that Laura considered herself bound by the laws of chaste marriage as decreed by Augustus Caesar. Wyatt's readers who identified the deer with Anne Boleyn (whom Wyatt knew and perhaps loved), would have read the lines as suggesting that the "hind" belongs to Henry VIII.

GASPARA STAMPA (1523–1554)

132

Quando io dimando nel mio pianto Amore,
Che cosí male il mio parlar ascolata,
Mille fate il dí, non una volta,
Ché mi fere e trafigge a tutte l'ore:
5   "Come esser può, s'io diedi l'alma e 'l core
al mio signor dal dí ch'a me l'ho tolta,
e se ogni cosa dentro a lui raccolta
è riso e gioia, è scema di dolore,
    ch'io senta gelosia fredda e temenza,
10 e d'allegrezza e gioia resti priva,
s'io vivo in lui, e in me di me son senza?"
    "Vo' che tu mora al bene ed al mal viva,"
mi risponde egli in ultima sentenza;
"Questa ti basti, e questo fa' che scriva."
—1554 (*Rime*, NO. 132 IN A. SALZA ED., 1913)

132

When in my weeping I inquire of Love[2]
(Who so unwillingly gives ear to me)
A thousand times a day—never just once—
Why he will wound and pierce me all the time:
5   "How can it be, since I gave heart and soul
To him,[3] the day I took them both from me;
If everything enclosed within his breast
Is only joy and laughter, never sorrow,
    How can I feel cold jealousy and fear
10 And be deprived of all my joyfulness,
Living in him, and never in myself?"
    "I bid you die to joy and live in grief,"
Love answers me in his hard final sentence:
"Let this suffice you, that it makes you write."
—1997 (TRANS. LAURA ANNA STORTONI AND MARY
PRENTICE LILLIE)

JOACHIM DU BELLAY (?1522–1560)

113

Si nostre vie est moins qu'une journée
En l'eternel, si l'an qui faict le tour
Chasse noz jours sans espoir de retour,
Si perissable est toute chose née,
5   Que songes-tu, mon ame emprisonée?
Pourquoy te plaist l'obscur de nostre jour
Si pour voler en un plus cler sejour,
Tu as au dos l'aele bien empanée?
    La, est le bien que tout esprit desire,
10 La, le repos ou tout le monde aspire,
La, est l'amour, la, le plaisir encore.
    La, ô mo name au plus hault ciel guide!
Tu y pouras recongnoistre l'Idée
De la beauté, qu'en ce monde j'adore.[1]
—1550

113

If this, our life, be less than but a day
In the eternal; if each circling year
Bears off our days, never to reappear;
If every creature born must death obey,
5   Why then, my prisoned soul, should you delay?
How can it please you thus to tarry here,
In darkness, when unto a brighter sphere,
Your well-plumed wings would carry you away?
    There is the good that man's mind hungers for;
10 There, the repose he seeks, forevermore;
There, love and joy abound, their bliss bestow.
    There, O my soul, as you reach heaven's height,
Beauty ideal will loom within your sight,
That beauty that I worship here below.
—2002 (TRANS. NORMAN R. SHAPIRO)

---

[2] *Love* The personified god of love, Cupid, Eros.

[3] *To him* Stampa refers to her beloved and social superior, Count Collatino di Collalto, on whose name, "high hill," she often puns, and who seems for a while to have reciprocated her love.

---

[1] *De la … j'adore* A Neoplatonic sonnet adapted from a sonnet by Bernardino Daniello.

PIERRE DE RONSARD (1524–1585)

Je vouldroy bien richement jaunissant
En pluye d'or goute à goute descendre
Dans le giron de ma belle Cassandre,
Lors qu'en ses yeux le somne va glissant.[1]
5   Puis je vouldroy bien en toreau blandissant[2]
Me transformer pour finement la prendre,
Quand elle va par l'herbe la plus tendre
Seule à l'escart mille fleurs ravissant.
      Je vouldroy bien afin d'aiser ma peine
10 Estre un Narcisse, & elle une fontaine
Pour m'y plonger une nuict à sejour:
      Et vouldroy bien que ceste nuict encore
Durast toujours sans que jamais l'Aurore[3]
D'un front nouveau nous r'allumast le jour.
—1552 (*Amours* I.20)

I would in rich and golden coloured rain,
      With tempting showers in pleasant sort descend
Into fair Phyllis' lap (my lovely friend)
When sleep her sense with slumber doth restrain.
5   I would be changed to a milk-white bull,
When midst the gladsome fields she should appear,
By pleasant sweetness to surprise my dear,
Whilst from their stalks she pleasant flowers did pull.
      I were content to weary out my pain,
10 To be Narcissus so she were a spring
To drown in her those woes my heart do wring:
      And, more, I wish transformed to remain:
That whilst I thus in pleasures' lap did lie,
I might refresh desire, which else would die.
—1593 (TRANS. THOMAS LODGE, *Phillis* 34)

Quand vous serez bien vielle, au soir à la
      chandelle,
Assise aupres du feu, devidant & filant,
Direz, chantant mes vers, en vous esmerveillant,
"Ronsard me celebroit du temps que j'estois belle."
5   Lors vous n'aurez servante oyant telle nouvelle,
Desja sous le labeur à demy sommeillant,
Qui au bruit de "Ronsard" ne s'aille resveillant,
Benissant vostre nom de louange immortelle.
      Je seray sous la terre, & fantaume sans os:
10 Par les ombres Myrtheux je prendray mon repos.
Vous serez au fouyer une vielle accroupie,
      Regrettant mon amour, & vostre fier disdain.
Vivez, si m'en croyez, n'attendez à demain:
Cueillez dés aujourdhuy les roses de la vie.
—1578 (SONNETS FOR HÉLÈNE II, 43)

When you are very old, by candle's flame,
      Spinning beside the fire, at end of day,
Singing my verse, admiring, you will say:
"When I was fair, Ronsard's muse I became."
5   Your servant then, some weary old beldame—
Whoever she may be—nodding away,
Hearing "Ronsard," will shake off sleep, and pray
Your name be blessed, to live in deathless fame.
      Buried, I shall a fleshless phantom be,
10 Hovering by the shadowed myrtle tree;
You, by the hearth, a pining crone, bent low,
      Whose pride once scorned my love, much to your
        sorrow.
Heed me, live for today, wait not the morrow:
Gather life's roses while still fresh they grow.
—2002 (TRANS. NORMAN R. SHAPIRO)

---

[1] *je vouldroy … glissant* In this poem, popular in England, Ronsard wishes to become golden rain like that into which Zeus changed himself so as to visit the imprisoned Danaë, into a white bull like the one Zeus became when he seduced and kidnapped young Europa, and a pool like the one in which Narcissus saw himself and fell in love.

[2] *blandissant* Later editions have "blanchissant"—"white."

[3] *l'Aurore* The dawn goddess.

SAMUEL DANIEL (1562–1619)

from *Delia*

6[1]

Fair is my love, and cruel as she's fair;
  Her brow shades frowns, although her eyes are
    sunny;
  Her smiles are lightning, though her pride despair;
  And her disdains are gall, her favours honey.
5 A modest maid, decked with a blush of honour,
  Whose feet do tread green paths of youth and love;
  The wonder of all eyes that look upon her:
  Sacred on earth, designed a saint above.
  Chastity and Beauty, which were deadly foes,
10 Live reconciled friends within her brow:
  And had she pity to conjoin° with those,   *join*
  Then who had heard the plaints I utter now?
  O had she not been fair, and thus unkind,
  My Muse had slept, and none had known my mind.
—1592

28[2]

Raising my hopes on hills of high desire,
  Thinking to scale the heaven of her heart,
  My slender means presumed too high a part;
  Her thunder of disdain forced me retire,
5 And threw me down to pain in all this fire,
  Where, lo, I languish in so heavy smart,
  Because th'attempt was far above my art:
  Her pride brooked not poor souls should come so
    nigh her.
  Yet I protest my high aspiring will
10 Was not to dispossess her of her right:
  Her sovereignty should have remained still,
  I only sought the bliss to have her sight.
  Her sight, contented thus to see me spill,
  Framed my desires fit for her eyes to kill.
—1592

---

[1] *6* The numbering here follows that in the edition edited by A.C.
Sprague (Cambridge, Mass., 1930). Because Daniel frequently
revised his poetry, numbering varies in the editions published during
his lifetime.

[2] *28* First printed in a collection of sonnets appended to the 1591
unauthorized edition of Sir Philip Sidney's *Astrophil and Stella*.

33

When men shall find thy flower, thy glory pass,
  And thou with careful° brow   *full of cares*
    sitting alone
  Received hast this message from thy glass,
  That tells thee truth, and says that all is gone;
5 Fresh shalt thou see in me the wounds thou madest,
  Though spent thy flame, in me the heat remaining:
  I that have loved thee thus before thou fadest,
  My faith shall wax, when thou art in thy waning.
  The world shall find this miracle in me,
10 That fire can burn when all the matter's spent:
  Then what my faith hath been thy self shalt see,
  And that thou wast unkind thou mayst repent.
  Thou mayst repent that thou hast scorned my tears,
  When winter snows upon thy golden hairs.
—1592

MICHAEL DRAYTON (1563–1631)

from *Idea*

6

How many paltry, foolish, painted things,
  That now in coaches trouble every street,
  Shall be forgotten, whom no poet sings,
  Ere they be well wrapped in their winding sheet?
5 Where I to thee eternity shall give,
  When nothing else remaineth of these days,
  And queens hereafter shall be glad to live
  Upon the alms of thy superfluous praise;
  Virgins and matrons reading these my rhymes,
10 Shall be so much delighted with thy story,
  That they shall grieve they lived not in these times,
  To have seen thee, their sex's only glory:
  So shalt thou fly above the vulgar throng,
  Still to survive in my immortal song.
—1619

61

Since there's no help, come let us kiss and part;
  Nay, I have done: you get no more of me,
  And I am glad, yea glad with all my heart,
  That thus so cleanly I myself can free;
5 Shake hands for ever, cancel all our vows,
  And when we meet at any time again,

Be it not seen in either of our brows
That we one jot of former love retain.
Now at the last gasp of Love's latest breath,
10 When his pulse failing, Passion speechless lies,
When Faith is kneeling by his bed of death,
And Innocence is closing up his eyes,
Now if thou would'st, when all have given him over,
From death to life, thou might'st him yet recover.
        —1619

63

Truce, gentle Love, a parley now I crave:
    Methinks 'tis long since first these wars begun.
Nor thou, nor I, the better yet can have;
Bad is the match, where neither party won.
5 I offer free conditions of fair peace,
My heart for hostage that it shall remain.
Discharge our forces, here let malice cease,
So for my pledge thou give me pledge again.
Or if no thing but death will serve thy turn,
10 Still thirsting for subversion of my state,
Do what thou canst, raze, massacre, and burn,
Let the world see the utmost of thy hate:
        I send defiance, since if overthrown,
        Thou vanquishing, the conquest is mine own.
        —1599

WILLIAM SHAKESPEARE (1564–1616)

from *Romeo and Juliet* (Act 1, Scene 5)

ROMEO. If I profane with my unworthiest hand
This holy shrine,[1] the gentle fine is this,
My lips, two blushing pilgrims, ready stand
To smooth that rough touch with a tender kiss.
5 JULIET. Good pilgrim, you do wrong your hand too
    much,
Which mannerly devotion shows in this;
For saints[2] have hands that pilgrims' hands do touch,
And palm to palm is holy palmers' kiss.[3]

---

[1] *holy shrine* Juliet's hand.

[2] *saints* That is, images or statues of saints, venerated by pilgrims.

[3] *palmers' kiss* Palmers were pilgrims who have been to the Holy Land; their emblem was the palm frond (hence Juliet's pun on "palm").

ROMEO.   Have not saints lips, and holy palmers too?
10 JULIET. Aye, pilgrim, lips that they must use in prayer.
ROMEO.   Oh then, dear saint, let lips do what hands do.
  They pray. Grant thou, lest faith turn to despair.
JULIET.   Saints do not move, though grant for prayers'
    sake.
ROMEO.   Then move not while my prayer's effect I take.
        [He kisses her]

    —1597 (WRITTEN C. 1595)

SIR JOHN DAVIES (1569–1626)

from *Gulling Sonnets*[4]

3

What eagle can behold her sun-bright eye,
    Her sun-bright eye that lights the world with
        love,
The world of Love wherein I live and die,
I live and die and diverse changes prove,
5 I changes prove, yet still the same am I,
The same am I and never will remove,
Never remove until my soul doth fly,
My soul doth fly and I surcease to move,
I cease to move which now am moved by you,
10 Am moved by you that move all mortal hearts,
All mortal hearts whose eyes your eyes doth view,
Your eyes doth view whence Cupid shoots his darts,
Whence Cupid shoots his darts and woundeth those
That honor you, and never were his foes.
—1594

JOHN DAVIES OF HEREFORD (1565–1618)

from *The Scourge of Villany*

The author loving these homely meats[5] specially, viz:
cream, pancakes, buttered pippin pies[6] (laugh, good

---

[4] *Gulling Sonnets* Davies's *Gulling Sonnets*, parodying the conventions and clichés of the sonnet form, circulated in manuscript.

[5] *meats* Foods, consumables; Davies, too, is writing parody.

[6] *pippin pies* Apple pies.

people) and tobacco; writ to that worthy and
virtuous gentlewoman, whom he calleth mistress, as
followeth:

If there were, oh! an Hellespont[1] of cream
  Between us, milk-white mistress, I would swim
To you, to show to both my love's extreme,
Leander-like—yea! dive from brim to brim.
5 But met I with a buttered pippin pie
Floating upon't, that would I make my boat
To waft me to you without jeopardy,
Though sea-sick I might be while it did float.
Yet if a storm should rise, by night or day,
10 Of sugar-snows and hail of caraways,
Then, if I found a pancake in my way,
It like a plank should bring me to your quays;
Which having found, if they tobacco kept,
The smoke should dry me well before I slept.
—1611

RICHARD BARNFIELD (1574–1620)

from *Cynthia*

14

Here, hold this glove (this milk-white
  cheverel° glove)   *leather*
  Not quaintly over-wrought with curious knots,
  Not decked° with golden spangs,° nor
    silver spots,   *decorated / decorative metal*
  Yet wholesome for thy hand as thou shalt prove.
5 Ah no (sweet boy)[2] place this glove near thy heart,
  Wear it, and lodge it still within thy breast,
  So shalt thou make me (most unhappy) blest.
So shalt thou rid my pain, and ease my smart:
How can that be (perhaps) thou wilt reply,
10 A glove is for the hand not for the heart,
  Nor can it well be proved by common art,

---

[1] *Hellespont* Older name for the Dardanelles, the strait between European and Asian Turkey. The Leander of line 4 is the young man in classical legend who swam across the Hellespont to meet his mistress Hero.

[2] *sweet boy* Barnfield's sonnets are the only extant ones in Renaissance England, other than Shakespeare's, in which a male speaker addresses another man in a homoerotic manner.

Nor reason's rule. To this, thus answer I:
  If thou from glove dost take away the "g,"
  Then glove is love: and so I send it thee.
—1595

17

Cherry-lipped Adonis[3] in his snowy shape,
  Might not compare with his pure ivory white,
  On whose fair front° a poet's pen may write,   *forehead*
  Whose roseate red excels the crimson grape,
5 His love-enticing delicate soft limbs,
  Are rarely° framed t' entrap poor gazing eyes: *wonderfully*
  His cheeks, the lily and carnation dyes
With lovely tincture, which Apollo's dims.[4]
His lips ripe strawberries in nectar wet,
10 His mouth a hue, his tongue a honey-comb,
  Where muses (like bees) make their mansion.
His teeth pure pearl in blushing coral set.
  Oh how can such a body sin-procuring,
  Be slow to love, and quick to hate, enduring?
—1595

GEORGE GASCOIGNE (1539–1578)

Gascoigne's Lullaby

Sing lullaby, as women do,
  Wherewith they bring their babes to rest,
And lullaby can I sing too
As womanly as can the best.
5 With lullaby they still the child,
And if I be not much beguiled,
Full many wanton babes have I
Which must be stilled with lullaby.

First lullaby my youthful years,
10 It is now time to go to bed,
For crooked age and hoary hairs
Have won the haven within my head:
With lullaby then youth be still,
With lullaby content thy will,

---

[3] *Adonis* The young man beloved by the goddess Venus.

[4] *Apollo* God of the sun: the beloved's color "dims" even the sun.

15   Since courage quails, and comes behind,
      Go sleep, and so beguile thy mind.

      Next lullaby my gazing eyes,
      Which wonted were to glance apace.°   *directly*
      For every glass may now suffice,
20   To show the furrows in my face:
      With lullaby then wink awhile,
      With lullaby your looks beguile:
      Let no fair face, nor beauty bright,
      Entice you eft° with vain delight.   *again*

25   And lullaby my wanton will,
      Let reasons rule now reign thy thought,
      Since all too late I find by skill,
      How dear I have thy fancies bought.
      With lullaby now take thine ease,
30   With lullaby thy doubts appease:
      For trust to this, if thou be still,
      My body shall obey thy will.

      Eke° lullaby my loving boy,   *also*
      My little Robin[1] take thy rest,
35   Since age is cold, and nothing coy,
      Keep close thy coin, for so is best:
      With lullaby be thou content,
      With lullaby thy lusts relent,
      Let others pay which hath mo° pence,   *more*
40   Thou art too poor for such expense.

      Thus lullaby my youth, mine eyes,
      My will, my ware, and all that was,
      I can no mo delays devise,
      But welcome pain, let pleasure pass:
45   With lullaby now take your leave,
      With lullaby your dreams deceive,
      And when you rise with waking eye,
      Remember Gascoigne's lullaby.

---

[1] *Robin* Slang for penis.

ANONYMOUS[2]

Ode[3]

That time and absence proves[4]
Rather helps than hurts to loves.

Absence, hear thou my protestation
      Against thy strength,
        Distance and length:
Do what you can for alteration,
5   For hearts of truest mettle
Absence doth join and time doth settle.

Who loves a mistress of such quality,
      He soon hath found
        Affection ground[5]
10   Beyond time, place, and all mortality;
      To hearts that cannot vary,
Absence is present, time doth tarry.

My senses want° their outward motions,   *lack*
      Which now within
15   Reason doth win,
Redoubled in her[6] secret notions,
      Like rich men that take pleasure
      In hiding, more than handling, treasure.

By absence, this good means I gain:
      That I can catch her,
        Where none can watch her,
In some close corner of my brain.
      There I embrace and kiss her,
And so I both enjoy and miss her.
—1611

---

[2] *Anonymous* The authorship is uncertain. This is one of a number of Renaissance love poems celebrating the triumph of the waking or dreaming imagination over the beloved's absence or, in some cases, rejection.

[3] *Ode* From Francis Davison et al., *A Poetical Rhapsody* (1611 ed.).

[4] *That time and absence proves* I.e., prove: a singular verb after a double subject was then common.

[5] *Affection ground* The wording is condensed, but the idea is that love for an admirable lady is a ground, a base, for an affection that does not change because of absence.

[6] *Redoubled in her* I.e., Reason's.

EDMUND SPENSER
1552? – 1599

Edmund Spenser has consistently been accorded a special place in the history of English literature. In the seventeenth century John Milton, as much impressed by *The Faerie Queene*'s subtle treatment of the moral virtues as by its aesthetic charm, called him "our sage and serious Spenser, whom I dare to name a better teacher than Scotus or Aquinas." In the nineteenth, Wordsworth wrote of "Sweet Spenser, moving through his clouded heaven / With the moon's beauty and the moon's soft pace." And in the twentieth and twenty-first centuries poets and critics have continued to hold Spenser and *The Faerie Queene* in extraordinarily high regard.

Spenser's career as a servant of the Crown was less glorious. He was not the moping failure some have thought him (he had steady work in Ireland helping the English govern its often rebellious and resentful population), but in England he was never the courtier that he seems to have wanted to be. His bid for more direct royal patronage was the first part of *The Faerie Queene* (1590). This is an allegorical epic poem with debts to Virgil, elements of Arthurian and Italian epic or romance, traces of medieval pilgrimage allegory, Chaucerian moments, and passages indebted to a range of other genres from the fabliau to the pastoral. The central if often absent figure is Prince Arthur, the future British king, who is seeking the always absent heroine, Gloriana, queen of Fairyland and an allegorical "mirror," Spenser told his friend Sir Walter Ralegh in a letter published at the end of the volume, of Queen Elizabeth in her public role as ruler. Modern scholars may perceive veiled criticisms of Elizabeth in the poetry, but the queen either did not notice or thought it wise to read the epic as purely complimentary, so she gave the author a generous yearly pension of fifty pounds.

Little is known with any certainty of Spenser's early life, although his writings provide some information. He was born, probably in London, to parents of modest means, and it was as an "impoverished" student that he entered the Merchant Taylors' School, headed by the scholar Richard Mulcaster, remembered today for his impassioned defense of the English language. There Spenser studied Latin, Greek, and possibly Hebrew; he also learned French and Italian. From there he went to Pembroke Hall (now Pembroke College) at Cambridge University, where he was registered as a "sizar," a poor student who was required to work for his keep, earning his bachelor's degree in 1573 and his M.A. in 1576. While at Pembroke, Spenser made friends with Gabriel Harvey, soon to be a prominent Cambridge don, who introduced him to useful patrons and whose correspondence with the young poet demonstrates a shared interest in poetic theory, genres, and metrics.

In 1579 Spenser produced his first significant, if pseudonymous, publication, *The Shepheardes Calender*, a set of illustrated pastoral poems for each month of the year and written, says a prefatory poem, by one "Immerito." The work, dedicated to Philip Sidney, comes with a preface and annotations by the still unidentified "E.K." In this innovative work, which saw a number of editions, Spenser exploits a genre that hearkened back to Theocritus and Virgil in the third and first centuries BCE but that had since added the potential for religious and political commentary because of the Christian associations of "pastor" and "flock." The book's presentation is fashionably Continental and the metrical variation innovative, yet the language is deliberately old-fashioned, reminiscent of Chaucer and with a name for the protagonist—Colin Clout—taken from the work of an earlier poet, John Skelton.

In that same year, 1579, Spenser was in the service, as secretary, of the Earl of Leicester, an important royal advisor and at one point suitor to Queen Elizabeth. There he would have met Sidney, Leicester's nephew, and Edward Dyer, both poets and both eventually knighted, whose friendship, or at least notice, would have seemed valuable. Sidney may have helped Spenser later gain an appointment as secretary to Lord Grey, the Lord Deputy of Ireland. It is not quite clear how Spenser regarded Grey's brutality against the Spanish troops who supported the Irish rebels, but his later tract, *A Vewe of the Present State of Ireland* (printed 1633), whatever the ambiguities of its dialogue form and a few residual doubts about its authorship, displays little regard for the Irish and even less for the insurgents. After Grey was recalled to England, Spenser remained in Ireland and continued to work as a civil servant, gaining considerable acreage and a small castle.

In 1589 Spenser traveled with Sir Walter Ralegh to England, where in 1590 he published the first three books of *The Faerie Queene*, on which he had been working for about a decade. Politically as well as poetically motivated, this Protestant, but hardly "Puritan," epic creates a romance world filled with monsters, giants, knights, and enchanters, allegorical personifications who enact a subtle, complex, and often elusive interplay between the Aristotelian or Christian virtues and their enemies, both those active out in the world and those operating within the leading figures' own souls. According to his letter to Ralegh, Spenser hoped to write twelve books, but only six were completed (the second set being published in the 1596 edition): the "legends" of holiness, temperance, chastity, friendship, justice, and courtesy, as well as a fragment on "Mutabilitie." Spenser won his pension, but Elizabeth's patronage seems to have gone no further, perhaps because his satirical "Mother Hubberds Tale," included in his *Complaints* (1591), angered the authorities.

In between the first and second installments of *The Faerie Queene* Spenser published his *Complaints*, a collection of poems; *Colin Clouts Come Home Againe* (1595), a sometimes satirical anti-court pastoral; *Astrophel*, an elegy for Philip Sidney (1596); and *Amoretti and Epithalamion* (1595), sonnets that commemorate Spenser's courtship of Elizabeth Boyle, followed by a magnificently stately marriage hymn celebrating their marriage. The sonnets, which depart from the Petrarchan tradition of adulterous or futile desire, are structured by allusions to the liturgical year; the twenty-four stanzas of the "Epithalamion" allude to the day (June 11, then the summer solstice), and its 365 long lines recall the year.

In 1597 Spenser became Sheriff of Cork, but later that year Irish rebels ransacked and burned his castle. He returned to London carrying dispatches for the Privy Council, but his time there was to be short. He died early in 1599 and is buried in Westminster Abbey, next to Chaucer. A memorial erected in 1620 reads, in part, "Heare lyes … the body of Edmond Spencer, the prince of poets in his tyme; whose divine spirit needs noe other witnesse then the works which he left behinde him."

⌘ ⌘ ⌘

The Faerie Queene

In a letter to his friend Sir Walter Ralegh, Spenser writes that his unfinished *Faerie Queene* aimed to "fashion" a gentleman or noble person who would combine the virtues represented by twelve knightly heroes. In his epic poem, each of the books features one of these knights, who represents a virtue and struggles to fight the specific vices that threaten his quest. The hero of Book 1's "Legend of Holinesse," is Saint George (the Redcrosse Knight), patron saint of England and, with God's help, slayer of a satanic dragon that has been threatening a royal family and its kingdom, Eden. In the legend as it came down to Spenser, George rescues the royal maiden and the kingdom by defeating the dragon but then leaves, soon to be martyred. In Spenser's Protestant version, however, the knight will marry the princess, Una (representing the One, the Truth, and the True Church), although not until his earthly service to the Fairy Queen, Gloriana (who represents, among other things, Queen Elizabeth), is finished. Then, at the end of human time, the marriage of Christ and his Church can be completed.

The somewhat chilly hero of Book 2 is Sir Guyon, Knight of Temperance, who with the intermittent guidance of a Palmer (usually a religious figure, but here signifying rectified reason) seeks not so much a middle way as a dynamic mixture of positive and negative energies, fire and water, excess and lack—a mixture that parallels the healthy body's balance of elements and the cosmos's own tense harmony. The villain is the seductively beautiful but murderous Acrasia ("Excess") who, like Homer's Circe, turns men to beasts. After a journey recalling that of Odysseus, Guyon arrives at her island, a pseudo-paradise of sensuous but sterile pleasures and largely artificial beauty.

The Garden of Adonis is the Bower's parallel and correction, made beautiful by Nature's own art. To this garden will come the lovely Amoret to be raised by Venus in "goodly womanhed." The Garden is the center, structurally and conceptually, of Book 3, the Legend of Chastity. For Spenser, Chastity (represented by the armed lady knight, Britomart) is an energetic love that embraces a sexuality culminating in faithful marriage. In all the books, the epic's chief hero is Prince Arthur, a Briton who is in love with Gloriana and who will, in Spenser's version of the tale, establish the royal line from which will eventually derive the Welsh Tudor dynasty.

Book 1 derives from a saint's legend, a genre that many Protestants contemptuously dismissed as medieval and Catholic. It is also a dynastic epic, as loosely defined in the Renaissance: its opening lines signal Spenser's aims, and his ambition to be a national poet, through paraphrasing the cancelled start of Virgil's *Aeneid* and the opening of Ariosto's *Orlando Furioso*. Spenser takes his structure of twelve books, each consisting of twelve cantos, from Virgil's *Aeneid*, but his rhyme scheme is distinctly his own. Each nine-line stanza (later referred to as the Spenserian stanza) consists of eight lines of iambic pentameter and a final line of iambic hexameter (an alexandrine) with an interlocking rhyme scheme (*ababbcbcc*). Structurally, the poem follows a pattern set by St. Bernard of Clairvaux (1090-1153) in a sermon that allegorizes the parable of the Prodigal Son: a young man on an impatient horse journeys with a number of personifications through Error, to Pride, to Despair, and finally to a house where he recovers and is ready for Heaven. Spenser also borrows heavily from Ariosto, Tasso's *Jerusalem Delivered*, Virgil, Chaucer, Arthurian legend, and Tudor anti-Catholic polemic, so that the poem incorporates epic, romance, legend, personification allegory, satire, and pastoral. The Bible figures too, for the narrative moves from a besieged Eden through a fall into error and eventually by way of a victory over the old dragon, Satan, to the promise of the New Jerusalem and the union of God and humanity at the end of time. George's very name, from the Greek for farmer, or "earth-worker," parallels that of Adam (Hebrew for "red earth"), because the Legend of Holinesse also narrates the conversion by God's grace of earthly flesh into Saint George of "merry" England.

Book 1 also allegorizes England's loss of the true Church to Catholicism—just when this had occurred, historically, was a matter of debate at the time, and Spenser is not clear on that point—and its recovery under the Protestant Tudors. In this regard, Spenser's poem exemplifies the anti-Catholicism common in his time and place. Yet he also incorporates a number of Catholic touches, from the hermit who instructs Redcrosse to elements of the Catholic Easter Eve liturgy that deepen the concluding betrothal ceremony. Indeed, in recent years Spenser has seemed less urgently Protestant, and although there can be no doubt that he feared and detested the might of Catholic Spain (allegorized by the giant Orgoglio) and what he saw as the mendaciously seductive powers of the Papacy (allegorized by the magician Archimago and the witch Duessa), his theology has been read as less rigidly Calvinist, with at least a little more room for a free human will than strict Protestants would have liked, and with an acceptance of formal and communal ceremony that would make radical Puritans wince.

In recent years, then, Spenser's moral and religious understanding has come to seem more flexible. Similarly, his treatment of the virtues that his knightly heroes represent has been seen as less illustrative or demonstrative and more interrogative or exploratory. In all the books, even Book 1 (which deals with a virtue hard to live by but easy for readers to value), Spenser is willing to show the problems and paradoxes attendant upon the six virtues he examines: holiness, temperance, chastity, friendship, justice, and courtesy. Although few at his time would deny the virtue of holiness, Spenser can still suggest that it might need, or lead to, the other virtues, and when he comes to the remaining five he is willing to show their limits and their need of correction by yet others. In all cases his knights, and especially the usually less than brilliant St. George, make terrible mistakes. Through these knights' errors Spenser implies that we live in a world that makes virtuous action difficult because perceiving what is good, or even simply knowing what is going on, is often harder than wanting to be good. Spenser's readers may (and perhaps should) find his allegory confusing, but his knights are usually just as confused. Eventually both hero and reader realize what is happening, but each experiences the error and puzzlement that, for Spenser, characterize human life.

The first three books of *The Faerie Queene* were published in 1590 with an appended letter to Sir Walter Ralegh in which Spenser outlines his designs for the epic; some modern editions print it as a preface and others, including this anthology, as the "annex" Spenser himself called it.

---

from *The Faerie Queene*

THE FIRST BOOKE OF THE FAERIE QUEENE
CONTAYNING THE LEGENDE OF THE KNIGHT OF THE
RED CROSSE, OR OF HOLINESSE

1

Lo I the man, whose Muse[1] whilome° did   *formerly*
    maske,
As time her taught, in lowly Shepheards weeds,°   *garments*
Am now enforst a far unfitter taske,
For trumpets sterne to chaunge mine Oaten reeds,[2]
5 And sing of Knights and Ladies gentle° deeds;   *noble*
Whose prayses having slept in silence long,
Me, all too meane,° the sacred Muse
    areeds°   *common | advises*
To blazon° broad° emongst her learned
    throng: *proclaim | abroad*
Fierce warres and faithfull loves shall moralize my song.

2

10 Helpe then, O holy Virgin chiefe of nine,
Thy weaker° Novice to performe thy will,   *weak*
Lay forth out of thine everlasting scryne[3]
The antique rolles, which there lye hidden still,
Of Faerie knights and fairest Tanaquill,[4]
15 Whom that most noble Briton Prince° so long   *Arthur*
Sought through the world, and suffered so much ill,
That I must rue his undeservèd wrong:
O helpe thou my weake wit, and sharpen my dull tong.

3

And thou most dreaded impe° of highest Jove,[5]   *child*
20 Faire Venus sonne, that with thy cruell dart
At that good knight so cunningly didst rove,°   *shoot*
That glorious fire it kindled in his hart,
Lay now thy deadly Heben° bow apart,   *ebony*
And with thy mother milde come to mine ayde:

---

[1] *Muse* One of the nine goddesses who preside over the arts and sciences. In line 10 it seems that Spenser is referring either to Clio, the Muse of history, or Calliope, the Muse of epic.

[2] *Oaten reeds* I.e, the shepherd's pipe, the symbol of pastoral poetry. Spenser exchanges these pipes for the trumpet, the symbol of heroic poetry.

[3] *scryne* Chest for valuables, especially sacred objects such as saints' relics.

[4] *Tanaquill* I.e., Gloriana, a symbolic representation of Queen Elizabeth I.

[5] *And thou … Jove* Here Cupid is the son of Jove, Roman King of the gods, and Venus, goddess of beauty and love. Cupid's father is sometimes said to be Hermes or Mars rather than Jove.

25 Come both, and with you bring triumphant Mart,[1]
   In loves and gentle jollities arrayd,
   After his murdrous spoiles and bloudy rage allayd.

4

   And with them eke,° O Goddesse heavenly bright,   *also*
30   Mirrour of grace and Majestie divine,
   Great Lady of the greatest Isle, whose light
   Like Phoebus lampe[2] throughout the world doth shine,
   Shed thy faire beames into my feeble eyne,°   *eyes*
   And raise my thoughts too humble and too vile,
35   To thinke of that true glorious type[3] of thine,
   The argument° of mine afflicted° stile:°   *topic/humble/work*
The which to heare, vouchsafe, O dearest dred[4] a-while.

Canto 1

The Patron of true Holinesse,
Foule Errour doth defeate:
Hypocrisie him to entrappe,
Doth to his home entreate.

1

A Gentle Knight was pricking° on the   *galloping*
     plaine,
   Y cladd in mightie armes and silver shielde,
   Wherein old dints of deepe wounds did remaine,
   The cruell markes of many a bloudy fielde;
5   Yet armes till that time did he never wield:[5]
   His angry steede did chide his foming bitt,
   As much disdayning to the curbe to yield:
   Full jolly° knight he seemd, and faire did sitt,   *handsome*
As one for knightly giusts° and fierce encounters   *jousts*
     fitt.

2

10 But on his brest a bloudie Crosse he bore,
   The deare remembrance of his dying Lord,

---

1 *Mart* Mars, god of war and one of Venus's lovers.

2 *Phoebus lampe* I.e., the sun (Phoebus Apollo is god of the sun).

3 *that … type* Gloriana.

4 *dred* Object of reverence.

5 *Y cladd …, wield* The knight wears the "whole armor of God" (Ephesians 13-17), worn by those who struggle against sin. Though the armor itself bears marks from many battles, this particular knight has never fought in it before.

   For whose sweete sake that glorious badge he wore,
   And dead as living ever him ador'd:
   Upon his shield the like was also scor'd,
15   For soveraine° hope, which in his helpe he had: *greatest*
   Right faithfull true he was in deede and word,
   But of his cheere° did seeme too solemne
     sad;°   *demeanor / serious*
Yet nothing did he dread, but ever was ydrad.°   *dreaded*

3

Upon a great adventure he was bond,
20   That greatest Gloriana to him gave,
   That greatest Glorious Queene of Faerie lond,
   To winne him worship,° and her grace to have,   *renown*
   Which of all earthly things he most did crave;
   And ever as he rode, his hart did earne°   *yearn*
25   To prove his puissance° in battell brave   *strength*
   Upon his foe, and his new force to learne;
Upon his foe, a Dragon horrible and stearne.

4

A lovely Ladie rode him faire beside,
   Upon a lowly Asse more white then snow,
30   Yet she much whiter, but the same did hide
   Under a vele, that wimpled° was full low,   *folded*
   And over all a blacke stole she did throw,
   As one that inly mournd: so was she sad,
   And heavie sat upon her palfrey slow:
35   Seemèd in heart some hidden care she had,
And by her in a line a milke white lambe she lad.

5

So pure and innocent, as that same lambe,
   She was in life and every vertuous lore,
   And by descent from Royall lynage came
40   Of ancient Kings and Queenes, that had of yore
   Their scepters stretcht from East to Westerne shore,
   And all the world in their subjection held;
   Till that infernall feend with foule uprore
   Forwasted° all their land, and them expeld: *lay waste*
45 Whom to avenge, she had this Knight from far compeld.

6

Behind her farre away a Dwarfe did lag,
   That lasie seemd in being ever last,
   Or wearied with bearing of her bag

Of needments at his backe. Thus as they past,
50 The day with cloudes was suddeine overcast,
And angry Jove an hideous storme of raine
Did poure into his Lemans lap[1] so fast,
That every wight° to shrowd° it did
    constrain,°   *creature / cover / impel*
And this faire couple eke to shroud themselves were
    fain.°   *eager*

7

55 Enforst to seeke some covert° nigh at hand,   *shelter*
A shadie grove not far away they spide,
That promist ayde° the tempest to withstand: *aid*
Whose loftie trees yclad with sommers pride,
Did spred so broad, that heavens light did hide,
60 Not perceable[2] with power of any starre:
And all within were pathes and alleies wide,
With footing worne, and leading inward farre:
Faire harbour that them seemes; so in they entred arre.

8

And foorth they passe, with pleasure forward led,
65 Joying to heare the birdes sweete harmony,
Which therein shrouded from the tempest dred,
Seemd in their song to scorne the cruell sky.
Much can° they prayse the trees so straight and hy,   *did*
The sayling Pine, the Cedar proud and tall,
70 The vine-prop Elme, the Poplar never dry,
The builder Oake, sole king of forrests all,
The Aspine good for staves, the Cypresse funerall.

9

The Laurell, meed° of mightie Conquerours   *reward*
And Poets sage, the Firre that weepeth[3] still,°   *continuously*
75 The Willow worne of forlorne Paramours,
The Eugh° obedient to the benders will,   *yew*
The Birch for shaftes,° the Sallow for the mill,   *lances*
The Mirrhe sweete bleeding in the bitter wound,
The warlike Beech, the Ash for nothing ill,
80 The fruitfull Olive, and the Platane° round,   *plane-tree*
The carver Holme,° the Maple seeldom inward
    sound.   *holly*

---

[1] *his Lemans lap* His beloved's lap; i.e., the earth.

[2] *perceable* Able to be perceived.

[3] *weepeth* I.e., by exuding resin.

10

Led with delight, they thus beguile the way,
Untill the blustring storme is overblowne;
When weening° to returne, whence they   *expecting*
    did stray,
85 They cannot finde that path, which first was showne,
But wander too and fro in wayes unknowne,
Furthest from end then, when they neerest weene,
That makes them doubt, their wits be not their owne:
So many pathes, so many turnings seene,
90 That which of them to take, in diverse doubt they been.

11

At last resolving forward still to fare,
Till that some end they finde or in or out,
That path they take, that beaten seemd most bare,
And like to lead the labyrinth about;°   *out from*
95 Which when by tract they hunted had throughout,
At length it brought them to a hollow cave,
Amid the thickest woods. The Champion stout
Eftsoones° dismounted from his courser
    brave,   *soon afterwards*
And to the Dwarfe a while his needlesse spere he gave.

12

100 Be well aware, quoth then that Ladie milde,
Least suddaine mischiefe ye too rash provoke:
The danger hid, the place unknowne and wilde,
Breedes dreadfull doubts: Oft fire is without smoke,
And perill without show: therefore your stroke
105 Sir knight with-hold, till further triall made.
Ah Ladie (said he) shame were to revoke°   *withdraw*
The forward footing for° an hidden shade: *because of*
Vertue gives her selfe light, through darkenesse for to
    wade.

13

Yea but (quoth she) the perill of this place
110 I better wot° then you, though now too late   *know*
To wish you backe returne with foule disgrace,
Yet wisedome warnes, whilest foot is in the gate,
To stay the steppe, ere forcèd to retrate.
This is the wandring wood, this Errours den,
115 A monster vile, whom God and man does hate:

Therefore I read° beware. Fly fly (quoth then   *declare*
The fearefull Dwarfe:) this is no place for living men.

14

But full of fire and greedy hardiment,°   *daring*
   The youthfull knight could not for ought be staide,
120 But forth unto the darksome hole he went,
   And looked in: his glistring armor made
   A litle glooming light, much like a shade,
   By which he saw the ugly monster plaine,
   Halfe like a serpent horribly displaide,
125 But th'other halfe did womans shape retaine,
Most lothsom, filthie, foule, and full of vile
    disdaine.°   *loathsomeness*

15

And as she lay upon the durtie ground,
   Her huge long taile her den all overspred,
   Yet was in knots and many boughtes° upwound,   *coils*
130 Pointed with mortall sting. Of her there bred
   A thousand yong ones, which she dayly fed,
   Sucking upon her poisonous dugs, each one
   Of sundry shapes, yet all ill favored:
   Soone as that uncouth° light upon them
    shone,   *unfamiliar*
135 Into her mouth they crept, and suddain all were gone.

16

Their dam° upstart, out of her den effraide,°   *mother / alarmed*
   And rushèd forth, hurling her hideous taile
   About her cursèd head, whose folds displaid
   Were stretcht now forth at length without
    entraile.°   *coil*
140 She lookt about, and seeing one in mayle
   Armèd to point,° sought backe to turne againe;   *completely*
   For light she hated as the deadly bale,°   *injury*
   Ay° wont° in desert darknesse to
    remaine,   *ever / accustomed*
Where plaine° none might her see, nor she see any
    plaine.   *plainly*

17

145 Which when the valiant Elfe[1] perceiv'd, he lept
   As Lyon fierce upon the flying pray,
   And with his trenchand° blade her boldly kept   *cutting*
   From turning backe, and forcèd her to stay:
   Therewith enrag'd she loudly gan to bray,
150 And turning fierce, her speckled taile advaunst,
   Threatning her angry sting, him to dismay:°   *defeat*
   Who nought aghast, his mightie hand°
    enhaunst: *raised up*
The stroke down from her head vnto her shoulder
    glaunst.

18

Much daunted with that dint, her sence was dazd,
155 Yet kindling rage, her selfe she gathered round,
   And all attonce° her beastly body raizd   *at once*
   With doubled forces high above the ground:
   Tho° wrapping up her wrethèd° sterne
    arownd,   *then / coiled*
   Lept fierce upon his shield, and her huge traine°   *tail*
160 All suddenly about his body wound,
   That hand or foot to stirre he strove in vaine:
God helpe the man so wrapt in Errours endlesse traine.

19

His Lady sad to see his sore constraint,
   Cride out, Now now Sir knight, shew what ye bee,
165 Add faith unto your force, and be not faint:
   Strangle her, else she sure will strangle thee.
   That when he heard, in great perplexitie,
   His gall° did grate for griefe and high
    disdaine,   *spirit / anger*
   And knitting all his force got one hand free,
170 Wherewith he grypt her gorge with so great paine,
That soone to loose her wicked bands did her constraine.

20

Therewith she spewd out of her filthy maw°   *mouth*
   A floud of poyson horrible and blacke,
   Full of great lumpes of flesh and gobbets raw,
175 Which stunck so vildly,° that it forst him slacke   *vilely*
   His grasping hold, and from her turne him backe:

---

[1] *valiant Elfe* I.e., the Redcrosse Knight (who is from Fairyland, and not yet discovered to be English).

Her vomit full of bookes and papers was,[1]
With loathly frogs and toades, which eyes did lacke,
And creeping sought way in the weedy gras:
180 Her filthy parbreake° all the place defilèd has.   *vomit*

21

As when old father Nilus° gins to swell   *Nile river*
  With timely° pride above the Aegyptian vale,   *seasonal*
  His fattie° waves do fertile slime outwell,   *rich | gush forth*
  And overflow each plaine and lowly dale:
185 But when his later spring gins to avale,°   *subside*
  Huge heapes of mudd he leaves, wherein there breed
  Ten thousand kindes of creatures, partly male
  And partly female of his fruitfull seed;
Such ugly monstrous shapes elswhere may no man
    reed.°   *see*

22

190 The same so sore annoyèd has the knight,
  That welnigh chokèd with the deadly stinke,
  His forces faile, ne can no longer fight.
  Whose corage when the feend perceiv'd to shrinke,
  She pourèd forth out of her hellish sinke
195 Her fruitfull cursèd spawne of serpents small,
  Deformèd monsters, fowle, and blacke as inke,
  Which swarming all about his legs did crall,
And him encombred sore, but could not hurt at all.

23

As gentle Shepheard in sweete even-tide,
200 When ruddy Phoebus gins to welke° in west,   *set*
  High on an hill, his flocke to vewen wide,
  Markes° which do byte their hasty supper best;   *notes*
  A cloud of combrous gnattes do him molest,
  All striving to infixe their feeble stings,
205 That from their noyance he no where can rest,
  But with his clownish° hands their tender wings   *rustic*
He brusheth oft, and oft doth mar their murmurings.

24

Thus ill bestedd,° and fearefull more of shame,   *situated*
  Then of the certaine perill he stood in,
210 Halfe furious unto his foe he came,
  Resolv'd in minde all suddenly to win,

---

[1] *Her vomit … was*   I.e., works of Roman Catholic propaganda.

Or soone to lose, before he once would lin;°   *cease*
  And strooke at her with more then manly force,
  That from her body full of filthie sin
215 He raft° her hatefull head without remorse;   *cut off*
A streame of cole black bloud forth gushed from her
    corse.

25

Her scattred brood, soone as their Parent deare
  They saw so rudely° falling to the ground,   *violently*
  Groning full deadly, all with troublous feare,
220 Gathred themselves about her body round,
  Weening° their wonted entrance to have found   *believing*
  At her wide mouth: but being there withstood
  They flockèd all about her bleeding wound,
  And suckèd up their dying mothers blood,
225 Making her death their life, and eke her hurt their good.

26

That detestable sight him much amazde,
  To see th'unkindly Impes° of heaven
    accurst,   *unnatural offspring*
  Devoure their dam; on whom while so he gazd,
  Having all satisfide their bloudy thurst,
230 Their bellies swolne he saw with fulnesse burst,
  And bowels gushing forth: well worthy end
  Of such as drunke her life, the which them nurst;
  Now needeth him no lenger labour spend,
His foes have slaine themselves, with whom he should
    contend.

27

235 His Ladie seeing all, that chaunst, from farre
  Approcht in hast to greet his victorie,
  And said, Faire knight, borne under happy starre,
  Who see your vanquisht foes before you lye:
  Well worthy be you of that Armorie,°   *armor*
240 Wherein ye have great glory wonne this day,
  And proov'd your strength on a strong enimie,
  Your first adventure: many such I pray,
And henceforth ever wish, that like succeed it may.

28

Then mounted he upon his Steede againe,
245 And with the Lady backward sought to wend;°   *travel*

That path he kept, which beaten was most plaine,
   Ne ever would to any by-way bend,
   But still did follow one unto the end,
   The which at last out of the wood them brought.
250 So forward on his way (with God to° frend°)   *as / friend*
   He passèd forth, and new adventure sought;
Long way he travellèd, before he heard of ought.

29

At length they chaunst to meet upon the way
   An agèd Sire, in long blacke weedes yclad,
255 His feete all bare, his beard all hoarie gray,
   And by his belt his booke he hanging had;
   Sober he seemde, and very sagely sad,°   *serious*
   And to the ground his eyes were lowly bent,
   Simple in shew, and voyde of malice bad,
260 And all the way he prayèd, as he went,
And often knockt his brest, as one that did repent.

30

He faire the knight saluted, louting° low,   *bowing*
   Who faire him quited,° as that courteous was: *returned*
   And after askèd him, if he did know
265 Of straunge adventures, which abroad did pas.
   Ah my deare Sonne (quoth he) how should, alas,
   Silly° old man, that lives in hidden cell,   *simple*
   Bidding his beades[1] all day for his trespas,
   Tydings of warre and worldly trouble tell?
270 With holy father sits not with such things to
      mell.°   *meddle*

31

But if of daunger which hereby doth dwell,
   And homebred evill ye desire to heare,
   Of a straunge man I can you tidings tell,
   That wasteth all this countrey farre and neare.
275 Of such (said he) I chiefly do inquere,
   And shall you well reward to shew the place,
   In which that wicked wight his dayes doth weare:°   *spend*
   For to all knighthood it is foule disgrace,
That such a cursèd creature lives so long a space.

32

280 Far hence (quoth he) in wastfull° wildernesse   *barren*
   His dwelling is, by which no living wight
   May ever passe, but thorough great distresse.
   Now (sayd the Lady) draweth toward night,
   And well I wote,° that of your later° fight   *know / recent*
285 Ye all forwearied be: for what so strong,
   But wanting rest will also want of might?
   The Sunne that measures heaven all day long,
At night doth baite° his steedes the Ocean   *refresh*
   waves emong.

33

Then with the Sunne take Sir, your timely rest,
290 And with new day new worke at once begin:
   Untroubled night they say gives counsell best.
   Right well Sir knight ye have advised bin,
   (Quoth then that agèd man;) the way to win
   Is wisely to advise:° now day is spent;   *consider*
295 Therefore with me ye may take up your In
   For this same night. The knight was well content:
So with that godly father to his home they went.

34

A little lowly Hermitage it was,
   Downe in a dale, hard by a forests side,
300 Far from resort of people, that did pas
   In travell to and froe: a little wyde°   *apart*
   There was an holy Chappell edifyde,°   *built*
   Wherein the Hermite dewly wont° to say   *was accustomed*
   His holy things each morne and eventyde:
305 Thereby a Christall streame did gently play,
Which from a sacred fountaine wellèd forth alway.

35

Arrivèd there, the little house they fill,
   Ne looke for entertainment, where none was:
   Rest is their feast, and all things at their will;
310 The noblest mind the best contentment has.
   With faire discourse the evening so they pas:
   For that old man of pleasing wordes had store,
   And well could file his tongue as smooth as glas;
   He told of Saintes and Popes, and evermore
315 He strowd an *Ave-Mary*[2] after and before.

---

[1] *Bidding his beades* I.e., praying with the aid of rosary beads.
These beads, each of which represents a prayer, are counted off as
each prayer is completed.

[2] *Ave-Mary* I.e., "Hail, Mary!," a prayer to the Virgin Mary.

36

The drouping Night thus creepeth on them fast,
  And the sad humour[1] loading their eye liddes,
  As messenger of Morpheus on them cast
  Sweet slombring deaw,° the which to sleepe   *dew*
    them biddes.
320 Unto their lodgings then his guestes he riddes:°   *leads*
  Where when all drownd in deadly° sleepe   *death-like*
    he findes,
  He to his study goes, and there amiddes
  His Magick bookes and artes of sundry kindes,
He seekes out mighty charmes, to trouble sleepy mindes.

37

325 Then choosing out few wordes most horrible,
  (Let none them read) thereof did verses frame,
  With which and other spelles like terrible,
  He bad awake blacke Plutoes griesly Dame,[2]
  And cursèd heaven, and spake reprochfull shame
330 Of highest God, the Lord of life and light;
  A bold bad man, that dar'd to call by name
  Great Gorgon,[3] Prince of darknesse and dead night,
At which Cocytus quakes, and Styx[4] is put to flight.

38

And forth he cald out of deepe darknesse dred
335 Legions of Sprights, the which like little flyes
  Fluttring about his ever damnèd hed,
  A-waite whereto their service he applyes,
  To aide his friends, or fray° his enimies: *frighten*
  Of those he chose out two, the falsest twoo,
340 And fittest for to forge true-seeming lyes;
  The one of them he gave a message too,
The other by him selfe staide other worke to doo.

39

He making speedy way through spersèd° ayre,   *dispersed*
  And through the world of waters wide and deepe,
345 To Morpheus house doth hastily repaire.

---

[1] *sad humour* Heavy moisture, sent by Morpheus, god of sleep.

[2] *Plutoes griesly Dame* Persephone, or Proserpine, wife of Pluto and goddess of the underworld.

[3] *Gorgon* Demogorgon, a pseudo-classical demon of the underworld, associated with the early days of creation.

[4] *Cocytus … Styx* Two rivers of the underworld.

Amid the bowels of the earth full steepe,
  And low, where dawning day doth never peepe,
  His dwelling is; there Tethys[5] his wet bed
  Doth ever wash, and Cynthia[6] still°   *continually*
    doth steepe
350 In silver deaw his ever-drouping hed,
  Whiles sad° Night over him her mantle black   *grave*
    doth spred.

40

Whose double gates he findeth lockèd fast,
  The one faire fram'd of burnisht Yvory,
  The other all with silver overcast;
355 And wakefull dogges before them farre do lye,
  Watching to banish Care their enimy,
  Who oft is wont to trouble gentle Sleepe.
  By them the Sprite doth passe in quietly,
  And unto Morpheus comes, whom drownèd deepe
360 In drowsie fit he findes: of nothing he takes keepe.°   *notice*

41

And more, to lulle him in his slumber soft,
  A trickling streame from high rocke tumbling downe
  And ever-drizling raine upon the loft,
  Mixt with a murmuring winde, much like the
    sowne°   *sound*
365 Of swarming Bees, did cast him in a swowne:°   *swoon*
  No other noyse, nor peoples troublous cryes,
  As still are wont t'annoy the wallèd towne,
  Might there be heard: but carelesse° Quiet lyes, *without care*
Wrapt in eternall silence farre from enemyes.

42

370 The messenger approching to him spake,
  But his wast° wordes returnd to him in vaine: *wasted*
  So sound he slept, that nought mought°   *might*
    him awake.
  Then rudely he him thrust, and pusht with paine,
  Whereat he gan to stretch: but he againe
375 Shooke him so hard, that forcèd him to speake.
  As one then in a dreame, whose dryer braine
  Is tost with troubled sights and fancies weake,
He mumbled soft, but would not all his silence breake.

---

[5] *Tethys* Goddess of the sea.

[6] *Cynthia* Goddess of the moon.

43

The Sprite then gan more boldly him to wake,
   And threatned unto him the dreaded name
380   Of Hecate:[1] whereat he gan to quake,
   And lifting up his lumpish head, with blame
   Halfe angry asked him, for what he came.
   Hither (quoth he) me Archimago[2] sent,
385   He that the stubborne Sprites can wisely tame,
   He bids thee to him send for his intent
A fit false dreame, that can delude the sleepers sent.

44

The God obayde, and calling forth straight way
   A diverse° dreame out of his prison darke,   *diverting*
390   Delivered it to him, and downe did lay
   His heavie head, devoide of carefull carke,[3]
   Whose sences all were straight benumbd and starke.
   He backe returning by the Yvorie dore,
   Remounted up as light as chearefull Larke,
395   And on his litle winges the dreame he bore
In hast unto his Lord, where he him left afore.

45

Who all this while with charmes and hidden artes,
   Had made a Lady of that other Spright,
   And fram'd of liquid ayre her tender partes
400   So lively, and so like in all mens sight,
   That weaker sence it could have ravisht quight:
   The maker selfe for all his wondrous witt,
   Was nigh beguilèd with so goodly sight:
   Her all in white he clad, and over it
405 Cast a blacke stole, most like to seeme for Una[4] fit.

46

Now when that ydle dreame was to him brought,
   Unto that Elfin knight he bad him fly,
   Where he slept soundly void of evill thought,
   And with false shewes abuse his fantasy,
410   In sort as he him schoolèd privily:

And that new creature borne without her dew,[5]
   Full of the makers guile, with usage sly
   He taught to imitate that Lady trew,
   Whose semblance she did carrie under feignèd
      hew.°   *figure*

47

415 Thus well instructed, to their worke they hast,
   And comming where the knight in slomber lay,
   The one upon his hardy head him plast,
   And made him dreame of loves and lustfull play,
   That nigh his manly hart did melt away,
420   Bathèd in wanton blis and wicked joy:
   Then seemèd him his Lady by him lay,
   And to him playnd,° how that false   *complained*
      wingèd boy,[6]
Her chast hart had subdewd, to learne Dame pleasures
      toy.°   *play*

48

And she her selfe of beautie soveraigne Queene,
425   Faire Venus seemde unto his bed to bring
   Her, whom he waking evermore did weene,
   To be the chastest flowre, that ay° did spring   *ever*
   On earthly braunch, the daughter of a king,
   Now a loose Leman to vile service bound:
430   And eke the Graces[7] seemèd all to sing,
   Hymen iô Hymen, dauncing all around,
Whilst freshest Flora[8] her with Yvie girlond crownd.

49

In this great passion of unwonted lust,
   Or wonted feare of doing ought amis,
435   He started up, as seeming to mistrust,
   Some secret ill, or hidden foe of his:
   Lo there before his face his Lady is,
   Under blake stole hyding her bayted hooke,
   And as halfe blushing offred him to kis,
440   With gentle blandishment and lovely looke,

---

[1] *Hecate* Greek goddess of the crossroads, often perceived as evil and linked to witchcraft.

[2] *Archimago* Meaning both arch-image maker and arch-magician in Latin.

[3] *carefull* I.e., full of care; *carke* Anxiety, distress.

[4] *Una* From *unus*, the Latin word for one or unity.

[5] *without her dew* I.e., unnaturally.

[6] *wingèd boy* I.e., Cupid.

[7] *the Graces* Handmaids of Venus who personify pleasure, courtesy, and beauty. Here they sing a hymn to Hymen, the god of weddings, in celebration of the pleasures of the marriage bed.

[8] *Flora* Goddess of flowers.

Most like that virgin true, which for her knight him
   took.

50

All cleane dismayd to see so uncouth sight,
   And halfe enragèd at her shamelesse guise,
   He thought have slaine her in his fierce
      despight:°   *indignation*
445 But hasty heat tempring with sufferance wise,
   He stayde his hand, and gan himselfe advise
   To prove his sense, and tempt her faignèd truth.
   Wringing her hands in wemens pitteous wise,
   Tho can° she weepe, to stirre up gentle
      ruth,   *did | compassion*
450 Both for her noble bloud, and for her tender youth.

51

And said, Ah Sir, my liege Lord and my love,
   Shall I accuse the hidden cruell fate,
   And mightie causes wrought in heaven above,
   Or the blind God, that doth me thus amate,°   *dismay*
455 For° hopèd love to winne me certaine hate?   *in place of*
   Yet thus perforce he bids me do, or die.
   Die is my dew:° yet rew° my wretched state   *due | pity*
   You, whom my hard avenging destinie
   Hath made judge of my life or death indifferently.

52

460 Your owne deare sake forst me at first to leave
   My Fathers kingdome,—There she stopt with teares;
   Her swollen hart her speach seemd to bereave,
   And then againe begun, My weaker yeares
   Captiv'd to fortune and frayle worldly feares,
465 Fly to your faith for succour and sure ayde:
   Let me not dye in languor° and long teares.   *distress*
   Why Dame (quoth he) what hath ye thus dismayd?
   What frayes° ye, that were wont to comfort   *frightens*
      me affrayd?

53

   Love of your selfe, she said, and deare° constraint   *dire*
470 Lets me not sleepe, but wast the wearie night
   In secret anguish and unpittied plaint,
   Whiles you in carelesse sleepe are drownèd quight.
   Her doubtfull words made that redoubted°
      knight   *distinguished*

475 Suspect her truth: yet since no untruth he knew,
   Her fawning love with foule disdainefull spight
   He would not shend,° but said, Deare dame   *reprove*
      I rew,
   That for my sake unknowne such griefe unto you grew.

54

Assure your selfe, it fell not all to ground;
   For all so deare as life is to my hart,
480 I deeme your love, and hold me to you bound;
   Ne let vaine feares procure your needlesse smart,°   *suffering*
   Where cause is none, but to your rest depart.
   Not all content, yet seemd she to appease
   Her mournefull plaintes, beguilèd° of her art,   *foiled*
485 And fed with words, that could not chuse but please,
   So slyding softly forth, she turnd as to her ease.

55

Long after lay he musing at her mood,
   Much griev'd to thinke that gentle Dame so
      light,°   *immoral*
   For whose defence he was to shed his blood.
490 At last dull wearinesse of former fight
   Having yrockt a sleepe his irkesome°
      spright,°   *weary | spirit*
   That troublous dreame gan freshly tosse his braine,
   With bowres, and beds, and Ladies deare delight:
   But when he saw his labour[1] all was vaine,
495 With that misformèd spright[1] he backe returnd againe.

CANTO 2

The guilefull great Enchaunter parts
   The Redcrosse Knight from Truth:
Into whose stead faire falshood steps,
   And workes him wofull ruth.

1

By this the Northerne wagoner[2] had set
   His sevenfold teme behind the stedfast starre,

---

[1] *that misinformèd spright* I.e., the spirit disguised as Una.

[2] *Northerne wagoner* Constellation, probably Ursa Major (in England also called "Charles's Wain," or cart), imagined as a farmer guiding a wagon. The "steadfast starre" that never sets in the ocean, however, is the North Star, in the nearby Ursa Minor.

That was in Ocean waves yet never wet,
　　But firme is fixt, and sendeth light from farre
5　　To all, that in the wide deepe wandring arre:
　　And chearefull Chaunticlere° with his note shrill　　*rooster*
　　Had warned once, that Phoebus fiery carre°　　*chariot*
　　In hast was climbing up the Easterne hill,
Full envious that night so long his roome did fill.

2

When those accursèd messengers of hell,
　　That feigning dreame, and that faire-forgèd Spright
　　Came to their wicked maister, and gan tell
　　Their bootelesse° paines, and ill succeeding night:　　*useless*
　　Who all in rage to see his skilfull might
15　　Deluded so, gan threaten hellish paine
　　And sad Proserpines wrath, them to affright.
　　But when he saw his threatning was but vaine,
He cast about, and searcht his balefull°　　*destructive*
　　bookes againe.

3

Eftsoones he tooke that miscreated faire,
20　　And that false other Spright, on whom he spred
　　A seeming body of the subtile aire,
　　Like a young Squire, in loves and lusty-hed
　　His wanton dayes that ever loosely led,
　　Without regard of armes and dreaded fight:
25　　Those two he tooke, and in a secret bed,
　　Covered with darknesse and misdeeming°　　*misleading*
　　night,
Them both together laid, to joy in vaine delight.

4

Forthwith he runnes with feignèd faithfull hast
　　Unto his guest, who after troublous sights
30　　And dreames, gan now to take more sound
　　repast,°　　*repose*
　　Whom suddenly he wakes with fearefull frights,
　　As one aghast with feends or damnèd sprights,
　　And to him cals, Rise rise unhappy Swaine,°　　*lover*
　　That here wex° old in sleepe, whiles wicked　　*grow*
　　wights
35　　Have knit themselves in Venus shamefull chaine;
Come see, where your false Lady doth her honour
　　staine.

5

All in amaze he suddenly up start
　　With sword in hand, and with the old man went;
　　Who soone him brought into a secret part,
40　　Where that false couple were full closely ment°　　*joined*
　　In wanton lust and lewd embracèment:
　　Which when he saw, he burnt with gealous fire,
　　The eye of reason was with rage yblent,°　　*blinded*
　　And would have slaine them in his furious ire,
45　But hardly was restreinèd of° that agèd sire.　　*by*

6

Returning to his bed in torment great,
　　And bitter anguish of his guiltie sight,
　　He could not rest, but did his stout heart eat,
　　And wast his inward gall with deepe despight,
50　　Yrkesome of life, and too long lingring night.
　　At last faire Hesperus[1] in highest skie
　　Had spent his lampe, and brought forth dawning light,
　　Then up he rose, and clad him hastily;
The Dwarfe him brought his steed: so both away do fly.

7

55　Now when the rosy-fingred Morning faire,
　　Weary of agèd Tithones[2] saffron bed,
　　Had spred her purple robe through deawy aire,
　　And the high hils Titan° discovered,　　*the sun*
　　The royall virgin shooke off drowsy-hed,
60　　And rising forth out of her baser bowre,
　　Lookt for her knight, who far away was fled,
　　And for her Dwarfe, that wont to wait each houre;
Then gan she waile and weepe, to see that woefull
　　stowre.°　　*plight*

8

And after him she rode with so much speede
65　　As her slow beast could make; but all in vaine:
　　For him so far had borne his light-foot steede,
　　Prickèd with wrath and fiery fierce disdaine,
　　That him to follow was but fruitlesse paine;
　　Yet she her weary limbes would never rest,

---

[1]　*Hesperus*　Venus as the morning or evening star.

[2]　*agèd Tithones*　Husband of the goddess of the dawn, Aurora. Aurora asked Jupiter to give the mortal Tithonus eternal life, but forgot to ask for eternal youth.

70 But every hill and dale, each wood and plaine
  Did search, sore grievèd in her gentle brest,
 He so ungently left her, whom she lovèd best.

9

 But subtill Archimago, when his guests
  He saw divided into double parts,
75 And Una wandring in woods and forrests,
  Th'end of his drift,° he praisd his divelish arts, *scheme*
  That had such might over true meaning harts;
  Yet rests not so, but other meanes doth make,
  How he may worke unto her further smarts:
80 For her he hated as the hissing snake,
 And in her many troubles did most pleasure take.

10

 He then devisde himselfe how to disguise;
  For by his mightie science° he could take *knowledge*
  As many formes and shapes in seeming wise,[1]
85 As ever Proteus[2] to himselfe could make:
  Sometime a fowle, sometime a fish in lake,
  Now like a foxe, now like a dragon fell,° *fierce*
  That of himselfe he oft for feare would quake,
  And oft would flie away. O who can tell
90 The hidden power of herbes, and might of Magicke
   spell?

11

 But now seemde best, the person to put on
  Of that good knight, his late beguilèd guest:
  In mighty armes he was yclad anon,
  And silver shield upon his coward brest
95 A bloudy crosse, and on his craven° crest° *cowardly | head*
  A bounch of haires discolourd diversly:
  Full jolly knight he seemde, and well addrest,° *armed*
  And when he sate upon his courser free,
 Saint George himself ye would have deemèd him to be.

12

100 But he the knight, whose semblaunt he did beare,
  The true Saint George was wandred far away,
  Still flying from his thoughts and gealous feare;
  Will was his guide, and griefe led him astray.

 At last him chaunst to meete upon the way
105 A faithlesse Sarazin[3] all arm'd to point,
  In whose great shield was writ with letters gay
 Sans foy:[4] full large of limbe and every joint
 He was, and carèd not for God or man a point.

13

 He had a faire companion of his way,
110 A goodly Lady clad in scarlot red,
  Purfled° with gold and pearle of rich
   assay,° *decorated | quality*
  And like a Persian mitre° on her hed *headdress*
  She wore, with crownes and owches° garnishèd, *brooches*
  The which her lavish lovers to her gave;
115 Her wanton palfrey all was overspred
  With tinsell trappings, woven like a wave,
 Whose bridle rung with golden bels and bosses°
   brave.° *studs | handsome*

14

 With faire disport° and courting dalliaunce *amusement*
  She intertainde her lover all the way:
120 But when she saw the knight his speare advaunce,
  She soone left off her mirth and wanton play,
  And bad her knight addresse him to the fray:
  His foe was nigh at hand. He prickt with pride
  And hope to winne his Ladies heart that day,
125 Forth spurrèd fast: adowne his coursers side
 The red bloud trickling staind the way, as he did ride.

15

 The knight of the Redcrosse when him he spide,
  Spurring so hote with rage dispiteous,° *merciless*
  Gan fairely couch his speare, and towards ride:
130 Soone meete they both, both fell and furious,
  That daunted with their forces hideous,
  Their steeds do stagger, and amazed stand,
  And eke themselves too rudely rigorous,
  Astonied with the stroke of their owne hand,
135 Do backe rebut,° and each to other yeeldeth land. *retreat*

16

 As when two rams stird with ambitious pride,
  Fight for the rule of the rich fleecèd flocke,

---

[1] *in seeming wise* In the matter of seeming; i.e., in appearance.

[2] *Proteus* Sea god able to change his shape at will.

[3] *Sarazin* I.e., Saracen, a Muslim (but representing Catholicism).

[4] *Sans foy* French: without faith.

Their hornèd fronts so fierce on either side
  Do meete, that with the terrour of the shocke
140 Astonied both, stand sencelesse as a blocke,
  Forgetfull of the hanging victory:
  So stood these twaine, unmovèd as a rocke,
  Both staring fierce, and holding idely
The broken reliques of their former cruelty.

17

145 The Sarazin sore daunted with the buffe
  Snatcheth his sword, and fiercely to him flies;
  Who well it wards, and quyteth° cuff with cuff: *requites*
  Each others equall puissaunce envies,
  And through their iron sides with cruell spies°   *glances*
150 Does seeke to perce: repining courage yields
  No foote to foe. The flashing fier flies
  As from a forge out of their burning shields,
And streames of purple bloud new dies the verdant
    fields.

18

Curse on that Crosse (quoth then the Sarazin)
155 That keepes thy body from the bitter fit;[1]
  Dead long ygoe I wote thou haddest bin,
  Had not that charme from thee forwarnèd° it: *prevented*
  But yet I warne thee now assurèd sitt,
  And hide thy head. Therewith upon his crest
160 With rigour so outrageous he smitt,
  That a large share it hewd out of the rest,
And glauncing downe his shield, from blame° him
    fairely blest.°   *harm / protected*

19

Who thereat wondrous wroth, the sleeping spark
  Of native vertue° gan eftsoones revive,   *strength*
165 And at his haughtie helmet making mark,
  So hugely stroke, that it the steele did rive,°   *rend*
  And cleft his head. He tumbling downe alive,
  With bloudy mouth his mother earth did kis,
  Greeting his grave: his grudging ghost did strive
170 With the fraile flesh; at last it flitted is,
Whither the soules do fly of men, that live amis.

20

The Lady when she saw her champion fall,
  Like the old ruines of a broken towre,
  Staid not to waile his woefull funerall,
175 But from him fled away with all her powre;
  Who after her as hastily gan scowre,°   *run*
  Bidding the Dwarfe with him to bring away
  The Sarazins shield, signe of the conqueroure.
  Her soone he overtooke, and bad to stay,
180 For present cause was none of dread her to dismay.

21

She turning backe with ruefull countenaunce,
  Cride, Mercy mercy Sir vouchsafe to show
  On silly Dame, subiect to hard mischaunce,
  And to your mighty will. Her humblesse low
185 In so ritch weedes° and seeming glorious show,   *clothes*
  Did much emmove his stout heroicke heart,
  And said, Deare dame, your suddein overthrow
  Much rueth° me; but now put feare apart,   *grieves*
And tell, both who ye be, and who that tooke your part.

22

190 Melting in teares, then gan she thus lament;
  The wretched woman, whom unhappy howre
  Hath now made thrall° to your commandèment,   *slave*
  Before that angry heavens list to lowre,°   *scowl*
  And fortune false betraide me to your powre,
195 Was, (O what now availeth that I was!)
  Borne the sole daughter of an Emperour,
  He that the wide West under his rule has,
And high hath set his throne, where Tiberis doth pas.[2]

23

He in the first flowre of my freshest age,
200 Betrothèd me unto the onely haire
  Of a most mighty king, most rich and sage;
  Was never Prince so faithfull and so faire,
  Was never Prince so meeke and debonaire;
  But ere my hopèd day of spousall shone,
205 My dearest Lord fell from high honours staire,

---

[1] *bitter fit* I.e., death.

[2] *where … pas* Rome (the seat of Roman Catholicism), through which the river Tiber runs. The prince to whom the lady claims to have been betrothed is Christ.

Into the hands of his accursèd fone,°   *foes*
And cruelly was slaine, that shall I ever mone.

24

His blessed body spoild of lively breath,
    Was afterward, I know not how, convaid
210   And fro me hid: of whose most innocent death
    When tidings came to me unhappy maid,
    O how great sorrow my sad soule assaid.°   *assailed*
    Then forth I went his woefull corse to find,
    And many yeares throughout the world I straid,
215   A virgin widow, whose deepe wounded mind
With love, long time did languish as the striken
      hind.°   *female deer*

25

At last it chauncèd this proud Sarazin
    To meete me wandring, who perforce° me led   *by force*
    With him away, but yet could never win
220   The Fort, that Ladies hold in soveraigne dread.
    There lies he now with foule dishonour dead,
    Who whiles he liv'de, was callèd proud Sans foy,
    The eldest of three brethren, all three bred
    Of one bad sire, whose youngest is Sans joy,°   *without joy*
225   And twixt them both was borne the bloudy bold Sans
      loy.°   *without law*

26

In this sad plight, friendlesse, unfortunate,
    Now miserable I Fidessa[1] dwell,
    Craving of you in pitty of my state,
    To do none ill, if please ye not do well.
230   He in great passion all this while did dwell,
    More busying his quicke eyes, her face to view,
    Then his dull eares, to heare what she did tell;
    And said, Faire Lady hart of flint would rew
The undeservèd woes and sorrowes, which ye shew.

27

235   Henceforth in safe assuraunce may ye rest,
    Having both found a new friend you to aid,
    And lost an old foe, that did you molest:
    Better new friend then an old foe is said.
    With chaunge of cheare the seeming simple maid

---

[1] *Fidessa* Fidelity.

240   Let fall her eyen, as shamefast to the earth,
    And yeelding soft, in that she nought gain-said,
    So forth they rode, he feining seemely merth,
    And she coy lookes: so dainty° they say maketh
      derth.°   *valuable / rare*

28

Long time they thus together traveilèd,
245   Till weary of their way, they came at last,
    Where grew two goodly trees, that faire did spred
    Their armes abroad, with gray mosse overcast,
    And their greene leaves trembling with every
      blast,°   *gust of wind*
    Made a calme shadow far in compasse round:
250   The fearefull Shepheard often there aghast°   *frightened*
    Under them never sat, ne wont there sound
His mery oaten pipe, but shund th'unlucky ground.

29

But this good knight soone as he them can° spie,   *did*
    For the coole shade him thither hastly got:
255   For golden Phoebus now ymounted hie,
    From fiery wheeles of his faire chariot
    Hurlèd his beame so scorching cruell hot,
    That living creature mote it not abide;
    And his new Lady it endured not.
260   There they alight, in hope themselves to hide
From the fierce heat, and rest their weary limbs a tide.

30

Faire seemely pleasaunce° each to other makes,   *pleasantry*
    With goodly purposes there as they sit:
    And in his falsèd° fancy he her takes   *deceived*
265   To be the fairest wight, that livèd yit;
    Which to expresse, he bends his gentle wit,
    And thinking of those braunches greene to frame
    A girlond for her dainty forehead fit,
    He pluckt a bough; out of whose rift there came
270   Small drops of gory bloud, that trickled downe the same.

31

Therewith a piteous yelling voyce was heard,
    Crying, O spare with guilty hands to teare
    My tender sides in this rough rynd embard,°   *enclosed*
    But fly, ah fly far hence away, for feare

275   Least° to you hap, that happened to me heare,   *lest*
       And to this wretched Lady, my deare love,
       O too deare love, love bought with death too deare.
       Astond he stood, and up his haire did hove,°   *raise*
       And with that suddein horror could no member move.

32

280   At last whenas the dreadfull passion
       Was overpast, and manhood well awake,
       Yet musing at the straunge occasiön,
       And doubting much his sence, he thus bespake;
       What voyce of damnèd Ghost from Limbo lake,[1]
285   Or guilefull spright wandring in empty aire,
       Both which fraile men do oftentimes mistake,°   *mislead*
       Sends to my doubtfull eares these speaches rare,
       And ruefull plaints, me bidding guiltlesse bloud to spare?

33

       Then groning deepe, Nor damned Ghost, (quoth he,)
290   Nor guilefull sprite, to thee these wordes doth speake,
       But once a man Fradubio,[2] now a tree,
       Wretched man, wretched tree; whose nature weake,
       A cruell witch her cursèd will to wreake,
       Hath thus transformd, and plast in open plaines,
295   Where Boreas[3] doth blow full bitter bleake,
       And scorching Sunne does dry my secret vaines:
       For though a tree I seeme, yet cold and heat me paines.

34

       Say on Fradubio then, or man, or tree,
       Quoth then the knight, by whose mischievous arts
300   Art thou misshapèd thus, as now I see?
       He oft finds med'cine, who his griefe imparts;
       But double griefs afflict concealing harts,
       As raging flames who striveth to suppresse.
       The author then (said he) of all my smarts,
305   Is one Duessa[4] a false sorceresse,
       That many errant° knights hath brought to   *wandering*
          wretchednesse.

---

[1] *Limbo lake* Part of hell to which the unbaptized are sent.

[2] *Fradubio* Italian: literally, Brother Doubt.

[3] *Boreas* North wind.

[4] *Duessa* Implies two, doubleness.

35

       In prime of youthly yeares, when corage hot
       The fire of love and joy of chevalree
       First kindled in my brest, it was my lot
310   To love this gentle Lady, whom ye see,
       Now not a Lady, but a seeming tree;
       With whom as once I rode accompanyde,
       Me chauncèd of a knight encountred bee,
       That had a like faire Lady by his syde,
315   Like a faire Lady, but did fowle Duessa hyde.

36

       Whose forgèd beauty he did take in hand,[5]
       All other Dames to have exceeded farre;
       I in defence of mine did likewise stand,
       Mine, that did then shine as the Morning starre:
320   So both to battell fierce arraungèd arre,
       In which his harder fortune was to fall
       Under my speare: such is the dye of warre:
       His Lady left as a prise martiall,
       Did yield her comely person, to be at my call.

37

325   So doubly lov'd of Ladies unlike° faire,   *differently*
       Th'one seeming such, the other such indeede,
       One day in doubt I cast° for to compare,   *resolved*
       Whether in beauties glorie did exceede;
       A Rosy girlond was the victors meede:
330   Both seemde to win, and both seemde won to bee,
       So hard the discord was to be agreede.
       Frælissa[6] was as faire, as faire mote bee,
       And ever false Duessa seemde as faire as shee.

38

       The wicked witch now seeing all this while
335   The doubtfull ballaunce equally to sway,
       What not by right, she cast to win by guile,
       And by her hellish science raisd streightway
       A foggy mist, that overcast the day,
       And a dull blast, that breathing on her face,
340   Dimmed her former beauties shining ray,
       And with foule ugly forme did her disgrace:
       Then was she faire alone, when none was faire in place.

---

[5] *take in hand* Maintain.

[6] *Frælissa* Frailty.

39

Then cride she out, Fye, fye, deformèd wight,
　Whose borrowed beautie now appeareth plaine
345　To have before bewitchèd all mens sight;
　O leave her soone, or let her soone be slaine.
　Her loathly visage viewing with disdaine,
　Eftsoones I thought her such, as she me told,
　And would have kild her; but with faignèd paine,
350　The false witch did my wrathfull hand with-hold;
So left her, where she now is turnd to treen mould.

40

Thensforth I tooke Duessa for my Dame,
　And in the witch unweeting° joyd long time,　　*unknowingly*
　Ne ever wist, but that she was the same,
355　Till on a day (that day is every Prime,[1]
　When Witches wont do penance for their crime)
　I chaunst to see her in her proper hew,
　Bathing her selfe in origane and thyme:
　A filthy foule old woman I did vew,
360　That ever to have toucht her, I did deadly rew.

41

Her neather partes misshapen, monstruous,
　Were hidd in water, that I could not see,
　But they did seeme more foule and hideous,
　Then womans shape man would beleeve to bee.
365　Thensforth from her most beastly companie
　I gan refraine, in minde to slip away,
　Soone as appeard safe opportunitie:
　For danger great, if not assur'd decay
I saw before mine eyes, if I were knowne to stray.

42

370　The divelish hag by chaunges of my cheare
　Perceiv'd my thought, and drownd in sleepie night,
　With wicked herbes and ointments did besmeare
　My bodie all, through charmes and magicke might,
　That all my senses were bereavèd quight:
375　Then brought she me into this desert waste,
　And by my wretched lovers side me pight,°　　*planted*
　Where now enclosd in wooden wals full faste,
Banisht from living wights, our wearie dayes we waste.

43

But how long time, said then the Elfin knight,
380　Are you in this misformèd house to dwell?
　We may not chaunge (quoth he) this evil plight,
　Till we be bathèd in a living well;[2]
　That is the terme prescribèd by the spell.
　O how, said he, mote I that well out find,
385　That may restore you to your wonted well?°　　*well-being*
　Time and suffisèd° fates to former kind　　*satisfied*
Shall us restore, none else from hence may us unbynd.

44

The false Duessa, now Fidessa hight,°　　*called*
　Heard how in vaine Fradubio did lament,
390　And knew well all was true. But the good knight
　Full of sad feare and ghastly dreriment,°　　*gloom*
　When all this speech the living tree had spent,
　The bleeding bough did thrust into the ground,
　That from the bloud he might be innocent,
395　And with fresh clay did close the wooden wound:
Then turning to his Lady, dead with feare her found.

45

Her seeming dead he found with feignèd feare,
　As all unweeting° of that well she knew,　　*unknowing*
　And paynd himselfe with busie care to reare
400　Her out of carelesse° swowne. Her eylids blew　　*unconscious*
　And dimmèd sight with pale and deadly hew
　At last she up gan lift: with trembling cheare
　Her up he tooke, too simple and too trew,
　And oft her kist. At length all passèd feare,
He set her on her steede, and forward forth did beare.

CANTO 3

Forsaken Truth long seekes her love,
　And makes the Lyon mylde,
Marres blind Devotions mart,° and fals　　trade
　In hand of leachour vylde.

---

[1]　*Prime*　First day of a new moon.

[2]　*Till … well*　See 1 John 4.14, which describes Christ as the Well of Life, a "well of water, springing up into eternal life," for those who believe in Christ and follow his teachings.

1

Nought there under heav'ns wilde hollownesse,
That moves more deare compassiön of mind,
Then beautie brought t'unworthy wretchednesse
Through envies snares or fortunes freakes unkind:
5 I, whether lately through her brightnesse blind,
Or through alleageance and fast fealtie,
Which I do owe unto all woman kind,
Feele my heart perst with so great agonie,
When such I see, that all for pittie I could die.

2

10 And now it is empassionèd so deepe,
For fairest Unaes sake, of whom I sing,
That my fraile eyes these lines with teares do steepe,
To thinke how she through guilefull handeling,
Though true as touch, though daughter of a king,
15 Though faire as ever living wight was faire,
Though nor in word nor deede ill meriting,
Is from her knight divorcèd in despaire
And her due loves deriv'd to that vile witches share.

3

Yet she most faithfull Ladie all this while
20 Forsaken, wofull, solitarie mayd
Farre from all peoples prease,° as in exile,   *press*
In wildernesse and wastfull deserts strayd,
To seeke her knight; who subtilly betrayd
Through that late vision, which th'Enchaunter
wrought,
25 Had her abandond. She of nought affrayd,
Through woods and wastnesse wide him daily sought;
Yet wishèd tydings none of him unto her brought.

4

One day nigh wearie of the yrkesome way,
From her unhastie beast she did alight,
30 And on the grasse her daintie limbes did lay
In secret shadow, farre from all mens sight:
From her faire head her fillet° she
undight,°   *headband | undid*
And laid her stole aside. Her angels face
As the great eye of heaven shyned bright,
35 And made a sunshine in the shadie place;
Did never mortall eye behold such heavenly grace.

5

It fortuned out of the thickest wood
A ramping Lyon rushed suddainly,
Hunting full greedie after salvage° blood;   *savage*
40 Soone as the royall virgin he did spy,
With gaping mouth at her ran greedily,
To have attonce devour'd her tender corse:
But to the pray when as he drew more ny,
His bloudie rage asswaged with remorse,
45 And with the sight amazd, forgat his furious forse.

6

In stead thereof he kist her wearie feet,
And lickt her lilly hands with fawning tong,
As he her wrongèd innocence did weet.°   *understand*
O how can beautie maister the most strong,
50 And simple truth subdue avenging wrong?
Whose yeelded pride and proud submissiön,
Still dreading death, when she had markèd long,
Her hart gan melt in great compassiön,
And drizling teares did shed for pure affection.

7

55 The Lyon Lord of everie beast in field,
Quoth she, his princely puissance doth abate,
And mightie proud to humble weake does yield,
Forgetfull of the hungry rage, which late
Him prickt, in pittie of my sad estate:°   *state*
60 But he my Lyon, and my noble Lord,
How does he find in cruell hart to hate
Her that him lov'd, and ever most adord,
As the God of my life? why hath he me abhord?

8

Redounding° teares did choke th'end of   *overflowing*
her plaint,
65 Which softly ecchoed from the neighbour wood;
And sad to see her sorrowfull constraint
The kingly beast upon her gazing stood;
With pittie calmd, downe fell his angry mood.
At last in close hart shutting up her paine,
70 Arose the virgin borne of heavenly brood,
And to her snowy Palfrey got againe,
To seeke her strayèd Champion, if she might
attaine.°   *overtake*

9

The Lyon would not leave her desolate,
   But with her went along, as a strong gard
75   Of her chast person, and a faithfull mate
   Of her sad troubles and misfortunes hard:
   Still° when she slept, he kept both watch and ward,   *always*
   And when she wakt, he waited diligent,
   With humble service to her will prepard:
80   From her faire eyes he tooke commaundèment,
And ever by her lookes conceivèd her intent.

10

Long she thus traveilèd through deserts wyde,
   By which she thought her wandring knight shold pas,
   Yet never shew of living wight espyde;
85   Till that at length she found the troden gras,
   In which the tract of peoples footing was,
   Under the steepe foot of a mountaine hore;°   *grey*
   The same she followes, till at last she has
   A damzell spyde slow footing her before,
90   That on her shoulders sad° a pot of water bore.   *stooped*

11

To whom approching she to her gan call,
   To weet, if dwelling place were nigh at hand;
   But the rude wench her answer'd nought at all,
   She could not heare, nor speake, nor understand;[1]
95   Till seeing by her side the Lyon stand,
   With suddaine feare her pitcher downe she threw,
   And fled away: for never in that land
   Face of faire Ladie she before did vew,
And that dread Lyons looke her cast in deadly hew.

12

100   Full fast she fled, ne ever lookt behynd,
   As if her life upon the wager lay,
   And home she came, whereas her mother blynd
   Sate in eternall night: nought could she say,
   But suddaine catching hold, did her dismay
105   With quaking hands, and other signs of feare:
   Who full of ghastly fright and cold affray,°   *fear*
   Gan shut the dore. By this arrivèd there
Dame Una, wearie Dame, and entrance did
    requere.°   *request*

13

Which when none yeelded, her unruly Page
110   With his rude° clawes the wicket open rent,   *rough*
   And let her in; where of his cruell rage
   Nigh dead with feare, and faint astonishment,
   She found them both in darkesome corner pent;
   Where that old woman day and night did pray
115   Upon her beades devoutly penitent;
   Nine hundred *Pater nosters*[2] every day,
And thrise nine hundred *Aves* she was wont to say.

14

And to augment her painefull pennance more,
   Thrise every weeke in ashes she did sit,
120   And next her wrinkled skin rough sackcloth wore,
   And thrise three times did fast from any bit:
   But now for feare her beads she did forget.
   Whose needlesse dread for to remove away,
   Faire Una framèd words and count'nance fit:
125   Which hardly° doen, at length she gan   *with difficulty*
    them pray,
That in their cotage small, that night she rest her may.

15

The day is spent, and commeth drowsie night,
   When every creature shrowded is in sleepe;
   Sad Una downe her laies in wearie plight,
130   And at her feet the Lyon watch doth keepe:
   In stead of rest, she does lament, and weepe
   For the late losse of her deare lovèd knight,
   And sighes, and grones, and evermore does steepe
   Her tender brest in bitter teares all night,
135 All night she thinks too long, and often lookes for light.

16

Now when Aldeboran was mounted hie
   Above the shynie Cassiopeias chaire,[3]
   And all in deadly sleepe did drowèd lie,
   One knockèd at the dore, and in would fare;
140   He knockèd fast,° and often curst, and sware,   *vigorously*

---

1 *She ... understand* The girl is both deaf and mute.

2 *Pater nosters* Latin: Our Fathers; i.e., repetitions of the Lord's Prayer.

3 *Aldeboran ... chaire* Aldeboran, a star in the constellation Taurus, rises above the northern constellation Cassiopeia.

That readie entrance was not at his call:
  For on his backe a heavy load he bare
  Of nightly stelths and pillage severall,
Which he had got abroad by purchase criminall.

17

His bleeding hart is in the vengers hand,
  Who streight him rent in thousand peeces small,
  And quite dismembred hath: the thirstie land
  Drunke up his life; his corse° left on the
      strand.°   *body / ground*
  His fearefull friends weare out the wofull night,
  Ne dare to weepe, nor seeme to understand
  The heavie hap,° which on them is alight,   *occurrence*
Affraid, least to themselves the like mishappen might.[3]

145 He was to weete° a stout and sturdie thiefe,   *wit*
  Wont to robbe Churches of their ornaments,
  And poore mens boxes of their due reliefe,
  Which given was to them for good intents;
  The holy Saints of their rich vestiments
150 He did disrobe, when all men carelesse slept,
  And spoild the Priests of their habiliments,°   *robes*
  Whiles none the holy things in safety kept;
Then he by cunning sleights in at the window crept.

21

Now when broad day the world discovered has,
  Up Una rose, up rose the Lyon eke,
  And on their former journey forward pas,
  In wayes unknowne, her wandring knight to seeke,
185 With paines farre passing that long wandring Greeke,
  That for his love refusèd deitie;[4]
  Such were the labours of this Lady meeke,
  Still seeking him, that from her still did flie,
Then furthest from her hope, when most she
      weenèd° nie.   *believed*

18

And all that he by right or wrong could find,
155 Unto this house he brought, and did bestow
  Upon the daughter of this woman blind,
  Abessa daughter of Corceca[1] slow,
  With whom he whoredome usd, that few did know,
  And fed her fat with feast of offerings,
160 And plentie, which in all the land did grow;
  Ne sparèd he to give her gold and rings:
And now he to her brought part of his stolen things.

22

190 Soone as she parted thence, the fearefull twaine,°   *pair*
  That blind old woman and her daughter deare
  Came forth, and finding Kirkrapine[5] there slaine,
  For anguish great they gan to rend their heare,°   *hair*
  And beat their brests, and naked flesh to teare.
195 And when they both had wept and wayld their fill,
  Then forth they ranne like two amazèd deare,
  Halfe mad through malice, and revenging will,
To follow her, that was the causer of their ill.

19

Thus long the dore with rage and threats he bet,°   *beat*
  Yet of those fearefull women none durst rize,
165 The Lyon frayèd° them, him in to let: *frightened*
  He would no longer stay him to advize,°   *consider*
  But open breakes the dore in furious wize,
  And entring is; when that disdainfull° beast   *indignant*
  Encountring fierce, him suddaine doth surprize,
170 And seizing cruell clawes on trembling brest,
Under his Lordly foot him proudly hath supprest.

23

Whom overtaking, they gan loudly bray,
200 With hollow howling, and lamenting cry,
  Shamefully at her rayling° all the way,   *insulting*
  And her accusing of dishonesty,°   *lewdness*
  That was the flowre of faith and chastity;

20

Him booteth not resist,[2] nor succour call,

---

1 *Abessa … Corceca* Abessa's name derives from the word abbess and associates her with Roman Catholic abbey, monasteries, and absence (from the Latin *abesse*, to be absent). Corceca suggests blindness of heart.

2 *Him … resist* It did no good for him to resist.

3 *least … might* I.e., lest the same mishap befall them.

4 *that long … deitie* Odysseus, King of Ithaca who, according to Homer's *Odyssey*, wandered for ten years seeking his home after the Trojan War. On the way, he was detained by the sea nymph Calypso, who offered him immortality if he would stay with her.

5 *Kirkrapine* Church robber.

And still amidst her rayling, she° did pray,   *Corceca*
That plagues, and mischiefs, and long misery
Might fall on her, and follow all the way,
And that in endlesse error° she might ever stray.   *roaming*

24

But when she saw her prayers nought prevaile,
She backe returnèd with some labour lost;
And in the way as she did weepe and waile,
A knight her met in mighty armes embost,°   *covered*
Yet knight was not for all his bragging bost,°   *boast*
But subtill Archimag, that Una sought
By traynes into new troubles to have tost:
Of that old woman tydings he besought,
If that of such a Ladie she could tellen ought.°   *anything*

25

Therewith she gan her passion to renew,
And cry, and curse, and raile, and rend her heare,
Saying, that harlot she too lately knew,
That causd her shed so many a bitter teare,
And so forth told the story of her feare:
Much seemèd he to mone her haplesse chaunce,
And after for that Ladie did inquere;
Which being taught, he forward gan advaunce
His fair enchaunted steed, and eke his charmèd launce.

26

Ere long he came, where Una traveild slow,
And that wilde Champion wayting her besyde:
Whom seeing such, for dread he durst not show
Himselfe too nigh at hand, but turnèd wyde
Unto an hill; from whence when she him spyde,
By his like seeming shield, her knight by name
She weend it was, and towards him gan ryde:
Approching nigh, she wist it was the same,
And with faire fearefull humblesse° towards   *humility*
    him shee came.

27

And weeping said, Ah my long lackèd Lord,
Where have ye bene thus long out of my sight?
Much fearèd I to have bene quite abhord,
Or ought° have done, that ye displeasen might,   *aught*

That should as death unto my deare° hart
    light:°   *heavy | descend*
For since mine eye your joyous sight did mis,
My chearefull day is turnd to chearelesse night,
And eke my night of death the shadow is;
But welcome now my light, and shining lampe of blis.

28

He thereto meeting[1] said, My dearest Dame,
Farre be it from your thought, and fro my will,
To thinke that knighthood I so much should shame,
As you to leave, that have me lovèd still,
And chose in Faery court of meere° goodwill,   *absolute*
Where noblest knights were to be found on earth:
The earth shall sooner leave her kindly° skill   *natural*
To bring forth fruit, and make eternall derth,°   *famine*
Then I leave you, my liefe,° yborne of   *beloved*
    heavenly berth.

29

And sooth to say, why I left you so long,
Was for to seeke adventure in strange place,
Where Archimago said a felon strong
To many knights did daily worke disgrace;
But knight he now shall never more deface:
Good cause of mine excuse; that mote° ye please   *may*
Well to accept, and evermore embrace
My faithfull service, that by land and seas
Have vowd you to defend. Now then your plaint
    appease.°   *cease*

30

His lovely words her seemd due recompence
Of all her passèd paines: one loving howre°   *hour*
For many yeares of sorrow can dispence:°   *compensate*
A dram of sweet is worth a pound of sowre:
She has forgot, how many a wofull stowre°   *time of turmoil*
For him she late endur'd; she speakes no more
Of past: true is, that true love hath no powre
To looken backe; his eyes be fixt before.
Before her stands her knight, for whom she
    toyld° so sore.   *toiled*

31

---

[1] *thereto meeting* Meeting her manner; i.e., answering in a like fashion.

Much like, as when the beaten marinere,
  That long hath wandred in the Ocean wide,
  Oft soust° in swelling Tethys saltish teare,   *soaked*
  And long time having tand his tawney hide
275 With blustring breath of heaven, that none can bide,
  And scorching flames of fierce Orions hound,[1]
  Soone as the port from farre he has espide,
  His chearefull whistle merrily doth sound,
And Nereus crownes with cups;[2] his mates him
    pledg° around.   *toast*

32

280 Such joy made Una, when her knight she found;
  And eke th'enchaunter joyous seemd no lesse,
  Then the glad marchant, that does vew from ground
  His ship farre come from watrie wildernesse,
  He hurles out vowes, and Neptune oft doth blesse:
285 So forth they past, and all the way they spent
  Discoursing of her dreadfull late distresse,
  In which he askt her, what the Lyon ment:
Who told her all that fell in journey as she went.

33

They had not ridden farre, when they might see
290 One pricking° towards them with hastie heat,   *galloping*
  Full strongly armd, and on a courser free,
  That through his fiercenesse fomed all with sweat,
  And the sharpe yron° did for anger eat,   *bit*
  When his hot ryder spurd his chauffed° side;   *chafed*
295 His looke was sterne, and seemèd still to threat
  Cruell revenge, which he in hart did hyde,
And on his shield Sans loy in bloudie lines was dyde.

34

When nigh he drew unto this gentle payre
  And saw the Red-crosse, which the knight did beare,
300 He burnt in fire, and gan eftsoones prepare
  Himselfe to battell with his couchèd speare.
  Loth was that other, and did faint through feare,
  To taste th'untryed dint of deadly steele;

But yet his Lady did so well him cheare,
305 That hope of new good hap he gan to feele;
  So bent his speare, and spurnd his horse with yron heele.

35

But that proud Paynim° forward came so fierce,   *pagan*
  And full of wrath, that with his sharp-head speare
  Through vainely crossèd shield[3] he quite did pierce,
310 And had his staggering steede not shrunke for feare,
  Through shield and bodie eke he should him beare:
  Yet so great was the puissance of his push,
  That from his saddle quite he did him beare:
  He tombling rudely downe to ground did rush,
315 And from his gorèd wound a well of bloud did gush.

36

Dismounting lightly from his loftie steed,
  He to him lept, in mind to reave° his life,   *take*
  And proudly said, Lo there the worthie meed°   *recompense*
  Of him, that slew Sans foy with bloudie knife;
320 Henceforth his ghost freed from repining strife,
  In peace may passen over Lethe[4] lake,
  When morning altars purgd with enemies life,
  The blacke infernall Furies[5] doen aslake:°   *appease*
Life from Sansfoy thou tookst, Sansloy shall from thee
    take.

37

325 Therewith in haste his helmet gan unlace,
  Till Una cride, O hold that heavie hand,
  Deare Sir, what ever that thou be in place:
  Enough is, that thy foe doth vanquisht stand
  Now at thy mercy: Mercie not withstand:
330 For he is one the truest knight alive,
  Though conquered now he lie on lowly land,
  And whilest him fortune favourd, faire did thrive
In bloudie field: therefore of life him not deprive.

38

---

[1] *Orions hound* Sirius, the dog star, brightest star in the constellation Canis Major. The ancient Egyptians, who observed the star shining for most of the summer months, believed its rays caused the extreme heat, hence the "dog days" of summer.

[2] *Nereus … cups* He toasts Nereus, a sea god.

[3] *vainely … shield* "Vainely" bearing the mere image of a cross and not accompanied by true faith, the shield does not offer Archimago protection.

[4] *Lethe* River in Hades whose waters bring forgetfulness.

[5] *Furies* Three terrible winged goddesses who punish those who commit unavenged crimes.

Her piteous words might not abate his rage,
335   But rudely rending up his helmet, would
Have slaine him straight: but when he sees his age,
And hoarie head of Archimago old,
His hastie hand he doth amazèd hold,
And halfe ashamèd, wondred at the sight:
340   For the old man well knew he, though untold,[1]
In charmes and magicke to have wondrous might,
Ne ever wont in field, ne in round lists[2] to fight.

39

And said, Why Archimago, lucklesse syre,
What doe I see? what hard mishap is this,
345   That hath thee hither brought to taste mine yre?
Or thine the fault, or mine the error is,
In stead of foe to wound my friend amis?
He answered nought, but in a traunce still lay,
And on those guilefull dazed eyes of his
350   The cloud of death did sit. Which doen away,
He left him lying so, ne would no lenger stay.

40

But to the virgin comes, who all this while
Amasèd stands, her selfe so mockt to see
By him, who has the guerdon° of his guile,   *recompense*
355   For so misfeigning her true knight to bee:
Yet is she now in more perplexitie,
Left in the hand of that same Paynim bold,
From whom her booteth not at all to flie;
Who by her cleanly° garment catching hold,   *pure*
360   Her from her Palfrey pluckt, her visage to behold.

41

But her fierce servant full of kingly awe
And high disdaine, whenas his soveraine Dame
So rudely handled by her foe he sawe,
With gaping jawes full greedy at him came,
365   And ramping° on his shield, did weene°   *charging / hope*
the same

Have reft away with his sharpe rending clawes:
But he was stout, and lust did now inflame
His corage more, that from his griping pawes
He hath his shield redeem'd, and foorth his sword he
drawes.

42

370   O then too weake and feeble was the forse
Of salvage beast, his puissance to withstand:
For he was strong, and of so mightie corse,
As ever wielded speare in warlike hand,
And feates of armes did wisely understand.
375   Eftsoones he perced through his chaufèd° chest   *angry*
With thrilling° point of deadly yron brand,   *piercing*
And launcht° his Lordly hart: with death opprest   *slit*
He roar'd aloud, whiles life forsooke his stubborne brest.

43

Who now is left to keepe the forlorne maid
380   From raging spoile of lawlesse victors will?
Her faithfull gard remov'd, her hope dismaid,
Her selfe a yeelded pray to save or spill.°   *ruin*
He now Lord of the field, his pride to fill,
With foule reproches, and disdainfull spight
385   Her vildly° entertaines, and will or nill,[3]   *vilely*
Beares her away upon his courser light:°   *quick*
Her prayers nought prevaile, his rage is more of might.

44

And all the way, with great lamenting paine,
And piteous plaints she filleth his dull° eares,   *deaf*
390   That stony hart could riven have in twaine,
And all the way she wets with flowing teares:
But he enrag'd with rancor, nothing heares.
Her servile beast[4] yet would not leave her so,
But followes her farre off, ne ought he feares,
395   To be partaker of her wandring woe,
More mild in beastly kind,° then that her beastly
foe.   *nature*

---

[1] *though untold* I.e., without being told.

[2] *round lists* Arenas in which tournaments were held.

[3] *will or nill* Expression meaning willingly or not; i.e., whether she
will or won't.

[4] *Her ... beast* I.e., her palfrey.

CANTO 4

To sinfull house of Pride, Duessa
Guides the faithfull knight,
Where brothers death to wreak° Sansjoy   avenge
Doth chalenge him to fight.

1

Young knight, what ever that dost armes professe,
  And through long labours huntest after fame,
  Beware of fraud, beware of ficklenesse,
  In choice, and change of thy deare lovèd Dame,
5 Least thou of her beleeve too lightly blame,
  And rash misweening doe thy hart remove:
  For unto knight there is no greater shame,
  Then lightnesse and inconstancie in love;
That doth this Redcrosse knights ensample°   example
  plainly prove.

2

10 Who after that he had faire Una lorne,°   deserted
  Through light misdeeming of her loialtie,
  And false Duessa in her sted had borne,
  Called Fidess', and so supposd to bee;
  Long with her traveild, till at last they see
15 A goodly building, bravely garnishèd,
  The house of mightie Prince it seemd to bee:
  And towards it a broad high way that led,
All bare through peoples feet, which thither traveilèd.

3

  Great troupes of people traveild thitherward
20 Both day and night, of each degree and place,
  But few returnèd, having scapèd hard,°   with difficulty
  With balefull° beggerie, or foule disgrace,   miserable
  Which ever after in most wretched case,
  Like loathsome lazars,° by the hedges lay.   lepers
25 Thither Duessa bad him bend his pace:
  For she is wearie of the toilesome way,
And also nigh consumèd is the lingring day.

4

  A stately Pallace built of squarèd bricke,
  Which cunningly was without morter laid,
30 Whose wals were high, but nothing strong, nor thick,

  And golden foile[1] all over them displaid,
  That purest skye with brightnesse they dismaid:
  High lifted up were many loftie towres,
  And goodly galleries farre over laid,
35 Full of faire windowes, and delightfull bowres;
And on the top a Diall° told the timely   clock, timepiece
  howres.

5

  It was a goodly heape° for to behould,   edifice
  And spake the praises of the workmans wit;
  But full great pittie, that so faire a mould
40 Did on so weake foundation ever sit:
  For on a sandie hill, that still did flit,°   shift
  And fall away, it mounted was full hie,
  That every breath of heaven shakèd it:
  And all the hinder parts, that few could spie,
45 Were ruinous and old, but painted cunningly.

6

  Arrivèd there they passèd in forth right;
  For still to all the gates stood open wide,
  Yet charge of them was to a Porter hight°   designated
  Cald Maluenù, who entrance none denide:
50 Thence to the hall, which was on every side
  With rich array and costly arras dight:°   decorated
  Infinite sorts of people did abide
  There waiting long, to win the wishèd sight
Of her, that was the Lady of that Pallace bright.

7

55 By them they passe, all gazing on them round,
  And to the Presence[2] mount; whose glorious vew
  Their frayle amazèd senses did confound:
  In living Princes court none ever knew
  Such endlesse richesse, and so sumptuous shew;
60 Ne Persia selfe, the nourse° of pompous pride   nurse
  Like ever saw. And there a noble crew
  Of Lordes and Ladies stood on every side
Which with their presence faire, the place much beautifide.

---

[1] *golden foile* Thin layer of gold.

[2] *Presence* Presence-chamber, where members of the royalty receive guests.

8

High above all a cloth of State was spred,
65   And a rich throne, as bright as sunny day,
    On which there sate most brave° embellished   *handsomely*
    With royall robes and gorgeous array,
    A mayden Queene, that shone as Titans ray,
    In glistring gold, and peerelesse pretious stone:
70   Yet her bright blazing beautie did assay
    To dim the brightnesse of her glorious throne,
As envying her selfe, that too exceeding shone.

9

Exceeding shone, like Phoebus fairest childe,[1]
    That did presume his fathers firie wayne,°   *chariot*
75   And flaming mouthes of steedes unwonted°   *unusually*
      wilde
    Through highest heaven with weaker hand to rayne;
    Proud of such glory and advancement vaine,
    While flashing beames do daze his feeble eyen,
    He leaves the welkin° way most beaten plaine,   *heavenly*
80   And rapt with whirling wheeles, inflames the skyen,
With fire not made to burne, but fairely for to shyne.

10

So proud she shynèd in her Princely state,
    Looking to heaven; for earth she did disdayne,
    And sitting high; for lowly she did hate:
85   Lo underneath her scornefull feete, was layne
    A dreadfull Dragon with an hideous trayne,°   *tail*
    And in her hand she held a mirrhour bright,
    Wherein her face she often vewèd fayne,°   *gladly*
    And in her selfe-lov'd semblance tooke delight;
90 For she was wondrous faire, as any living wight.

11

Of griesly Pluto she the daughter was,
    And sad Proserpina the Queene of hell;
    Yet did she thinke her pearelesse worth to pas
    That parentage, with pride so did she swell,
95   And thundring Jove, that high in heaven doth dwell,
    And wield the world, she claymèd for her syre,
    Or if that any else did Jove excell:

---

[1] *Phoebus ... childe* Phaeton, son of Apollo, tried to drive his father's chariot (by which the sun was pulled across the sky), but he lost control of the horses and was hurled down by Jove.

    For to the highest she did still aspyre,
Or if ought higher were then that, did it desyre.

12

100 And proud Lucifera men did her call,
    That made her selfe a Queene, and crownd to be,
    Yet rightfull kingdome she had none at all,
    Ne heritage of native soveraintie,
    But did usurpe with wrong and tyrannie
105   Upon the scepter, which she now did hold:
    Ne ruld her Realmes with lawes, but
      pollicie,°   *political cunning*
    And strong advizement of six wisards old,
That with their counsels bad her kingdome did uphold.

13

Soone as the Elfin knight in presence came,
110   And false Duessa seeming Lady faire,
    A gentle Husher,° Vanitie by name   *usher*
    Made rowme, and passage for them did prepaire:
    So goodly brought them to the lowest staire
    Of her high throne, where they on humble knee
115   Making obeyssance, did the cause declare,
    Why they were come, her royall state to see,
To prove° the wide report of her great Majestee.   *confirm*

14

With loftie eyes, halfe loth to looke so low,
    She thankèd them in her disdainefull wise,°   *fashion*
120   Ne other grace vouchsafèd them to show
    Of Princesse worthy, scarse them bad arise.
    Her Lordes and Ladies all this while devise°   *prepare*
    Themselves to setten forth to straungers sight:
    Some frounce° their curlèd haire in courtly guise,   *frizz*
125   Some prancke° their ruffes, and others trimly dight   *pleat*
Their gay attire: each others greater pride does spight.

15

Goodly they all that knight do entertaine,
    Right glad with him to have increast their crew:
    But to Duess' each one himselfe did paine
130   All kindnesse and faire courtesie to shew;
    For in that court whylome° her well they knew: *previously*
    Yet the stout Faerie mongst the middest° crowd   *central*
    Thought all their glorie vaine in knightly vew,

And that great Princesse too exceeding prowd,
135 That to strange knight no better countenance allowd.

16

Suddein upriseth from her stately place
  The royall Dame, and for her coche doth call:
  All hurtlen° forth, and she with Princely pace,   *rush*
  As faire Aurora in her purple° pall,°   *crimson | robe*
140   Out of the East the dawning day doth call:
  So forth she comes: her brightnesse brode° doth
     blaze;   *abroad*
  The heapes of people thronging in the hall,
  Do ride each other, upon her to gaze:
Her glorious glitterand light doth all mens eyes amaze.

17

145 So forth she comes, and to her coche does clyme,
  Adornèd all with gold, and girlonds gay,
  That seemd as fresh as Flora in her prime,
  And strove to match, in royall rich array,
  Great Junoes golden chaire, the which they say
150   The Gods stand gazing on, when she does ride
  To Joves high house through heavens bras-pavèd way
  Drawne of faire Pecocks, that excell in pride,
And full of Argus eyes[1] their tailes dispredden wide.

18

But this was drawne of six unequall beasts,
155   On which her six sage Counsellours did ryde,[2]
  Taught to obay their bestiall beheasts,
  With like conditions to their kinds° applyde: *natures*
  Of which the first, that all the rest did guyde,
  Was sluggish Idlenesse the nourse of sin;
160   Upon a slouthfull Asse he chose to ryde,
  Arayd in habit blacke, and amis[3] thin,
Like to an holy Monck, the service to begin.

19

And in his hand his Portesse° still he bare,   *prayer book*
  That much was worne, but therein little red,
165   For of devotion he had little care,
  Still drownd in sleepe, and most of his dayes ded;
  Scarse could he once uphold his heavie hed,
  To looken, whether it were night or day:
  May seeme the wayne was very evill led,
170   When such an one had guiding of the way,
That knew not, whether right he went, or else astray.

20

From worldy cares himselfe he did esloyne,°   *remove*
  And greatly shunnèd manly exercise,
  From every worke he chalengèd°
     essoyne,°   *claimed | exemption*
175   For contemplation sake: yet otherwise,
  His life he led in lawlesse riotie;°   *riot*
  By which he grew to grievous malady;
  For in his lustlesse limbs through evill guise
  A shaking fever raignd continually:
180 Such one was Idlenesse, first of this company.

21

And by his side rode loathsome Gluttony,
  Deformèd creature, on a filthie swyne,
  His belly was up-blowne with luxury,°   *indulgence*
  And eke with fatnesse swollen were his eyne,
185   And like a Crane[4] his necke was long and fyne,
  With which he swallowd up excessive feast,
  For want whereof poore people oft did pyne;
  And all the way, most like a brutish beast,
He spuèd° up his gorge, that° all did   *vomited | so that*
     him deteast.

22

190 In greene vine leaves he was right fitly clad;
  For other clothes he could not weare for heat,
  And on his head an yvie girland had,
  From under which fast trickled downe the sweat:
  Still as he rode, he somewhat still did eat,
195   And in his hand did beare a bouzing° can,   *drinking*
  Of which he supt so oft, that on his seat

---

[1] *full of Argus eyes* The monster Argus, who had one hundred eyes, was sent by Juno to watch Io, who was loved by Juno's husband, Jove. When Argus was killed, Juno placed his eyes in the tail-feathers of a peacock.

[2] *six unequal beasts* Lucifera, the personification of Pride, worst of the Seven Deadly Sins, leads her counselors, who personify the other six. They ride symbolically relevant animals.

[3] *amis* I.e., amice, priestly vestment.

[4] *Crane* Symbol of gluttony; it was thought the crane's long neck gave it increased pleasure in swallowing.

His dronken corse he scarse upholden can,
In shape and life more like a monster, then a man.

23

Unfit he was for any worldy thing,
200   And eke unhable once to stirre or go,
Not meet to be of counsell to a king,
Whose mind in meat and drinke was drownèd so,
That from his friend he seldome knew his fo:
Full of diseases was his carcas blew,
205   And a dry dropsie[1] through his flesh did flow:
Which by misdiet daily greater grew:
Such one was Gluttony, the second of that crew.

24

And next to him rode lustfull Lechery,
Upon a bearded Goat, whose rugged haire,
210   And whally° eyes (the signe of gelosy,)   *glaring*
Was like the person selfe, whom he did beare:
Who rough, and blacke, and filthy did appeare,
Unseemely man to please faire Ladies eye;
Yet he of Ladies oft was lovèd deare,
215   When fairer faces were bid standen by:°   *away*
O who does know the bent of womens fantasy?

25

In a greene gowne he clothèd was full faire,
Which underneath did hide his filthinesse,
And in his hand a burning hart he bare,
220   Full of vaine follies, and new fanglenesse:
For he was false, and fraught with ficklenesse,
And learnèd had to love with secret lookes,
And well could daunce, and sing with
ruefulnesse,°   *dejection*
And fortunes tell, and read in loving° bookes,   *erotic*
225   And thousand other wayes, to bait his fleshly hookes.

26

Inconstant man, that lovèd all he saw,
And lusted after all, that he did love,
Ne would his looser life be tide to law,
But joyd weake wemens hearts to tempt, and prove°   *test*
230   If from their loyall loves he might then move;

Which lewdnesse fild him with reprochfull paine
Of that fowle evill, which all men reprove,
That rots the marrow, and consumes the braine:[2]
Such one was Lecherie, the third of all this traine.

27

235   And greedy Avarice by him did ride,
Upon a Camell loaden all with gold;
Two iron coffers hong on either side,
With precious mettall full, as they might hold,
And in his lap an heape of coine he told;°   *counted*
240   For of his wicked pelfe° his God he made,   *riches*
And unto hell him selfe for money sold;
Accursèd usurie was all his trade,
And right and wrong ylike in equall ballaunce waide.

28

His life was nigh unto deaths doore yplast,
245   And thred-bare cote, and cobled shoes he ware,
Ne scarse good morsell all his life did tast,
But both from backe and belly still did spare,
To fill his bags, and richesse to compare;°   *obtain*
Yet chylde ne kinsman living had he none
250   To leave them to; but thorough daily care
To get, and nightly feare to lose his owne,
He led a wretched life unto him selfe unknowne.

29

Most wretched wight, whom nothing might suffise,
Whose greedy lust did lacke in greatest store,°   *plenty*
255   Whose need had end, but no end covetise,°   *covetousness*
Whose wealth was want, whose plenty made him pore,
Who had enough, yet wishèd ever more;
A vile disease, and eke in foote and hand
A grievous gout tormented him full sore,
260   That well he could not touch, nor go, nor stand:
Such one was Avarice, the fourth of this faire band.

30

And next to him malicious Envie rode,
Upon a ravenous wolfe, and still did chaw°   *chew*
Betweene his cankred° teeth a venemous tode,   *infected*
265   That all the poison ran about his chaw;°   *jaw*
But inwardly he chawèd his owne maw°   *guts*

---

[1] *dropsie* I.e., dropsy, disease in which fluid accumulates in the bodily tissue and causes bloating.

[2] *that fowle … braine* I.e., syphilis.

At neighbours wealth, that made him ever sad;
  For death it was, when any good he saw,
  And wept, that cause of weeping none he had,
270 But when he heard of harme, he wexèd wondrous glad.

31

All in a kirtle° of discolourd° say[1]   *tunic | multicolored*
  He clothed was, ypainted full of eyes;
  And in his bosome secretly there lay
  An hatefull Snake, the which his taile uptyes
275 In many folds, and mortall sting implyes.
  Still as he rode, he gnasht his teeth, to see
  Those heapes of gold with griple°
    Covetyse,°   *grasping | avarice*
  And grudgèd at the great felicitie
Of proud Lucifera, and his owne companie.

32

280 He hated all good workes and vertuous deeds,
  And him no lesse, that any like did use,°   *perform*
  And who with gracious bread the hungry feeds,
  His almes for want of faith he doth accuse;[2]
  So every good to bad he doth abuse:°   *misrepresent*
285 And eke the verse of famous Poets witt
  He does backebite, and spightfull poison spues
  From leprous mouth on all, that ever writt:
Such one vile Envie was, that fifte in row did sitt.

33

And him beside rides fierce revenging Wrath,
290 Upon a Lion, loth for to be led;
  And in his hand a burning brond° he hath,   *sword*
  The which he brandisheth about his hed;
  His eyes did hurle forth sparkles fiery red,
  And starèd sterne on all, that him beheld;
295 As ashes pale of hew and seeming ded;
  And on his dagger still his hand he held,
Trembling through hasty rage, when choler°   *anger*
  in him sweld.

34

His ruffin° raiment all was staind with blood,   *disordered*

Which he had spilt, and all to rags yrent,
300 Through unadvizèd rashnesse woxen°
  wood;°   *grew | mad*
  For of his hands he had no governement,°   *control*
  Ne car'd for bloud in his avengement:
  But when the furious fit was overpast,
  His cruell facts° he often would repent;   *deeds*
305 Yet wilfull man he never would forecast,°   *foresee*
How many mischieves should ensue his heedlesse hast.

35

Full many mischiefes follow cruell Wrath;
  Abhorrèd bloudshed, and tumultuous strife,
  Unmanly murder, and unthrifty° scath,°   *wasteful | damage*
310 Bitter despight,° with rancours rusty knife,   *contempt*
  And fretting griefe the enemy of life;
  All these, and many evils moe haunt ire,
  The swelling Splene,[3] and Frenzy raging rife,
  The shaking Palsey, and Saint Fraunces fire:[4]
315 Such one was Wrath, the last of this ungodly
  tire.°   *procession*

36

And after all, upon the wagon beame
  Rode Sathan, with a smarting whip in hand,
  With which he forward lasht the laesie teme,
  So oft as Slowth still in the mire did stand.
320 Huge routs° of people did about them band,   *crowds*
  Showting for joy, and still° before their way   *always*
  A foggy mist had covered all the land;
  And underneath their feet, all scattered lay
Dead sculs & bones of men, whose life had gone astray.

37

325 So forth they marchen in this goodly sort,
  To take the solace of the open aire,
  And in fresh flowring fields themselves to sport;
  Emongst the rest rode that false Lady faire,
  The fowle Duessa, next unto the chaire
330 Of proud Lucifera, as one of the traine:
  But that good knight would not so nigh repaire,°   *approach*

---

1 *say* Fine cloth, usually made of a mixture of silk and wool.

2 *His almes … accuse* Envy accuses those who give to the poor of doing so in an attempt to hide their lack of faith.

3 *Splene* I.e., spleen, ill-humor or violent temper.

4 *Saint Fraunces fire* Erysipelas; also known as wildfire or St. Anthony's fire, an inflammatory disease of the skin which produces a red rash.

Him selfe estraunging from their joyaunce vaine,
Whose fellowship seemd far unfit for warlike swaine.

38

335   So having solacèd themselves a space
With pleasaunce of the breathing° fields yfed   *fragrant*
They backe returned to the Princely Place;
Whereas° an errant knight in armes ycled,   *where*
And heathnish shield, wherein with letters red
Was writ Sans joy, they new arrivèd find:
340   Enflam'd with fury and fiers hardy-hed,°   *hardihood*
He seemd in hart to harbour thoughts unkind,
And nourish bloudy vengeaunce in his bitter mind.

39

Who when the shamèd shield of slaine Sans foy
He spide with that same Faery champions page,
345   Bewraying him, that did of late destroy
His eldest brother, burning all with rage
He to him leapt, and that same envious°
    gage°   *envied | token*
Of victors glory from him snatcht away:
But th'Elfin knight, which ought° that warlike°
    wage,°   *owned | of war | spoil*
350   Disdaind to loose the meed° he wonne in fray,   *prize*
And him rencountring fierce, reskewd° the
    noble pray.   *rescued*

40

Therewith they gan to hurtlen° greedily,   *rush*
Redoubted battaile ready to darrayne,°   *engage*
And clash their shields, and shake their swords on hy,
355   That with their sturre they troubled all the traine;
Till that great Queene upon eternall paine
Of high displeasure, that ensewen might,
Commaunded them their fury to refraine,
And if that either to that shield had right,
360   In equall lists they should the morrow next it fight.

41

Ah dearest Dame, (quoth then the Paynim bold,)
Pardon the errour of enragèd wight,
Whom great griefe made forget the raines to hold
Of reasons rule, to see this recreant° knight,   *faint-hearted*
365   No knight, but treachour° full of false despight   *traitor*

And shamefull treason, who through guile hath slayn
The prowest knight, that ever field did fight,
Even stout Sans foy (O who can then refrayn?)
Whose shield he beares renverst, the more to heape
    disdayn.[1]

42

370   And to augment the glorie of his guile,
His dearest love the faire Fidessa loe°   *look*
Is there possessèd of° the traytour vile,   *by*
Who reapes the harvest sowen by his foe,
Sowen in bloudy field, and bought with woe:
375   That brothers hand shall dearely well requight
So be,[2] O Queene, you equall favour showe.
Him litle answerd th'angry Elfin knight;
He never meant with words, but swords to plead his
    right.

43

But threw his gauntlet as a sacred pledge,
380   His cause in combat the next day to try:
So been they parted both, with harts on edge,
To be aveng'd each on his enimy.
That night they pas in joy and jollity,
Feasting and courting both in bowre and hall;
385   For Steward was excessive Gluttonie,
That of his plenty poured forth to all:
Which doen, the Chamberlain Slowth did to rest
    them call.

44

Now whenas darkesome night had all displayd
Her coleblacke curtein over brightest skye,
390   The warlike youthes on dayntie couches layd,
Did chace away sweet sleepe from sluggish eye,
To muse on meanes of hopèd victory.
But whenas Morpheus had with leaden mace
Arrested[3] all that courtly company,
395   Up-rose Duessa from her resting place,
And to the Paynims lodging comes with silent pace.

---

[1] *Whose … disdayn* Carrying a shield upside down was considered a great insult.

[2] *So be* If.

[3] *Arrested* I.e., put to sleep.

45

Whom broad awake she finds, in troublous fit,
  Forecasting, how his foe he might annoy,°   *harm*
  And him amoves° with speaches seeming fit: *arouses*
400 Ah deare Sans joy, next dearest to Sans foy,
  Cause of my new griefe, cause of my new joy,
  Joyous, to see his ymage in mine eye,
  And greev'd, to thinke how foe did him destroy,
  That was the flowre of grace and chevalrye;
405 Lo his Fidessa to thy secret faith I flye.

46

With gentle wordes he can° her fairely greet,   *did*
  And bad° say on the secret of her hart.   *bade*
  Then sighing soft, I learne that litle sweet
  Oft tempred is (quoth she) with muchell°
    smart:°   *much / pain*
410 For since my brest was launcht with lovely° dart   *of love*
  Of deare Sans foy, I never joyèd howre,
  But in eternall woes my weaker° hart   *too weak*
  Have wasted, loving him with all my powre,
  And for his sake have felt full many an heavie
    stowre.°   *turmoil*

47

415 At last when perils all I weenèd past,
  And hop'd to reape the crop of all my care,
  Into new woes unweeting I was cast,
  By this false faytor,° who unworthy ware   *imposter*
  His worthy shield, whom he with guilefull snare
420 Entrappèd slew, and brought to shamefull grave.
  Me silly° maid away with him he bare,   *helpless*
  And ever since hath kept in darksome cave,
  For that I would not yeeld, that to Sans-foy I gave.

48

But since faire Sunne hath sperst° that lowring
  clowd,   *dispersed*
425 And to my loathèd life now shewes some light,
  Under your beames I will me safely shrowd,
  From dreaded storme of his disdainfull spight:
  To you th'inheritance belongs by right
  Of brothers prayse, to you eke longs° his love.   *belongs*

430 Let not his love, let not his restlesse spright°   *spirit*
  Be unreveng'd, that calles to you above
  From wandring Stygian shores,[1] where it doth endlesse
    move.

49

Thereto said he, Faire Dame be nought dismaid
  For sorrowes past; their griefe is with them gone:
435 Ne yet of present perill be affraid;
  For needlesse feare did never vantage none,
  And helplesse hap it booteth not to mone.°   *bemoan*
  Dead is Sans-foy, his vitall° paines are past,   *living*
  Though greevèd ghost for vengeance deepe do grone:
440 He lives, that shall him pay his dewties° last,   *rites*
  And guiltie Elfin bloud shall sacrifice in hast.

50

O but I feare the fickle° freakes°   *unpredictable / whims*
  (quoth shee)
  Of fortune false, and oddes° of armes in field.   *advantages*
  Why dame (quoth he) what oddes can ever bee,
445 Where both do fight alike, to win or yield?
  Yea but (quoth she) he beares a charmèd shield,
  And eke enchaunted armes, that none can perce,
  Ne none can wound the man, that does them wield.
  Charmd or enchaunted (answerd he then ferce)°   *fiercely*
450 I no whit reck,° ne you the like need to   *care / recount*
    reherce.

51

But faire Fidessa, sithens fortunes guile,
  Or enimies powre hath now captivèd you,
  Returne from whence ye came, and rest a while
  Till morrow next, that I the Elfe subdew,
455 And with Sans-foyes dead dowry you endew.
  Ay me, that is a double death (she said)
  With proud foes sight my sorrow to renew:
  Where ever yet I be, my secrete aid
  Shall follow you. So passing forth she him obaid.

---

1 *Stygian shores* Shores of the river Styx, across which (according
to classical mythology) all souls had to travel to reach Hades. Those
who were not given a proper funeral were condemned to wander the
banks of the river for one hundred years.

CANTO 5: SUMMARY

The Redcrosse knight and Sans joy commence battle. Sans joy, enraged by the sight of his brother Sans foy's bloody shield (which Duessa has hung from a tree), nearly kills the Redcrosse knight, but he recovers and is about to deal a fatal blow when Sans joy suddenly vanishes in an enchanted dark cloud summoned by Duessa. The Redcrosse knight, bewildered, is nevertheless celebrated as the victor of the fight. He is taken back to the castle to have his wounds tended to. When darkness falls, Duessa leaves to meet Night, the queen of darkness, and enlists her help in avenging Sans foy and Sans joy (who are grandsons of Night). Night and Duessa retrieve Sans joy from where he lies hidden. They bring him to Hades, the underworld, where they seek out Aesculapius, a celebrated and immortal physician whom Jove has condemned to Hades as punishment for bringing Hippolytus, a wrongly murdered boy, back to life. The two treacherous women convince Aesculapius to heal Sans joy. Meanwhile, Redcrosse's companion, the dwarf, discovers Lucifera's dungeon of pride, in which the bodies of the proud lie in heaps, and reports his discovery to the knight. The two flee in the night, and Duessa returns to find them gone.

CANTO 6: SUMMARY

Sans loy attempts to seduce Una; when she refuses his advances he resolves to rape her. Her cries of terror bring to her rescue a group of fauns and satyrs (mythological woodland creatures who are men from the waist up, goats from the waist down). The fauns and satyrs rescue Una and take her to their forest dwelling. Although Una tries to teach them true religion, they assume her to be a goddess and begin to worship her. Eventually she is discovered by Satyrane, a virtuous knight who was borne of a human mother and a satyr father. At her request, he helps her to escape the idolatrous fauns and satyrs. After having fled the forest, Una and the knight meet a pilgrim on the road. They ask him for news of the Redcrosse knight, and the pilgrim (who is really Archimago in disguise) tells them he has seen that knight killed in combat by a pagan knight. Una and Satyrane seek out the pagan, who remains at a nearby fountain washing his wounds. The Satyrane begins to fight the pagan, who is actually Sans loy. Una flees in terror and is pursued by Archimago, still disguised as a pilgrim.

Canto 7

The Redcrosse knight is captive made
  By Gyaunt proud opprest,°   vanquished
Prince Arthur meets with Una greatly
  With those newes distrest.

1

What man so wise, what earthly wit so ware,°   wary
  As to descry° the crafty cunning
      traine,°   perceive / trickery
  By which deceipt doth maske in visour° faire,   mask
  And cast her colours dyed deepe in graine,
5 To seeme like Truth, whose shape she well can faine,
  And fitting gestures to her purpose frame;
  The guiltlesse man with guile to entertaine?
  Great maistresse of her art was that false Dame,
The false Duessa, cloked with Fidessaes name.

2

10 Who when returning from the drery Night,
  She fownd not in that perilous house of Pryde,
  Where she had left, the noble Redcrosse knight,
  Her hopèd pray,° she would no lenger bide,   prey
  But forth she went, to seeke him far and wide.
15 Ere long she fownd, whereas° he wearie sate,   where
  To rest him selfe, foreby a fountaine side,
  Disarmèd all of yron-coted Plate,
  And by his side his steed the grassy forage ate.

3

  He feedes upon the cooling shade, and bayes°   bathes
20 His sweatie forehead in the breathing wind,
  Which through the trembling leaves full gently playes
  Wherein the cherefull birds of sundry kind
  Do chaunt sweet musick, to delight his mind:
  The Witch approching gan him fairely° greet,   courteously
25 And with reproch of carelesnesse unkind
  Upbrayd, for leaving her in place unmeet,°   unfitting
With fowle words tempring faire, soure gall with hony
      sweet.

4

Unkindnesse past, they gan of solace treat,°   speak
  And bathe in pleasaunce of the joyous shade,

30 Which shieldèd them against the boyling heat,
  And with greene boughes decking a gloomy glade,
  About the fountaine like a girlond made;
  Whose bubbling wave did ever freshly well,
  Ne ever would through fervent sommer fade:°   dry up
35 The sacred Nymph, which therein wont to dwell,
Was out of Dianes favour, as it then befell.°   so happened

5

  The cause was this: one day when Phoebe[1] fayre
  With all her band was following the chace,°   hunt
  This Nymph, quite tyr'd with heat of scorching ayre,
40 Sat downe to rest in middest of the race:
  The goddesse wroth° gan fowly her disgrace,   angry
  And bad the waters, which from her did flow,
  Be such as she her selfe was then in place.
  Thenceforth her waters waxèd dull and slow,
45 And all that drunke thereof, did faint and feeble grow.

6

  Hereof this gentle knight unweeting was,
  And lying downe upon the sandie graile,°   gravel
  Drunke of the streame, as cleare as cristall glas;
  Eftsoones his manly forces gan to faile,
50 And mightie strong was turnd to feeble fraile.
  His chaunged powres at first them selves not felt,
  Till crudled° cold his corage gan assaile,   curdled
  And chearefull° bloud in faintnesse chill did melt,   lively
Which like a fever fit through all his body swelt.°   raged

7

55 Yet goodly court he made still to his Dame,
  Pourd° out in loosnesse on the grassy grownd,   stretched
  Both carelesse of his health, and of his fame:[2]
  Till at the last he heard a dreadfull sownd,
  Which through the wood loud bellowing, did rebownd,
60 That all the earth for terrour seemd to shake,
  And trees did tremble. Th'Elfe therewith astownd,
  Upstarted lightly° from his looser make,°   quickly / mate
And his unready weapons gan in hand to take.

8

But ere he could his armour on him dight,°   place

---

[1] *Phoebe* Diana, goddess of the moon, chastity, and the hunt.

[2] *fame* Good reputation or character.

65   Or get his shield, his monstrous enimy
    With sturdie steps came stalking in his sight,
    An hideous Geant horrible and hye,
    That with his talnesse seemd to threat the skye,
    The ground eke groned under him for dreed;
70   His living like saw never living eye,
    Ne durst behold: his stature did exceed
The hight of three the tallest sonnes of mortall seed.

9

The greatest Earth his uncouth mother was,
    And blustring Aeolus[1] his boasted sire,
75   Who with his breath, which through the world doth pas,
    Her hollow womb did secretly inspire,°   *blow in to*
    And fild her hidden caves with stormie yre,
    That she conceiv'd; and trebling the dew time,
    In which the wombes of women do expire,°   *bring forth*
80   Brought forth this monstrous masse of earthly slime,
Puft up with emptie wind, and fild with sinfull crime.

10

So growen great through arrogant delight
    Of th'high descent, whereof he was yborne,
    And through presumption of his matchlesse might,
85   All other powres and knighthood he did scorne.
    Such now he marcheth to this man forlorne,
    And left to losse: his stalking steps are stayde°   *supported*
    Upon a snaggy Oke, which he had torne
    Out of his mothers bowelles, and it made
90   His mortall° mace,° wherewith his foemen   *deadly / weapon*
    he dismayde.

11

That when the knight he spide, he gan advance
    With huge force and insupportable°
      mayne,°   *irresistable / strength*
    And towardes him with dreadfull fury praunce;
    Who haplesse, and eke hopelesse, all in vaine
95   Did to him pace, sad battaile to darrayne,°   *engage*
    Disarmd, disgrast, and inwardly dismayde,
    And eke so faint in every joynt and vaine,°   *vein*
    Through that fraile° fountaine, which him feeble made,
That scarsely could he weeld his bootlesse°   *useless*
    single blade.

---

1   *Aeolus* Keeper of the winds.

12

100   The Geaunt strooke so maynly° mercilesse,   *fiercely*
    That could have overthrowne a stony towre,
    And were not heavenly grace, that him did blesse,
    He had beene pouldred° all, as thin as
      flowre:°   *pulverized / flour*
    But he was wary of that deadly stowre,°   *danger*
105   And lightly lept from underneath the blow:
    Yet so exceeding was the villeins powre,
    That with the wind it did him overthrow,
And all his sences stound,° that still he lay   *stunned*
    full low.

13

As when that divelish yron Engin[2] wrought
110   In deepest Hell, and framd by Furies skill,
    With windy Nitre° and quick Sulphur
      fraught,°   *gunpowder / filled*
    And ramd with bullet round, ordaind to kill,
    Conceiveth fire, the heavens it doth fill
    With thundring noyse, and all the ayre doth choke,
115   That none can breath, nor see, nor heare at will,
    Through smouldry cloud of duskish° stincking   *dark*
    smoke,
That th'onely° breath° him daunts,°   *alone / smell / overcomes*
    who hath escapt the stroke.

14

So daunted when the Geaunt saw the knight,
    His heavie hand he heavèd up on hye,
120   And him to dust thought to have battred quight,
    Untill Duessa loud to him gan crye;
    O great Orgoglio,[3] greatest under skye,
    O hold thy mortall hand for Ladies sake,
    Hold for my sake, and do him not to dye,
125   But vanquisht thine eternall bondslave make,
And me thy worthy meed° unto° thy Leman   *prize / as*
    take.

15

He hearkned, and did stay from further harmes,
    To gayne so goodly guerdon, as she spake:
    So willingly she came into his armes,

---

2   *yron Engin* I.e., the cannon.
3   *Orgoglio* Italian: pride, disdain.

130 Who her as willingly to grace did take,
    And was possessèd of his new found make.
    Then up he tooke the slombred sencelesse corse,
    And ere he could out of his swowne awake,
    Him to his castle brought with hastie forse,
135 And in a Dongeon deepe him threw without remorse.

16

From that day forth Duessa was his deare,
    And highly honourd in his haughtie eye,
    He gave her gold and purple pall to weare,
    And triple crowne[1] set on her head full hye,
140 And her endowd with royall majestye:
    Then for to make her dreaded more of men,
    And peoples harts with awfull terrour tye,°   enthrall
    A monstrous beast[2] ybred in filthy fen
    He chose, which he had kept long time in darksome den.

17

145 Such one it was, as that renowmèd Snake
    Which great Alcides in Stremona slew,[3]
    Long fostred in the filth of Lerna lake,
    Whose many heads out budding ever new,
    Did breed him endlesse labour to subdew:
150 But this same Monster much more ugly was;
    For seven great heads out of his body grew,
    An yron brest, and backe of scaly bras,
    And all embrewd° in bloud, his eyes did shine   stained
        as glas.

18

His tayle was stretched out in wondrous length,
155 That to the house of heavenly gods it raught,°   reached
    And with extorted powre, and borrow'd strength,
    The ever-burning lamps[4] from thence it braught,
    And prowdly threw to ground, as things of naught;
    And underneath his filthy feet did tread
160 The sacred things, and holy heasts° foretaught.   doctrines

---

[1] triple crown Like that worn by the pope.

[2] beast The description of Duessa and her beast echo several passages in the Book of Revelation (esp. 17, 3, 12.3–4, 9).

[3] Such one ... slew Alcides (Hercules) had to kill the nine-headed Hydra of Lerna as one of his twelve labors. Each time he cut off one head, several more would grow in its place.

[4] ever-burning lamps I.e., the stars.

Upon this dreadfull Beast with sevenfold head
He set the false Duessa, for more aw and dread.

19

The wofull Dwarfe, which saw his maisters fall,
    Whiles he had keeping of his grasing steed,
165 And valiant knight become a caytive thrall,°   slave
    When all was past, tooke up his forlorne weed,
    His mightie armour, missing most at need;
    His silver shield, now idle maisterlesse;
    His poynant° speare, that many made to bleed,   piercing
170 The ruefull moniments of heavinesse,°   grief
    And with them all departes, to tell his great distresse.

20

He had not travaild long, when on the way
    He wofull Ladie, wofull Una met,
    Fast flying from the Paynims greedy pray,°   grasp
175 Whilest Satyrane him from pursuit did let:°   prevent
    Who when her eyes she on the Dwarf had set,
    And saw the signes, that deadly tydings spake,
    She fell to ground for sorrowfull regret,
    And lively° breath her sad brest did forsake,   of life
180 Yet might her pitteous hart be seene to pant and quake.

21

The messenger of so unhappie newes
    Would faine have dyde: dead was his hart within,
    Yet outwardly some little comfort shewes:
    At last recovering hart, he does begin
185 To rub her temples, and to chaufe her chin,
    And every tender part does tosse and turne:
    So hardly° he the flitted life does win,   with difficulty
    Unto her native prison to retourne:
    Then gins her grievèd ghost thus to lament and mourne.

22

190 Ye dreary instruments of dolefull sight,
    That doe this deadly spectacle behold,
    Why do ye lenger° feed on loathèd light,   longer
    Or liking° find to gaze on earthly mould,°   pleasing / shapes
    Sith cruell fates the carefull threeds unfould,
195 The which my life and love together tyde?
    Now let the stony dart of senselesse cold
    Perce to my hart, and pas through every side,
    And let eternall night so sad sight fro me hide.

23

O lightsome day, the lampe of highest Jove,
200   First made by him, mens wandring wayes to guyde,
When darknesse he in deepest dongeon drove,
Henceforth thy hated face for ever hyde,
And shut up heavens windowes shyning wyde:
For earthly sight can nought but sorow breed,
205   And late repentance, which shall long abyde.
Mine eyes no more on vanitie shall feed,
But seelèd up with death, shall have their deadly meed.

24

Then downe againe she fell unto the ground;
But he her quickly rearèd up againe:
210   Thrise did she sinke adowne in deadly swownd,
And thrise he her reviv'd with busie paine:
At last when life recover'd had the raine,
And over-wrestled his strong enemie,
With foltring tong, and trembling every vaine,
215   Tell on (quoth she) the wofull Tragedie,
The which these reliques sad present unto mine eie.

25

Tempestuous fortune hath spent all her spight,
And thrilling sorrow throwne his utmost dart;
Thy sad tongue cannot tell more heavy plight,
220   Then that I feele, and harbour in mine hart:
Who hath endur'd the whole, can beare each part.
If death it be, it is not the first wound,
That launchèd° hath my brest with bleeding   *pierced*
      smart.
Begin, and end the bitter balefull stound;[1]
225   If lesse, then that I feare, more favour I have found.

26

Then gan the Dwarfe the whole discourse declare,
The subtill traines of Archimago old;
The wanton loves of false Fidessa faire,
Bought with the bloud of vanquisht Paynim bold:
230   The wretched payre° transform'd to treen mould;   *pair*
The house of Pride, and perils round about;
The combat, which he with Sansjoy did hould;
The lucklesse conflict with the Gyant stout,
Wherein captiv'd, of life or death he stood in doubt.

27

235   She heard with patience all unto the end,
And strove to maister sorrowfull assay,°   *tribulation*
Which greater grew, the more she did contend,
And almost rent her tender hart in tway;°   *two*
And love fresh coles unto her fire did lay:
240   For greater love, the greater is the losse.
Was never Ladie lovèd dearer day,°   *life*
Then she did love the knight of the Redcrosse;
For whose deare sake so many troubles her did tosse.

28

At last when fervent sorrow slakèd was,
245   She up arose, resolving him to find
A live or dead: and forward forth doth pas,
All as the Dwarfe the way to her assynd:°   *indicated*
And evermore in constant carefull mind
She fed her wound with fresh renewèd bale;°   *misery*
250   Long tost with stormes, and bet° with bitter   *beaten*
      wind,
High over hils, and low adowne the dale,
She wandred many a wood, and measurd many a vale.

29

At last she chauncèd by good hap to meet
A goodly knight, faire marching by the way
255   Together with his Squire, arayèd meet:°   *suitably*
His glitterand armour shinèd farre away,
Like glauncing° light of Phoebus brightest ray;   *shining*
From top to toe no place appearèd bare,
That deadly dint of steele endanger may:
260   Athwart his brest a bauldrick[2] brave he ware,
That shynd, like twinkling stars, with stons most
      pretious rare.

30

And in the midst thereof one pretious stone
Of wondrous worth, and eke of wondrous mights,
Shapt like a Ladies head, exceeding shone,
265   Like Hesperus emongst the lesser lights,
And strove for to amaze the weaker sights;
Thereby his mortall blade full comely hong
In yvory sheath, ycarv'd with curious slights;°   *designs*

---

[1]   *stound*   Time of pain.

[2]   *bauldrick*   Belt or sash worn to support a sword.

Whose hilts were burnisht gold, and handle strong
270 Of mother pearle, and buckled with a golden tong.°   *pin*

31

His haughtie° helmet, horrid° all with gold,   *high | bristling*
     Both glorious brightnesse, and great terrour bred;
     For all the crest a Dragon did enfold
     With greedie pawes, and over all did spred
275 His golden wings: his dreadfull hideous hed
     Close couchèd on the bever,° seem'd to throw   *visor*
     From flaming mouth bright sparkles fierie red,
     That suddeine horror to faint harts did show;
And scaly tayle was stretcht adowne his backe full low.

32

280 Upon the top of all his loftie crest,°   *helmet*
     A bunch of haires discolourd° diversly,   *dyed*
     With sprinded pearle, and gold full richly drest,
     Did shake, and seem'd to daunce for jollity,
     Like to an Almond tree ymounted hye
285 On top of greene Selinis[1] all alone,
     With blossomes brave bedeckèd daintily;
     Whose tender locks do tremble every one
At every little breath, that under heaven is blowne.

33

His warlike shield all closely cover'd was,
290 Ne might of mortall eye be ever seene;
     Not made of steele, nor of enduring bras,
     Such earthly mettals soone consumèd bene:
     But all of Diamond perfect pure and cleene
     It framèd was, one massie entire mould,[2]
295 Hewen out of Adamant rocke with engines
          keene,°   *sharp*
     That point of speare it never percen could,
Ne dint of direfull sword divide the substance would.

34

The same to wight he never wont disclose,
     But° when as monsters huge he would dismay,   *except*
300 Or daunt unequall armies of his foes,
     Or when the flying° heavens he would affray;   *revolving*
     For so exceeding shone his glistring ray,

That Phoebus golden face it did attaint,°   *sully*
     As when a cloud his beames doth over-lay;
305 And silver Cynthia wexèd pale and faint,
As when her face is staynd with magicke arts constraint.[3]

35

No magicke arts hereof had any might,
     Nor bloudie wordes of bold Enchaunters call,
     But all that was not such, as seemd in sight,
310 Before that shield did fade, and suddeine fall:
     And when him list the raskall routes appall,
     Men into stones therewith he could transmew,°   *transform*
     And stones to dust, and dust to nought at all;
     And when him list the prouder lookes subdew,
315 He would them gazing blind, or turne to other
          hew.°   *shape*

36

Ne let it seeme, that credence this exceedes,
     For he that made the same, was knowne right well
     To have done much more admirable deedes.
     It Merlin was, which whylome did excell
320 All living wightes in might of magicke spell:
     Both shield, and sword, and armour all he wrought
     For this young Prince, when first to armes he
          fell;°   *came*
     But when he dyde, the Faerie Queene it brought
To Faerie lond, where yet it may be seene, if sought.[4]

37

325 A gentle youth, his dearely lovèd Squire
     His speare of heben° wood behind him bare,   *ebony*
     Whose harmefull head, thrice heated in the fire,
     Had riven many a brest with pikehead square;
     A goodly person, and could menage° faire   *manage*
330 His stubborne steed with curbèd canon bit,[5]
     Who under him did trample as the aire,

---

[1] *Selinis* Town in Italy.

[2] *one ... mould* I.e., one solid, unbroken piece of diamond.

[3] *with ... constraint* I.e., by a lunar eclipse, believed by some to be caused by magic.

[4] *But when ... sought* I.e., this knight's armor (and hence his virtues) can still be found in England. From the references to Merlin and the Faerie Queene, it is clear that the unnamed knight is Arthur.

[5] *canon bit* Type of round, smooth bit.

And chauft, that any on his backe should sit;
The yron rowels[1] into frothy fome he bit.

38

When as this knight nigh to the Ladie drew,
335   With lovely° court he gan her entertaine;   *kindly*
   But when he heard her answeres loth,° he knew *reluctant*
   Some secret sorrow did her heart distraine:°   *afflict*
   Which to allay, and calme her storming paine,
   Faire feeling words he wisely gan display,
340   And for her humour fitting purpose° faine,   *manner*
   To tempt the cause it selfe for to bewray;°   *reveal*
Wherewith emmov'd, these bleeding words she gan to
     say.

39

What worlds delight, or joy of living speach
   Can heart, so plung'd in sea of sorrowes deepe,
345   And heapèd with so huge misfortunes, reach?
   The carefull cold beginneth for to creepe,
   And in my heart his yron arrow steepe,
   Soone as I thinke upon my bitter bale:°   *sorrow*
   Such helplesse harmes yts better hidden keepe,
350   Then rip up griefe, where it may not availe,
My last left comfort is, my woes to weepe and waile.

40

Ah Ladie deare, quoth then the gentle knight,
   Well may I weene, your griefe is wondrous great;
   For wondrous great griefe groneth in my spright,
355   Whiles thus I heare you of your sorrowes treat.
   But wofull Ladie let me you intrete,
   For to unfold the anguish of your hart:
   Mishaps are maistred by advice discrete,
   And counsell mittigates the greatest smart;
360   Found never helpe, who never would his hurts impart.

41

O but (quoth she) great griefe will not be tould,
   And can more easily be thought, then said.
   Right so; (quoth he) but he, that never would,
   Could never: will to might gives greatest aid.
365   But griefe (quoth she) does greater grow displaid,
   If then it find not helpe, and breedes despaire.

Despaire breedes not (quoth he) where faith is
   staid.°   *firm*
   No faith so fast (quoth she) but flesh does
   paire.°   *impair*
Flesh may empaire (quoth he) but reason can repaire.

42

His goodly reason, and well guided speach
370   So deepe did settle in her gratious thought,
   That her perswaded to disclose the breach,
   Which love and fortune in her heart had wrought,
   And said; faire Sir, I hope good hap hath brought
   You to inquere the secrets of my griefe,
375   Or that your wisedome will direct my thought,
   Or that your prowesse can me yield reliefe:
Then heare the storie sad, which I shall tell you briefe.

43

The forlorne Maiden, whom your eyes have seene
380   The laughing stocke of fortunes mockeries,
   Am th'only daughter of a King and Queene,
   Whose parents deare, whilest equall destinies
   Did runne about,° and their felicities   *their course*
   The favourable heavens did not envy,
385   Did spread their rule through all the territories,
   Which Phison and Euphrates floweth by,
And Gehons[2] golden waves doe wash continually.

44

Till that their cruell cursèd enemy,
   An huge great Dragon horrible in sight,
390   Bred in the loathly lakes of Tartary,°   *Hell*
   With murdrous ravine,° and devouring might *violence*
   Their kingdome spoild, and countrey wasted quight:
   Themselves, for feare into his jawes to fall,
   He forst to castle strong to take their flight,
395   Where fast embard° in mightie brasen wall, *imprisoned*
He has them now foure yeres besiegd to make them
     thrall.

45

Full many knights adventurous and stout
   Have enterprizd that Monster to subdew;

---

[1] *rowels* Knobs on the ends of a horse's bit.

[2] *Phison ... Gehons* Three of the four rivers of Eden. Thus Una's parents were Adam and Eve, the rulers of Eden.

From every coast that heaven walks about,
400   Have thither come the noble Martiall crew,
That famous hard atchievements still pursew,
Yet never any could that girlond win,
But all still shronke,° and still he greater grew: *cowered*
All they for want of faith, or guilt of sin,
405 The pitteous pray of his fierce crueltie have bin.

46

At last yledd° with farre reported praise,   *led by*
   Which flying fame throughout the world had spred,
   Of doughtie° knights, whom Faery land did raise,   *worthy*
   That noble order hight° of Maidenhed,°   *named / virginity*
410   Forthwith to court of Gloriane I sped,
   Of Gloriane great Queene of glory bright,
   Whose kingdomes seat Cleopolis[1] is red,°   *called*
   There to obtaine some such redoubted knight,
That Parents deare from tyrants powre deliver might.

47

415 It was my chance (my chance was faire and good)
   There for to find a fresh unprovèd knight,
   Whose manly hands imbrew'd in guiltie blood
   Had never bene, ne ever by his might
   Had throwne to ground the unregarded right:
420   Yet of his prowesse proofe he since hath made
   (I witnesse am) in many a cruell fight;
   The groning ghosts of many one dismaide
Have felt the bitter dint of his avenging blade.

48

And ye the forlorne reliques of his powre,
425   His byting sword, and his devouring speare,
   Which have endurèd many a dreadfull stowre,
   Can speake his prowesse, that did earst you beare,
   And well could rule: now he hath left you heare,
   To be the record of his ruefull losse,
430   And of my dolefull disaventurous°
      deare:°   *unfortunate / dear one*
   O heavie record of the good Redcrosse,
Where have you left your Lord, that could so well you
      tosse?°   *wield*

49

Well hopèd I, and faire beginnings had,
   That he my captive° langour should redeeme,   *inescapable*
435   Till all unweeting, an Enchaunter bad
   His sence abusd, and made him to misdeeme
   My loyalty, not such as it did seeme;
   That rather death desire, then such despight.°   *treachery*
   Be judge ye heavens, that all things right esteeme,
440   How I him lov'd, and love with all my might,
So thought I eke of him, and thinke I thought aright.

50

Thenceforth me desolate he quite forsooke,
   To wander, where wilde fortune would me lead,
   And other bywaies he himselfe betooke,
445   Where never foot of living wight did tread,
   That brought not backe the balefull body dead;
   In which him chauncèd false Duessa meete,
   Mine onely foe, mine onely deadly dread,
   Who with her witchcraft and misseeming sweete,
450 Inveigled° him to follow her desires
      unmeete.°   *deceived / inappropriate*

51

At last by subtill sleights she him betraid
   Unto his foe, a Gyant huge and tall,
   Who him disarmèd, dissolute,° dismaid,   *weakened*
   Unwares surprisèd, and with mightie mall°   *mallet*
455   The monster mercilesse him made to fall,
   Whose fall did never foe before behold;
   And now in darkesome dungeon, wretched thrall,
   Remedilesse, for aie° he doth him hold;   *ever*
This is my cause of griefe, more great, then may be told.

52

460 Ere she had ended all, she gan to faint:
   But he her comforted and faire bespake,
   Certes, Madame, ye have great cause of plaint,
   That stoutest heart, I weene, could cause to quake.
   But be of cheare, and comfort to you take:
465   For till I have acquit° your captive knight,   *freed*
   Assure your selfe, I will you not forsake.
   His chearefull words reviv'd her chearelesse spright,
So forth they went, the Dwarfe them guiding ever
      right.

---

1 *Cleopolis* From Greek: famous city.

CANTO 8

Faire virgin to redeeme her deare
Brings Arthur to the fight,
Who slayes the Gyant, wounds the beast,
And strips Duessa quight.

1

A y me, how many perils doe enfold
   The righteous man, to make him daily fall?
Were not, that heavenly grace doth him uphold,
And stedfast truth acquite him out of all.
5 Her love is firme, her care continuall,
So oft as he through his owne foolish pride,
Or weaknesse is to sinfull bands° made thrall: *bonds*
Else should this Redcrosse knight in bands have dyde,
For whose deliverance she this Prince doth thither guide.

2

10 They sadly traveild thus, untill they came
   Nigh to a castle builded strong and hie:
   Then cryde the Dwarfe, lo yonder is the same,
   In which my Lord my liege° doth lucklesse lie,   *master*
   Thrall to that Gyants hatefull tyrannie:
15 Therefore, deare Sir, your mightie powres assay.
   The noble knight alighted by and by
   From loftie steede, and bad the Ladie stay,
To see what end of fight should him befall that day.

3

So with the Squire, th'admirer of his might,
20 He marchèd forth towards that castle wall;
   Whose gates he found fast shut, ne living wight
   To ward° the same, nor answere commers call.   *guard*
   Then tooke that Squire an horne of bugle°   *hunting horn*
     small,
   Which hong adowne his side in twisted gold,
25 And tassels gay. Wyde wonders over all
   Of that same hornes great vertues weren told,
Which had approvèd° bene in uses manifold.   *proven*

4

Was never wight, that heard that shrilling sound,
   But trembling feare did feele in every vaine:
30 Three miles it might be easie heard around,
   And Ecchoes three answerd it selfe againe:

No false enchauntment, nor deceiptfull traine
Might once abide the terror of that blast,
But presently was voide and wholly vaine:
35 No gate so strong, no locke so firme and fast,
But with that percing noise flew open quite, or
   brast.°   *burst*

5

The same before the Geants gate he blew,
   That all the castle quakèd from the ground,
   And every dore of freewill open flew.
40 The Gyant selfe dismaièd with that sownd,
   Where he with his Duessa dalliance°   *amorous toying*
     fownd,
   In hast came rushing forth from inner bowre,
   With staring countenance sterne, as one astownd,
   And staggering steps, to weet, what suddein stowre
45 Had wrought that horror strange, and dar'd his dreaded
     powre.

6

And after him the proud Duessa came,
   High mounted on her manyheaded beast,
   And every head with fyrie tongue did flame,
   And every head was crownèd on his creast,
50 And bloudie mouthèd with late cruell feast.
   That when the knight beheld, his mightie shild
   Upon his manly arme he soone addrest,°   *prepared*
   And at him fiercely flew, with courage fild,
And eger greedinesse° through every member   *readines*
   thrild.

7

55 Therewith the Gyant buckled° him to fight,   *engaged*
   Inflam'd with scornefull wrath and high disdaine,
   And lifting up his dreadfull club on hight,
   All arm'd with ragged snubbes° and knottie   *stumps*
     graine,
   Him thought at first encounter to haue slaine,
60 But wise and warie was that noble Pere,°   *peer*
   And lightly leaping from so monstrous maine,°   *force*
   Did faire avoide the violence him nere;
It booted nought, to thinke, such thunderbolts to
   beare.°   *withstand*

8

Ne shame he thought to shunne so hideous might:
The idle stroke, enforcing furious way,
Missing the marke of his misaymèd sight
Did fall to ground, and with his heavie sway
So deepely dinted in the driven clay,
That three yardes deepe a furrow up did throw:
The sad earth wounded with so sore assay,°   *assault*
Did grone full grievous underneath the blow,
And trembling with strange feare, did like an earthquake
show.

9

As when almightie Jove in wrathfull mood,
To wreake° the guilt of mortall sins is bent,   *punish*
Hurles forth his thundring dart with deadly
food,°   *hatred*
Enrold in flames, and smouldring°
dreriment,°   *suffocating / darknes*
Through riven cloudes and molten firmament;
The fierce threeforkèd engin° making way,   *weapon*
Both loftie towres and highest trees hath rent,
And all that might his angrie passage stay,
And shooting in the earth, casts up a mount of clay.

10

His boystrous° club, so buried in the ground,   *unwieldy*
He could not rearen up againe so light,°   *easily*
But that the knight him at avantage found,
And whiles he strove his combred° clubbe to
quight°   *encumbered / free*
Out of the earth, with blade all burning bright
He smote off his left arme, which like a blocke
Did fall to ground, depriv'd of native might;
Large streames of bloud out of the trunckèd
stocke°   *stump*
Forth gushèd, like fresh water streame from riven rocke.

11

Dismaièd with so desperate deadly wound,
And eke impatient of[1] unwonted paine,
He loudly brayd with beastly yelling sound,
That all the fields rebellowèd againe;
As great a noyse, as when in Cymbrian plaine[2]
An heard of Bulles, whom kindly° rage doth
sting,   *natural*
Do for the milkie mothers want complaine,
And fill the fields with troublous bellowing,
The neighbour woods around with hollow murmur
ring.

12

That when his deare Duessa heard, and saw
The evill stownd,° that daungerd her
estate,°   *peril / condition*
Unto his aide she hastily did draw
Her dreadfull beast, who swolne with bloud of late
Came ramping forth with proud presumpteous gate,
And threatned all his heads like flaming brands.°   *torches*
But him the Squire made quickly to retrate,
Encountring fierce with single sword in hand,
And twixt him and his Lord did like a bulwarke stand.

13

The proud Duessa full of wrathfull spight,
And fierce disdaine, to be affronted so,
Enforst her purple beast with all her might
That stop° out of the way to overthroe,   *obstacle*
Scorning the let° of so unequall foe: *hindrance*
But nathemore° would that courageous
swayne   *never the more*
To her yeeld passage, gainst his Lord to goe,
But with outrageous strokes did him restraine,
And with his bodie bard the way atwixt them twaine.

14

Then tooke the angrie witch her golden cup,
Which still she bore, replete with magick artes;
Death and despeyre did many thereof sup,
And secret poyson through their inner parts,
Th'eternall bale of heavie wounded harts;
Which after charmes and some enchauntments said,
She lightly sprinkled on his weaker° parts;   *too weak*

---

[1] *impatient of* Unable to endure.

[2] *Cymbrian plaine* Jutland, a peninsula comprising Northern Germany and most of Denmark and formerly inhabited by the ancient European tribe the Cimbri.

125   Therewith his sturdie courage soone was
              quayd,°   *quelled*
       And all his senses were with suddeine dread dismayd.

                               15
       So downe he fell before the cruell beast,
           Who on his necke his bloudie clawes did seize,
           That life nigh crusht out of his panting brest:
130   No powre he had to stirre, nor will to rize.
           That when the carefull knight gan well avise,°   *perceived*
           He lightly left the foe, with whom he fought,
           And to the beast gan turne his enterprise;
           For wondrous anguish in his hart it wrought,
135   To see his lovèd Squire into such thraldome brought.

                               16
       And high advauncing his bloud-thirstie blade,
           Stroke one of those deformèd heads so sore,
           That of his puissance proud ensample made;
           His monstrous scalpe downe to his teeth it tore,
140   And that misformèd shape mis-shapèd more:
           A sea of bloud gusht from the gaping wound,
           That her gay garments staynd with filthy gore,
           And overflowèd all the field around;
       That over shoes in bloud he waded on the ground.

                               17
145   Thereat he roarèd for exceeding paine,
           That to have heard, great horror would have bred,
           And scourging th'emptie ayre with his long traine,
           Through great impatience of his grievèd hed
           His gorgeous ryder from her loftie sted
150   Would have cast downe, and trod in durtie myre,
           Had not the Gyant soone her succoured;
           Who all enrag'd with smart and franticke yre,
       Came hurtling in full fierce, and forst the knight retyre.

                               18
       The force, which wont in two to be disperst,
155   In one alone left hand he now unites,
           Which is through rage more strong then both
              were erst;
           With which his hideous club aloft he dites,°   *raises*
           And at his foe with furious rigour smites,
       That strongest Oake might seeme to overthrow.

160   The stroke upon his shield so heavie lites,
           That to the ground it doubleth him full low
       What mortall wight could ever beare so monstrous
           blow?

                               19
       And in his fall his shield, that covered was,
           Did loose his vele° by chaunce, and open flew: *covering*
165   The light whereof, that heavens light did pas,°   *surpass*
           Such blazing brightnesse through the aier threw,
           That eye mote not the same endure to vew.
           Which when the Gyaunt spyde with staring eye,
           He downe let fall his arme, and soft withdrew
170   His weapon huge, that heavèd was on hye
       For to have slaine the man, that on the ground did lye.

                               20
       And eke the fruitfull-headed° beast, amaz'd   *many-headed*
           At flashing beames of that sunshiny shield,
           Became starke blind, and all his senses daz'd,
175   That downe he tumbled on the durtie field,
           And seem'd himselfe as conquerèd to yield.
           Whom when his maistresse proud perceiv'd to fall,
           Whiles yet his feeble feet for faintnesse reeld,
           Unto the Gyant loudly she gan call,
180   O helpe Orgoglio, helpe, or else we perish all.

                               21
       At her so pitteous cry was much amoov'd
           Her champion stout, and for to ayde his frend,°   *lover*
           Againe his wonted angry weapon proov'd:°   *tried*
           But all in vaine: for he has read his end
185   In that bright shield, and all their forces spend
           Themselves in vaine: for since that glauncing°   *gleaming*
              sight,
           He hath no powre to hurt, nor to defend;
           As where th'Almighties lightning brond does light,
       It dimmes the dazèd eyen, and daunts the senses quight.

                               22
190   Whom when the Prince, to battell new addrest,
           And threatning high his dreadfull stroke did see,
           His sparkling blade about his head he blest,°   *brandished*
           And smote off quite his right leg by the knee,
           That downe he tombled; as an agèd tree,

195   High growing on the top of rocky clift,
     Whose hartstrings with keene steele nigh hewen be,
     The mightie trunck halfe rent, with ragged rift°   *split*
   Doth roll adowne the rocks, and fall with fearefull
       drift.°   *force*

23

   Or as a Castle rearèd high and round,
200   By subtile° engins and malitious slight°   *clever / strategy*
     Is underminèd from the lowest ground
     And her foundation forst,° and feebled quight,   *broken*
     At last downe falles, and with her heapèd hight
     Her hastie ruine does more heavie make,
205   And yields it selfe unto the victours might;
     Such was this Gyaunts fall, that seemd to shake
   The stedfast globe of earth, as it for feare did quake.

24

   The knight then lightly leaping to the pray,
210   With mortall steele him smot againe so sore,
     That headlesse his unweldy bodie lay,
     All wallowd in his owne fowle bloudy gore,
     Which flowèd from his wounds in wondrous
       store,°   *plenty*
     But soone as breath out of his breast did pas,
     That huge great body, which the Gyaunt bore,
215   Was vanisht quite, and of that monstrous mas
   Was nothing left, but like an emptie bladder was.

25

   Whose grievous fall, when false Duessa spide,
     Her golden cup she cast unto the ground,
     And crownèd mitre rudely threw aside;
220   Such percing griefe her stubborne hart did wound,
     That she could not endure that dolefull stound,
     But leaving all behind her, fled away:
     The light-foot Squire her quickly turnd around,
     And by hard meanes enforcing her to stay,
225   So brought unto his Lord, as his deservèd pray.

26

   The royall Virgin, which beheld from farre,
     In pensive° plight, and sad perplexitie,   *apprehensive*
     The whole atchievement° of this doubtfull
       warre,   *progress*
     Came running fast to greet his victorie,

230   With sober gladnesse, and myld modestie,
     And with sweet joyous cheare him thus bespake;
     Faire braunch of noblesse, flowre of chevalrie,
     That with your worth the world amazèd make,
     How shall I quite° the paines, ye suffer for my   *requite*
       sake?

27

235 And you fresh bud of vertue springing fast,
     Whom these sad eyes saw nigh unto deaths dore,
     What hath poore Virgin for such perill past,
     Wherewith you to reward? Accept therefore
     My simple selfe, and service evermore;
240   And he that high does sit, and all things see
     With equall eyes, their merites to restore,°   *reward*
     Behold what ye this day have done for mee,
   And what I cannot quite, requite with usuree.°   *interest*

28

   But sith the heavens, and your faire handeling°   *actions*
245   Have made you maister of the field this day,
     Your fortune maister° eke with governing,   *secure*
     And well begun end all so well, I pray,
     Ne let that wicked woman scape away;
     For she it is, that did my Lord bethrall,
250   My dearest Lord, and deepe in dongeon lay,
     Where he his better dayes hath wasted all.
   O heare, how pitèous he to you for ayd does call.

29

   Forthwith he gave in charge unto his Squire,
     That scarlot whore to keepen carefully;
255   Whiles he himselfe with greedie° great desire   *eager*
     Into the Castle entred forcibly,
     Where living creature none he did espye;
     Then gan he lowdly through the house to call:
     But no man car'd to answere to his crye.
260   There raignd a solemne silence over all,
   Nor voice was heard, nor wight was seene in bowre or
       hall.

30

   At last with creeping crooked pace forth came
     An old old man, with beard as white as snow,
     That on a staffe his feeble steps did frame,°   *support*
265   And guide his wearie gate° both too and fro: *steps*

For his eye sight him faile̎d long ygo,
And on his arme a bounch of keyes he bore,
The which unuse̎d rust did overgrow:
Those were the keyes of every inner dore,
270   But he could not them use, but kept them still in store.

31

But very uncouth sight was to behold,
    How he did fashion his untoward° pace,   *awkward*
    For as he forward moov'd his footing old,
    So backward still was turnd his wrincled face,
275   Unlike to men, who ever as they trace,
    Both feet and face one way are wont to lead.
    This was the auncient keeper of that place,
    And foster father of the Gyant dead;
His name Ignaro[1] did his nature right aread.°   *make known*

32

280   His reverend haires and holy gravitie
    The knight much honord, as beseeme̎d well,°   *proper*
    And gently° askt, where all the people bee,   *politely*
    Which in that stately building wont to dwell.
    Who answerd him full soft, he could not tell.
285   Againe he askt, where that same knight was layd,
    Whom great Orgoglio with his puissaunce fell°   *deadly*
    Had made his caytive thrall; againe he sayde,
He could not tell: ne ever other answere made.

33

Then aske̎d he, which way he in might pas:
290   He could not tell, againe he answere̎d.
    Thereat the curteous knight displease̎d was,
    And said, Old sire, it seemes thou hast not red°   *noted*
    How ill it sits with that same silver hed
    In vaine to mocke, or mockt in vaine to bee:
295   But if thou be, as thou art pourtrahe̎d°   *represented*
    With natures pen, in ages grave degree,°   *dignity*
Aread° in graver wise, what I demaund of thee.   *state*

34

His answere likewise was, he could not tell.
    Whose senceless speach, and doted° ignorance   *foolish*
300   When as the noble Prince had marke̎d well,
    He ghest his nature by his countenaunce,
    And calmd his wrath with goodly temperance.

[1] *Ignaro* Ignorance.

Then to him stepping, from his arme did reach
Those keyes, and made himselfe free enterance.
305   Each dore he opened without any breach;°   *breakage*
There was no barre to stop, nor foe him to empeach.

35

There all within full rich arayd he found,
    With royall arras° and resplendent gold.   *tapestries*
    And did with store of every thing abound,
310   That greatest Princes presence° might behold.   *person*
    But all the floore (too filthy to be told)
    With bloud of guiltlesse babes, and innocents trew,
    Which there were slaine, as sheepe out of the fold,
    Defile̎d was, that dreadfull was to vew,
315   And sacred ashes over it was strowe̎d° new.   *scattered*

36

And there beside of marble stone was built
    An Altare,[2] carv'd with cunning imagery,
    On which true Christians bloud was often spilt,
    And holy Martyrs often doen° to dye,°   *put | death*
320   With cruell malice and strong tyranny:
    Whose blessed sprites from underneath the stone
    To God for vengeance cryde continually,
    And with great griefe were often heard to grone,
That hardest heart would bleede, to heare their piteous
        mone.

37

325   Through every rowme he sought, and every bowr,
    But no where could he find that wofull thrall:°   *slave*
    At last he came unto an yron doore,
    That fast was lockt, but key found not at all
    Emongst that bounch, to open it withall;
330   But in the same a little grate was pight,°   *placed*
    Through which he sent his voyce, and lowd did call
    With all his powre, to weet, if living wight
Were house̎d therewithin, whom he enlarge°   *liberate*
        might.

38

Therewith an hollow, dreary, murmuring voyce
335   These piteous plaints and dolours° did resound;   *laments*
    O who is that, which brings me happy choyce°   *chance*

[2] *Altare* See Revelation 6.9–10. The echo reinforces the association of Arthur with Christ.

Of death, that here lye dying every stound,°   *moment*
   Yet live perforce in balefull darkenesse bound?
   For now three Moones have chang'd thrice their
     hew,°   *shape*
340 And have beene thrice hid underneath the ground,
   Since I the heavens chearefull face did vew,
   O welcome thou, that doest of death bring tydings trew.

39

Which when that Champion heard, with percing point
   Of pitty deare his hart was thrill'd sore,
345 And trembling horrour ran through every joynt,
   For ruth of gentle knight so fowle forlore:
   Which shaking off, he rent that yron dore,
   With furious force, and indignation fell;
   Where entred in, his foot could find no flore,
350 But all a deepe descent, as darke as hell,
That breath'd ever forth a filthie banefull°   *poisonous*
   smell.

40

But neither darkenesse fowle, nor filthy bands,°   *bonds*
   Nor noyous° smell his purpose could withhold,   *noxious*
   (Entire affection hateth nicer° hands)   *too fastidious*
355 But that with constant zeale, and courage bold,
   After long paines and labours manifold,
   He found the meanes that Prisoner up to reare;
   Whose feeble thighes, unhable to uphold
   His pin'd° corse, him scarse to light could   *wasted*
     beare,
360 A ruefull spectacle of death and ghastly drere.

41

His sad dull eyes deepe sunck in hollow pits,
   Could not endure th'unwonted sunne to view;
   His bare thin cheekes for want of better bits,°   *sustenance*
   And empty sides deceiv'd° of their dew,°   *deprived / due*
365 Could make a stony hart his hap to rew;
   His rawbone armes, whose mighty brawn'd
     bowrs°   *muscles*
   Were wont to rive steele plates, and helmets hew,
   Were cleane consum'd, and all his vitall powres
Decayd, and all his flesh shronk up like withered flowres.

42

370 Whom when his Lady saw, to him she ran

With hasty joy: to see him made her glad,
   And sad to view his visage pale and wan,
   Who earst in flowres of freshest youth was clad.
   Tho when her well of teares she wasted had,
375 She said, Ah dearest Lord, what evill starre
   On you hath frownd, and pourd his influence bad,
   That of your selfe ye thus berobbèd arre,
And this misseeming hew your manly looks doth marre?

43

But welcome now my Lord, in wele or woe,
380 Whose presence I have lackt too long a day;
   And fie on Fortune mine avow'd foe,
   Whose wrathfull wreakes° them selves   *punishments*
     do now alay.
   And for these wrongs shall treble penaunce pay
   Of treble good: good growes of evils priefe.°   *endured*
385 The chearelesse man, whom sorrow did dismay,
   Had no delight to treaten° of his griefe;   *tell*
His long endurèd famine needed more reliefe.

44

Faire Lady, then said that victorious knight,
   The things, that grievous were to do, or beare,
390 Them to renew,° I wote,° breeds no delight: *relate / know*
   Best musicke breeds delight in loathing eare:
   But th'onely good, that growes of passèd feare,
   Is to be wise, and ware° of like agein.   *wary*
   This dayes ensample hath this lesson deare
395 Deepe written in my heart with yron pen,
That blisse may not abide in state of mortall men.

45

Henceforth sir knight, take to you wonted strength,
   And maister these mishaps with patient might;
   Loe where your foe lyes stretcht in monstrous length,
400 And loe that wicked woman in your sight,
   The roote of all your care, and wretched plight,
   Now in your powre, to let her live, or dye.
   To do her dye (quoth Una) were despight,°   *spiteful*
   And shame t'avenge so weake an enimy;
405 But spoile° her of her scarlot robe, and let her fly.   *strip*

46

So as she bad,° that witch they disaraid,   *ordered*
   And robd of royall robes, and purple pall,

And ornaments that richly were displaid;
  Ne sparèd they to strip her naked all.
410 Then when they had despoild her tire° and   *attire / headdress*
    call,°
  Such as she was, their eyes might her behold,
  That her misshapèd parts did them appall,
  A loathly, wrinckled hag, ill favoured, old,
Whose secret filth good manners biddeth not be told.

47

415 Her craftie head was altogether bald,
  And as in hate of honorable eld,°   *age*
  Was overgrowne with scurfe° and filthy scald;[1]   *scabs*
  Her teeth out of her rotten gummes were feld,°   *fallen*
  And her sowre breath abhominably smeld;
420 Her drièd dugs,° like bladders lacking wind,   *breasts*
  Hong downe, and filthy matter from them
    weld;°   *flowed*
  Her wrizled° skin as rough, as maple rind,°   *wrinkled / bark*
So scabby was, that would have loathd all womankind.

48

  Her neather parts, the shame of all her kind,
425 My chaster Muse for shame doth blush to write;
  But at her rompe she growing had behind
  A foxes taile, with dong all fowly dight;°   *covered*
  And eke her feete most monstrous were in sight;
  For one of them was like an Eagles claw,
430 With griping talaunts armd to greedy fight,
  The other like a Beares uneven° paw: *rough*
More ugly shape yet never living creature saw.

49

  Which when the knights beheld, amazd they were,
  And wondred at so fowle deformèd wight.
435 Such then (said Una) as she seemeth here,
  Such is the face of falshood, such the sight
  Of fowle Duessa, when her borrowed light
  Is laid away, and counterfesaunce° knowne.   *fraud*
  Thus when they had the witch disrobèd quight,
440 And all her filthy feature° open showne,   *form*
They let her goe at will, and wander wayes unknowne.

---

[1] *scald* Disease of the skin that causes scabbing and flaking, usually
on the scalp.

50

  She flying fast from heavens hated face,
  And from the world that her discovered wide,
  Fled to the wastfull° wildernesse apace,   *barren*
445 From living eyes her open shame to hide,
  And lurkt in rocks and caves long unespide.
  But that faire crew of knights, and Una faire
  Did in that castle afterwards abide,
  To rest them selves, and weary powres repaire,
450 Where store they found of all, that dainty was and rare.

CANTO 9

*His loves and lignage Arthur tells
    The knights knit friendly bands:
Sir Trevisan flies from Despayre,
    Whom Redcrosse knight withstands.*

1

O goodly golden chaine, wherewith yfere°   *together*
    The vertues linkèd are in lovely wize:°   *ways*
  And noble minds of yore allyed were,
  In brave poursuit of chevalrous emprize,
5 That none did others safety despize,
  Nor aid envy to him, in need that stands,
  But friendly each did others prayse devize
  How to advaunce with favourable hands,
As this good Prince redeemd the Redcrosse knight
    from bands.

2

  Who when their powres, empaird through labour long,
  With dew repast they had recurèd well,   *refreshed*
  And that weake captive wight now wexèd strong,
  Them list no lenger there at leasure dwell,
  But forward fare, as their adventures fell,
15 But ere they parted, Una faire besought
  That straunger knight his name and nation tell;
  Least so great good, as he for her had wrought,
Should die unknown, & buried be in thanklesse thought.

3

  Faire virgin (said the Prince) ye me require
20 A thing without° the compas of my wit: *beyond*
  For both the lignage and the certain Sire,

From which I sprong, from me are hidden yit.
For all so soone as life did me admit
Into this world, and shewèd heavens light,
25   From mothers pap I taken was unfit:[1]
And streight delivered to a Faery knight,
To be upbrought in gentle thewes° and   *manners*
    martiall might.

4

Unto old Timon[2] he me brought bylive,°   *directly*
Old Timon, who in youthly yeares hath beene
30   In warlike feates th'expertest man alive,
And is the wisest now on earth I weene;
His dwelling is low in a valley greene,
Under the foot of Rauran[3] mossy hore,°   *gray*
From whence the river Dee[4] as silver cleene°   *clear*
35   His tombling billowes rolls with gentle rore:
There all my dayes he traind me up in vertuous lore.

5

Thither the great Magicien Merlin came,
As was his use,° ofttimes to visit me: *habit*
For he had charge my discipline° to frame,   *education*
40   And Tutours nouriture° to oversee.   *upbringing*
Him oft and oft I askt in privitie,
Of what loines and what lignage I did spring:
Whose aunswere bad me still assurèd bee,
That I was sonne and heire unto a king,
45   As time in her just terme the truth to light should bring.

6

Well worthy impe, said then the Lady gent,°   *noble*
And Pupill fit for such a Tutours hand.
But what adventure, or what high intent
Hath brought you hither into Faery land,
50   Aread° Prince Arthur, crowne of Martiall band?   *declare*
Full hard it is (quoth he) to read aright
The course of heavenly cause, or understand
The secret meaning of th'eternall might,

---

[1] *From … unfit* He was taken from his mother's breast before he was weaned.

[2] *Timon* Honor.

[3] *Rauran* Hill in Wales.

[4] *Dee* River that flows along part of the boundary between England and Wales.

That rules mens wayes, and rules the thoughts of
    living wight.

7

55   For whither he through fatall° deepe foresight   *fated*
Me hither sent, for cause to me unghest,
Or that fresh bleeding wound, which day and night
Whilome° doth rancle in my riven brest,   *all the while*
With forcèd fury following his° behest,   *its*
60   Me hither brought by wayes yet never found,
You to have helpt I hold my selfe yet blest.
Ah curteous knight (quoth she) what secret wound
Could ever find, to grieve the gentlest hart on ground?

8

Deare Dame (quoth he) you sleeping sparkes awake,
65   Which troubled once, into huge flames will grow,
Ne ever will their fervent fury slake,
Till living moysture into smoke do flow,
And wasted life do lye in ashes low.
Yet sithens silence lesseneth not my fire,
70   But told it flames, and hidden it does glow,
I will revele, what ye so much desire:
Ah Love, lay downe thy bow, the whiles I may
    respire.°   *breathe*

9

It was in freshest flowre of youthly yeares,
When courage first does creepe in manly chest,
75   Then first the coale of kindly° heat appeares   *natural*
To kindle love in every living brest;
But me had warnd old Timons wise behest,
Those creeping flames by reason to subdew,
Before their rage grew to so great unrest,
80   As miserable lovers use° to rew,   *are used*
Which still wex° old in woe, whiles woe still   *grow*
    wexeth new.

10

That idle name of love, and lovers life,
As losse of time, and vertues enimy
I ever scornd, and joyd to stirre up strife,
85   In middest of their mournfull Tragedy,
Ay wont to laugh, when them I heard to cry,
And blow the fire, which them to ashes brent:°   *burned*
Their God° himselfe, griev'd at my libertie,   *Cupid*

Shot many a dart at me with fiers intent,
90 But I them warded all with wary government.°   *self-discipline*

11

But all in vaine: no fort can be so strong,
  Ne fleshly brest can armèd be so sound,
  But will at last be wonne with battrie long,
  Or unawares at disavantage found;
95 Nothing is sure, that growes on earthly ground:
  And who most trustes in arme of fleshly might,
  And boasts, in beauties chaine not to be bound,
  Doth soonest fall in disaventrous° fight,   *disastrous*
And yeeldes his caytive neck to victours most°
  despight.°   *greatest / malice*

12

100 Ensample make of him your haplesse joy,
  And of my selfe now mated,° as ye see;   *beaten*
  Whose prouder° vaunt° that proud   *too proud / boast*
    avenging boy
  Did soone pluck downe, and curbd my libertie.
  For on a day prickt° forth with jollitie   *spurred*
105 Of looser life, and heat of hardiment,
  Raunging the forest wide on courser free,
  The fields, the floods, the heavens with one consent
Did seeme to laugh on me, and favour mine intent.

13

For-wearied with my sports, I did alight
110 From loftie steed, and downe to sleepe me layd;
  The verdant gras my couch did goodly dight,°   *form*
  And pillow was my helmet faire displayd:
  Whiles every sence the humour[1] sweet embayd,°   *imbued*
  And slombring soft my hart did steale away,
115 Me seemèd, by my side a royall Mayd
  Her daintie limbes full softly down did lay:
So faire a creature yet saw never sunny day.

14

Most goodly glee and lovely blandishment°   *flattery*
  She to me made, and bad me love her deare,
120 For dearely sure her love was to me bent,
  As when just time expirèd° should appeare.   *had expired*
  But whether dreames delude, or true it were,

---

[1] *humour* Dew of sleep.

Was never hart so ravisht with delight,
  Ne living man like words did ever heare,
125 As she to me delivered all that night;
And at her parting said, She Queene of Faeries
  hight.°   *was called*

15

When I awoke, and found her place devoyd,°   *empty*
  And nought but pressèd gras, where she had lyen,
  I sorrowed all so much, as earst I joyd,
130 And washèd all her place with watry eyen.
  From that day forth I lov'd that face divine;
  From that day forth I cast in carefull° mind,   *care-filled*
  To seeke her out with labour, and long tyne,°   *affliction*
  And never vow to rest, till her I find,
135 Nine monethes I seeke in vaine yet ni'll° that   *never will*
  vow unbind.

16

Thus as he spake, his visage wexèd pale,
  And chaunge of hew great passion did bewray;°   *betray*
  Yet still he strove to cloke his inward bale,°   *sorrow*
  And hide the smoke, that did his fire display,
140 Till gentle Una thus to him gan say;
  O happy Queene of Faeries, that hast found
  Mongst many, one that with his prowesse may
  Defend thine honour, and thy foes confound:
True Loves are often sown, but seldom grow on ground.

17

145 Thine, O then, said the gentle Redcrosse knight,
  Next to that Ladies love, shalbe the place,
  O fairest virgin, full of heavenly light,
  Whose wondrous faith, exceeding earthly race,
  Was firmest fixt in mine extremest case,°   *plight*
150 And you, my Lord, the Patrone° of my life,   *protector*
  Of that great Queene may well gaine worthy grace:
  For onely worthy you through prowes priefe°   *proven*
Yf living man mote° worthy be, to be her
  liefe.°   *may / beloved*

18

So diversly discoursing of their loves,
155 The golden Sunne his glistring head gan shew,
  And sad remembraunce now the Prince amoves,
  With fresh desire his voyage to pursew:

Als Una earnd° her traveill to renew.   *yearned*
Then those two knights, fast friendship for to bynd,
60 And love establish each to other trew,
Gave goodly gifts, the signes of gratefull mynd,
And eke as pledges firme, right hands together joynd.

19

Prince Arthur gave a boxe of Diamond sure,°   *true*
Embowd° with gold and gorgeous ornament,   *wrapped*
65 Wherein were closd few drops of liquor pure,
Of wondrous worth, and vertue excellent,
That any wound could heale incontinent:°   *immediately*
Which to requite, the Redcrosse knight him gave
A booke, wherein his Saveours testament
70 Was writ with golden letters rich and brave;°   *handsome*
A worke of wondrous grace, and able soules to save.

20

Thus beene they parted, Arthur on his way
To seeke his love, and th'other for to fight
With Unaes foe, that all her realme did pray.°   *plunder*
75 But she now weighing the decayèd plight,
And shrunken synewes of her chosen knight,
Would not a while her forward course pursew,
Ne bring him forth in face of dreadfull fight,
Till he recovered had his former hew:
80 For him to be yet weake and wearie well she knew.

21

So as they traveild, lo they gan espy
An armèd knight towards them gallop fast,
That seemèd from some fearèd foe to fly,
Or other griesly thing, that him agast.
85 Still as he fled, his eye was backward cast,
As if his feare still followed him behind;
Als flew his steed, as he his bands had brast,°   *burst*
And with his wingèd heeles did tread the wind,
As he had beene a fole° of Pegasus his kind.   *foal*

22

90 Nigh as he drew, they might perceive his head
To be unarmd, and curld uncombèd heares
Upstaring stiffe, dismayd with uncouth° dread;   *unknown*
Nor drop of bloud in all his face appeares
Nor life in limbe: and to increase his feares,
95 In fowle reproch° of knighthoods faire degree,   *disgrace*

About his neck an hempen rope he weares,
That with his glistring armes does ill agree;
But he of rope or armes has now no memoree.

23

The Redcrosse knight toward him crossed fast,
200 To weet, what mister° wight was so dismayd: *sort of*
There him he finds all sencelesse and aghast,
That of him selfe he seemd to be afrayd;
Whom hardly he from flying forward stayd,
Till he these wordes to him deliver might;
205 Sir knight, aread who hath ye thus arayd,°   *afflicted*
And eke from whom make ye this hasty flight:
For never knight I saw in such misseeming°   *unseemly*
   plight.

24

He answerd nought at all, but adding new
Feare to his first amazment, staring wide
210 With stony° eyes, and hartlesse hollow hew,   *staring*
Astonisht stood, as one that had aspide
Infernall furies, with their chaines untide.
Him yet againe, and yet againe bespake
The gentle knight; who nought to him replide,
215 But trembling every joynt did inly quake,
And foltring tongue at last these words seemd forth to
   shake.

25

For Gods deare love, Sir knight, do me not stay;
For loe he comes, he comes fast after mee.
Eft° looking backe would faine have runne away;   *again*
220 But he him forst to stay, and tellen free
The secret cause of his perplexitie:°   *anxiety*
Yet nathemore° by his bold hartie speach,   *not at all*
Could his bloud-frosen hart emboldned bee,
But through his boldnesse rather feare did reach,
225 Yet forst, at last he made through silence suddein breach.

26

And am I now in safetie sure (quoth he)
From him, that would have forcèd me to dye?
And is the point of death now turnd fro mee,
That I may tell this haplesse history?
230 Feare nought: (quoth he) no daunger now is nye.
Then shall I you recount a ruefull cace,°   *occurrence*

(Said he) the which with this unlucky eye
   I late beheld, and had not greater grace
Me reft from it, had bene partaker of the place.

27

235 I lately chaunst (Would I had never chaunst)
   With a faire knight to keepen companee,
   Sir Terwin hight,° that well himselfe advaunst   *called*
   In all affaires, and was both bold and free,
   But not so happie as mote happie bee:
240   He lov'd, as was his lot, a Ladie gent,
   That him againe lov'd in the least degree:[1]
   For she was proud, and of too high intent,
And joyd to see her lover languish and lament.

28

From whom returning sad and comfortlesse,
245   As on the way together we did fare,
   We met that villen (God from him me blesse°)   *protect*
   That cursèd wight, from whom I scapt whyleare,°   *earlier*
   A man of hell, that cals himselfe Despaire:
   Who first us greets, and after faire areedes°   *relates*
250   Of tydings strange, and of adventures rare:
   So creeping close, as Snake in hidden weedes,
Inquireth of our states, and of our knightly deedes.

29

Which when he knew, and felt our feeble harts
   Embost° with bale, and bitter byting griefe,   *fatigued*
255   Which love had launchèd° with his deadly   *penetrated*
     darts,
   With wounding words and termes of foule repriefe
   He pluckt from us all hope of due reliefe,
   That earst° us held in love of lingring life;°   *first*
   Then hopelesse hartlesse, gan the cunning thiefe
260   Perswade us die, to stint° all further strife: *cease*
To me he lent this rope, to him a rustie knife.

30

With which sad instrument of hastie death,
   That wofull lover, loathing lenger light,
   A wide way made to let forth living breath.
265   But I more fearefull, or more luckie wight,
   Dismayd with that deformèd dismall sight,

Fled fast away, halfe dead with dying feare:°   *fear of*
   Ne yet assur'd of life by you, Sir knight,
   Whose like infirmitie like chaunce may beare:
270 But God you never let his charmèd speeches heare.

31

How may a man (said he) with idle speach
   Be wonne, to spoyle the Castle of his health?
   I wote (quoth he) whom triall late did teach,
   That like would not for all this worldes wealth:
275   His subtill tongue, like dropping honny, mealt'th°   *melts*
   Into the hart, and searcheth every vaine,
   That ere one be aware, by secret stealth
   His powre is reft, and weaknesse doth remaine.
O never Sir desire to try° his guilefull traine.°   *test / deceit*

32

280 Certes° (said he) hence shall I never rest,   *certainly*
   Till I that treachours art have heard and tride;
   And you Sir knight, whose name mote I request,
   Of grace° do me unto his cabin° guide.   *a favor / cave*
   I that hight Trevisan (quoth he) will ride
285   Against my liking backe, to doe you grace:
   But nor for gold nor glee° will I abide   *song*
   By you, when ye arrive in that same place;
For lever° had I die, then see his deadly face.   *rather*

33

Ere long they come, where that same wicked wight
290   His dwelling has, low in an hollow cave,
   Farre underneath a craggie clift ypight,°   *placed*
   Darke, dolefull, drearie, like a greedie grave,
   That still for carrion carcases doth crave:
   On top whereof aye° dwelt the ghastly Owle,[2]   *ever*
295   Shrieking his balefull note, which ever drave
   Farre from that haunt all other chearefull fowle;
And all about it wandring ghostes did waile and howle.

34

And all about old stockes° and stubs of trees,   *stumps*
   Whereon nor fruit, nor leafe was ever seene,
300   Did hang upon the ragged rocky knees;°   *crags*
   On which had many wretches hangèd beene,
   Whose carcases were scattered on the greene,

---

[1] *That him … degree*   I.e., did not return his love.

[2] *Owle*   Owls were believed to bring tidings of death.

And throwne about the cliffs. Arrivèd there,
　　That bare-head knight for dread and dolefull
　　　teene,°　　　　　　　　　　　　　　　　　　　*suffering*
305　Would faine have fled, ne durst approchen neare,
　　But th'other forst him stay, and comforted in feare.

35

That darkesome cave they enter, where they find
　　That cursèd man, low sitting on the ground,
　　Musing full sadly in his sullein mind;
310　His griesie° lockes, long growen, and unbound,　　*grizzled*
　　Disordred hong about his shoulders round,
　　And hid his face; through which his hollow eyne
　　Lookt deadly dull, and starèd as astound;
　　His raw-bone cheekes through penurie° and
　　　pine,°　　　　　　　　　　　　　　　*poverty / starvation*
315　Were shronke into his jawes, as he did never dine.

36

His garment nought but many ragged clouts,°　　*rags*
　　With thornes together pind and patchèd was,
　　The which his naked sides he wrapt abouts;
　　And him beside there lay upon the gras
320　A drearie corse, whose life away did pas,
　　All wallowd in his owne yet luke-warme blood,
　　That from his wound yet wellèd fresh alas;
　　In which a rustie knife fast fixèd stood,
　　And made an open passage for the gushing flood.

37

325　Which piteous spectacle, approving° trew　　*proving*
　　The wofull tale that Trevisan had told,
　　When as the gentle Redcrosse knight did vew,
　　With firie zeale he burnt in courage bold,
　　Him to avenge, before his bloud were cold,
330　And to the villein said, Thou damnèd wight,
　　The author of this fact,° we here behold,　　*act*
　　What justice can but judge against thee right,
　　With thine owne bloud to price° his bloud,　　*pay for*
　　　here shed in sight.

38

What franticke fit (quoth he) hath thus distraught
335　Thee, foolish man, so rash a doome to give?
　　What justice ever other judgement taught,
　　But he should die, who merites not to live?

None else to death this man despayring drive,°　　*drove*
　　But his owne guiltie mind deserving death.
340　Is then unjust to each his due to give?
　　Or let him die, that loatheth living breath?
　　Or let him die at ease, that liveth here uneath?°　　*with difficulty*

39

Who travels by the wearie wandring way,
　　To come unto his wishèd home in haste,
345　And meetes a flood, that doth his passage stay,
　　Is not great grace to helpe him over past,
　　Or free his feet, that in the myre sticke fast?
　　Most envious man, that grieves at neighbours good,
　　And fond,° that joyest in the woe thou hast,　　*foolish*
350　Why wilt not let him passe, that long hath stood
Upon the banke, yet wilt thy selfe not passe the flood?

40

He there does now enjoy eternall rest
　　And happie ease, which thou doest want and crave,
　　And further from it daily wanderest:
355　What if some litle paine the passage have,
　　That makes fraile flesh to feare the bitter wave?
　　Is not short paine well borne, that brings long ease,
　　And layes the soule to sleepe in quiet grave?
　　Sleepe after toyle, port after stormie seas,
360　Ease after warre, death after life does greatly please.

41

The knight much wondred at his suddeine wit,°　　*intelligence*
　　And said, The terme of life is limited,
　　Ne may a man prolong, nor shorten it;
　　The souldier may not move from watchfull sted,
365　Nor leave his stand, untill his Captaine bed.°　　*bid*
　　Who life did limit by almightie doome,
　　(Quoth he) knowes best the termes establishèd;
　　And he, that points the Centonell his roome,°　　*position*
　　Doth license him depart at sound of morning
　　　droome.°　　　　　　　　　　　　　　　　*drum*

42

370　Is not his deed, what ever thing is donne,
　　In heaven and earth? did not he all create
　　To die againe? all ends that was begonne.
　　Their times in his eternall booke of fate
　　Are written sure, and have their certaine date.

375 Who then can strive with strong necessitie,
    That holds the world in his still chaunging state,
    Or shunne the death ordaynd by destinie?
When houre of death is come, let none aske whence,
      nor why.

43

The lenger life, I wote the greater sin,
380   The greater sin, the greater punishment:
    All those great battels, which thou boasts to win,
    Through strife, and bloud-shed, and avengement,
    Now praysd, hereafter deare thou shalt repent:
    For life must life, and bloud must bloud repay.
385   Is not enough thy evill life forespent?°   *spent previously*
    For he, that once hath missed the right way,
The further he doth goe, the further he doth stray.

44

Then do no further goe, no further stray,
    But here lie downe, and to thy rest betake,
390   Th’ill to prevent, that life ensewen may.
    For what hath life, that may it lovèd make,
    And gives not rather cause it to forsake?
    Feare, sicknesse, age, losse, labour, sorrow, strife,
    Paine, hunger, cold, that makes the hart to quake;
395   And ever fickle fortune rageth rife,
All which, and thousands mo° do make a   *more*
      loathsome life.

45

Thou wretched man, of death hast greatest need,
    If in true ballance thou wilt weigh thy state:
    For never knight, that darèd warlike deede,
400   More lucklesse disaventures° did
      amate:°   *misfortunes / dismay*
    Witnesse the dongeon deepe, wherein of late
    Thy life shut up, for death so oft did call;
    And though good lucke prolongèd hath thy date,
    Yet death then, would the like mishaps forestall,
405 Into the which hereafter thou maiest happen fall.

46

Why then doest thou, O man of sin, desire
    To draw thy dayes forth to their last degree?
    Is not the measure of thy sinfull hire°   *work*
    High heapèd up with huge iniquitie,°   *sin*

410 Against the day of wrath,[1] to burden thee?
    Is not enough, that to this Ladie milde
    Thou falsèd° hast thy faith with perjurie,   *betrayed*
    And sold thy selfe to serve Duessa vilde,°   *vile*
With whom in all abuse thou hast thy selfe defilde?

47

415 Is not he just, that all this doth behold
    From highest heaven, and beares an equall° eye?   *impartial*
    Shall he thy sins up in his knowledge fold,
    And guiltie be of thine impietie?
    Is not his law, Let every sinner die:
420   Die shall all flesh? what then must needs be donne,
    Is it not better to doe willinglie,
    Then linger, till the glasse be all out ronne?
Death is the end of woes: die soone, O faeries sonne.

48

The knight was much enmovèd with his speach,
425   That as a swords point through his hart did perse,
    And in his conscience made a secret breach,
    Well knowing true all, that he did reherse,°   *recount*
    And to his fresh remembrance did reverse°   *recall*
    The ugly vew of his deformèd crimes,
430   That all his manly powres it did disperse,
    As° he were charmèd with inchaunted rimes,   *as if*
That oftentimes he quakt, and fainted oftentimes.

49

In which amazement, when the Miscreant
    Perceivèd him to waver weake and fraile,
435   Whiles trembling horror did his conscience dant,°   *daunt*
    And hellish anguish did his soule assaile,
    To drive him to despaire, and quite to quaile,
    He shew’d him painted in a table° plaine,   *picture*
    The damnèd ghosts, that doe in torments waile,
440   And thousand feends that doe them endlesse paine
With fire and brimstone, which for ever shall remaine.

50

The sight whereof so throughly him dismaid,
    That nought but death before his eyes he saw,
    And ever burning wrath before him laid,
445   By righteous sentence of th’Almighties law:

---

[1] *day of wrath* Judgment Day.

Then gan the villein him to overcraw,°   *overpower*
  And brought unto him swords, ropes, poison, fire,
  And all that might him to perdition draw;
  And bad him choose, what death he would desire:
450 For death was due to him, that had provokt Gods ire.

51

But when as none of them he saw him take,
  He to him raught° a dagger sharpe and keene,   *reached*
  And gave it him in hand: his hand did quake,
  And tremble like a leafe of Aspin greene,
455 And troubled bloud through his pale face was seene
  To come, and goe with tydings from the hart,
  As it a running messenger had beene.
  At last resolv'd to worke his finall smart,
He lifted up his hand, that backe againe did start.

52

460 Which when as Una saw, through every vaine
  The crudled° cold ran to her well of life,[1]   *curdled*
  As in a swowne: but soone reliv'd° againe,   *revived*
  Out of his hand she snatcht the cursèd knife,
  And threw it to the ground, enragèd rife,°   *deeply*
465 And to him said, Fie, fie, faint harted knight,
  What meanest thou by this reprochfull strife?
  Is this the battell, which thou vauntst to fight
With that fire-mouthèd Dragon, horrible and bright?

53

Come, come away, fraile, seely, fleshly wight,
470 Ne let vaine words bewitch thy manly hart,
  Ne divelish thoughts dismay thy constant spright.
  In heavenly mercies hast thou not a part?
  Why shouldst thou then despeire, that chosen art?
  Where justice growes, there grows eke greater grace,
475 The which doth quench the brond of hellish smart,
  And that accurst hand-writing doth deface,
Arise, Sir knight arise, and leave this cursèd place.

54

So up he rose, and thence amounted° streight.   *mounted*
  Which when the carle° beheld, and saw his guest   *villain*
480 Would safe depart, for° all his subtill sleight,   *in spite of*
  He chose an halter from among the rest,

---

[1] *well of life* Heart.

And with it hung himselfe, unbid° unblest.   *unprayed for*
  But death he could not worke himselfe thereby;
  For thousand times he so himselfe had drest,°   *prepared*
485 Yet nathelesse it could not doe° him die,   *make*
Till he should die his last, that is eternally.

CANTO 10

Her faithfull knight faire Una brings
    To house of Holinesse,
Where he is taught repentance, and
    The way to heavenly blesse.

1

What man is he, that boasts of fleshly might,
  And vaine assurance of mortality,
  Which all so soone, as it doth come to fight,
  Against spirituall foes, yeelds by and by,
5 Or from the field most cowardly doth fly?
  Ne let the man ascribe it to his skill,
  That thorough grace hath gainèd victory.
  If any strength we have, it is to ill,
But all the good is Gods, both power and eke will.

2

By that, which lately hapned, Una saw,
10 That this her knight was feeble, and too faint;
  And all his sinews woxen° weake and
    raw,°   *grown / inexperienced*
  Through long enprisonment, and hard
    constraint,°   *misfortune*
  Which he endurèd in his late restraint,
15 That yet he was unfit for bloudie fight:
  Therefore to cherish° him with diets daint,   *nourish / choice*
  She cast to bring him, where he chearen° might,   *be cheered*
Till he recouered had his° late decayèd plight.   *from his*

3

There was an auntient house not farre away,
20 Renowmd throughout the world for sacred lore,°   *wisdom*
  And pure unspotted life: so well they say
  It governd was, and guided evermore,
  Through wisedome of a matrone grave and
    hore;°   *venerable*
  Whose onely joy was to relieve the needes

25 Of wretched soules, and helpe the helpelesse pore:
　　All night she spent in bidding of her bedes,°　　　*beads*
　　And all the day in doing good and godly deedes.

4

　　Dame Cælia[1] men did her call, as thought
　　　　From heaven to come, or thither to arise,
30　　The mother of three daughters, well upbrought
　　　　In goodly thewes, and godly exercise:
　　　　The eldest two most sober, chast, and wise,
　　　　Fidelia and Speranza[2] virgins were,
　　　　Though spousd,° yet wanting wedlocks
　　　　　solemnize;　　　　　　　　　　*engaged*
35　　But faire Charissa[3] to a lovely° fere°　*loving / spouse*
　　Was linckèd, and by him had many
　　　　pledges° dere.　　　　　　　　*children*

5

　　Arrivèd there, the dore they find fast lockt;
　　　　For it was warely watchèd night and day,
　　　　For feare of many foes: but when they knockt,
40　　The Porter opened unto them streight way:
　　　　He was an agèd syre, all hory gray,
　　　　With lookes full lowly cast, and gate° full slow,　*gait*
　　　　Wont on a staffe his feeble steps to stay,
　　　　Hight Humilta.[4] They passe in stouping low;
45　　For streight & narrow was the way, which he did show.

6

　　Each goodly thing is hardest to begin,
　　　　But entred in a spacious court they see,
　　　　Both plaine, and pleasant to be walkèd in,
　　　　Where them does meete a francklin[5] faire and free,
50　　And entertaines with comely° courteous glee,　*appropriate*
　　　　His name was Zele,[6] that him right well became,
　　　　For in his speeches and behaviour hee
　　　　Did labour lively to expresse the same,
　　And gladly did them guide, till to the Hall they came.

1　*Cælia* Heavenly.
2　*Fidelia and Speranza* Faith and Hope.
3　*Charissa* Charity.
4　*Humilta* Humility.
5　*francklin* I.e., franklin; freeholder, one who owns his own land.
6　*Zele* Zeal.

7

There fairely them receives a gentle Squire,
　　Of milde demeanure, and rare courtesie,
　　Right cleanly clad in comely sad° attire;　　　*sober*
　　In word and deede that shew'd great modestie,
　　And knew his good° to all of each　*proper courtesy / rank*
　　　degree,
60　Hight Reverence. He them with speeches meet
　　Does faire entreat; no courting° nicetie,°　*courtly / flattery*
　　But simple true, and eke unfainèd sweet,
As might become a Squire so great persons to greet.

8

And afterwards them to his Dame he leades,
　　That agèd Dame, the Ladie of the place:
65　Who all this while was busie at her beades:
　　Which doen, she up arose with seemely grace,
　　And toward them full matronely did pace.
　　Where when that fairest Una she beheld,
70　Whom well she knew to spring from heavenly race,
　　Her hart with joy unwonted° inly sweld,　*unaccustomed*
As feeling wondrous comfort in her weaker eld.

9

And her embracing said, O happie earth,
　　Whereon thy innocent feet doe ever tread,
75　Most vertuous virgin borne of heavenly berth,
　　That to redeeme thy woefull parents head,
　　From tyrans rage, and ever-dying dread,[7]
　　Hast wandred through the world now long a day;
　　Yet ceasest not thy wearie soles to lead,
80　What grace hath thee now hither brought this way?
Or doen thy feeble feet unweeting hither stray?

10

Strange thing it is an errant knight to see
　　Here in this place, or any other wight,
　　That hither turnes his steps. So few there bee,
85　That chose the narrow path, or seeke the right:
　　All keepe the broad high way, and take delight
　　With many rather for to go astray,
　　And be partakers of their evill plight,
　　Then with a few to walke the rightest way;
90　O foolish men, why haste ye to your owne decay?

7　*ever-dying dread* Ever-present fear of death.

11

Thy selfe to see, and tyred limbs to rest,
　O matrone sage (quoth she) I hither came,
　And this good knight his way with me addrest,
　Led with thy prayses and broad-blazèd fame,
95　That up to heaven is blowne. The auncient Dame
　Him goodly greeted in her modest guise,
　And entertaynd them both, as best became,
　With all the court'sies, that she could devise.
Ne wanted ought, to shew her bounteous° or wise.　*generous*

12

100　Thus as they gan of sundry things devise,°　*discuss*
　Loe two most goodly virgins came in place,
　Ylinkèd arme in arme in lovely° wise,°　*loving / manner*
　With countenance demure, and modest grace,
　They numberd even steps and equall pace:
105　Of which the eldest, that Fidelia hight,
　Like sunny beames threw from her Christall face,
　That could have dazd the rash beholders sight,
And round about her head did shine like heavens light.

13

110　She was araièd all in lilly white,
　And in her right hand bore a cup of gold,
　With wine and water fild up to the hight,
　In which a Serpent did himselfe enfold,[1]
　That horrour made to all, that did behold;
115　But she no whit did chaunge her constant mood:
　And in her other hand she fast did hold
　A booke, that was both signd and seald with blood,
Wherein darke things were writ, hard to be understood.[2]

14

Her younger sister, that Speranza hight,
120　Was clad in blew, that her beseemèd well;
　Not all so chearefull seemèd she of sight,
　As was her sister; whether dread° did dwell,　*fear*
　Or anguish in her hart, is hard to tell:
　Upon her arme a silver anchor[3] lay,

Whereon she leanèd ever, as befell:°　*was appropriate*
125　And ever up to heaven, as she did pray,
Her stedfast eyes were bent, ne swarvèd other way.

15

They seeing Una, towards her gan wend,°　*proceed*
　Who them encounters with like courtesie;
　Many kind speeches they betwene them spend,
130　And greatly joy each other well to see:
　Then to the knight with shamefast° modestie　*humble*
　They turne themselves, at Unáes meeke request,
　And him salute with well beseeming glee:
　Who faire them quites,° as him beseemèd best,　*returns*
135 And goodly gan discourse of many a noble gest.°　*deed*

16

Then Una thus; But she your sister deare;
　The deare Charissa where is she become?
　Or wants she health, or busie is elsewhere?
　Ah no, said they, but forth she may not come:
140　For she of late is lightned of her wombe,
　And hath encreast the world with one sonne more,
　That her to see should be but troublesome.
　Indeede (quoth she) that should her trouble sore,
But thankt be God, and her encrease so evermore.

17

145 Then said the agèd Caelia, Deare dame,
　And you good Sir, I wote that of your toyle,
　And labours long, through which ye hither came,
　Ye both forwearied be: therefore a whyle
　I read° you rest, and to your bowres recoyle.°　*advise / retire*
150　Then called she a Groome, that forth him led
　Into a goodly lodge, and gan despoile°　*undress*
　Of puissant armes, and laid in easie bed;
His name was meeke Obedience rightfully arèd.　*understood*

18

Now when their wearie limbes with kindly rest,
155　And bodies were refresht with due repast,
　Faire Una gan Fidelia faire request,
　To have her knight into her schoolehouse plaste,
　That of her heauenly learning he might taste,
　And heare the wisedome of her words divine.
160　She graunted, and that knight so much agraste,°　*favored*

---

[1] *cup ... enfold*　The cup of wine and water is the sacrament of Holy Communion, and the serpent is an ancient symbol of renewal and rebirth.

[2] *A booke ... understood*　The New Testament.

[3] *silver anchor*　Symbol of hope.

That she him taught celestiall discipline,
And opened his dull eyes, that light mote in them shine.

19

And that her sacred Booke, with bloud ywrit,
   That none could read, except she did them teach,
165 She unto him disclosèd every whit,
   And heavenly documents° thereout did preach,   *doctrines*
   That weaker wit of man could never reach,
   Of God, of grace, of justice, of free will,
   That wonder was to heare her goodly speach:
170 For she was able, with her words to kill,
And raise againe to life the hart, that she did thrill.°   *pierce*

20

And when she list° poure out her larger°   *desired to | greater*
   spright,
   She would commaund the hastie Sunne to stay,
   Or backward turne his course from heavens hight;
175 Sometimes great hostes of men she could dismay,
   Dry-shod to passe, she parts the flouds in tway;
   And eke huge mountaines from their native seat
   She would commaund, themselves to beare away,
   And throw in raging sea with roaring threat.
180 Almightie God her gave such powre, and puissance
   great.

21

The faithfull knight now grew in litle space,
   By hearing her, and by her sisters lore,
   To such perfection of all heavenly grace,
   That wretched world he gan for to abhore,
185 And mortall life gan loath, as thing forlore,°   *confounded*
   Greev'd with remembrance of his wicked wayes,
   And prickt with anguish of his sinnes so sore,
   That he desirde to end his wretched dayes:
So much the dart of sinfull guilt the soule dismayes.

22

190 But wise Speranza gave him comfort sweet,
   And taught him how to take assurèd hold
   Upon her silver anchor, as was meet;
   Else had his sinnes so great, and manifold
   Made him forget all that Fidelia told.
195 In this distressèd doubtfull agonie,
   When him his dearest Una did behold,

Disdeining life, desiring leave° to die,   *permission*
She found her selfe assayld with great perplexitie.

23

And came to Caelia to declare her smart,
200 Who well acquainted with that commune plight,
   Which sinfull horror workes in wounded hart,
   Her wisely comforted all that she might,
   With goodly counsell and advisement right;
   And streightway sent with carefull diligence,
205 To fetch a Leach, the which had great insight
   In that disease of grievèd conscience,
And well could cure the same; His name was Patience.

24

Who comming to that soule-diseasèd knight,
   Could hardly him intreat, to tell his griefe:
210 Which knowne, and all that noyd° his heavie
   spright   *troubled*
   Well searcht,° eftsoones he gan apply reliefe   *examined*
   Of salves and med'cines, which had passing°   *superior*
   priefe,
   And thereto added words of wondrous might:
   By which to ease he him recurèd° briefe,°   *cured | quickly*
215 And much asswag'd the passion° of his plight,   *suffering*
That he his paine endur'd, as seeming now more light.

25

But yet the cause and root of all his ill,
   Inward corruption, and infected sin,
   Not purg'd nor heald, behind remainèd still,
220 And festring sore did rankle yet within,
   Close creeping twixt the marrow and the skin.
   Which to extirpe,° he laid him privily   *remove*
   Downe in a darkesome lowly place farre in,
   Whereas he meant his corrosives to apply,
225 And with streight° diet tame his stubborne malady.   *strict*

26

In ashes and sackcloth he did array
   His daintie corse, proud humors to abate,
   And dieted with fasting every day,
   The swelling of his wounds to mitigate,
230 And made him pray both earely and eke late:
   And ever as superfluous flesh did rot
   Amendment readie still at hand did wayt,

To pluck it out with pincers firie whot,°   *hot*
That soone in him was left no one corrupted jot.

27

235 And bitter Penance with an yron whip,
     Was wont him once to disple° every day: *discipline*
     And sharpe Remorse his hart did pricke and nip,
     That drops of bloud thence like a well did play;
     And sad Repentance usèd to embay°   *bathe*
240   His bodie in salt water smarting sore,
     The filthy blots of sinne to wash away.
So in short space they did to health restore
    The man that would not live, but earst° lay at   *now*
      deathes dore.

28

In which his torment often was so great,
245   That like a Lyon he would cry and rore,
     And rend his flesh, and his owne synewes eat.
     His owne deare Una hearing evermore
     His ruefull shriekes and gronings, often tore
     Her guiltlesse garments, and her golden heare,
250   For pitty of his paine and anguish sore;
     Yet all with patience wisely she did beare;
For well she wist, his crime could else be never cleare.

29

Whom thus recover'd by wise Patience,
    And trew Repentance they to Una brought:
255   Who joyous of his curèd conscience,
     Him dearely kist, and fairely° eke besought   *courteously*
     Himselfe to chearish, and consuming thought
     To put away out of his carefull brest.
     By this° Charissa, late in child-bed brought,   *this time*
260   Was woxen strong, and left her fruitfull nest;
To her faire Una brought this unacquainted guest.

30

She was a woman in her freshest age,
    Of wondrous beauty, and of bountie rare,
     With goodly grace and comely personage,
265   That was on earth not easie to compare;
     Full of great love, but Cupids wanton snare
     As hell she hated, chast in worke and will;
     Her necke and breasts were ever open bare,
     That ay thereof her babes might sucke their fill;
270 The rest was all in yellow robes arayèd still.

31

A multitude of babes about her hong,
    Playing their sports, that joyd her to behold,
     Whom still she fed, whiles they were weake & young,
     But thrust them forth still, as they wexèd old:
275   And on her head she wore a tyre° of gold,   *headdress*
     Adornd with gemmes and owches wondrous faire,
     Whose passing° price° uneath°   *surpassing / value / scarcely*
      was to be told;
     And by her side there sate a gentle paire
Of turtle doves, she sitting in an yvorie chaire.

32

280 The knight and Una entring, faire her greet,
     And bid her joy of that her happie brood;
     Who them requites with court'sies seeming meet,
     And entertaines with friendly chearefull mood.
     Then Una her besought, to be so good,
285   As in her vertuous rules to schoole her knight,
     Now after all his torment well withstood,
     In that sad house of Penaunce, where his spright
Had past the paines of hell, and long enduring night.

33

She was right joyous of her just request,
290   And taking by the hand that Faeries sonne,
     Gan him instruct in every good behest,
     Of love, and righteousnesse, and well to donne,[1]
     And wrath, and hatred warely to shonne,
     That drew on men Gods hatred, and his wrath,
295   And many soules in dolours had fordonne:°   *overcome*
     In which when him she well instructed hath,
From thence to heaven she teacheth him the
      ready° path.   *direct*

34

Wherein his weaker wandring steps to guide,
    An auncient matrone she to her does call,
300   Whose sober lookes her wisedome well descride:°   *revealed*
     Her name was Mercie, well knowne over all,
     To be both gratious, and eke liberall:
     To whom the carefull charge of him she gave,
     To lead aright, that he should never fall

---

1 *well to donne* Good deeds.

305 In all his wayes through this wide worldès
wave,°   *changing conditions*
That Mercy in the end his righteous soule might save.

35

The godly Matrone by the hand him beares°   *leads*
Forth from her presence, by a narrow way,
Scattred with bushy thornes, and ragged breares,°   *briars*
310 Which still before him she remov'd away,
That nothing might his ready passage stay:
And ever when his feet encombred were,
Or gan to shrinke, or from the right to stray,
She held him fast, and firmely did upbeare,
315 As carefull Nourse her child from falling oft does reare.

36

Eftsoones unto an holy Hospitall,°   *hostel*
That was fore° by the way, she did him bring,   *close*
In which seven Bead-men[1] that had vowèd all
Their life to service of high heavens king
320 Did spend their dayes in doing godly thing:
Their gates to all were open evermore,
That by the wearie way were travelling,
And one sate wayting ever them before,
To call in-commers by, that needy were and pore.

37

325 The first of them that eldest was, and best,°   *foremost*
Of all the house had charge and governement,
As Guardian and Steward of the rest:
His office was to give entertainement
And lodging, unto all that came, and went:
330 Not unto such, as could him feast againe,°   *in return*
And double quite,° for that he on them spent,   *repay*
But such, as want of harbour° did constraine: *shelter*
Those for Gods sake his dewty was to entertaine.

38

The second was as Almner[2] of the place,
335 His office was, the hungry for to feed,
And thristy give to drinke, a worke of grace:
He feard not once him selfe to be in need,

Ne car'd to hoord for those, whom he did breede:
The grace of God he layd up still in store,
340 Which as a stocke° he left unto his
seede;°   *inheritance / children*
He had enough, what need him care for more?
And had he lesse, yet some he would give to the pore.

39

The third had of their wardrobe custodie,
In which were not rich tyres,° nor garments gay,   *attire*
345 The plumes of pride, and wings of vanitie,
But clothes meet to keepe keene could° away,   *cold*
And naked nature seemely° to aray;   *appropriately*
With which bare wretched wights he dayly clad,
The images of God in earthly clay;
350 And if that no spare cloths to give he had,
His owne coate he would cut, and it distribute glad.

40

The fourth appointed by his office was,
Poore prisoners to relieve with gratious ayd,
And captives to redeeme with price° of bras,   *payment*
355 From Turkes and Sarazins, which them had
stayd;°   *taken prisoner*
And though they faultie° were, yet well he
wayd,°   *sinful / judged*
That God to us forgiveth every howre
Much more then that, why° they in bands° were
layd,°   *for which / bonds*
And he that harrowd hell with heavie stowre,
360 The faultie soules from thence brought to his heavenly
bowre.[3]

41

The fift had charge sicke persons to attend,
And comfort those, in point of death which lay;
For them most needeth comfort in the end,
When sin, and hell, and death do most dismay
365 The feeble soule departing hence away.
All is but lost, that living we bestow,°   *store up*
If not well ended at our dying day.

---

1 *seven Bead-men*   These men of prayer perform the seven works of charity, which are described in the following stanzas.

2 *Almner*   One who distributes alms.

3 *And he … bowre*   According to some Christian tradition, Christ descended into Hell after his crucifixion in order to release all the good Israelites who had lived before his earthly sufferings opened the gate of Heaven. In traditional terminology, this was known as the Harrowing of Hell, described in *The Golden Legend*.

O man have mind of that last bitter throw;° *throe*
For as the tree does fall, so lyes it ever low.

42

370 The sixt had charge of them now being dead,
In seemely sort their corses to engrave,° *bury*
And deck with dainty flowres their bridall bed,
That to their heavenly spouse both sweet and
   brave° *handsome*
They might appeare, when he their soules shall save.
375 The wondrous workemanship of Gods owne mould,
Whose face he made, all beasts to feare, and gave
All in his hand, even dead we honour should.
Ah dearest God me graunt, I dead be not defould.

43

The seventh now after death and buriall done,
380 Had charge the tender Orphans of the dead
And widowes ayd, least they should be undone:° *ruined*
In face of judgement[1] he their right would plead,
Ne ought° the powre of mighty men did dread *at all*
In their defence, nor would for gold or fee° *bribe*
385 Be wonne their rightfull causes downe to tread:
And when they stood in most necessitee,
He did supply their want, and gave them ever free.

44

There when the Elfin knight arrivèd was,
The first and chiefest of the seven, whose care
390 Was guests to welcome, towards him did pas:
Where seeing Mercie, that his steps up bare,
And alwayes led, to her with reverence rare
He humbly louted° in meeke lowlinesse, *bowed*
And seemely welcome for her did prepare:
395 For of their order she was Patronesse,
Albe° Charissa were their chiefest founderesse. *although*

45

There she awhile him stayes, him selfe to rest,
That to the rest more able he might bee:
During which time, in every good behest
400 And godly worke of Almes and charitee
She him instructed with great industree;
Shortly therein so perfect he became,

---

[1] *judgement* I.e., in a court of law.

That from the first unto the last degree,
His mortall life he learnèd had to frame
405 In holy righteousnesse, without rebuke or blame.

46

Thence forward by that painfull way they pas,
Forth to an hill, that was both steepe and hy;
On top whereof a sacred chappell was,
And eke a litle Hermitage thereby,
410 Wherein an agèd holy man did lye,° *live*
That day and night said his devotion,
Ne other worldly busines did apply;° *conduct*
His name was heavenly Contemplation;
Of God and goodnesse was his meditation.

47

415 Great grace that old man to him given had;
For God he often saw from heavens hight,
All° were his earthly eyen both blunt° *although / dim*
   and bad,
And through great age had lost their kindly sight,
Yet wondrous quick and persant° was his spright, *keen*
420 As Eagles eye, that can behold the Sunne:
That hill they scale with all their powre and might,
That his frayle thighes nigh wearie and fordonne
Gan faile, but by her helpe the top at last he wonne.

48

There they do finde that godly agèd Sire,
425 With snowy lockes adowne his shoulders shed,
As hoarie frost with spangles° doth attire *icicles*
The mossy braunches of an Oke halfe ded.
Each bone might through his body well be red,
And every sinew seene through his long fast:
430 For nought he car'd his carcas long unfed;
His mind was full of spirituall repast,
And pyn'd° his flesh, to keepe his body
   low° and chast. *starved / humble*

49

Who when these two approching he aspide,
At their first presence grew agrievèd sore,° *sorely*
435 That forst him lay his heavenly thoughts aside;
And had he not that Dame respected more,° *greatly*
Whom highly he did reverence and adore,
He would not once have movèd for the knight.

They him saluted standing far afore;° *away*
440 Who well them greeting, humbly did requight,° *return*
And askèd, to what end they clomb that tedious height.

50

What end (quoth she) should cause us take such paine,
But that same end, which every living wight
Should make his marke,° high heaven to attaine? *object*
445 Is not from hence the way, that leadeth right
To that most glorious house, that glistreth bright
With burning starres, and everliving fire,
Whereof the keyes are to thy hand behight° *granted*
By wise Fidelia? she doth thee require,
450 To shew it to this knight, according° his desire. *granting*

51

Thrise happy man, said then the father grave,
Whose staggering steps thy steady hand doth lead,
And shewes the way, his sinfull soule to save.
Who better can the way to heaven aread,° *counsel*
455 Then thou thy selfe, that was both borne and bred
In heavenly throne, where thousand Angels shine?
Thou doest the prayers of the righteous sead° *seed*
Present before the majestie divine,
And his avenging wrath to clemencie incline.

52

460 Yet since thou bidst, thy pleasure shalbe donne.
Then come thou man of earth, and see the way,
That never yet was seene of Faeries sonne,
That never leads the traveiler astray,
But after labours long, and sad delay,
465 Brings them to joyous rest and endlesse blis.
But first thou must a season fast and pray,
Till from her bands the spright assoilèd° is, *freed*
And have her strength recur'd° from fraile *recovered*
infirmitis.

53

That done, he leads him to the highest Mount;
470 Such one, as that same mighty man of God,
That bloud-red billowes like a wallèd front
On either side disparted° with his rod, *parted*
Till that his army dry-foot through them yod,° *went*
Dwelt fortie dayes upon; where writ in stone
475 With bloudy letters by the hand of God,

The bitter doome of death and balefull mone
He did receive, whiles flashing fire about him shone.[1]

54

Or like that sacred hill, whose head full hie,
Adornd with fruitfull Olives all arownd,[2]
480 Is, as it were for endlesse memory
Of that deare Lord, who oft thereon was fownd,
For ever with a flowring girlond crownd:
Or like that pleasaunt Mount,[3] that is for ay
Through famous Poets verse each where[4] renownd,
485 On which the thrise three learnèd Ladies play
Their heavenly notes, and make full many a lovely
lay.° *verse*

55

From thence, far off he unto him did shew
A litle path, that was both steepe and long,
Which to a goodly Citie led his vew;
490 Whose wals and towres were builded high and strong
Of perle and precious stone, that earthly tong
Cannot describe, nor wit of man can tell;
Too high a ditty° for my simple song; *theme*
The Citie of the great king hight it well,
495 Wherein eternall peace and happinesse doth dwell.

56

As he thereon stood gazing, he might see
The blessed Angels to and fro descend
From highest heaven, in gladsome companee,[5]
And with great joy into that Citie wend,
500 As commonly° as friend does with his frend. *familiarly*
Whereat he wondred much, and gan enquere,
What stately building durst so high extend

---

[1] *That done ... shone* References to Mount Sinai, upon which
Moses lived for 40 days before receiving the Ten Commandments
("bloody letters"), to Moses's parting of the Red Sea to allow the
Israelites to escape from Egypt, and to the burning bush through
which God spoke to Moses. See the Book of Exodus.

[2] *Or like ... arownd* The Mount of Olives, upon which Jesus
delivered the "Sermon on the Mount" (see Matthew 5–7).

[3] *that pleasaunt Mount* Mount Parnassus, sacred to the Nine
Muses.

[4] *each where* Everywhere.

[5] *The blessed ... companee* Jacob had a vision of a ladder that
connected earth and heaven. See Genesis 28.12.

Her loftie towres unto the starry sphere,
And what unknowen nation there empeopled were.

57

505 Faire knight (quoth he) Hierusalem° that is,   *Jerusalem*
The new Hierusalem, that God has built
For those to dwell in, that are chosen his,
His chosen people purg'd from sinfull guilt,
With pretious bloud, which cruelly was spilt
510 On cursèd tree, of that unspotted lam,°   *lamb*
That for the sinnes of all the world was kilt:
Now are they Saints all in that Citie sam,°   *same*
More deare unto their God, then younglings to their
     dam.

58

Till now, said then the knight, I weenèd well,
515 That great Cleopolis, where I have beene,
In which that fairest Faerie Queene doth dwell,
The fairest Citie was, that might be seene;
And that bright towre all built of christall cleene,
Panthea, seemd the brightest thing, that was:
520 But now by proofe all otherwise I weene;
For this great Citie that does far surpas,
And this bright Angels towre quite dims that towre of
     glas.

59

Most trew, then said the holy agèd man;
Yet is Cleopolis for earthly frame,°   *structure*
525 The fairest peece, that eye beholden can:
And well beseemes all knights of noble name,
That covet in th'immortall booke of fame
To be eternizèd, that same to haunt,
And doen their service to that soveraigne Dame,
530 That glorie does to them for guerdon graunt:
For she is heavenly borne, and heaven may justly
     vaunt.°   *boast*

60

And thou faire ymp, sprong out from English race,
How ever now accompted° Elfins sonne,   *considered*
Well worthy doest thy service for her grace,
535 To aide a virgin desolate foredonne.°   *undone*
But when thou famous victorie hast wonne,

And high emongst all knights hast hong thy shield,
Thenceforth the suit of earthly conquest shonne,°   *shun*
And wash thy hands from guilt of bloudy field:
540 For bloud can nought but sin, & wars but sorrowes yield.

61

Then seeke this path, that I to thee presage,°   *point out*
Which after all to heaven shall thee send;
Then peaceably thy painefull pilgrimage
To yonder same Hierusalem do bend,
545 Where is for thee ordaind a blessed end:
For thou emongst those Saints, whom thou doest see,
Shalt be a Saint, and thine owne nations frend
And Patrone: thou Saint George shalt callèd bee,
Saint George of mery England, the signe of victoree.

62

550 Unworthy wretch (quoth he) of so great grace,
How dare I thinke such glory to attaine?
These that have it attaind, were in like cace
(Quoth he) as wretched, and liv'd in like paine.
But deeds of armes must I at last be faine,°   *willing*
555 And Ladies love to leave so dearely bought?
What need of armes, where peace doth ay remaine,
(Said he) and battailes none are to be fought?
As for loose loves they are vaine, and vanish into nought.

63

O let me not (quoth he) then turne againe
560 Backe to the world, whose joyes so fruitlesse are;
But let me here for aye in peace remaine,
Or streight way on that last long voyage fare,
That nothing may my present hope empare.
That may not be (said he) ne maist thou yit
565 Forgo that royall maides bequeathèd care,
Who did her cause into thy hand commit,
Till from her cursèd foe thou have her freely quit.°   *released*

64

Then shall I soone, (quoth he) so God me grace,
Abet° that virgins cause disconsolate,   *support*
570 And shortly backe returne unto this place,
To walke this way in Pilgrims poore estate.
But now aread,° old father, why of late   *state*
Didst thou behight° me borne of English blood,   *call*

Whom all a Faeries sonne doen nominate?
575 That word shall I (said he) avouchen° good,   prove
Sith to thee is unknowne the cradle of thy brood.

65

For well I wote, thou springst from ancient race
  Of Saxon kings, that have with mightie hand
  And many bloudie battailes fought in place°   that place
580 High reard° their royall throne in Britane land,   erected
  And vanquisht them, unable to withstand:
  From thence a Faerie thee unweeting° reft,   secretly
  There as thou slepst in tender swadling band,
  And her base Elfin brood there for thee left.
585 Such men do Chaungelings call, so chaungd by Faeries
      theft.

66

Thence she thee brought into this Faerie lond,
  And in an heapèd furrow did thee hyde,
  Where thee a Ploughman all unweeting fond,
  As he his toylesome teme that way did guyde,
590 And brought thee up in ploughmans state to byde,
  Whereof Georgos[1] he thee gave to° name;   as
  Till prickt with courage, and thy forces pryde,
  To Faery court thou cam'st to seeke for fame,
And prove thy puissaunt armes, as seemes thee best
      became.°   suited

67

595 O holy Sire (quoth he) how shall I quight°   repay
  The many favours I with thee have found,
  That hast my name and nation red aright,
  And taught the way that does to heaven bound?
  This said, adowne he lookèd to the ground,
600 To have returnd, but dazèd were his eyne,
  Through passing° brightnesse, which did   exceeding
      quite confound
  His feeble sence, and too exceeding shyne.
So darke are earthly things compard to things divine.

68

At last whenas himselfe he gan to find,°   recover
605 To Una back he cast him to retire;
  Who him awaited still with pensive° mind.   apprehensive

---

[1] *Georgos* Farmer.

Great thankes and goodly meed° to that   recompense
    good syre,
He thence departing gave for his paines hyre.°   reward
So came to Una, who him joyd to see,
610 And after litle rest, gan him desire,
  Of her adventure° mindfull for to bee.   quest
So leave they take of Caelia, and her daughters three.

CANTO II

The knight with that old Dragon fights
    Two dayes incessantly:
The third him overthrowes, and gayns
    Most glorious victory.

1

High time now gan it wex[2] for Una faire,
  To thinke of those her captive Parents deare,
  And their forwasted kingdome to repaire:
  Whereto whenas they now approchèd neare,
5 With hartie words her knight she gan to cheare,
  And in her modest manner thus bespake;
  Deare knight, as deare, as ever knight was deare,
  That all these sorrowes suffer for my sake,
High heaven behold the tedious toyle, ye for me take.

2

10 Now are we come unto my native soyle,
  And to the place, where all our perils dwell;
  Here haunts that feend, and does his dayly spoyle,
  Therefore henceforth be at your keeping well,[3]
  And ever ready for your foeman fell.
15 The sparke of noble courage now awake,
  And strive your excellent selfe to excell;
  That shall ye evermore renowmèd make,
Above all knights on earth, that batteill undertake.

3

And pointing forth, lo yonder is (said she)
20 The brasen towre in which my parents deare
  For dread of that huge feend emprisond be
  Whom I from far see on the walles appeare

---

[2] *gan it wex* It began to grow.

[3] *at your keeping well* Well on your guard.

Whose sight my feeble soule doth greatly cheare:
And on the top of all I do espye
25 The watchman wayting tydings glad to heare,
That O my parents might I happily
Unto you bring, to ease you of your misery.

4

With that they heard a roaring hideous sound,
That all the ayre with terrour fillèd wide,
30 And seemd uneath° to shake the stedfast ground.   *almost*
Eftsoones that dreadfull Dragon they espide,
Where stretcht he lay upon the sunny side
Of a great hill, himselfe like a great hill.
But all so soone, as he from far descride
35 Those glistring armes, that heaven with light did fill,
He rousd himselfe full blith,° and hastned them
        untill.°   *gladly | towards*

5

Then bad the knight his Lady yede° aloofe,   *go*
And to an hill her selfe with draw aside,
From whence she might behold that battailles
        proof°   *outcome*
40 And eke be safe from daunger far descryde:°   *observed*
She him obayd, and turnd a little wyde.
Now O thou sacred Muse, most learnèd Dame,
Faire ympe of Phoebus, and his agèd bride,[1]
The Nourse of time, and everlasting fame,
45 That warlike hands ennoblest with immortall name;

6

O gently come into my feeble brest,
Come gently, but not with that mighty rage,
Wherewith the martiall troupes thou doest
        infest,°   *arouse*
And harts of great Heroës doest enrage,
50 That nought their kindled courage may aswage,
Soone as thy dreadfull trompe° begins to sownd;   *trumpet*
The God of warre with his fiers equipage
Thou doest awake, sleepe never he so sownd,
And scarèd nations doest with horrour sterne
        astownd.°   *astonish*

7

Faire Goddesse lay that furious fit° aside,   *music*
55 Till I of warres and bloudy Mars do sing,
And Briton fields with Sarazin bloud bedyde,
Twixt that great faery Queene and Paynim king,
That with their horrour heaven and earth did ring,
60 A worke of labour long, and endlesse prayse:
But now a while let downe that haughtie string,
And to my tunes thy second tenor rayse,
That I this man of God his godly armes may
        blaze.°   *proclaim*

8

By this the dreadfull Beast drew nigh to hand,
65 Halfe flying, and halfe footing in his hast,
That with his largenesse measurèd much land,
And made wide shadow under his huge wast;°   *girth*
As mountaine doth the valley overcast.
Approching nigh, he rearèd high afore
70 His body monstrous, horrible, and vast,
Which to increase his wondrous greatnesse more,
Was swolne with wrath, & poyson, & with bloudy gore.

9

And over, all with brasen scales was armd,
Like plated coate of steele, so couchèd° neare,°   *set | closely*
75 That nought mote perce, ne might his corse be harmd
With dint of sword, nor push of pointed speare;
Which as an Eagle, seeing pray appeare,
His aery plumes doth rouze, full rudely° dight,   *roughly*
So shakèd he, that horrour was to heare,
80 For as the clashing of an Armour bright,
Such noyse his rouzèd scales did send unto the knight.

10

His flaggy° wings when forth he did display,   *pendulous*
Were like two sayles, in which the hollow wynd
Is gathered full, and worketh speedy way:
85 And eke the pennes, that did his pineons°   *quills | wings*
        bynd,
Were like mayne-yards, with flying canvas lynd,
With which whenas him list the ayre to beat,
And there by force unwonted° passage find,   *unaccustomed*
The cloudes before him fled for terrour great,
90 And all the heavens stood still amazèd with his threat.

---

[1] *his agèd bride* Mnemosyne, or Memory, the mother of the Muses.

11

His huge long tayle wound up in hundred foldes,
   Does overspred his long bras-scaly backe,
   Whose wrathèd boughts° when ever he unfoldes,   *coils*
   And thicke entangled knots adown does slacke.
95   Bespotted all with shields° of red and blacke,   *scales*
   It sweepeth all the land behind him farre,
   And of three furlongs[1] does but litle lacke;
   And at the point two stings in-fixèd arre,
Both deadly sharpe, that sharpest steele exceeden farre.

12

100 But stings° and sharpest steele did far exceed   *spears*
   The sharpnesse of his cruell rending clawes;[2]
   Dead was it sure, as sure as death in deed,
   What ever thing does touch his ravenous pawes,
   Or what within his reach he ever drawes.
105 But his most hideous head my toung to tell
   Does tremble: for his deepe devouring jawes
   Wide gapèd, like the griesly mouth of hell,
Through which into his darke abisse all ravin° fell.   *prey*

13

And that more wondrous was, in either jaw
110 Three ranckes of yron teeth enraungèd were,
   In which yet trickling bloud and gobbets° raw   *chunks*
   Of late devourèd bodies did appeare,
   That sight thereof bred cold congealèd feare:
   Which to increase, and as atonce to kill,
115 A cloud of smoothering smoke and sulphur seare°   *searing*
   Out of his stinking gorge forth steemèd still,
That all the ayre about with smoke and stench did fill.

14

His blazing eyes, like two bright shining shields,
   Did burne with wrath, and sparkled living fyre;
120 As two broad Beacons, set in open fields,
   Send forth their flames farre off to every shyre,°   *district*
   And warning give, that enemies conspyre,
   With fire and sword the region to invade;
   So flam'd his eyne with rage and rancorous yre:

---

1 *furlong* Agricultural measurement presently equal to 220 yards;
originally the length of a furrow in a common field.

2 *but stings … clawes* I.e., the sharpness of his claws far exceeded
that of spears and the sharpest steel.

125 But farre within, as in a hollow glade,
   Those glaring lampes were set, that made a dreadfull
      shade.

15

So dreadfully he towards him did pas,
   Forelifting up aloft his speckled brest,
   And often bounding on the brusèd gras,
130 As for great joyance of his newcome guest.
   Eftsoones he gan advance his haughtie crest,
   As chauffèd° Bore his bristles doth upreare,   *angered*
   And shoke his scales to battell readie drest;
   That made the Redcrosse knight nigh quake for feare,
135 As bidding° bold defiance to his foeman neare.   *inviting*

16

The knight gan fairely couch° his steadie speare,   *aim*
   And fiercely ran at him with rigorous might:
   The pointed steele arriving rudely theare,
   His harder hide would neither perce, nor bight,
140 But glauncing by forth passèd forward right;
   Yet sore amovèd with so puissant push,
   The wrathfull beast about him turnèd light,°   *swiftly*
   And him so rudely passing by, did brush
With his long tayle, that horse and man to ground did
      rush.

17

145 Both horse and man up lightly rose againe,
   And fresh encounter towards him addrest:
   But th'idle° stroke yet backe recoyld in vaine,   *futile*
   And found no place his deadly point to rest.
   Exceeding rage enflam'd the furious beast,
150 To be avengèd of so great despight;°   *outrage*
   For never felt his imperceable brest
   So wondrous force, from hand of living wight;
Yet had he prov'd the powre of many a puissant knight.

18

Then with his waving wings displayèd wyde,
155 Himselfe up high he lifted from the ground,
   And with strong flight did forcibly divide
   The yielding aire, which nigh° too feeble found   *almost*
   Her flitting partes, and element unsound,
   To beare so great a weight: he cutting way
160 With his broad sayles, about him soarèd round:

At last low stouping with unweldie sway,°   *force*
Snatcht up both horse & man, to beare them quite away.

19

Long he them bore above the subject plaine,
   So farre as Ewghen[1] bow a shaft may send,
165   Till struggling strong did him at last constraine,
   To let them downe before his flightès end:
   As hagard° hauke presuming to contend   *wild*
   With hardie fowle, above his hable°
     might,°   *proper / strength*
   His wearie pounces° all in vaine doth spend,   *talons*
170   To trusse the pray too heavie for his flight;
Which comming downe to ground, does free it selfe
     by fight.

20

He so disseizèd of his gryping° grosse,°   *freed / grip / heavy*
   The knight his thrillant° speare againe assayd   *penetrating*
   In his bras-plated body to embosse,°   *plunge*
175   And three mens strength unto the stroke he layd;
   Wherewith the stiffe beame quaked, as affrayd,
   And glauncing from his scaly necke, did glyde
   Close under his left wing, then broad displayd.
   The percing steele there wrought a wound full wyde,
180 That with the uncouth° smart the Monster   *unknown*
     lowdly cryde.

21

He cryde, as raging seas are wont to rore,
   When wintry storme his wrathfull wreck does threat,
   The rolling billowes° beat the ragged shore,   *waves*
   As they the earth would shoulder from her seat,
185   And greedie gulfe does gape, as he would eat
   His neighbour element in his revenge:
   Then gin the blustring brethren° boldly threat,   *winds*
   To move the world from off his stedfast henge,°   *hinge*
And boystrous battell make, each other to avenge.

22

190 The steely head stucke fast still in his flesh,
   Till with his cruell clawes he snatcht the wood,
   And quite a sunder broke. Forth flowèd fresh
   A gushing river of blacke goarie blood,

---

[1] *Ewghen* Made of wood from the yew tree.

That drownèd all the land, whereon he stood;
195 The streame thereof would drive a water-mill.
   Trebly augmented was his furious mood
   With bitter sense of his deepe rooted ill,°   *wound*
That flames of fire he threw forth from his large nosethrill.

23

His hideous tayle then hurlèd he about,
200   And therewith all enwrapt the nimble thyes°   *thighs*
   Of his froth-fomy steed, whose courage stout
   Striving to loose the knot, that fast him tyes,
   Himselfe in streighter° bandes too rash
     implyes,°   *tighter / entangles*
   That to the ground he is perforce° constraynd   *thereby*
205   To throw his rider: who can quickly ryse
   From off the earth, with durty bloud distaynd,°   *dirtied*
For that reprochfull fall right fowly he disdaynd.

24

And fiercely tooke his trenchand° blade in hand,   *cutting*
   With which he stroke so furious and so fell,
210   That nothing seemd the puissance could withstand:
   Upon his crest the hardned yron fell,
   But his more hardned crest was armd so well,
   That deeper dint therein it would not make;
   Yet so extremely did the buffe° him quell,   *blow*
215   That from thenceforth he shund the like to take,
But when he saw them come, he did them still
     forsake.°   *avoid*

25

The knight was wrath to see his stroke beguyld,°   *foiled*
   And smote againe with more outrageous might;
   But backe againe the sparckling steele recoyld,
220   And left not any marke, where it did light;
   As if in Adamant° rocke it had bene pight.°   *hardest / pitched*
   The beast impatient of his smarting wound,
   And of so fierce and forcible despight,
   Thought with his wings to stye° above the ground;   *rise*
225 But his late wounded wing unserviceable found.

26

Then full of griefe and anguish vehement,
   He lowdly brayd, that like was never heard,
   And from his wide devouring oven sent
   A flake° of fire, that flashing in his beard,   *stream*

230   Him all amazd, and almost made affeard:
    The scorching flame sore swingèd° all his face,   *singed*
    And through his armour all his bodie seard,
    That he could not endure so cruell cace,
  But thought his armes to leave, and helmet to unlace.

27

235 Not that great Champion[1] of the antique world,
    Whom famous Poetes verse so much doth vaunt,
    And hath for twelve huge labours high extold,
    So many furies and sharpe fits did haunt,
    When him the poysoned garment did enchaunt
240   With Centaures bloud, and bloudie verses charm'd,
    As did this knight twelve thousand dolours daunt,
    Whom fyrie steele now burnt, that earst him arm'd,
  That erst him goodly arm'd, now most of all him harm'd.

28

   Faint, wearie, sore, emboylèd, grievèd, brent
245   With heat, toyle, wounds, armes, smart, & inward fire
    That never man such mischiefes did torment;
    Death better were, death did he oft desire,
    But death will never come, when needes require.
    Whom so dismayd when that his foe beheld,
250   He cast to suffer him no more respire,°   *live*
    But gan his sturdie sterne° about to weld,   *tail / swing*
  And him so strongly stroke, that to the ground him feld.

29

   It fortunèd (as faire it then befell)
    Behind his backe unweeting, where he stood,
255   Of auncient time there was a springing well,
    From which fast trickled forth a silver flood,
    Full of great vertues, and for med'cine good.
    Whylome, before that cursèd Dragon got
    That happie land, and all with innocent blood
260   Defyld those sacred waves, it rightly hot°   *was called*
  The well of life, ne yet his vertues had forgot.

30

For unto life the dead it could restore,
    And guilt of sinfull crimes cleane wash away,
    Those that with sicknesse were infected sore,
265   It could recure,° and agèd long decay   *heal*
    Renew, as one were borne that very day.
    Both Silo this, and Jordan did excell,
    And th'English Bath, and eke the german Spau,
    Ne can Cephise, nor Hebrus match this well:[2]
270 Into the same the knight backe overthrowèn, fell.

31

Now gan the golden Phoebus for to steepe
    His fierie face in billowes of the west,
    And his faint steedes watred in Ocean deepe,
    Whiles from their journall° labours they did rest,   *daily*
275   When that infernall Monster, having kest°   *cast*
    His wearie foe into that living well,
    Can° high advance his broad discoloured brest,   *did*
    Above his wonted pitch,° with countenance
      fell,°   *height / fierce*
  And clapt his yron wings, as victor he did dwell.°   *stay*

32

280 Which when his pensive Ladie saw from farre,
    Great woe and sorrow did her soule assay,
    As weening that the sad end of the warre,
    And gan to highest God entirely° pray,   *earnestly*
    That fearèd chance from her to turne away;
285   With folded hands and knees full lowly bent
    All night she watcht, ne once adowne would lay
    Her daintie limbs in her sad dreriment,°   *peril*
  But praying still did wake, and waking did lament.

33

The morrow next gan early to appeare,
290   That Titan rose to runne his daily race:
    But early ere the morrow next gan reare
    Out of the sea faire Titans deawy face,
    Up rose the gentle virgin from her place,

---

[1] *that great Champion* Hercules, who successfully completed twelve labors. His death occurred when his wife inadvertently presented him with a poisoned shirt. The pain was so intense that he caused a funeral pyre to be built so that he could cast himself upon it. He was, however, rescued from the pyre and brought to dwell on Mount Olympus, the home of the gods.

[2] *Both Silo … well* These waters have all been said to have healing powers. In John 9.7 a blind man is cured in the waters of the Siloam; Christ was baptized in the river Jordan; the supposedly medicinal waters of Bath and Spa were visited by those suffering from a variety of ailments; the waters of Cephise and Hebrus are praised in classical mythology for their purifying powers.

And lookèd all about, if she might spy
   Her lovèd knight to move his manly pace:
295   For she had great doubt of his safety,
Since late she saw him fall before his enemy.

34

At last she where he upstarted brave
   Out of the well, wherein he drenchèd lay;
300   As Eagle fresh out of the Ocean wave,
   Where he hath left his plumes all hoary gray,
   And deckt himselfe with feathers youthly gay,
   Like Eyas hauke° up mounts unto the skies,   *young hawk*
   His newly budded pineons to assay,
305   And marveiles at himselfe, still as he flies:
So new this new-borne knight to battell new did rise.

35

Whom when the damnèd feend so fresh did spy,
   No wonder if he wondred at the sight,
   And doubted, whether his late enemy
310   It were, or other new supplièd knight.
   He, now to prove his late renewèd might,
   High brandishing his bright deaw-burning[1] blade,
   Upon his crested scalpe so sore did smite,
   That to the scull a yawning wound it made:
315 The deadly dint his dullèd senses all dismaid.

36

I wote not, whether the revenging steele
   Were hardned with that holy water dew,
   Wherein he fell, or sharper edge did feele,
   Or his baptizèd hands now greater grew;
320   Or other secret vertue° did ensew;   *power*
   Else never could the force of fleshly arme,
   Ne molten mettall in his bloud embrew:°   *thrust*
   For till that stownd° could never wight him harme,   *time*
By subtilty, nor slight, nor might, nor mighty charme.

37

325 The cruell wound enragèd him so sore,
   That loud he yelded for exceeding paine;
   As hundred ramping Lyons seem'd to rore,
   Whom ravenous hunger did thereto constraine:

Then gan he tosse aloft his stretchèd traine,°   *tail*
330   And therewith scourge the buxome° aire so
      sore,°   *pliant | violently*
   That to his force to yeelden it was faine;
   Ne ought° his sturdie strokes might stand afore,   *aught*
That high trees overthrew, and rocks in peeces tore.

38

The same advauncing high above his head,
335   With sharpe intended° sting so rude him smot,   *extended*
   That to the earth him drove, as stricken dead,
   Ne living wight would have him life behot:°   *expected*
   The mortall sting his angry needle shot
   Quite through his shield, and in his shoulder
      seasd,°   *fastened*
340   Where fast it stucke, ne would there out be got:
   The griefe thereof him wondrous sore diseasd,
Ne might his ranckling paine with patience be appeasd.

39

But yet more mindfull of his honour deare,
   Then of the grievous smart, which him did wring,°   *vex*
345   From loathèd soile he can him lightly reare,
   And strove to loose the farre infixèd sting:
   Which when in vaine he tryde with struggeling,
   Inflam'd with wrath, his raging blade he heft,°   *raised*
   And strooke so strongly, that the knotty string
350   Of his huge taile he quite a sunder cleft,
Five joynts thereof he hewd, and but the stump him left.

40

Hart cannot thinke, what outrage, and what cryes,
   With foule enfouldred[2] smoake and flashing fire,
   The hell-bred beast threw forth unto the skyes,
   That all was coverèd with darknesse dire:
355   Then fraught° with rancour, and engorgèd ire,   *filled*
   He cast at once him to avenge for all,
   And gathering up himselfe out of the mire,°   *mud*
   With his uneven wings did fiercely fall
360 Upon his sunne-bright shield, and gript it fast withall.

41

Much was the man encombred with his hold,
   In feare to lose his weapon in his paw,

---

[1] *deaw-burning* I.e., the sword is so bright that its light, like that of the sun, burns up the dew.

[2] *enfouldred* Charged with lightning.

Ne wist yet, how his talants° to unfold;   talons
  Nor harder was from Cerberus greedie jaw
365 To plucke a bone, then from his cruell claw
  To reave° by strength the gripèd gage away: wrest
  Thrise he assayd it from his foot to draw,
  And thrise in vaine to draw it did assay,
It booted nought to thinke, to robbe him of his pray.

42

370 Tho° when he saw no power might prevaile,   then
  His trustie sword he cald to his last aid,
  Wherewith he fiercely did his foe assaile,
  And double blowes about him stoutly laid,
  That glauncing fire out of the yron plaid;°   danced
375 As sparckles from the Andvile° use to fly,   anvil
  When heavie hammers on the wedge° are
    swaid;°   i.e., anvil / struck
  Therewith at last he forst him to unty°   release
One of his grasping feete, him to defend thereby.

43

 The other foot, fast fixèd on his shield,
380 Whenas no strength, nor stroks mote° him   could
   constraine
  To loose, ne yet the warlike pledge to yield,
  He smot thereat with all his might and maine,
  That nought so wondrous puissance might sustaine;
  Upon the joynt the lucky steele did light,
385 And made such way, that hewd it quite in twaine;
  The paw yet missèd not his minisht° might,   diminished
But hong still on the shield, as it at first was pight.°   placed

44

 For griefe thereof, and divelish despight,
  From his infernall fournace forth he threw
390 Huge flames, that dimmèd all the heavens light,
  Enrold in duskish smoke and brimstone°
   blew;°   sulphur / blue
  As burning Aetna[1] from his boyling stew
  Doth belch out flames, and rockes in peeces broke,
  And ragged ribs of mountaines molten new,
395 Enwrapt in coleblacke clouds and filthy smoke,
That all the land with stench, and heaven with horror
  choke.

---

[1] *Aetna*   Volcano in eastern Sicily.

45

The heate whereof, and harmefull pestilence°   injury
  So sore him noyd,° that forst him to retire   vexed
  A little backward for his best defence,
400 To save his bodie from the scorching fire,
  Which he from hellish entrailes did expire.°   exhale
  It chaunst (eternall God that chaunce did guide)
  As he recoylèd backward, in the mire
  His nigh forwearied feeble feet did slide,
405 And downe he fell, with dread of shame sore terrifide.

46

There grew a goodly tree him faire beside,
  Loaden with fruit and apples rosie red,
  As they in pure vermilion had beene dide,
  Whereof great vertues over all were red:°   told
410 For happie life to all, which thereon fed,
  And life eke everlasting did befall:
  Great God it planted in that blessed sted°   place
  With his almightie hand, and did it call
The tree of life,[2] the crime of our first fathers fall.

47

415 In all the world like was not to be found,
  Save in that soile, where all good things did grow,
  And freely sprong out of the fruitfull ground,
  As incorrupted Nature did them sow,
  Till that dread Dragon[3] all did overthrow.
420 Another like faire tree eke grew thereby,
  Whereof who so did eat, eftsoones did know
  Both good and ill: O mornefull memory:
That tree through one mans fault hath doen us all to dy.

48

From that first tree forth flowd, as from a well,
425 A trickling streame of Balme, most soveraine°   powerful
  And daintie° deare,° which on the   particularly / precious
   ground still fell,
  And overflowèd all the fertill plaine,
  As it had deawèd bene with timely° raine: seasonal
  Life and long health that gratious° ointment   pleasing
   gave,

---

[2] *tree of life*   This tree grows in the Garden of Eden, from which
Adam and Eve were expelled for eating from the Tree of Knowledge.

[3] *that dread Dragon*   I.e., Satan.

430 And deadly woundes could heale, and reare againe
    The senselesse corse appointed for the grave.
    Into that same he fell: which did from death him save.

49

For nigh thereto the ever damnèd beast
    Durst not approch, for he was deadly° made,   *of death*
435 And all that life preservèd, did detest:
    Yet he it oft adventur'd to invade.
    By this the drouping day-light gan to fade
    And yeeld his roome to sad succeeding night,
    Who with her sable mantle gan to shade
440   The face of earth, and wayes of living wight,
And high her burning torch set up in heaven bright.

50

When gentle Una saw the second fall
    Of her deare knight, who wearie of long fight,
    And faint through losse of bloud, mov'd not at all,
445   But lay as in a dreame of deepe delight,
    Besmeard with pretious Balme, whose vertuous might
    Did heale his wounds, and scorching heat alay,
    Againe she stricken was with sore affright,
    And for his safetie gan devoutly pray;
450 And watch the noyous° night, and wait for   *harmful*
    joyous day.

51

The joyous day gan early to appeare,
    And faire Aurora from the deawy bed
    Of agèd Tithone gan her selfe to reare,
    With rosie cheekes, for shame as blushing red;
455   Her golden lockes for haste were loosely shed
    About her eares, when Una her did marke
    Clymbe to her charet, all with flowers spred;
    From heaven high to chase the chearelesse darke,
With merry note her loud salutes the mounting larke.

52

460 Then freshly up arose the doughtie knight,
    All healèd of his hurts and woundès wide,
    And did himselfe to battell readie dight;

Whose early foe awaiting him beside
    To have devourd, so soone as day he spyde,
465   When now he saw himselfe so freshly reare,
    As if late fight had nought him damnifyde,°   *hurt*
    He woxe° dismayd, and gan his fate to feare;   *grew*
Nathlesse with wonted rage he him advauncèd neare.

53

And in his first encounter, gaping wide,
470   He thought attonce him to have swallowd quight,
    And rusht upon him with outragious pride;
    Who him r'encountring fierce, as hauke in flight,
    Perforce° rebutted backe. The weapon bright   *forcibly*
    Taking advantage of his open jaw,
475   Ran through his mouth with so importune°   *exacting*
    might,
    That deepe emperst his darksome hollow maw,°   *mouth*
And back retyrd,° his life bloud forth with all   *withdrawn*
    did draw.

54

So downe he fell, and forth his life did breath,
    That vanisht into smoke and cloudès swift;
480   So downe he fell, that th'earth him underneath
    Did grone, as feeble so great load to lift;
    So downe he fell, as an huge rockie clift,
    Whose false° foundation waves have washt away,   *defective*
    With dreadfull poyse° is from the mayneland   *weight*
    rift,
485   And rolling downe, great Neptune doth dismay;
So downe he fell, and like an heapèd mountaine lay.

55

The knight himselfe even trembled at his fall,
    So huge and horrible a masse it seem'd;
    And his deare Ladie, that beheld it all,
490   Durst not approch for dread, which she
    misdeem'd,°   *misjudged*
    But yet at last, when as the direfull feend
    She saw not stirre, off-shaking vaine° affright,   *empty*
    She nigher drew, and saw that joyous end:
    Then God she praysd, and thankt her faithfull knight,
That had atchiev'd so great a conquest by his might.

CANTO 12

Faire Una to the Redcrosse knight
   Betrouthèd is with joy:
Though false Duessa it to barre°   *stop*
   Her false sleights doe imploy.

1

Behold I see the haven nigh at hand,
   To which I meane my wearie course to bend;
   Vere° the maine shete, and beare up with[1] the   *release*
     land,
   The which afore is fairely to be kend,°   *recognized*
5   And seemeth safe from stormes, that may offend;
   There this faire virgin wearie of her way
   Must landed be, now at her journeyes end:
   There eke my feeble barke° a while may stay,   *vessel*
Till merry° wind and weather call her thence away. *favorable*

2

10 Scarsely had Phoebus in the glooming° East   *glowing*
   Yet harnessèd his firie-footed teeme,
   Ne reard aboue the earth his flaming creast,°   *crest*
   When the last deadly smoke aloft did steeme,
   That signe of last outbreathèd life did seeme,
15 Unto the watchman on the castle wall;
   Who thereby dead that balefull° Beast did   *destructive*
     deeme,
   And to his Lord and Ladie lowd gan call,
To tell, how he had seene the Dragons fatall fall.

3

Uprose with hastie joy, and feeble speed
20 That agèd Sire, the Lord of all that land,
   And lookèd forth, to weet, if true indeede
   Those tydings were, as he did understand,
   Which whenas true by tryall he out fond,
   He bad to open wyde his brazen gate,
25 Which long time had bene shut, and out of hond[2]
   Proclaymèd joy and peace through all his state;
For dead now was their foe, which them
     forrayèd° late.   *pillaged*

4

Then gan triumphant Trompets sound on hie,
   That sent to heaven the ecchoèd report
30 Of their new joy, and happie victorie
   Gainst him, that had them long opprest with tort,° *injury*
   And fast imprisonèd in siegèd fort.
   Then all the people, as in solemne feast,
   To him assembled with one full consort,[3]
35 Rejoycing at the fall of that great beast,
From whose eternall bondage now they were releast.

5

Forth came that auncient Lord and agèd Queene,
   Arayd in antique robes downe to the ground,
   And sad habiliments right well beseene;°   *appropriate*
40 A noble crew about them waited round
   Of sage and sober Peres,° all gravely gownd;   *peers*
   Whom farre before did march a goodly band
   Of tall young men, all hable° armes to sownd,° *able | wield*
   But now they laurell braunches bore in hand;
45 Glad signe of victorie and peace in all their land.

6

Unto that doughtie° Conquerour they came,   *valiant*
   And him before themselves prostrating low,
   Their Lord and Patrone° loud did him proclame, *protector*
   And at his feet their laurell boughes did throw.
50 Soone after them all dauncing on a row
   The comely virgins came, with girlands dight,
   As fresh as flowres in medow greene do grow,
   When morning deaw upon their leaves doth light:
And in their hands sweet Timbrels° all   *tambourines*
     upheld on hight.

7

And them before, the fry° of children young   *group*
   Their wanton sports and childish mirth did play,
   And to the Maydens sounding tymbrels sung
   In well attunèd notes, a joyous lay,
   And made delightfull musicke all the way,
60 Untill they came, where that faire virgin stood;
   As faire Diana in fresh sommers day

---

[1] *beare up with* Steer toward.

[2] *out of hond* Immediately.

[3] *one full consort* All at once.

Beholds her Nymphes, enraung'd° in shadie   *spread out*
   wood,
Some wrestle, some do run, some bathe in christall flood.

8

So she beheld those maydens meriment
65 With chearefull vew; who when to her they came,
   Themselves to ground with gratious humblesse bent,
   And her ador'd by honorable name,°   *titles*
   Lifting to heaven her everlasting fame:
   Then on her head they set a girland greene,
70 And crownèd her twixt earnest and twixt game;
   Who in her selfe-resemblance well beseene,
Did seeme such, as she was, a goodly maiden Queene.

9

And after, all the raskall many ran,
  Heapèd together in rude° rabblement°   *disorganized / swarm*
75 To see the face of that victorious man:
   Whom all admired, as from heaven sent,
   And gazd upon with gaping wonderment.
   But when they came, where that dead Dragon lay,
   Stretcht on the ground in monstrous large extent,
80 The sight with idle feare did them dismay,
Ne durst approch him nigh, to touch, or once assay.

10

Some feard, and fled; some feard and well it faynd;°   *hid*
  One that would wiser seeme, then all the rest,
   Warnd him not touch, for yet perhaps remaynd
85 Some lingring life within his hollow brest,
   Or in his wombe might lurke some hidden nest
   Of many Dragonets, his fruitfull seed;
   Another said, that in his eyes did rest
   Yet sparckling fire, and bad thereof take heed;
90 Another said, he saw him move his eyes indeed.

11

One mother, when as her foolehardie chyld
  Did come too neare, and with his talents° play,   *claws*
   Halfe dead through feare, her litle babe
    revyld,°   *reprimanded*
   And to her gossips gan in counsell say;
95 How can I tell, but that his talants may
   Yet scratch my sonne, or rend his tender hand?
   So diversly themselves in vaine they fray;°   *frighten*

Whiles some more bold, to measure him nigh stand,
To prove how many acres he did spread of land.

12

100 Thus flockèd all the folke him round about,
  The whiles that hoarie° king, with all his   *gray-headed*
   traine,
   Being arrivèd, where that champion stout
   After his foes defeasance° did remaine,   *defeat*
   Him goodly greetes, and faire does entertaine,
105 With princely gifts of yvorie and gold,
   And thousand thankes him yeelds for all his paine.
   Then when his daughter deare he does behold,
Her dearely doth imbrace, and kisseth
   manifold.°   *many times*

13

And after to his Pallace he them brings,
110 With shaumes,[1] & trompets, & with Clarions sweet;
   And all the way the joyous people sings,
   And with their garments strowes the pavèd street:
   Whence mounting up, they find
    purveyance° meet   *provisions / fitting*
   Of all, that royall Princes court became,°   *suited*
115 And all the floore was underneath their feet
   Bespred with costly scarlot[2] of great name,
On which they lowly sit, and fitting
   purpose° frame.   *conversation*

14

What needs me tell their feast and goodly guize,°   *behavior*
  In which was nothing riotous nor vaine?
120 What needs of daintie dishes to devize,°   *recount*
   Of comely services, or courtly trayne?
   My narrow leaves cannot in them containe
   The large discourse of royall Princes state.
   Yet was their manner then but bare and plaine:
125 For th'antique world excesse and pride did hate;
Such proud luxurious pompe is swollen up but late.

15

Then when with meates and drinkes of every kinde
  Their fervent appetites they quenchèd had,

---

1 *shaumes* Older instruments resembling the oboe.

2 *scarlot* Rich type of cloth, usually of a vivid red color.

That auncient Lord gan fit occasion finde,
130   Of straunge adventures, and of perils sad,
Which in his travell him befallen had,
For to demaund of his renowmèd guest:
Who then with utt'rance grave, and count'nance sad
From point to point, as is before exprest,
135 Discourst his voyage long, according his request.

16

Great pleasure mixt with pittifull° regard,   *compassionate*
That godly King and Queene did passionate,°   *feel*
Whiles they his pittifull° adventures heard,   *deplorable*
That oft they did lament his lucklesse state,
140   And often blame the too importune° fate,   *exacting*
That heapd on him so many wrathfull wreakes:°   *injuries*
For never gentle knight, as he of late,
So tossèd was in fortunes cruell freakes;°   *vagaries*
And all the while salt teares bedeawd the hearers cheaks.

17

145 Then said that royall Pere in sober wise;
Deare Sonne, great beene the evils, which ye bore
From first to last in your late enterprise,
That I note,° whether prayse, or pitty more: *could not*
For never living man, I weene, so sore
150   In sea of deadly daungers was distrest;
But since now safe ye seisèd have the shore,
And well arrivèd are, (high God be blest)
Let us devize° of ease and everlasting rest.   *talk*

18

Ah dearest Lord, said then that doughty knight,
155   Of ease or rest I may not yet devize;
For by the faith, which I to armes have plight,
I bounden am streight after this emprize,°   *enterprise*
As that your daughter can ye well advize,
Backe to returne to that great Faerie Queene,
160   And her to serve six yeares in warlike wize,°   *ways*
Gainst that proud Paynim king, that workes her
teene:°   *sorrow*
Therefore I ought crave pardon, till I there have beene.

19

Unhappie falles that hard necessitie,
(Quoth he) the troubler of my happie peace,
165   And vowèd foe of my felicitie;

Ne I against the same can justly preace:°   *contend*
But since that band° ye cannot now release,   *bond*
Nor doen undo; (for vowes may not be vaine°)   *empty*
Soone as the terme of those six yeares shall cease,
170   Ye then shall hither backe returne againe,
The marriage to accomplish vowd betwixt you twain.

20

Which for my part I covet to performe,
In sort as through the world I did proclame,
That who so kild that monster most deforme,
175   And him in hardy battaile overcame,
Should have mine onely daughter to his Dame,
And of my kingdome heire apparaunt bee:
Therefore since now to thee perteines the same,
By dew desert of noble chevalree,
180   Both daughter and eke kingdome, lo I yield to thee.

21

Then forth he callèd that his daughter faire,
The fairest Un' his onely daughter deare,
His onely daughter, and his onely heyre;
Who forth proceeding with sad° sober cheare,   *serious*
185   As bright as doth the morning starre appeare
Out of the East, with flaming lockes bedight,°   *bedecked*
To tell that dawning day is drawing neare,
And to the world does bring long wishèd light;
So faire and fresh that Lady shewd her selfe in sight.

22

190 So faire and fresh, as freshest flowre in May;
For she had layd her mournefull stole° aside,   *cloak*
And widow-like sad wimple° throwne away,   *veil*
Wherewith her heavenly beautie she did hide,
Whiles on her wearie journey she did ride;
195   And on her now a garment she did weare,
All lilly white, withoutten spot, or pride,°   *adornment*
That seemd like silke and silver woven neare,°   *tightly*
But neither silke nor silver therein did appeare.

23

The blazing brightnesse of her beauties beame,
200   And glorious light of her sunshyny face
To tell, were as to strive against the streame.
My ragged rimes are all too rude and bace,
Her heavenly lineaments for to enchace.°   *portray*

Ne wonder; for her owne deare lovèd knight,
All° were she dayly with himselfe in place,   *although*
205 Did wonder much at her celestiall sight:
Oft had he seene her faire, but never so faire dight.

24

So fairely dight, when she in presence came,
She to her Sire made humble reverence,
210 And bowèd low, that her right well became,
And added grace unto her excellence:
Who with great wisedome, and grave eloquence
Thus gan to say. But eare he thus had said,
With flying speede, and seeming great
   pretence,°   *purpose*
215 Came running in, much like a man dismaid,
A Messenger with letters, which his message said.

25

All in the open hall amazèd stood,
At suddeinnesse of that unwarie° sight,   *unexpected*
And wondred at his breathlesse hastie mood.
220 But he for nought would stay his passage right,°   *straight*
Till fast before the king he did alight;
Where falling flat, great humblesse he did make,
And kist the ground, whereon his foot was pight;
Then to his hands that writ he did betake,°   *deliver*
225 Which he disclosing,° red thus, as the   *unfolding / said*
   paper spake.

26

To thee, most mighty king of Eden faire,
Her greeting sends in these sad lines addrest,
The wofull daughter, and forsaken heire
Of that great Emperour of all the West;
230 And bids thee be advizèd for the best,
Ere thou thy daughter linck in holy band
Of wedlocke to that new unknowen guest:
For he already plighted his right hand
Unto another love, and to another land.

27

235 To me sad mayd, or rather widow sad,
He was affiauncèd° long time before,   *engaged*
And sacred pledges he both gave, and had,
False erraunt knight, infamous, and forswore:

Witnesse the burning Altars,[1] which° he swore, *by which*
240 And guiltie° heavens of his bold perjury,   *polluted*
Which though he hath polluted oft of yore,
Yet I to them for judgement just do fly,
And them conjure t'avenge this shamefull injury.

28

Therefore since mine he is, or free or bond,
245 Or false or trew, or living or else dead,
Withhold, O soveraine Prince, your hasty hond
From knitting league with him, I you aread;
Ne weene° my right with strength adowne to *think*
   tread,
Through weakenesse of my widowhed, or woe:
250 For truth is strong, her rightfull cause to plead,
And shall find friends, if need requireth soe,
So bids thee well to fare, Thy neither friend, nor foe,
   Fidessa.

29

When he these bitter byting words had red,
The tydings straunge did him abashèd make,
255 That still he sate long time astonishèd
As in great muse,° ne word to creature spake. *perplexity*
At last his solemne silence thus he brake,
With doubtfull eyes fast fixèd on his guest;
Redoubted° knight, that for mine onely sake *respected*
260 Thy life and honour late adventurest,
Let nought be hid from me, that ought to be exprest.

30

What meane these bloudy vowes, and idle threats,
Throwne out from womanish impatient mind?
What heavens? what altars? what enragèd
   heates°   *passions*
265 Here heapèd up with termes of love unkind,° *unnatural*
My conscience cleare with guilty bands would bind?
High God be witnesse, that I guiltlesse ame.
But if your selfe, Sir knight, ye faultie find,
Or wrappèd be in loves of former Dame,
270 With crime do not it cover, but disclose the same.

---

[1] *burning Altars* In classical Greece and Rome, the union of two persons in marriage was confirmed by burning sacrifices.

31

To whom the Redcrosse knight this answere sent,
  My Lord, my King, be nought hereat dismayd,
  Till well ye wote by grave intendiment,°   *consideration*
  What woman, and wherefore doth me upbrayd
275 With breach of love, and loyalty betrayd.
  It was in my mishaps, as hitherward
  I lately traveild, that unwares I strayd
  Out of my way, through perils straunge and hard;
That day should faile me, ere I had them all declard.

32

280 There did I find, or rather I was found
  Of this false woman, that Fidessa hight,
  Fidessa hight the falsest Dame on ground,
  Most false Duessa, royall richly dight,
  That easie° was t'invegle° weaker sight: *eager | blind*
285 Who by her wicked arts, and wylie skill,
  Too false and strong for earthly skill or might,
  Unwares me wrought unto her wicked will,
And to my foe betrayd, when least I feared ill.

33

Then stepped forth the goodly royall Mayd,
290 And on the ground her selfe prostrating low,
  With sober countenaunce thus to him sayd;
  O pardon me, my soveraigne Lord, to show
  The secret treasons, which of late I know
  To have bene wroght by that false sorceresse.
295 She onely she it is, that earst° did throw   *once*
  This gentle knight into so great distresse,
That death him did awaite in dayly wretchednesse.

34

And now it seemes, that she suborned hath
  This craftie messenger with letters vaine,
300 To worke new woe and improvided°   *unforeseen | damage*
    scath,
  By breaking of the band betwixt us twaine;
  Wherein she used hath the practicke°   *cunning | care*
    paine°
  Of this false footman, clokt with simplenesse,
  Whom if ye please for to discover plaine,
305 Ye shall him Archimago find, I ghesse,
The falsest man alive; who tries shall find no lesse.

35

The king was greatly moved at her speach,
  And all with suddein indignation fraight,°   *laden*
  Bad on that Messenger rude hands to reach.
310 Eftsoones° the Gard, which on his state did wait,   *at once*
  Attacht° that faitor° false, and bound   *seized | imposter*
    him strait:
  Who seeming sorely chauffed at his band,
  As chained Beare, whom cruell dogs do bait,
  With idle force did faine them to withstand,
315 And often semblaunce made to scape out of their hand.

36

But they him layd full low in dungeon deepe,
  And bound him hand and foote with yron chains.
  And with continuall watch did warely keepe;
  Who then would thinke, that by his subtile trains
320 He could escape fowle death or deadly paines?
  Thus when that Princes wrath was pacifide,
  He gan renew the late forbidden banes,°   *banns*
  And to the knight his daughter deare he tyde,
With sacred rites and vowes for ever to abyde.

37

325 His owne two hands the holy knots did knit,
  That none but death for ever can devide;
  His owne two hands, for such a turne most fit,
  The housling° fire did kindle and provide,   *sacramental*
  And holy water thereon sprinckled wide;[1]
330 At which the bushy Teade° a groome did light,   *torch*
  And sacred lampe in secret chamber hide,
  Where it should not be quenched day nor night,
For feare of evill fates, but burnen ever bright.

38

Then gan they sprinckle all the posts with wine,[2]
335 And made great feast to solemnize that day;
  They all perfumde with frankincense divine,
  And precious odours fetcht from far away,
  That all the house did sweat with great aray:°   *festivities*
  And all the while sweete Musicke did apply

---

[1] *The housing ... wide* The king is blessing the marriage with sacramental fire and water, as was common in ancient Roman marriage rituals.

[2] *Then gan ... wine* Sprinkling doorways with wine was meant to bring fertility.

340   Her curious° skill, the warbling notes to play,   *complex*
      To drive away the dull Melancholy;
    The whiles one sung a song of love and jollity.

              39

    During the which there was an heavenly noise
      Heard sound through all the Pallace pleasantly,
345   Like as it had bene many an Angels voice,
      Singing before th'eternall maiesty,
      In their trinall triplicities[1] on hye;
    Yet wist no creature, whence that heavenly sweet
    Proceeded, yet each one felt secretly
350   Himselfe thereby reft of his sences meet,
  And ravishèd with rare impression in his sprite.

              40

    Great joy was made that day of young and old,
      And solemne feast proclaimd throughout the land,
      That their exceeding merth may not be told:
355   Suffice it heare by signes to understand
      The usuall joyes at knitting of loves band.
      Thrise happy man the knight himselfe did hold,
      Possessèd of his Ladies hart and hand,
      And ever, when his eye did her behold,
360   His heart did seeme to melt in pleasures manifold.

              41

    Her joyous presence and sweet company
      In full content he there did long enioy,
      Ne wicked envie, ne vile gealosy
      His deare delights were able to annoy:
365   Yet swimming in that sea of blisfull joy,
      He nought forgot, how he whilome had sworne,
      In case he could that monstrous beast destroy,
      Unto his Farie Queene backe to returne:
  The which he shortly did, and Una left to mourne.

              42

370 Now strike your sailes ye jolly Mariners,
      For we be come unto a quiet rode,°   *harbor*
      Where we must land some of our passengers,
    And light this wearie vessell of her lode.

Here she a while may make her safe abode,
375   Till she repairèd have her tackles spent,°   *worn out*
      And wants supplide. And then againe abroad
      On the long voyage whereto she is bent:
    Well may she speede and fairely finish her intent.

from THE THIRD BOOKE OF THE FAERIE QUEENE CONTAYNING THE LEGEND OF BRITOMARTIS[2] OR OF CHASTITIE

CANTO 6

The birth of faire Belphoebe and
Of Amoret is told.
The Gardins of Adonis fraught
With pleasures manifold.

              1

Well may I weene, faire Ladies, all this while
      Ye wonder, how this noble Damozell
    So great perfections did in her compile,
    Sith that in salvage° forests she did dwell,   *wild*
5   So farre from court and royall Citadell,
    The great schoolmistresse of all curtesy:
    Seemeth that such wild woods should far expell
    All civill usage and gentility,
And gentle sprite deforme with rude rusticity.

              2

10 But to this faire Belphoebe[3] in her berth
      The heavens so favourable were and free,°   *liberal*
      Looking with myld aspect upon the earth,
    In th'Horoscope of her nativitee,[4]
    That all the gifts of grace and chastitee
    On her they pourèd forth of plenteous horne;[5]
    Jove laught on Venus from his soveraigne see,°   *throne*

---

[1] *trinall triplicities* The triple triad (nine orders) of angels, which correspond to the nine spheres of the universe. Thus the music described is that of the spheres, an extraordinarily beautiful harmony that humankind has been unable to hear since the Fall.

[2] *Britomartis* Her name is a combination of the words Britain and Mars (god of war).

[3] *Belphoebe* Her name associates her with the goddess Diana (also called Phoebe).

[4] *The heavens … nativitee* I.e., the planets were favorably arranged at the time of her birth. Any combination of Jupiter (Jove) and Venus was believed to bring particular luck.

[5] *plenteous horne* Horn of plenty.

And Phoebus[1] with faire beames did her adorne,
And all the Graces[2] rockt her cradle being borne.

3

Her berth was of the wombe of Morning dew,[3]
20   And her conception of the joyous Prime,
        And all her whole creation did her shew
        Pure and unspotted from all loathly crime,
        That is ingenerate° in fleshly slime.   *innate*
        So was this virgin borne, so was she bred,
25   So was she traynèd up from time to time,[4]
        In all chast vertue, and true bounti-hed°   *goodness*
Till to her dew perfection she was ripenèd.

4

Her mother was the faire Chrysogonee,
        The daughter of Amphisa,[5] who by race
30   A Faerie was, yborne of high degree,
        She bore Belphoebe, she bore in like cace
        Faire Amoretta[6] in the second place:
        These two were twinnes, & twixt them two did share
        The heritage of all celestiall grace.
35   That all the rest it seem'd they robbèd bare
Of bountie,° and of beautie, and all vertues rare.   *goodness*

5

It were a goodly storie, to declare,
        By what straunge accident faire Chrysogone
        Conceiv'd these infants, and how them she bare,
40   In this wild forrest wandring all alone,
        After she had nine moneths fulfild and gone:
        For not as other wemens commune brood,
        They were enwombèd in the sacred throne

Of her chaste bodie, nor with commune food,
45   As other wemens babes, they suckèd vitall blood.

6

But wondrously they were begot, and bred
        Through influence of th'heavens fruitfull ray,
        As it in antique bookes is mentionèd.
        It was upon a Sommers shynie day,
50   When Titan[7] faire his beamès did display,
        In a fresh fountaine, farre from all mens vew,
        She bath'd her brest, the boyling heat t'allay;
        She bath'd with roses red, and violets blew,
And all the sweetest flowres, that in the forrest grew.

7

55   Till faint through irkesome wearinesse, adowne
        Upon the grassie ground her selfe she layd
        To sleepe, the whiles a gentle slombring swowne°   *sleep*
        Upon her fell all naked bare displayd;
        The sunne-beames bright upon her body playd,
60   Being through former bathing mollifide,°   *made soft*
        And pierst into her wombe, where they
            embayd°   *permeated*
        With so sweet sence° and secret power unspide,   *sensation*
That in her pregnant flesh they shortly fructifide.

8

Miraculous may seeme to him, that reades
65   So straunge ensample of conception;
        But reason teacheth that the fruitfull seades
        Of all things living, through impression
        Of the sunbeames in moyst complexion,
        Doe life conceive and quickned are by kynd:°   *nature*
70   So after Nilus° inundation,   *the Nile's*
        Infinite shapes of creatures men do fynd,
Informèd° in the mud, on which the Sunne   *formed*
        hath shynd.

9

Great father he of generation
        Is rightly cald, th'author of life and light;
75   And his faire sister[8] for creation
        Ministreth matter fit, which tempred right

---

[1] *Phoebus* I.e., Phoebus Apollo, god of the sun.

[2] *the Graces* Three sister goddesses who dispense the gifts of pleasure, beauty, and charm.

[3] *Her . . . dew* Cf. Psalm 110.3, describing the reign of the Messiah: "Thy people shall be willing in the day of thy power, in the beauties of holiness from the womb of the morning: thou hast the dew of thy youth."

[4] *from time to time* Continuously.

[5] *Chrysogonee* Golden-born (Danaë conceived when Jove came to her as a golden shower); *Amphisa* Of double nature.

[6] *Amoretta* Italian: little love.

[7] *Titan* The sun.

[8] *his faire sister* The moon.

With heate and humour,° breedes the living
   wight.°   *moisture / creature*
So sprong these twinnes in wombe of Chrysogone,
Yet wist° she nought thereof, but sore affright,   *knew*
80   Wondred to see her belly so upblone,
Which still increast, till she her terme had full outgone.

10

Whereof conceiving shame and foule disgrace,
  Albe° her guiltlesse conscience her cleard,   *although*
She fled into the wildernesse a space,
85   Till that unweeldy burden she had reard,°   *brought forth*
And shund dishonor, which as death she feard:
Where wearie of long travell, downe to rest
Her selfe she set, and comfortably cheard;[1]
There a sad cloud of sleepe her overkest,°   *covered*
90 And seizèd every sense with sorrow sore opprest.

11

It fortunèd, faire Venus having lost
  Her little sonne, the wingèd god of love,
Who for some light displeasure, which him crost,
Was from her fled, as flit° as ayerie Dove,   *quick*
95   And left her blisfull bowre of joy above,
(So from her often he had fled away,
When she for ought him sharpely did reprove,
And wandred in the world in strange aray,
Disguiz'd in thousand shapes, that none might him
   bewray.°)   *reveal*

12

100 Him for to seeke, she left her heavenly hous,
  The house of goodly formes and faire aspects,
Whence all the world derives the glorious
Features of beautie, and all shapes select,°   *choice*
With which high God his workmanship hath deckt;
105   And searchèd every way, through which his wings
Had borne him, or his tract° she mote°   *path / might*
   detect:
She promist kisses sweet, and sweeter things
Unto the man, that of him tydings to her brings.

13

First she him sought in Court, where most he used

110 Whylome° to haunt, but there she found   *previously*
   him not;
But many there she found, which sore accused
His falsehood, and with foule infamous blot
His cruell deedes and wicked wyles did spot:°   *reproach*
Ladies and Lords she every where mote heare
115 Complayning, how with his empoysned shot
Their wofull harts he wounded had
   whyleare,°   *a while earlier*
And so had left them languishing twixt hope and feare.

14

She then the Cities sought from gate to gate,
  And every one did aske, did he him see;
120 And every one her answerd, that too late°   *recently*
He had him seene, and felt the crueltie
Of his sharpe darts and whot° artillerie;   *hot*
And every one threw forth reproches rife
Of his mischievous deedes, and said, that hee
125 Was the disturber of all civill life,
The enimy of peace, and author of all strife.

15

Then in the countrey she abroad him sought,
  And in the rurall cottages inquired,
Where also many plaints to her were brought,
130 How he their heedlesse harts with love had fyred,
And his false venim through their veines inspyred;
And eke the gentle shepheard swaynes,°   *country laborers*
   which sat
Keeping their fleecie flockes, as they were hyred,
She sweetly heard complaine, both how and what
135 Her sonne had to them doen; yet she did smile thereat.

16

But when in none of all these she him got,
  She gan avize,° where else he mote him hyde: *reflect*
At last she her bethought, that she had not
Yet sought the salvage woods and forrests wyde,
140 In which full many lovely Nymphes abyde,
Mongst whom might be, that he did closely lye,
Or that the love of some of them him tyde:°   *bound*
For thy,[2] she thither cast° her course t'apply,   *resolved*
To search the secret haunts of Dianes company.

---

[1] *comfortably cheard* I.e., was cheered by this comfort.

[2] *For thy* Therefore.

17

145 Shortly unto the wastefull° woods she came,   *wild*
    Whereas she found the Goddesse with her crew,
    After late chace of their embrewèd° game,   *bloodstained*
    Sitting beside a fountaine in a rew,°   *row*
    Some of them washing with the liquid dew
150   From off their dainty limbes the dustie sweat,
    And soyle which did deforme their lively hew;
    Others lay shaded from the scorching heat;
The rest upon her person gave attendance great.

18

She having hong upon a bough on high
155   Her bow and painted quiver, had unlaste°   *untied*
    Her silver buskins° from her nimble thigh,   *boots*
    And her lancke° loynes ungirt, and brests   *slender*
       unbraste,
    After her heat the breathing cold to taste;
    Her golden lockes, that late in tresses bright
160   Embreaded° were for° hindring of   *braided | to prevent*
       her haste,
    Now loose about her shoulders hong undight,°   *unbound*
And were with sweet Ambrosia° all   *perfume*
      bespinckled light.

19

Soone as she Venus saw behind her backe,
    She was asham'd to be so loose surprized,
165   And woxe° halfe wroth against her damzels slacke,   *grew*
    That had not her thereof before avized,°   *warned*
    But suffred her so carelesly disguized
    Be overtaken. Soone her garments loose
    Upgath'ring, in her bosome she comprized,°   *gathered*
170   Well as she might, and to the Goddesse rose,
Whiles all her Nymphes did like a girlond her enclose.

20

Goodly° she gan faire Cytherea[1] greet,   *politely*
    And shortly askèd her, what cause her brought
    Into that wildernesse for her unmeet,°   *unsuitable*
175   From her sweet bowres, and beds with pleasures
      fraught:

That suddein change she strange adventure°   *chance*
    thought.
    To whom halfe weeping, she thus answerèd,
    That she her dearest sonne Cupido sought,
    Who in his frowardnesse° from her was fled;   *naughtiness*
180 That she repented sore, to have him angerèd.

21

Thereat Diana gan to smile, in scorne
    Of her vaine plaint, and to her scoffing sayd;
    Great pittie sure, that ye be so forlorne
    Of your gay sonne, that gives ye so good ayd
185   To your disports:° ill mote ye bene
      apayd.°   *amusements | repaid*
    But she was more engrievèd, and replide;
    Faire sister, ill beseemes it to upbrayd
    A dolefull heart with so disdainfull pride;
The like that mine, may be your paine another tide.°   *time*

22

190 As you in woods and wanton wildernesse
    Your glory set, to chace the salvage beasts,
    So my delight is all in joyfulnesse,
    In beds, in bowres, in banckets,° and in feasts: *banquets*
    And ill becomes you with your loftie creasts,°   *helmets*
195   To scorne the joy, that Jove is glad to seeke;
    We both are bound to follow heavens beheasts,
    And tend our charges with obeisance meeke:
Spare, gentle sister, with reproch my paine to eeke.°   *increase*

23

And tell me, if that ye my sonne have heard,
200   To lurke emongst your Nymphes in secret wize;
    Or keepe their cabins:° much I am affeard,   *caves*
    Least he like one of them him selfe disguize,
    And turne his arrowes to their exercize:
    So may he long himselfe full easie hide:
205   For he is faire and fresh in face and guize,
    As any Nymph (let not it be envyde),°   *begrudged*
So saying every Nymph full narrowly she eyde.

24

But Phoebe therewith sore was angered,
    And sharply said; Goe Dame, goe seeke your boy,

---

[1] *Cytherea* Venus, who, according to myth, first rose out of the sea near the island of Cythera.

210 Where you him lately left, in Mars[1] his bed;
     He comes not here, we scorne his foolish joy,
     Ne lend we leisure to his idle toy:°   *play*
     But if I catch him in this company,
     By Stygian lake[2] I vow, whose sad annoy°   *affliction*
215 The Gods doe dread, he dearely shall abye:°   *atone for it*
     Ile clip his wanton wings, that he no more shall fly.

25

     Whom when as Venus saw so sore displeased,
     She inly sory was, and gan relent,
     What she had said: so her she soone appeased,
220 With sugred words and gentle blandishment,°   *flattery*
     Which as a fountaine from her sweet lips went,
     And wellèd goodly forth, that in short space
     She was well pleasd, and forth her damzels sent,
     Through all the woods, to search from place to place,
225 If any tract° of him or tydings they mote trace. *trace*

26

     To search the God of love, her Nymphes she sent
     Throughout the wandring forrest every where:
     And after them her selfe eke with her went
     To seeke the fugitive, both farre and nere,
230 So long they sought, till they arrivèd were
     In that same shadie covert, whereas lay
     Faire Crysogone in slombry traunce whilere:
     Who in her sleepe (a wondrous thing to say)
     Unwares had borne two babes, as faire as
        springing° day.   *dawning*

27

235 Unwares she them conceiv'd, unwares she bore:
     She bore withouten paine, that she conceived
     Withouten pleasure: ne her need implore
     Lucinaes[3] aide: which when they both perceived,
     They were through wonder nigh° of sense
        bereaved,   *almost*
240 And gazing each on other, nought bespake:°   *spoke*

     At last they both agreed, her seeming grieved° *afflicted*
     Out of her heavy swowne not to awake,
     But from her loving side the tender babes to take.

28

     Up they them tooke, each one a babe uptooke,
245 And with them carried, to be fosterèd;
     Dame Phoebe to a Nymph her babe betooke,
     To be upbrought in perfect Maydenhed,°   *virginity*
     And of her selfe her name Belphoebe red:°   *declared*
     But Venus hers thence farre away convayd,
250 To be upbrought in goodly womanhed,
     And in her litle loves stead, which was strayd,
     Her Amoretta cald, to comfort her dismayd.

29

     She brought her to her joyous Paradize,
     Where most she wonnes,° when she on earth   *resides*
        does dwel.
255 So faire a place, as Nature can devize:
     Whether in Paphos, or Cytheron hill,
     Or it in Gnidus[4] be, I wote not well;
     But well I wote by tryall, that this same
     All other pleasant places doth excell,
260 And callèd is by her lost lovers name,[5]
     The Gardin of Adonis, farre renowmd by fame.

30

     In that same Gardin all the goodly flowres,
     Wherewith dame Nature doth her beautifie,
     And decks the girlonds° of her paramoures,   *garlands*
265 Are fetcht: there is the first seminarie°   *seed-plot*
     Of all things, that are borne to live and die,
     According to their kindes. Long worke it were,
     Here to account° the endlesse progenie   *enumerate*
     Of all the weedes, that bud and blossome there;
270 But so much as doth need, must needs be
        counted° here.   *listed*

---

1   *Mars*   God of war and Venus's lover.

2   *Stygian lake*   The Styx, a river of the underworld. Oaths made on
the Styx were especially sacred; even the gods would not break them.

3   *Lucinaes*   Goddess of childbirth.

4   *Paphos … Gnidus*   Locations of three major shrines to Venus.

5   *her … name*   Venus loved a beautiful boy named Adonis, who was
killed by a boar while hunting one day. His blood was transformed
into a flower, the anemone.

31

It sited° was in fruitfull soyle of old,   *located*
　　And girt in with two walles on either side;
　　The one of yron, the other of bright gold,
　　That none might thorough breake, nor over-stride:
275　And double gates it had, which opened wide,
　　By which both in and out men moten pas;
　　Th'one faire and fresh, the other old and dride:
　　Old Genius[1] the porter of them was,
Old Genius, the which a double nature has.

32

280　He letteth in, he letteth out to wend,°   *come*
　　All that to come into the world desire;
　　A thousand thousand naked babes attend
　　About him day and night, which doe require,
　　That he with fleshly weedes would them attire:
285　Such as him list,° such as eternall fate   *likes*
　　Ordainèd hath, he clothes with sinfull mire,[2]
　　And sendeth forth to live in mortall state,
Till they againe returne backe by the hinder gate.

33

After that they againe returnèd beene,
290　They in that Gardin planted be againe;
　　And grow afresh, as they had never seene
　　Fleshly corruption, nor mortall paine.
　　Some thousand yeares so doen they there remaine;
　　And then of him are clad with other hew,°   *form*
295　Or sent into the chaungefull world againe,
　　Till thither they returne, where first they grew:
So like a wheele around they runne from old to new.

34

Ne needs there Gardiner to set, or sow,
　　To plant or prune: for of their owne accord
300　All things, as they created were, doe grow,
　　And yet remember well the mightie word,
　　Which first was spoken by th'Almightie lord,
　　That bad them to increase and multiply:[3]
　　Ne doe they need with water of the ford,°   *stream*

305　Or of the clouds to moysten their roots dry;
　　For in themselves eternall moisture they imply.°   *contain*

35

Infinite shapes of creatures there are bred,
　　And uncouth° formes, which none yet   *unfamiliar*
　　　ever knew,
　　And every sort is in a sundry° bed   *separate*
310　Set by it selfe, and ranckt° in comely rew:°   *arranged / row*
　　Some fit for reasonable[4] soules t'indew,°   *assume*
　　Some made for beasts, some made for birds to weare,
　　And all the fruitfull spawne of fishes hew
　　In endlesse rancks along enraungèd were,
315　That seem'd the Ocean could not containe them there.

36

Daily they grow, and daily forth are sent
　　Into the world, it to replenish more;
　　Yet is the stocke not lessenèd, nor spent,
　　But still remaines in everlasting store,
320　As it at first created was of yore.
　　For in the wide wombe of the world there lyes,
　　In hatefull darkenesse and in deepe horrore,
　　An huge eternall Chaos, which supplyes
The substances of natures fruitfull progenyes.

37

All things from thence doe their first being fetch,
　　And borrow matter, whereof they are made,
　　Which when as forme and feature it does ketch,°   *take*
　　Becomes a bodie, and doth then invade°   *enter*
　　The state of life, out of the griesly shade.
330　That substance is eterne, and bideth so,
　　Ne when the life decayes, and forme does fade,
　　Doth it consume, and into nothing go,
But chaungèd is, and often altred to and fro.

38

The substance is not chaunged, nor alterèd,
335　But th'only forme and outward fashion;
　　For every substance is conditionèd°   *bound*
　　To change her hew, and sundry formes to don,
　　Meet for her temper and complexion:
　　For formes are variable and decay,

---

[1]　*Genius*   I.e., Janus, the Roman god of doors and gates.

[2]　*sinfull mire*   Flesh.

[3]　*increase and multiply*   See Genesis 1.28.

[4]　*reasonable*   Rational; i.e., human.

340   By course of kind,° and by occasion;   *nature*
       And that faire flowre of beautie fades away,
       As doth the lilly fresh before the sunny ray.

39

    Great enimy to it, and to all the rest,
       That in the Gardin of Adonis springs,
345   Is wicked Time, who with his scyth addrest,°   *armed*
       Does mow the flowring herbes and goodly things,
       And all their glory to the ground downe flings,
       Where they doe wither, and are fowly mard:°   *marred*
       He flyes about, and with his flaggy wings
350   Beates downe both leaves and buds without regard,
    Ne ever pittie may relent° his malice hard.   *soften*

40

    Yet pittie often did the gods relent,
       To see so faire things mard, and spoylèd quight:
       And their great mother Venus did lament
355   The losse of her deare brood, her deare delight:
       Her hart was pierst with pittie at the sight,
       When walking through the Gardin, them she spyde,
       Yet no'te she find redresse for such despight.
       For all that lives, is subject to that law:
360   All things decay in time, and to their end do draw.

41

    But were it not, that Time their troubler is,
       All that in this delightfull Gardin growes,
       Should happie be, and have immortall blis:
       For here all plentie, and all pleasure flowes,
365   And sweet love gentle fits° emongst them   *impulses*
         throwes,
       Without fell rancor, or fond° gealosie;   *foolish*
       Franckly each paramour his leman knowes,
       Each bird his mate, ne any does envie
       Their goodly meriment, and gay felicitie.

42

370   There is continuall spring, and harvest there
       Continuall, both meeting at one time:
       For both the boughes doe laughing blossomes beare,
       And with fresh colours decke the wanton Prime,
       And eke attonce the heavy trees they clime,
375   Which seeme to labour under their fruits lode:
       The whiles the joyous birdes make their pastime

    Emongst the shadie leaves, their sweet abode,
    And their true loves without suspition tell abrode.

43

    Right in the middest of that Paradise,
380   There stood a stately Mount, on whose round top
       A gloomy° grove of mirtle trees[1] did rise,   *shady*
       Whose shadie boughes sharpe steele did never lop,° *cut*
       Nor wicked beasts their tender buds did crop,
       But like a girlond compassèd the hight,
385   And from their fruitfull sides sweet gum did drop,
       That all the ground with precious deaw
         bedight,°   *bedecked*
    Threw forth most dainty odours, & most sweet delight.

44

    And in the thickest covert of that shade,
       There was a pleasant arbour, not by art,
390   But of the trees owne inclination made,
       Which knitting their rancke° braunches part   *dense*
         to part,
       With wanton yvie twyne entrayld°
         athwart,°   *entwined | across*
       And Eglantine,° and Caprifole°   *sweet-briar | honeysuckle*
         emong,
       Fashiond above within their inmost part,
395   That nether Phoebus beams could through them
         throng,
    Nor Aeolus sharp blast could worke them any wrong.

45

    And all about grew every sort of flowre,
       To which sad lovers were transformd of yore;
       Fresh Hyacinthus,[2] Phoebus paramoure,
400   And dearest love:
       Foolish Narcisse,[3] that likes the watry shore,
       Sad Amaranthus, made a flowre but late,°   *recently*
       Sad Amaranthus, in whose purple gore

---

[1] *mirtle trees* Myrtle was sacred to Venus.

[2] *Hyacinthus* Apollo accidentally killed his young lover Hyacinth, and the hyacinth flower sprang up from the drops of his blood.

[3] *Narcisse* Narcissus, who fell in love with his own reflection in a pool of water and pined away when he realized it. A narcissus sprang up at the poolside when he died.

Me seemes I see Amintas[1] wretched fate,
405   To whom sweet Poets verse hath given endlesse date.

46

There wont° faire Venus often to enioy   *was accustomed*
 Her deare Adonis joyous company,
 And reape sweet pleasure of the wanton boy;
 There yet, some say, in secret he does ly,
410   Lappèd in flowres and pretious spycery,°   *spices*
 By her hid from the world, and from the skill°   *knowledge*
 Of Stygian Gods, which doe her love envy;
 But she her selfe, when ever that she will,
Possesseth him, and of his sweetnesse takes her fill.

47

415   And sooth° it seemes they say: for he may not   *truly*
 For ever die, and ever buried bee
 In balefull night, where all things are forgot;
 All° be he subject to mortalitie,   *although*
 Yet is eterne in mutabilitie,
420   And by succession made perpetuall,
 Transformèd oft, and chaungèd diverslie:
 For him the Father of all formes they call;
Therefore needs mote he live, that living gives to all.

48

There now he liveth in eternall blis,
425   Joying° his goddesse, and of her enjoyd: *enjoying*
 Ne feareth he henceforth that foe of his,
 Which with his cruell tuske him deadly cloyd:°   *pierced*
 For that wilde Bore, the which him once
  annoyd,°   *harmed*
 She firmely hath emprisoned for ay,°   *ever*
430   That her sweet love his malice mote avoyd,
 In a strong rocky Cave, which is they say,
Hewen underneath that Mount, that none him losen
  may.

49

There now he lives in everlasting joy,
 With many of the Gods in company,
435   Which thither haunt, and with the wingèd boy
 Sporting himselfe in safe felicity:

Who when he hath with spoiles and cruelty
 Ransackt the world, and in the wofull harts
 Of many wretches set his triumphes hye,
440   Thither resorts, and laying his sad darts
Aside, with faire Adonis playes his wanton parts.

50

And his true love faire Psyche[2] with him playes,
 Faire Psyche to him lately reconcyld,
 After long troubles and unmeet upbrayes,°   *reproofs*
445   With which his mother Venus her revyld,°   *reproached*
 And eke himselfe her cruelly exyld:
 But now in stedfast love and happy state
 She with him lives, and hath him borne a chyld,
 Pleasure, that doth both gods and men aggrate,°   *gratify*
450   Pleasure, the daughter of Cupid and Psyche late.

51

Hither great Venus brought this infant faire,
 The younger daughter of Chrysogonee,
 And unto Psyche with great trust and care
 Committed her, yfosterèd to bee,
455   And traind up in true feminitee:
 Who no lesse carefully her tenderèd,°   *cared for*
 Then her owne daughter Pleasure, to whom shee
 Made her companion, and her lessonèd°   *taught*
In all the lore of love, and goodly womanhead.

52

460   In which when she to perfect ripenesse grew,
 Of grace and beautie noble Paragone,°   *model*
 She brought her forth into the worldès vew,
 To be th'ensample of true love alone,
 And Lodestarre° of all chaste affectione,   *guiding star*
465   To all faire Ladies, that doe live on ground.
 To Faery court she came, where many one
 Admyrd her goodly haveour,° and found   *bearing*
His feeble hart wide launchèd° with loves cruell   *cut*
  wound.

---

1   *Amintas*   Man who died for the love of a woman named Phillis and was changed into an Amaranthus flower.

2   *Psyche*   Wife of Cupid who, when she disobeyed his orders never to look at his face, was punished by Venus, who set her several seemingly impossible tasks. Finally the gods mercifully granted Psyche immortality, allowing her to become a suitable partner for Cupid. See Apoleius's *Golden Ass* (second century CE).

53

But she to none of them her love did cast,
470   Save to the noble knight Sir Scudamore,
    To whom her loving hart she linkèd fast
    In faithfull love, t'abide for ever more,
    And for his dearest sake endurèd sore,
    Sore trouble of an hainous enimy;
475   Who her would forcèd have to have forlore°   *abandoned*
    Her former love, and stedfast loyalty,
As ye may elsewhere read that ruefull history.

54

But well I weene, ye first desire to learne,
    What end unto that fearefull Damozell,
480   Which fled so fast from that same foster°
      stearne,°   *forester / cruel*
    Whom with his brethren Timias slew, befell:
    That was to weet, the goodly Florimell;
    Who wandring for to seeke her lover deare,
    Her lover deare, her dearest Marinell,
485   Into misfortune fell, as ye did heare,
And from Prince Arthur fled with wings of idle feare.[1]
—1590, 1596

Letter to Sir Walter Ralegh
on The Faerie Queene

Spenser's letter to Sir Walter Ralegh, an important colleague in England's efforts to govern the often rebellious Irish, was first published, together with a large number of dedicatory sonnets, as an explanatory "annex" to the 1590 *Faerie Queene*. The 1596 edition dropped it, possibly because Ralegh had recently earned the queen's displeasure or perhaps because, or so think many scholars, what the letter

says about the plot sits problematically alongside the poem itself. Nor is it clear how the "virtues" on which Spenser tells Ralegh he would base his projected twelve books in fact relate to those of Aristotle, particularly since Aristotelian tradition had been modified by a still lively Medieval Scholastic and Christian understanding of that Greek philosopher. The Letter reappeared near the end of the 1690 *Faerie Queene*, and since then it has been routinely printed with the poem, often as a preface even though Spenser wrote it as an appendix. Authorities on Spenser, who read the Letter with interest, caution, and sometimes puzzlement, disagree as to where it should be placed. In this edition we retain it as an "annex," but readers should remember that it is an anomaly—a prefatory afterword.

Letter to Sir Walter Ralegh
on The Faerie Queene

A Letter of the author's expounding his whole intention in the course of this work: which, for that it giveth great light to the reader, for the better understanding is hereunto annexed.[2]

To the right noble, and valorous, Sir Walter Ralegh, knight, Lord Warden of the Stanneries,[3] and Her Majesty's lieutenant of the County of Cornwall.

Sir: Knowing how doubtfully all Allegories may be construed, and this book of mine, which I have entitled the *Faery Queene*, being a continued allegory, or dark conceit,[4] I have thought good, as well for avoiding of jealous opinions and misconstructions, as also for your better light in reading thereof (being so by you commanded), to discover unto you the general intention and meaning which in the whole course thereof I have fashioned, without expressing of any particular purposes or by-accidents[5] therein occasioned. The general end therefore of all the book is to fashion a

---

1 *But well … feare* In Canto 1, Britomart, Arthur, and Timias (meaning honored), his squire, encounters the lovely Florimell (whose name combines the words flower and honey and who is associated with Beauty) fleeing from a cruel forester. Timias pursues and eventually slays the forester, along with his two brothers, though he is seriously wounded in the process. In Canto 4, we learned that Florimell is seeking her beloved, Marinell (whose name associates him with the sea). Marinell, however, has been told by his mother that a woman will cause him mortal harm and therefore has rejected Florimell's love.

2 *annexed* Added.

3 *Stanneries* Mines in Cornwall and Devon.

4 *dark conceit* Semi-concealed or difficult poetic notion, plan, or conception.

5 *by-accidents* Secondary narratives or descriptions.

gentleman or noble person in virtuous and gentle[1] discipline: which for that I conceived should be most plausible and pleasing being coloured with an historical fiction,[2] the which the most part of men delight to read rather for variety of matter than for profit of the ensample,[3] I chose the history of King Arthur, as most fit for the excellency of his person, being made famous by many men's former works, and also furthest from the danger of envy, and suspicion of present time.[4] In which I have followed all the antique poets historical: first Homer, who in the persons of Agamemnon and Ulysses hath ensampled[5] a good governor and a virtuous man, the one in his Ilias, the other in his Odysseus; then Virgil, whose like intention was to do[6] in the person of Æneas; after him Ariosto comprised them both in his Orlando; and lately Tasso dissevered them again and formed both parts in two persons, namely that part which they in philosophy call Ethice, or virtues of a private man, coloured[7] in his Rinaldo; the other named Politice in his Godfredo.[8] By ensample of which excellent poets, I labour to portrait[9] in Arthur, before he was king, the image of a brave knight perfected in the twelve private moral virtues as Aristotle hath devised, the which is the purpose of these first twelve books:[10] which if I find to be well accepted, I may be perhaps encouraged to frame the other part of politic virtues in his person after that he came to be king. To some, I

know, this method will seem unpleasant, who had rather have good discipline delivered plainly in way of precepts,[11] or sermoned at large, as they use, than thus cloudily enwrapped in allegorical devises. But such, meseems, should be satisfied with the use[12] of these days, seeing all things accounted by their shows and nothing esteemed of that is not delightful and pleasing to common sense.[13] For this cause is Xenophon preferred before Plato,[14] for that the one, in the exquisite depth of his judgement, formed a commonwealth such as it should be, but the other in the person of Cyrus and the Persians fashioned a government such as might best be: so much more profitable and gracious is doctrine by ensample than by rule. So have I laboured to do in the person of Arthur: whom I conceive, after his long education by Timon, to whom he was by Merlin delivered to be brought up so soon as he was born of the Lady Igrayne, to have seen in a dream or vision the Faery Queene, with whose excellent beauty ravished, he awaking resolved to seek her out, and so being by Merlin armed, and by Timon thoroughly instructed, he went to seek her forth in Faery Land. In that Faery Queene I mean glory in my general intention, but in my particular I conceive the most excellent and glorious person of our sovereign the Queene,[15] and her kingdom in Faery Land. And yet, in some places else[16] I do otherwise shadow[17] her. For considering she beareth two persons, the one of a most royal queene or empress, the other of a most virtuous and beautiful lady, this latter

---

[1] *fashion* Represent; also form, educate; *gentle* As befits the gentry class, the well-born.

[2] *historical fiction* Imaginary narrative, fiction.

[3] *ensample* Example, model.

[4] *suspicion of present time* Potential accusations related to current political controversies or government censorship.

[5] *ensampled* Exemplified.

[6] *like intention was to do* I.e., "intention was to do something similar."

[7] *coloured* Illustrated, demonstrated.

[8] *Ariosto* Lodovico Ariosto (1474–1533) wrote the epic romance *Orlando Furioso* (1532); *Tasso* Torquato Tasso (1544–95) published *Rinaldo*, a chivalric romance, in 1562, and *Gerusalemme Liberata* (which follows the epic adventures of Count Godfredo) in 1581.

[9] *portrait* Portray.

[10] *first twelve books* Evidently, Spenser planned for *The Faerie Queene* to comprise 12 books and then perhaps a sequel of another 12; so far as we know, he completed only six.

[11] *precepts* Principles, advice.

[12] *use* Custom.

[13] *shows* Outward appearances; *common sense* Popular opinion, or less pejoratively, the consensus.

[14] *Xenophon preferred before Plato* Spenser contrasts Xenophon's *Cyropaedia* (early 4th century BCE), with its narrative excitement, compelling characters, and greater political realism, to Plato's more abstract ideal *Republic* (c. 380 BCE).

[15] *our sovereign the Queene* Elizabeth I (reigned 1558–1603); Spenser exploits the older conception of the monarch's two bodies, one public and continuing, the other private, individual, and mortal.

[16] *places else* Other places.

[17] *shadow* Indirectly represent.

part in some places I do express in Belphœbe, fashioning her name according to your own excellent conceit of Cynthia[1] (Phoebe and Cynthia being both names of Diana). So in the person of Prince Arthur I set forth magnificence[2] in particular, which virtue for that (according to Aristotle and the rest) it is the perfection of all the rest and containeth in it them all, therefore in the whole course I mention the deeds of Arthur applicable to that virtue which I write of in that book. But of the 12 other virtues I make 12 other knights the patrons, for the more variety of the history: of which these three books contain three. The first of the Knight of the Redcrosse, in whom I express holiness. The second of Sir Guyon, in whom I set forth temperance.[3] The third of Britomart, a lady knight, in whom I picture chastity.[4] But because the beginning of the whole work seemeth abrupt and as depending upon other antecedents, it needs that ye know the occasion of these three knights' several adventures. For the method of a poet historical is not such as of an historiographer.[5] For an historiographer discourseth[6] of affairs orderly as they were done, accounting as well the times as the actions; but a poet thrusteth into the midst, even where it most concerneth him, and there recoursing to the things forepast,[7] and divining of things to come, maketh a pleasing analysis of all.

The beginning therefore of my history, if it were to be told by an historiographer, should be the twelfth

book, which is the last, where I devise that the Faery Queene kept her annual feast 12 days, upon which 12 several[8] days, the occasions of the 12 several adventures happened, which being undertaken by 12 several knights, are in these 12 books severally handled and discoursed. The first was this: In the beginning of the feast, there presented himself a tall clownish[9] young man, who falling before the Queen of Faries desired a boon[10] (as the manner then was), which during that feast she might not refuse: which was that he might have the achievement of any adventure which during that feast should happen; that being granted, he rested him on the floor, unfit through his rusticity for a better place. Soon after entered a fair lady in mourning weeds,[11] riding on a white ass, with a dwarf behind her leading a warlike steed that bore the arms of a knight, and his spear in the dwarf's hand. She, falling before the Queene of Faeries, complained that her father and mother, an ancient king and queene, had been by an huge dragon many years shut up in a brasen[12] castle, who thence suffered them not to issue;[13] and therefore besought the Faery Queene to assign her some one of her knights to take on him that exploit. Presently that clownish person, upstarting, desired that adventure, whereat the Queene much wondering and the lady much gainsaying,[14] yet he earnestly importuned[15] his desire. In the end the lady told him that unless that

---

[1] *Cynthia* Probably as an effort to soften her anger, Ralegh's poem *The Ocean to Cynthia* (1592?) praises the still-offended Queen Elizabeth. Cynthia, Phoebe, and Diana were all names for the Greco-Roman virgin goddess of the hunt and the moon.

[2] *magnificence* "Greatness in action," specifically a princely and protective liberality suiting a great ruler. How Magnificence relates to the Aristotelian "Magnanimity" (greatness of soul) has been debated, as has the relation of either virtue to Christian thinking, especially granted Medieval interpretations of Aristotle.

[3] *temperance* Moderation and self restraint, but also the dynamic fusion of opposites (one "tempers" a sword with fire and cold water).

[4] *chastity* Not to be confused with virginity; chastity includes faithful married sexuality.

[5] *historiographer* Writer of factual chronicles.

[6] *discourseth* Tells.

[7] *recoursing to things forepast* Returning to past events; like Homer and Virgil, Spenser begins his poem *in medias res* (in the middle) and then indicates what has come before.

[8] *several* Separate.

[9] *clownish* Rustic-looking.

[10] *boon* Favor.

[11] *weeds* Clothes.

[12] *brasen* Strong.

[13] *issue* Emerge.

[14] *gainsaying* Opposing.

[15] *importuned* Begged for.

armour which she brought would serve him (that is, the armour of a Christian man specified by Saint Paul, vi Ephes.),[1] that he could not succeed in that enterprise: which being forthwith put upon him with due furnitures[2] thereunto, he seemed the goodliest man in all that company, and was well liked of the lady. And soon after taking on him knighthood, and mounting on that strange courser,[3] he went forth with her on that adventure, where beginneth the first book, vz.[4] "A gentle knight was pricking on the plain," &c.

The second day there came in a palmer[5] bearing an infant with bloody hands, whose parents he complained to have been slain by an enchantress called Acrasia, and therefore craved of the Faery Queene to appoint him some knight to perform that adventure, which being assigned to Sir Guyon, he presently went forth with that same palmer, which is the beginning of the second book and the whole subject thereof. The third day there came in a groom,[6] who complained before the Faery Queene, that a vile enchanter called Busirane had in hand a most fair lady, called Amoret, whom he kept in most grievous torment because she would not yield him the pleasure of her body. Whereupon Sir Scudamour, the lover of that lady, presently took on him that adventure. But being unable to perform it by reason of the hard[7] enchantments, after long sorrow, in the end met with Britomart, who succoured[8] him, and rescued his love.

But by occasion hereof, many other adventures are intermedled, but rather as accidents than intendments,[9] as the love of Britomart, the overthrow of Marinell, the misery of Florimell, the virtuousness of Belphœbe, the lasciviousness[10] of Hellenora, and many the like.

Thus much, Sir, I have briefly overrun[11] to direct your understanding to the well-head of the history, that from thence gathering the whole intention of the conceit ye may, as in a handful, grip all the discourse, which otherwise may happily[12] seem tedious and confused. So humbly craving the continuance of your honourable favour towards me, and th'eternal establishment of your happiness, I humbly take leave.

23 January, 1589[13]

Yours most humbly affectionate,

Ed. Spenser

---

[1] *Saint Paul, vi Ephes.* Ephesians 6 in which Paul commands, "Put on the whole armor of God, that ye may be able to stand against the wiles of the devil." The parts specified are the loins girt about with truth; the breastplate of righteousness; feet shod with the gospel of peace; the shield of faith "wherewith ye shall be able to quench all the fiery darts of the wicked"; the helmet of salvation; and "the sword of the Spirit, which is the word of God."

[2] *due furnitures* Suitable equipment, supplies.

[3] *courser* Swift horse.

[4] *vz.* Latin: namely, to wit (Videlicet. Abbreviation: viz).

[5] *palmer* Pilgrim, especially one who has returned from the Holy Land.

[6] *groom* Manservant.

[7] *hard* Persistent, powerful.

[8] *succoured* Assisted.

[9] *accidents than intendments* Episodes not part of the main storylines.

[10] *lasciviousness* Unrestrained sensuality, especially lustful behavior.

[11] *overrun* Described rapidly.

[12] *happily* By chance.

[13] *23 January, 1589* By the modern (i.e., Gregorian) calendar, 3 February 1589; England did not abandon the old Julian Calendar until 1752, and in Spenser's day March 25 was still the official start of the new year.

IN CONTEXT

The Redcrosse Knight

This illustration of the Redcrosse Knight is from the 1590 edition of *The Faerie Queene*.

Christian Armor

The opening stanza of Book 1 presents a riddle: how can Redcrosse Knight's armor be dented and battle scarred when the Knight has yet to see battle? Spenser expected his readers to realize that the Knight's armor is allegorical, the Christian armor specified by Saint Paul in Ephesians 6.11–17. The idea of spiritual armor for the spiritual warfare of everyday life was a popular trope in Renaissance theology and literature, and one of the best known treatments appeared in the *Handbook of the Christian Soldier* by the great Dutch humanist Desiderius Eramsus (c. 1469–1546).

from Paul's Epistle to the Ephesians, 6.11–17 (Geneva Bible, modernized spelling)

Put on the whole armour of God, that ye may be able to stand against the assaults of the devil. For we wrestle not against flesh and blood, but against principalities, against powers, and against the worldly governors, the princess of the darkness of this world, against spiritual wickednesses, which are in the high places.

For this cause take unto you the whole armour of God, that ye may be able to resist in the evil day,
& having finished all things, stand fast.

Stand therefore, and your loins gird about with verity, & having on the breast plate of righteousness,
And your feet shod with the preparation of the Gospel of peace.

Above all, take the shield of faith, wherewith ye may quench all the fiery darts of the wicked,
And take the helmet of salvation, and the sword of the Spirit, which is the word of God.

from Desiderius Erasmus, *Enchiridion militis Christiani* [Handbook of the Christian Soldier] (1504), first translated into English in 1533, probably by William Tyndale. The following excerpt is a modern spelling version of the 1533 translation.

ON THE ARMOR OF THE CHRISTIAN KNIGHT

Wilt thou hear the instruments or artillery of Christian men's war? And the zeal of him (saith scripture) shall take harness, and shall harness his creature to avenge his enemies; he will put on justice for his breast plate, and take for his helmet sure and true judgement; he will take a shield of equity impenetrable or that cannot be pierced, yea and he will sharpen or fashion cruel wrath into a spear. Thou readest also in Isaiah he is armed with justice as with an habergeon,[1] and a sallet[2] of health upon his head; he is clothed with the vestures[3] of vengeance, and covered as it were with a cloak of zeal.

Now if thou list, go thee to the storehouse of Paul that valiant captain, certainly thou shalt also find there the armour of war, not carnal things but valiant in God to destroy fortresses and counsels, and every high thing that exalteth himself against the doctrine of God. Thou shalt find there the armour of God, by the which thou mayest resist in a woeful day. Thou shalt find the harness of justice on the right hand, and on the left thou shalt find the defense of thy sides' verity, and the habergeon of justice, the buckler[4] of faith wherewith thou mayest quench all the hot and fiery weapons of thy cruel adversary. Thou shalt find also the helmet of health and the sword of the spirit, which is the word of God, with the which all, if a man shall be diligently covered and fenced, he may boldly without fear bring forth the bold saying of Paul: who shall separate us from the love of God? shall tribulation? shall straitness or difficulty? shall hunger? shall nakedness? shall peril? shall persecution? shall a sword? Behold how mighty enemies and how much feared of all men he setteth at nought.

But hear also a certain greater thing, for it followeth. But in all things we have overcome by his help which loved us. And I am assured (saith he) that neither death nor life, nor angels, neither principates, neither virtues, neither present things, neither things to come, neither strength, neither highness, neither lowness, nor none other creature shall or may separate us from the love of God which is in Christ Jesu. O happy trust and confidence which the weapons or armour of light giveth to Paul, that is by interpretation a little man, which calleth himself the refuse or outcast of the world. Of such armour therefore abundantly shall holy scripture minister to thee, if thou wilt occupy thy time in it with all thy might: so that thou shalt not need our counsel or admonitions. Nevertheless, seeing it is thy mind, lest I should seem not to have obeyed thy request, I have forged for thee this little treatise called *Enchiridion*, that is to say, a certain little dagger, whom never lay out of thy hand, no not when thou art at meat, or

---

[1] *habergeon* Sleeveless coat or jacket of mail or scale armor.

[2] *sallet* Light headpiece, with the lower part curving out behind.

[3] *vestures* Clothing, apparel.

[4] *buckler* Small round shield.

in thy chamber. Insomuch that if at any time thou shalt be compelled to make a pilgrimage in these worldly occupations, and shalt be accumbered to bear about with the whole and complete armour and harness of holy scripture, yet commit not that the sutler[1] in wait at any season should come upon thee and find thee utterly unarmed, but at the least let it not grieve thee to have with them this little hanger,[2] which shall not be heavy to bear, nor unprofitable for thy defense, for it is very little, yet if thou use it wisely, and couple with it the buckler of faith, thou shalt be able to withstand the fierce and raging assault of thine enemy: so that thou shalt have no deadly wound.

Spirituality and *The Faerie Queene*

The Bible's Song of Solomon, a quasi-dialogue of lovers filled with sensuous metaphors, had long been read in both Jewish and Christian tradition as allegorizing the marriage between God and humanity, or God and the soul, or Christ and the Church (the body of all believers). For writers such as Spenser and Donne, the tradition further legitimized the crossover between the spiritual and the erotic found in much Renaissance art and literature.

Heading to the Song of Solomon (Geneva Bible, modernized spelling)

In this song, Salomon by most sweet and comfortable allegories and parables describeth the perfect love of Jesus Christ, the true Salomon and King of peace, and the faithful soul of his church which he hath sacrificed and appointed to be his spouse, holy, chaste, and without reprehension. So that here is declared the singular love of the bridegroom toward the bride, and his great and excellent benefits wherewith he doth enrich her of his pure bounty and grace without any of her deservings. Also the earnest affection of the church which is inflamed with the love of Christ desiring to be more and more joined to him in love, and not to be forsaken for any spot or blemish that is in her.

---

[1]   *sutler*   One who sells provisions to soldiers.

[2]   *hanger*   Short sword.

from *Amoretti* [1]

1

Happy ye leaves° when as those lilly hands,   *pages*
  which hold my life in their dead doing[2] might,
  shall handle you and hold in loves soft bands,°   *bonds*
  lyke captives trembling at the victors sight.
5 And happy lines, on which with starry light,
  those lamping° eyes will deigne sometimes to
    look   *blazing*
  and reade the sorrowes of my dying spright,°   *spirit*
  written with teares in harts close bleeding book.
And happy rymes bath'd in the sacred brooke,
10 of Helicon[3] whence she derivèd is,
  when ye behold that Angels blessèd looke,
  my soules long lackèd foode, my heavens blis.
Leaves, lines, and rymes, seeke her to please alone,
  whom if ye please, I care for other none.

3

The soverayne beauty which I doo admyre,
  witnesse the world how worthy to be prayzed:
  the light wherof hath kindled heavenly fyre,
  in my fraile spirit by her from basenesse raysed.
5 That being now with her huge brightnesse dazed,
  base thing I can no more endure to view:
  but looking still on her I stand amazed,
  at wondrous sight of so celestiall hew.°   *form*
So when my toung would speak her praises dew,°   *due*
10 it stoppèd is with thoughts astonishment:
  and when my pen would write her titles true,
  it ravisht is with fancies wonderment:
Yet in my hart I then both speake and write,
  The wonder that my wit cannot endite.

6

Be nought dismayd that her unmovèd mind
  doth still persist in her rebellious pride:
  such love not lyke to lusts of baser kynd,

  the harder wonne, the firmer will abide.
5 The duresull° Oake, whose sap is not yet dride,   *durable*
  is long ere it conceive the kindling fyre:
  but when it once doth burne, it doth divide,
  great heat, and makes his flames to heaven aspire.
So hard it is to kindle new desire,
10 in gentle brest that shall endure for ever:
  deepe is the wound, that dints° the parts entire   *strikes*
  with chast affects, that naught but death can sever.
Then thinke not long in taking litle paine,
  to knit the knot, that ever shall remaine.

15

Ye tradefull° Merchants, that with weary
  toyle,°   *engaged in trading / toil*
  do seeke most pretious things to make your gain;
  and both the Indias[4] of their treasures spoile,
  what needeth you to seeke so farre in vaine?
5 For loe° my love doth in her selfe containe   *behold*
  all this worlds riches that may farre be found,
  if Saphyres, loe her eies be Saphyres plaine,
  if Rubies, loe hir lips be Rubies sound:°   *pure*
If Pearles, hir teeth be pearles both pure and round;
10 if Yvorie, her forhead yvory weene;°   *seems*
  if Gold, her locks are finest gold on ground;
  if silver, her faire hands are silver sheene.°   *beautiful*
But that which fairest is, but few behold,
  her mind adornd with vertues manifold.

22

This holy season[5] fit to fast and pray,
  Men to devotion ought to be inclynd:
  therefore, I lykewise on so holy day,[6]
  for my sweet Saynt some service fit will find.
5 Her temple fayre is built within my mind,
  in which her glorious ymage placèd is,
  on which my thoughts doo day and night attend
  lyke sacred priests that never thinke amisse.
There I to her as th'author of my blisse,
10 will builde an altar to appease her yre:
  and on the same my hart will sacrifise,
  burning in flames of pure and chast desyre:

---

[1] *Amoretti*   Italian: little loves. This sonnet sequence is generally read as a description of Spenser's courtship of and marriage to Elizabeth Boyle (whom he had married in the previous year, 1594).

[2] *dead doing*   Death-dealing.

[3] *Helicon*   One of the mountains sacred to the Nine Muses, the goddesses of the arts and sciences. The sacred spring which flows from Helicon is the Hippocrene.

---

[4] *both the Indias*   I.e., the East and West Indies.

[5] *This holy season*   Lent.

[6] *holy day*   Ash Wednesday.

The which vouchsafe O goddesse to accept,
  amongst thy deerest relicks to be kept.

26

Sweet is the Rose, but growes upon a brere;°   *thorny bush*
  Sweet is the Junipere, but sharpe his bough;
  sweet is the Eglantine,° but pricketh nere;   *sweet-briar*
  sweet is the firbloome,[1] but his braunches rough.
5 Sweet is the Cypresse, but his rynd° is tough,   *bark*
  sweet is the nut, but bitter is his pill;°   *shell*
  sweet is the broome-flowre,[2] but yet sowre enough;
  and sweet is Moly,[3] but his root is ill.
  So every sweet with soure is tempred still,
10   that maketh it be coveted the more:
  for easie things that may be got at will,
  most sorts of men doe set but little store.
  Why then should I accoumpt° of little paine,   *think much*
  that endlesse pleasure shall unto me gaine.

34[4]

Lyke as a ship that through the Ocean wyde,
  by conduct of some star doth make her way,
  whenas a storme hath dimd her trusty guyde,
  out of her course doth wander far astray.
5 So I whose star, that wont with her bright ray,
  me to direct, with cloudes is overcast,
  doe wander now in darknesse and dismay,
  through hidden perils round about me plast.°   *placed*
  Yet hope I well, that when this storme is past
10 my Helice the lodestar[5] of my lyfe
  will shine again, and looke on me at last,
  with lovely light to cleare my cloudy grief,
  Till then I wander carefull° comfortlesse,   *full of cares*
  in secret sorow and sad pensivenesse.

37

What guyle is this, that those her golden tresses,

---

[1] *firbloome* Fruit of the fir tree.

[2] *broome-flowre* Large yellow flower of the broom shrub, a common English plant.

[3] *Moly* Mythical herb with a white flower and black root, taken by Odysseus to ward off the spells of the witch Circe.

[4] *34* From Petrarch's *Rima* 189, or one of the many adaptations.

[5] *Helice* The constellation Ursa Major; *lodestar* North Star, Polaris, in the constellation Ursa Major.

She doth attyre under a net of gold:
  and with sly° skill so cunningly them dresses,   *dexterous*
  that which is gold or heare,° may scarse be told?   *hair*
5 Is it that mens frayle eyes, which gaze too bold,
  she may entangle in that golden snare:
  and being caught may craftily enfold,
  theyr weaker harts, which are not wel aware?
  Take heed therefore, myne eyes, how ye doe stare
10 henceforth too rashly on that guilefull net,
  in which if ever ye entrappèd are,
  out of her bands° ye by no meanes shall get.   *bonds*
  Fondnesse° it were for any being free,   *foolishness*
  to covet fetters, though they golden bee.

54

Of this worlds Theatre in which we stay,
  My love lyke the Spectator ydly sits
  beholding me that all the pageants° play,   *parts*
  disguysing diversly my troubled wits.
5 Sometimes I joy when glad occasion fits,
  and mask in myrth lyke to a Comedy:
  soone after when my joy to sorrow flits,
  I waile and make my woes a Tragedy.
  Yet she beholding me with constant eye,
10 delights not in my merth nor rues° my smart:°   *pities / pain*
  but when I laugh she mocks, and when I cry
  she laughes, and hardens evermore her hart.
  What then can move her? if nor merth nor mone,°   *moan*
  she is no woman, but a sencelesse stone.

64

Comming to kisse her lyps, (such grace I found)
  Me seemd I smelt a gardin of sweet flowres:
  that dainty odours from them threw around
  for damzels fit to decke their lovers bowres.
5 Her lips did smell lyke unto Gillyflowers,°   *carnations*
  her ruddy cheekes lyke unto Roses red:
  her snowy browes lyke budded Bellamoures,[6]
  her lovely eyes lyke Pincks[7] but newly spred,
  Her goodly bosome lyke a Strawberry bed,
10 her neck lyke to a bounch of Cullambynes:°   *columbines*
  her brest lyke lillyes, ere theyr leaves be shed,

---

[6] *Bellamoures* Unidentified.

[7] *Pincks* Dianthus plants, the flowers of which can be red, white, pink, or variegated.

her nipples lyke yong blossomd Jessemynes,°   *jasmines*
Such fragrant flowres doe give most odorous smell,
    but her sweet odour did them all excell.

67[1]

Lyke as a huntsman after weary chace,
    Seeing the game from him escapt away,
    sits downe to rest him in some shady place,
    with panting hounds beguilèd of their pray:
5   So after long pursuit and vaine° assay,°   *fruitless / attempt*
    when I all weary had the chace forsooke,
    the gentle deare returnd the selfe-same way,
    thinking to quench her thirst at the next brooke.
There she beholding me with mylder looke,
10   sought not to fly, but fearelesse still did bide:
    till I in hand her yet halfe trembling tooke,
    and with her owne goodwill hir fyrmely tyde.
Strange thing me seemd to see a beast so wyld,
    so goodly wonne with her owne will beguyld.°   *deluded*

68

Most glorious Lord of lyfe that on this day,[2]
    Didst make thy triumph, over death and sin:
    and having harrowd hell didst bring away[3]
    captivity thence captive us to win:
5   This joyous day, deare Lord, with joy begin,
    and grant that we for whom thou diddest dye
    being with thy deare blood clene washt from sin,
    may live for ever in felicity.
And that thy love we weighing worthily,
10   may likewise love thee for the same againe:
    and for thy sake that all lyke deare[4] didst buy,
    with love may one another entertayne.
So let us love, deare love, lyke as we ought,
    love is the lesson which the Lord us taught.

69

The famous warriors of the anticke world,[5]
    Used Trophees to erect in stately wize:°   *ways*
    in which they would the records have enrold,
    of theyr great deeds and valarous emprize.
5   What trophee then shall I most fit devize,
    in which I may record the memory
    of my loves conquest, peerelesse beauties prise,
    adorn'd with honour, love, and chastity.
Even this verse vowd to eternity,
10   shall be thereof immortall moniment:
    and tell her prayse to all posterity,
    that may admire such worlds rare wonderment.
The happy purchase of my glorious spoile,
    gotten at last with labour and long toyle.

70

Fresh spring the herald of loves mighty king,
    In whose cote armour richly are displayd
    all sorts of flowers the which on earth do spring
    in goodly colours gloriously arrayd.
5   Goe to my love, where she is carelesse layd,
    yet in her winters bowre not well awake:
    tell her the joyous time wil not be staid°   *halted*
    unlesse she doe him by the forelock take.[6]
Bid her therefore her selfe soone ready make,
10   to wayt on love amongst his lovely crew:
    where every one that misseth then her make,°   *mate*
    shall be by him amearst° with penance dew.°   *immersed / due*
Make hast therefore sweet love, whilest it is prime,°   *spring*
    for none can call againe the passèd time.

74

Most happy letters fram'd by skilfull trade,°   *application*
    with which that happy name[7] was first desynd:
    the which three times thrise happy hath me made,
    with guifts of body, fortune and of mind.
5   The first my being to me gave by kind,°   *nature*
    from mothers womb deriv'd by dew° descent,   *due*
    the second is my sovereigne Queene most kind,
    that honour and large richesse to me lent.

---

[1]   *67*   An adaptation of the Italian poet Petrarch's *Rima* 190 (also adapted by Thomas Wyatt, Torquato Tasso, and Marguerite de Navarre). Spenser significantly changes Petrarch's original ending, turning Petrarch's lament into a happy celebration of the realization of his desires.

[2]   *this day*   Easter.

[3]   *having … away*   Before his Resurrection, Christ descended into Hell to rescue the good Israelites who had died before his birth—an event referred to as the Harrowing of Hell.

[4]   *lyke deare*   At the same cost. I.e., Christ redeemed all people at the same cost.

[5]   *anticke world*   I.e., antique world, classical Greece and Rome.

[6]   *by … take*   Seize the time or take the opportunity.

[7]   *that happy name*   Elizabeth, the name shared by Spenser's mother, Queen and wife.

The third my love, my lives last ornament,
10   by whom my spirit out of dust was raysed:°   raised
to speake her prayse and glory excellent,
of all alive most worthy to be praysed.
Ye three Elizabeths for ever live,
that three such graces[1] did unto me give.

75

One day I wrote her name upon the strand,°   shore
but came the waves and washèd it away:
agayne I wrote it with a second hand,
but came the tyde, and made my paynes his pray.°   prey
5   Vayne man, sayd she, that doest in vaine assay,°   attempt
a mortall thing so to immortalize.
for I my selve shall lyke to this decay,
and eek° my name bee wypèd out lykewize.   also
Not so, (quod° I) let baser things devize   said / plan
10   to dy in dust, but you shall live by fame:
my verse your vertues rare shall eternize,
and in the hevens wryte your glorious name.
Where whenas death shall all the world subdew,
our love shall live, and later life renew.

80

After so long a race as I have run
Through Faery land, which those six books[2] compile,
give leave to rest me being halfe fordonne,°   overcome
and gather to my selfe new breath awhile.
5   Then as a steed refreshèd after toyle,
out of my prison I will breake anew:
and stoutly will that second worke assoyle,°   discharge
with strong endevour and attention dew.°   due
Till then give leave to me in pleasant mew,°   seclusion
10   to sport my muse and sing my loves sweet praise:
the contemplation of whose heavenly hew,°   form
my spirit to an higher pitch will rayse.
But let her prayses yet be low and meane,°   common
fit for the handmayd of the Faery Queene.

82

Joy of my life, full oft for loving you
I blesse my lot, that was so lucky placed:
but then the more your owne mishap I rew,°   pity
that are so much by so meane° love   common / lowered
embased.°
5   For had the equall hevens so much you graced
in this as in the rest, ye mote invent
som hevenly wit, whose verse could have
enchased°   engraved
your glorious name in golden moniment.
But since ye deignd so goodly to relent
10   to me your thrall,° in whom is little worth,   bondage
that little that I am, shall all be spent,
in setting your immortall prayses forth.
Whose lofty argument° uplifting me,   theme
shall lift you up unto an high degree.

89

Lyke as the Culver° on the barèd bough,   dove
Sits mourning for the absence of her mate:
and in her songs sends many a wishfull vow,
for his returne that seemes to linger late.
5   So I alone now left disconsolate,
mourne to my selfe the absence of my love:
and wandring here and there all desolate,
seek with my playnts° to match that   laments
mournful dove
Ne joy of ought° that under heaven doth
hove,°   anything / dwell
10   can comfort me, but her owne joyous sight:
whose sweet aspect both God and man can move,
in her unspotted° pleasauns° to delight.   pure / pleasure
Dark is my day, whyles her fayre light I mis,
and dead my life that wants such lively° blis.   vital
—1594

---

[1]   *three such graces*   I.e., Three Graces, sister goddesses of beauty, mirth, and bounty.

[2]   *those six books*   The six completed books of *The Faerie Queene*.

Epithalamion[1]

Ye learnèd sisters[2] which have oftentimes
  Beene to me ayding, others to adorne:°   praise
Whom ye thought worthy of your gracefull rymes,
That even the greatest did not greatly scorne,
5 To heare theyr names sung in your simple layes,°   songs
But joyèd in theyr prayse.
And when ye list° your owne mishaps to mourne,   desire
Which death, or love, or fortunes wreck did rayse,
Your string could soone to sadder tenor turne,
10 And teach the woods and waters to lament
Your dolefull dreriment.°   misery
Now lay those sorrowfull complaints aside,
And having all your heads with girland crownd,
Helpe me mine owne loves prayses to resound,
15 Ne let the same of any be envide:
So Orpheus did for his owne bride,[3]
So I unto my selfe alone will sing,
The woods shall to me answer and my Eccho ring.

Early before the worlds light giving lampe,
20 His golden beame upon the hils doth spred,
Having disperst the nights unchearefull dampe,
Doe ye awake, and with fresh lusty hed[4]
Go to the bowre° of my beloved love,   bedroom
My truest turtle dove
25 Bid her awake; for Hymen[5] is awake,
And long since ready forth his maske° to
    move,   wedding procession

With his bright Tead° that flames with many a
    flake,°   torch / spark
And many a bachelor to waite on him,
In theyr fresh garments trim.
30 Bid her awake therefore and soone her dight,°   prepare
For lo the wishèd day is come at last,
That shall for al the paynes and sorrowes past,
Pay to her usury° of long delight,   interest
And whylest she doth her dight,
35 Doe ye to her of joy and solace sing,
That all the woods may answer and your eccho ring.

Bring with you all the Nymphes that you can heare[6]
Both of the rivers and the forrests greene:
And of the sea that neighbours to her neare,
40 Al with gay girlands goodly wel beseene.°   befit
And let them also with them bring in hand,
Another gay girland
For my fayre love of lillyes and of roses,
Bound true love wize[7] with a blew silke riband.° ribbon
45 And let them make great store of bridale poses,°   posies
And let them eeke° bring store of other flowers   also
To deck the bridale bowers.
And let the ground whereas her foot shall tread,
For feare the stones her tender foot should wrong
50 Be strewed with fragrant flowers all along,
And diapred° lyke the discolored°
    mead.°   adorned / multicoloured / meadow
Which done, doe at her chamber dore awayt,
For she will waken strayt,°   at once
The whiles doe ye this song unto her sing,
55 The woods shall to you answer and your Eccho ring.

Ye Nymphes of Mulla[8] which with carefull heed,
The silver scaly trouts doe tend full well,
And greedy pikes which use therein to feed,
(Those trouts and pikes all others doo excell)
60 And ye likewise which keepe the rushy lake,
Where none doo fishes take
Bynd up the locks the which hang scatterd light,

---

[1] *Epithalamion* Meaning "at the bedroom" (Greek), an epithalamion is a wedding song, normally written by an outsider to celebrate a marriage. Classical poets including Sappho and Catullus wrote poems in this genre, which always begin with an invocation of the Muses, proceed through a full description of the wedding ceremony and celebration, and end with a reference to the consummation of the marriage. In Spenser's poem, each of the twenty-four sections corresponds to an hour of the wedding day.

[2] *learnèd sisters* The Nine Muses, goddesses of the arts and sciences.

[3] *So … bride* One of the earliest and most celebrated poets of Greek mythology, Orpheus was famous for the magical power of his music and his passion for his wife, Eurydice, whom he attempted to rescue from the underworld after her death.

[4] *lusty hed* Vigor.

[5] *Hymen* God of marriage.

[6] *that you can heare* I.e., that can hear you.

[7] *true love wize* I.e., in a truelove's knot, an ornamental, double-looped knot.

[8] *Mulla* Poetic name of the River Awbeg in Ireland, near Spenser's home.

And in his waters which your mirror make,
Behold your faces as the christall bright,
65   That when you come whereas° my love doth lie,   *to where*
No blemish she may spie.
And eke ye lightfoot mayds which keepe the deere,
That on the hoary° mountayne use to towre,   *ancient*
And the wylde wolves which seeke them to devoure,
70   With your steele darts doo chace fro comming neer
Be also present heere,
To helpe to decke her and to help to sing,
That all the woods may answer and your eccho ring.

Wake now my love, awake; for it is time,
75   The Rosy Morne long since left Tithones[1] bed,
All ready to her silver coche° to clyme,   *coach*
And Phoebus[2] gins to shew his glorious hed.
Hark how the cheerefull birds do chaunt theyr laies
And carroll of loves praise.
80   The merry Larke hir mattins° sings aloft,   *morning prayers*
The thrush replyes, the Mavis descant[3] playes,
The Ouzell° shrills, the Ruddock°   *blackbird / robin*
        warbles soft,
So goodly all agree with sweet consent,
To this dayes merriment.
85   Ah my deere love why doe ye sleepe thus long,
When meeter° were that ye should now
        awake,   *more suitable*
T'awayt the comming of your joyous make,°   *mate*
And hearken to the birds lovelearnèd song,
The deawy leaves among.
90   For they of joy and pleasance to you sing,
That all the woods them answer & theyr eccho ring.

My love is now awake out of her dreame,
And her fayre eyes like stars that dimmèd were
With darksome cloud, now shew theyr goodly beams
95   More bright then Hesperus[4] his head doth rere.
Come now ye damzels, daughters of delight,
Helpe quickly her to dight,
But first come ye fayre houres which were begot

In Joves[5] sweet paradice, of Day and Night,
100 Which doe the seasons of the yeare allot,
And al that ever in this world is fayre
Doe make and still° repayre.°   *always / recreate*
And ye three handmayds of the Cyprian Queene,[6]
The which doe still adorne her beauties pride,
105 Helpe to addorne my beautifullest bride:
And as ye her array, still throw betweene°   *occasionally*
Some graces to be seene,
And as ye use° to Venus, to her sing,   *are accustomed*
The whiles the woods shal answer & your eccho ring.

110 Now is my love all ready forth to come,
Let all the virgins therefore well awayt,
And ye fresh boyes that tend upon her groome
Prepare your selves; for he is comming strayt.°   *immediately*
Set all your things in seemely° good aray°   *suitable / order*
115 Fit for so joyfull day,
The joyfulst day that ever sunne did see.
Faire Sun, shew forth thy favourable ray,
And let thy lifull° heat not fervent be   *life-giving*
For feare of burning her sunshyny face,
120 Her beauty to disgrace.
O fayrest Phoebus, father of the Muse,[7]
If ever I did honour thee aright,
Or sing the thing, that mote° thy mind delight,   *might*
Doe not thy servants simple boone° refuse,   *request*
125 But let this day let this one day be myne,
Let all the rest be thine.
Then I thy soverayne prayses loud wil sing,
That all the woods shal answer and theyr eccho ring.

Harke how the Minstrels gin to shrill aloud
130 Their merry Musick that resounds from far,
The pipe, the tabor,° and the trembling
        Croud,°   *drum / fiddle*
That well agree withouten breach° or jar.   *break*
But most of all the Damzels doe delite,
When they their tymbrels° smyte,   *tambourines*
135 And thereunto doe daunce and carrol sweet,

---

[1]   *Tithones*   I.e., Tithonus, husband of Aurora, goddess of the dawn.

[2]   *Phoebus*   Phoebus Apollo, god of the sun.

[3]   *Mavis*   Song thrush; *descant*   Accompaniment.

[4]   *Hesperus*   Morning star.

[5]   *Jove*   King of the gods.

[6]   *ye three … Queene*   The Cyprian Queen is Venus, goddess of love, and her handmaids are the Three Graces, who embody beauty, love, and pleasure.

[7]   *father … Muse*   Apollo was god of music and poetry.

That all the sences they doe ravish quite,
The whyles the boyes run up and downe the street,
Crying aloud with strong confusèd noyce,°   *noise*
As if it were one voyce.
140 Hymen[1] io° Hymen, Hymen they do shout,   *dear*
That even to the heavens theyr shouting shrill
Doth reach, and all the firmament doth fill,
To which the people standing all about,
As in approvance doe thereto applaud
145 And loud advaunce her laud,°   *praise*
And evermore they Hymen Hymen sing,
That al the woods them answer and theyr eccho ring.

Loe where she comes along with portly° pace   *majestic*
Lyke Phoebe[2] from her chamber of the East,
150 Arysing forth to run her mighty race,
Clad all in white, that seemes° a virgin best.   *suits*
So well it her beseemes that ye would weene°   *believe*
Some angell she had beene.
Her long loose yellow locks lyke golden wyre,
155 Sprinckled with perle, and perling flowres a
     tweene,°   *between*
Doe lyke a golden mantle her attyre,
And being crownèd with a girland greene,
Seeme lyke some mayden Queene.
Her modest eyes abashèd to behold
160 So many gazers, as on her do stare,
Upon the lowly ground affixèd are.
Ne dare lift up her countenance too bold,
But blush to heare her prayses sung so loud,
So farre from being proud.
165 Nathlesse doe ye still loud her prayses sing.
That all the woods may answer and your eccho ring.

Tell me ye merchants daughters did ye see
So fayre a creature in your towne before,
So sweet, so lovely, and so mild as she,
170 Adornd with beautyes grace and vertues store,
Her goodly eyes lyke Saphyres shining bright,
Her forehead yvory white,
Her cheekes lyke apples which the sun hath
     rudded,°   *reddened*
Her lips lyke cherryes charming men to byte,

175 Her brest like to a bowle of creame uncrudded,°   *unclotted*
Her paps° lyke lyllies budded,   *breasts*
Her snowie necke lyke to a marble towre,
And all her body like a pallace fayre,
Ascending uppe with many a stately stayre,
180 To honors seat and chastities sweet bowre.
Why stand ye still ye virgins in amaze,
Upon her so to gaze,
Whiles ye forget your former lay to sing,
To which the woods did answer and your eccho ring.

185 But if ye saw that which no eyes can see,
The inward beauty of her lively° spright,°   *living / spirit*
Garnisht with heavenly guifts of high degree,
Much more then would ye wonder at that sight,
And stand astonisht lyke to those which red°   *beheld*
190 Medusaes mazeful hed.[3]
There dwels sweet love and constant chastity,
Unspotted fayth and comely womanhood,
Regard of honour and mild modesty,
There vertue raynes as Queene in royal throne,
195 And giveth lawes alone.
The which the base affections doe obay,
And yeeld theyr services unto her will,
Ne thought of thing uncomely° ever may   *unseemly*
Thereto approch to tempt her mind to ill.
200 Had ye once seene these her celestial threasures,
And unrevealèd pleasures,
Then would ye wonder and her prayses sing,
That al the woods should answer and your echo ring.

Open the temple gates unto my love,
205 Open them wide that she may enter in,
And all the postes adorne as doth behove,
And all the pillours deck with girlands trim,
For to recyve this Saynt with honour dew,
That commeth in to you.
210 With trembling steps and humble reverence,
She commeth in, before th'almighties vew,
Of her ye virgins learne obedience,
When so ye come into those holy places,

---

1   *Hymen*   God of marriage.
2   *Phoebe*   Another name for Diana, virgin goddess of the moon.
3   *Medusaes mazeful hed*   Medusa was one of the Gorgons, three sister monsters, terrible to behold. Medusa's hair was made up of intertwined serpents, and when she was looked upon, her beholder would turn to stone. Renaissance commentators often read her as symbolizing amazing chastity.

To humble your proud faces:
215 Bring her up to th'high altar that she may
The sacred ceremonies there partake,
The which do endlesse matrimony make,
And let the roring Organs loudly play
The praises of the Lord in lively notes,
220 The whiles with hollow throates
The Choristers the joyous Antheme sing,
That al the woods may answere and their eccho ring.

Behold whiles she before the altar stands
Hearing the holy priest that to her speakes
225 And blesseth her with his two happy hands,
How the red roses flush up in her cheekes,
And the pure snow with goodly° vermill° stayne,   *fair / scarlet*
Like crimsin dyde in grayne,[1]
That even th'Angels which continually,
230 About the sacred Altare doe remaine,
Forget their service and about her fly,
Ofte peeping in her face that seemes more fayre,
The more they on it stare.
But her sad° eyes still fastened on the ground,   *dignified*
235 Are governèd with goodly modesty,
That suffers not one looke to glaunce awry,
Which may let in a little thought unsownd.
Why blush ye love to give to me your hand,
The pledge of all our band?°   *bond*
240 Sing ye sweet Angels, Alleluya sing,
That all the woods may answere and your eccho ring.

Now al is done; bring home the bride againe,
Bring home the triumph of our victory,
Bring home with you the glory of her gaine,° *having gained*
245 With joyance bring her and with jollity.
Never had man more joyfull day then this,
Whom heaven would heape with blis.
Make feast therefore now all this live long day,
This day for ever to me holy is,
250 Poure out the wine without restraint or stay,°   *pause*
Poure not by cups, but by the belly full,
Poure out to all that wull,°   *will*
And sprinkle all the postes and wals with wine,
That they may sweat, and drunken be withall.

255 Crowne ye God Bacchus[2] with a coronall,°   *garland*
And Hymen also crowne with wreathes of vine,
And let the Graces daunce unto the rest;
For they can doo it best:
The whiles the maydens doe theyr carroll sing,
260 To which the woods shal answer & theyr eccho ring.

Ring ye the bels, ye yong men of the towne,
And leave your wonted° labors for this day: *habitual*
This day is holy; doe ye write it downe,
That ye for ever it remember may.
265 This day the sunne is in his chiefest hight,
With Barnaby the bright,[3]
From whence declining daily by degrees,
He somewhat loseth of his heat and light,
When once the Crab[4] behind his back he sees.
270 But for this time it ill ordainèd was,
To chose the longest day in all the yeare,
And shortest night, when longest fitter weare:°   *were*
Yet never day so long, but late° would passe.   *finally*
Ring ye the bels, to make it weare° away,   *wear*
275 And bonefiers° make all day,   *bonfires*
And daunce about them, and about them sing:
That all the woods may answer, and your eccho ring.

Ah when will this long weary day have end,
And lende° me leave to come unto my love?   *grant*
280 How slowly do the houres theyr numbers spend?
How slowly does sad Time his feathers move?
Hast thee O fayrest Planet[5] to thy home
Within the Westerne fome:°   *ocean*
Thy tyred steedes long since have need of rest.
285 Long though it be, at last I see it gloome,°   *become dusk*
And the bright evening star with golden creast°   *crest*
Appeare out of the East.
Fayre childe of beauty, glorious lampe of love
That all the host of heaven in rankes doost lead,
290 And guydest lovers through the nightès dread,

---

1 *in grayne* Fast dyed.

2 *Bacchus* God of wine.

3 *Barnaby the bright* In the Julian Calendar St. Barnaby's Day,
June 11, was the longest day of the year.

4 *the Crab* Cancer, the constellation through which the sun passes
toward the end of July.

5 *fayrest Planet* The sun, which the god Apollo pulls in his horse-
drawn chariot.

How chearefully thou lookest from above,
And seemst to laugh atweene thy twinkling light
As joying in the sight
Of these glad many which for joy doe sing,
295 That all the woods them answer and their echo ring.

Now ceasse ye damsels your delights forepast;°   *past*
Enough is it, that all the day was youres:
Now day is doen, and night is nighing° fast: *coming*
Now bring the Bryde into the brydall boures.
300 Now night is come, now soone her disaray,
And in her bed her lay;
Lay her in lillies and in violets,
And silken courteins over her display,
And odourd sheetes, and Arras° coverlets,   *tapestry*
305 Behold how goodly my faire love does ly
In proud humility;
Like unto Maia,¹ when as Jove her tooke,
In Tempe,² lying on the flowry gras,
Twixt sleepe and wake, after she weary was,
310 With bathing in the Acidalian brooke.
Now it is night, ye damsels may be gon,
And leave my love alone,
And leave likewise your former lay to sing:
The woods no more shal answere, nor your echo ring.

315 Now welcome night, thou night so long expected,
that long daies labour doest at last defray,°   *repay*
And all my cares, which cruell love collected,
Hast sumd in one, and cancellèd for aye:°   *ever*
Spread thy broad wing over my love and me,
320 That no man may us see,
And in thy sable mantle us enwrap,
From feare of perrill and foule horror free.
Let no false treason seeke us to entrap,
Nor any dread disquiet once annoy
325 The safety of our joy:
But let the night be calme and quietsome,
Without tempestuous storms or sad afray:°   *fear*
Lyke as when Jove with fayre Alcmena³ lay,

When he begot the great Tirynthian groome:
330 Or lyke as when he with thy selfe° did lie,   *i.e., night*
And begot Majesty.
And let the mayds and yongmen cease to sing:
Ne let the woods them answer, nor theyr eccho ring.

Let no lamenting cryes, nor dolefull teares,
335 Be heard all night within nor yet without:
Ne let false whispers, breeding hidden feares,
Breake gentle sleepe with misconceivèd dout.
Let no deluding dreames, nor dreadful sights
Make sudden sad affrights;
340 Ne let house fyres, nor lightnings helpelesse harmes,
Ne let the Pouke,⁴ nor other evill sprights,
Ne let mischivous witches with theyr charmes,
Ne let hob Goblins, names whose sence we see not,
Fray us with things that be not.
345 Let not the shriech° Oule, nor the Storke be heard: *screech*
Nor the night Raven that still° deadly yels,⁵   *always*
Nor damnèd ghosts cald up with mighty spels,
Nor griesly° vultures make us once affeard: *ghastly*
Ne let th'unpleasant Quyre° of Frogs still croking   *choir*
350 Make us to wish theyr choking.
Let none of these theyr drery accents sing;
Ne let the woods them answer, nor theyr eccho ring.

But let stil Silence trew night watches keepe,
That sacred peace may in assurance rayne,
355 And tymely sleep, when it is tyme to sleepe,
May poure his limbs forth on your pleasant playne,
The whiles an hundred little wingèd loves,⁶
Like divers° fethered doves,   *diverse*
Shall fly and flutter round about your bed,
360 And in the secret darke, that none reproves,
Their prety stealthes shal worke, & snares shal spread
To filch away sweet snatches of delight,
Conceald through covert night.
Ye sonnes of Venus, play your sports at will,
365   For greedy pleasure, carelesse of your toyes,°   *games*
Thinks more upon her paradise of joyes,

---

¹ *Maia* Eldest daughter of Atlas, who gave birth to Mercury after being seduced by Jove.

² *Tempe* Vale of Tempe, in Thessaly.

³ *Alcmena* Mother of Hercules, with whom Jove lay for three nights.

⁴ *Pouke* Puck, or Robin Goodfellow, a mischievous fairy.

⁵ *Let not … yels* The owl was said to be a harbinger of death and the raven to be a bad omen; the stork, according to Chaucer, was an avenger of adultery.

⁶ *wingèd loves* Cupids.

Then what ye do, albe it good or ill.
All night therefore attend your merry play,
For it will soone be day:
470 Now none doth hinder you, that say or sing,
Ne will the woods now answer, nor your Eccho ring.

Who is the same, which at my window peepes?
Or whose is that faire face, that shines so bright,
Is it not Cinthia,[1] she that never sleepes,
475 But walkes about high heaven al the night?
O fayrest goddesse, do thou not envy
My love with me to spy:
For thou likewise didst love, though now unthought,
And for a fleece of woll,° which privily,   *wool*
480 The Latmian shephard[2] once unto thee brought,
His pleasures with thee wrought.
Therefore to us be favorable now;
And sith° of wemens labours thou hast charge,   *since*
And generation goodly dost enlarge,
485 Encline they will t'effect our wishfull vow,
And the chast wombe informe° with timely seed   *impregnate*
That may our comfort breed:
Till which we cease our hopefull hap° to
    sing,   *hoped for good fortune*
Ne let the woods us answere, nor our Eccho ring.

490 And thou great Juno,[3] which with awful might
The lawes of wedlock still dost patronize,
And the religion° of the faith first plight   *worship*
With sacred rites hast taught to solemnize:
And eeke for comfort often callèd art
495 Of women in their smart,°   *pain*
Eternally bind thou this lovely band,
And all thy blessings unto us impart.
And thou glad Genius, in whose gentle hand,
The bridale bowre and geniall° bed remaine,   *nuptial*

400 Without blemish or staine,
And the sweet pleasures of theyr loves delight.
With secret ayde doest succour° and supply,   *assist*
Till they bring forth the fruitfull progeny,
Send us the timely fruit of this same night.
405 And thou fayre Hebe,[4] and thou Hymen free,
Grant that it may so be.
Til which we cease your further prayse to sing,
Ne any woods shal answer, nor your Eccho ring.

And ye high heavens, the temple of the gods,
410 In which a thousand torches flaming bright
Doe burne, that to us wretched earthly clods:
In dreadfull darknesse lend desirèd light;
And all ye powers which in the same remayne,
More then we men can fayne,°   *desire*
415 Poure out your blessing on us plentiously,
And happy influence upon us raine,
That we may raise a large posterity,
Which from the earth, which they may long possesse,
With lasting happinesse,
420 Up to your haughty° pallaces may mount,   *lofty*
And for the guerdon° of theyr glorious merit   *reward*
May heavenly tabernacles there inherit,
Of blessed Saints for to increase the count.
So let us rest, sweet love, in hope of this,
425 And cease till then our tymely joyes to sing,
The woods no more us answer, nor our eccho ring.

Song made in lieu of many ornaments,
With which my love should duly have bene dect,°   *decked*
Which cutting off through hasty accidents,
430 Ye would not stay your dew time to expect,°   *await*
But promist both to recompens,
Be unto her a goodly ornament,
And for short time an endlesse moniment.
—1594

---

[1] *Cinthia* Diana, goddess of the moon and childbirth.

[2] *Latmian shephard* Endymion, whom Diana loved.

[3] *Juno* Goddess of marriage and wife of Jove.

[4] *Hebe* Goddess of youth and spring.

Sir Philip Sidney
1554 – 1586

Sir Philip Sidney remains not only a famous writer but an example of the complete Renaissance courtier. He was the author of the sonnet sequence *Astrophil and Stella*, of the prose romance *Arcadia* and of *An Apology for Poetry* (also known as *A Defence of Poesy*), the first extended work of literary criticism in English. Sidney's writings are witty, eloquent, and imaginative in their marriage of English style and the Renaissance genres and ideals embraced by artists in Italy, France, and Spain. Sidney was also a courtier, diplomat, and gentleman-soldier renowned for his courtesy; according to a probably

apocryphal story, when wounded on the battlefield and offered water, he saw a thirsty foot-soldier eying the bottle longingly and told him to take it, saying "Thy necessity is yet greater than mine."

Sidney was born on 30 November 1554, the eldest son of Sir Henry Sidney and Lady Mary Dudley. Although his family was not rich by the standards of the nobility, his birth placed him in an élite circle: his father, at one point Viceroy of Ireland, had been a friend of Edward VI; his godfather was Philip II of Spain, for whom he was named; and his uncle, Robert Dudley, was the powerful Earl of Leicester, the royal favorite who had courted Elizabeth and whom the Queen certainly loved. Sidney's education befitted one of his class. He entered Shrewsbury School in 1564, was taught there by the learned Thomas Ashton, and in 1568 entered Christ Church, Oxford, where he remained until he was 17. He left without a degree, as was often done, and was sent on a tour of Europe to learn about the languages and circumstances of other countries. This trip was to be highly beneficial for the young Sidney: it sparked a fascination with Continental ideas, and the important figures he befriended in the political, philosophical, and scholarly worlds helped shape his mind and career.

Sidney's cosmopolitanism also earned him some favor at court. In 1572 he was a junior member of a special embassy to France's Charles IX. While in Paris, Sidney witnessed the horrifying St. Bartholomew's Day massacre in which many Huguenots (French Protestants) were slaughtered. The event left its mark on him, confirming his passionate, if hardly narrow-minded, Protestantism. He continued his travels around Europe, studying for a while at the University of Padua and visiting Vienna, Frankfurt and Prague. He returned to England in May 1575, finding service with the Queen and gaining a reputation as an excellent diplomat.

Although Sidney's writing took second place to his political service, he influenced the literary world by encouraging other writers such as Edward Dyer, Fulke Greville (who later wrote his biography), and the young Edmund Spenser, who dedicated his *Shepheardes Calender* (1579) to him. Sidney's own first known work is *The Lady of May* (1578), a masque he composed for a royal visit; it featured the Queen herself.

Knowing his talent as a persuasive writer, the political faction headed by the Earl of Leicester and Sir Francis Walsingham, an important royal advisor and director of the secret service whose daughter was to marry Sidney, asked Philip to write a letter to Elizabeth opposing her marriage plans. Throughout the 1570s Spain had been gathering political and military power, so as a counterbalance some in England and France suggested an alliance between the two nations to be cemented by a match between Elizabeth and the Duke of Alençon, brother of the French king (who had himself once courted the English queen). In his letter Sidney reminds the queen of the duke's role in the murder of Huguenots and urges her not to marry a foreign and Catholic prince. It used to be thought that Elizabeth was highly displeased at this gesture: John Stubbs, Puritan gentleman, printed a pamphlet that contained similar advice and was severely punished. Sidney, however, was doing his duty as a courtier, and there is no evidence that the Queen resented his letter. He did fall out with the Earl of Oxford in a tennis-court quarrel and, given the Earl's murderous proclivities, seems to have thought it safer to stay with his sister Mary and her husband, the Earl of Pembroke, at their Wiltshire manor for a year. There he composed verses, translated a few Huguenot texts and some psalms, and wrote *A Defence of Poesy* (published in 1595). In this last, Sidney sets out a more wide-ranging and substantial theory of literature and criticism than any that had yet appeared in English, lightened by urbane humor and touches of self-mockery and with elements of paradox (Sidney smilingly claims to prove the distorting power of self-love by showing how he, a poet, can praise poetry). By "poetry" Sidney means fictions, products of the imagination, which he insists are more psychologically compelling than the historian's facts or the philosopher's moral abstractions. He also comments on particular authors and works, and compares modern English literature to that of ancient Greece and Rome. His assessment of the English play *Gorboduc* is the first sustained critical discussion of a literary work in English.

In writing his poetic work *Astrophil and Stella*, and despite his claim not to be a "pickpurse of another's wit," Sidney had before him a major Continental model—the Petrarchan sonnet sequence. Although Sidney's own contribution to, and revision of, the genre was not printed until five years after his death, the sonnets had been circulating in manuscript. Their publication in 1591 launched a brief but intense fashion for sonnet sequences. Sidney's longest work, *The Countess of Pembroke's Arcadia*, a pastoral romance with elements of epic and drama, recounts the romantic and martial adventures of two Greek princes, Musidorus and Pyrocles. Mixed in with the five books of prose narrative are a number of pastoral poems that sometimes experiment with classical meters. Ostensibly begun as entertainment for the author's sister, Sidney revised what is now called "The Old Arcadia" (lost until 1908), increasing the work's epic possibilities and political significance; he was part way through this version, now called "The New Arcadia," when he died. In 1590 his sister Mary published *The Countess of Pembroke's Arcadia*, a hybrid volume with the revised first part and the unrevised later part; it was this version that became popular and influential in England and even on the Continent.

In the early 1580s Sidney was knighted, named Joint Master of the Ordnance, and later charged with helping the English prepare an expedition to aid the Dutch in their revolt against Spain. In 1585 he was appointed Governor of Flushing, a town in the Netherlands that the English used as a base of operations, where he participated in several successful armed forays against the Spanish. On 22 September 1586, during a skirmish with Spanish forces outside the Dutch town of Zutphen, Sidney was shot in the thigh. The wound became gangrenous, and Sidney died of the infection on 17 October 1586. A flurry of grieving poetry was to follow and in February 1587 the body was brought home and given a magnificent funeral—an occasion designed in part to stir public patriotism and encourage support for the struggle against Spain. A fine poet had died but a legend had been born.

⌘⌘⌘

from *Astrophil and Stella*

1

Loving in truth, and fain° in verse my love   *desiring*
   to show,
That she, dear she,[1] might take some pleasure of my
   pain,
Pleasure might cause her read, reading might make
   her know,
Knowledge might pity win, and pity grace obtain,
5 I sought fit words to paint the blackest face of woe,
Studying inventions fine, her wits to entertain,
Oft turning others' leaves, to see if thence would flow
Some fresh and fruitful showers upon my sun-burned
   brain.
But words came halting forth, wanting Invention's
   stay;°   *support*
10 Invention, Nature's child, fled step-dame Study's blows,
And others' feet still seemed but strangers in my way.
Thus, great with child to speak, and helpless in my throes,
Biting my truant pen, beating myself for spite,
"Fool," said my Muse to me, "look in thy heart and
   write."

2

Not at first sight, nor with a dribbèd° shot,   *faulty*
Love[2] gave the wound which while I breathe
   will bleed.
But known worth did in mine[3] of time proceed,
'Till by degrees it had full conquest got.
5 I saw and liked, I liked but lovèd not,
I loved, but straight did not what Love decreed.
At length to Love's decrees I—forced—agreed,
Yet with repining at so partial° lot.   *unequal*
Now even that footstep of lost liberty
10 Is gone, and now like slave-born Muscovite.
I call it praise to suffer tyranny;
And now employ the remnant of my wit.
To make myself believe that all is well,
While with a feeling skill I paint my hell.

7

When Nature made her chief work, Stella's eyes,
In colour black, why wrapped she beams so bright?
Would she in beamy black, like painter wise,
Frame daintiest lustre mixed of shades and light?
5 Or did she else that sober hue devise,
In object[4] best to knit and strength our sight,
Lest if no veil these brave gleams did disguise,
They, sun-like, should more dazzle than delight?
Or would she her miraculous power show,
10 That whereas black seems beauty's contrary,
She e'en in black doth make all beauties flow?
Both so, and thus, she, minding° Love,   *remembering*
   should be
Placed ever there, gave him this mourning
   weed°   *garment*
To honour all their deaths who for her bleed.

18

With what sharp checks I in myself am shent[5]
When into Reason's audit I do go,
And by just counts myself a bankrout° know   *bankrupt*
Of all those goods which Heaven to me hath lent.
5 Unable quite to pay even Nature's rent,
Which unto it by birthright I do owe.
And which is worse, no good excuse can show,
But that my wealth I have most idly spent.
My youth doth waste, my knowledge brings forth toys,[6]
10 My wit doth strive those passions to defend,
Which for reward spoil it with vain annoys.[7]
I see my course to lose myself doth bend.
I see, and yet no greater sorrow take
Than that I lose no more for Stella's sake.

20

Fly, fly, my friends, I have my death wound; fly!
See there that boy, that murdering boy° I say,   *Cupid*
Who like a thief, hid in dark bush doth lie,
Till bloody bullet get him wrongful prey.
5 So tyrant he no fitter place could spy,

---

1 *That she, dear she* In the 1591 edition, this phrase is "That the
dear she."

2 *Love* Cupid.

3 *mine* Subterranean passage dug under an enemy fortress.

4 *In object* With the goal.

5 *sharp checks* Reproaches; *shent* Disgraced.

6 *toys* Frivolous pieces of writing.

7 *annoys* Irritations.

Nor so fair level[1] in so secret stay,
As that sweet black which veils the heav'nly eye:
There himself with his shot he close doth lay.
Poor passenger,° pass now thereby I did,   *passer-by*
10 And stayed pleased with the prospect of the place,
While that black hue from me the bad guest hid:
But straight I saw motions of lightning grace,
And then descried the glist'ring of his dart:
But ere I could fly hence, it pierced my heart.

21

Your words, my friend, (right healthful caustics[2]) blame
My young mind marred, whom Love doth
        windlass° so,   *ensnare*
That mine own writings like bad servants show
My wits, quick in vain thoughts, in virtue lame;
5   That Plato[3] I read for nought, but if° he tame   *unless*
Such doltish gyres;° that to my birth I owe   *circles*
Nobler desires, lest else that friendly foe,
Great expectation, were a train of shame.
For since mad March great promise made of me,
10 If now the May of my years much decline,
What can be hoped my harvest time will be?
Sure you say well, "Your wisdom's golden mine,
Dig deep with learning's spade." Now tell me this,
Hath this world aught so fair as Stella is?

22

In highest way of heav'n the Sun did ride,
Progressing then from fair twins' golden place:[4]
Having no scarf of clouds before his face,
But shining forth of heat in his chief pride;
5   When some fair ladies by hard promise tied,
On horseback met him in his furious race,
Yet each prepared with fan's well-shading grace
From that foe's wounds° their tender skins   *sunburn*
        to hide.
Stella alone with face unarmed marched.

10 Either to do like him which open shone,
Or careless of the wealth because her own:
Yet were the hid and meaner beauties parch'd,
Her daintiest bare went free; the cause was this,
The Sun, which others burned, did her but kiss.

23

The curious wits seeing dull pensiveness
Bewray° itself in my long settled eyes,   *reveal*
Whence those same fumes of melancholy rise,
With idle pains, and missing aim, do guess.
5   Some that know how my spring I did address,
Deem that my Muse some fruit of knowledge plies:
Others, because the Prince° my service tries,   *the Queen*
Think that I think state errors to redress.
But harder judges judge ambition's rage,
10 Scourge of itself, still climbing slipp'ry place,
Holds my young brain cativ'd° in golden cage.   *captive*
Oh fools, or over-wise, alas the race
Of all my thoughts hath neither stop nor start,
But only Stella's eyes and Stella's heart.

24

Rich fools there be, whose base and filthy heart
Lies hatching still the goods wherein they flow:
And damning their own selves to Tantal's smart,[5]
Wealth breeding want, more blist° more   *blessed*
        wretched grow.
5   Yet to those fools heav'n such wit doth impart
As what their hands do hold, their heads do know,
And knowing love, and loving, lay apart,
As sacred things, far from all danger's show.
But that rich fool[6] who by blind Fortune's lot
10 The richest gem of love and life enjoys,
And can with foul abuse such beauties blot;
Let him, deprived of sweet but unfelt joys,
(Exiled for aye° from those high treasures, which   *ever*
He knows not) grow in only folly rich.

---

[1] *so fair level* So well take aim.

[2] *right healthful caustics* Truly life-giving corrosives.

[3] *Plato* Plato likened reason to a charioteer of the passions.

[4] *fair twins' golden place* Gemini, the sign from which the sun emerges in June.

[5] *Tantal's smart* The torment of Tantalus, the miser, who was condemned to perpetual thirst even amid water.

[6] *that rich fool* Lord Rich, the husband of Penelope Devereaux (Sidney's Stella).

25

The wisest scholar[1] of the wight° most wise   *man*
By Phoebus' doom,[2] with sugared sentence says,
That Virtue, if it once met with our eyes,
Strange flames of love it in our souls would raise;
5 But for that man with pain his truth descries,
While he each thing in sense's balance weighs,
And so nor will, nor can behold those skies
Which inward sun to *heroic* mind displays,
Virtue of late with virtuous care to stir°   *encourage*
10 Love of herself, took Stella's shape, that she
To mortal eyes might sweetly shine in her.
It is most true, for since I her did see,
Virtue's great beauty in that face I prove,
And find th'effect, for I do burn in love.

26

Though dusty° wits dare scorn astrology,   *earthbound*
And fools can think those lamps° of purest light   *stars*
Whose numbers, ways, greatness, eternity,
Promising wonders, wonder do invite,
5 To have for no cause birthright in the sky,
But for to spangle the black weeds of night:
Or for some brawl,° which in that   *country dance*
   chamber high,
They should still dance to please a gazer's sight;
For me, I do Nature unidle know,
10 And know great causes, great effects procure:
And know those bodies high reign on the low.
And if these rules did fail, proof° makes me sure,   *experience*
Who oft fore-judge my after-following race,
By only those two stars in Stella's face.

27

Because I oft in dark abstracted guise
Seem most alone in greatest company,
With dearth of words, or answers quite awry,
To them that would make speech of speech arise,
5 They deem, and of their doom the rumour flies,
That poison foul of bubbling pride doth lie
So in my swelling breast that only I
Fawn on myself, and others do despise:

Yet pride I think doth not my soul possess,
10 Which looks too oft in his unflatt'ring glass:°   *mirror*
But one worse fault, ambition, I confess,
That makes me oft my best friends overpass,
Unseen, unheard, while though to highest place
Bends all his powers, even° unto Stella's grace.   *only*

31

With how sad steps, oh Moon, thou climb'st the skies,
How silently, and with how wan° a face.   *pale*
What, may it be, that even in heav'nly place
That busy archer° his sharp arrows tries?   *Cupid*
5 Sure, if that long-with-love-acquainted eyes
Can judge of love, thou feel'st a lover's case;
I read it in thy looks; thy languished grace
To me that feel the like, thy state descries.°   *reveals*
Then ev'n of fellowship, oh Moon, tell me
10 Is constant love deemed there but want of wit?
Are beauties there as proud as here they be?
Do they above love to be loved, and yet
Those lovers scorn whom that love doth possess?
Do they call virtue there ungratefulness?

34

Come, let me write. "And to what end?" To ease
A burdened heart. "How can words ease, which are
The glasses of thy daily vexing care?"
Oft cruel fights well-pictured forth do please.
5 "Art not ashamed to publish[3] thy disease?"
Nay, that may breed my fame, it is so rare.
"But will not wise men think thy words fond ware?"[4]
Then be they close,° and so none shall displease.   *concealed*
"What idler thing than speak and not be heard?"
10 What harder thing than smart and not to speak?
Peace, foolish wit, with wit my wit is marred.
Thus write I while I doubt[5] to write, and wreak
My harms on ink's poor loss. Perhaps some find
Stella's great pow'rs that so confuse my mind.

39

Come, Sleep! O Sleep, the certain knot of peace,
The baiting place of wit, the balm of woe,

---

1 *wisest scholar* Plato was the pupil of Socrates.

2 *By Phoebus' doom* Judged most wise by the oracle of Apollo at Delphi.

3 *publish* Make public.

4 *fond ware* Frivolities.

5 *doubt* Hesitate.

The poor man's wealth, the prisoner's release,
Th' indifferent° judge 'tween the high and low.   *impartial*
5 With shield of proof shield me from out the press
Of those fierce darts Despair at me doth throw.
O make in me those civil wars to cease;
I will good tribute pay, if thou do so.
Take thou of me smooth pillows, sweetest bed,
10 A chamber deaf to noise and blind to light,
A rosy garland, and a weary head.
And if these things, as being thine by right,
Move not thy heavy grace, thou shalt in me,
Livelier than elsewhere, Stella's image see.

41

Having this day my horse, my hand, my lance
Guided so well, that I obtained the prize,
Both by the judgment of the English eyes,
And of some sent from that sweet enemy France;[1]
5 Horsemen my skill in horsemanship advance,
Town-folks my strength; a daintier°   *more discerning*
   judge applies
His praise to sleight,° which from good use   *dexterity*
   doth rise;
Some lucky wits impute it but to chance;
Others, because of both sides I do take
10 My blood from them who did excel in this,[2]
Think Nature me a man of arms did make.
How far they shot awry! The true cause is,
Stella looked on, and from her heav'nly face
Sent forth the beams, which made so fair my race.

45

Stella oft sees the very face of woe
Painted in my beclouded stormy face,
But cannot skill[3] to pity my disgrace,
Not though thereof the cause herself she know.
5 Yet hearing late a fable which did show
Of lovers never known a grievous case,

Pity thereof gate° in her breast such place   *got*
That, from that sea derived, tears' spring did flow.
Alas, if fancy, drawn by imagined things,
10 Though false, yet with free scope more grace doth breed
Than servant's[4] wrack, where new doubts honor brings,
Then think, my dear, that you in me do read
Of lover's ruin some sad tragedy:
I am not I; pity the tale of me.

47

What, have I thus betrayed my liberty?
Can those black beams such burning marks[5] engrave
In my free side? or am I born a slave,
Whose neck becomes[6] such yoke of tyranny?
5 Or want° I sense to feel my misery?   *lack*
Or sprite,° disdain of such disdain to have,   *spirit*
Who for long faith, though daily help I crave,
May get no alms but scorn of beggery?
Virtue awake, beauty but beauty is;
10 I may, I must, I can, I will, I do
Leave following that, which it is gain to miss.
Let her go. Soft, but here she comes. "Go to,
Unkind, I love you not." Oh me, that eye
Doth make my heart give to my tongue the lie.

48

Soul's joy, bend not those morning stars from me,
Where Virtue is made strong by Beauty's might,
Where Love is chasteness, Pain doth learn delight,
And Humbleness grows one with Majesty.
5 Whatever may ensue, oh let me be
Copartner of the riches of that sight:
Let not mine eyes be hell-driv'n from that light:
Oh look, oh shine, oh let me die and see.
For though I oft my self of them bemoan,
10 That through my heart their beamy darts be gone,
Whose cureless wounds ev'n now most freshly bleed:
Yet since my death-wound is already got,
Dear killer, spare not thy sweet cruel shot:
A kind of grace it is to slay with speed.

---

1 *that sweet enemy France* French emissaries sent by the Duke of Anjou to negotiate a match with Queen Elizabeth. Sidney participated in a tournament at court to honor the delegation in April, 1581.

2 *both sides … this* Both sides of Sidney's family were distinguished in war and chivalry.

3 *cannot skill* Is unable.

---

4 *servant's* I.e., the lover's.

5 *burning marks* Permanent scars seared into him by Stella's eyes.

6 *becomes* Is suited to.

49

I on my horse, and Love on me doth try
Our horsemanships, while by strange work I prove
A horseman to my horse, a horse to Love;
And now man's wrongs in me, poor beast,
    descry.°   *discover*
5 The reins wherewith my rider doth me tie,
Are humbled thoughts, which bit of reverence move,
Curbed in with fear, but with gilt boss[1] above
Of hope, which makes it seem fair to the eye.
The wand° is will; thou, fancy, saddle art,[2]   *crop*
10 Girt° fast by memory; and while I spur   *fastened*
My horse, he spurs with sharp desire my heart:
He sits me fast, however I do stir:
And now hath made me to his hand so right,[3]
That in the manage[4] myself takes delight.

50

Stella, the fullness of my thoughts of thee
Cannot be stayed within my panting breast,
But they do swell and struggle forth of me,
Till that in words thy figure be expressed.
5 And yet as soon as they so formed be,
According to my Lord Love's own behest:
With sad eyes I their weak proportion see,
To portrait° that which in this world is best.   *portray*
So that I cannot choose but write my mind,
10 And cannot choose but put out what I write,
While these poor babes[5] their death in birth do find:
And now my pen these lines had dashed quite,
But that they stopped his fury from the same,
Because their forefront bare sweet Stella's name.[6]

51

Pardon mine ears, both I and they do pray,°   *ask earnestly*
So may your tongue still fluently proceed,
To them that do such entertainment need,
So may you still have somewhat new to say.

On silly me do not the burden lay
Of all the grave conceits[7] your brain doth breed;
But find some Hercules to bear, instead
Of Atlas tired, your wisdom's heav'nly sway.
10 For me, while you discourse of courtly tides,
Of cunning fishers in most troubled streams,[8]
Of straying ways, when valiant error guides:
Meanwhile my heart confers with Stella's beams,
And is even irked that so sweet comedy,[9]
By such unsuited speech should hindered be.

52

A strife is grown between Virtue and Love,
While each pretends° that Stella must be his.   *declares*
Her eyes, her lips, her all, saith Love, do this
Since they do wear his badge, most firmly prove.
5 But Virtue thus that title doth disprove:
That Stella (oh dear name) that Stella is
That virtuous soul, sure heir of heav'nly bliss,
Not this fair outside, which our hearts doth move.
And therefore, though her beauty and her grace
10 Be Love's indeed, in Stella's self he may
By no pretense claim any manner° place.   *kind of*
Well, Love, since this demur our suit doth stay,[10]
Let Virtue have that Stella's self; yet thus,
That Virtue but that body grant to us.

53

In martial sports I had my cunning tried,
And yet to break more staves° did me address: *lances*
While, with the people's shouts, I must confess,
Youth, luck, and praise, ev'n filled my veins with pride;
5 When Cupid having me his slave descried,°   *discerned*
In Mars's livery, prancing in the press:[11]
"What now, Sir Fool," said he; I would no less.[12]
"Look here, I say." I look'd and Stella spied,
Who hard by made a window send forth light.

---

[1] *gilt boss* Metal knob on the bit.

[2] *thou, fancy, saddle art* You, imagination, are the saddle.

[3] *to his hand so right* Respond so sensitively to his hand.

[4] *the manage* The process of training, management.

[5] *these poor babes* The poems.

[6] *Because their ... name* Because Stella is the first word of the sonnet, it preserves the poem from destruction.

---

[7] *grave conceits* Serious ideas.

[8] *cunning fishers ... streams* Courtiers currying favor amid political turmoil.

[9] *sweet comedy* Pleasant reflections.

[10] *demur* Objection; *stay* Halt.

[11] *livery* Uniform; *press* Throng.

[12] *I would no less* I would like the same attention that you give Mars.

₁₀ My heart then quaked, then dazzled were mine eyes;
One hand forgot to rule,[1] th'other to fight.
Nor trumpet's sound I heard, nor friendly cries;
My foe came on, and beat the air for me,[2]
Till that her blush taught me my shame to see.

54

Because I breathe not love to every one,
Nor do not use set colours[3] for to wear,
Nor nourish special locks of vowed hair,[4]
Nor give each speech the full point of a groan,
₅ The courtly nymphs,[5] acquainted with the moan
Of them, who in their lips Love's
      standard° bear;   *distinctive flag*
"What he?" say they of me. "Now I dare swear,
He cannot love. No, no, let him alone."
And think so still, so Stella know my mind.
₁₀ Profess indeed I do not Cupid's art;
But you, fair maids, at length this true shall find:
That his right° badge is worn but in the heart;   *true*
Dumb swans, not chatt'ring pies,[6] do lovers prove;
They love indeed, who quake to say they love.

55

Muses, I oft invoked your holy aid,
With choicest flow'rs my speech t'engarland so
That it, despised in true but naked show,[7]
Might win some grace in your sweet skill arrayed.
₅ And oft whole troops of saddest words I stayed,°   *held back*
Striving abroad a-foraging to go,
Until by your inspiring I might know
How their black banner° might be best displayed. *sad aspect*
But now I mean no more your help to try,
₁₀ Nor other sug'ring of my speech to prove,
But on her name incessantly to cry:
For let me but name her whom I do love,

---

1. *to rule* To control the horse.

2. *beat the air for me* Struck at the empty air instead of me.

3. *set colours* The usual colors of a lover.

4. *nourish special … hair* Keep special locks of hair given as a pledge.

5. *courtly nymphs* Women at court.

6. *dumb* Silent; *pies* Magpies.

7. *despised in … show* Despised for being plain, though sincere.

So sweet sounds straight mine ear and heart do hit,
That I well find no eloquence like it.

61

Oft with true sighs, oft with uncallèd tears,
Now with slow words, now with dumb eloquence,
I Stella's eyes assail, invade her ears,
But this at last is her sweet-breathed defense:
₅ That who indeed in-felt affection bears,
So captives to his saint both soul and sense,
That wholly hers, all selfness° he forbears;   *self-centeredness*
Thence his desires he learns, his life's course thence.
Now, since her chaste mind hates this love in me,
₁₀ With chastened mind I straight must show that she
Shall quickly me from what she hates remove.
O Doctor[8] Cupid, thou for me reply,
Driven else to grant, by angel's sophistry,[9]
That I love not without I leave to love.

69

O joy too high for my low style to show!
O bliss fit for a nobler state than me!
Envy, put out thine eyes, lest thou do see
What oceans of delight in me do flow.
₅ My friend, that oft saw, through all masks, my woe,
Come, come, and let me pour myself on thee.
Gone is the winter of my misery,
My spring appears, O see what here doth grow.
For Stella hath with words where faith doth shine,
₁₀ Of her high heart given me the monarchy.
I, I, O I may say that she is mine!
And though she give but thus condition'ly
This realm of bliss, while virtuous course I take,
No kings be crowned but they some covenants make.

71

Who will in fairest book of Nature know
How Virtue may best lodged in beauty be,
Let him but learn of love to read in thee,
Stella, those fair lines which true goodness show.
₅ There shall he find all vices' overthrow,
Not by rude force, but sweetest sovereignty
Of reason, from whose light those night-birds fly,

---

8. *Doctor* One who is well educated and highly knowledgeable.

9. *sophistry* Clever but fallacious reasoning.

That inward sun in thine eyes shineth so.
And not content to be Perfection's heir,
10 Thyself, dost strive all minds that way to move,
Who mark in thee what is in thee most fair.
So while thy beauty draws thy heart to love,
As fast thy virtue bends that love to good.
"But ah," Desire still cries, "Give me some food."

94

Grief find the words, for thou hast made my brain
So dark with misty vapours, which arise
From out thy heavy mould, that inbent[1] eyes
Can scarce discern the shape of mine own pain.
5   Do thou then (for thou canst), do thou complain,°   *lament*
For my poor soul, which now that sickness tries,[2]
Which ev'n to sense, sense of itself denies,
Though harbingers of death lodge there his train.
Or if thy love of plaint° yet mine forbears,   *lamentation*
10 As of a caitiff[3] worthy so to die,
Yet wail thyself, and wail with causeful tears,
That though in wretchedness thy life doth lie,
Yet growest more wretched than thy nature bears,
By being placed in such a wretch as I.

95

Yet Sighs, dear Sighs, indeed true friends you are,
That do not leave your least friend at the worst,
But as you with my breast I oft have nursed,
So grateful now you wait upon my care.
5   Faint coward Joy no longer tarry dare,
Seeing Hope yield when this woe strake° him first: *struck*
Delight protests he is not for th'accursed,
Though oft himself my mate-in-arms he sware.[4]
Nay Sorrow comes with such main rage, that he
10 Kills his own children, Tears, finding that they
By love were made apt to consort with me.
Only, true Sighs, you do not go away;
Thank may you have for such a thankful part,
Thank-worthiest yet when you shall break my heart.

96

Thought, with good cause thou lik'st so well the Night,
Since kind or chance gives both one livery,[5]
Both sadly black, both blackly darkened be,
Night barred from sun, thou from thy own sunlight;
5   Silence in both displays his sullen might,
Slow Heaviness in both holds one degree—[6]
That full of doubts, *thou* of perplexity;
Thy tears express Night's native moisture right.[7]
In both a mazeful° solitariness: *bewildering*
10 In Night of sprites° the ghastly powers to stir,   *spirits*
In thee, or sprites or sprited ghastliness.
But, but (alas) Night's side the odds hath, fur,°[8]   *far*
For that° at length yet doth invite some rest,   *night*
Thou, though still tired, yet still dost it° detest.   *rest*

97

Dian,[9] that fain would cheer her friend the Night,
Shows her oft at the full her fairest face,
Bringing with her those starry nymphs, whose
          chase°   *arrows*
From heav'nly standing hits each mortal wight.[10]
5   But ah, poor Night, in love with Phoebus'[11] light,
And endlessly despairing of his grace,
Herself (to show no other joy hath place)
Silent and sad in mourning weeds doth dight:[12]
Ev'n so (alas) a lady, Dian's peer,
10 With choice delights and rarest company
Would fain° drive clouds from out my heavy cheer.   *gladly*
But woe is me, though Joy itself were she,
She could not show my blind brain ways of joy,
While I despair my[13] Sun's sight to enjoy.

---

[5] *kind* Nature; *livery* Aspect.

[6] *one degree* Similar sway.

[7] *Thy tears ... right* Thought's tears reveal night's natural dampness.

[8] *fur* Far. (Spelled by Sidney this way to rhyme with "stir.")

[9] *Dian* Diana, goddess of the moon.

[10] *standing* Position; *wight* Man.

[11] *Phoebus'* The sun god's.

[12] *weeds* Clothes; *dight* Dress.

[13] *despair my* Despair of my.

---

[1] *inbent* Inward-looking.

[2] *sickness tries* Lovesickness triumphs.

[3] *caitiff* Despicable person.

[4] *sware* Swore he was.

98

Ah bed, the field where joy's peace some do see,
The field where all my thoughts to war be trained,°   *drawn*
How is thy grace by my strange fortune stained!
How thy lee° shores by my sighs stormed be!   *sheltered*
5 With sweet soft shades° thou oft invitest me   *shadows*
To steal some rest, but wretch I am constrained
(Spurred with Love's spur, though galled and shortly
    reined[1]
With Care's hard hand) to turn and toss in thee.
While the black horrors of the silent night
10 Paint woe's black face so lively to my sight,
That tedious leisure marks each wrinkled line.
But when Aurora leads out Phoebus' dance,[2]
Mine eyes then only wink,° for spite perchance,   *close*
That worms should have their Sun, and I want mine.

99

When far-spent night persuades each mortal eye,
To whom nor° art nor nature granteth light,   *neither*
To lay his then mark-wanting° shafts of sight,   *aimless*
Closed with their quivers, in sleep's armory;
5 With windows° ope then most my mind doth lie,   *eyes*
Viewing the shape of darkness and delight,
Takes in that sad hue, which the inward night
Of his mazed powers[3] keeps perfect harmony.
But when birds charm,[4] and that sweet air which is
10 Morn's messenger, with rose enamel'd skies,
Calls each wight° to salute the flower of bliss: *person*
In tomb of lids then buried are mine eyes,
Forced by their lord, who is ashamed to find
Such light in sense,[5] with such a darkened mind.

100

Oh tears, no° tears, but rain from Beauty's skies,   *not*
Making those lilies and those roses[6] grow,
Which aye° most fair, now more than most   *always*
    fair show,

While graceful Pity Beauty beautifies.
5 Oh honeyed sighs, which from that breast do rise,
Whose pants do make unspilling cream to flow,
Winged with whose breath, so pleasing zephyrs blow,
As can refresh the hell where my soul fries.
Oh plaints° conserved in such a sugared phrase   *complaints*
10 That Eloquence itself envies your praise
While sobbed-out words a perfect music give.
Such tears, sighs, plaints, no sorrow is, but joy:
Or if such heav'nly signs must prove annoy,
All mirth farewell, let me in sorrow live.

101

Stella is sick, and in that sickbed lies
Sweetness, that breathes and pants as oft as she;
And Grace, sick too, such fine conclusions[7] tries
That Sickness brags itself best graced to be.[8]
5 Beauty is sick, but sick in so fair guise
That is that paleness Beauty's white we see;
And Joy, which is inseparate° from those eyes,   *inseparable*
Stella now learns (strange case) to weep in thee.
Love moves[9] thy pain, and like a faithful page,
10 As thy looks stir, runs up and down to make
All folks pressed° at thy will thy pain t'assuage.   *eager*
Nature with care sweats for her darling's sake,
Knowing worlds pass, ere she enough can find
Of such heav'n stuff,° to clothe so heav'nly mind.   *matter*

102

Where be those roses gone, which sweetened so our eyes?
Where those red cheeks, which oft with fair increase
    did frame
The height of honour in the kindly° badge   *pleasant*
    of shame?
Who hath the crimson weeds° stol'n from my   *clouds*
    morning skies?
5 How doth the colour fade of those vermilion° dyes   *scarlet*
Which Nature's self did make, and self
    engrained° the same?   *dyed fast*
I would know by what right this paleness overcame
That hue, whose force my heart still unto thraldom ties.

---

1 *galled* Sore, chafed; *shortly reined* Reined in tight.

2 *Aurora* Goddess of the dawn; *Phoebus' dance* The sun's dance, daylight.

3 *mazed powers* Bewildered thoughts.

4 *charm* Sing in chorus.

5 *light in sense* Light available to the senses.

6 *those lilies and those roses* The colors of Stella's cheeks.

---

7 *fine conclusions* Delicate trials.

8 *best graced to be* In the most graced of states.

9 *moves* Is animated by.

Galen's adoptive sons,[1] who by a beaten way
10   Their judgments hackney on, the fault of sickness lay;
But feeling proof makes me say they mistake it fur:°   *far*
It is but Love, which makes his paper perfect white
To write therein more fresh the story of delight,
While Beauty's reddest ink Venus for him doth stir.

103

Oh happy Thames, that didst my Stella bear,
I saw thyself with many a smiling line
Upon thy cheerful face,[2] Joy's livery° wear,   *uniform*
While those fair planets[3] on thy streams did shine.
5   The boat for joy could not to dance forbear,
While wanton winds with beauties so divine
Ravished, stayed not, till in her golden hair
They did themselves (oh sweetest prison) twine.
And fain° those Aeol's youths[4] there would their stay *gladly*
10   Have made, but, forced by Nature still to fly,
First did with puffing kiss those locks display:°   *blow about*
She so disheveled, blushed; from window I
With sight thereof cried out, "oh fair disgrace;
Let Honour's self to thee grant highest place."

104

Envious wits,° what hath been mine offence,   *minds*
That with such poisonous care my looks you mark,
That to each word, nay, sigh of mine you hark,
As grudging me my sorrow's eloquence?
5   Ah, is it not enough that I am thence?[5]
Thence, so far thence, that scarcely any spark
Of comfort dare come to this dungeon dark,
Where rigorous exile locks up all my sense?
But if I by a happy window pass,
10   If I but stars[6] upon mine armour bear

---

[1] *Galen's adoptive sons* Doctors; followers of Aelius Galenus (131?–201? CE), probably the most accomplished medical researcher of the Roman period.

[2] *many a ... face* Water is conceived as having a human face elsewhere by Sidney; in the *Countess of Pembroke's Arcadia*, for example, he describes blood as filling "the wrinkles of the sea's visage."

[3] *fair planets* Stella's eyes.

[4] *Aeol's youths* Breezes; sons of Aeolus, ruler of the winds in Greek mythology.

[5] *thence* Away from where I want to be.

[6] *stars* Stella's emblems.

—Sick, thirsty, glad (though but of empty glass):
Your moral notes straight my hid meaning tear
From out my ribs, and puffing prove that I
Do Stella love. Fools, who doth it deny?

105

Unhappy sight, and hath she vanished by
So near, in so good time, so free° a place?   *open*
Dead glass,[7] dost thou thy object so embrace,
As what my heart still sees thou canst not spy?
5   I swear by her I love and lack, that I
Was not in fault, who bend thy dazzling race[8]
Only unto the heav'n of Stella's face,
Counting but dust what in the way did lie.
But cease, mine eyes; your tears do witness well
10   That you, guiltless thereof, your nectar missed:
Cursed be the page from whom the bad torch fell,
Cursed be the night which did your strife° resist,   *objective*
Cursed be the coachman which did drive so fast,
With no worse curse than absence makes me taste.

106

Oh absent presence, Stella is not here;
False flattering Hope, that with so fair a face
Bare me in hand,[9] that in this orphan place,
Stella, I say my Stella, should appear:
5   What say'st thou now? Where is that dainty cheer
Thou told'st mine eyes should help their famished case?
But thou art gone, now that self-felt disgrace
Doth make me most to wish thy comfort near.
But here I do store of[10] fair ladies meet,
Who may with charm° of conversation sweet   *harmony*
10   Make in my heavy mould new thought to grow:
Sure they prevail as much with me, as he
That bade his friend, but then new maimed, to be
Merry with him, and not think of his woe.

107

Stella, since thou so right a princess art
Of all the powers which life bestows on me,

---

[7] *Dead glass* Astrophil's eyes.

[8] *dazzling race* Lantern, torch.

[9] *Bare me in hand* Deceived me.

[10] *store of* Many.

That ere by them aught undertaken be[1]
They first resort unto that sovereign part;[2]
5   Sweet, for a while give respite to my heart,
Which pants as though it still should leap to thee,
And on my thoughts give thy lieutenancy°   authority
To this great cause,[3] which needs both use°   experience
      and art.
And as a queen, who from her presence sends
10   Whom she employs, dismiss from thee my wit,
Till it have wrought what thy own will attends.[4]
On servants' shame oft master's blame doth sit;
Oh let not fools in me thy works° reprove,   actions
And scorning say, "See what it is to love."

108

When Sorrow (using mine own fire's might)
Melts down his lead into my boiling breast,
Through that dark furnace to my heart oppressed
There shines a joy from thee, my only light;
5   But soon as thought of thee breeds my delight,
And my young soul flutters to thee, his nest,
Most rude Despair, my daily unbidden guest,
Clips straight my wings, straight wraps me in his night,
And makes me then bow down my head and say,
10   "Ah, what doth Phoebus' gold° that wretch avail   sunlight
Whom iron doors do keep from use of[5] day?"
So strangely (alas) thy works in me prevail,[6]
That in my woes for thee thou art my joy,
And in my joys for thee my only annoy.
—1591

from *The Defence of Poesy*

… Poesy therefore is an art of imitation: for so Aristotle termeth it in the word μίμησις,[7] that is to say, a representing, counterfeiting, or figuring forth—to speak metaphorically, a speaking picture—with this end, to teach and delight.

Of this there have been three general kinds. The chief, both in antiquity and excellency, were they that did imitate the unconceivable excellencies of God. Such were David in his Psalms; Solomon in his Song of Songs, in his Ecclesiastes and Proverbs; Moses and Deborah in their Hymns; and the writer of Job: which, beside other, the learned Immanuel Tremellius and Franciscus Junius[8] do entitle the poetical part of the Scripture. Against these none will speak that hath the Holy Ghost in due holy reverence. (In this kind, though in a full wrong divinity, were Orpheus, Amphion, Homer in his hymns, and many other, both Greeks and Romans.) And this poesy must be used by whosoever will follow St. James's counsel in singing psalms when they are merry,[9] and I know is used with the fruit of comfort by some, when, in sorrowful pangs of their death-bringing sins, they find the consolation of the never-leaving goodness.

The second kind is of them that deal with matters philosophical; either moral, as Tyrteus, Phocylides, Cato; or natural, as Lucretius and Virgil's Georgics; or astronomical, as Manilius and Pontanus; or historical, as Lucan:[10] which who mislike, the fault is in their judgment quite out of taste, & not in the sweet food of sweetly uttered knowledge.

---

1   *ere by … be*   Before they undertake anything.

2   *resort unto … part*   Refer to your sovereign direction.

3   *this great cause*   Perhaps the composition of the *Arcadia*.

4   *wrought*   Created; *attends*   Waits for.

5   *use of*   Enjoying.

6   *thy works … prevail*   Your actions rule me.

---

7   μίμησις   Greek: mimesis, the concept of poetry as primarily imitative. (See Aristotle's *Poetics* 1.2.)

8   *Immanuel … Junius*   Two theologians who produced a Latin translation of the Hebrew and Greek Bible first published in 1575.

9   *whosoever … merry*   "Is any among you afflicted? Let him pray. Is any merry? Let him sing psalms" (James 5.13).

10   *Cato*   Dionysus Cato (234–149 BCE), author of *The Distichs*, a collection of proverbial wisdom used in moral education; *Lucretius*   First-century BCE Epicurean poet, author of *De Rerum Natura* (*On the Nature of Things*); *Georgics*   Virgil's instructive poems on farming; *Manilius*   First-century CE Stoic, author of the *Astronomica*, an astrological poem; *Pontanus*   Fifteenth-century Italian humanist Giovanni Pontano, author of an astrological poem entitled *Urania*; *Lucan*   Roman poet of the first century CE who never finished his epic *Pharsalia*, on Rome's civil wars.

But because this second sort is wrapped within the fold of the proposed subject, and takes not the free course of his own invention, whether they properly be poets or no let grammarians dispute, and go to the third, indeed right poets, of whom chiefly this question ariseth: betwixt whom and these second is such a kind of difference as betwixt the meaner sort of painters, who counterfeit only such faces as are set before them, and the more excellent, who, having no law but wit, bestow that in colours upon you which is fittest for the eye to see: as the constant, though lamenting look of Lucretia[1] when she punished in herself another's fault, wherein he painteth not Lucretia whom he never saw, but painteth the outward beauty of such a virtue. For these third be they which most properly do imitate to teach & delight, and to imitate borrow nothing of what is, hath been, or shall be; but range, only reined with learned discretion, into the divine consideration of what may be and should be. These be they that, as the first and most noble sort may justly be termed *vates*, so these are waited on in the excellentest languages and best understandings with the fore-described name of poets. For these indeed do merely make to imitate; and imitate both to delight & teach; and delight, to move men to take that goodness in hand, which without delight they would fly as from a stranger; and teach, to make them know that goodness whereunto they are moved—which being the noblest scope to which ever any learning was directed, yet want there not idle tongues to bark at them.

These be subdivided into sundry more special denominations. The most notable be the heroic, lyric, tragic, comic, satiric, iambic, elegiac, pastoral, and certain others, some of these being termed according to the matter they deal with, some by the sort of verse they liked best to write in; for indeed the greatest part of poets have apparelled their poetical inventions in that numbrous kind of writing which is called verse—indeed but apparelled, verse being but an ornament and no cause to poetry, since there have been many most excellent poets that never versified, and now swarm many versifiers that need never answer to the name of poets. For Xenophon, who did imitate so excellently as to give us *effigiem iusti imperii*, the portraiture of a just empire, under the name of Cyrus (as Cicero saith of him), made therein an absolute heroical poem. So did Heliodorus in his sugared invention of that picture of love in Theagenes & Chariclea;[2] and yet both these wrote in prose, which I speak to show that it is not rhyming and versing that makes a poet (no more than a long gown makes an advocate,[3] who, though he pleaded in armour, should be an advocate and no soldier). But it is that feigning notable images of virtues, vices, or what else, with that delightful teaching, which must be the right describing note to know a poet by. Although indeed the senate of poets hath chosen verse as their fittest raiment, meaning, as in matter they passed all in all, so in manner to go beyond them: not speaking (table-talk fashion or like men in a dream) words as they chanceably fall from the mouth, but peising[4] each syllable of each word by just proportion, according to the dignity of the subject.

Now, therefore, it shall not be amiss first to weigh this latter sort of poetry by his works, and then by his parts; and if in neither of these anatomies he be condemnable, I hope we shall obtain a more favorable sentence.

This purifying of wit—this enriching of memory, enabling of judgment, and enlarging of conceit—which commonly we call learning, under what name soever it come forth, or to what immediate end soever it be directed, the final end is to lead and draw us to as high a perfection as our degenerate souls, made worse by their clayey lodgings, can be capable of.

This, according to the inclination of man, bred many-formed impressions. For some, that thought this felicity principally to be gotten by knowledge, and no knowledge to be so high or heavenly as acquaintance with the stars, gave themselves to astronomy. Others, persuading themselves to be demigods if they knew the causes of things, became natural and supernatural philosophers. Some an admirable delight drew to music, and some the certainty of demonstration to the mathematics. But all, one and other, having scope to know, & by knowledge to lift up

---

[1] *Lucretia* Beautiful wife of Tarquinius Collatinus, a Roman noble, whose suicide after she was raped by Sextus Tarquinius, a Roman prince, led to political revolt and the creation of the Roman Republic.

[2] *Theagenes & Chariclea* Lovers in *The Aethiopica* by Heliodorus.

[3] *advocate* Lawyer.

[4] *peising* Weighing.

the mind from the dungeon of the body to the enjoying his own divine essence.

But when by the balance of experience it was found that the astronomer, looking to the stars, might fall in a ditch, that the inquiring philosopher might be blind in himself, & the mathematician might draw forth a straight line with a crooked heart, then lo, did proof, the overruler of opinions, make manifest that all these are but serving sciences, which, as they have each a private end in themselves, so yet are they all directed to the highest end of the mistress-knowledge, by the Greeks called ἀρχίτεκτονικη,[1] which stands, as I think, in the knowledge of a man's self, in the ethic and politic consideration, with the end of well-doing and not of well-knowing only—even as the saddler's next end is to make a good saddle, but his further end to serve a nobler faculty, which is horsemanship, so the horseman's to soldiery, and the soldier not only to have the skill, but to perform the practise of a soldier. So that, the ending end of all earthly learning being virtuous action, those skills that most serve to bring forth that have a most just title to be princes over all the rest.

Wherein, if we can, show we the poet is worthy to have it before any other competitors, among whom principally to challenge it step forth the moral philosophers, whom me thinketh I see coming towards me with a sullen gravity, as though they could not abide vice by daylight, rudely clothed for to witness outwardly their contempt of outward things, with books in their hands against glory, whereto they set their names, sophistically speaking against subtlety, and angry with any man in whom they see the foul fault of anger. These men casting largess as they go, of definitions, divisions, and distinctions, with a scornful interrogative do soberly ask whether it be possible to find any path so ready to lead a man to virtue as that which teacheth what virtue is, & teacheth it not only by delivering forth his very being, his causes and effects, but also by making known his enemy, vice, which must be destroyed, and his cumbersome servant, passion, which must be mastered; by showing the generalities that

containeth it and the specialties that are derived from it; lastly, by plain setting down how it extendeth itself out of the limits of a man's own little world to the government of families and maintaining of public societies.

The historian scarcely gives leisure to the moralist to say so much, but that he, laden with old mouse-eaten records, authorizing himself for the most part upon other histories, whose greatest authorities are built upon the notable foundation hearsay, having much ado to accord differing writers & to pick truth out of partiality; better acquainted with a thousand years ago than with the present age, and yet better knowing how this world goeth than how his own wit runneth; curious for antiquities and inquisitive of novelties; a wonder to young folks and a tyrant in table talk, denieth, in a great chafe,[2] that any man for teaching of virtue, and virtuous actions, is comparable to him. "I am *testis temporum, lux veritatis, vita memoriae, magistra vitae, nuncia vetustatis.*[3] The philosopher," saith he, "teacheth a disputative virtue, but I do an active. His virtue is excellent in the dangerless Academy of Plato, but mine showeth forth her honorable face in the battles of Marathon, Pharsalia, Poitiers, and Agincourt.[4] He teacheth virtue by certain abstract considerations, but I only follow the footing of them that have gone before you. Old-aged experience goeth beyond the fine-witted philosopher, but I give the experience of many ages. Lastly, if he make the songbook, I put the learner's hand to the lute; and if he be the guide, I am the light." Then he would allege you innumerable examples, confirming story by stories, how much the wisest senators and princes have been directed by the credit of history, as Brutus, Alphonsus of Aragon,[5] and who not, if need be.

---

[2] *chafe* Temper, passion.

[3] *testis … vetustatis* Latin: The witness of time, the light of truth, the life of memory, the instructor of life, the herald of old age (Cicero, *De Oratore*, 2.9.36).

[4] *Marathon* Site of the Greeks' victory over the Persians in 490 BCE; *Pharsalia* Site of Pompey's loss to Caesar in 48 BCE; *Poitiers* Site of the French defeat by Edward, England's Black Prince, in 1356; *Agincourt* Battlefield on which the French were again defeated by the English in 1415.

[5] *Brutus* Roman politician who conspired to assassinate Caesar, and was inspired to do so by the history of his ancestor, Junius Brutus, who defeated the Tarquin kings; *Alphonsus of Aragon* King

---

[1] ἀρχίτεκτονικη Greek: architectonics (the science of architecture, or more broadly, of structure) is perhaps the closest modern equivalent to this Greek word.

At length the long line of their disputation maketh a point in this, that the one giveth the precept, & the other the example.

Now whom shall we find (since the question stands for the highest form in the school of learning) to be moderator? Truly as me seemeth, the poet; and if not a moderator, even the man that ought to carry the title from them both, & much more from all the other serving sciences. Therefore compare we the poet with the historian & with the moral philosopher; and if he go beyond them both, no other human skill can match him. For as for the divine, with all reverence it is ever to be excepted, not only for having his scope as far beyond any of these as eternity exceeds a moment, but even for passing each of these in themselves. And for the lawyer, though *Ius*[1] be the daughter of Justice, the chief of virtues, yet because he seeketh to make men good rather *formidine poenae* than *virtutis amore*;[2] or, to say righter, doth not endeavour to make men good, but that their evil hurt not others; having no care so he be a good citizen, how bad a man he might be. Therefore, as our wickedness maketh him necessary, and necessity maketh him honorable, so he is not in the deepest truth to stand in rank with these who all endeavour to take naughtiness away and plant goodness even in the secretest cabinet of our souls. And these four are all that any way deal in the consideration of men's manners, which being the supreme knowledge, they that best breed it deserve the best commendation.

The philosopher, therefore, and the historian are they which would win the goal, the one by precept, the other by example. But both, not having both, do both halt.[3] For the philosopher, setting down with thorny arguments the bare rule, is so hard of utterance and so misty to be conceived, that one that hath no other guide but him shall wade in him till he be old before he shall find sufficient cause to be honest. For his knowledge standeth so upon the abstract and general that happy is that man who may understand him, and more happy that can apply what he doth understand. On the other side, the historian, wanting the precept, is so tied, not to what should be but to what is, to the particular truth of things and not to the general reason of things, that his example draweth no necessary consequence, and therefore a less fruitful doctrine.

Now doth the peerless poet perform both: for whatsoever the philosopher says should be done, he gives a perfect picture of it by someone by whom he presupposes it was done, so as he coupleth the general notion with the particular example. A perfect picture I say, for he yieldeth to the powers of the mind an image of that whereof the philosopher bestoweth but a wordish description, which doth neither strike, pierce, nor possess the sight of the soul so much as that other doth. For as in outward things, to a man that had never seen an elephant or a rhinoceros, who should tell him most exquisitely all their shape, colour, bigness, and particular marks, or of a gorgeous palace an architect, who, declaring the full beauties, might well make the hearer able to repeat, as it were by rote, all he had heard, yet should never satisfy his inward conceit with being witness to itself of a true lively knowledge; but the same man, as soon as he might see those beasts well painted, or that house well in model, should straightaways grow without need of any description, to a judicial comprehending of them: so no doubt the philosopher with his learned definitions—be it of virtues or vices, matters of public policy or private government— replenisheth the memory with many infallible grounds of wisdom, which, notwithstanding, lie dark before the imaginative and judging power, if they be not illuminated or figured forth by the speaking picture of poesy. . . .

For conclusion, I say the philosopher teacheth, but he teacheth obscurely, so as the learned only can understand him; that is to say, he teacheth them that are already taught. But the poet is the food for the tenderest stomachs; the poet is indeed the right popular philosopher, whereof Aesop's tales give good proof, whose pretty allegories, stealing under the formal tales of beasts, makes many, more beastly than beasts, begin to hear the sound of virtue from those dumb speakers.

But now it may be alleged that if this imagining of

---

of Aragon who carried the histories of Livy and Caesar with him into battle and who, according to Jacques Amyot, recovered from a severe illness upon being read aloud the deeds of Alexander the Great.

[1] *Ius* Latin: Right.

[2] *formidine amore* Latin: By fear of punishment than by love of virtue (Horace, *Epistles,* 1.6.52–53).

[3] *halt* Limp; proceed unsteadily or imperfectly.

matters be so fit for the imagination, then must the historian needs surpass, who bringeth you images of true matters, such as indeed were done, and not such as fantastically or falsely may be suggested to have been done. Truly Aristotle himself, in his discourse of poesy, plainly determines this question, saying that poetry is φιλοσοφωτερων and σπουδαιοτερον that is to say, it is more philosophical and more studiously serious than history. His reason is, because poesy dealeth with καθόλου;[1] that is to say, with the universal consideration, and the history with καθ' ἕκαστον,[2] the particular. Now, saith he, the universal ways what is fit to be said or done, either in likelihood or necessity (which the poesy considers in his imposed names), and the particular only marketh whether Alcibiades[3] did, or suffered, this or that. Thus far Aristotle: which reason of his (as all his) is most full of reason. For indeed, if the question were whether it were better to have a particular act truly or falsely set down, there is no doubt which is to be chosen, no more than whether you had rather have Vespasian's[4] picture right as he was, or, at the painter's pleasure, nothing resembling. But if the question be for your own use and learning, whether it be better to have it set down as it should be, or as it was, then certainly is more doctrinable the feigned Cyrus in Xenophon than the true Cyrus in Justin, and the feigned Aeneas in Virgil than the right Aeneas in Dares Phrygius:[5] as to a lady that desired to fashion her countenance to the best grace, a painter should more benefit her to portrait a most sweet face, writing Canidia upon it, than to paint Canidia as she was, who, Horace sweareth, was full ill-favored.[6]

If the poet do his part aright, he will show you in Tantalus,[7] Atreus, and such like, nothing that is not to be shunned; in Cyrus, Aeneas, Ulysses, each thing to be followed; where the historian, bound to tell things as things were, cannot be liberal (without he will be poetical) of a perfect pattern, but, as in Alexander or Scipio himself, show doings, some to be liked, some to be misliked. And then how will you discern what to follow but by your own discretion, which you had without reading Quintus Curtius.[8] And whereas a man may say, though in universal consideration of doctrine the poet prevaileth, yet that the history, in his saying such a thing was done, doth warrant a man more in that he shall follow—the answer is manifest: that, if he stand upon that was (as if he should argue, because it rained yesterday, therefore it should rain today), then indeed hath it some advantage to a gross conceit. But if he know an example only informs a conjectured likelihood, and so go by reason, the poet doth so far exceed him as he is to frame his example to that which is most reasonable (be it in warlike, politic, or private matters), where the historian in his bare *was* hath many times that which we call fortune to overrule the best wisdom. Many times he must tell events whereof he can yield no cause; or, if he do, it must be poetically.

For that a feigned example hath as much force to teach as a true example (for as for to move, it is clear, since the feigned may be tuned to the highest key of passion) let us take one example wherein an historian and a poet did concur. Herodotus and Justin doth both testify that Zopirus, King Darius's faithful servant, seeing his master long resisted by the rebellious Babylonians, feigned himself in extreme disgrace of his king; for verifying of which he caused his own nose and ears to be cut off, and so flying to the Babylonians was received, and for his known valour so far credited that he did find means to deliver them over to Darius. Much like matter doth Livy record of Tarquinius and his son.[9] Xenophon excellently

---

[1] καθόλου Greek: universal, Catholic (in the sense of universal or worldwide).

[2] καθ'ἕκαστον Greek: detailed, or particular account or list.

[3] *Alcibiades* Greek statesman and friend of Achilles. (See *Poetics* 9.145.)

[4] *Vespasian* First-century CE Roman emperor, reported to have been very ugly.

[5] *Justin* Marcus Justinus, whose c. second-century BCE *Histories* provide an account of Cyrus' actions; *Dares Phrygius* Supposed author of an account of the Trojan War, probably in fact written after the second century CE.

[6] *Horace … ill-favored* Cf. *Epodes* 5, in which Horace attacks the Roman prostitute Canidia; she had apparently rejected him.

[7] *Tantalus* When invited to dine with the gods, Tantalus served them pieces of his own murdered son, Pelops.

[8] *Quintus Curtius* Roman historian who wrote a multi-volume biography of Alexander the Great.

[9] *Livy … son* Tarquinius Superbus, last king of Rome (534–510 BCE), and his son, who pretended to be an ally of the Gabians in order to deliver them over to his father. See Titus Livius's *Early*

feigneth such another stratagem performed by Abradates in Cyrus' behalf.[1] Now would I fain know, if occasion be presented unto you to serve your prince by such an honest dissimulation, why you do not as well learn it of Xenophon's fiction as of the others verity; and truly so much the better, as you shall save your nose by the bargain: for Abradates did not counterfeit so far. So then the best of the historian is subject to the poet; for whatsoever action, or faction, whatsoever counsel, policy, or war stratagem the historian is bound to recite, that may the poet (if he list[2]) with his imitation make his own, beautifying it both for further teaching, and more delighting, as it please him: having all, from Dante's heaven to his hell, under the authority of his pen.[3] Which if I be asked what poets have done so, as I might well name some, so yet say I, and say again, I speak of the art, and not of the artificer.

Now to that which commonly is attributed to the praise of history, in respect of the notable learning, is got by marking the success, as though therein a man should see virtue exalted & vice punished—truly that commendation is peculiar to poetry, and far off from history. For indeed poetry ever sets Virtue so out in her best colours, making Fortune her well-waiting handmaid, that one must needs be enamoured of her. Well may you see Ulysses in a storm and in other hard plights, but they are but exercises of patience and magnanimity, to make them shine the more in the near following prosperity. And of the contrary part, if evil men come to the stage, they ever go out (as the tragedy writer answered to one that misliked the show of such persons) so manacled as they little animate folks to follow them. But the history, being captived to the truth of a foolish world, is many times a terror from well-doing, and an encouragement to unbridled wickedness. For see we not valiant Miltiades[4] rot in his fetters? The just Phocion[5] and the accomplished Socrates put to death like traitors? The cruel Severus[6] live prosperously? The excellent Severus[7] miserably murdered? Sulla and Marius[8] dying in their beds? Pompey and Cicero[9] slain then, when they would have thought exile a happiness? See we not virtuous Cato[10] driven to kill himself, and rebel Caesar so advanced that his name yet, after 1600 years, lasteth in the highest honor? And mark but even Caesar's own words of the forenamed Sulla (who in that only did honestly, to put down his dishonest tyranny), *literas nescivet*,[11] as if want of learning caused him to do well. He meant it not by poetry, which, not content with earthly plagues, deviseth new punishments in hell for tyrants, nor yet by philosophy, which teacheth *occidendos esse*; but no doubt by skill in history, for that indeed can afford you Cypselus, Periander, Phalaris, Dionysius,[12] and I know not how many more of the same kennel, that speed well enough in their abominable injustice of usurpation.

I conclude, therefore, that he excelleth history, not only in furnishing the mind with knowledge, but in setting it forward to that which deserves to be called and accounted good: which setting forward, and moving to well-doing, indeed setteth the laurel crown upon the poets as victorious,

---

History of Rome.

[1] *Xenophon ... behalf* Abradates, the fifth-century BCE viceroy of Shushan who gave his allegiance to Cyrus, King of Persia. See Xenophon's *Cyropaedia*.

[2] *list* Desires.

[3] *from Dante's ... pen* Reference to Dante's *Divine Comedy*, which describes its narrator's journey through hell, purgatory, and heaven.

[4] *Miltiades* Fifth-century BCE Athenian general who was imprisoned by his own people after leading a failed naval attack.

[5] *Phocion* Athenian statesman (402–318 BCE).

[6] *cruel Severus* Lucius Septimius Severus, second-century BCE Roman emperor known for his cruelty.

[7] *excellent Severus* Alexander Severus (208–235 CE), noble and virtuous Roman emperor who was nevertheless killed by his troops.

[8] *Sulla and Marius* Lucius Sulla (138–78 BCE) and Gaius Marius (157–83 BCE), two rival Roman generals and politicians whose disputes brought civil war to Rome.

[9] *Pompey* Gnaeus Pompeius, first-century BCE Roman general who was murdered after opposing Caesar in battle; *Cicero* Marcus Tullius Cicero was murdered by order of Marcus Antonius.

[10] *Cato* Marcus Porcius Cato (95–46 BCE), Roman aristocrat who opposed both Pompey and Caesar and who committed suicide rather than submit to Caesar's authority.

[11] *literas nescivet* Latin: he knew nothing of letters (Suetonius, *Life of Caesar*, ch. 77).

[12] *occidentos esse* Latin: they are to be killed; *Cypselus, Periander, Phalaris, Dionysius* Tyrannical rulers remembered for the brutality of their crimes and the impunity with which those crimes were committed.

not only of the historian, but over the philosopher, howsoever in teaching it may be questionable. . . .

That imitation whereof poetry is, hath the most conveniency to nature of all other, insomuch that, as Aristotle saith, those things which in themselves are horrible, as cruel battles, unnatural monsters, are made in poetical imitation delightful.[1] Truly, I have known men that even with reading *Amadis de Gaule*[2] (which God knoweth wanteth much of a perfect poesy) have found their hearts moved to the exercise of courtesy, liberality, and especially courage. Who readeth Aeneas carrying old Anchises on his back, that wisheth not it were his fortune to perform so excellent an act? Whom doth not those words of Turnus move, the tale of Turnus having planted his image in the imagination,

> *Fugientam haec terra videbit?*
> *Usque adeone mori miserum est?*[3]

Where the philosophers, as they scorn to delight, so must they be content little to move—saving wrangling whether *virtus*[4] be the chief or the only good, whether the contemplative or the active life do excel—which Plato and Boethius well knew, and therefore made mistress Philosophy very often borrow the masking raiment of poesy.[5] For even those hard-hearted evil men who think virtue a school name, and know no other good but *indulgere genio*,[6] and therefore despise the austere admonitions of the philosopher, and feel not the inward reason they stand upon, yet will be content to be delighted—which is all the good-fellow poet seemeth to promise—and so steal to see the form of goodness, (which seen, they cannot but love) ere themselves be aware, as if they took a medicine of cherries. . . .

Now in his parts, kinds, or species (as you list to term them), it is to be noted that some poesies have coupled together two or three kinds, as the tragical and comical, whereupon is risen the tragicomical. Some, in the manner, have mingled prose and verse, as Sannazaro[7] and Boethius; some have mingled matters heroical and pastoral. But that cometh all to one in this question; for, if severed they be good, the conjunction cannot be hurtful. Therefore, perchance forgetting some and leaving some as needless to be remembered, it shall not be amiss in a word to cite the special kinds, to see what faults may be found in the right use of them.

Is it then the Pastoral poem which is misliked? (For perchance where the hedge is lowest[8] they will soonest leap over.) Is the poor pipe[9] disdained, which sometimes out of Meliboeus' mouth can show the misery of people under hard lords and ravening soldiers, and again, by Tityrus,[10] what blessedness is derived to them that lie lowest from the goodness of them that sit highest; sometimes, under the pretty tales of wolves and sheep, can include the whole considerations of wrongdoing and patience; sometimes show that contentions for trifles can get but a trifling victory: where perchance a man may see that even Alexander & Darius, when they strove who should be cock of this world's dunghill, the benefit they got was that the after-livers may say

> *Haec memini & victum frustra contendere Thyrsin:*
> *Ex illo Corydon, Corydon est tempore nobis.*[11]

---

[1] *as Aristotle … delightful* Cf. *Poetics* Part 4.

[2] *Amadis de Gaule* Spanish chivalric romance written by Vasco de Lobeyra.

[3] *Fugientam … est* Latin. In Virgil's *Aeneid*, Turnus, when attempting to defend his home from the invading Trojans, cries, "Shall this land see him [Turnus] run away? / Is it so hard to die?" (*Aeneid* 12.645–46).

[4] *virtus* Latin word that carries with it the sense of courage and strength of purpose as well as the quality we now use the word "virtue" to denote.

[5] *which … poesy* Both Plato and Boethius were philosophers who believed in the superiority of a contemplative life.

[6] *indulgere genio* Latin: To indulge your appetite; i.e., self-indulgence (Persius, *Satires* 5.151).

[7] *Sannazaro* Italian poet Jacopo Sannazaro, author of the pastoral romance *Arcadia*, which mixes poetry and prose.

[8] *lowest* Pastoral poetry was considered the lowest and least technically advanced of the poetic genres.

[9] *pipe* Shepherd's pipe, the symbol of pastoral poetry.

[10] *Meliboeus … Tityrus* Meliboeus and Tityrus are two shepherds in Virgil's *Eclogues*.

[11] *Haec … nobis* Latin: These things I remember, how Thyrsis, vanquished, strove in vain. From that time it is Corydon, Corydon with us. From Virgil, *Eclogues* 7.69–70, in which the pastoral poets Thyrsis and Corydon challenge one another to a singing contest—an event which, Sidney says, is comparable to the victory of Alexander the Great over Darius of Persia.

Or is it the lamenting Elegiac, which in a kind heart would move rather pity than blame; who bewails with the great philosopher Heraclitus[1] the weakness of mankind and the wretchedness of the world; who surely is to be praised either for compassionate accompanying just causes of lamentations, or for rightly painting out how weak be the passions of woefulness? Is it the bitter but wholesome Iambic,[2] who rubs the galled mind, in making shame the trumpet of villainy, with bold and open crying out against naughtiness? Or the Satiric, who

Omne vafer vitium ridenti tangit amico;[3]

who sportingly never leaveth till he make a man laugh at folly, and at length ashamed, to laugh at himself, which he cannot avoid without avoiding the folly; who, while

circum praecordia ludit,[4]

giveth us to feel how many headaches a passionate life bringeth us to; how, when all is done,

Est Ulubris, animus si nos non deficit aequus.[5]

No, perchance it is the Comic, whom naughty play-makers and stage-keepers have justly made odious. To the arguments of abuse I will after answer. Only thus much now is to be said, that the comedy is an imitation of the common errors of our life, which he representeth in the most ridiculous and scornful sort that may be, so as it is impossible that any beholder can be content to be such a one. Now, as in geometry the oblique must be known as well as the right, and in arithmetic the odd as well as the even, so in the actions of our life who seeth not the filthiness of evil wanteth a great folly to perceive the beauty of virtue. This doth the comedy handle so in our private and domestical matters as with hearing it we get, as it were, an experience what is to be looked for of a niggardly Demea, of a crafty Davus, of a flattering Gnatho, of a vain-glorious Thraso;[6] and not only to know what effects are to be expected, but to know who be such, by the signifying badge given them by the comedian. And little reason hath any man to say that men learn the evil by seeing it so set out, since, as I said before, there is no man living but, by the force truth hath in nature, no sooner seeth these men play their parts, but wisheth them *in pistrinum;*[7] although perchance the sack of his own faults lie so behind his back that he seeth not himself to dance the same measure;[8] whereto yet nothing can more open his eyes than to see his own actions contemptibly set forth.

So that the right use of comedy will, I think, by nobody be blamed; and much less of the high and excellent Tragedy, that openeth the greatest wounds, and showeth forth the ulcers that are covered with tissue; that maketh kings fear to be tyrants, and tyrants manifest their tyrannical humours; that, with stirring the affects of admiration and commiseration, teacheth the uncertainty of this world, and upon how weak foundations gilded roofs are builded; that maketh us know.

---

[1] *Heraclitus* Fifth-century BCE Greek philosopher who believed that everything in the universe is subject to constant change and strife.

[2] *Iambic* Verse form typically used in satire and direct attacks.

[3] *Omne ... amico* Latin: The crafty man probes every fault while making his friends laugh (Persius, *Satires* 1.116–17).

[4] *Circum praecordia ludit* Latin: He plays about the heart (Persius, *Satires*, 1.117).

[5] *Est ... aequus* Latin: What you are seeking] is at Ulubrae, if a well-balanced mind does not fail us (Adaptation of Horace, *Epistles*, 1.11.30). Ulubrae was a small, notoriously dull town bordered by marshlands.

[6] *Demea ... Thraso* Four stock characters from the plays of Terence.

[7] *in pistrinum* Latin: in the mill (where Roman slaves and criminals were forced to work as punishment).

[8] *the sack ... measure* Reference to one of Aesop's fables, in which every person is given two sacks to carry. One, which is slung behind the back, out of sight, contains one's own faults. The other, hung in front of one's neck, contains all the faults of others.

Qui sceptra saevus duro imperio regit
Timet timentes; metus in auctorem redit.[1]

… But it is not the tragedy they do mislike; for it were too absurd to cast out so excellent a representation of whatsoever is most worthy to be learned.

Is it the Lyric that most displeaseth, who with his tuned lyre and well-accorded voice giveth praise, the reward of virtue, to virtuous acts; who gives moral precepts, and natural problems; who sometimes raiseth up his voice to the height of the heavens in singing the lauds of the immortal God? Certainly I must confess mine own barbarousness, I never heard the old song of Percy and Douglas[2] that I found not my heart moved more than with a trumpet. …

There rests the Heroical[3]—whose very name, I think, should daunt all backbiters. For by what conceit can a tongue be directed to speak evil of that which draweth with him no less champions than Achilles, Cyrus, Aeneas, Turnus, Tydeus, Rinaldo[4]—who doth not only teach and move to a truth, but teacheth and moveth to the most high and excellent truth; who maketh magnanimity and justice shine through all misty fearfulness and foggy desires. …

But truly I imagine it falleth out with these poet-whippers, as with some good women, who often are sick, but in faith they cannot tell where; so the name of poetry is odious to them, but neither his cause nor effects, neither the sum that contains him, nor the particularities descending from him, give any fast handle to their carping dispraise. …

But because we have ears as well as tongues, and that the lightest reasons that may be will seem to weigh greatly, if nothing be put in the counterbalance, let us hear, and, as well as we can, ponder what objections be made against this art, which may be worthy either of yielding or answering.

First, truly I note not only in these μισομουσι, poet-haters, but in all that kind of people who seek a praise by dispraising others, that they do prodigally spend a great many wandering words in quips and scoffs, carping and taunting at each thing which, by stirring the spleen, may stay the brain from a thorough-beholding the worthiness of the subject. Those kind of objections, as they are full of a very idle easiness, since there is nothing of so sacred a majesty but that an itching tongue may rub itself upon it, so deserve they no other answer, but, instead of laughing at the jest, to laugh at the jester. … Marry, these other pleasant fault-finders, who will correct the verb before they understand the noun, and confute others knowledge before they confirm their own, I would have them only remember that scoffing cometh not of wisdom; so as the best title in true English they get with their merriments is to be called good fools, for so have our grave forefathers ever termed that humorous kind of jesters.

But that which giveth greatest scope to their scorning humour is rhyming and versing. It is already said (and, as I think, truly said) it is not rhyming and versing that makes poesy. One may be a poet without versing, and a versifier without poetry. But yet, presuppose it were inseparable (as indeed it seemeth Scaliger[5] judgeth), truly it were an inseparable commendation. For if *oratio* next to *ratio*, speech next to reason, be the greatest gift bestowed upon mortality, that cannot be praiseless which doth most polish that blessing of speech; which considers each word, not only (as a man may say) by his forcible quality, but by his best measured quantity, carrying even in themselves a harmony—without, perchance, number, measure, order, proportion be in our time grown odious. But lay aside the just praise it hath by being the only fit speech for music (music, I say, the most divine striker of the senses), thus much is undoubtedly true, that if reading be foolish without remembering, memory being the only treasure of knowledge, those words which are fittest for memory are likewise most convenient for knowledge. Now, that verse far exceedeth prose in the knitting up of the memory, the

---

[1]   *Qui … redit*   Latin: The cruel man who rules his kingdom with harsh sway / Fears those who fear him; terror returns upon the author (Seneca, *Oedipus* 3.705–06).

[2]   *old song … Douglas*   *The Ballad of Chevy Chase.*

[3]   *Heroical*   Epic.

[4]   *Turnus*   Great adversary of Aeneas in Virgil's *Aeneid*; *Tydeus*   Hero of Statius's *Thebaid*; *Rinaldo*   Hero of Ariosto's *Orlando Furioso.*

[5]   *Scaliger*   Julius Caesar Scaliger, Italian scholar of the sixteenth century who wrote *Seven Books on Poetry.*

reason is manifest: the words (besides their delight, which hath a great affinity to memory) being so set as one cannot be lost but the whole work fails; which accusing itself, calleth the remembrance back to itself, and so most strongly confirmeth it. ...

Now then go we to the most important imputations laid to the poor poets. For aught I can yet learn, they are these. First, that there being many other more fruitful knowledges, a man might better spend his time in them than in this. Secondly, that it is the mother of lies. Thirdly, that it is the nurse of abuse, infecting us with many pestilent desires; with a siren's sweetness drawing the mind to the serpent's tail of sinful fancies (and herein, especially, comedies give the largest field to ear,[1] as Chaucer saith); how, both in other nations and in ours, before poets did soften us, we were full of courage, given to martial exercises, the pillars of man-like liberty, and not lulled asleep in shady idleness with poets' pastimes. And lastly and chiefly, they cry out with open mouth, as if they had shot Robin Hood, that Plato banished them out of his commonwealth. Truly this is much, if there be much truth in it.

First, to the first. That a man might better spend his time, is a reason indeed; but it doth, as they say, but *petere principium*.[2] For if it be as I affirm, that no learning is so good as that which teacheth and moveth to virtue; and that none can both teach and move thereto so much as poesy, then is the conclusion manifest that ink and paper cannot be to a more profitable purpose employed. And certainly, though a man should grant their first assumption, it should follow (methinks) very unwillingly, that good is not good, because better is better. But I still and utterly deny that there is sprung out of the earth a more fruitful knowledge.

To the second, therefore, that they should be the principal liars, I answer paradoxically, but truly, I think truly, that of all writers under the sun, the poet is the least liar; and, though he would, as a poet can scarcely be a liar. The astronomer, with his cousin the geometrician, can hardly escape, when they take upon them to measure the

height of the stars. How often, think you, do the physicians lie, when they aver things good for sicknesses, which afterwards send Charon[3] a great number of souls drowned in a potion before they come to his ferry? And no less of the rest, which take upon them to affirm. Now, for the poet, he nothing affirms, and therefore never lieth. For, as I take it, to lie is to affirm that to be true which is false. So as the other artists, and especially the historian, affirming many things, can, in the cloudy knowledge of mankind, hardly escape from many lies. But the poet, as I said before, never affirmeth. The poet never maketh any circles about your imagination, to conjure you to believe for true what he writes. He citeth not authorities of other histories, but even for his entry calleth the sweet Muses to inspire unto him a good invention; in truth, not labouring to tell you what is or is not, but what should or should not, be. And therefore, though he recount things not true, yet because he telleth them not for true, he lieth not—without we will say that Nathan lied in his speech before alleged to David; which as a wicked man durst scarce say, so think I none so simple would say that Aesop lied in the tales of his beasts; for who thinks Aesop wrote it for actually true were well worthy to have his name chronicled among the beasts he writeth of. What child is there that, coming to a play and seeing "Thebes" written in great letters upon an old door, doth believe that it is Thebes? If then a man can arrive to the child's age to know that the poets' persons and doings are but pictures what should be, and not stories what have been, they will never give the lie to things not affirmatively but allegorically and figuratively written. And therefore, as in history, looking for truth, they may go away full fraught with falsehood, so in poesy, looking but for fiction, they shall use the narration but as an imaginative ground-plot of a profitable invention. But hereto is replied that the poets give names to men they write of, which argueth a conceit of an actual truth, and so, not being true, proves a falsehood. And doth the lawyer lie then, when under the names of *John-a-stiles* and *John-a-nokes*[4] he putteth his case? But that is easily answered. Their naming of men is

---

[1] *comedies ... ear* See "The Knight's Tale" 1.28, in Chaucer's *Canterbury Tales*: "a large feeld to ere" ("ere" meaning "to plow").

[2] *petere principium* Latin: to beg the question.

[3] *Charon* Greek mythological ferryman of the underworld who transports the souls of the dead across the River Styx.

[4] *John ... nokes* Fictitious names, like John Doe.

but to make their picture the more lively, and not to build any history: painting men, they cannot leave men nameless. We see we cannot play at chess but that we must give names to our chessmen; and yet, methinks, he were a very partial champion of truth that would say we lied for giving a piece of wood the reverend title of a bishop. The poet nameth Cyrus and Aeneas no other way than to show what men of their fames, fortunes, and estates should do.

Their third is, how much it abuseth men's wit, training it to wanton sinfulness and lustful love. For indeed that is the principal, if not only, abuse I can hear alleged. They say the comedies rather teach than reprehend amorous conceits. They say the lyric is larded with passionate sonnets, the elegiac weeps the want of his mistress, and that even to the heroical, Cupid hath ambitiously climbed. Alas, Love, I would thou couldst as well defend thyself as thou canst offend others. I would those on whom thou doest attend could either put thee away, or yield good reason why they keep thee. But grant love of beauty to be a beastly fault (although it be very hard, since only man, and no beast, hath that gift to discern beauty); grant that lovely name of Love to deserve all hateful reproaches (although even some of my masters the philosophers spent a good deal of their lamp-oil in setting forth the excellency of it); grant, I say, whatsoever they will have granted, that not only love, but lust, but vanity, but (if they list) scurrility, possesseth many leaves of the poets' books; yet, think I, when this is granted, they will find their sentence may with good manners put the last words foremost, and not say that poetry abuseth man's wit, but that man's wit abuseth poetry.

For I will not deny but that man's wit may make poesy, which should be εἰκαστικὴ[1] (which some learned have defined, "figuring forth good things"), to be φανταστικὴ[2] (which doth, contrariwise, infect the fancy with unworthy objects), as the painter should give to the eye either some excellent perspective, or some fine picture fit for building or fortification, or containing in it some notable example (as Abraham sacrificing his son Isaac,

Judith killing Holofernes, David fighting with Goliath),[3] may leave those, and please an ill-pleased eye with wanton shows of better hidden matters. But what, shall the abuse of a thing, make the right use odious? Nay, truly, though I yield that poesy may not only be abused, but that, being abused, by the reason of his sweet charming force, it can do more hurt than any other army of words: yet shall it be so far from concluding that the abuse should give reproach to the abused, that, contrariwise, it is a good reason that whatsoever, being abused, doth most harm, being rightly used (and upon the right use, each thing receives his title), doth most good. Do we not see skill of physic, the best rampire[4] to our often-assaulted bodies, being abused, teach poison, the most violent destroyer? Doth not knowledge of law, whose end is to even & right all things, being abused, grow the crooked fosterer of horrible injuries? Doth not (to go to the highest) God's word, abused, breed heresy, and his name, abused, become blasphemy? Truly, a needle cannot do much hurt, and as truly (with leave of ladies be it spoken) it cannot do much good: with a sword thou mayst kill thy father, and with a sword thou mayst defend thy prince and country. So that, as in their calling poets fathers of lies they said nothing, so in this their argument of abuse they prove the commendation.

They allege herewith, that before poets began to be in price, our nation had set their hearts' delight upon action, and not imagination: rather doing things worthy to be written, than writing things fit to be done. What that before-time was, I think scarcely Sphinx[5] can tell, since no memory is so ancient that hath not the precedent of poetry. And certain it is that, in our plainest homeliness, yet never was the Albion nation[6] without poetry. Marry, this argument, though it be levelled against poetry, yet is it indeed a chainshot[7] against all learning, or "bookish-

---

[1] εἰκαστικὴ Greek: representing real things.

[2] φανταστικὴ Greek: representing imaginary things.

[3] *as Abraham … Goliath* See Genesis 22, Judith 2–14, and 1 Samuel 17, respectively.

[4] *rampire* Rampart; bulwark.

[5] *Sphinx* Mythical creature with the head of a woman and the body of a lion who posed riddles to humans.

[6] *Albion nation* England.

[7] *chainshot* Weapon used in naval warfare to destroy ships; it consists of two cannon balls joined by a chain.

ness," as they commonly term it. ...

But now indeed my burden is great, that Plato's name is laid upon me, whom, I must confess, of all philosophers, I have ever esteemed most worthy of reverence; and with good reason, since of all philosophers he is the most poetical. Yet if he will defile the fountain out of which his flowing streams have proceeded, let us boldly examine with what reasons he did it. First, truly, a man might maliciously object that Plato, being a philosopher, was a natural enemy of poets. For indeed, after the philosophers had picked out of the sweet mysteries of poetry the right discerning true points of knowledge, they forthwith, putting it in method, and making a school-art of that which the poets did only teach by a divine delightfulness, beginning to spurn at their guides like ungrateful apprentices, were not content to set up shop for themselves, but sought by all means to discredit their masters; which by the force of delight being barred them, the less they could overthrow them, the more they hated them. For indeed, they found for Homer seven cities strove who should have him for their citizen; where so many cities banished philosophers as not fit members to live among them. ...

St. Paul himself setteth a watch-word upon philosophy, indeed upon the abuse.[1] So doth Plato upon the abuse, not upon poetry. Plato found fault that the poets of his time filled the world with wrong opinions of the gods, making light tales of that unspotted essence, and therefore would not have the youth depraved with such opinions. Herein may much be said. Let this suffice: the poets did not induce such opinions, but did imitate those opinions already induced; for all the Greek stories can well testify that the very religion of that time stood upon many, and many-fashioned, gods, not taught so by poets, but followed according to their nature of imitation. Who list may read in Plutarch the discourses of Isis and Osiris, of the cause why Oracles ceased, of the divine providence, & see whether the theology of that nation stood not upon such dreams which the poets indeed superstitiously observed—and truly (since they had not the light of Christ) did much better in it than the philosophers, who,

shaking off superstition, brought in atheism. Plato therefore (whose authority I had much rather justly construe than unjustly resist) meant not in general of poets, in those words of which Julius Scaliger saith, *Qua authoritate barbari quidam atque hispidi abuti velint ad poetas e republica exigendos;*[2] but only meant to drive out those wrong opinions of the Deity (whereof now, without further law, Christianity hath taken away all the hurtful belief), perchance (as he thought) nourished by then-esteemed poets. ...

Of the other side, who would show the honors have been by the best sort of judgments granted them, a whole sea of examples would present themselves: Alexanders, Caesars, Scipios, all favorers of poets; Laelius,[3] called the Roman Socrates, himself a poet, so as part of *Heautontimorumenos* in Terence was supposed to be made by him; and even the Greek Socrates, whom Apollo confirmed to be the only wise man, is said to have spent part of his old time in putting Aesop's fables into verses. And therefore, full evil should it become his scholar Plato to put such words in his master's mouth against poets. But what need more? Aristotle writes the Art of Poesy; and why, if it should not be written? Plutarch teacheth the use to be gathered of them;[4] and how, if they should not be read? And who reads Plutarch's either history or philosophy shall find he trimmeth both their garments with guards of poesy. But I list not to defend poesy with the help of his underling historiography. Let it suffice to have showed it is a fit soil for praise to dwell upon; and what dispraise may set upon it, is either easily overcome, or transformed into just commendation.

So that, since the excellencies of it may be so easily and so justly confirmed, and the low-creeping objections so soon trodden down—it not being an art of lies, but of true doctrine; not of effeminateness, but of notable stirring of courage; not of abusing man's wit, but of strengthening man's wit; not banished, but honored, by

---

[1] *St. Paul ... abuse* See Colossus 2.8: "Beware lest any man spoil you through philosophy and vain deceit, after the tradition of men, after the rudiments of the world, and not after Christ."

[2] *Qua ... exigendos* Latin: By the abuse of which authority [i.e., Plato's] some barbarous and crude men seek to expel poets from the Republic (Scaliger, *Poetics* 5.a.1).

[3] *Laelius* Roman soldier and politician Gaius Laelius (d. 160 BCE).

[4] *Plutarch ...them* See Plutarch's *Moralia* 17, "How the Young Man Should Study Poetry."

Plato—let us rather plant more laurels for to engarland the poets' heads (which honor of being laureate, as besides them only triumphant captains were, is a sufficient authority to show the price they ought to be held in) than suffer the ill-favored breath of such wrong-speakers once to blow upon the clear springs of poesy.

But since I have run so long a career in this matter, methinks, before I give my pen a full stop, it shall be but a little more lost time to enquire why England, the mother of excellent minds, should be grown so hard a stepmother to poets, who certainly in wit ought to pass all other, since all only proceedeth from their wit, being indeed makers of themselves, not takers of others. How can I but exclaim

Musa, mihi causas memoria, quo numine laeso?[1]

Sweet poesy, that hath anciently had kings, emperors, senators, great captains, such as—besides a thousands others—David, Adrian, Sophocles, Germanicus, not only to favor poets, but to be poets; and of our nearer times can present for her patrons a Robert, King of Sicily, the great King Francis of France, King James of Scotland; such cardinals as Bembus and Bibbiena; such famous preachers and teachers as Beza and Melanchthon; so learned philosophers as Fracastorius and Scaliger; so great orators as Pontanus and Muretus; so piercing wits as George Buchanan; so grave counsellors as, besides many, but before all, that Hospital of France,[2] than whom (I think)

that realm never brought forth a more accomplished judgment, more firmly built upon virtue: I say these, with numbers of others, not only to read others' poesies, but to poetize for others' reading—that poesy, thus embraced in all other places, should only find in our time a hard welcome in England. I think the very earth lamenteth it, and therefore decks our soil with fewer laurels than it was accustomed. For heretofore poets have in England also flourished, and which is to be noted, even in those times when the trumpet of Mars[3] did sound loudest. And now that an over-faint quietness should seem to strew the house for poets, they are almost in as good reputation as the mountebanks[4] at Venice. Truly even that, as of the one side it giveth great praise to poesy, which like Venus (but to better purpose) had rather be troubled in the net with Mars than enjoy the homely quiet of Vulcan:[5] so serves it for a piece of a reason why they are less grateful to idle England, which now can scarce endure the pain of a pen. . . .

Our tragedies and comedies (not without cause cried out against), observing rules neither of honest civility, nor skilful poetry—excepting *Gorboduc*[6] (again, I say, of those that I have seen), which notwithstanding as it is full of stately speeches and well-sounding phrases, climbing to the height of Seneca's style, and as full of notable morality, which it doth most delightfully teach, and so obtain the very end of poesy, yet in truth it is very defectuous in the circumstances, which grieveth me, because it might not remain as an exact model of all tragedies. For it is faulty both in place and time, the two necessary companions of all corporal actions. For where the stage should always represent but one place, and the uttermost time

[1] *Musa ... laeso* Latin: O Muse, tell me the cause by which the divine has been offended? (*Aeneid* 1.8).

[2] *David* King David of Israel; *Adrian* Roman emperor Hadrian (76–138 CE), a patron of the arts and also a writer; *Germanicus* Roman general (d. 19 CE), known for conquering Germany and said to have written verse; *Robert* King Robert II of Anjou (1275–1343), patron to Petrarch; *Francis* King Francis I of France (1494–1547), under whose patronage many French poets flourished; *James* King James VI of Scotland (later James I of England), author, and patron of other poets; *Bembus* The Roman Catholic cardinal, philosopher, and poet Pietro Bembo (1470–1547); *Bibbiena* Cardinal and author of the comedy *Calandria* (1513); *Beza* Theodore Beza (1519–1605), Calvinist reformer, theologian, and author; *Melanchthon* Philip Melanchthon (1497–1560), theologian, author, and friend and supporter of Martin Luther; *Fracastorius* The Italian physician Girolamo Fracastoro, known for writing the *Naugerius* (1555); *Pontanus* The

poet Giovanni Pontano (1426–1503); *Muretus* The French humanist Marc-Antoine de Muret (1526–85); *George Buchanan* Scottish humanist, poet, and playwright (1506–82); *Hospital of France* Michel de L'Hôpital (1505–73), reformist French Chancellor and Latin poet.

[3] *Mars* Roman god of war.

[4] *mountebanks* Charlatans.

[5] *Venus ... Vulcan* Vulcan, the Roman god of fire, forged a net to catch his wife, Venus, goddess of love and beauty, in adultery with Mars.

[6] *Gorboduc* 1561 tragedy by Thomas Norton and Thomas Sackville.

presupposed in it should be, both by Aristotle's precept and common reason, but one day, there is both many days and places inartificially imagined.

But if it be so in *Gorboduc*, how much more in all the rest, where you shall have Asia of the one side, and Africa of the other, and so many other under-kingdoms that the player, when he cometh in, must ever begin with telling where he is, or else the tale will not be conceived? Now you shall have three ladies walk to gather flowers: and then we must believe the stage to be a garden. By and by we hear news of shipwreck in the same place: and then we are to blame if we accept it not for a rock. Upon the back of that comes out a hideous monster with fire and smoke: and then the miserable beholders are bound to take it for a cave. While in the meantime two armies fly in, represented with four swords & bucklers: and then what hard heart will not receive it for a pitched field?

Now, of time they are much more liberal: for ordinary it is that two young princes[1] fall in love; after many traverses[2] she is got with child, delivered of a fair boy; he is lost, groweth a man, falls in love, and is ready to get another child; and all this is in two hours' space: which, how absurd it is in sense, even sense may imagine, and art hath taught, and all ancient examples justified—and at this day, the ordinary players in Italy will not err in. Yet will some bring in an example of *Eunuchus* in Terence, that containeth matter of two days, yet far short of twenty years. True it is, and so was it to be played in two days, and so fitted to the time it set forth. And though Plautus[3] have in one place done amiss, let us hit with him, & not miss with him.

But they will say, how then shall we set forth a story which containeth both many places and many times? And do they not know that a tragedy is tied to the laws of poesy, and not of history; not bound to follow the story, but having liberty either to feign a quite new matter or to frame the history to the most tragical conveniency? Again, many things may be told which cannot be showed, if they know the difference betwixt reporting and representing. …

But besides these gross absurdities, how all their plays be neither right tragedies, nor right comedies, mingling kings and clowns, not because the matter so carrieth it, but thrust in the clown by head and shoulders to play a part in majestical matters with neither decency nor discretion, so as neither the admiration and commiseration, nor the right sportfulness, is by their mongrel tragicomedy obtained. I know Apuleius[4] did somewhat so, but that is a thing recounted with space of time, not represented in one moment; and I know the ancients have one or two examples of tragicomedies, as Plautus hath *Amphitryo*;[5] but, if we mark them well, we shall find that they never, or very daintily, match hornpipes and funerals. So falleth it out that, having indeed no right comedy, in that comical part of our tragedy we have nothing but scurrility, unworthy of any chaste ears, or some extreme show of doltishness, indeed fit to lift up a loud laughter, and nothing else: where the whole tract of a comedy should be full of delight, as the tragedy should be still maintained in a well-raised admiration.   But our comedians think there is no delight without laughter, which is very wrong; for though laughter may come with delight, yet cometh it not of delight, as though delight should be the cause of laughter; but well may one thing breed both together. Nay, rather in themselves they have, as it were, a kind of contrariety: for delight we scarcely do but in things that have a conveniency to ourselves, or to the general nature; laughter almost ever cometh of things most disproportioned to ourselves and nature. Delight hath a joy in it, either permanent or present. Laughter hath only a scornful tickling.

For example, we are ravished with delight to see a fair woman, and yet are far from being moved to laughter. We laugh at deformed creatures, wherein certainly we cannot delight. We delight in good chances, we laugh at mischances. We delight to hear the happiness of our friends and country, at which he were worthy to be laughed at

---

[1] *princes* I.e., children of kings, both male and female.

[2] *traverses* Trials; tribulations.

[3] *Plautus* Roman writer whose play *The Menaechmi or the Twin Brothers* provided the basis for Shakespeare's *Comedy of Errors*.

[4] *Apuleius* Author of the Latin work *The Golden Ass* (translated into English in 1566 by William Adlington).

[5] *Amphitryo* Tragicomedy by the Roman playwright Plautus, in which the gods trick Alcmena, the heroine, into sleeping with Jupiter.

that would laugh; we shall, contrarily, laugh sometimes to find a matter quite mistaken and go down the hill against the bias[1] in the mouth of some such men—as for the respect of them one shall be heartily sorry, he cannot choose but laugh, and so is rather pained than delighted with laughter. ...

But I have lavished out too many words of this play matter. I do it because, as they are excelling parts of poesy, so is there none so much used in England, and none can be more pitifully abused; which, like an unmannerly daughter showing a bad education, causeth her mother Poesy's honesty to be called in question.

Other sort of poetry almost have we none, but that lyrical kind of songs and sonnets: which, Lord, if He gave us so good minds, how well it might be employed, and with how heavenly fruits, both private and public, in singing the praises of the immortal beauty: the immortal goodness of that God who giveth us hands to write and wits to conceive; of which we might well want words, but never matter; of which we could turn our eyes to nothing, but we should ever have new-budding occasions. But truly many of such writings as come under the banner of unresistible love, if I were a mistress, would never persuade me they were in love: so coldly they apply fiery speeches, as men that had rather read lovers' writings—and so caught up certain swelling phrases which hang together like a man that once told me the wind was at northwest and by south, because he would be sure to name winds enough—than that in truth they feel those passions. ...

Now, of versifying there are two sorts, the one ancient, the other modern. The ancient marked the quantity of each syllable, and according to that, framed his verse; the modern, observing only number (with some regard of the accent) the chief life of it standeth in that like sounding of the words, which we call rhyme. Whether of these be the more excellent, would bear many speeches: the ancient no doubt more fit for music, both words and time observing quantity, and more fit lively to express divers passions by the low or lofty sound of the well-weighed syllable; the latter likewise with his rhyme striketh a certain music to the ear, and, in fine, since it doth delight, though by an other way, it obtains the same purpose, there being in either sweetness, and wanting in neither majesty. Truly the English, before any vulgar language[2] I know, is fit for both sorts: for, for the ancient, the Italian is so full of vowels that it must ever be cumbered with elisions; the Dutch so of the other side, with consonants, that they cannot yield the sweet sliding fit for a verse; the French in his whole language hath not one word that hath his accent in the last syllable, saving two, called *antepenultima*; and little more hath the Spanish, and therefore very gracelessly may they use dactyls. The English is subject to none of these defects. Now for rhyme, though we do not observe quantity, yet we observe the accent very precisely, which other languages either cannot do, or will not do so absolutely. That *caesura*, or breathing place in the midst of the verse, neither Italian nor Spanish have, the French and we never almost fail of. Lastly, even the very rhyme itself, the Italian cannot put it in the last syllable, by the French named the masculine rhyme, but still in the next to the last, which the French call the female, or the next before that, which the Italian term *sdrucciola*. The example of the former, is *buono, suono*, of the *sdrucciola*, is *femina, semina*. The French, of the other side, hath both the male, as *bon, son*; and the female, as *plaise, taise*; but the *sdrucciola* he hath not: where the English hath all three, as due, true; father, rather; motion, potion[3]—with much more which might be said, but that already I find the triflingness of this discourse is much too much enlarged. ...

—1595

---

[1] *go down ... bias* End disastrously.

[2] *vulgar language* Vernacular.

[3] *motion, potion* Pronounced with three syllables.

IN CONTEXT

The Abuse of Poesy

The attacks against which Sidney and others were defending poetry have important roots in ancient philosophy. They stem in particular from the Platonic arguments that storytelling is in some ways morally akin to lying, and that in so far as fictions are to be allowed (whether spoken, written in prose, or acted upon the stage) they should embody human notions of moral justice, with the wicked shown to be punished, and so on. In the sixteenth century some Protestants expanded upon these arguments from Plato, contending that the representation of wickedness in artistic form was itself immoral—regardless of whether wickedness was represented as leading in the end to reward or punishment. The most famous of these attacks was *The School of Abuse* by Stephen Gosson (1554–1624). Gosson, who had himself been a playwright as well as a writer of pamphlets, and who would later become a clergyman, was commissioned by the authorities in London to write an attack on what were perceived to be the excesses and immoralities of the commercial drama. Gosson's style of attack itself ran to excess—as is evident in the excerpt below.

from Plato, *The Republic* (c. 375 BCE)[1]

In this excerpt the philosopher Socrates (who is assumed to be speaking for Plato) is discussing with Adeimantus the education of a leader. In the course of the discussion he puts forward the argument that the sorts of stories that poets and dramatists are allowed to recount should be restricted, and that certain subjects should be censored.

from BOOK 2:
…

SOCRATES.   You know also that the beginning is the most important part of any work, especially in the case of a young and tender thing; for that is the time at which the character is being formed and the desired impression is more readily taken.

ADEIMANTUS.   Quite true.

SOCRATES.   And shall we just carelessly allow children to hear any casual tales which may be devised by casual persons, and to receive into their minds ideas for the most part the very opposite of those which we should wish them to have when they are grown up?

ADEIMANTUS.   We cannot.

SOCRATES.   Then the first thing will be to establish a censorship of the writers of fiction, and let the censors receive any tale of fiction which is good, and reject the bad; and we will desire mothers and nurses to tell their children the authorized ones only. Let them fashion the mind with such tales, even more fondly than they mold the body with their hands; but most of those which are now in use must be discarded.

ADEIMANTUS.   Of what tales are you speaking?

---

[1]   *The Republic*   Translated by Benjamin Jowett (1894).

SOCRATES.   You may find a model of the lesser in the greater, for they are necessarily of the same type, and there is the same spirit in both of them.

ADEIMANTUS.   Very likely, but I do not as yet know what you would term the greater.

SOCRATES.   Those which are narrated by Homer and Hesiod,[1] and the rest of the poets, who have ever been the great story-tellers.

ADEIMANTUS.   But which stories do you mean; and what fault do you find with them?

SOCRATES.   A fault which is most serious—the fault of telling a lie, and, what is more, a bad lie.

ADEIMANTUS.   But when is this fault committed?

SOCRATES.   Whenever an erroneous representation is made of the nature of gods and heroes —as when a painter paints a portrait not having the shadow of a likeness to the original. […] God, if He be good, is not the author of all things, as the many assert, but He is the cause of a few things only, and not of most things that occur to men. For few are the goods of human life, and many are the evils, and the good is to be attributed to God alone; of the evils the causes are to be sought elsewhere, and not in Him.

ADEIMANTUS.   That appears to me to be most true.

SOCRATES.   Then we must not listen to Homer or to any other poet who is guilty of the folly of saying that two casks lie at the threshold of Zeus,[2] full of lots, one of good, the other of evil lots, and that he to whom Zeus gives a mixture of the two sometimes meets with evil fortune, at other times with good; but that he to whom is given the cup of unmingled ill, him wild hunger drives o'er the beauteous earth. And if anyone assert that the violation of oaths and treaties, which was really the work of Pandarus,[3] was brought about by Athene[4] and Zeus, or that the strife and contention of the gods was instigated by Themis[5] and Zeus, he shall not have our approval; neither will we allow our young men to hear the words of Aeschylus,[6] that God plants guilt among men when he desires utterly to destroy a house. And if a poet writes of the sufferings of Niobe—the subject of the tragedy in which these iambic verses occur—or of the house of Pelops,[7] or of the Trojan war or on any similar theme, either we must not permit him to say that these are the works of God, or if they are of God, he must devise some explanation of them such as we are seeking; he must say that God did what was just and right, and they were the better for being punished; but that those who are punished are miserable, and that God is the author of their misery, the poet is not to be permitted to say; though he may say that the wicked are miserable because they require to be punished, and are benefitted by receiving punishment from God; but that God being good is the author of evil to anyone is to be strenuously denied, and not to be said or sung or heard in verse or prose by anyone whether old or young in any well-ordered commonwealth. Such a fiction is suicidal, ruinous, impious.

---

[1] *Homer*   Eighth-century BCE Greek poet credited with authoring the epic poems *The Iliad* and *The Odyssey*; *Hesiod*   Eighth-century BCE Greek poet known for *Works and Days* and *The Theogeny*.

[2] *Zeus*   King of the Greek gods.

[3] *Pandarus*   Trojan warrior in Homer's *Iliad* who broke the truce between Greece and Troy by wounding Menelaus, the king of Sparta.

[4] *Athene*   Athena, the Greek goddess of wisdom and warfare and the protectress of Athens.

[5] *Themis*   In Greek mythology, a Titan and the goddess of order and justice.

[6] *Aeschylus*   Athenian tragic dramatist of the fifth century BCE.

[7] *Niobe*   Queen of Thebes who boasted of her fruitfulness, angering the gods Apollo and Artemis and causing them to murder her children; *Pelops*   Son of Tantalus who won his wife, Hippodamia, by defeating her father, the king of Pisa, in a chariot race. To ensure his victory, Pelops bribed the king's charioteer to betray his master. After the race, Pelops was unable to pay the reward, and threw the charioteer in the lake instead. Before drowning, the charioteer cursed the house of Pelops.

from Stephen Gosson, *The School of Abuse* (1579)

I must confess that poets are the whetstones of wit, notwithstanding that wit is dearly bought. Where honey and gall are mixed, it will be hard to sever the one from the other. The deceitful physician giveth sweet syrups to make his poison go down the smoother; the juggler casteth a mist to work the close; the Siren's song[1] is the sailor's wreck; the fowler's whistle, the bird's death; the wholesome bait, the fish's bane; the Harpies[2] have virgins' faces and vultures' talons; Hyena speaks like a friend, and devours like a foe; the calmest seas hide dangerous rocks; the wolf jets in weathers fells. Many good sentences are spoken by Davus[3] to shadow his knavery, and written by poets as ornaments to beautify their works and set their trumpery to sale without suspect.

But if you look well to Epeus's horse, you find in his bowels the destruction of Troy;[4] open the sepulchre of Semiramis,[5] whose title promiseth such wealth to the kings of Persia, you shall see nothing but dead bones; rip up the golden ball that Nero[6] consecrated to Jupiter Capitolinus, you shall have it stuffed with the shavings of his beard; pull off the vizard that poets mask in, you shall disclose their reproach, bewray their vanity, loath their wantonness, lament their folly, and perceive their sharp sayings to be placed as pearls in dunghills, fresh pictures on rotten walls, chaste matrons' apparel on common courtesans. These are the cups of Circe that turn reasonable creatures into brute beasts, the balls of Hippomenes that hinder the course of Atalanta,[7] and the blocks of the Devil that are cast in our ways to cut off the race of toward wits. No marvel though Plato shut them out of his school and banished them quite from his commonwealth as effeminate writers, unprofitable members, and utter enemies to virtue.

The Romans were very desirous to imitate the Greeks, and yet very loath to receive their poets. Insomuch that Cato[8] layeth it in the dish of Marcus the noble as a foul reproach that in the time of his consulship he brought Ennius the poet into his province. Tully,[9] accustomed to read them with great diligence in his youth, but when he waxed graver in study, elder in years, riper in judgment, he accompted them the fathers of lies, the pipes of vanity, and schools of abuse. Maximus Tyrius[10] taketh

---

[1] *Siren's song*   In Greek mythology the Sirens—creatures that were half woman, half bird—would sing in a captivating fashion that would lead sailors to destroy themselves, whether by jumping overboard or by running their ships aground.

[2] *Harpies*   Greek mythological creatures with women's faces and bodies, wings, and sharp claws.

[3] *Davus*   Servant in *Andria*, a comedy by the Roman second-century BCE dramatist Terence.

[4] *Epeus's horse ... Troy*   According to Greek legend, the Greeks pretended to retreat after having attacked the city of Troy for many years, but they left behind a huge wooden horse, supposedly as a gift. When the Trojans moved the horse inside the city walls, Greek warriors who had hidden themselves inside the structure attacked the Trojans and conquered the city. Epeus had taken the lead in constructing the horse.

[5] *Semiramis*   Mythical Assyrian queen who was said to have conquered many lands and founded the city of Babylon.

[6] *Nero*   Tyrannical Roman emperor of the first century CE.

[7] *cups of Circe*   In Homer's *Odyssey*, the enchantress Circe gives Odysseus's men a potion that turns them into swine; *balls of Hippomenes*   According to Greek mythology, Atalanta was a huntress who was famous for her speed, and who would only marry the suitor who could beat her in a race. Hippomenes did so by dropping three golden apples, which Atalanta stopped to retrieve.

[8] *Cato*   The Roman statesman Cato the Younger (95-46 BCE), whose great-grandfather, the statesman Cato the Elder (Marcus Porcius Cato), brought the poet Ennius from Sardinia to Rome.

[9] *Tully*   Marcus Tullius Cicero, a great Roman orator and politician (106-43 BCE).

[10] *Maximus Tyrius*   See Oration 26 of the *Philosophical Orations* of Maximus of Tyre, a second-century CE Greek philosopher.

upon him to defend the discipline of these doctors under the name of Homer, wresting the rashness of Ajax to valor, the cowardice of Ulysses to policy,[1] the dotage of Nestor to grave counsel, and the battle of Troy to the wonderful conflict of the four elements, where Juno, which is counted the air, sets in her foot to take up the strike and steps boldly betwixt them to part the fray. It is a pageant worth the sight, to behold how he labors with mountains to bring forth mice, much like to some of those players that come to the scaffold[2] with drum and trumpet to proffer skirmish, and when they have sounded alarm, off go the pieces to encounter a shadow, or conquer a paper monster. You will smile, I am sure, if you read it, to see how this moral philosopher toils to draw the lion's skin upon Aesop's ass, Hercules' shoes on a child's feet, amplifying that which the more it is stirred, the more it stinks, the less it is talked of, the better it is liked, and as wayward children, the more they be flattered, the worse they are, or as cursed sores with often touching wax angry, and run the longer without healing. He attributeth the beginning of virtue to Minerva, if friendship to Venus, and the root of all handicrafts to Vulcan, but if he had broke his arm as well as his leg when he fell out of heaven into Lemnos,[3] either Apollo must have played the bonesetter, or every occupation been laid a-water.[4]

---

[1] *policy* Political cunning.

[2] *scaffold* Stage.

[3] *Lemnos* Island in the northern part of the Aegean Sea.

[4] *laid a-water* Made of no effect.

ELIZABETH I, QUEEN OF ENGLAND
1533 – 1603

One of the most famous monarchs in European history, Queen Elizabeth I presided over a vigorous culture that saw notable accomplishments in the arts, voyages of discovery, the "Elizabethan settlement" that created the Church of England, and the defeat of military threats from Spain. Her shrewd political mind helped sustain her country in a time of occasional famine, widespread poverty, intermittent plague, and deep religious and political divisions; she also, if sometimes reluctantly, supported the beginnings of an empire that would flourish over the next 350 years. Elizabeth was also a precocious writer, penning translations even in her childhood and later composing poetry and speeches.

Elizabeth was the product of a controversial union, that of Henry VIII and Anne Boleyn. Some months before giving birth on 7 September 1533 Boleyn became the king's second wife. In 1534, Pope Clement VII, who had waffled for a few years, officially confirmed his refusal to annul Henry's marriage to his first wife, Catherine of Aragon. Henry responded by declaring himself head of the English Church, but many in and out of the government refused to recognize either his right to do this or the validity of his new marriage. A significant portion of the population therefore considered Elizabeth illegitimate, and throughout her reign many of those loyal to the Roman Catholic Church continued to dispute her right to the throne.

At first Henry designated Elizabeth as his heir. However, after her mother fell from favor and was executed in 1536, Elizabeth's political fortunes turned (much as they had for her older half-sister, Mary). Henry married Jane Seymour and had a son, Edward, who was named King after Henry died in 1547. Orphaned, Elizabeth was cared for by Henry's last wife, Catherine Parr, and her new husband, Thomas Seymour. Catherine made sure that Elizabeth received a fine education, hiring a number of prominent tutors, including the distinguished humanist Roger Ascham.

Young Edward VI proved to be sickly, dying in 1553 before his sixteenth birthday. Various political maneuvers ensued, but eventually Elizabeth's half-sister Mary was crowned Queen. Mary I was a staunch Catholic who wanted to undo the reforms of her father as well as the explicitly Protestant changes made by Edward, and she attempted to convince Elizabeth to convert to Catholicism. Whether from sincere reluctance or awareness that she was the Protestant hope, or both, Elizabeth was prudently ambiguous about her religious beliefs, so on 17 March 1554, fearful of plots against her throne, Mary had her imprisoned in the Tower of London. There she stayed for two months before being transferred into custody at Woodstock Castle, a dilapidated hunting lodge in Oxfordshire, where she remained for almost a year.

When Mary died on 17 November 1558, childless in her marriage to Philip II of Spain, Elizabeth was named Queen. She was crowned on 15 January 1559, after elaborate London celebrations, in Westminster Abbey. As Queen, Elizabeth proved to be a strong and cunning leader. Early in her reign she worked hard to solidify her rule, thwarting assassination attempts and Catholic plots to install her cousin, Mary Stuart, as queen. Elizabeth took a more moderate approach to England's religious conflicts than had her predecessors. She reinstated the reforms instituted by her father and brother, but she eschewed Edward's Calvinist militancy as well as Mary's punitive conservatism. She also displayed her acumen in domestic politics, manipulating her advisors as a means of maintaining her own control and playing the Petrarchan mistress or virgin goddess to encourage her courtiers' and subjects' loyalty and affection. Internationally, although she did send money and men to help Henri IV to the French throne and to help the Dutch expel the Spanish, she largely withdrew England from costly involvement in foreign conflicts. Ireland was another matter, and Elizabeth's government engaged in an often bloody struggle to suppress Irish revolts against English rule.

Throughout the first half of her reign, Elizabeth was under pressure from advisors and Parliament to marry and produce an heir. She resisted, no doubt aware that any spouse would exert considerable influence over her. She entertained many suitors, English and foreign, but declared that she preferred being married to England.

Elizabeth's writings provide glimpses into her mind, although as a princess or queen she knew she was always on stage and without real privacy. Her lines written on a window frame during her captivity at Woodstock (1555) cry for justice, for example, while "On Monsieur's Departure" (c. 1581; "Monsieur" is almost certainly her suitor the Duc d'Anjou, brother to the French king) shows her romantic side—or its political simulation. In her so-called "Golden Speech," her farewell speech to Parliament given on 30 November 1601, Elizabeth speaks frankly about the burdens of queenship: "to be a king and wear a crown is a thing more glorious to them that see it than it is pleasant to them that bear it." The queen also translated various works, including passages from Boethius' *Consolation of Philosophy*, and made the first English translation of Horace's "Art of Poetry."

Elizabeth overcame the uncertainty that surrounded her accession to become enormously popular, even with many Catholics; she came to be known to her subjects as "Good Queen Bess." She died on 24 March 1603 at almost seventy, having ruled England for nearly 45 years. She was buried in Westminster Abbey and was succeeded by James VI of Scotland, the Protestant son of Mary Stuart, who reigned as James I.

⌘ ⌘ ⌘

Written on a Wall at Woodstock[1]

Oh fortune, thy wresting[2] wavering state
   Hath fraught with cares my troubled wit,
Whose witness this present prison late
Could bear, where once was joy's loan quit.[3]
5 Thou causedst the guilty to be loosed

From bands where innocents were enclosed,
And caused the guiltless to be reserved,
And freed those that death had well deserved.
But herein can be nothing wrought,
10 So God send to my foes as they have thought.
—C. 1554–55

---

[1] *Wall* This poem is variously noted as being written on a wall, a shutter, and a window frame. Writing poetry or proverbs on these surfaces was not uncommon in the period; *Woodstock* Elizabeth, under suspicion for involvement in Sir Thomas Wyatt the Younger's plots against Mary, was placed under house arrest at Woodstock.

[2] *wresting* Struggling, twisting.

[3] *joy's loan quit* The lease of joy repaid.

Written in Her French Psalter[4]

No crooked leg, no bleared eye,
   No part deformed out of kind,

---

[4] *Psalter* Translation or version of the Book of Psalms. This poem is inscribed in the last leaf of Elizabeth's French psalter.

Nor yet so ugly half can be
    As is the inward suspicious mind.
—1565

The Doubt of Future Foes[1]

The doubt of future foes exiles my present joy,
    And wit me warns to shun such snares as
        threaten mine annoy,
For falsehood now doth flow, and subjects' faith
    doth ebb,
Which should not be if reason ruled or wisdom
    weaved the web.
5 But clouds of joys untried do cloak aspiring minds,
Which turn to rain of late repent by changed
    course of winds.
The top of hope supposed the root upreared shall be,
And fruitless all their grafted guile, as shortly ye shall see.
Their dazzled eyes with pride, which great ambition
    blinds,
10 Shall be unsealed by worthy wights° whose   *people*
    foresight falsehood finds.
The daughter of debate[2] that discord aye doth sow
Shall reap no gain where former rule still peace hath
    taught to grow.
No foreign banished wight shall anchor in this port;
Our realm brooks° not seditious sects, let   *tolerates*
    them elsewhere resort.
15 My rusty sword through rest[3] shall first his edge employ
To poll° their tops that seek such change or   *crop or cut*
    gape for future joy.
—c. 1568–71

---

[1] *Doubt* Dread or fear; *Future Foes* This poem was written in response to the threat to Elizabeth's rule from Mary, Queen of Scots. Mary believed she had a legitimate claim to the throne of England and became the focal point of Catholic protests against Elizabeth. This was probably written shortly after Mary's flight from Scotland to England in 1568, as it appeared in commonplace books early in the 1570s, though the poem has been understood as a response to Mary's execution in 1587.

[2] *The daughter of debate* Mary, Queen of Scots.

[3] *rusty sword through rest* The sword is rusty because unused.

On Monsieur's Departure[4]

I grieve, and dare not show my discontent,
    I love, and yet am forced to seem to hate,
I do, yet dare not say I ever meant,
I seem stark mute, but inwardly do prate.
5   I am and not, I freeze and yet am burned,
      Since from myself another self I turned.

My care is like my shadow in the sun,
Follows me flying, flies when I pursue it,
Stands and lies by me, doth what I have done.
10 His too familiar care doth make me rue° it.   *regret*
    No means I find to rid him from my breast,
    Till by the end of things it be suppressed.

Some gentler passion slide into my mind,
For I am soft and made of melting snow,
15 Or be more cruel, love, and so be kind.
Let me or float or[5] sink, be high or low,
    Or let me live with some more sweet content,
    Or die, and so forget what love ere meant.
—c. 1582

When I Was Fair and Young[6]

When I was fair and young, and favour graced me,
    Of many was I sought their mistress for to be,
But I did scorn them all and answered them therefore,
"Go, go, go, seek some other where. Importune me no
    more."

5 How many weeping eyes I made to pine with woe,
How many sighing hearts I have no skill to show,
But I the prouder grew and still this spake therefore,
"Go, go, go, seek some other where. Importune
    me no more."

---

[4] *On Monsieur's Departure* This poem was written in response to the final departure of Elizabeth's French suitor, François, duc d'Anjou, in 1582.

[5] *or ... or* Either ... or.

[6] *When I Was Fair and Young* The date of this poem is uncertain, and some editors have doubted its authenticity.

Then spake fair Venus' son,[1] that proud victorious boy,
Saying, "You dainty dame, for that you be so coy,
I will so pluck your plumes as you shall say no more,
'Go, go, go, seek some other where. Importune
    me no more.'"

When he had spoke these words, such change grew in
    my breast
That neither night nor day since that I could take any
    rest.
Wherefore I did repent that I had said before,
"Go, go, go, seek some other where. Importune me no
    more."
—1589–90

To Our Most Noble and Virtuous Queen Katherine, Elizabeth Her Humble Daughter Wishes Perpetual Felicity and Everlasting Joy[2]

Not only knowing the affectionate will and fervent zeal which your highness hath toward all godly learning, as also my duty toward you (most gracious and sovereign princess), but knowing also that pusillanimity[3] and idleness are most repugnant unto a reasonable creature and that (as the philosopher[4] saith) even as an instrument of iron or of other metal waxeth soon rusty unless it be continually occupied,[5] even so shall the wit of a man or woman wax dull and unapt to do or understand anything perfectly unless it be always occupied upon some manner of study, which things considered hath moved so small a portion as God hath lent me to prove what I could do. And therefore have I as for assay[6]

or beginning (so following the right noble saying of the proverb aforesaid) translated this little book out of French rhyme into English prose, joining the sentences together as well as the capacity of my simple wit and small learning could extend themselves. The which book is entitled, or named, *The Mirror or Glass of the Sinful Soul*, wherein is contained how she[7] (beholding and contemplating what she is) doth perceive how of herself and of her own strength she can do nothing that good is, or prevaileth for her salvation, unless it be through the grace of God, whose mother, daughter, sister, and wife by the scriptures she proveth herself to be. Trusting also that through His incomprehensible love, grace, and mercy she (being called from sin to repentance) doth faithfully hope to be saved. And although I know that as for my part which I have wrought in it (as well spiritual as manual) there is nothing done as it should be, nor else worthy to come in your grace's hands, but rather all unperfect and uncorrect, yet do I trust also that albeit it is like a work which is but new begun and shaped, that the file of your excellent wit and godly learning in the reading of it (if so it vouchsafe your highness to do) shall rub out, polish, and mend (or else cause to mend) the words (or rather the order of my writing), the which I know in many places to be rude, and nothing done as it should be. But I hope that after having been in your grace's hands there shall be nothing in it worthy of reprehension and that in the meanwhile no other (but your highness only) shall read it or see it, lest my faults be known of many. Then shall they be better excused (as my confidence is in your grace's accustomed benevolence) than if I should bestow a whole year in writing or inventing ways to excuse them.

Praying God almighty, the maker and creator of all things, to grant unto your highness this same New Year's day a lucky and prosperous year with prosperous issue and continuance of many years in good health and continual joy and all to His honour, praise, and glory.
—1548 (31 DECEMBER 1544)

---

[1] *Venus' son* Cupid.

[2] *To Our Most ... Joy* This is the prefatory letter to Elizabeth's English translation of Marguerite de Navarre's *Miroir de l'Ame Récheresse*, given as a New Year's gift to Catherine Parr, Henry VIII's last wife.

[3] *pusillanimity* Lack of courage and strength of mind.

[4] *the philosopher* Aristotle, but the thought is proverbial.

[5] *occupied* Used.

[6] *assay* Attempt.

[7] *she* Marguerite de Navarre.

To the Troops at Tilbury[1]

My loving people, we have been persuaded by some that are careful of our safety to take heed how we commit ourself to armed multitudes for fear of treachery, but I assure you, I do not desire to live to distrust my faithful and loving people. Let tyrants fear. I have always so behaved myself that under God I have placed my chiefest strength and safeguard in the loyal hearts and good will of my subjects. And therefore I am come amongst you as you see at this time not for my recreation and disport, but being resolved in the midst and heat of the battle to live or die amongst you all, to lay down for God and for my kingdom and for my people my honour and my blood even in the dust. I know I have the body of a weak and feeble woman, but I have the heart and stomach of a king, and of a king of England too, and think foul scorn that Parma[2] or Spain or any prince of Europe should dare invade the borders of my realm, to which, rather than any dishonour shall grow by me, I myself will take up arms; I myself will be your general, judge, and rewarder of every one of your virtues in the field. I know already for your forwardness you have deserved rewards and crowns, and we do assure you in the word of a prince, they shall be duly paid you.

In the meantime my lieutenant-general[3] shall be in my stead, than whom never prince commanded a more noble or worthy subject. Not doubting but by your obedience to my general, by your concord in the camp and your valour in the field, we shall shortly have a famous victory over these enemies of God, of my kingdom, and of my people.

—1588

---

[1] *To the Troops at Tilbury* In July 1588, the Spanish Armada sailed toward England intending to invade. As the Armada entered the English Channel it was attacked by an English fleet led by Sir Francis Drake. Although at this point in the fighting the Spanish ships had been dissipated, there were fears they would regroup; as preparations continued at Tilbury, one observer noted that Elizabeth "rode through all the squadrons of her army as armed Pallas attended by noble footmen" before she gave this speech.

[2] *Parma* Duke of Parma, who was regent of the Spanish Netherlands at the time.

[3] *lieutenant-general* Robert Dudley, the Earl of Leicester and Elizabeth's favorite, who would die a few months later.

Two Letters from Elizabeth to Catherine de Bourbon, Sister of Henri IV of France[4]

Madame,

If my paper had the color of my heart, I would not dare to show it to you, the color black suiting too ill with the young. It is, I thank God, in no way for myself that I feel regret, but for him[5] for whom I wish the greatest good, [and] upon whom I see so many misfortunes fall that I feel them too much to [want to] be part of them. And in response to your desire to be able to serve me in place of [or perhaps "close to"] the king your brother, nothing you could do for me would so please me as to purchase for him so much honor and security that whatever harm he has wished to do to himself may not crush him through his forgetting the care of those of the true religion[6] who for so many years have consumed their means [and] poured out their blood to safeguard his cause. Not only does he owe this in good conscience, policy of state invites him to it, which is so uncertainly grounded on marshlands that he needs to grasp some very strong poles to get himself out. Remind him, Madam my good sister, in God's honor, that he must keep so much reputation even among his enemies that at no price should he abandon those devoted to him just to please wickedness. Rest assured that if you do this you will oblige me to remain

Your most faithful sister. ER.

—1593 (AUGUST 25)

---

[4] *Henry IV of France* Henri de Navarre became Henri IV, King of France, upon the assassination in 1589 of his childless cousin, Henri III. Because Navarre was the leader of the Huguenot (Protestant) side in a three-sided civil war among supporters of Henri III, Huguenots, and ultra-papist supporters of the Duc de Guise, his accession merely led to further fighting. To prevent more bloodshed and to strengthen his position, Navarre announced his conversion to Catholicism in the summer of 1593; his sincerity has been doubted, but perhaps unjustly, and there is in fact no firm evidence that he ever said "Paris is worth a mass." His conversion had been widely anticipated, but after hearing the news Elizabeth wrote to him in an anguish of reproach, making sure that the letter circulated widely. A little later she also wrote Henri's still Protestant sister, Catherine. Catherine was herself an experienced politician, having at times served her brother as regent in his ancestral domains.

[5] *him* Henri IV.

[6] *those of the true religion* Huguenots.

Madam,

As I am sending this gentleman[1] to the King, I have been unable to restrain my pen from revealing to you one of the urgent reasons for sending him at once: he must serve as tablets to remind him[2] of the important reasons why he must have consideration for those of the Religion,[3] not only for the danger to their lives, bodies, and goods when he was not too near his [current] dignity to reward them for it, but for his own salvation and the firm maintenance of his state. For if his enemies see him even slightly leaning on them, they make sport of him, knowing he has lost all other hope. Behold here, Madame, my boldness in minding somebody else's business: if this is a sin, I merit pardon for acknowledging it. Nevertheless, I beg you to add your urging [to mine]. And rest assured always to have in me

Your most faithful sister. ER.

—1593 (NOVEMBER)

On Marriage[4]

I may say unto you that from my years of understanding, sith[5] I first had consideration of myself to be born a servitor of Almighty God, I happily chose this kind of life in which I yet live, which I assure you for mine own part hath hitherto best contented myself and I trust hath been most acceptable to God. From the which, if either ambition of high estate[6] offered to me in marriage by the pleasure and appointment of my prince[7]—whereof I have

some records in this presence,[8] as you our Lord Treasurer[9] well know; or if the eschewing of the danger of mine enemies or the avoiding of the period of death, whose messenger or rather continual watchman, the prince's indignation, was not little time daily before mine eyes— by whose means, although I know or justly may suspect, yet I will not now utter; or if the whole cause were in my sister herself, I will not now burden her therewith, because I will not charge the dead: if any of these I say, I had not now remained in this estate wherein you see me. But so constant have I always continued in this determination—although my youth and words may seem to some hardly to agree together—yet is it most true that at this day I stand free from any other meaning that either I have had in times past or have at this present. With which trade of life I am so thoroughly acquainted that I trust God, who hath hitherto therein preserved and led me by the hand, will not now of His goodness suffer me to go alone....

Nevertheless—if any of you be in suspect —whensoever it may please God to incline my heart to another kind of life, ye may well assure yourselves my meaning is not to do or determine anything wherewith the realm may or shall have just cause to be discontented. And therefore put that clean out of your heads. For I assure you—what credit my assurance may have with you I cannot tell, but what credit it shall deserve to have the sequence shall declare—I will never in that matter conclude anything that shall be prejudicial to the realm, for the weal,[10] good, and safety whereof I will never shun to spend my life. And whomsoever my chance shall be to light upon, I trust he shall be as careful for the realm and you—I will not say as myself, because I cannot so certainly determine of any other; but at the least ways, by my good will and desire he shall be such as shall be as careful for the preservation of the realm and you as myself.

And albeit it might please Almighty God to con-

---

[1] *gentleman* Presumably a messenger or diplomat.

[2] *him* I.e., Henri.

[3] *those of the Religion* Huguenots.

[4] *On Marriage* Elizabeth addressed this speech to Parliament in the second year of her reign. It was expected that she would marry and produce a child to be heir to the throne.

[5] *sith* Since.

[6] *estate* Rank.

[7] *my prince* Likely a reference to Mary I, Elizabeth's half-sister, who, during her time as monarch, could have offered her sister's hand in marriage to a consort.

[8] *whereof I ... this presence* Possible reference to a marriage proposal made by Emmanuel Philibert, Duke of Savoy, during Mary's reign.

[9] *Lord Treasurer* The third Marquis of Winchester, William Paulet, who was Mary's Lord Treasurer as well as Elizabeth's.

[10] *weal* Wealth.

tinue me still in this mind to live out of the state of marriage, yet it is not to be feared but He will so work in my heart and in your wisdoms as good provision by His help may be made in convenient time, whereby the realm shall not remain destitute of an heir that may be a fit governor, and peradventure[1] more beneficial to the realm than such offspring as may come of me. For, although I be never so careful of your well doings and mind ever so to be, yet may my issue grow out of kind and become perhaps ungracious. And in the end, this shall be for me sufficient, that a marble stone shall declare that a Queen, having reigned such a time, lived and died a virgin.

—1559

On Mary, Queen of Scots[2]

The bottomless graces and immeasurable benefits bestowed upon me by the Almighty are and have been such, as I must not only acknowledge them but admire them, accounting them as well miracles as benefits; not so much in respect of His Divine Majesty —with whom nothing is more common than to do things rare and singular—as in regard of our weakness, who cannot sufficiently set forth His wonderful works and graces, which to me have been so many, so diversely folded and embroidered one upon another, as in no sort am I able to express them.

And although there liveth not any that may more justly acknowledge themselves infinitely bound unto God than I, whose life He hath miraculously preserved at sundry times (beyond my merit) from a multitude of perils and dangers, yet is not that the cause for which I count myself the deepliest bound to give Him my humblest thanks, or to yield Him greatest recognition; but this which I shall tell you hereafter, which will

deserve the name of wonder, if rare things and seldom seen be worthy of account. Even this it is: that as I came to the crown with the willing hearts of subjects, so do I now, after twenty-eight years' reign, perceive in you no diminution of good wills, which, if haply I should want,[3] well might I breathe but never think I lived.

And now, albeit I find my life hath been full dangerously sought, and death contrived by such as no desert procured it, yet am I thereof so clear from malice— which hath the property to make men glad at the falls and faults of their foes, and make them seem to do for other causes, when rancour is the ground—as I protest it is and hath been my grievous thought that one, not different in sex, of like estate,[4] and my near kin, should be fallen into so great a crime. Yea, I had so little purpose to pursue her with any colour of malice, that as it is not unknown to some of my Lords here—for now I will play the blab[5]—I secretly wrote her a letter upon the discovery of sundry treasons, that if she would confess them, and privately acknowledge them by her letters unto myself, she never should need be called for them into so public question. Neither did I [have] it of mind to circumvent her, for then I knew as much as she could confess; and so did I write.

And if, even yet, now the matter is made but too apparent, I thought she truly would repent—as perhaps she would easily appear in outward show to do—and that for her none other would take the matter upon them; or that we were but as two milkmaids, with pails upon our arms; or that there were no more dependency upon us, but mine own life were only in danger, and not the whole estate of your religion and well doings; I protest—wherein you may believe me, for although I may have many vices, I hope I have not accustomed my tongue to be an instrument of untruth—I would most willingly pardon and remit this offence. Or if by my death other nations and kingdoms might truly say that this realm had attained an ever prosperous and flourishing estate, I would (I assure you) not desire to live, but gladly give my life, to the end my death might procure

---

[1] *peradventure* By chance.

[2] *On Mary, Queen of Scots* Mary, Queen of Scots had been a prisoner for the last ten years and apparently had conspired to have Elizabeth I (her cousin) deposed. In 1586 Elizabeth became aware of a new plot to depose her on Mary's behalf; the conspirators were executed. The following is Elizabeth's response to a petition to execute Mary was well.

[3] *haply* By chance; *want* Lack.

[4] *estate* Rank.

[5] *blab* Tattler.

you a better prince.[1] And for your sakes it is that I desire to live: to keep you from a worse. For, as for me, I assure you I find no great cause I should be fond to live. I take no such pleasure in it that I should much wish it, nor conceive such terror in death that I should greatly fear it. And yet I say not but, if the stroke were coming, perchance flesh and blood would be moved with it, and seek to shun it.

I have had good experience and trial of this world. I know what it is to be a subject, what to be a sovereign, what to have good neighbours, and sometime meet evil-willers. I have found treason in trust, seen great benefits little regarded, and instead of gratefulness, courses[2] of purpose to cross. These former remembrances, present feeling, and future expectation of evils (I say) have made me think an evil is much the better the less while it dureth,[3] and so them happiest that are soonest hence;[4] and taught me to bear with a better mind these treasons, than is common to my sex—yea, with a better heart perhaps than is in some men. Which I hope you will not merely impute to my simplicity or want of understanding, but rather that I thus conceived—that had their purposes taken effect, I should not have found the blow, before I had felt it; nor, though my peril should have been great, my pain should have been but small and short. Wherein, as I would be loath to die so bloody a death, so doubt I not but God would have given me grace to be prepared for such an event; which, when it shall chance, I refer to His good pleasure.

And now, as touching their treasons and conspiracies, together with the contriver of them. I will not so prejudicate myself and this my realm as to say or think that I might not, without the last statute,[5] by the ancient laws of this land have proceeded against her; which was not made particularly to prejudice her, though perhaps it might then be suspected in respect of the disposition of such as depend that way. It was so far from being intended to entrap her, that it was rather an admonition to warn the danger thereof. But sith[6] it is made, and in the force of a law, I thought good, in that which might concern her, to proceed according thereunto rather than by course of common law.[7] Wherein, if you the judges have not deceived me, or that the books you brought me were not false—which God forbid—I might as justly have tried her by the ancient laws of the land.

But you lawyers are so nice[8] and so precise in sifting and scanning every word and letter, that many times you stand more upon form than matter, upon syllables than the sense of the law. For, in this strictness and exact following of common form,[9] she must have been indicted in Staffordshire, been arraigned at the bar, holden up her hand, and then been tried by a jury: a proper course, forsooth,[10] to deal in that manner with one of her estate! I thought it better, therefore, for avoiding of these and more absurdities, to commit the cause to the inquisition of a good number of the greatest and most noble personages of this realm, of the judges and others of good account, whose sentence I must approve.

And all little enough: for we princes, I tell you, are set on stages, in the sight and view of all the world duly observed. The eyes of many behold our actions; a spot is soon spied in our garments, a blemish quickly noted in our doings. It behoveth[11] us, therefore, to be careful that our proceedings be just and honourable.

But I must tell you one thing more: that in this late Act of Parliament you have laid an hard hand on me—that I must give direction for her death, which cannot be but most grievous, and an irksome burden to me. And lest you might mistake mine absence from this Parliament—which I had almost forgotten: although there be no cause why I should willingly come amongst

---

[1] *prince* I.e., ruler.

[2] *courses* Paths.

[3] *dureth* Lasts.

[4] *hence* Gone.

[5] *the last statute* I.e., the Act for the Queen's Safety (1584–85), which called for the execution of anyone involved in a plot to usurp the Queen; it was created with Mary in mind.

[6] *sith* Since.

[7] *by course of common law* I.e., through a criminal trial in a common law court, which would have been inappropriate for the Queen of Scotland.

[8] *nice* Particular.

[9] *common form* I.e., the form of common law.

[10] *forsooth* In truth.

[11] *behoveth* Is fitting for.

multitudes (for that amongst many, some may be evil), yet hath it not been the doubt of any such danger or occasion that kept me from thence, but only the great grief to hear this cause spoken of, especially that such one of state and kin should need so open a declaration, and that this nation should be so spotted with blots of disloyalty. Wherein, the less is my grief for that I hope the better part is mine; and those of the worse not much to be accounted of, for that in seeing my destruction they might have spoiled their own souls.

And even now I could tell you that which would make you sorry. It is a secret; and yet I will tell it you (although it be known I have the property to keep counsel but too well, often times to mine own peril). It is not long since mine eyes did see it written that an oath was taken within few days either to kill me or to be hanged themselves; and that to be performed ere one month were ended. Hereby I see your danger in me, and neither can or will be so unthankful or careless of your consciences as to take no care for your safety.

I am not unmindful of your oath made in the Association,[1] manifesting your great good wills and affections, taken and entered into upon good conscience and true knowledge of the guilt, for safeguard of my person; done (I protest God) before I ever heard it, or ever thought of such a matter, till a thousand hands, with many obligations, were showed me at Hampton Court, signed and subscribed with the names and seals of the greatest of this land. Which, as I do acknowledge as a perfect argument of your true hearts and great zeal to my safety, so shall my bond be stronger tied to greater care for all your good.

But, for that this matter is rare, weighty and of great consequence, and I think you do not look for any present resolution—the rather for that, as it is not my manner in matters of far less moment to give speedy answer without due consideration, so in this of such importance—I think it very requisite with earnest prayer to beseech His Divine Majesty so to illuminate mine understanding and inspire me with His grace, as I may do and determine that which shall serve to the establishment of His Church, preservation of your estates, and prosperity of this Commonwealth under my charge. Wherein, for that I know delay is dangerous, you shall have with all conveniency our resolution delivered by our message. And whatever any prince may merit of their subjects, for their approved testimony of their unfeigned sincerity, either by governing justly, void of all partiality, or sufferance of any injuries done (even to the poorest), that I do assuredly promise inviolably to perform, for requital of your so many deserts.[2]
—1586

On Mary's Execution[3]

Full grievous is the way whose going on and end breeds cumber[4] for the hire of a laborious journey. I have strived more this day than ever in my life whether I should speak or use silence. If I speak and not complain, I shall dissemble; if I hold my peace, your labour taken were full vain.

For me to make my moan were strange and rare, for I suppose you shall find few that, for their own particular, will cumber you with such a care. Yet such, I protest, hath been my greedy desire and hungry will that of your consultation might have fallen out some other means to work my safety, joined with your assurance, than that for which you are become so earnest suitors, as I protest I must needs use complaint[5]—though not of you, but unto you, and of the cause; for that I do perceive, by your advices, prayers, and desires, there falleth out this accident, that only my injurer's bane[6] must be my life's surety.[7]

---

[1] *oath ... Association* In October 1582, the Queen's Council signed a Bond of Association, in which they swore to arrest and execute without trial anyone who attempted to usurp the throne or kill the Queen; the oath was intended as a threat to Mary.

[2] *requital of ... many deserts* Repayment of so many things you deserve.

[3] *On Mary's Execution* Speech delivered to a Parliamentary delegation who asked for Elizabeth's signature on Mary's death warrant and argued that an execution was the only way to ensure Elizabeth's safety.

[4] *cumber* Encumbrance; burden.

[5] *use complaint* Show regret.

[6] *bane* Death.

[7] *surety* Security.

But if any there live so wicked of nature to suppose that I prolonged this time only pro forma,[1] to the intent to make a show of clemency, thereby to set my praises to the wire-drawers[2] to lengthen them the more, they do me so great a wrong as they can hardly recompense. Or if any person there be that think or imagine that the least vainglorious thought hath drawn me further herein, they do me as open injury as ever was done to any living creature—as He that is the maker of all thoughts knoweth best to be true. Or if there be any that think that the Lords, appointed in commission, durst do no other,[3] as fearing thereby to displease or to be suspected to be of a contrary opinion to my safety, they do but heap upon me injurious conceits. For, either those put in trust by me to supply my place have not performed their duty towards me, or else they have signified unto you all that my desire was that everyone should do according to his conscience, and in the course of these proceedings should enjoy both freedom of voice and liberty of opinion, and what they would not openly, they might privately to myself declare. It was of a willing mind and great desire I had, that some other means might be found out, wherein I should have taken more comfort than in any other thing under the sun.

And since now it is resolved that my surety cannot be established without a princess's head, I have just cause to complain that I, who have in my time pardoned so many rebels, winked at so many treasons, and either not produced[4] them or altogether slipped them over with silence, should now be forced to this proceeding, against such a person. I have besides, during my reign, seen and heard many opprobrious[5] books and pamphlets against me, my realm and state, accusing me to be a tyrant. I thank them for their alms. I believe therein their meaning was to tell me news: and news it is to me indeed. I would it were as strange to hear of their impiety. What will they not now say, when it shall be spread that for the safety of her life a maiden queen could be content to spill the blood even of her own kinswoman? I may therefore full well complain that any man should think me given to cruelty; whereof I am so guiltless and innocent as I should slander God if I should say He gave me so vile a mind. Yea, I protest, I am so far from it that for mine own life I would not touch her. Neither hath my care been so much bent how to prolong mine, as how to preserve both: which I am right sorry is made so hard, yea so impossible.

I am not so void of judgment as not to see mine own peril; nor yet so ignorant as not to know it were in nature a foolish course to cherish a sword to cut mine own throat; nor so careless as not to weigh that my life daily is in hazard. But this I do consider, that many a man would put his life in danger for the safeguard of a king. I do not say that so will I; but I pray you think that I have thought upon it.

But sith[6] so many hath both written and spoken against me, I pray you give me leave to say somewhat for myself, and, before you return to your countries, let you know for what a one you have passed so careful thoughts. And, as I think myself infinitely beholding unto you all that seek to preserve my life by all the means you may, so I protest that there liveth no prince—nor ever shall be—more mindful to requite so good deserts.[7] Wherein, as I perceive you have kept your old wont[8] in a general seeking the lengthening of my days, so am I sure that never shall I requite it, unless I had as many lives as you all; but forever I will acknowledge it while there is any breath left me. Although I may not justify, but may justly condemn, my sundry faults and sins to God, yet for my care in this government let me acquaint you with my intents.

When first I took the sceptre,[9] my title made me not forget the giver, and therefore [I] began as it became me, with such religion as both I was born in, bred in, and, I trust, shall die in; although I was not so simple as not to know what danger and peril so great an alteration might

---

[1] *pro forma* As a formality.

[2] *wire-drawers* Those who make wire, which requires pulling metal into narrow ribbons.

[3] *durst do no other* I.e., dare to give no other opinion.

[4] *produced* Acted on.

[5] *opprobrious* Reproachful.

[6] *sith* Since.

[7] *requite so good deserts* Repay such good things as you deserve.

[8] *wont* Desire.

[9] *sceptre* Ornamental rod; a symbol of royal authority.

procure me—how many great princes of the contrary opinion would attempt all they might against me, and generally what enmity I should thereby breed unto myself. Which all I regarded not, knowing that He, for whose sake I did it, might and would defend me. Rather marvel that I am, than muse that I should not be if it were not God's holy hand that continueth me beyond all other expectation.

I was not simply trained up, nor in my youth spent my time altogether idly; and yet, when I came to the crown, then entered I first into the school of experience, bethinking myself of those things that best fitted a king—justice, temper, magnanimity, judgment. As for the two latter, I will not boast. But for the two first, this may I truly say: among my subjects I never knew a difference of person, where right was one; nor never to my knowledge preferred for favour what I thought not fit for worth; nor bent mine ears to credit a tale that first was told me; nor was so rash to corrupt my judgment with my censure, ere I heard the cause. I will not say but many reports might fortune[1] be brought me by such as must hear the matter, whose partiality might mar the right; for we princes cannot hear all causes ourselves. But this dare I boldly affirm: my verdict went with the truth of my knowledge.

But full well wished Alcibiades his friend, that he should not give any answer till he had recited the letters of the alphabet.[2] So have I not used over-sudden resolutions in matters that have touched me full near: you will say that with me, I think. And therefore, as touching your counsels and consultations, I conceive them to be wise, honest, and conscionable; so provident and careful for the safety of my life (which I wish no longer than may be for your good), that though I never can yield you of recompense your due, yet shall I endeavour myself to give you cause to think your good will not ill bestowed, and strive to make myself worthy for such

subjects. And as for your petition: your judgment I condemn not, neither do I mistake your reasons, but pray you to accept my thankfulness, excuse my doubtfulness, and take in good part my answer-answerless. Wherein I attribute not so much to my own judgment, but that I think many particular persons may go before me, though by my degree I go before them. Therefore, if I should say, I would not do what you request, it might peradventure be more than I thought; and to say I would do it, might peradventure breed peril of that you labour to preserve, being more than in your own wisdoms and discretions would seem convenient, circumstances of place and time being duly considered.[3] —1586

The Golden Speech[4]

Mr. Speaker,[5] we have heard your declaration and perceive your care of our state, by falling into the consideration of a grateful acknowledgement of such benefits as you have received, and that your coming is to present thanks unto us, which I accept with no less joy than your loves can have desire to offer such a present.

I do assure you that there is no prince that loveth his subjects better, or whose love can countervail[6] our love. There is no jewel, be it of never so rich a price, which I prefer before this jewel—I mean your love—for I do more esteem it than any treasure or riches: for that we know how to prize, but love and thanks I count inestimable. And though God has raised me high, yet this I count

---

[1] *fortune* Happen to.

[2] *Alcibiades* Skilled Athenian general and political strategist who changed sides twice during the Peloponnesian War with Sparta. As a result he had many enemies, and was assassinated; *But full … the alphabet* The "friend" referred to here is Alcibiades's teacher Socrates; however, this advice actually comes from the philosopher Athenodoros, who gave it to his student Augustus Caesar.

[3] *Therefore, if … considered* Elizabeth did not agree to sign Mary's death warrant until another assassination plot was discovered, in February 1587.

[4] *The Golden Speech* This text is based on a transcription by one of the members of parliament, Hayward Townshend. This parliamentary speech was Elizabeth's most celebrated, and in it she states her recognition of the people's right—and even duty—to raise grievances over royal policies. Here, Elizabeth addresses grievances raised over monopolies, which, because they favored certain individuals, were often economically detrimental to many.

[5] *Mr. Speaker* The speaker of the house at the time was Sir John Croke (1553–1620).

[6] *countervail* Equal.

the glory of my crown: that I have reigned with your loves. This makes me that I do not so much rejoice that God hath made me to be a queen, as to be a queen over so thankful a people. Therefore I have cause to wish nothing more than to content the subjects, and that is a duty which I owe. Neither do I desire to live longer days than that I may see your prosperity, and that is my only desire. And as I am that person that still yet under God hath delivered you, so I trust by the almighty power of God that I still shall be His instrument to preserve you from envy, peril, dishonour, shame, tyranny, and oppression, partly by means of your intended helps, which we take very acceptably, because it manifests the largeness of your loves and loyalties unto your sovereign.

Of myself I must say this: I never was any greedy, scraping grasper, nor a strait,[1] fast-holding prince, nor yet a waster; my heart was never set on worldly goods, but only for my subjects' good. What you do bestow on me I will not hoard up, but receive it to bestow on you again. Yea, mine own properties I account yours, to be expended for your good. Therefore render unto them, I beseech you, Mr. Speaker, such thanks as you imagine my heart yieldeth, but my tongue cannot express.

Mr. Speaker, I would wish you and the rest to stand up, for I shall yet trouble you with longer speech.[2]

Mr. Speaker, you give me thanks, but I doubt me[3] I have more cause to thank you all than you me: and I charge you to thank them of the Lower House[4] from me, for had I not received a knowledge from you, I might have fallen into the lapse of an error only for lack of true information.

Since I was queen, yet never did I put my pen to any grant but that upon pretext and semblance made unto me that it was both good and beneficial to the subjects in general, though a private profit to some of my ancient servants who had deserved well. But the contrary being found by experience, I am exceedingly beholding to such subjects as would move the same at

first. And I am not so simple to suppose but that there be some of the Lower House whom these grievances never touched, and from them I think they speak out of zeal to their countries[5] and not out of spleen or malevolent affection, as being parties grieved. And I take it exceedingly grateful from them, because it gives us to know that no respects or interests had moved them other than the minds they bear to suffer no diminution of our honour and our subjects' love unto us, the zeal of which affection, tending to ease my people and knit their hearts unto me, I embrace with a princely care.

Far above all earthly treasure I esteem my people's love, more than which I desire not to merit. That my grants should be grievous to my people and oppressions to be privileged under colour of our patents, our kingly dignity shall not suffer it. Yea, when I heard it, I could give no rest to my thoughts until I had reformed it. Shall they think to escape unpunished that have thus oppressed you and have been respectless of their duty and regardless of our honour? No, Mr. Speaker, I assure you, were it not more for conscience' sake than for any glory or increase of love that I desire, these errors, troubles, vexations, and oppressions done by these varlets[6] and lewd persons, not worthy the name of subjects, should not escape without condign[7] punishment. But I perceive they dealt with me like physicians who, ministering a drug, make it more acceptable by giving it a good aromatical savour, or, when they give pills, do gild[8] them all over.

I have ever used to set the last judgement day before my eyes and so to rule as I shall be judged to answer before a higher judge. To whose judgement seat I do appeal that never thought was cherished in my heart that tended not unto my people's good. And if my kingly bounty have been abused and my grants turned to the hurt of my people, contrary to my will and meaning, or if any in authority under me have neglected or perverted what I have committed to them, I hope

---

[1] *strait* Severe, strict.

[2] Townshend's transcription here indicates that all listeners have been kneeling so far.

[3] *doubt me* Do not doubt.

[4] *Lower House* House of Commons.

[5] *countries* Counties.

[6] *varlets* Knaves, rogues.

[7] *condign* Appropriate, deserved.

[8] *gild* Cover with gold.

God will not lay their culps[1] and offenses to my charge. And though there were danger in repealing our grants, yet what danger would not I rather incur for your own good, than I would suffer them still to continue?

I know the title of a king is a glorious title, but assure yourself that the shining glory of princely authority hath not so dazzled the eyes of our understanding but we well know and remember that we also are to yield an account of our actions before the great judge. To be a king and wear a crown is a thing more glorious to them that see it than it is pleasant to them that bear it. For myself, I was never so much enticed with the glorious name of a king or royal authority of a queen as delighted that God hath made me His instrument to maintain His truth and glory, and to defend this kingdom, as I said, from peril, dishonour, tyranny, and oppression.

There will never queen sit in my seat with more zeal to my country or care to my subjects, and that will sooner with willingness venture her life for your good and safety than myself. For it is not my desire to live nor reign longer than my life and reign shall be for your good. And though you have had and may have many princes more mighty and wise sitting in this seat, yet you never had or shall have any that will be more careful and loving.

Should I ascribe anything to myself and my sexly weakness, I were not worthy to live then, and of all most unworthy of the mercies I have had from God, who hath ever yet given me a heart which never yet feared foreign or home enemies. I speak it to give God the praise as a testimony before you, and not to attribute anything unto myself. For I, O Lord, what am I, whom practices and perils past should not fear? Or what can I do? That I should speak for any glory, God forbid.

This, Mr. Speaker, I pray you deliver unto the House, to whom heartily recommend me. And so I commit you all to your best fortunes and further counsels. And I pray you, Mr. Comptroller, Mr. Secretary, and you of my Council, that before these gentlemen depart into their countries, you bring them all to kiss my hand.

—30 NOVEMBER 1601

---

[1] *culps* Guilt, sins.

IN CONTEXT

The Defeat of the Spanish Armada

Tensions between England and Spain rose through the 1580s primarily as a result of raids on Spanish shipping and the looting of Spanish settlements in the Americas (largely by Sir Francis Drake), and religious differences between Catholic Spain and Protestant England. Finally, on 30 May 1588, Philip II of Spain launched an Armada of 130 ships, which, together with the army of Philip's nephew the Duke of Parma (then stationed across the English Channel in Flanders), was to invade and conquer England. The English fleet (under Lord Howard and Drake) of 197 smaller and more maneuverable ships engaged the Spanish in a battle that began on 29 July and extended over many days, culminating in a Spanish defeat at Gravesend and made more decisive by a gale that drove the remnants of the Spanish fleet north, up the English coast. Meanwhile an English army of 22,000 troops had gathered at Tilbury (east of London on the Thames). Under the command of Robert Dudley, the Earl of Leicester, it prepared to engage the army of the Duke of Parma—but with the defeat of the Armada was never called upon to fight. Leicester, the Queen's favorite, died of natural causes only 28 days later.

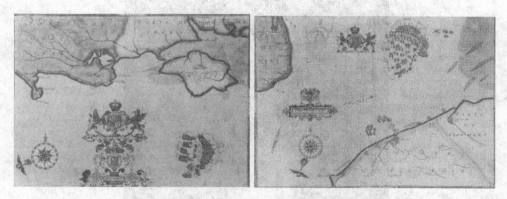

These engravings (by Augustine Ryther, based on illustrations by Robert Adams to the 1588 book *Expeditionis Hispanorum*), depict battles between the English fleet and the Spanish Armada on 4 August off the Isle of Wight (left) and on 8 August off Gravelines, Flanders (right).

The Ark Royal, flagship of the English fleet, commanded by Lord Howard against the Armada in 1588.

Sir William Segar, *Robert Dudley, Earl of Leicester*, c. 1583.

Culture: A Portfolio

CONTEXTS

As in any period, the culture of the sixteenth and early seventeenth centuries was not monolithic and uniform: the "high" culture of the nobility was largely foreign to the rural laborers (although the élite was often familiar with popular culture), various cultural phenomena were peculiar to the citizens and merchants in the social class below the nobility and gentry, or to the yeomen in the social class above the laborers, and so on. It varied substantially by gender: the culture of women was different from that of men, and women were effectively excluded from participation in many activities. Culture varied too from place to place: the culture of London (and to a lesser extent that of other cities, such as Bristol and York) differed from that of the rural areas of England or that of smaller centers, and that of Scotland, of Wales, and of other regions was different again. Of necessity, then, the following can provide only limited impressions of the culture of Britain during this period.

⌘ ⌘ ⌘

Music

Over the sixteenth and early seventeenth centuries, home performance from printed or manuscript music began to play a much larger role in daily life than it had in earlier periods. The work of composers and musicians such as John Dowland (1563–1626), William Byrd (1539–1623) and Thomas Campion (1567–1620) was highly regarded, and their compositions, whether for stringed instruments such as the lute (in Dowland's case), or keyboard instruments such as the virginal and the harpsichord (as with Byrd) began to be printed and distributed. Among the common people music continued to play an integral part of daily life; most communities possessed shared knowledge of a body of popular song, as this excerpt from Walton's *Compleat Angler* (1653) indicates.

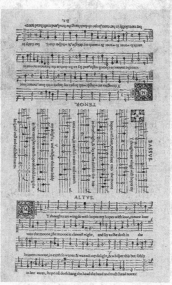

from John Dowland, *First Booke of Songs or Ayres*, 1597.

The book of songs, each written for four-part singing, was printed to allow each of the four singers to face his or her own part.

Advertisement for William Byrd, *Parthenia*, a collection of songs by William Byrd and others, c. 1611.

from Izaak Walton, *The Compleat Angler, or, The Contemplative Man's Recreation* (1653)

PISCATOR.[1]   I pray, do us a courtesy that shall stand you and your daughter in nothing, and yet we will think ourselves something in your debt. It is but to sing a song that was sung by your daughter when I last passed over this meadow, about eight or nine days since.

---
[1] *Piscator* Latin: Fisher.

MILK-WOMAN: What song was it, pray? Was it "Come Shepherds, deck your herds"? or "As at noon Dulcina rested"? or "Phillida flouts me"? or "Chevy Chace"? or "Johnny Armstrong"? or "Troy Town?

PISCATOR.   No, it is none of those; it is a song that your daughter sung the first part, and you sung the answer to it.

MILK-WOMAN.   Come, Maudlin, sing the first part to the gentleman with a merry heart; and I'll sing the second when you have done.

[The song that follows is Christopher Marlowe's "Come live with me and be my love."]

Painting

The emphasis throughout this period was on portraiture; in the sixteenth century, it was common for portraits to depict the subject's face naturalistically so as to suggest three dimensions, while the portrayal of the rest of the figure was rendered in a flatter, decorative fashion. (The portrait of Edward Alleyn below is a good example.)

Some of the best-known "English" paintings of the period were painted by leading artists from the Continent: Hans Holbein the Younger (1497–1543) became court painter to Henry VIII, and Anthony Van Dyck court painter to Charles I. Among sixteenth- and early seventeenth-century painters of English nationality, Nicholas Hilliard may have been the best known—for his *Treatise Concerning the Art of Limning* as well as for his miniature cameos and other portraits. ("Limning," as a later seventeenth-century definition explains, is an "Art whereby in Water Colours, we strive to resemble Nature in every thing to the life.")

The two passages ending this section present contrasting attitudes of the subjects of portraits as to how they should be painted. The quotation attributed to Oliver Cromwell is the source of the famous phrase "warts and all" (Cromwell did indeed have several warts on his face, and they are shown in the Lely portrait.)

Rowland Lockey, copy of Hans Holbein the Younger, *Sir Thomas More and his Family*, detail, 1593, original c. 1527.

The original of this large portrait (the full picture includes eleven figures) is now lost; it is the first known example by a northern European artist of a large group portrait in which the figures are all shown standing (rather than most or all being shown kneeling).

Nicholas Hilliard, *A Youth Leaning Against a Tree Among Roses*, c. 1590.

from Nicholas Hilliard, *A Treatise Concerning the Art of Limning* (1624)

I wish it were so that none should meddle with limning but gentlemen alone, for that it is a kind of gentle painting of less subjection than any other; for one may leave when he will, his colours nor his work taketh any harm by it. Moreover it is secret, a man may use it and scarcely be perceived of his own folk; it is sweet and cleanly to use, and it is a thing apart from all other painting or drawing, and tendeth not to common men's use, either for furnishing of houses or any patterns for tapestries, or building, or any other work whatsoever, and yet it excelleth all other painting whatsoever in sundry points, in giving the true lustre to pearl and precious stone, and worketh the metals gold or silver with themselves, which so enricheth and ennobleth the work that it seemeth to be the thing itself.

from *A Letter to F.P. Verney from the Countess of Sussex* (1639)

Sweet Mr. Verney, the picture came very well, many hearty thanks to you for it. The frame is a little hurt, the gilt being rubbed off. The picture is very ill favoured, makes me quite out of love with myself, the face is so big and so fat that it pleases me not at all. It looks like one of the winds puffing—but truly I think it is like the original. If ever I come to London before Sir Vandyck go, I will get him to mend my picture, for though I be ill favoured I think that makes me worse than I am.

Oliver Cromwell, Instructions to His Painter, as Reported by George Vertue, *Notebooks* (c. 1720)

Mr. Lilly,[1] I desire you would use all your skill to paint my picture truly like me and not flatter me at all but [pointing to his own face] remark all these roughnesses, pimples, warts and everything as you see me; otherwise I will never pay a farthing for it.

---

[1] *Mr. Lilly* I.e., Peter Lely (1618–80), later Sir Peter Lely.

Sir Peter Lely, *Portrait of Oliver Cromwell*, c. 1653.

Games and Pastimes

Considerable attention was paid to games and pastimes in the sixteenth century. Skill in archery was considered to be of particular importance to the defence of the realm—so much so that Henry VIII passed several statutes to enforce its practice and ensure that "every man having a man-child or men-children in his house, shall provide, ordain, and have in his house for every man-child being of the age of seven years and above, till he come to the age of seventeen years, a bow and two shafts to induce and learn them, and bring them up in shooting." The statutes appear to have been widely ignored, and it is probable that archery became slowly less popular over this period.

Sports, games, and entertainments pursued purely for pleasure, on the other hand, clearly gained in popularity. Bear-baiting is of special interest because of the surprising degree to which connections existed between bear-baiting and the theater in the late-sixteenth and early-seventeenth centuries. Philip Henslowe, a prominent theater manager, and Edward Alleyn, a leading actor, were from 1594 onwards two of the leading figures in the sport. For some years they controlled both the Bear Garden and the Paris Garden, the two sites for bear-baiting in London, and they eventually built a new theater, the Hope, designed to house both bear-baiting and stage plays. Both Elizabeth I and James I encouraged the practice, and royal exhibitions of bear-baiting (at venues such as Whitehall and Greenwich Park) to entertain foreign visitors were frequent occurrences; though the monarch is never recorded to have attended public performances of plays during this period, Elizabeth is known to have visited the Paris Garden in 1599.

Though most sports, games and pastimes were heavily male-oriented, there are some exceptions among the more gentle pastimes. Queen Elizabeth is known to have played draughts (checkers) and chess with Roger Ascham, and Arthur Saul dedicated *The Famous Game of Chess-Play* (1614) to Lucy, Countess of Bedford.

Frontispiece, Gervase Markham, *The Art of Archery*, 1634. The woodcut depicts Charles I.

A Game of Tennis, early seventeenth century. The early version of the game was played indoors with short-handled racquets and leather balls packed with hair. (The modern game of "lawn tennis" dates from the nineteenth century.)

THE NOBLE ARTE OF
VENERIE OR HVNTING.

VVherein is handled and set out the Vertues, Nature, and Properties of fiuetene sundrie Chaces togither, with the order and maner how to Hunte and kill euery one of them.

Translated and collected for the pleasure of all Noblemen and Gentlemen, out of the best approued Authors, which haue written any thing concerning the same: And reduced into such order and proper termes as are vsed here, in this noble Realme of England.

The Contentes vvhereof shall more playnely appeare in the Page next follovyng.

Title page, George Turberville, *The Noble Art of Venerie or Hunting*, 1575.

The Booke of Faulconrie or Hauking, FOR THE ONELY DE-
light and pleasure of all Noblemen and Gentlemen: Collected out of the best aucthors, asvvell Italians as Frenchmen, and some English practises withall concernyng Faulconrie, the contentes whereof are to be seene in the next page folowyng. By *George Turberuile* Gentleman.
NOCET EMPTA DOLORE VOLVPTAS.

Imprinted at London for Christopher Barker, at the signe of the Grashopper in Paules Churchyarde. *Anno.* 1575.

Title page, George Turberville, *The Book of Falconry or Hawking*, 1575.

Anonymous, *Edward Alleyn*, detail (early
seventeenth century).

In addition to being one of the most important
bear-baiting impresarios of the age, Alleyn
(1566–1626) was widely considered to be the era's
greatest actor. Among his leading parts were the title
roles in *Tamburlaine* and *Doctor Faustus*; in 1592
Thomas Nashe wrote that no one "could ever
perform more in action than famous Ned Allen."

Title page, *The Famous Game of
Chess-Play.*

Food and Drink

In this as in many other things, the sixteenth and
early-seventeenth century point of comparison was
often Italy. The first of the passages below gives an
early impression of the comparison from an Italian
point of view, the second a seventeenth-century view
from an English gentleman. Moryson's comment
that the English eat "more flesh" than the Italians
may be something of an understatement: the 1589
records preserved of the food and drink purchased
for a well-off bachelor in London show a diet of
almost nothing but meat. On May 11, for example,
the following were purchased for the midday dinner:

a piece of beef	xviiid.
a loin of veal	iis.
2 chickens	xiiiid.
oranges	iid
for dressings ye veal & chickens & sauce	xiid

The following items were purchased for supper
the same day:

a shoulder of mutton	xvid.
2 rabbits	xd.
for dressing ye mutton, rabbits & a pigges pettie toes	viiid.
cold beef	viiid.
cheese	iid.

The diet of commoners, in contrast, included a good
deal of bread and cheese but relatively little meat
through much of the year. Even in towns most
families kept chickens (and sometimes pigs) and
maintained a small plot of land. Animals were
slaughtered in the late autumn, and salted or
smoked meat was consumed in the winter. At all
levels of society the Church requirement that fish be
eaten on Fridays was observed; for those living at
any significant distance from the sea, salt rather than
fresh fish was usually the only option. Neither
potatoes nor tomatoes were yet a part of the English
diet, and green vegetables do not seem to have
figured very prominently in most people's diet; fruit
was common, however.

Many remarked on the liberal consumption of beer and ale throughout the sixteenth century and into the seventeenth, and clearly women as well as men were known to frequent taverns. Indeed, if the the catalogue of tavern types in John Skelton's account of "The Tunning of Elynour Rumming" (with its account of "wenches unlaced" and "housewives unbraced") is to be believed even in part, that was far from a rare occurrence. As the early seventeenth-century watercolor reproduced below illustrates, wine was often the preferred drink of the better-off classes of society. Beginning in the late 1560s the smoking of tobacco—described below by William Harrison—also became common. By the early 1600s there was also a strong reaction against the "stinking smoke" of tobacco—expressed most powerfully in James I's *A Counterblast to Tobacco* (an excerpt from which is included elsewhere in this anthology).

from An Anonymous Venetian Official Traveling in England, *A Relation, or Rather a True Account, of the Island of England* (1497)

The English are, for the most part, both men and women of all ages, handsome and well-proportioned; though not quite so much so, in my opinion, as it had been asserted to me, before your magnificence went to that kingdom; and I have understood from persons acquainted with these countries, that the Scotch are much handsomer; and that the English are great lovers of themselves, and of everything belonging to them; they think that there are no other men than themselves, and no other world but England; and whenever they see a handsome foreigner, they say that "he looks like an Englishman," and that "it is a great pity that he should not be an Englishman;" and when they partake of any delicacy with a foreigner, they ask him, "whether such a thing is made in *their* country?" They take great pleasure in having a quantity of excellent victuals, and also in remaining a long time at table, being very sparing of wine when they drink it at their own expense. And this, it is said, they do in order to induce their other English guests to drink wine in moderation also; not considering it any

inconvenience for three or four persons to drink out of the same cup. Few people keep wine in their own houses, but buy it, for the most part, at a tavern; and when they mean to drink a great deal, they go to the tavern, and this is done not only by the men, but by ladies of distinction. The deficiency of wine, however, is amply supplied by the abundance of ale and beer, to the use of which these people are become so habituated, that, at an entertainment where there is plenty of wine, they will drink them in preference to it, and in great quantities.

from Fynes Moryson, *Itinerary* (1617)

England abounds in cattle of all kinds, and particularly hath very great oxen, the flesh whereof is so tender, as no meat is more desired ... The flesh of hogs and swine is more savoury than in any other parts, excepting the bacon of Westphalia. ...English husbandmen eat barley and rye brown bread, and prefer it to white bread as abiding longer in the stomach, and not so soon digested with their labour. ...

The Italian Sansovino is much deceived, writing, that in general the English eat and cover the table at least four times in the day; for howsoever those that journey and some sickly men staying at home may perhaps take a small breakfast, yet in general the English eat but two meals (of dinner and supper) each day. And I profess for myself and other Englishmen, passing through Italy so famous for temperance, that we often observed, that, howsoever we might have a pullet and some flesh[1] prepared for us, eating it with a moderate proportion of bread, the Italians at the same time, with a charger[2] full of herbs for a salad, and with roots,[3] like meats of small price, would each of them eat two or three penny-worth of bread. And since all fulness is ill, and that of bread worst, I think we were more temperate in our diet, though eating more flesh, than they eating so much more bread than we did. ...

I observed a custom in all those Italian cities and towns through which I passed that is not used in any

---

[1] *a pullet and some flesh* A chicken and some red meat.

[2] *charger* Large plate or dish.

[3] *roots* I.e., root vegetables such as carrots, parsnips, or beetroot.

other country that I saw in my travels, neither do I think that any other nation in Christendom use it, but only Italy. The Italians … do always at their meals use a little fork when they cut their meat. … The reason for this their curiosity[1] is because the Italian cannot endure by any means to have his dish touched by fingers, seeing that all men's fingers are not alike clean.

Anonymous, Miniature watercolor depicting eating and drinking, c. 1610.

The weight of eche peny white Lofe according to the pryce of Cocket. An.51.H.3.	The weigt of the halfe peny wheaton Lofe drawne fro the corse coket. A.51.H.3	The weight of the peny wheaton Lofe drawne frō the corse Cocket An.51.H.3.	The weight of the peny houfhold Lofe drawne frō the corse Cocket, An.51.H.3.
viii ʒ q.	vi.ʒ.iij.ठ.	rij.ʒ.q.i.ठ.	rvi.ʒ.ठi.
viij.ʒ.iij ठ.	vi.ʒ.ij.ठ.	rij.ʒ.iiij.ठ.	rvi.ʒ.q.i.ठ.
viij.ʒ.j ठ.	vi.ʒ.	rij.ʒ.	rvi.ʒ.ij.ठ.
vij.ʒ.iij.q.iij.ठ.	v.ʒ.iij.q.iiij.ठ.	ri.ʒ.iij.q.iij.ठ.	ठv.ʒ.iij.q.i.ठ.
vij.ʒ iij.q ij.ठ.	v.ʒ.ij.q.ij.ठ.	rj.ʒ.iij.q.j.ठ.	ठv.ʒ.ठi.iij.ठ.
vij.ʒ.iij q.	v.ʒ.iij.q.j.ठ.	rj.ʒ.ठi.ij.ठ.	ठv.ʒ.ठi.
vij.ʒ.ठi iij ठ.	v.ʒ.iij.q.	rj.ʒ.ठi.	ठv.ʒ.q.j.ठ.
vij ʒ.ठi.ij.ठ.	v.ʒ.ठi.iij.ठ.	ठj.ʒ.q.j.ठ.	ठv.ʒ.iiij.ठ.
vij.ʒ ठi.	v.ʒ.ठi.ij.ठ.	ठj.ʒ.iij.ij.ठ.	ठv.ʒ.
vij.ʒ.q.iij.ठ.	v.ʒ.ठi.j.ठ.	ठj.ʒ.ij.ठ.	riiij.ʒ.iij.q.j.ठ.

The Assize of Bread, London, 1600. The chart sets out the prices to be charged for different sorts of loaves of bread, depending on the price of wheat at the time.

---

[1] *curiosity*   Curious or unusual behavior.

---

from Sarah Longe, *Mrs. Sarah Longe Her Receipt Book* (manuscript c. 1610)

> Medieval recipes (or "receipts") are typically as vague as is Longe about cooking times, but many published recipes from the late sixteenth and early seventeenth centuries include references to time ("cook it a quarter of an hour … " etc.).

To make cherry marmalet

Take 5 pound of cherries, you must weigh them with their stones in them, after stone them, then take one pound of sugar such as you make marmalet with, and put your cherries and your sugar both together into the pan, or skillet which you will make it in, but beat your sugar very well, and so let it boil as you do other marmalets, and when you think it is boiled enough, put it into your boxes or glasses as fast as you can.

from William Harrison, *Chronologie* (1573)

In these days, the taking-in of the smoke of the Indian herb called tobacco by an instrument formed like a little ladle, whereby it passeth from the mouth into the head and stomach, is greatly taken up and used in England, against rheums and some other diseases engendered in the lungs.

Children and Education

There was little support for compulsory or state-supported education in the British Isles before the late-seventeenth century, except in Scotland, but with the tide of Protestantism came much greater interest in education. The Convocation of Canterbury in 1529 ordered all parish priests to teach children to read and write, and, while it is certain not all did so, it may be that close to half of the population were at least barely literate by the end of the sixteenth century. Under the Tudors, Parliament expressed its support for educational ideals, and acted to regulate grammar schools in such matters as the prescribing of textbooks. (Lily's *Short Introduction of Grammar* remained the standard for Latin grammar until well into the nineteenth century.) Boys from well-off families aged five to seven attended a Petty (from the French "petit," or small) School; they then attended a grammar school from ages seven through fourteen; only a few would follow on to one of the two universities. Boys (and often girls) of noble birth were educated by a tutor at home; girls of other social classes were generally not provided with any formal education. Male children of laborers and poor townsfolk were also effectively denied an education for, although schools were officially open to all boys, in practice the fees that were charged (often a pound or more per year, even in the mid-sixteenth century) put education out of reach of those of modest means.

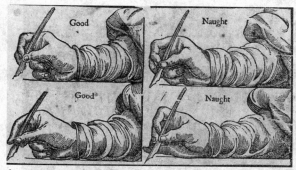

from John Baidon, *New Book containg All Sorts of Hands* (revised edition 1611), first published c. 1570), woodcut, "How you ought to hold your pen."

Anonymous woodcut, a Petty School (early seventeenth century).

A hornbook from the early seventeenth century. Hornbooks typically included the letters of the alphabet and the text of the Lord's Prayer, framed in wood and covered by a thin layer of transparent horn.

Edward IV Grammar School, Stratford-upon-Avon.

Attributed to the Master of the Countess of Warwick, *Lord Cobham and his Family*, 1567. Cobham's wife is shown opposite him; her sister is to the left. The age of each child is painted above the head.

Anthony Van Dyck, *George and Francis Villiers*, 1635. After their father, the Duke of Buckingham, was assassinated, these children were raised in the household of Charles I. Francis was killed in battle during the Civil War; following the Restoration George became a leading politician. (George is portrayed by John Dryden in "Absalom and Architophel" in the character of Zimri, "stiff in opinions, always in the wrong.")

Artist unknown, *Portrait of John Donne*, c. 1595.

Sir Peter Lelly, *George Villiers, Second Duke of Buckingham*, c. 1675.

The Supernatural and the Miraculous

The supernatural was the subject of ongoing controversy in the sixteenth and early seventeenth centuries. Belief in astrology, in witchcraft, and in a wide range of supernatural or miraculous occurrences was widespread throughout society. Though repeated efforts were made by writers such as Joseph Hall to associate such "superstitions"[1] with the uneducated or simple of mind, Elizabeth I is known to have had her own astrologer, and (as the account below records) James I regarded witchcraft with the utmost seriousness. The writings on witchcraft of George Gifford, from which an excerpt appears below, give an

almost anthropological analysis of how allegations of witchcraft took root and grew in a community.

ASTROLOGASTER,
OR,
THE FIGVRE-CASTER.

Rather the Arraignment of Artlesse Astrologers, and Fortune-tellers, that cheat many ignorant people vnder the pretence of foretelling things to come, of telling things that are past, finding out things that are lost, expounding Dreames, calculating Deaths and Natiuities, once againe brought to the Barre.

By Iohn Melton.

Cicero. *Stultorum plena sunt omnia.*

Imprinted at London by *Barnard Alsop*, for *Edward Blackmore*, and are to be sold in *Paules* Churchyard, at the Signe of the *Blazing-Starre.* 1620.

Title page, John Melton, *Astrologastor, or, the Figurecaster*, 1620. Included in the text of Melton's book is the following reference to the stage:

Another [astrologer] will foretell of lightning and thunder that shall happen such a day, when there are no such inflammations seen, except[2] men go to the Fortune in Golding Lane, to see the tragedy of *Doctor Faustus*. There indeed a man may behold shag-haired devils run roaring over the stage with squibs[3] in their mouths, while drummers make thunder in the tiring-house,[4] and the twelve-penny hirelings make artificial lightning in their heavens.

---

[1] *superstitions* The word "superstition" first appeared in the fifteenth century, and it gained wide currency in the sixteenth; Richard Hooker in his *Ecclesiastical Polity*, 1597 defines it thus: "superstition is, when things are either abhorred or observed, with a zealous or fearful, but erroneous relation to God." As time went on the term started to be less and less frequently applied to perceived Christian heresies, and to become reserved more and more for denoting (and ridiculing) supernatural beliefs outside of a Christian context.

[2] *except* Unless.

[3] *squibs* Fireworks.

[4] *tiring-house* Room in which actors dressed for the stage.

from Reginald Scot, *The Discovery of Witchcraft* (1584)

Who they be that are called witches, with a manifest declaration of the cause that moveth men so commonly to think, and witches themselves to believe that they can hurt children, cattle, &c. with words and imaginations: and of cozening witches.

One sort of such as are said to be witches, are women which be commonly old, lame, blear-eyed, pale, foul, and full of wrinkles; poor, and sullen, superstitious, and papists; or such as know no religion: in whose drowsy minds the devil hath gotten a fine seat; so as, what mischief, mischance, calamity, or slaughter is brought to pass, they are easily persuaded the same is done by themselves; imprinting in their minds an earnest and constant imagination hereof. They are lean and deformed, showing melancholy in their faces, to the horror of all that see them. They are doting, scolds, mad, devilish; and not much differing from them that are thought to be possessed with spirits; so firm and steadfast in their opinions, as whosoever shall only have respect to the constancy of their words uttered, would easily believe they were true indeed.

These miserable wretches are so odious unto all their neighbors, and so feared, as few dare offend them, or deny them any thing they ask: whereby they take upon them; yea, and sometimes think, that they can do such things as are beyond the ability of human nature. These go from house to house, and from door to door for a pot full of milk, yeast, drink, pottage, or some such relief; without the which they could hardly live: neither obtaining for their service and pains, nor by their art, nor yet at the devil's hands (with whom they are said to make a perfect and visible bargain) either beauty, money, promotion, wealth, worship, pleasure, honor, knowledge, learning, or any other benefit whatsoever.

from George Gifford, *A Discourse of the Subtle Practices of Devils by Witches and Sorcerers* (1587)

In a later text, *A Dialogue Concerning Witches and Witchcraft* (1593), Gifford summarized the purpose of the work from which the following excerpt is taken: "certain years now past ... I published a small Treatise concerning witches, to lay open some of Satan's sleights, and subtle practices, lest the ignoranter sort should be carried awry and seduced more and more by them."

Some woman doth fall out bitterly with her neighbour: there followeth some great hurt, either that God hath permitted the devil to vex him: or otherwise. There is a suspicion conceived. Within few years after she is in some jar with an other. He is also plagued. This is noted of all. Great fame is spread of the matter. Mother W. is a witch. She hath bewitched goodman B. Two hogs which died strangely: or else he is taken lame. Well, mother W. doth begin to be very odious and terrible unto many. Her neighbours dare say nothing but yet in their hearts they wish she were hanged. Shortly after another falleth sick and doth pine, he can have no stomach unto his meat, now he can not sleep. The neighbours come to visit him. "Well, neighbour," sayeth one, "do ye not suspect some naughty dealing: did ye never anger mother W.?" "Truly neighbour" (sayth he), "I have not liked the woman a long time. I can not tell how I should displease her, unless it were this other day, my wife prayed her, and so did I, that she would keep her hens out of my garden. We spake her as fair as we could for our lives. I think verily she hath bewitched me." Every body sayeth now that mother W. is a witch in deed, and hath bewitched the good man E. He cannot eat his meat. It is out of all doubt: for there were (those) which saw a weasel run from her house-ward into his yard even a little before he fell sick. The sick man dieth, and taketh it upon his death that he is bewitched: then is mother W. apprehended, and sent to prison.

from Joseph Hall, *Characters of Virtues and Vices* (1608)

> Joseph Hall (1574–1656) was a moral philosopher well known for his attempts to reconcile the ideas of the ancient Stoics with those of Christianity. In later life he was appointed Bishop of Exeter (in 1627) and became heavily embroiled in the conflicts between Anglican and Puritan factions.

Superstition is godless religion, devout impiety. The superstitious is fond in observation, servile in fear; he worships God but as he lists; he gives God what he asks not, more than he asks, and all but what he should give, and makes more sins than the Ten Commandments. This man dares not stir forth till his breast be crossed and his face sprinkled. If but an hare cross him the way, he returns; or if his journey began, unawares, on the dismal day; or, if he stumbled at the threshold. If he see a snake unkilled, he fears a mischief; if the salt fall towards him, he looks pale and red, and is not quiet till one of the waiters have poured wine on his lap; and when he sneezeth, thinks them not his friends that uncover not. In the morning, he listens whether the crow crieth even or odd, and by that token presages of the weather. If he hear but a raven croak from the next roof, he makes his will; or if a bittour[1] fly over his head by night: but if his troubled fancy shall second his thoughts with the dream of a fair garden, or green rushes, or the salutation of a dead friend, he takes leave of the world, and says he cannot live. He will never set to sea but on a Sunday.... When he lies sick on his deathbed, no sin troubles him so much, as that he did once eat flesh on a Friday: no repentance can expiate that; the rest need none. There is no dream of his without an interpretation, without a prediction; and if the event answer not his exposition, he expounds it according to the event.... Old wives and stars are his counsellors: his nightspell is his guard; and charms, his physicians.... This man is strangely credulous, and calls impossible things miraculous: if he hear that some sacred block speaks, moves, weeps, smiles, his bare feet carry him thither with an offering; and if a danger miss him in the way, his saint hath the thanks. Some ways he will not go, and some he dares not; either there are bugs, or he feigneth them; every lantern is a ghost, and every noise is of chains. He knows not why, but his custom is to go a little about, and to leave the cross still on the right hand. One event is enough to make a rule: out of these rules he concludes fashions, proper to himself; and nothing can turn him out of his own course.

from Sir John Harington, "Account of an Audience with King James I" (1604), as recorded in *Nugae Antiquae*

Soon upon this, the Prince his Highness did enter, and in much good humour asked if I was "cousin to Lord Harrington of Exton?" I humbly replied [that] His Majesty did me some honour in enquiring my kin to one whom he had so late honoured and made a baron; and moreover did add, "we were both branches of the same tree." Then he enquired much of learning, and showed me his own in such sort, as made me remember my examiner at Cambridge aforetime. He sought much to know my advances in philosophy, and uttered profound sentences of Aristotle, and such like writers, which I had never read, and which some are bold enough to say, others do not understand: but this I must pass by. The Prince did now press my reading to him part of a canto in Ariosto; praised my utterance, and said he had been informed of many, as to my learning, in the time of the Queen. He asked me what I thought pure wit was made of; and whom it did best become? Whether a King should not be the best clerk in his own country; and, if this land did not entertain good opinion of his learning and wisdom. His Majesty did much press for my opinion touching the power of Satan in matter of witchcraft; and asked me, with much gravity, if I did "truly understand, why the devil did work more with ancient women than others."

More serious discourse did next ensue, wherein I wanted room to continue, and sometime room to escape; for the Queen was not forgotten, nor Davison[2] neither. His Highness told me her death was visible in

---

[1] *bittour* Bittern (a species of large heron).

[2] *Davison* William Davison (c. 1541–1608), a courtier.

Scotland before it did really happen, being, as he said, "spoken of in secret by those whose power of sight presented to them a bloody head dancing in the air." He then did remark much on this gift, and said he had sought out of certain books a sure way to attain knowledge of future chances. Hereat, he named many books, which I did not know, nor by whom written; but advised me not to consult some authors which would lead me to evil consultations. I told his Majesty, "the power of Satan had, I much feared, damaged my bodily frame; but I had not farther will to court his friendship, for my soul's hurt." We next discoursed somewhat on religion, when at length he said: "Now, Sir, you have seen my wisdom in some sort, and I have pried into yours. I pray you, do me justice in your report, and in good season, I will not fail to add to your understanding, in such points as I may find you lack amendment." I made courtesy hereat, and withdrew down the passage, and out at the gate, amidst the many varlets and lordly servants who stood around.

Title page, *True and Wonderfull: A Discourse Relating a Strange and Monstrous Serpent (or Dragon) Lately Discovered*, 1614.

At Maidstone in Kent there was one Margaret Mere, daughter to Richard Mere of the said town of Maidstone, who being unmarried, played the naughty pack,[1] and was gotten with child, being delivered of the same child the 24th day of October last past, in the year of our Lord 1568 at seven of the clock in the afternoon of the same day, being Sunday. Which child, being a man child, had first the mouth slitted on the right side like a leopard's mouth, terrible to behold, the left arm lying upon the breast, fast thereto joined, having as it were stumps on the hands, the left leg growing upward toward the head, and the right leg bending toward the left leg, the foot thereof growing into the buttock of the said left leg. In the middest of the back there was a broad lump of flesh in fashion like a rose, in the middest whereof was a hole, which voided like an issue. This said child was born alive, and lived 24 hours, and then departed this life. Which may be a terror as well to all such workers of filthiness and iniquity, as to those ungodly livers. Who (if in them any fear of God be) may move them to repentance and amendment of life. Which God for Christ's sake grant both to them and us. Amen.

Witnesses hereof were these: William Plomer, John Squier Glasier, John Sadler Goldsmith, beside diverse other credible persons both men and women.

Crime

In the late sixteenth century many publications offered accounts of crimes. Some, such as Robert Greene's *Notable Discovery of Coosenage, Now Daily Practised by Sundry lewd persons, called Connie-Catchers, and Cross-Biters* (1593) aimed to warn the populace of the methods adopted by petty crooks and confidence tricksters. Others provided lurid accounts of violent crime. As the excerpt below from the pamphlet describing the murder of Richard

---

1 *played the naughty pack* Engaged in immoral behavior (slang term of unknown origin).

Hobson illustrates, these were often colored with religious or political bias.

THE BELMAN
OF LONDON.
Bringing to light the moſt notorious villanies that are now practiſed
in the KINGDOME.
Profitable for Gentlemen, Lawyers, Merchants, Citizens, Farmers, Maſters of Houſholds, and all ſortes of ſervants, to marke, and delightfull for all men to Reade.

Lege, Perlege, Relege.

Printed at London for NATHANIEL BVTTER. 1 6 0 8.

Title page, Thomas Dekker, *The Belman*[1] *of London,* 1608.

With the temporary closing of the theaters in 1603 due to the plague, the playwright Thomas Dekker turned to writing pamphlets. In *The Belman of London* he promised to the reader that he would "bring to light a number of more notable enormities (daily hatched in this Realm) than ever have yet been published to the open eye of the world."

from "A True Report of the Late Horrible Murder Committed by William Sherwood, upon Richard Hobson, Gentleman, both Prisoners in the Queen's Bench, for the profession of Popery, the 18th of June, 1581"

I am the more loath at this time, to lay open unto the view of the whole world that late foul murder committed by Sherwood, because I would not speak much of them which be gone, and be thought to bite them by the back which are dead, and so be like unto those papists which being hot in cruelty did not only curse the dead continually, but did take up and burn the bones of diverse good men into ashes, to signify unto the world that no drink could cool their thirst but blood, no sacrifice could content them but the warm heart blood of martyrs and the death of the saints of God. But my intent is this: for as much as their scabs now break out, and that their cruelty seeketh no corners[2] but setteth itself upon a stage to be beheld of all men, to give all good Christians warning that as they shall hear of their naughtiness,[3] and see it so, they will learn to spew them out of their stomachs forever. . . .

But to be brief: the day grew on, which was the 28th of June about 8 of the clock in the morning, at which time he had determined to murder his fellow papist, and that the matter might more easy be brought to pass, he caused the night before the keeper to remove all Hobson's weapons, so that the next morning, as Hobson was coming down through Sherwood's chamber, from his prayers, Sherwood shutting his chamber door, assailed him with a knife, and a stool trestle, astonishing him, afterwards gave him a large wound, keeping him down and struggling till he bled to death, Hobson often crying, "Help, Father Throckmorton, he killeth me with his knife!" Master Throckmorton and others, hearing this noise, came upon Sherwood and by force broke up his doors, found the young man all to befouled in his own blood, and gasping for breath: who after a few faint words, yielded his soul into the hands of God. Sherwood perceived a great many busy about Hobson, began to practice to escape, but by heed taking of one Master

---

[1] *Belman* Man employed to walk the streets of a town making public announcements, or simply "calling the hours."

[2] *corners* I.e., places to hide.

[3] *naughtiness* Wickedness, evil.

Smith's man, he was brought to the marshal's hands, and imbrued in his fellow's blood: who being examined, he denied that manifest murder, which by witness was proved, and he being brought to the slain body, the blood which was settled, issued out afresh. Thus he slew this young man, in deed and cause miserably, in form and fashion cruelly and beastly.

Let us advisedly now weigh and consider what manner of razor this is that cutteth so sharp: if they be thus unable to master their passions, and thus like bloodsuckers do open them against their own fellow prisoners, what shall we look for at their hands? ...

Print Culture

Mechanical print technology originated in Germany in the mid-fifteenth century and the printing press was introduced to the British Isles by William Caxton in 1476. The illustrations that follow give some sense of the range of print culture in the sixteenth and early seventeenth centuries beyond what has been presented under the headings above.

from Jan van der Straet, *Nova Reperta*. This engraving by a Flemish artist of a printing shop was one of a series published in Antwerp in the 1580s; no comparable illustration of the technology of printing from Elizabethan England is known.

Title page, attributed to Anthony Fitzherbert, *The Book of Husbandry*, c. 1523.

In 1598 the eleventh edition of this work was published; it appears to have been one of the most popular books of the age. In all probability the primary audience for the work was the yeoman farmer; laborers were in most cases illiterate. The book offers advice on such matters as whether to plough with horses or oxen, how to sow oats or barley, how to make simple farm implements, and how to care for animals, including how to treat their diseases. Advice on highway repair is also included; throughout the sixteenth century husbandmen were required to devote several days per year to road work in their area. Gender roles were strictly differentiated; women are advised to clean the house, feed the animals, prepare meals, and make butter and cheese. In only a few areas are the roles allowed to overlap; the wife is advised to go to market if her husband is unable to do so, and to assist him in filling "the muck wain or dung cart." Each spouse is advised to provide an honest account to the other of money spent.

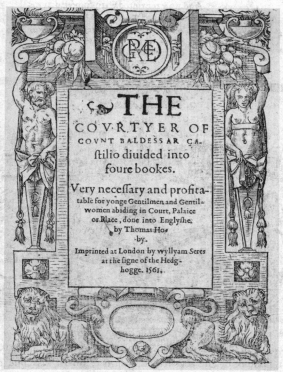

Title page, Baldassare Castiglione, *The Courtier*, translated by Thomas Hoby (first English edition, 1561). Castiglione's work (often referred to as *The Book of the Courtier*), was first published in Venice in 1528. It quickly became influential throughout Europe in its many translations.

Crispin van de Passe the Elder, engraving after a drawing by Isaac Oliver, *Queen Elizabeth*, 1603. This engraving is thought to have been published in commemoration of the Queen's death.

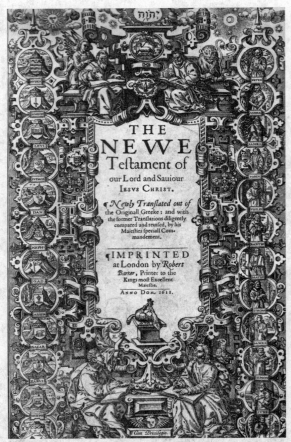

Title page, *New Testament, King James Bible*
(first edition, 1611).

Title page, John Taylor, *The Fearful Summer: or London's
Calamity* (1625, reprinted 1636). The plague of 1665 remains the
most famous of the seventeenth century, but it was one of
many—including those of 1603, 1625 and 1636.

AEMILIA LANYER
1569 – 1645

Aemilia Lanyer published her one book of poetry at a time when it was unusual for an English woman to publish her writing, especially under her full name. It was even more unusual for a middle-class woman to approach publication as a means of making money; to choose herself female patrons; and to make carefully planned use of poems addressed to them in order to raise the status of her work. Lanyer did all of these things.

Because Lanyer was not born into the nobility, many of the details of her personal life are sketchy, cobbled together from court and church records, information gleaned from her poems, and the professional journals of Simon Forman, an astrologer whom she consulted in 1597. She was born to Baptista Bassano and Margaret Johnson, a couple in a common-law marriage, in January 1569. Her father was an Italian musician in the courts of Edward VI and Elizabeth I, so although Aemilia Bassano was not of noble birth, she had access to aristocratic circles and was probably educated along with the young ladies of the court, likely in classical literature and rhetoric.

At age 18, Aemilia Bassano became the mistress of Henry Carey, Lord Hunsdon, who was then serving as Lord Chamberlain to Queen Elizabeth. The affair continued for five years, until she became pregnant. To avoid embarrassment, Carey married her off to another court musician, Alfonso Lanyer, on 18 October 1592, and provided her with an annual stipend of £40. Lanyer bore a son in early 1593, and named him Henry. Lanyer's marriage to Alfonso was not happy: according to Simon Forman's journals, "her husband hath dealt hardly with her and spent and consumed her goods and she is now … in debt." The couple had one child together in December 1598, named Odillya, who died at the age of ten months.

Despite her domestic situation, Lanyer maintained her connection with aristocratic families, particularly with a circle of intellectual court women, to whom she later dedicated many poems. Some time before 1609, she stayed with Margaret Clifford, Countess of Cumberland, and her daughter Anne at the estate where they were then living, Cookham Dean. The visit influenced Lanyer profoundly, as she relates in "The Description of Cooke-ham," the first "country house" poem published in English. While at Cookham Dean, she says, she experienced a spiritual awakening, inspired by the piety of the countess.

In 1611, at age 42, she published her volume of verse, *Salve Deus Rex Judæorum* (*Hail, God, King of the Jews*). Although the book focuses on virtue and religion, topics considered appropriate for a woman, it is nevertheless a radical (although not unprecedented) work for its time. Among its topics is the traditional and misogynistic maltreatment of women. The title poem, a lively narrative of the passion of Christ, interrupts its story once to argue that Eve, and, by extension, womankind, have been unjustly made to bear the chief responsibility for eating the fruit of the forbidden tree: that sin pales in comparison to the sin of the men who deliberately sentenced Christ to death. She commends the intervention of Pilate's wife and contrasts the behavior of Christ's male disciples, who forsook or denied him, with that of the women who stayed with him to the end.

After her husband died in 1613, Lanyer founded a school for the children of nobility and other wealthy families as a means of supporting herself. The only details concerning the remainder of her life come from court records, which indicate that she had considerable legal troubles, first concerning her school, then regarding the estate of her son, Henry, who died in October 1633. Lanyer died at age 76, and was buried 3 April 1645, at St. James Church, Clerkenwell.

⌘⌘⌘

To the Virtuous Reader

Often have I heard that it is the property[1] of some women not only to emulate the virtues and perfections of the rest, but also by all their powers of ill-speaking to eclipse the brightness of their deserved fame; now contrary to this custom, which men I hope unjustly lay to their charge, I have written this small volume or little book, for the general use of all virtuous ladies and gentlewomen of this kingdom; and in commendation of some particular persons of our own sex, such as for the most part are so well known to myself and others, that I dare undertake fame dares not to call any better. And this have I done to make known to the world that all women deserve not to be blamed, though some forgetting they are women themselves, and in danger to be condemned by the words of their own mouths, fall into so great an error, as to speak unadvisedly against the rest of their sex; which if it be true, I am persuaded they can show their own imperfection in nothing more; and therefore could wish (for their own ease, modesties and credit) they would refer such points of folly to be practised by evil-disposed men, who forgetting they were born of women, nourished of women, and that if it were not by the means of women, they would be quite extinguished out of the world, and a final end of them all, do like vipers deface the wombs wherein they were bred,[2] only to give way and utterance to their want of discretion and goodness. Such as these, were they that dishonoured Christ, his apostles and prophets, putting them to shameful deaths. Therefore we are not to regard any imputations, that they undeservedly lay upon us, no otherwise than to make use of them to our own benefits, as spurs to virtue, making us fly all occasions that may colour their unjust speeches to pass current.[3] Especially considering that they have tempted even the patience of God himself, who gave power to wise and virtuous women to bring down their pride and arrogance. As was cruel Cesarius by the discreet counsel of noble Deborah,[4] judge and prophetess of Israel, and resolution of Jael,[5] wife of Heber the Kenite; wicked Haman, by the divine prayers and prudent proceedings of beautiful Hester;[6] blasphemous Holofernes, by the invincible courage, rare wisdom, and confident carriage of Judith;[7] and the unjust judges, by the innocence of chaste Susanna;[8] with infinite others, which for brevity's sake I will omit. As also in respect it pleased our Lord and Saviour Jesus Christ, without the assistance of man, being free from original and all other sins, from the time of his conception till the hour of his death, to be begotten of a woman, born of a woman, nourished of a woman, obedient to a woman; and that he healed women, pardoned women, comforted women, yea, even when he was in his greatest agony and bloody sweat, going to be crucified, and also in the last hour of his death, took care to dispose of a woman; after his resurrection, appeared first to a woman, sent a woman to declare his most glorious resurrection to the rest of his disciples. Many other examples I could allege of diverse faithful and virtuous women, who have in all ages not only been confessors, but also endured most cruel martyrdom for their faith in Jesus Christ. All which is sufficient to enforce all good Christians and honourable-minded men to speak reverently of our sex, and especially of all virtuous and good women. To the modest censures of both which I refer these my imperfect endeavours, knowing that according to their own excellent dispositions they will rather cherish, nourish, and increase the least spark of virtue where they find it, by their favourable and best interpretations, than quench it by wrong constructions. To whom I wish with all increase of virtue, and desire their best opinions.

---

[1] *property* Habit.

[2] *vipers ... bred* It was thought that at birth the viper's young bit through the sides of the mother in order to be born, killing her.

[3] *pass current* Seem legitimate.

[4] *Deborah* Ruler of Israel who defeated the army of Sisera (Cesarius), a Canaanite general (see Judges 4).

[5] *Jael* Woman who killed Sisera by driving a tent peg through his head (see Judges 4).

[6] *Hester* Jewish queen (also called Esther) who saved the Jews from a genocidal plot concocted by Haman by appealing to Xerxes, King of Persia (see Esther 3–7).

[7] *Judith* Woman who killed the Babylonian general Holofernes by cutting off his head (see Judith 8–12).

[8] *Susanna* Woman who resisted the advances of two judges, who then unjustly charged her with adultery (see Daniel and Susanna 13).

from *Salve Deus Rex Judæorum*

"Invocation"

Sith° *Cynthia*[1] is ascended to that rest   *since*
Of endless joy and true eternity,
That glorious place that cannot be expressed
By any wight° clad in mortality,   *creature*
5 In her almighty love so highly blest,
And crowned with everlasting sovereignty;
    Where saints and angels do attend her throne,
    And she gives glory unto God alone.

To thee, great Countess,[2] now I will apply
10 My pen, to write thy never dying fame;
That when to heaven thy blessed soul shall fly,
These lines on earth record thy reverend name:
And to this task I mean my muse to tie,
Though wanting skill I shall but purchase blame:
15   Pardon (dear Lady) want of woman's wit
    To pen thy praise, when few can equal it.

*   *   *

"Eve's Apology in Defense of Women"

745 Now Pontius Pilate[3] is to judge the cause
Of faultless Jesus, who before him stands,
Who neither hath offended prince, nor laws,
Although he now be brought in woeful bands.
O noble governor, make thou yet a pause,
750 Do not in innocent blood inbrue° thy hands;[4]   *defile*
    But hear the words of thy most worthy wife,
    Who sends to thee, to beg her Savior's life.[5]

Let barb'rous cruelty far depart from thee,
And in true justice take affliction's part;
755 Open thine eyes, that thou the truth may'st see.
Do not the thing that goes against thy heart,
Condemn not him that must thy Savior be;
But view his holy life, his good desert.°   *merit*
    Let not us women glory in men's fall.[6]
760   Who had power given to overrule us all.

Till now your indiscretion sets us free.
And makes our former fault much less appear;
Our mother Eve, who tasted of the tree,[7]
Giving to Adam what she held most dear,
765 Was simply good, and had no power to see;
The after-coming harm did not appear:
    The subtle serpent that our sex betrayed
    Before our fall so sure a plot had laid.

That undiscerning ignorance perceived
770 No guile or craft that was by him intended;
For had she known of what we were bereaved,[8]
To his request she had not condescended.
But she, poor soul, by cunning was deceived;
No hurt therein her harmless heart intended:
775   For she alleged° God's word, which he[9] denies,   *affirmed*
    That they should die, but even as gods be wise.

But surely Adam cannot be excused;
Her fault though great, yet he was most to blame;
What weakness offered, strength might have refused,
780 Being lord of all, the greater was his shame.
Although the serpent's craft had her abused,
God's holy word ought all his actions frame,°   *shape*
    For he was lord and king of all the earth,
    Before poor Eve had either life or breath,

---

[1] *Cynthia* Goddess of the moon, often identified with Queen Elizabeth I, who died in 1603.

[2] *Countess* Margaret Clifford, Countess of Cumberland (1560–1616), Lanyer's patroness.

[3] *Pontius Pilate* Roman governor of Judea, who presided over the trial of Jesus (see Matthew 27.11–26).

[4] *Do … hands* Reference to Matthew 27.24, in which Pilate washes his hands to demonstrate that he does not consider himself responsible for what happens to Jesus.

[5] *hear … life* Pilate received a message from his wife, urging him not to convict Jesus (see Matthew 27.19).

[6] *men's fall* Fall into a sin, by crucifying Christ, greater than Eve's "original" sin.

[7] *Eve … tree* According to Genesis 3.6, Eve ate the fruit of the tree of the knowledge of good and evil. She shared the fruit with Adam, and as a consequence the two were banished from the Garden of Eden.

[8] *bereaved* Robbed (of eternal life).

[9] *he* I.e., the serpent (see Genesis 3.4–5).

785 Who being framed° by God's eternal hand   *formed*
    The perfectest man that ever breathed on earth;
    And from God's mouth received that strait° command, *strict*
    The breach whereof he knew was present death;
    Yea, having power to rule both sea and land,
790 Yet with one apple won to lose that breath[1]
        Which God had breathed in his beauteous face,
        Bringing us all in danger and disgrace.

    And then to lay the fault on Patience' back,
    That we (poor women) must endure it all.
795 We know right well he did discretion lack,
    Being not persuaded thereunto at all.
    If Eve did err, it was for knowledge sake;
    The fruit being fair persuaded him to fall:
        No subtle serpent's falsehood did betray him;
800   If he would eat it, who had power to stay° him?   *stop*

    Not Eve, whose fault was only too much love,
    Which made her give this present to her dear,
    That what she tasted he likewise might prove,°   *experience*
    Whereby his knowledge might become more clear;
805 He never sought her weakness to reprove
    With those sharp words which he of God did hear;
        Yet men will boast of knowledge, which he took
        From Eve's fair hand, as from a learned book.

    If any evil did in her remain,
810 Being made of him,[2] he was the ground of all.
    If one of many worlds[3] could lay a stain
    Upon our sex, and work so great a fall
    To wretched man by Satan's[4] subtle train,
    What will so foul a fault amongst you all?
815   Her weakness did the serpent's words obey,
        But you in malice God's dear Son betray,

    Whom, if unjustly you condemn to die,
    Her sin was small to what you do commit;
    All mortal sins that do for vengeance cry
820 Are not to be compared unto it.
    If many worlds would altogether try
    By all their sins the wrath of God to get,
        This sin of yours surmounts them all as far
        As doth the sun another little star.[5]

825 Then let us have our liberty again,
    And challenge° to yourselves no sovereignty.   *attribute*
    You came not in the world without our pain,
    Make that a bar against your cruelty;
    Your fault being greater, why should you disdain
830 Our being your equals, free from tyranny?
        If one weak woman simply did offend,
        This sin of yours hath no excuse nor end,

    To which, poor souls, we never gave consent.
    Witness, thy wife, O Pilate, speaks for all,
835 Who did but dream, and yet a message sent
    That thou shouldest have nothing to do at all
    With that just man[6] which, if thy heart relent,
    Why wilt thou be a reprobate[7] with Saul[8]
        To seek the death of him that is so good,
840   For thy soul's health to shed his dearest blood?

The Description of Cooke-ham[9]

Farewell (sweet Cooke-ham) where I first obtained
Grace from that grace where perfect grace remained;
And where the muses gave their full consent,

---

[1] *breath* God breathed life into Adam (see Genesis 2.7).

[2] *made ... him* According to Genesis 2.21–22, Eve was made from one of Adam's ribs.

[3] *many worlds* As the first man, Adam was the father of all humans. Human beings were sometimes likened to individual worlds in the literature of the time.

[4] *Satan's* Belonging to the serpent, traditionally identified with Satan.

[5] *sun ... star* As the sun outshines the other stars in the sky, so the sin of killing Jesus is greater in magnitude. In earlier understandings of astronomy, the sun was thought to be much larger than the stars.

[6] *just man* I.e., Jesus.

[7] *a reprobate* Damned.

[8] *Saul* King of Israel, who tried to kill David (see 1 Samuel 19.9–24).

[9] *Cooke-ham* Cookham Dean, a country house in Berkshire, UK, leased by the brother of Lanyer's patroness, Margaret Clifford, Countess of Cumberland.

I should have power the virtuous to content;
5   Where princely palace willed me to indite°   *write*
The sacred story of the soul's delight.[1]
Farewell (sweet place) where virtue then did rest,
And all delights did harbour in her breast;
Never shall my sad eyes again behold
10 Those pleasures which my thoughts did then unfold;
Yet you (great lady) mistress of that place,[2]
From whose desires did spring this work of grace,
Vouchsafe° to think upon these pleasures past   *are prepared*
As fleeting, worldly joys that could not last,
15 Or as dim shadows of celestial pleasures,
Which are desired above all earthly treasures.
Oh how (methought) against you thither came
Each part did seem some new delight to frame!
The house received all ornaments to grace it,
20 And would endure no foulness to deface it.
The walks put on their summer liveries,°   *uniforms*
And all things else did hold like similes:
The trees with leaves, with fruits, with flowers clad,
Embraced each other, seeming to be glad,
25 Turning themselves to beauteous canopies
To shade the bright sun from your brighter eyes;
The crystal streams with silver spangles graced,
While by the glorious sun they were embraced;
The little birds in chirping notes did sing,
30 To entertain both you and that sweet spring;
And Philomela[3] with her sundry lays,
Both you and that delightful place did praise.
Oh, how methought each plant, each flower, each tree
Set forth their beauties then to welcome thee;
35 The very hills right humbly did descend,
When you to tread upon them did intend.
And as you set your feet, they still did rise,
Glad that they could receive so rich a prize.
The gentle winds did take delight to be
40 Among those woods that were so graced by thee

And in sad murmur uttered pleasing sound,
That pleasure in that place might more abound;
The swelling banks delivered all their pride,
When such a phoenix once they had espied.
45 Each arbour, bank, each seat, each stately tree
Thought themselves honoured in supporting thee.
The pretty birds would oft come to attend thee,
Yet fly away for fear they should offend thee;
The little creatures in the burrow by
50 Would come abroad to sport them in your eye;[4]
Yet fearful of the bow in your fair hand
Would run away when you did make a stand.
Now let me come unto that stately tree,
Wherein such goodly prospects you did see;
55 That oak that did in height his fellows pass,
As much as lofty trees, low-growing grass;
Much like a comely cedar, straight and tall,
Whose beauteous stature far exceeded all;
How often did you visit this fair tree,
60 Which seeming joyful in receiving thee,
Would like a palm tree spread his arms abroad,
Desirous that you there should make abode;
Whose fair green leaves much like a comely veil
Defended Phoebus[5] when he would assail;
65 Whose pleasing boughs did lend a cool fresh air,
Joying his happiness when you were there;
Where being seated, you might plainly see
Hills, vales and woods, as if on bended knee
They had appeared, your honour to salute,
70 Or to prefer° some strange unlooked-for suit;°   *proffer / request*
All interlaced with brooks and crystal springs,
A prospect fit to please the eyes of kings;
And thirteen shires appear all in your sight,
Europe could not afford much more delight.
75 What was there then but gave you all content,
While you the time in meditation spent,
Of their creator's power, which there you saw
In all his creatures held a perfect law,
And in their beauties did you plain descry°   *discern*
80 His beauty, wisdom, grace, love, majesty.

---

[1] *sacred … delight   Salve Deus Rex Judaeorum*, to which this poem is appended.

[2] *you … place* Margaret Clifford, Countess of Cumberland (1560-1616).

[3] *Philomela* Nightingale. In Greek mythology, Philomela was a woman who was changed into a nightingale.

[4] *sport … eye* Entertain you.

[5] *Phoebus* Sun. "Phoebus" is an epithet for Apollo, Greek and Roman god of the sun.

In these sweet woods how often did you walk
With Christ and his apostles there to talk;
Placing his holy writ° in some fair tree,   *scripture*
To meditate what you therein did see;
85   With Moses you did mount his holy hill,[1]
To know his pleasure and perform his will.
With lovely David you did often sing,
His holy hymns to heaven's eternal king.[2]
And in sweet music did your soul delight,
90   To sound his praises, morning, noon and night.
With blessed Joseph you did often feed
Your pined brethren when they stood in need.[3]
And that sweet lady sprung from Clifford's race,
Of noble Bedford's blood, fair stem of grace,
95   To honourable Dorset now espoused,[4]
In whose fair breast true virtue then was housed;
Oh, what delight did my weak spirits find
In those pure parts of her well-framed mind;
And yet it grieves me that I cannot be
100   Near unto her, whose virtues did agree
With those fair ornaments of outward beauty,
Which did enforce from all both love and duty.
Unconstant fortune, thou art most to blame,
Who casts us down into so low a frame,°   *state*
105   Where our great friends we cannot daily see,
So great a difference is there in degree.°   *social status*
Many are placed in those orbs of state,
Parters° in honour, so ordained by fate,   *dividers*
Nearer in show, yet farther off in love,
110   In which the lowest always are above.
But whither am I carried in conceit?°   *thought*
My wit too weak to conster° of the great.   *understand*

Why not? although we are but born of earth,
We may behold the heavens, despising death;
115   And loving heaven that is so far above,
May in the end vouchsafe° us entire love.   *grant*
Therefore sweet memory, do thou retain
Those pleasures past, which will not turn again;
Remember beauteous Dorset's[5] summer sports,[6]
120   So far from being touched by ill reports;
Wherein myself did always bear a part,
While reverend love presented my true heart;
Those recreations let me bear in mind,
Which her sweet youth and noble thoughts did find;
125   Whereof deprived, I evermore must grieve,
Hating blind fortune, careless to relieve.
And you, sweet Cooke-ham, whom these ladies leave,
I now must tell the grief you did conceive
At their departure; when they went away,
130   How everything retained a sad dismay;
Nay long before, when once an inkling came,
Methought each thing did unto sorrow frame;
The trees that were so glorious in our view,
Forsook both flowers and fruit, when once they knew
135   Of your depart, their very leaves did wither,
Changing their colours as they grew together.
But when they saw this had no power to stay you,
They often wept, though speechless, could not pray you;
Letting their tears in your fair bosoms fall,
140   As if they said: "Why will ye leave us all?"
This being vain, they cast their leaves away,
Hoping that pity would have made you stay;
Their frozen tops, like age's hoary hairs,
Shows their disasters, languishing in fears;
145   A swarthy rivelled rine[7] all overspread
Their dying bodies, half-alive, half-dead.
But your occasions called you so away,
That nothing there had power to make you stay;
Yet did I see a noble, grateful mind,
150   Requiting each according to their kind;
Forgetting not to turn and take your leave
Of these sad creatures, powerless to receive

---

[1] *Moses … hill* In Exodus 24.9 Moses climbs Mount Sinai in order to see God.

[2] *With … king* David was then supposed to be the author of most or all of Psalms, songs written in praise of God.

[3] *With … need* Reference to Genesis 42.25, in which Joseph, as governor of Egypt, provides his deceitful brothers with food in order to save them from starvation.

[4] *sweet lady … espoused* Margaret Clifford's daughter, Lady Anne Clifford (1589–1675), married Richard Sackville, Earl of Dorset (1589–1624). Lady Anne's maternal grandfather was Francis Russell, Earl of Bedford (1527–85). A selection from her diary is in this anthology.

[5] *Dorset* Lady Anne Clifford.

[6] *summer sports* E.g., country dances and outdoor games.

[7] *rivelled rine* Wrinkled bark.

Your favour, when with grief you did depart,
Placing their former pleasures in your heart;
155 Giving great charge to noble memory,
There to preserve their love continually;
But specially the love of that fair tree,
That first and last you did vouchsafe to see;
In which it pleased you oft to take the air,
160 With noble Dorset, then a virgin fair;
Where many a learned book was read and scanned;
To this fair tree, taking me by the hand,
You did repeat the pleasures which had passed,
Seeming to grieve they could no longer last.
165 And with a chaste, yet loving kiss took leave,
Of which sweet kiss I did it soon bereave;°   rob
Scorning a senseless creature should possess
So rare a favour, so great happiness.
No other kiss it could receive from me,
170 For fear to give back what it took of thee;
So I, ungrateful creature, did deceive it,
Of that which you vouchsafed in love to leave it.
And though it oft had giv'n me much content,
Yet this great wrong I never could repent;
175 But of the happiest made it most forlorn,
To show that nothing's free from fortune's scorn,
While all the rest with this most beauteous tree,
Made their sad consort sorrow's harmony.
The flowers that on the banks and walks did grow,
180 Crept in the ground, the grass did weep for woe.
The winds and waters seemed to chide together,
Because you went away, they knew not whither.
And those sweet brooks that ran so fair and clear,
With grief and trouble wrinkled did appear.
185 Those pretty birds that wonted° were to sing,   accustomed
Now neither sing, nor chirp, nor use their wing;
But with their tender feet on some bare spray,°   branch
Warble forth sorrow, and their own dismay.
Fair Philomela leaves her mournful ditty,
190 Drowned in dead sleep, yet can procure no pity;
Each arbour, bank, each seat, each stately tree
Looks bare and desolate now, for want of thee;

Turning green tresses° into frosty grey,   hair
While in cold grief they wither all away.
195 The sun grew weak, his beams no comfort gave,
While all green things did make the earth their grave;
Each briar, each bramble, when you went away,
Caught fast your clothes, thinking to make you stay;
Delightful Echo,[1] wonted to reply
200 To our last words, did now for sorrow die;
The house cast off each garment that might grace it,
Putting on dust and cobwebs to deface it.
All desolation then there did appear,
When you were going whom they held so dear.
205 This last farewell to Cooke-ham here I give;
When I am dead thy name in this may live,
Wherein I have performed her noble hest,°   command
Whose virtues lodge in my unworthy breast,
And ever shall, so long as life remains,
210 Tying my heart to her by those rich chains.

To the Doubtful[2] Reader

Gentle reader, if thou desire to be resolved,[3] why I give this title, *Salve Deus Rex Judæorum*,[4] know for certain, that it was delivered unto me in sleep many years before I had any intent to write in this manner, and was quite out of my memory, until I had written the Passion of Christ, when immediately it came into my remembrance, what I had dreamed long before; and thinking it a significant token, that I was appointed to perform this work, I gave the very same words I received in sleep as the fittest title I could devise for this book.
—1611

---

1. *Echo* Nymph in Greek mythology who was prevented by a curse from saying anything other than what others said.

2. *Doubtful* Curious.

3. *be resolved* Understand.

4. *Salve ... Judæorum* Latin: Hail, God, King of the Jews.

Sir Walter Ralegh
1554 – 1618

Sir Walter Ralegh was one of the leading courtiers, adventurers, and literary figures of the Elizabethan era. Intermittently regarded as a hero and a traitor in his lifetime, Ralegh profited richly and suffered considerably from his proximity to Elizabeth I—but fared considerably worse after James I replaced Elizabeth on the throne. Known for his gallantry, for his fighting ability, for his effort at colonization in Virginia, and for bringing the practice of smoking tobacco into European culture, Ralegh was also the author of literary work that ranged from love poetry to exploration narratives to an unfinished history of the world.

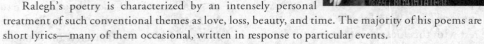

Born into the lesser gentry at Hayes Barton, Devon, Ralegh went to France in 1569 to fight for the Huguenots in the French religious civil wars. By 1572, he was studying at Oriel College, Oxford, only to leave over a year later without a degree. Ralegh finished his education in the Inns of Court, including Lyon's Inn and the Middle Temple, and it was during these years that his first poem was probably printed. It is often difficult to date or even attribute Ralegh's poems accurately, for like many courtiers, Ralegh generally circulated his verses in manuscript.

Ralegh's poetry is characterized by an intensely personal treatment of such conventional themes as love, loss, beauty, and time. The majority of his poems are short lyrics—many of them occasional, written in response to particular events.

After embarking with his stepbrother, Humphrey Gilbert, on an unsuccessful colonizing expedition to North America in 1578, Ralegh spent a year and a half fighting in Ireland. He returned to England in 1581 and caught the Queen's attention, eventually emerging as her new favorite and reaping substantial rewards, including a monopoly over wine licences in 1583 and a knighthood in 1585. A grant of 42,000 Irish acres on which to establish English colonists, made in 1587, brought Ralegh back to Ireland several times, and he was responsible for bringing an acquaintance, Edmund Spenser, back to England and introducing him to the Queen in 1589.

Ralegh's rapid rise to prominence at Elizabeth I's court was abruptly halted in 1592 after the discovery of his secret marriage to Elizabeth Throckmorton, one of the Queen's attendants. The Queen had him imprisoned in the Tower of London for several months—the occasion for his long poem, *The Ocean to Cynthia*, Ralegh's lament over Elizabeth's displeasure. This, Ralegh's most ambitious and sprawling poem, is a work that exists only in fragments, the longest of them over five hundred lines long. Five years elapsed before Ralegh was again in the Queen's good graces, a period during which he traveled to Guiana (1595), published a report on his adventures entitled *The Discoverie of the Large, Rich, and Bewtiful Empyre of Guiana* (1596), developed his Irish plantations, and participated in the attack on Cadiz (1596). Always critical of Spain's colonial and naval power, Ralegh never lost interest in North America, sponsoring reconnaissance and colonizing expeditions in the late 1580s to the areas now known as Virginia and the Carolinas.

Following James I's accession in 1603, Ralegh returned to the Tower of London for nearly thirteen years after a dubious treason conviction for allegedly supporting Arabella Stuart's claim to the throne. Rarely idle, Ralegh kept abreast of the political and intellectual climate during his imprisonment by entertaining numerous visitors (including James's son, Prince Henry), conducting scientific experiments, compounding drugs, and writing. His most notable work from this period is *The Historie of the World* (1614), a three-volume overview of world events from creation to the second century BCE. Ralegh was released in 1617 to make a second journey to Guiana in search of the gold mine that he claimed to have found on his first voyage. Returning empty-handed in 1618, he was imprisoned under his former sentence for disobeying James's orders to avoid any acts of violence against the Spanish, and then beheaded. Despite a reputation for unorthodoxy and even atheism, Ralegh made a pious if showy end and replied, when asked if he should not face east (toward Jerusalem), "What matter how the head lie, so the heart be right?"

⌘ ⌘ ⌘

A Vision Upon This Conceit of the Fairy Queen[1]

Methought I saw the grave where Laura[2] lay,
Within that temple where the vestal flame[3]
Was wont to burn: and, passing by that way,
To see that buried dust of living fame,
5 Whose tomb fair Love and fairer Virtue kept,
All suddenly I saw the Faery Queen,°   *Elizabeth I*
At whose approach the soul of Petrarch wept;
And from thenceforth those graces[4] were not seen,
For they this Queen attended; in whose stead
10 Oblivion laid him down on Laura's hearse.
Hereat the hardest stones were seen to bleed,
And groans of buried ghosts the heavens did pierce:
Where Homer's spright° did tremble all for grief,   *spirit*
And cursed the access[5] of that celestial thief.[6]
—1590

---

[1] *A Vision … Queen* Ralegh's poem was printed in the first edition of Spenser's *The Fairie Queene* (1590).

[2] *Laura* The subject of Petrarch's love poems of the fourteenth century.

[3] *vestal flame* Reference to the Roman goddess of the hearth, Vesta, whose temple was maintained by vestal virgins guarding an eternal flame.

[4] *those graces* I.e., "Fair Love and fairer Virtue."

[5] *access* To achieve an honour or office (accession).

[6] *Homer's spright … celestial thief* The Queen has usurped Laura's reputation for purity and chastity, and Spenser has stolen Petrarch's artistic legacy and even threatened the place of Homer in the literary pantheon; *Homer* Author of *The Iliad* and *The Odyssey*.

Detail from a portrait of Sir Walter Ralegh and His Son, 1602 (artist unknown).

Sir Walter Ralegh to His Son[7]

Three things there be that prosper up apace°   *quickly*
And flourish, whilst they grow asunder° far,   *apart*
But on a day, they meet all in one place,
And when they meet, they one another mar;°   *damage*

---

[7] *Sir Walter Ralegh to His Son* Ralegh's son, Wat, had a reputation for being wild. He died during his father's second voyage to Guiana.

5 And they be these: the wood, the weed, the wag.[1]
The wood is that which makes the gallow tree;
The weed is that which strings the hangman's bag;
The wag, my pretty knave, betokeneth thee.
Mark well, dear boy, whilst these assemble not,
10 Green springs the tree, hemp grows, the wag is wild,
But when they meet, it makes the timber rot,
It frets the halter, and it chokes the child.
Then bless thee, and beware, and let us pray
We part not with thee at this meeting day.
—c. 1600

The Nymph's Reply to the Shepherd [2]

If all the world and love were young,
And truth in every shepherd's tongue,
These pretty pleasures might me move
To live with thee and be thy love.

5 Time drives the flocks from field to fold
When rivers rage and rocks grow cold,
And Philomel[3] becometh dumb;
The rest complains of cares to come.

The flowers do fade, and wanton° fields   *unrestrained, unruly*
10 To wayward winter reckoning yields;
A honey tongue, a heart of gall,°   *bitterness, rancor*
Is fancy's spring, but sorrow's fall.

Thy gowns, thy shoes, thy beds of roses,
Thy cap, thy kirtle,° and thy posies   *tunic or skirt*
15 Soon break, soon wither, soon forgotten—
In folly ripe, in reason rotten.

Thy belt of straw and ivy buds,
Thy coral clasps and amber studs,

All these in me no means can move
20 To come to thee and be thy love.

But could youth last and love still breed,
Had joys no date nor age no need,[4]
Then these delights my mind might move
To live with thee and be thy love.
—1600

The Lie

Go, soul, the body's guest,
Upon a thankless errand;
Fear not to touch the best;
The truth shall be thy warrant.
5 Go, since I needs must die,
And give the world the lie.

Say to the court, it glows
And shines like rotten wood;
Say to the church, it shows
10 What's good, and doth no good.
If church and court reply,
Then give them both the lie.

Tell potentates° they live   *powerful rulers*
Acting by others' action;
15 Not loved unless they give,
Not strong but by a faction.
If potentates reply,
Give potentates the lie.

Tell men of high condition,
20 That manage the estate,°   *the state or body politic*
Their purpose is ambition,
Their practice only hate.
And if they once reply,
Then give them all the lie.

25 Tell them that brave it most,[5]
They beg for more by spending,

---

1 *wag* Joker, mischievous boy.

2 *The Nymph's … Shepherd* Response to Christopher Marlowe's "The Passionate Shepherd to His Love."

3 *Philomel* I.e., the nightingale doesn't sing. In classical mythology, Philomela, the daughter of the King of Athens, was transformed into a nightingale after being pursued and raped by her brother-in-law, Tereus, King of Thrace.

4 *Had joys … no need* If joys had no ending, and aging did not bring with it its own needs.

5 *brave it most* Dress extravagantly.

Who, in their greatest cost,
Seek nothing but commending.
And if they make reply,
30   Then give them all the lie.

Tell zeal it wants° devotion;   lacks
Tell love it is but lust;
Tell time it is but motion;
Tell flesh it is but dust.
35   And wish them not reply,
For thou must give the lie.

Tell age it daily wasteth;°   fades, diminishes
Tell honour how it alters;
Tell beauty how she blasteth;
40   Tell favour how it falters.
And as they shall reply,
Give every one the lie.

Tell wit° how much it wrangles   intelligence, understanding
In tickle points of niceness;[1]
45   Tell wisdom she entangles
Herself in overwiseness.
And when they do reply,
Straight give them both the lie.

Tell physic° of her boldness;°   medicine / presumption
50   Tell skill it is pretension;
Tell charity of coldness;
Tell law it is contention.
And as they do reply,
So give them still the lie.

55   Tell fortune of her blindness;
Tell nature of decay;
Tell friendship of unkindness;
Tell justice of delay.
And if they will reply,
60   Then give them all the lie.

Tell arts[2] they have no soundness,

But vary by esteeming;[3]
Tell schools[4] they want profoundness,
And stand too much on seeming.
65   If arts and schools reply,
Give arts and schools the lie.

Tell faith it's fled the city;
Tell how the country erreth;
Tell manhood shakes off pity
70   And virtue least preferreth.[5]
And if they do reply,
Spare not to give the lie.

So when thou hast, as I
Commanded thee, done blabbing—
75   Although to give the lie
Deserves no less than stabbing—[6]
Stab at thee he that will,
No stab the soul can kill.
—1608 (WRITTEN C. 1592)

Nature That Washed Her Hands in Milk

Nature that washed her hands in milk
And had forgot to dry them,
Instead of earth[7] took snow and silk,
At love's request to try° them,   test
5   If she a mistress could compose
To please love's fancy out of those.[8]

---

[1] wrangles ... niceness   To waste time with trivial, or overly subtle matters.

[2] arts   The seven liberal arts: grammar, rhetoric, logic, arithmetic, geometry, astronomy, and music; soundness   Freedom from weakness, based on fact.

[3] they have ... esteeming   They have no basis in solid and unchanging fact; they are subject to opinion.

[4] schools   Systems of philosophy.

[5] Tell manhood ... virtue least preferreth   Tell humanity that it refuses to feel pity, and that it prefers virtue less than all other things.

[6] Deserves no less than stabbing   To accuse someone of lying would likely cause a duel.

[7] Instead of earth   The Bible recounts the creation of Adam out of the dust of the earth. See Genesis 2.7.

[8] To please love's fancy out of those   At the request of love, Nature attempted to make a mistress out of snow and silk.

Her eyes he would° should be of light,   wanted
A violet breath and lips of jelly,
Her hair not black nor over-bright,
10   And of the softest down her belly;
As for her inside he would have it
Only of wantonness° and wit.°   sexual appetite / intelligence,
                                                      understanding

At love's entreaty, such a one
Nature made, but with her beauty
15   She hath framed a heart of stone,
So as love by ill destiny
Must die for her whom nature gave him
Because her darling would not save him.

But time, which nature doth despise,
20   And rudely gives her love the lie,[1]
Makes hope a fool, and sorrow wise,
His hands doth neither wash nor dry,
But being made of steel and rust,
Turns snow, and silk, and milk to dust.

25   The light, the belly, lips, and breath
He dims, discolors, and destroys,
With those he feeds, but fills not death,
Which sometimes were the food of joys;
Yea, time doth dull each lively wit
30   And dries all wantonness with it.

Oh cruel time which takes in trust
Our youth, our joys, and all we have,
And pays us but with age and dust,
Who in the dark and silent grave,
35   When we have wandered all our ways,
Shuts up the story of our days.[2]
                        —EARLY 17TH CENTURY

---

[1]   *gives … the lie*   Offers a challenge; in this period, to a duel.

[2]   *Oh cruel time … shuts up the story of our days*   The night before he died, Ralegh wrote this final stanza, with alterations, in his Bible. He changed the first three words to "Even such is time," and added a final couplet, "But from which earth and grave and dust / The Lord shall raise me up, I trust."

---

from *The Discovery of the Large, Rich, and Beautiful Empire of Guiana,*[3] *with a relation of the great and golden City of Manoa,*[4] *which the Spaniards call El Dorado …*

To the Right Honourable my singular good Lord and kinsman Charles Howard,[5] *Knight of the Garter, Baron, and Councillor, and of the Admirals of England the most renowned; and to the Right Honourable Sir Robert Cecil,*[6] *Knight, Councillor in her Highness's Privy Councils.*

PART 1, PREFACE

For your Honours' many honourable and friendly parts, I have hitherto only returned promises; and now, for answer of both your adventures,[7] I have sent you a bundle of papers, which I have divided between your Lordship and Sir Robert Cecil, in these two respects chiefly; first, for that it is reason that wasteful factors,[8] when they have consumed such stocks as they had in trust, do yield some colour[9] for the same in their account; secondly, for that I am assured that whatsoever shall be done, or written, by me, shall need a double protection

---

[3]   *Empire of Guiana*   Ralegh's Guiana is located predominately in the Orinoco basin of present-day eastern Venezuela.

[4]   *Manoa*   The European myth of El Dorado, "the gilded one," resulted from conflated reports of several indigenous peoples' practices. Once a year, a king, or a chief, was anointed with gold dust and paddled to the center of a lake, believed to be in an upland area beside the golden city of Manoa, where he would make gold offerings. The location of El Dorado, or Manoa, was variously held to be in Colombia, Surinam, Guyana, and Venezuela.

[5]   *Charles Howard*   Baron Howard of Effingham (1536–1624), Earl of Nottingham, Lord High Admiral, Commander-in-chief of the English fleet against the Spanish Armada in 1588. Howard contributed a ship, the *Lion's Whelp*, to Ralegh's expedition.

[6]   *Sir Robert Cecil*   Earl of Salisbury (1563–1612), Secretary of State. Although an ally of Ralegh's at the time of the Guiana expedition, Cecil would later turn James I against Ralegh by suggesting his involvement in the plot to place Arabella Stuart on the throne.

[7]   *adventures*   Commercial investments in Ralegh's voyage.

[8]   *factors*   Those who buy or sell for others, agents.

[9]   *colour*   Specious or plausible reason, pretext.

and defence. The trial that I had of both your loves, when I was left of all but of malice and revenge, makes me still presume that you will be pleased (knowing what little power I had to perform aught,[1] and the great advantage of forewarned enemies) to answer that out of knowledge, which others shall but object out of malice. In my more happy times as I did especially honour you both, so I found that your loves sought me out in the darkest shadow of adversity, and the same affection which accompanied my better fortune soared not away from me in my many miseries; all which though I cannot requite, yet I shall ever acknowledge; and the great debt which I have no power to pay, I can do no more for a time but confess to be due. It is true that as my errors were great, so they have yielded very grievous effects; and if aught might have been deserved in former times, to have counterpoised[2] any part of offences, the fruit thereof, as it seemeth, was long before fallen from the tree, and the dead stock only remained. I did therefore, even in the winter of my life, undertake these travails,[3] fitter for bodies less blasted with misfortunes, for men of greater ability, and for minds of better encouragement, that thereby, if it were possible, I might recover but the moderation of excess, and the least taste of the greatest plenty formerly possessed. If I had known other way to win, if I had imagined how greater adventures might have regained, if I could conceive what farther means I might yet use but even to appease so powerful displeasure,[4] I would not doubt but for one year more to hold fast my soul in my teeth till it were performed. Of that little remain I had, I have wasted in effect all herein. I have undergone many constructions;[5] I have been accompanied with many sorrows, with labour, hunger, heat, sickness, and peril; it appeareth, notwithstanding, that I made no other bravado of going to the sea, than was meant, and that I was never hidden in

Cornwall, or elsewhere, as was supposed. They have grossly belied me that forejudged that I would rather become a servant to the Spanish king than return; and the rest were much mistaken, who would have persuaded that I was too easeful and sensual to undertake a journey of so great travail. But if what I have done receive the gracious construction of a painful pilgrimage, and purchase the least remission,[6] I shall think all too little, and that there were wanting to the rest many miseries. But if both the times past, the present, and what may be in the future, do all by one grain of gall[7] continue in eternal distaste, I do not then know whether I should bewail myself, either for my too much travail and expense, or condemn myself for doing less than that which can deserve nothing. From myself I have deserved no thanks, for I am returned a beggar, and withered; but that I might have bettered my poor estate, it shall appear from the following discourse, if I had not only respected her Majesty's future honour and riches. ...

from PART 5

... To speak of what passed homeward were tedious, either to describe or name any of the rivers, islands, or villages of the Tivitivas, which dwell on trees; we will leave all those to the general map. And to be short, when we were arrived at the sea-side, then grew our greatest doubt, and the bitterest of all our journey forepassed; for I protest before God, that we were in a most desperate estate. For the same night which we anchored in the mouth of the river of Capuri, where it falleth into the sea, there arose a mighty storm, and the river's mouth was at least a league broad, so as we ran before night close under the land with our small boats, and brought the galley as near as we could. But she had as much ado to live as could be, and there wanted little of her sinking, and all those in her; for mine own part, I confess I was very doubtful which way to take, either to go over in the pestered[8] galley, there being but six foot water over the sands for two leagues together, and that also in the

---

[1] *aught* Anything.

[2] *counterpoised* Bring to or keep in a state of balance.

[3] *travails* Labor.

[4] *powerful displeasure* Ralegh's secret marriage to Elizabeth Throckmorton in 1592 incurred Queen Elizabeth's wrath; he was imprisoned in the Tower of London for several months and did not regain the queen's favor for some years.

[5] *constructions* Trials.

[6] *remission* Pardon.

[7] *gall* Bitterness, rancor.

[8] *pestered* Troubled.

channel, and she drew five; or to adventure in so great a billow, and in so doubtful weather, to cross the seas in my barge. The longer we tarried the worse it was, and therefore I took Captain Gifford, Captain Caulfield, and my cousin Greenvile into my barge; and after it cleared up about midnight we put ourselves to God's keeping, and thrust out into the sea, leaving the galley at anchor, who durst not adventure but by daylight. And so, being all very sober and melancholy, one faintly cheering another to shew courage, it pleased God that the next day about nine o'clock, we descried[1] the island of Trinidad; and steering for the nearest part of it, we kept the shore till we came to Curiapan, where we found our ships at anchor, than which there was never to us a more joyful sight.

Now that it hath pleased God to send us safe to our ships, it is time to leave Guiana to the sun, whom they worship, and steer away towards the north. I will, therefore, in a few words finish the discovery thereof. Of the several nations which we found upon this discovery I will once again make repetition, and how they are affected. At our first entrance into Amana, which is one of the outlets of the Orinoco, we left on the right hand of us in the bottom of the bay, lying directly against Trinidad, a nation of inhuman Cannibals, which inhabit the rivers of Guanipa and Berbeese.[2] In the same bay there is also a third river, which is called Areo, which riseth on Paria side towards Cumana, and that river is inhabited with the Wikiri, whose chief town upon the said river is Sayma. In this bay there are no more rivers but these three before rehearsed and the four branches of Amana, all which in the winter thrust so great abundance of water into the sea, as the same is taken up fresh two or three leagues from the land. In the passages towards Guiana, that is, in all those lands which the eight branches of the Orinoco fashion into islands, there are but one sort of people, called Tivitivas, but of two castes, as they term them, the one called Ciawani, the other Waraweeti,[3] and those war one with another.

On the hithermost[4] part of the Orinoco, as at Toparimaca and Winicapora, those are of a nation called Nepoios, and are the followers of Carapana, lord of Emeria. Between Winicapora and the port of Morequito, which standeth in Aromaia, and all those in the valley of Amariocapana are called Orenoqueponi, and did obey Morequito and are now followers of Topiawari. Upon the river of Caroli are the Canuri, which are governed by a woman who is inheritrix[5] of that province; who came far off to see our nation, and asked me divers questions of her Majesty, being much delighted with the discourse of her Majesty's greatness, and wondering at such reports as we truly made of her Highness' many virtues. And upon the head of Caroli and on the lake of Cassipa are the three strong nations of the Cassipagotos. Right south into the land are the Capurepani and Emparepani, and beyond those, adjoining to Macureguarai, the first city of Inca, are the Iwarawakeri. All these are professed enemies to the Spaniards, and to the rich Epuremei also. To the west of Caroli are divers nations of Cannibals and of those Ewaipanoma without heads. Directly west are the Amapaias and Anebas, which are also marvellous rich in gold. The rest towards Peru we will omit. On the north of the Orinoco, between it and the West Indies, are the Wikiri, Saymi, and the rest before spoken of, all mortal enemies to the Spaniards. On the south side of the main mouth of the Orinoco are the Arawaks; and beyond them, the Cannibals; and to the south of them, the Amazons.

To make mention of the several beasts, birds, fishes, fruits, flowers, gums, sweet woods, and of their several religions and customs, would for the first require as many volumes as those of Gesnerus,[6] and for the next another bundle of Decades.[7] The religion of the Epuremei is the same which the Incas, emperors of Peru, used, which may

---

[1] *descried* Caught sight of.

[2] *Berbeese* Berbice River in eastern Guyana.

[3] *Ciawani ... Waraweeti* Warao sub-groups, now called Siawani and Waraowitu.

[4] *hithermost* Nearest.

[5] *inheritrix* Female heiress.

[6] *Gesnerus* Conrad Gesner (1516–65), Swiss zoologist, author of *Historia animalium* (1551), a compilation of information, both ancient and contemporary, concerning animals.

[7] *bundle of Decades* Richard Eden's *The Decades of the Newe World of West India* (1555), was a translation of Pietro Martire d'Anghiera's *De Orbe Novo* (1511–30); the first printed book to use the name "America" is the anonymous *Of the newe landes* (1520).

be read in Cieza[1] and other Spanish stories; how they believe the immortality of the soul, worship the sun, and bury with them alive their best beloved wives and treasure, as they likewise do in Pegu[2] in the East Indies, and other places. The poni bury not their wives with them, but their jewels, hoping to enjoy them again. The Arawaks dry the bones of their lords, and their wives and friends drink them in powder. In the graves of the Peruvians the Spaniards found their greatest abundance of treasure. The like, also, is to be found among these people in every province. They have all many wives, and the lords five-fold to the common sort. Their wives never eat with their husbands, nor among the men, but serve their husbands at meals and afterwards feed by themselves. Those that are past their younger years make all their bread and drink, and work their cotton-beds, and do all else of service and labour; for the men do nothing but hunt, fish, play, and drink, when they are out of the wars.

I will enter no further into discourse of their manners, laws, and customs. And because I have not myself seen the cities of Inca I cannot avow on my credit what I have heard, although it be very likely that the emperor Inca hath built and erected as magnificent palaces in Guiana as his ancestors did in Peru; which were for their riches and rareness most marvellous, and exceeding all in Europe, and, I think, of the world, China excepted, which also the Spaniards, which I had, assured me to be true, as also the nations of the borderers, who, being but savages to those of the inland, do cause much treasure to be buried with them. For I was informed of one of the caciques of the valley of Amariocapana which had buried with him a little before our arrival a chair of gold most curiously wrought, which was made either in Macureguarai adjoining or in Manoa. But if we should have grieved them in their religion at the first, before they had been taught better, and have digged up their graves, we had lost them all. And therefore I held my first resolution, that her Majesty should either accept or refuse the enterprise before anything should be done that might in any sort hinder the

same. And if Peru had so many heaps of gold, whereof those Incas were princes, and that they delighted so much therein, no doubt but this which now liveth and reigneth in Manoa hath the same humour,[3] and, I am assured, hath more abundance of gold within his territory than all Peru and the West Indies.

For the rest, which myself have seen, I will promise these things that follow, which I know to be true. Those that are desirous to discover and to see many nations may be satisfied within this river, which bringeth forth so many arms and branches leading to several countries and provinces, above 2,000 miles east and west and 800 miles south and north, and of these the most either rich in gold or in other merchandises. The common soldier shall here fight for gold, and pay himself, instead of pence, with plates of half-a-foot broad, whereas he breaketh his bones in other wars for provant[4] and penury. Those commanders and chieftains that shoot at honour and abundance shall find there more rich and beautiful cities, more temples adorned with golden images, more sepulchres[5] filled with treasure, than either Cortés[6] found in Mexico or Pizarro[7] in Peru. And the shining glory of this conquest will eclipse all those so far-extended beams of the Spanish nation. There is no country which yieldeth more pleasure to the inhabitants, either for those common delights of hunting, hawking, fishing, fowling, and the rest, than Guiana doth; it hath so many plains, clear rivers, and abundance of pheasants, partridges, quails, rails, cranes, herons, and all other fowl; deer of all sorts, porks, hares, lions, tigers, leopards, and divers other sorts of beasts, either for chase or food. It hath a kind of beast called cama or anta,[8] as big as an English beef, and in great plenty. To speak of the several sorts of every kind I fear would be troublesome to the reader, and therefore I will omit them, and conclude that both for health, good

---

[1] *Cieza* Pedro Cieza de Leon (1518?–60), Spanish soldier and explorer, author of *Chronicle of Peru* (1553?).

[2] *Pegu* Capital of the United Burmese kingdom during the sixteenth century.

[3] *humour* State of mind.

[4] *provant* Allowance of food.

[5] *sepulchres* Tombs.

[6] *Cortés* Hernán Cortés (1485–1547), Spanish conquistador, conqueror of Mexico.

[7] *Pizarro* Francisco Pizarro (1476–1541), Spanish conquistador, conqueror of Peru.

[8] *anta* Tapir.

air, pleasure, and riches, I am resolved it cannot be equalled by any region either in the east or west. Moreover the country is so healthful, as of an hundred persons and more, which lay without shift most sluttishly, and were every day almost melted with heat in rowing and marching, and suddenly wet again with great showers, and did eat of all sorts of corrupt fruits, and made meals of fresh fish without seasoning, of tortugas,[1] of lagartos or crocodiles, and of all sorts good and bad, without either order or measure, and besides lodged in the open air every night, we lost not any one, nor had one ill-disposed to my knowledge; nor found any calentura[2] or other of those pestilent diseases which dwell in all hot regions, and so near the equinoctial line.

Where there is store of gold it is in effect needless to remember other commodities for trade. But it hath, towards the south part of the river, great quantities of brazil-wood,[3] and divers berries that dye a most perfect crimson and carnation; and for painting, all France, Italy, or the East Indies yield none such. For the more the skin is washed, the fairer the colour appeareth, and with which even those brown and tawny women spot themselves and colour their cheeks. All places yield abundance of cotton, of silk, of balsamum,[4] and of those kinds most excellent and never known in Europe, of all sorts of gums, of Indian pepper; and what else the countries may afford within the land we know not, neither had we time to abide the trial and search. The soil besides is so excellent and so full of rivers, as it will carry sugar, ginger, and all those other commodities which the West Indies have.

The navigation is short, for it may be sailed with an ordinary wind in six weeks, and in the like time back again; and by the way neither lee-shore,[5] enemies' coast, rocks, nor sands. All which in the voyages to the West Indies and all other places we are subject unto; as the channel of Bahama, coming from the West Indies, cannot well be passed in the winter, and when it is at the best, it is a perilous and a fearful place; the rest of the Indies for calms and diseases very troublesome, and the sea about the Bermudas a hellish sea for thunder, lightning, and storms.

This very year (1595) there were seventeen sail of Spanish ships lost in the channel of Bahama, and the great Philip, like to have sunk at the Bermudas, was put back to St. Juan de Puerto Rico; and so it falleth out in that navigation every year for the most part. Which in this voyage are not to be feared; for the time of year to leave England is best in July, and the summer in Guiana is in October, November, December, January, February, and March, and then the ships may depart thence in April, and so return again into England in June. So as they shall never be subject to winter weather, either coming, going, or staying there: which, for my part, I take to be one of the greatest comforts and encouragements that can be thought on, having, as I have done, tasted in this voyage by the West Indies so many calms, so much heat, such outrageous gusts, such weather, and contrary winds.

To conclude, Guiana is a country that hath yet her maidenhead,[6] never sacked, turned, nor wrought;[7] the face of the earth hath not been torn, nor the virtue and salt of the soil spent by manurance. The graves have not been opened for gold, the mines not broken with sledges, nor their images pulled down out of their temples. It hath never been entered by any army of strength, and never conquered or possessed by any Christian prince. It is besides so defensible, that if two forts be builded in one of the provinces which I have seen, the flood setteth in so near the bank, where the channel also lieth, that no ship can pass up but within a pike's length of the artillery, first of the one, and afterwards of the other. Which two forts will be a sufficient guard both to the empire of Inca, and to an hundred other several kingdoms, lying within the said river, even to the city of Quito in Peru.

There is therefore great difference between the easiness of the conquest of Guiana, and the defence of it being conquered, and the West or East Indies. Guiana

---

[1] *tortugas* Turtles.

[2] *calentura* Disease experienced by sailors in the tropics, characterized by fever and delirium.

[3] *brazil-wood* Brownish hardwood used to make a red dye.

[4] *balsamum* Aromatic resin of the balsam tree used for medicines.

[5] *lee-shore* Shore on which the wind blows.

[6] *maidenhead* Literally, hymen; i.e., Guiana is still a virgin country.

[7] *wrought* Worked.

hath but one entrance by the sea, if it hath that, for any vessels of burden. So as whosoever shall first possess it, it shall be found unaccessible for any enemy, except he come in wherries, barges, or canoes, or else in flat-bottomed boats; and if he do offer to enter it in that manner, the woods are so thick 200 miles together upon the rivers of such entrance, as a mouse cannot sit in a boat unhit from the bank. By land it is more impossible to approach; for it hath the strongest situation of any region under the sun, and it is so environed with impassable mountains on every side, as it is impossible to victual any company in the passage. Which hath been well proved by the Spanish nation, who since the conquest of Peru have never left five years free from attempting this empire, or discovering some way into it; and yet of three-and-twenty several gentlemen, knights, and noblemen, there was never any that knew which way to lead an army by land, or to conduct ships by sea, anything near the said country. Orellana,[1] of whom the river of the Amazon taketh name, was the first, and Don Antonio de Berreo, whom we displanted, the last: and I doubt much whether he himself or any of his yet know the best way into the said empire. It can therefore hardly be regained, if any strength be formerly set down, but in one or two places, and but two or three crumsters[2] or galleys built and furnished upon the river within. The West Indies have many ports, watering places, and landings; and nearer than 300 miles to Guiana, no man can harbour a ship, except he know one only place, which is not learned in haste, and which I will undertake there is not any one of my companies that knoweth, whosoever hearkened most after it.

Besides, by keeping one good fort, or building one town of strength, the whole empire is guarded; and whatsoever companies shall be afterwards planted within the land, although in twenty several provinces, those shall be able all to reunite themselves upon any occasion either by the way of one river, or be able to march by land

without either wood, bog, or mountain. Whereas in the West Indies there are few towns or provinces that can succour or relieve one the other by land or sea. By land the countries are either desert, mountainous, or strong enemies. By sea, if any man invade to the eastward, those to the west cannot in many months turn against the breeze and eastern wind. Besides, the Spaniards are therein so dispersed as they are nowhere strong, but in Nueva Espana only; the sharp mountains, the thorns, and poisoned prickles, the sandy and deep ways in the valleys, the smothering heat and air, and want of water in other places are their only and best defence; which, because those nations that invade them are not victualled or provided to stay, neither have any place to friend adjoining, do serve them instead of good arms and great multitudes.

The West Indies were first offered her Majesty's grandfather[3] by Columbus, a stranger, in whom there might be doubt of deceit; and besides it was then thought incredible that there were such and so many lands and regions never written of before. This Empire is made known to her Majesty by her own vassal,[4] and by him that oweth to her more duty than an ordinary subject; so that it shall ill sort with the many graces and benefits which I have received to abuse her Highness, either with fables or imaginations. The country is already discovered, many nations won to her Majesty's love and obedience, and those Spaniards which have latest and longest laboured about the conquest, beaten out, discouraged, and disgraced, which among these nations were thought invincible. Her Majesty may in this enterprise employ all those soldiers and gentlemen that are younger brethren, and all captains and chieftains that want employment, and the charge will be only the first setting out in victualling and arming them; for after the first or second year I doubt not but to see in London a Contractation-House[5] of more receipt for Guiana than there is now in Seville

---

[1] *Orellana* Francesco de Orellana was the first Spaniard to descend the entire length of the Amazon river in 1541–42. Orellana renamed the river "Amazon" from "Marañon" after encountering a group of female warriors.

[2] *crumsters* Merchant ships used as warships that accompanied Spanish galleons. The crumster could carry a great deal of cargo and firepower.

[3] *her Majesty's grandfather* Bartholomew Columbus, brother of Christopher, approached Henry VII of England to raise money for Columbus's western route to India, but Columbus had already contracted his services to Queen Isabella of Spain.

[4] *vassal* Humble servant.

[5] *Contractation-House* Seville's Casa de Contractacion controlled all aspects of the Spanish trade with the Americas.

for the West Indies.

And I am resolved that if there were but a small army afoot in Guiana, marching towards Manoa, the chief city of Inca, he would yield to her Majesty by composition so many hundred thousand pounds yearly as should both defend all enemies abroad, and defray all expenses at home; and that he would besides pay a garrison of three or four thousand soldiers very royally to defend him against other nations. For he cannot but know how his predecessors, yea, how his own great uncles, Guascar and Atabalipa,[1] sons to Guiana-Capac, emperor of Peru, were, while they contended for the empire, beaten out by the Spaniards, and that both of late years and ever since the said conquest, the Spaniards have sought the passages and entry of his country; and of their cruelties used to the borderers he cannot be ignorant. In which respects no doubt but he will be brought to tribute with great gladness; if not, he hath neither shot nor iron weapon in all his empire, and therefore may easily be conquered.

And I further remember that Berreo confessed to me and others, which I protest before the Majesty of God to be true, that there was found among the prophecies in Peru, at such time as the empire was reduced to the Spanish obedience, in their chiefest temples, amongst divers others which foreshadowed the loss of the said empire, that from Inglatierra[2] those Incas should be again in time to come restored, and delivered from the servitude of the said conquerors. And I hope, as we with these few hands have displanted the first garrison, and driven them out of the said country, so her Majesty will give order for the rest, and either defend it, and hold it as tributary,[3] or conquer and keep it as empress of the same. For whatsoever prince shall possess it, shall be greatest; and if the King of Spain enjoy it, he will become unresistible. Her Majesty hereby shall confirm and strengthen the opinions of all nations as touching her great and princely actions. And where the south border of Guiana reacheth to the dominion and empire of the Amazons, those women shall hereby hear the name of a virgin, which is not only able

to defend her own territories and her neighbours, but also to invade and conquer so great empires and so far removed.

To speak more at this time I fear would be but troublesome: I trust in God, this being true, will suffice, and that he which is King of all Kings, and Lord of Lords, will put it into her heart which is Lady of Ladies to possess it. If not, I will judge those men worthy to be kings thereof, that by her grace and leave will undertake it of themselves.

—1596

Letter to His Wife[4]

You shall now receive (my deare wife) my last words in these last lines. My love I send you that you may keep it when I am dead, and my councell that you may remember it when I am no more. I would not by my will present you with sorrowes (dear Besse) let them go to the grave with me and be buried in the dust. And seeing that it is not Gods will that I should see you any more in this life, beare it patiently, and with a heart like thy selfe.

First, I send you all the thankes which my heart can conceive, or my words can rehearse for your many travailes, and care taken for me, which though they have not taken effect as you wished, yet my debt to you is not the lesse: but I pay it I never shall in this world.

Secondly, I beseech you for the love you beare me living, do not hide your selfe many dayes, but by your travailes seeke to helpe your miserable fortunes and the right of your poor childe. Thy mourning cannot availe me, I am but dust.

Thirdly, you shall understand, that my land was conveyed *bona fide*[5] to my childe; the writings were

original spelling

---

[1] *Atabalipa* Atahualpa.

[2] *Inglatierra* England.

[3] *tributary* I.e., tributary nation, one which pays tribute in the form of goods or money to a sovereign nation.

[4] *Letter to His Wife* The following letter was written after Ralegh had been convicted of attempting to conspire against the Crown, and sent to the Tower of London; he believed he would be executed the next day. That did not happen, but he did remain imprisoned in the Tower for most of the rest of his life, and was finally executed in 1618.

[5] *bona fide* Latin: in good faith.

drawne[1] at midsumer was twelve months, my honest cosen Brett can testify so much, and Dolberry too, can remember somewhat therein. And I trust my blood will quench their malice that have cruelly murthered me: and that they will not seek also to kill thee and thine with extreme poverty.

To what friend to direct thee I know not, for all mine have left me in the true time of tryall. And I perceive that my death was determined from the first day. Most sorry I am God knowes that being thus surprised with death I can leave you in no better estate. God is my witnesse I meant you all my office of wines or all that I could have purchased by selling it, halfe of my stuffe, and all my jewels, but some one for the boy, but God hath prevented all my resolutions. That great God that ruleth all in all, but if you live free from want, care for no more, for the rest is but vanity. Love God, and begin betimes to repose your selfe upon him, have travailed and wearied your thoughts over all sorts of worldly cogitations, you shall but sit downe by sorrowe in the end.

Teach your son also to love and feare God while he is yet young, that the feare of God may grow with him, and then God will be a husband to you, and a father to him; a husband and a father which cannot be taken from you.

Baily oweth me 200 pounds, and Adrian Gilbert 600. In Jersey I also have much owing me besides. The arrearages of the wines will pay my debts. And howsoever you do, solues sake,[2] pay all poore men. When I am gone, no doubt you shall be sought for my many, for the world thinkes that I was very rich. But take heed of the pretences of men, and their affections, for they last not but in honest and worthy men, and no greater misery

can befall you in this life, than to become a prey, and afterwards to be despised. I speake not this (God knowes) to dissuade you from marriage, for it will be best for you, both in respect of the world and of God. As for me, I am no more yours, nor you mine, death hath cut us asunder: and God hath divided me from the world, and your from me.

Remember your poor childe for his father's sake, who chose you, and loved you in his happiest times. Get those letters (if it be possible) which I write to the Lords, wherein I sued for my life: God is my witnesse it was for you and yours that I desired life, but it is true that I disdained my self for begging of it: for know it (my deare wife) that your son is the son of a true man, and one who in his owne respect despiseth death and all his misshapen & ugly formes.

I cannot write much, God he knows how hardly I steale time while others sleep, and it is also time that I should separate my thoughts from the world. Begg my dead body which living was denied thee; and either lay it at Sherburne (and if the land continue) or in Exeter-Church, by my Father and Mother; I can say no more, time and death call me away.

The everlasting God, powerfull, infinite, and omnipotent God, That Almighty God, who is goodnesse it selfe, the true life and true light keep thee and thine: have mercy on me, and teach me to forgive my persecutors and false accusers, and send us to meet in his glorious Kingdome. My deare wife farewell. Blesse my poore boy. Pray for me, and let my good God hold you both in his arms.

Written with the dying hand of sometimes thy Husband, but now alasse overthrowne.

Yours that was, but now not my own.

Walter Rawleigh

—1603

---

[1]   *the writings were drawne*   The documents were made out.

[2]   *solues sake*   So long as you are solvent.

Francis Bacon
1561 – 1626

Philosopher, essayist, jurist, politician, naturalist, classicist, historian, and utopian fantasist, Francis Bacon had an extraordinary capacity to range throughout the world of learning while keeping a focus on the practical uses of knowledge, able not only to master the traditions of the past but also

to combine, manipulate, and consolidate old concepts into fruitful new ideas. His essays, memorable distillations of his wide reading and worldly experience, are still widely read and enjoyed. His philosophical writings, in both Latin and English, aim at nothing less than the reformation of humanity's approach to understanding nature and society. Ironically, it can be hard for us now, reading from the other side of the revolution he helped accelerate, to appreciate the full impact of Bacon's philosophy. He did not fully develop what some call "the scientific method" or anticipate the crucial role of mathematics in later scientific developments. What he did accomplish, in his philosophy and in his often terse style (deliberately free, usually, from flights of metaphor or fancy), was to anchor the mind more firmly in experience and to lend momentum to a new sense of worldly inquiry and expectation. It would be unfair to hold him responsible, as some have done, for the dangers and excesses inherent in modern science and its assumptions; indeed, in *The New Atlantis* Bacon himself hints presciently that increased power over nature should be accompanied by increased love and gratitude.

"I had rather studied books than men," Bacon concluded late in his life, but his origins made vast ambitions in both the political and intellectual spheres seem almost inevitable. His father, Sir Nicholas Bacon, was Lord Keeper of the Great Seal, one of the most powerful ministers in the Elizabethan government. His mother, Ann Cook, was an erudite and devout Calvinist who instilled in her son a deep sense of purpose and a passion for knowledge. Cambridge student at twelve, Assistant to the Ambassador to France at sixteen, barrister and Member of Parliament by the age of twenty-three, Bacon achieved much early, but his father's untimely death in 1579 left him short of funds and without direct influence at court. He was not well liked by Elizabeth, and it was not until the accession of James I that his star began to rise. Knighted in 1603, he was appointed Solicitor General in 1607, Attorney General in 1613, Privy Councillor in 1616, Lord Keeper of the Seal in 1617, and finally Lord Chancellor in 1618, acquiring along the way the titles of Baron Verulam and Viscount St. Albans. "By indignities men come to dignities," Bacon wrote in his essay "Of Great Place"—conscious, no doubt, of the reputation for sycophancy and scheming he had acquired in his quest for power and position—and "the standing is slippery." In 1621, Bacon lost his political footing. Caught on the wrong side of a dispute between Parliament and his ally the Duke of Buckingham, he pleaded guilty to accepting bribes and was expelled for life from public office. The bribes do not seem to have dulled Bacon's keen legal mind: John Aubrey could report fifty years later that "there are fewer of his decrees reversed than of any other Chancellor." Bacon was variously denounced as a spendthrift, a calculating politician, and a homosexual who had married the heiress Alice Barnham in 1606 merely for money (and had disinherited her in his last will), but he was also respected as an able administrator and advisor and a consummate orator whose audiences, Ben Jonson testified, were unwilling to accept that his speeches must end.

Until his death in 1626 (reputedly from a chill caught while investigating the preservative properties of snow), Bacon concentrated on expanding and refining his intellectual project. A third edition of his *Essays* appeared in 1625 with a new subtitle, *Counsels, Civil and Moral*. Bacon was the first to import the term "essai" into English from Montaigne for this new form, but as the subtitle indicates, his orientation was more public and impersonal than Montaigne's, based more in the tradition of the commonplace book and the manual of conduct than in discursive meditation. The first edition of 1597 was composed of terse, aphoristic observations organized under ten topics. The final edition of 1625 had grown to 58 essays. The overall style is one of brevity, curtness, and sagacity, with fluid transitions between subjects. Bacon employs to great effect aphoristic devices such as observations in parallel series of twos and threes, and he is fond of antitheses, "the case exaggerated both ways, with the utmost force of the wit," which have the effect of encouraging a balanced consideration of the issues by the reader. A notable exception is "Of Gardens," in which Bacon, an avid gardener, indulges in a didactic and uncharacteristically opinionated exhortation concerning his lifelong passion.

To the end of his life Bacon pursued another passion, his grand design for the renewal of knowledge, the Great Instauration, which he had already outlined in the preface to his aphoristic Latin treatise *Novum Organum* (New Instrument) in 1620. Only a few of the many volumes he conceived for this project were actually completed, though others exist in partial form, or as prefaces or proposals. He wrote many of these in Latin, still considered the international language of scholarship. Bacon now expanded and translated *The Advancement of Learning*, which had appeared in English in 1605, as *De Augmentis*. Its vital innovation was a reclassification of knowledge so as to separate theology from natural philosophy. Bacon was no atheist, but he insisted that the deductive, syllogistic methods applied by the Aristotelian Schoolmen to theological speculation would not succeed in unlocking nature's secrets. Rather than perceiving the natural world through the lens of unproven axioms and generalizations, we must begin with nature itself, gathering facts, sorting and analyzing them using inductive methods, and only then deriving principles which may be used to enhance further investigation: "Nature cannot be commanded except by being obeyed."

In fact, the pure induction favored by Bacon did not suffice for fruitful experimental investigation; the scientific method still needs room for intuitive guesses and intermediate deduction. But if Bacon's methodology and philosophy was not in accord with twenty-first century practices, he was certainly rhetorically skillful and inspiring on the topic to a degree unmatched by his contemporaries. His *New Atlantis*, a fragment written in 1610 and published after his death in 1626, imagines in vivid and beguiling detail a utopian community of dynamic technical and spiritual progress founded upon bureaucratic and co-operative science. The power of Bacon's prose fired the imagination of seventeenth-century English readers and sparked widespread public interest in scientific undertakings. In 1662, the Royal Society, the first concrete realization of Bacon's dream of a scientific bureaucracy, acclaimed him as their model and prophet; a century later, Diderot adopted Bacon's classification of learning and dedicated the Encyclopedia to him, as did Kant his *Critique of Pure Reason*. Bacon's ambition, announced in *The Advancement of Learning*, to "ring a bell to call other wits together," has been fulfilled.

⌘⌘⌘

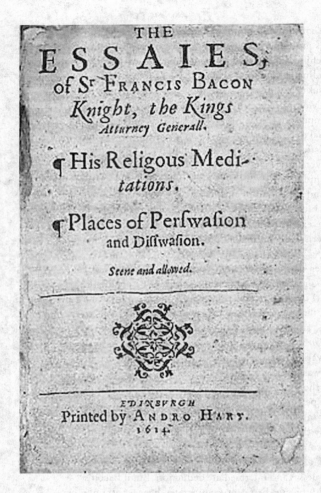

Title page of the 1614 edition of Bacon's *Essays*.

from *Essays*

OF TRUTH

"What is truth?" said jesting Pilate,[1] and would not stay for an answer. Certainly there be that delight in giddiness, and count it a bondage to fix a belief; affecting free-will in thinking, as well as in acting. And though the sects of philosophers of that kind[2] be gone, yet there remain certain discoursing wits, which are of the same veins, though there be not so much blood in them, as was in those of the ancients. But it is not only the difficulty and labor which men take in finding out of truth, nor again that when it is found it imposeth upon men's thoughts, that doth bring lies in favor; but a natural though corrupt love of the lie itself. One of the later school of the Grecians examineth the matter,[3] and is at a stand to think what should be in it, that men should love lies, where neither they make for pleasure, as with poets, nor for advantage, as with the merchant; but for the lie's sake. But I cannot tell: this same truth is a naked and open day-light, that doth not show the masks and mummeries and triumphs[4] of the world half so stately and daintily as candle-lights. Truth may perhaps come to the price of a pearl, that showeth best by day; but it will not rise to the price of a diamond or carbuncle,[5] that showeth best in varied lights. A mixture of a lie doth ever add pleasure.

Doth any man doubt, that if there were taken out of men's minds vain opinions, flattering hopes, false valuations, imaginations as one would, and the like, but it would leave the minds of a number of men poor shrunken things, full of melancholy and indisposition,[6] and unpleasing to themselves? One of the fathers, in

---

[1] *What is truth* Cf. John 18.38; *Pilate* Pontius Pilate, Roman governor of Judea from 26–36 CE, who presided over Christ's trial.

[2] *of that kind* I.e., Skepticism, a mid-fourth century BCE philosophy positing the uncertainty of all knowledge.

[3] *One of … matter* See the *Philopseudes* (*The Lover of Lies*) by Lucian of Samosata (c. 120–180 CE).

[4] *masks* I.e., masques, elaborate court pageants; *mummeries* Popular plays or ceremonies; *triumphs* Ceremonial processions of victorious military commanders and their forces.

[5] *carbuncle* Ruby.

[6] *melancholy* Brooding sadness; in Bacon's day the word could also denote neurosis; *indisposition* Hesitancy or reluctance.

great severity, called poesy *vinum daemonum*,[1] because it filleth the imagination; and yet it is but with the shadow of a lie. But it is not the lie that passeth through the mind, but the lie that sinketh in and settleth in it, that doth the hurt; such as we spake of before. But howsoever these things are thus in men's depraved judgments and affections, yet truth, which only doth judge itself, teacheth that the inquiry of truth, which is the love-making, or wooing of it, the knowledge of truth, which is the presence of it, and the belief of truth, which is the enjoying of it, is the sovereign good of human nature.

The first creature of God, in the works of the days, was the light of the sense; the last, was the light of reason; and His sabbath work[2] ever since, is the illumination of his Spirit. First He breathed light upon the face of the matter or chaos; then He breathed light into the face of man; and still He breatheth and inspireth light into the face of His chosen. The poet that beautified the sect that was otherwise inferior to the rest[3] saith yet excellently well: "It is a pleasure to stand upon the shore, and to see ships tossed upon the sea; a pleasure to stand in the window of a castle, and to see a battle and the adventures thereof below: but no pleasure is comparable to the standing upon the vantage ground of Truth" (a hill not to be commanded, and where the air is always clear and serene), "and to see the errors, and wanderings, and mists, and tempests, in the vale below";[4] so always that this prospect be with pity, and not with swelling or pride. Certainly, it is heaven upon earth to have a man's mind move in charity, rest in Providence, and turn upon the poles of truth.

To pass from theological, and philosophical truth to the truth of civil business; it will be acknowledged even by those that practise it not that clear and round[5] dealing is the honor of man's nature; and that mixture of falsehood is like alloy in coin of gold and silver, which may make the metal work the better, but it embaseth[6] it. For these winding and crooked courses are the goings of the serpent, which goeth basely upon the belly, and not upon the feet. There is no vice that doth so cover a man with shame as to be found false and perfidious. And therefore Montaigne[7] saith prettily, when he inquired the reason, why the word of the lie should be such a disgrace and such an odious charge? Saith he, "If it be well weighed, to say that a man lieth, is as much to say, as that he is brave towards God and a coward towards men."[8] For a lie faces God, and shrinks from man. Surely the wickedness of falsehood and breach of faith cannot possibly be so highly expressed, as in that it shall be the last peal to call the judgments of God upon the generations of men; it being foretold, that when Christ cometh, "He shall not find faith upon the earth."[9]

Of Marriage and Single Life

He that hath wife and children hath given hostages to fortune; for they are impediments to great enterprises, either of virtue or mischief. Certainly the best works, and of greatest merit for the public, have proceeded from the unmarried or childless men; which both in affection and means have married and endowed the public. Yet it were great reason that those that have children should have greatest care of future times; unto which they know they must transmit their dearest pledges. Some there are, who though they lead a single life, yet their thoughts do end with themselves, and account future times impertinences.[10] Nay, there are

---

[1] *One of ... fathers* St. Augustine (354–430 CE) or St. Jerome (340?–420 CE); *vinum daemonum* Latin: wine of devils. This reference likely combines passages from St. Jerome's Epistle 146 and St. Augustine's *Confessions* 1.16.26.

[2] *sabbath work* God's work on the seventh ("sabbath") day, here imagined as the ongoing period of divine rest after the initial six days' work of creation. Bacon's paradox is that God "works" daily even if rigorous Puritans objected to all labor on the Sabbath.

[3] *The poet* Lucretius (c. 99–c. 55 BCE), Roman poet who expressed the Epicurean world view in his *De Rerum Natura* (*On the Nature of Things*); *the sect ... rest* The Epicureans, philosophers who taught that the highest pursuit involved avoiding pain and pursuing pleasures, which they identified with the practice of virtue.

[4] *"It is ... below"* Cf. Lucretius's *De Rerum Natura* 2.1–13.

[5] *round* Honest.

[6] *alloy* Metal added to strengthen gold or silver; *embaseth* Makes less pure.

[7] *Montaigne* Michel de Montaigne (1533–1592), French writer commonly credited as the originator of the personal essay.

[8] *"If it ... men"* Cf. Montaigne's *Essays* 2.18, "Of Giving the Lie."

[9] *"He shall ... earth"* Cf. Luke 18.8.

[10] *impertinences* Things that are trivial and irrelevant.

some other that account wife and children but as bills of charges. Nay more, there are some foolish rich covetous men, that take a pride in having no children, because they may be thought so much the richer. For perhaps they have heard some talk, "Such an one is a great rich man," and another except[1] to it, "Yea, but he hath a great charge of children"; as if it were an abatement[2] to his riches. But the most ordinary cause of a single life is liberty, especially in certain self-pleasing and humorous minds, which are so sensible of every restraint, as they will go near to think their girdles and garters[3] to be bonds and shackles.

Unmarried men are best friends, best masters, best servants; but not always best subjects; for they are light to run away; and almost all fugitives are of that condition. A single life doth well with churchmen; for charity will hardly water the ground where it must first fill a pool. It is indifferent for judges and magistrates; for if they be facile[4] and corrupt, you shall have a servant five times worse than a wife. For soldiers, I find the generals commonly in their hortatives[5] put men in mind of their wives and children; and I think the despising of marriage amongst the Turks maketh the vulgar soldier more base. Certainly wife and children are a kind of discipline of humanity; and single men, though they may be many times more charitable, because their means are less exhaust, yet, on the other side, they are more cruel and hardhearted (good to make severe inquisitors), because their tenderness is not so oft called upon. Grave natures, led by custom, and therefore constant, are commonly loving husbands; as was said of Ulysses, *vetulam suam praetulit immortalitati.*[6] Chaste women are often proud and froward,[7] as presuming upon the merit of their chastity. It is one of the best bonds both of chastity and obedience in the wife, if she

think her husband wise; which she will never do if she find him jealous. Wives are young men's mistresses; companions for middle age; and old men's nurses. So as a man may have a quarrel to marry when he will. But yet he was reputed one of the wise men,[8] that made answer to the question, when a man should marry?—"A young man not yet, an elder man not at all." It is often seen that bad husbands have very good wives; whether it be that it raiseth the price of their husband's kindness when it comes; or that the wives take a pride in their patience. But this never fails, if the bad husbands were of their own choosing, against their friends' consent; for then they will be sure to make good their own folly.

OF STUDIES
(1597 version)

Studies serve for pastimes, for ornaments and for abilities. Their chiefe use for pastime is in privateness and retiring; for ornamente is in discourse, and for abilitie is in judgement. For expert men can execute, but learned men are fittest to judge or censure.

To spend too much time in them is slouth, to use them too much for ornament is affectation: to make judgement wholly by their rules, is the humour of a Scholler.

They perfect *Nature*, and are perfected by experience.

Craftie men contemn them, simple men admire them, wise men use them: For they teach not their owne use, but that is a wisedome without them: and above them wonne by observation.

Reade not to contradict, nor to believe, but to waigh and consider.

Some bookes are to bee tasted, others are to bee swallowed, and some few to bee chewed and disgested: That is, some bookes are to be read only in partes; others to be read, but cursorily, and some few to be read wholly and with diligence and attention.

---

[1] *except* Object.

[2] *abatement* Reduction.

[3] *humorous* Fanciful, whimsical; *girdles* Belts; *garters* Bands that keep stockings from coming down.

[4] *facile* Yielding, compliant.

[5] *hortatives* Speeches meant to exhort or encourage.

[6] *Ulysses* Wily, well-traveled character of Greek legend, his story is told variously in the *Iliad*, the *Odyssey* and the *Aeneid; vetulam … immortalitati* Latin: he preferred his old wife to immortality.

[7] *froward* Headstrong and obstinate.

[8] *he … wise men* Thales (b. seventh century BCE), one of the Seven Sages of ancient Greece. When a young man was asked by his mother when he would marry, he reputedly responded, "I'm too young," and when an older man, responded to the same question, "I am too old."

original spelling

original spelling

Reading maketh a full man, conference a readye man, and writing an exacte man. And therefore if a man write little, he had neede have a great memorie, if he conferre little, he had neede have a present wit, and if he reade little, hee had neede have much cunning, to seeme to know that he doth not.

Histories make men wise, Poets wittie: the Mathematickes subtle, naturall Phylosophie deepe: Morall grave, Logicke and Rhetoricke able to contend.

OF STUDIES
(1625 version)

Studies serve for delight, for ornament, and for ability. Their chief use for delight, is in privateness and retiring; for ornament, is in discourse;[1] and for ability, is in the judgment and disposition of business. For expert men can execute, and perhaps judge of particulars, one by one; but the general counsels, and the plots and marshalling of affairs, come best from those that are learned. To spend too much time in studies is sloth; to use them too much for ornament, is affectation; to make judgment wholly by their rules, is the humor of a scholar. They perfect nature, and are perfected by experience: for natural abilities are like natural plants, that need pruning by study; and studies themselves do give forth directions too much at large, except they be bounded in by experience. Crafty men contemn[2] studies, simple men admire them, and wise men use them; for they teach not their own use; but that is a wisdom without them, and above them, won by observation. Read not to contradict and confute; nor to believe and take for granted; nor to find talk and discourse; but to weigh and consider. Some books are to be tasted, others to be swallowed, and some few to be chewed and digested; that is, some books are to be read only in parts; others to be read but not curiously;[3] and some few to be read wholly, and with diligence and attention. Some books also may be read by deputy,[4] and

extracts made of them by others; but that would be only in the less important arguments, and the meaner[5] sort of books; else distilled books are like common distilled waters, flashy[6] things. Reading maketh a full man; conference a ready man; and writing an exact man. And therefore, if a man write little, he had need have a great memory; if he confer little, he had need have a present wit: and if he read little, he had need have much cunning, to seem to know that he doth not. Histories make men wise; poets witty; the mathematics subtle; natural philosophy deep; moral grave; logic and rhetoric able to contend. *Abeunt studia in mores.*[7] Nay there is no stond or impediment in the wit, but may be wrought[8] out by fit studies; like as diseases of the body may have appropriate exercises. Bowling is good for the stone and reins;[9] shooting for the lungs and breast; gentle walking for the stomach; riding for the head; and the like. So if a man's wit be wandering, let him study the mathematics; for in demonstrations, if his wit be called away never so little, he must begin again. If his wit be not apt to distinguish or find differences, let him study the schoolmen;[10] for they are *cymini sectores.*[11] If he be not apt to beat over matters, and to call up one thing to prove and illustrate another, let him study the lawyers' cases. So every defect of the mind, may have a special receipt.[12]

OF LOVE

The stage is more beholding to love, than the life of man. For as to the stage, love is ever matter of comedies, and now and then of tragedies; but in life it doth much mischief; sometimes like a siren, sometimes

---

[1] *retiring* Removing oneself from public life; *discourse* Conversation.

[2] *crafty* Artful, cunning; *contemn* Scorn.

[3] *curiously* Carefully, attentively.

[4] *by deputy* Second-hand, as in extracts or commentaries.

[5] *meaner* More common, less significant.

[6] *distilled waters* Medicinal waters made from plant and vegetable essences; *flashy* Dull, tasteless.

[7] *Abeunt ... mores* Latin: Studies influence manners; see Ovid's *Heroides* 15.83.

[8] *stond* Obstacle; *wrought* Worked.

[9] *stone and reins* Kidney stones and the kidneys.

[10] *schoolmen* Medieval scholastic theologians and philosophers, whose practices were characterized by systematic rigor.

[11] *cymini sectores* Latin: dividers of cumin seeds. I.e., close and careful arguers; hair-splitters.

[12] *receipt* Recipe, prescription.

like a fury.[1] You may observe, that amongst all the great and worthy persons whereof the memory remaineth, either ancient or recent, there is not one that hath been transported to the mad degree of love: which shows that great spirits and great business do keep out this weak passion. You must except nevertheless Marcus Antonius, the half-partner of the empire of Rome, and Appius Claudius, the decemvir[2] and lawgiver; whereof the former was indeed a voluptuous man, and inordinate;[3] but the latter was an austere and wise man: and therefore it seems (though rarely) that love can find entrance not only into an open heart, but also into a heart well fortified, if watch be not well kept. It is a poor saying of Epicurus, *Satis magnum alter alteri theatrum sumus;*[4] as if man, made for the contemplation of heaven and all noble objects, should do nothing but kneel before a little idol, and make himself a subject, though not of the mouth (as beasts are), yet of the eye; which was given him for higher purposes.

It is a strange thing to note the excess of this passion, and how it braves the nature and value of things, by this: that the speaking in a perpetual hyperbole is comely[5] in nothing but in love. Neither is it merely in the phrase; for whereas it hath been well said that the arch-flatterer, with whom all the petty flatterers have intelligence,[6] is a man's self; certainly the lover is more. For there was never proud man thought so absurdly well of himself, as the lover doth of the person loved; and therefore it was well said, that "it is impossible to love and to be wise."[7] Neither doth this weakness appear to others only, and not to the party loved; but to the loved most of all, except the love be reciproque.[8] For it is a true rule, that love is ever rewarded either with the reciproque or with an inward and secret contempt. By how much the more men ought to beware of this passion, which loseth not only other things, but itself. As for the other losses, the poet's relation doth well figure them; that he that preferred Helena, quitted the gifts of Juno and Pallas.[9] For whosoever esteemeth too much of amorous affection quitteth both riches and wisdom.

This passion hath his floods in very times of weakness, which are great prosperity and great adversity, though this latter hath been less observed: both which times kindle love, and make it more fervent, and therefore show it to be the child of folly. They do best, who if they cannot but admit love, yet make it keep quarter,[10] and sever it wholly from their serious affairs, and actions of life; for if it check[11] once with business, it troubleth men's fortunes, and maketh men that they can no ways be true to their own ends. I know not how, but martial men are given to love: I think it is but as they are given to wine; for perils commonly ask to be paid in pleasures. There is in man's nature a secret inclination and motion towards love of others, which if it be not spent upon some one or a few, doth naturally spread itself towards many, and maketh men become humane and charitable; as it is seen sometime in friars. Nuptial love maketh mankind; friendly love perfecteth it; but wanton love corrupteth and embaseth[12] it.

—1625

---

[1] *siren* One of the mythical sea nymphs who lure sailors to destruction with their sweet singing voices; *fury* One of the three winged goddesses of Greek mythology who punish those who commit unavenged crimes.

[2] *Marcus Antonius* Roman general (83–30 BCE) known for his disastrous love affair with Cleopatra, the Egyptian queen; *Appius Claudius* Leader of the Roman Republic (c. fifth century BCE), whose love affair with Verginia led to his murder (by her father), which incited a commoner revolt; *decemvir* One of ten officials responsible for administration in the Roman Republic. This term literally means "man of ten."

[3] *voluptuous* Devoted to sensuality or pleasure; *inordinate* Disorderly.

[4] *Epicurus* Ancient Greek philosopher (341–270 BCE) who founded Epicureanism, the philosophy that advocated avoiding pain and pursuing pleasure, which he linked to virtue; *Satis magnum … sumus* Latin: Each of us is enough of an audience for another. See Seneca, *Epistles,* 7.2.

[5] *comely* Pleasing.

[6] *intelligence* Communication.

[7] *it is … wise* Classical saying most notably quoted in Bacon's time in Erasmus's *Adagia.*

[8] *reciproque* Reciprocal.

[9] *he … Helena* Paris, who chose Venus's prize (the love of Helen) over the power and riches offered by Juno and the wisdom offered by Minerva; *Helena* Helen of Troy, reputedly the most beautiful woman in the world, whose abduction by Paris spurred the Trojan War between Greece and Troy; *quitted* Renounced; *Juno* Queen of the Gods and wife of Jupiter in the Roman pantheon; *Pallas* Athena in the Greek tradition, or Minerva in the Roman, goddess of wisdom.

[10] *keep quarter* Keep to its own place.

[11] *check* Collides.

[12] *embaseth* Degrades.

Christopher Marlowe
1564 – 1593

Christopher Marlowe's small body of work—seven plays, as well as a number of poems written during six productive years—profoundly influenced the course of English Renaissance drama. His plays set precedents for English history plays, tragedy, and heroic drama, while his newly supple and powerful blank verse (unrhymed iambic pentameter) impressed Ben Jonson as Marlowe's "mighty line." Had his writing career not been cut so short by a lethal tavern brawl he might have rivaled Shakespeare as the finest dramatist of his age.

Marlowe was born in Canterbury on 26 February 1564, in the same year as Shakespeare. His father was a shoemaker and a bondsman but also an actor; his mother was the daughter of a clergyman—and both theater and theology would help shape him. Despite his father's fairly humble occupation, Marlowe was well educated, first at King's School, in Canterbury, and then at Cambridge University's Corpus Christi College. His education at Cambridge, which was paid for by a foundation set up by Matthew Parker, Archbishop of Canterbury, included history, philosophy, and the theology of the Protestant Reformation, one version of which, despite a large and sometimes surreptitiously active Catholic minority, was now the orthodoxy of the officially established Church of England. In 1584 he earned his B.A.

During the latter part of his time at Cambridge, Marlowe frequently disappeared for extended periods. It is likely, some historians believe, that Marlowe had been recruited as a spy by Queen Elizabeth's Privy Council, which had longstanding fears of subversive Catholic activity at home and abroad. He spent time in the French city of Rheims, a refuge for many English Catholic expatriates, and perhaps helped uncover a Catholic plot to assassinate Elizabeth. This theory is strengthened by the actions of the Council upon Marlowe's return to England. Marlowe applied for his M.A., a degree normally granted automatically upon application once a certain amount of time had elapsed since the granting of a B.A., but the university refused him on multiple grounds. Not only had Marlowe failed to pursue ordination after his theological studies (as was expected of theology students); he had also spent considerable time among Catholics in France, and was therefore suspected of Catholic sympathies. Marlowe asked the Privy Council to intercede on his behalf and it obliged by sending a letter to the Cambridge authorities indicating that Marlowe "had done Her Majesty good service, & deserved to be rewarded for his faithful dealing." Moreover, says the letter severely, "it was not Her Majesty's pleasure that anyone employed, as [Marlowe] had been, in matters touching the benefit of his country, should be defamed by those that are ignorant in th' affairs he went about." Marlowe was granted his M.A. in 1587.

In the same year, Marlowe left Cambridge and moved to London to pursue his career as a playwright. His London years were marked by violence. In 1589 he spent two weeks in Newgate Prison, charged with the murder of one William Bradley, although he was acquitted and released, and in 1592 court records indicate that he was implicated in a street fight in which another man was killed. Through these same years, however, Marlowe's career soared. He had the luxury of being hired by the Lord Admiral's Company, which meant that the finest of London's actors would perform his plays. His first major plays, including *Tamburlaine the Great*—a grandiloquently written and violence-filled play—were produced in 1587 and were wildly popular. Over the next six years Marlowe completed at least five more plays: *The Jew of Malta* (c.1589), *Edward II* (c.1592), *The Massacre of Paris* (printed c. 1593), *Dido, Queen of Carthage* (printed in 1594), and *The Tragical History of Doctor Faustus* (?1593). In recent decades *Edward II* has drawn critical notice for its ambivalent portrayal of homoerotic love in conflict with political and marital duty, while the darkly comic *Jew of Malta*, whose Christians are quite as wicked as the Jewish protagonist, is significant in understanding early modern English views of the Jew as "other." *Faustus*, however, remains the most widely read and performed of Marlowe's plays. Based on an old Czech and German legend, the play presents a scholar who sells his soul to the devil in exchange for knowledge and power. As always, this proves a bad bargain: Faustus fritters away his power on pointless magic tricks and must, eventually, disappear in anguish into Hell. Marlowe's sympathies are hard to identify: the play may be read as orthodox (the anti-Catholic humor would not displease audiences or ecclesiastical authorities in England) but it may also raise difficult questions about free will and an implacable God.

Marlowe is also known for his poetry, including translations from Lucan's *Pharsalia* and Ovid's *Amores*. His most famous English poems are the unfinished "Hero and Leander," a tragic love story lightened by witty rhymes, outrageous metaphors, and a view of erotic love at once skeptical and sympathetic, and "The Passionate Shepherd to His Love," a poem based in part on Virgil's homoerotic Second Eclogue (Marlowe's version was soon treated as entirely heterosexual but recent criticism has noted its ambiguity in this regard). Unfortunately, piecing together Marlowe's *oeuvre* is a complicated matter. We have, for example, two quite different versions of *Doctor Faustus* (1604 and 1616).

Marlowe's death on 30 May 1593 has been the subject of much controversy. According to the coroner's report, Marlowe and a number of his acquaintances were dining at Eleanor Bull's House, a tavern just outside London. A heated argument arose between Marlowe and a fellow diner, Ingram Frizer, over the bill. The report states that Marlowe attacked Frizer with a knife and injured him on the back of the head. Frizer wrested the knife from Marlowe's grasp and sank its blade two inches into Marlowe's skull, just above the right eye. Marlowe died instantly. Was there a conspiracy behind this? Marlowe had maintained connections from his spying days and at the time of his death was in the presence of men with connections to his former employer, Sir Francis Walsingham, who as Secretary of State was responsible for the government's intelligence operations. Marlowe had recently been arrested on charges of atheism (an imprecisely defined offence which could be laid against anyone expressing unorthodox theological opinions) and was due to go on trial in a few days. Some scholars have speculated that members of the government feared that Marlowe would identify other "atheists" in high positions or perhaps reveal espionage secrets should he appear in a court of law, and so had him assassinated.

Marlowe was buried in an unmarked grave on the grounds of St. Nicholas's Church, Deptford, on 1 June 1593. Not until July 2002, more than 400 years after he died, was he memorialized in the prestigious Poet's Corner of Westminster Abbey.

⌘ ⌘ ⌘

Hero and Leander

O n Hellespont,[1] guilty of true-loves' blood,
In view and opposite, two cities stood,
Sea-borderers, disjoined by Neptune's[2] might;
The one Abydos,[3] the other Sestos[4] hight.°   *named*
5   At Sestos Hero dwelt; Hero the fair,
Whom young Apollo[5] courted for her hair,
And offered as a dower his burning throne,
Where she should sit for men to gaze upon.
The outside of her garments were of lawn,[6]
10   The lining purple silk, with gilt stars drawn;
Her wide sleeves green, and bordered with a grove
Where Venus in her naked glory strove
To please the careless and disdainful eyes
Of proud Adonis, that before her lies;[7]
15   Her kirtle° blue, whereon was many a stain,   *skirt*
Made with the blood of wretched lovers slain.
Upon her head she ware° a myrtle wreath,   *wore*
From whence her veil reached to the ground beneath.
Her veil was artificial flowers and leaves,
20   Whose workmanship both man and beast deceives;
Many would praise the sweet smell as she passed,
When 'twas the odor which her breath forth cast;
And there for honey, bees have sought in vain,
And, beat from thence, have lighted there again.
25   About her neck hung chains of pebble-stone,
Which, lightened° by her neck, like diamonds shone. *lit up*
She ware no gloves, for neither sun nor wind
Would burn or parch her hands, but to her mind[8]
Or° warm or cool them, for they took delight   *either*
30   To play upon those hands, they were so white.

Buskins° of shells all silvered usèd she,   *boots*
And branched with blushing coral to the knee,
Where sparrows perched, of hollow pearl and gold,
Such as the world would wonder to behold;
35   Those with sweet water oft her handmaid fills,
Which, as she went, would chirrup through the bills.
Some say, for her the fairest Cupid pined,
And looking in her face, was strooken° blind.   *struck*
But this is true: so like was one the other,
40   As he imagined Hero was his mother;[9]
And oftentimes into her bosom flew,
About her naked neck his bare arms threw,
And laid his childish head upon her breast,
And with still° panting rocked, there took his rest. *continual*
45   So lovely fair was Hero, Venus' nun,[10]
As Nature wept, thinking she was undone,
Because she took more from her than she left
And of such wondrous beauty her bereft;
Therefore, in sign her treasure suffered wrack,
50   Since Hero's time hath half the world been black.
Amorous Leander, beautiful and young,
(Whose tragedy divine Musaeus[11] sung)
Dwelt at Abydos; since him dwelt there none
For whom succeeding times make greater moan.
55   His dangling tresses that were never shorn,
Had they been cut and unto Colchos[12] borne,
Would have allured the vent'rous youth of Greece
To hazard more than for the Golden Fleece.
Fair Cynthia[13] wished his arms might be her sphere;° *orbit*
60   Grief makes her pale, because she moves not there.
His body was as straight as Circe's wand;[14]
Jove might have sipped out nectar from his hand.
Even as delicious meat is to the taste,
So was his neck in touching, and surpassed

---

[1] *Hellespont*   Narrow strait in Turkey between the Aegean Sea and the Marmara sea, now called the Dardanelles. One bank lies in Europe, one in Asia.

[2] *Neptune*   Roman god of the sea.

[3] *Abydos*   Ancient city on the Asian bank.

[4] *Sestos*   Ancient city on the European bank.

[5] *Apollo*   Greek and Roman sun god.

[6] *lawn*   Fine linen.

[7] *bordered ... lies*   Description of an embroidered pattern depicting the story of Venus and Adonis, told by both the Roman writer Ovid in his *Metamorphoses* (1 CE) and by Shakespeare in his *Venus and Adonis* (1593).

[8] *to her mind*   As she chose.

[9] *Hero ... mother*   Cupid's mother was Venus, Roman goddess of love and beauty.

[10] *Venus' nun*   Hero was a priestess of Venus.

[11] *Musaeus*   Greek poet (fifth century CE) who wrote an early version of the Hero and Leander story.

[12] *Colchos*   Colchis, a country now in western Georgia, where the Argonauts (the "vent'rous youths") were said to have found the Golden Fleece.

[13] *Cynthia*   Moon.

[14] *Circe's wand*   In Homer's *Odyssey*, Circe turns Odysseus's crew into pigs with her wand.

65 The white of Pelops' shoulder.[1] I could tell ye
How smooth his breast was, and how white his belly,
And whose immortal fingers did imprint
That heavenly path, with many a curious° dint,   *artful*
That runs along his back; but my rude[2] pen
70 Can hardly blazon forth the loves of men,
Much less of powerful gods; let it suffice
That my slack° muse sings of Leander's eyes,   *weak*
Those orient° cheeks and lips, exceeding his   *lustrous*
That leapt into the water for a kiss
75 Of his own shadow, and despising many,
Died ere he could enjoy the love of any.[3]
Had wild Hippolytus[4] Leander seen,
Enamored of his beauty had he been;
His presence made the rudest peasant melt,
80 That in the vast uplandish country dwelt;
The barbarous Thracian soldier, moved with naught,
Was moved with him, and for his favor sought.
Some swore he was a maid in man's attire,
For in his looks were all that men desire:
85 A pleasant smiling cheek, a speaking° eye,   *expressive*
A brow for love to banquet royally;
And such as knew he was a man, would say,
"Leander, thou art made for amorous play;
Why art thou not in love, and loved of all?
90 Though thou be fair, yet be not thine own thrall."
    The men of wealthy Sestos every year,
For his sake whom their goddess held so dear,
Rose-cheeked Adonis,[5] kept a solemn feast.
Thither resorted many a wandering guest
95 To meet their loves; such as had none at all
Came lovers home from this great festival;
For every street, like to a firmament,
Glistered with breathing stars, who, where they went,

Frighted the melancholy earth, which deemed
100 Eternal heaven to burn, for so it seemed
As if another Phaëton[6] had got
The guidance of the sun's rich chariot.
But, far above the loveliest, Hero shined,
And stole away th' enchanted gazer's mind;
105 For like sea nymphs'[7] inveigling harmony,
So was her beauty to the standers by.
Nor that night-wandering pale and watery star[8]
(When yawning dragons draw her thirling° car   *hurtling*
From Latmos' mount[9] up to the gloomy sky,
110 Where, crowned with blazing light and majesty,
She proudly sits) more over-rules the flood
Than she the hearts of those that near her stood.
Even as when gaudy nymphs pursue the chase,°   *hunt*
Wretched Ixion's shaggy-footed race,[10]
115 Incensed with savage heat, gallop amain
From steep pine-bearing mountains to the plain,
So ran the people forth to gaze upon her,
And all that viewed her were enamored on her.
And as in fury of a dreadful fight,
120 Their fellows being slain or put to flight,
Poor soldiers stand with fear of death dead-strooken,
So at her presence all, surprised and tooken,
Await the sentence of her scornful eyes;
He whom she favors lives, the other dies.
125 There might you see one sigh, another rage,
And some, their violent passions to assuage,
Compile sharp satires; but alas, too late,
For faithful love will never turn to hate.
And many, seeing great princes were denied,
130 Pined as they went, and thinking on her, died.
On this feast day, oh, cursèd day and hour!
Went Hero thorough° Sestos, from her tower   *through*
To Venus' temple, where unhappily,
As after chanced, they did each other spy.
135 So fair a church as this had Venus none;

---

[1] *Pelops' shoulder* In Ovid, Pelops was cut into pieces by his father, Tantalus, and served to the gods. The gods put him back together, except for his shoulder, which had already been eaten. They fashioned a new one out of ivory for him.

[2] *rude* Lacking in elegance.

[3] *his … any* Reference to Narcissus, who fell in love with his own reflection in the water and drowned.

[4] *Hippolytus* Exceedingly beautiful young man in Greek mythology.

[5] *Adonis* Beautiful boy beloved by Aphrodite, Greek goddess of love.

[6] *Phaëton* Son of the Greek sun god Apollo. Phaëton drives the sun chariot so badly that Zeus blasts him from the sky.

[7] *sea nymphs* I.e., the Sirens.

[8] *night-wandering … star* Moon.

[9] *Latmos' mount* Diana, the Greek moon goddess, nightly visited her sleeping beloved Eudymion on Mount Latmos.

[10] *Ixion's … race* Centaurs, fathered by Ixion, who was condemned to be bound to a burning wheel for all eternity.

The walls were of discolored° jasper stone,   *multicolored*
Wherein was Proteus[1] carvèd, and o'erhead
A lively° vine of green sea-agate spread,   *lifelike*
Where, by one hand, light-headed Bacchus[2] hung,
140 And with the other, wine from grapes out-wrung.
Of crystal shining fair the pavement was;
The town of Sestos called it Venus' glass;°   *mirror*
There might you see the gods in sundry shapes,
Committing heady riots, incest, rapes:
145 For know that underneath this radiant floor
Was Danaë's statue in a brazen tower,
Jove slyly stealing from his sister's bed
To dally with Idalian Ganymede,
And for his love Europa bellowing loud,
150 And tumbling with the rainbow in a cloud;[3]
Blood-quaffing Mars heaving the iron net
Which limping Vulcan and his Cyclops set;[4]
Love kindling fire to burn such towns as Troy;[5]
Silvanus weeping for the lovely boy[6]
155 That now is turned into a cypress tree,
Under whose shade the wood-gods love to be.
And in the midst a silver altar stood;
There Hero sacrificing turtles'[7] blood,
Vailed° to the ground, veiling her eyelids close,   *bowed*
160 And modestly they opened as she rose;
Thence flew love's arrow with the golden head,
And thus Leander was enamorèd.
Stone still he stood, and evermore he gazed,
Till with the fire that from his countenance blazed,

---

[1] *Proteus* Greek lesser sea god able to change his shape rapidly.

[2] *Bacchus* Greek god of wine.

[3] *Danaë's ... cloud* Chronicle of the amorous exploits of Zeus (called Jove in Roman mythology). He impregnated Danaë as a shower of gold while she was locked in a tower, married his sister Juno, kidnapped the beautiful young man Ganymede on Mount Ida, seduced Europa while in the form of a bull, and had a tryst with Iris, goddess of the rainbow (although this last conquest is a Renaissance addition to the myth).

[4] *Blood ... set* Vulcan, god of fire, used a net to catch his wife Venus in an affair with Mars, god of war. The Cyclopes were his assistants.

[5] *Love ... Troy* Paris's abduction of Helen of Troy caused the Trojan Wars.

[6] *lovely boy* Cyparissus, who was turned into a cypress tree by Apollo.

[7] *turtles* Turtledoves, a symbol of fidelity.

165 Relenting Hero's gentle heart was strook;
Such force and virtue° hath an amorous look.   *power*
    It lies not in our power to love or hate,
For will in us is overruled by fate.
When two are stripped, long ere the course[8] begin
170 We wish that one should lose, the other win;
And one especially do we affect°   *prefer*
Of two gold ingots, like in each respect.
The reason no man knows, let it suffice,
What we behold is censured° by our eyes.   *judged*
175 Where both deliberate, the love is slight;
Who ever loved, that loved not at first sight?[9]
    He kneeled, but unto her devoutly prayed.
Chaste Hero to herself thus softly said,
"Were I the saint he worships, I would hear him,"
180 And as she spake those words, came somewhat near him.
He started up; she blushed as one ashamed,
Wherewith Leander much more was inflamed.
He touched her hand; in touching it she trembled:
Love deeply grounded hardly is dissembled.[10]
185 These lovers parlèd° by the touch of hands;   *spoke*
True love is mute, and oft amazèd stands.
Thus, while dumb signs their yielding hearts entangled,
The air with sparks of living fire was spangled,
And Night, deep drenched in misty Acheron,[11]
190 Heaved up her head, and half the world upon
Breathed darkness forth. (Dark night is Cupid's day.)
And now begins Leander to display
Love's holy fire, with words, with sighs and tears,
Which like sweet music entered Hero's ears,
195 And yet at every word she turned aside
And always cut him off as he replied.
At last, like to a bold sharp sophister,[12]
With cheerful hope thus he accosted her:
    "Fair creature, let me speak without offense;
200 I would my rude words had the influence
To lead thy thoughts as thy fair looks do mine;
Then shouldst thou be his prisoner, who is thine.

---

[8] *course* I.e., race course.

[9] *Who ... sight?* Shakespeare quotes this line in *As You Like It* 3.5.87.

[10] *hardly is dissembled* Is difficult to disguise.

[11] *Acheron* River in the underworld.

[12] *sophister* Here, student or scholar adept at rhetoric.

Be not unkind and fair—misshapen stuff[1]
Are of behavior boisterous and rough.
205 O shun me not, but hear me ere you go;
God knows I cannot force° love, as you do.   *compel*
My words shall be as spotless as my youth,
Full of simplicity and naked truth.
This sacrifice, whose sweet perfume descending
210 From Venus' altar to your footsteps bending,°   *turning*
Doth testify that you exceed her far
To whom you offer and whose nun you are.
Why should you worship her? Her you surpass
As much as sparkling diamonds flaring° glass.   *gaudy*
215 A diamond set in lead his worth retains;
A heavenly nymph, beloved of human swains,
Receives no blemish but ofttimes more grace;
Which makes me hope, although I am but base—
Base in respect of[2] thee, divine and pure—
220 Dutiful service may thy love procure;
And I in duty will excel all other,
As thou in beauty dost exceed Love's mother.
Nor heaven, nor thou, were made to gaze upon;
As heaven preserves all things, so save thou one.
225 A stately builded ship, well rigged and tall,
The ocean maketh more majestical:
Why vowest thou then to live in Sestos here,
Who on Love's seas more glorious wouldst appear?
Like untuned golden strings all women are,
230 Which, long time lie untouched, will harshly jar.[3]
Vessels of brass, oft handled, brightly shine;
What difference betwixt the richest mine
And basest mold,° but use? for both not used   *earth*
Are of like worth. Then treasure is abused
235 When misers keep it; being put to loan,[4]
In time it will return us two for one.
Rich robes themselves and others do adorn;
Neither themselves nor others, if not worn.
Who builds a palace and rams up the gate
240 Shall see it ruinous and desolate.
Ah, simple Hero, learn thyself to cherish;
Lone women, like to empty houses, perish.

___

[1] *misshapen stuff* Human beings.
[2] *in respect of* Compared to.
[3] *harshly jar* Be out of tune.
[4] *put to loan* Invested.

Less sins the poor rich man that starves himself
In heaping up a mass of drossy pelf,[5]
245 Than such as you: his golden earth remains,
Which after his decease some other gains.
But this fair gem, sweet in the loss alone,
When you fleet hence[6] can be bequeathed to none.
Or if it could, down from th' enameled° sky   *multi-colored*
250 All heaven would come to claim this legacy,
And with intestine broils[7] the world destroy
And quite confound Nature's sweet harmony.
Well therefore by the gods decreed it is,
We human creatures should enjoy that bliss.
255 One is no number;[8] maids are nothing then
Without the sweet society of men.
Wilt thou live single still? One shalt thou be,
Though never-singling Hymen[9] couple thee.
Wild savages, that drink of running springs,
260 Think water far excels all earthly things;
But they that daily taste neat° wine despise it.   *pure*
Virginity, albeit some highly prize it,
Compared with marriage, had you tried them both,
Differs as much as wine and water doth.
265 Base bullion for the stamp's sake we allow:[10]
Even so for men's impression do we you;
By which alone, our reverend fathers[11] say,
Women receive perfection every way.
This idol which you term Virginity,
270 Is neither essence,° subject to the eye—   *real*
No, nor to any one exterior sense;
Nor hath it any place of residence,
Nor is 't of earth or mold° celestial,   *form*
Or capable of any form at all.
275 Of that which hath no being do not boast:
Things that are not at all are never lost.
Men foolishly do call it virtuous:

___

[5] *drossy pelf* Gold ore that has not yet been refined.
[6] *fleet hence* Die.
[7] *intestine broils* Civil wars.
[8] *One … number* Aristotelian mathematical idea.
[9] *Hymen* Greek god of weddings.
[10] *Base … allow* We allow poorer metal to gain worth by being stamped as coins.
[11] *reverend fathers* Early Christian theologians.

What virtue is it that is born with us?[1]
Much less can honor be ascribed thereto:
280 Honor is purchased by the deeds we do.
Believe me, Hero, honor is not won
Until some honorable deed be done.
Seek you for chastity, immortal fame,
And know that some have wronged Diana's name?[2]
285 Whose name is it, if she be false or not,
So she be fair, but some vile tongues will blot?
But you are fair, aye me! so wondrous fair,
So young, so gentle, and so debonair,°   pleasant
As Greece will think, if thus you live alone,
290 Some one or other keeps you as his own.
Then, Hero, hate me not, nor from me fly
To follow swiftly-blasting infamy.
Perhaps thy sacred priesthood makes thee loath.
Tell me, to whom madest thou that heedless oath?"
295   "To Venus," answered she, and as she spake,
Forth from those two tralucent cisterns[3] brake
A stream of liquid pearl, which down her face
Made milk-white paths whereon the gods might
    trace°   follow
To Jove's[4] high court. He thus replied:
300 "The rites in which Love's beauteous empress most delights
Are banquets, Doric music,[5] midnight revel,
Plays, masques, and all that stern age counteth evil.
Thee as a holy idiot doth she scorn;
For thou, in vowing chastity, hast sworn
305 To rob her name and honor, and thereby
Commit'st a sin far worse than perjury—
Even sacrilege against her Deity,
Through regular and formal purity.
To expiate which sin, kiss and shake hands;
310 Such sacrifice as this Venus demands."
    Thereat she smiled and did deny him so
As, put° thereby, yet might he hope for mo.° put aside / more
Which makes him quickly reinforce his speech

And her in humble manner thus beseech:
315   "Though neither gods nor men may thee deserve,
Yet for her sake whom you have vowed to serve,
Abandon fruitless, cold Virginity,
The gentle Queen of Love's sole enemy.
Then shall you most resemble Venus' nun,
320 When Venus' sweet rites are performed and done.
Flint-breasted Pallas[6] joys in single life,
But Pallas and your mistress are at strife.
Love, Hero, then, and be not tyrannous,
But heal the heart that thou hast wounded thus,
325 Nor stain thy youthful years with avarice;
Fair fools delight to be accounted nice.°   shy
The richest corn° dies, if it be not reaped;   grain
Beauty alone is lost, too warily kept."
    These arguments he used, and many more,
330 Wherewith she yielded, that was won before.[7]
Hero's looks yielded, but her words made war:
Women are won when they begin to jar.°   argue
Thus, having swallowed Cupid's golden hook,
The more she strived, the deeper was she strook.
335 Yet, evilly feigning anger, strove she still
And would be thought to grant against her will.
So having paused a while, at last she said:
"Who taught thee rhetoric to deceive a maid?
Aye me, such words as these should I abhor,
340 And yet I like them for the orator."
    With that, Leander stooped to have embraced her,
But from his spreading arms away she cast her,° herself
And thus bespake him: "Gentle youth, forbear
To touch the sacred garments which I wear.
345   "Upon a rock, and underneath a hill,
Far from the town, where all is whist° and still, hushed
Save that the sea, playing on yellow sand,
Sends forth a rattling murmur to the land,
Whose sound allures the golden Morpheus[8]
350 In silence of the night to visit us,
My turret stands, and there, God knows, I play
With Venus' swans and sparrows[9] all the day.

---

[1] *What ... us?* Virtues can only be acquired. One is not born with them.

[2] *Seek ... name?* Even Diana, the goddess of chastity, could not prove her chastity when it was slandered.

[3] *tralucent cisterns* Translucent eyes.

[4] *Jove* Chief in the pantheon of Roman gods (Greek Zeus).

[5] *Doric music* Form of music with a military feel to it. This may not be the association that Leander (or Marlowe) had intended.

[6] *Pallas* Athena, Greek goddess of wisdom, was, in one of her roles, a goddess of war, and was thus depicted dressed in armor.

[7] *that ... before* I.e., she was, privately, already convinced.

[8] *Morpheus* Greek god of dreams, whose gift was golden slumbers.

[9] *swans and sparrows* Venus's chariot was drawn by swans and sparrows.

A dwarfish beldame° bears me company,   *old woman*
That hops about the chamber where I lie
355   And spends the night, that might be better spent,
In vain discourse and apish° merriment.   *foolish*
Come thither." As she spake this, her tongue tripped,
For unawares "Come thither" from her slipped;
And suddenly her former color changed
360   And here and there her eyes through anger ranged.
And like a planet, moving several ways,[1]
At one self° instant, she, poor soul, assays°   *same / tries*
Loving, not to love at all, and every part
Strove to resist the motions of her heart;
365   And hands so pure, so innocent, nay, such
As might have made heaven stoop to have a touch,
Did she uphold to Venus, and again
Vowed spotless chastity, but all in vain.
Cupid beat down her prayers with his wings;
370   Her vows above the empty air he flings.
All deep enraged, his sinewy° bow he bent,   *strong*
And shot a shaft that burning from him went,
Wherewith she, strooken, looked so dolefully
As made Love sigh to see his tyranny.
375   And as she wept, her tears to pearl he turned,
And wound them on his arm, and for her mourned.
Then towards the palace of the Destinies,[2]
Laden with languishment and grief, he flies,
And to those stern nymphs humbly made request
380   Both might enjoy each other and be blessed.
But with a ghastly dreadful countenance,
Threatening a thousand deaths at every glance,
They answered Love, nor would vouchsafe so much
As one poor word, their hate to him was such.
385   Harken a while, and I will tell you why:
Heaven's wingèd herald, Jove-born Mercury,[3]
The selfsame day that he asleep had laid
Enchanted Argus,[4] spied a country maid

Whose careless hair, instead of pearl t' adorn it,
390   Glistered with dew, as one that seemed to scorn it;[5]
Her breath as fragrant as the morning rose,
Her mind pure, and her tongue untaught to glose.°   *flatter*
Yet proud she was, for lofty pride that dwells
In towered courts is oft in shepherds' cells,
395   And too-too well the fair vermilion[6] knew,
And silver tincture of her cheeks, that drew
The love of every swain. On her, this god
Enamored was, and with his snaky rod[7]
Did charm her nimble feet and made her stay;
400   The while upon a hillock down he lay,
And sweetly on his pipe began to play,
And with smooth speech, her fancy to assay,
Till in his twining arms he locked her fast,
And then he wooed with kisses, and at last,
405   As shepherds do, her on the ground he laid,
And tumbling in the grass, he often strayed
Beyond the bounds of shame, in being bold
To eye those parts which no eye should behold;
And, like an insolent commanding lover,
410   Boasting his parentage, would needs discover
The way to new Elysium;[8] but she,
Whose only dower was her chastity,
Having striven in vain, was now about to cry
And crave the help of shepherds that were nigh.
415   Herewith he stayed his fury,° and began   *passion*
To give her leave to rise. Away she ran;
After went Mercury, who used such cunning
As she, to hear his tale, left off her running.
Maids are not won by brutish force and might,
420   But speeches full of pleasure and delight.
And knowing Hermes courted her, was glad
That she such loveliness and beauty had
As could provoke his liking, yet was mute,
And neither would deny nor grant his suit.
425   Still vowed he love; she, wanting no excuse
To feed him with delays, as women use,°   *do*
Or thirsting after immortality

---

[1] *several ways* In older astronomy, the planets moved around the earth within their own orbits and were also affected by the movement of other heavenly bodies; *several* Different.

[2] *Destinies* Fates, three female entities in Greek mythology who controlled the destiny of all humans.

[3] *Mercury* Roman messenger god, called Hermes by the Greeks. Mercury was depicted with winged feet.

[4] *Enchanted Argus* Monster placed by Juno as a guard over Io to keep her away from Jupiter. Mercury put Argus to sleep.

[5] *it* Pearls, jewelry.

[6] *vermilion* Red.

[7] *snaky rod* Caduceus, held by Mercury. Now the symbol for medicine.

[8] *Elysium* Section of the underworld in Greek mythology reserved for heroes. In the Renaissance could apply to Paradise.

(All women are ambitious naturally),
Imposed upon her lover such a task
430　As he ought not perform, nor yet she ask.
A draft of flowing nectar she requested,
Wherewith the king of gods and men is feasted.
He, ready to accomplish what she willed,
Stole some from Hebe[1] (Hebe Jove's cup filled)
435　And gave it to his simple rustic love,
Which being known (as what is hid from Jove?)
He inly° stormed and waxed more furious　　　*inwardly*
Than for the fire filched by Prometheus,[2]
And thrusts him down from heaven. He, wandering here,
440　In mournful terms, with sad and heavy cheer,[3]
Complained to Cupid. Cupid, for his sake,
To be revenged on Jove did undertake;
And those on whom heaven, earth, and hell relies
(I mean the adamantine° Destinies)　　　*immovable*
445　He wounds with love and forced them equally
To dote upon deceitful Mercury.
They offered him the deadly fatal knife
That shears the slender threads of human life;[4]
At his fair feathered feet the engines laid
450　Which th' earth from ugly Chaos' den upweighed.[5]
These he regarded not, but did entreat
That Jove, usurper of his father's seat,
Might presently be banished into hell
And agèd Saturn in Olympus dwell.
455　They granted what he craved, and once again
Saturn and Ops began their golden reign.
Murder, rape, war, lust, and treachery
Were with Jove closed in Stygian empery.
But long this blessèd time continued not;
460　As soon as he his wishèd purpose got,
He, reckless of his promise, did despise
The love of th' everlasting Destinies.
They seeing it, both Love and him abhorred,

And Jupiter unto his place restored.[6]
465　And but that Learning, in despite of Fate,
Will mount aloft and enter heaven gate,
And to the seat of Jove itself advance,
Hermes had slept in hell with Ignorance.
Yet as a punishment they added this,
470　That he and Poverty should always kiss.[7]
And to this day is every scholar poor;
Gross gold from them runs headlong to the boor.
Likewise the angry sisters, thus deluded,
To venge themselves on Hermes, have concluded
475　That Midas' brood[8] shall sit in Honor's chair,
To which the Muses' sons are only heir.
And fruitful wits, that inaspiring[9] are
Shall discontent run into regions far;
And few great lords in virtuous deeds shall joy,
480　But be surprised with every garish toy,
And still enrich the lofty servile clown,°　　　*boor*
Who, with encroaching guile, keeps learning down.
Then muse not[10] Cupid's suit no better sped,
Seeing in their loves the Fates were injurèd.
485　　By this, sad Hero, with love unacquainted,
Viewing Leander's face, fell down and fainted.
He kissed her and breathed life into her lips,
Wherewith, as one displeased, away she trips.
Yet as she went, full often looked behind,
490　And many poor excuses did she find
To linger by the way, and once she stayed,
And would have turned again, but was afraid,

---

[6]　*These he regarded … his place restored*　Mythical story in which Mercury rejects the gifts of the Fates, requesting instead that Jove be overthrown as king of the gods and thrown down into Hades. Jove's father, Saturn, the original ruler of heaven during the Golden Age, returns with his wife Ops and begins a second Golden Age, where all the negative elements associated with Jove ("Murder, rape, war, lust and treachery") are similarly banished to Hades (the "Stygian empery"). The second Golden Age does not last long, for Mercury quickly forgets the Fates, who restore Jove to his throne.

[7]　*Learning … kiss*　Myth invented by Marlowe. Mercury (referred to here by his Greek name Hermes) is identified as god of learning. Mercury sleeps "in hell with Ignorance," yet Learning is so great a power that it raises him up to heaven ("the seat of Jove") despite the wishes of the Fates. The Fates punish Mercury for his inconstancy, linking Learning with Poverty.

[8]　*Midas' brood*　I.e., the rich and the foolish.

[9]　*inaspiring*　I.e., those that do not aspire toward wealth.

[10]　*muse not*　Do not wonder that.

---

[1]　*Hebe*　Greek goddess of youth, cupbearer for the gods.

[2]　*Prometheus*　Greek Titan who stole fire from the gods.

[3]　*terms*　Condition; *cheer*　Expression.

[4]　*knife … life*　The Fate Atropos caused a human death by cutting the thread of life.

[5]　*engines … upweighed*　The Fates were also said to be in charge of the pillars that held the world up ("upweighed") out of Chaos, the primeval disordered matter from which the gods first came.

In offering parley to be counted light.[1]
So on she goes, and in her idle flight
495 Her painted fan of curlèd plumes let fall,
Thinking to train° Leander therewithal.   *lure*
He, being a novice, knew not what she meant
But stayed, and after her a letter sent,
Which joyful Hero answered in such sort
500 As he had hope to scale the beauteous fort
Wherein the liberal Graces[2] locked their wealth,
And therefore to her tower he got by stealth.
Wide open stood the door; he need not climb,
And she herself before the pointed° time   *appointed*
505 Had spread the board,[3] with roses strewed the room,
And oft looked out, and mused he did not come.
At last he came; O who can tell the greeting
These greedy lovers had at their first meeting?
He asked, she gave, and nothing was denied;
510 Both to each other quickly were affied.°   *betrothed*
Look how their hands, so were their hearts united,
And what he did, she willingly requited.
(Sweet are the kisses, the embracements sweet,
When like desires and affections meet,
515 For from the earth to heaven is Cupid raised
Where fancy is in equal balance peised.)°   *weighed*
Yet she this rashness suddenly repented
And turned aside and to herself lamented,
As if her name and honor had been wronged
520 By being possessed of him for whom she longed.
Ay, and she wished, albeit not from her heart,
That he would leave her turret and depart.
The mirthful god of amorous pleasure smiled
To see how he this captive nymph beguiled,
525 For hitherto he did but fan the fire
And kept it down that it might mount the higher.
Now waxed she jealous lest his love abated,
Fearing her own thoughts made her to be hated.
Therefore unto him hastily she goes
530 And, like light Salmacis,[4] her body throws
Upon his bosom where, with yielding eyes,

She offers up herself a sacrifice
To slake his anger; if he were displeased,
O what god would not therewith be appeased?
535 Like Aesop's cock,[5] this jewel he enjoyed,
And as a brother with his sister toyed,
Supposing nothing else was to be done,
Now he her favor and good will had won.
But know you not that creatures wanting sense°   *intelligence*
540 By nature have a mutual appetence,°   *attraction*
And wanting organs to advance a step,
Moved by love's force, unto each other leap?
Much more in subjects having intellect
Some hidden influence breeds like effect.
545 Albeit Leander, rude° in love and raw,   *unsophisticated*
Long dallying with Hero, nothing saw
That might delight him more, yet he suspected
Some amorous rites or other were neglected.
Therefore unto his body, hers he clung;
550 She, fearing on the rushes[6] to be flung,
Strived with redoubled strength; the more she strived,
The more a gentle, pleasing heat revived,
Which taught him all that elder lovers know.
And now the same gan° so to scorch and glow,   *began*
555 As, in plain terms, yet cunningly, he craved it.
(Love always makes those eloquent that have it.)
She, with a kind of granting, put him by it,
And, ever as he thought himself most nigh it,
Like to the tree of Tantalus,[7] she fled,
560 And, seeming lavish, saved her maidenhead.
Ne'er king more sought to keep his diadem°   *crown*
Than Hero this inestimable gem.
Above our life we love a steadfast friend;
Yet, when a token of great worth we send,
565 We often kiss it, often look thereon,
And stay the messenger that would be gone.
No marvel then, though Hero would not yield
So soon to part from that she dearly held.
Jewels being lost are found again, this never;
570 'Tis lost but once, and once lost, lost forever.

---

[1] *In offering … light* By conversing to be considered improper.

[2] *Graces* Three Greek goddesses of joy, charm and beauty.

[3] *spread the board* Set the table.

[4] *Salmacis* Nymph who falls in love with Hermaphroditus. He rejects her, but she clings to him and prays that they will never be parted. The gods grant her wish by fusing their two bodies together.

[5] *Aesop's cock* In Aesop's "The Cock and the Jewel" a rooster finds a jewel but sees no value in it, preferring barleycorns.

[6] *rushes* Floors in Renaissance houses and castles were often strewn with reeds.

[7] *Tantalus* Tantalus was cursed to stand under a tree whose fruit remained just out of reach and to stand in water, unable to drink.

Now had the Morn espied her lover's steeds,[1]
Whereat she starts, puts on her purple weeds,°   *clothes*
And, red for anger that he stayed so long,
All headlong throws herself the clouds among.
75 And now Leander, fearing to be missed,
Embraced her suddenly, took leave, and kissed;
Long was he taking leave, and loath to go,
And kissed again, as lovers use to do.
Sad Hero wrung him by the hand and wept,
80 Saying, "Let your vows and promises be kept."
Then, standing at the door, she turned about,
As loath to see Leander going out.
And now the sun that through th' horizon peeps,
As pitying these lovers, downward creeps,
85 So that in silence of the cloudy night,
Though it was morning, did he take his flight.
But what the secret trusty night concealed,
Leander's amorous habit° soon revealed.   *clothing*
With Cupid's myrtle[2] was his bonnet° crowned;   *hat*
90 About his arms the purple riband° wound   *ribbon*
Wherewith she wreathed her largely spreading hair;
Nor could the youth abstain but he must wear
The sacred ring wherewith she was endowed
When first religious chastity she vowed;
95 Which made his love through Sestos to be known,
And thence unto Abydos sooner blown
Than he could sail, for incorporeal Fame,
Whose weight consists in nothing but her name,
Is swifter than the wind, whose tardy plumes
00 Are reeking water and dull earthly fumes.[3]
Home when he came, he seemed not to be there,
But like exilèd air thrust from his sphere,
Set in a foreign place, and straight from thence,
Alcides-like,[4] by mighty violence
05 He would have chased away the swelling main
That him from her unjustly did detain.
Like as the sun in a diameter[5]
Fires and inflames objects removèd far,
And heateth kindly, shining lat'rally,

610 So beauty sweetly quickens when 'tis nigh,
But being separated and removed,
Burns where it cherished, murders where it loved.[6]
Therefore, even as an index to a book,
So to his mind was young Leander's look.
615 O none but gods have power their love to hide:
Affection by the count'nance is descried.[7]
The light of hidden fire itself discovers,
And love that is concealed betrays poor lovers.
His secret flame apparently° was seen;   *clearly*
620 Leander's father knew where he had been,
And for the same mildly rebuked his son,
Thinking to quench the sparkles new begun.
But love, resisted once, grows passionate,
And nothing more than counsel lovers hate.
625 For as a hot, proud horse highly disdains
To have his head controlled, but breaks the reins,
Spits forth the ringled° bit, and with his hooves   *ringed*
Checks° the submissive ground; so he that loves,   *paws*
The more he is restrained, the worse he fares.
630 What is it now but mad Leander dares?[8]
"O Hero, Hero!" thus he cried full oft,
And then he got him to a rock aloft,
Where, having spied her tower, long stared he on't
And prayed the narrow toiling Hellespont
635 To part in twain, that he might come and go;
But still the rising billows answered "No!"
With that he stripped him to the ivory skin,
And crying, "Love, I come!" leapt lively in.
Whereat the sapphire-visaged god[9] grew proud,
640 And made his capering Triton[10] sound aloud;
Imagining that Ganymede,[11] displeased,
Had left the heavens, therefore on him seized.
Leander strived; the waves about him wound
And pulled him to the bottom, where the ground
645 Was strewed with pearl, and in low coral groves

---

[1] *lover's steeds* Horses that pull the sun's chariot.

[2] *myrtle* Plant symbolic of love, which Cupid wears on his head.

[3] *Are … fumes* I.e., are as fleeting as mist.

[4] *Alcides-like* Like Hercules.

[5] *in a diameter* I.e., shining directly.

---

[6] *being separated … loved* I.e., inaccessible love can be a destructive force.

[7] *Affection … descried* Love is visible on the face.

[8] *but mad … dares?* That Leander won't do?

[9] *sapphire-visaged god* Neptune.

[10] *Triton* Son of Neptune, who blew on a conch shell to raise the waves.

[11] *Ganymede* Young man abducted by Jove and taken to the heavens to be the gods' cupbearer.

Sweet singing mermaids sported with their loves
On heaps of heavy gold and took great pleasure
To spurn in careless sort the shipwrack treasure;
For here the stately azure palace stood
650 Where kingly Neptune and his train abode.
The lusty god embraced him, called him love,
And swore he never should return to Jove.
But when he knew it was not Ganymede,
For under water he was almost dead,
655 He heaved him up, and looking on his face,
Beat down the bold waves with his triple mace,[1]
Which mounted up, intending to have kissed him,
And fell in drops like tears because they missed him.
Leander being up, began to swim,
660 And, looking back, saw Neptune follow him;
Whereat aghast, the poor soul gan to cry,
"O let me visit Hero ere I die!"
The god put Helle's bracelet[2] on his arm,
And swore the sea should never do him harm.
665 He clapped his plump cheeks, with his tresses played,
And, smiling wantonly, his love bewrayed.°   exposed
He watched his arms, and as they opened wide,
At every stroke betwixt them he would slide
And steal a kiss, and then run out and dance
670 And, as he turned, cast many a lustful glance
And throw him gaudy toys to please his eye,
And dive into the water and there pry
Upon his breast, his thighs, and every limb,
And up again and close beside him swim,
675 And talk of love. Leander made reply,
"You are deceived; I am no woman, I."
Thereat smiled Neptune, and then told a tale
How that a shepherd, sitting in a vale,
Played with a boy so lovely fair and kind,
680 As for his love both earth and heaven pined;
That of the cooling river durst not drink,
Lest water nymphs should pull him from the brink.
And when he sported in the fragrant lawns,

Goat-footed satyrs and up-staring fawns[3]
685 Would steal him thence. Ere half this tale was done
"Ay me!" Leander cried, "th' enamored sun
That now should shine on Thetis' glassy bower[4]
Descends upon my radiant Hero's tower.
O that these tardy arms of mine were wings!"
690 And as he spake, upon the waves he springs.
Neptune was angry that he gave no ear,
And in his heart revenging malice bare.
He flung at him his mace, but as it went
He called it in, for love made him repent.
695 The mace returning back, his own hand hit,
As meaning to be venged for darting it.
When this fresh bleeding wound Leander viewed,
His color went and came, as if he rued
The grief which Neptune felt. In gentle breasts
700 Relenting thoughts, remorse, and pity rests;
And who have hard hearts and obdurate minds
But vicious, harebrained, and illit'rate hinds?°   boors
The god, seeing him with pity to be moved,
Thereon concluded that he was beloved.
705 (Love is too full of faith, too credulous,
With folly and false hope deluding us.)
Wherefore Leander's fancy to surprise,
To the rich ocean for gifts he flies.
'Tis wisdom to give much; a gift prevails
710 When deep persuading oratory fails.
By this[5] Leander, being near the land,
Cast down his weary feet and felt the sand.
Breathless albeit he were, he rested not
Till to the solitary tower he got,
715 And knocked and called; at which celestial noise
The longing heart of Hero much more joys
Than nymphs and shepherds when the timbrel[6] rings,
Or crooked dolphin when the sailor sings.[7]
She stayed not for her robes, but straight arose
720 And, drunk with gladness, to the door she goes;

---

[1] *triple mace* Three-pointed trident.

[2] *Helle's bracelet* Fleeing a cruel stepmother on a flying ram, Helle fell into the Hellespont and in most versions drowns. She gave her name to the Hellespont. The bracelet appears to be Marlowe's invention.

[3] *Goat-footed … fawns* Fauns; wood creatures who divined the future by looking up at the stars.

[4] *Thetis' glassy bower* Sea. Thetis was a sea nymph.

[5] *By this* By this time.

[6] *timbrel* Tambourine.

[7] *crooked dolphin … sings* Arion, the musician, was saved from drowning by a dolphin (swimming in leaps, hence "crooked") that was charmed by his music.

Where, seeing a naked man, she screeched for fear
(Such sights as this to tender maids are rare)
And ran into the dark herself to hide.
Rich jewels in the dark are soonest spied.
725 Unto her was he led, or rather drawn
By those white limbs which sparkled through the lawn.
The nearer that he came, the more she fled,
And, seeking refuge, slipped into her bed.
Whereon Leander sitting, thus began,
730 Through numbing cold, all feeble, faint, and wan:
    "If not for love, yet, love, for pity's sake
Me in thy bed and maiden bosom take;
At least vouchsafe these arms some little room,
Who, hoping to embrace thee, cheerly° swum.   *gladly*
735 This head was beat with many a churlish billow,[1]
And therefore let it rest upon thy pillow."
Herewith affrighted Hero shrunk away
And in her lukewarm place Leander lay;
Whose lively heat, like fire from heaven fet,°   *fetched*
740 Would animate gross clay, and higher set
The drooping thoughts of base declining souls
Than dreary° Mars carousing nectar bowls.   *gory*
His hands he cast upon her like a snare;
She, overcome with shame and sallow fear,
745 Like chaste Diana when Actaeon spied her,[2]
Being suddenly betrayed, dived down to hide her,
And as her silver body downward went,
With both her hands she made the bed a tent,
And in her own mind thought herself secure,
750 O'ercast with dim and darksome coverture.°   *covering*
And now she lets him whisper in her ear,
Flatter, entreat, promise, protest, and swear;
Yet ever as he greedily assayed
To touch those dainties, she the Harpy[3] played,
755 And every limb did, as a soldier stout,
Defend the fort and keep the foeman out.
For though the rising ivory mount he scaled,
Which is with azure circling lines empaled,°   *surrounded*
Much like a globe (a globe may I term this,

760 By which love sails to regions full of bliss),
Yet there with Sisyphus[4] he toiled in vain,
Till gentle parley did the truce obtain.
Wherein Leander on her quivering breast,
Breathless spoke something, and sighed out the rest;
765 Which so prevailed, as he, with small ado,
Enclosed her in his arms and kissed her, too.
And every kiss to her was as a charm,
And to Leander as a fresh alarm,[5]
So that the truce was broke, and she, alas,
770 Poor silly° maiden, at his mercy was.   *defenseless*
Love is not full of pity, as men say,
But deaf and cruel, where he means to prey.
Even as a bird which in our hands we wring
Forth plungeth and oft flutters with her wing,
775 She trembling strove; this strife of hers, like that
Which made the world,[6] another world begat
Of unknown joy. Treason was in her thought,
And cunningly to yield herself she sought.
Seeming not won, yet won she was, at length.
780 (In such wars women use but half their strength.)
Leander now, like Theban Hercules,[7]
Entered the orchard of th' Hesperides,
Whose fruit none rightly can describe but he
That pulls or shakes it from the golden tree.[8]
785 And now she wished this night were never done,
And sighed to think upon th' approaching sun,
For much it grieved her that the bright daylight
Should know the pleasure of this blessèd night,
And them like Mars and Erycine[9] displayed,
790 Both in each other's arms chained as they laid.
Again she knew not how to frame her look
Or speak to him who in a moment took

---

1 *churlish billow* Angry wave.

2 *Diana ... spied her* The hunter Actaeon was punished for seeing Diana while she was bathing in a woodland pool.

3 *Harpy* Monster, half-bird, half-woman. Although a banquet was set for the mythical character Phineus, the harpies continually stole the food out of his hands before he could put it in his mouth.

4 *Sisyphus* Sisyphus was forever condemned to roll a stone up a hill; as he brought it to the top, it would roll down again.

5 *alarm* Call to arms.

6 *like ... world* The Greek philosopher Empedocles held that the world was created out of the tension between love and strife.

7 *Hercules* Hercules's eleventh task was to steal the golden apples of the Hesperides, nymphs who tended a beautiful garden.

8 Some scholars have suggested that an error occurred during the first printing of this poem, in which two pages of Marlowe's original manuscript were reversed. If this is the case, lines 775–84 were intended to follow line 762.

9 *Erycine* Another name for Venus, caught in bed with Mars by her husband Vulcan.

That which so long so charily° she kept;　　　*carefully*
And fain by stealth away she would have crept
795　And to some corner secretly have gone,
Leaving Leander in the bed alone.
But as her naked feet were whipping out,
He on the sudden clinged her so about
That mermaid-like unto the floor she slid:
800　One half appeared, the other half was hid.
Thus near the bed she blushing stood upright;
And from her countenance behold ye might
A kind of twilight break, which through the hair,
As from an orient cloud, glims° here and there,　　　*glimmers*
805　And round about the chamber this false morn
Brought forth the day before the day was born.
So Hero's ruddy cheek Hero betrayed,
And her all naked to his sight displayed,
Whence his admiring eyes more pleasure took
810　Than Dis[1] on heaps of gold fixing his look.
By this Apollo's golden harp began
To sound forth music to the Ocean,
Which watchful Hesperus[2] no sooner heard
But he the day's bright-bearing car prepared,
815　And ran before, as harbinger of light,
And with his flaring beams mocked ugly Night
Till she, o'ercome with anguish, shame, and rage,
Danged° down to hell her loathsome carriage.　　　*threw*
Desunt nonnulla.[3]
　—1598

[1] *Dis* Another name for Pluto, god of the underworld.

[2] *Hesperus* Evening star, the planet Venus.

[3] *Desunt nonnulla* "Something is missing." Inserted by the first printer. Marlowe does not include the tragic end of the story as related by other authors. It is possible that he died before finishing the poem.

The Passionate Shepherd to His Love

Come live with me and be my love,
And we will all the pleasures prove°　　　*experience*
That valleys, groves, hills, and fields,
Woods, or steepy mountain yields.

5　And we will sit upon the rocks,
Seeing the shepherds feed their flocks,
By shallow rivers to whose falls
Melodious birds sing madrigals.[4]

And I will make thee beds of roses
10　And a thousand fragrant posies,
A cap of flowers, and a kirtle°　　　*skirt*
Embroidered all with leaves of myrtle;

A gown made of the finest wool
Which from our pretty lambs we pull;
15　Fair linèd slippers for the cold,
With buckles of the purest gold;

A belt of straw and ivy buds,
With coral clasps and amber studs:
And if these pleasures may thee move,
20　Come live with me, and be my love.

The shepherd swains° shall dance and sing　　　*rustic lovers*
For thy delight each May morning:
If these delights thy mind may move,
Then live with me and be my love.
　—1599

[4] *madrigals* Part-songs for several voices, often with pastoral or amatory associations.

The Tragical History of Doctor Faustus

*T*he *Tragical History of Doctor Faustus* is a work that employs belief from both the medieval and modern worlds. At its core is a story, of which there are various medieval versions, of a man selling his soul to the devil. Yet the play is plotted in a way that differs strikingly from the conventions of most medieval drama with, for example, a progression of scenes structured to suggest the passage of time in the real world. (Whereas in most medieval plays characters may exit at the end of one scene and reappear immediately at the beginning of the next in a different place or at a different time, Marlowe and Shakespeare broke new ground in the early 1590s, always providing for some passage of time in such circumstances.) The play posits sinister magical worlds that may seem far-fetched to the modern mind; in the late sixteenth century the lines that now divide what we term "science" from "superstition" had barely begun to be drawn and—again like Shakespeare—Marlowe mixes the comic and the tragic in ways that may jar on some modern sensibilities. Yet its treatment of the connections between the worlds of religion, magic, and science; of the connections between knowledge and power; and of the bitter fruits of excessive ambition resonate deeply with modern readers and modern audiences. So too does the material of the story itself, which has been recast by many authors in the intervening centuries—most notably by Goethe in the eighteenth century (*Faust*, 1790) and by Thomas Mann in the twentieth century (*Dr. Faustus*, 1947).

Not surprisingly, a somewhat uneasy relationship exists between *Dr. Faustus* and traditional Christian doctrine, Protestant or Catholic. However much the ambition of Faustus leads to damning sin, we are made to sense something attractive in his soaring visions. And in numerous other respects, too, the play puts forward religious notions from outside the mainstream (that hell may also be a state of mind, for example, and that there may be legitimate ties between the practices of magic and those of Christianity). Yet the play remains a memorable and provocative literary exploration of Christian doctrine. Do we have free will? What are the limits of God's forgiveness?

Marlowe's *Dr. Faustus* exists in two substantially different versions. There has been a great deal of scholarly discussion of the differences between the two, and debate over which is closest to what Marlowe himself wrote.

Marlowe probably completed the play in 1592 or early 1593 (he died on 30 May of that year). We know that between September of 1594 and October of 1597 the play was performed 25 times at the Rose Theatre by the Admiral's Men, with Edward Alleyn playing Faustus. The same company added the play to their repertory again when they opened the Fortune Theatre as their new house in late 1602. (Payment of £4 was made at this time on behalf of the Admiral's Men to two individuals "for there adicyones in doctor fostes.")

The first printed text that has come down to us is that of 1604 (commonly known as the "A" text). A much longer version was published in 1616; it included numerous new scenes (the majority of them comic) and a variety of other revisions throughout. Some of these revisions were evidently forced by the 1606 "Act to restrain Abuses of Players," which forbad actors "in any Stage play ... jestingly or prophanely" from speaking or using "the holy Name of God or of Christ Jesus, or of the Holy Ghoste or of the Trinitie, which are not to be spoken but with feare and reverence." Thus Faustus's characterization of God as "unpleasant, harsh, contemptible, and vile" 1.1.110 is cut from the 1616 (or "B") text; similarly, his vision of Christ's blood and the frowns of an angry God (5.2.70–77) are radically altered. The reasons for and the source of the various other differences between the A and B texts remain in dispute among scholars. Michael Keefer, whose edition of the play appears in these pages, has argued persuasively not only that the "A" text is "shorter, harsher, more focused, and more disturbing" than the 1616 "B" text but also that it is much closer to the play as it was performed in the 1590s. The edition here has been adapted from Keefer's edition, which is based on the 1604 "A" text. For the text of all the 1616 revisions, together with a full scholarly discussion of the differences between the two versions, readers are invited to consult Keefer's full edition of the play, which appears as part of the Broadview Editions series.

The Tragical History of Doctor Faustus
("A" Text)

DRAMATIS PERSONAE

John Faustus, *doctor of theology*
Wagner, *a student, and Faustus's servant; also speaks the part of Chorus*
Good Angel   5
Evil Angel
Valdes and Cornelius, *magicians*
Three Scholars, *colleagues of Faustus at Wittenberg University*
Mephastophilis, *a devil*   10
Clown (Robin)
Rafe, *another clown*
Lucifer
Belzebub
The Seven Deadly Sins   15
Pope
Cardinal of Lorraine
Friar
Vintner
Charles V, Emperor of Germany
Knight
Alexander the Great and his Paramour, *spirits*
Horse-courser
Duke of Vanholt and his Duchess
Helen of Troy, a spirit
Old Man
Devils, Friars, Attendants

PROLOGUE

(*Enter Chorus.*)

CHORUS. Not marching now in fields of Thracimene
Where Mars did mate[1] the Carthaginians,
Nor sporting in the dalliance of love
In courts of kings where state is overturn'd,
Nor in the pomp of proud audacious deeds
Intends our muse to vaunt° his heavenly verse. *display proudly*
Only this, gentlemen: we must perform
The form of Faustus' fortunes, good or bad.
To patient judgments we appeal our plaud,[2]
And speak for Faustus in his infancy:
Now is he born, his parents base of stock,
In Germany, within a town call'd Rhodes;[3]
Of riper years to Wittenberg[4] he went,
Whereas his kinsmen chiefly brought him up.
So soon he profits in divinity,
The fruitful plot of scholarism grac'd,
That shortly he was grac'd[5] with doctor's name,
Excelling all whose sweet delight disputes[6]

---

[1] *Mars did mate* Mars "allied himself with" or "rivaled." Hannibal's Carthaginian army inflicted a crushing defeat upon the Romans at the battle of Lake Trasummenus in 217 BCE.

[2] *appeal our plaud* Appeal for our applause.

[3] *Rhodes* Roda (now Stadtroda), near Weimar.

[4] *Wittenberg* The University of Wittenberg was famous under Martin Luther as a Protestant center of learning.

[5] *grac'd* At Cambridge it was and still is by the "grace" or decree of the university Senate that degrees are conferred; Marlowe's name appears in the Grace Book in 1584 and 1587 for the B.A. and M.A. degrees respectively.

[6] *whose ... disputes* It is possible to construe "disputes" as a verb; more probably the expression is elliptical and means "whose sweet delight consists in disputes."

In heavenly matters of theology,
20 Till swoll'n with cunning[1] of a self-conceit,
His waxen wings[2] did mount above his reach
And melting heavens conspir'd his overthrow.
For falling to a devilish exercise,
And glutted now with learning's golden gifts,
25 He surfeits upon cursed necromancy;
Nothing so sweet as magic is to him,
Which he prefers before his chiefest bliss:
And this the man that in his study sits.

(*Exit.*)

ACT 1, SCENE 1[3]

(*Faustus in his study.*)

FAUSTUS.   Settle thy studies, Faustus, and begin
To sound the depth of that thou wilt profess.[4]
Having commenc'd,[5] be a divine in show,
Yet level at the end of every art,[6]
5 And live and die in Aristotle's works:
Sweet *Analytics*,[7] 'tis thou hast ravish'd me—
Bene disserere est finis logices.[8]
Is to dispute well logic's chiefest end?
Affords this art no greater miracle?
10 Then read no more, thou hast attain'd the end.
A greater subject fitteth Faustus' wit:°   *understanding*

---

[1] *cunning* Knowledge, erudition, cleverness; sometimes with negative connotations.

[2] *waxen wings* Allusion to the story of Icarus (cf. Ovid, *Metamorphoses* 8.183–235): escaping with his father Daedalus from Minos's island kingdom of Crete, Icarus ignored his father's warning about the wings he had made for them and flew too close to the sun.

[3] *Act 1, Scene 1* Neither the 1604 nor the 1616 texts of the play contains any act or scene divisions; all such divisions in modern editions of the play are therefore editorial.

[4] *profess* Affirm faith in or allegiance to.

[5] *commenc'd* Taken a degree.

[6] *level ... art* Take aim at the final purpose or limit of every discipline.

[7] *Analytics* Name of two treatises on logic by Aristotle, whose works still dominated the university curriculum.

[8] *Bene ... logices* Latin: To argue well is the end or purpose of logic (a definition derived not from Aristotle but from Cicero).

Bid *on kai me on*[9] farewell; Galen[10] come,
Seeing *ubi desinit philosophus, ibi incipit medicus*.[11]
Be a physician Faustus, heap up gold,
15 And be eterniz'd for some wondrous cure!
Summum bonum medicinae sanitas:[12]
The end of physic° is our bodies' health.   *medicine*
Why Faustus, hast thou not attain'd that end?
Is not thy common talk sound aphorisms?[13]
20 Are not thy bills hung up as monuments,
Whereby whole cities have escap'd the plague,
And thousand desperate maladies been eas'd?
Yet art thou still but Faustus, and a man.
Couldst thou make men to live eternally,
25 Or being dead, raise them to life again,
Then this profession were to be esteem'd.
Physic farewell; where is Justinian?
*Si una eademque res legatur duobus,
alter rem, alter valorem rei*,[14] *etc.*
30 A petty case of paltry legacies!
Exhereditare filium non potest pater, nisi—[15]
Such is the subject of the *Institute*[16]
And universal body of the law.
This study fits a mercenary drudge
35 Who aims at nothing but external trash—

---

[9] *on kai me on* Transliteration of Greek words meaning "being and not being," the subject of an ancient Greek philosophical treatise.

[10] *Galen* Claudius Galenus (c. 130–200 CE), most famous of ancient writers on medicine.

[11] *ubi ... medicus* Latin: where the philosopher leaves off, there the physician begins. Freely translated from Aristotle, *Sense and Sensibilia* 436a.

[12] *Summum ... sanitas* Latin: The supreme good of medicine is health. Translated from Aristotle, *Nicomachean Ethics* 1094a.

[13] *sound aphorisms* Reliable medical precepts.

[14] *Si ... rei* Latin: If one and the same thing is bequeathed to two persons, one of them shall have the thing, the other the value of the thing. Derived in part from 2.20 of the *Institutes*, a compilation of Roman law carried out at the command of the emperor Justinian in the sixth century.

[15] *Exhereditare ... nisi*— Latin: A father cannot disinherit his son except—. An incomplete formulation of a rule from Justinian's *Institutes* 2.12.

[16] *Institute* "Institute" here means "founding principle," and may refer also to Justinian's *Institutes*.

Too servile[1] and illiberal for me.
When all is done, divinity is best:
Jerome's Bible,[2] Faustus, view it well.
Stipendium peccati mors est.[3] Ha! *Stipendium, etc.*
40   The reward of sin is death? That's hard.
Si peccasse negamus, fallimur,
et nulla est in nobis veritas.[4]
If we say that we have no sin
We deceive ourselves, and there's no truth in us.
45   Why then belike we must sin,
And so consequently die.
Ay, we must die, an everlasting death.
What doctrine call you this? *Che sarà, sarà,*
What will be, shall be? Divinity, adieu!
50   These metaphysics[5] of magicians
And necromantic books are heavenly!
Lines,[6] circles,[7] seals, letters and characters:[8]
Ay, these are those that Faustus most desires,
O, what a world of profit and delight,
55   Of power, of honor, of omnipotence,

Is promis'd to the studious artisan![9]
All things that move between the quiet poles[10]
Shall be at my command. Emperors and kings
Are but obey'd in their several provinces,
60   Nor can they raise the wind, or rend the clouds;[11]
But his dominion that exceeds° in this   excels
Stretcheth as far as doth the mind of man!
A sound magician is a mighty god:
Here tire, my brains, to get° a deity!   beget

(*Enter Wagner.*)

65   Wagner, commend me to my dearest friends,
The German Valdes and Cornelius;
Request them earnestly to visit me.
WAGNER.   I will, sir.

(*Exit.*)

FAUSTUS.   Their conference will be a greater help to me
70   Than all my labors, plod I ne'er so fast.

(*Enter the Good Angel and the Evil Angel.*)

GOOD ANGEL.   O Faustus, lay that damned book aside,
And gaze not on it, lest it tempt thy soul
And heap God's heavy wrath upon thy head!
Read, read the Scriptures; that is blasphemy.
75   EVIL ANGEL.   Go forward, Faustus, in that famous art
Wherein all nature's treasury is contain'd:
Be thou on earth as Jove[12] is in the sky,
Lord and commander of these elements![13]

(*Exeunt Angels.*)

---

1   *Too servile*   To contrast the liberal arts with "servile" or "mechanical" studies and practices is an Elizabethan commonplace.

2   *Jerome's Bible*   Vulgate, prepared mainly by St. Jerome in the fourth century, was the Latin text of the Bible used by the Roman Catholic church.

3   *Stipendium ... est*   This is the first of several quotations from the Latin Vulgate Bible. This quotation is the first half of Romans 6.23, a verse which in the Geneva Bible (1560) is translated as follows: "For the wages of sin is death: but the gift of God is eternal life through Jesus Christ our Lord."

4   *Si peccasse ... veritas*   1 John 1.8. Faustus has again quoted only the first half of an antithetical statement: he notices the condemnation of sinners by the law of God, but not the conditional promise of divine mercy which immediately follows in 1 John 1.9. In the Geneva Bible, 1 John 1.8–9 is rendered as follows: "If we say that we have no sin, we deceive our selves, and truth is not in us. If we acknowledge our sins, he is faithful and just, to forgive us our sins, and to cleanse us from all unrighteousness."

5   *metaphysics*   Science of the supernatural.

6   *lines*   Reference to the occult art of geomancy, or divination by means of astrologically determined patterns of points and lines.

7   *circles*   Magic circles protected the practitioner of ceremonial magic from evil spirits.

8   *seals, letters and characters*   Talismanic symbols of the planets and of the angels, spiritual intelligences, and daemons that were believed to govern them.

9   *artisan*   Practitioner of an art.

10   *quiet poles*   This could refer either to the poles of the outermost celestial sphere or, more probably, to those of the earth.

11   *raise ... clouds*   Blasphemous echo of Jeremiah 10.13 (which speaks of God's power over clouds, lightning and wind).

12   *Jove*   The substitution of the supreme god of the pagan Roman pantheon for the Christian God is common in Renaissance texts and in Elizabethan poetry.

13   *these elements*   Earth, water, air and fire, here used as a metonymy for the world contained by the sphere of the moon which these elements were thought to constitute.

FAUSTUS.   How am I glutted with conceit[1] of this!
80 Shall I make spirits fetch me what I please,
Resolve me of all ambiguities,
Perform what desperate enterprise I will?
I'll have them fly to India for gold,
Ransack the ocean for orient pearl
85 And search all corners of the new found world
For pleasant fruits and princely delicates;
I'll have them read me strange philosophy
And tell the secrets of all foreign kings;
I'll have them wall all Germany with brass
90 And make swift Rhine[2] circle fair Wittenberg;
I'll have them fill the public schools with silk
Wherewith the students shall be bravely[3] clad;
I'll levy soldiers with the coin they bring,
And chase the Prince of Parma[4] from our land
95 And reign sole king of all our provinces;
Yea, stranger engines for the brunt° of war   assault, onset
Than was the fiery keel at Antwerp's bridge[5]
I'll make my servile spirits to invent.
Come, German Valdes and Cornelius,
100 And make me blest with your sage conference!

(*Enter Valdes and Cornelius.*)

Valdes, sweet Valdes, and Cornelius,
Know that your words have won me at the last
To practise magic and concealed arts:
Yet not your words only, but mine own fantasy,

105 That will receive no object, for my head
But ruminates on necromantic skill.[6]
Philosophy is odious and obscure;
Both law and physic are for petty wits;
Divinity is basest of the three,
110 Unpleasant, harsh, contemptible and vile;
'Tis magic, magic, that hath ravish'd me.
Then, gentle friends, aid me in this attempt,
And I, that have with concise syllogisms[7]
Gravell'd° the pastors of the German church   confounded
115 And made the flowering pride of Wittenberg
Swarm to my problems as the infernal spirits
On sweet Musaeus[8] when he came to hell,
Will be as cunning as Agrippa was,
Whose shadows[9] made all Europe honor him.
120 VALDES.   Faustus, these books, thy wit, and our experience
Shall make all nations canonize us.
As Indian Moors[10] obey their Spanish lords,
So shall the subjects[11] of every element
Be always serviceable to us three:
125 Like lions shall they guard us when we please,
Like Almain rutters[12] with their horsemen's staves,°   lances
Or Lapland giants trotting by our sides;
Sometimes like women, or unwedded maids,
Shadowing° more beauty in their airy brows   harboring
130 Than has the white breasts of the queen of love.[13]
From Venice shall they drag huge Argosies,[14]

---

[1] *conceit* Thought, notion.

[2] *Rhine* River in Germany.

[3] *bravely* Splendidly. University regulations forbade students to wear fine clothing: their scholars' gowns were to be made of woolen cloth in somber colors, and silk-lined hoods could only be worn by the holders of doctoral degrees.

[4] *Prince of Parma* Alessandro Farnese, Duke of Parma, a grandson of the emperor Charles V and the foremost general of his time. Parma served as Spanish governor of the Netherlands from 1578 until his death in 1592; he was hated by Protestants as a tyrant. He commanded the force that the Spanish Armada was to have transported across the Channel in 1588 for the invasion of England.

[5] *fiery ... bridge* On 4 April 1585 the Netherlanders sent two fire-ships loaded with explosives against the pontoon bridge over the river Scheldt which formed part of Parma's siegeworks around Antwerp; one of them reached its target and destroyed part of the bridge, killing many Spanish soldiers. Parma had the bridge rebuilt, and Antwerp subsequently surrendered.

[6] *Yet ... skill* Faustus is saying that his imagination is so preoccupied with thoughts of magic that he can think of no other subjects.

[7] *syllogisms* Particular form of argument from logic.

[8] *Musaeus* Legendary pre-Homeric Greek poet, a pupil of Orpheus. In Virgil's *Aeneid*, Musaeus is represented as standing in the midst of a crowd of spirits in the underworld, head and shoulders above the rest.

[9] *Agrippa ... shadows* Henricus Cornelius Agrippa of Nettesheim (1486–1535), said to be "the greatest conjurer in Christendom." Agrippa distinguished between two kinds of necromancy: *necyomantia*, the reviving of corpses by means of a blood sacrifice, and *scyomantia*, in which only the shadow of a dead person is invoked.

[10] *Indian Moors* Native peoples of the Americas.

[11] *subjects* Spirits. "Subjects" carries the additional implication of subjection to a sovereign will (here, that of the magician).

[12] *Almain rutters* German soldiers.

[13] *queen of love* Venus, Roman goddess of love.

[14] *Argosies* Richly laden merchant ships.

And from America the golden fleece[1]
That yearly stuffs old Philip's treasury,[2]
If learned Faustus will be resolute.
135 FAUSTUS.   Valdes, as resolute am I in this
As thou to live, therefore object it not.
CORNELIUS.   The miracles that magic will perform
Will make thee vow to study nothing else.
He that is grounded in[3] astrology,
140 Enrich'd with tongues,[4] well seen in minerals,[5]
Hath all the principles magic doth require.
Then doubt not, Faustus, but to be renown'd
And more frequented° for this mystery   *sought out*
Than heretofore the Delphian oracle.[6]
145 The spirits tell me they can dry the sea
And fetch the treasure of all foreign wrecks,
Ay, all the wealth that our forefathers hid
Within the massy° entrails of the earth.   *heavy, massive*
Then tell me Faustus, what shall we three want?
150 FAUSTUS.   Nothing, Cornelius. O, this cheers my soul!
Come, show me some demonstrations magical,
That I may conjure in some lusty grove
And have these joys in full possession.
VALDES.   Then haste thee to some solitary grove,
155 And bear wise Bacon's and Albanus' works,[7]
The Hebrew Psalter, and New Testament;
And whatsoever else is requisite
We will inform thee ere our conference cease.
CORNELIUS.   Valdes, first let him know the words of art,
160 And then, all other ceremonies learn'd,
Faustus may try his cunning by himself.
VALDES.   First I'll instruct thee in the rudiments,

And then wilt thou be perfecter than I.
FAUSTUS.   Then come and dine with me, and after meat
165 We'll canvas every quiddity[8] thereof.
For ere I sleep I'll try what I can do;
This night I'll conjure though I die therefore.

(*Exeunt.*)

ACT 1, SCENE 2

(*Enter two scholars.*)

FIRST SCHOLAR.   I wonder what's become of Faustus, that
was wont to make our schools ring with *sic probo*.[9]
SECOND SCHOLAR.   That shall we presently° know, for   *at once*
see: here comes his boy.

(*Enter Wagner.*)

5 FIRST SCHOLAR.   How now sirrah,[10] where's thy master?
WAGNER.   God in heaven knows.
SECOND SCHOLAR.   Why, dost not thou know?
WAGNER.   Yes, I know, but that follows not.
FIRST SCHOLAR.   Go to sirrah, leave your jesting, and tell
10 us where he is.
WAGNER.   That follows not necessary by force of argu-
ment, which you, being licentiate,[11] should stand
upon;[12] therefore acknowledge your error and be atten-
tive.
15 SECOND SCHOLAR.   Why, didst thou not say thou
knew'st?
WAGNER.   Have you any witness on't?
FIRST SCHOLAR.   Yes, sirrah, I heard you.
WAGNER.   Ask my fellow if I be a thief!
20 SECOND SCHOLAR.   Well, you will not tell us.

---

[1] *golden fleece*   In Greek mythology, Jason and his crew sailed in the
Argo on a quest for the Golden Fleece.

[2] *golden ... treasury*   Annual fleet that shipped gold and silver from
the Americas to Spain.

[3] *grounded in*   Firmly established in.

[4] *enrich'd with tongues*   Improved by knowledge of (ancient)
languages.

[5] *well ... minerals*   Well versed in the properties of minerals.

[6] *Delphian oracle*   Oracle of Apollo at Delphi, the most famous and
authoritative of ancient Greek oracles.

[7] *wise Bacon's and Albanus' works*   Roger Bacon (c. 1214–94), an
English Franciscan philosopher, was reputed also to have been a
magician "Albanus" is an error for Pietro d'Abano or Petrus de
Aponus (c. 1250–1316), a physician who was posthumously
convicted of sorcery and burned in effigy by the Inquisition.

[8] *canvass every quiddity*   Discuss every essential particular.

[9] *sic probo*   Latin: thus I prove; the cry of triumph with which
Faustus would have clinched his victories in disputation.

[10] *sirrah*   Term of address that expresses the speaker's contempt, the
addressee's social inferiority, or both.

[11] *licentiate*   Licensed by an academic degree to proceed to further
studies.

[12] *stand upon*   Insist on.

WAGNER. Yes sir, I will tell you; yet if you were not dunces[1] you would never ask me such a question, for is not he *corpus naturale*, and is not that *mobile*?[2] Then wherefore should you ask me such a question? But that
25 I am by nature phlegmatic, slow to wrath and prone to lechery (to love I would say), it were not for you to come within forty foot of the place of execution[3]— although I do not doubt but to see you both hanged the next sessions. Thus having triumphed over you, I will
30 set my countenance like a precisian,[4] and begin to speak thus: Truly, my dear brethren, my master is within at dinner with Valdes and Cornelius, as this wine if it could speak would inform your worships; and so the Lord bless you, preserve you, and keep you,[5] my dear
35 brethren, my dear brethren.

(*Exit.*)

FIRST SCHOLAR. Nay then, I fear he is fallen into that damned art, for which they two are infamous through the world.
SECOND SCHOLAR. Were he a stranger, and not allied to
40 me, yet should I grieve for him. But come, let us go and inform the Rector, and see if he by his grave counsel can reclaim him.
FIRST SCHOLAR. O, but I fear me nothing can reclaim him.
45 SECOND SCHOLAR. Yet let us try what we can do.

(*Exeunt.*)

----

[1] *dunces* Renaissance humanists opposed both the hair-splitting complexity of scholastic logic. As a result, the name of Johannes Duns Scotus (c. 1265 –1308), one of the most subtle medieval logicians, came to connote sophistical quibbling and, by extension, stupidity.

[2] *corpus naturale … mobile* Latin: a body that is natural or subject to change—an adaptation of Aristotle's statement of the subject-matter of physics.

[3] *place of execution* Scene of action; in this case, the dining-room.

[4] *precisian* Puritan, one who is precise and scrupulous about religious observances. Having parodied the logic of scholastic disputation, Wagner proceeds to parody the discourse of excessive piety.

[5] *the Lord … keep you* Numbers 6.24. In quoting these words as an exit line, Wagner is mocking the language with which religious services were (and are) commonly brought to a close.

ACT I, SCENE 3

(*Enter Faustus to conjure.*)

FAUSTUS. Now that the gloomy shadow of the earth,
Longing to view Orion's drizzling look,[6]
Leaps from th'antarctic world[7] unto the sky
And dims the welkin° with her pitchy breath,   sky
5 Faustus, begin thine incantations,
And try if devils will obey thy hest,°   command
Seeing thou hast pray'd and sacrific'd to them.
Within this circle is Jehovah's name,
Forward and backward anagrammatiz'd,[8]
10 The breviated° names of holy saints,   abbreviated
Figures of every adjunct to[9] the heavens,
And characters of signs and erring stars[10]
By which the spirits are enforc'd to rise;
Then fear not, Faustus, but be resolute,
15 And try the uttermost magic can perform.
*Sint mihi dei Acherontis propitii! Valeat numen triplex
Iehovae! Ignei, aerii, aquatici spiritus salvete! Orientis princeps
Belzebub, inferni ardentis monarcha, et Demogorgon, propitia-
mus vos ut appareat et surgat Mephastophilis. Quid tu moraris?*
20 *Per Iehovam, Gehennam et consecratam aquam quam nunc
spargo, signumque crucis quod nunc facio, et per vota nostra,
ipse nunc surgat nobis dicatus Mephastophilis.*[11]

----

[6] *Orion's drizzling look* Constellation of Orion associated in classical poetry with winter storms.

[7] *th'antarctic world* If one believes the sun to revolve around the earth, and lives in the northern hemisphere, then the sun will be conceived of as shining on the southern hemisphere when it is night in the northern, and re-emerging from "th'antarctic world" at dawn.

[8] *anagrammatiz'd* Cabalist mystics believed that hidden meanings were present in every possible recombination of letters in the Hebrew scriptures, and practitioners of Cabalistic magic saw the names of God in particular as containing occult secrets of divine power and knowledge.

[9] *adjunct to* Heavenly body attached to.

[10] *characters … stars* Diagrams representing the constellations of the zodiac (one Latin term for which was *signa*) and the planets.

[11] *Sint … Mephastophilis* Latin: May the gods of Acheron be propitious to me. Away with the threefold divinity of Jehovah! Hail, spirits of fire, air, and water! Belzebub, Prince of the East, monarch of burning hell, and Demogorgon, we invoke your favor that Mephastophilis may appear and ascend. Why do you delay? By Jehovah, Gehenna, and the holy water which I now sprinkle, by the sign of the cross which I now make, and by our vows, may Mephastophilis himself now rise to serve us!; *Mephastophilis* Compound of

(Enter a devil.)

I charge thee to return and change thy shape.
Thou art too ugly to attend on me;
25   Go, and return an old Franciscan friar:
That holy shape becomes a devil best.

(Exit devil.)

I see there's virtue[1] in my heavenly words,
Who would not be proficient in this art?
How pliant is this Mephastophilis,
30   Full of obedience and humility:
Such is the force of magic and my spells!
Now, Faustus, thou art conjurer laureate[2]
That canst command great Mephastophilis!
Quin redis, Mephastophilis, fratris imagine![3]

(Enter Mephastophilis.)

35   MEPHASTOPHILIS.   Now, Faustus, what wouldst thou
            have me do?
    FAUSTUS. I charge thee wait upon me whilst I live
    To do whatever Faustus shall command,
    Be it to make the moon drop from her sphere
    Or the ocean to overwhelm the world.
40   MEPHASTOPHILIS.   I am a servant to great Lucifer,[4]
    And may not follow thee without his leave;
    No more than he commands must we perform.
    FAUSTUS. Did not he charge thee to appear to me?
    MEPHASTOPHILIS. No, I came hither of my own accord.
45   FAUSTUS. Did not my conjuring speeches raise thee?
            Speak.

MEPHASTOPHILIS.   That was the cause, but yet *per accidens*,[5]
    For when we hear one rack[°] the name of God,   °torture
    Abjure the Scriptures and his saviour Christ,
    We fly, in hope to get his glorious[6] soul;
50   Nor will we come unless he use such means
    Whereby he is in danger to be damn'd.
    Therefore the shortest cut for conjuring
    Is stoutly[7] to abjure the Trinity,[8]
    And pray devoutly to the prince of hell.
55   FAUSTUS. So Faustus hath already done,
    And holds this principle:
    There is no chief but only Belzebub,
    To whom Faustus doth dedicate himself.
    This word "damnation" terrifies not him,
60   For he confounds hell in Elysium:[9]
    His ghost be with the old philosophers!
    But leaving these vain trifles of men's souls,
    Tell me, what is that Lucifer thy lord?
    MEPHASTOPHILIS.   Arch-regent and commander of all spirits.
65   FAUSTUS. Was not that Lucifer an angel once?
    MEPHASTOPHILIS. Yes Faustus, and most dearly lov'd
            of God.
    FAUSTUS. How comes it then that he is prince of devils?
    MEPHASTOPHILIS. O, by aspiring pride and insolence,
    For which God threw him from the face of heaven.
70   FAUSTUS. And what are you that live with Lucifer?
    MEPHASTOPHILIS. Unhappy spirits that fell with Lucifer,
    Conspir'd against our God with Lucifer,
    And are for ever damn'd with Lucifer.
    FAUSTUS. Where are you damn'd?
75   MEPHASTOPHILIS.   In hell.
    FAUSTUS. How comes it then that thou art out of hell?
    MEPHASTOPHILIS. Why this is hell, nor am I out of it:
    Think'st thou that I who saw the face of God
    And tasted the eternal joys of heaven

---

three Greek words indicating negation (*me*), light (*phos*), and loving (*philis*); in its original form, the name thus means "not-light-loving"—perhaps parodying the Latin "Lucifer," or "light-bearer."

[1] *virtue* Power.

[2] *laureate* Crowned with laurel; of proved distinction.

[3] *Quin ... imagine* Latin: Why do you not return, Mephastophilis, in the shape of a friar!

[4] *Lucifer* The name appears in Isaiah 14.12.

[5] *per accidens* Scholastics distinguished between an efficient cause, i.e., an agent which itself produced an effect, and a cause *per accidens*, which was related to the final effect only in having provided an occasion for the intervention of some external agent.

[6] *glorious* Splendid; possibly also boastful.

[7] *stoutly* Courageously, resolutely.

[8] *Trinity* In orthodox Christian belief, the three persons (God the Father, Son, and Holy Spirit) of the Godhead.

[9] *confounds ... Elysium* Identifies Hell with Elysium; confuses the two; undoes Hell through belief in Elysium (in ancient Greece, the place in the afterworld reserved for heroes).

80 Am not tormented with ten thousand hells
In being depriv'd of everlasting bliss?
O Faustus, leave these frivolous demands,
Which strike a terror to my fainting soul.
FAUSTUS.   What, is great Mephastophilis so passionate
85 For being deprived of the joys of heaven?
Learn thou of Faustus manly fortitude
And scorn those joys thou never shalt possess.
Go, bear these tidings to great Lucifer:
Seeing Faustus hath incurr'd eternal death
90 By desperate thoughts against Jove's deity,
Say he surrenders up to him his soul,
So[1] he will spare him four and twenty years,
Letting him live in all voluptuousness,
Having thee ever to attend on me
95 To give me whatsoever I shall ask,
To tell me whatsoever I demand,
To slay mine enemies and aid my friends,
And always be obedient to my will.
Go, and return to mighty Lucifer,
100 And meet me in my study at midnight,
And then resolve me of thy master's mind.
MEPHASTOPHILIS.   I will, Faustus.

(*Exit.*)

FAUSTUS.   Had I as many souls as there be stars
I'd give them all for Mephastophilis!
105 By him I'll be a great emperor of the world,
And make a bridge thorough[2] the moving air
To pass the ocean with a band of men;
I'll join the hills that bind the Afric shore,
And make that country continent to[3] Spain,
110 And both contributory to my crown;
The emperor shall not live but by my leave,
Nor any potentate of Germany.
Now that I have obtain'd what I desire,
I'll live in speculation of this art
115 Till Mephastophilis return again.

(*Exit.*)

---

[1]   *So*   On condition that.

[2]   *thorough*   I.e., through.

[3]   *continent to*   Continuous with.

ACT 1, SCENE 4

(*Enter Wagner and the Clown.*)[4]

WAGNER.   Sirrah boy, come hither.
CLOWN.   How, "boy"? Swowns[5] boy, I hope you have
seen many boys with such pickadevaunts[6] as I have.
"Boy," quotha?
5 WAGNER.   Tell me sirrah, hast thou any comings in?[7]
CLOWN.   Ay, and goings out[8] too, you may see else.
WAGNER.   Alas, poor slave: see how poverty jesteth in his
nakedness. The villain is bare, and out of service,[9] and so
hungry that I know he would give his soul to the devil
10 for a shoulder of mutton, though it were blood raw.
CLOWN.   How, my soul to the devil for a shoulder of
mutton though 'twere blood raw? Not so, good friend:
b'urlady[10] I had need have it well roasted, and good
sauce to it, if I pay so dear.
15 WAGNER.   Well, wilt thou serve me, and I'll make thee
go like *Qui mihi discipulus?*[11]
CLOWN.   How, in verse?
WAGNER.   No sirrah, in beaten silk[12] and stavesacre.[13]
CLOWN.   How, how, knave's acre? Ay, I thought that
20 was all the land his father left him. Do ye hear, I would
be sorry to rob you of your living.
WAGNER.   Sirrah, I say in stavesacre!

---

[4]   *Clown*   Boorish rustic, a fool. This character is presumably to be
identified with the Robin of 2.2 and 3.2.

[5]   *Swowns*   Contraction of "God's wounds" (a mild oath).

[6]   *pickadevaunts*   Short beards trimmed to a point; apparently from
the French *piqué devant*, "peaked in front," possibly with an obscene
double entendre.

[7]   *comings in*   Earnings.

[8]   *goings out*   Expenses; a punning reference to the fact that the
Clown is bursting out of his tattered clothes.

[9]   *out of service*   Unemployed.

[10]   *b'urlady*   Contraction of "by Our Lady."

[11]   *Qui mihi discipulus*   Latin: You who are my pupil. The opening
words of a didactic poem which appeared in the standard elementary
Latin textbook used in Elizabethan schools.

[12]   *beaten silk*   Embroidered silk; with a punning suggestion that
Wagner will thrash his servant.

[13]   *stavesacre*   Preparation against lice made from the seeds of a plant
related to the delphinium.

CLOWN. Oho, oho, stavesacre! Why then belike,[1] if I were your man I should be full of vermin.

WAGNER. So thou shalt, whether thou beest with me or no. But sirrah, leave your jesting, and bind yourself presently unto me for seven years,[2] or I'll turn all the lice about thee into familiars,[3] and they shall tear thee to pieces.

CLOWN. Do you hear, sir? You may save that labor: they are too familiar with me already, swowns they are as bold with my flesh as if they had paid for my meat and drink.

WAGNER. Well, do you hear, sirrah? Hold, take these guilders.

CLOWN. Gridirons, what be they?

WAGNER. Why, French crowns.

CLOWN. Mass, but for the name of French crowns, a man were as good have as many English counters.[4] And what should I do with these?

WAGNER. Why now, sirrah, thou art at an hour's warning whensoever or wheresoever the devil shall fetch thee.

CLOWN. No, no; here, take your gridirons again.

WAGNER. Truly, I'll none of them.

CLOWN. Truly, but you shall.

WAGNER. Bear witness I gave them him!

CLOWN. Bear witness I give them you again!

WAGNER. Well, I will cause two devils presently to fetch thee away. Baliol,[5] and Belcher!

CLOWN. Let your Balio and Belcher come here, and I'll knock them, they were never so knocked since they were

devils! Say I should kill one of them, what would folks say? "Do ye see yonder tall[6] fellow in the round slop,[7] he has killed the devil": so I should be called "kill-devil" all the parish over.

(*Enter two devils, and the clown runs up and down crying.*)

WAGNER. Balio and Belcher, spirits away!

(*Exeunt.*)

CLOWN. What, are they gone? A vengeance on them, they have vile long nails. There was a he-devil and a she-devil. I'll tell you how you shall know them: all he-devils has horns,[8] and all she-devils has clefts[9] and cloven feet.

WAGNER. Well sirrah, follow me.

CLOWN. But do you hear: If I should serve you, would you teach me to raise up Banios and Belcheos?

WAGNER. I will teach thee to turn thyself to anything: to a dog, or a cat, or a mouse, or a rat, or any thing.

CLOWN. How? A Christian fellow to a dog or a cat, a mouse or a rat? No, no, sir. If you turn me into anything, let it be in the likeness of little pretty frisking flea, that I may be here and there and everywhere: O, I'll tickle the pretty wenches' plackets,[10] I'll be amongst them i'faith!

WAGNER. Well sirrah, come.

CLOWN. But do you hear, Wagner?

WAGNER. How? Baliol and Belcher!

CLOWN. O Lord! I pray sir, let Banio and Belcher go sleep.

WAGNER. Villain, call me Master Wagner, and see that you walk attentively, and let your right eye be always diametrally fixed upon my left heel, that thou mayest *quasi vestigiis nostris insitere.*[11]

(*Exit.*)

---

[1] *belike* In all likelihood.

[2] *seven years* Standard period of time for an apprenticeship or a contract of indentured labor.

[3] *familiars* Attendant spirits of witches and sorcerers, who took the form of animals.

[4] *guilders … English counters* Wagner professes to give the Clown Dutch guilders. Observing, it would seem, that the coins have holes punched in them, the Clown mis-hears the word as "grid-irons"—whereupon Wagner re-identifies the coins as French crowns. A proclamation of 1587 authorized members of the public to strike holes in French crowns, which in the late 1580s and early 1590s were notoriously debased, and often counterfeit. From the sixteenth until the early nineteenth century, English merchants issued privately minted counters or tokens which circulated without having any officially accepted value; "counter" often denoted a debased or counterfeit coin; *Mass* An oath: "by the Mass."

[5] *Baliol* Deformation of "Belial," a name which occurs in the Bible (e.g., 2 Cor. 6.15).

[6] *tall* Valiant, handsome.

[7] *round slop* Baggy breeches.

[8] *horns* Standard demonic equipment, perhaps with an overtone of cuckoldry.

[9] *clefts* Vulvas.

[10] *plackets* Pockets in women's skirts; metaphorically, a woman's genitals.

[11] *quasi vestigiis nostris insitere* Latin: as if walking in our footsteps.

CLOWN. God forgive me, he speaks Dutch fustian.[1]
Well, I'll follow him, I'll serve him, that's flat.

(*Exit.*)

ACT 2, SCENE 1

(*Enter Faustus in his study.*)

FAUSTUS. Now Faustus, must thou needs be damn'd,
And canst thou not be saved.
What boots° it then to think of God or heaven?   avails
Away with such vain fancies, and despair,
5 Despair in God, and trust in Belzebub.
Now go not backward: no Faustus, be resolute.
Why waverest thou? O, something soundeth in mine ears:
"Abjure this magic, turn to God again."
Ay, and Faustus will turn to God again.
10 To God? He loves thee not;
The god thou serv'st is thine own appetite,
Wherein is fix'd the love of Belzebub:
To him I'll build an altar and a church,
And offer lukewarm blood of new-born babes!

(*Enter Good Angel, and Evil.*)

15 GOOD ANGEL. Sweet Faustus, leave that execrable art.
FAUSTUS. Contrition, prayer, repentance: what of these?
GOOD ANGEL. O, they are means to bring thee unto
heaven.
EVIL ANGEL. Rather illusions, fruits of lunacy,
That makes men foolish that do trust them most.
20 GOOD ANGEL. Sweet Faustus, think of heaven and
heavenly things.
EVIL ANGEL. No Faustus, think of honor and of
wealth.

(*Exeunt Angels.*)

FAUSTUS. Of wealth?

Why, the signory° of Emden[2] shall be mine!   *lordship, rule*
When Mephastophilis shall stand by me
25 What God can hurt me?[3] Faustus, thou art safe;
Cast° no more doubts. Come, Mephastophilis,   *emit, ponder*
And bring glad tidings[4] from great Lucifer!
Is't not midnight? Come Mephastophilis,
Veni, veni, Mephastophilis![5]

(*Enter Mephastophilis.*)

30 Now tell me, what says Lucifer thy lord?
MEPHASTOPHILIS. That I shall wait on Faustus whilst
he lives,
So he will buy my service with his soul.
FAUSTUS. Already Faustus hath hazarded that for thee.
MEPHASTOPHILIS. But now thou must bequeath it
solemnly,
35 And write a deed of gift with thine own blood,
For that security craves great Lucifer.
If thou deny it I will back to hell.
FAUSTUS. Stay Mephastophilis, and tell me,
What good will my soul do thy lord?
40 MEPHASTOPHILIS. Enlarge his kingdom.
FAUSTUS. Is that the reason why he tempts us thus?
MEPHASTOPHILIS. *Solamen miseris socios habuisse
doloris.*[6]
FAUSTUS. Why, have you any pain that tortures others?
MEPHASTOPHILIS. As great as have the human souls of
men.
45 But tell me, Faustus, shall I have thy soul?
And I will be thy slave and wait on thee,
And give thee more than thou hast wit to ask.
FAUSTUS. Ay Mephastophilis, I give it thee.
MEPHASTOPHILIS. Then stab this arm courageously,
50 And bind thy soul, that at some certain day
Great Lucifer may claim it as his own:

---

[2] *Emden* Prosperous port in northwest Germany which conducted
an extensive trade with England.

[3] *When … me?* Blasphemous distortion of Romans 8.31: "If God
be on our side, who can be against us?"

[4] *glad tidings* Cf. Luke 2.10: "I bring you glad tidings of great joy."

[5] *Veni, veni, Mephastophilis!* Latin: Come, O come, Mephastophilis!—a blasphemous echo of the twelfth-century Advent hymn
Veni, veni, Emmanuel (Come, O Come Redeemer).

[6] *Solamen … doloris* Latin: It is a comfort to the wretched to have
had companions in misfortune.

---

[1] *fustian* Bombast, nonsense. Fustian was a coarse cloth made of
cotton and flax; the word was metaphorically applied to inflated or
inappropriately lofty language.

And then be thou as great as Lucifer!
FAUSTUS.   Lo Mephastophilis, for love of thee
    I cut mine arm, and with my proper° blood   *own*
55 Assure my soul to be great Lucifer's,
    Chief lord and regent of perpetual night.
    View here the blood that trickles from mine arm,
    And let it be propitious for my wish.
MEPHASTOPHILIS.   But Faustus, thou must
60 Write it in manner of a deed[1] of gift.
FAUSTUS.   Ay, so I will. But Mephastophilis,
    My blood congeals, and I can write no more.
MEPHASTOPHILIS.   I'll fetch thee fire to dissolve it
        straight.

        (*Exit.*)

FAUSTUS. What might the staying of my blood portend?
65 Is it unwilling I should write this bill?°   *contract*
    Why streams it not, that I may write afresh?
    "Faustus gives to thee his soul": ah, there it stay'd.
    Why should'st thou not? Is not thy soul thine own?
    Then write again: "Faustus gives to thee his soul."

        (*Enter Mephastophilis with a chafer[2] of coals.*)

70 MEPHASTOPHILIS.   Here's fire: come Faustus, set it on.
FAUSTUS.   So: now the blood begins to clear again;
    Now will I make an end immediately.
MEPHASTOPHILIS.   (*Aside.*) O, what will not I do to
        obtain his soul!
FAUSTUS.   *Consummatum est:*[3] this bill is ended,
75 And Faustus hath bequeath'd his soul to Lucifer.
    But what is this inscription on mine arm?
    Homo fuge![4] Whither should I fly?
    If unto God he'll throw thee down to hell.
    My senses are deceiv'd: here's nothing writ.
80 O yes, I see it plain! Even here is writ

---

[1] *deed* Legally binding document.

[2] *chafer* Saucepan or chafing-dish.

[3] *Consummatum est* "It is finished." According to the Gospel of John, these were the last words of Jesus on the cross (John 19.30).

[4] *Homo fuge* Latin: Man, flee! The words occur in the Vulgate text of 1 Timothy 6.11, but this line as a whole alludes more distinctly to Psalm 139.7–8: "Whither shall I go from thy spirit? or whither shall I flee from thy presence? If I ascend into heaven, thou art there: if I lie down in hell, thou art there."

Homo fuge; yet shall not Faustus fly.
MEPHASTOPHILIS.   I'll fetch him somewhat to delight
        his mind.

        (*Exit. Enter with devils, giving crowns and rich apparel
        to Faustus, and dance, and then [the devils] depart.*)

FAUSTUS.   Speak Mephastophilis: what means this show?
MEPHASTOPHILIS.   Nothing, Faustus, but to delight
        thy mind,
85 And let thee see what magic can perform.
FAUSTUS.   But may I raise such spirits when I please?
MEPHASTOPHILIS.   Ay Faustus, and do greater things
        than these.
FAUSTUS.   Then there's enough for a thousand souls!
    Here Mephastophilis, receive this scroll,
90 A deed of gift, of body and of soul:
    But yet conditionally, that thou perform
    All articles prescrib'd between us both.
MEPHASTOPHILIS.   Faustus, I swear by hell and Lucifer
    To effect all promises between us made.
95 FAUSTUS.   Then hear me read them.
    On these conditions following:
    First, that Faustus may be a spirit in form and substance;
    Secondly, that Mephastophilis shall be his servant, and at
        his command;
    Thirdly, that Mephastophilis shall do for him, and bring
        him whatsoever;
100 *Fourthly, that he shall be in his chamber or house*
        invisible;
    Lastly, that he shall appear to the said John Faustus at all
        times, in what form or shape soever he please;
    I, John Faustus of Wittenberg, Doctor, by these presents[5]
    do give both body and soul to Lucifer, Prince of the East,
    and his minister Mephastophilis, and furthermore grant
105 *unto him that four and twenty years being expired, and*
    these articles above written being inviolate, full power to
    fetch or carry the said John Faustus, body and soul, flesh,
    blood, or goods, into their habitation wheresoever.
                                    By me, John Faustus.

MEPHASTOPHILIS.   Speak Faustus, do you deliver this as
        your deed?
110 FAUSTUS.   Ay, take it, and the devil give thee good on't.

---

[5] *these presents* Legal articles being presented.

MEPHASTOPHILIS.   So. Now, Faustus, ask me what
    thou wilt.
FAUSTUS.   First will I question with thee about hell.
  Tell me, where is the place that men call hell?
MEPHASTOPHILIS.   Under the heavens.
15 FAUSTUS.   Ay, so are all things else; but whereabouts?
MEPHASTOPHILIS.   Within the bowels of these elements,
  Where we are tortur'd and remain forever.
  Hell hath no limits, nor is circumscrib'd
  In one self° place, but where we are is hell,   *single, particular*
20   And where hell is there must we ever be;
  And to be short, when all the world dissolves
  And every creature shall be purify'd,
  All places shall be hell that is not heaven.
FAUSTUS.   Come, I think hell's a fable.
25 MEPHASTOPHILIS.   Ay, think so still, till experience
    change thy mind.
FAUSTUS.   Why, think'st thou then that Faustus shall
    be damn'd?
MEPHASTOPHILIS.   Ay, of necessity, for here's the scroll
  Wherein thou hast given thy soul to Lucifer.
FAUSTUS.   Ay, and body too, but what of that?
30   Think'st thou that Faustus is so fond° to imagine *foolish*
  That after this life there is any pain?
  Tush, these are trifles and mere old wives' tales.
MEPHASTOPHILIS.   But I am an instance to prove the
    contrary,
  For I tell thee I am damn'd, and now in hell.
35 FAUSTUS.   Nay, and this be hell, I'll willingly be damn'd!
  What, sleeping, eating, walking and disputing?
  But leaving this, let me have a wife, the fairest maid in
  Germany, for I am wanton and lascivious, and cannot
  live without a wife.
40 MEPHASTOPHILIS.   How, a wife? I prithee Faustus, talk
    not of a wife.
FAUSTUS.   Nay, sweet Mephastophilis, fetch me one,
  for I will have one.
MEPHASTOPHILIS.   Well, thou wilt have one. Sit there
45   till I come; I'll fetch thee a wife in the devil's name.

(*Enter a devil dressed like a woman, with fireworks.*)[1]

MEPHASTOPHILIS.   Tell, Faustus: how dost thou like
    thy wife?
FAUSTUS.   A plague on her for a hot whore!

(*Exit devil.*)

MEPHASTOPHILIS.   Tut, Faustus, marriage is but a
    ceremonial toy.°   *trifle*
  If thou lov'st me, think no more of it.
150   I'll cull thee out the fairest courtesans
  And bring them every morning to thy bed.
  She whom thine eye shall like, thy heart shall have,
  Be she as chaste as was Penelope,[2]
  As wise as Saba,[3] or as beautiful
155   As was bright Lucifer before his fall.
  Hold, take this book: peruse it thoroughly.
  The iterating of these lines brings gold;
  The framing of this circle on the ground
  Brings whirlwinds, tempests, thunder and lightning.
160   Pronounce this thrice devoutly to thyself,
  And men in armor shall appear to thee,
  Ready to execute what thou desir'st.
FAUSTUS.   Thanks, Mephastophilis; yet fain would I have
  a book wherein I might behold all spells and incanta-
165   tions, that I might raise up spirits when I please.
MEPHASTOPHILIS.   Here they are in this book.

(*There turn to them.*)

FAUSTUS.   Now would I have a book where I might see
  all characters[4] and planets of the heavens, that I might
  know their motions and dispositions.
170 MEPHASTOPHILIS.   Here they are too.

(*Turn to them.*)

FAUSTUS.   Nay, let me have one book more, and then I
  have done, wherein I might see all plants, herbs, and
  trees that grow upon the earth.
MEPHASTOPHILIS.   Here they be.

---

[1] *fireworks* In the comic sequences of sixteenth-century pageants
and plays, fireworks were often attached to the costumes of devils
and clowns in ways designed to make fun of sexual and excretory
functions.

[2] *Penelope* Faithful wife of Odysseus, hero of the Trojan War and
Homer's *Odyssey*.

[3] *Saba* Queen of Sheba, who in 1 Kings 10.1–13 comes to
Jerusalem to test King Solomon's knowledge of God.

[4] *characters* Talismanic symbols of the planets and of the spiritual
powers that govern them.

175 FAUSTUS. O, thou art deceived.
MEPHASTOPHILIS. Tut, I warrant thee.[1]

(*Turn to them. Exeunt.*)

ACT 2, SCENE 2[2]

(*Enter Robin the ostler with a book in his hand.*)

ROBIN. O, this is admirable! Here I ha' stolen one of
Doctor Faustus' conjuring books, and i'faith I mean to
search some circles[3] for my own use: now will I make all
the maidens in our parish dance at my pleasure stark
5 naked before me, and so by that means I shall see more
than I ever felt, or saw yet.

(*Enter Rafe, calling Robin.*)

RAFE. Robin, prithee come away! There's a gentleman
tarries to have his horse, and he would have his things
rubbed and made clean: he keeps such a chafing with
10 my mistress about it, and she has sent me to look thee
out; prithee come away!
ROBIN. Keep out, keep out, or else you are blown up,
you are dismembered. Rafe! Keep out, for I am about a
roaring[4] piece of work.
15 RAFE. Come, what dost thou with that same book?
Thou canst not read.
ROBIN. Yes, my master and mistress shall find that I can
read: he for his forehead,[5] she for her private study.[6]
She's born to bear with[7] me, or else my art fails.
20 RAFE. Why Robin, what book is that?
ROBIN. What book? Why, the most intolerable book for
conjuring that e'er was invented by any brimstone devil!

RAFE. Canst thou conjure with it?
ROBIN. I can do all these things easily with it: first, I can
25 make thee drunk with hippocras[8] at any tavern in
Europe for nothing; that's one of my conjuring works.
RAFE. Our master parson says that's nothing.
ROBIN. True, Rafe. And more, Rafe, if thou hast any
mind to Nan Spit our kitchen maid, then turn her and
30 wind her[9] to thine own use, as often as thou wilt, and at
midnight.
RAFE. O brave Robin, shall I have Nan Spit, and to
mine own use? On that condition I'll feed thy devil with
horse-bread[10] as long as he lives, of free cost.
35 ROBIN. No more, sweet Rafe: let's go and make clean
our boots which lie foul upon our hands; and then to
our conjuring, in the devil's name!

(*Exeunt.*)

ACT 2, SCENE 3

(*Enter Faustus in his study, and Mephastophilis.*)

FAUSTUS. When I behold the heavens then I repent
And curse thee, wicked Mephastophilis,
Because thou hast depriv'd me of those joys.
MEPHASTOPHILIS. Why Faustus,
5 Think'st thou heaven is such a glorious thing?
I tell thee 'tis not half so fair as thou
Or any man that breathes on earth.
FAUSTUS. How prov'st thou that?
MEPHASTOPHILIS.   'Twas made for man,
10 Therefore is man more excellent.
FAUSTUS. If it were made for man, 'twas made for me:
I will renounce this magic and repent.

---

[1] *I warrant thee* I assure you.

[2] *Act 2, Scene 2* In both the 1604 and the 1616 texts of the play
this scene, together with the scene numbered Act 3, Scene 2 in the
present edition, appear in succession.

[3] *circles* Magic circles, and also women's vaginas.

[4] *roaring* Noisy, riotous.

[5] *forehead* Deceived husbands or cuckolds were said to wear horns
on their foreheads.

[6] *private study* With a quibble on private parts.

[7] *to bear with* To put up with; also (another bawdy quibble) to lie
under, to bear the weight of his body.

[8] *hippocras* Wine flavored with spices.

[9] *Nan Spit … wind her* One of the humblest occupations in the
kitchen of a large household or inn was that of the turnspit, whose
job was to stand by the open fireplace and crank the horizontally
mounted spit on which roasting meat was impaled. Robin tempts
Rafe with the thought of sexually impaling and "turning" this
kitchen maid—of treating her, in effect, as she treats a roast of meat.

[10] *horse-bread* Bread made of beans, bran, etc. for horses—but
apparently sometimes eaten also by the very poor. Rafe seems to be
aware of the popular superstition according to which familiar spirits
took the form of animals, and were fed like pets by the witches to
whom they attached themselves.

(*Enter Good Angel and Evil Angel.*)

GOOD ANGEL.   Faustus, repent yet, God will pity thee.
EVIL ANGEL.   Thou art a spirit, God cannot pity thee.
15 FAUSTUS.   Who buzzeth° in mine ears I am a spirit? *whispers*
     Be I a devil, yet God may pity me.
     Ay, God will pity me if I repent.
EVIL ANGEL.   Ay, but Faustus never shall repent.

(*Exeunt Angels.*)

FAUSTUS.   My heart's so harden'd I cannot repent.
20   Scarce can I name salvation, faith, or heaven,
     But fearful echoes thunders in mine ears,
     "Faustus, thou art damn'd!" Then swords and knives,
     Poison, guns, halters,[1] and envenom'd steel
     Are laid before me to dispatch myself,
25   And long ere this I should have done the deed
     Had not sweet pleasure conquer'd deep despair.
     Have I not made blind Homer sing to me
     Of Alexander's love and Oenone's death?[2]
     And hath not he that built the walls of Thebes
30   With ravishing sound of his melodious harp[3]
     Made music with my Mephastophilis?
     Why should I die, then, or basely despair?
     I am resolv'd: Faustus shall ne'er repent.
     Come Mephastophilis, let us dispute again,
35   And reason of divine astrology.[4]
     Speak, are there many spheres above the moon?
     Are celestial bodies but one globe,

As is the substance of this centric earth?[5]
MEPHASTOPHILIS.   As are the elements, such are the
     heavens,
40   Even from the moon unto the empyreal orb,
     Mutually folded on each other's spheres,
     And jointly move upon one axle-tree
     Whose termine is term'd the world's wide pole.
     Nor are the names of Saturn, Mars, or Jupiter
45   Feign'd, but are erring stars.
FAUSTUS.   But tell me, have they all one motion, both
     situ et tempore?[6]
MEPHASTOPHILIS.   All jointly move from east to west in
     four and twenty hours upon the poles of the world, but
50   differ in their motions upon the poles of the zodiac.
FAUSTUS.   These slender questions Wagner can decide:
     Hath Mephastophilis no greater skill?
     Who knows not the double notion of the planets?[7]
     The first is finish'd in a natural day,
55   The second thus: Saturn in thirty years,
     Jupiter in twelve, Mars in four, the Sun, Venus, and
     Mercury in a year, the Moon in twenty-eight days.[8]

---

[1] *halters* Hangman's nooses.

[2] *Alexander's … death* These are matters which Homer left unsung; Faustus would have been the first to hear them from his lips. Paris (also named Alexandros), a son of King Priam and Queen Hecuba of Troy, was cast out by his parents (for it was prophesied that he should cause the destruction of Troy) and brought up among the shepherds of Mount Ida, where he won the love of Oenone. Asked by Hera, Athena, and Aphrodite to award a golden apple to the most beautiful goddess, he succumbed to Aphrodite's bribe of the love of the fairest woman alive, abandoned Oenone and abducted Helen from Sparta, thus provoking the Trojan War. Later, having been wounded by a poisoned arrow, he could have been healed only by Oenone; after jealously refusing to cure him, she was overwhelmed with remorse and threw herself onto his funeral pyre.

[3] *he … harp* Amphion and his brother built the walls of Thebes; the music of Amphion's lyre magically moved huge stones into place.

[4] *astrology* Not clearly distinguished from astronomy until the seventeenth century.

[5] *the substance of this centric earth* The elements (earth, water, air, and fire) that make up "the substance of this centric earth" were thought to be concentrically disposed; so also, in the old geocentric cosmology, were the spheres that governed the motions of those wandering or "erring" stars, the planets. Mephastophilis says there are nine spheres: those of the planets, including the moon and the sun; the firmament, to which the fixed stars are attached; and the empyrean, the outermost and motionless sphere of the universe. (He apparently conflates the *primum mobile*, thought of by some astronomers as a distinct sphere that imparts motion to the heavens, with the firmament.) All of this is utterly commonplace. The systems developed by ancient astronomers were enormously more complex: Eudoxus (fourth century BCE) required twenty-seven, and Ptolemy (second century CE) more than eighty variously revolving spheres, including epicyclic and eccentric ones, to explain the motions of the planets.

[6] *situ et tempore* Latin: in position and time; i.e., in the direction of their revolutions around the earth and in the time these take.

[7] *poles … planets* The apparent diurnal motion of the planetary spheres "upon one axle-tree" (the northern "termine" of which nearly coincides with the star Polaris) is of course due, in post-Copernican terms, to the earth's rotation upon its axis. The second component of the planets' apparent "double motion" is an effect of the differences between the earth's period of revolution around the sun and theirs.

[8] *first … days* The periods of planetary revolution given by Faustus correspond for the most part to the then-accepted figures: Saturn 28 years, Jupiter 12 years, Mars 2 years, Venus, Mercury, and, of course, the sun 1 year, and the moon 1 month. The actual—as opposed to apparent—periods for the inner planets are of course much less: $7\frac{1}{2}$ and 3 months respectively.

Tush, these are freshmen's suppositions! But tell me, hath every sphere a dominion or *intelligentia?*[1]

60 MEPHASTOPHILIS.   Ay.

FAUSTUS.   How many planets or spheres are there?

MEPHASTOPHILIS.   Nine: the seven planets, the firmament, and the empyreal heaven.

FAUSTUS.   But is there not *coelum igneum, et crystallinum?*[2]

65 MEPHASTOPHILIS.   No, Faustus, they be but fables.

FAUSTUS.   Resolve me then in this one question: Why are not conjunctions, oppositions, aspects,[3] eclipses all at one time, but in some years we have more, in some less?

70 MEPHASTOPHILIS.   *Per inaequalem motum respectu totius.*[4]

FAUSTUS.   Well, I am answered. Now tell me who made the world.

MEPHASTOPHILIS.   I will not.

FAUSTUS.   Sweet Mephastophilis, tell me.

MEPHASTOPHILIS.   Move° me not, Faustus.   *anger*

75 FAUSTUS.   Villain, have I not bound thee to tell me any thing?

MEPHASTOPHILIS.   Ay, that is not against our kingdom. This is. Thou are damn'd, think thou of hell.

FAUSTUS.   Think, Faustus, upon God that made the world!

MEPHASTOPHILIS.   Remember this.

(*Exit.*)

80 FAUSTUS.   Ay, go accursed spirit to ugly hell:
'Tis thou hast damn'd distressed Faustus' soul.
Is't not too late?

(*Enter Good Angel and Evil Angel.*)

EVIL ANGEL.   Too late.

GOOD ANGEL.   Never too late, if Faustus can repent.

85 EVIL ANGEL.   If thou repent, devils shall tear thee in pieces.

GOOD ANGEL.   Repent, and they shall never raze° thy skin.   *graze*

(*Exeunt Angels.*)

FAUSTUS.   Ah Christ, my Saviour,
Seek to save distressed Faustus' soul!

(*Enter Lucifer, Belzebub, and Mephastophilis.*)

LUCIFER.   Christ cannot save thy soul, for he is just;
90 There's none but I have interest in[5] the same.

FAUSTUS.   O, what art thou that look'st so terribly?

LUCIFER.   I am Lucifer, and this is my companion prince in hell.

FAUSTUS.   O Faustus, they are come to fetch away thy soul!

LUCIFER.   We come to tell thee thou dost injure us.
95 Thou talk'st of Christ, contrary to thy promise.

BELZEBUB.   Thou should'st not think of God.

LUCIFER.   Think of the devil.

BELZEBUB.   And of his dam° too.   *woman*

FAUSTUS.   Nor will I henceforth:[6] pardon me in this,
100 And Faustus vows never to look to heaven,
Never to name God or to pray to him,
To burn his Scriptures, slay his ministers,
And make my spirits pull his churches down.

LUCIFER.   So shalt thou show thyself an obedient servant,
105 and we will highly gratify thee for it.

BELZEBUB.   Faustus, we are come from hell to show thee some pastime. Sit down, and thou shalt behold the Seven Deadly Sins appear to thee in their own proper shapes and likeness.

110 FAUSTUS.   That sight will be as pleasing unto me as Paradise was to Adam, the first day of his creation.

LUCIFER.   Talk not of Paradise, or creation, but mark the show.
Go, Mephastophilis, fetch them in.

(*Enter the Seven Deadly Sins.*)

---

[1] *dominion or intelligentia*   It was widely believed that the planets were moved or guided by angels or intelligences.

[2] *coelum igneum, et crystallinum*   Latin: a fiery, and a crystalline heaven.

[3] *conjunctions … aspects*   Astrological terms referring respectively to the apparent proximity of two planets, to their positioning on opposite sides of the sky, and to any other angular relation between their positions.

[4] *Per inaequalem motum respectu totius*   Latin: Through an unequal motion with respect to the whole.

[5] *interest in*   Legal claim upon.

[6] *Nor … henceforth*   I.e., think of God.

BELZEBUB.   Now Faustus, question them of their names
115 and dispositions.

FAUSTUS.   That shall I soon: what art thou, the first?

PRIDE.   I am Pride. I disdain to have any parents. I am
like Ovid's flea,[1] I can creep into every corner of a
wench: sometimes like a periwig I sit upon her brow;
120 next like a necklace I hang about her neck; then like a
fan of feathers I kiss her lips; and then, turning myself
to a wrought smock, do what I list. But fie, what a smell
is here? I'll not speak a word more, unless the ground be
perfumed and covered with a cloth of arras.[2]

125 FAUSTUS.   Thou art a proud knave indeed. What art
thou, the second?

COVETOUSNESS.   I am Covetousness, begotten of an old
churl in an old leathern bag; and might I have my wish,
I would desire that this house and all the people in it
130 were turned to gold, that I might lock you up in my
good chest. O, my sweet gold!

FAUSTUS.   What art thou, the third?

WRATH.   I am Wrath. I had neither father nor mother;
I leapt out of a lion's mouth when I was scarce half an
135 hour old, and ever since I have run up and down the
world with this case[3] of rapiers, wounding myself when
I had nobody to fight withal. I was born in hell, and
look to it: for some of you shall be my father.

FAUSTUS.   What art thou, the fourth?

140 ENVY.   I am Envy, begotten of a chimney-sweeper and an
oyster wife.[4] I cannot read, and therefore wish all books
were burned; I am lean with seeing others eat. O, that
there would come a famine through all the world, that
all might die, and I live alone: then thou should'st see
145 how fat I would be. But must thou sit and I stand?
Come down, with a vengeance![5]

FAUSTUS.   Away, envious rascal! What art thou, the fifth?

GLUTTONY.   Who I, sir? I am Gluttony. My parents are
all dead, and the devil a penny they have left me, but a
150 bare pension, and that buys me thirty meals a day and
ten bevers:[6] a small trifle to suffice nature. O, I come of
a royal parentage: my grandfather was a gammon of
bacon,[7] my grand-mother a hogshead[8] of claret[9] wine.
My god-fathers were these: Peter Pickleherring[10] and
155 Martin Martlemas-beef.[11] O, but my godmother she was
a jolly gentlewoman, and well-beloved in every good
town and city: her name was Mistress Margery March-
beer.[12] Now, Faustus, thou hast heard all my progeny,
wilt thou bid me to supper?

160 FAUSTUS.   No, I'll see thee hanged: thou wilt eat up all
my victuals.

GLUTTONY.   Then the devil choke thee.

FAUSTUS.   Choke thyself, glutton! What art thou, the
sixth?

165 SLOTH.   I am Sloth. I was begotten on a sunny bank,
where I have lain ever since, and you have done me
great injury to bring me from thence. Let me be carried
thither again by Gluttony and Lechery. I'll not speak
another word for a king's ransom.

170 FAUSTUS.   What are you, mistress minx,[13] the seventh
and last?

LECHERY.   Who I, sir? I am one that loves an inch of raw
mutton[14] better than an ell[15] of fried stock-fish,[16] and
the first letter of my name begins with Lechery.

175 LUCIFER.   Away, to hell, to hell.

---

[6] *bevers*   Drinks; also light meals or snacks.

[7] *gammon of bacon*   Bottom piece of a flitch of bacon.

[8] *hogshead*   Wine-barrel of a standard size, holding (in modern
terms) 225 liters or 63 American gallons—the equivalent of 25 cases
of a dozen bottles of wine.

[9] *claret*   Light red wine from the Bordeaux region.

[10] *Pickleherring*   Clown figure associated with carnival festivities and
popular farces.

[11] *Martlemas-beef*   Martinmas, or St. Martin's Day (November 11),
was the traditional time to slaughter cattle that could not be fed over
the winter, and to commence the production of salt beef; it was
therefore also a time for feasting on "green" or unsalted beef.

[12] *March-beer*   Strong beer brewed in March.

[13] *minx*   Hussy, wanton woman.

[14] *raw mutton*   Metaphor for prostitutes; the expression here takes
on a phallic meaning.

[15] *ell*   Measure of length (equal in England to some forty-five
inches), commonly contrasted to an inch.

[16] *stock-fish*   Unsalted dried fish, sometimes abusively associated
with the flaccid male organ.

---

[1] *Ovid's flea*   *Elegia de pulice*, a poem written in imitation of Ovid,
was wrongly ascribed to him. In it is a line addressed to the flea:
"You go wherever you wish; nothing, savage, is hidden from you."

[2] *cloth of arras*   Tapestry fabric of the kind woven at Arras in
Flanders; to use it as a floor covering would be grossly ostentatious.

[3] *case*   Pair.

[4] *begotten … wife*   I.e., filthy and foul-smelling woman.

[5] *with a vengeance*   With a curse on you.

(*Exeunt the Sins.*)

Now Faustus, how dost thou like this?
FAUSTUS.   O, this feeds my soul.
LUCIFER.   Tut, Faustus, in hell is all manner of delight.
FAUSTUS.   O, might I see hell, and return again, how
180   happy were I then!
LUCIFER.   Thou shalt. I will send for thee at midnight. In
      mean time, take this book, peruse it thoroughly, and
      thou shalt turn thyself into what shape thou wilt.
FAUSTUS.   Great thanks, mighty Lucifer:
185   This will I keep as chary° as my life.   *carefully*
LUCIFER.   Farewell, Faustus, and think on the devil.
FAUSTUS.   Farewell, great Lucifer. Come, Mephastophilis.

(*Exeunt all.*)

ACT 3, CHORUS.

(*Enter the Chorus [Wagner].*)

WAGNER.   Learned Faustus,
      To know the secrets of astronomy
      Graven in the book of Jove's high firmament,
      Did mount him up to scale Olympus' top,[1]
5   Where sitting in a chariot burning bright,[2]
      Drawn by the strength of yoked dragons' necks,
      He views the clouds, the planets and the stars,
      The tropics, zones, and quarters[3] of the sky,
      From the bright circle of the horned moon
10   Even to the height of *primum mobile*;[4]
      And whirling round with this circumference
      Within the concave compass of the pole,
      From east to west his dragons swiftly glide,

---

[1]   *to scale Olympus' top*   I.e., to ascend to the dwelling-place of the gods, on the top of Mount Olympus.

[2]   *chariot ... bright*   Parodic echo of the vision of the divine chariot-throne in Ezekiel 1.13–28.

[3]   *tropics ... quarters*   Tropics of Cancer and Capricorn, the arctic and antarctic circles and the equator divided the celestial sphere into five belts or zones; traditional astronomy also quartered the celestial sphere with two other circles that passed through its north and south poles: the solstitial colure, which intersects the two tropics at the solstitial points (those at which the ecliptic meets the tropics); and the equinoctial colure, which intersects the equator at the equinoctial points (those at which the ecliptic crosses the equator).

[4]   *From ... mobile*   From the lowest to the highest of the spheres.

And in eight days did bring him home again.
15   Not long he stay'd within his quiet house
      To rest his bones after his weary toil,
      But new exploits do hale him out again,
      And mounted then upon a dragon's back
      That with his wings did part the subtle° air,   *rarified*
20   He now is gone to prove cosmography,[5]
      That measures coasts and kingdoms of the earth.
      And as I guess, will first arrive at Rome
      To see the Pope, and manner of his court,
      And take some part of holy Peter's[6] feast,
25   The which this day is highly solemniz'd.

(*Exit.*)

ACT 3, SCENE 1

(*Enter Faustus and Mephastophilis.*)

FAUSTUS.   Having now, my good Mephastophilis,
      Pass'd with delight the stately town of Trier,[7]
      Environ'd round with airy mountain tops,
      With walls of flint, and deep entrenched lakes,
5   Not to be won by any conquering prince;
      From Paris next, coasting the realm of France,
      We saw the river Main fall into Rhine,
      Whose banks are set with groves of fruitful vines;
      Then up to Naples, rich Campania,[8]
10   Whose buildings, fair and gorgeous to the eye
      (The streets are straightforth and pav'd with finest brick),
      Quarters the town in four equivalents.
      There saw we learned Maro's[9] golden tomb,

---

[5]   *to prove cosmography*   To put geography to the test. Cosmography was sometimes thought of as a science that maps the universe as a whole, thus incorporating geography and astronomy.

[6]   *holy Peter*   St. Peter.

[7]   *Trier*   City on the Moselle River, capital of an electoral state of the Holy Roman Empire, which under the rule of Elector-Archbishop Johann von Schönenburg was subjected during the 1580s and 1590s to a violent wave of witch-hunts.

[8]   *Campania*   In ancient usage, the plain surrounding the city of Capua; since medieval times, Naples has been the principal city of this region. (In modern Italy the name Campania is applied to a much larger area.)

[9]   *Maro*   Virgil, or Publius Vergilius Maro, died at Naples in 19 BCE. In part because his fourth Eclogue was interpreted as a prophecy of the coming of Christ, he acquired a reputation during the medieval period as a necromancer. His supposed (continued)

The way[1] he cut, an English mile in length,

15   Thorough a rock of stone in one night's space.

From thence to Venice, Padua, and the rest,

In midst of which a sumptuous temple stands,

That threats the stars[2] with her aspiring top.

Thus hitherto hath Faustus spent his time.

20   But tell me now, what resting place is this?

Hast thou, as erst° I did command,   *first*

Conducted me within the walls of Rome?

MEPHASTOPHILIS.   Faustus, I have, and because we will not be unprovided,

I have taken up his Holiness' privy chamber[3] for our use.

25 FAUSTUS.   I hope his Holiness will bid us welcome.

MEPHASTOPHILIS.   Tut, 'tis no matter, man, we'll be bold with his good cheer.

And now my Faustus, that thou may'st perceive

What Rome containeth to delight thee with,

Know that this city stands upon seven hills

30   That underprop the groundwork of the same;

Just through the midst runs flowing Tiber's stream,

With winding banks that cut it in two parts,

Over the which four stately bridges lean,

That make safe passage to each part of Rome.

35   Upon the bridge call'd Ponte Angelo

Erected is a castle passing strong,[4]

Within those walls such stores of ordnance are,

And double cannons,[5] fram'd of carved brass,

As match the days within one complete year—

40   Besides the gates and high pyramides[6]

Which Julius Caesar brought from Africa.

FAUSTUS.   Now, by the kingdoms of infernal rule,

Of Styx, Acheron, and the fiery lake

Of ever-burning Phlegethon,[7] I swear

45   That I do long to see the monuments

And situation of bright splendent Rome.

Come therefore, let's away.

MEPHASTOPHILIS.   Nay Faustus, stay: I know you'd fain see the Pope,

And take some part of° holy Peter's feast,   *in*

50   Where thou shalt see a troop of bald-pate friars

Whose *summum bonum*[8] is in belly-cheer.

FAUSTUS.   Well, I am content to compass° then some sport,   *contrive*

And by their folly make us merriment.

Then charm me, that I may be invisible,

55   To do what I please

Unseen of any whilst I stay in Rome.

(*Mephastophilis charms him.*)[9]

MEPHASTOPHILIS.   So, Faustus: now

Do what thou wilt, thou shalt not be discern'd.

(*Sound a sennet.*[10] *Enter the Pope and the Cardinal of Lorraine*[11] *to the banquet, with Friars attending.*)

POPE.   My lord of Lorraine, will't please you draw near?

60 FAUSTUS.   Fall to, and the devil choke you and you spare.[12]

---

tomb stands on the promontory of Posilipo on the Bay of Naples, at the Naples end of a tunnel, nearly half a mile in length, which cuts through the promontory—and which, as Petrarch wrote, "the insipid masses conclude was made by Virgil with magical incantations."

1 *way*   Road. The tunnel is in fact some seven yards wide.

2 *sumptuous … stars*   Saint Mark's in Venice. The "aspiring top" would have to be that of the campanile, which stands at some distance from the church.

3 *privy chamber*   Bedchamber.

4 *castle … strong*   Papal fortress of Castel San Angelo.

5 *double cannons*   Cannons of very large caliber.

6 *pyramides*   Obelisk, in this case the one brought to Rome from Egypt by the emperor Caligula (not Julius Caesar), and moved to its present site in the Piazza San Pietro in 1586. The word is singular, not plural.

7 *Styx, Acheron … Phlegethon*   Three of the four rivers of Hades, the Greek underworld.

8 *summum bonum*   Latin: highest good.

9 *Mephastophilis charms him*   According to Henslowe's *Diary* the Admiral's Men owned a "robe for to go invisible," a prop which may have been used here.

10 *sennet*   Flourish on the trumpet to announce a ceremonial entrance.

11 *Cardinal of Lorraine*   This position was held during the sixteenth century by several members of the powerful Guise family: Jean de Guise (1498–1550); Charles de Guise (1524–74), who helped foment the wars of religion that convulsed France for decades after 1562 and acquired a reputation for dissimulation and cruelty; and Louis de Guise (1555–88), who along with his brother, Henri, third Duc de Guise (1550–88), was assassinated by King Henri III. As leaders of the pro-Spanish and ultra-Catholic Ligue, and thus major figures in the Spanish-led campaign against Protestantism, Louis and Henri de Guise were feared and detested in England.

12 *and you spare*   If you eat sparingly.

POPE.   How now, who's that which spake? Friars, look
     about!
FRIAR.   Here's nobody, if it like[1] your Holiness.
POPE.   My lord, here is a dainty dish was sent me from
     the Bishop of Milan.
65 FAUSTUS.   I thank you, sir.

(*Snatch it.*)

POPE.   How now, who's that which snatched the meat
     from me? Will no man look? My lord, this dish was sent
     me from the Cardinal of Florence.
FAUSTUS.   You say true, I'll ha' it.

(*Snatch it.*)

70 POPE.   What, again! My lord, I'll drink to your grace.
FAUSTUS.   I'll pledge your grace.

(*Snatch it.*)

LORRAINE.   My lord, it may be some ghost newly crept
     out of purgatory come to beg a pardon of your Holiness.
POPE.   It may be so. Friars, prepare a dirge[2] to lay the
75   fury of this ghost. Once again, my lord, fall to. (*The
     Pope crosses himself.*[3])
FAUSTUS.   What, are you crossing your self? Well, use
     that trick no more, I would advise you.

(*Cross again.*)

FAUSTUS. Well, there's the second time. Aware the
80   third, I give you fair warning.

(*Cross again, and Faustus hits him a box of the ear, and
they all run away.*)

Come on, Mephastophilis, what shall we do?

MEPHASTOPHILIS.   Nay, I know not; we shall be cursed
     with bell, book and candle.[4]
FAUSTUS.   How? Bell, book and candle, candle, book
     and bell,
85   Forward and backward, to curse Faustus to hell.
Anon you shall hear a hog grunt, a calf bleat, and an
     ass bray,
Because it is Saint Peter's holy day!

(*Enter all the Friars to sing the dirge.*)

FRIAR.   Come brethren, let's about our business with
     good devotion.

(*They sing this:*)

Cursed be he that stole away his Holiness' meat from the table.
90   *Maledicat dominus!*[5]
Cursed be he that struck his Holiness a blow on the face.
          Maledicat dominus!
Cursed be he that took Friar Sandelo a blow on the pate.
          Maledicat dominus!
95 *Cursed be he that disturbeth our holy dirge.*
          Maledicat dominus!
Cursed be he that took away his Holiness' wine.
Maledicat dominus! Et omnes sancti![6] *Amen.*

(*Faustus and Mephastophilis beat the Friars and fling
fireworks among them, and so exeunt.*)

ACT 3, SCENE 2

(*Enter Robin and Rafe with a silver goblet.*)

ROBIN.   Come Rafe, did I not tell thee we were for ever
     made by this Doctor Faustus' book? *Ecce signum*,[7] here's

---

1   *like* Please.

2   *dirge* Originally "dirige," the first word of the Latin antiphon at
matins in the Office of the Dead ("Dirige, Domine, Deus meus, in
conspectu tuo viam meum": "Direct, O Lord, my God, my way in
thy sight").

3   *crosses himself* Makes the sign of the cross, the preliminary to
Roman Catholic prayer.

4   *bell, book and candle* At the end of the ritual of excommunication, which is performed to debar a member of the Church from the
sacraments, the bell is tolled, the book closed, and the candle
extinguished. That ritual is confused here with the office of exorcism, performed to banish evil spirits.

5   *Maledicat dominus* Latin: May the Lord curse him.

6   *et omnes sancti!* Latin: and (may) all the saints (curse him).

7   *Ecce signum* Latin: Behold the sign.

a simple purchase for horse-keepers! Our horses shall eat no hay as long as this lasts.

(*Enter the Vintner.*)

5 RAFE. But Robin, here comes the Vintner.

ROBIN. Hush, I'll gull[1] him supernaturally. Drawer,[2] I hope all is paid. God be with you; come Rafe.

VINTNER. Soft,[3] sir; a word with you. I must yet have a goblet paid from you ere you go.

10 ROBIN. I a goblet? Rafe, I a goblet? I scorn you, and you are but a etc.[4] I a goblet? Search me!

VINTNER. I mean so, sir, with your favor.

(*Searches Robin.*)

ROBIN. How say you now?

VINTNER. I must say somewhat to your fellow. You, sir.

15 RAFE. Me, sir? Me, sir! Search your fill! Now, sir, you may be ashamed to burden honest men with a matter of truth.

VINTNER. Well, t'one of you hath this goblet about you.

ROBIN. You lie, drawer, 'tis afore me. Sirrah you, I'll
20 teach ye to impeach[5] honest men: stand by, I'll scour you for a goblet. Stand aside, you had best, I charge you in the name of Belzebub! Look to the goblet, Rafe.[6]

VINTNER. What mean you, sirrah?

ROBIN. I'll tell you what I mean.

(*He reads.*)

25 *Sanctabulorum periphrasticon*—Nay, I'll tickle you, Vintner! Look to the goblet, Rafe. *Polypragmos Belseborams framanto pacostiphos tostu Mephastophilis, etc.*[7]

(*Enter Mephastophilis; sets squibs[8] at their backs; they run about.*)

VINTNER. *O nomine Domine!* What mean'st thou, Robin? Thou hast no goblet!

30 RAFE. *Peccatum peccatorum!* Here's thy goblet, good Vintner!

ROBIN. *Misericordia pro nobis!*[9] What shall I do? Good devil, forgive me now, and I'll never rob thy library more!

35 MEPHASTOPHILIS. Monarch of hell, under whose black survey
   Great potentates do kneel with awful fear,
   Upon whose altars thousand souls do lie,
   How am I vexed with these villains' charms!
   From Constantinople am I hither come
40 Only for pleasure of these damned slaves.

ROBIN. How, from Constantinople? You have had a great journey, will you take sixpence in your purse to pay for your supper, and be gone?

MEPHASTOPHILIS. Well villains, for your presumption,
45 I transform thee into an ape, and thee into a dog, and so be gone!

(*Exit.*)

ROBIN. How, into an ape? That's brave, I'll have fine sport with the boys; I'll get nuts and apples enow.[10]

RAFE. And I must be a dog.

50 ROBIN. I'faith, thy head will never be out of the pottage pot.

(*Exeunt.*)

---

1 *gull* Trick.

2 *Drawer* An insult: Robin pretends to mistake the Vintner (or innkeeper) for his employee, the tapster or drawer who serves the customers.

3 *Soft* Softly, slowly; here carrying an imperative force, as in "not so fast!"

4 *etc.* Substitute for a scatological or obscene expression.

5 *impeach* Accuse.

6 *Look … Rafe* Robin and Rafe are apparently passing the goblet back and forth between them.

7 *Sanctabulorum … Mephastophilis, etc.* Robin's incantation is gibberish, though some of it comes close to deviating into sense. The Greek *periphrastikos* means "circumlocutory." In Greek *polypragmosyne* means "curiosity" or "meddlesomeness," and a *polypragmon* is a "busybody." The first four words of the invocation might then be translated as "Busy-body Belseborams … of beating-around-the-bush holy-molydoms!"

8 *squibs* Fireworks.

9 *O … nobis* Garbled scraps of liturgical Latin.

10 *enow* Enough.

ACT 4, CHORUS

(*Enter Chorus.*)

CHORUS.   When Faustus had with pleasure ta'en the view
    Of rarest things and royal courts of kings,
    He stay'd his course, and so returned home,
    Where such as bear his absence but with grief,
5   I mean his friends and nearest companions,
    Did gratulate his safety with kind words,
    And in their conference of what befell
    Touching his journey through the world and air
    They put forth questions of astrology,
10   Which Faustus answer'd with such learned skill
    As[1] they admir'd and wonder'd at his wit.
    Now is his fame spread forth in every land;
    Amongst the rest of Emperor is one,
    Carolus the Fifth,[2] at whose palace now
15   Faustus is feasted 'mongst his noblemen.
    What there he did in trial of his art
    I leave untold, your eyes shall see perform'd.

(*Exit.*)

ACT 4, SCENE 1

(*Enter Emperor, Faustus, and a Knight, with attendants.*)

EMPEROR.   Master Doctor Faustus, I have heard strange
report of thy knowledge in the black art, how that none
in my empire, nor in the whole world, can compare
with thee for the rare[3] effects of magic: they say thou
5 hast a familiar spirit, by whom thou canst accomplish
what thou list.[4] This therefore is my request: that thou
let me see some proof of thy skill, that mine eyes may be
witnesses to confirm what mine ears have heard reported; and here I swear to thee, by the honor of mine
10 imperial crown, that whatever thou doest, thou shalt be
no ways prejudiced or endamaged.[5]
KNIGHT.   (*Aside.*) I'faith, he looks much like a conjurer.
FAUSTUS.   My gracious sovereign, though I must confess
myself far inferior to the report men have published,
15 and nothing answerable[6] to the honor of your imperial
Majesty, yet for that[7] love and duty binds me thereunto,
I am content to do whatsoever your Majesty shall
command me.
EMPEROR.   Then Doctor Faustus, mark what I shall say.
20 As I was sometime solitary set
    Within my closet,[8] sundry thoughts arose
    About the honor of mine ancestors:
    How they had won by prowess such exploits,
    Got riches, subdu'd so many kingdoms,
25   As we that do succeed,[9] or they that shall
    Hereafter possess our throne shall,
    I fear me, never attain to that degree
    Of high renown and great authority;
    Amongst which kings is Alexander the Great,
30   Chief spectacle of the world's pre-eminence,[10]
    The bright shining of whose glorious acts
    Lightens the world with his reflecting beams,
    As when I hear but motion° made of him   *mention*
    It grieves my soul I never saw the man.
35   If therefore thou, by cunning of thine art,
    Canst raise this man from hollow vaults below
    Where lies entomb'd this famous conqueror,
    And bring with him his beauteous paramour,[11]
    Both in their right shapes, gesture, and attire
40   They us'd to wear during their time of life,
    Thou shalt both satisfy my just desire
    And give me cause to praise thee whilst I live.
FAUSTUS.   My gracious lord, I am ready to accomplish
your request, so far forth as by art and power of my
45 spirit I am able to perform.
KNIGHT.   (*Aside.*) I'faith that's just nothing at all.

---

[1] *As* That.

[2] *Carolus the Fifth* Charles V (1500–58), King of Spain and Holy
Roman Emperor from 1518 and 1519 respectively until his
abdication in 1555. The historical Doctor Faustus never made an
appearance at the imperial court. Contemporary *magi*, however, had
connections with the courts of both the emperor Maximilian
(Charles V's grandfather and immediate predecessor) and Charles V.

[3] *rare* Remarkable, extraordinary.

[4] *what thou list* Whatever you wish.

[5] *endamaged* Harmed.

[6] *nothing answerable* Quite unequal.

[7] *for that* Because.

[8] *closet* Study, inner chamber.

[9] *succeed* Follow in dynastic succession.

[10] *pre-eminence* Pre-eminent people.

[11] *paramour* Mistress, consort (i.e., Roxane of Oxyartes).

FAUSTUS. But if it like your Grace, it is not in my ability to present before your eyes the true substantial bodies of those two deceased princes, which long since are con-
50 sumed to dust.

KNIGHT. (*Aside.*) Ay, marry[1] Master Doctor, now there's a sign of grace in you when you will confess the truth.

FAUSTUS. But such spirits as can lively resemble Alexander and his paramour shall appear before your Grace, in
55 that manner that they best lived in, in their most flourishing estate, which I doubt not shall sufficiently content your imperial Majesty.

EMPEROR. Go to,[2] Master Doctor, let me see them presently.[3]

60 KNIGHT. Do you hear, Master Doctor? You bring Alexander and his paramour before the Emperor?

FAUSTUS. How then, sir?

KNIGHT. I'faith, that's as true as Diana turned me to a stag.

65 FAUSTUS. No sir, but when Actaeon[4] died, he left the horns for you. Mephastophilis, be gone.

(*Exit Mephastophilis.*)

KNIGHT. Nay, and[5] you go to conjuring, I'll be gone.

(*Exit Knight.*)

FAUSTUS. I'll meet with[6] you anon for interrupting me so. Here they are, my gracious lord.

(*Enter Mephastophilis with Alexander and his paramour.*)

70 EMPEROR. Master Doctor, I heard this lady while she lived had a wart or mole in her neck. How shall I know whether it be so or no?

FAUSTUS. Your highness may boldly go and see.

---

[1] *marry* Here, expression used to give emphasis to a statement.

[2] *Go to* Normally an expression of incredulity, it appears here to express mild demurral, or perhaps encouragement, with the same range of meanings as "Come, come."

[3] *presently* At once.

[4] *Diana … Actaeon* Actaeon, a hunter, witnessed the goddess Diana and her nymphs bathing; the goddess transformed him into a stag and he was torn to pieces by his own dogs.

[5] *and* If.

[6] *meet with* Get even with.

(*Emperor does so; then spirits exeunt.*)

EMPEROR. Sure these are no spirits, but the true sub-
75 stantial bodies of these two deceased princes.[7]

FAUSTUS. Will't please your highness now to send for the knight that was so pleasant with me here of late?

EMPEROR. One of you call him forth.

(*Enter the Knight with a pair of horns on his head.*)

How now, sir knight? Why, I had thought thou had'st
80 been a bachelor, but now I see thou hast a wife, that not only gives thee horns but makes thee wear them. Feel on thy head!

KNIGHT. Thou damned wretch and execrable dog, Bred in the concave of some monstrous rock,
85 How dar'st thou thus abuse a gentleman? Villain, I say, undo what thou hast done!

FAUSTUS. O not so fast, sir; there's no haste but good.[8] Are you remembered how you crossed me in my conference with the Emperor? I think I have met with you for
90 it.

EMPEROR. Good Master Doctor, at my entreaty release him. He hath done penance sufficient.

FAUSTUS. My gracious lord, not so much for the injury[9] he offered me here in your presence, as to delight you
95 with some mirth, hath Faustus worthily requited this injurious knight; which being all I desire, I am content to release him of his horns. And sir knight, hereafter speak well of scholars. Mephastophilis, transform him straight.[10] Now, my good lord, having done my duty, I
100 humbly take my leave.

EMPEROR. Farewell, Master Doctor; yet ere you go, expect from me a bounteous reward.

(*Exeunt Emperor, Knight, and attendants.*)

ACT 4, SCENE 2

FAUSTUS. Now Mephastophilis, the restless course

---

[7] *princes* Used in this period to refer, not to a male ruler, but any ruler.

[8] *there's … good* Common proverb: "No haste but good (speed)."

[9] *injury* Insult.

[10] *straight* At once.

That time doth run with calm and silent foot,
Shortening my days and thread of vital life,
Calls for the payment of my latest years.
5   Therefore, sweet Mephastophilis,
Let us make haste to Wittenberg.
MEPHASTOPHILIS.   What, will you go on horseback, or
      on foot?
FAUSTUS.   Nay, till I am past this fair and pleasant green
I'll walk on foot.

(*Enter a Horse-courser.*)[1]

10   HORSE-COURSER.   I have been all this day seeking one
Master Fustian; mass,[2] see where he is. God save you,
Master Doctor.
FAUSTUS.   What, horse-courser, you are well met.
HORSE-COURSER.   Do you hear, sir? I have brought you
15   forty dollars for your horse.
FAUSTUS.   I cannot sell him. If thou lik'st him for fifty,
take him.
HORSE-COURSER.   Alas sir, I have no more. I pray you,
speak for me.
20   MEPHASTOPHILIS.   I pray you, let him have him. He is
an honest fellow, and he has a great charge,[3] neither wife
nor child.
FAUSTUS.   Well, come, give me your money. My boy will
deliver him to you. But I must tell you one thing before
25   you have him: ride him not into the water at any hand.[4]
HORSE-COURSER.   Why sir, will he not drink of all
waters?
FAUSTUS.   O yes, he will drink of all waters, but ride him
not into the water. Ride him over hedge or ditch, or
30   where thou wilt, but not into the water.
HORSE-COURSER.   Well, sir, now am I a made man for
ever! I'll not leave[5] my horse for forty. If he had but the
quality of hey ding ding, hey ding ding, I'd make a
brave living on him: he has a buttock so slick as an eel.[6]

---

[1]   *Horse-courser*   Horse dealer.

[2]   *Fustian*   Clownish deformation of "Faustus"; bombast, nonsense;
mass   Contraction of "By the Mass."

[3]   *charge*   Burden (of family responsibilities).

[4]   *at any hand*   Under any circumstances.

[5]   *leave*   Sell.

[6]   *hey ding ding … eel*   "Hey ding-a-ding" is a common refrain in
popular songs. The phrase has sexual overtones, and "buttock so
slick as an eel" implies sexual potency; thus, the "brave living" that

35   Well, God-bye[7] sir, your boy will deliver him me. But
hark ye sir, if my horse be sick or ill at ease, if I bring his
water[8] to you, you'll tell me what it is?
FAUSTUS.   Away, you villain! What, dost thou think I am
a horse-doctor?

(*Exit Horse-courser.*)

40   What art thou, Faustus, but a man condemn'd to die?
Thy fatal time[9] doth draw to final end;
Despair doth drive distrust into my thoughts.
Confound these passions with a quiet sleep:
Tush, Christ did call the thief upon the cross.[10]
45   Then rest thee, Faustus, quiet in conceit.

(*Sleeps in his chair. Enter Horse-courser all wet, crying.*)

HORSE-COURSER.   Alas, alas, Doctor Fustian, quotha?
Mass, Doctor Lopus[11] was never such a doctor: has given
me a purgation,[12] has purged me of forty dollars, I shall
never see them more. But yet like an ass as I was, I
50   would not be ruled by him, for he bade me I should ride
him into no water. Now I, thinking my horse had some
rare quality that he would not have had me know of, I
like a venturous youth rid him into the deep pond at the
town's end. I was no sooner in the middle of the pond,
55   but my horse vanished away, and I sat upon a bottle[13] of
hay, never so near drowning in my life! But I'll seek out
my doctor, and have my forty dollars again, or I'll make

---

the horse-courser anticipates will presumably come from stud fees.

[7]   *God-bye*   Contraction of "God be with you."

[8]   *water*   Urine.

[9]   *fatal time*   Time allotted by fate.

[10]   *the thief … cross*   See Luke 23.43.

[11]   *Doctor Lopus*   Doctor Roderigo Lopez, a Portuguese *marrano*, or
Christianized Jew, and personal physician to Queen Elizabeth. Lopez
incurred the enmity of the Earl of Essex, who in January 1594
accused him of high treason; he was tried (and convicted) on
February 28 on charges that included attempting to poison the
queen, and was executed on June 7—more than a year after Marlowe's death. Although Lopez was well-known even before his
appointment as the queen's physician in 1586 (he had previously
been household physician to the Earl of Leicester), the past-tense
allusion to him suggests that in its present form this scene must have
been written after Marlowe's death.

[12]   *purgation*   Emetic.

[13]   *bottle*   From the French "botte," meaning bundle.

it dearest[1] horse. O, yonder is his snipper-snapper.[2] Do you hear? you, hey-pass,[3] where's your master?

60 MEPHASTOPHILIS. Why sir, what would you? You cannot speak with him.

HORSE-COURSER. But I will speak with him.

MEPHASTOPHILIS. Why, he's fast asleep; come some other time.

65 HORSE-COURSER. I'll speak with him now, or I'll break his glass windows[4] about his ears.

MEPHASTOPHILIS. I tell thee, he hath not slept this eight nights.

HORSE-COURSER. And he have not slept this eight
70 weeks I'll speak with him.

MEPHASTOPHILIS. See where he is, fast asleep.

HORSE-COURSER. Ay, this is he. God save ye Master Doctor! Master Doctor, Master Doctor Fustian, forty dollars, forty dollars for a bottle of hay!

75 MEPHASTOPHILIS. Why, thou seest he hears thee not.

HORSE-COURSER. So ho, ho! So ho, ho![5] (*Hallow in his ear.*) No, will you not wake? I'll make you wake ere I go!

(*Pull him by the leg, and pull it away.*)

Alas, I am undone! What shall I do?

80 FAUSTUS. O my leg, my leg! Help, Mephastophilis! Call the officers, my leg, my leg!

MEPHASTOPHILIS. Come villain, to the constable.

HORSE-COURSER. O Lord, sir: let me go, and I'll give you forty dollars more.

85 MEPHASTOPHILIS. Where be they?

HORSE-COURSER. I have none about me; come to my ostry,[6] and I'll give them you.

MEPHASTOPHILIS. Be gone, quickly.

(*Horse-courser runs away.*)

FAUSTUS. What, is he gone? Farewell he, Faustus has his
90 leg again, and the horse-courser, I take it, a bottle of hay

---

1 *dearest* Most expensive. If the horse-courser can't have his money back, he'll take revenge.

2 *snipper-snapper* Conceited young fellow, smart-aleck.

3 *hey-pass* Expression used by fairground conjurors or jugglers.

4 *glass windows* Spectacles.

5 *So ho, ho* Huntsman's cry.

6 *ostry* Hostelry, inn.

---

for his labor. Well, this trick shall cost him forty dollars more.

(*Enter Wagner.*)

How now, Wagner, what's the news with thee?

WAGNER. Sir, the Duke of Vanholt doth earnestly
95 entreat your company.

FAUSTUS. The Duke of Vanholt! An honorable gentleman, to whom I must be no niggard[7] of my cunning. Come Mephastophilis, let's away to him.

(*Exeunt.*)

ACT 4, SCENE 3

(*Enter to them the Duke, and the Duchess; the Duke speaks.*)

DUKE. Believe me, Master Doctor, this merriment hath much pleased me.

FAUSTUS. My gracious lord, I am glad it contents you so well. But it may be, madam, you take no delight in this.
5 I have heard that great-bellied[8] women do long for some dainties or other: what is it, madam? Tell me, and you shall have it.

DUCHESS. Thanks, good Master Doctor, and for I see your courteous intent to pleasure me, I will not hide
10 from you the thing my heart desires; and were it now summer, as it is January, and the dead time of winter, I would desire no better meat[9] than a dish of ripe grapes.

FAUSTUS. Alas, madam, that's nothing. Mephastophilis, be gone.

(*Exit Mephastophilis.*)

15 Were it a greater thing than this, so it would content you, you should have it.

(*Enter Mephastophilis with the grapes.*)

Here they be, madam, will't please you to taste on them?

DUKE. Believe me, Master Doctor, this makes me
20 wonder above the rest, that being in the dead time of

---

7 *niggard* Parsimonious person, one who shares only grudgingly.

8 *great-bellied* Pregnant.

9 *meat* Food.

winter, and in the month of January, how you should
come by these grapes.

FAUSTUS. If it like your Grace, the year is divided into
two circles over the whole world, that when it is here
25   winter with us, in the contrary circle it is summer with
them, as in India, Saba, and farther countries in the
east;[1] and by means of a swift spirit that I have, I had
them brought hither, as ye see. How do you like them,
madam, be they good?

30   DUCHESS. Believe me, Master Doctor, they be the best
grapes that e'er I tasted in my life before.

FAUSTUS. I am glad they content you so, madam.

DUKE. Come, madam, let us in, where you must well
reward this learned man for the kindness he hath
35   showed to you.

DUCHESS. And so I will, my lord, and whilst I live rest
beholden for this courtesy.

FAUSTUS. I humbly thank your Grace.

DUKE. Come Master Doctor, follow us, and receive your
40   reward.

(*Exeunt.*)

ACT 5, SCENE 1

(*Enter Wagner alone.*)

WAGNER. I think my master means to die shortly,
For he hath given to me all his goods;
And yet methinkes[2] if that death were near
He would not banquet and carouse and swill
5   Amongst the students, as even now he doth,
Who are at supper with such belly-cheer
As Wagner ne'er beheld in all his life.
See where they come: belike the feast is ended.

(*Exit. Enter Faustus with two or three scholars.*)

FIRST SCHOLAR. Master Doctor Faustus, since our
10   conference about fair ladies, which was the beautiful'st
in all the world, we have determined with[3] our selves

that Helen of Greece was the admirablest lady that ever
lived. Therefore, Master Doctor, if you will do us so
much favor as to let us see that peerless dame of Greece,
15   whom all the world admires for majesty, we should
think ourselves much beholding unto you.

FAUSTUS. Gentlemen,
For that[4] I know your friendship is unfeign'd
(And Faustus' custom is not to deny
20   The just requests of those that wish him well),
You shall behold that peerless dame of Greece
No otherways for pomp and majesty
Than when Sir Paris cross'd the seas with her
And brought the spoils to rich Dardania.[5]
25   Be silent then, for danger is in words.

(*Music sounds, and Helen passeth over the stage.*)

SECOND SCHOLAR. Too simple is my wit to tell her
praise,
Whom all the world admires for majesty.

THIRD SCHOLAR. No marvel though the angry Greeks
pursued[6]
With ten years' war the rape° of such a queen,   abduction
30   Whose heavenly beauty passeth all compare.

FIRST SCHOLAR. Since we have seen the pride of
nature's works,
And only paragon of excellence,

(*Enter an old man.*)

Let us depart, and for this glorious deed
Happy and blest be Faustus evermore.
35   FAUSTUS. Gentlemen, farewell, the same I wish to you.

(*Exeunt scholars.*)

OLD MAN. Ah, Doctor Faustus, that I might prevail
To guide thy steps unto the way of life,
By which sweet path thy may'st attain the goal
That shall conduct thee to celestial rest.
40   Break heart, drop blood, and mingle it with tears,
Tears falling from repentant heaviness

---

[1] *two circles … east* The two "circles" should of course be the
northern and southern hemispheres. Saba is the land of the Queen
of Sheba, now Yemen.

[2] *methinkes* Modernized spelling would upset the rhythm of this
line.

[3] *determined with* Settled among.

[4] *for that* Because.

[5] *Dardania* Troy, referred to here by the name of the founder of
the Trojan dynasty, Dardanus.

[6] *pursued* Sought to avenge.

Of thy most vile and loathsome filthiness,
The stench whereof corrupts the inward soul
With such flagitious[1] crimes of heinous sins
45 As no commiseration may expel
But mercy, Faustus, of thy Saviour sweet,
Whose blood alone must wash away thy guilt.[2]
FAUSTUS. Where art thou, Faustus?[3] wretch, what hast
      thou done?
Damn'd art thou, Faustus, damn'd, despair and die!
50 Hell claims his right, and with a roaring voice
Says, "Faustus, come, thine hour is almost come!"

(*Enter Mephastophilis, who gives him a dagger.*)

And Faustus now will come to do thee right.
OLD MAN.   Ah stay, good Faustus, stay thy desperate steps:
I see an angel hovers o'er thy head,
55 And with a vial full of precious grace[4]
Offers to pour the same into thy soul:
Then call for mercy and avoid despair.
FAUSTUS.   Ah sweet friend, I feel thy words
To comfort my distressed soul.
60 Leave me awhile to ponder on my sins.
OLD MAN.   I go, sweet Faustus, but with heavy cheer,
Fearing the ruin of thy hopeless soul.

(*Exit.*)

FAUSTUS.   Accursed Faustus, where is mercy now?
I do repent, and yet I do despair:
65 Hell strives with grace for conquest in my breast;
What shall I do to shun the snares of death?
MEPHASTOPHILIS.   Thou traitor, Faustus, I arrest thy soul
For disobedience to my sovereign lord.
Revolt,[5] or I'll in piece-meal tear thy flesh!

70 FAUSTUS.   I do repent I e'er offended him.
Sweet Mephastophilis, entreat thy lord
To pardon my unjust presumption,
And with my blood again I will confirm
My former vow I made to Lucifer.
75 MEPHASTOPHILIS.   Do it then quickly, with unfeigned
      heart,
Lest greater danger do attend thy drift.[6]
FAUSTUS.   Torment, sweet friend, that base and
      crooked age
That durst dissuade me from thy Lucifer,
With greatest torments that our hell affords.
80 MEPHASTOPHILIS.   His faith is great, I cannot touch his
      soul.
But what I may afflict his body with
I will attempt, which is but little worth.
FAUSTUS.   One thing, good servant, let me crave of thee
To glut the longing of my heart's desire:
85 That I might have unto° my paramour   *as*
That heavenly Helen which I saw of late,
Whose sweet embracings may extinguish clean
These thoughts that do dissuade me from my vow,
And keep mine oath I made to Lucifer.
90 MEPHASTOPHILIS.   Faustus, this, or what else thou
      shalt desire
Shall be perform'd in the twinkling of an eye.

(*Enter Helen.*)

FAUSTUS.   Was this the face that launch'd a thousand ships
And burnt the topless° towers of Ilium?°   *soaring / Troy*
Sweet Helen, make me immortal with a kiss;
95 Her lips suck forth my soul, see where it flies!
Come Helen, come, give me my soul again;
Here will I dwell, for heaven be in these lips,
And all is dross that is not Helena.

(*Enter old man.*)

I will be Paris, and for love of thee
100 Instead of Troy shall Wittenberg be sack'd,
And I will combat with weak Menelaus[7]

---

[1] *flagitious* Extremely wicked, infamous.

[2] *no ... guilt* Cf. Revelation 1.5: "Jesus Christ ... loved us, and washed us from our sins in his own blood." *The Prayer-Book of Queen Elizabeth* (1559) specifies that if a person in "extremity of sickness ... do truly repent him of his sins, and steadfastly believe that Jesus Christ ... shed his blood for his redemption" (135), this is the equivalent of taking communion.

[3] *Where ... Faustus?* Cf. Genesis 3.9: "The Lord God called to the man, and said unto him, Where art thou?"

[4] *vial ... grace* The old man here individualizes an image from Revelation 5.8, in which elders worshiping before the throne of God carry "golden vials full of odors, which are the prayers of saints."

[5] *Revolt* Reverse your course of action.

[6] *drift* Conscious or unconscious tendency or aim.

[7] *weak Menelaus* Book 3 of Homer's *Iliad* recounts the duel between Alexandros or Paris and Menelaus. Paris challenged all the best of the Achaeans to single combat, but recoiled in fear from Menelaus. Having agreed that Helen and her possessions should go to the victor, Paris was defeated, but saved from death by Aphrodite,

And wear thy colours on my plumed crest;
Yea, I will wound Achilles in the heel
And then return to Helen for a kiss.
105 O, thou art fairer than the evening air
Clad in the beauty of a thousand stars;
Brighter art thou than flaming Jupiter
When he appear'd to hapless Semele,[1]
More lovely than the monarch of the sky
110 In wanton Arethusa's[2] azur'd arms,
And none but thou shalt be my paramour.

(*Exeunt.*)

OLD MAN.   Accursed Faustus, miserable man,
That from thy soul exclud'st the grace of heaven
And fliest the throne of his tribunal seat!

(*Enter the devils.*)

115 Satan begins to sift me[3] with his pride;
As in this furnace God shall try my faith,
My faith, vile hell, shall triumph over thee!
Ambitious fiends, see how the heaven smiles
At your repulse, and laughs your state to scorn:
120 Hence, hell, for hence I fly unto my God.

(*Exeunt.*)

ACT 5, SCENE 2

(*Enter Faustus with the scholars.*)

FAUSTUS.   Ah, gentlemen!
FIRST SCHOLAR.   What ails Faustus?
FAUSTUS.   Ah, my sweet chamber-fellow, had I lived
with thee, then had I lived still, but now I die eternally.
5 Look, comes he not, comes he not?

SECOND SCHOLAR.   What means Faustus?
THIRD SCHOLAR.   Belike he is grown into some sickness,
by being over-solitary.
FIRST SCHOLAR.   If it be so, we'll have physicians to cure
10 him. 'Tis but a surfeit,[4] never fear, man.
FAUSTUS.   A surfeit of deadly sin, that hath damned both
body and soul.
SECOND SCHOLAR.   Yet Faustus, look up to heaven;
remember, God's mercies are infinite.
15 FAUSTUS.   But Faustus' offence can ne'er be pardoned:
the serpent that tempted Eve may be saved, but not
Faustus. Ah gentlemen, hear me with patience, and
tremble not at my speeches. Though my heart pants and
quivers to remember that I have been a student here
20 these thirty years, O would I had never seen Wittenberg,
never read book: and what wonders I have done, all
Germany can witness, yea all the world, for which
Faustus hath lost both Germany and the world, yea
heaven itself, heaven the seat of God, the throne of the
25 blessed, the kingdom of joy, and must remain in hell for
ever—hell, ah, hell, for ever! Sweet friends, what shall
become of Faustus, being in hell for ever?
THIRD SCHOLAR.   Yet Faustus, call on God.
FAUSTUS.   On God, whom Faustus hath abjured? on
30 God, whom Faustus hath blasphemed? Ah my God, I
would weep, but the devil draws in my tears. Gush forth
blood instead of tears, yea life and soul! Oh, he stays my
tongue; I would lift up my hands, but see, they hold
them, they hold them!
35 ALL.   Who, Faustus?
FAUSTUS.   Lucifer and Mephastophilis. Ah, gentlemen,
I gave them my soul for my cunning.[5]
ALL.   God forbid!
FAUSTUS.   God forbade it indeed, but Faustus hath done
40 it: for the vain pleasure of four and twenty years hath
Faustus lost eternal joy and felicity. I writ them a bill
with mine own blood, the date is expired, the time will
come, and he will fetch me!
FIRST SCHOLAR.   Why did not Faustus tell of this before,
45 that divines might have prayed for thee?
FAUSTUS.   Oft have I thought to have done so, but the
devil threatened to tear me in pieces if I named God, to
fetch both body and soul if I once gave ear to divinity,

---

who carried him in a mist into his own bedchamber. There,
although shamed in Helen's eyes as in everyone else's, he promptly
took her to bed.

[1] *hapless Semele* One of Jupiter's human mistresses, she was
persuaded by Juno to ask him to come to her in the same form in
which he embraced Juno in heaven, and was consumed by fire.

[2] *Arethusa* Nymph who, bathing in the river Alpheus, aroused the
river-god's lust; fleeing from him, she was transformed into a
fountain. No classical myth links her with Jupiter or the sun-god.

[3] *sift me* Cf. Christ's words to Peter at the last supper: "Simon,
Simon, behold, Satan hath desired to have you, and he may sift you
as wheat" (Luke 22.31).

[4] *surfeit* Excessive indulgence in food or drink, and the resulting
disorder of the system.

[5] *cunning* Knowledge.

and now 'tis too late: gentlemen, away, lest you perish
50 with me.

SECOND SCHOLAR.   O what may we do to save Faustus?

FAUSTUS.   Talk not of me, but save yourselves, and
depart.

THIRD SCHOLAR.   God will strengthen me, I will stay
55 with Faustus.

FIRST SCHOLAR.   Tempt not God, sweet friend, but let
us into the next room, and there pray for him.

FAUSTUS.   Ah, pray for me, pray for me; and what noise
soever[1] ye hear, come not unto me, for nothing can
60 rescue me.

SECOND SCHOLAR.   Pray thou, and we will pray that
God may have mercy upon thee.

FAUSTUS.   Gentlemen, farewell. If I live till morning, I'll
visit you; if not, Faustus is gone to hell.

65 ALL.   Faustus, farewell.

(*Exeunt scholars. The clock strikes eleven.*)

FAUSTUS.   Ah Faustus,
Now hast thou but one bare hour to live,
And then thou must be damn'd perpetually.
Stand still, you ever-moving spheres of heaven.
70 That time may cease, and midnight never come!
Fair nature's eye, rise, rise again, and make
Perpetual day, or let this hour be but a year,
A month, a week, a natural day,
That Faustus may repent, and save his soul.
75 *O lente lente currite noctis equi!*[2]
The stars move still, time runs, the clock will strike,
The devil will come, and Faustus must be damn'd.
O, I'll leap up to my God: who pulls me down?
See, see where Christ's blood streams in the firmament:
80 One drop would save my soul, half a drop! Ah, my Christ,
Ah rend not my heart for the naming of my Christ,[3]
Yet I will call on him, oh spare me Lucifer!
Where is it now? 'tis gone,
And see where God stretcheth out his arm
85 And bends his ireful brows!

Mountains and hills, come, come, and fall on me
And hide me from the heavy wrath of God.[4]
No, no?
Then will I headlong run into the earth.
90 Earth, gape! O no, it will not harbor me.
You stars that reign'd at my nativity,
Whose influence hath allotted death and hell,
Now draw up Faustus like a foggy mist
Into the entrails of yon laboring cloud,
95 That when you vomit forth into the air
My limbs may issue from your smoky mouths,
So that my soul may but ascend to heaven.

(*The watch° strikes.*)   clock

Ah, half the hour is past: 'twill all be past anon.
Oh God, if thou wilt not have mercy on my soul,
100 Yet for Christ's sake, whose blood hath ransom'd me,
Impose some end to my incessant pain:
Let Faustus live in a hell a thousand years,
A hundred thousand, and at last be sav'd.
O, no end is limited to damned souls.[5]
105 Why wert thou not a creature wanting soul?
Or why is this immortal that thou hast?
Ah, Pythagoras' metempsychosis,[6] were that true
This soul should fly from me, and I be chang'd
Unto some brutish beast.
110 All beasts are happy, for when they die
Their souls are soon dissolv'd in elements,
But mine must live still to be plagu'd in hell.
Curst be the parents that engender'd me;
No Faustus, curse thyself, curse Lucifer
115 That hath depriv'd thee of the joys of heaven!

(*The clock strikes twelve.*)

O it strikes, it strikes, now body, turn to air
Or Lucifer will bear thee quick° to hell!   alive

(*Thunder and lightning.*)
O soul, be changed into little water drops
And fall into the ocean, ne'er be found;
120 My God, my God, look not so fierce on me!

---

[1]   *soever* I.e., whatsoever.

[2]   *O lente … equi* Latin: O gallop slowly, slowly, you horses of the
night! Ovid, *Amores* 1.8.40.

[3]   *rend … Christ* Cf. Joel 2.12–13, where, faced by a terrifying
prospect of destruction that makes the earth quake and the heavens
tremble, and that darkens the sun, moon and stars, the Israelites are
exhorted to "rend their hearts in repentance."

[4]   *Mountains … God* Cf. Luke 23.30, Revelation 6.16, Hosea 10.8.

[5]   *no end … souls* I.e., damnation is endless.

[6]   *metempsychosis* Doctrine of the transmigration of souls.

(Enter devils.)

Adders and serpents, let me breathe awhile!
Ugly hell gape not, come not Lucifer,
I'll burn my books, ah Mephastophilis!

(Exeunt with him.)

EPILOGUE

(Enter Chorus.)

CHORUS.　Cut is the branch that might have grown full
　　straight,

And burned is Apollo's laurel bough
That sometime grew within this learned man:
Faustus is gone, regard his hellish fall,
Whose fiendful fortune may exhort the wise
Only to wonder[1] at unlawful things,
Whose deepness doth entice such forward wits
To practice more than heavenly power permits.

(Exit.)

Terminat hora diem, terminat Author opus.[2]
—1604, 1616

In Context

Dr. Faustus

from Anonymous, *The History of the Damnable Life, and Deserved Death of Dr. John Faustus* (1592)

Though much of the story of Marlowe's *Dr. Faustus* and of its principal source, the prose *History of the Damnable Life, and Deserved Death of Dr. John Faustus*, are obviously legendary or mythic in nature, there was indeed a historical Dr. Faustus. Like Marlowe himself, the historical Faustus was, in Michael Keefer's words, "a transgressor both of sexual and of ideological codes."

　　The historical Faustus was Georgius of Helmstadt (c. 1466–c. 1537), a magician from the village of Helmstadt who attended the University of Heidelberg from 1483 until 1489 or thereabouts, and who by 1507 had established himself as a magician styling himself as "Magister Georgius Sabellicus, the younger Faustus, Chief of Necromancers, Astrologer, the Second Magus, Palmist, Diviner by Earth and Fire, Second in the Art of Divination by Water." Georgius Faustus seems to have had a very mixed career; he was hired in 1520 to cast the horoscope of the Bishop of Bamberg, and consulted in 1536 by a close associate of Erasmus's to predict the fortunes of an expedition to the new world—but he was also accused of being a braggart, a blasphemer, and worse. (When, in 1507, Faustus for a time took an appointment as a schoolmaster, he was accused of having indulged "in the most abominable kind of fornication with the boys," and fled to escape punishment.)

　　There was no suggestion during the life of the historical Faustus of a pact with the devil. Even before his death, however, the historical figure had evidently become something of a magnet for anecdotes of all sorts about sorcerers, charlatans, and demons. Interestingly, Martin Luther seems to have played a key role in the formation of the Faustus legend; the earliest record that survives of many of the anecdotes about Faustus is the written record of the "table talk" of Luther in the 1530s.

1　*Only to wonder*　To be content with wondering.

2　*Terminat ... opus*　Latin: The hour ends the day; the author ends his work.

The direct source of the legend of Faustus selling his soul to the devil is the *Historia von D. Johann Fausten* of 1587, translated into English as *The History of the Damnable Life, and Deserved Death of Dr. John Faustus* in 1592. Marlowe evidently drew on this work extensively for his *Dr. Faustus;* a few key passages are reproduced below, with parallel passages from the play noted.

from CHAPTER 1.   John Faustus, born in the town of Rhode, lying in the province of Weimar in Germ[any], his father a poor husbandman and not [able] well to bring him up: but having an uncle at Wittenberg, a rich man and without issue, took this J. Faustus from his father and made him his heir, in so much that his father was no more troubled with him, for he remained with his uncle at Wittenberg, where he was kept at the university in the same city to study divinity. But Faustus, being of a naughty mind and otherwise addicted, applied not his studies, but took himself to other exercises: the which his uncle oftentimes hearing, rebuked him for it, as Eli oft times rebuked his children for sinning against the Lord: even so this good man labored to have Faustus apply his study of divinity, that he might come to the knowledge of God and his laws. But it is manifest that many virtuous parents have wicked children, as Cain, Reuben, Absolom and such like have been to their parents: so this Faustus having godly parents, and seeing him to be of a toward wit, were very desirous to bring him up in those virtuous studies, namely, of divinity: but he gave himself secretly to study necromancy and conjuration, in so much that few or none could perceive his profession.

But to the purpose: Faustus continued at study in the university, and was by the Rectors and sixteen Masters afterwards examined how he had profited in his studies; and being found by them that none for his time were able to argue with him in divinity, or for the excellency of his wisdom to compare with him, with one consent they made him Doctor of Divinity. But Doctor Faustus, within short time after he had obtained his degree, fell into such fantasies and deep cogitations that he was marked of many, and of the most part of the students was called the Speculator; and sometime he would throw the scriptures from him as though he had no care of his former profession: so that he began a very ungodly life, as hereafter more at large may appear; for the old proverb saith, Who can hold that will away? So who can hold Faustus from the devil, that seeks after him with all his endeavor? For he accompanied himself with divers that were seen in those devilish arts, and that had the Chaldean, Persian, Hebrew, Arabian, and Greek tongues, using figures, characters, conjurations, incantations, with many other ceremonies belonging to these infernal arts, as necromancy, charms, soothsaying, witchcraft, enchantment, being delighted with their books, words, and names so well that he studied day and night therein: in so much that he could not abide to be called doctor of divinity, but waxed a worldly man, and named himself an astrologian, and a mathematician: and for a shadow sometimes a physician, and did great cures, namely with herbs, roots, waters, drinks, receipts, and clisters. And without doubt he was passing wise, and excellent perfect in the holy scriptures: but he that knoweth his master's will and doth it not, is worthy to be beaten with many stripes. It is written, No man can serve two masters, and Thou shalt not tempt the Lord thy God: but Faustus threw all this in the wind, and made his soul of no estimation, regarding more his worldly pleasure than the joys to come: therefore at the day of judgment there is no hope of his redemption.

CHAPTER 2. You have heard before, that all Faustus' mind was set to study the arts of necromancy and conjuration, the which exercise he followed day and night: and taking to him the wings of an eagle, thought to fly over the whole world, and to know the secrets of heaven and earth; for his speculation was so wonderful, being expert in using his *vocabula,* figures, characters, conjurations, and other ceremonial actions, that in all the haste he put in practice to bring the devil before him. And taking his way to a thick wood near to Wittenberg, called in the German tongue *Spisser Waldt...,* he came into the same wood towards evening into a cross way, where he made with a wand a circle in the dust, and within that many more circles and characters: and thus he passed away the time, until it was nine or ten of the clock in the night, then began Doctor Faustus to call for Mephostophiles the spirit, and to charge him in the name of Beelzebub to appear there personally without any long stay: then presently the devil began so great a rumor in the wood, as if heaven and earth would have come together with wind, the trees bowing their tops to the ground; then fell the devil to bleat as if the whole wood had been full of lions, and suddenly about the circle ran the devil as if a thousand wagons had been running together on paved stones.... Faustus commanded that the next morning at twelve of the clock he should appear to him at his house, but the devil would in no wise grant. Faustus began again to conjure him in the name of Beelzebub, that he should fulfil his request: whereupon the spirit agreed, and so they departed each one his way.

from CHAPTER 3.   Doctor Faustus having commanded the spirit to be with him, at his hour appointed he came and appeared in his chamber, demanding of Faustus what his desire was: then began Doctor Faustus anew with him to conjure him that he should be obedient unto him, and to answer him certain articles, and to fulfil them in all points.

1.   That the spirit should serve him and be obedient unto him in all things that he asked of him from that hour until the hour of his death.
2.   Farther, any thing that he desired of him he should bring it to him.
3.   Also, that in all Faustus his demands or interrogations the spirit should tell him nothing but that which is true.

Hereupon the spirit answered and laid his case forth, that he had no power of himself, until he had first given his prince (that was ruler over him) to understand thereof, and to know if he could obtain so much of his lord: Therefore speak farther that I may do thy whole desire to my prince: for it is not in my power to fulfil without his leave....

Doctor Faustus upon this arose where he sat, and said, I will have my request, and yet I will not be damned. The spirit answered, Then shalt thou want thy desire, and yet art thou mine notwithstanding: if any man would detain thee it is in vain, for thine infidelity hath confounded thee.

Hereupon spake Faustus: Get thee hence from me, and take Saint Valentine's farewell and Crisam with thee, yet I conjure thee that thou be here at evening, and bethink thyself on that I have asked thee, and ask thy prince's counsel therein. Mephostophiles the spirit, thus answered, vanished away, leaving Faustus in his study, where he sat pondering with himself how he might obtain his request of the devil without loss of his soul: yet fully he was resolved in himself rather than to want his pleasure, to do whatsoever the spirit and his lord should condition upon.

from CHAPTER 4.   Faustus continuing in his devilish cogitations, never moving out of the place where the spirit left him (such was his fervent love to the devil), the night approaching, this swift flying spirit appeared to Faustus, offering himself with all submission to his service, with full authority from his prince to do whatsoever he would request, if so be Faustus would promise to be his: This answer I bring thee, and an answer must thou make by me again, yet will I hear what is thy desire, because thou hast sworn me to be here at this time. Doctor Faustus gave him this answer, though faintly (for his soul's sake): That his request was none other but to become a devil, or at least a limb of him, and that the spirit should agree unto these articles as followeth.

1.   That he might be a spirit in shape and quality.
2.   That Mephostophiles should be his servant, and at his commandment.
3.   That Mephostophiles should bring him any thing, and do for him whatsoever.
4.   That at all times he should be in his house, invisible to all men, except only to himself, and at his commandment to show himself.

5. Lastly, that Mephostophiles should at all times appear at his command, in what form or shape soever he would.

Upon these points the spirit answered Doctor Faustus, that all this should be granted him and fulfilled, and more if he would agree unto him upon certain articles as followeth.

First, that Doctor Faustus should give himself to his lord Lucifer, body and soul.
Secondly, for confirmation of the same, he should make him a writing, written with his own blood.
Thirdly, that he would be an enemy to all Christian people.
Fourthly, that he would deny his Christian belief.
Fifthly, that he let not any man change his opinion, if so be any man should go about to dissuade or withdraw him from it.

Further, the spirit promised Faustus to give him certain years to live in health and pleasure, and when such years were expired, that then Faustus should be fetched away, and if he should hold these articles and conditions, then he should have all whatsoever his heart would wish or desire; and that Faustus should quickly perceive himself to be a spirit in all manner of actions whatsoever. Hereupon Doctor Faustus his mind was so inflamed that he forgot his soul, and promised Mephostophiles to hold all things as he had mentioned them: he thought the devil was not so black as they use to paint him, nor hell so hot as the people say, etc.

from CHAPTER 6.   *How Doctor Faustus set his blood in a saucer on warm ashes, and writ as followeth.* ... [N]ow have I, Doctor John Faustus, unto the hellish prince of Orient and his messenger Mephostophiles, given both body and soul, upon such condition that they shall learn me, and fulfil my desire in all things, as they have promised and vowed unto me, with due obedience unto me, according to the articles mentioned between us.

Further, I covenant and grant them by these presents, that at the end of 24 years next ensuing the date of this present letter ... I give them full power to do with me at their pleasure, to rule, to send, fetch, or carry me or mine, be it either body, soul, flesh, blood, or goods, into their habitation, be it wheresoever: and hereupon, I defy God and his Christ, all the host of heaven, and all living creatures that bear the shape of God, yea all that lives; and again I say it, and it shall be so. And to the more strengthening of this writing, I have written it with mine own hand and blood....

from Henricus Cornelius Agrippa, *De Occulta Philosophia* (Of Occult Philosophy),[1] 1533

Early in *Dr. Faustus* Faustus imagines that he "will be as cunning as Agrippa was, / Whose shadows made all Europe honour him." Agrippa (1486–1535) was a contemporary of the historical Dr. Faustus, and the two names were often linked in sixteenth century attacks on magic. Agrippa's *De Occulta Philosophia* is an encyclopaedic survey of magical beliefs and practices which also expounds a magical form of Christianity; Agrippa draws on Hermetic, Cabalistic, and Neoplatonic writings as well as on the canonical scriptures in developing his own notions of rebirth and deification. Not surprisingly, his efforts to associate non-Christian magical practices and traditions with the Christian scriptures were widely denounced. The groundbreaking Protestant thinker Jean Calvin termed him an atheist (1550), and André Thevet described his doctrines as "mortal poison" in 1584.

---

[1] *Of Occult Philosophy*   Translated by Michael Keefer, originally published as part of Appendix 3 to Keefer's edition of *Dr. Faustus* (Peterborough: Broadview, 1991, second edition 2006).

from AUTHOR'S PREFACE

I do not doubt but that the title of our book, *Of Occult Philosophy, or of Magic*, may by its rarity entice a large number to read it, among whom some twisted, feeble-minded people, and also many ill-disposed and hostile to my talents, will approach: these, in their rash ignorance taking the name of magic in the worse sense, will cry out, hardly having beheld the title, that I teach forbidden arts, sow the seed of heresy, am an offence to pious ears and to outstanding minds a stumbling block; that I am a sorcerer, a superstitious man, and a demoniac, because I am a magician. To these people I would reply that *magus* among learned men does not signify a sorcerer, nor a superstitious man, nor one possessed, but one who is a wise man, a priest, a prophet. The Sibyls were magicians; hence they prophesied most plainly of Christ. And indeed the Magi knew by the wonderful secrets of the world that Christ the author of the world itself was born, and were the first of all to come and worship him. And the name itself of magic was accepted by philosophers, extolled by theologians, and was also not displeasing to the gospel itself. Yet I believe those censors to be of such steadfast arrogance that they will forbid themselves the Sibyls and the holy magicians, and even the gospel itself, sooner than that the name of magic should be admitted into favour; to such a degree are they careful of their conscience, that neither Apollo, nor all the Muses, nor an angel from heaven would be able to deliver me from their curse. And I advise them now that they neither read, nor understand, nor remember our treatise, for it is harmful, it is poisonous, the gate of Acheron is in this book, it speaks stones: let them take heed lest it beat out their brains. …

Dr. Faustus

The title pages of the 1604 and 1616 editions of *Dr. Faustus* are reproduced below.

WILLIAM SHAKESPEARE
1564 – 1616

The plays of Shakespeare are foundational works of Western culture; in the English-speaking world they have influenced subsequent literary culture more broadly and more deeply than any other group of texts except the books of the Bible. The language and imagery of the plays; their ways of telling stories; their innovative dramatic qualities; the characters that populate them (and the ways in which these characters are created); the issues and ideas the plays explore (and the ways in which they explore them)—all these have powerfully shaped English literature and culture over the past four centuries. And this shaping influence has continually touched popular culture as well as more "elevated" literary and academic worlds. From the eighteenth century on Shakespeare's plays have held the stage with far greater frequency than those of any other playwright, and in the twentieth century many have been made into popular films (some of the best of which are films in Japanese and in Russian). Even outside the English-speaking world the plays of Shakespeare receive unparalleled exposure; in the Netherlands, for example, his plays have been performed in the late twentieth and early twenty-first centuries more than twice as often as those of any other playwright. In 2000 he headed the list both on the BBC "person of the millennium" poll and on the *World Almanac*'s poll listing the 10 "most influential people of the second millennium." The fact that a playwright, a member of the popular entertainment industry, has continued to enjoy this kind of cultural status—ranked above the likes of Newton, Churchill, Galileo, and Einstein—is worth pausing over. Why are these plays still performed, read, watched, filmed, studied, and appropriated four centuries after they were written? What is the source of his ongoing cultural currency?

There are many ways to answer this question. One is surely that the plays tell great stories. Fundamental, psychologically sophisticated stories, about love, death, growing up, families, communities, guilt, revenge, jealousy, order and disorder, self-knowledge and identity. Another, just as surely, is that they tell them with extraordinary verbal facility in almost all respects: Shakespeare is generally regarded as unsurpassed in his choice of individual words and his inventiveness in conjuring up striking images; in his structuring of the rhythm of poetic lines; in balancing sentences rhetorically; in shaping long speeches; and in crafting sparkling dialogue. A third is that the characters within the stories are uniquely engaging and memorable. In large part this can be attributed to Shakespeare's ingenuity: within the English literary tradition he more or less invented the psychologically realistic literary character; within the European literary tradition he more or less also invented the strong, independent female character. The bare bones of his characters are typically provided by other sources, but the flesh and blood is of Shakespeare's making. Fourth, and perhaps most important of all, Shakespeare's plays tell their stories in ways that are open-ended emotionally and intellectually: no matter how neatly the threads of story may be knitted together at the end, the threads of idea and emotion in Shakespeare's plays are never tied off. It is this openness of the plays, their availability for reinterpretation, that enables them to be endlessly re-staged, rewritten, re-interpreted—and to yield fresh ideas and fresh feelings time and time again.

Given the centrality of Shakespeare to Western culture, the wish of many readers to know far more than we do about his life is understandable. In fact we do know a fair amount about the facts of his life—given late sixteenth- and early seventeenth-century norms, perhaps more than we might expect to know of someone of his class and background. But we know a good deal less of Shakespeare than we do of some other leading writers of his era—Ben Jonson, for example, or John Donne. And, perhaps most frustrating of all, we know almost nothing of an intimate or personal nature about Shakespeare.

Shakespeare (whose surname also appears on various documents as Shakespear, Shakspere, Shaxpere, and Shagspere) was baptized in Stratford-upon-Avon on 26 April 1564. Reasonable conjecture, given the customs of the time, suggests that he was born two-to-four days earlier; the date that has been most frequently advanced is 23 April (the same day of the year on which he died in 1616, and also the day on which St. George, England's patron saint, is traditionally honored). His father, John, was a glove-maker and also a local politician: first an alderman and then bailiff, a position equivalent to mayor. Some scholars have argued that he had remained a Catholic in newly-Protestant England, and that Shakespeare thus grew up in a clandestinely Catholic home; though the evidence for this is suggestive, it is not conclusive. (If Shakespeare had grown up Catholic, that background might lead readers to see some of his history plays in a different perspective, and might lend even greater poignancy to images such as that of the "bare ruined choirs" of Sonnet 73, with its suggestion of the destruction of the monasteries destroyed by Henry VIII following the break with Rome.)

Stratford-upon-Avon had a good grammar school, which is generally presumed to have provided William's early education, though no records exist to confirm this. Not surprisingly, he did not go on to university, which at the time would have been unusual for a person from the middle class. (Even Ben Jonson, one of the finest classicists of the period, did not attend university.) Shakespeare's first exposure to theater was probably through the troupes of traveling players that regularly toured the country at that time.

On 28 November 1562, when Shakespeare was eighteen, he was married to Anne Hathaway, who was eight years his senior. Six months later, in May of 1583, Anne gave birth to their first daughter, Susanna; given the timing, it seems reasonable to speculate that an unexpected pregnancy may have prompted a sudden marriage. In February 1585, twins, named Hamnet (Shakespeare's only son, who was to die at the age of eleven) and Judith, were born. Some time later, probably within the next three years, Shakespeare moved to London, leaving his young family behind. There has been considerable speculation as to his reasons for leaving Stratford-upon Avon, but no solid evidence has been found to support any of the numerous theories. Certainly London was then (as now) a magnet for ambitious young men, and in the late 1580s it was effectively the only English city conducive to the pursuit of a career as a writer or in the theater.

It is not known exactly when Shakespeare joined the professional theater in London, but by 1592 several of his plays had reached the stage–the three parts of *Henry VI*, probably *The Comedy of Errors* and *Titus Andronicus*, possibly others. The earliest extant mention of him in print occurs in 1592: a sarcastic jibe by an embittered older playwright, Robert Greene. Greene calls Shakespeare "an upstart crow beautified with our feathers," probably referring to Shakespeare's work on the series of *Henry VI* plays, which may well have involved the revision of material by other writers who had originally worked on the play. In any case, from 1594 on, Will Shakespeare is listed as a member of the company called The Lord Chamberlain's Men (later called The King's Men, when James I became their patron).

Professional theater in London did not become firmly established until 1576, when the first permanent playhouses opened. By the late 1580s four theaters were in operation—an unprecedented level of activity, and one that in all probability helped to nurture greater sophistication on the part of audiences. Certainly it was a hothouse that nurtured an extraordinary growth of theatrical agility on the part of Elizabethan playwrights. Shakespeare, as both playwright and actor in The Lord Chamberlain's Men, was afforded opportunities of forging, testing and reworking his written work in the heat of rehearsals and performances—opportunities that were not open to other playwrights.[1] And in Christopher Marlowe he had a rival playwright of a most extraordinary sort. It seems safe to conjecture that the two learned a good deal about play construction from each other. In the late 1580s and early 1590s they both adopt virtually simultaneously the practice of having their characters express their intentions in advance of the unfolding action, thereby encouraging the formation of audience expectations; they also begin to make it a practice to interpose some other action between the exit and the re-entry of any character, thereby further fostering the creation of a sense of temporal and spatial illusion of a sort quite new to the English stage.

In his early years in London Shakespeare also established himself as a non-dramatic poet—and sought aristocratic patronage in doing so. In the late sixteenth century the writing of poetry was accorded considerable respect, the writing of plays a good deal less. It was conventional for those not of aristocratic birth themselves to seek a patron for their writing—as Shakespeare evidently did with the Earl of Southampton, a young noble to whom he dedicated two substantial poems of mythological narrative, *Venus and Adonis* (1593) and *The Rape of Lucrece* (1594). (It is a measure of the enormity of Shakespeare's achievement that these poems, which would be regarded as major works of almost any other writer of the period, are an afterthought in most considerations of Shakespeare's work.) Before the end of the century Shakespeare was also circulating his sonnets, as we know from the praise of Francis Meres, who wrote in 1598 that the "sweet, witty soul" of the classical poet of love, Ovid, "lives in mellifluous and honey-tongued Shakespeare, witness his Venus and Adonis, his Lucrece, his sugared sonnets among his private friends, etc." Such circulation among "private friends" was common practice at the time, and was not necessarily followed by publication. When Shakespeare's sonnets were finally published, in 1609, the dedication was from the printer rather than the author, suggesting that Shakespeare may not have authorized their publication.

There are thirty-eight extant plays by Shakespeare (if *Two Noble Kinsmen* is included in the total). Unlike most other playwrights of the age, he wrote in every major dramatic genre. His history plays (most of them written in the 1590s) include *Richard III, Henry IV, Part 1 and Part 2,* and *Henry V.* He wrote comedies throughout his playwriting years; the succession of comedies that date from the years 1595–1601, including *Much Ado About Nothing, As You Like It* and *Twelfth Night,* may represent his most successful work in this genre, though some have argued that *The Merchant of Venice* (c. 1596) and the "dark comedies" which date from between 1601 and 1604 (including *All's Well That Ends Well* and *Measure for Measure*) resonate even more deeply. The period of the "dark comedies" substantially overlaps with the period in which Shakespeare wrote a succession of great tragedies. *Hamlet* may have been written as early as 1598–99, but *Othello, King Lear,* and *Macbeth* were written in succession between 1601 and1606. Several of his last plays are romance-comedies—notably *Cymbeline, The Winter's Tale* and *The Tempest* (all of which date from the period 1608–11).

Shakespeare was a shareholder in The Lord Chamberlain's Men, and it was in that capacity rather than as a playwright or actor that he made a good deal of money. There was at the time no equivalent

---

[1] From the nineteenth century onwards (though, perhaps tellingly, never before that), the suggestion has occasionally been put forward that Shakespeare never wrote the plays attributed to him, and that someone else–perhaps Francis Bacon, perhaps Edward de Vere, 17th Earl of Oxford–was actually the author. These conspiracy theories have sometimes gained popular currency, but scholars have never found any reason whatsoever to credit any of them. One of the many reasons such theories lack credibility follows from our sure knowledge that Shakespeare was an actor in many of the plays that bear his name as author. If Shakespeare had not written the plays himself it would surely have been impossibly difficult to conceal that fact from all the members of the rest of the company, in rehearsal as well as in performance, over the course of many, many years.

to modern laws of copyright, or to modern conventions of payment to the authors of published works. Nineteen of Shakespeare's plays were printed individually during Shakespeare's lifetime, but it is clear that many of these publications did not secure his co-operation. It has often been hypothesized that some of the printers of the most obviously defective texts (referred to by scholars as "bad quartos") are pirated editions dictated from memory to publishers by actors; there is some evidence to support this theory, though even if correct it leaves many textual issues unresolved.

The first publication of Shakespeare's collected works did not occur until 1623, several years after his death, when two of his fellow actors, John Heminges and Henry Condell, arranged to have printed the First Folio, a carefully prepared volume (by the standards of the time) that included thirty-six of Shakespeare's plays. Eighteen of these were appearing for the first time, and four others for the first time in a reliable edition. (*Two Noble Kinsmen*, which was written in collaboration with a younger playwright, John Fletcher, and *Pericles*, of which it appears Shakespeare was not the sole author, were both excluded, although the editors did include *Henry VIII*, which is now generally believed to have been another work in which Fletcher had a hand.)

A vital characteristic of Shakespeare's plays is their extraordinary richness of language. After several centuries of forging a new tongue out of its polyglot sources, the English language in the sixteenth century had entered a period of steady growth in its range, as vocabulary expanded to meet the needs of an increasingly complex society. Yet its structure over this same time (no doubt in connection with the spread of print culture) was becoming increasingly stable. When we compare the enormous difference between the language of Chaucer, who was writing in the late fourteenth century, and that of Shakespeare, writing in the late sixteenth century, it is remarkable to see how greatly the language changed over those two centuries—considerably more than it has changed in the four centuries from Shakespeare's time to our own. English was still effectively a new language in his time, with immense and largely unexplored possibilities for conveying subtleties of meaning. More than any other, Shakespeare embarked on that exploration; his reading was clearly very wide,[1] as was his working vocabulary. But he expanded the language as well as absorbing it; a surprising number of the words Shakespeare used are first recorded as having been used in his work.

The popular image of Shakespeare's last few years is that first expressed by Nicholas Rowe in 1709:

> The latter part of his life was spent, as all men of good sense wish theirs may be, in ease, retirement, and the conversation of his friends. He had the good fortune to gather together an estate equal to his occasion, and, in that, to his wish; and is said to have spent some years before his death at his native Stratford.

We know for a fact that around 1610 Shakespeare moved from London to Stratford, where his family had continued to live throughout the years he had spent in London, and the move has often been referred to as a "retirement." Shakespeare did not immediately give up playwriting, however: *The Tempest* (1611), *Henry VIII* (c. 1612) and *Two Noble Kinsmen* (c. 1613) all date from after his move to Stratford. By the time he left London Shakespeare was indeed a relatively wealthy man, with

---

[1] In his early years in London Shakespeare may well have acquired much of his reading material from Richard Field, a man from Stratford-upon-Avon of about Shakespeare's age who was in the book trade. Field printed Shakespeare's early poems, *Venus and Adonis* and *The Rape of Lucrece,* and it is certainly possible that the two men had some understanding by which Shakespeare borrowed some of the books he read, which otherwise might have been prohibitively expensive. (Among the works printed by Field was a multi-volume Thomas North translation of Plutarch's *Lives,* of which Shakespeare made extensive use.) Shakespeare also lodged for a time in London with a French Huguenot family named Montjoy, whose home may have been the source for some of the French books that his plays demonstrate a familiarity with. And he may also have had the use of the libraries of one or more of his aristocratic patrons.

substantial investments both in real estate and in the tithes of the town (an arrangement that would be comparable to buying government bonds today).

After 1613 we have no record of any further writing; he died on 23 April 1616, aged 52. In his will, Shakespeare left his extensive property to the sons of his daughter, Susanna (described in her epitaph as "witty above her sex"). To his wife, he left his "second-best bed"—a bequest which many have found both puzzling and provocative. He was buried as a respectable citizen in the chancel of the parish church, where his gravestone is marked not with a name, but a simple poem:

> Good friend, for Jesus' sake forbear
> To dig the dust enclosed here.
> Blest be the man that spares these stones,
> And curst be he that moves my bones.

Shakespeare's work appears to have been extremely well regarded in his lifetime; soon after his death a consensus developed that his work—his plays in particular—constitute the highest achievement in English literature. In some generations he has been praised most highly for the depth of his characterization, in others for the dense brilliance of his imagery, in others for the extraordinary intellectual suggestiveness of the ideas that his characters express (and occasionally embody). But in every generation since the mid-seventeenth century a consensus has remained that Shakespeare stands without peer among English authors.

In most generations the study of Shakespeare has also helped to shape the development of literary criticism and theory. From John Dryden and Samuel Johnson to Samuel Taylor Coleridge to Northrop Frye, works central to the development of literary theory and criticism have had Shakespeare as their subject. And in the past 50 years Shakespeare has been a vital test case in the development of feminist literary theory, of post-colonial theory, and of political, cultural, and new historicist criticism: just as with each generation people of the theater develop new ways of playing Shakespeare that yield fresh insight, so too do scholars develop new ways of reading texts through reading Shakespeare.

The Sonnets

Begun in the 1590s, intermittently revised, and with some of its contents already circulating, Shakespeare's *Sonnets* was printed in 1609 under obscure circumstances. Did Shakespeare authorize publication by the printer Thomas Thorpe? Did he organize the sonnets himself? Is there a pattern to them? The 154 sonnets, concluding with two light poems on Cupid, are followed by a long "Lover's Complaint" in a female voice. How does this poem fit the volume, and do we know with any certainty that Shakespeare is the author of it as well?

The volume's structure parallels that of sonnet collections in the 1590s, such as Samuel Daniel's *Delia* and Spenser's *Epithalamion and Amoretti*. Is Shakespeare merely following this example or subtly commenting on it? Who is the "W.H." whom the printer Thorpe calls "the only begetter" of the sonnets? No one knows. Nor, despite sometimes wild speculation, do we know the identity of the beautiful but faithless young man to whom many of the sonnets are addressed (or if there is only one young man), or that of the "dark lady" whom the lover treats with erotic admiration and moral contempt, or that of the rival poet to whom some sonnets allude. Is the lady always the same woman? Sonnet 145 seems to pun on "Hathaway," maiden name of Shakespeare's wife, Anne. Who is the presumed speaker of these sonnets? Several sonnets pun on the "Will"—a useful name, for it could also denote a faculty of the soul, sexual desire, and even the genitals.

For many years the sonnets received little attention or respect. The second edition of Shake-speare's poems, a shabby volume published by John Benson (1640), feminizes some pronouns, runs some sonnets together, and plagiarizes some commentary; it did the sonnets' reputation no good, and it was not until relatively recently that their splendor and power was fully acknowledged.

One source of older generations' unease with the sonnets was the passion with which the speaker addresses a younger man. It is conventional to think that the first 126 sonnets are to or about this youth and most of the remainder to or about a "dark lady," but many of the sonnets leave the gender of the addressee unspecified. Some of those undeniably involving the young man are clearly expressive of strong homoerotic desire, but the extent to which such desire is acted upon is much less clear. Sonnet 20 seems to say that a sexual relation between the speaker and his friend is impossible, but for some recent critics the poem's puns hint at the opposite. However we read them, such ardent expressions of love and longing for a fellow man are unusual, although not unparalleled, in the literature either of Renaissance England or the Continent.

Also unusual is the lover's sexually reciprocated but problematic love for a compliant if unfaithful woman. This is another respect in which Shakespeare makes a show of revising the Petrarchan tradition familiar to him from Renaissance poetry, in which the love of the male wooer was typically not reciprocated by his female beloved. Much as Shakespeare was clearly indebted to the Petrarchan tradition, he departed from it in a variety of ways.

In form, Petrarch and most other Italian poets had made it a practice to divide their sonnets formally into an octave followed by a sestet. Henry Howard, Earl of Surrey, had been instrumental in the development of an "English" sonnet pattern of three quatrains followed by a couplet. Shakespeare varies the structure of his sonnets in a number of ways, but generally employs rhyme schemes deriving from the "English" pattern (most commonly: *abab cdcd efef gg*).

Whether or not we read *Sonnets* as a sequence, certain recurrent motifs are worth noticing: desire and "will" in every sense, the ruinous passage of time together with the physical and poetic means of surmounting its ravages, the cyclical and poignant beauty of the natural world, and the paradoxes involved in loving the unworthy. Just as notable is the language, which offers an astonishing array of puns, syntactic or lexical ambiguities, and metaphors that evolve through associative connections with a logic just below the surface sense of the verse. Note, for example, how Sonnet 60 moves from ocean waves, to crooked eclipses that must involve the moon (which affects the ocean), to the (curved) plow that makes agricultural furrows, that parallels the wrinkles of bent age, and to Time's curved scythe. Shakespeare can also be funny, though—as witness Sonnet 135's bawdy insinuations, or the resigned (bitter? amused?) puns in Sonnet 138 on lying to and lying with a lover.

⌘ ⌘ ⌘

Sonnets

1

Fr-rom fairest creatures we desire increase,°   *progeny*
    That thereby beauty's rose might never die,
But as the riper should by time[1] decease
His tender° heir might bear his memory: *young*
5 But thou, contracted[2] to thine own bright eyes,
Feed'st thy light's flame with self-substantial fuel,[3]
Making a famine where abundance lies,[4]
Thyself thy foe, to thy sweet self too cruel.
Thou that art now the world's fresh° ornament,   *unspoiled*
10 And only herald to the gaudy[5] spring,
Within thine own bud buriest thy content,[6]
And, tender churl, mak'st waste in niggarding.[7]
        Pity the world, or else this glutton[8] be,
        To eat the world's due, by the grave and thee.[9]

2

When forty[10] winters shall besiege thy brow,
    And dig deep trenches in thy beauty's field,
Thy youth's proud livery,° so gazed on now,   *uniform*
Will be a tattered weed° of small worth held: *garment*
5 Then being asked, where all thy beauty lies,
Where all the treasure of thy lusty° days,   *vigorous*
To say, within thine own deep-sunken eyes,

Were an all-eating shame and thriftless[11] praise.
How much more praise deserved thy beauty's use[12]
10 If thou couldst answer, "This fair child of mine
Shall sum my count, and make my old excuse,"[13]
Proving his beauty by succession° thine: *legal inheritance*
        This were to be new made when thou art old,
        And see thy blood warm when thou feel'st it cold.

12

When I do count the clock[14] that tells the time,
    And see the brave° day sunk in hideous   *splendid*
        night;
When I behold the violet past prime,
And sable curls all silvered o'er with white:
5 When lofty trees I see barren of leaves,
Which erst from heat did canopy the herd,[15]
And summer's green all girded° up in sheaves   *bundled*
Borne on the bier with white and bristly beard:[16]
Then of thy beauty do I question make,
10 That thou among the wastes of time must go,
Since sweets and beauties do themselves forsake,[17]
And die as fast as they see others grow,
        And nothing 'gainst time's scythe can make defence
        Save breed° to brave° him, when he   *reproduce / defy*
            takes thee hence.

15

When I consider° everything that grows   *consider that*
    Holds in perfection but a little moment;
That this huge stage presenteth naught but shows[18]

---

[1] *But* But rather that; *riper* Older; *by time* Because of the passage of time.

[2] *contracted* Betrothed; also confined.

[3] *Feed'st ... fuel* Like a candle, you consume your own substance with self-love; cf. the story of Narcissus in Ovid, *Metamorphoses* 3.464 ("I am burned by love of myself / I produce and am consumed by flames").

[4] *Making ... lies* Cf. *Metamorphoses* 3.466 ("my very abundance makes me poor").

[5] *only* Chief; *gaudy* Brightly colored, but not in the modern pejorative sense.

[6] *content* Contentment; also, essence.

[7] *churl* Here, miser; *mak'st ... niggarding* Cf. *Romeo and Juliet* 1.1.223; *niggarding* Behaving in a miserly fashion.

[8] *this glutton* This kind of glutton.

[9] *To ... thee* What should belong to the world will be consumed first by yourself, then by death.

[10] *forty* Number signifying many and, in Shakespeare's time, corresponding to late middle age.

[11] *thriftless* Wasteful or unprofitable.

[12] *deserved ... use* Would thy beauty's use deserve; *use* Proper employment, also engagement for profit, as in money on loan.

[13] *sum my count* Display the total of my assets; *make ... excuse* Justify or make reparation for my old age.

[14] *count the clock* Count the sounds of the clock.

[15] *erst* Formerly; *canopy the herd* Provide shade for livestock.

[16] *bier* Barrow or litter for carrying crops, but more often associated with the bearing of a corpse to the grave; *white ... beard* As on wheat or barley after harvest.

[17] *sweets* Pleasures, or people or things affording pleasure; *themselves forsake* Lose their essence through time.

[18] *this huge stage* The world as stage was a common notion in the Renaissance; cf. Shakespeare's *As You Like It* 2.7.139–40: "All the world's a stage / And all the men and women merely players"; *shows* Theatrical displays.

Whereon the stars in secret influence[1] comment;
When I perceive that men as plants increase,
Cheered and checked even by the self-same sky,
Vaunt° in their youthful sap, at height decrease,   *exult*
And wear their brave state out of memory:[2]
Then the conceit of this inconstant stay[3]
Sets you, most rich in youth, before my sight,
Where wasteful[4] time debateth with decay
To change your day of youth to sullied[5] night:
    And all in war with time for love of you
    As he takes from you, I engraft[6] you new.

16

But wherefore° do not you a mightier way   *why*
Make war upon this bloody tyrant, time,
And fortify yourself in your decay
With means more blessed than my barren rhyme?
Now stand you on the top of happy hours,
And many maiden gardens, yet unset,°   *unplanted*
With virtuous wish would bear your living flowers,
Much liker[7] than your painted counterfeit:
So should the lines of life that life repair,[8]
Which this, time's pencil or my pupil pen,
Neither in inward worth nor outward fair,°   *beauty*
Can make you live yourself in eyes of men:
    To give away yourself[9] keeps yourself still,°   *always*
    And you must live drawn by your own sweet skill.

18

Shall I compare thee to a summer's day?
Thou art more lovely and more temperate:

---

[1] *secret influence*   The supposed life effects of the stars on human life and temperament.

[2] *wear … memory*   Decay until their glory fades from memory.

[3] *conceit* Thought; conception; *inconstant stay* Constant state ("stay") of inconstancy, or change, as in the aging process.

[4] *wasteful* In the sense of wasting or destructive.

[5] *sullied* Tarnished; made gloomy or dull.

[6] *engraft* Insert a scion, or shoot, from one tree into the bark of another, from which it gains sustenance.

[7] *liker* More like you.

[8] *lines of life* Bloodlines of your descendants, or the outlines of you reflected in them; *repair* Restore.

[9] *give away yourself* Marry.

Rough winds do shake the darling buds of May,
And summer's lease hath all too short a date:
Sometime too hot the eye of heaven shines,
And often is his gold complexion dimmed;
And every fair° from fair sometime declines,   *beauty*
By chance, or nature's changing course, untrimmed:
But thy eternal summer shall not fade,
Nor lose possession of that fair thou ow'st,°   *own*
Nor shall death brag thou wander'st in his shade
When in eternal lines to time thou grow'st:
    So long as men can breathe or eyes can see,
    So long lives this, and this gives life to thee.

19

Devouring time, blunt thou the lion's paws,
And make the earth devour her own sweet brood;
Pluck the keen teeth from the fierce tiger's jaws,
And burn the long-lived Phoenix in her blood;[10]
Make glad and sorry seasons as thou fleet'st,
And do whate'er thou wilt, swift-footed time,
To the wide world and all her fading sweets:°   *pleasures*
But I forbid thee one most heinous crime,
O carve not with thy hours my love's fair brow,
Nor draw no lines there with thine antique[11] pen;
Him in thy course untainted[12] do allow
For beauty's pattern to succeeding men.
    Yet do thy worst, old Time, despite thy wrong,
    My love shall in my verse ever live young.

20

A woman's face with nature's own hand painted
Hast thou, the master mistress of my passion;
A woman's gentle heart, but not acquainted
With shifting change, as is false women's fashion;
An eye more bright than theirs, less false in rolling,[13]
Gilding the object whereupon it gazeth;
A man in hue,° all hues in his controlling,   *appearance*
Which steals men's eyes and women's souls amazeth;
And for a woman wert thou first created,

---

[10] *Phoenix* Mythical bird that after living five or six centuries burns itself in a nest of spices and then rises from the ashes renewed to begin another cycle; *in her blood* Alive.

[11] *antique* Ancient.

[12] *untainted* Unmarked, unhurt.

[13] *rolling* Glancing at lovers.

10   Till nature as she wrought thee fell a-doting,
      And by addition[1] me of thee defeated,
      By adding one thing to my purpose nothing:
          But since she pricked[2] thee out for women's pleasure,
          Mine be thy love, and thy love's use[3] their treasure.

23

A s an unperfect actor[4] on the stage,
      Who with his fear is put besides[5] his part;
Or some fierce thing, replete with too much rage,
Whose strength's abundance weakens his own heart;
5   So I, for fear of trust,[6] forget to say
The perfect ceremony[7] of love's right,°   *due*
And in mine own love's strength seem to decay,
O'ercharged with burden of mine own love's might:
O let my books be then the eloquence
10   And dumb presagers[8] of my speaking breast,
Who plead for love, and look for recompense,
More than that tongue that more hath more expressed:
          O learn to read what silent love hath writ!
          To hear with eyes belongs to love's fine wit.[9]

29

W hen in disgrace with fortune and men's eyes
      I all alone beweep my outcast state,
And trouble deaf heav'n with my bootless° cries,   *unavailing*
And look upon myself, and curse my fate,
5   Wishing me like to one more rich in hope,
Featured like him,[10] like him with friends possessed,
Desiring this man's art° and that man's scope,   *skill*
With what I most enjoy contented least;
Yet in these thoughts myself almost despising,
10   Haply° I think on thee, and then my state,   *by chance*

---

¹ *by addition* I.e., of male genitals.

² *pricked* Selected; "prick" was also slang for penis.

³ *love's use* Sexual pleasure and probably the suggestion of reproduction and increase, with a pun on "usury."

⁴ *unperfect actor* Actor who does not remember his lines accurately.

⁵ *is put besides* Loses track of, forgets.

⁶ *for ... trust* Afraid to trust myself, or perhaps afraid of not being trusted.

⁷ *perfect ceremony* Precise words demanded by the situation.

⁸ *dumb presagers* Silent signals.

⁹ *belongs ... wit* Is characteristic of love's subtle intelligence.

¹⁰ *featured like him* With physical attractions like his.

Like to the lark at break of day arising,
From sullen° earth sings hymns at   *dark, gloomy*
          heaven's gate;
      For thy sweet love remembered such wealth brings
      That then I scorn to change my state with kings.

30

W hen to the sessions° of sweet silent   *judicial sittings*
      thought
I summon up remembrance of things past,[11]
I sigh the lack of many a thing I sought,
And with old woes new wail my dear time's waste;
5   Then can I drown an eye (unused to flow)
For precious friends hid in death's dateless night,
And weep afresh love's long since cancelled woe,
And moan th'expense° of many a vanished sight.   *loss*
Then can I grieve at grievances foregone,°   *past*
10   And heavily from woe to woe tell° o'er   *count*
The sad account of fore-bemoanéd moan,
Which I new pay, as if not paid before;
          But if the while I think on thee, dear friend,
          All losses are restored, and sorrows end.

33

F ull many a glorious morning have I seen
      Flatter the mountain tops with sovereign eye,
Kissing with golden face the meadows green,
Gilding pale streams with heavenly alchemy;
5   Anon° permit the basest clouds to ride   *soon*
With ugly rack[12] on his celestial face,
And from the forlorn world his visage hide,
Stealing unseen to west with this disgrace:
Even so my sun one early morn did shine
10   With all triumphant splendour on my brow;
But out alack,[13] he was but one hour mine,
The region cloud[14] hath masked him from me now.
          Yet him for this, my love no whit[15] disdaineth:

---

¹¹ *summon* Call to court; *remembrance ... past* Cf. Geneva Bible (1560), *Wisdom* 11.10: "For their grief was double with mourning, and the remembrance of things past."

¹² *rack* Mass of clouds driven by the wind in the upper air.

¹³ *out alack* An expression of sharp regret.

¹⁴ *region cloud* Clouds of the upper air.

¹⁵ *no whit* Not the least bit.

Suns of the world may stain,[1] when heaven's sun
    staineth.

35

No more be grieved at that which thou hast done;
  Roses have thorns, and silver fountains mud;
Clouds and eclipses stain both moon and sun,
And loathsome canker° lives in sweetest bud.   *caterpillar*

5 All men make faults, and even I, in this,
Authorizing thy trespass with compare,°   *comparisons*
Myself corrupting, salving thy amiss,[2]
Excusing these sins more than these sins are:[3]
For to thy sensual fault I bring in sense;[4]

10 Thy adverse party is thy advocate,[5]
And 'gainst myself a lawful plea commence:
Such civil war is in my love and hate
    That I an accessary needs must be
    To that sweet thief which sourly robs from me.

36

Let me confess that we two must be twain,°   *separate*
  Although our undivided loves are one;
So shall those blots° that do with me remain,   *disgraces*
Without thy help, by me be borne alone.

5 In our two loves there is but one respect,[6]
Though in our lives a separable spite;[7]
Which, though it alter not love's sole effect,[8]
Yet doth it steal sweet hours from love's delight.
I may not evermore acknowledge[9] thee,

10 Lest my bewailed guilt should do thee shame,
Nor thou with public kindness honour me,
Unless thou take[10] that honour from thy name:

But do not so;[11] I love thee in such sort,
As thou being mine, mine is thy good report.

55

Not marble, nor the gilded monuments
  Of princes, shall outlive this powerful rhyme;
But you shall shine more bright in these contents[12]
Than unswept stone, besmeared with sluttish time.[13]

5 When wasteful war shall statues overturn
And broils° root out the work of masonry,   *violent quarrels*
Nor Mars[14] his sword, nor war's quick° fire,   *vigorous*
    shall burn
The living record of your memory:
'Gainst death, and all oblivious[15] enmity,

10 Shall you pace forth; your praise shall still find room
Even in the eyes of all posterity
That wear this world out to the ending doom.[16]
    So till the judgement that yourself arise,[17]
    You live in this, and dwell in lovers' eyes.

60

Like as the waves make towards the pebbled shore,
  So do our minutes hasten to their end,
Each changing place with that which goes before,
In sequent toil all forwards do contend.

5 Nativity, once in the main° of light,   *broad expanse*
Crawls to maturity; wherewith being crowned
Crooked eclipses 'gainst his glory fight,
And time, that gave, doth now his gift confound.°   *ruin*
Time doth transfix° the flourish set on youth,   *pierce*

10 And delves the parallels[18] in beauty's brow;
Feeds on the rarities of nature's truth,
And nothing stands[19] but for his scythe to mow.

---

1 *stain* Lose luster or brightness.

2 *salving thy amiss* Excusing or explaining away your wrong.

3 *Excusing ... are* My making excuses for your sins is worse than the actual sins themselves.

4 *bring in sense* Add spurious reasoning.

5 *adverse party* Legal opponent; *advocate* Legal defender.

6 *one respect* A single, and hence mutual, regard.

7 *a separable spite* An injury or misfortune capable of separating us.

8 *love's sole effect* Our unity in love.

9 *acknowledge* Greet or recognize in public.

10 *Unless thou take* Without taking.

11 *do not so* Do not display such public kindness toward me.

12 *these contents* The contents of these poems.

13 *Than ... time* Than in dust-covered stone dirtied by the passage of time, which is dirty and grimy ("sluttish") in its effects.

14 *Mars* Roman god of war.

15 *oblivious* Bringing about oblivion.

16 *ending doom* Last Judgment at the end of the world.

17 *That ... arise* When you yourself are resurrected.

18 *delves the parallels* Digs the trenches, i.e., forms the wrinkled lines; cf. Sonnet 2.2: "... dig deep trenches in thy beauty's field."

19 *stands* Grows to full height, as a plant ready for harvest.

And yet to times in hope my verse shall stand,
Praising thy worth, despite his cruel hand.

64

When I have seen by time's fell hand defaced
  The rich proud cost[1] of outworn buried age;[2]
When sometime lofty towers I see down razed,
And brass eternal slave to mortal rage;[3]
5 When I have seen the hungry ocean gain
Advantage on the kingdom of the shore,
And the firm soil win of the wat'ry main,°   *ocean*
Increasing store° with loss, and loss with store;   *gain*
When I have seen such interchange of state,
10 Or state itself confounded,° to decay,   *ruined*
Ruin hath taught me thus to ruminate:
That time will come and take my love away.
    This thought is as a death, which cannot choose
    But weep[4] to have that which it fears to lose.

65

Since brass, nor stone, nor earth, nor boundless sea,
  But sad mortality o'er-sways° their power,   *overcomes*
How with this rage[5] shall beauty hold a plea,[6]
Whose action is no stronger than a flower?
5 O how shall summer's honey breath hold out
Against the wrackful° siege of batt'ring days   *destructive*
When rocks impregnable are not so stout,
Nor gates of steel so strong, but time decays?
O fearful meditation! Where, alack,
10 Shall time's best jewel from time's chest lie hid?
Or what strong hand can hold his swift foot back,
Or who his spoil° o'er beauty can forbid?   *plunder*
    O none, unless this miracle have might:
    That in black ink my love may still shine bright.

71

No longer mourn for me when I am dead
  Than you shall hear[7] the surly sullen bell[8]
Give warning to the world that I am fled
From this vile world, with vilest worms to dwell:
5 Nay, if you read this line, remember not
The hand that writ it, for I love you so
That I in your sweet thoughts would be forgot,
If thinking on me then should make you woe.[9]
O if (I say) you look upon this verse,
10 When I, perhaps, compounded am with clay,
Do not so much as my poor name rehearse,°   *utter*
But let your love even° with my life decay;   *along*
    Lest the wise world should look into your moan,[10]
    And mock you with me[11] after I am gone.

73

That time of year thou mayst in me behold,
  When yellow leaves, or none, or few do hang
Upon those boughs which shake against the cold,
Bare ruined choirs[12] where late the sweet birds sang;
5 In me thou seest the twilight of such day
As after sunset fadeth in the west,
Which by and by black night doth take away,
Death's second self[13] that seals up all in rest;
In me thou seest the glowing of such fire
10 That on the ashes of his youth doth lie,
As the deathbed, whereon it must expire,
Consumed with that which it was nourished by;
    This thou perceiv'st, which makes thy love more
      strong,
    To love that well, which thou must leave°   *lose*
      ere long.

---

1 *rich ... cost* Prideful and extravagant splendor.

2 *outworn ...age* Antiquity worn out and obscured by time.

3 *Brass ... rage* Brass, known for its durability, but also subject ultimately to the fatally destructive effects of time.

4 *cannot ... weep* Can only weep.

5 *with this rage* Against this destructive action.

6 *hold a plea* Present a legal case.

7 *you shall hear* The span of time during which you hear.

8 *surly ... bell* Passing-bell, rung solemnly from the church to announce a death, customarily one chime for each year of the deceased's lifespan.

9 *make you woe* Cause you grief.

10 *look ... moan* Question the cause of your grief.

11 *with me* Along with me, and perhaps in the same manner.

12 *choirs* Parts of churches designated for singers.

13 *Death's second self* Sleep.

74

But be contented when that fell° arrest   *cruel*
Without all bail shall carry me away.[1]
My life hath in this line[2] some interest,
Which for memorial still[3] with thee shall stay.
5   When thou reviewest this, thou dost review
The very part was consecrate to thee.
The earth can have but earth, which is his due;
My spirit is thine, the better part of me.
So then thou hast but° lost the dregs of life,   *only*
10 The prey of worms, my body being dead,
The coward conquest of a wretch's knife,
Too base of thee to be remembered.
        The worth of that is that which it contains,[4]
        And that is this, and this with thee remains.

80

O how I faint° when I of you do write,   *lose heart*
Knowing a better spirit[5] doth use your name,
And in the praise thereof spends all his might,
To make me tongue-tied speaking of your fame.
5   But since your worth, wide as the ocean is,
The humble as the proudest sail doth bear,°   *carry along*
My saucy bark,[6] inferior far to his,
On your broad main° doth wilfully appear.   *ocean*
Your shallowest help will hold me up afloat,
10 Whilst he upon your soundless° deep doth   *immeasurable*
        ride;
Or, being wracked, I am a worthless boat,
He of tall building, and of goodly pride.
        Then if he thrive, and I be cast away,
        The worst was this: my love was my decay.

87

Farewell—thou art too dear[7] for my possessing,
And like enough thou know'st thy estimate.°   *value*
The charter of thy worth gives thee releasing;[8]
My bonds in thee are all determinate.°   *expired*
5   For how do I hold thee but by thy granting,
And for that riches where is my deserving?[9]
The cause of this fair gift in me is wanting,
And so my patent° back again is swerving.   *title to property*
Thyself thou gav'st, thy own worth then not knowing,
Or me to whom thou gav'st it else mistaking;
10 So thy great gift, upon misprision° growing,   *error*
Comes home again, on better judgement making.
        Thus have I had thee as a dream doth flatter:
        In sleep a king, but waking no such matter.

93

So shall I live supposing thou art true
Like a deceived husband; so love's face
May still seem love to me, though altered new—
Thy looks with me, thy heart in other place.
5   For there can live no hatred in thine eye,
Therefore in that I cannot know thy change.[10]
In many's looks the false heart's history
Is writ in moods and frowns and wrinkles strange;
But heav'n in thy creation did decree
10 That in thy face sweet love should ever dwell;
Whate'er thy thoughts or thy heart's workings be,
Thy looks should nothing thence but sweetness tell.
        How like Eve's apple doth thy beauty grow
        If thy sweet virtue answer not thy show![11]

---

[1]   *But be … away*   Some modern editors punctuate these lines with a semi-colon after "contented" and a comma after "away."

[2]   *in this line*   I.e., in this verse.

[3]   *for memorial still*   As a remembrance always.

[4]   *The worth of that … contains*   The value of the body is that it contains the spirit.

[5]   *a better spirit*   A rival poet of superior gifts, referred to in Sonnet 79.

[6]   *bark*   Small boat.

[7]   *too dear*   Both "too expensive" and "too much loved."

[8]   *The character … releasing*   The document stating your value releases you (from any associated debts).

[9]   *for that riches … deserving?*   How do I deserve the rich reward (of being granted your affection)?

[10]   *in that … change*   From your eye I cannot know that your heart has changed.

[11]   *How like … thy show*   How much your beauty grows to resemble the attractiveness of the apple to Eve (i.e., that it will lead to the downfall of the one attracted to it) if your virtue does not match your appearance.

94

They that have power to hurt and will do none,
    That do not do the thing they most do show,[1]
Who, moving others, are themselves as stone,
Unmovèd, cold, and to temptation slow—[2]
5   They rightly do inherit heaven's graces,
And husband° nature's riches from
        expense;°   *conserve / spending*
They are the lords and owners of their faces,
Others but stewards° of their excellence.   *managers*
The summer's flower is to the summer sweet
10 Though to itself it only live and die,
But if that flower with base infection meet
The basest weed outbraves his dignity;[3]
        For sweetest things turn sourest by their deeds:
        Lilies that fester smell far worse than weeds.

97

How like a winter hath my absence been
    From thee, the pleasure of the fleeting year!
What freezings have I felt, what dark days seen,
What old December's bareness everywhere!
5   And yet this time removed[4] was summer's time,
The teeming autumn big with[5] rich increase
Bearing the wanton burden of the prime,[6]
Like widowed wombs after their lords' decease:
Yet this abundant issue° seemed to me   *offspring*
10 But hope of orphans, and unfathered fruit;
For summer and his pleasures wait on thee,[7]
And thou away, the very birds are mute;
        Or if they sing, 'tis with so dull a cheer
        That leaves look pale, dreading the winter's near.

98

From you have I been absent in the spring,
    When proud pied° April, dressed in all his
        trim,°   *particolored / adornment*
Hath put a spirit of youth in everything,
That° heavy Saturn[8] laughed, and leaped   *such that*
        with him.
5   Yet nor the lays° of birds, nor the sweet smell   *songs*
Of different flowers in odour and in hue,
Could make me any summer's story tell,
Or from their proud lap[9] pluck them where they grew;
Nor did I wonder at the lily's white,
10 Nor praise the deep vermilion in the rose;
They were but° sweet, but figures of delight,   *merely*
Drawn after you, you pattern of all those.
        Yet seemed it winter still, and, you away,
        As with your shadow I with these did play.

105

Let not my love be called idolatry,
    Nor my beloved as an idol show,[10]
Since all alike my songs and praises be
To one, of one, still such, and ever so.
5   Kind is my love today, tomorrow kind,[11]
Still constant in a wondrous excellence.
Therefore my verse, to constancy confined,
One thing expressing, leaves out difference.
"Fair, kind, and true" is all my argument,
10 "Fair, kind, and true" varying to other words,
And in this change is my invention spent,[12]
Three themes in one, which wondrous scope affords.
Fair, kind, and true have often lived alone,
Which three till now never kept seat in one.

---

1   *the thing they most do show*   It is not entirely clear what this thing is, but it probably relates to romantic or sexual activity; "though they inspire love, they do not reciprocate," is one possible paraphrase.

2   *to temptation slow*   Slow to respond to temptation.

3   *But if that flower ... dignity*   The most common weed will outshine a lovely flower that has been infected by disease.

4   *time removed*   Time of my absence.

5   *big with*   Great with, about to give birth to.

6   *burden*   Contents of a womb; *prime* Spring.

7   *wait on thee*   Hold themselves in abeyance until you are present.

8   *Saturn*   Planetary God associated astrologically with the melancholy humor.

9   *their proud lap*   The rich earth that nurtures them.

10   *as an idol show*   Seem to be (perhaps also with a pun on "idle"—"be called an insignificant creature of appearances").

11   *Kind ... kind*   Both "of one sort today, and the same tomorrow," and "kind" in the sense of "having a gentle and sympathetic nature."

12   *varying ... spent*   My inventiveness is used up in finding other words (to express the same thought).

106

When in the chronicle of wasted time[1]
I see descriptions of the fairest wights,[2]
And beauty making beautiful old rhyme,
In praise of ladies dead, and lovely knights;
5   Then in the blazon[3] of sweet beauties best,
Of hand, of foot, of lip, of eye, of brow,
I see their antique pen would have expressed
Even such a beauty as you master° now: *possess*
So all their praises are but prophecies
10   Of this our time, all you prefiguring;
And for° they looked but with divining eyes   *since*
They had not skill enough your worth to sing;
        For we which now behold these present days
        Have eyes to wonder, but lack tongues to praise.

109

O never say that I was false of heart,
Though absence seemed my flame to qualify;
As easy might I from myself depart
As from my soul which in thy breast doth lie:
5   That is my home of love; if I have ranged,
Like him that travels I return again,
Just to the time,[4] not with the time exchanged,[5]
So that myself bring water for my stain;[6]
Never believe, though in my nature reigned
10   All frailties that besiege all kinds of blood,
That it could so preposterously be stained,°   *corrupted*
To leave for nothing all thy sum of good:
        For nothing this wide universe I call,
        Save thou, my rose; in it thou art my all.

110

Alas, 'tis true, I have gone here and there,
And made myself a motley to the view,[7]
Gored[8] mine own thoughts, sold cheap what is most
        dear,
Made old offences of affections new.[9]
5   Most true it is that I have looked on truth°   *constancy*
Askance and strangely;° but by all above,   *coldly*
These blenches[10] gave my heart another youth,[11]
And worse essays[12] proved thee my best of love.
Now all is done, save what shall have no end;
10   Mine appetite I never more will grind°   *whet*
On newer proof,° to try° an older friend,   *experience / test*
A god in love, to whom I am confined:°   *devoted*
        Then give me welcome, next my heaven the best,
        Even to thy pure and most most loving breast.

116

Let me not to the marriage of true minds
Admit impediments;[13] love is not love
Which alters when it alteration finds,
Or bends with the remover[14] to remove.
5   O no, it is an ever-fixed mark,
That looks on tempests and is never shaken;
It is the star to every wand'ring bark,°   *boat*
Whose worth's unknown, although his height be taken.[15]
Love's not Time's fool, though rosy lips and cheeks

---

[1]   *wasted time*   Time gone by, with "chronicles" suggesting previous eras, or "olden times."

[2]   *fairest wights*   Most beautiful people, again with an archaic flavor by Shakespeare's time.

[3]   *blazon*   Description catalogue of a beloved's body.

[4]   *Just ... time*   Exactly on time.

[5]   *not ... exchanged*   Not changed during the time spent away.

[6]   *So ... stain*   So that my return, unchanged, might erase the fault of my absence; *water*   Possibly, tears of repentence.

[7]   *motley*   Fool (from the motley, or particolored clothing traditionally worn by jesters); *to the view*   In appearance, in the eyes of society.

[8]   *Gored*   Altered, as a garment is altered by inserting a gore, or wedge-shaped piece of cloth, and perhaps even mutilated, like a person gored by a horned animal.

[9]   *Made ... new*   Committed infidelity by pursuing new relationships.

[10]   *blenches*   Flinchings or deviations (from constancy).

[11]   *gave ... youth*   Rejuvenated my affections for you.

[12]   *worse essays*   Experiments with inferior loves.

[13]   *impediments*   Cf. the marriage service in the Book of Common Prayer (c. 1552): "If any of you know cause, or just impediment, why these two persons should not be joined together in holy Matrimony, ye are to declare it."

[14]   *remover*   One who changes, e.g., ceases to love.

[15]   *Whose ... taken*   Referring to the "star" of the previous line, most likely the North Star, whose altitude can be reckoned for navigation purposes using a sextant, but whose essence remains unknown.

10 Within his bending sickle's compass° come; *sweep*
Love alters not with his brief hours and weeks,
But bears it out even to the edge of doom.
  If this be error and upon me proved,
  I never writ, nor no man ever loved.

117

A ccuse me thus: that I have scanted[1] all
  Wherein I should your great deserts repay,
Forgot upon your dearest love to call,
Whereto all bonds do tie me day by day;
5 That I have frequent been with unknown minds,
And given to time your own dear-purchased right;[2]
That I have hoisted sail to all the winds
Which should transport me farthest from your sight.
Book° both my wilfulness and errors down, *record*
10 And on just proof surmise accumulate;[3]
Bring me within the level° of your frown, *aim*
But shoot not at me in your wakened hate:
  Since my appeal says[4] I did strive to prove° *test*
  The constancy and virtue of your love.

127

I n the old age[5] black was not counted fair,° *beautiful*
  Or if it were, it bore not beauty's name;
But now is black beauty's successive° heir, *legitimate*
And beauty slandered with a bastard shame:[6]
5 For since each hand hath put on nature's power,[7]
Fairing the foul with art's false borrowed face,
Sweet beauty hath no name, no holy bower,[8]
But is profaned, if not lives in disgrace.
Therefore my mistress' eyes are raven black,
10 Her eyes so suited,° and they mourners seem *attired*

At such who, not born fair, no beauty lack,[9]
Sland'ring creation with a false esteem;[10]
  Yet so they mourn, becoming of[11] their woe,
  That every tongue says beauty should look so.

128

H ow oft when thou, my music, music play'st
  Upon that blessed wood[12] whose motion sounds
With thy sweet fingers, when thou gently sway'st° *direct*
The wiry concord[13] that mine ear confounds,° *dazzles*
5 Do I envy those jacks° that nimble leap, *keys*
To kiss the tender inward° of thy hand, *palm*
Whilst my poor lips, which should that harvest reap,
At the wood's boldness by thee blushing stand?
To be so tickled they would change their state
10 And situation with those dancing chips,[14]
O'er whom thy fingers walk with gentle gait,
Making dead wood more blessed than living lips.
  Since saucy jacks[15] so happy are in this,
  Give them thy fingers, me thy lips to kiss.

129

Th'expense of spirit in a waste° of shame *desolation*
  Is lust in action; and till action, lust
Is perjured, murd'rous, bloody, full of blame,
Savage, extreme, rude, cruel, not to trust;° *be trusted*
5 Enjoyed no sooner but despised straight;
Past reason hunted, and no sooner had,
Past reason hated as a swallowed bait,
On purpose laid to make the taker mad;
Mad in pursuit, and in possession so,
10 Had, having, and in quest to have, extreme;
A bliss in proof,° and proved, a very woe; *experience*

---

[1] *scanted* Provided grudgingly or insufficently for.

[2] *given ...right* Spent elsewhere the time you had a right to expect I should spend with you.

[3] *on ... accumulate* On the basis of my proven misdeeds, add others on suspicion.

[4] *my appeal says* My defense is that.

[5] *the old age* Earlier times.

[6] *beauty...shame* The former (fair) conception of beauty has been discredited as illegitimate and false.

[7] *each...power* Everyone has assumed the power to mimic natural beauty (through cosmetics).

[8] *name* Legitimate title; *holy bower* Sacred dwelling-place.

[9] *who ... lack* (1) Who, lacking natural beauty, have acquired it artificially; (2) Who, not being of fair coloration, are in accord with current ideals of beauty.

[10] *Sland'ring ... esteem* Devaluing natural beauty with false praise accorded to the artificial.

[11] *becoming of* Suiting well.

[12] *blessed wood* Probably a virginal, a small, legless harpsichord on which the strings were plucked rather than struck.

[13] *wiry concord* Harmony produced by the plucking of the strings.

[14] *dancing chips* The keys.

[15] *saucy jacks* Common slang for impertinent fellows, but here referring also to the aforementioned keys.

Before, a joy proposed; behind, a dream.
    All this the world well knows, yet none knows well
    To shun the heaven that leads men to this hell.

130

My mistress' eyes are nothing like the sun;
  Coral is far more red than her lips' red;
If snow be white, why then her breasts are dun;
If hairs be wires, black wires grow on her head;
5   I have seen roses damasked,° red and white,   *parti-colored*
But no such roses see I in her cheeks;
And in some perfumes is there more delight
Than in the breath that from my mistress reeks.
I love to hear her speak, yet well I know
10 That music hath a far more pleasing sound;
I grant I never saw a goddess go;°   *walk*
My mistress when she walks treads on the ground.
    And yet, by heaven, I think my love as rare
    As any she[1] belied with false compare.

135

Whoever hath her wish,[2] thou hast thy Will,[3]
  And Will to boot, and Will in
      overplus;°   *superabundance*
More than enough am I, that vex thee still,
To thy sweet will making addition thus.
5   Wilt thou, whose will is large and spacious,
Not once vouchsafe to hide my will in thine?
Shall will in others seem right gracious,
And in my will no fair acceptance shine?
The sea, all water, yet receives rain still,
10 And in abundance addeth to his store;
So thou, being rich in Will, add to thy Will
One will of mine, to make thy large Will more:
    Let no unkind,° no fair beseechers kill;   *unkindness*
    Think all but one,[4] and me in that one Will.

136

If thy soul check[5] thee that I come so near,
  Swear to thy blind soul[6] that I was thy Will,
And will, thy soul knows, is admitted there;
Thus far for love my love-suit sweet fulfil.
5   Will will fulfil the treasure of thy love,
Ay, fill it full with wills, and my will one;
In things of great receipt° with ease we prove   *capacity*
Among a number one is reckoned none.
Then in the number let me pass untold,
10 Though in thy store's account I one must be.
For nothing hold° me, so it please thee hold   *regard*
That nothing, me, a something sweet to thee.
    Make but my name thy love, and love that still;°   *always*
    And then thou lov'st me, for my name is Will.

138

When my love swears that she is made of truth,
  I do believe her, though I know she lies,
That she might think me some untutored youth
Unlearnèd in the world's false subtleties.
5   Thus vainly thinking that she thinks me young,
Although she knows my days are past the best,
Simply I credit her false-speaking tongue;
On both sides thus is simple truth suppressed.
But wherefore says she not she is unjust?°   *unfaithful*
10 And wherefore say not I that I am old?
O love's best habit is in seeming trust,
And age in love[7] loves not t'° have years told: *to*
    Therefore I lie with her, and she with me,
    And in our faults by lies we flattered be.

143

Lo, as a careful housewife[8] runs to catch
  One of her feathered creatures broke away,
Sets down her babe, and makes all swift dispatch°   *haste*

---

[1] *any she* Any woman.

[2] *Whoever ... wish* No matter what other women may wish for or attain.

[3] *Will* In Shakespeare's time, the word could also refer to sexual desire and even to the genitals.

[4] *Think ... one* Think of all your suitors as one.

[5] *check* Restrain or rebuke.

[6] *blind soul* Blind by nature, being enclosed within the body, or blinded by passion.

[7] *age in love* An older person in love, or in matters of love.

[8] *careful* Attentive, but also perhaps "full of cares," or anxious; *housewife* Pronounced "hussif" in Shakespeare's time.

In pursuit of the thing she would have stay;
5 Whilst her neglected child holds her in chase,[1]
Cries to catch her whose busy care is bent°   determined
To follow that which flies before her face,
Not prizing° her poor infant's discontent: considering
So run'st thou after that which flies from thee,
10 Whilst I, thy babe, chase thee afar behind.
But if thou catch thy hope,[2] turn back to me,
And play the mother's part, kiss me, be kind:
    So will I pray that thou mayst have thy Will,
    If thou turn back and my loud crying still.°   soothe

144

Two loves I have, of comfort and despair,
Which, like two spirits, do suggest° me
    still:°   tempt / always
The better angel is a man right fair,
The worser spirit a woman coloured ill.[3]
5 To win me soon to hell[4] my female evil
Tempteth my better angel from my side,
And would corrupt my saint to be a devil,
Wooing his purity with her foul pride;
And whether that[5] my angel be turned fiend
10 Suspect I may, yet not directly° tell;   exactly
But being both from me both to each friend,[6]
I guess one angel in another's hell.
    Yet this shall I ne'er know, but live in doubt,
    Till my bad angel fire my good one out.[7]

146

Poor soul, the centre of my sinful earth,
…[8] these rebel powers that thee array;[9]
Why dost thou pine[10] within and suffer dearth,
Painting thy outward walls so costly gay?
5 Why so large cost, having so short a lease,
Dost thou upon thy fading mansion spend?
Shall worms, inheritors of this excess,
Eat up thy charge?[11] Is this thy body's end?
Then soul, live thou upon thy servant's loss,
10 And let that[12] pine to aggravate thy store;[13]
Buy terms[14] divine in selling hours of dross;°   scum
Within be fed, without° be rich no more: externally
    So shalt thou feed on death, that feeds on men,
    And death once dead, there's no more dying then.

147

My love is as a fever, longing still°   continually
For that which longer nurseth the disease,
Feeding on that which doth preserve the ill,
Th'uncertain° sickly appetite to please: fitful
20 My reason, the physician to my love,
Angry that his prescriptions are not kept,
Hath left me, and I, desperate, now approve°   accept that
Desire is death, which physic did except.[15]
Past cure I am, now reason is past care,
25 And frantic mad with ever more unrest;
My thoughts and my discourse as madmen's are,

---

[1] *holds … chase* Chases after her.

[2] *thy hope* The object of your hope.

[3] *coloured ill* Of a dark or ugly complexion or temperament.

[4] *hell* For the equation of hell with sexual intercourse, cf. Sonnet 129.14: "… the heaven that leads men to this hell."

[5] *whether that* Whether or not.

[6] *being … friend* Both spirits being apart from me and together (and friendly) with each other.

[7] *fire … out* Expel or reject my good angel; to "fire out" meant to drive someone or something away from a place by setting a fire, as, e.g., in fox hunting; *fire* Possibly "fever," with perhaps a glancing reference to venereal disease.

[8] *…* The earliest printed version repeats the words "my sinful earth," an apparent misprint; Shakespeare's words are not known. Possible substitutions include "Rebuke," "Foiled by," or "Fooled by."

[9] *these rebel … thee array* I.e., the body that clothes you (which rebels against your soul).

[10] *pine* Dwindle from longing.

[11] *thy charge* Your expense; also, a possession for which you are responsible.

[12] *that* I.e., the body.

[13] *aggravate thy store* Increase your riches.

[14] *terms* Periods of time; also agreements.

[15] *Desire … except* The sexual desire objected to by my physician is deadly.

At random[1] from the truth vainly expressed:[2]
　　For I have sworn thee fair, and thought thee bright,
　　Who art as black as hell, as dark as night.

153

Cupid laid by his brand,[3] and fell asleep;
A maid of Dian's[4] this advantage° found,　　　*opportunity*
And his love-kindling fire did quickly steep°　　　*plunge*
In a cold valley-fountain[5] of that ground,
5　　Which borrowed from this holy fire of love
A dateless° lively heat still° to endure,　　　*endless / always*
And grew° a seething bath, which yet men prove　　　*grew into*
Against strange maladies a sovereign° cure:　　　*potent*
But at my mistress' eye love's brand new fired,[6]
10　　The boy for trial needs would[7] touch my breast;
I, sick withal, the help of bath desired,
And thither hied,[8] a sad distempered guest,

But found no cure; the bath for my help lies
Where Cupid got new fire: my mistress' eye.

154

The little love-god° lying once asleep,　　　*Cupid*
Laid by his side his heart-inflaming brand,[9]
Whilst many nymphs, that vowed chaste life to keep,[10]
Came tripping by; but in her maiden hand
5　　The fairest votary[11] took up that fire
Which many legions of true hearts had warmed;
And so the general of hot desire[12]
Was, sleeping, by a virgin hand disarmed.
This brand she quenched in a cool well by,°　　　*nearby*
10　　Which from love's fire took heat perpetual,
Growing° a bath and healthful remedy　　　*growing into*
For men diseased; but I, my mistress' thrall,
　　Came there for cure, and this by that I prove:
　　Love's fire heats water, water cools not love.

—1609

---

[1] *At random*　Wandering.

[2] *vainly expressed*　Expressing myself foolishly or fecklessly.

[3] *Cupid ... brand*　Cupid, Roman god of love, often pictured as a small boy carrying a torch (brand) used to kindle erotic love in the hearts of mortals; *laid by*　Set aside.

[4] *maid of Dian's*　Diana, Roman goddess of the moon and the hunt, known for her chastity, was attended by young virgin nymphs (maids).

[5] *cold valley-fountain*　One of the cool springs associated with the dwelling-place of Diana.

[6] *new fired*　Reignited.

[7] *for trial*　To test the flame; *needs would*　Wanted to.

[8] *thither hied*　Hastened there.

[9] *heart-inflaming brand*　Torch used by Cupid to kindle erotic love in the hearts of mortals.

[10] *nymphs ... keep*　Attendants of the chaste goddess Diana, who themselves took a vow of chastity.

[11] *fairest votary*　Most beautiful of those vowed to chastity.

[12] *general ... desire*　Cupid, pictured as the commander of erotic passion.

On this and the following page appear facsimile reproductions of two pages from the 1609 quarto edition of Shakespeare's sonnets. The facsimile pages include some sonnets that may be compared with annotated texts in modernized spelling appearing elsewhere in these pages, and others that are provided here only in this facsimile form, without mediation.

SHAKE-SPEARES

70

THat thou are blam'd shall not be thy defect,
  For slanders marke was euer yet the faire,
The ornament of beauty is suspect,
A Crow that flies in heauens sweetest ayre.
So thou be good,slander doth but approue,
Their worth the greater beeing woo'd of time,
For Canker vice the sweetest buds doth loue,
And thou present'st a pure vnstayined prime.
Thou hast past by the ambush of young daies,
Either not assayld,or victor beeing charg'd,
Yet this thy praise cannot be soe thy praise,
To tye vp enuy,euermore inlarged,
    If some suspect of ill maskt not thy show,
    Then thou alone kingdomes of hearts shouldst owe.'

71

NOe Longer mourne for me when I am dead,
  Then you shall heare the surly sullen bell
Giue warning to the world that I am fled
From this vile world with vildest wormes to dwell:
Nay if you read this line,remember not,
The hand that writ it,for I loue you so,
That I in your sweet thoughts would be forgot,
If thinking on me then should make you woe.
O if(I say)you looke vpon this verse,
When I (perhaps) compounded am with clay,
Do not so much as my poore name reherse;
But let your loue euen with my life decay.
    Least the wise world should looke into your mone,
    And mocke you with me after I am gon.

72

O Least the world should taske you to recite,
  What merit liu'd in me that you should loue
After my death(deare loue)for get me quite,
For you in me can nothing worthy proue.
Vnlesse you would deuise some vertuous lye,

                                            To

SONNETS.

To doe more for me then mine owne defert,
And hang more praife vpon deceafed I,
Then nigard truth would willingly impart.
O leaft your true loue may feeme falce in this,
That you for loue fpeake well of me vntrue,
My name be buried where my body is,
And liue no more to fhame nor me, nor you.
   For I am fhamd by that which I bring forth,
   And fo fhould you, to loue things nothing worth.

73

THat time of yeeare thou maift in me behold,
   When yellow leaues, or none, or few doe hange
Vpon thofe boughes which fhake againft the could,
Bare rn'wd quiers, where late the fweet birds fang.
In me thou feeft the twi-light of fuch day,
As after Sun-fet fadeth in the Weft,
Which by and by blacke night doth take away,
Deaths fecond felfe that feals vp all in reft.
In me thou feeft the glowing of fuch fire,
That on the afhes of his youth doth lye,
As the death bed, whereon it muft expire,
Confum'd with that which it was nurrifht by.
   This thou perceu'ft, which makes thy loue more ftrong,
   To loue that well, which thou muft leaue ere long.

74

BVt be contented when that fell areft,
   With out all bayle fhall carry me away,
My life hath in this line fome intereft,
Which for memoriall ftill with thee fhall ftay.
When thou reueweft this, thou doeft reuew,
The very part was confecrate to thee,
The earth can haue but earth, which is his due,
My fpirit is thine the better part of me,
So then thou haft but loft the dregs of life,
The pray of wormes, my body being dead,
The coward conqueft of a wretches knife,

To

BEN JONSON
1572 – 1637

Ben Jonson was an innovator in poetry, drama, and criticism. In 1616 he became the first Englishman to edit and publish not just his own poetry but his own drama. King James I awarded him a pension and he was, in effect, England's Poet Laureate although there was as yet no such official position. He presided over a literary following that in one poem he calls the "tribe of Ben," members of which included some of the best Cavalier poets. Like Shakespeare a pioneer in the transition from verse to prose in comic dialogue, with a particular talent for shaping social and moral satire into comedy, Jonson also preferred to create his own plots rather than to borrow stories from earlier sources, as was

a common practice. With inventive and lyrical virtuosity, he also accumulated a supple and diverse body of poetry. His reputation came to be partially eclipsed by that of Shakespeare, for his humanist erudition and the frequent comic realism of his drama made him seem flat and pedantic beside what was read as Shakespeare's genial inspiration (what Milton called his "native woodnotes wild")—a writer for scholars, to be respected and admired sooner than loved and enjoyed. The twentieth century, though, felt an affinity for what appeared to be the anticipatory modern elements in Jonson—his "plain style," his acute social observation, and his audacity in manipulating dramatic and classical conventions. T.S. Eliot, one of the first to sense this affinity, called Jonson's works "a part of our literary inheritance that craves further expression."

Jonson's grounding in the classics began in adolescence at Westminster School under the noted scholar and antiquarian William Camden, a lifelong friend whom Jonson later praised as the teacher "to whom I owe all that I am in arts." After brief stints as an apprentice bricklayer and a soldier, Jonson (like Shakespeare) joined the developing theater world as an actor. *Every Man in his Humour* (1598), in which Shakespeare acted, established Jonson as master of the new "comedy of humors," which lampoons eccentricities of character, called "humors" because diagnosable as an imbalance of the four humors that make up the body and affect the mind. Jonson also announced himself as an innovator with a mission. His prologue to the play—one of many such overt statements and justifications of his art that he eventually learned to dramatize more indirectly—sets out what remained the core of his dramatic philosophy; in it he advocates direct and realistic language ("deeds and language such as men do use") and a return to classical unities of time and space, eschewing the elaborate fantasies and distortions common in Elizabethan comedy and even more common in Jacobean romance and tragicomedy. A more satirical sequel, *Every Man out of his Humour* (1599), proved so popular that Jonson took the unorthodox step of personally supervising its publication, thereby establishing a double precedent—the play as property of its author rather than of the acting company, and the popular stage play as literary document.

Jonson's high opinion of his art proved justified; his plays *Volpone* (1606) and *The Alchemist* (1610) remain two of the best-loved comedies in British literature. *Volpone* chronicles a scheming miser's deception of a series of legacy hunters; in *The Alchemist*, various vain and gullible types are exploited by three servants posing as musicians in their master's absence. Both are comedies of intrigue, and in both Jonson set new standards in incisive, naturalistic dialogue and intricate plot construction. (Coleridge judged the plot of *The Alchemist* "absolute perfection.") These comedies show Jonson able to turn his ferocious satirical gifts to a coherent purpose, what he called "high moral" comedy, and, in the case of *The Alchemist*, to attain perfect classical unities of time and space: its action takes place in real time in a set built to actual size.

Jonson also scored hits with *Epicoene* (1612), a sportive exploration of sexual politics, and *Bartholomew Fair* (1614), a broad, slice-of-life portrait of London holiday street life. His attempts at tragedy, *Sejanus* (1603) and *Catiline* (1612), were judged too ponderous and pedantic, though Jonson, who well understood the power of print, was convinced his reading public would overleap what he saw as the deficiencies of his playgoing audiences. In the case of *Catiline*, he was right: though never a performance success, it was the most-quoted English play of the seventeenth century.

Posterity has since consigned Jonson's tragedies to relative obscurity but has shown increased regard for the limpid and clever verse he contributed to the Jacobean court masques. These were entertainments, commissioned to celebrate special events, that were danced and acted by members of the court. They featured increasingly elaborate costumes, scenery, and special effects, all designed by Jonson's collaborator, the court architect Inigo Jones. Such spectacles as the *Masque of Blackness* (1605) and the *Masque of Beauty* (1608) played off antique myths, providing a venue for Jonson to display his classical learning and sharpen his lyrical gifts. Jonson also introduced, in such flattering yet admonitory court masques as *Pleasure Reconciled to Virtue* and *Love Restored* (1612), the intriguing device of the "antimasque," a more rough-and-tumble moment with comic images of irrationality or grotesquerie that the surrounding masque both absorbs and exorcizes. Between them, Jonson and Jones took the masque from transitory amusement into a high art that in its multimedia form in some ways anticipates the opera and even film.

Jonson considered himself above all a poet. His poetry follows his dramas and masques in the 1616 folio of his collected works, which was the culmination of his career to that point, "the ripest of my studies." When, in his "Epistle to the Countess of Rutland" (1600), he introduced his "strange poems, which as yet / Had not their form touched by an English wit," Jonson was referring to such classical forms as the ode, epistle, epitaph, and epigram that he intended to revive or invigorate with a more crystalline yet colloquial style. His two best-loved lyrics, "To Celia" and "Drink to Me Only With Thine Eyes," written for *Volpone*, are not mere translations of Catullus and Philostrates; they are quintessentially Jonsonian, bringing to mind Oscar Wilde's assertion that Jonson "made the poets of Greece and Rome terribly modern."

These classical poetic genres were well suited to the intensely personal and yet social nature of Jonson's poetry, and it is here that his turbulent life and personality are reflected most vividly. We see in his many commissioned occasional pieces the cultivation of the aristocratic patronage on which he depended—as in "To Penshurst," his eloquent tribute to the estate of the Sidney family. We witness his capacity for generous friendship in his epigrams to John Donne and his preface to Shakespeare's First Folio, and his capacity for grief in the restrained eloquence of his epitaphs on his young son and infant daughter. We even glean hints of his legendary appetite for food and drink in "Inviting a Friend to Supper," which celebrates the sort of literary camaraderie Jonson found (and read about in his beloved Horace) in his early years, at the Mermaid Tavern, where he held court with a coterie of wits and fellow writers. Other early literary friends included Ralegh, Bacon, Chapman, Beaumont, and Fletcher, while later in his career, he mentored younger poets such as Herrick, Suckling, and Carew, presiding over a literary cult of sorts, the "sons [or sometimes "tribe"] of Ben," at the Devil Tavern in the 1620s. Jonson had enemies, too; he could be vain, arrogant and quarrelsome, especially in defense of his literary principles and reputation, as in his legendary feud with his rival playwrights Dekker and Marston early in his career. Indeed, in 1598 he got into a fight with an actor and killed him (a crime for which he was branded and sent for a while to prison, where he became a Catholic, reconverting some years later).

The royal pension bestowed on him in 1616 enabled Jonson to leave the stage and concentrate largely on his poetry for a decade. In 1618, he traveled to Scotland, where he visited the poet William Drummond, who left a record of their conversations and Jonson's often imperious opinions. The following year he was awarded an honorary M.A. from Oxford. Such triumphs and his "tribe" or "sons" notwithstanding, the 1620s brought a gradual decline in Jonson's health and fortunes. A fire destroyed his library, along with several manuscripts, in 1623. The death of King James in 1625 left him without a place at court, necessitating a return to the stage in 1626 with *The Staple of News,* a satire on the emerging newspaper business; it was not well-received. In fact, he was never again to attain success as a playwright; Dryden was later to refer to these late plays as "Jonson's dotages." His masque-writing career ended with the culmination in 1631 of a long-running feud with Inigo Jones. Even though disabled and confined to his house after a stroke in 1628, however, and though no longer the influential lion of his youth, Jonson did not lack for admirers or companionship. When he died in August 1637, most of London's literary and social elite attended his funeral.

Ben Jonson did not leave the world of letters as he found it. His assertion of ownership and careful editing of his own works affected the development of modern authorship and certainly influenced the publication of Shakespeare's First Folio. His satirical comedies provided a significant model for Restoration and eighteenth-century drama, and even for later comic writers in other genres such as Fielding and Dickens. In numerous justificatory prologues to his plays, and in his commonplace book, *Timber, or Discoveries,* he left behind a striking record of a writer's mind at work. And, just as important, the muscular yet supple "plain style" of his poetry was pivotal in deflecting a late Elizabethan taste for the highly wrought and decorative towards a more direct and colloquial manner that became one major strand of late seventeenth-century (and modern) aesthetics.

⌘ ⌘ ⌘

To the Reader

Pray thee take care, that tak'st my book in hand,
    To read it well: that is, to understand.
—1616

To My Book

It will be looked for, book, when some but see
    Thy title, *Epigrams,* and named of me,
Thou should'st be bold, licentious, full of gall,
    Wormwood and sulphur, sharp and toothed withal;[1]
5   Become a petulant thing, hurl ink and wit
    As madmen stones, not caring whom they hit.
Deceive their malice who could wish it so,
    And by thy wiser temper let men know
Thou are not covetous of least self-fame
10   Made from the hazard of another's shame;

Much less with lewd, profane and beastly phrase,
    To catch the world's loose laughter or vain gaze.
He that departs with his own honesty
    For vulgar praise, doth it too dearly buy.
—1616

On Something that Walks Somewhere

At court I met it, in clothes brave enough
    To be a courtier, and looks grave enough
To seem a statesman: as I near it came,
    It made me a great face; I asked the name.
5   "A lord," it cried, "buried in flesh and blood,
    And such from whom let no man hope least good,
For I will do none; and as little ill,
    For I will dare none." Good lord, walk dead still.
—1616

---

[1] *Thou should'st ... toothed withal*   Characteristics of late Elizabethan verse satire, a mode of poetry with which epigrams were associated.

To William Camden[1]

Camden, most reverend head, to whom I owe
  All that I am in arts, all that I know
(How nothing's that?), to whom my country owes
    The great renown and name[2] wherewith she goes;
5 Than thee the age sees not that thing more grave,
    More high, more holy, that she more would crave.
What name, what skill, what faith hast thou in things!
    What sight in searching the most antique springs!
What weight, and what authority in thy speech!
10   Man scarce can make that doubt, but thou canst teach.
Pardon free truth, and let thy modesty,
    Which conquers all, be once overcome by thee.
Many of thine this better could than I;
    But for their powers, accept my piety.
—1616

On My First Daughter

Here lies, to each her parents' ruth,
  Mary, the daughter of their youth;
Yet, all heaven's gifts being heaven's due,
It makes the father less to rue.
5 At six months' end she parted hence
With safety of her innocence;
Whose soul heaven's queen (whose name she bears)
In comfort of her mother's tears,
Hath placed amongst her virgin train:
10 Where, while that severed doth remain,[3]
This grave partakes the fleshly birth;
Which cover lightly, gentle earth.
—1616

To John Donne[4]

Donne, the delight of Phoebus[5] and each muse,
  Who, to thy one, all other brains refuse;[6]
Whose every work of thy most early wit
    Came forth example, and remains so yet;
5 Longer a-knowing than most wits do live,
    And which no affection praise enough can give!
To it, thy language, letters, arts, best life,
    Which might with half mankind maintain a strife;
All which I meant to praise, and yet I would,
10   But leave, because I cannot as I should.
—1616

On My First Son

Farewell, thou child of my right hand,[7] and joy;
  My sin was too much hope of thee, loved boy.
Seven years thou wert lent to me, and I thee pay,
    Exacted by thy fate, on the just day.[8]
5 Oh, could I lose all father, now! For why
    Will man lament the state he should envy?
To have so soon 'scaped world's and flesh's rage,
    And, if no other misery, yet age?
Rest in soft peace, and, asked, say here doth lie
10   Ben Jonson his best piece of poetry;
For whose sake, henceforth, all his vows be such,
    As what he loves may never like too much.
—1616 (WRITTEN 1603)

---

[4] *To John Donne*   For biographical information on Donne, see the introduction to the selection of his works; for some of Jonson's informal opinions on Donne, see the selection from his "Conversations with William Drummond."

[5] *Phoebus*   Apollo, god of poetry.

[6] *refuse*   Jonson's syntax here is compact: Apollo and the Muses refuse to bestow on other brains the gifts they've given Donne, or they reject all brains in favor of his.

[7] *right hand*   The name "Benjamin," which was also the name of Jonson's dead son, means "son of the right hand" in Hebrew (see Genesis 35), implying right-handedness, and good luck, also being placed in a position of privilege and paternal favor.

[8] *Seven years ... just day*   Jonson's first son (b. 1596) died at the age of seven, and seven years was the traditional length of time for which loans were extended.

---

[1] *Camden*   William Camden (1551–1623), historian and schoolmaster; Jonson's teacher at Westminster School.

[2] *name*   Punning reference to Camden's great historical work *Britannia* (1586).

[3] *that severed doth remain*   Her soul, severed from the body, remains in heaven.

On Lucy, Countess of Bedford[1]

This morning, timely rapt with holy fire,
   I thought to form unto my zealous muse
What kind of creature I could most desire
   To honour, serve and love, as poets use.
5 I meant to make her fair, and free,° and wise,   *generous*
   Of greatest blood, and yet more good than great;
I meant the day-star[2] should not brighter rise,
   Nor lend like influence from his lucent° seat.   *shining*
I meant she should be courteous, facile,° sweet,   *affable*
10   Hating that solemn vice of greatness, pride;
I meant each softest virtue there should meet,
   Fit in that softer bosom to reside.
Only a learnèd and a manly soul
   I purposed her; that should, with even powers,
15 The rock, the spindle and the shears control
   Of destiny,[3] and spin her own free hours.
Such when I meant to feign, and wished to see,
   My muse bade, *Bedford* write, and that was she.
—1616

Inviting a Friend to Supper

Tonight, grave sir, both my poor house and I
   Do equally desire your company:
Not that we think us worthy such a guest,
   But that your worth will dignify our feast
5 With those that come; whose grace may make that seem
   Something, which else could hope for no esteem.
It is the fair acceptance, sir, creates
   The entertainment perfect, not the cates.°   *food*
Yet shall you have, to rectify your palate,
10   An olive, capers, or some better salad
Ushering the mutton; with a short-legged hen,

If we can get her, full of eggs, and then
Lemons, and wine for sauce; to these, a coney°   *rabbit*
   Is not to be despaired of, for our money;
15 And though fowl now be scarce, yet there are clerks,[4]
   The sky not falling, think we may have larks.[5]
I'll tell you of more, and lie, so you will come:
   Of partridge, pheasant, woodcock, of which some
May yet be there; and godwit, if we can;
20   Knat, rail and ruff, too.[6] Howsoe'er, my man
Shall read a piece of Virgil, Tacitus,
   Livy, or of some better book to us,
Of which we'll speak our minds, amidst our meat;
   And I'll profess no verses to repeat;
25 To this, if aught appear which I not know of,
   That will the pastry, not my paper, show of.[7]
Digestive cheese and fruit there sure will be;
   But that which most doth take my muse and me
Is a pure cup of rich Canary wine,[8]
30   Which is the Mermaid's[9] now, but shall be mine;
Of which had Horace or Anacreon[10] tasted,
   Their lives, as do their lines, till now had lasted.
Tobacco,[11] nectar, or the Thespian Spring[12]
   Are all but Luther's beer[13] to this I sing.

---

[1] *Lucy, Countess of Bedford* (1581–1627), friend and patron of Ben Jonson and other writers, including John Donne, Samuel Daniel, and Michael Drayton.

[2] *day-star* Often the morning star or planet Venus, but sometimes, as here, the sun (the next line indicates that this day-star is figured as masculine).

[3] *rock … of destiny* Referring to the three Fates of classical myth: Clotho spun the thread of life (a "rock" is a distaff), Lachesis measured its length on her spindle, and Atropos cut the thread. Jonson's ideal patron controls her own destiny, and so spins for herself her "free" (unmeasured) hours.

[4] *clerks* Pronounced "clarks."

[5] *larks* Playing on a proverb: "if the sky falls, we shall have larks." Here, some "clerks" (knowledgeable people) think Jonson's supper will feature larks even if the sky does not fall. Not figurative: to "have larks" in the sense of to "have fun" first appears in the nineteenth century.

[6] *knat … too* All edible birds. Jonson is not offering his guest an expensive feast: by the standards of the gentry of the time, the food on offer is simple and inexpensive, though well chosen.

[7] *if aught appear … show of* That is, if Jonson's own poems do make a surprise appearance, it will only be because they are on paper used to wrap the pastries.

[8] *Canary wine* Light, sweet wine from the Canary Islands, off the west coast of Africa.

[9] *Mermaid's* The Mermaid Tavern in Cheapside, Jonson's favorite place to meet friends and drink.

[10] *Horace or Anacreon* Respectively, a Roman and an ancient Greek lyric poet; both wrote in praise of wine.

[11] *Tobacco* Tobacco was described as being "drunk" rather than "smoked" in the period.

[12] *Thespian Spring* Stream at the foot of Mount Helicon sacred to the classical Muses.

[13] *Luther's beer* Beer brewed in Germany and thought to be weaker than and inferior to English beer.

35   Of this we will sup free, but moderately;
    And we will have no Poley or Parrot[1] by;
Nor shall our cups make any guilty men,
    But at our parting we will be as when
We innocently met. No simple word
40   That shall be uttered at our mirthful board
Shall make us sad next morning, or affright
    The liberty that we'll enjoy tonight.

—1616

To Penshurst[2]

Thou art not, Penshurst, built to envious show
    Of touch° or marble, nor canst boast a row   *black stone*
Of polished pillars, or a roof of gold;
    Thou hast no lantern[3] whereof tales are told,
5   Or stair, or courts; but standst an ancient pile,
    And these grudged at, art reverenced the while.
Thou joy'st in better marks, of soil, of air,
    Of wood, of water; therein thou art fair.
Thou hast thy walks for health as well as sport:
10   Thy Mount, to which the dryads° do resort,   *wood nymphs*
Where Pan and Bacchus[4] their high feasts have made,
    Beneath the broad beech and the chestnut shade;
That taller tree, which of a nut was set

At his great birth,[5] where all the Muses met.
15   There, in the writhèd° bark, are cut the names   *twisted*
    Of many a sylvan,[6] taken with his flames;
And thence the ruddy satyrs oft provoke
    The lighter fauns to reach thy lady's oak.[7]
Thy copse, too, named of Gamage,[8] thou hast there,
20   That never fails to serve thee seasoned° deer   *of suitable age*
When thou wouldst feast or exercise thy friends.
    The lower land, that to the river bends,
Thy sheep, thy bullocks, kine and calves do feed;
    The middle grounds thy mares and horses breed.
25   Each bank doth yield thee conies,° and the tops,   *rabbits*
    Fertile of wood, Ashour and Sidney's copse,[9]
To crown thy open table, doth provide
    The purpled pheasant with the speckled side;
The painted partridge lies in every field,
30   And for thy mess° is willing to be killed.   *meal*
And if the high-swoll'n Medway[10] fail thy dish,
    Thou hast thy ponds that pay thee tribute fish:
Fat, agèd carps, that run into thy net;
    And pikes, now weary their own kind to eat,[11]
35   As loath the second draught or cast to stay,
    Officiously,° at first, themselves betray;   *obligingly*
Bright eels, that emulate them, and leap on land
    Before the fisher, or into his hand.
Then hath thy orchard fruit, thy garden flowers,
40   Fresh as the air and new as are the hours:
The early cherry, with the later plum,
    Fig, grape and quince, each in his time doth come;
The blushing apricot and woolly peach
    Hang on thy walls, that every child may reach.
45   And though thy walls be of the country° stone,   *local*
    They're reared with no man's ruin, no man's groan;
There's none that dwell about them wish them down,

---

1   *Poley or Parrot*   Two well known government spies or informers; Robert Poley (or Pooly) and Henry Parrot. Pooly was present when Christopher Marlowe was fatally stabbed in a Deptford tavern. Jonson also plays on these men's names: a "Polly" or Parrot is a talkative bird.

2   *To Penshurst*   Penshurst Place, in Kent, was the home of Sir Robert Sidney, Viscount Lisle (1563–1626) and his wife, Barbara Gamage (c. 1559–1621); Robert was the younger brother of Sir Philip Sidney (1554–86) and, in 1618, was made Earl of Leicester. Penshurst had been given to the Sidney family by King Edward VI in 1552, but, as Jonson points out, parts of the manor were much older: the Great Hall was built in 1340–41, and remains today as one of England's finest examples of fourteenth-century domestic architecture.

3   *lantern*   Windowed turret or similar structure; the new, lavish manors with which Jonson compares Penshurst featured such "talked about" architectural features.

4   *Pan and Bacchus*   Greek gods: Pan was the half man, half goat deity of the pastoral world; Bacchus was the god of wine. Both were also associated with song and poetic inspiration, and their presence is an implicit tribute to the Sidneys as a family of poets (Philip in particular; see line 14) and patrons of poetry.

5   *his great birth*   Sir Philip Sidney (b. 1554).

6   *sylvan*   Rural lover, inspired by the flames of love (or by the passions in Sidney's love poetry).

7   *satyrs … lady's oak*   Satyrs and fauns are ancient woodland deities: the satyrs challenge the (smaller) fauns in races to an oak tree named for a Lady Leicester who went into labor while sitting under it.

8   *Gamage*   Named for Barbara Gamage, Lady Leicester.

9   *tops … copse*   Like other parts of the estate, nature in the "tops" (high grounds) bears the names of people.

10   *Medway*   River near the estate.

11   *And pikes … to eat*   Pikes were reputed to be particularly voracious fish.

But all come in, the farmer and the clown,°   *rustic*
And no one empty-handed, to salute
50   Thy lord and lady, though they have no suit.°   *request*
Some bring a capon, some a rural cake,
     Some nuts, some apples; some that think they make
The better cheeses, bring 'em; or else send
     By their ripe daughters, whom they would commend
55 This way to husbands; and whose baskets bear
     An emblem of themselves, in plum or pear.
But what can this (more than express their love)
     Add to thy free provisions, far above
The need of such? whose liberal board doth flow
60   With all that hospitality doth know!
Where comes no guest but is allowed to eat
     Without his fear, and of thy lord's own meat;
Where the same beer and bread and self-same wine
     That is his lordship's shall be also mine;
65 And I not fain to sit, as some this day
     At great men's tables, and yet dine away.
Here no man tells° my cups, nor, standing by,   *counts*
     A waiter, doth my gluttony envy,
But gives me what I call, and lets me eat;
70   He knows below he shall find plenty of meat,
Thy tables hoard not up for the next day.
     Nor, when I take my lodging, need I pray
For fire or lights or livery:° all is there,   *provisions*
     As if thou then wert mine, or I reigned here;
75 There's nothing I can wish, for which I stay.°   *wait*
     That found King James, when, hunting late this way
With his brave son, the Prince,[1] they saw thy fires
     Shine bright on every hearth as the desires
Of thy Penates[2] had been set on flame
80   To entertain them; or the country came
With all their zeal to warm their welcome here.
     What (great, I will not say, but) sudden cheer
Didst thou then make 'em! and what praise was heaped
     On thy good lady then! who therein reaped

85 The just reward of her high housewifery:
     To have her linen, plate, and all things nigh
When she was far; and not a room but dressed
     As if it had expected such a guest!
These, Penshurst, are thy praise, and yet not all.
90   Thy lady's noble, fruitful, chaste withal;
His children thy great lord may call his own,
     A fortune in this age but rarely known.
They are and have been taught religion; thence
     Their gentler spirits have sucked innocence.
95 Each morn and even they are taught to pray
     With the whole household, and may every day
Read in their virtuous parents' noble parts
     The mysteries of manners, arms, and arts.
Now, Penshurst, they that will proportion° thee   *compare*
100   With other edifices, when they see
Those proud, ambitious heaps, and nothing else,
     May say, their lords have built, but thy lord dwells.
—1616 (WRITTEN 1611/12)

Song: To Celia [3]

D rink to me only, with thine eyes,
     And I will pledge with mine;
Or leave a kiss but in the cup,
     And I'll not look for wine.
5 The thirst that from the soul doth rise
     Doth ask a drink divine;
But might I of Jove's nectar sup,
     I would not change for thine.
I sent thee late a rosy wreath,
10   Not so much honouring thee
As giving it a hope that there
     It could not withered be.
But thou thereon didst only breathe,
     And sent'st it back to me;
15 Since when it grows, and smells, I swear,
     Not of itself, but thee.
—1616

---

[1] *the Prince*   Prince Henry; he died in November 1612.

[2] *Penates*   Roman household divinities.

[3] *Song: To Celia*   Much of this poem consists of Jonson's translations of prose fragments by the ancient Greek writer Philostratus.

To the Memory of My Beloved, The Author, Mr. William Shakespeare, And What He Hath Left Us[1]

To draw no envy, Shakespeare, on thy name,
Am I thus ample to thy book and fame;
While I confess thy writings to be such
    As neither man nor Muse can praise too much:
5 'Tis true, and all men's suffrage. But these ways
    Were not the paths I meant unto thy praise:
For silliest ignorance on these may light,
    Which, when it sounds at best, but echoes right;
Or blind affection, which doth ne'er advance
10   The truth, but gropes, and urgeth all by chance;
Or crafty malice might pretend this praise,
    And think to ruin where it seemed to raise.
These are as some infamous bawd or whore
    Should praise a matron: what could hurt her more?
15 But thou art proof against them, and indeed
    Above the ill fortune of them, or the need.
I therefore will begin. Soul of the age!
    The applause, delight, the wonder of our stage!
My Shakespeare, rise: I will not lodge thee by
20   Chaucer or Spenser, or bid Beaumont[2] lie
A little further, to make thee a room;
    Thou art a monument without a tomb,
And art alive still while thy book doth live,
    And we have wits to read, and praise to give.
25 That I not mix thee so, my brain excuses:
    I mean with great, but disproportioned, Muses;
For if I thought my judgement were of years
    I should commit thee surely with thy peers:
And tell how far thou didst our Lyly outshine,
30   Or sporting Kyd, or Marlowe's mighty line.[3]
And though thou hadst small Latin, and less Greek,[4]
    From thence to honour thee I would not seek
For names, but call forth thundering Aeschylus,
Euripides, and Sophocles[5] to us,
35 Pacuvius, Accius, him of Cordova dead,[6]
    To life again, to hear thy buskin[7] tread
And shake a stage; or, when thy socks[8] were on,
    Leave thee alone for the comparison
Of all that insolent Greece or haughty Rome
40   Sent forth, or since did from their ashes come.
Triumph, my Britain, thou hast one to show
    To whom all scenes of Europe homage owe.
He was not of an age, but for all time!
    And all the Muses still were in their prime
45 When like Apollo he came forth to warm
    Our ears, or like a Mercury[9] to charm!
Nature herself was proud of his designs,
    And joyed to wear the dressing of his lines,
Which were so richly spun and woven so fit
50   As, since, she will vouchsafe no other wit.
The merry Greek, tart Aristophanes,
    Neat Terence, witty Plautus,[10] now not please,
But antiquated and deserted lie
    As they were not of nature's family.
55 Yet must I not give nature all: thy art,
    My gentle Shakespeare, must enjoy a part.
For though the poet's matter nature be,
    His art doth give the fashion. And that he
Who casts to write a living line must sweat
60   (Such as thine are) and strike the second heat
Upon the Muses' anvil: turn the same
    (And himself with it) that he thinks to frame;
Or for the laurel he may gain a scorn:
    For a good poet's made, as well as born;
65 And such wert thou.[11] Look how the father's face
    Lives in his issue: even so, the race

---

[1] *To the Memory … Left Us*   Published in the first folio edition of Shakespeare's *Works* (1623).

[2] *Beaumont*   Playwright Francis Beaumont (1584–1616), buried, like Chaucer and Spenser, in Westminster Abbey.

[3] *our Lyly … mighty line*   Playwrights John Lyly (c. 1554–1606), Thomas Kyd (1558–94), and Christopher Marlowe (1564–93).

[4] *small Latin, and less Greek*   By Jonson's standards, this means something less than erudite and expert fluency.

[5] *Aeschylus, Euripides, and Sophocles*   Ancient Greek dramatists.

[6] *Pacuvius … Cordova dead*   Ancient Roman playwrights. No works are extant by Pacuvius or Accius; "him of Cordova" is Seneca.

[7] *buskin*   Boot worn by actors in Greek tragedies, and so a metonym for tragic drama.

[8] *socks*   Shoes worn by actors in Greek and Roman comedies, and so a metonym for comic drama.

[9] *Apollo … Mercury*   Gods of poetry and eloquence.

[10] *tart Aristophanes … Plautus*   Aristophanes was a Greek dramatist known for satirical comedies; Plautus and Terence were both Roman playwrights known for comedies.

[11] *thy art … wert thou*   Jonson in fact seems to have resented the ease with which Shakespeare wrote: see his comments in the "Conversations with Drummond" and *Timber, or, Discoveries*.

Of Shakespeare's mind and manners brightly shines
    In his well-turned and true-filed lines:
In each of which he seems to shake a lance,
70   As brandished at the eyes of ignorance.
Sweet swan of Avon! What a sight it were
    To see thee in our waters yet appear,
And make those flights upon the banks of Thames
    That so did take Eliza, and our James![1]
75 But stay, I see thee in the hemisphere
    Advanced, and made a constellation there!
Shine forth, thou star of poets, and with rage
    Or influence chide or cheer the drooping stage;
Which, since thy flight from hence, hath mourned
    like night
80 And despairs day, but for thy volume's light.
    —1623

Ode to Himself[2]

Come leave the loathèd stage,
    And the more loathsome age,
Where pride and impudence, in faction knit,
    Usurp the chair of wit:
5 Indicting and arraigning every day
    Something they call a play.
    Let their fastidious, vain
    Commission of the brain
Run on, and rage, sweat, censure, and condemn:
10 They were not made for thee, less thou for them.

    Say that thou pour'st them wheat,
    And they will acorns eat:
'Twere simple fury, still, thyself to waste
    On such as have no taste:
15 To offer them a surfeit of pure bread,
    Whose appetites are dead.
    No, give them grains their fill,
    Husks, draff° to drink and swill.   *dregs*

If they love lees, and leave the lusty wine,
20 Envy them not, their palate's with the swine.

    No doubt some mouldy tale,
    Like Pericles,[3] and stale
As the shrieve's crusts,[4] and nasty as his fish-
    Scraps out of every dish
25 Thrown forth, and raked into the common tub,
    May keep up the play-club:
    There, sweepings do as well
    As the best ordered meal.
For, who the relish of these guests will fit,
30 Needs set them but the alms-basket of wit.

    And much good do't you then:
    Brave plush and velvet-men;
Can feed on orts:° and safe in your stage-clothes,   *scraps*
    Dare quit, upon your oaths,
35 The stagers and the stage-wrights too (your peers)
    Of larding your large ears
    With their foul comic socks,
    Wrought upon twenty blocks:
Which if they are torn, and turned, and patched enough,
40 The gamesters share your guilt, and you their stuff.

    Leave things so prostitute,
    And take the Alcaic lute;
Or thine own Horace or Anacreon's lyre;
    Warm thee by Pindar's[5] fire:
45 And though thy nerves be shrunk, and blood be cold,
    Ere years have made thee old,
    Strike that disdainful heat
    Throughout, to their defeat:

[1] *Eliza ... James* I.e., Queen Elizabeth I and King James I of England.

[2] *Ode to Himself* Written in response to the poor reception of his play *The New Inn*, which was hissed off stage in 1629. Jonson first published this ode with the printed version of the play in 1631; the version here, slightly revised, appeared in his 1640 *Works*.

[3] *Pericles* Usually read as a reference to the play by Shakespeare, performed in 1607–08; Jonson would have disapproved of the play (a romance with a very loose structure, based on old narrative elements), but he also refers to the taste of his audience, which apparently still preferred to watch a play first performed two decades earlier.

[4] *shrieve's crusts* Sheriff's crusts; referring to the leftover food collected to feed poor prisoners.

[5] *Alcaic ... Pindar's* Jonson tells himself to return to classical literary genres, as represented by such renowned ancient poets as the Greeks Alcaeus, Pindar, and Anacreon, and the Roman Horace.

As curious fools, and envious of thy strain,
50   May, blushing, swear no palsy's in thy brain.

But when they hear thee sing
The glories of thy King,
His zeal to God, and his just awe o'er men:
They may, blood-shaken, then,
55   Feel such a flesh-quake to possess their powers
As they shall cry, "Like ours
In sound of peace or wars,
No harp e'er hit the stars,
In tuning forth the acts of his sweet reign:
60   And raising Charles's chariot 'bove his Wain."[1]
—1631, 1640

My Picture Left in Scotland

I now think Love is rather deaf than blind,
For else it could not be,
That she
Whom I adore so much, should so slight me,
5   And cast my suit behind:
I'm sure my language to her was as sweet,
And every close[2] did meet
In sentence of as subtle feet,
As hath the youngest he
10   That sits in shadow of Apollo's tree.

Oh, but my conscious fears,
That fly my thoughts between,
Tell me that she hath seen
My hundreds of gray hairs
15   Told seven and forty years,
Read so much waist, as she cannot embrace
My mountain belly, and my rocky face,
And all these, through her eyes, have stopped her ears.
—1640 (WRITTEN 1619)

To the Immortal Memory and Friendship of That Noble Pair, Sir Lucius Cary and Sir H. Morison[3]

The Turn[4]

Brave infant of Saguntum,[5] clear°   *explain*
Thy coming forth in that great year
When the prodigious Hannibal did crown
His rage with razing your immortal town.
5   Thou, looking then about,
Ere thou wert half got out,
Wise child, didst hastily return,
And mad'st thy mother's womb thine urn.
How summed° a circle didst thou leave
mankind   *complete*
10   Of deepest lore, could we the centre find!

The Counter-Turn

Did wiser nature draw thee back
From out the horror of that sack?
Where shame, faith, honour, and regard of right
Lay trampled on; the deeds of death and night
15   Urged, hurried forth, and hurled
Upon the affrighted world:
Sword, fire, and famine with fell fury met,
And all on utmost ruin set;

---

[3] *Noble Pair ... Morison* Sir Lucius Cary (1609/10–43), second Viscount Falkland, famed for his learning and for the intellectual and literary circle that met at his estate of Great Tew, outside of Oxford. A peaceable, moderate Royalist who fell into despair with the outbreak of civil war, Cary would die in battle when he more or less deliberately exposed himself to enemy fire. Sir Henry Morison (1608–29), Cary's brother-in-law, probably died of smallpox.

[4] *The Turn* This poem is one of the earliest attempts in English to imitate the Greek Pindaric ode., and the most successful. Pindar (518–438 BCE) composed choral odes that commemorate winners at the Olympic games. His language is allusive and his form and meter complex. His structure is tripartite: the chorus sings a "strophe" (Jonson's "turn") while moving in one direction, then reverses direction and sings a structurally identical "antistrophe" (Jonson's "counter-turn"), then stops and sings the "epode" (Jonson's "stand"), which differs structurally from the other parts.

[5] *infant of Saguntum* According to the Roman writer Pliny, an infant born in Sagunto (in Spain) while it was being sacked by the Carthaginian general Hannibal in 219 BCE returned immediately to its mother's womb.

---

[1] *Charles ... his Wain* "Charles's Wain" is the constellation the Big Dipper, named for Charlemagne; a "wain" is a chariot or cart. Jonson's poetry will elevate King Charles above the stars.

[2] *close* Conclusion of a musical theme or phrase

As, could they but life's miseries foresee,
20   No doubt all infants would return like thee?

The Stand

For what is life, if measured by the space,
Not by the act?
Or maskèd man, if valued by his face
Above his fact?
25   Here's one outlived his peers
And told forth fourscore years;
He vexèd time, and busied the whole state;
Troubled both foes and friends,
But ever to no ends;
30   What did this stirrer,° but die late?   *agitator*
How well at twenty had he fallen or stood!
For three of his fourscore he did no good.

The Turn

He entered well by virtuous parts,
Got up and thrived with honest arts;
35   He purchased friends and fame and honours then,
And had his noble name advanced with men;
But weary of that flight,
He stooped in all men's sight
To sordid flatteries, acts of strife,
40   And sunk in that dead sea of life
So deep, as he did then death's waters sup,
But that the cork of title buoyed him up.

The Counter-Turn

Alas, but Morison fell young!
He never fell: thou fall'st, my tongue.
45   He stood, a soldier to the last right end,
A perfect patriot, and a noble friend;
But most, a virtuous son.
All offices were done
By him so ample, full, and round,
50   In weight, in measure, number, sound,
As, though his age imperfect might appear,
His life was of humanity the sphere.

The Stand

Go now, and tell out days summed up with fears,
And make them years;
55   Produce thy mass of miseries on the stage,
To swell thine age;
Repeat of things a throng,
To show thou hast been long,
Not lived; for life doth her great actions spell
60   By what was done and wrought
In season, and so brought
To light: her measures are, how well
Each syllabe answered, and was formed, how fair;
These make the lines of life, and that's her air.

The Turn

65   It is not growing like a tree
In bulk, doth make man better be;
Or standing long an oak, three hundred year,
To fall a log at last, dry, bald, and sere:
A lily of a day
70   Is fairer far, in May,
Although it fall and die that night;
It was the plant and flower of light.
In small proportions we just beauty see,
And in short measures life may perfect be.

The Counter-Turn

75   Call, noble Lucius, then for wine,
And let thy looks with gladness shine;
Accept this garland, plant it on thy head;
And think, nay know, thy Morison's not dead.
He leaped the present age,
80   Possessed with holy rage
To see that bright eternal day,
Of which we priests and poets say
Such truths as we expect for happy men;
And there he lives with memory, and Ben

The Stand

85   Jonson, who sung this of him, ere he went
Himself to rest,
Or taste a part of that full joy he meant

To have expressed
In this bright asterism;°   constellation
90 Where it were friendship's schism
    (Were not his Lucius long with us to tarry)
    To separate these twi-
    Lights, the Dioscuri;[1]
    And keep the one half from his Harry.
95 But fate doth so alternate the design,
    Whilst that in heaven, this light on earth must shine.

The Turn

    And shine as you exalted are;
    Two names of friendship, but one star:
    Of hearts the union. And those not by chance
100 Made, or indentured, or leased out to advance
    The profits for a time.
    No pleasures vain did chime,
    Of rhymes, or riots, at your feasts,
    Orgies of drink, or feigned protests:
105 But simple love of greatness, and of good;
    That knits brave minds and manners, more than blood.

The Counter-Turn

    This made you first to know the why
    You liked; then after to apply
    That liking; and approach so one the t'other,
110 Till either grew a portion of the other:
    Each styled, by his end,
    The copy of his friend.
    You lived to be the great surnames
    And titles by which all made claims
115 Unto the virtue. Nothing perfect done
    But as a Cary, or a Morison.

The Stand

    And such a force the fair example had,
    As they that saw
    The good and durst not practise it, were glad
120 That such a law
    Was left yet to mankind;
    Where they might read and find

Friendship in deed was written, not in words;
And with the heart, not pen,
125 Of two so early men
    Whose lines her rolls were, and records.
    Who, ere the first down bloomèd on the chin,
    Had sowed these fruits, and got the harvest in.
    —1640 (WRITTEN 1629?)

Karolin's Song[2]

Though I am young, and cannot tell
    Either what Death or Love is well,
Yet I have heard they both bear darts,
    And both do aim at human hearts;
5 And then again, I have been told,
    Love wounds with heat, as Death with cold;
So that I fear they do but bring
    Extremes to touch, and mean one thing.

As in a ruin we it call
10 One thing to be blown up, or fall;
Or to our end, like way may have,
    By flash of lightning, or a wave:
So Love's inflamèd shaft or brand,
    May kill as soon as Death's cold hand;
15 Except Love's fires the virtue have
    To fright the frost out of the grave.
—1640

Hymn to Cynthia[3]

Queen and huntress, chaste and fair,
    Now the sun is laid to sleep,
Seated in thy silver chair,
    State in wonted manner keep:

---

[1] *Dioscuri* Castor and Pollux, twins set among the stars as the constellation Gemini.

[2] *Karolin's Song* From Jonson's final, unfinished play *The Sad Shepherd* (1640), 1.5; the speaker, Karolin, is a kind but naive shepherd.

[3] *Hymn to Cynthia* From Jonson's play *Cynthia's Revels* (1601), 5.6. Cynthia is Diana, goddess of the moon, of chastity, and of hunting; in the literature of the English Renaissance generally, and in this poem, Diana is also a figure for Queen Elizabeth.

5   Hesperus[1] entreats thy light,
       Goddess excellently bright.

       Earth, let not thy envious shade
       Dare itself to interpose;
       Cynthia's shining orb was made
10   Heaven to clear, when day did close:
           Bless us then with wishèd sight,
           Goddess excellently bright.

       Lay thy bow of pearl apart,
       And thy crystal-shining quiver;
15   Give unto the flying hart°   deer
       Space to breathe, how short soever:
           Thou that mak'st a day of night,
           Goddess excellently bright.
       —1601

Clerimont's Song[2]

Still° to be neat, still to be dressed,   *always*
As you° were going to a feast;   *as if you*
Still to be powdered, still perfumed:
Lady, it is to be presumed,
5   Though Art's hid causes are not found,
All is not sweet, all is not sound.

Give me a look, give me a face,
That makes simplicity a grace;
Robes loosely flowing, hair as free:
10 Such sweet neglect more taketh me,
Than all the adulteries of Art;
They strike mine eyes, but not my heart.
—1609

---

[1] *Hesperus*   The planet Venus (when it appears after sunset); in the play, the song is sung by Hesperus.

[2] *Clerimont's Song* From Jonson's play *Epicoene: or, The Silent Woman* (1609), 1.1; in the play, the song is written by Clerimont, a young male gallant, about a woman named Lady Haughty.

JOHN DONNE
1572 – 1631

John Donne was an innovator: his work represented something new in poetry, and his contemporaries knew it. Donne set out to startle his readers with his disdain for convention, writing poems that challenged expectations about what was appropriate in poetic subject, form, tone, language, and imagery. He was not afraid of being difficult, or ambiguous, or contradictory from one poem to

another: like the speaker of his "Holy Sonnet 19," in Donne "contraries meet in one." Some critics and readers try to smooth out these "contraries" by separating Donne's works into the secular verse written by "Jack Donne" (Donne's own phrase), the witty young man-about-London whose love poems combine erotic energy with high-minded argument; and the religious verse written later in life by Dr. John Donne, Dean of St. Paul's Cathedral, the learned Anglican minister famous for his electrifying sermons. But this neat division is complicated by the fact that many of his poems are impossible to date. Donne wrote primarily for manuscript circulation: only a handful of his poems were printed before he died. Some religious poetry may therefore have been written earlier than once thought, and some love lyrics later. In any case, Donne frequently blurs any differences between the sacred and the secular, erotic love and divine love: he can present erotic love as a form of religious experience, and religious devotion as an erotic experience. Donne's voice, moreover, ranges across a multitude of roles and postures, from misogynist cynicism and self-mocking sophistry to tender idealism and devout if still painfully self-conscious religious passion.

With his colloquial language, rough meter, sometimes swaggeringly masculine persona, and elaborately worked out philosophical (or wittily pseudo-philosophical) conceits, Donne's poetry breaks with the late Elizabethan poets: even when expressing difficult or ambiguous thoughts, they tended to prefer lines of smooth and highly decorated elegance. Donne's new manner caught the imagination of many poets, and his work was immensely influential for much of the seventeenth century. Times and tastes change, however, and what had been thought wit in 1600 by 1700 had come to seem mere fancy, unrestrained by judgment. In 1693, for example, John Dryden argued that Donne "affects the metaphysics … where nature only should reign," claiming that his love poetry "perplexes [women's minds] … with nice speculations of philosophy, when he should engage their hearts." In the eighteenth century, Samuel Johnson labeled Donne and his followers "Metaphysical Poets" who "ransacked" nature to create startling and strained conceits. (Because of the objections of scholars who point out that the term is misleading, the long-popular term "metaphysical" is currently losing ground.) Thanks to further shifts in sensibility, and thanks also to the praise of T.S. Eliot, who found in Donne's difficulty and intellectual dazzle a model for modernist poetic practice, Donne's work moved again in the twentieth century to the center of the English poetic canon.

Born in London in 1572, Donne was the son of a prosperous ironmonger. The family was Catholic at a time when the government viewed all Catholics with suspicion and prosecuted those it thought seditious. Donne's mother, Elizabeth, was related to Thomas More, beheaded as a traitor for refusing to support Henry VIII's rejection of the Pope's authority. Two of her uncles lived in exile; another, a Jesuit, was incarcerated; and in 1593 Donne's brother Henry died of a fever while imprisoned for harboring a priest. Thus, Donne well understood religious persecution, which is why some have speculated that his conversion to the Church of England, however sincere, must have felt at times like a betrayal. First educated by Jesuits, at age eleven Donne entered Oxford, and then studied at Cambridge. He took no degree, perhaps because graduation required accepting the Church of England's thirty-nine "articles of religion." In 1592 he began legal studies at Lincoln's Inn, and over the next few years wrote many of the love lyrics that were known at first to a few friends and then, especially in the next century, found a large readership. A set of five satires mocking English life, laws, and mores (including those of courtiers) also dates from these years; they helped intensify a fashion in the late 1590s for biting verse satire. The most powerful, "Satire III," explores with surprising candor, if no conclusion, the risks and dilemmas of choosing a version of Christianity to follow.

After taking part in the 1596 and 1597 anti-Spanish expeditions to Cadiz and the Azores, in 1598 Donne was appointed secretary to Sir Thomas Egerton, Lord Keeper of the Great Seal. By now his future seemed assured—he had distanced himself from the Roman Catholic Church and had served in Parliament. In 1601, however, he nearly wrecked his prospects by a secret marriage to Egerton's 17-year-old-niece, Ann More. When the marriage was discovered, Donne wrote to her father, Sir George More, begging that Ann not "feel the terror of your sudden anger," but Sir George disinherited his daughter and had Donne dismissed from his position and briefly imprisoned. Years of poverty and unemployment lay before the couple and their family (Ann eventually had twelve children, seven of whom survived). Donne found some support, however, from various friends and patrons, among them Sir Robert Drury, for whom he wrote two long "Anniversary" poems (1611-1612) lamenting the death of Sir Robert's daughter, Elizabeth.

During this difficult period Donne finally renounced his Roman Catholicism and within a few years published two anti-Catholic tracts: *Pseudo-Martyr* (1610), which argues that Catholics should take the Oath of Allegiance to the crown, and the satirical *Ignatius his Conclave* (1611), which describes a meeting of Jesuits in Hell. King James was pleased but insisted that Donne be ordained before receiving an appointment. Donne complied and was shortly thereafter made a royal chaplain and a Reader in Divinity at Lincoln's Inn. He soon suffered a personal loss, however, when his wife died during childbirth at age 33, a sorrow to which Donne probably alludes in his seventeenth "Holy Sonnet," when he mentions that "she whom I loved hath paid her last debt." Most of his "Holy Sonnets," however (including "Death be not Proud"), seem to have been written before his ordination and reflect earlier hopes and anguish. In 1621 Donne was appointed Dean of St. Paul's, and attracted large audiences for his intellectually challenging and emotionally stirring sermons, many of which were published, both during and after his life.

During a grave illness in the mid-1620s, Donne wrote his popular *Devotions Upon Emergent Occasions* (1624), a series of prose meditations that include his famous assertion of human interconnectedness ("No man is an island"). Donne survived, but he never lost his fascination with death. He delivered his last sermon, "Death's Duel," early in 1631 before Charles I. His audience, it was later said, sensed that he was in effect preaching his own funeral sermon; he died that March. Donne is buried at St. Paul's Cathedral; his monument is modeled on a portrait of himself taken while he was still alive and dressed for the occasion in his shroud. His collected *Poems* were printed in 1633 and was reprinted several times before his reputation faded with the coming of the Restoration and a new generation's taste for neoclassical poetry.

⌘ ⌘ ⌘

Hymn to God My God, in My Sickness

Since I am coming to that holy room,[1]
  Where, with thy choir of saints for evermore,
I shall be made thy music; as I come
  I tune the instrument here at the door,
5 And what I must do then, think here before;

Whilst my physicians by their love are grown
  Cosmographers,[2] and I their map, who lie
Flat on this bed, that by them may be shown
  That this is my south-west discovery,
10 Per fretum febris, by these straits[3] to die;

I joy, that in these straits I see my west;
  For, though those currents yield return to none,
What shall my west hurt me? As west and east
  In all flat maps (and I am one) are one,[4]
15 So death doth touch the resurrection.

Is the Pacific Sea my home? Or are
  The eastern riches?[5] Is Jerusalem?
Anian, and Magellan, and Gibraltar?[6]
  All straits, and none but straits, are ways to them,
20 Whether where Japhet dwelt, or Cham, or Shem.[7]

We think that Paradise and Calvary,
  Christ's cross and Adam's tree, stood in one place;[8]

Look, Lord, and find both Adams[9] met in me;
  As the first Adam's sweat surrounds my face,
25 May the last Adam's blood my soul embrace.

So, in his purple wrapped, receive me, Lord,
  By these his thorns give me his other crown;
And as to others' souls I preached thy word,
  Be this my text, my sermon to mine own:
30 Therefore° that he may raise, the Lord   *So*
    throws down.
—1635

from *Songs and Sonnets*[10]

The Good-Morrow

I wonder by my troth, what thou, and I
  Did, till we loved? were we not weaned till then?
But sucked on country pleasures, childishly?
Or snorted we in the seven sleepers' den?[11]
5 'Twas so; but° this, all pleasures fancies be   *except for*
If ever any beauty I did see,
  Which I desired, and got, 'twas but a dream of thee.

And now good-morrow to our waking souls,
Which watch not one another out of fear;
10 For love, all love of other sights controls,
And makes one little room, an every where.
Let sea-discoverers to new worlds have gone,
Let maps[12] to others, worlds on worlds have shown,
Let us possess one world,[13] each hath one, and is one.

15 My face in thine eye, thine in mine appears,
And true plain hearts do in the faces rest,
Where can we find two better hemispheres,
Without sharp North, without declining West?

---

[1] *that holy room* I.e., heaven.

[2] *Cosmographers* Scientists who map the universe.

[3] *Per fretum febris* Latin: Through the straits of fever; *straits* Narrow water channels; also, perilous circumstances.

[4] *As west … are one* As the edges of a flat map of the earth would meet if the map were made round like a globe.

[5] *eastern riches* I.e., wealth of East Asia.

[6] *Anian* Strait thought to separate North America from China, a part of the imagined Northwest Passage; *Magellan* Strait at the tip of South America, connecting the Atlantic and Pacific oceans; *Gibraltar* Strait at the mouth of the Mediterranean Sea. (One would pass through it if sailing to Jerusalem from England.)

[7] *Japhet … Shem* Japhet, Cham, and Shem, Noah's three sons, survived the Great Flood described in Genesis 10. Each was thought to have fathered the population of a continent: Japhet repopulated Europe; Cham, Africa; and Shem, Asia.

[8] *Paradise and … one place* It was often suggested that Christ's crucifixion took place in the region where the forbidden tree of Eden had once stood.

[9] *both Adams* Adam and Jesus Christ, who is referred to as "the last Adam" in Corinthians 15.45. Also see Corinthians 15.22: "For as in Adam all die, even so in Christ shall all be made alive."

[10] *Sonnets* Donne uses the term as a general one for love poems or love songs, rather than referring specifically to the 14-line sonnet; his secular love poetry includes no traditional 14-line sonnets.

[11] *seven sleepers den* In early Christian legend, seven youths walled up in a cave during a persecution who slept for nearly 200 years.

[12] *maps* Probably astronomical maps.

[13] *one world* Many manuscript versions have "our world."

What ever dies, was not mixed equally;[1]
20 If our two loves be one, or, thou and I
Love so alike that none do slacken, none can die.
—1633

Song ("Go, and catch a falling star")

Go, and catch a falling star,
   Get with child a mandrake root,[2]
Tell me, where all past years are,
      Or who cleft the Devil's foot,
5 Teach me to hear mermaids singing,
      Or to keep off envy's stinging,
            And find
            What wind
Serves to advance an honest mind.

10 If thou be'st born to strange sights,
      Things invisible to see,
Ride ten thousand days and nights,
      Till age snow white hairs on thee,
Thou, when thou return'st, wilt tell me
15 All strange wonders that befell thee,
            And swear,
            No where
Lives a woman true, and fair.

If thou find'st one, let me know,
20   Such a pilgrimage were sweet;
Yet do not, I would not go,
      Though at next door we might meet;
Though she were true, when you met her,
And last, till you write your letter,
25   Yet she
            Will be
False, ere I come, to two, or three.
—1633

Woman's Constancy

Now thou hast loved me one whole day,
   To-morrow when thou leavest, what wilt thou say?
Wilt thou then antedate some new-made vow?
      Or, say that now
5 We are not just those persons, which we were?
Or, that oaths made in reverential fear
Of Love, and his wrath, any may forswear?
Or, as true deaths, true marriages untie,
So lovers' contracts, images of those,
10 Bind but till sleep, death's image, them unloose?
         Or, your own end to justify,
For having purposed change, and falsehood, you
Can have no way but falsehood to be true?
Vain lunatic,[3] against these 'scapes I could
15   Dispute, and conquer, if I would;
            Which I abstain to do,
For by to-morrow, I may think so too.
—1633

The Sun Rising

Busy old fool, unruly Sun,
   Why dost thou thus,
Through windows, and through curtains call on us?
Must to thy motions lovers' seasons run?
5   Saucy pedantic wretch, go chide
         Late schoolboys and sour prentices,
      Go tell court-huntsmen that the King will ride,
      Call country ants to harvest offices;
Love, all alike, no season knows, nor clime,
10 Nor hours, days, months, which are the rags of time.

         Thy beams, so reverend, and strong
            Why shouldst thou think?
I could eclipse and cloud them with a wink,
But that I would not lose her sight so long:
15   If her eyes have not blinded thine,
         Look, and tomorrow late, tell me,

---

[1] *Whatever … equally* Classical medical theory held that disease was the result of improper balance among the body's elements.

[2] *mandrake root* Plant whose forked root resembles a human body.

---

[3] *lunatic* Under the control of the moon, thus inconstant, subject to change.

Whether both the Indias of spice and mine[1]
  Be where thou leftst them, or lie here with me.
Ask for those kings whom thou saw'st yesterday,
20 And thou shalt hear, All here in one bed lay.

    She's all states, and all princes, I,
    Nothing else is.
Princes do but play us; compared to this,
All honor's mimic, all wealth alchemy.[2]
25   Thou sun art half as happy as we,
    In that the world's contracted thus:
    Thine age asks ease, and since thy duties be
    To warm the world, that's done in warming us.
Shine here to us, and thou art everywhere;
30 This bed thy center is, these walls, thy sphere.
    —1633

The Canonization

For God's sake hold your tongue, and let me love,
  Or chide my palsy, or my gout,
My five gray hairs, or ruined fortune flout,
    With wealth your state, your mind with arts improve,
      Take you a course, get you a place,[3]
      Observe his honour, or his grace,[4]
And the King's real, or his stamped face
    Contemplate;[5] what you will, approve,[6]
    So you will let me love.

10   Alas, alas, who's injured by my love?
    What merchant's ships have my sighs drowned?
Who says my tears have overflowed his ground?
    When did my colds a forward spring remove?
    When did the heats which my veins fill

15   Add one more to the plaguy bill?[7]
Soldiers find wars, and lawyers find out still
    Litigious men, which quarrels move,
    Though she and I do love.

Call us what you will, we are made such by love;
20   Call her one, me another fly,[8]
We're tapers too, and at our own cost die,[9]
    And we in us find the eagle and the dove.[10]
      The phoenix riddle[11] hath more wit
      By us; we two being one, are it.
25 So, to one neutral thing both sexes fit,
    We die and rise the same, and prove
    Mysterious by this love.

We can die by it, if not live by love,
    And if unfit for tombs and hearse
30 Our legend be, it will be fit for verse;
    And if no piece of chronicle° we prove,   *history*
      We'll build in sonnets° pretty rooms;[12]   *love poems*
      As well a well wrought urn becomes
The greatest ashes, as half-acre tombs,
35   And by these hymns, all shall approve
    Us canonized for love.

And thus invoke us: You whom reverend love
    Made one another's hermitage;
You, to whom love was peace, that now is rage;

---

[1] *Indias of spice and mine* The East Indies (source of spice and perfume) and West Indies (source of gold and precious metals).

[2] *alchemy* Here, flashy rubbish.

[3] *course ... place* Take a course of action; get yourself a position.

[4] *his honour ... his grace* Cultivate contacts with political or religious dignitaries.

[5] *stamped face / Contemplate* Look at the king's face stamped on coins: in effect, "go think about money."

[6] *what you will, approve* Do whatever you want.

[7] *plaguy bill* Weekly list of those who had died of the plague.

[8] *me another fly* Call her a fly (butterfly or moth), and call me one too.

[9] *We're tapers ... die* "To die" was slang for reaching orgasm, and each sexual act was popularly believed to shorten one's life by one day. The two lovers are compared to moths attracted to a candle, and to the self-consuming candle (taper) itself: moths, candle, and lovers all pay for doing what they do by their very nature.

[10] *eagle and the dove* Symbols of (masculine) strength and (feminine) gentleness, now united in the lovers.

[11] *phoenix riddle* Only one mythical phoenix ever lived at a time; the bird mysteriously renewed itself by rising from the ashes of its own funeral pyre. The "riddle" of its unisex existence makes better sense (has "more wit") when compared with the two lovers: like the phoenix, they combine "both sexes" to make "one neutral thing" which dies, then rises the same (with the traditional play on the sexual resonances of dying and rising).

[12] *rooms* In Italian, "stanza" means "room."

40   Who did the whole world's soul contract,[1]
            and drove
        Into the glasses of your eyes
            (So made such mirrors, and such spies,
    That they did all to you epitomize)
45   Countries, towns, courts: beg from above
        A pattern of your love.
    —1633

Song ("Sweetest love, I do not go")

Sweetest love, I do not go
        For weariness of thee,
Nor in hope the world can show
        A fitter love for me;
5   But since that I
Must die at last, 'tis best
To use my self in jest
            Thus by feigned deaths[2] to die.

Yesternight the sun went hence,
10   And yet is here today,
He hath no desire nor sense,
        Nor half so short a way:
            Then fear not me,
But believe that I shall make
15   Speedier journeys, since I take
            More wings and spurs than he.

O how feeble is man's power,
        That if good fortune fall,
Cannot add another hour,
20   Nor a lost hour recall!
            But come bad chance,
And we join to it our strength,
And we teach it art and length,
            Itself o'er us to advance.

25   When thou sigh'st, thou sigh'st not wind,
        But sigh'st my soul away,
When thou weep'st, unkindly kind,
        My life's blood doth decay.

            It cannot be
30   That thou lov'st me, as thou say'st,
    If in thine my life thou waste,
        Thou art the best of me.

    Let not thy divining heart
            Forethink me any ill,
35   Destiny may take thy part,
        And may thy fears fulfil;
            But think that we
    Are but turned aside to sleep;
    They who one another keep
40   Alive, ne'er parted be.
    —1633

Air and Angels

Twice or thrice had I loved thee,
        Before I knew thy face or name;
So in a voice, so in a shapeless flame,[3]
Angels affect us oft, and worshipped be;
5   Still when, to where thou wert, I came,
Some lovely glorious nothing I did see.
        But since my soul, whose child love is,
Takes limbs of flesh, and else could nothing do,
        More subtle than the parent is
10   Love must not be, but take a body too;
        And therefore what thou wert, and who,
            I bid Love ask, and now
That it assume thy body, I allow,
And fix itself in thy lip, eye, and brow.

15   Whilst thus to ballast love, I thought,
And so more steadily to have gone,
With wares which would sink admiration,
I saw I had love's pinnace[4] overfraught;
        Ev'ry thy hair for love to work upon
20   Is much too much, some fitter must be sought;
        For, nor in nothing, nor in things
Extreme, and scatt'ring bright, can love inhere;
        Then as an angel, face and wings
Of air, not pure as it, yet pure doth wear,

---

1   *contract* Manuscript versions have "extract."

2   *feigned deaths* Separations from the beloved.

3   *shapeless flame* Unsteady, or suddenly flaring, flame.

4   *pinnace* Small, light ship, unsuited for carrying the figurative cargo of the beloved's many beauties.

25   So thy love may be my love's sphere;
        Just such disparity
As is 'twixt air and angels' purity,
'Twixt women's love, and men's will ever be.
    —1633

Break of Day[1]

'Tis true, 'tis day; what though it be?
  O wilt thou therefore rise from me?
Why should we rise because 'tis light?
Did we lie down because 'twas night?
5 Love, which in spite of darkness brought us hither,
Should in despite of light keep us together.

Light hath no tongue, but is all eye;
If it could speak as well as spy,
This were the worst that it could say,
10 That being well, I fain would stay,
And that I loved my heart and honor so,
That I would not from him, that had them, go.

Must business thee from hence remove?
Oh that's the worst disease of love,
15 The poor, the foul, the false, love can
Admit, but not the busied man.
He which hath business, and makes love, doth do
Such wrong, as when a married man doth woo.
    —1612, 1633

The Anniversary

All kings, and all their favourites,
  All glory of honours, beauties, wits,
The sun itself, which makes times, as they pass,
Is elder by a year, now, than it was
5 When thou and I first one another saw:
All other things to their destruction draw,
    Only our love hath no decay;
This, no tomorrow hath, nor yesterday,

Running it never runs from us away,
10 But truly keeps his first, last, everlasting day.

Two graves must hide thine and my corse,°   *corpse*
  If one might, death were no divorce:
Alas, as well as other princes, we
(Who prince enough in one another be)
15 Must leave at last in death, these eyes, and ears,
Oft fed with true oaths, and with sweet salt tears;
    But souls where nothing dwells but love
(All other thoughts being inmates) then shall prove
This, or a love increased there above,
20 When bodies to their graves, souls from their
    graves remove.

And then we shall be throughly° blest,   *thoroughly*
  But we no more than all the rest,
Here upon earth, we're kings, and none but we
Can be such kings, nor of such subjects be;
25 Who is so safe as we? where none can do
Treason to us, except one of us two.
    True and false fears let us refrain,
Let us love nobly, and live, and add again
Years and years unto years, till we attain
30 To write threescore: this is the second of our reign.
    —1633

Twicknam Garden[2]

Blasted with sighs, and surrounded with tears,
  Hither I come to seek the spring,
    And at mine eyes, and at mine ears,
Receive such balms, as else cure everything;
5   But O, self traitor, I do bring
The spider[3] love, which transubstantiates all,
    And can convert manna to gall,

---

[1] *Break of Day* First printed, with a musical setting, in William Corkine's *Second Book of Airs* (1612). The speaker is a woman.

[2] *Twicknam Garden* Twickenham Park (pronounced, and often in the period spelled, Twicknam) was the home of Lucy, Countess of Bedford (1581–1627), a friend and patron of Donne and other writers, including Ben Jonson, Samuel Daniel, and Michael Drayton.

[3] *spider* Spiders were believed to transform everything they ate into poison.

And that this place may thoroughly be thought
   True Paradise, I have the serpent[1] brought.

10 'Twere wholesomer for me, that winter did
   Benight the glory of this place,
   And that a grave frost did forbid
These trees to laugh and mock me to my face;
   But that I may not this disgrace
15 Endure, nor leave this garden, Love, let me
   Some senseless piece of this place be;
Make me a mandrake, so I may groan here,[2]
   Or a stone fountain weeping out my year.

Hither with crystal vials, lovers come,
20   And take my tears, which are love's wine,
   And try° your mistress' tears at home,   *test*
For all are false, that taste not just like mine;
   Alas, hearts do not in eyes shine,
Nor can you more judge woman's thoughts by tears,
25   Than by her shadow, what she wears.
O perverse sex, where none is true but she,
   Who's therefore true, because her truth kills me.
—1633

A Valediction: of Weeping

Let me pour forth
  My tears before thy face, whil'st I stay here,
For thy face coins them, and thy stamp they bear,
And by this mintage they are something worth,
5   For thus they be
   Pregnant of thee;
Fruits of much grief they are, emblems of more,
When a tear falls, that thou falls which it bore,
So thou and I are nothing then, when on a diverse shore.

10   On a round ball[3]
A workman that hath copies by, can lay

An Europe, Afric, and an Asia,[4]
And quickly make that, which was nothing, All,
   So doth each tear,
15   Which thee doth wear,
A globe, yea world by that impression grow,
Till thy tears mixed with mine do overflow
This world, by waters sent from thee, my heaven
   dissolved so.

   O more than Moon,
20 Draw not up seas to drown me in thy sphere,
Weep me not dead, in thine arms, but forbear
To teach the sea what it may do too soon;
   Let not the wind
   Example find,
25 To do me more harm than it purposeth;
Since thou and I sigh one another's breath,
Who e'r sighs most is cruellest, and hastes the
   other's death.[5]
—1633

The Flea

Mark but this flea, and mark in this,
How little that which thou deny'st me is;
It sucked me first,[6] and now sucks thee,
And in this flea our two bloods mingled be;[7]
5 Thou know'st that[8] this cannot be said
A sin, nor shame, nor loss of maidenhead,
   Yet this enjoys before it woo,
   And pampered swells with one blood made of two,
   And this, alas, is more than we would do.

10 Oh stay, three lives in one flea spare,
Where we almost, nay more than married are:
This flea is you and I, and this
Our marriage bed, and marriage temple is;

---

[1] *serpent*   Emblem of envy, and of temptation.

[2] *mandrake ... groan here*   Plant whose forked root was thought to resemble the human body, and reputed to shriek or groan; the printed edition has "grow," but many manuscripts have "groan," which better parallels the weeping fountain in the next line.

[3] *round ball*   Blank globe, on which printed maps could be placed to make a world.

[4] *Asia*   Pronounced in the period as a three-syllable word.

[5] *Who e'r sighs ... death*   According to folklore, sighing shortened life (each sigh was said to cost one drop of blood).

[6] *It sucked me first*   "Me it sucked first" in many manuscripts.

[7] *mingled be*   The speaker's subsequent argument hinges on the traditional belief that blood mixed during sexual intercourse.

[8] *Thou know'st that*   "Confess it" in many manuscripts.

Though parents grudge, and you, we're met

15   And cloistered in these living walls of jet.°   *black stone*
     Though use° make you apt to kill me,   *habit*
     Let not to that, self murder added be,
     And sacrilege, three sins in killing three.

Cruel and sudden, hast thou since
20   Purpled thy nail in blood of innocence?
Wherein could this flea guilty be,
Except in that drop which it sucked from thee?
Yet thou triumph'st, and say'st that thou
Find'st not thy self, nor me the weaker now;
25   'Tis true, then learn how false, fears be;
     Just so much honor, when thou yield'st to me,
     Will waste, as this flea's death took life from thee.
—1633

A Nocturnal upon St. Lucy's Day,
Being the Shortest Day[1]

'Tis the year's midnight, and it is the day's,
     Lucy's, who scarce seven hours herself unmasks;
The sun is spent, and now his flasks°   *the stars*
Send forth light squibs, no constant rays;
5   The world's whole sap is sunk:
The general balm[2] the hydroptic° earth hath drunk,   *thirsty*
Whither, as to the bed's-feet, life is shrunk,
Dead and interred; yet all these seem to laugh,
Compared with me, who am their epitaph.

10   Study me then, you who shall lovers be
At the next world, that is, at the next spring:
     For I am every dead thing,
     In whom Love wrought new alchemy.
          For his art did express°   *extract*
15   A quintessence even from nothingness,
From dull privations, and lean emptiness;
He ruined me, and I am re-begot
Of absence, darkness, death; things which are not.

All others, from all things, draw all that's good,

20   Life, soul, form, spirit, whence they being have;
     I, by love's limbeck,[3] am the grave
     Of all that's nothing. Oft a flood
          Have we two wept, and so
Drowned the whole world, us two; oft did we grow
25   To be two chaoses, when we did show
Care to aught else; and often absences
Withdrew our souls, and made us carcasses.

But I am by her death (which word wrongs her)
Of the first nothing the elixir grown;
30   Were I a man, that I were one
     I needs must know; I should prefer,
          If I were any beast,
Some ends, some means; yea plants, yea stones detest,
And love; all, all some properties invest;
35   If I an ordinary nothing were,
As shadow, a light and body must be here.

But I am none; nor will my sun renew.
You lovers, for whose sake the lesser sun
     At this time to the Goat[4] is run
40   To fetch new lust, and give it you,
          Enjoy your summer all;
Since she enjoys her long night's festival,
Let me prepare towards her, and let me call
This hour her vigil, and her eve, since this
45   Both the year's, and the day's deep midnight is.
—1633

The Bait

Come live with me, and be my love,
     And we will some new pleasures prove
Of golden sands, and crystal brooks,
With silken lines, and silver hooks.

5   There will the river whispering run
Warmed by thy eyes, more than the sun.
And there the enamoured fish will stay,
Begging themselves they may betray.

---

1   *St Lucy's Day, Being the Shortest Day*   December 13, the shortest
day of the year in the old Julian calendar.

2   *general balm*   The innate, vital sap believed to preserve all things.

3   *limbeck*   Retort, or still (apparatus for distillation).

4   *Goat*   The constellation Capricorn, into whose sign the sun enters
at the winter solstice; goats were associated with lust.

When thou wilt swim in that live bath,
10   Each fish, which every channel hath,
Will amorously to thee swim,
Gladder to catch thee, than thou him.

If thou, to be so seen, be'st loth,
15   By sun or moon, thou dark'nest both,
And if myself have leave to see,
I need not their light, having thee.

Let others freeze with angling reeds,
And cut their legs with shells and weeds,
Or treacherously poor fish beset,
20   With strangling snare, or windowy net.

Let coarse bold hands, from slimy nest
The bedded fish in banks out-wrest,
Or curious traitors, sleave-silk[1] flies,
Bewitch poor fishes' wand'ring eyes.

25   For thee, thou need'st no such deceit,
For thou thyself art thine own bait;
That fish, that is not catched thereby,
Alas, is wiser far than I.
—1633

The Apparition

When by thy scorn, O murd'ress, I am dead,
And that thou thinkst thee free
From all solicitation from me,
Then shall my ghost come to thy bed,
5   And thee, feigned vestal,[2] in worse arms shall see;
Then thy sick taper will begin to wink,
And he, whose thou art then, being tired before,
Will, if thou stir, or pinch to wake him, think
          Thou call'st for more,
10   And in false sleep will from thee shrink,
And then, poor aspen° wretch, neglected thou   *trembling*

Bathed in a cold quicksilver sweat[3] wilt lie,
          A verier ghost than I;
What I will say, I will not tell thee now,
15   Lest that preserve thee; and since my love is spent,
I'd rather thou shouldst painfully repent,
Than by my threatnings rest still innocent.
—1633

A Valediction: Forbidding Mourning

As virtuous men pass mildly away,
     And whisper to their souls to go,
Whilst some of their sad friends do say,
     The breath goes now, and some say, no:

5   So let us melt, and make no noise,
     No tear-floods, nor sigh-tempests move,
'Twere profanation of our joys,
     To tell the laity our love.

Moving of the earth° brings harms and fears,   *earthquakes*
10   Men reckon what it did and meant,
But trepidation of the spheres,[4]
     Though greater far, is innocent.

Dull sublunary[5] lovers' love
     (Whose soul is sense) cannot admit
15   Absence, because it doth remove
     Those things which elemented it.

But we by a love, so much refined
     That our selves know not what it is,
Inter-assured of the mind,
20   Care less, eyes, lips, and hands to miss.

Our two souls therefore, which are one,
     Though I must go, endure not yet

---

1   *sleave-silk*   Silk in the form of fine filaments.

2   *feigned vestal*   Pretended virgin. The original has "fained," the common variant spelling in the period; many editions retain "fained" (eager, glad).

3   *quicksilver sweat*   Shiny coating of sweat; from quicksilvering, the application of a thin coat of an alloy using mercury (quicksilver). That mercury was also used to relieve the symptoms of syphilis adds to Donne's insult.

4   *trepidation of the spheres*   The precession of the equinox, thought to be caused by movements in the celestial spheres.

5   *sublunary*   Beneath the moon, hence corruptible and subject to change (because subject to the consequences of the Fall from Paradise).

A breach, but an expansion,
    Like gold to airy thinness beat.

25 If they be two, they are two so
    As stiff twin compasses[1] are two:
Thy soul, the fixed foot, makes no show
    To move, but doth, if the other do.

And though it in the center sit,
30   Yet when the other far doth roam,
It leans, and hearkens after it,
    And grows erect, as that comes home.

Such wilt thou be to me, who must
    Like the other foot, obliquely run;
35 Thy firmness makes my circle just,
    And makes me end, where I begun.
       —1633

The Ecstasy

Where, like a pillow on a bed,
    A pregnant bank swelled up, to rest
The violet's reclining head,
    Sat we two, one another's best.
5 Our hands were firmly cemented
    With a fast balm, which thence did spring;
Our eye-beams twisted, and did thread
    Our eyes upon one double string.
So to engraft our hands, as yet
10   Was all our means to make us one,
And pictures in our eyes to get°   *beget*
    Was all our propagation.
As 'twixt two equal armies, Fate
    Suspends uncertain victory,
15 Our souls (which to advance their state,
    Were gone out) hung 'twixt her and me.
And whilst our souls negotiate there,
    We like sepulchral statues lay;
All day, the same our postures were,
20   And we said nothing, all the day.
If any, so by love refined,
    That he soul's language understood,

And by good love were grown all mind,
    Within convenient distance stood,
25 He (though he knew not which soul spake,
    Because both meant, both spake the same)
Might thence a new concoction take,[2]
    And part far purer than he came.
This ecstasy doth unperplex
30   (We said) and tell us what we love;
We see by this, it was not sex;
    We see, we saw not what did move:
But as all several souls contain
    Mixture of things, they know not what,
35 Love, these mixed souls doth mix again,
    And makes both one, each this, and that.
A single violet transplant,
    The strength, the colour, and the size
(All which before was poor and scant)
40   Redoubles still, and multiplies.
When love with one another so
    Interinanimates two souls,
That abler soul, which thence doth flow,
    Defects of loneliness controls.
45 We then, who are this new soul, know
    Of what we are composed, and made,
For the atomies of which we grow
    Are souls, whom no change can invade.
But O alas, so long, so far
50   Our bodies why do we forbear?
They're ours, though they're not we, we are
    The intelligences, they the sphere.
We owe them thanks, because they thus
    Did us, to us, at first convey,
55 Yielded their forces, sense, to us,
    Nor are dross to us, but allay.°   *alloy*
On man heaven's influence works not so,
    But that it first imprints the air;
So soul into the soul may flow,
60   Though it to body first repair.
As our blood labours to beget
    Spirits, as like souls as it can,
Because such fingers need to knit
    That subtle knot, which makes us man:
65 So must pure lovers' souls descend
    To affections, and to faculties,
Which sense may reach and apprehend,

---

1 *twin compasses* Single drawing compass (with twin "feet").

2 *new concoction take* Be even further refined.

Else a great prince in prison lies.
To our bodies turn we then, that so
70   Weak men on love revealed may look;
Love's mysteries in souls do grow,
      But yet the body is his book.
And if some lover, such as we,
      Have heard this dialogue of one,
75 Let him still mark us, he shall see
      Small change when we're to bodies gone.
      —1633

The Relic

W hen my grave is broke up again
      Some second guest to entertain
      (For graves have learned that woman-head[1]
      To be to more than one a bed)
5   And he that digs it, spies
A bracelet of bright° hair about the bone,   *fair*
      Will he not let us alone,
And think that there a loving couple lies,
Who thought that this device might be some way
10 To make their souls, at the last busy day,
Meet at this grave, and make a little stay?

      If this fall in a time, or land,
      Where mis-devotion doth command,[2]
      Then he that digs us up will bring
15   Us to the Bishop, and the King,
          To make us relics; then
Thou shalt be a Mary Magdalen, and I
          A something else thereby;
All women shall adore us, and some men;
20 And since at such times miracles are sought,
I would have that age by this paper taught
What miracles we harmless lovers wrought.

      First, we loved well and faithfully,
      Yet knew not what we loved, nor why,
25   Difference of sex no more we knew,
          Than our guardian angels do;
          Coming and going, we

Perchance might kiss, but not between those meals;
          Our hands ne'er touched the seals,
30 Which nature, injured by late law,[3] sets free:
These miracles we did; but now, alas,
All measure, and all language, I should pass,
Should I tell what a miracle she was.
      —1633

from *Elegies*

Elegy 1. Jealousy[4]

F ond° woman, which wouldst have thy   *foolish*
      husband die,
And yet complain'st of his great jealousy.
If swollen with poison, he lay in his last bed,
His body with a sere-bark° covered,   *dry crust*
5 Drawing his breath as thick and short as can
The nimblest crocheting[5] musician,
Ready with loathsome vomiting to spew
His soul out of one hell into a new,
Made deaf with his poor kindred's howling cries,
10 Begging with few feigned tears great legacies,
Thou wouldst not weep, but jolly and frolic be,
As a slave which to-morrow should be free.
Yet weep'st thou when thou seest him hungerly
Swallow his own death, heart's-bane jealousy.
15 Oh give him many thanks, he's courteous,
That in suspecting kindly warneth us.
We must not, as we used, flout openly
In scoffing riddles his deformity;
Nor at his board, together being sat,
20 With words, nor touch, scarce looks, adulterate.
Nor when he, swol'n and pampered with great fare,
Sits down and snorts, caged in his basket chair,
Must we usurp his own bed any more,
Nor kiss and play in his house, as before.
25 Now I see many dangers; for that is
His realm, his castle, and his diocese.
But if, as envious men which would revile

---

[1] *woman-head* Womanishness (a play on "maidenhead").

[2] *If this fall … command* That is, in a time or place where people prayed to saints and venerated relics: in effect, were Roman Catholic.

[3] *late law* Human law, which came after the original "law" of nature.

[4] *Elegy 1. Jealousy* Numbered "Elegy 4" in some modern editions.

[5] *crotcheting* Crotchets are grace notes; in effect, "quick-fingered."

Their prince, or coin his gold, themselves exile
Into another country, and do it there,
30 We play in another house, what should we fear?
There we will scorn his household policies,
His silly plots and pensionary spies,°   servants
As the inhabitants of Thames' right side[1]
Do London's mayor, or Germans, the Pope's pride.[2]
—1633

Elegy 8. The Comparison[3]

A s the sweet sweat of roses in a still,
    As that which from chafed musk cat's pores
        doth trill,°   flow
As the almighty balm° of the early East,   morning dew
Such are the sweat drops of my mistress' breast,
5 And on her neck her skin such lustre sets,
They seem no sweat drops, but pearl carcanets.°   necklaces
Rank sweaty froth thy mistress' brow defiles,
Like spermatic issue of ripe menstruous boils,
Or like that scum, which, by need's lawless law
10 Enforced, Sanserra's starved men did draw
From parboiled shoes, and boots, and all the rest
Which were with any sovereign fatness blest,[4]
And like vile lying stones in saffroned tin,[5]
Or warts, or weals, they hang upon her skin.
15 Round as the world's her head, on every side,
Like to that fatal ball which fell on Ide,[6]

Or that whereof God had such jealousy,
As, for the ravishing thereof we die.[7]
Thy head[8] is like a rough-hewn statue of jet,°   black stone
20 Where marks for eyes, nose, mouth, are yet scarce set;
Like the first Chaos, or flat seeming face
Of Cynthia,° where the earth's shadows her   the moon
    embrace.
Like Proserpine's white beauty-keeping chest,[9]
Or Jove's best fortune's urn,[10] is her fair breast.
25 Thine's like worm eaten trunks, clothed in seal's skin,
Or grave, that's dirt without, and stink within.
And like that slender stalk, at whose end stands
The woodbine quivering, are her arms and hands,
Like rough-barked elmboughs, or the russet skin
30 Of men late scourged for madness, or for sin,
Like sun-parched quarters on the city gate,[11]
Such is thy tanned skin's lamentable state.
And like a bunch of ragged carrots stand
The short swoll'n fingers of thy gouty hand.
35 Then like the chemic's masculine equal° fire,   evenly heating
Which in the limbeck's[12] warm womb doth inspire
Into the earth's worthless dirt a soul of gold,
Such cherishing heat her best loved part doth hold.
Thine's like the dread mouth of a fired gun,
40 Or like hot liquid metals newly run
Into clay moulds, or like to that Aetna[13]
Where round about the grass is burnt away.
Are not your kisses then as filthy, and more,
As a worm sucking an envenomed sore?
45 Doth not thy fearful hand in feeling quake,

---

[1] *Thames' right side* Southwark, where the theaters were, was outside the jurisdiction of London authorities.

[2] *Pope's pride* Germany was the birthplace of the Reformation, which challenged the authority of the Pope.

[3] *Elegy 8. The Comparison* Numbered "Elegy 2" in some modern editions.

[4] *From parboiled shoes ... fatness blest* The King's Catholic army laid siege to the Protestants of Sancerre, France, for nine months in 1573; the town's inhabitants were reduced to eating anything made out of leather.

[5] *lying stones in saffroned tin* Artificial jewels set in false gold (gilded tin).

[6] *fatal ball that fell on Ide* The golden apple inscribed "To the fairest" that Eris, goddess of discord, brought to a wedding in revenge for not being invited. Hera, Athena, and Aphrodite competed for the prize, and Paris, a herdsman on Mount Ida (near Troy), had to choose the winner. His choice of Aphrodite led to the Trojan war. The elegy invites the reader to compare that beauty

competition with the one it offers.

[7] *ravishing ... we die* The forbidden fruit of the Tree of the Knowledge of Good and Evil in Eden.

[8] *Thy head* That is, the head of thy mistress, as opposed to "her head" (the speaker's mistress) of line 15. The poem proceeds to contrast the qualities of the speaker's "her" with those of "thy" or "thine" mistress.

[9] *beauty-keeping chest* In classical story, Psyche was required to travel to the underworld and ask Prosperina (Persephone) to place in a box a gift of beauty for Venus.

[10] *Jove's best fortune's urn* From Homer, *Iliad*: Zeus (Jove) kept two urns in his palace, one filled with good gifts, the other with evil ones.

[11] *Like sun-parched ... city gate* The dessicated body parts of "quartered" criminals, impaled as warning to would-be offenders on city gates.

[12] *limbeck* Alchemical still or retort.

[13] *Aetna* Volcano in Sicily.

As one which gath'ring flowers, still fears a snake?
Is not your last act harsh, and violent,
As when a plough a stony ground doth rent?
So kiss good turtles,° so devoutly nice   turtledoves
50 Are priests in handling reverent sacrifice,
And such in searching wounds the surgeon is
As we, when we embrace, or touch, or kiss.
Leave her, and I will leave comparing thus,
She, and comparisons are odious.

—1633

Elegy 19. To His Mistress Going to Bed[1]

Come Madam, come, all rest my powers defy,
Until I labour, I in labour lie.
The foe oft-times, having the foe in sight,
Is tired with standing though they never fight.
5   Off with that girdle, like heaven's zone glistering,
But a far fairer world encompassing.
Unpin that spangled breastplate,[2] which you wear
That the eyes of busy fools may be stopped there.
Unlace your self: for that harmonious chime[3]
10 Tells me from you that now 'tis your bed time.
Off with that happy busk,° which I envy,   corset
That still can be, and still can stand so nigh.
Your gown's going off, such beauteous state reveals,
As when from flowr'y meads the hill's shadow steals.
15 Off with that wiry coronet and show
The hairy diadem which on you doth grow.
Now off with those shoes, and then softly tread
In this love's hallowed temple, this soft bed.
In such white robes, Heaven's angels used to be
20 Received by men: thou, angel, bringst with thee
A heaven like Mahomet's Paradise,[4] and though

Ill spirits walk in white, we easily know
By this these angels from an evil sprite:
Those set our hairs, but these our flesh upright.
25   Licence my roving hands, and let them go,
Behind, before, above, between, below.[5]
Oh my America, my newfound land,
My kingdom, safeliest when with one man manned,
My mine of precious stones: my empery,°   empire
30 How blest am I in this discovering thee!
To enter in these bonds, is to be free;
Then where my hand is set, my seal shall be.
      Full nakedness, all joys are due to thee;
As souls unbodied, bodies unclothed must be
35 To taste whole joys. Gems which you women use
Are like Atlanta's balls,[6] cast in men's views,
That when a fool's eye lighteth on a gem,
His earthly soul may covet theirs, not them.
Like pictures, or like books' gay coverings, made
40 For lay-men,[7] are all women thus arrayed;
Themselves are mystic books, which only we
(Whom their imputed grace[8] will dignify)
Must see revealed. Then since I may know,
As liberally as to a midwife show
45 Thyself: cast all, yea, this white linen hence,
There is no penance, much less innocence.[9]
      To teach thee, I am naked first; why then
What needst thou have more covering than a man.

—1654

---

[1] *Elegy 19. To His Mistress Going to Bed*   Censoring authorities refused to let the publisher include this elegy in early collections of Donne's poems; it was first printed in an anthology, *The Harmony of the Muses* (1654), and did not appear in an edition of Donne's poems until 1669. It is numbered "Elegy 8" in some modern editions.

[2] *spangled breastplate*   The stomacher; it covered the chest and was often richly ornamented.

[3] *chime*   The lady wears a chiming watch.

[4] *Mahomet's Paradise*   Heaven of erotic bliss. The sensual aspects of the Islamic version of Paradise are described in the Koran sura 55, 54–56, sura 56, 12–40, and sura 76, 12–22.

[5] *Behind, before … below*   The order of the words in this line varies in the manuscripts and printed editions.

[6] *Atlanta's balls*   In classical legend, Atalanta said she would only marry a man who could defeat her in footrace. Her suitor Hippomenes won the challenge by dropping three golden balls as he ran; Atalanta stopped to pick them up. The speaker here reverses the story's gender dynamic.

[7] *lay-men*   Referring to the traditional use of images to instruct non-clerics ("lay-men") who could not read the Bible itself; and to the ornate bindings commissioned by wealthy owners to cover books they probably would never read. The speaker proceeds to argue that women are like these kinds of pictures or books: externally beautiful, but only a favored few may "read" what lies inside.

[8] *imputed grace*   Theological term associated with Protestantism: the justifying grace ascribed to a person through Christ's righteousness.

[9] *this white … innocence*   The color white is associated with both penitence and innocence. In some manuscripts and in the 1654 and 1669 printed editions, this line reads "There is no penance due to innocence," a more theologically conventional reading. Some manuscripts read "Here is no penance, much less innocence."

from *Satires*

Satire 3

Kind pity chokes my spleen; brave scorn forbids
 Those tears to issue which swell my eye-lids;
I must not laugh, nor weep sins, and be wise,
Can railing then cure these worn maladies?
5 Is not our mistress, fair Religion,
As worthy of all our soul's devotion,
As virtue was to the first blinded age?
Are not heaven's joys as valiant to assuage
Lusts, as earth's honour was to them?[1] Alas,
10 As we do them in means, shall they surpass
Us in the end, and shall thy father's spirit
Meet blind philosophers in heaven, whose merit
Of strict life may be imputed faith,[2] and hear
Thee, whom he taught so easy ways and near
15 To follow, damned? Oh if thou dar'st, fear this;
This fear great courage, and high valour is.
Dar'st thou aid mutinous Dutch,[3] and dar'st thou lay
Thee in ships, wooden sepulchers, a prey
To leaders' rage, to storms, to shot, to dearth?
20 Dar'st thou dive seas, and dungeons of the earth?
Hast thou courageous fire to thaw the ice
Of frozen North discoveries? and thrice
Colder than salamanders,[4] like divine
Children in the oven,[5] fires of Spain, and the line,[6]
25 Whose countries' limbecks to our bodies be,[7]

Canst thou for gain bear? and must every he
Which cries not "Goddess" to thy Mistress, draw,
Or eat thy poisonous words? courage of straw!
Oh desperate coward, wilt thou seem bold, and
30 To thy foes and his (who made thee to stand
Sentinel in his world's garrison) thus yield,
And for forbidden wars, leave the appointed field?
Know thy foes: the foul devil, whom thou
Striv'st to please, for hate, not love, would allow
35 Thee fain his whole realm to be quit; and as
The world's all parts wither away and pass,
So the world's self, thy other loved foe, is
In her decrepit wane, and thou loving this,
Dost love a withered and worn strumpet; last,
40 Flesh (itself's death) and joys which flesh can taste,
Thou lovest; and thy fair goodly soul, which doth
Give this flesh power to taste joy, thou dost loathe.
Seek true religion. Oh where? Mirreus[8]
Thinking her unhoused here, and fled from us,
45 Seeks her at Rome;[9] there, because he doth know
That she was there a thousand years ago;
He loves her rags so, as we here obey
The statecloth[10] where the Prince sat yesterday.
Crants to such brave loves will not be enthralled,
50 But loves her only, who at Geneva is called
Religion,[11] plain, simple, sullen, young,
Contemptuous, yet unhandsome: as among
Lecherous humors, there is one that judges
No wenches wholesome, but coarse country drudges.
55 Graius stays still at home here,[12] and because
Some preachers, vile ambitious bauds, and laws
Still new like fashions, bid him think that she
Which dwells with us, is only perfect, he
Embraceth her whom his godfathers will
60 Tender to him, being tender, as wards still

---

[1] *them* The virtuous ancients who lived in the "blinded age" before the Christian revelation; their motive for virtue was earthly fame.

[2] *imputed faith* The speaker daringly uses a key term from Protestant theology to suggest that ancient philosophers might be "saved" as a result of their own merits, which might constitute an "imputed faith."

[3] *mutinous Dutch* The (Protestant) Dutch had been in revolt against their (Catholic) Spanish occupiers since 1568.

[4] *salamanders* Reputed to be so naturally cold that they could extinguish fires by contact.

[5] *Children in the oven* children who survived in the fiery furnace into which Nebuchadnezzar cast them. See Daniel 3.11–30.

[6] *fires of Spain, and the line* The tropical heat of the Spanish Main and the equatorial line; possibly also a reference to the "fires" of the Spanish inquisition.

[7] *limbecks to our bodies be* Because they make our bodies sweat: a limbeck is an alchemical still.

---

[8] *Mirreus* Some of the proper names the poem assigns to characters who hold various opinions (Mirreus, Graius, Graccus, Phrygius) have classical resonances; "Crants" (l. 49) sounds vaguely Dutch or German; but none appears to hold any particular significance.

[9] *Seeks her at Rome* Mirreus finds "true religion" in Catholicism.

[10] *statecloth* The canopy over the throne, or chair of state, respected as an emblem of the monarch's power.

[11] *But loves … called / Religion* "Crants" seeks "true religion" in the austere Protestantism of Genevan Calvinism.

[12] *Graius stays still at home here* "Graius" settles for the Church of England, but does so only because those around him do likewise.

Take such wives as their guardians offer, or
Pay values.[1] Careless Phrygius doth abhor
All, because all cannot be good, as one
Knowing some women whores, dares marry none.
65 Graccus loves all as one, and thinks that so
As women do in diverse countries go
In diverse habits, yet are still one kind,
So doth, so is Religion; and this blind-
ness too much light breeds; but unmoved thou
70 Of force must one, and forced but one allow;
And the right; ask thy father which is she,
Let him ask his; though truth and falsehood be
Near twins, yet truth a little elder is;
Be busy to seek her, believe me this,
75 He's not of none, nor worst, that seeks the best.
To adore, or scorn an image, or protest,
May all be bad; doubt wisely; in strange way
To stand inquiring right, is not to stray;
To sleep, or run wrong, is. On a huge hill,
80 Cragged and steep, Truth stands, and he that will
Reach her, about must, and about must go;
And what the hill's suddenness resists, win so;
Yet strive so, that before age, death's twilight,
Thy soul rest, for none can work in that night.
85 To will implies delay, therefore now do.
Hard deeds, the body's pains; hard knowledge too
The mind's endeavours reach, and mysteries
Are like the sun, dazzling, yet plain to all eyes.
Keep the truth which thou hast found; men do not
        stand
90 In so ill case here, that God hath with his hand
Signed kings blank-charters[2] to kill whom they hate,
Nor are they vicars, but hangmen to fate.
Fool and wretch, wilt thou let thy soul be tied
To man's laws, by which she shall not be tried
95 At the last day? Will it then boot thee
To say a Philip, or a Gregory,
A Harry, or a Martin taught thee this?[3]

Is not this excuse for mere contraries
Equally strong? Cannot both sides say so?
100 That thou mayest rightly obey power, her bounds
        know;
Those passed, her nature and name is changed; to be
Then humble to her is idolatry;
As streams are, Power is; those blest flowers that dwell
At the rough stream's calm head, thrive and do well,
105 But having left their roots, and themselves given
To the stream's tyrannous rage, alas are driven
Through mills, and rocks, and woods, and at last,
        almost
Consumed in going, in the sea are lost:
So perish souls, which more choose men's unjust
110 Power from God claimed, than God himself to trust.
—1633

from *Verse Letters*

To Sir Henry Wotton[4]

Sir, more than kisses, letters mingle souls;
For thus, friends absent speak. This ease controls
The tediousness of my life: but for these
I could ideate nothing which could please,
5 But I should wither in one day, and pass
To a bottle° of hay, that am a lock of grass.   bundle
Life is a voyage, and in our life's ways
Countries, courts, towns are rocks, or remoras;[5]
They break or stop all ships, yet our state's such,
10 That though than pitch they stain worse, we must
        touch.
If in the furnace of the even line,°   the equator
Or under the adverse icy pole thou pine,
Thou know'st two temperate regions, girded in,
Dwell there: But Oh, what refuge canst thou win
15 Parched in the court, and in the country frozen?
Shall cities, built of both extremes, be chosen?

---

[1] *Pay values*   A ward who refused a marriage arranged by his or her guardian had to pay the guardian a compensatory fine.

[2] *blank-charters*   Originally, legal papers that recorded a promise to supply the king with money: the amount of money was left blank, to be filled in by the king after it was signed. Here, warrants to have people killed, with the space for the victim's name left blank.

[3] *A Philip … thee this*   Respectively, King Philip II of Spain, Pope Gregory (either XIII or XIV), King Henry VIII, and Martin Luther: the group balances two Roman Catholic leaders against two

Reformation leaders.

[4] *To Sir Henry Wotton*   Administrator, diplomat, poet and writer, Sir Henry Wotton (1568–1639) met Donne at Oxford and was a close friend. This poem appears to have been written in the late 1590s, when both men were looking to win positions at court.

[5] *remoras*   Parasitical fish that could attach themselves to the bottom of ships and were thought to slow them down.

Can dung or garlic be a perfume? Or can
A scorpion and torpedo[1] cure a man?
Cities are worst of all three; of all three
20   (O knotty riddle) each is worst equally.
Cities are sepulchres; they who dwell there
Are carcasses, as if no such there were.
And courts are theatres, where some men play
Princes, some slaves, all to one end, and of one clay.
25   The country is a desert, where no good,
Gained (as habits, not born), is understood.
There men become beasts, and prone to more evils;
In cities blocks, and in a lewd court, devils.
As in the first chaos, confusedly,
30   Each element's qualities were in the other three,
So pride, lust, covetise,° being several   covetousness
To these three places, yet all are in all,
And mingled thus, their issue is incestuous.
Falsehood is denizened.[2] Virtue is barbarous.
35   Let no man say there, "Virtue's flinty wall
Shall lock vice in me, I'll do none, but know all."
Men are sponges, which to pour out, receive,
Who know false play, rather than lose, deceive.
For in best understandings sin began,
40   Angels sinned first, then devils, and then man.
Only perchance beasts sin not; wretched we
Are beasts in all, but white integrity.
I think if men, which in these place live,
Durst look in themselves, and themselves retrieve,
45   They would like strangers greet themselves, seeing then
Utopian youth, grown old Italian.[3]
      Be then thine own home, and in thyself dwell;
Inn anywhere; continuance maketh hell.
And seeing the snail, which everywhere doth roam,
50   Carrying his own house still, still is at home,
Follow (for he is easy paced) this snail,
Be thine own palace, or the world's thy jail.
And in the world's sea, do not like cork sleep
Upon the water's face; nor in the deep
55   Sink like a lead without a line; but as
Fishes glide, leaving no print where they pass,

Nor making sound, so closely thy course go,
Let men dispute, whether thou breathe, or no.
Only in this be no Galenist;[4] to make
60   Courts' hot ambitions wholesome, do not take
A dram of country's dullness; do not add
Correctives, but, as chemics, purge the bad.
But, sir, I advise not you, I rather do
Say o'er those lessons, which I learned of you:
65   Whom, free from German schisms, and lightness
Of France, and fair Italy's faithlessness,
Having from these sucked all they had of worth,
And brought home that faith which you carried forth,
I throughly° love; but if myself I've won   thoroughly
70   To know my rules, I have, and you have
                              DONNE.

—1633

An Anatomy of the World

Wherein, by occasion of the untimely death of mistress
Elizabeth Drury,[5] the frailty and the decay of this whole
world is represented.

THE FIRST ANNIVERSARY

When that rich soul which to her heaven is gone,
      Whom all they celebrate, who know they have
         one,
(For who is sure he hath a soul, unless
It see, and judge, and follow worthiness,
5   And by deeds praise it? he who doth not this,
May lodge an inmate soul, but 'tis not his.)
When that Queen ended here her progress time,[6]

---

[1]   *torpedo*   Also known as the numbfish or crampfish; the electric ray.

[2]   *denizened*   Naturalized (as in a "naturalized citizen").

[3]   *Utopian youth … Italian*   That is, an ideal youth turned old and depraved (from proverbial expressions concerning Italianate Englishmen, and Machiavelli).

[4]   *Galenist*   Follower of the ancient Roman doctor Galen, who believed that illness was a result of imbalance among the body's four "humors" and who cured an imbalance of one quality with a dose of its opposite.

[5]   *Elizabeth Drury*   The daughter of Sir Robert Drury; she died in December 1610, aged 14. Donne had never met her, but his sister Anne knew the family and possibly encouraged Donne to write the poem in hopes (ultimately successful) of patronage. A year later, Donne wrote a second poem to commemorate Elizabeth, *The Second Anniversary*. They are two of the few poems Donne published in his lifetime.

[6]   *progress time*   Monarch's ceremonial journey through the kingdom.

And, as t' her standing house, to heaven did climb,
Where, loth to make the saints attend her long,
10   She's now a part both of the choir, and song,
This world, in that great earthquake languished;
For in a common bath of tears it bled,
Which drew the strongest vital spirits out:
But succoured then with a perplexed doubt,
15   Whether the world did lose or gain in this,
(Because since now no other way there is
But goodness, to see her, whom all would see,
All must endeavour to be good as she,)
This great consumption to a fever turned,
20   And so the world had fits; it joyed, it mourned;
And, as men think, that agues physic are,
And th' ague being spent, give over care,
So thou, sick world, mistak'st thyself to be
Well, when alas, thou'rt in a lethargy.
25   Her death did wound and tame thee then, and then
Thou mightst have better spared the sun, or man.
That wound was deep, but 'tis more misery,
That thou hast lost thy sense and memory.
'Twas heavy then to hear thy voice of moan,
30   But this is worse, that thou art speechless grown.
Thou has forgot thy name thou hadst; thou wast
Nothing but she, and her thou hast o'erpast.
For as a child kept from the font,[1] until
A prince, expected long, come to fulfil
35   The ceremonies, thou unnamed hadst laid,
Had not her coming, thee her palace made:
Her name defined thee, gave thee form, and frame,
And thou forget'st to celebrate thy name.
Some months she hath been dead (but being dead,
40   Measures of times are all determined)
But long she hath been away, long, long, yet none
Offers to tell us who it is that's gone.
But as in states doubtful of future heirs,
When sickness without remedy impairs
45   The present prince, they're loth it should be said,
The prince doth languish, or the prince is dead:
So mankind feeling now a general thaw,
A strong example gone, equal to law,
The cement which did faithfully compact
50   And glue all virtues, now resolved, and slacked,
Thought it some blasphemy to say sh' was dead;
Or that our weakness was discovered

In that confession; therefore spoke no more
Than tongues, the soul being gone, the loss deplore.
55   But though it be too late to succour thee,
Sick world, yea dead, yea putrefied, since she
Thy intrinsic balm, and thy preservative,
Can never be renewed, thou never live,
I (since no man can make thee live) will try,
60   What we may gain by thy anatomy.
Her death hath taught us dearly, that thou art
Corrupt and mortal in thy purest part.
Let no man say, the world itself being dead,
'Tis labour lost to have discovered
65   The world's infirmities, since there is none
Alive to study this dissection;
For there's a kind of world remaining still,
Though she which did inanimate and fill
The world, be gone, yet in this last long night,
70   Her ghost doth walk; that is, a glimmering light,
A faint weak love of virtue and of good
Reflects from her, on them which understood
Her worth; and though she have shut in all day,
The twilight of her memory doth stay;
75   Which, from the carcass of the old world, free,
Creates a new world; and new creatures be
Produced: the matter and the stuff of this,
Her virtue, and the form our practice is.
And though to be thus elemented, arm
80   These creatures, from home-born intrinsic harm,
(For all assumed unto this dignity,
So many weedless paradises be,
Which of themselves produce no venomous sin,
Except some foreign serpent bring it in)
85   Yet, because outward storms the strongest break,
And strength itself by confidence grows weak,
This new world may be safer, being told
The dangers and diseases of the old:
For with due temper men do then forgo,
90   Or covet things, when they their true worth know.
There is no health; physicians say that we
At best, enjoy but a neutrality.
And can there be worse sickness, than to know
That we are never well, nor can be so?
95   We are born ruinous: poor mothers cry,
That children come not right, nor orderly,
Except they headlong come, and fall upon
An ominous precipitation.

---

[1] *font*   Baptismal font.

How witty's ruin! how importunate
100 Upon mankind! it laboured to frustrate
Even God's purpose: and made woman, sent
For man's relief, cause of his languishment.
They were to good ends, and they are so still,
But accessory, and principal in ill.
105 For that first marriage was our funeral:
One woman at one blow, then killed us all,
And singly, one by one, they kill us now.
We do delightfully ourselves allow
To that consumption; and profusely blind,
110 We kill ourselves,[1] to propagate our kind.
And yet we do not that; we are not men:
There is not now that mankind, which was then,
When as the sun, and man, did seem to strive,
(Joint tenants of the world) who should survive.
115 When stag, and raven, and the long-lived tree,
Compared with man, died in minority;
When, if a slow-paced star had stol'n away
From the observer's marking, he might stay
Two or three hundred years to see't again,
120 And then make up his observation plain;
When, as the age was long, the size was great:
Man's growth confessed, and recompensed the meat:
So spacious and large, that every soul
Did a fair kingdom, and large realm control:
125 And when the very stature thus erect,
Did that soul a good way towards heaven direct.
Where is this mankind now? who lives to age,
Fit to be made Methusalem[2] his page?
Alas, we scarce live long enough to try
130 Whether a new made clock run right, or lie.
Old grandsires talk of yesterday with sorrow,
And for our children we reserve tomorrow.
So short is life, that every peasant strives,
In a torn house, or field, to have three lives.[3]
135 And as in lasting, so in length is man
Contracted to an inch, who was a span;
For had a man at first in forests strayed,
Or shipwrecked in the sea, one would have laid
A wager, that an elephant, or whale,

140 That met him, would not hastily assail
A thing so equal to him: now alas,
The fairies and the pygmies well may pass
As credible; mankind decays so soon,
We're scarce our fathers' shadows cast at noon.
145 Only death adds to our length: nor are we grown
In stature to be men, till we are none.
But this were light, did our less volume hold
All the old text; or had we changed to gold
Their silver; or disposed into less glass
150 Spirits of virtue, which then scattered was.
But 'tis not so: we're not retired, but damped;
And as our bodies, so our minds are cramped:
'Tis shrinking, not close weaving that hath thus,
In mind and body both bedwarfed us.
155 We seem ambitious, God's whole work to undo;
Of nothing he made us, and we strive too,
To bring ourselves to nothing back; and we
Do what we can, to do 't so soon as he.
With new diseases on ourselves we war,
160 And with new physic, a worse engine far.
Thus man, this world's vice-emperor, in whom
All faculties, all graces are at home;
And if in other creatures they appear,
They're but man's ministers, and legates there,
165 To work on their rebellions, and reduce
Them to civility, and to man's use.
This man, whom God did woo, and loth t'attend
Till man came up, did down to man descend,
This man, so great, that all that is, is his,
170 Oh what a trifle, and poor thing he is!
If man were anything, he's nothing now:
Help, or at least some time to waste, allow
T' his other wants, yet when he did depart
With her whom we lament, he lost his heart.
175 She, of whom th' ancients seemed to prophesy,
When they called virtues by the name of she;
She in whom virtue was so much refined,
That for allay unto so pure a mind
She took the weaker sex, she that could drive
180 The poisonous tincture,[4] and the stain of Eve,
Out of her thoughts, and deeds; and purify
All, by a true religious alchemy;
She, she is dead; she's dead: when thou know'st this,
Thou know'st how poor a trifling thing man is.

---

[1]   *we kill ourselves*   Sex was believed to shorten life.

[2]   *Methusalem*   I.e., Methuselah, who lived 969 years (Genesis 5.27).

[3]   *three lives*   Probably referring to certain kinds of leases, which lasted until the death of three named leasees.

[4]   *poisonous tincture*   Original sin.

185   And learn'st thus much by our anatomy,
The heart being perished, no part can be free.
And that except thou feed (not banquet)[1] on
The supernatural food, religion,
Thy better growth grows withered, and scant;
190   Be more than man, or thou'rt less than an ant.
Then, as mankind, so is the world's whole frame
Quite out of joint, almost created lame:
For, before God had made up all the rest,
Corruption entered, and depraved the best:
195   It seized the angels, and then first of all
The world did in her cradle take a fall,
And turned her brains, and took a general maim
Wronging each joint of th' universal frame.
The noblest part, man, felt it first; and then
200   Both beasts and plants, cursed in the curse of man.
So did the world from the first hour decay,
That evening was beginning of the day,
And now the springs and summers which we see,
Like sons of women after fifty be.
205   And new philosophy calls all in doubt,
The element of fire is quite put out;[2]
The sun is lost, and th' earth, and no man's wit
Can well direct him where to look for it.[3]
And freely men confess that this world's spent,
210   When in the planets, and the firmament
They seek so many new; they see that this
Is crumbled out again to his atomies.
'Tis all in pieces, all coherence gone;
All just supply, and all relation:
215   Prince, subject, father, son, are things forgot,
For every man alone thinks he hath got
To be a phoenix, and that there can be
None of that kind, of which he is, but he.
This is the world's condition now, and now
220   She that should all parts to reunion bow,
She that had all magnetic force alone,
To draw, and fasten sundered parts in one;

She whom wise nature had invented then
When she observed that every sort of men
225   Did in their voyage in this world's sea stray,
And needed a new compass for their way;
She that was best, and first original
Of all fair copies; and the general
Steward to Fate; she whose rich eyes, and breast,
230   Gilt the West Indies, and perfumed the East;
Whose having breathed in this world, did bestow
Spice on those isles, and bade them still smell so,
And that rich Indy which doth gold inter,
Is but as single money, coined from her:
235   She to whom this world must itself refer,
As suburbs, or the microcosm of her,
She, she is dead; she's dead: when thou know'st this,
Thou know'st how lame a cripple this world is.
And learn'st thus much by our anatomy,
240   That this world's general sickness doth not lie
In any humour, or one certain part;
But as thou sawest it rotten at the heart,
Thou seest a hectic fever hath got hold
Of the whole substance, not to be controlled,
245   And that thou hast but one way, not to admit
The world's infection, to be none of it.
For the world's subtlest immaterial parts
Feel this consuming wound, and age's darts.
For the world's beauty is decayed, or gone,
250   Beauty, that's colour, and proportion.
We think the heavens enjoy their spherical,
Their round proportion embracing all.[4]
But yet their various and perplexed course,
Observed in diverse ages, doth enforce
255   Men to find out so many eccentric parts,
Such diverse down-right lines, such overthwarts,
As disproportion that pure form. It tears
The firmament in eight and forty shares,
And in these constellations then arise

---

[1] *banquet*   That is, feed rather than snack or nibble: a banquet in the period could refer to an appetizer or dessert course.

[2] *The element of fire … put out*   The astronomer Johannes Kepler (1571–1630) disproved the traditional belief that the earth was surrounded by a sphere of fire.

[3] *The sun is lost … look for it*   Referring to the cosmological uncertainty created by the new, heliocentric theories of Copernicus, Brahe, and Kepler.

[4] *Their round proportion embracing all*   Beginning in line 251, Donne points to changes in astronomical models as a sign of universal change. Plato had suggested that planetary orbits were perfect circles (lines 251–52); Ptolemy had constructed a more complex model, still geocentric, that accounted for observed movements (line 253 forward). Ptolemy's model was itself under challenge in Donne's time by the work of astronomers such as Copernicus.

260 New stars,[1] and old do vanish from our eyes:
As though heaven suffered earthquakes, peace or war,
When new towns rise, and old demolished are.
They have impaled within a zodiac
The free-born sun, and keep twelve signs awake
265 To watch his steps; the goat and crab control,
And fright him back, who else to either pole
(Did not these tropics fetter him) might run:
For his course is not round; nor can the sun
Perfect a circle, or maintain his way
270 One inch direct; but where he rose today
He comes no more, but with a cozening line,
Steals by that point, and so is serpentine:
And seeming weary with his reeling thus,
He means to sleep, being now fall'n nearer us.
275 So, of the stars which boast that they do run
In circle still, none ends where he begun.
All their proportion's lame, it sinks, it swells.
For of meridians, and parallels,
Man hath weaved out a net, and this net thrown
280 Upon the heavens, and now they are his own.
Loth to go up the hill, or labour thus
To go to heaven, we make heaven come to us.
We spur, we rein the stars, and in their race
They're diversely content t' obey our pace.
285 But keeps the earth her round proportion still?
Doth not a Tenerife,[2] or higher hill
Rise so high like a rock, that one might think
The floating moon would shipwreck there, and sink?
Seas are so deep, that whales being struck today,
290 Perchance tomorrow, scarce at middle way
Of their wished journey's end, the bottom, die.
And men, to sound depths, so much line untie,
As one might justly think that there would rise
At end thereof, one of th' Antipodes:
295 If under all, a vault infernal be,
(Which sure is spacious, except that we
Invent another torment, that there must
Millions into a strait hot room be thrust)

Then solidness, and roundness have no place.
300 Are these but warts, and pock-holes in the face
Of th' earth? Think so: but yet confess, in this
The world's proportion disfigured is,
That those two legs whereon it doth rely,
Reward and punishment are bent awry.
305 And, oh, it can no more be questioned,
That beauty's best, proportion, is dead,
Since even grief itself, which now alone
Is left us, is without proportion.
She by whose lines proportion should be
310 Examined, measure of all symmetry,
Whom had that ancient[3] seen, who thought souls made
Of harmony, he would at next have said
That harmony was she, and thence infer,
That souls were but resultances from her,
315 And did from her into our bodies go,
As to our eyes, the forms from objects flow:
She, who if those great Doctors[4] truly said
That the Ark to man's proportions was made,
Had been a type for that, as that might be
320 A type of her in this, that contrary
Both elements, and passions lived at peace
In her, who caused all civil war to cease.
She, after whom what form soe'er we see
Is discord, and rude incongruity;
325 She, she is dead, she's dead; when thou know'st this
Thou know'st how ugly a monster this world is:
And learn'st thus much by our anatomy,
That here is nothing to enamour thee:
And that, not only faults in inward parts,
330 Corruptions in our brains, or in our hearts,
Poisoning the fountains, whence our actions spring,
Endanger us: but that if everything
Be not done fitly and in proportion,
To satisfy wise, and good lookers-on,
335 (Since most men be such as most think they be)
They're loathsome too, by this deformity.
For good, and well, must in our actions meet;
Wicked is not much worse than indiscreet.
But beauty's other second element,
340 Colour, and lustre now, is as near spent.

---

[1] *new stars* Brahe and Kepler had observed the appearance of new stars, and Galileo had discovered the moons of Jupiter; these observations all challenged belief in the unchangeableness of the firmament above the moon.

[2] *Tenerife* Mountain on the island of Teneriffe, in the Canary Islands; it rises over 12,000 feet, but was often considered much higher in the period.

---

[3] *that ancient* Probably the ancient Greek mathematician and philosopher Pythagoras (born c. 560 BCE).

[4] *great Doctors* Church doctors or fathers, the patristic writers; Augustine and Ambrose both make this claim.

And had the world his just proportion,
Were it a ring still, yet the stone is gone.
As a compassionate turquoise[1] which doth tell
By looking pale, the wearer is not well,
As gold falls sick[2] being stung with mercury,
All the world's parts of such complexion be.
When nature was most busy, the first week,
Swaddling the new born earth, God seemed to like
That she should sport herself sometimes, and play,
To mingle, and vary colours every day:
And then, as though she could not make enow,
Himself his various rainbow did allow.
Sight is the noblest sense of any one,
Yet sight hath only colour to feed on,
And colour is decayed: summer's robe grows
Dusky, and like an oft dyed garment shows.
Our blushing red, which used in cheeks to spread,
Is inward sunk, and only our souls are red.
Perchance the world might have recovered,
If she whom we lament had not been dead:
But she, in whom all white, and red, and blue
(Beauty's ingredients) voluntary grew,
As in an unvexed paradise; from whom
Did all things verdure, and their lustre come,
Whose composition was miraculous,
Being all colour, all diaphanous,
(For air, and fire but thick gross bodies were
And liveliest stones but drowsy, and pale to her),
She, she, is dead; she's dead: when thou know'st this,
Thou know'st how wan a ghost this our world is:
And learn'st thus much by our anatomy,
That it should more affright, than pleasure thee.
And that, since all fair colour then did sink,
'Tis now but wicked vanity, to think
To colour vicious deeds with good pretense,
Or with bought colours to elude men's sense.
Nor in aught more this world's decay appears,
Than that her influence the heaven forbears,
Or that the elements do not feel this,
The father, or the mother barren is.
The clouds conceive not rain, or do not pour
In the due birth time, down the balmy shower.

Th' air doth not motherly sit on the earth,
To hatch her seasons, and give all things birth.
385 Spring-times were common cradles, but are tombs;
And false conceptions fill the general wombs.
Th' air shows such meteors, as none can see,
Not only what they mean, but what they be.
Earth such new worms, as would have troubled much
390 Th' Egyptian Mages[3] to have made more such.
What artist now dares boast that he can bring
Heaven hither, or constellate anything,
So as the influence of those stars may be
Imprisoned in an herb, or charm, or tree,
395 And do by touch, all which those stars could do?
The art is lost, and correspondence too.
For heaven gives little, and the earth takes less,
And man least knows their trade, and purposes.
If this commerce 'twixt heaven and earth were not
400 Embarred, and all this traffic quite forgot,
She, for whose loss we have lamented thus,
Would work more fully and powerfully on us.
Since herbs, and roots by dying, lose not all,
But they, yea ashes too, are medicinal,
405 Death could not quench her virtue so, but that
It would be (if not followed) wondered at:
And all the world would be one dying swan,
To sing her funeral praise, and vanish then.
But as some serpents' poison hurteth not,
410 Except it be from the live serpent shot,
So doth her virtue need her here, to fit
That unto us; she working more than it.
But she, in whom to such maturity
Virtue was grown, past growth, that it must die,
415 She, from whose influence all impressions came,
But, by receivers' impotencies, lame,
Who, though she could not transubstantiate
All states to gold, yet gilded every state,
So that some princes have some temperance;
420 Some counsellors some purpose to advance
The common profit; and some people have
Some stay, no more than kings should give, to crave;
Some women have some taciturnity,
Some nunneries, some grains of chastity.
425 She that did thus much, and much more could do,

---

1 *compassionate turquoise* Turquoise was reputed to change lustre
according to the health of the wearer.

2 *gold falls sick* Gold amalgam, a mixture of gold with mercury, is
paler than gold.

3 *Egyptian Mages* From Exodus 7.10–12; Donne refers to the new
snakes ("worms") that explorers in Africa and America were encountering.

But that our age was iron, and rusty too,
She, she is dead; she 's dead; when thou know'st this,
Thou know'st how dry a cinder this world is.
And learn'st thus much by our anatomy,
430   That 'tis in vain to dew, or mollify
It with thy tears, or sweat, or blood: nothing
Is worth our travail, grief, or perishing,
But those rich joys, which did possess her heart,
Of which she's now partaker, and a part.
435   But as in cutting up a man that's dead,
The body will not last out to have read
On every part, and therefore men direct
Their speech to parts, that are of most effect;
So the world's carcass would not last, if I
440   Were punctual in this anatomy.
Nor smells it well to hearers, if one tell
Them their disease, who fain would think they're well.
Here therefore be the end: and, blessed maid,
Of whom is meant whatever hath been said,
445   Or shall be spoken well by any tongue,
Whose name refines coarse lines, and makes prose song,
Accept this tribute, and his first year's rent,
Who till his dark short taper's end be spent,
As oft as thy feast sees this widowed earth,
450   Will yearly celebrate thy second birth,
That is, thy death. For though the soul of man
Be got when man is made, 'tis born but then
When man doth die. Our body's as the womb,
And as a midwife death directs it home.
455   And you her creatures, whom she works upon
And have your last, and best concoction
From her example, and her virtue, if you
In reverence to her, do think it due,
That no one should her praises thus rehearse,
460   As matter fit for chronicle, not verse,
Vouchsafe to call to mind, that God did make
A last, and lasting'st piece, a song. He spake
To Moses, to deliver unto all,
That song: because he knew they would let fall
465   The Law, the prophets, and the history,
But keep the song[1] still in their memory.
Such an opinion (in due measure) made
Me this great office boldly to invade.
Nor could incomprehensibleness deter
470   Me, from thus trying to imprison her.

---

[1] *the song*   See Deuteronomy 31.19, 31–43.

Which when I saw that a strict grave could do,
I saw not why verse might not do so too.
Verse hath a middle nature: heaven keeps souls,
The grave keeps bodies, verse the fame enrols.
—1611

from *Holy Sonnets*

2[2]

As due by many titles I resign
Myself to thee, O God, first I was made
By thee, and for Thee, and when I was decayed
Thy blood bought that, the which before was Thine;
5   I am Thy son, made with Thyself to shine,
Thy servant, whose pains Thou hast still repaid,
Thy sheep, Thine image, and, till I betrayed
Myself, a temple of Thy Spirit divine;
Why doth the devil then usurp on me?
10   Why doth he steal, nay ravish, that's Thy right?
Except Thou rise and for Thine own work fight,
Oh I shall soon despair, when I do see
That Thou lov'st mankind well, yet wilt not choose me,
And Satan hates me, yet is loth to lose me.
—1633

5[3]

I am a little world made cunningly
Of elements, and an angelic sprite,
But black sin hath betrayed to endless night
My world's both parts, and (oh) both parts must die.
5   You which beyond that heaven which was most high
Have found new spheres, and of new lands can write,
Pour new seas in mine eyes, that so I might
Drown my world with my weeping earnestly,
Or wash it, if it must be drowned no more:
10   But oh it must be burnt; alas the fire
Of lust and envy have burnt it heretofore,
And made it fouler; let their flames retire,
And burn me O Lord, with a fiery zeal
Of Thee and Thy house, which doth in eating heal.
—1635

---

[2] 2 Numbered as Sonnet 1 in some modern editions.

[3] 5 Numbered as Sonnet 2 (of those added in 1635) in some modern editions.

6 [1]

This is my play's last scene, here heavens appoint
    My pilgrimage's last mile; and my race
Idly, yet quickly run, hath this last pace,
My span's last inch, my minute's last point,
5 And gluttonous death will instantly unjoint
My body and soul, and I shall sleep a space,
But my ever-waking part shall see that face
Whose fear already shakes my every joint:
Then, as my soul, to heaven her first seat, takes flight,
10 And earth-born body in the earth shall dwell,
So, fall my sins, that all may have their right,
To where they're bred, and would press me, to hell.
Impute me righteous,[2] thus purged of evil,
For thus I leave the world, the flesh, and devil.
    —1633

7 [3]

At the round earth's imagined corners, blow
    Your trumpets, angels, and arise, arise
From death, you numberless infinities
Of souls, and to your scattered bodies go,
5 All whom the flood did, and fire shall o'erthrow,
All whom war, dearth, age, agues, tyrannies,
Despair, law, chance, hath slain, and you whose eyes
Shall behold God and never taste death's woe.[4]
But let them sleep, Lord, and me mourn a space,
10 For if above all these my sins abound,
'Tis late to ask abundance of Thy grace
When we are there; here on this lowly ground,
Teach me how to repent; for that's as good
As if Thou hadst sealed my pardon with Thy blood.
    —1633

9 [5]

If poisonous minerals, and if that tree,
    Whose fruit threw death on else immortal us,
If lecherous goats, if serpents envious
Cannot be damned, alas, why should I be?
5 Why should intent or reason, born in me,
Make sins, else equal, in me more heinous?
And mercy being easy, and glorious
To God, in His stern wrath, why threatens He?
But who am I, that dare dispute with Thee?
10 O God, oh! of Thine only worthy blood
And my tears, make a heavenly Lethean flood,[6]
And drown in it my sins' black memory.
That Thou remember them, some claim as debt,
I think it mercy, if Thou wilt forget.
    —1633

10 [7]

Death be not proud, though some have called thee
    Mighty and dreadful, for thou are not so;
For those whom thou think'st thou dost overthrow
Die not, poor death, nor yet canst thou kill me.
5 From rest and sleep, which but thy pictures be,
Much pleasure; then from thee, much more must flow,
And soonest our best men with thee do go,
Rest of their bones, and soul's delivery.
Thou art slave to fate, chance, kings, and desperate men,
10 And dost with poison, war, and sickness dwell;
And poppy, or charms, can make us sleep as well
And better than thy stroke; why swell'st thou then?
One short sleep past, we wake eternally,
And death shall be no more; death, thou shalt die.
    —1633

---

1   6   Numbered as Sonnet 3 in some modern editions.

2   *Impute me righteous*   Key idea of Protestant theology: justifying grace is imputed to a person through Christ's righteousness.

3   7   Numbered as Sonnet 4 in some modern editions.

4   *Shall behold … death's woe*   Referring to those mentioned in Luke 9.27, who will "not taste of death, till they have seen the kingdom of God."

5   9   Numbered as Sonnet 5 in some modern editions.

6   *Lethean flood*   In classical myth, Lethe is a river in the underworld; those who drink from it forget their earthly life.

7   10   Numbered as Sonnet 6 in some modern editions.

13[1]

What if this present were the world's last night?
    Mark in my heart, O soul, where thou dost dwell,
The picture of Christ crucified, and tell
Whether that countenance can thee affright,
5 Tears in His eyes quench the amazing light,
Blood fills His frowns, which from His pierced head fell,
And can that tongue adjudge thee unto hell,
Which prayed forgiveness for His foes' fierce spite?
No, no; but as in my idolatry
10 I said to all my profane mistresses,
Beauty, of pity, foulness only is
A sign of rigour:[2] so I say to thee,
To wicked spirits are horrid shapes assigned,
This beauteous form assures a piteous mind.
                                                —1633

14[3]

Batter my heart, three personed God; for you
    As yet but knock, breathe, shine, and seek to mend;
That I may rise and stand, o'erthrow me, and bend
Your force, to break, blow, burn and make me new.
5 I, like an usurped town, to another due,
Labour to admit You, but oh, to no end:
Reason Your viceroy in me, me should defend,
But is captived, and proves weak or untrue.
Yet dearly I love You, and would be loved fain,
10 But am betrothed unto your enemy:
Divorce me, untie, or break that knot again,
Take me to You, imprison me, for I
Except You enthral me, never shall be free,
Nor ever chaste, except You ravish me.
                                                —1633

18[4]

Show me, dear Christ, Thy spouse, so bright and clear.
    What, is it she which on the other shore
Goes richly painted?[5] or which, robbed and tore,
Laments and mourns in Germany and here?[6]
5 Sleeps she a thousand, then peeps up one year?
Is she self-truth and errs? now new, now outwore?
Doth she, and did she, and shall she evermore
On one, on seven, or on no hill appear?[7]
Dwells she with us, or like adventuring knights
10 First travail we to seek and then make love?
Betray, kind husband, Thy spouse to our sights,
And let mine amorous soul court Thy mild dove,
Who is most true and pleasing to Thee then
When she's embraced and open to most men.
                                                —1899

19[8]

Oh, to vex me, contraries meet in one:
    Inconstancy unnaturally hath begot
A constant habit; that when I would not
I change in vows, and in devotion.
5 As humorous is my contrition
As my profane love, and as soon forgot:
As riddlingly distempered, cold and hot,
As praying, as mute; as infinite, as none.
I durst not view heaven yesterday; and today
10 In prayers and flattering speeches I court God:
Tomorrow I quake with true fear of His rod.
So my devout fits come and go away
Like a fantastic ague: save that here
Those are my best days, when I shake with fear.
                                                —1899

---

[1] *13* Numbered as Sonnet 9 in some modern editions.

[2] *A sign of rigour*   That is, beauty is a sign of pity (compassion for the lover and his desires), ugliness a sign of rigor (denial of the lover his desires).

[3] *14* Numbered as Sonnet 10 in some modern editions.

[4] *18* Numbered as Sonnet 2 (of the Westmoreland manuscript sonnets) in some modern editions.

[5] *Goes richly painted*   The Roman Catholic Church.

[6] *Laments … and here*   The Protestant or perhaps, more specifically, Calvinist Church.

[7] *On one … hill appear*   Solomon's Temple stood on one hill, Mount Moriah (see 2 Chronicles 3.1); Rome has seven hills; Geneva, the center of Calvinism, has none.

[8] *19* Numbered as Sonnet 3 (of the Westmoreland manuscript sonnets) in some modern editions.

Good Friday, 1613. Riding Westward

Let man's soul be a sphere, and then, in this,
    The intelligence that moves, devotion is,[1]
And as the other spheres, by being grown
Subject to foreign motions, lose their own,
5   And being by others hurried every day,
Scarce in a year their natural form obey:
Pleasure or business, so our souls admit
For their First Mover, and are whirled by it.
Hence is't, that I am carried towards the West
10 This day, when my soul's form bends towards the East.
There I should see a sun, by rising set,
And by that setting endless day beget;
But that Christ on this cross did rise and fall,
Sin had eternally benighted all.
15 Yet dare I almost be glad, I do not see
That spectacle of too much weight for me.
Who sees God's face, that is self life, must die;
What a death were it then to see God die?
It made His own lieutenant, Nature, shrink,
20 It made His footstool crack, and the sun wink.
Could I behold those hands which span the poles,
And tune all spheres at once, pierced with those holes?
Could I behold that endless height which is
Zenith to us, and to our antipodes,
25 Humbled below us? or that blood which is
The seat of all our souls, if not of His,
Made dirt of dust, or that flesh which was worn
By God, for His apparel, ragged and torn?
If on these things I durst not look, durst I
30 Upon His miserable mother cast mine eye,
Who was God's partner here, and furnished thus
Half of that sacrifice, which ransomed us?
Though these things, as I ride, be from mine eye,
They are present yet unto my memory,
35 For that looks towards them; and thou look'st
        towards me,

O Saviour, as Thou hang'st upon the tree;
I turn my back to Thee, but to receive
Corrections, till Thy mercies bid Thee leave.
O think me worth Thine anger, punish me,
40 Burn off my rusts, and my deformity,
Restore Thine image, so much, by Thy grace,
That Thou may'st know me, and I'll turn my face.
—1633

A Hymn to God the Father

1

Wilt Thou forgive that sin where I begun,
    Which is my sin, though it were done before?
Wilt Thou forgive those sins through which I run,
    And do them still, though still I do deplore?
5   When Thou hast done, Thou hast not done,
            For I have more.

2

Wilt Thou forgive that sin which I have won
    Others to sin? and made my sin their door?
Wilt Thou forgive that sin which I did shun
10   A year, or two, but wallowed in, a score?
        When Thou hast done, Thou hast not done,
            For I have more.

3

I have a sin of fear, that when I have spun
    My last thread, I shall perish on the shore;
15 But swear by Thyself, that at my death Thy sun
    Shall shine as he shines now, and heretofore;
        And, having done that, Thou hast done,
            I have no more.[2]
—1633

---

[1] *The intelligence ... devotion is* Donne invokes traditional cosmography, in which each heavenly sphere was controlled by its "intelligence" or spirit.

[2] *I have no more* "I fear no more" in the printed version; "have" in the manuscripts.

from *Devotions* [1]

MEDITATION 17

Nunc Lento Sonitu Dicunt, Morieris
Now, this bell tolling softly for another, says to me:
Thou must die

Perchance he for whom this bell tolls may be so ill, as that he knows not it tolls for him; and perchance I may think myself so much better than I am, as that they who are about me, and see my state, may have caused it to toll for me, and I know not that. The Church is catholic, universal, so are all her actions; all that she does belongs to all. When she baptizes a child, that action concerns me; for that child is thereby connected to that body which is my head too, and ingrafted into that body whereof I am a member. And when she buries a man, that action concerns me: all mankind is of one author, and is one volume; when one man dies, one chapter is not torn out of the book, but translated into a better language; and every chapter must be so translated; God employs several translators; some pieces are translated by age, some by sickness, some by war, some by justice; but God's hand is in every translation, and His hand shall bind up all our scattered leaves again for that library where every book shall lie open to one another. As therefore the bell that rings to a sermon calls not upon the preacher only, but upon the congregation to come, so this bell calls us all; but how much more me, who am brought so near the door by this sickness. There was a contention as far as a suit (in which both piety and dignity, religion and estimation, were mingled), which of the religious orders should ring to prayers first in the morning; and it was determined, that they should ring first that rose earliest. If we understand aright the dignity of this bell that tolls for our evening prayer, we would be glad to make it ours by rising early, in that application, that it might be ours as well as his, whose indeed it is. The bell doth toll for him that thinks it doth; and though it intermit again, yet from that minute that that occasion wrought upon him, he is united to God. Who casts not up his eye to the sun when it rises? but who takes off his eye from a comet when that breaks out? Who bends not his ear to any bell which upon any occasion rings? but who can remove it from that bell which is passing a piece of himself out of this world? No man is an island, entire of itself; every man is a piece of the continent, a part of the main. If a clod be washed away by the sea, Europe is the less, as well as if a promontory were, as well as if a manor of thy friend's or of thine own were: any man's death diminishes me, because I am involved in mankind, and therefore never send to know for whom the bells tolls; it tolls for thee. Neither can we call this a begging of misery, or a borrowing of misery, as though we were not miserable enough of ourselves, but must fetch in more from the next house, in taking upon us the misery of our neighbours. Truly it were an excusable covetousness if we did, for affliction is a treasure, and scarce any man hath enough of it. No man hath affliction enough that is not matured and ripened by it, and made fit for God by that affliction. If a man carry treasure in bullion, or in a wedge of gold, and have none coined into current money, his treasure will not defray him as he travels. Tribulation is treasure in the nature of it, but it is not current money in the use of it, except we get nearer and nearer our home, heaven, by it. Another man may be sick too, and sick to death, and this affliction may lie in his bowels, as gold in a mine, and be of no use to him; but this bell, that tells me of his affliction, digs out and applies that gold to me: if by this consideration of another's danger I take mine own into contemplation, and so secure myself, by making my recourse to my God, who is our only security.

—1624

[1] *Devotions*   Donne wrote *Devotions* (1624) during his convalescence from a dangerous illness. The book consists of 23 "stations," each consisting of a meditation, an expostulation, and a concluding prayer. Each of the meditations explores a stage of his illness (that is, a stage in the story of the little world of the body), by looking for correspondences to and implications of that stage in the larger world.

LADY MARY WROTH
c. 1587 – c. 1653

Lady Mary Wroth wrote the first work of prose fiction and the first amatory sonnet sequence published by a woman in English. Her court romance, *The Countess of Montgomery's Urania* (1621) exploits multiple Renaissance genres—sonnet, ballad, madrigal, pastoral narrative and song, among others—with penetrating observation, worldly skepticism, and emotional subtlety. Wroth's work was admired by a number of poets of her day—Ben Jonson, who dedicated his play *The Alchemist* (1610) to her, proclaimed that her verse had made him "a better lover, and much better poet"—and although her reputation faded into oblivion during the ensuing centuries, today Mary Wroth is recognized as a significant Jacobean writer and pioneer.

Born Mary Sidney, probably in 1587, Wroth was a member of an illustrious political and literary family that included her uncle, Sir Philip Sidney, her aunt, Mary Sidney Herbert, Countess of Pembroke (herself a poet and patron of poets), and her father, Sir Robert Sidney, a statesman and minor poet. Educated by tutors, Mary was already an accomplished scholar, musician, and dancer by the time of her arranged marriage in 1604 to a wealthy landowner, Sir Robert Wroth. The union was not a happy one, but it did propel Lady Mary further into the life of the Jacobean court, where she performed in Ben Jonson's *Masque of Blackness* in 1605 and *Masque of Beauty* in 1608, and, in her family's tradition, bestowed friendship and patronage on poets such as Jonson and George Chapman.

On her husband's death in 1614, Wroth was left with an infant son (who died in 1616) and crushing debts. She was also free to pursue more openly a long-time illicit affair with her cousin, William Herbert, with whom she eventually had two illegitimate children. This affair, and financial constraints, may have limited Wroth's access to court and spurred her to write more seriously. She polished her sonnets, already circulating in manuscript as early as 1605, and in 1621 appended them to a 558-page prose romance, *Urania*, dedicated to the Countess of Montgomery. Because of its fictionalized allusions to actual court personages and events, the book offended those who saw themselves depicted too transparently. One such person, Sir William Denny, complained to the King and circulated a scathing poem criticizing Wroth as a "hermaphrodite" and "monster," an "oyster" gaping open to every tide. Denny's attack sparked a wittily vigorous reply in which Wroth mimicked the exact form of Denny's verse, rewriting his lines one by one. But in the end the attacks on her found their mark; she withdrew the edition of *Urania* and published no more work during her lifetime. (A second part of *Urania*, a few other poems, and a pastoral drama, *Love's Victory*, remained unpublished until our own time.)

Scandalous elements aside, *Urania* is a groundbreaking work because it uses a genre traditionally written by men—the episodic pastoral narrative of Philip Sidney's *Arcadia* and the digressive adventures of the Alexandrian romance—in untraditional ways to examine the social situation of women in actual court society. Wroth's prose is plainer than Sidney's and her outlook even more skeptical of romantic ideals. ("Credit no thing" is a typical warning.) Centering on the friendship of the shepherdess Urania (modeled on the Countess of Montgomery) with the princess Pamphilia (modeled on Wroth herself) and Pamphilia's frustrated love for the faithless Amphilanthus (whose name means "lover of two"), the story branches into multiple episodes and characters, interspersed with over fifty poems and songs in various genres. While celebrating the power of female desire, Wroth does not shrink from depicting the casual brutality of relations between the sexes: women seduced and abandoned, the indignity of forced marriages, the tortures of jealousy and deception.

In *Pamphilia to Amphilanthus*, the sequence of 83 sonnets and 20 songs that follows *Urania*, Wroth, no doubt influenced by her famous uncle's *Astrophil and Stella*, again applies herself to a genre traditionally (although by now by no means exclusively) reserved for males. She again deftly employs a somewhat outdated convention—the Petrarchan sonnet—in ways that highlight love's tensions and contradictions. Pamphilia addresses not her beloved, as in many Petrarchan sonnets, but herself ("I with my spirit talk and cry"), as well as Cupid, Time, Fortune, and other personifications of her trials. As Paula Payne observes, "Astrophil is writing to win his love, but Pamphilia is writing to discover her self." If so, she may in this regard be more genuinely and interestingly Petrarchan than some of Petrarch's later and lesser followers. The climax of *Pamphilia to Amphilanthus* is a technical *tour de force*, a "corona" of fourteen sonnets in which the last line of the first becomes the first line of the next. The line that begins and ends it ("In this strange labyrinth how shall I turn?") is emblematic of Wroth's skill in combining the elegant detachment of the Petrarchan form with a heightened emotional urgency: love, it turns out, is not the "thread" that she had expected to lead her from the labyrinth, for the "corona" leaves her there.

Mary Wroth lived her final decades in obscurity, struggling with debt, and died probably in 1653. In the youthful portrait of her which survives, she is pictured holding, not the gloves or fan customary in female portraits of the time, but an archlute—symbol of the poet.

⌘ ⌘ ⌘

from *Pamphilia to Amphilanthus*

1.

When night's black mantle could most darkness prove,° *display*
And sleep death's Image did my senses hire° *engage*
From knowledge of my self, then thoughts did move
Swifter than those most swiftness need require:
5 In sleep, a Chariot drawn by winged desire
I saw: where sat bright Venus Queen of love,
And at her feet her son,[1] still adding fire
To burning hearts which she did hold above,
But one heart flaming more than all the rest
10 The goddess held, and put it to my breast,
Dear son, now shoot said she: thus must we win;
He her obeyed, and martyred my poor heart,
I, waking hoped as dreams it would depart
Yet since: O me: a lover I have been.

6.

My pain, still smothered in my grieved breast,
Seeks for some ease, yet cannot passage find
To be discharged of this unwelcome guest;
When most I strive, more fast his burdens bind,
5 Like to a ship, on Goodwins[2] cast by wind
The more she strives, more deep in sand is pressed
Till she be lost; so am I, in this kind° *manner*
Sunk, and devoured, and swallowed by unrest,
Lost, shipwrecked, spoiled, debarred of smallest hope
10 Nothing of pleasure left; save° thoughts have scope, *unless*
Which wander may: Go then, my thoughts, and cry
Hope's perished; Love tempest-beaten; Joy lost;
Killing despair hath all these blessings crossed
Yet faith still cries, Love will not falsify.

7.

Love leave° to urge, thou know'st thou hast the
hand;° *cease / upper hand*
'Tis cowardice, to strive where none resist:
Pray thee leave off, I yield unto thy band;° *bond*

---

[1] *her son* Cupid, customarily pictured as a winged infant carrying a bow and a quiver of arrows for piercing hearts, and torches to set them ablaze.

[2] *Goodwins* The Goodwins, or Goodwin Sands, a dangerous shoal off the coast of Kent proverbially associated with shipwrecks in Wroth's time.

Do not thus, still, in thine own power persist,
Behold I yield: let forces be dismissed;
I am thy subject, conquered, bound to stand,
Never thy foe, but did thy claim assist
Seeking thy due of those who did withstand;
But now, it seems, thou would'st I should thee love;
I do confess, 'twas thy will made me choose;
And thy fair shows[1] made me a lover prove
When I my freedom did, for pain, refuse.
Yet this Sir God,[2] your boyship I despise;
Your charms I obey, but love not want of eyes.[3]

13.

Dear, famish not what you your self gave food;
Destroy not what your glory is to save;
Kill not that soul to which you spirit gave;
In pity, not disdain your triumph stood;
An easy thing it is to shed the blood
Of one, who at your will, yields to the grave;
But more you may true worth[4] by mercy crave
When you preserve, not spoil, but nourish good;
Your sight is all the food I do desire;
Then sacrifice me not in hidden fire,
Or stop the breath which did your praises move:
Think but how easy 'tis a sight to give;
Nay ev'n desert; since by it I do live,
I but chameleon-like[5] would live, and love.

14.

Am I thus conquered? have I lost the powers
That to withstand, which joys° to ruin me?   *delights*
Must I be still while it my strength devours
And captive leads me prisoner, bound, unfree?
Love first shall leave men's fancies to them free,
Desire shall quench love's flames, spring hate°   *shall hate*
    sweet showers,   *sweet showers,*
Love shall loose all his darts, have sight, and see
His shame, and wishings hinder happy hours;
Why should we not love's purblind° charms   *almost blind*
    resist?

Must we be servile, doing what he list?°   *wishes*
No, seek some host to harbour thee: I fly°   *flee from*
Thy babish° tricks, and freedom do profess;   *babyish*
But O my hurt, makes my lost heart confess
I love, and must: So farewell liberty.

15.

Truly poor Night thou welcome art to me:
I love thee better in this sad attire
Than that which raiseth some men's fancies higher
Like painted outsides which foul inward be;
I love thy grave, and saddest looks to see,
Which seems° my soul, and dying heart entire,   *resembles*
Like to the ashes of some happy fire
That flamed in joy, but quenched in misery:
I love thy count'nance, and thy sober pace
Which evenly goes, and as of loving grace
To us, and me among the rest oppressed
Gives quiet, peace to my poor self alone,
And freely grants day leave when thou art gone
To give clear light to see all ill° redressed.   *misery*

22.

Like to the Indians, scorched with the sun,
The sun which they do as their God adore
So am I used by love, for ever more
I worship him, less favors have I won,
Better are they who thus to blackness run,
And so can only whiteness' want deplore
Than I who pale, and white am with grief's store,°   *abundance*
Nor can have hope, but to see hopes undone;
Besides, their sacrifice received's in sight
Of their chose saint: mine hid as worthless rite;
Grant me to see where I my offerings give,
Then let me wear the mark of Cupid's might
In heart as they in skin of Phoebus' light[6]
Not ceasing offerings to love while I Live.

23.

When every one to pleasing pastime hies°   *hastens*
Some hunt, some hawk, some play, while some
    delight
In sweet discourse, and music shows joy's might
Yet I my thoughts do far above these prize.

---

[1] *shows* Displays (of power).

[2] *Sir God* Mocking address to Cupid.

[3] *want of eyes* Blindness, a proverbial attribute of love, and of Cupid.

[4] *worth* Pun on "Wroth," which was pronounced "worth."

[5] *chameleon-like* The chameleon could survive for long periods without food, and was thus reputed to live on air.

[6] *as … light* As Indians, "scorched with the sun," show "in their skins" the mark of Phoebus, the sun-god.

The joy which I take, is that free from eyes[1]
I sit, and wonder at this daylike night
So to dispose themselves, as void° of right;   *bereft*
And leave true pleasure for poor vanities;
When others hunt, my thoughts I have in chase;
If hawk,[2] my mind at wished end doth fly,
Discourse,[3] I with my spirit talk, and cry
While others, music choose as greatest grace.
O God, say I, can these fond° pleasures move?   *foolish*
Or music be but in sweet thoughts of love?

35.

False hope which feeds but to destroy, and spill
What it first breeds;[4] unnatural to the birth
Of thine own womb; conceiving but to kill,
And plenty gives to make the greater dearth,
So Tyrants do who falsely ruling earth
Outwardly grace them, and with profit's fill
Advance those who appointed are to death
To make their greater fall to please their will.
Thus shadow they their wicked vile intent
Colouring evil with a show of good
While in fair shows° their malice so is spent;   *spectacles*
Hope kills the heart, and tyrants shed the blood.
For hope deluding brings us to the pride°   *peak*
Of our desires the farther down to slide.
—1621

from *A Crown of Sonnets Dedicated to Love*

77

In this strange labyrinth how shall I turn?
Ways° are on all sides while the way I miss: *paths*
  If to the right hand, there in love I burn;
  Let me go forward, therein danger is;
If to the left, suspicion hinders bliss;
  Let me turn back, shame cries I ought return,
  Nor faint, though crosses° with my fortunes kiss; *troubles*
  Stand still is harder, although sure to mourn.[5]
Thus let me take the right, or left-hand way,

Go forward, or stand still, or back retire:
I must these doubts endure without allay°   *relief*
Or help, but travail[6] find for my best hire.
Yet that which most my troubled sense doth move,
Is to leave all, and take the thread of Love.[7]
—1621

Railing Rhymes Returned upon the Author by Mistress Mary Wroth

Hermaphrodite[8] in sense in Art a monster
As by your railing rhymes the world may
    conster°   *construe*
Your spiteful words against a harmless book
Shows that an ass much like the sire doth look
Men truly noble fear no touch of blood
Nor question make of others much more good
Can such comparisons seem the want° of wit   *lack*
When oysters have inflamed your blood with it
But it appears your guiltiness gaped wide
And filled with Dirty doubt your brain's swollen tide
Both friend and foe in deed you use alike
And your mad wit in sherry equal strike
These slanderous flying flames raised from the pot[9]
You know are false and raging makes you hot
How easily now do you receive your own
Turned on your self from whence the squib was thrown
When these few lines not thousands writ at least
Mainly thus prove your self the drunken beast
This is far less to you than you have done
A Thread but of your own all words worse spun
By which you lively see in your own glass[10]
How hard it is for you to lie and pass
Thus you have made yourself a lying wonder
Fools and their pastimes should not part asunder.
—1983 (WRITTEN C. 1621)

---

[1] *eyes* The eyes, or gaze, of others.

[2] *If hawk* If they (others) hawk.

[3] *Discourse* When others discourse.

[4] *spill … breeds* As in a miscarriage.

[5] *although sure to mourn* Although sure to make me mourn.

[6] *travail* Hard work, but also with a pun on "travel."

[7] *thread of Love* Referring to the myth of Ariadne, who gave her beloved Theseus a spool of thread to unwind behind him as he traveled through the labyrinth of the Minotaur; by following the thread he could find his way back out.

[8] *Hermaphrodite* Possessing both male and female sexual organs; often used pejoratively to describe a mannish woman or an effeminate man.

[9] *pot* Drinking vessel.

[10] *glass* Mirror, but here perhaps also drinking-glass.

IN CONTEXT

The Occasion of "Railing Rhymes"

Wroth's "Railing Rhymes" was written in response to the following attack by Lord Denny.

Edward Denny, Baron of Waltham, To Pamphilia from the father-in-law of Seralius[1] (c. 1621)

Hermaphrodite in show, in deed a monster
As by thy words and works all men may conster°   construe
Thy wrathful spite conceived an Idle° book   worthless
Brought forth a fool which like the dam doth look
5   Wherein thou strikes at some man's noble blood
Of kin to thine[2] if thine be counted good
Whose vain comparison for want° of wit   lack
Takes up the oystershell to play with it
Yet common oysters such as thine gape wide
10   And take in pearls or worse at every tide
Both friend and foe to thee are even alike
Thy wit runs mad not caring who it strike
These slanderous flying f[l]ames rise from the pot
For potted wits inflamed are raging hot
15   How easy wer't to pay thee with thine own
Returning that which thou thyself hast thrown
And write a thousand lies of thee at least
And by thy lines describe a drunken beast
This were no more to thee than thou hast done
20   A Thread but of thine own which thou hast spun
By which thou plainly seest in thine own glass
How easy 'tis to bring a lie to pass
Thus hast thou made thyself a lying wonder
Fools and their Babbles seldom part asunder
25   Work o th' Works leave idle books alone
For wise and worthier women have writ none.
—1983 (WRITTEN C. 1621)

---

[1] *Seralius* A character in Wroth's court pastoral *The Countess of Montgomery's Urania* (1621), whose satirical resemblance to Denny's son-in-law was transparent enough to suggest embarrassing parallels to a recent Denny family scandal. Denny wrote angry letters to Wroth demanding withdrawal of her book and circulated this poem questioning her honesty and the appropriateness of a woman pursuing the vocation of writing.

[2] *Of kin to thine* As good, or noble, as yours.

THOMAS HOBBES
1588 – 1679

Thomas Hobbes was active in the study of geometry, optics, physics, psychology, language, and religion, but he is best known as the author of *Leviathan*, a seminal work of political and moral philosophy. His writings have remained the subject of controversy—not least of all his contention that the life of one who exists in a state of nature is "solitary, poor, nasty, brutish, and short." In his own time Hobbes had to contend with more severe criticism by the Royalists, the Parliamentarians, and the Church, all of which at various times found his writings to be seditious; the reading of his

works was at one time banned by both the Church and Oxford University. Many objected to his materialist assertions that a person attains knowledge only by way of sensory impressions and not by divine transference (Hobbes said "the universe is corporeal; all that is real is material, and what is not material is not real"), and that moral behavior is best only because it is rational to live a moral life and not because God wills people to do so.

Hobbes was born in Wiltshire, England, in the year of the Spanish Armada (1588); rumors had it that his premature birth had been brought on by his mother's fear of an attack. He was raised after the age of seven by his uncle, who took responsibility when Thomas Hobbes Sr., a parson, fled the family after a violent argument with another vicar. Hobbes appears not to have suffered intellectually from this upheaval, however—he translated Euripides's *Medea* from Greek to Latin during his formative years and entered Oxford University at the age of 15. After graduation he became tutor to the son of William Cavendish, Baron Hardwick (later the Earl of Devonshire), and indeed he would spend most of his life as a tutor. Hobbes accompanied the younger Cavendish on a European tour in 1610, and on this and subsequent trips overseas he met and befriended such important thinkers as Galileo and René Descartes (Hobbes wrote a famous refutation of Descartes's *Meditations*), all of whom influenced his theories of mathematics and natural science.

Hobbes continued translating throughout his life, first publishing Thucydides's *Eight Books of the Peloponnesian War* in 1629, long after he had completed the translation. The purpose of the book, he says in the introduction, is to "instruct and enable men, by the knowledge of actions past, to bear themselves prudently in the present and providently towards the future." In one of the first texts authored and published by Hobbes, *Elements of Law, Natural and Politic* (1642), which he called a "scientific treatment of politics," he responded to the political and civil unrest during the reign of Charles I by arguing for the right of the monarchy to absolute power. The contentious nature of the book and its appearance at the time of the King's dissolution of Parliament and the beginning of the Civil War caused Hobbes to flee to Paris, where he lived in exile for over a decade, there tutoring the future king, Charles II, and beginning his work on an important philosophical trilogy concerning politics (*De Cive*, 1642), matter (*De Corpore*, 1655), and human nature (*De Homine*, 1658).

The crux of the argument in *Leviathan* (1651) has its basis in the upheaval of the Civil War in England (1642–48). The work outlines Hobbes's theories about the necessity for a civilized society to live under the rule of government and abide obediently by its laws in order to exist in security. A sovereign power, Hobbes thought, is in the best position to make decisions regarding the welfare of its people and should be given absolute authority to rule over its constituents. He did not, however, specify that the "sovereign power" need be a king or queen, and because of this, when *Leviathan* appeared, Hobbes found himself in danger on the Continent, as the Royalists, who were also living in exile, interpreted his political stance as supportive of Cromwell's reign.

Leviathan's argument was founded on a defense of reason, which Hobbes saw as having as a natural goal self-preservation and the avoidance of war and violent death. Rather than living in a state of nature (i.e., without laws), people are better able in the long term to protect themselves against the threat of anarchy and civil war by banding together and giving themselves up to sovereign rule. They are then obliged to abide unquestioningly by the sovereign's laws, and, in essence, to let government become the "voice of the people." While Hobbes's doctrines were from one angle supportive of the sovereign power of the monarch, they were revolutionary in deriving justifications for that power from the common interests of the people and not from any divine right.

Hobbes lived to 91, an extraordinary age for someone of his day. He did not cease work in his final decade, but wrote his autobiography, translated Homer's *Iliad* and *Odyssey*, and completed work on *Behemoth* (authorized version published 1682), a history of the Civil War period in the form of a dialogue.

⌘ ⌘ ⌘

Frontispiece to the 1651 edition of *Leviathan*.

from *Leviathan;*[1] *Or the Matter, Form, & Power of a Commonwealth, Ecclesiastical and Civil*

THE INTRODUCTION

Nature (the art whereby God hath made and governs the world) is by the art of man, as in many other things, so in this also imitated, that it can make an artificial animal. For seeing life is but a motion of limbs, the beginning whereof is in some principal part within, why may we not say that all automata (engines that move themselves by springs and wheels as doth a watch) have an artificial life? For what is the heart, but a spring; and the nerves, but so many strings; and the joints, but so many wheels, giving motion to the whole body, such as was intended by the Artificer? Art goes yet further, imitating that rational and most excellent work of nature, man. For by art is created that great Leviathan called a Commonwealth, or State (in Latin, *Civitas*), which is but an artificial man, though of greater stature

---

[1] *Leviathan* From Job 41: an enormous primordial sea serpent whose strength is immeasurable and the existence of which attests to God's power and will. The 1651 edition of Hobbes's book pictured the Leviathan as sovereign power, personified by a giant monarch made up of small figures of men.

and strength than the natural, for whose protection and defense it was intended; and in which the sovereignty is an artificial soul, as giving life and motion to the whole body. The magistrates and other officers of judicature and execution, artificial joints. Reward and punishment (by which fastened to the seat of the sovereignty, every joint and member is moved to perform his duty) are the nerves that do the same in the body natural. The wealth and riches of all the particular members are the strength. *Salus populi* (the people's safety) its business. Counsellors, by whom all things needful for it to know are suggested unto it, are the memory. Equity and laws, an artificial reason and will. Concord, health. Sedition. sickness. And civil war, death. Lastly, the pacts and covenants by which the parts of this body politic were at first made, set together, and united, resemble that fiat,[1] or the "Let us make man,"[2] pronounced by God in the Creation.

To describe the nature of this artificial man, I will consider: first, the matter thereof, and the artificer, both which is Man. Secondly, how, and by what covenants it is made; what are the rights and just power or authority of a sovereign; and what it is that preserveth and dissolveth it. Thirdly, what is a Christian Commonwealth. Lastly, what is the Kingdom of Darkness.

Concerning the first, there is a saying much usurped of late that wisdom is acquired, not by reading of books, but of men. Consequently whereunto, those persons, that for the most part can give no other proof of being wise, take great delight to show what they think they have read in men by uncharitable censures of one another behind their backs. But there is another saying, not of late understood, by which they might learn truly to read one another, if they would take the pains, and that is *nosce teipsum*, read thyself, which was not meant, as it is now used, to countenance either the barbarous state of men in power towards their inferiors or to encourage men of low degree to a saucy behavior towards their betters, but to teach us that for the similitude of the thoughts and passions of one man to the thoughts and passions of another, whosoever looketh into himself and considereth what he doth when he does think, opine, reason, hope, fear, etc., and upon what grounds, he shall thereby read and know

what are the thoughts and passions of all other men upon the like occasions. I say the similitude of passions, which are the same in all men, desire, fear, hope, etc., not the similitude of the objects of the passions, which are the things desired, feared, hoped, etc.; for these the constitution individual and particular education do so vary, and they are so easy to be kept from our knowledge that the characters of man's heart, blotted and confounded as they are with dissembling, lying, counterfeiting, and erroneous doctrines are legible only to him that searcheth hearts. And though by men's actions we do discover their design sometimes; yet to do it without comparing them with our own and distinguishing all circumstances by which the case may come to be altered is to decipher without a key and be for the most part deceived by too much trust or by too much diffidence, as he that reads is himself a good or evil man.

But let one man read another by his actions never so perfectly, it serves him only with his acquaintance, which are but few. He that is to govern a whole nation must read in himself, not this or that particular man, but mankind, which though it be hard to do, harder than to learn any language or science; yet when I shall have set down my own reading orderly and perspicuously, the pains left another will be only to consider if he also find not the same in himself. For this kind of doctrine admitteth no other demonstration.

CHAPTER 13: OF THE NATURAL CONDITION OF MANKIND AS CONCERNING THEIR FELICITY AND MISERY

Nature hath made men so equal in the faculties of body and mind, as that, though there be found one man sometimes manifestly stronger in body or of quicker mind than another, yet when all is reckoned together, the difference between man and man is not so considerable as that one man can thereupon claim to himself any benefit to which another may not pretend as well as he. For as to the strength of body, the weakest has strength enough to kill the strongest, either by secret machination or by confederacy with others that are in the same danger with himself.

And as to the faculties of the mind, setting aside the arts grounded upon words, and especially that skill of proceeding upon general and infallible rules, called

---

[1] *fiat*   Decree. Latin: let there be.

[2] *"Let us make man"*   From Genesis 1.26.

science, which very few have and but in few things, as being not a native faculty born with us, nor attained, as prudence, while we look after somewhat else, I find yet a greater equality amongst men than that of strength. For prudence is but experience, which equal time equally bestows on all men in those things they equally apply themselves unto. That which may perhaps make such equality incredible is but a vain conceit of one's own wisdom, which almost all men think they have in a greater degree than the vulgar, that is, than all men but themselves and a few others, whom by fame or for concurring with themselves, they approve. For such is the nature of men that howsoever they may acknowledge many others to be more witty or more eloquent or more learned, they will hardly believe there be many so wise as themselves, for they see their own wit at hand and other men's at a distance. But this proveth rather that men are in that point equal, than unequal. For there is not ordinarily a greater sign of the equal distribution of anything than that every man is contented with his share.

From this equality of ability ariseth equality of hope in the attaining of our ends. And therefore if any two men desire the same thing, which nevertheless they cannot both enjoy, they become enemies, and in the way to their end (which is principally their own conservation, and sometimes their delectation only) endeavour to destroy or subdue one another. And from hence it comes to pass that where an invader hath no more to fear than another man's single power, if one plant, sow, build, or possess a convenient seat, others may probably be expected to come prepared with forces united to dispossess and deprive him, not only of the fruit of his labour, but also of his life or liberty. And the invader again is in the like danger of another.

And from this diffidence of one another, there is no way for any man to secure himself so reasonable as anticipation, that is, by force or wiles, to master the persons of all men he can so long till he see no other power great enough to endanger him; and this is no more than his own conservation requireth, and is generally allowed. Also, because there be some that, taking pleasure in contemplating their own power in the acts of conquest, which they pursue farther than their security requires, if others, that otherwise would be glad to be at ease within modest bounds, should not by invasion increase their power, they would not be able,

long time, by standing only on their defence, to subsist. And by consequence, such augmentation of dominion over men being necessary to a man's conservation, it ought to be allowed him.

Again, men have no pleasure (but on the contrary a great deal of grief) in keeping company where there is no power able to overawe them all. For every man looketh that his companion should value him at the same rate he sets upon himself, and upon all signs of contempt or undervaluing naturally endeavours, as far as he dares (which amongst them that have no common power to keep them in quiet is far enough to make them destroy each other), to extort a greater value from his contemners,[1] by damage; and from others, by the example.

So that in the nature of man, we find three principal causes of quarrel. First, competition; secondly, diffidence; thirdly, glory.

The first maketh men invade for gain; the second, for safety; and the third, for reputation. The first use violence to make themselves masters of other men's persons, wives, children, and cattle; the second, to defend them; the third, for trifles, as a word, a smile, a different opinion, and any other sign of undervalue, either direct in their persons or by reflection in their kindred, their friends, their nation, their profession, or their name.

Hereby it is manifest that during the time men live without a common power to keep them all in awe, they are in that condition which is called war; and such a war as is of every man against every man. For war consisteth not in battle only, or the act of fighting, but in a tract of time, wherein the will to contend by battle is sufficiently known; and therefore the notion of *time* is to be considered in the nature of war, as it is in the nature of weather. For as the nature of foul weather lieth not in a shower or two of rain, but in an inclination thereto of many days together, so the nature of war consisteth not in actual fighting, but in the known disposition thereto during all the time there is no assurance to the contrary. All other time is peace.

Whatsoever therefore is consequent to a time of war, where every man is enemy to every man, the same consequent to the time wherein men live without other security than what their own strength and their own invention shall furnish them withal. In such condition

---

[1] *his contemners* Those who scorn him.

there is no place for industry, because the fruit thereof is uncertain; and consequently no culture of the earth; no navigation, nor use of the commodities that may be imported by sea; no commodious building; no instruments of moving and removing such things as require much force; no knowledge of the face of the earth; no account of time; no arts; no letters; no society; and which is worst of all, continual fear, and danger of violent death; and the life of man, solitary, poor, nasty, brutish, and short.

It may seem strange to some man that has not well weighed these things that nature should thus dissociate and render men apt to invade and destroy one another; and he may therefore, not trusting to this inference, made from the passions, desire perhaps to have the same confirmed by experience. Let him therefore consider with himself; when taking a journey, he arms himself and seeks to go well accompanied; when going to sleep, he locks his doors; when even in his house he locks his chests; and this when he knows there be laws and public officers, armed to revenge all injuries shall be done him; what opinion he has of his fellow subjects, when he rides armed; of his fellow citizens, when he locks his doors; and of his children, and servants, when he locks his chests. Does he not there as much accuse mankind by his actions as I do by my words? But neither of us accuse man's nature in it. The desires and other passions of man are in themselves no sin. No more are the actions that proceed from those passions till they know a law that forbids them; which, till laws be made, they cannot know; nor can any law be made till they have agreed upon the person that shall make it.

It may peradventure be thought there was never such a time nor condition of war as this; and I believe it was never generally so, over all the world; but there are many places where they live so now. For the savage people in many places of America, except the government of small families, the concord whereof dependeth on natural lust, have no government at all, and live at this day in that brutish manner, as I said before. Howsoever, it may be perceived what manner of life there would be, where there were no common power

to fear, by the manner of life which men that have formerly lived under a peaceful government use to degenerate into a civil war.

But though there had never been any time wherein particular men were in a condition of war one against another; yet in all times kings and persons of sovereign authority, because of their independency, are in continual jealousies, and in the state and posture of gladiators, having their weapons pointing and their eyes fixed on one another, that is, their forts, garrisons, and guns upon the frontiers of their kingdoms, and continual spies upon their neighbours, which is a posture of war. But because they uphold thereby the industry of their subjects, there does not follow from it that misery which accompanies the liberty of particular men.

To this war of every man against every man, this also is consequent: that nothing can be unjust. The notions of right and wrong, justice and injustice, have there no place. Where there is no common power, there is no law; where no law, no injustice. Force and fraud are in war the two cardinal virtues. Justice and injustice are none of the faculties neither of the body nor mind. If they were, they might be in a man that were alone in the world, as well as his senses and passions. They are qualities that relate to men in society, not in solitude. It is consequent also to the same condition that there be no propriety,[1] no dominion, no *mine* and *thine* distinct, but only that to be every man's that he can get, and for so long as he can keep it. And thus much for the ill condition which man by mere nature is actually placed in, though with a possibility to come out of it, consisting partly in the passions, partly in his reason.

The passions that incline men to peace are fear of death, desire of such things as are necessary to commodious living, and a hope by their industry to obtain them. And reason suggesteth convenient articles of peace upon which men may be drawn to agreement. These articles are they which otherwise are called the laws of nature, whereof I shall speak more particularly in the two following chapters.

—1651

---

[1] *propriety*   Private property.

ROBERT HERRICK
1591 – 1674

Of the "sons of Ben" who basked in the genius of Ben Jonson in 1620s London, Robert Herrick is the poet most familiar to modern readers—more so, to many readers, than Jonson himself. "Gather ye Rosebuds while ye may," the opening line of Herrick's "To the Virgins, to make much of Time," is the most famous version of a classical refrain, while poems such as "Delight in Disorder" and "The Hock Cart" are fixtures in anthologies. That Herrick's fame rests on a few crystalline lyrics obscures the fact that he possessed a fairly varied repertoire. Herrick emulated Jonson (whom he called "Saint Ben") not only in editing and publishing his own complete works but also in cultivating and "Englishing" a number of classical poets. Herrick's *Hesperides* (1648) contains epigrams, epistles,

Robert Herrick
HIS AUTOGRAPHS, AND SEAL.

odes, eclogues, and other lyric forms—over 1,400 poems in all—on a variety of themes. The pastoral features prominently in *Hesperides*, as does the amorous (158 poems are addressed to 14 separate mistresses, most of whom seem to be the products of Herrick's literary imagination) and the political; poems such as "Upon Julia's Clothes" express an aesthetics of sensuality. The best of these poems had been circulating in manuscript for decades before they were published, and some had become popular songs, set to music by Henry Lawes and others.

Hesperides appeared during a period of political upheaval and civil war, and achieved little notice in Herrick's lifetime. Its often light bucolic tone did not match the seriousness of the time; its occasional indecency offended some; and *His Noble Numbers*, the religious verse appended to it, seemed flat and undistinguished. No separate volume of Herrick's poetry was published again until 1810, but once his poetry had been rediscovered the romantic attraction to pastoral and rural themes made Herrick popular with nineteenth-century anthologists. If subsequent critics have never quite endorsed Algernon Charles Swinburne's extravagant praise of Herrick as "the greatest song-writer ever born of English race," recent consensus has raised his status among mid-seventeenth- century poets thanks to a deeper appreciation of his cunning and delicate artistry, the clever scope and organization of *Hesperides*, and the political implications of his celebration of traditional rites and pastimes.

The son of a London goldsmith, Herrick apprenticed in that craft before attending Cambridge, from which he graduated in 1617. After years spent mostly in London, cultivating patrons and literary friendships with Ben Jonson and others, he moved to Devonshire to become vicar of Dean Prior in 1629. Ousted from his living by the triumphant Parliamentary forces in 1647, Herrick, in "His Returne to London," shed no tears for "the dull confines of the drooping West," indeed lamenting the economic necessity that had condemned him to such "a long and irksome banishment." He returned to Dean Prior at his own request after the Restoration in 1660, however, to live out the remainder of his bachelor's life ministering to his "rude" flock.

In "Discontents in Devon," Herrick confesses his ambivalence toward country life: "I ne'er invented such / Ennobled numbers for the Presse / Then where I loath'd so much." In fact, the Epicurean bent of Herrick's classical models had prepared him well for versifying the joys of the natural world and infusing them with the echoes of what Puritans (doubtless correctly) thought the residual paganism he found in rural festivals and rituals, as he does impeccably in "Corinna's Gone A-Maying." In "The Argument of His Book," his verse preface to *Hesperides*, he announces himself as a poet of nature (as it was perceived in his day), ceremony, and "Times trans-shifting," linking natural cycles and the transience of nature's creatures to the inevitability of aging and death. Just as the title of his book recalls the island garden of classical myth (a sea-guarded place of golden apples, maidens, and a vigilant dragon), Herrick views nature and the natural cycles of work and play, including festivals and holidays, as providing shelter against the ravages of time, mortality, and civil strife. An ardent Royalist, Herrick would also have approved of the political role such rural festivals played in reinforcing traditional hierarchies and social stability. Not surprisingly, these holidays (including "Sunday sports") had been espoused and encouraged in the *Book of Sports* issued by the Stuart kings, but deplored and condemned by the Puritans as profanations of the Sabbath and excuses for drunkenness. Herrick's conservative politics and his natural Epicureanism leave no doubt as to his stand on the issue. From his classical models, Herrick had learned to express a carefully cultivated simplicity of outlook that sets him apart from the smooth urbanity and self-conscious sophistication of the Cavalier poets and the strenuous spiritual strivings of the metaphysical poets. For Herrick, or at least for the persona he constructs, mortality must either be confronted by seizing and enjoying the pleasures of today (*Carpe diem*, as the Romans put it) or transcended by achieving poetic immortality. Although he seems to have been a sincere Christian and wrote some fine religious verse, "To live merrily, and to trust to Good Verses," the memorable title of one of his lyrics, might be cited as Herrick's ultimate advice to posterity.

⌘ ⌘ ⌘

The Argument[1] of His Book

I sing of brooks, of blossoms, birds, and bowers,
  Of April, May, of June, and July flowers.
I sing of Maypoles, hock carts, wassails, wakes,[2]
Of bridegrooms, brides, and of their bridal cakes.
5 I write of youth, of love, and have access
  By these, to sing of cleanly° wantonness.   innocent
I sing of dews, of rains, and piece by piece,
Of balm, of oil, of spice, and ambergris.[3]
I sing of times trans-shifting; and I write
10 How roses first came red, and lilies white.

I write of groves, of twilights, and I sing
The court of Mab,[4] and of the fairy king.
I write of hell; I sing (and ever shall)
Of Heaven, and hope to have it after all.
—1648

Delight in Disorder

A sweet disorder in the dress
  Kindles in clothes a wantonness:
A lawn[5] about the shoulders thrown
Into a fine distractiòn;
5 An erring lace, which here and there
Enthralls the crimson stomacher:[6]

---

1 *Argument* Summary of the subject matter of a book or poem.

2 *hock carts* Wagons carrying the last of the harvest, associated with rural festivals; *wassails* Toasts drunk to the health of others, especially on Twelfth Night or Christmas Eve; *wakes* Annual parish festivals.

3 *ambergris* Waxy secretion produced by sperm whales, used in making perfume, and very valuable.

4 *Mab* Queen of the Fairies.

5 *lawn* Shawl or scarf of finely woven cotton or linen.

6 *stomacher* Decorative garment worn over the breast and stomach and secured by lacing.

A cuff neglectful, and thereby
Ribbons to flow confusedly:
A winning wave, deserving note,
10 In the tempestuous petticoat;
A careless shoestring, in whose tie
I see a wild civility:
Do more bewitch me than when art
Is too precise in every part.
—1648

His Farewell to Sack

Farewell, thou thing, time-past so known, so dear
To me as blood to life and spirit; near,
Nay, thou more near than kindred, friend, man, wife,
Male to the female, soul to body, life
5 To quick action, or the warm soft side
Of the resigning yet resisting bride.
The kiss of virgins; first-fruits of the bed;
Soft speech, smooth touch, the lips, the maidenhead;
These and a thousand sweets could never be
10 So near or dear as thou wast once to me.
O thou, the drink of gods and angels! Wine
That scatterest spirit and lust;° whose purest shine   *pleasure*
More radiant than the summer's sunbeams shows,
Each way illustrious, brave;° and like to those   *splendid*
15 Comets we see by night, whose shagg'd[1] portents
Foretell the coming of some dire events,
Or some full flame which with a pride aspires,°   *rises*
Throwing about his wild and active fires.
'Tis thou, above nectar, O divinest soul!
20 (Eternal in thyself) that canst control
That which subverts whole nature: grief and care,
Vexation of the mind, and damned despair.
'Tis thou alone who with thy mystic fan[2]
Work'st more than wisdom, art, or nature can
25 To rouse the sacred madness, and awake
The frost-bound blood and spirits, and to make

Them frantic with thy raptures, flashing through
The soul like lightning, and as active too.
'Tis not Apollo[3] can, or those thrice three
30 Castalian sisters[4] sing, if wanting thee.
Horace, Anacreon[5] both had lost their fame
Had'st thou not filled them with thy fire and flame.
Phoebean splendor! and thou Thespian spring![6]
Of which sweet swans° must drink before they sing   *poets*
35 Their true-paced numbers° and their holy lays°   *verses / songs*
Which makes them worthy° cedar and the bays.[7]   *worthy of*
But why? why longer do I gaze upon
Thee with the eye of admiration?
Since I must leave thee, and enforced must say
40 To all thy witching beauties, Go, Away.
But if thy whimpering looks do ask me why,
Then know that nature bids thee go, not I.
'Tis her erroneous self has made a brain
Uncapable of such a sovereign
45 As is thy powerful self. Prithee not smile,
Or smile more inly,° lest thy looks beguile   *inwardly*
My vows denounced° in zeal, which thus   *announced*
        much show thee,
That I have sworn but by thy looks to know thee.
Let others drink thee freely, and desire
50 Thee and their lips espoused, while I admire
And love thee but not taste thee. Let my muse
Fail of thy former helps,° and only use   *supports*
Her inadulterate strength. What's done by me
Hereafter shall smell of the lamp,[8] not thee.
—1648

---

[1] *shagg'd* Shaggy or ragged, as the tail of a comet.

[2] *mystic fan* Winnowing fan for grain, sacred emblem in the rites of Dionysus, Greek god of wine.

[3] *Apollo* Greek sun god, and god of poetry and music.

[4] *Castalian sisters* The nine muses in Greek mythology, who presided over the various arts and sciences. The Castalian spring on Mount Parnassus was sacred to them and to Apollo.

[5] *Horace* Roman poet (65–8 BCE) noted for his satires and odes; *Anacreon* Greek lyric poet (c. 570–480 BCE) celebrated for his drinking songs.

[6] *Phoebean* Bright as the sun, from Phoebus, a common epithet for Apollo; *Thespian spring* Hippocrene spring near Thespiae in Boeotia, sacred to the muses.

[7] *cedar* Cedar oil, used to preserve manuscripts; *the bays* Laurel crown for poetic achievement; poetic renown.

[8] *smell of the lamp* Labored and turgid, the product of study, not inspiration.

Corinna's Going A-Maying[1]

Get up! get up for shame! the blooming morn
Upon her wings presents the god unshorn.[2]
   See how Aurora[3] throws her fair
   Fresh-quilted colors through the air:
5   Get up, sweet slug-a-bed, and see
   The dew bespangling herb and tree.
Each flower has wept, and bowed toward the east
Above an hour since, yet you not dressed;
   Nay, not so much as out of bed?
10   When all the birds have matins[4] said,
   And sung their thankful hymns: 'tis sin,
   Nay, profanation to keep in,
Whenas a thousand virgins on this day
Spring, sooner than the lark, to fetch in May.[5]

15 Rise, and put on your foliage, and be seen
To come forth, like the springtime, fresh and green,
   And sweet as Flora.[6] Take no care
   For jewels for your gown or hair;
   Fear not; the leaves will strew
20   Gems in abundance upon you;
Besides, the childhood of the day has kept,
Against° you come, some orient pearls unwept;   *until*
   Come and receive them[7] while the light
   Hangs on the dew-locks of the night,
25   And Titan° on the eastern hill   *the sun*
   Retires himself, or else stands still

Till you come forth. Wash, dress, be brief in praying:
Few beads[8] are best, when once we go a-Maying.

Come, my Corinna, come; and coming, mark
30 How each field turns° a street; each street a park   *becomes*
   Made green and trimmed with trees; see how
   Devotion gives each house a bough,
   Or branch: each porch, each door, ere this,
   An ark, a tabernacle is,
35 Made up of whitethorn neatly interwove;[9]
As if here were those cooler shades of love.
   Can such delights be in the street
   And open fields, and we not see 't?
   Come, we'll abroad;° and let's obey   *go out*
40   The proclamation[10] made for May,
And sin no more, as we have done, by staying;
But, my Corinna, come, let's go a-Maying.

There's not a budding boy, or girl, this day
But is got up and gone to bring in May;
45   A deal° of youth, ere this, is come   *multitude*
   Back, and with whitethorn laden, home.
   Some have dispatched their cakes and cream,
   Before that we have left to dream:[11]
And some have wept, and wooed, and plighted troth,
50 And chose their priest, ere we can cast off sloth.
   Many a green-gown[12] has been given,
   Many a kiss, both odd and even;
   Many a glance, too, has been sent
   From out the eye, love's firmament;
55 Many a jest told of the keys betraying
This night, and locks picked; yet we're not a-Maying.

---

1 *A-Maying* Celebrating May Day, especially by gathering spring flowers and greenery.

2 *god unshorn* Apollo, the sun god of classical mythology, often pictured with long, brilliant, streaming hair, suggesting the rays of the sun, and also often identified with the advent of spring.

3 *Aurora* Roman goddess of the dawn.

4 *matins* Morning prayers.

5 *fetch in May* Bring in the month of May; also a pun on "may" as a common word for the blossoms of the hawthorn, which were gathered ("fetched in") on May Day and whose white or pinkish hue was suggestive of virginity.

6 *Flora* Roman goddess of flowers and spring.

7 *receive them* According to English rural tradition, young girls could ensure their future beauty by washing themselves in the dew of the hawthorn on May Day.

8 *beads* Prayers, or beads of a rosary.

9 *Devotion ... interwove* According to ancient rural custom (eventually tailored to Christian belief), hawthorn boughs were placed above a doorway on May Day to confer blessing on the dwelling.

10 *proclamation* Referring to a royal "Declaration concerning lawful sports" (1613, 1633), which encouraged traditional pastimes such as maypoles and May games to counter puritan Sabbatarianism.

11 *Before ... dream* Before we have ceased to dream, i.e., awoken.

12 *green-gown* Gown grass-stained from amorous sport.

Come, let us go while we are in our prime,
And take the harmless folly of the time.
    We shall grow old apace, and die
    Before we know our liberty.
    Our life is short, and our days run
    As fast away as does the sun;
And as a vapor or a drop of rain,
Once lost, can ne'er be found again,
    So when or you or I are made
    A fable, song, or fleeting shade,
All love, all liking, all delight
Lies drowned with us in endless night.
Then while time serves, and we are but decaying,
Come, my Corinna, come, let's go a-Maying.
—1648

To the Virgins, to Make Much of Time

Gather ye rosebuds while ye may,
    Old time is still a-flying;[1]
And this same flower that smiles today,
    Tomorrow will be dying.

The glorious lamp of heaven, the sun,
    The higher he's a-getting;
The sooner will his race be run,[2]
    And nearer he's to setting.

That age is best, which is the first,
    When youth and blood are warmer;
But being spent, the worse, and worst
    Times still succeed the former.

Then be not coy, but use your time,
    And while ye may, go marry;
For having lost but once your prime,
    You may for ever tarry.
—1648

The Hock-Cart,[3] or Harvest Home

*To the Right Honorable, Mildmay,
Earl of Westmoreland*[4]

Come, sons of summer, by whose toil,
    We are the lords of wine and oil;
By whose tough labors, and rough hands,
We rip up first, then reap our lands.
5 Crowned with the ears of corn, now come,
And, to the pipe, sing harvest home.
Come forth, my Lord, and see the cart
Dressed up with all the country art.
See, here a maukin,[5] there a sheet,
10 As spotless pure, as it is sweet,
The horses, mares, and frisking fillies,
(Clad, all, in linen, white as lilies).
The harvest swains,° and wenches bound   peasant lads
For joy, to see the hock-cart crowned.
15 About the cart, hear how the rout°   crowd
Of rural younglings raise the shout,
Pressing before, some coming after,
Those with a shout and these with laughter.
Some bless the cart, some kiss the sheaves;
20 Some prank° them up with oaken leaves: dress
Some cross° the fill-horse,°   sit astride / shaft-horse
    some with great
Devotion stroke the home-borne wheat:
While other rustics, less attent°   attentive
To prayers, than to merriment,
25 Run after with their breeches rent.
    Well, on, brave boys, to your Lord's hearth,
Glittering with fire; where, for your mirth,
Ye shall see first the large and chief
Foundation of your feast, fat beef:
30 With upper stories, mutton, veal,
And bacon,° (which makes full the meal)   pork
With several dishes standing by,
As here a custard, there a pie,

---

[3] *Hock-Cart* The hock-cart, or "high cart" (because piled high), was the last wagon load of the harvest.

[4] *Mildmay ... Westmoreland* Mildmay Fane was Herrick's friend and patron; he published a collection of his own poetry, *Otia Sacra* (1648).

[5] *maukin* Rag doll, made of cloths.

---

[1] *Old ... a-flying* Paraphrase of the Latin *tempus fugit* ("time flies").

[2] *his race be run* The sun's movement was pictured in Greek mythology as the chariot of Phoebus Apollo racing across the sky.

And here all tempting frumenty.[1]

35 And for to make the merry cheer,
If smirking wine be wanting here,
There's that, which drowns all care, stout beer:
Which freely drink to your Lord's health,
Then to the plough, (the common-wealth),
40 Next to your flails, your fanes, your vats;[2]
Then to the maids with wheaten° hats: *straw*
To the rough sickle, and crook'd sythe,
Drink, frolic boys, till all be blithe.

    Feed, and grow fat; and as ye eat,
45 Be mindful, that the laboring neat,°   *oxen*
As you, may have their fill of meat.
And know, besides, ye must revoke°   *recall*
The patient ox unto the yoke,
And all go back unto the plow
50 And harrow, though they're hanged up now.

And, you must know, your Lord's word's true,
Feed him ye must, whose food fills you,
And that this pleasure is like rain,
Not sent ye for to drown your pain,
55 But for to make it spring again.
—1648

Upon Julia's Clothes

Whenas° in silks my Julia goes,   *whenever*
    Then, then, methinks, how sweetly flows
That liquefaction of her clothes.

Next, when I cast mine eyes and see
5 That brave° vibration each way free,   *beautiful*
Oh, how that glittering taketh me!
—1648

---

[1] *frumenty* Hulled wheat boiled in milk and flavored with sugar and spices.

[2] *fanes* Winnowing fans; *vats* Storage barrels.

George Herbert
1593 – 1633

Although his contribution to English poetry consists of a single volume, *The Temple*, George Herbert stands in the first rank of the poets of the seventeenth century and, indeed, of all English lyric poets. Born into wealth and privilege, he chose instead a life dedicated to the power of faith and poetry, dying a humble country parson. An early friend and poetic disciple of John Donne, he left behind Donne's learned abstruseness and fashioned instead a modestly artful music that overleaps sectarian boundaries. Immensely influential on the devotional poets of his own century, Herbert in the eighteenth century was celebrated perhaps more for his piety than his poetry. (John Wesley, for instance, turned a number of Herbert's lyrics into hymns, some of which are still sung.) In the nineteenth century his reputation waned, though he was deeply admired by a few major figures, including Coleridge, Emerson, and Hopkins. In the twentieth century Herbert rejoined the poetic mainstream when T.S. Eliot, in his influential 1921 essay "The Metaphysical Poets," lamented the modern "dissociation of sensibility" and praised Herbert as one of the last poets to have consummated a true fusion of feeling and intellect.

George Herbert was born in 1593, the fifth son of a prominent landowning family in the Welsh Border Country. His eldest brother, Edward, Lord Herbert of Cherbury, was a noted philosopher and

diplomat. Raised by their widowed mother Magdalen, an intelligent and strong-willed woman, the Herbert children benefitted from a sound education and a lively environment that included a close family friendship with John Donne. George Herbert attended Westminster School in London and later Trinity College at Cambridge, where he stayed on as a tutor and lecturer. His appointment as Public Orator there in 1620 made him spokesman for the University. Able, urbane, and ambitious, Herbert aspired to political prominence, and was named as Member of Parliament in 1624. Soon after, however, with the ascension of a new monarch and the fall from favor of influential friends such as Francis Bacon, Herbert's political fortunes dimmed and his health began to fail. A devoted Anglican all his life, he began to turn more seriously toward the Church, and was ordained deacon in 1624. When his mother died in 1627, John Donne delivered her funeral oration, and Herbert commemorated her with a collection of Latin and Greek verse, *Memoriae Matris Sacrum*.

For the next few years Herbert seems to have lived quietly with friends, nursing his health, pursuing his religious vocation, and writing much of the devotional poetry in English for which he was to become famous. He married in 1629, was ordained a priest in 1630, and devoted his remaining years to his small country parish at Bemerton, near Salisbury. Herbert died in 1633, releasing for publication on his deathbed *The Temple*, a meticulously crafted compilation of devotional and meditative verse that was to achieve immediate popularity, running through at least eleven editions in the seventeenth century alone.

Herbert had been writing poetry as early as 1610, when, in two sonnets sent as a gift to his mother, he declared his intention to consecrate his poetic gifts to the glory of God rather than to erotic or romantic love. With the exception of some occasional pieces and a collection of polemical Latin epigrams written during his tenure as Public Orator, he remained true to his word.

As a collection, *The Temple* is an intricately structured whole, with numerous correspondences and connections among its almost 170 poems. Herbert establishes resonant patterns that link the physical space of the church with the interior space of the human heart, and the cycle of the church year with the spiritual journey of both the individual believer and humanity as a whole. The poems themselves reflect the subtle spiritual struggles of the everyday inner life. Herbert shows the influence of John Donne in his affinity for plain diction and the rhythms of colloquial speech, but he consciously avoids the elaborate conceits, scholarly allusions, and self-dramatizing spiritual anguish found in Donne's devotional verse. Simplicity, or the artfulness of seeming artless, is one of the central themes of Herbert's poetry, and generations of readers and poets have admired Herbert's exquisite craftsmanship, emotional directness, modest wit, elegance and concision of language, and ability to create connections among poetic form, language, and meaning.

⌘ ⌘ ⌘

The Altar

A broken ALTAR, Lord thy servant rears,
Made of a heart, and cemented with tears:[1]
   Whose parts are as thy hand did frame;
   No workman's tool hath touched the same.[2]
5   A HEART alone
      Is such a stone,
      As nothing but
      Thy pow'r doth cut.
      Wherefore° each part   *accordingly*
10   Of my hard heart
      Meets in this frame,
      To praise thy name.
   That, if I chance to hold my peace,
   These stones to praise thee may not cease.[3]
15 O let thy blessed SACRIFICE be mine,
And sanctify this ALTAR to be thine.
   —1633

Redemption

Having been tenant long to a rich Lord,
  Not thriving, I resolved to be bold,
   And make a suit unto him, to afford°   *grant*
A new small-rented lease, and cancel th' old.
5 In heaven at his manor I him sought:
   They told me there, that he was lately gone
   About some land, which he had dearly bought
Long since on earth, to take possession.
I straight returned, and knowing his great birth,
10   Sought him accordingly in great resorts;
   In cities, theatres, gardens, parks, and courts:
At length I heard a ragged noise and mirth
   Of thieves and murderers: there I him espied,
   Who straight, *Your suit is granted*, said, and died.
   —1633

---

[1] *A broken … tears* Cf. Psalms 51.17.

[2] *No … same* Cf. Exodus 20.25.

[3] *That … cease* From Luke 19.40.

Easter Wings

Lord, who createdst man in wealth and store,
Though foolishly he lost the same,
Decaying more and more,
Till he became
Most poor:
With thee
O let me rise
As larks, harmoniously,
And sing this day thy victories:
Then shall the fall further the flight in me.

My tender age in sorrow did begin:
And still with sicknesses and shame
Thou didst so punish sin,
That I became
Most thin.
With thee
Let me combine,
And feel this day thy victory:
For, if I imp¹ my wing on thine,
Affliction shall advance the flight in me.

—1633

Affliction (1)

When first thou didst entice to thee my heart,
    I thought the service brave:°   *splendid*
So many joys I writ down for my part,
    Besides what I might have
5   Out of my stock of natural delights,
Augmented with thy gracious benefits.

I looked on thy furniture so fine,
    And made it fine to me:
Thy glorious household-stuff did me entwine,
10   And 'tice° me unto thee.   *entice*
Such stars I counted mine: both heav'n and earth
Paid me my wages in a world of mirth.

What pleasures could I want, whose King I served?
    Where joys my fellows were.
15 Thus argued into hopes, my thoughts reserved

No place for grief or fear.
Therefore my sudden² soul caught at³ the place,
And made her youth and fierceness seek thy face,

At first thou gav'st me milk and sweetnesses;
20   I had my wish and way:
My days were strawed⁴ with flow'rs and happiness;
        There was no month but May.
But with my years sorrow did twist and grow,
And made a party° unawares° for woe.   *faction / unwittingly*

25 My flesh began unto my soul in pain,
        Sicknesses cleave my bones;
Consuming agues° dwell in ev'ry vein,   *fevers*
        And tune my breath to groans.
Sorrow was all my soul; I scarce believed,
30 Till grief did tell me roundly, that I lived.

---

¹ *imp* Graft feathers from one falcon onto the wing of another, a technique used in falconry to mend damaged wings and improve flight.

² *sudden* Rash, impetuous.

³ *caught at* Eagerly sought.

⁴ *strawed* Strewn.

When I got health, thou took'st away my life,
    And more; for my friends die:
My mirth and edge was lost; a blunted knife
    Was of more use than I.
35 Thus thin and lean without a fence or friend,
I was blown through with ev'ry storm and wind.

Whereas my birth and spirit rather took
    The way that takes the town;
Thou didst betray me to a ling'ring book,
40   And wrap me in a gown.[1]
I was entangled in the world of strife,
Before I had the power to change my life.

Yet, for I threat'ned oft the siege to raise,
    Not simp'ring all mine age,
45 Thou often didst with academic praise
    Melt and dissolve my rage.
I took thy sweet'ned pill, till I came where
I could not go away, nor persevere.

Yet lest perchance I should too happy be
50   In my unhappiness,
Turning my purge to food, thou throwest me
    Into more sicknesses.
Thus doth thy power cross-bias[2] me, not making
Thine own gift good, yet me from my ways taking.

55 Now I am here, what thou wilt do with me
    None of my books will show:
I read, and sigh, and wish I were a tree;
    For sure then I should grow
To fruit or shade: at least some bird would trust
60 Her household to me, and I should be just.

Yet, though thou troublest me, I must be meek;
    In weakness must be stout.
Well, I will change the service,[3] and go seek
Some other master out.
65 Ah my dear God! though I am clean forgot,
Let me not love thee, if I love thee not.
—1633

Prayer (1)

Prayer the Church's banquet, Angels' age,
  God's breath in man returning to his birth,
The soul in paraphrase, heart in pilgrimage,
The Christian plummet sounding heav'n and earth;
5 Engine[4] against th' Almighty, sinners' tower,[5]
  Reversed thunder, Christ-side-piercing spear,[6]
The six-days world transposing in an hour,
A kind of tune, which all things hear and fear;
Softness, and peace, and joy, and love, and bliss,
10   Exalted Manna,[7] gladness of the best,
Heaven in ordinary,[8] man well dressed,
The milky way, the bird of Paradise,[9]
  Church-bells beyond the stars heard, the soul's blood,
The land of spices; something understood.
—1633

Jordan[10] (1)

Who says that fictions only and false hair
  Become° a verse? Is there in truth no beauty?   *befit*
Is all good structure in a winding stair?

---

1 *book … gown* Symbolic book and gown of Herbert's academic life at Cambridge.

2 *cross-bias* Deflect from straight or intended course (a metaphor from the game of bowls as well as a play on Christ's cross).

3 *service* As in domestic service; see also line 2 above.

---

4 *Engine* Instrument of war, such as a catapult or battering-ram; also, a device, a stratagem.

5 *sinners' tower* Alluding to the tower of Babel, in Genesis 11.1–9, and also, perhaps, to the siege tower as an engine of war.

6 *Christ … spear* From John 19.34.

7 *Manna* Food supplied by God to the Israelites in Exodus 16.15.

8 *ordinary* Everyday clothing.

9 *bird of Paradise* Tropical bird mistakenly believed to reside constantly in the air.

10 *Jordan* The river associated with entry into the Promised Land and Christ's baptism, here meant also to suggest the purity and simplicity of Christian poetry as opposed to the artificiality of secular verse.

May no lines pass, except they do their duty
5   Not to a true, but painted chair?[1]

Is it no verse, except enchanted groves
And sudden arbours shadow coarse-spun[2] lines?
Must purling[3] streams refresh a lover's loves?
Must all be veiled, while he that reads, divines,   *interprets*
10   Catching the sense at two removes?

Shepherds are honest people; let them sing:
Riddle who list, for me, and pull for Prime:[4]
I envy no man's nightingale or spring;
Nor let them punish me with loss of rhyme,
15   Who plainly say, *My God, My King*.
   —1633

Church-Monuments

While that my soul repairs to her devotion,
   Here I intomb my flesh, that it betimes°   *soon*
May take acquaintance of this heap of dust;
To which the blast of death's incessant motion,
5 Fed with the exhalation of our crimes,
Drives all at last. Therefore I gladly trust

My body to this school, that it may learn
To spell his elements,[5] and find his birth
Written in dusty heraldry and lines:
10 Which dissolution sure doth best discern,[6]
Comparing dust with dust, and earth with earth.
These laugh at jet°and marble put for signs,   *black stone*

To sever the good fellowship of dust,
And spoil the meeting. What shall point out them,

15 When they shall bow, and kneel, and fall down flat
To kiss those heaps, which now they have in trust?
Dear flesh, while I do pray, learn here thy stem[7]
And true descent; that when thou shalt grow fat,

And wanton in thy cravings, thou mayst know,
20 That flesh is but the glass,[8] which holds the dust
That measures all our time; which also shall
Be crumbled into dust. Mark here below
How tame these ashes are, how free from lust,
That thou mayst fit thyself against thy fall.[9]
   —1633

The Windows

Lord, how can man preach thy eternal word?
   He is a brittle crazy° glass: *cracked*
Yet in thy temple thou dost him afford
    This glorious and transcendent place,
5   To be a window, through thy grace.

But when thou dost anneal[10] in glass thy story,
    Making thy life to shine within
The holy Preacher's; then the light and glory
    More rev'rend grows, and more doth win:
10   Which else shows wat'rish, bleak, and thin.

Doctrine and life, colours and light, in one
    When they combine and mingle, bring
A strong regard and awe: but speech alone
    Doth vanish like a flaring thing,
15   And in the ear, not conscience ring.
   —1633

---

[1] *painted chair* The meaning here is uncertain. This may be a reference to the ideas of Plato regarding the reality of ideal forms. Some have suggested a reference to the English Royal Throne is intended.

[2] *sudden* Unexpected; *shadow* Camouflage; *coarse-spun* Shoddy.

[3] *purling* Rippling; babbling.

[4] *Riddle who list* Let those who enjoy riddling do so; *pull for Prime* Draw for a winning hand at Primero, a fashionable card game.

[5] *elements* Letters of the alphabet.

[6] *Which ... discern* The body best comprehends its own decay.

---

[7] *stem* Line of ancestry.

[8] *flesh is ... glass* A play on "All flesh is grass," Isaiah 40.6, with "glass" here meaning "hourglass."

[9] *against thy fall* Against the individual body's fall into death, but also the original Fall of humankind into sin and death. See Genesis 3.19: "… for dust thou art, and unto dust thou shalt return."

[10] *anneal* Apply heat to stained glass to fix the colors painted on it.

Denial

When my devotions could not pierce
     Thy silent ears;
Then was my heart broken, as was my verse:
     My breast was full of fears
5   And disorder:

     My bent thoughts, like a brittle bow,
        Did fly asunder:
Each took his way; some would to pleasures go,
     Some to the wars and thunder
10   Of alarms.

     As good go anywhere, they say,
        As to benumb
Both knees and heart, in crying night and day,
     Come, come my God, O come,
15   But no hearing.

     O that thou shouldst give dust a tongue
        To cry to thee,
And then not hear it crying! all day long
     My heart was in my knee,
20   but no hearing.

     Therefore my soul lay out of sight,
        Untuned, unstrung:
My feeble spirit, unable to look right,
     Like a nipped blossom, hung
25   Discontented.

     O cheer and tune my heartless breast,
        Defer no time;[1]
That so thy favours granting my request,
     They and my mind may chime,
30   And mend my rhyme.

—1633

Virtue

Sweet day, so cool, so calm, so bright,
    The bridal° of the earth and sky: *wedding*
The dew shall weep thy fall tonight;
        For thou must die.

5 Sweet rose, whose hue angry and brave°   *beautiful; splendid*
Bids the rash gazer wipe his eye:
Thy root is ever in its grave,
        And thou must die.

Sweet spring, full of sweet days and roses,
10 A box where sweets compacted lie;
My music shows ye have your closes,[2]
        And all must die.

Only a sweet and virtuous soul,
Like seasoned timber, never gives;°   *gives way*
15 But though the whole world turn to coal,[3]
        Then chiefly lives.

—1633

Man

My God, I heard this day,
That none doth build a stately habitation,
    But he that means to dwell therein.
    What house more stately hath there been,
5 Or can be, than is Man? to° whose creation   *next to*
    All things are in decay.

    For Man is ev'ry thing,
And more: He is a tree, yet bears no fruit;
    A beast, yet is, or should be more:
    Reason and speech we only bring.
10 Parrots may thank us, if they are not mute,
    They go upon the score.[4]

---

[1] *Defer no time*   Wait no longer.

[2] *closes*   Conclusions of phrases or themes in music.

[3] *turn to coal*   Be destroyed by fire, as predicted in the Bible.

[4] *They ... score*   They are in our debt.

Man is all symmetry,
Full of proportions, one limb to another,
15   And all to all the world besides:
    Each part may call the farthest, brother:
For head with foot hath private amity,
    And both with moons and tides.

    Nothing hath got so far,
20 But Man hath caught and kept it, as his prey.
    His eyes dismount° the highest star: *bring down*
    He is in little° all the sphere.°   *miniature / world*
Herbs gladly cure our flesh; because that they
    Find their acquaintance there.

25   For us the winds do blow,
The earth doth rest, heav'n move, and fountains flow.
    Nothing we see, but means our good,
    As our delight, or as our treasure:
The whole is, either our cupboard of food,
30   Or cabinet of pleasure.

    The stars have us to bed;
Night draws the curtain, which the sun withdraws;
    Music and light attend our head.
    All things unto our flesh are kind°   *akin*
35 In their descent° and being; to our mind   *becoming*
    In their ascent° and cause.   *origin*

    Each thing is full of duty:
Waters united are our navigation;
    Distinguished,[1] our habitation;
    Below, our drink; above, our meat;
40 Both are our cleanliness. Hath one° such beauty?   *one thing*
    Then how are all things neat?°   *excellent*

    More servants wait on Man,
Than he'll take notice of: in ev'ry path
    He treads down that which doth befriend him,
45   When sickness makes him pale and wan.[2]
O mighty love! Man is one world, and hath
    Another to attend him.

Since then, my God, thou hast
50 So brave° a Palace built; O dwell in it,   *splendid*
    That it may dwell with thee at last!
    Till then, afford us so much wit;
That, as the world serves us, we may serve thee,
    And both thy servants be.
—1633

Jordan (2)

When first my lines of heav'nly joys made mention,
    Such was their lustre, they did so excel,
That I sought out quaint words, and trim invention;
My thoughts began to burnish, sprout, and swell,
5 Curling with metaphors a plain intention,
    Decking° the sense, as if it were to sell.   *adorning*

Thousands of notions in my brain did run,
Off'ring their service, if I were not sped:°   *successful*
I often blotted what I had begun;
10 This was not quick° enough, and that was dead.   *lively*
Nothing could seem too rich to clothe the sun,
Much less those joys which trample on his head.

As flames do work and wind, when they ascend,
So did I weave my self into the sense.
15 But while I bustled, I might hear a friend
Whisper, *How wide is all this long pretence!*
There is in love a sweetness ready penned;
Copy out only that, and save expense.
—1633

Time

Meeting with Time, slack° thing, said I,   *remiss*
    Thy scythe is dull; whet it for shame.
No marvel Sir, he did reply,
If it at length deserve some blame:
5   But where one man would have me grind it,
    Twenty for one[3] too sharp do find it.

---

1 *Distinguished* Separated.

2 *He treads ... wan* Referring to the herbs mentioned above that "gladly cure our flesh."

3 *Twenty for one* Twenty men for every one.

Perhaps some such of old did pass,
Who above all things loved this life;
To whom thy scythe a hatchet was,
10   Which now is but a pruning-knife.
        Christ's coming hath made man thy debtor,
        Since by thy cutting he grows better.

And in his blessing thou art blessed;
For where thou only wert° before   *were*
15   An executioner at best;
Thou art a gard'ner now, and more,
        An usher to convey our souls
        Beyond the utmost stars and poles.

And this is that makes life so long,
20   While it detains us from our God.
Ev'n pleasures here increase the wrong,
And length of days lengthen the rod.°   *punishment*
        Who wants° the place, where God doth dwell,   *lacks*
        Partakes already half of hell.

25   Of what strange length must that needs be,
Which ev'n eternity excludes!
Thus far Time heard me patiently:
Then chafing said, This man deludes:
        What do I here before his door?
30   He doth not crave less time, but more.
—1633

The Bunch of Grapes [1]

Joy, I did lock thee up: but some bad man
        Hath let thee out again:
And now, methinks, I am where I began
        Sev'n years ago: one vogue and vein,
5   One air of thoughts usurps my brain.
I did toward Canaan draw; but now I am
Brought back to the Red Sea, the sea of shame.[2]

For as the Jews of old by God's command
        Travelled, and saw no town:
10   So now each Christian hath his journeys spanned:[3]
        Their story pens and sets us down.
        A single deed is small renown.
God's works are wide, and let in future times;
His ancient justice overflows our crimes.

15   Then have we too our guardian fires and clouds;[4]
        Our Scripture-dew drops fast:
We have our sands and serpents, tents and shrouds;[5]
        Alas! our murmurings come not last.
        But where's the cluster? where's the taste
20   Of mine inheritance? Lord, if I must borrow,
Let me as well take up their joy, as sorrow.

But can he want the grape, who hath the wine?
        I have their fruit and more.
Blessèd be God, who prospered Noah's vine,[6]
25   And make it bring forth grapes good store.
        But much more him I must adore,
Who of the law's sour juice sweet wine did make,
Ev'n God himself, being pressed for my sake.
—1633

The Collar

I struck the board,° and cried, No more.   *table*
        I will abroad.°   *go abroad; depart*
    What? shall I ever° sigh and pine?   *always*
My lines and life are free; free as the road,
5   Loose as the wind, as large as store.°   *abundance*
            Shall I be still in suit?[7]
    Have I no harvest but a thorn
    To let me blood,° and not restore   *bleed*
What I have lost with cordial fruit?
10   Sure there was wine
Before my sighs did dry it: there was corn

---

[1] *Bunch of Grapes*   Cluster of grapes brought by scouts to Moses from the Promised Land of Canaan as evidence of its fertility: see Numbers 13.23.

[2] *I did … shame*   On the brink of attaining the Promised Land, the Israelites were condemned by the Lord for their faithlessness to wander the desert for 40 years (thus returning in the direction of the Red Sea): see Numbers 14.22–35.

[3] *spanned*   Limited.

[4] *guardian … clouds*   Cf. Exodus 13.21.

[5] *shrouds*   Shelters.

[6] *Noah's vine*   Vineyard planted by Noah with the Lord's blessing after the Flood: see Genesis 9.20.

[7] *in suit*   In attendance.

Before my tears did drown it.
Is the year only lost to me?
    Have I no bays° to crown it?   *laurel wreaths*
15 No flowers, no garlands gay? All blasted?
        All wasted?
    Not so, my heart: but there is fruit,
        And thou hast hands.[1]
    Recover all thy sigh-blown age
20 On double pleasures: leave thy cold dispute
Of what is fit, and not. Forsake thy cage,
        Thy rope of sands,[2]
Which petty thoughts have made, and made to thee
    Good cable, to enforce and draw,
25   And be thy law,
    While thou didst wink[3] and wouldst not see.
        Away; take heed:
        I will abroad.
Call in thy death's head° there: tie up thy fears.   *skull*
30   He that forbears°   *neglects*
    To suit and serve his need,
        Deserves his load.
But as I raved and grew more fierce and wild
        At every word,
35 Me thoughts I heard one calling, *Child:*
        And I replied, *My Lord.*

—1633

The Pulley

When God at first made man,
    Having a glass of blessings standing by,
Let us (said he) pour on him all we can:
Let the world's riches, which dispersed lie,
5   Contract into a span.[4]

So strength first made a way;
Then beauty flowed, then wisdom, honour, pleasure:
When almost all was out, God made a stay,°   *paused*
Perceiving that alone of all his treasure
10   Rest in the bottom lay.

For if I should (said he)
Bestow this jewel also on my creature,
He would adore my gifts instead of me,
And rest in Nature, not the God of Nature:
15   So both should losers be.

Yet let him keep the rest,
But keep them with repining° restlessness: *fretful*
Let him be rich and weary, that at least,
If goodness lead him not, yet weariness
20   May toss him to my breast.

—1633

The Flower

How fresh, O Lord, how sweet and clean
    Are thy returns! ev'n as the flowers in spring;
To which, besides their own demean,[5]
The late-past frosts tributes of pleasure bring.
5   Grief melts away
        Like snow in May,
    As if there were no such cold thing.

Who would have thought my shrivelled heart
Could have recovered greenness? It was gone
10   Quite underground; as flowers depart
To see their mother-root, when they have blown;°   *bloomed*
        Where they together
        All the hard weather,
    Dead to the world, keep house unknown.

15 These are thy wonders, Lord of power,
Killing and quick'ning,[6] bringing down to hell
    And up to heaven in an hour;

---

[1] *but ... hands* An echo of the disobedience that led to the original Fall; see Genesis 3.22: " lest he put forth his hand, and take also of the tree of life."

[2] *rope of sands* Delusive security. To "twist a rope of sand" is also a proverbial expression of futility.

[3] *wink* Shut one's eyes.

[4] *span* Distance between the tip of the thumb and little finger of an extended hand.

[5] *demean* Demesne, or estate, where a tenant might pay tributes to the landlord.

[6] *quick'ning* Bringing to life.

Making a chiming of a passing-bell.[1]
        We say amiss,
20   This or that is:
Thy word is all, if we could spell.°   *comprehend*

O that I once past changing were,
Fast in thy Paradise, where no flower can wither!
        Many a spring I shoot up fair,
25 Off'ring° at heav'n, growing and groaning thither:
            Nor doth my flower
            Want° a spring-shower,   *lack*
        My sins and I joining together:

        But while I grow in a straight line,
30 Still upwards bent, as if heav'n were mine own,
        Thy anger comes, and I decline:
What° frost to that? what pole is not the zone,
            Where all things burn,
            When thou dost turn,
35   And the least frown of thine is shown?

        And now in age I bud again,
After so many deaths I live and write;
        I once more smell the dew and rain,
And relish versing: O my only light,
40   It cannot be
            That I am he
        On whom thy tempests fell all night.

        These are thy wonders, Lord of love,
To make us see we are but flowers that glide:[2]
45   Which when we once can find and prove,[3]
Thou hast a garden for us, where to bide.
            Who° would be more,   *those who*
            Swelling through store,°   *abundance; wealth*
        Forfeit their Paradise by their pride.
—1633

---

[1] *passing-bell* Bell tolled to mark a death.

[2] *flowers that glide* Flowers that pass away silently, imperceptibly. Cf. Job 14.2: "Man cometh forth like a flower, and is cut down; he fleeteth also like a shadow, and continueth not."

[3] *prove* Confirm through experience.

Discipline

Throw away thy rod,
  Throw away thy wrath:
      O my God,
Take the gentle path.

5 For my heart's desire
Unto thine is bent:
      I aspire
To a full consent.

Not a word or look
10 I affect to own,
      But by book,
And thy book alone.

Though I fail, I weep:
Though I halt in pace,
15   Yet I creep
To the throne of grace.

Then let wrath remove;°   *depart*
Love will do the deed:
      For with love
20 Stony hearts will bleed.

Love is swift of foot;
Love's a man of war,[4]
      And can shoot,
And can hit from far.

25 Who can scape° his bow?   *escape*
That which wrought° on thee,   *worked*
      Brought thee low,
Needs must work on me.

Throw away thy rod;
30 Though man frailties hath,
      Thou art God:
Throw away thy wrath.
—1633

---

[4] *Love's … war* Cf. Exodus 15.3: "The Lord is a man of war." Also, an armed naval vessel.

Death

Death, thou wast once an uncouth hideous thing,
            Nothing but bones,
        The sad effect of sadder groans:
Thy mouth was open, but thou couldst not sing.

5   For we considered thee as at some six
            Or ten years hence,
        After the loss of life and sense,
Flesh being turned to dust, and bones to sticks.

We looked on this side of thee, shooting short;
10   Where we did find
        The shells of fledge[1] souls left behind,
Dry dust, which sheds no tears, but may extort.

But since our Saviour's death did put some blood
            Into thy face;
15   Thou art grown fair and full of grace,
Much in request, much sought for, as a good.

For we do now behold thee gay and glad,
            As at doomsday;
        When souls shall wear their new array,°   clothing
20 And all thy bones with beauty shall be clad.

Therefore we can go die as sleep, and trust
            Half that we have
        Unto an honest faithful grave;
Making our pillows either down, or dust.
—1633

Love (3)

Love bade me welcome: yet my soul drew back,
            Guilty of dust and sin.
But quick-eyed Love, observing me grow slack[2]
            From my first entrance in,
5   Drew nearer to me, sweetly questioning,
            If I lacked anything.
A guest, I answered, worthy to be here:
            Love said, You shall be he.
I the unkind, ungrateful? Ah my dear,
10   I cannot look on thee.
Love took my hand, and smiling did reply,
            Who made the eyes but I?
Truth Lord, but I have marred them: let my shame
            Go where it doth deserve.
15 And know you not, says Love, who bore the blame?
            My dear, then I will serve.
You must sit down, says Love, and taste my meat:[3] So
            I did sit and eat.

—1633

---

[2] *grow slack* Become hesitant or uncertain.

[3] *My dear ... my meat* Cf. Luke 12.37: "Blessed are those servants, whom the Lord when he cometh shall find watching: verily I say unto you, that he shall gird himself, and make them to sit down to meat, and will come forth and serve them."

---

[1] *fledge* Ready to fly.

Andrew Marvell
1621 – 1678

In his life as well as in his writing, Andrew Marvell is elusive. Famous long after his death as a spokesman for political and religious liberty, the intensely private Marvell kept his personal opinions largely to himself. His verse is complex, full of paradoxes and ironies, and is frequently mediated through naive or ambivalent personae who present debates or balance competing claims. His poem "An Horation Ode upon Cromwell's Return from Ireland" oscillates between praise for (and veiled criticism of) both Oliver Cromwell, who choreographed the abolition of the monarchy in 1649, and admiration for King Charles I, who was executed in the process. (Later, he would satirize the restored monarchy of Charles II.) A poet who wrote seductive and titillating love poetry, Marvell was also a politician who lampooned the government in satires for which he was renowned in his day. Even after death, mystery surrounded his life; in order to keep creditors of his estate at bay a few years later, his housekeeper, Mary Palmer, claimed to have been the author's wife and published his *Miscellaneous Poems* (1681), which included a preface by "Mary Marvell" guaranteeing the poems to be the "exact copies of my late dear husband."

Marvell, the son of Anne Pease and the Reverend Andrew Marvell, was born in 1621 in Winestead, but was raised primarily in Hull. At age twelve he was admitted to the University of Cambridge, where he studied for the following seven years and where he published his first poems, written in Latin and Greek. Before he had completed his degree, his father drowned and Marvell left England to travel on the Continent, perhaps to wait out the period of the Civil War (1642–47). In a letter of 1653 proposing that Marvell be given the post of Assistant Latin Secretary to the Council of State, Milton mentioned that Marvell had been abroad for four years and that on this journey he had learned to speak Dutch, French, Italian, and Spanish. (He did not win the appointment at that time, but it was awarded to him four years later.) In 1650 Marvell wrote "An Horation Ode Upon Cromwell's Return from Ireland," one of his best known and most widely studied poems. Written in a complex style that marks much of his subsequent work, the "Ode" defies definitive interpretation but instead raises many political and ideological questions. Scholars continue to disagree over Marvell's allegiance to Cromwell, whose armies had just completed a bloody mission in Ireland.

Later in 1650 Marvell began working as a tutor to the twelve-year-old daughter of Thomas, Lord Fairfax, the retired Commander-in-Chief of the Parliamentary Army. In the poem "Upon Appleton House," Marvell celebrates the architecture and inhabitants of the Fairfax home. It is likely that during his two years on this estate he composed many of his most famous works, including much of his pastoral poetry and the poems "The Definition of Love" and "Dialogue Between the Soul and the Body." In the sensuous and witty *carpe diem* poem "To His Coy Mistress," also likely written in this period, Marvell's speaker tries to convince his love of the brevity of life and the need to seize the moment of passion.

In 1653, the year in which Cromwell declared himself Lord Protector of England, Marvell was appointed tutor to a ward of Cromwell, William Dutton. Along with Milton and Dryden, Marvell took part in Cromwell's 1659 funeral procession, but despite his ties to the republican regime his political career flourished upon the restoration of a Royalist Parliament. In 1659 he was elected Member of Parliament for Hull, a seat he would maintain until his death. While in office, Marvell was outspoken in his contempt for Charles II, who was restored to the monarchy in 1660; in his 1667 satire *The Last Instructions to a Painter*, he ridiculed the King and his government for their ineffectuality. Marvell took part in a diplomatic mission to Holland in 1662–63 and another to Russia, Sweden, and Denmark in 1665; these operations served to strengthen his criticism of corruption in the government, which he recorded in numerous pamphlets and newsletters and circulated to his constituents.

When Marvell died of complications from a fever in 1678, there was still an outstanding government reward offered for the name of the man who had written "An Account of the Growth of Popery and Arbitrary Government in England" a year earlier. More satires and poems were published posthumously as a result of Mary Palmer's efforts, but they fell into relative obscurity in the following century as readers began to perceive his metaphysical conceits as cold and discordant. The nineteenth century saw something of a revival of his poetry; Wordsworth praised his work, and Tennyson recognized him as "the green poet" for his sensuous pastoral poems. In the twentieth century Marvell's reputation was firmly re-established by T.S. Eliot, who championed him as one of the finest of the "metaphysical" poets.

⌘ ⌘ ⌘

The Coronet

When for the thorns with which I long, too long,
   With many a piercing wound,
     My Saviour's head have crowned,
I seek with garlands to redress that wrong:
5   Through every garden, every mead,°   *meadow*
I gather flowers (my fruits are only flowers),[1]
     Dismantling all the fragrant towers[2]
That once adorned my shepherdess's head.
And now, when I have summed up all my store,
10   Thinking (so I myself deceive)
      So rich a chaplet thence to weave
As never yet the King of Glory wore:

15 Alas! I find the serpent old
     That, twining in his speckled breast,
     About the flowers disguised does fold,
With wreaths of fame and interest.
Ah, foolish man, that wouldst debase with them,
And mortal glory, Heaven's diadem!
But thou[3] who only couldst the serpent tame,
20 Either his slippery knots at once untie,
And disentangle all his winding snare:
Or shatter too with him my curious frame,[4]
And let these wither, so that he may die,
Though set with skill, and chosen out with care:
25 That they, while thou on both their spoils dost tread,
May crown thy feet, that could not crown thy head.
    —1681 (PROBABLY WRITTEN IN THE 1640S)

---

[1] *fruits ... flowers* With verbal play on "fruits" as accomplishments, the "fruits" of his efforts (spiritual and literary); and on "flowers" as poems or poetic tropes (anthologies in the period could gather "flowers of poetry" or "flowers of rhetoric").

[2] *fragrant towers* Floral garlands; but also the secular love poems the poet had made for his beloved.

---

[3] *thou* Christ.

[4] *curious frame* Clever or ingenious structure: the floral garland or chaplet within the fiction of the poem, and the "Coronet" that is the poem itself.

Bermudas

Where the remote Bermudas ride,
 In the ocean's bosom unespied,
From a small boat, that rowed along,
The listening winds received this song:
5   "What should we do but sing his praise
That led us through the watery maze,
Unto an isle so long unknown,[1]
And yet far kinder than our own?
Where He the huge sea-monsters wracks,[2]
10 That lift the deep upon their backs,
He lands us on a grassy stage,
Safe from the storms, and prelate's rage.[3]
He gave us this eternal spring,
Which here enamels every thing,
15 And sends the fowls to us in care,
On daily visits through the air.
He hangs in shades the orange bright,
Like golden lamps in a green night,
And does in the pom'granates close°   *enclose*
20 Jewels more rich than Ormus[4] shows.

He makes the figs our mouths to meet,
And throws the melons at our feet;
But apples plants of such a price,
No tree could ever bear them twice;
25 With cedars chosen by His hand,
From Lebanon, He stores the land,
And makes the hollow seas that roar,
Proclaim the ambergris[5] on shore;
He cast (of which we rather boast)
30 The Gospel's pearl upon our coast,
And in these rocks for us did frame
A temple where to sound His name.
Oh let our voice His praise exalt,
Till it arrive at heaven's vault,
35 Which, thence (perhaps) rebounding, may
Echo beyond the Mexique Bay."
Thus sung they, in the English boat,
An holy and a cheerful note;
And all the way, to guide their chime,
40 With falling oars they kept the time.
—1681 (PROBABLY WRITTEN C. 1653–54)

---

[1] *Unto an isle ... unknown* Although the Spanish had landed on (and named) Bermuda in 1515, English seafarers first reached the island in 1609, when an expedition on its way to Jamestown landed there during a storm; Shakespeare is thought to have drawn on accounts of their "miraculous" survival for *The Tempest*. An English colony was founded on the island soon after, and early accounts, such as Lewis Hughes's *A letter, sent to England from the Summer Islands* (1615) and John Smith's *General History of Virginia, the Summer Isles, and New England* (1624), stressed Bermuda's paradisal qualities. Bermuda was sometimes called Somers' or Summer Island, after Sir George Somers, the admiral of the first English expedition that landed there.

[2] *wracks* Casts ashore; Marvell is probably referring to a mock-heroic poem by Edmund Waller, "The Battle of the Summer Islands" (1645), which describes attempts by the colonists to kill two stranded whales.

[3] *prelate's rage* This phrase situates the poem in the 1630s, when religious Independents (Congregationalists) left England as a result of attempts by William Laud, Archbishop of Canterbury, to impose uniformity in Church practice. In the early 1650s, Marvell lived in the house of the John Oxenbridge, a religious Independent who had twice been to Bermuda, and who in 1655 would become Governor of the Somers Islands Company. This poem was written at least in part as a compliment to Oxenbridge.

[4] *Ormus* Hormuz, near the entrance to the Persian Gulf, an international market proverbial for the riches on display.

A Dialogue between the Soul and Body

SOUL

O, who shall from this dungeon raise
 A soul, enslaved so many ways?
With bolts of bones, that fettered stands
In feet, and manacled in hands.
5 Here blinded with an eye; and there
Deaf with the drumming of an ear.
A soul hung up, as 'twere, in chains
Of nerves, and arteries, and veins,
Tortured, besides each other part,
10 In a vain head, and double heart.

BODY

O, who shall me deliver whole,
From bonds of this tyrannic soul?
Which, stretched upright, impales me so,

---

[5] *ambergris* Wax-like substance secreted by sperm whales, valuable for its use in perfume.

That mine own precipice[1] I go;
15   And warms and moves this needless frame
(A fever could but do the same),
And, wanting where its spite to try,
Has made me live to let me die,
A body that could never rest,
20   Since this ill spirit it possessed.

SOUL

What magic could me thus confine
Within another's grief to pine?
Where, whatsoever it complain,
I feel, that cannot feel, the pain.
25   And all my care itself employs,
That to preserve, which me destroys:
Constrained not only to endure
Diseases, but, what's worse, the cure:
And ready oft the port to gain,[2]
30   Am shipwrecked into health again.

BODY

But physic yet could never teach
The maladies thou me dost reach:
Whom first the cramp of hope does tear,
And then the palsy shakes of fear;
35   The pestilence of love does heat,
Or hatred's hidden ulcer eat;
Joy's cheerful madness does perplex,
Or sorrow's other madness vex;
Which knowledge forces me to know,
40   And memory will not forgo.
What but a soul could have the wit
To build me up for sin so fit?
So architects do square and hew,
Green trees that in the forest grew.[3]

—1681 (PROBABLY WRITTEN AFTER 1652)

---

[1]   *mine own precipice*   The body complains that, being upright, it is
a moving precipice.

[2]   *the port to gain*   That is, the death of the body, which "lands" the
soul in eternal life.

[3]   *What but … forest grew*   These last four lines are crossed out by
hand in an important copy of Marvell's 1681 *Poems* that contains
several additional poems in manuscript; the annotator has also added
the words "desunt multa" ("much is missing").

The Nymph Complaining for the Death of Her Fawn

The wanton troopers[4] riding by
Have shot my fawn, and it will die.
Ungentle men! They cannot thrive
To kill thee. Thou ne'er didst alive
5   Them any harm; alas, nor could
Thy death yet do them any good.
I'm sure I never wished them ill;
Nor do I for all this, nor will:
But if my simple prayers may yet
10   Prevail with heaven to forget
Thy murder, I will join my tears
Rather than fail. But, O my fears!
It cannot die so. Heaven's King
Keeps register of every thing:
15   And nothing may we use in vain.
Even beasts must be with justice slain,
Else men are made their deodands.[5]
Though they should wash their guilty hands
In this warm life-blood which doth part
20   From thine, and wound me to the heart,
Yet could they not be clean: their stain
Is dyed in such a purple grain.
There is not such another in
The world, to offer for their sin.
25   Unconstant Sylvio, when yet
I had not found him counterfeit,
One morning (I remember well),
Tied in this silver chain and bell
Gave it to me: nay, and I know
30   What he said then, I'm sure I do.
Said he, "Look how your huntsman here
Hath taught a fawn to hunt his dear."[6]
But Sylvio soon had me beguiled.

---

[4]   *troopers*   Cavalry soldiers; the word was first used of soldiers in the
Scottish ("Covenanting") army that invaded England in 1640, and
during the civil wars was associated with Parliamentary soldiers.

[5]   *deodands*   Literally, "things given to God": possessions (including
animals) that caused a person's death and were therefore forfeited to
the king to be used for pious purposes, for example, to be given to
the poor and hungry; the nymph suggests that people who unjustly
cause an animal's death should be treated likewise.

[6]   *dear*   Sylvio makes the obvious pun on "deer."

This waxèd tame, while he grew wild,
35 And quite regardless of my smart,
Left me his fawn, but took his heart.
    Thenceforth I set myself to play
My solitary time away
With this: and very well content,
40 Could so mine idle life have spent.
For it was full of sport, and light
Of foot and heart, and did invite
Me to its game; it seemed to bless
Itself in me. How could I less
45 Than love it? O, I cannot be
Unkind to a beast that loveth me.
    Had it lived long, I do not know
Whether it too might have done so
As Sylvio did; his gifts might be
50 Perhaps as false, or more, than he.
But I am sure, for aught that I
Could in so short a time espy,
Thy love was far more better then°   *than*
The love of false and cruel men.
55   With sweetest milk and sugar first
I it at mine own fingers nursed.
And as it grew, so every day
It waxed more white and sweet than they.
It had so sweet a breath! And oft
60 I blushed to see its foot more soft
And white (shall I say than my hand?
Nay, any lady's of the land).
    It is a wondrous thing, how fleet
'Twas on those little silver feet.
65 With what a pretty skipping grace,
It oft would challenge me the race:
And, when 't had left me far away,
'Twould stay, and run again, and stay.
For it was nimbler much than hinds;
70 And trod, as on the foúr[1] winds.
    I have a garden of my own,
But so with roses overgrown,
And lilies, that you would it guess
To be a little wilderness.
75 And all the springtime of the year
It only lovèd to be there.

Among the beds of lilies, I
Have sought it oft, where it should lie;
Yet could not, till itself would rise,
80 Find it, although before mine eyes.
For, in the flaxen lilies' shade,
It like a bank of lilies laid.
Upon the roses it would feed,
Until its lips e'en seem to bleed:
85 And then to me 'twould boldly trip,
And print those roses on my lip.
But all its chief delight was still
On roses thus itself to fill:
And its pure virgin limbs to fold
90 In whitest sheets of lilies cold.
Had it lived long, it would have been
Lilies without, roses within.
    O help! O help! I see it faint:
And die as calmly as a saint.
95 See how it weeps. The tears do come
Sad, slowly, dropping like a gum.
So weeps the wounded balsam: so
The holy frankincense doth flow.
The brotherless Heliades[2]
100 Melt in such amber tears as these.
    I in a golden vial will
Keep these two crystal tears; and fill
It till it do o'erflow with mine;
Then place it in Diana's[3] shrine.
105   Now my sweet fawn is vanished to
Whither the swans and turtles° go: *turtledoves*
In fair Elysium to endure,
With milk-white lambs, and ermines pure.
O do not run too fast: for I
110 Will but bespeak thy grave, and die.
    First, my unhappy statue shall
Be cut in marble; and withal,
Let it be weeping too: but there
The engraver sure his art may spare,
115 For I so truly thee bemoan,

---

[2] *Heliades* Daughters of Helios, the sun; while weeping over the death of their brother Phaethon they were transformed into poplar trees that wept amber tears (a story from Ovid's *Metamorphoses*).

[3] *Diana* Roman goddess of chastity, the moon, and hunting; according to a story in Ovid's *Metamorphoses*, her pet stag was killed during a hunt.

---

[1] *foúr* Pronounced as two syllables.

That I shall weep, though I be stone:[1]
Until my tears, still dropping, wear
My breast, themselves engraving there.
There at my feet shalt thou be laid,
20 Of purest alabaster made:
For I would have thine image be
White as I can, though not as thee.
—c. 1681

To His Coy Mistress

Had we but world enough, and time,
This coyness Lady were no crime.
We would sit down, and think which way
To walk, and pass our long love's day.
5 Thou by the Indian Ganges' side
Shouldst rubies find: I by the tide
Of Humber[2] would complain. I would
Love you ten years before the Flood:
And you should, if you please, refuse
10 Till the conversion of the Jews.[3]
My vegetable love[4] should grow
Vaster than empires, and more slow.
An hundred years should go to praise
Thine eyes, and on thy forehead gaze.
15 Two hundred to adore each breast:
But thirty thousand to the rest.
An age at least to every part,
And the last age should show your heart:

For Lady you deserve this state;
20 Nor would I love at lower rate.
But at my back I always hear
Time's wingèd chariot hurrying near:
And yonder all before us lie
Deserts of vast eternity.
25 Thy beauty shall no more be found;
Nor, in thy marble vault, shall sound
My echoing song: then worms shall try[5]
That long-preserved virginity:
And your quaint honour turn to dust;
30 And into ashes all my lust.
The grave's a fine and private place,
But none, I think, do there embrace.
Now, therefore, while the youthful glew
Sits on thy skin like morning dew,[6]
35 And while thy willing soul transpires
At every pore with instant fires,
Now let us sport us while we may;
And now, like amorous birds of prey,
Rather at once our time devour,
40 Than languish in his slow-chapped[7] power.
Let us roll all our strength, and all
Our sweetness, up into one ball:
And tear our pleasures with rough strife,
Thorough° the iron gates[8] of life.   through

[1] *I shall weep, though I be stone* Like Niobe, who continued to weep after she was turned into stone by Zeus. Niobe wept for the loss of her many children, who died as punishment for Niobe's excessive maternal pride (she had boasted that she was a more impressive mother than Latona, who only had two children, Apollo and Artemis/Diana). From Ovid's *Metamorphoses*.

[2] *Humber* River in northern England; it flowed alongside Hull, Marvell's home town.

[3] *conversion of the Jews* Event supposed to usher in the final Millenium leading to the end of time. Jews were officially readmitted to England in 1655 (after being expelled in 1290), primarily as a result of widespread millenarian hopes that their return would speed up the process of conversion.

[4] *vegetable love* His love (or its physical manifestation) would grow slowly and steadily: Aristotle had defined the vegetative part of the soul as that characterized only by growth.

[5] *try* Test, and taste.

[6] *youthful glew / ... morning dew* One of the more famous textual problems in English literature. The 1681 printed edition has "youthful hew / ... morning glew." The version of the 1681 text with manuscript corrections changes this reading to "youthful glew / ... morning dew." Another manuscript, a transcription of the entire poem dated 1672, reads "youthful glue / ... morning dew." Many modern editions conflate the first line of the 1681 edition with the second line from the two manuscript versions, producing the decorous "youthful hue/ ... morning dew." But the original manuscript reading does seem to have been "glew," a word then read by one transcriber as "glue," and changed by a puzzled 1681 printer to "hew." "Glew" appears to mean sweat, which sits on the Lady's skin like dewdrops (and is evaporating from her pores in lines 35-36). The image might seem unusual, but is in keeping with the violent, passionate physicality of the poem's final section. "Glew" might be a northern dialect spelling of "glow," a word that could imply sexual ardour.

[7] *slow-chapped* Slowly devouring; "chaps" are jaws.

[8] *gates* "Grates" in the 1681 printed edition with manuscript corrections. But many editors see "gates of life" as a typically Marvellian inversion of the Biblical "gates of death" (Psalm 9.13).

45 Thus, though we cannot make our sun
Stand still,[1] yet we will make him run.
—1681

The Picture of Little T.C.[2] in a Prospect of Flowers

1

See with what simplicity
This nymph begins her golden days!
In the green grass she loves to lie,
And there with her fair aspect tames
5 The wilder flowers, and gives them names:[3]
But only with the roses plays;
            And them does tell
What colour best becomes them, and what smell.

2

Who can foretell for what high cause
10 This Darling of the Gods was born!
Yet this is she whose chaster laws
The wanton Love shall one day fear,
And, under her command severe,
See his bow broke and ensigns torn,
15   Happy, who can
Appease this virtuous enemy of man!

3

O, then let me in time compound,[4]
And parley with those conquering eyes;
Ere they have tried their force to wound,

20 Ere, with their glancing wheels, they drive
In triumph over hearts that strive,
And them that yield but more despise.
            Let me be laid,
Where I may see thy glories from some shade.

4

25 Meantime, whilst every verdant thing
Itself does at thy beauty charm,
Reform the errors of the spring;
Make that the tulips may have share
Of sweetness, seeing they are fair;
30 And roses of their thorns disarm:
            But most procure
That violets may a longer age endure.

5

But, O young beauty of the woods,
Whom Nature courts with fruits and flowers,
35 Gather the flowers, but spare the buds;
Lest Flora[5] angry at thy crime,
To kill her infants in their prime,
Do quickly make the example yours;
            And, ere we see,
40 Nip in the blossom all our hopes and thee.
—1681 (PROBABLY WRITTEN IN THE EARLY 1650S)

The Mower against Gardens

Luxurious man, to bring his vice in use,
    Did after him the world seduce,
And from the fields the flowers and plants allure,
    Where nature was most plain and pure.
5 He first enclosed within the gardens square
    A dead and standing pool of air,
And a more luscious earth for them did knead,
    Which stupefied them while it fed.
The pink grew then as double as his mind;
10   The nutriment did change the kind.
With strange perfumes he did the roses taint,
    And flowers themselves were taught to paint.
The tulip, white, did for complexion seek,

---

[1] *sun / Stand still* Referring ultimately to Joshua 10.12–14, when Joshua made the sun and moon stand still while his army slaughtered the Amorites; but also invoking a traditional trope of love poetry in which lovers ask for time to slow down or stop when in one another's company.

[2] *T.C.* Probably Theophila Cornewall (b. 1644), whose mother was a member of a family, the Skinners, with whom Marvell was familiar. "Darling of the Gods" (line 10) is a literal translation of "Theophila."

[3] *gives them names* Associating "T.C." with Eve, traditionally said to have named the flowers in Eden (*Paradise Lost*, 11.277).

[4] *compound* "Come to terms with." The word also had a political resonance in the period: Royalists "compounded" by paying a fine to avoid confiscation of their estates.

[5] *Flora* Roman goddess of flowers.

And learned to interline its cheek:
15   Its onion root they then so high did hold,
        That one was for a meadow sold.[1]
     Another world was searched, through oceans new,
        To find the *Marvel of Peru*.[2]
     And yet these rarities might be allowed
20   To man, that sovereign thing and proud,
     Had he not dealt between the bark and tree,[3]
        Forbidden mixtures there to see.
     No plant now knew the stock from which it came;
        He grafts upon the wild the tame:
25   That the uncertain and adulterate fruit
        Might put the palate in dispute.
     His green seraglio has its eunuchs too,
        Lest any tyrant him outdo.
     And in the cherry he does nature vex,
30   To procreate without a sex.[4]
     'Tis all enforced, the fountain and the grot,
        While the sweet fields do lie forgot:
     Where willing Nature does to all dispense
        A wild and fragrant innocence:
35   And fauns and fairies do the meadows till,
        More by their presence than their skill.
     Their statues, polished by some ancient hand,
        May to adorn the gardens stand:
     But howsoe'er the figures do excel,
40   The gods themselves with us[5] do dwell.
        —1681 (PROBABLY WRITTEN IN THE EARLY 1650S)

---

[1] *for a meadow sold* Referring to the speculative bubble of the "tulip mania" in Holland in the 1630s, during which spectacular prices were paid for some bulbs.

[2] *Marvel of Peru* Much prized multi-colored tropical flower of South America (and possibly with a pun on the poet's name).

[3] *between the bark and tree* "To deal between the bark and the tree" was a proverbial expression for interfering activity, often to interfering between husband and wife; the proverb is here made literal through its reference to grafting.

[4] *And in the cherry ... a sex* Probably referring to attempts to create, through grafting, stoneless cherries (hence "eunuchs").

[5] *with us* With mowers (not with gardeners).

Damon the Mower

1

Hark how the Mower Damon sung,
    With love of Juliana stung!
While everything did seem to paint
The scene more fit for his complaint.
5   Like her fair eyes the day was fair,
But scorching like his am'rous care.
Sharp like his scythe his sorrow was,
And withered like his hopes the grass.

2

"Oh what unusual heats are here,
10   Which thus our sunburned meadows sear!
The grasshopper its pipe gives o'er;
And hamstringed[6] frogs can dance no more.
But in the brook the green frog wades;
And grasshoppers seek out the shades.
15   Only the snake, that kept within,
Now glitters in its second skin.

3

"This heat the sun could never raise,
Nor Dog Star[7] so inflame the days.
It from an higher beauty groweth,
20   Which burns the fields and mower both:
Which mads the dog, and makes the sun
Hotter than his own Phaëton.[8]
Not Jùly causeth these extremes,
But Juliana's scorching beams.

4

25   "Tell me where I may pass the fires
Of the hot day, or hot desires.
To what cool cave shall I descend,

---

[6] *hamstringed* Lamed or disabled (figuratively) by the heat.

[7] *Dog Star* Sirius; associated with the "dog days" of July and August, the period when Sirius rises at the same time as the sun.

[8] *Phaëton* Son of the sun god, who set part of the world on fire when driving his father's chariot.

Or to what gelid° fountain bend?   cold
Alas! I look for ease in vain,
30   When remedies themselves complain.
No moisture but my tears do rest,
Nor cold but in her icy breast.

5

"How long wilt thou, fair shepherdess,
Esteem me, and my presents less?
35   To thee the harmless snake I bring,
Disarmèd of its teeth and sting;
To thee chameleons, changing hue,
And oak leaves tipped with honey dew.
Yet thou, ungrateful, hast not sought
40   Nor what they are, nor who them brought.

6

"I am the Mower Damon, known
Through all the meadows I have mown.
On me the morn her dew distils
Before her darling daffodils.
45   And, if at noon my toil me heat,
The sun himself licks off my sweat.
While, going home, the evening sweet
In cowslip-water bathes my feet.

7

"What, though the piping shepherd stock
50   The plains with an unnumbered flock,
This scythe of mine discovers wide
More ground than all his sheep do hide.
With this the golden fleece[1] I shear
Of all these closes° every year.   enclosed fields
55   And though in wool more poor than they,
Yet am I richer far in hay.

8

"Nor am I so deformed to sight,
If in my scythe I lookèd right;

In which I see my picture done,
60   As in a crescent moon the sun.
The deathless fairies takes me oft
To lead them in their dances soft:
And, when I tune myself to sing,
About me they contract their ring.

9

65   "How happy might I still have mowed,
Had not Love here his thistles sowed!
But now I all the day complain,
Joining my labour to my pain;
And with my scythe cut down the grass,
70   Yet still my grief is where it was:
But, when the iron blunter grows,
Sighing, I whet my scythe and woes."

10

While thus he threw his elbow round,
Depopulating all the ground,
75   And, with his whistling scythe, does cut
Each stroke between the earth and root,
The edgèd steel by careless chance
Did into his own ankle glance;
And there among the grass fell down,
80   By his own scythe, the mower mown.

11

"Alas!" said he, "these hurts are slight
To those that die by love's despite.
With shepherd's-purse, and clown's-all-heal,[2]
The blood I staunch, and wound I seal.
85   Only for him no cure is found,
Whom Juliana's eyes do wound.
'Tis death alone that this must do:
For Death thou art a mower too."
—1681 (PROBABLY WRITTEN IN THE EARLY 1650S)

---

[1] *golden fleece* The golden hay he mows, which he implies is
superior to the regular fleece of the shepherd's sheep; but also
associating himself with the ancient hero Jason, who sought and
obtained the Golden Fleece.

---

[2] *shepherd's-purse, and clown's-all-heal* Herbs traditionally used to
stop bleeding and to heal wounds; a "clown" is a country dweller.

The Garden

1

How vainly men themselves amaze
To win the palm, the oak, or bays,[1]
And their uncessant labours see
Crowned from some single herb or tree,
5 Whose short and narrow vergèd shade
Does prudently their toils upbraid,
While all flow'rs and all trees do close
To weave the garlands of repose.

2

Fair Quiet, have I found thee here,
10 And Innocence, thy sister dear!
Mistaken long, I sought you then
In busy companies of men.
Your sacred plants, if here below,
Only among the plants will grow.
15 Society is all but rude,
To this delicious solitude.

3

No white nor red[2] was ever seen
So am'rous as this lovely green.
Fond lovers, cruel as their flame,
20 Cut in these trees their mistress' name.
Little, alas, they know, or heed,
How far these beauties hers exceed!
Fair trees! wheres'e'er your barks I wound,
No name shall but your own be found.

4

25 When we have run our passions' heat,
Love hither makes his best retreat.
The gods, that mortal beauty chase,
Still in a tree did end their race.
Apollo hunted Daphne so,
30 Only that she might laurel grow.

5

And Pan[3] did after Syrinx speed,
Not as a nymph, but for a reed.

What wondrous life is this I lead!
Ripe apples drop about my head;
35 The luscious clusters of the vine
Upon my mouth do crush their wine;
The nectarine, and curious peach,
Into my hands themselves do reach;
Stumbling on melons, as I pass,
40 Ensnared with flow'rs, I fall on grass.

6

Meanwhile the mind, from pleasures less,
Withdraws into its happiness:
The mind, that ocean where each kind
Does straight its own resemblance find;[4]
45 Yet it creates, transcending these,
Far other worlds, and other seas,
Annihilating all that's made
To a green thought in a green shade.

7

Here at the fountain's sliding foot,
50 Or at some fruit-tree's mossy root,
Casting the body's vest aside,
My soul into the boughs does glide:
There like a bird it sits, and sings,
Then whets,° and combs its silver wings;   preens
55 And, till prepared for longer flight,
Waves in its plumes the various light.

---

1 *the palm, the oak, or bays* Wreaths or garlands; the traditional rewards signifying military (palm leaves), civic or political (oak leaves), or poetic (laurel, or bay, leaves) achievement.

2 *white nor red* Colors traditionally associated with female beauty.

3 *Apollo … Pan* The speaker invokes two classical myths associated with erotic pursuit and the transformation of desire into art. Daphne, chased by Apollo, the god of poetry, was transformed into the laurel tree that became Apollo's sacred emblem. Syrinx, chased by Pan, god of flocks and shepherds, was transformed into a reed, the basis of the pan-pipe, emblem of pastoral poetry. The speaker naively (or mischievously) claims that these gods were really seeking the plants these women transformed into, not the women themselves, and thus asserts the superiority in beauty of plants to women.

4 *that ocean … own resemblance find* Alluding to the Renaissance belief that the ocean contains a counterpart for every plant and animal on land.

8

Such was that happy garden-state,
While man there walked without a mate:
After a place so pure, and sweet,
60   What other help could yet be meet?[1]
But 'twas beyond a mortal's share
To wander solitary there:
Two Paradises 'twere in one
To live in Paradise alone.

9

65   How well the skilful gardener drew
Of flowers and herbs this dial[2] new,
Where from above the milder sun
Does through a fragrant zodiac run;
And, as it works, the industrious bee
70   Computes its time as well as we.
How could such sweet and wholesome hours
Be reckoned but with herbs and flowers!

—1681 (PROBABLY WRITTEN IN THE EARLY 1650S)

An Horatian Ode upon Cromwell's Return from Ireland [3]

The forward[4] youth that would appear[5]
Must now forsake his Muses dear,

Nor in the shadows sing
His numbers[6] languishing:
5   'Tis time to leave the books in dust,
And oil the unused armour's rust:
Removing from the wall
The corslet[7] of the hall.
So restless Cromwell could not cease
10   In the inglorious arts of peace,
But through adventurous war
Urged his active star:
And, like the three-forked lightning, first
Breaking the clouds where it was nursed,
15   Did thorough° his own side   *through*
His fiery way divide.[8]
(For 'tis all one to courage high
The emulous or enemy:
And with such to enclose
20   Is more than to oppose.)
Then burning through the air he went,
And palaces and temples rent:
And Caesar's head at last
Did through his laurels blast.[9]
25   'Tis madness to resist or blame
The force of angry heaven's flame:
And, if we would speak true,
Much to the man is due,
Who, from his private gardens, where
30   He lived reserved and austere,
As if his highest plot
To plant the bergamot,[10]

---

1   *help … meet*   Alluding to Genesis 2.18: "And the Lord God said, It is not good that the man should be alone; I will make him an help meet for him."

2   *dial*   Floral sundial; sometimes read literally (Renaissance gardens did contain floral sundials), but the speaker also likens the entire garden to a sundial, in that it keeps seasonal time as the sun moves through its twelve-part zodiac.

3   *An Horatian Ode upon Cromwell's Return from Ireland*   In May 1650, Oliver Cromwell returned from a military expedition to Ireland, where he had defeated Royalist armies in several bloody battles. At the time he was second-in-command of Parliament's New Model Army, but in June 1650 Sir Thomas Fairfax resigned, and Cromwell became Commander-in-Chief in July, just prior to the invasion of Scotland this poem anticipates in lines 125ff. This poem was typeset for inclusion in the 1681 *Poems,* but the pages on which it was printed were removed before publication ("cancelled") from all but two extant copies.

4   *forward*   Prompt, ready, eager, spirited.

5   *appear*   Emerge to play a role in public life.

6   *numbers*   Metrical numbers: the youth can no longer spend time in the shadows writing love ("languishing") poetry.

7   *corslet*   Piece of armour that covered the body: the youth's "hall" or house had one, hanging on the wall.

8   *side … divide*   Referring to Cromwell's rise to power through the ranks and past "emulous" (envious) rivals.

9   *And Caesar's head … blast*   Comparing Charles I to Caesar, and Cromwell to a bolt of lightning: Roman emperors wore laurel wreaths; lightning was thought not to strike laurel trees; but Cromwell's bolt blasted through this protection. Note that Cromwell is figured as Caesar in line 100, and that lines 81-82 remind readers of the historical clash between the Imperial Caesar and the Roman republic.

10   *bergamot*   Variety of pear traditionally known as the pear of kings: a "plot" to "plant" (bury) this fruit was not as innocent sounding as it might seem.

Could by industrious valour climb
To ruin the great work of time,
35   And cast the kingdoms[1] old
    Into another mould.
Though justice against fate complain,
And plead the ancient rights[2] in vain:
    But those do hold or break
40   As men are strong or weak.
Nature, that hateth emptiness,
Allows of penetration less:[3]
    And therefore must make room
    Where greater spirits come.
45 What field of all the Civil Wars,
Where his were not the deepest scars?
    And Hampton[4] shows what part
    He had of wiser art:
Where, twining subtle fears with hope,
50 He wove a net of such a scope,
    That Charles himself might chase
    To Carisbrooke's narrow case:°   *box, prison*
That thence the royal actor borne
The tragic scaffold might adorn:[5]
55   While round the armed bands
    Did clap their bloody hands.
He nothing common did or mean

Upon that memorable scene:
    But with his keener eye[6]
60   The axe's edge did try:
Nor called the gods with vulgar spite
To vindicate his helpless right,
    But bowed his comely head,
    Down, as upon a bed.[7]
65 This was that memorable hour
Which first assured the forced power.
    So when they did design
    The Capitol's first line,
A bleeding head where they begun,
70 Did fright the architects to run;
    And yet in that the State
    Foresaw its happy fate.[8]
And now the Irish are ashamed
To see themselves in one year tamed:[9]
75   So much one man can do,
    That does both act and know.
They can affirm his praises best,
And have, though overcome, confessed
    How good he is, how just,
80   And fit for highest trust:[10]
Nor yet grown stiffer with command,

---

[1] *kingdoms* Charles was King of three countries: England, Scotland, and Ireland.

[2] *ancient rights* Not the "divine right" of kings, but the place of the monarch in the "ancient" constitution, a place abolished by the English Republic.

[3] *Nature, that hateth … less* Nature abhors a vacuum, but it also will not let two objects occupy the same place simultaneously: one needs to go.

[4] *Hampton* Hampton Court Palace, where Charles stayed until, fearful of assassination, he fled to Carisbrooke Castle (see line 52) on the Isle of Wight in November 1647. Charles expected to be safe in the Isle of Wight, but the Governor held him prisoner and he was eventually returned to London for trial. The poem voices contemporary rumors that Cromwell had slyly organized the whole train of events; these rumors are now thought to be groundless.

[5] *The tragic scaffold might adorn* The execution of the King (the "royal actor") is presented through a sustained theatrical metaphor. Marvell probably assumed that readers would remember that Charles was beheaded on a scaffold set up outside the Banqueting House, where plays and court entertainments were staged before the war: many of these entertainments, the court masques, celebrated royal power and featured members of the court on stage.

[6] *keener eye* I.e., keener than the blade with which he was to be executed.

[7] *He nothing … a bed* Charles (the "He" of line 56, though the poem requires the reader to pause a moment to identify the referent) won admiration for his dignified manner throughout his trial and execution.

[8] *And yet … fate* The "Capitol" is the ancient Roman temple of Jupiter Capitolium: according to Roman historians, workers digging the temple's foundation found a man's undecayed (hence "bleeding") head, which Roman authorities interpreted as a good omen: in Latin, the word head (*caput*) is related to capital, so the head was read as a sign that the temple would be the capital of a great empire. The poem implies that under Cromwell another empire will be founded on another bleeding head.

[9] *And now … tamed* Cromwell's ferocious campaign against the Irish lasted from August 1649 to May 1650.

[10] *They … trust* The Irish; few if any Irish, then or now, would "confess" any goodness or justice to Cromwell in his campaign in Ireland.

But still in the Republic's hand:[1]
   How fit he is to sway
   That can so well obey.
85 He to the Commons' feet presents
A kingdom, for his first year's rents:
   And, what he may, forbears
   His fame, to make it theirs:
And has his sword and spoils ungirt,
90 To lay them at the public's skirt.[2]
   So when the falcon high
   Falls heavy from the sky,
She, having killed, no more does search
But on the next green bough to perch,
95   Where, when he first does lure,
   The falconer has her sure.
What may not then our isle presume
While Victory his crest does plume?
   What may not others fear
100   If thus he crowns each year?
A Caesar, he, ere long to Gaul,[3]
To Italy a Hannibal,[4]

And to all states not free
   Shall climacteric be.[5]
105 The Pict[6] no shelter now shall find
Within his parti-coloured[7] mind,
   But from this valour sad[8]
   Shrink underneath the plaid:
Happy, if in the tufted brake
110 The English hunter him mistake,
   Nor lay his hounds in near
   The Caledonian° deer.   *Scottish*
But thou, the Wars' and Fortune's son,
March indefatigably on,
115   And for the last effect
   Still keep thy sword erect:
Besides the force it has to fright
The spirits of the shady night,[9]
   The same arts that did gain
120   A power, must it maintain.
—1681 (BUT CANCELLED FROM MOST COPIES; WRITTEN
1650)

---

[1] *in … hand* The next four stanzas figure Cromwell as a falcon (see line 91) under the control of the House of Commons, the Republic's representative body: as a bird of prey he hunts kingdoms, but dutifully brings them back to the "falconer" rather than claiming them for himself.

[2] *public's skirt* He lays his sword, and trophies, at the feet of the "body politic."

[3] *A Caesar … Gaul* Julius Caesar subdued Gaul (France); the poem implies that Cromwell before long might do likewise.

[4] *Hannibal* Carthaginian general who invaded Italy in 218 BCE, and left, undefeated, fifteen years later. He was later defeated by a Roman army, but the reference is probably not meant ironically: the power to invade, to "be a Hannibal" to Italy, is the key point.

[5] *climacteric be* Be the cause of a critical or crucial moment in the lives of those states.

[6] *Pict* Scot, from the name of the ancient Celtic people who inhabited Scotland when the Romans occupied Britain; the name, with its link to picture and painting, also puns on "parti-coloured" in the next line.

[7] *parti-coloured* Varied in color; the Scots were regarded in the period as politically fickle, prone to change and to variety of opinion.

[8] *sad* Referring to Cromwell's "valor": steadfast and grave; also dark or soberly colored (in contrast with the "parti-coloured" Scots).

[9] *Besides … night* Cold iron, and the cross-shaped hilt of a sword, were both thought to have the power to protect against evil spirits.

KATHERINE PHILIPS
1632 – 1664

Katherine Philips, known also by her *nom de plume* "Orinda" whom some called "the Matchless Orinda," was the first Englishwoman to enjoy widespread public acclaim as a poet during her lifetime. Despite prejudice against seeing women's secular works in print, her male peers recognized Philips as a poet of the first rank. As early as 1651, Henry Vaughan paid tribute to her "new miracles in Poetrie," and in 1663 Abraham Cowley proclaimed her verse "then Man more strong, and more then Woman sweet." In the guise of her literary persona Orinda, Philips dramatized, within her self-devised Society of Friendship, the ideals—and the realities and tribulations—of Platonic love with wit, elegance, and clarity. Thus the Society—whether fully or partly imaginary—helped establish a literary standard for her generation and Orinda herself a model for the female writers who followed her. Toward the end of her fairly short life Philips also broke new ground as a playwright and

translator: although other women had written or translated dramas, her translation of Corneille's neoclassical *Pompey* was the first rhymed version of a French tragedy in English and the first English play written by a woman to be performed on the professional stage.

Orinda was born Katherine Fowler in London on 1 January 1632, into a prosperous middle-class family with strong Puritan leanings. Friendships made at the boarding school she attended from 1640 to about 1645 probably influenced Philips's eventual shift to the Royalist cause. Certainly at school she began to write verse within a coterie of friends and to cultivate a taste for the French romances and Cavalier plays from which she would later choose many of the pet names she gave members of her Society of Friendship.

In 1648, Philips, then 16, married James Philips and moved with him to Cardigan in Wales, which was to remain her family home for the rest of her life. Since her husband was a prominent Parliamentarian, however, she accompanied him occasionally on trips to London, where she befriended a circle of Cavalier writers gathered around the composer Henry Lawes and devoted to the memory of William Cartwright, who had died in 1643. It was her prefatory poem to the 1651 edition of Cartwright's works, in fact, that marked Philips's first appearance in print, and she contributed her "To the much honoured Henry Lawes" and "Mutuall Affection between Orinda and Lucasia" (later retitled as "Friendship's Mysterys") to Lawes's *Second Book of Ayres* in 1655. By this time, her poems were being read in manuscript as public chronicles of a literary and social clique.

The Society of Friendship had its origins in the cult of Neoplatonic love imported from the continent in the 1630s by Charles I's French wife, Henrietta Maria. Adherents indulged in elaborate rhetoric about the mingling of souls, and often adopted pseudonyms drawn from French pastoral romances or Cavalier dramas. With her literary gifts, however, and her intuitive sense of the value of deep friendships in a time of war and social schism, Philips enriched this convention as a cultural ideal of harmony and personal friendships to set against the faithless, war-torn public world. At the same time many of her poems (which she herself evidently valued highly) address public, political events.

During the 1650s the Society of Friendship probably numbered at least 20 people of both sexes, but Philips's literary energies were concentrated on her two closest female friends, Mary Aubrey ("Rosania")—until the latter's marriage in 1652 caused an estrangement—and then, in the succeeding decade, Anne Owen Lewis ("Lucasia"). The degree to which these friendships and the poetry that sprang from them include an erotic component is a subject of debate among scholars; what is agreed is that these poems have always attracted the keenest critical attention from readers of Philips's works. Initially strongly influenced by John Donne, Philips eventually matched the best of the Cavalier lyricists in freshness of wit, elegant invention, and pleasing rhythm.

Hoping to bolster her husband's political fortunes after the Restoration in 1660, Philips wrote many Royalist occasional pieces and became a friend of Sir Charles Cotterell, Master of Ceremonies to the King. She dubbed him "Poliarchus" and carried on a lively correspondence with him that was published after her death. While visiting the newly married Anne Owen in Ireland in 1662, Philips translated Corneille's *Mort de Pompée* from French alexandrines into fine English heroic couplets. The play was an instant success in Dublin and London in 1663, introducing Philips to wider celebrity as a playwright. (She left a second Corneille translation, *Horace*, unfinished, however.)

A supposedly illicit edition of Philips's poems appeared early in 1664. Germaine Greer and others have suggested that Philips engineered the publication of this edition in such a way that she could disown it. In any event, the publisher, Richard Marriott, withdrew the edition before Philips (who rushed to London to deal with the situation) had time to compel him to do so. It was during this same visit to London that Philips contracted smallpox; she died in June of that year, seemingly at the height of her powers. An authorized volume of her collected verse, published by Henry Herringman in 1667, exerted enormous influence on female poets of the succeeding generations, such as Anne Killigrew and Anne Finch, the Countess of Winchilsea. Praised for her modesty and Christian virtue as well as for her poetry, Philips, in her brief career as playwright, helped to pave the way for the acceptance of the somewhat less modest and less virtuous Aphra Behn. Finally, as Orinda, she asserted a female claim to what had been so often thought an exclusively male sphere: ideal friendship. As she claims in "A Friend":

> … for men t'exclude
> Women from friendship's capacity,
> Is a design injurious and rude,
> Only maintain'd by partial tyranny.
> Love is allow'd to us, and Innocence,
> And noblest friendships do proceed from thence.

⌘ ⌘ ⌘

A Married State

A married state affords but little ease
　The best of husbands are so hard to please.
This in wives' careful° faces you may spell°　　　　*careworn / discern*
Though they dissemble° their misfortunes well.　　　　*conceal*
5　A virgin state is crowned with much content;°　　　　*contentment*
It's always happy as it's innocent.
No blustering husbands to create your fears;
No pangs of childbirth to extort your tears;
No children's cries for to offend your ears;
10　Few worldly crosses° to distract your prayers:　　　*difficulties*
Thus are you freed from all the cares that do
Attend on matrimony and a husband too.
Therefore Madam, be advised by me
Turn, turn apostate to° loves levity.　　　　*reject, forsake*
15　Suppress wild nature if she dare rebel.

There's no such thing as leading apes in hell.[1]
—c. 1648

Upon the Double Murder of King Charles
In Answer to a Libelous Rhyme made by V. P.[2]

I think not on the state, nor am concerned
Which way soever that great helm is turned,
But as that son whose father's danger nigh
Did force his native dumbness, and untie
5 His fettered organs:[3] so here is a cause
That will excuse the breach of nature's laws.
Silence were now a sin: nay passion now
Wise men themselves for merit would allow.
What noble eye could see, (and careless pass)
10 The dying lion kicked by every ass?[4]
Hath Charles so broke God's laws, he must not have
A quiet crown, nor yet a quiet grave?
Tombs have been sanctuaries; thieves lie here
Secure from all their penalty and fear.
15 Great Charles his double misery was this,
Unfaithful friends, ignoble enemies;
Had any heathen been this prince's foe,
He would have wept to see him injured so.
His title was his crime, they'd reason good
20 To quarrel at the right they had withstood.
He broke God's laws, and therefore he must die,
And what shall then become of thee and I?
Slander must follow treason; but yet stay,°   *stop*

25 Take not our reason with our king away.
Though you have seized upon all our defense,
Yet do not sequester° our common sense.   *confiscate*
But I admire not at this new supply:
No bounds will hold those who at scepters fly.
Christ will be King, but I ne'er understood,
30 His subjects built his kingdom up with blood
(Except their own) or that he would dispense
With his commands, though for his own defense.
Oh! to what height of horror are they come
Who dare pull down a crown, tear up a tomb![5]
—1667

On the Third of September, 1651[6]

A s when the glorious magazine of light[7]
Approaches to his canopy of night,
He with new splendor clothes his dying rays,
And double brightness to his beams conveys;
5 As if to brave° and check his ending fate,   *defy*
Puts on his highest looks in 's lowest state;
Dressed in such terror as to make us all
Be anti-Persians,[8] and adore his fall;
Then quits the world, depriving it of day,
10 While every herb and plant does droop away:
So when our gasping English royalty
Perceived her period° now was drawing nigh,   *end*
She summons her whole strength to give one blow,
To raise her self, or pull down others too.
15 Big with revenge and hope, she now spake more
Of terror than in many months before;
And musters her attendants, or to save
Her from, or wait upon° her to the grave: *escort / follow*
Yet but enjoyed the miserable fate
20 Of setting majesty, to die in state.
Unhappy Kings! who cannot keep a throne,
Nor be so fortunate to fall alone!

---

[1] *leading apes in hell*   The proverbial fate of spinsters after death.

[2] *V.P.*   Vavasor Powell (1617–70), an itinerant Nonconformist preacher and one of the Fifth Monarchists, who believed in the imminent Second Coming and the illegitimacy of earthly kings. The verses alluded to by Philips have not survived.

[3] *that son … fettered organs*   Referring to the ancient Greek tale in which Croesus, King of Lydia, was saved from summary execution during the sack of Sardis by his mute son, who, speaking for the first time, identified his father as King and thus a man to be taken alive (Herodotus 1.85).

[4] *dying lion kicked by every ass*   The dying Lion in Aesop's fable "The Sick Lion," who is assaulted in his helplessness by the various beasts, his subjects. On being finally kicked in the face by the Ass, the Lion proclaims, "This is a double death." Aesop's moral reads, "Only cowards insult dying majesty." The Scottish lion was also the dominant figure on the Stuart coat of arms.

[5] *tear up a tomb*   Deface the honor and memory of the dead king.

[6] *Third of September, 1651*   The date of the Battle of Worcester, in which Oliver Cromwell decisively defeated Charles II and the Royalist cause, bringing the English Civil War to an end.

[7] *magazine of light*   The sun, pictured as a storehouse of light.

[8] *anti-Persians* Anti-sun, referring to the ancient Persian worship of Mithra, later identified with the sun.

Their weight sinks others: Pompey could not fly,
But half the world must bear him company;[1]
25 Thus captive Sampson could not life conclude,
Unless attended with a multitude.[2]
Who'd trust to greatness now, whose food is air,[3]
Whose ruin sudden, and whose end despair?
Who would presume upon his glorious birth,
30 Or quarrel for a spacious share of earth,
That sees such diadems become thus cheap,
And heroes tumble in the common heap
O! give me virtue then, which sums up° all, *encompasses*
And firmly stands when crowns and scepters fall.
—1667

To My Excellent Lucasia, on Our Friendship

17th. July 1651[4]

I did not live until this time
  Crowned my felicity,
When I could say without a crime,
  I am not thine, but thee.
5 This carcass° breathed, and walked, and slept, *body*
  So that the world believed
There was a soul the motions kept;
  But they were all deceived.
For as a watch by art° is wound *mechanical skill*
10   To motion, such was mine:
But never had Orinda found
  A soul till she found thine;

---

1 *Pompey…company* The Roman general Pompey fled to Egypt after being defeated by Julius Caesar at Pharsalus (48 BCE), where 15,000 of his men were killed. Pompey's defeat and subsequent assassination in Egypt brought an end to the Civil War of the Triumvirate.

2 *captive Samson … multitude* Captured and blinded by the Philistines, the biblical hero Samson brought down the pillars of the temple at Gaza, killing thousands of his enemies along with himself. See Book of Judges 16.

3 *whose food is air* Who is changeable and inconstant as the chameleon, which had the ability to endure long periods without food, and was thus reputed to live on air.

4 *Lucasia … 1651* Philips met her close friend Anne Owen (Lucasia) in 1651.

Which now inspires, cures and supplies,
  And guides my darkened breast:
15 For thou art all that I can prize,
  My joy, my life, my rest.
Nor bridegroom's nor crowned conqueror's mirth
  To mine compared can be:
They have but pieces of this earth,
20   I've all the world in thee.
Then let our flame still light and shine,
  (And no bold° fear control) *strong*
As innocent as our design,° *intent*
  Immortal as our soul.
—1667

Friendship's Mystery, To My Dearest Lucasia

Come, my *Lucasia*, since we see
  That Miracles Mens faith do move,
By wonder and by prodigy[5]
  To the dull angry world let's prove
5 There's a Religion in our Love.

For though we were design'd t' agree,
  That Fate no liberty destroyes,
But our Election is as free
  As Angels, who with greedy choice
10 Are yet determin'd to their joyes.

Our hearts are doubled by the loss,
  Here Mixture is Addition grown;
We both diffuse, and both ingross:
  And we whose minds are so much one,
15 Never, yet ever are alone.

We court our own Captivity
  Than Thrones more great and innocent:
'Twere banishment to be set free,
  Since we wear fetters whose intent
20 Not Bondage is, but Ornament.

---

5 *prodigy* Miracle or extraordinary event.

original spelling

Divided joyes are tedious found,
    And griefs united easier grow:
We are our selves but by rebound,
    And all our Titles shuffled so,
25 Both Princes, and both Subjects too.

Our Hearts are mutual Victims laid,
    While they (such power in Friendship lies)
Are Altars, Priests, and Off'rings made:
    And each Heart which thus kindly dies,
30 Grows deathless by the Sacrifice.
—1667

On the Death of My First and Dearest Child, Hector Philips[1]

1

Twice forty months of wedlock I did stay,[2]
    Then had my vows crowned with a lovely boy,
And yet in forty days he dropt away,
    O swift vicissitude of human joy.

2

5 I did but see him and he disappeared,
    I did but pluck the rosebud and it fell,
A sorrow unforeseen and scarcely feared,
    For ill can mortals their afflictions spell.

3

And now (sweet babe) what can my trembling heart
10 Suggest to right my doleful fate or thee,
Tears are my Muse and sorrow all my Art,
    So piercing groans must be thy eulogy.

4

Thus whilst no eye is witness of my moan,
    I grieve thy loss (ah boy too dear to live)

15 And let the unconcerned world alone,
    Who neither will, nor can refreshment give.

5

An off'ring too for thy sad tomb I have,
    Too just a tribute to thy early hearse,
Receive these gasping numbers to thy grave,
20 The last of thy unhappy mother's verse.
—1667 (WRITTEN 1655)

Friendship in Emblem,[3] or the Seal, To My Dearest Lucasia

The hearts thus intermixed speak
    A love that no bold shock can break;
For joined and growing, both in one,
Neither can be disturbed alone.

5 That means a mutual knowledge too;
    For what is't either heart can do,
Which by its panting sentinel°   *guard*
It does not to the other tell?

That friendship hearts so much refines,
10 It nothing but itself designs:
The hearts are free from lower ends,
For each point to the other tends.

They flame, 'tis true, and several ways,
But still those flames do so much raise,
15 That while to either they incline
They yet are noble and divine.

From smoke or hurt those flames are free,
From grossness° or mortality: *vulgarity*
The hearts (like Moses' bush[4] presumed)
20 Warmed and enlightened, not consumed.

---

[1] *Hector Philips* According to a manuscript copy of this poem, Philips's son Hector was born 23 April 1655 and died about ten days later, on 2 May. She would have one other child, a daughter named Katherine, the following year.

[2] *Twice forty ... stay* Philips was married in August 1648, almost seven years before Hector was born.

[3] *Emblem* Drawing expressing an allegory, or representing a quality. Often these were accompanied by a motto and some lines of verse; this poem describes the symbolic elements in an emblem of friendship.

[4] *Moses' bush* The Angel of the Lord appears to Moses in a burning bush, which, miraculously, is not consumed by the fire (see Exodus 3.2–5).

The compasses that stand above
Express this great immortal Love;
For friends, like them, can prove this true,
They are, and yet they are not, two.

25   And in their posture is expressed
Friendship's exalted interest:
Each follows where the other leans,
And what each does, the other means.

And as when one foot does stand fast,
30   And t'other circles seeks to cast,
The steady part does regulate
And make the wanderer's motion straight.

So friends are only two in this,
T'reclaim each other when they miss:
35   For whose'er will grossly fall,
Can never be a friend at all.

And as that useful instrument
For even lines was ever meant;
So friendship from good angels springs,
40   To teach the world heroic things.

As these are found out in design
To rule and measure ev'ry line;
So friendship governs actions best,
Prescribing law to all the rest.

45   And as in nature nothing's set
So just as lines and numbers met;
So compasses for these b'ing made,
Do friendship's harmony persuade.

And like to them, so friends may own
50   Extension, not division:
Their points, like bodies, separate;
But head, like souls, knows no such fate.

And as each part so well is knit,
That their embraces ever fit:
55   So friends are such by destiny,
And no third can the place supply.

There needs no motto to the seal:
But that we may the mine reveal
To the dull eye, it was thought fit
60   That friendship only should be writ.

But as there is degrees of bliss,
So there's no friendship meant by this,
But such as will transmit to fame
Lucasia's and Orinda's name.
—1664 (WRITTEN C. 1653)

JOHN MILTON
1608 – 1674

John Milton aspired to be a writer for the ages—and he succeeded. Almost within his lifetime, Milton was widely considered England's greatest poet and a writer whose only serious rivals were the ancient masters Homer and Virgil. His influence on subsequent English poetry is probably second only to that of Shakespeare: for centuries, major poets struggled to define themselves in relation to Milton's achievement in a literary psychodrama of admiration, emulation, exasperation, and denial. No other English writer appears to have assimilated so thoroughly all the literature, culture, and history that had come before him. Milton first mastered the European artistic tradition, and then out

of it made something new, producing magnificent and innovative poems in all the major genres. In addition, had Milton not published a line of verse he would still hold a place in literary history by virtue of his prose. Even though he dismissed these books as the product of "his left hand," Milton was a significant prose writer and a formidable polemicist, in Latin as well as English, producing a wide range of works on political, social, religious, educational, and historical issues.

Of all the major writers in English, Milton was probably the most deeply engaged in the politics of his time. Milton's poetry has consequently been read in light of his active involvement in political, religious, and social revolution. But the nature of Milton's literary engagement with these issues continues to be debated: Milton, like Shakespeare, rarely if ever offers easy answers. Over the centuries, Milton has been championed as both a pillar of religious orthodoxy and as the great dissenter, a religious radical or even heretic. He has been called a proto-feminist and the great patriarchal bogeyman, a radical political egalitarian and a man who did not believe in democracy. His is the greatest voice of "Puritanism" in English literature, but to think of him in anything like the modern sense of "puritanical" is to go immediately off-track. While a profoundly religious man, Milton by the end of his life had almost no use for institutional religion or theological tradition. While a "Puritan," he was also a spokesman for revolution, freedom of the will (which Protestant theory usually denied), and political, social, intellectual, and personal liberty. Thomas Jefferson copied out 48 excerpts from Milton's works into his commonplace book, almost all of them having to do with liberty. Milton's works have been called the culmination of Renaissance humanism and a monument to dead ideas; and they have been celebrated as ushering in the modern world in their complex treatment of human agency, human love, and human political relations.

No writer before Milton fashioned himself quite so insistently and self-consciously as an author: in text after text, Milton invites us to read connections between his life and his writing, and then challenges or complicates our ability to do so. Born the eldest son of a successful scrivener in London in 1608, Milton was surrounded by words from an early age; he began writing seriously at the age of ten. In 1618 he was admitted to Christ's College, Cambridge, where he would remain the next seven years, graduating M.A. in 1632. While Milton did very well in his studies, he also complained repeatedly about the inadequacies of the educational curriculum and requirements: he described his frustration with traditional approaches to education in his treatise *On Education* (1644). Milton entered Cambridge expecting to become a minister in the Church of England (he would later change his mind, probably in the 1630s). In his university writings, however, he talks about himself as a poet and as a scholar, and never as a prospective minister. But he did develop a reputation for erudition and literary skill: during his university years he wrote several poems he would later publish, including the companion poems "L'Allegro" and "Il Penseroso."

After he left Cambridge, Milton spent the next six years in "studious retirement," living with his parents, reading extensively, preparing himself for his vocation—and trying to discover what that vocation was. He published his first poem, an epitaph for Shakespeare included in Shakespeare's second folio (1632); he accepted commissions for two aristocratic entertainments (*Arcades* and *A Maske*, popularly known as *Comus*). He kept a close eye on the changing political and religious conditions of England over the 1630s. Finally, in 1638, he published "Lycidas," one of the most extraordinary poems in English, simultaneously a eulogy for a drowned classmate, a denunciation of current Anglican Church leadership, and a confident assertion of his own poetic vocation, all mediated through the conventions of classical pastoral elegy. Writing "Lycidas" seemed to be the trigger that propelled Milton from his retirement into an active engagement with the world. In 1638 and 1639, he traveled abroad, spending considerable time in Italy, where he was much taken with the intellectual and cultural life. Had not rumors of the impending English Civil War called him home in late 1639, Milton's travels would likely have lasted much longer.

Milton continued to train himself towards his goal of becoming a great poet in the classical tradition of Virgil, becoming familiar with Spanish, Dutch, and Hebrew as well as Latin and Greek, French and Italian, and with the leading works of history, science and philosophy as well as of literature. But after returning to England in 1639 he devoted himself over the next twenty years very largely to the cause of political and religious change. Most of his publications during this period consist of prose polemic, including some anti-episcopal tracts in the early 1640s, several others arguing for an increased freedom to divorce, *Areopagitica* (1644), and works of political theory and argument that hold a central place among the writings of the English civil wars: *The Tenure of Kings and Magistrates* (1649), *Eikonoklastes* (1649), *Defensio pro populo Anglicano* (1651), *Defensio secunda* (1654), and *The Ready and Easy Way to Establish a Free Commonwealth* (1659). Milton's skill as a polemicist brought him to the attention of the revolutionary government, and in the 1650s he served as Secretary for Foreign Tongues in the government of Oliver Cromwell—a job that entailed writing a wide variety of official documents and letters (Latin remained the most important "foreign tongue" for international communication).

Of his prose works, the most widely read in the modern era has been *Areopagitica* (1644), Milton's extended defense of literary and intellectual freedom. The occasion for the work was the effort by Parliament to require books to be licensed prior to publication. Milton did not advocate complete freedom of the press. But his arguments for the necessity of letting readers make up their own minds, of letting arguments fight it out in the public sphere, continue to be cited in legal cases today. At the time, however, Milton was far better known, notorious even, for his books advocating a right to divorce. In June of 1642 Milton (then thirty-six) married Mary Powell, a young woman from a Royalist family. The two proved to be a less than perfect match, and she returned to her family's home in Buckinghamshire two months later. They were eventually reconciled, but many readers see a connection between their apparent difficulties and Milton's publication of *The Doctrine and Discipline of Divorce* (1642), in which he argues that the purpose of marriage is to provide companionship based on affection and like-mindedness, and that divorce should be allowed when a marriage fails to do so. The scandal Milton provoked in England with these arguments was supplanted only by the European-wide scandal he created by defending the execution of King Charles I.

While Milton might not have had time to write much poetry in the 1640s, he did publish the poetry he had written up to the outbreak of war. In 1645, a year that saw some of the bloodiest fighting of the war, Humphrey Moseley, the most prominent literary publisher of the day, produced

The Poems of Mr. John Milton, Both English and Latin. In addition to "On the Morning of Christ's Nativity," "On Shakespeare," "L'Allegro" and "Il Penseroso," "Lycidas," and *A Maske*, the collection included twenty-two other poems in English, including ten sonnets (six of them written in Italian), and twelve Latin poems.

Milton's wife Mary died during childbirth in 1652, and one of the couple's four children died shortly thereafter. At about the same time Milton entirely lost his sight; the sonnet "When I consider how my light is spent" (often referred to as "On His Blindness") was written later that same year. His two daughters were among those who served thereafter as scribes; all of his subsequent works were dictated. In 1656 Milton married Katherine Woodcock; two years later, in 1658, she also died of complications arising from childbirth.

With the Restoration in 1660, Milton went into hiding from the authorities. Eventually he suffered a brief imprisonment, but his freedom was negotiated by friends (notable among them the poet Andrew Marvell). His existence for the final fourteen years of his life was one of relative isolation—but these were also the years of his greatest poetic achievement. Rising early each day and beginning to dictate as soon as his scribe or secretary joined him, he had begun in the late 1650s to compose *Paradise Lost*, a sweeping re-telling of the Biblical story of humanity's expulsion from Paradise; the epic was initially published in 1667 in ten books, and then reissued in a revised twelve-book edition in 1674. Since the early eighteenth century *Paradise Lost* has been almost universally accorded a central place in the English literary canon. Two other major works followed: *Paradise Regained* (1671), which presents in blank verse the story of the temptation of Jesus and of his defeat of Satan; and *Samson Agonistes* (1671), which recounts in the form of a poetic drama the story of the blind and anguished Samson, struggling to understand God's will.

In 1663 Milton married Elizabeth Minshul, who became a scribe, caregiver, and inspiration to him in the last decade of his life. Though *Paradise Lost* sold moderately well from its first publication, and though Milton came to be regarded by many as a "classic" even during his lifetime, his anti-monarchical political views precluded any official honors; when he died in 1674 he was buried not in Westminster Abbey but beside his father in Saint Giles's Church, Cripplegate.

⌘ ⌘ ⌘

L'Allegro [1]

Hence loathèd Melancholy
Of Cerberus,[2] and blackest Midnight born,
In Stygian[3] cave forlorn
'Mongst horrid shapes, and shrieks, and sights unholy,
5 Find out some uncouth cell,
Where brooding Darkness spreads his jealous wings,
And the night-raven sings;
There under ebon shades, and low-browed rocks,

As ragged as thy locks,
10 In dark Cimmerian[4] desert ever dwell.
But come thou goddess fair and free,
In heaven yclept° Euphrosyne,[5]   *named*
And by men, heart-easing Mirth,
Whom lovely Venus at a birth
15 With two sister Graces more
To ivy-crownèd Bacchus bore;[6]

---

1 *L'Allegro* Italian: the merry or happy man.

2 *Cerberus* In classical myth, the three-headed dog that guards the entrance to the underworld.

3 *Stygian* Hellishly black; from Styx, a river that in classical myth leads to the underworld.

4 *Cimmerian* Densely dark (from the Cimmerians, a people fabled in classical story to live in perpetual darkness).

5 *Euphrosyne* Classical personification of Joy and one of the three Graces.

6 *heart-easing Mirth ... Bacchus bore* Milton makes the three Graces the daughters of Venus (goddess of love) and Bacchus (god of wine); Euphrosyne's two sisters were Aglaia (Brightness) and Thalia (Bloom).

Or whether (as some sager sing)
The frolic wind that breathes the spring,
Zephyr with Aurora[1] playing,
20 As he met her once a-Maying,[2]
There on beds of violets blue,
And fresh-blown roses washed in dew,
Filled her with thee a daughter fair,
So buxom, blithe, and debonair.[3]
25 Haste thee nymph, and bring with thee
Jest and youthful jollity,
Quips and cranks, and wanton wiles,[4]
Nods, and becks,° and wreathèd smiles,   *beckonings*
Such as hang on Hebe's[5] cheek,
30 And love to live in dimple sleek;
Sport that wrinkled Care derides,
And Laughter holding both his sides.
Come, and trip it as ye go
On the light fantastic toe,
35 And in thy right hand lead with thee,
The mountain nymph, sweet Liberty;
And if I give thee honour due,
Mirth, admit me of thy crew
To live with her, and live with thee,
40 In unreprovèd° pleasures free;   *free of blame*
To hear the lark begin his flight,
And singing startle the dull night,
From his watch-tower in the skies,
Till the dappled dawn doth rise;
45 Then to come in spite of sorrow,
And at my window bid good morrow, [6]

Through the sweet-briar, or the vine,
Or the twisted eglantine.
While the cock with lively din,
50 Scatters the rear of darkness thin,
And to the stack,° or the barn door,   *haystack*
Stoutly struts his dames before,
Oft list'ning how the hounds and horn
Cheerly rouse the slumb'ring morn,
55 From the side of some hoar° hill,   *grey*
Through the high wood echoing shrill.
Sometime walking not unseen
By hedgerow elms, on hillocks green,
Right against the eastern gate,
60 Where the great sun begins his state,
Robed in flames, and amber light,
The clouds in thousand liveries dight,°   *clothed*
While the ploughman near at hand,
Whistles o'er the furrowed land,
65 And the milkmaid singeth blithe,
And the mower whets his scythe,
And every shepherd tells his tale[7]
Under the hawthorn in the dale.
Straight mine eye hath caught new pleasures
70 Whilst the landscape round it measures.
Russet lawns, and fallows grey,
Where the nibbling flocks do stray,
Mountains on whose barren breast
The labouring clouds do often rest:
75 Meadows trim with daisies pied,
Shallow brooks, and rivers wide,
Towers, and battlements it sees
Bosomed high in tufted trees,
Where perhaps some beauty lies,
80 The cynosure[8] of neighbouring eyes.
Hard by, a cottage chimney smokes,
From betwixt two agèd oaks,
Where Corydon and Thyrsis[9] met,
Are at their savoury dinner set
85 Of herbs, and other country messes,
Which the neat-handed Phyllis dresses;

---

[1] *Zephyr … Aurora* Classical personifications of the west wind and of the dawn.

[2] *a-Maying* Celebrating the arrival of May; May Day was celebrated with various traditional pastimes. Sterner Puritans opposed such revelry as pagan.

[3] *buxom, blithe, and debonair* These three adjectives had overlapping meanings in the period, and were often grouped with one another: *buxom* Easy-going, lively; *blithe* Merry, jolly; *debonair* Affable, kindly, gracious.

[4] *Quips* Witty sayings; *cranks* Plays on words; *wanton wiles* Playful games and tricks.

[5] *Hebe* Classical personification of youth.

[6] *to come … bid good morrow* That is, L'Allegro comes to his window and bids the day good morrow (though some readers think it is the lark who bids good morrow to L'Allegro): the same, deliberately agentless syntax has L'Allegro "oft list'ning" and "sometime walking" in subsequent lines.

---

[7] *tells his tale* A double meaning: "tells his story" and/or "counts his flock."

[8] *cynosure* Center of attraction or interest.

[9] *Corydon … Thyrsis* With "Phyllis" and "Thestylis" five lines below, traditional names in classical pastoral poetry.

And then in haste her bower she leaves,
With Thestylis to bind the sheaves;
Or if the earlier season lead
90 To the tanned haycock in the mead,
Sometimes with secure delight
The upland hamlets will invite,
When the merry bells ring round,
And the jocund rebecks[1] sound
95 To many a youth, and many a maid,
Dancing in the chequered shade;
And young and old come forth to play
On a sunshine holiday,
Till the livelong daylight fail,
100 Then to the spicy nut-brown ale,
With stories told of many a feat,
How Fairy Mab[2] the junkets[3] eat,
She was pinched, and pulled she said,
And he by Friar's Lantern[4] led
105 Tells how the drudging Goblin[5] sweat,
To earn his cream-bowl duly set,
When in one night, ere glimpse of morn,
His shadowy flail hath threshed the corn,
That ten day-labourers could not end;
110 Then lies him down the lubber fiend,
And stretched out all the chimney's length,
Basks at the fire his hairy strength;
And crop-full[6] out of doors he flings,
Ere the first cock his matin rings.
115 Thus done the tales, to bed they creep,
By whispering winds soon lulled asleep.
Towered cities please us then,
And the busy hum of men,
Where throngs of knights and barons bold,
120 In weeds of peace[7] high triumphs hold,
With store of ladies, whose bright eyes

Rain influence, and judge the prize
Of wit, or arms, while both contend
To win her grace, whom all commend.
125 There let Hymen[8] oft appear
In saffron robe, with taper clear,[9]
And pomp, and feast, and revelry,
With masque, and antique pageantry,
Such sights as youthful poets dream
130 On summer eves by haunted stream.
Then to the well-trod stage anon,
If Jonson's learnèd sock[10] be on,
Or sweetest Shakespeare, fancy's child,
Warble his native wood-notes wild,
135 And ever against eating cares,
Lap me in soft Lydian airs,[11]
Married to immortal verse
Such as the meeting soul may pierce
In notes, with many a winding bout
140 Of linkèd sweetness long drawn out,
With wanton heed, and giddy cunning,
The melting voice through mazes running;
Untwisting all the chains that tie
The hidden soul of harmony.
145 That Orpheus self[12] may heave his head
From golden slumber on a bed
Of heaped Elysian[13] flowers, and hear
Such strains as would have won the ear
Of Pluto, to have quite set free
150 His half-regained Eurydice.[14]

---

1 *rebecks* Three-stringed fiddles.

2 *Fairy Mab* In English folklore, the Queen of the Fairies.

3 *junkets* Dishes of sweet curds and cream.

4 *Friar's Lantern* Folkloric name for the will-o'-the-wisp.

5 *Goblin* Robin Goodfellow or Hobgoblin; usually a mischievous trickster, he might help with household chores, as here, if propitiated with an offering of cream.

6 *crop-full* Filled to the brim (here, with cream).

7 *weeds of peace* Showy tournament outfits, as opposed to real, wartime armor.

8 *Hymen* Classical god of weddings.

9 *taper clear* Candle or torch; it was a good omen for the marriage if the flame burned without smoke ("clear").

10 *sock* Slipper worn by comic actors in ancient Greece (as opposed to the buskin worn by actors in tragedies): L'Allegro suggests going to the theater if one of Ben Jonson's erudite comedies is playing.

11 *Lydian airs* Soft, convivial songs or melodies ("Lydian" is one of the Greek musical modes).

12 *Orpheus self* That is, Orpheus's self, or Orpheus himself. For Orpheus, see note below.

13 *Elysian* From Elysian Fields or Elysium, the resting place of dead heroes in classical myth.

14 *Orpheus … Eurydice* In classical myth, Orpheus was the musician who traveled to the underworld to reclaim his wife, Eurydice, after she died. Touched by the beauty of Orpheus's playing, Pluto, god of the underworld, agreed to release her. But he made the condition that Orpheus had to leave the underworld without looking back to

These delights, if thou canst give,
Mirth with thee, I mean to live.
—1645 (WRITTEN C. 1631?)

Il Penseroso[1]

Hence vain deluding joys,
      The brood of folly without father bred,
How little you bestead,[2]
      Or fill the fixèd mind with all your toys;
5 Dwell in some idle brain,
      And fancies fond with gaudy shapes possess,
As thick and numberless
      As the gay motes that people the sunbeams,
Or likest hovering dreams
10   The fickle pensioners of Morpheus' train.[3]
But hail thou goddess, sage and holy,
Hail divinest Melancholy,
Whose saintly visage is too bright
To hit the sense of human sight;
15 And therefore to our weaker view,
O'erlaid with black staid Wisdom's hue.
Black, but such as in esteem, Prince
Memnon's sister[4] might beseem,
Or that starred Ethiop queen[5] that strove
20 To set her beauty's praise above
The sea-nymphs, and their powers offended.
Yet thou art higher far descended,
Thee bright-haired Vesta[6] long of yore,

To solitary Saturn[7] bore;
25 His daughter she (in Saturn's reign,
Such mixture was not held a stain)
Oft in glimmering bowers, and glades
He met her, and in secret shades
Of woody Ida's[8] inmost grove,
30 While yet there was no fear of Jove.
Come pensive nun, devout and pure,
Sober, steadfast, and demure,
All in a robe of darkest grain,
Flowing with majestic train,
35 And sable stole of cypress lawn,[9]
Over thy decent shoulders drawn.
Come, but keep thy wonted state,
With even step, and musing gait,
And looks commercing with the skies,
40 Thy rapt soul sitting in thine eyes:
There held in holy passion still,
Forget thyself to marble, till
With a sad leaden downward cast,
Thou fix them on the earth as fast.
45 And join with thee calm Peace, and Quiet,
Spare Fast, that oft with gods doth diet,
And hears the Muses in a ring,
Ay round about Jove's altar sing.
And add to these retired Leisure,
50 That in trim gardens takes his pleasure;
But first, and chiefest, with thee bring,
Him that yon soars on golden wing,
Guiding the fiery-wheelèd throne,[10]
The cherub Contemplation,
55 And the mute Silence hist° along,   summon
'Less Philomel[11] will deign a song,

---

see if Eurydice was following; at the last minute, he looked, and lost
her once again (hence she is "half-regained").

[1] *Il Penseroso*   The pensive or contemplative man (Italian).

[2] *bestead*   Help, avail, be of service.

[3] *Morpheus' train*   Dreams are the attendants of Morpheus, the god
of sleep.

[4] *Memnon's sister*   In classical story, Memnon was an Ethiopian
prince who fought on the side of the Trojans in the Trojan war; his
sister was named Himera.

[5] *starred Ethiop queen*   Cassiopaeia; in classical myth she was changed
into a constellation (hence "starred") as punishment for claiming to
be more beautiful than the sea nymphs.

[6] *Vesta*   Classical goddess of hearth and home.

[7] *Saturn*   In classical myth, father of Jove (mentioned below);
traditionally "solitary," he was associated with melancholics (hence
the adjective "saturnine") even though his was the Golden Age.

[8] *Ida*   Mount Ida, in Crete, the traditional site from which Saturn
ruled, before his son Jove overthrew him.

[9] *cypress lawn*   Lawn is a fine linen, usually white, but "cypress
lawn" is black.

[10] *fiery-wheeled throne*   Apparently referring to the Biblical vision of
Ezekiel (Ezekiel 10) of a chariot guided by cherubim (angels).

[11] *Philomel*   The nightingale, from a classical story in which a young
woman, Philomela, is transformed into the sweet-singing bird after
being raped and silenced by having her tongue cut out (hence
"saddest plight").

In her sweetest, saddest plight,
Smoothing the rugged brow of night,
While Cynthia[1] checks her dragon yoke,
60 Gently o'er th' accustomed oak;
Sweet bird that shunn'st the noise of folly,
Most musical, most melancholy!
Thee chauntress oft the woods among,
I woo to hear thy even-song;
65 And missing thee, I walk unseen
On the dry smooth-shaven green,
To behold the wandering moon,
Riding near her highest noon,[2]
Like one that had been led astray
70 Through the heaven's wide pathless way;
And oft, as if her head she bowed,
Stooping through a fleecy cloud.
Oft on a plat° of rising ground,   *patch*
I hear the far-off curfew sound,
75 Over some wide-watered shore,
Swinging slow with sullen roar;
Or if the air will not permit,
Some still removèd place will fit,
Where glowing embers through the room
80 Teach light to counterfeit a gloom,
Far from all resort of mirth,
Save the cricket on the hearth,
Or the bellman's° drowsy charm,   *night watchman*
To bless the doors from nightly harm:
85 Or let my lamp at midnight hour,
Be seen in some high lonely tower,
Where I may oft outwatch the Bear,[3]
With thrice great Hermes,[4] or unsphere
The spirit of Plato[5] to unfold
90 What worlds, or what vast regions hold
The immortal mind that hath forsook
Her mansion in this fleshly nook:

And of those daemons[6] that are found
In fire, air, flood, or underground,
95 Whose power hath a true consent
With planet, or with element.
Sometime let gorgeous Tragedy
In sceptred pall come sweeping by,
Presenting Thebes, or Pelops' line,[7]
100 Or the tale of Troy divine.
Or what (though rare) of later age,
Ennobled hath the buskined stage.[8]
But, O sad virgin, that thy power
Might raise Musaeus[9] from his bower,
105 Or bid the soul of Orpheus sing
Such notes as warbled to the string,
Drew iron tears down Pluto's cheek,
And made hell grant what love did seek.[10]
Or call up him[11] that left half-told
110 The story of Cambuscan bold,
Of Camball, and of Algarsife,
And who had Canace to wife,
That owned the virtuous ring and glass,
And of the wondrous horse of brass,
115 On which the Tartar king did ride;[12]

---

1 *Cynthia* Classical goddess of the moon, here imagined as driving across the night sky in a chariot drawn by a dragon.

2 *highest noon* Highest point, apogee.

3 *the Bear* The constellation Ursa Major.

4 *thrice great Hermes* Hermes Trismegistus, the reputed author of the classical *Corpus Hermeticum*, a collection of mystical ("Hermetic") writings that Il Penseroso stays up all night to read.

5 *Plato* Il Penseroso contemplates reading the works of Plato, whose spirit is imagined as inhabiting a heavenly sphere or star.

6 *daemons* From neo-Platonic or Hermetic philosophy, spirits that inhabit the four "elements" of fire, air, water, and earth.

7 *Thebes, or Pelops' line* Two royal families whose stories provided subject matter for classical tragedies: the house of Thebes was that of Oedipus and his family; the house of Pelops was the family of Atreus, Agamemnon, Orestes, Electra, and Iphigenia.

8 *buskined stage* Tragedies, from the footwear worn by Greek tragic actors; Milton implies that good tragedies were rare in his (as opposed to the classical) period.

9 *Musaeus* In classical myth, a great singer, sometimes called the son of Orpheus.

10 *Orpheus ... seek* In classical myth, Orpheus was the master musician who traveled to the underworld to reclaim his wife, Eurydice, after she died. Touched by the beauty of Orpheus's playing, Pluto, god of the underworld, agreed to release her. But he made the condition that Orpheus had to leave the underworld without looking back to see if Eurydice was following; at the last minute, he looked, and lost her once again (hence she is "half-regained").

11 *him* I.e., Geoffrey Chaucer.

12 *story of ... ride* The romance of Cambuscan, his children Camball, Algarsife, and Canace, and the gifts of a brass horse and a magic ring, is told in Chaucer's unfinished "Squire's Tale" in the *Canterbury Tales*, and continued by Spenser in Book 4 of *The Faerie*

And if aught else, great bards beside,
In sage and solemn tunes have sung,
Of tourneys and of trophies hung;
Of forest, and enchantments drear,
120 Where more is meant than meets the ear.[1]
Thus Night oft see me in thy pale career,
Till civil-suited Morn appear,
Not tricked and frounced as she was wont,
With the Attic boy[2] to hunt,
125 But kerchiefed in a comely cloud,
While rocking winds are piping loud,
Or ushered with a shower still,
When the gust hath blown his fill,
Ending on the rustling leaves,
130 With minute drops from off the eaves.
And when the sun begins to fling
His flaring beams, me goddess bring
To archèd walks of twilight groves,
And shadows brown that Sylvan[3] loves
135 Of pine, or monumental oak,
Where the rude axe with heavèd stroke,
Was never heard the nymphs to daunt,
Or fright them from their hallowed haunt.
There in close covert by some brook,
140 Where no profaner eye may look,
Hide me from day's garish eye,
While the bee with honied thigh,
That at her flowery work doth sing,
And the waters murmuring
145 With such consort as they keep,
Entice the dewy-feathered Sleep;
And let some strange mysterious dream,
Wave at his wings in airy stream,
Of lively portraiture displayed,
150 Softly on my eyelids laid.
And as I wake, sweet music breathe
Above, about, or underneath,
Sent by some spirit to mortals good,
Or th' unseen genius° of the wood.   *guardian spirit*

155 But let my due° feet never fail,   *dutiful*
To walk the studious cloister's[4] pale,°   *enclosure*
And love the high embowèd roof,
With antique pillars' massy proof,
And storied windows[5] richly dight,°   *decorated*
160 Casting a dim religious light.
There let the pealing organ blow,
To the full-voiced choir below,
In service high, and anthems clear,
As may with sweetness, through mine ear,
165 Dissolve me into ecstasies,
And bring all heaven before mine eyes.
And may at last my weary age
Find out the peaceful hermitage,
The hairy gown and mossy cell,
170 Where I may sit and rightly spell,[6]
Of every star that heaven doth shew,
And every herb that sips the dew;
Till old experience do attain
To something like prophetic strain.
175 These pleasures Melancholy give,
And I with thee will choose to live.
—1645 (WRITTEN C.1631?)

Lycidas

In this monody[7] the author bewails a learned friend,[8]
unfortunately drowned in his passage from Chester on the
Irish Seas, 1637. And by occasion foretells the ruin of our
corrupted clergy then in their height.[9]

Queene.

[1] *more is meant than meets the ear*   Milton apparently refers to *The
Faerie Queene* and Spenser's allegorical method.

[2] *Attic boy*   In classical myth, Aurora (Dawn) loved Cephalus, an
Athenian (Attic) youth.

[3] *Sylvan*   Sylvanus, Roman god of forests.

---

[4] *cloister*   Covered walk; here, probably a university, not a monastic, cloister.

[5] *storied windows*   Pictorial stained glass windows.

[6] *spell*   Study, decipher.

[7] *monody*   Lament sung by one voice.

[8] *friend*   Edward King (1612–37), a fellow student of Milton's at
Cambridge.

[9] *In this … height*   Milton added this headnote to the version in his
Poems (1645), published when the success of Parliament in the Civil
Wars made it possible to publish a comment about the "corrupted
clergy." When the poem was first published, in a 1638 collection of
poems dedicated to the memory of Edward King, English bishops,
under the leadership of Archbishop William Laud, were indeed at
the "height" of their power.

Yet once more, O ye laurels, and once more
Ye myrtles brown, with ivy[1] never sere,°   *withered*
I come to pluck your berries harsh and crude,
And with forced fingers rude,
5 Shatter your leaves before the mellowing year.
Bitter constraint, and sad occasion dear,
Compels me to disturb your season due:
For Lycidas[2] is dead, dead ere his prime,
Young Lycidas, and hath not left his peer:
10 Who would not sing for Lycidas? he knew
Himself to sing, and build the lofty rhyme.
He must not float upon his watery bier
Unwept, and welter[3] to the parching wind,
Without the meed° of some melodious tear.   *honor*
15   Begin then, sisters of the sacred well,[4]
That from beneath the seat of Jove[5] doth spring,
Begin, and somewhat loudly sweep the string.
Hence with denial vain, and coy excuse,
So may some gentle muse
20 With lucky words favour my destined urn,
And as he passes turn,
And bid fair peace be to my sable shroud.
For we were nursed upon the self-same hill,[6]
Fed the same flock; by fountain, shade, and rill.°   *brook*
25   Together both, ere the high lawns[7] appeared
Under the opening eyelids of the morn,
We drove afield, and both together heard

What time the grey-fly winds[8] her sultry horn,
Battening° our flocks with the fresh dews[9]   *feeding*
     of night,
30 Oft till the star that rose, at evening, bright
Toward heaven's descent had sloped his westering
     wheel.
Meanwhile the rural ditties were not mute,
Tempered to the oaten flute,
Rough satyrs[10] danced, and fauns with cloven heel,
35 From the glad sound would not be absent long,
And old Damoetas[11] loved to hear our song.
     But O the heavy change, now thou art gone,
Now thou art gone, and never must return!
Thee shepherd, thee the woods, and desert caves,
40 With wild thyme and the gadding vine o'ergrown,
And all their echoes mourn.
The willows, and the hazel copses green,
Shall now no more be seen,
Fanning their joyous leaves to thy soft lays.°   *songs*
45 As killing as the canker to the rose,
Or taint-worm to the weanling herds that graze,
Or frost to flowers, that their gay wardrobe wear,
When first the whitethorn blows;°   *blooms*
Such, Lycidas, thy loss to shepherd's ear.
50   Where were ye nymphs when the remorseless deep
Closed o'er the head of your loved Lycidas?
For neither were ye playing on the steep,
Where your old bards, the famous Druids[12] lie,
Nor on the shaggy top of Mona high,
55 Nor yet where Deva spreads her wizard stream:
Ay me, I fondly dream!
Had ye been there ... for what could that have done?
What could the Muse herself that Orpheus bore,
The Muse herself, for her enchanting son

---

1 *laurels ... myrtles ... ivy*   These three evergreens were emblems of poetic achievement: laurel was sacred to Apollo, so a laurel wreath was the traditional crown of poets; myrtle was sacred to Venus, and so was an emblem of love poetry; ivy was linked with Bacchus, god of wine, and so was associated with poetic ecstasy or inspiration. By saying that he needs to pluck these berries before they are ripe, the speaker implies that he thinks himself unready to write the poetry these plants honored.

2 *Lycidas*   Traditional name in classical and Renaissance pastoral literature.

3 *welter*   Roll or tumble about.

4 *sisters of the sacred well*   The nine Muses; their well is the emblematic source of artistic inspiration.

5 *seat of Jove*   Probably Mt. Olympus, from beneath which one of the muses' sacred springs flowed; possibly Mt. Helicon, the site of another sacred spring.

6 *nursed upon the self-same hill*   Milton uses pastoral conventions to indicate that he and "Lycidas" went to the same school.

7 *lawns*   Open spaces between woods, glades.

8 *winds*   Blows its horn (that is, buzzes).

9 *dews*   Grasses still covered in dew.

10 *satyrs*   Part human, part animal creatures associated with lechery and wildness; when translated from the pastoral fiction, these are Milton's fellow undergraduates at Cambridge.

11 *Damoetas*   Conventional pastoral name, and here a teacher or mentor figure, possibly alluding to a real tutor at Cambridge.

12 *Druids*   The speaker asks if the sea nymphs failed to save King because they were playing in places associated with the Druids, ancient Celtic minstrel-poets or, here, "bards": Bardsey (the "steep" island where they "lie" buried), the island of Mona (Anglesey), and the river Dee (here, Latinized as "Deva") in Chester.

60 Whom universal nature did lament,
When by the rout that made the hideous roar,
His gory visage down the stream was sent,
Down the swift Hebrus to the Lesbian shore.[1]
        Alas! What boots it with uncessant care
65 To tend the homely slighted shepherd's trade,
And strictly meditate the thankless Muse,
Were it not better done as others use,
To sport with Amaryllis in the shade,
Or with the tangles of Neaera's[2] hair?
70 Fame is the spur that the clear spirit doth raise
(That last infirmity of noble mind)
To scorn delights, and live laborious days;
But the fair guerdon° when we hope to find,   *reward*
And think to burst out into sudden blaze,
75 Comes the blind Fury[3] with th' abhorrèd shears,
And slits the thin-spun life. But not the praise,
Phoebus[4] replied, and touched my trembling ears;
Fame is no plant that grows on mortal soil,
Nor in the glistering foil
80 Set off to the world, nor in broad rumour lies,
But lives and spreads aloft by those pure eyes,
And perfect witness of all-judging Jove;
As he pronounces lastly on each deed,
Of so much fame in heaven expect thy meed.
85   O fountain Arethuse,[5] and thou honoured flood,
Smooth-sliding Mincius[6] crowned with vocal reeds,
That strain I heard was of a higher mood:

But now my oat[7] proceeds,
And listens to the herald of the sea°   *Triton*
90 That came in Neptune's plea,
He asked the waves, and asked the felon winds,
What hard mishap hath doomed this gentle swain?
And questioned every gust of rugged wings[8]
That blows from off each beakèd promontory;
95 They knew not of his story,
And sage Hippotades[9] their answer brings,
That not a blast was from his dungeon strayed,
The air was calm, and on the level brine,
Sleek Panope[10] with all her sisters played.
100 It was that fatal and perfidious bark
Built in th' eclipse, and rigged with curses dark,
That sunk so low that sacred head of thine.
      Next Camus,[11] reverend sire, went footing slow,
His mantle hairy, and his bonnet sedge,
105 Inwrought with figures dim, and on the edge
Like to that sanguine flower inscribed with woe.[12]
Ah! who hath reft (quoth he) my dearest pledge?
Last came, and last did go,
The pilot of the Galilean lake,[13]
110 Two massy keys he bore of metals twain
(The golden opes, the iron shuts amain),
He shook his mitred locks,[14] and stern bespake,
How well could I have spared for thee, young swain,
Enow° of such as for their bellies' sake,   *enough*

---

1 *What could the Muse … shore* Orpheus was the greatest musician/poet in the classical tradition; his mother was the Muse Calliope. He met his death at the hands of Maenads, a group of women in an ecstatic frenzy. Orpheus's severed bleeding head ("gory visage") floated down the Hebrus river across the sea and to the island of Lesbos, where the Muses buried it.

2 *Amaryllis … Neaera* Conventional names in pastoral poetry for young women.

3 *Fury* In classical myth, the three Fates respectively spun the thread of life, measured it, and then cut it; the Fate with the cutting shears was named Atropos, or Destiny. The speaker compares her to one of the Furies, another group of mythological sisters, who were snaky-haired agents of vengeance.

4 *Phoebus* Apollo, god of poetry.

5 *Arethuse* Fountain on an island near Sicily, associated with pastoral poetry; named for the nymph Arethusa, who was transformed into the fountain while being chased by the river god Alpheus (see below, line 132).

6 *Mincius* River in Mantua, where the Roman poet Virgil was born.

7 *oat* Oaten flute (of l. 33); metaphorically, the speaker's song (poem).

8 *wings* Winds, imagined as birdlike.

9 *Hippotades* Aeolus, the classical keeper of winds.

10 *Panope* The chief nymph of fifty sea-nymph sisters, the Nereides.

11 *Camus* Personification of the River Cam, in Cambridge.

12 *sanguine flower … woe* The hyacinth. In classical myth, it sprang from the blood of Hyacinthus, a youth beloved of Apollo; the god recorded his grief by marking the flower with the letters AI AI ("alas").

13 *pilot of the Galilean lake* Usually identified as St. Peter, speaking as the founder of the Christian Church; he mourns the loss of a young man who had intended to enter the ministry. He holds the keys of the kingdom of Heaven, from Matthew 16.19. Thee pilot is sometimes identified as Christ. But as a (ship) pilot on Galilee, Peter would here appear to be paired with Christ, mentioned in line 173 below as "Him that walked the waves."

14 *mitred locks* Peter, the first bishop, wears the bishop's mitre (a tall, cleft headdress), and shakes his head.

115 Creep and intrude, and climb into the fold?°   *sheepfold*
Of other care they little reckoning make,
Than how to scramble at the shearers' feast,
And shove away the worthy bidden guest.
Blind mouths! that scarce themselves know how
    to hold
120 A sheep-hook, or have learned aught else the least
That to the faithful herdman's art belongs!
What recks it them?[1] What need they? They are sped;[2]
And when they list,[3] their lean and flashy songs
Grate on their scrannel[4] pipes of wretched straw,
125 The hungry sheep look up, and are not fed,
But swoll'n with wind, and the rank mist they draw,
Rot inwardly, and foul contagion spread:
Besides what the grim wolf[5] with privy paw[6]
Daily devours apace, and nothing said,[7]
130 But that two-handed engine[8] at the door,
Stands ready to smite once, and smite no more.
    Return Alpheus,[9] the dread voice is past,
That shrunk thy streams; return Sicilian Muse,[10]

And call the vales, and bid them hither cast
135 Their bells, and flowrets of a thousand hues.
Ye valleys low where the mild whispers use,
Of shades and wanton winds, and gushing brooks,
On whose fresh lap the swart star[11] sparely looks,
Throw hither all your quaint enamelled eyes,
140 That on the green turf suck the honied showers,
And purple all the ground with vernal flowers.
Bring the rathe° primrose that forsaken dies,   *early blooming*
The tufted crow-toe, and pale jessamine,
The white pink, and the pansy freaked° with jet,   *streaked*
145 The glowing violet,
The musk-rose, and the well-attired woodbine,
With cowslips wan that hang the pensive head,
And every flower that sad embroidery wears:
Bid amaranthus all his beauty shed,
150 And daffodillies fill their cups with tears,
To strew the laureate[12] hearse where Lycid lies.
For so to interpose a little ease,
Let our frail thoughts dally with false surmise
(Ay me!) Whilst thee the shores, and sounding seas
155 Wash far away, where'er thy bones are hurled,
Whether beyond the stormy Hebrides
Where thou perhaps under the whelming tide
Visit'st the bottom of the monstrous world;
Or whether thou to our moist vows denied,
160 Sleep'st by the fable of Bellerus[13] old,
Where the great vision of the guarded mount[14]
Looks toward Namancos and Bayona's hold;°   *fortress*
Look homeward angel now, and melt with ruth.
And, O ye dolphins, waft the hapless youth.
165   Weep no more, woeful shepherds weep no more,
For Lycidas your sorrow is not dead,
Sunk though he be beneath the watery floor,
So sinks the day-star° in the ocean bed,   *the sun*
And yet anon repairs his drooping head,

---

[1] *What recks it them* What do they care?

[2] *They are sped* They have done well.

[3] *when they list* When they choose, or please.

[4] *scrannel* Shriveled, thin; an unusual word, probably provincial dialect, apparently chosen for its appropriately ugly sound.

[5] *wolf* Usually identified as an allusion to the threat posed by Catholicism.

[6] *with privy paw* With secret or hidden steps; possibly also an allusion to the Privy Council, and implying that the government under Charles I was helping the Church push a Catholic agenda.

[7] *nothing said* In the manuscript version of this poem, Milton originally wrote "nothing" but then crossed it out and wrote "little"; "nothing" appears in the 1645 edition.

[8] *two-handed engine* The specific reference here continues to be debated. Probably, in one respect, a sword: in *Paradise Lost*, the Archangel Michael wields a "huge two-handed" sword (6.251), which likely refers to the two-edged swords mentioned in Revelation 1.16 and Psalm 149.6. But as an emblem for divine agency or judgment, the "sword of God" can also be interpreted as manifesting itself in many different objects, institutions, or ideas (such as the two keys of line 110 above).

[9] *Alphaeus* River in Greece, and the god of the river (see l. 85 above). The speaker invites the return of sources that inspire the pastoral mode.

[10] *Sicilian Muse* Probably Arethusa (see l. 85 above). Sicily was associated with the pastoral mode: the poet Theocritus (fl. 280 BCE), the creator of pastoral poetry, was Sicilian.

[11] *swart star* Sirius, the Dog Star, associated with the hottest weeks of the year.

[12] *laureate* Decorated with laurel (see line 1).

[13] *Bellerus* Milton apparently invents the name from Bellarium, the Latin name for Land's End in Cornwall, the south-west tip of England.

[14] *guarded mount* St. Michael's Mount in Cornwall, from which the Archangel was traditionally said to guard England; here, Michael looks out toward two places in Spain, but is asked to look "homeward" in pity for Lycidas.

170 And tricks his beams, and with new spangled ore,
Flames in the forehead of the morning sky:
So Lycidas sunk low, but mounted high,
Through the dear might of Him that walked the waves,
Where other groves, and other streams along,
175 With nectar pure his oozy locks he laves,
And hears the unexpressive nuptial song,
In the blest kingdoms meek of joy and love.
There entertain him all the saints above,
In solemn troops, and sweet societies
180 That sing, and singing in their glory move,
And wipe the tears for ever from his eyes.
Now Lycidas the shepherds weep no more;
Henceforth thou art the genius° of the shore, *guardian spirit*
In thy large recompense, and shalt be good
185 To all that wander in that perilous flood.

    Thus sang the uncouth swain to th' oaks and rills,
While the still morn went out with sandals grey,
He touched the tender stops of various quills,° *reeds (flutes)*
With eager thought warbling his Doric[1] lay:
190 And now the sun had stretched out all the hills,
And now was dropped into the western bay;
At last he rose, and twitched his mantle blue:[2]
Tomorrow to fresh woods, and pastures new.[3]
—1638, 1645

Sonnets

7

How soon hath Time the subtle thief of youth,
Stol'n on his wing my three and twenti'th year!
My hasting days fly on with full career,
But my late spring no bud or blossom shew'th.
5 Perhaps my semblance might deceive the truth,
That I to manhood am arriv'd so near,
And inward ripeness doth much less appear,
That some more timely-happy spirits indu'th.
Yet be it less or more, or soon or slow,
10   It shall be still° in strictest measure ev'n,   *always*

---

[1] *Doric* Musical mode.

[2] *blue* Color traditionally associated with hope.

[3] *Thus song … new* The final eight lines, rhyming ABABABCC, reflect the form of an *ottava rima* stanza, one pattern associated with epic narrative poetry.

To that same lot, however mean, or high,
Toward which Time leads me, and the will of Heav'n;
   All is, if I have grace to use it so,
   As ever in my great task-master's eye.
—1645 (WRITTEN EITHER 1631 OR 1632)

16[4]

TO THE LORD GENERAL CROMWELL[5]

Cromwell, our chief of men, who through a cloud
  Not of war only, but detractions rude,
Guided by faith and matchless fortitude,
To peace and truth thy glorious way hast plough'd,
5 And on the neck of crowned Fortune proud
Hast rear'd God's trophies, and his work pursu'd,
While Darwen stream[6] with blood of Scots imbru'd,
And Dunbar field,[7] resounds thy praises loud,
And Worcester's[8] laureate wreath; yet much remains
10 To conquer still: peace hath her victories
No less renown'd than war. New foes arise
Threat'ning to bind our souls with secular chains:[9]
Help us to save free Conscience from the paw
Of hireling[10] wolves whose Gospel is their maw.
—1694 (WRITTEN 1652)

---

[4] *16* Not published in Milton's lifetime. It is numbered sonnet 16 in Milton's manuscript version, though some modern editions give the number 16 to "When I consider how my light is spent" (Sonnet 19 here). The manuscript dates the poem May 1652, and has a scratched-out subtitle: "On the proposals of certain ministers at the Committee for Propagation of the Gospel."

[5] *To the Lord General Cromwell* Oliver Cromwell (1599–1658), at the time Commander-in-Chief of the Parliamentary Army, and subsequently Lord Protector.

[6] *Darwen stream* The river near Preston, where Cromwell defeated a Scottish army in August 1648.

[7] *Dunbar field* Where Cromwell routed the Scottish army in September 1650.

[8] *Worcester* Where Cromwell defeated the Royalist Army of Charles II, who was crowned in Scotland when in exile after the death of his father.

[9] *To conquer … secular chains* Referring to the proposals mentioned in the poem's manuscript subtitle (see note above) that sought to reinstall a state-controlled church.

[10] *hireling* Milton disapproved of compulsory tithes, believing that congregations should be able to hire ministers of their own choosing: to him, ministers in a state church are hired state employees.

18[1]
ON THE LATE MASSACRE IN PIEDMONT [2]

Avenge O Lord the slaughtered saints, whose bones
  Lie scattered on the Alpine mountains cold,
  Even them who kept thy truth so pure of old
  When all our fathers worshipped stocks and stones,
5 Forget not: in thy book record their groans
    Who were thy sheep and in their ancient fold
    Slain by the bloody Piedmontese that rolled
    Mother with infant down the rocks. Their moans
  The vales redoubled to the hills, and they
10   To heaven. Their martyred blood and ashes sow
    O'er all the Italian fields where still doth sway
  The triple tyrant:[3] that from these may grow
    A hundredfold, who having learnt thy way
    Early may fly the Babylonian woe.
—C. 1673 (WRITTEN 1655)

19[4]

When I consider how my light is spent,
  Ere half my days,[5] in this dark world and wide,
  And that one talent[6] which is death to hide,
  Lodged with me useless, though my soul more bent
5 To serve therewith my maker, and present
    My true account, lest he returning chide,
    Doth God exact day-labour, light denied,
    I fondly ask; but patience to prevent
  That murmur, soon replies, God doth not need
10   Either man's work or his own gifts, who best
    Bear his mild yoke, they serve him best, his state
  Is kingly. Thousands at his bidding speed
    And post[7] o'er land and ocean without rest:
    They also serve who only stand and wait.
—1673 (WRITTEN C. 1652–55)

23[8]

Methought I saw my late espoused saint[9]
  Brought to me, like Alcestis,[10] from the grave,
  Whom Jove's great son to her glad husband gave,
  Rescued from death by force, though pale and faint.
5 Mine, as whom washed from spot of child-bed taint
    Purification in the old Law[11] did save,
    And such as yet once more I trust to have
    Full sight of her in Heaven without restraint,
  Came vested all in white, pure as her mind;
10 Her face was veiled,[12] yet to my fancied sight
    Love, sweetness, goodness, in her person shined
    So clear as in no face with more delight.
  But Oh! as to embrace me she inclined,
  I waked, she fled, and day brought back my night.
—1673 (WRITTEN BETWEEN 1652 AND 1658)

---

[1] *18* Some modern editions number this sonnet 15, the number assigned it in the 1673 edition of Milton's *Poems*.

[2] *Massacre in Piedmont* In April 1655, a Catholic army under the command of the Duke of Savoy began a persecution of the Vaudois or Waldensians, a Protestant sect that lived in the mountainous Piedmont region of Italy, near the Swiss border. The Waldensians had broken away from the Catholic Church in the twelfth century. But seventeenth-century Protestants thought they represented a much older tradition, and regarded them as having retained the beliefs of the primitive Church.

[3] *triple tyrant* The Pope, from the three-crowned papal mitre or headdress.

[4] *19* Numbered sonnet 16 in some modern editions. The title "On his blindness" was added in the eighteenth century, and appears in some modern editions.

[5] *half my days* The source of much debate on the date of this poem: Milton was born in December 1608, and it is not clear by what standard he judges the normal length of a life. He was totally blind by early 1652.

[6] *talent* Alluding to the parable of the talents in Matthew 25.14-30.

[7] *post* Ride.

[8] *23* Numbered sonnet 19 in some modern editions.

[9] *late espoused saint* Milton's first wife, Mary Powell, died in May 1652, shortly after giving birth to their daughter Deborah. His second wife, Katherine Woodcock, died in February 1658, several months after giving birth to their daughter Katherine. The sonnet could refer to either wife, or even both (on the grounds that if Milton had wanted to make the reference clear, he could have).

[10] *Alcestis* In classical story, Alcestis sacrificed her life to save her husband, Admetus; Hercules, the son of Jove, repays Admetus's hospitality to him by forcing Death (in a wrestling match) to return her alive. The story is told in the play *Alcestis* by Euripedes.

[11] *Purification in the old Law* Referring to the rites of purification after childbirth detailed in Leviticus 12 (the old Law of the Old Testament, as opposed to the new Law of the New Testament).

[12] *veiled* Like Alcestis, when she returned; but also from the reader.

from *Areopagitica:*
A Speech of Mr. John Milton
for the Liberty of Unlicensed Printing,
to the Parliament of England[1]

They who to states and governors of the Commonwealth direct their speech, High Court of Parliament, or, wanting such access in a private condition, write that which they foresee may advance the public good; I suppose them, as at the beginning of no mean endeavour, not a little altered and moved inwardly in their minds: some with doubt of what will be the success, others with fear of what will be the censure; some with hope, others with confidence of what they have to speak. And me perhaps each of these dispositions, as the subject was whereon I entered, may have at other times variously affected; and likely might in these foremost expressions now also disclose which of them swayed most, but that the very attempt of this address thus made, and the thought of whom it hath recourse to, hath got the power within me to a passion, far more welcome than incidental to a preface....

If ye be thus resolved, as it were injury to think ye were not, I know not what should withhold me from presenting ye with a fit instance wherein to show both that love of truth which ye eminently profess, and that uprightness of your judgment which is not wont to be partial to yourselves; by judging over again that Order which ye have ordained to regulate printing: that no book, pamphlet, or paper shall be henceforth printed, unless the same be first approved and licensed by such, or at least one of such, as shall thereto be appointed. For that part which preserves justly every man's copy to himself, or provides for the poor, I touch not, only wish they be not made pretences to abuse and persecute honest and painful men, who offend not in either of these particulars. But that other clause of licensing books, which we thought had died with his brother quadragesimal and matrimonial[2] when the prelates expired, I shall now attend with such a homily, as shall lay before ye, first the inventors of it to be those whom ye will be loath to own; next what is to be thought in general of reading, whatever sort the books be; and that this Order avails nothing to the suppressing of scandalous, seditious, and libellous books, which were mainly intended to be suppressed. Last, that it will be primely to the discouragement of all learning, and the stop of Truth, not only by disexercising and blunting our abilities in what we know already, but by hindering and cropping the discovery that might be yet further made both in religious and civil wisdom.

I deny not, but that it is of greatest concernment in the Church and Commonwealth to have a vigilant eye how books demean themselves as well as men; and thereafter to confine, imprison, and do sharpest justice on them as malefactors. For books are not absolutely dead things, but do contain a potency of life in them to be as active as that soul was whose progeny they are; nay, they do preserve as in a vial the purest efficacy and extraction of that living intellect that bred them. I know they are as lively, and as vigorously productive, as those fabulous dragon's teeth;[3] and being sown up and down, may chance to spring up armed men. And yet, on the other hand, unless wariness be used, as good almost kill a man as kill a good book. Who kills a man kills a reasonable creature, God's image; but he who destroys

---

[1] *Areopagitica ... England* Milton's title invokes the *Areopagite Discourse* (c. 355 BCE) by the Greek orator Isocrates, who advocated a return to the days when the Athenian court of the Areopagus (a kind of Supreme Court) was a model of virtue, wisdom, and responsibility. Milton might also expect his readers to remember that Saint Paul delivered an oration on the Areopagus, the hill outside Athens that gave its name to the court that met there (Acts 17.19-34). Milton's text is in the form of an oration to Parliament, the entity the speaker addresses throughout. His motive for writing was a Parliamentary order (June 1643) that banned the publication of any book that had not been licensed before publication: what Milton attacks here is pre-publication censorship, not censorship in general (he does *not* argue for complete freedom of the press). Milton's main strategy is to embarrass Parliament by linking their attempt to control the press to the similar powers wielded by the monarchical government they were battling to overthrow.

[2] *quadragesimal and matrimonial* Referring to powers formerly held by bishops to award dispensations, here specifically those governing dietary restrictions in Lent ("quadragesimal" refers to Lent's forty days) and marriage licenses. Milton's point, a recurring one, is that with this new order, Parliament was giving itself the kind of controlling powers it had abolished when it abolished episcopacy.

[3] *dragon's teeth* In Greek mythology, the teeth of a dragon slain by the hero Cadmus bred armed men when sown in the ground.

a good book, kills reason itself, kills the image of God, as it were in the eye. Many a man lives a burden to the earth; but a good book is the precious life-blood of a master spirit, embalmed and treasured up on purpose to a life beyond life. 'Tis true, no age can restore a life, whereof perhaps there is no great loss; and revolutions of ages do not oft recover the loss of a rejected truth, for the want of which whole nations fare the worse.

We should be wary therefore what persecutions we raise against the living labours of public men, how we spill that seasoned life of man, preserved and stored up in books; since we see a kind of homicide may be thus committed, sometimes a martyrdom, and if it extend to the whole impression, a kind of massacre; whereof the execution ends not in the slaying of an elemental life, but strikes at that ethereal and fifth essence, the breath of reason itself, slays an immortality rather than a life....

Good and evil we know in the field of this world grow up together almost inseparably; and the knowledge of good is so involved and interwoven with the knowledge of evil, and in so many cunning resemblances hardly to be discerned, that those confused seeds which were imposed upon Psyche[1] as an incessant labour to cull out, and sort asunder, were not more intermixed. It was from out the rind of one apple tasted, that the knowledge of good and evil, as two twins cleaving together, leaped forth into the world. And perhaps this is that doom which Adam fell into of knowing good and evil, that is to say of knowing good by evil. As therefore the state of man now is; what wisdom can there be to choose, what continence to forbear without the knowledge of evil? He that can apprehend and consider vice with all her baits and seeming pleasures, and yet abstain, and yet distinguish, and yet prefer that which is truly better, he is the true wayfaring Christian. I cannot praise a fugitive and cloistered virtue, unexercised and unbreathed, that never sallies out and sees her adversary, but slinks out of the race, where that immortal garland is to be run for, not without dust and heat. Assuredly we bring not innocence into the world, we bring impurity much rather; that which purifies us

is trial, and trial is by what is contrary. That virtue therefore which is but a youngling in the contemplation of evil, and knows not the utmost that vice promises to her followers, and rejects it, is but a blank virtue, not a pure; her whiteness is but an excremental[2] whiteness. Which was the reason why our sage and serious poet Spenser, whom I dare be known to think a better teacher than Scotus or Aquinas, describing true temperance under the person of Guyon, brings him in with his Palmer through the cave of Mammon, and the bower of earthly bliss, that he might see and know, and yet abstain.[3] Since therefore the knowledge and survey of vice is in this world so necessary to the constituting of human virtue, and the scanning of error to the confirmation of truth, how can we more safely, and with less danger, scout into the regions of sin and falsity than by reading all manner of tractates and hearing all manner of reason? And this is the benefit which may be had of books promiscuously read....

If we think to regulate printing, thereby to rectify manners, we must regulate all recreations and pastimes, all that is delightful to man. No music must be heard, no song be set or sung, but what is grave and Doric.[4] There must be licensing dancers, that no gesture, motion, or deportment be taught our youth but what by their allowance shall be thought honest; for such Plato was provided of; it will ask more than the work of twenty licensers to examine all the lutes, the violins, and the guitars in every house; they must not be suffered to prattle as they do, but must be licensed what they may say. And who shall silence all the airs and madrigals that whisper softness in chambers? The windows also, and the balconies must be thought on; there are shrewd

---

[2] *excremental* Superficial.

[3] *Which was the reason ... yet abstain* Milton here famously misremembers *The Faerie Queene*. Guyon, the Knight of Temperance in Book 2, does resist the temptation offered by the Bower of Bliss (2.12.42ff.) with the aid of the Palmer (a pilgrim who has been to the Holy Land, and in Spenser a figure for the reason that restrains passion). But Guyon's settled habits of temperance allow him to withstand the temptations of Mammon's cave on his own (2.7.2, 2.8.3).

[4] *Doric* One of the "modes" of ancient music; in his *Republic*, Plato (cited later in the paragraph) used "Doric" to describe poetry that was manly and dignified.

---

[1] *Psyche* Apuleius (born 125 CE) tells the story of Cupid and Psyche in *The Golden Ass*; Psyche's impossible task was set her by her mother-in-law, Venus.

books, with dangerous frontispieces, set to sale; who shall prohibit them, shall twenty licensers? The villages also must have their visitors to inquire what lectures the bagpipe and the rebeck[1] reads, even to the ballatry and the gamut of every municipal fiddler, for these are the countryman's Arcadias, and his Montemayors.[2]

Next, what more national corruption, for which England hears ill abroad, than household gluttony: who shall be the rectors of our daily rioting? And what shall be done to inhibit the multitudes that frequent those houses where drunkenness is sold and harboured? Our garments also should be referred to the licensing of some more sober workmasters to see them cut into a less wanton garb. Who shall regulate all the mixed conversation of our youth, male and female together, as is the fashion of this country? Who shall still appoint what shall be discoursed, what presumed, and no further? Lastly, who shall forbid and separate all idle resort, all evil company? These things will be, and must be; but how they shall be least hurtful, how least enticing, herein consists the grave and governing wisdom of a state.

To sequester out of the world into Atlantic and Utopian polities which never can be drawn into use will not mend our condition; but to ordain wisely as in this world of evil, in the midst whereof God hath placed us unavoidably. Nor is it Plato's licensing of books will do this, which necessarily pulls along with it so many other kinds of licensing, as will make us all both ridiculous and weary, and yet frustrate; but those unwritten, or at least unconstraining, laws of virtuous education, religious and civil nurture, which Plato there mentions as the bonds and ligaments of the commonwealth, the pillars and the sustainers of every written statute; these they be which will bear chief sway in such matters as these, when all licensing will be easily eluded. Impunity and remissness, for certain, are the bane of a commonwealth; but here the great art lies, to discern in what the law is to bid restraint and punishment, and in what

things persuasion only is to work.

If every action which is good or evil in man at ripe years were to be under pittance and prescription and compulsion, what were virtue but a name, what praise could be then due to well-doing, what gramercy to be sober, just, or continent? Many there be that complain of Divine Providence for suffering Adam to transgress; foolish tongues! When God gave him reason, he gave him freedom to choose, for reason is but choosing; he had been else a mere artificial Adam, such an Adam as he is in the motions. We ourselves esteem not of that obedience, or love, or gift, which is of force: God therefore left him free, set before him a provoking object, ever almost in his eyes; herein consisted his merit, herein the right of his reward, the praise of his abstinence. Wherefore did he create passions within us, pleasures round about us, but that these rightly tempered are the very ingredients of virtue?...

And lest some should persuade ye, Lords and Commons, that these arguments of learned men's discouragement at this your Order are mere flourishes, and not real, I could recount what I have seen and heard in other countries, where this kind of inquisition tyrannizes; when I have sat among their learned men, for that honour I had, and been counted happy to be born in such a place of philosophic freedom, as they supposed England was, while themselves did nothing but bemoan the servile condition into which learning amongst them was brought; that this was it which had damped the glory of Italian wits; that nothing had been there written now these many years but flattery and fustian. There it was that I found and visited the famous Galileo,[3] grown old a prisoner to the Inquisition, for thinking in astronomy otherwise than the Franciscan and Dominican licensers thought.

And though I knew that England then was groaning loudest under the prelatical yoke, nevertheless I took it as a pledge of future happiness, that other nations were so persuaded of her liberty. Yet was it beyond my hope

---

[1] bagpipe and the rebeck   Viewed as rustic instruments; a rebeck is a three-stringed fiddle.

[2] the countryman's Arcadias, and his Montemayors   That is, popular music is the rural equivalent to sophisticated prose romances, such as Sir Philip Sidney's Arcadia (1590) and Jorge de Montemayor's Diana (c. 1559).

[3] There it was ... Galileo   Milton visited Italy in 1638-39; there seems no reason to doubt his claim to have visited Galileo, who is the only contemporary Milton names in Paradise Lost (5.262). Galileo at the time was under house arrest for having published his Dialogue Concerning the Two Chief World Systems.

that those worthies were then breathing in her air, who should be her leaders to such a deliverance, as shall never be forgotten by any revolution of time that this world hath to finish. When that was once begun, it was as little in my fear that, what words of complaint I heard among learned men of other parts uttered against the Inquisition, the same I should hear by as learned men at home uttered in time of Parliament against an order of licensing; and that so generally that, when I had disclosed myself a companion of their discontent, I might say, if without envy, that he whom an honest quaestorship had endeared to the Sicilians was not more by them importuned against Verres,[1] than the favourable opinion which I had among many who honour ye, and are known and respected by ye, loaded me with entreaties and persuasions, that I would not despair to lay together that which just reason should bring into my mind, toward the removal of an undeserved thraldom upon learning. That this is not therefore the disburdening of a particular fancy, but the common grievance of all those who had prepared their minds and studies above the vulgar pitch to advance truth in others, and from others to entertain it, thus much may satisfy. ...

Truth indeed came once into the world with her Divine Master, and was a perfect shape most glorious to look on: but when He ascended, and His Apostles after Him were laid asleep, then straight arose a wicked race of deceivers, who, as that story goes of the Egyptian Typhon with his conspirators, how they dealt with the good Osiris,[2] took the virgin Truth, hewed her lovely form into a thousand pieces, and scattered them to the four winds. From that time ever since, the sad friends of Truth, such as durst appear, imitating the careful search that Isis made for the mangled body of Osiris, went up and down gathering up limb by limb, still as they could find them. We have not yet found them all, Lords and Commons, nor ever shall do, till her Master's second coming; He shall bring together every joint and mem-

ber, and shall mold them into an immortal feature of loveliness and perfection. Suffer not these licensing prohibitions to stand at every place of opportunity, forbidding and disturbing them that continue seeking, that continue to do our obsequies to the torn body of our martyred saint.

We boast our light; but if we look not wisely on the Sun itself, it smites us into darkness. Who can discern those planets that are oft combust, and those stars of brightest magnitude that rise and set with the Sun, until the opposite motion of their orbs bring them to such a place in the firmament, where they may be seen evening or morning? The light which we have gained was given us, not to be ever staring on, but by it to discover onward things more remote from our knowledge. It is not the unfrocking of a priest, the unmitring of a bishop, and the removing him from off the Presbyterian shoulders, that will make us a happy nation. No, if other things as great in the Church, and in the rule of life both economical and political, be not looked into and reformed, we have looked so long upon the blaze that Zwinglius and Calvin[3] hath beaconed up to us, that we are stark blind. There be who perpetually complain of schisms and sects, and make it such a calamity that any man dissents from their maxims. 'Tis their own pride and ignorance which causes the disturbing, who neither will hear with meekness, nor can convince; yet all must be suppressed which is not found in their syntagma.[4] They are the troublers, they are the dividers of unity, who neglect and permit not others to unite those dissevered pieces which are yet wanting to the body of Truth. To be still searching what we know not by what we know, still closing up truth to truth as we find it (for all her body is homogeneal and proportional), this is the golden rule in theology as well as in arithmetic, and makes up the best harmony in a Church; not the forced and outward union of cold and neutral, and inwardly divided minds.

Lords and Commons of England, consider what nation it is whereof ye are, and whereof ye are the governors: a nation not slow and dull, but of a quick, ingenious and piercing spirit, acute to invent, subtle and

---

[1] *he ... Verres* Cicero (106-43 BCE), whose forensic oratory drove the corrupt Gaius Verres from office.

[2] *Typhon ... Osiris* Milton's source for this allegory about the search for the divided body of truth is likely Plutarch's essay "On Isis and Osiris." Typhon (the Egyptian god Set) tore up and scattered the body of Osiris; Isis, Osiris's sister, collected the pieces and put them back together.

[3] *Zwinglius and Calvin* Ulrich Zwingli (1484-1531) and John Calvin (1509-64), two leading figures of the Protestant Reformation.

[4] *syntagma* Systematic treatise or body of doctrine.

sinewy to discourse, not beneath the reach of any point, the highest that human capacity can soar to. Therefore the studies of Learning in her deepest sciences have been so ancient and so eminent among us, that writers of good antiquity and ablest judgment have been persuaded that even the school of Pythagoras and the Persian wisdom took beginning from the old philosophy of this island. And that wise and civil Roman, Julius Agricola, who governed once here for Caesar, preferred the natural wits of Britain before the laboured studies of the French.[1] Nor is it for nothing that the grave and frugal Transylvanian sends out yearly from as far as the mountainous borders of Russia, and beyond the Hercynian wilderness, not their youth, but their staid men, to learn our language and our theologic arts.[2]

Yet that which is above all this, the favour and the love of Heaven, we have great argument to think in a peculiar manner propitious and propending towards us. Why else was this nation chosen before any other, that out of her, as out of Sion, should be proclaimed and sounded forth the first tidings and trumpet of Reformation to all Europe? And had it not been the obstinate perverseness of our prelates against the divine and admirable spirit of Wycliffe,[3] to suppress him as a schismatic and innovator, perhaps neither the Bohemian Huss and Jerome,[4] no nor the name of Luther or of Calvin, had been ever known: the glory of reforming all our neighbours had been completely ours. But now, as our obdurate clergy have with violence demeaned the matter, we are become hitherto the latest and backwardest scholars, of whom God offered to have made us the teachers. Now once again by all concurrence of signs, and by the general instinct of holy and devout men, as they daily and solemnly express their thoughts, God is decreeing to begin some new and great period in his Church, even to the reforming of Reformation itself: what does He then but reveal himself to His servants, and as His manner is, first to his Englishmen? I say, as his manner is, first to us, though we mark not the method of His counsels, and are unworthy.

Behold now this vast city: a city of refuge, the mansion house of liberty, encompassed and surrounded with His protection; the shop of war hath not there more anvils and hammers waking, to fashion out the plates and instruments of armed Justice in defence of beleaguered Truth, than there be pens and heads there, sitting by their studious lamps, musing, searching, revolving new notions and ideas wherewith to present, as with their homage and their fealty, the approaching Reformation: others as fast reading, trying all things, assenting to the force of reason and convincement. What could a man require more from a nation so pliant and so prone to seek after knowledge? What wants there to such a towardly and pregnant soil but wise and faithful labourers, to make a knowing people, a nation of prophets, of sages, and of worthies? We reckon more than five months yet to harvest; there need not be five weeks; had we but eyes to lift up, the fields are white already.[5]

Where there is much desire to learn, there of necessity will be much arguing, much writing, many opinions; for opinion in good men is but knowledge in the making. Under these fantastic terrors of sect and schism, we wrong the earnest and zealous thirst after knowledge and understanding which God hath stirred up in this city. What some lament of, we rather should rejoice at, should rather praise this pious forwardness among men, to reassume the ill-reputed care of their Religion into their own hands again. A little generous prudence, a little forbearance of one another, and some grain of charity might win all these diligences to join, and unite in one general and brotherly search after Truth; could we but forgo this prelatical tradition of crowding free consciences and Christian liberties into canons and precepts of men. I doubt not, if some great and worthy stranger should come among us, wise to discern the mold and temper of a people, and how to govern it,

---

[1] *And that wise ... the French* Citing a story that appears in the Roman historian Tacitus, *Agricola*, 21.

[2] *Nor is it ... theologic arts* Many theologians from strongly Protestant Transylvania came to study during this period in Western European universities.

[3] *Wycliffe* John Wycliffe (c. 1324-84), an early Church reformer associated with the Lollard movement, often regarded as a proto-Protestant.

[4] *Huss and Jerome* John Huss (c. 1383-1415), founder of an influential reform movement in Bohemia, also often regarded as proto-Protestant; Jerome of Prague (d. 1416) was a disciple of both Wycliffe and Huss.

[5] *We reckon ... white already* Milton here adapts John 4.35.

observing the high hopes and aims, the diligent alacrity of our extended thoughts and reasonings, in the pursuance of truth and freedom, but that he would cry out as Pyrrhus did,[1] admiring the Roman docility and courage: If such were my Epirots, I would not despair the greatest design that could be attempted, to make a Church or Kingdom happy.

Yet these are the men cried out against for schismatics and sectaries; as if, while the temple of the Lord was building, some cutting, some squaring the marble, others hewing the cedars, there should be a sort of irrational men who could not consider there must be many schisms and many dissections made in the quarry and in the timber, ere the house of God can be built. And when every stone is laid artfully together, it cannot be united into a continuity, it can but be contiguous in this world; neither can every piece of the building be of one form; nay rather the perfection consists in this, that, out of many moderate varieties and brotherly dissimilitudes that are not vastly disproportional, arises the goodly and the graceful symmetry that commends the whole pile and structure.

Let us therefore be more considerate builders, more wise in spiritual architecture, when great reformation is expected. For now the time seems come, wherein Moses the great prophet may sit in heaven rejoicing to see that memorable and glorious wish of his fulfilled, when not only our seventy Elders, but all the Lord's people, are become prophets. No marvel then though some men, and some good men too perhaps, but young in goodness, as Joshua then was, envy them. They fret, and out of their own weakness are in agony, lest these divisions and subdivisions will undo us. The adversary again applauds, and waits the hour: When they have branched themselves out, saith he, small enough into parties and partitions, then will be our time. Fool! he sees not the firm root, out of which we all grow, though into branches: nor will beware until he see our small divided maniples[2] cutting through at every angle of his ill-united and unwieldy brigade. And that we are to hope better of all these supposed sects and schisms, and that we shall

not need that solicitude, honest perhaps though over-timorous of them that vex in this behalf, but shall laugh in the end at those malicious applauders of our differences, I have these reasons to persuade me.

First, when a city shall be as it were besieged and blocked about, her navigable river infested, inroads and incursions round, defiance and battle oft rumoured to be marching up even to her walls and suburb trenches, that then the people, or the greater part, more than at other times, wholly taken up with the study of highest and most important matters to be reformed, should be disputing, reasoning, reading, inventing, discoursing, even to a rarity and admiration, things not before discoursed or written of, argues first a singular goodwill, contentedness and confidence in your prudent foresight and safe government, Lords and Commons; and from thence derives itself to a gallant bravery and well-grounded contempt of their enemies, as if there were no small number of as great spirits among us, as his was, who when Rome was nigh besieged by Hannibal, being in the city, bought that piece of ground at no cheap rate, whereon Hannibal himself encamped his own regiment.

Next, it is a lively and cheerful presage of our happy success and victory. For as in a body, when the blood is fresh, the spirits pure and vigorous, not only to vital but to rational faculties, and those in the acutest and the pertest operations of wit and subtlety, it argues in what good plight and constitution the body is so when the cheerfulness of the people is so sprightly up, as that it has not only wherewith to guard well its own freedom and safety, but to spare, and to bestow upon the solidest and sublimest points of controversy and new invention, it betokens us not degenerated, nor drooping to a fatal decay, but casting off the old and wrinkled skin of corruption to outlive these pangs and wax young again, entering the glorious ways of truth and prosperous virtue, destined to become great and honourable in these latter ages. Methinks I see in my mind a noble and puissant nation rousing herself like a strong man after sleep, and shaking her invincible locks. Methinks I see her as an eagle mewing[3] her mighty youth, and kindling her undazzled eyes at the full midday beam; purging and unscaling her long-abused sight at the fountain itself of heavenly radiance; while the whole noise of timorous

[1] *Pyrrhus did* Pyrrhus, King of Epirus (his people are the "Epirots" mentioned later in the paragraph) defeated a Roman army in 280 BCE.

[2] *maniples* Infantry companies in the Roman Army.

[3] *mewing* Renewing, from a term in falconry meaning to moult.

and flocking birds, with those also that love the twilight, flutter about, amazed at what she means, and in their envious gabble would prognosticate a year of sects and schisms.

What would ye do then? Should ye suppress all this flowery crop of knowledge and new light sprung up and yet springing daily in this city? should ye set an oligarchy of twenty engrossers[1] over it, to bring a famine upon our minds again, when we shall know nothing but what is measured to us by their bushel? Believe it, Lords and Commons, they who counsel ye to such a suppressing do as good as bid ye suppress yourselves; and I will soon show how. If it be desired to know the immediate cause of all this free writing and free speaking, there cannot be assigned a truer than your own mild and free and humane government. It is the liberty, Lords and Commons, which your own valorous and happy counsels have purchased us, liberty which is the nurse of all great wits; this is that which hath rarefied and enlightened our spirits like the influence of heaven; this is that which hath enfranchised, enlarged and lifted up our apprehensions degrees above themselves.

Ye cannot make us now less capable, less knowing, less eagerly pursuing of the truth, unless ye first make yourselves, that made us so, less the lovers, less the founders of our true liberty. We can grow ignorant again, brutish, formal and slavish, as ye found us; but you then must first become that which ye cannot be, oppressive, arbitrary and tyrannous, as they were from whom ye have freed us. That our hearts are now more capacious, our thoughts more erected to the search and expectation of greatest and exactest things, is the issue of your own virtue propagated in us; ye cannot suppress that, unless ye reinforce an abrogated and merciless law, that fathers may dispatch at will their own children. And who shall then stick closest to ye, and excite others? not he who takes up arms for coat and conduct and his four nobles of Danegelt.[2] Although I dispraise not the defence of just immunities, yet love my peace better, if

that were all. Give me the liberty to know, to utter, and to argue freely according to conscience, above all liberties. …

For who knows not that Truth is strong, next to the Almighty? She needs no policies, nor stratagems, nor licensings to make her victorious; those are the shifts and the defences that error uses against her power. Give her but room, and do not bind her when she sleeps, for then she speaks not true, as the old Proteus[3] did, who spake oracles only when he was caught and bound, but then rather she turns herself into all shapes, except her own, and perhaps tunes her voice according to the time, as Micaiah did before Ahab,[4] until she be adjured into her own likeness. Yet is it not impossible that she may have more shapes than one. What else is all that rank of things indifferent, wherein Truth may be on this side or on the other, without being unlike herself? What but a vain shadow else is the abolition of those ordinances, that handwriting nailed to the cross? What great purchase is this Christian liberty which Paul so often boasts of? His doctrine is, that he who eats or eats not, regards a day or regards it not, may do either to the Lord. How many other things might be tolerated in peace, and left to conscience, had we but charity, and were it not the chief stronghold of our hypocrisy to be ever judging one another?

I fear yet this iron yoke of outward conformity hath left a slavish print upon our necks; the ghost of a linen decency[5] yet haunts us. We stumble and are impatient at the least dividing of one visible congregation from another, though it be not in fundamentals; and through our forwardness to suppress, and our backwardness to recover any enthralled piece of truth out of the grip of custom, we care not to keep truth separated from truth, which is the fiercest rent and disunion of all. We do not see that, while we still affect by all means a rigid external formality, we may as soon fall again into a gross conforming stupidity, a stark and dead congealment of wood and hay and stubble, forced and frozen together,

---

[1] *engrossers* Monopolists.

[2] *coat and conduct* Tax that provided clothing and transportation of new troops; *noble* Coin worth six shillings eight pence; *Danegelt* Tax known as "ship money," originally levied to support the building of ships with which to oppose invading Danes but controversially resurrected by King Charles I.

[3] *Proteus* Shape-shifting sea deity in Greek mythology.

[4] *Micaiah … Ahab* See 1 Kings 22.9–28.

[5] *linen decency* Referring to the clerical vestments (with linen sleeves) that Archbishop William Laud insisted ministers wear in the interest of conformity.

which is more to the sudden degenerating of a Church than many subdichotomies of petty schisms.

Not that I can think well of every light separation, or that all in a Church is to be expected gold and silver and precious stones: it is not possible for man to sever the wheat from the tares, the good fish from the other fry; that must be the angels' ministry at the end of mortal things. Yet if all cannot be of one mind—as who looks they should be?—this doubtless is more wholesome, more prudent, and more Christian that many be tolerated, rather than all compelled. I mean not tolerated popery, and open superstition, which, as it extirpates all religions and civil supremacies, so itself should be extirpate, provided first that all charitable and compassionate means be used to win and regain the weak and the misled: that also which is impious or evil absolutely either against faith or manners no law can possibly permit, that intends not to unlaw itself: but those neighbouring differences, or rather indifferences, are what I speak of, whether in some point of doctrine or of discipline, which, though they may be many, yet need not interrupt the unity of Spirit, if we could but find among us the bond of peace.

In the meanwhile if any one would write, and bring his helpful hand to the slow-moving Reformation which we labour under, if Truth have spoken to him before others, or but seemed at least to speak, who hath so bejesuited us that we should trouble that man with asking licence to do so worthy a deed? and not consider this, that if it come to prohibiting, there is not aught more likely to be prohibited than truth itself; whose first appearance to our eyes, bleared and dimmed with prejudice and custom, is more unsightly and unplausible than many errors, even as the person is of many a great man slight and contemptible to see to. And what do they tell us vainly of new opinions, when this very opinion of theirs, that none must be heard, but whom they like, is the worst and newest opinion of all others; and is the chief cause why sects and schisms do so much abound, and true knowledge is kept at distance from us; besides yet a greater danger which is in it? ...

And as for regulating the press, let no man think to have the honour of advising ye better than yourselves have done in that Order published next before this, "that no book be printed, unless the printer's and the author's name, or at least the printer's, be registered."[1] Those which otherwise come forth, if they be found mischievous and libellous, the fire and the executioner will be the timeliest and the most effectual remedy that man's prevention can use. For this authentic Spanish policy of licensing books, if I have said aught, will prove the most unlicensed book itself within a short while; and was the immediate image of a Star Chamber decree[2] to that purpose made in those very times when that Court did the rest of those her pious works, for which she is now fallen from the stars with Lucifer. Whereby ye may guess what kind of state prudence, what love of the people, what care of religion or good manners there was at the contriving, although with singular hypocrisy it pretended to bind books to their good behaviour.
—1644

---

[1] *And as for regulating ... be registered*   Milton cites a Parliamentary Order of January 29, 1642.

[2] *Star Chamber decree*   Referring to the 1637 Star Chamber decree for licensing books; the Court of Star Chamber at Westminster Palace was associated with efforts to maintain royal authority before the war, and had been abolished by Parliament in 1641. Milton punningly links the "fallen" Star Chamber with Lucifer, the "morning star" (Isaiah 14.12) and "fallen" angel.

Paradise Lost

While there is some evidence that Milton drafted parts of *Paradise Lost* in the 1640s, he appears to have written most of the poem between about 1658 and about 1663. He thus composed his great epic of human loss followed by the restoration of hope across the Restoration of 1660, an event that marked the collapse of the English Republic and Milton's own hopes for a reformed political and religious structure. *Paradise Lost* was first published in 1667 as a work of ten books. Milton subsequently re-divided the poem (with the original Books 7 and 10 each split into two) and republished it in 1674 as a work in twelve books, thus more closely mirroring the form of Virgil's *Aeneid*. Since Milton had gone completely blind in the early 1650s, he wrote the work through dictation. Interestingly, the one surviving manuscript (which includes only Book 1) reveals that he nevertheless revised with a view to spelling and punctuation.

The epic, written in blank verse (i.e., unrhymed lines of iambic pentameter), draws heavily on classical inspiration and is highly allusive. Scholars estimate that Milton draws on more than 1500 books in *Paradise Lost*, but his primary touchstones are Homer's *Iliad* and *Odyssey*, Virgil's *Aeneid*, Ovid's *Metamorphoses*, Spenser's *Faerie Queene*, and such central works of epic and romance of the European Renaissance as Ludovico Ariosto's *Orlando Furioso*, Torquato Tasso's *Jersualem Delivered*, and Guillaume Du Bartas's *Divine Weeks* (Milton in fact borrows many whole phrases from Joshua Sylvester's 1608 translation of Du Bartas). Milton takes his title from the account in Genesis of the expulsion of humankind from Paradise after Adam and Eve eat from the forbidden Tree of Knowledge. As a retelling of the Biblical Fall, *Paradise Lost* is the best known and most influential literary version of this foundational story of innocence and experience, temptation and expulsion, desire and its consequences.

The poem's dramatic first two books focus not on humanity but on the defeated but still rebellious Satan, cast down from Heaven with his traitor legions for daring to war on God. Satan and his fellows explore Hell, make a home of sorts, and decide to continue their fight with God not in open warfare, but through subverting and corrupting God's new creation, humankind. The rest of *Paradise Lost* follows the enactment of Satan's plan, though in true epic fashion the poem flashes back to the story's beginnings and looks forward to its end, which in this case means the beginning and end of time itself. Critical discussion of the poem has often concerned the extent to which Satan appears to be the driving force behind the epic, sometimes taking as a starting point William Blake's remark that the "reason Milton wrote in fetters when he wrote of Angels & God, and at liberty when of Devils & Hell, is because he was a true Poet and of the Devil's party without knowing it." As a character, Satan is indeed dramatically compelling, if also arguably repellent in his pride and thirst for power: Milton opens his epic by confronting us with the power of the adversary he believed we faced in everyday life. But many readers also find that Satan recedes and shrinks over the whole course of the poem, while Adam and Eve gain in complexity and stature through their conversations with one another and with the angels Raphael and Michael.

The theological heart of *Paradise Lost* is the extended conversation in Book 3 between God and the Son. God addresses the problem of foreknowledge and free will by explaining the central importance in Milton's world of choice and freedom. God anticipates Satan's subsequent actions, yet promises mercy and grace through the Son should humanity fall. In its broad outlines, the theology Milton presents is conventional Christian thought; in some respects though, Milton is less orthodox. His God, for example, is not a Calvinist: there is no predestination in Milton's heaven, because all will hear the call of the Divine, and all those who choose to be saved will be saved. Milton also appears to make the Son subordinate to (rather than co-eternal with) the Father, though scholars argue over the implications (and importance to the poem) of this conception of the divine.

The most frequently debated issue in *Paradise Lost* is probably Milton's depiction of Adam and Eve. Modern readers can feel uncomfortable with the explicit subordination of women in some passages, particularly those that draw on St. Paul's injunctions from the New Testament. Are these moments to be taken as representing the views of Adam, of Raphael, of Milton, or of God? In other passages, however, *Paradise Lost* gives Eve a greater personal, political, and theological equality than she had ever been accorded: in Book 10 in particular, Eve's actions give her a good claim to be the poem's true hero. She even gives names to some of God's creation, a sign of power and capacity to rule that the Bible itself reserves only for Adam. On the subject of Eve, the poem speaks with two voices, and Milton invites readers to work through the implications of the ways Adam and Eve are presented as man and woman, as husband and wife, as humanity in general, and even as different aspects of the individual human psyche.

Despite its daunting erudition and older poetics, *Paradise Lost* still speaks powerfully and directly to modern readers. As Johnson, Coleridge, and many others have pointed out, the verbal acrobatics of the poem may occasionally frustrate, but vested in them is also the capacity to astonish. And the rich poetic texture of the full poem retains the capacity to provoke intellectual inquiry not only concerning theology and gender, but also concerning the human condition, religious faith, responsibility and heroism, politics and hierarchy, and the limits that may exist on the pursuit of knowledge and freedom.

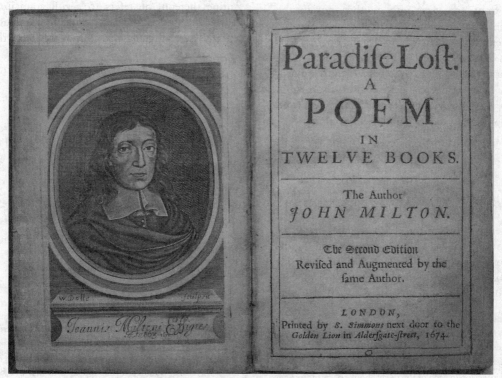

Title page of the 1674 edition of *Paradise Lost*.

from *Paradise Lost*

THE VERSE

The measure is English heroic verse without rhyme,[1] as that of Homer in Greek, and Virgil in Latin; rhyme being no necessary adjunct or true ornament of poem or good verse, in longer works especially, but the invention of a barbarous age, to set off wretched matter and lame metre; graced indeed since by the use of some famous modern poets, carried away by custom, but much to their own vexation, hindrance, and constraint to express many things otherwise, and for the most part worse then else they would have expressed them. Not without cause therefore some both Italian, and Spanish poets of prime note have rejected rhyme both in longer and shorter works, as have also long since our best English tragedies, as a thing of itself, to all judicious ears, trivial, and of no true musical delight; which consists only in apt numbers, fit quantity of syllables, and the sense variously drawn out from one verse into another, not in the jingling sound of like endings, a fault avoided by the learned ancients both in poetry and all good oratory. This neglect then of rhyme so little is to be taken for a defect, though it may seem so perhaps to vulgar readers, that it rather is to be esteemed an example set, the first in English, of ancient liberty recovered to heroic poem from the troublesome and modern bondage of rhyming.

ARGUMENT TO BOOK 1[2]

This first book proposes first in brief the whole subject, man's disobedience, and the loss thereupon of Paradise wherein he was placed: then touches the prime cause of his fall, the serpent, or rather Satan in the serpent; who revolting from God, and drawing to his side many legions of angels, was by the command of God driven out of Heaven with all his crew into the great

deep. Which action past over, the poem hastes into the midst of things, presenting Satan with his angels now fallen into Hell, described here, not in the center (for Heaven and Earth may be supposed as yet not made, certainly not yet accurst) but in a place of utter darkness, fitliest called Chaos: here Satan with his angels lying on the burning lake, thunder-struck and astonished, after a certain space recovers, as from confusion, calls up him who next in order and dignity lay by him; they confer of their miserable fall. Satan awakens all his legions, who lay till then in the same manner confounded; they rise, their numbers, array of battle, their chief leaders named, according to the idols known afterwards in Canaan and the countries adjoining. To these Satan directs his speech, comforts them with hope yet of regaining Heaven, but tells them lastly of a new world and new kind of creature to be created, according to an ancient prophesy or report in Heaven; for that angels were long before this visible creation, was the opinion of many ancient Fathers. To find out the truth of this prophesy, and what to determine thereon, he refers to a full council. What his associates thence attempt. Pandemonium the palace of Satan rises, suddenly built out of the deep: the infernal peers there sit in council.

BOOK 1

Of Mans First Disobedience, and the Fruit
Of that Forbidden Tree, whose mortal tast
Brought Death into the World, and all our woe,
With loss of *Eden,* till one greater Man[3]
5 Restore us, and regain the blissful Seat,
Sing Heav'nly Muse,[4] that on the secret° top *hidden*
Of *Oreb,* or of *Sinai,*[5] didst inspire
That Shepherd,[6] who first taught the chosen Seed,[7]

— original spelling —

---

[1] *English … rhyme* Verse suited to the treatment of heroic or elevated themes; i.e., blank verse in iambic pentameter.

[2] *Argument to Book 1* The Arguments are Milton's own prose summaries of the action in each of the twelve books of *Paradise Lost.* They did not appear in the first edition, but Milton added them in 1668, apparently at the request of his printer.

[3] *one greater Man* Christ, in this poem, or here, the Son of God.

[4] *Heav'nly Muse* Urania, Muse of astronomy and hence religious poetry.

[5] *Of Oreb, or of Sinai* God delivered the Ten Commandments to Moses on the summit either of Mount Horeb (Deuteronomy 4.10) or Mount Sinai (Exodus 19.10).

[6] *That Shepherd* Moses, who was tending the sheep of his father-in-law, Jethro, when God first appeared to him as a burning bush (Exodus 3.1–4).

[7] *the chosen Seed* The Jewish people. See Deuteronomy 6.6–8.

In the Beginning how the Heav'ns and Earth
10 Rose out of *Chaos*. Or if *Sion* Hill[1]
Delight thee more, and *Siloa's* Brook[2] that flow'd
Fast by the Oracle of God; I thence
Invoke thy[3] aid to my adventrous Song,
That with no middle° flight intends to soar   *mediocre*
15 Above th' *Aonian* Mount,[4] while it pursues
Things unattempted yet in Prose or Rhime.
And chiefly Thou O Spirit, that dost prefer
Before all Temples th' upright heart and pure,
Instruct me, for Thou know'st; Thou from the first
20 Wast present, and with mighty wings outspread
Dove-like satst brooding on the vast Abyss
And mad'st it pregnant:[5] What in me is dark
Illumine, what is low raise and support;
That to the highth of this great Argument
25 I may assert th' Eternal Providence,
And justifie the wayes of God to men.

Say first—for Heav'n hides nothing from thy view,
Nor the deep tract of Hell—say first what cause
Moved our grand parents,[6] in that happy state,[7]
30 Favoured of Heav'n so highly, to fall off
From their Creator, and transgress His will
For one restraint,[8] lords of the world besides.
Who first seduced them to that foul revolt?
Th' infernal Serpent; he it was whose guile,
35 Stirred up with envy and revenge, deceived
The mother of mankind, what time[9] his pride

original spelling

Had cast him out from Heav'n, with all his host
Of rebel angels, by whose aid, aspiring
To set himself in glory above his peers,
40 He trusted to have equalled the Most High,
If he opposed, and with ambitious aim
Against the throne and monarchy of God,
Raised impious war in Heav'n and battle proud,
With vain attempt. Him the Almighty Power
45 Hurled headlong flaming from th' ethereal sky,
With hideous ruin and combustion, down
To bottomless perdition, there to dwell
In adamantine° chains and penal fire,   *unbreakable*
Who dared defy th' Omnipotent to arms.
50 Nine times the space that measures day and night
To mortal men, he, with his horrid crew,
Lay vanquished, rolling in the fiery gulf,
Confounded, though immortal. But his doom
Reserved him to more wrath;[10] for now the thought
55 Both of lost happiness and lasting pain
Torments him: round he throws his baleful eyes,
That witnessed huge affliction and dismay,
Mixed with obdurate pride and steadfast hate.
At once, as far as angels ken,° he views   *can see*
60 The dismal situation waste and wild.
A dungeon horrible, on all sides round,
As one great furnace flamed; yet from those flames
No light; but rather darkness visible
Served only to discover sights of woe,
65 Regions of sorrow, doleful shades, where peace
And rest can never dwell, hope never comes
That comes to all, but torture without end
Still urges, and a fiery deluge,° fed   *downpour*
With ever-burning sulphur unconsumed.
70 Such place Eternal Justice has prepared
For those rebellious; here their prison ordained
In utter darkness, and their portion set,
As far removed from God and light of Heav'n
As from the centre thrice to the utmost pole.[11]
75 Oh how unlike the place from whence they fell!
There the companions of his fall, overwhelmed

---

[1] *Sion Hill* Mount Zion, a sacred mountain, site of Solomon's temple and a seat of religious and secular law (Isaiah 2.3).

[2] *Siloa's Brook* The pool of Siloam in the Temple at Jerusalem, mentioned first in Nehemiah 3.15, then used by Jesus to restore a blind man's sight in John 9.1–12.

[3] *thy* I.e., Urania/God.

[4] *th' Aonian Mount* Helicon, a mountain in central Greece sacred to the Muses, and one of their homes.

[5] *O Spirit … pregnant* The Holy Spirit, specifically in its generative aspect.

[6] *our grand parents* Adam and Eve.

[7] *in that happy state* Simultaneously the state of innocence and the state, or country, of Eden.

[8] *one restraint* God's admonition against eating from the Tree of Knowledge of Good and Evil (Genesis 2.17).

[9] *what time* "When" or "by which time."

---

[10] *Reserved him to more wrath* Gave Satan yet more pain.

[11] *As far removed … utmost pole* In Homer, Hades was as far below Earth as Heaven was above; in Virgil, Tartarus was twice as far below. Milton overdoes his classical predecessors by placing Hell three times as far from Heaven as Earth is.

With floods and whirlwinds of tempestuous fire,
He soon discerns; and, weltering° by his side,   *rolling*
One next himself in power, and next in crime,
80   Long after known in Palestine, and named
Beelzebub.[1] To whom th' arch-enemy,
And thence in Heaven called Satan,[2] with bold words
Breaking the horrid silence, thus began:—
    "If thou beest he—but O how fall'n! How changed
85   From him who, in the happy realms of light
Clothed with transcendent brightness, didst outshine
Myriads, though bright!—if he whom mutual league,
United thoughts and counsels, equal hope
And hazard in the glorious enterprise
90   Joined with me once, now misery hath joined
In equal ruin; into what pit thou seest
From what height fall'n: so much the stronger proved
He with his thunder; and till then who knew
The force of those dire arms? Yet not for those,
95   Nor what the potent Victor in his rage
Can else inflict, do I repent, or change,
Though changed in outward lustre, that fixed mind,
And high disdain from sense of injured merit,
That with the mightiest raised me to contend,
100   And to the fierce contentions brought along
Innumerable force of Spirits armed,
That dared dislike His reign, and, me preferring,
His utmost power with adverse power opposed
In dubious° battle on the plains of Heaven,   *uncertain*
105   And shook His throne. What though the field be lost?
All is not lost—the unconquerable will,
And study of revenge, immortal hate,
And courage never to submit or yield:
And what is else not to be overcome?
110   That glory never shall His wrath or might
Extort from me. To bow and sue for grace
With suppliant knee, and deify His power
Who, from the terror of this arm, so late
Doubted His empire—that were low indeed;
115   That were an ignominy and shame beneath
This downfall; since, by fate, the strength of gods,
And this empyreal° substance, cannot fail;   *celestial*

Since, through experience of this great event,
In arms not worse, in foresight much advanced,
120   We may with more successful hope resolve
To wage by force or guile eternal war,
Irreconcilable to our grand foe,
Who now triumphs, and in th' excess of joy
Sole reigning holds the tyranny of Heaven."
125   So spake th' apostate[3] angel, though in pain,
Vaunting° aloud, but racked with deep despair;   *bragging*
And him thus answered soon his bold compeer:[4]
    "O Prince, O Chief of many thronèd powers
That led th' embattled seraphim[5] to war
130   Under thy conduct, and, in dreadful deeds
Fearless, endangered Heav'n's perpetual king,
And put to proof his high supremacy,
Whether upheld by strength, or chance, or fate,
Too well I see and rue the dire event
135   That, with sad overthrow and foul defeat,
Hath lost us Heav'n, and all this mighty host
In horrible destruction laid thus low,
As far as gods and heavenly essences
Can perish: for the mind and spirit remains
140   Invincible, and vigour soon returns,
Though all our glory extinct, and happy state
Here swallowed up in endless misery.
But what if He our conqueror (whom I now
Of force[6] believe almighty, since no less
145   Than such could have o'erpow'red such force as ours)
Have left us this our spirit and strength entire,
Strongly to suffer and support our pains,
That we may so suffice His vengeful ire,
Or do Him mightier service as His thralls
150   By right of war, whatever His business be,
Here in the heart of Hell to work in fire,
Or do His errands in the gloomy deep?
What can it then avail though yet we feel
Strength undiminished, or eternal being

---

1   *Beelzebub*   Hebrew for Lord of the Flies, the name is an alteration of Baal, historically the chief male god of Phoenicia and Canaan.

2   *And thence in Heaven called Satan*   Satan is the English transliteration of the Hebrew word for "adversary."

3   *apostate*   One who has abandoned one's faith.

4   *compeer*   Fellow comrade.

5   *embattled seraphim*   Rebelling or persecuted seraphim. Seraphim are the highest-ranked angels in traditional angelology.

6   *Of force*   Of necessity, per force.

155 To undergo eternal punishment?"[1]
Whereto with speedy words the archfiend replied:
  "Fall'n cherub, to be weak is miserable,
Doing or suffering: but of this be sure—
To do aught° good never will be our task,   *nothing*
160 But ever to do ill our sole delight,
As being the contrary to His high will
Whom we resist. If then His Providence
Out of our evil seek to bring forth good,
Our labour must be to pervert that end,
165 And out of good still to find means of evil;
Which oft times may succeed so as perhaps
Shall grieve Him, if I fail not, and disturb
His inmost counsels from their destined aim.
But see! The angry Victor hath recalled
170 His ministers of vengeance and pursuit
Back to the gates of Heav'n: the sulphurous hail,
Shot after us in storm, o'erblown has laid
The fiery surge[2] that from the precipice
Of Heav'n received us falling;[3] and the thunder,
175 Winged with red lightning and impetuous rage,
Perhaps hath spent his shafts, and ceases now
To bellow through the vast and boundless deep.
Let us not slip° th' occasion, whether scorn   *miss*
Or satiate° fury yield it from our Foe.   *satisfied*
180 Seest thou yon dreary plain, forlorn and wild,
The seat of desolation, void of light,
Save what the glimmering of these livid flames
Casts pale and dreadful? Thither let us tend[4]
From off the tossing of these fiery waves;
185 There rest, if any rest can harbour there;
And, re-assembling our afflicted powers,
Consult how we may henceforth most offend
Our enemy, our own loss how repair,
How overcome this dire calamity,
190 What reinforcement we may gain from hope,

If not, what resolution from despair."
  Thus Satan, talking to his nearest mate,
With head uplift above the wave, and eyes
That sparkling blazed; his other parts besides
195 Prone on the flood, extended long and large,
Lay floating many a rood,[5] in bulk as huge
As whom the fables name of monstrous size,
Titanian or Earth-born, that warred on Jove,
Briareos or Typhon,[6] whom the den
200 By ancient Tarsus[7] held, or that sea-beast
Leviathan,[8] which God of all His works
Created hugest that swim th' ocean stream.
Him, haply slumbering on the Norway foam,
The pilot of some small night-foundered[9] skiff,
205 Deeming some island, oft, as seamen tell,
With fixèd anchor in his scaly rind,
Moors by his side under the lee, while night
Invests the sea, and wishèd morn delays.
So stretched out huge in length the arch-fiend lay,
210 Chained on the burning lake; nor ever thence
Had ris'n, or heaved his head, but that the will
And high permission of all-ruling Heaven
Left him at large to his own dark designs,
That with reiterated crimes he might
215 Heap on himself damnation, while he sought
Evil to others, and enraged might see
How all his malice served but to bring forth
Infinite goodness, grace, and mercy, shown
On Man by him seduced, but on himself
220 Treble° confusion, wrath, and vengeance poured. *tripled*
Forthwith upright he rears from off the pool
His mighty stature; on each hand the flames
Driven backward slope their pointing spires, and rolled
In billows, leave i' th' midst a horrid vale.
225 Then with expanded wings he steers his flight

---

1 *What can it … eternal punishment*   What good can it do that we don't feel any weaker, or that since we're immortal our punishment can never end?

2 *surge*   Surf, especially a rolling swell.

3 *the sulphurous hail … received us falling*   Satan is pointing out that the fiery lake they fell into in Hell was the product of the fiery hail Heaven shot after them, which passed them and filled the basin below them.

4 *Thither let us tend*   Let us go there.

5 *rood*   Unit of linear measurement from 5.5 to 8 yards long.

6 *Titanian … Typhon*   In Greek mythology, the Titans (children of the sky and earth) and the giants, including Briareos and Typhon, fought and were defeated by Zeus (Jupiter/Jove).

7 *Tarsus*   Ancient city in Southern Turkey.

8 *Leviathan*   Mythological sea creature, supposed to be the largest creature in all creation; mentioned in Job 41.1–8 to illustrate the enormity of God's power, and mentioned in Isaiah 27 as defeated by the promised Messiah.

9 *night-foundered*   Sinking at night.

Aloft, incumbent on the dusky air,
That felt unusual weight; till on dry land
He lights°—if it were land that ever burned   *alights*
With solid, as the lake with liquid fire,
230   And such appeared in hue as when the force
Of subterranean wind transports a hill
Torn from Pelorus, or the shattered side
Of thundering Etna,[1] whose combustible
And fuelled entrails, thence conceiving fire,
235   Sublimed with mineral fury, aid the winds,
And leave a singèd bottom all involved
With stench and smoke. Such resting found the sole
Of unblessèd feet. Him followed his next mate;
Both glorying to have scaped the Stygian[2] flood
240   As gods, and by their own recovered strength,
Not by the suff'rance of supernal° power.   *celestial*
     "Is this the region, this the soil, the clime,"
Said then the lost archangel, "this the seat
That we must change for Heav'n? This mournful gloom
245   For that celestial light? Be it so, since He
Who now is sovereign can dispose and bid
What shall be right: farthest from Him is best
Whom reason has equalled, force has made supreme
Above His equals. Farewell, happy fields,
250   Where joy forever dwells! Hail, horrors! Hail,
Infernal world! And thou, profoundest Hell,
Receive thy new possessor—one who brings
A mind not to be changed by place or time.
The mind is its own place, and in itself
255   Can make a Heav'n of Hell, a Hell of Heav'n.
What matter where, if I be still the same,
And what I should be, all but less than He
Whom thunder hath made greater? Here at least
We shall be free; th' Almighty hath not built
260   Here for His envy, will not drive us hence:
Here we may reign secure; and, in my choice,
To reign is worth ambition, though in Hell:
Better to reign in Hell than serve in Heav'n.
But wherefore let we then our faithful friends,
265   Th' associates and co-partners of our loss,

Lie thus astonished on th' oblivious pool,
And call them not to share with us their part
In this unhappy mansion, or once more
With rallied arms to try what may be yet
270   Regained in Heaven, or what more lost in Hell?"
     So Satan spake; and him Beelzebub
Thus answered: "Leader of those armies bright
Which, but th' Omnipotent, none could have foiled!
If once they hear that voice, their liveliest pledge
275   Of hope in fears and dangers—heard so oft
In worst extremes, and on the perilous edge
Of battle, when it raged, in all assaults
Their surest signal—they will soon resume
New courage and revive, though now they lie
280   Grovelling and prostrate on yon lake of fire,
As we erewhile, astounded and amazed;
No wonder, fall'n such a pernicious height!"
     He scarce had ceased when the superior fiend
Was moving toward the shore; his ponderous shield,
285   Ethereal temper,° massy, large, and round,   *strength*
Behind him cast.[3] The broad circumference
Hung on his shoulders like the moon, whose orb
Through optic glass[4] the Tuscan artist[5] views
At ev'ning, from the top of Fesolé,[6]
290   Or in Valdarno,[7] to descry new lands,
Rivers, or mountains, in her spotty globe.
His spear—to equal which the tallest pine
Hewn on Norwegian hills, to be the mast
Of some great ammiral,[8] were but a wand
295   He walked with, to support uneasy steps
Over the burning marl,° not like those steps   *soil*
On Heaven's azure; and the torrid clime
Smote on him sore besides, vaulted with fire.
Natheless° he so endured, till on the beach   *nevertheless*
300   Of that inflamèd sea he stood, and called
His legions—angel forms, who lay entranced
Thick as autumnal leaves that strew the brooks

---

[1]   *Pelorus ... thundering Etna*   Cape Pelorus in Sicily, located near volcanic Mount Etna.

[2]   *Stygian*   I.e., like the river Styx, a river that the dead must cross in order to enter the underworld. The word connotes the river's location in the underworld, but also implies bleakness and darkness.

[3]   *Behind him cast*   Satan wears his shield slung across his back.

[4]   *optic glass*   Telescope.

[5]   *the Tuscan artist*   Galileo (1564–1652), the only contemporary mentioned in the poem.

[6]   *Fesolé*   Fiesole, a town just outside Florence, Italy.

[7]   *Valdarno*   Arno Valley, the valley in which Florence is located.

[8]   *ammiral*   Admiral's flagship. This spelling was standard at the time, and refers specifically to a first-rate ship of the fleet.

In Vallombrosa,[1] where th' Etrurian shades
High over-arched embower;[2] or scattered sedge
305 Afloat, when with fierce winds Orion[3] armed
Hath vexed the Red Sea coast, whose waves o'erthrew
Busiris and his Memphian chivalry,[4]
While with perfidious hatred they pursued
The sojourners of Goshen,[5] who beheld
310 From the safe shore their floating carcasses
And broken chariot wheels. So thick bestrewn,
Abject and lost, lay these, covering the flood,
Under amazement of their hideous change.
He called so loud that all the hollow deep
315 Of Hell resounded: "Princes, potentates,
Warriors, the flower of Heav'n once yours; now lost,
If such astonishment as this can seize
Eternal spirits! Or have ye chos'n this place
After the toil of battle to repose
320 Your wearied virtue, for the ease you find
To slumber here, as in the vales of Heav'n?
Or in this abject posture have ye sworn
To adore the conqueror who now beholds
Cherub and seraph rolling in the flood
325 With scattered arms and ensigns,° till anon   flags
His swift pursuers from Heaven-gates discern
Th' advantage, and descending, tread us down
Thus drooping, or with linkèd thunderbolts
Transfix us to the bottom of this gulf?
330 Awake, arise, or be forever fall'n!"
      They heard, and were abashed, and up they sprung
Upon the wing, as when men wont to watch
On duty, sleeping found by whom they dread,
Rouse and bestir themselves ere well awake.
335 Nor did they not perceive the evil plight
In which they were, or the fierce pains not feel;

Yet to their General's voice they soon obeyed
Innumerable. As when the potent rod
Of Amram's son, in Egypt's evil day,
340 Waved round the coast, up-called a pitchy cloud
Of locusts, warping on the eastern wind,
That o'er the realm of impious Pharaoh hung
Like Night, and darkened all the land of Nile;[6]
So numberless were those bad angels seen
345 Hovering on wing under the cope° of Hell,   vault, canopy
'Twixt upper, nether,° and surrounding fires;   lower
Till, as a signal giv'n, th' uplifted spear
Of their great sultan waving to direct
Their course, in even balance down they light
350 On the firm brimstone, and fill all the plain:
A multitude like which the populous North
Poured never from her frozen loins to pass
Rhene or the Danaw,[7] when her barbarous sons
Came like a deluge on the south, and spread
355 Beneath Gibraltar to the Libyan sands.
Forthwith, form every squadron and each band,
The heads and leaders thither haste where stood
Their great commander—godlike shapes, and forms
Excelling human; princely dignities;
360 And powers that erst° in Heav'n sat on thrones, formerly
Though on their names in heav'nly records now
Be no memorial, blotted out and razed
By their rebellion from the books of life.[8]
Nor had they yet among the sons of Eve
365 Got them new names, till, wand'ring ov'r the earth,
Through God's high sufferance for the trial of man,
By falsities and lies the greatest part
Of mankind they corrupted to forsake
God their Creator, and th' invisible
370 Glory of Him that made them to transform
Oft to the image of a brute, adorned
With gay religions full of pomp and gold,
And devils to adore for deities:
Then were they known to men by various names,
375 And various idols through the heathen world.

---

[1] *Vallombrosa* Valley near Florence famous for its arboreal displays; literally, valley of shadow or shadowed valley.

[2] *where th' Etrurian … embower* Where the leaves of Etruria arch high and densely overhead. Etruria was an ancient region in west-central Italy, the seat of the Etruscan empire.

[3] *Orion* Great hunter whom Diana loved but killed in error and then had made into a constellation in the Northern sky; its appearance above the horizon heralds winter.

[4] *Busiris and his Memphian chivalry* Pharaoh and his horsemen or charioteers, stymied by Moses's parting of the Red Sea (Exodus 14.21–31).

[5] *sojourners of Goshen* Israelites who fled Egypt with Moses.

---

[6] *As when the potent … land of Nile* Moses was the son of Amram; God's command to him to reach out with his staff (or rod) summoned the plague of locusts to afflict Egypt (Exodus 10.12–20).

[7] *Rhene or the Danaw* Rhine and Danube Rivers.

[8] *books of life* Books in which are written all the names of God's faithful (Exodus 32.32–33).

Say, Muse, their names then known, who first, who last,
Roused from the slumber on that fiery couch,
At their great emperor's call, as next in worth
Came singly where he stood on the bare strand,
380　While the promiscuous crowd stood yet aloof?
The chief were those who, from the pit of Hell
Roaming to seek their prey on Earth, dared fix
Their seats, long after, next the seat of God,
Their altars by His altar, gods adored
385　Among the nations round, and dared abide
Jehovah thundering out of Sion, throned
Between the cherubim; yea, often placed
Within His sanctuary itself their shrines,
Abominations; and with cursèd things
390　His holy rites and solemn feasts profaned,
And with their darkness dared affront His light.
First, Moloch,[1] horrid king, besmeared with blood
Of human sacrifice, and parents' tears;
Though, for the noise of drums and
　　　　timbrels° loud,　　　　　　　　　　*small hand drums*
395　Their children's cries unheard that passed through fire
To his grim idol. Him the Ammonite[2]
Worshiped in Rabba and her watery plain,
In Argob and in Basan, to the stream
Of utmost Arnon.[3] Nor content with such
400　Audacious neighbourhood, the wisest heart
Of Solomon he led by fraud to build
His temple right against the temple of God
On that opprobrious hill, and made his grove
The pleasant valley of Hinnom,[4] Tophet[5] thence
405　And black Gehenna[6] called, the type of Hell.

Next Chemos,[7] th' obscene dread of Moab's[8] sons,
From Aroar to Nebo and the wild
Of southmost Abarim; in Hesebon
And Horonaim, Seon's realm, beyond
410　The flow'ry dale of Sibma clad with vines,
And Eleale to th' Asphaltic Pool:[9]
Peor[10] his other name, when he enticed
Israel in Sittim,[11] on their march from Nile,
To do him wanton rites, which cost them woe.
415　Yet thence his lustful orgies he enlarged
Even to that hill of scandal, by the grove
Of Moloch homicide, lust hard by hate,
Till good Josiah[12] drove them thence to Hell.
With these came they who, from the bordering flood
420　Of old Euphrates to the brook that parts
Egypt from Syrian ground, had general names
Of Baalim[13] and Ashtaroth[14]—those male,
These feminine. For spirits, when they please,
Can either sex assume, or both; so soft
425　And uncompounded° is their essence pure,　　　　*unalloyed*
Not tried or manacled with joint or limb,
Nor founded on the brittle strength of bones,
Like cumbrous flesh; but, in what shape they choose,
Dilated or condensed, bright or obscure,
430　Can execute their airy purposes,
And works of love or enmity fulfil.
For those the race of Israel oft forsook
Their living strength,[15] and unfrequented left

---

[1]　*Moloch*　Heathen god worshipped by sacrificing children in ovens or flame; his name means king or monarch.

[2]　*Ammonite*　Biblical enemies of the Israelites.

[3]　*Rabba … Argob … Basan … Arnon*　Lands east of the Dead Sea, in present-day Jordan.

[4]　*Hinnom*　Valley west and southwest of Jerusalem, mentioned in the Bible as a place of child sacrifice.

[5]　*Tophet*　City in the valley Hinnom where children of the Israelites were sacrificed in flame.

[6]　*Gehenna*　Because of the sacrifice of Israelite children at Tophet in Hinnom, Gehenna (a transliteration of the Hebrew for the place-name) became the New Testament word for Hell.

[7]　*Chemos*　God of war worshipped by the Moabites.

[8]　*Moab*　Biblical country east of the Dead Sea. The place names that follow are all associated with Moab in various books of the Old Testament.

[9]　*Asphaltic Pool*　Dead Sea.

[10]　*Peor*　Diminutive form of Baal-Peor, a Moabite god who appeared both as a sun god and moon goddess.

[11]　*Sittim*　Site of the last camp of the Israelites before they entered Canaan and were suborned by Baal-Peor (Numbers 25).

[12]　*Josiah*　Biblical King of Judah who renewed his people's covenant with God and ruined heathen temples (2 Kings 23).

[13]　*Baalim*　Hebrew: collective term for Phoenician and Canaanite sun gods.

[14]　*Ashtaroth*　Collective term for variants of Ashtoreth, or Ishtar, a goddess of love, fertility, and war worshipped throughout the Middle East; her classical equivalent is Venus.

[15]　*living strength*　I.e., God.

His righteous altar, bowing lowly down
435 To bestial gods; for which their heads as low
Bowed down in battle, sunk before the spear
Of despicable foes. With these in troop
Came Astoreth, whom the Phoenicians called
Astarte, queen of Heaven, with crescent horns;
440 To whose bright image nightly by the moon
Sidonian[1] virgins paid their vows and songs;
In Sion also not unsung, where stood
Her temple on th' offensive mountain, built
By that uxorious king whose heart, though large,
445 Beguiled by fair idolatresses, fell
To idols foul.[2] Thammuz came next behind,
Whose annual wound in Lebanon allured
The Syrian damsels to lament his fate
In amorous ditties all a summer's day,
450 While smooth Adonis from his native rock
Ran purple to the sea, supposed with blood
Of Thammuz yearly wounded:[3] the love-tale
Infected Sion's daughters with like heat,
Whose wanton passions in the sacred porch
455 Ezekiel saw, when, by the vision led,
His eye surveyed the dark idolatries
Of alienated Judah.[4] Next came one
Who mourned in earnest, when the captive ark
Maimed his brute image, head and hands lopped off,
460 In his own temple, on the groundsel-edge,° *threshold*
Where he fell flat and shamed his worshippers:[5]
Dagon his name, sea-monster, upward man
And downward fish; yet had his temple high
Reared in Azotus, dreaded through the coast
465 Of Palestine, in Gath and Ascalon,

And Accaron[6] and Gaza's frontier bounds.
Him followed Rimmon,[7] whose delightful seat
Was fair Damascus, on the fertile banks
Of Abbana and Pharphar, lucid streams.
470 He also against the house of God was bold:
A leper once he lost, and gained a king—
Ahaz,[8] his sottish conqueror, whom he drew
God's altar to disparage and displace
For one of Syrian mode, whereon to burn
475 His odious offerings, and adore the gods
Whom he had vanquished. After these appeared
A crew who, under names of old renown,
Osiris, Isis, Orus,[9] and their train,
With monstrous shapes and sorceries abused
480 Fanatic Egypt and her priests to seek
Their wandering gods disguised in brutish forms[10]
Rather than human. Nor did Israel scape
Th' infection, when their borrowed gold composed
The calf in Oreb;[11] and the rebel king
485 Doubled that sin in Bethel and in Dan,[12]
Lik'ning his maker to the grazèd ox,
Jehovah, who in one night, when he passed
From Egypt marching, equalled with one stroke

---

[1] *Sidonian* From Sidonia, a Biblical country north of the Dead Sea, between modern day Lebanon and Syria.

[2] *that uxorious king … idols foul* King Solomon.

[3] *Thammuz came next … yearly wounded* Thammuz's consort of Astarte, identified with the Greek god Adonis. His sacred river runs reddish-purple yearly with silt, marking his feast and commemorating his mortal wounding by a wild boar.

[4] *Whose wanton passions … alienated Judah* See Ezekiel's vision of faithless Israelites in Ezekiel 8.9–15.

[5] *the captive ark … worshippers* After the Philistines captured the Ark of the Covenant and brought it back to the temple of Dagon, the statue of Dagon fell and broke into pieces (1 Samuel 5.1–5).

[6] *Azotus* Philistine city northeast of Gaza, also called Ashdod; *Gath* Now thought to be located at modern Tel es-Safi, west of Jerusalem; *Ascalon* Now called Ashkelon, located southwest of Ashdod; *Accaron* Modern Tel Miqne, located approximately twenty-five miles west of Jerusalem; these four cities plus Gaza were the five major cities of the Philistines.

[7] *Rimmon* Ancient Syrian storm god.

[8] *Ahaz* Also known as Ahaziah, a wicked apostate king of the Israelites (1 Kings 22.51–53, 2 Kings 1.1–17).

[9] *Osiris* Ancient Egyptian chief god, judge of the dead; *Isis* Wife of Osiris and goddess of fertility; *Orus* Horus, ancient Egyptian God of the sun, revenge, and war, son of Osiris and Isis.

[10] *disguised in brutish forms* Ancient Egyptian gods were depicted as having animal heads.

[11] *The calf in Oreb* While waiting for Moses to return from his mountaintop meeting with God, his brother Aaron crafted a golden calf, and the Israelites began to worship it as an idol (Exodus 32).

[12] *the rebel king … and in Dan* Jeroboam is the rebel king who, with the ten tribes of Israel, overthrew King Rehoboam, the son of Solomon (1 Kings 11). He set up two golden bull idols, saying "It is too much for you to go up to Jerusalem. Here are your gods, O Israel, who brought you up out of Egypt" (1 Kings 12.28).

Both her first-born and all her bleating gods.[1]

490 Belial[2] came last; than whom a Spirit more lewd
Fell not from Heaven, or more gross to love
Vice for itself. To him no temple stood
Or altar smoked; yet who more oft than he
In temples and at altars, when the priest

495 Turns atheist, as did Eli's sons,[3] who filled
With lust and violence the house of God?
In courts and palaces he also reigns,
And in luxurious cities, where the noise
Of riot ascends above their loftiest tow'rs,

500 And injury and outrage; and, when night
Darkens the streets, then wander forth the sons
Of Belial,[4] flown° with insolence and wine.   *delirious*
Witness the streets of Sodom,[5] and that night
In Gibeah, when the hospitable door

505 Exposed a matron, to avoid worse rape.[6]
These were the prime in order and in might:
The rest were long to tell; though far renowned
Th' Ionian° gods—of Javan's[7] issue held   *Greek*
Gods, yet confessed later than Heav'n and Earth,

510 Their boasted parents; Titan, Heav'n's first-born,
With his enormous brood, and birthright seized
By younger Saturn: he from mightier Jove,
His own and Rhea's son, like measure found;
So Jove usurping reigned. These, first in Crete

515 And Ida[8] known, thence on the snowy top
Of cold Olympus ruled the middle air,

Their highest Heav'n; or on the Delphian cliff,[9]
Or in Dodona,[10] and through all the bounds
Of Doric° land; or who with Saturn old   *Greek*

520 Fled over Adria to th' Hesperian fields,
And o'er the Celtic roamed the utmost isles.[11]
All these and more came flocking; but with looks
Downcast and damp; yet such wherein appeared
Obscure some glimpse of joy to have found their chief

525 Not in despair, to have found themselves not lost
In loss itself; which on his count'nance cast
Like doubtful hue. But he, his wonted pride
Soon recollecting, with high words, that bore
Semblance of worth, not substance, gently raised

530 Their fainting courage, and dispelled their fears.
Then straight commands that, at the warlike sound
Of trumpets loud and clarions, be upreared
His mighty standard. That proud honour claimed
Azazel[12] as his right, a cherub tall:

535 Who forthwith from the glittering staff unfurled
Th' imperial ensign; which, full high advanced,
Shone like a meteor streaming to the wind,
With gems and golden lustre rich emblazed,
Seraphic arms and trophies; all the while

540 Sonorous metal blowing martial sounds:
At which the universal host up-sent
A shout that tore Hell's concave,[13] and beyond
Frighted the reign of chaos and old night.
All in a moment through the gloom were seen

545 Ten thousand banners rise into the air,
With orient° colours waving: with them rose   *exotic*
A forest huge of spears; and thronging helms
Appeared, and serried° shields in thick array   *crowded*
Of depth immeasurable. Anon they move

550 In perfect phalanx to the Dorian mood[14]

---

[1] *Jehovah … her bleating gods*   Jehovah in one night ravaged Egypt and its gods by slaying Egypt's firstborn sons (see Exodus 12:29–33).

[2] *Belial*   Personification of defilement, fornication, and wealth. Here a devil; originally a Hebrew word for worthlessness.

[3] *Eli's sons*   Eli, the man who raised Samuel in the temple; he had two sons who were lustful and who seduced members of the congregation (1 Samuel 2.12–25).

[4] *sons / Of Belial*   I.e., drunken rioters and lechers.

[5] *Sodom*   Biblical city that epitomized wickedness and debauchery, destroyed by God (Genesis 19.27–28).

[6] *that night … worse rape*   Biblical incident in which a group who demanded to rape an Israelite man traveling through Gibeah settled instead for raping and killing his concubine, whose master then killed her. See Judges 19.16–30.

[7] *Javan*   Grandson of Noah.

[8] *Ida*   Highest mountain in Crete.

[9] *Delphian cliff*   Site of ancient Greece's most important Oracle.

[10] *Dodona*   The most ancient Greek oracular site.

[11] *Adria*   The Adriatic Sea; *Hesperian fields* Italy; *Celtic* France; *utmost isles* Far reaches of Scotland and Ireland.

[12] *Azazel*   Hebrew: scapegoat. Mentioned in Leviticus 16, this name refers either to the scapegoat ritual given to Aaron, the scapegoat itself, or the entity to whom the scapegoat is sacrificed.

[13] *Hell's concave*   Roof of Hell seen from underneath resembles an inverted bowl.

[14] *the Dorian mood*   Greek musical mode associated with martial valor.

Of flutes and soft recorders—such as raised
To height of noblest temper heroes old
Arming to battle, and instead of rage
Deliberate valour breathed, firm, and unmoved
555 With dread of death to flight or foul retreat;
Nor wanting power to mitigate and swage[1]
With solemn touches troubled thoughts, and chase
Anguish and doubt and fear and sorrow and pain
From mortal or immortal minds. Thus they,
560 Breathing united force with fixed thought,
Moved on in silence to soft pipes that charmed
Their painful steps o'er the burnt soil. And now
Advanced in view they stand—a horrid front
Of dreadful length and dazzling arms, in guise
565 Of warriors old, with ordered spear and shield,
Awaiting what command their mighty chief
Had to impose. He through the armèd files
Darts his experienced eye, and soon traverse°   *crosswise*
The whole battalion views—their order due,
570 Their visages and stature as of gods;
Their number last he sums. And now his heart
Distends with pride, and, hardening in his strength,
Glories: for never, since created Man,
Met such embodied force as, named with these,
575 Could merit more than that small infantry
Warred on by cranes—[2] though all the giant brood
Of Phlegra[3] with th' heroic race were joined
That fought at Thebes and Ilium,° on each side   *Troy*
Mixed with auxiliar gods; and what resounds
580 In fable or romance of Uther's son,[4]
Begirt with British and Armoric° knights;   *Breton*
And all who since, baptized or infidel,
Jousted in Aspramont, or Montalban,
Damasco, or Marocco, or Trebisond,[5]
585 Or whom Bizerta[6] sent from Afric shore

When Charlemagne with all his peerage fell
By Fontarabbia.[7] Thus far these beyond
Compare of mortal prowess, yet observed
Their dread commander. He, above the rest
590 In shape and gesture proudly eminent,
Stood like a tow'r. His form had yet not lost
All her original brightness, nor appeared
Less than archangel ruined, and th' excess
Of glory obscured: as when the sun new-ris'n
595 Looks through the horizontal misty air
Shorn of his beams, or, from behind the moon,
In dim eclipse, disastrous twilight sheds
On half the nations, and with fear of change
Perplexes monarchs.[8] Dark'n'd so, yet shone
600 Above them all th' archangel: but his face
Deep scars of thunder had entrenched, and care
Sat on his faded cheek, but under brows
Of dauntless courage, and considerate pride
Waiting revenge. Cruel his eye, but cast
605 Signs of remorse and passion, to behold
The fellows of his crime, the followers rather
(Far other once beheld in bliss), condemned
Forever now to have their lot in pain—
Millions of spirits for his fault amerced
610 Of Heav'n,[9] and from eternal splendours flung
For his revolt—yet faithful how they stood,
Their glory withered; as, when Heaven's fire
Has scathed° the forest oaks or mountain pines,   *blasted*
With singèd top their stately growth, though bare,
615 Stands on the blasted heath. He now prepared
To speak; whereat their doubled ranks they bend
From wing to wing, and half enclose him round
With all his peers: attention held them mute.
Thrice he assayed, and thrice, in spite of scorn,
620 Tears, such as angels weep, burst forth: at last
Words interwove with sighs found out their way:

---

1 *swage* I.e., assuage: to appease.

2 *that small infantry / Warred on by cranes* Pygmies. Allusion to the fabled battle between cranes and tiny pygmies often mentioned in classical texts and after.

3 *Phlegra* Location of the battle between rebellious giants and Zeus.

4 *Uther's son* King Arthur, son of Uther Pendragon.

5 *Aspramont … Montalban … Damasco … Marocco … Trebisond* Sites associated with the Crusades.

6 *Bizerta* Departure point from which Moorish fleets invaded southern Europe.

7 *When Charlemagne … By Fontarabbia* Charlemagne (742–814) did not die at Fontarabia, in Northern Spain, but his troops under the command of Roland (Charlemagne's general) were defeated at Roncesvalles, 40 miles from Fontarabia, in 778.

8 *from behind the moon … Perplexes monarchs* Eclipses are traditionally harbingers of disaster or of death, especially of the deaths of monarchs, who were routinely identified with the sun.

9 *amerced / Of Heav'n* Both those banished from Heaven, and those punished by Heaven.

"O myriads of immortal spirits! O powers
Matchless, but with th' Almighty; and that strife
Was not inglorious, though th' event was dire,
625 As this place testifies, and this dire change,
Hateful to utter. But what power of mind,
Foreseeing or presaging, from the depth
Of knowledge past or present, could have feared
How such united force of gods, how such
630 As stood like these, could ever know repulse?
For who can yet believe, though after loss,
That all these puissant° legions, whose exile   *powerful*
Hath emptied Heaven, shall fail to re-ascend,
Self-raised, and repossess their native seat?
635 For me, be witness all the host of Heav'n,
If counsels different, or danger shunned
By me, have lost our hopes. But He who reigns
Monarch in Heav'n till then as one secure
Sat on His throne, upheld by old repute,
640 Consent or custom, and His regal state
Put forth at full, but still His strength concealed—
Which tempted our attempt, and wrought our fall.
Henceforth His might we know, and know our own,
So as not either to provoke, or dread
645 New war provoked: our better part remains
To work in close design, by fraud or guile,
What force effected not; that He no less
At length from us may find, who overcomes
By force hath overcome but half His foe.
650 Space may produce new worlds; whereof so rife
There went a fame° in Heav'n that He ere long   *rumor*
Intended to create, and therein plant
A generation whom His choice regard
Should favour equal to the sons of Heav'n.
655 Thither, if but to pry, shall be perhaps
Our first eruption—thither, or elsewhere;
For this infernal pit shall never hold
Celestial spirits in bondage, nor th' abyss
Long under darkness cover. But these thoughts
660 Full counsel must mature. Peace is despaired;
For who can think submission? War, then, war
Open or understood, must be resolved."
  He spake; and, to confirm his words, outflew
Millions of flaming swords, drawn from the thighs
665 Of mighty cherubim; the sudden blaze
Far round illumined Hell. Highly they raged

Against the highest and fierce with graspèd arms
Clashed on their sounding shields the din of war,
Hurling defiance toward the vault of Heav'n.
670   There stood a hill not far, whose grisly top
Belched fire and rolling smoke; the rest entire
Shone with a glossy scurf[1]—undoubted sign
That in his womb was hid metallic ore,
The work of sulphur. Thither, winged with speed,
675 A numerous brigade hastened: as when bands
Of pioneers,[2] with spade and pickaxe armed,
Forerun the royal camp, to trench a field,
Or cast a rampart. Mammon led them on—
Mammon, the least erected[3] spirit that fell
680 From Heav'n; for even in Heav'n his looks and thoughts
Were always downward bent, admiring more
The riches of Heav'n's pavement, trodden gold,
Than aught divine or holy else enjoyed
In vision beatific. By him first
685 Men also, and by his suggestion taught,
Ransacked the centre,[4] and with impious hands
Rifled the bowels of their mother Earth
For treasures better hid. Soon had his crew
Op'nd into the hill a spacious wound,
690 And digged out ribs of gold. Let none admire
That riches grow in Hell; that soil may best
Deserve the precious bane. And here let those
Who boast in mortal things, and wondering tell
Of Babel,[5] and the works of Memphian kings,[6]
695 Learn how their greatest monuments of fame
And strength and art are easily outdone
By spirits reprobate, and in an hour
What in an age they, with incessant toil
And hands innumerable, scarce perform.

---

[1] *scurf* Scaly crust.

[2] *pioneers* Advance body of foot-soldiers who prepare for the main body of the army.

[3] *least erected* Lowest-ranked. Mammon is concerned with worldly or material goods and wealth.

[4] *Ransacked the centre* Mined the Earth; "centre" extends the Ptolemaic metaphor.

[5] *Babel* Tower built by men who wished to reach Heaven. For their presumption, God caused them all to speak in different languages, so that they could not communicate well enough to continue to build the city. See Genesis 11.1–9.

[6] *Memphian kings* Egyptian Pharaohs.

700 Nigh on the plain, in many cells prepared,
That underneath had veins of liquid fire
Sluiced from the lake, a second multitude
With wondrous art founded the massy° ore,   *heavy*
Sev'ring each kind, and scummed the bullion dross.
705 A third as soon had formed within the ground
A various mould, and from the boiling cells
By strange conveyance filled each hollow nook;
As in an organ, from one blast of wind,
To many a row of pipes the soundboard breathes.
710 Anon out of the earth a fabric huge
Rose like an exhalation, with the sound
Of dulcet symphonies and voices sweet—
Built like a temple, where pilasters[1] round
Were set, and Doric pillars overlaid
715 With golden architrave;° nor did there want   *filigree*
Cornice or frieze, with bossy° sculptures graven;   *embossed*
The roof was fretted° gold. Not Babylon   *engraved*
Nor great Alcairo° such magnificence   *Cairo*
Equalled in all their glories, to enshrine
720 Belus or Serapis[2] their gods, or seat
Their kings, when Egypt with Assyria strove
In wealth and luxury. Th' ascending pile
Stood fixed her stately height, and straight the doors,
Op'ning their brazen folds, discover, wide
725 Within, her ample spaces o'er the smooth
And level pavement: from the arched roof,
Pendant° by subtle magic, many a row   *hanging*
Of starry lamps and blazing cressets,° fed   *torches*
With naptha and asphaltus,° yielded light   *pitch*
730 As from a sky. The hasty multitude
Admiring entered; and the work some praise,
And some the architect. His hand was known
In Heav'n by many a towered structure high,
Where sceptred angels held their residence,
735 And sat as princes, whom the supreme King
Exalted to such power, and gave to rule,
Each in his hierarchy, the orders bright.
Nor was his name unheard or unadored
In ancient Greece; and in Ausonian° land   *Italian*
740 Men called him Mulciber;[3] and how he fell
From Heav'n they fabled, thrown by angry Jove

Sheer o'er the crystal battlements: from morn
To noon he fell, from noon to dewy eve,
A summer's day, and with the setting sun
745 Dropt from the zenith, like a falling star,
On Lemnos, th' Aegaean isle.[4] Thus they relate,
Erring; for he with this rebellious rout
Fell long before; nor aught availed him now
To have built in Heav'n high tow'rs; nor did he 'scape
750 By all his engines, but was headlong sent,
With his industrious crew, to build in Hell.
Meanwhile the wingèd heralds, by command
Of sovereign power, with awful ceremony
And trumpet's sound, throughout the host proclaim
755 A solemn council forthwith to be held
At Pandemonium,[5] the high capital
Of Satan and his peers. Their summons called
From every band and squarèd regiment
By place or choice the worthiest: they anon
760 With hundreds and with thousands trooping came
Attended. All access was thronged; the gates
And porches wide, but chief the spacious hall
(Though like a covered field, where champions bold
Wont ride in armed, and at the Soldan's° chair   *Sultan's*
765 Defied the best of paynim° chivalry   *pagan*
To mortal combat, or career° with lance),   *joust*
Thick swarmed, both on the ground and in the air,
Brushed with the hiss of rustling wings. As bees
In springtime, when the sun with Taurus rides,[6]
770 Pour forth their populous youth about the hive
In clusters; they among fresh dews and flowers
Fly to and fro, or on the smoothèd plank,
The suburb of their straw-built citadel,
New rubbed with balm, expatiate, and confer
775 Their state-affairs: so thick the airy crowd
Swarmed and were straightened; till, the signal giv'n,
Behold a wonder! They but now who seemed
In bigness to surpass Earth's giant sons,
Now less than smallest dwarfs, in narrow room

---

1 *pilasters* Pillars fixed to the wall.

2 *Belus* Baal; *Serapis* Egyptian bull god.

3 *Mulciber* Vulcan, or Hephaestus, the gods' blacksmith.

4 *and how he fell … Aegaean isle* In some accounts, Hephaestus was thrown out of Heaven for attempting to protect his mother, Hera, from Zeus's (Jove's) anger.

5 *Pandemonium* Literally, all demonhood or all demons; the word is Milton's invention.

6 *when the sun with Taurus rides* Springtime, when the sun is in the astrological house of Taurus, the bull.

780 Throng numberless—like that pygmean race
Beyond the Indian mount; or faery elves,
Whose midnight revels, by a forest-side
Or fountain, some belated peasant[1] sees,
Or dreams he sees, while overhead the moon
785 Sits arbitress, and nearer to the earth
Wheels her pale course: they, on their mirth and dance
Intent, with jocund music charm his ear;
At once with joy and fear his heart rebounds.
Thus incorporeal spirits to smallest forms
790 Reduced their shapes immense, and were at large,
Though without number still, amidst the hall
Of that infernal court. But far within,
And in their own dimensions like themselves,
The great seraphic lords and cherubim
795 In close recess and secret conclave sat,
A thousand demi-gods on golden seats,
Frequent° and full. After short silence then,   *many*
And summons read, the great consult began.

THE END OF THE FIRST BOOK

ARGUMENT TO BOOK 2

The consultation begun, Satan debates whether another battle be to be hazarded for the recovery of Heaven: some advise it, others dissuade. A third proposal is preferred, mentioned before by Satan, to search the truth of that prophesy or tradition in Heaven concerning another world, and another kind of creature equal or not much inferior to themselves, about this time to be created; their doubt who shall be sent on this difficult search; Satan their chief undertakes alone the voyage, is honoured and applauded. The council thus ended, the rest betake them several ways and to several employments, as their inclinations lead them, to entertain the time till Satan return. He passes on his journey to Hell gates, finds them shut, and who sat there to guard them, by whom at length they are opened, and discover to him the great gulf between Hell and Heaven; with what difficulty he passes through, directed by Chaos, the power of that place, to the sight of this new world which he sought.

BOOK 2

High on a throne of royal state, which far
Outshone the wealth of Ormuz and of Ind,[2]
Or where the gorgeous east with richest hand
Showers on her kings barbaric pearl and gold,
5 Satan exalted sat, by merit raised
To that bad eminence; and, from despair
Thus high uplifted beyond hope, aspires
Beyond thus high, insatiate to pursue
Vain war with Heav'n; and, by success untaught,
10 His proud imaginations thus displayed:
   "Powers and dominions, deities of Heav'n!
For, since no deep° within her gulf can hold   *depth*
Immortal vigour, though oppressed and fallen,
I give not Heav'n for lost: from this descent
15 Celestial virtues rising will appear
More glorious and more dread than from no fall,
And trust themselves to fear no second fate!
Me though just right, and the fixed laws of Heav'n,
Did first create your leader—next, free choice
20 With what besides in council or in fight
Hath been achieved of merit—yet this loss,
Thus far at least recovered, hath much more
Established in a safe, unenvied throne,
Yielded with full consent. The happier state
25 In Heav'n, which follows dignity, might draw
Envy from each inferior; but who here
Will envy whom the highest place exposes
Foremost to stand against the Thunderer's aim
Your bulwark, and condemns to greatest share
30 Of endless pain? Where there is, then, no good
For which to strive, no strife can grow up there
From faction: for none sure will claim in Hell
Precedence; none whose portion is so small
Of present pain that with ambitious mind
35 Will covet more! With this advantage, then,
To union, and firm faith, and firm accord,
More than can be in Heav'n, we now return
To claim our just inheritance of old,
Surer to prosper than prosperity
40 Could have assured us; and by what best way,
Whether of open war or covert guile,

---

[1] *belated peasant* I.e., a peasant out late.

[2] *Ormuz* Straight of Hormuz, a waterway linking the Persian Gulf with the Gulf of Oman—traditionally and still a critical waterway for trade and shipping; *Ind* India.

We now debate. Who can advise may speak."
    He ceased; and next him Moloch, sceptred king,
Stood up—the strongest and the fiercest spirit
45 That fought in Heav'n, now fiercer by despair.
His trust was with th' eternal to be deemed
Equal in strength, and rather than be less
Cared not to be at all; with that care lost
Went all his fear: of God, or Hell, or worse,
50 He recked not, and these words thereafter spake:
    "My sentence is for open war. Of wiles,
More unexpert, I boast not: them let those
Contrive who need, or when they need; not now.
For, while they sit contriving, shall the rest—
55 Millions that stand in arms, and longing wait
The signal to ascend—sit lingering here,
Heav'n's fugitives, and for their dwelling-place
Accept this dark opprobrious den of shame,
The prison of His tyranny who reigns
60 By our delay? No! Let us rather choose,
Armed with Hell-flames and fury, all at once
O'er Heav'n's high towers to force resistless[1] way,
Turning our tortures into horrid arms
Against the Torturer; when, to meet the noise
65 Of His almighty engine,[2] He shall hear
Infernal thunder, and, for lightning, see
Black fire and horror shot with equal rage
Among His angels, and His throne itself
Mixed with Tartarean° sulphur and strange fire,   *hellish*
70 His own invented torments. But perhaps
The way seems difficult, and steep to scale
With upright wing against a higher foe!
Let such bethink them, if the sleepy drench
Of that forgetful lake[3] benumb not still,
75 That in our proper motion we ascend
Up to our native seat; descent and fall
To us is adverse. Who but felt of late,
When the fierce Foe hung on our broken rear
Insulting,[4] and pursued us through the deep,
80 With what compulsion and laborious flight

We sunk thus low? Th' ascent is easy, then;
Th' event is feared! Should we again provoke
Our stronger, some worse way His wrath may find
To our destruction, if there be in Hell
85 Fear to be worse destroyed! What can be worse
Than to dwell here, driven out from bliss, condemned
In this abhorred deep to utter woe!
Where pain of unextinguishable fire
Must exercise us without hope of end
90 The vassals of His anger, when the scourge
Inexorably, and the torturing hour,
Calls us to penance? More destroyed than thus,
We should be quite abolished, and expire.
What fear we then? What doubt we to incense
95 His utmost ire? Which, to the height enraged,
Will either quite consume us, and reduce
To nothing this essential—happier far
Than miserable to have eternal being—
Or, if our substance be indeed divine,
100 And cannot cease to be, we are at worst
On this side nothing;[5] and by proof we feel
Our power sufficient to disturb his Heav'n,
And with perpetual inroads[6] to alarm,
Though inaccessible, his fatal throne:
105 Which, if not victory, is yet revenge."
    He ended frowning, and his look denounced
Desperate revenge, and battle dangerous
To less than gods. On th' other side up rose
Belial, in act more graceful and humane.
110 A fairer person lost not Heav'n; he seemed
For dignity composed, and high exploit.
But all was false and hollow; though his tongue
Dropped manna,[7] and could make the worse appear
The better reason, to perplex and dash
115 Maturest counsels: for his thoughts were low—
To vice industrious,[8] but to nobler deeds

---

[1] *resistless* I.e., cannot be resisted.

[2] *engine* I.e., war machine.

[3] *Of that forgetful lake* Lethe, river of oblivion in Hades.

[4] *hung on our broken rear / Insulting* Followed close behind our broken rear ranks, attacking us and exulting; the scatological joke of "broken rear" is intentional.

[5] *What doubt we ... this side nothing* Why do we care if we anger God more? We're immortal, and either God can't hurt us, or He will just completely erase us from existence—either way, we are no worse off than we are right now.

[6] *perpetual inroads* Constant attacks.

[7] *though his tongue / Dropped manna* Though he spoke as sweetly as could be.

[8] *To vice industrious* Quick to commit vice, and hardworking when doing so.

Timorous and slothful. Yet he pleased the ear,
And with persuasive accent thus began:
  "I should be much for open war, O peers,
120 As not behind in hate, if what was urged
Main reason to persuade immediate war
Did not dissuade me most, and seem to cast
Ominous conjecture on the whole success;
When he who most excels in fact of arms,
125 In what he counsels and in what excels
Mistrustful, grounds his courage on despair
And utter dissolution, as the scope
Of all his aim, after some dire revenge.
First, what revenge? The tow'rs of Heav'n are filled
130 With armèd watch,° that render all access   guards
Impregnable: oft on the bordering deep
Encamp their legions, or with obscure wing
Scout far and wide into the realm of night,
Scorning¹ surprise. Or, could we break our way
135 By force, and at our heels all Hell should rise
With blackest insurrection to confound
Heav'n's purest light, yet our great Enemy,
All incorruptible, would on His throne
Sit unpolluted, and th' ethereal mould,
140 Incapable of stain, would soon expel
Her mischief, and purge off the baser fire,²
Victorious. Thus repulsed, our final hope
Is flat despair: we must exasperate
Th' almighty Victor to spend all his rage;
145 And that must end us; that must be our cure—
To be no more. Sad cure! For who would lose,
Though full of pain, this intellectual° being,   sentient
Those thoughts that wander through eternity,
To perish rather, swallowed up and lost
150 In the wide womb of uncreated night,
Devoid of sense and motion? And who knows,
Let this be good, whether our angry Foe
Can give it, or will ever? How He can
Is doubtful; that He never will is sure.
155 Will He, so wise, let loose at once His ire,
Belike through impotence or unaware,

To give His enemies their wish, and end
Them in His anger whom His anger saves
To punish endless? 'Wherefore cease we, then?'
160 Say they who counsel war; 'we are decreed,
Reserved, and destined to eternal woe;
Whatever doing, what can we suffer more,
What can we suffer worse?' Is this, then, worst—
Thus sitting, thus consulting, thus in arms?
165 What when we fled amain,° pursued   at full speed
     and struck
With Heav'n's afflicting thunder, and besought
The deep to shelter us? This Hell then seemed
A refuge from those wounds. Or when we lay
Chained on the burning lake? That sure was worse.
170 What if the breath that kindled those grim fires,
Awaked, should blow them into sevenfold rage,
And plunge us in the flames; or from above
Should intermitted° vengeance arm again   paused
His red right hand to plague us? What if all
175 Her stores were op'n'd, and this firmament
Of Hell should spout her cataracts of fire,
Impendent° horrors, threatening hideous fall   hanging
One day upon our heads; while we perhaps,
Designing or exhorting glorious war,
180 Caught in a fiery tempest, shall be hurled,
Each on his rock transfixed,° the sport and prey pinned
Of racking° whirlwinds, or forever sunk   torturing
Under yon boiling ocean, wrapt in chains,
There to converse with everlasting groans,
185 Unrespited, unpitied, unreprieved,
Ages of hopeless end?³ This would be worse.
War, therefore, open or concealed, alike
My voice dissuades; for what can force or guile
With Him, or who deceive His mind, whose eye
190 Views all things at one view? He from Heav'n's height
All these our motions vain sees and derides,
Not more almighty to resist our might
Than wise to frustrate all our plots and wiles.
Shall we, then, live thus vile—the race of Heav'n
195 Thus trampled, thus expelled, to suffer here
Chains and these torments? Better these than worse,
By my advice; since fate inevitable
Subdues us, and omnipotent decree,
The Victor's will. To suffer, as to do,

---

¹ *Scorning* Making impossible.

² *th' ethereal mould … purge off the baser fire* The pure "consuming fire" of God (Exodus 24.17, Numbers 11.1, Deuteronomy 4.24) would quickly defeat and exterminate the merely "flaming fire" of the rebel angels (Exodus 3.2, Psalm 104.4, Hebrews 1.7).

---

³ *Ages of hopeless end* An ages-long hopeless fate.

200 Our strength is equal; nor the law unjust
That so ordains. This was at first resolved,
If we were wise, against so great a foe
Contending, and so doubtful what might fall.
I laugh when those who at the spear are bold
205 And venturous, if that fail them, shrink, and fear
What yet they know must follow—to endure
Exile, or ignominy, or bonds, or pain,
The sentence of their conqueror. This is now
Our doom; which if we can sustain and bear,
210 Our supreme Foe in time may much remit
His anger, and perhaps, thus far removed,
Not mind us not offending, satisfied
With what is punished; whence these raging fires
Will slacken, if His breath stir not their flames.
215 Our purer essence then will overcome
Their noxious vapour; or, inured, not feel;
Or, changed at length, and to the place conformed
In temper and in nature, will receive
Familiar the fierce heat; and, void of pain,
220 This horror will grow mild, this darkness light;
Besides what hope the never-ending flight
Of future days may bring, what chance, what change
Worth waiting—since our present lot appears
For happy though but ill, for ill not worst,
225 If we procure not to ourselves more woe."
　　　　Thus Belial, with words clothed in reason's garb,
Counselled ignoble ease and peaceful sloth,
Not peace; and after him thus Mammon spoke:
　　　　"Either to disenthrone the King of Heaven
230 We war, if war be best, or to regain
Our own right lost. Him to unthrone we then
May hope, when everlasting fate shall yield
To fickle chance, and chaos judge the strife.
The former, vain to hope, argues as vain
235 The latter; for what place can be for us
Within Heav'n's bound, unless Heav'n's Lord Supreme
We overpower? Suppose He should relent
And publish° grace to all, on promise made　　　　*grant*
Of new subjection; with what eyes could we
240 Stand in His presence humble, and receive
Strict laws imposed, to celebrate His throne
With warbled hymns, and to His godhead sing
Forced hallelujahs, while He lordly sits
Our envied Sovereign, and His altar breathes

245 Ambrosial odours and ambrosial[1] flowers,
Our servile offerings? This must be our task
In Heav'n, this our delight. How wearisome
Eternity so spent in worship paid
To Whom we hate! Let us not then pursue
250 By force impossible, by leave obtained
Unacceptable,[2] though in Heav'n, our state
Of splendid vassalage;° but rather seek　　　　*servitude*
Our own good from ourselves, and from our own
Live to ourselves, though in this vast recess,
255 Free and to none accountable, preferring
Hard liberty before the easy yoke
Of servile pomp. Our greatness will appear
Then most conspicuous when great things of small,
Useful of hurtful, prosperous of adverse,
260 We can create, and in what place soe'er°　　　　*whatsoever*
Thrive under evil, and work ease out of pain
Through labour and endurance. This deep world
Of darkness do we dread? How oft amidst
Thick clouds and dark doth Heav'n's all-ruling Sire
265 Choose to reside, His glory unobscured,
And with the majesty of darkness round
Covers His throne, from whence deep thunders roar.[3]
Must'ring their rage, and Heav'n resembles Hell!
As He our darkness, cannot we His light
270 Imitate when we please? This desert soil
Wants not her hidden lustre, gems and gold;
Nor want we skill or art from whence to raise
Magnificence; and what can Heav'n show more?
Our torments also may, in length of time,
275 Become our elements, these piercing fires
As soft as now severe, our temper changed
Into their temper; which must needs remove
The sensible[4] of pain. All things invite
To peaceful counsels, and the settled state
280 Of order, how in safety best we may

---

[1] *ambrosial* Ambrosia is the mythical food of the Greek and Roman gods.

[2] *Let us not then pursue ... by leave obtained / Unacceptable* Let us not try and take by considerable force of arms a servitude we would find disgusting and hateful.

[3] *How oft amidst / Thick clouds ... from whence deep thunders roar* See, for example Exodus 13 and 14, Leviticus 16.2, Numbers 9–16.

[4] *The sensible* Those who feel.

Compose our present evils, with regard
Of what we are and where, dismissing quite
All thoughts of war. Ye have what I advise."
    He scarce had finished, when such murmur filled
285 Th' assembly as when hollow rocks retain
The sound of blustering winds, which all night long
Had roused the sea, now with hoarse cadence lull
Seafaring men o'erwatched,[1] whose bark° by   *boat*
    chance
Or pinnace,° anchors in a craggy bay   *ship*
290 After the tempest. Such applause was heard
As Mammon ended, and his sentence pleased,
Advising peace: for such another field
They dreaded worse than Hell; so much the fear
Of thunder and the sword of Michael[2]
295 Wrought still within them; and no less desire
To found this nether empire, which might rise,
By policy and long process of time,
In emulation opposite to Heav'n.
Which when Beelzebub perceived—than whom,
300 Satan except, none higher sat—with grave
Aspect he rose, and in his rising seemed
A pillar of state. Deep on his front° engraven   *forehead*
Deliberation sat, and public care;
And princely counsel in his face yet shone,
305 Majestic, though in ruin. Sage he stood
With Atlantean[3] shoulders, fit to bear
The weight of mightiest monarchies; his look
Drew audience and attention still as night
Or summer's noontide air, while thus he spoke:
310   "Thrones and imperial powers, offspring of Heav'n,
Ethereal virtues; or these titles now
Must we renounce, and, changing style, be called
Princes of Hell? For so the popular vote
Inclines—here to continue, and build up here
315 A growing empire; doubtless; while we dream,
And know not that the King of Heav'n hath doomed
This place our dungeon, not our safe retreat
Beyond His potent arm, to live exempt
From Heav'n's high jurisdiction, in new league

320 Banded against His throne, but to remain
In strictest bondage, though thus far removed,
Under th' inevitable curb, reserved
His captive multitude. For He, to be sure,
In height or depth, still first and last will reign
325 Sole king, and of His kingdom lose no part
By our revolt, but over Hell extend
His empire, and with iron sceptre rule
Us here, as with His golden those in Heav'n.
What sit we then projecting peace and war?
330 War hath determined us and foiled with loss
Irreparable; terms of peace yet none
Vouchsafed or sought; for what peace will be given
To us enslaved, but custody severe,
And stripes° and arbitrary punishment   *lashes*
335 Inflicted? And what peace can we return,
But, to our power,[4] hostility and hate,
Untamed reluctance, and revenge, though slow,
Yet ever plotting how the Conqueror least
May reap His conquest, and may least rejoice
340 In doing what we most in suffering feel?
Nor will occasion want, nor shall we need
With dangerous expedition to invade
Heaven, whose high walls fear no assault or siege,
Or ambush from the deep. What if we find
345 Some easier enterprise? There is a place
(If ancient and prophetic fame in Heav'n
Err not)—another world, the happy seat
Of some new race called Man, about this time
To be created like to us, though less
350 In power and excellence, but favoured more
Of Him who rules above; so was His will
Pronounced among the gods, and by an oath
That shook Heav'n's whole circumference confirmed.
Thither let us bend all our thoughts, to learn
355 What creatures there inhabit, of what mould°   *form*
Or substance, how endued, and what their power
And where their weakness: how attempted best,
By force or subtlety. Though Heav'n be shut,
And Heav'n's high Arbitrator sit secure
360 In His own strength, this place may lie exposed,
The utmost border of His kingdom, left
To their defence who hold it: here, perhaps,
Some advantageous act may be achieved

---

[1] *o'erwatched* Worn out from having to forgo sleep for watchfulness.

[2] *Michael* Archangel Michael, a general of God's army.

[3] *Atlantean* The Titan Atlas carried the world on his broad shoulders.

[4] *to our power* To our utmost ability.

By sudden onset°—either with Hell-fire   *assault*
365 To waste His whole creation, or possess
All as our own, and drive, as we were driven,
The puny habitants; or, if not drive,
Seduce them to our party, that their God
May prove their Foe, and with repenting hand
370 Abolish His own works. This would surpass
Common revenge, and interrupt His joy
In our confusion, and our joy upraise
In His disturbance; when his darling sons,
Hurled headlong to partake with us, shall curse
375 Their frail original, and faded bliss—
Faded so soon! Advise if this be worth
Attempting, or to sit in darkness here
Hatching vain empires." Thus Beelzebub
Pleaded his devilish counsel—first devised
380 By Satan, and in part proposed: for whence,
But from the author of all ill, could spring
So deep a malice, to confound the race
Of mankind in one root, and earth with Hell
To mingle and involve, done all to spite
385 The great Creator? But their spite still serves
His glory to augment. The bold design
Pleased highly those infernal states,[1] and joy
Sparkled in all their eyes: with full assent
They vote: whereat his speech he thus renews:
390   "Well have ye judged, well ended long debate,
Synod[2] of gods, and, like to what ye are,
Great things resolved, which from the lowest deep
Will once more lift us up, in spite of fate,
Nearer our ancient seat—perhaps in view
395 Of those bright confines, whence, with neighbouring
     arms,
And opportune excursion, we may chance
Re-enter Heav'n; or else in some mild zone
Dwell, not unvisited of Heav'n's fair light,
Secure, and at the bright'ning orient beam[3]
400 Purge off this gloom: the soft delicious air,
To heal the scar of these corrosive fires,
Shall breathe her balm. But, first, whom shall we send
In search of this new world? Whom shall we find
Sufficient? Who shall tempt with wandering feet

405 The dark, unbottomed, infinite abyss,
And through the palpable obscure[4] find out
His uncouth° way, or spread his airy flight,   *unknown*
Upborne with indefatigable wings
Over the vast abrupt, ere he arrive
410 The happy isle? What strength, what art, can then
Suffice, or what evasion bear him safe,
Through the strict sentries and stations thick
Of angels watching round? Here he had need
All circumspection: and we now no less
415 Choice in our suffrage; for on whom we send
The weight of all, and our last hope, relies."
     This said, he sat; and expectation held
His look suspense,[5] awaiting who appeared
To second, or oppose, or undertake
420 The perilous attempt. But all sat mute,
Pondering the danger with deep thoughts; and each
In other's count'nance read his own dismay,
Astonished. None among the choice and prime
Of those Heav'n-warring champions could be found
425 So hardy[6] as to proffer or accept,
Alone, the dreadful voyage; till, at last,
Satan, whom now transcendent glory raised
Above his fellows, with monarchal pride
Conscious of highest worth, unmoved thus spake:
430   "O progeny of Heav'n! Empyreal thrones!
With reason hath deep silence and demur
Seized us, though undismayed. Long is the way
And hard, that out of Hell leads up to light.
Our prison strong, this huge convex° of fire,   *dome*
435 Outrageous° to devour, immures us round   *eager*
Ninefold; and gates of burning adamant,[7]
Barred over us, prohibit all egress.
These passed, if any pass, the void profound
Of unessential[8] night receives him next,
440 Wide-gaping, and with utter loss of being
Threatens him, plunged in that abortive gulf.
If thence he scape, into whatever world,

---

1 *states* Heads of state or estates, the hierarchs of Hell.

2 *Synod* Council or assembly, especially of church officials.

3 *bright'ning orient beam* Lightening of the eastern horizon; dawn.

4 *the palpable obscure* Darkness so complete one can feel it.

5 *expectation held / His look suspense* His look was suspenseful as he waited for their response.

6 *hardy* Tough, or also possibly "foolhardy."

7 *adamant* Unbreakable shining metal.

8 *unessential* Having no substance, absolutely empty.

Or unknown region, what remains him less
Than unknown dangers, and as hard escape?
445 But I should ill become this throne, O peers,
And this imperial sov'reignty, adorned
With splendour, armed with power, if aught proposed
And judged of public moment° in the shape   *importance*
Of difficulty or danger, could deter
450 Me from attempting. Wherefore do I assume
These royalties, and not refuse to reign,
Refusing to accept as great a share
Of hazard as of honour, due alike
To him who reigns, and so much to him due
455 Of hazard more as he above the rest
High honoured sits? Go, therefore, mighty powers,
Terror of Heav'n, though fallen; intend at[1] home,
While here shall be our home, what best may ease
The present misery, and render Hell
460 More tolerable; if there be cure or charm
To respite, or deceive, or slack the pain
Of this ill mansion: intermit no watch[2]
Against a wakeful foe, while I abroad
Through all the coasts of dark destruction seek
465 Deliverance for us all. This enterprise
None shall partake with me." Thus saying rose
The monarch, and prevented all reply;
Prudent, lest from his resolution raised
Others among the chief might offer now,
470 Certain to be refused, what erst° they feared,   *formerly*
And, so refused, might in opinion stand
His rivals, winning cheap the high repute
Which he through hazard huge must earn. But they
Dreaded not more th' adventure than his voice
475 Forbidding; and at once with him they rose.
Their rising all at once was as the sound
Of thunder heard remote. Towards him they bend
With awful reverence prone, and as a God
Extol him equal to the high'st in Heav'n.
480 Nor failed they to express how much they praised
That for the general safety he despised
His own: for neither do the spirits damned
Lose all their virtue; lest bad men should boast
Their specious° deeds on earth, which glory   *worthless*
     excites,

485 Or close ambition varnished o'er with zeal.
Thus they their doubtful consultations dark
Ended, rejoicing in their matchless chief:
As, when from mountaintops the dusky clouds
Ascending, while the north wind sleeps, o'erspread
490 Heav'n's cheerful face, the louring element[3]
Scowls o'er the darkened landscape snow or shower,
If chance the radiant sun, with farewell sweet,
Extend his ev'ning beam, the fields revive,
The birds their notes renew, and bleating herds
495 Attest their joy, that hill and valley rings.
O shame to men! Devil with devil damned
Firm concord holds;[4] men only disagree
Of creatures rational, though under hope
Of heavenly grace, and, God proclaiming peace,
500 Yet live in hatred, enmity, and strife
Among themselves, and levy cruel wars
Wasting the earth, each other to destroy:
As if (which might induce us to accord)
Man had not hellish foes enow° besides,   *enough*
505 That day and night for his destruction wait!
     The Stygian° council thus dissolved; and forth *hellish*
In order came the grand infernal peers:
Midst came their mighty paramount, and seemed
Alone th' antagonist of Heaven, nor less
510 Than Hell's dread emperor, with pomp supreme,
And God-like imitated state: him round[5]
A globe of fiery seraphim enclosed
With bright emblazonry, and horrent arms.[6]
Then of their session ended they bid cry
515 With trumpet's regal sound the great result:
Toward the four winds four speedy cherubim
Put to their mouths the sounding alchemy,[7]
By herald's voice explained; the hollow abyss
Heard far and wide, and all the host of Hell
520 With deaf'ning shout returned them loud acclaim.
Thence more at ease their minds, and somewhat raised
By false presumptuous hope, the rangèd powers

---

[1] *intend at* Turn your thoughts to.

[2] *intermit no watch* Do not interrupt your vigilance.

---

[3] *louring element* Darkening sky.

[4] *Devil … holds* Devils hold firm to their contracts with each other.

[5] *him round* Around him.

[6] *bright emblazonry … horrent arms* Bright heraldry and bared weapons.

[7] *the sounding alchemy* Trumpets, metal that sings.

Disband; and, wand'ring, each his several way
Pursues, as inclination or sad choice
525 Leads him perplexed, where he may likeliest find
Truce to his restless thoughts, and entertain
The irksome hours, till his great chief return.
Part° on the plain, or in the air sublime,   *some*
Upon the wing or in swift race contend,
530 As at th' Olympian games or Pythian fields;[1]
Part curb their fiery steeds, or shun the goal
With rapid wheels,[2] or fronted° brigades form: *ranked*
As when, to warn proud cities, war appears
Waged in the troubled sky, and armies rush
535 To battle in the clouds; before each van° *foremost division*
Prick forth the airy knights, and couch° their spears, *set*
Till thickest legions close; with feats of arms
From either end of Heav'n the welkin° burns.   *sky*
Others, with vast Typhoean rage, more fell,[3]
540 Rend up both rocks and hills, and ride the air
In whirlwind; Hell scarce holds the wild uproar:
As when Alcides,° from Oechalia crowned   *Hercules*
With conquest, felt th' envenomed robe, and tore
Through pain up by the roots Thessalian pines,
545 And Lichas from the top of Oeta threw
Into th' Euboic sea.[4] Others, more mild,
Retreated in a silent valley, sing
With notes angelical to many a harp
Their own heroic deeds, and hapless fall
550 By doom of battle, and complain that fate
Free virtue should enthral to force or chance.
Their song was partial;[5] but the harmony
(What could it less when spirits immortal sing?)
Suspended Hell, and took with ravishment

555 The thronging audience. In discourse more sweet
(For eloquence the soul, song charms the sense)[6]
Others apart sat on a hill retired,
In thoughts more elevate, and reasoned high
Of Providence, foreknowledge, will, and fate—
560 Fixed fate, free will, foreknowledge absolute,
And found no end, in wandering mazes lost.
Of good and evil much they argued then,
Of happiness and final misery,
Passion and apathy, and glory and shame:
565 Vain wisdom all, and false philosophy!
Yet, with a pleasing sorcery, could charm
Pain for a while or anguish, and excite
Fallacious hope, or arm th' obdured breast[7]
With stubborn patience as with triple steel.
570 Another part, in squadrons and gross bands,
On bold adventure to discover wide
That dismal world, if any clime° perhaps   *region*
Might yield them easier habitation, bend
Four ways their flying march, along the banks
575 Of four infernal rivers, that disgorge
Into the burning lake their baleful streams—
Abhorred Styx, the flood of deadly hate;
Sad Acheron of sorrow, black and deep;
Cocytus, named of lamentation loud
580 Heard on the rueful stream; fierce Phlegeton,
Whose waves of torrent fire inflame with rage.
Far off from these, a slow and silent stream,
Lethe,[8] the river of oblivion, rolls
Her watery labyrinth, whereof who drinks
585 Forthwith his former state and being forgets—
Forgets both joy and grief, pleasure and pain.
Beyond this flood a frozen continent
Lies dark and wild, beat with perpetual storms
Of whirlwind and dire hail, which on firm land
590 Thaws not, but gathers heap,[9] and ruin seems
Of ancient pile; all else deep snow and ice,

---

[1] *Pythian fields* Fields below the Temple of the Oracle at Delphi, site of games honoring Apollo's victory over Python, the great serpent that was ravaging the area.

[2] *shun ... wheels* Avoid crashing their chariots into the goalposts they must pass close to in order to score in their games.

[3] *Typhoean* Monstrous, from Typhon the monstrous giant whom Zeus threw into Hades. Some said he lay under Mt. Aetna and caused eruptions; *more fell* Nastier, more evil.

[4] *from Oechalia ... th' Euboic sea* Hercules, after returning from victory in Oechalia, a region in Greece, was presented as a gift a cloak dipped in burning venom. Once he put it on, the pain drove him into a violent rage and he threw Lichas, the innocent and unknowing giver of the fatal gift, into the Euboean Sea.

[5] *partial* Sung in parts, or harmony.

---

[6] *For eloquence ... sense* Eloquence charms the soul, song charms the senses.

[7] *th' obdured breast* Hardened heart.

[8] *Acheron* River of woe; *Cocytus* River of lamentation; *Phlegeton* River of fire; *Lethe* River from which the dead drink to forget their prior lives; these are four of the five rivers of the underworld in Greek mythology, the fifth being the Styx.

[9] *gathers heap* Gathers into heaps.

A gulf profound as that Serbonian bog
Betwixt Damiata and Mount Casius old,[1]
Where armies whole have sunk: the parching air
595 Burns frore,° and cold performs th' effect of fire.   *frostily*
Thither, by harpy-footed furies[2] haled,°   *dragged*
At certain revolutions all the damned
Are brought; and feel by turns the bitter change
Of fierce extremes, extremes by change more fierce,
600 From beds of raging fire to starve° in ice   *i.e., freeze*
Their soft ethereal warmth, and there to pine
Immovable, infixed, and frozen round
Periods of time, thence hurried back to fire.
They ferry over this Lethean sound[3]
605 Both to and fro, their sorrow to augment,
And wish and struggle, as they pass, to reach
The tempting stream,[4] with one small drop to lose
In sweet forgetfulness all pain and woe,
All in one moment, and so near the brink;
610 But fate withstands, and, to oppose th' attempt,
Medusa with Gorgonian terror[5] guards
The ford, and of itself the water flies
All taste of living wight,° as once it fled   *person*
The lip of Tantalus.[6] Thus roving on
615 In confused march forlorn, th' adventurous bands,
With shuddering horror pale, and eyes aghast,
Viewed first their lamentable lot, and found
No rest. Through many a dark and dreary vale
They passed, and many a region dolorous,
620 O'er many a frozen, many a fiery alp,
Rocks, caves, lakes, fens, bogs, dens, and shades
        of death—
A universe of death, which God by curse

Created evil, for evil only good;
Where all life dies, death lives, and nature breeds,
625 Perverse, all monstrous, all prodigious things,
Abominable, inutterable, and worse
Than fables yet have feigned or fear conceived,
Gorgons, and hydras, and chimeras dire.
        Meanwhile the adversary of God and man,
630 Satan, with thoughts inflamed of highest design,
Puts on swift wings, and toward the gates of Hell
Explores his solitary flight: sometimes
He scours the right hand coast, sometimes the left;
Now shaves with level wing the deep, then soars
635 Up to the fiery concave towering high.
As when far off at sea a fleet descried
Hangs in the clouds, by equinoctial winds
Close sailing from Bengala, or the isles
Of Ternate and Tidore,[7] whence merchants bring
640 Their spicy drugs; they on the trading flood,
Through the wide Ethiopian to the Cape,[8]
Ply stemming nightly toward the pole: so seemed
Far off the flying fiend. At last appear
Hell-bounds, high reaching to the horrid roof,
645 And thrice threefold the gates; three folds were brass,
Three iron, three of adamantine rock,
Impenetrable, impaled° with circling fire,   *fenced*
Yet unconsumed. Before the gates there sat
On either side a formidable shape.
650 The one seemed woman to the waist, and fair,
But ended foul in many a scaly fold,
Voluminous and vast—a serpent armed
With mortal sting. About her middle round
A cry° of Hell-hounds never-ceasing barked   *pack*
655 With wide Cerberean[9] mouths full loud, and rung
A hideous peal; yet, when they list,° would   *wanted to*
    creep,
If aught disturbed their noise, into her womb,
And kennel there; yet there still barked and howled
Within unseen. Far less abhorred than these

---

[1] *that Serbonian bog … Mount Casius old* Lake Serbonis (modern Lake Bardawil), located in northern Egypt, is surrounded by quicksand.

[2] *harpy-footed furies* Talon-footed furies. The infernal snake-haired Furies, and Harpies (taloned birds with heads of women) were agents of retribution in classical myth.

[3] *sound* Expanse of water.

[4] *The tempting stream* Lethe, the river of forgetfulness.

[5] *Medusa with Gorgonian terror* Medusa and her sisters were Gorgons, monsters of Greek myth, and Medusa specifically was so terrible that her sight turned men to stone.

[6] *The lip of Tantalus* In Greek myth, Tantalus was condemned to be immersed in water that receded when he tried to drink and was overhung by fruit on a branch that retreated from his reach.

[7] *Bengala … Ternate … Tidore* Three eastern Indian ports, source of spices and exotic trade riches.

[8] *the wide Ethiopian to the Cape* The Indian Ocean to the Cape of Good Hope.

[9] *Cerberean* Cerberus, guardian of the underworld in classical mythology, was a dog with three heads.

560 Vexed Scylla,[1] bathing in the sea that parts
Calabria from the hoarse Trinacrian° shore;   *Sicilian*
Nor uglier follow the night-hag, when, called
In secret, riding through the air she comes,
565 Lured with the smell of infant blood, to dance
With Lapland witches, while the labouring moon
Eclipses at their charms. The other shape—
If shape it might be called that shape had none
Distinguishable in member, joint, or limb;
Or substance might be called that shadow seemed,
70 For each seemed either—black it stood as night,
Fierce as ten furies, terrible as Hell,
And shook a dreadful dart:° what seemed his head   *javelin*
The likeness of a kingly crown had on.
Satan was now at hand, and from his seat
75 The monster moving onward came as fast
With horrid strides; Hell trembled as he strode.
Th' undaunted fiend what this might be
        admired—°
                                wondered
Admired, not feared (God and His Son except,
Created thing naught valued he nor shunned),
80 And with disdainful look thus first began:
"Whence and what art thou, execrable shape,
That dar'st, though grim and terrible, advance
Thy miscreated front athwart my way
To yonder gates? Through them I mean to pass,
85 That be assured, without leave asked of thee.
Retire; or taste thy folly, and learn by proof,
Hell-born, not to contend with spirits of Heav'n."
    To whom the goblin,° full of wrath, replied: *monster*
"Are thou that traitor angel? Are thou he,
90 Who first broke peace in Heav'n and faith, till then
Unbroken, and in proud rebellious arms
Drew after him the third part of Heaven's sons,
Conjured against the highest—for which both thou
And they, outcast from God, are here condemned
95 To waste eternal days in woe and pain?
And reckon'st thou thyself with spirits of Heav'n
Hell-doomed, and breath'st defiance here and scorn,
Where I reign king, and, to enrage thee more,
Thy king and lord? Back to thy punishment,
00 False fugitive; and to thy speed add wings,

Lest with a whip of scorpions[2] I pursue
Thy lingering, or with one stroke of this dart
Strange horror seize thee, and pangs unfelt before."
    So spake the grisly terror, and in shape,
705 So speaking and so threat'ning, grew tenfold,
More dreadful and deform. On th' other side,
Incensed with indignation, Satan stood
Unterrified, and like a comet burned,
That fires the length of Ophiuchus[3] huge
710 In th' arctic sky, and from his horrid hair
Shakes pestilence and war.[4] Each at the head
Levelled his deadly aim; their fatal hands
No second stroke intend; and such a frown
Each cast at th' other as when two black clouds,
715 With Heav'n's artillery[5] fraught, came rattling on
Over the Caspian, then stand front to front
Hovering a space, till winds the signal blow
To join their dark encounter in mid-air.
So frowned the mighty combatants that Hell
720 Grew darker at their frown; so matched they stood;
For never but once more was either like
To meet so great a foe. And now great deeds
Had been achieved, whereof all Hell had rung,
Had not the snaky sorceress, that sat
725 Fast by Hell-gate and kept the fatal key,
Risen, and with hideous outcry rushed between.
    "O father, what intends thy hand," she cried,
"Against thy only son? What fury, O son,
Possesses thee to bend that mortal dart
730 Against thy father's head? And know'st for whom?
For Him who sits above, and laughs the while
At thee, ordained His drudge to execute
Whate'er His wrath, which He calls justice, bids—
His wrath, which one day will destroy ye both!"
735 She spake, and at her words the hellish pest
Forbore: then these to her Satan returned:
    "So strange thy outcry, and thy words so strange

---

2 *with a whip of scorpions* Mirrors the words of King Rheoboam, son of Solomon in 1 Kings 12.11, whose promise of harshness sparked a civil war.

3 *Ophiuchus* The constellation Serpent Bearer, visible in the northern sky from June to October.

4 *from his horrid hair ... war* Comets, with their long luminous tails, or hair, were believed to be harbingers of disaster.

5 *Heav'n's artillery* Lightning.

---

1 *Scylla* Nymph transformed by Circe, the Greek enchantress, into a dreadful monster with a lower body composed of savage dogs.

Thou interposest, that my sudden hand,
Prevented, spares to tell thee yet by deeds
740 What it intends, till first I know of thee
What thing thou art, thus double-formed, and why,
In this infernal vale first met, thou call'st
Me father, and that phantasm call'st my son.
I know thee not, nor ever saw till now
745 Sight more detestable than him and thee."
        T' whom thus the portress[1] of Hell-gate replied:
"Hast thou forgot me, then; and do I seem
Now in thine eye so foul? Once deemed so fair
In Heaven, when at th' assembly, and in sight
750 Of all the seraphim with thee combined
In bold conspiracy against Heaven's King,
All on a sudden miserable pain
Surprised thee, dim thine eyes and dizzy swum
In darkness, while thy head flames thick and fast
755 Threw forth, till on the left side op'ning wide,
Likest to thee in shape and count'nance bright,
Then shining heav'nly fair, a goddess armed,
Out of thy head I sprung.[2] Amazement seized
All th' host of Heav'n; back they recoiled afraid
760 At first, and called me Sin, and for a sign
Portentous held me; but, familiar grown,
I pleased, and with attractive graces won
The most averse—thee chiefly, who, full oft
Thyself in me thy perfect image viewing,
765 Becam'st enamored; and such joy thou took'st
With me in secret that my womb conceived
A growing burden. Meanwhile war arose,
And fields were fought in Heav'n: wherein remained
(For what could else?) to our Almighty Foe
770 Clear victory; to our part loss and rout
Through all the Empyrean. Down they fell,
Driven headlong from the pitch° of Heaven,   *field
    down
Into this deep; and in the general fall
I also: at which time this powerful key
775 Into my hands was given, with charge to keep
These gates for ever shut, which none can pass
Without my op'ning. Pensive here I sat
Alone; but long I sat not, till my womb,

Pregnant by thee, and now excessive grown,
780 Prodigious motion felt and rueful throes.
At last this odious offspring whom thou seest,
Thine own begotten, breaking violent way,
Tore through my entrails, that, with fear and pain
Distorted, all my nether shape thus grew
785 Transformed: but he my inbred enemy
Forth issued, brandishing his fatal dart,
Made to destroy. I fled, and cried out Death!
Hell trembled at the hideous name, and sighed
From all her caves, and back resounded Death!
790 I fled; but he pursued (though more, it seems,
Inflamed with lust than rage), and, swifter far,
Me overtook, his mother, all dismayed,
And, in embraces forcible and foul
Engendering with me, of that rape begot
795 These yelling monsters, that with ceaseless cry
Surround me, as thou saw'st—hourly conceived
And hourly born, with sorrow infinite
To me; for, when they list, into the womb
That bred them they return, and howl, and gnaw
800 My bowels, their repast; then, bursting forth
Afresh, with conscious terrors vex me round,
That rest or intermission none I find.
Before mine eyes in opposition sits
Grim Death, my son and foe, who set them on,
805 And me, his parent, would full soon devour
For want of other prey, but that he knows
His end with mine involved, and knows that I
Should prove a bitter morsel, and his bane,
Whenever that shall be: so fate pronounced.
810 But thou, O father, I forewarn thee, shun
His deadly arrow; neither vainly hope
To be invulnerable in those bright arms,
Though tempered heavenly; for that mortal
    dint,°   *power
Save He who reigns above, none can resist."
815   She finished; and the subtle fiend his lore
Soon learned, now milder, and thus answered smooth:
"Dear daughter—since thou claim'st me for thy sire,
And my fair son here show'st me, the dear pledge
Of dalliance had with thee in Heav'n, and joys
820 Then sweet, now sad to mention, through dire change
Befall'n us unforeseen, unthought-of-know,
I come no enemy, but to set free

---

1 *portress* Female doorkeeper.

2 *Out of thy head I sprung* Cf. Athena's birth from the head of Zeus
in classical myth.

From out this dark and dismal house of pain
Both him and thee, and all the heav'nly host
825 Of spirits that, in our just pretences armed,
Fell with us from on high. From them I go
This uncouth errand sole, and one for all
Myself expose, with lonely steps to tread
Th' unfounded deep, and through the void immense
830 To search, with wandering quest, a place foretold
Should be—and, by concurring signs, ere now
Created vast and round—a place of bliss
In the purlieus° of Heav'n; and therein placed   outskirts
A race of upstart creatures, to supply
835 Perhaps our vacant room, though more removed,
Lest Heav'n, surcharged with potent multitude,
Might hap to move new broils.[1] Be this, or aught
Than this more secret, now designed, I haste
To know; and, this once known, shall soon return,
840 And bring ye to the place where thou and Death
Shall dwell at ease, and up and down unseen
Wing silently the buxom° air, embalmed   healthy
With odours. There ye shall be fed and filled
Immeasurably; all things shall be your prey."
845 He ceased; for both seemed highly pleased, and Death
Grinned horrible a ghastly smile, to hear
His famine should be filled, and blessed his maw
Destined to that good hour. No less rejoiced
His mother bad, and thus bespake her sire:
850   "The key of this infernal pit, by due
And by command of Heav'n's all-powerful King,
I keep, by Him forbidden to unlock
These adamantine gates; against all force
Death ready stands to interpose his dart,
855 Fearless to be o'ermatched by living might.
But what owe I to His commands above,
Who hates me, and hath hither thrust me down
Into this gloom of Tartarus profound,
To sit in hateful office° here confined,   duty
860 Inhabitant of Heav'n and heav'nly born—
Here in perpetual agony and pain,
With terrors and with clamours compassed round
Of mine own brood, that on my bowels feed?
Thou art my father, thou my author, thou
865 My being gav'st me; whom should I obey
But thee? Whom follow? Thou will bring me soon

To that new world of light and bliss, among
The gods who live at ease, where I shall reign
At thy right hand voluptuous, as beseems
870 Thy daughter and thy darling, without end."
    Thus saying, from her side the fatal key,
Sad instrument of all our woe, she took;
And, towards the gate rolling her bestial train,
Forthwith the huge portcullis high up-drew,
875 Which, but herself, not all the Stygian powers
Could once have moved; then in the key-hole turns
Th' intricate wards,[2] and every bolt and bar
Of massy iron or solid rock with ease
Unfast'ns. On a sudden op'n fly,
880 With impetuous recoil and jarring sound,
Th' infernal doors, and on their hinges grate
Harsh thunder, that the lowest bottom shook
Of Erebus.[3] She op'nd; but to shut
Excelled her power: the gates wide op'n stood,
885 That with extended wings a bannered host,
Under spread ensigns° marching, might pass   flags
    through
With horse and chariots ranked in loose array;
So wide they stood, and like a furnace-mouth
Cast forth redounding° smoke and ruddy flame. copious
890 Before their eyes in sudden view appear
The secrets of the hoary deep—a dark
Illimitable ocean, without bound,
Without dimension; where length, breadth, and height,
And time, and place, are lost; where eldest Night
895 And Chaos, ancestors of nature, hold
Eternal anarchy, amidst the noise
Of endless wars, and by confusion stand.
For Hot, Cold, Moist, and Dry,[4] four champions
    fierce,
Strive here for mastery, and to battle bring
900 Their embryon atoms:[5] they around the flag
Of each his faction, in their several clans,
Light-armed or heavy, sharp, smooth, swift, or slow,
Swarm populous, unnumbered as the sands

---

1 *Might hap to move new broils* Might chance to begin new wars.

2 *wards* The tumblers and pin assemblies of a lock, which mate
with and are turned by the teeth of a key.

3 *Erebus* Upper region of Hades.

4 *Hot, Cold, Moist, and Dry* Personifications of the four classical
elements: fire, air, water, and earth.

5 *Their embryon atoms* Their primeval matter.

Of Barca or Cyrene's torrid soil,[1]
905 Levied to side with warring winds, and poise
Their lighter wings. To whom these most adhere
He rules a moment: Chaos umpire sits,
And by decision more embroils the fray
By which he reigns: next him, high arbiter,
910 Chance governs all. Into this wild abyss,
The womb of Nature, and perhaps her grave,
Of neither sea, nor shore, nor air, nor fire,
But all these in their pregnant causes mixed
Confus'dly, and which thus must ever fight,
915 Unless th' Almighty Maker them ordain
His dark materials to create more worlds—
Into this wild abyss the wary fiend
Stood on the brink of Hell and looked a while,
Pondering his voyage; for no narrow frith°   *fjord*
920 He had to cross. Nor was his ear less pealed°   *deafened*
With noises loud and ruinous (to compare
Great things with small) than when Bellona[2] storms
With all her battering engines, bent to raze
Some capital city; or less than if this frame
925 Of Heav'n were falling, and these elements
In mutiny had from her axle torn
The steadfast Earth. At last his sail-broad vans°   *wings*
He spread for flight, and, in the surging smoke
Uplifted, spurns the ground; thence many a league,
930 As in a cloudy chair, ascending rides
Audacious; but, that seat soon failing, meets
A vast vacuity. All unawares,
Fluttering his pennons° vain, plumb down[3] he drops *wings*
Ten thousand fathom deep, and to this hour
935 Down had been falling, had not, by ill chance,
The strong rebuff of some tumultuous cloud,
Instinct[4] with fire and nitre, hurried him
As many miles aloft. That fury stayed—
Quenched in a boggy Syrtis,[5] neither sea,
940 Nor good dry land—nigh foundered,[6] on he fares,

Treading the crude consistence, half on foot,
Half flying; behoves him now both oar and sail.
As when a griffon[7] through the wilderness
With wingèd course, o'er hill or moory dale,
945 Pursues the Arimaspian,[8] who by stealth
Had from his wakeful custody purloined
The guarded gold; so eagerly the fiend
O'er bog or steep, through strait, rough, dense, or rare,
With head, hands, wings, or feet, pursues his way,
950 And swims, or sinks, or wades, or creeps, or flies.
At length a universal hubbub wild
Of stunning sounds, and voices all confused,
Borne through the hollow dark, assaults his ear
With loudest vehemence. Thither he plies
955 Undaunted, to meet there whatever power
Or spirit of the nethermost abyss
Might in that noise reside, of whom to ask
Which way the nearest coast of darkness lies
Bordering on light; when straight behold the throne
960 Of Chaos, and his dark pavilion spread
Wide on the wasteful° deep! With him enthroned   *empty*
Sat sable-vested night, eldest of things,
The consort of his reign; and by them stood
Orcus and Ades, and the dreaded name
965 Of Demogorgon;[9] Rumour next, and Chance,
And Tumult, and Confusion, all embroiled,
And Discord with a thousand various mouths.
      T' whom Satan, turning boldly, thus: "Ye powers
And spirits of this nethermost abyss,
970 Chaos and ancient Night, I come no spy
With purpose to explore or to disturb
The secrets of your realm; but, by constraint°   *necessity*
Wandering this darksome desert, as my way
Lies through your spacious empire up to light,
975 Alone and without guide, half lost, I seek,
What readiest path leads where your gloomy bounds
Confine° with Heav'n; or, if some other place,   *meet*

---

[1] *Barca or Cyrene's torrid soil* Barca and Cyrene are cities in the Libyan desert surrounded by sand dunes.

[2] *Bellona* Goddess of war in the Roman pantheon.

[3] *plumb down* Straight down.

[4] *Instinct* Shot through.

[5] *Syrtis* Pair of quicksand gulfs on either side of Tripoli; see Book 5 of Pliny the Elder's *Natural History*.

[6] *nigh foundered* Nearly sunk.

[7] *griffon* Fabled beast with the head and wings of an eagle, the body of a lion, a voracious appetite for horses, and a penchant for hoarding gold and treasure.

[8] *Arimaspian* Member of the Arimaspi tribe, said by Herodotus to pilfer the griffons' treasure.

[9] *Orcus* Pluto, Roman god of the underworld; *Ades* Hades, Greek god of the underworld; *Demogorgon* Greek god of the underworld who predates Hades.

From your dominion won, th' ethereal King
Possesses lately, thither to arrive
980 I travel this profound.° Direct my course: deep
Directed, no mean recompense° it brings   reward
To your behoof,° if I that region lost,   benefit
All usurpation thence expelled, reduce
To her original darkness and your sway
985 (Which is my present journey), and once more
Erect the standard° there of ancient Night.   flag
Yours be th' advantage all, mine the revenge!"
      Thus Satan; and him thus the anarch old,[1]
With faltering speech and visage incomposed,
990 Answered: "I know thee, stranger, who thou art—
That mighty leading angel, who of late
Made head against Heav'n's King, though overthrown.
I saw and heard; for such a numerous host
Fled not in silence through the frighted deep,
995 With ruin upon ruin, rout on rout,
Confusion worse confounded; and Heav'n-gates
Poured out by millions her victorious bands,
Pursuing. I upon my frontiers here
Keep residence; if all I can will serve
1000 That little which is left so to defend,
Encroached on still through our intestine broils[2]
Weakening the sceptre of old Night: first, Hell,
Your dungeon, stretching far and wide beneath;
Now lately Heav'n and Earth, another world
1005 Hung o'er my realm, linked in a golden chain
To that side Heav'n from whence your legions fell!
If that way be your walk, you have not far;
So much the nearer danger. Go, and speed;
Havoc, and spoil, and ruin, are my gain."
1010 He ceased; and Satan stayed not to reply,
But, glad that now his sea should find a shore,
With fresh alacrity and force renewed
Springs upward, like a pyramid of fire,
Into the wild expanse, and through the shock
1015 Of fighting elements, on all sides round
Environed, wins his way; harder beset
And more endangered than when Argo passed
Through Bosporus betwixt the jostling rocks,
Or when Ulysses on the larboard shunned
1020 Charybdis,[3] and by th' other whirlpool steered.
So he with difficulty and labour hard
Moved on, with difficulty and labour he;
But, he once passed, soon after, when man fell,
Strange alteration! Sin and Death amain,[4]
1025 Following his track (such was the will of Heav'n)
Paved after him a broad and beaten way
Over the dark abyss, whose boiling gulf
Tamely endured a bridge of wondrous length,
From Hell continued, reaching th' utmost orb
1030 Of this frail world; by which the spirits perverse
With easy intercourse[5] pass to and fro
To tempt or punish mortals, except whom
God and good angels guard by special grace.
But now at last the sacred influence
1035 Of light appears, and from the walls of Heav'n
Shoots far into the bosom of dim Night
A glimmering dawn. Here Nature first begins
Her farthest verge,° and Chaos to retire,   border
As from her outmost works, a broken foe,
1040 With tumult less and with less hostile din;
That Satan with less toil, and now with ease,
Wafts on the calmer wave by dubious light,
And, like a weather-beaten vessel, holds
Gladly the port, though shrouds° and tackle torn;   sails
1045 Or in the emptier waste, resembling air,
Weighs his spread wings, at leisure to behold
Far off th' empyreal Heav'n, extended wide
In circuit, undetermined square or round,[6]
With opal towers and battlements adorned
1050 Of living sapphire, once his native seat;
And, fast by, hanging in a golden chain,
This pendent world, in bigness as a star

---

1 *the anarch old* The old anarchist, i.e., Chaos.

2 *intestine broils* Civil wars.

3 *Argo* The ship of Jason and the Argonauts of Greek legend, sailors who faced many challenges in their travels; *the jostling rocks* Huge floating rocks that clashed and ground on one another were a peril passed by Jason and the Argonauts; *Ulysses* Subject of Homer's *Odyssey* and a character in his *Iliad*, a famous wandering king, sailor, and hero; *larboard* The port or left side of a ship; *Charybdis* Terrible whirlpool circumnavigated by Ulysses.

4 *amain* Moving at full speed.

5 *intercourse* Movement.

6 *undetermined square or round* In other words, the overall shape of Heaven is indiscernible.

Of smallest magnitude close by the moon.[1]
Thither, full fraught with mischievous revenge,
1055   Accursed, and in a cursed hour, he hies.°   goes

THE END OF THE SECOND BOOK

ARGUMENT TO BOOK 3

God sitting on His throne sees Satan flying towards this world, then newly created; shows him to the Son who sat at His right hand; foretells the success of Satan in perverting mankind; clears His own justice and wisdom from all imputation, having created man free and able enough to have withstood his tempter; yet declares His purpose of grace towards Him, in regard he fell not of his own malice, as did Satan, but by him seduced. The Son of God renders praises to His Father for the manifestation of His gracious purpose towards man; but God again declares, that grace cannot be extended towards man without the satisfaction of Divine Justice; man hath offended the Majesty of God by aspiring to Godhead, and therefore with all his progeny devoted to death must die, unless some one can be found sufficient to answer for his offence, and undergo his punishment. The Son of God freely offers himself a ransom for man: the Father accepts Him, ordains His incarnation, pronounces His exaltation above all names in Heaven and Earth; commands all the angels to adore Him; they obey, and hymning to their harps in full choir, celebrate the Father and the Son. Meanwhile Satan alights upon the bare convex of this world's outermost orb; where wandering he first finds a place since called the Limbo of Vanity; what persons and things fly up thither; thence comes to the gate of Heaven, described ascending by stairs, and the waters above the firmament that flow about it: his passage thence to the orb of the Sun; he finds there Uriel the regent of that orb, but first changes himself into the shape of a meaner angel; and pretending a zealous desire to behold the new creation and man whom God had placed here, inquires of him the place of his habitation, and is directed; alights first on Mount Niphates.

from BOOK 3

Hail, holy light, offspring of Heav'n first-born,
    Or of th' eternal coeternal beam
May I express thee unblamed? Since God is light,[2]
And never but in unapproached° light   incomparable
5   Dwelt from eternity, dwelt then in thee
Bright effluence of bright° essence increate.[3]
Or hear'st thou rather pure ethereal stream,
Whose fountain° who shall tell? Before the sun,   source
Before the Heav'ns thou wert, and at the voice
10 Of God, as with a mantle, didst invest
The rising world of waters dark and deep,
Won from the void and formless infinite.
Thee I re-visit now with bolder wing,
Escaped the Stygian pool, though long detained
15 In that obscure sojourn, while in my flight
Through utter and through middle darkness borne,
With other notes than to th' Orphean[4] lyre
I sung of Chaos and eternal Night;
Taught by the heavenly Muse to venture down
20 The dark descent, and up to re-ascend,
Though hard and rare: thee I revisit safe,
And feel thy sovereign vital lamp; but thou
Revisit'st not these eyes,[5] that roll in vain
To find thy piercing ray, and find no dawn;
25 So thick a drop serene[6] hath quenched their orbs,
Or dim suffusion veiled. Yet not the more
Cease I to wander, where the Muses haunt,
Clear spring, or shady grove, or sunny hill,
Smit° with the love of sacred song; but chief   smitten
30 Thee, Sion, and the flowery brooks beneath,
That wash thy hallowed feet, and warbling flow,
Nightly I visit: nor sometimes forget
So were I equalled with them in renown,
Thy sov'reign command, that Man should find grace;
35 Blind Thamyris, and blind Maeonides,

[1] *in bigness as a star / Of smallest magnitude close by the moon*   Refers to the perceived size of the smallest star in the sky compared to the moon (not the actual size of a star compared to the moon); in other words, very, very small.

[2] *May I express thee unblam'd*   May I call you that without being blamed; *God is light*   See 1 John 1.5.

[3] *increate*   Not created, always existing.

[4] *Orphean*   Orpheus, a musician-hero of Greek myth, visited the underworld to retrieve his wife Eurydice. The notes of his lyre won him safe passage.

[5] *Revisit'st not these eyes*   Milton became totally blind in 1652.

[6] *drop serene*   Gutta serena, the eye disease Milton had.

And Tiresias, and Phineus,[1] prophets old:
Then feed on thoughts, that voluntary move
Harmonious numbers; as the wakeful bird[2]
Sings darkling,° and in shadiest covert hid   *in the dark*
40 Tunes her nocturnal note. Thus with the year
Seasons return; but not to me returns
Day, or the sweet approach of even or morn,
Or sight of vernal° bloom, or summer's rose,   *spring*
Or flocks, or herds, or human face divine;
45 But cloud instead, and ever-during dark
Surrounds me, from the cheerful ways of men
Cut off, and for the book of knowledge fair
Presented with a universal blank
Of Nature's works to me expunged and razed,
50 And Wisdom at one entrance quite shut out.[3]
So much the rather thou, celestial Light,
Shine inward, and the mind through all her powers
Irradiate; there plant eyes, all mist from thence
Purge and disperse, that I may see and tell
55 Of things invisible to mortal sight.
        Now had the Almighty Father from above,
From the pure empyrean where He sits
High throned above all height, bent down His eye
His own works and their works at once to view:
60 About Him all the sanctities of Heaven[4]
Stood thick as stars, and from His sight received
Beatitude past utterance; on his right
The radiant image of His glory sat,
His only Son; on earth He first beheld
65 Our two first parents, yet° the only two   *thus far*
Of mankind in the happy garden placed
Reaping immortal fruits of joy and love,
Uninterrupted joy, unrivalled love,
In blissful solitude; He then surveyed
70 Hell and the gulf between, and Satan there

Coasting[5] the wall of Heav'n on this side night
In the dun° air sublime, and ready now   *dusky*
To stoop° with wearied wings, and willing feet,   *swoop*
On the bare outside of this world, that seemed
75 Firm land embosomed,° without firmament,   *enclosed*
Uncertain which, in ocean or in air.
Him God beholding from His prospect high,
Wherein past, present, future, He beholds,
Thus to His only Son foreseeing spake:
80   "Only begotten Son, seest Thou what rage
Transports Our adversary? whom no bounds
Prescribed no bars of Hell, nor all the chains
Heaped on him there, nor yet the main abyss
Wide interrupt, can hold; so bent he seems
85 On desperate revenge, that shall redound
Upon his own rebellious head. And now,
Through all restraint broke loose, he wings his way
Not far off Heav'n, in the precincts of light,
Directly towards the new created world,
90 And man there placed, with purpose to assay
If him by force he can destroy, or, worse,
By some false guile pervert; and shall pervert;
For man will hearken to his glozing° lies,   *flattering*
And easily transgress the sole command,
95 Sole pledge of his obedience: so will fall
He and his faithless progeny: Whose fault?
Whose but his own? Ingrate, he had of Me
All he could have; I made him just and right,
Sufficient to have stood, though free to fall.
100 Such I created all th' ethereal powers
And spirits, both them who stood, and them who
        failed;
Freely they stood who stood, and fell who fell.
Not free, what proof could they have given sincere
Of true allegiance, constant faith, or love,
105 Where only what they needs must do appeared,
Not what they would? What praise could they receive?
What pleasure I, from such obedience paid,
When Will and Reason (Reason also is choice)
Useless and vain, of freedom both despoiled,
110 Made passive both, had served necessity,
Not me? They therefore, as to right belonged,
So were created, nor can justly accuse
Their Maker, or their making, or their fate,

---

[1] *Thamyris* Ancient Greek poet deprived of his sight by the Muses
for competing with them; *Maeonides* Homer, the blind author of
The Odyssey and *The Iliad*; *Tiresias* Greek prophet blinded either
by Hera or by Diana; *Phineus* Prophet blinded by the gods for
telling too many truthful prophecies.

[2] *wakeful bird* Nightingale.

[3] *And Wisdom at one entrance quite shut out* Information cannot be
received as one sense has ceased to operate.

[4] *sanctities of Heaven* Saints.

---

[5] *Coasting* Following the coast of.

As if predestination over-ruled
115 Their will disposed by absolute decree
Or high foreknowledge; they themselves decreed
Their own revolt, not I: if I foreknew,
Foreknowledge had no influence on their fault,
Which had no less proved certain unforeknown.
120 So without least impulse or shadow of fate,
Or aught by me immutably foreseen,
They trespass, authors to themselves in all
Both what they judge and what they choose; for so
I formed them free, and free they must remain,
125 Till they enthral themselves: I else must change
Their nature, and revoke the high decree
Unchangeable, eternal, which ordained
Their freedom, they themselves ordained their fall.
The first sort by their own suggestion fell,
130 Self-tempted, self-depraved: Man falls deceived
By the other first: Man therefore shall find grace,
The other none: In mercy and justice both,
Through Heav'n and earth, so shall My glory excel,
But mercy, first and last, shall brightest shine."
135   Thus while God spake, ambrosial fragrance filled
All Heaven, and in the blessèd spirits elect[1]
Sense of new joy ineffable diffused.
Beyond compare the Son of God was seen
Most glorious; in Him all His Father shone
140 Substantially expressed; and in His face
Divine compassion visibly appeared,
Love without end, and without measure grace,
Which uttering, thus He to His Father spake:
"O Father, gracious was that word which closed
145 Thy sovereign sentence, that man should find grace;
For which both Heav'n and earth shall high extol
Thy praises, with the innumerable sound
Of hymns and sacred songs, wherewith Thy throne
Encompassed shall resound Thee ever blest.
150 For should Man finally be lost, should Man,
Thy creature late so loved, thy youngest son,
Fall circumvented thus by fraud, though joined
With his own folly? That be from Thee far,
That far be from Thee, Father, who art Judge
155 Of all things made, and judgest only right.
Or shall the adversary thus obtain
His end, and frustrate Thine? Shall he fulfil

His malice, and Thy goodness bring to nought,
Or proud return, though to his heavier doom,
160 Yet with revenge accomplished, and to Hell
Draw after him the whole race of mankind,
By him corrupted? Or wilt Thou Thyself
Abolish Thy creation, and unmake
For him, what for Thy glory Thou hast made?
165 So should Thy goodness and Thy greatness both
Be questioned and blasphemed without defence."
    To whom the great Creator thus replied:
"O Son, in whom My soul hath chief delight,
Son of My bosom, Son who art alone
170 My word, My wisdom, and effectual might,
All hast Thou spoken as My thoughts are, all
As My eternal purpose hath decreed;
Man shall not quite be lost, but saved who will;
Yet not of will in him, but grace in Me
175 Freely vouchsafed;[2] once more I will renew
His lapsed powers, though forfeit; and enthralled
By sin to foul exorbitant desires;
Upheld by Me, yet once more he shall stand
On even ground against his mortal foe;
180 By Me upheld, that he may know how frail
His fallen condition is, and to Me owe
All his deliv'rance, and to none but Me.
Some I have chosen of peculiar grace,
Elect above the rest; so is My will:
185 The rest shall hear Me call, and oft be warned
Their sinful state, and to appease betimes
Th' incensèd deity, while offered grace
Invites; for I will clear their senses dark,[3]
What may suffice, and soften stony hearts
190 To pray, repent, and bring obedience due.
To prayer, repentance, and obedience due,
Though but endeavoured with sincere intent,
Mine ear shall not be slow, Mine eye not shut.
And I will place within them as a guide,
195 My umpire Conscience; whom if they will hear,
Light after light, well used, they shall attain,
And to the end, persisting, safe arrive.
This My long sufferance, and My day of grace,
They who neglect and scorn, shall never taste;

---

[1] *spirits elect* Unfallen angels.

[2] *vouchsafed* Given by oath.

[3] *their senses dark* Cf. 1 Corinthians 13.12: "For now we see through a glass, darkly."

300 But hard be hardened, blind be blinded more,
That they may stumble on, and deeper fall;
And none but such from mercy I exclude.
But yet all is not done; Man disobeying,
Disloyal, breaks his fealty,° and sins   *faith, loyalty*
305 Against the high supremacy of Heav'n,
Affecting Godhead, and, so losing all,
To expiate his treason hath nought left,
But to destruction sacred and devote,
He, with his whole posterity, must die,
310 Die he or justice must; unless for him
Some other able, and as willing, pay
The rigid satisfaction, death for death.
Say, heavenly powers, where shall we find such love?
Which of you will be mortal, to redeem
315 Man's mortal crime, and just the unjust to save,
Dwells in all Heaven charity so dear?"
        He asked, but all the heav'nly choir stood mute,
And silence was in Heav'n: on man's behalf
Patron or intercessor none appeared,
320 Much less that dared upon his own head draw
The deadly forfeiture, and ransom set.
And now without redemption all mankind
Must have been lost, adjudged to death and Hell
By doom severe, had not the Son of God,
325 In whom the fullness dwells of love divine,
His dearest mediation thus renewed:
        "Father, Thy word is past, Man shall find grace;
And shall grace not find means, that finds her way,
The speediest of Thy winged messengers,
330 To visit all Thy creatures, and to all
Comes unprevented, unimplor'd, unsought?
Happy for Man, so coming; he her aid
Can never seek, once dead in sins, and lost;
Atonement for himself, or offering meet,
335 Indebted and undone, hath none to bring;
Behold Me then: Me for him, life for life
I offer: on Me let Thine anger fall;
Account Me Man; I for his sake will leave
Thy bosom, and this glory next to Thee
340 Freely put off, and for him lastly die
Well pleased; on Me let Death wreak all his rage.
Under his gloomy power I shall not long
Lie vanquished. Thou hast giv'n Me to possess
Life in Myself for ever; by Thee I live;

245 Though now to Death I yield, and am his due,
All that of Me can die, yet, that debt paid,
Thou wilt not leave Me in the loathsome grave
His prey, nor suffer my unspotted soul
For ever with corruption there to dwell;
250 But I shall rise victorious, and subdue
My vanquisher, spoiled of his vaunted spoil.
Death his death's wound shall then receive, and stoop
Inglorious, of his mortal sting disarmed;[1]
I through the ample air in triumph high
255 Shall lead Hell captive maugre[2] Hell, and show
The powers of darkness bound. Thou, at the sight
Pleased, out of Heaven shall look down and smile,
While, by Thee raised, I ruin all My foes;
Death last, and with his carcass glut the grave;
260 Then, with the multitude of My redeemed,
Shall enter Heaven, long absent, and return,
Father, to see Thy face, wherein no cloud
Of anger shall remain, but peace assured
And reconcilement: wrath shall be no more
265 Thenceforth, but in Thy presence joy entire."
        His words here ended; but His meek aspect
Silent yet spake, and breathed immortal love
To mortal men, above which only shone
Filial obedience:[3] as a sacrifice
270 Glad to be offered, He attends the will
Of His great Father. Admiration seized
All Heav'n, what this might mean, and whither tend,
Wondering; but soon th' Almighty thus replied:
        "O Thou in Heav'n and earth the only peace
275 Found out for mankind under wrath, O Thou
My sole complacence![4] Well Thou know'st how dear
To Me are all My works; nor Man the least,
Though last created, that for him I spare
Thee from My bosom and right hand, to save,
280 By losing Thee a while, the whole race lost.
Thou, therefore, whom Thou only canst redeem,
Their nature also to Thy nature join;
And be Thyself Man among men on earth,
Made flesh, when time shall be, of virgin seed,

---

1 *Death ... his mortal sting disarmed* See 1 Corinthians 15.55.

2 *maugre* In spite of.

3 *Filial obedience* Proper for a child/parent relationship.

4 *complacence* Here, source of satisfaction.

285 By wondrous birth; be Thou in Adam's room[1]
The head of all mankind, though Adam's son.
As in him perish all men, so in Thee,
As from a second root, shall be restored
As many as are restored, without Thee none.

290 His crime makes guilty all his sons; Thy merit,
Imputed, shall absolve them who renounce
Their own both righteous and unrighteous deeds,
And live in Thee transplanted, and from Thee
Receive new life. So Man, as is most just,

295 Shall satisfy for Man, be judged and die,
And dying rise, and rising with Him raise
His brethren, ransomed with His own dear life.
So heavenly love shall outdo hellish hate,
Giving to death, and dying to redeem,

300 So dearly to redeem what hellish hate
So easily destroyed, and still destroys
In those who, when they may, accept not grace.
Nor shalt Thou, by descending to assume
Man's nature, lessen or degrade Thine own.

305 Because Thou hast, though throned in highest bliss
Equal to God, and equally enjoying
God-like fruition, quitted all, to save
A world from utter loss, and hast been found
By merit more than birthright Son of God,

310 Found worthiest to be so by being good,
Far more than great or high; because in Thee
Love hath abounded more than glory abounds;
Therefore Thy humiliation shall exalt
With Thee Thy manhood also to this throne:

315 Here shalt thou sit incarnate, here shalt reign
Both God and Man, Son both of God and Man,
Anointed universal King; all power
I give Thee; reign forever, and assume
Thy merits; under Thee, as Head Supreme,

320 Thrones, princedoms, powers, dominions, I reduce:
All knees to Thee shall bow, of them that bide°   live
In Heav'n, or earth, or under earth in Hell.
When Thou, attended gloriously from Heav'n,
Shalt in the sky appear, and from Thee send

325 The summoning arch-angels to proclaim
Thy dread tribunal; forthwith from all winds,
The living, and forthwith the cited dead
Of all past ages, to the general doom

Shall hasten; such a peal shall rouse their sleep.
330 Then, all Thy saints assembled, Thou shalt judge
Bad men and angels; they, arraigned, shall sink
Beneath Thy sentence; Hell, her numbers full,
Thenceforth shall be forever shut. Meanwhile
The world shall burn, and from her ashes spring

335 New Heav'n and earth, wherein the just shall dwell,
And, after all their tribulations long,
See golden days, fruitful of golden deeds,
With joy and peace triumphing, and fair truth.
Then Thou Thy regal sceptre shall lay by,

340 For regal sceptre then no more shall need,
God shall be all in all.[2] But, all ye gods,
Adore Him, who to compass all this dies;
Adore the Son, and honour Him as Me."
     No sooner had th' Almighty ceased, but all

345 The multitude of angels, with a shout
Loud as from numbers without number, sweet
As from blest voices, uttering joy, Heav'n rung
With jubilee, and loud hosannas[3] filled
Th' eternal regions: lowly reverent

350 Towards either throne[4] they bow, and to the ground
With solemn adoration down they cast
Their crowns inwove with amarant[5] and gold;
Immortal amarant, a flower which once
In Paradise, fast° by the tree of life,   near

355 Began to bloom; but soon for man's offence
To Heav'n removed, where first it grew, there grows,
And flowers aloft shading the fount of life,
And where the river of bliss through midst of Heav'n
Rolls o'er Elysian° flowers her amber   paradisiacal
     stream;

360 With these that never fade the spirits elect
Bind their resplendent locks enwreathed with beams;
Now in loose garlands thick thrown off, the bright
Pavement, that like a sea of jasper shone,
Empurpled with celestial roses smiled.

365 Then, crowned again, their golden harps they took,

---

[1] *in Adam's room* Instead of Adam.

[2] *When thou, attended … be all in all* This account of the end of all things is a paraphrased of the Book of Revelation.

[3] *hosannas* Shouts of fervent and worshipful praise.

[4] *either throne* Both the throne of God and the throne of the Son of God.

[5] *amarant* Amaranthus, a red flower with large leaves that symbolizes undying love.

Harps ever tuned, that glittering by their side
Like quivers hung, and with preamble sweet
Of charming symphony they introduce
Their sacred song, and waken raptures high;
70   No voice exempt, no voice but well could join
Melodious part, such concord is in Heav'n....

ARGUMENT TO BOOK 4

Satan now in prospect of Eden, and nigh the place
where he must now attempt the bold enterprise which
he undertook alone against God and man, falls into
many doubts with himself, and many passions, fear,
envy, and despair; but at length confirms himself in evil,
journeys on to Paradise, whose outward prospect and
situation is described, overleaps the bounds, sits in the
shape of a cormorant on the Tree of Life, as highest in
the garden to look about him. The garden described;
Satan's first sight of Adam and Eve; his wonder at their
excellent form and happy state, but with resolution to
work their fall; overhears their discourse, thence gathers
that the Tree of Knowledge was forbidden them to eat
of, under penalty of death; and thereon intends to
found his temptation, by seducing them to transgress:
then leaves them a while, to know further of their state
by some other means. Meanwhile Uriel descending on
a sunbeam warns Gabriel, who had in charge the gate of
Paradise, that some evil spirit had escaped the deep, and
passed at noon by his sphere in the shape of a good
angel down to Paradise, discovered after by his furious
gestures in the Mount. Gabriel promises to find him out
ere morning. Night coming on, Adam and Eve
discourse of going to their rest: their bower described;
their evening worship. Gabriel drawing forth his bands
of night watch to walk the round of Paradise, appoints
two strong angels to Adam's bower, least the evil spirit
should be there doing some harm to Adam or Eve
sleeping; there they find him at the ear of Eve, tempting
her in a dream, and bring him, though unwilling, to
Gabriel; by whom questioned, he scornfully answers,
prepares resistance, but hindered by a sign from Heaven,
flies out of Paradise.

BOOK 4

O, for that warning voice, which he, who saw
Th' Apocalypse, heard cry in Heaven aloud,
Then when the Dragon, put to second rout,[1]
Came furious down to be revenged on men,
5   Woe to the inhabitants on earth! That now,
While time was,[2] our first parents had been warned
The coming of their secret foe, and 'scaped,
Haply so 'scaped his mortal snare: For now
Satan, now first inflamed with rage, came down,
10   The tempter ere th' accuser of mankind,
To wreak on innocent frail man his loss
Of that first battle, and his flight to Hell:
Yet, not rejoicing in his speed, though bold
Far off and fearless, nor with cause to boast,
15   Begins his dire attempt; which nigh the birth
Now rolling boils in his tumultuous breast,
And like a devilish engine back recoils
Upon himself; horror and doubt distract
His troubled thoughts, and from the bottom stir
20   The Hell within him; for within him Hell
He brings, and round about him, nor from Hell
One step, no more than from himself, can fly
By change of place: Now conscience wakes despair,
That slumbered; wakes the bitter memory
25   Of what he was, what is, and what must be
Worse; of worse deeds worse sufferings must ensue.
Sometimes towards Eden, which now in his view
Lay pleasant, his grieved look he fixes sad;
Sometimes towards Heav'n, and the full-blazing sun,
30   Which now sat high in his meridian tower:
Then, much revolving,° thus in sighs began: *pondering*
    "O thou that with surpassing glory crowned
Lookest from thy sole dominion like the God
Of this new world; at whose sight all the stars
35   Hide their diminished heads; to thee I call,
But with no friendly voice, and add thy name,
Of sun to tell thee how I hate thy beams,
That bring to my remembrance from what state
I fell, how glorious once above thy sphere;

---

[1]   *O, for that ... to second rout*   See the Book of Revelation, specifically Revelation 1.10.

[2]   *That now / While time was*   If that had happened now, while there was still time.

40 Till Pride and worse Ambition threw me down
Warring in Heav'n against Heav'n's matchless King:
Ah, wherefore! He deserved no such return°   *repayment*
From me, whom He created what I was
In that bright eminence, and with His good
45 Upbraided none; nor was His service hard.
What could be less than to afford Him praise,
The easiest recompense, and pay Him thanks,
How due! Yet all His good proved ill in me,
And wrought but malice; lifted up so high
50 I 'sdained° subjection, and thought one   *disdained*
      step higher
Would set me highest, and in a moment quit
The debt immense of endless gratitude,
So burdensome still paying, still to owe,
Forgetful what from Him I still received,
55 And understood not that a grateful mind
By owing owes not, but still pays, at once
Indebted and discharged; what burden then
O, had His powerful destiny ordained
Me some inferior angel, I had stood
60 Then happy; no unbounded hope had raised
Ambition! Yet why not some other power
As great might have aspired, and me, though
      mean,°   *lowly*
Drawn to his part; but other powers as great
Fell not, but stand unshaken, from within
65 Or from without, to all temptations armed.
Hadst thou the same free will and power to stand?
Thou hadst: whom hast thou then or what to accuse,
But Heav'n's free love dealt equally to all?
Be then his love accursed, since love or hate,
70 To me alike, it deals eternal woe.
Nay, cursed be thou; since against His thy will
Chose freely what it now so justly rues.
Me miserable! which way shall I fly
Infinite wrath, and infinite despair?
75 Which way I fly is Hell; myself am Hell;
And, in the lowest deep, a lower deep
Still threatening to devour me opens wide,
To which the Hell I suffer seems a Heav'n.
O, then, at last relent: Is there no place
80 Left for repentance, none for pardon left?
None left but by submission; and that word
Disdain forbids me, and my dread of shame

Among the spirits beneath, whom I seduced
With other promises and other vaunts
85 Than to submit, boasting I could subdue
Th' Omnipotent. Ay me! They little know
How dearly I abide° that boast so vain,   *bear*
Under what torments inwardly I groan,
While they adore me on the throne of Hell.
90 With diadem and sceptre high advanced,
The lower still I fall, only supreme
In misery: such joy ambition finds.
But say I could repent, and could obtain,
By act of grace, my former state; how soon
95 Would height recall high thoughts, how soon unsay
What feigned submission swore? Ease would recant
Vows made in pain, as violent and void.
For never can true reconcilement grow,
Where wounds of deadly hate have pierced so deep:
100 Which would but lead me to a worse relapse
And heavier fall: so should I purchase dear
Short intermission bought with double smart.
This knows my punisher; therefore as far
From granting He, as I from begging, peace;
105 All hope excluded thus, behold, instead
Of us outcast, exiled, His new delight,
Mankind created, and for Him this world.
So farewell, hope; and with hope farewell, fear;
Farewell, remorse: all good to me is lost;
110 Evil, be thou my good; by thee at least
Divided empire with Heav'n's King I hold,
By thee, and more than half perhaps will reign;
As man ere long, and this new world, shall know."
      Thus while he spake, each passion dimmed his
            face
115 Thrice changed with pale, ire, envy, and despair;
Which marred his borrowed visage,[1] and betrayed
Him counterfeit, if any eye beheld.
For heav'nly minds from such distempers foul
Are ever clear. Whereof he soon aware,
120 Each perturbation smoothed with outward calm,
Artificer of fraud; and was the first
That practised falsehood under saintly show,

---

[1] *his borrowed visage* Satan had disguised himself as a "stripling cherub" at the end of Book 3, to fool the angel Uriel into telling him where Earth was.

Deep malice to conceal, couched[1] with revenge:
Yet not enough had practised to deceive
125 Uriel[2] once warned; whose eye pursued him down
The way he went, and on the Assyrian mount[3]
Saw him disfigured more than could befall
Spirit of happy sort; his gestures fierce
He marked and mad demeanour, then alone,
130 As he supposed, all unobserved, unseen.
So on he fares, and to the border comes
Of Eden, where delicious Paradise,
Now nearer, crowns with her enclosure green,
As with a rural mound, the champaign head
135 Of a steep wilderness,[4] whose hairy° sides   *forested*
With thicket overgrown, grotesque and wild,
Access denied; and overhead up grew
Insuperable height of loftiest shade,
Cedar, and pine, and fir, and branching palm,
140 A sylvan scene, and, as the ranks ascend,
Shade above shade, a woody theatre
Of stateliest view. Yet higher than their tops
The verdurous wall of Paradise upsprung;
Which to our general sire° gave prospect large   *i.e., Adam*
145 Into his nether empire neighbouring round.
And higher than that wall a circling row
Of goodliest trees, laden with fairest fruit,
Blossoms and fruits at once of golden hue,
Appeared, with gay enamelled° colours mixed: *vivid*
150 On which the sun more glad impressed his beams
Than in fair evening cloud, or humid bow,[5]
When God hath showered the earth; so lovely seemed
That landskip:° And of pure now purer air   *landscape*
Meets his approach, and to the heart inspires
155 Vernal delight and joy, able to drive
All sadness but despair: now gentle gales,
Fanning their odoriferous wings, dispense
Native perfumes, and whisper whence they stole
Those balmy spoils. As when to them who fail

160 Beyond the Cape of Hope, and now are past
Mozambique, off at sea northeast winds blow
Sabean[6] odours from the spicy shore
Of Araby the blest; with such delay
Well pleased they slack their course, and many a
      league
165 Cheered with the grateful smell old ocean smiles:
So entertained those odorous sweets the fiend,
Who came their bane; though with them better
      pleased
Than Asmodeus with the fishy fume
That drove him, though enamoured, from the spouse
170 Of Tobit's son, and with a vengeance sent
From Media post to Egypt,[7] there fast bound.
      Now to th' ascent of that steep savage hill
Satan had journeyed on, pensive and slow;
But further way found none, so thick entwined,
175 As one continued brake,° the undergrowth   *thicket*
Of shrubs and tangling bushes had perplexed
All path of man or beast that passed that way.
One gate there only was, and that looked east
On the other side: which when the arch-felon saw,
180 Due entrance he disdained; and, in contempt,
At one flight bound high over-leaped all bound
Of hill or highest wall, and sheer within
Lights on his feet. As when a prowling wolf,
Whom hunger drives to seek new haunt for prey,
185 Watching where shepherds pen their flocks at eve
In hurdled cotes[8] amid the field secure,
Leaps o'er the fence with ease into the fold:
Or as a thief, bent to unhoard the cash
Of some rich burgher,° whose substantial   *merchant*
      doors,
190 Cross-barred and bolted fast, fear no assault,
In at the window climbs, or o'er the tiles:°   *shingles*
So clomb° this first grand thief into God's fold;   *climbed*

---

1 *couched* Lying closely next to.

2 *Uriel* Angel standing guard on the sun; the name literally means "fire of God."

3 *the Assyrian mount* Mount Niphates in Syria, named in Book 3 as Satan's landing place.

4 *champaign ... wilderness* Pastoral meadow at the foot of a steep and wooded slope.

5 *humid bow* Rainbow.

---

6 *Sabean* Exotic; from Sheba, modern-day Yemen.

7 *Than Asmodeus ... post to Egypt* Story from the Apocryphal Book of Tobit, in which the son of Tobit, to win the hand of Sara, defeats the incubus Asmodeus by burning the liver of a certain fish to call the archangel Raphael, who "took the devil, and bound him in the desert of upper Egypt" (Tobit 8.3).

8 *hurdled cotes* Temporary shelters.

So since into his church lewd hirelings[1] climb.
Thence up he flew, and on the tree of life,
195 The middle tree and highest there that grew,
Sat like a cormorant; yet not true life
Thereby regained, but sat devising death
To them who lived; nor on the virtue thought
Of that life-giving plant, but only used
200 For prospect[2] what well used had been the pledge
Of immortality. So little knows
Any, but God alone, to value right
The good before him, but perverts best things
To worst abuse, or to their meanest use.
205 Beneath him with new wonder now he views,
To all delight of human sense exposed,
In narrow room, nature's whole wealth, yea more,
A Heav'n on Earth: For blissful paradise
Of God the garden was, by Him in the east
210 Of Eden planted; Eden stretched her line
From Auran° eastward to the royal towers   *Israel*
Of great Seleucia,° built by Grecian kings,   *Iraq*
Of where the sons of Eden long before
Dwelt in Telassar:[3] In this pleasant soil
215 His far more pleasant garden God ordained;
Out of the fertile ground He caused to grow
All trees of noblest kind for sight, smell, taste;
And all amid them stood the tree of life,
High eminent, blooming ambrosial fruit
220 Of vegetable gold; and next to life,
Our death, the tree of knowledge, grew fast by,
Knowledge of good bought dear by knowing ill.
Southward through Eden went a river large,
Nor changed his course, but through the shaggy hill
225 Passed underneath engulfed; for God had thrown
That mountain as His garden-mould high raised
Upon the rapid current, which, through veins
Of porous earth with kindly thirst up-drawn,
Rose a fresh fountain, and with many a rill
230 Watered the garden; thence united fell
Down the steep glade, and met the nether flood,
Which from his darksome passage now appears,
And now, divided into four main streams,

Runs diverse, wandering many a famous realm
235 And country, whereof here needs no account;
But rather to tell how, if art could tell,
How from that sapphire fount the crisped brooks,
Rolling on orient pearl and sands of gold,
With mazy error° under pendant shades   *meander*
240 Ran nectar, visiting each plant, and fed
Flowers worthy of Paradise, which not nice° art   *careful*
In beds and curious knots, but nature boon
Poured forth profuse on hill, and dale, and plain,
Both where the morning sun first warmly smote
245 The open field, and where the unpierced shade
Imbrowned° the noontide bowers: Thus   *darkened*
    was this place
A happy rural seat of various view;
Groves whose rich trees wept odorous gums and balm,
Others whose fruit, burnished with golden rind,
250 Hung amiable, Hesperian fables[4] true,
If true, here only, and of delicious taste:
Betwixt them lawns, or level downs, and flocks
Grazing the tender herb, were interposed,
Or palmy hillock; or the flowery lap
255 Of some irriguous° valley spread her store,   *watered*
Flowers of all hue, and without thorn the rose:
Another side, umbrageous grots[5] and caves
Of cool recess, o'er which the mantling° vine   *climbing*
Lays forth her purple grape, and gently creeps
260 Luxuriant; meanwhile murmuring waters fall
Down the slope hills, dispersed, or in a lake,
That to the fringèd bank with myrtle crowned
Her crystal mirror holds, unite their streams.
The birds their choir apply;[6] airs, vernal airs,
265 Breathing the smell of field and grove, attune
The trembling leaves, while universal Pan,
Knit with the Graces and the Hours[7] in dance,
Led on the eternal spring. Not that fair field

---

1 *hirelings* Ministers supported by obligatory tithes or taxes. Milton did not believe in a salaried clergy.

2 *used / For prospect* Used as a perch.

3 *Telassar* Province in southeast Syria.

4 *Hesperian fables* In classical mythology, nymphs called the Hesperides, guarded a tree of golden apples.

5 *umbrageous grots* Shadowy grottos.

6 *their choir apply* Sing.

7 *Pan* Classical god of nature; *Graces* Aglaia, Euphrosyne, and Thalia, sister goddesses of charm and beauty; *Hours* Horae, various goddesses of the hours, seasons, and other aspects of time.

Of Enna,[1] where Proserpine gathering flowers,
70 Herself a fairer flower by gloomy Dis
Was gathered, which cost Ceres all that pain
To seek her through the world;[2] nor that sweet grove
Of Daphne by Orontes,[3] and the inspired
Castilian spring,[4] might with this Paradise
75 Of Eden strive; nor that Nyseian[5] isle
Girt with the river Triton,[6] where old Cham,
Whom Gentiles Ammon call and Libyan Jove,[7]
Hid Amalthea, and her florid son
Young Bacchus, from his stepdame Rhea's eye;[8]
80 Nor where Abassin° kings their issue guard,   *Abyssinian*
Mount Amara, though this by some supposed
True Paradise under the Ethiop line[9]
By Nilus' head,[10] enclosed with shining rock,
A whole day's journey high, but wide remote
85 From this Assyrian garden, where the fiend
Saw, undelighted, all delight, all kind
Of living creatures, new to sight, and strange
Two of far nobler shape, erect and tall,
Godlike erect, with native honour clad

290 In naked majesty seemed lords of all:
And worthy seemed; for in their looks divine
The image of their glorious Maker shone,
Truth, wisdom, sanctitude severe and pure
(Severe, but in true filial freedom placed),
295 Whence true authority in men; though both
Not equal, as their sex not equal seemed;
For contemplation he and valour formed;
For softness she and sweet attractive grace;
He for God only, she for God in him:
300 His fair large front and eye sublime declared
Absolute rule; and hyacinthine[11] locks
Round from his parted forelock manly hung
Clustering, but not beneath his shoulders broad:
She, as a veil, down to the slender waist
305 Her unadornèd golden tresses wore
Dishevelled, but in wanton ringlets waved
As the vine curls her tendrils, which implied
Subjection, but required with gentle sway,
And by her yielded, by him best received,
310 Yielded with coy submission, modest pride,
And sweet, reluctant, amorous delay.
Nor those mysterious parts were then concealed;
Then was not guilty shame, dishonest shame
Of nature's works, honour dishonourable,
315 Sin-bred, how have ye troubled all mankind
With shows instead, mere shows of seeming pure,
And banished from man's life his happiest life,
Simplicity and spotless innocence!
So passed they naked on, nor shunned the sight
320 Of God or angel; for they thought no ill:
So hand in hand they passed, the loveliest pair,
That ever since in love's embraces met;
Adam the goodliest man of men since born
His sons, the fairest of her daughters Eve.
325 Under a tuft of shade that on a green
Stood whispering soft, by a fresh fountain side
They sat them down; and, after no more toil
Of their sweet gardening labour than sufficed

---

[1] *Enna* Meadow in Sicily.

[2] *Proserpine ... world* Proserpine, the daughter of the goddess of agriculture and the harvest, Ceres, was kidnapped by the god of the underworld, Dis (Hades or Pluto). Proserpine's mother went into mourning, thereby bringing winter to the land. Dis agreed to return Proserpine to her mother for half the year; hence, the seasons of summer and winter.

[3] *that sweet ... by Orontes* Daphne was a Naiad, a spirit charged with safekeeping of rivers, streams, and brooks. She was willingly transformed into a laurel tree to avoid Apollo's amorous pursuit; this event was supposed to have happened near the river Orontes, where it crosses through Syria, and to have resulted in a peaceful grotto beneath the transfigured laurel, now sacred to Apollo.

[4] *inspired / Castilian spring* Spring of the Muses on Mount Parnassus.

[5] *Nyseian* Nyseia, an ancient Mediterranean country.

[6] *the river Triton* Modern-day Gazanos River.

[7] *Cham ... Ammon ... Jove* Cham (the Biblical Ham, son of Noah) was sometimes said to be the same as the pagan Ammon and the Lybian version of Jove.

[8] *Hid Amalthea ... stepdame Rhea's eye* Amalthea was impregnated by Ammon, King of Libya and gave birth to Bacchus, god of wine. Since she needed to be hidden from Rhea, Ammon's wife and Uranus's daughter, she was hidden on Nyseia.

[9] *the Ethiop line* The equator.

[10] *By Nilus' head* By the head of the Nile River.

---

[11] *hyacinthine* Dark colored and shiny, lustrous and thick. The hyacinth is a rich-colored and many-bloomed flower; Hyacinthus was a handsome youth in classical mythology, unintentionally killed by his lover Apollo, who turned him into the flower.

To recommend cool Zephyr,[1] and made ease
330 More easy, wholesome thirst and appetite
More grateful, to their supper-fruits they fell,
Nectarine fruits which the compliant boughs
Yielded them, side-long as they sat recline
On the soft downy bank damasked with flowers:
335 The savoury pulp they chew, and in the rind,
Still as they thirsted, scoop the brimming stream;
Nor gentle purpose, nor endearing smiles
Wanted, nor youthful dalliance, as beseems
Fair couple, linked in happy nuptial league,[2]
340 Alone as they. About them frisking played
All beasts of the earth, since wild, and of all chase
In wood or wilderness, forest or den;
Sporting the lion ramped, and in his paw
Dandled the kid; bears, tigers, ounces, pards,[3]
345 Gambolled before them; the unwieldy elephant,
To make them mirth, used all his might, and
        wreathed
His lithe proboscis; close the serpent sly,
Insinuating, wove with Gordian twine[4]
His braided train, and of his fatal guile
350 Gave proof unheeded; others on the grass
Couched, and now filled with pasture gazing sat,
Or bedward ruminating; for the sun,
Declined, was hasting now with prone career
To th' ocean isles, and in the ascending scale
355 Of Heav'n the stars that usher evening rose:
When Satan still in gaze, as first he stood,
Scarce thus at length failed speech recovered sad.
    "O Hell! What do mine eyes with grief behold!
Into our room of bliss thus high advanced
360 Creatures of other mould, earth-born perhaps,
Not spirits, yet to heav'nly spirits bright
Little inferior; whom my thoughts pursue
With wonder, and could love, so lively shines

In them divine resemblance, and such grace
365 The hand that formed them on their shape hath
        poured.
Ah! Gentle pair, ye little think how nigh
Your change approaches, when all these delights
Will vanish, and deliver ye to woe;
More woe, the more your taste is now of joy;
370 Happy, but for so happy ill secured
Long to continue, and this high seat your Heav'n
Ill fenced for Heav'n to keep out such a foe
As now is entered; yet no purposed foe
To you, whom I could pity thus forlorn,
375 Though I unpitied: League with you I seek,
And mutual amity, so strait, so close,
That I with you must dwell, or you with me
Henceforth; my dwelling haply may not please,
Like this fair Paradise, your sense; yet such
380 Accept your Maker's work; He gave it me,
Which I as freely give: Hell shall unfold,
To entertain you two, her widest gates,
And send forth all her kings; there will be room,
Not like these narrow limits, to receive
385 Your numerous offspring; if no better place,
Thank Him who puts me loath to this revenge
On you who wrong me not for Him who wronged.
And should I at your harmless innocence
Melt, as I do, yet public reason just,
390 Honour and empire with revenge enlarged,
By conquering this new world, compels me now
To do what else, though damned, I should abhor."
    So spake the fiend, and with necessity,
The tyrant's plea, excused his devilish deeds.
395 Then from his lofty stand on that high tree
Down he alights among the sportful herd
Of those four-footed kinds, himself now one,
Now other, as their shape served best his end
Nearer to view his prey, and, unespied,
400 To mark what of their state he more might learn,
By word or action marked. About them round
A lion now he stalks with fiery glare;
Then as a tiger, who by chance hath spied
In some purlieu[5] two gentle fawns at play,
405 Straight couches close, then, rising, changes oft

[1] *Zephyr* West wind, synonymous with a gentle and pleasant breeze.
[2] *happy nuptial league* Marriage.
[3] *Dandled* Playfully dangled; *kid* Baby goat; *ounces* Lynxes; *pards* Leopards.
[4] *Gordian twine* Inextricable knot, after the Gordian knot of legend, which no one was able to untie. It was undone only by Alexander the Great, who did not attempt to untie it, but instead sliced it in half with his sword.
[5] *purlieu* Forest outskirts.

His couchant° watch, as one who chose   *crouching*
   his ground,
Whence rushing, he might surest seize them both,
Gripped in each paw: when, Adam first of men
To first of women Eve thus moving speech,
10 Turned him, all ear to hear new utterance flow:
   "Sole partner, and sole part, of all these joys,
Dearer thyself than all; needs must the power
That made us, and for us this ample world,
Be infinitely good, and of His good
15 As liberal and free as infinite;
That raised us from the dust,[1] and placed us here
In all this happiness, who at His hand
Have nothing merited, nor can perform
Aught whereof He hath need; He who requires
20 From us no other service than to keep
This one, this easy charge, of all the trees
In Paradise that bear delicious fruit
So various, not to taste that only tree
Of knowledge, planted by the tree of life;[2]
25 So near grows death to life, whate'er death is,
Some dreadful thing no doubt; for well thou knowest
God hath pronounced it death to taste that tree,
The only sign of our obedience left,
Among so many signs of power and rule
30 Conferred upon us, and dominion giv'n
Over all other creatures that possess
Earth, air, and sea. Then let us not think hard
One easy prohibition, who enjoy
Free leave so large to all things else, and choice
35 Unlimited of manifold delights:
But let us ever praise Him, and extol
His bounty, following our delightful task,
To prune these growing plants, and tend these
   flowers,
Which were it toilsome, yet with thee were sweet."
40   To whom thus Eve replied: "O thou for whom
And from whom I was formed, flesh of thy flesh,
And without whom am to no end, my guide
And head! What thou hast said is just and right.
For we to Him indeed all praises owe,
45 And daily thanks; I chiefly, who enjoy
So far the happier lot, enjoying thee

Pre-eminent by so much odds, while thou
Like consort to thyself canst nowhere find.
That day I oft remember, when from sleep
450 I first awaked, and found myself reposed
Under a shade of flowers, much wondering where
And what I was, whence thither brought, and how.
Not distant far from thence a murmuring sound
Of waters issued from a cave, and spread
455 Into a liquid plain, then stood unmoved
Pure as th' expanse of Heav'n; I thither went
With unexperienced thought, and laid me down
On the green bank, to look into the clear
Smooth lake, that to me seemed another sky.
460 As I bent down to look, just opposite
A shape within the wat'ry gleam appeared,
Bending to look on me: I started back,
It started back; but pleased I soon returned,
Pleased it returned as soon with answering looks
465 Of sympathy and love:[3] There I had fixed
Mine eyes till now, and pined with vain desire,
Had not a voice thus warned me; 'What thou seest,
What there thou seest, fair creature, is thyself;
With thee it came and goes: but follow me,
470 And I will bring thee where no shadow stays
Thy coming, and thy soft embraces—he
Whose image thou art; him thou shalt enjoy
Inseparably thine, to him shalt bear
Multitudes like thyself, and thence be called
475 Mother of human race.' What could I do,
But follow straight, invisibly thus led?
Till I espied thee, fair indeed and tall,
Under a platane;[4] yet methought less fair,
Less winning soft, less amiably mild,
480 Than that smooth wat'ry image: back I turned;[5]
Thou following cryedst aloud, 'Return, fair Eve;

---

1 *raised us from the dust* See Genesis 2.7.

2 *not to taste ... tree of life* See Genesis 2.16–17.

3 *As I bent down ... sympathy and love* The narrative here mirrors the classical myth of Narcissus, a beautiful youth who became captivated by his own reflection and wasted away.

4 *platane* Plane tree.

5 *back I turned* The narrative here mirrors the myth of Eurydice, lost when her husband Orpheus took her back from the underworld, but violated his agreement with Pluto by looking back to see if she were following. It also suggests the Biblical story of Lot's wife, who looked back at the destruction of Sodom and Gomorrah and was transformed into a pillar of salt (Genesis 19.26).

Whom flyest thou?[1] Whom thou flyest, of him thou
       art,
His flesh, his bone; to give thee being I lent
Out of my side to thee, nearest my heart,
485   Substantial life, to have thee by my side
Henceforth an individual solace dear;
Part of my soul I seek thee, and thee claim
My other half:' With that thy gentle hand
Seized mine: I yielded, and from that time see
490   How beauty is excelled by manly grace,
And wisdom, which alone is truly fair."
       So spake our general mother, and with eyes
Of conjugal attraction unreproved,
And meek surrender, half-embracing leaned
495   On our first father; half her swelling breast
Naked met his, under the flowing gold
Of her loose tresses hid: he in delight
Both of her beauty, and submissive charms,
Smiled with superior love, as Jupiter
500   On Juno smiles, when he impregns the clouds
That shed May flowers; and pressed her matron lip
With kisses pure. Aside the devil turned
For envy; yet with jealous leer malign
Eyed them askance, and to himself thus plained.[2]
505   "Sight hateful, sight tormenting! Thus these two,
Imparadised in one another's arms,
The happier Eden, shall enjoy their fill
Of bliss on bliss; while I to Hell am thrust,
Where neither joy nor love, but fierce desire,
510   Among our other torments not the least,
Still unfulfilled with pain of longing pines.
Yet let me not forget what I have gained
From their own mouths: all is not theirs, it seems;
One fatal tree there stands, of knowledge called,
515   Forbidden them to taste: knowledge forbidd'n
Suspicious, reasonless. Why should their Lord
Envy them that? Can it be sin to know?
Can it be death? And do they only stand
By ignorance? Is that their happy state,
520   The proof of their obedience and their faith?
O fair foundation laid whereon to build
Their ruin! Hence I will excite their minds
With more desire to know, and to reject

Envious commands, invented with design
525   To keep them low, whom knowledge might exalt
Equal with gods: aspiring to be such,
They taste and die: What likelier can ensue
But first with narrow search I must walk round
This garden, and no corner leave unspied;
530   A chance but chance may lead where I may meet
Some wandering spirit of Heav'n by fountain side,
Or in thick shade retired, from him to draw
What further would be learned. Live while ye may,
Yet happy pair; enjoy, till I return,
535   Short pleasures, for long woes are to succeed!"
       So saying, his proud step he scornful turned,
But with sly circumspection, and began
Through wood, through waste, o'er hill, o'er dale, his
       roam
Meanwhile in utmost longitude, where Heav'n
540   With earth and ocean meets, the setting sun
Slowly descended, and with right aspect
Against the eastern gate of Paradise
Levelled his evening rays: it was a rock
Of alabaster, piled up to the clouds,
545   Conspicuous far, winding with one ascent
Accessible from earth, one entrance high;
The rest was craggy cliff that overhung
Still as it rose, impossible to climb.
Betwixt these rocky pillars Gabriel[3] sat,
550   Chief of the angelic guards, awaiting night;
About him exercised heroic games
The unarmed youth of Heav'n, but nigh at hand
Celestial armoury, shields, helms, and spears,
Hung high with diamond flaming, and with gold.
555   Thither came Uriel, gliding through the even
On a sun-beam, swift as a shooting star
In autumn thwarts the night, when vapours fired[4]
Impress the air, and shows the mariner
From what point of his compass to beware
560   Impetuous winds: He thus began in haste.
       "Gabriel, to thee thy course by lot hath given
Charge and strict watch, that to this happy place
No evil thing approach or enter in.
This day at height of noon came to my sphere

---

1   *Whom flyest thou?*   From whom are you running?

2   *plained*   Complained, lamented.

3   *Gabriel*   Archangel, messenger of God. His name means "strength of God."

4   *vapours fired*   Shooting stars.

565 A spirit, zealous, as he seemed, to know
More of th' Almighty's works, and chiefly Man,
God's latest image: I described° his way   *noted*
Bent all on speed, and marked his airy gait;
But in the mount that lies from Eden north,
570 Where he first lighted, soon discerned his looks
Alien from Heav'n, with passions foul obscured:
Mine eye pursued him still, but under shade
Lost sight of him. One of the banished crew,
I fear, hath ventured from the deep, to raise
575 New troubles; him thy care must be to find."
    To whom the wingèd warrior thus returned:
"Uriel, no wonder if thy perfect sight,
Amid the sun's bright circle where thou sitst,
See far and wide: in at this gate none pass
580 The vigilance here placed, but such as come
Well known from Heav'n; and since meridian°   *noon*
    hour
No creature thence: If spirit of other sort,
So minded, have o'er-leaped these earthly bounds
On purpose, hard thou knowest it to exclude
585 Spiritual substance with corporeal bar.
But if within the circuit of these walks,
In whatsoever shape he lurk, of whom
Thou tellest, by morrow dawning I shall know."
    So promised he; and Uriel to his charge
590 Returned on that bright beam, whose point now
    raised
Bore him slope downward to the sun now fall'n
Beneath th' Azores;[1] whether the prime orb,
Incredible how swift, had thither rolled
Diurnal, or this less voluble° earth,   *revolving*
595 By shorter flight to th' east, had left him there[2]
Arraying with reflected purple and gold
The clouds that on his western throne attend.
Now came still evening on, and twilight grey
Had in her sober livery all things clad;
600 Silence accompanied; for beast and bird,
They to their grassy couch, these to their nests
Were slunk, all but the wakeful nightingale;

She all night long her amorous descant sung;
Silence was pleased. Now glowed the firmament
605 With living sapphires: Hesperus,[3] that led
The starry host, rode brightest, till the moon,
Rising in clouded majesty, at length
Apparent queen unveiled her peerless light,
And o'er the dark her silver mantle threw.
610   When Adam thus to Eve: "Fair consort, the hour
Of night, and all things now retired to rest,
Mind us of like repose; since God hath set
Labour and rest, as day and night, to men
Successive; and the timely dew of sleep,
615 Now falling with soft slumbrous weight, inclines
Our eye-lids: other creatures all day long
Rove idle, unemployed, and less need rest;
Man hath his daily work of body or mind
Appointed, which declares his dignity,
620 And the regard of Heav'n on all his ways;
While other animals unactive range,
And of their doings God takes no account.
Tomorrow, ere fresh morning streak the east
With first approach of light, we must be risen,
625 And at our pleasant labour, to reform
Yon flowery arbours, yonder alleys green,
Our walk at noon, with branches overgrown,
That mock our scant manuring, and require
More hands than ours to lop their wanton growth:
630 Those blossoms also, and those dropping gums,
That lie bestrown, unsightly and unsmooth,
Ask riddance, if we mean to tread with ease;
Meanwhile, as nature wills, night bids us rest."
    To whom thus Eve, with perfect beauty adorned:
635 "My author and disposer, what thou bidst
Unargued I obey: So God ordains;
God is thy law, thou mine: to know no more
Is woman's happiest knowledge, and her praise.
With thee conversing I forget all time;
640 All seasons, and their change, all please alike.
Sweet is the breath of morn, her rising sweet,
With charm of earliest birds: pleasant the sun,
When first on this delightful land he spreads
His orient beams, on herb, tree, fruit, and flower,
645 Glistering with dew; fragrant the fertile earth
After soft showers; and sweet the coming on

---

[1] *Azores* Islands located in the Atlantic Ocean off the coast of Portugal.

[2] *whether the prime orb … had left him there* Whether the sun, with amazing speed, circled the earth every day or the earth, less rapid ("voluble"), circled the sun.

[3] *Hesperus* The evening star.

Of grateful ev'ning mild; then silent night,
With this her solemn bird, and this fair moon,
And these the gems of Heaven, her starry train:
650   But neither breath of morn, when she ascends
With charm of earliest birds; nor rising sun
On this delightful land; nor herb, fruit, flower,
Glist'ring with dew; nor fragrance after showers;
Nor grateful ev'ning mild; nor silent night,
655   With this her solemn bird, nor walk by moon,
Or glittering starlight, without thee is sweet.
But wherefore all night long shine these? For whom
This glorious sight, when sleep hath shut all eyes?"
        To whom our general ancestor replied:
660   "Daughter of God and man, accomplished Eve,
These have their course to finish round the earth,
By morrow ev'ning, and from land to land
In order, though to nations yet unborn,
Ministring light prepared, they set and rise;
665   Lest total darkness should by night regain
Her old possession, and extinguish life
In nature and all things; which these soft fires
Not only enlighten, but with kindly heat
Of various influence foment[1] and warm,
670   Temper or nourish, or in part shed down
Their stellar virtue on all kinds that grow
On earth, made hereby apter to receive
Perfection from the sun's more potent ray.
These then, though unbeheld in deep of night,
675   Shine not in vain; nor think, though men were none,
That Heav'n would want spectators, God want praise:
Millions of spiritual creatures walk the earth
Unseen, both when we wake, and when we sleep:
All these with ceaseless praise His works behold
680   Both day and night: how often from the steep
Of echoing hill or thicket have we heard
Celestial voices to the midnight air,
Sole, or responsive each to other's note,
Singing their great Creator? Oft in bands
685   While they keep watch, or nightly rounding walk,
With heav'nly touch of instrumental sounds
In full harmonic number joined, their songs
Divide the night, and lift our thoughts to Heaven."
Thus talking, hand in hand alone they passed
690   On to their blissful bower: it was a place

Chosen by the Sovereign Planter,[2] when He framed
All things to Man's delightful use; the roof
Of thickest covert was inwoven shade
Laurel and myrtle, and what higher grew
695   Of firm and fragrant leaf; on either side
Acanthus, and each odorous bushy shrub,
Fenced up the verdant wall; each beauteous flower,
Iris all hues, roses, and jessamine,°   jasmine
Reared high their flourished heads between, and
        wrought
700   Mosaic; underfoot the violet,
Crocus, and hyacinth, with rich inlay
Broidered the ground, more coloured than with stone
Of costliest emblem. Other creature here,
Bird, beast, insect, or worm, durst enter none,
705   Such was their awe of Man. In shadier bower
More sacred and sequestered, though but feigned,
Pan or Sylvanus never slept, nor Nymph
Nor Faunus[3] haunted. Here, in close recess,
With flowers, garlands, and sweet-smelling herbs,
710   Espousèd° Eve decked first her nuptial bed;   married
And heav'nly choirs the hymenaean[4] sung,
What day the genial angel to our sire
Brought her in naked beauty more adorned,
More lovely than Pandora, whom the Gods
715   Endowed with all their gifts, and O! Too like
In sad event, when to the unwiser son
Of Japhet brought by Hermes,[5] she ensnared
Mankind with her fair looks, to be avenged
On him who had stole Jove's authentic° fire.   primal
720   Thus, at their shady lodge arrived, both stood,
Both turned, and under open sky adored
The God that made both sky, air, earth, and Heaven,
Which they beheld, the moon's resplendent globe,

---

[1] *foment* Excite, cause to develop.

[2] *the Sovereign Planter* God.

[3] *Sylvanus* Roman god of forests, fields, and herding; *Nymph*
Nature spirit; *Faunus* Roman god of nature and fertility.

[4] *hymenaean* Wedding song.

[5] *Pandora* Created and given to Epimetheus, the brother of
Prometheus, to punish Prometheus for having stolen fire from the
gods and given it to humans. Pandora's dowry was a jar that, when
opened, released all the ills and cares of the world to roam free and
plague humankind. However, one thing remained, Hope; *the
unwiser son / Of Japhet* Prometheus, whose father (the Titan
Iapetus) was identified with Noah's son Japhet; *Hermes* Greek
messenger god; Roman Mercury.

And starry pole: "Thou also madest the night,
25 Maker omnipotent, and Thou the day,
Which we, in our appointed work employed,
Have finished, happy in our mutual help
And mutual love, the crown of all our bliss
Ordained by Thee; and this delicious place
30 For us too large, where Thy abundance wants
Partakers, and uncropt falls to the ground.
But Thou hast promised from us two a race
To fill the earth, who shall with us extol
Thy goodness infinite, both when we wake,
35 And when we seek, as now, thy gift of sleep."
      This said unanimous, and other rites
Observing none, but adoration pure
Which God likes best, into their inmost bower
Handed they went; and, eased the putting off
40 These troublesome disguises[1] which we wear,
Straight side by side were laid; nor turned, I ween,
Adam from his fair spouse, nor Eve the rites
Mysterious of connubial love refused:
Whatever hypocrites austerely talk
45 Of purity, and place, and innocence,
Defaming as impure what God declares
Pure, and commands to some,[2] leaves free to all.
Our Maker bids increase;[3] who bids abstain
But our destroyer, foe to God and man?
50 Hail, wedded love, mysterious law, true source
Of human offspring, sole propriety
In Paradise of all things common else!
By thee adulterous lust was driv'n from men
Among the bestial herds to range; by thee
55 Founded in reason, loyal, just, and pure,
Relations dear, and all the charities
Of father, son, and brother, first were known.
Far be it, that I should write thee sin or blame,
Or think thee unbefitting holiest place,
60 Perpetual fountain of domestic sweets,
Whose bed is undefiled and chaste pronounced,
Present, or past, as saints and patriarchs used.
Here love his golden shafts employs, here lights
His constant lamp, and waves his purple wings,
65 Reigns here and revels; not in the bought smile

---

[1] *These troublesome disguises* Clothes.

[2] *commands to some* See 1 Corinthians 7.2.

[3] *Our Maker bids increase* See Genesis 9.7.

Of harlots, loveless, joyless, unendeared,
Casual fruition; nor in court-amours,
Mixed dance, or wanton mask, or midnight ball,
Or serenade, which the starved lover sings
770 To his proud fair, best quitted with disdain.
These, lulled by nightingales, embracing slept,
And on their naked limbs the flowery roof
Showered roses, which the morn repaired. Sleep on,
Blest pair! And, O! Yet happiest, if ye seek
775 No happier state, and know to know no more!
      Now had night measured with her shadowy cone
Halfway up hill this vast sublunar vault,[4]
And from their ivory port the cherubim
Forth issuing at th' accustomed hour stood armed
780 To their night watches in warlike parade,
When Gabriel to his next in power thus spake.
      "Uzziel,[5] half these draw off, and coast the south
With strictest watch; these other wheel the north,[6]
Our circuit meets full west." As flame they part
785 Half wheeling to the shield, half to the spear.[7]
From these, two strong and subtle spirits he called
That near him stood, and gave them thus in charge.
      "Ithuriel and Zephon,[8] with winged speed
Search through this garden, leave unsearched no nook,
790 But chiefly where those two fair creatures lodge,
Now laid perhaps asleep secure of° harm.   *unsuspecting*
This evening from the sun's decline arrived
Who° tells of some infernal spirit seen   *One who*
Hitherward bent (who could have thought?) escaped
795 The bars of Hell, on errand bad no doubt:
Such where ye find, seize fast, and hither bring."

---

[4] *night measured … vault* With the sun below the horizon, the earth's globe casts a conical shadow that arches across the horizon. This shadow has ascended halfway to its zenith (midnight), which makes the time 9:00 pm.

[5] *Uzziel* "My strength is God" (Hebrew). A human name in the Bible, but an angel in rabbinic tradition.

[6] *coast the south / … wheel the north* Starting at the eastern gate, Uzziel sends half his troops to check the garden perimeter to the south, the other half to the north; they will meet again due west.

[7] *to the shield … to the spear* To the left (shield hand) and right (spear hand).

[8] *Ithuriel and Zephon* "Discovery of God" and "Searcher" respectively (Hebrew). Their names reflect their roles in the narrative. Zephon is a biblical name (human, not an angel); Ithuriel is not biblical, but appears in apocryphal traditions.

So saying, on he led his radiant files,
Dazzling the moon; these to the bower direct
In search of whom they sought: him there they found
800 Squat like a toad, close at the ear of Eve;
Assaying by his devilish art to reach
The organs of her fancy, and with them forge
Illusions as he list,° phantasms and dreams,   *desires*
Or if, inspiring° venom, he might taint   *breathing*
805 Th' animal spirits that from pure blood arise
Like gentle breaths from rivers pure, thence raise
At least distempered,° discontented thoughts, *unbalanced*
Vain hopes, vain aims, inordinate desires
Blown up with high conceits° engend'ring pride.   *ideas*
810 Him thus intent Ithuriel with his spear
Touched lightly; for no falsehood can endure
Touch of celestial temper, but returns
Of force to its own likeness: up he starts
Discovered and surprised. As when a spark
815 Lights on a heap of nitrous powder,° laid   *gunpowder*
Fit for the tun° some magazine° to store   *cask / storehouse*
Against a rumored war, the smutty° grain   *black*
With sudden blaze diffused, enflames the air:
So started up in his own shape the fiend.
820 Back stepped those two fair angels half amazed
So sudden to behold the grisly king;
Yet thus, unmoved with fear, accost him soon.

    "Which of those rebel spirits adjudged to Hell
Com'st thou, escaped thy prison, and transformed,
825 Why sat'st thou like an enemy in wait
Here watching at the head of these that sleep?"

    "Know ye not then," said Satan, filled with scorn,
"Know ye not me? Ye knew me once no mate
For you, there sitting where ye durst not soar;
830 Not to know me argues° yourselves unknown,   *indicates*
The lowest of your throng; or if ye know,
Why ask ye, and superfluous begin
Your message, like to end as much in vain?"
To whom thus Zephon, answering scorn with scorn.
835 "Think not, revolted spirit, thy shape the same,
Or undiminished brightness, to be known
As when thou stood'st in Heaven upright and pure;
That glory then, when thou no more wast good,
Departed from thee, and thou resemblest now
840 Thy sin and place of doom obscure° and foul.   *dark*

But come, for thou, be sure, shalt give account
To him who sent us, whose charge is to keep
This place inviolable, and these from harm."
    So spake the cherub, and his grave rebuke
845 Severe in youthful beauty, added grace
Invincible: abashed the Devil stood,
And felt how awful° goodness is, and saw   *awe-inspiring*
Virtue in her shape how lovely, saw, and pined
His loss; but chiefly to find here observed
850 His lustre visibly impaired; yet seemed
Undaunted. "If I must contend," said he,
"Best with the best, the sender not the sent,
Or all at once; more glory will be won,
Or less be lost." "Thy fear," said Zephon bold,
855 "Will save us trial what the least can do
Single against thee wicked, and thence weak."
    The fiend replied not, overcome with rage;
But like a proud steed reined, went haughty on,
Champing his iron curb: to strive or fly
860 He held it vain; awe from above had quelled
His heart, not else dismayed. Now drew they nigh
The western point, where those half-rounding guards
Just met, and closing stood in squadron joined
Awaiting next command. To whom their chief
865 Gabriel from the front thus called aloud.
    "O friends, I hear the tread of nimble feet
Hasting this way, and now by glimpse discern
Ithuriel and Zephon through the shade,°   *trees*
And with them comes a third of regal port,°   *bearing*
870 But faded splendor wan;° who by his gait   *gloomy*
And fierce demeanour seems the Prince of Hell,
Not likely to part hence without contest;
Stand firm, for in his look defiance lours."°   *scowls*
    He scarce had ended, when those two approached
875 And brief related whom they brought, where found,
How busied, in what form and posture couched.
    To whom with stern regard thus Gabriel spake.
"Why hast thou, Satan, broke the bounds prescribed
To thy transgressions, and disturbed the charge
880 Of others, who approve not to transgress
By thy example, but have power and right
To question thy bold entrance on this place;
Employed it seems to violate sleep, and those
Whose dwelling God hath planted here in bliss?"

85 To whom thus Satan with contemptuous brow.
"Gabriel, thou hadst in Heaven th' esteem of wise,[1]
And such I held thee; but this question asked
Puts me in doubt. Lives there who loves his pain?
Who would not, finding way, break loose from Hell,
90 Though thither doomed? Thou wouldst thyself, no doubt,
And boldly venture to whatever place
Farthest from pain, where thou might'st hope to change
Torment with ease, and soonest recompense°   *repay*
Dole° with delight, which in this place I sought;   *Sorrow*
95 To thee no reason; who know'st only good,
But evil hast not tried: and wilt object
His will who bound us? Let him surer bar
His iron gates, if he intends our stay
In that dark durance:° thus much what was   *confinement*
      asked.
100 The rest is true, they found me where they say;
But that implies not violence or harm."
      Thus he in scorn. The warlike angel moved,°   *angry*
Disdainfully half smiling thus replied.
"O loss of one in Heaven to judge of wise,°   *wisdom*
905 Since Satan fell, whom folly overthrew,
And now returns him from his prison 'scaped,
Gravely in doubt whether to hold them wise
Or not, who ask what boldness brought him hither
Unlicensed from his bounds in Hell prescribed;
910 So wise he judges it to fly from pain
However,° and to 'scape his punishment.   *In whatever way*
So judge thou still, presumptuous, till the wrath,
Which thou incurr'st by flying, meet thy flight
Sevenfold, and scourge that wisdom back to Hell,
915 Which taught thee yet no better, that no pain
Can equal anger infinite provoked.
But wherefore thou alone? Wherefore with thee
Came not all Hell broke loose? Is pain to them
Less pain, less to be fled, or thou than they
920 Less hardy to endure? Courageous chief,
The first in flight from pain, hadst thou alleged
To thy deserted host this cause of flight,
Thou surely hadst not come sole fugitive."
      To which the fiend thus answered frowning stern.
925 "Not that I less endure, or shrink from pain,
Insulting angel, well thou know'st I stood°   *withstood*
Thy fiercest, when in battle to thy aide

The blasting volleyed thunder made all speed
And seconded thy else° not dreaded spear.   *otherwise*
930 But still thy words at random, as before,
Argue thy inexperience what behooves°   *is proper*
From° hard assays° and ill successes past   *After / attempts*
A faithful leader, not to hazard all
Through ways of danger by himself untried,
935 I therefore, I alone first undertook
To wing the desolate abyss, and spy
This new created world, whereof in Hell
Fame° is not silent, here in hope to find   *Rumor*
Better abode, and my afflicted powers°   *downcast forces*
940 To settle here on earth, or in mid air;
Though for possession put to try° once more   *test*
What thou and thy gay[2] legions dare against;
Whose easier business were to serve their Lord
High up in Heaven, with songs to hymn his throne,
945 And practiced distances[3] to cringe, not fight."
      To whom the warrior angel, soon replied.
"To say and straight unsay, pretending first
Wise to fly pain, professing next the spy,
Argues no leader, but a liar traced,°   *discovered*
950 Satan, and couldst thou faithful add? O name,
O sacred name of faithfulness profaned!
Faithful to whom? To thy rebellious crew?
Army of fiends, fit body to fit head;
Was this your discipline and faith engaged,
955 Your military obedience, to dissolve
Allegiance to th' acknowledged Power Supreme?
And thou sly hypocrite, who now wouldst seem
Patron of liberty, who more than thou
Once fawned, and cringed, and servilely adored
960 Heaven's awful° Monarch? Wherefore but   *awe-inspiring*
      in hope
To dispossess him, and thyself to reign?
But mark what I areed° thee now, avant;°   *advise / depart*
Fly thither whence thou fled'st: if from this hour
Within these hallowed limits thou appear,
965 Back to th' infernal pit I drag thee chained,
And seal thee so, as henceforth not to scorn
The facile° gates of Hell too slightly barred."   *yielding*
      So threatened he, but Satan to no threats

---

[1] *esteem of wise* Reputation of being wise.

[2] *gay* Showy; like courtiers.

[3] *practiced distances* I.e., they practiced judging distance by courtly
bowing, not sword fighting.

Gave heed, but waxing° more in rage replied.   *growing*

970   "Then when I am thy captive talk of chains,
Proud limitary° cherub, but ere then   *boundary-guarding*
Far heavier load thyself expect to feel
From my prevailing arm, though Heaven's King
Ride on thy wings, and thou with thy compeers,° *fellows*
975   Used to the yoke, draw'st his triumphant wheels
In progress through the road of Heaven star-paved."[1]
    While thus he spake, th' angelic squadron bright
Turned fiery red, sharp'ning in mooned horns
Their phalanx,[2] and began to hem him round
980   With ported[3] spears, as thick as when a field
Of Ceres[4] ripe for harvest waving bends
Her bearded grove of ears, which way the wind
Sways them; the careful° plowman doubting *apprehensive*
    stands
Lest on the threshing floor his hopeful sheaves
985   Prove chaff.[5] On th' other side Satan alarmed[6]
Collecting all his might dilated° stood,   *inflated*
Like Tenerife or Atlas[7] unremoved:°   *immovable*
His stature reached the sky, and on his crest
Sat Horror plumed; nor wanted° in his grasp   *lacked*
990   What seemed both spear and shield: now dreadful deeds
Might have ensued, nor only Paradise
In this commotion, but the starry cope°   *canopy*
Of Heaven perhaps, or all the elements
At least had gone to rack,° disturbed and torn   *ruin*
995   With violence of this conflict, had not soon
Th' Eternal to prevent such horrid fray
Hung forth in Heaven his golden scales, yet seen

Betwixt Astrea and the Scorpion sign,[8]
Wherein all things created first he weighed,
1000   The pendulous round Earth with balanced air
In counterpoise, now ponders° all events,   *weighs*
Battles and realms: in these he put two weights
The sequel° each of parting and of fight;   *consequences*
The latter quick up flew,[9] and kicked the beam;
1005   Which Gabriel spying, thus bespake the fiend.
    "Satan, I know thy strength, and thou know'st mine,
Neither our own but given; what folly then
To boast what arms can do, since thine no more
Than Heaven permits, nor mine, though doubled now
1010   To trample thee as mire:° for proof look up,   *mud*
And read thy lot° in yon celestial sign   *fate*
Where thou art weighed, and shown how light, how weak,
If thou resist." The fiend looked up and knew
His mounted scale aloft: nor more; but fled
1015   Murmuring, and with him fled the shades of night.

THE END OF THE FOURTH BOOK

ARGUMENT TO BOOK 5

Morning approached, Eve relates to Adam her
troublesome dream; he likes it not, yet comforts
her: they come forth to their day labours: their morning
hymn at the door of their bower. God to render man
inexcusable sends Raphael to admonish him of his
obedience, of his free estate, of his enemy near at hand;
who he is, and why his enemy, and whatever else may
avail Adam to know. Raphael comes down to Paradise,
his appearance described, his coming discerned by Adam
afar off sitting at the door of his bower; he goes out to
meet him, brings him to his lodge, entertains him with
the choicest fruits of Paradise got together by Eve; their
discourse at table: Raphael performs his message, minds
Adam of his state and of his enemy; relates at Adam's

---

[1]   *progress … star-paved*   Triumphal procession: Satan compares angels serving the divine to the prisoners who pulled the chariots of triumphant generals in the classical world.

[2]   *sharp'ning … phalanx*   The angels surround Satan in a crescent-shaped military formation.

[3]   *ported*   Held at the ready, slanted in front of them.

[4]   *Ceres*   Classical goddess of agriculture. Here, grain.

[5]   *chaff*   Husks. The useless, discarded parts of grain.

[6]   *alarmed*   Called to arms.

[7]   *Tenerife*   Mountain in the Canary Islands, reputed in Milton's time the highest in the world; *Atlas*   Mountain in Morocco, and the name of the Titan from Greek myth sentenced to hold up the world as punishment for rebelling against the gods.

[8]   *golden scales … sign*   Milton identifies these heavenly scales with the autumnal zodiac sign Libra, which lies between Virgo (associated with Astrea, the goddess of Justice) and Scorpio.

[9]   *The latter … flew*   The scale representing fighting (desired by Satan) is lighter, and thus found wanting (cf. Daniel 5.27). The scale representing the consequences of preventing the fight weighs more, and is thus more desirable. In a similar scene from Homer's *Iliad*, Zeus balances the fates of the Trojans and the Greeks, but in that scene, it is the loser's scale that sinks down, to death.

request who that enemy is, and how he came to be so, beginning from his first revolt in Heaven, and the occasion thereof; how he drew his legions after him to the parts of the North, and there incited them to rebel with him, persuading all but only Abdiel a seraph, who in argument dissuades and opposes him, then forsakes him.

Argument to Book 6

Raphael continues to relate how Michael and Gabriel were sent forth to battle against Satan and his angels. The first fight described: Satan and his powers retire under night: he calls a council, invents devilish engines, which in the second day's fight put Michael and his angels to some disorder; but they at length pulling up mountains overwhelmed both the force and machines of Satan: yet the tumult not so ending, God on the third day sends Messiah His Son, for whom He had reserved the glory of that victory: He in the power of His Father coming to the place, and causing all His legions to stand still on either side, with His chariot and thunder driving into the midst of His enemies, pursues them unable to resist towards the wall of Heaven; which opening, they leap down with horror and confusion into the place of punishment prepared for them in the deep: Messiah returns with triumph to His Father.

Argument to Book 7

Raphael at the request of Adam relates how and wherefore this world was first created; that God, after the expelling of Satan and his angels out of Heaven, declared His pleasure to create another world and other creatures to dwell therein; sends His Son with glory and attendance of angels to perform the work of creation in six days: the angels celebrate with hymns the performance thereof, and His re-ascension into Heaven.

from Book 7

Descend from Heav'n, Urania,[1] by that name
If rightly thou art called, whose voice divine

---

[1] *Urania* Classical Muse of astronomy and later, of religious poetry.

Following, above th' Olympian hill I soar,
Above the flight of Pegasean[2] wing!
5   The meaning, not the name, I call: for thou
Nor of the Muses nine, nor on the top
Of old Olympus dwell'st; but, Heavenly-born,
Before the hills appeared, or fountain flowed,
Thou with eternal wisdom didst converse,
10   Wisdom thy sister, and with her didst play
In presence of th' Almighty Father, pleased
With thy celestial song. Up led by thee
Into the Heav'n of Heav'ns I have presumed,
An earthly guest, and drawn empyreal air,
15   Thy tempering: with like safety guided down
Return me to my native element:
Lest from this flying steed unreined (as once
Bellerophon,[3] though from a lower clime).°   region
Dismounted, on the Aleian field[4] I fall,
20   Erroneous° there to wander, and forlorn.   directionless
Half yet remains unsung, but narrower bound
Within the visible diurnal sphere;
Standing on earth, not rapt° above the pole,   transported
More safe I sing with mortal voice, unchanged
25   To hoarse or mute, though fall'n on evil days,
On evil days though fall'n, and evil tongues;
In darkness, and with dangers compassed round,
And solitude; yet not alone, while thou
Visitest my slumbers nightly, or when morn
30   Purples the east: still govern thou my song,
Urania, and fit audience find, though few.
But drive far off the barbarous dissonance
Of Bacchus and his revellers, the race
Of that wild rout that tore the Thracian bard
35   In Rhodope, where woods and rocks had ears
To rapture, till the savage clamour drowned
Both harp and voice; nor could the Muse defend

---

[2] *Pegasean* Referring to Pegasus, winged horse of Greek myth, a symbol of poetic effort. A strike of his hoof was said to have started the sacred spring of the Muses on Mount Helicon.

[3] *Bellerophon* Rider of Pegasus, who was thrown by the winged horse when he tried to fly to the summit of Mount Olympus. Cursed because of his arrogance, he lived out the rest of his days blind and alone; no mortal dared befriend him for fear of drawing the negative attention of the gods.

[4] *Aleian field* Bellerophon's landing site.

Her son.[1] So fail not thou, who thee implores:
For thou art heav'nly, she an empty dream....

ARGUMENT TO BOOK 8

Adam inquires concerning celestial motions, is doubtfully answered, and exhorted to search rather things more worthy of knowledge: Adam assents, and still desirous to detain Raphael, relates to him what he remembered since his own creation, his placing in Paradise, his talk with God concerning solitude and fit society, his first meeting and nuptials with Eve, his discourse with the angel thereupon; who after admonitions repeated departs.

ARGUMENT TO BOOK 9

Satan having compassed the Earth, with meditated guile returns as a mist by night into Paradise, enters into the serpent sleeping. Adam and Eve in the morning go forth to their labours, which Eve proposes to divide in several places, each labouring apart: Adam consents not, alleging the danger, lest that enemy, of whom they were forewarned, should attempt her found alone: Eve loath to be thought not circumspect or firm enough, urges her going apart, the rather desirous to make trial of her strength; Adam at last yields; the serpent finds her alone; his subtle approach, first gazing, then speaking, with much flattery extolling Eve above all other creatures. Eve wondering to hear the serpent speak, asks how he attained to human speech and such understanding not till now; the serpent answers, that by tasting of a certain tree in the garden he attained both to speech and reason, till then void of both: Eve requires him to bring her to that tree, and finds it to be the Tree of Knowledge forbidden: the Serpent now grown bolder, with many wiles and arguments induces her at length to eat; she pleased with the taste deliberates awhile whether to impart thereof to Adam or not, at last brings him of the fruit, relates what persuaded her to eat thereof: Adam at first amazed, but perceiving her lost, resolves through vehemence of love to perish with her; and extenuating the trespass, eats also of the fruit: the effects thereof in them both; they seek to cover their nakedness, then fall to variance and accusation of one another.

BOOK 9

No more of talk where God or angel guest
    With man, as with his friend, familiar used,
To sit indulgent, and with him partake
Rural repast; permitting him the while
Venial discourse unblamed. I now must change   5
Those notes to tragic; foul distrust, and breach
Disloyal on the part of man, revolt,
And disobedience: on the part of Heav'n
Now alienated, distance and distaste,
Anger and just rebuke, and judgement given,   10
That brought into this world a world of woe,
Sin and her shadow Death, and Misery
Death's harbinger. Sad task, yet argument
Not less but more heroic than the wrath
Of stern Achilles on his foe pursued   15
Thrice fugitive about Troy wall;[2] or rage
Of Turnus for Lavinia disespoused;[3]
Or Neptune's ire, or Juno's, that so long
Perplexed the Greek, and Cytherea's son:[4]
If answerable style I can obtain   20

---

[1] *tore the Thracian bard ... the Muse defend / Her son*   These lines allude to the death of Orpheus who, disconsolate after losing his wife for the second time, wandered Thrace playing tunes so sad they made wild animals, stones, and trees weep. He met a frenzied group of Maenads, female followers of Bacchus, whose screams drowned out the song of Orpheus so that they would not be affected by it. They then tore him apart, and not even Orpheus's mother, the Muse Calliope, could stop them. It was said that his head floated down the river, still singing.

[2] *Achilles ... Troy wall*   Achilles, a Greek hero at Troy, chased the Trojan hero Hector three times around the walls of Troy before bringing him down, and then dragged the corpse around the city to dispirit its defenders.

[3] *Turnus for Lavinia disespoused*   Turnus, a chieftain of the Rutuli people, is the foremost suitor for the hand of Lavinia, daughter of King Latinus, when Aeneas arrives in the latter half of *The Aeneid*. Latinus chooses to grant Lavinia's hand to Aeneas. Turnus then declares war, is slaughtered, and his people are defeated.

[4] *Or Neptune's ire ... Cytherea's son*   Neptune, god of the sea, tormented Odysseus ("the Greek"); Juno tormented Aeneas, the son of Venus (who is also known as Cythera, after Cyprus, her purported first home).

Of my celestial patroness, who deigns[1]
Her nightly visitation unimplored,
And dictates to me slumbering; or inspires
Easy my unpremeditated verse:
25 Since first this subject for heroic song
Pleased me long choosing, and beginning late;
Not sedulous° by nature to incite   *active*
Wars, hitherto the only argument
Heroic deemed chief mastery to dissect
30 With long and tedious havoc fabled knights
In battles feigned; the better fortitude
Of patience and heroic martyrdom
Unsung; or to describe races and games,
Or tilting furniture,[2] emblazoned shields,
35 Impresas quaint,[3] caparisons° and steeds,   *horse armor*
Bases and tinsel trappings, gorgeous knights
At joust and tournament; then marshalled feast
Served up in hall with sewers° and   *servers*
    seneschals; °   *stewards*
The skill of artifice or office mean,[4]
40 Not that which justly gives heroic name
To person, or to poem. Me, of these
Nor skilled nor studious, higher argument
Remains; sufficient of itself to raise
That name, unless an age too late, or cold
45 Climate, or years damp my intended wing
Depressed; and much they may, if all be mine,
Not hers, who brings it nightly to my ear.
        The sun was sunk, and after him the star
Of Hesperus, whose office is to bring
50 Twilight upon the earth, short arbiter
Twixt day and night, and now from end to end
Night's hemisphere had veiled the horizon round:
When Satan, who late fled before the threats
Of Gabriel out of Eden, now improved[5]
55 In meditated fraud and malice, bent
On man's destruction, maugre what might hap
Of heavier on himself, fearless returned
By night he fled, and at midnight returned

From compassing° the earth; cautious of day,   *circling*
60 Since Uriel, regent of the sun, descried
His entrance, and forewarned the cherubim
That kept their watch; thence full of anguish driven,
The space of seven continued nights he rode
With darkness; thrice the equinoctial line
65 He circled; four times crossed the car of night
From pole to pole, traversing each colure;[6]
On the eighth returned; and, on the coast averse°   *opposite*
From entrance or cherubic watch, by stealth
Found unsuspected way. There was a place,
70 Now not, though sin, not time, first wrought the change,
Where Tigris,[7] at the foot of Paradise,
Into a gulf shot under ground, till part
Rose up a fountain by the tree of life:
In with the river sunk, and with it rose
75 Satan, involved in rising mist; then sought
Where to lie hid; sea he had searched, and land,
From Eden over Pontus and the pool
Maeotis, up beyond the river Ob;
Downward as far antarctic; and in length,
80 West from Orontes to the ocean barred
At Darien; thence to the land where flows
Ganges and Indus:[8] Thus the orb he roamed
With narrow search; and with inspection deep
Considered every creature, which of all
85 Most opportune might serve his wiles; and found
The serpent subtlest beast of all the field.
Him after long debate, irresolute
Of thoughts revolved, his final sentence° chose   *decision*
Fit vessel, fittest imp° of fraud, in whom   *shoot, slip*
90 To enter, and his dark suggestions hide
From sharpest sight: for, in the wily snake
Whatever sleights, none would suspicious mark,

---

1 *deigns* Chooses to give.

2 *tilting furniture* Lances or heavy spears.

3 *Impresas quaint* Complex heraldic designs.

4 *skill of artifice or office mean* Skill of craftsman or manual worker.

5 *improved* Strengthened, better able to carry out.

---

6 *colure* Conventional cartographic dissection of the globe by two longitudinal lines, perpendicular at the poles and dividing the earth into four sections like the segments of an orange.

7 *Tigris* Tigris River, originating in eastern Turkey and flowing southeast through Iraq to join the Euphrates River before spilling into the Persian Gulf.

8 *Pontus* The Black Sea; *the pool / Maeotis* Sea of Azov, the northern arm of the Black Sea; *river Ob* River in Siberia, in northeastern Russia; *Orontes* River originating in northern Lebanon and flowing north through Syria and Turkey to empty into the Mediterranean Sea; *Darien* Panama, in South America; *Ganges and Indus* Ganges and Indus Rivers, the principal rivers of India.

As from his wit and native subtlety
Proceeding; which, in other beasts observed,
95 Doubt might beget of diabolic pow'r
Active within, beyond the sense of brute.
Thus he resolved, but first from inward grief
His bursting passion into plaints thus poured:
      "O Earth, how like to Heav'n, if not preferred
100 More justly, seat worthier of gods, as built
With second thoughts, reforming what was old!
For what God, after better, worse would build?
Terrestrial Heav'n, danced round by other Heav'ns
That shine, yet bear their bright officious lamps,
105 Light above light, for thee alone, as seems,
In thee concentring all their precious beams
Of sacred influence! As God in Heav'n
Is centre, yet extends to all; so thou,
Centring, receivest from all those orbs: in thee,
110 Not in themselves, all their known virtue appears
Productive in herb, plant, and nobler birth
Of creatures animate with gradual life
Of growth, sense, reason, all summed up in man.
With what delight could I have walked thee round,
115 If I could joy in aught, sweet interchange
Of hill, and valley, rivers, woods, and plains,
Now land, now sea and shores with forest crowned,
Rocks, dens, and caves! But I in none of these
Find place or refuge; and the more I see
120 Pleasures about me, so much more I feel
Torment within me, as from the hateful siege
Of contraries: all good to me becomes
Bane, and in Heav'n much worse would be my state.
But neither here seek I, no nor in Heav'n
125 To dwell, unless by mastering Heav'n's Supreme;
Nor hope to be myself less miserable
By what I seek, but others to make such
As I, though thereby worse to me redound:°   return
For only in destroying I find ease
130 To my relentless thoughts; and, him destroyed,
Or won to what may work his utter loss,
For whom all this was made, all this will soon
Follow, as to him linked in weal° or woe;   prosperity
In woe then; that destruction wide may range:
135 To me shall be the glory sole among
The infernal powers, in one day to have marred
What He, Almighty styled, six nights and days

Continued making; and who knows how long
Before had been contriving? Though perhaps
140 Not longer than since I, in one night, freed
From servitude inglorious well nigh half
Th' angelic name, and thinner left the throng
Of His adorers: He, to be avenged,
And to repair His numbers thus impaired,
145 Whether such virtue spent of old now failed
More angels to create, if they at least
Are His created, or, to spite us more,
Determined to advance into our room
A creature formed of earth, and him endow,
150 Exalted from so base original,
With Heav'nly spoils, our spoils. What He decreed,
He effected; Man He made, and for him built
Magnificent this world, and earth his seat,
Him lord pronounced; and, O indignity!
155 Subjected to his service angel-wings,
And flaming ministers to watch and tend
Their earthly charge: of these the vigilance
I dread; and, to elude, thus wrapt in mist
Of midnight vapour glide obscure, and pry
160 In every bush and brake, where hap may find
The serpent sleeping; in whose mazy folds
To hide me, and the dark intent I bring.
O foul descent! That I, who erst contended
With Gods to sit the highest, am now constrained
165 Into a beast; and, mixed with bestial slime,
This essence to incarnate and imbrute,
That to the height of deity aspired!
But what will not ambition and revenge
Descend to? Who aspires, must down as low
170 As high he soared; obnoxious, first or last,
To basest things. Revenge, at first though sweet,
Bitter ere long, back on itself recoils:
Let it; I reck° not, so it light well aimed,   care
Since higher I fall short, on him who next
175 Provokes my envy, this new favourite
Of Heav'n, this man of clay, son of despite,
Whom, us the more to spite, his Maker raised
From dust: spite then with spite is best repaid."
      So saying, through each thicket dank or dry,
180 Like a black mist low-creeping, he held on
His midnight-search, where soonest he might find
The serpent; him fast-sleeping soon he found

In labyrinth of many a round self-rolled,
His head the midst, well stored with subtle wiles:
85 Not yet in horrid shade or dismal den,
Nor nocent° yet; but, on the grassy herb,   *harmful*
Fearless unfeared he slept: in at his mouth
The devil entered; and his brutal sense,
In heart or head, possessing, soon inspired
90 With act intelligential; but his sleep
Disturbed not, waiting close th' approach of morn.
Now, when as sacred light began to dawn
In Eden on the humid flowers, that breathed
Their morning incense, when all things that breathe
95 From the Earth's great altar send up silent praise
To the Creator, and His nostrils fill
With grateful smell, forth came the human pair,
And joined their vocal worship to the choir
Of creatures wanting voice; that done, partake
00 The season prime for sweetest scents and airs:
Then commune, how that day they best may ply
Their growing work: for much their work out-grew
The hands' dispatch of two gardening so wide,
And Eve first to her husband thus began:
05   "Adam, well may we labour still to dress
This garden, still to tend plant, herb, and flower,
Our pleasant task enjoined; but, till more hands
Aid us, the work under our labour grows
Luxurious by restraint; what we by day
10 Lop overgrown, or prune, or prop, or bind,
One night or two with wanton growth derides
Tending to wild. Thou therefore now advise,
Or hear what to my mind first thoughts present:
Let us divide our labours; thou, where choice
15 Leads thee, or where most needs, whether to wind
The woodbine round this arbour, or direct
The clasping ivy where to climb; while I,
In yonder spring of roses intermixed
With myrtle, find what to redress till noon:
20 For, while so near each other thus all day
Our task we choose, what wonder if so near
Looks intervene and smiles, or object new
Casual discourse draw on; which intermits
Our day's work, brought to little, though begun
25 Early, and th' hour of supper comes unearned?"
      To whom mild answer Adam thus returned:
"Sole Eve, associate sole, to me beyond

Compare above all living creatures dear!
Well hast thou motioned, well thy thoughts
      employed,
230 How we might best fulfil the work which here
God hath assigned us; nor of me shalt pass
Unpraised: for nothing lovelier can be found
In woman, than to study household good,
And good works in her husband to promote.
235 Yet not so strictly hath our Lord imposed
Labour, as to debar° us when we need   *constrain*
Refreshment, whether food, or talk between,
Food of the mind, or this sweet intercourse
Of looks and smiles; for smiles from Reason flow,
240 To brute denied, and are of Love the food;
Love, not the lowest end of human life.
For not to irksome toil, but to delight,
He made us, and delight to reason joined.
These paths and bowers doubt not but our joint hands
245 Will keep from wilderness with ease, as wide
As we need walk, till younger hands ere long
Assist us; But, if much converse perhaps
Thee satiate, to short absence I could yield:
For solitude sometimes is best society,
250 And short retirement urges sweet return.
But other doubt possesses me, lest harm
Befall thee severed from me; for thou knowest
What hath been warned us, what malicious foe
Envying our happiness, and of his own
255 Despairing, seeks to work us woe and shame
By sly assault; and somewhere nigh at hand
Watches, no doubt, with greedy hope to find
His wish and best advantage, us asunder;
Hopeless to circumvent us joined, where each
260 To other speedy aid might lend at need:
Whether his first design be to withdraw
Our fealty from God, or to disturb
Conjugal love, than which perhaps no bliss
Enjoyed by us excites his envy more;
265 Or this, or worse, leave not the faithful side
That gave thee being, still shades thee, and protects.
The wife, where danger or dishonour lurks,
Safest and seemliest by her husband stays,
Who guards her, or with her the worst endures."
270   To whom the virgin majesty of Eve,
As one who loves, and some unkindness meets,

With sweet austere composure thus replied:
    "Offspring of Heaven and Earth, and all Earth's
        lord!
That such an enemy we have, who seeks
275 Our ruin, both by thee informed I learn,
And from the parting Angel[1] over-heard,
As in a shady nook I stood behind,
Just then returned at shut of evening flowers.
But, that thou shouldst my firmness therefore doubt
280 To God or thee, because we have a foe
May tempt it, I expected not to hear.
His violence thou fearest not, being such
As we, not capable of death or pain,
Can either not receive, or can repel.
285 His fraud is then thy fear; which plain infers
Thy equal fear, that my firm faith and love
Can by his fraud be shaken or seduced;
Thoughts, which how found they harbour in thy
       breast,
Adam, mis-thought of her to thee so dear?"
290   To whom with healing words Adam replied:
"Daughter of God and Man, immortal Eve!
For such thou art; from sin and blame entire:
Not diffident of thee do I dissuade
Thy absence from my sight, but to avoid
295 Th' attempt itself, intended by our foe.
For he who tempts, though in vain, at least asperses[2]
The tempted with dishonour foul; supposed
Not incorruptible of faith, not proof
Against temptation: Thou thyself with scorn
300 And anger wouldst resent the offered wrong,
Though ineffectual found: misdeem not then,
If such affront I labour to avert
From thee alone, which on us both at once
The enemy, though bold, will hardly dare;
305 Or daring, first on me th' assault shall light.
Nor thou his malice and false guile contemn;
Subtle he needs must be, who could seduce
Angels; nor think superfluous others' aid.
I, from the influence of thy looks, receive
310 Access in every virtue; in thy sight

More wise, more watchful, stronger, if need were
Of outward strength; while shame, thou looking on,
Shame to be overcome or over-reached,
Would utmost vigour raise, and raised unite.
315 Why shouldst not thou like sense within thee feel
When I am present, and thy trial choose
With me, best witness of thy virtue tried?"
    So spake domestic Adam in his care
And matrimonial love; but Eve, who thought
320 Less attributed to her faith sincere,
Thus her reply with accent sweet renewed:
    "If this be our condition, thus to dwell
In narrow circuit straitened by a foe,
Subtle or violent, we not endued
325 Single with like defence, wherever met;
How are we happy, still in fear of harm?
But harm precedes not sin: only our foe,
Tempting, affronts us with his foul esteem
Of our integrity: his foul esteem
330 Sticks no dishonour on our front, but turns
Foul on himself; then wherefore shunned or feared
By us? Who rather double honour gain
From his surmise proved false; find peace within,
Favour from Heav'n, our witness, from the event.
335 And what is faith, love, virtue, unassayed
Alone, without exterior help sustained?
Let us not then suspect our happy state
Left so imperfect by the Maker wise,
As not secure to single or combined.
340 Frail is our happiness, if this be so,
And Eden were no Eden, thus exposed."
    To whom thus Adam fervently replied.
"O woman, best are all things as the will
Of God ordained them: His creating hand
345 Nothing imperfect or deficient left
Of all that he created, much less Man,
Or aught that might his happy state secure,
Secure from outward force; within himself
The danger lies, yet lies within his power:
350 Against his will he can receive no harm.
But God left free the Will; for what obeys
Reason, is free; and Reason He made right,
But bid her well beware, and still erect;[3]

---

1   *the parting Angel* Raphael, the angel who visits Adam and Eve in Books Four through Eight, and warns them of the danger they are about to face.

2   *asperses* Bespatters, besprinkles, here someone's reputation.

3   *bid her ... still erect* Advised her to be careful, and to remain vigilant.

355 Lest, by some fair-appearing good surprised,
She dictate false; and mis-inform the will
To do what God expressly hath forbid.
Not then mistrust, but tender love, enjoins,
That I should mind thee oft; and mind thou me.
Firm we subsist, yet possible to swerve;
360 Since Reason not impossibly may meet
Some specious object by the foe suborned,
And fall into deception unaware,
Not keeping strictest watch, as she was warned.
Seek not temptation then, which to avoid
365 Were better, and most likely if from me
Thou sever trial will come unsought.
Wouldst thou approve thy constancy, approve
First thy obedience; the other who can know,
Not seeing thee attempted, who attest?
370 But, if thou think, trial unsought may find
Us both securer than thus warned thou seemest,
Go; for thy stay, not free, absents thee more;
Go in thy native innocence, rely
On what thou hast of virtue; summon all!
375 For God towards thee hath done his part, do thine."
        So spake the patriarch of mankind; but Eve
Persisted; yet submiss, though last, replied:
        "With thy permission then, and thus forewarned
Chiefly by what thy own last reasoning words
380 Touched only; that our trial, when least sought,
May find us both perhaps far less prepared,
The willinger I go, nor much expect
A foe so proud will first the weaker seek;
So bent, the more shall shame him his repulse."
385 Thus saying, from her husband's hand her hand
Soft she withdrew; and, like a wood-nymph light,
Oread or dryad, or of Delia's[1] train,
Betook her to the groves; but Delia's self
In gait surpassed, and goddess-like deport,°   *composure*
390 Though not as she with bow and quiver armed,
But with such gard'ning tools as art yet rude,
Guiltless of fire, had formed, or angels brought.
To Pales, or Pomona, thus adorned,
Likest she seemed, Pomona when she fled

395 Vertumnus,[2] or to Ceres in her prime,
Yet virgin of Proserpina from Jove.
Her long with ardent look his eye pursued
Delighted, but desiring more her stay.
Oft he to her his charge of quick return
400 Repeated; she to him as oft engaged
To be returned by noon amid the bower,
And all things in best order to invite
Noontide repast, or afternoon's repose.
O much deceived, much failing, hapless Eve,
405 Of thy presumed return! Event perverse!
Thou never from that hour in Paradise
Foundst either sweet repast, or sound repose;
Such ambush, hid among sweet flowers and shades,
Waited with hellish rancour imminent
410 To intercept thy way, or send thee back
Despoiled of innocence, of faith, of bliss!
For now, and since first break of dawn, the fiend,
Mere serpent in appearance, forth was come;
And on his quest, where likeliest he might find
415 The only two of mankind, but in them
The whole included race, his purposed prey.
In bower and field he sought, where any tuft
Of grove or garden-plot more pleasant lay,
Their tendance, or plantation for delight;
420 By fountain or by shady rivulet
He sought them both, but wished his hap might find
Eve separate; he wished, but not with hope
Of what so seldom chanced; when to his wish,
Beyond his hope, Eve separate he spies,
425 Veiled in a cloud of fragrance, where she stood,
Half spied, so thick the roses blushing round
About her glowed, oft stooping to support
Each flower of slender stalk, whose head, though gay
Carnation, purple, azure, or specked with gold,
430 Hung drooping unsustained; them she upstays
Gently with myrtle band, mindless the while
Herself, though fairest unsupported flower,
From her best prop so far, and storm so nigh.
Nearer he drew, and many a walk traversed
435 Of stateliest covert, cedar, pine, or palm;
Then voluble and bold, now hid, now seen,
Among thick-woven arborets, and flowers

---

1 *Oread ... dryad* Nature spirits from Greek mythology; *Delia*
Roman virgin goddess of the moon and the hunt.

2 *Pales ... Pomona ... Vertumnus* Goddess of pastures, goddess of
orchards, and god of gardens and the change of seasons, respectively.

Imbordered on each bank, the hand of Eve:
Spot more delicious than those gardens feigned
440 Or of revived Adonis,[1] or renowned
Alcinous,[2] host of old Laertes' son;
Or that, not mystick, where the sapient king
Held dalliance with his fair Egyptian spouse.[3]
Much he the place admired, the person more.
445 As one who long in populous city pent,
Where houses thick and sewers annoy the air,
Forth issuing on a summer's morn, to breathe
Among the pleasant villages and farms
Adjoined, from each thing met conceives delight;
450 The smell of grain, or tedded grass, or kine,[4]
Or dairy, each rural sight, each rural sound;
If chance, with nymph-like step, fair virgin pass,
What pleasing seemed, for her now pleases more;
She most, and in her look sums all delight:
455 Such pleasure took the serpent to behold
This flowery plat,° the sweet recess of   ° *plot, patch of ground*
      Eve
Thus early, thus alone: Her heav'nly form
Angelic, but more soft, and feminine,
Her graceful innocence, her every air
460 Of gesture, or least action, overawed
His malice, and with rapine sweet bereaved
His fierceness of the fierce intent it brought:
That space the evil one abstracted stood
From his own evil, and for the time remained
465 Stupidly good; of enmity disarmed,
Of guile, of hate, of envy, of revenge:
But the hot Hell that always in him burns,
Though in mid Heav'n, soon ended his delight,
And tortures him now more, the more he sees
470 Of pleasure, not for him ordained: then soon
Fierce hate he recollects, and all his thoughts
Of mischief, gratulating, thus excites:

"Thoughts, whither have ye led me! With what
      sweet
Compulsion thus transported, to forget
475 What hither brought us! Hate, not love; nor hope
Of Paradise for Hell, hope here to taste
Of pleasure; but all pleasure to destroy,
Save what is in destroying; other joy
To me is lost. Then, let me not let pass
480 Occasion which now smiles; behold alone
The woman, opportune to all attempts,
Her husband, for I view far round, not nigh,
Whose higher intellectual more I shun,
And strength, of courage haughty, and of limb
485 Heroic built, though of terrestrial mould;
Foe not informidable! Exempt from wound,
I not; so much hath Hell debased, and pain
Enfeebled me, to what I was in Heav'n.
She fair, divinely fair, fit love for Gods!
490 Not terrible, though terror be in love
And beauty, not approached by stronger hate,
Hate stronger, under show of love well feigned;
The way which to her ruin now I tend."
      So spake the enemy of mankind, enclosed
495 In serpent, inmate bad, and toward Eve
Addressed his way: not with indented wave,
Prone on the ground, as since; but on his rear,
Circular base of rising folds, that towered
Fold above fold, a surging maze! His head
500 Crested aloft, and carbuncle[5] his eyes;
With burnished neck of verdant gold, erect
Amidst his circling spires, that on the grass
Floated redundant: pleasing was his shape
And lovely; never since of serpent-kind
505 Lovelier, not those that in Illyria changed,
Hermione and Cadmus, or the god
In Epidaurus; nor to which transformed
Ammonian Jove, or Capitoline, was seen;
He with Olympias; this with her who bore
510 Scipio, the height of Rome.[6] With tract oblique

---

[1] *Adonis* Beloved of Venus, goddess of love. He was slain by a boar but was turned to a flower. He became a cult figure. His "gardens" were miniature gardens, symbols, says Erasmus, of evanescence.

[2] *Alcinous* Alcinous, King of the Phaeacians, owned a fabulous garden visited by Odysseus, son of Laertes, in Homer's *Odyssey*.

[3] *the sapient king ... spouse* Solomon the Wise and the daughter of the King of Egypt (see 1 Kings).

[4] *tedded* Mown, as for hay; *kine* Cattle.

[5] *carbuncle* Ruby.

[6] *those that in Illyria ... Rome Hermione and Cadmus* Citizens of Illyria changed into serpents: he for killing a sacred snake, she out of love for Cadmus; *the God / In Epidaurus* Aesculapius, god of healing, who appeared at his temple in Epidaurus in the form of a snake; *Ammonian Jove, or Capitoline* Both names refer to Jove, but

At first, as one who sought access, but feared
To interrupt, sidelong he works his way.
As when a ship, by skilful steersmen wrought
Nigh river's mouth or foreland, where the wind
15 Veers oft, as oft so steers, and shifts her sail:
So varied he, and of his tortuous train
Curled many a wanton wreath in sight of Eve,
To lure her eye; she, busied, heard the sound
Of rustling leaves, but minded not, as used
20 To such disport before her through the field,
From every beast; more duteous at her call,
Than at Circean call the herd disguised.[1]
He, bolder now, uncalled before her stood,
But as in gaze admiring: oft he bowed
25 His turret crest, and sleek enamelled neck,
Fawning; and licked the ground whereon she trod.
His gentle dumb expression turned at length
The eye of Eve to mark his play; he, glad
Of her attention gained, with serpent-tongue
30 Organic, or impulse of vocal air,
His fraudulent temptation thus began:
    "Wonder not, sov'reign mistress, if perhaps
Thou canst, who art sole wonder! Much less arm
Thy looks, the heaven of mildness, with disdain,
35 Displeased that I approach thee thus, and gaze
Insatiate; I thus single; nor have feared
Thy awful brow, more awful thus retired.
Fairest resemblance of thy Maker fair,
Thee all things living gaze on, all things thine
40 By gift, and thy celestial beauty adore
With ravishment beheld! There best beheld,
Where universally admired; but here
In this enclosure wild, these beasts among,
Beholders rude, and shallow to discern
45 Half what in thee is fair, one man except,
Who sees thee? And what is one? Who should be seen
A goddess among gods, adored and served
By angels numberless, thy daily train."

So glozed the tempter, and his proem[2] tuned:
550 Into the heart of Eve his words made way,
Though at the voice much marvelling; at length,
Not unamazed, she thus in answer spake:
    "What may this mean? Language of man
        pronounced
By tongue of brute, and human sense expressed?
555 The first, at least, of these I thought denied
To beasts; whom God, on their creation-day,
Created mute to all articulate sound:
The latter I demur; for in their looks
Much reason, and in their actions, oft appears.
560 Thee, serpent, subtlest beast of all the field
I knew, but not with human voice endued;
Redouble then this miracle, and say,
How cam'st thou speakable of mute, and how
To me so friendly grown above the rest
565 Of brutal kind, that daily are in sight?
Say, for such wonder claims attention due."
    To whom the guileful tempter thus replied,
"Empress of this fair world, resplendent Eve!
Easy to me it is to tell thee all
570 What thou commandest; and right thou shouldst be
        obeyed:
I was at first as other beasts that graze
The trodden herb, of abject thoughts and low,
As was my food; nor aught but food discerned
Or sex, and apprehended nothing high:
575 Till, on a day roving the field, I chanced
A goodly tree far distant to behold
Loaden with fruit of fairest colours mixed,
Ruddy and gold: I nearer drew to gaze;
When from the boughs a savoury odour blown,
580 Grateful to appetite, more pleased my sense
Than smell of sweetest fennel, or the teats
Of ewe or goat dropping with milk at even,
Unsucked of lamb or kid, that tend their play.
To satisfy the sharp desire I had
585 Of tasting those fair apples, I resolved
Not to defer; hunger and thirst at once,
Powerful persuaders, quickened at the scent
Of that alluring fruit, urged me so keen.
About the mossy trunk I wound me soon;
590 For, high from ground, the branches would require

---

different instances of his shape-shifting to impregnate (continued)
women with famous conqueror children; *Olympias ... Scipio*
Olympias was Alexander the Great's mother, and Scipio was a great
Roman conqueror-hero. Both men were supposed to have been
begotten by Jove in the form of a snake.

[1] *Circean call the herd disguised* Circe was a sorceress who transformed men into animals.

[2] *glozed* Flattered; *proem* Prelude or introduction.

Thy utmost reach or Adam's: Round the tree
All other beasts that saw, with like desire
Longing and envying stood, but could not reach.
Amid the tree now got, where plenty hung
595   Tempting so nigh, to pluck and eat my fill
I spared not; for, such pleasure till that hour,
At feed or fountain, never had I found.
Sated at length, ere long I might perceive
Strange alteration in me, to degree
600   Of reason in my inward powers; and speech
Wanted not long; though to this shape retained.
Thenceforth to speculations high or deep
I turned my thoughts, and with capacious mind
Considered all things visible in Heav'n,
605   Or Earth, or middle; all things fair and good:
But all that fair and good in thy divine
Semblance, and in thy beauty's heav'nly ray,
United I beheld; no fair to thine
Equivalent or second, which compelled
610   Me thus, though importune perhaps, to come
And gaze, and worship thee of right declared
Sov'reign of creatures, universal dame!"
        So talked the spirited sly snake; and Eve,
Yet more amazed, unwary thus replied,
615   "Serpent, thy overpraising leaves in doubt
The virtue of that fruit, in thee first proved:
But say, where grows the tree? From hence how far?
For many are the trees of God that grow
In Paradise, and various, yet unknown
620   To us; in such abundance lies our choice,
As leaves a greater store of fruit untouched,
Still hanging incorruptible, till men
Grow up to their provision, and more hands
Help to disburden nature of her birth."
625   To whom the wily adder, blithe and glad:
"Empress, the way is ready, and not long;
Beyond a row of myrtles, on a flat,
Fast by a fountain, one small thicket past
Of blowing myrrh and balm: if thou accept
630   My conduct, I can bring thee thither soon."
        "Lead then," said Eve. He, leading, swiftly rolled
In tangles, and made intricate seem straight,
To mischief swift. Hope elevates, and joy
Brightens his crest; as when a wandering fire,
635   Compact of unctuous vapour, which the night

Condenses, and the cold environs round,
Kindled through agitation to a flame,
Which oft, they say, some evil spirit attends,
Hovering and blazing with delusive light,
640   Misleads th' amazed night-wanderer from his way
To bogs and mires, and oft through pond or pool;
There swallowed up and lost, from succour far.
So glistered the dire snake, and into fraud
Led Eve, our credulous mother, to the tree
645   Of prohibition, root of all our woe;
Which when she saw, thus to her guide she spake:
        "Serpent, we might have spared our coming
                hither,
Fruitless to me, though fruit be here to excess,
The credit of whose virtue rest with thee;
650   Wondrous indeed, if cause of such effects.
But of this tree we may not taste nor touch;
God so commanded, and left that command
Sole daughter of His voice; the rest, we live
Law to ourselves; our reason is our law."
655   To whom the tempter guilefully replied:
"Indeed! Hath God then said that of the fruit
Of all these garden-trees ye shall not eat,
Yet lords declared of all in earth or air?"
        To whom thus Eve, yet sinless: "Of the fruit
660   Of each tree in the garden we may eat;
But of the fruit of this fair tree amidst
The garden, God hath said, 'ye shall not eat
Thereof, nor shall ye touch it, lest ye die.'"
        She scarce had said, though brief, when now more
                bold
665   The tempter, but with show of zeal and love
To Man, and indignation at his wrong,
New part puts on; and, as to passion moved,
Fluctuates disturbed, yet comely and in act
Raised, as of some great matter to begin.
670   As when of old some orator renowned,
In Athens or free Rome, where eloquence
Flourished, since mute to some great cause addressed,
Stood in himself collected; while each part,
Motion, each act, won audience ere the tongue;
675   Sometimes in height began, as no delay
Of preface brooking, through his zeal of right:
So standing, moving, or to height up grown,
The tempter, all impassioned, thus began:

"O sacred, wise, and wisdom-giving plant,
580 Mother of science!° Now I feel thy power   *knowledge*
Within me clear; not only to discern
Things in their causes, but to trace the ways
Of highest agents, deemed however wise.
Queen of this universe! Do not believe
585 Those rigid threats of death: ye shall not die:
How should you? By the fruit? It gives you life
To knowledge; by the threat'ner? Look on me,
Me, who have touched and tasted; yet both live,
And life more perfect have attained than fate
590 Meant me, by vent'ring higher than my lot.
Shall that be shut to Man, which to the beast
Is open? Or will God incense His ire
For such a petty trespass and not praise
Rather your dauntless virtue, whom the pain
595 Of death denounced, whatever thing death be,
Deterred not from achieving what might lead
To happier life, knowledge of good and evil;
Of good, how just? Of evil, if what is evil
Be real, why not known, since easier shunned?
700 God therefore cannot hurt ye, and be just;
Not just, not God; not feared then, nor obeyed:
Your fear itself of death removes the fear.
Why then was this forbid? Why, but to awe;
Why, but to keep ye low and ignorant,
705 His worshippers? He knows that in the day
Ye eat thereof, your eyes that seem so clear,
Yet are but dim, shall perfectly be then
Opened and cleared, and ye shall be as gods,
Knowing both good and evil, as they know.
710 That ye shall be as gods, since I as man,
Internal man, is but proportion meet;
I, of brute, human; ye, of human, gods.
So ye shall die perhaps, by putting off
Human, to put on gods; death to be wished,
715 Though threatened, which no worse than this can
        bring.
And what are gods, that man may not become
As they, participating godlike food?
The gods are first, and that advantage use
On our belief, that all from them proceeds:
720 I question it; for this fair earth I see,
Warmed by the sun, producing every kind;
Them, nothing: if they all things, who enclosed

Knowledge of good and evil in this tree,
That whoso eats thereof, forthwith attains
725 Wisdom without their leave? And wherein lies
The offence, that man should thus attain to know?
What can your knowledge hurt Him, or this tree
Impart against His will, if all be His?
Or is it envy? And can envy dwell
730 In heav'nly breasts? These, these, and many more
Causes import your need of this fair fruit.
Goddess human, reach then, and freely taste!"
    He ended; and his words, replete with guile,
Into her heart too easy entrance won:
735 Fixed on the fruit she gazed, which to behold
Might tempt alone; and in her ears the sound
Yet rung of his persuasive words, impregned
With reason, to her seeming, and with truth:
Meanwhile the hour of noon drew on, and waked
740 An eager appetite, raised by the smell
So savoury of that fruit, which with desire,
Inclinable now grown to touch or taste,
Solicited her longing eye; yet first
Pausing a while, thus to herself she mused:
745   "Great are thy virtues, doubtless, best of fruits,
Though kept from man, and worthy to be admired;
Whose taste, too long forborne, at first assay
Gave elocution to the mute, and taught
The tongue not made for speech to speak thy praise:
750 Thy praise He also, who forbids thy use,
Conceals not from us, naming thee the tree
Of knowledge, knowledge both of good and evil;
Forbids us then to taste! But His forbidding
Commends thee more, while it infers the good
755 By thee communicated, and our want:
For good unknown sure is not had; or, had
And yet unknown, is as not had at all.
In plain then, what forbids He but to know,
Forbids us good, forbids us to be wise?
760 Such prohibitions bind not. But, if death
Bind us with after-bands, what profits then
Our inward freedom? In the day we eat
Of this fair fruit, our doom is, we shall die!
How dies the serpent? He hath eaten and lives,
765 And knows, and speaks, and reasons, and discerns,
Irrational till then. For us alone
Was death invented? Or to us denied

This intellectual food, for beasts reserved?
For beasts it seems: yet that one beast which first
770 Hath tasted envies not, but brings with joy
The good befallen him, author unsuspect,
Friendly to man, far from deceit or guile.
What fear I then? Rather, what know to fear
Under this ignorance of good and evil,
775 Of God or death, of law or penalty?
Here grows the cure of all, this fruit divine,
Fair to the eye, inviting to the taste,
Of virtue to make wise: what hinders then
To reach, and feed at once both body and mind?"
780   So saying, her rash hand in evil hour
Forth reaching to the fruit, she plucked, she ate!
Earth felt the wound; and nature from her seat,
Sighing through all her works, gave signs of woe,
That all was lost. Back to the thicket slunk
785 The guilty serpent; and well might; for Eve,
Intent now wholly on her taste, nought else
Regarded; such delight till then, as seemed,
In fruit she never tasted, whether true
Or fancied so, through expectation high
790 Of knowledge; nor was godhead from her thought.
Greedily she engorged without restraint,
And knew not eating death. Satiate at length,
And heightened as with wine, jocund and boon,
Thus to herself she pleasingly began:
795   "O sov'reign, virtuous, precious of all trees
In Paradise! Of operation blest
To sapience, hitherto obscured, infamed.
And thy fair fruit let hang, as to no end
Created; but henceforth my early care,
800 Not without song, each morning, and due praise,
Shall tend thee, and the fertile burden ease
Of thy full branches offered free to all;
Till, dieted by thee, I grow mature
In knowledge, as the gods, who all things know;
805 Though others envy what they cannot give:
For, had the gift been theirs, it had not here
Thus grown. Experience, next, to thee I owe,
Best guide; not following thee, I had remained
In ignorance; thou openest wisdom's way,
810 And givest access, though secret she retire.
And I perhaps am secret: Heav'n is high,
High, and remote to see from thence distinct

Each thing on Earth; and other care perhaps
May have diverted from continual watch
815 Our great Forbidder, safe with all His spies
About Him. But to Adam in what sort
Shall I appear? Shall I to him make known
As yet my change, and give him to partake
Full happiness with me, or rather not,
820 But keeps the odds of knowledge in my power
Without copartner? So to add what wants
In female sex, the more to draw his love,
And render me more equal; and perhaps,
A thing not undesirable, sometime
825 Superior; for, inferior, who is free?
This may be well: but what if God have seen,
And death ensue? Then I shall be no more!
And Adam, wedded to another Eve,
Shall live with her enjoying, I extinct;
830 A death to think! Confirmed then I resolve,
Adam shall share with me in bliss or woe:
So dear I love him, that with him all deaths
I could endure, without him live no life."
    So saying, from the tree her step she turned;
835 But first low reverence done, as to the power
That dwelt within, whose presence had infused
Into the plant sciential sap, derived
From nectar, drink of Gods. Adam the while,
Waiting desirous her return, had wove
840 Of choicest flowers a garland, to adorn
Her tresses, and her rural labours crown;
As reapers oft are wont their harvest-queen.
Great joy he promised to his thoughts, and new
Solace in her return, so long delayed:
845 Yet oft his heart, divine of something ill,
Misgave him; he the faltering measure felt;
And forth to meet her went, the way she took
That morn when first they parted: by the tree
Of knowledge he must pass; there he her met,
850 Scarce from the tree returning; in her hand
A bough of fairest fruit, that downy smiled,
New gathered, and ambrosial smell diffused.
To him she hasted; in her face excuse
Came prologue, and apology too prompt;
855 Which, with bland words at will, she thus addressed:
    "Hast thou not wondered, Adam, at my stay?
Thee I have missed, and thought it long, deprived

Thy presence; agony of love till now
Not felt, nor shall be twice; for never more
60 Mean I to try, what rash untried I sought,
The pain of absence from thy sight. But strange
Hath been the cause, and wonderful to hear:
This tree is not, as we are told, a tree
Of danger tasted, nor to evil unknown
65 Op'ning the way, but of divine effect
To open eyes, and make them gods who taste;
And hath been tasted such. The serpent wise,
Or not restrained as we, or not obeying,
Hath eaten of the fruit; and is become,
70 Not dead, as we are threatened, but thenceforth
Endued with human voice and human sense,
Reasoning to admiration; and with me
Persuasively hath so prevailed, that I
Have also tasted, and have also found
75 Th' effects to correspond; opener mine eyes,
Dim erst, dilated spirits, ampler heart,
And growing up to godhead; which for thee
Chiefly I sought, without thee can despise.
For bliss, as thou hast part, to me is bliss;
80 Tedious, unshared with thee, and odious soon.
Thou therefore also taste, that equal lot
May join us, equal joy, as equal love;
Lest, thou not tasting, different degree
Disjoin us, and I then too late renounce
85 Deity for thee, when fate will not permit."
    Thus Eve with countenance blithe her story told;
But in her cheek distemper flushing glowed.
On th' other side Adam, soon as he heard
The fatal trespass done by Eve, amazed,
90 Astonied° stood and blank, while horror chill   *astonished*
Ran through his veins, and all his joints relaxed;
From his slack hand the garland wreathed for Eve
Down dropt, and all the faded roses shed:
Speechless he stood and pale, till thus at length
95 First to himself he inward silence broke.
    "O fairest of creation, last and best
Of all God's works, creature in whom excelled
Whatever can to sight or thought be formed,
Holy, divine, good, amiable, or sweet!
00 How art thou lost! How on a sudden lost,
Defaced, deflowered, and now to death devote!
Rather, how hast thou yielded to transgress

The strict forbiddance, how to violate
The sacred fruit forbidden! Some cursed fraud
905 Of enemy hath beguiled thee, yet unknown,
And me with thee hath ruined; for with thee
Certain my resolution is to die:
How can I live without thee! How forego
Thy sweet converse, and love so dearly joined,
910 To live again in these wild woods forlorn!
Should God create another Eve, and I
Another rib afford, yet loss of thee
Would never from my heart; no. No, I feel
The link of nature draw me: flesh of flesh,
915 Bone of my bone thou art, and from thy state
Mine never shall be parted, bliss or woe."
    So having said, as one from sad dismay
Recomforted, and after thoughts disturbed
Submitting to what seemed remediless,
920 Thus in calm mood his words to Eve he turned.
    "Bold deed thou hast presumed, advent'rous Eve,
And peril great provoked, who thus hast dared,
Had it been only coveting to eye
That sacred fruit, sacred to abstinence,
925 Much more to taste it under ban to touch.
But past who can recall, or done undo?
Not God omnipotent, nor fate; yet so
Perhaps thou shalt not die, perhaps the fact
Is not so heinous now, foretasted fruit,
930 Profaned first by the serpent, by him first
Made common, and unhallowed, ere our taste;
Nor yet on him found deadly; yet he lives;
Lives, as thou saidst, and gains to live, as man,
Higher degree of life; inducement strong
935 To us, as likely tasting to attain
Proportional ascent; which cannot be
But to be gods, or angels, demi-gods.
Nor can I think that God, Creator wise,
Though threat'ning, will in earnest so destroy
940 Us His prime creatures, dignified so high,
Set over all His works; which in our fall,
For us created, needs with us must fail,
Dependent made; so God shall uncreate,
Be frustrate, do, undo, and labour lose;
945 Not well conceived of God, who, though His power
Creation could repeat, yet would be loth
Us to abolish, lest the adversary

Triumph, and say; 'Fickle their state whom God
Most favours; who can please Him long? Me first
950 He ruined, now Mankind; whom will He next?'
Matter of scorn, not to be given the foe.
However I with thee have fixed my lot,
Certain to undergo like doom: If death
Consort with thee, death is to me as life;
955 So forcible within my heart I feel
The bond of nature draw me to my own;
My own in thee, for what thou art is mine;
Our state cannot be severed; we are one,
One flesh; to lose thee were to lose myself."
960   So Adam; and thus Eve to him replied:
"O glorious trial of exceeding love,
Illustrious evidence, example high!
Engaging me to emulate; but, short
Of thy perfection, how shall I attain,
965 Adam, from whose dear side I boast me sprung,
And gladly of our union hear thee speak,
One heart, one soul in both; whereof good proof
This day affords, declaring thee resolved,
Rather than death, or aught than death more dread,
970 Shall separate us, linked in love so dear,
To undergo with me one guilt, one crime,
If any be, of tasting this fair fruit;
Whose virtue for of good still good proceeds,
Direct, or by occasion, hath presented
975 This happy trial of thy love, which else
So eminently never had been known?
Were it I thought death menaced would ensue
This my attempt, I would sustain alone
The worst, and not persuade thee, rather die
980 Deserted, than oblige thee with a fact
Pernicious to thy peace; chiefly assured
Remarkably so late of thy so true,
So faithful, love unequalled: but I feel
Far otherwise th' event; not death, but life
985 Augmented, opened eyes, new hopes, new joys,
Taste so divine, that what of sweet before
Hath touched my sense, flat seems to this, and harsh.
On my experience, Adam, freely taste,
And fear of death deliver to the winds."
990   So saying, she embraced him, and for joy
Tenderly wept; much won, that he his love
Had so ennobled, as of choice to incur

Divine displeasure for her sake, or death.
In recompense for such compliance bad
995 Such recompense best merits from the bough
She gave him of that fair enticing fruit
With liberal hand: he scrupled° not to eat,   *hesitated*
Against his better knowledge; not deceived,
But fondly overcome with female charm.
1000 Earth trembled from her entrails, as again
In pangs; and Nature gave a second groan;
Sky loured; and, muttering thunder, some sad drops
Wept at completing of the mortal sin
Original: while Adam took no thought,
1005 Eating his fill; nor Eve to iterate
Her former trespass feared, the more to soothe
Him with her loved society; that now,
As with new wine intoxicated both,
They swim in mirth, and fancy that they feel
1010 Divinity within them breeding wings,
Wherewith to scorn the earth: but that false fruit
Far other operation first displayed,
Carnal desire inflaming; he on Eve
Began to cast lascivious eyes; she him
1015 As wantonly repaid; in lust they burn:
Till Adam thus 'gan° Eve to dalliance move: *began*
    "Eve, now I see thou art exact of taste,
And elegant, of sapience no small part;
Since to each meaning savour we apply,
1020 And palate call judicious; I the praise
Yield thee, so well this day thou hast purveyed.
Much pleasure we have lost, while we abstained
From this delightful fruit, nor known till now
True relish, tasting; if such pleasure be
1025 In things to us forbidden, it might be wished,
For this one tree had been forbidden ten.
But come, so well refreshed, now let us play,
As meet is, after such delicious fare;
For never did thy beauty, since the day
1030 I saw thee first and wedded thee, adorned
With all perfections, so inflame my sense
With ardour to enjoy thee, fairer now
Than ever; bounty of this virtuous tree!"
    So said he, and forbore not glance or toy
1035 Of amorous intent; well understood
Of Eve, whose eye darted contagious fire.
Her hand he seized; and to a shady bank,

Thick over-head with verdant roof embowered,
He led her nothing loth; flowers were the couch,
1040 Pansies, and violets, and asphodel,
And hyacinth; Earth's freshest softest lap.
There they their fill of love and love's disport
Took largely, of their mutual guilt the seal,
The solace of their sin; till dewy sleep
1045 Oppressed them, wearied with their amorous play,
Soon as the force of that fallacious fruit,
That with exhilarating vapour bland
About their spirits had played, and inmost powers
Made err, was now exhaled; and grosser sleep,
1050 Bred of unkindly fumes, with conscious dreams
Encumbered, now had left them; up they rose
As from unrest; and, each the other viewing,
Soon found their eyes how opened, and their minds
How darkened; innocence, that as a veil
1055 Had shadowed them from knowing ill, was gone;
Just confidence, and native righteousness,
And honour, from about them, naked left
To guilty shame; he covered, but his robe
Uncovered more. So rose the Danite strong,
1060 Herculean Samson, from the harlot-lap
Of Philistean Delilah, and waked
Shorn of his strength.[1] They destitute and bare
Of all their virtue, silent, and in face
Confounded, long they sat, as strucken mute:
1065 Till Adam, though not less than Eve abashed,
At length gave utterance to these words constrained:
    "O Eve, in evil hour thou didst give ear
To that false worm,° of whomsoever taught   *snake*
To counterfeit Man's voice; true in our fall,
1070 False in our promised rising; since our eyes
Opened we find indeed, and find we know
Both good and evil; good lost, and evil got;
Bad fruit of knowledge, if this be to know;
Which leaves us naked thus, of honour void,
1075 Of innocence, of faith, of purity,
Our wonted ornaments now soiled and stained,
And in our faces evident the signs
Of foul concupiscence;° whence evil store;   *lust*
Even shame, the last of evils; of the first

1080 Be sure then. How shall I behold the face
Henceforth of God or angel, erst with joy
And rapture so oft beheld? Those heav'nly shapes
Will dazzle now this earthly with their blaze
Insufferably bright. O! Might I here
1085 In solitude live savage; in some glade
Obscured, where highest woods, impenetrable
To star or sun-light, spread their umbrage° broad   *shadows*
And brown as evening: Cover me, ye pines!
Ye cedars, with innumerable boughs
1090 Hide me, where I may never see them more!—
But let us now, as in bad plight, devise
What best may for the present serve to hide
The parts of each from other, that seem most
To shame obnoxious, and unseemliest seen;
1095 Some tree, whose broad smooth leaves together sewed,
And girded on our loins, may cover round
Those middle parts; that this newcomer, Shame,
There sit not, and reproach us as unclean."
        So counselled he, and both together went
1100 Into the thickest wood; there soon they chose
The fig tree; not that kind for fruit renowned,
But such as at this day, to Indians known,
In Malabar or Decan spreads her arms
Branching so broad and long, that in the ground
1105 The bended twigs take root, and daughters grow
About the mother tree, a pillared shade
High overarched, and echoing walks between:
There oft the Indian herdsman, shunning heat,
Shelters in cool, and tends his pasturing herds
1110 At loop-holes cut through thickest shade: Those leaves
They gathered, broad as Amazonian targe;°   *shield*
And, with what skill they had, together sewed,
To gird their waist; vain covering, if to hide
Their guilt and dreaded shame! O, how unlike
1115 To that first naked glory! Such of late
Columbus found the American, so girt
With feathered cincture; ° naked else, and wild   *belt*
Among the trees on isles and woody shores.
Thus fenced, and, as they thought, their shame in part
1120 Covered, but not at rest or ease of mind,
They sat them down to weep; nor only tears
Rained at their eyes, but high winds worse within
Began to rise, high passions, anger, hate,
Mistrust, suspicion, discord; and shook sore

---

[1] *So rose the ... of his strength*   The Biblical hero Samson, whose strength lay in his hair, was undone when it was shorn by his wife, the Philistine Delilah (Judges 16).

1125 Their inward state of mind, calm region once
And full of peace, now tossed and turbulent:
For understanding ruled not, and the will
Heard not her lore; both in subjection now
To sensual appetite, who from beneath
1130 Usurping over sov'reign reason claimed
Superior sway. From thus distempered breast,
Adam, estranged in look and altered style,
Speech intermitted thus to Eve renewed:
    "Would thou hadst hearkened to my words, and
        stayed
1135 With me, as I besought thee, when that strange
Desire of wandering, this unhappy morn,
I know not whence possessed thee; we had°   *would have*
    then
Remained still happy; not, as now, despoiled
Of all our good; shamed, naked, miserable!
1140 Let none henceforth seek needless cause to approve
The faith they owe; when earnestly they seek
Such proof, conclude, they then begin to fail."
        To whom, soon moved with touch of blame, thus
            Eve:
"What words have passed thy lips, Adam severe!
1145 Imputest thou that to my default, or will
Of wandering, as thou call'st it, which who knows
But might as ill have happened thou being by,
Or to thyself perhaps? Hadst thou been there,
Or here the attempt, thou couldst not have discerned
1150 Fraud in the serpent, speaking as he spake;
No ground of enmity between us known,
Why he should mean me ill, or seek to harm.
Was I to have never parted from thy side?
As good have grown there still a lifeless rib.
1155 Being as I am, why didst not thou, the head,
Command me absolutely not to go,
Going into such danger, as thou saidst?
Too facile then, thou didst not much gainsay;
Nay, didst permit, approve, and fair dismiss.
1160 Hadst thou been firm and fixed in thy dissent,
Neither had I transgressed, nor thou with me."
        To whom, then first incensed, Adam replied:
"Is this the love, is this the recompense
Of mine to thee, ingrateful Eve! Expressed
1165 Immutable, when thou wert lost, not I;
Who might have lived, and joyed immortal bliss,

Yet willingly chose rather death with thee?
And am I now upbraided as the cause
Of thy transgressing? Not enough severe,
1170 It seems, in thy restraint: what could I more
I warned thee, I admonished thee, foretold
The danger, and the lurking enemy
That lay in wait; beyond this, had been force;
And force upon free will hath here no place.
1175 But confidence then bore thee on; secure
Either to meet no danger, or to find
Matter of glorious trial; and perhaps
I also erred, in overmuch admiring
What seemed in thee so perfect, that I thought
1180 No evil durst attempt thee; but I rue
The error now, which is become my crime,
And thou the accuser. Thus it shall befall
Him, who, to worth in women overtrusting,
Lets her will rule: restraint she will not brook;°   *accept*
1185 And, left to herself, if evil thence ensue,
She first his weak indulgence will accuse."
        Thus they in mutual accusation spent
The fruitless hours, but neither self-condemning;
And of their vain contest appeared no end.

THE END OF THE NINTH BOOK

ARGUMENT TO BOOK 10

Man's transgression known, the guardian angels
forsake Paradise, and return up to Heaven to
approve their vigilance, and are approved, God declaring
that the entrance of Satan could not be by them
prevented. He sends His Son to judge the transgressors,
who descends and gives sentence accordingly; then in
pity clothes them both, and reascends. Sin and Death
sitting till then at the gates of Hell, by wondrous
sympathy feeling the success of Satan in this new world,
and the sin by Man there committed, resolve to sit no
longer confined in Hell, but to follow Satan their sire up
to the place of Man: to make the way easier from Hell
to this world to and fro, they pave a broad highway or
bridge over Chaos, according to the track that Satan first
made; then preparing for Earth, they meet him proud of
his success returning to Hell; their mutual gratulation.

Satan arrives at Pandemonium, in full assembly relates with boasting his success against man; instead of applause is entertained with a general hiss by all his audience, transformed with himself also suddenly into serpents, according to his doom given in Paradise; then deluded with show of the forbidden Tree springing up before them, they greedily reaching to take of the fruit, chew dust and bitter ashes. The proceedings of Sin and Death; God foretells the final victory of His Son over them, and the renewing of all things; but for the present commands His angels to make several alterations in the heavens and elements. Adam more and more perceiving his fallen condition heavily bewails, rejects the condolement of Eve; she persists and at length appeases him: then to evade the curse likely to fall on their offspring, proposes to Adam violent ways, which he approves not, but conceiving better hope, puts her in mind of the late promise made them, that her seed should be revenged on the serpent, and exhorts her with him to seek peace of the offended Deity, by repentance and supplication.

BOOK 10

Meanwhile the heinous and despiteful act
Of Satan done in Paradise, and how
He, in the serpent, had perverted Eve,
Her husband she, to taste the fatal fruit,
5   Was known in Heaven; for what can 'scape the eye
Of God all-seeing, or deceive his heart
Omniscient, who in all things wise and just,
Hindered not Satan to attempt the mind
Of man, with strength entire, and free will armed,
10   Complete to have discovered and repulsed
Whatever wiles of foe or seeming friend.
For still° they knew, and ought to have   *always*
    still remembered
The high injunction not to taste that fruit,
Whoever tempted; which they not obeying,
15   Incurred, what could they less, the penalty,
And manifold in sin, deserved to fall.
Up into Heaven from Paradise in haste
Th' angelic guards ascended, mute and sad
For man, for of his state by this° they knew,   *this time*
20   Much wond'ring how the subtle fiend had stolen
Entrance unseen. Soon as th' unwelcome news

From Earth arrived at Heaven gate, displeased
All were who heard, dim sadness did not spare
That time celestial visages, yet mixed
25   With pity, violated not their bliss.
About the new-arrived, in multitudes
Th' ethereal people ran, to hear and know
How all befell: they towards the throne supreme
Accountable made haste to make appear
30   With righteous plea, their utmost vigilance,[1]
And easily approved;° when the most high   *accepted*
Eternal Father from his secret cloud,
Amidst in thunder uttered thus his voice.
    "Assembled angels, and ye powers returned
35   From unsuccessful charge, be not dismayed,
Nor troubled at these tidings from the earth,
Which your sincerest care could not prevent,
Foretold so lately what would come to pass,
When first this tempter crossed the gulf from Hell.
40   I told ye then he should prevail and speed°   *succeed*
On his bad errand, man should be seduced
And flattered out of all, believing lies
Against his Maker; no decree of mine
Concurring to necessitate his fall,
45   Or touch with lightest moment[2] of impulse
His free will, to her own inclining left
In even scale. But fallen he is, and now
What rests° but that the mortal sentence pass   *remains*
On his transgression, death denounced°   *proclaimed*
    that day,
50   Which he presumes already vain° and void,   *in vain*
Because not yet inflicted, as he feared,
By some immediate stroke; but soon shall find
Forbearance no acquaintance[3] ere day end.
Justice shall not return as bounty scorned.[4]
55   But whom send I to judge them? Whom but thee
Vicegerent[5] Son, to thee I have transferred
All judgment whether in Heaven, or Earth, or Hell.

---

[1] *they towards ... vigilance*   The "accountable" angels hasten to plea that they had exercised the utmost vigilance in guarding Eden.

[2] *moment*   Small weight or counterweight, to tip the balance.

[3] *Forbearance no acquaintance*   Proverbial; a debt has not been repaid just because payment has not yet been requested.

[4] *Justice ... scorned*   My justice shall not be scorned like my generosity (bounty) has been.

[5] *Vicegerent*   Exercising the powers of a deputy to a sovereign.

Easy it might be seen that I intend
Mercy colleague with justice, sending thee
60   Man's friend his mediator, his designed
Both ransom and redeemer voluntary,
And destined man himself to judge man fallen."
     So spake the Father, and unfolding bright
Toward the right hand his glory, on the Son
65   Blazed forth unclouded deity; he full
Resplendent all his Father manifest
Expressed, and thus divinely answered mild.
     "Father Eternal, thine is to decree,
Mine both in Heaven and Earth to do thy will
70   Supreme, that thou in me thy Son beloved
May'st ever rest well pleased. I go to judge
On Earth these thy transgressors, but thou know'st,
Whoever judged, the worst on me must light,°   *fall*
When time shall be, for so I undertook
75   Before thee; and not repenting, this obtain
Of right, that I may mitigate their doom
On me derived,[1] yet I shall temper so
Justice with mercy, as may illustrate most°   *best*
Them fully satisfied, and thee appease.
80   Attendance none shall need, nor train,°   *retinue*
     where none
Are to behold the judgment, but the judged,
Those two; the third best absent is condemned,
Convict° by flight, and rebel to all law;   *Convicted*
Conviction to the serpent none belongs."
85   Thus saying, from his radiant seat he rose
Of high collateral[2] glory: him Thrones and Powers,
Princedoms, and Dominations ministrant
Accompanied to Heaven gate, from whence
Eden and all the coast° in prospect lay.   *surrounding area*
90   Down he descended strait;° the speed of gods   *immediately*
Time counts not,[3] though with swiftest minutes winged.
Now was the sun in western cadence° low   *sinking*
From noon, and gentle airs due at their hour
To fan the earth now waked, and usher in
95   The evening cool, when he from wrath more cool

Came the mild judge and intercessor both
To sentence man: the voice of God they heard
Now walking in the garden, by soft winds
Brought to their ears, while day declined; they heard,
100   And from his presence hid themselves among
The thickest trees, both man and wife, till God
Approaching, thus to Adam called aloud.
     "Where art thou Adam, wont with joy to meet
My coming seen far off? I miss thee here,
105   Not pleased, thus entertained with solitude,
Where obvious duty erewhile appeared unsought:
Or come I less conspicuous, or what change
Absents thee, or what chance detains? Come forth."
He came, and with him Eve, more loath, though first
110   To offend, discount'nanced both, and discomposed;
Love was not in their looks, either to God
Or to each other, but apparent guilt,
And shame, and perturbation, and despair,
Anger, and obstinacy, and hate, and guile.
115   Whence Adam falt'ring long, thus answered brief:
     "I heard thee in the garden, and of thy voice
Afraid, being naked, hid myself." To whom
The gracious judge without revile° replied.   *reproach*
     "My voice thou oft hast heard, and hast not feared,
120   But still rejoiced, how is it now become
So dreadful to thee? That thou art naked, who
Hath told thee? Hast thou eaten of the tree
Whereof I gave thee charge thou should'st not eat?"
     To whom thus Adam sore beset replied.
125   "O Heaven! In evil strait this day I stand
Before my judge, either to undergo
Myself the total crime, or to accuse
My other self, the partner of my life;
Whose failing, while her faith to me remains,
130   I should conceal, and not expose to blame
By my complaint; but strict necessity
Subdues me, and calamitous constraint
Lest on my head both sin and punishment,
However insupportable, be all
135   Devolved;[4] though should I hold my peace, yet thou
Would'st easily detect what I conceal.
This woman whom thou mad'st to be my help,
And gav'st me as thy perfect gift, so good,
So fit, so acceptable, so divine,

---

[1]   *On me derived*   I.e., their eventual punishment will be largely diverted onto the redeemer Son.

[2]   *collateral*   Side-by-side: one of Milton's many ways of expressing the complex and (apparently to him) not quite equivalent relationship between Father and Son.

[3]   *Time counts not*   I.e., their speed is so fast it cannot be measured.

[4]   *Devolved*   Caused to fall upon.

140 That from her hand I could suspect no ill,
And what she did, whatever in itself,
Her doing seemed to justify the deed;
She gave me of the tree, and I did eat."[1]
           To whom the sov'reign presence thus replied.
145 "Was she thy God, that her thou did'st obey
Before his voice, or was she made thy guide,
Superior, or but equal, that to her
Thou did'st resign thy manhood, and the place
Wherein God set thee above her made of thee,
150 And for thee, whose perfection far excelled
Hers in all real dignity: adorned
She was indeed, and lovely to attract
Thy love, not thy subjection, and her gifts
Were such as under government well seemed,
155 Unseemly to bear rule, which was thy part°   *role*
And person,° hadst thou known thyself aright." *character*
           So having said, he thus to Eve in few:°   *few words*
"Say woman, what is this which thou hast done?"
           To whom sad Eve with shame nigh overwhelmed,
160 Confessing soon, yet not before her judge
Bold or loquacious, thus abashed replied:
"The serpent me beguiled and I did eat."[2]
           Which when the Lord God heard, without delay
To judgment he proceeded on th' accused
165 Serpent though brute,° unable to transfer   *animal*
The guilt on him who made him instrument
Of mischief, and polluted from the end°   *purpose*
Of his creation; justly then accursed,
As vitiated in nature: more to know
170 Concerned not man (since he no further knew)
Nor altered his offence; yet God at last
To Satan first in sin his doom applied
Though in mysterious terms,[3] judged as then best:
And on the serpent thus his curse let fall.
175   "Because thou hast done this, thou art accurst
Above all cattle, each beast of the field;
Upon thy belly groveling thou shalt go,
And dust shalt eat all the days of thy life.
Between thee and the woman I will put
180 Enmity, and between thine and her seed;
Her seed shall bruise thy head, thou bruise his heel."

So spake this oracle, then verified
When Jesus son of Mary second Eve,
Saw Satan fall like lightning down from heaven,[4]
185 Prince of the Air; then rising from his grave
Spoiled Principalities and Powers, triumphed
In open show, and with ascension bright
Captivity led captive through the air,
The realm itself of Satan long usurped,
190 Whom he shall tread at last under our feet;
Even he who now foretold his fatal bruise,
And to the woman thus his sentence turned.
           "Thy sorrow I will greatly multiply
By thy conception; children thou shalt bring
195 In sorrow forth, and to thy husband's will
Thine shall submit, he over thee shall rule."
           On Adam last thus judgment he pronounced.
"Because thou hast hearkened to the voice of thy wife,
And eaten of the tree concerning which
200 I charged thee, saying, 'Thou shalt not eat thereof,'
Cursed is the ground for thy sake, thou in sorrow
Shalt eat thereof all the days of thy life;
Thorns also and thistles it shall bring thee forth
Unbid, and thou shalt eat th' herb of th' field,
205 In the sweat of thy face shalt thou eat bread,
Till thou return unto the ground, for thou
Out of the ground wast taken, know thy birth,
For dust thou art, and shalt to dust return."
           So judged he man, both Judge and Saviour sent,
210 And th' instant stroke of death denounced that day
Removed far off; then pitying how they stood
Before him naked to the air, that now
Must suffer change, disdained not to begin
Thenceforth the form of servant to assume,
215 As when he washed his servants' feet,[5] so now
As father of his family he clad
Their nakedness with skins of beasts, or slain,
Or as the snake with youthful coat repaid;
And thought not much to clothe his enemies:
220 Nor he their outward only with the skins
Of beasts, but inward nakedness, much more
Opprobrious, with his robe of righteousness,
Arraying covered from his Father's sight.
To him with swift ascent he up returned,

---

[1] *O Heaven ... eat* Adam's reply expands greatly on Genesis 3.12.

[2] *The serpent ... eat* Eve's reply reproduces that in Genesis 3.13.

[3] *mysterious terms* Mystical or typological (prefigurative) terms.

[4] *Saw Satan ... from heaven* See Luke 10.18–19.

[5] *As when ... servants' feet* See John 13.5.

225 Into his blissful bosom reassumed
In glory as of old, to him appeased
All, though all-knowing, what had past with man
Recounted, mixing intercession sweet.
Meanwhile ere thus was sinned and judged on Earth,
230 Within the gates of Hell sat Sin and Death,
In counterview within the gates, that now
Stood open wide, belching outrageous flame
Far into Chaos, since the fiend passed through,
Sin opening, who thus now to Death began.
235   "O Son, why sit we here each other viewing
Idly, while Satan our great author thrives
In other worlds, and happier seat provides
For us his offspring dear? It cannot be
But that success attends him; if mishap,
240 Ere this he had returned, with fury driven
By his avengers, since no place like this
Can fit his punishment, or their revenge.
Methinks I feel new strength within me rise,
Wings growing, and dominion given me large
245 Beyond this deep; whatever draws me on,
Or sympathy, or some connatural force
Powerful at greatest distance to unite
With secret amity things of like kind
By secretest conveyance. Thou my shade
250 Inseparable must with me along:
For Death from Sin no power can separate.
But lest the difficulty of passing back
Stay his return perhaps over this gulf
Impassable, impervious, let us try
255 Advent'rous work, yet to thy power and mine
Not unagreeable, to found a path
Over this main¹ from Hell to that new world
Where Satan now prevails, a monument
Of merit high to all th' infernal host,
260 Easing their passage hence, for intercourse,
Or transmigration,° as their lot shall lead.   *migration*
Nor can I miss the way, so strongly drawn
By this new felt attraction and instinct."
        Whom thus the meager shadow answered soon.
265 "Go whither fate and inclination strong
Leads thee, I shall not lag behind, nor err
The way, thou leading, such a scent I draw
Of carnage, prey innumerable, and taste

The savour of death from all things there that live:
270 Nor shall I to the work thou enterprisest
Be wanting, but afford thee equal aid."
        So saying, with delight he snuffed the smell
Of mortal change on Earth. As when a flock
Of ravenous fowl, though many a league remote,
275 Against the day of battle, to a field,
Where armies lie encamped, come flying, lured
With scent of living carcasses designed
For death, the following day, in bloody fight.
So scented the grim feature,° and upturned   *form*
280 His nostril wide into the murky air,
Sagacious² of his quarry from so far.
Then both from out Hell gates into the waste
Wide anarchy of Chaos damp and dark
Flew diverse, and with power (their power was great)
285 Hovering upon the waters; what they met
Solid or slimy, as in raging sea
Tossed up and down, together crowded drove
From each side shoaling towards the mouth of Hell.
As when two polar winds blowing adverse
290 Upon the Cronian° Sea, together drive   *Arctic*
Mountains of ice, that stop th' imagined way
Beyond Petsora eastward, to the rich
Cathaian Coast.³ The aggregated soil
Death with his mace petrific, cold and dry,
295 As with a trident smote, and fixed as firm
As Delos⁴ floating once; the rest his look
Bound with Gorgonian rigor⁵ not to move,
And with asphaltic slime; broad as the gate,
Deep to the roots of Hell the gathered beach°   *stony ridge*
300 They fastened, and the mole° immense   *causeway*
     wrought on
Over the foaming deep high arched, a bridge
Of length prodigious joining to the wall
Immovable of this now fenceless world
Forfeit to Death; from hence a passage broad,

---

¹ *main* The "ocean" of Chaos.

² *Sagacious* Acutely aware of (by scent).

³ *imagined way … Coast* Northwest passage between Siberia (site of the Pechora river) and China.

⁴ *Delos* Fabled floating island in the Aegean Sea, chained in place by Neptune.

⁵ *Gorgonian rigor* In Greek myth, the beautiful but serpent-haired Medusa, one of the mythical Gorgons, turned those who gazed on her into stone.

05 Smooth, easy, inoffensive down to Hell.
So, if great things to small may be compared,
Xerxes, the liberty of Greece to yoke,
From Susa his Memnonian palace high
Came to the sea, and over Hellespont
10 Bridging his way, Europe with Asia joined,
And scourged with many a stroke th' indignant waves.[1]
Now had they brought the work by wondrous art
Pontifical,[2] a ridge of pendent rock
Over the vexed abyss, following the track
15 Of Satan, to the self same place where he
First lighted from his wing, and landed safe
From out of Chaos to the outside bare
Of this round world: with pins of adamant
And chains they made all fast, too fast they made
20 And durable; and now in little space
The confines met of empyrean Heaven
And of this world, and on the left hand Hell
With long reach interposed; three sev'ral ways
In sight, to each of these three places led.
25 And now their way to Earth they had descried,
To Paradise first tending, when behold
Satan in likeness of an angel bright
Betwixt the Centaur and the Scorpion steering
His zenith,[3] while the sun in Aries rose:
30 Disguised he came, but those his children dear
Their parent soon discerned, though in disguise.
He after Eve seduced, unminded slunk
Into the wood fast by, and changing shape
To observe the sequel, saw his guileful act
35 By Eve, though all unweeting, seconded
Upon her husband, saw their shame that sought
Vain covertures; but when he saw descend
The Son of God to judge them terrified
He fled, not hoping to escape, but shun
40 The present, fearing guilty what his wrath

---

[1] *Bridging his way … waves* In order to invade Greece, Xerxes of Persia created a bridge across the Hellespont by laying his ships side by side; when the sea destroyed the bridge he ordered that the waters be whipped.

[2] *Pontifical* Bridge-building (but punning on the Papal title "Pontifex").

[3] *Satan … zenith* Satan had entered the serpent by its mouth; he appears in the sky exiting the tail of the constellation of the serpent Anguis, located between the archer Sagittarius (Milton's "Centaur") and Scorpio.

Might suddenly inflict; that past, returned
By night, and listening where the hapless pair
Sat in their sad discourse, and various plaint,
Thence gathered his own doom, which understood
345 Not instant, but of future time. With joy
And tidings fraught, to Hell he now returned,
And at the brink of Chaos, near the foot
Of this new wondrous pontifice, unhoped
Met who to meet him came, his offspring dear.
350 Great joy was at their meeting, and at sight
Of that stupendous bridge his joy increased.
Long he admiring stood, till Sin, his fair
Enchanting daughter, thus the silence broke.
"O Parent, these are thy magnific deeds,
355 Thy trophies, which thou viewest as not thine own,
Thou art their author and prime architect:
For I no sooner in my heart divined,
My heart, which by a secret harmony
Still moves with thine, joined in connection sweet,
360 That thou on Earth hadst prospered, which thy looks
Now also evidence, but straight I felt
Though distant from the worlds between, yet felt
That I must after thee with this thy son;
Such fatal consequence unites us three:
365 Hell could no longer hold us in her bounds,
Nor this unvoyageable gulf obscure
Detain from following thy illustrious track.
Thou hast achieved our liberty, confined
Within Hell gates till now, thou us empow'red
370 To fortify thus far, and overlay
With this portentous bridge the dark abyss.
Thine now is all this world, thy virtue hath won
What thy hands builded not, thy wisdom gained
With odds what war hath lost, and fully avenged
375 Our foil in Heaven; here thou shalt monarch reign,
There didst not; there let him still victor sway,
As battle hath adjudged, from this new world
Retiring, by his own doom alienated,
And henceforth monarchy with thee divide
380 Of all things parted by th' empyreal bounds,
His quadrature,[4] from thy orbicular world,
Or try thee now more dang'rous to his throne."
      Whom thus the Prince of Darkness answered glad.

---

[4] *quadrature* See Revelation 21.16, where Heaven is described as laid out "four-square."

"Fair daughter, and thou son and grandchild both,
385 High proof ye now have given to be the race
Of Satan (for I glory in the name,[1]
Antagonist of Heaven's Almighty King)
Amply have merited of me, of all
Th' infernal empire, that so near Heaven's door
390 Triumphal with triumphal act have met,
Mine with this glorious work, and made one realm
Hell and this world, one realm, one continent
Of easy thoroughfare. Therefore while I
Descend through darkness, on your road with ease
395 To my associate powers, them to acquaint
With these successes, and with them rejoice,
You two this way, among these numerous orbs
All yours, right down to Paradise descend;
There dwell and reign in bliss, thence on the Earth
400 Dominion exercise and in the air,
Chiefly on man, sole lord of all declared,
Him first make sure your thrall, and lastly kill.
My substitutes I send ye, and create
Plenipotent° on Earth, of matchless might   *Fully powerful*
405 Issuing from me: on your joint vigor now
My hold of this new kingdom all depends,
Through Sin to Death exposed by my exploit.
If your joint power prevails, th' affairs of Hell
No detriment need fear, go and be strong."
410   So saying he dismissed them,[2] they with speed
Their course through thickest constellations held
Spreading their bane: the blasted stars looked wan
And planets, planet-struck, real eclipse
Then suffered. Th' other way Satan went down
415 The causey° to hell gate: on either side   *causeway*
Disparted Chaos overbuilt exclaimed,
And with rebounding surge the bars assailed,
That scorned his indignation: through the gate,
Wide open and unguarded, Satan passed,
420 And all about found desolate; for those
Appointed to sit there had left their charge,
Flown to the upper world; the rest were all
Far to the inland retired, about the walls
Of Pandemonium; city and proud seat
425 Of Lucifer, so by allusion called
Of that bright star to Satan paragoned;°   *compared*

There kept their watch the legions, while the grand
In council sat, solicitous° what chance   *anxious to discover*
Might intercept their emperor sent; so he
430 Departing gave command, and they observed.
As when the Tartar from his Russian foe,
By Astracan,[3] over the snowy plains,
Retires; or Bactrin Sophy,[4] from the horns
Of Turkish crescent, leaves all waste beyond
435 The realm of Aladule, in his retreat
To Tauris or Casbeen:[5] So these, the late
Heav'n-banished host, left desert utmost Hell[6]
Many a dark league, reduced in careful watch
Round their metropolis; and now expecting
440 Each hour their great adventurer, from the search
Of foreign worlds: he through the midst unmarked,
In show plebeian angel militant
Of lowest order, passed; and from the door
Of that plutonian[7] hall, invisible
445 Ascended his high throne; which, under state°   *canopy*
Of richest texture spread, at th' upper end
Was placed in regal lustre. Down a while
He sat, and round about him saw unseen:
At last, as from a cloud, his fulgent° head   *shining*
450 And shape star-bright appeared, or brighter; clad
With what permissive glory since his fall
Was left him, or false glitter. All amazed
At that so sudden blaze the Stygian throng
Bent their aspect, and whom they wished beheld,
455 Their mighty chief returned: loud was th' acclaim:
Forth rushed in haste the great consulting peers,
Raised from their dark divan, and with like joy
Congratulant approached him; who with hand
Silence and with these words attention won:
460 "Thrones, dominations, princedoms, virtues, powers;
For in possession such, not only of right,
I call ye, and declare ye now; returned
Successful beyond hope, to lead ye forth
Triumphant out of this infernal pit

---

1 *name* "Satan" means "adversary" in Hebrew.

2 *them* Sin and Death, now on their way to Earth.

3 *Astracan* Modern Astrakhan, a city in the southwest of Russia near the Caspian Sea, originally founded by the Tartars.

4 *Bactrin Sophy* Shah of Persia.

5 *Aladule* Armenia; *Tauris … Casbeen* Cities in northern Iran.

6 *left desert utmost Hell* Left the outermost reaches of Hell deserted.

7 *plutonian* Both richly decorated and morbid, deathly; after Pluto, god of the underworld.

465 Abominable, accursed, the house of woe,
And dungeon of our tyrant: now possess,
As lords, a spacious world, to our native Heaven
Little inferior, by my adventure hard
With peril great achieved. Long were to tell
470 What I have done; what suffered; with what pain
Voyaged th' unreal, vast, unbounded deep
Of horrible confusion; over which
By Sin and Death a broad way now is paved,
To expedite your glorious march; but I
475 Toiled out my uncouth passage, forced to ride
Th' intractable abyss, plunged in the womb
Of unoriginal night and Chaos wild;
That, jealous of their secrets, fiercely opposed
My journey strange, with clamorous uproar
480 Protesting fate supreme; thence how I found
The new created world, which fame in Heav'n
Long had foretold, a fabric wonderful
Of absolute perfection, therein Man
Placed in a Paradise, by our exile
485 Made happy. Him by fraud I have seduced
From his Creator; and, the more to increase
Your wonder, with an apple; He, thereat
Offended worth your laughter, hath given up
Both His beloved Man, and all His world,
490 To Sin and Death a prey, and so to us,
Without our hazard, labour, or alarm;
To range in, and to dwell, and over man
To rule, as over all He should have ruled.
True is, me also He hath judged, or rather
495 Me not, but the brute serpent in whose shape
Man I deceived: that which to me belongs,
Is enmity which He will put between
Me and mankind; I am to bruise his heel;
His seed, when is not set, shall bruise my head:[1]
500 A world who would not purchase with a bruise,
Or much more grievous pain? Ye have the account
Of my performance: What remains, ye gods,
But up, and enter now into full bliss?"

So having said, a while he stood, expecting
505 Their universal shout, and high applause,
To fill his ear; when, contrary, he hears
On all sides, from innumerable tongues,
A dismal universal hiss, the sound

Of public scorn; he wondered, but not long
510 Had leisure, wondering at himself now more,
His visage drawn he felt to sharp and spare;
His arms clung to his ribs; his legs entwining
Each other, till supplanted down he fell
A monstrous serpent on his belly prone,
515 Reluctant, but in vain; a greater power
Now ruled him, punished in the shape he sinned,
According to his doom: he would have spoke,
But hiss for hiss returnèd with forkèd tongue
To forkèd tongue; for now were all transformed
520 Alike, to serpents all, as accessories
To his bold riot: dreadful was the din
Of hissing through the hall, thick swarming now
With complicated monsters head and tail,
Scorpion, and asp, and amphisbaena[2] dire,
525 Cerastes[3] horned, hydrus,[4] and elops[5] drear,
And dipsas[6] (not so thick swarmed once the soil
Bedropt with blood of gorgon,[7] or the isle
Ophiusa[8]); but still greatest he the midst,
Now dragon grown, larger than whom the sun
530 Engendered in the Pythian Vale or slime,
Huge python, and his power no less he seemed
Above the rest still to retain; they all
Him followed, issuing forth to th' open field,
Where all yet left of that revolted rout,
535 Heav'n-fall'n, in station stood or just array;
Sublime with expectation when to see
In triumph issuing forth their glorious chief;
They saw, but other sight instead: a crowd
Of ugly serpents; horror on them fell,
540 And horrid sympathy; for, what they saw,
They felt themselves, now changing; down their arms,
Down fell both spear and shield; down they as fast;
And the dire hiss renewed, and the dire form

---

2   *amphisbaena*   Mythical serpent with a head at each end of its body.

3   *Cerastes*   Legendary four-horned serpent.

4   *hydrus*   Hydra, venomous many-headed serpent of classical myth.

5   *elops*   Mythical sea snake.

6   *dipsas*   Snake whose venom reputedly caused ravenous thirst.

7   *not so thick … blood of gorgon*   When Perseus slew Medusa, the Gorgon, snakes sprang from every drop of her blood that touched the earth.

8   *Ophiusa*   Literally "land of snakes," the island of Rhodes, renowned in legend for its many snakes.

---

1   *I am to bruise … bruise my head*   See Genesis 3.15.

Catched by contagion; like in punishment,
545   As in their crime. Thus was the applause they meant
Turned to exploding hiss, triumph to shame
Cast on themselves from their own mouths. There
      stood
A grove hard by, sprung up with this their change,
His will Who reigns above, to aggravate
550   Their penance, laden with fair fruit, like that
Which grew in Paradise, the bait of Eve
Used by the tempter: on that prospect strange
Their earnest eyes they fixed, imagining
For one forbidden tree a multitude
555   Now ris'n, to work them further woe or shame;
Yet, parched with scalding thirst and hunger fierce,
Though to delude them sent, could not abstain;
But on they rolled in heaps, and, up the trees
Climbing, sat thicker than the snaky locks
560   That curled Megaera:[1] greedily they plucked
The fruitage fair to sight, like that which grew
Near that bituminous lake where Sodom flamed;
This more delusive, not the touch, but taste
Deceived; they, fondly thinking to allay
565   Their appetite with gust, instead of fruit
Chewed bitter ashes, which the offended taste
With spattering noise rejected: oft they assayed,
Hunger and thirst constraining; drugged as oft,
With hatefullest disrelish writhed their jaws,
570   With soot and cinders filled; so oft they fell
Into the same illusion, not as man
Whom they triumphed once lapsed. Thus were they
      plagued
And worn with famine, long and ceaseless hiss,
Till their lost shape, permitted, they resumed;
575   Yearly enjoined, some say, to undergo,
This annual humbling certain numbered days,
To dash their pride, and joy, for man seduced.
However some tradition they dispersed
Among the heathen of their purchase got,
580   And fabled how the serpent, whom they called
Ophion with Eurynome, the wide-
Encroaching Eve perhaps, had first the rule
Of high Olympus, thence by Saturn driven

And Ops, ere yet Dictæan Jove was born.[2]
585   Meanwhile in Paradise the hellish pair
Too soon arrived, Sin there in power before,
Once actual, now in body, and to dwell
Habitual habitant; behind her Death
Close following pace for pace, not mounted yet
590   On his pale horse:[3] to whom Sin thus began.
      "Second of Satan sprung, all conquering Death,
What thinkst thou of our empire now, though earned
With travail difficult, not better far
Than still at Hell's dark threshold to have sat watch,
595   Unnamed, undreaded, and thyself half starved?"
      Whom thus the Sin-born Monster answered soon.
"To me, who with eternal famine pine,
Alike is Hell, or Paradise, or Heaven,
There best, where most with ravin° I may meet;   prey
600   Which here, though plenteous, all too little seems
To stuff this maw, this vast unhide-bound corpse."
      To whom th' incestuous mother thus replied.
"Thou therefore on these herbs, and fruits, and flowers
Feed first, on each beast next, and fish, and fowl,
605   No homely morsels, and whatever thing
The scythe of Time mows down, devour unspared,
Till I in man residing through the race,
His thoughts, his looks, words, actions all infect,
And season him thy last and sweetest prey."
610   This said, they both betook them several ways,
Both to destroy, or unimmortal make
All kinds, and for destruction to mature
Sooner or later; which th' Almighty seeing,
From his transcendent seat the saints among,
615   To those bright orders uttered thus his voice.
      "See with what heat these dogs of Hell advance
To waste and havoc yonder world, which I
So fair and good created, and had still
Kept in that state, had not the folly of man
620   Let in these wasteful Furies, who impute
Folly to me, so doth the Prince of Hell

---

[1]   *Megaera* One of the classical Furies, avenging underworld
goddesses.

[2]   *Ophion with ... was born* To explain their annual metamorphoses
(Milton suggests), the devils spread stories in the ancient world of
primordial serpents, such as Ophion (from the Greek word for
serpent), who with Eurynome (daughter of the Ocean) ruled
Olympus before being driven out by Saturn and his wife Rhea (Ops),
parents to Jove (Zeus), who was raised in a cave in Crete near Mount
Dicte.

[3]   *pale horse* See Revelation 6.8.

And his adherents, that with so much ease
I suffer them to enter and possess
A place so heavenly, and conniving seem
25 To gratify my scornful enemies,
That laugh, as if transported with some fit
Of passion, I to them had quitted° all,   *handed over*
At random yielded up to their misrule;
And know not that I called and drew them thither
30 My Hell-hounds, to lick up the draff and filth
Which man's polluting sin with taint hath shed
On what was pure, till crammed and gorged, nigh burst
With sucked and glutted offal, at one sling
Of thy victorious arm, well-pleasing Son,
35 Both Sin, and Death, and yawning grave at last
Through Chaos hurled, obstruct the mouth of Hell
Forever, and seal up his ravenous jaws.
Then Heaven and Earth renewed shall be made pure
To sanctity that shall receive no stain:
40 Till then the curse pronounced on both precedes."
      He ended, and the heavenly audience loud
Sung halleluja, as the sound of seas,
Through multitude that sung: "Just are thy ways,
Righteous are thy decrees on all thy works;
45 Who can extenuate thee? Next, to the Son,
Destined restorer of mankind, by whom
New Heaven and Earth shall to the ages rise,
Or down from Heaven descend." Such was their song,
While the Creator calling forth by name
50 His mighty angels gave them several charge,
As sorted best with present things. The sun
Had first his precept so to move, so shine,
As might affect the Earth with cold and heat
Scarce tolerable, and from the north to call
55 Decrepit winter, from the south to bring
Solstitial summer's heat. To the blank° moon   *pale*
Her office they prescribed, to th' other five
Their planetary motions and aspects
In sextile, square, and trine, and opposite,[1]
60 Of noxious efficacy, and when to join
In synod unbenign, and taught the fixed
Their influence malignant when to shower,

Which of them rising with the sun, or falling,
Should prove tempestuous: to the winds they set
665 Their corners, when with bluster to confound
Sea, air, and shore, the thunder when to roll
With terror through the dark aerial hall.
Some say he bid his angels turn askance
The poles of Earth twice ten degrees and more
670 From the sun's axle; they with labour pushed
Oblique the centric globe: some say the sun
Was bid turn reins from th' equinoctial road
Like distant breadth to Taurus with the seven
Atlantic sisters, and the Spartan Twins
675 Up to the Tropic Crab; thence down amain
By Leo and the Virgin and the Scales,
As deep as Capricorn, to bring in change
Of seasons to each clime;[2] else had the spring
Perpetual smiled on Earth with vernant flowers,
680 Equal in days and nights, except to those
Beyond the polar circles; to them day
Had unbenighted shone, while the low sun
To recompense his distance, in their sight
Had rounded still th' horizon, and not known
685 Or east or west, which had forbid the snow
From cold Estotiland, and south as far
Beneath Magellan.[3] At that tasted fruit
The sun, as from Thyestean banquet,[4] turned
His course intended; else how had the world
690 Inhabited, though sinless, more than now,
Avoided pinching cold and scorching heat?
These changes in the heavens, though slow, produced

---

[1] *sextile … opposite* Terms for the four "aspects" or degrees of planetary position: respectively, 60°, 90°, 120°, and 180°. In astrology, planetary aspect shaped planetary influence: as a consequence of the Fall, the angels teach the planets and stars how to exert malignant influences, including weather.

[2] *Some say … each clime* Seasonal change is caused by the tilt of the earth's axis about 23° ("twice ten degrees and more") relative to the sun. Milton presents both ways of achieving the identical effect, without deciding between them: the angels either tilted the earth from its formerly "centric" (centered) orbit around the "sun's axle" (if the universe is heliocentric), or they shifted the sun's circuit around the earth so that it moved at an oblique angle to the celestial equator, through the path Milton then traces through the Zodiac (if the universe were geocentric).

[3] *except to those … Magellan* In the eternal spring before the Fall, days and nights were always equal in length except at the poles, where the sun would never set and there would be no snow even in northern Labrador ("Estotiland") or south of the Strait of Magellan.

[4] *Thyestean banquet* Referring to Seneca's tragedy *Thyestes*, where the sun changes course to avoid the sight of Thyestes unknowingly eating his sons.

Like change on sea and land, sideral[1] blast,
Vapour, and mist, and exhalation hot,
695 Corrupt and pestilent: now from the north
Of Norumbega, and the Samoed shore
Bursting their brazen dungeon, armed with ice
And snow and hail and stormy gust and flaw,
Boreas and Caecias and Argestes loud
700 And Thrascias rend the woods and seas upturn;
With adverse blast upturns them from the south
Notus and Afer black with thund'rous clouds
From Serraliona; thwart of these as fierce
Forth rush the Levant and the ponent° winds   *western*
705 Eurus and Zephyr with their lateral noise,
Sirocco, and Libecchio.[2] Thus began
Outrage from lifeless things; but Discord first
Daughter of Sin, among th' irrational,
Death introduced through fierce antipathy:
710 Beast now with beast 'gan war, and fowl with fowl,
And fish with fish; to graze the herb° all leaving,   *grass*
Devoured each other; nor stood much in awe
Of Man, but fled him; or, with countenance grim,
Glared on him passing. These were from without
715 The growing miseries, which Adam saw
Already in part, though hid in gloomiest shade,
To sorrow abandoned, but worse felt within;
And, in a troubled sea of passion tossed,
Thus to disburden sought with sad complaint:
720   "O miserable of happy! Is this the end
Of this new glorious world, and me so late
The glory of that glory, who now become
Accursed, of blessèd? Hide me from the face
Of God,[3] whom to behold was then my height
725 Of happiness: yet well, if here would end
The misery; I deserved it, and would bear
My own deservings; but this will not serve:

All that I eat or drink, or shall beget,
Is propagated curse. O voice, once heard
730 Delightfully, 'increase and multiply,'[4]
Now death to hear! For what can I increase,
Or multiply, but curses on my head?
Who of all ages to succeed, but, feeling
The evil on him brought by me, will curse
735 My head? 'Ill fare our ancestor impure,
For this we may thank Adam!' But his thanks
Shall be the execration: so, besides
Mine own that bide upon me, all from me
Shall with a fierce reflux on me rebound;
740 On me, as on their natural centre, light
Heavy, though in their place. O fleeting joys
Of Paradise, dear bought with lasting woes!
Did I request Thee, Maker, from my clay
To mould me man? Did I solicit Thee
745 From darkness to promote me, or here place
In this delicious garden? As my will
Concurred not to my being, it were but right
And equal to reduce me to my dust;
Desirous to resign and render back
750 All I received; unable to perform
Thy terms too hard, by which I was to hold
The good I sought not. To the loss of that,
Sufficient penalty, why hast Thou added
The sense of endless woes? Inexplicable
755 Thy justice seems; yet to say truth, too late,
I thus contest; then should have been refused
Those terms whatever, when they were proposed:
Thou didst accept them; wilt thou enjoy the good,
Then cavil[5] the conditions? And though God
760 Made thee without thy leave, what if thy son
Prove disobedient, and reproved, retort,
'Wherefore didst thou beget me? I sought it not.'
Wouldst thou admit for his contempt of thee
That proud excuse? Yet him not thy election°   *choice*
765 But natural necessity begot.
God made thee of choice His own, and of His own
To serve Him, thy reward was of His grace,
Thy punishment then justly is at His will.
Be it so, for I submit, His doom is fair,
770 That dust I am, and shall to dust return.

---

[1] *sideral* Usually "sidereal": pertaining to stars. Apparently referring to winds or storms on earth thought to be caused by these post-Fall changes in the heavens.

[2] *Norumbega ... Libecchio* A catalogue of winds let loose by the Fall, some associated with far-flung geographical points of origin. Boreas, Caecias, Argestes, and Thrascias are northern winds, from North America ("Norumbega") and Siberia ("Samoed shore"). They clash with the southern winds Notus and Afer, from Sierra Leone, and various cross-winds from the east and west named Levant, Eurus, Zephyr, Sirocco, and Libecchio.

[3] *Hide me from the face / Of God* See Psalm 27.9.

[4] *increase and multiply* See Genesis 9.7.

[5] *cavil* Raise unnecessary objections.

O welcome hour whenever! Why delays
His hand to execute what His decree
Fixed on this day? Why do I overlive,
Why am I mocked with death, and lengthened out
775 To deathless pain? How gladly would I meet
Mortality my sentence, and be earth
Insensible! How glad would lay me down
As in my mother's lap! There I should rest,
And sleep secure; His dreadful voice no more
780 Would thunder in my ears; no fear of worse
To me, and to my offspring, would torment me
With cruel expectation. Yet one doubt
Pursues me still, lest all I cannot die;
Lest that pure breath of life, the spirit of man
785 Which God inspired, cannot together perish
With this corporeal clod; then, in the grave,
Or in some other dismal place, who knows
But I shall die a living death? O thought
Horrid, if true! Yet why? It was but breath
790 Of life that sinned; what dies but what had life
And sin? The body properly had neither,
All of me then shall die: let this appease
The doubt, since human reach no further knows.
For though the Lord of all be infinite,
795 Is His wrath also? Be it, man is not so,
But mortal doomed. How can He exercise
Wrath without end on man, whom death must end?
Can He make deathless death? That were to make
Strange contradiction, which to God Himself
800 Impossible is held; as argument
Of weakness, not of power. Will He draw out,
For anger's sake, finite to infinite,
In punished man, to satisfy His rigour,
Satisfied never? That were to extend
805 His sentence beyond dust and nature's law;
By which all causes else, according still
To the reception of their matter, act;
Not to the extent of their own sphere. But say
That death be not one stroke, as I supposed,
810 Bereaving sense, but endless misery
From this day onward; which I feel begun
Both in me, and without me; and so last
To perpetuity; ay me, that fear
Comes thundering back with dreadful revolution
815 On my defenceless head; both death and I

Am found eternal, and incorporate both;
Nor I on my part single; in me all
Posterity stands cursed: fair patrimony
That I must leave ye, sons; o were I able
820 To waste it all myself, and leave ye none!
So disinherited, how would you bless
Me, now your curse! Ah, why should all mankind,
For one man's fault, thus guiltless be condemned,
It guiltless? But from me what can proceed,
825 But all corrupt; both mind and will depraved
Not to do only, but to will the same
With me? How can they then acquitted stand
In sight of God? Him, after all disputes,
Forced I absolve: all my evasions vain,
830 And reasonings, though through mazes, lead me still
But to my own conviction: first and last
On me, me only, as the source and spring
Of all corruption, all the blame lights due;
So might the wrath. Fond wish! Couldst thou support
835 That burden, heavier than the earth to bear;
Than all the world much heavier, though divided
With that bad woman? Thus, what thou desirest,
And what thou fearest, alike destroys all hope
Of refuge, and concludes thee miserable
840 Beyond all past example and future;
To Satan only like both crime and doom.
O Conscience! Into what abyss of fears
And horrors hast thou driven me; out of which
I find no way, from deep to deeper plunged!"
845   Thus Adam to himself lamented loud,
Through the still night; not now, as ere man fell,
Wholesome, and cool, and mild, but with black air
Accompanied; with damps, and dreadful gloom;
Which to his evil conscience represented
850 All things with double terror: on the ground
Outstretched he lay, on the cold ground; and oft
Cursed his creation; Death as oft accused
Of tardy execution, since denounced
The day of his offence. "Why comes not Death,"
855 Said he, "with one thrice-acceptable stroke
To end me? Shall Truth fail to keep her word,
Justice divine not hasten to be just?
But death comes not at call; justice divine
Mends not her slowest pace for prayers or cries,
860 O woods, O fountains, hillocks, dales, and bowers!

With other echo late I taught your shades
To answer, and resound far other song."
Whom thus afflicted when sad Eve beheld,
Desolate where she sat, approaching nigh,
865 Soft words to his fierce passion she assayed:
But her with stern regard he thus repelled.

    "Out of my sight, thou serpent! That name best
Befits thee with him leagued, thyself as false
And hateful; nothing wants, but that thy shape,
870 Like his, and colour serpentine, may show
Thy inward fraud; to warn all creatures from thee
Henceforth; lest that too heav'nly form, pretended
To hellish falsehood, snare them! But for thee
I had persisted happy; had not thy pride
875 And wandering vanity, when least was safe,
Rejected my forewarning, and disdained
Not to be trusted; longing to be seen,
Though by the Devil himself; him overweening
To over-reach; but, with the serpent meeting,
880 Fooled and beguiled; by him thou, I by thee
To trust thee from my side; imagined wise,
Constant, mature, proof against all assaults;
And understood not all was but a show,
Rather than solid virtue; all but a rib
885 Crooked by nature, bent, as now appears,
More to the part sinister, from me drawn;
Well if thrown out, as supernumerary
To my just number found. O why did God,
Creator wise, that peopled highest Heav'n
890 With spirits masculine,[1] create at last
This novelty on earth, this fair defect
Of nature, and not fill the world at once
With men, as angels, without feminine;
Or find some other way to generate
895 Mankind? This mischief had not been befallen,
And more that shall befall; innumerable
Disturbances on earth through female snares,
And strait conjunction with this sex: for either
He never shall find out fit mate, but such
900 As some misfortune brings him, or mistake;
Or whom he wishes most shall seldom gain
Through her perverseness, but shall see her gained
By a far worse; or, if she love, withheld

By parents; or his happiest choice too late
905 Shall meet, already linked and wedlock-bound
To a fell adversary, his hate or shame:
Which infinite calamity shall cause
To human life, and household peace confound."
    He added not, and from her turned; but Eve,
910 Not so repulsed, with tears that ceased not flowing
And tresses all disordered, at his feet
Fell humble; and, embracing them, besought
His peace, and thus proceeded in her plaint:
    "Forsake me not thus, Adam, witness Heav'n
915 What love sincere, and reverence in my heart
I bear thee, and unweeting° have offended,   *unwitting*
Unhappily deceived! Thy suppliant
I beg, and clasp thy knees; bereave me not,
Whereon I live, thy gentle looks, thy aid,
920 Thy counsel, in this uttermost distress,
My only strength and stay: forlorn of thee,
Whither shall I betake me, where subsist?
While yet we live, scarce one short hour perhaps,
Between us two let there be peace; both joining,
925 As joined in injuries, one enmity
Against a foe by doom express[2] assigned us,
That cruel serpent. On me exercise not
Thy hatred for this misery befallen;
On me already lost, me than thyself
930 More miserable! Both have sinned; but thou
Against God only; I against God and thee;
And to the place of judgement will return,
There with my cries importune Heaven; that all
The sentence, from thy head removed, may light
935 On me, sole cause to thee of all this woe;
Me, me only, just object of His ire!"
    She ended weeping; and her lowly plight,
Immoveable, till peace obtained from fault
Acknowledged and deplored, in Adam wrought
940 Commiseration. Soon his heart relented
Towards her, his life so late, and sole delight,
Now at his feet submissive in distress;
Creature so fair his reconcilement seeking,
His counsel, whom she had displeased, his aid:
945 As one disarmed, his anger all he lost,
And thus with peaceful words upraised her soon:

---

[1] *that peopled ... masculine* Adam's anger against Eve leads him to forget that angels have no gender (as Raphael had informed him).

[2] *doom express* Specific judgment.

"Unwary, and too desirous, as before,
So now of what thou know'st not, who desir'st
The punishment all on thyself; alas!
50 Bear thine own first, ill able to sustain
His full wrath, whose thou feelest as yet least part,
And my displeasure bearest so ill. If prayers
Could alter high decrees, I to that place
Would speed before thee, and be louder heard,
55 That on my head all might be visited;
Thy frailty and infirmer sex forgiv'n,
To me committed, and by me exposed.
But rise, let us no more contend, nor blame
Each other, blamed enough elsewhere; but strive
60 In offices of love, how we may light'n
Each other's burden, in our share of woe;
Since this day's death denounced, if aught I see,
Will prove no sudden, but a slow-paced evil;
A long day's dying, to augment our pain;
65 And to our seed (O hapless seed!) derived."
    To whom thus Eve, recovering heart, replied:
"Adam, by sad experiment I know
How little weight my words with thee can find,
Found so erroneous; thence by just event
70 Found so unfortunate. Nevertheless,
Restored by thee, vile as I am, to place
Of new acceptance, hopeful to regain
Thy love, the sole contentment of my heart
Living or dying, from thee I will not hide
75 What thoughts in my unquiet breast are risen,
Tending to some relief of our extremes,
Or end; though sharp and sad, yet tolerable,
As in our evils, and of easier choice.
If care of our descent perplex us most,
80 Which must be born to certain woe, devoured
By Death at last; and miserable it is
To be to others cause of misery,
Our own begotten, and of our loins to bring
Into this cursèd world a woeful race,
85 That after wretched life must be at last
Food for so foul a monster; in thy power
It lies, yet ere conception to prevent
The race unblest, to being yet unbegot.
Childless thou art, childless remain: so Death
90 Shall be deceived his glut, and with us two
Be forced to satisfy his rav'nous maw.

But if thou judge it hard and difficult,
Conversing, looking, loving, to abstain
From love's due rights, nuptial embraces sweet;
995 And with desire to languish without hope,
Before the present object languishing
With like desire; which would be misery
And torment less than none of what we dread;
Then, both ourselves and seed at once to free
1000 From what we fear for both, let us make short,
Let us seek Death, or he not found, supply
With our own hands his office on ourselves;
Why stand we longer shivering under fears,
That show no end but death, and have the power,
1005 Of many ways to die the shortest choosing,
Destruction with destruction to destroy."
    She ended here, or vehement despair
Broke off the rest: so much of death her thoughts
Had entertained, as dyed her cheeks with pale.
1010 But Adam, with such counsel nothing swayed,
To better hopes his more attentive mind
Labouring had raised; and thus to Eve replied:
    "Eve, thy contempt of life and pleasure seems
To argue in thee something more sublime
1015 And excellent than what thy mind contemns;
But self-destruction therefore sought, refutes
That excellence thought in thee; and implies,
Not thy contempt, but anguish and regret
For loss of life and pleasure overloved.
1020 Or if thou covet death as utmost end
Of misery, so thinking to evade
The penalty pronounced; doubt not but God
Hath wiselier armed His vengeful ire, than so
To be forestalled; much more I fear lest Death,
1025 So snatched, will not exempt us from the pain
We are by doom to pay; rather, such acts
Of contumacy° will provoke the highest   *contempt*
To make death in us live. Then let us seek
Some safer resolution, which methinks
1030 I have in view, calling to mind with heed
Part of our sentence, that thy seed shall bruise
The serpent's head; piteous amends! Unless
Be meant, whom I conjecture, our grand foe,
Satan; who, in the serpent, hath contrived
1035 Against us this deceit: to crush his head
Would be revenge indeed, which will be lost

By death brought on ourselves, or childless days
Resolved, as thou proposest; so our foe
Shall 'scape his punishment ordained, and we
1040　Instead shall double ours upon our heads.
No more be mentioned then of violence
Against ourselves; and wilful barrenness,
That cuts us off from hope; and savours only
Rancour and pride, impatience and despite,°   *ill-will*
1045　Reluctance° against God and His just yoke   *resistance*
Laid on our necks. Remember with what mild
And gracious temper He both heard, and judged,
Without wrath or reviling; we expected
Immediate dissolution, which we thought
1050　Was meant by death that day; when lo, to thee
Pains only in child-bearing were foretold,
And bringing forth; soon recompensed with joy,
Fruit of thy womb: On me the curse aslope
Glanced on the ground; with labour I must earn
1055　My bread; what harm? Idleness had been worse;
My labour will sustain me; and, lest cold
Or heat should injure us, His timely care
Hath, unbesought, provided; and His hands
Clothed us unworthy, pitying while He judged;
1060　How much more, if we pray Him, will His ear
Be open, and His heart to pity incline,
And teach us further by what means to shun
The inclement seasons, rain, ice, hail, and snow!
Which now the sky, with various face, begins
1065　To show us in this mountain; while the winds
Blow moist and keen, shattering the graceful locks
Of these fair spreading trees; which bids us seek
Some better shroud, some better warmth to cherish
Our limbs benumbed, ere this diurnal star
1070　Leave cold the night, how we His gathered beams
Reflected may with matter sere foment;[1]
Or, by collision of two bodies, grind
The air attrite to fire; as late the clouds
Jostling, or pushed with winds, rude in their shock,
1075　Tine[2] the slant lightning; whose thwart flame, driv'n
　　　down
Kindles the gummy bark of fir or pine;

---

[1] *with matter sere foment*　With dry material, focus the beams of light (so as to make fire).

[2] *Tine*　Branch, as of a fork; i.e., forked lightning is coming through the clouds.

And sends a comfortable heat from far,
Which might supply the sun. Such fire to use,
And what may else be remedy or cure
1080　To evils which our own misdeeds have wrought,
He will instruct us praying, and of grace
Beseeching Him; so as we need not fear
To pass commodiously this life, sustained
By Him with many comforts, till we end
1085　In dust, our final rest and native home.
What better can we do than, to the place
Repairing where He judged us, prostrate fall
Before Him reverent; and there confess
Humbly our faults, and pardon beg, with tears
1090　Watering the ground, and with our sighs the air
Frequenting, sent from hearts contrite, in sign
Of sorrow unfeigned, and humiliation meek?
Undoubtedly He will relent, and turn
From His displeasure; in whose look serene,
1095　When angry most He seemed and most severe,
What else but favour, grace, and mercy shone?"
　　So spake our father penitent; nor Eve
Felt less remorse: they, forthwith to the place
Repairing where He judged them, prostrate fell
1100　Before Him reverent; and both confessed
Humbly their faults, and pardon begged; with tears
Watering the ground, and with their sighs the air
Frequenting, sent from hearts contrite, in sign
Of sorrow unfeigned, and humiliation meek.

THE END OF THE TENTH BOOK

ARGUMENT TO BOOK 11

The Son of God presents to His Father the prayers of our first parents now repenting, and intercedes for them: God accepts them, but declares that they must no longer abide in Paradise; sends Michael with a band of cherubim to dispossess them; but first to reveal to Adam future things: Michael's coming down. Adam shows to Eve certain ominous signs; he discerns Michael's approach, goes out to meet him: the Angel denounces their departure. Eve's lamentation. Adam pleads, but submits: the Angel leads him up to a high hill, sets before him in vision what shall happen till the Flood.

ARGUMENT TO BOOK 12

The angel Michael continues from the Flood to relate what shall succeed; then, in the mention of Abraham, comes by degrees to explain, who that Seed of the Woman shall be, which was promised Adam and Eve in the Fall; His incarnation, death, resurrection, and ascension; the state of the Church till His second coming. Adam greatly satisfied and recomforted by these relations and promises descends the hill with Michael; wakens Eve, who all this while had slept, but with gentle dreams composed to quietness of mind and submission. Michael in either hand leads them out of Paradise, the fiery sword waving behind them, and the cherubim taking their stations to guard the place.

from BOOK 12

...

    So spake th' archangel Michael;[1] then paused,
As at the world's great period;[2] and our sire,
Replete with joy and wonder, thus replied:
    "O goodness infinite, goodness immense!
470 That all this good of evil shall produce,
And evil turn to good; more wonderful
Than that which by creation first brought forth
Light out of darkness! Full of doubt I stand,
Whether I should repent me now of sin
475 By me done, and occasioned; or rejoice
Much more, that much more good thereof shall
      spring;
To God more glory, more goodwill to men
From God, and over wrath grace shall abound.
But say, if our Deliverer up to Heaven
480 Must re-ascend, what will betide the few
His faithful, left among the unfaithful herd,
The enemies of truth? Who then shall guide
His people, who defend? Will they not deal
Worse with His followers than with Him they dealt?"
485   "Be sure they will," said th' angel; "but from
      Heaven
He to His own a comforter will send,

The promise of the Father, who shall dwell
His Spirit within them; and the law of faith,
Working through love, upon their hearts shall write,
490 To guide them in all truth; and also arm
With spiritual armour, able to resist
Satan's assaults, and quench his fiery darts;
What man can do against them, not afraid,
Though to the death; against such cruelties
495 With inward consolations recompensed,
And oft supported so as shall amaze
Their proudest persecutors: for the Spirit,
Poured first on His apostles, whom He sends
To evangelize the nations, then on all
500 Baptized, shall them with wondrous gifts endue
To speak all tongues, and do all miracles,
As did their Lord before them. Thus they win
Great numbers of each nation to receive
With joy the tidings brought from Heav'n. At length
505 Their ministry performed, and race well run,
Their doctrine and their story written left,
They die; but in their room, as they forewarn,
Wolves shall succeed for teachers, grievous wolves,[3]
Who all the sacred mysteries of Heav'n
510 To their own vile advantages shall turn
Of lucre and ambition; and the truth
With superstitions and traditions taint,
Left only in those written records pure,
Though not but by the Spirit understood.
515 Then shall they seek to avail themselves of names,
Places, and titles, and with these to join
Secular power; though feigning still to act
By spiritual, to themselves appropriating
The Spirit of God, promised alike and giv'n
520 To all believers; and, from that pretence,
Spiritual laws by carnal power shall force
On every conscience; laws which none shall find
Left them enrolled, or what the Spirit within
Shall on the heart engrave. What will they then
525 But force the Spirit of Grace itself, and bind
His consort Liberty; what, but unbuild
His living temples, built by faith to stand,
Their own faith, not another's? For, on earth,
Who against faith and conscience can be heard
530 Infallible? Yet many will presume:

---

[1] *So spake th' archangel Michael* Michael has just assured Adam of humanity's eventual redemption and salvation.

[2] *world's great period* End of the world.

[3] *grievous wolves* See Acts 20.29.

Whence heavy persecution shall arise
On all, who in the worship persevere
Of Spirit and Truth; the rest, far greater part,
Will deem in outward rites and specious forms
535 Religion satisfied; Truth shall retire
Bestuck with slanderous darts, and works of faith
Rarely be found. So shall the world go on,
To good malignant, to bad men benign;
Under her own weight groaning; till the day
540 Appear of respiration to the just,
And vengeance to the wicked, at return
Of him so lately promised to thy aid,
The woman's seed; obscurely then foretold,
Now ampler known thy Saviour and thy Lord;
545 Last, in the clouds, from Heav'n to be revealed
In glory of the Father, to dissolve
Satan with his perverted world; then raise
From the conflagrant mass, purged and refined,
New heav'ns, new earth, ages of endless date,
550 Founded in righteousness, and peace, and love;
To bring forth fruits, joy and eternal bliss."
      He ended; and thus Adam last replied:
"How soon hath thy prediction, seer blest,
Measured this transient world, the race of time,
555 Till time stand fixed! Beyond is all abyss,
Eternity, whose end no eye can reach.
Greatly instructed I shall hence depart;
Greatly in peace of thought; and have my fill
Of knowledge, what this vessel can contain;
560 Beyond which was my folly to aspire.
Henceforth I learn that to obey is best,
And love with fear the only God; to walk
As in His presence; ever to observe
His Providence; and on Him sole depend,
565 Merciful over all His works, with good
Still overcoming evil, and by small
Accomplishing great things, by things deemed weak
Subverting worldly strong, and worldly wise
By simply meek: that suffering for truth's sake
570 Is fortitude to highest victory,
And, to the faithful, death the gate of life.
Taught this by His example, whom I now
Acknowledge my Redeemer ever blest."
      To whom thus also th' angel last replied:
575 "This having learned, thou hast attained the sum

Of wisdom; hope no higher, though all the stars
Thou knewest by name, and all th' ethereal powers,
All secrets of the deep, all Nature's works,
Or works of God in Heaven, air, earth, or sea,
580 And all the riches of this world enjoyedst,
And all the rule, one empire; only add
Deeds to thy knowledge answerable; add faith,
Add virtue, patience, temperance; add love,
By name to come called charity, the soul
585 Of all the rest: then wilt thou not be loth
To leave this Paradise, but shalt possess
A Paradise within thee, happier far.
Let us descend now therefore from this top
Of speculation; for the hour precise
590 Exacts our parting hence; and see the guards,
By me encamped on yonder hill, expect
Their motion; at whose front a flaming sword,
In signal of remove, waves fiercely round:[1]
We may no longer stay. Go, waken Eve;
595 Her also I with gentle dreams have calmed
Portending good, and all her spirits composed
To meek submission: thou, at season fit,
Let her with thee partake what thou hast heard;
Chiefly what may concern her faith to know,
600 The great deliverance by her seed to come
(For by the woman's seed) on all mankind:
That ye may live, which will be many days,
Both in one faith unanimous, though sad,
With cause, for evils past; yet much more cheered
605 With meditation on the happy end."
      He ended, and they both descend the hill;
Descended, Adam to the bower, where Eve
Lay sleeping, ran before; but found her waked;
And thus with words not sad she him received:
610 "Whence thou returnest, and whither wentest, I
      know;
For God is also in sleep; and dreams advise,
Which He hath sent propitious, some great good
Presaging, since with sorrow and heart's distress
Wearied I fell asleep: but now lead on;
615 In me is no delay; with thee to go,
Is to stay here; without thee here to stay,
Is to go hence unwilling; thou to me
Art all things under Heav'n, all places thou,

---

[1] *a flaming sword ... waves fiercely round*   See Genesis 3.24.

Who for my wilful crime art banished hence.
520 This further consolation yet secure
I carry hence; though all by me is lost,
Such favour I unworthy am vouchsafed,
By me the promised seed shall all restore."
525 So spake our mother Eve; and Adam heard
Well pleased, but answered not: for now, too nigh
Th' archangel stood; and, from the other hill
To their fixed station, all in bright array
The cherubim descended; on the ground
Gliding meteorous, as ev'ning mist
530 Ris'n from a river o'er the marish° glides,   *marsh*
And gathers ground fast at the labourer's heel
Homeward returning. High in front advanced,
The brandished sword of God before them blazed,
Fierce as a comet; which with torrid heat,
535 And vapour as the Libyan air adust,
Began to parch that temperate clime; whereat

In either hand the hastening angel caught
Our lingering parents, and to the eastern gate
Led them direct, and down the cliff as fast
640 To the subjected plain; then disappeared.
They, looking back, all the eastern side beheld
Of Paradise, so late their happy seat,
Waved over by that flaming brand; the gate
With dreadful faces thronged, and fiery arms.
645 Some natural tears they dropt, but wiped them soon;
The world was all before them, where to choose
Their place of rest, and Providence their guide.
They, hand in hand, with wand'ring steps and slow,
Through Eden took their solitary way.

THE END

—1667, 1674

IN CONTEXT

Illustrating *Paradise Lost*

The first illustrated edition of *Paradise Lost* was that of 1688—the fourth published edition. Twelve illustrations appear in the edition (one per book). Of these, seven are attributed to John Baptist Medina and one to Bernard Lens; four are anonymous.

Many illustrated editions of the poem appeared in the eighteenth and nineteenth centuries; among the most notable are those illustrated by Francis Hayman (c. 1707–76), by William Blake (1757–1827), and by John Martin (1789–1854). Two illustrations from each of these editions are reproduced below, together with two from the 1688 edition.

Illustrations to Book 5 and Book 12 (1688).

Francis Hayman, illustrations to Book 2 and Book 4 (1749).

William Blake, illustrations to Book 6 and Book 9 (1808).

John Martin, illustrations to Book 1 and Book 9 (1824).

THE RESTORATION AND
THE EIGHTEENTH CENTURY

Between 1660, when the Stuart monarchy was restored, and the close of the eighteenth century, the people of England (then more commonly referred to as "English" than "British," despite the official creation of Great Britain with the 1707 Act of Union) underwent numerous changes—in how they earned their living, by whom they were ruled, and how they responded to that government, in where they tended to live, and in the ways they envisioned themselves and their relationship with the world around them.

Over the course of the eighteenth century the population of the nation doubled to roughly ten million, with the most significant growth occurring in London, where the population grew from half a million in 1700 to over a million in 1800. Approximately one-tenth of the nation's population resided in its capital city, which in the seventeenth century had already become the largest city in Europe. Regional migration (from Scotland and Ireland as well as from other parts of the nation) accounted for much of this growth, but international immigrants—from Germany, Poland, Africa, and the Caribbean, for example—made up a significant portion of the city's new residents, and often formed discrete communities. More than half the city's inhabitants were women, many of whom, seeking employment as domestic help, joined the large numbers of those who left their rural homes to earn a living in the city. While developments in medicine and sanitation improved the quality of life and lowered the death rate, the English population remained quite young (with the percentage of the population over 60 never reaching higher than 8 per cent), particularly in London. In the rural areas large tracts of land were enclosed for the cultivation of crops or for grazing livestock as agriculture increasingly shifted from subsistence farming into a business and demands for food from the growing urban population increased.

On average, the English people were significantly wealthier at the end of this period than they had been at its beginning. The national income increased more than fivefold—from 43 million to 222 million pounds. Industrial and financial revolutions spurred the further growth of a hitherto small though highly significant class of people, the merchant middle class, and led to a demand for a plethora of new goods that these people imported, manufactured, and sold. From a nation of farmers England was increasingly becoming, in Adam Smith's famous phrase, "a nation of shopkeepers."

Samuel Scott, "Entrance to the Fleet River" (c. 1750). Scott's style was influenced by that of Canaletto, the Italian master of city painting who lived in London intermittently from 1746 to 1755. The entrance to the Fleet River from the Thames in London is now hidden from view by the Thames Embankment.

Of London's million people, a growing percentage (though still a small one by modern standards) was literate, able to afford books, and in possession of the leisure time necessary for reading. In 1782, bookseller James Lackington claimed that the reading public had quadrupled since the early 1770s. While a substantial proportion of publications continued to be collections of sermons or devotion manuals, the new reading public also demanded news in the form of newspapers and periodicals, and fiction in a new, capacious form, the novel. The first provincial paper was launched in 1701, and by 1760 over 150 had been started. The first public libraries were founded in 1725 in Bath and Edinburgh, and by 1800 there were 122 libraries in London and 268 more in the rest of the country.

In the eighteenth century the term "British" became more and more far-reaching. For centuries the Scots had periodically fought the English to preserve their independence, but with the 1707 Act of Union that struggle ended. The kingdom of Scotland joined with that of England and Wales, and the Scottish people became subjects of the new Great Britain. Because several colonies along the eastern seaboard of North America declared independence during this period, students of American history often have the sense that Britain was a shrinking colonial power during this era; in fact the opposite is true. After the Treaty of Utrecht that ended the War of Spanish Succession, the people of the Hudson Bay Territory, as well as those of Acadia and Newfoundland (in what are now eastern provinces of Canada), became colonial British subjects. The same thing happened to the remaining inhabitants of Canada and many of those of India after the 1763 Treaty of Paris, which ended the Seven Years' War (now sometimes referred to as the first of the world wars). That treaty formalized England's supremacy in Canada and paved the way for an extensive British Empire in India. Under it, England also received control of Grenada, France's American territory east of the Mississippi, and the Spanish colony of Florida.

With the restoration of the monarchy in the late seventeenth century, the English people attempted to move beyond centuries of religious strife that had culminated in a bitter civil war. The animosity between the established Anglican Church, the Nonconformists and descendants of the former "Puritans," and the "papists," which had dominated political life, did not disappear (laws discriminating against religious minorities, such as Catholics, remained in place), but increasingly these religious debates were subsumed into broader political debates between parties with established party ideologies. Whereas previously any formal opposition to the government was apt to be regarded as treason (as it was in the case of Algernon Sidney and William Russell in 1683), during the eighteenth century the concept of a legitimate ongoing opposition to government began to take root. Political parties were born, and Parliament and the press became arenas for sanctioned political debate. By 1800 England could boast a political system that was the envy of its neighbors for its stability, effectiveness, and perceived fairness.

RELIGION, GOVERNMENT, AND PARTY POLITICS

The period began, however, with an attempt to reverse, rather than embrace, change. When Charles II landed at Dover, returning from exile in France and restoring the Stuart monarchy, many English people hoped they could return to the old order that had been shattered by civil war. Charles was crowned King in 1661, but the new monarch governed as if this were the eleventh, rather than the first, year of his rule—symbolically erasing the intervening years of civil war, Commonwealth, and Interregnum. The Act of Oblivion formally forgave many (though not all) convicted rebels, furthering the illusion that the turmoil of the preceding years could be erased. With the restoration of the monarchy came that of the established church, but Charles II promised some changes from the disastrous rule of Charles I before the civil war, including increased tolerance of Protestant dissenters and a monarchy that would rule in conjunction with Parliament, rather than in opposition to it. Underlying religious and constitutional issues continued to threaten the stability of the nation, however. Charles was ostensibly a member of the Anglican Church, but his brother, James, Duke of York, remained staunchly and publicly Catholic, with the avowed aim of establishing his faith as the national one. Though Charles had many children, he produced none with his wife; as a result, James remained next in line for the throne. These issues came to a head with the "Popish Plot" of 1678, in which Titus Oates presented perjured testimony suggesting that a Jesuit plot existed to assassinate the King and reestablish Catholic rule in England. A sharp divide arose between Successionists, who supported Charles II and his brother James, and Exclusionists, who sought to exclude James from the line of succession and to appoint James, Duke of Monmouth (one of the King's Protestant illegitimate children), in his place. To restore order Charles asserted his absolute monarchical authority, dissolving Parliament and preventing the passage of the Exclusion Bill. (It is this assertion of royal authority that Poet Laureate John Dryden celebrates in his 1681 poem *Absalom and Achitophel*.)

J.M. Wright, "Charles II" (1661).

The division between Successionists and Exclusionists led to a more lasting one between England's emerging political parties—the Whigs and the Tories. The Tories, made up primarily of landed gentry and rural clergymen, developed out of the Successionist faction; Tories (whose party name was a former term for Irish-Catholic or Royalist bandits) were characterized by their support for the monarchy and for continuing all the privileges of the Anglican Church—that is to say, by a desire to maintain the status quo. From the Exclusionist faction emerged the opposing Whig party, which represented the new moneyed interests (of big landowners and merchants), as well as Dissenters. The Whigs (a previous name for Scottish Covenanters) supported stronger Parliamentary authority, the interests and development of commerce, and somewhat more religious tolerance. These parties established themselves more and more securely in the British political arena as the eighteenth century progressed.

As many Protestants had feared, the Catholic James II did indeed come to the throne when Charles died in 1685. James promised to honor the supremacy of the Anglican Church, but soon began to back away from that promise—suspending the Test Act (which had required all holders of office to take Communion in an Anglican church) and installing Catholics in senior positions in the army, the universities, and the government. The birth of James's son raised in many minds the specter of a Catholic dynasty of rulers, and plans to remove the monarch began to take shape. Secret negotiations resulted in William of Orange, husband of James's elder, Protestant daughter Mary, marching on London with a small army in what became known as the Glorious (or Bloodless) Revolution of 1688. At William's approach James fled to exile in France—though he retained some loyal supporters in England (who were referred to as "Jacobites," from *Jacobus*, the Latin form of "James"). Parliament sanctioned the joint crowning of King William III and Queen Mary II, announcing that, rather than having conquered anything or overthrown anyone, William had simply arrived, found the throne vacant, and installed himself as its rightful occupant. (In fact Mary, as a direct descendant, was first offered the Crown, but she was too dutiful a wife to reign without her husband.) Despite the best efforts of Parliament to paper over the dynastic change, Jacobites continued through the first half of the eighteenth century to affirm that James's son and grandson (known to others as the "Old Pretender" and the "Young Pretender," respectively) were the legitimate rulers of the nation, and major Jacobite uprisings threatened the peace in 1715 and 1745.

AN *Jul 9 F. d*

ARGUMENT,

Shewing, that a

Standing Army

Is inconſiſtent with

A Free Government, and abſolutely deſtructive to the Conſtitution of the Engliſh Monarchy.

Cervus Equum pugna melior communibus herbis
Pellebat, donec minor in certamine longo
Imploravit opes hominis frænumq; recepit.
Sed poſtquam victor violens diſceſſit ab hoſte,
Non Equitem dorſo, non frænum depulit ore.

Horat. Epiſt. 10.

LONDON;
Printed in the Year 1697.

Title page of an anonymous 1697 pamphlet. The issue of whether or not the government should be allowed to retain a standing army was a highly contentious one in the last years of the seventeenth century—and one that revived many of the strong feelings of the Civil War and Interregnum; until William III's 1697 decision to maintain a permanent army in the wake of the Peace of Ryswick, the only English ruler to have maintained a standing army in peacetime was Oliver Cromwell.

The reign of William and Mary restored a Protestant monarchy, and it was one that promised increased tolerance. The Toleration Act of 1689 granted religious freedoms to some Dissenters (though not to Catholics) if they swore their allegiance to the Crown. Jews during this period were allowed to worship (London's first synagogue was built in 1701) but were deprived of most civil rights. A Bill of Rights reaffirmed the powers of Parliament and limited the control of the Crown. The reign of the successor to William and Mary, Mary's sister Anne (who reigned from 1702 to 1714), marked a period of commercial growth and expansion abroad. During the war with France known variously as Queen Anne's War and the War of the Spanish Succession (1702–13), England won a number of victories under John Churchill, Duke of Marlborough, which brought the nation new territory in North America, as well as control over the slave trade from Africa to the Caribbean and Spanish America. Anne's reign was the first in which a Tory government ruled (from 1710 to 1714), much to the joy of Tory writers Jonathan Swift, Alexander Pope, John Gay, and others. However, a rivalry between two important Tory ministers—Robert Harley, Earl of Oxford, and Henry St. John, Viscount Bolingbroke—weakened the party, and when George I (James II's Protestant grandson and the first British king from the house of Hanover) ascended the throne in 1714, the Whigs resumed control of Parliament.

The reigns of the first three Hanoverian kings, George I, II, and III, took the nation through the second decade of the nineteenth century and marked a period of continued economic growth, industrialization, expansion of foreign trade—and an important development in the growth of Parliamentary power. Both George I and II were born in Germany and were unfamiliar with the language, culture, or government of their new country. As a result, they intervened little in the day-to-day affairs of the nation. In the absence of a strong monarchy, the political scene was dominated from 1721 to 1742 by Robert Walpole, a Whig minister who had risen to power after the economic bubble and subsequent stock market crash of 1720 known as the "South Sea Bubble." Many government ministers were among the thousands ruined through overheated speculation in the South Sea Company's shares, but

Walpole remained untainted by the ensuing scandal, and consolidated his hold on the reins of government. The unprecedented degree of power with which he aggrandized himself earned him the derogatory nickname among his opponents of "prime minister"— an insult that had become an official title by the time Walpole left office. The centralization of power proved to have considerable benefits; under his corrupt but firm and efficient rule the government enjoyed a long period of stability. Walpole cultivated commerce and avoided conflict as much as possible.

If Walpole was anxious to maintain the peace, others saw a willingness to wage war as a necessity if Britain wished to continue to increase its wealth and power. Subsequent prime ministers—William Pitt most prominent among them—entered the nation into a series of wars fought to protect their foreign trade against encroachments by France, Spain, and Austria. It was under Pitt (and under George III, who took the throne in 1760 and reigned until 1820) that Britain emerged as the world's most significant colonial power. But George's reign was hardly one of untroubled success. The loss of the American colonies in 1783 was a blow to both British commerce and British pride, and religious intolerance continued to cause problems at home; a partial repeal of the penal laws, which had restricted the freedoms of Catholics, led to the Gordon Riots of 1780, in which a reactionary Protestant mob ruled the streets for ten days, defacing Catholic public buildings, and even threatening known Catholics. George himself suffered from mental instability (likely caused by a metabolic disorder called porphyria), and descriptions of his bouts of madness—such as that given by Frances Burney in her journal—were a source of concern for many of his subjects.

Empiricism, Skepticism, and Religious Dissent

The eighteenth century was an age of great scientific advancement, during which the English people increasingly seemed to possess the capacity to uncover laws governing the universe. Sir Isaac Newton (1642–1727) was the hero of the age, and vast numbers of scientific advances were either directly or indirectly attributed to him. As Alexander Pope says in a famous couplet, "Nature and Nature's laws lay hid in Night; / God said Let Newton be! and all was Light." In *Principia Mathematica* (1687), *Optics* (1704), and other works, Newton laid out the laws of gravity, celestial mechanics, and optics. Perhaps as important as the discoveries themselves was the scientific approach to causes and effects that Newton exemplified. In the first of the four rules in the *Principia* for arriving at knowledge he puts the matter succinctly: "We are to admit no more causes of natural things than such as are both true and sufficient to explain the appearances.... Nature is pleased with simplicity, and affects not the pomp of superfluous causes."

Other scientific advances included improvements in navigation, the successful determination of the shape of the earth and the measurement of its distance from the sun, and improved knowledge of physical and chemical properties—for example, Robert Boyle determined that the pressure and volume of a gas are inversely proportionate (Boyle's Law). In 1752 Benjamin Franklin demonstrated that lightning is an electrical discharge; Franklin, a colonial British subject who lived for much of his adult life in England, was admitted to the Royal Society the following year in recognition of his scientific achievements. Later in the century Linnaeus's system of taxonomy was accepted among naturalists, and increased study of fossils led to the discovery, through the examination of lava-based soil from volcanic eruptions, that the earth was much older than the 6000 years allowed by biblical tradition. Largely as a follow-up to these geological discoveries, comprehensive theories of evolution began to be put forward in the last decades of the century.

More than ever before, citizens felt they could understand the world through logic, reasoning, and close attention to detail, rather than through faith. A plethora of new instruments for observing, measuring, and quantifying (most notably, the microscope and the telescope) opened up whole new realms of the universe, from microscopic organisms to other planets, for examination. The influential Royal Society of London for the Improving of Natural Knowledge, founded in 1662, helped to organize scientific enquiry and championed empiricism—the belief that through observation, experimentation, and experience humans could ascertain the truth. The Royal Society also helped to spread knowledge of scientific discoveries and advances; the British Museum, for example, was founded in 1759 with the donation of the private collection of a former president of the Royal Society, physician and botanist Sir Hans Sloane. In all walks of life Britons began to experience a desire to keep records of the observed minutiae of their everyday lives. Notable among them was Samuel Pepys, a naval administrator in London who rose to be secretary of the Admiralty, systematically restructured the navy, and became president of the Royal Society—yet is nevertheless remembered primarily as a diarist. His diary provides a unique record of the daily goings-on of his native city, including details of business, religion, science, literature, theater, and music; Pepys brought to the diary form the same sort of passion for detail that James Boswell would later bring to his biography of Samuel Johnson. For the nearly ten years (1660–69) that Pepys kept his diary, he related all that he saw around him, compressing remarkable detail into each page through use of his own private shorthand. When it was finally decoded and certain selections published in 1825, the diary gave readers an extraordinary glimpse of life during the Restoration, including such momentous events as the landing of Charles II at Dover in 1660 and the Great Fire of London in 1666.

Another member of the Royal Society whose career was founded on a fascination for detail was antiquarian and biographer John Aubrey. Aubrey's desire to preserve as complete a record of the past as possible led him to write a natural history of Wiltshire (his home county), a survey of ancient sites across Britain (including Avebury, some twenty miles from Stonehenge, which he is credited with "discovering"), and a scrappy collection of notes which, collected and published after his death as *Brief Lives*, brought together biographical sketches of some of the dominant figures of his time (including John Milton and Francis Bacon). His studies in archaeological history were unique at their time; similarly, his studies in folklore led him to write the first English work entirely devoted to that topic. And Aubrey's inquiry into the ways in which practices and conventions such as prices, weights, measures, dress, handwriting, navigation, and astronomy have changed over time anticipated the strategies followed in modern historical research.

Rather as a turn toward personal observation increasingly marked secular life in the late seventeenth and eighteenth centuries, so too did many people advocate a turn inward in spiritual life, to one's own conscience and personal faith in God. One such thinker was John Bunyan, a preacher who staunchly defended the primacy of one's own conscience over the dictates of organized religion. In 1660 the Anglican Church began to move against dissenting sects, jailing nonconformist preachers such as Bunyan. Though he was offered release if he promised to stop preaching, Bunyan chose to remain in jail, continuing to preach and write religious manuals and a spiritual autobiography, *Grace Abounding to the Chief of Sinners* (1666), while in prison. He defended his calling and, by remaining loyal to his beliefs, inspired many of his converts to do the same. Released after 12 years, Bunyan was yet again imprisoned in 1675; it was during this second sentence that he wrote *The Pilgrim's Progress*, a religious allegory in which Christian is a traveler putting this world resolutely behind him in order to achieve the perilous journey to salvation and the next world. It became the most popular work of prose fiction of the seventeenth century.

The ways of thinking of Bunyan, on one hand, and of Aubrey and Pepys, on the other, epitomize two approaches to interpreting the world—approaches that continued to clash throughout the seventeenth century. The ever-growing belief that through close observation the order of the universe could be uncovered was often at odds with religious beliefs, particularly as a result of the influential theories of philosopher John Locke. Locke, sometimes referred to as the "Newton of the mind," took Newton's theories and scientific reasoning and applied them to epistemological questions, asking how we come to know and understand. In his *Essay Concerning Human Understanding* (1690), Locke (drawing on Aristotle) advances the theory that the mind is a *tabula rasa* (blank slate) at birth and acquires ideas through experience. The theory had enormous implications for the study of the human mind and for educational practice, but its impact on theology was also profound. If we have no innate ideas concerning our own existence or the world around us, no more do we possess any innate notions as to the existence of God. Instead, in Locke's view, we must arrive at the idea of God through a chain of reasoning. Through intuiting knowledge of our own existence as humans and of the world around us, we proceed to a knowledge of the existence of God through the logical necessity of a "First Cause" to account for our existence. By emphasizing the role that external evidence can play in finding a path to theological truth, Locke brought about an explosion in Deism, or natural theology. Locke's theories, like those of Newton, offered rational grounds for belief in God. For many, the perfectly ordered universe gave in its very being evidence of the God who had created it, for this order could not have arisen out of chaos without a creator (the cosmological argument), nor could it have been designed with such incomparable artistry (the argument from design). (Joseph Addison poetically summed up this belief in the periodical *The Spectator*, saying the planets are in reason's ear "Forever singing as they shine / The hand that made us is divine.") Popular throughout the later eighteenth century was the concept of God as a mechanic or mathematician who does not necessarily need to intervene in the working of his creation, which he has ordered so that it runs smoothly on its own.

Empiricism brought about new forms of religious belief, but for many the logical end of empiricist thinking was a profound religious skepticism. As geological discoveries challenged the truth of the Scriptures, and as the mysteries of the universe seemed ready to be solved one by one, some began to feel that there might no longer be room for God in this rational, enlightened universe. The leading skeptic of his day was David Hume. As Boswell famously recorded it, Hume was asked on his deathbed if "it was not possible that there might be a future state" after death, to which Hume replied that "it was possible that a piece of coal put upon the fire would not burn." Despite his evident lack of faith in the existence of any afterlife, Hume was not a full-fledged atheist; he stated repeatedly that he accepted the argument from design. "I infer an infinitely perfect architect from the infinite art and contrivance which is displayed in the whole fabric of the universe," he declared. Yet Hume was rightly regarded as the foe of many common manifestations of Christian belief,

including belief in divine Providence as well as faith in an afterlife. In his *Natural History of Religion* (1757), Hume took an almost anthropological approach to religious belief, examining the histories of various religions through the ages and concluding that religions tend to arise from passion, fear, imagination, or desire, and that they are products of various cultures and thus evolve slowly over time. He claimed that any member of humanity who seeks the protection of faith tends to do so "from a consciousness of his imbecility and misery, rather than from any reasoning." And, both in his major work *An Enquiry Concerning Human Understanding* and in his most controversial essay, "Of Miracles," Hume voices a thoroughgoing skepticism concerning supernatural claims:

> It is a general maxim worthy of our attention, "That no testimony is sufficient to establish a miracle, unless the testimony be of such a kind that its falsehood would be more miraculous than the fact which it endeavors to establish. …" When anyone tells me, that he saw a dead man restored to life, I immediately consider with myself whether it be more probable that this person should either deceive or be deceived, or that the fact which he relates should really have happened. I weigh the one miracle against the other; and according to the superiority which I discover, I pronounce my decision, and always reject the greater miracle.

Hume's skepticism was shared by many freethinkers, but Samuel Johnson doubtless represented the majority view in his disdain for Hume, and in his unwavering belief in miracles. In his *Life of Johnson* Boswell records Johnson's view that "although God has made Nature to operate by certain fixed laws, yet it is not unreasonable to think that he may suspend those laws in order to establish a system highly advantageous to mankind."

In the face of increasing skepticism, many Christian apologists sought to defend their beliefs by using the same rational tools employed by the freethinkers. Various mathematical and logistical arguments were also published, endeavoring to provide scientific support for the truth of the scriptures. Joseph Butler, for example, argued for the truth of revelation using historical evidence in *The Analogy of Religion Natural and Revealed to the Constitution and Course of Nature* (1736). Others responded by disregarding the rational arguments of skeptics altogether, turning instead to powerful appeals to the emotions in their efforts to reaffirm faith. Methodism, an evangelical movement that originated within the Church of England, is perhaps the most important example here. Led by John Wesley, Methodism spread rapidly in new industrial villages and poorer areas. Methodist preachers spoke their gospel to common people—often out in the fields or in barns because they were barred from preaching in churches. With its emphasis on faith as the only path to salvation, its strong reliance on hymns, and its fervent and energetic sermons, Methodism won many converts.

Throughout the century the debate over free-thinking was a heated one in England—citizens heard freethinkers denounced from pulpits, read attacks on them in the press, and even saw them pilloried or imprisoned for blasphemy. Despite public alarm, however, these blasphemous thinkers made up a very small minority of the population, and posed little real threat to the established Church. As Johnson famously said to Boswell, "Sir, there is a great cry about infidelity; but there are, in reality, very few infidels." The Church continued as an arm of the state, serving as both political body and spiritual leader. "Papists" were a minority, despite the fears their presence evoked among Protestants.

More and more homes contained copies of at least a few books—most commonly the Bible, a prayer book, and John Bunyan's *The Pilgrim's Progress*. After those three, James Thomson's *Seasons* may well have been the most popular book of the age. Many homes would also have held copies of devotional manuals such as William Law's *A Serious Call* and a few of the most popular fictional works of the time, many of which—such as Daniel Defoe's *Robinson Crusoe*, for example—contained a strong moral message.

INDUSTRY, COMMERCE, AND THE MIDDLE CLASS

While religious and secular debates continued, the scientific advances that had helped to incite them changed the physical face of the nation. The first crude steam engine was invented in 1698 by Thomas Savery,

a military engineer, as a means of removing water from mines. In *The Miner's Friend; or, an Engine to Raise Water by Fire, Described* (1702), however, Savery includes a chapter on "The Uses that this Engine may be applied Unto" that shows a dawning awareness of the far-reaching possibilities for such a device:

> (1) It may be of great use for palaces, for the nobilities or gentlemen's houses: for by a cistern on the top of a house, you may with a great deal of ease and little charge, throw what quantity of water you have occasion for to the top of any house; which water in its fall makes you what sorts of fountains you please and supply any room in the house. And it is of excellent use in case of fire, of which more hereafter. (2) Nothing can be more fit for serving cities and towns with water, except a crank-work by the force of a river.... (3) As for draining fens and marshes ... it is much cheaper, and every way easier, especially where coals are water borne, to continue the discharge of any quantities of water by our engine than it can be done by any horse engines what so ever. (4) I believe it may be made very useful to ships, but I dare not meddle with that matter; and leave it to the judgment of those who are the best judges of maritime affairs.

The steam engine—particularly following Thomas Newcomen's pioneering use of pistons in 1712 and James Watt's invention of a condenser (patented in 1769) to make its functioning more efficient—was the driving force behind an Industrial Revolution in Britain that both literally and figuratively gathered steam throughout the eighteenth century. And the fuel that fed it, coal, took a central place in British life. Coal had begun to be used extensively as a heating fuel in the later Middle Ages, as the forests were depleted, and its domestic use accelerated during the "Little Ice Age" that brought colder-than-average winters to Britain through most of the seventeenth and eighteenth centuries. The industrial use of coal grew rapidly throughout the era as well; by 1700 Britain was mining and burning far more coal than the rest of the world. In the early years of the eighteenth century, Daniel Defoe marveled at the "prodigious fleets of ships which come constantly in with coals for this increasing city [London]," and at the vast numbers of coal pits and the "prodigious heaps, I may say mountains of coal which are dug up at every pit" in Newcastle. But if coal made possible warmer dwellings and industrial growth, it was most certainly a mixed blessing. The life of a miner was nasty, brutish, and short. The mines themselves were extraordinarily dangerous, and the mine operators in Newcastle created what may have been the first industrial slums. London by 1700 was already a blackened city; according to the essayist Thomas Nourse, "when men think to take the sweet air, they suck into their lungs this sulphurous stinking powder." Nourse concluded that "of all the cities perhaps of Europe, there is not a more nasty and a more unpleasant place."

London firefighters, c. 1720. The machine is filled by hand at the front as the pumping mechanism is operated at the sides.

If coal mining and the steam engine both accelerated the Industrial Revolution, so too did modifications in factory design and in the production process, which enabled goods to be produced more quickly and in larger quantities. And with the industrial revolution came a financial revolution. Today investment banking has become the epitome of a respectable profession, but before the late seventeenth century moneylending was for the most part both informal and disreputable. With the founding of the Bank of England in 1694 the country took a decisive step toward the provision for loans at stable interest rates and toward the creation of a permanent national debt (the bank's primary purpose was to lend to the government, not to individuals or private companies). Also vital to financing the growth of business and industry was the rise of equity financing,

the division of a company's ownership into equal shares made available for sale to the general public. Though the London Stock Exchange did not exist on any formally regulated basis until 1801, the exchange dates its existence to 1698, when one John Casting began to issue a list of the current prices of company shares and of commodities on a regular basis from "this Office in Jonathan's Coffee-house." The invention of paper money and of checks also helped to facilitate economic fluidity, and virtual free trade resulted from the breaking of a number of government monopolies in the late seventeenth century. Put together, these developments placed Britain firmly on the road toward the system that would come to be known as "capitalism" (the word "capitalism" was not coined until the mid-nineteenth century, but the *Oxford English Dictionary* records the first use of "capital" as occurring in 1708 with the issuance of "An Act for Enlarging the Capital Stock of the Bank of England"). By the early eighteenth century it had become relatively respectable to make money with money, and for the first time moneyed interests dominated landed ones. By the end of the century Britain was the richest nation in the world.

With the extension of trade and the development of more—and more sophisticated—manufactured goods, the nation found itself with a new driving force—one of relentless growth, expansion, and mercantilism. Goods and people could more easily move throughout the nation thanks to developments in transportation. The first Turnpike Trust was passed in 1663, and by 1770 there were 519 trusts, covering nearly 15,000 miles of road. In such trusts, a group of people (usually including a treasurer, a surveyor, and many of the landowners through whose property the road passed) would be granted (by an Act of Parliament) responsibility for managing the road, and would earn money for its upkeep through the establishment and maintenance of toll gates. A canal system was also begun, first to extend natural waterways and then to connect different river systems, bringing more inland coalfields and manufacturing districts within reach. Boats and coaches began for the first time to keep regular schedules, and time-keeping became an exact science as British clock-makers worked to meet the needs of their nation. A new group of consumers was established, as the merchant class began producing goods not only designed for the aristocracy, but for fellow members of the middle class, who struggled to keep up with the ever-changing dictates of fashion. And for the first time periodicals and newspapers were filled with advertisements for consumer goods.

A booming leisure industry was created to feed the demands of the growing middle class, particularly in London, where urban entertainment flourished. For the first time women from middle-class families entered the public sphere, and the result was something of a cultural revolution. Before 1700 these women (for example merchants' or doctors' wives and daughters) could attend few public social activities, even in larger provincial towns—the only places at which it was proper to be seen included the church, county fairs, and races. By the last decades of the century, however, such a woman's social calendar could include concerts, plays, lectures, debates, balls, exhibitions, and assemblies. Significant architectural changes occurred to feed this leisure industry: shopping streets were laid out, old public buildings were rebuilt, therapeutic spas and bath houses were constructed, and massive pleasure gardens, such as those at Vauxhall and Ranelagh, were laid out. With the advent of town planning, it became fashionable to design town centers in an octagonal pattern, which facilitated movement into the business center at the town core.

The growing power of the middle class and the influence of its values and ideals were evident in the changes that occurred in the theater between the Restoration and the mid-eighteenth century. The theaters, which had been closed in 1642 by Puritan decree, were reopened with the restoration of the monarchy in 1660. Charles II, returning from exile in France (the theater center of Europe) and anxious to signal a new era, indulged the public's keen appetite for the theater by licensing two public London theaters. In the atmosphere and layout of the playhouses and in the plays performed, Restoration theater showed a marked difference from its Elizabethan predecessor. While in Elizabethan theater almost every stratum of society could be found, except royalty, this was no longer true of the Restoration playhouses, which, for the first time in history, the King attended. Restoration playhouses were much smaller and more exclusive; while the Globe Theatre sat between two and three thousand people, Restoration playhouses held between two and three hundred. Prices were therefore significantly higher, and beyond the means of most citizens. The audience consisted almost entirely of young and well-to-do fashionable people from the western end of London (the "Town"), who were closely affiliated with the court. As a group they were united in their Royalist leanings and love of wit, and mostly shared an attitude of skepticism and cynicism coupled with anti-Puritanism. Authors wrote with this audience in mind; they fed their audience's desire for singing, dancing, elaborate costumes, glittering sets, and brilliant spectacles. They also wrote an extraordinary number of scathingly witty and entertaining comedies; the Restoration and early eighteenth century was something of a golden age for the English stage. Among the many comedies from this period that have continued to be revived into our own age are William Wycherley's *The Country Wife* (1675), Aphra Behn's *The Rover* (1677), John Vanbrugh's *The Relapse* (1677), William Congreve's *The Way of the World* (1700), and Susanna Centlivre's *A Bold Stroke for a Wife* (1718), as well as John Gay's ballad opera *The Beggar's Opera*.

While the fashionable set flocked to the theater in these years, members of the respectable middle classes, who leaned more toward Puritan religious notions and who typically resided in the original city of London (now the East End)—while people of rank lived in what was then the separate city of Westminster (now the West End)—tended to avoid the theaters, which were situated in the luminal area between London and Westminster. By the end of the seventeenth century Puritan opposition to the stage was again becoming more vocal. Jeremy Collier's famous attack on contemporary theater, *A Short View of the Immorality and Profaneness of the English Stage* (1698), was effectively answered in principle by Congreve's "Amendments Upon Mr. Collier's False and Imperfect Citations, etc." and John Dennis's "The Usefulness of the Stage," but the sorts of views that Collier had expressed continued to gain ground among the populace at large, and Congreve, like other playwrights, hastened to pay lip service to the new climate of opinion by, for instance, replacing "Oh God" with "Oh Heaven" in his characters' lines. Collier's anger was chiefly drawn by bad (that is, irreligious) language and by the representation of either clergymen or ladies as less than exemplary. In 1737 Parliament passed a new Licensing Act, restricting London theater to two tightly controlled venues. Some modern readers may find the raucous, grossly physical and demeaning satire of such pieces as *A Vision of the Golden Rump* (the play which made Walpole's case for the need for censorship) offensive in itself, but to the eighteenth-century censor the point was the attack on Robert Walpole.

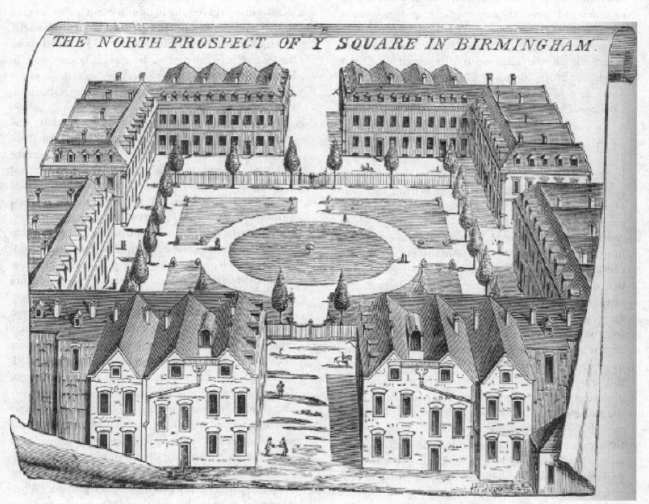

"The North Prospect of the Square in Birmingham," engraving (1732).
The Square, an exclusive residential complex, began to be constructed around 1700.

As a result of the Licensing Act restrictions, writers who a generation earlier might have been drawn to the stage began increasingly to try their hand at the novel. The drama that remained gave prominent place to moralizing and sentimentality, and placed considerable emphasis on decorum. The theater continued to sparkle intermittently (the mid-eighteenth century was the era of renowned actor, theater manager, and playwright David Garrick), but it was not until the last quarter of the century that satirical social comedy made a brilliant comeback on the stage with plays such as Oliver Goldsmith's *She Stoops to Conquer* (1773), Richard Sheridan's *The School for Scandal* (1777), and Hannah Cowley's *The Belle's Stratagem* (1780).

ETHICAL DILEMMAS IN A CHANGING NATION

In the Middle Ages and through much of the sixteenth century most Britons saw themselves as living in an age of decline or of stasis, and even in the seventeenth century a sense of the world as a place in which continual improvements were to be expected was limited to the well-educated. But in the eighteenth century a sense of the inevitability of progress—a sense that would crest in the nineteenth and early twentieth centuries—became more and more general. Prosperity unquestionably played its part in fostering this change; so too did various technological and medical advancements. Increased sanitation and improvements in hygiene had reduced the death rate, particularly in the army. The use of citrus to prevent scurvy was discovered in 1754, and James Cook had sailed around the globe without a single sailor dying of it. (Tragically, though, Cook's expeditions spread suffering and death through venereal disease to various populations in the South Pacific, most notably in Tahiti.) Improvements in preventative medicine had also reduced the death rate, and the first preventative injections began in England with inoculation against smallpox, a process popularized largely by the unflagging efforts of woman-of-letters Lady Mary Wortley Montagu, who had observed the practice in Turkey. Many new hospitals were founded, while increased understanding of the workings of the nervous system and of psychological or physiological disorders brought about more humane treatment for those suffering from mental diseases—who were formerly believed to be possessed by demonic spirits, and were therefore locked up in terrible conditions and even put on display for visitors, as at St. Mary's of Bethlehem ("Bedlam"). St. Luke's Hospital in London, where poet Christopher Smart was an early inmate, was founded in 1751. Increased investigations into the relationship between the body and mind led to detailed studies of hypochondria, depression, and hysteria. George Chine's *The English Malady* (1733) investigated the complaint (believed to be especially common in England) known as "the vapors" or "spleen," a vague melancholia and malaise from which James Boswell, amongst others, suffered.

While most English people believed that new advances benefited society, an understanding of them was growing to be beyond the grasp of the average educated individual. The numerous scientific and technological developments led inevitably toward greater specialization, and the new disciplines of physics, astronomy, and chemistry grew increasingly complex. Until the eighteenth century most educated gentlemen could keep up to date with discoveries and theories in all areas of knowledge, but this was now no longer the case. While many writers, such as Margaret Cavendish in her 1666 work *Description of a New Blazing World* (a precursor of the genre we now call "science fiction"), enjoyed speculating about where the path of the new knowledge might lead, for others the effect was far more disorienting. Swift's satire of poorly formulated and ill-conceived experimental science in Book Three of *Gulliver's Travels*, for example, gives voice to the widely shared sense that some of the new lines of inquiry were not only incomprehensible, but also ridiculous. As the world broadened, it became increasingly difficult for individuals to understand the complex societal machine of which they formed a small part—and this broadening was often perceived as a threat to social coherence. When Alexander Pope, in his *Essay on Man*, attacks scientists who are too absorbed in minutiae to see the bigger picture, he reflects a common belief that individuals must keep the interests of society as a whole in mind.

Any references to "the average educated individual" in this period are of course still very far from denoting the whole population. One of the new notions of the

Reformation was the idea that education should be universal—for all classes of society, and for females as well as for males. John Knox, the Scottish Protestant leader, was the first to give practical shape to such radical notions, formulating in the 1560s a plan for incorporating schools into every church. Implementation of such a plan occurred only slowly and fitfully; the Scottish Highlands lagged behind the rest of Britain in levels of education as a result of the lack of books in Gaelic. But by the late eighteenth century the system had put down deep roots, and Scotland was the only area in Europe in which over half of the citizenry was formally educated.

In England it was coming to be considered proper that female members of the gentry should be tutored, and boarding schools, although decried by the intelligentsia, were increasingly popular for middle-class girls. But the idea of universal education for all women and men was given serious consideration only by a few, and higher education for women remained a subject for jokes. Some women did strongly protest the philosophical and theological assumptions that denied that women have the capacity to improve their minds. Mary Astell's 1694 *A Serious Proposal to the Ladies* (probably the most famous of such early proto-feminist texts) was not only an important call for the education of women but also one of the first works to inquire into the degree to which humans' search for truth may be influenced by prejudice. In this she challenges Locke's theory that we are born as blank slates; Astell argues instead that people are born into families, towns, cities, and countries that provide pre-existing conditions and help to shape human prejudices. In a similar vein Bathsua Makin, in her *Essay to Revive the Ancient Education of Gentlewomen* (1673) had already declared, "Custom, when it is inveterate, has a mighty influence: it has the force of nature itself. The barbarous custom to breed women low is grown general amongst us, and has prevailed so far, that it is verily believed (especially amongst a sort of debauched sots) that women are not endued with such reason as men; nor capable of improvement by education, as they are. It is looked upon as a monstrous thing to pretend the contrary.... To offer to the world the liberal education of women is to deface the image of God in man." At least a few men

shared such views—Daniel Defoe, for example, refers to the denial of learning to women as "one of the most barbarous customs in the world"—but it would be two hundred years before such views became those of the majority.

Susana Highmore Duncombe, *Vignette with Two Ladies Conversing in a Park, with Athena Chasing Away Cupid* (c. 1785). Duncombe's parents held advanced views regarding the education of young women; she learned French, Latin, and Italian, was taught to draw by her father (the painter Joseph Highmore, also remembered as illustrator of Richardson's *Pamela*), and published both translations of Italian poets and her own verse.

The new celebration of mercantilism—and the acceptance of selfishness that this mercantilism implied—posed moral dilemmas that Enlightenment habits of thought encouraged many individuals to explore. If people allowed themselves to be driven by their own self-interest, would they ignore the greater good of society as a whole? How should other peoples (as well as other individual people) be treated? These questions became more complex and vexing as England expanded geographically and its citizens found themselves part of an ever-larger community. With the Seven Years' War Britain became a major colonial power, and its position in relation to the rest of the world changed dramatically. This too was generally assumed to be "progress," both for England and for the areas it came to control. The appropriation of wealth from India and the Indies, for example, was justified by citing England's supposed cultural and technological superiority, from which it was supposed that the indigenous populations would themselves benefit, and by arguing that the British were saving the Hindus from the oppressive Muslim Mughal emperors. But some English people voiced different beliefs concerning the morality of colonial expansion and trade. While many saw the future of the nation as dependent on aggressive expansion of trade and the colonial empire, others supported international trade but were morally opposed to expansion. Many writers—including Jonathan Swift and Samuel Johnson—have left memorable denunciations of colonial land-grabbing and many more of involvement in the slave trade.

English participation in the slave trade had begun to grow significantly in the seventeenth century, and by the mid-eighteenth century close to 50,000 slaves were being transported across the Atlantic annually by British ships. But by that time stirrings of conscience about the morality of the practice of slavery were also evident. Here is how Samuel Johnson (as reported by Boswell) thought the matter through:

> It must be agreed that in most ages many countries have had part of their inhabitants in a state of slavery; yet it may be doubted whether slavery can ever be supposed the natural condition of man. It is impossible not to conceive that men in their original state were equal; and very difficult to imagine how one would be subjected to another but by violent compulsion. An individual may, indeed, forfeit his liberty by a crime; but he cannot by that crime forfeit the liberty of his children. What is true of a criminal seems true likewise of a captive. A man may accept life from a conquering enemy on condition of perpetual servitude; but it is very doubtful whether he can entail that servitude on his descendants; for no man can stipulate without commission for another. The condition which he himself accepts, his son or grandson would have rejected.

As Johnson's thoughts suggest, the questioning of the moral grounds for slavery arose to a significant extent from the consideration of broader inquiries concerning human nature. Many theorists of the time, such as

Anthony Ashley Cooper, the third Earl of Shaftesbury, claimed people naturally attained the greatest possible level of happiness by being good to others. Because humanity is inherently sociable, that argument went, those acts and characteristics that are most virtuous are also those that are best for society as a whole. In Pope's *Essay on Man* (1733–34), for example, self-interest is seen as beneficial (through God's foresight) to others as well as to the self. Each individual's "ruling passion" causes him or her to seek "a sev'ral goal"; thus, by gratifying one's own desires, one also works together as part of a larger framework. David Hume also argued, though from a rather different standpoint, that the cultivation of virtue would advance the general good; Hume emphasized the importance of the feelings or "sentiments"—what we would today call the emotions—in leading us to a sense of what is right—and emphasized, too, the role that habit can play in cultivating patterns of good behavior.

There were some, however, who took a more pessimistic view of human nature and society. Bernard Mandeville, the most controversial of early eighteenth-century moral theorists, saw self-interest purely as selfishness, a quality that, in the natural state of human beings, would not allow for the interests of others. Ethical behavior, in Mandeville's view, is in essence a by-product of our vanity. It arises purely from the human desire to be recognized and praised. There is no place in Mandeville's world for appeals to conscience; morality is only driven by pride and shame. According to Mandeville, a wealthy society depends on people having and indulging their vices, such as greed and vanity, because these lead to full employment and a buoyant economy—whereas a pious, self-denying society will lead to unemployment and general poverty. In other words, general Puritan reform would bring economic collapse. Mandeville's defense of the financial benefits of the consumer society is in many ways strikingly modern.

The ideas of Adam Smith concerning human nature are in some respects closely connected with those of Mandeville, but Smith's understanding of both morality and economics is more complex and nuanced. Even as Smith puts forward the notion that self-interest can work to the benefit of all through the mechanism of the "invisible hand," Smith does not see selfishness itself as a virtue. He accepts that altruism exists, recognizing that, however selfish "man may be supposed, there are evidently some principles in his nature that interest him in the fortune of others and render their happiness necessary to him, though he derives nothing from it except the pleasure of seeing it." And Smith devotes considerable effort to discussing the ways in which selfishness acts *against* the public interest, and must be curbed. Though "civil government" was said to have been instituted "for the security of property," he concluded that it had been "in reality instituted for the defense of the rich against the poor, or of those who have some property against those who have none at all." Far from giving free rein to commercial interests, Smith concluded that the interests of business people "is never exactly the same with that of the public," and that they "have generally an interest to deceive and even to oppress the public."

Most people accepted the more optimistic view of human nature, and the theories such as those of Shaftesbury and Hume led to a growing cult of senti-ment, in which people celebrated what they saw as their natural sympathetic responses to human suffering (and, to a lesser extent, to human joy). Social reform movements grew as the English people sought the pleasure that charitable acts would bring them. As the growing trend of social improvement became not only

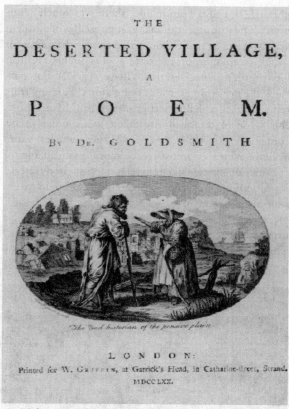

Title page, Oliver Goldsmith's *The Deserted Village* (1770).

A View of the Poor House of Datchworth, detail from an engraving in Philip Thicknesse's *Four Persons Found Starved to Death, at Datchworth* (1769).

Outrage against extremes of hardship and inequality caused by such "rural improvement" practices as enclosure (of formerly common land) and engross-ment (the practice of replacing a larger number of rural tenants with a much smaller number) was stirred in the 1760s by a variety of works, among them Thicknesse's shocking account of an incident in Hertfordshire, and Oliver Goldsmith's long poem lamenting the disappearance of rural and village society in the face of the greed of wealthy land-owners: "the man of wealth and pride / Takes up a space that many poor supplied."

popular, but also fashionable, there was much sentimental posturing, and many supposedly benevolent actions were, in reality, motivated by selfish desires for social acceptance or prestige. Works such as Oliver Goldsmith's "The Deserted Village" (1770), however, show the deepening sense of obligation that many truly felt toward their fellow citizens. (Goldsmith also shows this sense of responsibility taken to extremes in his comedy *The Good-Natured Man* [1768], which features a hero who is almost pathologically incapable of considering his own needs in relation to anybody else's.)

Questions concerning the goodness of human nature were also linked with debates concerning the best form of government—debates that attained particular urgency with the American and French Revolutions. Thomas Paine's *Common Sense* (1776) brought the issues of the goodness of government to the forefront for many eighteenth-century citizens of both England and the colonies. For Paine, an Englishman with limited formal education who moved to the colony of Pennsylvania in 1774, when he was 37, government was at best a necessary evil to be endured, and its dictatorial tendencies must be curbed. The constitution of England was, according to Paine, an amalgam of republican elements with the remains of monarchical and despotic ones. The very idea of a monarch, in his view, went against the principle of human equality: and "'tis a form of government which the word of God bears testimony against, and blood will attend it." Blood was shed over such issues only on the American side of the Atlantic, but *Common Sense* went through five editions in London, with editions also appearing in Newcastle and Edinburgh.

A Coffee House, engraving, 1668. The first London coffee house opened in 1652.

PRINT CULTURE

Whatever British people's opinions on issues of morality, philosophy, government, or technology, they soon found themselves with a multitude of new forums in which to express those opinions, thanks to the booming print trade. The religious controversies of the seventeenth-century English civil wars had done much to fuel a desire for printed information, whether in the form of prophecies, sermons, news, or political controversy. Censorship under the Licensing Act, which had loosened under Charles I at the approach of the civil war, was briefly revived following the Restoration, but in 1695 the old Licensing Act was allowed to lapse. Newfound freedom of the press sparked a rise in writing of all kinds, whether political or religious treatises, satires, or debates. The production of newspapers, journals, miscellanies (what we would call anthologies, with mostly contemporary content), and pamphlets increased greatly, and printed materials began to sell in unprecedented numbers. Short or serial publications were cheaper than novels or volumes of poetry and made information accessible to a much larger portion of the population. Defoe's *Robinson Crusoe* (1719), for example, was far more widely read after it was reprinted in the *Original London Post* in installments three times a week.

Gradually, a new reading public emerged. Though reading had always been a social activity, with literate members of a family reading the Bible or news to others, for example, in the eighteenth century reading and writing became activities that occurred in public spaces that were often designed solely for that purpose. With the rise of coffee houses—of which it was estimated London had roughly 3,000 by the end of the eighteenth century—British subjects could come together to read and debate. Libraries and literary clubs provided alternative spaces for such activities, and ones in which women were welcome (as they were not in coffee houses). Literary clubs such as the Scriblerus Club of Alexander Pope, John Gay, Jonathan Swift, Thomas Parnell, and John Arbuthnot or Dr. Johnson's Literary Club (both all male) originated in the eighteenth century. Many of these groups, such as that gathered informally around Samuel Richardson, were of mixed company or made up predominantly of women, such as the bluestocking society organized by Elizabeth Montagu. (Though this society included men, the term "bluestocking" soon came to be a derisive term for a bookish woman.) During the period, people frequently read aloud, and many guides were published to instruct people in the best practices of reading to others. The anxiety that Frances Burney describes in her journal at being asked to read to Queen Charlotte demonstrates the importance placed on this new art.

With new print technology and the development of the newspaper, as well as the new popularity of the essay as a literary form and the new social space of the city (where the majority of the reading public was located) came the rise of the periodical—of which by far the most influential was Richard Steele's *The Tatler* and his and Joseph Addison's *The Spectator*. These periodicals organized themselves around the coffee-house culture and embraced the conversation and public debate that they fostered. *The Spectator* (1711–14) advertised itself as being organized around the meetings of a fictitious club, the Spectator Club, which claimed to comprise a country gentleman, a London merchant, a retired soldier, a clergyman, a lawyer, and a gentleman born to a hereditary estate. Addison claimed that each copy of *The Spectator* was read by as many as twenty people as a result of coffee-shop circulation. With this large an audience, Addison greatly influenced the beliefs of his society and the ways in which that society saw itself. He popularized the theories of Newton and Locke, bringing them to the average gentleman (and also explicitly aiming to include strong female representation among his readership), and substantially influenced the aesthetic tastes of his day. Anthologies, miscellanies, and periodicals also provided a forum for women writers. Future bluestocking Elizabeth Carter worked for the *Gentleman's Magazine*, and there were numerous women who occasionally contributed to such magazines. Several specifically female periodicals were also published, such as *The Female Tatler*, Eliza Haywood's *The Female Spectator*, and Charlotte Lennox's *The Lady's Museum*. These offered a public space for women writers, editors, and critics.

As a result of these changes in print culture, the individual reader had a sense of him or herself as part of a larger reading community in which debate was freely engaged, and conversation between various readers and writers was a central part of most publications. Writers frequently responded to, continued, or revised one another's work. Collaborative work became popular, and frequently arose out of literary groups. Meanwhile, booksellers produced anthologies of both poems and prose, such as Dodsley's *Collection of Poems* (1748–58).

During this period criticism came into its own as a separate genre. Though writers had always commented on and responded to one another's work, they often did so more privately. In manuscript culture, for example, texts would be annotated with marginal comments arguing with, supporting, or even summarizing an author's points. Thomas More's *Utopia* contains printed marginal notes of this sort, probably written by his friend and supporter Erasmus. With the decline of manuscript circulation, this sort of private literary conversation became public, separate works of criticism became more common, and Dryden included critical introductions in his own work. With this genre of writing about literature and about authors themselves, some literary personalities approached the status of celebrities. Samuel Johnson, for example, observed to Boswell a few years before his death, "I believe there is hardly a day in which there is not something about me in the newspapers."

All these developments in print culture marked a dramatic change from the previous century, when publishing one's own work had been seen as "vulgar"; it had been thought that the lofty aims of art or high-culture conversation transcended material concerns such as money or a desire for fame. Some seventeenth-century authors had circulated their works in manuscript for years (even if after that they took steps to publish them), and many works were not published at all during an author's lifetime. In the eighteenth century some authors still continued the practice of publishing anonymously, particularly in the first half of the century, even if their identity was commonly known. Samuel Johnson, a bookseller's son who famously declared, "No man but a blockhead ever wrote, except for money," did not sign his name on any of his early work.

Because writers often played with the new print culture, using various means to disguise their authorship, the question of attribution can be a difficult one for scholars of the eighteenth century. Readers at the time generally assumed they could solve the mysteries of authorship, but they were frequently incorrect. Authors carefully avoided publishing any autobiographical or blatantly self-promotional material. Letters were occasionally saved and prepared for post-humous publication by their authors, but in 1739 Pope startled his peers by becoming one of the first literary figures to oversee the publication of his own letters. Pope avoided much of the scandal that this would ordinarily have caused through employing intricate subterfuge. Throughout his career he had an antagonistic relationship with the notoriously immoral publisher Edmund Curll, who frequently attacked Pope in print and published pirated copies of his works and those of his friends, such as Jonathan Swift, John Gay, and Lady Mary Wortley Montagu. Pope arranged for some of his correspondence to fall into Curll's hands, and when the publisher printed this supposedly pirated edition, Pope was justified in releasing the official edition of his letters—an edition that he had significantly doctored (while pretending candor and sincerity) to present himself in a more favorable light.

While it became increasingly socially acceptable for people of high rank to publish their writing, advances in print technology and changes in the publishing industry also made it possible for men and women from various backgrounds to earn a living through writing. Before the eighteenth century, those who wished to support themselves by writing would have had to find themselves a rich aristocratic patron who would support them, and to whom they would dedicate their works. During the Restoration, Aphra Behn and John Dryden also supported themselves by writing for the stage, and in the eighteenth century Alexander Pope was the first to earn a living by subscription writing. His success marked a change in the writing and publishing industries. With subscription printing, all subscribers would make financial contributions in exchange for having their names appear on a page inside the work, just as the patron's name would have previously; in this way, a system of what Terry Eagleton refers to as "collective patronage" came into effect. By contributing money up front, subscribers helped defray the initial cost of printing. An author's friends often formed the bulk of subscribers, though many others might become subscribers either out of something akin to charity or for the prestige that came with illustrious publications. Dryden's *The Works of Virgil* (1697), which set the standard for the Latin translations that were highly esteemed and successful during this century, was one of the first works by an English poet to be financed in this manner, though in the seventeenth century much legal, scientific, and theological publishing was done in this way. Publishers (who usually doubled as and were known as new booksellers) also formed "congers," or partnerships, to share the costs of elaborate or expensive new works and of existing copyrights (because the copyright of works by dead authors could be sold on from one publisher to another).

The concept of copyright as we know it today first took shape in the early eighteenth century. In England from the sixteenth century onwards, the rights acquired by stationers or printers upon securing from the Stationers' Company a license to print books had been generally assumed to be property rights, with the understanding being that, as with other sorts of property, ownership was ongoing; English practice severely restricted the reproduction of literary works other than by their "owner." No formal copyright protection existed in English law, however, and from time to time editions would find their way into the English market from Scotland or Ireland (where intellectual property was less restricted). English publishers began to agitate to have perpetual "copy right" formalized in law, and the British Parliament eventually decided (in the 1709 Statute of Anne) to recognize and protect copyright. But rather than declaring copyright to be a property right held in perpetuity, Parliament restricted it to 14 years from publication (renewable in certain circumstances for a further 14 years)—after which anyone could publish competing editions of a work. Remarkably, publishers who had "owned" popular works refused to concede, and managed to persuade a succession of judges that the Statute of Anne had improperly authorized the uncompensated confiscation of private property. In

defiance of what was seemingly set out in law, they succeeded for another 65 years in maintaining control over what we would now term "works in the public domain." Ironically, then, the Statute of Anne ushered in what William St. Clair has termed an "age of high monopoly" in the book trade. Together with the ending of official state censorship in 1695 and the gradual withdrawal of some other controls on the content of printed matter in the first half of the eighteenth century, the secure conditions under which British publishers operated fostered the production of large, beautifully produced volumes—and something of a golden era for the spread of Enlightenment culture. But the same conditions that favored the publication of expensive works of history and philosophy with a limited market slowed the spread of popular literature in book form—and the growth of a reading public. It was not until a 1774 legal case finally brought an end to the near-monopoly conditions that books started to become smaller and cheaper. That in turn led to a huge surge in reading across all social classes. In 1791, bookseller James Lackington described the degree to which things had changed: "According to the best estimation I have been able to make, I suppose that more than four times the number of books are sold now than were sold twenty years since.... In short, all ranks and degrees now READ."

An explosive growth in periodicals and newspapers, however, began much earlier. And with it came changes in the community of writers. A new term, "Grub Street," was used to describe the multitude of freelance writers who contributed for pay to the popular press. Many of these writers had little education, worked for meager wages, and lived in rundown apartments on London's Grub Street. With this profusion of "hack" writers (one of whom was Samuel Johnson in his early career), many feared that literature was becoming mired in trivial, everyday concerns. Alexander Pope was without a doubt the writer who most viciously satirized hack writers; his satirical masterpiece *The Dunciad* (1742) depicted a kingdom of dunces that included nearly every minor writer or publisher with whose work Pope had found fault.

Eighteenth-century theories of aesthetics sought to define what should be the lofty aims of true art (in order to separate the "true" art from the masses of popular writing), and often advocated avoiding the "low" details of the surrounding everyday world. Early in the eighteenth century John Gay wrote poetry of the tradespeople and messengers in the streets of London, with the often dirty or pungent details of their business. Later, in his essay on the theater, Oliver Goldsmith argued that the single word "low" as a term of contempt had made comedy virtually impossible. When he introduced bailiffs into a tea-party of his hero and heroine in *The Good-Natured Man* the audience was outraged, rather as if he had personally introduced them to actual bailiffs. Not only were certain aspects of satire out of bounds, but poets also felt that general principles, abstract propositions, or sensitive feelings were more worthy of their art than the material world. The empiricism of Locke and Hume shaped aesthetic theories according to which the artist's role was to embody sensory messages (through which individuals receive information about the outside world) in the imagery of his or her work. According to Locke, the mind passively receives impressions through our senses from external objects, and then combines these received simple ideas into complex ideas. Edmund Burke, in his *Enquiry into the Origin of Our Ideas of the Sublime and the Beautiful* (1757), follows Locke in asserting that the senses are the origin of all our ideas and pleasures. The reader experiences the work as a series of sensations, and its value lies in the emotional effect it produces and the way in which the artist produces this effect. In his treatise, Burke forms a distinction between the sublime and the beautiful—either of which, he maintains, may be the aim of a literary work. Our emotional response to something beautiful is a positive pleasure, or a social pleasure. Ideas that excite terror, on the other hand, and give us impressions of pain and danger, are sources of the sublime. We are impressed and astonished without being troubled by receiving ideas of pain and danger when we are in no actual danger ourselves, and thus we derive delight as a result of our desire for self-preservation.

Theories such as Burke's endeavored to link principles of aesthetics to those of morality and psychology. Such was also the case with the influential aesthetic theories of Henry Home, Lord Kames. For

Thomas Hickey, *Edmund Burke and Charles James Fox* (c. 1775). A friend in early life of Burke (who is best remembered for his later, conservative views), Fox went on to become a leader in Whig politics in the late eighteenth and early nineteenth centuries.

Kames, what we find beautiful in works of art is what improves us morally; for example, tragedy appeals to us in large part because it develops our sympathy for others. It is the nature of fine arts, Kames says in his *Elements of Criticism* (1762), to raise pleasurable emotions. Kames also expanded the definition of the fine arts to include practices not formerly considered, such as gardening (that is, landscape gardening or large-scale garden design, an artistic pursuit that flourished in the eighteenth century). According to Kames, the characteristics of gardens, such as their (loosely) regulated patterns, their color, and their utility, can raise pleasurable emotions such as gaiety, melancholy, surprise, wonder, or a sense of grandeur.

Increasingly as the eighteenth century progressed, those who valued the sublime in art sought the work of a wide variety of ancient societies as models. Alongside the well-established admiration for the complex social organization of ancient Greece and Rome, critics and

Paul Sandby, *Dolbadarn Castle and Llanberris Lake*, c. 1770. In the second half of the eighteenth century interest in travel to the more remote and wild regions of Britain (notably the Lake District, North Wales, and the Highlands of Scotland) greatly increased; Thomas Pennant's *Tour in Scotland* (1772), for example, went through five editions before 1790. Sandby's painting shows the ruins of a thirteenth-century castle set among craggy peaks in North Wales, viewed by a touring party.

artists began to celebrate the natural genius of what they saw as primitive and uneducated writers from uncivilized ages. These writers were seen as having created through spontaneous impulse, unimpeded by the conventions of civilization. Influential critics such as Sir William Temple also admired "exotic" cultures such as those of China and Peru. The Goths became another important model, as did the Celts and the Druids, and interest in medieval English literature increased greatly; the works of Chaucer found renewed popularity, and Alfred the Great became an object of admiration. It was during the eighteenth century that a field of genuine medieval scholarship arose, though romantic medievalism was also popular among poets; Thomas Gray was among the prominent poets who looked to medieval literature for inspiration. William Collins, for his part, purported to draw from ancient Persian writing in his *Persian Eclogues* (1742). All things Oriental exploded into fashion in the eighteenth century; the Orient became, in the minds of many English people, a place that embodied all the characteristics found lacking in British society. This led to admiration for the Orient as

an ideal, uncorrupted place of wealth and leisure, but it did not provide the average reader with any understanding of the complex realities of these foreign cultures. Sir William Temple garnered much critical interest when he published an old Icelandic fragment, and Scottish poet James Macpherson captured public attention when he claimed to have discovered and translated primitive epics from the Scottish Highlands written about the legendary hero Ossian. Though *Ossian* was later discovered to have been almost entirely composed by Macpherson himself on the slenderest dependence on traditional ballads, the impact the work had upon the reading public testified to the high demand for works colored with the romantic appeal of antiquity.

POETRY

While many writers turned to the exotic or primitive as a source of inspiration or a means of indicating special knowledge (which would distinguish them from the masses of hack writers), there was in general a continued emphasis on Greek and Roman cultures as representing the origins of true art and literature. In the early part of the eighteenth century in particular, a knowledge of Greek and Latin languages and literature was seen as prerequisite for anyone who attempted to write in English. Allusions to Homer and Roman poets Horace, Virgil, Juvenal, and Ovid occur throughout the works of poets such as Dryden, Pope, and Swift, who saw themselves as the eighteenth-century disciples of these venerated ancient poets. In fact, because of the similarities between the creative and political climates of the early eighteenth century and those of ancient Rome during the reign of Augustus Caesar, the first few decades of the century are often referred to as the "Augustan Age." In the political climate that these poets saw as relatively stable, in comparison to the turmoil of the mid-seventeenth century following the Restoration, poetry was able to flourish—just as during the reign of Augustus Caesar, the first Roman emperor, patrons in this period of peace following Rome's civil war had increasingly used their wealth and leisure to enjoy and support the arts. In the Restoration and early eighteenth century, many leading literary figures tried their hands

Thomas Gainsborough, *Robert Andrews and his Wife, Frances* (c. 1748–49). Gainsborough is now regarded as one of the great artists of rural life in the eighteenth century. During his lifetime (1727–88) his portraits were far more in demand than were his landscapes of rural life; the latter came to be far more appreciated after his death. This canvas, which combines the two genres, is unfinished; a small area remains blank on Mrs. Andrews's lap.

at translations of the ancient poets. Dryden was the first writer of the period to tackle this sort of work on a large scale, producing English versions of the works of Virgil, Juvenal, and parts of Horace and Homer. Pope, as an aspiring poet, translated Homer's *Iliad* and *Odyssey*, and later produced imitations or freely updated adaptations of many poems by Horace. Poets combined these influences with important ones from the English tradition, including Chaucer, Shakespeare, Spenser, and Milton. (Because they attempted to fuse new elements with the classical, Pope, Dryden, and others were often referred to as "neoclassical" writers.)

Like the ancients, these neoclassical poets sought to convey truths about the world around them by investigating general aspects of human character or striking aspects of the natural realm. In contrast to earlier poets such as Donne and Milton, eighteenth-century poets sought a simplicity of language with

which to convey pleasurable images of nature and the sublime to their readers. Nevertheless, the classical influence often resulted in Latinate syntax and diction, and highly allusive content. Eighteenth-century poetry is also highly visual, frequently relying on detailed descriptions and often personifying abstract aspects of human nature or elements of the physical world.

As in classical Rome, so in Restoration and eighteenth-century Britain, satire was a prominent poetic form and the most common path used by poets to comment on the particulars of their daily lives. Eighteenth-century poets looked back to Juvenal and Horace, the great classical satirists, and imitations of their models provided a forum for sharp yet elegantly styled attacks on the government. Despite this reliance on the ancients, poetry was intimately connected to current political and social events, and wielded a good deal of power. The more witty and technically masterful the poem, the more damaging the satire, and those who perfected the mode could ruin entire careers and ministries. Political satire in both poetry and prose could also cause trouble for writers in the politically charged climate in the late seventeenth and early eighteenth centuries. If well-written, however, such work often had the effect of silencing enemies. When Daniel Defoe was placed in the pillory after pleading guilty to charges of libel for his 1703 *The Shortest Way with the Dissenters* (a pamphlet parodying extremist High Churchman and facetiously advocating the mass torture of Dissenters), he turned the event to his advantage with his "Hymn to the Pillory," denouncing those who sentenced him. The government so admired his skill in doing this that the ministry hired him to publish a newspaper (the *Review*) that would report the news from a point of view that was sympathetic to the government. Another satirical art form that developed in the eighteenth century in conjunction with poetic satire was the political cartoon or caricature. Until the eighteenth and early nineteenth centuries cartoons were usually published anonymously to protect their authors from charges of libel. Nevertheless, the cartoon became a popular and often savage form of propaganda and of satire.

Poetic satire began as a means of political commentary, but it soon branched out to include almost all aspects of public life, and on occasion the minutiae of private life as well. Samuel Garth's *The Dispensary* (1699), for example, used the mock epic form to satirize the war between doctors and apothecaries over who would dispense medicine. Mock epic was a popular form for such ventures; its contrast between elevated style and mundane content accentuates the frivolity of whatever petty disputes or political intrigues are described. Pope's *The Rape of the Lock* (1712) is probably the most celebrated example of such a genre. Epic conventions such as the description of the battle scene become ridiculous when used to treat trivialities such as the theft of a piece of hair. By using the heroic couplet, writers could pair elevated and common subject matter in one rhyme. In these types of satire, poets had a very clear sense of their audience, which was often very small (in the case of *The Rape of the Lock*, the original audience was only two families, though in print the poem sold extremely well), and spoke directly to it.

(This close relationship between writer and audience can cause difficulty for the contemporary reader who cannot be familiar with the highly specific references to people, events, and places of eighteenth-century London.)

After Pope, who stretched the heroic couplet in new directions, using it with unprecedented virtuosity, the form became less common. Blank verse, the form of James Thomson's *The Seasons* (1727) and William Cowper's *The Task* (1785), was an increasingly popular form that gave writers greater flexibility while still providing a set structure. More "common" poetic forms such as the ballad, hymn, and various stanzaic forms also gained in popularity as the century progressed.

While the neoclassical poets of the early part of the eighteenth century felt that "low" details of common life had little place in poetry (except in the realm of satire), in the later part of the century realism and attention to detail manifested themselves as well in various works, usually set outside the London scene. Wordsworth, in his 1800 preface to *Lyrical Ballads*, expressed concern that the novel had taken and sensationalized subjects and language that poetry needed to reclaim. He disliked the classical and what he felt to be the artificial tone of the important body of eighteenth-century poetry dealing with rural life and the world of work. These poems that dealt with the details of common life often took the form of the georgic, a genre named after Virgil's *Georgics*, which Addison defined as "some part of the science of husbandry [i.e., farming] put into a pleasing dress, and set off with all the beauties and embellishments of poetry." Unlike the pastoral, the most common type of poem in the sixteenth and seventeenth centuries dealing with nature, the georgic did not idealize nature or rural life, and was not highly stylized. Instead, georgics were digressive, often didactic, and unusually detailed, typically taking one very specific aspect of rustic life as a topic. William Somerville's *The Chase* (1735) described hunting, fishing, and sports, while Christopher Smart's *The Hop Garden* (1752) and James Grainger's *The Sugar Cane* (1764)—set in the West Indies—dealt with specificities of agriculture. John Dyer's *The Fleece* (1757) was the first such poem to include scenes in an industrial setting, linking traditional husbandry with the new commercialism. Often georgics used burlesque or subtle mockery in their treatment of their subjects, as in John Gay's *Wine* (1708), *Rural Sports* (1713), and *The Shepherd's Week* (1714). James Thomson's *The Seasons* (1730, following the individual appearances of the four poems, "Spring," "Summer," "Autumn," and "Winter," which, combined, make up the larger work), the most famous work to come out of this tradition, remained popular throughout this period and indeed through the nineteenth century.

The authors of many of these poems lacked first-hand experience of rural labor, but rural poets also began to find their own voice in this period. Appearing in the same year as *The Seasons* was *The Thresher's Labour*, a poem by Stephen Duck, a farm laborer taken up by patrons, which was commissioned as a poem "on his own labors." In contrast to Thomson's poem, *The Thresher's Labour* presents a harsher view of the agricultural cycle as a relentless master. Another poet writing of her own experience was Mary Collier; Collier's *The Woman's Labour* (1739)—written, without patrons, in response to Duck's poem—objected to his depiction of women workers as less important to rural labor than men.

George Stubbs, *Haymakers*, 1785. Stubbs (1724–1806), is known primarily for his equestrian pictures—scenes of hunting and horseracing. He was also active in other genres of painting, however; in the 1780s he began to concentrate largely on portrayals of daily life in rural England.

Some poets writing about the countryside directly challenged the vision of rural happiness so common in pastoral poetry. George Crabbe's *The Village* (1783) is one such poem. With its damning portraits of the failure both of individuals and of institutions to alleviate the suffering of the poor, and its diagnosis of social evils, it brought heightened realism to the genre. Charles Churchill found a similar parody of the pastoral helpful for political satire; his satirical portrait of Scotland, *The Prophecy of Famine: A Scots Pastoral* (1763), parodies the conventions of the pastoral, conveying Churchill's political concerns against a backdrop of waste and disease.

Close observation of nature could sometimes play a part in the introspective poetry of meditation, as in some work by Anne Finch, Countess of Winchilsea. Clergyman Thomas Parnell favored religious subject matter in his "Meditating on the Wounds of Christ" (1722), "On Divine Love" (1722), and "Hymn to Contentment" (1714). These poems, examining one aspect of human nature, often take the form of the hymn or ode. (William Collins's *Odes on Several Descriptive and Allegorical Subjects* [1746], which includes "Ode to Pity" and "Ode to Fear," is an important example.) A school of so-called graveyard poets might claim particular poems by several of these poets, though its leading representatives are Robert Blair's *The Grave* (1743) and Edward Young's *Night Thoughts* (1742–46). The meditative verse of these poets is suffused with melancholy and often features solitary, brooding figures who wander at night, a type largely inspired by Milton's *Il Penseroso* (1645). Gray's *Elegy Written in a Country Churchyard* (1751), which also employs aspects of this genre, features an isolated poet meditating on the generalities of life and death and lamenting the loss of poetic power and authority. Poetry's loss of force in contemporary society was a common complaint among these poets, and their works evince a lyrical nostalgia for the days when the poet's rich language and imagination held sway. Many were concerned that the true art of poetry would be lost without the flights of imagination and fantastical language they saw as the markers of poetry.

THEATER

Following the restoration of the monarchy, English theater showed the influence of the French productions that the court had enjoyed while in exile. William Wycherley and Sir George Etherege composed comedies of wit like those of Molière, but with a narrow focus on the follies of a small class of people, the fashionable wits and beaux who were the theater's primary audience. They treated the particulars of the social life of the time, and satirized the more ridiculous and self-serving aspects of upper-class behavior; as in Molière's work, the humor of these plays relies on exaggeration and a highly stylized view of life, in which comic repartee and artful contrivance dominate. Referred to as "comedies of manners" or "social comedies," these plays often feature a witty, unprincipled, yet charismatic and charming libertine. The libertine-hero is ambivalently presented, generally an object of unmixed admiration to his own male circle and the available young women in the play, though more or less open to criticism from the audience. In Etherege's *The Man of Mode* (1676) the rake-hero gets off scot-free, rewarded for his heartless infidelities to other women with the hand of the witty and virginal heroine; Behn's rake-hero in *The Rover* (1677) is similarly rewarded, though he is not a cruel character and may be seen as having been (twice) genuinely in love in the course of the action. (After this play Behn arranged the offstage death of her witty heroine, in order to free the hero for fresh adventures in a sequel.) In Wycherley's *The Country Wife* (1675) a tradesman who marries for love may appear colorless beside the out-and-out rake whose continuing, obsessive pursuit of women leaves him isolated from his peers. Etherege, Behn, and Wycherley belonged to the earlier generation of Restoration playwrights. In the next generation, Vanbrugh (e.g., in *The Relapse* [1696]) and Congreve (e.g., in *The Way of the World* [1700]) opened the possibility of a charismatic rake not only marrying for love but attempting fidelity afterwards. These comedies are highly physical, with duels, disguises, and highly erotic scenes; their language is full of wordplay and sexual innuendo.

In Restoration theater women were hired for the first time to play the female parts. Their presence on stage (and the wide popularity that many of them achieved through the audience's knowledge or supposed knowledge about their private lives—as with Nell Gwynn, who eventually left the stage to become Charles II's mistress) incited playwrights to create provocative roles for them. The degree to which coarse or sexually suggestive language and behavior was being depicted on the stage in the late seventeenth century became a particular focus of complaint, and the portrayal of women was the most common source of outrage. Jeremy Collier's view was that

> Obscenity in any company is a rustic, uncreditable talent, but among women 'tis particularly rude. Such talk would be very affrontive in conversation and not endured by any lady of reputation. Whence then comes it to pass that those liberties which disoblige so much in conversation should entertain upon the stage? Do women leave all the regards to decency and conscience behind them when they come to the playhouse? In this respect the stage is faulty to a scandalous degree of nauseousness and aggravation.

Women were not only present on the stage; they were also writing plays for the stage for the first time in history. (Some women had written closet dramas before this, but none had been performed in a public theater.) Aphra Behn was one of the most successful dramatists of the age; her career began with *The Forced Marriage* (1670), a tragi-comedy about sexual relations and power struggles between the sexes. Behn had been preceded by a year by Frances Boothby's *Marcela* (1669). Delarivier Manley, Mary Pix, and Catharine Trotter soon followed in her footsteps, though all four women were considered morally suspect for embracing such an inherently public career. Susanna Centlivre, a leading professional playwright of the next generation, did not attract the censure her predecessors had. Her many published plays include the highly successful *The Busy Body* (1709).

Most of these women wrote more frequently in the genre of sophisticated farcical comedy than in the highly stylized tragedies that were popular at the time (Centlivre's one tragedy, *The Cruel Gift*, was written in collaboration with Nicholas Rowe). Set in remote times and places with spectacular scenes and effects, such tragedies tended to center on warrior/lovers torn between conflicting obligations in agonizing dilemmas. In this sort of heroic tragedy, the heroic couplet (written in iambic pentameter), championed by Dryden, was the meter of choice. While the heroic-couplet tragedy swiftly grew to enormous popularity, its downfall was just as sudden. George Villiers's famous burlesque *The Rehearsal* (1671), written in parody of Dryden and of the genre of heroic tragedy in general, was said to have helped hasten its end. From this point on, blank-verse tragedies, such as Thomas Otway's *Venice Preserved* (1682), gradually became more popular. In the theater, as in poetry, the eighteenth-century interest in (and admiration for) classical culture was prominent; the most popular tragedy of the time was Joseph Addison's *Cato* (1713). Adaptations and imitations of Shakespearean dramas were also common; Dryden's *All for Love* (1678), a revision of Shakespeare's *Antony and Cleopatra*, was the most successful of such adaptations in the period. The "she-tragedy," which detailed the dramatic fall of a heroine, was a popular new form of tragedy that appealed to the audience's sense of pity, especially for helpless women. These she-tragedies were removed from the current political and social scene, but featured historical settings that were often more precise or more recent than those of the heroic drama.

In the eighteenth century a new form of theatrical entertainment, the opera, came to England from Italy and became both a popular form of entertainment and a source of much derision. Critics could not comprehend the audience's desire to forego "legitimate" theater for entertainment featuring songs in languages they did not understand. In a *Spectator* article on the subject, Addison derisively declares that these operas seem to be written according to a rule "that nothing is capable of being well set to music that is not nonsense." With John Gay's *The Beggar's Opera* (1728), however, a new genre of opera was born—the ballad opera, to which the modern musical can trace its roots. Written in mockery of the rise of Italian opera in England, Gay's work derives its music from ballads and folk-songs. *The Beggar's Opera* became an instant success, inspiring numerous imitations and parodies, as well as a line of merchandise that included playing cards, fans, plates, and paintings.

One effect of Gay's play was to lessen the popularity of the Italian opera; another was to incur the displeasure of minister Robert Walpole: *The Beggar's Opera* was taken as a satire on the Prime Minister (though Gay never admitted to any such intention). Nevertheless, it was one of many real or supposed theatrical attacks on Walpole during his time in office. Henry Fielding's

Pasqual (1736) was one of a series of works with which he targeted Walpole. Perceiving these satires as a threat to the authority of his ministry, Walpole sought to bring them to an end. He pushed through the Theatrical Licensing Act of 1737, the result of which was that the Lord Chamberlain had to approve plays before they could be produced. The political threat posed by the theater was curbed, and Walpole's control over his reputation was asserted.

William Hogarth, *The Laughing Audience* (1733). This etching depicts the audience at a theatrical performance. The three figures in the front are seated in the orchestra. Behind them (and separated by a spiked partition), commoners in the pit laugh uproariously—with the exception of one being jostled by an orange seller. One gentleman in the balcony has eyes only for a competing orange seller, while the interests of another are also engaged elsewhere.

Revivals of earlier plays, which had always been staples of the stage, helped to take the place of new plays. Those new plays that were produced tended to replace political with domestic concerns and biting wit with sentimentality and melodrama; theatrical productions were required to be much more respectful of conventional views, and playwrights had to be acutely aware of the public temper at any given time. The taste for decorum, overt moralizing, and warm human sentiments evident in the new sentimental comedies offered opportunities for female playwrights, who were seen as having authority in these emotional, domestic realms. Elizabeth Griffith and Frances Sheridan—and Elizabeth Inchbald and Joanna Baillie a few decades later—could argue for their inherent expertise in the matters depicted in their plays. Following a lengthy vogue for sentimental comedy in the mid-eighteenth century, new "laughing" comedies such as Oliver Goldsmith's *She Stoops to Conquer* (1773), Richard Brinsley Sheridan's *The School for Scandal* (1778), and Hannah Cowley's *The Belle's Stratagem* (1780) sought to reclaim comedy for satire and fun, though at least the threat of tears was still likely to accompany the laughter, and protagonists were lauded for their private, emotional virtue as well as teased about faults or follies.

The Novel

With the rise of the reading public, the decline of literary patronage, and the increasing power and range of the influence of "booksellers," literature for the first time became a market commodity. As Daniel Defoe put it, writing "is become a very considerable branch of the English Commerce. The booksellers are the master manufacturers or employers. The several writers, authors, copiers, sub-writers, and all other operators with pen and ink are the workmen employed by the said master manufacturers." Literature was not only more popular and more widely disseminated, it was also to an unprecedented degree subject to economic laws, in which supply was determined by popular demand.

The growth and diversification of the reading public are two frequently cited reasons for the sudden rise of the popular form of the novel. As the century progressed, the influence of an educated elite who maintained an interest in (and knowledge of) classical letters declined; more and more, reading became a leisure activity undertaken for pleasure. Many of the new readers were females from well-off families. These readers sought increasingly realistic (rather than romantic-fantastical), detailed works that spoke to their own lives and the world around them. The periodical essay, in which the minute details of ordinary lives were described and analyzed, was instrumental in creating tastes to which the novel then catered. Articles gave practical information about domestic and public life and sought to improve the minds and morals of their readers while simultaneously providing entertainment. Novels also represented the new values and lifestyles of eighteenth-century Britain, in which older, rural, land-centered lifestyles were being replaced. The vast majority of novels were either entirely set in London or involved travel to that city. Defoe's *The Fortunes and Misfortunes of Moll Flanders* (1722) features a woman in London underground society without a family, education, or social position. It describes the specifics of the London criminal world as well as the potential for rehabilitation. When Moll is transported to the New World as a convicted felon (where, under the "Transportation Act" of 1718, regular shiploads of criminals were sent), she becomes both rich and penitent. Frances Burney's novel *Evelina, or the History of a Young Lady's Entrance into the World* (1778), like some of the articles in Eliza Haywood's *The Female Tatler*, opened up the intimate details of a female world to the public eye, giving male readers a glimpse of what it meant to be female and vulnerable.

The modern conception of "realism," often considered the novel's most defining characteristic, was not explicitly formulated as an aesthetic principle until the nineteenth and twentieth centuries, but owes its origin to the ideas of Descartes and Locke, who worked to advance the theory that truth can be discovered through the individual's senses. This new emphasis on individual experience and perception of reality lies at the heart of the eighteenth-century novel. Previous forms (such as the epic or pastoral elegy) demanded fidelity to certain set rules of the genre, and the author's skill was judged by his or her ability to adhere to accepted traditional models. In contrast, the primary aim of novels was the depiction of individual experience. In order to give primacy to an individual perception of reality, authors did not rely on allusions to or inspiration from classical sources, but sought their material in the actual, familiar world of daily experience. Daniel Defoe and Samuel Richardson were notable in that they did not take their plots from mythology, history, or pre-existing legend or literature.

The rise of the epistolary form is another important thread in the development of the novel. Aphra Behn pioneered epistolary fiction in the Restoration; her *Love Letters between a Nobleman and his Sister* (meaning, in this case, sister-in-law) (1684–87), is an epistolary novel that also provides a subjective account of contemporary political events. (The form was also used by Mary Davys in a work published in 1725, but the epistolary novel did not gain wide popularity as a genre until well into the eighteenth century.) The century's countless newspapers generally had correspondents who wrote in from their various locations, summarizing local events, and publishers of periodicals often found letters—fictitious or otherwise—to be a popular method of creating a sense of sociability and of literary conversation. Late seventeenth-century writers had begun to explore various themes and concerns through collections of fictitious letters; Margaret Cavendish's *Sociable Letters* (1664), for example, imagines the written communication of two women living a short distance from one another, mixing discursive, serious letters (frequently critiquing marriage) with more comic, anecdotal letters. Travel narratives too began frequently to be cast as a series of letters from the traveler to those at home, describing his or her experiences. Richardson's first novel, *Pamela* (1740), developed out of a small book of sample letters Richardson wrote in order to educate his readers in the art of letter-writing; eventually he reworked the "sample" and incorporated it into a much larger prose narrative.

Behn's *Oroonoko* (1688) shows the influence of various forms of non-fiction on the development of the novel. Part novel or romance, part history, and part travel narrative, of novella length, it includes an extended description of natives and slaves in Africa and Guiana, economic details of colonial trade, and various of Behn's observations from the time she spent in Surinam in 1663 and 1664. As such works suggest, the development of the novel as a popular genre was a many-faceted process. The term "novel" can be misleading for the contemporary reader; by thinking of the various long prose narratives of the eighteenth century as novels, we unify them into one genre in a way that contemporary readers did not. The use of the term "novel," which identifies the genre only by its newness, was not in common use until the end of the seventeenth century, and when it was used, it typically denoted a short, romantic tale. (Its first use was to describe the various short tales within Boccaccio's fifteenth-century *Decameron*.) In the eighteenth century a variety of other names as well were given to what we now call novels, including "romance," "history," "adventure," "memoir," and "tale." The current conception of the novel—as a long prose fiction presenting more or less realistic characters—did not solidify until the time of Jane Austen and Sir Walter Scott. Aphra Behn, Daniel Defoe, and Samuel Richardson—each of whom has been named as the "founder" of the modern novel—each conceived of their fiction in very different terms, came to the novel from different writing backgrounds, and had different goals for their work. Samuel Richardson and Henry Fielding each significantly influenced the development of the novel, but these two men wrote in diametrically opposed styles and created works with what they saw as opposing aims. Richardson boasted that his epistolary mode allowed him to provide "familiar letters written as it were to the moment."

In response to Richardson's *Pamela; or, Virtue Rewarded* (1741), Fielding, one of the leading comic playwrights in England in the early part of the century, but at that point a writer who had not previously attempted prose fiction, wrote the anonymous *An Apology for the Life of Mrs. Shamela Andrews* (1741) to mock Richardson's style. Both *Shamela* and Eliza Haywood's *Anti-Pamela; or, Feigned Innocence Detected* (1741) question Richardson's representation of sexuality and class while mocking his style and the generic conventions he establishes for his novel. In contrast to Richardson's prurience and lack of humor, both works adopt a playful ironic tone that mockingly exposes

PAMELA:

OR,

VIRTUE Rewarded.

In a SERIES of

FAMILIAR LETTERS

FROM A

Beautiful Young DAMSEL,
To her PARENTS.

Now first Published

In order to cultivate the Principles of
VIRTUE and RELIGION in the Minds of
the YOUTH of BOTH SEXES.

A Narrative which has its Foundation in TRUTH
and NATURE; and at the same time that it agreeably entertains, by a Variety of *curious* and *affecting*
INCIDENTS, is intirely divested of all those Images,
which, in too many Pieces calculated for Amusement
only, tend to *inflame* the Minds they should *instruct.*

In Two VOLUMES.

VOL. I.

LONDON:

Printed for C. RIVINGTON, in *St. Paul's Church-
Yard*; and J. OSBORN, in *Pater-noster Row.*

MDCCXLI.

Title page, *Pamela; or Virtue Rewarded* (1741).

John Michael Wright, *Astraea Returns to Earth*, 1660. This prophecy of the Roman poet Virgil of a golden age ruled over by Astraea, virgin goddess of Justice, is alluded to in the painting. A cherub holds the image of the new monarch, Charles II, as Astraea returns to earth.

Jan Siberechts, *Landscape with Rainbow, Henley-on-Thames*, c. 1690. Siberechts came to London from Flanders around 1675, and played an influential part in the development of an English tradition of landscape art.

Edward Haytley, *View of the Temple Pond at Beachborough Manor*, 1744–46.

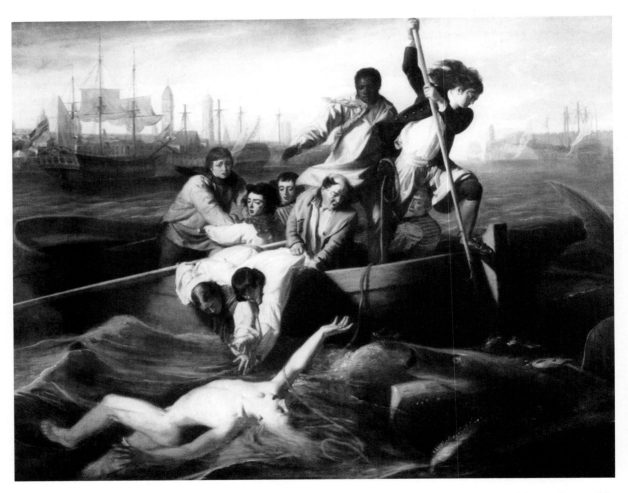

John Singleton Copley, *Brook Watson and the Shark*, 1778. Copley (1738–1814) and Benjamin West were the leading British historical artists of the second half of the eighteenth century. This painting depicts a 1749 incident in the West Indies. Watson, a 14-year-old British orphan, was attacked while swimming in Havana harbor; his shipmates came to the rescue and Watson lost a leg but survived. Copley, born and raised in the British colony of Massachusetts, moved to London in 1774 at the age of 28, and never returned to America.

Sir Joshua Reynolds, *Mrs. Susanna Hoare and Child*, 1763–64. The goldsmith Richard Hoare began banking out of his shop in Cheapside in 1672, and the Hoare family became established landed gentry in the eighteenth century. Hoare & Company still operates today as a private bank.

Joseph Wright of Derby, *Sir Brooke Boothby*, 1781. Boothby, sometimes described as epitomizing the "Man of Feeling," was a friend of Jean-Jacques Rousseau and was instrumental in making Rousseau's *Confessions* available in England. The word "Rousseau" appears on the spine of the book that Boothby holds in this portrait.

George Stubbs, *The Reapers*, 1785. This is one of two paired images; a detail of the other, *The Haymakers*, appears on the cover of this volume.

Angelica Kauffmann, *The Artist in the Character of Design Listening to the Inspiration of Poetry*, 1782. The Swiss-born Kauffmann moved to London in 1766, and established herself as a highly successful artist; she was a founding member of the Royal Academy of Arts.

William Hogarth, *Heads of Six of Hogarth's Servants*, c. 1750–55. For an artist to make his servants the subject of his art was highly unusual in the mid eighteenth century. The picture, which Hogarth hung in his studio, is a composite—the figures are painted from unrelated studies rather than posed together.

Joseph Wright of Derby, *An Experiment on a Bird in the Air Pump*, 1768. In the early 1660s, Royal Society member Robert Boyle used a pump like this one for several experiments involving air and air pressure; the most striking was his experiment examining the effects of air deprivation on animals. Boyle describes the experiment on a hen-sparrow:

> *When we put her into the receiver … she seemed to be dead within seven minutes … but upon the speedy turning of the key, the fresh air flowing in began slowly to revive her, so that after some pantings she opened her eyes and regained her feet, and in about ½ of an hour after, threatened to make an escape at the top of the glass, which had been unstoppered to let the fresh air upon her. But the receiver being closed the second time, she was killed with violent convulsions within five minutes….*

By the 1760s, the air deprivation experiment was a mainstay of traveling lecturers, who performed demonstrations in natural philosophy for the entertainment and education of the general public. Wright's painting depicts such an experiment and the varied reactions of its viewers.

Benjamin West, *The Death of General Wolfe*, 1770. In 1750, General James Wolfe led British troops to a decisive victory over the French forces at Quebec City, dying from battle wounds in the hour of his success. Reproduced again and again in prose, poetry, and painting, his story became a beloved popular legend. Of the many imaginings of the dramatic scene, West's was by far the most famous—it was, in fact, the most reproduced of any image in eighteenth-century England. The work depicts the moment at which the dying Wolfe, concerned only with the outcome of the battle, was informed that the English were winning; upon hearing this, he reportedly expressed his satisfaction, and died.

Anonymous, *Portrait of Dido Elizabeth Belle and Lady Elizabeth Murray*, c. 1777. From the collection of the Earl of Mansfield, Scone Palace, Perth, Scotland. In its portrayal of a black woman and a white woman as equals—or at least near equals—this double portrait is highly unusual for its time. On the left sits Dido Elizabeth Belle, the mixed-race daughter of British admiral John Lindsay and Maria Belle, an African slave. Almost immediately after her birth, Dido was sent to England to be raised by her great-uncle, Lord Chief Justice Mansfield. Growing up with her cousin, Lady Elizabeth Murray (on the right), Dido occupied an unconventional position in the Mansfield household, treated much better than a servant but not as well as Elizabeth (although, because Elizabeth was a legitimate heir and Dido was illegitimate, this unequal treatment might have occurred even if both had been white). Dido and Elizabeth were close companions and moved in the same social circles.

Lord Mansfield is well known for his influential decision on Somerset's Case (1772), a dispute in which the recaptured slave James Somersett, with the help of abolitionist activists, challenged the legality of slavery in England. Mansfield ruled in Somersett's favor; the language he uses limits the decision to the particular case, but many interpreted his verdict to mean that slavery was outlawed on English soil (although not in the colonies); the ruling thus had a considerable impact on behavior. Mansfield had great affection and admiration for his great-niece Dido, and it has been speculated that his relationship to her may have influenced his progressive ruling.

AN

APOLOGY

FOR THE

LIFE

OF

Mrs. SHAMELA ANDREWS.

In which, the many notorious FALSHOODS and
MISREPRSENTATIONS of a Book called

P A M E L A,

Are exposed and refuted; and all the matchless
ARTS of that young Politician, set in a true and
just Light.

Together with

A full Account of all that passed between her
and Parson *Arthur Williams*; whose Character
is represented in a manner something different
from what he bears in *PAMELA*. The
whole being exact Copies of authentick Papers
delivered to the Editor.

Necessary to be had in all FAMILIES.

By Mr. *CONNY KEYBER.*

LONDON:

Printed for A. DODD, at the *Peacock*, without *Temple-bar.*
M. DCC. XLI.

Title page, *An Apology for the Life of Mrs. Shamela Andrews* (1741).

Pamela's virtue as feigned. Fielding's *Joseph Andrews* (1742), written about a hero who turns out to be Pamela's brother, works in a similar fashion, using the picaresque, ironic, and anti-romantic style of Cervantes's *Don Quixote* as a model.

These works demonstrate the ways in which novels and the cultural discourse surrounding them were in dialogue with one another as the generic shape of the novel gradually began to solidify. From its outset the novel was often a remarkably self-conscious form, however, and even as the genre was taking shape some writers were keen to play with its nascent conventions. Laurence Sterne's *Tristram Shandy*, in particular, does this with typographical oddities, direct addresses by author to reader about his difficulties in writing, and chapters printed out of order. Its chronology moves backward as well as forward. The narrator plays with the language through puns and *double entendres*, and frequently interrupts himself for digressions so lengthy that he professes to have difficulty keeping track of his own story. In this novel the narrator's private reality takes control of both the content and the form of the novel. Charlotte Lennox's *The Female Quixote* (1752), another work influenced by Cervantes, comments on the interrelationships between romance, female desire and social position, and the novel. Her heroine is, like Don Quixote, a dreamer who treats her life as if it were a plot from one of the numerous chivalric romances she reads. Lennox's novel demonstrates the mistakes that can be made if one thinks of life as resembling a popular romance; it also highlights the differences between the emerging novel and a genre from which most novel writers sought to distance themselves—the popular romance.

Many works that were, at the time, written in reaction to the genre of the novel are now regarded as being novels themselves. Jonathan Swift distrusted the individualist psychology, adjustable morals, and the faith in class mobility and commercialism that the novel represented; his *Gulliver's Travels* (1726)—which is not a novel, but follows an earlier form of non-naturalistic prose fiction—in some respects, as in the middle-class ordinariness of its protagonist, forecasts the direction of the emergent novel, and in some respects reads like a burlesque of the form. Gulliver can be seen as a parody of the typical, middle-class fictional subject; while the authority of narratives by early novelists, particularly Defoe, relied on the assumed fitness of a merchant class or low-life narrator (such as Robinson Crusoe, Moll Flanders, or Colonel Jack) to record modern life, Swift employs a naive narrator to obliquely advance social criticisms. Later in the eighteenth century, Samuel Johnson, who observed that novels were written "chiefly to the young, the ignorant, and the idle," felt these readers in particular required moral instruction and not the false optimism of a happy-ever-after ending. His *Rasselas* (1759) reacts against the moral ambiguities of the novel by offering a strictly moral and elaborately inconclusive tale meant to educate his readers by forcing them to think.

Women made up an increasing percentage of the novel's new writers, and as they struggled for literary authority they influenced the development of various modes of fiction. Of these female writers, Eliza Haywood (whom Fielding used as the basis of a stage figure named "Mrs. Novel") was the most prolific producer of novel titles before the late eighteenth century. Her first novel, *Love in Excess* (1719), published in the same year as *Robinson Crusoe*, was one of only two works to rival it in popularity. Although her later novels are less erotically charged, Haywood's reputation remained colored by her early work; along with Delarivier Manley and Aphra Behn, she was known for bawdy, sensational novels whose plots foregrounded sexual intrigue. Manley was famous for publishing "secret histories," such as *The New Atlantis* (1709)—for which she was arrested—which detailed scandals about contemporary political figures, passed off as fiction. John Cleland's *Fanny Hill; or, Memoirs of a Woman of Pleasure* (1749) may be one of the most famous of numerous scandalous texts—many disseminated by notorious bookseller Edmund Curll—that celebrated libertine attitudes of sexual behavior. Haywood's *Fantomina* (1725) and *The History of Miss Betsy Thoughtless* (1751), though they featured far less in the line of seduction or rape, were to some people even more shocking, since it was female sexuality they foregrounded, rather than male.

The new taste for sentiment made itself felt in fiction as in poetry and the theater. The "sentimental" in fiction may mean stories designed to fill the reader with anguished pity, or stories glorifying the sentimental as morally worthy. Sarah Fielding's *The Adventures of David Simple* (1744) was, like Richardson's *Pamela*, designed to display the elevated, refined, humanitarian feelings of its central characters, while the still fairly heavy incidence of seduction, rape, and false accusation is performed by palpably evil characters, and the moral design of the fiction is obvious. When Fielding added her *Volume the Last* to *David Simple* in 1753, she produced a disturbing tear-jerker in which the good characters are routed and largely destroyed by the bad ones. Sarah Scott's *The History of Sir George Ellison* (1770) claimed to depict "the life of a man more ordinarily good"; while Sir George succeeds in materially reforming at least the small section of the world around him, the sentimental character is often seen in vain opposition to a cruel world to which he or she could not be reconciled. Henry Mackenzie's *The Man of Feeling* (1771), for example, shows a character of sentiment too sensitive for the world. This sentiment was considered edifying and instructive as well as touching; as Johnson told Boswell of Samuel Richardson, "You must read him for the sentiment." The ideal characteristics of both sentimental heroes and heroines were traditionally feminine ones, such as sensitivity, compassion, and private virtue. Some women writers led and some opposed the movement to establish the sentimental, sensitive, often victimized heroine as the ideal model of femininity, often using heroines of this type to engage with political issues. Novels such as Frances Sheridan's *Memoirs of Miss Sidney Bidulph* (1761), or Elizabeth Griffith's three novels about women in unhappy marriages, explore women's virtue and vice, their status in the home, and their use of domestic power within the larger social structure. Often these works also express concern about the double standard of sexual morality.

Courtship novels were also a convenient mode for examining sentiment, sensibility, gender roles, and behavior. Frances Burney's *Cecilia* (1782), Elizabeth Inchbald's *A Simple Story* (1791), and Charlotte Smith's *Emmeline, the Orphan of the Castle* (1788) and *Celestina* (1791) all use the tale of a young girl's emergence into social life and the rituals of courtship to convey opinions on manners, fashions, morals, and changing sexual and national politics. An element of subversion is often built into the courtship genre, as the heroine looks critically upon the process she is undergoing. Jane Austen, who was an avid reader of Charlotte Smith's work, was strongly influenced by Smith's *Emmeline* when she wrote her *Sense and Sensibility* (1811); that novel marks a turn away from the cult of sensibility (upon which *Emmeline* relies) and toward a reassertion of rationalism.

Just as some poets began to feel that realism had robbed their art of its power and creativity, some novelists came to feel the novel's strict fidelity to realistic narrative to be stifling. Horace Walpole, frustrated with the confines of realism and rationalism, attempted in his *Castle of Otranto* (1764) to combine the realism of the novel's psychological representation with the imaginative resources of old romance, in which the supernatural and marvelous were allowed full play. Written as a trifle and in a spirit of pure fun, *Otranto* is now taken seriously as the first Gothic novel; it created a form that became predominant at the turn of the century. Popular Gothic works included Clara Reeve's *The Old English Baron* (1777), William Beckford's *Vathek* (1786), Matthew Lewis's *The Monk* (1796), William Godwin's *Caleb Williams* (1794) and *St. Leon* (1799), and the numerous novels of renowned Gothic novelist Ann Radcliffe, including *The Mysteries of Udolpho* (1794) and *The Italian* (1797). These novels investigated human responses to seemingly supernatural occurrences, things known (thanks to the advances of science and natural history) to be impossible. In an Enlightenment era, the Gothic examined dark mysteries, and their darkness was even more menacing in contrast to the light that had been thrown on the world around them. The "horror" Gothic associated with Matthew or "Monk" Lewis was strong on graveyard elements and corpses risen from the dead, while the "terror" Gothic associated primarily with Ann Radcliffe turned on the emotions awakened in a rational and balanced person by the threat of the supernatural or the unexplained. The generally formulaic plots of Gothic novels often involve the usurpation of a title or estate, a hidden crime, or a secret pact with the devil. They tend to feature stereotypical characters and take place in worlds temporally or geographically distanced from England. Many of the elements of Gothic fiction had been present decades earlier in other genres, such as Alexander Pope's heroic epistle *Eloisa to Abelard* (1717). Like a typical terror Gothic, the poem featured a heroine physically confined, isolated, and subjected to harrowing emotions. The surrounding landscape is highly symbolic, reflecting the psychological world of the character, which dominates the work, and the heroine's plight is rendered in highly expressive rhetoric full of rhapsodic feeling. The Gothic often expresses darker elements of marriage and family life: where the courtship novel offers an attractive young man, the Gothic novel offers a cruel patriarch. Gothic novels provided an ominous view of homes, which tend to be confining, isolating, and ill-omened structures whose occupants are threatened by insanity and hysteria. Forbidden themes (such as incest, necrophilia, and murder) are allowed to surface. The structures themselves often embodied the political and social tensions resulting from the integration of ancient or historical time, preserved in castles or abbeys, into a world which is in other respects modern. The Gothic setting of Charlotte Smith's *Emmeline, the Orphan of the Castle*, for example, allows Smith to explore social concerns such as English laws of primogeniture and women's social status and identity within the frame of a courtship novel. Her novel illustrates the ways in which the frightening, distorted world of the Gothic could also serve as a forum for social commentary—as it also does in William Godwin's *Caleb Williams* and in Eliza Fenwick's *Secresy* (1795).

As the British Empire expanded and Britons increasingly looked out beyond the borders of Europe, the scope of the British novel responded to this broader perspective. Restoration tragedy had favored exotic settings including the empires of the Mughals and the Aztecs. In the early eighteenth century, fiction writers like Daniel Defoe and Penelope Aubin made use of both the "East Indies" (roughly today's East Asia) and the West. *Robinson Crusoe* famously takes place on an uninhabited island in the Atlantic; Behn's *Oroonoko* takes its readers to the racially mixed society of Surinam; in Johnson's *Rasselas* the central characters come from Africa and journey through Egypt. An English appetite for non-fiction about the colonies was fed by Mary Rowlandson's narrative of her captivity and ransom by

the Algonquin Native Americans, *A True History of the Captivity and Restoration of Mrs. Mary Rowlandson* (1682) and by *The Female American; or, The Adventures of Unca Eliza Winkfield* (1767), which is a novel in the guise of autobiography. Its narrator, the daughter of a Native-American princess and an English settler, is, like Robinson Crusoe, shipwrecked on an island in the Atlantic. This trans-Atlantic examination of issues of race, gender, and empire depicts a feminist utopian society in the cross-racial community its narrator discovers on her island. Fiction in which characters and settings spanned the Atlantic became common. Frances Brooke published *The History of Emily Montague* (1768), set in what is now Quebec, after living there for several years. Among those who more than once set a novel at least partly in the colonies were Charlotte Lennox, who had an American childhood, and Susanna Rowson, who became on balance more American than English, while Phebe Gibbes and Charlotte Smith took an interest in the colonies without ever having gone there. Smith's interest was political, and was shared with other radical or Jacobin writers: the protagonist of Robert Bage's *Hermsprong, or, Man as He Is Not* (1796) is by no means the only English radical hero to have been shaped by an upbringing among Native Americans. Rowson's *Reuben and Rachel* (1798) amounts at least in its earlier parts to an American melting-pot or birth-of-the-nation novel, while Elizabeth Hamilton's *Translations of the Letters of a Hindoo Rajah* (1796) continues the examination of Indian culture that Gibbes had launched in *Hartly House, Calcutta*, in 1789 (another novel which was widely taken for non-fiction).

Not only did the imaginary realms of fiction extend out into the world; the books themselves increasingly traveled outside Britain. Popular works such as novels by Fielding and Richardson would be shipped to the colonies or pirated by American printers. Across the continent, British literature was becoming more widely translated, read, and admired. *The Tatler* and *The Spectator* were read as far north as the Scottish Highlands, in addition to being sent across the Atlantic to the North American colonies. *Robinson Crusoe* was one of the first works of British literature to be widely acclaimed on the continent; in Germany and France the novel was more widely read than Chaucer, Shakespeare, or Milton at the time of its publication. The value of these older English writers also began to be more widely recognized internationally, however, as eighteenth-century poets, dramatists, and critics acknowledged their debt to these predecessors, extolling their merits and making international readers aware of the influence their contributions had made to contemporary writing. Johnson's *Dictionary* also contributed to the international recognition of British authors. In his account of the English language, Johnson's quotations from leading English authors from previous centuries not only illustrated the wealth and variety of usage, but were instrumental in the creation of a canon of works of established value. As the *Dictionary* gained international renown, so, too, did the authors Johnson quoted.

The Development of the English Language

One effect of the growth of print culture was to slow down the rate at which change in the language occurred; another was to make people more aware of the variations that did exist. Many came to the view that change in the language was in itself something to be resisted on principle, on the grounds that change allowed "corruptions" to be introduced to the language, and would make literary works of their present generation less accessible to future generations. In the late seventeenth century Dryden had expressed his desire that the English "might all write with the same certainty of words, and purity of phrase, to which the Italians first arrived, and after them the French"—in other words, a "purity" of linguistic standards set and enforced by the state, as the Accademia della Crusca had done in Italy since 1592 and the Académie française had done in France since 1635. Swift echoed Dryden in 1712 with "A Proposal for Correcting, Improving, and Ascertaining the English Tongue," which exerted considerable influence on educated opinion. Like Dryden, Swift called for the production of dictionaries and books of grammar that would codify practice and identify corrupt linguistic practices to be weeded out, and that would act as a retarding force against change. Swift wanted to "fix" the English language in two

senses: "fix" in the sense of "repair damage" (he believed that numerous corruptions had been introduced to the language since the civil wars), and also "fix" in the sense of "set in a fixed position." In his view, it was "better that a language should not be wholly perfect, than that it should be perpetually changing."

Before the Restoration, books of grammar in England were generally books on the grammar of Latin. In the late sixteenth century, two short grammars of English had been published, and several more had followed in the first half of the seventeenth. In the late seventeenth century, though, and even more so in the eighteenth century, this trickle became a flood. Perhaps the most influential was Robert Lowth's *Short Introduction to English Grammar* (1762), which did much to establish a tradition of focusing such works largely on errors in grammar and usage. In the view of grammarians such as Thomas Sheridan (father of the playwright Richard), such errors carried moral weight: the "revival of the art of speaking, and the study of language," in Sheridan's view, might be expected to contribute "in great measure" to remedying the "evils of immorality, ignorance, and false taste." At the other end of the spectrum was Joseph Priestley, the theologian and scientist (discoverer of sulphur dioxide, ammonia, and the gas that was later given the name oxygen); Priestley's *Rudiments of English Grammar* (1761) staunchly resisted the prescriptive, maintaining in startlingly modern terms that "the custom of speaking is the original and only just standard of a language."

In the late eighteenth century the prescriptivists won the day over issues of grammar, and began to entrench a good many distinctions, rules, and standards of correctness that remain with us today. Among these were the creation of distinctions in meaning between the verbs "lie" and "lay," between "between" and "among," and between "shall" and "will"; the prohibition on degrees of such "absolute" qualities as roundness and perfection; and the prohibition of double negatives.

English dictionaries (the first of which had appeared in 1604) included only "hard words" through the seventeenth century. The first dictionary to aim at comprehensiveness was Nathaniel Bailey's *Universal Etymological English Dictionary* (1721). Bailey's work went through 27 editions before the end of the century, but it was Samuel Johnson's *Dictionary* (1755) that had the more lasting impact. The decisions Johnson made in writing his *Dictionary*—to include illustrative quotations and to break down definitions of each head word into distinct senses—became conventional for all later dictionaries. Perhaps Johnson's most controversial decision was to make the dictionary primarily descriptive rather than prescriptive in nature; though Johnson noted certain "improprieties and absurdities, which it is the duty of the lexicographer to correct or proscribe," he saw the main purpose of his dictionary as being to record how the language was being and had been used, not to dictate how it should be used.

Johnson agreed with Swift that the pre-Restoration language represented "the wheels of English undefiled," but he disagreed as to the appropriate response. Not only was he willing to record usages of which he disapproved in his dictionary; he also strenuously resisted calls for the establishment of a formal authority to regulate the language, approving of the way in which "Englishmen have always been moved by a spirit of personal liberty in the use of their language." In similar fashion Priestley declared that an academy regulating the language would be "unsuitable to the genius of a free nation." It was this nationalistic argument more than anything that swayed the English in the late eighteenth century against the French and Italian models.

Language, of course, continued to change throughout the period, albeit at a rather slower pace than in the sixteenth and early seventeenth centuries. It often changed in ways of which the prescriptivists disapproved —and often resisted change in directions they wished it to follow. Swift and many other prescriptivists had conceived a violent disapproval of the supposedly excessive number of monosyllabic words in English. Swift disapproved strongly of the shortening of words such as "drudged" and "fledged" into a single syllable (initially through the substitution of an apostrophe for the *e* before the final *d*) where formerly such words had been pronounced as two. He disapproved too of the creation of shortened forms of longer words, such as *pozz* for *positive* and *mob* for *mobile*. (This last was long a particular pet peeve of Swift's, but late in life he finally admitted defeat in the face of the linguistic mob that adopted the shortened form.) But English has remained a language possessing a substantially larger percentage of monosyllabic words than do other European languages.

Perhaps the most important structural change in the late seventeenth and eighteenth centuries was the spread of progressive verb forms, and in particular the development of the passive progressive. Where in the seventeenth century one would say "The church is building," in the eighteenth people began to say "The church is being built." This development occurred organically, and (despite what seems to us to be its obvious usefulness) was widely resisted by grammarians.

There were also a number of more superficial changes in the written forms of English. There remained no agreed-upon standards regarding capitalization and italics, but it was common practice to employ both liberally. Many writers made it a practice to capitalize all abstract nouns, and some capitalized virtually all nouns. No conventions existed for the treatment of quotations in print (quotation marks were not commonly used in the modern style before the nineteenth century); some writers used dashes and paragraph breaks to aid the reader, while others left the reader to infer who was saying what, purely on the basis of interpolated phrases such as *he said, she replied*, and so on.

The spread of dictionaries—and of publishing itself—helped to "fix" English spelling, but it largely became fixed in a form that represented the English that had been spoken before the great shift in English pronunciation that had occurred in the fifteenth to seventeenth centuries. Thus were preserved the *t* in *castle*, the *k* in *knight*, the *gh* in *through*, and so on.

The American Revolution was accompanied by dissatisfaction in the new nation at using the language of the defeated imperial power. Noah Webster was among those who preferred to call the language used in the United States "American," and in 1789 Webster introduced a range of spelling changes designed both to rationalize spelling and to make the American variety distinctive from the English; the American spellings of *color, favor, honor, traveling*, and *theater* all took root as a result of Webster's initiative. (Over the following decades Webster came to acknowledge that he had lost the battle to call "American" a separate language, however; his 1828 dictionary was entitled *An American Dictionary of the English Language*.)

Above all, perhaps, the late seventeenth and eighteenth centuries were a period of growth for the English language. Words continued to be imported from other languages, perhaps most notably from French; it was a sign of the times that many now found these imports objectionable. In 1711, for example, Addison expressed his hope that "superintendents of our language" might be appointed "to hinder any words of a foreign coin from passing among us; and in particular to prohibit any French phrases from becoming current in our kingdom, when those of our own stamp are altogether as valuable." Even in the face of resistance such as this, *ballet* and *champagne* made their way across the Channel and entered English during this period, as did *connoisseur*, *dentist*, *negligee*, and *publicity*, along with a host of others. But the greatest growth came not in imports from France but in the coining of new scientific terms (often from Latin or Greek roots), from *abdomen* and *atom*, to *corolla* and *cortex*, to *genus* and *gravity*, on to *zoology*, and including thousands of more specialized terms that have never come into general circulation but have nonetheless contributed to the expansion in the communicative capacity of the English language.

HISTORY OF THE LANGUAGE
AND OF PRINT CULTURE

In an effort to provide for readers a direct sense of the development of the language and of print culture, examples of texts in their original form and illustrations have been provided for each period. A list of these within the Restoration and the Eighteenth Century, arranged chronologically, appears below.

An overview of developments in language during this period appears on pp. 1035–37, and a "Contexts" section on various aspects of "Print and Stage Culture" appears on pp. 1451–67.

The London Gazette, Sept 3–10, 1666, pp. 1099–1102.

"An Argument Shewing, that a Standing Army is inconsistent with a Free Government," title page of 1697 pamphlet, p. 1004.

John Wilmot, Earl of Rochester, "A Letter from Artemesia in the Town to Chloe in the Country," passage in original spelling and punctuation, p. 1201; facsimile page from a late eighteenth-century edition of *Rochester's Life*, p. 1206.

Daniel Defoe, *Robinson Crusoe*, illustrations from various editions, pp. 1235–37.

Anne Finch, Countess of Winchelsea, "By neer resemblance that Bird betray'd," poem in original spelling and punctuation, pp. 1252–53.

Alexander Pope, *The Rape of the Lock*, illustrations from the 1714 edition, pp. 1381, 1383, 1386, 1388, 1391.

Eliza Haywood, *Fantomina*, passage in original spelling and punctuation, pp. 1438–39.

Jonathan Swift, *Gulliver's Travels*, illustration from frontispiece to 1726 edition, p. 1272; maps from the 1726 edition, pp. 1272, 1302, 1333; passages in original spelling and punctuation, pp. 1323–25.

Samuel Richardson, *Pamela: or, Virtue Rewarded*, facsimile of 1741 title page, p. 1030.

Henry Fielding, *An Apology for the Life of Mrs. Shamela Andrews*, facsimile of 1741 title page, p. 1031.

Hester Thrale Piozzi, *Hester Thrale's Journal*, passage in original spelling and punctuation (www.broadviewpress.com/babl).

John Dryden
1631 – 1700

Few authors of the Restoration were as prolific as was John Dryden, and few rival his vigor, intellect and craftsmanship. Throughout his literary career, Dryden maintained a conscious awareness of his public role as an author, and his works give a fine sense of the changing moral, political and intellectual enthusiasms of his day. He is perhaps best known for his poetic and dramatic works, yet he was with some justice referred to by Samuel Johnson as "the father of English criticism." He was, according to his contemporary William Congreve, "an improving writer to the last."

Born 9 August 1631, in Aldwinkle All Saints, Northamptonshire, Dryden grew up in the uneasy period of Civil War and Parliamentary Revolution. He was the son of Erasmus Dryden and Mary Pickering; both sides of Dryden's family were Puritans who were allied with the Parliamentary party against the King. He attended Westminster School where he received a humanist education, firmly grounded in the ideals of ancient Greece and Rome. His first poem, *Upon the Death of Lord Hastings* (a school-mate of Dryden's), was published in 1649 while he was still at Westminster. The following

year, he was admitted to Trinity College, Cambridge. He graduated in 1654, the same year his father died, and left Dryden a small estate upon which to build his adult livelihood. Little is known about the years immediately following his departure from Cambridge, but there is evidence to suggest that (likely through the influence of his cousin, Sir Gilbert Pickering, Cromwell's Lord Chamberlain) Dryden found employment as an administrator in Oliver Cromwell's Protectorate.

The publication in 1659 of Dryden's *Heroic Stanzas to the Glorious Memory of Cromwell* effectively began his literary career. Always supportive of authority and troubled by civic unrest, Dryden celebrated the return of Charles II the following year with his poem *Astraea Redux*, a poem that confirmed his mastery of the heroic couplet. In it he expounded for the first time in his works the notion of a parallel between England and ancient Rome. Dryden's reputation as a prominent man of letters quickly gained ground; he was elected a Fellow of the Royal Society in 1662.

Dryden's first play, the comedy *The Wild Gallant* (1662), did little to herald the author's future success as a playwright. According to Samuel Pepys the play was "so poor a thing as I never saw in my life almost … the King did not seem pleased at all." Dryden soon found success with *The Indian Queen* (1664), co-authored with Sir Robert Howard, a principal investor in the King's Company and also a brother-in-law; Dryden had married Lady Elizabeth Howard the previous year. *The Indian Queen* featured the music of Dryden's contemporary Henry Purcell, and marked the beginning of Dryden's interest in developing the genre of heroic tragedy for the Restoration audience. Later heroic tragedies such as *The Indian Emperor* (1665), *Tyrannick Love* (1669), *The Conquest of Granada* (1670), and *Aureng-Zebe* (1675) featured sensational plots, extravagant pageantry, and noble heroes torn between love and honor. Consciously artificial and bombastic, these plays repeatedly demonstrated Dryden's mastery of the heroic rhyming couplet; he finally confessed, in the prologue for *Aureng-Zebe*, that he had "grown weary of his long-lov'd mistress, Rhyme." His next play, *All For Love* (1677), presented the story of Antony and Cleopatra using more flexible and natural blank verse.

Although Dryden had argued in his *Essay of Dramatic Poesy* (1668) that English plays could succeed even when they did not follow the classical unities of time, place, and action, he valued the unities highly, and *All for Love* observes them, in his own words "more exactly than, perhaps the English theatre requires." Its precise construction was far more in accord with the neoclassical spirit of the age than was Shakespeare's sprawling rendition of the same story, and *All for Love* enjoyed enormous success through to the late eighteenth century. Although seldom produced today, *All For Love* remains a milestone in the corpus of English tragedy, and is considered a masterpiece of the Restoration stage.

Dryden attained notoriety as well as fame amongst play-goers for his heroic tragedies; the King's Company produced a dramatic parody of Drydenesque heroic drama in *The Rehearsal* (1671), by George Villiers, Duke of Buckingham (and collaborators). Dryden's comedies also received a mixed reception: this genre did not seem to offer him the same degree of inspiration he found in serious drama. *Marriage à la Mode* (1671), however, felt by Dryden to be the best of his comic works, was a considerable success. It embodies much of the gaiety and exuberance of Restoration comedy, yet extends Dryden's exploration of the heroic form through its serious sub-plot.

Outside of the theater, Dryden continued to chronicle important public occasions in verse. In 1668 he succeeded William Davenant as Poet Laureate, and in 1670 was also appointed Historiographer Royal. These appointments not only afforded him a degree of financial security; they also established him as the leading public author of the English realm.

For the next decade Dryden devoted most of his artistry to works for the stage, but political and personal debate also drew him to satire. An ongoing rivalry with fellow author Thomas Shadwell prompted the satirical invective *Mac Flecknoe* (1678). Drawing on an obvious animosity towards his subject and a long-established mastery of classical history and literature, Dryden rendered Shadwell's ascension to the "throne of dullness" with great deftness and wit. With its playful use of heroic style, and its ironic grandiosity, the poem exemplifies the mock-epic form; it would influence Alexander Pope's *The Rape of the Lock* (1712) and *The Dunciad* (1728).

In 1681, Dryden responded to the atmosphere of political turbulence occasioned by the Popish Plot and the controversy over the line of succession with the majestic satire *Absalom and Achitophel*. By drawing a biblical parallel to contemporary events and personalities Dryden succeeded in offering the public a reasoned (if far from impartial) examination of the exclusion debate, while endowing the poem with such satiric invention that the fever of the moment was exposed as ridiculous. Especially popular in its day for its clever portraiture of contemporary figures and controlled allegorical representation of events, *Absalom and Achitophel* established Dryden as the leading satirical poet of the day.

Known as a public man of letters and as a commentator on the political and social events of his day, Dryden seldom offered personal revelation in his poetry. The majority of his poems are "occasional" writings, inspired by particular events or current debates. His two poems on the subject of religion, *Religio Laici* (1682) and *The Hind and the Panther* (1687) are his most personal. The ideal balance between religious faith and political authority had long been of interest to Dryden. In *Religio Laici*, a discursive statement of his beliefs, he defends the Church of England as a necessary intercessor against the excesses of private guidance in religious matters. In 1685, with the ascension of James II to the throne, Dryden himself converted to Catholicism. Although regarded by many as an opportunist and hypocrite for his conversion, Dryden refused to change his religious views when the Glorious Revolution of 1688 placed the Protestant William III and Mary II on the throne. As a result, Dryden was stripped of his laureateship and pension and entered a period of great personal and financial difficulty.

Without the security of public office and income, Dryden turned once again to the stage; producing works such as *Don Sebastian* (1690), *Amphitryon* (1690) and the opera *King Arthur* (1691), a successful collaboration with Henry Purcell. Far from slowing his literary efforts in later years, Dryden rejuvenated his career as a translator, publishing the satires of Juvenal and Persius (1693), and Virgil (1697). His final major work demonstrated strength of mind and continued vigor in his last years, combining his talents as poet, critic and translator in *Fables Ancient and Modern* (1700). *Fables* contains a number of adaptations of tales from Homer, Ovid, Chaucer, and Boccaccio, as well as several original fables. Its preface also provided occasion for one of Dryden's most important critical essays.

Throughout his life Dryden wrote prefaces, dedications and critical essays that interpreted and refined tradition in English literature. He sought to give precision to what he perceived as an unruly and languid English poetic form and championed the application of critical and historical principles to the creation and appreciation of artistic work. Of his critical works, the most noteworthy are *An Essay of Dramatic Poesy* (1668), an extended discussion on the nature of dramatic writing and of the degree to which classical principles should be applied; and The Preface to *Fables Ancient and Modern*, wherein Dryden defends his editorial influence as a translator, and offers a spirited defense of Chaucer's poetry. Although the critical preface did not originate with Dryden, no previous English author had developed the form as fully or as skillfully as he did.

In the first year of the new century Dryden succumbed to the gout that had long afflicted him; he refused amputation of an inflamed toe until the infection had spread beyond remedy. On 1 May 1700, it was reported in a London newspaper that "John Dryden Esq., departed his life, who for his poetry &c. excelled all others this age produced." He was buried in Westminster Abbey on 13 May 1700.

Absalom and Achitophel

Published in 1681, *Absalom and Achitophel* was composed in celebration of what Dryden saw as King Charles II's recent assertion of monarchical authority and recovery of political control. The previous years had been characterized by widespread political turmoil and the looming threat of civil war, which had begun with the "Popish Plot" of 1678. That year, Catholic convert Titus Oates testified to the existence of a Jesuit plot to assassinate the king, destroy London, and kill the Protestants in order to reestablish Catholic rule in England. Though this plot was later discovered to be a fabrication, at the time it created mass panic, particularly when the murdered body of prominent London Justice of the Peace Sir Edmund Berry Godfrey was discovered. Fears of Catholic invasion reinforced existing divisions between King Charles and his opponents and fueled the already bitter controversy concerning the successor to the English throne.

Though Charles had many illegitimate children, he had produced none with his wife; as a result, his Catholic brother, James, the Duke of York, would succeed him to the throne—a fact that dismayed many Protestants and divided the country into Successionists, who supported Charles and his brother James, and Exclusionists, who sought to pass a bill excluding James from the line of succession and appointing in his place James, Duke of Monmouth (a Protestant and one of the king's illegitimate children). Order was only restored when Charles dissolved Parliament, prevented the passage of the Exclusion Bill, and arrested opposition leader Lord Shaftesbury, who had tried twice to pass the bill.

Written while Shaftesbury was in jail awaiting trial, *Absalom and Achitophel* is often described as a "miniature epic" of the Popish plot, and the resulting exclusion debate, presented within the framework of the biblical story King David's betrayal by his wayward son, Absalom, in 2 Samuel. Readers at the time would have been familiar with this story, and indeed various writers and politicians had already drawn parallels between Charles II and David, between Absalom and Monmouth, and between England and Israel. Dryden, however, used these established metaphors to exploit the biblical tale for a broad range of satiric possibilities that had been overlooked by other writers.

Dryden casts Shaftesbury in the role of Achitophel, Absalom's evil counselor who incites him to rebel against his father. Achitophel is made more evil by his association, in the poem, with Satan; conversely, David is seen as closer to the divine for having been anointed by God. Monmouth (as Absalom), led by Shaftesbury (Achitophel), tempts the English to abandon their King—an event which, described in epic language and within the framework of a biblical narrative, is portrayed as catastrophic, not merely for the English Parliament, but for all humanity. The happy resolution of events which Dryden foresees, however, will, according to the poem's closing lines, usher in an age of peace and justice.

In using his wit to demonstrate his loyalty to the king (without glossing over all the King's faults, particularly his promiscuity), to garner support for the Successionists, and to ridicule his enemies (without dealing too harshly with Monmouth, whom Charles still loved) Dryden was fulfilling some of the most difficult tasks of his office as Poet Laureate, while simultaneously succeeding in entertaining his audience.

⌘ ⌘ ⌘

Absalom and Achitophel: A Poem

In pious times, ere priestcraft did begin,
Before polygamy was made a sin;
When man on many multiplied his kind,
Ere one to one was cursedly confined;
5   When nature prompted and no law denied
Promiscuous use of concubine and bride;
Then Israel's monarch[1] after Heaven's own heart,
His vigorous warmth did variously impart
To wives and slaves; and, wide as his command,
10   Scattered his Maker's image through the land.
Michal,[2] of royal blood, the crown did wear,
A soil ungrateful to the tiller's care:
Not so the rest; for several mothers bore
To godlike David several sons before.
15   But since like slaves his bed they did ascend,
No true succession could their seed attend.
Of all this numerous progeny was none
So beautiful, so brave, as Absalom:[3]
Whether, inspired by some diviner lust,

20   His father got him with a greater gust,°   *pleasure*
Or that his conscious destiny made way,
By manly beauty, to imperial sway.
Early in foreign fields he won renown,
With kings and states allied to Israel's crown:[4]
25   In peace the thoughts of war he could remove,
And seemed as he were only born for love.
Whate'er he did, was done with so much ease,
In him alone 'twas natural to please;
His motions all accompanied with grace;
30   And paradise was opened in his face.
With secret joy indulgent David viewed
His youthful image in his son renewed:
To all his wishes nothing he denied;
And made the charming Annabel[5] his bride.
35   What faults he had (for who from faults is free?)
His father could not, or he would not see.
Some warm excesses which the law forbore,
Were construed youth that purged by boiling o'er:
And Amnon's murder,[6] by a specious name,

---

[1]   *Israel's monarch*   David, King of Israel (here representing Charles II).

[2]   *Michal*   One of David's wives, here representing Catherine of Braganza, Charles's Queen. See 2 Samuel 6.12-23.

[3]   *Absalom*   David's son; here, James, Duke of Monmouth, Charles II's illegitimate son.

[4]   *early in foreign … Israel's crown*   Monmouth fought as a soldier for France against Holland in 1672–73, and for Holland against France in 1678.

[5]   *Annabel*   Anne, Countess of Buccleuch (1651–1732).

[6]   *Amnon's murder*   In 2 Samuel 13.28–29, Absalom murders his half-brother Amnon for the rape of his sister Tamar.

Was called a just revenge for injured fame.
Thus praised and loved the noble youth remained,
While David, undisturbed, in Sion[1] reigned.
But life can never be sincerely° blest;   completely
Heav'n punishes the bad, and proves° the best.   tests
The Jews,[2] a headstrong, moody, murm'ring race,
As ever tried th' extent and stretch of grace;
God's pampered people, whom, debauched with ease,
No king could govern, nor no God could please
(Gods they had tried of every shape and size
That god-smiths could produce, or priests devise);
These Adam-wits,[3] too fortunately free,
Began to dream they wanted liberty;
And when no rule, no precedent was found,
Of men by laws less circumscribed and bound,
They led their wild desires to woods and caves,
And thought that all but savages were slaves.
They who, when Saul[4] was dead, without a blow,
Made foolish Ishbosheth[5] the crown forgo;
Who banished David did from Hebron[6] bring,
And with a general shout proclaimed him king:
Those very Jews, who, at their very best,
Their humor more than loyalty expressed,
Now wondered why so long they had obeyed
An idol monarch, which their hands had made;
Thought they might ruin him they could create,
Or melt him to that golden calf,[7] a state.°   republic
But these were random bolts; no formed design
Nor interest made the factious crowd to join:
The sober part of Israel, free from stain,
Well knew the value of a peaceful reign;
And, looking backward with a wise affright,
Saw seams of wounds, dishonest° to the sight: shameful

In contemplation of whose ugly scars
They cursed the memory of civil wars.
75 The moderate sort of men, thus qualified,
Inclined the balance to the better side;
And David's mildness managed it so well,
The bad found no occasion to rebel.
But when to sin our biased nature leans,
80 The careful Devil is still at hand with means;
And providently pimps for ill desires:
The Good Old Cause[8] revived, a plot requires.
Plots, true or false, are necessary things,
To raise up commonwealths and ruin kings.
85   Th' inhabitants of old Jerusalem
Were Jebusites;[9] the town so called from them;
And theirs the native right.
But when the chosen people[10] grew more strong,
The rightful cause at length became the wrong;
90 And every loss the men of Jebus bore,
They still were thought God's enemies the more.
Thus worn and weakened, well or ill content,
Submit they must to David's government:
Impoverished and deprived of all command,
95 Their taxes doubled as they lost their land;
And, what was harder yet to flesh and blood,
Their gods disgraced, and burnt like common wood.
This set the heathen priesthood[11] in a flame;
For priests of all religions are the same:
100 Of whatsoe'er descent their godhead be,
Stock, stone, or other homely pedigree,
In his defense his servants are as bold,
As if he had been born of beaten gold.
The Jewish rabbins,[12] though their enemies,
105 In this conclude them honest men and wise:
For 'twas their duty, all the learned think,
T' espouse his cause, by whom they eat and drink.
From hence began that Plot,[13] the nation's curse,

---

[1] *Sion* Jerusalem; here, London.

[2] *Jews* I.e., the English.

[3] *Adam-wits* False reasoners.

[4] *Saul* Former king of Israel; here, Oliver Cromwell, Lord Protector of England, Scotland, and Ireland from 1649 to 1658.

[5] *Ishbosheth* Here, Cromwell's son Richard, who succeeded his father as Lord Protector (from 1658 to 1659). See 2 Samuel 3–4.

[6] *Hebron* Here, Scotland, where Charles II had been crowned in 1651, prior to his ascension to the English throne in 1660. See 2 Samuel 5.1–5.

[7] *golden calf* The image worshiped by the Jews as Moses was on Mount Sinai (Exodus 32).

---

[8] *The Good Old Cause* Slogan of the Puritan rebellion; here it refers to the Commonwealth of 1649–53.

[9] *Jebusites* Jebus was the original name of Jerusalem. Jebusites inhabited Jerusalem before Benjamin's tribe. Here Dryden refers to Roman Catholics.

[10] *chosen people* Originally, the Jews; in this context, the Protestants.

[11] *heathen priesthood* Roman Catholic clergy.

[12] *rabbins* Here, Anglican priests.

[13] *that Plot* The Popish Plot of 1678.

Bad in itself, but represented worse;
110   Raised in extremes, and in extremes decried;
With oaths affirmed, with dying vows denied;
Not weighed or winnowed[1] by the multitude;
But swallowed in the mass, unchewed and crude.
Some truth there was, but dashed and brewed with lies,
115   To please the fools, and puzzle all the wise.
Succeeding times did equal folly call,
Believing nothing, or believing all.
Th' Egyptian rites the Jebusites embraced,
Where gods were recommended by their taste.[2]
120   Such sav'ry deities must needs be good,
As served at once for worship and for food.
By force they could not introduce these gods,
For ten to one in former days was odds;
So fraud was used (the sacrificer's trade):
125   Fools are more hard to conquer than persuade.
Their busy teachers mingled with the Jews,
And raked for converts even the court and stews:°   *brothels*
Which Hebrew priests the more unkindly took,
Because the fleece[3] accompanies the flock.
130   Some thought they God's anointed[4] meant to slay
By guns, invented since full many a day:
Our author swears it not; but who can know
How far the Devil and Jebusites may go?
This Plot, which failed for want of common sense,
135   Had yet a deep and dangerous consequence:
For, as when raging fevers boil the blood,
The standing lake soon floats into a flood,
And ev'ry hostile humor, which before
Slept quiet in its channels, bubbles o'er;
140   So several factions from this first ferment
Work up to foam, and threat the government.
Some by their friends, more by themselves thought wise,
Opposed the pow'r to which they could not rise.
Some had in courts been great, and thrown from thence,
145   Like fiends were hardened in impenitence;
Some, by their monarch's fatal mercy, grown
From pardoned rebels kinsmen to the throne,

Were raised in pow'r and public office high;
Strong bands, if bands ungrateful men could tie.
150   Of these the false Achitophel[5] was first;
A name to all succeeding ages cursed:
For close designs, and crooked counsels fit;
Sagacious, bold, and turbulent of wit;
Restless, unfixed in principles and place;
155   In pow'r unpleased, impatient of disgrace:
A fiery soul, which, working out its way,
Fretted the pygmy body to decay,[6]
And o'er-informed the tenement of clay.
A daring pilot in extremity;
160   Pleased with the danger, when the waves went high,
He sought the storms; but, for a calm unfit,
Would steer too nigh the sands, to boast his wit.
Great wits are sure to madness near allied,
And thin partitions do their bounds divide;
165   Else why should he, with wealth and honor blest,
Refuse his age the needful hours of rest?
Punish a body which he could not please;
Bankrupt of life, yet prodigal of ease?
And all to leave what with his toil he won,
170   To that unfeathered two-legged thing,[7] a son;
Got, while his soul did huddled° notions try;   *disordered*
And born a shapeless lump, like anarchy.[8]
In friendship false, implacable in hate,
Resolved to ruin or to rule the state.
175   To compass this the triple bond[9] he broke.
The pillars of the public safety shook,
And fitted Israel for a foreign yoke;[10]
Then seized with fear, yet still affecting fame,
Usurped a patriot's all-atoning name.
180   So easy still it proves in factious times,
With public zeal to cancel private crimes.
How safe is treason, and how sacred ill,

---

[1] *winnowed* Separated from inferior elements.

[2] *Egyptian rites … taste* Refers to the Roman Catholic doctrine of transubstantiation, and the consumption of bread and wine during Mass.

[3] *fleece* Tithes.

[4] *God's annointed* The king.

[5] *Achitophel* Evil counselor of Absalom; see 2 Samuel. Here, Anthony Ashley Cooper (1621–83), First Earl of Shaftesbury.

[6] *A fiery … decay* Shaftesbury's body was twisted and stunted as a result of illness.

[7] *unfeathered two-legged thing* Dryden refers to Plato's definition of a human as "a featherless biped."

[8] *a son … anarchy* Dryden's allusion is uncertain.

[9] *triple bond* The 1668 alliance of England, Sweden, and Holland against France.

[10] *foreign yoke* That of France.

Where none can sin against the people's will!
Where crowds can wink, and no offense be known,
185 Since in another's guilt they find their own!
Yet fame deserved, no enemy can grudge;
The statesman we abhor, but praise the judge.
In Israel's courts ne'er sat an Abbethdin[1]
With more discerning eyes, or hands more clean;
190 Unbribed, unsought, the wretched to redress;
Swift of dispatch, and easy of access.
Oh, had he been content to serve the crown,
With virtues only proper to the gown;
Or had the rankness of the soil been freed
195 From cockle,° that oppressed the noble seed;   weeds
David for him his tuneful harp had strung,
And Heav'n had wanted one immortal song.[2]
But wild Ambition loves to slide, not stand,
And Fortune's ice prefers to Virtue's land.
200 Achitophel, grown weary to possess
A lawful fame, and lazy happiness,
Disdained the golden fruit[3] to gather free,
And lent the crowd his arm to shake the tree.
Now, manifest of crimes contrived long since,
205 He stood at bold defiance with his prince;
Held up the buckler[4] of the people's cause
Against the crown, and skulked behind the laws.
The wished occasion of the Plot he takes;
Some circumstances finds, but more he makes.
210 By buzzing emissaries fills the ears
Of list'ning crowds with jealousies° and fears   suspicions
Of arbitrary counsels brought to light,
And proves the king himself a Jebusite.
Weak arguments! which yet he knew full well
215 Were strong with people easy to rebel.
For, governed by the moon, the giddy Jews
Tread the same track when she the prime renews;[5]
And once in twenty years, their scribes record,

By natural instinct they change their lord.
220 Achitophel still wants a chief, and none
Was found so fit as warlike Absalom:
Not that he wished his greatness to create
(For politicians neither love nor hate),
But, for he knew his title not allowed,
225 Would keep him still depending on the crowd,
That kingly pow'r, thus ebbing out, might be
Drawn to the dregs of a democracy.[6]
Him he attempts with studied arts to please,
And sheds his venom in such words as these:
230   "Auspicious prince, at whose nativity
Some royal planet ruled the southern sky;
Thy longing country's darling and desire;
Their cloudy pillar and their guardian fire:[7]
Their second Moses, whose extended wand
235 Divides the seas, and shows the promised land;
Whose dawning day in every distant age
Has exercised the sacred prophet's rage:°   inspiration
The people's prayer, the glad diviners' theme,
The young men's vision, and the old men's dream![8]
240 Thee, savior, thee, the nation's vows confess,
And, never satisfied with seeing, bless:
Swift unbespoken pomps[9] thy steps proclaim,
And stammering babes are taught to lisp thy name.
How long wilt thou the general joy detain,
245 Starve and defraud the people of thy reign?
Content ingloriously to pass thy days
Like one of Virtue's fools that feeds on praise;
Till thy fresh glories, which now shine so bright,
Grow stale and tarnish with our daily sight.
250 Believe me, royal youth, thy fruit must be
Or gathered ripe, or rot upon the tree.
Heav'n has to all allotted, soon or late,
Some lucky revolution of their fate;
Whose motions if we watch and guide with skill
255 (For human good depends on human will),
Our Fortune rolls as from a smooth descent,
And from the first impression takes the bent;

---

[1] *an Abbethdin* A senior justice of the Jewish civil court. Shaftesbury was Lord Chancellor from 1672–73.

[2] *And Heav'n ... immortal song* Refers to Psalms 3 and 4, and also to 2 Samuel 18.33.

[3] *the golden fruit* The forbidden fruit in the Garden of Eden.

[4] *buckler* Small round shield.

[5] *For ... renews* Dryden refers to the constitutional crises of 1640, 1660, and 1680 as following the lunar cycle, which lasts approximately 20 years.

[6] *democracy* Popular government (here used pejoratively).

[7] *Their cloudy pillar and their guardian fire* During the Exodus, Moses led the Israelites across the Red Sea, following a pillar of cloud by day and a pillar of fire by night.

[8] *young men's ... dream* Cf. Joel 2.28.

[9] *unbespoken pomps* Spontaneous honors or processions.

But, if unseized, she glides away like wind,
And leaves repenting Folly far behind.
260　Now, now she meets you with a glorious prize,
And spreads her locks before her as she flies.[1]
Had thus old David, from whose loins you spring,
Not dared, when Fortune called him, to be king,
At Gath[2] an exile he might still remain,
265　And heaven's anointing oil had been in vain.
Let his successful youth your hopes engage;
But shun th' example of declining age;
Behold him setting in his western skies,
The shadows lengthening as the vapors rise.
270　He is not now, as when on Jordan's sand[3]
The joyful people thronged to see him land,
Cov'ring the beach, and black'ning all the strand;
But, like the Prince of Angels, from his height
Comes tumbling downward with diminished light;[4]
275　Betrayed by one poor plot to public scorn
(Our only blessing since his cursed return),
Those heaps of people which one sheaf did bind,
Blown off and scattered by a puff of wind.
What strength can he to your designs oppose,
280　Naked of friends, and round beset with foes?
If Pharaoh's[5] doubtful succor he should use,
A foreign aid would more incense the Jews:
Proud Egypt would dissembled friendship bring;
Foment the war, but not support the king:
285　Nor would the royal party e'er unite
With Pharaoh's arms t' assist the Jebusite;
Or if they should, their interest soon would break,
And with such odious aid make David weak.
All sorts of men by my successful arts,
290　Abhorring kings, estrange their altered hearts
From David's rule: and 'tis the general cry,
'Religion, commonwealth, and liberty.'

If you, as champion of the public good,
Add to their arms a chief of royal blood,
295　What may not Israel hope, and what applause
Might such a general gain by such a cause?
Not barren praise alone, that gaudy flow'r
Fair only to the sight, but solid pow'r;
And nobler is a limited command,
300　Giv'n by the love of all your native land,
Than a successive title, long and dark,
Drawn from the moldy rolls of Noah's ark."
　　What cannot praise effect in mighty minds,
When flattery soothes, and when ambition blinds!
305　Desire of pow'r, on earth a vicious weed,
Yet, sprung from high, is of celestial seed:
In God 'tis glory; and when men aspire,
'Tis but a spark too much of heavenly fire.
Th' ambitious youth, too covetous of fame,
310　Too full of angels' metal[6] in his frame,
Unwarily was led from virtue's ways,
Made drunk with honor, and debauched with praise.
Half loath, and half consenting to the ill
(For loyal blood within him struggled still),
315　He thus replied: "And what pretense have I
To take up arms for public liberty?
My father governs with unquestioned right;
The faith's defender, and mankind's delight,
Good, gracious, just, observant of the laws:
320　And heav'n by wonders has espoused his cause.
Whom has he wronged in all his peaceful reign?
Who sues for justice to his throne in vain?
What millions has he pardoned of his foes,
Whom just revenge did to his wrath expose?
325　Mild, easy, humble, studious of our good,
Inclined to mercy, and averse from blood;
If mildness ill with stubborn Israel suit,
His crime is God's beloved attribute.
What could he gain, his people to betray,
330　Or change his right for arbitrary sway?
Let haughty Pharaoh curse with such a reign
His fruitful Nile, and yoke a servile train.
If David's rule Jerusalem displease,
The Dog Star[7] heats their brains to this disease.

---

[1]　*But, if unseized ... flies*　Traditionally, Fortune (or Opportunity) is represented as a woman with flowing hair that can be seized as she approaches. She is bald behind, however, and once past cannot be grasped.

[2]　*Gath*　Here, Brussels, where Charles II spent the last years of his exile.

[3]　*Jordan's sand*　Here, Dover Beach, where Charles II landed in 1660.

[4]　*Comes ... light*　Lucifer, once the light-bearer, was cast out of heaven for rebelling against God.

[5]　*Pharaoh*　Ruler of Egypt; here, Louis XIV of France.

[6]　*angels' metal*　Pun on both *metal* (mettle) and *angel* (a gold coin).

[7]　*Dog Star*　Sirius, which rises and sets with the mid-summer sun and is therefore associated with "midsummer madness" or the "dog days."

Why then should I, encouraging the bad,
Turn rebel and run popularly mad?
Were he a tyrant, who, by lawless might
Oppressed the Jews, and raised the Jebusite,
Well might I mourn; but nature's holy bands
Would curb my spirits and restrain my hands:
The people might assert their liberty,
But what was right in them were crime in me.
His favor leaves me nothing to require,
Prevents my wishes, and outruns desire.
What more can I expect while David lives?
All but his kingly diadem he gives:
And that"—But there he paused; then sighing, said—
"Is justly destined for a worthier head.
For when my father from his toils shall rest
And late augment the number of the blest,
His lawful issue shall the throne ascend,
Or the collat'ral line,[1] where that shall end.
His brother, though oppressed with vulgar spite,
Yet dauntless, and secure of native right,
Of every royal virtue stands possessed;
Still dear to all the bravest and the best.
His courage foes, his friends his truth proclaim;
His loyalty the king, the world his fame.
His mercy ev'n th' offending crowd will find,
For sure he comes of a forgiving kind.°   *family*
Why should I then repine at heaven's decree,
Which gives me no pretense to royalty?
Yet O that fate, propitiously inclined,
Had raised my birth, or had debased my mind;
To my large soul not all her treasure lent,
And then betrayed it to a mean descent!
I find, I find my mounting spirits bold,
And David's part disdains my mother's mold.
Why am I scanted by a niggard° birth?   *stingy*
My soul disclaims the kindred of her earth;
And, made for empire, whispers me within,
'Desire of greatness is a godlike sin.'"
    Him staggering° so when hell's dire agent   *wavering*
        found,
While fainting Virtue scarce maintained her ground,
He pours fresh forces in, and thus replies:
    "Th' eternal god, supremely good and wise,

Imparts not these prodigious gifts in vain:
What wonders are reserved to bless your reign!
Against your will, your arguments have shown,
380 Such virtue's only giv'n to guide a throne.
Not that your father's mildness I contemn,
But manly force becomes the diadem.
'Tis true he grants the people all they crave;
And more, perhaps, than subjects ought to have:
385 For lavish grants suppose a monarch tame,
And more his goodness than his wit proclaim.
But when should people strive their bonds to break,
If not when kings are negligent or weak?
Let him give on till he can give no more,
390 The thrifty Sanhedrin[2] shall keep him poor;
And every shekel which he can receive,
Shall cost a limb of his prerogative.[3]
To ply him with new plots shall be my care;
Or plunge him deep in some expensive war;
395 Which when his treasure can no more supply,
He must, with the remains of kingship, buy.
His faithful friends our jealousies and fears
Call Jebusites, and Pharaoh's pensioners;
Whom when our fury from his aid has torn,
400 He shall be naked left to public scorn.
The next successor, whom I fear and hate,
My arts have made obnoxious to the state;
Turned all his virtues to his overthrow,
And gained our elders[4] to pronounce a foe.
405 His right, for sums of necessary gold,
Shall first be pawned, and afterward be sold;
Till time shall ever-wanting David draw,
To pass your doubtful title into law:
If not, the people have a right supreme
410 To make their kings; for kings are made for them.
All empire is no more than pow'r in trust,
Which, when resumed, can be no longer just.
Succession, for the general good designed,
In its own wrong a nation cannot bind;
415 If altering that the people can relieve,

---

[2] *Sanhedrin* The highest Jewish judicial council; here, Parliament.

[3] *prerogative* The Royal prerogative, or special privileges, which Parliament sought to limit by controlling the Crown's money supply.

[4] *elders* Shaftesbury's supporters were members of the gentry and aristocracy.

---

[1] *collat'ral line* The line of succession through Charles's brother James, or his descendants.

Better one suffer than a nation grieve.[1]
The Jews well know their pow'r: ere Saul they chose,
God was their king, and God they durst depose.[2]
Urge now your piety, your filial name,
420   A father's right and fear of future fame;
The public good, that universal call,
To which even heav'n submitted, answers all.
Nor let his love enchant your generous mind;
'Tis Nature's trick to propagate her kind.
425   Our fond begetters, who would never die,
Love but themselves in their posterity.
Or let his kindness by th' effects be tried,
Or let him lay his vain pretense aside.
God said he loved your father; could he bring
430   A better proof than to anoint him king?
It surely showed he loved the shepherd well,
Who gave so fair a flock as Israel.
Would David have you thought his darling son?
What means he then, to alienate[3] the crown?
435   The name of godly he may blush to bear:
'Tis after God's own heart to cheat his heir.
He to his brother gives supreme command;
To you a legacy of barren land,[4]
Perhaps th' old harp, on which he thrums his lays,°   *ballads*
440   Or some dull Hebrew ballad in your praise.
Then the next heir, a prince severe and wise,
Already looks on you with jealous eyes;
Sees through the thin disguises of your arts,
And marks your progress in the people's hearts.
445   Though now his mighty soul its grief contains,
He meditates revenge who least complains;
And, like a lion, slumb'ring in the way,
Or sleep dissembling, while he waits his prey,
His fearless foes within his distance draws,
450   Constrains his roaring, and contracts his paws;

Till at the last, his time for fury found,
He shoots with sudden vengeance from the ground;
The prostrate vulgar[5] passes o'er and spares,
But with a lordly rage his hunters tears.
455   Your case no tame expedients will afford:
Resolve on death, or conquest by the sword,
Which for no less a stake than life you draw;
And self-defense is nature's eldest law.
Leave the warm people no considering time;
460   For then rebellion may be thought a crime.
Prevail° yourself of what occasion gives,   *avail*
But try your title while your father lives;
And that your arms may have a fair pretense,
Proclaim you take them in the king's defense;
465   Whose sacred life each minute would expose
To plots, from seeming friends, and secret foes.
And who can sound the depth of David's soul?
Perhaps his fear his kindness may control.
He fears his brother, though he loves his son,
470   For plighted vows too late to be undone.
If so, by force he wishes to be gained,
Like women's lechery, to seem constrained.°   *forced*
Doubt not; but when he most affects the frown,
Commit a pleasing rape upon the crown.
475   Secure his person to secure your cause:
They who possess the prince, possess the laws."
    He said, and this advice above the rest
With Absalom's mild nature suited best:
Unblamed of life (ambition set aside),
480   Not stained with cruelty, nor puffed with pride,
How happy had he been, if destiny
Had higher placed his birth, or not so high!
His kingly virtues might have claimed a throne,
And blest all other countries but his own.
485   But charming greatness since so few refuse,
'Tis juster to lament him than accuse.
Strong were his hopes a rival to remove,
With blandishments to gain the public love;
To head the faction while their zeal was hot,
490   And popularly prosecute the Plot.
To further this, Achitophel unites
The malcontents of all the Israelites;
Whose differing parties he could wisely join,
For several ends, to serve the same design:

---

[1] *Better one ... grieve* Cf. John 11.50, in which the high priest Caiaphas says to the Pharisees about Jesus, "it is expedient for us that one man should die for the people, and that the whole nation perish not."

[2] *The Jews ... durst depose* Before Saul, Israel was ruled by judges. Cromwell, the first Lord Protector, replaced the Rump Parliament in 1653.

[3] *alienate* Transfer into ownership of another person.

[4] *To you ... land* Charles II promoted James to general in 1678 and banished Monmouth to Holland in the following year.

---

[5] *vulgar* Commoners.

The best (and of the princes some were such),
Who thought the pow'r of monarchy too much;
Mistaken men, and patriots in their hearts;
Not wicked, but seduced by impious arts.
By these the springs of property were bent,
And wound so high, they cracked the government.
The next for interest sought t' embroil the state,
To sell their duty at a dearer rate;
And make their Jewish markets of the throne,
Pretending public good, to serve their own.
Others thought kings an useless heavy load,
Who cost too much, and did too little good.
These were for laying honest David by,
On principles of pure good husbandry.°   *management*
With them joined all th' haranguers of the throng,
That thought to get preferment by the tongue.
Who follow next, a double danger bring,
Not only hating David, but the king:
The Solymaean rout,[1] well-versed of old
In godly faction, and in treason bold;
Cow'ring and quaking at a conqu'ror's sword,
But lofty to a lawful prince restored;
Saw with disdain an ethnic[2] plot begun,
And scorned by Jebusites to be outdone.
Hot Levites[3] headed these; who, pulled before
From th' ark, which in the Judges' days they bore,
Resumed their cant, and with a zealous cry
Pursued their old belov'd theocracy:[4]
Where Sanhedrin[5] and priest enslaved the nation,
And justified their spoils by inspiration:[6]
For who so fit for reign as Aaron's race,[7]
If once dominion they could found in grace?

These led the pack; though not of surest scent,
Yet deepest-mouthed° against the government.   *loudest*
A numerous host of dreaming saints succeed,
530 Of the true old enthusiastic breed:[8]
'Gainst form and order they their pow'r employ,
Nothing to build, and all things to destroy.
But far more numerous was the herd of such,
Who think too little, and who talk too much.
535 These out of mere instinct, they knew not why,
Adored their fathers' God and property;
And, by the same blind benefit of fate,
The Devil and the Jebusite did hate:
Born to be saved, even in their own despite,
540 Because they could not help believing right.
Such were the tools; but a whole Hydra[9] more
Remains, of sprouting heads too long to score.
Some of their chiefs were princes of the land:
In the first rank of these did Zimri[10] stand;
545 A man so various, that he seemed to be
Not one, but all mankind's epitome:
Stiff in opinions, always in the wrong;
Was everything by starts, and nothing long;
But, in the course of one revolving moon,
550 Was chemist, fiddler, statesman, and buffoon:
Then all for women, painting, rhyming, drinking,
Besides ten thousand freaks° that died in thinking.   *whims*
Blest madman, who could every hour employ,
With something new to wish, or to enjoy!
555 Railing° and praising were his usual themes;   *criticizing*
And both (to show his judgment) in extremes:
So over-violent, or over-civil,
That every man, with him, was God or Devil.
In squandering wealth was his peculiar art:
560 Nothing went unrewarded but desert.
Beggared by fools, whom still he found too late,
He had his jest, and they had his estate.
He laughed himself from court; then sought relief

---

[1] *Solymaean rout* London rabble.

[2] *ethnic* Gentile; here, Roman Catholic.

[3] *Levites* Ancient Hebrew tribe, especially those who were Assistants to the Priestly class. During the exile of the Jews, the Levites carried the Ark of the Covenant. Here Dryden refers to Presbyterian clergymen who lost their church benefices with the Act of Conformity in 1662.

[4] *theocracy* System of government by God, or by priestly order; here, the Commonwealth.

[5] *Sanhedrin* Supreme Jewish Council and highest court of Jerusalem.

[6] *inspiration* Members of non-conforming sects sometimes claimed divine inspiration, or direct contact with God.

[7] *Aaron's race* The priests of Israel, who were descendants of Aaron.

[8] *enthusiastic breed* Here, religious enthusiasts, used pejoratively.

[9] *Hydra* In Greek mythology the Hydra was a many-headed serpent that would sprout new heads whenever one was severed.

[10] *Zimri* George Villiers, Second Duke of Buckingham, a prominent Whig and supporter of Shaftesbury. He was the author of *The Rehearsal*, which satirized the heroic play and ridiculed Dryden. For biblical Zimris, see Numbers 25.6–15, 1 Kings 8–20, and 2 Kings 9.31.

By forming parties, but could ne'er be chief;
565 For, spite of him, the weight of business fell
On Absalom and wise Achitophel:
Thus, wicked but in will, of means bereft,
He left not faction, but of that was left.
        Titles and names 'twere tedious to rehearse
570 Of lords, below the dignity of verse.
Wits, warriors, Commonwealth's men, were the best;
Kind husbands, and mere nobles, all the rest.
And therefore, in the name of dullness, be
The well-hung Balaam[1] and cold Caleb,[2] free;
575 And canting Nadab[3] let oblivion damn,
Who made new porridge for the paschal lamb.[4]
Let friendship's holy band some names assure;
Some their own worth, and some let scorn secure.
Nor shall the rascal rabble here have place,
580 Whom kings no titles gave, and God no grace:
Not bull-faced Jonas,[5] who could statutes draw
To mean rebellion, and make treason law.
But he, though bad, is followed by a worse,
The wretch who heav'n's anointed dared to curse:
585 Shimei,[6] whose youth did early promise bring
Of zeal to God and hatred to his king,
Did wisely from expensive sins refrain,
And never broke the Sabbath, but for gain;
Nor ever was he known an oath to vent,
590 Or curse, unless against the government.
Thus heaping wealth, by the most ready way
Among the Jews, which was to cheat and pray,
The city, to reward his pious hate
Against his master, chose him magistrate.

595 His hand a vare° of justice did uphold;   *staff*
His neck was loaded with a chain of gold.
During his office, treason was no crime;
The sons of Belial[7] had a glorious time;
For Shimei, though not prodigal of pelf,[8]
600 Yet loved his wicked neighbor as himself.
When two or three were gathered to declaim
Against the monarch of Jerusalem,
Shimei was always in the midst of them;
And if they cursed the king when he was by,
605 Would rather curse than break good company.
If any durst his factious friends accuse,
He packed a jury of dissenting Jews;
Whose fellow-feeling in the godly cause
Would free the suff'ring saint from human laws.
610 For laws are only made to punish those
Who serve the king, and to protect his foes.
If any leisure time he had from pow'r
(Because 'tis sin to misemploy an hour),
His business was, by writing, to persuade
615 That kings were useless, and a clog to trade;
And, that his noble style he might refine,
No Rechabite[9] more shunned the fumes of wine.
Chaste were his cellars, and his shrieval board°   *sheriff's table*
The grossness of a city feast abhorred:
620 His cooks, with long disuse, their trade forgot;
Cool was his kitchen, though his brains were hot,
Such frugal virtue malice may accuse,
But sure 'twas necessary to the Jews:
For towns once burnt[10] such magistrates require
625 As dare not tempt God's providence by fire.
With spiritual food he fed his servants well,
But free from flesh that made the Jews rebel;
And Moses' laws he held in more account,
For forty days of fasting in the mount.[11]
630 To speak the rest, who better are forgot,

---

[1] *Balaam*   Probably Theophilus Hastings, Earl of Huntingdon, who initially supported Shaftesbury, but returned his support to the King in 1681. See Numbers 13–14.

[2] *Caleb*   Arthur Capel, Earl of Essex. See Number 13–14.

[3] *Nadab*   William, Lord Howard of Escrick, a dissenting preacher. See Leviticus 10.1–2.

[4] *Who ... lamb*   Howard was said to have taken the sacrament with hot ale, known as "porridge," instead of wine.

[5] *Jonas*   Sir William Jones, prosecutor of those accused in the Popish Plot, and then supporter of the Exclusion Bill against the succession of James, Duke of York.

[6] *Shimei*   In 2 Samuel 16.5–14, Shimei curses David as he flees from Absalom's rebellion. Here, Slingsby Bethel, a London sheriff responsible for packing juries in order to thwart the prosecution of Shaftesbury and his supporters.

[7] *Belial*   Fallen angel, a minister of Satan. Here, wicked or dissolute persons in general. Possibly also a pun on Balliol College, which was friendly to the Whigs during the Oxford Parliament of 1681.

[8] *prodigal of pelf*   Free with money.

[9] *Rechabite*   Jewish sect that abstained from wine drinking.

[10] *towns once burnt*   Reference to the Great Fire of London in 1666.

[11] *And Moses' laws ... fasting on the mount*   Moses received God's commandments during a forty-day fast on Mount Sinai (Exodus 34.28).

Would tire a well-breathed witness of the Plot.
Yet, Corah,[1] thou shalt from oblivion pass:
Erect thyself, thou monumental brass,
High as the serpent of thy metal made,[2]
635 While nations stand secure beneath thy shade.
What though his birth were base, yet comets rise
From earthy vapors, ere they shine in skies.
Prodigious actions may as well be done
By weaver's issue,[3] as by prince's son.
640 This arch-attestor for the public good
By that one deed ennobles all his blood.
Who ever asked the witnesses' high race
Whose oath with martyrdom did Stephen[4] grace?
Ours was a Levite, and as times went then,
645 His tribe were God Almighty's gentlemen.
Sunk were his eyes, his voice was harsh and loud,
Sure signs he neither choleric° was nor proud: *hot-tempered*
His long chin proved his wit; his saintlike grace
A church vermilion, and a Moses' face.[5]
650 His memory, miraculously great,
Could plots, exceeding man's belief, repeat;
Which therefore cannot be accounted lies,
For human wit could never such devise.
Some future truths are mingled in his book;
655 But where the witness failed, the prophet spoke:
Some things like visionary flights appear;
The spirit caught him up, the Lord knows where,
And gave him his rabbinical degree,
Unknown to foreign university.[6]
660 His judgment yet his mem'ry did excel;
Which pieced his wondrous evidence so well,
And suited to the temper of the times,

Then groaning under Jebusitic crimes.
Let Israel's foes suspect his heav'nly call,
665 And rashly judge his writ apocryphal;[7]
Our laws for such affronts have forfeits made:
He takes his life, who takes away his trade.
Were I myself in witness Corah's place,
The wretch who did me such a dire disgrace
670 Should whet my memory, though once forgot,
To make him an appendix of my plot.
His zeal to heav'n made him his prince despise,
And load his person with indignities;
But zeal peculiar privilege affords,
675 Indulging latitude to deeds and words;
And Corah might for Agag's[8] murder call,
In terms as coarse as Samuel used to Saul.
What others in his evidence did join
(The best that could be had for love or coin),
680 In Corah's own predicament will fall;
For *witness* is a common name to all.
     Surrounded thus with friends of every sort,
Deluded Absalom forsakes the court:
Impatient of high hopes, urged with renown,
685 And fired with near possession of a crown.
Th' admiring crowd are dazzled with surprise,
And on his goodly person feed their eyes:
His joy concealed, he sets himself to show,
On each side bowing popularly low;
690 His looks, his gestures, and his words he frames,
And with familiar ease repeats their names.
Thus formed by nature, furnished out with arts,
He glides unfelt into their secret hearts.
Then, with a kind compassionating look,
695 And sighs, bespeaking pity ere he spoke,
Few words he said; but easy those and fit,
More slow than Hybla-drops,[9] and far more sweet.
    "I mourn, my countrymen, your lost estate;
Though far unable to prevent your fate:
700 Behold a banished man, for your dear cause
Exposed a prey to arbitrary laws!
Yet oh! that I alone could be undone,

---

[1] *Corah* Rebellious Levite; here, Titus Oates, the chief manufacturer of the Popish Plot.

[2] *the serpent of thy metal made* Moses erected a brass serpent to cure Jews suffering from snake bites (Numbers 21.4–9); metal also refers to Oates's "mettle," his spirit, or ambition.

[3] *By weaver's issue* By the child of a weaver. (Oates's father was a weaver.)

[4] *Stephen* The first Christian martyr; he was stoned by false witnesses (Acts 6–7).

[5] *Moses' face* Moses's face shone with divine illumination after receiving God's commandments (Exodus 34.29–30).

[6] *And gave him … foreign university* Oates falsely claimed to have a Doctor of Divinity degree from the University of Salamanca.

---

[7] *apocryphal* Excluded from the Holy Canon.

[8] *Agag* Likely refers to Lord Stafford, accused by Oates and executed in 1680. For Samuel's denouncement of Saul see 1 Samuel 15.

[9] *Hybla-drops* Celebrated Sicilian honey noted for its sweetness.

Cut off from empire, and no more a son!
Now all your liberties a spoil are made;
705 Egypt and Tyrus[1] intercept your trade,
And Jebusites your sacred rites invade.
My father, whom with reverence yet I name,
Charmed into ease, is careless of his fame;
And, bribed with petty sums of foreign gold,
710 Is grown in Bathsheba's[2] embraces old;
Exalts his enemies, his friends destroys;
And all his pow'r against himself employs.
He gives, and let him give, my right away;
But why should he his own, and yours betray?
715 He only, he can make the nation bleed,
And he alone from my revenge is freed.
Take then my tears (with that he wiped his eyes),
'Tis all the aid my present pow'r supplies:
No court-informer can these arms accuse;
720 These arms may sons against their fathers use:
And 'tis my wish, the next successor's reign
May make no other Israelite complain."

    Youth, beauty, graceful action seldom fail;
But common interest always will prevail;
725 And pity never ceases to be shown
To him who makes the people's wrongs his own.
The crowd (that still° believe their kings oppress) *always*
With lifted hands their young Messiah bless:
Who now begins his progress to ordain
730 With chariots, horsemen, and a num'rous train;
From east to west his glories he displays,[3]
And, like the sun, the promised land surveys.
Fame runs before him as the morning star,
And shouts of joy salute him from afar:
735 Each house receives him as a guardian god,
And consecrates the place of his abode:
But hospitable treats did most commend
Wise Issachar,[4] his wealthy western friend.

---

[1] *Egypt and Tyrus* Here, France and Holland.

[2] *Bathsheba* The Duchess of Portsmouth, Louise-Renée de Kéroualle, a mistress of Charles II who was popularly considered a French spy.

[3] *From ... displays* Monmouth journeyed through western England in order to rally support.

[4] *Issachar* Thomas Thynne of Longleat, a wealthy Whig supporter who entertained Monmouth on his western journey. See Genesis 49.14–15.

This moving court, that caught the people's eyes,
740 And seemed but pomp, did other ends disguise:
Achitophel had formed it, with intent
To sound the depths, and fathom, where it went,
The people's hearts; distinguish friends from foes,
And try their strength, before they came to blows.
745 Yet all was colored with a smooth pretense
Of specious love, and duty to their prince.
Religion, and redress of grievances,
Two names that always cheat and always please,
Are often urged; and good King David's life
750 Endangered by a brother and a wife.[5]
Thus, in a pageant show, a plot is made,
And peace itself is war in masquerade.
O foolish Israel! never warned by ill,
Still the same bait, and circumvented still!
755 Did ever men forsake their present ease,
In midst of health imagine a disease;
Take pains contingent mischiefs to foresee,
Make heirs for monarchs, and for God decree?
What shall we think! Can people give away
760 Both for themselves and sons, their native sway?
Then they are left defenseless to the sword
Of each unbounded, arbitrary lord:
And laws are vain, by which we right enjoy,
If kings unquestioned can those laws destroy.
765 Yet if the crowd be judge of fit and just,
And kings are only officers in trust,
Then this resuming cov'nant was declared
When kings were made, or is forever barred.
If those who gave the scepter could not tie
770 By their own deed their own posterity,
How then could Adam bind his future race?
How could his forfeit on mankind take place?
Or how could heavenly justice damn us all,
Who ne'er consented to our father's fall?
775 Then kings are slaves to those whom they command,
And tenants to their people's pleasure stand.
Add, that the pow'r for property allowed
Is mischievously seated in the crowd;
For who can be secure of private right,
780 If sovereign sway may be dissolved by might?
Nor is the people's judgment always true:

---

[5] *Endangered ... wife* Titus Oates accused Charles's Queen Catherine and his brother James of conspiring to murder him.

The most may err as grossly as the few;
And faultless kings run down, by common cry,
For vice, oppression, and for tyranny.
5   What standard is there in a fickle rout,
Which, flowing to the mark, runs faster out?
Nor only crowds, but Sanhedrins may be
Infected with this public lunacy,
And share the madness of rebellious times,
0   To murder monarchs for imagined crimes.[1]
If they may give and take whene'er they please,
Not kings alone (the Godhead's images),
But government itself at length must fall
To nature's state, where all have right to all.
5   Yet, grant our lords the people kings can make,
What prudent men a settled throne would shake?
For whatsoe'er their sufferings were before,
That change they covet makes them suffer more.
All other errors but disturb a state,
0   But innovation is the blow of fate.
If ancient fabrics nod, and threat to fall,
To patch the flaws, and buttress up the wall,
Thus far 'tis duty; but here fix the mark;
For all beyond it is to touch our ark.[2]
5   To change foundations, cast the frame anew,
Is work for rebels, who base ends pursue,
At once divine and human laws control,
And mend the parts by ruin of the whole.
The tamp'ring world is subject to this curse,
0   To physic their disease into a worse.
　　　Now what relief can righteous David bring?
How fatal 'tis to be too good a king!
Friends he has few, so high the madness grows:
Who dare be such, must be the people's foes:
5   Yet some there were, ev'n in the worst of days;
Some let me name, and naming is to praise.
　　　In this short file Barzillai[3] first appears;
Barzillai, crowned with honor and with years:
Long since, the rising rebels he withstood
0   In regions waste, beyond the Jordan's flood:

Unfortunately brave to buoy the State;
But sinking underneath his master's fate:
In exile with his godlike prince he mourned;
For him he suffered, and with him returned.
825   The court he practiced, not the courtier's art:
Large was his wealth, but larger was his heart:
Which well the noblest objects knew to choose,
The fighting warrior, and recording Muse.
His bed could once a fruitful issue boast;
830   Now more than half a father's name is lost.
His eldest hope,[4] with every grace adorned,
By me (so Heav'n will have it) always mourned,
And always honored, snatched in manhood's prime
B' unequal fates, and Providence's crime:
835   Yet not before the goal of honor won,
All parts fulfilled of subject and of son;
Swift was the race, but short the time to run.
O narrow circle, but of pow'r divine,
Scanted in space, but perfect in thy line!
840   By sea, by land, thy matchless worth was known,
Arms thy delight, and war was all thy own:
Thy force, infused, the fainting Tyrians[5] propped;
And haughty Pharaoh found his fortune stopped.
Oh ancient honor! Oh unconquered hand,
845   Whom foes unpunished never could withstand!
But Israel was unworthy of thy name:
Short is the date of all immoderate fame.
It looks as Heav'n our ruin had designed,
And durst not trust thy fortune and thy mind.
850   Now, free from earth, thy disencumbered soul
Mounts up, and leaves behind the clouds and starry pole:
From thence thy kindred legions mayst thou bring,
To aid the guardian angel of thy king. Here stop my
　　Muse, here cease thy painful flight;
855   No pinions° can pursue immortal height:　　　　　*wings*
Tell good Barzillai thou canst sing no more,
And tell thy soul she should have fled before:
Or fled she with his life, and left this verse
To hang on her departed patron's hearse?
860   Now take thy steepy flight from heav'n, and see
If thou canst find on earth another *he:*
Another *he* would be too hard to find;
See then whom thou canst see not far behind.

---

[1]   *To … crimes*   Allusion to the execution of Charles I in 1649.

[2]   *to touch our ark*   To touch the Ark of the Covenant is to commit
sacrilege.

[3]   *Barzillai*   A loyal supporter of David during Absalom's rebellion
(2 Samuel 19.31–39). Here, James Butler, Duke of Ormond, a loyal
supporter of both Charles I and Charles II.

---

[4]   *eldest hope*   Ormond's son, Thomas, Earl of Ossory, died in 1680.

[5]   *Tyrians*   Here, the Dutch.

Zadoc[1] the priest, whom, shunning pow'r and place,
865 His lowly mind advanced to David's grace:
With him the Sagan[2] of Jerusalem,
Of hospitable soul, and noble stem;
Him of the western dome,[3] whose weighty sense
Flows in fit words and heavenly eloquence.
870 The prophets' sons,[4] by such example led,
To learning and to loyalty were bred:
For colleges on bounteous kinds depend,
And never rebel was to arts a friend.
To these succeed the pillars of the laws,
875 Who best could plead, and best can judge a cause.
Next them a train of loyal peers ascend;
Sharp-judging Adriel,[5] the Muses' friend,
Himself a Muse—in Sanhedrin's debate
True to his prince, but not a slave of state:
880 Whom David's love with honors did adorn,
That from his disobedient son were torn.[6]
Jotham[7] of piercing wit, and pregnant thought,
Indued by nature, and by learning taught
To move assemblies, who but only tried
885 The worse a while, then chose the better side;
Nor chose alone, but turned the balance too;
So much the weight of one brave man can do.
Hushai,[8] the friend of David in distress,
In public storms, of manly steadfastness:
890 By foreign treaties he informed his youth,

And joined experience to his native truth.
His frugal care supplied the wanting throne,
Frugal for that, but bounteous of his own:
'Tis easy conduct when exchequers flow,
895 But hard the task to manage well the low;
For sovereign power is too depressed or high,
When kings are forced to sell, or crowds to buy.
Indulge one labor more, my weary Muse,
For Amiel:[9] who can Amiel's praise refuse?
900 Of ancient race by birth, but nobler yet
In his own worth, and without title great:
The Sanhedrin long time as chief he ruled,
Their reason guided, and their passion cooled:
So dext'rous was he in the crown's defense,
905 So formed to speak a loyal nation's sense,
That, as their band was Israel's tribes in small,
So fit was he to represent them all.
Now rasher charioteers the seat ascend,
Whose loose careers his steady skill commend:
910 They like th' unequal ruler of the day,
Misguide the seasons, and mistake the way;[10]
While he withdrawn at their mad labor smiles,
And safe enjoys the sabbath of his toils.
    These were the chief, a small but faithful band
915 Of worthies, in the breach who dared to stand,
And tempt th' united fury of the land.
With grief they viewed such powerful engines bent,
To batter down the lawful government:
A numerous faction, with pretended frights,
920 In Sanhedrins to plume° the regal rights;   pluck
The true successor from the court removed:[11]
The Plot, by hireling witnesses, improved.
These ills they saw, and, as their duty bound,
They showed the king the danger of the wound:
925 That no concessions from the throne would please,
But lenitives[12] fomented the disease;
That Absalom, ambitious of the crown,

---

[1] *Zadoc*   David demanded that Zadoc and the Levites remain behind when he left the city during Absalom's rebellion (2 Samuel 8.17). Here Zadoc represents William Sancroft, Archbishop of Canterbury.

[2] *Sagan*   The second-highest temple official. Here, Henry Compton, Bishop of London.

[3] *Him of the western dome*   John Dolben, Dean of Westminster.

[4] *The prophet's sons*   Students of Westminster School, where Dryden had been a King's Scholar.

[5] *Adriel*   John Sheffield, Earl of Mulgrave. He was a patron and friend of Dryden's.

[6] *That from ... were torn*   In 1679, two high offices, Governor of Hull and Lord Lieutenant of Yorkshire, were transferred from Monmouth to Mulgrave.

[7] *Jotham*   George Saville, Marquis of Halifax. Formerly associated with Shaftesbury, he helped defeat the Exclusion Bill in the House of Lords. See Judges 9.1–21.

[8] *Hushai*   Laurence Hyde, Earl of Rochester and First Lord of the Treasury from 1679–85. He was another of Dryden's patrons. See 2 Samuel 16.

---

[9] *Amiel*   Edward Seymour, Speaker of the House of Commons from 1673–78.

[10] *Misguide ... way*   An allusion to Phaethon, son of Apollo, who almost set the world afire when he could not control his father's chariot, which pulled the sun across the sky.

[11] *The true ... removed*   The Duke of York was banished from England for six months in 1679.

[12] *lenitives*   Soothing medicines.

Was made the lure to draw the people down;
That false Achitophel's pernicious hate
930 Had turned° the Plot to ruin Church and State: *manipulated*
The council violent, the rabble worse;
That Shimei taught Jerusalem to curse.
　　　With all these loads of injuries oppressed,
And long revolving, in his careful breast,
935 Th' event of things, at last, his patience tired,
Thus from his royal throne, by Heav'n inspired,
The godlike David spoke: with awful fear
His train their Maker in their master hear.
　　　"Thus long have I, by native mercy swayed,
940 My wrongs dissembled, my revenge delayed:
So willing to forgive th' offending age,
So much the father did the king assuage.
But now so far my clemency they slight,
Th' offenders question my forgiving right.
945 That one was made for many, they contend;
But 'tis to rule; for that's a monarch's end.
They call my tenderness of blood, my fear;
Though manly tempers can the longest bear.
Yet, since they will divert my native course,
950 'Tis time to show I am not good by force.
Those heaped affronts that haughty subjects bring,
Are burdens for a camel, not a king:
Kings are the public pillars of the State,
Born to sustain and prop the nation's weight:
955 If my young Samson[1] will pretend a call
To shake the column, let him share the fall:
But, oh, that yet he would repent and live!
How easy 'tis for parents to forgive!
With how few tears a pardon might be won
960 From nature, pleading for a darling son!
Poor pitied youth, by my paternal care
Raised up to all the height his frame could bear:
Had God ordained his fate for empire born,
He would have giv'n his soul another turn:
965 Gulled° with a patriot's name, whose modern sense *tricked*
Is one that would by law supplant his prince:
The people's brave, the politician's tool;
Never was patriot yet, but was a fool.
Whence comes it that religion and the laws

970 Should more be Absalom's than David's cause?
His old instructor, ere he lost his place,
Was never thought indued with so much grace.
Good heav'ns, how faction can a patriot paint!
My rebel ever proves my people's saint:
975 Would *they* impose an heir upon the throne?
Let Sanhedrins be taught to give their own.
A king's at least a part of government,
And mine as requisite as their consent;
Without my leave a future king to choose,
980 Infers a right the present to depose:
True, they petition me to approve their choice;
But Esau's hands suit ill with Jacob's voice.[2]
My pious subjects for my safety pray,
Which to secure, they take my pow'r away.
985 From plots and treasons Heav'n preserve my years,
But save me most from my petitioners.
Unsatiate as the barren womb or grave;
God cannot grant so much as they can crave.
What then is left but with a jealous eye
990 To guard the small remains of royalty?
The law shall still direct my peaceful sway,
And the same law teach rebels to obey:
Votes shall no more established power control—
Such votes as make a part exceed the whole:
995 No groundless clamors shall my friends remove,
Nor crowds have pow'r to punish ere they prove:
For gods and godlike kings, their care express,
Still to defend their servants in distress.
O that my pow'r to saving were confined:
1000 Why am I forced, like Heav'n, against my mind,
To make examples of another kind?
Must I at length the sword of justice draw?
O curst effects of necessary law!
How ill my fear they by my mercy scan!°　　*judge*
1005 Beware the fury of a patient man.
Law they require, let Law then show her face,
They could not be content to look on Grace,
Her hinder parts, but with a daring eye
To tempt the terror of her front and die.[3]

---

[1] *Samson* Biblical hero of enormous strength who killed himself by pulling down the Temple pillars while he stood under them. See Judges 13–16.

[2] *But Esau's ... voice* In Genesis 27 Jacob disguised himself as his brother Esau by covering his hands with rough goat skin in order to receive his father's blessings.

[3] *To tempt ... die* Moses was not allowed to see the face of God (Exodus 33.20–23).

1010 By their own arts, 'tis righteously decreed,
Those dire artificers of death shall bleed.
Against themselves their witnesses will swear,
Till viper-like their mother Plot they tear:
And suck for nutriment that bloody gore,
1015 Which was their principle of life before.
Their Belial with their Belzebub[1] will fight;
Thus on my foes, my foes shall do me right:
Nor doubt th' event; for factious crowds engage,
In their first onset, all their brutal rage.
1020 Then let 'em take an unresisted course,
Retire and traverse, and delude their force:

But when they stand all breathless, urge the fight,
And rise upon 'em with redoubled might:
For lawful pow'r is still superior found,
1025 When long driv'n back, at length it stands the ground."
    He said. Th' Almighty, nodding, gave consent;
And peals of thunder shook the firmament.
Henceforth a series of new time began,
The mighty years in long procession ran:
1030 Once more the godlike David was restored,
And willing nations knew their lawful lord.
    —1681

━━━━━━━━━━
━━━━━━━━━━

Mac Flecknoe

The first of Dryden's satires, *Mac Flecknoe*, with its bawdy raillery against dull writers and ignorant, unimaginative readers, is often considered his liveliest and most humorous poem. Its primary target is Thomas Shadwell, a rival dramatist of Dryden who wrote "humor-comedy," a genre, perfected by Ben Jonson and popular during the Renaissance, in which characters are seen to be ruled by one dominant mood, or humor. Dryden's comedies of wit employed a style almost directly opposed to Shadwell's. More pertinently, Shadwell was politically a Whig, one of the party Dryden attacked in *Absalom and Achitophel*. For several years the two men had engaged in an ongoing quarrel —primarily conducted in prefaces of their respective plays—over the relative merits of their respective works. With *Mac Flecknoe*, Dryden moved the quarrel from the realm of polite literary debate to a more pointed attack and used his disagreement with Shadwell to voice his dissatisfaction with the literary society of his day.

In the poem, Shadwell has been chosen by the Irish poet Richard Flecknoe (a minor poet of the previous generation whose name was, at least for Dryden, synonymous with bad poetry) as heir to his kingdom of dullness—thus becoming "Mac," or the "son of" Flecknoe. In elevated language and an epic form, the poem proclaims a new ruler of the kingdom of dullness and provides a description of the coronation ceremony that takes as its model that of Charles II. Shadwell's royal procession though the city also satirically echoes the entry of Christ into Jerusalem. In this ironic vision of a world in which dullness is a virtue, and wit and sense are scourges of the earth, Shadwell comes to embody the void of cultural values that Dryden saw around him.

Though the poem may have been completed as early as 1678, Dryden made no move to publish it, most likely out of respect for Shadwell, and though the manuscript was circulated for several years it did not appear publicly until a pirated edition was published in 1682. Ironically, Shadwell was chosen to replace Dryden as Poet Laureate in 1688.

---

[1] *Belzebub* Devil, one of Satan's ministers.

Mac Flecknoe
Or, a Satire upon the True-Blue-Protestant Poet, T.S.

All human things are subject to decay,
 And when fate summons, monarchs must obey.
This Flecknoe found, who, like Augustus,[1] young
Was called to empire, and had governed long;
5 In prose and verse, was owned, without dispute,
Through all the realms of Nonsense, absolute.
This aged prince, now flourishing in peace,
And blest with issue of a large increase,
Worn out with business, did at length debate
10 To settle the succession of the state;
And, pondering which of all his sons was fit
To reign, and wage immortal war with wit,
Cried: "'Tis resolved; for nature pleads that he
Should only rule, who most resembles me.
15 Sh—— alone my perfect image bears,
Mature in dullness from his tender years:
Sh—— alone, of all my sons, is he
Who stands confirmed in full stupidity.
The rest to some faint meaning make pretense,
20 But Sh—— never deviates into sense.
Some beams of wit on other souls may fall,
Strike through, and make a lucid interval;
But Sh——'s genuine night admits no ray,
His rising fogs prevail upon the day.
25 Besides, his goodly fabric[2] fills the eye,
And seems designed for thoughtless majesty:
Thoughtless as monarch oaks that shade the plain,
And, spread in solemn state, supinely reign.
Heywood and Shirley[3] were but types[4] of thee,
30 Thou last great prophet of tautology.[5]
Even I, a dunce of more renown than they,
Was sent before but to prepare thy way;[6]

And, coarsely clad in Norwich drugget,[7] came
To teach the nations in thy greater name.
35 My warbling lute, the lute I whilom° strung,   *formerly*
When to King John of Portugal[8] I sung,
Was but the prelude to that glorious day,
When thou on silver Thames didst cut thy way,
With well-timed oars before the royal barge,
40 Swelled with the pride of thy celestial charge;
And big with hymn, commander of a host,
The like was ne'er in Epsom blankets[9] tossed.
Methinks I see the new Arion[10] sail,
The lute still trembling underneath thy nail.
45 At thy well-sharpened thumb from shore to shore
The treble squeaks for fear, the basses roar;
Echoes from Pissing Alley[11] Sh—— call,
And Sh—— they resound from Aston Hall.
About thy boat the little fishes throng,
50 As at the morning toast° that floats along.   *sewage*
Sometimes, as prince of thy harmonious band,
Thou wield'st thy papers in thy threshing hand,
St. Andre's feet[12] ne'er kept more equal time,
Not ev'n the feet of thy own *Psyche's* rhyme;
55 Though they in number as in sense excel:
So just, so like tautology, they fell,
That, pale with envy, Singleton[13] forswore
The lute and sword, which he in triumph bore,
And vowed he ne'er would act Villerius[14] more."

---

[1] *Augustus* Octavius (later Augustus) Caesar became the first Roman emperor at the age of 32.

[2] *goodly fabric* Allusion to Shadwell's corpulence.

[3] *Heywood and Shirley* Thomas Heywood (1570?–1641), and James Shirley (1596–1666), popular dramatists prior to the closing of the theatres in 1642. They were not well known in Dryden's age.

[4] *types* Prefigurings, or imperfect symbols.

[5] *tautology* Unintentional repetition of the same meaning.

[6] *prepare thy way* John the Baptist is said to have been sent to prepare the way for Christ (Matthew 3.3).

[7] *Norwich drugget* Drugget is a coarse woolen cloth. Shadwell was from Norfolk.

[8] *King John of Portugal* Flecknoe boasted of this King's patronage.

[9] *Epsom blankets* Reference to two different plays by Shadwell, *Epsom Wells* and *The Virtuoso*. In the latter, the character of Sir Samuel Hearty is tossed in a blanket.

[10] *Arion* In Greek mythology, Arion was a celebrated musician who was saved from drowning by music-loving dolphins.

[11] *Pissing Alley* Route from London's Strand to the Thames.

[12] *St. Andre's* French dancer who choreographed Shadwell's opera *Psyche*. Dryden's suggestion here is that the metrical feet of Shadwell's poetry would be just as regular as a dancer's steps to the music—a comparison not intended as a compliment. The "threshing hand" of Shadwell is suggested to be beating out a mechanical rhythm.

[13] *Singleton* John Singleton, a musician at the Theatre Royal.

[14] *Villerius* Character in William Davenant's opera *The Siege of Rhodes*.

60 Here stopped the good old sire, and wept for joy
In silent raptures of the hopeful boy.
All arguments, but most his plays, persuade.
That for anointed dullness he was made.

   Close to the walls which fair Augusta[1] bind
65 (The fair Augusta much to fears inclined),[2]
An ancient fabric,° raised to inform the sight,   *building*
There stood of yore, and Barbican[3] it hight:°   *was called*
A watchtower once; but now, so fate ordains,
Of all the pile an empty name remains.
70 From its old ruins brothel houses rise,
Scenes of lewd loves, and of polluted joys,
Where their vast courts the mother-strumpets keep,
And, undisturbed by watch, in silence sleep.
Near these a Nursery[4] erects its head,
75 Where queens are formed, and future heroes bred;
Where unfledged actors learn to laugh and cry,
Where infant punks° their tender voices try,   *prostitutes*
And little Maximins[5] the gods defy.
Great Fletcher never treads in buskins here,
80 Nor greater Jonson dares in socks appear;[6]
But gentle Simkin[7] just reception finds
Amidst this monument of vanished minds:
Pure clinches° the suburbian Muse affords,   *puns*
And Panton[8] waging harmless war with words.
85 Here Flecknoe, as a place to fame well known,
Ambitiously design'd his Sh——'s throne;
For ancient Dekker[9] prophesied long since,

That in this pile would reign a mighty prince,
Born for a scourge of wit, and flail of sense;
90 To whom true dullness should some *Psyches* owe,
But worlds of *Misers* from his pen should flow;
Humorists and *Hypocrites*[10] it should produce,
Whole Raymond families, and tribes of Bruce.[11]
   Now Empress Fame had published the renown
95 Of Sh——'s coronation through the town.
Roused by report of Fame, the nations meet,
From near Bunhill, and distant Watling Street.[12]
No Persian carpets spread the imperial way,
But scattered limbs of mangled poets lay;
100 From dusty shops neglected authors come,
Martyrs of pies, and relics of the bum.[13]
Much Heywood, Shirley, Ogilby[14] there lay,
But loads of Sh—— almost choked the way.
Bilked stationers for yeomen stood prepared,
105 And Herringman was captain of the guard.[15]
The hoary prince in majesty appeared,
High on a throne of his own labors reared.
At his right hand our young Ascanius[16] sate,
Rome's other hope, and pillar of the state.
110 His brows thick fogs, instead of glories, grace,
And lambent dullness played around his face.
As Hannibal did to the altars come,
Sworn by his sire a mortal foe to Rome,[17]

---

for his plays about life in London. Jonson satirized him in *The Poetaster*.

[10] *Misers … Humorists and Hypocrites*   Titles of early plays by Shadwell.

[11] *Raymond … Bruce*   Characters in Shadwell's plays.

[12] *Bunhill … Watling Street*   Both Bunhill and Watling Street are within half a mile of the Nursery and are located within the inner City.

[13] *Martyrs or pies … bum*   Unsold books were sold for scrap paper, here used as wrapping paper for pieshops, or bakeries, and as toilet paper.

[14] *Ogilby*   John Ogilby (1600–76), a poet and translator of Homer and Virgil.

[15] *Bilked stationers … the guard*   Publishers who lost money. Henry Herringman published both Dryden and Shadwell.

[16] *Ascanius*   Son of Aeneas who was marked by the gods by a flickering flame around his head in Virgil's *Aeneid*.

[17] *As Hannibal … Rome*   According to Livy, the Carthaginian general Hannibal was forced by his father to swear an oath against Rome as a young boy.

---

[1] *Augusta*   London.

[2] *The fair Augusta … inclined*   The line alludes to fears and suspicions aroused by the Popish Plot.

[3] *Barbican*   Fortification, or gatehouse in the ancient wall surrounding the city. The area was a disreputable district in Dryden's day.

[4] *Nursery*   School for young actors founded by Lady Davenant in 1671.

[5] *Maximins*   Raging emperor in Dryden's *Tyrannic Love*.

[6] *Great Fletcher … socks appear*   John Fletcher (1579–1625), playwright noted for his tragedies, and Ben Jonson (1573–1637), noted for his comedies. Buskins were high boots worn by tragic actors and socks were the slippers, or soft shoes, of Athenian comic actors.

[7] *Simkin*   Common simple character in a farce.

[8] *Panton*   Common farce character known for being a punster.

[9] *Dekker*   Thomas Dekker (1572?–1632), prolific dramatist known

So Sh—— swore, nor should his vow be vain,
115   That he till death true dullness would maintain;
And, in his father's right, and realm's defense,
Ne'er to have peace with wit, nor truce with sense.
The king himself the sacred unction[1] made,
As king by office, and as priest by trade.
120   In his sinister° hand, instead of ball,   *left*
He placed a mighty mug of potent ale;
Love's Kingdom[2] to his right he did convey,
At once his scepter, and his rule of sway;
Whose righteous lore the prince had practiced young,
125   And from whose loins recorded *Psyche*[3] sprung.
His temples, last, with poppies[4] were o'erspread,
That nodding seemed to consecrate his head.
Just at that point of time, if Fame not lie,
On his left hand twelve reverend owls[5] did fly.
130   So Romulus, 'tis sung, by Tiber's brook,[6]
Presage of sway from twice six vultures took.[7]
The admiring throng loud acclamations make,
And omens of his future empire take.
The sire then shook the honors of his head,
135   And from his brows damps of oblivion shed
Full on the filial dullness: long he stood,
Repelling from his breast the raging God;
At length burst out in this prophetic mood:
    "Heavens bless my son, from Ireland let him reign
140   To far Barbadoes on the western main;
Of his dominion may no end be known,
And greater than his father's be his throne;
Beyond *Love's Kingdom* let him stretch his pen!"
He paused, and all the people cried, "Amen."
145   Then thus continued he: "My son, advance

Still in new impudence, new ignorance.
Success let others teach, learn thou from me
Pangs without birth, and fruitless industry.
Let *Virtuosos* in five years be writ;
150   Yet not one thought accuse thy toil of wit.
Let gentle George[8] in triumph tread the stage,
Make Dorimant betray, and Loveit rage;
Let Cully, Cockwood, Fopling, charm the pit,
And in their folly show the writer's wit.
155   Yet still thy fools shall stand in thy defense,
And justify their author's want of sense.
Let 'em be all by thy own model made
Of dullness, and desire no foreign aid;
That they to future ages may be known,
160   Not copies drawn, but issue of thy own.
Nay, let thy men of wit too be the same,
All full of thee, and differing but in name.
But let no alien S—dl—y[9] interpose,
To lard with wit thy hungry *Epsom* prose.
165   And when false flowers of rhetoric thou wouldst cull,
Trust nature, do not labor to be dull;
But write thy best, and top; and, in each line,
Sir Formal's[10] oratory will be thine:
Sir Formal, though unsought, attends thy quill,
170   And does thy northern dedications fill.[11]
Nor let false friends seduce thy mind to fame,
By arrogating Jonson's hostile name.
Let father Flecknoe fire thy mind with praise,
And uncle Ogilby thy envy raise.
175   Thou art my blood, where Jonson has no part:
What share have we in nature, or in art?
Where did his wit on learning fix a brand,
And rail at arts he did not understand?
Where made he love in Prince Nicander's[12] vein,
180   Or swept the dust in *Psyche's* humble strain?

---

[1]   *sacred unction*   Sacramental oil used to anoint the monarch in coronation ceremonies.

[2]   *Love's Kingdom*   Play by Flecknoe (1664).

[3]   *Psyche*   Opera by Shadwell.

[4]   *poppies*   Alludes to Shadwell's use of opium as well as to the mental dullness that is associated with its use (and, in Dryden's view, with Shadwell's writing).

[5]   *twelve reverend owls*   Symbols of darkness or dullness.

[6]   *Romulus ... Tiber's brook*   Romulus and Remus were the co-founders of Rome, through which the Tiber River runs.

[7]   *from twice six vultures took*   According to Plutarch, Romulus chose the site of Rome upon seeing twelve vultures to his brother Remus's six.

[8]   *George*   Sir George Etherege (1636–92), a comedic dramatist. The names in the next couplet refer to characters from his plays.

[9]   *S—dl—y*   Sir Charles Sedley (1638–1701), poet and playwright. Dryden alludes to the rumor that Sedley contributed more than the prologue to Shadwell's *Epsom Wells*.

[10]   *Sir Formal's*   Sir Formal Trifle, "The Orator" from Shadwell's *The Virtuoso*.

[11]   *northern dedications fill*   Both Shadwell and Flecknoe dedicated several works to the Duke and Duchess of Newcastle.

[12]   *Prince Nicander's*   A character in *Psyche*.

Where sold he bargains,[1] 'whip-stitch,[2] kiss my arse,'
Promised a play and dwindled to a farce?
When did his Muse from Fletcher scenes purloin,
As thou whole Eth'rege dost transfuse to thine?
185　But so transfused, as oil on water's flow,
His always floats above, thine sinks below.
This is thy province, this thy wondrous way,
New humors to invent for each new play:
This is that boasted bias of thy mind,
190　By which one way, to dullness, 'tis inclined;
Which makes thy writings lean on one side still,
And, in all changes, that way bends thy will.
Nor let thy mountain-belly make pretense
Of likeness; thine's a tympany[3] of sense.
195　A tun° of man in thy large bulk is writ,　　　*large cask*
But sure thou'rt but a kilderkin° of wit.　　　*small cask*
Like mine, thy gentle numbers feebly creep;
Thy tragic Muse gives smiles, thy comic sleep.
With whate'er gall thou sett'st thyself to write,
200　Thy inoffensive satires never bite.
In thy felonious heart though venom lies,
It does but touch thy Irish pen,[4] and dies.
Thy genius calls thee not to purchase fame
In keen iambics,[5] but mild anagram.
205　Leave writing plays, and choose for thy command
Some peaceful province in acrostic[6] land.
There thou may'st wings display and altars raise,[7]
And torture one poor word ten thousand ways.
Or, if thou wouldst thy different talent suit,
210　Set thy own songs, and sing them to thy lute."

He said: but his last words were scarcely heard
For Bruce and Longville had a trap prepared,[8]
And down they sent the yet declaiming bard.
Sinking he left his drugget robe behind,
215　Borne upwards by a subterranean wind.
The mantle fell to the young prophet's part,[9]
With double portion of his father's art.
—1682 (WRITTEN C. 1679)

To the Memory of Mr. Oldham[10]

Farewell, too little and too lately known,
　Whom I began to think and call my own;
For sure our souls were near allied, and thine
Cast in the same poetic mould with mine.[11]
5　One common note on either lyre did strike,
And knaves and fools we both abhorred alike:
To the same goal did both our studies drive,
The last set out the soonest did arrive.
Thus Nisus fell upon the slippery place,
10　While his young friend performed and won the race.[12]
O early ripe! to thy abundant store
What could advancing age have added more?
It might (what Nature never gives the young)
Have taught the numbers[13] of thy native tongue;
15　But satire needs not those, and wit will shine
Through the harsh cadence of a rugged line:

---

[1]　*sold he bargains*　To "sell bargains" is to respond to an innocent question with a coarse response.

[2]　*whip-stitch*　A nonsense phrase frequently used by Sir Samuel Hearty in *The Virtuoso.*

[3]　*tympany*　A swelling of the abdomen due to excess gas.

[4]　*Irish pen*　Although neither Flecknoe, nor Shadwell were Irish, Dryden uses the term as a common seventeenth-century reference to barbarity and poverty.

[5]　*iambics*　Sharp satire was often written in iambic meter.

[6]　*acrostic*　A poem in which the first letter of every line spells out the name of the person, or thing that is the subject of the verse.

[7]　*wings display and altars raise*　Dryden refers to the style of emblematic verse used by George Herbert in *Easter Wings* and *The Altar.* In this form of poetry, the lines of the poem create the visual shape of the subject.

[8]　*Bruce and Longville ... prepared*　In *The Virtuoso*, Bruce and Longville open a trap-door underneath Sir Formal Trifle as he makes a speech.

[9]　*The mantle ... prophet's part*　In 2 Kings 2.8–14, the prophet Elijah is carried to heaven in a chariot of fire as his mantle falls to his successor Elisha.

[10]　*Mr. Oldham*　John Oldham, (1653–83) English poet known for his 1681 *Satires upon the Jesuits* (which was, like Dryden's *Absalom and Achitophel*, inspired by the Popish plot) and for his translations of classical poems. Dryden, who greatly admired his work, published this poem as a memorial, prefixed to the *Remains of Mr. John Oldham in Verse and Prose* (1684).

[11]　*For sure ... mine*　An echo of lines 204–5 of Oldham's "David's Lamentation": "Oh, dearer than my soul! if I can call it mine, / For sure we had the same, 'twas very thine."

[12]　*Thus ... race*　In his *Aeneid*, Virgil tells the story of Nisus, who slips in a pool of blood during a foot race, impeding a rival and thus enabling his friend Euryalus to win.

[13]　*numbers*　Metrical patterns.

A noble error, and but seldom made,
When poets are by too much force betrayed.
Thy generous fruits, though gathered ere their prime
20   Still showed a quickness;[1] and maturing time
But mellows what we write to the dull sweets of rhyme.
Once more, hail and farewell;[2] farewell though young,
But ah too short, Marcellus[3] of our tongue;
Thy brows with ivy, and with laurels bound;[4]
25   But fate and gloomy night encompass thee around.
     —1684

A Song for St. Cecilia's Day[5]

1

From harmony, from heavenly harmony
This universal frame° began: *structure*
     When Nature underneath a heap
          Of jarring atoms lay,
5   And could not heave her head,
The tuneful voice was heard from high:
     "Arise, ye more than dead."
Then cold, and hot, and moist, and dry,[6]
In order to their stations leap,
10   And Music's power obey.
From harmony, from heavenly harmony

---

[1] *quickness*   Liveliness; also, an acidity or sharpness (either of taste or of speech).

[2] *hail and farewell*   Translation of the Latin "ave atque vale," from Roman poet Catullus's elegy for his brother.

[3] *Marcellus*   Nephew and adopted son (and heir) of Augustus, Marcellus had a great military career but died at the age of twenty. Book 6 of Virgil's *Aeneid* ends with Aeneas being shown a vision of Marcellus: "… hov'ring mists around his brows are spread, / And night, with sable shades, involves his head."

[4] *Thy … bound*   Ivy denotes immortality, while laurels are awarded to victors.

[5] *A Song … Day*   St. Cecilia, the patron saint of music, was celebrated in England on November 22 of each year. In London the Musical Society would commission as an original composition an ode for the occasion. This is the first of two odes composed by Dryden in honor of St. Cecilia; the second, *Alexander's Feast*, was written ten years later. Both were later set to music by Handel. (G.B. Draghi composed the original music to which the ode was set in 1687.)

[6] *cold … dry*   Refers to the Epicurean conception of atoms of the activity of atoms of the four elements: earth, fire, water, and air.

This universal frame began:
     From harmony to harmony
Through all the compass of the notes it ran,
15   The diapason[7] closing full in man.

2

What passion cannot Music raise and quell!
     When Jubal[8] struck the corded shell,
     His listening brethren stood around,
     And, wondering, on their faces fell
20   To worship that celestial sound.
Less than a god they thought there could not dwell
          Within the hollow of that shell
          That spoke so sweetly and so well.
What passion cannot Music raise and quell!

3

25   The trumpet's loud clangor
               Excites us to arms,
          With shrill notes of anger,
               And mortal alarms.
          The double double double beat
30   Of the thundering drum
Cries: "Hark! the foes come;
Charge, charge, 'tis too late to retreat."

4

          The soft complaining flute
          In dying notes discovers
35   The woes of hopeless lovers,
Whose dirge is whispered by the warbling lute.

5

          Sharp violins proclaim
Their jealous pangs, and desperation,
Fury, frantic indignation,
40   Depth of pains, and height of passion,
          For the fair, disdainful dame.

6

          But O! what art can teach,

---

[7] *diapason*   The combination of all the notes or parts of the harmony.

[8] *Jubal*   "The father of all such as handle the harp and organ" (Genesis 4.21).

What human voice can reach,
The sacred organ's praise?
45   Notes inspiring holy love,
Notes that wing their heavenly ways
To mend the choirs above.

7

Orpheus[1] could lead the savage race;
And trees unrooted left their place,
50   Sequacious of[2] the lyre;
But bright Cecilia raised the wonder higher:
When to her organ vocal breath was given,
An angel heard, and straight appeared,
Mistaking earth for heaven.

GRAND CHORUS

55   *As from the power of sacred lays*
The spheres began to move,
And sung the great Creator's praise
To all the blest above;
So, when the last and dreadful hour
60   *This crumbling pageant shall devour,*
The trumpet shall be heard on high,[3]
The dead shall live, the living die,
And Music shall untune the sky.
—1687

from *An Essay of Dramatic Poesy*

It was that memorable day[4] in the first summer of the late war, when our navy engaged the Dutch; a day wherein the two most mighty and best appointed fleets which any age had ever seen, disputed the command of the greater half of the globe, the commerce of nations, and the riches of the universe. While these vast floating bodies, on either side, moved against each other in parallel lines, and our countrymen, under the happy conduct of his Royal Highness, went breaking, by little and little, into the line of the enemies; the noise of the cannon from both navies reached our ears about the City,[5] so that all men being alarmed with it, and in a dreadful suspense of the event which we knew was then deciding, every one went following the sound as his fancy led him; and leaving the town almost empty, some took towards the park, some cross the river, others down it; all seeking the noise in the depth of silence.

Among the rest, it was the fortune of Eugenius, Crites, Lisideius, and Neander,[6] to be in company together; three of them persons whom their wit and quality have made known to all the town; and whom I have chose to hide under these borrowed names, that they may not suffer by so ill a relation as I am going to make of their discourse.

Taking then a barge which a servant of Lisideius had provided for them, they made haste to shoot the bridge, and left behind them that great fall of waters which hindered them from hearing what they desired: after which, having disengaged themselves from many vessels which rode at anchor in the Thames, and almost blocked up the passage towards Greenwich, they ordered the watermen to let fall their oars more gently; and then, every one favouring his own curiosity with a strict silence, it was not long ere they perceived the air break about them like the noise of distant thunder, or of swallows in a chimney: those little undulations of sound, though almost vanishing before they reached them, yet still seeming to retain somewhat of their first horror, which they had betwixt the fleets. After they had attentively listened till such time as the sound by little and little went from them, Eugenius, lifting up his head, and taking notice of it, was the first who congratulated to the rest that happy omen of our Nation's victory: adding, we had but this to desire in confirmation of it, that we might hear no more of that noise, which was now leaving the English coast. When the rest had concurred in the same opinion, Crites, a person of a

---

[1] *Orpheus*   According to Ovid's *Metamorphoses*, Orpheus was able to charm trees, stones and wild beasts into following him by the beautiful playing of his lyre.

[2] *Sequacious of*   Following.

[3] *The ... high*   1 Corinthians 15.52 describes the "last trump" as heralding the Resurrection and Last Judgement.

[4] *memorable day*   3 June 1665, when the English defeated the Dutch.

[5] *the City*   London.

[6] *Eugenius*   Charles Sackville (1638–1706), son of Richard, fifth Earl of Dorset; *Crites* Sir Robert Howard (1626–98); *Lisideius* Sir Charles Sedley (c. 1639–1701); *Neander* Dryden himself.

sharp judgment, and somewhat too delicate a taste in wit, which the world have mistaken in him for ill-nature, said, smiling to us, that if the concernment of this battle had not been so exceeding great, he could scarce have wished the victory at the price he knew he must pay for it, in being subject to the reading of so many ill verses as he was sure would be made upon it. Adding that no argument could 'scape some of those eternal rhymers, who watch a battle with more diligence than the ravens and birds of prey; and the worst of them surest to be first in upon the quarry: while the better able either out of modesty writ not at all, or set that due value upon their poems, as to let them be often called for and long expected!

"There are some of those impertinent people you speak of," answered Lisideius, "who to my knowledge are already so provided, either way, that they can produce not only a panegyric upon the victory, but, if need be, a funeral elegy on the Duke; and after they have crowned his valour with many laurels, at last deplore the odds under which he fell, concluding that his courage deserved a better destiny." All the company smiled at the conceit of Lisideius; but Crites, more eager than before, began to make particular exceptions against some writers, and said, the public magistrate ought to send betimes to forbid them; and that it concerned the peace and quiet of all honest people, that ill poets should be as well silenced as seditious preachers.

"In my opinion," replied Eugenius, "you pursue your point too far; for as to my own particular, I am so great a lover of poesy, that I could wish them all re-warded, who attempt but to do well; at least, I would not have them worse used than Sylla the Dictator[1] did one of their brethren heretofore: *Quern in concione vidimus* (says Tully) *cum ei libellum malus poeta de populo subjecisset, quod epigramma in eum fecisset tantummodo alternis versiculis longiusculis, statim ex its rebus quas tunc vendebat jubere ei praemium tribui, sub ea*

conditione ne quid postea scriberet."[2]

"I could wish with all my heart," replied Crites, "that many whom we know were as bountifully thanked upon the same condition—that they would never trouble us again. For amongst others, I have a mortal apprehension of two poets,[3] whom this victory, with the help of both her wings, will never be able to escape."

"'Tis easy to guess whom you intend," said Lisideius; "and without naming them, I ask you, if one of them does not perpetually pay us with clenches[4] upon words, and a certain clownish kind of raillery? if now and then he does not offer at a catachresis[5] or Clevelandism,[6] wresting and torturing a word into another meaning: in fine, if he be not one of those whom the French would call *un mauvais buffon*; one that is so much a well-willer to the satire, that he spares no man; and though he cannot strike a blow to hurt any, yet ought to be pun-ished for the malice of the action, as our witches are justly hanged, because they think themselves so; and suffer deservedly for believing they did mischief, because they meant it."

"You have described him," said Crites, "so exactly, that I am afraid to come after you with my other extremity of poetry. He is one of those who, having had some advantage of education and converse, knows better than the other what a poet should be, but puts it into practice more unluckily than any man; his style and matter are everywhere alike: he is the most calm, peace-able writer you ever read: he never disquiets your passions with the least concernment, but still leaves you in as even a temper as he found you; he is a very

---

[1] *Sylla the Dictator* Lucius Cornelius Sulla (c. 138–78 BCE), a Roman general and self-proclaimed dictator of the Roman Empire in 82 BCE. Sulla's dictatorship was notorious for its cruelty and illegal activity.

[2] *Quem in concione ... scriberet* Latin: Whom we saw in a gather-ing, when an amateurish poet of the people handed up a book to him with every other line a bit longer; immediately from those wares which he was then selling, he ordered a reward to be given to him but on the condition that he would not write afterwards (Cicero, *Pro Archia* 10. 25); *Tully* Marcus Tullius Cicero (c. 106– 43 BCE), Roman orator, politician and philosopher.

[3] *two poets* Likely Robert Wild and Richard Flecknoe (satirized by Dryden in *Mac Flecknoe*).

[4] *clenches* Puns.

[5] *catachresis* The misapplication of a word or phrase, or a strained figure of speech.

[6] *Clevelandism* Named for metaphysical poet John Cleveland (1613–58).

Leveller[1] in poetry: he creeps along with ten little words in every line, and helps out his numbers with *For to*, and *Unto*, and all the pretty expletives he can find, till he drags them to the end of another line; while the sense is left tired half way behind it: he doubly starves all his verses, first for want of thought, and then of expression; his poetry neither has wit in it, nor seems to have it; like him in Martial:

Pauper videri Cinna *vult, est pauper.*[2]

"He affects plainness, to cover his want of imagination: when he writes the serious way, the highest flight of his fancy is some miserable antithesis, or seeming contradiction; and in the comic he is still reaching at some thin conceit, the ghost of a jest, and that too flies before him, never to be caught; these swallows which we see before us on the Thames are the just resemblance of his wit: you may observe how near the water they stoop, how many proffers they make to dip, and yet how seldom they touch it; and when they do, 'tis but the surface: they skim over it but to catch a gnat, and then mount into the air and leave it."

"Well, gentlemen," said Eugenius, "you may speak your pleasure of these authors; but though I and some few more about the town may give you a peaceable hearing, yet assure yourselves, there are multitudes who would think you malicious and them injured: especially him who you first described; he is the very Withers[3] of the city: they have bought more editions of his works than would serve to lay under all their pies at the Lord Mayor's Christmas. When his famous poem first came out in the year 1660, I have seen them reading it in the midst of 'Change time; nay so vehement they were at it, that they lost their bargain by the candles' ends; but what will you say, if he has been received amongst the great ones? I can assure you he is, this day, the envy of a great Person who is lord in the art of quibbling; and who does not take it well, that any man should intrude so far into his province."

"All I would wish," replied Crites, "is that they who love his writings, may still admire him, and his fellow poet: *Qui Bavium non odit, &c.*,[4] is curse sufficient."

"And farther," added Lisideius, "I believe there is no man who writes well, but would think himself[5] very hardly dealt with, if their admirers should praise anything of his: *Nam quos contemnimus, eorum quoque laudes contemnimus.*"[6]

"There are so few who write well in this age," says Crites, "that methinks any praises should be welcome; they neither rise to the dignity of the last age, nor to any of the Ancients: and we may cry out of the writers of this time, with more reason than Petronius[7] of his, *Pace vestra liceat dixisse, primi omnium eloquentiam perdidistis*:[8] you have debauched the true old poetry so far, that Nature, which is the soul of it, is not in any of your writings."

"If your quarrel," said Eugenius, "to those who now write, be grounded only on your reverence to antiquity, there is no man more ready to adore those great Greeks and Romans than I am: but on the other side, I cannot think so contemptibly of the age I live in, or so dishonourably of my own country, as not to judge we equal the Ancients in most kinds of poesy, and in some surpass them; neither know I any reason why I may not be as zealous for the reputation of our age, as we find the Ancients themselves in reference to those who lived before them. For you hear your Horace saying,

Indignor quidquam reprehendi, non quia crasse Compositum, illepideve putetur, sed quia nuper.[9]

---

[1] *Leveller* Derogatory term for political radicals in favor of the abolition of social or economic inequalities. (Before the Restoration the term was used by members of that party to describe themselves.)

[2] *Pauper ... pauper* Latin: "Cinna wishes to appear a pauper, and he is" (*Epigrams* 8.19).

[3] *Withers* Reference to poet George Wither (1588-1667).

[4] *Qui Bavium ... &c.* Latin: Who does not hate Boevius, etc. (Virgil, *Eclogues* 3.90).

[5] *but would think himself* I.e., who would not think himself.

[6] *Nam quos ... contemnimus* Latin For we detest those people who admire what we despise (source unknown).

[7] *Petronius* Notable Roman author and satirist (c. 27–66 CE); his sole surviving work is the *Satyricon*.

[8] *Pace vestra ... perdidists* Latin: If I may say it, you [rhetoricians] are the first to have lost the eloquence of all who went before (*Satyricon* 2).

[9] *Indignor ... nuper* Latin: It angers me when something is blamed, not for being poorly written or inelegant, but for being new (Horace, *Epistles* 2.1.76–77).

And after:

> *Si meliora dies, ut vina, poemata reddit,*
> *Scire velim, pretium chartis quotus arroget annus?*[1]

"But I see I am engaging in a wide dispute, where the arguments are not like to reach close on either side; for Poesy is of so large an extent, and so many both of the Ancients and Moderns have done well in all kinds of it, that in citing one against the other, we shall take up more time this evening than each man's occasions will allow him: therefore I would ask Crites to what part of poesy he would confine his arguments, and whether he would defend the general cause of the Ancients against the Moderns, or oppose any age of the Moderns against this of ours?"

Crites, a little while considering upon this demand, told Eugenius he approved his propositions, and if he pleased, he would limit their dispute to dramatic poesy; in which he thought it not difficult to prove, either that the Ancients were superior to the Moderns, or the last age to this of ours. ...

Crites, being desired by the company to begin, spoke on behalf of the Ancients, in this manner:

"If confidence presage a victory, Eugenius, in his own opinion, has already triumphed over the Ancients: nothing seems more easy to him, than to overcome those whom it is our greatest praise to have imitated well; for we do not only build upon their foundation, but by their models. Dramatic poesy had time enough, reckoning from Thespis[2] (who first invented it) to Aristophanes,[3] to be born, to grow up, and to flourish in maturity. It has been observed of arts and sciences, that in one and the same century they have arrived to a great perfection; and no wonder, since every age has a kind of universal genius, which inclines those that live in it to some particular studies: the work then being pushed on by many hands, must of necessity go forward.

"Is it not evident, in these last hundred years (when the study of philosophy[4] has been the business of all the Virtuosi in Christendom), that almost a new nature has been revealed to us?—that more errors of the school have been detected, more useful experiments in philosophy have been made, more noble secrets in optics, medicine, anatomy, astronomy, discovered, than in all those credulous and doting ages from Aristotle to us?—so true is it, that nothing spreads more fast than science,[5] when rightly and generally cultivated.

"Add to this, the more than common emulation that was in those times of writing well; which though it be found in all ages and all persons that pretend to the same reputation, yet Poesy, being then in more esteem than now it is, had greater honours decreed to the professors of it, and consequently the rivalship was more high between them; they had judges ordained to decide their merit, and prizes to reward it; and historians have been diligent to record of Aeschylus, Euripides, Sophocles, Lycophron,[6] and the rest of them, both who they were that vanquished in these wars of the theatre, and how often they were crowned: while the Asian kings and Grecian commonwealths scarce afforded them a nobler subject than the unmanly luxuries of a debauched court, or giddy intrigues of a factious city. *Alit aemulatio ingenia* (says Paterculus[7]) *et nunc invidia, nunc admiratio incitationem accendit*: Emulation is the spur of wit; and sometimes envy, sometimes admiration, quickens our endeavours.

"But now, since the rewards of honour are taken away, that virtuous emulation is turned into direct malice; yet so slothful, that it contents itself to condemn and cry down others, without attempting to do better: 'tis a reputation too unprofitable, to take the necessary pains for it; yet, wishing they had it is incitement enough to hinder others from it. And this, in short, Eugenius, is the reason why you have now so few good poets, and so many severe judges. Certainly, to imitate

---

[1] *Si ... annus*   Latin: If poems improve with every passing day, as wine does, I should like to know which year is best for literature (Horace, *Epistles* 2.1.34–35).

[2] *Thespis*   The first reported actor upon the stage in ancient Greece (in the sixth century BCE).

[3] *Aristophanes*   Greek comic poet (c. 446–385 BCE); his plays are the only surviving examples of ancient Greek "Old Comedy," characterized by high-spirited satire of popular persons and events, as well as buffoonery and "low" humor.

[4] *philosophy*   I.e., science.

[5] *science*   I.e., knowledge.

[6] *Aeschylus, Euripides, Sophocles, Lycophron*   Ancient Greek tragedians.

[7] *Paterculus*   Marcus Velleius Paterculus (c. 19 BCE–c. 31 CE), Roman historian known for his *Historiae Romanae*.

the Ancients well, much labour and long study is required; which pains, I have already shown, our poets would want encouragement to take, if yet they had ability to go through with it. Those Ancients have been faithful imitators and wise observers of that Nature which is so torn and ill represented in our plays; they have handed down to us a perfect resemblance of her; which we, like ill copiers, neglecting to look on, have rendered monstrous, and disfigured. But, that you may know how much you are indebted to those your masters, and be ashamed to have so ill requited them, I must remember you, that all the rules by which we practise the drama at this day (either such as relate to the justness and symmetry of the plot, or the episodical ornaments, such as descriptions, narrations, and other beauties, which are not essential to the play) were delivered to us from the observations which Aristotle made, of those poets, which either lived before him, or were his contemporaries: we have added nothing of our own, except we have the confidence to say our wit is better; of which none boast in this our age, but such as understand not theirs. Of that book which Aristotle has left us, περὶ τῆς Ποιητικῆς,[1] Horace his *Art of Poetry* is an excellent comment, and I believe, restores to us that Second Book of his concerning *Comedy*, which is wanting in him.

"Out of these two have been extracted the famous rules, which the French call *des trois unitez*, or, the three unities, which ought to be observed in every regular play; namely, of time, place, and action.

"The unity of time they comprehend in twenty-four hours, the compass of a natural day, or as near as it can be contrived; and the reason of it is obvious to every one—that the time of the feigned action, or fable of the play, should be proportioned as near as can be to the duration of that time in which it is represented: since therefore, all plays are acted on the theatre in a space of time much within the compass of twenty-four hours, that play is to be thought the nearest imitation of nature, whose plot or action is confined within that time; and, by the same rule which concludes this general proportion of time, it follows, that all the parts of it are to be equally subdivided; as namely, that one act take not up the supposed time of half a day, which is out of

proportion to the rest; since the other four are then to be straitened within the compass of the remaining half: for it is unnatural that one act, which being spoke or written is not longer than the rest, should be supposed longer by the audience; 'tis therefore the poet's duty, to take care that no act should be imagined to exceed the time in which it is represented on the stage; and that the intervals and inequalities of time be supposed to fall out between the acts.

"This rule of time, how well it has been observed by the Ancients, most of their plays will witness; you see them in their tragedies (wherein to follow this rule, is certainly most difficult) from the very beginning of their plays, falling close into that part of the story which they intend for the action or principal object of it, leaving the former part to be delivered by narration: so that they set the audience, as it were, at the post where the race is to be concluded; and, saving them the tedious expectation of seeing the poet set out and ride the beginning of the course, you behold him not till he is in sight of the goal, and just upon you.

"For the second unity, which is that of place, the Ancients meant by it, that the scene ought to be continued through the play, in the same place where it was laid in the beginning: for the stage on which it is represented being but one and the same place, it is unnatural to conceive it many; and those far distant from one another. I will not deny but, by the variation of painted scenes, the fancy, which in these cases will contribute to its own deceit, may sometimes imagine it several places, with some appearance of probability; yet it still carries the greater likelihood of truth, if those places be supposed so near each other, as in the same town or city; which may all be comprehended under the larger denomination of one place; for a greater distance will bear no proportion to the shortness of time which is allotted in the acting, to pass from one of them to another; for the observation of this, next to the Ancients, the French are to be most commended. They tie themselves so strictly to the unity of place, that you never see in any of their plays, a scene changed in the middle of an act: if the act begins in a garden, a street, or a chamber, 'tis ended in the same place; and that you may know it to be the same, the stage is so supplied with persons, that it is never empty all the time: he that

---

[1] περὶ τῆς Ποιητικῆς   *Poetics* of Aristotle.

enters the second, has business with him who was on before; and before the second quits the stage, a third appears who has business with him. This Corneille calls *la liaison des scenes*, the continuity or joining of the scenes; and 'tis a good mark of a well-contrived play, when all the persons are known to each other, and every one of them has some affairs with all the rest.

"As for the third unity, which is that of action, the Ancients meant no other by it than what the logicians do by their *finis*, the end or scope of any action; that which is the first in intention, and last in execution: now the poet is to aim at one great and complete action, to the carrying on of which all things in his play, even the very obstacles, are to be subservient; and the reason of this is as evident as any of the former.

"For two actions, equally laboured and driven on by the writer, would destroy the unity of the poem; it would be no longer one play, but two: not but that there may be many actions in a play, as Ben Johnson has observed in his *Discoveries*; but they must be all subservient to the great one, which our language happily expresses in the name of *underplots*: such as in Terence's *Eunuch*[1] is the difference and reconcilement of Thais and Phaedria, which is not the chief business of the play, but promotes the marriage of Chaerea and Chremes's sister, principally intended by the poet. There ought to be but one action, says Corneille,[2] that is, one complete action which leaves the mind of the audience in a full repose; but this cannot be brought to pass but by many other imperfect actions, which conduce to it, and hold the audience in a delightful suspense of what will be.

"If by these rules (to omit many other drawn from the precepts and practice of the Ancients) we should judge our modern plays, 'tis probable that few of them would endure the trial: that which should be business of a day, takes up in some of them an age; instead of one action, they are the epitomes of a man's life; and for one spot of ground (which the stage should represent) we are sometimes in more countries than the map can show us."…

[Neander:] "But to return from whence I have digressed: I dare boldly affirm these two things of the English drama; first, that we have many plays of ours as regular as any of theirs,[3] and which, besides, have more variety of plot and characters; and secondly, that in most of the irregular plays of Shakespeare or Fletcher[4] (for Ben Jonson's are for the most part regular) there is a more masculine fancy and greater spirit in the writing, than there is in any of the French. I could produce, even in Shakespeare's and Fletcher's works, some plays which are almost exactly formed; as *The Merry Wives of Windsor*, and *The Scornful Lady*: but because (generally speaking) Shakespeare, who writ first, did not perfectly observe the laws of comedy, and Fletcher, who came nearer to perfection, yet through carelessness made many faults; I will take the pattern of a perfect play from Ben Jonson, who was a careful and learned observer of the dramatic laws, and from all his comedies I shall select *The Silent Woman*; of which I will make a short examen, according to those rules which the French observe."

As Neander was beginning to examine *The Silent Woman*, Eugenius, looking earnestly upon him; "I beseech you, Neander," said he, "gratify the company, and me in particular, so far, as before you speak of the play, to give us a character of the author; and tell us frankly your opinion, whether you do not think all writers, both French and English, ought to give place to him."

"I fear," replied Neander, "that in obeying your commands I shall draw a little envy on myself. Besides, in performing them, it will be first necessary to speak somewhat of Shakespeare and Fletcher, his rivals in poesy; and one of them, in my opinion, at least his equal, perhaps his superior.

"To begin, then, with Shakespeare. He was the man who of all modern, and perhaps ancient poets, had the largest and most comprehensive soul. All the images of Nature were still present to him, and he drew them, not laboriously, but luckily; when he describes any thing, you more than see it, you feel it too. Those who accuse him to have wanted learning, give him the greater

---

[1] *Terence's Eunuch* P. Terentius Afer, or Terence (185–159 BCE), a Roman comic playwright and author of *Eunuchus* (161 BCE).

[2] *Corneille* Pierre Corneille (1606–84), a French playwright.

[3] *of theirs* I.e., those of the French.

[4] *Fletcher* John Fletcher (1579–1625), a Jacobean poet and playwright, known for his tragicomedies and comedies of manners, who often collaborated with Francis Beaumont (1584–1616).

commendation: he was naturally learned; he needed not the spectacles of books to read Nature; he looked inwards, and found her there. I cannot say he is every where alike; were he so, I should do him injury to compare him with the greatest of mankind. He is many times flat, insipid; his comic wit degenerating into clenches, his serious swelling into bombast. But he is always great, when some great occasion is presented to him; no man can say he ever had a fit subject for his wit, and did not then raise himself as high above the rest of poets,

Quantum lenta solent inter viburna cupressi.[1]

The consideration of this made Mr. Hales[2] of Eton say, that there was no subject of which any poet ever writ, but he would produce it much better treated of in Shakespeare; and however others are now generally preferred before him, yet the age wherein he lived, which had contemporaries with him Fletcher and Jonson, never equalled them to him in their esteem: and in the last King's court, when Ben's reputation was at highest, Sir John Suckling, and with him the greater part of the courtiers, set our Shakespeare far above him.

"Beaumont and Fletcher, of whom I am next to speak, had, with the advantage of Shakespeare's wit, which was their precedent, great natural gifts, improved by study: Beaumont especially being so accurate a judge of plays, that Ben Jonson, while he lived, submitted all his writings to his censure, and, 'tis thought, used his judgment in correcting, if not contriving, all his plots. What value he had for him, appears by the verses he writ to him; and therefore I need speak no farther of it. The first play that brought Fletcher and him in esteem was their *Philaster*: for before that, they had written two or three very unsuccessfully, as the like is reported of Ben Jonson, before he writ *Every Man in his Humour*. Their plots were generally more regular than Shakespeare's, especially those which were made before Beaumont's death; and they understood and imitated the conversation of gentlemen much better; whose wild debaucher-

ies, and quickness of wit in repartees, no poet can ever paint as they have done. Humour, which Ben Jonson derived from particular persons, they made it not their business to describe: they represented all the passions very lively, but above all, love. I am apt to believe the English language in them arrived to its highest perfection: what words have since been taken in, are rather superfluous than ornamental. Their plays are now the most pleasant and frequent entertainments of the stage; two of theirs being acted through the year for one of Shakespeare's or Jonson's: the reason is, because there is a certain gaiety in their comedies, and pathos in their more serious plays, which suits generally with all men's humours. Shakespeare's language is likewise a little obsolete, and Ben Jonson's wit comes short of theirs.

"As for Jonson, to whose character I am now arrived, if we look upon him while he was himself (for his last plays were but his dotages), I think him the most learned and judicious writer which any theatre ever had. He was a most severe judge of himself, as well as others. One cannot say he wanted wit, but rather that he was frugal of it. In his works you find little to retrench or alter. Wit, and language, and honour also in some measure, we had before him; but something of art was wanting to the drama, till he came. He managed his strength to more advantage than any who preceded him. You seldom find him making love in any of his scenes, or endeavouring to move the passions; his genius was too sullen and saturnine to do it gracefully, especially when he knew he came after those who had performed both to such an height. Humour was his proper sphere; and in that he delighted most to represent mechanic people.[3] He was deeply conversant in the Ancients, both Greek and Latin, and he borrowed boldly from them: there is scarce a poet or historian among the Roman authors of those times whom he has not translated in *Sejanus* and *Catiline*. But he has done his robberies so openly, that one may see he fears not to be taxed by any law. He invades authors like a monarch; and what would be theft in other poets, is only victory in him. With the spoils of these writers he so represents old Rome to us, in its rites, ceremonies, and customs, that if one of their poets had written either of his tragedies, we had seen less of it than in him. If there was any fault

---

[1] *Quantum … cupressi* Latin: As do cypresses among pliant shrubs (Virgil, *Eclogues* 1.25).

[2] *Mr. Hales* John Hales (1584–1656), who claimed he had heard Ben Jonson speak of Shakespeare's lack of learning.

[3] *mechanic people* Members of the working class; tradespeople.

in his language, 'twas that he weaved it too closely and laboriously, in his serious plays: perhaps too, he did a little too much Romanize our tongue, leaving the words which he translated almost as much Latin as he found them: wherein, though he learnedly followed the idiom of their language, he did not enough comply with the idiom of ours. If I would compare him with Shakespeare, I must acknowledge him the more correct poet, but Shakespeare the greater wit. Shakespeare was the Homer, or father of our dramatic poets; Jonson was the Virgil, the pattern of elaborate writing; I admire him, but I love Shakespeare. To conclude of him; as he has given us the most correct plays, so in the precepts which he has laid down in his *Discoveries*, we have as many and profitable rules for perfecting the stage, as any wherewith the French can furnish us.

"Having thus spoken of the author, I proceed to the examination of his comedy, *The* Silent Woman.

Examen of The Silent Woman

"To begin first with the length of the action; it is so far from exceeding the compass of a natural day, that it takes not up an artificial one. 'Tis all included in the limits of three hours and an half, which is no more than is required for the presentment on the stage. A beauty perhaps not much observed; if it had, we should not have looked on the Spanish translation of *Five Hours* with so much wonder. The scene of it is laid in London; the latitude of place is almost as little as you can imagine; for it lies all within the compass of two houses, and after the first act, in one. The continuity of scenes is observed more than in any of our plays, except his own *Fox* and *Alchymist*. They are not broken above twice or thrice at most in the whole comedy; and in the two best of Corneille's plays, the *Cid* and *Cinna*, they are interrupted once apiece. The action of the play is entirely one; the end or aim of which is the settling Morose's estate on Dauphine. The intrigue of it is the greatest and most noble of any pure unmixed comedy in any language; you see it in many persons of various characters and humours, and all delightful: as first, Morose, or an old man, to whom all noise but his own talking is offensive. Some who would be thought critics, say this

humour of his is forced: but to remove that objection, we may consider him first to be naturally of a delicate hearing, as many are, to whom all sharp sounds are unpleasant; and secondly, we may attribute much of it to the peevishness of his age, or the wayward authority of an old man in his own house, where he may make himself obeyed; and this the poet seems to allude to in his name Morose. Besides this, I am assured from diverse persons, that Ben Jonson was actually acquainted with such a man, one altogether as ridiculous as he is here represented. Others say, it is not enough to find one man of such an humour; it must be common to more, and the more common the more natural. To prove this, they instance in the best of comical characters, Falstaff: there are many men resembling him; old, fat, merry, cowardly, drunken, amorous, vain, and lying. But to convince these people, I need but tell them, that humour is the ridiculous extravagance of conversation, wherein one man differs from all others. If then it be common, or communicated to many, how differs it from other men's? or what indeed causes it to be ridiculous so much as the singularity of it? As for Falstaff, he is not properly one humour, but a miscellany of humours or images, drawn from so many several men: that wherein he is singular is his wit, or those things he says *praeter expectatum*, unexpected by the audience; his quick evasions, when you imagine him surprised, which, as they are extremely diverting of themselves, so receive a great addition from his person; for the very sight of such an unwieldy old debauched fellow is a comedy alone. And here, having a place so proper for it, I cannot but enlarge somewhat upon this subject of humour into which I am fallen. The ancients had little of it in their comedies; for the τὸ γελοῖον[1] of the Old Comedy, of which Aristophanes was chief, was not so much to imitate a man, as to make the people laugh at some odd conceit, which had commonly somewhat of unnatural or obscene in it. Thus, when you see Socrates brought upon the stage, you are not to imagine him made ridiculous by the imitation of his actions, but rather by making him perform something very unlike himself; something so childish and absurd, as by comparing it with the gravity of true Socrates, makes a ridiculous

---

[1] τὸ γελοῖον   Greek: the laughable.

object for the spectators. In their New Comedy[1] which succeeded, the poets sought indeed to express the ἦθος[2] as in their tragedies the πάθος[3] of mankind. But this ἦθος contained only the general characters of men and manners; as old men, lovers, serving-men, courtezans, parasites, and such other persons as we see in their comedies; all which they made alike: that is, one old man or father, one lover, one courtezan, so like another, as if the first of them had begot the rest of every sort: *Ex homine hunc natum dicas.*[4] The same custom they observed likewise in their tragedies. As for the French, though they have the word *humeur* among them, yet they have small use of it in their comedies or farces; they being but ill imitations of the *ridiculum*, or that which stirred up laughter in the Old Comedy. But among the English 'tis otherwise: where by humour is meant some extravagant habit, passion, or affection, particular (as I said before) to some one person, by the oddness of which, he is immediately distinguished from the rest of men; which being lively and naturally represented, most frequently begets that malicious pleasure in the audience which is testified by laughter; as all things which are deviations from common customs are ever the aptest to produce it: though by the way this laughter is only accidental, as the person represented is fantastic or bizarre; but pleasure is essential to it, as the limitation of what is natural. The description of these humours, drawn from the knowledge and observation of particular persons, was the peculiar genius and talent of Ben Jonson; to whose play I now return.

"Besides Morose, there are at least nine or ten different characters and humours in *The Silent Woman*; all which persons have several concernments of their own, yet are all used by the poet, to the conducting of the main design to perfection. I shall not waste time in commending the writing of this play; but I will give you

my opinion, that there is more wit and acuteness of fancy in it than in any of Ben Jonson's. Besides, that he has here described the conversation of gentlemen in the persons of True-Wit, and his friends, with more gaiety, air, and freedom, than in the rest of his comedies. For the contrivance of the plot, 'tis extreme elaborate, and yet withal easy; for the λύσις, or untying of it, 'tis so admirable, that when it is done, no one of the audience would think the poet could have missed it; and yet it was concealed so much before the last scene, that any other way would sooner have entered into your thoughts. But I dare not take upon me to commend the fabric of it, because it is altogether so full of art, that I must unravel every scene in it to commend it as I ought. And this excellent contrivance is still the more to be admired, because 'tis comedy, where the persons are only of common rank, and their business private, not elevated by passions or high concernments, as in serious plays. Here every one is a proper judge of all he sees, nothing is represented but that with which he daily converses: so that by consequence all faults lie open to discovery, and few are pardonable. 'Tis this which Horace has judiciously observed:

Creditur, ex medio quia res arcessit, habere
Sudoris minimum; sed habet Comedia tanto
Plus oneris, quanto veniae minus.[5]

But our poet who was not ignorant of these difficulties, had prevailed himself of all advantages; as he who designs a large leap takes his rise from the highest ground. One of these advantages is that which Corneille has laid down as the greatest which can arrive to any poem, and which he himself could never compass above thrice in all his plays; viz. the making choice of some signal and long-expected day, whereon the action of the play is to depend. This day was that designed by Dauphine for the settling of his uncle's estate upon him; which to compass, he contrives to marry him. That the marriage had been plotted by him long beforehand, is made evident by what he tells True-Wit in the second act, that

---

[1] *New Comedy* Originating in ancient Greece and Rome in the fourth and third centuries BCE, New Comedy began to replace the farcical satires of Old Comedy with a wittier and more romantic form. Menander, Plautus and Terence were writers associated with this style.

[2] ἦθος Greek: character.

[3] πάθος Greek: passion of mankind.

[4] *Ex homine ... dicas* Latin: You would say he was born of the other man (Terence, *Eunuch*, 460).

[5] *Creditur ... minus* Latin: It is believed that comedy demands the least effort because it draws its subjects from the ordinary; but the less indulgence it has, the greater the work it needs (Horace, *Epistles* 2. 1.168–170).

in one moment he had destroyed what he had been raising many months.

"There is another artifice of the poet, which I cannot here omit, because by the frequent practice of it in his comedies he has left it to us almost as a rule; that is, when he has any character of humour wherein he would show a *coup de Maistre*, or his highest skill, he recommends it to your observation by a pleasant description of it before the person first appears. Thus, in *Bartholomew Fair* he gives you the pictures of Numps and Cokes, and in this those of Daw, Lafoole, Morose, and the Collegiate Ladies; all which you hear described before you see them. So that before they come upon the stage, you have a longing expectation of them, which prepares you to receive them favourably; and when they are there, even from their first appearance you are so far acquainted with them, that nothing of their humour is lost to you.

"I will observe yet one thing further of this admirable plot; the business of it rises in every act. The second is greater than the first; the third than the second; and so forward to the fifth. There too you see, till the very last scene, new difficulties arising to obstruct the action of the play; and when the audience is brought into despair that the business can naturally be effected, then, and not before, the discovery is made. But that the poet might entertain you with more variety all this while, he reserves some new characters to show you, which he opens not till the second and third act. In the second Morose, Daw, the Barber, and Otter; in the third the Collegiate Ladies: all which he moves afterwards in bywalks, or under-plots, as diversions to the main design, lest it should grow tedious, though they are still naturally joined with it, and somewhere or other subservient to it. Thus, like a skillful chess-player, by little and little he draws out his men, and makes his pawns of use to his greater persons.

"If this comedy and some others of his were translated into French prose (which would now be no wonder to them, since Moliere has lately given them plays out of verse, which have not displeased them), I believe the controversy would soon be decided betwixt the two nations, even making them the judges. But we need not call our heroes to our aid; be it spoken to the honour of the English, our nation can never want in any age such who are able to dispute the empire of wit with any people in the universe. And though the fury of a civil war, and power for twenty years together abandoned to a barbarous race of men, enemies of all good learning, had buried the Muses under the ruins of monarchy; yet, with the restoration of our happiness, we see revived Poesy lifting up its head, and already shaking off the rubbish which lay so heavy on it. We have seen since his Majesty's return, many dramatic poems which yield not to those of any foreign nation, and which deserve all laurels but the English. I will set aside flattery and envy: it cannot be denied but we have had some little blemish either in the plot or writing of all those plays which have been made within these seven years (and perhaps there is no nation in the world so quick to discern them, or so difficult to pardon them, as ours): yet if we can persuade ourselves to use the candour[1] of that poet, who, though the most severe of critics, has left us this caution by which to moderate our censures—

… ubi plura nitent in carmine, non ego paucis Offendar maculis;[2]

if, in consideration of their many and great beauties, we can wink at some slight and little imperfections, if we, I say, can be thus equal to ourselves, I ask no favour from the French. And if I do not venture upon any particular judgment of our late plays, 'tis out of the consideration which an ancient writer gives me: *vivorum, ut magna admiratio, ita censura difficilis:*[3] betwixt the extremes of admiration and malice, 'tis hard to judge uprightly of the living. Only I think it may be permitted me to say, that as it is no lessening to us to yield to some plays, and those not many, of our own nation in the last age, so can it be no addition to pronounce of our present poets, that they have far surpassed all the Ancients, and the modern writers of other countries."

—1668

---

[1] *candour* Generosity in judgement.

[2] *ubi … maculis* Latin: where many beauties shine in a poem, I will not be bothered by little faults (Horace, *The Art of Poetry* 2.351–52).

[3] *vivorum … difficilis* Latin: admiration for the living is great, censure is difficult (Velleius Paterculus, *Historia Romana* 2.36.3).

Samuel Pepys
1633 — 1703

On 1 January 1660, a young civil servant named Samuel Pepys (pronounced "peeps") took pen in hand and began recording what has become one of the most important sources of information on the Restoration in London. Covering almost 10 years, from 1660 to 1669, Pepys's *Diary* offers an invaluable record of such momentous events as the Restoration of the Stuart monarchy in 1660, the Plague of 1665, and the Great Fire of London in 1666. Far from being a document of public record,

however, Pepys's *Diary* records with tantalizing detail hundreds of scenes from his own personal and private life. As such, the *Diary* offers an uncensored and unaffected view of one man's tastes, preoccupations, desires, and pleasures in an age of social and political turbulence. Writing in shorthand, and often employing foreign words and phrases, particularly when describing his amorous affairs, Pepys evidently never intended his *Diary* to be read by any eyes but his own (it was not deciphered and published until more than a century after his death).

Samuel Pepys was born in London in 1633, above his father's prosperous tailor shop. The fifth of eleven children (only three of whom survived childhood), Pepys grew up amidst the Puritan home atmosphere of his parents John and Margaret Pepys. Distressed from an early age by a stone in his urinary system, Pepys wrote decades later: "I remember not my life without the pain of the stone in the kidneys … till I was about twenty years of age." He was educated at St. Paul's School in London, and then attended Magdalene College, Cambridge as a scholarship student, taking his B.A. in 1654. A year later he married Elizabeth St. Michel, a penniless, fifteen-year-old French Protestant. As later entries in his *Diary* would reveal, Pepys found the marriage satisfactory, despite his criticisms of Elizabeth's unintellectual nature and alleged failures in domestic management—and despite the fact that it was a childless union (still a frequent source of marital discord at the time). As the *Diary* also reveals, Pepys engaged in a number of adulterous affairs. Nevertheless, the marriage was affectionate, and Pepys never remarried after his wife's death in 1669.

Shortly after his marriage, Pepys entered the personal service of his influential cousin Edward Montagu (later Earl of Sandwich). Commander of the Commonwealth fleet, Montagu engaged Pepys to manage his personal affairs while he was away at sea. In 1658, likely through Montagu's influence, Pepys became a clerk of the Exchequer and began his future in public administration. At the same time, the symptoms of his urinary ailment were recurring with agonizing frequency. Pepys agreed to a life-threatening surgical procedure to remove the offending kidney stone, and to his absolute delight the surgery was a success. In later years he celebrated the anniversary of this event with an annual dinner of thanksgiving with his friends and family. His continued good health is celebrated in the opening line of his *Diary* over a year later: "Blessed be God, at the end of the last year I was in very good health, without any sense of my old pain, but upon taking of cold."

As Pepys began his *Diary*, England was in tumult. Oliver Cromwell's death in 1658 had opened a period of Parliamentary upheaval and civil unrest. Pepys secured his future in public office through this difficult time by further attaching himself to the affairs of his cousin Montagu. Although Pepys and his cousin had long been supporters of Cromwell, the events following the Protector's death converted both to the Royalist cause. In 1660, Pepys went to sea as secretary to his cousin, returning on the flagship that carried King Charles II home to England. Having made valuable contacts with influential persons during the voyage, Pepys secured a high position as Clerk of the Acts with the royal navy, and distinguished himself significantly by reducing the cost of naval maintenance. His success in this post earned him accolades as "the right hand of the navy."

Having solidified his position in public office, Pepys enjoyed the security of home and income it afforded, and was able to indulge in many of his interests to a new degree. The pages of his *Diary* abound with tales of his frequent trips to the theater, not to mention his infatuations and illicit affairs with the actresses (who appeared on the English stage for the first time when Charles II reopened the London theaters). Pepys reveals his taste in fashion and his obvious love of social gatherings involving food and drink. He indulged his deep love of music, often singing with friends in his home, at taverns and coffeehouses, or playing his lute in the solitude of his room. Keenly observant by nature, and insatiably curious, Pepys began attending weekly meetings of the Royal Society to see experiments and hear lectures by leading minds of the day. He took a keen, though amateur, interest in scientific matters, and eventually he was appointed the Society's President, serving from 1684 to 1685.

Of all the events described by Pepys in his *Diary*, none illustrates more dramatically the value of first-hand commentary than his account of the Great Fire of 1666. Starting in a baker's shop in Pudding Lane on 2 September, the fire spread through the close-packed streets of London with terrifying speed. Citizens watched helplessly as their homes were consumed; the inferno raged for four days, during which 80 per cent of the city was reduced to rubble. By the end over 13,000 houses, 89 churches, 52 guild halls and the Cathedral of St. Paul's had burned in a disaster of unprecedented proportions. Pepys's contemporary (and fellow member of the Royal Society), architect Christopher Wren, was instrumental in the reconstruction of the city, including the provision of the designs for the new St. Paul's. (One interesting aspect of the reconstruction is that the fire prompted the introduction of the world's first set of building standards.)

By 1669 Pepys's eyesight had begun to trouble him a great deal. He became convinced that he was going blind, and reluctantly gave up maintaining his *Diary*. On 31 May 1669 he concluded his final entry: "And so I betake myself to that course, which is almost as much as to see myself go into my grave: for which, and all the discomforts that will accompany my being blind, the good God prepare me!" His fears proved unjustified, as he lived another thirty-four years without going blind, yet he never felt able to resume his confidential daily record. Soon after he finished with his *Diary*, Pepys and his wife embarked on a visit to France and Holland. Elizabeth fell ill during the journey, and after struggling home to London she died later that year at the age of twenty-nine.

Following the death of his wife, Pepys found distraction in his work at the Navy Office. In 1673, when the Test Act forced the Duke of York (Charles's Catholic brother James) to resign as Lord High Admiral, Pepys was installed in the newly created post of Secretary of the Admiralty by the King. He immediately enacted widespread reforms in naval operations, making the entire fleet more efficient than before. His efforts were interrupted in 1679 when he was falsely charged with, and imprisoned for, involvement in the Popish Plot (a plan that Titus Oates, an anti-Catholic protester, largely invented: he claimed that Jesuits were plotting to assassinate the King and hasten the succession of the openly Catholic James II). Although acquitted of any wrongdoing, Pepys was not re-installed in office until 1684. He continued in this official capacity when James II, an admirer of his talents, acceded to the throne in 1685. However, James's flight to France in 1688 heralded the end of Pepys's naval career. He officially discharged his last duty in 1689, and died in Clapham on 26 May 1703, after a lengthy illness.

⌘ ⌘ ⌘

from *The Diary*

MAY 1660[1]

21. So into my naked bed and slept till 9 o'clock, and then John Goods waked me, [by] and by the captain's boy brought me four barrels of Mallows oysters, which Captain Tatnell had sent me from Murlace.[2] The weather foul all this day also. After dinner, about writing one thing or other all day, and setting my papers in order, having been so long absent. At night Mr. Pierce, Purser (the other Pierce and I having not spoken to one another since we fell out about Mr. Edward), and Mr. Cook[3] sat with me in my cabin and supped with me, and then I went to bed. By letters that came hither in my absence, I understand that the Parliament had ordered all persons to be secured, in order to a trial, that did sit as judges in the late King's death[4] and all the officers too attending the Court. Sir John Lenthall moving in the House that all that had borne arms against the King should be exempted from pardon, he was called to the bar of the House, and after a severe reproof he was degraded his knighthood.[5] At Court I find that all things grow high. The old clergy talk as being sure of their lands again, and laugh at the Presbytery; and it is believed that the sales of the King's and Bishops' lands will never be confirmed by Parliament,[6] there being nothing now in any man's power to hinder them and the King[7] from doing what they have a mind, but everybody willing to submit to anything. We expect every day to have the King and Duke[8] on board as soon as it is fair. My Lord do nothing now, but offers all things to the pleasure of the Duke as Lord High Admiral. So that I am at a loss what to do.

22. Up very early, and now beginning to be settled in my wits again, I went about setting down my last four days' observations this morning. After that, was trimmed by a barber that has not trimmed me yet, my Spaniard being on shore. News brought that the two Dukes are coming on board, which, by and by, they did, in a Dutch boat, the Duke of York in yellow trimmings, the Duke of Gloucester[9] in grey and red. My Lord[10] went in a boat to meet them, the Captain, myself, and others, standing at the entering port. So soon as they were entered we shot the guns off round the fleet. After that they went to view the ship all over, and were most exceedingly pleased with it. They seem to be both very fine gentlemen. After that done, upon the quarter-deck table under the awning, the Duke of York and my Lord,

---

[1] *May 1660* In March 1660, Pepys accompanied his patron Edward Montagu, soon to become the 1st Earl of Sandwich, then recently reappointed General at Sea, on a mission to retrieve Charles II from the Netherlands, where he had been exiled during Oliver Cromwell's protectorate (1651–58). On 8 May 1660, the English Parliament formally named Charles II king, and Montagu was officially charged with bringing Charles home. This entry is thus written onboard ship.

[2] *naked bed* Reference to the then-common habit of sleeping naked; a bed in which one sleeps without undergarments; *John Goods* One of the Earl of Sandwich's servants; *Mallows* St. Malo, a port city in the Brittany region in the northwest of France; *Murlace* Morlaix, a village in Brittany.

[3] *Mr. Pierce … the other Pierce* The ship's purser was Andrew Pearse; the "other" Pearse is James, the ship's surgeon; *Purser* Naval officer charged with supplies and accounts onboard a ship; *Mr. Edward* Edward Montagu, the Earl of Sandwich's son, then twelve years old. A few days earlier when they were spending time as tourists on shore, Pepys had left the boy with Pearse to look after him, and the two spent the night in another town without leaving Pepys any indication of where they had gone; *Mr. Cook* Another of Sandwich's servants.

[4] *late King's death* King Charles I, father of Charles II, was executed on 30 January 1649 during the English Civil War.

[5] *Sir John Lenthall … degraded his knighthood* Lenthall was elected Member of Parliament in 1645 and knighted by Cromwell in 1658. The House's rebuke, apparently provoked by Lenthall's blanket condemnation of Cromwell's supporters, may have been politically motivated; the House did not, however, revoke his title, which ceased to exist at the end of Cromwell's protectorate.

[6] *The old … by Parliament* Church and crown lands had been sold during Cromwell's rule, but most property was recovered by its original owners; *Presbytery* Clerical court.

[7] *King* Charles II.

[8] *Duke* James Stuart, Duke of York and Lord High Admiral. In 1685, he would become King of England and Ireland (as James II) and King of Scotland (as James VII).

[9] *Duke of Gloucester* Henry Stuart, youngest son of Charles I.

[10] *My Lord* Earl of Sandwich.

Mr. Coventry[1] and I spent an hour at allotting to every ship their service in their return to England; which having done, they went to dinner, where the table was very full: the two Dukes at the upper end, my Lord Opdam[2] next on one side, and my Lord on the other. Two guns given to every man while he was drinking the King's health, and so likewise to the Duke's health. I took down Monsieur d'Esquier[3] to the great cabin below, and dined with him in state alone with only one or two friends of his. All dinner the harper[4] belonging to Captain Sparling played to the Dukes. After dinner, the Dukes and my Lord to see the Vice and Rear-Admirals, and I in a boat after them. After that done, they made to the shore in the Dutch boat that brought them, and I got into the boat with them; but the shore was so full of people to expect their coming, as that it was as black (which otherwise is white sand), as every one could stand by another. When we came near the shore my Lord left them and came into his own boat, and General Pen[5] and I with him; my Lord being very well pleased with this day's work. By the time we came on board again, news is sent us that the King is on shore; so my Lord fired all his guns round twice, and all the fleet after him, which in the end fell into disorder, which seemed very handsome. The gun over against my cabin I fired myself to the King, which was the first time that he had been saluted by his own ships since this change; but holding my head too much over the gun, I had almost spoiled my right eye. Nothing in the world but going of guns almost all this day. In the evening we began to remove[6] cabins; I to the carpenter's cabin, and Dr. Clerke with me, who came on board this afternoon, having been twice ducked in the sea today coming from

shore, and Mr. North and John Pickering[7] the like. Many of the King's servants came on board tonight; and so many Dutch of all sorts came to see the ship till it was quite dark, that we could not pass by one another, which was a great trouble to us all. This afternoon Mr. Downing[8] (who was knighted yesterday by the King) was here on board, and had a ship for his passage into England, with his lady and servants. By the same token he called me to him when I was going to write the order, to tell me that I must write him Sir G. Downing. My Lord lay in the roundhouse[9] tonight. This evening I was late writing a French letter myself by my Lord's order to Monsieur Kragh, Embassador de Denmarke à la Haye,[10] which my Lord signed in bed. After that I to bed, and the Doctor, and sleep well.

23. The Doctor and I waked very merry, only my eye was very red and ill in the morning from yesterday's hurt. In the morning came infinity of people on board from the King to go along with him. My Lord, Mr. Crew,[11] and others, go on shore to meet the King as he comes off from shore, where Sir R. Stayner[12] bringing His Majesty into the boat, I hear that His Majesty did with a great deal of affection kiss my Lord upon his first meeting. The King, with the two Dukes and Queen of Bohemia, Princess Royal, and Prince of Orange,[13] came

---

[1] *Mr. Coventry* Sir William Coventry served as secretary to the Duke of York following negotiations to restore Charles II to the throne. He and Pepys became well-acquainted and attached.

[2] *Lord Opdam* Jacob Obdam served as the supreme commander of the Dutch navy.

[3] *Monsieur d'Esquier* Sandwich's assistant.

[4] *harper* Harp player.

[5] *General Pen* Sir William Penn, an English admiral and, as of 1660, Commissioner of the Navy Board.

[6] *remove* I.e., remove to.

[7] *Dr. Clerke* Timothy Clarke, physician; *Mr. North and John Pickering* Sir Charles North and John Pickering, both sons of barons related to the Montagu family by marriage.

[8] *Mr. Downing* Sir George Downing, a diplomat sent by Cromwell to the Netherlands in 1657 to unite the Protestant countries in Europe and follow the activities of exiled supporters of the King. However, in 1660, he renounced his former allegiances and reconciled with Charles II, who, as Pepys notes, knighted him.

[9] *roundhouse* Set of cabins in the ship's rear part.

[10] *Monsieur Kragh … la Haye* Otto Krag, one of two Danish ambassadors to Charles II.

[11] *Mr. Crew* John Crew, a Member of Parliament who worked to restore Charles II to the throne.

[12] *Sir R. Stayner* Richard Stayner, a naval commander and friend of Montagu, who had the distinction of being knighted by both Cromwell and, after the Restoration, Charles II.

[13] *Queen of Bohemia* Sister of Charles I—and therefore aunt to the King and to the Duke of York; *Princess Royal* Sister to the King and to the Duke of York; *Prince of Orange* Son of the Princess Royal, William (who much later would become king) was nine years old in 1660.

on board, where I in their coming in kissed the King's, Queen's, and Princess's hands, having done the other before. Infinite shooting off of the guns and that in a disorder on purpose, which was better than if it had been otherwise. All day nothing but Lords and persons of honour on board, that we were exceeding full. Dined in a great deal of state, the royal company by themselves in the coach,[1] which was a blessed sight to see. I dined with Dr. Clerke, Dr. Quarterman, and Mr. Darcy[2] in my cabin. This morning Mr. Lucy came on board, to whom and his company of the King's guard in another ship my Lord did give three dozen of bottles of wine. He made friends between Mr. Pierce and me. After dinner the king and Duke altered the name of some of the ships, viz.[3] the *Nazeby* into *Charles*; the *Richard*, *James*; the *Speakers*, *Mary*; the *Dunbar* (which was not in company with us), the *Henry*; *Winsly*, *Happy Return*; *Wakefield*, *Richmond*; *Lambert*, the *Henrietta*; *Cheriton*, the *Speedwell*; *Bradford*, the *Success*. That done, the Queen, Princess Royal, and Prince of Orange took leave of the King, and the Duke of York went on board the *London*, and the Duke of Gloucester, the *Swiftsure*. Which done, we weighed anchor, and with a fresh gale and most happy weather we set sail for England. All the afternoon the King walked here and there, up and down (quite contrary to what I thought him to have been), very active and stirring. Upon the quarter-deck he fell into discourse of his escape from Worcester,[4] where it made me ready to weep to hear the stories that he told of his difficulties that he had passed through, as his travelling four days and three nights on foot, every step up to his knees in dirt, with nothing but a green coat

and a pair of country breeches on, and a pair of country shoes that made him so sore all over his feet that he could scarce stir. Yet he was forced to run away from a miller and other company that took them for rogues. His sitting at table at one place, where the master of the house, that had not seen him in eight years, did know him, but kept it private; when at the same table there was one that had been of his own regiment at Worcester, could not know him, but made him drink the King's health, and said that the King was at least four fingers higher than he.[5] At another place he was by some servants of the house made to drink, that they might know him not to be a Roundhead,[6] which they swore he was. In another place at his inn, the master of the house, as the King was standing with his hands upon the back of a chair by the fire-side, kneeled down and kissed his hand, privately, saying that he would not ask him who he was, but bid God bless him whither he was going. Then the difficulty of getting a boat to get into France, where he was fain[7] to plot with the master thereof to keep his design from the four men and a boy (which was all his ship's company), and so got to Fécamp in France. At Rouen he looked so poorly that the people went into the rooms before he went away to see whether he had not stole something or other. In the evening I went up to my Lord to write letters for England, which he sent away with word of our coming, by Mr. Edw. Pickering.[8] The King supped alone in the coach; after that I got a dish, and we four supped in my cabin, as at noon. About bed-time my Lord Bartelett (who I had offered my service to before) sent for me to get him a bed, who with much ado I did get to bed to my Lord Middlesex[9]

---

[1] *the coach* I.e., the ship.

[2] *Dr. Quarterman* William Quartermaine, personal physician to Charles II; *Mr. Darcy* Marmaduke Darcy, companion to Charles II during his exile.

[3] *viz.* Abbreviation of the Latin *videlicet*, meaning "namely" or "that is to say." Ship names reflecting glory on the Commonwealth (e.g. the battle of Nazeby, a roundhead victory, and Richard, Oliver Cromwell's son) are giving way to royalist names, e.g. Charles and James.

[4] *Worcester* Site of an attempt by Charles II to regain the crown in 1651; Charles's forces were decisively defeated, and a £1000 reward was offered for Charles's arrest. The king's escape to France (the story of which was preserved for posterity by Pepys) was thus a thoroughly dangerous one, shadowed by the possibility of capture and execution.

[5] *the King … higher than he* Charles II was 1.88 meters (or 6′ 2″) in height, a size that distinguished him from other seventeenth-century men, who were generally significantly shorter. The king's conspicuous height made his escape after the Battle of Worcester all the more difficult.

[6] *Roundhead* Supporter of Parliament during the Civil War, named for their tendency to cut their hair close to their heads.

[7] *fain* Forced by circumstance.

[8] *Mr. Edw. Pickering* Edward Pickering, a relative of Sandwich's, whose tendency to gossip made him widely reviled.

[9] *Lord Bartelett* Apparently a mistake for Lord Berkeley, one of the six lords assigned to present a congratulatory speech to the restored king; *Lord Middlesex* Charles Sackville, also a member of the delegation sent to congratulate and welcome the King.

in the great cabin below, but I was cruelly troubled before I could dispose of him, and quit myself of him. So to my cabin again, where the company still was, and were talking more of the King's difficulties; as how he was fain to eat a piece of bread and cheese out of a poor boy's pocket; how, at a Catholic house, he was fain to lie in the priest's hole[1] a good while in the house for his privacy. After that our company broke up, and the Doctor and I to bed. We have all the Lords Commissioners on board us, and many others. Under sail all night, and most glorious weather.

OCTOBER 1660[2]

20. This morning one came to me to advise with me where to make me a window into my cellar in lieu of one which Sir W. Batten[3] had stopped up, and going down into my cellar to look I stepped into a great heap of ———, by which I found that Mr. Turner's house of office[4] is full and comes into my cellar, which do trouble me, but I shall have it helped. To my Lord's by land, calling at several places about business, where I dined with my Lord and Lady;[5] when he was very merry, and did talk very high how he would have a French cook, and a master of his horse, and his lady and child to wear black patches;[6] which methought was strange, but he is become a perfect courtier; and, among other things, my Lady saying that she could get a good merchant for her

daughter Jem.,[7] he answered, that he would rather see her with a pedlar's[8] pack at her back, so she married a gentleman, than she should marry a citizen. This afternoon, going through London, and called at Crowe's the upholster's, in Saint Bartholomew's, I saw the limbs of some of our new traitors set upon Aldersgate, which was a sad sight to see; and a bloody week this and the last have been, there being ten hanged, drawn, and quartered.[9] Home, and after writing a letter to my uncle by the post, I went to bed.

NOVEMBER 1660

10. Up early. Sir Wm. Batten and I to make up an account of the wages of the officers and mariners at sea, ready to present to the Committee of Parliament this afternoon. Afterwards came the Treasurer and Comptroller,[10] and sat all the morning with us till the business was done. So we broke up, leaving the thing to be wrote over fair and carried to Trinity House for Sir Wm. Batten's hand.[11] When staying very long I found (as appointed) the Treasurer and Comptroller at Whitehall,[12] and so we went with a foul copy[13] to the Parliament house, where we met with Sir Thos. Clarges and Mr. Spry, and after we had given them good satisfaction we parted. The Comptroller and I to the coffee-

---

[1] *Catholic house* Charles II was repeatedly aided by Catholics. The King converted to Catholicism on his deathbed; *priest's hole* Hiding place for Catholic priests, particularly necessary in Elizabethan and Jacobean England during intense periods of persecution.

[2] *October 1660* Pepys spent much of October 1660 making household repairs, bringing his house into accordance with his newly attained status and wealth.

[3] *Sir W. Batten* Sir William Batten, admiral and Surveyor of the Navy.

[4] ——— Samuel politely notes stepping into the toilet waste that has apparently collected in his neighbor's home; *Mr. Turner* Thomas Turner, General Clerk at the Navy Office; *house of office* Toilet.

[5] *Lady* Jemima Montagu, Countess of Sandwich, wife of Edward Montagu.

[6] *black patches* Artificial beauty spots, placed on the face. These became fashionable in the court of Charles I, though they were just as often ridiculed.

[7] *Jem.* Jemima Montagu, later Carteret, daughter of the Earl and Countess of Sandwich.

[8] *pedlar* Itinerant street seller. Sandwich would rather his daughter married an upper-class man, even if poor, than someone bourgeois ("citizen") even if rich.

[9] *traitors set … and quartered* On 13 October 1660, ten men involved in the execution of Charles I were hanged, drawn, and quartered. The limbs "upon Aldersgate" are the butchered quarters of these men, nailed up on one of the gateways to the City of London as an awful warning. Pepys, a witness to the event, writes in his entry for the day: "Thus it was my chance to see the King beheaded at Whitehall, and to see the first blood shed in revenge for the blood of the King at Charing Cross."

[10] *Comptroller* Head accountant.

[11] *Trinity House … Batten's hand* Batten was Master of Trinity House, the authority responsible for lighthouses and other markers for marine navigation.

[12] *Whitehall* Main residence of English monarchs from 1530 to 1698, when most of the palace was destroyed by fire.

[13] *foul copy* Draft.

house, where he showed me the state of his case; how the King did owe him about 6000*l.* But I do not see great likelihood for them to be paid, since they begin already in Parliament to dispute the paying of the just sea-debts, which were already promised to be paid, and will be the undoing of thousands if they be not paid. So to Whitehall to look but could not find Mr. Fox, and then to Mr. Moore[1] at Mr. Crew's, but missed of him also. So to Paul's Churchyard, and there bought Montelion,[2] which this year do not prove so good as the last was; so after reading it I burnt it. After reading of that and the comedy of the Rump,[3] which is also very silly, I went to bed. This night going home, Will[4] and I bought a goose.

20. About two o'clock my wife[5] wakes me, and comes to bed, and so both to sleep and the wench to wash.[6] I rose and with Will to my Lord's by land, it being a very hard frost, the first we have had this year. There I stayed with my Lord and Mr. Shepley,[7] looking over my Lord's accounts and to set matters straight between him and Shepley, and he did commit the viewing of these accounts to me, which was a great joy to me to see that my Lord do look upon me as one to put trust in. Hence to the organ, where Mr. Child[8] and one Mr. Mackworth (who plays finely upon the violin) were playing, and so we played till dinner and then dined, where my Lord in a very good humour and kind to me. After dinner to the

Temple,[9] where I met Mr. Moore and discoursed with him about the business of putting out[10] my Lord's 3,000*l.*, and that done, Mr. Shepley and I to the new Play-house near Lincoln's-Inn Fields (which was formerly Gibbon's tennis-court), where the play of *Beggar's Bush*[11] was newly begun; and so we went in and saw it, it was well acted: and here I saw the first time one Moone,[12] who is said to be the best actor in the world, lately come over with the King, and indeed it is the finest play-house, I believe, that ever was in England. From thence, after a pot of ale with Mr. Shepley at a house hard by, I went by link home, calling a little by the way at my father's and my uncle Fenner's,[13] where all pretty well, and so home, where I found the house in a washing pickle, and my wife in a very joyful condition when I told her that she is to see the Queen next Thursday, which puts me in mind to say that this morning I found my Lord in bed late, he having been with the King, Queen, and Princess, at the Cockpit all night, where General Monk[14] treated them; and after supper a play, where the King did put a great affront upon Singleton's[15] music, he bidding them stop and bade the French music play, which, my Lord says, do much outdo all ours. But while my Lord was rising, I went to Mr. Fox's, and there did leave the gilt tankard

[9] *Temple*   Area in central London where many legal offices and associations are located.

[10] *putting out*   Investing.

[11] *new Play-house ... tennis-court*   King's House, which first opened on 8 November 1660; *Beggar's Bush*   Beaumont and Fletcher's 1647 comedy, revived in November 1660. The old form of tennis ("royal tennis") was played in a large indoor arena, suitable for conversion into a theater.

[12] *Moone*   Michael Mohun, a celebrated London actor, who had previously held a commission in the king's army.

[13] *link*   Lighted torch, here carried by a hired boy to guide people through the dark streets; *my father*   John Pepys, a tailor; *uncle Fenner*   Thomas Fenner, a master blacksmith, husband of Katherine Kite, sister of Samuel's mother.

[14] *Queen*   Henrietta-Maria Stuart, wife of Charles I and mother of Charles II and James II, thus known as the Queen-Mother during Charles's reign; *Princess*   Henrietta Stuart, youngest daughter of Charles I; *the Cockpit*   Theater at Whitehall named from its former use in the cruel sport of cock-fighting; *General Monk*   George Monk, 1st Duke of Albemarle, who played an integral part in the restoration of Charles II.

[15] *Singleton*   John Singleton, musician to the king.

[1] *Mr. Fox*   Sir Stephen Fox, Paymaster of the Forces and friend of Charles II; *Mr. Moore*   Henry Moore, Sandwich's lawyer.

[2] *Paul's Churchyard*   Center of London's book trade; *Montelion*   John Phillips, under the pen name Montelion, published an annual series of parody astrological almanacs full of royalist political satire.

[3] *the Rump*   Rump Parliament is the name given to the Parliament after it was purged, in December 1648, of members against the resolution to try Charles I for high treason. The term "Rump Parliament" has since come to mean a parliament remaining after the legitimate parliament has disbanded.

[4] *Will*   Will Hewer, Pepys's chief clerk.

[5] *my wife*   Elizabeth Pepys.

[6] *wench*   Jane Birch, the Pepys's maid; *wash*   I.e., begin the laundry.

[7] *Mr. Shepley*   Sandwich's servant.

[8] *Mr. Child*   William Child, organist and Master of the king's Wind Music.

for Mrs. Fox, and then to the counting-house to him, who hath invited me and my wife to dine with him on Thursday next, and so to see the Queen and Princesses.

January 1660/61

3. Early in the morning to the Exchequer,[1] where I told over what money I had of my Lord's and my own there, which I found to be 970*l*. Thence to Will's, where Spicer[2] and I eat our dinner of a roast leg of pork which Will did give us, and after that to the Theatre, where was acted *Beggars' Bush*, it being very well done; and here the first time that ever I saw women come upon the stage.[3] From thence to my father's, where I found my mother gone by Bird, the carrier, to Brampton, upon my uncle's great desire, my aunt[4] being now in despair of life. So home.

July 1662[5]

12. Up by five o'clock, and put things in my house in order to be laid up, against my workmen come on Monday to take down the top of my house, which trouble I must go through now, but it troubles me much to think of it. So to my office,[6] where till noon we sat, and then I to dinner and to the office all the afternoon with much business. At night with Cooper[7] at arithmetic, and then came Mr. Creed[8] about my Lord's accounts to even them, and he gone I to supper and to bed.

18. Up very early, and got atop of my house, seeing the design of my work, and like it very well, and it comes into my head to have my dining-room wainscoted,[9] which will be very pretty. By-and-by by water to Deptford,[10] to put several things in order, being myself now only left in town, and so back again to the office, and there doing business all the morning and the afternoon also till night, and then comes Cooper for my mathematics, but, in good earnest, my head is so full of business that I cannot understand it as otherwise I should do. At night to bed, being much troubled at the rain coming into my house, the top being open.

19. Up early and to some business, and my wife coming to me I stayed long with her discoursing about her going into the country, and as she is not very forward so am I at a great loss whether to have her go or no because of the charge, and yet in some considerations I would be glad she was there, because of the dirtiness of my house and the trouble of having of a family there. So to my office, and there all the morning, and then to dinner and my brother Tom[11] dined with me only to see me. In the afternoon I went upon the river to look after some tar[12] I am sending down and some coals, and so home again; it raining hard upon the water, I put ashore and sheltered myself, while the King came by in his barge, going down towards the Downs[13] to meet the Queen: the Duke being gone yesterday. But methought it lessened my esteem of a king, that he should not be able to command the rain. Home, and Cooper coming (after I had dispatched several letters) to my mathematics, and so at night to bed in a chamber at Sir W. Pen's, my own house being so foul that I cannot lie there any longer, and there the chamber lies so as that I come into it over my leads[14] without going about, but yet I am not fully content with it, for there will be much trouble to have servants running over the leads to and fro.

---

[1] *Exchequer* Government treasury.

[2] *Spicer* Jack Spicer, a clerk in the Exchequer.

[3] *the first time … the stage* Women were first allowed on the stage following the Restoration.

[4] *my mother* Margaret Pepys; *my uncle* Robert Pepys, oldest brother of Samuel's father, who resided in Brampton in Cambridge-shire; *my aunt* Anne Pepys, Robert's wife.

[5] *July 1662* In July of 1662, Pepys undertook a household renovation, with workmen removing the roof of the house in order to build additional stories.

[6] *my office* Navy Office, site of the Navy Board.

[7] *Cooper* Richard Cooper, sailing master, then unemployed, who Pepys hired to teach him mathematics.

[8] *Mr. Creed* John Creed, deputy treasurer to the Earl of Sandwich in the spring of 1660 and Pepys's rival for Sandwich's patronage.

[9] *wainscoted* Lined with wood panel-work.

[10] *Deptford* Location of royal dockyards, downriver from the City of London.

[11] *my brother Tom* Thomas Pepys, a tailor.

[12] *tar* Used as a timber preservative for ships.

[13] *the Downs* Part of the sea near the English Channel used as a base for ships patrolling the North Sea.

[14] *leads* Roof.

MAY 1663

9. … At noon dined at home with a heavy heart … and after dinner went out to my brother's, and thence to Westminster, where at Mr. Jervas's, my old barber, I did try two or three periwigs,[1] meaning to wear one; and yet I have no stomach [for it] but that the pains of keeping my hair clean is so great. He trimmed me, and at last I parted, but my mind was almost altered from my first purpose, from the trouble that I foresee will be in wearing them also. Thence by water home and to the office, where busy late, and so home to supper and bed. …

10. *Lord's Day*.[2] Up betimes, and put on a black cloth suit, with white lynings[3] under all, as the fashion is to wear, to appear under the breeches. So being ready walked to St. James's,[4] where I sat talking with Mr. Coventry, while he made himself ready, about several businesses of the Navy, and afterwards, the Duke being gone out, he and I walked to Whitehall together over the Park. …

OCTOBER 1663

29. Up, it being my Lord Mayor's day,[5] Sir Anthony Bateman. This morning was brought home my new velvet cloak, that is, lined with velvet, a good cloth the outside, the first that ever I had in my life, and I pray God it may not be too soon now that I begin to wear it. I had it this day brought, thinking to have worn it to dinner, but I thought it would be better to go without it because of the crowd, and so I did not wear it. We met a little at the office, and then home again and got me ready to go forth, my wife being gone forth by my consent before to see her father and mother, and taken

her cook maid[6] and little girl to Westminster with her for them to see their friends. This morning in dressing myself and wanting a band,[7] I found all my bands that were newly made clean so ill smoothed that I crumpled them, and flung them all on the ground, and was angry with Jane, which made the poor girl mighty sad, so that I were troubled for it afterwards. At noon I went forth, and by coach to Guildhall[8] (by the way calling at Mr. Rawlinson's),[9] and there was admitted, and meeting with Mr. Proby[10] (Sir R. Ford's son), and Lieutenant-Colonel Baron, a city commander, we went up and down to see the tables; where under every salt[11] there was a bill of fare,[12] and at the end of the table the persons proper for the table. Many were the tables, but none in the Hall but the Mayor's and the Lords of the Privy Council[13] that had napkins or knives, which was very strange. We went into the Buttry,[14] and there stayed and talked, and then into the Hall again: and there wine was offered and they drunk, I only drinking some hypocras, which do not break my vow,[15] it being, to the best of my present judgment, only a mixed compound drink, and not any wine.[16] If I am mistaken, God forgive me! but I hope and do think I am not. By and by met with Creed; and we, with the others, went within the several Courts, and there saw the tables prepared for the Ladies and Judges and Bishops: all great sign of a great dinner to come. By and by about one

---

[6] *cook maid*   Kitchen maid.

[7] *band*   Neckband for a shirt, a necessary component of seventeenth-century gentlemanly attire.

[8] *Guildhall*   City of London's Town Hall.

[9] *Mr. Rawlinson's*   Dan Rawlinson was the host of the Mitre, a London tavern.

[10] *Mr. Proby*   Peter Proby, merchant. His father-in-law, Sir Richard Ford, was among those sent to request Charles II's return to England.

[11] *salt*   Large salt-cellar.

[12] *bill of fare*   Menu.

[13] *Privy Council*   Body of royal advisors, made up of senior members of Parliament, both present and past.

[14] *Buttry*   Room for storing liquor.

[15] *my vow*   In July 1663, Samuel made a vow to abstain from "all strong drink," including wine.

[16] *Hippocras … not any wine*   Pepys was wrong. Hippocras is spiced wine.

---

[1] *periwigs*   Wigs, especially formal ones, commonly worn by men and women in the seventeenth century.

[2] *Lord's Day*   Sunday.

[3] *lynings*   Underclothes.

[4] *St. James's*   St. James's Palace, the primary residence of James Stuart, near St. James's Park.

[5] *Lord Mayor's day*   Day on which London's Lord Mayor holds a dinner and a lavish pageant.

o'clock, before the Lord Mayor came, come into the Hall, from the room where they were first led into, the Lord Chancellor (Archbishop before him), with the Lords of the Council, and other Bishops, and they to dinner. Anon comes the Lord Mayor, who went up to the lords, and then to the other tables to bid welcome; and so all to dinner. I sat near Proby, Baron, and Creed at the Merchant Strangers' table; where ten good dishes to a messe,[1] with plenty of wine of all sorts, of which I drunk none; but it was very unpleasing that we had no napkins nor change of trenchers,[2] and drunk out of earthen pitchers and wooden dishes. It happened that after the lords had half dined, came the French Ambassador, up to the lords' table, where he was to have sat; but finding the table set, he would not sit down nor dine with the Lord Mayor, who was not yet come, nor have a table to himself, which was offered; but in a discontent went away again. After I had dined, I and Creed rose and went up and down the house, and up to the ladys' room, and there stayed gazing upon them. But though there were many and fine, both young and old, yet I could not discern one handsome face there; which was very strange, nor did I find the lady that young Dawes married so pretty as I took her for,[3] I having here an opportunity of looking much upon her very near. I expected music, but there was none but only trumpets and drums, which displeased me. The dinner, it seems, is made by the Mayor and two Sheriffs[4] for the time being, the Lord Mayor paying one half, and they the other. And the whole, Proby says, is reckoned to come to about 7 or 800l. at most. Being wearied with looking upon a company of ugly women, Creed and I went away, and took coach and through Cheapside,[5] and there saw the pageants, which were very silly, and thence to the Temple, where meeting Greatorex, he and we to Hercules Pillars, there to show me the manner of his

going about of draining of fenns,[6] which I desired much to know, but it did not appear very satisfactory to me, as he discoursed it, and I doubt[7] he will fail in it. Thence I by coach home, and there found my wife come home, and by and by came my brother Tom, with whom I was very angry for not sending me a bill with my things, so as that I think never to have more work done by him if ever he serves me so again, and so I told him. The consideration of laying out 32l. 12s. this very month in his very work troubles me also, and one thing more, that is to say, that Will having been at home all the day,[8] I doubt is the occasion that Jane has spoken to her mistress tonight that she sees she cannot please us and will look out to provide herself elsewhere, which do trouble both of us, and we wonder also at her, but yet when the rogue is gone I do not fear but the wench will do well. To the office a little, to set down my journal, and so home late to supper and to bed. The Queen[9] mends apace, they say; but yet talks idle still.

31. Up and to the office, where we sat all the morning, and at noon home to dinner, where Creed came and dined with me, and after dinner he and I upstairs, and I showed him my velvet cloak and other things of clothes, that I have lately bought, which he likes very well, and I took his opinion as to some things of clothes, which I purpose to wear, being resolved to go a little handsomer than I have hitherto. Thence to the office; where busy till night, and then to prepare my monthly account, about which I stayed till 10 or 11 o'clock at night, and to my great sorrow find myself 43l. worse than I was the last month, which was then 760l., and now it is but 717l. But it hath chiefly arisen from my layings-out in clothes for myself and wife; viz., for her

---

[1] *messe* Meal course.

[2] *trenchers* Plates.

[3] *the lady ... her for* Earlier in the year, Samuel expressed envy toward Sir John Dawes, who, despite being "a simple man," had managed to marry a wealthy, "well-bred and handsome lady."

[4] *Sheriffs* Judicial officers immediately subordinate to the Lord Mayor.

[5] *Cheapside* London market street, often the site of important parades.

[6] *Greatorex* Robert Greatorex, inventor and maker of mathematical instruments, a long-time friend of Pepys; *Hercules Pillars* Tavern near the Temple district; *fenns* Marshes.

[7] *doubt* Suspect.

[8] *Will having ... the day* Will Hewer had been living with the Pepys family, causing some conflict in the household; the day before this entry, Samuel resolved to find him lodging elsewhere.

[9] *The Queen* Catherine of Braganza, daughter of John IV of Portugal and queen consort to Charles II. In October 1663, the Queen suffered a prolonged illness, perhaps the result of a miscarriage, her poor health made worse by her unhappiness with Charles's affairs, known publicly and therefore profoundly shameful to her.

about 12*l.*, and for myself 55*l.*, or thereabouts; having made myself a velvet cloak, two new cloth suits, black, plain both; a new shag[1] gown, trimmed with gold buttons and twist, with a new hat, and silk tops for my legs, and many other things, being resolved henceforward to go like myself. And also two periwigs, one whereof cost me 3*l.*, and the other 40*s.*—I have worn neither yet, but will begin next week, God willing. So that I hope I shall not need now to lay out more money a great while, I having laid out in clothes for myself and wife, and for her closet and other things without, these two months, this and the last, besides household expenses of victuals, &c., above 110*l.* But I hope I shall with more comfort labour to get more, and with better success than when, for want of clothes, I was forced to sneak like a beggar. Having done this I went home, and after supper to bed, my mind being eased in knowing my condition, though troubled to think that I have been forced to spend so much....

NOVEMBER 1663

3. Up and to the office, where busy all the morning, and at noon to the Coffee-house, and there heard a long and most passionate discourse between two doctors of physic, of which one was Dr. Allen, whom I knew at Cambridge, and a couple of apothecaries;[2] these maintaining chemistry against them Galenical physic;[3] and the truth is, one of the apothecaries whom they charged most, did speak very prettily, that is, his language and sense good, though perhaps he might not be so knowing a physician as to offer to contest with them. At last they came to some cooler terms, and broke up. I home, and there Mr. Moore coming by my appointment dined with me, and after dinner came Mr. Goldsborough, and

we discoursed about the business of his mother,[4] but could come to no agreement in it but parted dissatisfied. By and by comes Chapman, the periwig-maker, and upon my liking it, without more ado I went up, and there he cut off my hair, which went a little to my heart at present to part with it; but, it being over, and my periwig on, I paid him 3*l.* for it; and away went he with my own hair to make up another of, and I by and by, after I had caused all my maids to look upon it; and they conclude it do become me; though Jane was mightily troubled for my parting of my own hair, and so was Besse, I went abroad to the Coffeehouse, and coming back went to Sir W. Pen and there sat with him and Captain Cocke[5] till late at night, Cocke talking of some of the Roman history very well, he having a good memory. Sir W. Pen observed mightily, and discoursed much upon my cutting off my hair, as he do of every thing that concerns me, but it is over, and so I perceive after a day or two it will be no great matter.

8. *Lord's Day.* Up, and it being late, to church[6] without my wife, and there I saw Pembleton come into the church and bring his wife with him, a good comely plain woman, and by and by my wife came after me all alone, which I was a little vexed at. I found that my coming in a periwig did not prove so strange to the world as I was afraid it would, for I thought that all the church would presently have cast their eyes all upon me, but I found no such thing. Here an ordinary lazy sermon of Mr. Mill's, and then home to dinner, and there Tom came and dined with us; and after dinner to talk about a new black cloth suit that I have a making, and so at church time to church again, where the Scot[7] preached, and I slept most of the time. Thence home, and I spent most of the evening upon Fuller's *Church*

---

[1] *shag* Velvet-like luxury fabric.

[2] *apothecaries* Makers and sellers of medicine.

[3] *Galenical physic* Galenical medicine (the approach still favored by most doctors at the time) treated disease with foods thought to balance the bodily humors, which were believed to control the health of the human body; the chemistry-based approach of the apothecaries would have somewhat more closely resembled that of modern scientific medicine.

[4] *Mr. Goldsborough ... his mother* Goldsborough's mother owed £10 to Samuel's uncle's estate.

[5] *Captain Cocke* George Cocke, a merchant who supplied goods to the navy.

[6] *church* St. Olave, an Anglican church.

[7] *the Scot* Young Scottish preacher who occasionally delivered the sermon at St. Olave.

History and Barckly's *Argeny*,[1] and so after supper to prayers and to bed, a little fearing my pain coming back again, myself continuing as costive as ever, and my physic[2] ended, but I had sent a porter today for more and it was brought me before I went to bed, and so with pretty good content to bed.

OCTOBER 1664

30. *Lord's Day*. Up, and this morning put on my new, fine, coloured cloth suit, with my cloak lined with plush, which is a dear and noble suit, costing me about 17*l*.[3] To church, and then home to dinner, and after dinner to a little music with my boy,[4] and so to church with my wife, and so home, and with her all the evening reading and at music with my boy with great pleasure, and so to supper, prayers, and to bed.

JUNE 1665

2. Lay troubled in mind abed a good while, thinking of my Tangier and victualling business,[5] which I doubt will fall. Up and to the Duke of Albemarle,[6] but missed him. Thence to the Harp and Ball and to Westminster Hall, where I visited "the flowers"[7] in each place, and so met with Mr. Creed, and he and I to Mrs. Croft's to drink and did, but saw not her daughter Borroughes. I away home, and there dined and did business. In the afternoon went with my tallies, made a fair end with Colvill

and Viner,[8] delivering them 5000*l*. tallies to each and very quietly had credit given me upon other tallies of Mr. Colvill for 2000*l*. and good words for more, and of Mr. Viner too. Thence to visit the Duke of Albemarle, and thence my Lady Sandwich and Lord Crew. Thence home, and there met an express from Sir W. Batten at Harwich, that the fleet is all sailed from Solebay,[9] having spied the Dutch fleet at sea, and that, if the calms hinder not, they must needs now be engaged with them.[10] Another letter also come to me from Mr. Hater, committed by the Council this afternoon to the Gatehouse, upon the misfortune of having his name used by one, without his knowledge or privity, for the receiving of some powder that he had bought.[11] Up to Court about these two, and for the former was led up to my Lady Castlemayne's[12] lodgings, where the King and she and others were at supper, and there I read the letter and returned; and then to Sir G. Carteret[13] about Hater, and shall have him released tomorrow, upon my giving bail for his appearance, which I have promised to do. Sir G. Carteret did go on purpose to the King to ask this, and it was granted. So home at past 12, almost one o'clock in the morning. To my office till past two, and then home to supper and to bed.

6. Waked in the morning before 4 o'clock with great pain to piss, and great pain in pissing by having, I think, drank too great a draught of cold drink before going to bed. But by and by to sleep again, and then rose and to the office, where very busy all the morning, and at noon to dinner with Sir G. Carteret to his house with all our

---

[1] *Fuller's Church History* Thomas Fuller's *The Church-History of Britain* (1655); *Barckly's Argeny* John Barclay's *Argenis* (1621), a royalist historical allegory.

[2] *costive* Constipated; *physic* Purging medicine.

[3] *17l.* Some historians have noted the expense, remarking that a typical salary for a household servant would have been £2 or £3 per year.

[4] *my boy* Thomas Edwards, a servant in the Pepys household.

[5] *Tangier* Port city in northern Morocco, site of a British naval base; *victualling business* Food provision, here presumably for the navy. Later that year, Pepys was named Surveyor-General of Victualling for the navy, a highly lucrative position.

[6] *Duke of Albemarle* While James Stuart was at sea commanding the British in the Second Anglo-Dutch War, the Duke of Albemarle was performing the administrative duties of the Lord High Admiral.

[7] *"the flowers"* I.e., the pretty women.

[8] *tallies* Wooden sticks marked with notches representing debts or payments; *Colvill and Viner* John Colvill and Robert Viner, bankers, coin-makers, and financiers.

[9] *Solebay* English port town on the North Sea.

[10] *the fleet … with them* Second Anglo-Dutch War (1665–67), between England and the Dutch Republic, was beginning.

[11] *Mr. Hater* Thomas Hayter, one of Pepys's favorite clerks; *the Gatehouse* London prison; *privity* I.e., legal consent; *some powder … had bought* Hayter was accused of embezzling gunpowder from the King.

[12] *Lady Castlemayne* Barbara Palmer, Countess of Castlemaine, was a mistress of Charles II; her beauty and ability to manipulate the king resulted in a series of scandals in the court.

[13] *Sir G. Carteret* George Carteret, Treasurer of the Navy and a politician of considerable influence.

Board, where a good pasty[1] and brave discourse. But our great fear was some fresh news of the fleet, but not from the fleet, all being said to be well and beaten the Dutch, but I do not give much belief to it, and indeed the news come from Sir W. Batten at Harwich, and writ so simply that we all made good mirth of it. Thence to the office, where upon Sir G. Carteret's accounts, to my great vexation there being nothing done by the Controller[2] to right the King herein. I thence to my office and wrote letters all the afternoon, and in the evening by coach to Sir Ph. Warwicke's[3] about my Tangier business to get money, and so to my Lady Sandwich's, who, poor lady, expects every hour to hear of my Lord;[4] but in the best temper, neither confident nor troubled with fear, that I ever did see in my life. She tells me my Lord Rochester is now declaredly out of hopes of Mrs. Mallett,[5] and now she is to receive notice in a day or two how the King stands inclined to the giving leave for my Lord Hinchingbroke[6] to look after her, and that being done to bring it to an end shortly. Thence by coach home, and to my office a little, and so before 12 o'clock home and to bed.

7. This morning my wife and mother rose about two o'clock; and with Mercer,[7] Mary, the boy, and W. Hewer, as they had designed, took boat and down to refresh themselves on the water to Gravesend.[8] Lay till 7 o'clock, then up and to the office upon Sir G. Carteret's accounts again, where very busy; thence abroad and to the 'Change,[9] no news of certainty being yet come from the fleet. Thence to the Dolphin Tavern, where Sir J. Minnes, Lord Brunkard, Sir Thomas Harvy,[10] and myself dined, upon Sir G. Carteret's charge, and very merry we were, Sir Thomas Harvy being a very droll.[11] Thence to the office, and meeting Creed away with him to my Lord Treasurer's, there thinking to have met the goldsmiths, at Whitehall, but did not, and so appointed another time for my Lord to speak to them to advance us some money. Thence, it being the hottest day that ever I felt in my life, and it is confessed so by all other people the hottest they ever knew in England in the beginning of June, we to the New Exchange, and there drunk whey,[12] with much entreaty getting it for our money, and [they] would not be entreated to let us have one glass more. So took water and to Fox-Hall, to the Spring garden,[13] and there walked an hour or two with great pleasure, saving our minds ill at ease concerning the fleet and my Lord Sandwich, that we have no news of them, and ill reports run up and down of his being killed, but without ground. Here stayed pleasantly walking and spending but 6d. till nine at night, and then by water to Whitehall, and there I stopped to hear news of the fleet, but none come, which is strange, and so by water home, where, weary with walking and with the mighty heat of the weather, and for my wife's not coming home, I staying walking in the garden till twelve at night, when it begun to lighten[14] exceedingly, through the greatness of the heat. Then despairing of her coming home, I to bed. This day, much against my will, I did in Drury Lane[15] see two or three houses marked with a red cross upon the doors, and "Lord have mercy upon us" writ

[1] *Board* Navy Board, which administered the royal navy; *pasty* Meat pie, in the shape of a turnover.

[2] *Controller* Comptroller; manager of the royal accounts.

[3] *Sir Ph. Warwicke* Philip Warwick, secretary to the Lord Treasurer.

[4] *expects every … my Lord* Sandwich served as Lieutenant Admiral in the Second Anglo-Dutch War.

[5] *Lord Rochester* John Wilmot, 2nd Earl of Rochester, renowned libertine and important satirical poet; *Mrs. Mallet* Elizabeth Malet, a great beauty, according to Pepys, attracted Rochester's attention but refused his offer of marriage; he responded to her refusal by kidnapping the young woman in May 1665 and causing a scandal. Eventually, Elizabeth forgave him, and she married Rochester in 1667, becoming Countess of Rochester.

[6] *Lord Hinchingbroke* Edward Montagu, Sandwich's son.

[7] *Mercer* Mary Mercer, a companion to Mrs. Pepys.

[8] *Gravesend* Town on the Thames.

[9] *the 'Change* Royal Exchange, a commerce center built in 1565. It was sometimes known as the "Old Exchange."

[10] *Sir J. Minnes … Sir Thomas Harvy* Members of the Navy Board.

[11] *droll* Joker.

[12] *New Exchange* Built in 1608–09, the Exchange served as a commercial center, clustering many sellers of luxury goods; *whey* Liquid remainder of curdled milk, usually a by-product of cheese making.

[13] *Fox-Hall … Spring garden* New Spring Gardens, later known as Vauxhall Gardens.

[14] *it begun to lighten* I.e., there was thunder and lightning.

[15] *Drury Lane* London street of brothels, taverns, and theaters.

there; which was a sad sight to me, being the first of the kind that, to my remembrance, I ever saw. It put me into an ill conception of myself and my smell, so that I was forced to buy some roll-tobacco to smell to and chaw, which took away the apprehension.[1]

8. About five o'clock my wife come home, it having lightened all night hard, and one great shower of rain. She come and lay upon the bed; I up and to the office, where all the morning. Alone at home to dinner, my wife, mother, and Mercer dining at W. Joyce's;[2] I giving her a caution to go round by the Half Moone to his house, because of the plague.[3] I to my Lord Treasurer's by appointment of Sir Thomas Ingram's, to meet the goldsmiths;[4] where I met with the great news at last newly come, brought by Bab May[5] from the Duke of York, that we have totally routed the Dutch; that the Duke himself, the Prince,[6] my Lord Sandwich, and Mr. Coventry are all well: which did put me into such joy that I forgot almost all other thoughts. The particulars I shall set down by and by. By and by comes Alderman Maynell and Mr. Viner, and there my Lord Treasurer did entreat them to furnish me with money upon my tallies, Sir Philip Warwicke before my Lord declaring the King's changing of the hand from Mr. Povy[7] to me, whom he called a very sober person, and one whom the Lord Treasurer would own in all things that I should concern myself with them in the business of money. They did at present declare they could not part with money at present. My Lord did press them very hard, and I hope upon their considering we shall get some of them. Thence with great joy to the Cocke-pitt;[8] where the Duke of Albermarle, like a man out of himself with content, new-told me all; and by and by comes a letter from Mr. Coventry's own hand to him, which he never opened (which was a strange thing), but did give it me to open and read, and consider what was fit for our office to do in it, and leave the letter with Sir W. Clerke; which upon such a time and occasion was a strange piece of indifference, hardly pardonable. I copied out the letter, and did also take minutes out of Sir W. Clerke's other letters; and the sum of the news is:

VICTORY OVER THE DUTCH,[9] JUNE 3RD, 1665.

This day they engaged; the Dutch neglecting greatly the opportunity of the wind they had of us, by which they lost the benefit of their fire-ships. The Earl of Falmouth, Muskerry, and Mr. Richard Boyle killed on board the Duke's ship, the *Royall Charles*, with one shot: their blood and brains flying in the Duke's face; and the head of Mr. Boyle striking down the Duke, as some say. Earl of Marlborough, Portland, Rear-Admiral Sansum (to Prince Rupert) killed, and Capt. Kirby and Ableson. Sir John Lawson wounded on the knee; hath had some bones taken out, and is likely to be well again. Upon receiving the hurt, he sent to the Duke for another to command the *Royall Oake*. The Duke sent Jordan out of the *St. George*, who did brave things in her. Capt. Jer. Smith of the *Mary* was second to the Duke, and stepped between him and Captain Seaton of the *Urania* (76 guns and 400 men), who had sworn to board the Duke; killed him, 200 men, and took the ship; himself losing 99 men, and never an officer saved but himself and lieutenant. His master indeed is saved, with his leg cut off: Admiral Opdam blown up, Trump killed, and said by Holmes; all the rest of their admirals, as they say, but Everson (whom they dare not trust for his

---

[1] *ill conception … the apprehension* Body odor was considered an early sign of the plague, and tobacco was thought to protect from the disease.

[2] *W. Joyce* William Joyce, a relative of the Pepys family.

[3] *plague* The Great Plague (1665–66) killed an estimated 20 per cent of the English population.

[4] *Sir Thomas Ingram* Politician who served with Pepys on the committee governing Tangier; *goldsmiths* Francis Meynell and Thomas Viner, makers of English coins.

[5] *Bab May* Baptist May, a royal courtier.

[6] *the Prince* Prince Rupert of the Rhine, who served as a squadron commander during the Second Anglo-Dutch War.

[7] *Mr. Povy* Thomas Povey, appointed First Treasurer for Tangier in 1663. The position was reassigned to Pepys in May 1665, following Povy's failure to keep accounts in order.

[8] *Cocke-pitt* Cockpit, part of the Royal Palace at Whitehall so named from its former use in the cruel sport of cock-fighting.

[9] *Victory over the Dutch* The Battle of Lowestoft on 13 June (New Style) 1665 was a decisive success for the English in the Second Anglo-Dutch War, though the English failed to take full advantage of the Dutch defeat. The war ended in a Dutch victory.

affection to the Prince of Orange[1]), are killed: we having taken and sunk, as is believed, about 24 of their best ships; killed and taken near 8 or 10,000 men, and lost, we think, not above 700. A great[er] victory never known in the world. They are all fled, some 43 got into the Texell,[2] and others elsewhere, and we in pursuit of the rest.

Thence, with my heart full of joy; home, and to my office a little; then to my Lady Pen's, where they are all joyed and not a little puffed up at the good success of their father; and good service indeed is said to have been done by him.[3] Had a great bonfire at the gate; and I with my Lady Pen's people and others to Mrs. Turner's[4] great room, and then down into the street. I did give the boys 4s. among them, and mighty merry. So home to bed, with my heart at great rest and quiet, saving that the consideration of the victory is too great for me presently to comprehend.

15. Up, and put on my new stuff suit with close knees, which becomes me most nobly, as my wife says. At the office all day. At noon, put on my first laced band, all lace; and to Kate Joyce's[5] to dinner, where my mother, wife, and abundance of their friends, and good usage. Thence, wife and Mercer and I to the Old Exchange, and there bought two lace bands more, one of my seamstress, whom my wife concurs with me to be a pretty woman. So down to Deptford and Woolwich,[6] my boy and I. At Woolwich, discoursed with Mr. Sheldon[7] about my bringing my wife down for a month or two to his house,

which he approves of, and, I think, will be very convenient. So late back, and to the office, wrote letters, and so home to supper and to bed. This day the newsbook (upon Mr. Moore's showing L'Estrange Captain Ferrers's letter[8]) did do my Lord Sandwich great right as to the late victory. The Duke of York not yet come to town. The towne grows very sickly, and people to be afeard of it; there dying this last week of the plague 112, from 43 the week before, whereof but [one] in Fanchurch-street, and one in Broad-street, by the Treasurer's office.

29. Up and by water to Whitehall, where the Court full of wagons and people ready to go out of town. To the Harp and Ball, and there drank and talked with Mary, she telling me in discourse that she lived lately at my neighbour's, Mr. Knightly, which made me forbear further discourse. This end of the town every day grows very bad of the plague. The Mortality Bill is come to 267;[9] which is about ninety more than the last: and of these but four in the City,[10] which is a great blessing to us. Thence to Creed, and with him up and down about Tangier business, to no purpose. Took leave again of Mr. Coventry; though I hope the Duke has not gone to stay, and so do others too. So home, calling at Somersett House,[11] where all are packing up too: the Queen-Mother setting out for France this day to drink Bourbon waters this year, she being in a consumption; and intends not to come till winter come twelvemonths.[12] So by coach home, where at the office all the morning, and

---

[8] *L'Estrange* Roger L'Estrange published *The Public Intelligencer*, the precursor of the *London Gazette*; *Captain Ferrers's letter* Ferrer, a captain in Sandwich's regiment, wrote a letter praising the Earl's actions in the Battle of Lowestoft.

[9] *Mortality Bill … to 267* The London Bills of Mortality were an official source of mortality statistics, issued to inform the population about plague outbreaks. In the week ending 27 June, the total number of deaths in London was 684, of which 267 were caused by the plague.

[10] *City* I.e., City of London, the part of the city falling within London's ancient boundaries. The financial and commercial centers were located in the City.

[11] *Somersett House* Palace used by Charles II.

[12] *consumption* Extreme wasting of the body, typically due to tuberculosis; *intends … twelvemonths* In fact, the Queen Mother never again returned to England; she died in August 1669, at her French chateau.

---

[1] *whom they … of Orange* William III was born in the Dutch Republic and would become head of state there before he became King of England; his family thus had Dutch supporters.

[2] *Texell* Island belonging to the Netherlands. The final naval battle of the First Anglo-Dutch War took place there.

[3] *good service … by him* When Charles II granted William Penn a charter for governing the American province to be called Pennsylvania, his service during the Battle of Lowestoft was specifically cited in the document.

[4] *Mrs. Turner* Jane Turner, Samuel's cousin.

[5] *Kate Joyce* Samuel's cousin.

[6] *Deptford and Woolwich* Sites of royal dockyards outside the City.

[7] *Mr. Sheldon* Financial manager of the Woolwich Dockyard, living in Woolwich.

at noon Mrs. Hunt[1] dined with us. Very merry, and she a very good woman. To the office, where busy a while putting some things in my office in order, and then to letters till night. About 10 o'clock home, the days being sensibly shorter before I have once kept a summer's day by shutting up office by daylight; but my life hath been still as it was in winter almost. But I will for a month try what I can do by daylight. So home to supper and to bed.

JULY 1665

30. *Lord's Day*. Up, and in my night gown, cap and neckcloth, undressed all day long, lost not a minute, but in my chamber, setting my Tangier accounts to rights. Which I did by night to my very heart's content, not only that it is done, but I find everything right, and even beyond what, after so long neglecting them, I did hope for. The Lord of Heaven be praised for it! Will was with me today, and is very well again. It was a sad noise to hear our bell to toll and ring so often today, either for deaths or burials; I think five or six times. At night weary with my day's work, but full of joy at my having done it, I to bed, being to rise betimes tomorrow to go to the wedding at Dagenhams.[2] So to bed, fearing I have got some cold sitting in my loose garments all this day.

31. Up, and very betimes by six o'clock at Deptford, and there find Sir G. Carteret, and my Lady ready to go: I being in my new coloured silk suit, and coat trimmed with gold buttons and gold broad lace round my hands, very rich and fine. By water to the Ferry, where, when we come, no coach there; and tide of ebb so far spent as the horse-boat could not get off on the other side the river to bring away the coach. So we were fain to stay there in the unlucky Isle of Doggs,[3] in a chill place, the morning cool, and wind fresh, above two if not three hours to our great discontent. Yet being upon a pleasant errand, and seeing that it could not be helped, we did bear it very patiently; and it was worth my observing, I thought, as ever anything, to see how upon these two

scores, Sir G. Carteret, the most passionate man in the world, and that was in greatest haste to be gone, did bear with it, and very pleasant all the while, at least not troubled much so as to fret and storm at it. Anon the coach comes: in the meantime there coming a News thither with his horse to go over, that told us he did come from Islington this morning; and that Proctor the vintner[4] of the Miter in Wood-street, and his son, are dead this morning there, of the plague; he having laid out abundance of money there, and was the greatest vintner for some time in London for great entertainments. We, fearing the canonical hour[5] would be past before we got thither, did with a great deal of unwillingness send away the license and wedding ring. So that when we come, though we drove hard with six horses, yet we found them gone from home; and going towards the church, met them coming from church, which troubled us. But, however, that trouble was soon over; hearing it was well done: they being both in their old clothes; my Lord Crew giving her,[6] there being three coach fulls of them. The young lady mighty sad,[7] which troubled me; but yet I think it was only her gravity in a little greater degree than usual. All saluted[8] her, but I did not till my Lady Sandwich did ask me whether I had saluted her or no. So to dinner, and very merry we were; but yet in such a sober way as never almost any wedding was in so great families: but it was much better. After dinner company divided, some to cards, others to talk. My Lady Sandwich and I up to settle accounts, and pay her some money. And mighty kind she is to me, and would fain have had me gone down for company with her to Hinchingbroke;[9] but for my life I cannot. At night to supper, and so to talk; and which, methought, was the most extraordinary thing, all of us to prayers as usual, and the young bride and bridegroom too and so

---

[1] *Mrs. Hunt* Neighbor of the Pepys family.

[2] *wedding at Dagenhams* Between Jemima Montagu, Sandwich's daughter, and Sir George Carteret's son Philip; *Dagenhams* Village on the Thames.

[3] *Isle of Doggs* I.e., Isle of dogs, an area of East London

[4] *vintner* Wine-seller.

[5] *canonical hour* Interval between 8:00 a.m. and 12:00 p.m., the only hours during which the Church of England would perform weddings.

[6] *Lord Crew giving her* I.e., giving her away in marriage (because her father was at sea with the navy).

[7] *sad* I.e., serious.

[8] *saluted* Kissed.

[9] *Hinchingbroke* In Hertfordshire, country seat of the Earls of Sandwich.

after prayers, soberly to bed; only I got into the bridegroom's chamber while he undressed himself, and there was very merry, till he was called to the bride's chamber, and into bed they went. I kissed the bride in bed, and so the curtains drawn with the greatest gravity that could be, and so good night. But the modesty and gravity of this business[1] was so decent, that it was to me indeed ten times more delightful than if it had been twenty times more merry and jovial. Whereas I feared I must have sat up all night, we did here all get good beds, and I lay in the same I did before with Mr. Brisband, who is a good scholar and sober man; and we lay in bed, getting him to give me an account of home, which is the most delightful talk a man can have of any traveller: and so to sleep. My eyes much troubled already with the change of my drink. Thus I ended this month with the greatest joy that ever I did any in my life, because I have spent the greatest part of it with abundance of joy, and honour, and pleasant journeys, and brave entertainments, and without cost of money; and at last live to see the business ended with great content on all sides. This evening with Mr. Brisband, speaking of enchantments and spells; I telling him some of my charms; he told me this of his own knowledge, at Bourdeaux, in France. The words these:

> *Voici un corps mort,*
> *Raide comme un bâton,*
> *Froid comme marbre,*
> *Léger comme un esprit,*
> *Levons te au nom de Jesus Christ.*[2]

He saw four little girls, very young ones, all kneeling, each of them, upon one knee; and one begun the first line, whispering in the ear of the next, and the second to the third, and the third to the fourth, and she to the first. Then the first begun the second line, and so round quite through, and, putting each one finger only to a boy that lay flat upon his back on the ground, as if he was dead; at the end of the words, they did with their four fingers raise this boy as high as they could reach, and he[3] being there, and wondering at it, as also being afeard to see it, for they would have had him to have bore a part in saying the words, in the room of one of the little girls that was so young that they could hardly make her learn to repeat the words, did, for fear there might be some sleight used in it by the boy, or that the boy might be light, call the cook of the house, a very lusty fellow, as Sir G. Carteret's cook, who is very big, and they did raise him in just the same manner. This is one of the strangest things I ever heard, but he tells it me of his own knowledge, and I do heartily believe it to be true. I enquired of him whether they were Protestant or Catholic girls; and he told me they were Protestant, which made it the more strange to me. Thus we end this month, as I said, after the greatest glut of content that ever I had; only under some difficulty because of the plague, which grows mightily upon us, the last week being about 1700 or 1800 of the plague. My Lord Sandwich at sea with a fleet of about 100 sail, to the Northward, expecting De Ruyter, or the Dutch East India fleet.[4] My Lord Hinchingbroke coming over from France, and will meet his sister at Scott's-hall.[5] Myself having obliged both these families in this business very much; as both my Lady, and Sir G. Carteret and his Lady do confess exceedingly, and the latter do also now call me cousin, which I am glad of. So God preserve us all friends long, and continue health among us.

---

[1]   *this business*   Lord Hinchingbroke is Lord Sandwich's son and heir, and so brother of the recent bride, and "this business" is the wedding. Pepys has done a service to both families by helping to bring about the marriage between them, and Carteret calls him cousin because he is a distant cousin of the Montagu family (that of Lord and Lady Sandwich).

[2]   *Voici un … Jesus Christ*   French: "Here lies a dead body, / Stiff as a stick, / Cold as marble, / Light as a spirit, / Rise in the name of Jesus Christ." This chant—similar to the present-day "light as a feather, stiff as a board"—is part of a game in which one person lies on the floor while others gather round the body, each placing one finger under it. When the chant is recited, the body is supposed to levitate. The game was especially popular during times of plague outbreak.

[3]   *he*   Mr. Brisband.

[4]   *De Ruyter*   Michiel Adriaenszoon de Ruyter, perhaps the most famous Dutch admiral and an integral force in both Anglo-Dutch Wars; *Dutch East India fleet*   The Dutch East India Company, established in 1602, was a trading concern so powerful as to establish colonies and wage war. The company had a fleet of nearly five thousand ships. (In contrast, the English East India Company, chartered in 1600, had a fleet of some 2,690 ships.)

[5]   *Scott's-hall*   Country manor in southeast England.

AUGUST 1665

15. Up by 4 o'clock and walked to Greenwich,[1] where called at Captain Cocke's and to his chamber, he being in bed, where something put my last night's dream into my head, which I think is the best that ever was dreamt, which was that I had my Lady Castlemayne in my arms and was admitted to use all the dalliance I desired with her, and then dreamt that this could not be awake, but that it was only a dream; but that since it was a dream, and that I took so much real pleasure in it, what a happy thing it would be if when we are in our graves (as Shakespeare resembles it[2]) we could dream, and dream but such dreams as this, that then we should not need to be so fearful of death, as we are this plague time. Here I hear that news is brought Sir G. Carteret that my Lord Hinchingbroke is not well, and so cannot meet us at Cranborne tonight. So I to Sir G. Carteret's; and there was sorry with him for our disappointment. So we have put off our meeting there till Saturday next. Here I stayed talking with Sir G. Carteret, he being mighty free with me in his business, and among other things hath ordered Rider and Cutler[3] to put into my hands copper to the value of 5,000*l.* (which Sir G. Carteret's share it seems come to in it), which is to raise part of the money he is to lay out for a purchase for my Lady Jemimah. Thence he and I to Sir J. Minnes's[4] by invitation, where Sir W. Batten and my Lady, and my Lord Bruncker,[5] and all of us dined upon a venison pasty and other good meat, but nothing well dressed. But my pleasure lay in getting some bills signed by Sir G. Carteret, and promise of present payment from Mr. Fenn,[6] which do rejoice my heart, it being one of the heaviest things I had upon me, that so much of the little I have should lie (*viz.* near 1000*l.*) in the King's hands. Here very merry and (Sir G. Carteret being gone presently after dinner) to Captain Cocke's, and there merry, and so broke up

and I by water to the Duke of Albemarle, with whom I spoke a great deal in private, they being designed to send a fleet of ships privately to the Streights.[7] No news yet from our fleet, which is much wondered at, but the Duke says for certain guns have been heard to the northward very much. It was dark before I could get home, and so land at Church-yard stairs, where, to my great trouble, I met a dead corpse of the plague, in the narrow ally just bringing down[8] a little pair of stairs. But I thank God I was not much disturbed at it. However, I shall beware of being late abroad again.

SEPTEMBER 1665

7. Up by 5 of the clock, mighty full of fear of an ague,[9] but was obliged to go, and so by water, wrapping myself up warm, to the Tower, and there sent for the Weekly Bill,[10] and find 8,252 dead in all, and of them 6,878 of the plague; which is a most dreadful number, and shows reason to fear that the plague hath got that hold that it will yet continue among us. Thence to Brainford, reading *The Villaine*,[11] a pretty good play, all the way. There a coach of Mr. Povy's stood ready for me, and he at his house ready to come in, and so we together merrily to Swakely,[12] Sir R. Viner's. A very pleasant place, bought by him of Sir James Harrington's lady. He took us up and down with great respect, and showed us all his house and grounds; and it is a place not very modern in the garden nor house, but the most uniform in all that ever I saw; and some things to excess. Pretty to see over the screen of the hall (put up by Sir J. Harrington, a Long Parliamentman) the King's head,

---

[1] *Greenwich* For safety during the plague, London's navy office relocated from the City to Greenwich, near Deptford.

[2] *Shakespeare resembles it* See *Hamlet* 3.1.65–66.

[3] *Rider and Cutler* Merchants who sold supplies to the navy.

[4] *Sir J. Minnes* John Mennes, Comptroller of the Navy.

[5] *Lord Bruncker* William Brouncker, a mathematician and natural philosopher.

[6] *Mr. Fenn* John Fenn, paymaster to the Navy Treasurer.

[7] *the Streights* Strait of Gibraltar, which connects the Atlantic Ocean and the Mediterranean Sea.

[8] *just bringing down* I.e., just being brought down.

[9] *ague* Illness.

[10] *the Tower* Tower of London, used as a prison for high-status inmates; *Weekly Bill* I.e., Bill of Mortality.

[11] *Brainford* Brentford, a few miles outside the City; *The Villaine* Play by Thomas Porter, first performed in 1662 and published the following year, which borrows heavily from Shakespeare's *Othello*.

[12] *Swakely* Viner's country house.

and my Lord of Essex on one side, and Fairfax[1] on the other; and upon the other side of the screen, the parson of the parish, and the lord of the manor and his sisters. The window-cases, door-cases, and chimneys of all the house are marble. He showed me a black boy that he had, that died of a consumption, and being dead, he caused him to be dried in an oven, and lies there entire in a box. By and by to dinner, where his lady I find yet handsome, but hath been a very handsome woman; now is old, hath brought him near 100,000*l.* and now he lives, no man in England in greater plenty, and commands both King and Council with his credit he gives them. Here was a fine lady a merchant's wife at dinner with us, and who should be here in the quality of a woman but Mrs. Worship's daughter, Dr. Clerke's niece, and after dinner Sir Robert led us up to his long gallery, very fine, above stairs (and better, or such, furniture I never did see), and there Mrs. Worship did give us three or four very good songs, and sings very neatly, to my great delight. After all this, and ending the chief business to my content about getting a promise of some money of him, we took leave, being exceedingly well treated here, and a most pleasant journey we had back, Povy and I, and his company most excellent in anything but business, he here giving me an account of as many persons at Court as I had a mind or thought of enquiring after. He tells me by a letter he showed me, that the King is not, nor hath been of late, very well, but quite out of humour; and, as some think, in a consumption, and weary of everything. He showed me my Lord Arlington's house that he was born in, in a town called Harlington: and so carried me through a most pleasant country to Brainford, and there put me into my boat, and good night. So I wrapt myself warm, and by water got to Woolwich[2] about one in the morning, my wife and all in bed.

10. *Lord's Day.* Walked home; being forced thereto by one of my watermen falling sick yesterday, and it was God's great mercy I did not go by water with them yesterday, for he fell sick on Saturday night, and it is to be feared of the plague. So I sent him away to London with his fellow; but another boat come to me this morning, whom I sent to Blackewall for Mr. Andrews.[3] I walked to Woolwich, and there find Mr. Hill,[4] and he and I all the morning at music and a song he hath set of three parts, methinks, very good. Anon comes Mr. Andrews, though it be a very ill day, and so after dinner we to music and sang till about 4 or 5 o'clock, it blowing very hard, and now and then raining, and wind and tide being against us, Andrews and I took leave and walked to Greenwich. My wife before I come out telling me the ill news that she hears that her father is very ill, and then I told her I feared of the plague, for that the house is shut up. And so she much troubled she did desire me to send them something; and I said I would, and will do so.

But before I come out there happened news to come to the by an express from Mr. Coventry, telling me the most happy news of my Lord Sandwich's meeting with[5] part of the Dutch; his taking two of their East India ships, and six or seven others, and very good prizes and that he is in search of the rest of the fleet, which he hopes to find upon the Wellbancke,[6] with the loss only of the *Hector*, poor Captain Cuttle. This news do so overjoy me that I know not what to say enough to express it, but the better to do it I did walk to Greenwich, and there sending away Mr. Andrews, I to Captain Cocke's, where I find my Lord Bruncker and his mistress, and Sir J. Minnes. Where we supped (there was also Sir W. Doyly and Mr. Evelyn[7]); but the receipt of this news did put us all into such an ecstasy of joy, that it inspired into Sir J. Minnes and Mr. Evelyn such

---

1 *Long Parliamentman*   Lasting from 1640 until 1648, the so-called Long Parliament was called by Charles I. Its name derives from an Act of Parliament decreeing that it could only be dissolved through the agreement of its members, rather than by the King's will; *Fairfax* Thomas Fairfax, 3rd Lord Fairfax of Cameron, was the Parliamentarians' commander-in-chief during the English Civil War.

2 *Woolwich* I.e., Mr. Sheldon's house in Woolwich, where Elizabeth was staying to avoid the plague.

3 *Mr. Andrews* Thomas Andrews, a merchant who sold supplies to the naval base in Tangier.

4 *Mr. Hill* Thomas Hill, merchant and amateur musician, a close friend of Pepys.

5 *meeting with* I.e., engaging in combat with.

6 *Wellbancke* Area of the North Sea between northern England and the Netherlands.

7 *Sir W. Doyly and Mr. Evelyn* Two of the four commissioners responsible for the navy's medical services during the Second Anglo-Dutch War. Like Pepys, John Evelyn was a diarist.

a spirit of mirth, that in all my life I never met with so merry a two hours as our company this night was. Among other humours, Mr. Evelyn's repeating of some verses made up of nothing but the various acceptations of may and can, and doing it so aptly upon occasion of something of that nature, and so fast, did make us all die almost with laughing, and did so stop the mouth of Sir J. Minnes in the middle of all his mirth (and in a thing agreeing with his own manner of genius), that I never saw any man so out-done in all my life; and Sir J. Minnes's mirth too to see himself out-done, was the crown of all our mirth. In this humour we sat till about ten at night, and so my Lord and his mistress home, and we to bed, it being one of the times of my life wherein I was the fullest of true sense of joy.

14. Up, and walked to Greenwich, and there fitted myself in several businesses to go to London, where I have not been now a pretty while. But before I went from the office news is brought by word of mouth that letters are just now brought from the fleet of our taking a great many more of the Dutch fleet, in which I did never more plainly see my command of my temper in my not admitting myself to receive any kind of joy from it till I had heard the certainty of it, and therefore went by water directly to the Duke of Albemarle, where I find a letter of the 12th from Solebay, from my Lord Sandwich, of the fleet's meeting with about eighteen more of the Dutch fleet, and his taking of most of them; and the messenger says they had taken three after the letter was wrote and sealed; which being twenty-one, and the fourteen took the other day, is forty-five sail; some of which are good, and others rich ships, which is so great a cause of joy in us all that my Lord and everybody is highly joyed thereat. And having taken a copy of my Lord's letter, I away back again to the Bear at the Bridge foot,[1] being full of wind and out of order, and there called for a biscuit and a piece of cheese and gill of sack,[2] being forced to walk over the Bridge, toward the 'Change, and the plague being all thereabouts. Here my news was highly welcome, and I did wonder to see the 'Change so full, I believe 200 people; but not a man or

merchant of any fashion, but plain men all. And Lord! to see how I did endeavour all I could to talk with as few as I could, there being now no observation of shutting up of houses infected, that to be sure we do converse and meet with people that have the plague upon them. I to Sir Robert Viner's, where my main business was about settling the business of Debusty's[3] 5000*l*. tallies, which I did for the present to enable me to have some money, and so home, buying some things for my wife in the way. So home, and put up several things to carry to Woolwich, and upon serious thoughts I am advised by W. Griffin to let my money and plate[4] rest there, as being as safe as any place, nobody imagining that people would leave money in their houses now, when all their families are gone. So for the present that being my opinion, I did leave them there still. But, Lord! to see the trouble that it puts a man to, to keep safe what with pain a man hath been getting together, and there is good reason for it. Down to the office, and there wrote letters to and again about this good news of our victory, and so by water home late. Where, when I come home I spent some thoughts upon the occurrences of this day, giving matter for as much content on one hand and melancholy on another, as any day in all my life. For the first; the finding of my money and plate, and all safe at London, and speeding in my business of money this day. The hearing of this good news to such excess, after so great a despair of my Lord's doing anything this year; adding to that, the decrease of 500 and more, which is the first decrease we have yet had in the sickness since it begun: and great hopes that the next week it will be greater. Then, on the other side, my finding that though the Bill in general is abated, yet the City within the walls is increased, and likely to continue so, and is close to our house there. My meeting dead corpses of the plague, carried to be buried close to me at noon-day through the City in Fanchurch-street. To see a person sick of the sores,[5] carried close by me by Gracechurch in a hackney-

---

[1] *the Bear at the Bridge foot* Tavern at the foot of London Bridge.

[2] *gill of sack* Fourth of a pint of fortified white wine.

[3] *Debusty* Lawrence Debussy, merchant.

[4] *W. Griffin* Employee of the navy office; *plate* Gold or silver tableware.

[5] *sick of the sores* Sores were a common mark of the plague, and contact with open sores was a source of the disease's spread. Beginning in 1604, anyone in public found to have a plague sore could be whipped or even hanged.

coach.[1] My finding the Angell tavern, at the lower end of Tower-hill, shut up, and more than that, the alehouse at the Tower-stairs, and more than that, the person was then dying of the plague when I was last there, a little while ago, at night, to write a short letter there, and I overheard the mistress of the house sadly saying to her husband somebody was very ill, but did not think it was of the plague. To hear that poor Payne, my waiter, hath buried a child, and is dying himself. To hear that a labourer I sent but the other day to Dagenhams, to know how they did there, is dead of the plague; and that one of my own watermen, that carried me daily, fell sick as soon as he had landed me on Friday morning last, when I had been all night upon the water (and I believe he did get his infection that day at Brainford), and is now dead of the plague. To hear that Captain Lambert and Cuttle are killed in the taking these ships; and that Mr. Sidney Montague[2] is sick of a desperate fever at my Lady Carteret's, at Scott's-hall. To hear that Mr. Lewes[3] hath another daughter sick. And, lastly, that both my servants, W. Hewer and Tom Edwards, have lost their fathers, both in St. Sepulchre's parish, of the plague this week, do put me into great apprehensions of melancholy, and with good reason. But I put off the thoughts of sadness as much as I can, and the rather to keep my wife in good heart and family also. After supper (having eat nothing all this day) upon a fine tench[4] of Mr. Shelden's taking, we to bed.

SEPTEMBER 1666

1. Up and at the office all the morning, and then dined at home. Got my new closet[5] made mighty clean against tomorrow. Sir W. Penn and my wife and Mercer and I to *Polichenelly*,[6] but were there horribly frighted to see young Killigrew[7] come in with a great many more young sparks; but we hid ourselves, so as we think they did not see us. By and by they went away, and then we were at rest again; and so the play being done, we to Islington and there eat and drank and mighty merry—and so home, singing; and after a letter or two at the office, to bed.

2. *Lord's day.* Some of our maids sitting up late last night to get things ready against our feast today, Jane called us up, about 3 in the morning, to tell us of a great fire they saw in the City.[8] So I rose, and slipped on my nightgown and went to her window, and thought it to be on the back side of Mark Lane at the furthest; but being unused to such fires as followed, I thought it far enough off, and so went to bed again and to sleep. About 7 rose again to dress myself, and there looked out at the window and saw the fire not so much as it was, and further off. So to my closet to set things to rights after yesterday's cleaning. By and by Jane comes and tells me that she hears that above 300 houses have been burned down tonight by the fire we saw, and that it was now burning down all Fish Street by London Bridge. So I made myself ready presently, and walked to the Tower and there got up upon one of the high places, Sir J. Robinson's[9] little son going up with me; and there I did see the houses at that end of the bridge all on fire, and an infinite great fire on this and the other side the end of the bridge—which, among other people, did trouble me for poor little Michell[10] and our Sarah on the Bridge. So down, with my heart full of trouble, to the Lieutenant of the Tower, who tells me that it begun this morning in the King's baker's house in Pudding Lane, and that it hath burned down St. Magnes Church and most part of Fish Street already. So I down to the water-side and there got a boat and through bridge, and there saw

---

[1] *hackney-coach*   Hired coach.

[2] *Mr. Sidney Montague*   The Earl of Sandwich's father.

[3] *Mr. Lewes*   Civil servant in navy administration.

[4] *tench*   Carp-like fish.

[5] *closet*   Small private room.

[6] *Polichenelly*   Puppet play based on the Italian *commedia dell'arte* character of Polichinello.

[7] *young Killigrew*   Possibly Henry Killigrew, younger brother to dramatist Thomas Killigrew.

[8] *the City*   I.e., the City of London, the part of the city falling within London's ancient boundaries. The financial and commercial centers were located in the City.

[9] *Sir J. Robinson*   Sir John Robinson was lieutenant of the Tower of London.

[10] *Michell*   William Michell and his wife Betty kept a brandy shop near London Bridge. Betty had been one of Pepys's old flames, and is referred to earlier in the *Diary* as his "second wife," Sarah.

a lamentable fire. Poor Michell's house, as far as the Old Swan,[1] already burned that way and the fire running further, that in a very little time it got as far as the Steelyard while I was there. Everybody endeavouring to remove their goods, and flinging into the River or bringing them into lighters[2] that lay off. Poor people staying in their houses as long as till the very fire touched them, and then running into boats or clambering from one pair of stair by the water-side to another. And among other things, the poor pigeons I perceive were loath to leave their houses, but hovered about the windows and balconies till they were some of them burned, their wings, and fell down.

Having stayed, and in an hour's time seen the fire rage every way, and nobody to my sight endeavouring to quench it, but to remove their goods and leave all to the fire; and having seen it get as far as the Steel-yard, and the wind mighty high and driving it into the city, and everything, after so long a drought, proving combustible, even the very stones of churches, and among other things, the poor steeple by which pretty Mrs. ——[3] lives, and whereof my old school-fellow Elborough is parson, taken fire in the very top and there burned till it fall down—I to Whitehall with a gentleman with me who desired to go off from the Tower to see the fire in my boat—to Whitehall, and there up to the King's closet in the chapel, where people came about me and I did give them an account dismayed them all; and word was carried in to the King, so I was called for and did tell the King and Duke of York what I saw, and that unless his Majesty did command houses to be pulled down, nothing could stop the fire. They seemed much troubled, and the King commanded me to go to my Lord Mayor from him and command him to spare no houses but to pull down before the fire every way. The Duke of York bid me tell him that if he would have any more soldiers, he shall; and so did my Lord Arlington afterward, as a great secret. Here meeting with Captain Cocke, I in his coach, which he lent me, and Creed with me, to Paul's;[4] and there walked along Watling Street as

well as I could, every creature coming away loaden with goods to save—and here and there sick people carried away in beds. Extraordinary good goods carried in carts and on backs. At last met my Lord Mayor in Canning Street, like a man spent, with a handkerchief about his neck. To the King's message, he cried like a fainting woman, "Lord, what can I do? I am spent. People will not obey me. I have been pulling down houses. But the fire overtakes us faster than we can do it." That he needed no more soldiers; and that for himself, he must go and refresh himself, having been up all night. So he left me, and I him, and walked home—seeing people all almost distracted and no manner of means used to quench the fire. The houses too, so very thick thereabouts, and full of matter for burning, as pitch and tar, in Thames Street—and warehouses of oil and wines and brandy and other things. Here I saw Mr. Isaac Houblon, that handsome man—prettily dressed and dirty at his door at Dowgate, receiving some of his brother's things whose houses were on fire; and as he says, have been removed twice already, and he doubts (as it soon proved) that they must be in a little time removed from his house also—which was a sad consideration. And to see the churches all filling with goods, by people who themselves should have been quietly there at this time.

By this time it was about 12 o'clock, and so home and there find my guests, which was Mr. Wood and his wife, Barbary Shelden, and also Mr. Moone—she mighty fine, and her husband, for aught I see, a likely[5] man. But Mr. Moone's design and mine, which was to look over my closet and please him with the sight thereof, which he hath long desired, was wholly disappointed, for we were in great trouble and disturbance at this fire, not knowing what to think of it. However, we had an extraordinary good dinner, and as merry as at this time we could be.

While at dinner, Mrs. Batelier came to enquire after Mr. Woolfe and Stanes (who it seems are related to them), whose houses in Fish Street are all burned, and they in a sad condition. She would not stay in the fright.

As soon as dined, I and Moone away and walked through the City, the streets full of nothing but people and horses and carts loaded with goods, ready to run over one another, and removing goods from one burned

[1] *Old Swan* Tavern in Thames Street.

[2] *lighters* Barges.

[3] *Mrs. ——* Mrs. Horsely, a pretty woman whom Pepys admired and pursued unsuccessfully.

[4] *Paul's* St. Paul's Cathedral.

[5] *likely* Capable.

house to another—they now removing out of Canning Street (which received goods in the morning) into Lumbard Street and further; and among others, I now saw my little goldsmith Stokes receiving some friend's goods, whose house itself was burned the day after. We parted at Paul's, he home and I to Paul's Wharf, where I had appointed a boat to attend me; and took in Mr. Carcasse and his brother, whom I met in the street, and carried them below and above bridge, to and again, to see the fire, which was now got further, both below and above, and no likelihood of stopping it. Met with the King and Duke of York in their barge, and with them to Queenhithe[1] and there called Sir Rd. Browne[2] to them. Their order was only to pull down houses apace, and so below bridge at the waterside; but little was or could be done, the fire coming upon them so fast. Good hopes there was of stopping it at the Three Cranes above, and at Buttolph's Wharf below bridge, if care be used; but the wind carries it into the City, so as we know not by the water-side what it doth there. River full of lighters and boats taking in goods, and good goods swimming in the water; and only, I observed that hardly one lighter or boat in three that had the goods of a house in, but there was a pair of virginals[3] in it. Having seen as much as I could now, I away to Whitehall by appointment, and there walked to St. James's Park, and there met my wife and Creed and Wood and his wife and walked to my boat, and there upon the water again, and to the fire up and down, it still increasing and the wind great. So near the fire as we could for smoke; and all over the Thames, with one's face in the wind you were almost burned with a shower of firedrops—this is very true—so as houses were burned by these drops and flakes of fire, three or four, nay five or six houses, one from another. When we could endure no more upon the water, we to a little alehouse on the Bankside over against the Three Cranes, and there stayed till it was dark almost and saw the fire grow; and as it grew darker, appeared more and more, and in corners and upon steeples and between churches and houses, as far as we could see up the hill of the City, in a most horrid malicious bloody flame, not

like the fine flame of an ordinary fire. Barbary[4] and her husband away before us. We stayed till, it being darkish, we saw the fire as only one entire arch of fire from this to the other side the bridge, and in a bow up the hill, for an arch of above a mile long. It made me weep to see it. The churches, houses, and all on fire and flaming at once, and a horrid noise the flames made, and the cracking of houses at their ruin. So home with a sad heart, and there find everybody discoursing and lamenting the fire; and poor Tom Hater came with some few of his goods saved out of his house, which is burned upon Fish Street hill. I invited him to lie at my house, and did receive his goods: but was deceived in his lying there,[5] the noise coming every moment of the growth of the fire, so as we were forced to begin to pack up our own goods and prepare for their removal. And did by moonshine (it being brave,[6] dry, and moonshine and warm weather) carry much of my goods into the garden, and Mr. Hater and I did remove my money and iron chests into my cellar—as thinking that the safest place. And got my bags of gold into my office ready to carry away, and my chief papers of accounts also there, and my tallies into a box by themselves. So great was our fear, as Sir W. Batten had carts come out of the country to fetch away his goods this night. We did put Mr. Hater, poor man, to bed a little; but he got but very little rest, so much noise being in my house, taking down of goods.

3. About 4 o'clock in the morning, my Lady Batten sent me a cart to carry away all my money and plate and best things to Sir W. Rider's at Bednall Green; which I did, riding myself in my nightgown in the cart; and Lord, to see how the streets and the highways are crowded with people, running and riding and getting of carts at any rate to fetch away things. I find Sir W. Rider tired with being called up all night and receiving things from several friends. His house full of goods—and much of Sir W. Batten and Sir W. Penn's. I am eased at my heart to have my treasure so well secured. Then home with much ado to find a way. Nor any sleep all this night to me nor my

---

[1] *Queenhithe* Harbor in Thames Street.

[2] *Sir Rd. Browne* I.e., Sir Richard Browne, a former Lord Mayor.

[3] *pair of virginals* Popular table-sized harpsichord.

[4] *Barbary* Actress Elizabeth Knepp, whom Pepys called "Barbary" because of her singing of *Barbary Allen*.

[5] *deceived in his lying there* Pepys felt mistaken to have extended the offer as the fire advanced.

[6] *brave* Fine.

poor wife. But then, and all this day, she and I and all my people labouring to get away the rest of our things, and did get Mr. Tooker to get me a lighter to take them in, and we did carry them (myself some) over Tower Hill, which was by this time full of people's goods, bringing their goods thither. And down to the lighter, which lay at the next quay above the Tower dock. And here was my neighbour's wife, Mrs. ——,[1] with her pretty child and some few of her things, which I did willingly give way to be saved with mine. But there was no passing with anything through the postern, the crowd was so great.

The Duke of York came this day by the office and spoke to us, and did ride with his guard up and down the City to keep all quiet (he being now General, and having the care of all).

This day, Mercer being not at home, but against her mistress's order gone to her mother's, and my wife going thither to speak with W. Hewer, met her there and was angry; and her mother saying that she was not an apprentice girl, to ask leave every time she goes abroad, my wife with good reason was angry, and when she came home, bid her be gone again. And so she went away, which troubled me; but yet less than it would, because of the condition we are in fear of coming into in a little time, of being less able to keep one in her quality. At night, lay down a little upon a quilt of W. Hewer in the office (all my own things being packed up or gone); and after me, my poor wife did the like—we having fed upon the remains of yesterday's dinner, having no fire nor dishes, nor any opportunity of dressing anything.

4. Up by break of day to get away the remainder of my things, which I did by a lighter at the Iron-gate; and my hands so few, that it was the afternoon before we could get them all away.

Sir W. Penn and I to Tower Street, and there met the fire burning three or four doors beyond Mr. Howell's; whose goods, poor man (his trays and dishes, shovels &c., were flung all along Tower Street in the kennels,[2] and people working therewith from one end to the other), the fire coming on in that narrow street, on both sides, with infinite fury. Sir W. Batten, not knowing how to remove his wine, did dig a pit in the garden and laid it in there; and I took the opportunity of laying all the papers of my office that I could not otherwise dispose of. And in the evening Sir W. Penn and I did dig another and put our wine in it, and I my parmesan cheese as well as my wine and some other things.

The Duke of York was at the office this day at Sir W. Penn's, but I happened not to be within. This afternoon, sitting melancholy with Sir W. Penn in our garden and thinking of the certain burning of this office without extraordinary means, I did propose for the sending up of all our workmen from Woolwich and Deptford yards (none whereof yet appeared), and to write to Sir W. Coventry to have the Duke of York's permission to pull down houses rather than lose this office, which would much hinder the King's business. So Sir W. Penn he went down this night, in order to the sending them up tomorrow morning; and I wrote to Sir W. Coventry about the business, but received no answer.

This night Mrs. Turner (who, poor woman, was removing her goods all this day—good goods, into the garden, and knew not how to dispose of them)—and her husband supped with my wife and I at night in the office, upon a shoulder of mutton from the cook's, without any napkin or anything, in a sad manner but were merry. Only, now and then walking into the garden and saw how horridly the sky looks, all on fire in the night, was enough to put us out of our wits; and indeed it was extremely dreadful—for it looks just as if it was at us, and the whole heaven on fire. I after supper walked in the dark down to Tower Street, and there saw it all on fire at the Trinity house on that side and the Dolphin tavern on this side, which was very near us—and the fire with extraordinary vehemence. Now begins the practice of blowing up of houses in Tower Street, those next the Tower, which at first did frighten people more than anything; but it stopped the fire where it was done—it bringing down the houses to the ground in the same places they stood, and then it was easy to quench what little fire was in it, though it kindled nothing almost. W. Hewer this day went to see how his mother did, and comes late home, but telling us how he hath been forced to remove her to Islington, her house in Pye Corner being burned. So that it is got so

1 *Mrs. ——* Mrs. Buckworth.

2 *kennels* Gutters.

far that way and all the Old Bailey,[1] and was running down to Fleet Street. And Paul's is burned, and all Cheapside. I wrote to my father this night; but the post–house being burned, the letter could not go.

5. I lay down in the office again upon W. Hewer's quilt, being mighty weary and sore in my feet with going[2] till I was hardly able to stand. About 2 in the morning my wife calls me up and tells of new cries of "Fire!"—it being come to Barking Church, which is the bottom of our lane. I up; and finding it so, resolved presently to take her away; and did, and took my gold (which was about 2350*l*.), W. Hewer, and Jane down by Poundy's boat to Woolwich. But Lord, what a sad sight it was by moonlight to see the whole City almost on fire—that you might see it plain at Woolwich, as if you were by it. There when I came, I find the gates shut, but no guard kept at all; which troubled me, because of discourses now begun that there is plot in it and that the French had done it.[3] I got the gates open, and to Mr. Shelden's, where I locked up my gold and charged my wife and W. Hewer never to leave the room without one of them in it night nor day. So back again, by the way seeing my goods well in the lighters at Deptford and watched well by people. Home, and whereas I expected to have seen our house on fire, it being now about 7 o'clock, it was not. But to the fire, and there find greater hopes than I expected; for my confidence of finding our office on fire was such, that I durst not ask anybody how it was with us, till I came and saw it not burned. But going to the fire, I find, by the blowing up of houses and the great help given by the workmen out of the King's yards, sent up by Sir W. Penn, there is a good stop given to it, as well at Mark Lane end as ours—it having only burned the dial[4] of Barking Church, and part of the porch, and was there quenched. I up to the top of Barking steeple, and there saw the saddest sight of desolation that I ever saw. Everywhere great fires. Oil cellars and brimstone and other things burning. I became afeared to stay there long;

and therefore down again as fast as I could, the fire being spread as far as I could see it, and to Sir W. Penn's and there eat a piece of cold meat, having eaten nothing since Sunday but the remains of Sunday's dinner.

Here I met with Mr. Young and Whistler; and having removed all my things, and received good hopes that the fire at our end is stopped, they and I walked into the town and find Fanchurch Street, Gracious Street, and Lumbard Street all in dust. The Exchange a sad sight, nothing standing there of all the statues or pillars but Sir Tho. Gresham's[5] picture in the corner. Walked into Moorfields (our feet ready to burn, walking through the town among the hot coals) and find that full of people, and poor wretches carrying their goods there, and everybody keeping his goods together by themselves (and a great blessing it is to them that it is fair weather for them to keep abroad[6] night and day); drank there, and paid twopence for a plain penny loaf.

Thence homeward, having passed through Cheapside and Newgate Market, all burned—and seen Anthony Joyce's house in fire. And took up (which I keep by me) a piece of glass of Mercer's chapel in the street, where much more was, so melted and buckled with the heat of the fire, like parchment. I also did see a poor cat taken out of a hole in the chimney joining to the wall of the Exchange, with the hair all burned off the body and yet alive. So home at night, and find there good hopes of saving our office—but great endeavours of watching all night and having men ready; and so we lodged them in the office, and had drink and bread and cheese for them. And I lay down and slept a good night about midnight— though when I rose, I hear that there had been a great alarm of French and Dutch being risen—which proved nothing. But it is a strange thing to see how long this time did look since Sunday, having been always full of variety of actions, and little sleep, that it looked like a week or more. And I had forgot almost the day of the week.

MAY 1668

17. *Lord's Day.* Up, and put on my new stuff-suit with a shoulder-belt, according to the new fashion, and the

---

[1]   *Old Bailey*   The area in which the Old Bailey, London's central criminal court, was located.

[2]   *going*   Walking.

[3]   *French had done it*   Pepys refers to rumors that the French had set the fire and were invading.

[4]   *dial*   Clock-face.

[5]   *Sir Tho. Gresham's*   I.e., Sir Thomas Gresham, who founded the Royal Exchange in 1568.

[6]   *abroad*   Outdoors.

bands of my vest and tunic laced with silk lace of the colour of my suit. And so, very handsome, to church, where a dull sermon and of a stranger, and so home; and there I find W. Howe,[1] and a younger brother of his, come to dine with me; and there comes Mercer, and brings with her Mrs. Gayet, which pleased me mightily; and here was also W. Hewer, and mighty merry; and after dinner to sing psalms. But Lord! to hear what an excellent bass this younger brother of W. Howe's sings, even to my astonishment, and mighty pleasant. By and by Gayet goes away, being a Catholic, to her devotions, and Mercer to church; but we continuing an hour or two singing, and so parted; and I to Sir W. Pen's, and there sent for a hackney-coach and he and she[2] and I out to take the gyre.[3] We went to Stepney,[4] and there stopped at the Trinity House, he to talk with the servants there against tomorrow, which is a great day for the choice of a new Master. And thence to Mile End,[5] and there eat and drank, and so home; and I supped with them—that is, eat some butter and radishes, which is my excuse for not eating of any other of their victuals, which I hate because of their sluttery:[6] and so home, and made my boy read to me part of Dr. Wilkins's new book of the *Real Character*;[7] and so to bed.

MAY 1669[8]

31. Up very betimes, and so continued all the morning, with W. Hewer, upon examining and stating my accounts, in order to the fitting myself to go abroad beyond sea, which the ill condition of my eyes, and my

---

[1] *W. Howe*   Sandwich's clerk.

[2] *she*   Lady Penn.

[3] *take the gyre*   I.e., walk around.

[4] *Stepney*   Village outside the City of London.

[5] *Mile End*   Between Stepney and the City of London.

[6] *sluttery*   Filthiness.

[7] *Dr. Wilkins… Real Character*   John Wilkins, a clergyman, writer, and scientific thinker, wrote *An Essay towards a Real Character and a Philosophical Language* (1688), in which he proposed a universal language to be used for international communication by diplomats, merchants, and travelers.

[8] *May 1669*   At this point, Pepys began to notice the deterioration of his eyesight, which he attributed to the long hours he spent working and writing.

neglect for a year or two, hath kept me behindhand in, and so as to render it very difficult now and troublesome to my mind to do it; but I this day made a satisfactory entrance therein. Dined at home, and in the afternoon by water to Whitehall, calling by the way at Michell's, where I have not been many a day till just the other day; and now I met her mother there and knew her husband to be out of town. And here *je* did *baiser elle*, but had not opportunity *para hacer*[9] some with her as I would have offered if *je* had had it. And thence had another meeting with the Duke of York, at Whitehall, on yesterday's work and made a good advance: and so being called by my wife, we to the park, Mary Batelier,[10] and a Dutch gentleman, a friend of hers, being with us. Thence to "The World's End," a drinking-house by the park; and there merry, and so home late.

And thus ends all that I doubt I shall ever be able to do with my own eyes in the keeping of my journal, I being not able to do it any longer, having done now so long as to undo my eyes almost every time that I take a pen in my hand; and, therefore, whatever comes of it, I must forbear: and, therefore, resolve, from this time forward, to have it kept by my people in long-hand, and must therefore be contented to set down no more than is fit for them and all the world to know; or if there be anything, which cannot be much, now my amours to Deb.[11] are past, and my eyes hindering me in almost all other pleasures, I must endeavour to keep a margin in my book open, to add, here and there, a note in short-hand with my own hand.

And so I betake myself to that course, which is almost as much as to see myself go into my grave: for which, and all the discomforts that will accompany my being blind, the good God prepare me!

S.P.

MAY 31, 1669

---

[9] *je did baiser elle*   French: I did kiss her; *para hacer*   Spanish: To do.

[10] *Mary Batelier*   Neighbor of the Pepys family.

[11] *Deb.*   Deborah Willet was hired to accompany and attend to Pepys's wife Elizabeth in 1668. Samuel became infatuated with her, and the two had an affair. When Elizabeth learned of the relationship, she threatened to attack Deb, and Pepys was forced to renounce her.

IN CONTEXT

Other Accounts of the Great Fire

The painting above is of the Dutch school, after Jan Griffien the Elder; it dates from c. 1675.
The old St. Paul's Cathedral is in the center of the picture.

The Great Fire of London, 1666

from *The London Gazette* (3–10 Sept 1666)

Reproduced on the following four pages is the issue of *The London Gazette* that reported on
the fire. As with most newspapers of the time, four pages constituted the entire publication.

THE LONDON GAZETTE.

Published by Authority.

From Monday, Septemb 3, to Monday, Septemp 10, 1666.

Whitehall, Sept. 8.

THE ordinary course of this paper having been interrupted by a sad and lamentable accident of Fire lately hapned in the City of *London* : it hath been thought fit for satisfying the minds of so many of His Majesties good Subjects who must needs be concerned for the Issue of so great an accident, to give this short, but true Accompt of it.

On the second instant, at one of the clock in the Morning, there hapned to break out, a sad in deplorable Fire in *Pudding-lane*, neer *New Fish-street*, which falling out at that hour of the night, and in a quarter of the Town so close built with wooden pitched houses spread itself so far before day, and with such distraction to the inhabitants and Neighbours, that care was not taken for the timely preventing the further diffusion of it, by pulling down houses, as ought to have been ; so that this lamentable Fire in a short time became too big to be mastred by any Engines or working neer it.   It fell out most unhappily too, That a violent Easterly wind fomented it, and kept it burning all that day, and the night following spreading itself up to *Grace-church-street* and downwards from *Cannon-street* to the Water-side, as far as the *Three Cranes in the Vintrey.*

The people in all parts about it, distracted by the vastness of it, and their particular care to carry away their Goods, many attempts were made to prevent the spreading of it by pulling down Houses, and making great Intervals, but all in vain, the Fire seizing upon the Timber and Rubbish, and so continuing it set even through those spaces, and raging in a bright flame all Monday and Teusday, not withstanding His Majesties own, and His Royal Highness's indefatigable and personal pains to apply all possible remedies to prevent it, calling upon and helping the people with their Guards ; and a great number of Nobility and Gentry unweariedly assisting therein, for which they were requited with a thousand blessings from the poor distressed people. By the favour of God the Wind slackened a little on Teusday night & the Flames meeting with brick buildings at the *Temple*, by little and little it was observed to lose its force on that side, so that on Wednesday morning we began to hope well, and his Royal Highness never despairing or slackening his personal care wrought so well that day, assisted in some parts by the Lords of the Council before and behind it that a stop was put to it at the *Temple*

Church, neer *Holborn-bridge*, Pie-corner, *Aldersgate*, *Cripple-gate*, neer the lower end of *Coleman-street*, at the end of *Basin-hall-street* by the *Postern* at the upper end of *Bishopsgate-street* and *Leadenhall-street*, at the *Standard* in *Cornhill* at the church in *Fenchurch street*, neer *Cloth-workers Hall* in *Mincing-lane*, at the middle of *Mark-lane*, and at the *Tower-dock.*

On Thursday by the blessing of God it was wholly beat down and extinguished. But so as that Evening it unhappily burst out again a fresh at the *Temple*, by the falling of some sparks (as is supposed) upon a Pile of Wooden buildings ; but his Royal Highness who watched there that whole night in Person, by the great labours and diligence used, and especially by applying Powder to blow up the Houses about it, before day most happily mastered it.

Divers Strangers, Dutch and French were, during the fire, apprehended, upon suspicion that they contributed mischievously to it, who are all imprisoned, and Informations prepared to make a severe inquisition here upon by my Lord Chief Justice *Keeling*, assisted by some of the Lords of the Privy Council ; and some principal Members of the City, notwithstanding which suspicion, the manner of the burning all along in a Train, and so blowen forwards in all its way by strong Winds, make us conclude the whole was an effect of an unhappy chance, or to speak better, the heavy hand of God upon us for our sins, shewing us the terrour of his Judgement in thus raising the Fire, and immediately after his miraculous and never to be acknowledged Mercy, in putting a stop to it when we were in the last despair, and that all attempts for quenching it however industriously pursued seemed insufficient.   His Majesty then sat hourly in Councel, and ever since hath continued making rounds about the City in all parts of it where the danger and mischief was greatest, till this morning that he hath sent his Grace the Duke of *Albermarle*, whom he hath called for to assist him in this great occasion, to put his happy and successful hand to the finishing this memorable deliverance.

About the *Tower* the seasonable orders given for plucking down the Houses to secure the Magazines of Powder was more especially successful, that part being up the Wind, notwithstanding which it came almost to the very Gates of it.   So as by this early provision the general Stores of War lodged in the *Tower* were entirely saved : And we have further this intimate cause to give God thanks, that the Fire did not happen where his Majesties Naval Stores are kept. So as though it has pleased God to visit us with his own hand, he hath not, by disfurnishing us with the means of carrying on the War, subjected us to our enemies.

It must be observed, that this fire happened in a part of the Town, vvhere tho the commodities vvere not very rich, yet they vvere so bulky that they could not vvell be removed, so that the Inhabitants of that part where it first began have sustained very great loss, but by the best enquiry vve can make, the other parts of the Town where the Commodities vvere of greater value, took the Alarum so early, that they saved most of their goods of value; which possibly may have diminished the loss, tho some think, that if the whole industry of the Inhabitants had been applyed to the stopping of the fire, and not to the saving of their particular *Goods*, the success might have been much better, not only to the publick, but to many of them in their own particulars.

Through this sad Accident it is easie to be imagined how many persons were necessitated to remove themselves and Goods into the open fields, where they were forced to continue some time, which could not but work compassion in the beholders, but his Majesties care was most signal in this occasion, who besides his personal pains was frequent in consulting all wayes for relieving those distressed persons, which produced so good effect, as well as by his Majesties Proclamations and the Orders issued to the Neighbour Justices of the Peace to encourage the sending in provisions to the Markets, which are publickly known, as by other directions, that when his Majesty, fearing lest other Orders might not yet have been sufficient, had commanded the Victualler of his Navy to send bread into *Moore-fields* for relief of the poor, which for the more speedy supply he sent in Bisket out of the Sea Stores; it was found that the Markets had been already so well supplyd that the people, being un-accustomed to that kind of Bread declined it, and so it was returned in greater part to his Majestys Stores again vvithout any use made of it.

And we cannot but observe to the confutation of all his Majesties enemies, who endeavour to perswade the vvorld abroad of great parties, and disaffection at home against his Majesties Government; that a greater instance of the affections of this City could never been given then hath now been given in this sad and deplorable Accident vvhen if at any time disorder might have been expected from the losses, distraction, and almost desperation of some people in their private fortune, thousands of people not having had habitations to cover them. And yet in all this time it hath been so far from any appearance of designs or attempts against his Majesties Government, that his Majesty and his Royal Brother, out of their care to stop and prevent the fire, frequently exposing their persons with very small attendants in all parts of the Town—sometimes even to be intermixed with those who laboured in the business, yet never the less there hath not been observed so much as a mur-

muring word to fall from any, but on the contrary, even those persons, whose losses rendered their conditions most desperate, and to be fit objects of others prayers, beholding those frequent instances of his Majesties care of his people, forgot their own misery, and filled the streets with their prayers for his Majesty, vvhose trouble they seemed to compassionate before their own.

A FARTHUR ACCOUNT OF THIS LAMENTABLE FIRE.

This dismal fire broke out at a baker's shop in *Pudding-lane*, by *Fish-street*, in the lower part of the city, near Thames-street (among wooden houses ready to take fire & full of combustible goods) in *Billinsgate-ward*; which ward in a few hours was laid in ashes. As it began in the dead of the night when everybody was asleep, the darkness greatly increased the horror of the calamity; it rapidly rushed down the hill to the bridge; crossed *Thames-street* to *St. Mangus* church at the foot of the bridge; but having scaled and captured its fort, shot large volumes of flames into every place about it. The fire drifted back to the city again & roared with great violence through *Thames-street* aided by the combustible matter deposited there with such a fierce wind at its back as to strike with horror its beholders.

Fire! Fire! Fire! doth resound in every street, some starting out of their sleep & peeping through the windows half-dressed. Some in night dresses rushing wildly about the streets crying piteously & praying to God for assistance, women carrying children in their arms & the men looking quite bewildered. Many cripples were also seen hobbling about not knowing which way to go to get free from the flames which were raging all round them. No man that had the sence of human miseries could unconcertedly behold the frightful destruction made in one of the noblest Cities in the world.

What a confusion! the Lord Mayor of the city came with his officers, & *London* so famous for its wisdom can find neither hands nor brains to prevent its utter ruin. London must fall to the ground in ashes & who can prevent it? The fire raged mastery, & burnt dreadfully; by the fierce Easterly wind it spread quickly in all directions, overturning all so furiously that the whole city is brought into a desolation. That night most of the citizens had taken their last sleep; & when they went to sleep they little thought that when their ears were unlocked that such an enemy had invaded their City, & that they should see him with such fury break through their doors, & enter their rooms with such threatening countenance.

It commenced on the Lord's day morning, never was there the like Sabbath in *London*: many churches were in flames that day; God seemed to come down and preach himself in them, as he did in *Sinai* when the mount burnt with fire: such warm preaching those churches never had before

THE LONDON GAZETTE.

& in other churches ministers had preached their farewell sermons.

Goods were moved hastily from the lower part of the City to the upper part, & some hopes were retained on Sunday that the fire would not reach them; they could scarcely imagine that a fire half a mile off could reach their houses. All means to stop it proved ineffectual; the wind blew so hard that flakes of flames & burning matters were carried across the streets & spread the fire in all directions, & when the evening came on the fire was more visible & dreadful & instead of the dark curtains of night which used to spread over the City the curtains had changed to yellow & at a distance the whole City appeared to be on fire, little sleep was taken that night, men busy in all directions pulling down & blowing up houses to stop its progress, but all to no purpose, for it made the most furious onset & drove back all opposers. Many were upon their knees in the night, pouring out tears before the Lord; interceding for poor London in the day of its calamity; but all in vain.

Sunday night the fire had got into *Cannon-street* & levelled it with the ground.

On Monday, *Grace-church-street* was all in flames & *Lombard-street* & *Fen-church-street*. The burning was in the shape of a bow, & a fearful bow it was!

Then the flames broke in on *Cornhill* that large & spacious street, & rapidly crossed the way by the train of wood that laid in the streets untaken away, which had been pulled from the houses to prevent its spreading & burned to the tops of the highest houses & to the bottom of the lowest cellars.

The *Royal Exchange* was next invaded & burned quickly through all its galleries; by and bye down fell all the Kings upon their faces & the building on the top of them with such a noise as was dreadful; then the citizens trembled & fled away lest they should be devoured also.

Monday night was a dreadful night! The fire burst into *Cheapside* in four directions with such a dazzling glare and roaring noise by the falling of so many houses at one time, as to amaze any one who witnessed it.

On Tuesday the fire burned up the very bowels of *London* from *Bow-lane*, *Bread-street*, *Friday-street*, and *Old Change* the flames came up almost together.

Then the fire got on to *Paternoster Row*, *Newgate-street*, the *Old Bailey* and *Ludgate hill* & rushed down into *Fleet-street*. St. *Paul's church* though all of stone outward, and naked of houses about it strangely caught fire at the top; the lead melted & run down as snow before the burning sun and the massy stones, with a hideous noise fell on the pavement.

Tuesday night was more dreadful than Monday night, for the flames having consumed the greatest part of the city; threatened the suburbs, and the poor were preparing to fly as well as they could with their luggage into the countries and villages.

On Wednesday the Lord had pity on them; the wind hushed & the fire burnt gently; then the citizens began to gather a little heart.

The following list of buildings destroyed in this terrible disaster hath been taken:—

13,200 Houses
    87 Churches
     6 Chapels
The Royal Exchange
The Custom House
Jail at Newgate
Three City gates
The Guildhall and
Four bridges.

Edenburg Aug 29 Scarce a day passes wherein some Prizes are not bough in by our Privateers, amongst the rest one of them of six guns has lately ziesed on a very rich Prize laden with Spices bound for *Denmark*, and in her (as 'tis said) a Natural Son of the King of *Denmark*.

Southwold Sept 2 A French vessel called the *Hope* of *Quellebœuf*, laden with 1750 firkins of Butter and 400 Pigs of Lead, was put ashore about a league to the south-ward of this Town, and split in pieces; but the Goods are most of them saved and preserved for the owners, it being one of those vessels that bought over the Lord Douglas' Regiment and was permitted to lade home.

Plymouth Sept. 2. Yesterday arrived here *Ostenders* laden with salt &c. from *Rochells*, from whence they came the 16 of *August* last, and report the D. *de Beaufort* was then in there with his Fleet of about 40 sayl, great and small, Men of War and Fireships, whereof 3 Dutch; and were making all the preparations they could for the Sea, but their going out was uncertain.

Pendennis Sept 3. On Friday morning arrived here *La Signoria de la Grafia*, a Venetian Vessell, hired by Mr *Abraham Walwyn*, who laded Currans and Oyle at *Zanti* and *Gallipoli*, and were bound for *London*; by the way the *Venetians*, *Maltesians*, and other Italians with whom she was mann'd designed the destruction of the Merchant and those belonging to them; intending afterwards to carry off the ship with its fraight; and in execution of their purpose had fallen upon the Merchant whom they wounded in several places, and had undoubtly kill'd him, but that Captain *Lucy* in the *Victory*, a Privateer, came by providence to its rescue, and seizing their principals secured them from further attempts.

Weymouth Sept 3. On the first instant a small French vessel with Ballast, taken by one of our Frigots, was sent in hither and by the way ran on ground in the storm, but by the assistance of several persons she got off, being robb'd whilst' he lay there of all her Rigging Sayles, and Tackle.

Dublin Aug 28. On the 25 instant his Grace the Lord Lieutenant came safe to *Kilkenny*, intending from thence to visit all the most considerable places in *Munster*. The Lord Chancellour is well recovered, and was yesterday abroad and intends speedily to follow. All countries are in very

THE LONDON GAZETTE.

good order, the Toryes no more heard of, and the Militia is generally settled in a very good posture.

Norwich September 5. The account of our Bill of Mortality for this last week runs thus, buried of all Diseases 162. Whereof of the Plague 147, Besides at the Pest house 12.

Portsmouth Septemb 7. Yesterday, his Grace the Lord General passed hence for *London*, leaving the Fleet refitted after the late Storm ready to put to Sea again vvith the first fair vvind.

NOtice *is hereby given, That Sir* Robert Viner *is now settld in the* Affrican *house near the middle of* Broad-street London, *where he intends to manage his affairs (as formerly in* Lumbard-street*) having by the good providence of God been entirely preserved by a timely and safe removal of all his concerns, almost twenty-four hours before the furious fire entered* Lumbard-street.

Also Alderman Meynell, *and Alderman* Backwell, *with divers others of* Lumbard Street, *being likewise preserved in their estates, do intend to settle in a few daies in or near* Broard Street.

THE *General Post-office is for the present held at the two Black Pillars in* Bridges Street, *over against the* Fleece Tavern, Covent Garden, *till a more convenient place can be found in* London.

Royal Charles in St. *Helen's* Road, Sept 2. On the 30th past, by six in the morning, our Fleet weighed Anchor at *Sole* Bay, but it proving a calm, and the tide against us, we were forced to come again to an Anchor before we had made a league of vvay, and so rid that day without farther intelligence of the Enemy.

The 31 by 7 in the morning we were under sayl, and stood a course towards the *Long-sandhead*, till about 11 at noon, when off *Balsey Cliffe*, we discovered the Enemy bearing S. and by E, whereupon we steered S.E., being assured by our Pilots to be clear of the Galopes, but yet we past not so well, but that this Ship struck upon the sand, but was so fortunate to get off again without prejudice; Which stop brought us into better

order to steer after the Enemy with the White Squadron in the Van and the Blew in the Rear, till 12 at night, keeping the Wind, at which time we guess the Dutch were tacked, seeing them neer us, and some of our sternmost ships and the Enemy firing, which made us tack also and stand to the northward.

Sept 1. We saw the Vice-Admiral of the Blew to the Leeward with some few ships, and finding the Dutch were gone away from us towards *Calais*, we stood a Course after them, and found some of them merely Anchored, and others standing in, but at our approach they all got Under sayle, and stood for *Bullogne* Road, haling in close to the shore, being sure to weather us if we pass the Point, the Wind then E. by N. and E.N.E. as much as we could carry our Topsails half-mast high: Whereupon we lay by short of the place till all our Fleet came up; but then the storm growing greater, and having no hopes, by reason of the ill-weather, of attempting further upon the enemy; who durst not adventure out of the shelter of the shoar. It was found best to lay bye and bring the Fleet together, and the next day to betake ourselves to St. *Helen's* Bay—the place appointed for our Rendezvous, as the most proper station to hinder the Enemies conjunction with the French, we being ready with the first fair wind to seek out the enemy.

In the storm two of our ships struck upon the *Riprap* Sands viz. the *Andrew* and the *Happy Return*, but we got well off again; The rest of our Fleet in good condition. What loss the enemy sustained by the storm we know not, only we are assured, they were forced to blow up one of their greatest ships; another a Flagship wholly disabled was seen driving before the vvind, and that several others of them were much damnified and disabled; and of the rest four vve could see run upon the Sands, and with great difficulty got off again.

Dover Sept 8 This afternoon the *Dutch* Fleet weighed from *Bullen Road*, and are now standing towards their own coast.

London Printed by Tho. Newcomb. 1666.

Aphra Behn
1640 – 1689

Long recognized as the first professional woman writer in England, Aphra Behn is also known for a life of adventure and espionage, for libertine sexual views, and for helping to lay the foundation for the cause of women's rights. Behn was one of the most prolific dramatists of the Restoration period and has been credited with introducing into her plays to an unprecedented degree aspects of the life of the time not previously considered fit material for the stage. Her most successful work, *Oroonoko*, has come to be recognized as an important narrative of slavery. Much as Behn was successful and influential in her own day, by the late nineteenth century she was almost forgotten; the open treatment of sexuality in her work was condemned as too "coarse" to be deserving of a broad audience. In the twentieth century, however, her literary reputation soared, and she has been

Mrs. Behn.

championed by feminists for creating a place for women in the writing world. Virginia Woolf wrote in *A Room of One's Own*: "All women together ought to let flowers fall upon the tomb of Aphra Behn, [...] for it was she who earned them the right to speak their minds."

Behn's parentage is not known with any certainty. Some believe she was born to a barber and his wife, the Amies, in Wye, Kent, but scholars now generally accept that she was born to a family called Johnson just outside Canterbury. In the late 1650s the family moved to Surinam in South America, where her father had been given an administrative post. He died on the voyage, but the family remained in Surinam until about 1663. Her stay in the then-British colony exposed Behn to what would become the setting of *Oroonoko* more than twenty years later; it is believed that she also began writing plays during this period. She married shortly after her return to England. Virtually nothing is known of Mr. Behn, who was a merchant of Dutch/German heritage. He may have died in 1664, possibly of the bubonic plague; at any rate, no record of him after this point has come down to us. Some time during this period, Behn was introduced to the court of Charles II. She was considered a witty conversationalist, and her travels to the colonies made her much sought after. Her knowledge of several languages, including Dutch, proved useful and in 1666 she became a spy for the King in Antwerp. She was Agent 160, also known as Astrea, a name she used later as a *non de plume*. She incurred a great deal of debt while working in the King's service, and when she returned to London in 1667 she may have been put briefly in debtors' prison.

Single and forced to earn a living, Behn became a writer out of necessity. She wrote in one of her prefaces that she was "forced to write for bread and not ashamed to own it." With the Restoration the theaters had been re-opened and women were for the first time appearing on the commercial stage in England, as they did in France. Behn was able to find a niche in a newly burgeoning theater world that was looking for new works to produce. Her first play was *The Forc'd Marriage* (1670). Its central theme—the human damage caused when parents forced their offspring, particularly daughters, to marry against their free choice—was present in many of her later plays as well. Behn would often use her plays to attack what she considered the wrongs of society. In the prefaces of the printed versions of her plays she would answer her critics and put forward her ideas on the position of women.

The world of Restoration drama was one tolerant of iconoclasm, and in that context it is less surprising than it might otherwise be that Behn became one of the most established dramatists of the time, writing approximately 20 plays in as many years. The years 1676–83 were her most successful period of writing, and from this period *The Rover* (1677) remains the play she is most known for. Like many of her plays, *The Rover* was a social comedy, involving a good deal of sexual adventure (and misadventure). It was said to be one of the King's favorite plays and it was frequently produced through to the end of the century.

Two years after the success of *The Rover*, Behn followed with a similar play, *The Feigned Courtesans*, which also proved to be extremely popular. In this play Behn again raises the issue of women with limited marital options; Marcella and Cornelia pose as prostitutes in order to avoid an arranged marriage for Marcella and the convent for Cornelia. The women use their wits to marry the husbands of their own choosing. In using the "oldest profession in the world" in this dramatic fashion, Behn makes a pointed commentary on the treatment of women as commodities in society at large.

Between 1683 and 1688 Behn did not produce as many plays, and instead turned her attention to other genres (poetry, letters, and novels). The most widely read and discussed of Behn's non-dramatic works is *Oroonoko: or, The Royal Slave*, published in 1688. Now widely regarded as one of the most important prose fiction narratives of the period in English literature, *Oroonoko* caused little stir initially; its great fame came later (and was inextricably involved) with that of Thomas Southerne's dramatic adaptation (1695). From not long thereafter until well into the nineteenth century *Oroonoko* remained a literary touchstone of the anti-slavery movement. The work details the journey of Oroonoko from royal prince to slave in Surinam, where he leads a failed slave uprising. It is not certain how much of the narrative is based on actual events; while Behn was in Surinam, it is possible that she encountered a figure like Oroonoko.

Behn's last few years were filled with poverty and illness. She was aging, and no longer sought after for her witty repartee. Although it is known that she died on 16 April 1689, few of the details are known. The epitaph on her tombstone in Westminster Abbey reads as follows: "Here lies a proof that wit can never be / Defence enough against mortality."

⌘ ⌘ ⌘

The Disappointment [1]

O ne day the amorous Lysander,[2]
By an impatient passion swayed,
Surprised fair Cloris,[3] that loved maid,
Who could defend herself no longer.
5   All things did with his love conspire;
The gilded planet° of the day,   *sun*

In his gay chariot drawn by fire,
Was now descending to the sea,
And left no light to guide the world,
10   But what from Cloris' brighter eyes was hurled.

In a lone thicket made for love,
Silent as yielding maid's consent,
She with a charming languishment,
Permits his force, yet gently strove;
15   Her hands his bosom softly meet,
But not to put him back designed,
Rather to draw him on inclined;
Whilst he lay trembling at her feet,

---

[1]   *The Disappointment*   Cf. "The Imperfect Enjoyment," by Behn's contemporary, John Wilmot, Earl of Rochester. "The Disappointment" was first published alongside Rochester's poem in his 1680 volume *Poems on Several Occasions*.

[2]   *Lysander*   Common name for a shepherd in pastoral poetry.

[3]   *Cloris*   Common name for a shepherdess in pastoral poetry.

Resistance 'tis in vain to show;
20 She wants the power to say—"Ah! What d'ye do?"

Her bright eyes sweet, and yet severe,
Where love and shame confus'dly strive,
Fresh vigour to Lysander give;
And breathing faintly in his ear,
25 She cried—"Cease, cease—your vain desire,
Or I'll call out—what would you do?
My dearer honour ev'n to you
I cannot, must not give—retire,
Or take this life, whose chiefest part
30 I gave you with the conquest of my heart."

But he as much unused to fear,
As he was capable of love,
The blessed minutes to improve,
Kisses her mouth, her neck, her hair;
35 Each touch her new desire alarms,
His burning trembling hand he pressed
Upon her swelling snowy breast,
While she lay panting in his arms.
All her unguarded beauties lie
40 The spoils and trophies of the enemy.

And now without respect or fear,
He seeks the object of his vows,
(His love no modesty allows)
By swift degrees advancing—where
45 His daring hand that altar seized,
Where gods of love do sacrifice:
That awful throne, that paradise
Where rage is calmed, and anger pleased,
That fountain where delight still flows,
50 And gives the universal world repose.

Her balmy lips encount'ring his,
Their bodies, as their souls, are joined;
Where both in transports unconfined
Extend themselves upon the moss.
55 Cloris half dead and breathless lay;
Her soft eyes cast a humid light,
Such as divides the day and night;
Or falling stars, whose fires decay:

And now no signs of life she shows,
60 But what in short-breathed sighs returns and goes.

He saw how at her length she lay;
He saw her rising bosom bare;
Her loose thin robes, through which appear
A shape designed for love and play;
65 Abandoned by her pride and shame
She does her softest joys dispense,
Offering her virgin innocence
A victim to love's sacred flame;
While the o'er-ravished shepherd lies
70 Unable to perform the sacrifice.

Ready to taste a thousand joys,
The too transported hapless swain
Found the vast pleasure turned to pain;
Pleasure which too much love destroys.
75 The willing garments by he laid,
And heaven all opened to his view,
Mad to possess, himself he threw
On the defenceless lovely maid.
But oh what envious gods conspire
80 To snatch his power, yet leave him the desire!

Nature's support (without whose aid
She can no human being give)
Itself now wants the art to live;
Faintness its slackened nerves invade;
85 In vain th'enraged youth essayed
To call its fleeting vigour back,
No motion 'twill from motion take;
Excess of love his love betrayed.
In vain he toils, in vain commands;
90 The insensible fell weeping in his hand.

In this so amorous cruel strife,
Where love and fate were too severe,
The poor Lysander in despair
Renounced his reason with his life.
95 Now all the brisk and active fire
That should the nobler part inflame,
Served to increase his rage and shame,
And left no spark for new desire:

Not all her naked charms could move
100   Or calm that rage that had debauched his love.

Cloris returning from the trance
Which love and soft desire had bred,
Her timorous hand she gently laid
(Or guided by design or chance)
105   Upon that fabulous Priapus,[1]
That potent god, as poets feign;
But never did young shepherdess,
Gath'ring of fern upon the plain,
More nimbly draw her fingers back,
110   Finding beneath the verdant leaves, a snake,

Then Cloris her fair hand withdrew,
Finding that god of her desires
Disarmed of all his awful fires,
And cold as flow'rs bathed in the morning dew.
115   Who can the nymph's confusion guess?
The blood forsook the hinder place,
And strewed with blushes all her face,
Which both disdain and shame expressed:
And from Lysander's arms she fled,
120   Leaving him fainting on the gloomy bed.

Like lightning through the grove she hies,
Or Daphne from the Delphic god,[2]
No print upon the grassy road
She leaves, t'instruct pursuing eyes.
125   The wind that wantoned in her hair,
And with her ruffled garments played,
Discovered in the flying maid
All that the gods e'er made, of fair.
So Venus, when her love was slain,
130   With fear and haste flew o'er the fatal plain.[3]

The nymph's resentments none but I
Can well imagine or condole:
But none can guess Lysander's soul,
But those who swayed his destiny.
135   His silent griefs swell up to storms,
And not one god his fury spares;
He cursed his birth, his fate, his stars
But more the shepherdess's charms,
Whose soft bewitching influence
140   Had damned him to the hell of impotence.
—1680

══════════

Oroonoko: or, The Royal Slave. A True History

In the opening lines of *Oroonoko*, the narrator promises to give us a true history: "I was myself an eyewitness, to a great part, of what you will find here set down." This promise is not to be taken at face value, as it is highly contested how closely we ought to associate Aphra Behn's own experiences with those of her narrator, and equally uncertain whether the account of Oroonoko's life is purely fiction or possibly inspired by a real person or event. Oroonoko's name itself is almost certainly an invention; it could be derived from the name Oorondates used in Ancient Greek literature, inspired by the Orinoco river where an English population settled in South America, or taken from the oronoko variety of tobacco, which was grown on the plantations of Surinam.

Even if Oroonoko's story is likely imagined, Behn's depiction of its setting in Surinam, although certainly romanticized, is historically genuine, and is far more realistic and detailed than was typical of fiction at the time. Surinam was the site of a British colony between 1650 and 1667, after which

---

[1] *Priapus*   Greek god of fertility, who is usually depicted with an enormous, erect phallus.

[2] *Daphne … god*   The nymph Daphne fled from the god Apollo's advances and was transformed into a laurel tree in her escape.

[3] *Venus … plain*   When Adonis was slain by a wild boar, Venus, the goddess of love, rushed to his side to help him.

it became a possession of the Dutch. Most of the Europeans mentioned by name in *Oroonoko* were actual members of the colony's upper classes during this time. Their primary goal as colonists was the cultivation of coffee, sugar cane, and other trade goods for export, and most of this work was done by African slaves under appalling conditions of violence and deprivation. The Englishman George Warren lamented in his 1667 *Impartial Description of Surinam* that slaves

> are sold like dogs, and no better esteem'd but for their work-sake, which they perform all the week, with the severest usages for the slightest fault ... [T]heir lodging is a hard board, and their black skins their covering. These wretched miseries not seldom drive them to desperate attempts for the recovery of their liberty, endeavouring to escape.

Although there is no record of a large scale rebellion similar to the one the title character Oroonoko incites, some slaves did manage to escape the plantations, and the raids conducted by these refugees were a significant threat to colonists' safety. Behn's portrait of Surinam as plagued by unstable violent tension between races and classes is true to the political realities of the colony.

Despite a few dissenting voices that existed at the time of *Oroonoko*'s publication, on the whole popular opinion in Britain was not yet against slavery. While *Oroonoko* would later acquire a reputation as an abolitionist text, it was not initially perceived as one, and it cannot be taken for granted that Behn herself opposed slavery in all of its forms—in fact, evidence suggests that she might have been married to a slave trader. Her engagement with the issue is nonetheless progressive for its time, especially in its sympathetic portrayal of a black African hero and heroine; Oroonoko and Imoinda are much more virtuous than the general population of slaves—and, notably, than the majority of the white characters. On the subject of race, *Oroonoko* is also unusual in that, through its retelling of Oroonoko and Imoinda's initial love affair in their homeland, it provides one of the first accounts of West African native life attempted by a European writer. Although her depiction is far more fanciful than factual, a few aspects are true; for example, as she reports, warring tribes did sell their captives to the British as slaves. For the most part, however, Behn combines personal invention with whatever inaccurate information she might have been able to gather, manufacturing an intricate West African civilization that never actually existed. Her representation of native life in Surinam as an uncomplicated golden age is equally distorted.

While *Oroonoko*'s treatment of race is certainly of interest, it may not have been the political issue foremost in Behn's mind at the time of her writing. She composed *Oroonoko* in 1688, which was a period of upheaval for the British government due to James II's precarious position as king. As a Catholic advocating religious freedom, and as an absolutist monarch attempting to ignore the will of Parliament, James was faced with rapidly growing opposition from most of his subjects. The Glorious Revolution was approaching, and later in 1688, after *Oroonoko* was published, it would result in James's forced abdication of the throne. Behn was a vehement royalist who remained supportive of James II, and it is worth considering in the context of these events what Oroonoko might represent as a virtuous, legitimate prince deprived of his rightful class position. *Oroonoko*'s most hypocritical characters claim to be Christian but act otherwise, and this, too, can be read as an indictment of the revolutionaries, since James's Parliamentarian enemies supported the power of the Anglican Church.

Whatever immediate political intentions Behn might originally have had, the story's popular success did not arrive until after the Glorious Revolution had passed. In 1695, Thomas Southerne adapted Behn's story to the stage, and his play *Oroonoko: A Tragedy* was performed frequently for the next hundred years. Although Behn's work shared in the play's success—her book was reprinted shortly after Southerne's play was first performed—Southerne's reinterpretation came to color subsequent readings of the original. *Oroonoko: A Tragedy* differed from its predecessor in its increased emphasis on the romance between Oroonoko and the beautiful Imoinda, who was transformed from a black African into a white woman in Southerne's text and in nearly all of the other stage adaptations that followed. Southerne's first audiences were, it seemed, much more interested in the story's emotional qualities than in any political aspects; it was only as the abolitionist movement gained momentum in Britain that *Oroonoko*'s potential as an ideological engagement with slavery was acknowledged. When abolitionism became popular in the late 1700's and early 1800's, stage versions of *Oroonoko* proliferated and were performed as contributions to the slavery debate. John Ferriar's 1778 adaptation *The Prince of Angola*, for instance, was presented as a reworking of the plot to accurately portray the injustices of slavery in South America. *The Prince of Angola*, described on its title page as "a tragedy, altered from the play of *Oroonoko* [a]nd adapted to the circumstances of the present times," corrected what Ferriar saw as pro-slavery tendencies in both Southerne's text and Behn's original. In most eyes, however, all versions of *Oroonoko* including Behn's became synonymous with anti-slavery sentiment—so much so that, while it was very successful elsewhere, all its stage incarnations were banned in the slave-trading port of Liverpool.

Valued alternately as superbly descriptive travel narrative, sensational tragedy, political allegory, and early abolitionist argument, *Oroonoko* has presented very different faces according to the contexts in which it has been read and reinterpreted. This is no less true for modern readers, who will find much that is problematically colonialist in its treatment of race, romance, and leadership, but will also find much that remains affecting and challenging.

Oroonoko: or, The Royal Slave.
A True History

I do not pretend, in giving you the history of this royal slave, to entertain my reader with the adventures of a feigned hero, whose life and fortunes fancy may manage at the poet's pleasure; nor in relating the truth, design to adorn it with any accidents, but such as arrived in earnest to him. And it shall come simply into the world, recommended by its own proper merits, and natural intrigues; there being enough of reality to support it, and to render it diverting, without the addition of invention.

I was myself an eyewitness, to a great part, of what you will find here set down; and what I could not be witness of, I received from the mouth of the chief actor in this history, the hero himself, who gave us the whole transactions of his youth; and though I shall omit, for brevity's sake, a thousand little accidents of his life, which, however pleasant to us, where history was scarce, and adventures very rare, yet might prove tedious and heavy to my reader, in a world where he finds diversions for every minute, new and strange. But we who were perfectly charmed with the character of this great man, were curious to gather every circumstance of his life.

The scene of the last part of his adventures lies in a colony in America, called Surinam,[1] in the West Indies.

But before I give you the story of this gallant slave, 'tis fit I tell you the manner of bringing them to these new colonies; for those they make use of there, are not natives of the place; for those we live with in perfect amity, without daring to command them; but on the contrary, caress them with all the brotherly and friendly affection in the world; trading with them for their fish, venison, buffaloes, skins, and little rarities; as marmosets, a sort of monkey as big as a rat or weasel, but of a marvellous and delicate shape, and has face and hands like an human creature; and cousheries, a little beast in the form and fashion of a lion, as big as a kitten; but so

---

[1] *Surinam*   The first Dutch settlers arrived in Surinam (previously allocated as part of the territory of Guiana in South America and now called the Republic of Suriname) in the late 1500s. The Dutch West India Company took control of the territory in 1621, and it became officially a Dutch colony (Dutch Guiana) in 1667. Unable to find enough laborers among the native Indian tribes to support their rich sugar plantations, the Dutch brought in vast numbers of slaves from West Africa. There were frequent and violent slave uprisings, with many slaves being killed and others fleeing to the country's interior. In Voltaire's *Candide*, a native of Surinam says: "When we work in the sugar mills and catch our finger in the millstone, they cut off our hand; when we try to run away, they cut off our leg: both things have happened to me. It is at this price that you eat sugar in Europe."

exactly made in all parts like that noble beast, that it is it in miniature. Then for little parakeets, great parrots, macaws, and a thousand other birds and beasts of wonderful and surprising forms, shapes, and colours. For skins of prodigious snakes, of which there are some threescore[1] yards in length; as is the skin of one that may be seen at His Majesty's Antiquaries, where are also some rare flies,[2] of amazing forms and colours, presented to them by myself, some as big as my fist, some less; and all of various excellencies, such as art cannot imitate. Then we trade for feathers, which they order into all shapes, make themselves little short habits of them, and glorious wreaths for their heads, necks, arms and legs, whose tinctures are inconceivable. I had a set of these presented to me, and I gave them to the King's Theatre, and it was the dress of the *Indian Queen*,[3] infinitely admired by persons of quality, and were inimitable. Besides these, a thousand little knacks, and rarities in nature, and some of art, as their baskets, weapons, aprons, etc. We dealt with them with beads of all colours, knives, axes, pins and needles, which they used only as tools to drill holes with in their ears, noses and lips, where they hang a great many little things, as long beads, bits of tin, brass, or silver, beat thin, and any shining trinket. The beads they weave into aprons about a quarter of an ell[4] long, and of the same breadth; working them very prettily in flowers of several colours of beads; which apron they wear just before them, as Adam and Eve did the fig leaves, the men wearing a long strip of linen, which they deal with us for. They thread these beads also on long cotton threads, and make girdles to tie their aprons to, which come twenty times, or more, about the waist, and then cross, like a shoulder-belt, both ways, and round their necks, arms and legs. This adornment, with their long black hair, and the face painted in little specks or flowers here and there, makes them a wonderful figure to behold. Some of the beauties which indeed are finely shaped, as almost all are, and who have pretty features, are very charming and novel; for they have all that is called beauty, except the colour, which is a reddish yellow; or after a new oiling, which they often use to themselves, they are of the colour of a new brick, but smooth, soft and sleek. They are extreme modest and bashful, very shy, and nice[5] of being touched. And though they are all thus naked, if one lives forever among them, there is not to be seen an indecent action, or glance; and being continually used to see one another so unadorned, so like our first parents before the fall, it seems as if they had no wishes; there being nothing to heighten curiosity, but all you can see, you see at once, and every moment see; and where there is no novelty, there can be no curiosity. Not but I have seen a handsome young Indian, dying for love of a very beautiful young Indian maid; but all his courtship was, to fold his arms, pursue her with his eyes, and sighs were all his language; while she, as if no such lover were present, or rather, as if she desired none such, carefully guarded her eyes from beholding him, and never approached him, but she looked down with all the blushing modesty I have seen in the most severe and cautious of our world. And these people represented to me an absolute idea of the first state of innocence, before man knew how to sin; and 'tis most evident and plain, that simple nature is the most harmless, inoffensive and virtuous mistress. 'Tis she alone, if she were permitted, that better instructs the world than all the inventions of man; religion would here but destroy that tranquillity they possess by ignorance, and laws would but teach them to know offence, of which now they have no notion. They once made mourning and fasting for the death of the English governor, who had given his hand to come on such a day to them, and neither came, nor sent, believing, when once a man's word was past, nothing but death could or should prevent his keeping it. And when they saw he was not dead, they asked him, what name they had for a man who promised a thing he did not do? The governor told them, such a man was a liar, which was a word of infamy to a gentleman. Then one of them replied, "Governor, you are a liar, and guilty of that infamy." They have a native justice, which knows no fraud; and they understand no vice, or cunning, but when they are taught by the white men.

---

[1] *threescore* Sixty.

[2] *flies* Butterflies.

[3] *Indian Queen* This semi-opera (play that combined music and the spoken word), written by John Dryden and Sir Robert Howard, featured ornate costumes, in particular a dress made from exotic feathers.

[4] *ell* Unit of measurement equal to 45 inches.

[5] *nice* Reluctant.

They have plurality of wives, which, when they grow old, they serve those that succeed them, who are young, but with a servitude easy and respected; and unless they take slaves in war, they have no other attendants.

Those on that continent where I was, had no king; but the oldest war captain was obeyed with great resignation.

A war captain is a man who has led them on to battle with conduct, and success, of whom I shall have occasion to speak more hereafter, and of some other of their customs and manners, as they fall in my way.

With these people, as I said, we live in perfect tranquility, and good understanding, as it behooves us to do; they knowing all the places where to seek the best food of the country, and the means of getting it; and for very small and invaluable trifles, supply us with what 'tis impossible for us to get; for they do not only in the wood, and over the savannahs, in hunting, supply the parts of hounds, by swiftly scouring through those almost impassable places, and by the mere activity of their feet, run down the nimblest deer, and other eatable beasts, but in the water, one would think they were gods of the rivers, or fellow citizens of the deep, so rare an art they have in swimming, diving, and almost living in water, by which they command the less swift inhabitants of the floods. And then for shooting, what they cannot take, or reach with their hands, they do with arrows, and have so admirable an aim, that they will split almost a hair; and at any distance that an arrow can reach, they will shoot down oranges, and other fruit, and only touch the stalk with the darts' points, that they may not hurt the fruit. So that they being, on all occasions, very useful to us, we find it absolutely necessary to caress[1] them as friends, and not to treat them as slaves; nor dare we do other, their numbers so far surpassing ours in that continent.

Those then whom we make use of to work in our plantations of sugar are negroes, black slaves altogether, which are transported thither in this manner.

Those who want slaves, make a bargain with a master, or captain of a ship, and contract to pay him so much apiece, a matter of twenty pound a head for as many as he agrees for, and to pay for them when they shall be delivered on such a plantation. So that when there arrives a ship laden with slaves, they who have so contracted, go aboard, and receive their number by lot; and perhaps in one lot that may be for ten, there may happen to be three or four men, the rest, women and children; or be there more or less of either sex, you are obliged to be contented with your lot.

Coramantien,[2] a country of blacks so called, was one of those places in which they found the most advantageous trading for these slaves; and thither most of our great traders in that merchandise trafficked; for that nation is very warlike and brave, and having a continual campaign, being always in hostility with one neighbouring prince or other, they had the fortune to take a great many captives; for all they took in battle, were sold as slaves, at least, those common men who could not ransom themselves. Of these slaves so taken, the general only has all the profit; and of these generals, our captains and masters of ships buy all their freights.

The King of Coramantien was himself a man of a hundred and odd years old, and had no son, though he had many beautiful black wives; for most certainly, there are beauties that can charm of that colour. In his younger years he had had many gallant men to his sons, thirteen of which died in battle, conquering when they fell; and he had only left him for his successor, one grandchild, son to one of these dead victors; who, as soon as he could bear a bow in his hand, and a quiver at his back, was sent into the field, to be trained up by one of the oldest generals, to war; where, from his natural inclination to arms, and the occasions given him, with the good conduct of the old general, he became, at the age of seventeen, one of the most expert captains, and bravest soldiers, that ever saw the field of Mars;[3] so that he was adored as the wonder of all that world, and the darling of the soldiers. Besides, he was adorned with a native beauty so transcending all those of his gloomy race, that he struck an awe and reverence, even in those that knew not his quality; as he did in me, who beheld him with surprise and wonder, when afterwards he arrived in our world.

He had scarce arrived at his seventeenth year, when fighting by his side, the general was killed with an arrow

---

[1] *caress* Treat with kindness.

[2] *Coramantien* Region on the west coast of Africa (now Ghana), where the British held a fort and slave market.

[3] *Mars* Roman god of war.

in his eye, which the Prince Oroonoko (for so was this gallant Moor[1] called) very narrowly avoided; nor had he, if the general, who saw the arrow shot, and perceiving it aimed at the Prince, had not bowed his head between, on purpose to receive it in his own body rather than it should touch that of the Prince, and so saved him.

'Twas then, afflicted as Oroonoko was, that he was proclaimed general in the old man's place; and then it was, at the finishing of that war, which had continued for two years, that the Prince came to court, where he had hardly been a month together, from the time of his fifth year to that of seventeen; and 'twas amazing to imagine where it was he learned so much humanity, or, to give his accomplishments a juster name, where 'twas he got that real greatness of soul, those refined notions of true honour, that absolute generosity, and that softness that was capable of the highest passions of love and gallantry, whose objects were almost continually fighting men, or those mangled, or dead, who heard no sounds, but those of war and groans. Some part of it we may attribute to the care of a Frenchman of wit and learning, who finding it turn to very good account to be a sort of royal tutor to this young Black, and perceiving him very ready, apt, and quick of apprehension, took a great pleasure to teach him morals, language and science, and was for it extremely beloved and valued by him. Another reason was, he loved, when he came from war, to see all the English gentlemen that traded thither; and did not only learn their language, but that of the Spaniards also, with whom he traded afterwards for slaves.

I have often seen and conversed with this great man, and been a witness to many of his mighty actions, and do assure my reader, the most illustrious courts could not have produced a braver man, both for greatness of courage and mind, a judgment more solid, a wit more quick, and a conversation more sweet and diverting. He knew almost as much as if he had read much: he had heard of, and admired the Romans; he had heard of the late civil wars in England, and the deplorable death of our great monarch,[2] and would discourse of it with all the sense, and abhorrence of the injustice imaginable. He had an extreme good and graceful mien, and all the civility of a well-bred great man. He had nothing of barbarity in his nature, but in all points addressed himself as if his education had been in some European court.

This great and just character of Oroonoko gave me an extreme curiosity to see him, especially when I knew he spoke French and English, and that I could talk with him. But though I had heard so much of him, I was as greatly surprised when I saw him as if I had heard nothing of him, so beyond all report I found him. He came into the room, and addressed himself to me, and some other women, with the best grace in the world. He was pretty tall, but of a shape the most exact that can be fancied; the most famous statuary[3] could not form the figure of a man more admirably turned from head to foot. His face was not of that brown, rusty black which most of that nation are, but a perfect ebony, or polished jet. His eyes were the most awful[4] that could be seen, and very piercing; the white of them being like snow, as were his teeth. His nose was rising and Roman, instead of African and flat. His mouth, the finest shaped that could be seen, far from those great turned lips, which are so natural to the rest of the Negroes. The whole proportion and air of his face was so noble, and exactly formed, that, bating[5] his colour, there could be nothing in nature more beautiful, agreeable and handsome. There was no one grace wanting, that bears the standard of true beauty. His hair came down to his shoulders, by the aids of art, which was, by pulling it out with a quill, and keeping it combed, of which he took particular care. Nor did the perfections of his mind come short of those of his person; for his discourse was admirable upon almost any subject; and whoever had heard him speak, would have been convinced of their errors, that all fine wit is confined to the white men, especially to those of

---

[1]   *Moor*   Originally a native of North Africa of mixed Berber and Arab ancestry. Because Moors were regarded as being dark skinned, the term was often used to refer to black people in general.

[2]   *civil wars … monarch*   In the 1640s King Charles I and the Royalists, his supporters, fought the Parliamentarians, led by Oliver Cromwell. The King was eventually captured and was executed in 1649.

[3]   *statuary*   Sculptor.

[4]   *awful*   Awe-inspiring.

[5]   *bating*   Excepting.

Christendom; and would have confessed that Oroonoko was as capable even of reigning well, and of governing as wisely, had as great a soul, as politic maxims,[1] and was as sensible of power as any Prince civilized in the most refined schools of humanity and learning, or the most illustrious courts.

This Prince, such as I have described him, whose soul and body were so admirably adorned, was (while yet he was in the court of his grandfather) as I said, as capable of love, as 'twas possible for a brave and gallant man to be; and in saying that, I have named the highest degree of love; for sure, great souls are most capable of that passion.

I have already said the old general was killed by the shot of an arrow, by the side of this Prince, in battle, and that Oroonoko was made general. This old dead hero had one only daughter left of his race, a beauty that, to describe her truly, one need say only, she was female to the noble male; the beautiful black Venus,[2] to our young Mars; as charming in her person as he, and of delicate virtues. I have seen an hundred white men sighing after her, and making a thousand vows at her feet, all vain, and unsuccessful; and she was, indeed, too great for any but a prince of her own nation to adore.

Oroonoko coming from the wars (which were now ended) after he had made his court to his grandfather, he thought in honour he ought to make a visit to Imoinda, the daughter of his foster father, the dead general; and to make some excuses to her, because his preservation was the occasion of her father's death; and to present her with those slaves that had been taken in this last battle, as the trophies of her father's victories. When he came, attended by all the young soldiers of any merit, he was infinitely surprised at the beauty of this fair Queen of Night, whose face and person was so exceeding all he had ever beheld; that lovely modesty with which she received him, that softness in her look, and sighs, upon the melancholy occasion of this honour that was done by so great a man as Oroonoko, and a prince of whom she had heard such admirable things; the awfulness wherewith she received him, and the sweetness of her words and behaviour while he stayed, gained a perfect conquest over his fierce heart, and made

him feel the victor could be subdued. So that having made his first compliments, and presented her a hundred and fifty slaves in fetters, he told her with his eyes that he was not insensible of her charms; while Imoinda, who wished for nothing more than so glorious a conquest, was pleased to believe she understood that silent language of newborn love, and from that moment, put on all her additions to beauty.

The Prince returned to court with quite another humour[3] than before; and though he did not speak much of the fair Imoinda, he had the pleasure to hear all his followers speak of nothing but the charms of that maid, insomuch that, even in the presence of the old King, they were extolling her, and heightening, if possible, the beauties they had found in her, so that nothing else was talked of, no other sound was heard in every corner where there were whisperers, but "Imoinda! Imoinda!"

'Twill be imagined Oroonoko stayed not long before he made his second visit, nor, considering his quality, not much longer before he told her, he adored her. I have often heard him say, that he admired by what strange inspiration he came to talk things so soft, and so passionate, who never knew love, nor was used to the conversation of women; but (to use his own words) he said, most happily, some new and till then unknown power instructed his heart and tongue in the language of love, and at the same time, in favour of him, inspired Imoinda with a sense of his passion. She was touched with what he said, and returned it all in such answers as went to his very heart, with a pleasure unknown before. Nor did he use those obligations ill that love had done him, but turned all his happy moments to the best advantage; and as he knew no vice, his flame aimed at nothing but honour, if such a distinction may be made in love, and especially in that country, where men take to themselves as many as they can maintain, and where the only crime and sin with woman is to turn her off, to abandon her to want, shame and misery. Such ill morals are only practised in Christian countries, where they prefer the bare name of religion, and, without virtue or morality, think that's sufficient. But Oroonoko was none of those professors; but as he had right notions of honour, so he made her such propositions as were not

---

[1] *politic maxims* Judicious opinion in matters of policy.

[2] *Venus* Roman goddess of love.

[3] *humour* Disposition.

only and barely such, but, contrary to the custom of his country, he made her vows she should be the only woman he would possess while he lived; that no age or wrinkles should incline him to change, for her soul would be always fine, and always young; and he should have an eternal idea in his mind of the charms she now bore, and should look into his heart for that idea, when he could find it no longer in her face.

After a thousand assurances of his lasting flame, and her eternal empire over him, she condescended to receive him for her husband, or rather, received him, as the greatest honour the gods could do her.

There is a certain ceremony in these cases to be observed, which I forgot to ask him how performed; but 'twas concluded on both sides that, in obedience to him, the grandfather was to be first made acquainted with the design; for they pay a most absolute resignation to the monarch, especially when he is a parent also.

On the other side, the old King, who had many wives, and many concubines, wanted not court flatterers to insinuate in his heart a thousand tender thoughts for this young beauty, and who represented her to his fancy as the most charming he had ever possessed in all the long race of his numerous years. At this character his old heart, like an extinguished brand, most apt to take fire, felt new sparks of love, and began to kindle, and now grown to his second childhood, longed with impatience to behold this gay thing, with whom, alas, he could but innocently play. But how he should be confirmed she was this wonder, before he used his power to call her to court (where maidens never came, unless for the king's private use) he was next to consider; and while he was so doing, he had intelligence brought him, that Imoinda was most certainly mistress to the Prince Oroonoko. This gave him some chagrin; however, it gave him also an opportunity, one day, when the Prince was a-hunting, to wait on a man of quality, as his slave and attendant, who should go and make a present to Imoinda, as from the Prince; he should then, unknown, see this fair maid, and have an opportunity to hear what message she would return the Prince for his present, and from thence gather the state of her heart, and degree of her inclination. This was put in execution, and the old monarch saw, and burnt; he found her all he had heard, and would not delay his happiness, but found he should

have some obstacle to overcome her heart; for she expressed her sense of the present the Prince had sent her, in terms so sweet, so soft and pretty, with an air of love and joy that could not be dissembled, insomuch that 'twas past doubt whether she loved Oroonoko entirely. This gave the old King some affliction, but he salved it with this, that the obedience the people pay their king, was not at all inferior to what they paid their gods, and what love would not oblige Imoinda to do, duty would compel her to.

He was therefore no sooner got to his apartment, but he sent the royal veil to Imoinda, that is, the ceremony of invitation; he sends the lady, he has a mind to honour with his bed, a veil, with which she is covered and secured for the King's use; and 'tis death to disobey, besides, held a most impious disobedience.

'Tis not to be imagined the surprise and grief that seized this lovely maid at this news and sight. However, as delays in these cases are dangerous, and pleading worse than treason, trembling, and almost fainting, she was obliged to suffer herself to be covered and led away.

They brought her thus to court; and the King, who had caused a very rich bath to be prepared, was led into it, where he sat under a canopy in state, to receive this longed for virgin, whom he having commanded should be brought to him, they (after disrobing her) led her to the bath, and making fast the doors, left her to descend. The King, without more courtship, bade her throw off her mantle and come to his arms. But Imoinda, all in tears, threw herself on the marble on the brink of the bath, and besought him to hear her. She told him, as she was a maid, how proud of the divine glory she should have been of having it in her power to oblige her king; but as by the laws he could not, and from his royal goodness would not take from any man his wedded wife, so she believed she should be the occasion of making him commit a great sin, if she did not reveal her state and condition, and tell him she was another's, and could not be so happy to be his.

The King, enraged at this delay, hastily demanded the name of the bold man that had married a woman of her degree without his consent. Imoinda, seeing his eyes fierce, and his hands tremble, whether with age or anger, I know not, but she fancied the last, almost repented she had said so much, for now she feared the storm would fall on the Prince; she therefore said a thousand things to appease the raging of his flame, and to prepare him to hear who it was with calmness; but before she spoke, he imagined who she meant, but would not seem to do so, but commanded her to lay aside her mantle and suffer herself to receive his caresses; or, by his gods, he swore, that happy man whom she was going to name should die, though it were even Oroonoko himself. "Therefore," said he, "deny this marriage, and swear thyself a maid."

"That," replied Imoinda, "by all our powers I do, for I am not yet known to my husband."[1]

"'Tis enough," said the King, "'tis enough to satisfy both my conscience, and my heart." And rising from his seat, he went and led her into the bath, it being in vain for her to resist.

In this time the Prince, who was returned from hunting, went to visit his Imoinda, but found her gone, and not only so, but heard she had received the royal veil. This raised him to a storm, and in his madness they had much ado to save him from laying violent hands on himself. Force first prevailed, and then reason. They urged all to him that might oppose his rage; but nothing weighed so greatly with him as the King's old age, incapable of injuring him with Imoinda.[2] He would give way to that hope, because it pleased him most, and flattered best his heart. Yet this served not altogether to make him cease his different passions, which sometimes raged within him, and sometimes softened into showers. 'Twas not enough to appease him, to tell him, his grandfather was old, and could not that way injure him, while he retained that awful duty which the young men are used there to pay to their grave relations. He could not be convinced he had no cause to sigh and mourn for the loss of a mistress he could not with all his strength and courage retrieve. And he would often cry, "Oh my friends! Were she in walled cities, or confined from me in fortifications of the greatest strength; did enchantments or monsters detain her from me, I would venture through any hazard to free her. But here, in the arms of a feeble old man, my youth, my violent love, my trade

in arms, and all my vast desire of glory avail me nothing. Imoinda is as irrecoverably lost to me, as if she were snatched by the cold arms of death. Oh! she is never to be retrieved. If I would wait tedious years, till fate should bow the old King to his grave, even that would not leave me Imoinda free; but still that custom that makes it so vile a crime for a son to marry his father's wives or mistress would hinder my happiness, unless I would either ignobly set an ill precedent to my successors, or abandon my country, and fly with her to some unknown world, who never heard our story."

But it was objected to him, that his case was not the same; for Imoinda being his lawful wife, by solemn contract, 'twas he was the injured man, and might, if he so pleased, take Imoinda back, the breach of the law being on his grandfather's side; and that if he could circumvent him, and redeem her from the otan, which is the palace of the King's women, a sort of seraglio,[3] it was both just and lawful for him so to do.

This reasoning had some force upon him, and he should have been entirely comforted, but for the thought that she was possessed by his grandfather. However, he loved so well that he was resolved to believe what most favoured his hope, and to endeavour to learn from Imoinda's own mouth, what only she could satisfy him in, whether she was robbed of that blessing,[4] which was only due to his faith and love. But as it was very hard to get a sight of the women, for no men ever entered into the otan, but when the King went to entertain himself with some one of his wives or mistresses, and 'twas death at any other time for any other to go in, so he knew not how to contrive to get a sight of her.

While Oroonoko felt all the agonies of love, and suffered under a torment the most painful in the world, the old King was not exempted from his share of affliction. He was troubled for having been forced by an irresistible passion to rob his son of a treasure he knew could not but be extremely dear to him, since she was the most beautiful that ever had been seen; and had besides, all the sweetness and innocence of youth and modesty, with a charm of wit surpassing all. He found that, however she was forced to expose her lovely person

---

1. *not yet ... my husband* I.e., the marriage has not been consummated.

2. *incapable ... with Imoinda* I.e., the King will not be able to consummate his liaison with Imoinda due to his age.

3. *seraglio* Harem.

4. *that blessing* I.e., Imoinda's virginity.

to his withered arms, she could only sigh and weep there, and think of Oroonoko, and oftentimes could not forbear speaking of him, though her life were, by custom, forfeited by owning her passion. But she spoke not of a lover only, but of a prince dear to him to whom she spoke; and of the praises of a man, who, till now, filled the old man's soul with joy at every recital of his bravery, or even his name. And 'twas this dotage on our young hero that gave Imoinda a thousand privileges to speak of him without offending, and this condescension in the old King that made her take the satisfaction of speaking of him so very often.

Besides, he many times enquired how the Prince bore himself; and those of whom he asked, being entirely slaves to the merits and virtues of the Prince, still answered what they thought conduced best to his service, which was, to make the old King fancy that the Prince had no more interest in Imoinda, and had resigned her willingly to the pleasure of the King, that he diverted himself with his mathematicians, his fortifications, his officers, and his hunting.

This pleased the old lover, who failed not to report these things again to Imoinda, that she might, by the example of her young lover, withdraw her heart and rest better contented in his arms. But however she was forced to receive this unwelcome news, in all appearance, with unconcern, and content, her heart was bursting within, and she was only happy when she could get alone, to vent her griefs and moans with sighs and tears.

What reports of the Prince's conduct were made to the King, he thought good to justify as far as possibly he could by his actions; and when he appeared in the presence of the King, he showed a face not at all betraying his heart; so that in a little time the old man, being entirely convinced that he was no longer a lover of Imoinda, he carried him with him, in his train to the otan, often to banquet with his mistress. But as soon as he entered, one day, into the apartment of Imoinda, with the King, at the first glance from her eyes, notwithstanding all his determined resolution, he was ready to sink in the place where he stood, and had certainly done so, but for the support of Aboan, a young man, who was next to him, which, with his change of countenance, had betrayed him, had the King chanced to look that

way. And I have observed, 'tis a very great error in those who laugh when one says, a Negro can change colour; for I have seen them as frequently blush, and look pale, and that as visibly as ever I saw in the most beautiful white. And 'tis certain that both these changes were evident, this day, in both these lovers. And Imoinda, who saw with some joy the change in the Prince's face, and found it in her own, strove to divert the King from beholding either, by a forced caress, with which she met him, which was a new wound in the heart of the poor dying Prince. But as soon as the King was busied in looking on some fine thing of Imoinda's making, she had time to tell the Prince with her angry, but love-darting eyes, that she resented his coldness, and bemoaned her own miserable captivity. Nor were his eyes silent, but answered hers again, as much as eyes could do, instructed by the most tender, and most passionate heart that ever loved. And they spoke so well, and so effectually, as Imoinda no longer doubted, but she was the only delight, and the darling of that soul she found pleading in them its right of love, which none was more willing to resign than she. And 'twas this powerful language alone that in an instant conveyed all the thoughts of their souls to each other, that they both found there wanted but opportunity to make them both entirely happy. But when he saw another door opened by Onahal, a former old wife of the King's who now had charge of Imoinda, and saw the prospect of a bed of state made ready with sweets and flowers for the dalliance of the King, who immediately led the trembling victim from his sight, into that prepared repose. What rage! What wild frenzies seized his heart! Which forcing to keep within bounds, and to suffer without noise, it became the more insupportable and rent his soul with ten thousand pains. He was forced to retire to vent his groans, where he fell down on a carpet, and lay struggling a long time, and only breathing now and then, "O Imoinda!" When Onahal had finished her necessary affair within, shutting the door, she came forth to wait, till the King called; and hearing someone sighing in the other room, she passed on, and found the Prince in that deplorable condition which she thought needed her aid. She gave him cordials, but all in vain, till finding the nature of his disease, by his sighs, and naming Imoinda. She told him he had not so much cause as he imagined to afflict himself; for if he knew the King so well as she did, he would not lose a moment in jealousy, and that she was confident that Imoinda bore, at this minute, part in his affliction. Aboan was of the same opinion, and both together, persuaded him to reassume his courage; and all sitting down on the carpet, the Prince said so many obliging things to Onahal, that he half persuaded her to be of his party. And she promised him she would thus far comply with his just desires, that she would let Imoinda know how faithful he was, what he suffered, and what he said.

This discourse lasted till the King called, which gave Oroonoko a certain satisfaction; and with the hope Onahal had made him conceive, he assumed a look as gay as 'twas possible a man in his circumstances could do; and presently after, he was called in with the rest who waited without. The King commanded music to be brought, and several of his young wives and mistresses came all together by his command, to dance before him, where Imoinda performed her part with an air and grace so passing all the rest, as her beauty was above them, and received the present, ordained as a prize. The Prince was every moment more charmed with the new beauties and graces he beheld in this fair one; and while he gazed and she danced, Onahal was retired to a window with Aboan.

This Onahal, as I said, was one of the cast[1] mistresses of the old King; and 'twas these (now past their beauty) that were made guardians, or governants[2] to the new, and the young ones, and whose business it was, to teach them all those wanton arts of love with which they prevailed and charmed heretofore in their turn and who now treated the triumphing happy ones with all the severity, as to liberty and freedom, that was possible, in revenge of those honours they rob them of envying them those satisfactions, those gallantries and presents, that were once made to themselves, while youth and beauty lasted, and which they now saw pass regardless by, and paid only to the bloomings. And certainly, nothing is more afflicting to a decayed beauty than to behold in itself declining charms, that were once adored, and to find those caresses paid to new beauties to which once she laid a claim to hear them whisper as she passes by, "That once was a delicate woman." These aban-

doned ladies therefore endeavour to revenge all the despites[3] and decays of time on these flourishing happy ones. And 'twas this severity that gave Oroonoko a thousand fears he should never prevail with Onahal to see Imoinda. But, as I said, she was now retired to a window with Aboan.

This young man was not only one of the best quality, but a man extremely well made, and beautiful; and coming often to attend the King to the otan, he had subdued the heart of the antiquated Onahal, which had not forgot how pleasant it was to be in love. And though she had some decays in her face, she had none in her sense and wit; she was there agreeable still, even to Aboan's youth, so that he took pleasure in entertaining her with discourses of love. He knew also, that to make his court to these she-favourites was the way to be great, these being the persons that do all affairs and business at court. He had also observed that she had given him glances more tender and inviting than she had done to others of his quality. And now, when he saw that her favour could so absolutely oblige the Prince, he failed not to sigh in her ear, and to look with eyes all soft upon her, and give her hope that she had made some impressions on his heart. He found her pleased at this, and making a thousand advances to him, but the ceremony ending, and the King departing, broke up the company for that day, and his conversation.

Aboan failed not that night to tell the Prince of his success, and how advantageous the service of Onahal might be to his amour with Imoinda. The Prince was overjoyed with this good news, and besought him, if it were possible, to caress her, so as to engage her entirely, which he could not fail to do, if he complied with her desires. "For then," said the Prince, "her life lying at your mercy, she must grant you the request you make in my behalf." Aboan understood him, and assured him he would make love so effectually, that he would defy the most expert mistress of the art, to find out whether he dissembled it or had it really. And 'twas with impatience they waited the next opportunity of going to the otan.

The wars came on, the time of taking the field approached, and 'twas impossible for the Prince to delay his going at the head of his army to encounter the enemy; so that every day seemed a tedious year, till he saw his Imoinda, for he believed he could not live, if he were forced away without being so happy. 'Twas with impatience therefore, that he expected the next visit the King would make; and, according to his wish, it was not long.

The parley of the eyes of these two lovers had not passed so secretly, but an old jealous lover could spy it; or rather, he wanted not flatterers who told him they observed it. So that the Prince was hastened to the camp, and this was the last visit he found he should make to the otan; he therefore urged Aboan to make the best of this last effort, and to explain himself so to Onahal, that she, deferring her enjoyment of her young lover no longer, might make way for the Prince to speak to Imoinda.

The whole affair being agreed on between the Prince and Aboan, they attended the King, as the custom was, to the otan, where, while the whole company was taken up in beholding the dancing and antic[1] postures the women royal made, to divert the King, Onahal singled out Aboan, whom she found most pliable to her wish. When she had him where she believed she could not be heard, she sighed to him, and softly cried, "Ah, Aboan! When will you be sensible of my passion? I confess it with my mouth, because I would not give my eyes the lie; and you have but too much already perceived they have confessed my flame. Nor would I have you believe that because I am the abandoned mistress of a king I esteem myself altogether divested of charms. No, Aboan; I have still a rest[2] of beauty enough engaging, and have learned to please too well, not to be desirable. I can have lovers still, but will have none but Aboan."

"Madam," replied the half-feigning youth, "you have already, by my eyes, found you can still conquer; and I believe 'tis in pity of me, you condescend to this kind confession. But, Madam, words are used to be so small a part of our country courtship, that 'tis rare one can get so happy an opportunity as to tell one's heart; and those few minutes we have are forced to be snatched for more certain proofs of love than speaking and sighing; and such I languish for."

He spoke this with such a tone, that she hoped it true, and could not forbear believing it; and being wholly transported with joy, for having subdued the finest of all the King's subjects to her desires, she took from her ears two large pearls and commanded him to wear them in his. He would have refused them, crying, "Madam, these are not the proofs of your love that I expect; 'tis opportunity, 'tis a lone hour only, that can make me happy."

But forcing the pearls into his hand, she whispered softly to him, "Oh! Do not fear a woman's invention, when love sets her a-thinking." And pressing his hand, she cried, "This night you shall be happy. Come to the gate of the orange groves, behind the otan, and I will be ready, about midnight, to receive you." 'Twas thus agreed, and she left him, that no notice might be taken of their speaking together.

The ladies were still dancing, and the King, laid on a carpet, with a great deal of pleasure, was beholding them, especially Imoinda, who that day appeared more lovely than ever, being enlivened with the good tidings Onahal had brought her of the constant passion the Prince had for her. The Prince was laid on another carpet, at the other end of the room, with his eyes fixed on the object of his soul; and as she turned, or moved, so did they; and she alone gave his eyes and soul their motions. Nor did Imoinda employ her eyes to any other use, than in beholding with infinite pleasure the joy she produced in those of the Prince. But while she was more regarding him than the steps she took, she chanced to fall, and so near him as that leaping with extreme force from the carpet, he caught her in his arms as she fell; and 'twas visible to the whole presence, the joy wherewith he received her. He clasped her close to his bosom, and quite forgot that reverence that was due to the mistress of a king, and that punishment that is the reward of a boldness of this nature; and had not the presence of mind of Imoinda (fonder of his safety, than her own) befriended him in making her spring from his arms and fall into her dance again, he had, at that instant, met his death; for the old King, jealous to the last degree, rose up in rage, broke all the diversion, and led Imoinda to her apartment, and sent out word to the Prince to go immediately to the camp, and that if he were found another night in court, he should suffer the death ordained for disobedient offenders.

---

[1] *antic* Bizarre.

[2] *rest* Remnant.

You may imagine how welcome this news was to Oroonoko, whose unseasonable transport and caress of Imoinda was blamed by all men that loved him; and now he perceived his fault, yet cried, that for such another moment, he would be content to die.

All the otan was in disorder about this accident; and Onahal was particularly concerned, because on the Prince's stay depended her happiness, for she could no longer expect that of Aboan. So that, e'er they departed, they contrived it so that the Prince and he should come both that night to the grove of the otan, which was all of oranges and citrons, and that there they should wait her orders.

They parted thus, with grief enough, till night, leaving the King in possession of the lovely maid. But nothing could appease the jealousy of the old lover. He would not be imposed on, but would have it that Imoinda made a false step on purpose to fall into Oroonoko's bosom, and that all things looked like a design on both sides, and 'twas in vain she protested her innocence. He was old and obstinate, and left her more than half assured that his fear was true.

The King going to his apartment, sent to know where the Prince was, and if he intended to obey his command. The messenger returned, and told him he found the Prince pensive, and altogether unpreparing for the campaign, that he lay negligently on the ground, and answered very little. This confirmed the jealousy of the King, and he commanded that they should very narrowly and privately watch his motions, and that he should not stir from his apartment, but one spy or other should be employed to watch him. So that the hour approaching, wherein he was to go to the citron grove, and taking only Aboan along with him, he leaves his apartment, and was watched to the very gate of the otan, where he was seen to enter, and where they left him, to carry back the tidings to the King.

Oroonoko and Aboan were no sooner entered but Onahal led the Prince to the apartment of Imoinda, who, not knowing anything of her happiness, was laid in bed. But Onahal only left him in her chamber to make the best of his opportunity, and took her dear Aboan to her own, where he showed the height of complaisance for his Prince, when, to give him an opportunity, he suffered himself to be caressed in bed by Onahal.

The Prince softly wakened Imoinda, who was not a little surprised with joy to find him there, and yet she trembled with a thousand fears. I believe he omitted saying nothing to this young maid, that might persuade her to suffer him to seize his own, and take the rights of love; and I believe she was not long resisting those arms where she so longed to be; and having opportunity, night and silence, youth, love and desire, he soon prevailed, and ravished in a moment what his old grandfather had been endeavouring for so many months.

'Tis not to be imagined the satisfaction of these two young lovers, nor the vows she made him, that she remained a spotless maid till that night, and that what she did with his grandfather had robbed him of no part of her virgin honour, the gods in mercy and justice having reserved that for her plighted lord, to whom of right it belonged. And 'tis impossible to express the transports he suffered, while he listened to a discourse so charming from her loved lips, and clasped that body in his arms, for whom he had so long languished; and nothing now afflicted him, but his sudden departure from her; for he told her the necessity and his commands, but should depart satisfied in this, that since the old King had hitherto not been able to deprive him of those enjoyments which only belonged to him, he believed for the future he would be less able to injure him. So that, abating the scandal of the veil, which was no otherwise so, than that she was wife to another, he believed her safe, even in the arms of the King, and innocent; yet would he have ventured at the conquest of the world, and have given it all, to have had her avoided that honour of receiving the royal veil. 'Twas thus, between a thousand caresses, that both bemoaned the hard fate of youth and beauty, so liable to that cruel promotion; 'twas a glory that could well have been spared here, though desired, and aimed at by all the young females of that kingdom.

But while they were thus fondly employed, forgetting how time ran on, and that the dawn must conduct him far away from his only happiness, they heard a great noise in the otan, and unusual voices of men, at which the Prince, starting from the arms of the frighted Imoinda, ran to a little battle-axe he used to wear by his side; and having not so much leisure as to put on his habit,[1] he opposed himself against some who were already opening the door, which they did with so much violence, that Oroonoko was not able to defend it, but was forced to cry out with a commanding voice, "Whoever ye are that have the boldness to attempt to approach this apartment thus rudely, know that I, the Prince Oroonoko, will revenge it with the certain death of him that first enters. Therefore stand back, and know this place is sacred to love, and me this night; tomorrow 'tis the King's."

This he spoke with a voice so resolved and assured, that they soon retired from the door, but cried, "'Tis by the King's command we are come; and being satisfied by thy voice, O Prince, as much as if we had entered, we can report to the King the truth of all his fears, and leave thee to provide for thy own safety, as thou art advised by thy friends."

At these words they departed, and left the Prince to take a short and sad leave of his Imoinda, who trusting in the strength of her charms, believed she should appease the fury of a jealous king by saying she was surprised, and that it was by force of arms he got into her apartment. All her concern now was for his life, and therefore she hastened him to the camp, and with much ado, prevailed on him to go. Nor was it she alone that prevailed; Aboan and Onahal both pleaded, and both assured him of a lie that should be well enough contrived to secure Imoinda. So that, at last, with a heart sad as death, dying eyes, and sighing soul, Oroonoko departed, and took his way to the camp.

It was not long after the King in person came to the otan, where beholding Imoinda with rage in his eyes, he upbraided her wickedness and perfidy, and threatening her royal lover, she fell on her face at his feet, bedewing the floor with her tears and imploring his pardon for a fault which she had not with her will committed, as Onahal, who was also prostrate with her, could testify that, unknown to her, he had broke into her apartment, and ravished her. She spoke this much against her conscience; but to save her own life, 'twas absolutely necessary she should feign this falsity. She knew it could not injure the Prince, he being fled to an army that would stand by him against any injuries that should assault him. However, this last thought of Imoinda's

being ravished changed the measures of his revenge, and whereas before he designed to be himself her executioner, he now resolved she should not die. But as it is the greatest crime in nature amongst them to touch a woman, after having been possessed by a son, a father, or a brother, so now he looked on Imoinda as a polluted thing, wholly unfit for his embrace; nor would he resign her to his grandson, because she had received the royal veil. He therefore removed her from the otan, with Onahal, whom he put into safe hands, with order they should be both sold off, as slaves, to another country, either Christian, or heathen; 'twas no matter where.

This cruel sentence, worse than death, they implored might be reversed; but their prayers were vain, and it was put in execution accordingly, and that with so much secrecy, that none, either without or within the otan, knew anything of their absence, or their destiny.

The old King, nevertheless, executed this with a great deal of reluctance; but he believed he had made a very great conquest over himself when he had once resolved, and had performed what he resolved. He believed now, that his love had been unjust, and that he could not expect the gods, or Captain of the Clouds (as they call the unknown power) should suffer a better consequence from so ill a cause. He now begins to hold Oroonoko excused, and to say, he had reason for what he did; and now everybody could assure the King, how passionately Imoinda was beloved by the Prince; even those confessed it now who said the contrary before his flame was abated. So that the King being old and not able to defend himself in war, and having no sons of all his race remaining alive, but only this, to maintain him on the throne, and looking on this as a man disobliged, first by the rape of his mistress, or rather, wife; and now by depriving him wholly of her, he feared, might make him desperate, and do some cruel thing, either to himself, or his old grandfather, the offender, he began to repent him extremely of the contempt he had, in his rage, put on Imoinda. Besides, he considered he ought in honour to have killed her for this offence, if it had been one. He ought to have had so much value and consideration for a maid of her quality, as to have nobly put her to death, and not to have sold her like a common slave, the greatest revenge, and the most disgraceful of any, and to which they a thousand times prefer death,

---

[1] *habit* Clothing.

and implore it as Imoinda did, but could not obtain that honour. Seeing therefore it was certain that Oroonoko would highly resent this affront, he thought good to make some excuse for his rashness to him, and to that end he sent a messenger to the camp with orders to treat with him about the matter, to gain his pardon, and to endeavour to mitigate his grief, but that by no means he should tell him she was sold, but secretly put to death; for he knew he should never obtain his pardon for the other.

When the messenger came, he found the Prince upon the point of engaging with the enemy, but as soon as he heard of the arrival of the messenger he commanded him to his tent, where he embraced him, and received him with joy, which was soon abated, by the downcast looks of the messenger, who was instantly demanded the cause by Oroonoko, who, impatient of delay, asked a thousand questions in a breath, and all concerning Imoinda. But there needed little return, for he could almost answer himself of all he demanded from his sighs and eyes. At last, the messenger casting himself at the Prince's feet and kissing them with all the submission of a man that had something to implore which he dreaded to utter, he besought him to hear with calmness what he had to deliver to him, and to call up all his noble and heroic courage to encounter with his words, and defend himself against the ungrateful things he must relate. Oroonoko replied, with a deep sigh, and a languishing voice, "I am armed against their worst efforts—for I know they will tell me, Imoinda is no more—and after that, you may spare the rest." Then, commanding him to rise, he laid himself on a carpet under a rich pavilion, and remained a good while silent, and was hardly heard to sigh. When he was come a little to himself, the messenger asked him leave to deliver that part of his embassy which the Prince had not yet divined, and the Prince cried, "I permit thee." Then he told him the affliction the old King was in for the rashness he had committed in his cruelty to Imoinda, and how he deigned to ask pardon for his offence, and to implore the Prince would not suffer that loss to touch his heart too sensibly which now all the gods could not restore him, but might recompense him in glory which he begged he would pursue; and that death, that common revenger of all injuries, would soon even the

account between him and a feeble old man.

Oroonoko bade him return his duty to his lord and master, and to assure him there was no account of revenge to be adjusted between them; if there were, 'twas he was the aggressor, and that death would be just, and, maugre[1] his age, would see him righted; and he was contented to leave his share of glory to youths more fortunate, and worthy of that favour from the gods. That henceforth he would never lift a weapon, or draw a bow, but abandon the small remains of his life to sighs and tears, and the continual thoughts of what his lord and grandfather had thought good to send out of the world, with all that youth, that innocence, and beauty.

After having spoken this, whatever his greatest officers, and men of the best rank could do, they could not raise him from the carpet, or persuade him to action and resolutions of life, but commanding all to retire, he shut himself into his pavilion all that day, while the enemy was ready to engage; and wondering at the delay, the whole body of the chief of the army then addressed themselves to him, and to whom they had much ado to get admittance. They fell on their faces at the foot of his carpet, where they lay, and besought him with earnest prayers and tears, to lead them forth to battle, and not let the enemy take advantages of them, and implored him to have regard to his glory, and to the world that depended on his courage and conduct. But he made no other reply to all their supplications but this, that he had now no more business for glory; and for the world, it was a trifle not worth his care. "Go," continued he, sighing, "and divide it amongst you; and reap with joy what you so vainly prize, and leave me to my more welcome destiny."

They then demanded what they should do, and whom he would constitute in his room,[2] that the confusion of ambitious youth and power might not ruin their order, and make them a prey to the enemy. He replied, he would not give himself the trouble, but wished them to choose the bravest man amongst them, let his quality or birth be what it would, "For, O my friends!" said he, "it is not titles make men brave, or good, or birth that bestows courage and generosity, or makes the owner happy. Believe this, when you behold

---

[1] *maugre* Despite.

[2] *constitute ... room* I.e., appoint as his successor.

Oroonoko, the most wretched, and abandoned by fortune of all the creation of the gods." So turning himself about, he would make no more reply to all they could urge or implore.

The army beholding their officers return unsuccessful, with sad faces, and ominous looks, that presaged no good luck, suffered a thousand fears to take possession of their hearts, and the enemy to come even upon them, before they would provide for their safety by any defence; and though they were assured by some, who had a mind to animate them, that they should be immediately headed by the Prince, and that in the meantime Aboan had orders to command as general, yet they were so dismayed for want of that great example of bravery that they could make but a very feeble resistance; and at last, downright, fled before the enemy, who pursued them to the very tents, killing them. Nor could all Aboan's courage, which that day gained him immortal glory, shame them into a manly defence of themselves. The guards that were left behind, about the Prince's tent, seeing the soldiers flee before the enemy, and scatter themselves all over the plain, in great disorder, made such outcries as roused the Prince from his amorous slumber, in which he had remained buried for two days, without permitting any sustenance to approach him. But, in spite of all his resolutions, he had not the constancy of grief to that degree as to make him insensible of the danger of his army; and in that instant he leapt from his couch, and cried, "Come, if we must die, let us meet death the noblest way; and 'twill be more like Oroonoko to encounter him at an army's head, opposing the torrent of a conquering foe, than lazily, on a couch, to wait his lingering pleasure, and die every moment by a thousand wrecking thoughts; or be tamely taken by an enemy and led a whining, lovesick slave, to adorn the triumphs of Jamoan, that young victor, who already is entered beyond the limits I had prescribed him."

While he was speaking, he suffered his people to dress him for the field; and sallying out of his pavilion, with more life and vigour in his countenance than ever he showed, he appeared like some divine power descended to save his country from destruction; and his people had purposely put him on all things that might make him shine with most splendour, to strike a rever-

end awe into the beholders. He flew into the thickest of those that were pursuing his men, and being animated with despair, he fought as if he came on purpose to die, and did such things as will not be believed that human strength could perform, and such as soon inspired all the rest with new courage and new order. And now it was that they began to fight indeed, and so, as if they would not be outdone even by their adored hero, who turning the tide of the victory, changing absolutely the fate of the day, gained an entire conquest; and Oroonoko having the good fortune to single out Jamoan, he took him prisoner with his own hand, having wounded him almost to death.

This Jamoan afterwards became very dear to him, being a man very gallant and of excellent graces, and fine parts, so that he never put him amongst the rank of captives, as they used to do, without distinction, for the common sale or market, but kept him in his own court, where he retained nothing of the prisoner but the name, and returned no more into his own country, so great an affection he took for Oroonoko; and by a thousand tales and adventures of love and gallantry, flattered[1] his disease of melancholy and languishment, which I have often heard him say had certainly killed him, but for the conversation of this Prince and Aboan, and the French governor he had from his childhood, of whom I have spoken before, and who was a man of admirable wit, great ingenuity and learning, all which he had infused into his young pupil. This Frenchman was banished out of his own country for some heretical notions he held; and though he was a man of very little religion, he had admirable morals, and a brave soul.

After the total defeat of Jamoan's army, which all fled, or were left dead upon the place, they spent some time in the camp, Oroonoko choosing rather to remain a while there in his tents, than enter into a palace, or live in a court where he had so lately suffered so great a loss. The officers therefore, who saw and knew his cause of discontent, invented all sorts of diversions and sports to entertain their Prince: so that what with those amusements abroad, and others at home, that is, within their tents, with the persuasions, arguments and care of his friends and servants that he more peculiarly prized, he wore off in time a great part of that chagrin and torture

---

[1] *flattered* Cheered away.

of despair which the first effects of Imoinda's death had given him; insomuch as having received a thousand kind embassies from the King, and invitations to return to court, he obeyed, though with no little reluctance; and when he did so, there was a visible change in him, and for a long time he was much more melancholy than before. But time lessens all extremes, and reduces them to mediums and unconcern; but no motives or beauties, though all endeavoured it, could engage him in any sort of amour, though he had all the invitations to it, both from his own youth and others' ambitions and designs.

Oroonoko was no sooner returned from this last conquest, and received at court with all the joy and magnificence that could be expressed to a young victor, who was not only returned triumphant, but beloved like a deity, when there arrived in the port an English ship.

This person had often before been in these countries, and was very well known to Oroonoko, with whom he had trafficked for slaves, and had used to do the same with his predecessors.

This commander was a man of a finer sort of address and conversation, better bred, and more engaging than most of that sort of men are; so that he seemed rather never to have been bred out of a court, than almost all his life at sea. This captain therefore was always better received at court, than most of the traders to those countries were, and especially by Oroonoko, who was more civilized, according to the European mode, than any other had been, and took more delight in the white nations, and, above all, men of parts and wit. To this captain he sold abundance of his slaves, and for the favour and esteem he had for him, made him many presents, and obliged him to stay at court as long as possibly he could. Which the captain seemed to take as a very great honour done him, entertaining the Prince every day with globes and maps, and mathematical discourses and instruments, eating, drinking, hunting and living with him with so much familiarity, that it was not to be doubted, but he had gained very greatly upon the heart of this gallant young man. And the captain, in return of all these mighty favours, besought the Prince to honour his vessel with his presence, some day or other, to dinner, before he should set sail, which he condescended to accept, and appointed his day. The captain, on his part, failed not to have all things in a readiness, in the most magnificent order he could possibly. And the day being come, the captain, in his boat, richly adorned with carpets and velvet cushions, rowed to the shore to receive the Prince, with another longboat, where was placed all his music and trumpets, with which Oroonoko was extremely delighted; who met him on the shore, attended by his French governor, Jamoan, Aboan, and about an hundred of the noblest of the youths of the court. And after they had first carried the Prince on board, the boats fetched the rest off, where they found a very splendid treat, with all sorts of fine wines, and were as well entertained, as 'twas possible in such a place to be.

The Prince having drunk hard of punch, and several sorts of wine, as did all the rest (for great care was taken, they should want nothing of that part of the entertainment) was very merry, and in great admiration of the ship, for he had never been in one before, so that he was curious of beholding every place, where he decently might descend. The rest, no less curious, who were not quite overcome with drinking, rambled at their pleasure fore and aft, as their fancies guided them: so that the captain, who had well laid his design before, gave the word and seized on all his guests; they clapping great irons suddenly on the Prince when he was leaped down in the hold to view that part of the vessel, and locking him fast down, secured him. The same treachery was used to all the rest; and all in one instant, in several places of the ship, were lashed fast in irons and betrayed to slavery. That great design over, they set all hands to work to hoist sail; and with as treacherous and fair a wind they made from the shore with this innocent and glorious prize, who thought of nothing less than such an entertainment.

Some have commended this act, as brave in the captain; but I will spare my sense of it, and leave it to my reader to judge as he pleases.

It may be easily guessed in what manner the Prince resented this indignity, who may be best resembled to a lion taken in a toil; so he raged, so he struggled for liberty, but all in vain; and they had so wisely managed his fetters, that he could not use a hand in his defence, to quit himself of a life that would by no means endure slavery; nor could he move from the place where he was tied to any solid part of the ship against which he might have beat his head, and have finished his disgrace that way, so that being deprived of all other means, he resolved to perish for want of food. And pleased at last with that thought, and toiled and tired by rage and indignation, he laid himself down, and sullenly resolved upon dying, and refused all things that were brought him.

This did not a little vex the captain, and the more so because he found almost all of them of the same humour, so that the loss of so many brave slaves, so tall and goodly to behold, would have been very considerable. He therefore ordered one to go from him (for he would not be seen himself) to Oroonoko, and to assure him he was afflicted for having rashly done so inhospitable a deed, and which could not be now remedied, since they were far from shore; but since he resented it in so high a nature, he assured him he would revoke his resolution, and set both him and his friends ashore on the next land they should touch at; and of this the messenger gave him his oath, provided he would resolve to live. And Oroonoko, whose honour was such as he never had violated a word in his life himself, much less a solemn asseveration,[1] believed in an instant what this man said, but replied he expected for a confirmation of this to have his shameful fetters dismissed. This demand was carried to the captain, who returned him answer that the offence had been so great which he had put upon the Prince, that he durst not trust him with liberty while he remained in the ship, for fear lest by a valour natural to him, and a revenge that would animate that valour, he might commit some outrage fatal to himself and the King his master, to whom his vessel did belong. To this Oroonoko replied, he would engage his honour to behave himself in all friendly order and manner, and obey the command of the captain, as he was lord of the King's vessel, and general of those men under his command.

This was delivered to the still doubting captain, who could not resolve to trust a heathen he said, upon his parole, a man that had no sense or notion of the God that he worshipped. Oroonoko then replied he was very sorry to hear that the captain pretended to the knowledge and worship of any gods who had taught him no better principles, than not to credit as he would be

credited; but they told him the difference of their faith occasioned that distrust: for the captain had protested to him upon the word of a Christian, and sworn in the name of a great God, which if he should violate, he would expect eternal torment in the world to come. "Is that all the obligation he has to be just to his oath?" replied Oroonoko. "Let him know I swear by my honour, which to violate, would not only render me contemptible and despised by all brave and honest men, and so give myself perpetual pain, but it would be eternally offending and diseasing all mankind, harming, betraying, circumventing and outraging all men; but punishments hereafter are suffered by oneself; and the world takes no cognizances whether this god have revenged them, or not, 'tis done so secretly, and deferred so long; while the man of no honour suffers every moment the scorn and contempt of the honester world, and dies every day ignominiously in his fame, which is more valuable than life. I speak not this to move belief, but to show you how you mistake, when you imagine that he who will violate his honour, will keep his word with his gods." So turning from him with a disdainful smile, he refused to answer him when he urged him to know what answer he should carry back to his captain, so that he departed without saying any more.

The captain pondering and consulting what to do, it was concluded that nothing but Oroonoko's liberty would encourage any of the rest to eat, except the Frenchman, whom the captain could not pretend to keep prisoner, but only told him he was secured because he might act something in favour of the Prince, but that he should be freed as soon as they came to land. So that they concluded it wholly necessary to free the Prince from his irons that he might show himself to the rest, that they might have an eye upon him, and that they could not fear a single man.

This being resolved, to make the obligation the greater, the captain himself went to Oroonoko, where, after many compliments, and assurances of what he had already promised, he receiving from the Prince his parole, and his hand, for his good behaviour, dismissed his irons, and brought him to his own cabin, where, after having treated and reposed him a while, for he had neither eaten nor slept in four days before, he besought him to visit those obstinate people in chains, who refused all manner

---

[1] *asseveration* Promise; oath.

of sustenance, and entreated him to oblige them to eat, and assure them of their liberty the first opportunity.

Oroonoko, who was too generous not to give credit to his words, showed himself to his people, who were transported with excess of joy at the sight of their darling Prince, falling at his feet, and kissing and embracing them, believing, as some divine oracle, all he assured them. But he besought them to bear their chains with that bravery that became those whom he had seen act so nobly in arms, and that they could not give him greater proofs of their love and friendship, since 'twas all the security the captain (his friend) could have against the revenge, he said, they might possibly justly take, for the injuries sustained by him. And they all, with one accord, assured him they could not suffer enough when it was for his repose and safety.

After this they no longer refused to eat, but took what was brought them and were pleased with their captivity, since by it they hoped to redeem the Prince, who, all the rest of the voyage, was treated with all the respect due to his birth, though nothing could divert his melancholy; and he would often sigh for Imoinda, and think this a punishment due to his misfortune, in having left that noble maid behind him that fatal night in the otan, when he fled to the camp.

Possessed with a thousand thoughts of past joys with this fair young person, and a thousand griefs for her eternal loss, he endured a tedious voyage, and at last arrived at the mouth of the river of Surinam, a colony belonging to the King of England, and where they were to deliver some part of their slaves. There the merchants and gentlemen of the country going on board to demand those lots of slaves they had already agreed on, and amongst those the overseers of those plantations where I then chanced to be, the captain, who had given the word, ordered his men to bring up those noble slaves in fetters, whom I have spoken of; and having put them, some in one, and some in other lots, with women and children (which they call pickaninnies), they sold them off as slaves to several merchants and gentlemen, not putting any two in one lot, because they would separate them far from each other; not daring to trust them together, lest rage and courage should put them upon contriving some great action, to the ruin of the colony.

Oroonoko was first seized on and sold to our over-seer, who had the first lot, with seventeen more of all sorts and sizes, but not one of quality with him. When he saw this, he found what they meant; for, as I said, he understood English pretty well; and being wholly unarmed and defenceless, so as it was in vain to make any resistance, he only beheld the captain with a look all fierce and disdainful, upbraiding him with eyes, that forced blushes on his guilty cheeks, he only cried in passing over the side of the ship, "Farewell, Sir! 'Tis worth my suffering to gain so true a knowledge both of you and of your gods by whom you swear." And desiring those that held him to forbear their pains, and telling them he would make no resistance, he cried, "Come, my fellow slaves, let us descend, and see if we can meet with more honour and honesty in the next world we shall touch upon." So he nimbly leapt into the boat, and showing no more concern, suffered himself to be rowed up the river with his seventeen companions.

The gentleman that bought him was a young Cornish gentleman, whose name was Trefry; a man of great wit, and fine learning, and was carried into those parts by the Lord ——, Governor, to manage all his affairs.[1] He reflecting on the last words of Oroonoko to the captain, and beholding the richness of his vest, no sooner came into the boat, but he fixed his eyes on him; and finding something so extraordinary in his face, his shape and mien, a greatness of look, and haughtiness in his air, and finding he spoke English, had a great mind to be enquiring into his quality and fortune; which, though Oroonoko endeavoured to hide by only confessing he was above the rank of common slaves, Trefry soon found he was yet something greater than he confessed, and from that moment began to conceive so vast an esteem for him, that he ever after loved him as his dearest brother, and showed him all the civilities due to so great a man.

Trefry was a very good mathematician, and a linguist, could speak French and Spanish; and in the three days they remained in the boat (for so long were they going from the ship to the plantation) he entertained Oroonoko so agreeably with his art and discourse, that he was no less pleased with Trefry, than he was with the

---

[1] *Trefry ... affairs* John Trefry was hired by the then-governor of Surinam, Lord Willoughby, to be his agent at his plantation at Parham.

Prince; and he thought himself, at least, fortunate in this, that since he was a slave, as long as he would suffer himself to remain so, he had a man of so excellent wit and parts for a master. So that before they had finished their voyage up the river, he made no scruple of declaring to Trefry all his fortunes and most part of what I have here related, and put himself wholly into the hands of his new friend, whom he found resenting all the injuries were done him, and was charmed with all the greatnesses of his actions, which were recited with that modesty and delicate sense, as wholly vanquished him, and subdued him to his interest. And he promised him on his word and honour, he would find the means to reconduct him to his own country again; assuring him, he had a perfect abhorrence of so dishonourable an action, and that he would sooner have died, than have been the author of such a perfidy. He found the Prince was very much concerned to know what became of his friends, and how they took their slavery; and Trefry promised to take care about the enquiring after their condition, and that he should have an account of them.

Though, as Oroonoko afterwards said, he had little reason to credit the words of a backearary,[1] yet he knew not why, but he saw a kind of sincerity and awful truth in the face of Trefry; he saw an honesty in his eyes, and he found him wise and witty enough to understand honour, for it was one of his maxims, "A man of wit could not be a knave or villain."

In their passage up the river they put in at several houses for refreshment, and ever when they landed numbers of people would flock to behold this man; not but their eyes were daily entertained with the sight of slaves, but the fame of Oroonoko was gone before him, and all people were in admiration of his beauty. Besides, he had a rich habit on, in which he was taken, so different from the rest, and which the captain could not strip him of because he was forced to surprise his person in the minute he sold him. When he found his habit made him liable, as he thought, to be gazed at the more, he begged Trefry to give him something more befitting a slave, which he did, and took off his robes. Nevertheless, he shone through all and his osenbrigs (a sort of brown holland suit he had on) could not conceal the graces of his looks and mien; and he had no less admir-

ers than when he had his dazzling habit on. The royal youth appeared in spite of the slave, and people could not help treating him after a different manner without designing it; as soon as they approached him they venerated and esteemed him; his eyes insensibly commanded respect, and his behaviour insinuated it into every soul. So that there was nothing talked of but this young and gallant slave, even by those who yet knew not that he was a prince.

I ought to tell you, that the Christians never buy any slaves but they give them some name of their own, their native ones being likely very barbarous, and hard to pronounce; so that Mr. Trefry gave Oroonoko that of Caesar, which name will live in that country as long as that (scarce more) glorious one of the great Roman, for 'tis most evident, he wanted no part of the personal courage of that Caesar, and acted things as memorable, had they been done in some part of the world replenished with people and historians that might have given him his due. But his misfortune was to fall in an obscure world, that afforded only a female pen to celebrate his fame, though I doubt not but it had lived from others' endeavours, if the Dutch, who, immediately after his time, took that country, had not killed, banished, and dispersed all those that were capable of giving the world this great man's life,[2] much better than I have done. And Mr. Trefry, who designed it, died before he began it, and bemoaned himself for not having undertook it in time.

For the future therefore, I must call Oroonoko Caesar, since by that name only he was known in our western world, and by that name he was received on shore at Parham House, where he was destined a slave. But if the King himself (God bless him) had come ashore, there could not have been greater expectations by all the whole plantation, and those neighbouring ones, than was on ours at that time; and he was received more like a governor than a slave. Notwithstanding, as the custom was, they assigned him his portion of land, his house, and his business, up in the plantation.

But as it was more for form than any design to put him to his task, he endured no more of the slave but the name, and remained some days in the house, receiving

1 *backearary* From the word "buckra," meaning white man.

2 *the Dutch … life* The Dutch took control of Surinam from the British in 1667.

all visits that were made him, without stirring towards that part of the plantation where the Negroes were.

At last, he would needs go view his land, his house, and the business assigned him. But he no sooner came to the houses of the slaves, which are like a little town by itself, the Negroes all having left work, but they all came forth to behold him, and found he was that prince who had, at several times, sold most of them to these parts; and, from a veneration they pay to great men, especially if they know them, and from the surprise and awe they had at the sight of him, they all cast themselves at his feet, crying out, in their language, "Live, O King! Long live, O King!" And kissing his feet, paid him even divine homage.

Several English gentlemen were with him, and what Mr. Trefry had told them, was here confirmed of which he himself before had no other witness than Caesar himself. But he was infinitely glad to find his grandeur confirmed by the adoration of all the slaves.

Caesar, troubled with their over-joy, and over-ceremony, besought them to rise, and to receive him as their fellow slave, assuring them, he was no better. At which they set up with one accord a most terrible and hideous mourning and condoling, which he and the English had much ado to appease. But at last they prevailed with them, and they prepared all their barbarous music, and everyone killed and dressed something of his own stock (for every family has their land apart, on which, at their leisure times, they breed all eatable things) and clubbing it together, made a most magnificent supper, inviting their grandee captain, their Prince, to honour it with his presence, which he did, and several English with him, where they all waited on him, some playing, others dancing before him all the time, according to the manners of their several nations, and with unwearied industry, endeavouring to please and delight him.

While they sat at meat Mr. Trefry told Caesar, that most of these young slaves were undone in love, with a fine she slave, whom they had had about six months on their land. The Prince, who never heard the name of love without a sigh, nor any mention of it without the curiosity of examining further into that tale, which of all discourses was most agreeable to him, asked, how they came to be so unhappy, as to be all undone for one fair slave? Trefry, who was naturally amorous, and loved to talk of love as well as anybody, proceeded to tell him, they had the most charming black that ever was beheld on their plantation, about fifteen or sixteen years old, as he guessed; that, for his part, he had done nothing but sigh for her ever since she came; and that all the white beauties he had seen, never charmed him so absolutely as this fine creature had done; and that no man, of any nation, ever beheld her, that did not fall in love with her; and that she had all the slaves perpetually at her feet; and the whole country resounded with the fame of Clemene, for so, said he, we have christened her. But she denies us all with such a noble disdain, that 'tis a miracle to see that she, who can give such eternal desires, should herself be all ice, and all unconcern. She is adorned with the most graceful modesty that ever beautified youth, the softest sigher—that, if she were capable of love, one would swear she languished for some absent happy man, and so retired, as if she feared a rape even from the God of Day,[1] or that the breezes would steal kisses from her delicate mouth. Her task of work some sighing lover every day makes it his petition to perform for her, which she accepts blushing, and with reluctance, for fear he will ask her a look for a recompense, which he dares not presume to hope, so great an awe she strikes into the hearts of her admirers. "I do not wonder," replied the Prince, "that Clemene should refuse slaves, being as you say so beautiful, but wonder how she escapes those who can entertain her as you can do. Or why, being your slave, you do not oblige her to yield."

"I confess," said Trefry, "when I have, against her will, entertained her with love so long, as to be transported with my passion, even above decency, I have been ready to make use of those advantages of strength and force nature has given me. But oh! she disarms me, with that modesty and weeping so tender and so moving, that I retire, and thank my stars she overcame me." The company laughed at his civility to a slave, and Caesar only applauded the nobleness of his passion and nature, since that slave might be noble, or, what was better, have true notions of honour and virtue in her. Thus passed they this night, after having received, from the slaves, all imaginable respect and obedience.

----

[1]   *the God of Day* Apollo, god of light, here represented by the sun.

The next day Trefry asked Caesar to walk, when the heat was allayed, and designedly carried him by the cottage of the fair slave, and told him, she whom he spoke of last night lived there retired. "But," says he, "I would not wish you to approach, for, I am sure, you will be in love as soon as you behold her." Caesar assured him, he was proof against all the charms of that sex, and that if he imagined his heart could be so perfidious to love again, after Imoinda, he believed he should tear it from his bosom. They had no sooner spoke, but a little shock dog,[1] that Clemene had presented her, which she took great delight in, ran out, and she, not knowing anybody was there, ran to get it in again, and bolted out on those who were just speaking of her. When seeing them, she would have run in again, but Trefry caught her by the hand, and cried, "Clemene, however you fly a lover, you ought to pay some respect to this stranger" (pointing to Caesar). But she, as if she had resolved never to raise her eyes to the face of a man again, bent them the more to the earth, when he spoke, and gave the Prince the leisure to look the more at her. There needed no long gazing, or consideration, to examine who this fair creature was. He soon saw Imoinda all over her; in a minute he saw her face, her shape, her air, her modesty, and all that called forth his soul with joy at his eyes, and left his body destitute of almost life. It stood without motion, and, for a minute, knew not that it had a being. And, I believe, he had never come to himself, so oppressed he was with over-joy, if he had not met with this allay, that he perceived Imoinda fall dead in the hands of Trefry. This awakened him, and he ran to her aid, and caught her in his arms, where, by degrees, she came to herself; and 'tis needless to tell with what transports, what ecstasies of joy, they both a while beheld each other, without speaking, then snatched each other to their arms, then gaze again, as if they still doubted whether they possessed the blessing they grasped. But when they recovered their speech, 'tis not to be imagined what tender things they expressed to each other, wondering what strange fate had brought them again together. They soon informed each other of their fortunes, and equally bewailed their fate; but, at the same time, they mutually protested, that even fetters and slavery were soft and easy, and would be supported with joy and pleasure, while they could be so happy to possess each other, and to be able to make good their vows. Caesar swore he disdained the empire of the world, while he could behold his Imoinda, and she despised grandeur and pomp, those vanities of her sex, when she could gaze on Oroonoko. He adored the very cottage where she resided, and said, that little inch of the world would give him more happiness than all the universe could do, and she vowed, it was a palace, while adorned with the presence of Oroonoko.

Trefry was infinitely pleased with this novel,[2] and found this Clemene was the fair mistress of whom Caesar had before spoke, and was not a little satisfied, that heaven was so kind to the Prince, as to sweeten his misfortunes by so lucky an accident, and leaving the lovers to themselves, was impatient to come down to Parham House (which was on the same plantation) to give me an account of what had happened. I was as impatient to make these lovers a visit, having already made a friendship with Caesar, and from his own mouth learned what I have related, which was confirmed by his Frenchman, who was set on shore to seek his fortunes, and of whom they could not make a slave, because a Christian, and he came daily to Parham Hill to see and pay his respects to his pupil Prince. So that concerning and interesting myself in all that related to Caesar, whom I had assured of liberty as soon as the governor arrived, I hasted presently to the place where the lovers were, and was infinitely glad to find this beautiful young slave (who had already gained all our esteems, for her modesty and her extraordinary prettiness) to be the same I had heard Caesar speak so much of. One may imagine then, we paid her a treble respect; and though from her being carved in fine flowers and birds all over her body, we took her to be of quality before, yet, when we knew Clemene was Imoinda, we could not enough admire her.

I had forgot to tell you, that those who are nobly born of that country are so delicately cut and raced[3] all over the fore part of the trunk of their bodies, that it looks as if it were japanned,[4] the works being raised like high point round the edges of the flowers. Some are

---

[1] *shock dog* Small, long-haired dog.

[2] *novel* Story.

[3] *raced* Engraved; i.e., tattooed.

[4] *japanned* Lacquered in the Japanese style.

only carved with a little flower, or bird, at the sides of the temples, as was Caesar; and those who are so carved over the body, resemble our ancient Picts,[1] that are figured in the chronicles, but these carvings are more delicate.

From that happy day Caesar took Clemene for his wife, to the general joy of all people, and there was as much magnificence as the country would afford at the celebration of this wedding. And in a very short time after she conceived with child, which made Caesar even adore her, knowing he was the last of his great race. This new accident made him more impatient of liberty, and he was every day treating with Trefry for his and Clemene's liberty, and offered either gold, or a vast quantity of slaves, which should be paid before they let him go, provided he could have any security that he should go when his ransom was paid. They fed him from day to day with promises, and delayed him, till the Lord Governor should come, so that he began to suspect them of falsehood, and that they would delay him till the time of his wife's delivery, and make a slave of that too, for all the breed is theirs to whom the parents belong. This thought made him very uneasy, and his sullenness gave them some jealousies[2] of him, so that I was obliged, by some persons who feared a mutiny (which is very fatal sometimes in those colonies that abound so with slaves that they exceed the whites in vast numbers), to discourse with Caesar, and to give him all the satisfaction I possibly could. They knew he and Clemene were scarce an hour in a day from my lodgings, that they ate with me, and that I obliged them in all things I was capable of: I entertained him with the lives of the Romans, and great men, which charmed him to my company, and her, with teaching her all the pretty works[3] that I was mistress of, and telling her stories of nuns, and endeavouring to bring her to the knowledge of the true God. But of all discourses Caesar liked that the worst, and would never be reconciled to our notions of the Trinity, of which he ever made a jest; it was a riddle, he said, would turn his brain to conceive, and one could not make him understand what faith was.

However, these conversations failed not altogether so well to divert him, that he liked the company of us women much above the men, for he could not drink, and he is but an ill companion in that country that cannot. So that obliging him to love us very well, we had all the liberty of speech with him, especially myself, whom he called his Great Mistress; and indeed my word would go a great way with him. For these reasons, I had opportunity to take notice to him, that he was not well pleased of late, as he used to be, was more retired and thoughtful, and told him, I took it ill he should suspect we would break our words with him, and not permit both him and Clemene to return to his own kingdom, which was not so long away, but when he was once on his voyage he would quickly arrive there. He made me some answers that showed a doubt in him, which made me ask him, what advantage it would be to doubt? It would but give us a fear of him, and possibly compel us to treat him so as I should be very loath to behold: that is, it might occasion his confinement. Perhaps this was not so luckily spoke of me, for I perceived he resented that word, which I strove to soften again in vain. However, he assured me, that whatsoever resolutions he should take, he would act nothing upon the white people. And as for myself, and those upon that plantation where he was, he would sooner forfeit his eternal liberty, and life itself, than lift his hand against his greatest enemy on that place. He besought me to suffer no fears upon his account, for he could do nothing that honour should not dictate, but he accused himself for having suffered slavery so long; yet he charged that weakness on love alone, who was capable of making him neglect even glory itself, and, for which, now he reproaches himself every moment of the day. Much more to this effect he spoke, with an air impatient enough to make me know he would not be long in bondage, and though he suffered only the name of a slave, and had nothing of the toil and labour of one, yet that was sufficient to render him uneasy, and he had been too long idle, who used to be always in action, and in arms. He had a spirit all rough and fierce, and that could not be tamed to lazy rest, and though all endeavours were used to exercise himself in such actions and sports as this

---

[1]   *Picts*   From the Latin *pictii*, meaning painted, an ancient people of northern Britain who were said to have been ornately tattooed.

[2]   *jealousies*   Apprehensions; suspicions.

[3]   *works*   Kinds of needlework.

world afforded, as running, wrestling, pitching the bar,[1] hunting and fishing, chasing and killing tigers of a monstrous size, which this continent affords in abundance, and wonderful snakes, such as Alexander is reported to have encountered at the river of Amazons, and which Caesar took great delight to overcome; yet these were not actions great enough for his large soul, which was still panting after more renowned action.

Before I parted that day with him, I got, with much ado, a promise from him to rest yet a little longer with patience, and wait the coming of the Lord Governor, who was every day expected on our shore. He assured me he would, and this promise he desired me to know was given perfectly in complaisance to me, in whom he had an entire confidence.

After this, I neither thought it convenient to trust him much out of our view, nor did the country who feared him; but with one accord it was advised to treat him fairly, and oblige him to remain within such a compass, and that he should be permitted, as seldom as could be, to go up to the plantations of the Negroes, or, if he did, to be accompanied by some that should be rather in appearance attendants than spies. This care was for some time taken, and Caesar looked upon it as a mark of extraordinary respect, and was glad his discontent had obliged them to be more observant to him. He received new assurance from the overseer, which was confirmed to him by the opinion of all the gentlemen of the country, who made their court to him. During this time that we had his company more frequently than hitherto we had had, it may not be unpleasant to relate to you the diversions we entertained him with, or rather he us.

My stay was to be short in that country, because my father died at sea, and never arrived to possess the honour was designed him (which was lieutenant-general of six and thirty islands, besides the continent of Surinam), nor the advantages he hoped to reap by them, so that though we were obliged to continue on our voyage, we did not intend to stay upon the place. Though, in a word, I must say thus much of it, that certainly had his late Majesty, of sacred memory, but seen and known what a vast and charming world he had been master of

in that continent, he would never have parted so easily with it to the Dutch. 'Tis a continent whose vast extent was never yet known, and may contain more noble earth than all the universe besides; for, they say, it reaches from east to west, one way as far as China, and another to Peru. It affords all things both for beauty and use; 'tis there eternal spring, always the very months of April, May and June. The shades are perpetual, the trees, bearing at once all degrees of leaves and fruit, from blooming buds to ripe autumn, groves of oranges, lemons, citrons, figs, nutmegs, and noble aromatics, continually bearing their fragrancies. The trees appearing all like nosegays adorned with flowers of different kind; some are all white, some purple, some scarlet, some blue, some yellow; bearing, at the same time, ripe fruit and blooming young, or producing every day new. The very wood of all these trees have an intrinsic value above common timber, for they are, when cut, of different colours, glorious to behold, and bear a price considerable, to inlay withal. Besides this, they yield rich balm, and gums, so that we make our candles of such an aromatic substance, as does not only give a sufficient light, but, as they burn, they cast their perfumes all about. Cedar is the common firing, and all the houses are built with it. The very meat we eat, when set on the table, if it be native, I mean of the country, perfumes the whole room, especially a little beast called an armadillo, a thing which I can liken to nothing so well as a rhinoceros. 'Tis all in white armour so jointed, that it moves as well in it, as if it had nothing on. This beast is about the bigness of a pig of six weeks old. But it were endless to give an account of all the diverse wonderful and strange things that country affords, and which we took a very great delight to go in search of, though those adventures are oftentimes fatal and at least dangerous. But while we had Caesar in our company on these designs we feared no harm, nor suffered any.

As soon as I came into the country, the best house in it was presented me, called St. John's Hill. It stood on a vast rock of white marble, at the foot of which the river ran a vast depth down, and not to be descended on that side. The little waves still dashing and washing the foot of this rock, made the softest murmurs and purlings in the world, and the opposite bank was adorned with such

---

[1] *pitching the bar* Throwing a heavy rod was considered both a game and a form of exercise.

vast quantities of different flowers eternally blowing,[1] and every day and hour new, fenced behind them with lofty trees of a thousand rare forms and colours, that the prospect was the most ravishing that sands can create. On the edge of this white rock, towards the river, was a walk or grove of orange and lemon trees, about half the length of the Mall[2] here, whose flowery and fruity branches meet at the top, and hindered the sun, whose rays are very fierce there, from entering a beam into the grove, and the cool air that came from the river made it not only fit to entertain people in, at all the hottest hours of the day, but refreshed the sweet blossoms, and made it always sweet and charming, and sure the whole globe of the world cannot show so delightful a place as this grove was. Not all the gardens of boasted Italy can produce a shade to out-vie this, which nature had joined with art to render so exceeding fine. And 'tis a marvel to see how such vast trees, as big as English oaks, could take footing on so solid a rock, and in so little earth, as covered that rock, but all things by nature there are rare, delightful and wonderful. But to our sports.

Sometimes we would go surprising,[3] and in search of young tigers[4] in their dens, watching when the old ones went forth to forage for prey, and oftentimes we have been in great danger, and have fled apace for our lives, when surprised by the dams. But once, above all other times, we went on this design, and Caesar was with us, who had no sooner stolen a young tiger from her nest, but going off, we encountered the dam,[5] bearing a buttock of a cow, which he had torn off with his mighty paw, and going with it towards his den. We had only four women, Caesar, and an English gentleman, brother to Harry Martin, the great Oliverian.[6] We found there was no escaping this enraged and ravenous beast. However, we women fled as fast as we could from it, but our heels had not saved our lives, if Caesar had not laid down his cub, when he found the tiger quit her prey to make the more speed towards him, and taking Mr. Martin's sword desired him to stand aside, or follow the ladies. He obeyed him, and Caesar met this monstrous beast of might, size, and vast limbs, who came with open jaws upon him, and fixing his awful stern eyes full upon those of the beast, and putting himself into a very steady and good aiming posture of defence, ran his sword quite through his breast down to his very heart, home to the hilt of the sword. The dying beast stretched forth her paw, and going to grasp his thigh, surprised with death in that very moment, did him no other harm than fixing her long nails in his flesh very deep, feebly wounded him, but could not grasp the flesh to tear off any. When he had done this, he hollowed to us to return, which, after some assurance of his victory, we did, and found him lugging out the sword from the bosom of the tiger, who was laid in her blood on the ground. He took up the cub, and with an unconcern, that had nothing of the joy or gladness of a victory, he came and laid the whelp at my feet. We all extremely wondered at his daring, and at the bigness of the beast, which was about the height of an heifer, but of mighty, great, and strong limbs.

Another time, being in the woods, he killed a tiger, which had long infested that part, and borne away abundance of sheep and oxen, and other things, that were for the support of those to whom they belonged. Abundance of people assailed this beast, some affirming they had shot her with several bullets quite through the body, at several times, and some swearing they shot her through the very heart, and they believed she was a devil rather than a mortal thing. Caesar had often said, he had a mind to encounter this monster, and spoke with several gentlemen who had attempted her, one crying, I shot her with so many poisoned arrows, another with his gun in this part of her, and another in that. So that he remarking all these places where she was shot, fancied still he should overcome her, by giving her another sort of a wound than any had yet done, and one day said (at the table) "What trophies and garlands ladies will you make me, if I bring you home the heart of this ravenous beast, that eats up all your lambs and pigs?" We all promised he should be rewarded at all our hands. So taking a bow, which he chose out of a great many, he went up in the wood, with two gentlemen, where he

---

[1] *blowing* Blooming.
[2] *Mall* Tree-lined promenade in St. James's Park, London.
[3] *surprising* Raiding.
[4] *tigers* Pumas (cougars).
[5] *dam* Behn confuses the tiger's gender in the following message.
[6] *Oliverian* Martin owned Surinam plantations and had been a supporter of Oliver Cromwell.

imagined this devourer to be. They had not passed very far in it, but they heard her voice, growling and grumbling, as if she were pleased with something she was doing. When they came in view, they found her muzzling in the belly of a new ravished sheep, which she had torn open, and seeing herself approached, she took fast hold of her prey, with her forepaws, and set a very fierce raging look on Caesar, without offering to approach him, for fear, at the same time, of losing what she had in possession. So that Caesar remained a good while, only taking aim, and getting an opportunity to shoot her where he designed. 'Twas some time before he could accomplish it, and to wound her, and not kill her, would but have enraged her more, and endangered him. He had a quiver of arrows at his side, so that if one failed he could be supplied. At last, retiring a little, he gave her opportunity to eat, for he found she was ravenous, and fell to as soon as she saw him retire, being more eager of her prey than of doing new mischiefs. When he going softly to one side of her, and hiding his person behind certain herbage that grew high and thick, he took so good aim, that, as he intended, he shot her just into the eye, and the arrow was sent with so good a will, and so sure a hand, that it stuck in her brain, and made her caper, and become mad for a moment or two, but being seconded by another arrow, he fell dead upon the prey. Caesar cut him open with a knife, to see where those wounds were that had been reported to him, and why he did not die of them. But I shall now relate a thing that possibly will find no credit among men, because 'tis a notion commonly received with us, that nothing can receive a wound in the heart and live; but when the heart of this courageous animal was taken out, there were seven bullets of lead in it, and the wounds seamed up with great scars, and she lived with the bullets a great while, for it was long since they were shot. This heart the conqueror brought up to us, and 'twas a very great curiosity, which all the country came to see, and which gave Caesar occasion of many fine discourses, of accidents in war, and strange escapes.

At other times he would go a-fishing, and discoursing on that diversion, he found we had in that country a very strange fish, called, a numb eel[1] (an eel of which I have eaten) that while it is alive, it has a quality so cold, that those who are angling, though with a line of never so great a length, with a rod at the end of it, it shall, in the same minute the bait is touched by this eel, seize him or her that holds the rod with benumbedness, that shall deprive them of sense, for a while. And some have fallen into the water, and others dropped as dead on the banks of the rivers where they stood, as soon as this fish touches the bait. Caesar used to laugh at this, and believed it impossible a man could lose his force at the touch of a fish, and could not understand that philosophy,[2] that a cold quality should be of that nature. However, he had a great curiosity to try whether it would have the same effect on him it had on others, and often tried, but in vain. At last, the sought for fish came to the bait, as he stood angling on the bank; and instead of throwing away the rod, or giving it a sudden twitch out of the water, whereby he might have caught both the eel, and have dismissed the rod, before it could have too much power over him for experiment sake, he grasped it but the harder, and fainting fell into the river. And being still possessed of the rod, the tide carried him senseless as he was a great way, till an Indian boat took him up, and perceived, when they touched him, a numbness seize them, and by that knew the rod was in his hand, which, with a paddle (that is, a short oar) they struck away, and snatched it into the boat, eel and all. If Caesar were almost dead, with the effect of this fish, he was more so with that of the water, where he had remained the space of going a league,[3] and they found they had much ado to bring him back to life. But, at last, they did, and brought him home, where he was in a few hours well recovered and refreshed; and not a little ashamed to find he should be overcome by an eel, and that all the people, who heard his defiance, would laugh at him. But we cheered him up, and he, being convinced, we had the eel at supper; which was a quarter of an ell about, and most delicate meat, and was of the more value, since it cost so dear as almost the life of so gallant a man.

About this time we were in many mortal fears about some disputes the English had with the Indians, so that we could scarce trust ourselves, without great numbers, to go to any Indian towns, or place, where they abode,

---

[1] *numb eel* Electric eel.

[2] *philosophy* Scientific phenomenon.

[3] *league* Approximately three miles.

for fear they should fall upon us, as they did immediately after my coming away, and that it was in the possession of the Dutch, who used them not so civilly as the English, so that they cut in pieces all they could take, getting into houses, and hanging up the mother, and all her children about her, and cut a footman I left behind me, all in joints, and nailed him to trees.

This feud began while I was there, so that I lost half the satisfaction I proposed, in not seeing and visiting the Indian towns. But one day, bemoaning of our misfortunes upon this account, Caesar told us, we need not fear, for if we had a mind to go, he would undertake to be our guard. Some would, but most would not venture. About eighteen of us resolved, and took barge, and, after eight days, arrived near an Indian town. But approaching it, the hearts of some of our company failed, and they would not venture on shore, so we polled who would, and who would not. For my part, I said, if Caesar would, I would go. He resolved, so did my brother, and my woman, a maid of good courage. Now none of us speaking the language of the people, and imagining we should have a half diversion in gazing only and not knowing what they said, we took a fisherman that lived at the mouth of the river, who had been a long inhabitant there, and obliged him to go with us. But because he was known to the Indians, as trading among them, and being, by long living there, become a perfect Indian in colour, we, who resolved to surprise them, by making them see something they never had seen (that is, white people) resolved only myself, my brother, and woman should go. So Caesar, the fisherman, and the rest, hiding behind some thick reeds and flowers, that grew on the banks, let us pass on towards the town, which was on the bank of the river all along. A little distant from the houses, or huts, we saw some dancing, others busied in fetching and carrying of water from the river. They had no sooner spied us, but they set up a loud cry, that frighted us at first. We thought it had been for those that should kill us, but it seems it was of wonder and amazement. They were all naked, and we were dressed, so as is most commode[1] for the hot countries, very glittering and rich, so that we appeared extremely fine. My own hair was cut short, and I had a taffeta cap, with black feathers, on my head. My brother

was in a stuff[2] suit, with silver loops and buttons, and abundance of green ribbon. This was all infinitely surprising to them, and because we saw them stand still, till we approached them, we took heart and advanced, came up to them, and offered them our hands, which they took, and looked on us round about, calling still for more company, who came swarming out, all wondering, and crying out "*tepeeme*," taking their hair up in their hands, and spreading it wide to those they called out to, as if they would say (as indeed it signified) "numberless wonders," or not to be recounted, no more than to number the hair of their heads. By degrees they grew more bold, and from gazing upon us round, they touched us, laying their hands upon all the features of our faces, feeling our breasts and arms, taking up one petticoat, then wondering to see another, admiring our shoes and stockings, but more our garters, which we gave them, and they tied about their legs, being laced with silver lace at the ends, for they much esteem any shining things. In fine,[3] we suffered them to survey us as they pleased, and we thought they would never have done admiring us. When Caesar, and the rest, saw we were received with such wonder, they came up to us, and finding the Indian trader whom they knew (for 'tis by these fishermen, called Indian traders, we hold a commerce with them; for they love not to go far from home, and we never go to them), when they saw him therefore they set up a new joy, and cried, in their language, "Oh! here's our *tiguamy*, and we shall now know whether those things can speak." So advancing to him, some of them gave him their hands, and cried, "*Amora tiguamy*," which is as much as, "How do you," or "Welcome friend," and all, with one din, began to gabble to him, and asked if we had sense, and wit? If we could talk of affairs of life, and war, as they could do? If we could hunt, swim, and do a thousand things they use? He answered them, we could. Then they invited us into their houses, and dressed venison and buffalo for us, and, going out, gathered a leaf of a tree, called a sarumbo leaf, of six yards long, and spread it on the ground for a tablecloth, and cutting another in pieces instead of plates, setting us on little bow Indian stools, which they cut out of one entire piece of wood, and

---

[1] *commode* Suitable.

[2] *stuff* Wool.

[3] *In fine* In the end.

paint, in a sort of japan work. They serve everyone their mess on these pieces of leaves, and it was very good, but too high seasoned with pepper. When we had eaten, my brother and I took out our flutes, and played to them, which gave them new wonder, and I soon perceived, by an admiration that is natural to these people, and by the extreme ignorance and simplicity of them, it were not difficult to establish any unknown or extravagant religion among them, and to impose any notions or fictions upon them. For seeing a kinsman of mine set some paper afire, with a burning-glass, a trick they had never before seen, they were like to have adored him for a god, and begged he would give them the characters or figures of his name, that they might oppose it against winds and storms, which he did, and they held it up in those seasons, and fancied it had a charm to conquer them, and kept it like a holy relic. They are very superstitious, and called him the great *peeie*, that is, prophet. They showed us their Indian *peeie*, a youth of about sixteen years old, as handsome as nature could make a man. They consecrate a beautiful youth from his infancy, and all arts are used to complete him in the finest manner, both in beauty and shape. He is bred to all the little arts and cunning they are capable of, to all the legerdemain[1] tricks, and sleight of hand, whereby he imposes upon the rabble, and is both a doctor in physic and divinity. And by these tricks makes the sick believe he sometimes eases their pains, by drawing from the afflicted part little serpents, or odd flies, or worms, or any strange thing; and though they have besides undoubted good remedies, for almost all their diseases, they cure the patient more by fancy than by medicines, and make themselves feared, loved, and reverenced. This young *peeie* had a very young wife, who seeing my brother kiss her, came running and kissed me; after this, they kissed one another, and made it a very great jest, it being so novel, and new admiration and laughing went round the multitude, that they never will forget that ceremony, never before used or known. Caesar had a mind to see and talk with their war captains, and we were conducted to one of their houses, where we beheld several of the great captains, who had been at council. But so frightful a vision it was to see them no fancy can create; no such dreams can represent so dreadful a

spectacle. For my part I took them for hobgoblins, or fiends, rather than men. But however their shapes appeared, their souls were very humane and noble, but some wanted their noses, some their lips, some both noses and lips, some their ears, and others cut through each cheek, with long slashes, through which their teeth appeared; they had several other formidable wounds and scars, or rather dismemberings. They had *comitias*, or little aprons before them, and girdles of cotton, with their knives naked, stuck in it, a bow at their backs, and a quiver of arrows on their thighs, and most had feathers on their heads of diverse colours. They cried "*Amora tigame*" to us at our entrance, and were pleased we said as much to them. They feted us, and gave us drink of the best sort, and wondered, as much as the others had done before, to see us. Caesar was marvelling as much at their faces, wondering how they should all be so wounded in war; he was impatient to know how they all came by those frightful marks of rage or malice, rather than wounds got in noble battle. They told us, by our interpreter, that when any war was waging, two men chosen out by some old captain, whose fighting was past, and who could only teach the theory of war, these two men were to stand in competition for the generalship, or Great War Captain, and being brought before the old judges, now past labour, they are asked, what they dare do to show they are worthy to lead an army? When he, who is first asked, making no reply, cuts off his nose, and throws it contemptibly on the ground, and the other does something to himself that he thinks surpasses him, and perhaps deprives himself of lips and an eye. So they slash on till one gives out, and many have died in this debate. And 'tis by a passive valour they show and prove their activity, a sort of courage too brutal to be applauded by our black hero; nevertheless he expressed his esteem of them.

In this voyage Caesar begot so good an understanding between the Indians and the English, that there were no more fears, or heartburnings during our stay, but we had a perfect, open, and free trade with them. Many things remarkable, and worthy reciting, we met with in this short voyage, because Caesar made it his business to search out and provide for our entertainment, especially to please his dearly adored Imoinda, who was a sharer in all our adventures; we being resolved to make her chains

---

[1] *legerdemain* Magic.

as easy as we could, and to compliment the Prince in that manner that most obliged him.

As we were coming up again, we met with some Indians of strange aspects, that is, of a larger size, and other sort of features, than those of our country. Our Indian slaves, that rowed us, asked them some questions, but they could not understand us, but showed us a long cotton string, with several knots on it, and told us, they had been coming from the mountains so many moons as there were knots. They were habited in skins of a strange beast, and brought along with them bags of gold dust, which, as well as they could give us to understand, came streaming in little small channels down the high mountains, when the rains fell, and offered to be the convoy to anybody, or persons, that would go to the mountains. We carried these men up to Parham, where they were kept till the Lord Governor came. And because all the country was mad to be going on this golden adventure, the governor, by his letters, commanded (for they sent some of the gold to him) that a guard should be set at the mouth of the river of Amazons (a river so called, almost as broad as the river of Thames), and prohibited all people from going up that river, it conducting to those mountains of gold. But we going off for England before the project was further prosecuted, and the governor being drowned in a hurricane,[1] either the design died, or the Dutch have the advantage of it. And 'tis to be bemoaned what His Majesty lost by losing that part of America.

Though this digression is a little from my story, however since it contains some proofs of the curiosity and daring of this great man, I was content to omit nothing of his character.

It was thus, for some time we diverted him. But now Imoinda began to show she was with child, and did nothing but sigh and weep for the captivity of her lord, herself, and the infant yet unborn, and believed, if it were so hard to gain the liberty of two, 'twould be more difficult to get that for three. Her griefs were so many darts in the great heart of Caesar, and taking his opportunity one Sunday, when all the whites were overtaken in drink, as there were abundance of several trades, and

slaves for four years,[2] that inhabited among the Negro houses, and Sunday was their day of debauch (otherwise they were a sort of spies upon Caesar), he went pretending out of goodness to them, to feast amongst them, and sent all his music, and ordered a great treat for the whole gang, about three hundred Negroes. And about a hundred and fifty were able to bear arms, such as they had, which were sufficient to do execution with spirits accordingly. For the English had none but rusty swords, that no strength could draw from a scabbard, except the people of particular quality, who took care to oil them and keep them in good order. The guns also, unless here and there one, or those newly carried from England, would do no good or harm, for 'tis the nature of that county to rust and eat up iron, or any metals, but gold and silver. And they are very inexpert at the bow, which the Negroes and Indians are perfect masters of.

Caesar, having singled out these men from the women and children, made a harangue to them of the miseries, and ignominies of slavery; counting up all their toils and sufferings, under such loads, burdens, and drudgeries, as were fitter for beasts than men; senseless brutes, than human souls. He told them it was not for days, months, or years, but for eternity; there was no end to be of their misfortunes. They suffered not like men who might find a glory, and fortitude in oppression, but like dogs that loved the whip and bell, and fawned the more they were beaten. That they had lost the divine quality of men, and were become insensible asses, fit only to bear. Nay worse, an ass, or dog, or horse having done his duty, could lie down in retreat, and rise to work again, and while he did his duty endured no stripes, but men, villainous, senseless men, such as they, toiled on all the tedious week till Black Friday, and then, whether they worked or not, whether they were faulty or meriting, they promiscuously, the innocent with the guilty, suffered the infamous whip, the sordid stripes, from their fellow slaves till their blood trickled from all parts of their body, blood whose every drop ought to be revenged with a life of some of those tyrants that impose it. "And why," said he, "my dear friends and fellow sufferers, should we be slaves to an unknown

---

1. *drowned in a hurricane* Lord Willoughby died at sea in 1666.

2. *slaves for four years* Europeans could bind themselves to service in the colonies by contract, or indenture. Criminals were also shipped to the colonies to serve out sentences as laborers.

people? Have they vanquished us nobly in fight? Have they won us in honourable battle? And are we, by the chance of war, become their slaves? This would not anger a noble heart, this would not animate a soldier's soul. No, but we are bought and sold like apes, or monkeys, to be the sport of women, fools and cowards, and the support of rogues, renegades, that have abandoned their own countries, for raping, murders, thefts and villainies. Do you not hear every day how they upbraid each other with infamy of life, below the wildest savages, and shall we render obedience to such a degenerate race, who have no one human virtue left, to distinguish them from the vilest creatures? Will you, I say, suffer the lash from such hands?"

They all replied, with one accord, "No, no, no; Caesar has spoke like a great captain, like a great king."

After this he would have proceeded, but was interrupted by a tall Negro of some more quality than the rest. His name was Tuscan, who bowing at the feet of Caesar, cried, "My lord, we have listened with joy and attention to what you have said, and, were we only men, would follow so great a leader through the world. But oh! consider, we are husbands and parents too, and have things more dear to us than life: our wives and children unfit for travel, in these impassable woods, mountains and bogs. We have not only difficult lands to overcome, but rivers to wade, and monsters to encounter, ravenous beasts of prey—." To this, Caesar replied, that honour was the first principle in nature that was to be obeyed; but as no man would pretend to that, without all the acts of virtue, compassion, charity, love, justice and reason, he found it not inconsistent with that, to take an equal care of their wives and children, as they would of themselves, and that he did not design, when he led them to freedom, and glorious liberty, that they should leave that better part of themselves to perish by the hand of the tyrant's whip. But if there were a woman among them so degenerate from love and virtue to choose slavery before the pursuit of her husband, and with the hazard of her life, to share with him in his fortunes, that such an one ought to be abandoned, and left as a prey to the common enemy.

To which they all agreed—and bowed. After this, he spoke of the impassable woods and rivers, and convinced them, the more danger, the more glory. He told

them that he had heard of one Hannibal a great captain, had cut his way through mountains of solid rocks,[1] and should a few shrubs oppose them, which they could fire before them? No, 'twas a trifling excuse to men resolved to die, or overcome. As for bogs, they are with a little labour filled and hardened, and the rivers could be no obstacle, since they swam by nature, at least by custom, from their first hour of their birth. That when the children were weary they must carry them by turns, and the woods and their own industry would afford them food. To this they all assented with joy.

Tuscan then demanded, what he would do? He said, they would travel towards the sea; plant a new colony, and defend it by their valour; and when they could find a ship, either driven by stress of weather, or guided by providence that way, they would seize it, and make it a prize, till it had transported them to their own countries. At least, they should be made free in his kingdom, and be esteemed as his fellow sufferers, and men that had the courage, and the bravery to attempt, at least, for liberty. And if they died in the attempt it would be more brave, than to live in perpetual slavery.

They bowed and kissed his feet at this resolution, and with one accord vowed to follow him to death. And that night was appointed to begin their march; they made it known to their wives, and directed them to tie their hamaca[2] about their shoulder and under their arm like a scarf, and to lead their children that could go,[3] and carry those that could not. The wives who pay an entire obedience to their husbands obeyed, and stayed for them, where they were appointed. The men stayed but to furnish themselves with what defensive arms they could get, and all met at the rendezvous, where Caesar made a new encouraging speech to them, and led them out.

But, as they could not march far that night, on Monday early, when the overseers went to call them all together, to go to work, they were extremely surprised to find not one upon the place, but all fled with what baggage they had. You may imagine this news was not only suddenly spread all over the plantation, but soon

---

[1] *Hannibal … rocks* Hannibal, the commander of the Carthaginians, crossed the Alps in 218 BCE on a mission to invade Rome.

[2] *hamaca* Hammock.

[3] *go* Walk.

reached the neighbouring ones, and we had by noon about six hundred men, they call the militia of the county, that came to assist us in the pursuit of the fugitives. But never did one see so comical an army march forth to war. The men, of any fashion,[1] would not concern themselves, though it were almost the common cause, for such revoltings are very ill examples, and have very fatal consequences oftentimes in many colonies. But they had a respect for Caesar, and all hands were against the Parhamites, as they called those of Parham plantation, because they did not, in the first place, love the Lord Governor, and secondly, they would have it, that Caesar was ill used, and baffled with.[2] And 'tis not impossible but some of the best in the country was of his counsel in this flight, and depriving us of all the slaves, so that they of the better sort would not meddle in the matter. The deputy governor, of whom I have had no great occasion to speak, and who was the most fawning fair-tongued fellow in the world, and one that pretended the most friendship to Caesar, was now the only violent man against him; and though he had nothing, and so need fear nothing, yet talked and looked bigger than any man. He was a fellow whose character is not fit to be mentioned with the worst of the slaves. This fellow would lead his army forth to meet Caesar, or rather to pursue him. Most of their arms were of those sort of cruel whips they call cat with nine tails; some had rusty useless guns for show, others old basket-hilts,[3] whose blades had never seen the light in this age, and others had long staffs, and clubs. Mr. Trefry went along, rather to be a mediator than a conqueror, in such a battle; for he foresaw, and knew, if by fighting they put the Negroes into despair, they were a sort of sullen fellows, that would drown, or kill themselves, before they would yield, and he advised that fair means was best. But Byam[4] was one that abounded in his own wit, and would take his own measures.

It was not hard to find these fugitives, for as they fled they were forced to fire and cut the woods before

them, so that night or day they pursued them by the light they made, and by the path they had cleared. But as soon as Caesar found he was pursued, he put himself in a posture of defence, placing all the women and children in the rear, and himself, with Tuscan by his side, or next to him, all promising to die or conquer. Encouraged thus, they never stood to parley, but fell on pell-mell upon the English, and killed some, and wounded a good many, they having recourse to their whips, as the best of their weapons. And as they observed no order, they perplexed the enemy so sorely, with lashing them in the eyes. And the women and children, seeing their husbands so treated, being of fearful cowardly dispositions, and hearing the English cry out, "Yield and live, yield and be pardoned," they all ran in amongst their husbands and fathers, and hung about them, crying out, "Yield, yield, and leave Caesar to their revenge," that by degrees the slaves abandoned Caesar, and left him only Tuscan and his heroic Imoinda, who, grown big as she was, did nevertheless press near her lord, having a bow, and a quiver full of poisoned arrows, which she managed with such dexterity, that she wounded several, and shot the governor into the shoulder, of which wound he had like to have died, but that an Indian woman, his mistress, sucked the wound, and cleansed it from the venom. But however, he stirred not from the place till he had parleyed with Caesar, who he found was resolved to die fighting, and would not be taken; no more would Tuscan, or Imoinda. But he, more thirsting after revenge of another sort, than that of depriving him of life, now made use of all his art of talking, and dissembling, and besought Caesar to yield himself upon terms, which he himself should propose, and should be sacredly assented to and kept by him. He told him, it was not that he any longer feared him, or could believe the force of two men, and a young heroine, could overcome all them, with all the slaves now on their side also, but it was the vast esteem he had for his person, the desire he had to serve so gallant a man, and to hinder himself from the reproach hereafter, of having been the occasion of the death of a prince, whose valour and magnanimity deserved the empire of the world. He protested to him, he looked upon this action, as gallant and brave, however tending to the prejudice of his lord and master, who would by it

---

[1] *fashion*   Rank.

[2] *baffled with*   Cheated.

[3] *basket-hilts*   Old-fashioned swords with basket-shaped guards on their hilts.

[4] *Byam*   William Byam, deputy governor of Surinam under Lord Willoughby.

have lost so considerable a number of slaves, that this flight of his should be looked on as a heat of youth, and rashness of a too forward courage, and an unconsidered impatience of liberty, and no more; and that he laboured in vain to accomplish that which they would effectually perform, as soon as any ship arrived that would touch on his coast. "So that if you will be pleased," continued he, "to surrender yourself, all imaginable respect shall be paid you; and yourself, your wife, and child, if it be here born, shall depart free out of our land." But Caesar would hear of no composition, though Byam urged, if he pursued, and went on in his design, he would inevitably perish, either by great snakes, wild beasts, or hunger, and he ought to have regard to his wife, whose condition required ease, and not the fatigues of tedious travel, where she could not be secured from being devoured. But Caesar told him, there was no faith in the white men, or the gods they adored, who instructed them in principles so false, that honest men could not live amongst them; though no people professed so much, none performed so little; that he knew what he had to do, when he dealt with men of honour, but with them a man ought to be eternally on his guard, and never to eat and drink with Christians without his weapon of defence in his hand, and, for his own security, never to credit one word they spoke. As for the rashness and inconsiderateness of his action he would confess the governor is in the right, and that he was ashamed of what he had done, in endeavouring to make those free, who were by nature slaves, poor wretched rogues, fit to be used as Christians' tools; dogs, treacherous and cowardly, fit for such masters, and they wanted only but to be whipped into the knowledge of the Christian gods to be the vilest of all creeping things, to learn to worship such deities as had not power to make them just, brave, or honest. In fine, after a thousand things of this nature, not fit here to be recited, he told Byam, he had rather die than live upon the same earth with such dogs. But Trefry and Byam pleaded and protested together so much, that Trefry believing the governor to mean what he said, and speaking very cordially himself, generously put himself into Caesar's hands, and took him aside, and persuaded him, even with tears, to live, by surrendering himself, and to name his conditions. Caesar was overcome by his wit and

reasons, and in consideration of Imoinda, and demanding what he desired, and that it should be ratified by their hands in writing, because he had perceived that was the common way of contract between man and man, amongst the whites. All this was performed, and Tuscan's pardon was put in, and they surrender to the governor, who walked peaceably down into the plantation with them, after giving order to bury their dead. Caesar was very much toiled with the bustle of the day, for he had fought like a Fury,[1] and what mischief was done he and Tuscan performed alone, and gave their enemies a fatal proof that they durst do anything, and feared no mortal force.

But they were no sooner arrived at the place, where all the slaves receive their punishments of whipping, but they laid hands on Caesar and Tuscan, faint with heat and toil; and, surprising them, bound them to two several stakes, and whipped them in a most deplorable and inhumane manner, rending the very flesh from their bones, especially Caesar, who was not perceived to make any moan, or to alter his face, only to roll his eyes on the faithless governor, and those he believed guilty, with fierceness and indignation. And, to complete his rage, he saw every one of those slaves, who, but a few days before, adored him as something more than mortal, now had a whip to give him some lashes, while he strove not to break his fetters, though, if he had, it were impossible. But he pronounced a woe and revenge from his eyes, that darted fire, that 'twas at once both awful and terrible to behold.

When they thought they were sufficiently revenged on him, they untied him, almost fainting with loss of blood, from a thousand wounds all over his body, from which they had rent his clothes, and led him bleeding and naked as he was, and loaded him all over with irons, and then rubbed his wounds, to complete their cruelty, with Indian pepper, which had like to have made him raving mad, and, in this condition, made him so fast to the ground that he could not stir, if his pains and wounds would have given him leave. They spared Imoinda, and did not let her see this barbarity committed towards her lord, but carried her down to Parham, and shut her up, which was not in kindness to her, but

---

[1] *Fury* One of the three Greek, and later Roman, avenging deities, who were terrifying in their aspects and behavior.

for fear she should die with the sight, or miscarry, and then they should lose a young slave, and perhaps the mother.

You must know, that when the news was brought on Monday morning, that Caesar had betaken himself to the woods, and carried with him all the Negroes, we were possessed with extreme fear, which no persuasions could dissipate, that he would secure himself till night, and then, that he would come down and cut all our throats. This apprehension made all the females of us fly down the river, to be secured, and while we were away, they acted this cruelty. For I suppose I had authority and interest enough there, had I suspected any such thing, to have prevented it, but we had not gone many leagues, but the news overtook us that Caesar was taken, and whipped like a common slave. We met on the river with Colonel Martin, a man of great gallantry, wit, and goodness, and, whom I have celebrated in a character of my new comedy,[1] by his own name, in memory of so brave a man. He was wise and eloquent, and, from the fineness of his parts, bore a great sway over the hearts of all the colony. He was a friend to Caesar, and resented this false dealing with him very much. We carried him back to Parham, thinking to have made an accommodation; when we came, the first news we heard was, that the governor was dead of a wound Imoinda had given him, but it was not so well. But it seems he would have the pleasure of beholding the revenge he took on Caesar, and before the cruel ceremony was finished, he dropped down, and then they perceived the wound he had on his shoulder was by a venomed arrow, which, as I said, his Indian mistress healed, by sucking the wound.

We were no sooner arrived, but we went up to the plantation to see Caesar, whom we found in a very miserable and inexpressible condition, and I have a thousand times admired how he lived, in so much tormenting pain. We said all things to him, that trouble, pity, and good nature could suggest, protesting our innocence of the fact, and our abhorrence of such cruelties, making a thousand professions of services to him, and begging as many pardons for the offenders, till we said so much, that he believed we had no hand in his ill treatment, but told us, he could never pardon Byam.

As for Trefry, he confessed he saw his grief and sorrow, for his suffering, which he could not hinder, but was like to have been beaten down by the very slaves, for speaking in his defence. But for Byam, who was their leader, their head—and should, by his justice, and honour, have been an example to them—for him, he wished to live, to take a dire revenge of him, and said, "It had been well for him, if he had sacrificed me, instead of giving me the contemptible whip." He refused to talk much, but begging us to give him our hands, he took them, and protested never to lift up his, to do us any harm. He had a great respect for Colonel Martin, and always took his counsel, like that of a parent, and assured him, he would obey him in anything, but his revenge on Byam. "Therefore," said he, "for his own safety, let him speedily dispatch me, for if I could dispatch myself, I would not, till that justice were done to my injured person, and the contempt of a soldier. No, I would not kill myself, even after a whipping, but will be content to live with that infamy, and be pointed at by every grinning slave, till I have completed my revenge; and then you shall see that Oroonoko scorns to live with the indignity that was put on Caesar." All we could do could get no more words from him, and we took care to have him put immediately into a healing bath, to rid him of his pepper, and ordered a chirurgeon[2] to anoint him with healing balm, which he suffered, and in some time he began to be able to walk and eat. We failed not to visit him every day, and, to that end, had him brought to an apartment at Parham.

The governor was no sooner recovered, and had heard of the menaces of Caesar, but he called his council, who (not to disgrace them, or burlesque the government there) consisted of such notorious villains as Newgate never transported,[3] and possibly originally were such, who understood neither the laws of God or man, and had no sort of principles to make them worthy the name of men. But, at the very council table, would contradict and fight with one another, and swear so bloodily that 'twas terrible to hear, and see them. (Some of them were afterwards hanged, when the Dutch took

---

[1] *character of my new comedy* George Marteen, in *The Younger Brother, or the Amorous Jilt* (1696).

[2] *chirurgeon* Surgeon.

[3] *Newgate ... transported* London prison from which criminals were sometimes shipped out to the colonies.

possession of the place; others sent off in chains.) But calling these special rulers of the nation together, and requiring their counsel in this weighty affair, they all concluded, that (damn them) it might be their own cases, and that Caesar ought to be made an example to all the Negroes, to fright them from daring to threaten their betters, their lords and masters, and, at this rate, no man was safe from his own slaves, and concluded, *nemine contradicente*,[1] that Caesar should be hanged.

Trefry then thought it time to use his authority, and told Byam his command did not extend to his lord's plantation, and that Parham was as much exempt from the law as Whitehall;[2] and that they ought no more to touch the servants of the lord—(who there represented the King's person) than they could those about the King himself; and that Parham was a sanctuary, and though his lord were absent in person, his power was still in being there, which he had entrusted with him, as far as the dominions of his particular plantations reached, and all that belonged to it; the rest of the country, as Byam was lieutenant to his lord, he might exercise his tyranny upon. Trefry had others as powerful, or more, that interested themselves in Caesar's life, and absolutely said, he should be defended. So turning the governor, and his wise council, out of doors (for they sat at Parham House) we set a guard upon our landing place, and would admit none but those we called friends to us and Caesar.

The governor having remained wounded at Parham, till his recovery was completed, Caesar did not know but he was still there, and indeed, for the most part, his time was spent there, for he was one that loved to live at other people's expense, and if he were a day absent, he was then present there, and used to play, and walk, and hunt, and fish, with Caesar. So that Caesar did not at all doubt, if he once recovered strength, but he should find an opportunity of being revenged on him. Though, after such a revenge, he could not hope to live, for if he escaped the fury of the English mobile,[3] who perhaps would have been glad of the occasion to have killed him, he was resolved not to survive his whipping, yet he had, some tender hours, a repenting softness, which he called

his fits of coward, wherein he struggled with love for the victory of his heart, which took part with his charming Imoinda there, but, for the most part, his time was passed in melancholy thought, and black designs. He considered, if he should do this deed, and die either in the attempt, or after it, he left his lovely Imoinda a prey, or at best a slave, to the enraged multitude; his great heart could not endure that thought. "Perhaps," said he, "she may be first ravished by every brute, exposed first to their nasty lusts, and then a shameful death." No, he could not live a moment under that apprehension, too insupportable to be borne. These were his thoughts, and his silent arguments with his heart, as he told us afterwards, so that now resolving not only to kill Byam, but all those he thought had enraged him, pleasing his great heart with the fancied slaughter he should make over the whole face of the plantation. He first resolved on a deed, that (however horrid it at first appeared to us all) when we had heard his reasons, we thought it brave and just. Being able to walk, and, as he believed, fit for the execution of his great design, he begged Trefry to trust him into the air, believing a walk would do him good, which was granted him, and taking Imoinda with him, as he used to do in his more happy and calmer days, he led her up into a wood, where, after (with a thousand sighs, and long gazing silently on her face, while tears gushed, in spite of him, from his eyes), he told her his design first of killing her, and then his enemies, and next himself, and the impossibility of escaping, and therefore he told her the necessity of dying. He found the heroic wife faster pleading for death than he was to propose it, when she found his fixed resolution, and, on her knees, besought him, not to leave her a prey to his enemies. He (grieved to death) yet pleased at her noble resolution, took her up, and embracing her, with all the passion and languishment of a dying lover, drew his knife to kill this treasure of his soul, this pleasure of his eyes. While tears trickled down his cheeks, hers were smiling with joy she should die by so noble a hand, and be sent in her own country (for that's their notion of the next world) by him she so tenderly loved, and so truly adored in this, for wives have a respect for their husbands equal to what any other people pay a deity, and when a man finds any occasion to quit his wife, if he love her, she dies by his hand, if not, he sells her, or

---

[1] *nemine contradicente* Latin: unanimously.

[2] *Whitehall* Whitehall Palace, then the king's residence in London.

[3] *mobile* Populace.

suffers some other to kill her. It being thus, you may believe the deed was soon resolved on, and 'tis not to be doubted, but the parting, the eternal leave-taking of two such lovers, so greatly born, so sensible,[1] so beautiful, so young, and so fond, must be very moving, as the relation of it was to me afterwards.

All that love could say in such cases, being ended, and all the intermitting irresolutions being adjusted, the lovely, young, and adored victim lays herself down, before the sacrificer, while he, with a hand resolved, and a heart breaking within, gave the fatal stroke, first, cutting her throat, and then severing her, yet smiling, face from that delicate body, pregnant as it was with fruits of tenderest love. As soon as he had done, he laid the body decently on leaves and flowers, of which he made a bed, and concealed it under the same coverlid of nature, only her face he left yet bare to look on. But when he found she was dead, and past all retrieve, never more to bless him with her eyes, and soft language, his grief swelled up to rage; he tore, he raved, he roared, like some monster of the wood, calling on the loved name of Imoinda. A thousand times he turned the fatal knife that did the deed, toward his own heart, with a resolution to go immediately after her, but dire revenge, which now was a thousand times more fierce in his soul than before, prevents him, and he would cry out, "No, since I have sacrificed Imoinda to my revenge, shall I lose that glory which I have purchased so dear, as at the price of the fairest, dearest, softest creature that ever nature made? No, no!" Then, at her name, grief would get the ascendant of rage, and he would lie down by her side, and water her face with showers of tears, which never were wont to fall from those eyes. And however bent he was on his intended slaughter, he had not power to stir from the sight of this dear object, now more beloved, and more adored than ever.

He remained in this deploring condition for two days, and never rose from the ground where he had made his sad sacrifice. At last, rousing from her side, and accusing himself with living too long, now Imoinda was dead, and that the deaths of those barbarous enemies were deferred too long, he resolved now to finish the great work; but offering to rise, he found his strength so decayed, that he reeled to and fro, like boughs assailed by contrary winds, so that he was forced to lie down again, and try to summon all his courage to his aid. He found his brains turn round, and his eyes were dizzy, and objects appeared not the same to him as they were wont to do; his breath was short, and all his limbs surprised with a faintness he had never felt before. He had not eaten in two days, which was one occasion of this feebleness, but excess of grief was the greatest; yet still he hoped he should recover vigour to act his design, and lay expecting it yet six days longer, still mourning over the dead idol of his heart, and striving every day to rise, but could not.

In all this time you may believe we were in no little affliction for Caesar, and his wife. Some were of opinion he was escaped never to return; others thought some accident had happened to him. But however, we failed not to send out a hundred people several ways to search for him. A party, of about forty, went that way he took, among whom was Tuscan, who was perfectly reconciled to Byam. They had not gone very far into the wood, but they smelt an unusual smell, as of a dead body, for stinks must be very noisome that can be distinguished among such a quantity of natural sweets, as every inch of that land produces. So that they concluded they should find him dead, or somebody that was so. They passed on towards it, as loathsome as it was, and made such a rustling among the leaves that lie thick on the ground, by continual falling, that Caesar heard he was approached, and though he had, during the space of these eight days, endeavoured to rise, but found he wanted strength, yet looking up, and seeing his pursuers, he rose, and reeled to a neighbouring tree, against which he fixed his back. And being within a dozen yards of those that advanced, and saw him, he called out to them, and bid them approach no nearer, if they would be safe, so that they stood still, and hardly believing their eyes, that would persuade them that it was Caesar that spoke to them, so much was he altered. They asked him, what he had done with his wife, for they smelt a stink that almost struck them dead. He, pointing to the dead body, sighing, cried, "Behold her there."

They put off the flowers that covered her with their sticks, and found she was killed, and cried out, "Oh monster! that hast murdered thy wife." Then asking him, why he did so cruel a deed.

---

[1] *sensible* Sensitive.

He replied, he had no leisure to answer impertinent questions. "You may go back," continued he, "and tell the faithless governor, he may thank fortune that I am breathing my last, and that my arm is too feeble to obey my heart, in what it had designed him." But his tongue faltering, and trembling, he could scarce end what he was saying.

The English taking advantage by his weakness, cried, "Let us take him alive by all means."

He heard them; and, as if he had revived from a fainting, or a dream, he cried out, "No, gentlemen, you are deceived, you will find no more Caesars to be whipped, no more find a faith in me. Feeble as you think me, I have strength yet left to secure me from a second indignity." They swore all anew, and he only shook his head, and beheld them with scorn.

Then they cried out, "Who will venture on this single man? Will nobody?"

They stood all silent while Caesar replied, "Fatal will be the attempt to the first adventurer, let him assure himself," and, at that word, held up his knife in a menacing posture. "Look ye, ye faithless crew," said he, "'tis not life I seek, nor am I afraid of dying," and, at that word, cut a piece of flesh from his own throat, and threw it at them, "yet still I would live if I could, till I had perfected my revenge. But oh! it cannot be. I feel life gliding from my eyes and heart, and, if I make not haste, I shall yet fall a victim to the shameful whip." At that, he ripped up his own belly, and took his bowels and pulled them out, with what strength he could, while some, on their knees imploring, besought him to hold his hand.

But when they saw him tottering, they cried out, "Will none venture on him?"

A bold English cried, "Yes, if he were the devil" (taking courage when he saw him almost dead) and swearing a horrid oath for his farewell to the world he rushed on. Caesar with his armed hand met him so fairly, as stuck him to the heart, and he fell dead at his feet.

Tuscan seeing that, cried out, "I love thee, oh Caesar, and therefore will not let thee die, if possible." And, running to him, took him in his arms, but, at the same time, warding a blow that Caesar made at his bosom, he received it quite through his arm, and Caesar having not the strength to pluck the knife forth, though

he attempted it, Tuscan neither pulled it out himself, nor suffered it to be pulled out, but came down with it sticking in his arm, and the reason he gave for it was, because the air should not get into the wound. They put their hands across, and carried Caesar between six of them, fainted as he was, and they thought dead, or just dying, and they brought him to Parham, and laid him on a couch, and had the chirurgeon immediately to him, who dressed his wounds, and sewed up his belly, and used means to bring him to life, which they effected. We ran all to see him; and, if before we thought him so beautiful a sight, he was now so altered, that his face was like a death's head blacked over, nothing but teeth, and eyeholes. For some days we suffered nobody to speak to him, but caused cordials to be poured down his throat, which sustained his life, and in six or seven days he recovered his senses. For, you must know, that wounds are almost to a miracle cured in the Indies, unless wounds in the legs, which rarely ever cure.

When he was well enough to speak, we talked to him, and asked him some questions about his wife, and the reasons why he killed her. And he then told us what I have related of that resolution, and of his parting, and he besought us, we would let him die, and was extremely afflicted to think it was possible he might live. He assured us, if we did not despatch him, he would prove very fatal to a great many. We said all we could to make him live, and gave him new assurances, but he begged we would not think so poorly of him, or of his love to Imoinda, to imagine we could flatter him to life again; but the chirurgeon assured him, he could not live, and therefore he need not fear. We were all (but Caesar) afflicted at this news; and the sight was gashly.[1] His discourse was sad; and the earthly smell about him so strong, that I was persuaded to leave the place for some time (being myself but sickly, and very apt to fall into fits of dangerous illness upon any extraordinary melancholy). The servants, and Trefry, and the chirurgeons, promised all to take what possible care they could of the life of Caesar, and I, taking boat, went with other company to Colonel Martin's, about three days' journey down the river, but I was no sooner gone, but the governor taking Trefry, about some pretended earnest business, a day's journey up the river, having communi-

---

[1] *gashly* Ghastly.

cated his design to one Banister,[1] a wild Irishman, and one of the council, a fellow of absolute barbarity, and fit to execute any villainy, but was rich. He came up to Parham, and forcibly took Caesar, and had him carried to the same post where he was whipped, and causing him to be tied to it, and a great fire made before him, he told him, he should die like a dog, as he was. Caesar replied, this was the first piece of bravery that ever Banister did, and he never spoke sense till he pronounced that word, and, if he would keep it, he would declare, in the other world, that he was the only man, of all the whites, that ever he heard speak truth. And turning to the men that bound him, he said, "My friends, am I to die, or to be whipped?"

And they cried, "Whipped! no; you shall not escape so well."

And then he replied, smiling, "A blessing on thee," and assured them, they need not tie him, for he would stand fixed, like a rock, and endure death so as should encourage them to die. "But if you whip me," said he, "be sure you tie me fast."

He had learned to take tobacco, and when he was assured he should die, he desired they would give him a pipe in his mouth, ready lighted, which they did, and the executioner came, and first cut off his members, and threw them into the fire. After that, with an ill-favoured knife, they cut his ears, and his nose, and burned them; he still smoked on, as if nothing had touched him. Then they hacked off one of his arms, and still he bore up, and held his pipe. But at the cutting off the other arm, his head sunk, and his pipe dropped, and he gave up the ghost, without a groan, or a reproach. My mother and sister were by him all the while, but not suffered to save him, so rude and wild were the rabble, and so inhuman were the justices, who stood by to see the execution, who after paid dearly enough for their insolence. They cut Caesar in quarters, and sent them to several of the chief plantations. One quarter was sent to Colonel Martin, who refused it, and swore, he had rather see the quarters of Banister, and the governor himself, than those of Caesar, on his plantations, and that he could govern his Negroes without terrifying and grieving them with frightful spectacles of a mangled king.

Thus died this great man, worthy of a better fate, and a more sublime wit than mine to write his praise. Yet, I hope, the reputation of my pen is considerable enough to make his glorious name to survive to all ages, with that of the brave, the beautiful, and the constant Imoinda.

—1688

---

[1] *Banister*   Major James Banister, who succeeded Byam as deputy governor of Surinam.

WILLIAM WYCHERLEY
1641 – 1716

Though he produced only four plays, William Wycherley is recognized as one of the leading playwrights of the Restoration period. Wycherley was born in Clive, near Shrewsbury, England, into a privileged family; his father was Daniel Wycherley, High Steward in the household of John Paulet, marquess of Winchester, at Basing House in Hampshire. Wycherley's father was a Royalist, and he sent Wycherley to France to be educated. While in France, Wycherley converted from Protestantism to Catholicism under the influence of his mentors, Madame and Marquis de Montausier. It was a theological shift of a sort that he was to make a number of times throughout his life, often changing his religion in order to suit his environment.

Wycherley's father brought him back to England in 1659, not long before the Restoration of Charles II, and enrolled him in Queen's College at Oxford University. For this he had to become a

Protestant again. He left Oxford very quickly, without graduating, and began to study law. However, his attentions were focused less on work than on the court of Charles II, the new monarch, where his status as an eligible bachelor quickly made him a court favorite. Wycherley soon gave up on the law; he joined the navy, and went off to fight the Dutch. Through his favor with the court, he quickly became a Captain, but he resigned his commission within a week, turning to playwriting instead. Between 1671 and 1677, he published four plays: *Love in a Wood, or St. James's Park* (1671), a farce that takes place largely in the dark; *The Gentleman Dancing-Master* (1672), a comedy depicting a resourceful fourteen-year-old who deceives her father in order to marry the man she loves; *The Country Wife* (1675); and *The Plain Dealer* (1676), an adaptation of Molière's *Le Misanthrope* that centers on a man who prides himself on his inability to tell a lie.

The Country Wife, Wycherley's best-known work, is a witty, ribald portrait of the London society in which he lived. It was first produced by the King's Company and performed at Drury Lane's Theatre Royal, likely on 12 January 1675. The play features broadly drawn characters and a plot full of misunderstandings, secrets, and *double entendres*, all elements that were typical of Restoration comedies. It was considered so bawdy that from the mid-eighteenth century it ceased to be performed in its original form. The famous actor David Garrick gutted the play of its sexual content and produced a tamer version called *The Country Girl* in 1766. The original text was not produced again on the English stage until 1924.

In the late 1670s Wycherley turned away from the stage and was engaged by Charles II as royal tutor. He was to be paid very well to teach the King's illegitimate son, James Scott (later Earl of Monmouth), and then offered a life-long pension once his services were no longer needed. However, his favor with the court ended abruptly in 1680 with his disastrous marriage to Laetitia-Isabella, the recent widow of the Earl of Drogheda. He had entered into this marriage as a means of paying off his sizeable debts; Laetitia-Isabella was a wealthy heiress. But his plan backfired badly. He had intended to keep his marriage to Laetitia-Isabella a secret; as a tutor he was an entirely unsuitable match for a woman of the nobility, and for such a gentleman to marry such an heiress against her family's wishes was seen as tantamount to robbery. Unfortunately for her, word of Wycherley's transgression quickly got out, and he was banished from the court of Charles II and from his position as royal tutor. The marriage itself was also a failure, but after one very unhappy year Isabella suddenly died in 1681. Her estate became tied up in litigation; Wycherley received nothing but her debts, and in 1682 was imprisoned as a debtor.

Wycherley's fortunes turned again when James II ascended the throne in 1685. The new monarch took a liking to the former playwright, believing that he had modeled the character of Manly in *The Plain Dealer* on him. Flattered, he had Wycherley released from debtors' prison, paid him a pension of £200 per year, and offered to settle all his debts. In gratitude to the King, who was deeply Catholic, Wycherley re-converted. Unfortunately, he felt too embarrassed to reveal the total amount of his debt to the King, and thus continued to owe money after his release from prison. During these years, Wycherley wrote no plays; he did write a number of poems, none of which are considered to be of the same caliber as his dramatic works. He also struck up an association with the young Alexander Pope, who revised and edited his poems.

Toward the end of his life, Wycherley married a young girl, Elizabeth Jackson, in order to keep his estate out of the hands of his nephew and sole heir, who he felt had treated him badly. He was married to her for eleven days before his death at age 76 on 31 December 1716. He was buried in St. Paul's Church, Covent Garden, London.

⌘ ⌘ ⌘

The Country Wife

PROLOGUE

Spoken by Mr. Hart[1]

Poets, like cudgeled bullies, never do
   At first or second blow submit to you
But will provoke you still, and ne'er have done,
Till you are weary first with laying on.
5 The late so baffled scribbler of this day,
Though he stands trembling, bids me boldly say
What we before most plays are used to do;
For poets out of fear first draw on you,
In a fierce prologue the still pit[2] defy,
10 And, ere you speak, like Kastrill[3] give the lie.[4]

15 But though our Bayes's[5] battles oft I've fought,
And with bruised knuckles their dear conquest bought;
Nay, never yet feared odds upon the stage,
In prologue dare not hector with the age,
But would take quarter from your saving hands,
Though Bayes within all yielding countermands,
Says you confed'rate wits no quarter give,
Therefore his play shan't ask your leave to live.
Well, let the vain, rash fop, by huffing so,
20 Think to obtain the better terms of you;
But we, the actors, humbly will submit,
Now, and at any time, to a full pit;
Nay, often we anticipate your rage,
And murder poets for you on our stage;
25 We set no guards upon our tiring room,[6]
But when with flying colors[7] there you come,
We patiently, you see, give up to you
Our poets, virgins, nay, our matrons too.

---

[1] *Mr. Hart*   Charles Hart (d. 1683), actor, the first to play Mr. Horner.

[2] *pit*   Fashionable men—"gallants" and "beaux"—sat in the pit and set themselves up as hard-to-please critics.

[3] *Kastrill*   Character in Ben Jonson's *The Alchemist*.

[4] *give the lie*   Accuse a person of lying, to his or her face.

[5] *Bayes's*   Playwright's (i.e., Wycherley's). This is the name of the playwright-character mocked in the Duke of Buckingham's *The Rehearsal*.

[6] *tiring room*   Dressing room.

[7] *with flying colors*   I.e., like a besieging army, with flags or ensigns held aloft.

DRAMATIS PERSONAE

[MEN]
    Mr. Horner
    Mr. Harcourt
    Mr. Dorilant
    Mr. Pinchwife
    Mr. Sparkish
    Sir Jaspar Fidget
    A boy
    [Dr.] Quack
    [Clasp, a bookseller]
    [A parson]
    Waiters, servants, and attendants
[WOMEN]
    Mrs. Margery Pinchwife
    Mrs.[1] Alithea
    My Lady Fidget
    Mrs. Dainty Fidget
    Mrs. Squeamish
    Old Lady Squeamish
    Lucy, Alithea's maid

THE SCENE: LONDON.

Indignor quicquam reprehendi, non quia crasse
Compositum illepideve putetur, sed quia nuper,
Nec veniam antiquis, sed honorem et praemia posci.[2]
Horat.

ACT 1, SCENE 1. [Horner's lodging.]

(*Enter Horner and Quack following him at a distance.*)

HORNER. (Aside.) A quack is as fit for a pimp as a midwife for a bawd; they are still but in their way both helpers of nature.—Well my dear doctor, hast thou done what I desired?

QUACK. I have undone you forever with the women and reported you throughout the whole Town[3] as bad as an eunuch with as much trouble as if I had made you one in earnest.

HORNER. But have you told all the midwives you know, the orange wenches[4] at the playhouses, the City husbands, and old fumbling keepers[5] of this end of the Town? For they'll be the readiest to report it.

QUACK. I have told all the chambermaids, waiting women, tirewomen,[6] and old women of my acquaintance, nay, and whispered it as a secret to 'em and to the whisperers of Whitehall,[7] so that you need not doubt 'twill spread, and you will be as odious to the handsome young women as—

HORNER. As the small pox. Well—

QUACK. And to the married women of this end of the Town as—

HORNER. As the great ones,[8] nay, as their own husbands.

QUACK. And to the City dames as Aniseed Robin[9] of filthy and contemptible memory, and they will frighten their children with your name, especially their females.

HORNER. And cry, "Horner's coming to carry you away!" I am only afraid 'twill not be believed. You told 'em 'twas by an English-French disaster and an English-French chirurgeon,[10] who has given me at once, not only a cure, but an antidote for the future against that damned malady and that worse distemper, love, and all other women's evils.

QUACK. Your late journey into France has made it the more credible, and your being here a fortnight before you appeared in public looks as if you apprehended the shame, which I wonder you do not. Well, I have been

1   *Mrs.* "Mistress," used for both married and unmarried women.

2   *Indignor … posci* Latin: I am impatient that any work is censured, not because it is thought to be coarse or inelegant in style, but because it is modern, and that what is claimed for the ancients should be, not indulgence, but honor and rewards (Horace, *Epistles* 2.1.76-78).

3   *Town* The fashionable world; London.

4   *orange wenches* Women who sold oranges at the playhouses, and who were often prostitutes as well.

5   *keepers* Men who kept mistresses.

6   *tirewomen* Ladies' maids in charge of attire.

7   *Whitehall* English royal palace and the area around it in Westminster.

8   *the great ones* Great (or French) pox; i.e., syphilis.

9   *Aniseed Robin* Notorious hermaphrodite.

10 *English-French disaster … English-French chirurgeon* French pox caught by an Englishman, treated by an English doctor practicing in France.

hired by young gallants to belie 'em t'other way, but you are the first would be thought a man unfit for women.

40 HORNER. Dear Mr. Doctor, let vain rogues be contented only to be thought abler men than they are; generally 'tis all the pleasure they have, but mine lies another way.

QUACK. You take, methinks, a very preposterous way to
45 it and as ridiculous as if we operators in physic should put forth bills to disparage our medicaments with hopes to gain customers.

HORNER. Doctor, there are quacks in love as well as physic who get but the fewer and worse patients for
50 their boasting; a good name is seldom got by giving it one's self, and women no more than honor are compassed by bragging. Come, come, doctor, the wisest lawyer never discovers[1] the merits of his cause till the trial; the wealthiest man conceals his riches, and the
55 cunning gamester his play; shy husbands and keepers, like old rooks,[2] are not to be cheated but by a new unpracticed trick: false friendship will pass now no more than false dice upon 'em, no, not in the City.

(*Enter boy.*)

BOY. There are two ladies and a gentleman coming up.
60 HORNER. A pox! some unbelieving sisters of my former acquaintance, who, I am afraid, expect their sense should be satisfied of the falsity of the report.

(*Enter Sir Jaspar Fidget, Lady Fidget, and Dainty.*)

No—this formal fool and women!
QUACK. His wife and sister.
65 SIR JASPAR. My coach breaking just now before your door, sir, I look upon as an occasional[3] reprimand to me, sir, for not kissing your hands, sir, since your coming out of France, sir, and so my disaster, sir, has been my good fortune, sir, and this is my wife and sister,
70 sir.
HORNER. What then, sir?

SIR JASPAR. My lady and sister, sir.—Wife, this is Master Horner.
LADY FIDGET. Master Horner, husband!
75 SIR JASPAR. My lady, my Lady Fidget, sir.
HORNER. So, sir.
SIR JASPAR. Won't you be acquainted with her, sir? (*Aside.*) So the report is true, I find by his coldness or aversion to the sex, but I'll play the wag with him.—
80 Pray salute[4] my wife, my lady, sir.
HORNER. I will kiss no man's wife, sir, for him, sir; I have taken my eternal leave, sir, of the sex already, sir.
SIR JASPAR. (*Aside.*) Ha, ha, ha, I'll plague him yet.—Not know my wife, sir?
85 HORNER. I do know your wife, sir: she's a woman, sir, and consequently a monster, sir, a greater monster than a husband, sir.
SIR JASPAR. A husband! How, sir?
HORNER. (*Makes horns.*[5]) So, sir. But I make no more
90 cuckolds, sir.
SIR JASPAR. Ha, ha, ha, Mercury, Mercury.[6]
LADY FIDGET. Pray Sir Jaspar, let us be gone from this rude fellow.
DAINTY. Who, by his breeding, would think he had ever
95 been in France?
LADY FIDGET. Faugh, he's but too much a French fellow, such as hate women of quality and virtue for their love to their husbands, Sir Jaspar; a woman is hated by 'em as much for loving her husband as for
100 loving their money. But pray, let's be gone.
HORNER. You do well, madam, for I have nothing that you came for. I have brought over not so much as a bawdy picture, new postures,[7] nor the second part of the *École des filles*,[8] nor—
105 QUACK. (*Apart to Horner.*) Hold for shame, sir. What d'ye mean? You'll ruin yourself forever with the sex.

---

[4] *salute* To greet with a kiss.

[5] *horns* Sign of a cuckold, a man whose wife is having an affair.

[6] *Mercury* God associated with wit (who wears a hat with wings resembling cuckold's horns); also, substance used to treat venereal disease.

[7] *new postures* Cf. *The Sixteen Postures*, by Giuliano Romano (1492–1546), drawings of sixteen sexual positions accompanied by sonnets by Pietro Aretino (1492–1556).

[8] *École des filles* Notoriously bawdy dialogues by Michel Millot (1655); the "second part," like the "new postures," was nonexistent.

---

[1] *discovers* Reveals.

[2] *rooks* Cheaters.

[3] *occasional* Timely; arising from the occasion.

SIR JASPAR.   Ha, ha, ha, he hates women perfectly, I find.

DAINTY.   What pity 'tis he should.

LADY FIDGET.   Aye, he's a base rude fellow for it, but
110 affectation makes not a woman more odious to them
than virtue.

HORNER.   Because your virtue is your greatest affectation, madam.

LADY FIDGET.   How, you saucy fellow, would you
115 wrong my honor?

HORNER.   If I could.

LADY FIDGET.   How d'ye mean, sir?

SIR JASPAR.   Ha, ha, ha, no, he can't wrong your ladyship's honor, upon my honor; he, poor man—hark you
120 in your ear—a mere eunuch.

LADY FIDGET.   Oh filthy French beast! Faugh, faugh!
Why do we stay? Let's be gone; I can't endure the sight
of him.

SIR JASPAR.   Stay but till the chairs¹ come; they'll be here
125 presently.

LADY FIDGET.   No, no.

SIR JASPAR.   Nor can I stay longer: 'tis—let me see, a
quarter and a half quarter of a minute past eleven; the
Council² will be sat; I must away. Business must be
130 preferred always before love and ceremony with the
wise, Mr. Horner.

HORNER.   And the impotent, Sir Jaspar.

SIR JASPAR.   Aye, aye, the impotent Master Horner, ha,
ha, ha!

135 LADY FIDGET.   What, leave us with a filthy man alone in
his lodgings?

SIR JASPAR.   He's an innocent man now, you know. Pray
stay, I'll hasten the chairs to you.—Mr. Horner, your
servant. I should be glad to see you at my house. Pray,
140 come and dine with me and play at cards with my wife
after dinner; you are fit for women at that game yet, ha,
ha! (*Aside.*) 'Tis as much a husband's prudence to
provide innocent diversion for a wife as to hinder her
unlawful pleasures, and he had better employ her than
145 let her employ herself.—Farewell. (*Exit.*)

HORNER.   Your servant, Sir Jaspar.

LADY FIDGET.   I will not stay with him, faugh!

HORNER.   Nay madam, I beseech you stay, if it be but to

see I can be as civil to ladies yet as they would desire.

150 LADY FIDGET.   No, no, faugh, you cannot be civil to
ladies.

DAINTY.   You as civil as ladies would desire!

LADY FIDGET.   No, no, no, faugh, faugh, faugh!

(*Exeunt Lady Fidget and Dainty.*)

QUACK.   Now I think, I, or you yourself rather, have
155 done your business with the women.

HORNER.   Thou art an ass. Don't you see already upon
the report and my carriage, this grave man of business
leaves his wife in my lodgings, invites me to his house
and wife, who before would not be acquainted with me
160 out of jealousy?

QUACK.   Nay, by this means you may be the more
acquainted with the husbands, but the less with the
wives.

HORNER.   Let me alone; if I can but abuse the husbands,
165 I'll soon disabuse the wives. Stay—I'll reckon you up
the advantages I am like to have by my stratagem: first,
I shall be rid of all my old acquaintances, the most
insatiable sorts of duns that invade our lodgings in a
morning. And next to the pleasure of making a new
170 mistress is that of being rid of an old one and of all old
debts: love, when it comes to be so, is paid the most
unwillingly.

QUACK.   Well, you may be so rid of your old acquaintances, but how will you get any new ones?

175 HORNER.   Doctor, thou wilt never make a good
chemist,³ thou art so incredulous and impatient. Ask but
all the young fellows of the Town if they do not lose
more time, like huntsmen, in starting the game than in
running it down; one knows not where to find 'em, who
180 will or will not. Women of quality are so civil, you can
hardly distinguish love from good breeding, and a man
is often mistaken. But now I can be sure, she that shows
an aversion to me loves the sport, as those women that
are gone, whom I warrant to be right. And then the next
185 thing is, your women of honor, as you call 'em, are only
chary of their reputations, not their persons, and 'tis
scandal they would avoid, not men. Now may I have by
the reputation of an eunuch the privileges of one and be

---

¹   *chairs* Sedans, portable chairs borne by chairmen.

²   *Council* Possibly the Common Council, the administrative body
of the City of London.

³   *chemist* Alchemist, who needs both credulity and patience to see
his experiments through.

seen in a lady's chamber in a morning as early as her
190 husband, kiss virgins before their parents or lovers, and
may be, in short, the *passe-partout* of the Town. Now,
doctor.

QUACK. Nay, now you shall be the doctor, and your
process is so new that we do not know but it may
195 succeed.

HORNER. Not so new neither: *probatum est*,[1] doctor.

QUACK. Well, I wish you luck and many patients whilst
I go to mine. (*Exit.*)

(*Enter Harcourt and Dorilant to Horner.*)

HARCOURT. Come, your appearance at the play yester-
200 day has, I hope, hardened you for the future against the
women's contempt and the men's raillery, and now
you'll abroad as you were wont.

HORNER. Did I not bear it bravely?[2]

DORILANT. With a most theatrical impudence, nay,
205 more than the orange wenches show there or a drunken
vizard mask[3] or a great bellied[4] actress, nay, or the most
impudent of creatures, an ill poet, or what is yet more
impudent, a second-hand critic.

HORNER. But what say the ladies? Have they no pity?

210 HARCOURT. What ladies? The vizard masks, you know,
never pity a man when all's gone though in their service.

DORILANT. And for the women in the boxes, you'd
never pity them when 'twas in your power.

HARCOURT. They say 'tis pity, but all that deal with
215 common women should be served so.

DORILANT. Nay I dare swear, they won't admit you to
play at cards with them, go to plays with 'em, or do the
little duties which other shadows of men are wont to do
for 'em.

220 HORNER. Who do you call shadows of men?

DORILANT. Half men.

HORNER. What, boys?

DORILANT. Aye, your old boys, old *beaux garçons*,[5] who
like superannuated stallions are suffered to run, feed,
225 and whinny with the mares as long as they live, though
they can do nothing else.

HORNER. Well, a pox on love and wenching; women
serve but to keep a man from better company. Though
I can't enjoy them, I shall you the more. Good fellow-
230 ship and friendship are lasting, rational, and manly
pleasures.

HARCOURT. For all that, give me some of those pleasures you call effeminate, too; they help to relish one
another.

235 HORNER. They disturb one another.

HARCOURT. No, mistresses are like books: if you pore
upon them too much, they doze you and make you
unfit for company, but if used discreetly, you are the
fitter for conversation[6] by 'em.

240 DORILANT. A mistress should be like a little country
retreat near the Town, not to dwell in constantly but
only for a night and away, to taste the Town the better
when a man returns.

HORNER. I tell you, 'tis as hard to be a good fellow, a
245 good friend, and a lover of women as 'tis to be a good
fellow, a good friend, and a lover of money. You cannot
follow both; then choose your side. Wine gives you
liberty; love takes it away.

DORILANT. Gad, he's in the right on't.

250 HORNER. Wine gives you joy; love, grief and tortures,
besides the chirurgeon's. Wine makes us witty; love,
only sots.[7] Wine makes us sleep; love breaks it.

DORILANT. By the world, he has reason, Harcourt.

HORNER. Wine makes—

255 DORILANT. Aye, wine makes us—makes us princes; love
makes us beggars, poor rogues, egad—and wine—

HORNER. So, there's one converted.—No, no, love and
wine, oil and vinegar.

HARCOURT. I grant it: love will still be uppermost.

260 HORNER. Come, for my part I will have only those
glorious manly pleasures of being very drunk and very
slovenly.

---

[1] *probatum est* Tried and tested (literally, it is approved [Lat.]).

[2] *bravely* Excellently.

[3] *vizard mask* Masked prostitute.

[4] *great bellied* Pregnant.

[5] *beaux garçons* Fops (literally, pretty boys [Fr.]).

[6] *conversation* Social (or sexual) intercourse.

[7] *sots* Fools.

(*Enter boy.*)

BOY. Mr. Sparkish is below, sir.

HARCOURT. What, my dear friend! a rogue that is fond of me only, I think, for abusing him.

DORILANT. No, he can no more think the men laugh at him than that women jilt him, his opinion of himself is so good.

HORNER. Well, there's another pleasure by drinking, I thought not of: I shall lose his acquaintance because he cannot drink, and you know 'tis a very hard thing to be rid of him, for he's one of those nauseous offerers at wit who, like the worst fiddlers, run themselves into all companies.

HARCOURT. One that by being in the company of men of sense would pass for one.

HORNER. And may so to the short-sighted world, as a false jewel amongst true ones is not discerned at a distance; his company is as troublesome to us as a cuckold's when you have a mind to his wife's.

HARCOURT. No, the rogue will not let us enjoy one another, but ravishes our conversation, though he signifies no more to't than Sir Martin Mar-all's[1] gaping and awkward thrumming upon the lute does to his man's voice and music.

DORILANT. And to pass for a wit in Town shows himself a fool every night to us that are guilty of the plot.

HORNER. Such wits as he are, to a company of reasonable men, like rooks to the gamesters, who only fill a room at the table but are so far from contributing to the play that they only serve to spoil the fancy of those that do.

DORILANT. Nay, they are used like rooks, too— snubbed, checked, and abused—yet the rogues will hang on.

HORNER. A pox on 'em and all that force Nature and would be still what she forbids 'em; affectation is her greatest monster.

HARCOURT. Most men are the contraries to that they would seem: your bully, you see, is a coward with a long sword; the little humbly fawning physician with his ebony cane is he that destroys men.

DORILANT. The usurer, a poor rogue possessed of moldy bonds and mortgages, and we they call spend-thrifts are only wealthy who lay out his money upon daily new purchases of pleasure.

HORNER. Aye, your arrantest cheat is your trustee or executor; your jealous man, the greatest cuckold; your churchman, the greatest atheist; and your noisy pert rogue of a wit, the greatest fop, dullest ass, and worst company, as you shall see. For here he comes.

(*Enter Sparkish to them.*)

SPARKISH. How is't, sparks, how is't? Well faith, Harry, I must rally thee a little, ha, ha, ha, upon the report in Town of thee, ha, ha, ha. I can't hold i'faith. Shall I speak?

HORNER. Yes, but you'll be so bitter then.

SPARKISH. Honest Dick and Frank here shall answer for me; I will not be extreme bitter, by the universe.

HARCOURT. We will be bound in ten thousand pound bond, he shall not be bitter at all.

DORILANT. Nor sharp, nor sweet.

HORNER. What, not downright insipid?

SPARKISH. Nay then, since you are so brisk and provoke me, take what follows: you must know, I was discours-ing and rallying with some ladies yesterday, and they happened to talk of the fine new signs in Town.

HORNER. Very fine ladies, I believe.

SPARKISH. Said I, "I know where the best new sign is." "Where?" says one of the ladies. "In Covent Garden,"[2] I replied. Said another, "In what street?" "In Russell Street," answered I. "Lord," says another, "I'm sure there was ne'er a fine new sign there yesterday." "Yes, but there was," said I again, "and it came out of France and has been there a fortnight."

DORILANT. A pox, I can hear no more, prithee.

HORNER. No, hear him out; let him tune his crowd[3] a while.

HARCOURT. The worst music, the greatest preparation.

SPARKISH. Nay faith, I'll make you laugh. "It cannot

---

[1] *Sir Martin Mar-all* Foolish hero of John Dryden's play of that name (1667), who mimes a serenade to his mistress even after his hidden servant has stopped singing and playing his lute.

[2] *Covent Garden* Fashionable residential district that also housed the first theaters of the period.

[3] *crowd* Fiddle.

be," says a third lady. "Yes, yes," quoth I again. Says a fourth lady—

HORNER.   Look to't, we'll have no more ladies.

SPARKISH.   No? Then mark, mark, now. Said I to the
345   fourth, "Did you never see Mr. Horner? He lodges in Russell Street, and he's a sign of a man, you know, since he came out of France." He, ha, he!

HORNER.   But the devil take me if thine be the sign of a jest.

350 SPARKISH.   With that they all fell a-laughing till they bepissed themselves. What, but it does not move you, me-thinks? Well, I see one had as good go to law without a witness as break a jest without a laugher on one's side.—Come, come, sparks, but where do we
355   dine? I have left at Whitehall an earl to dine with you.

DORILANT.   Why, I thought thou hadst loved a man with a title better than a suit with a French trimming to't.

HARCOURT.   Go, to him again.

360 SPARKISH.   No sir, a wit to me is the greatest title in the world.

HORNER.   But go dine with your earl, sir; he may be exceptious.[1] We are your friends and will not take it ill to be left, I do assure you.

365 HARCOURT.   Nay, faith he shall go to him.

SPARKISH.   Nay, pray gentlemen.

DORILANT.   We'll thrust you out if you wonnot. What, disappoint anybody for us?

SPARKISH.   Nay, dear gentlemen, hear me.

370 HORNER.   No, no, sir, by no means; pray go, sir.

SPARKISH.   Why, dear rogues—

DORILANT.   No, no.

(They all thrust him out of the room.)

ALL.   Ha, ha, ha.

(Sparkish returns.)

SPARKISH.   But sparks, pray hear me. What, d'ye think
375   I'll eat then with gay shallow fops and silent coxcombs? I think wit as necessary at dinner as a glass of good wine, and that's the reason I never have any stomach when I eat alone. Come, but where do we dine?

---

[1]   *exceptious*   Likely to take offense.

HORNER.   Ev'n where you will.

380 SPARKISH.   At Chateline's.[2]

DORILANT.   Yes, if you will.

SPARKISH.   Or at the Cock.[3]

DORILANT.   Yes, if you please.

SPARKISH.   Or at the Dog and Partridge.[4]

385 HORNER.   Aye, if you have a mind to't, for we shall dine at neither.

SPARKISH.   Pshaw, with your fooling we shall lose the new play, and I would no more miss seeing a new play the first day than I would miss sitting in the wits' row;[5]
390   therefore, I'll go fetch my mistress and away. *(Exit.)*

(Enter Pinchwife.)

HORNER.   Who have we here, Pinchwife?

PINCHWIFE.   Gentlemen, your humble servant.

HORNER.   Well Jack, by thy long absence from the Town, the grumness[6] of thy countenance, and the
395   slovenliness of thy habit, I should give thee joy, should I not, of marriage?

PINCHWIFE.   *(Aside.)*   Death, does he know I'm married, too? I thought to have concealed it from him at least.—My long stay in the country will excuse my
400   dress, and I have a suit of law that brings me up to Town that puts me out of humor; besides, I must give Sparkish tomorrow five thousand pound to lie with my sister.[7]

HORNER.   Nay, you country gentlemen, rather than not
405   purchase, will buy anything, and he is a cracked title,[8] if we may quibble. Well, but am I to give thee joy? I heard thou wert married.

PINCHWIFE.   What then?

HORNER.   Why, the next thing that is to be heard is

---

[2]   *Chateline's*   Fashionable French restaurant in Covent Garden.

[3]   *the Cock*   Out of many taverns by that name, this probably refers to a less fashionable one in Bow Street, Covent Garden, frequented by Wycherley.

[4]   *the Dog and Partridge*   An unfashionable tavern in Fleet Street.

[5]   *wits' row*   Near the front of the theater pit.

[6]   *grumness*   Moroseness; gloominess.

[7]   *Sparkish ... sister*   Pinchwife is providing his sister with a dowry to enable her to marry Sparkish.

[8]   *cracked title*   Either Sparkish's patrimony or his genealogy is of questionable value.

410 thou'rt a cuckold.

PINCHWIFE. (*Aside.*) Insupportable name.

HORNER. But I did not expect marriage from such a whoremaster as you: one that knew the Town so much and women so well.

415 PINCHWIFE. Why, I have married no London wife.

HORNER. Pshaw, that's all one: that grave circumspection in marrying a country wife is like refusing a deceitful pampered Smithfield[1] jade to go and be cheated by a friend in the country.

420 PINCHWIFE. (*Aside.*) A pox on him and his simile.—At least we are a little surer of the breed there, know what her keeping has been, whether foiled[2] or unsound.[3]

HORNER. Come, come, I have known a clap[4] gotten in Wales, and there are cozens,[5] justices, clerks, and 425 chaplains in the country; I won't say coachmen. But she's handsome and young?

PINCHWIFE. (*Aside.*) I'll answer as I should do.—No, no, she has no beauty but her youth, no attraction but her modesty: wholesome, homely, and housewifely, 430 that's all.

DORILANT. He talks as like a grazier[6] as he looks.

PINCHWIFE. She's too awkward, ill-favored, and silly[7] to bring to Town.

HARCOURT. Then methinks you should bring her to be 435 taught breeding.

PINCHWIFE. To be taught! No sir, I thank you, good wives and private soldiers should be ignorant. [*Aside.*] I'll keep her from your instructions, I warrant you.

HARCOURT. (*Aside.*) The rogue is as jealous as if his wife 440 were not ignorant.

HORNER. Why, if she be ill-favored, there will be less danger here for you than by leaving her in the country: we have such variety of dainties that we are seldom hungry.

445 DORILANT. But they have always coarse, constant, swingeing[8] stomachs in the country.

HARCOURT. Foul feeders indeed.

DORILANT. And your hospitality is great there.

HARCOURT. Open house, every man's welcome.

450 PINCHWIFE. So, so, gentlemen.

HORNER. But prithee, why wouldst thou marry her? If she be ugly, ill-bred, and silly, she must be rich then.

PINCHWIFE. As rich as if she brought me twenty thousand pound out of this Town, for she'll be as sure not to 455 spend her moderate portion as a London baggage would be to spend hers, let it be what it would; so 'tis all one. Then because she's ugly, she's the likelier to be my own, and being ill-bred, she'll hate conversation and, since silly and innocent, will not know the difference betwixt 460 a man of one-and-twenty and one of forty.

HORNER. Nine—to my knowledge. But if she be silly, she'll expect as much from a man of forty-nine as from him of one-and-twenty. But methinks wit is more necessary than beauty, and I think no young woman 465 ugly that has it and no handsome woman agreeable without it.

PINCHWIFE. 'Tis my maxim: he's a fool that marries, but he's a greater that does not marry a fool. What is wit in a wife good for but to make a man a cuckold?

470 HORNER. Yes, to keep it from his knowledge.

PINCHWIFE. A fool cannot contrive to make her husband a cuckold.

HORNER. No, but she'll club with a man that can, and what is worse, if she cannot make her husband a cuck-475 old, she'll make him jealous and pass for one, and then 'tis all one.

PINCHWIFE. Well, well, I'll take care for one: my wife shall make me no cuckold though she had your help, Mr. Horner. I understand the Town, sir.

480 DORILANT. (*Aside.*) His help!

HARCOURT. (*Aside.*) He's come newly to Town, it seems, and has not heard how things are with him.

HORNER. But tell me, has marriage cured thee of whoring, which it seldom does?

485 HARCOURT. 'Tis more than age can do.

HORNER. No, the word is, "I'll marry and live honest."[9] But a marriage vow is like a penitent gamester's oath

---

1   *Smithfield* City market, known for its sharp practices.

2   *foiled* Injured (of a horse); deflowered (of a woman).

3   *unsound* Unhealthy, particularly suffering from venereal disease.

4   *a clap* Gonorrhea.

5   *cozens* Cheats.

6   *grazier* One who grazes cattle.

7   *silly* Innocent, unsophisticated, usually rustic.

8   *swingeing* Huge.

9   *honest* Faithful.

and entering into bonds and penalties to stint himself to such a particular small sum at play for the future, which makes him but the more eager, and not being able to hold out, loses his money again and his forfeit to boot.

DORILANT. Aye, aye, a gamester will be a gamester whilst his money lasts, and a whoremaster, whilst his vigor.

HARCOURT. Nay, I have known 'em, when they are broke and can lose no more, keep a-fumbling with the box[1] in their hands to fool with only and hinder other gamesters.

DORILANT. That had wherewithal to make lusty stakes.

PINCHWIFE. Well gentlemen, you may laugh at me, but you shall never lie with my wife. I know the Town.

HORNER. But prithee, was not the way you were in better? Is not keeping better than marriage?

PINCHWIFE. A pox on't, the jades would jilt me; I could never keep a whore to myself.

HORNER. So then you only married to keep a whore to yourself. Well but let me tell you, women, as you say, are, like soldiers, made constant and loyal by good pay rather than by oaths and covenants. Therefore, I'd advise my friends to keep rather than marry since, too, I find by your example it does not serve one's turn, for I saw you yesterday in the eighteen-penny place[2] with a pretty country wench.

PINCHWIFE. (Aside.) How the devil! Did he see my wife then? I sat there that she might not be seen, but she shall never go to a play again.

HORNER. What, dost thou blush at nine-and-forty for having been seen with a wench?

DORILANT. No faith, I warrant 'twas his wife, which he seated there out of sight, for he's a cunning rogue and understands the Town.

HARCOURT. He blushes; then 'twas his wife, for men are now more ashamed to be seen with them in public than with a wench.

PINCHWIFE. (Aside.) Hell and damnation! I'm undone since Horner has seen her and they know 'twas she.

HORNER. But prithee, was it thy wife? She was exceedingly pretty. I was in love with her at that distance.

PINCHWIFE. You are like never to be nearer to her. Your servant, gentlemen. (Offers to go.)

HORNER. Nay, prithee stay.

PINCHWIFE. I cannot; I will not.

HORNER. Come, you shall dine with us.

PINCHWIFE. I have dined already.

HORNER. Come, I know thou hast not. I'll treat thee, dear rogue; thou shalt spend none of thy Hampshire money today.

PINCHWIFE. (Aside.) Treat me! So he uses me already like his cuckold.

HORNER. Nay, you shall not go.

PINCHWIFE. I must, I have business at home. (Exit.)

HARCOURT. To beat his wife: he's as jealous of her as a Cheapside[3] husband of a Covent Garden[4] wife.

HORNER. Why, 'tis as hard to find an old whoremaster without jealousy and the gout as a young one without fear or the pox.

As gout in age from pox in youth proceeds,
So wenching past, then jealousy succeeds:
The worst disease that love and wenching breeds.

(Exeunt.)

ACT 2, SCENE 1. [Pinchwife's lodging.]

(Margery Pinchwife and Alithea, Pinchwife peeping behind at the door.)

MARGERY. Pray sister,[5] where are the best fields and woods to walk in in London?

ALITHEA. A pretty question. Why sister, Mulberry Garden[6] and St. James's Park[7] and, for close[8] walks, the New Exchange.[9]

---

1   box   Dice cup (double entendre).

2   eighteen-penny place   Middle gallery in the theater, away from the gallants in the pit and boxes.

3   Cheapside   Business district.

4   Covent Garden   Area associated with prostitutes.

5   sister   I.e., sister-in-law. Alithea is Pinchwife's sister.

6   Mulberry Garden   Fashionable promenade within St. James's Park, at the site of the current Buckingham Palace.

7   St. James's Park   Very fashionable London district at the western end of Pall Mall.

8   close   Indoor.

9   New Exchange   Meeting place for bankers and merchants, as well as the location of a gallery of fashionable shops, located on the Strand in London. The original Exchange burned down in the fire of 1666.

MARGERY.   Pray sister, tell my why my husband looks so grum here in Town and keeps me up so close and will not let me go a-walking nor let me wear my best gown yesterday?

10 ALITHEA.   Oh, he's jealous, sister.

MARGERY.   Jealous, what's that?

ALITHEA.   He's afraid you should love another man.

MARGERY.   How should he be afraid of my loving another man when he will not let me see any but

15 himself?

ALITHEA.   Did he not carry you yesterday to a play?

MARGERY.   Aye, but we sat amongst ugly people; he would not let me come near the gentry, who sat under us, so that I could not see 'em. He told me none but

20 naughty women sat there, whom they toused and moused, but I would have ventured for all that.

ALITHEA.   But how did you like the play?

MARGERY.   Indeed I was aweary of the play, but I liked hugeously the actors; they are the goodliest, properest

25 men, sister.

ALITHEA.   Oh, but you must not like the actors, sister.

MARGERY.   Ay, how should I help it, sister? Pray sister, when my husband comes in, will you ask leave for me to go a-walking?

30 ALITHEA.   (Aside.) A-walking, ha, ha! Lord, a country gentlewoman's leisure is the drudgery of a foot post,[1] and she requires as much airing as her husband's horses.

(Enter Pinchwife.)

But here comes your husband; I'll ask, though I'm sure he'll not grant it.

35 MARGERY.   He says he won't let me go abroad for fear of catching the pox.[2]

ALITHEA.   Fie, the small pox you should say.

MARGERY.   Oh my dear, dear bud, welcome home. Why dost thou look so froppish? Who has nangered[3] thee?

40 PINCHWIFE.   You're a fool.

(Margery goes aside and cries.)

ALITHEA.   Faith so she is, for crying for no fault, poor, tender creature!

PINCHWIFE.   What, you would have her as impudent as yourself, as arrant a jill-flirt,[4] a gadder, a magpie, and, to

45 say all, a mere[5] notorious Town woman?

ALITHEA.   Brother, you are my only censurer, and the honor of your family shall sooner suffer in your wife there than in me, though I take the innocent liberty of the Town.

50 PINCHWIFE.   Hark you, mistress, do not talk so before my wife. The innocent liberty of the Town!

ALITHEA.   Why pray, who boasts of any intrigue with me? What lampoon has made my name notorious? What ill women frequent my lodgings? I keep no

55 company with any women of scandalous reputations.

PINCHWIFE.   No, you keep the men of scandalous reputations company.

ALITHEA.   Where? Would you not have me civil? answer 'em in a box at the plays? in the Drawing Room[6] at

60 Whitehall? in St. James's Park? Mulberry Garden? or—

PINCHWIFE.   Hold, hold, do not teach my wife where the men are to be found; I believe she's the worse for your Town documents[7] already. I bid you keep her in ignorance as I do.

65 MARGERY.   Indeed, be not angry with her, bud; she will tell me nothing of the Town, though I ask her a thousand times a day.

PINCHWIFE.   Then you are very inquisitive to know, I find?

70 MARGERY.   Not I, indeed, dear. I hate London. Our place-house[8] in the country is worth a thousand of't. Would I were there again!

PINCHWIFE.   So you shall, I warrant, but were you not talking of plays and players when I came in?—You are

75 her encourager in such discourses.

MARGERY.   No indeed, dear, she chid me just now for liking the playermen.

PINCHWIFE.   (Aside.) Nay, if she be so innocent as to own to me her liking them, there is no hurt in't.—

---

1   foot post   One who delivers the mail (post) on foot.

2   pox   Smallpox. In Town usage, "pox" referred to venereal disease.

3   froppish   Fretful; peevish; nangered   Angered (baby talk).

4   jill-flirt   Female flit; wanton.

5   mere   No less than.

6   Drawing Room   Reception room at the royal palace.

7   documents   Lessons.

8   place-house   Chief residence of an estate.

80 Come my poor rogue, but thou lik'st none better than
me?

MARGERY.   Yes indeed, but I do: the playermen are finer
folks.

PINCHWIFE.   But you love none better then me?

85 MARGERY.   You are mine own dear bud, and I know
you; I hate a stranger.

PINCHWIFE.   Aye my dear, you must love me only and
not be like the naughty Town women, who only hate
their husbands and love every man else, love plays, visits,

90 fine coaches, fine clothes, fiddles, balls, treats, and so
lead a wicked Town life.

MARGERY.   Nay, if to enjoy all these things be a Town
life, London is not so bad a place, dear.

PINCHWIFE.   How! If you love me, you must hate

95 London.

ALITHEA.   (Aside.)   The fool has forbid me discovering to
her the pleasures of the Town, and he is now setting her
agog upon them himself.

MARGERY.   But husband, do the Town women love the

100 playermen, too?

PINCHWIFE.   Yes, I warrant you.

MARGERY.   Ay, I warrant you.

PINCHWIFE.   Why, you do not, I hope?

MARGERY.   No, no, bud, but why have we no playermen

105 in the country?

PINCHWIFE.   Hah! Mrs. Minx, ask me no more to go to
a play.

MARGERY.   Nay, why, love? I did not care for going, but
when you forbid me, you make me, as 't were, desire it.

110 ALITHEA.   (Aside.)   So 'twill be in other things, I warrant.

MARGERY.   Pray, let me go to a play, dear.

PINCHWIFE.   Hold your peace; I wonnot.

MARGERY.   Why, love?

PINCHWIFE.   Why, I'll tell you.

115 ALITHEA.   (Aside.)   Nay, if he tell her, she'll give him
more cause to forbid her that place.

MARGERY.   Pray, why, dear?

PINCHWIFE.   First, you like the actors, and the gallants
may like you.

120 MARGERY.   What, a homely country girl? No, bud,
nobody will like me.

PINCHWIFE.   I tell you, yes, they may.

MARGERY.   No, no, you jest. I won't believe you; I will
go.

125 PINCHWIFE.   I tell you then that one of the lewdest
fellows in Town, who saw you there, told me he was in
love with you.

MARGERY.   Indeed! Who, who, pray, who was't?

PINCHWIFE.   (Aside.)   I've gone too far and slipped before

130 I was aware. How overjoyed she is!

MARGERY.   Was it any Hampshire gallant, any of our
neighbors? I promise you, I am beholding to him.

PINCHWIFE.   I promise you, you lie, for he would but
ruin you as he has done hundreds. He has no other love

135 for women but that. Such as he look upon women like
basilisks, but to destroy 'em.

MARGERY.   Ay, but if he loves me, why should he ruin
me? Answer me to that. Methinks he should not; I
would do him no harm.

140 ALITHEA.   Ha, ha, ha.

PINCHWIFE.   'Tis very well, but I'll keep him from doing
you any harm, or me either.

(Enter Sparkish and Harcourt.)

But here comes company. Get you in, get you in.

MARGERY.   But pray, husband, is he a pretty gentleman

145 that loves me?

PINCHWIFE.   In baggage, in. (Thrusts her in; shuts the
door.) What, all the lewd libertines of the Town brought
to my lodging by this easy coxcomb! S'death,[1] I'll not
suffer it.

150 SPARKISH.   Here Harcourt, do you approve my choice?
—Dear little rogue, I told you I'd bring you acquainted
with all my friends, the wits, and—

(Harcourt salutes her.)

PINCHWIFE.   Aye, they shall know her as well as you
yourself will, I warrant you.

155 SPARKISH.   This is one of those, my pretty rogue, that are
to dance at your wedding tomorrow, and him you must
bid welcome ever to what you and I have.

PINCHWIFE.   (Aside.)   Monstrous!

SPARKISH.   Harcourt, how dost thou like her, faith?—

160 Nay dear, do not look down; I should hate to have a
wife of mine out of countenance at any thing.

PINCHWIFE.   Wonderful!

---

1   S'death   God's death (an oath).

SPARKISH. Tell me, I say, Harcourt, how dost thou like her? Thou hast stared upon her enough to resolve me.

HARCOURT. So infinitely well that I could wish I had a mistress, too, that might differ from her in nothing but her love and engagement to you.

ALITHEA. Sir, Master Sparkish has often told me that his acquaintance were all wits and railleurs,[1] and now I find it.

SPARKISH. No, by the universe, madam, he does not rally now; you may believe him. I do assure you, he is the honestest, worthiest, true-hearted gentleman—a man of such perfect honor, he would say nothing to a lady he does not mean.

PINCHWIFE. (*Aside.*) Praising another man to his mistress!

HARCOURT. Sir, you are so beyond expectation obliging, that—

SPARKISH. Nay, egad, I am sure you do admire her extremely; I see't in your eyes.—He does admire you, madam.—By the world, don't you?

HARCOURT. Yes, above the world or the most glorious part of it, her whole sex, and till now I never thought I should have envied you, or any man about to marry, but you have the best excuse for marriage I ever knew.

ALITHEA. Nay, now, sir, I'm satisfied you are of the society of the wits and railleurs since you cannot spare your friend, even when he is but too civil to you, but the surest sign is since you are an enemy to marriage, for that I hear you hate as much as business or bad wine.

HARCOURT. Truly madam, I never was an enemy to marriage till now because marriage was never an enemy to me before.

ALITHEA. But why, sir, is marriage an enemy to you now? because it robs you of your friend here? For you look upon a friend married as one gone into a monastery, that is, dead to the world.

HARCOURT. 'Tis indeed because you marry him. I see, madam, you can guess my meaning. I do confess heartily and openly I wish it were in my power to break the match. By heavens, I would!

SPARKISH. Poor Frank!

ALITHEA. Would you be so unkind to me?

HARCOURT. No, no, 'tis not because I would be unkind to you.

SPARKISH. Poor Frank! No, gad, 'tis only his kindness to me.

PINCHWIFE. (*Aside.*) Great kindness to you, indeed. Insensible fop, let a man make love[2] to his wife to his face!

SPARKISH. Come, dear Frank, for all my wife there that shall be, thou shalt enjoy me sometimes, dear rogue. By my honor, we men of wit condole for our deceased brother in marriage as much as for one dead in earnest. I think that was prettily said of me, hah, Harcourt? But come, Frank, be not melancholy for me.

HARCOURT. No, I assure you I am not melancholy for you.

SPARKISH. Prithee Frank, dost think my wife that shall be there a fine person?

HARCOURT. I could gaze upon her till I became as blind as you are.

SPARKISH. How, as I am! How?

HARCOURT. Because you are a lover, and true lovers are blind, stock-blind.

SPARKISH. True, true, but by the world, she has wit, too, as well as beauty. Go, go with her into a corner and try if she has wit; talk to her anything; she's bashful before me.

HARCOURT. Indeed, if a woman wants[3] wit in a corner, she has it nowhere.

ALITHEA. (*Aside to Sparkish.*) Sir, you dispose of me a little before your time.

SPARKISH. Nay, nay, madam, let me have an earnest of your obedience, or—Go, go, madam.

(*Harcourt courts Alithea aside.*)

PINCHWIFE. How, sir! if you are not concerned for the honor of a wife, I am for that of a sister. He shall not debauch her. Be a pander to your own wife, bring men to her, let 'em make love before your face, thrust 'em into a corner together, then leave 'em in private! Is this your Town wit and conduct?

SPARKISH. Ha, ha, ha, a silly wise rogue would make one laugh more than a stark fool, ha, ha! I shall burst. Nay, you shall not disturb 'em. I'll vex thee, by the world. (*Struggles with Pinchwife to keep him from Harcourt and Alithea.*)

---

1 *railleurs* Those who banter or mock, a fashionable French word.

2 *make love* Pay court.

3 *wants* Lacks or needs.

ALITHEA.   The writings are drawn, sir, settlements made;
'tis too late, sir, and past all revocation.

HARCOURT.   Then so is my death.

250 ALITHEA.   I would not be unjust to him.

HARCOURT.   Then why to me so?

ALITHEA.   I have no obligation to you.

HARCOURT.   My love.

ALITHEA.   I had his before.

255 HARCOURT.   You never had it: he wants, you see,
jealousy, the only infallible sign of it.

ALITHEA.   Love proceeds from esteem; he cannot distrust
my virtue. Besides, he loves me, or he would not marry
me.

260 HARCOURT.   Marrying you is no more sign of his love
than bribing your woman, that he may marry you, is a
sign of his generosity. Marriage is rather a sign of
interest than love, and he that marries a fortune, covets
a mistress, not loves her. But if you take marriage for a
265 sign of love, take it from me immediately.

ALITHEA.   No, now you have put a scruple in my head.
But in short, sir, to end our dispute, I must marry him:
my reputation would suffer in the world else.

HARCOURT.   No, if you do marry him, with your
270 pardon, madam, your reputation suffers in the world,
and you would be thought in necessity for a cloak.

ALITHEA.   Nay, now you are rude, sir.—Mr. Sparkish,
pray come hither; your friend here is very troublesome
and very loving.

275 HARCOURT.   (*Aside to Alithea.*)   Hold, hold—

PINCHWIFE.   D'ye hear that?

SPARKISH.   Why, d'ye think I'll seem to be jealous, like
a country bumpkin?

PINCHWIFE.   No, rather be a cuckold, like a credulous
280 cit.[1]

HARCOURT.   Madam, you would not have been so little
generous[2] as to have told him.

ALITHEA.   Yes, since you could be so little generous as to
wrong him.

285 HARCOURT.   Wrong him! No man can do't; he's beneath an injury: a bubble,[3] a coward, a senseless idiot, a

wretch so contemptible to all the world but you that—

ALITHEA.   Hold, do not rail at him, for since he is like to
be my husband, I am resolved to like him. Nay, I think
290 I am obliged to tell him you are not his friend.—Master
Sparkish, Master Sparkish.

SPARKISH.   What, what? Now, dear rogue, has not she
wit?

HARCOURT.   (*Speaks surlily.*)   Not so much as I thought
295 and hoped she had.

ALITHEA.   Mr. Sparkish, do you bring people to rail at
you?

HARCOURT.   Madam—

SPARKISH.   How! No, but if he does rail at me, 'tis but in
300 jest, I warrant, what we wits do for one another and
never take any notice of it.

ALITHEA.   He spoke so scurrilously of you I had no
patience to hear him; besides, he has been making love
to me.

305 HARCOURT.   (*Aside.*)   True, damned, tell-tale woman.

SPARKISH.   Pshaw, to show his parts.[4] We wits rail and
make love often but to show our parts; as we have no
affections, so we have no malice, we—

ALITHEA.   He said you were a wretch, below an injury.

310 SPARKISH.   Pshaw.

HARCOURT.   [*Aside.*]   Damned, senseless, impudent,
virtuous jade! Well, since she won't let me have her,
she'll do as good: she'll make me hate her.

ALITHEA.   A common bubble.

315 SPARKISH.   Pshaw.

ALITHEA.   A coward.

SPARKISH.   Pshaw, pshaw.

ALITHEA.   A senseless, driveling idiot.

SPARKISH.   How! Did he disparage my parts? Nay, then
320 my honor's concerned. I can't put up that, sir.—By the
world, brother, help me to kill him. (*Aside.*) I may draw[5]
now, since we have the odds of him; 'tis a good occasion, too, before my mistress. (*Offers to draw.*)

ALITHEA.   Hold, hold!

325 SPARKISH.   What, what?

ALITHEA.   (*Aside.*)   I must not let 'em kill the gentleman
neither, for his kindness[6] to me. I am so far from hating

---

[1]   *cit* A businessman, as opposed to a gentleman. The City was the
section of London in which trade was conducted; hence, a "cit" is a
denizen of the City.

[2]   *generous* Noble.

[3]   *bubble* Dupe.

[4]   *parts* Personal qualities.

[5]   *draw* Withdraw a sword.

[6]   *kindness* Affection.

him that I wish my gallant had his person and understanding. Nay, if my honor—

330 SPARKISH. I'll be thy death.

ALITHEA. Hold, hold! Indeed, to tell the truth, the
gentleman said after all that what he spoke was but out
of friendship to you.

SPARKISH. How! Say I am, I am a fool, that is, no wit,
335 out of friendship to me?

ALITHEA. Yes, to try whether I was concerned enough
for you, and made love to me only to be satisfied of my
virtue, for your sake.

HARCOURT. (*Aside.*) Kind however—

340 SPARKISH. Nay, if it were so, my dear rogue, I ask thee
pardon, but why would not you tell me so, faith?

HARCOURT. Because I did not think on't, faith.

SPARKISH. Come, Horner does not come, Harcourt,
let's be gone to the new play.—Come, madam.

345 ALITHEA. I will not go if you intend to leave me alone
in the box and run into the pit, as you use to do.

SPARKISH. Pshaw, I'll leave Harcourt with you in the
box to entertain you, and that's as good. If I sat in the
box, I should be thought no judge but of trim-
350 mings.—Come away, Harcourt, lead her down.

(*Exeunt Sparkish, Harcourt, and Alithea.*)

PINCHWIFE. Well, go thy ways, for the flower of the
true Town fops, such as spend their estates before they
come to 'em and are cuckolds before they're married.
But let me go look to my own freehold.—How—

(*Enter My Lady Fidget, Dainty, and Mistress Squeamish.*)

355 LADY FIDGET. Your servant, sir. Where is your lady? We
are come to wait upon her to the new play.

PINCHWIFE. New play!

LADY FIDGET. And my husband will wait upon you
presently.

360 PINCHWIFE. (*Aside.*) Damn your civility.—Madam, by
no means, I will not see Sir Jaspar here till I have waited
upon him at home, nor shall my wife see you till she has
waited upon your ladyship at your lodgings.

LADY FIDGET. Now we are here, sir—

365 PINCHWIFE. No, madam.

DAINTY. Pray, let us see her.

MRS. SQUEAMISH. We will not stir till we see her.

PINCHWIFE. (*Aside.*) A pox on you all. (*Goes to the door
and returns.*)

370 She has locked the door and is gone abroad.

LADY FIDGET. No, you have locked the door, and she's
within.

DAINTY. They told us below she was here.

PINCHWIFE. [*Aside.*] Will nothing do?—Well it must
375 out then: to tell you the truth, ladies, which I was afraid
to let you know before lest it might endanger your lives,
my wife has just now the small pox come out upon her.
Do not be frightened, but pray, be gone ladies. You shall
not stay here in danger of your lives. Pray get you gone,
380 ladies.

LADY FIDGET. No, no, we have all had 'em.

MRS. SQUEAMISH. Alack, alack.

DAINTY. Come, come, we must see how it goes with
her. I understand the disease.

385 LADY FIDGET. Come.

PINCHWIFE. (*Aside.*) Well, there is no being too hard for
women at their own weapon, lying; therefore, I'll quit
the field. (*Exit.*)

MRS. SQUEAMISH. Here's an example of jealousy.

390 LADY FIDGET. Indeed, as the world goes, I wonder there
are no more jealous, since wives are so neglected.

DAINTY. Pshaw, as the world goes, to what end should
they be jealous?

LADY FIDGET. Faugh, 'tis a nasty world.

395 MRS. SQUEAMISH. That men of parts, great acquaintance, and quality should take up with and spend themselves and fortunes in keeping little playhouse creatures,
faugh!

LADY FIDGET. Nay, that women of understanding, great
400 acquaintance, and good quality should fall a-keeping,
too, of little creatures, faugh!

MRS. SQUEAMISH. Why, 'tis the men of quality's fault:
they never visit women of honor and reputation as they
used to do and have not so much as common civility for
405 ladies of our rank but use us with the same indifferency
and ill breeding as if we were all married to 'em.

LADY FIDGET. She says true. 'Tis an arrant shame
women of quality should be so slighted; methinks birth,
birth, should go for something. I have known men
410 admired, courted, and followed for their titles only.

MRS. SQUEAMISH. Aye, one would think men of honor

should not love, no more than marry, out of their own rank.

DAINTY. Fie, fie upon 'em, they are come to think
crossbreeding for themselves best, as well as for their
dogs and horses.

LADY FIDGET. They are dogs and horses for't.

MRS. SQUEAMISH. One would think if not for love, for
vanity a little.

DAINTY. Nay, they do satisfy their vanity upon us
sometimes and are kind to us in their report, tell all the
world they lie with us.

LADY FIDGET. Damned rascals, that we should be only
wronged by 'em! To report a man has had a person,
when he has not had a person, is the greatest wrong in
the whole world that can be done to a person.

MRS. SQUEAMISH. Well, 'tis an arrant shame noble
persons should be so wronged and neglected.

LADY FIDGET. But still 'tis an arranter shame for a noble
person to neglect her own honor and defame her own
noble person with little inconsiderable fellows, faugh!

DAINTY. I suppose the crime against our honor is the
same with a man of quality as with another.

LADY FIDGET. How! No, sure the man of quality is
likest one's husband, and therefore, the fault should be
the less.

DAINTY. But then the pleasure should be the less.

LADY FIDGET. Fie, fie, fie, for shame sister! Whither
shall we ramble? Be continent in your discourse, or I
shall hate you.

DAINTY. Besides, an intrigue is so much the more
notorious for the man's quality.

MRS. SQUEAMISH. 'Tis true, nobody takes notice of a
private man, and therefore, with him 'tis more secret,
and the crime's the less when 'tis not known.

LADY FIDGET. You say true. I'faith, I think you are in
the right on't. 'Tis not an injury to a husband till it be
an injury to our honors, so that a woman of honor loses
no honor with a private person, and to say truth—

DAINTY. (*Apart to Mrs. Squeamish.*) So the little fellow
is grown a private person—with her—

LADY FIDGET. But still my dear, dear honor.

(*Enter Sir Jaspar, Horner, Dorilant.*)

SIR JASPAR. Aye, my dear, dear of honor, thou hast still
so much honor in thy mouth—

HORNER. (*Aside.*) That she has none elsewhere—

LADY FIDGET. Oh, what d'ye mean to bring in these
upon us?

DAINTY. Faugh, these are as bad as wits!

MRS. SQUEAMISH. Faugh!

LADY FIDGET. Let us leave the room.

SIR JASPAR. Stay, stay, faith, to tell you the naked truth.

LADY FIDGET. Fie, Sir Jaspar, do not use that word
"naked."

SIR JASPAR. Well, well, in short, I have business at
Whitehall and cannot go to the play with you; therefore,
would have you go—

LADY FIDGET. With those two to a play?

SIR JASPAR. No, not with t'other, but with Mr. Horner;
there can be no more scandal to go with him than with
Mr. Tattle or Master Limberham.[1]

LADY FIDGET. With that nasty fellow! No—no.

SIR JASPAR. Nay prithee dear, hear me. (*Whispers to Lady
Fidget.*)

(*Horner, Dorilant drawing near Squeamish and Dainty.*)

HORNER. Ladies.

DAINTY. Stand off.

MRS. SQUEAMISH. Do not approach us.

DAINTY. You herd with the wits; you are obscenity all
over.

MRS. SQUEAMISH. And I would as soon look upon a
picture of Adam and Eve without fig leaves as any of
you, if I could help it; therefore, keep off and do not
make us sick.

DORILANT. What a devil are these?

HORNER. Why, these are pretenders to honor, as critics
to wit, only by censuring others, and as every raw,
peevish, out-of-humored, affected, dull, tea-drinking,
arithmetical[2] fop sets up for a wit by railing at men of
sense, so these for honor, by railing at the Court and
ladies of as great honor as quality.

SIR JASPAR. Come Mr. Horner, I must desire you to go
with these ladies to the play, sir.

HORNER. I, sir!

SIR JASPAR. Aye, aye, come, sir.

HORNER. I must beg your pardon, sir, and theirs. I will
not be seen in women's company in public again for the

---

1 *Limberham* Limber-jointed or weak-kneed person.

2 *arithmetical* Precise.

world.

SIR JASPAR. Ha, ha, strange aversion!

MRS. SQUEAMISH. No, he's for women's company in private.

SIR JASPAR. He—poor man—he! Ha, ha, ha.

DAINTY. 'Tis a greater shame amongst lewd fellows to be seen in virtuous women's company than for the women to be seen with them.

HORNER. Indeed madam, the time was I only hated virtuous women, but now I hate the other, too. I beg your pardon, ladies.

LADY FIDGET. You are very obliging, sir, because we would not be troubled with you.

SIR JASPAR. In sober sadness he shall go.

DORILANT. Nay, if he wonnot, I am ready to wait upon the ladies, and I think I am the fitter man.

SIR JASPAR. You, sir! no, I thank you for that. Master Horner is a privileged man amongst the virtuous ladies; 'twill be a great while before you are so. He, he, he, he's my wife's gallant, he, he, he. No, pray withdraw, sir, for as I take it, the virtuous ladies have no business with you.

DORILANT. And I am sure, he can have none with them. 'Tis strange a man can't come amongst virtuous women now but upon the same terms as men are admitted into the Great Turk's seraglio,[1] but heavens keep me from being an ombre[2] player with 'em. But where is Pinchwife? (*Exit.*)

SIR JASPAR. Come, come, man. What, avoid the sweet society of womankind? that sweet, soft, gentle, tame, noble creature woman, made for man's companion—

HORNER. So is that soft, gentle, tame, and more noble creature a spaniel, and has all their tricks: can fawn, lie down, suffer beating, and fawn the more, barks at your friends when they come to see you, makes your bed hard, gives you fleas and the mange sometimes, and all the difference is, the spaniel's the more faithful animal and fawns but upon one master.

SIR JASPAR. He, he, he.

MRS. SQUEAMISH. Oh, the rude beast!

DAINTY. Insolent brute!

LADY FIDGET. Brute! Stinking, mortified, rotten French wether,[3] to dare—

SIR JASPAR. Hold, an't[4] please your ladyship.—For shame, Master Horner, your mother was a woman. (*Aside.*) Now shall I never reconcile 'em.—Hark you, madam, take my advice in your anger: you know you often want one to make up your drolling pack of ombre players, and you may cheat him easily, for he's an ill gamester and consequently loves play. Besides, you know, you have but two old civil gentlemen (with stinking breaths, too) to wait upon you abroad. Take in the third into your service. The other are but crazy, and a lady should have a supernumerary gentleman-usher, as a supernumerary coach-horse, lest sometimes you should be forced to stay at home.

LADY FIDGET. But are you sure he loves play and has money?

SIR JASPAR. He loves play as much as you and has money as much as I.

LADY FIDGET. Then I am contented to make him pay for his scurrility; money makes up in a measure all other wants in men. (*Aside.*) Those whom we cannot make hold for gallants, we make fine.[5]

SIR JASPAR. (*Aside.*) So, so, now to mollify, to wheedle him.—Master Horner, will you never keep civil company? Methinks 'tis time now, since you are only fit for them. Come, come, man, you must e'en fall to visiting our wives, eating at our tables, drinking tea with our virtuous relations after dinner, dealing cards to 'em, reading plays and gazettes to 'em, picking fleas out of their shocks[6] for 'em, collecting receipts,[7] new songs, women, pages, and footmen for 'em.

HORNER. I hope they'll afford me better employment, sir.

SIR JASPAR. He, he, he! 'Tis fit you know your work before you come into your place, and since you are unprovided of a lady to flatter and a good house to eat at, pray frequent mine and call my wife "mistress," and she shall call you "gallant," according to the custom.

HORNER. Who, I?

---

1 *Great Turk's seraglio* Harem of the Ottoman sultan.

2 *ombre* Card game.

3 *wether* Eunuch.

4 *an't* And it; i.e., if it.

5 *fine* Pun, meaning both "elegant" and "thin, whittled away."

6 *shocks* Lapdogs.

7 *receipts* Recipes or prescriptions.

SIR JASPAR. Faith, thou shalt for my sake; come, for my sake only.

HORNER. For your sake—

580 SIR JASPAR. Come, come, here's a gamester for you; let him be a little familiar sometimes. Nay, what if a little rude? Gamesters may be rude with ladies, you know.

LADY FIDGET. Yes, losing gamesters have a privilege with women.

585 HORNER. I always thought the contrary, that the winning gamester had most privilege with women, for when you have lost your money to a man, you'll lose anything you have, all you have, they say, and he may use you as he pleases.

590 SIR JASPAR. He, he, he! Well, win or lose, you shall have your liberty with her.

LADY FIDGET. As he behaves himself and for your sake, I'll give him admittance and freedom.

HORNER. All sorts of freedom, madam?

595 SIR JASPAR. Aye, aye, aye, all sorts of freedom thou canst take, and so go to her; begin thy new employment. Wheedle her, jest with her, and be better acquainted one with another.

HORNER. (Aside.) I think I know her already, therefore,
600 may venture with her, my secret for hers.

(Horner and Lady Fidget whisper.)

SIR JASPAR. Sister, Cuz,[1] I have provided an innocent playfellow for you there.

DAINTY. Who, he!

MRS. SQUEAMISH. There's a playfellow indeed.

605 SIR JASPAR. Yes, sure. What, he is good enough to play at cards, blindman's buff, or the fool with sometimes.

MRS. SQUEAMISH. Faugh, we'll have no such playfellows.

DAINTY. No sir, you shan't choose playfellows for us, we
610 thank you.

SIR JASPAR. Nay, pray hear me. (Whispering to them.)

LADY FIDGET. [Aside to Horner.] But poor gentleman, could you be so generous? so truly a man of honor, as for the sakes of us women of honor, to cause your self to
615 be reported no man? no man! and to suffer your self the greatest shame that could fall upon a man, that none might fall upon us women by your conversation. But indeed, sir, as perfectly, perfectly the same man as before

your going into France, sir, as perfectly, perfectly, sir?

620 HORNER. As perfectly, perfectly, madam. Nay, I scorn you should take my word; I desire to be tried only, madam.

LADY FIDGET. Well, that's spoken again like a man of honor; all men of honor desire to come to the test. But
625 indeed, generally you men report such things of yourselves one does not know how or whom to believe, and it is come to that pass, we dare not take your words, no more than your tailors, without some staid servant of yours be bound with you. But I have so strong a faith in
630 your honor, dear, dear, noble sir, that I'd forfeit mine for yours at any time, dear sir.

HORNER. No madam, you should not need to forfeit it for me: I have given you security already to save you harmless, my late reputation being so well known in the
635 world, madam.

LADY FIDGET. But if upon any future falling out or upon a suspicion of my taking the trust out of your hands to employ some other, you yourself should betray your trust, dear sir? I mean, if you'll give me leave to
640 speak obscenely, you might tell, dear sir.

HORNER. If I did, nobody would believe me: the reputation of impotency is as hardly recovered again in the world as that of cowardice, dear madam.

LADY FIDGET. Nay then, as one may say, you may do
645 your worst, dear, dear, sir.

SIR JASPAR. Come, is your ladyship reconciled to him yet? Have you agreed on matters? For I must be gone to Whitehall.

LADY FIDGET. Why indeed, Sir Jaspar, Master Horner
650 is a thousand, thousand times a better man than I thought him.—Cousin Squeamish, Sister Dainty, I can name him now. Truly not long ago, you know, I thought his very name obscenity, and I would as soon have lain with him as have named him.

655 SIR JASPAR. Very likely, poor madam.

DAINTY. I believe it.

MRS. SQUEAMISH. No doubt on't.

SIR JASPAR. Well, well, that your ladyship is as virtuous as any she, I know, and him all the Town knows, he, he,
660 he. Therefore, now you like him, get you gone to your business together. Go, go, to your business, I say, pleasure, whilst I go to my pleasure, business.

LADY FIDGET. Come then, dear gallant.

---

[1] *Cuz* Cousin.

HORNER.   Come away, my dearest mistress.

665   SIR JASPAR.   So, so, why 'tis as I'd have it. (*Exit.*)

HORNER.   And as I'd have it.

LADY FIDGET.   Who for his business from his wife will run
Takes the best care to have her business done.

(*Exeunt.*)

ACT 3, SCENE 1. [Pinchwife's lodging.]

(*Alithea and Margery.*)

ALITHEA.   Sister, what ails you, you are grown melancholy?

MARGERY.   Would it not make anyone melancholy to
see you go every day fluttering about abroad, whilst I
5   must stay at home like a poor lonely, sullen bird in a
cage?

ALITHEA.   Aye sister, but you came young and just from
the nest to your cage, so that I thought you liked it and
could be as cheerful in't as others that took their flight
10   themselves early and are hopping abroad in the open air.

MARGERY.   Nay, I confess I was quiet enough till my
husband told me what pure[1] lives the London ladies live
abroad, with their dancing, meetings, and junketings,
and dressed every day in their best gowns, and I warrant
15   you, play at ninepins every day of the week, so they do.

(*Enter Pinchwife.*)

PINCHWIFE.   Come, what's here to do? You are putting
the Town pleasures in her head and setting her a-
longing.

ALITHEA.   Yes, after ninepins! You suffer none to give
20   her those longings, you mean, but yourself.

PINCHWIFE.   I tell her of the vanities of the Town like a
confessor.

ALITHEA.   A confessor! just such a confessor as he that by
forbidding a silly ostler to grease the horses' teeth,[2]
25   taught him to do't.

PINCHWIFE.   Come Mistress Flippant, good precepts are
lost when bad examples are still before us: the liberty
you take abroad makes her hanker after it and out of

humor at home, poor wretch! She desired not to come
30   to London; I would bring her.

ALITHEA.   Very well.

PINCHWIFE.   She has been this week in Town and never
desired, till this afternoon, to go abroad.

ALITHEA.   Was she not at a play yesterday?

35   PINCHWIFE.   Yes, but she ne'er asked me; I was myself
the cause of her going.

ALITHEA.   Then if she ask you again, you are the cause
of her asking, and not my example.

PINCHWIFE.   Well, tomorrow night I shall be rid of you,
40   and the next day before 'tis light, she and I'll be rid of
the Town and my dreadful apprehensions.—Come, be
not melancholy, for thou shalt go into the country after
tomorrow, dearest.

ALITHEA.   Great comfort.

45   MARGERY.   Pish, what d'ye tell me of the country for?

PINCHWIFE.   How's this! What, pish at the country?

MARGERY.   Let me alone; I am not well.

PINCHWIFE.   Oh, if that be all—what ails my dearest?

MARGERY.   Truly I don't know, but I have not been well
50   since you told me there was a gallant at the play in love
with me.

PINCHWIFE.   Hah—

ALITHEA.   That's by my example too.

PINCHWIFE.   Nay, if you are not well but are so con-
55   cerned because a lewd fellow chanced to lie and say he
liked you, you'll make me sick, too.

MARGERY.   Of what sickness?

PINCHWIFE.   Oh, of that which is worse than the plague,
jealousy.

60   MARGERY.   Pish, you jeer. I'm sure there's no such
disease in our receipt-book at home.

PINCHWIFE.   No, thou never met'st with it, poor innocent. (*Aside.*) Well, if thou cuckold me, 'twill be my
own fault, for cuckolds and bastards are generally
65   makers of their own fortune.

MARGERY.   Well but pray, bud, let's go to a play tonight.

PINCHWIFE.   'Tis just done; she comes from it.—But
why are you so eager to see a play?

MARGERY.   Faith dear, not that I care one pin for their
70   talk there, but I like to look upon the playermen and
would see, if I could, the gallant you say loves me; that's
all, dear bud.

PINCHWIFE.   Is that all, dear bud?

ALITHEA.   This proceeds from my example.

---

[1]   *pure*   Fine; wonderful (a ruralism).

[2]   *grease the horses's teeth*   Ruse by which horses cannot eat what
their owners have paid for.

75 MARGERY. But if the play be done, let's go abroad, however, dear bud.

PINCHWIFE. Come, have a little patience, and thou shalt go into the country on Friday.

MARGERY. Therefore, I would see first some sights to 80 tell my neighbors of. Nay, I will go abroad, that's once.[1]

ALITHEA. I'm the cause of this desire, too.

PINCHWIFE. But now I think on't, who was the cause of Horner's coming to my lodging today? That was you.

ALITHEA. No, you, because you would not let him see 85 your handsome wife out of your lodging.

MARGERY. Why, oh Lord! Did the gentleman come hither to see me indeed?

PINCHWIFE. No, no.—You are not cause of that damned question, too, Mistress Alithea? (*Aside.*) Well, 90 she's in the right of it: he is in love with my wife—and comes after her. 'Tis so. But I'll nip his love in the bud, lest he should follow us into the country and break his chariot[2] wheel near our house on purpose for an excuse to come to't. But I think I know the Town.

95 MARGERY. Come, pray bud, let's go abroad before 'tis late, for I will go, that's flat and plain.

PINCHWIFE. (*Aside.*) So! The obstinacy already of a Town wife, and I must, whilst she's here, humor her like one.—Sister, how shall we do, that she may not be 100 seen or known?

ALITHEA. Let her put on her mask.

PINCHWIFE. Pshaw, a mask makes people but the more inquisitive and is as ridiculous a disguise as a stage beard; her shape, stature, habit will be known, and if we 105 should meet with Horner, he would be sure to take acquaintance with us, must wish her joy, kiss her, talk to her, leer upon her, and the devil and all. No, I'll not use her to a mask; 'tis dangerous, for masks have made more cuckolds than the best faces that ever were known.

110 ALITHEA. How will you do then?

MARGERY. Nay, shall we go? The Exchange will be shut, and I have a mind to see that.

PINCHWIFE. So—I have it. I'll dress her up in the suit we are to carry down to her brother, little Sir James; 115 nay, I understand the Town tricks. Come, let's go dress her. A mask! No—a woman masked, like a covered dish, gives a man curiosity and appetite, when, it may be, uncovered, 'twould turn his stomach. No, no.

ALITHEA. Indeed, your comparison is something a 120 greasy one. But I had a gentle gallant used to say, a beauty masked, like the sun in eclipse, gathers together more gazers than if it shined out.

(*Exeunt.*)

ACT 3, SCENE 2. The New Exchange.

(*Enter Horner, Harcourt, Dorilant. [Clasp at his booth.]*)

DORILANT. Engaged to women, and not sup with us?

HORNER. Aye, a pox on 'em all.

HARCOURT. You were much a more reasonable man in the morning and had as noble resolutions against 'em as 5 a widower of a week's liberty.

DORILANT. Did I ever think to see you keep company with women in vain?

HORNER. In vain! No, 'tis since I can't love 'em, to be revenged on 'em.

10 HARCOURT. Now your sting is gone, you looked in the box amongst all those women like a drone in the hive: all upon you, shoved and ill-used by 'em all, and thrust from one side to t'other.

DORILANT. Yet he must be buzzing amongst 'em still, 15 like other old beetle-headed, lickerish drones. Avoid 'em and hate 'em as they hate you.

HORNER. Because I do hate 'em and would hate 'em yet more, I'll frequent 'em. You may see by marriage, nothing makes a man hate a woman more than her 20 constant conversation. In short, I converse with 'em, as you do with rich fools, to laugh at 'em and use 'em ill.

DORILANT. But I would no more sup with women unless I could lie with 'em, than sup with a rich cox-comb unless I could cheat him.

25 HORNER. Yes, I have known thee sup with a fool for his drinking; if he could set out your hand[3] that way only, you were satisfied, and if he were a wine-swallowing mouth, 'twas enough.

HARCOURT. Yes, a man drinks often with a fool, as he 30 tosses with a marker, only to keep his hand in ure.[4] But do the ladies drink?

---

1 *that's once* That's final, or positive; once and for all.

2 *chariot* Light four-wheeled vehicle.

3 *set out your hand* Furnish you.

4 *tosses … ure* Throws dice with a scorekeeper (i.e., one who doesn't play for money) to keep in practice.

HORNER. Yes sir, and I shall have the pleasure at least of laying 'em flat with a bottle and bring as much scandal that way upon 'em as formerly t'other.

35 HARCOURT. Perhaps you may prove as weak a brother amongst 'em that way as t'other.

DORILANT. Faugh, drinking with women is as unnatural as scolding with 'em, but 'tis a pleasure of decayed fornicators and the basest way of quenching love.

40 HARCOURT. Nay, 'tis drowning love instead of quenching it. But leave us for civil women, too!

DORILANT. Aye, when he can't be the better for 'em. We hardly pardon a man that leaves his friend for a wench, and that's a pretty lawful call.

45 HORNER. Faith, I would not leave you for 'em if they would not drink.

DORILANT. Who would disappoint his company at Lewis's[1] for a gossiping?

HARCOURT. Faugh, wine and women good apart, 50 together as nauseous as sack[2] and sugar. But hark you, sir, before you go, a little of your advice; an old maimed general, when unfit for action, is fittest for counsel. I have other designs upon women than eating and drinking with them. I am in love with Sparkish's mistress, 55 whom he is to marry tomorrow. Now how shall I get her?

(*Enter Sparkish, looking about.*)

HORNER. Why, here comes one will help you to her.

HARCOURT. He! He, I tell you, is my rival and will hinder my love.

50 HORNER. No, a foolish rival and a jealous husband assist their rivals' designs, for they are sure to make their women hate them, which is the first step to their love for another man.

HARCOURT. But I cannot come near his mistress but in 55 his company.

HORNER. Still the better for you, for fools are most easily cheated when they themselves are accessories, and he is to be bubbled of his mistress, as of his money, the common mistress, by keeping him company.

70 SPARKISH. Who is that, that is to be bubbled? Faith, let me snack;[3] I han't met with a bubble since Christmas. Gad, I think bubbles are like their brother woodcocks, go out with the cold weather.

HARCOURT. (*Apart to Horner.*) A pox! He did not hear 75 all, I hope.

SPARKISH. Come, you bubbling rogues, you. Where do we sup?—Oh Harcourt, my mistress tells me you have been making fierce love to her all the play long, ha, ha—but I—

80 HARCOURT. I make love to her?

SPARKISH. Nay, I forgive thee, for I think I know thee, and I know her, but I am sure I know myself.

HARCOURT. Did she tell you so? I see all women are like these of the Exchange, who, to enhance the price of 85 their commodities, report to their fond[4] customers offers which were never made 'em.

HORNER. Aye, women are as apt to tell before the intrigue as men after it and so show themselves the vainer sex. But hast thou a mistress, Sparkish? 'Tis as 90 hard for me to believe it as that thou ever hadst a bubble, as you bragged just now.

SPARKISH. Oh your servant, sir. Are you at your raillery, sir? But we were some of us beforehand with you today at the play. The wits were something bold with you, sir. 95 Did you not hear us laugh?

HARCOURT. Yes, but I thought you had gone to plays to laugh at the poet's wit, not at your own.

SPARKISH. Your servant, sir. No, I thank you. Gad, I go to a play as to a country treat: I carry my own wine to 100 one and my own wit to t'other, or else I'm sure I should not be merry at either, and the reason why we are so often louder than the players is because we think we speak more wit and so become the poet's rivals in his audience. For to tell you the truth, we hate the silly 105 rogues, nay, so much that we find fault even with their bawdy upon the stage whilst we talk nothing else in the pit as loud.

HORNER. But why shouldst thou hate the silly poets? Thou hast too much wit to be one, and they, like 110 whores, are only hated by each other, and thou dost scorn writing, I'm sure.

---

1 *Lewis's* Presumably a tavern or eating house.
2 *sack* Wine.
3 *snack* Share; take part.
4 *fond* Foolish.

SPARKISH. Yes, I'd have you to know, I scorn writing, but women, women, that make men do all foolish things, make 'em write songs, too; everybody does it. 'Tis e'en as common with lovers as playing with fans, and you can no more help rhyming to your Phyllis than drinking to your Phyllis.

HARCOURT. Nay, poetry in love is no more to be avoided than jealousy.

DORILANT. But the poets damned your songs, did they?

SPARKISH. Damn the poets! They turned 'em into burlesque, as they call it; that burlesque is a hocus-pocus trick they have got, which by the virtue of "*hictius doctius*,[1] topsey turvey," they make a wise and witty man in the world a fool upon the stage, you know not how, and 'tis, therefore, I hate 'em too, for I know not but it may be my own case, for they'll put a man into a play for looking asquint. Their predecessors were contented to make serving men only their stage fools, but these rogues must have gentlemen, with a pox to 'em, nay, knights. And indeed, you shall hardly see a fool upon the stage but he's a knight, and to tell you the truth, they have kept me these six years from being a knight in earnest, for fear of being knighted in a play and dubbed a fool.

DORILANT. Blame 'em not; they must follow their copy, the age.

HARCOURT. But why shouldst thou be afraid of being in a play, who expose yourself everyday in the playhouses and as public places?

HORNER. 'Tis but being on the stage instead of standing on a bench in the pit.

DORILANT. Don't you give money to painters to draw you like? And are you afraid of your pictures at length in a playhouse where all your mistresses may see you?

SPARKISH. A pox! Painters don't draw the small pox or pimples in one's face. Come, damn all your silly authors whatever, all books and booksellers, by the world, and all readers, courteous or uncourteous.

HARCOURT. But who comes here, Sparkish?

(*Enter Pinchwife and his wife in man's clothes; Alithea; Lucy, her maid.*)

SPARKISH. Oh hide me! There's my mistress, too. (*Hides himself behind Harcourt.*)

HARCOURT. She sees you.

SPARKISH. But I will not see her; 'tis time to go to Whitehall, and I must not fail the Drawing Room.

HARCOURT. Pray, first carry me and reconcile me to her.

SPARKISH. Another time, faith, the King will have supped.

HARCOURT. Not with the worse stomach for thy absence. Thou art one of those fools that think their attendance at the King's meals as necessary as his physicians', when you are more troublesome to him than his doctors or his dogs.

SPARKISH. Pshaw, I know my interest, sir. Prithee hide me.

HORNER. Your servant, Pinchwife.—What, he knows us not!

PINCHWIFE. (*To his wife aside.*) Come along.

MARGERY. Pray, have you any ballads? Give me sixpenny worth.

CLASP. We have no ballads.

MARGERY. Then give me *Covent Garden Drollery*,[2] and a play or two.—Oh here's *Tarugo's Wiles* and *The Slighted Maiden*.[3] I'll have them.

PINCHWIFE. (*Apart to her.*) No, plays are not for your reading. Come along. Will you discover yourself?

HORNER. Who is that pretty youth with him, Sparkish?

SPARKISH. I believe his wife's brother, because he's something like her, but I never saw her but once.

HORNER. Extremely handsome. I have seen a face like it, too. Let us follow 'em.

(*Exeunt Pinchwife, Margery; Alithea, Lucy, Horner, Dorilant following them.*)

HARCOURT. Come Sparkish, your mistress saw you and will be angry you go not to her; besides, I would fain be reconciled to her, which none but you can do, dear friend.

SPARKISH. Well that's a better reason, dear friend. I

---

[1] *hictius doctius* Standard part of the magician's (juggler's) repertoire; perhaps from *hicce est doctus* (Latin: this is the doctor).

[2] *Covent Garden Drollery* Miscellany of songs, poems, prologues and epilogues by various writers, including Wycherley, published in 1672.

[3] *Tarugo's Wiles* Comedy by Sir Thomas St. Serfe (1668); *The Slighted Maiden* Tragicomedy by Sir Robert Staplyton (1663).

would not go near her now for hers or my own sake, but I can deny you nothing, for though I have known thee a great while, never go,[1] if I do not love thee as well as a new acquaintance.

HARCOURT. I am obliged to you indeed, dear friend. I would be well with her only to be well with thee still, for these ties to wives usually dissolve all ties to friends. I would be contented she should enjoy you a-nights, but I would have you to my self a-days, as I have had, dear friend.

SPARKISH. And thou shalt enjoy me a-days, dear, dear friend, never stir,[2] and I'll be divorced from her sooner than from thee. Come along.

HARCOURT. (*Aside.*) So we are hard put to't when we make our rival our procurer, but neither she nor her brother would let me come near her now. When all's done, a rival is the best cloak to steal to a mistress under without suspicion, and when we have once got to her as we desire, we throw him off like other cloaks.

(*Exit Sparkish, Harcourt following him. Re-enter Pinchwife, Margery in man's clothes.*)

PINCHWIFE. (*To Alithea [offstage].*) Sister, if you will not go, we must leave you. (*Aside.*) The fool, her gallant, and she will muster up all the young saunterers of this place, and they will leave their dear seamstresses to follow us. What a swarm of cuckolds and cuckold-makers are here?—Come let's be gone, Mistress Margery.

MARGERY. Don't you believe that, I han't half my belly full of sights yet.

PINCHWIFE. Then walk this way.

MARGERY. Lord, what a power of brave signs are here! Stay—the Bull's Head, the Ram's Head, and the Stag's Head, dear—

PINCHWIFE. Nay, if every husband's proper sign here were visible, they would be all alike.

MARGERY. What d'ye mean by that, bud?

PINCHWIFE. 'Tis no matter—no matter, bud.

MARGERY. Pray tell me, nay, I will know.

PINCHWIFE. They would be all bulls', stags', and rams' heads.

(*Exeunt Pinchwife, Margery. Re-enter Sparkish, Harcourt, Alithea, Lucy at the other door.*)

SPARKISH. Come dear madam, for my sake, you shall be reconciled to him.

ALITHEA. For your sake, I hate him.

HARCOURT. That's something too cruel, madam, to hate me for his sake.

SPARKISH. Aye indeed, madam, too, too cruel to me to hate my friend for my sake.

ALITHEA. I hate him because he is your enemy, and you ought to hate him, too, for making love to me, if you love me.

SPARKISH. That's a good one! I hate a man for loving you! If he did love you, 'tis but what he can't help, and 'tis your fault not his, if he admires you. I hate a man for being of my opinion! I'll ne'er do't, by the world.

ALITHEA. Is it for your honor or mine to suffer a man to make love to me, who am to marry you tomorrow?

SPARKISH. Is it for your honor or mine to have me jealous? That he makes love to you is a sign you are handsome, and that I am not jealous is a sign you are virtuous. That, I think, is for your honor.

ALITHEA. But 'tis your honor, too, I am concerned for.

HARCOURT. But why, dearest madam, will you be more concerned for his honor than he is himself? Let his honor alone for my sake and his. He, he, has no honor—

SPARKISH. How's that?

HARCOURT. But what my dear friend can guard himself.

SPARKISH. Oh ho—that's right again.

HARCOURT. Your care of his honor argues his neglect of it, which is no honor to my dear friend here; therefore, once more, let his honor go which way it will, dear madam.

SPARKISH. Aye, aye, were it for my honor to marry a woman whose virtue I suspected and could not trust her in a friend's hands?

ALITHEA. Are you not afraid to lose me?

HARCOURT. He afraid to lose you, madam! No, no—you may see how the most estimable and most glorious creature in the world is valued by him. Will you not see it?

---

[1] *never go* Don't worry.

[2] *never stir* As above, don't worry.

SPARKISH.   Right, honest Frank, I have that noble value for her that I cannot be jealous of her.

270 ALITHEA.   You mistake him: he means you care not for me nor who has me.

SPARKISH.   Lord madam, I see you are jealous. Will you wrest a poor man's meaning from his words?

ALITHEA.   You astonish me, sir, with your want of
275 jealousy.

SPARKISH.   And you make me giddy, madam, with your jealousy and fears and virtue and honor; gad, I see virtue makes a woman as troublesome as a little reading or learning.

280 ALITHEA.   Monstrous!

LUCY. (*Behind.*)   Well, to see what easy husbands these women of quality can meet with! A poor chambermaid can never have such ladylike luck. Besides, he's thrown away upon her; she'll make no use of her fortune, her
285 blessing. None to a gentleman for a pure cuckold, for it requires good breeding to be a cuckold.

ALITHEA.   I tell you then plainly: he pursues me to marry me.

SPARKISH.   Pshaw—

290 HARCOURT.   Come madam, you see you strive in vain to make him jealous of me; my dear friend is the kindest creature in the world to me.

SPARKISH.   Poor fellow.

HARCOURT.   But his kindness only is not enough for
295 me, without your favor; your good opinion, dear madam, 'tis that must perfect my happiness. Good gentleman, he believes all I say; would you would do so. Jealous of me! I would not wrong him nor you for the world.

(*Alithea walks carelessly to and fro.*)

300 SPARKISH.   Look you there, hear him, hear him, and do not walk away so.

HARCOURT.   I love you, madam, so—

SPARKISH.   How's that! Nay—now you begin to go too far indeed.

305 HARCOURT.   So much, I confess, I say I love you, that I would not have you miserable and cast yourself away upon so unworthy and inconsiderable a thing as what you see here. (*Clapping his hand on his breast, points at Sparkish.*)

310 SPARKISH.   No, faith, I believe thou wouldst not, now his meaning is plain. But I knew before thou wouldst not wrong me nor her.

HARCOURT.   No, no, heavens forbid the glory of her sex should fall so low as into the embraces of such a con-
315 temptible wretch, the last of mankind—my dear friend here—I injure him. (*Embracing Sparkish.*)

ALITHEA.   Very well.

SPARKISH.   No, no, dear friend, I knew it.—Madam, you see he will rather wrong himself than me in giving
320 himself such names.

ALITHEA.   Do not you understand him yet?

SPARKISH.   Yes, how modestly he speaks of himself, poor fellow.

ALITHEA.   Methinks he speaks impudently of yourself,
325 since—before yourself, too, insomuch that I can no longer suffer his scurrilous abusiveness to you, no more than his love to me. (*Offers to go.*)

SPARKISH.   Nay, nay, madam, pray stay. His love to you! Lord madam, has he not spoke yet plain enough?

330 ALITHEA.   Yes indeed, I should think so.

SPARKISH.   Well then, by the world, a man can't speak civilly to a woman now but presently[1] she says he makes love to her. Nay madam, you shall stay, with your pardon, since you have not yet understood him, till he
335 has made an éclaircissement[2] of his love to you, that is, what kind of love it is.—Answer to thy catechism. Friend, do you love my mistress here?

HARCOURT.   Yes, I wish she would not doubt it.

SPARKISH.   But how do you love her?

340 HARCOURT.   With all my soul.

ALITHEA.   I thank him, methinks he speaks plain enough now.

SPARKISH. (*To Alithea.*)   You are out[3] still.—But with what kind of love, Harcourt?

345 HARCOURT.   With the best and truest love in the world.

SPARKISH.   Look you there then: that is with no matrimonial love, I'm sure.

ALITHEA.   How's that, do you say matrimonial love is not best?

---

[1] *presently* Instantly or immediately.

[2] *éclaircissement* Clarification.

[3] *out* Mistaken.

SPARKISH. [*Aside.*] Gad, I went too far ere I was aware.—But speak for thyself, Harcourt: you said you would not wrong me nor her.

HARCOURT. No, no, madam, e'en take him for Heaven's sake—

SPARKISH. Look you there, madam.

HARCOURT. Who should in all justice be yours, he that loves you most. (*Claps his hand on his breast.*)

ALITHEA. Look you there, Mr. Sparkish. Who's that?

SPARKISH. Who should it be? Go on, Harcourt.

HARCOURT. Who loves you more than women, titles, or fortune fools. (*Points at Sparkish.*)

SPARKISH. Look you there: he means me still, for he points at me.

ALITHEA. Ridiculous!

HARCOURT. Who can only match your faith and constancy in love.

SPARKISH. Aye.

HARCOURT. Who knows, if it be possible, how to value so much beauty and virtue.

SPARKISH. Aye.

HARCOURT. Whose love can no more be equaled in the world than that heavenly form of yours.

SPARKISH. No—

HARCOURT. Who could no more suffer a rival than your absence and yet could no more suspect your virtue than his own constancy in his love to you.

SPARKISH. No—

HARCOURT. Who, in fine, loves you better than his eyes that first made him love you.

SPARKISH. Aye.—Nay madam, faith you shan't go till—

ALITHEA. Have a care lest you make me stay too long—

SPARKISH. But till he has saluted[1] you, that I may be assured you are friends after his honest advice and declaration. Come pray, madam, be friends with him.

(*Enter Pinchwife, Margery.*)

ALITHEA. You must pardon me, sir, that I am not yet so obedient to you.

PINCHWIFE. What, invite your wife to kiss men? Monstrous! Are you not ashamed? I will never forgive you.

SPARKISH. Are you not ashamed that I should have more confidence in the chastity of your family than you

have? You must not teach me: I am a man of honor, sir, though I am frank and free. I am frank, sir—

PINCHWIFE. Very frank, sir, to share your wife with your friends.

SPARKISH. He is an humble, menial friend, such as reconciles the differences of the marriage bed. You know man and wife do not always agree. I design him for that use, therefore, would have him well with my wife.

PINCHWIFE. A menial friend—you will get a great many menial friends by showing your wife as you do.

SPARKISH. What then, it may be I have a pleasure in't, as I have to show fine clothes at a playhouse the first day[2] and count money before poor rogues.

PINCHWIFE. He that shows his wife or money will be in danger of having them borrowed sometimes.

SPARKISH. I love to be envied and would not marry a wife that I alone could love; loving alone is as dull as eating alone. Is it not a frank age, and I am a frank person? And to tell you the truth, it may be I love to have rivals in a wife: they make her seem to a man still but as a kept mistress, and so good night, for I must to Whitehall.—Madam, I hope you are now reconciled to my friend, and so I wish you a good night, madam, and sleep if you can, for tomorrow you know I must visit you early with a canonical gentleman.[3]—Good night, dear Harcourt. (*Exit.*)

HARCOURT. Madam, I hope you will not refuse my visit tomorrow, if it should be earlier, with a canonical gentleman, than Mr. Sparkish's.

PINCHWIFE. (*Coming between Alithea and Harcourt.*) This gentlewoman is yet under my care; therefore, you must yet forbear your freedom with her, sir.

HARCOURT. Must, sir—

PINCHWIFE. Yes, sir, she is my sister.

HARCOURT. 'Tis well she is, sir—for I must be her servant, sir.—Madam—

PINCHWIFE. Come away, sister. We had been gone if it had not been for you and so avoided these lewd rake-hells who seem to haunt us.

(*Enter Horner, Dorilant to them.*)

HORNER. How now, Pinchwife?

PINCHWIFE. Your servant.

---

[2] *the first day* I.e., the first performance of a play.

[3] *canonical gentleman* Clergyman.

[1] *saluted* Kissed.

HORNER. What, I see a little time in the country makes a man turn wild and unsociable and only fit to converse with his horses, dogs, and his herds.

PINCHWIFE. I have business, sir, and must mind it. Your business is pleasure; therefore, you and I must go different ways.

HORNER. Well, you may go on, but this pretty young gentleman—— (*Takes hold of Margery.*)

HARCOURT. The lady—

DORILANT. And the maid—

HORNER. Shall stay with us, for I suppose their business is the same with ours, pleasure.

PINCHWIFE. (*Aside.*) 'Sdeath, he knows her, she carries it so sillily, yet if he does not, I should be more silly to discover it first.

ALITHEA. Pray let us go, sir.

PINCHWIFE. Come, come—

HORNER. (*To Margery.*) Had you not rather stay with us?—Prithee Pinchwife, who is this pretty young gentleman?

PINCHWIFE. One to whom I'm a guardian. (*Aside.*) I wish I could keep her out of your hands—

HORNER. Who is he? I never saw any thing so pretty in all my life.

PINCHWIFE. Pshaw, do not look upon him so much. He's a poor bashful youth; you'll put him out of countenance. Come away, brother. (*Offers to take her away.*)

HORNER. Oh your brother!

PINCHWIFE. Yes, my wife's brother.—Come, come, she'll stay supper for us.

HORNER. I thought so, for he is very like her I saw you at the play with, whom I told you I was in love with.

MARGERY. (*Aside.*) Oh jiminy! Is this he that was in love with me? I am glad on't, I vow, for he's a curious fine gentleman, and I love him already, too. (*To Mr. Pinchwife.*) Is this he, bud?

PINCHWIFE. (*To his wife.*) Come away, come away.

HORNER. Why, what haste are you in? Why won't you let me talk with him?

PINCHWIFE. Because you'll debauch him. He's yet young and innocent, and I would not have him debauched for anything in the world. (*Aside.*) How she gazes on him! The devil—

HORNER. Harcourt, Dorilant, look you here: this is the likeness of that dowdy he told us of, his wife. Did you ever see a lovelier creature? The rogue has reason to be jealous of his wife, since she is like him, for she would make all that see her in love with her.

HARCOURT. And as I remember now, she is as like him here as can be.

DORILANT. She is indeed very pretty, if she be like him.

HORNER. Very pretty? a very pretty commendation! She is a glorious creature, beautiful beyond all things I ever beheld.

PINCHWIFE. So, so.

HARCOURT. More beautiful than a poet's first mistress of imagination.

HORNER. Or another man's last mistress of flesh and blood.

MARGERY. Nay, now you jeer, sir. Pray don't jeer me—

PINCHWIFE. Come, come. (*Aside.*) By heavens, she'll discover herself!

HORNER. I speak of your sister, sir.

PINCHWIFE. Aye, but saying she was handsome, if like him, made him blush. (*Aside.*) I am upon a rack—

HORNER. Methinks he is so handsome, he should not be a man.

PINCHWIFE. [*Aside.*] Oh there 'tis out! He has discovered her! I am not able to suffer any longer. (*To his wife.*) Come, come away, I say—

HORNER. Nay by your leave, sir, he shall not go yet.—Harcourt, Dorilant, let us torment this jealous rogue a little.

HARCOURT AND DORILANT. How?

HORNER. I'll show you.

PINCHWIFE. Come, pray let him go. I cannot stay fooling any longer. I tell you his sister stays supper for us.

HORNER. Does she? Come then we'll all go sup with her and thee.

PINCHWIFE. No, now I think on't, having stayed so long for us, I warrant she's gone to bed. (*Aside.*) I wish she and I were well out of their hands.—Come, I must rise early tomorrow, come.

HORNER. Well then, if she be gone to bed, I wish her and you a good night.—But pray, young gentleman, present my humble service to her.

MARGERY. Thank you heartily, sir.

PINCHWIFE. (*Aside.*) S'death, she will discover herself yet in spite of me.—He is something more civil to you, for your kindness to his sister, than I am, it seems.

HORNER. Tell her, dear sweet little gentleman, for all

25 your brother there, that you have revived the love I had for her at first sight in the playhouse.

MARGERY. But did you love her indeed and indeed?

PINCHWIFE. (*Aside.*) So, so.—Away, I say.

HORNER. Nay, stay. Yes, indeed and indeed, pray do
30 you tell her so and give her this kiss from me. (*Kisses her.*)

PINCHWIFE. (*Aside.*) Oh heavens! What do I suffer! Now 'tis too plain he knows her and yet—

HORNER. And this and this— (*Kisses her again.*)
35 MARGERY. What do you kiss me for? I am no woman.

PINCHWIFE. (*Aside.*) So—there 'tis out.—Come, I cannot, nor will stay any longer.

HORNER. Nay, they shall send your lady a kiss, too. Here Harcourt, Dorilant, will you not?

(*They kiss her.*)

40 PINCHWIFE. (*Aside.*) How! Do I suffer this? Was I not accusing another just now for this rascally patience in permitting his wife to be kissed before his face? Ten thousand ulcers gnaw away their lips.—Come, come.

HORNER. Good night, dear little gentleman.—Madam,
45 good night.—Farewell, Pinchwife. (*Apart to Harcourt and Dorilant.*) Did not I tell you I would raise his jealous gall?

(*Exeunt Horner, Harcourt, and Dorilant.*)

PINCHWIFE. So they are gone at last.—Stay, let me see first if the coach be at this door. (*Exit.*)

(*Horner, Harcourt, Dorilant return.*)

50 HORNER. What, not gone yet? Will you be sure to do as I desired you, sweet sir?

MARGERY. Sweet sir, but what will you give me then?

HORNER. Anything. Come away into the next walk.

(*Exit Horner, haling away Margery.*)

ALITHEA. Hold, hold, what d'ye do?
55 LUCY. Stay, stay, hold—

(*Alithea, Lucy struggling with Harcourt and Dorilant.*)

HARCOURT. Hold, madam, hold. Let him present him; he'll come presently. Nay, I will never let you go till you answer my question.

LUCY. For God's sake, sir, I must follow 'em.
560 DORILANT. No, I have something to present you with, too. You shan't follow them.

Pinchwife returns.

PINCHWIFE. Where? how? what's become of—? Gone! Whither?

LUCY. He's only gone with the gentleman, who will give
565 him something, an't please your worship.

PINCHWIFE. Something—give him something, with a pox! Where are they?

ALITHEA. In the next walk only, brother.

PINCHWIFE. Only! Only! Where? Where? (*Exit and
570 returns presently, then goes out again.*)

HARCOURT. What's the matter with him? Why so much concerned?—But dearest madam—

ALITHEA. Pray let me go, sir. I have said and suffered enough already.

575 HARCOURT. Then you will not look upon nor pity my sufferings?

ALITHEA. To look upon 'em, when I cannot help 'em, were cruelty, not pity; therefore, I will never see you more.

580 HARCOURT. Let me then, madam, have my privilege of a banished lover: complaining or railing and giving you but a farewell reason why, if you cannot condescend to marry me, you should not take that wretch my rival.

ALITHEA. He only, not you, since my honor is engaged
585 so far to him, can give me a reason why I should not marry him, but if he be true and what I think him to me, I must be so to him. Your servant, sir.

HARCOURT. Have women only constancy when 'tis a vice and, like Fortune, only true to fools?

590 DORILANT. (*To Lucy, who struggles to get from him.*) Thou shalt not stir, thou robust creature. You see I can deal with you; therefore, you should stay the rather and be kind.

(*Enter Pinchwife.*)

PINCHWIFE. Gone, gone, not to be found! quite gone!
595 Ten thousand plagues go with 'em! Which way went they?

ALITHEA.   But into t'other walk, brother.

LUCY.   Their business will be done presently sure, an't please your worship; it can't be long in doing, I'm sure on't.

ALITHEA.   Are they not there?

PINCHWIFE.   No, you know where they are, you infamous wretch, eternal shame of your family, which you do not dishonor enough yourself, you think, but you must help her to do it, too, thou legion of bawds!

ALITHEA.   Good brother!

PINCHWIFE.   Damned, damned sister!

ALITHEA.   Look you here, she's coming.

(*Enter Margery in man's clothes, running with her hat under her arm, full of oranges and dried fruit, Horner following.*)

MARGERY.   Oh dear bud, look you here what I have got! See.

PINCHWIFE. (*Aside, rubbing his forehead.*)   And what I have got here, too, which you can't see.[1]

MARGERY.   The fine gentleman has given me better things yet.

PINCHWIFE. Has he so? (*Aside.*) Out of breath and colored—I must hold yet.

HORNER.   I have only given your little brother an orange, sir.

PINCHWIFE. (*To Horner.*)   Thank you, sir. (*Aside.*) You have only squeezed my orange, I suppose, and given it me again, yet I must have a City patience. (*To his wife.*) Come, come away.

MARGERY.   Stay, till I have put up my fine things, bud.

(*Enter Sir Jaspar Fidget.*)

SIR JASPAR.   Oh, Master Horner, come, come, the ladies stay for you. Your mistress, my wife, wonders you make not more haste to her.

HORNER.   I have stayed this half hour for you here, and 'tis your fault I am not now with your wife.

SIR JASPAR.   But pray, don't let her know so much; the truth on't is I was advancing a certain project to his Majesty about—I'll tell you.

HORNER.   No, let's go and hear it at your house.—Good night, sweet little gentleman. One kiss more. (*Kisses her.*) You'll remember me now, I hope.

DORILANT.   What, Sir Jaspar, will you separate friends? He promised to sup with us, and if you take him to your house, you'll be in danger of our company, too.

SIR JASPAR.   Alas gentlemen, my house is not fit for you: there are none but civil women there, which are not for your turn. He, you know, can bear with the society of civil women, now, ha, ha, ha. Besides he's one of my family;[2] he's—he, he, he.

DORILANT.   What is he?

SIR JASPAR.   Faith, my eunuch, since you'll have it, he, he, he.

(*Exit Sir Jaspar Fidget and Horner.*)

DORILANT.   I rather wish thou wert his, or my cuckold.—Harcourt, what a good cuckold is lost there for want of a man to make him one; thee and I cannot have Horner's privilege, who can make use of it.

HARCOURT.   Aye, to poor Horner 'tis like coming to an estate at threescore,[3] when a man can't be the better for't.

PINCHWIFE.   Come.

MARGERY.   Presently, bud.

DORILANT.   Come, let us go, too. (*To Alithea.*) Madam, your servant. (*To Lucy.*) Good night, strapper.

HARCOURT.   Madam, though you will not let me have a good day or night, I wish you one, but dare not name the other half of my wish.

ALITHEA.   Good night, sir, forever.

MARGERY.   I don't know where to put this. Here, dear bud, you shall eat it. Nay, you shall have part of the fine gentleman's good things, or treat as you call it, when we come home.

PINCHWIFE.   Indeed I deserve it, since I furnished the best part of it. (*Strikes away the orange.*)
The gallant treats, presents, and gives the ball,
But 'tis the absent cuckold pays for all.

---

[1]   *Aside … can't see*   Reference to cuckold's horns.

[2]   *family*   Household.

[3]   *threescore*   Sixty (years of age).

ACT 4, SCENE 1. Pinchwife's house in the morning.

(*Lucy, Alithea dressed in new clothes.*)

LUCY. Well madam, now have I dressed you and set you out with so many ornaments and spent upon you ounces of essence and pulvillio,[1] and all this for no other purpose but as people adorn and perfume a corpse for a stinking second-hand grave, such or as bad I think Master Sparkish's bed.

ALITHEA. Hold your peace.

LUCY. Nay madam, I will ask you the reason why you would banish poor Master Harcourt forever from your sight? How could you be so hard-hearted?

ALITHEA. 'Twas because I was not hard-hearted.

LUCY. No, no, 'twas stark love and kindness, I warrant.

ALITHEA. It was so: I would see him no more because I love him.

LUCY. Hey day, a very pretty reason.

ALITHEA. You do not understand me.

LUCY. I wish you may yourself.

ALITHEA. I was engaged to marry, you see, another man, whom my justice will not suffer me to deceive or injure.

LUCY. Can there be a greater cheat or wrong done to a man than to give him your person without your heart? I should make a conscience of it.

ALITHEA. I'll retrieve it for him after I am married awhile.

LUCY. The woman that marries to love better will be as much mistaken as the wencher that marries to live better. No madam, marrying to increase love is like gaming to become rich: alas, you only lose what little stock you had before.

ALITHEA. I find by your rhetoric you have been bribed to betray me.

LUCY. Only by his merit that has bribed your heart, you see, against your word and rigid honor. But what a devil is this honor? 'Tis sure a disease in the head, like the megrim[2] or falling sickness,[3] that always hurries people away to do themselves mischief. Men lose their lives by it; women, what's dearer to 'em, their love, the life of life.

ALITHEA. Come, pray talk you no more of honor nor Master Harcourt. I wish the other would come to secure my fidelity to him and his right in me.

LUCY. You will marry him then?

ALITHEA. Certainly, I have given him already my word and will my hand, too, to make it good when he comes.

LUCY. Well, I wish I may never stick pin more, if he be not an arrant natural[4] to t'other fine gentleman.

ALITHEA. I own he wants the wit of Harcourt, which I will dispense withal for another want he has, which is want of jealousy, which men of wit seldom want.

LUCY. Lord madam, what should you do with a fool to your husband? You intend to be honest, don't you? Then that husbandly virtue, credulity, is thrown away upon you.

ALITHEA. He only that could suspect my virtue should have cause to do it; 'tis Sparkish's confidence in my truth that obliges me to be so faithful to him.

LUCY. You are not sure his opinion may last.

ALITHEA. I am satisfied 'tis impossible for him to be jealous after the proofs I have had of him. Jealousy in a husband, Heaven defend me from it! It begets a thousand plagues to a poor woman: the loss of her honor, her quiet, and her—

LUCY. And her pleasure.

ALITHEA. What d'ye mean, impertinent?

LUCY. Liberty is a great pleasure, madam.

ALITHEA. I say loss of her honor, her quiet, nay, her life sometimes, and what's as bad almost, the loss of this Town; that is, she is sent into the country, which is the last ill usage of a husband to a wife, I think.

LUCY. (*Aside.*) Oh does the wind lie there?—Then of necessity, madam, you think a man must carry his wife into the country if he be wise. The country is as terrible I find to our young English ladies as a monastery to those abroad. And on my virginity, I think they would rather marry a London gaoler than a high sheriff of a county, since neither can stir from his employment. Formerly women of wit married fools for a great estate, a fine seat, or the like, but now 'tis for a pretty seat only in Lincoln's Inn Fields, St. James's Fields, or the Pall Mall.[5]

(*Enter to them Sparkish and Harcourt dressed like a parson.*)

SPARKISH. Madam, your humble servant, a happy day to you and to us all.

HARCOURT. Amen.

ALITHEA. Who have we here?

85 SPARKISH. My chaplain, faith. Oh madam, poor Harcourt remembers his humble service to you and, in obedience to your last commands, refrains coming into your sight.

ALITHEA. Is not that he?

90 SPARKISH. No, fie, no, but to show that he ne'er intended to hinder our match, has sent his brother here to join our hands. When I get me a wife, I must get her a chaplain, according to the custom; this is his brother and my chaplain.

95 ALITHEA. His brother?

LUCY. (*Aside.*) And your chaplain, to preach in your pulpit then.

ALITHEA. His brother!

SPARKISH. Nay, I knew you would not believe it.—I

100 told you, sir, she would take you for your brother Frank.

ALITHEA. Believe it!

LUCY. (*Aside.*) His brother! Ha, ha, he, he has a trick left still it seems.

SPARKISH. Come my dearest, pray let us go to church

105 before the canonical hour[1] is past.

ALITHEA. For shame! You are abused still.

SPARKISH. By the world, 'tis strange now you are so incredulous.

ALITHEA. 'Tis strange you are so credulous.

110 SPARKISH. Dearest of my life, hear me: I tell you this is Ned Harcourt of Cambridge;[2] by the world, you see he has a sneaking college look. 'Tis true he's something like his brother Frank, and they differ from each other no more than in their age, for they were twins.

115 LUCY. Ha, ha, he.

ALITHEA. Your servant, sir. I cannot be so deceived, though you are. But come let's hear, how do you know what you affirm so confidently?

SPARKISH. Why, I'll tell you all. Frank Harcourt coming

120 to me this morning to wish me joy and present his

service to you, I asked him if he could help me to a parson, whereupon he told me he had a brother in Town who was in orders,[3] and he went straight away and sent him you see there to me.

125 ALITHEA. Yes, Frank goes, and puts on a black coat, then tells you he is Ned; that's all you have for't.

SPARKISH. Pshaw, pshaw, I tell you by the same token, the midwife put her garter about Frank's neck to know 'em asunder, they were so like.

130 ALITHEA. Frank tells you this, too.

SPARKISH. Aye, and Ned there too; nay, they are both in a story.

ALITHEA. So, so, very foolish.

SPARKISH. Lord, if you won't believe one, you had best

135 try him by your chambermaid there, for chambermaids must needs know chaplains from other men, they are so used to 'em.[4]

LUCY. Let's see: nay, I'll be sworn he has the canonical smirk and the filthy, clammy palm of a chaplain.

140 ALITHEA. Well, most reverend doctor, pray let us make an end of this fooling.

HARCOURT. With all my soul, divine, heavenly creature, when you please.

ALITHEA. He speaks like a chaplain indeed.

145 SPARKISH. Why, was there not, "soul," "divine," "heavenly," in what he said?

ALITHEA. Once more, most impertinent blackcoat, cease your persecution and let us have a conclusion of this ridiculous love.

150 HARCOURT. (*Aside.*) I had forgot, I must suit my style to my coat, or I wear it in vain.

ALITHEA. I have no more patience left; let us make once an end of this troublesome love, I say.

HARCOURT. So be it, seraphic lady, when your honor

155 shall think it meet and convenient so to do.

SPARKISH. Gad, I'm sure none but a chaplain could speak so, I think.

ALITHEA. Let me tell you, sir, this dull trick will not serve your turn. Though you delay our marriage, you

160 shall not hinder it.

HARCOURT. Far be it from me, munificent patroness, to delay your marriage. I desire nothing more than to marry you presently, which I might do, if you yourself

---

[1] *canonical hour* Twelve o'clock noon, the hour after which marriages could not legally be performed.

[2] *of Cambridge* I.e., of Cambridge University.

[3] *in orders* I.e., Holy Orders—reference to a clergyman.

[4] *chambermaids ... used to 'em* Alleged promiscuity between chambermaids and the clergy was a standard joke of the time.

would, for my noble, good-natured, and thrice generous
patron here would not hinder it.

SPARKISH. No, poor man, not I, faith.

HARCOURT. And now, madam, let me tell you plainly,
nobody else shall marry you, by heavens. I'll die first, for
I'm sure I should die[1] after it.

LUCY. [*Aside.*] How his love has made him forget his
function, as I have seen it in real parsons.

ALITHEA. That was spoken like a chaplain, too! Now
you understand him, I hope.

SPARKISH. Poor man, he takes it heinously to be refused.
I can't blame him; 'tis putting an indignity upon him
not to be suffered. But you'll pardon me, madam, it
shan't be; he shall marry us. Come away, pray madam.

LUCY. Ha, ha, he, more ado! 'Tis late.

ALITHEA. Invincible stupidity, I tell you he would marry
me as your rival, not as your chaplain.

SPARKISH. (*Pulling her away.*) Come, come, madam.

LUCY. I pray, madam, do not refuse this reverend divine
the honor and satisfaction of marrying you, for I dare
say, he has set his heart upon't, good doctor.

ALITHEA. What can you hope or design by this?

HARCOURT. [*Aside.*] I could answer her, a reprieve for
a day only often revokes a hasty doom; at worst, if she
will not take mercy on me and let me marry her, I have
at least the lover's second pleasure, hindering my rival's
enjoyment, though but for a time.

SPARKISH. Come, madam, 'tis e'en twelve o'clock, and
my mother charged me never to be married out of the
canonical hours. Come, come. Lord, here's such a deal
of modesty, I warrant, the first day.

LUCY. Yes, an't please your worship, married women
show all their modesty the first day, because married
men show all their love the first day.

(*Exeunt.*)

ACT 4, SCENE 2. A bedchamber.

(*Pinchwife, Margery.*)

PINCHWIFE. Come tell me, I say.

MARGERY. Lord, han't I told it an hundred times over?

PINCHWIFE. (*Aside.*) I would try, if in the repetition of
the ungrateful tale, I could find her altering it in the
least circumstance, for if her story be false, she is so
too.——Come, how was't, baggage?

MARGERY. Lord, what pleasure you take to hear it, sure!

PINCHWIFE. No, you take more in telling it, I find, but
speak. How was't?

MARGERY. He carried me up into the house next to the
Exchange.

PINCHWIFE. So, and you two were only in the room.

MARGERY. Yes, for he sent away a youth that was there,
for some dried fruit and China oranges.[2]

PINCHWIFE. Did he so? Damn him for it——and for——

MARGERY. But presently came up the gentlewoman of
the house.

PINCHWIFE. Oh 'twas well she did. But what did he do
whilst the fruit came?

MARGERY. He kissed me an hundred times and told me
he fancied he kissed my fine sister, meaning me, you
know, whom he said he loved with all his soul and bid
me be sure to tell her so and to desire her to be at her
window by eleven of the clock this morning, and he
would walk under it at that time.

PINCHWIFE. (*Aside.*) And he was as good as his word,
very punctual. A pox reward him for't.

MARGERY. Well, and he said if you were not within, he
would come up to her, meaning me, you know, bud,
still.

PINCHWIFE. (*Aside.*) So——he knew her certainly, but for
this confession I am obliged to her simplicity.——But
what, you stood very still when he kissed you?

MARGERY. Yes, I warrant you. Would you have had me
discovered myself?

PINCHWIFE. But you told me he did some beastliness to
you, as you called it. What was't?

MARGERY. Why, he put——

PINCHWIFE. What?

MARGERY. Why he put the tip of his tongue between
my lips and so muzzled[3] me——and I said I'd bite it.

PINCHWIFE. An eternal canker seize it, for a dog!

MARGERY. Nay, you need not be so angry with him
neither, for to say truth, he has the sweetest breath I ever
knew.

PINCHWIFE. The devil——you were satisfied with it then
and would do it again.

---

[1] *die* To suffer *la petite mort* ("the little death") of sexual orgasm.

[2] *China oranges* Sweet, thin-skinned oranges, a delicacy originally from China.

[3] *muzzled* French kissed.

MARGERY.   Not unless he should force me.

PINCHWIFE.   Force you, changeling! I tell you no
50   woman can be forced.

MARGERY.   Yes, but she may sure, by such a one as he,
for he's a proper, goodly strong man; 'tis hard, let me
tell you, to resist him.

PINCHWIFE. [*Aside*.]   So, 'tis plain she loves him, yet she
55   has not love enough to make her conceal it from me,
but the sight of him will increase her aversion for me
and love for him, and that love instruct her how to
deceive me and satisfy him, all idiot as she is. Love, 'twas
he gave women first their craft, their art of deluding; out
60   of Nature's hands they came plain, open, silly, and fit
for slaves, as she and Heaven intended 'em, but damned
Love—well—I must strangle that little monster whilst
I can deal with him.—Go fetch pen, ink, and paper out
of the next room.

65   MARGERY.   Yes bud. (*Exit*.)

PINCHWIFE.   Why should women have more invention
in love than men? It can only be because they have more
desires, more soliciting passions, more lust, and more of
the Devil.

(*Margery returns.*)

70   Come minx, sit down and write.

MARGERY.   Aye, dear bud, but I can't do't very well.

PINCHWIFE.   I wish you could not at all.

MARGERY.   But what should I write for?

PINCHWIFE.   I'll have you write a letter to your lover.

75   MARGERY.   Oh Lord, to the fine gentleman a letter!

PINCHWIFE.   Yes, to the fine gentleman.

MARGERY.   Lord, you do but jeer; sure you jest.

PINCHWIFE.   I am not so merry. Come write as I bid
you.

80   MARGERY.   What, do you think I am a fool?

PINCHWIFE. [*Aside*.]   She's afraid I would not dictate any
love to him; therefore, she's unwilling.—But you had
best begin.

MARGERY.   Indeed and indeed, but I won't, so I won't.

85   PINCHWIFE.   Why?

MARGERY.   Because he's in Town; you may send for him
if you will.

PINCHWIFE.   Very well, you would have him brought to
you. Is it come to this? I say take the pen and write, or
90   you'll provoke me.

MARGERY.   Lord, what d'ye make a fool of me for?
Don't I know that letters are never writ but from the
country to London and from London into the country?
Now he's in Town, and I am in Town, too; therefore, I
95   can't write to him, you know.

PINCHWIFE. (*Aside*.)   So, I am glad it is no worse; she is
innocent enough yet.—Yes, you may when your husband bids you write letters to people that are in Town.

MARGERY.   Oh may I so! Then I'm satisfied.

100   PINCHWIFE.   Come begin. (*Dictates*.) "Sir"—

MARGERY.   Shan't I say, "Dear Sir"? You know one says
always something more than bare "Sir."

PINCHWIFE.   Write as I bid you, or I will write whore
with this penknife in your face.

105   MARGERY.   Nay, good bud. (*She writes*.) "Sir"—

PINCHWIFE.   "Though I suffered last night your nauseous, loathed kisses and embraces"—Write.

MARGERY.   Nay, why should I say so? You know I told
you he had a sweet breath.

110   PINCHWIFE.   Write!

MARGERY.   Let me but put out "loathed."

PINCHWIFE.   Write I say!

MARGERY.   Well then. (*Writes*.)

PINCHWIFE.   Let's see what have you writ. (*Takes the
115   paper and reads*.) "Though I suffered last night your
kisses and embraces"—Thou impudent creature! Where
is "nauseous" and "loathed"?

MARGERY.   I can't abide to write such filthy words.

PINCHWIFE. (*Holds up penknife*.)   Once more, write as
120   I'd have you and question it not, or I will spoil thy
writing with this. I will stab out those eyes that cause my
mischief.

MARGERY.   Oh Lord, I will! [*Writes*.]

PINCHWIFE.   So—so—let's see now! (*Reads*.) "Though
125   I suffered last night your nauseous, loathed kisses, and
embraces." Go on: "Yet I would not have you presume
that you shall ever repeat them." So—

(*She writes.*)

MARGERY.   I have writ it.

PINCHWIFE.   On then: "I then concealed myself from
130   your knowledge to avoid your insolencies."

(*She writes.*)

MARGERY.   So—

PINCHWIFE.   "The same reason now I am out of your hands"—

(*She writes.*)

MARGERY.   So—

35 PINCHWIFE.   "Makes me own to you my unfortunate though innocent frolic of being in man's clothes"—

(*She writes.*)

MARGERY.   So—

PINCHWIFE.   "That you may forever more cease to pursue her who hates and detests you"—

(*She writes on.*)

40 MARGERY.   So—h— (*Sighs.*)

PINCHWIFE.   What, do you sigh?—"detests you—as much as she loves her husband and her honor."

MARGERY.   I vow, husband, he'll ne'er believe I should write such a letter.

45 PINCHWIFE.   What, he'd expect a kinder from you? Come now, your name only.

MARGERY.   What, shan't I say "Your most faithful, humble servant till death"?

PINCHWIFE.   No, tormenting fiend. (*Aside.*) Her style, I 50 find, would be very soft.—Come wrap it up now whilst I go fetch wax and a candle[1] and write on the back side "For Mr. Horner." (*Exit.*)

MARGERY.   "For Mr. Horner." So, I am glad he has told me his name. Dear Mr. Horner, but why should I send 55 thee such a letter that will vex thee and make thee angry with me?—Well, I will not send it.—Aye, but then my husband will kill me, for I see plainly he won't let me love Mr. Horner.—But what care I for my husband?—I won't so, I won't send poor Mr. Horner such a let-60 ter.—But then my husband— But oh, what if I writ at bottom, "My husband made me write it"?—Aye, but then my husband would see't.—Can one have no shift?[2] Ah, a London woman would have had a hundred

presently. Stay—what if I should write a letter and wrap 165 it up like this and write upon't, too?—Aye, but then my husband would see't.—I don't know what to do.—But yet y'vads[3] I'll try, so I will, for I will not send this letter to poor Mr. Horner, come what will on't. (*She writes and repeats what she hath writ.*) "Dear, sweet Mr. 170 Horner"—so—"My husband would have me send you a base, rude, unmannerly letter, but I won't,"—so— "and would have me forbid you loving me, but I won't,"—so—"and would have me say to you, I hate you, poor Mr. Horner, but I won't tell a lie for 175 him,"—there—"for I'm sure if you and I were in the country at cards together,"—so—"I could not help treading on your toe under the table"—so—"or rubbing knees with you and staring in your face till you saw me"—very well—"and then looking down and blushing 180 for an hour together."—so—"But I must make haste before my husband come, and now he has taught me to write letters, you shall have longer ones from me who am, dear, dear, poor dear Mr. Horner, your most humble friend and servant to command till death, 185 Margery Pinchwife." Stay, I must give him a hint at bottom—so—now wrap it up just like t'other—so— now write "For Mr. Horner."—But oh now what shall I do with it? For here comes my husband.

(*Enter Pinchwife.*)

PINCHWIFE. (*Aside.*)   I have been detained by a sparkish 190 coxcomb who pretended a visit to me, but I fear 'twas to my wife.—What, have you done?

MARGERY.   Aye, aye, bud, just now.

PINCHWIFE.   Let's see't. What d'ye tremble for? What, you would not have it go?

195 MARGERY.   Here. (*Aside.*) No, I must not give him that; so I had been served if I had given him this.

(*He opens and reads the first letter.*)

PINCHWIFE.   Come, where's the wax and seal?

MARGERY. (*Aside.*)   Lord, what shall I do now? Nay, then I have it.—Pray let me see't. Lord, you think me so 200 arrant a fool, I cannot seal a letter? I will do't, so I will. (*Snatches the letter from him, changes it for the other, seals it, and delivers it to him.*)

---

[1]   *wax and a candle*   Pinchwife will melt the wax on the folded letter and press the end of the candle into the wax. When the wax has cooled, the letter will be sealed.

[2]   *shift*   Change of clothes.

[3]   *y'vads*   In faith (rustic expression).

PINCHWIFE.   Nay, I believe you will learn that and other things, too, which I would not have you.

205   MARGERY.   So, han't I done it curiously?[1] (*Aside.*) I think I have: there's my letter going to Mr. Horner, since he'll needs have me send letters to folks.

PINCHWIFE.   'Tis very well, but I warrant, you would not have it go now?

210   MARGERY.   Yes indeed, but I would, bud, now.

PINCHWIFE.   Well, you are a good girl then. Come let me lock you up in your chamber till I come back, and be sure you come not within three strides of the window when I am gone, for I have a spy in the street.

(*Exit Margery. Pinchwife locks the door.*)

215   At least 'tis fit she think so. If we do not cheat women, they'll cheat us, and fraud may be justly used with secret enemies, of which a wife is the most dangerous. And he that has a handsome one to keep, and a frontier town, must provide against treachery rather than open force.

220   Now I have secured all within, I'll deal with the foe without with false intelligence.

(*Holds up the letter and exits.*)

ACT 4, SCENE 3. Horner's lodging.

(*Quack and Horner.*)

QUACK.   Well sir, how fadges[2] the new design? Have you not the luck of all your brother projectors,[3] to deceive only yourself at last?

HORNER.   No, good domine[4] doctor, I deceive you, it

5   seems, and others too, for the grave matrons and old rigid husbands think me as unfit for love as they are. But their wives, sisters, and daughters know, some of 'em, better things already.

QUACK.   Already!

10   HORNER.   Already, I say. Last night I was drunk with half a dozen of your civil persons, as you call 'em, and people of honor and so was made free of their society

and dressing rooms forever hereafter and am already come to the privileges of sleeping upon their pallets,

15   warming smocks, tying shoes and garters, and the like, doctor, already, already, doctor.

QUACK.   You have made use of your time, sir.

HORNER.   I tell thee, I am now no more interruption to 'em when they sing or talk bawdy than a little, squab,

20   French page who speaks no English.

QUACK.   But do civil persons and women of honor drink and sing bawdy songs?

HORNER.   Oh amongst friends, amongst friends. For your bigots in honor are just like those in religion: they

25   fear the eye of the world more than the eye of Heaven and think there is no virtue but railing at vice and no sin but giving scandal. They rail at a poor, little, kept player[5] and keep themselves some young, modest pulpit comedian to be privy to their sins in their closets,[6] not

30   to tell 'em of them in their chapels.

QUACK.   Nay, the truth on't is, priests amongst the women now have quite got the better of us lay confessors, physicians.

HORNER.   And they are rather their patients, but—

(*Enter Lady Fidget, looking about her.*)

35   Now we talk of women of honor, here comes one. Step behind the screen there and but observe if I have not particular privileges with the women of reputation already, doctor, already.

LADY FIDGET.   Well Horner, am not I a woman of

40   honor? You see I'm as good as my word.

HORNER.   And you shall see, madam, I'll not be behind-hand with you in honor, and I'll be as good as my word, too, if you please but to withdraw into the next room.

LADY FIDGET.   But first, my dear sir, you must promise

45   to have a care of my dear honor.

HORNER.   If you talk a word more of your honor, you'll make me incapable to wrong it. To talk of honor in the mysteries of love is like talking of Heaven or the Deity in an operation of witchcraft: just when you are employ-

50   ing the Devil, it makes the charm impotent.

LADY FIDGET.   Nay, fie, let us not be smutty! But you talk of mysteries and bewitching to me; I don't under-stand you.

---

1   *curiously*   Skillfully.

2   *fadges*   Prospers.

3   *projectors*   Schemers.

4   *domine*   Master (of a profession).

5   *player*   Actress.

6   *closets*   Small private rooms, generally within bedchambers.

HORNER. I tell you, madam, the word "money" in a mistress's mouth at such a nick of time is not a more disheartening sound to a younger brother than that of "honor" to an eager lover like myself.

LADY FIDGET.   But you can't blame a lady of my reputation to be chary.

HORNER.   Chary! I have been chary of it already by the report I have caused of myself.

LADY FIDGET. Aye, but if you should ever let other women know that dear secret, it would come out. Nay, you must have a great care of your conduct, for my acquaintance are so censorious (oh 'tis a wicked censorious world, Mr. Horner), I say, are so censorious and detracting that perhaps they'll talk to the prejudice of my honor, though you should not let them know the dear secret.

HORNER. Nay madam, rather than they shall prejudice your honor, I'll prejudice theirs, and to serve you, I'll lie with 'em all, make the secret their own, and then they'll keep it. I am a Machiavel[1] in love, madam.

LADY FIDGET.   Oh no, sir, not that way.

HORNER. Nay, the devil take me if censorious women are to be silenced any other way.

LADY FIDGET.   A secret is better kept, I hope, by a single person than a multitude; therefore, pray do not trust anybody else with it, dear, dear Mr. Horner. (*Embracing him.*)

(*Enter Sir Jaspar Fidget.*)

SIR JASPAR.   How now!

LADY FIDGET. (*Aside.*) Oh my husband—prevented— and what's almost as bad, found with my arms about another man. That will appear too much. What shall I say?—Sir Jaspar, come hither. I am trying if Mr. Horner were ticklish, and he's as ticklish as can be. I love to torment the confounded toad. Let you and I tickle him.

SIR JASPAR. No, your ladyship will tickle him better without me, I suppose. But is this your buying china? I thought you had been at the china house?

HORNER. (*Aside.*) China house, that's my cue; I must take it.—A pox, can't you keep your impertinent wives at home? Some men are troubled with the husbands, but I with the wives. But I'd have you to know, since I cannot be your journeyman by night, I will not be your drudge by day, to squire your wife about and be your man of straw, or scarecrow, only to pies and jays[2] that would be nibbling at your forbidden fruit. I shall be shortly the hackney gentleman-usher of the Town.

SIR JASPAR. (*Aside.*) He, he, he, poor fellow, he's in the right on't, faith: to squire women about for other folks is as ungrateful an employment as to tell money for other folks.—He, he, he, ben't angry, Horner—

LADY FIDGET. No, 'tis I have more reason to be angry, who am left by you to go abroad indecently alone or, what is more indecent, to pin myself upon such ill-bred people of your acquaintance, as this is.

SIR JASPAR.   Nay prithee, what has he done?

LADY FIDGET.   Nay, he has done nothing.

SIR JASPAR. But what d'ye take ill if he has done nothing?

LADY FIDGET. Ha, ha, ha! Faith, I can't but laugh, however. Why, d'ye think, the unmannerly toad would not come down to me to the coach. I was fain to come up to fetch him or go without him, which I was resolved not to do, for he knows china very well and has himself very good, but will not let me see it, lest I should beg some. But I will find it out and have what I came for yet.

(*Exit Lady Fidget, and locks the door, followed by Horner to the door.*)

HORNER. (*Apart to Lady Fidget.*) Lock the door, madam.—So, she has got into my chamber and locked me out. Oh the impertinency of womankind! Well Sir Jaspar, plain dealing is a jewel: if ever you suffer your wife to trouble me again here, she shall carry you home a pair of horns, by my Lord Mayor she shall; though I cannot furnish you myself, you are sure yet I'll find a way.

SIR JASPAR. (*Aside.*) Ha, ha, he, at my first coming in and finding her arms about him, tickling him it seems, I was half jealous, but now I see my folly.—He, he, he, poor Horner.

HORNER. Nay, though you laugh now, 'twill be my turn ere long. Oh women, more impertinent, more cunning, and more mischievous than their monkeys and to me almost as ugly.—Now is she throwing my things

---

[1] *Machiavel* Unscrupulous villain, from Niccolò Machiavelli, author of a treatise on political power, *The Prince.*

[2] *pies and jays* Birds; magpies and jackdaws.

about and rifling all I have, but I'll get into her the back
way and so rifle her for it.

SIR JASPAR. Ha, ha, ha, poor angry Horner.

HORNER. Stay here a little. I'll ferret her out to you
140 presently, I warrant. (*Exit at the other door.*)

SIR JASPAR. Wife, my Lady Fidget, wife, he is coming
into you the back way.

(*Sir Jaspar calls through the door to his wife; she answers
from within.*)

LADY FIDGET. Let him come, and welcome, which way
he will.

145 SIR JASPAR. He'll catch you and use you roughly and be
too strong for you.

LADY FIDGET. Don't you trouble yourself; let him if he
can.

QUACK. (*Behind.*) This indeed I could not have believed
150 from him nor any but my own eyes.

(*Enter Mistress Squeamish.*)

MRS. SQUEAMISH. Where's this woman-hater, this toad,
this ugly, greasy, dirty sloven?

SIR JASPAR. [*Aside.*] So the women all will have him
ugly. Methinks he is a comely person, but his wants
155 make his form contemptible to 'em, and 'tis e'en as my
wife said yesterday, talking of him, that a proper handsome eunuch was as ridiculous a thing as a gigantic
coward.

MRS. SQUEAMISH. Sir Jaspar, your servant. Where is the
160 odious beast?

SIR JASPAR. He's within in his chamber with my wife;
she's playing the wag with him.

MRS. SQUEAMISH. Is she so? And he's a clownish[1] beast:
he'll give her no quarter; he'll play the wag with her
165 again, let me tell you. Come, let's go help her. What,
the door's locked?

SIR JASPAR. Aye, my wife locked it.

MRS. SQUEAMISH. Did she so? Let us break it open
then.

170 SIR JASPAR. No, no, he'll do her no hurt.

MRS. SQUEAMISH. No. (*Aside.*) But is there no other
way to get into 'em? Whither goes this? I will disturb
'em.

(*Exit Squeamish at another door. Enter Old Lady Squeamish.*)

OLD LADY SQUEAMISH. Where is this harlotry, this
175 impudent baggage, this rambling tomrig?[2]—Oh Sir
Jaspar, I'm glad to see you here. Did you not see my
vild[3] grandchild come in hither just now?

SIR JASPAR. Yes.

OLD LADY SQUEAMISH. Aye, but where is she then?
180 Where is she? Lord, Sir Jaspar, I have e'en rattled myself
to pieces in pursuit of her. But can you tell what she
makes here? They say below, no woman lodges here.

SIR JASPAR. No.

OLD LADY SQUEAMISH. No—what does she here then?
185 Say if it be not a woman's lodging, what makes she here?
But are you sure no woman lodges here?

SIR JASPAR. No, nor no man neither: this is Mr.
Horner's lodging.

OLD LADY SQUEAMISH. Is it so? Are you sure?

190 SIR JASPAR. Yes, yes.

OLD LADY SQUEAMISH. So then there's no hurt in't, I
hope. But where is he?

SIR JASPAR. He's in the next room with my wife.

OLD LADY SQUEAMISH. Nay, if you trust him with your
195 wife, I may with my Biddy. They say he's a merry,
harmless man now, e'en as harmless a man as ever came
out of Italy with a good voice[4] and as pretty harmless
company for a lady as a snake without his teeth.

SIR JASPAR. Aye, aye, poor man.

(*Enter Mrs. Squeamish.*)

200 MRS. SQUEAMISH. I can't find 'em.—Oh are you here,
Grandmother? I followed, you must know, my Lady
Fidget hither; 'tis the prettiest lodging, and I have been
staring on the prettiest pictures.

(*Enter Lady Fidget with a piece of china in her hand and
Horner following.*)

LADY FIDGET. And I have been toiling and moiling for
205 the prettiest piece of china, my dear.

---

1 *clownish* Unsophisticated.

2 *tomrig* Strumpet, tomboy.

3 *vild* Archaic form of "vile."

4 *man … good voice* Castrato, a male singer castrated as a youth to
preserve a soprano or alto voice.

HORNER. Nay, she has been too hard for me, do what I could.

MRS. SQUEAMISH. Oh Lord, I'll have some china, too. Good Mr. Horner, don't think to give other people china and me none. Come in with me, too.

HORNER. Upon my honor I have none left now.

MRS. SQUEAMISH. Nay, nay, I have known you deny your china before now, but you shan't put me off so. Come—

HORNER. This lady had the last there.

LADY FIDGET. Yes indeed, madam, to my certain knowledge he has no more left.

MRS. SQUEAMISH. Oh but it may be he may have some you could not find.

LADY FIDGET. What, d'ye think if he had had any left, I would not have had it too? For we women of quality never think we have china enough.

HORNER. Do not take it ill. I cannot make china for you all, but I will have a roll-waggon[1] for you, too, another time.

MRS. SQUEAMISH. Thank you, dear toad.

LADY FIDGET. (*To Horner, aside.*) What do you mean by that promise?

HORNER. (*Apart to Lady Fidget.*) Alas, she has an innocent, literal understanding.

OLD LADY SQUEAMISH. Poor Mr. Horner. He has enough to do to please you all, I see.

HORNER. Aye madam, you see how they use me.

OLD LADY SQUEAMISH. Poor gentleman, I pity you.

HORNER. I thank you, madam. I could never find pity but from such reverend ladies as you are; the young ones will never spare a man.

MRS. SQUEAMISH. Come, come, beast, and go dine with us, for we shall want a man at ombre after dinner.

HORNER. That's all their use of me, madam, you see.

MRS. SQUEAMISH. Come sloven, I'll lead you to be sure of you. (*Pulls him by the cravat.*[2])

OLD LADY SQUEAMISH. Alas, poor man, how she tugs him. Kiss, kiss her! That's the way to make such nice[3] women quiet.

HORNER. No madam, that remedy is worse than the torment; they know I dare suffer anything rather than do it.

OLD LADY SQUEAMISH. Prithee, kiss her, and I'll give you her picture in little[4] that you admired so last night, prithee do.

HORNER. Well, nothing but that could bribe me. I love a woman only in effigy and good painting as much as I hate them. I'll do't, for I could adore the Devil well painted. (*Kisses Mrs. Squeamish.*)

MRS. SQUEAMISH. Faugh, you filthy toad! Nay, now I've done jesting.

OLD LADY SQUEAMISH. Ha, ha, ha, I told you so.

MRS. SQUEAMISH. Faugh, a kiss of his—

SIR JASPAR. Has no more hurt in't than one of my spaniel's.

MRS. SQUEAMISH. Nor no more good neither.

QUACK. (*Behind.*) I will now believe anything he tells me.

(*Enter Pinchwife.*)

LADY FIDGET. Oh Lord, here's a man, Sir Jaspar! My mask, my mask. I would not be seen here for the world.

SIR JASPAR. What, not when I am with you?

LADY FIDGET. No, no, my honor—let's be gone.

MRS. SQUEAMISH. Oh Grandmother, let us be gone. Make haste, make haste. I know not how he may censure us.

LADY FIDGET. Be found in the lodging of anything like a man? Away.

(*Exeunt Sir Jaspar, Lady Fidget, Old Lady Squeamish, Mrs. Squeamish.*)

QUACK. (*Behind.*) What's here, another cuckold? He looks like one, and none else sure have any business with him.

HORNER. Well, what brings my dear friend hither?

PINCHWIFE. Your impertinency.

HORNER. My impertinency! Why, you gentlemen that have got handsome wives think you have a privilege of saying anything to your friends and are as brutish as if you were our creditors.

PINCHWIFE. No sir, I'll ne'er trust you anyway.

HORNER. But why not, dear Jack? Why diffide[5] in me

---

[1] *roll-waggon* Cylindrical-shaped Chinese vase.

[2] *cravat* Neckerchief.

[3] *nice* Fastidious; delicate.

[4] *picture in little* Miniature.

[5] *diffide* Lack confidence.

thou knowst so well?

PINCHWIFE. Because I do know you so well.

HORNER. Han't I been always thy friend, honest Jack, always ready to serve thee, in love or battle, before thou wert married and am so still?

PINCHWIFE. I believe so; you would be my second[1] now indeed.

HORNER. Well then, dear Jack, why so unkind, so grum, so strange to me? Come, prithee kiss me, dear rogue. Gad, I was always, I say, and am still as much thy servant as—

PINCHWIFE. As I am yours, sir. What, you would send a kiss to my wife, is that it?

HORNER. So there 'tis. A man can't show his friendship to a married man but presently he talks of his wife to you. Prithee, let thy wife alone and let thee and I be all one, as we were wont. What, thou art as shy of my kindness as a Lombard Street[2] alderman of a courtier's civility at Locket's.[3]

PINCHWIFE. But you are over-kind to me, as kind as if I were your cuckold already, yet I must confess you ought to be kind and civil to me since I am so kind, so civil to you as to bring you this. Look you there, sir. (*Delivers him a letter.*)

HORNER. What is't?

PINCHWIFE. Only a love letter, sir.

HORNER. From whom? (*Reads.*) How, this is from your wife!—hum—and hum—

PINCHWIFE. Even from my wife, sir. Am I not wondrous kind and civil to you now, too? (*Aside.*) But you'll not think her so.

HORNER. (*Aside.*) Hah, is this a trick of his or hers?

PINCHWIFE. The gentleman's surprised, I find. What, you expected a kinder letter?

HORNER. No faith, not I. How could I?

PINCHWIFE. Yes, yes, I'm sure you did. A man so well made as you are must needs be disappointed if the women declare not their passion at first sight or opportunity.

HORNER. [*Aside.*] But what should this mean? Stay, the postscript: "Be sure you love me whatsoever my husband says to the contrary, and let him not see this, lest

he should come home and pinch me or kill my squirrel." It seems he knows not what the letter contains.

PINCHWIFE. Come, ne'er wonder at it so much.

HORNER. Faith, I can't help it.

PINCHWIFE. Now I think I have deserved your infinite friendship and kindness and have showed myself sufficiently an obliging kind friend and husband. Am I not so, to bring a letter from my wife to her gallant?

HORNER. Aye, the devil take me, art thou the most obliging, kind friend and husband in the world, ha, ha.

PINCHWIFE. Well, you may be merry, sir, but in short I must tell you, sir, my honor will suffer no jesting.

HORNER. What dost thou mean?

PINCHWIFE. Does the letter want a comment? Then know, sir, though I have been so civil a husband as to bring you a letter from my wife, to let you kiss and court her to my face, I will not be a cuckold, sir, I will not.

HORNER. Thou art mad with jealousy. I never saw thy wife in my life but at the play yesterday, and I know not if it were she or no. I court her, kiss her!

PINCHWIFE. I will not be a cuckold, I say; there will be danger in making me a cuckold.

HORNER. Why, wert thou not well cured of thy last clap?

PINCHWIFE. I wear a sword.

HORNER. It should be taken from thee lest thou shouldst do thyself a mischief with it. Thou art mad, man.

PINCHWIFE. As mad as I am and as merry as you are, I must have more reason from you ere we part, I say again, though you kissed and courted last night my wife in man's clothes, as she confesses in her letter.

HORNER. (*Aside.*) Hah!

PINCHWIFE. Both she and I say you must not design it again, for you have mistaken your woman, as you have done your man.

HORNER. (*Aside.*) Oh I understand something now.— Was that thy wife? Why wouldst thou not tell me 'twas she? Faith, my freedom with her was your fault, not mine.

PINCHWIFE. (*Aside.*) Faith, so 'twas.

HORNER. Fie, I'd never do't to a woman before her husband's face, sure.

PINCHWIFE. But I had rather you should do't to my wife before my face than behind my back, and that you shall never do.

---

[1] *second* In a duel, the friend who stands by a principal.

[2] *Lombard Street* In the City.

[3] *Locket's* Fashionable eating-house.

HORNER. No, you will hinder me.

PINCHWIFE. If I would not hinder you, you see by her letter, she would.

HORNER. Well, I must e'en acquiesce then and be contented with what she writes.

PINCHWIFE. I'll assure you 'twas voluntarily writ; I had no hand in't, you may believe me.

HORNER. I do believe thee, faith.

PINCHWIFE. And believe her too, for she's an innocent creature, has no dissembling in her, and so fare you well, sir.

HORNER. Pray however, present my humble service to her and tell her I will obey her letter to a tittle and fulfill her desires be what they will or with what difficulty soever I do't, and you shall be no more jealous of me, I warrant her, and you—

PINCHWIFE. Well then, fare you well, and play with any man's honor but mine, kiss any man's wife but mine, and welcome. (*Exit.*)

HORNER. Ha, ha, ha, doctor.

QUACK. It seems he has not heard the report of you or does not believe it.

HORNER. Ha, ha, now doctor, what think you?

QUACK. Pray let's see the letter. (*Reads.*) Hum—"for"—"dear"—"love you"—

HORNER. I wonder how she could contrive it! What say'st thou to't? 'Tis an original.

QUACK. So are your cuckolds, too, originals, for they are like no other common cuckolds, and I will henceforth believe it not impossible for you to cuckold the Grand Signior[1] amidst his guards of eunuchs, that I say.

HORNER. And I say for the letter, 'tis the first love letter that ever was without flames, darts, fates, destinies, lying, and dissembling in't.

(*Enter Sparkish pulling in Pinchwife.*)

SPARKISH. Come back! You are a pretty brother-in-law, neither go to church nor to dinner with your sister bride.

PINCHWIFE. My sister denies her marriage and you see is gone away from you dissatisfied.

SPARKISH. Pshaw, upon a foolish scruple that our parson was not in lawful orders and did not say all the Common Prayer,[2] but 'tis her modesty only, I believe. But let women be never so modest the first day, they'll be sure to come to themselves by night, and I shall have enough of her then. In the meantime, Harry Horner, you must dine with me; I keep my wedding at my aunt's in the Piazza.[3]

HORNER. Thy wedding! What stale maid has lived to despair of a husband, or what young one of a gallant?

SPARKISH. Oh your servant, sir. This gentleman's sister then—no stale maid.

HORNER. I'm sorry for't.

PINCHWIFE. (*Aside.*) How comes he so concerned for her?

SPARKISH. You sorry for't! Why, do you know any ill by her?

HORNER. No, I know none but by thee; 'tis for her sake, not yours, and another man's sake that might have hoped, I thought—

SPARKISH. Another man, another man, what is his name?

HORNER. Nay, since 'tis past, he shall be nameless. (*Aside.*) Poor Harcourt, I am sorry thou hast missed her.

PINCHWIFE. (*Aside.*) He seems to be much troubled at the match.

SPARKISH. Prithee, tell me.—Nay, you shan't go, brother.

PINCHWIFE. I must of necessity, but I'll come to you to dinner. (*Exit.*)

SPARKISH. But Harry, what, have I a rival in my wife already? But with all my heart, for he may be of use to me hereafter, for though my hunger is now my sauce and I can fall on heartily without. But the time will come, when a rival will be as good sauce for a married man to a wife as an orange to veal.

HORNER. Oh thou damned rogue, thou hast set my teeth on edge with thy orange.

SPARKISH. Then let's to dinner. There I was with you again. Come.

HORNER. But who dines with thee?

SPARKISH. My friends and relations, my brother Pinchwife, you see, of your acquaintance.

HORNER. And his wife?

---

1 *Grand Signior* Sultan of Turkey.

2 *Common Prayer* Marriage service within the Anglican *Book of Common Prayer*.

3 *Piazza* Arcade around two sides of Covent Garden.

SPARKISH.   No, gad, he'll ne'er let her come amongst us good fellows. Your stingy country coxcomb keeps his wife from his friends as he does his little firkin of ale for his own drinking, and a gentleman can't get a smack on't. But his servants, when his back is turned, broach it at their pleasure and dust it away, ha, ha, ha. Gad, I am witty, I think, considering I was married today, by the world, but come——

HORNER.   No, I will not dine with you unless you can fetch her, too.

SPARKISH.   Pshaw, what pleasure canst thou have with women now, Harry?

HORNER.   My eyes are not gone. I love a good prospect[1] yet and will not dine with you unless she does too. Go fetch her, therefore, but do not tell her husband 'tis for my sake.

SPARKISH.   Well, I'll go try what I can do. In the meantime, come away to my aunt's lodging; 'tis in the way to Pinchwife's.

HORNER. [Apart to Quack.]   The poor woman has called for aid and stretched forth her hand, doctor; I cannot but help her over the pale[2] out of the briars.

(Exeunt.)

ACT 4, SCENE 4. Pinchwife's house.

(Margery alone leaning on her elbow. A table, pen, ink, and paper.)

MARGERY.   Well 'tis e'en so: I have got the London disease they call love; I am sick of my husband and for my gallant. I have heard this distemper called a fever, but methinks 'tis liker an ague,[3] for when I think of my husband, I tremble and am in a cold sweat and have inclinations to vomit, but when I think of my gallant, dear Mr. Horner, my hot fit comes, and I am all in a fever indeed, and as in other fevers, my own chamber is tedious to me, and I would fain be removed to his, and then methinks I should be well. Ah poor Mr. Horner! Well, I cannot, will not stay here; therefore, I'll make an end of my letter to him, which shall be a finer letter than my last, because I have studied it like anything. Oh sick! sick! (Takes the pen and writes.)

(Enter Mr. Pinchwife, who, seeing her writing, steals softly behind her and looking over her shoulder, snatches the paper from her.)

PINCHWIFE.   What, writing more letters?

MARGERY.   Oh Lord, bud, why d'ye fright me so?

(She offers to run out; he stops her and reads.)

PINCHWIFE.   How's this! Nay, you shall not stir, madam. "Dear, dear, dear, Mr. Horner"—very well—I have taught you to write letters to good purpose, but let's see't. "First I am to beg your pardon for my boldness in writing to you, which I'd have you to know I would not have done, had not you said first you loved me so extremely, which if you do, you will never suffer me to lie in the arms of another man, whom I loathe, nauseate, and detest." Now you can write these filthy words! But what follows? "Therefore, I hope you will speedily find some way to free me from this unfortunate match, which was never, I assure you, of my choice, but I'm afraid 'tis already too far gone; however, if you love me, as I do you, you will try what you can do, but you must help me away before tomorrow, or else, alas, I shall be forever out of your reach for I can defer no longer our—" (The letter concludes.) "Our"? What is to follow "our"? Speak! What? Our journey into the country, I suppose. Oh woman, damned woman! And Love, damned Love, their old tempter! For this is one of his miracles: in a moment he can make those blind that could see and those see that were blind, those dumb that could speak and those prattle who were dumb before, nay, what is more than all, make these dough-baked,[4] senseless, indocile animals, women, too hard for us, their politic lords and rulers, in a moment. But make an end of your letter, and then I'll make an end of you thus and all my plagues together. (Draws his sword.)

MARGERY.   Oh Lord, oh Lord, you are such a passionate man, bud!

(Enter Sparkish.)

---

[1]   prospect   Scene; landscape.

[2]   pale   Fence.

[3]   ague   Fever.

[4]   dough-baked   Half-baked; foolish.

SPARKISH. How now, what's here to do?

PINCHWIFE. This fool here now!

SPARKISH. What, drawn upon your wife? You should
50 never do that but at night in the dark when you can't
hurt her. This is my sister-in-law, is it not? (*Pulls aside
her handkerchief.*) Aye faith, e'en our country Margery,
one may know her. Come, she and you must go dine
with me; dinner's ready, come. But where's my wife? Is
55 she not come home yet? Where is she?

PINCHWIFE. Making you a cuckold. 'Tis that they all do
as soon as they can.

SPARKISH. What, the wedding day? No, a wife that
designs to make a cully of her husband will be sure to let
60 him win the first stake of love, by the world. But come,
they stay dinner for us; come, I'll lead down, our
Margery.

MARGERY. No sir, go, we'll follow you.

SPARKISH. I will not wag without you.

65 PINCHWIFE. This coxcomb is a sensible torment to me
amidst the greatest in the world.

SPARKISH. Come, come, Madam Margery.

PINCHWIFE. No, I'll lead her my way. What, would you
treat your friends with mine, for want of your own wife?
70 (*Leads her to the other door and locks her in and returns.
Aside.*) I am contented my rage should take breath.

SPARKISH. I told Horner this.

PINCHWIFE. Come now.

SPARKISH. Lord, how shy you are of your wife, but let
75 me tell you, brother, we men of wit have amongst us a
saying that cuckolding, like the small pox, comes with
a fear, and you may keep your wife as much as you will
out of danger of infection, but if her constitution incline
her to't, she'll have it sooner or later, by the world, say
80 they.

PINCHWIFE. (*Aside.*) What a thing is a cuckold, that
every fool can make him ridiculous.—Well sir, but let
me advise you, now you are come to be concerned
because you suspect the danger, not to neglect the
85 means to prevent it, especially when the greatest share of
the malady will light upon your own head, for

Hows'e'er the kind wife's belly comes to swell,
The husband breeds[1] for her and first is ill.

ACT 5, SCENE 1. Pinchwife's house.

(*Enter Pinchwife and Margery. A table and candle.*)

PINCHWIFE. Come, take the pen and make an end of
the letter, just as you intended. If you are false in a tittle,
I shall soon perceive it and punish you with this as you
deserve. (*Lays his hand on his sword.*)
5 Write what was to follow. Let's see. "You must make
haste and help me away before tomorrow, or else I shall
be forever out of your reach, for I can defer no longer
our—" What follows "our"?

MARGERY. Must all out then, bud? (*Margery takes the
10 pen and writes.*) Look you there then.

PINCHWIFE. Let's see. "For I can defer no longer
our—wedding. Your slighted Alithea." What's the
meaning of this, my sister's name to't? Speak, unriddle!

MARGERY. Yes indeed, bud.

15 PINCHWIFE. But why her name to't? Speak—speak, I
say!

MARGERY. Aye, but you'll tell her then again. If you
would not tell her again—

PINCHWIFE. I will not. I am stunned; my head turns
20 round. Speak.

MARGERY. Won't you tell her indeed and indeed?

PINCHWIFE. No. Speak, I say.

MARGERY. She'll be angry with me, but I had rather she
should be angry with me than you, bud, and to tell you
25 the truth, 'twas she made me write the letter and taught
me what I should write.

PINCHWIFE. [*Aside.*] Hah! I thought the style was
somewhat better than her own.—But how could she
come to you to teach you, since I had locked you up
30 alone?

MARGERY. Oh, through the keyhole, bud.

PINCHWIFE. But why should she make you write a letter
for her to him, since she can write herself?

MARGERY. Why, she said because—for I was unwilling
35 to do it.

PINCHWIFE. Because what? Because?

MARGERY. Because lest Mr. Horner should be cruel and
refuse her, or vain afterwards and show the letter, she
might disown it, the hand not being hers.

40 PINCHWIFE. (*Aside.*) How's this? Hah! Then I think I
shall come to myself again. This changeling could not
invent this lie. But if she could, why should she? She

---

[1] *breeds* Grows the cuckold's horns.

might think I should soon discover it. Stay—now I think on't, too, Horner said he was sorry she had married Sparkish, and her disowning her marriage to me makes me think she has evaded it for Horner's sake. Yet why should she take this course? But men in love are fools; women may well be so.—But hark you, madam, your sister went out in the morning and I have not seen her within since.

MARGERY.   Alackaday, she has been crying all day above, it seems, in a corner.

PINCHWIFE.   Where is she? Let me speak with her.

MARGERY.   (*Aside.*)   Oh Lord, then he'll discover all.— Pray hold, bud. What, d'ye mean to discover me? She'll know I have told you then. Pray bud, let me talk with her first.

PINCHWIFE.   I must speak with her to know whether Horner ever made her any promise and whether she be married to Sparkish or no.

MARGERY.   Pray dear bud, don't till I have spoken with her and told her that I have told you all, for she'll kill me else.

PINCHWIFE.   Go then, and bid her come out to me.

MARGERY.   Yes, yes, bud.

PINCHWIFE.   Let me see—

MARGERY.   [*Aside.*]   I'll go, but she is not within to come to him. I have just got time to know of Lucy, her maid, who first set me on work, what lie I shall tell next, for I am e'en at my wit's end. (*Exit.*)

PINCHWIFE.   Well, I resolve it: Horner shall have her. I'd rather give him my sister than lend him my wife, and such an alliance will prevent his pretensions to my wife, sure. I'll make him of kin to her, and then he won't care for her.

(*Margery returns.*)

MARGERY.   Oh Lord, bud, I told you what anger you would make me with my sister.

PINCHWIFE.   Won't she come hither?

MARGERY.   No no, alackaday, she's ashamed to look you in the face, and she says if you go in to her, she'll run away downstairs and shamefully go herself to Mr. Horner, who has promised her marriage, she says, and she will have no other, so she won't—

PINCHWIFE.   Did he so—promise her marriage? Then she shall have no other. Go tell her so, and if she will come and discourse with me a little concerning the means, I will about it immediately. Go.

(*Exit Margery.*)

His estate is equal to Sparkish's, and his extraction as much better than his as his parts are, but my chief reason is I'd rather be of kin to him by the name of brother-in-law than that of cuckold.

(*Enter Margery.*)

Well, what says she now?

MARGERY.   Why, she says she would only have you lead her to Horner's lodging—with whom she first will discourse the matter before she talk with you, which yet she cannot do, for, alack poor creature, she says she can't so much as look you in the face; therefore, she'll come to you in a mask, and you must excuse her if she make you no answer to any question of yours till you have brought her to Mr. Horner, and if you will not chide her nor question her, she'll come out to you immediately.

PINCHWIFE.   Let her come. I will not speak a word to her nor require a word from her.

MARGERY.   Oh, I forgot: besides, she says, she cannot look you in the face though through a mask; therefore, would desire you to put out the candle.

PINCHWIFE.   I agree to all; let her make haste.

(*Exit Margery; [Pinchwife] puts out the candle.*)

There, 'tis out. My case is something better: I'd rather fight with Horner for not lying with my sister than for lying with my wife, and of the two, I had rather find my sister too forward than my wife. I expected no other from her free education, as she calls it, and her passion for the Town. Well, wife and sister are names which make us expect love and duty, pleasure and comfort, but we find 'em plagues and torments and are equally, though differently, troublesome to their keeper, for we have as much ado to get people to lie with our sisters as to keep 'em from lying with our wives.

(*Enter Margery masked and in hoods and scarves and a nightgown*[1] *and petticoat of Alithea's, in the dark.*)

20 What, are you come, sister? Let us go then, but first let me lock up my wife. Mistress Margery, where are you?
MARGERY. Here, bud.
PINCHWIFE. Come hither, that I may lock you up.

(*Margery gives him her hand, but when he lets her go, she steals softly on the other side of him.*)

Get you in. (*Locks the door.*) Come, sister, where are you
25 now?

([*She*] *is led away by him for his sister Alithea.*)

ACT 5, SCENE 2. Horner's lodging.

(*Quack, Horner.*)

QUACK. That, all alone, not so much as one of your cuckolds here nor one of their wives? They use to take their turns with you as if they were to watch you.
HORNER. Yes, it often happens that a cuckold is but his
5 wife's spy and is more upon family duty when he is with her gallant abroad hindering his pleasure than when he is at home with her playing the gallant. But the hardest duty a married woman imposes upon a lover is keeping her husband company always.
10 QUACK. And his fondness wearies you almost as soon as hers.
HORNER. A pox, keeping a cuckold company after you have had his wife is as tiresome as the company of a country squire to a witty fellow of the Town when he
15 has got all his money.
QUACK. And as at first a man makes a friend of the husband to get the wife, so at last you are fain to fall out with the wife to be rid of the husband.
HORNER. Aye, most cuckold-makers are true courtiers:
20 when once a poor man has cracked his credit for 'em, they can't abide to come near him.
QUACK. But at first to draw him in, are so sweet, so kind, so dear, just as you are to Pinchwife. But what becomes of that intrigue with his wife?
25 HORNER. A pox, he's as surly as an alderman that has

been bit,[2] and since he's so coy, his wife's kindness is in vain, for she's a silly innocent.
QUACK. Did she not send you a letter by him?
HORNER. Yes, but that's a riddle I have not yet solved.
30 Allow the poor creature to be willing, she is silly, too, and he keeps her up so close—
QUACK. Yes, so close that he makes her but the more willing and adds but revenge to her love, which two, when met, seldom fail of satisfying each other one way
35 or other.
HORNER. What, here's the man we are talking of, I think.

(*Enter Pinchwife leading in his wife masked, muffled, and in her sister's gown.*)

HORNER. Pshaw.
QUACK. Bringing his wife to you is the next thing to
40 bringing a love letter from her.
HORNER. What means this?
PINCHWIFE. The last time, you know, sir, I brought you a love letter; now you see a mistress. I think you'll say I am a civil man to you.
45 HORNER. Aye, the devil take me, will I say thou art the civilest man I ever met with, and I have known some. I fancy I understand thee now better than I did the letter, but hark thee in thy ear—
PINCHWIFE. What?
50 HORNER. Nothing but the usual question, man. Is she sound,[3] on thy word?
PINCHWIFE. What, you take her for a wench and me for a pimp?
HORNER. Pshaw, wench and pimp, paw[4] words. I know
55 thou art an honest fellow and hast a great acquaintance among the ladies and perhaps hast made love for me rather than let me make love to thy wife—
PINCHWIFE. Come sir, in short, I am for no fooling.
HORNER. Nor I neither. Therefore, prithee, let's see her
60 face presently; make her show, man. Art thou sure I don't know her?
PINCHWIFE. I am sure you do know her.
HORNER. A pox, why dost thou bring her to me then?

---

[2] *bit* Cheated.

[3] *sound* Healthy; here, free of venereal disease.

[4] *paw* Obscene.

[1] *nightgown* Evening dress.

PINCHWIFE.   Because she's a relation of mine.

65 HORNER.   Is she, faith, man? Then thou art still more
civil and obliging, dear rogue.

PINCHWIFE.   Who desired me to bring her to you.

HORNER.   Then she is obliging, dear rogue.

PINCHWIFE.   You'll make her welcome, for my sake, I
70 hope.

HORNER.   I hope she is handsome enough to make
herself welcome. Prithee, let her unmask.

PINCHWIFE.   Do you speak to her; she would never be
ruled by me.

75 HORNER.   Madam—

(*Margery whispers to Horner.*)

She says she must speak with me in private. Withdraw,
prithee.

PINCHWIFE. (*Aside.*)   She's unwilling, it seems, I should
know all her undecent conduct in this business.—Well
80 then, I'll leave you together and hope when I am gone
you'll agree; if not, you and I shan't agree, sir.

HORNER. [*Aside.*]   What means the fool?—If she and I
agree, 'tis no matter what you and I do.

(*Whispers to Margery, who makes signs with her hand for
[Pinchwife] to be gone.*)

PINCHWIFE.   In the meantime, I'll fetch a parson and
85 find out Sparkish and disabuse him. You would have me
fetch a parson, would you not? [*Aside.*] Well then, now
I think I am rid of her and shall have no more trouble
with her. Our sisters and daughters, like usurers' money,
are safest when put out, but our wives, like their writ-
90 ings, never safe but in our closets under lock and key.
(*Exit.*)

(*Enter Boy.*)

BOY.   Sir Jaspar Fidget, sir, is coming up.

HORNER. [*Aside to Quack.*]   Here's the trouble of a
cuckold now we are talking of. A pox on him! Has he
95 not enough to do to hinder his wife's sport, but he must
other women's, too?—Step in here, madam.

(*Exit Margery. Enter Sir Jaspar.*)

SIR JASPAR.   My best and dearest friend.

HORNER. [*Aside to Quack.*]   The old style, doctor.—
Well, be short, for I am busy. What would your imperti-
100 nent wife have now?

SIR JASPAR.   Well guessed i'faith, for I do come from her.

HORNER.   To invite me to supper. Tell her I can't come.
Go.

SIR JASPAR.   Nay, now you are out, faith, for my lady
105 and the whole knot of the virtuous gang, as they call
themselves, are resolved upon a frolic of coming to you
tonight in a masquerade and are all dressed already.

HORNER.   I shan't be at home.

SIR JASPAR.   Lord, how churlish he is to women! Nay,
110 prithee don't disappoint 'em; they'll think 'tis my fault.
Prithee, don't. I'll send in the banquet and the fiddles,
but make no noise on't, for the poor virtuous rogues
would not have it known for the world that they go a-
masquerading, and they would come to no man's ball
115 but yours.

HORNER.   Well, well—get you gone and tell 'em if they
come, 'twill be at the peril of their honor and yours.

SIR JASPAR.   He, he, he—we'll trust you for that. Farewell. (*Exit.*)

120 HORNER.   Doctor, anon you too shall be my guest,
But now I'm going to a private feast.

[*Exeunt.*]

ACT 5, SCENE 3. The Piazza of Covent Garden.

(*Sparkish, Pinchwife.*)

SPARKISH. (The letter in his hand.)   But who would have
thought a woman could have been false to me? By the
world, I could not have thought it.

PINCHWIFE.   You were for giving and taking liberty; she
5 has taken it only, sir, now you find in that letter. You
are a frank person, and so is she, you see there.

SPARKISH.   Nay, if this be her hand, for I never saw it.

PINCHWIFE.   'Tis no matter whether that be her hand or
no. I am sure this hand, at her desire, led her to Mr.
10 Horner, with whom I left her just now to go fetch a
parson to 'em at their desire, too, to deprive you of her
forever, for it seems yours was but a mock marriage.

SPARKISH.   Indeed, she would needs have it that 'twas
Harcourt himself in a parson's habit that married us, but

15 I'm sure he told me 'twas his brother Ned.

PINCHWIFE. Oh there 'tis out, and you were deceived, not she, for you are such a frank person. But I must be gone. You'll find her at Mr. Horner's; go and believe your eyes. (*Exit.*)

20 SPARKISH. Nay, I'll to her and call her as many crocodiles, sirens, harpies,[1] and other heathenish names as a poet would do a mistress who had refused to hear his suit, nay more, his verses on her. But stay, is not that she following a torch at t'other end of the Piazza, and from 25 Horner's certainly? 'Tis so.

(*Enter Alithea following a torch and Lucy behind.*)

You are well met, madam, though you don't think so. What, you have made a short visit to Mr. Horner, but I suppose you'll return to him presently; by that time the parson can be with him.

30 ALITHEA. Mr. Horner and the parson, sir!

SPARKISH. Come madam, no more dissembling, no more jilting, for I am no more a frank person.

ALITHEA. How's this?

LUCY. (*Aside.*) So 'twill work, I see.

35 SPARKISH. Could you find out no easy country fool to abuse? None but me, a gentleman of wit and pleasure about the Town? But it was your pride to be too hard for a man of parts, unworthy, false woman, false as a friend that lends a man money to lose, false as dice, who 40 undo those that trust all they have to 'em.

LUCY. (*Aside.*) He has been a great bubble by his similes, as they say.

ALITHEA. You have been too merry, sir, at your wedding dinner, sure.

45 SPARKISH. What, d'ye mock me too?

ALITHEA. Or you have been deluded.

SPARKISH. By you.

ALITHEA. Let me understand you.

SPARKISH. Have you the confidence—I should call it 50 something else, since you know your guilt—to stand my just reproaches? You did not write an impudent letter to Mr. Horner, who I find now has clubbed with you in deluding me with his aversion for women, that I might not, forsooth, suspect him for my rival?

55 LUCY. (*Aside.*) D'ye think the gentleman can be jealous now, madam?

ALITHEA. I write a letter to Mr. Horner!

SPARKISH. Nay madam, do not deny it; your brother showed it me just now and told me likewise he left you 60 at Horner's lodging to fetch a parson to marry you to him, and I wish you joy, madam, joy, joy, and to him, too, much joy and to myself, more joy for not marrying you.

ALITHEA. (*Aside.*) So I find my brother would break off 65 the match, and I can consent to't, since I see this gentleman can be made jealous.—Oh Lucy, by his rude usage and jealousy, he makes me almost afraid I am married to him. Art thou sure 'twas Harcourt himself and no parson that married us?

70 SPARKISH. No madam, I thank you. I suppose that was a contrivance too of Mr. Horner's and yours to make Harcourt play the parson, but I would as little as you have him one now, no, not for the world, for shall I tell you another truth? I never had any passion for you till 75 now, for now I hate you. 'Tis true I might have married your portion, as other men of parts of the Town do sometimes, and so, your servant, and to show my unconcernedness, I'll come to your wedding and resign you with as much joy as I would a stale wench to a new 80 cully, nay, with as much joy as I would after the first night, if I had been married to you. There's for you, and so, your servant, servant. (*Exit.*)

ALITHEA. How was I deceived in a man!

LUCY. You'll believe, then, a fool may be made jealous 85 now? For that easiness in him that suffers him to be led by a wife will likewise permit him to be persuaded against her by others.

ALITHEA. But marry Mr. Horner? My brother does not intend it, sure. If I thought he did, I would take thy 90 advice and Mr. Harcourt for my husband, and now I wish that if there be any over-wise woman of the Town, who, like me, would marry a fool for fortune, liberty, or title: first, that her husband may love play and be a cully[2] to all the Town but her and suffer none but 95 Fortune to be mistress of his purse; then, if for liberty, that he may send her into the country under the conduct of some housewifely mother-in-law; and if for title, may the world give 'em none but that of cuckold.

LUCY. And for her greater curse, madam, may he not

1 *harpies* According to Greek mythology, sirens lured sailors to destruction and harpies were monstrous creatures with claws and wings appended to a woman's body.

2 *cully* Person who is easily deceived.

100 deserve it.

ALITHEA.   Away, impertinent!—Is not this my old Lady Lanterlu's?[1]

LUCY.   Yes, madam. (*Aside.*) And here I hope we shall find Mr. Harcourt.

(*Exeunt.*)

ACT 5, SCENE 4. Horner's lodging.

(*Horner, Lady Fidget, Dainty, Mrs. Squeamish. A table, banquet, and bottles.*)

HORNER.   (*Aside.*) A pox, they are come too soon— before I have sent back my new mistress! All I have now to do is to lock her in that they may not see her.

LADY FIDGET.   That we may be sure of our welcome, we
5 have brought our entertainment with us and are re- solved to treat thee, dear toad——

DAINTY.   And that we may be merry to purpose, have left Sir Jaspar and my old Lady Squeamish quarreling at home at backgammon.

10 MRS. SQUEAMISH.   Therefore, let us make use of our time, lest they should chance to interrupt us.

LADY FIDGET.   Let us sit then.

HORNER.   First that you may be private, let me lock this door and that, and I'll wait upon you presently.

15 LADY FIDGET.   No sir, shut 'em only and your lips forever, for we must trust you as much as our women.[2]

HORNER.   You know all vanity's killed in me; I have no occasion for talking.

LADY FIDGET.   Now ladies, supposing we had drank
20 each of us our two bottles, let us speak the truth of our hearts.

DAINTY AND MRS. SQUEAMISH.   Agreed.

LADY FIDGET.   By this brimmer,[3] for truth is nowhere else to be found. (*Aside to Horner.*) Not in thy heart,
25 false man.

HORNER.   (*Aside to Lady Fidget.*)   You have found me a true man, I'm sure.

LADY FIDGET. (*Aside to Horner.*)   Not every way.——But let us sit and be merry. (*Sings.*)

---

[1] *Lady Lanterlu's* Lanterloo, or loo, a popular card game; from *lanturelu*, French for twaddle.

[2] *women* Waiting-women.

[3] *brimmer* Full glass.

1.

30 Why should our damned tyrants oblige us to live
On the pittance of pleasure which they only give?
   We must not rejoice
   With wine and with noise.
In vain we must wake in a dull bed alone,
35 Whilst to our warm rival the bottle they're gone.
   Then lay aside charms
   And take up these arms.[4]

2.

'Tis wine only gives 'em their courage and wit;
Because we live sober to men, we submit.
40   If for beauties you'd pass,
   Take a lick of the glass;
'Twill mend your complexions, and when they are gone,
The best red we have is the red of the grape.
   Then sisters lay't on
45   And damn a good shape.

DAINTY.   Dear brimmer! Well, in token of our openness and plain dealing, let us throw our masks over our heads.

HORNER.   So 'twill come to the glasses anon.

50 MRS. SQUEAMISH.   Lovely brimmer! Let me enjoy him first.

LADY FIDGET.   No, I never part with a gallant till I've tried him. Dear brimmer that mak'st our husbands short-sighted——

55 DAINTY.   And our bashful gallants bold——

MRS. SQUEAMISH.   And for want of a gallant, the butler lovely in our eyes. Drink, eunuch.

LADY FIDGET.   Drink, thou representative of a husband. Damn a husband——

60 DAINTY.   And as it were a husband, an old keeper——

MRS. SQUEAMISH.   And an old grandmother——

HORNER.   And an English bawd and a French chirur- geon.

LADY FIDGET.   Aye, we have all reason to curse 'em.

65 HORNER.   For my sake, ladies.

LADY FIDGET.   No, for our own, for the first spoils all young gallant's industry——

DAINTY.   And the other's art makes 'em bold only with common women——

70 MRS. SQUEAMISH.   And rather run the hazard of the vile distemper amongst them than of a denial amongst us.

---

[4] *arms* The glasses.

DAINTY.   The filthy toads choose mistresses now as they do stuffs,[1] for having been fancied and worn by others—

MRS. SQUEAMISH.   For being common and cheap—

LADY FIDGET.   Whilst women of quality, like the richest stuffs, lie untumbled and unasked for.

HORNER.   Aye, neat and cheap and new often they think best.

DAINTY.   No sir, the beasts will be known by a mistress longer than by a suit—

MRS. SQUEAMISH.   And 'tis not for cheapness neither—

LADY FIDGET.   No, for the vain fops will take up druggets[2] and embroider 'em. But I wonder at the depraved appetites of witty men; they used to be out of the common road and hate imitation. Pray tell me, beast, when you were a man, why you rather chose to club with a multitude in a common house for an entertainment than to be the only guest at a good table.

HORNER.   Why faith, ceremony and expectation are unsufferable to those that are sharp bent;[3] people always eat with the best stomach at an ordinary,[4] where every man is snatching for the best bit—

LADY FIDGET.   Though he get a cut over the fingers. But I have heard people eat most heartily of another man's meat, that is, what they do not pay for.

HORNER.   When they are sure of their welcome and freedom, for ceremony in love and eating is as ridiculous as in fighting: falling on[5] briskly is all should be done in those occasions.

LADY FIDGET.   Well then, let me tell you, sir, there is nowhere more freedom than in our houses, and we take freedom from a young person as a sign of good breeding, and a person may be as free as he pleases with us, as frolic, as gamesome, as wild as he will.

HORNER.   Han't I heard you all declaim against wild men?

LADY FIDGET.   Yes, but for all that, we think wildness in a man as desirable a quality as in a duck or rabbit. A tame man, faugh!

HORNER.   I know not, but your reputations frightened me as much as your faces invited me.

LADY FIDGET.   Our reputation! Lord, why should you not think that we women make use of our reputation as you men of yours, only to deceive the world with less suspicion? Our virtue is like the stateman's religion, the Quaker's word, the gamester's oath, and the great man's honor: but to cheat those that trust us.

MRS. SQUEAMISH.   And that demureness, coyness, and modesty that you see in our faces in the boxes at plays is as much a sign of a kind woman as a vizard-mask in the pit.

DAINTY.   For I assure you, women are least masked when they have the velvet vizard on.

LADY FIDGET.   You would have found us modest women in our denials only—

MRS. SQUEAMISH.   Our bashfulness is only the reflection of the men's—

DAINTY.   We blush when they are shame-faced.

HORNER.   I beg your pardon, ladies, I was deceived in you devilishly. But why that mighty pretense to honor?

LADY FIDGET.   We have told you, but sometimes 'twas for the same reason you men pretend business often: to avoid ill company, to enjoy the better and more privately those you love.

HORNER.   But why would you ne'er give a friend a wink then?

LADY FIDGET.   Faith, your reputation frightened us as much as ours did you, you were so notoriously lewd—

HORNER.   And you so seemingly honest.

LADY FIDGET.   Was that all that deterred you?

HORNER.   And so expensive— (You allow freedom, you say?)

LADY FIDGET.   Aye, aye.

HORNER.   That I was afraid of losing my little money, as well as my little time, both which my other pleasures required.

LADY FIDGET.   Money, faugh! You talk like a little fellow now. Do such as we expect money?

HORNER.   I beg your pardon, madam, I must confess I have heard that great ladies, like great merchants, set but the higher prices upon what they have because they are not in necessity of taking the first offer.

DAINTY.   Such as we make sale of our hearts?

MRS. SQUEAMISH.   We bribed for our love? Faugh!

HORNER.   With your pardon, ladies, I know, like great men in offices, you seem to exact flattery and attendance

---

[1]   *stuffs*   Material for clothing; cloth.

[2]   *druggets*   Coarse woven material.

[3]   *sharp bent*   Hungry.

[4]   *ordinary*   Dining room in a public house or tavern.

[5]   *falling on*   Commencing.

only from your followers, but you have receivers[1] about you and such fees to pay, a man is afraid to pass your grants;[2] besides, we must let you win at cards, or we lose your hearts, and if you make an assignation, 'tis at a goldsmith's, jeweler's, or china house, where for your honor you deposit to him, he must pawn his to the punctual cit, and so paying for what you take up, pays for what he takes up.

DAINTY.   Would you not have us assured of our gallant's love?

MRS. SQUEAMISH.   For love is better known by liberality than by jealousy—

LADY FIDGET.   For one may be dissembled, the other not. (*Aside.*) But my jealousy can be no longer dissembled, and they are telling-ripe.——Come, here's to our gallants in waiting, whom we must name, and I'll begin: this is my false rogue. (*Claps him on the back.*)

MRS. SQUEAMISH.   How!

HORNER.   So all will out now—

MRS. SQUEAMISH. (*Aside to Horner.*) Did you not tell me 'twas for my sake only you reported yourself no man?

DAINTY. (*Aside.*) Oh wretch! Did you not swear to me 'twas for my love and honor you passed for that thing you do?

HORNER.   So, so.

LADY FIDGET.   Come, speak ladies. This is my false villain.

MRS. SQUEAMISH.   And mine too.

DAINTY.   And mine.

HORNER.   Well then, you are all three my false rogues too, and there's an end on't.

LADY FIDGET.   Well then, there's no remedy, sister sharers. Let us not fall out but have a care of our honor. Though we get no presents, no jewels of him, we are savers of our honor, the jewel of most value and use, which shines yet to the world unsuspected, though it be counterfeit.

HORNER.   Nay and is e'en as good as if it were true, provided the world think so, for honor, like beauty now, only depends on the opinion of others.

LADY FIDGET.   Well Harry Common, I hope you can be true to three. Swear. But 'tis no purpose to require your oath, for you are as often forsworn as you swear to new

women.

HORNER.   Come, faith madam, let us e'en pardon one another, for all the difference I find betwixt we men and you women, we forswear ourselves at the beginning of an amour, you, as long as it lasts.

(*Enter Sir Jaspar Fidget and Old Lady Squeamish.*)

SIR JASPAR.   Oh my Lady Fidget, was this your cunning, to come to Mr. Horner without me? But you have been no where else, I hope?

LADY FIDGET.   No, Sir Jaspar.

OLD LADY SQUEAMISH.   And you came straight hither, Biddy?

MRS. SQUEAMISH.   Yes indeed, Lady Grandmother.

SIR JASPAR.   'Tis well, 'tis well. I knew when once they were thoroughly acquainted with poor Horner, they'd ne'er be from him. You may let her masquerade it with my wife and Horner, and I warrant her reputation safe.

(*Enter boy.*)

BOY.   Oh sir, here's the gentleman come whom you bid me not suffer to come up without giving you notice, with a lady, too, and other gentlemen.

HORNER.   Do you all go in there, whilst I send 'em away.——And boy, do you desire 'em to stay below till I come, which shall be immediately.

(*Exeunt Sir Jaspar, [Old] Lady Squeamish, Lady Fidget, Dainty, Mrs. Squeamish.*)

BOY.   Yes sir. (*Exit.*)

(*Exit Horner at the other door, and returns with Margery.*)

HORNER.   You would not take my advice to be gone home before your husband came back. He'll now discover all, yet pray, my dearest, be persuaded to go home and leave the rest to my management; I'll let you down the back way.

MARGERY.   I don't know the way home, so I don't.

HORNER.   My man shall wait upon you.

MARGERY.   No, don't you believe that I'll go at all. What, are you weary of me already?

---

[1] *receivers* Servants who must be paid for cooperation and silence.

[2] *pass your grants* Accept your favors.

HORNER. No my life, 'tis that I may love you long, 'tis
to secure my love and your reputation with your husband; he'll never receive you again else.

MARGERY. What care I? D'ye think to frighten me with
that? I don't intend to go to him again; you shall be my
husband now.

HORNER. I cannot be your husband, dearest, since you
are married to him.

MARGERY. Oh, would you make me believe that? Don't
I see every day at London here, women leave their first
husbands and go and live with other men as their wives?
Pish, pshaw, you'd make me angry, but that I love you
so mainly.

HORNER. So, they are coming up. In again, in, I hear
'em.

(*Exit Margery.*)

Well, a silly mistress is like a weak place, soon got, soon
lost; a man has scarce time for plunder. She betrays her
husband first to her gallant and then her gallant to her
husband.

(*Enter Pinchwife, Alithea, Harcourt, Sparkish, Lucy, and
a parson.*)

PINCHWIFE. Come madam, 'tis not the sudden change
of your dress, the confidence of your asseverations, and
your false witness there shall persuade me I did not
bring you hither just now; here's my witness, who
cannot deny it, since you must be confronted.—Mr.
Horner, did not I bring this lady to you just now?

HORNER. (*Aside.*) Now must I wrong one woman for
another's sake, but that's no new thing with me, for in
these cases I am still on the criminal's side against the
innocent.

ALITHEA. Pray speak, sir.

HORNER. (*Aside.*) It must be so. I must be impudent
and try my luck; impudence uses to be too hard for
truth.

PINCHWIFE. What, you are studying an evasion or
excuse for her. Speak, sir.

HORNER. No, faith, I am something backward only to
speak in women's affairs or disputes.

PINCHWIFE. She bids you speak.

ALITHEA. Aye, pray sir, do, pray satisfy him.

HORNER. Then truly, you did bring that lady to me just
now.

PINCHWIFE. Oh ho!

ALITHEA. How, sir!

HARCOURT. How, Horner!

ALITHEA. What mean you, sir? I always took you for a
man of honor.

HORNER. (*Aside.*) Aye, so much a man of honor that I
must save my mistress, I thank you, come what will
on't.

SPARKISH. So if I had had her, she'd have made me
believe, the moon had been made of a Christmas pie.

LUCY. (*Aside.*) Now could I speak, if I durst, and solve
the riddle, who am the author of it.

ALITHEA. Oh unfortunate woman! [*To Harcourt.*] A
combination against my honor, which most concerns
me now, because you share in my disgrace, sir, and it is
your censure, which I must now suffer, that troubles
me, not theirs.

HARCOURT. Madam, then have no trouble; you shall
now see 'tis possible for me to love, too, without being
jealous. I will not only believe your innocence myself,
but make all the world believe it. (*Apart to Horner.*)
Horner, I must now be concerned for this lady's honor.

HORNER. And I must be concerned for a lady's honor,
too.

HARCOURT. This lady has her honor, and I will protect
it.

HORNER. My lady has not her honor, but has given it
me to keep, and I will preserve it.

HARCOURT. I understand you not.

HORNER. I would not have you.

MARGERY. (*Peeping in behind.*) What's the matter with
'em all?

PINCHWIFE. Come, come, Mr. Horner, no more
disputing. Here's the parson; I brought him not in vain.

HARCOURT. No sir, I'll employ him, if this lady please.

PINCHWIFE. How, what d'ye mean?

SPARKISH. Aye, what does he mean?

HORNER. Why, I have resigned your sister to him; he
has my consent.

PINCHWIFE. But he has not mine, sir. A woman's
injured honor, no more than a man's, can be repaired or
satisfied by any but him that first wronged it, and you
shall marry her presently, or— (*Lays his hand on his
sword.*)

(*Enter Margery.*)

MARGERY. Oh Lord, they'll kill poor Mr. Horner! Besides, he shan't marry her whilst I stand by and look
320 on; I'll not lose my second husband so.

PINCHWIFE. What do I see?

ALITHEA. My sister in my clothes!

SPARKISH. Hah!

MARGERY. (*To Pinchwife.*) Nay, pray now don't quarrel
325 about finding work for the parson; he shall marry me to Mr. Horner, for now I believe you have enough of me.

HORNER. Damned, damned, loving changeling.

MARGERY. Pray sister, pardon me for telling so many lies of you.

330 HARCOURT. I suppose the riddle is plain now.

LUCY. No, that must be my work, good sir, hear me. (*Kneels to Pinchwife, who stands doggedly, with his hat over his eyes.*)

PINCHWIFE. I will never hear woman again, but make
335 'em all silent thus— (*Offers to draw upon his wife.*)

HORNER. No, that must not be.

PINCHWIFE. You then shall go first; 'tis all one to me. (*Offers to draw on Horner, stopped by Harcourt.*)

HARCOURT. Hold—

(*Enter Sir Jaspar Fidget, Lady Fidget, Old Lady Squeamish, Dainty, Mrs. Squeamish.*)

340 SIR JASPAR. What's the matter, what's the matter, pray what's the matter, sir? I beseech you communicate, sir.

PINCHWIFE. Why, my wife has communicated, sir, as your wife may have done, too, sir, if she knows him, sir.

SIR JASPAR. Pshaw, with him, ha, ha, he!

345 PINCHWIFE. D'ye mock me, sir? A cuckold is a kind of wild beast, have a care, sir.

SIR JASPAR. No, sure you mock me, sir. He cuckold you! It can't be, ha, ha, he. Why, I'll tell you, sir. (*Offers to whisper.*)

350 PINCHWIFE. I tell you again, he has whored my wife and yours, too, if he knows her, and all the women he comes near. 'Tis not his dissembling, his hypocrisy can wheedle me.

SIR JASPAR. How! Does he dissemble? Is he a hypocrite?
355 Nay, then—how—wife—sister, is he a hypocrite?

OLD LADY SQUEAMISH. A hypocrite! A dissembler! Speak, young harlotry, speak. How!

SIR JASPAR. Nay, then—oh my head too—oh thou libidinous lady!

360 OLD LADY SQUEAMISH. Oh thou harloting harlotry, hast thou done't then?

SIR JASPAR. Speak, good Horner. Art thou a dissembler, a rogue? Hast thou—

HORNER. Soh—

365 LUCY. (*Apart to Horner.*) I'll fetch you off and her too, if she will but hold her tongue.

HORNER. (*Apart to Lucy.*) Canst thou? I'll give thee—

LUCY. (*To Mr. Pinchwife.*) Pray have but patience to hear me, sir, who am the unfortunate cause of all this
370 confusion. Your wife is innocent, I only culpable, for I put her upon telling you all these lies concerning my mistress in order to the breaking off the match between Mr. Sparkish and her to make way for Mr. Harcourt.

SPARKISH. Did you so, eternal rotten tooth? Then it
375 seems my mistress was not false to me; I was only deceived by you.—Brother that should have been, now, man of conduct, who is a frank person now? To bring your wife to her lover—hah!

LUCY. I assure you, sir, she came not to Mr. Horner out
380 of love, for she loves him no more—

MARGERY. Hold! I told lies for you, but you shall tell none for me, for I do love Mr. Horner with all my soul, and nobody shall say me nay. Pray don't you go to make poor Mr. Horner believe to the contrary. 'Tis spitefully
385 done of you, I'm sure.

HORNER. (*Aside to Margery.*) Peace, dear idiot.

MARGERY. Nay, I will not peace.

PINCHWIFE. Not till I make you.

(*Enter Dorilant, Quack.*)

DORILANT. Horner, your servant. I am the doctor's
390 guest; he must excuse our intrusion.

QUACK. But what's the matter, gentlemen? For Heaven's sake, what's the matter?

HORNER. Oh 'tis well you are come. 'Tis a censorious world we live in. You may have brought me a reprieve,
395 or else I had died for a crime I never committed, and these innocent ladies had suffered with me; therefore, pray satisfy these worthy, honorable, jealous gentlemen that—(*Whispers.*)

QUACK. Oh I understand you. Is that all?—Sir Jasper,
400 by heavens and upon the word of a physician, sir,—

(*Whispers to Sir Jaspar.*)

SIR JASPAR.   Nay, I do believe you truly.—Pardon me, my virtuous lady and dear of honor.

OLD LADY SQUEAMISH.   What, then all's right again.

405 SIR JASPAR.   Aye, aye, and now let us satisfy him, too.

(*They whisper with Pinchwife.*)

PINCHWIFE.   An eunuch! Pray no fooling with me.

QUACK.   I'll bring half the chirurgeons in Town to swear it.

PINCHWIFE.   They! They'll swear a man that bled to
10   death through his wounds died of an apoplexy.[1]

QUACK.   Pray hear me, sir. Why, all the Town has heard the report of him.

PINCHWIFE.   But does all the Town believe it?

QUACK.   Pray inquire a little and first of all these.

15 PINCHWIFE.   I'm sure when I left the Town he was the lewdest fellow in't.

QUACK.   I tell you, sir, he has been in France since. Pray ask but these ladies and gentlemen, your friend Mr. Dorilant.—Gentlemen and ladies, han't you all heard
20   the late sad report of poor Mr. Horner?

ALL LADIES.   Aye, aye, aye.

DORILANT.   Why, thou jealous fool, dost thou doubt it? He's an arrant French capon.[2]

MARGERY.   'Tis false, sir, you shall not disparage poor
25   Mr. Horner, for to my certain knowledge—

LUCY.   Oh hold!

MRS. SQUEAMISH.   (*Aside to Lucy.*)   Stop her mouth!

LADY FIDGET.   (*To Pinchwife.*)   Upon my honor, sir, 'tis as true—

30 DAINTY.   D'ye think we would have been seen in his company—

MRS. SQUEAMISH.   Trust our unspotted reputations with him?

LADY FIDGET.   (*Aside to Horner.*)   This you get and we,
35   too, by trusting your secret to a fool.

HORNER.   Peace, madam. (*Aside to Quack.*) Well Doctor, is not this a good design that carries a man on unsuspected and brings him off safe?

PINCHWIFE.   (*Aside.*)   Well, if this were true, but my
40   wife—

(*Dorilant whispers with Margery.*)

ALITHEA.   Come brother, your wife is yet innocent, you see, but have a care of too strong an imagination, lest like an over-concerned, timorous gamester, by fancying an unlucky cast, it should come. Women and Fortune
445   are truest still to those that trust 'em.

LUCY.   And any wild thing grows but the more fierce and hungry for being kept up and more dangerous to the keeper.

ALITHEA.   There's doctrine for all husbands, Mr. Har-
450   court.

HARCOURT.   And I edify, madam, so much that I am impatient till I am one.

DORILANT.   And I edify so much by example I will never be one.

455 SPARKISH.   And because I will not disparage my parts, I'll ne'er be one.

HORNER.   And I, alas, can't be one.

PINCHWIFE.   But I must be one against my will, to a country wife, with a country murrain[3] to me.

460 MARGERY.   (*Aside.*)   And I must be a country wife still, too, I find, for I can't, like a City one, be rid of my musty husband and do what I list.

HORNER.   Now sir, I must pronounce your wife innocent, though I blush whilst I do it, and I am the only
465   man by her now exposed to shame, which I will straight drown in wine, as you shall your suspicion, and the ladies' troubles we'll divert with a ballet.—Doctor, where are your maskers?

LUCY.   Indeed, she's innocent, sir. I am her witness, and
470   her end of coming out was but to see her sister's wedding, and what she has said to your face of her love to Mr. Horner was but the usual innocent revenge on a husband's jealousy, was it not? Madam, speak.

MARGERY.   (*Aside to Lucy and Horner.*)   Since you'll have
475   me tell more lies.—Yes indeed, bud.

PINCHWIFE.   For my own sake, fain I would all believe: Cuckolds, like lovers, should themselves deceive. But— (*Sighs.*)
His honor is least safe (too late I find)
480 Who trusts it with a foolish wife or friend.

(*A dance of cuckolds.*)

---

[1]   *apoplexy* Stroke.

[2]   *capon* Domestic male fowl which has been castrated so that it will fatten for eating.

[3]   *murrain* Infection, of livestock.

HORNER.   Vain fops but court and dress and keep a pother
To pass for women's men with one another,
But he who aims by women to be prized,
First by the men, you see, must be despised.

[Exeunt.]

EPILOGUE

Spoken by Mrs. Knepp[1]

Now you, the vigorous, who daily here
O'er vizard mask in public domineer,
And what you'd do to her, if in place where;
Nay, have the confidence to cry, "Come out!"
5   Yet when she says, "Lead on!" you are not stout;
But to your well-dressed brother straight turn round
And cry, "Pox on her, Ned, she can't be sound!"
Then slink away, a fresh one to engage,
With so much seeming heat and loving rage,
10   You'd frighten listening actress on the stage;
Till she at last has seen you huffing come,
And talk of keeping in the tiring room,
Yet cannot be provoked to lead her home.
Next, you Falstaffs[2] of fifty, who beset

15   Your buckram maidenheads,[3] which your friends get;
And whilst to them you of achievements boast,
They share the booty and laugh at your cost.
In fine, you essenced boys, both old and young,
Who would be thought so eager, brisk, and strong,
20   Yet do the ladies, not their husbands, wrong;
Whose purses for your manhood make excuse,
And keep your Flanders mares for show, not use;
Encouraged by our woman's man today,
A Horner's part may vainly think to play;
25   And may intrigues so bashfully disown,
That they may doubted be by few or none;
May kiss the cards at picquet, ombre, loo,[4]
And so be thought to kiss the lady too;
But, gallants, have a care, faith, what you do.
30   The world, which to no man his due will give,
You by experience know you can deceive;
And men may still believe you vigorous,
But then we women—there's no cozening[5] us.

FINIS

—1675

---

1   *Mrs. Knepp*   Mary Knep or Knipp (died c. 1680), actress, first to play Lady Fidget.

2   *Falstaffs*   Reference to a character in Shakespeare's *Merry Wives of Windsor, 1 Henry IV* and *2 Henry IV.*

3   *buckram maidenheads*   Cf. Shakespeare's *1 Henry IV,* 2.4.

4   *picquet, ombre, loo*   Card games.

5   *cozening*   Cheating.

JOHN WILMOT, EARL OF ROCHESTER
1647 – 1680

John Wilmot, Earl of Rochester, so embodied the role of a Restoration rake that his writing risks being eclipsed by his notoriety. Although historically considered a minor writer, Rochester was a dynamic participant in the literary milieu of his day: a contributor to plays by John Fletcher and John Howard; an influential stage patron who was blamed by many for instigating a 1679 attack on Dryden, his arch rival, in Covent Garden; and a poet known and feared for his relentless satire and lampooning of contemporary court figures and mores.

Born in April 1647 at Ditchley, Oxfordshire, Wilmot became the second Earl of Rochester in 1658 after his Royalist father died in exile. (His mother favored the other side in the great political split of the time.) Rochester entered Wadham College, Oxford, in January 1660, but left within two years to embark on a three-year tour of Europe. He returned to the court of Charles II at the age of 17 and soon provided plenty of grist for the London gossip mills by abducting his future wife, Elizabeth Malet, in 1665—an impetuous plan that earned the young Earl several weeks in the Tower while plague ravaged the city. After his release in June 1665, Rochester volunteered for service against the Dutch by joining the English fleet under the command of the Earl of Sandwich. His courage earned him a reward of £750 from the King, who later made Rochester a Gentleman of the Bedchamber. Rochester eventually married Malet (who also wrote poetry) in January 1667, and the couple had four children; their relationship is believed to have been happy despite his frequent absences and affairs. A well-known philanderer and drinker, Rochester fathered an illegitimate daughter with one of his mistresses, the actress Elizabeth Barry, and he claimed to have been continually drunk for five years during his early twenties.

Rochester's relationship with Charles II was mercurial; the Earl was often in disgrace, but the King was seemingly unable to remain angry with him, in spite of his irreverent behavior and verse. In one serious breach of court etiquette, Rochester struck Thomas Killigrew in the King's presence in 1669, but the King was seen walking amicably with Rochester the day after the incident. In 1674, Rochester mistakenly gave the King a copy of verses concerning Charles II's sexual exploits, a manuscript that included such lines as, "Poor prince! thy prick, like thy buffoons at Court, / Will govern thee because it makes thee sport. / 'Tis sure the sauciest prick that e'er did swive, / The proudest, peremptoriest prick alive." For that offence Rochester was briefly banished from the Court, but the King granted him the lucrative Rangership of Woodstock Park only a few months later. In one of his more infamous adventures, a drunken Rochester, accompanied by equally inebriated friends, smashed the King's phallic glass sundials in Whitehall's Privy Garden, shouting as he did so, "What! Dost thou stand here to —— Time?"

Like many Court poets, Rochester circulated his work in manuscript and did not pursue publication. A collection of his poems that contained many false attributions appeared only months after his death in July 1680. (A second collection appeared in 1691, with several poems missing stanzas to avoid, according to the publisher, offending the reader.) It was not until the late twentieth century that reliable and unexpurgated texts of all Rochester's known work were published; in all, there are approximately 75 authentic Rochester poems in existence. Many of them are remarkably explicit sexually, even by today's standards; more generally, his verse is characterized by his unsparing honesty about the most personal of subjects (including love, religious belief or unbelief, and sexual failure and embarrassment). He also writes of his disinclination to trust anything beyond personal, usually physical, experience. In its style Rochester's verse is often (though by no means always) as polished and elegant as it is rude in its content.

At the end of his short life, his health ruined by alcoholism and venereal disease, the former skeptic retired to the country in April 1680 and underwent a surprising conversion to Christianity after listening to his mother's chaplain read Isaiah 53. He had already summoned clergyman Gilbert Burnet, his first biographer, to his London home in October 1679 after reading Burnet's *History of the Reformation*. Burnet recorded the details of their theological debates in his book, published after Rochester's death, entitled *Some Passages of the Life and Death of the Right Honourable John, Earl of Rochester*, but many doubted the validity of Rochester's deathbed conversion, claiming either that he was unbalanced due to illness or that Burnet's account was biassed. His mother honored his request to burn his papers—an act which has no doubt contributed to the difficulty of determining an accurate Rochester canon. Authentic or not, his celebrated conversion has only added to the Rochester legend; his story was gladly seized upon by those wishing to transform him into a lesson in morality, the paradigm of the reformed rake.

⌘⌘⌘

A Satire on Charles II[1]

I' th' isle of Britain, long since famous grown
  For breeding the best cunts in Christendom
There reigns, and oh! long may he reign and thrive,
The easiest King and best-bred man alive.
5 Him no ambition moves to get renown
Like the French fool,[2] that wanders up and down
Starving his people, hazarding[3] his crown.
Peace is his aim, his gentleness is such,
And love he loves, for he loves fucking much.

10 Nor are his high desires above his strength:
His scepter and his prick are of a length;[4]
And she may sway the one who plays with th'other,
And make him little wiser than his brother.[5]

Poor prince! thy prick, like thy buffoons at Court,
15 Will govern thee because it makes thee sport.
'Tis sure the sauciest prick that e'er did swive,[6]
The proudest, peremptoriest prick alive.
Though safety, law, religion, life lay on't,
'Twould break through all to make its way to cunt.
20 Restless he rolls about from whore to whore,
A merry monarch, scandalous and poor.

To Carwell,[7] the most dear of all his dears,
The best relief of his declining years,
Oft he bewails his fortune, and her fate:
25 To love so well, and be beloved so late.
For though in her he settles well his tarse,[8]
Yet his dull, graceless bollocks hang an arse.[9]
This you'd believe, had I but time to tell ye
The pains it costs to poor, laborious Nelly,[10]
30 Whilst she employs hands, fingers, mouth, and thighs,

---

[1] *A Satire on Charles II* Rochester was banished from court as a result of the King having read this poem. The circumstances are described in a letter dated 20 January 1674: "My lord Rochester fled from Court some time since for delivering (by mistake) into the King's hands a terrible lampoon of his own making against the King, instead of another the King asked for."

[2] *the French fool* King Louis XIV (1638–1715).

[3] *hazarding* Putting at risk.

[4] *of a length* I.e., of the same length.

[5] *his brother* James (later King James II).

[6] *swive* Engage in sexual intercourse.

[7] *Carwell* Louise de Kéroualle, Duchess of Portsmouth.

[8] *tarse* Penis.

[9] *hang an arse* Are slow or sluggish.

[10] *Nelly* Nell Gwyn, an actress and Charles II's best-known mistress. There were extensive rivalries among Charles's various mistresses, including Lady Castlemaine, Frances Stuart, Lucy Walters and Moll Davis, as well as Gwyn and de Kéroualle.

Ere she can raise the member she enjoys.
    All monarchs I hate, and the thrones they sit on,
    From the hector[1] of France to the cully[2] of Britain.
—1673/74

A Satire against Reason and Mankind

Were I (who to my cost already am
    One of those strange prodigious creatures, man)
A spirit free to choose for my own share,
What case of flesh and blood I pleased to wear;
5   I'd be a dog, a monkey, or a bear.
Or any thing but that vain animal
Who is so proud of being rational.
The senses are too gross, and he'll contrive
A sixth to contradict the other five:
10 And before certain instinct will prefer
Reason, which fifty times for one does err.
Reason, an *ignis fatuus*[3] of the mind,
Which leaving light of nature, sense, behind;
Pathless and dangerous wand'ring ways it takes,
15 Through error's fenny° bogs and thorny
      brakes:°   *swampy / briars*
Whilst the misguided follower climbs with pain
Mountains of whimsies heaped in his own brain;
Stumbling from thought to thought, falls headlong down
Into doubt's boundless sea, where like to drown,
20 Books bear him up a while, and make him try
To swim with bladders[4] of philosophy:
In hopes still to o'ertake th'escaping light,
The vapour dances in his dazzled sight,
Till spent, it leaves him to eternal night.
25 Then old age and experience hand in hand,
Lead him to death, and make him understand,
After a search so painful and so long
That all his life he has been in the wrong.
Huddled in dirt the reasoning engine lies,
30 Who was so proud, so witty and so wise.

Pride drew him in (as cheats their bubbles° catch)   *victims*
And made him venture to be made a wretch.
His wisdom did his happiness destroy,
Aiming to know that world he should enjoy;
35 And wit was his vain frivolous pretence,
Of pleasing others at his own expense:
For wits are treated just like common whores,
First they're enjoyed and then kicked out of doors.
The pleasure past, a threat'ning doubt remains,
40 That frights th'enjoyer with succeeding pains:
Women and men of wit are dangerous tools,
And ever fatal to admiring fools.
Pleasure allures, and when the fops escape,
'Tis not that they're belov'd, but fortunate;
45 And therefore what they fear, at heart they hate.
    But now methinks some formal band and beard
Takes me to task. Come on, sir, I'm prepared:
Then by your favour anything that's writ
Against this gibing, jingling knack called wit,
50 Likes me abundantly, but you take care
Upon this point not to be too severe.
Perhaps my muse were fitter for this part,
For, I profess, I can be very smart
On wit, which I abhor with all my heart.
55 I long to lash it in some sharp essay,
But your grand indiscretion bids me stay,
And turns my tide of ink another way.
What rage ferments in your degenerate mind,
To make you rail at reason and mankind?
60 Blest glorious man! to whom alone kind Heaven
An everlasting soul has freely given:
Whom his Creator took such care to make,
That from Himself He did the image take:
And this fair frame in shining reason dressed,
65 To dignify his nature above beast.
Reason, by whose aspiring influence
We take a flight beyond material sense;
Dive into mysteries, then soaring pierce
The flaming limits of the universe:
70 Search Heaven and Hell, find out what's acted there,
And give the world true grounds of hope and fear.
    Hold mighty man, I cry; all this we know,
From the pathetic pen of Ingelo,[5]

---

1 *hector* Noisy, blustery fellow, bully.

2 *cully* One who is deceived.

3 *ignis fatuus* Latin: foolish fire; also called will-o'-the-wisp. A phosphorescent light that hovers above marshy ground and is believed to be caused by the spontaneous combustion of inflammable gases emitted from decaying matter. Travelers attempting to follow this light would frequently become lost.

4 *bladders* Inflated and used as a float.

5 *Ingelo* Reverend Nathaniel Ingelo, author of the allegorical romance *Bentivolio and Urania* (1660).

From Patrick's Pilgrim, Sibbes' Soliloquies;[1]
75　And 'tis this very reason I despise.
This supernatural gift, that makes a mite
Think he's the image of the infinite;
Comparing his short life, void of all rest,
To the eternal, and the ever blest.
80　This busy puzzling stirrer up of doubt,
That frames deep mysteries, then finds them out;
Filling with frantic crowds of thinking fools
Those reverend bedlams,[2] colleges and schools;
Born on whose wings each heavy sot can pierce
85　The limits of the boundless universe.
So charming ointments make an old witch fly,
And bear a crippled carcass through the sky.
'Tis this exalted power whose business lies
In nonsense and impossibilities.
90　This made a whimsical philosopher
Before the spacious world his tub prefer.[3]
And we have modern cloistered coxcombs, who
Retire to think, 'cause they have nought to do:
But thoughts are given for action's government,
95　Where action ceases, thought's impertinent.
Our sphere of action is life's happiness,
And he who thinks beyond, thinks like an ass.
Thus whilst against false reasoning I inveigh,
I own right reason, which I would obey;
100　That reason which distinguishes by sense,
And gives us rules of good and ill from thence:
That bounds desires with a reforming will,
To keep them more in vigour, not to kill.
Your reason hinders, mine helps to enjoy,
105　Renewing appetites yours would destroy.
My reason is my friend, yours is a cheat,
Hunger calls out, my reason bids me eat;
Perversely yours your appetites does mock,
They ask for food, that answers what's a clock.
110　This plain distinction, Sir, your doubt secures,
'Tis not true reason I despise, but yours.

Thus I think reason righted, but for man,
I'll ne'er recant, defend him if you can.
For all his pride and his philosophy,
115　'Tis evident beasts are in their degree,
As wise at least, and better far than he.
Those creatures are the wisest who attain
By surest means, the ends at which they aim:
If therefore Jowler[4] finds and kills his hares,
120　Better than Meeres[5] supplies committee chairs;
Though one's a statesman, th'other but a hound,
Jowler in justice would be wiser found.
You see how far man's wisdom here extends;
Look next if human nature makes amends:
125　Whose principles most generous are and just,
And to whose morals you would sooner trust.
Be judge yourself, I'll bring it to the test,
Which is the basest creature, man or beast.
Birds feed on birds, beasts on each other prey,
130　But savage man alone does man betray:
Pressed by necessity they kill for food,
Man undoes man to do himself no good.
With teeth and claws by nature armed, they hunt
Nature's allowance to supply their want.
135　But man with smiles, embraces, friendship, praise,
Inhumanly his fellow's life betrays;
With voluntary pains works his distress,
Not through necessity, but wantonness.
For hunger or for love they fight and tear,
140　Whilst wretched man is still in arms for fear:
For fear he arms, and is of arms afraid,
By fear to fear successively betrayed.
Base fear! The source whence his best passion came,
His boasted honour, and his dear bought fame:
145　That lust of power, to which he's such a slave,
And for the which alone he dares be brave,
To which his various projects are designed,
Which makes him generous, affable and kind;
For which he takes such pains to be thought wise
150　And screws his actions in a forced disguise;
Leading a tedious life in misery
Under laborious mean hypocrisy:
Look to the bottom of his vast design,

---

[1] *Patrick's Pilgrim* Reference to *The Parable of the Pilgrim* (1665) by Simon Patrick, Bishop of Chichester and Ely; *Sibbes' Soliloquies* Sermons of Richard Sibbes (1577–1635), a Puritan apologist.

[2] *reverend bedlams* I.e., monasteries. "Bedlam," so called after London's Bedlam (originally, the Hospital of St. Mary of Bethlehem), a hospital for the mentally and emotionally ill.

[3] *whimsical ... prefer* Reference to the Greek Cynic philosopher Diogenes (c. 412-323 BCE), who is said to have temporarily resided in a large tub.

---

[4] *Jowler* Common name for a hunting dog.

[5] *Meeres* Sir Thomas Meeres (1635–1715), an industrious Lincoln MP who was a leading figure in the campaign against the Test Act, which imposed legal sanctions on Catholics and Dissenters.

Wherein man's wisdom, power and glory join;
55 The good he acts, the ill he does endure,
'Tis all from fear to make himself secure.
Merely for safety after fame we thirst;
For all men would be cowards if they durst.
And honesty's against all common sense;
60 Men must be knaves, 'tis in their own defence.
Mankind's dishonest, if you think it fair
Among known cheats to play upon the square,
You'll be undone—
Nor can weak truth your reputation save;
65 The knaves will all agree to call you knave.
Wronged shall he live, insulted o'er, oppressed,
Who dares be less a villain than the rest.
        Thus, sir, you see what human nature craves,
Most men are cowards, all men should[1] be knaves.
70 The difference lies, as far as I can see,
Not in the thing itself, but the degree:
And all the subject matter of debate,
Is only who's a knave of the first rate.

ADDITION[2]
All this with indignation have I hurled
75 At the pretending part of the proud world,
Who swollen with selfish vanity, devise
False freedoms, holy cheats and formal lies,
Over their fellow slaves to tyrannize.
        But if in court so just a man there be,
80 (In court a just man yet unknown to me)
Who does his needful flattery direct,
Not to oppress and ruin, but protect.
(Since flattery, which way so ever laid,
Is still a tax on that unhappy trade)
85 If so upright a statesman you can find,
Whose passions bend to his unbiased mind;
Who does his arts and policies apply,
To raise his country, not his family.
Nor while his pride owned avarice withstands,
90 Receives close bribes through friends' corrupted hands.
        Is there a churchman who on God relies,
Whose life his faith and doctrine justifies;
Not one blown up with vain prelatic[3] pride,

Who for reproof of sins does man deride;
195 Whose envious heart makes preaching a pretence,
With his obstreperous saucy eloquence,
To chide at kings, and rail at men of sense.
Who from his pulpit vents more peevish lies,
More bitter railings, scandals, calumnies,
200 Than at a gossiping are thrown about
When the good wives get drunk and then fall out.
None of that sensual tribe, whose talents lie
In avarice, pride, sloth and gluttony,
Who hunt good livings,° but abhor good lives,   *jobs*
205 Whose lust exalted to that height arrives,
They act° adultery with their own wives;   *perform*
And ere a score of years completed be,
Can from the lofty pulpit proudly see
Half a large parish their own progeny.
210 Nor doting bishop, who would be adored
For domineering at the council board,
A greater fop in business at fourscore,[4]
Fonder of serious toys, affected more
Than the gay glittering fool at twenty proves,
215 With all his noise, his tawdry clothes and loves.
But a meek humble man of honest sense,
Who preaching peace does practice continence;° *chastity*
Whose pious life's a proof he does believe
Mysterious truths, which no man can conceive.
220 If upon earth there dwell such God-like men,
I'll here recant my paradox to them;
Adore those shrines of virtue, homage pay,
And, with the rabble world, their laws obey.
If such there be, yet grant me this at least,
225 Man differs more from man, than man from beast.
—1679

Love and Life: A Song

All my past life is mine no more;
The flying hours are gone,
Like transitory dreams giv'n o'er°   *finished*
Whose images are kept in store
5 By memory alone.

Whatever is to come is not;
How can it then be mine?

---

[1] *should* I.e., wish to.

[2] *ADDITION* This second part was originally circulated separately.

[3] *prelatic* Characteristic of bishops.

[4] *fourscore* Eighty (four times a "score," or twenty).

The present moment's all my lot,[1]
And that as fast as it is got
10   Phyllis[2] is wholly thine.

Then talk not of inconstancy,
False hearts, and broken vows,
If I, by miracle can be
This livelong minute true to thee,
15   'Tis all that heav'n allows.
          —1680

The Disabled Debauchee

As some brave admiral, in former war,
Deprived of force, but pressed with courage still,
Two rival fleets, appearing from afar,
Crawls to the top of an adjacent hill;

5   From whence (with thoughts full of concern) he views
The wise, and daring conduct of the fight,
And each bold action, to his mind renews,
His present glory, and his past delight;

From his fierce eyes, flashes of rage he throws,
10   As from black clouds, when lightning breaks away,
Transported, thinks himself amidst his foes,
And absent, yet enjoys the bloody day;

So when my days of impotence approach,
And I'm by pox° and wine's unlucky chance,   syphilis
15   Forced from the pleasing billows of debauch,
On the dull shore of lazy temperance,

My pains at least some respite shall afford,
Whilst I behold the battles you maintain,
When fleets of glasses sail above the board,°   table
20   From whose broadsides[3] volleys of wit shall rain.

Nor let the sight of honourable scars,
Which my too forward valour did procure,
Frighten new-listed° soldiers from the wars,   newly enlisted
Past joys have more than paid what I endure.

25   Should any youth (worth being drunk) prove nice,[4]
And from his fair inviter meanly shrink,
'Twill please the ghost of my departed vice,[5]
If at my counsel, he repent and drink.

Or should some cold-complexioned[6] sot forbid,
30   With his dull morals, our night's brisk alarms,[7]
I'll fire his blood by telling what I did,
When I was strong, and able to bear arms.

I'll tell of whores attacked, their lords at home,
Bawds' quarters[8] beaten up, and fortress won,
35   Windows demolished, watches[9] overcome,
And handsome ills, by my contrivance done.

Nor shall our love-fits, Chloris,[10] be forgot,
When each the well-looked linkboy,[11] strove t' enjoy,
And the best kiss, was the deciding lot,
40   Whether the boy fucked you, or I the boy.

With tales like these, I will such thoughts inspire,
As to important mischief shall incline.
I'll make him long some ancient church to fire,
And fear no lewdness he's called to by wine.

45   Thus, statesmanlike, I'll saucily impose,
And safe from action valiantly advise,

---

1   *Whatever … my lot*   Several critics read these lines as a paraphrase of a passage in Hobbes's *Leviathan*: "The present only has a being in nature; things past have a being in the memory only, but things to come have no being at all, the future being but a fiction of the mind."

2   *Phyllis*   Woman's name, common in pastoral poetry.

3   *broadsides*   Sides of a ship from which guns were fired; also sheets printed with news, ballads, proclamations, etc.

4   *nice*   Fastidiousp; fussy.

5   *vice*   Character in morality plays.

6   *cold-complexioned*   Reference to the medieval and Renaissance belief in the four humors, four liquids that constitute a person's temperament and physicality. Someone with a high proportion of the cold and moist phlegm would be considered phlegmatic, or calm and unemotional.

7   *alarms*   Signals calling men to arms or warning of danger.

8   *Bawd's quarters*   Houses kept by men or women for the purposes of prostitution.

9   *watches*   Watchmen or sentinels hired to keep order during the night.

10   *Chloris*   Woman's name, common in pastoral poetry.

11   *linkboy*   Boy hired to accompany people through the streets carrying a lighted link, or torch.

Sheltered in impotence, urge you to blows,
And being good for nothing else, be wise.
—1680

A Letter from Artemisia[1] in the Town
to Chloe in the Country

Chloe, in verse by your command I write;
  Shortly you'll bid me ride astride, and fight.
These talents better with our sex agree,
Than lofty flights of dang'rous poetry.
5 Amongst the men, I mean the men of wit
(At least they passed for such before they writ),
How many bold adventurers for the bays,[2]
(Proudly designing large returns of praise)
Who durst that stormy, pathless world explore,
10 Were soon dashed back, and wrecked on the dull
     shore,
Broke of that little stock, they had before?
How would a woman's tottering bark° be tossed,   *ship*
Where stoutest ships (the men of wit) are lost?
When I reflect on this, I straight grow wise,
15 And my own self thus gravely I advise.
Dear Artemisia, poetry's a snare;
Bedlam[3] has many mansions: have a care.
Your muse diverts you, makes the reader sad;
You fancy, you're inspired, he thinks you mad.
20 Consider too, 'twill be discreetly done,
To make your self the fiddle° of the town,   *jester*
To find th' ill-humoured pleasure at their need,
Cursed if you fail, and scorned, though you succeed.
Thus, like an arrant° woman, as I am,   *notorious*
25 No sooner well convinced writing's a shame,
That whore is scarce a more reproachful name
Than poetess:
Like men that marry, or like maids that woo,
'Cause 'tis the very worst thing they can do,

30 Pleased with the contradiction and the sin,
Methinks I stand on thorns till I begin.
Y' expect at least to hear what loves have passed
In this lewd town since you and I met last.
What change has happened of intrigues, and whether
35 The old ones last, and who and who's together.
But how, my dearest Chloe, shall I set
My pen to write, what I would fain° forget,   *willingly*
Or name that lost thing (love) without a tear
Since so debauched by ill-bred customs here?
40 Love, the most gen'rous passion of the mynde,
The softest refuge Innocence can fynde,
The safe directour of unguided youth,
Fraught with kind wishes, and secur'd by Trueth,
That Cordiall[4] dropp Heavn'n in our Cup has
     throwne,
45 To make the nauseous draught of life goe downe,
On which one onely blessing God might rayse
In lands of Atheists Subsidyes of prayse
(For none did e're soe dull, and stupid prove,
But felt a God, and blest his pow'r in Love)
50 This onely Joy, for which poore Wee were made,
Is growne like play,° to be an Arrant Trade;   *gaming*
The Rookes° creepe in, and it has gott of late   *swindlers*
As many little Cheates, and Trickes, as that.
But what yet more a Womans heart would vexe,
55 'Tis cheifely carry'd on by our own Sexe,
Our silly Sexe, who borne, like Monarchs, free,
Turne Gipsyes for a meaner Liberty,[5]
And hate restraint, though but from Infamy.[6]
They call whatever is not Common, nice,°   *fastidious*
60 And deafe to Natures rule, or Loves advice,
Forsake the pleasure, to pursue the Vice.
To an exact perfection they have wrought
The action, love, the passion is forgot.
'Tis below wit, they tell you, to admire,
65 And ev'n without approving they desire.
Their private wish obeys the public voice,
'Twist good and bad, whimsy decides, not choice.

(right margin, vertical: original spelling*)*

---

[1] *Artemisia* Pen name, chosen perhaps as an allusion to a queen of Helicarnassus in Asia Minor. Artemisia joined Xerxes's forces during the Persian invasion of mainland Greece by commanding a small squadron of ships.

[2] *bays* Wreaths of laurel or bay leaves given in recognition of distinction in poetry.

[3] *Bedlam* Colloquial term for a hospital for the mentally ill, from the Hospital of Saint Mary of Bethlehem in London.

[4] *Cordiall* Invigorating medicine.

[5] *Turne … Liberty* Turn into licentious and dishonorable people in order to be free in demeaning ways. The itinerant Romany people have been subject to systematic discrimination throughout Europe; as this line illustrates, the label that they have usually been given, "gypsies," has tended to have pejorative connotations.

[6] *Infamy* Disgraceful act.

Fashions grow up for taste, at forms they strike;
They know what they would have, not what they like.

70 Bovey's[1] a beauty, if some few agree
To call him so, the rest to that degree
Affected are, that with their ears they see.
Where I was visiting the other night,
Comes a fine lady with her humble knight,
75 Who had prevailed on her, through her own skill,
At his request, though much against his will,
To come to London.
As the coach stopped, we heard her voice, more loud
Than a great-bellied woman's in a crowd,
80 Telling the knight that her affairs require
He for some hours obsequiously retire.
I think she was ashamed to have him seen;
(Hard fate of husbands) the gallant had been,
Though a diseased, ill-favoured fool, brought in.
85 "Dispatch," says she, "that business you pretend,
Your beastly visit to your drunken friend;
A bottle ever makes you look so fine!
Methinks I long to smell you stink of wine.
Your country drinking breath's enough, to kill
90 Sour ale corrected with a lemon pill.
Prithee farewell—we'll meet again anon."
The necessary thing bows, and is gone.
She flies upstairs, and all the haste does show
That fifty antic° postures will allow,   *ludicrous*
95 And then bursts out—"Dear madam, am not I
The altered'st creature breathing? Let me die,
I find my self ridiculously grown
Embarassé with being out of town,
Rude and untaught like any Indian queen;
100 My country nakedness is strangely seen."
How is love governed? Love, that rules the state,
And pray, who are the men most worn° of late?   *fashionable*
When I was married fools were *à la mode,*°   *in fashion*
The men of wit were then held *incommode,*°   *unsuitable*
105 Slow of belief, and fickle in desire,
Who ere they'll be persuaded, must inquire
As if they came to spy, not to admire.
With searching wisdom fatal to their ease,
They still find out why what may, should not please;
110 Nay, take themselves for injured when we dare

Make 'em think better of us than we are;
And if we hide our frailties from their sights,
Call us deceitful jilts[2] and hypocrites.
They little guess who at our arts are grieved,
115 The perfect joy of being well deceived.
Inquisitive as jealous cuckolds[3] grow,
Rather than not be knowing, they will know
What, being known, creates their certain woe.
Women should these of all mankind avoid,
120 For wonder by clear knowledge is destroyed.
Woman, who is an arrant bird of night,
Bold in the dusk, before a fool's dull sight,
Should fly when reason brings the glaring light.
But the kind easy fool, apt to admire
125 Himself, trusts us; his follies all conspire
To flatter his and favour our desire.
Vain of his proper merit, he with ease
Believes we love him best who best can please.
On him our gross, dull, common flatt'ries pass,
130 Ever most joyful when most made an ass.
Heavy to apprehend, though all mankind
Perceive us false, the fop concerned is blind,
Who, doting on himself,
Thinks everyone that sees him of his mind.

135 These are true women's men.—Here forced to cease
Through want of breath, not will, to hold her peace,
She to the window runs, where she had spied
Her much esteemed dear friend, the monkey, tied.
With forty smiles, as many antic bows,
140 As if 't had been the lady of the house,
The dirty, chatt'ring monster she embraced,
And made it this fine tender speech at last:
"Kiss me, thou curious miniature of man.
How odd thou art. How pretty. How Japan.[4]
145 Oh I could live and die with thee." Then on
For half an hour in compliment she run.
I took this time to think what nature meant,
When this mixed thing into the world she sent,
So very wise, yet so impertinent.
150 One who knew everything, who, God thought fit,
Should be an ass through choice, not want of wit;
Whose foppery, without the help of sense,

---

1 *Bovey's* Possibly a reference to Sir Ralph Bovey, a contemporary of Rochester.

2 *jilts* Here, harlot or strumpet.

3 *cuckolds* Husbands of unfaithful wives.

4 *Japan* Fashionable, relating to the interest in Japanese goods.

Could ne'er have rose to such an excellence.
Nature's as lame in making a true fop
55 As a philosopher; the very top
And dignity of folly we attain
By studious search and labour of the brain,
By observation, counsel, and deep thought;
God never made a coxcomb° worth a groat.[1]   *conceited fop*
60 We owe that name to industry and arts:
An eminent fool must be a fool of parts;
And such a one was she, who had turned o'er
As many books as men, loved much, read more,
Had a discerning wit; to her was known
65 Everyone's fault and merit but her own.
All the good qualities that ever blessed
A woman, so distinguished from the rest,
Except discretion only, she possessed.
"But now, *mon cher*, dear Pug,"[2] she cries, "*adieu*,"
70 And the discourse broke off does thus renew.

You smile to see me, whom the world perchance
Mistakes to have some wit, so far advance
The interest of fools, that I approve
Their merit more than men's of wit, in love.
75 But in our sex too many proofs there are
Of such whom wits undo and fools repair.
This in my time was so observed a rule,
Hardly a wench in town but had her fool.
The meanest common slut, who long was grown
80 The jest and scorn of every pit buffoon[3]
Had yet left charms enough to have subdued
Some fop or other fond° to be thought lewd.   *eager*
Foster could make an Irish lord a Nokes,[4]
And Betty Morris[5] had her city cokes.°   *dupes*
85 A woman's ne'er so ruined but she can
Be still revenged on her undoer, man.
How lost so e'er she'll find some lover more

A lewd abandoned fool than she a whore.
That wretched thing Corinna, who had run
190 Through all the several ways of being undone,
Cozened° at first by love and living then   *deceived*
By turning the too-dear-bought trick on men.[6]
Gay were the hours, and winged with joys they flew,
When first the town her early beauties knew,
195 Courted, admired, and loved, with presents fed,
Youth in her looks and pleasure in her bed,
Till fate, or her ill angel, thought it fit
To make her dote upon a man of wit,
Who found 'twas dull to love above a day,
200 Made his ill-natured jest, and went away.
Now scorned by all, forsaken and oppressed,
She's a *memento mori* ° to the rest.   *reminder of death*
Diseased, decayed, to take up half a crown,
Must mortgage her long scarf and mantua gown.
205 Poor creature! who, unheard of as a fly,
In some dark hole must all the winter lie,
And want and dirt endure a whole half year,
That for one month she tawdry may appear.
In Easter term she gets her a new gown,
210 When my young master's worship comes to town,
From pedagogue[7] and mother just set free,
The heir and hopes of a great family,
Which, with strong ale and beef, the country rules,
And ever since the Conquest[8] have been fools.
215 And now with careful prospect to maintain
This character, lest crossing of the strain
Should mend the booby° breed, his friends   *useless, stupid*
    provide
A cousin of his own to be his bride;
And thus set out—
220 With an estate, no wit, and a young wife
(The solid comforts of a coxcomb's life),
Dung-hill and pease forsook, he comes to town,
Turns spark,[9] learns to be lewd, and is undone.
Nothing suits worse with vice than want of sense;
225 Fools are still wicked at their own expense.
This o'ergrown schoolboy lost-Corinna wins,
And at first dash to make an ass begins:

---

[1] *groat* Silver coin equal to four pence.

[2] *Pug* Name at this date for a monkey rather than a dog.

[3] *pit buffoon* The pit, or the floor of the theater, was the preferred seating area for the fashionable men of London. This part of the audience was noted for its noisy and disruptive behavior; a "pit buffoon" would be such an audience member.

[4] *Foster* Foster may be a lower-class woman mentioned by John Muddyman in a 1671 letter to Rochester; *James Nokes* Actor in the Duke's Company who regularly played the role of a fool.

[5] *Betty Morris* Probably a prostitute. Betty Morris is also mentioned in Wilmot's "An Allusion to Horace" (111).

[6] *turning … men* Becoming a prostitute.

[7] *young master's … pedagogue* University student in London during term break.

[8] *the Conquest* Norman Conquest of England, 1066 CE.

[9] *spark* Young man of smart dress and manners.

Pretends to like a man who has not known
The vanities nor vices of the town;
230 Fresh in his youth and faithful in his love,
Eager of joys, which he does seldom prove,
Healthful and strong, he does no pains endure,
But what the fair one he adores can cure.
Grateful for favours does the sex esteem,
235 And libels none for being kind to him.
Then of the lewdness of the times complains,
Rails at the wits and atheists and maintains
'Tis better than good sense, than pow'r or wealth,
To have a love untainted, youth, and health.
240 The unbred puppy, who had never seen
A creature look so gay or talk so fine,
Believes, then falls in love, and then in debt,
Mortgages all, ev'n to th' ancient seat,°   estate
To buy this mistress a new house for life;
245 To give her plate° and jewels, robs his wife;   silver
And when to the height of fondness he is grown,
'Tis time to poison him, and all's her own.
Thus meeting in her common¹ arms his fate,
He leaves her bastard heir to his estate;
250 And as the race of such an owl deserves,
His own dull lawful progeny he starves.
Nature, who never made a thing in vain,
But does each insect to some end ordain,
Wisely contrived kind-keeping fools, no doubt,
255 To patch up vices men of wit wear out.
Thus she ran on two hours, some grains of sense
Still mixed with volleys of impertinence.
But now 'tis time, I should some pity show
To Chloe, since I cannot choose but know
260 Readers must reap the dullness writers sow.
By the next post such stories I will tell
As joined with these shall to a volume swell,
As true as heaven, more infamous than hell;
But you are tired, and so am I. Farewell.
—1680

The Imperfect Enjoyment²

Naked she lay, clasped in my longing arms,
I filled with love, and she all over charms,
Both equally inspired with eager fire,
Melting through kindness,³ flaming in desire;
5   With arms, legs, lips, close clinging to embrace,
She clips me to her breast, and sucks me to her face.
The nimble tongue (Love's lesser lightning) played
Within my mouth, and to my thoughts conveyed
Swift orders that I should prepare to throw,
10   The all-dissolving thunderbolt below.
My fluttering soul, sprung with the pointed kiss,
Hangs hovering o'er her balmy brinks of bliss.
But whilst her busy hand would guide that part,
Which should convey my soul up to her heart,
15   In liquid raptures I dissolve all o'er,
Melt into sperm, and spend° at every pore: ejaculate
A touch from any part of her had done 't,
Her hand, her foot, her very look's a cunt.
Smiling, she chides in a kind murmuring noise,
20   And from her body wipes the clammy joys;
When with a thousand kisses, wandering o'er
My panting bosom, "Is there then no more?"
She cries. "All this to love and rapture's due,
Must we not pay a debt to pleasure too?"
25   But I, the most forlorn, lost man alive,
To show my wished obedience vainly strive,
I sigh alas! and kiss, but cannot swive.°   copulate
Eager desires confound my first intent,
Succeeding shame does more success prevent,
30   And rage at last confirms me impotent.
Ev'n her fair hand, which might bid heat return
To frozen age, and make cold hermits burn,
Applied to my dead cinder, warms no more
Than fire to ashes, could past flames restore.
35   Trembling, confused, despairing, limber, dry,
A wishing, weak, unmoving lump I lie.
This dart of love, whose piercing point oft tried,
With virgin blood, ten thousand maids have dyed;
Which nature still directed with such art,

---

² *The Imperfect Enjoyment* Stemming from Ovid's *Amores*, the
tradition of seventeenth-century "imperfect enjoyment" poems
includes works by Aphra Behn and George Etherege, as well as by
several French poets.

³ *kindness* Instinct.

---

¹ *common* Also used by other men.

40 That it through every cunt reached every heart.
Stiffly resolved, 'twould carelessly invade
Woman or man, nor ought its fury stayed,
Where'er it pierced, a cunt it found or made.
Now languid lies in this unhappy hour,
45 Shrunk up and sapless, like a withered flower.
Thou treacherous, base, deserter of my flame,
False to my passion, fatal to my fame;
Through what mistaken magic dost thou prove
So true to lewdness, so untrue to love?
50 What oyster, cinder,[1] beggar, common whore,
Didst thou e'er fail in all thy life before?
When vice, disease, and scandal lead the way,
With what officious haste dost thou obey?
Like a rude, roaring hector[2] in the streets,
55 That scuffles, cuffs, and ruffles all he meets,
But if his king or country claim his aid,
The rakehell° villain shrinks and hides his head;   *debauched*
Ev'n so thy brutal valor is displayed,
Breaks every stew,° does each small whore invade,   *brothel*
60 But when great Love the onset does command,
Base recreant[3] to thy prince, thou dar'st not stand.

Worst part of me, and henceforth hated most,
Through all the town, a common fucking post,
On whom each whore relieves her tingling cunt,
65 As hogs on gates do rub themselves and grunt.
May'st thou to ravenous chancres° be a prey,   *syphilitic ulcers*
Or in consuming weepings waste away.
May strangury and stone[4] thy days attend,
May'st thou ne'er piss, who didst refuse to spend,
70 When all my joys did on false thee depend.
And may ten thousand abler pricks agree,
To do the wronged Corinna[5] right for thee.
—1680

Impromptu on Charles II

God bless our good and gracious King,
Whose promise none relies on;
Who never said a foolish thing,
Nor ever did a wise one.
—1707

---

1 *oyster, cinder* Some of the poorest women on the streets, oyster women and cinder women were considered potential prostitutes.

2 *hector* Rowdy young man.

3 *recreant* One who is unfaithful to his or her duty.

4 *strangury and stone* Diseases characterized by painful and slow urination.

5 *Corinna* Woman's name, common in pastoral poetry.

IN CONTEXT

The Lessons of Rochester's Life

ADVERTISEMENT.

ALL the lewd and profane poems and libels
of the late Lord Rochester having been (contrary
to his dying request, and in defiance of religion,
government, and common decency) published to
the world; and (for the easier and surer propagation of vice) printed in penny-books, and cried
about the streets of this honourable city, without
any offence or dislike taken at them: it is humbly
hoped that this short discourse, which gives a true
account of the death and repentance of that noble
lord, may likewise (for the sake of his name) find
find a favourable reception among such persons;
though the influence of it cannot be supposed to
reach as far as the poison of the other books is
spread; which, by the strength of their own viru-
lent corruption, are capable of doing more mischief
than all the plays, and fairs, and stews, in and
about this town can do together.

Advertisement and opening page, Robert Parson's "Sermon Preached
at Rochester's Funeral," facsimile page from a volume c. 1780 entitled
Rochester's Life, which brought together Samuel Johnson's "Preface" to
Rochester's works, Gilbert Burnet's account of *The Life and Death of
John Rochester*, and Parson's sermon. Material of this sort concerning
Rochester continued to be republished through the eighteenth century.

Daniel Defoe
1660 – 1731

In 1660 Daniel Foe was born to Alice and James Foe; his father was an eminent London and area tradesman and tallow chandler. His parents were Puritan Dissenters or Nonconformists (individuals who separated themselves from the national church) and at the age of ten, shortly after his mother's death, Daniel was sent to a private Nonconformist school in Dorking, and then to a notable academy for Dissenters run by Dr. Charles Morton. While in attendance at school, he was tutored according to a more unconventional curriculum than was commonplace; the study of Greek and Latin was underplayed in favor of a strong education in science, philosophy, civil law, and modern history.

By 1679, while many of his classmates prepared for careers in the ministry, Foe entered his

father's world of trade. In his early twenties, he became a partner in a haberdashery, and quickly expanded his interests as a wholesaler of wine, tobacco, textiles, and other commodities. Foe was married in 1684 to Mary Tuffley, the daughter of a London merchant family. Mary Foe would live to bear her husband eight children, and the marriage survived over fifty years of political turbulence, personal danger, and financial ruin. It was shortly after his marriage that Foe began involving himself, often to his own personal and professional peril, in the capricious world of English politics.

An ardent Whig and a Dissenter, Foe strongly opposed the Catholic James II, and chose to fight in the failed Monmouth Rebellion of 1685. In consequence he was forced to spend much of the next two years in hiding; during this time he continued to speak in anonymous pamphlets against the King's religious policies. When the Glorious Revolution brought the Protestant William III to the throne in 1688, Foe offered his services to the new king—as an author and also as a secret agent. Ironically, Foe's business ventures met with disaster partly due to William's policies; when the new king went to war with France he lost many lucrative trading connections. These problems, compounded by the failure of some risky ventures into ship insurance, forced him to declare bankruptcy in 1692.

Never allowing his energy and pride to fail him, Foe began to focus on writing for his livelihood. It was at this period that he began to add the French *de* to his surname, as he launched into a long and prolific career as an essayist, poet, and novelist. In 1697 Defoe completed his first substantial book, *An Essay upon Projects*, followed four years later by his more popular *The True-Born Englishman*, in which he attacked "loyal" and "native" Britons who condemned their king for being a foreigner. The unexpected death of William III in 1702 once again brought Defoe's fortunes into doubt, as Queen Anne launched a new assault on Nonconformists. Undeterred, Defoe anonymously published *The Shortest Way with Dissenters*, a deliberately crafted hoax in which he mimicked the rhetoric of High Tory officials in an exaggerated argument for the extermination of all Dissenters. It did not take long for his enemies to discover the identity of the pamphlet's author, and a warrant was issued for Defoe's arrest. After four months of hiding, Defoe was arrested and sentenced to stand three times in the pillory, and to serve an indefinite period of time in Newgate Prison "at the Queen's pleasure." While in prison Defoe managed to arrange for publication of a mock ode, *Hymn to the Pillory* (1703), which was popularly sold in the streets; to the author's surprise, as he stood in the pillory he was pelted with flowers rather than with putrid vegetables.

In spite of his rise in popularity with the common reader, Defoe was in a bad state. His indefinite prison sentence had ruined his new business (as a partner in a brick and tile factory) and his ability to provide for his large family had grown extraordinarily limited. It was an ambitious Tory politician, Robert Harley, who brought about a change in Defoe's fortunes. Harley approached Defoe with an offer to work as a literary secret agent for the Tory cause; in return Harley arranged to pay some of Defoe's fines and debts, and secured his release from jail. Disillusioned with his Whig allies, Defoe accepted, and as a result of Harley's influence was released from prison in November, 1703.

From 1703 to 1714 Defoe served his Tory benefactors as a pamphleteer and political spy, traveling throughout England and Scotland and sending reports back to Harley on how the counties felt about the government. From 1704 to 1713 he wrote and edited the thrice-weekly periodical *A Review of the Affairs of France: and of All Europe, as Influenc'd by That Nation,* which offered commentary on foreign and domestic affairs, and published numerous other works, including his ambitious political poem in twelve books, *The History of the Union of Great Britain* (1709).

With the death of Queen Anne in 1714, the political tide turned once again, and the newly installed Whig leaders quickly realized the value of Defoe's position, engaging him to deliver "Tory" political messages infiltrated with the voice of the opposing Whig point of view. Although it has been said that Defoe's changing allegiances demonstrated a lack of principled politics, it has also plausibly been argued that his ability to take on the voice of another with conviction allowed him to play against both Whig and Tory extremes throughout the course of his party employment, and that his aim had generally been to advocate a reasonable and moderate course between partisan extremes.

It was not until the last decade of his life that Defoe turned to writing fiction. In 1719 he published what purported to be the true account of the strange and surprising adventures of one Robinson Crusoe, a mariner of York. Based on the actual accounts of William Selkirk, a castaway for four years on the remote island of Juan Fernandez, *Robinson Crusoe* was the first of Defoe's "true histories" in which the author imaginatively relayed the events and memoirs of a fictitious character's life, all the while creating a convincing air of truth behind every detail. *Robinson Crusoe* proved so popular that Defoe issued two sequels to the story, *The Farther Adventures of Robinson Crusoe* (1719), and *Reflections During the Life and Surprising Adventures of Robinson Crusoe* (1720). In the next five years he followed the success of these fictional "memoirs" with such works as *The Life, Adventures, and Pyracies of the Famous Captain Singleton* (1720), *The Fortunes and Misfortunes of the Famous Moll Flanders* (1721), *Colonel Jack* (1722), *A Journal of the Plague Year* (1722), and *Roxana* (1724). With these works Defoe secured his position as a leading popular author. His reputation among his contemporaries never rivaled that of Pope, Dryden, or other leading poets, but in the centuries since his work has arguably been at least as influential; Defoe is universally acknowledged as a founding figure in the history of the English novel.

In the final years of his life Defoe continued to publish considerable works of non-fiction according to his interests, including *A Tour Through the Whole Island of Great Britain* (1724–27), *The Great Law of Subordination Considered* (1724), and *The Complete English Tradesman* (1726). Becoming increasingly interested in the supernatural, he also published *The Political History of the Devil* (1726) and *An Essay on the History and Reality of Apparitions* (1727). Despite the success of his fictional narratives and his furious rate of publication, Defoe continued to struggle financially. In the last months before his death, he was forced into hiding in order to avoid debtor's prison. In an effort to hide his whereabouts, Defoe returned to the parish of his birth, where he died on 24 April 1731. He is buried in Bunhill Fields, where his grave lies amongst other notable Dissenters of his century, including John Bunyan, Isaac Watts, and William Blake.

⌘ ⌘ ⌘

A True Relation of the Apparition of One Mrs. Veal the Next Day after her Death to One Mrs. Bargrave at Canterbury the 8th of September, 1705[1]

THE PREFACE

This relation is matter of fact, and attended with such circumstances as may induce any reasonable man to believe it. It was sent by a gentleman, a justice of peace at Maidstone, in Kent, and a very intelligent person, to his friend in London, as it is here worded; which discourse is attested by a very sober and understanding gentlewoman, a kinswoman of the said gentleman's, who lives in Canterbury, within a few doors of the house in which the within-named Mrs. Bargrave lives; who believes his kinswoman to be of so discerning a spirit as not to be put upon by any fallacy; and who positively assured him that the whole matter, as it is related and laid down, is really true; and what she herself had in the same words, as near as may be, from Mrs. Bargrave's own mouth, who, she knows, had no reason to invent and publish such a story, or any design to forge and tell a lie, being a woman of much honesty and virtue, and her whole life a course, as it were, of piety. The use which we ought to make of it is to consider that there is a life to come after this, and a just God, who will retribute to every one according to the deeds done in the body; and therefore to reflect upon our past course of life we have led in the world; that our time is short and uncertain; and that if we would escape the punishment of the ungodly, and receive the reward of the righteous, which is the laying hold of eternal life, we ought, for the time to come, to return to God by a speedy repentance, ceasing to do evil and learning to do well: to seek after God early, if happily he may be found

of us, and lead such lives for the future, as may be well pleasing in his sight.

A Relation of the Apparition of Mrs. Veal

This thing is so rare in all its circumstances, and on so good authority, that my reading and conversation has not given me anything like it; it is fit to gratify the most ingenious and serious inquirer. Mrs. Bargrave is the person to whom Mrs. Veal appeared after her death; she is my intimate friend, and I can avouch for her reputation for these last fifteen or sixteen years on my own knowledge, and I can confirm the good character she had from her youth to the time of my acquaintance. Though, since this relation, she is calumniated by some people that are friends to the brother of this Mrs. Veal, who appeared; who think the relation of this appearance to be a reflection, and endeavour what they can to blast Mrs. Bargrave's reputation, and to laugh the story out of countenance. But by the circumstances thereof, and the cheerful disposition of Mrs. Bargrave, notwithstanding the ill-usage of a very wicked husband, there is not yet the least sign of dejection in her face; nor did I ever hear her let fall a desponding or murmuring expression; nay, not when actually under her husband's barbarity, which I have been witness to, and several other persons of undoubted reputation.

Now you must know that Mrs. Veal was a maiden[2] gentlewoman of about thirty years of age, and for some years last past had been troubled with fits, which were perceived coming on her by her going off from her discourse very abruptly to some impertinence. She was maintained by an only brother, and kept his house in Dover. She was a very pious woman, and her brother a very sober man to all appearance; but now he does all he can to null or quash the story. Mrs. Veal was intimately acquainted with Mrs. Bargrave from her childhood. Mrs. Veal's circumstances were then mean; her father did not take care of his children as he ought, so that they were exposed to hardships; and Mrs. Bargrave, in those days, had as unkind a father, though she wanted neither for food nor clothing, whilst Mrs. Veal wanted for both. So that it was in the power of Mrs. Bargrave to be very much her friend in several instances, which

---

[1] *A True ... 1705*   First published as an anonymous pamphlet, this work was originally thought to be an entirely fictional account, possibly written to support Charles Drelincourt's *Defense Against the Fears of Death*, which is repeatedly praised by Mrs. Veal. In the late nineteenth century, however, evidence came to light that the story was based, at least in part, on alleged fact. Defoe scholar George Aitkin published a Latin note recording an interview with a real Mrs. Bargrave, and other contemporary records of Mrs. Bargrave's story were discovered, including an account printed in the *Loyal Post*. Here Defoe gives his own account of the strange appearance of Mrs. Veal, using the perspective of a fictional friend.

[2] *Mrs. Veal ... maiden*   At this date the title Mrs. or mistress did not imply marriage.

mightily endeared Mrs. Veal; insomuch that she would often say, "Mrs. Bargrave, you are not only the best, but the only friend I have in the world, and no circumstance of life shall ever dissolve my friendship." They would often condole each other's adverse fortunes, and read together *Drelincourt upon Death*,[1] and other good books. And so, like two Christian friends, they comforted each other under their sorrow.

Sometime after, Mr. Veal's friends got him a place in the custom-house at Dover, which occasioned Mrs. Veal, by little and little, to fall off from her intimacy with Mrs. Bargrave, though there was never any such thing as a quarrel. But an indifference came on by degrees, till at last Mrs. Bargrave had not seen her in two years and a half; though above a twelvemonth of the time Mrs. Bargrave hath been absent from Dover, and this last half year has been in Canterbury about two months of the time, dwelling in a house of her own.

In this house, on the 8th of September, 1705, she was sitting alone in the forenoon, thinking over her unfortunate life, and arguing herself into a due resignation to Providence, though her condition seemed hard. And said she, "I have been provided for hitherto, and doubt not but I shall be still; and am well satisfied that my afflictions shall end when it is most fit for me." And then took up her sewing-work, which she had no sooner done but she hears a knocking at the door. She went to see who was there, and this proved to be Mrs. Veal, her old friend, who was in a riding-habit. At that moment of time the clock struck twelve at noon.

"Madam," says Mrs. Bargrave, "I am surprised to see you; you have been so long a stranger," but told her she was glad to see her, and offered to salute[2] her; which Mrs. Veal complied with till their lips almost touched; and then Mrs. Veal drew her hand across her own eyes and said, "I am not very well," and so waived it. She told Mrs. Bargrave she was going a journey, and had a great mind to see her first. "But," says Mrs. Bargrave, "how came you to take a journey alone? I am amazed at it, because I know you have a fond brother." "Oh!" says Mrs. Veal, "I gave my brother the slip and came away, because I had so great a desire to see you before I took

my journey." So Mrs. Bargrave went in with her, into another room within the first, and Mrs. Veal sat her down in an elbow-chair,[3] in which Mrs. Bargrave was sitting when she heard Mrs. Veal knock. Then says Mrs. Veal, "My dear friend, I am come to renew our old friendship again, and beg your pardon for my breach of it; and if you can forgive me, you are the best of women." "O," says Mrs. Bargrave, "do not mention such a thing. I have not had an uneasy thought about it; I can easily forgive it." "What did you think of me?" said Mrs. Veal. Says Mrs. Bargrave, "I thought you were like the rest of the world, and that prosperity had made you forget yourself and me." Then Mrs. Veal reminded Mrs. Bargrave of the many friendly offices she did her in former days, and much of the conversation they had with each other in the times of their adversity; what books they read, and what comfort, in particular, they received from *Drelincourt's Book of Death*, which was the best, she said, on that subject ever wrote. She also mentioned Dr. Sherlock,[4] and two Dutch books which were translated, wrote upon death, and several others. But Drelincourt, she said, had the clearest notions of death, and of the future state, of any who had handled that subject. Then she asked Mrs. Bargrave whether she had Drelincourt. She said, "Yes." Says Mrs. Veal, "Fetch it." And so Mrs. Bargrave goes up stairs and brings it down. Says Mrs. Veal, "Dear Mrs. Bargrave, if the eyes of our faith were as open as the eyes of our body, we should see numbers of angels about us for our guard. The notions we have of heaven now are nothing like what it is, as Drelincourt says; therefore be comforted under your afflictions, and believe that the Almighty has a particular regard to you, and that your afflictions are marks of God's favour; and when they have done the business they are sent for, they shall be removed from you. And, believe me, my dear friend, believe what I say to you, one minute of future happiness will infinitely reward you for all your sufferings. For I can never believe" (and claps her hand upon her knee with great earnestness, which indeed ran through most of her discourse) "that ever God will suffer you to spend all your days in this afflicted state. But be assured that your afflictions shall leave you, or you them, in a short time."

---

1   *Drelincourt upon Death*   French Protestant pastor and devotional writer Charles Drelincourt's *The Christian Defense against the Fears of Death* (1651).

2   *salute*   Kiss.

3   *elbow-chair*   Armchair.

4   *Dr. Sherlock*   William Sherlock (1640–1707), Church of England clergyman and author of *Practical Discourse Upon Death* (1689).

She spake in that pathetical and heavenly manner, that Mrs. Bargrave wept several times, she was so deeply affected with it. Then Mrs. Veal mentioned Dr. Horneck's *Ascetic*,[1] at the end of which he gives an account of the lives of the primitive Christians. Their pattern she recommended to our imitation, and said their conversation was not like this of our age. "For now," says she, "there is nothing but frothy, vain discourse, which is far different from theirs. Theirs was to edification, and to build one another up in faith; so that they were not as we are, nor are we as they were. But," says she, "we ought to do as they did. There was an hearty friendship among them; but where is it now to be found?" Says Mrs. Bargrave, "It is hard indeed to find a true friend in these days." Says Mrs. Veal, "Mr. Norris[2] has a fine copy of verses called *Friendship in Perfection*, which I wonderfully admire. Have you seen the book?" says Mrs. Veal. "No," says Mrs. Bargrave, "but I have the verses of my own writing out." "Have you?" says Mrs. Veal, "Then fetch them." Which she did from above stairs, and offered them to Mrs. Veal to read, who refused, and waived the thing, saying holding down her head would make it ache, and then desired Mrs. Bargrave to read them to her, which she did. As they were admiring friendship, Mrs. Veal said, "Dear Mrs. Bargrave, I shall love you for ever. In these verses there is twice used the word Elysium. Ah!" says Mrs. Veal, "these poets have such names for heaven." She would often draw her hand across her own eyes, and say, "Mrs. Bargrave, do not you think I am mightily impaired by my fits?" "No," says Mrs. Bargrave, "I think you look as well as ever I knew you."

After all this discourse, which the apparition put in much finer words than Mrs. Bargrave said she could pretend to, and as much more than she can remember (for it cannot be thought that an hour and three quarters' conversation could all be retained, though the main of it she thinks she does). She said to Mrs. Bargrave she would have her write a letter to her brother, and tell him she would have him give rings to such and such, and that there was a purse of gold in her cabinet, and that she would have two broad pieces given to her cousin Watson. Talking at this rate, Mrs. Bargrave thought that a fit was coming upon her, and so placed herself in a chair just before her knees, to keep her from falling to the ground if her fits should occasion it: for the elbow-chair, she thought, would keep her from falling on either side. And to divert Mrs. Veal, as she thought, she took hold of her gown sleeve several times, and commended it. Mrs. Veal told her it was a scoured[3] silk, and newly made up. But for all this, Mrs. Veal persisted in her request, and told Mrs. Bargrave she must not deny her, and she would have her tell her brother all their conversation, when she had opportunity. "Dear Mrs. Veal," says Mrs. Bargrave, "this seems so impertinent that I cannot tell how to comply with it; and what a mortifying story will our conversation be to a young gentleman?" "Well," says Mrs. Veal, "I must not be denied." "Why," says Mrs. Bargrave, "it is much better, methinks, to do it yourself." "No," says Mrs. Veal, "though it seems impertinent to you now, you will see more reason for it hereafter." Mrs. Bargrave then, to satisfy her importunity, was going to fetch a pen and ink; but Mrs. Veal said, "Let it alone now, and do it when I am gone; but you must be sure to do it." Which was one of the last things she enjoined her at parting; and so she promised her.

Then Mrs. Veal asked for Mrs. Bargrave's daughter. She said she was not at home. "But if you have a mind to see her," says Mrs. Bargrave, "I'll send for her." "Do," says Mrs. Veal. On which she left her and went to a neighbour's to see for her; and by the time Mrs. Bargrave was returning, Mrs. Veal was got without the door in the street, in the face of the beast-market on a Saturday, which is market-day, and stood ready to part as soon as Mrs. Bargrave came to her. She asked her why she was in such haste. She said she must be going, though perhaps she might not go her journey till Monday; and told Mrs. Bargrave she hoped she should see her again at her cousin Watson's before she went whither she was a-going. Then she said she would take her leave of her, and walked from Mrs. Bargrave in her view, till a turning interrupted the sight of her, which was three quarters after one in the afternoon.

Mrs. Veal died the 7th of September at twelve o'clock at noon, of her fits, and had not above four hours' senses before her death, in which time she

---

[1] *Dr. Horneck's Ascetic* Church of England clergyman Anthony Horneck's *The Happy Ascetic* (1681).

[2] *Mr. Norris* Clergyman and philosopher John Norris (1657–1712).

[3] *scoured* Treated with detergent.

received the sacrament. The next day after Mrs. Veal's appearing, being Sunday, Mrs. Bargrave was mightily indisposed with a cold and a sore throat, that she could not go out that day; but on Monday morning she sent a person to Captain Watson's to know if Mrs. Veal was there. They wondered at Mrs. Bargrave's inquiry, and sent her word that she was not there, nor was expected. At this answer Mrs. Bargrave told the maid she had certainly mistook the name, or made some blunder. And though she was ill, she put on her hood and went herself to Captain Watson's, though she knew none of the family, to see if Mrs. Veal was there or not. They said they wondered at her asking, for that she had not been in town; they were sure, if she had, she would have been there. Says Mrs. Bargrave, "I am sure she was with me on Saturday almost two hours." They said it was impossible, for they must have seen her if she had. In comes Captain Watson, while they were in dispute, and said that Mrs. Veal was certainly dead, and her escutcheons were making.[1] This strangely surprised Mrs. Bargrave, who went to the person immediately who had the care of them, and found it true. Then she related the whole story to Captain Watson's family, and what gown she had on, and how striped; and that Mrs. Veal told her it was scoured. Then Mrs. Watson cried out, "You have seen her indeed, for none knew but Mrs. Veal and myself that gown was scoured!" And Mrs. Watson owned that she described the gown exactly. "For," said she, "I helped her to make it up." This, Mrs. Watson blazed all about the town, and avouched the demonstration of the truth of Mrs. Bargrave's seeing Mrs. Veal's apparition. And Captain Watson carried two gentlemen immediately to Mrs. Bargrave's house to hear the relation of her own mouth. And then it spread so fast that gentlemen and persons of quality, the judicious and sceptical part of the world, flocked in upon her, which at last became such a task that she was forced to go out of the way. For they were, in general, extremely satisfied of the truth of the thing, and plainly saw that Mrs. Bargrave was no hypochondriac; for she always appears with such a cheerful air and pleasing mien that she has gained the favour and esteem of all the gentry, and it is thought a great favour if they can but get the relation from her own mouth. I should have told you before that

Mrs. Veal told Mrs. Bargrave that her sister and brother-in-law were just come down from London to see her. Says Mrs. Bargrave, "How came you to order matters so strangely?" "It could not be helped," says Mrs. Veal. And her brother and sister did come to see her, and entered the town of Dover just as Mrs. Veal was expiring. Mrs. Bargrave asked her whether she would drink some tea. Says Mrs. Veal, "I do not care if I do; but I'll warrant you, this mad fellow" (meaning Mrs. Bargrave's husband) "has broke all your trinkets." "But," says Mrs. Bargrave, "I'll get something to drink in for all that." But Mrs. Veal waived it, and said, "It is no matter, let it alone." And so it passed.

All the time I sat with Mrs. Bargrave, which was some hours, she recollected fresh sayings of Mrs. Veal. And one material thing more she told Mrs. Bargrave, that old Mr. Breton allowed Mrs. Veal ten pounds a year, which was a secret, and unknown to Mrs. Bargrave till Mrs. Veal told it her. Mrs. Bargrave never varies in her story, which puzzles those who doubt of the truth, or are unwilling to believe it. A servant in the neighbour's yard adjoining to Mrs. Bargrave's house heard her talking to somebody an hour of the time Mrs. Veal was with her. Mrs. Bargrave went out to her next neighbour's the very moment she parted with Mrs. Veal, and told her what ravishing conversation she had with an old friend, and told the whole of it. *Drelincourt's Book of Death* is, since this happened, bought up strangely. And it is to be observed that notwithstanding all the trouble and fatigue Mrs. Bargrave has undergone upon this account, she never took the value of a farthing, nor suffered her daughter to take anything of anybody, and therefore can have no interest in telling the story.

But Mr. Veal does what he can to stifle the matter, and said he would see Mrs. Bargrave; but yet it is certain matter of fact that he has been at Captain Watson's since the death of his sister, and yet never went near Mrs. Bargrave. And some of his friends report her to be a liar, and that she knew of Mr. Breton's ten pounds a year. But the person who pretends to say so has the reputation of a notorious liar among persons whom I know to be of undoubted credit. Now Mr. Veal is more of a gentleman than to say she lies, but says a bad husband has crazed her. But she needs only present herself, and it will effectually confute that pretense. Mr. Veal says he asked his sister on her deathbed whether she

---

[1] *her escutcheons were making* Her funeral ornaments were being made.

had a mind to dispose of anything, and she said, "No." Now, the things which Mrs. Veal's apparition would have disposed of were so trifling, and nothing of justice aimed at in their disposal, that the design of it appears to me to be only in order to make Mrs. Bargrave so to demonstrate the truth of her appearance as to satisfy the world of the reality thereof, as to what she had seen and heard, and to secure her reputation among the reasonable and understanding part of mankind. And then again, Mr. Veal owns that there was a purse of gold, but it was not found in her cabinet, but in a comb-box. This looks improbable, for that Mrs. Watson owned that Mrs. Veal was so very careful of the key of the cabinet that she would trust nobody with it. And if so, no doubt she would not trust her gold out of it. And Mrs. Veal's often drawing her hand over her eyes, and asking Mrs. Bargrave whether her fits had not impaired her, looks to me as if she did it on purpose to remind Mrs. Bargrave of her fits, to prepare her not to think it strange that she should put her upon writing to her brother to dispose of rings and gold, which looked so much like a dying person's bequest; and it took accordingly with Mrs. Bargrave as the effects of her fits coming upon her, and was one of the many instances of her wonderful love to her, and care of her, that she should not be affrighted; which indeed appears in her whole management, particularly in her coming to her in the daytime, waiving the salutation, and when she was alone; and then the manner of her parting, to prevent a second attempt to salute her.

Now, why Mr. Veal should think this relation a reflection, as 'tis plain he does, by his endeavouring to stifle it, I cannot imagine, because the generality believe her to be a good spirit, her discourse was so heavenly. Her two great errands were to comfort Mrs. Bargrave in her affliction, and to ask her forgiveness for the breach of friendship, and with a pious discourse to encourage her. So that, after all, to suppose that Mrs. Bargrave could hatch such an invention as this from Friday noon till Saturday noon, supposing that she knew of Mrs. Veal's death the very first moment, without jumbling circumstances, and without any interest too, she must be more witty, fortunate, and wicked too, than any indifferent person, I dare say, will allow. I asked Mrs. Bargrave several times if she was sure she felt the gown. She answered modestly, "If my senses be to be relied on,

I am sure of it." I asked her if she heard a sound when she clapped her hand upon her knee? She said she did not remember she did; but said she appeared to be as much a substance as I did, who talked with her. "And I may," said she, "be as soon persuaded that your apparition is talking to me now, as that I did not really see her." For I was under no manner of fear, and received her as a friend, and parted with her as such. "I would not," says she, "give one farthing to make anyone believe it. I have no interest in it; nothing but trouble is entailed upon me for a long time, for aught I know; and had it not come to light by accident, it would never have been made public." But now she says she will make her own private use of it, and keep herself out of the way as much as she can; and so she has done since. She says she had a gentleman who came thirty miles to her to hear the relation, and that she had told it to a room full of people at a time. Several particular gentlemen have had the story from Mrs. Bargrave's own mouth.

This thing has very much affected me, and I am as well satisfied as I am of the best-grounded matter of fact. And why we should dispute matter of fact because we cannot solve things of which we can have no certain or demonstrative notions, seems strange to me. Mrs. Bargrave's authority and sincerity alone would have been undoubted in any other case.

—1706

Robinson Crusoe

Defoe's work, often considered one of the earliest English novels, is based in part on the experiences of Alexander Selkirk, a sailor who, after a disagreement with his captain concerning some repairs to the ship, refused to sail any farther and was set down on the Island of Juan Fernandez, off the coast of Chile, in 1704. He survived the four and a half years on the island before his rescue in much the same manner as Crusoe does for his twenty-eight years.

In Defoe's novel, Crusoe chooses to devote his life to the sea (despite the disapproval of his father, who has encouraged him to study law). A ship he has enlisted on is later seized by Moorish pirates, who take Crusoe and the other sailors to North Africa to work as slaves. On a fishing expedition Crusoe and a young slave boy break free and sail down the African coast, where a Portuguese captain picks them up. Crusoe purchases the slave boy from him and is then released in Brazil, where he establishes himself as a plantation owner. The excerpt below recounts what happens next.

from *Robinson Crusoe*

from CHAPTER 3[1]

… To come, then, by the just degrees to the particulars of this part of my story. You may suppose that, having now lived almost four years in the Brasils, and beginning to thrive and prosper very well upon my plantation, I had not only learned the language, but had contracted acquaintance and friendship among my fellow-planters, as well as among the merchants at St. Salvadore,[2] which was our port; and that, in my discourses among them, I had frequently given them an account of my two voyages to the coast of Guinea,[3] the manner of trading with the negroes there, and how easy it was to purchase upon the coast for trifles—such as beads, toys, knives, scissors, hatchets, bits of glass, and the like—not only gold-dust, Guinea grains,[4] elephants' teeth, &c., but negroes for the service of the Brasils, in great numbers.

They listened always very attentively to my discourses on these heads, but especially to that part which related to the buying negroes, which was a trade at that time not only not far entered into, but as far as it was, had been carried on by the assientos,[5] or permission of the kings of Spain and Portugal, and engrossed[6] in the public, so that few negroes were brought, and those excessive dear.

It happened, being in company with some merchants and planters of my acquaintance and talking of those things very earnestly, three of them came to me next morning, and told me they had been musing very much upon what I had discoursed with them of the last night, and they came to make a secret proposal to me; and, after enjoining me secrecy,[7] they told me that they had a mind to fit out a ship to go to Guinea, that they had all plantations as well as I, and were straitened for nothing so much as servants; that as it was a trade that could not be carried on, because they could not publicly sell the negroes when they came home, so they desired to make but one voyage, to bring the negroes on shore privately and divide them among their own plantations; and, in a word, the question was whether I would go their super-cargo[8] in the ship to manage the trading part upon the coast of Guinea. And they offered me that I should have my equal share of the negroes, without providing any part of the stock.

This was a fair proposal, it must be confessed, had it been made to any one that had not had a settlement and plantation of his own to look after, which was in a fair way of coming to be very considerable, and with a good stock upon it. But for me that was thus entered and established, and had nothing to do but to go on as I had begun for three or four years more, and to have sent for the other hundred pound from England, and who in that time, and with that little addition, could scarce have failed of being worth three or four thousand pounds sterling, and that increasing too; for me to think of such a voyage was the most preposterous thing that ever man in such circumstances could be guilty of.

But I that was born to be my own destroyer could no more resist the offer than I could restrain my first rambling designs, when my father's good counsel was lost upon me. In a word, I told them I would go with all my heart, if they would undertake to look after my plantation in my absence and would dispose of it to

---

[1] *Chapter 3*   Defoe's original text did not contain chapter divisions, but these divisions, inserted after the original publication, are now commonly used and are here provided for reference.

[2] *St. Salvadore*   Salvador da Bahia, then capital of Brazil.

[3] *Guinea*   Region of West Africa.

[4] *Guinea grains*   Seeds of a West African plant, used as a substitute for black pepper.

[5] *assientos*   Spanish: contracts. Refers to agreements granting exclusive rights to the slave trade in the Spanish colonies. Since receiving an assiento in 1713, the British held a legal monopoly on the sale of slaves in the area; even a private operation to obtain slaves for oneself would have been illegal.

[6] *engrossed*   Held by exclusive possession.

[7] *enjoining me secrecy*   I.e., requesting that I keep the conversation secret.

[8] *go their super-cargo*   Travel as the officer who oversees the cargo and its exchange.

such as I should direct if I miscarried. This they all engaged to do, and entered into writings or covenants to do so; and I made a formal will, disposing of my plantation and effects in case of my death, making the captain of the ship that had saved my life, as before, my universal heir, but obliging him to dispose of my effects as I had directed in my will, one half of the produce being to himself, and the other to be shipped to England.

In short, I took all possible caution to preserve my effects and keep up my plantation; had I used half as much prudence to have looked into my own interest, and have made a judgment of what I ought to have done, and not to have done, I had certainly never gone away from so prosperous an undertaking, leaving all the probable views of a thriving circumstance, and gone upon a voyage to sea, attended with all its common hazards; to say nothing of the reasons I had to expect particular misfortunes to myself.[1]

But I was hurried on, and obeyed blindly the dictates of my fancy rather than my reason; and accordingly, the ship being fitted out, and the cargo furnished, and all things done as by agreement by my partners in the voyage, I went on board in an evil hour: the first of September, 1659, being the same day eight year that I went from my father and mother at Hull, in order to act the rebel to their authority, and the fool to my own interests.

Our ship was about 120 tun burden,[2] carried 6 guns and 14 men besides the master, his boy, and myself. We had on board no large cargo of goods, except of such toys as were fit for our trade with the negroes, such as beads, bits of glass, shells, and odd trifles, especially little looking-glasses, knives, scissors, hatchets, and the like.

The same day I went on board we set sail, standing away to the northward upon our own coast, with design to stretch over for the African coast, when they came about 10 or 12 degrees of northern latitude, which it seems was the manner of their course in those days. We had very good weather, only excessive hot, all the way

upon our own coast, till we came to the height of Cape St. Augustino;[3] from whence keeping farther off at sea we lost sight of land, and steered as if we were bound for the isle Fernand de Noronha,[4] holding our course N.E. by N. and leaving those isles on the east; in this course we passed the line[5] in about 12 days' time, and were by our last observation in 7 degrees 22 min. northern latitude, when a violent tornado or hurricane took us quite out of our knowledge. It began from the south-east, came about to the north-west, and then settled into the north-east, from whence it blew in such a terrible manner that for twelve days together we could do nothing but drive and, scudding away before it, let it carry us whither ever fate and the fury of the winds directed; and during these twelve days, I need not say that I expected every day to be swallowed up, nor indeed did any in the ship expect to save their lives.

In this distress, we had, besides the terror of the storm, one of our men die of the calenture,[6] and one man and the boy washed overboard. About the 12th day, the weather abating a little, the master made an observation as well as he could, and found that he was in about 11 degrees north latitude, but that he was 22 degrees of longitude difference west from Cape St. Augustino; so that he found he was upon the coast of Guiana, or the north part of Brasil, beyond the river Amazones, toward that of the river Orinoque,[7] commonly called the Great River; and began to consult with me what course he should take, for the ship was leaky and very much disabled, and he was going directly back to the coast of Brasil.

I was positively against that, and, looking over the charts of the sea-coast of America with him, we concluded there was no inhabited country for us to have recourse to till we came within the circle of the Caribbee Islands, and therefore resolved to stand away for

---

[1] *the reasons ... to myself* Crusoe's earlier experiences have led him to believe that he is subject to an "evil influence" causing him to embark on adventures against his better judgment, and that these are fated to end in disaster.

[2] *tun burden* Measurement of a ship's capacity based on the weight of tuns (large wine casks). Crusoe's ship would have been able to carry 115 modern tons.

[3] *Cape St. Augustino* Town on the easternmost portion of Brazil's coastline.

[4] *Fernand de Noronha* About 370 miles north of Cape St. Augustino.

[5] *the line* The equator.

[6] *calenture* Heatstroke, often accompanied by hallucinations.

[7] *Orinoque* Orinoco River, the mouth of which is located near the top of the continent, north of the Amazon.

Barbadoes,[1] which, by keeping off at sea to avoid the indraft of the Bay or Gulf of Mexico, we might easily perform, as we hoped, in about fifteen days' sail; whereas we could not possibly make our voyage to the coast of Africa without some assistance both to our ship and to ourselves.

With this design we changed our course, and steered away N.W. by W. in order to reach some of our English islands, where I hoped for relief; but our voyage was otherwise determined, for being in the latitude of 12 deg. 18 min. a second storm came upon us, which carried us away with the same impetuosity westward and drove us so out of the very way of all human commerce that, had all our lives been saved as to the sea, we were rather in danger of being devoured by savages than ever returning to our own country.

In this distress, the wind still blowing very hard, one of our men early in the morning cried out, *Land*; and we had no sooner run out of the cabin to look out in hopes of seeing whereabouts in the world we were, but the ship struck upon a sand, and in a moment, her motion being so stopped, the sea broke over her in such a manner that we expected we should all have perished immediately, and we were immediately driven into our close quarters to shelter us from the very foam and spray of the sea.

It is not easy for anyone who has not been in the like condition to describe or conceive the consternation of men in such circumstances; we knew nothing where we were, or upon what land it was we were driven, whether an island or the main, whether inhabited or not inhabited; and as the rage of the wind was still great, though rather less than at first, we could not so much as hope to have the ship hold many minutes without breaking in pieces, unless the winds by a kind of miracle should turn immediately about. In a word, we sat looking upon one another and expecting death every moment, and every man acting accordingly, as preparing for another world, for there was little or nothing more for us to do in this; that which was our present comfort, and all the comfort we had, was that, contrary to our expectation, the ship did not break yet, and that the master said the wind began to abate.

Now, though we thought that the wind did a little abate, yet the ship having thus struck upon the sand, and sticking too fast for us to expect her getting off, we were in a dreadful condition indeed, and had nothing to do but to think of saving our lives as well as we could; we had a boat at our stern just before the storm, but she was first staved by dashing against the ship's rudder, and in the next place she broke away, and either sunk or was driven off to sea, so there was no hope from her; we had another boat on board, but how to get her off into the sea was a doubtful thing; however, there was no room to debate, for we fancied the ship would break in pieces every minute, and some told us she was actually broken already.

In this distress, the mate of our vessel laid hold of the boat, and with the help of the rest of the men, they got her flung over the ship's side and, getting all into her, let go and committed ourselves, being eleven in number, to God's mercy and the wild sea; for though the storm was abated considerably, yet the sea went dreadful high upon the shore, and might be well called *den wild zee*,[2] as the Dutch call the sea in a storm.

And now our case was very dismal indeed; for we all saw plainly that the sea went so high that the boat could not live, and that we should be inevitably drowned. As to making sail, we had none, nor, if we had, could we have done anything with it; so we worked at the oar towards the land, though with heavy hearts, like men going to execution; for we all knew that when the boat came nearer the shore, she would be dashed in a thousand pieces by the breach of the sea. However, we committed our souls to God in the most earnest manner; and, the wind driving us towards the shore, we hastened our destruction with our own hands, pulling as well as we could towards land.

What the shore was, whether rock or sand, whether steep or shoal, we knew not; the only hope that could rationally give us the least shadow of expectation was if we might happen into some bay or gulf, or the mouth of some river, where by great chance we might have run our boat in, or got under the lee of the land, and perhaps made smooth water. But there was nothing of this appeared; but as we made nearer and nearer the shore, the land looked more frightful than the sea.

---

[1] *Caribbee Islands* Chain of islands between South America and Puerto Rico; *Barbadoes* One of several English island colonies in this chain.

[2] *den wild zee* Dutch: the wild sea.

After we had rowed—or rather driven—about a league and a half,[1] as we reckoned it, a raging wave, mountain-like, came rolling astern of us and plainly bade us expect the *coup de grace*.[2] In a word, it took us with such a fury that it overset the boat at once; and, separating us as well from the boat, as from one another, gave us no time to say, O God! for we were all swallowed up in a moment.

Nothing can describe the confusion of thought which I felt when I sunk into the water; for though I swam very well, yet I could not deliver myself from the waves so as to draw breath till that wave, having driven me, or rather carried me, a vast way on towards the shore, and, having spent itself, went back and left me upon the land almost dry, but half-dead with the water I took in. I had so much presence of mind as well as breath left that, seeing myself nearer the main land than I expected, I got upon my feet and endeavoured to make on towards the land as fast as I could, before another wave should return and take me up again. But I soon found it was impossible to avoid it; for I saw the sea come after me as high as a great hill and as furious as an enemy which I had no means or strength to contend with; my business was to hold my breath, and raise myself upon the water if I could; and so, by swimming, to preserve my breathing and pilot myself towards the shore, if possible; my greatest concern now being that the sea, as it would carry me a great way towards the shore when it came on, might not carry me back again with it when it gave back towards the sea.

The wave that came upon me again buried me at once 20 or 30 foot deep in its own body; and I could feel myself carried with a mighty force and swiftness towards the shore a very great way; but I held my breath and assisted myself to swim still forward with all my might. I was ready to burst with holding my breath when, as I felt myself rising up, so to my immediate relief I found my head and hands shoot out above the surface of the water; and though it was not two seconds of time that I could keep myself so, yet it relieved me greatly, gave me breath and new courage. I was covered again with water a good while, but not so long but I held it out; and, finding the water had spent itself and began to return, I struck forward against the return of the waves, and felt ground again with my feet. I stood still a few moments to recover breath, and till the water went from me, and then took to my heels and ran with what strength I had farther towards the shore. But neither would this deliver me from the fury of the sea, which came pouring in after me again, and twice more I was lifted up by the waves and carried forwards as before, the shore being very flat.

The last time of these two had well near been fatal to me; for the sea, having hurried me along as before, landed me—or rather dashed me—against a piece of rock, and that with such force as it left me senseless, and indeed helpless, as to my own deliverance; for the blow, taking my side and breast, beat the breath, as it were, quite out of my body; and, had it returned again immediately, I must have been strangled in the water; but I recovered a little before the return of the waves, and, seeing I should be covered again with the water, I resolved to hold fast by a piece of the rock, and so to hold my breath, if possible, till the wave went back; now, as the waves were not so high as at first, being nearer land, I held my hold till the wave abated, and then fetched another run, which brought me so near the shore that the next wave, though it went over me, yet did not so swallow me up as to carry me away, and the next run I took, I got to the main land, where, to my great comfort, I clambered up the cliffs of the shore and sat me down upon the grass, free from danger, and quite out of the reach of the water.

I was now landed, and safe on shore, and began to look up and thank God that my life was saved in a case wherein there was, some minutes before, scarce any room to hope. I believe it is impossible to express to the life what the ecstasies and transports of the soul are, when it is so saved, as I may say, out of the very grave; and I do not wonder now at that custom, *viz.*[3] that when a malefactor[4] who has the halter about his neck is tied up and just going to be turned off,[5] and has a reprieve brought to him; I say, I do not wonder that they bring a surgeon with it to let his blood that very moment they tell him of it, that the surprise may not drive the animal spirits from the heart and overwhelm him:

---

[1] *about a … half* More than five miles.

[2] *coup de grace* French: merciful killing blow.

[3] *viz.* Abbreviation of the Latin *videlicet*, meaning "namely; that is to say."

[4] *malefactor* Criminal.

[5] *turned off* Hanged.

For sudden joys, like griefs, confound at first.[1]

I walked about on the shore, lifting up my hands, and my whole being, as I may say, wrapped up in the contemplation of my deliverance, making a thousand gestures and motions which I cannot describe, reflecting upon all my comrades that were drowned, and that there should not be one soul saved but myself; for, as for them, I never saw them afterwards, or any sign of them, except three of their hats, one cap, and two shoes that were not fellows.

I cast my eyes to the stranded vessel, when, the breach and froth of the sea being so big, I could hardly see it, it lay so far off, and considered, Lord! how was it possible I could get on shore?

After I had solaced my mind with the comfortable part of my condition, I began to look round me to see what kind of place I was in and what was next to be done; and I soon found my comforts abate, and that, in a word, I had a dreadful deliverance: for I was wet, had no clothes to shift me,[2] nor anything either to eat or drink to comfort me; neither did I see any prospect before me but that of perishing with hunger or being devoured by wild beasts; and that which was particularly afflicting to me was that I had no weapon, either to hunt and kill any creature for my sustenance, or to defend myself against any other creature that might desire to kill me for theirs. In a word, I had nothing about me but a knife, a tobacco-pipe, and a little tobacco in a box; this was all my provision, and this threw me into such terrible agonies of mind that for a while I ran about like a madman; night coming upon me, I began with a heavy heart to consider what would be my lot if there were any ravenous beasts in that country, seeing at night they always come abroad for their prey.

All the remedy that offered to my thoughts at that time was to get up into a thick bushy tree, like a fir, but thorny, which grew near me, and where I resolved to sit all night, and consider the next day what death I should die, for as yet I saw no prospect of life; I walked about a furlong[3] from the shore to see if I could find any fresh water to drink, which I did, to my great joy; and having

drank and put a little tobacco into my mouth to prevent hunger, I went to the tree and, getting up into it, endeavoured to place myself so that if I should sleep I might not fall; and, having cut me a short stick, like a truncheon, for my defence, I took up my lodging, and having been excessively fatigued, I fell fast asleep and slept as comfortably as, I believe, few could have done in my condition, and found myself more refreshed with it than I think I ever was on such an occasion.

Chapter 4

When I waked it was broad day, the weather clear, and the storm abated, so that the sea did not rage and swell as before. But that which surprised me most was that the ship was lifted off in the night from the sand where she lay, by the swelling of the tide, and was driven up almost as far as the rock which I at first mentioned, where I had been so bruised by the wave dashing me against it. This being within about a mile from the shore where I was, and the ship seeming to stand upright still, I wished myself on board, that at least I might save some necessary things for my use.

When I came down from my apartment in the tree, I looked about me again, and the first thing I found was the boat, which lay as the wind and the sea had tossed her up upon the land, about two miles on my right hand. I walked as far as I could upon the shore to have got to her, but found a neck or inlet of water between me and the boat which was about half a mile broad, so I came back for the present, being more intent upon getting at the ship, where I hoped to find something for my present subsistence.

A little after noon I found the sea very calm, and the tide ebbed so far out that I could come within a quarter of a mile of the ship. And here I found a fresh renewing of my grief; for I saw evidently that if we had kept on board we had been all safe—that is to say, we had all got safe on shore, and I had not been so miserable as to be left entirely destitute of all comfort and company, as I now was. This forced tears to my eyes again; but as there was little relief in that, I resolved, if possible, to get to the ship; so I pulled off my clothes—for the weather was hot to extremity—and took the water. But when I came to the ship my difficulty was still greater to know how to get on board; for, as she lay aground, and high out of

---

[1] *For sudden … at first* From Robert Wild's poem "Poetica Licentia" (1672).

[2] *shift me* Dress myself in.

[3] *furlong* 220 yards.

the water, there was nothing within my reach to lay hold of. I swam round her twice, and the second time I spied a small piece of rope, which I wondered I did not see at first, hung down by the fore-chains, so low as that with great difficulty I got hold of it, and by the help of that rope I got up into the forecastle of the ship. Here I found that the ship was bulged,[1] and had a great deal of water in her hold, but that she lay so on the side of a bank of hard sand, or rather earth, that her stern lay lifted up upon the bank, and her head low almost to the water. By this means all her quarter was free, and all that was in that part was dry; for you may be sure my first work was to search and to see what was spoiled and what was free. And first I found that all the ship's provisions were dry and untouched by the water; and, being very well disposed to eat, I went to the bread room and filled my pockets with biscuit, and ate it as I went about other things, for I had no time to lose. I also found some rum in the great cabin, of which I took a large dram, and which I had indeed need enough of to spirit me for what was before me. Now I wanted nothing but a boat to furnish myself with many things which I foresaw would be very necessary to me.

It was in vain to sit still and wish for what was not to be had; and this extremity roused my application. We had several spare yards,[2] and two or three large spars of wood, and a spare topmast or two in the ship; I resolved to fall to work with these, and I flung as many of them overboard as I could manage for their weight, tying every one with a rope, that they might not drive away. When this was done I went down the ship's side and, pulling them to me, I tied four of them together at both ends as well as I could, in the form of a raft, and, laying two or three short pieces of plank upon them crossways, I found I could walk upon it very well, but that it was not able to bear any great weight, the pieces being too light. So I went to work, and with a carpenter's saw I cut a spare topmast into three lengths, and added them to my raft with a great deal of labour and pains. But the hope of furnishing myself with necessaries encouraged me to go beyond what I should have been able to have done upon another occasion.

My raft was now strong enough to bear any reasonable weight. My next care was what to load it with, and how to preserve what I laid upon it from the surf of the sea; but I was not long considering this. I first laid all the planks or boards upon it that I could get, and, having considered well what I most wanted, I got three of the seamen's chests, which I had broken open and emptied, and lowered them down upon my raft; the first of these I filled with provisions—*viz.* bread, rice, three Dutch cheeses, five pieces of dried goat's flesh (which we lived much upon), and a little remainder of European corn, which had been laid by for some fowls which we brought to sea with us, but the fowls were killed. There had been some barley and wheat together; but, to my great disappointment, I found afterwards that the rats had eaten or spoiled it all. As for liquors, I found several cases of bottles belonging to our skipper, in which were some cordial waters, and, in all, about five or six gallons of rack.[3] These I stowed by themselves, there being no need to put them into the chest, nor any room for them. While I was doing this, I found the tide began to flow, though very calm, and I had the mortification to see my coat, shirt, and waistcoat, which I had left on shore upon the sand, swim away; as for my breeches, which were only linen, and open-kneed, I swam on board in them and my stockings. However, this set me upon rummaging for clothes, of which I found enough, but took no more than I wanted for present use, for I had other things which my eye was more upon—as, first, tools to work with on shore. And it was after long searching that I found out the carpenter's chest, which was, indeed, a very useful prize to me, and much more valuable than a shipload of gold would have been at that time. I got it down to my raft, whole as it was, without losing time to look into it, for I knew in general what it contained.

My next care was for some ammunition and arms. There were two very good fowling-pieces[4] in the great cabin, and two pistols. These I secured first, with some powder-horns[5] and a small bag of shot, and two old rusty swords. I knew there were three barrels of powder

---

[1] *bulged* Warping or bulging would cause gaps to open between the planks and make the ship take on water.

[2] *yards* Wooden spars that support and extend sails already hung on masts.

[3] *rack* Arrack, a name given by Europeans to liquor made by natives, especially that made from fermented rice, sugar, or coco-palm.

[4] *fowling-piece* Light gun (used for shooting birds).

[5] *powder-horns* Flasks for holding gunpowder.

in the ship, but knew not where our gunner had stowed them; but with much search I found them, two of them dry and good, the third had taken water. Those two I got to my raft with the arms. And now I thought myself pretty well freighted, and began to think how I should get to shore with them, having neither sail, oar, nor rudder; and the least capful of wind would have overset all my navigation.

I had three encouragements: 1. a smooth, calm sea; 2. the tide rising, and setting in to the shore; 3. what little wind there was blew me towards the land: and thus, having found two or three broken oars belonging to the boat, and, besides the tools which were in the chest, I found two saws, an axe, and a hammer, and with this cargo I put to sea. For a mile or thereabouts my raft went very well, only that I found it drive a little distant from the place where I had landed before; by which I perceived that there was some indraft of the water, and consequently I hoped to find some creek or river there, which I might make use of as a port to get to land with my cargo.

As I imagined, so it was. There appeared before me a little opening of the land, and I found a strong current of the tide set into it, so I guided my raft as well as I could to keep in the middle of the stream; but here I had like to have suffered a second shipwreck—which, if I had, I think verily would have broken my heart; for, knowing nothing of the coast, my raft ran aground at one end of it upon a shoal, and, not being aground at the other end, it wanted but a little that all my cargo had slipped off towards that end that was afloat, and so fallen into the water. I did my utmost, by setting my back against the chests, to keep them in their places, but could not thrust off the raft with all my strength; neither durst I stir from the posture I was in; but, holding up the chests with all my might, I stood in that manner near half-an-hour, in which time the rising of the water brought me a little more upon a level; and a little after, the water still rising, my raft floated again, and I thrust her off with the oar I had into the channel, and then, driving up higher, I at length found myself in the mouth of a little river, with land on both sides and a strong current of tide running up. I looked on both sides for a proper place to get to shore; for I was not willing to be driven too high up the river, hoping in time to see some ships at sea, and therefore resolved to place myself as near the coast as I could.

At length I spied a little cove on the right shore of the creek, to which with great pain and difficulty I guided my raft, and at last got so near that, reaching ground with my oar, I could thrust her directly in. But here I had like to have dipped all my cargo into the sea again; for that shore lying pretty steep—that is to say sloping—there was no place to land, but where one end of my float, if it ran on shore, would lie so high, and the other sink lower, as before, that it would endanger my cargo again. All that I could do was to wait till the tide was at the highest, keeping the raft with my oar like an anchor, to hold the side of it fast to the shore, near a flat piece of ground, which I expected the water would flow over; and so it did. As soon as I found water enough—for my raft drew about a foot of water—I thrust her upon that flat piece of ground, and there fastened, or moored, her by sticking my two broken oars into the ground, one on one side near one end, and one on the other side near the other end; and thus I lay till the water ebbed away and left my raft and all my cargo safe on shore.

My next work was to view the country and seek a proper place for my habitation, and where to stow my goods to secure them from whatever might happen. Where I was, I yet knew not; whether on the continent or on an island; whether inhabited or not inhabited; whether in danger of wild beasts or not. There was a hill not above a mile from me, which rose up very steep and high, and which seemed to overtop some other hills, which lay as in a ridge from it northward. I took out one of the fowling-pieces, and one of the pistols, and a horn of powder; and, thus armed, I travelled for discovery up to the top of that hill, where, after I had with great labour and difficulty got to the top, I saw my fate to my great affliction—viz. that I was in an island environed every way with the sea: no land to be seen except some rocks, which lay a great way off, and two small islands, less than this, which lay about three leagues to the west.

I found also that the island I was in was barren, and, as I saw good reason to believe, uninhabited except by wild beasts, of whom, however, I saw none. Yet I saw abundance of fowls, but knew not their kinds; neither when I killed them could I tell what was fit for food and what not. At my coming back, I shot at a great bird which I saw sitting upon a tree on the side of a great wood. I believe it was the first gun that had been fired there since the creation of the world. I had no sooner fired than from all parts of the wood there arose an innumerable number of fowls of many sorts, making a confused screaming and crying, and every one according to his usual note, but not one of them of any kind that I knew. As for the creature I killed, I took it to be a kind of hawk, its colour and beak resembling it, but it had no talons, or claws, more than common. Its flesh was carrion,[1] and fit for nothing.

Contented with this discovery, I came back to my raft and fell to work to bring my cargo on shore, which took me up the rest of that day. What to do with myself at night I knew not, nor indeed where to rest, for I was afraid to lie down on the ground, not knowing but some wild beast might devour me, though, as I afterwards found, there was really no need for those fears.

However, as well as I could I barricaded myself round with the chest and boards that I had brought on shore, and made a kind of hut for that night's lodging. As for food, I yet saw not which way to supply myself, except that I had seen two or three creatures like hares run out of the wood where I shot the fowl.

I now began to consider that I might yet get a great many things out of the ship which would be useful to me, and particularly some of the rigging and sails, and such other things as might come to land; and I resolved to make another voyage on board the vessel, if possible. And as I knew that the first storm that blew must necessarily break her all in pieces, I resolved to set all other things apart till I had got everything out of the ship that I could get. Then I called a council—that is to say in my thoughts—whether I should take back the raft; but this appeared impracticable: so I resolved to go as before, when the tide was down; and I did so, only that I stripped before I went from my hut, having nothing on but my chequered shirt, a pair of linen drawers, and a pair of pumps on my feet.

I got on board the ship as before, and prepared a second raft; and, having had experience of the first, I neither made this so unwieldy, nor loaded it so hard, but yet I brought away several things very useful to me. As first, in the carpenter's stores I found two or three

bags full of nails and spikes, a great screw-jack,[2] a dozen or two of hatchets, and, above all, that most useful thing called a grindstone. All these I secured, together with several things belonging to the gunner, particularly two or three iron crows,[3] and two barrels of musket bullets, seven muskets, another fowling-piece with some small quantity of powder more, a large bagful of small shot, and a great roll of sheet-lead; but this last was so heavy I could not hoist it up to get it over the ship's side.

Besides these things, I took all the men's clothes that I could find, and a spare fore-topsail, a hammock, and some bedding; and with this I loaded my second raft and brought them all safe on shore, to my very great comfort.

I was under some apprehension during my absence from the land that at least my provisions might be devoured on shore. But when I came back I found no sign of any visitor; only there sat a creature like a wild cat upon one of the chests, which, when I came towards it, ran away a little distance and then stood still. She sat very composed and unconcerned, and looked full in my face, as if she had a mind to be acquainted with me. I presented my gun at her, but, as she did not understand it, she was perfectly unconcerned at it, nor did she offer to stir away; upon which I tossed her a bit of biscuit—though, by the way, I was not very free of it, for my store was not great. However, I spared her a bit, I say, and she went to it, smelled at it, and ate it, and looked (as if pleased) for more; but I thanked her and could spare no more, so she marched off.

Having got my second cargo on shore—though I was fain to open the barrels of powder and bring them by parcels, for they were too heavy, being large casks—I went to work to make me a little tent with the sail and some poles which I cut for that purpose. And into this tent I brought everything that I knew would spoil either with rain or sun; and I piled all the empty chests and casks up in a circle round the tent, to fortify it from any sudden attempt, either from man or beast.

When I had done this, I blocked up the door of the tent with some boards within, and an empty chest set up on end without; and, spreading one of the beds upon

---

[2] *screw-jack* Portable device used for lifting heavy objects. By turning a handle connected to a screw and a rack, the object is lifted from below.

[3] *crows* I.e., crowbars.

[1] *carrion* I.e., flesh unfit for food.

the ground, laying my two pistols just at my head and my gun at length by me, I went to bed for the first time, and slept very quietly all night, for I was very weary and heavy; for the night before I had slept little, and had laboured very hard all day to fetch all those things from the ship and to get them on shore.

I had the biggest magazine of all kinds now that ever was laid up, I believe, for one man. But I was not satisfied still; for while the ship sat upright in that posture I thought I ought to get everything out of her that I could; so every day at low water I went on board and brought away something or other; but particularly the third time I went I brought away as much of the rigging as I could, as also all the small ropes and rope-twine I could get, with a piece of spare canvas, which was to mend the sails upon occasion, and the barrel of wet gunpowder. In a word, I brought away all the sails, first and last; only that I was fain to cut them in pieces and bring as much at a time as I could, for they were no more useful to be sails, but as mere canvas only.

But that which comforted me more still was that, last of all, after I had made five or six such voyages as these and thought I had nothing more to expect from the ship that was worth my meddling with—I say, after all this, I found a great hogshead[1] of bread, three large runlets[2] of rum, or spirits, a box of sugar, and a barrel of fine flour. This was surprising to me because I had given over expecting any more provisions, except what was spoiled by the water. I soon emptied the hogshead of the bread and wrapped it up, parcel by parcel, in pieces of the sails, which I cut out; and, in a word, I got all this safe on shore also.

The next day I made another voyage, and now, having plundered the ship of what was portable and fit to hand out, I began with the cables. Cutting the great cable into pieces such as I could move, I got two cables and a hawser[3] on shore, with all the ironwork I could get; and, having cut down the spritsail-yard and the mizzen-yard,[4] and everything I could to make a large raft, I loaded it with all these heavy goods and came away. But my good luck began now to leave me; for this raft was so unwieldy and so overladen that, after I had entered the little cove where I had landed the rest of my goods, not being able to guide it so handily as I did the other, it overset and threw me and all my cargo into the water. As for myself, it was no great harm, for I was near the shore; but as to my cargo, it was a great part of it lost, especially the iron, which I expected would have been of great use to me; however, when the tide was out I got most of the pieces of the cable ashore, and some of the iron, though with infinite labour; for I was fain to dip for it into the water, a work which fatigued me very much. After this, I went every day on board and brought away what I could get.

I had been now thirteen days on shore and had been eleven times on board the ship, in which time I had brought away all that one pair of hands could well be supposed capable to bring; though I believe verily, had the calm weather held, I should have brought away the whole ship, piece by piece. But preparing the twelfth time to go on board, I found the wind began to rise. However, at low water I went on board, and though I thought I had rummaged the cabin so effectually that nothing more could be found, yet I discovered a locker with drawers in it, in one of which I found two or three razors and one pair of large scissors, with some ten or a dozen of good knives and forks. In another I found about thirty-six pounds value in money—some European coin, some Brasil, some pieces of eight, some gold, and some silver.

I smiled to myself at the sight of this money: "O drug!" said I, aloud, "what art thou good for? Thou art not worth to me—no, not the taking off the ground; one of those knives is worth all this heap; I have no manner of use for thee—e'en remain where thou art, and go to the bottom as a creature whose life is not worth saving." However, upon second thoughts I took it away; and, wrapping all this in a piece of canvas, I began to think of making another raft. But while I was preparing this, I found the sky overcast, and the wind began to rise, and in a quarter of an hour it blew a fresh gale from the shore. It presently occurred to me that it was in vain to pretend[5] to make a raft with the wind offshore, and that it was my business to be gone before the tide of flood began, otherwise I might not be able to reach the shore at all. Accordingly, I let myself down

---

[1] *hogshead*   Large cask.

[2] *runlet*   Vessel for storing liquid; cask.

[3] *hawser*   Large rope used for mooring and warping.

[4] *spritsail-yard … mizzen-yard*   Wooden spars that support and extend the spritsail and mizzen sail.

[5] *pretend*   Attempt.

into the water and swam across the channel, which lay between the ship and the sands—and even that with difficulty enough, partly with the weight of the things I had about me, and partly the roughness of the water; for the wind rose very hastily, and before it was quite high water it blew a storm.

But I had got home to my little tent, where I lay with all my wealth about me, very secure. It blew very hard all night, and in the morning when I looked out, behold, no more ship was to be seen! I was a little surprised, but recovered myself with the satisfactory reflection that I had lost no time, nor abated any diligence, to get everything out of her that could be useful to me; and that, indeed, there was little left in her that I was able to bring away if I had had more time.

I now gave over any more thoughts of the ship, or of anything out of her, except what might drive on shore from her wreck; as, indeed, diverse pieces of her after-wards did. But those things were of small use to me.

My thoughts were now wholly employed about securing myself against either savages, if any should appear, or wild beasts, if any were in the island; and I had many thoughts of the method how to do this, and what kind of dwelling to make—whether I should make me a cave in the earth, or a tent upon the earth; and, in short, I resolved upon both; the manner and description of which, it may not be improper to give an account of.

I soon found the place I was in was not fit for my settlement, because it was upon a low, moorish ground, near the sea, and I believed it would not be wholesome, and more particularly because there was no fresh water near it; so I resolved to find a more healthy and more convenient spot of ground.

I consulted several things in my situation, which I found would be proper for me: 1st, health and fresh water, I just now mentioned; 2ndly, shelter from the heat of the sun; 3rdly, security from ravenous creatures, whether man or beast; 4thly, a view to the sea, that if God sent any ship in sight, I might not lose any advantage for my deliverance, of which I was not willing to banish all my expectation yet.

In search of a place proper for this, I found a little plain on the side of a rising hill whose front towards this little plain was steep as a house-side, so that nothing could come down upon me from the top. On the one side of the rock there was a hollow place, worn a little

way in, like the entrance or door of a cave, but there was not really any cave or way into the rock at all.

On the flat of the green just before this hollow place I resolved to pitch my tent. This plain was not above a hundred yards broad, and about twice as long, and lay like a green before my door; and, at the end of it, descended irregularly every way down into the low ground by the seaside. It was on the north-northwest side of the hill, so that it was sheltered from the heat every day till it came to a west-and-by-south sun, or thereabouts, which, in those countries, is near the setting.

Before I set up my tent I drew a half-circle before the hollow place which took in about ten yards in its semi-diameter from the rock, and twenty yards in its diameter from its beginning and ending.

In this half-circle I pitched two rows of strong stakes, driving them into the ground till they stood very firm like piles, the biggest end being out of the ground above five feet and a half, and sharpened on the top. The two rows did not stand above six inches from one another.

Then I took the pieces of cable which I had cut in the ship and laid them in rows, one upon another, within the circle, between these two rows of stakes, up to the top, placing other stakes in the inside, leaning against them, about two feet and a half high, like a spur to a post; and this fence was so strong that neither man nor beast could get into it or over it. This cost me a great deal of time and labour, especially to cut the piles in the woods, bring them to the place, and drive them into the earth.

The entrance into this place I made to be not by a door, but by a short ladder to go over the top; which ladder, when I was in, I lifted over after me; and so I was completely fenced in and fortified, as I thought, from all the world, and consequently slept secure in the night, which otherwise I could not have done; though, as it appeared afterwards, there was no need of all this caution from the enemies that I apprehended danger from.

Into this fence or fortress, with infinite labour, I carried all my riches, all my provisions, ammunition, and stores, of which you have the account above; and I made a large tent, which, to preserve me from the rains that in one part of the year are very violent there, I made double—one smaller tent within, and one larger tent above it—and covered the uppermost with a large tarpaulin, which I had saved among the sails.

And now I lay no more for a while in the bed which I had brought on shore, but in a hammock, which was indeed a very good one, and belonged to the mate of the ship.

Into this tent I brought all my provisions and everything that would spoil by the wet; and, having thus enclosed all my goods, I made up the entrance, which till now I had left open, and so passed and repassed, as I said, by a short ladder.

When I had done this, I began to work my way into the rock, and, bringing all the earth and stones that I dug down out through my tent, I laid them up within my fence, in the nature of a terrace, so that it raised the ground within about a foot and a half; and thus I made me a cave, just behind my tent, which served me like a cellar to my house.

It cost me much labour and many days before all these things were brought to perfection; and therefore I must go back to some other things which took up some of my thoughts. At the same time it happened, after I had laid my scheme for the setting up my tent and making the cave, that, a storm of rain falling from a thick, dark cloud, a sudden flash of lightning happened, and after that a great clap of thunder, as is naturally the effect of it. I was not so much surprised with the lightning as I was with the thought which darted into my mind as swift as the lightning itself—Oh, my powder! My very heart sank within me when I thought that at one blast all my powder might be destroyed; on which, not my defence only, but the providing my food, as I thought, entirely depended. I was nothing near so anxious about my own danger—though had the powder took fire I should never have known who had hurt me.

Such impression did this make upon me that after the storm was over I laid aside all my works, my building and fortifying, and applied myself to make bags and boxes, to separate the powder and to keep it a little and a little in a parcel, in the hope that, whatever might come, it might not all take fire at once; and to keep it so apart that it should not be possible to make one part fire another. I finished this work in about a fortnight; and I think my powder, which in all was about two hundred and forty pounds weight, was divided in not less than a hundred parcels. As to the barrel that had been wet, I

did not apprehend any danger from that, so I placed it in my new cave, which in my fancy I called my kitchen; and the rest I hid up and down in holes among the rocks, so that no wet might come to it, marking very carefully where I laid it.

In the interval of time while this was doing, I went out once at least every day with my gun, as well to divert myself as to see if I could kill anything fit for food; and, as near as I could, to acquaint myself with what the island produced. The first time I went out I presently discovered that there were goats in the island, which was a great satisfaction to me; but then it was attended with this misfortune to me—*viz.* that they were so shy, so subtle, and so swift of foot, that it was the most difficult thing in the world to come at them; but I was not discouraged at this, not doubting but I might now and then shoot one, as it soon happened; for after I had found their haunts a little, I laid wait in this manner for them: I observed if they saw me in the valleys, though they were upon the rocks, they would run away, as in a terrible fright; but if they were feeding in the valleys and I was upon the rocks, they took no notice of me; from whence I concluded that, by the position of their optics, their sight was so directed downward that they did not readily see objects that were above them; so afterwards I took this method—I always climbed the rocks first, to get above them, and then had frequently a fair mark.

The first shot I made among these creatures, I killed a she-goat, which had a little kid by her which she gave suck to, which grieved me heartily; for when the old one fell, the kid stood stock still by her, till I came and took her up; and not only so, but when I carried the old one with me, upon my shoulders, the kid followed me quite to my enclosure; upon which I laid down the dam, and took the kid in my arms, and carried it over my pale,[1] in hopes to have bred it up tame; but it would not eat; so I was forced to kill it and eat it myself. These two supplied me with flesh a great while, for I ate sparingly and saved my provisions—my bread especially—as much as possibly I could.

Having now fixed my habitation, I found it absolutely necessary to provide a place to make a fire in, and fuel to burn: and what I did for that, and also how I enlarged my cave, and what conveniences I made, I shall give a full account of in its place. But I must now give

---

[1] *pale* Fence.

some little account of myself and of my thoughts about living, which, it may well be supposed, were not a few.

I had a dismal prospect of my condition; for as I was not cast away upon that island without being driven, as is said, by a violent storm, quite out of the course of our intended voyage, and a great way—*viz.* some hundreds of leagues—out of the ordinary course of the trade of mankind, I had great reason to consider it as a determination of Heaven that in this desolate place, and in this desolate manner, I should end my life. The tears would run plentifully down my face when I made these reflections; and sometimes I would expostulate with myself why Providence should thus completely ruin His creatures and render them so absolutely miserable; so without help, abandoned, so entirely depressed, that it could hardly be rational to be thankful for such a life.

But something always returned swift upon me to check these thoughts and to reprove me; and particularly one day, walking with my gun in my hand by the seaside, I was very pensive upon the subject of my present condition, when reason, as it were, expostulated with me the other way, thus: "Well, you are in a desolate condition, it is true; but pray remember, where are the rest of you? Did not you come, eleven of you in the boat? Where are the ten? Why were they not saved, and you lost? Why were you singled out? Is it better to be here or there?" And then I pointed to the sea. All evils are to be considered with the good that is in them, and with what worse attends them.

Then it occurred to me again how well I was furnished for my subsistence, and what would have been my case if it had not happened (which was a hundred thousand to one) that the ship floated from the place where she first struck and was driven so near to the shore that I had time to get all these things out of her. What would have been my case if I had been forced to have lived in the condition in which I at first came on shore, without necessaries of life, or necessaries to supply and procure them? "Particularly," said I, aloud (though to myself), "what should I have done without a gun, without ammunition, without any tools to make anything, or to work with; without clothes, bedding, a tent, or any manner of covering?" and that now I had all these to sufficient quantity and was in a fair way to provide myself in such a manner as to live without my gun when my ammunition was spent: so that I had a

tolerable view of subsisting, without any want, as long as I lived; for I considered from the beginning how I would provide for the accidents that might happen, and for the time that was to come, even not only after my ammunition should be spent, but even after my health and strength should decay.

I confess I had not entertained any notion of my ammunition being destroyed at one blast—I mean my powder being blown up by lightning—and this made the thoughts of it so surprising to me when it lightened and thundered, as I observed just now.

And now being about to enter into a melancholy relation of a scene of silent life, such, perhaps, as was never heard of in the world before, I shall take it from its beginning and continue it in its order. It was by my account the 30th of September when, in the manner as above said, I first set foot upon this horrid island; when the sun, being to us in its autumnal equinox, was almost over my head; for I reckoned myself, by observation, to be in the latitude of nine degrees, twenty-two minutes north of the line.

After I had been there about ten or twelve days, it came into my thoughts that I should lose my reckoning of time for want of books and pen and ink, and should even forget the Sabbath days; but to prevent this, I cut with my knife upon a large post, in capital letters—and making it into a great cross, I set it up on the shore where I first landed—"I came on shore here on the 30th September 1659."

Upon the sides of this square post I cut every day a notch with my knife, and every seventh notch was as long again as the rest, and every first day of the month as long again as that long one; and thus I kept my calendar, or weekly, monthly, and yearly reckoning of time.

In the next place, we are to observe that among the many things which I brought out of the ship in the several voyages which, as above mentioned, I made to it, I got several things of less value, but not at all less useful to me, which I omitted setting down before; as, in particular, pens, ink, and paper; several parcels in the captain's, mate's, gunner's and carpenter's keeping; three or four compasses; some mathematical instruments, dials, perspectives, charts, and books of navigation; all which I huddled together, whether I might want them or no; also, I found three very good Bibles, which came to me in my cargo from England, and which I had packed up among my things; some Portuguese books also; and among them two or three Popish prayer-books, and several other books, all which I carefully secured. And I must not forget that we had in the ship a dog and two cats, of whose eminent history I may have occasion to say something in its place; for I carried both the cats with me; and, as for the dog, he jumped out of the ship of himself, and swam on shore to me the day after I went on shore with my first cargo, and was a trusty servant to me many years; I wanted nothing that he could fetch me, nor any company that he could make up to me; I only wanted to have him talk to me, but that would not do. As I observed before, I found pens, ink, and paper, and I husbanded them to the utmost; and I shall show that while my ink lasted, I kept things very exact, but after that was gone I could not, for I could not make any ink by any means that I could devise.

And this put me in mind that I wanted many things notwithstanding all that I had amassed together; and of these, ink was one; as also a spade, pickaxe, and shovel, to dig or remove the earth; needles, pins, and thread; as for linen, I soon learned to want that without much difficulty.

This want of tools made every work I did go on heavily, and it was near a whole year before I had entirely finished my little pale, or surrounded my habitation. The piles, or stakes, which were as heavy as I could well lift, were a long time in cutting and preparing in the woods, and more, by far, in bringing home; so that I spent sometimes two days in cutting and bringing home one of those posts, and a third day in driving it into the ground; for which purpose I got a heavy piece of wood at first, but at last bethought myself of one of the iron crows; which, however, though I found it, made driving those posts or piles very laborious and tedious work. But what need I have been concerned at the tediousness of anything I had to do, seeing I had time enough to do it in? Nor had I any other employment if that had been over, at least that I could foresee, except the ranging the island to seek for food, which I did, more or less, every day.

I now began to consider seriously my condition and the circumstances I was reduced to, and I drew up the state of my affairs in writing, not so much to leave them to any that were to come after me—for I was likely to

have but few heirs—as to deliver my thoughts from daily poring over them and afflicting my mind; and as my reason began now to master my despondency, I began to comfort myself as well as I could, and to set the good against the evil, that I might have something to distinguish my case from worse; and I stated very impartially, like debtor and creditor, the comforts I enjoyed against the miseries I suffered, thus:

EVIL.	GOOD.
I am cast upon a horrible desolate island, void of all hope of recovery.	But I am alive, and not drowned, as all my ship's company was.
I am singled out and separated, as it were, from all the world to be miserable.	But I am singled out, too, from all the ship's crew to be spared from death; and He that miraculously saved me from death, can deliver me from this condition.
I am divided from mankind, a solitaire, one banished from human society.	But I am not starved and perishing on a barren place, affording no substance.
I have no clothes to cover me.	But I am in a hot climate, where, if I had clothes, I could hardly wear them.
I am without any defence, or means to resist any violence of man or beast.	But I am cast on an island, where I see no wild beasts to hurt me, as I saw on the coast of Africa; and what if I had been shipwrecked there?
I have no soul to speak to, or relieve me.	But God wonderfully sent the ship in near enough to the shore, that I have gotten out so many necessary things as will either supply my wants, or enable me to supply myself, even as long as I live.

Upon the whole, here was an undoubted testimony that there was scarce any condition in the world so miserable, but there was something *negative* or something *positive* to be thankful for in it; and let this stand as a direction from the experience of the most miserable of all conditions in this world: that we may always find in it something to comfort ourselves from, and to set, in the description of good and evil, on the credit side of the account.

Having now brought my mind a little to relish my condition, and given over looking out to sea to see if I could spy a ship—I say, giving over these things, I begun to apply myself to arrange my way of living, and to make things as easy to me as I could.

I have already described my habitation, which was a tent under the side of a rock, surrounded with a strong pale of posts and cables. But I might now rather call it a wall, for I raised a kind of wall up against it of turfs, about two feet thick on the outside; and after some time (I think it was a year and a half) I raised rafters from it, leaning to the rock, and thatched or covered it with boughs of trees and such things as I could get to keep out the rain, which I found at some times of the year very violent.

I have already observed how I brought all my goods into this pale, and into the cave which I had made behind me. But I must observe, too, that at first this was a confused heap of goods, which, as they lay in no order, so they took up all my place. I had no room to turn myself, so I set myself to enlarge my cave and work farther into the earth; for it was a loose sandy rock, which yielded easily to the labour I bestowed on it: and so when I found I was pretty safe as to beasts of prey, I worked sideways, to the right hand, into the rock; and then, turning to the right again, worked quite out, and made me a door to come out on the outside of my pale or fortification.

This gave me not only egress and regress, as it was a back way to my tent and to my storehouse, but gave me room to store my goods.

And now I began to apply myself to make such necessary things as I found I most wanted, particularly a chair and a table; for without these I was not able to enjoy the few comforts I had in the world. I could not write or eat, or do several things, with so much pleasure without a table.

So I went to work; and here I must needs observe that, as reason is the substance and origin of the mathematics, so by stating and squaring everything by reason, and by making the most rational judgment of things, every man may be, in time, master of every mechanic art. I had never handled a tool in my life; and yet, in time, by labour, application, and contrivance, I found at last that I wanted nothing but I could have made it, especially if I had had tools. However, I made abundance of things, even without tools; and some with no more tools than an adze and a hatchet, which perhaps were never made that way before, and that with infinite labour. For example, if I wanted a board, I had no other way but to cut down a tree, set it on an edge before me, and hew it flat on either side with my axe, till I brought it to be thin as a plank, and then dub it smooth with my adze. It is true, by this method I could make but one board out of a whole tree; but this I had no remedy for but patience, any more than I had for the prodigious deal of time and labour which it took me up to make a plank or board: but my time or labour was little worth, and so it was as well employed one way as another.

However, I made me a table and a chair, as I observed above, in the first place; and this I did out of the short pieces of boards that I brought on my raft from the ship. But when I had wrought out some boards as above, I made large shelves, of the breadth of a foot and a half, one over another all along one side of my cave, to lay all my tools, nails, and ironwork on; and, in a word, to separate everything at large into their places, that I might come easily at them. I knocked pieces into the wall of the rock to hang my guns and all things that would hang up; so that, had my cave been to be seen, it looked like a general magazine of all necessary things; and had everything so ready at my hand that it was a great pleasure to me to see all my goods in such order, and especially to find my stock of all necessaries so great.

And now it was that I began to keep a journal of every day's employment; for, indeed, at first I was in too much hurry—and not only hurry as to labour, but in too much discomposure of mind—and my journal would have been full of many dull things; for example, I must have said thus: "Sept. the 30th. After I had got to shore, and escaped drowning, instead of being thankful to God for my deliverance, having first vomited, with the great quantity of salt water which had got into my stomach, and recovering myself a little, I ran about the shore wringing my hands and beating my head and face, exclaiming at my misery, and crying out, 'I was undone, undone!' till, tired and faint, I was forced to lie down on the ground to repose, but durst not sleep for fear of being devoured."

Some days after this, and after I had been on board the ship, and got all that I could out of her, yet I could not forbear getting up to the top of a little mountain and looking out to sea, in hopes of seeing a ship; then fancy at a vast distance I spied a sail—please myself with the hopes of it—and then after looking steadily, till I was almost blind, lose it quite, and sit down and weep like a child, and thus increase my misery by my folly.

But having gotten over these things in some measure, and having settled my household staff and habitation, made me a table and a chair, and all as handsome about me as I could, I began to keep my journal; of which I shall here give you the copy (though in it will be told all these particulars over again) as long as it lasted; for having no more ink, I was forced to leave it off.

CHAPTER 5

The Journal

September 30, 1659. I, poor miserable Robinson Crusoe, being shipwrecked during a dreadful storm in the offing, came on shore on this dismal, unfortunate island, which I called "The Island of Despair"; all the rest of the ship's company being drowned, and myself almost dead.

All the rest of the day I spent in afflicting myself at the dismal circumstances I was brought to—*viz.* I had neither food, house, clothes, weapon, nor place to fly to—and, in despair of any relief, saw nothing but death before me, either that I should be devoured by wild beasts, murdered by savages, or starved to death for want of food. At the approach of night I slept in a tree for fear of wild creatures; but slept soundly, though it rained all night.

October 1. In the morning I saw, to my great surprise, the ship had floated with the high tide, and was driven on shore again much nearer the island; which, as it was some comfort, on one hand—for, seeing her set upright, and not broken to pieces, I hoped, if the wind

abated, I might get on board, and get some food and necessaries out of her for my relief—so, on the other hand, it renewed my grief at the loss of my comrades, who I imagined, if we had all stayed on board, might have saved the ship, or, at least, that they would not have been all drowned as they were; and that, had the men been saved, we might perhaps have built us a boat out of the ruins of the ship to have carried us to some other part of the world. I spent great part of this day in perplexing myself on these things; but at length, seeing the ship almost dry, I went upon the sand as near as I could, and then swam on board. This day also it continued raining, though with no wind at all.

From the 1st of October to the 24th. All these days entirely spent in many several voyages to get all I could out of the ship, which I brought on shore every tide of flood upon rafts. Much rain also in the days, though with some intervals of fair weather; but it seems this was the rainy season.

Oct. 20. I overset my raft, and all the goods I had got upon it; but, being in shoal water, and the things being chiefly heavy, I recovered many of them when the tide was out.

Oct. 25. It rained all night and all day, with some gusts of wind, during which time the ship broke in pieces, the wind blowing a little harder than before, and was no more to be seen, except the wreck of her, and that only at low water. I spent this day in covering and securing the goods which I had saved, that the rain might not spoil them.

Oct. 26. I walked about the shore almost all day to find out a place to fix my habitation, greatly concerned to secure myself from any attack in the night, either from wild beasts or men. Towards night, I fixed upon a proper place, under a rock, and marked out a semicircle for my encampment, which I resolved to strengthen with a work, wall, or fortification, made of double piles, lined within with cables, and without with turf.

From the 26th to the 30th I worked very hard in carrying all my goods to my new habitation, though some part of the time it rained exceedingly hard.

The 31st, in the morning, I went out into the island with my gun to seek for some food and discover the country, when I killed a she-goat, and her kid followed me home, which I afterwards killed also, because it would not feed.

November 1. I set up my tent under a rock and lay there for the first night; making it as large as I could, with stakes driven in to swing my hammock upon.

Nov. 2. I set up all my chests and boards, and the pieces of timber which made my rafts, and with them formed a fence round me, a little within the place I had marked out for my fortification.

Nov. 3. I went out with my gun and killed two fowls like ducks, which were very good food. In the afternoon went to work to make me a table.

Nov. 4. This morning I began to order my times of work, of going out with my gun, time of sleep, and time of diversion—*viz.* every morning I walked out with my gun for two or three hours, if it did not rain; then employed myself to work till about eleven o'clock; then ate what I had to live on; and from twelve to two I lay down to sleep, the weather being excessively hot; and then, in the evening, to work again. The working part of this day and of the next were wholly employed in making my table, for I was yet but a very sorry workman, though time and necessity made me a complete natural mechanic soon after, as I believe they would do anyone else.

Nov. 5. This day went abroad with my gun and my dog and killed a wild cat; her skin pretty soft, but her flesh good for nothing. Every creature that I killed I took off the skins, and preserved them. Coming back by the seashore I saw many sorts of sea-fowls, which I did not understand; but was surprised, and almost frightened, with two or three seals, which, while I was gazing at, not well knowing what they were, got into the sea and escaped me for that time.

Nov. 6. After my morning walk I went to work with my table again, and finished it, though not to my liking; nor was it long before I learned to mend[1] it.

Nov. 7. Now it began to be settled fair weather. The 7th, 8th, 9th, 10th, and part of the 12th (for the 11th was Sunday) I took wholly up to make me a chair, and with much ado brought it to a tolerable shape, but never to please me; and even in the making I pulled it in pieces several times. *Note.* I soon neglected my keeping Sundays; for, omitting my mark for them on my post, I forgot which was which.

Nov. 13. This day it rained, which refreshed me exceedingly, and cooled the earth; but it was accompanied with terrible thunder and lightning, which frightened me dreadfully, for fear of my powder. As soon as it was over, I resolved to separate my stock of powder into as many little parcels as possible, that it might not be in danger.

Nov. 14, 15, 16. These three days I spent in making little square chests, or boxes, which might hold about a pound, or two pounds at most, of powder; and so, putting the powder in, I stowed it in places as secure and remote from one another as possible. On one of these three days I killed a large bird that was good to eat, but I knew not what to call it.

Nov. 17. This day I began to dig behind my tent into the rock, to make room for my further conveniency. *Note.* Three things I wanted exceedingly for this work—*viz.* a pickaxe, a shovel, and a wheelbarrow or basket—so I desisted from my work and began to consider how to supply that want, and make me some tools. As for the pickaxe, I made use of the iron crows, which were proper enough, though heavy; but the next thing was a shovel or spade; this was so absolutely necessary, that, indeed, I could do nothing effectually without it; but what kind of one to make I knew not.

Nov. 18. The next day in searching the woods I found a tree of that wood, or like it, which in the Brasils they call the iron-tree, for its exceeding hardness. Of this, with great labour, and almost spoiling my axe, I cut a piece, and brought it home, too, with difficulty enough, for it was exceeding heavy. The excessive hardness of the wood, and my having no other way, made me a long while upon this machine, for I worked it effectually by little and little into the form of a shovel or spade; the handle exactly shaped like ours in England, only that the board part having no iron shod upon it at bottom, it would not last me so long; however, it served well enough for the uses which I had occasion to put it to; but never was a shovel, I believe, made after that fashion, or so long in making.

I was still deficient, for I wanted a basket or a wheelbarrow. A basket I could not make by any means, having no such things as twigs that would bend to make wicker-ware—at least, none yet found out; and as to a

---

[1] *mend* Improve.

wheelbarrow, I fancied I could make all but the wheel; but that I had no notion of; neither did I know how to go about it; besides, I had no possible way to make the iron gudgeons[1] for the spindle or axis of the wheel to run in. So I gave it over, and so, for carrying away the earth which I dug out of the cave, I made me a thing like a hod,[2] which the labourers carry mortar in when they serve the bricklayers. This was not so difficult to me as the making the shovel: and yet this and the shovel, and the attempt which I made in vain to make a wheelbarrow, took me up no less than four days—I mean always excepting my morning walk with my gun, which I seldom failed, and very seldom failed also bringing home something fit to eat.

Nov. 23. My other work having now stood still because of my making these tools, when they were finished I went on; and, working every day as my strength and time allowed, I spent eighteen days entirely in widening and deepening my cave, that it might hold my goods commodiously. *Note.* During all this time I worked to make this room or cave spacious enough to accommodate me as a warehouse or magazine, a kitchen, a dining-room, and a cellar. As for my lodging, I kept to the tent; except that sometimes, in the wet season of the year, it rained so hard that I could not keep myself dry, which caused me afterwards to cover all my place within my pale with long poles, in the form of rafters, leaning against the rock, and load them with flags[3] and large leaves of trees, like a thatch.

December 10. I began now to think my cave or vault finished, when on a sudden (it seems I had made it too large) a great quantity of earth fell down from the top on one side; so much that, in short, it frighted me, and not without reason, too, for if I had been under it, I had never wanted a gravedigger. I had now a great deal of work to do over again, for I had the loose earth to carry out; and, which was of more importance, I had the ceiling to prop up, so that I might be sure no more would come down.

Dec. 11. This day I went to work with it accordingly, and got two shores, or posts, pitched upright to the top, with two pieces of boards across over each post.

This I finished the next day; and, setting more posts up with boards, in about a week more I had the roof secured, and the posts, standing in rows, served me for partitions to part off the house.

Dec. 17. From this day to the 20th I placed shelves and knocked up nails on the posts to hang everything up that could be hung up; and now I began to be in some order within doors.

Dec. 20. Now I carried everything into the cave and began to furnish my house and set up some pieces of boards like a dresser, to order my victuals upon; but boards began to be very scarce with me; also, I made me another table.

Dec. 24. Much rain all night and all day. No stirring out.

Dec. 25. Rain all day.

Dec. 26. No rain, and the earth much cooler than before, and pleasanter.

Dec. 27. Killed a young goat and lamed another, so that I caught it and led it home in a string; when I had it at home, I bound and splintered up its leg, which was broke. *N.B.*[4] I took such care of it that it lived, and the leg grew well and as strong as ever; but by my nursing it so long it grew tame, and fed upon the little green at my door, and would not go away. This was the first time that I entertained a thought of breeding up some tame creatures, that I might have food when my powder and shot was all spent.

Dec. 28, 29, 30, 31. Great heats and no breeze, so that there was no stirring abroad, except in the evening, for food; this time I spent in putting all my things in order within doors.

January 1. Very hot still, but I went abroad early and late with my gun, and lay still in the middle of the day. This evening, going farther into the valleys which lay towards the centre of the island, I found there were plenty of goats, though exceedingly shy, and hard to come at; however, I resolved to try if I could not bring my dog to hunt them down.

Jan. 2. Accordingly, the next day I went out with my dog and set him upon the goats, but I was mistaken, for they all faced about upon the dog, and he knew his danger too well, for he would not come near them.

Jan. 3. I began my fence or wall; which, being still jealous of my being attacked by somebody, I resolved to

---

[1] *gudgeons* Pivots on which the wheels turn.

[2] *hod* Receptacle for carrying mortar, bricks, coal, etc., on the shoulder.

[3] *flags* Rushes.

[4] *N.B.* For *nota bene* (Latin: note well).

make very thick and strong. *N.B.* This wall being described before, I purposely omit what was said in the journal; it is sufficient to observe that I was no less time than from the 2nd of January to the 14th of April working, finishing, and perfecting this wall, though it was no more than about twenty-four yards in length, being a half-circle from one place in the rock to another place about eight yards from it, the door of the cave being in the centre behind it.

All this time I worked very hard, the rains hindering me many days—nay, sometimes weeks together—but I thought I should never be perfectly secure till this wall was finished; and it is scarce credible what inexpressible labour everything was done with, especially the bringing piles out of the woods and driving them into the ground; for I made them much bigger than I needed to have done.

When this wall was finished and the outside double fenced, with a turf wall raised up close to it, I perceived myself that if any people were to come on shore there, they would not perceive anything like a habitation; and it was very well I did so—as may be observed hereafter, upon a very remarkable occasion.

During this time I made my rounds in the woods for game every day when the rain permitted me, and made frequent discoveries in these walks of something or other to my advantage; particularly, I found a kind of wild pigeons, which build not as wood-pigeons, in a tree, but rather as house-pigeons, in the holes of the rocks; and taking some young ones, I endeavoured to breed them up tame, and did so; but when they grew older they flew away, which perhaps was at first for want of feeding them, for I had nothing to give them. However, I frequently found their nests and got their young ones, which were very good meat.

And now, in the managing my household affairs, I found myself wanting in many things which I thought at first it was impossible for me to make; as, indeed, with some of them it was. For instance, I could never make a cask to be hooped. I had a small runlet or two, as I observed before, but I could never arrive at the capacity of making one by them, though I spent many weeks about it. I could neither put in the heads, or join the staves so true to one another as to make them hold water; so I gave that also over.

In the next place, I was at a great loss for candles; so that as soon as ever it was dark, which was generally by seven o'clock, I was obliged to go to bed. I remembered the lump of beeswax with which I made candles in my African adventure, but I had none of that now. The only remedy I had was that when I had killed a goat I saved the tallow, and with a little dish made of clay, which I baked in the sun (to which I added a wick of some oakum) I made me a lamp; and this gave me light, though not a clear, steady light, like a candle. In the middle of all my labours it happened that, rummaging my things, I found a little bag which, as I hinted before, had been filled with corn for the feeding of poultry—not for this voyage, but before, as I suppose, when the ship came from Lisbon. The little remainder of corn that had been in the bag was all devoured by the rats, and I saw nothing in the bag but husks and dust; and being willing to have the bag for some other use (I think it was to put powder in, when I divided it for fear of the lightning, or some such use), I shook the husks of corn out of it on one side of my fortification, under the rock.

It was a little before the great rains just now mentioned that I threw this stuff away, taking no notice, and not so much as remembering that I had thrown anything there, when, about a month after, or thereabouts, I saw some few stalks of something green shooting out of the ground, which I fancied might be some plant I had not seen; but I was surprised and perfectly astonished when, after a little longer time, I saw about ten or twelve ears come out, which were perfect green barley, of the same kind as our European—nay, as our English barley.

It is impossible to express the astonishment and confusion of my thoughts on this occasion. I had hitherto acted upon no religious foundation at all; indeed, I had very few notions of religion in my head, nor had entertained any sense of anything that had befallen me otherwise than as chance, or, as we lightly say, what pleases God, without so much as inquiring into the end of Providence in these things, or His order in governing events for the world. But after I saw barley grow there, in a climate which I knew was not proper for corn,[1] and especially that I knew not how it came

---

[1] *corn* I.e., grain.

there, it startled me strangely, and I began to suggest that God had miraculously caused His grain to grow without any help of seed sown, and that it was so directed purely for my sustenance on that wild, miserable place.

This touched my heart a little, and brought tears out of my eyes, and I began to bless myself, that such a prodigy of nature should happen upon my account; and this was the more strange to me because I saw near it still, all along by the side of the rock, some other straggling stalks, which proved to be stalks of rice, and which I knew because I had seen it grow in Africa when I was ashore there.

I not only thought these the pure productions of Providence for my support, but, not doubting that there was more in the place, I went all over that part of the island where I had been before, peering in every corner, and under every rock, to see for more of it, but I could not find any. At last it occurred to my thoughts that I shook a bag of chickens' meat[1] out in that place; and then the wonder began to cease; and I must confess my religious thankfulness to God's providence began to abate too, upon the discovering that all this was nothing but what was common—though I ought to have been as thankful for so strange and unforeseen a providence as if it had been miraculous; for it was really the work of Providence to me, that should order or appoint that ten or twelve grains of corn should remain unspoiled, when the rats had destroyed all the rest, as if it had been dropped from heaven; as also, that I should throw it out in that particular place, where, it being in the shade of a high rock, it sprang up immediately; whereas, if I had thrown it anywhere else at that time, it had been burnt up and destroyed.

I carefully saved the ears of this corn, you may be sure, in their season, which was about the end of June; and, laying up every corn, I resolved to sow them all again, hoping in time to have some quantity sufficient to supply me with bread. But it was not till the fourth year that I could allow myself the least grain of this corn to eat, and even then but sparingly, as I shall say afterwards, in its order; for I lost all that I sowed the first season by not observing the proper time; for I sowed it just before the dry season, so that it never came up at all, at least not as it would have done; of which in its place.

Besides this barley, there were, as above, twenty or thirty stalks of rice, which I preserved with the same care and for the same use, or to the same purpose—to make me bread, or rather food; for I found ways to cook it without baking, though I did that also after some time. But to return to my journal.

I worked excessive hard these three or four months to get my wall done; and the 14th of April I closed it up, contriving to go into it not by a door but over the wall, by a ladder, that there might be no sign on the outside of my habitation.

April 16. I finished the ladder; so I went up the ladder to the top, and then pulled it up after me and let it down in the inside. This was a complete enclosure to me; for within I had room enough, and nothing could come at me from without, unless it could first mount my wall.

The very next day after this wall was finished I had almost had all my labour overthrown at once, and myself killed. The case was thus: as I was busy in the inside, behind my tent, just at the entrance into my cave, I was terribly frighted with a most dreadful, surprising thing indeed; for all on a sudden I found the earth come crumbling down from the roof of my cave, and from the edge of the hill over my head, and two of the posts I had set up in the cave cracked in a frightful manner. I was heartily scared, but thought nothing of what was really the cause, only thinking that the top of my cave was fallen in, as some of it had done before. And for fear I should be buried in it I ran forward to my ladder, and not thinking myself safe there neither, I got over my wall for fear of the pieces of the hill which I expected might roll down upon me. I was no sooner stepped down upon the firm ground than I plainly saw it was a terrible earthquake, for the ground I stood on shook three times at about eight minutes' distance, with three such shocks as would have overturned the strongest building that could be supposed to have stood on the earth; and a great piece of the top of a rock which stood about half a mile from me next the sea fell down with such a terrible noise as I never heard in all my life. I perceived also the very sea was put into violent motion by it; and I believe the shocks were stronger under the water than on the island.

---

[1] *meat* Food.

I was so much amazed with the thing itself, having never felt the like, nor discoursed with anyone that had, that I was like one dead or stupefied; and the motion of the earth made my stomach sick, like one that was tossed at sea. But the noise of the falling of the rock awakened me, as it were, and, rousing me from the stupefied condition I was in, filled me with horror; and I thought of nothing then but the hill falling upon my tent and all my household goods, and burying all at once; and this sunk my very soul within me a second time.

After the third shock was over and I felt no more for some time, I began to take courage; and yet I had not heart enough to go over my wall again, for fear of being buried alive, but sat still upon the ground, greatly cast down and disconsolate, not knowing what to do. All this while I had not the least serious religious thought; nothing but the common "Lord have mercy upon me!" And when it was over that went away too.

While I sat thus, I found the air overcast and grow cloudy, as if it would rain. Soon after that the wind arose by little and little, so that in less than half-an-hour it blew a most dreadful hurricane. The sea was all on a sudden covered over with foam and froth; the shore was covered with the breach of the water; the trees were torn up by the roots; and a terrible storm it was. This held about three hours, and then began to abate; and in two hours more it was quite calm, and began to rain very hard.

All this while I sat upon the ground, very much terrified and dejected, when on a sudden it came into my thoughts that these winds and rain being the consequences of the earthquake, the earthquake itself was spent and over, and I might venture into my cave again. With this thought my spirits began to revive; and the rain also helping to persuade me, I went in and sat down in my tent. But the rain was so violent that my tent was ready to be beaten down with it, and I was forced to go into my cave, though very much afraid and uneasy, for fear it should fall on my head.

This violent rain forced me to a new work—*viz.* to cut a hole through my new fortification, like a sink, to let the water go out, which would else have flooded my cave. After I had been in my cave for some time, and found still no more shocks of the earthquake follow, I began to be more composed. And now, to support my spirits, which indeed wanted it very much, I went to my little store and took a small sup of rum; which, however,

I did then and always very sparingly, knowing I could have no more when that was gone.

It continued raining all that night and great part of the next day, so that I could not stir abroad; but, my mind being more composed, I began to think of what I had best do; concluding that if the island was subject to these earthquakes there would be no living for me in a cave, but I must consider of building a little hut in an open place which I might surround with a wall, as I had done here, and so make myself secure from wild beasts or men; for I concluded, if I stayed where I was, I should certainly one time or other be buried alive.

With these thoughts I resolved to remove my tent from the place where it stood, which was just under the hanging precipice of the hill; and which, if it should be shaken again, would certainly fall upon my tent; and I spent the two next days, being the 19th and 20th of April, in contriving where and how to remove my habitation.

The fear of being swallowed up alive made me that I never slept in quiet; and yet the apprehension of lying abroad without any fence was almost equal to it; but still, when I looked about, and saw how everything was put in order, how pleasantly concealed I was, and how safe from danger, it made me very loath to remove.

In the meantime, it occurred to me that it would require a vast deal of time for me to do this, and that I must be contented to venture where I was till I had formed a camp for myself, and had secured it so as to remove to it. So with this resolution I composed myself for a time, and resolved that I would go to work with all speed to build me a wall with piles and cables, &c., in a circle, as before, and set my tent up in it when it was finished; but that I would venture to stay where I was till it was finished, and fit to remove. This was the 21st.

April 22. The next morning I begin to consider of means to put this resolve into execution; but I was at a great loss about my tools. I had three large axes, and abundance of hatchets (for we carried the hatchets for traffic with the Indians); but, with much chopping and cutting knotty hard wood, they were all full of notches, and dull; and though I had a grindstone, I could not turn it and grind my tools too. This cost me as much thought as a statesman would have bestowed upon a grand point of politics, or a judge upon the life and death of a man. At length I contrived a wheel with a string, to turn it with my foot, that I might have both my hands at liberty. *Note.* I had never seen any such thing in England, or at least, not to take notice how it was done, though since I have observed, it is very common there; besides that, my grindstone was very large and heavy. This machine cost me a full week's work to bring it to perfection.

April 28, 29. These two whole days I took up in grinding my tools, my machine for turning my grindstone performing very well.

April 30. Having perceived my bread had been low a great while, now I took a survey of it, and reduced myself to one biscuit cake a day, which made my heart very heavy.

May 1. In the morning, looking towards the sea side, the tide being low, I saw something lie on the shore bigger than ordinary, and it looked like a cask; when I came to it, I found a small barrel and two or three pieces of the wreck of the ship, which were driven on shore by the late hurricane; and, looking towards the wreck itself, I thought it seemed to lie higher out of the water than it used to do. I examined the barrel which was driven on shore, and soon found it was a barrel of gunpowder; but it had taken water, and the powder was caked as hard as a stone; however, I rolled it farther on shore for the present, and went on upon the sands, as near as I could to the wreck of the ship, to look for more.

When I came down to the ship I found it strangely removed. The forecastle, which lay before buried in sand, was heaved up at least six feet, and the stern (which was broke in pieces and parted from the rest by the force of the sea, soon after I had left rummaging her) was tossed, as it were, up, and cast on one side; and the sand was thrown so high on that side next her stern, that whereas there was a great place of water before, so that I could not come within a quarter of a mile of the wreck without swimming I could now walk quite up to her when the tide was out. I was surprised with this at first, but soon concluded it must be done by the earthquake; and as by this violence the ship was more broke open than formerly, so many things came daily on shore which the sea had loosened, and which the winds and water rolled by degrees to the land.

This wholly diverted my thoughts from the design of removing my habitation, and I busied myself mightily, that day especially, in searching whether I could make any way into the ship; but I found nothing was to be expected of that kind, for all the inside of the ship was choked up with sand. However, as I had learned not to despair of anything, I resolved to pull everything to pieces that I could of the ship, concluding that everything I could get from her would be of some use or other to me.

—1719

IN CONTEXT

Illustrating *Robinson Crusoe*

The first edition of *Robinson Crusoe* (1719) included only one illustration as a frontispiece; This illustration was reprinted numerous times over several decades—though there were some variants, such as that in the sixth edition of 1722. (Whereas the 1719 image shows a ship in full sail in good weather, the 1722 version portrays a ship floundering during a storm.) By the 1770s the book was neither widely read nor much esteemed in England, though it remained popular in France; in *Emile* (1762) Jean-Jacques Rousseau praised it as the finest work available on "natural education." In the 1780s and 1790s illustrated editions of *Robinson Crusoe* began to be issued with some frequency—as would remain the case throughout the nineteenth and twentieth centuries. The Clark and Pine image continued to exert an influence on many illustrators, but others departed from it entirely. A frequent focus of later illustrations is Crusoe becoming acquainted (after twenty-four years of solitude) with another human—the native whom he christens "Friday." The description of Friday in Defoe's text reads as follows:

He was a comely, handsome fellow, perfectly well made, with straight, strong limbs, not too large; tall, and well-shaped; and, as I reckon, about twenty-six years of age. He had a very good countenance, not a fierce and surly aspect, but seemed to have something very manly in his face; and yet he had all the sweetness and softness of a European in his countenance, too, especially when he smiled. His hair was long and black, not curled like wool; his forehead very high and large; and a great vivacity and sparkling sharpness in his eyes. The colour of his skin was not quite black, but very tawny; and yet not an ugly, yellow, nauseous tawny, as the Brasilians and Virginians, and other natives of America are, but of a bright kind of a dun olive-colour, that had in it something very agreeable, though not very easy to describe. His face was round and plump; his nose small, not flat, like the negroes; a very good mouth, thin lips, and his fine teeth well set, and as white as ivory.

(John?) Clark and John Pine, frontispiece, 1719 edition.

Charles Ansell and Inigo Barlow,
frontispiece, 1790.

George Cruikshank and Augustus Fox,
frontispiece, 1831.

Alexander Fraser and Charles G. Lewis, *Robinson Crusoe reading the Bible to his Man
Friday*, 1835.

John Butler Yeats, *Crusoe landing on the island*, 1895.

Charles Edmund Brock, *This Friday admired very much*, 1898.

from *A Journal of the Plague Year*[1]

It was now mid-July, and the plague, which had chiefly raged at the other end of the town, and, as I said before, in the parishes of St. Giles, St. Andrew's, Holborn, and towards Westminster, began to now come eastward towards the part where I lived. It was to be observed, indeed, that it did not come straight on towards us; for the city, that is to say, within the walls, was indifferently healthy still; nor was it got then very much over the water into Southwark; for though there died that week 1268 of all distempers, whereof it might

be supposed above 900 died of the plague, yet there was but twenty-eight in the whole city, within the walls, and but nineteen in Southwark, Lambeth parish included; whereas in the parishes of St. Giles and St. Martin-in-the-Fields alone there died 421.

But we perceived the infection kept chiefly in the out-parishes, which being very populous, and fuller also of poor, the distemper found more to prey upon than in the city, as I shall observe afterwards. We perceived, I say, the distemper to draw our way, *viz.*[2] by the parishes of Clarkenwell, Cripplegate, Shoreditch, and Bishopsgate; which last two parishes joining to Aldgate, Whitechapel, and Stepney, the infection came at length to spread its utmost rage and violence in those parts, even when it abated at the western parishes where it began.

It was very strange to observe that in this particular week, from the 4th to the 11th of July, when, as I have

---

[1] *A Journal ... Year*   This piece of historical fiction was written in the early 1720s, when an outbreak of the plague threatened London. In the piece, the text's narrator (who resembles Defoe's uncle, Henry Foe, a London saddler in the parish of Aldgate) reflects back upon journal entries he wrote during 1665, the year of the great outbreak of bubonic plague in London, hoping to provide beneficial information for future generations.

[2] *viz.*   Abbreviation of the Latin *videlicet*, meaning "namely; that is to say."

observed, there died near 400 of the plague in the two parishes of St. Martin and St. Giles-in-the-Fields only, there died in the parish of Aldgate but four, in the parish of Whitechapel three, in the parish of Stepney but one.

Likewise in the next week, from the 11th of July to the 18th, when the week's bill[1] was 1761, yet there died no more of the plague, on the whole Southwark side of the water, than sixteen.

But this face of things soon changed, and it began to thicken in Cripplegate parish especially, and in Clarkenwell; so that by the second week in August, Cripplegate parish alone buried 886, and Clarkenwell 155. Of the first, 850 might well be reckoned to die of the plague; and of the last, the bill itself said 145 were of the plague.

During the month of July and while, as I have observed, our part of the town seemed to be spared in comparison of the west part, I went ordinarily about the streets, as my business required, and particularly went generally once in a day, or in two days, into the city, to my brother's house, which he had given me charge of, and to see if it was safe; and, having the key in my pocket, I used to go into the house and over most of the rooms, to see that all was well; for though it be something wonderful to tell that any should have hearts so hardened in the midst of such a calamity as to rob and steal, yet certain it is that all sorts of villainies, and even levities and debaucheries, were then practised in the town as openly as ever—I will not say quite as frequently, because the numbers of people were many ways lessened.

But the city itself began now to be visited too, I mean within the walls; but the number of people there were indeed extremely lessened by so great a multitude having been gone into the country; and even all this month of July they continued to flee, though not in such multitudes as formerly. In August, indeed, they fled in such a manner that I began to think there would be really none but magistrates and servants left in the city.

As they fled now out of the city, so I should observe that the Court removed early, *viz.* in the month of June, and went to Oxford, where it pleased God to preserve them; and the distemper did not, as I heard of, so much

as touch them, for which I cannot say that I ever saw they showed any great token of thankfulness, and hardly anything of reformation, though they did not want being told that their crying vices might without breach of charity be said to have gone far in bringing that terrible judgement upon the whole nation.

The face of London was now indeed strangely altered: I mean the whole mass of buildings, city, liberties, suburbs, Westminster, Southwark, and altogether; for as to the particular part called the city, or within the walls, that was not yet much infected. But in the whole the face of things, I say, was much altered. Sorrow and sadness sat upon every face; and though some parts were not yet overwhelmed, yet all looked deeply concerned; and, as we saw it apparently coming on, so every one looked on himself and his family as in the utmost danger. Were it possible to represent those times exactly to those that did not see them, and give the reader due ideas of the horror that everywhere presented itself, it must make just impressions upon their minds and fill them with surprise. London might well be said to be all in tears; the mourners did not go about the streets indeed, for nobody put on black or made a formal dress of mourning for their nearest friends; but the voice of mourners was truly heard in the streets. The shrieks of women and children at the windows and doors of their houses, where their dearest relations were perhaps dying, or just dead, were so frequent to be heard as we passed the streets that it was enough to pierce the stoutest heart in the world to hear them. Tears and lamentations were seen almost in every house, especially in the first part of the visitation; for towards the latter end men's hearts were hardened, and death was so always before their eyes that they did not so much concern themselves for the loss of their friends, expecting that themselves should be summoned the next hour.

Business led me out sometimes to the other end of the town, even when the sickness was chiefly there; and as the thing was new to me, as well as to everybody else, it was a most surprising thing to see those streets which were usually so thronged now grown desolate, and so few people to be seen in them that, if I had been a stranger and at a loss for my way, I might sometimes have gone the length of a whole street (I mean of the by-streets) and seen nobody to direct me except watchmen

---

[1] *the week's bill* I.e., the Bill of Mortality, a record of all London deaths published weekly.

set at the doors of such houses as were shut up, of which I shall speak presently.

One day, being at that part of the town on some special business, curiosity led me to observe things more than usually, and indeed I walked a great way where I had no business. I went up Holborn, and there the street was full of people, but they walked in the middle of the great street, neither on one side or other, because, as I suppose, they would not mingle with anybody that came out of houses, or meet with smells and scent from houses that might be infected.

The Inns of Court were all shut up; nor were very many of the lawyers in the Temple, or Lincoln's Inn, or Gray's Inn, to be seen there. Everybody was at peace; there was no occasion for lawyers; besides, it being in the time of the vacation too, they were generally gone into the country. Whole rows of houses in some places were shut close up, the inhabitants all fled, and only a watchman or two left.

When I speak of rows of houses being shut up, I do not mean shut up by the magistrates, but that great numbers of persons followed the Court, by the necessity of their employments and other dependences; and as others retired, really frighted with the distemper, it was a mere desolating of some of the streets. But the fright was not yet near so great in the city, abstractly so called, and particularly because, though they were at first in a most inexpressible consternation, yet as I have observed that the distemper intermitted often at first, so they were, as it were, alarmed and unalarmed again, and this several times, till it began to be familiar to them; and that even when it appeared violent, yet seeing it did not presently spread into the city, or the east and south parts, the people began to take courage, and to be, as I may say, a little hardened. It is true a vast many people fled, as I have observed, yet they were chiefly from the west end of the town, and from that we call the heart of the city: that is to say, among the wealthiest of the people, and such people as were unencumbered with trades and business. But of the rest, the generality stayed and seemed to abide the worst; so that in the place we call the Liberties, and in the suburbs, in Southwark, and in the east part, such as Wapping, Ratcliff, Stepney, Rotherhithe, and the like, the people generally stayed, except here and there a few wealthy families, who, as above, did not depend upon their business.

It must not be forgot here that the city and suburbs were prodigiously full of people at the time of this visitation, I mean at the time that it began; for though I have lived to see a further increase, and mighty throngs of people settling in London more than ever, yet we had always a notion that the numbers of people which—the wars being over, the armies disbanded, and the royal family and the monarchy being restored[1]—had flocked to London to settle in business, or to depend upon and attend the Court for rewards of services, preferments, and the like, was such that the town was computed to have in it above a hundred thousand people more than ever it held before; nay, some took upon them to say it had twice as many, because all the ruined families of the royal party flocked hither. All the old soldiers set up trades here, and abundance of families settled here. Again, the Court brought with them a great flux of pride, and new fashions. All people were grown gay and luxurious, and the joy of the Restoration had brought a vast many families to London.

… But I must go back again to the beginning of this surprising time. While the fears of the people were young, they were increased strangely by several odd accidents which, put altogether, it was really a wonder the whole body of the people did not rise as one man and abandon their dwellings, leaving the place as a space of ground designed by Heaven for an Aceldama,[2] doomed to be destroyed from the face of the earth, and that all that would be found in it would perish with it. I shall name but a few of these things; but sure they were so many, and so many wizards and cunning people[3] propagating them, that I have often wondered there was any (women especially) left behind.

In the first place, a blazing star or comet appeared for several months before the plague, as there did the

---

1   *royal family … restored*   In 1660 the monarchy was restored after twenty years of turmoil, including civil war and the protectorate of Cromwell. Charles Stuart and his court returned from exile in France and Charles assumed the throne as Charles II.

2   *Aceldama*   Scene of slaughter or mass death; place with terrible associations. (From the field of that name near Jerusalem, which was purchased by priests with the money Judas received—and later returned to them—for betraying Jesus. The field was used as a burial ground for strangers.)

3   *cunning people*   People who possessed magical knowledge and skill.

year after another, a little before the fire.[1] The old women and the phlegmatic hypochondriac part of the other sex, whom I could almost call old women too, remarked (especially afterward, though not till both those judgements were over) that those two comets passed directly over the city, and that so very near the houses that it was plain they imported something peculiar to the city alone; that the comet before the pestilence was of a faint, dull, languid colour, and its motion very heavy, solemn, and slow; but that the comet before the fire was bright and sparkling, or, as others said, flaming, and its motion swift and furious; and that, accordingly, one foretold a heavy judgement, slow but severe, terrible and frightful, as was the plague; but the other foretold a stroke, sudden, swift, and fiery as the conflagration. Nay, so particular some people were that as they looked upon that comet preceding the fire, they fancied that they not only saw it pass swiftly and fiercely, and could perceive the motion with their eye, but even they heard it; that it made a rushing, mighty noise, fierce and terrible, though at a distance, and but just perceivable.

I saw both these stars and, I must confess, had so much of the common notion of such things in my head that I was apt to look upon them as the forerunners and warnings of God's judgements; and especially when, after the plague had followed the first. I yet saw another of the like kind. I could not but say God had not yet sufficiently scourged the city.

But I could not at the same time carry these things to the height that others did, knowing, too, that natural causes are assigned by the astronomers for such things, and that their motions and even their revolutions are calculated, or pretended to be calculated, so that they cannot be so perfectly called the forerunners or fore-tellers, much less the procurers, of such events as pestilence, war, fire, and the like.

But let my thoughts and the thoughts of the philosophers be, or have been, what they will, these things had a more than ordinary influence upon the minds of the common people, and they had almost universal melancholy apprehensions of some dreadful calamity and judgement coming upon the city; and this principally from the sight of this comet, and the little alarm that

was given in December by two people dying at St. Giles's, as above.

The apprehensions of the people were likewise strangely increased by the error of the times; in which, I think, the people, from what principle I cannot imagine, were more addicted to prophecies and astrological conjurations, dreams, and old wives' tales than ever they were before or since. Whether this unhappy temper was originally raised by the follies of some people who got money by it—that is to say, by printing predictions and prognostications—I know not; but certain it is, books frighted them terribly, such as *Lilly's Almanack*, *Gadbury's Astrological Predictions*, *Poor Robin's Almanack*, and the like; also several pretended religious books, one entitled, *Come out of her, my People, lest you be Partaker of her Plagues*; another called *Fair Warning*; another, *Britain's Remembrancer*; and many such, all, or most part of which, foretold, directly or covertly, the ruin of the city. Nay, some were so enthusiastically bold as to run about the streets with their oral predictions, pretending they were sent to preach to the city; and one in particular, who, like Jonah to Nineveh, cried in the streets, "Yet forty days, and London shall be destroyed."[2]

... When the plague at first seized a family—that is to say, when anybody of the family had gone out and unwarily or otherwise catched the distemper and brought it home—it was certainly known by the family before it was known to the officers, who, as you will see by the order, were appointed to examine into the circumstances of all sick persons when they heard of their being sick.

In this interval between their being taken sick and the examiners coming, the master of the house had leisure and liberty to remove himself or all his family, if he knew whither to go, and many did so. But the great disaster was that many did thus after they were really infected themselves, and so carried the disease into the houses of those who were so hospitable as to receive them; which, it must be confessed, was very cruel and ungrateful.

And this was, in part, the reason of the general notion, or scandal rather, which went about of the

---

[1] *the fire* The Great Fire of London, in September 1666.

[2] *Yet forty ... destroyed* From Jonah 3.4, in which the prophet Jonah warns the people of Nineveh of their impending doom. They then repent and mend their evil ways, and God spares them.

temper of people infected—namely, that they did not take the least care or make any scruple of infecting others, though I cannot say but there might be some truth in it too, but not so general as was reported. What natural reason could be given for so wicked a thing at a time when they might conclude themselves just going to appear at the bar of Divine Justice I know not. I am very well satisfied that it cannot be reconciled to religion and principle any more than it can be to generosity and humanity, but I may speak of that again.

I am speaking now of people made desperate by the apprehensions of their being shut up, and their breaking out by stratagem or force, either before or after they were shut up, whose misery was not lessened when they were out, but sadly increased. On the other hand, many that thus got away had retreats to go to and other houses, where they locked themselves up and kept hid till the plague was over; and many families, foreseeing the approach of the distemper, laid up stores of provisions sufficient for their whole families, and shut themselves up, and that so entirely that they were neither seen or heard of till the infection was quite ceased, and then came abroad sound and well. I might recollect several such as these, and give you the particulars of their management; for doubtless it was the most effectual secure step that could be taken for such whose circumstances would not admit them to remove, or who had not retreats abroad proper for the case; for in being thus shut up they were as if they had been a hundred miles off. Nor do I remember that any one of those families miscarried. Among these, several Dutch merchants were particularly remarkable, who kept their houses like little garrisons besieged, suffering none to go in or out or come near them, particularly one in a court in Throgmorton Street whose house looked into Draper's Garden.[1]

But I come back to the case of families infected and shut up by the magistrates. The misery of those families is not to be expressed; and it was generally in such houses that we heard the most dismal shrieks and outcries of the poor people, terrified and even frighted to death by the sight of the condition of their dearest relations, and by the terror of being imprisoned as they were.

I remember, and while I am writing this story I think I hear the very sound of it, a certain lady had an only daughter, a young maiden about nineteen years old, and who was possessed of a very considerable fortune. They were only lodgers in the house where they were. The young woman, her mother, and the maid had been abroad on some occasion, I do not remember what, for the house was not shut up; but about two hours after they came home the young lady complained she was not well; in a quarter of an hour more she vomited and had a violent pain in her head. "Pray God," says her mother, in a terrible fright, "my child has not the distemper!" The pain in her head increasing, her mother ordered the bed to be warmed, and resolved to put her to bed, and prepared to give her things to sweat, which was the ordinary remedy to be taken when the first apprehensions of the distemper began.

While the bed was airing the mother undressed the young woman, and just as she was laid down in the bed, she, looking upon her body with a candle, immediately discovered the fatal tokens on the inside of her thighs. Her mother, not being able to contain herself, threw down her candle and shrieked out in such a frightful manner that it was enough to place horror upon the stoutest heart in the world; nor was it one scream or one cry, but the fright having seized her spirits, she fainted first, then recovered, then ran all over the house, up the stairs and down the stairs, like one distracted, and indeed really was distracted, and continued screeching and crying out for several hours void of all sense, or at least government of her senses, and, as I was told, never came thoroughly to herself again. As to the young maiden, she was a dead corpse from that moment, for the gangrene which occasions the spots had spread over her whole body, and she died in less than two hours. But still the mother continued crying out, not knowing anything more of her child, several hours after she was dead. It is so long ago that I am not certain, but I think the mother never recovered, but died in two or three weeks after.

This was an extraordinary case, and I am therefore the more particular in it because I came so much to the knowledge of it; but there were innumerable such-like cases, and it was seldom that the weekly bill came in but there were two or three put in, "frighted"; that is, that may well be called frighted to death. But besides those

[1] *Draper's Garden*   Park next to Draper's Hall, the headquarters of a London livery company located in the heart of London.

who were so frighted as to die upon the spot, there were great numbers frighted to other extremes, some frighted out of their senses, some out of their memory, and some out of their understanding. ...

I went all the first part of the time freely about the streets, though not so freely as to run myself into apparent danger, except when they dug the great pit in the churchyard of our parish of Aldgate. A terrible pit it was, and I could not resist my curiosity to go and see it. As near as I may judge, it was about forty feet in length, and about fifteen or sixteen feet broad, and, at the time I first looked at it, about nine feet deep; but it was said they dug it near twenty feet deep afterwards in one part of it, till they could go no deeper for the water; for they had, it seems, dug several large pits before this. For though the plague was long a-coming to our parish, yet, when it did come, there was no parish in or about London where it raged with such violence as in the two parishes of Aldgate and Whitechapel.

I say they had dug several pits in another ground when the distemper began to spread in our parish, and especially when the dead-carts began to go about, which was not, in our parish, till the beginning of August. Into these pits they had put perhaps fifty or sixty bodies each; then they made larger holes wherein they buried all that the cart brought in a week, which, by the middle to the end of August, came to from 200 to 400 a week; and they could not well dig them larger, because of the order of the magistrates confining them to leave no bodies within six feet of the surface; and the water coming on at about seventeen or eighteen feet, they could not well, I say, put more in one pit. But now, at the beginning of September, the plague raging in a dreadful manner, and the number of burials in our parish increasing to more than was ever buried in any parish about London of no larger extent, they ordered this dreadful gulf to be dug—for such it was, rather than a pit.

They had supposed this pit would have supplied them for a month or more when they dug it, and some blamed the churchwardens for suffering such a frightful thing, telling them they were making preparations to bury the whole parish, and the like; but time made it appear the churchwardens knew the condition of the parish better than they did; for, the pit being finished the 4th of September, I think, they began to bury in it the 6th; and by the 20th, which was just two weeks,

they had thrown into it 1,114 bodies when they were obliged to fill it up, the bodies being then come to lie within six feet of the surface. I doubt not but there may be some ancient persons alive in the parish who can justify the fact of this, and are able to show even in what place of the churchyard the pit lay better than I can. The mark of it also was many years to be seen in the churchyard on the surface, lying in length parallel with the passage which goes by the west wall of the church-yard out of Houndsditch, and turns east again into Whitechapel, coming out near the Three Nuns' Inn.

It was about the 10th of September that my curiosity led, or rather drove, me to go and see this pit again, when there had been near 400 people buried in it; and I was not content to see it in the day-time, as I had done before, for then there would have been nothing to have been seen but the loose earth; for all the bodies that were thrown in were immediately covered with earth by those they called the buriers, which at other times were called bearers;[1] but I resolved to go in the night and see some of them thrown in.

There was a strict order to prevent people coming to those pits, and that was only to prevent infection. But after some time that order was more necessary, for people that were infected and near their end, and delirious also, would run to those pits, wrapt in blankets or rugs, and throw themselves in, and, as they said, bury themselves. I cannot say that the officers suffered any willingly to lie there; but I have heard that in a great pit in Finsbury, in the parish of Cripplegate, it lying open then to the fields, for it was not then walled about, many came and threw themselves in, and expired there, before they threw any earth upon them; and that when they came to bury others and found them there, they were quite dead, though not cold.

This may serve a little to describe the dreadful condition of that day, though it is impossible to say anything that is able to give a true idea of it to those who did not see it, other than this—that it was indeed very, very, very dreadful, and such as no tongue can express.

---

[1] *buriers ... bearers* Bearers carried dead bodies to the pits at night, while during the day they brought the sick to plague-hospitals. Buriers, on the other hand (which the narrator confuses with bearers) arranged and buried the bodies in pits.

I got admittance into the churchyard by being acquainted with the sexton[1] who attended; who, though he did not refuse me at all, yet earnestly persuaded me not to go, telling me very seriously (for he was a good, religious, and sensible man) that it was indeed their business and duty to venture, and to run all hazards, and that in it they might hope to be preserved; but that I had no apparent call to it but my own curiosity, which, he said, he believed I would not pretend was sufficient to justify my running that hazard. I told him I had been pressed in my mind to go, and that perhaps it might be an instructing sight that might not be without its uses. "Nay," says the good man, "if you will venture upon that score, name of God go in; for, depend upon it, 'twill be a sermon to you, it may be the best that ever you heard in your life. 'Tis a speaking sight," says he, "and has a voice with it, and a loud one, to call us all to repentance"; and with that he opened the door and said, "Go, if you will."

His discourse had shocked my resolution a little, and I stood wavering for a good while, but just at that interval I saw two links[2] come over from the end of the Minories,[3] and heard the bellman,[4] and then appeared a dead-cart, as they called it, coming over the streets; so I could no longer resist my desire of seeing it, and went in. There was nobody, as I could perceive at first, in the churchyard, or going into it, but the buriers and the fellow that drove the cart, or rather led the horse and cart; but when they came up to the pit they saw a man go to and again, muffled up in a brown cloak, and making motions with his hands under his cloak, as if he was in great agony, and the buriers immediately gathered about him, supposing he was one of those poor delirious or desperate creatures that used to pretend,[5] as I have said, to bury themselves. He said nothing as he walked about, but two or three times groaned very deeply and loud, and sighed as he would break his heart.

When the buriers came up to him they soon found

he was neither a person infected and desperate, as I have observed above, or a person distempered in mind, but one oppressed with a dreadful weight of grief indeed, having his wife and several of his children all in the cart that was just come in with him, and he followed in an agony and excess of sorrow. He mourned heartily, as it was easy to see, but with a kind of masculine grief that could not give itself vent by tears, and, calmly defying the buriers to let him alone, said he would only see the bodies thrown in and go away, so they left importuning him. But no sooner was the cart turned round and the bodies shot into the pit promiscuously, which was a surprise to him, for he at least expected they would have been decently laid in, though indeed he was afterwards convinced that was impracticable——I say, no sooner did he see the sight but he cried out aloud, unable to contain himself. I could not hear what he said, but he went backward two or three steps and fell down in a swoon. The buriers ran to him and took him up, and in a little while he came to himself, and they led him away to the Pie Tavern over against the end of Houndsditch, where, it seems, the man was known, and where they took care of him. He looked into the pit again as he went away, but the buriers had covered the bodies so immediately with throwing in earth, that though there was light enough—for there were lanterns, and candles in them, placed all night round the sides of the pit upon heaps of earth, seven or eight, or perhaps more—yet nothing could be seen.

This was a mournful scene indeed, and affected me almost as much as the rest; but the other was awful and full of terror. The cart had in it sixteen or seventeen bodies; some were wrapt up in linen sheets, some in rags, some little other than naked, or so loose that what covering they had fell from them in the shooting out of the cart, and they fell quite naked among the rest; but the matter was not much to them, or the indecency much to anyone else, seeing they were all dead, and were to be huddled together into the common grave of mankind, as we may call it; for here was no difference made, but poor and rich went together. There was no other way of burials, neither was it possible there should, for coffins were not to be had for the prodigious numbers that fell in such a calamity as this.

It was reported by way of scandal upon the buriers that if any corpse was delivered to them decently wound

[1] *sexton*   Church official whose duties include caring for the church and its grounds and overseeing the digging of graves.

[2] *links*   Torches; here, the boys hired to carry those torches.

[3] *the Minories*   An Aldgate street.

[4] *bellman*   Person who would ring a bell to announce the approach of the cart for burying the dead. In other times, the bellman would walk through the streets announcing the time and weather.

[5] *pretend*   Try.

up, as we called it then, in a winding-sheet tied over the head and feet, which some did, and which was generally of good linen—I say, it was reported that the buriers were so wicked as to strip them in the cart and carry them quite naked to the ground. But as I cannot easily credit anything so vile among Christians, and at a time so filled with terrors as that was, I can only relate it and leave it undetermined. ...

We had at this time a great many frightful stories told us of nurses and watchmen who looked after the dying people; that is to say, hired nurses who attended infected people, using them barbarously, starving them, smothering them, or by other wicked means hastening their end—that is to say, murdering of them; and watchmen, being set to guard houses that were shut up when there has been but one person left, and perhaps that one lying sick, that they have broke in and murdered that body, and immediately thrown them out into the dead-cart! And so they have gone scarce cold to the grave.

I cannot say but that some such murders were committed, and I think two were sent to prison for it, but died before they could be tried; and I have heard that three others, at several times, were excused for murders of that kind; but I must say I believe nothing of its being so common a crime as some have since been pleased to say, nor did it seem to be so rational where the people were brought so low as not to be able to help themselves, for such seldom recovered, and there was no temptation to commit a murder, at least none equal to the fact, where they were sure persons would die in so short a time, and could not live.

That there were a great many robberies and wicked practices committed even in this dreadful time I do not deny. The power of avarice was so strong in some that they would run any hazard to steal and to plunder; and, particularly in houses where all the families or inhabitants have been dead and carried out, they would break in at all hazards, and without regard to the danger of infection, take even the clothes off the dead bodies and the bed-clothes from others where they lay dead.

This, I suppose, must be the case of a family in Houndsditch, where a man and his daughter, the rest of the family being, as I suppose, carried away before by the dead-cart, were found stark naked, one in one chamber and one in another, lying dead on the floor, and the clothes of the beds, from whence 'tis supposed they were rolled off by thieves, stolen and carried quite away.

It is indeed to be observed that the women were in all this calamity the most rash, fearless, and desperate creatures, and as there were vast numbers that went about as nurses to tend those that were sick, they committed a great many petty thieveries in the houses where they were employed; and some of them were publicly whipped for it, when perhaps they ought rather to have been hanged for examples, for numbers of houses were robbed on these occasions, till at length the parish officers were sent to recommend nurses to the sick, and always took an account whom it was they sent, so as that they might call them to account if the house had been abused where they were placed.

But these robberies extended chiefly to wearing-clothes, linen, and what rings or money they could come at when the person died who was under their care, but not to a general plunder of the houses; and I could give you an account of one of these nurses, who, several years after, being on her deathbed, confessed with the utmost horror the robberies she had committed at the time of her being a nurse, and by which she had enriched herself to a great degree. But as for murders, I do not find that there was ever any proof of the facts in the manner as it has been reported, except as above. ...

It was under this John Hayward's[1] care, and within his bounds, that the story of the piper, with which people have made themselves so merry, happened, and he assured me that it was true. It is said that it was a blind piper; but, as John told me, the fellow was not blind, but an ignorant, weak, poor man, and usually walked his rounds about ten o'clock at night and went piping along from door to door, and the people usually took him in at public-houses where they knew him, and would give him drink and victuals, and sometimes farthings; and he in return would pipe and sing and talk simply, which diverted the people; and thus he lived. It was but a very bad time for this diversion while things were as I have told, yet the poor fellow went about as

---

[1] *John Hayward* A friend of the narrator's brother and an under-sexton (i.e., gravedigger and bearer of the dead) for the parish of St. Stephen.

usual, but was almost starved; and when anybody asked how he did he would answer, the dead cart had not taken him yet, but that they had promised to call for him next week.

It happened one night that this poor fellow, whether somebody had given him too much drink or no—John Hayward said he had not drink in his house, but that they had given him a little more victuals than ordinary at a public-house in Coleman Street—and the poor fellow, having not usually had a bellyful for perhaps not a good while, was laid all along upon the top of a bulk or stall, and fast asleep, at a door in the street near London Wall, towards Cripplegate; and that upon the same bulk or stall the people of some house, in the alley of which the house was a corner, hearing a bell which they always rang before the cart came, had laid a body really dead of the plague just by him, thinking, too, that this poor fellow had been a dead body, as the other was, and laid there by some of the neighbours.

Accordingly, when John Hayward with his bell and the cart came along, finding two dead bodies lie upon the stall, they took them up with the instrument they used and threw them into the cart, and all this while the piper slept soundly.

From hence they passed along and took in other dead bodies, till, as honest John Hayward told me, they almost buried him alive in the cart; yet all this while he slept soundly. At length the cart came to the place where the bodies were to be thrown into the ground, which, as I do remember, was at Mount Mill; and as the cart usually stopped some time before they were ready to shoot out the melancholy load they had in it, as soon as the cart stopped the fellow awaked and struggled a little to get his head out from among the dead bodies, when, raising himself up in the cart, he called out. "Hey! where am I?" This frighted the fellow that attended about the work; but after some pause John Hayward, recovering himself, said, "Lord, bless us! There's somebody in the cart not quite dead!" So another called to him and said, "Who are you?" The fellow answered, "I am the poor piper. Where am I?" "Where are you?" says Hayward. "Why, you are in the dead-cart, and we are going to bury you." "But I an't dead though, am I?" says the piper, which made them laugh a little, though, as John said, they were heartily frighted at first; so they helped

the poor fellow down, and he went about his business.

I know the story goes he set up his pipes in the cart and frighted the bearers and others so that they ran away; but John Hayward did not tell the story so, nor say anything of his piping at all; but that he was a poor piper, and that he was carried away as above, I am fully satisfied of the truth of.

It is to be noted here that the dead-carts in the city were not confined to particular parishes, but one cart went through several parishes, according as the number of dead presented; nor were they tied to carry the dead to their respective parishes, but many of the dead taken up in the city were carried to the burying-ground in the out-parts for want of room.

I have already mentioned the surprise that this judgement was at first among the people. I must be allowed to give some of my observations on the more serious and religious part. Surely never city, at least of this bulk and magnitude, was taken in a condition so perfectly unprepared for such a dreadful visitation, whether I am to speak of the civil preparations or religious. They were, indeed, as if they had had no warning, no expectation, no apprehensions, and consequently the least provision imaginable was made for it in a public way. For example, the Lord Mayor and sheriffs had made no provision as magistrates for the regulations which were to be observed. They had gone into no measures for relief of the poor. The citizens had no public magazines or storehouses for corn or meal for the subsistence of the poor, which if they had provided themselves, as in such cases is done abroad, many miserable families who were now reduced to the utmost distress would have been relieved, and that in a better manner than now could be done.

The stock of the city's money I can say but little to. The Chamber of London was said to be exceedingly rich, and it may be concluded that they were so, by the vast sums of money issued from thence in the rebuilding the public edifices after the fire of London, and in building new works, such as, for the first part, the Guildhall, Blackwell Hall, part of Leadenhall, half the Exchange, the Session House, the Compter, the prisons of Ludgate, Newgate, &c., several of the wharfs and stairs and landing-places on the river, all which were either burned down or damaged by the Great Fire of

London, the next year after the plague; and of the second sort, the Monument, Fleet Ditch with its bridges, and the Hospital of Bethlem or Bedlam,[1] &c. But possibly the managers of the city's credit at that time made more conscience of breaking in upon the orphan's money to show charity to the distressed

citizens than the managers in the following years did to beautify the city and re-edify the buildings; though, in the first case, the losers would have thought their fortunes better bestowed, and the public faith of the city have been less subjected to scandal and reproach. —1722

ANNE FINCH, COUNTESS OF WINCHILSEA
1661 – 1720

Though she published only one volume of verse in her lifetime, Anne Finch managed her texts very carefully. (Her husband transcribed them formally in successive bound volumes.) She is justly regarded as one of the more significant of early eighteenth-century poets; her poems on married life, on women's friendship, and on nature have earned her a distinctive place in British literary history.

Finch was born into a distinguished family as the third child of Sir William Kingsmill and Anne Haslewood, but her childhood was marked by tragedy; her father died when she was only a few months old, her mother when she was three, and her stepfather when she was ten. Her father made provisions in his will for the education of his children, and Finch's work indicates that she was unusually learned—familiar with the classics, Greek and Roman mythology, English history and literature, some French and Italian (languages and literature), and the Bible. In 1682 Finch became a Maid of Honor to Mary of Modena, wife of James, Duke of York (who would later become King James II). At court, she met and, in 1684, married Captain Heneage Finch (1657–1726), who was gentleman to the bedchamber to the Duke of York. They both remained in service until the Glorious Revolution of 1688, when James II was deposed and fled to France. Finch's husband was accused of having plotted on James's behalf, and was arrested. He was acquitted after a year, but he remained a nonjuror—one who refused to take an oath of allegiance to the new monarchs William and Mary—and so was prevented from re-entering public life. Consequently, the Finches retired in 1690 to the country, to Eastwell Park in Kent, the home of her husband's nephew, the Earl of Winchilsea. When he died in 1712 Heneage Finch became the Earl of Winchilsea, which made Anne a Countess. They did not return permanently to London until 1708—and they continued even then to spend a good deal of time at Eastwell.

The couple appear to have lived contentedly in retirement in Kent, and much of Finch's best work dates from this period. Finch had been writing since the 1680s but she appears not to have circulated any of her works until the 1690s. Charles Gildon's 1701 *New Collection of Poems on Several Occasions* contains four of her pieces, and three pastorals appear in Jacob Tonson's *Poetical Miscellanies* (1709). The dramatist Nicolas Rowe praised her poetry in Gildon's collection, and Swift directed "Apollo Outwitted" to her in 1709. It was not until 1713, however, that Finch published *Miscellany Poems on Several Occasions, Written By a Lady*. She had become a Countess the year before the volume appeared, but as her poem "The Introduction" makes clear, publishing a book of poems was still a bold move for a woman. (Indeed, this was one of only a very few poetry collections published by a woman in the early part of the century.)

Finch's poetry is in large part written in heroic couplets, as was the fashion at the time. It reflects a sensitivity to nature, a delicacy towards political allegiances, and an appreciation of close personal relationships. While she can be extremely critical of marriage (and in particular its effect on women), her own marriage appears to have been happy. Her husband, whom she addresses as Daphnis or Flavio in her verse, was supportive of her writing and even transcribed poems for her. Finch did, however, suffer from what today we would categorize as depression and seems to have been quite ill in 1715. Her piece "The Spleen," which contemplates and analyses depression, was her best known poem during her life. After her death in 1720 (the exact cause of which is unknown), her poetry continued to appear in collections for a time, but interest in her work waned in the latter half of the eighteenth-century. Wordsworth revived interest in Finch when, in his 1815 "Essay, Supplementary to the Preface," he noted that she was one of only two poets between the publication of Milton's *Paradise Lost* and Thomson's *The Seasons* (the other was Pope) to present a "new image of external nature." To see Finch primarily as a nature poet, however, is not to see her whole. Her range of genres and tones is unusually wide, and it is as much for her keen observations of the human as of the natural world that she is still read and remembered.

⌘ ⌘ ⌘

from *The Spleen* [1]
A Pindaric Poem

What art thou, Spleen, which every thing dost ape?
　　Thou Proteus [2] to abused mankind,
　　Who never yet thy real cause could find,
Or fix thee to remain in one continued shape.
5　　Still varying thy perplexing form,
　　Now a dead sea thou'lt represent,
　　A calm of stupid discontent,
Then, dashing on the rocks wilt rage into a storm.
　　Trembling sometimes thou dost appear,
10　　Dissolved into a panic fear;
　　On sleep intruding dost thy shadows spread,
　　Thy gloomy terrors round the silent bed,
And crowd with boding° dreams the melancholy
　　　　head;　　　　　　　　　　　　　　　*foreboding*
　　Or, when the midnight hour is told,
15　　And drooping lids thou still dost waking hold,
　　Thy fond delusions cheat the eyes,
　　Before them antic spectres° dance,　　　*ghosts*
Unusual fires their pointed heads advance,
　　And airy phantoms rise.
20　　Such was the monstrous vision seen,
When Brutus (now beneath his cares oppressed,
And all Rome's fortunes rolling in his breast,
　　Before Philippi's latest field,

Before his fate did to Octavius lead) [3]
25　　Was vanquished by the Spleen.

　　Falsely, the mortal part we blame
　　Of our depressed, and ponderous frame,
　　Which, till the first degrading sin [4]
　　Let thee, its dull attendant, in,
30　　Still with the other did comply,
Nor clogged the active soul, disposed to fly,
And range the mansions of its native sky.
　　Nor, whilst in his own heaven he dwelt,
　　Whilst man his paradise possessed,
35　His fertile garden in the fragrant East, [5]
　　And all united odors smelt,
　　No armed sweets, until thy reign,
　　Could shock the sense, or in the face
　　A flushed, unhandsome color place.
40　Now the jouquille [6] o'ercomes the feeble brain;
We faint beneath the aromatic pain,
Till some offensive scent thy powers appease,
And pleasure we resign for short, and nauseous ease.
. . . .

　　In vain to chase thee every art we try,
　　In vain all remedies apply,
130　　In vain the Indian leaf° infuse,　　*tea*

---

[3] *Brutus ... Octavius* In Shakespeare's *Julius Caesar*, Brutus sees visions the night before Octavius kills him at Philippi.

[4] *first ... sin* Original sin, which was thought to cause decay and illness.

[5] *garden ... East* The Garden of Eden was thought to lie in the East.

[6] *jouquille* Sweet-smelling form of narcissus.

---

[1] *Spleen* Melancholy or depression.

[2] *Proteus* Greek sea god who changes his shape at will.

Or the parched Eastern berry° bruise; *coffee*
Some pass, in vain, those bounds, and nobler liquors use.
    Now harmony, in vain, we bring,
    Inspire the flute, and touch the string.
35   From harmony no help is had;
Music but soothes thee, if too sweetly sad,
And if too light, but turns thee gaily mad.
    Though the physician's greatest gains,
    Although his growing wealth he sees
40   Daily increased by ladies' fees,
Yet dost thou baffle all his studious pains.
    Not skilful Lower[1] thy source could find,
Or through the well-dissected body trace
    The secret, the mysterious ways,
45 By which thou dost surprise, and prey upon the mind.
    Though in the search, too deep for humane thought,
      With unsuccessful toil he wrought,
    'Till thinking thee to've catched, himself by thee
      was caught,
    Retained thy prisoner, thy acknowledged slave,
50 And sunk beneath thy chain to a lamented grave.
—1701

The Introduction

Did I, my lines intend for public view,
How many censures, would their faults pursue,
Some would, because such words they do affect,
Cry they're insipid, empty, uncorrect.
5 And many, have attained, dull and untaught
The name of wit, only by finding fault.
True judges, might condemn their want of wit,
And all might say, they're by a woman writ.
Alas! a woman that attempts the pen,
10 Such an intruder on the rights of men,
Such a presumptuous creature, is esteemed,
The fault, can by no virtue be redeemed.
They tell us, we mistake our sex and way;
Good breeding, fashion, dancing, dressing, play
15 Are the accomplishments we should desire;
To write, or read, or think, or to enquire
Would cloud our beauty, and exhaust our time,
And interrupt the conquests of our prime;
Whilst the dull manage,° of a servile house *management*

Is held by some, our outmost art, and use.
20   Sure 'twas not ever thus, nor are we told
Fables, of women that excelled of old;
To whom, by the diffusive hand of heaven
Some share of wit, and poetry was given.
25 On that glad day, on which the Ark returned,[2]
The holy pledge, for which the land had mourned,
The joyful tribes, attend it on the way,
The Levites° do the sacred charge convey, *Judaic priests*
Whilst various instruments, before it play;
30 Here, holy virgins in the concert join,
The louder notes, to soften, and refine,
And with alternate verse, complete the hymn divine.
Lo! the young poet,[3] after God's own heart,
By Him inspired, and taught the muses' art,
35 Returned from conquest, a bright chorus meets,
That sing his slain ten thousand in the streets.[4]
In such loud numbers they his acts declare,
Proclaim the wonders, of his early war,
That Saul upon the vast applause does frown,[5]
40 And feels, its mighty thunder shake the crown.
What, can the threatened judgment now prolong?
Half of the kingdom is already gone;
The fairest half, whose influence guides the rest,
Have David's empire, o're their hearts confessed.
45   A woman here, leads fainting Israel on,
She fights, she wins, she triumphs with a song,
Devout, majestic, for the subject fit,
And far above her arms, exalts her wit,
Then, to the peaceful, shady palm withdraws,
50 And rules the rescued nation, with her laws.[6]
How are we fallen, fallen by mistaken rules?
And education's, more than nature's fools,
Debarred from all improvements of the mind,
And to be dull, expected and designed;
55 And if some one would soar above the rest,
With warmer fancy, and ambition pressed,
So strong, the opposing faction still appears,

---

1 *Lower* Richard Lower (1631–91), noted London physician.

2 *On ... returned* When David returned the ark of the covenant he was accompanied by musicians and singers (1 Chronicles 15).

3 *young poet* David was held to be author of the psalms.

4 *sing ... streets* See 1 Samuel 18.5–9.

5 *Saul upon the vast applause does frown* Saul, unpopular king of Israel, feared that the people, led by the women, would come to want David chosen to replace him. See 1 Samuel 18.6–9.

6 *A woman ... laws* Deborah, a judge in Israel (Judges 4).

The hopes to thrive, can ne'er outweigh the fears,
Be cautioned then my Muse, and still retired;
60 Nor be despised, aiming to be admired;
Conscious of wants, still with contracted wing,
To some few friends, and to thy sorrows sing;
For groves of laurel,[1] thou wert never meant;
Be dark enough thy shades, and be thou there content.
—1713

A Letter to Daphnis, April 2, 1685

This to the crown, and blessing of my life,
    The much loved husband, of a happy wife;
To him, whose constant passion found the art
To win a stubborn, and ungrateful heart;
5   And to the world, by tend'rest proof discovers
They err, who say that husbands can't be lovers.
With such return of passion, as is due,
Daphnis I love, Daphnis my thoughts pursue,
Daphnis, my hopes, my joys, are bounded all in you:
10 Ev'n I, for Daphnis, and my promise sake,
What I in woman censure, undertake.
But this from love, not vanity, proceeds;
You know who writes; and I who 'tis that reads.
Judge not my passion, by my want of skill,
15 Many love well, though they express it ill;
And I your censure could with pleasure bear,
Would you but soon return, and speak it here.
—1713

To Mr. F., Now Earl of W.
*Who going abroad, had desired Ardelia to
write some verses upon whatever subject
she thought fit, against his return in the evening*

No sooner, Flavio, was you gone,
    But, your injunction thought upon,
        Ardelia took the pen;
Designing to perform the task,
5   Her Flavio did so kindly ask,
        Ere he returned again.

Unto Parnassus[2] straight she sent,
And bid the messenger, that went
        Unto the muses' court,
10 Assure them, she their aid did need,
And begged they'd use their utmost speed,
        Because the time was short.

The hasty summons was allowed;
And being well-bred, they rose and bowed,
15   And said, they'd post away;[3]
That well they did Ardelia know,
And that no female's voice below
        They sooner would obey:

That many of that rhyming train,
20 On like occasions, sought in vain
        Their industry t'excite;
But for Ardelia all they'd leave:
Thus flattering can the muse deceive,
        And wheedle us to write.

25 Yet, since there was such haste required;
To know the subject 'twas desired,
        On which they must infuse;
That they might temper words and rules,
And with their counsel carry tools,
30   As country-doctors use.

Wherefore to cut off all delays,
'Twas soon replied, a husband's praise
        (Though in these looser times)
Ardelia gladly would rehearse
35 A husband's, who indulged her verse,
        And now required her rhymes.

A husband! echoed all around:
And to Parnassus sure that sound
        Had never yet been sent;
40 Amazement in each face was read,
In haste the affrighted sisters fled,
        And unto council went.

---

1 *groves of laurel*   Laurel was sacred to Apollo, the god of the arts, and is thus awarded to poets.

2 *Parnassus*   Greek mountain, sacred to Apollo and the Muses, and the home of the latter.

3 *they'd post away*   They would use relays of horses to travel faster.

Erato cried, since Grizel's[1] days,
Since Troy-town[2] pleased, and Chivey-chace,[3]
    No such design was known;
And 'twas their business to take care,
It reached not to the public ear,
    Or got about the town:

Nor came where evening beaux were met
O'er billets-doux° and chocolate,   *love letters*
    Lest it destroyed the house;°   *playhouse*
For in that place, who could dispense°   *excuse*
(That wore his clothes with common sense)
    With mention of a spouse?

'Twas put unto the vote at last,
And in the negative it past,
    None to her aid should move;
Yet since Ardelia was a friend,
Excuses 'twas agreed to send,
    Which plausible might prove:

That Pegasus[4] of late had been
So often rid through thick and thin,
    With neither fear nor wit;
In panegyric been so spurred
He could not from the stall be stirred,
    Nor would endure the bit.

Melpomene[5] had given a bond,
By the new house[6] alone to stand,
    And write of war and strife;

70 Thalia,[7] she had taken fees,
And stipends from the patentees,°   *theater proprietors*
    And durst not for her life.

Urania[8] only liked the choice;
Yet not to thwart the public voice,
75   She whisp'ring did impart:
They need no foreign aid invoke,
No help to draw a moving stroke,
    Who dictate from the heart.

Enough! the pleased Ardelia cried;
80 And slighting every Muse beside,
    Consulting now her breast,
Perceived that every tender thought,
Which from abroad she'd vainly sought,
    Did there in silence rest:

85 And should unmoved that post maintain,
Till in his quick return again,
    Met in some neighb'ring grove,
(Where vice nor vanity appear)
Her Flavio them alone might hear,
90   In all the sounds of love.

For since the world does so despise
Hymen's[9] endearments and its ties,
    They should mysterious be;
Till we that pleasure too possess
95 (Which makes their fancied happiness)
    Of stolen secrecy.
—1713

---

[1] *Erato* Muse of love poetry, one of the nine daughters of Zeus and Mnemosyne (Memory); *Grizel's* Griselda, the proverbial patient wife.

[2] *Troy-town* English ballad about the ancient city that was the site of a war between the Trojans and the Greeks.

[3] *Chivey-chace* "Chevy Chase," a fifteenth-century ballad.

[4] *Pegasus* Winged horse of Greek myth.

[5] *Melpomene* Muse of tragedy.

[6] *the new house* I.e., the new playhouse, probably the Haymarket Theatre (also confusingly known as the Queen's Theatre or the Opera House), which was licensed in December 1704 and opened in April 1705. The new theater's focus was to be opera, and since all operas of the time were virtual tragedies (essentially tragic plots with happy endings), the association with the Muse of tragedy is a natural one. The other theaters—run by the patentees, or proprietors—were most successful with comedy.

[7] *Thalia* Muse of comedy.

[8] *Urania* Muse of astronomy and heavenly love.

[9] *Hymen* God of marriage.

The Unequal Fetters

Could we stop the time that's flying
   Or recall it when 'tis past,
Put far off the day of dying
   Or make youth forever last,
5 To love would then be worth our cost.

But since we must lose those graces,
   Which at first your hearts have won,
And you seek for in new faces
   When our spring of life is done,
10 It would but urge our ruin on.

Free as nature's first intention
   Was to make us, I'll be found,
Nor by subtle man's invention
   Yield to be in fetters bound
15 By one that walks a freer round.

Marriage does but slightly tie Men,
   Whil'st close prisoners we remain,
They, the larger slaves of Hymen,
   Still are begging love again
20 At the full length of all their chain.
     —1713

By neer resemblance that Bird betray'd [1]

By neer resemblance see that Bird betray'd
  Who takes the well wrought Arras[2] for a shade.
There hopes to pearch and with a chearfull Tune
O're-passe the scortchings of the sultry Noon
5 But soon repuls'd by the obdurate Scean
How swift she turns but turns alas in vain
That piece a Grove this shews an ambient sky
Where immitated Fowl their pinnions° ply   *wings*
Seeming to mount in flight and aiming still more high.

original spelling (left margin)

10 All she outstripps and with a moment's pride
Their understation silent does deride.
Till the dash'd cealing strikes her to the ground
No intercepting shrub to break the fall is found
Recovering breath the window next she gaines
15 Nor fears a stop from the transparent Panes.

O man what inspiration was thy Guide
Who taught thee Light and Air thus to divide
To lett in all the usefull beames of Day
Yett force as subtil winds without thy Sash to stay
20 T'extract from Embers by a strange device
Then pollish fair these flakes of sollid Ice
Which silver'd o're redouble all in place
And give thee back thy well or ill-complexion'd Face.
To colors blown exceed the gloomy Bowl
25 Which did the Wines full excellence controul
These shew the Body whilest you taste the soul.
Its Colour Sparkles motion letts thee see
Though yett th'excesse the Preacher warns to flee
Least men att length as clearly spy through thee.

30 But we degresse and leave th'imprison'd wretch
Now sinking low now on a loftyer stretch
Flutt'ring in endlesse cercles of dismay
Till some kind hand directs the certain way
Which through the casement an escape affoards
35 And leads to ample space the only Heav'n of Birds.

So here confin'd and but of female Clay
As much my soul mistook the rightful way
Whilst the soft breeze of Pleasure's tempting air
Made her° believe Felicity was there   *the soul*
40 And basking in the warmth of early time
To vain Amusements dedicate her Prime
Ambition then alur'd her tow'ring Eye
For Paradice she heard was plac'd on high
Then thought the Court was all its glorious show
45 Was sure above the rest and Paradice below
There plac'd too soon the flaming sword[3] appear'd
Remov'd those Powers,[4] whom justly she rever'd

original spelling (right margin)

---

[1] *By neer … betray'd* Originally titled "Some occasional Reflections Digested (tho' not with great regularity) into a Poeme," this poem—a part of which is better known under the title "The Bird and the Arras"—appears in the original manuscript as it is printed here. It was later broken into three separate poems for publication in 1713.

[2] *Arras* Tapestry hung from a wall.

[3] *flaming sword* Cf. Genesis 3.24, in which God barred the way behind Adam and Eve when expelling them from Eden: "So he drove out the man; and he placed at the east of the garden of Eden Cherubims, and a flaming sword which turned every way, to keep the way of the tree of life."

[4] *those powers* King James II and his queen, Mary of Modena.

Adher'd too in their Wreck, and in their Ruin shar'd.
Now by the Wheels inevitable round[1]
50 With them thrown prostrate to the humble ground
No more she take's (instructed by that fall)
For fixt or worth her thought this rowling Ball
Nor feed a hope that boasts but mortal birth,
Or springs from man though fram'd of Royal earth
55 Tow'rds a more certain station she aspires
Unshaken by Revolts; and owns no lesse desires
But all in vain are Pray'rs extatick thoughts
Recover'd moments and retracted faults
Retirement which the World morossenesse calls
60 Abandon'd pleasures in Monastick walls
These but att distance towards that purpose tend
The lowly means to an exalted end
Which He must perfect who alotts her stay
And that accomplish'd will direct the way.
65 Pitty her restlesse cares and weary strife
And point some Issue to escaping Life
Which so dismiss'd no Pen or human speech
Th'ineffable Recesse can ever teach
Th'Expanse the Light the Harmony the Throng
70 The Brides attendance and the Bridal song
The numerous Mantions and th'immortal Tree
No Eye unpurg'd by Death must ever see
Or waves which through that wond'rous Citty rowl
Rest then content my too impatient Soul
75 Observe but here the easie Precepts given
Then wait with chearfull hope, till Heaven be known
        in Heaven.

—1713

A Nocturnal Reverie

In such a night, when every louder wind
Is to its distant cavern safe confined;
And only gentle Zephyr[2] fans his wings,
And lonely Philomel,° still waking, sings;   *nightingale*
5 Or from some tree, famed for the owl's delight,
She, hollowing clear, directs the wand'rer right:
In such a night, when passing clouds give place,
Or thinly veil the heaven's mysterious face;

10 When in some river, overhung with green,
The waving moon and trembling leaves are seen;
When freshened grass now bears itself upright,
And makes cool banks to pleasing rest invite,
Whence springs the woodbind, and the bramble-rose,
And where the sleepy cowslip sheltered grows;
15 Whilst now a paler hue the foxglove takes,
Yet chequers still with red the dusky brakes
When scattered glow-worms, but in twilight fine,
Show trivial beauties watch their hour to shine;
Whilst Salisb'ry[3] stands the test of every light,
20 In perfect charms, and perfect virtue bright:
When odours, which declined repelling day,
Through temp'rate air uninterrupted stray;
When darkened groves their softest shadows wear,
And falling waters we distinctly hear;
25 When through the gloom more venerable shows
Some ancient fabric,° awful in repose,   *building*
While sunburnt hills their swarthy looks conceal,
And swelling haycocks thicken up the vale:
When the loosed horse now, as his pasture leads,
30 Comes slowly grazing through th' adjoining meads,
Whose stealing pace, and lengthened shade we fear,
Till torn up forage in his teeth we hear:
When nibbling sheep at large pursue their food,
And unmolested kine° rechew the cud;   *cattle*
35 When curlews cry beneath the village walls,
And to her straggling brood the partridge calls;
Their shortlived jubilee the creatures keep,
Which but endures, whilst tyrant-man does sleep;
When a sedate content the spirit feels,
40 And no fierce light disturb, whilst it reveals;
But silent musings urge the mind to seek
Something, too high for syllables to speak;
Till the free soul to a compos'dness charmed,
Finding the elements of rage disarmed,
45 O'er all below a solemn quiet grown,
Joys in th' inferior world, and thinks it like her own:
In such a night let me abroad remain,
Till morning breaks, and all's confused again;
Our cares, our toils, our clamours are renewed,
50 Or pleasures, seldom reached, again pursued.

—1713

---

1 *Wheels … round* Revolution of the wheel of fortune.

2 *Zephyr* God of the west wind.

3 *Salisb'ry* Anne Tufton, Countess of Salisbury.

JONATHAN SWIFT
1667 – 1745

In *The Life of the Rev. Dr. Jonathan Swift* (1784), Thomas Sheridan called him "a man whose original genius and uncommon talents have raised him, in the general estimation, above all the writers of the age"—a list that included Defoe, Dryden, and Pope. If Swift's talents did indeed raise him above most writers of his time, he was entirely at one with his age in his penchant for satire, so notably illustrated in his most famous work, *Gulliver's Travels*. His aim in *Gulliver's Travels*, as he put it in a letter to Alexander Pope, was "to vex the world, not to divert it." Yet he understood that even the most pointed satire would often miss its mark. He once commented that satire "is a sort of glass, wherein beholders do generally discover everybody's face but their own." He held the glass up to hypocrites and bombasts of many forms, but he particularly loathed religious and political tyranny. *A Tale of a Tub* and "A Modest Proposal" are enduring protests against such oppression.

Swift was born in Ireland to Abigail Errick Swift; his English father died before he was born. At the age of one, Swift was kidnapped and taken to England by his nursemaid; he was not re-united with his mother until after he had reached the age of three. He studied at Kilkenny School and then moved on to Trinity College at the University of Dublin when he was fourteen. When he completed his education, he made what he thought would be a permanent move to England. There he took employment as secretary to retired politician, Sir William Temple, through whom Swift made several lifelong friends.

During the 1690s Swift composed urban pastoral poetry, odes, and two early satires. *The Battle of the Books* was written in defense of Temple and against the "moderns" who were, in Swift's view, unwisely neglecting "ancient" modes of learning. In *A Tale of a Tub*, Swift mocked the religious and intellectual foolishness of the sort that prompts absurd flights of fancy. The narrative focuses on the adventures of three brothers of different religious persuasions, representing Roman Catholicism, Anglicanism, and Calvinism, but chapters of narrative alternate with inventively irrelevant digressions, including the famous "Digression in Praise of Digressions."

Swift seemed destined to keep returning, for one reason or another, to Ireland. He studied for the Anglican priesthood in Dublin from 1694 to 1696 before returning to Temple's service, but after his employer's death in 1699 he traveled to Ireland as secretary and chaplain to Earl Berkeley and was then appointed Vicar of Laracor in the Dublin area. He returned to England in 1707 as an emissary of the Irish clergy, seeking a reduction in tax on their incomes. Queen Anne had little sympathy, however; the pious but literal-minded queen had misread *A Tale of a Tub* as an attack on established religion rather than a defense of it. Swift's poem "The Windsor Prophecy" did not help matters, as the attack on the Duchess of Somerset, a Whiggish favorite of the Queen, further consolidated her opposition both to his causes and to him personally. Lacking promotion in England, Swift had little choice but to return to Ireland, where he was installed as Dean of St. Patrick's Cathedral in 1713. He was never to achieve his goal of holding high religious office in London.

In the early 1700s Swift began to distinguish himself by his political pamphleteering and his comical literary hoaxes, some of them published in Richard Steele's periodical *The Tatler* (which also published some of his best-known poems). In 1708, for example, he composed "An Argument Against Abolishing Christianity in England." Whatever his relation to authority in general, Swift was all his life a defender of the established religion, and his argument was really aimed against the Whig attempt to abolish certain forms of discrimination against Roman Catholics and Dissenters by repealing the Test Act, which imposed certain civil disabilities on those who refused Church of England sacraments. Swift's strategy was to conflate arguments against the Test Act with arguments against the Church itself, while opening a disturbing split in his argument between real or primitive Christianity (which is irrelevant, he says, because nobody practices it) and nominal Christianity.

While in Temple's service, Swift had tutored Temple's eight-year-old ward, Esther Johnson (or "Stella," as he would come to call her), and when she came of age he convinced her and a companion to live near him in Dublin. While separated from her when he was in England, he wrote her a series of letters that was published much later as *Journal to Stella* (written 1710–13). In the *Journal* Swift adopted a private, often obscure language—a "nursery talk" full of neologisms, irregular spellings, and novel grammatical usages. Swift's and Johnson's relationship endured to the end of her life in 1728 and was marked by an annual birthday poem; the survivors are some of his most charming poems. The dynamics of his emotional life remain obscure: he conducted a simultaneous relationship with "Vanessa" (Esther Vanhomrigh), who was a more rebellious character than Johnson and who followed him, without invitation, to Ireland from England. This relationship too produced a remarkable poem, *Cadenus and Vanessa*, in which Swift relates the story of their friendship from his own point of view, leaving its ending open.

Swift counted among his friends many of the leading lights of London's literary scene, including Joseph Addison (until politics divided the two), Alexander Pope, and John Gay, and counted his "banishment" to Ireland as "the greatest unhappiness" of his life. Although he made a number of return visits to England, after 1727 his home was "wretched Dublin, in miserable Ireland." Swift also suffered from undiagnosed Ménières disease, a debilitating inner-ear disease causing dizziness, headaches, depression, and deafness.

A preoccupation with death and decay lends a sharply pessimistic tone to Swift's later satires. Rereading these works several years later, Samuel Johnson despaired at ever discovering "by what depravity of intellect [Swift] took delight in revolting ideas from which almost every other mind shrinks with disgust." Swift was often accused of misanthropy, but in a letter to Alexander Pope he endeavored to counter the charge, insisting that while he had "ever hated all nations, professions, and communities," he did indeed love "individuals." Swift has often also been accused of misogyny on account of such poems as "The Lady's Dressing Room," in which a man is abruptly cured of his passion when he discovers his beloved's bedroom to be disgustingly squalid.

If Swift was embittered by Ireland, the nation, which remained entirely subject to English rule, was to benefit greatly by its association with him. Swift wrote numerous pamphlets and tracts in opposition to British policy, among them *A Modest Proposal* (1729), a brilliantly macabre send-up of English hard-heartedness toward the Irish and of the number-crunching approach to public policy, which puts economic utility first. In his *Proposal*, Swift recommends that the Irish could solve their problems of famine and overpopulation by raising their children for export as a food source for the English.

Swift often proudly anticipated public opposition to his views. Foreseeing the hostile reaction to his founding of St. Patrick's Hospital, Ireland's first mental asylum, he wrote *Verses on the Death of Dr. Swift* (1739), which predicts and responds to hostilities and objections. His legacy, he hoped, would be based not on fashionable and worldly expectations, but on his commitment to identifying and rooting out abuses. Translated from the Latin, the epitaph on his tomb in St. Patrick's Cathedral reads: "*Here is laid the body of Jonathan Swift, Doctor of Divinity, Dean of this Cathedral Church, where fierce indignation can no longer rend the heart. Go, traveller, and imitate if you can this earnest and dedicated champion of liberty. He died on the 19th day of October 1745 AD. Aged 78 years."*

⌘ ⌘ ⌘

The Progress of Beauty

When first Diana[1] leaves her bed,
   Vapours and steams[2] her looks disgrace,
A frowzy° dirty-coloured red   *shabby*
Sits on her cloudy wrinkled face:
5 But, by degrees, when mounted high,
   Her artificial face appears
Down from her window in the sky,
   Her spots are gone, her visage clears.
'Twixt earthly females and the moon,
10 All parallels exactly run;
If Celia should appear too soon,
   Alas, the nymph° would be undone!   *beautiful woman*
To see her from her pillow rise,
   All reeking in a cloudy steam,
15 Cracked lips, foul teeth, and gummy eyes,
   Poor Strephon,[3] how would he blaspheme!
Three colours, black, and red, and white,
   So graceful in their proper place,
Remove them to a different light,
20 They form a frightful hideous face:
For instance, when the lily skips
   Into the precincts of the rose,
And takes possession of the lips,
   Leaving the purple to the nose.
25 So, Celia went entire to bed,
   All her complexions safe and sound;
But, when she rose, white, black, and red,
   Though still in sight, had changed their ground.
The black, which would not be confined,
30 A more inferior station seeks,
Leaving the fiery red behind,
   And mingles in her muddy cheeks.

But Celia can with ease reduce,
   By help of pencil, paint, and brush,
35 Each colour to its place and use,
   And teach her cheeks again to blush.
She knows her early self no more;
   But filled with admiration stands,
As other painters oft adore
40 The workmanship of their own hands.
Thus, after four important hours,
   Celia's the wonder of her sex:
Say, which among the heav'nly pow'rs
   Could cause such marvellous effects?
45 Venus,[4] indulgent to her kind,
   Gave women all their hearts could wish,
When first she taught them where to find
   White lead and Lusitanian dish.[5]
Love with white lead cements his wings;
50 White lead was sent us to repair
Two brightest, brittlest, earthly things,
   A lady's face, and China-ware.[6]
She ventures now to lift the sash,
   The window is her proper sphere:
55 Ah, lovely nymph! be not too rash,
   Nor let the beaux approach too near:
Take pattern by your sister star,
   Delude at once, and bless our sight;
When you are seen, be seen from far,
60 And chiefly choose to shine by night.
But, art no longer can prevail,
   When the materials all are gone;
The best mechanic hand must fail,
   Where nothing's left to work upon.
65 Matter, as wise logicians say,
   Cannot without a form subsist;
And form, say I as well as they,

---

[1] *Diana* Goddess of the moon.

[2] *Vapours* Exhalations from the organs, believed in the eighteenth century to cause a variety of physical and psychological ailments; *steams* Bad breath, perspiration, or other bodily excretions.

[3] *Strephon* Name commonly used in pastoral poetry for a young man in love.

[4] *Venus* Goddess of love and beauty.

[5] *White lead* Toxic lead-based pigment used as a cosmetic foundation; *Lusitanian dish* Cosmetic from Portugal.

[6] *China-ware* White lead was also used to glaze and repair porcelain.

Must fail, if matter brings no grist.°   *substance*
And this is fair Diana's case;
70   For all astrologers maintain,
Each night, a bit drops off her face,
When mortals say she's in her wane;
While Partrige[1] wisely shows the cause
Efficient of the moon's decay,
75   That Cancer with his pois'nous claws,[2]
Attacks her in the Milky Way:
But Gadbury,[3] in art profound,
From her pale cheeks pretends to show,
That swain° Endymion[4] is not found,   *lover*
80   Or else, that Mercury's[5] her foe.
But, let the cause be what it will,
In half the month she looks so thin,
That Flamstead[6] can, with all his skill,
See but her forehead and her chin.
85   Yet, as she wastes, she grows discreet,
'Till midnight never shows her head;
So rotting Celia strolls the street,
When sober folks are all a-bed:
For sure if this be Luna's° fate,   *the moon's*
90   Poor Celia, but of mortal race,
In vain expects a longer date
To the materials of her face.
When mercury her tresses mows,
To think of black-lead combs is vain;
95   No painting can restore a nose,
Nor will her teeth return again.
Ye pow'rs, who over love preside!
Since mortal beauties drop so soon,
If you would have us well supplied,
100   Send us new nymphs with each new moon.
—1719

---

[1]   *Partrige*   English astrologer John Partridge (1644–c. 1714).

[2]   *Cancer with ... pois'nous claws*   The constellation Cancer is a crab.

[3]   *Gadbury*   English astrologer John Gadbury (1627–1704).

[4]   *Endymion*   Beautiful Greek youth of myth, lover to the moon.

[5]   *Mercury's*   Planet with astrological meaning, associated with the Roman god of the same name. Also a pun on the side effects of mercury poisoning; mercury compounds were used to treat venereal disease, and could cause tooth and hair loss, as well as rotting of the soft tissues of the face.

[6]   *Flamstead*   Astronomer John Flamsteed (1646–1719), director of the Royal Observatory.

A Description of a City Shower

Careful observers may foretell the hour
(By sure prognostics) when to dread a shower.
While rain depends,° the pensive cat gives o'er   *is imminent*
Her frolics, and pursues her tail no more.
5   Returning home at night you find the sink°   *sewer*
Strike your offended sense with double stink.
If you be wise, then go not far to dine,
You spend in coach-hire more than save in wine.
A coming shower your shooting[7] corns presage,
10   Old aches throb, your hollow tooth will rage.
Sauntering in coffee-house is Dulman seen;
He damns the climate and complains of spleen.[8]

Meanwhile the south,° rising with dabbled[9]
        wings,   *south wind*
A sable cloud athwart the welkin° flings,   *sky*
15   That swilled more liquor than it could contain,
And like a drunkard gives it up again.
Brisk Susan whips her linen from the rope,
While the first drizzling shower is borne
        aslope:°   *on an incline*
Such is that sprinkling which some careless quean°   *hussy*
20   Flirts° on you from her mop, but not so clean: *flicks*
You fly, invoke the gods; then, turning, stop
To rail; she, singing, still whirls on her mop.
Nor yet the dust had shunned the unequal strife,
But, aided by the wind, fought still for life,
25   And wafted with its foe by violent gust,
'Twas doubtful which was rain, and which was dust.
Ah! Where must needy poet seek for aid,
When dust and rain at once his coat invade?
Sole coat, where dust cemented by the rain
30   Erects the nap,[10] and leaves a cloudy stain.

Now in contiguous drops the flood comes down,
Threatening with deluge this devoted° town.   *doomed*
To shops in crowds the daggled° females fly,   *bespattered*
Pretend to cheapen° goods, but nothing buy.   *bargain for*

---

[7]   *shooting*   I.e., beset by shooting pain.

[8]   *spleen*   Said to be the origin of melancholy feelings, "the spleen" was often used synonymously with "melancholia."

[9]   *dabbled*   Splashed with water or mud.

[10]   *nap*   Rough surface layer of projecting threads on wooly surfaces.

35　The templar spruce,[1] while every spout's abroach,°*streaming*
　　Stays till 'tis fair, yet seems to call a coach.
　　The tucked-up seamstress walks with hasty strides,
　　While streams run down her oiled umbrella's sides.
　　Here various kinds by various fortunes led,
40　Commence acquaintance underneath a shed.
　　Triumphant Tories, and desponding Whigs,
　　Forget their feuds,[2] and join to save their wigs.
　　Boxed in a chair° the beau impatient sits,　　　*sedan chair*
　　While spouts run clattering o'er the roof by fits,
45　And ever and anon with frightful din
　　The leather sounds;[3] he trembles from within.
　　So when Troy chairmen bore the wooden steed,
　　Pregnant with Greeks, impatient to be freed
　　(Those bully Greeks, who, as the moderns do,
50　Instead of paying chairmen, run them through),
　　Laocoon[4] struck the outside with his spear,
　　And each imprisoned hero quaked for fear.

　　　　Now from all parts the swelling kennels[5] flow,
　　And bear their trophies with them as they go:
55　Filths of all hues and odours seem to tell
　　What streets they sailed from, by the sight and smell.
　　They, as each torrent drives with rapid force
　　From Smithfield or St. Pulchre's shape their course,
　　And in huge confluent join at Snow Hill ridge,
60　Fall from the conduit prone to Holborn Bridge.[6]
　　Sweepings from butchers' stalls, dung, guts, and blood,
　　Drowned puppies, stinking sprats,[7] all drenched in mud,

Dead cats and turnip-tops come tumbling down the
　　flood.[8]
—1710

Stella's Birthday [9]
WRITTEN IN THE YEAR 1718 [10]

Stella this day is thirty-four[11]
(We shan't dispute a year or more);
However, Stella, be not troubled,
Although thy size and years are doubled
5　Since first I saw thee at sixteen,[12]
The brightest virgin on the green.
So little is thy form declined,
Made up so largely in thy mind.

　　Oh, would it please the gods to split
10　Thy beauty, size, and years, and wit,
No age could furnish out a pair
Of nymphs so graceful, wise, and fair,
With half the lustre of your eyes,
With half your wit, your years, and size.
15　And then before it grew too late,

---

[1] *templar* Law student; *spruce* Smartly dressed.

[2] *Triumphant Tories … feuds* In 1710 the Whig ministry fell and a Tory majority was elected to the House of Commons for the first time.

[3] *leather sounds* I.e., the rain pounds on the leather roof of the sedan chair.

[4] *Laocoon* Trojan priest who, according to Virgil's *Aeneid*, was suspicious of the horse and struck it with his spear. See *Aeneid* 2.40-53.

[5] *kennels* Open gutters that ran down the middle of streets. These were also used as sewers, into which all sorts of refuse could be dumped.

[6] *From Smithfield … Holborn Bridge* The drainage from the Smithfield cattle and sheep markets, which flowed down Cow Lane, met that from St. Sepulchre's Church, which flowed down Snow Hill, at the Holborn Conduit. The combined sewage ran into the Fleet River at Holborn Bridge.

[7] *sprats* Small fish.

[8] *Sweepings from … flood* According to the note, now attributed to Swift, in Falkner's edition of Swift's *Works* (1735), this concluding triplet, with an alexandrine as the final line, is an imitation of a form popular with John Dryden and other Restoration poets. Swift claims his mockery of the established form (which he saw as the "mere effect of haste, idleness, and want of money") finally brought about its demise.

[9] *Stella's Birthday* This is the first of the series of poems Swift wrote to his dear friend Esther Johnson ("Stella") every year on her birthday (March 13) until her death in 1728. Swift plays upon the convention that the Poet Laureate would write a birthday ode for the monarch each year.

[10] *1718* Before 1751, when the calendar was reformed, the new year officially began on March 25, the Feast of the Annunciation. Because many people also recognized January 1 as the start of the new year, the year was often written according to both systems when the date fell between January 1 and March 24. Swift's poem was written in February or March of what we would recognize as 1719.

[11] *thirty-four* Johnson was really thirty-eight.

[12] *at sixteen* Johnson was actually eight when the two first met at Moor Park, Sir William's estate in Surrey. On his next visit to Moor Park, however, when she was 16, Swift first noticed that Johnson had bloomed into, as he said, a "beautiful, graceful, and agreeable" young woman.

How should I beg of gentle fate
(That either nymph might have her swain°)   lover
To split my worship too in twain.
—1728

Stella's Birthday (1727)[1]

This day, whate'er the fates decree,
   Shall still be kept with joy by me;
This day then, let us not be told
That you are sick, and I grown old,
5   Nor think on our approaching ills,
And talk of spectacles and pills.
Tomorrow will be time enough
To hear such mortifying stuff.
Yet, since from reason may be brought
10   A better and more pleasing thought,
Which can, in spite of all decays,
Support a few remaining days,
From not the gravest of divines,°   clergymen, theologians
Accept for once some serious lines.

15   Although we now can form no more
Long schemes of life, as heretofore,
Yet you, while time is running fast,
Can look with joy on what is past.

Were future happiness and pain[2]
20   A mere contrivance of the brain,
As atheists argue, to entice,
And fit their proselytes° for vice   converts
(The only comfort they propose,
To have companions in their woes);
25   Grant this the case, yet sure 'tis hard,
That virtue, styled its own reward,
And by all sages understood
To be the chief of human good,
Should acting, die, nor leave behind
30   Some lasting pleasure in the mind,
Which by remembrance will assuage
Grief, sickness, poverty, and age,

And strongly shoot a radiant dart,
To shine through life's declining part.

35   Say, Stella, feel you no content,
Reflecting on a life well spent?
Your skilful hand employed to save
Despairing wretches from the grave;[3]
And then supporting with your store,
40   Those whom you dragged from death before
(So Providence on mortals waits,
Preserving what it first creates);
Your generous boldness to defend
An innocent and absent friend;
45   That courage which can make you just,
To merit humbled in the dust;
The detestation you express
For vice in all its glittering dress;
That patience under torturing pain,
50   Where stubborn Stoics would complain.

Shall these like empty shadows pass,
Or forms reflected from a glass?
Or mere chimeras[4] in the mind,
That fly and leave no marks behind?
55   Does not the body thrive and grow
By food of twenty years ago?
And, had it not been still supplied,
It must a thousand times have died.
Then who with reason can maintain,
60   That no effects of food remain?
And is not virtue in mankind
The nutriment that feeds the mind?
Upheld by each good action past,
And still continued by the last;
65   Then who with reason can pretend
That all effects of virtue end?

Believe me, Stella, when you show
That true contempt for things below,
Nor prize your life for other ends
70   Than merely to oblige your friends,
Your former actions claim their part,
And join to fortify your heart.

---

[1] *Stella's Birthday (1727)* The last of Swift's birthday poems to Esther Johnson ("Stella"), who died in 1728.

[2] *future happiness and pain* Reward or punishment in an afterlife.

[3] *Your skilful ... grave* Johnson frequently nursed Swift when he was ill. She also helped care for the poor in her neighborhood.

[4] *chimeras* Wild fantasies; unreal creatures.

For virtue, in her daily race,
Like Janus[1] bears a double face,
75 Looks back with joy where she has gone,
And therefore goes with courage on.
She at your sickly couch will wait,
And guide you to a better state.

O then, whatever heaven intends,
80 Take pity on your pitying friends;
Nor let your ills affect your mind,
To fancy they can be unkind.
Me, surely me, you ought to spare,
Who gladly would your sufferings share,
85 Or give my scrap of life to you,
And think it far beneath your due;
You, to whose care so oft I owe,
That I'm alive to tell you so.
                    —1728

The Lady's Dressing Room[2]

Five hours (and who can do it less in?)
By haughty Celia spent in dressing;
The goddess from her chamber issues,
Arrayed in lace, brocade,[3] and tissues.
5   Strephon,[4] who found the room was void,
And Betty[5] otherwise employed,
Stole in, and took a strict survey
Of all the litter as it lay;
Whereof, to make the matter clear,
10 An *inventory* follows here.

And first, a dirty smock appeared,
Beneath the armpits well besmeared.
Strephon, the rogue, displayed it wide,
And turned it round on every side.
15 In such a case few words are best,
And Strephon bids us guess the rest,
But swears how damnably the men lie
In calling Celia sweet and cleanly.

Now listen while he next produces
20 The various combs for various uses,
Filled up with dirt so closely fixed,
No brush could force a way betwixt;
A paste of composition rare,
Sweat, dandruff, powder, lead,[6] and hair,
25 A forehead cloth with oil upon't
To smooth the wrinkles on her front;
Here alum flower[7] to stop the steams
Exhaled from sour unsavoury streams;
There night-gloves made of Tripsy's[8] hide,
30 Bequeathed by Tripsy when she died,
With puppy water,[9] beauty's help,
Distilled from Tripsy's darling whelp.
Here gallipots° and vials placed,   *small ointment jars*
Some filled with washes, some with paste,
35 Some with pomatum,° paints, and slops,   *hair ointment*
And ointments good for scabby chops.
Hard by a filthy basin stands,
Fouled with the scouring of her hands;
The basin takes whatever comes,
40 The scrapings of her teeth and gums,
A nasty compound of all hues,
For here she spits, and here she spews.

But oh! it turned poor Strephon's bowels,
When he beheld and smelt the towels;
45 Begummed, bemattered, and beslimed;
With dirt, and sweat, and ear-wax grimed.
No object Strephon's eye escapes,
Here petticoats in frowzy heaps,

---

[1] *Janus* Roman god of gates, doorways, and beginnings and endings, after whom the month of January was named. He was depicted with two faces that looked in opposite directions, both forward and backward.

[2] *The Lady's Dressing Room* This poem provoked a biting response from Lady Mary Wortley Montagu. See her poem "The Reasons that Induced Dr. S. to Write a Poem called The Lady's Dressing Room."

[3] *brocade* Fabric with a woven, raised pattern, usually in gold or silver.

[4] *Strephon* Name used commonly in pastoral poetry for a young swain.

[5] *Betty* Name used commonly to denote a servant.

[6] *powder* Used on the hair, not the face; *lead* White lead, a mixture used as a white face paint to lighten the skin.

[7] *alum flower* I.e., alum powder. The astringent mineral was used as an antiperspirant.

[8] *Tripsey* Celia's lapdog.

[9] *puppy water* Puppy urine, formerly used as a cosmetic.

Nor be the handkerchiefs forgot,
50　All varnished o'er with snuff and snot.
The stockings why should I expose,
Stained with the moisture of her toes;
Or greasy coifs and pinners[1] reeking,
Which Celia slept at least a week in?
55　A pair of tweezers next he found
To pluck her brows in arches round,
Or hairs that sink the forehead low,
Or on her chin like bristles grow.

　　The virtues we must not let pass
60　Of Celia's magnifying glass;
When frighted Strephon cast his eye on't,
It showed the visage of a giant:
A glass that can to sight disclose
The smallest worm in Celia's nose,
65　And faithfully direct her nail
To squeeze it out from head to tail;
For catch it nicely by the head,
It must come out alive or dead.

　　Why, Strephon, will you tell the rest?
70　And must you needs describe the chest?
That careless wench! No creature warn her
To move it out from yonder corner,
But leave it standing full in sight,
For you to exercise your spite!
75　In vain the workman showed his wit
With rings and hinges counterfeit
To make it seem in this disguise
A cabinet to vulgar eyes,
Which Strephon ventured to look in,
80　Resolved to go through thick and thin;
He lifts the lid; there need no more,
He smelt it all the time before.

　　As from within Pandora's box,
When Epimethus oped the locks,
85　A sudden universal crew
Of human evils upward flew,
He still was comforted to find

That hope at last remained behind.[2]

　　So Strephon, lifting up the lid
90　To view what in the chest was hid,
The vapours flew from out the vent,
But Strephon cautious never meant
The bottom of the pan to grope,
And foul his hands in search of hope.

95　　O ne'er may such a vile machine°　　　　　structure
Be once in Celia's chamber seen!
O may she better learn to keep
"Those secrets of the hoary deep"![3]

　　As mutton cutlets, prime of meat,
100　Which though with art you salt and beat,
As laws of cookery require,
And roast them at the clearest fire,
If from adown the hopeful chops
The fat upon a cinder drops,
105　To stinking smoke it turns the flame,
Poisoning the flesh from whence it came,
And up exhales a greasy stench,
For which you curse the careless wench;
So things which must not be expressed,
110　When *plumped* into the reeking chest,
Send up an excremental smell
To taint the parts from which they fell,
The petticoats and gown perfume,
And waft a stink round every room.

115　　Thus finishing his grand survey,
The swain° disgusted slunk away,　　　　　lover
Repeating in his amorous fits,
"Oh! Celia, Celia, Celia shits!"

　　But Vengeance, goddess never sleeping,
120　Soon punished Strephon for his peeping.
His foul imagination links
Each dame he sees with all her stinks,

---

[1]　*coifs*　Close fitting caps; *pinners*　Coifs with long flaps hanging
down on either side.

[2]　*As from … behind*　Pandora, the first woman, according to Greek
mythology, was given a box or jar that contained all the evils of the
world. It was in fact Pandora, not her husband Epimetheus, who
opened the box or jar and released all the evils of the world. Only
hope remained inside.

[3]　*Those … deep*　See Milton's *Paradise Lost*, 2.891.

And, if unsavoury odours fly,
Conceives a lady standing by.
125 All women his description fits,
And both ideas jump like wits,[1]
By vicious fancy coupled fast,
And still appearing in contrast.

    I pity wretched Strephon, blind
130 To all the charms of womankind.
Should I the queen of love refuse
Because she rose from stinking ooze?[2]
To him that looks behind the scene,
Statira's but some pocky quean.[3]

135   When Celia in her glory shows,
If Strephon would but stop his nose,
Who now so impiously blasphemes
Her ointments, daubs, and paints and creams,
Her washes, slops, and every clout°   cloth, rag
140 With which she makes so foul a rout,
He soon would learn to think like me,
And bless his ravished eyes to see
Such order from confusion sprung,
Such gaudy tulips raised from dung.
            —1732

Verses on the Death of Dr Swift, D.S.P.D.[4]
OCCASIONED BY READING A MAXIM IN ROCHEFOUCAULD[5]

*Dans l'adversité de nos meilleurs amis nous trouvons
quelque chose, qui ne nous deplaist pas.*

In the adversity of our best friends, we find
something that doth not displease us.

---

[1]   *jump like wits* Agree, coincide. An allusion to the proverb "Good wits jump"—i.e., "Great minds think alike."

[2]   *queen ... ooze* Venus, the goddess of love, arose from the sea.

[3]   *Statira* One of the heroines of Nathaniel Lee's *Rival Queens* (1677); *pocky* Covered in pockmarks, as a result either of syphilis or of smallpox; *quean* Harlot.

[4]   *D.S.P.D.* Dean of St. Patrick's Cathedral, Dublin.

[5]   *Maxim in Rochefoucauld* François de la Rochefoucauld, whose *Reflections or Moral Aphorisms and Maxims* (1665) is made up of famously cynical, humorous observations.

As Rochefoucauld his maxims drew
    From nature, I believe 'em true:
They argue° no corrupted mind   indicate
In him; the fault is in mankind.

5   This maxim more than all the rest
Is thought too base for human breast:
"In all distresses of our friends
We first consult our private ends,
While Nature, kindly bent to ease us,
10 Points out some circumstance to please us."

    If this perhaps your patience move°   exasperates
Let reason and experience prove.

    We all behold with envious eyes
Our equal raised above our size;
15 Who would not at a crowded show
Stand high himself, keep others low?
I love my friend as well as you,
But would not have him stop my view.
Then let me have the higher post;
20 I ask but for an inch at most.

    If in a battle you should find
One whom you love of all mankind
Had some heroic action done,
A champion killed, or trophy won,
25 Rather than thus be overtopped,
Would you not wish his laurels[6] cropped?

    Dear honest Ned is in the gout,
Lies racked with pain, and you without:
How patiently you hear him groan!
30 How glad the case is not your own!

    What poet would not grieve to see
His brethren write as well as he?
But rather than they should excel,
He'd wish his rivals all in hell.

35   Her end when Emulation misses,
She turns to envy, stings, and hisses:

---

[6]   *laurels* In ancient Greece, laurel wreaths were given to victorious athletes, pre-eminent poets, and war heroes.

The strongest friendship yields to pride,
Unless the odds be on our side.

Vain humankind! Fantastic race!
40 Thy various follies, who can trace?
Self-love, ambition, envy, pride,
Their empire in our hearts divide:
Give others riches, power, and station,
'Tis all on me a usurpation.
45 I have no title to aspire;
Yet, when you sink, I seem the higher.
In Pope,[1] I cannot read a line,
But with a sigh, I wish it mine:
When he can in one couplet fix
50 More sense than I can do in six,
It gives me such a jealous fit,
I cry, "Pox take him, and his wit."

Why must I be outdone by Gay[2]
In my own humorous biting way?

55 Arbuthnot[3] is no more my friend,
Who dares to irony pretend,
Which I was born to introduce,
Refined it first, and showed its use.

St. John, as well as Pulteney,[4] knows
60 That I had some repute for prose;
And, till they drove me out of date,
Could maul a minister of state.
If they have mortified my pride,
And made me throw my pen aside;
65 If with such talents Heaven hath blest 'em,
Have I not reason to detest 'em?[5]

To all my foes, dear Fortune, send
Thy gifts, but never to my friend:
I tamely can endure the first,
70 But this° with envy makes me burst.   *the latter*

Thus much may serve by way of proem;°   *preamble*
Proceed we therefore to our poem.

The time is not remote when I
Must by the course of nature die;
75 When, I foresee, my special friends
Will try to find their private ends;
Though it is hardly understood
Which way my death can do them good,
Yet thus, methinks, I hear 'em speak:
80 "See how the Dean begins to break!
Poor gentleman, he droops apace;°   *swiftly*
You plainly find it in his face.
That old vertigo in his head[6]
Will never leave him till he's dead.
85 Besides, his memory decays:
He recollects not what he says;
He cannot call his friends to mind;
Forgets the place where last he dined;
Plies you with stories o'er and o'er,
90 He told them fifty times before.
How does he fancy we can sit
To hear his out-of-fashioned wit?
But he takes up with younger folks,
Who for his wine will bear his jokes.
95 Faith, he must make his stories shorter,
Or change his comrades once a quarter:
In half the time, he talks them round;
There must another set be found.

"For poetry, he's past his prime;
100 He takes an hour to find a rhyme.
His fire is out, his wit decayed,
His fancy sunk, his muse a jade.[7]

---

[1] *Pope* Alexander Pope (1688–1744), essayist, critic, satirist, and poet.

[2] *Gay* Poet and dramatist John Gay (1685–1732).

[3] *Arbuthnot* John Arbuthnot (1667–1735), Queen Anne's physician, satirist, and essayist.

[4] *St. John … Pulteney* Henry St. John, Lord Bolingbroke (1678–1751), was a Tory politician who was involved in the opposition to Sir Robert Walpole's Whig government. Among the opposition's members were a few disenchanted Whigs, including William Pulteney. The two helped put out a political paper, the *Craftsman*, that was in the style of Swift's own political pamphlets.

[5] *In Pope … detest 'em* Pope, Gay, and Arbuthnot were dear friends of Swift's. Along with Thomas Parnell, Swift himself, and occasionally Robert Harley, Earl of Oxford, they formed the

Scriblerus Club, meeting from 1713 to 1714 with the purpose of satirizing "false tastes in learning."

[6] *old vertigo … head* Swift suffered from what is now known as Ménière's disease, characterized by dizziness, vertigo, ringing and pressure in the ears, and hearing loss.

[7] *jade* Worn out, ill-tempered cart horse, here presented in contrast to the winged horse Pegasus, who in Greek mythology was associated with the Muses and poetic inspiration.

I'd have him throw away his pen,
But there's no talking to some men."

105　　And then their tenderness appears
By adding largely to my years:
"He's older than he would be reckoned,
And well remembers Charles the Second.[1]

　　"He hardly drinks a pint of wine,
110　And that, I doubt,° is no good sign.　　　　　*think*
His stomach° too begins to fail;　　　　　*appetite*
Last year we thought him strong and hale,°　　*healthy*
But now he's quite another thing;
I wish he may hold out till spring."

115　　Then hug themselves and reason thus:
"It is not yet so bad with us."

　　In such a case they talk in tropes,°　　*figures of speech*
And by their fears express their hopes.
Some great misfortune to portend,°　　　　*foretell*
120　No enemy can match a friend.
With all the kindness they profess,
The merit of a lucky guess
(When daily "How-d'ye's"° come of course,　*how do you's*
And servants answer, "Worse and worse")
125　Would please 'em better than to tell
That, God be praised, the Dean is well.
Then he who prophesied the best
Approves° his foresight to the rest:　　　　*demonstrates*
"You know, I always feared the worst,
130　And often told you so at first."
He'd rather choose that I should die
Than his prediction prove a lie.
No one foretells I shall recover,
But all agree to give me over.

135　　Yet should some neighbour feel a pain
Just in the parts where I complain,
How many a message would he send?
What hearty prayers that I should mend?
Enquire what regimen I kept,
140　What gave me ease, and how I slept?
And more lament, when I was dead,
Than all the snivellers round my bed.

My good companions, never fear,
For though you may mistake a year,
145　Though your prognostics run too fast,
They must be verified at last.

　　Behold the fatal day arrive!
"How is the Dean?"—"He's just alive."
Now the departing prayer is read;
150　"He hardly breathes."—"The Dean is dead."
Before the passing-bell[2] begun,
The news through half the town has run.
"O may we all for death prepare!
What has he left? And who's his heir?"
155　"I know no more than what the news is:
'Tis all bequeathed to public uses."
"To public use! A perfect whim!
What had the public done for him?
Mere envy, avarice, and pride!
160　He gave it all—but first he died.
And had the Dean, in all the nation,
No worthy friend, no poor relation?
So ready to do strangers good,
Forgetting his own flesh and blood?"

165　　Now Grub Street[3] wits are all employed;
With elegies the town is cloyed:
Some paragraph in every paper
To curse the Dean or bless the Drapier.[4]

　　The doctors, tender of their fame,
170　Wisely on me lay all the blame:
"We must confess his case was nice,°　　　*difficult*
But he would never take advice.
Had he been ruled, for aught appears,
He might have lived these twenty years;
175　For when we opened him, we found
That all his vital parts were sound."

---

[1] *well remembers … Second*   Swift was 18 when Charles II died in 1685.

[2] *passing-bell*   Bell tolled after a person's death.

[3] *Grub Street*   Street in London in which lived many writers who sold their services on a freelance basis. Gradually this became a term synonymous with "hack writers."

[4] *Drapier*   Under the name of M.B., a drapier, Swift had written a series of public letters persuading the Irish people to resist the British government's plan to introduce a new copper coin, Wood's halfpence, which would further debase Irish currency. For this he became a national hero.

From Dublin soon to London spread;
'Tis told at court, "The Dean is dead."

Kind Lady Suffolk, in the spleen,[1]
180 Runs laughing up to tell the Queen.
The Queen, so gracious, mild, and good,
Cries, "Is he gone? 'Tis time he should.
He's dead, you say? Why, let him rot;
I'm glad the medals were forgot.[2]
185 I promised them, I own, but when?
I only was a princess then,
But now, as consort of the King,
You know 'tis quite a different thing."

Now Chartres, at Sir Robert's levee,[3]
190 Tells with a sneer the tidings heavy.
"Why, is he dead without his shoes?"[4]
Cries Bob. "I'm sorry for the news.
Oh, were the wretch but living still,
And in his place my good friend Will;[5]
195 Or had a miter° on his head,   bishop's headdress
Provided Bolingbroke were dead!"

Now Curll[6] his shop from rubbish drains;
Three genuine tomes of Swift's remains.
And then, to make them pass the glibber,[7]
200 Revised by Tibbalds, Moore, and Cibber.[8]

He'll treat me as he does my betters:
Publish my will, my life, my letters;
Revive the libels born to die,
Which Pope must bear, as well as I.

205 Here shift the scene to represent
How those I love, my death lament.
Poor Pope will grieve a month, and Gay
A week, and Arbuthnot a day.

St. John himself will scarce forbear
210 To bite his pen and drop a tear.
The rest will give a shrug and cry,
"I'm sorry; but we all must die."
Indifference clad in wisdom's guise,
All fortitude of mind supplies;
215 For how can stony bowels melt
In those who never pity felt?
When *we* are lashed, *they* kiss the rod,[9]
Resigning to the will of God.

The fools, my juniors by a year,
220 Are tortured with suspense and fear—
Who wisely thought my age a screen,
When death approached, to stand between.
The screen removed, their hearts are trembling;
They mourn for me without dissembling.

225 My female friends, whose tender hearts
Have better learnt to act their parts,
Receive the news in doleful dumps,
"The Dean is dead (*and what is trumps?*),
Then Lord have mercy on his soul.
230 (*Ladies, I'll venture for the vole.*[10])
Six deans they say must bear the pall.
(*I wish I knew which king to call.*)"
"Madam, your husband will attend
The funeral of so good a friend?"
235 "No, madam, 'tis a shocking sight;
And he's engaged tomorrow night!

---

[1] *Lady Suffolk* Mistress of George II and close friend of Swift; *in the spleen* Depressed; melancholy (here meant ironically).

[2] *medals were forgot* When Queen Caroline was still Princess of Wales she had promised Swift some medals; he had yet to receive them.

[3] *Chartres* Colonel Francis Chartres, a moneylender, informer, and runner for Sir Robert Walpole. Chartres was a notorious scoundrel who was referred to as the "Rape-Master General" after having been convicted, at the age of 70, of having raped his maid. He was sentenced to death but pardoned by Sir Robert; *levee* Morning assembly or reception of visitors.

[4] *dead … shoes* I.e., he died in bed, as opposed to being hanged (when he would have "died in his shoes").

[5] *Will* William Pulteney.

[6] *Curll* Edmund Curll, a bookseller who published pirated, forged, and falsely ascribed works, often scavenging memoirs, letters, and other personal documents after a person's death. Arbuthnot wrote that Curll's biographies were "one of the new terrors of death."

[7] *pass the glibber* Sell more easily.

[8] *Tibbalds* Lewis Theobold, a dramatist and editor of Shakespeare whom Pope had cast as King of the Dunces in his *Dunciad* (1728); *Moore* James Moore Smythe, another author and enemy of Pope;

Cibber Colley Cibber, who was appointed Poet Laureate in 1730, and in 1743 was crowned next King of the Dunces in the new edition of Pope's *Dunciad*.

[9] *kiss the rod* Accept the punishment submissively.

[10] *vole* In the card game quadrille, a vole occurs when one wins all the tricks.

My Lady Club would take it ill
If he should fail her at quadrille.
He loved the Dean (*I lead a heart*),
240   But dearest friends, they say, must part.
His time was come; he ran his race;[1]
We hope he's in a better place."

    Why do we grieve that friends should die?
No loss more easy to supply.
245   One year is past; a different scene;
No further mention of the Dean,
Who now, alas, no more is missed
Than if he never did exist.
Where's now this favourite of Apollo?[2]
250   Departed, and his works must follow,
Must undergo the common fate;
His kind of wit is out of date.
Some country squire to Lintot[3] goes,
Inquires for Swift in verse and prose.
255   Says Lintot, "I have heard the name;
He died a year ago."—"The same."
He searches all his shop in vain.
"Sir, you may find them in Duck Lane;[4]
I sent them with a load of books
260   Last Monday to the pastry-cook's.[5]
To fancy they could live a year!
I find you're but a stranger here.
The Dean was famous in his time,
And had a kind of knack at rhyme.
265   His way of writing now is past;
The town hath got a better taste.
I keep no antiquated stuff,
But spick and span I have enough.
Pray, do but give me leave to show 'em;

270   Here's Colley Cibber's birthday poem.[6]
This ode you never yet have seen,
By Stephen Duck,[7] upon the Queen.
Then here's a letter finely penned
Against the *Craftsman* and his friend;
275   It clearly shows that all reflection
On ministers is disaffection.
Next, here's Sir Robert's vindication,[8]
And Mr. Henley's last oration.[9]
The hawkers° have not got 'em yet;   *street sellers*
280   Your honour please to buy a set?

    "Here's Woolston's tracts,[10] the twelfth edition;
'Tis read by every politician:
The country members,[11] when in town,
To all their boroughs send them down.
285   You never met a thing so smart;
The courtiers have them all by heart;
Those maids of honour (who can read)
Are taught to use them for their creed.
The reverend author's good intention
290   Hath been rewarded with a pension.
He doth an honour to his gown
By bravely running priestcraft down;
He shows, as sure as God's in Gloucester,[12]
That Jesus was a grand impostor,
295   That all his miracles were cheats,

---

1   *His time … his race* See 2 Timothy 4.6–7: "For I am now ready to be offered, and the time of my departure is at hand. I have fought a great fight, I have finished my course, I have kept my faith."

2   *Apollo* God of music and poetry.

3   *Lintot* Benard Lintot (1675–1736), London bookseller who had published some of Pope and Gay's work, and with whom Pope had quarreled.

4   *Duck Lane* Street at the center of the secondhand book business where used and remaindered books were often sent.

5   *pastry-cook's* Waste paper was used for wrapping pies or lining baking sheets and tins.

6   *Colley … poem* Cibber, as Poet Laureate, was expected to compose a birthday ode to the monarch each year.

7   *Stephen Duck* Referred to as the "thresher poet," Duck was a farm laborer turned poet who had gained favor with Queen Caroline and was even considered a possible candidate for Poet Laureate. He was a popular target for both Pope and Swift's ridicule.

8   [Swift's note] Walpole hires a set of party scribblers who do nothing else but write in his defense.

9   *Henley's last oration* John Henley was an independent preacher known as "Orator Henley." He gave lectures on a variety of matters, both theological and mundane, for which he charged a shilling for admission. Henley also edited the *Hyp Doctor*, a paper established in opposition to the *Craftsman*.

10   *Woolston's tracts* Rev. Thomas Woolston was a freethinker who was tried for blasphemy in 1729, and whose sensational *Discourses on the Miracles of Our Savior* became extremely popular. He never received a pension, though Swift here predicts he would.

11   *members* I.e., of Parliament.

12   *as sure … Gloucester* Proverbial. Gloucester was filled with monasteries.

Performed as jugglers do their feats.
The church had never such a writer;
A shame he hath not got a miter!"

Suppose me dead, and then suppose
A club assembled at the Rose,[1]
Where, from discourse of this and that,
I grow the subject of their chat;
And, while they toss my name about,
With favour some, and some without,
One quite indifferent in the cause
My character impartial draws:

"The Dean, if we believe report,
Was never ill received at court.
As for his works in verse and prose,
I own myself no judge of those,
Nor can I tell what critics thought 'em;
But this I know, all people bought 'em,
As with a moral view designed
To cure the vices of mankind.
His vein, ironically grave,
Exposed the fool and lashed the knave;
To steal a hint was never known,
But what he writ was all his own.

"He never thought an honour done him
Because a duke was proud to own him;
Would rather slip aside and choose
To talk with wits in dirty shoes;
Despised the fools with stars and garters,[2]
So often seen caressing Chartres.
He never courted men in station,
Nor persons had in admiration;
Of no man's greatness was afraid,
Because he sought for no man's aid.
Though trusted long in great affairs,
He gave himself no haughty airs;
Without regarding private ends,
Spent all his credit for his friends;
And only chose the wise and good—

No flatterers, no allies in blood;[3]
335 But succoured virtue in distress,
And seldom failed of good success,
As numbers in their hearts must own,
Who, but for him, had been unknown.

"With princes kept a due decorum,
340 But never stood in awe before 'em;
And to her Majesty, God bless her,
Would speak as free as to her dresser.[4]
She thought it his peculiar whim,
Nor took it ill as come from him.
345 He followed David's lesson just,
'In princes never put thy trust.'[5]
And, would you make him truly sour,
Provoke him with a slave in power:
The Irish senate, if you named,
350 With what impatience he declaimed!
Fair LIBERTY was all his cry;
For her he stood prepared to die;
For her he boldly stood alone;
For her he oft exposed his own.
355 Two kingdoms, just as factions led,
Had set a price upon his head,
But not a traitor could be found
To sell him for six hundred pound.[6]

"Had he but spared his tongue and pen,
360 He might have rose like other men;
But power was never in his thought,
And wealth he valued not a groat.[7]
Ingratitude he often found,
And pitied those who meant the wound,

---

[1] *the Rose* Fashionable tavern located across from the Drury Lane Theatre and frequented by playgoers.

[2] *stars and garters* Insignia of the Order of the Garter, the oldest and highest award for loyalty and military merit. Walpole received the Order in 1726.

[3] *allies in blood* Relatives.

[4] *dresser* Person who attends the Queen in her bedchamber and helps to dress her; here, most likely a reference specifically to Swift's friend Lady Suffolk.

[5] *David's ... trust* Cf. Psalm 146.3.

[6] *Two kingdoms ... pound* In 1713 the Queen offered £300 to the person who could discover the author of a pamphlet entitled *Public Spirit of the Whigs*. In 1724 the Irish government offered a similar reward for the identity of the author of *The Drapier's Fourth Letter*. In both cases Swift's identity as author was widely known, but nobody came forward to identify him.

[7] *not a groat* I.e., not a bit. A groat was a silver coin equal in value to four pence, and was often referred to metaphorically to signify any very small sum.

365 But kept the tenor of his mind
To merit well of humankind,
Nor made a sacrifice of those
Who still were true, to please his foes.
He laboured many a fruitless hour
370 To reconcile his friends in power;
Saw mischief by a faction brewing,
While they pursued each other's ruin.
But, finding vain was all his care,
He left the court in mere° despair.[1]   *utter*

375   "And, oh, how short are human schemes!
Here ended all our golden dreams.
What St. John's skill in state affairs,
What Ormonde's[2] valour, Oxford's cares,
To save their sinking country lent,
380 Was all destroyed by one event.[3]
Too soon that precious life was ended,
On which alone our weal° depended.   *well-being*
When up a dangerous faction starts,
With wrath and vengeance in their hearts;[4]
385 By solemn league and covenant bound,[5]
To ruin, slaughter, and confound;
To turn religion to a fable,
And make the government a Babel;
Pervert the law, disgrace the gown,
390 Corrupt the senate, rob the crown,
To sacrifice old England's glory,
And make her infamous in story.°   *history*
When such a tempest shook the land,
How could unguarded virtue stand?

395   "With horror, grief, despair the Dean
Beheld the dire destructive scene:
His friends in exile or the Tower,[6]
Himself within the frown of power,
Pursued by base, envenomed pens,
400 Far to the land of slaves and fens;[7]
A servile race in folly nursed,
Who truckle° most when treated worst.   *submit*

"By innocence and resolution
He bore continual persecution,
405 While numbers to preferment rose,
Whose merits were, to be his foes.
When *ev'n his own familiar friends,*
Intent upon their private ends,
Like renegadoes now he feels,
410 *Against him lifting up their heels.*[8]

"The Dean did by his pen defeat
An infamous destructive cheat;[9]
Taught fools their interest to know,
And gave them arms to ward the blow.
415 Envy hath owned it was his doing
To save that helpless land from ruin,
While they who at the steerage stood,[10]
And reaped the profit, sought his blood.

"To save them from their evil fate,
420 In him was held a crime of state.
A wicked monster on the bench,[11]
Whose fury blood could never quench,
As vile and profligate a villain

---

[1] *To reconcile … despair* The quarrel between two of Swift's close friends, Lord Bolingbroke and Robert Harley, Earl of Oxford, had divided the Tory ministry. The quarrel escalated until Queen Anne died on 1 August 1714 and the Whigs were restored to power.

[2] *Ormonde* James Butler, Duke of Ormonde, who was Captain-General of the English armies from 1712 until 1714, when he went into exile.

[3] *one event* The death of the Queen, who had supported the Tories.

[4] *dangerous faction … hearts* The Whig party. After regaining power they commenced impeaching, banishing, and harassing those who had opposed them. Many libels were written against Swift in England, and it was even rumored there was a reward offered for his arrest.

[5] *solemn … bound* Reference to the Solemn League and Covenant, which, in 1643, established Presbyterianism and provided for the suppression of Roman Catholicism.

[6] *the Tower* Tower of London, where the Earl of Oxford was sent by the Whigs. Bolingbroke had been exiled.

[7] *land … fens* Ireland.

[8] *ev'n his own … their heels* See Psalm 41.9.

[9] *infamous … cheat* England's plan to introduce Wood's copper half-pence into Ireland.

[10] *they who … stood* Those who managed Ireland's affairs (literally, those who were at the helm).

[11] *wicked … bench* William Whitshed, Chief Justice of Ireland, who in 1720 presided over the trial of the printer of Swift's anonymous pamphlet *The Universal Use of Irish Manufacture* and, in 1724, over that of the printer of Swift's fourth *Drapier's Letter*. In both cases he tried unsuccessfully to force the jury to return a verdict of guilty.

As modern Scroggs, or old Tresilian,[1]
25   Who long all justice had discarded,
Nor feared he God, nor man regarded,[2]
Vowed on the Dean his rage to vent,
And make him of his zeal repent.
But Heaven his innocence defends;
30   The grateful people stand his friends:
Not strains of law, nor judges' frown,
Nor topics° brought to please the crown,   *obscure points of law*
Nor witness hired, nor jury picked,
Prevail to bring him in convict.

35   "In exile, with a steady heart,
He spent his life's declining part;
Where folly, pride, and faction sway,
Remote from St. John, Pope, and Gay.

    "His friendship there, to few confined,
40   Were always of the middling kind:
No fools of rank, a mongrel breed,
Who fain would pass for lords indeed;
Where titles give no right or power,
And peerage is a withered flower,
45   He would have held it a disgrace
If such a wretch had known his face.
On rural squires, that kingdom's bane,
He vented oft his wrath in vain;
Biennial squires[3] to market brought,
50   Who sell their souls and votes for naught;
The nation stripped, go joyful back
To rob the church, their tenants rack,[4]
Go snacks[5] with thieves and rapparees,°   *highwaymen*
And keep the peace[6] to pick up fees;

455   In every job to have a share,
A jail or barrack to repair,
And turn the tax for public roads
Commodious to their own abodes.

    "Perhaps I may allow the Dean
460   Had too much satire in his vein,
And seemed determined not to starve it,
Because no age could more deserve it.
Yet malice never was his aim;
He lashed the vice but spared the name.
465   No individual could resent
Where thousands equally were meant.
His satire points at no defect
But what all mortals may correct;
For he abhorred that senseless tribe
470   Who call it humour when they jibe:
He spared a hump or crooked nose
Whose owners set not up for beaux.
True, genuine dullness moved his pity,
Unless it offered to be witty.
475   Those who their ignorance confessed,
He ne'er offended with a jest;
But laughed to hear an idiot quote
A verse from Horace, learned by rote.

    "He knew an hundred pleasant stories,
480   With all the turns of Whigs and Tories;
Was cheerful to his dying day,
And friends would let him have his way.

    "He gave the little wealth he had
To build a house for fools and mad,[7]
485   And showed, by one satiric touch,
No nation wanted it so much.
That kingdom he hath left his debtor,
I wish it soon may have a better."
—1739 (WRITTEN IN 1731)

---

[1] *Scroggs* Sir William Scroggs, Lord Chief Justice who was involved in the trials surrounding the Popish Plot and who, in 1680, was impeached for misconduct; *Tresilian* Sir Robert Tresilian, who was Chief Justice in 1381 and who tried John Ball and his followers after the Peasant's Revolt. He was impeached and hanged for treason.

[2] *Nor ... regarded* See Luke 18.2.

[3] *Biennial squires* Members of the Irish Parliament, who met only once every two years and had little real power.

[4] *rack* Force to pay exorbitantly high rent, nearly equal to the value of the land (referred to as "rack-rent").

[5] *Go snacks* Share.

[6] *keep the peace* Serve as magistrates.

[7] *To build ... mad* In his will, Swift left a considerable sum to the city for the construction of Ireland's first mental hospital. St. Patrick's opened in 1757 and is still functioning today.

Gulliver's Travels

A cruel satire; a biting political allegory; a parodic travel narrative; a fantastical adventure with elements of proto-science fiction—*Gulliver's Travels* is each of these. It has appealed to a remarkably wide range of audiences over several centuries; it is a prominent focus of scholarly commentary, a presence in popular culture, and (in bowdlerized form) even a common children's book. The *Travels* was among the most popular bestsellers of its time; as Samuel Johnson would later record in his "Life of Swift," upon its first publication the book was "received with such avidity, that the price of the first edition was raised before a second could be made." It has never been out of print since.

On the surface, *Gulliver's Travels* appears as a parodic adventure story. Parodies of this kind were fairly common in the eighteenth century—no doubt in part because travel narratives themselves were so popular. Such works enticed readers with exciting adventures, exotic settings realistically described—and, almost invariably, a seafaring protagonist who embodied British colonial values. While he worked on his *Travels*, Swift complained about reading extensively in the genre, which he described as an "abundance of trash."

However much Swift may have detested typical travel narratives, mocking them was not the only object of his wit in this work; the parody travel narrative provides a structure for a much wider-ranging satire, a primary focus of which is early eighteenth-century British politics. A central figure here was the powerful Whig Robert Walpole, who possessed varying degrees of power throughout the 1710s and had become established in a position of political dominance by 1721—the year Swift began work on the *Travels*. Governing primarily through the influence he wielded as a favorite of the king and operating through political intrigue rather than through official channels, Walpole epitomized what Tories such as Swift considered the despicable corruption of government. Many of Walpole's political enemies were Swift's friends. Among these were Tories Lord Bolingbroke and Lord Oxford, who had negotiated an initially popular peace treaty with the French; branding this treaty as pro-French and pro-Catholic, Walpole had Oxford and Bolingbroke impeached for treason. This event is a particular object of the satire in *Gulliver's Travels*, especially in Book 1, but Swift also attacks Walpole and the state of British politics more generally. Among his targets are the enmity displayed by the English towards France (and vice versa), England's exploitative attitude toward Ireland, and the endless bickering between the High and Low tendencies within the Church of England.

Another subject of satire in the *Travels* is one Swift had previously attacked in his *Battle of the Books*: the rejection of ancient in favor of modern knowledge. He was particularly suspicious of the previous fifty years' developments in natural philosophy, in which Aristotle's classical methods had been largely replaced by an emphasis on experimentation. The Royal Society of London for Improving Natural Knowledge, an organization of experimenters at the forefront of these changes, is caricatured in *Gulliver's Travels*; many of the experiments conducted at the Academy of Lagado in Book 3 are strikingly similar to some that were performed by Royal Society members. Members of the Royal Society attempted blood transfusion on dogs, and made use of bellows in experiments on the breathing of several animals. Scientific developments also influenced the text in other ways; the imagery of differing scale that Swift employs in Books 1 and 2 is deeply indebted to the invention of the microscope and the telescope in the previous century.

While scholars generally agree on the overall targets of the satire in *Gulliver's Travels*, there is no consensus as to what precise claims Swift is making in the text. Part of this ambiguity stems from the impossibility of equating the author's opinions with those of the narrator—a fictional character whose sanity at the end of the final book may be questioned. It has also proved impossible to establish a tidy allegorical correspondence between the story and any of the political events that inspired it; *Gulliver's Travels'* commentary on human nature cannot be reduced to a clever description of historical circumstances. In an angry letter to a translator who had altered the *Travels'* political content for publication in France, Swift said of his own work:

> If the books of Mr. Gulliver are calculated only for the British Isles, that traveler should pass for a very pitiful writer. The same vices, and the same follies reign everywhere, at least, in all the civilized countries of Europe, and the author who writes only for one city, one province, one realm, or even one century, so little deserves to be translated, that he does not deserve to be read. The partisans of this Gulliver, who remain in very great numbers here, maintain that his book will last as long as our language, for it derives its merit not from certain modes or manners of thinking and speaking, but from a series of observations on the imperfections, the follies, and the vices of man.

A NOTE ON THE TEXT

The manuscript of *Travels into Several Remote Nations of the World, in Four Parts*—as *Gulliver's Travels* was originally titled—was delivered in secret to London printer Benjamin Motte on an autumn night in 1726. The manuscript, which was later destroyed, was probably not in the handwriting of its author, whose real name did not appear on it; he had attributed the book to his protagonist, Lemuel Gulliver, and negotiated with the publisher by mail, posing as Gulliver's fictional cousin. Swift often published anonymously or under pseudonyms—even though, as in this case, it usually became widely known that he was the true author of the work. But even a thin cloak of anonymity allowed him to dissociate himself from the work on aesthetic grounds if he ever wished to do so—and also provided a means of protecting himself from legal retribution in case his barbed political content provoked a response from its powerful victims.

Unfortunately, Swift's efforts to distance himself from his work have left a legacy of confusion over textual matters. Because he did not communicate with Motte directly on the project, Swift was unable to review and correct the proofs, as would have been the usual practice. He spread the word that the printer had produced a "mangled and murdered" edition, full not only of typographical errors but also of more significant alterations. Did Motte, perhaps himself in fear of the law, edit out the most politically offensive passages? It may be that the first edition really was not representative of Swift's manuscript, but it is more likely that Swift created—or at least greatly exaggerated—the rumors of textual corruption as part of the charade to dissociate himself from the text. In 1735 Swift participated in the revision and correction of the text for a new printing by Dublin publisher George Faulkner; because of Swift's own complaints about the original printing, this later version is often used as the basis for modern editions of *Gulliver's Travels*. The following text, however, is based on the 1726 version, which was the first to amuse and unsettle the readers of early eighteenth-century London.

from *Gulliver's Travels*

Illustration of *Captain Lemuel Gulliver*,
printed as a frontispiece to the 1726 edition.

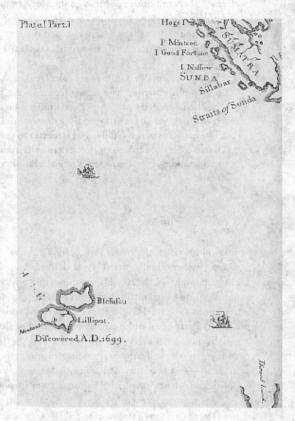

Map showing Lilliput as southwest of Sumatra,
printed in the 1726 edition with no accompanying
caption at the beginning of Part 1.

PART 1 – A VOYAGE TO LILLIPUT

CHAPTER 1

*(The author gives some account of himself and family; his
first inducements to travel. He is shipwrecked and
swims for his life; gets safe on shore in the country of
Lilliput; is made a prisoner and carried up the
country.)*

My father had a small estate in Nottinghamshire; I
was the third of five sons. He sent me to Emmanuel College in Cambridge at fourteen years old, where

I resided three years and applied myself close to my
studies; but the charge of maintaining me, although I
had a very scanty allowance, being too great for a narrow
fortune, I was bound apprentice to Mr. James Bates, an
eminent surgeon in London, with whom I continued
four years. And my father now and then sending me
small sums of money, I laid them out in learning
navigation and other parts of the mathematics useful to
those who intend to travel, as I always believed it would
be, some time or other, my fortune to do. When I left
Mr. Bates, I went down to my father, where, by the
assistance of him and my uncle John, and some other
relations, I got forty pounds, and a promise of thirty

pounds a year to maintain me at Leyden.[1] There I studied physic two years and seven months, knowing it would be useful in long voyages.

Soon after my return from Leyden, I was recommended by my good master Mr. Bates to be surgeon to the *Swallow*, Captain Abraham Pannel commander, with whom I continued three years and a half, making a voyage or two into the Levant[2] and some other parts. When I came back I resolved to settle in London, to which Mr. Bates, my master, encouraged me, and by him I was recommended to several patients. I took part of a small house in the Old Jury;[3] and, being advised to alter my condition,[4] I married Mrs.[5] Mary Burton, second daughter to Mr. Edmund Burton, hosier,[6] in Newgate Street, with whom I received four hundred pounds for a portion.[7]

But my good master Bates dying in two years after, and I having few friends, my business began to fail; for my conscience would not suffer me to imitate the bad practice of too many among my brethren. Having therefore consulted with my wife and some of my acquaintance, I determined to go again to sea. I was surgeon successively in two ships, and made several voyages, for six years, to the East and West Indies, by which I got some addition to my fortune. My hours of leisure I spent in reading the best authors, ancient and modern, being always provided with a good number of books; and when I was ashore, in observing the manners and dispositions of the people, as well as learning their language, wherein I had a great facility by the strength of my memory.

The last of these voyages not proving very fortunate, I grew weary of the sea, and intended to stay at home with my wife and family. I removed from the Old Jury to Fetter Lane, and from thence to Wapping, hoping to get business among the sailors; but it would not turn to account.[8] After three years expectation that things would mend, I accepted an advantageous offer from Captain William Prichard, master of the *Antelope*, who was making a voyage to the South Sea. We set sail from Bristol, May 4, 1699, and our voyage at first was very prosperous.

It would not be proper, for some reasons, to trouble the reader with the particulars of our adventures in those seas; let it suffice to inform him that in our passage from thence to the East Indies, we were driven by a violent storm to the north-west of Van Diemen's Land.[9] By an observation, we found ourselves in the latitude of 30 degrees 2 minutes south. Twelve of our crew were dead by immoderate labour and ill food; the rest were in a very weak condition. On the fifth of November, which was the beginning of summer in those parts, the weather being very hazy, the seamen spied a rock within half a cable's length[10] of the ship, but the wind was so strong that we were driven directly upon it, and immediately split. Six of the crew, of whom I was one, having let down the boat into the sea, made a shift to get clear of the ship and the rock. We rowed, by my computation, about three leagues,[11] till we were able to work no longer, being already spent with labour while we were in the ship. We therefore trusted ourselves to the mercy of the waves, and in about half an hour the boat was overset by a sudden flurry from the north. What became of my companions in the boat, as well as of those who escaped on the rock, or were left in the vessel, I cannot tell; but conclude they were all lost. For my own part, I swam as fortune directed me, and was pushed forward by wind and tide. I often let my legs drop, and could feel no bottom; but when I was almost gone, and able to struggle no longer, I found myself within my depth; and by this time the storm was much abated. The declivity was so small that I walked near a mile before I got to the shore, which I conjectured was about eight o'clock in the evening. I then advanced forward near half a mile,

---

[1] *Leyden*   University in Holland noted for the study of medicine ("physic").

[2] *the Levant*   Countries and islands of the eastern Mediterranean.

[3] *Old Jury*   I.e., the "Old Jewry," a street in London inhabited largely by Jewish people before their expulsion in the thirteenth century.

[4] *alter my condition*   I.e., from the single to the married state or "condition."

[5] *Mrs.*   Pronounced "mistress," this title was applied to both married and unmarried women.

[6] *hosier*   One who makes or sells stockings, socks, or men's clothing generally.

[7] *portion*   Dowry.

[8] *turn to account*   Result in profit.

[9] *Van Diemen's Land*   Tasmania.

[10] *cable's length*   600 feet.

[11] *three leagues*   Nine nautical miles.

but could not discover any sign of houses or inhabitants; at least, I was in so weak a condition that I did not observe them. I was extremely tired, and with that, and the heat of the weather, and about half a pint of brandy that I drank as I left the ship, I found myself much inclined to sleep. I lay down on the grass, which was very short and soft, where I slept sounder than ever I remembered to have done in my life, and, as I reckoned, about nine hours; for when I awaked, it was just daylight. I attempted to rise, but was not able to stir: for, as I happened to lie on my back, I found my arms and legs were strongly fastened on each side to the ground; and my hair, which was long and thick, tied down in the same manner. I likewise felt several slender ligatures across my body, from my armpits to my thighs. I could only look upwards; the sun began to grow hot, and the light offended my eyes. I heard a confused noise about me, but in the posture I lay, could see nothing except the sky. In a little time I felt something alive moving on my left leg, which advancing gently forward over my breast, came almost up to my chin; when, bending my eyes downwards as much as I could, I perceived it to be a human creature not six inches high,[1] with a bow and arrow in his hands and a quiver at his back. In the mean time, I felt at least forty more of the same kind (as I conjectured) following the first. I was in the utmost astonishment, and roared so loud that they all ran back in a fright; and some of them, as I was afterwards told, were hurt with the falls they got by leaping from my sides upon the ground. However, they soon returned, and one of them, who ventured so far as to get a full sight of my face, lifting up his hands and eyes by way of admiration,[2] cried out in a shrill but distinct voice, *Hekinah Degul.* The others repeated the same words several times, but then I knew not what they meant. I lay all this while, as the reader may believe, in great uneasiness. At length, struggling to get loose, I had the fortune to break the strings, and wrench out the pegs that fastened my left arm to the ground; for, by lifting it up to my face, I discovered the methods they had taken to bind me, and at the same time with a violent pull, which gave me excessive pain, I a little loosened the strings that tied down my hair on the left side, so

that I was just able to turn my head about two inches. But the creatures ran off a second time, before I could seize them; whereupon there was a great shout in a very shrill accent, and after it ceased I heard one of them cry aloud, *Tolgo phonac*; when in an instant I felt above a hundred arrows discharged on my left hand, which pricked me like so many needles; and besides they shot another flight into the air, as we do bombs in Europe, whereof many, I suppose, fell on my body (though I felt them not), and some on my face, which I immediately covered with my left hand. When this shower of arrows was over, I fell a groaning with grief and pain; and then striving again to get loose, they discharged another volley larger than the first, and some of them attempted with spears to stick me in the sides; but by good luck I had on a buff jerkin,[3] which they could not pierce. I thought it the most prudent method to lie still, and my design was to continue so till night, when, my left hand being already loose, I could easily free myself. And as for the inhabitants, I had reason to believe I might be a match for the greatest army they could bring against me, if they were all of the same size with him that I saw. But fortune disposed otherwise of me. When the people observed I was quiet, they discharged no more arrows; but by the noise increasing, I knew their numbers were greater; and about four yards from me, over against my right ear, I heard a knocking for above an hour, like that of people at work; when turning my head that way, as well as the pegs and strings would permit me, I saw a stage erected about a foot and a half from the ground, capable of holding four of the inhabitants, with two or three ladders to mount it: from whence one of them, who seemed to be a person of quality, made me a long speech, whereof I understood not one syllable. But I should have mentioned that before the principal person began his oration, he cried out three times, *Langro dehul san* (these words and the former were afterwards repeated and explained to me); whereupon, immediately, about fifty of the inhabitants came and cut the strings that fastened the left side of my head, which gave me the liberty of turning it to the right, and of observing the person and gesture of him that was to speak. He appeared to be of a middle age, and taller than any of the other three who attended him, whereof one was a page that held up his train, and

---

[1] *six inches high*   Everything in Lilliput is about one twelfth of the size it would be in Gulliver's world.

[2] *by way of admiration*   In wonder.

[3] *buff jerkin*   Military jacket made of thick leather.

seemed to be somewhat longer than my middle finger; the other two stood one on each side to support him. He acted every part of an orator, and I could observe many periods[1] of threatenings, and others of promises, pity, and kindness. I answered in a few words, but in the most submissive manner, lifting up my left hand, and both my eyes to the sun, as calling him for a witness; and being almost famished with hunger, having not eaten a morsel for some hours before I left the ship, I found the demands of nature so strong upon me, that I could not forbear showing my impatience (perhaps against the strict rules of decency) by putting my finger frequently to my mouth, to signify that I wanted food. The *Hurgo* (for so they call a great lord, as I afterwards learnt) understood me very well. He descended from the stage and commanded that several ladders should be applied to my sides, on which above a hundred of the inhabitants mounted and walked towards my mouth, laden with baskets full of meat, which had been provided and sent thither by the king's orders, upon the first intelligence he received of me. I observed there was the flesh of several animals, but could not distinguish them by the taste. There were shoulders, legs, and loins, shaped like those of mutton, and very well dressed, but smaller than the wings of a lark. I ate them by two or three at a mouthful, and took three loaves at a time, about the bigness of musket bullets. They supplied me as fast as they could, showing a thousand marks of wonder and astonishment at my bulk and appetite. I then made another sign, that I wanted drink. They found by my eating that a small quantity would not suffice me; and, being a most ingenious people, they slung up, with great dexterity, one of their largest hogsheads,[2] then rolled it towards my hand and beat out the top; I drank it off at a draught, which I might well do, for it did not hold half a pint, and tasted like a small wine[3] of Burgundy, but much more delicious. They brought me a second hogshead, which I drank in the same manner, and made signs for more; but they had none to give me. When I had performed these wonders, they shouted for joy, and danced upon my breast, repeating several times as they

did at first, *Hekinah degul*. They made me a sign that I should throw down the two hogsheads, but first warning the people below to stand out of the way, crying aloud, *Borach mevolah*; and when they saw the vessels in the air, there was a universal shout of *Hekinah degul*. I confess I was often tempted, while they were passing backwards and forwards on my body, to seize forty or fifty of the first that came in my reach, and dash them against the ground. But the remembrance of what I had felt, which probably might not be the worst they could do, and the promise of honour I made them—for so I interpreted my submissive behaviour—soon drove out these imaginations. Besides, I now considered myself as bound, by the laws of hospitality, to a people who had treated me with so much expense and magnificence. However, in my thoughts I could not sufficiently wonder at the intrepidity of these diminutive mortals, who durst venture to mount and walk upon my body, while one of my hands was at liberty, without trembling at the very sight of so prodigious a creature as I must appear to them. After some time, when they observed that I made no more demands for meat, there appeared before me a person of high rank from his Imperial Majesty. His Excellency, having mounted on the small of my right leg, advanced forwards up to my face with about a dozen of his retinue; and producing his credentials under the Signet Royal, which he applied close to my eyes, spoke about ten minutes without any signs of anger, but with a kind of determinate resolution, often pointing forwards, which, as I afterwards found, was towards the capital city, about half a mile distant; whither it was agreed by his Majesty in council that I must be conveyed. I answered in few words, but to no purpose, and made a sign with my hand that was loose, putting it to the other (but over his excellency's head for fear of hurting him or his train) and then to my own head and body, to signify that I desired my liberty. It appeared that he understood me well enough, for he shook his head by way of disapprobation, and held his hand in a posture to show that I must be carried as a prisoner. However, he made other signs to let me understand that I should have meat and drink enough, and very good treatment. Whereupon I once more thought of attempting to break my bonds; but again, when I felt the smart of their arrows upon my face and hands, which were all in blisters, and many of the darts

---

[1] *periods* Sentences.

[2] *hogsheads* Large casks.

[3] *small wine* Wine of low alcoholic content; diluted wine.

still sticking in them, and observing likewise that the number of my enemies increased, I gave tokens to let them know that they might do with me what they pleased. Upon this, the *Hurgo* and his train withdrew with much civility and cheerful countenances. Soon after I heard a general shout, with frequent repetitions of the words, *Peplom selan*, and I felt great numbers of people on my left side relaxing the cords to such a degree that I was able to turn upon my right, and to ease myself with making water;[1] which I very plentifully did, to the great astonishment of the people, who, conjecturing by my motion what I was going to do, immediately opened to the right and left on that side, to avoid the torrent which fell with such noise and violence from me. But before this, they had daubed my face and both my hands with a sort of ointment, very pleasant to the smell, which, in a few minutes, removed all the smart of their arrows. These circumstances, added to the refreshment I had received by their victuals and drink, which were very nourishing, disposed me to sleep. I slept about eight hours, as I was afterwards assured; and it was no wonder, for the physicians, by the Emperor's order, had mingled a sleepy potion in the hogsheads of wine.

It seems that upon the first moment I was discovered sleeping on the ground after my landing, the Emperor had early notice of it by an express;[2] and determined in council, that I should be tied in the manner I have related (which was done in the night while I slept), that plenty of meat and drink should be sent to me, and a machine prepared to carry me to the capital city.

This resolution perhaps may appear very bold and dangerous, and I am confident would not be imitated by any prince in Europe on the like occasion. However, in my opinion, it was extremely prudent as well as generous: for, supposing these people had endeavoured to kill me with their spears and arrows while I was asleep, I should certainly have awaked with the first sense of smart, which might so far have roused my rage and strength as to have enabled me to break the strings wherewith I was tied; after which, as they were not able to make resistance, so they could expect no mercy.

These people are most excellent mathematicians, and arrived to a great perfection in mechanics by the countenance and encouragement of the Emperor, who is a renowned patron of learning. This prince has several machines fixed on wheels, for the carriage of trees and other great weights. He often builds his largest men of war, whereof some are nine feet long, in the woods where the timber grows, and has them carried on these engines[3] three or four hundred yards to the sea. Five hundred carpenters and engineers were immediately set at work to prepare the greatest engine they had. It was a frame of wood raised three inches from the ground, about seven feet long and four wide, moving upon twenty-two wheels. The shout I heard was upon the arrival of this engine, which, it seems, set out in four hours after my landing. It was brought parallel to me as I lay, but the principal difficulty was to raise and place me in this vehicle. Eighty poles, each of one foot high, were erected for this purpose, and very strong cords, of the bigness of packthread,[4] were fastened by hooks to many bandages which the workmen had girt round my neck, my hands, my body, and my legs. Nine hundred of the strongest men were employed to draw up these cords, by many pulleys fastened on the poles; and thus, in less than three hours, I was raised and slung into the engine, and there tied fast. All this I was told; for, while the operation was performing, I lay in a profound sleep, by the force of that soporiferous medicine infused into my liquor. Fifteen hundred of the Emperor's largest horses, each about four inches and a half high, were employed to draw me towards the metropolis, which, as I said, was half a mile distant.

About four hours after we began our journey, I awaked by a very ridiculous accident; for the carriage being stopped a while, to adjust something that was out of order, two or three of the young natives had the curiosity to see how I looked when I was asleep; they climbed up into the engine, and advancing very softly to my face, one of them, an officer in the guards, put the sharp end of his half-pike a good way up into my left nostril, which tickled my nose like a straw and made me sneeze violently; whereupon they stole off unperceived, and it was three weeks before I knew the cause of my waking so suddenly. We made a long march the remaining part of the day, and rested at night with five hundred guards on each side of me, half with torches, and

---

1 *making water* Urinating.

2 *express* Messenger.

3 *engines* Mechanical devices.

4 *packthread* Strong twine.

half with bows and arrows, ready to shoot me if I should offer to stir. The next morning at sunrise we continued our march, and arrived within two hundred yards of the city gates about noon. The Emperor and all his court came out to meet us, but his great officers would by no means suffer His Majesty to endanger his person by mounting on my body.

At the place where the carriage stopped there stood an ancient temple, esteemed to be the largest in the whole kingdom, which, having been polluted some years before by an unnatural murder, was, according to the zeal of those people, looked upon as profane, and therefore had been applied to common use, and all the ornaments and furniture carried away. In this edifice it was determined I should lodge. The great gate fronting to the north was about four feet high and almost two feet wide, through which I could easily creep. On each side of the gate was a small window not above six inches from the ground: into that on the left side, the King's smith conveyed fourscore and eleven chains, like those that hang to a lady's watch in Europe, and almost as large, which were locked to my left leg with six-and-thirty padlocks. Over against this temple, on the other side of the great highway, at twenty feet distance, there was a turret at least five feet high. Here the Emperor ascended, with many principal lords of his court, to have an opportunity of viewing me, as I was told, for I could not see them. It was reckoned that above a hundred thousand inhabitants came out of the town upon the same errand; and, in spite of my guards, I believe there could not be fewer than ten thousand, at several times, who mounted my body by the help of ladders. But a proclamation was soon issued to forbid it upon pain of death. When the workmen found it was impossible for me to break loose, they cut all the strings that bound me; whereupon I rose up, with as melancholy a disposition as ever I had in my life. But the noise and astonishment of the people at seeing me rise and walk are not to be expressed. The chains that held my left leg were about two yards long, and gave me not only the liberty of walking backwards and forwards in a semicircle, but, being fixed within four inches of the gate, allowed me to creep in, and lie at my full length in the temple.

CHAPTER 2

(The Emperor of Lilliput, attended by several of the nobility, comes to see the author in his confinement. The Emperor's person and habit described. Learned men appointed to teach the author their language. He gains favour by his mild disposition. His pockets are searched, and his sword and pistols taken from him.)

When I found myself on my feet, I looked about me, and must confess I never beheld a more entertaining prospect. The country around appeared like a continued garden, and the enclosed fields, which were generally forty feet square, resembled so many beds of flowers. These fields were intermingled with woods of half a stang,[1] and the tallest trees, as I could judge, appeared to be seven feet high. I viewed the town on my left hand, which looked like the painted scene of a city in a theatre.

I had been for some hours extremely pressed by the necessities of nature; which was no wonder, it being almost two days since I had last disburdened myself. I was under great difficulties between urgency and shame. The best expedient I could think on, was to creep into my house, which I accordingly did; and shutting the gate after me, I went as far as the length of my chain would suffer, and discharged my body of that uneasy load. But this was the only time I was ever guilty of so uncleanly an action; for which I cannot but hope the candid reader will give some allowance, after he has maturely and impartially considered my case, and the distress I was in. From this time my constant practice was, as soon as I rose, to perform that business in open air, at the full extent of my chain; and due care was taken every morning, before company came, that the offensive matter should be carried off in wheel-barrows by two servants appointed for that purpose. I would not have dwelt so long upon a circumstance that perhaps, at first sight, may appear not very momentous, if I had not thought it necessary to justify my character in point of cleanliness to the world; which, I am told, some of my maligners have been pleased, upon this and other occasions, to call in question.

When this adventure was at an end, I came back out of my house, having occasion for fresh air. The Emperor

---

[1] *stang* Quarter of an acre.

was already descended from the tower and advancing on horseback towards me, which had like to have cost him dear; for the beast, though very well trained, yet wholly unused to such a sight, which appeared as if a mountain moved before him, reared up on its hinder feet: but that prince, who is an excellent horseman, kept his seat till his attendants ran in and held the bridle, while His Majesty had time to dismount. When he alighted, he surveyed me round with great admiration, but kept beyond the length of my chain. He ordered his cooks and butlers, who were already prepared, to give me victuals and drink, which they pushed forward in a sort of vehicles upon wheels till I could reach them. I took these vehicles and soon emptied them all; twenty of them were filled with meat, and ten with liquor; each of the former afforded me two or three good mouthfuls, and I emptied the liquor of ten vessels, which was contained in earthen vials, into one vehicle, drinking it off at a draught; and so I did with the rest. The Empress, and young princes of the blood, of both sexes, attended by many ladies, sat at some distance in their chairs; but upon the accident that happened to the Emperor's horse, they alighted and came near his person, which I am now going to describe. He is taller by almost the breadth of my nail than any of his court, which alone is enough to strike an awe into the beholders. His features are strong and masculine, with an Austrian lip[1] and arched nose, his complexion olive, his countenance[2] erect, his body and limbs well proportioned, all his motions graceful, and his deportment majestic. He was then past his prime, being twenty-eight years and three quarters old, of which he had reigned about seven in great felicity, and generally victorious. For the better convenience of beholding him, I lay on my side, so that my face was parallel to his, and he stood but three yards off: however, I have had him since many times in my hand, and therefore cannot be deceived in the description. His dress was very plain and simple, and the fashion of it between the Asiatic and the European, but he had on his head a light helmet of gold, adorned with jewels, and a plume on the crest. He held

his sword drawn in his hand to defend himself if I should happen to break loose; it was almost three inches long; the hilt and scabbard were gold enriched with diamonds. His voice was shrill, but very clear and articulate, and I could distinctly hear it when I stood up. The ladies and courtiers were all most magnificently clad, so that the spot they stood upon seemed to resemble a petticoat spread upon the ground, embroidered with figures of gold and silver. His Imperial Majesty spoke often to me, and I returned answers: but neither of us could understand a syllable. There were several of his priests and lawyers present (as I conjectured by their habits) who were commanded to address themselves to me; and I spoke to them in as many languages as I had the least smattering of, which were High and Low Dutch,[3] Latin, French, Spanish, Italian, and Lingua Franca,[4] but all to no purpose. After about two hours the court retired, and I was left with a strong guard to prevent the impertinence, and probably the malice, of the rabble, who were very impatient to crowd about me as near as they durst; and some of them had the impudence to shoot their arrows at me as I sat on the ground by the door of my house, whereof one very narrowly missed my left eye. But the colonel ordered six of the ringleaders to be seized, and thought no punishment so proper as to deliver them bound into my hands, which some of his soldiers accordingly did, pushing them forward with the butt-ends of their pikes into my reach. I took them all in my right hand, put five of them into my coat-pocket; and as to the sixth, I made a countenance as if I would eat him alive. The poor man squalled terribly, and the colonel and his officers were in much pain, especially when they saw me take out my penknife: but I soon put them out of fear; for, looking mildly, and immediately cutting the strings he was bound with, I set him gently on the ground, and away he ran. I treated the rest in the same manner, taking them one by one out of my pocket, and I observed both the soldiers and people were highly delighted at this mark of my clemency, which was represented very much to my advantage at court.

---

1. *Austrian lip*   A thick lower lip. This and the arched nose were features that were characteristic of Austria's Hapsburg family. The entire description of the Emperor may be a satiric representation of King George, who was stocky and ungainly.

2. *countenance*   Bearing.

3. *High and Low Dutch*   German and Dutch.

4. *Lingua Franca*   A mixed jargon, based primarily on Italian but containing elements of many Romance languages, used primarily by traders in the eastern Mediterranean.

Towards night I got with some difficulty into my house, where I lay on the ground, and continued to do so about a fortnight; during which time the Emperor gave orders to have a bed prepared for me. Six hundred beds of the common measure were brought in carriages and worked up in my house; a hundred and fifty of their beds, sewn together, made up the breadth and length, and these were four double, which, however, kept me but very indifferently from the hardness of the floor, that was of smooth stone. By the same computation they provided me with sheets, blankets, and coverlets, tolerable enough for one who had been so long inured to hardships as I.

As the news of my arrival spread through the kingdom, it brought prodigious numbers of rich, idle, and curious people to see me; so that the villages were almost emptied, and great neglect of tillage and household affairs must have ensued, if His Imperial Majesty had not provided, by several proclamations and orders of state, against this inconveniency. He directed that those who had already beheld me should return home, and not presume to come within fifty yards of my house without license from the court; whereby the secretaries of state got considerable fees.

In the meantime the Emperor held frequent councils to debate what course should be taken with me; and I was afterwards assured by a particular friend, a person of great quality, who was as much in the secret as any, that the court was under many difficulties concerning me. They apprehended[1] my breaking loose; that my diet would be very expensive, and might cause a famine. Sometimes they determined to starve me, or at least to shoot me in the face and hands with poisoned arrows, which would soon dispatch me; but again they considered that the stench of so large a carcass might produce a plague in the metropolis, and probably spread through the whole kingdom. In the midst of these consultations, several officers of the army went to the door of the great council-chamber, and two of them, being admitted, gave an account of my behaviour to the six criminals above-mentioned; which made so favourable an impression in the breast of His Majesty and the whole board in my behalf that an imperial commission was issued out, obliging all the villages nine hundred yards round the city to deliver in every morning six beeves,[2] forty sheep, and other victuals for my sustenance, together with a proportionable quantity of bread, and wine, and other liquors; for the due payment of which His Majesty gave assignments[3] upon his treasury; for this prince lives chiefly upon his own demesnes; seldom, except upon great occasions, raising any subsidies upon his subjects, who are bound to attend him in his wars at their own expense. An establishment was also made of six hundred persons to be my domestics, who had board-wages allowed for their maintenance, and tents built for them very conveniently on each side of my door. It was likewise ordered that three hundred tailors should make me a suit of clothes, after the fashion of the country; that six of His Majesty's greatest scholars should be employed to instruct me in their language; and lastly, that the Emperor's horses, and those of the nobility and troops of guards, should be frequently exercised in my sight, to accustom themselves to me. All these orders were duly put in execution, and in about three weeks I made a great progress in learning their language, during which time the Emperor frequently honoured me with his visits, and was pleased to assist my masters in teaching me. We began already to converse together in some sort; and the first words I learnt were to express my desire that he would please give me my liberty; which I every day repeated on my knees. His answer, as I could comprehend it, was that this must be a work of time, not to be thought on without the advice of his council, and that first I must *lumos kelmin peso desmar lon emposo*; that is, swear a peace with him and his kingdom; however, that I should be used with all kindness. And he advised me to acquire, by my patience and discreet behaviour, the good opinion of himself and his subjects. He desired I would not take it ill if he gave orders to certain proper officers to search me; for probably I might carry about me several weapons, which must needs be dangerous things, if they answered the bulk of so prodigious a person. I said His Majesty should be satisfied, for I was ready to strip myself, and turn up my pockets before him. This I delivered part in words and part in signs. He replied that by the laws of the kingdom I must be searched by two of his officers; that he knew this could not be done without my con-

---

[1]   *apprehended*   Feared; were apprehensive of.

[2]   *beeves*   Oxen.

[3]   *assignments*   Legal documents transferring funds or property.

sent and assistance; and he had so good an opinion of my generosity and justice as to trust their persons in my hands; that whatever they took from me should be returned when I left the country, or paid for at the rate which I would set upon them. I took up the two officers in my hands, put them first into my coat-pockets, and then into every other pocket about me, except my two fobs, and another secret pocket which I had no mind should be searched, wherein I had some little necessaries that were of no consequence to any but myself. In one of my fobs[1] there was a silver watch, and in the other a small quantity of gold in a purse. These gentlemen, having pen, ink, and paper about them, made an exact inventory of everything they saw; and when they had done, desired I would set them down, that they might deliver it to the Emperor. This inventory I afterwards translated into English, and is, word for word, as follows.

Imprimis,[2] in the right coat-pocket of the great Man-Mountain (for so I interpret the words *Quinbus Flestrin*), after the strictest search, we found only one great piece of coarse cloth, large enough to be a foot-cloth for Your Majesty's chief room of state. In the left pocket we saw a huge silver chest, with a cover of the same metal, which we, the searchers, were not able to lift. We desired it should be opened, and one of us, stepping into it, found himself up to the mid leg in a sort of dust, some part whereof flying up to our faces, set us both a sneezing for several times together. In his right waistcoat-pocket we found a prodigious bundle of white thin substances, folded one over another, about the bigness of three men, tied with a strong cable and marked with black figures; which we humbly conceive to be writings, every letter almost half as large as the palm of our hands. In the left there was a sort of engine, from the back of which were extended twenty long poles, resembling the palisades before Your Majesty's court; wherewith we conjecture the Man-Mountain combs his head; for we did not always trouble him with questions because we found it a great difficulty to make him understand us. In the large pocket on the right side of his middle cover (so I translate the word *ranfulo*, by which they meant my breeches) we saw a hollow pillar of iron, about the length of a man, fastened to a strong piece of timber larger than the pillar; and upon one side of the pillar were huge pieces of iron sticking out, cut into strange figures, which we know not what to make of. In the left pocket, another engine of the same kind. In the smaller pocket on the right side were several round flat pieces of white and red metal, of different bulk; some of the white, which seemed to be silver, were so large and heavy that my comrade and I could hardly lift them. In the left pocket were two black pillars irregularly shaped: we could not, without difficulty, reach the top of them as we stood at the bottom of his pocket. One of them was covered, and seemed all of a piece, but at the upper end of the other there appeared a white round substance, about twice the bigness of our heads. Within each of these was enclosed a prodigious plate of steel; which, by our orders, we obliged him to show us, because we apprehended they might be dangerous engines. He took them out of their cases and told us that in his own country his practice was to shave his beard with one of these, and cut his meat with the other. There were two pockets which we could not enter: these he called his fobs; they were two large slits cut into the top of his middle cover, but squeezed close by the pressure of his belly. Out of the right fob hung a great silver chain with a wonderful kind of engine at the bottom. We directed him to draw out whatever was at the end of that chain, which appeared to be a globe, half silver, and half of some transparent metal; for, on the transparent side, we saw certain strange figures circularly drawn, and thought we could touch them, till we found our fingers stopped by the lucid substance. He put this engine into our ears, which made an incessant noise like that of a water-mill, and we conjecture it is either some unknown animal, or the god that he worships; but we are more inclined to the latter opinion because he assured us (if we understood him right, for he expressed himself very imperfectly) that he seldom did any thing without consulting it. He called it his oracle and said it pointed out the time for every action of his life. From the left fob he took out a net almost large enough for a fisherman, but contrived to open and shut like a purse, and served him for the same use: we found therein several massy pieces of yellow metal, which, if they be real gold, must be of immense value.

---

[1] *fobs* Small pockets in the waistband of pants, used for carrying valuables.

[2] *Imprimis* Latin: In the first place.

Having thus, in obedience to Your Majesty's commands, diligently searched all his pockets, we observed a girdle about his waist made of the hide of some prodigious animal, from which, on the left side, hung a sword of the length of five men; and on the right, a bag or pouch divided into two cells, each cell capable of holding three of Your Majesty's subjects. In one of these cells were several globes, or balls, of a most ponderous metal, about the bigness of our heads, and requiring a strong hand to lift them. The other cell contained a heap of certain black grains, but of no great bulk or weight, for we could hold above fifty of them in the palms of our hands.

This is an exact inventory of what we found about the body of the Man-Mountain, who used us with great civility and due respect to Your Majesty's commission. Signed and sealed on the fourth day of the eighty-ninth moon of your Majesty's auspicious reign.

CLEFREN FRELOCK, MARSI FRELOCK

When this inventory was read over to the Emperor, he directed me, although in very gentle terms, to deliver up the several particulars. He first called for my scimitar, which I took out, scabbard and all. In the meantime he ordered three thousand of his choicest troops (who then attended him) to surround me at a distance, with their bows and arrows just ready to discharge; but I did not observe it, for mine eyes were wholly fixed upon His Majesty. He then desired me to draw my scimitar, which, although it had got some rust by the sea water, was, in most parts, exceeding bright. I did so, and immediately all the troops gave a shout between terror and surprise; for the sun shone clear, and the reflection dazzled their eyes as I waved the scimitar to and fro in my hand. His Majesty, who is a most magnanimous prince, was less daunted than I could expect; he ordered me to return it into the scabbard and cast it on the ground as gently as I could, about six feet from the end of my chain. The next thing he demanded was one of the hollow iron pillars, by which he meant my pocket pistols. I drew it out and, at his desire, as well as I could, expressed to him the use of it; and charging it only with

powder, which, by the closeness of my pouch, happened to escape wetting in the sea (an inconvenience against which all prudent mariners take special care to provide), I first cautioned the Emperor not to be afraid, and then I let it off in the air. The astonishment here was much greater than at the sight of my scimitar. Hundreds fell down as if they had been struck dead, and even the Emperor, although he stood his ground, could not recover himself for some time. I delivered up both my pistols in the same manner as I had done my scimitar, and then my pouch of powder and bullets, begging him that the former might be kept from fire, for it would kindle with the smallest spark and blow up his imperial palace into the air. I likewise delivered up my watch, which the Emperor was very curious to see, and commanded two of his tallest yeomen of the guards to bear it on a pole upon their shoulders, as draymen[1] in England do a barrel of ale. He was amazed at the continual noise it made and the motion of the minute-hand, which he could easily discern; for their sight is much more acute than ours. He asked the opinions of his learned men about it, which were various and remote, as the reader may well imagine without my repeating; although indeed I could not very perfectly understand them. I then gave up my silver and copper money, my purse with nine large pieces of gold, and some smaller ones; my knife and razor, my comb and silver snuff-box, my handkerchief and journal-book. My scimitar, pistols, and pouch were conveyed in carriages to His Majesty's stores, but the rest of my goods were returned me.

I had, as I before observed, one private pocket which escaped their search, wherein there was a pair of spectacles (which I sometimes use for the weakness of mine eyes), a pocket perspective,[2] and some other little conveniences; which, being of no consequence to the Emperor, I did not think myself bound in honour to discover, and I apprehended they might be lost or spoiled if I ventured them out of my possession.

---

[1] *draymen* At breweries, the workers who transport loads of beer, usually on low carts (or "drays").

[2] *perspective* Telescope.

CHAPTER 3

(*The author diverts the Emperor, and his nobility of both
sexes, in a very uncommon manner. The diversions of
the court of Lilliput described. The author has his
liberty granted him upon certain conditions.*)

My gentleness and good behaviour had gained so far
on the Emperor and his court, and indeed upon
the army and people in general, that I began to conceive
hopes of getting my liberty in a short time. I took all
possible methods to cultivate this favourable disposition.
The natives came, by degrees, to be less apprehensive of
any danger from me. I would sometimes lie down and
let five or six of them dance on my hand, and at last the
boys and girls would venture to come and play at hide-
and-seek in my hair. I had now made a good progress in
understanding and speaking the language. The Emperor
had a mind one day to entertain me with several of the
country shows, wherein they exceed all nations I have
known, both for dexterity and magnificence. I was
diverted with none so much as that of the rope-dancers,
performed upon a slender white thread extended about
two feet and twelve inches from the ground. Upon
which I shall desire liberty, with the reader's patience, to
enlarge a little.

This diversion is only practised by those persons who
are candidates for great employments, and high favour,
at court. They are trained in this art from their youth,
and are not always of noble birth or liberal education. When a great office is vacant, either by death or
disgrace (which often happens), five or six of those
candidates petition the Emperor to entertain His
Majesty and the court with a dance on the rope; and
whoever jumps the highest, without falling, succeeds in
the office. Very often the chief ministers themselves are
commanded to show their skill, and to convince the
Emperor that they have not lost their faculty. Flimnap,[1]
the Treasurer, is allowed to cut a caper on the straight
rope, at least an inch higher than any other lord in the
whole empire. I have seen him do the summerset[2]
several times together, upon a trencher[3] fixed on a rope

which is no thicker than a common packthread in
England. My friend Reldresal, Principal Secretary for
Private Affairs, is, in my opinion (if I am not partial) the
second after the Treasurer. The rest of the great officers
are much upon a par.

These diversions are often attended with fatal
accidents, whereof great numbers are on record. I myself
have seen two or three candidates break a limb. But the
danger is much greater when the ministers themselves
are commanded to show their dexterity; for, by contending to excel themselves and their fellows, they strain
so far that there is hardly one of them who has not
received a fall, and some of them two or three. I was
assured that, a year or two before my arrival, Flimnap
would infallibly have broke his neck if one of the King's
cushions, that accidentally lay on the ground, had not
weakened the force of his fall.[4]

There is likewise another diversion, which is only
shown before the Emperor and Empress, and first
minister, upon particular occasions. The Emperor lays
on the table three fine silken threads[5] of six inches long.
One is blue, the other red, and the third green. These
threads are proposed as prizes for those persons whom
the Emperor has a mind to distinguish by a peculiar
mark of his favour. The ceremony is performed in His
Majesty's great chamber of state, where the candidates
are to undergo a trial of dexterity very different from the
former, and such as I have not observed the least resemblance of in any other country of the new or old
world. The Emperor holds a stick in his hands, both
ends parallel to the horizon, while the candidates
advancing, one by one, sometimes leap over the stick,
sometimes creep under it backward and forward several
times, according as the stick is advanced or depressed. Sometimes the Emperor holds one end of the
stick, and his first minister the other; sometimes the
minister has it entirely to himself. Whoever performs his
part with most agility, and holds out the longest in
leaping and creeping, is rewarded with the blue-col-

---

[1] *Flimnap*   Thought to represent Whig Minister Robert Walpole,
who was notorious for his dexterous political acrobatics.

[2] *summerset*   Somersault.

[3] *trencher*   Flat board or platter.

[4] *Flimnap ... fall*   Walpole fell from power in 1717, but by
cultivating the friendship of the Duchess of Kendal, one of the
King's mistresses, he was restored to the King's favor.

[5] *three fine silken threads*   These blue, red, and green ribbons are the
colors, respectively, of the Order of the Garter, the Order of the
Bath, and the Order of the Thistle. These highly coveted awards
were conferred by the king for loyal service; Walpole was made a
knight of the Garter in 1726.

oured silk; the red is given to the next, and the green to the third, which they all wear girt twice round about the middle; and you see few great persons about this court who are not adorned with one of these girdles.

The horses of the army and those of the royal stables, having been daily led before me, were no longer shy, but would come up to my very feet without starting. The riders would leap them over my hand as I held it on the ground, and one of the Emperor's huntsmen, upon a large courser, took my foot, shoe and all; which was indeed a prodigious leap. I had the good fortune to divert the Emperor one day after a very extraordinary manner. I desired he would order several sticks of two feet high, and the thickness of an ordinary cane, to be brought me; whereupon His Majesty commanded the master of his woods to give directions accordingly, and the next morning six woodmen arrived with as many carriages, drawn by eight horses to each. I took nine of these sticks and, fixing them firmly in the ground in a quadrangular figure, two feet and a half square, I took four other sticks and tied them parallel at each corner, about two feet from the ground. Then I fastened my handkerchief to the nine sticks that stood erect and extended it on all sides, till it was tight as the top of a drum, and the four parallel sticks, rising about five inches higher than the handkerchief, served as ledges on each side. When I had finished my work, I desired the Emperor to let a troop of his best horses, twenty-four in number, come and exercise upon this plain. His Majesty approved of the proposal, and I took them up, one by one, in my hands, ready mounted and armed, with the proper officers to exercise them. As soon as they got into order they divided into two parties, performed mock skirmishes, discharged blunt arrows, drew their swords, fled and pursued, attacked and retired, and in short discovered the best military discipline I ever beheld. The parallel sticks secured them and their horses from falling over the stage; and the Emperor was so much delighted that he ordered this entertainment to be repeated several days, and once was pleased to be lifted up and give the word of command; and with great difficulty persuaded even the Empress herself to let me hold her in her close chair[1] within two yards of the stage, when she was able to take a full view of the whole performance. It was my good fortune that no ill accident happened in these entertainments; only once a fiery horse, that belonged to one of the captains, pawing with his hoof struck a hole in my handkerchief, and his foot slipping, he overthrew his rider and himself; but I immediately relieved them both, and, covering the hole with one hand, I set down the troop with the other, in the same manner as I took them up. The horse that fell was strained in the left shoulder, but the rider got no hurt; and I repaired my handkerchief as well as I could; however, I would not trust to the strength of it anymore in such dangerous enterprises.

About two or three days before I was set at liberty, as I was entertaining the court with this kind of feat, there arrived an express to inform His Majesty that some of his subjects, riding near the place where I was first taken up, had seen a great black substance lying on the ground, very oddly shaped, extending its edges round as wide as His Majesty's bedchamber, and rising up in the middle as high as a man; that it was no living creature, as they at first apprehended, for it lay on the grass without motion, and some of them had walked round it several times; that, by mounting upon each other's shoulders, they had got to the top, which was flat and even, and, stamping upon it, they found that it was hollow within; that they humbly conceived it might be something belonging to the Man-Mountain, and if His Majesty pleased, they would undertake to bring it with only five horses. I presently knew what they meant, and was glad at heart to receive this intelligence. It seems, upon my first reaching the shore after our shipwreck I was in such confusion that, before I came to the place where I went to sleep, my hat, which I had fastened with a string to my head while I was rowing, and had stuck on all the time I was swimming, fell off after I came to land; the string, as I conjecture, breaking by some accident which I never observed, but thought my hat had been lost at sea. I entreated His Imperial Majesty to give orders it might be brought to me as soon as possible, describing to him the use and the nature of it, and the next day the wagoners arrived with it, but not in a very good condition. They had bored two holes in the brim, within an inch and half of the edge, and fastened two hooks in the holes; these hooks were tied by a long cord to the harness, and thus my hat was dragged along for above half an English mile; but, the ground in that country being extremely smooth and level, it received

---

[1] *close chair*   Closed sedan chair, normally carried on poles.

less damage than I expected.

Two days after this adventure, the Emperor, having ordered that part of his army which quarters in and about his metropolis to be in readiness, took a fancy of diverting himself in a very singular manner. He desired I would stand like a colossus,[1] with my legs as far asunder as I conveniently could. He then commanded his general (who was an old experienced leader, and a great patron of mine) to draw up the troops in close order and march them under me; the foot[2] by twenty-four abreast, and the horse by sixteen, with drums beating, colours flying, and pikes advanced. This body consisted of three thousand foot, and a thousand horse. His Majesty gave orders, upon pain of death, that every soldier in his march should observe the strictest decency with regard to my person, which however could not prevent some of the younger officers from turning up their eyes as they passed under me; and, to confess the truth, my breeches were at that time in so ill a condition that they afforded some opportunities for laughter and admiration.

I had sent so many memorials and petitions for my liberty that His Majesty at length mentioned the matter, first in the cabinet and then in a full council, where it was opposed by none except Skyresh Bolgolam,[3] who was pleased, without any provocation, to be my mortal enemy. But it was carried against him by the whole board, and confirmed by the Emperor. That minister was *Galbet*, or Admiral of the Realm, very much in his master's confidence, and a person well versed in affairs, but of a morose and sour complexion. However, he was at length persuaded to comply; but prevailed that the articles and conditions upon which I should be set free, and to which I must swear, should be drawn up by himself. These articles were brought to me by Skyresh

Bolgolam in person, attended by two under-secretaries and several persons of distinction. After they were read, I was demanded to swear to the performance of them, first in the manner of my own country, and afterwards in the method prescribed by their laws; which was to hold my right foot in my left hand, and to place the middle finger of my right hand on the crown of my head, and my thumb on the tip of my right ear. But because the reader may be curious to have some idea of the style and manner of expression peculiar to that people, as well as to know the article upon which I recovered my liberty, I have made a translation of the whole instrument, word for word, as near as I was able, which I here offer to the public.

Golbasto Momarem Evlame Gurdilo Shefin Mully Ully Gue, Most Mighty Emperor of Lilliput, Delight and Terror of the universe, whose dominions extend five thousand *blustrugs* (about twelve miles in circumference) to the extremities of the globe; Monarch of all Monarchs, taller than the sons of men, whose feet press down to the centre, and whose head strikes against the sun; at whose nod the princes of the earth shake their knees; pleasant as the spring, comfortable as the summer, fruitful as autumn, dreadful as winter. His Most Sublime Majesty proposes to the Man-Mountain, lately arrived at our celestial dominions, the following articles, which by a solemn oath he shall be obliged to perform.

First, the Man-Mountain shall not depart from our dominions without our license under our great seal.

Second, he shall not presume to come into our metropolis without our express order, at which time the inhabitants shall have two hours warning to keep within doors.

Third, the said Man-Mountain shall confine his walks to our principal high roads, and not offer to walk or lie down in a meadow or field of corn.

Fourthly, as he walks the said roads, he shall take the utmost care not to trample upon the bodies of any of our loving subjects, their horses or carriages, nor take any of our subjects into his hands without their own consent.

Fifthly, if an express requires extraordinary dispatch, the Man-Mountain shall be obliged to carry in his pocket the messenger and horse, a six days' journey once in every moon, and return the said messenger back (if so required) safe to our Imperial Presence.

---

[1] *colossus* A larger-than-life statue of a human. The most famous colossus was the bronze statue of Apollo, which was over one hundred feet high and stood astride the harbor of the city of Rhodes. It was one of the seven ancient wonders of the world; an earthquake destroyed it in 224 BCE.

[2] *foot* Foot soldiers.

[3] *Skyresh Bolgolam* Possibly the Earl of Nottingham, who was First Lord of the Admiralty from 1681 to 1684. Though Nottingham was himself a Tory, he was an enemy of Swift because he frequently opposed the Earl of Oxford's Tory government. He was nicknamed "Dismal" because of his sour demeanor. See Swift's poem "Toland's Invitation to Dismal."

Sixthly, he shall be our ally against our enemies in the island of Blefuscu, and do his utmost to destroy their fleet, which is now preparing to invade us.

Seventhly, that the said Man-Mountain shall, at his times of leisure, be aiding and assisting to our workmen, in helping to raise certain great stones towards covering the wall of the principal park and other our royal buildings.

Eighthly, that the said Man-Mountain shall, in two moons' time, deliver in an exact survey of the circumference of our dominions by a computation of his own paces round the coast.

Lastly, that, upon his solemn oath to observe all the above articles, the said Man-Mountain shall have a daily allowance of meat and drink sufficient for the support of 1724 of our subjects, with free access to our Royal Person, and other marks of our favour. Given at our palace at Belfaborac the twelfth day of the ninety-first moon of our reign.

I swore and subscribed to these articles with great cheerfulness and content, although some of them were not so honourable as I could have wished, which proceeded wholly from the malice of Skyresh Bolgolam, the High Admiral; whereupon my chains were immediately unlocked, and I was at full liberty. The Emperor himself, in person, did me the honour to be by at the whole ceremony. I made my acknowledgements by prostrating myself at His Majesty's feet, but he commanded me to rise, and after many gracious expressions, which, to avoid the censure of vanity, I shall not repeat, he added that he hoped I should prove a useful servant, and well deserve all the favours he had already conferred upon me, or might do for the future.

The reader may please to observe that in the last article of the recovery of my liberty, the Emperor stipulates to allow me a quantity of meat and drink sufficient for the support of 1724 Lilliputians. Some time after, asking a friend at court how they came to fix on that determinate number, he told me that His Majesty's mathematicians, having taken the height of my body by the help of a quadrant, and finding it to exceed theirs in the proportion of twelve to one, they concluded from the similarity of their bodies that mine must contain at least 1724 of theirs, and consequently would require as much food as was necessary to support that number of Lilliputians—by which the reader may

conceive an idea of the ingenuity of that people, as well as the prudent and exact economy of so great a prince.

CHAPTER 4

(*Mildendo, the metropolis of Lilliput, described, together with the Emperor's palace. A conversation between the author and a principal secretary, concerning the affairs of that empire. The author's offers to serve the Emperor in his wars.*)

The first request I made after I had obtained my liberty was that I might have license to see Mildendo, the metropolis; which the Emperor easily granted me, but with a special charge to do no hurt either to the inhabitants or their houses. The people had notice by proclamation of my design to visit the town. The wall which encompassed it is two feet and a half high, and at least eleven inches broad, so that a coach and horses may be driven very safely round it, and it is flanked with strong towers at ten feet distance. I stepped over the great western gate and passed very gently, and sidling,[1] through the two principal streets, only in my short waistcoat, for fear of damaging the roofs and eaves of the houses with the skirts of my coat. I walked with the utmost circumspection, to avoid treading on any stragglers who might remain in the streets, although the orders were very strict that all people should keep in their houses, at their own peril. The garret windows and tops of houses were so crowded with spectators that I thought in all my travels I had not seen a more populous place. The city is an exact square, each side of the wall being five hundred feet long. The two great streets, which run across and divide it into four quarters, are five feet wide. The lanes and alleys, which I could not enter, but only view them as I passed, are from twelve to eighteen inches. The town is capable of holding five hundred thousand souls. The houses are from three to five stories; the shops and markets well provided.

The Emperor's palace is in the centre of the city where the two great streets meet. It is enclosed by a wall of two feet high and twenty feet distance from the buildings. I had His Majesty's permission to step over this wall, and, the space being so wide between that and

---

[1] *sidling* Moving sideways.

the palace, I could easily view it on every side. The outward court is a square of forty feet, and includes two other courts: in the inmost are the royal apartments, which I was very desirous to see, but found it extremely difficult; for the great gates, from one square into another, were but eighteen inches high and seven inches wide. Now the buildings of the outer court were at least five feet high, and it was impossible for me to stride over them without infinite damage to the pile,[1] though the walls were strongly built of hewn stone, and four inches thick. At the same time the Emperor had a great desire that I should see the magnificence of his palace, but this I was not able to do till three days after, which I spent in cutting down with my knife some of the largest trees in the royal park, about a hundred yards distant from the city. Of these trees I made two stools, each about three feet high, and strong enough to bear my weight. The people having received notice a second time, I went again through the city to the palace with my two stools in my hands. When I came to the side of the outer court, I stood upon one stool and took the other in my hand; this I lifted over the roof, and gently set it down on the space between the first and second court, which was eight feet wide. I then stepped over the building very conveniently from one stool to the other, and drew up the first after me with a hooked stick. By this contrivance I got into the inmost court, and, lying down upon my side, I applied my face to the windows of the middle stories, which were left open on purpose, and discovered the most splendid apartments that can be imagined. There I saw the Empress and the young princes in their several lodgings, with their chief attendants about them. Her Imperial Majesty was pleased to smile very graciously upon me, and gave me out of the window her hand to kiss.

But I shall not anticipate the reader with further descriptions of this kind, because I reserve them for a greater work, which is now almost ready for the press, containing a general description of this empire from its first erection through a long series of princes, with a particular account of their wars and politics, laws, learning, and religion; their plants and animals; their peculiar manners and customs, with other matters very curious and useful; my chief design at present being only to relate such events and transactions as happened to the public or to myself during a residence of about nine months in that empire.

One morning, about a fortnight after I had obtained my liberty, Reldresal, Principal Secretary (as they style him) of Private Affairs, came to my house attended only by one servant. He ordered his coach to wait at a distance, and desired I would give him an hour's audience, which I readily consented to on account of his quality and personal merits, as well as of the many good offices he had done me during my solicitations at court. I offered to lie down that he might the more conveniently reach my ear, but he chose rather to let me hold him in my hand during our conversation. He began with compliments on my liberty; said he might pretend to some merit in it; but, however, added that if it had not been for the present situation of things at court, perhaps I might not have obtained it so soon. For, said he, as flourishing a condition as we may appear to be in to foreigners, we labour under two mighty evils: a violent faction at home, and the danger of an invasion by a most potent enemy from abroad. As to the first, you are to understand that for about seventy moons past there have been two struggling parties in this empire, under the names of *Tramecksan* and *Slamecksan*,[2] from the high and low heels of their shoes, by which they distinguish themselves. It is alleged, indeed, that the high heels are most agreeable to our ancient constitution; but, however this be, His Majesty has determined to make use only of low heels in the administration of the government, and all offices in the gift of the crown, as you cannot but observe; and particularly that his Majesty's imperial heels are lower at least by a *drurr* than any of his court (*drurr* is a measure about the fourteenth part of an inch). The animosities between these two parties run so high that they will neither eat, nor drink, nor talk with each other. We compute the *Tramecksan*, or high heels, to exceed us in number, but the power is wholly on our side. We apprehend His Imperial High-

---

[1]   *pile*   Edifice.

[2]   *Tramecksan and Slamecksan*   Tory and Whig. Though both parties were Anglican, the Tories were the High Church party (which retained many elements of the Roman Catholic Church), while the Whigs were Low Church (which did not). George I and his ministry were Whigs, but in the last years of Queen Anne's reign a Tory ministry had ruled.

ness,[1] the heir to the crown, to have some tendency towards the high heels; at least, we can plainly discover that one of his heels is higher than the other, which gives him a hobble in his gait. Now, in the midst of these intestine disquiets, we are threatened with an invasion from the island of Blefuscu,[2] which is the other great empire of the universe, almost as large and powerful as this of His Majesty. For as to what we have heard you affirm, that there are other kingdoms and states in the world inhabited by human creatures as large as yourself, our philosophers[3] are in much doubt, and would rather conjecture that you dropped from the moon, or one of the stars, because it is certain that a hundred mortals of your bulk would in a short time destroy all the fruits and cattle of His Majesty's dominions. Besides, our histories of six thousand moons make no mention of any other regions than the two great empires of Lilliput and Blefuscu. Which two mighty powers have, as I was going to tell you, been engaged in a most obstinate war for six-and-thirty moons past. It began upon the following occasion. It is allowed on all hands that the primitive way of breaking eggs before we eat them was upon the larger end; but His present Majesty's grandfather, while he was a boy, going to eat an egg, and breaking it according to the ancient practice, happened to cut one of his fingers. Whereupon the Emperor his father published an edict commanding all his subjects, upon great penalties, to break the smaller end of their eggs. The people so highly resented this law that our histories tell us there have been six rebellions raised on that account; wherein one Emperor lost his life, and another his crown.[4] These civil commotions were constantly fomented by the monarchs of Blefuscu; and when they were quelled, the exiles always fled for refuge to that empire. It is computed that eleven thousand persons have at several times suffered death rather than submit to break their eggs at the smaller end. Many hundred large volumes have been published upon this controversy, but the books of the Big-Endians have been long forbidden, and the whole party rendered incapable by law of holding employments.[5] During the course of these troubles, the emperors of Blefuscu did frequently expostulate by their ambassadors, accusing us of making a schism in religion by offending against a fundamental doctrine of our great prophet Lustrog, in the fifty-fourth chapter of the *Blundecral* (which is their Alcoran). This, however, is thought to be a mere strain upon the text; for the words are these: "that all true believers break their eggs at the convenient end." And which is the convenient end, seems, in my humble opinion, to be left to every man's conscience, or at least in the power of the chief magistrate to determine. Now, the Big-Endian exiles have found so much credit in the Emperor of Blefuscu's court, and so much private assistance and encouragement from their party here at home, that a bloody war has been carried on between the two empires for six-and-thirty moons, with various success; during which time we have lost forty capital ships and a much greater number of smaller vessels, together with thirty thousand of our best seamen and soldiers; and the damage received by the enemy is reckoned to be somewhat greater than ours. However, they have now equipped a numerous fleet, and are just preparing to make a descent upon us; and His Imperial Majesty, placing great confidence in your valour and strength, has commanded me to lay this account of his affairs before you.

I desired the Secretary to present my humble duty to the Emperor, and to let him know that I thought it would not become me, who was a foreigner, to interfere with parties, but I was ready, with the hazard of my life, to defend his person and state against all invaders.

CHAPTER 5

(*The author, by an extraordinary stratagem, prevents an invasion. A high title of honour is conferred upon him. Ambassadors arrive from the Emperor of Blefuscu and sue for peace. The Empress's apartment on fire by an accident; the author instrumental in saving the rest of the palace.*)

---

1 *His Imperial Highness*   The Prince of Wales, later King George II. Though he seemed to have Tory leanings, as King he allowed the Whigs to retain power.

2 *Blefuscu*   France.

3 *philosophers*   Scientists.

4 *It began … his crown*   This is an allegorical description of the struggle between Catholics (Big-Endians) and Protestants (Little-Endians), beginning with Henry VIII, who broke with the Catholic Church. This struggle was a factor in the civil strife that saw Charles I beheaded and James II deposed.

5 *whole party … employments*   Catholics were prevented by the Test Acts of 1673 from holding office.

The empire of Blefuscu is an island situated to the north-east of Lilliput, from which it is parted only by a channel of eight hundred yards wide. I had not yet seen it, and upon this notice of an intended invasion, I avoided appearing on that side of the coast, for fear of being discovered by some of the enemy's ships, who had received no intelligence of me, all intercourse between the two empires having been strictly forbidden during the war, upon pain of death, and an embargo laid by our Emperor upon all vessels whatsoever. I communicated to His Majesty a project I had formed of seizing the enemy's whole fleet, which, as our scouts assured us, lay at anchor in the harbour, ready to sail with the first fair wind. I consulted the most experienced seamen upon the depth of the channel, which they had often plumbed; who told me that in the middle, at high-water, it was seventy *glumgluffs* deep, which is about six feet of European measure; and the rest of it fifty *glum-gluffs* at most. I walked towards the north-east coast over against Blefuscu, where, lying down behind a hillock, I took out my small perspective glass and viewed the enemy's fleet at anchor, consisting of about fifty men of war and a great number of transports. I then came back to my house and gave orders (for which I had a warrant) for a great quantity of the strongest cable and bars of iron. The cable was about as thick as packthread and the bars of the length and size of a knitting-needle. I trebled the cable to make it stronger, and for the same reason I twisted three of the iron bars together, bending the extremities into a hook. Having thus fixed fifty hooks to as many cables, I went back to the north-east coast and, putting off my coat, shoes, and stockings, walked into the sea in my leather jerkin, about half an hour before high water. I waded with what haste I could, and swam in the middle about thirty yards till I felt ground. I arrived at the fleet in less than half an hour. The enemy was so frightened when they saw me that they leaped out of their ships and swam to shore, where there could not be fewer than thirty thousand souls. I then took my tackling and, fastening a hook to the hole at the prow of each, I tied all the cords together at the end. While I was thus employed, the enemy discharged several thousand arrows, many of which stuck in my hands and face, and, beside the excessive smart, gave me much disturbance in my work. My greatest apprehension was for mine eyes, which I should have infallibly lost if I had not suddenly thought of an expedient. I kept, among other little necessaries, a pair of spectacles in a private pocket, which, as I observed before, had escaped the Emperor's searchers. These I took out and fastened as strongly as I could upon my nose, and thus armed, went on boldly with my work in spite of the enemy's arrows, many of which struck against the glasses of my spectacles, but without any other effect further than a little to discompose them. I had now fastened all the hooks, and, taking the knot in my hand, began to pull; but not a ship would stir, for they were all too fast held by their anchors, so that the boldest part of my enterprise remained. I therefore let go the cord and, leaving the hooks fixed to the ships, I resolutely cut with my knife the cables that fastened the anchors, receiving about two hundred shots in my face and hands. Then I took up the knotted end of the cables, to which my hooks were tied, and with great ease drew fifty of the enemy's largest men of war after me.

The Blefuscudians, who had not the least imagination of what I intended, were at first confounded with astonishment. They had seen me cut the cables, and thought my design was only to let the ships run adrift or fall foul on each other; but when they perceived the whole fleet moving in order, and saw me pulling at the end, they set up such a scream of grief and despair as it is almost impossible to describe or conceive. When I had got out of danger, I stopped awhile to pick out the arrows that stuck in my hands and face, and rubbed on some of the same ointment that was given me at my first arrival, as I have formerly mentioned. I then took off my spectacles, and, waiting about an hour till the tide was a little fallen, I waded through the middle with my cargo and arrived safe at the royal port of Lilliput.

The Emperor and his whole court stood on the shore, expecting the issue of this great adventure. They saw the ships move forward in a large half-moon, but could not discern me, who was up to my breast in water. When I advanced to the middle of the channel they were yet more in pain because I was under water to my neck. The Emperor concluded me to be drowned, and that the enemy's fleet was approaching in a hostile manner. But he was soon eased of his fears; for the channel growing shallower every step I made, I came in a short time within hearing, and, holding up the end of the cable by which the fleet was fastened, I cried in a loud voice, "Long live the most puissant king of Lilliput!" This great prince received me at my landing with all possible encomiums,[1] and created me a *Nardac* upon the spot, which is the highest title of honour among them.

His Majesty desired I would take some other opportunity of bringing all the rest of his enemy's ships into his ports. And so unmeasureable is the ambition of princes that he seemed to think of nothing less than reducing the whole empire of Blefuscu into a province, and governing it, by a viceroy; of destroying the Big-Endian exiles and compelling that people to break the smaller end of their eggs, by which he would remain the sole monarch of the whole world. But I endeavoured to divert him from this design by many arguments drawn from the topics of policy as well as justice; and I plainly protested that I would never be an instrument of bringing a free and brave people into slavery. And, when the matter was debated in council, the wisest part of the ministry were of my opinion.

This open bold declaration of mine was so opposite to the schemes and politics of His Imperial Majesty that he could never forgive me. He mentioned it in a very artful manner at council, where I was told that some of the wisest appeared, at least by their silence, to be of my opinion; but others, who were my secret enemies, could not forbear some expressions which by a side-wind[2] reflected on me. And from this time began an intrigue between His Majesty and a junto[3] of ministers maliciously bent against me, which broke out in less than two months, and had like to have ended in my utter destruction. Of so little weight are the greatest services to princes, when put into the balance with a refusal to gratify their passions.

About three weeks after this exploit there arrived a solemn embassy from Blefuscu with humble offers of a peace, which was soon concluded upon conditions very advantageous to our Emperor, wherewith I shall not trouble the reader. There were six ambassadors with a train of about five hundred persons, and their entry was very magnificent, suitable to the grandeur of their master and the importance of their business. When their treaty[4] was finished, wherein I did them several good offices by the credit I now had, or at least appeared to have, at court, their Excellencies, who were privately told how much I had been their friend, made me a visit in form.[5] They began with many compliments upon my valour and generosity, invited me to that kingdom in the Emperor their master's name, and desired me to show them some proofs of my prodigious strength, of which they had heard so many wonders; wherein I readily obliged them, but shall not trouble the reader with the particulars.

When I had for some time entertained Their Excellencies to their infinite satisfaction and surprise, I desired they would do me the honour to present my most humble respects to the Emperor their master, the renown of whose virtues had so justly filled the whole world with admiration, and whose royal person I resolved to attend, before I returned to my own country. Accordingly, the next time I had the honour to see our Emperor, I desired his general license to wait on the Blefuscudian monarch, which he was pleased to grant me, as I could perceive, in a very cold manner; but could not guess the reason till I had a whisper from a certain person that Flimnap and Bolgolam had represented my intercourse with those ambassadors as a mark of disaffection, from which I am sure my heart was wholly free. And this was the first time I began to conceive some imperfect idea of courts and ministers.

It is to be observed that these ambassadors spoke to me by an interpreter, the languages of both empires differing as much from each other as any two in Europe, and each nation priding itself upon the antiquity, beauty, and energy of their own tongue, with an avowed contempt for that of their neighbour. Yet our Emperor, standing upon the advantage he had got by the seizure of their fleet, obliged them to deliver their credentials, and make their speech, in the Lilliputian tongue. And it must be confessed that from the great intercourse of trade and commerce between both realms, from the continual reception of exiles which is mutual among them, and from the custom, in each empire, to send

---

[1] *encomiums* Panegyrics; expressions of praise.

[2] *by a side-wind* Indirectly.

[3] *junto* Political body; faction.

[4] *treaty* The Treaty of Utrecht, negotiated by Tory ministers, ended England's war with France in 1713. These same ministers, including Bolingbroke and Oxford, were later accused of weakness by the Whigs and driven from public life.

[5] *visit in form* Formal diplomatic visit.

their young nobility and richer gentry to the other, in order to polish themselves by seeing the world and understanding men and manners, there are few persons of distinction, or merchants, or seamen, who dwell in the maritime parts, but what can hold conversation in both tongues; as I found some weeks after, when I went to pay my respects to the Emperor of Blefuscu, which, in the midst of great misfortunes, through the malice of my enemies, proved a very happy adventure to me, as I shall relate in its proper place.

The reader may remember that when I signed those articles upon which I recovered my liberty, there were some which I disliked upon account of their being too servile; neither could anything but an extreme necessity have forced me to submit. But being now a *Nardac* of the highest rank in that empire, such offices were looked upon as below my dignity, and the Emperor (to do him justice) never once mentioned them to me. However, it was not long before I had an opportunity of doing His Majesty, at least as I then thought, a most signal[1] service. I was alarmed at midnight with the cries of many hundred people at my door; by which, being suddenly awaked, I was in some kind of terror. I heard the word *Burglum* repeated incessantly; several of the Emperor's court, making their way through the crowd, entreated me to come immediately to the palace, where Her Imperial Majesty's apartment was on fire, by the carelessness of a maid of honour, who fell asleep while she was reading a romance. I got up in an instant; and orders being given to clear the way before me, and it being likewise a moonshine night, I made a shift to get to the palace without trampling on any of the people. I found they had already applied ladders to the walls of the apartment, and were well provided with buckets, but the water was at some distance. These buckets were about the size of large thimbles, and the poor people supplied me with them as fast as they could, but the flame was so violent that they did little good. I might easily have stifled it with my coat, which I unfortunately left behind me for haste, and came away only in my leather jerkin. The case seemed wholly desperate and deplorable; and this magnificent palace would have infallibly been burnt down to the ground, if, by a presence of mind unusual to me, I had not suddenly thought of an expedient. I had the evening before drunk plentifully of a most delicious wine called *glimigrim* (the Blefuscudians call it *flunec*, but ours is esteemed the better sort), which is very diuretic. By the luckiest chance in the world, I had not discharged myself of any part of it. The heat I had contracted by coming very near the flames, and by labouring to quench them, made the wine begin to operate by urine, which I voided in such a quantity, and applied so well to the proper places, that in three minutes the fire was wholly extinguished, and the rest of that noble pile, which had cost so many ages in erecting, preserved from destruction.

It was now daylight, and I returned to my house without waiting to congratulate with the Emperor because, although I had done a very eminent piece of service, yet I could not tell how His Majesty might resent the manner by which I had performed it: for, by the fundamental laws of the realm, it is capital[2] in any person, of what quality soever, to make water within the precincts of the palace. But I was a little comforted by a message from His Majesty that he would give orders to the Grand Justiciary for passing my pardon in form; which, however, I could not obtain. And I was privately assured that the Empress,[3] conceiving the greatest abhorrence of what I had done, removed to the most distant side of the court, firmly resolved that those buildings should never be repaired for her use; and, in the presence of her chief confidents, could not forbear vowing revenge.

CHAPTER 6

(*Of the inhabitants of Lilliput; their learning, laws, and customs; the manner of educating their children. The author's way of living in that country. His vindication of a great lady.*)

Although I intend to leave the description of this empire to a particular treatise, yet in the meantime I am content to gratify the curious reader with some general ideas. As the common size of the natives is somewhat under six inches high, so there is an exact

---

[1] *signal* Notable.

[2] *capital* A capital crime, punishable by death.

[3] *the Empress* Here a reference to Queen Anne, who was supposedly so offended by the coarseness of Swift's work *A Tale of a Tub* that she refused to grant him a bishopric.

proportion in all other animals, as well as plants and trees. For instance, the tallest horses and oxen are between four and five inches in height; the sheep an inch and half, more or less; their geese about the bigness of a sparrow; and so the several gradations downwards till you come to the smallest, which to my sight were almost invisible. But nature has adapted the eyes of the Lilliputians to all objects proper for their view; they see with great exactness, but at no great distance. And, to show the sharpness of their sight towards objects that are near, I have been much pleased with observing a cook pulling[1] a lark, which was not so large as a common fly, and a young girl threading an invisible needle with invisible silk. Their tallest trees are about seven feet high—I mean some of those in the great royal park, the tops whereof I could but just reach with my fist clenched. The other vegetables are in the same proportion, but this I leave to the reader's imagination.

I shall say but little at present of their learning, which for many ages has flourished in all its branches among them: but their manner of writing is very peculiar, being neither from the left to the right, like the Europeans; nor from the right to the left, like the Arabians; nor from up to down, like the Chinese; nor from down to up, like the Cascagians;[2] but aslant, from one corner of the paper to the other, like ladies in England.

They bury their dead with their heads directly downward because they hold an opinion that in eleven thousand moons they are all to rise again; in which period the earth (which they conceive to be flat) will turn upside down, and by this means they shall, at their resurrection, be found ready standing on their feet. The learned among them confess the absurdity of this doctrine, but the practice still continues, in compliance to the vulgar.

There are some laws and customs in this empire very peculiar; and if they were not so directly contrary to those of my own dear country, I should be tempted to say a little in their justification. It is only to be wished they were as well executed. The first I shall mention relates to informers. All crimes against the state are punished here with the utmost severity; but, if the person accused makes his innocence plainly to appear

upon his trial, the accuser is immediately put to an ignominious death; and out of his goods or lands the innocent person is quadruply recompensed for the loss of his time, for the danger he underwent, for the hardship of his imprisonment, and for all the charges he has been at in making his defence. Or, if that fund be deficient, it is largely supplied by the crown. The Emperor also confers on him some public mark of his favour, and proclamation is made of his innocence through the whole city.

They look upon fraud as a greater crime than theft, and therefore seldom fail to punish it with death; for they allege that care and vigilance, with a very common understanding, may preserve a man's goods from thieves, but honesty has no defence against superior cunning. And, since it is necessary that there should be a perpetual intercourse of buying and selling, and dealing upon credit, where fraud is permitted and connived at,[3] or has no law to punish it, the honest dealer is always undone, and the knave gets the advantage. I remember when I was once interceding with the Emperor for a criminal who had wronged his master of a great sum of money, which he had received by order and ran away with; and, happening to tell His Majesty, by way of extenuation, that it was only a breach of trust, the Emperor thought it monstrous in me to offer as a defence the greatest aggravation of the crime; and truly I had little to say in return, farther than the common answer that different nations had different customs; for, I confess, I was heartily ashamed.

Although we usually call reward and punishment the two hinges upon which all government turns, yet I could never observe this maxim to be put in practice by any nation except that of Lilliput. Whoever can there bring sufficient proof that he has strictly observed the laws of his country for seventy-three moons has a claim to certain privileges, according to his quality[4] or condition of life, with a proportionable sum of money out of a fund appropriated for that use. He likewise acquires the title of *Snilpall*, or *Legal*, which is added to his name, but does not descend to his posterity. And these people thought it a prodigious defect of policy among us when I told them that our laws were enforced only by penalties, without any mention of reward. It is upon this

---

[1] *pulling* Plucking.

[2] *Cascagians* Invented by Swift.

[3] *connived at* Indulged or overlooked.

[4] *quality* Rank; position.

account that the image of Justice, in their courts of judicature, is formed with six eyes, two before, as many behind, and on each side one, to signify circumspection; with a bag of gold open in her right hand, and a sword sheathed in her left, to show she is more disposed to reward than to punish.

In choosing persons for all employments, they have more regard to good morals than to great abilities; for, since government is necessary to mankind, they believe that the common size of human understanding is fitted to some station or other; and that Providence never intended to make the management of public affairs a mystery to be comprehended only by a few persons of sublime genius, of which there seldom are three born in an age; but they suppose truth, justice, temperance, and the like, to be in every man's power; the practice of which virtues, assisted by experience and a good intention, would qualify any man for the service of his country, except where a course of study is required. But they thought the want of moral virtues was so far from being supplied by superior endowments of the mind that employments could never be put into such dangerous hands as those of persons so qualified; and, at least, that the mistakes committed by ignorance in a virtuous disposition would never be of such fatal consequence to the public weal[1] as the practices of a man whose inclinations led him to be corrupt, and who had great abilities to manage, to multiply, and defend his corruptions.

In like manner, the disbelief of a Divine Providence renders a man incapable of holding any public station; for, since Kings avow themselves to be the deputies of Providence, the Lilliputians think nothing can be more absurd than for a prince to employ such men as disown the authority under which he acts.

In relating these and the following laws, I would only be understood to mean the original institutions, and not the most scandalous corruptions, into which these people are fallen by the degenerate nature of man. For, as to that infamous practice of acquiring great employments by dancing on the ropes, or badges of favour and distinction by leaping over sticks and creeping under them, the reader is to observe that they were first introduced by the grandfather of the Emperor now reigning, and grew to the present height by the gradual increase of party and faction.

Ingratitude is among them a capital crime, as we read it to have been in some other countries; for they reason thus, that whoever makes ill returns to his benefactor must needs be a common enemy to the rest of mankind, from whom he has received no obligation, and therefore such a man is not fit to live.

Their notions relating to the duties of parents and children differ extremely from ours. For, since the conjunction of male and female is founded upon the great law of nature, in order to propagate and continue the species, the Lilliputians will needs have it that men and women are joined together, like other animals, by the motives of concupiscence; and that their tenderness towards their young proceeds from the like natural principle, for which reason they will never allow that a child is under any obligation to his father for begetting him, or to his mother for bringing him into the world; which, considering the miseries of human life, was neither a benefit in itself, nor intended so by his parents, whose thoughts, in their love encounters, were otherwise employed. Upon these and the like reasonings, their opinion is that parents are the last of all others to be trusted with the education of their own children; and therefore they have in every town public nurseries, where all parents, except cottagers[2] and labourers, are obliged to send their infants of both sexes to be reared and educated when they come to the age of twenty moons, at which time they are supposed to have some rudiments of docility.[3] These schools are of several kinds, suited to different qualities and both sexes. They have certain professors well skilled in preparing children for such a condition of life as befits the rank of their parents, and their own capacities as well as inclinations. I shall first say something of the male nurseries, and then of the female.

The nurseries for males of noble or eminent birth are provided with grave and learned professors and their several deputies. The clothes and food of the children are plain and simple. They are bred up in the principles of honour, justice, courage, modesty, clemency, religion, and love of their country; they are always employed in some business, except in the times of eating and sleeping, which are very short, and two hours for diversions consisting of bodily exercises. They are dressed by men

---

[1]   *public weal*   Public well-being; common good.

[2]   *cottagers*   Country dwellers.

[3]   *docility*   Ability to be taught.

till four years of age, and then are obliged to dress themselves, although their quality be ever so great; and the women attendant, who are aged proportionably to ours at fifty, perform only the most menial offices. They are never suffered to converse with servants, but go together in smaller or greater numbers to take their diversions, and always in the presence of a professor or one of his deputies, whereby they avoid those early bad impressions of folly and vice to which our children are subject. Their parents are suffered to see them only twice a year; the visit is not to last above an hour; they are allowed to kiss the child at meeting and parting, but a professor, who always stands by on those occasions, will not suffer them to whisper, or use any fondling expressions, or bring any presents of toys, sweetmeats,[1] and the like.

The pension from each family for the education and entertainment[2] of a child, upon failure of due payment, is levied by the Emperor's officers.

The nurseries for children of ordinary gentlemen, merchants, traders, and handicrafts are managed proportionably after the same manner; only those designed for trades are put out apprentices at eleven years old, whereas those of persons of quality continue in their exercises till fifteen, which answers to twenty-one with us; but the confinement is gradually lessened for the last three years.

In the female nurseries, the young girls of quality are educated much like the males, only they are dressed by orderly servants of their own sex, but always in the presence of a professor or deputy, till they come to dress themselves, which is at five years old. And if it be found that these nurses ever presume to entertain the girls with frightful or foolish stories, or the common follies practised by chambermaids among us, they are publicly whipped thrice about the city, imprisoned for a year, and banished for life to the most desolate part of the country. Thus the young ladies are as much ashamed of being cowards and fools as the men and despise all personal ornaments, beyond decency and cleanliness; neither did I perceive any difference in their education made by their difference of sex, only that the exercises of the females were not altogether so robust; and that some rules were given them relating to domestic life; and a smaller compass of learning was enjoined them. For their maxim is that among peoples of quality, a wife should be always a reasonable and agreeable companion, because she cannot always be young. When the girls are twelve years old, which among them is the marriageable age, their parents or guardians take them home, with great expressions of gratitude to the professors, and seldom without tears of the young lady and her companions.

In the nurseries of females of the meaner sort, the children are instructed in all kinds of works proper for their sex and their several degrees:[3] those intended for apprentices are dismissed at seven years old, the rest are kept to eleven.

The meaner families who have children at these nurseries are obliged, besides their annual pension, which is as low as possible, to return to the steward of the nursery a small monthly share of their gettings, to be a portion for the child; and therefore all parents are limited in their expenses by the law. For the Lilliputians think nothing can be more unjust than that people, in subservience to their own appetites, should bring children into the world, and leave the burden of supporting them on the public. As to persons of quality, they give security to appropriate a certain sum for each child, suitable to their condition; and these funds are always managed with good husbandry and the most exact justice.

The cottagers and labourers keep their children at home, their business being only to till and cultivate the earth, and therefore their education is of little consequence to the public; but the old and diseased among them are supported by hospitals, for begging is a trade unknown in this empire.

And here it may perhaps divert the curious reader to give some account of my domestic[4] and my manner of living in this country during a residence of nine months and thirteen days. Having a head mechanically turned, and being likewise forced by necessity, I had made for myself a table and chair, convenient enough, out of the largest trees in the royal park. Two hundred seamstresses were employed to make me shirts, and linen for my bed and table, all of the strongest and coarsest kind they could get; which, however, they were forced to quilt together in several folds, for the thickest was some

---

[1] *sweetmeats* Sweet foods, such as pastries, cakes, or candies.

[2] *entertainment* Sustenance; maintenance.

[3] *several degrees* Various social stations.

[4] *domestic* Household arrangements.

degrees finer than lawn.[1] Their linen is usually three inches wide, and three feet make a piece. The seamstresses took my measure as I lay on the ground, one standing at my neck and another at my mid-leg, with a strong cord extended that each held by the end, while a third measured the length of the cord with a rule of an inch long. Then they measured my right thumb, and desired no more; for, by a mathematical computation that twice round the thumb is once round the wrist, and so on to the neck and the waist, and by the help of my old shirt, which I displayed on the ground before them for a pattern, they fitted me exactly. Three hundred tailors were employed in the same manner to make me clothes; but they had another contrivance for taking my measure. I kneeled down, and they raised a ladder from the ground to my neck; upon this ladder one of them mounted, and let fall a plumb-line from my collar to the floor, which just answered the length of my coat; but my waist and arms I measured myself. When my clothes were finished, which was done in my house (for the largest of theirs would not have been able to hold them), they looked like the patchwork made by the ladies in England, only that mine were all of a colour.

I had three hundred cooks to dress my victuals in little convenient huts built about my house, where they and their families lived and prepared me two dishes apiece. I took up twenty waiters in my hand and placed them on the table; a hundred more attended below on the ground, some with dishes of meat, and some with barrels of wine and other liquors slung on their shoulders; all which the waiters above drew up as I wanted, in a very ingenious manner, by certain cords—as we draw the bucket up a well in Europe. A dish of their meat was a good mouthful, and a barrel of their liquor a reasonable draught. Their mutton yields to ours, but their beef is excellent. I have had a sirloin so large that I have been forced to make three bites of it, but this is rare. My servants were astonished to see me eat it bones and all, as in our country we do the leg of a lark. Their geese and turkeys I usually ate at a mouthful, and I confess they far exceed ours. Of their smaller fowl I could take up twenty or thirty at the end of my knife.

One day His Imperial Majesty, being informed of my way of living, desired that himself and his royal consort, with the young princes of the blood of both sexes, might have the happiness (as he was pleased to call it) of dining with me. They came accordingly, and I placed them in chairs of state on my table, just over against me, with their guards about them. Flimnap, the Lord High Treasurer, attended there likewise, with his white staff;[2] and I observed he often looked on me with a sour countenance, which I would not seem to regard, but ate more than usual, in honour to my dear country, as well as to fill the court with admiration. I have some private reasons to believe that this visit from His Majesty gave Flimnap an opportunity of doing me ill offices to his master. That minister had always been my secret enemy, though he outwardly caressed me more than was usual to the moroseness of his nature. He represented to the Emperor the low condition of his treasury: that he was forced to take up money at a great discount; that exchequer bills[3] would not circulate under nine per cent below par; that I had cost His Majesty above a million and a half of *sprugs* (their greatest gold coin, about the bigness of a spangle); and, upon the whole, that it would be advisable in the Emperor to take the first fair occasion of dismissing me.

I am here obliged to vindicate the reputation of an excellent lady who was an innocent sufferer upon my account. The Treasurer took a fancy to be jealous of his wife, from the malice of some evil tongues, who informed him that Her Grace had taken a violent affection for my person; and the court scandal ran for some time that she once came privately to my lodging. This I solemnly declare to be a most infamous falsehood, without any grounds farther than that Her Grace was pleased to treat me with all innocent marks of freedom and friendship. I own she came often to my house, but always publicly, nor ever without three more in the coach, who were usually her sister, and young daughter, and some particular acquaintance; but this was common to many other ladies of the court. And I still appeal to my servants round, whether they at any time saw a coach at my door without knowing what persons were in it. On those occasions, when a servant had given me notice, my custom was to go immediately to the door and, after paying my respects, to take up the coach and two horses very carefully in my hands (for, if there were

---

[1]   *lawn* Type of very fine linen.

[2]   *white staff* The lord treasurer's symbol of office.

[3]   *exchequer bills* Bills of credit issued by Parliament.

six horses, the postillion[1] always unharnessed four) and place them on a table, where I had fixed a movable rim quite round, of five inches high, to prevent accidents. And I have often had four coaches and horses at once on my table full of company, while I sat in my chair leaning my face towards them; and when I was engaged with one set, the coachmen would gently drive the others round my table. I have passed many an afternoon very agreeably in these conversations. But I defy the Treasurer, or his two informers (I will name them, and let them make the best of it), Clustril and Drunlo, to prove that any person ever came to me *incognito*, except the Secretary Reldresal, who was sent by express command of His Imperial Majesty, as I have before related. I should not have dwelt so long upon this particular if it had not been a point wherein the reputation of a great lady is so nearly concerned, to say nothing of my own; though I then had the honour to be a *Nardac*, which the Treasurer himself is not; for all the world knows that he is only a *Clumglum*, a title inferior by one degree, as that of a marquis is to a duke in England; yet I allow he preceded me in right of his post. These false informations, which I afterwards came to the knowledge of by an accident not proper to mention, made the Treasurer show his lady for some time an ill countenance, and me a worse; and although he was at last undeceived and reconciled to her, yet I lost all credit with him, and found my interest decline very fast with the Emperor himself, who was indeed too much governed by that favourite.

CHAPTER 7

(The author, being informed of a design to accuse him of high treason, makes his escape to Blefuscu. His reception there.)

Before I proceed to give an account of my leaving this kingdom, it may be proper to inform the reader of a private intrigue which had been for two months forming against me.

I had been hitherto, all my life, a stranger to courts, for which I was unqualified by the meanness of my condition.[2] I had indeed heard and read enough of the dispositions of great princes and ministers, but never expected to have found such terrible effects of them in so remote a country, governed, as I thought, by very different maxims from those in Europe.

When I was just preparing to pay my attendance on the Emperor of Blefuscu, a considerable person at court (to whom I had been very serviceable at a time when he lay under the highest displeasure of His Imperial Majesty) came to my house very privately at night in a close chair, and, without sending his name, desired admittance. The chairmen were dismissed. I put the chair, with his lordship in it, into my coat-pocket: and, giving orders to a trusty servant to say I was indisposed and gone to sleep, I fastened the door of my house, placed the chair on the table, according to my usual custom, and sat down by it. After the common salutations were over, observing His Lordship's countenance full of concern, and inquiring into the reason, he desired I would hear him with patience, in a matter that highly concerned my honour and my life. His speech was to the following effect, for I took notes of it as soon as he left me.

You are to know (said he) that several committees of council have been lately called in the most private manner on your account; and it is but two days since His Majesty came to a full resolution.

You are very sensible that Skyresh Bolgolam (*Galbet*, or High Admiral) has been your mortal enemy almost ever since your arrival. His original reasons I know not, but his hatred is increased since your great success against Blefuscu, by which his glory as Admiral is much obscured. This lord, in conjunction with Flimnap the High Treasurer, whose enmity against you is notorious on account of his lady; Limtoc the General; Lalcon the Chamberlain; and Balmuff the Grand Justiciary, have prepared articles of impeachment against you, for treason and other capital crimes.[3]

This preface made me so impatient, being conscious of my own merits and innocence, that I was going to interrupt, when he entreated me to be silent, and thus proceeded:

Out of gratitude for the favours you have done me, I procured information of the whole proceedings and a

---

[1] *postillion* One who guides the first pair of horses.

[2] *meanness ... condition* Low rank.

[3] *treason ... crimes* After the Whigs regained power, both Oxford and Bolingbroke were accused of being Jacobite sympathizers and were impeached for treason.

copy of the articles, wherein I venture my head for your service.

Articles of Impeachment against QUINBUS FLESTRIN (the Man-Mountain.)

ARTICLE 1

Whereas, by a statute made in the reign of His Imperial Majesty Calin Deffar Plune, it is enacted that whoever shall make water within the precincts of the royal palace shall be liable to the pains and penalties of high-treason; notwithstanding, the said Quinbus Flestrin, in open breach of the said law, under colour of extinguishing the fire kindled in the apartment of His Majesty's most dear imperial consort, did maliciously, traitorously, and devilishly, by discharge of his urine, put out the said fire kindled in the said apartment, lying and being within the precincts of the said royal palace, against the statute in that case provided, etc., against the duty, etc.

ARTICLE 2

That the said Quinbus Flestrin, having brought the imperial fleet of Blefuscu into the royal port, and being afterwards commanded by His Imperial Majesty to seize all the other ships of the said empire of Blefuscu, and reduce that empire to a province, to be governed by a viceroy from hence, and to destroy and put to death not only all the Big-Endian exiles, but likewise all the people of that empire who would not immediately forsake the Big-Endian heresy, he, the said Flestrin, like a false traitor against His Most Auspicious, Serene, Imperial Majesty, did petition to be excused from the said service, upon pretence of unwillingness to force the consciences, or destroy the liberties and lives of an innocent people.

ARTICLE 3

That, whereas certain ambassadors arrived from the court of Blefuscu to sue for peace in His Majesty's court, he, the said Flestrin, did, like a false traitor, aid, abet, comfort, and divert the said ambassadors, although he knew them to be servants to a prince who was lately an open enemy to His Imperial Majesty, and in an open war against His said Majesty.

ARTICLE 4

That the said Quinbus Flestrin, contrary to the duty of a faithful subject, is now preparing to make a voyage to the court and empire of Blefuscu, for which he has received only verbal license from His Imperial Majesty; and, under colour of the said license, does falsely and traitorously intend to take the said voyage, and thereby to aid, comfort, and abet the Emperor of Blefuscu, so late an enemy, and in open war with His Imperial Majesty aforesaid.

There are some other articles, but these are the most important, of which I have read you an abstract.

In the several debates upon this impeachment, it must be confessed that His Majesty gave many marks of his great lenity, often urging the services you had done him, and endeavouring to extenuate your crimes. The Treasurer and Admiral insisted that you should be put to the most painful and ignominious death, by setting fire to your house at night, and the General was to attend with twenty thousand men, armed with poisoned arrows, to shoot you on the face and hands. Some of your servants were to have private orders to strew a poisonous juice on your shirts and sheets, which would soon make you tear your own flesh and die in the utmost torture. The General came into the same opinion, so that for a long time there was a majority against you. But His Majesty resolving, if possible, to spare your life, at last brought off[1] the Chamberlain.

Upon this incident, Reldresal, Principal Secretary for Private Affairs, who always approved himself your true friend, was commanded by the Emperor to deliver his opinion, which he accordingly did; and therein justified the good thoughts you have of him. He allowed your crimes to be great, but that still there was room for mercy, the most commendable virtue in a prince, and for which His Majesty was so justly celebrated. He said the friendship between you and him was so well known to the world that perhaps the most honourable board might think him partial; however, in obedience to the command he had received, he would freely offer his sentiments. That if His Majesty, in consideration of your services, and pursuant to his own merciful disposition, would please to spare your life, and only give orders to

---

[1] *brought off* Won over from his former position.

put out both your eyes, he humbly conceived that by this expedient justice might in some measure be satisfied, and all the world would applaud the lenity of the Emperor, as well as the fair and generous proceedings of those who have the honour to be his counsellors. That the loss of your eyes would be no impediment to your bodily strength, by which you might still be useful to His Majesty; that blindness is an addition to courage, by concealing dangers from us; that the fear you had for your eyes was the greatest difficulty in bringing over the enemy's fleet; and it would be sufficient for you to see by the eyes of the ministers, since the greatest princes do no more.

This proposal was received with the utmost disapprobation by the whole board. Bolgolam, the Admiral, could not preserve his temper, but, rising up in fury, said he wondered how the Secretary durst presume to give his opinion for preserving the life of a traitor; that the services you had performed were, by all true reasons of state, the great aggravation of your crimes; that you, who were able to extinguish the fire by discharge of urine in Her Majesty's apartment (which he mentioned with horror) might, at another time, raise an inundation by the same means, to drown the whole palace; and the same strength which enabled you to bring over the enemy's fleet might serve, upon the first discontent, to carry it back; that he had good reasons to think you were a Big-Endian in your heart; and, as treason begins in the heart before it appears in overt acts, so he accused you as a traitor on that account, and therefore insisted you should be put to death.

The Treasurer was of the same opinion. He showed to what straits His Majesty's revenue was reduced by the charge of maintaining you, which would soon grow insupportable; that the Secretary's expedient of putting out your eyes was so far from being a remedy against this evil that it would probably increase it, as is manifest from the common practice of blinding some kind of fowls, after which they fed the faster, and grew sooner fat; that His sacred Majesty and the council, who are your judges, were in their own consciences fully convinced of your guilt, which was a sufficient argument to condemn you to death, without the formal proofs required by the strict letter of the law.

But His Imperial Majesty, fully determined against capital punishment, was graciously pleased to say that

since the council thought the loss of your eyes too easy a censure, some other way may be inflicted hereafter. And your friend the Secretary, humbly desiring to be heard again, in answer to what the Treasurer had objected concerning the great charge His Majesty was at in maintaining you, said that his Excellency, who had the sole disposal of the Emperor's revenue, might easily provide against that evil by gradually lessening your establishment; by which, for want of sufficient food, you would grow weak and faint, and lose your appetite, and consequently decay and consume in a few months; neither would the stench of your carcass be then so dangerous, when it should become more than half diminished; and immediately upon your death five or six thousand of His Majesty's subjects might, in two or three days, cut your flesh from your bones, take it away by cart-loads, and bury it in distant parts to prevent infection, leaving the skeleton as a monument of admiration to posterity.

Thus, by the great friendship of the Secretary, the whole affair was compromised. It was strictly enjoined that the project of starving you by degrees should be kept a secret; but the sentence of putting out your eyes was entered on the books; none dissenting except Bolgolam the Admiral, who, being a creature of the Empress, was perpetually instigated by Her Majesty to insist upon your death, she having borne perpetual malice against you on account of that infamous and illegal method you took to extinguish the fire in her apartment.

In three days your friend the Secretary will be directed to come to your house and read before you the articles of impeachment; and then to signify the great lenity and favour of His Majesty and council, whereby you are only condemned to the loss of your eyes, which His Majesty does not question you will gratefully and humbly submit to; and twenty of His Majesty's surgeons will attend, in order to see the operation well performed, by discharging very sharp-pointed arrows into the balls of your eyes as you lie on the ground.

I leave to your prudence what measures you will take, and to avoid suspicion I must immediately return in as private a manner as I came.

His Lordship did so, and I remained alone, under many doubts and perplexities of mind.

It was a custom introduced by this prince and his

ministry (very different, as I have been assured, from the practice of former times) that after the court had decreed any cruel execution, either to gratify the monarch's resentment or the malice of a favourite, the Emperor always made a speech to his whole council, expressing his great lenity and tenderness, as qualities known and confessed by all the world. This speech was immediately published throughout the kingdom; nor did anything terrify the people so much as those encomiums on His Majesty's mercy, because it was observed that the more these praises were enlarged and insisted on, the more inhuman was the punishment, and the sufferer more innocent. Yet, as to myself, I must confess, having never been designed for a courtier either by my birth or education, I was so ill a judge of things that I could not discover the lenity and favour of this sentence, but conceived it (perhaps erroneously) rather to be rigorous than gentle. I sometimes thought of standing my trial, for, although I could not deny the facts alleged in the several articles, yet I hoped they would admit of some extenuation. But having in my life perused many state trials, which I ever observed to terminate as the judges thought fit to direct, I durst not rely on so dangerous a decision in so critical a juncture, and against such powerful enemies. Once I was strongly bent upon resistance, for, while I had liberty the whole strength of that empire could hardly subdue me, and I might easily with stones pelt the metropolis to pieces; but I soon rejected that project with horror, by remembering the oath I had made to the Emperor, the favours I received from him, and the high title of *Nardac* he conferred upon me. Neither had I so soon learned the gratitude of courtiers to persuade myself that his Majesty's present severities acquitted me of all past obligations.

At last I fixed upon a resolution, for which it is probable I may incur some censure, and not unjustly; for I confess I owe the preserving of mine eyes, and consequently my liberty, to my own great rashness and want of experience; because, if I had then known the nature of princes and ministers, which I have since observed in many other courts, and their methods of treating criminals less obnoxious than myself, I should,

with great alacrity and readiness, have submitted to so easy a punishment. But hurried on by the precipitancy of youth, and having his Imperial Majesty's license to pay my attendance upon the Emperor of Blefuscu, I took this opportunity, before the three days were elapsed, to send a letter to my friend the Secretary, signifying my resolution of setting out that morning for Blefuscu,[1] pursuant to the leave I had got; and, without waiting for an answer, I went to that side of the island where our fleet lay. I seized a large man of war, tied a cable to the prow, and, lifting up the anchors, I stripped myself, put my clothes (together with my coverlet, which I carried under my arm) into the vessel, and, drawing it after me, between wading and swimming arrived at the royal port of Blefuscu, where the people had long expected me. They lent me two guides to direct me to the capital city, which is of the same name. I held them in my hands till I came within two hundred yards of the gate, and desired them to signify my arrival to one of the secretaries, and let him know I there waited His Majesty's command. I had an answer in about an hour, that His Majesty, attended by the royal family and great officers of the court, was coming out to receive me. I advanced a hundred yards. The Emperor and his train alighted from their horses, the Empress and ladies from their coaches, and I did not perceive they were in any fright or concern. I lay on the ground to kiss His Majesty's and the Empress's hands. I told His Majesty that I was come according to my promise, and with the license of the Emperor my master, to have the honour of seeing so mighty a monarch, and to offer him any service in my power, consistent with my duty to my own prince; not mentioning a word of my disgrace because I had hitherto no regular information of it, and might suppose myself wholly ignorant of any such design; neither could I reasonably conceive that the Emperor would discover the secret while I was out of his power; wherein, however, it soon appeared I was deceived.

I shall not trouble the reader with the particular account of my reception at this court, which was suitable to the generosity of so great a prince; nor of the difficulties I was in for want of a house and bed, being forced to lie on the ground, wrapped up in my coverlet.

---

[1] *setting out ... Blefuscu* Similarly, Bolingbroke fled to France in order to avoid his trial for treason.

CHAPTER 8

(The author, by a lucky accident, finds means to leave Blefuscu; and, after some difficulties, returns safe to his native country.)

Three days after my arrival, walking out of curiosity to the northeast coast of the island, I observed, about half a league off in the sea, somewhat that looked like a boat overturned. I pulled off my shoes and stockings, and, wading two or three hundred yards, I found the object to approach nearer by force of the tide; and then plainly saw it to be a real boat, which I supposed might by some tempest have been driven from a ship. Whereupon I returned immediately towards the city, and desired His Imperial Majesty to lend me twenty of the tallest vessels he had left after the loss of his fleet, and three thousand seamen under the command of his Vice Admiral. This fleet sailed round while I went back the shortest way to the coast where I first discovered the boat. I found the tide had driven it still nearer. The seamen were all provided with cordage, which I had beforehand twisted to a sufficient strength. When the ships came up, I stripped myself and waded till I came within a hundred yards of the boat, after which I was forced to swim till I got up to it. The seamen threw me the end of the cord, which I fastened to a hole in the fore-part of the boat, and the other end to a man of war. But I found all my labour to little purpose; for, being out of my depth, I was not able to work. In this necessity I was forced to swim behind, and push the boat forwards, as often as I could, with one of my hands; and the tide favouring me, I advanced so far that I could just hold up my chin and feel the ground. I rested two or three minutes, and then gave the boat another shove, and so on till the sea was no higher than my armpits; and now, the most laborious part being over, I took out my other cables, which were stowed in one of the ships, and fastened them first to the boat, and then to nine of the vessels which attended me. The wind being favourable, the seamen towed, and I shoved, until we arrived within forty yards of the shore; and, waiting till the tide was out, I got dry to the boat, and by the assistance of two thousand men with ropes and engines, I made a shift to turn it on its bottom, and found it was but little damaged.

I shall not trouble the reader with the difficulties I was under by the help of certain paddles, which cost me ten days making, to get my boat to the royal port of Blefuscu, where a mighty concourse of people appeared upon my arrival, full of wonder at the sight of so prodigious a vessel. I told the Emperor that my good fortune had thrown this boat in my way to carry me to some place whence I might return into my native country, and begged His Majesty's orders for getting materials to fit it up, together with his license to depart, which, after some kind expostulations, he was pleased to grant.

I did very much wonder, in all this time, not to have heard of any express relating to me from our Emperor to the court of Blefuscu. But I was afterward given privately to understand that his Imperial Majesty, never imagining I had the least notice of his designs, believed I was only gone to Blefuscu in performance of my promise, according to the license he had given me, which was well known at our court, and would return in a few days, when the ceremony was ended. But he was at last in pain at my long absence; and after consulting with the Treasurer and the rest of that cabal, a person of quality was dispatched with the copy of the articles against me. This envoy had instructions to represent to the monarch of Blefuscu the great lenity of his master, who was content to punish me no farther than with the loss of mine eyes; that I had fled from justice; and if I did not return in two hours, I should be deprived of my title of *Nardac* and declared a traitor. The envoy further added that in order to maintain the peace and amity between both empires, his master expected that his brother of Blefuscu would give orders to have me sent back to Lilliput, bound hand and foot, to be punished as a traitor.

The Emperor of Blefuscu, having taken three days to consult, returned an answer consisting of many civilities and excuses. He said that, as for sending me bound, his brother knew it was impossible; that, although I had deprived him of his fleet, yet he owed great obligations to me for many good offices I had done him in making the peace; that however, both Their Majesties would soon be made easy, for I had found a prodigious vessel on the shore, able to carry me on the sea, which he had given orders to fit up, with my own assistance and direction; and he hoped in a few weeks both empires would be freed from so insupportable an encumbrance.

With this answer the envoy returned to Lilliput, and the Monarch of Blefuscu related to me all that had passed, offering me at the same time (but under the strictest confidence) his gracious protection if I would continue in his service; wherein, although I believed him sincere, yet I resolved never more to put any confidence in princes or ministers where I could possibly avoid it; and therefore, with all due acknowledgments for his favourable intentions, I humbly begged to be excused. I told him that since fortune, whether good or evil, had thrown a vessel in my way, I was resolved to venture myself on the ocean, rather than be an occasion of difference between two such mighty monarchs. Neither did I find the Emperor at all displeased; and I discovered, by a certain accident, that he was very glad of my resolution, and so were most of his ministers.

These considerations moved me to hasten my departure somewhat sooner than I intended; to which the court, impatient to have me gone, very readily contributed. Five hundred workmen were employed to make two sails to my boat, according to my directions, by quilting thirteen folds of their strongest linen together. I was at the pains of making ropes and cables by twisting ten, twenty, or thirty of the thickest and strongest of theirs. A great stone that I happened to find, after a long search by the seashore, served me for an anchor. I had the tallow of three hundred cows for greasing my boat, and other uses. I was at incredible pains in cutting down some of the largest timber-trees for oars and masts, wherein I was, however, much assisted by His Majesty's ship-carpenters, who helped me in smoothing them after I had done the rough work.

In about a month, when all was prepared, I sent to receive His Majesty's commands and to take my leave. The Emperor and royal family came out of the palace; I lay down on my face to kiss his hand, which he very graciously gave me—so did the Empress and young Princes of the Blood. His Majesty presented me with fifty purses of two hundred *sprugs* apiece, together with his picture at full length, which I put immediately into one of my gloves to keep it from being hurt. The ceremonies at my departure were too many to trouble the reader with at this time.

I stored the boat with the carcasses of a hundred oxen and three hundred sheep, with bread and drink proportionable, and as much meat ready dressed as four hundred cooks could provide. I took with me six cows and two bulls alive, with as many ewes and rams, intending to carry them into my own country and propagate the breed. And to feed them on board I had a good bundle of hay and a bag of corn.[1] I would gladly have taken a dozen of the natives, but this was a thing the Emperor would by no means permit; and, besides a diligent search into my pockets, His Majesty engaged my honour not to carry away any of his subjects, although with their own consent and desire.

Having thus prepared all things as well as I was able, I set sail on the twenty-fourth day of September, 1701, at six in the morning; and when I had gone about four leagues to the northward, the wind being at southeast, at six in the evening I descried a small island about half a league to the north-west. I advanced forward and cast anchor on the lee-side of the island, which seemed to be uninhabited. I then took some refreshment and went to my rest. I slept well and, as I conjectured, at least six hours, for I found the day broke in two hours after I awaked. It was a clear night. I ate my breakfast before the sun was up; and, heaving anchor, the wind being favourable, I steered the same course that I had done the day before, wherein I was directed by my pocket compass. My intention was to reach, if possible, one of those islands which I had reason to believe lay to the northeast of Van Diemen's Land. I discovered nothing all that day; but upon the next, about three in the afternoon, when I had by my computation made twenty-four leagues from Blefuscu, I descried a sail steering to the southeast; my course was due east. I hailed her, but could get no answer; yet I found I gained upon her, for the wind slackened. I made all the sail I could, and in half an hour she spied me, then hung out her ancient[2] and discharged a gun. It is not easy to express the joy I was in upon the unexpected hope of once more seeing my beloved country, and the dear pledges[3] I left in it. The ship slackened her sails, and I came up with her between five and six in the evening, September 26th;

---

[1]   *corn* Cereal grain such as wheat, barley, or rye.

[2]   *ancient* Flag; insignia.

[3]   *pledges* Children (i.e., Gulliver's children).

but my heart leaped within me to see her English colours. I put my cows and sheep into my coat-pockets and got on board with all my little cargo of provisions. The vessel was an English merchantman, returning from Japan by the North and South Seas;[1] the Captain, Mr. John Biddel of Deptford, a very civil man and an excellent sailor. We were now in the latitude of 30 degrees south; there were about fifty men in the ship; and here I met an old comrade of mine, one Peter Williams, who gave me a good character to the Captain. This gentleman treated me with kindness, and desired I would let him know what place I came from last, and whither I was bound; which I did in a few words, but he thought I was raving, and that the dangers I underwent had disturbed my head; whereupon I took my black cattle and sheep out of my pocket, which, after great astonishment, clearly convinced him of my veracity. I then showed him the gold given me by the Emperor of Blefuscu, together with His Majesty's picture at full length, and some other rarities of that country. I gave him two purses of two hundreds *sprugs* each and promised, when we arrived in England, to make him a present of a cow and a sheep big with young.

I shall not trouble the reader with a particular account of this voyage, which was very prosperous for the most part. We arrived in the Downs[2] on the 13th of April, 1702. I had only one misfortune, that the rats on board carried away one of my sheep; I found her bones in a hole, picked clean from the flesh. The rest of my cattle I got safe ashore, and set them a grazing in a bowling-green at Greenwich, where the fineness of the grass made them feed very heartily, though I had always feared the contrary; neither could I possibly have preserved them in so long a voyage if the Captain had not allowed me some of his best biscuit, which, rubbed to powder and mingled with water, was their constant food. The short time I continued in England, I made a considerable profit by showing my cattle to many persons of quality and others; and before I began my second voyage, I sold them for six hundred pounds. Since my last return I find the breed is considerably increased, especially the sheep, which I hope will prove much to the advantage of the woollen manufacture by the fineness of the fleeces.

I stayed but two months with my wife and family, for my insatiable desire of seeing foreign countries would suffer me to continue no longer. I left fifteen hundred pounds with my wife, and fixed her in a good house at Redriff. My remaining stock I carried with me, part in money and part in goods, in hopes to improve my fortunes. My eldest uncle John had left me an estate in land, near Epping, of about thirty pounds a-year, and I had a long lease of the Black Bull in Fetter Lane, which yielded me as much more, so that I was not in any danger of leaving my family upon the parish.[3] My son Johnny, named so after his uncle, was at the grammar school, and a towardly[4] child. My daughter Betty (who is now well married, and has children) was then at her needlework. I took leave of my wife, and boy and girl, with tears on both sides, and went on board the *Adventure*, a merchant-ship of three hundred tons, bound for Surat,[5] Captain John Nicholas of Liverpool, Commander. But my account of this voyage must be referred to the second part of my travels.

PART 2 – A VOYAGE TO BROBDINGNAG

CHAPTER 1

(*A great storm described; the longboat sent to fetch water; the author goes with it to discover the country. He is left on shore, is seized by one of the natives and carried to a farmer's house. His reception, with several accidents that happened there. A description of the inhabitants.*)

Having been condemned by nature and fortune to active and restless life, in two months after my return I again left my native country, and took shipping in the Downs on the 20th day of June, 1702, in the *Adventure*, Captain John Nicholas, a Cornish man, Commander, bound for Surat. We had a very prosperous gale till we arrived at the Cape of Good Hope, where we landed for fresh water, but discovering a leak, we unshipped our goods and wintered there; for the Captain falling sick of an ague, we could not leave the Cape till the end of March. We then set sail, and had a

---

[1]   *North and South Seas*   North and South Pacific.

[2]   *the Downs*   Area of water off the coast of Kent.

[3]   *upon the parish*   The parish was responsible for taking care of the poor.

[4]   *towardly*   Promising.

[5]   *Surat*   Port in India, located on the Gulf of Cambay.

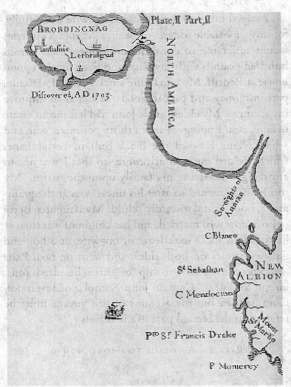

Map showing Brobdingnag in relation to North America, printed in the 1726 edition with no accompanying caption at the beginning of Part 2.

good voyage till we passed the Straits of Madagascar; but having got northward of that island, and to about five degrees south latitude, the winds, which in those seas are observed to blow a constant equal gale between the north and west from the beginning of December to the beginning of May, on the 19th of April began to blow with much greater violence and more westerly than usual, continuing so for twenty days together, during which time we were driven a little to the east of the Molucca Islands and about three degrees northward of the Line,[1] as our Captain found by an observation he took the 2nd of May, at which time the wind ceased, and it was a perfect calm, whereat I was not a little rejoiced. But he, being a man well experienced in the navigation of those seas, bid us all prepare against a storm, which accordingly happened the day following:

for the southern wind, called the southern monsoon, began to set in.

Finding it was likely to overblow, we took in our spritsail and stood by to hand the foresail; but making foul weather, we looked the guns were all fast, and handed the mizzen. The ship lay very broad off, so we thought it better spooning before the sea than trying or hulling. We reefed the foresail and set him, and hauled aft the foresheet; the helm was hard a-weather. The ship wore bravely. We belayed the fore-downhaul; but the sail was split, and we hauled down the yard, and got the sail into the ship, and unbound all the things clear of it. It was a very fierce storm; the sea broke strange and dangerous. We hauled off upon the lanyard of the whipstaff, and helped the man at the helm. We would not get down our topmast, but let all stand, because she scudded before the sea very well, and we knew that the topmast being aloft, the ship was the wholesomer, and made better way through the sea, seeing we had sea-room. When the storm was over, we set foresail and mainsail, and brought the ship to. Then we set the mizzen, main topsail, and the fore topsail. Our course was east-northeast, the wind was at southwest. We got the starboard tacks aboard; we cast off our weather braces and lifts; we set in the lee braces, and hauled forward by the weather-bowlings,[2] and hauled them tight, and belayed them, and hauled over the mizzen tack to windward, and kept her full and by as near as she would lie.[3]

During this storm, which was followed by a strong wind west-southwest, we were carried, by my computation, about five hundred leagues to the east, so that the oldest sailor on board could not tell in what part of the world we were. Our provisions held out well, our ship was staunch, and our crew all in good health; but we lay in the utmost distress for water. We thought it best to hold on the same course, rather than turn more northerly, which might have brought us to the northwest part of Great Tartary[4] and into the Frozen Sea.[5]

---

2. *weather-bowlings* I.e., bowlines.

3. *Finding it.... would lie* This paragraph is meant to satirize the then-prevalent use of nautical jargon in popular accounts of voyages. It is taken almost verbatim from Samuel Sturmy's *Mariner's Magazine*.

4. *Great Tartary* Siberia.

5. *Frozen Sea* Arctic Ocean.

---

1. *Line* Equator.

On the 16th day of June, 1703, a boy on the top-mast discovered land. On the 17th, we came in full view of a great island or continent (for we knew not whether), on the south side whereof was a small neck of land jutting out into the sea, and a creek too shallow to hold a ship of above one hundred tons. We cast anchor within a league of this creek, and our captain sent a dozen of his men well armed in the long-boat, with vessels for water, if any could be found. I desired his leave to go with them, that I might see the country and make what discoveries I could. When we came to land we saw no river or spring, nor any sign of inhabitants. Our men therefore wandered on the shore to find out some fresh water near the sea, and I walked alone about a mile on the other side, where I observed the country all barren and rocky. I now began to be weary, and seeing nothing to entertain my curiosity, I returned gently down towards the creek; and the sea being full in my view, I saw our men already got into the boat, and rowing for life to the ship. I was going to holler after them, although it had been to little purpose, when I observed a huge creature walking after them in the sea as fast as he could; he waded not much deeper than his knees, and took prodigious strides, but our men had the start of him half a league, and the sea thereabouts being full of sharp-pointed rocks, the monster was not able to overtake the boat. This I was afterwards told, for I durst not stay to see the issue of the adventure; but ran as fast as I could the way I first went, and then climbed up a steep hill, which gave me some prospect of the country. I found it fully cultivated; but that which first surprised me was the length of the grass, which, in those grounds that seemed to be kept for hay, was about twenty feet high.[1]

I fell into a high road, for so I took it to be, though it served to the inhabitants only as a footpath through a field of barley. Here I walked on for some time, but could see little on either side, it being now near harvest, and the corn rising at least forty feet. I was an hour walking to the end of this field, which was fenced in with a hedge of at least one hundred and twenty feet high, and the trees so lofty that I could make no computation of their altitude. There was a stile to pass from this field into the next. It had four steps, and a stone to cross over when you came to the uppermost. It was impossible for me to climb this stile because every step was six foot high, and the upper stone above twenty. I was endeavouring to find some gap in the hedge when I discovered one of the inhabitants in the next field advancing towards the stile, of the same size with him whom I saw in the sea pursuing our boat. He appeared as tall as an ordinary spire-steeple, and took about ten yards at every stride, as near as I could guess. I was struck with the utmost fear and astonishment, and ran to hide myself in the corn, from whence I saw him at the top of the stile looking back into the next field on the right hand, and heard him call in a voice many degrees louder than a speaking-trumpet; but the noise was so high in the air that at first I certainly thought it was thunder. Whereupon seven monsters like himself came towards him with reaping hooks in their hands, each hook about the largeness of six scythes. These people were not so well clad as the first, whose servants or labourers they seemed to be; for, upon some words he spoke, they went to reap the corn in the field where I lay. I kept from them at as great a distance as I could, but was forced to move with extreme difficulty, for the stalks of the corn were sometimes not above a foot distant, so that I could hardly squeeze my body betwixt them. However, I made a shift to go forward till I came to a part of the field where the corn had been laid[2] by the rain and wind. Here it was impossible for me to advance a step, for the stalks were so interwoven that I could not creep through, and the beards of the fallen ears so strong and pointed that they pierced through my clothes into my flesh. At the same time I heard the reapers not a hundred yards behind me. Being quite dispirited with toil, and wholly overcome by grief and despair, I lay down between two ridges and heartily wished I might there end my days. I bemoaned my desolate widow and fatherless children; I lamented my own folly and wilfulness in attempting a second voyage, against the advice of all my friends and relations. In this terrible agitation of mind I could not forbear thinking of Lilliput, whose inhabitants looked upon me as the greatest prodigy that ever appeared in the world; where I was able to draw an imperial fleet in my hand, and perform those other actions which will be recorded

---

[1] *twenty feet high* While in Lilliput the scale to our world is roughly 1 to 12, in Brobdingnag it is approximately (though less consistently) 12 to 1.

[2] *laid* Knocked flat.

forever in the chronicles of that empire, while posterity shall hardly believe them, although attested by millions. I reflected what a mortification it must prove to me to appear as inconsiderable in this nation as one single Lilliputian would be among us. But this I conceived was to be the least of my misfortunes; for, as human creatures are observed to be more savage and cruel in proportion to their bulk, what could I expect but to be a morsel in the mouth of the first among these enormous barbarians that should happen to seize me? Undoubtedly philosophers are in the right when they tell us that nothing is great or little otherwise than by comparison. It might have pleased fortune to have let the Lilliputians find some nation where the people were as diminutive with respect to them as they were to me. And who knows but that even this prodigious race of mortals might be equally overmatched in some distant part of the world, whereof we have yet no discovery.

Scared and confounded as I was, I could not forbear going on with these reflections when one of the reapers, approaching within ten yards of the ridge where I lay, made me apprehend that with the next step I should be squashed to death under his foot, or cut in two with his reaping-hook. And therefore, when he was again about to move, I screamed as loud as fear could make me. Whereupon the huge creature trod short, and, looking round about under him for some time, at last espied me as I lay on the ground. He considered awhile, with the caution of one who endeavours to lay hold on a small dangerous animal in such a manner that it shall not be able either to scratch or bite him, as I myself have sometimes done with a weasel in England. At length he ventured to take me behind, by the middle, between his forefinger and thumb, and brought me within three yards of his eyes, that he might behold my shape more perfectly. I guessed his meaning, and my good fortune gave me so much presence of mind that I resolved not to struggle in the least as he held me in the air above sixty feet from the ground, although he grievously pinched my sides for fear I should slip through his fingers. All I ventured was to raise mine eyes towards the sun, and place my hands together in a supplicating posture, and to speak some words in a humble melancholy tone, suitable to the condition I then was in. For I apprehended every moment that he would dash me against the ground, as we usually do any little hateful

animal which we have a mind to destroy. But my good star would have it that he appeared pleased with my voice and gestures, and began to look upon me as a curiosity, much wondering to hear me pronounce articulate words, although he could not understand them. In the meantime I was not able to forbear groaning and shedding tears and turning my head towards my sides, letting him know, as well as I could, how cruelly I was hurt by the pressure of his thumb and finger. He seemed to apprehend my meaning; for, lifting up the lappet[1] of his coat, he put me gently into it, and immediately ran along with me to his master, who was a substantial[2] farmer, and the same person I had first seen in the field.

The farmer, having (as I suppose by their talk) received such an account of me as his servant could give him, took a piece of a small straw, about the size of a walking-staff, and therewith lifted up the lappets of my coat, which it seems he thought to be some kind of covering that nature had given me. He blew my hairs aside to take a better view of my face. He called his hinds[3] about him and asked them, as I afterwards learned, whether they had ever seen in the fields any little creature that resembled me. He then placed me softly on the ground upon all four, but I got immediately up and walked slowly backward and forward, to let those people see I had no intent to run away. They all sat down in a circle about me, the better to observe my motions. I pulled off my hat and made a low bow towards the farmer; I fell on my knees, and lifted up my hands and eyes, and spoke several words as loud as I could; I took a purse of gold out of my pocket and humbly presented it to him. He received it on the palm of his hand, then applied it close to his eye to see what it was, and afterwards turned it several times with the point of a pin (which he took out of his sleeve), but could make nothing of it. Whereupon I made a sign that he should place his hand on the ground. I then took the purse, and, opening it, poured all the gold into his palm. There were six Spanish pieces of four pistoles each, beside twenty or thirty smaller coins. I saw him wet the tip of his little finger upon his tongue and take

---

[1]   *lappet*   Flap or fold; lapel.

[2]   *substantial*   Well established, well-to-do.

[3]   *hinds*   Servants, farm workers.

up one of my largest pieces, and then another, but he seemed to be wholly ignorant what they were. He made me a sign to put them again into my purse, and the purse again into my pocket, which, after offering it to him several times, I thought it best to do.

The farmer by this time was convinced I must be a rational creature. He spoke often to me, but the sound of his voice pierced my ears like that of a water mill, yet his words were articulate enough. I answered as loud as I could in several languages, and he often laid his ear within two yards of me, but all in vain, for we were wholly unintelligible to each other. He then sent his servants to their work and, taking his handkerchief out of his pocket, he doubled and spread it on his left hand, which he placed flat on the ground with the palm upward, making me a sign to step into it, as I could easily do, for it was not above a foot in thickness. I thought it my part to obey, and, for fear of falling, laid myself at full length upon the handkerchief, with the remainder of which he lapped me up to the head for further security, and in this manner carried me home to his house. There he called his wife, and showed me to her, but she screamed and ran back, as women in England do at the sight of a toad or a spider. However, when she had a while seen my behaviour, and how well I observed the signs her husband made, she was soon reconciled, and by degrees grew extremely tender of me.

It was about twelve at noon, and a servant brought in dinner. It was only one substantial dish of meat (fit for the plain condition of a husbandman[1]) in a dish of about four-and-twenty foot diameter. The company were the farmer and his wife, three children, and an old grandmother. When they were sat down, the farmer placed me at some distance from him on the table, which was thirty feet high from the floor. I was in a terrible fright, and kept as far as I could from the edge, for fear of falling. The wife minced a bit of meat, then crumbled some bread on a trencher and placed it before me. I made her a low bow, took out my knife and fork, and fell to eat, which gave them exceeding delight. The mistress sent her maid for a small dram cup, which held about two gallons, and filled it with drink; I took up the vessel with much difficulty in both hands, and in a most respectful manner drank to her ladyship's health, expressing the words as loud as I could in English,

which made the company laugh so heartily that I was almost deafened with the noise. This liquor tasted like a small[2] cider, and was not unpleasant. Then the master made me a sign to come to his trencher side; but as I walked on the table, being in great surprise all the time, as the indulgent reader will easily conceive and excuse, I happened to stumble against a crust, and fell flat on my face, but received no hurt. I got up immediately, and observing the good people to be in much concern, I took my hat (which I held under my arm out of good manners) and waving it over my head, made three huzzas to show I had got no mischief by my fall. But advancing forward towards my master (as I shall henceforth call him), his youngest son, who sat next to him, an arch boy of about ten years old, took me up by the legs and held me so high in the air, that I trembled every limb; but his father snatched me from him, and at the same time gave him such a box on the left ear as would have felled an European troop of horse to the earth, ordering him to be taken from the table. But being afraid the boy might owe me a spite, and well remembering how mischievous all children among us naturally are to sparrows, rabbits, young kittens, and puppy dogs, I fell on my knees and, pointing to the boy, made my master to understand, as well as I could, that I desired his son might be pardoned. The father complied, and the lad took his seat again, whereupon I went to him and kissed his hand, which my master took, and made him stroke me gently with it.

In the midst of dinner, my mistress's favourite cat leaped into her lap. I heard a noise behind me like that of a dozen stocking-weavers at work, and, turning my head, I found it proceeded from the purring of that animal, who seemed to be three times larger than an ox, as I computed by the view of her head and one of her paws while her mistress was feeding and stroking her. The fierceness of this creature's countenance altogether discomposed me, though I stood at the farther end of the table, above fifty feet off, and although my mistress held her fast for fear she might give a spring and seize me in her talons. But it happened there was no danger, for the cat took not the least notice of me when my master placed me within three yards of her. And as I have been always told, and found true by experience in my travels, that flying or discovering fear before a fierce

---

[1]   *husbandman* Farmer.

[2]   *small* Weak, of low alcohol content.

animal is a certain way to make it pursue or attack you, so I resolved in this dangerous juncture to show no manner of concern. I walked with intrepidity five or six times before the very head of the cat, and came within half a yard of her; whereupon she drew herself back, as if she were more afraid of me. I had less apprehension concerning the dogs, whereof three or four came into the room, as it is usual in farmers' houses; one of which was a mastiff, equal in bulk to four elephants, and another a greyhound, somewhat taller than the mastiff but not so large.

When dinner was almost done, the nurse came in with a child of a year old in her arms, who immediately spied me and began a squall that you might have heard from London Bridge to Chelsea, after the usual oratory of infants, to get me for a plaything. The mother, out of pure indulgence, took me up and put me towards the child, who presently seized me by the middle and got my head into his mouth, where I roared so loud that the urchin was frightened and let me drop, and I should infallibly have broke my neck if the mother had not held her apron under me. The nurse, to quiet her babe, made use of a rattle which was a kind of hollow vessel filled with great stones, and fastened by a cable to the child's waist; but all in vain; so that she was forced to apply the last remedy by giving it suck. I must confess no object ever disgusted me so much as the sight of her monstrous breast, which I cannot tell what to compare with so as to give the curious reader an idea of its bulk, shape, and colour. It stood prominent six feet, and could not be less than sixteen in circumference. The nipple was about half the bigness of my head, and the hue both of that and the dug[1] so varied with spots, pimples, and freckles, that nothing could appear more nauseous: for I had a near sight of her, she sitting down the more conveniently to give suck, and I standing on the table. This made me reflect upon the fair skins of our English ladies, who appear so beautiful to us only because they are of our own size, and their defects not to be seen but through a magnifying glass, where we find by experiment that the smoothest and whitest skins look rough, and coarse, and ill-coloured.

I remember when I was at Lilliput the complexion of those diminutive people appeared to me the fairest in the world; and, talking upon this subject with a person of learning there, who was an intimate friend of mine, he said that my face appeared much fairer and smoother when he looked on me from the ground than it did upon a nearer view, when I took him up in my hand and brought him close, which he confessed was at first a very shocking sight. He said he could discover great holes in my skin, that the stumps of my beard were ten times stronger than the bristles of a boar, and my complexion made up of several colours altogether disagreeable—although I must beg leave to say for myself that I am as fair as most of my sex and country, and very little sunburnt by all my travels. On the other side, discoursing of the ladies in that Emperor's court, he used to tell me one had freckles, another too wide a mouth, a third too large a nose; nothing of which I was able to distinguish. I confess this reflection was obvious enough, which however I could not forbear, lest the reader might think those vast creatures were actually deformed; for I must do them the justice to say, they are a comely race of people, and particularly the features of my master's countenance, although he was but a farmer, when I beheld him from the height of sixty feet, appeared very well proportioned.

When dinner was done my master went out to his labourers and, as I could discover by his voice and gesture, gave his wife strict charge to take care of me. I was very much tired and disposed to sleep, which my mistress perceiving, she put me on her own bed and covered me with a clean white handkerchief, but larger and coarser than the mainsail of a man-of-war.

I slept about two hours, and dreamt I was at home with my wife and children, which aggravated my sorrows when I awaked and found myself alone in a vast room between two and three hundred feet wide, and above two hundred high, lying in a bed twenty yards wide. My mistress was gone about her household affairs, and had locked me in. The bed was eight yards from the floor. Some natural necessities required me to get down; I durst not presume to call, and if I had, it would have been in vain with such a voice as mine at so great a distance from the room where I lay to the kitchen where the family kept. While I was under these circumstances, two rats crept up the curtains and ran smelling backwards and forwards on the bed. One of them came up almost to my face, whereupon I rose in a fright and

---

[1] *dug* Breast.

drew out my hanger[1] to defend myself. These horrible animals had the boldness to attack me on both sides, and one of them held his forefeet at my collar, but I had the good fortune to rip up his belly before he could do me any mischief. He fell down at my feet, and the other, seeing the fate of his comrade, made his escape, but not without one good wound on the back, which I gave him as he fled, and made the blood run trickling from him. After this exploit I walked gently to and fro on the bed to recover my breath and loss of spirits. These creatures were of the size of a large mastiff, but infinitely more nimble and fierce, so that if I had taken off my belt before I went to sleep, I must have infallibly been torn to pieces and devoured. I measured the tail of the dead rat and found it to be two yards long, wanting an inch; but it went against my stomach to drag the carcass off the bed, where it lay still bleeding. I observed it had yet some life, but with a strong slash across the neck I thoroughly dispatched it.

Soon after my mistress came into the room, who seeing me all bloody, ran and took me up in her hand. I pointed to the dead rat, smiling and making other signs to show I was not hurt, whereat she was extremely rejoiced, calling the maid to take up the dead rat with a pair of tongs and throw it out of the window. Then she set me on a table, where I showed her my hanger all bloody and, wiping it on the lappet of my coat, returned it to the scabbard. I was pressed to do more than one thing, which another could not do for me, and therefore endeavoured to make my mistress understand that I desired to be set down on the floor; which after she had done, my bashfulness would not suffer me to express myself farther than by pointing to the door and bowing several times. The good woman with much difficulty at last perceived what I would be at and, taking me up again in her hand, walked into the garden, where she set me down. I went on one side about two hundred yards and, beckoning to her not to look or to follow me, I hid myself between two leaves of sorrel, and there discharged the necessities of nature.

I hope the gentle reader will excuse me for dwelling on these and the like particulars, which, however insignificant they may appear to groveling, vulgar minds, yet will certainly help a philosopher to enlarge his thoughts and imagination, and apply them to the benefit of public as well as private life, which was my sole design in presenting this and other accounts of my travels to the world; wherein I have been chiefly studious of truth, without affecting any ornaments of learning or of style. But the whole scene of this voyage made so strong an impression on my mind, and is so deeply fixed in my memory, that in committing it to paper I did not omit one material circumstance; however, upon a strict review I blotted out several passages of less moment which were in my first copy, for fear of being censured as tedious and trifling, whereof travellers are often, perhaps not without justice, accused.

CHAPTER 2

(A description of the farmer's daughter. The author carried to a market town, and then to the metropolis. The particulars of his journey.)

My mistress had a daughter of nine years old, a child of towardly parts[2] for her age, very dexterous at her needle and skilful in dressing her baby.[3] Her mother and she contrived to fit up the baby's cradle for me against night: the cradle was put into a small drawer of a cabinet, and the drawer placed upon a hanging shelf for fear of the rats. This was my bed all the time I stayed with those people, though made more convenient by degrees as I began to learn their language and make my wants known. This young girl was so handy that after I had once or twice pulled off my clothes before her, she was able to dress and undress me, though I never gave her that trouble when she would let me do either myself. She made me seven shirts, and some other linen, of as fine cloth as could be got, which indeed was coarser than sackcloth; and these she constantly washed for me with her own hands. She was likewise my schoolmistress to teach me the language: when I pointed to anything, she told me the name of it in her own tongue, so that in a few days I was able to call for whatever I had a mind to. She was very good-natured, and not above forty feet high, being little for her age. She gave me the name of *Grildrig*, which the family took up, and afterwards the whole kingdom. The word imports what the Latins call

---

[1] *hanger* Short sword hung from the belt.

[2] *towardly parts* Promising abilities.

[3] *baby* Doll.

nanunculus, the Italians *homunceletino*,[1] and the English *mannikin*. To her I chiefly owe my preservation in that country: we never parted while I was there; I called her my *Glumdalclitch*, or little nurse, and should be guilty of great ingratitude if I omitted this honourable mention of her care and affection towards me, which I heartily wish it lay in my power to requite as she deserves, instead of being the innocent but unhappy instrument of her disgrace, as I have too much reason to fear.

It now began to be known and talked of in the neighbourhood that my master had found a strange animal in the field, about the bigness of a *splacknuck*, but exactly shaped in every part like a human creature, which it likewise imitated in all its actions: seemed to speak in a little language of its own, had already learned several words of theirs, went erect upon two legs, was tame and gentle, would come when it was called, do whatever it was bid, had the finest limbs in the world, and a complexion fairer than a nobleman's daughter of three years old. Another farmer who lived hard by, and was a particular friend of my master, came on a visit on purpose to inquire into the truth of this story. I was immediately produced and placed upon a table, where I walked as I was commanded, drew my hanger, put it up again, made my reverence to my master's guest, asked him in his own language how he did, and told him he was welcome, just as my little nurse had instructed me. This man, who was old and dim-sighted, put on his spectacles to behold me better, at which I could not forbear laughing very heartily, for his eyes appeared like the full moon shining into a chamber at two windows. Our people, who discovered the cause of my mirth, bore me company in laughing, at which the old fellow was fool enough to be angry and out of countenance. He had the character of a great miser, and, to my misfortune, he well deserved it by the cursed advice he gave my master to show me as a sight upon a market-day in the next town, which was half an hour's riding, about two-and-twenty miles from our house. I guessed there was some mischief when I observed my master and his friend whispering together, sometimes pointing at me; and my fears made me fancy that I overheard and understood some of their words. But the next morning Glumdalclitch, my little nurse, told me

the whole matter, which she had cunningly picked out from her mother. The poor girl laid me on her bosom and fell a-weeping with shame and grief. She apprehended some mischief would happen to me from rude vulgar folks, who might squeeze me to death, or break one of my limbs by taking me in their hands. She had also observed how modest I was in my nature, how nicely I regarded my honour, and what an indignity I should conceive it to be exposed for money as a public spectacle to the meanest of the people. She said her papa and mamma had promised that Grildrig should be hers, but now she found they meant to serve her as they did last year, when they pretended to give her a lamb, and yet as soon as it was fat sold it to a butcher. For my own part, I may truly affirm that I was less concerned than my nurse. I had a strong hope, which never left me, that I should one day recover my liberty: and as to the ignominy of being carried about for a monster, I considered myself to be a perfect stranger in the country, and that such a misfortune could never be charged upon me as a reproach if ever I should return to England, since the King of Great Britain himself, in my condition, must have undergone the same distress.

My master, pursuant to the advice of his friend, carried me in a box the next market day to the neighbouring town, and took along with him his little daughter, my nurse, upon a pillion[2] behind him. The box was close on every side, with a little door for me to go in and out and a few gimlet holes[3] to let in air. The girl had been so careful as to put the quilt of her baby's bed into it for me to lie down on. However, I was terribly shaken and discomposed in this journey, though it was but of half an hour, for the horse went about forty feet at every step and trotted so high that the agitation was equal to the rising and falling of a ship in a great storm, but much more frequent. Our journey was somewhat farther than from London to St. Alban's.[4] My master alighted at an inn which he used to frequent; and after consulting awhile with the inn-keeper, and making some necessary preparations, he hired the *grultrud*, or crier, to give notice through the town of a strange

---

[1] *Latins … homunceletino* These words are Swift's own inventions.

[2] *pillion* Cushion attached to the back of a saddle on which a second person could sit.

[3] *gimlet holes* Holes made by a gimlet, a sharp piercing or boring tool.

[4] *from London to St. Alban's* A distance of approximately 20 miles.

creature to be seen at the Sign of the Green Eagle, not so big as a *splacknuck* (an animal in that country very finely shaped, about six feet long), and in every part of the body resembling a human creature; could speak several words and perform a hundred diverting tricks.

I was placed upon a table in the largest room of the inn, which might be near three hundred feet square. My little nurse stood on a low stool close to the table to take care of me and direct what I should do. My master, to avoid a crowd, would suffer only thirty people at a time to see me. I walked about on the table as the girl commanded; she asked me questions, as far as she knew my understanding of the language reached, and I answered them as loud as I could. I turned about several times to the company, paid my humble respects, said they were welcome, and used some other speeches I had been taught. I took up a thimble filled with liquor, which Glumdalclitch had given me for a cup, and drank their health. I drew out my hanger and flourished with it after the manner of fencers in England. My nurse gave me a part of a straw, which I exercised as a pike, having learnt the art in my youth. I was that day shown to twelve sets of company, and as often forced to act over again the same fopperies, till I was half dead with weariness and vexation; for those who had seen me made such wonderful reports that the people were ready to break down the doors to come in. My master for his own interest would not suffer any one to touch me except my nurse; and, to prevent danger, benches were set round the table at such a distance as to put me out of every body's reach. However, an unlucky schoolboy aimed a hazelnut directly at my head, which very narrowly missed me; otherwise, it came with so much violence that it would have infallibly knocked out my brains, for it was almost as large as a small pumpion.[1] But I had the satisfaction to see the young rogue well beaten and turned out of the room.

My master gave public notice that he would show me again the next market day, and in the meantime he prepared a convenient vehicle for me, which he had reason enough to do, for I was so tired with my first journey, and with entertaining company for eight hours together, that I could hardly stand upon my legs or speak a word. It was at least three days before I recovered my strength; and that I might have no rest at home, all the neighbouring gentlemen from a hundred miles round, hearing of my fame, came to see me at my master's own house. There could not be fewer than thirty persons with their wives and children (for the country is very populous), and my master demanded the rate of a full room whenever he showed me at home, although it were only to a single family, so that for some time I had but little ease every day of the week (except Wednesday, which is their Sabbath), although I were not carried to the town.

My master, finding how profitable I was likely to be, resolved to carry me to the most considerable cities of the kingdom. Having therefore provided himself with all things necessary for a long journey, and settled his affairs at home, he took leave of his wife; and upon the 17th of August, 1703, about two months after my arrival, we set out for the metropolis, situated near the middle of that empire, and about three thousand miles distance from our house. My master made his daughter Glumdalclitch ride behind him. She carried me on her lap in a box tied about her waist. The girl had lined it on all sides with the softest cloth she could get, well quilted underneath, furnished it with her baby's bed, provided me with linen and other necessaries, and made everything as convenient as she could. We had no other company but a boy of the house, who rode after us with the luggage.

My master's design was to show me in all the towns by the way, and to step out of the road for fifty or a hundred miles to any village or person of quality's house where he might expect custom. We made easy journeys of not above seven or eight score miles a-day, for Glumdalclitch, on purpose to spare me, complained she was tired with the trotting of the horse. She often took me out of my box at my own desire, to give me air and show me the country, but always held me fast by leading strings.[2] We passed over five or six rivers many degrees broader and deeper than the Nile or the Ganges, and there was hardly a rivulet so small as the Thames at London Bridge. We were ten weeks in our journey, and I was shown in eighteen large towns, besides many villages and private families.

On the 26th day of October we arrived at the metropolis, called in their language *Lorbrulgrud*, or

---

[1] *pumpion* Pumpkin.

[2] *leading-strings* Strings that were attached to small children in order to guide and support them while they were learning to walk.

Pride of the Universe. My master took a lodging in the principal street of the city, not far from the royal palace, and put out bills[1] in the usual form, containing an exact description of my person and parts. He hired a large room between three and four hundred feet wide. He provided a table sixty feet in diameter, upon which I was to act my part, and palisadoed[2] it round three feet from the edge, and as many high, to prevent my falling over. I was shown ten times a day to the wonder and satisfaction of all people. I could now speak the language tolerably well, and perfectly understood every word that was spoken to me. Besides, I had learnt their alphabet, and could make a shift to explain a sentence here and there; for Glumdalclitch had been my instructor while we were at home, and at leisure hours during our journey. She carried a little book in her pocket, not much larger than a Sanson's *Atlas*;[3] it was a common treatise for the use of young girls, giving a short account of their religion. Out of this she taught me my letters and interpreted the words.

CHAPTER 3

(*The author sent for to court. The Queen buys him of his master the farmer, and presents him to the King. He disputes with His Majesty's great scholars. An apartment at court provided for the author. He is in high favour with the Queen. He stands up for the honour of his own country. His quarrels with the Queen's dwarf.*)

The frequent labours I underwent every day made in a few weeks a very considerable change in my health: the more my master got by me, the more insatiable he grew. I had quite lost my stomach, and was almost reduced to a skeleton. The farmer observed it and, concluding I must soon die, resolved to make as good a hand of me as he could. While he was thus reasoning and resolving with himself, a *sardral*, or gentleman usher, came from court, commanding my master to carry me immediately thither for the diversion of the Queen and her ladies. Some of the latter had already been to see me and reported strange things of my beauty, behaviour, and good sense. Her Majesty and those who attended her were beyond measure delighted with my demeanour. I fell on my knees and begged the honour of kissing her Imperial foot; but this gracious princess held out her little finger towards me after I was set on the table, which I embraced in both my arms, and put the tip of it with the utmost respect to my lip. She made me some general questions about my country and my travels, which I answered as distinctly and in as few words as I could. She asked whether I could be content to live at court. I bowed down to the board of the table, and humbly answered that I was my master's slave, but, if I were at my own disposal, I should be proud to devote my life to Her Majesty's service. She then asked my master whether he was willing to sell me at a good price. He, who apprehended I could not live a month, was ready enough to part with me, and demanded a thousand pieces of gold, which were ordered him on the spot, each piece being about the bigness of eight hundred moidores;[4] but, allowing for the proportion of all things between that country and Europe, and the high price of gold among them, was hardly so great a sum as a thousand guineas would be in England. I then said to the Queen, since I was now Her Majesty's most humble creature and vassal, I must beg the favour that Glumdalclitch, who had always tended me with so much care and kindness, and understood to do it so well, might be admitted into her service and continue to be my nurse and instructor. Her Majesty agreed to my petition and easily got the farmer's consent, who was glad enough to have his daughter preferred at court, and the poor girl herself was not able to hide her joy. My late master withdrew, bidding me farewell and saying he had left me in a good service; to which I replied not a word, only making him a slight bow.

The Queen observed my coldness and, when the farmer was gone out of the apartment, asked me the reason. I made bold to tell Her Majesty that I owed no other obligation to my late master than his not dashing out the brains of a poor harmless creature, found by chance in his fields; which obligation was amply recompensed by the gain he had made in showing me through half the kingdom, and the price he had now sold me for. That the life I had since led was laborious enough to kill

---

[1] *bills* Advertisements.

[2] *palisadoed* Enclosed; fenced in.

[3] *Sanson's Atlas* A book approximately 20 inches by 20 inches. Sanson was a French cartographer whose atlases were made in the largest possible book size.

[4] *moidores* Portuguese gold coins.

an animal of ten times my strength. That my health was much impaired by the continual drudgery of entertaining the rabble every hour of the day; and that if my master had not thought my life in danger, Her Majesty would not have got so cheap a bargain. But as I was out of all fear of being ill-treated under the protection of so great and good an Empress, the Ornament of Nature, the Darling of the World, the Delight of her Subjects, the Phoenix of the Creation, so I hoped my late master's apprehensions would appear to be groundless, for I already found my spirits revive by the influence of her most august presence.

This was the sum of my speech, delivered with great improprieties and hesitation. The latter part was altogether framed in the style peculiar to that people, whereof I learned some phrases from Glumdalclitch while she was carrying me to court.

The Queen, giving great allowance for my defectiveness in speaking, was, however, surprised at so much wit and good sense in so diminutive an animal. She took me in her own hand and carried me to the King, who was then retired to his cabinet.[1] His Majesty, a prince of much gravity, and austere countenance, not well observing my shape at first view, asked the Queen after a cold manner how long it was since she grew fond of a *splacknuck*; for such it seems he took me to be, as I lay upon my breast in Her Majesty's right hand. But this princess, who has an infinite deal of wit and humour, set me gently on my feet upon the scrutore[2] and commanded me to give His Majesty an account of myself, which I did in a very few words; and Glumdalclitch, who attended at the cabinet door and could not endure I should be out of her sight, being admitted, confirmed all that had passed from my arrival at her father's house.

The King, although he be as learned a person as any in his dominions, had been educated in the study of philosophy,[3] and particularly mathematics; yet when he observed my shape exactly, and saw me walk erect, before I began to speak, conceived I might be a piece of clockwork (which is in that country arrived to a very great perfection) contrived by some ingenious artist.[4]

But when he heard my voice, and found what I delivered to be regular and rational, he could not conceal his astonishment. He was by no means satisfied with the relation I gave him of the manner I came into his kingdom, but thought it a story concerted between Glumdalclitch and her father, who had taught me a set of words to make me sell at a better price. Upon this imagination, he put several other questions to me, and still received rational answers no otherwise defective than by a foreign accent and an imperfect knowledge in the language, with some rustic phrases which I had learned at the farmer's house, and did not suit the polite style of a court.

His Majesty sent for three great scholars, who were then in their weekly waiting (according to the custom in that country). These gentlemen, after they had a while examined my shape with much nicety, were of different opinions concerning me. They all agreed that I could not be produced according to the regular laws of nature because I was not framed with a capacity of preserving my life, either by swiftness, or climbing of trees, or digging holes in the earth. They observed by my teeth, which they viewed with great exactness, that I was a carnivorous animal; yet most quadrupeds being an overmatch for me, and field mice, with some others, too nimble, they could not imagine how I should be able to support myself, unless I fed upon snails and other insects, which they offered, by many learned arguments, to evince that I could not possibly do. One of these virtuosi seemed to think that I might be an embryo, or abortive birth. But this opinion was rejected by the other two, who observed my limbs to be perfect and finished; and that I had lived several years, as it was manifest from my beard, the stumps whereof they plainly discovered through a magnifying glass. They would not allow me to be a dwarf because my littleness was beyond all degrees of comparison; for the Queen's favourite dwarf, the smallest ever known in that kingdom, was near thirty feet high. After much debate, they concluded unanimously that I was only *relplum scalcath*, which is interpreted literally, *lusus naturae*,[5] a determination exactly agreeable to the modern philosophy of Europe, whose professors, disdaining the old evasion of occult causes, whereby the followers of Aristotle endea-

---

[1] *cabinet*   Boudoir, private chamber or apartment.

[2] *scrutore*   Escritoire, a small writing desk.

[3] *philosophy*   Science, or natural philosophy.

[4] *artist*   Artisan, craftsman.

[5] *lusus naturae*   Freak of nature. Swift here is criticizing those who referred to all things unfamiliar as resulting from "occult causes."

voured in vain to disguise their ignorance, have invented this wonderful solution of all difficulties, to the unspeakable advancement of human knowledge.

After this decisive conclusion, I entreated to be heard a word or two. I applied myself to the King, and assured His Majesty that I came from a country which abounded with several millions of both sexes, and of my own stature; where the animals, trees, and houses were all in proportion, and where, by consequence, I might be as able to defend myself and to find sustenance as any of His Majesty's subjects could do here; which I took for a full answer to those gentlemen's arguments. To this they only replied with a smile of contempt, saying that the farmer had instructed me very well in my lesson. The King, who had a much better understanding, dismissing his learned men, sent for the farmer, who by good fortune was not yet gone out of town. Having therefore first examined him privately, and then confronted him with me and the young girl, His Majesty began to think that what we told him might possibly be true. He desired the Queen to order that a particular care should be taken of me; and was of opinion that Glumdalclitch should still continue in her office of tending me, because he observed we had a great affection for each other. A convenient apartment was provided for her at court; she had a sort of governess appointed to take care of her education, a maid to dress her, and two other servants for menial offices; but the care of me was wholly appropriated to herself. The Queen commanded her own cabinet-maker to contrive a box that might serve me for a bedchamber, after the model that Glumdalclitch and I should agree upon. This man was a most ingenious artist and, according to my direction, in three weeks finished for me a wooden chamber of sixteen feet square and twelve high, with sash-windows, a door, and two closets, like a London bedchamber. The board that made the ceiling was to be lifted up and down by two hinges, to put in a bed ready furnished by Her Majesty's upholsterer, which Glumdalclitch took out every day to air, made it with her own hands, and, letting it down at night, locked up the roof over me. A nice[1] workman, who was famous for little curiosities, undertook to make me two chairs, with backs and frames, of a substance not unlike ivory, and two tables, with a cabinet to put my things in. The room was quilted on all sides, as well as the floor and the ceiling, to prevent any accident from the carelessness of those who carried me, and to break the force of a jolt when I went in a coach. I desired a lock for my door to prevent rats and mice from coming in. The smith, after several attempts, made the smallest that ever was seen among them, for I have known a larger at the gate of a gentleman's house in England. I made a shift to[2] keep the key in a pocket of my own, fearing Glumdalclitch might lose it. The Queen likewise ordered the thinnest silks that could be gotten, to make me clothes, not much thicker than an English blanket, very cumbersome till I was accustomed to them. They were after the fashion of the kingdom, partly resembling the Persian and partly the Chinese, and are a very grave and decent habit.

The Queen became so fond of my company that she could not dine without me. I had a table placed upon the same at which Her Majesty ate, just at her left elbow, and a chair to sit on. Glumdalclitch stood on a stool on the floor near my table, to assist and take care of me. I had an entire set of silver dishes and plates, and other necessaries, which, in proportion to those of the Queen, were not much bigger than what I have seen in a London toy-shop for the furniture of a baby-house: these my little nurse kept in her pocket in a silver box and gave me at meals as I wanted them, always cleaning them herself. No person dined with the Queen but the two princesses royal, the eldest sixteen years old, and the younger at that time thirteen and a month. Her Majesty used to put a bit of meat upon one of my dishes, out of which I carved for myself, and her diversion was to see me eat in miniature. For the Queen (who had indeed but a weak stomach) took up at one mouthful as much as a dozen English farmers could eat at a meal, which to me was for some time a very nauseous sight. She would crunch the wing of a lark, bones and all, between her teeth, although it were nine times as large as that of a full-grown turkey; and put a bit of bread into her mouth as big as two twelve-penny loaves. She drank out of a golden cup, above a hogshead at a draught. Her knives were twice as long as a scythe set straight upon the handle. The spoons, forks, and other instruments were all in the same proportion. I remember when Glumdalclitch carried me, out of curiosity, to see some of the

---

[1]   *nice*   Precise.

[2]   *made a shift to*   Contrived to, succeeded with difficulty in.

tables at court, where ten or a dozen of those enormous knives and forks were lifted up together, I thought I had never till then beheld so terrible a sight.

It is the custom that every Wednesday (which, as I have observed, is their Sabbath) the King and Queen, with the royal issue of both sexes, dine together in the apartment of His Majesty, to whom I was now become a great favourite; and at these times my little chair and table were placed at his left hand, before one of the salt-cellars. This prince took a pleasure in conversing with me, inquiring into the manners, religion, laws, government, and learning of Europe; wherein I gave him the best account I was able. His apprehension was so clear, and his judgment so exact, that he made very wise reflections and observations upon all I said. But I confess that after I had been a little too copious in talking of my own beloved country, of our trade and wars by sea and land, of our schisms in religion and parties in the state, the prejudices of his education prevailed so far that he could not forbear taking me up in his right hand, and stroking me gently with the other, after a hearty fit of laughing, asked me whether I were a Whig or Tory. Then, turning to his first minister, who waited behind him with a white staff near as tall as the mainmast of the *Royal Sovereign*,[1] he observed how contemptible a thing was human grandeur, which could be mimicked by such diminutive insects as I. "And yet," says he, "I dare engage,[2] these creatures have their titles and distinctions of honour; they contrive little nests and burrows that they call houses and cities; they make a figure in dress and equipage; they love, they fight, they dispute, they cheat, they betray!" And thus he continued on, while my colour came and went several times with indignation to hear our noble country, the mistress of arts and arms; the scourge of France; the arbitress of Europe; the seat of virtue, piety, honour, and truth; the pride and envy of the world, so contemptuously treated.

But as I was not in a condition to resent injuries, so upon mature thoughts I began to doubt whether I was injured or no. For, after having been accustomed several months to the sight and converse of this people, and observed every object upon which I cast mine eyes to be of proportionable magnitude, the horror I had at first

conceived from their bulk and aspect was so far worn off that if I had then beheld a company of English lords and ladies in their finery and birthday clothes,[3] acting their several parts in the most courtly manner of strutting, and bowing, and prating, to say the truth, I should have been strongly tempted to laugh as much at them as this King and his grandees did at me. Neither indeed could I forbear smiling at myself when the Queen used to place me upon her hand towards a looking-glass, by which both our persons appeared before me in full view together; and there could be nothing more ridiculous than the comparison, so that I really began to imagine myself dwindled many degrees below my usual size.

Nothing angered and mortified me so much as the Queen's dwarf, who, being of the lowest stature that was ever in that country (for I verily think he was not full thirty feet high) became so insolent at seeing a creature so much beneath him that he would always affect to swagger and look big as he passed by me in the Queen's antechamber, while I was standing on some table talking with the lords or ladies of the court, and he seldom failed of a smart word or two upon my littleness, against which I could only revenge myself by calling him brother, challenging him to wrestle, and such repartees as are usually in the mouths of court pages. One day at dinner this malicious little cub was so nettled with something I had said to him that, raising himself upon the frame of Her Majesty's chair, he took me up by the middle as I was sitting down, not thinking any harm, and let me drop into a large silver bowl of cream, and then ran away as fast as he could. I fell over head and ears, and if I had not been a good swimmer it might have gone very hard with me; for Glumdalclitch in that instant happened to be at the other end of the room, and the Queen was in such a fright that she wanted presence of mind to assist me. But my little nurse ran to my relief and took me out, after I had swallowed above a quart of cream. I was put to bed: however, I received no other damage than the loss of a suit of clothes, which was utterly spoiled. The dwarf was soundly whipped, and, as a further punishment, forced to drink up the bowl of cream into which he had thrown me; neither was he ever restored to favour; for soon after the Queen bestowed him on a lady of high quality, so that I saw

---

[1] *Royal Sovereign*   One of the tallest ships in the English navy, with a main mast over 100 feet high.

[2] *dare engage*   Believe.

[3] *birthday clothes*   Dress worn by courtiers for the monarch's birthday celebration.

him no more, to my very great satisfaction; for I could not tell to what extremities such a malicious urchin might have carried his resentment.

He had before served me a scurvy trick, which set the Queen a laughing, although at the same time she was heartily vexed, and would have immediately cashiered[1] him if I had not been so generous as to intercede. Her Majesty had taken a marrow bone upon her plate and, after knocking out the marrow, placed the bone again in the dish erect, as it stood before; the dwarf, watching his opportunity, while Glumdalclitch was gone to the side-board, mounted the stool that she stood on to take care of me at meals, took me up in both hands and, squeezing my legs together, wedged them into the marrow bone above my waist, where I stuck for some time and made a very ridiculous figure. I believe it was near a minute before any one knew what was become of me, for I thought it below me to cry out. But, as princes seldom get their meat hot, my legs were not scalded, only my stockings and breeches in a sad condition. The dwarf at my entreaty had no other punishment than a sound whipping.

I was frequently rallied[2] by the Queen upon account of my fearfulness, and she used to ask me whether the people of my country were as great cowards as myself. The occasion was this. The kingdom is much pestered with flies in summer, and these odious insects, each of them as big as a Dunstable[3] lark, hardly gave me any rest while I sat at dinner, with their continual humming and buzzing about mine ears. They would sometimes alight upon my victuals and leave their loathsome excrement or spawn behind, which to me was very visible, though not to the natives of that country, whose large optics were not so acute as mine in viewing smaller objects. Sometimes they would fix upon my nose or forehead, where they stung me to the quick, smelling very offensively; and I could easily trace that viscous matter, which our naturalists tell us enables those creatures to walk with their feet upwards upon a ceiling. I had much ado to defend myself against these detestable animals, and could not forbear starting when they came on my face. It was the common practice of the dwarf to catch a number of these insects in his hand, as schoolboys do among us, and let them out suddenly under my nose, on purpose to frighten me and divert the Queen. My remedy was to cut them in pieces with my knife as they flew in the air, wherein my dexterity was much admired.

I remember one morning when Glumdalclitch had set me in a box upon a window, as she usually did in fair days to give me air (for I durst not venture to let the box be hung on a nail out of the window, as we do with cages in England), after I had lifted up one of my sashes, and sat down at my table to eat a piece of sweet cake for my breakfast, above twenty wasps, allured by the smell, came flying into the room, humming louder than the drones of as many bagpipes. Some of them seized my cake and carried it piecemeal away; others flew about my head and face, confounding me with the noise and putting me in the utmost terror of their stings. However, I had the courage to rise and draw my hanger, and attack them in the air. I dispatched four of them, but the rest got away, and I presently shut my window. These insects were as large as partridges; I took out their stings, found them an inch and a half long and as sharp as needles. I carefully preserved them all and, having since shown them with some other curiosities in several parts of Europe, upon my return to England I gave three of them to Gresham College,[4] and kept the fourth for myself.

CHAPTER 4

(The country described. A proposal for correcting modern maps. The King's palace, and some account of the metropolis. The author's way of travelling. The chief temple described.)

I now intend to give the reader a short description of this country, as far as I travelled in it, which was not above two thousand miles round Lorbrulgrud, the metropolis. For the Queen, whom I always attended, never went farther when she accompanied the King in his progresses, and there staid till His Majesty returned from viewing his frontiers. The whole extent of this prince's dominions reaches about six thousand miles in length, and from three to five in breadth. From whence

---

[1] *cashiered*   Dismissed from service.

[2] *rallied*   Teased.

[3] *Dunstable*   City north of London. Larks were a popular food.

[4] *Gresham College*   The home of the Royal Society of England (a prestigious scientific organization) and of their museum.

I cannot but conclude that our geographers of Europe are in a great error by supposing nothing but sea between Japan and California; for it was ever my opinion that there must be a balance of earth to counterpoise the great continent of Tartary; and therefore they ought to correct their maps and charts by joining this vast tract of land to the northwest parts of America, wherein I shall be ready to lend them my assistance.

The kingdom is a peninsula, terminated to the northeast by a ridge of mountains thirty miles high, which are altogether impassable by reason of the volcanoes upon the tops. Neither do the most learned know what sort of mortals inhabit beyond those mountains, or whether they be inhabited at all. On the three other sides it is bounded by the ocean. There is not one seaport in the whole kingdom, and those parts of the coasts into which the rivers issue are so full of pointed rocks, and the sea generally so rough, that there is no venturing with the smallest of their boats; so that these people are wholly excluded from any commerce with the rest of the world. But the large rivers are full of vessels and abound with excellent fish, for they seldom get any from the sea because the sea fish are of the same size with those in Europe, and consequently not worth catching; whereby it is manifest that nature, in the production of plants and animals of so extraordinary a bulk, is wholly confined to this continent, of which I leave the reasons to be determined by philosophers. However, now and then they take a whale that happens to be dashed against the rocks, which the common people feed on heartily. These whales I have known so large that a man could hardly carry one upon his shoulders; and sometimes for curiosity they are brought in hampers to Lorbrulgrud; I saw one of them in a dish at the King's table, which passed for a rarity, but I did not observe he was fond of it; for I think indeed the bigness disgusted him, although I have seen one somewhat larger in Greenland.

The country is well inhabited, for it contains fifty-one cities, near a hundred walled towns, and a great number of villages. To satisfy my curious reader, it may be sufficient to describe Lorbrulgrud. This city stands upon almost two equal parts on each side the river that passes through. It contains above eighty thousand houses and about six hundred thousand inhabitants. It is in length three *glomglungs* (which make about fifty-

four English miles), and two and a half in breadth, as I measured it myself in the royal map made by the King's order, which was laid on the ground on purpose for me, and extended a hundred feet. I paced the diameter and circumference several times barefoot and, computing by the scale, measured it pretty exactly.

The King's palace is no regular edifice, but a heap of buildings about seven miles round. The chief rooms are generally two hundred and forty feet high, and broad and long in proportion. A coach was allowed to Glumdalclitch and me, wherein her governess frequently took her out to see the town or go among the shops; and I was always of the party, carried in my box, although the girl at my own desire would often take me out and hold me in her hand, that I might more conveniently view the houses and the people as we passed along the streets. I reckoned our coach to be about a square of Westminster-hall,[1] but not altogether so high: however, I cannot be very exact. One day the governess ordered our coachman to stop at several shops, where the beggars, watching their opportunity, crowded to the sides of the coach and gave me the most horrible spectacle that ever a European eye beheld. There was a woman with a cancer in her breast, swelled to a monstrous size, full of holes, in two or three of which I could have easily crept and covered my whole body. There was a fellow with a wen[2] in his neck larger than five woolpacks,[3] and another with a couple of wooden legs, each about twenty feet high. But the most hateful sight of all was the lice crawling on their clothes. I could see distinctly the limbs of these vermin with my naked eye, much better than those of a European louse through a microscope, and their snouts, with which they rooted like swine. They were the first I had ever beheld, and I should have been curious enough to dissect one of them if I had had proper instruments, which I unluckily left behind me in the ship, although, indeed, the sight was so nauseous that it perfectly turned my stomach.

Besides the large box in which I was usually carried, the Queen ordered a smaller one to be made for me, of about twelve feet square and ten high, for the conve-

---

1. *Westminster-hall*   Massive hall where the law courts then sat, now part of the English Parliament. It is approximately 290 feet long and 68 feet wide. Swift seems to mean the square of this area.

2. *wen*   Protuberance.

3. *woolpacks*   Large bags for transporting wool.

nience of traveling, because the other was somewhat too large for Glumdalclitch's lap, and cumbersome in the coach; it was made by the same artist, whom I directed in the whole contrivance. This travelling-closet was an exact square, with a window in the middle of three of the squares, and each window was latticed with iron wire on the outside, to prevent accidents in long journeys. On the fourth side, which had no window, two strong staples were fixed, through which the person that carried me, when I had a mind to be on horseback, put a leathern belt, and buckled it about his waist. This was always the office of some grave trusty servant, in whom I could confide, whether I attended the King and Queen in their progresses, or were disposed to see the gardens, or pay a visit to some great lady or minister of state in the court, when Glumdalclitch happened to be out of order;[1] for I soon began to be known and esteemed among the greatest officers—I suppose more upon account of Their Majesties' favour than any merit of my own. In journeys, when I was weary of the coach, a servant on horseback would buckle on my box and place it upon a cushion before him; and there I had a full prospect of the country on three sides from my three windows. I had in this closet a field bed and a hammock hung from the ceiling, two chairs and a table, neatly screwed to the floor to prevent being tossed about by the agitation of the horse or the coach. And, having been long used to sea voyages, those motions, although sometimes very violent, did not much discompose me.

Whenever I had a mind to see the town, it was always in my traveling closet, which Glumdalclitch held in her lap in a kind of open sedan, after the fashion of the country, borne by four men and attended by two others in the Queen's livery. The people, who had often heard of me, were very curious to crowd about the sedan, and the girl was complaisant enough to make the bearers stop, and to take me in her hand that I might be more conveniently seen.

I was very desirous to see the chief temple, and particularly the tower belonging to it, which is reckoned the highest in the kingdom. Accordingly, one day my nurse carried me thither, but I may truly say I came back disappointed; for the height is not above three thousand feet, reckoning from the ground to the highest pinnacle top, which, allowing for the difference between the size of those people and us in Europe, is no great matter for admiration, nor at all equal in proportion (if I rightly remember) to Salisbury steeple.[2] But, not to detract from a nation to which, during my life, I shall acknowledge myself extremely obliged, it must be allowed that whatever this famous tower wants in height, is amply made up in beauty and strength. For the walls are near a hundred feet thick, built of hewn stone, whereof each is about forty feet square, and adorned on all sides with statues of gods and emperors cut in marble, larger than the life, placed in their several niches. I measured a little finger which had fallen down from one of these statues and lay unperceived among some rubbish, and found it exactly four feet and an inch in length. Glumdalclitch wrapped it up in her handkerchief and carried it home in her pocket to keep among other trinkets, of which the girl was very fond, as children at her age usually are.

The King's kitchen is indeed a noble building, vaulted at top, and about six hundred feet high. The great oven is not so wide by ten paces as the cupola at St. Paul's[3]—for I measured the latter on purpose after my return. But if I should describe the kitchen grate, the prodigious pots and kettles, the joints of meat turning on the spits, with many other particulars, perhaps I should be hardly believed; at least a severe critic would be apt to think I enlarged a little, as travellers are often suspected to do. To avoid which censure, I fear I have run too much into the other extreme, and that if this treatise should happen to be translated into the language of Brobdingnag (which is the general name of that kingdom) and transmitted thither, the King and his people would have reason to complain that I had done them an injury by a false and diminutive representation.

His Majesty seldom keeps above six hundred horses in his stables; they are generally from fifty-four to sixty foot high. But when he goes abroad on solemn days, he is attended, for state, by a military guard of five hundred horse, which indeed I thought was the most splendid sight that could be ever beheld, till I saw part of his

---

[1] *out of order* Indisposed.

[2] *Salisbury steeple* The 404 foot high steeple of Salisbury Cathedral is the tallest in England.

[3] *the cupola at St. Paul's* The dome of St. Paul's Cathedral, London, is approximately 112 feet in diameter.

army in battalia,[1] whereof I shall find another occasion to speak.

CHAPTER 5

(Several adventurers that happened to the author. The execution of a criminal. The author shows his skill in navigation.)

I should have lived happy enough in that country if my littleness had not exposed me to several ridiculous and troublesome accidents, some of which I shall venture to relate. Glumdalclitch often carried me into the gardens of the court in my smaller box, and would sometimes take me out of it, and hold me in her hand or set me down to walk. I remember, before the dwarf left the Queen, he followed us one day into those gardens, and my nurse having set me down, he and I being close together near some dwarf apple trees, I must needs show my wit by a silly allusion between him and the trees, which happens to hold in their language as it does in ours. Whereupon, the malicious rogue, watching his opportunity, when I was walking under one of them, shook it directly over my head, by which a dozen apples, each of them near as large as a Bristol barrel,[2] came tumbling about my ears; one of them hit me on the back as I chanced to stoop, and knocked me down flat on my face; but I received no other hurt, and the dwarf was pardoned at my desire, because I had given the provocation.

Another day, Glumdalclitch left me on a smooth grassplot to divert myself while she walked at some distance with her governess. In the meantime, there suddenly fell such a violent shower of hail that I was immediately by the force of it struck to the ground; and when I was down the hailstones gave me such cruel bangs all over the body, as if I had been pelted with tennis balls; however, I made a shift to creep on all four and shelter myself by lying flat on my face on the lee-side of a border of lemon thyme, but so bruised from head to foot that I could not go abroad in ten days. Neither is this at all to be wondered at because, nature

in that country observing the same proportion through all her operations, a hailstone is near eighteen hundred times as large as one in Europe; which I can assert upon experience, having been so curious as to weigh and measure them.

But a more dangerous accident happened to me in the same garden when my little nurse, believing she had put me in a secure place (which I often entreated her to do, that I might enjoy my own thoughts), and having left my box at home to avoid the trouble of carrying it, went to another part of the garden with her governess and some ladies of her acquaintance. While she was absent and out of hearing, a small white spaniel that belonged to one of the chief gardeners, having got by accident into the garden, happened to range near the place where I lay. The dog, following the scent, came directly up and, taking me in his mouth, ran straight to his master, wagging his tail, and set me gently on the ground. By good fortune he had been so well taught that I was carried between his teeth without the least hurt, or even tearing my clothes. But the poor gardener, who knew me well and had a great kindness for me, was in a terrible fright. He gently took me up in both his hands and asked me how I did, but I was so amazed and out of breath that I could not speak a word. In a few minutes I came to myself, and he carried me safe to my little nurse, who by this time had returned to the place where she left me, and was in cruel agonies when I did not appear, nor answer when she called. She severely reprimanded the gardener on account of his dog; but the thing was hushed up and never known at court, for the girl was afraid of the Queen's anger, and truly, as to myself, I thought it would not be for my reputation that such a story should go about.

This accident absolutely determined Glumdalclitch never to trust me abroad for the future out of her sight. I had been long afraid of this resolution and therefore concealed from her some little unlucky adventures that happened in those times when I was left by myself. Once, a kite[3] hovering over the garden made a stoop[4] at me, and if I had not resolutely drawn my hanger and run under a thick espalier,[5] he would have certainly

---

[1] *in battalia* In their battle array.

[2] *Bristol barrel* A barrel holding roughly 40 gallons. Barrels varied in size depending on where they came from, and those from Bristol, a major industrial center, were among the largest.

[3] *kite* Bird of prey of the falcon family.

[4] *stoop* Swoop.

[5] *espalier* Trees trained to grow upon lattice-work or stakes.

carried me away in his talons. Another time, walking to the top of a fresh mole-hill, I fell to my neck in the hole through which that animal had cast up the earth, and coined some lie, not worth remembering, to excuse myself for spoiling my clothes. I likewise broke my right shin against the shell of a snail, which I happened to stumble over as I was walking alone and thinking on poor England.

I cannot tell whether I were more pleased or mortified to observe in those solitary walks that the smaller birds did not appear to be at all afraid of me, but would hop about within a yard distance, looking for worms and other food, with as much indifference and security as if no creature at all were near them. I remember a thrush had the confidence to snatch out of my hand, with his bill, a piece of cake that Glumdalclitch had just given me for my breakfast. When I attempted to catch any of these birds, they would boldly turn against me, endeavouring to peck my fingers, which I durst not venture within their reach; and then they would hop back, unconcerned, to hunt for worms or snails, as they did before. But one day I took a thick cudgel and threw it with all my strength so luckily at a linnet that I knocked him down and, seizing him by the neck with both my hands, ran with him in triumph to my nurse. However, the bird—who had only been stunned—recovering himself, gave me so many boxes with his wings on both sides of my head and body, though I held him at arm's length and was out of the reach of his claws, that I was twenty times thinking to let him go. But I was soon relieved by one of our servants, who wrung off the bird's neck, and I had him next day for dinner, by the Queen's command. This linnet, as near as I can remember, seemed to be somewhat larger than an English swan.

The Maids of Honour often invited Glumdalclitch to their apartments, and desired she would bring me along with her, on purpose to have the pleasure of seeing and touching me. They would often strip me naked from top to toe and lay me at full length in their bosoms; wherewith I was much disgusted because, to say the truth, a very offensive smell came from their skins; which I do not mention or intend to the disadvantage of those excellent ladies, for whom I have all manner of respect; but I conceive that my sense was more acute in proportion to my littleness, and that those illustrious

persons were no more disagreeable to their lovers, or to each other, than people of the same quality are with us in England. And, after all, I found their natural smell was much more supportable than when they used perfumes, under which I immediately swooned away. I cannot forget that an intimate friend of mine in Lilliput took the freedom in a warm day, when I had used a good deal of exercise, to complain of a strong smell about me, although I am as little faulty that way as most of my sex; but I suppose his faculty of smelling was as nice[1] with regard to me as mine was to that of this people. Upon this point, I cannot forbear doing justice to the Queen my mistress and Glumdalclitch my nurse, whose persons were as sweet as those of any lady in England.

That which gave me most uneasiness among these Maids of Honour (when my nurse carried me to visit then) was to see them use me without any manner of ceremony, like a creature who had no sort of consequence. For they would strip themselves to the skin and put on their smocks in my presence, while I was placed on their toilet[2] directly before their naked bodies, which I am sure to me was very far from being a tempting sight, or from giving me any other emotions than those of horror and disgust. Their skins appeared so coarse and uneven, so variously coloured, when I saw them near, with a mole here and there as broad as a trencher, and hairs hanging from it thicker than packthreads, to say nothing farther concerning the rest of their persons. Neither did they at all scruple, while I was by, to discharge what they had drank, to the quantity of at least two hogsheads, in a vessel that held above three tuns. The handsomest among these Maids of Honour, a pleasant, frolicsome girl of sixteen, would sometimes set me astride upon one of her nipples, with many other tricks, wherein the reader will excuse me for not being over particular. But I was so much displeased that I entreated Glumdalclitch to contrive some excuse for not seeing that young lady any more.

One day a young gentleman who was nephew to my nurse's governess came and pressed them both to see an execution. It was of a man who had murdered one of that gentleman's intimate acquaintance. Glumdalclitch was prevailed on to be of the company, very much against her inclination, for she was naturally tender-

---

[1] *nice* Sharp.

[2] *toilet* Dressing table.

hearted; and, as for myself, although I abhorred such kind of spectacles, yet my curiosity tempted me to see something that I thought must be extraordinary. The malefactor was fixed in a chair upon a scaffold erected for that purpose, and his head cut off at one blow with a sword of about forty feet long. The veins and arteries spouted up such a prodigious quantity of blood, and so high in the air, that the great *jet d'eau* at Versailles[1] was not equal to it for the time it lasted; and the head, when it fell on the scaffold floor, gave such a bounce as made me start, although I was at least half an English mile distant.

The Queen, who often used to hear me talk of my sea voyages, and took all occasions to divert me when I was melancholy, asked me whether I understood how to handle a sail or an oar, and whether a little exercise of rowing might not be convenient for my health? I answered that I understood both very well. For although my proper employment had been to be surgeon or doctor to the ship, yet often, upon a pinch, I was forced to work like a common mariner. But I could not see how this could be done in their country, where the smallest wherry[2] was equal to a first-rate man of war among us; and such a boat as I could manage would never live in any of their rivers. Her Majesty said, if I would contrive[3] a boat, her own joiner[4] should make it, and she would provide a place for me to sail in. The fellow was an ingenious workman and, by my instructions, in ten days finished a pleasure boat with all its tackling, able conveniently to hold eight Europeans. When it was finished, the Queen was so delighted that she ran with it in her lap to the King, who ordered it to be put into a cistern full of water, with me in it, by way of trial; where I could not manage my two sculls, or little oars, for want of room. But the Queen had before contrived another project. She ordered the joiner to make a wooden trough of three hundred feet long, fifty broad, and eight deep; which, being well pitched to prevent leaking, was placed on the floor along the wall in an outer room of the palace. It had a cock[5] near the bottom to let out the water when it began to grow stale; and two servants could easily fill it in half an hour. Here I often used to row for my own diversion, as well as that of the Queen and her ladies, who thought themselves well entertained with my skill and agility. Sometimes I would put up my sail, and then my business was only to steer while the ladies gave me a gale with their fans; and when they were weary some of their pages would blow my sail forward with their breath, while I showed my art by steering starboard or larboard as I pleased. When I had done, Glumdalclitch always carried back my boat into her closet[6] and hung it on a nail to dry.

In this exercise I once met an accident which had like to have cost me my life; for, one of the pages having put my boat into the trough, the governess who attended Glumdalclitch very officiously[7] lifted me up to place me in the boat; but I happened to slip through her fingers, and should infallibly have fallen down forty feet upon the floor if, by the luckiest chance in the world, I had not been stopped by a corking-pin that stuck in the good gentlewoman's stomacher,[8] the head of the pin passing between my shirt and the waistband of my breeches. And thus I was held by the middle in the air until Glumdalclitch ran to my relief.

Another time, one of the servants, whose office it was to fill my trough every third day with fresh water, was so careless as to let a huge frog (not perceiving it) slip out of his pail. The frog lay concealed till I was put into my boat, but then, seeing a resting-place, climbed up and made it lean so much on one side that I was forced to balance it with all my weight on the other to prevent overturning. When the frog was got in, it hopped at once half the length of the boat, and then over my head, backward and forward, daubing my face and clothes with its odious slime. The largeness of its features made it appear the most deformed animal that can be conceived. However, I desired Glumdalclitch to let me deal with it alone. I banged it a good while with one of my sculls, and at last forced it to leap out of the boat.

---

1 *jet ... Versailles* The largest fountain in Louis XIV's palace gardens at Versailles sprayed its water nearly 70 feet in the air.

2 *wherry* Small, light rowboat.

3 *contrive* Devise; invent.

4 *joiner* Carpenter.

5 *cock* Tap; spout.

6 *closet* Small, private inner chamber.

7 *officiously* Eagerly; dutifully.

8 *stomacher* Ornamental chest-covering for women, often decorated with jewels; *corking-pin* Large pin.

But the greatest danger I ever underwent in that kingdom was from a monkey who belonged to one of the clerks of the kitchen. Glumdalclitch had locked me up in her closet while she went somewhere upon business or a visit. The weather being very warm, the closet window was left open, as well as the windows and the door of my bigger box, in which I usually lived because of its largeness and conveniency. As I sat quietly meditating at my table, I heard something bounce in at the closet window and skip about from one side to the other, whereat, although I was much alarmed, yet I ventured to look out, but not stirring from my seat; and then I saw this frolicsome animal frisking and leaping up and down, till at last he came to my box, which he seemed to view with great pleasure and curiosity, peeping in at the door and every window. I retreated to the farther corner of my room, or box; but the monkey, looking in at every side, put me in such a fright that I wanted presence of mind to conceal myself under the bed, as I might easily have done. After some time spent in peeping, grinning, and chattering, he at last espied me and, reaching one of his paws in at the door, as a cat does when she plays with a mouse, although I often shifted place to avoid him, he at length seized the lappet of my coat (which being made of that country silk, was very thick and strong) and dragged me out. He took me up in his right forefoot and held me as a nurse does a child she is going to suckle, just as I have seen the same sort of creature do with a kitten in Europe; and when I offered to struggle he squeezed me so hard that I thought it more prudent to submit. I have good reason to believe that he took me for a young one of his own species, by his often stroking my face very gently with his other paw. In these diversions he was interrupted by a noise at the closet door, as if somebody were opening it, whereupon he suddenly leaped up to the window at which he had come in, and thence upon the leads and gutters, walking upon three legs and holding me in the fourth, till he clambered up to a roof that was next to ours. I heard Glumdalclitch give a shriek at the moment he was carrying me out. The poor girl was almost distracted;[1] that quarter of the palace was all in an uproar; the servants ran for ladders; the monkey was seen by hundreds in the court, sitting upon the ridge of a building, holding me like a baby in one of his fore-

paws and feeding me with the other by cramming into my mouth some victuals he had squeezed out of the bag on one side of his chaps,[2] and patting me when I would not eat; whereat many of the rabble below could not forbear laughing; neither do I think they justly ought to be blamed, for without question the sight was ridiculous enough to everybody but myself. Some of the people threw up stones, hoping to drive the monkey down, but this was strictly forbidden, or else very probably my brains had been dashed out.

The ladders were now applied, and mounted by several men; which the monkey observing, and finding himself almost encompassed, not being able to make speed enough with his three legs, let me drop on a ridge tile and made his escape. Here I sat for some time, five hundred yards from the ground, expecting every moment to be blown down by the wind, or to fall by my own giddiness, and come tumbling over and over from the ridge to the eaves. But an honest lad, one of my nurse's footmen, climbed up and, putting me into his breeches pocket, brought me down safe.

I was almost choked with the filthy stuff the monkey had crammed down my throat, but my dear little nurse picked it out of my mouth with a small needle, and then I fell a vomiting, which gave me great relief. Yet I was so weak and bruised in the sides with the squeezes given me by this odious animal that I was forced to keep my bed a fortnight. The King, Queen, and all the court sent every day to inquire after my health, and Her Majesty made me several visits during my sickness. The monkey was killed, and an order made that no such animal should be kept about the palace.

When I attended the King after my recovery, to return him thanks for his favours, he was pleased to rally me a good deal upon this adventure. He asked me what my thoughts and speculations were while I lay in the monkey's paw, how I liked the victuals he gave me, his manner of feeding, and whether the fresh air on the roof had sharpened my stomach. He desired to know what I would have done upon such an occasion in my own country. I told His Majesty that in Europe we had no monkeys except such as were brought for curiosity from other places, and so small that I could deal with a dozen of them together if they presumed to attack me. And as for that monstrous animal with whom I was so lately

---

[1] *distracted* Frantic.

[2] *chaps* Cheeks.

engaged (it was indeed as large as an elephant), if my fears had suffered me to think so far as to make use of my hanger (looking fiercely, and clapping my hand on the hilt, as I spoke) when he poked his paw into my chamber, perhaps I should have given him such a wound as would have made him glad to withdraw it with more haste than he put it in. This I delivered in a firm tone, like a person who was jealous lest his courage should be called in question. However, my speech produced nothing else beside a loud laughter, which all the respect due to His Majesty from those about him could not make them contain. This made me reflect how vain an attempt it is for a man to endeavour to do himself honour among those who are out of all degree of equality or comparison with him. And yet I have seen the moral of my own behaviour very frequent in England since my return; where a little contemptible varlet, without the least title to birth, person, wit, or common sense, shall presume to look with importance, and put himself upon a foot with the greatest persons of the kingdom.

I was every day furnishing the court with some ridiculous story, and Glumdalclitch, although she loved me to excess, yet was arch enough to inform the Queen whenever I committed any folly that she thought would be diverting to Her Majesty. The girl, who had been out of order, was carried by her governess to take the air about an hour's distance, or thirty miles from town. They alighted out of the coach near a small footpath in a field, and, Glumdalclitch setting down my travelling box, I went out of it to walk. There was a cow dung in the path, and I must need try my activity by attempting to leap over it. I took a run, but unfortunately jumped short, and found myself just in the middle up to my knees. I waded through with some difficulty, and one of the footmen wiped me as clean as he could with his handkerchief, for I was filthily bemired, and my nurse confined me to my box till we returned home, where the Queen was soon informed of what had passed, and the footmen spread it about the court, so that all the mirth for some days was at my expense.

CHAPTER 6

(*Several contrivances of the author to please the King and Queen. He shows his skill in music. The King inquires into the state of England, which the author relates to him. The King's observations thereon.*)

I used to attend the King's levee[1] once or twice a week, and had often seen him under the barber's hand, which indeed was at first very terrible to behold, for the razor was almost twice as long as an ordinary scythe. His Majesty, according to the custom of the country, was only shaved twice a-week. I once prevailed on the barber to give me some of the suds or lather, out of which I picked forty or fifty of the strongest stumps of hair. I then took a piece of fine wood and cut it like the back of a comb, making several holes in it at equal distances with as small a needle as I could get from Glumdalclitch. I fixed in the stumps so artificially,[2] scraping and sloping them with my knife toward the points, that I made a very tolerable comb; which was a seasonable supply,[3] my own being so much broken in the teeth that it was almost useless; neither did I know any artist in that country so nice and exact as would undertake to make me another.

And this puts me in mind of an amusement wherein I spent many of my leisure hours. I desired the Queen's woman to save for me the combings of Her Majesty's hair, whereof in time I got a good quantity; and consulting with my friend the cabinet-maker, who had received general orders to do little jobs for me, I directed him to make two chair-frames, no larger than those I had in my box, and to bore little holes with a fine awl round those parts where I designed the backs and seats; through these holes I wove the strongest hairs I could pick out, just after the manner of cane chairs in England. When they were finished, I made a present of them to Her Majesty; who kept them in her cabinet and used to show them for curiosities, as indeed they were the wonder of everyone that beheld them. The Queen would have me sit upon one of these chairs, but I absolutely refused to obey her, protesting I would rather

---

1 *levee* Morning reception of visitors, which was sometimes held as one dressed for the day.

2 *artificially* With artifice; skillfully.

3 *seasonable supply* Opportune provision.

die a thousand deaths than place a dishonourable part of my body on those precious hairs that once adorned Her Majesty's head. Of these hairs (as I had always a mechanical genius) I likewise made a neat little purse, about five feet long, with Her Majesty's name deciphered in gold letters, which I gave to Glumdalclitch, by the Queen's consent. To say the truth, it was more for show than use, being not of strength to bear the weight of the larger coins, and therefore she kept nothing in it but some little toys that girls are fond of.

The King, who delighted in music, had frequent concerts at court, to which I was sometimes carried, and set in my box on a table to hear them; but the noise was so great that I could hardly distinguish the tunes. I am confident that all the drums and trumpets of a royal army, beating and sounding together just at your ears, could not equal it. My practice was to have my box removed from the place where the performers sat, as far as I could, then to shut the doors and windows of it, and draw the window curtains, after which I found their music not disagreeable.

I had learned in my youth to play a little upon the spinet.[1] Glumdalclitch kept one in her chamber, and a master attended twice a week to teach her: I called it a spinet because it somewhat resembled that instrument, and was played upon in the same manner. A fancy came into my head that I would entertain the King and Queen with an English tune upon this instrument. But this appeared extremely difficult, for the spinet was near sixty feet long, each key being almost a foot wide, so that with my arms extended I could not reach to above five keys, and to press them down required a good smart stroke with my fist, which would be too great a labour and to no purpose. The method I contrived was this: I prepared two round sticks about the bigness of common cudgels; they were thicker at one end than the other, and I covered the thicker ends with pieces of a mouse's skin, that by rapping on them I might neither damage the tops of the keys nor interrupt the sound. Before the spinet a bench was placed about four feet below the keys, and I was put upon the bench. I ran sideling upon it, that way and this, as fast as I could, banging the proper keys with my two sticks, and made a shift to play a jig, to the great satisfaction of both their majesties; but it was the most violent exercise I ever underwent; and

yet I could not strike above sixteen keys, nor consequently play the bass and treble together as other artists do, which was a great disadvantage to my performance.

The King, who, as I before observed, was a prince of excellent understanding, would frequently order that I should be brought in my box and set upon the table in his closet. He would then command me to bring one of my chairs out of the box and sit down within three yards' distance upon the top of the cabinet, which brought me almost to a level with his face. In this manner I had several conversations with him. I one day took the freedom to tell His Majesty that the contempt he discovered towards Europe and the rest of the world did not seem answerable to those excellent qualities of mind that he was master of; that reason did not extend itself with the bulk of the body; on the contrary, we observed in our country that the tallest persons were usually the least provided with it; that, among other animals, bees and ants had the reputation of more industry, art, and sagacity than many of the larger kinds; and that, as inconsiderable as he took me to be, I hoped I might live to do His Majesty some signal service. The King heard me with attention, and began to conceive a much better opinion of me than he had ever before. He desired I would give him as exact an account of the government of England as I possibly could because, as fond as princes commonly are of their own customs (for so he conjectured of other monarchs, by my former discourses), he should be glad to hear of anything that might deserve imitation.

Imagine with thyself, courteous reader, how often I then wished for the tongue of Demosthenes or Cicero,[2] that might have enabled me to celebrate the praise of my own dear native country in a style equal to its merits and felicity.

I began my discourse by informing His Majesty that our dominions consisted of two islands, which composed three mighty kingdoms under one sovereign, beside our plantations[3] in America. I dwelt long upon the fertility of our soil and the temperature[4] of our climate. I then spoke at large upon the constitution of an English Parliament, partly made up of an illustrious body called the House of Peers—persons of the noblest

---

[1] *spinet* Musical instrument resembling a harpsichord.

[2] *Demosthenes or Cicero* Greek and Roman orators.

[3] *plantations* Colonies.

[4] *temperature* Temperate nature.

blood and of the most ancient and ample patrimonies. I described that extraordinary care always taken of their education in arts and arms to qualify them for being counsellors both to the King and kingdom; to have a share in the legislature; to be members of the Highest Court of Judicature, whence there can be no appeal; and to be champions always ready for the defence of their prince and country by their valour, conduct, and fidelity. That these were the ornament and bulwark of the kingdom, worthy followers of their most renowned ancestors, whose honour had been the reward of their virtue, from which their posterity were never once known to degenerate. To these were joined several holy persons, as part of that assembly under the title of bishops, whose peculiar business is to take care of religion and of those who instruct the people therein. These were searched and sought out through the whole nation, by the prince and his wisest counsellors, among such of the priesthood as were most deservedly distinguished by the sanctity of their lives and the depth of their erudition, who were indeed the spiritual fathers of the clergy and the people.

That the other part of the Parliament consisted of an assembly called the House of Commons, who were all principal gentlemen freely picked and culled out by the people themselves, for their great abilities and love of their country, to represent the wisdom of the whole nation. And that these two bodies made up the most august assembly in Europe, to whom, in conjunction with the prince, the whole legislature is committed.

I then descended to the Courts of Justice, over which the judges, those venerable sages and interpreters of the law, presided for determining the disputed rights and properties of men, as well as for the punishment of vice and protection of innocence. I mentioned the prudent management of our treasury, the valour and achievements of our forces by sea and land. I computed the number of our people by reckoning how many millions there might be of each religious sect or political party among us. I did not omit even our sports and pastimes, or any other particular which I thought might redound to the honour of my country. And I finished all with a brief historical account of affairs and events in England for about a hundred years past.

This conversation was not ended under five audiences, each of several hours; and the King heard the whole with great attention, frequently taking notes of what I spoke, as well as memorandums of what questions he intended to ask me.

When I had put an end to these long discourses, His Majesty, in a sixth audience, consulting his notes, proposed many doubts, queries, and objections upon every article. He asked what methods were used to cultivate the minds and bodies of our young nobility, and in what kind of business they commonly spent the first and teachable parts of their lives. What course was taken to supply that assembly when any noble family became extinct. What qualifications were necessary in those who are to be created new lords. Whether the humour[1] of the prince, a sum of money to a court lady, or a design of strengthening a party opposite to the public interest ever happened to be the motive in those advancements. What share of knowledge these lords had in the laws of their country, and how they came by it, so as to enable them to decide the properties of their fellow subjects in the last resort. Whether they were always so free from avarice, partialities, or want that a bribe, or some other sinister view, could have no place among them. Whether those holy lords I spoke of were always promoted to that rank upon account of their knowledge in religious matters, and the sanctity of their lives; had never been compliers with the times while they were common priests, or slavish prostitute chaplains to some nobleman whose opinions they continued servilely to follow after they were admitted into that assembly?

He then desired to know what Arts were practised in electing those whom I called Commoners. Whether, a Stranger with a strong Purse might not influence the vulgar Voters to chuse him before their own Landlord, or the most considerable Gentleman in the Neighbourhood. How it came to pass, that People were so violently bent upon getting into this Assembly, which I allowed to be a great Trouble and Expence, often to the Ruin of their Families, without any Salary or Pension: Because this appeared such an exalted strain of Virtue and publick Spirit, that his Majesty seemed to doubt it might possibly not be always sincere: And he desired to know whether such zealous Gentlemen could have any Views of refunding themselves for the Charges and Trouble they were at, by sacrificing the Publick Good to

original spelling

---

[1]   *humour* Idle fancy.

the Designs of a weak and vicious Prince, in Conjunction with a corrupted Ministry. He multiplied his Questions, and sifted[1] me thoroughly upon every part of this Head,[2] proposing numberless Enquiries and Objections, which I think it not prudent or convenient to repeat.

Upon what I said in relation to our Courts of Justice, His Majesty desired to be satisfied in several points, and this I was the better able to do, having been formerly almost ruined by a long suit in Chancery,[3] which was decreed for me with costs. He asked what time was usually spent in determining between right and wrong, and what degree of expense. Whether advocates and orators had liberty to plead in causes manifestly known to be unjust, vexatious, or oppressive. Whether party in religion or politics were observed to be of any weight in the scale of justice. Whether those pleading orators were persons educated in the general knowledge of equity, or only in provincial, national, and other local customs. Whether they or their judges had any part in penning those laws which they assumed the liberty of interpreting, and glossing upon at their pleasure. Whether they had ever, at different times, pleaded for and against the same cause, and cited precedents to prove contrary opinions. Whether they were a rich or a poor corporation. Whether they received any pecuniary reward for pleading or delivering their opinions. And particularly, whether they were ever admitted as members in the lower senate.

He fell next upon the management of our Treasury, and said he thought my memory had failed me, because I computed our taxes at about five or six millions a year, and when I came to mention the issues,[4] he found they sometimes amounted to more than double; for the notes he had taken were very particular in this point because he hoped, as he told me, that the knowledge of our conduct might be useful to him, and he could not be deceived in his calculations. But if what I told him were true, he was still at a loss how a kingdom could run out of its estate, like a private person. He asked me who were our creditors, and where we found money to pay

them. He wondered to hear me talk of such chargeable and expensive wars; that certainly we must be a quarrelsome people, or live among very bad neighbours, and that our generals must needs be richer than our kings.[5] He asked what business we had out of our own islands, unless upon the score of trade or treaty, or to defend the coasts with our fleet. Above all, he was amazed to hear me talk of a mercenary standing army[6] in the midst of peace, and among a free people. He said, if we were governed by our own consent in the persons of our representatives, he could not imagine of whom we were afraid, or against whom we were to fight; and would hear my opinion whether a private man's house might not be better defended by himself, his children and family than by half-a-dozen rascals, picked up at a venture in the streets for small wages, who might get a hundred times more by cutting their throats.

He laughed at my odd kind of Arithmetick, as he was pleased to call it, in reckoning the Numbers of our People by a Computation drawn from the several Sects among us in Religion and Politicks. He said, he knew no Reason, why those who entertain Opinions prejudicial to the Publick, should be obliged to Change, or should not be obliged to Conceal them. And as it was Tyranny in any Government to require the first, so it was Weakness not to enforce the second: for a Man may be allowed to keep Poisons in his closet, but not to vend them about for Cordials.[7]

He observed that among the diversions of our nobility and gentry, I had mentioned gaming.[8] He desired to know at what age this entertainment was usually taken up and when it was laid down; how much of their time it employed; whether it ever went so high as to affect their fortunes; whether mean, vicious people, by their dexterity in that art, might not arrive at great riches, and sometimes keep our very nobles in depend-

---

1 *sifted* Investigated; questioned.

2 *Head* Topic.

3 *Chancery* Court of the Lord Chancellor, ranking below only the House of Lords in legal authority.

4 *issues* Expenditures.

5 *our generals ... kings* One of Swift's enemies, the Duke of Marlborough, amassed an enormous fortune while serving as Captain General.

6 *standing army* A standing army without the approval of Parliament had been illegal since the declaration of the Bill of Rights in 1689, but one still existed. Swift and the Tories were strongly opposed to this.

7 *Cordials* Medicines, food, or beverages (usually alcoholic) that stimulate or invigorate the heart; restoratives.

8 *gaming* Gambling.

ence, as well as habituate them to vile companions, wholly take them from the improvement of their minds, and force them, by the losses they received, to learn and practise that infamous dexterity upon others.

He was perfectly astonished with the historical account I gave him of our affairs during the last century, protesting it was only a heap of conspiracies, rebellions, murders, massacres, revolutions, banishments—the very worst effects that avarice, faction, hypocrisy, perfidiousness, cruelty, rage, madness, hatred, envy, lust, malice, and ambition could produce.

His Majesty in another audience, was at the Pains to recapitulate the Sum of all I had spoken, compared the Questions he made with the Answers I had given; then taking me into his Hands, and stroking me gently, delivered himself in these Words, which I shall never forget, nor the manner he spoke them in: "My little friend *Grildrig*; you have made a most admirable Panegyrick upon your Country. You have clearly proved that Ignorance, Idleness, and Vice are the proper Ingredients for qualifying a Legislator. That Laws are best explained, interpreted, and applied by those whose Interest and Abilities lye in perverting, confounding, and eluding them. I observe among you some Lines of an Institution, which in its Original might have been tolerable, but these half erased, and the rest wholly blurred and blotted by Corruptions. It doth not appear from all you have said how any one Virtue is required towards the Procurement of any one Station among you, much less that Men are ennobled on Account of their Virtue, that Priests are advanced for their Piety or Learning, Soldiers for their Conduct or Valour, Judges for their Integrity, Senators for the Love of their Country, or Counsellors for their Wisdom. As for yourself (continued the King) who have spent the greatest part of your Life in travelling, I am well disposed to hope you may hitherto have escaped many Vices of your Country. But by what I have gathered from your own Relation, and the Answers I have with much Pains wringed and extorted from you, I cannot but conclude the Bulk of your Natives, to be the most pernicious Race of little odious Vermin that Nature ever suffered to crawl upon the Surface of the Earth.

original spelling

CHAPTER 7

(*The author's love of his country. He makes a proposal of much advantage to the King, which is rejected. The King's great ignorance in politics. The learning of that country very imperfect and confined. The laws, and military affairs, and parties in the state.*)

Nothing but an extreme love of truth could have hindered me from concealing this part of my story. It was in vain to discover my resentments, which were always turned into ridicule, and I was forced to rest with patience while my noble and beloved country was so injuriously treated. I am as heartily sorry as any of my readers can possibly be that such an occasion was given, but this prince happened to be so curious and inquisitive upon every particular that it could not consist either with gratitude or good manners to refuse giving him what satisfaction I was able. Yet thus much I may be allowed to say in my own vindication, that I artfully eluded many of his questions, and gave to every point a more favourable turn by many degrees than the strictness of truth would allow. For I have always borne that laudable partiality to my own country which Dionysius Halicarnassensis,[1] with so much justice, recommends to an historian. I would hide the frailties and deformities of my political mother and place her virtues and beauties in the most advantageous light. This was my sincere endeavour in those many discourses I had with that monarch, although it unfortunately failed of success.

But great allowances should be given to a King who lives wholly secluded from the rest of the world, and must therefore be altogether unacquainted with the manners and customs that most prevail in other nations, the want of which knowledge will ever produce many prejudices, and a certain narrowness of thinking, from which we and the politer countries of Europe are wholly exempted. And it would be hard indeed if so remote a prince's notions of virtue and vice were to be offered as a standard for all mankind.

To confirm what I have now said, and further to show the miserable effects of a confined education, I shall here insert a passage which will hardly obtain

---

[1] *Dionysius Halicarnassensis*   Dionysius Halicarnassus was a Greek historian who wrote a twenty-volume history of Rome that extolled the Romans' virtues and accomplishments in an effort to reconcile the Greeks to the idea of being enslaved.

belief. In hopes to ingratiate myself further into His Majesty's favour, I told him of an invention discovered between three and four hundred years ago, to make a certain powder, into a heap of which, the smallest spark of fire falling, would kindle the whole in a moment, although it were as big as a mountain, and make it all fly up in the air together, with a noise and agitation greater than thunder. That a proper quantity of this powder rammed into a hollow tube of brass or iron, according to its bigness, would drive a ball of iron or lead with such violence and speed as nothing was able to sustain its force. That the largest balls thus discharged would not only destroy whole ranks of an army at once, but batter the strongest walls to the ground; sink down ships, with a thousand men in each, to the bottom of the sea; and, when linked together by a chain, would cut through masts and rigging, divide hundreds of bodies in the middle, and lay all waste before them. That we often put this powder into large hollow balls of iron and discharged them by an engine into some city we were besieging, which would rip up the pavements, tear the houses to pieces, burst and throw splinters on every side, dashing out the brains of all who came near. That I knew the ingredients very well, which were cheap and common; I understood the manner of compounding them, and could direct his workmen how to make those tubes, of a size proportionable to all other things in His Majesty's kingdom, and the largest need not be above a hundred feet long; twenty or thirty of which tubes, charged with the proper quantity of powder and balls, would batter down the walls of the strongest town in his dominions in a few hours, or destroy the whole metropolis, if ever it should pretend to dispute his absolute commands. This I humbly offered to His Majesty as a small tribute of acknowledgment in turn for so many marks that I had received of his royal favour and protection.

The King was struck with horror at the description I had given of those terrible engines and the proposal I had made. He was amazed how so impotent and grovelling an insect as I (these were his expressions) could entertain such inhuman ideas, and in so familiar a manner as to appear wholly unmoved at all the scenes of blood and desolation which I had painted as the common effects of those destructive machines; whereof (he said) some evil genius, enemy to mankind, must have been the first contriver. As for himself, he protested that

although few things delighted him so much as new discoveries in art or in nature, yet he would rather lose half his kingdom than be privy to such a secret, which he commanded me, as I valued my life, never to mention any more.

A strange effect of narrow principles and short views! That a prince possessed of every quality which procures veneration, love, and esteem; of strong parts, great wisdom, and profound learning; endued with admirable talents for government, and almost adored by his subjects, should, from a nice, unnecessary scruple, whereof in Europe we can have no conception, let slip an opportunity put into his hands that would have made him absolute master of the lives, the liberties, and the fortunes of his people! Neither do I say this with the least intention to detract from the many virtues of that excellent King, whose character, I am sensible, will on this account be very much lessened in the opinion of an English reader: but I take this defect among them to have risen from their ignorance, by not having hitherto reduced politics into a science, as the more acute wits of Europe have done. For, I remember very well, in a discourse one day with the King, when I happened to say there were several thousand books among us written upon the art of government, it gave him (directly contrary to my intention) a very mean opinion of our understandings. He professed both to abominate and despise all mystery, refinement, and intrigue, either in a prince or a minister. He could not tell what I meant by secrets of state, where an enemy or some rival nation were not in the case. He confined the knowledge of governing within very narrow bounds: to common sense and reason, to justice and lenity, to the speedy determination of civil and criminal causes, with some other obvious topics which are not worth considering. And he gave it for his opinion that whoever could make two ears of corn or two blades of grass to grow upon a spot of ground where only one grew before would deserve better of mankind, and do more essential service to his country, than the whole race of politicians put together.

The learning of this people is very defective, consisting only in morality, history, poetry, and mathematics, wherein they must be allowed to excel. But the last of these is wholly applied to what may be useful in life—to the improvement of agriculture and all mechanical arts—so that among us it would be little esteemed. And as to ideas, entities, abstractions, and transcendentals, I could never drive the least conception into their heads.

No law in that country must exceed in words the number of letters in their alphabet, which consists only of two and twenty. But indeed few of them extend even to that length. They are expressed in the most plain and simple terms, wherein those people are not mercurial enough to discover above one interpretation. And to write a comment upon any law is a capital crime. As to the decision of civil causes, or proceedings against criminals, their precedents are so few that they have little reason to boast of any extraordinary skill in either.

They have had the art of printing as well as the Chinese, time out of mind. But their libraries are not very large; for that of the King, which is reckoned the largest, does not amount to above a thousand volumes placed in a gallery of twelve hundred feet long, from whence I had liberty to borrow what books I pleased. The Queen's joiner had contrived in one of Glumdalclitch's rooms a kind of wooden machine five-and-twenty foot high, formed like a standing ladder; the steps were each fifty feet long. It was indeed a moveable pair of stairs, the lowest end placed at ten feet distance from the wall of the chamber. The book I had a mind to read was put up leaning against the wall. I first mounted to the upper step of the ladder and, turning my face towards the book, began at the top of the page, and so walking to the right and left about eight or ten paces according to the length of the lines, till I had gotten a little below the level of mine eyes, and then descending gradually till I came to the bottom; after which I mounted again and began the other page in the same manner, and so turned over the leaf, which I could easily do with both my hands, for it was as thick and stiff as a pasteboard, and in the largest folios not above eighteen or twenty feet long.

Their style is clear, masculine, and smooth, but not florid; for they avoid nothing more than multiplying unnecessary words or using various expressions. I have perused many of their books, especially those in history and morality. Among the rest, I was much diverted with a little old treatise which always lay in Glumdalclitch's bed chamber, and belonged to her governess, a grave, elderly gentlewoman who dealt in writings of morality and devotion. The book treats of the weakness of human kind, and is in little esteem, except among the women and the vulgar. However, I was curious to see what an author of that country could say upon such a subject. This writer went through all the usual topics of European moralists: showing how diminutive, contemptible, and helpless an animal was man in his own nature; how unable to defend himself from inclemencies of the air or the fury of wild beasts; how much he was excelled by one creature in strength, by another in speed, by a third in foresight, by a fourth in industry. He added, that nature was degenerated in these latter declining ages of the world, and could now produce only small abortive births in comparison of those in ancient times. He said it was very reasonable to think not only that the species of men were originally much larger, but also that there must have been giants in former ages; which, as it is asserted by history and tradition, so it has been confirmed by huge bones and skulls, casually dug up in several parts of the kingdom, far exceeding the common dwindled race of men in our days. He argued that the very laws of nature absolutely required we should have been made in the beginning of a size more large and robust, not so liable to destruction from every little accident of a tile falling from a house, or a stone cast from the hand of a boy, or being drowned in a little brook. From this way of reasoning, the author drew several moral applications, useful in the conduct of life but needless here to repeat. For my own part, I could not avoid reflecting how universally this talent was spread, of drawing lectures in morality, or indeed rather matter of discontent and repining, from the quarrels we raise with nature. And I believe, upon a strict inquiry, those quarrels might be shown as ill-grounded among us as they are among that people.

As to their military affairs, they boast that the King's army consists of a hundred and seventy-six thousand foot and thirty-two thousand horse: if that may be called an army which is made up of tradesmen in the several cities, and farmers in the country, whose commanders are only the nobility and gentry, without pay or reward. They are indeed perfect enough in their exercises and under very good discipline, wherein I saw no great merit; for how should it be otherwise, where every farmer is under the command of his own landlord, and every citizen under that of the principal men in his own city, chosen after the manner of Venice, by ballot?[1]

I have often seen the militia of Lorbrulgrud drawn out to exercise in a great field near the city, of twenty miles square. They were in all not above twenty-five thousand foot and six thousand horse, but it was impossible for me to compute their number, considering the space of ground they took up. A cavalier mounted on a large steed might be about ninety feet high. I have seen this whole body of horse, upon a word of command, draw their swords at once and brandish them in the air. Imagination can figure nothing so grand, so surprising, and so astonishing! It looked as if ten thousand flashes of lightning were darting at the same time from every quarter of the sky.

I was curious to know how this prince, to whose dominions there is no access from any other country, came to think of armies, or to teach his people the practice of military discipline. But I was soon informed both by conversation and reading their histories. For in the course of many ages, they have been troubled with the same disease to which the whole race of mankind is subject: the nobility often contending for power, the people for liberty, and the King for absolute dominion. All which, however happily tempered by the laws of that kingdom, have been sometimes violated by each of the three parties, and have more than once occasioned civil wars, the last whereof was happily put an end to by this prince's grandfather in a general composition;[2] and the militia, then settled with common consent, has been ever since kept in the strictest duty.

CHAPTER 8

(*The King and Queen make a progress to the frontiers. The author attends them. The manner in which he leaves the country very particularly related. He returns to England.*)

I had always a strong impulse that I should some time recover my liberty, though it was impossible to conjecture by what means, or to form any project with the least hope of succeeding. The ship in which I sailed was the first ever known to be driven within sight of that coast, and the King had given strict orders that if at any time another appeared, it should be taken ashore and with all its crew and passengers brought in a tumbril[3] to Lorbrulgrud. He was strongly bent to get me a woman of my own size, by whom I might propagate the breed; but I think I should rather have died than undergone the disgrace of leaving a posterity to be kept in cages like tame canary-birds, and perhaps in time sold about the kingdom to persons of quality for curiosities. I was indeed treated with much kindness: I was the favourite of a great King and Queen and the delight of the whole court, but it was upon such a foot as ill became the dignity of humankind. I could never forget those domestic pledges I had left behind me. I wanted to be among people with whom I could converse upon even terms, and walk about the streets and fields without being afraid of being trod to death like a frog or a young puppy. But my deliverance came sooner than I expected, and in a manner not very common; the whole story and circumstances of which I shall faithfully relate.

I had now been two years in this country; and about the beginning of the third, Glumdalclitch and I attended the King and Queen in a progress to the south coast of the kingdom. I was carried, as usual, in my travelling-box, which, as I have already described, was a very convenient closet of twelve feet wide. And I had ordered a hammock to be fixed by silken ropes from the four corners at the top, to break the jolts when a servant carried me before him on horseback, as I sometimes desired; and would often sleep in my hammock while we were upon the road. On the roof of my closet, not directly over the middle of the hammock, I ordered the joiner to cut out a hole of a foot square, to give me air in hot weather as I slept; which hole I shut at pleasure with a board that drew backward and forward through a groove.

When we came to our journey's end, the King thought proper to pass a few days at a palace he has near Flanflasnic, a city within eighteen English miles of the seaside. Glumdalclitch and I were much fatigued. I had gotten a small cold, but the poor girl was so ill as to be confined to her chamber. I longed to see the ocean, which must be the only scene of my escape, if ever it should happen. I pretended to be worse than I really

---

[1] *if that may ... by ballot* This description of the army strongly resembles the idea for a trained militia of citizens advocated by Swift and the Tories.

[2] *composition* Treaty or mutual agreement for the settlement of political differences.

[3] *tumbril* Cart resembling a wheelbarrow that was used in farming; a dung cart.

was, and desired leave to take the fresh air of the sea with a page whom I was very fond of, and who had sometimes been trusted with me. I shall never forget with what unwillingness Glumdalclitch consented, nor the strict charge she gave the page to be careful of me, bursting at the same time into a flood of tears, as if she had some foreboding of what was to happen. The boy took me out in my box about half an hour's walk from the palace towards the rocks on the sea-shore. I ordered him to set me down and, lifting up one of my sashes,[1] cast many a wistful melancholy look towards the sea. I found myself not very well, and told the page that I had a mind to take a nap in my hammock, which I hoped would do me good. I got in, and the boy shut the window close down to keep out the cold. I soon fell asleep, and all I can conjecture is that while I slept, the page, thinking no danger could happen, went among the rocks to look for birds' eggs, having before observed him from my window searching about and picking up one or two in the clefts. Be that as it will, I found myself suddenly awaked with a violent pull upon the ring which was fastened at the top of my box for the conveniency of carriage. I felt my box raised very high in the air, and then borne forward with prodigious speed. The first jolt had like to have shaken me out of my hammock, but afterward the motion was easy enough. I called out several times, as loud as I could raise my voice, but all to no purpose. I looked towards my windows and could see nothing but the clouds and sky. I heard a noise just over my head like the clapping of wings, and then began to perceive the woeful condition I was in; that some eagle had got the ring of my box in his beak, with an intent to let it fall on a rock, like a tortoise in a shell, and then pick out my body and devour it. For the sagacity and smell of this bird enables him to discover his quarry at a great distance, although better concealed than I could be within a two-inch board.

In a little time I observed the noise and flutter of wings to increase very fast, and my box was tossed up and down like a sign in a windy day. I heard several bangs or buffets, as I thought, given to the eagle (for such I am certain it must have been that held the ring of my box in his beak), and then all on a sudden felt myself falling perpendicularly down for above a minute, but with such incredible swiftness that I almost lost my breath. My fall was stopped by a terrible squash[2] that sounded louder to my ears than the cataract of Niagara; after which I was quite in the dark for another minute, and then my box began to rise so high that I could see light from the tops of the windows. I now perceived I was fallen into the sea. My box, by the weight of my body, the goods that were in, and the broad plates of iron fixed for strength at the four corners of the top and bottom, floated about five feet deep in water. I did then, and do now, suppose that the eagle which flew away with my box was pursued by two or three others, and forced to let me drop while he defended himself against the rest, who hoped to share in the prey. The plates of iron fastened at the bottom of the box (for those were the strongest) preserved the balance while it fell, and hindered it from being broken on the surface of the water. Every joint of it was well grooved, and the door did not move on hinges, but up and down like a sash, which kept my closet so tight that very little water came in. I got with much difficulty out of my hammock, having first ventured to draw back the slip-board on the roof already mentioned, contrived on purpose to let in air, for want of which I found myself almost stifled.

How often did I then wish myself with my dear Glumdalclitch, from whom one single hour had so far divided me! And I may say with truth that in the midst of my own misfortunes I could not forbear lamenting my poor nurse, the grief she would suffer for my loss, the displeasure of the Queen, and the ruin of her fortune. Perhaps many travellers have not been under greater difficulties and distress than I was at this juncture, expecting every moment to see my box dashed to pieces, or at least overset by the first violent blast or rising wave. A breach in one single pane of glass would have been immediate death, nor could any thing have preserved the windows but the strong lattice wires placed on the outside against accidents in travelling. I saw the water ooze in at several crannies, although the leaks were not considerable, and I endeavoured to stop them as well as I could. I was not able to lift up the roof of my closet, which otherwise I certainly should have done, and sat on the top of it, where I might at least preserve myself some hours longer than by being shut up (as I may call it) in the hold. Or if I escaped these dangers for a day or two, what could I expect but a

---

[1] *sashes*   I.e., window-sashes.

[2] *squash*   Splash.

miserable death of cold and hunger? I was four hours under these circumstances, expecting and indeed wishing every moment to be my last.

I have already told the reader that there were two strong staples fixed upon that side of my box which had no window, and into which the servant, who used to carry me on horseback, would put a leathern belt, and buckle it about his waist. Being in this disconsolate state, I heard, or at least thought I heard, some kind of grating noise on that side of my box where the staples were fixed; and soon after I began to fancy that the box was pulled or towed along the sea; for I now and then felt a sort of tugging, which made the waves rise near the tops of my windows, leaving me almost in the dark. This gave me some faint hopes of relief, although I was not able to imagine how it could be brought about. I ventured to unscrew one of my chairs, which were always fastened to the floor; and, having made a hard shift to screw it down again directly under the slipping-board that I had lately opened, I mounted on the chair and, putting my mouth as near as I could to the hole, I called for help in a loud voice, and in all the languages I understood. I then fastened my handkerchief to a stick I usually carried and, thrusting it up the hole, waved it several times in the air, that if any boat or ship were near, the seamen might conjecture some unhappy mortal to be shut up in the box.

I found no effect from all I could do, but plainly perceived my closet to be moved along; and in the space of an hour or better, that side of the box where the staples were, and had no windows, struck against something that was hard. I apprehended it to be a rock, and found myself tossed more than ever. I plainly heard a noise upon the cover of my closet, like that of a cable, and the grating of it as it passed through the ring. I then found myself hoisted up, by degrees, at least three feet higher than I was before. Whereupon I again thrust up my stick and handkerchief, calling for help till I was almost hoarse. In return to which, I heard a great shout repeated three times, giving me such transports of joy as are not to be conceived but by those who feel them. I now heard a trampling over my head, and somebody calling through the hole with a loud voice, in the English tongue, "If there be any body below, let them speak." I answered, I was an Englishman, drawn by ill fortune into the greatest calamity that ever any creature underwent, and begged, by all that was moving, to be delivered out of the dungeon I was in. The voice replied, I was safe, for my box was fastened to their ship, and the carpenter should immediately come and saw a hole in the cover large enough to pull me out. I answered, that was needless and would take up too much time; for there was no more to be done, but let one of the crew put his finger into the ring and take the box out of the sea into the ship, and so into the captain's cabin. Some of them, upon hearing me talk so wildly, thought I was mad; others laughed; for indeed it never came into my head that I was now got among people of my own stature and strength. The carpenter came, and in a few minutes sawed a passage about four feet square, then let down a small ladder, upon which I mounted, and thence was taken into the ship in a very weak condition.

The sailors were all in amazement, and asked me a thousand questions, which I had no inclination to answer. I was equally confounded at the sight of so many pigmies, for such I took them to be, after having so long accustomed mine eyes to the monstrous objects I had left. But the Captain, Mr. Thomas Wilcocks, an honest worthy Shropshire man, observing I was ready to faint, took me into his cabin, gave me a cordial to comfort me, and made me turn in upon his own bed, advising me to take a little rest, of which I had great need. Before I went to sleep, I gave him to understand that I had some valuable furniture in my box, too good to be lost: a fine hammock, a handsome field-bed, two chairs, a table, and a cabinet; that my closet was hung on all sides, or rather quilted, with silk and cotton; that if he would let one of the crew bring my closet into his cabin, I would open it there before him and show him my goods. The Captain, hearing me utter these absurdities, concluded I was raving; however (I suppose to pacify me), he promised to give order as I desired and, going upon deck, sent some of his men down into my closet, whence (as I afterwards found) they drew up all my goods and stripped off the quilting; but the chairs, cabinet, and bedstead, being screwed to the floor, were much damaged by the ignorance of the seamen, who tore them up by force. Then they knocked off some of the boards for the use of the ship, and when they had got all they had a mind for, let the hull drop into the sea, which by reason of many breaches made in the bottom and sides, sunk to rights.[1] And indeed, I was glad not to have been a spectator of the havoc they made, because I am confident it would have sensibly touched me by bringing former passages into my mind, which I had rather forgot.

I slept some hours, but perpetually disturbed with dreams of the place I had left and the dangers I had escaped. However, upon waking I found myself much recovered. It was now about eight o'clock at night, and the Captain ordered supper immediately, thinking I had already fasted too long. He entertained me with great kindness, observing me not to look wildly or talk inconsistently; and, when we were left alone, desired I would give him a relation of my travels, and by what accident I came to be set adrift in that monstrous wooden chest. He said that about twelve o'clock at noon, as he was looking through his glass, he spied it at a distance and thought it was a sail, which he had a mind to make,[2] being not much out of his course, in hopes of buying some biscuit, his own beginning to fall short. That upon coming nearer and finding his error, he sent out his longboat to discover what it was; that his men came back in a fright, swearing they had seen a swimming house. That he laughed at their folly and went himself in the boat, ordering his men to take a strong cable along with them. That the weather being calm, he rowed round me several times, observed my windows and wire lattices that defended them. That he discovered two staples upon one side, which was all of boards, without any passage for light. He then commanded his men to row up to that side and, fastening a cable to one of the staples, ordered them to tow my chest, as they called it, toward the ship. When it was there he gave directions to fasten another cable to the ring fixed in the cover, and to raise up my chest with pulleys, which all the sailors were not able to do above two or three feet. He said they saw my stick and handkerchief thrust out of the hole, and concluded that some unhappy man must be shut up in the cavity. I asked whether he or the crew had seen any prodigious birds in the air about the time he first discovered me. To which he answered that, discoursing this matter with the sailors while I was asleep, one of them said he had observed three eagles flying towards the north, but remarked nothing of their being larger than the usual size (which I suppose must be imputed to the great height they were at), and he could not guess the reason of my question. I then asked the Captain how far he reckoned we might be from land. He said by the best computation he could make we were at least a hundred leagues. I assured him that he must be mistaken by almost half, for I had not left the country whence I came above two hours before I dropped into the sea. Whereupon he began again to think that my brain was disturbed, of which he gave me a hint, and advised me to go to bed in a cabin he had provided. I assured him I was well refreshed with his good entertainment and company, and as much in my senses as ever I was in my life. He then grew serious, and desired to ask me freely whether I were not troubled in my mind by the consciousness of some enormous crime, for which I was punished at the command of some prince, by exposing me in that chest, as great criminals in other countries have been forced to sea in a leaky vessel without provisions; for although he should be sorry to have taken so ill[3] a man into his ship, yet he would engage his word to set me safe ashore in the first port where we arrived. He added that his suspicions were much increased by some very absurd speeches I had delivered at first to his sailors, and afterwards to himself, in relation to my closet or chest, as well as by my odd looks and behaviour while I was at supper.

I begged his patience to hear me tell my story, which I faithfully did from the last time I left England to the moment he first discovered me. And as truth always forces its way into rational minds, so this honest worthy gentleman, who had some tincture of learning and very good sense, was immediately convinced of my candour and veracity. But further to confirm all I had said, I entreated him to give order that my cabinet should be brought, of which I had the key in my pocket (for he had already informed me how the seamen disposed of my closet). I opened it in his own presence and showed him the small collection of rarities I made in the country from which I had been so strangely delivered. There was the comb I had contrived out of the stumps of the King's beard, and another of the same materials, but fixed into a paring of Her Majesty's thumbnail, which served for the back. There was a collection of needles and pins from a foot to half a yard long; four wasp-

---

[1] *sunk to rights*   Sunk straight down, all at once.

[2] *make*   Reach.

[3] *ill*   Evil.

stings, like joiner's tacks; some combings of the Queen's hair; a gold ring which one day she made me a present of in a most obliging manner, taking it from her little finger and throwing it over my head like a collar. I desired the Captain would please to accept this ring in return for his civilities, which he absolutely refused. I showed him a corn that I had cut off with my own hand from a Maid of Honour's toe; it was about the bigness of Kentish pippin,[1] and grown so hard that when I returned to England I got it hollowed into a cup and set in silver. Lastly, I desired him to see the breeches I had then on, which were made of a mouse's skin.

I could force nothing on him but a footman's tooth, which I observed him to examine with great curiosity, and found he had a fancy for it. He received it with abundance of thanks, more than such a trifle could deserve. It was drawn by an unskilful surgeon in a mistake from one of Glumdalclitch's men, who was afflicted with the toothache, but it was as sound as any in his head. I got it cleaned and put it into my cabinet. It was about a foot long, and four inches in diameter.

The Captain was very well satisfied with this plain relation I had given him, and said he hoped when we returned to England, I would oblige the world by putting it on paper and making it public. My answer was that we were overstocked with books of travels; that nothing could now pass which was not extraordinary; wherein I doubted some authors less consulted truth than their own vanity or interest, or the diversion of ignorant readers; that my story could contain little beside common events, without those ornamental descriptions of strange plants, trees, birds, and other animals, or of the barbarous customs and idolatry of savage people, with which most writers abound. However, I thanked him for his good opinion and promised to take the matter into my thoughts.

He said he wondered at one thing very much, which was, to hear me speak so loud, asking me whether the King or Queen of that country were thick of hearing. I told him it was what I had been used to for above two years past, and that I admired[2] as much at the voices of him and his men, who seemed to me only to whisper, and yet I could hear them well enough. But, when I spoke in that country, it was like a man talking in the streets to another looking out from the top of a steeple, unless when I was placed on a table or held in any person's hand. I told him I had likewise observed another thing, that when I first got into the ship and the sailors stood all about me, I thought they were the most little contemptible creatures I had ever beheld. For indeed, while I was in that prince's country I could never endure to look in a glass, after mine eyes had been accustomed to such prodigious objects, because the comparison gave me so despicable a conceit[3] of myself. The Captain said that while we were at supper, he observed me to look at every thing with a sort of wonder, and that I often seemed hardly able to contain my laughter, which he knew not well how to take, but imputed it to some disorder in my brain. I answered, it was very true; and I wondered how I could forbear, when I saw his dishes of the size of a silver three-pence, a leg of pork hardly a mouthful, a cup not so big as a nut-shell; and so I went on, describing the rest of his household stuff and provisions after the same manner. For, although the Queen had ordered a little equipage of all things necessary for me while I was in her service, yet my ideas were wholly taken up with what I saw on every side of me, and I winked at[4] my own littleness as people do at their own faults. The captain understood my raillery very well, and merrily replied with the old English proverb that he doubted[5] mine eyes were bigger than my belly, for he did not observe my stomach so good, although I had fasted all day; and, continuing in his mirth, protested he would have gladly given a hundred pounds to have seen my closet in the eagle's bill, and afterwards in its fall from so great a height into the sea; which would certainly have been a most astonishing object, worthy to have the description of it transmitted to future ages; and the comparison of Phaëton[6] was so obvious that he could not forbear applying it, although I did not much admire the conceit.

---

[1] *pippin* Small apple.

[2] *admired* Marveled.

[3] *conceit* Opinion; notion.

[4] *winked at* Overlooked.

[5] *doubted* Suspected.

[6] *Phaëton* Son of Helios (later Apollo, the Greek sun god) who one day attempted to drive the chariot of the sun for his father, but instead drove too close to the earth and nearly scorched it. He was struck down by Zeus's thunderbolt and drowned in the river Eridanus.

The Captain, having been at Tonquin,[1] was in his return to England driven northeastward to the latitude of 44 degrees, and longitude of 143. But meeting a trade wind two days after I came on board him, we sailed southward a long time and, coasting New Holland,[2] kept our course west-southwest, and then south-south-west till we doubled the Cape of Good Hope. Our voyage was very prosperous, but I shall not trouble the reader with a journal of it. The Captain called in at one or two ports and sent in his longboat for provisions and fresh water, but I never went out of the ship till we came into the Downs, which was on the third day of June, 1706, about nine months after my escape. I offered to leave my goods in security for payment of my freight, but the captain protested he would not receive one farthing. We took a kind leave of each other, and I made him promise he would come to see me at my house in Redriff. I hired a horse and guide for five shillings, which I borrowed of the Captain.

As I was on the road, observing the littleness of the houses, the trees, the cattle, and the people, I began to think myself in Lilliput. I was afraid of trampling on every traveller I met, and often called aloud to have them stand out of the way, so that I had like to have gotten one or two broken heads for my impertinence.

When I came to my own house, for which I was forced to inquire, one of the servants opening the door, I bent down to go in (like a goose under a gate) for fear of striking my head. My wife run out to embrace me, but I stooped lower than her knees, thinking she could otherwise never be able to reach my mouth. My daughter kneeled to ask my blessing, but I could not see her till she arose, having been so long used to stand with my head and eyes erect to above sixty feet; and then I went to take her up with one hand by the waist. I looked down upon the servants, and one or two friends who were in the house, as if they had been pigmies and I a giant. I told my wife she had been too thrifty, for I found she had starved herself and her daughter to nothing. In short, I behaved myself so unaccountably that they were all of the Captain's opinion when he first saw me, and concluded I had lost my wits. This I mention as an instance of the great power of habit and prejudice.

In a little time, I and my family and friends came to a right understanding; but my wife protested I should never go to sea any more, although my evil destiny so ordered that she had not power to hinder me, as the reader may know hereafter. In the meantime, I here conclude the second part of my unfortunate voyages.

PART 4 —
A VOYAGE TO THE COUNTRY OF THE HOUYHNHNMS[3]

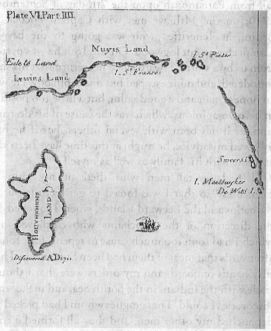

Map showing the location of "Houyhnhnms Lands," printed in the 1726 edition with no accompanying caption at the beginning of Part 4.

CHAPTER I

(*The author sets out as Captain of a ship. His men conspire against him, confine him a long time to his cabin, and set him on shore in an unknown land. He travels up into the country. The Yahoos, a strange sort of animal, described. The author meets two Houyhnhnms.*)

---

[1] *Tonquin* I.e., Tonkin, city in present-day Vietnam, at this time part of China.

[2] *New Holland* Australia.

[3] *Houyhnhnms* Pronounced "hwhin-hims," the name is meant to mimic the sound of a horse's whinny.

I continued at home with my wife and children about five months, in a very happy condition, if I could have learned the lesson of knowing when I was well. I left my poor wife big with child[1] and accepted an advantageous offer made me to be Captain of the *Adventure*, a stout merchantman of 350 tons; for I understood navigation well and, being grown weary of a surgeon's employment at sea, which, however, I could exercise upon occasion, I took a skilful young man of that calling, one Robert Purefoy, into my ship. We set sail from Portsmouth upon the 7th day of September, 1710; on the 14th we met with Captain Pocock of Bristol, at Teneriffe,[2] who was going to the bay of Campeche[3] to cut logwood. On the 16th he was parted from us by a storm; I heard since my return that his ship foundered, and none escaped but one cabin boy. He was an honest man and a good sailor, but a little too positive in his own opinions, which was the cause of his destruction, as it has been with several others. For if he had followed my advice, he might at this time have been safe at home with his family as well as myself.

I had several men who died in my ship of calentures,[4] so that I was forced to get recruits out of Barbados and the Leeward Islands, where I touched[5] by the direction of the merchants who employed me; which I had soon too much cause to repent, for I found afterwards that most of them had been buccaneers. I had fifty hands onboard, and my orders were that I should trade with the Indians in the South Sea, and make what discoveries I could. These rogues whom I had picked up debauched my other men, and they all formed a conspiracy to seize the ship and secure me; which they did one morning, rushing into my cabin and binding me hand and foot, threatening to throw me overboard if I offered to stir. I told them I was their prisoner and would submit. This they made me swear to do, and then they unbound me, only fastening one of my legs with a chain near my bed, and placed a sentry at my door with his piece charged, who was commanded to shoot me

dead if I attempted my liberty. They sent me down victuals and drink, and took the government of the ship to themselves. Their design was to turn pirates and plunder the Spaniards, which they could not do till they got more men. But first they resolved to sell the goods in the ship, and then go to Madagascar for recruits, several among them having died since my confinement. They sailed many weeks and traded with the Indians, but I knew not what course they took, being kept a close prisoner in my cabin and expecting nothing less than to be murdered, as they often threatened me.

Upon the 9th day of May, 1711, one James Welch came down to my cabin and said he had orders from the Captain to set me ashore. I expostulated with him, but in vain; neither would he so much as tell me who their new Captain was. They forced me into the longboat, letting me put on my best suit of clothes, which were as good as new, and take a small bundle of linen, but no arms except my hanger; and they were so civil as not to search my pockets, into which I conveyed what money I had, with some other little necessaries. They rowed about a league and then set me down on a strand.[6] I desired them to tell me what country it was. They all swore they knew no more than myself, but said that the Captain (as they called him) was resolved, after they had sold the lading,[7] to get rid of me in the first place where they could discover land. They pushed off immediately, advising me to make haste for fear of being overtaken by the tide, and so bade me farewell.

In this desolate condition I advanced forward, and soon got upon firm ground, where I sat down on a bank to rest myself and consider what I had best do. When I was a little refreshed I went up into the country, resolving to deliver myself to the first savages I should meet, and purchase my life from them by some bracelets, glass rings, and other toys,[8] which sailors usually provide themselves with in those voyages, and whereof I had some about me. The land was divided by long rows of trees, not regularly planted, but naturally growing; there was great plenty of grass and several fields of oats. I walked very circumspectly, for fear of being surprised, or suddenly shot with an arrow from behind or on either

---

[1]   *big with child*   Pregnant.

[2]   *Teneriffe*   Largest of the Canary Islands.

[3]   *Bay of Campeche*   The southernmost part of the Gulf of Mexico.

[4]   *calentures*   Tropical fever, common among sailors, which causes delirium.

[5]   *touched*   Landed for a short stay.

[6]   *strand*   Shore.

[7]   *lading*   Freight; cargo.

[8]   *toys*   Trinkets.

side. I fell into a beaten road, where I saw many tracks of human feet, and some of cows, but most of horses. At last I beheld several animals in a field, and one or two of the same kind sitting in trees. Their shape was very singular and deformed, which a little discomposed me, so that I lay down behind a thicket to observe them better. Some of them, coming forward near the place where I lay, gave me an opportunity of distinctly marking their form. Their heads and breasts were covered with a thick hair, some frizzled and others lank; they had beards like goats, and a long ridge of hair down their backs and the fore parts of their legs and feet; but the rest of their bodies was bare, so that I might see their skins, which were of a brown buff colour. They had no tails, nor any hair at all on their buttocks, except about the anus, which I presume nature had placed there to defend them as they sat on the ground, for this posture they used, as well as lying down, and often stood on their hind feet. They climbed high trees as nimbly as a squirrel, for they had strong extended claws before and behind, terminating in sharp points, and hooked. They would often spring, and bound, and leap with prodigious agility. The females were not so large as the males; they had long lank hair on their heads but none on their faces, nor anything more than a sort of down on the rest of their bodies, except about the anus and pudenda. The dugs hung between their fore feet and often reached almost to the ground as they walked. The hair of both sexes was of several colours: brown, red, black, and yellow. Upon the whole, I never beheld in all my travels so disagreeable an animal, or one against which I naturally conceived so strong an antipathy. So that, thinking I had seen enough, full of contempt and aversion, I got up and pursued the beaten road, hoping it might direct me to the cabin of some Indian. I had not got far when I met one of these creatures full in my way, and coming up directly to me. The ugly monster, when he saw me, distorted several ways every feature of his visage, and stared as at an object he had never seen before; then, approaching nearer, lifted up his forepaw, whether out of curiosity or mischief I could not tell; but I drew my hanger and gave him a good blow with the flat side of it, for I durst not strike with the edge, fearing the inhabitants might be provoked against me if they should come to know that I had killed or maimed any of their cattle. When the beast felt the smart, he drew

back, and roared so loud that a herd of at least forty came flocking about me from the next field, howling and making odious faces; but I ran to the body of a tree and, leaning my back against it, kept them off by waving my hanger. Several of this cursed brood, getting hold of the branches behind, leaped up into the tree, whence they began to discharge their excrements on my head; however, I escaped pretty well by sticking close to the stem of the tree, but was almost stifled with the filth, which fell about me on every side.

In the midst of this distress, I observed them all to run away on a sudden as fast as they could; at which I ventured to leave the tree and pursue the road, wondering what it was that could put them into this fright. But looking on my left hand, I saw a horse walking softly in the field; which, my persecutors having sooner discovered, was the cause of their flight. The horse started a little when he came near me, but soon, recovering himself, looked full in my face with manifest tokens of wonder; he viewed my hands and feet, walking round me several times. I would have pursued my journey, but he placed himself directly in the way, yet looking with a very mild aspect, never offering the least violence. We stood gazing at each other for some time; at last I took the boldness to reach my hand towards his neck with a design to stroke it, using the common style and whistle of jockeys when they are going to handle a strange horse. But this animal seemed to receive my civilities with disdain, shook his head and bent his brows, softly raising up his right forefoot to remove my hand. Then he neighed three or four times, but in so different a cadence that I almost began to think he was speaking to himself in some language of his own.

While he and I were thus employed, another horse came up, who applying himself to the first in a very formal manner, they gently struck each other's right hoof before, neighing several times by turns, and varying the sound, which seemed to be almost articulate. They went some paces off, as if it were to confer together, walking side by side, backward and forward, like persons deliberating upon some affair of weight, but often turning their eyes towards me, as it were to watch that I might not escape. I was amazed to see such actions and behaviour in brute beasts, and concluded with myself that if the inhabitants of this country were endued with a proportionable degree of reason, they must needs be the wisest people upon earth. This thought gave me so much comfort that I resolved to go forward until I could discover some house or village, or meet with any of the natives, leaving the two horses to discourse together as they pleased. But the first, who was a dapple gray, observing me to steal off, neighed after me in so expressive a tone that I fancied myself to understand what he meant; whereupon I turned back and came near to him to expect[1] his farther commands; but concealing my fear as much as I could, for I began to be in some pain how this adventure might terminate; and the reader will easily believe I did not much like my present situation.

The two horses came up close to me, looking with great earnestness upon my face and hands. The gray steed rubbed my hat all round with his right forehoof, and discomposed it so much that I was forced to adjust it better by taking it off and settling it again; whereat both he and his companion (who was a brown bay) appeared to be much surprised. The latter felt the lappet of my coat, and, finding it to hang loose about me, they both looked with new signs of wonder. He stroked my right hand, seeming to admire the softness and colour, but he squeezed it so hard between his hoof and his pastern[2] that I was forced to roar; after which they both touched me with all possible tenderness. They were under great perplexity about my shoes and stockings, which they felt very often, neighing to each other, and using various gestures not unlike those of a philosopher, when he would attempt to solve some new and difficult phenomenon.

Upon the whole, the behaviour of these animals was so orderly and rational, so acute and judicious, that I at last concluded they must needs be magicians who had thus metamorphosed themselves upon some design and, seeing a stranger in the way, resolved to divert themselves with him; or perhaps were really amazed at the sight of a man so very different in habit, feature, and complexion from those who might probably live in so remote a climate. Upon the strength of this reasoning, I ventured to address them in the following manner: "Gentlemen, if you be conjurers, as I have good cause to believe, you can understand my language; therefore I

make bold to let your worships know that I am a poor distressed Englishman, driven by his misfortunes upon your coast; and I entreat one of you to let me ride upon his back, as if he were a real horse, to some house or village where I can be relieved. In return of which favour, I will make you a present of this knife and bracelet" (taking them out of my pocket). The two creatures stood silent while I spoke, seeming to listen with great attention, and when I had ended they neighed frequently towards each other, as if they were engaged in serious conversation. I plainly observed that their language expressed the passions very well, and the words might, with little pains, be resolved into an alphabet more easily than the Chinese.

I could frequently distinguish the word *Yahoo*, which was repeated by each of them several times; and although it was impossible for me to conjecture what it meant, yet while the two horses were busy in conversation, I endeavoured to practise this word upon my tongue; and as soon as they were silent, I boldly pronounced *Yahoo* in a loud voice, imitating at the same time, as near as I could, the neighing of a horse; at which they were both visibly surprised, and the gray repeated the same word twice, as if he meant to teach me the right accent; wherein I spoke after him as well as I could, and found myself perceivably to improve every time, although very far from any degree of perfection. Then the bay tried me with a second word, much harder to be pronounced; but reducing it to the English orthography, may be spelt thus, *Houyhnhnm*. I did not succeed in this so well as in the former; but after two or three farther trials I had better fortune; and they both appeared amazed at my capacity.

After some further discourse, which I then conjectured might relate to me, the two friends took their leaves, with the same compliment of striking each other's hoof, and the gray made me signs that I should walk before him; wherein I thought it prudent to comply till I could find a better director. When I offered to slacken my pace, he would cry "*Hhuun, hhuun*." I guessed his meaning, and gave him to understand as well as I could that I was weary, and not able to walk faster; upon which he would stand awhile to let me rest.

---

[1] *expect* Wait for.

[2] *pastern* The part between the lower leg and the hoof, the equivalent of the ankle.

CHAPTER 2

(The author conducted by a Houyhnhnm to his house. The house described. The author's reception. The food of the Houyhnhnms. The author in distress for want of meat. Is at last relieved. His manner of feeding in this country.)

Having travelled about three miles, we came to a long kind of building, made of timber stuck in the ground and wattled[1] across; the roof was low and covered with straw. I now began to be a little comforted, and took out some toys, which travellers usually carry for presents to the savage Indians of America and other parts, in hopes the people of the house would be thereby encouraged to receive me kindly. The horse made me a sign to go in first; it was a large room with a smooth clay floor, and a rack and manger extending the whole length on one side. There were three nags and two mares, not eating, but some of them sitting down upon their hams, which I very much wondered at; but wondered more to see the rest employed in domestic business. The last seemed but ordinary cattle;[2] however, this confirmed my first opinion, that a people who could so far civilize brute animals must needs excel in wisdom all the nations of the world. The gray came in just after, and thereby prevented any ill treatment which the others might have given me. He neighed to them several times in a style of authority, and received answers.

Beyond this room there were three others, reaching the length of the house, to which you passed through three doors opposite to each other, in the manner of a vista.[3] We went through the second room towards the third. Here the gray walked in first, beckoning me to attend.[4] I waited in the second room, and got ready my presents for the master and mistress of the house; they were two knives, three bracelets of false pearls, a small looking-glass, and a bead necklace. The horse neighed three or four times, and I waited to hear some answers in a human voice, but I heard no other returns than in the same dialect, only one or two a little shriller than

his. I began to think that this house must belong to some person of great note among them, because there appeared so much ceremony before I could gain admittance. But, that a man of quality should be served all by horses, was beyond my comprehension. I feared my brain was disturbed by my sufferings and misfortunes. I roused myself and looked about me in the room where I was left alone; this was furnished like the first, only after a more elegant manner. I rubbed my eyes often, but the same objects still occurred. I pinched my arms and sides to awake myself, hoping I might be in a dream. I then absolutely concluded that all these appearances could be nothing else but necromancy and magic. But I had no time to pursue these reflections, for the gray horse came to the door and made me a sign to follow him into the third room, where I saw a very comely mare, together with a colt and foal, sitting on their haunches upon mats of straw, not unartfully made, and perfectly neat and clean.

The mare, soon after my entrance, rose from her mat, and coming up close, after having nicely observed my hands and face, gave me a most contemptuous look; then turning to the horse, I heard the word *Yahoo* often repeated betwixt them; the meaning of which word I could not then comprehend, although it was the first I had learned to pronounce. But I was soon better informed, to my everlasting mortification; for the horse, beckoning to me with his head, and repeating the word *hhuun, hhuun*, as he did upon the road, which I understood was to attend him, led me out into a kind of court, where was another building at some distance from the house. Here we entered, and I saw three of those detestable creatures, which I first met after my landing, feeding upon roots and the flesh of some animals, which I afterwards found to be that of asses and dogs, and now and then a cow dead by accident or disease. They were all tied by the neck with strong withes,[5] fastened to a beam; they held their food between the claws of their forefeet, and tore it with their teeth.

The master horse ordered a sorrel nag, one of his servants, to untie the largest of these animals and take him into the yard. The beast and I were brought close together, and by our countenances diligently compared both by master and servant, who thereupon repeated

---

[1] *wattled*   Made of woven sticks or branches.

[2] *cattle*   Horses.

[3] *vista*   Long and narrow passage.

[4] *attend*   Wait.

[5] *withes*   Shackles or bands made of twigs twisted together.

several times the word *Yahoo*. My horror and astonishment are not to be described when I observed in this abominable animal a perfect human figure: the face of it indeed was flat and broad, the nose depressed, the lips large, and the mouth wide; but these differences are common to all savage nations, where the lineaments of the countenance are distorted by the natives suffering their infants to lie grovelling on the earth, or by carrying them on their backs, nuzzling with their face against the mothers' shoulders. The forefeet of the Yahoo differed from my hands in nothing else but the length of the nails, the coarseness and brownness of the palms, and the hairiness on the backs. There was the same resemblance between our feet, with the same differences; which I knew very well, though the horses did not because of my shoes and stockings; the same in every part of our bodies except as to hairiness and colour, which I have already described.

The great difficulty that seemed to stick with the two horses was to see the rest of my body so very different from that of a Yahoo, for which I was obliged to my clothes, whereof they had no conception. The sorrel nag offered me a root, which he held (after their manner, as we shall describe in its proper place) between his hoof and pastern; I took it in my hand, and, having smelt it, returned it to him again as civilly as I could. He brought out of the Yahoos' kennel a piece of ass's flesh, but it smelt so offensively that I turned from it with loathing. He then threw it to the Yahoo, by whom it was greedily devoured. He afterwards showed me a wisp of hay and a fetlock full of oats, but I shook my head to signify that neither of these were food for me. And indeed I now apprehended that I must absolutely starve if I did not get to some of my own species; for as to those filthy Yahoos, although there were few greater lovers of mankind, at that time, than myself, yet I confess I never saw any sensitive being so detestable on all accounts; and the more I came near them the more hateful they grew, while I stayed in that country. This the master horse observed by my behaviour, and therefore sent the *Yahoo* back to his kennel. He then put his forehoof to his mouth, at which I was much surprised, although he did it with ease, and with a motion that appeared perfectly natural, and made other signs to know what I would eat; but I could not return him such an answer as he was able to apprehend; and if he had understood me, I did

not see how it was possible to contrive any way for finding myself nourishment. While we were thus engaged, I observed a cow passing by, whereupon I pointed to her and expressed a desire to go and milk her. This had its effect; for he led me back into the house and ordered a mare-servant to open a room, where a good store of milk lay in earthen and wooden vessels, after a very orderly and cleanly manner. She gave me a large bowlful, of which I drank very heartily, and found myself well refreshed.

About noon, I saw coming towards the house a kind of vehicle drawn like a sledge by four Yahoos. There was in it an old steed, who seemed to be of quality; he alighted with his hind feet forward, having by accident got a hurt in his left forefoot. He came to dine with our horse, who received him with great civility. They dined in the best room, and had oats boiled in milk for the second course, which the old horse ate warm, but the rest cold. Their mangers were placed circular in the middle of the room and divided into several partitions, round which they sat on their haunches upon bosses of straw. In the middle was a large rack with angles answering to every partition of the manger; so that each horse and mare ate their own hay, and their own mash of oats and milk, with much decency and regularity. The behaviour of the young colt and foal appeared very modest, and that of the master and mistress extremely cheerful and complaisant to their guest. The gray ordered me to stand by him, and much discourse passed between him and his friend concerning me, as I found by the stranger's often looking on me, and the frequent repetition of the word Yahoo.

I happened to wear my gloves, which the master gray observing, seemed perplexed, discovering signs of wonder what I had done to my forefeet. He put his hoof three or four times to them, as if he would signify that I should reduce them to their former shape, which I presently did, pulling off both my gloves and putting them into my pocket. This occasioned farther talk; and I saw the company was pleased with my behaviour, whereof I soon found the good effects. I was ordered to speak the few words I understood; and while they were at dinner, the master taught me the names for oats, milk, fire, water, and some others, which I could readily pronounce after him, having from my youth a great facility in learning languages.

When dinner was done, the master horse took me aside, and by signs and words made me understand the concern he was in that I had nothing to eat. Oats in their tongue are called *hlunnh*. This word I pronounced two or three times; for although I had refused them at first, yet, upon second thoughts, I considered that I could contrive to make of them a kind of bread, which might be sufficient, with milk, to keep me alive till I could make my escape to some other country, and to creatures of my own species. The horse immediately ordered a white mare servant of his family to bring me a good quantity of oats in a sort of wooden tray. These I heated before the fire as well as I could, and rubbed them till the husks came off, which I made a shift to winnow from the grain. I ground and beat them between two stones, then took water and made them into a paste or cake, which I toasted at the fire and ate warm with milk. It was at first a very insipid diet, though common enough in many parts of Europe, but grew tolerable by time; and having been often reduced to hard fare in my life, this was not the first experiment I had made how easily nature is satisfied. And I cannot but observe that I never had one hour's sickness while I stayed in this island. It is true, I sometimes made a shift to catch a rabbit or bird by springes[1] made of Yahoo's hairs; and I often gathered wholesome herbs, which I boiled and ate as salads with my bread; and now and then, for a rarity, I made a little butter, and drank the whey. I was at first at a great loss for salt, but custom soon reconciled me to the want of it; and I am confident that the frequent use of salt among us is an effect of luxury, and was first introduced only as a provocative to drink, except where it is necessary for preserving flesh in long voyages, or in places remote from great markets; for we observe no animal to be fond of it but man, and as to myself, when I left this country it was a great while before I could endure the taste of it in anything that I ate.

This is enough to say upon the subject of my diet, wherewith other travellers fill their books, as if the readers were personally concerned whether we fare well or ill. However, it was necessary to mention this matter, lest the world should think it impossible that I could find sustenance for three years in such a country, and among such inhabitants.

When it grew towards evening, the master horse ordered a place for me to lodge in; it was but six yards from the house and separated from the stable of the Yahoos. Here I got some straw and, covering myself with my own clothes, slept very sound. But I was in a short time better accommodated, as the reader shall know hereafter, when I come to treat more particularly about my way of living.

CHAPTER 3

(*The author studies to learn the language. The Houyhn-hnm, his master, assists in teaching him. The language described. Several Houyhnhnms of quality come out of curiosity to see the author. He gives his master a short account of his voyage.*)

My principal endeavour was to learn the language, which my master (for so I shall henceforth call him), and his children, and every servant of his house, were desirous to teach me; for they looked upon it as a prodigy, that a brute animal should discover such marks of a rational creature. I pointed to everything and inquired the name of it, which I wrote down in my journal-book when I was alone, and corrected my bad accent by desiring those of the family to pronounce it often. In this employment, a sorrel nag, one of the under servants, was very ready to assist me.

In speaking, they pronounced through the nose and throat, and their language approaches nearest to the High Dutch, or German, of any I know in Europe; but is much more graceful and significant.[2] The Emperor Charles V made almost the same observation when he said that if he were to speak to his horse, it should be in High Dutch.[3]

The curiosity and impatience of my master were so great that he spent many hours of his leisure to instruct me. He was convinced (as he afterwards told me) that I must be a Yahoo; but my teachableness, civility, and cleanliness astonished him; which were qualities altogether opposite to those animals. He was most perplexed

---

[1] *springes* Snares.

[2] *significant* Expressive.

[3] *Emperor Charles ... High Dutch* Charles V, Emperor of Rome, King of Spain, and ruler of parts of Italy and the Netherlands, apparently said that he would speak to his God in Spanish, his mistress in Italian, and his horse in German.

about my clothes, reasoning sometimes with himself whether they were a part of my body; for I never pulled them off till the family were asleep, and got them on before they waked in the morning. My master was eager to learn whence I came; how I acquired those appearances of reason, which I discovered in all my actions; and to know my story from my own mouth, which he hoped he should soon do by the great proficiency I made in learning and pronouncing their words and sentences. To help my memory, I formed all I learned into the English alphabet and writ the words down with the translations. This last, after some time, I ventured to do in my master's presence. It cost me much trouble to explain to him what I was doing; for the inhabitants have not the least idea of books or literature.

In about ten weeks time I was able to understand most of his questions, and in three months could give him some tolerable answers. He was extremely curious to know from what part of the country I came, and how I was taught to imitate a rational creature; because the Yahoos (whom he saw I exactly resembled in my head, hands, and face, that were only visible), with some appearance of cunning, and the strongest disposition to mischief, were observed to be the most unteachable of all brutes. I answered that I came over the sea, from a far place, with many others of my own kind, in a great hollow vessel made of the bodies of trees; that my companions forced me to land on this coast and then left me to shift for myself. It was with some difficulty, and by the help of many signs, that I brought him to understand me. He replied that I must needs be mistaken, or that I *said the thing which was not*; for they have no word in their language to express lying or falsehood. He knew it was impossible that there could be a country beyond the sea, or that a parcel of brutes could move a wooden vessel whither they pleased upon water. He was sure no Houyhnhnm alive could make such a vessel, nor would trust Yahoos to manage it.

The word Houyhnhnm in their tongue signifies a horse and, in its etymology, the perfection of nature. I told my master that I was at a loss for expression, but would improve as fast as I could, and hoped, in a short time, I should be able to tell him wonders. He was pleased to direct his own mare, his colt and foal, and the servants of the family to take all opportunities of instructing me; and every day, for two or three hours, he

was at the same pains himself. Several horses and mares of quality in the neighbourhood came often to our house upon the report spread of a wonderful Yahoo that could speak like a Houyhnhnm, and seemed, in his words and actions, to discover some glimmerings of reason. These delighted to converse with me; they put many questions, and received such answers as I was able to return. By all these advantages I made so great a progress that in five months from my arrival I understood whatever was spoken, and could express myself tolerably well.

The Houyhnhnms, who came to visit my master out of a design of seeing and talking with me, could hardly believe me to be a right Yahoo because my body had a different covering from others of my kind. They were astonished to observe me without the usual hair or skin, except on my head, face, and hands; but I discovered that secret to my master upon an accident which happened about a fortnight before.

I have already told the reader that every night when the family were gone to bed, it was my custom to strip and cover myself with my clothes. It happened one morning early that my master sent for me by the sorrel nag, who was his valet. When he came I was fast asleep, my clothes fallen off on one side, and my shirt above my waist. I awaked at the noise he made, and observed him to deliver his message in some disorder; after which he went to my master, and in a great fright gave him a very confused account of what he had seen. This I presently discovered; for, going as soon as I was dressed to pay my attendance upon his honour, he asked me the meaning of what his servant had reported, that I was not the same thing when I slept as I appeared to be at other times; that his valet assured him, some part of me was white, some yellow, at least not so white, and some brown.

I had hitherto concealed the secret of my dress in order to distinguish myself, as much as possible, from that cursed race of Yahoos; but now I found it in vain to do so any longer. Besides, I considered that my clothes and shoes would soon wear out, which already were in a declining condition, and must be supplied by some contrivance from the hides of Yahoos, or other brutes; whereby the whole secret would be known. I therefore told my master that in the country from whence I came, those of my kind always covered their bodies with the hairs of certain animals prepared by art, as well for decency as to avoid the inclemencies of air, both hot and cold; of which, as to my own person, I would give him immediate conviction, if he pleased to command me; only desiring his excuse if I did not expose those parts that nature taught us to conceal. He said my discourse was all very strange, but especially the last part; for he could not understand why nature should teach us to conceal what nature had given; that neither himself nor family were ashamed of any parts of their bodies; but, however, I might do as I pleased. Whereupon I first unbuttoned my coat and pulled it off. I did the same with my waistcoat. I drew off my shoes, stockings, and breeches. I let my shirt down to my waist, and drew up the bottom, fastening it like a girdle about my middle to hide my nakedness.

My master observed the whole performance with great signs of curiosity and admiration. He took up all my clothes in his pastern, one piece after another, and examined them diligently; he then stroked my body very gently, and looked round me several times; after which, he said it was plain I must be a perfect Yahoo; but that I differed very much from the rest of my species in the softness, whiteness, and smoothness of my skin; my want of hair in several parts of my body; the shape and shortness of my claws behind and before; and my affectation of walking continually on my two hinder feet. He desired to see no more, and gave me leave to put on my clothes again, for I was shuddering with cold.

I expressed my uneasiness at his giving me so often the appellation of Yahoo, an odious animal for which I had so utter a hatred and contempt. I begged he would forbear applying that word to me, and make the same order in his family and among his friends whom he suffered to see me. I requested likewise that the secret of my having a false covering to my body might be known to none but himself, at least as long as my present clothing should last; for as to what the sorrel nag, his valet, had observed, his honour might command him to conceal it.

All this my master very graciously consented to; and thus the secret was kept till my clothes began to wear out, which I was forced to supply by several contrivances that shall hereafter be mentioned. In the meantime, he desired I would go on with my utmost diligence to learn their language, because he was more astonished at my capacity for speech and reason than at the figure of my body, whether it were covered or not; adding that he waited with some impatience to hear the wonders which I promised to tell him.

Thenceforward he doubled the pains he had been at to instruct me; he brought me into all company, and made them treat me with civility; because, as he told them privately, this would put me into good humour, and make me more diverting.

Every day when I waited on him, beside the trouble he was at in teaching, he would ask me several questions concerning myself, which I answered as well as I could, and by these means he had already received some general ideas, though very imperfect. It would be tedious to relate the several steps by which I advanced to a more regular conversation; but the first account I gave of myself in any order and length was to this purpose:

That I came from a very far country, as I already had attempted to tell him, with about fifty more of my own species; that we travelled upon the seas in a great hollow vessel made of wood, and larger than his honour's house. I described the ship to him in the best terms I could, and explained, by the help of my handkerchief displayed, how it was driven forward by the wind. That upon a quarrel among us, I was set on shore on this coast, where I walked forward, without knowing whither, till he delivered me from the persecution of those execrable Yahoos. He asked me who made the ship, and how it was possible that the Houyhnhnms of my country would leave it to the management of brutes? My answer was that I durst proceed no further in my relation unless he would give me his word and honour that he would not be offended, and then I would tell him the wonders I had so often promised. He agreed; and I went on by assuring him that the ship was made by creatures like myself, who in all the countries I had travelled, as well as in my own, were the only governing rational animals; and that upon my arrival hither, I was as much astonished to see the Houyhnhnms act like rational beings as he or his friends could be in finding some marks of reason in a creature he was pleased to call a Yahoo; to which I owned my resemblance in every part, but could not account for their degenerate and brutal nature. I said farther, that if good fortune ever restored me to my native country, to relate my travels hither, as I resolved to do, everybody would believe that I said the thing that was not, that I invented the story out of my own head; and (with all possible respect to himself, his family, and friends, and under his promise of not being offended) our countrymen would hardly think it probable that a Houyhnhnm should be the presiding creature of a nation, and a Yahoo the brute.

CHAPTER 4

(The Houyhnhnm's notion of truth and falsehood. The author's discourse disapproved by his master. The author gives a more particular account of himself and the accidents of his voyage.)

My master heard me with great appearances of uneasiness in his countenance; because doubting or not believing are so little known in this country that the inhabitants cannot tell how to behave themselves under such circumstances. And I remember in frequent discourses with my master concerning the nature of manhood[1] in other parts of the world, having occasion to talk of lying and false representation, it was with much difficulty that he comprehended what I meant, although he had otherwise a most acute judgment. For he argued thus: that the use of speech was to make us understand one another, and to receive information of facts; now if anyone *said the thing which was not*, these ends were defeated, because I cannot properly be said to understand him; and I am so far from receiving information that he leaves me worse than in ignorance; for I am led to believe a thing black when it is white, and short when it is long. And these were all the notions he had concerning that faculty of lying, so perfectly well understood, and so universally practiced, among human creatures.

To return from this digression; when I asserted that the Yahoos were the only governing animals in my country, which my master said was altogether past his conception, he desired to know whether we had Houyhnhnms among us, and what was their employment? I told him we had great numbers; that in summer they grazed in the fields and in winter were kept in houses with hay and oats, where Yahoo servants were employed to rub their skins smooth, comb their manes, pick their feet, serve them with food, and make their beds. I understand you well, said my master; it is now

very plain from all you have spoken that whatever share of reason the Yahoos pretend to, the Houyhnhnms are your masters; I heartily wish our Yahoos would be so tractable. I begged his honour would please to excuse me from proceeding any further, because I was very certain that the account he expected from me would be highly displeasing. But he insisted in commanding me to let him know the best and the worst. I told him he should be obeyed. I owned that the Houyhnhnms among us, whom we called horses, were the most generous[2] and comely animals we had; that they excelled in strength and swiftness; and, when they belonged to persons of quality, were employed in travelling, racing, or drawing chariots; they were treated with much kindness and care, till they fell into diseases or became foundered[3] in the feet; but then they were sold, and used to all kind of drudgery till they died; after which their skins were stripped and sold for what they were worth, and their bodies left to be devoured by dogs and birds of prey. But the common race of horses had not so good fortune, being kept by farmers and carriers, and other mean people, who put them to greater labour, and fed them worse. I described, as well as I could, our way of riding; the shape and use of a bridle, a saddle, a spur, and a whip; of harness and wheels. I added that we fastened plates of a certain hard substance, called iron, at the bottom of their feet to preserve their hoofs from being broken by the stony ways on which we often travelled.

My master, after some expressions of great indignation, wondered how we dared to venture upon a Houyhnhnm's back; for he was sure that the weakest servant in his house would be able to shake off the strongest Yahoo; or, by lying down and rolling on his back, squeeze the brute to death. I answered that our horses were trained up from three or four years old to the several uses we intended them for; that if any of them proved intolerably vicious, they were employed for carriages; that they were severely beaten while they were young for any mischievous tricks; that the males, designed for the common use of riding or draught, were generally castrated about two years after their birth, to take down their spirits and make them more tame and gentle; that they were indeed sensible of rewards and

---

[1] *nature of manhood* Human nature.

[2] *generous* Noble; of noble birth.

[3] *foundered* Lamed.

punishments, but his honour would please to consider that they had not the least tincture of reason, any more than the Yahoos in this country.

It put me to the pains of many circumlocutions to give my master a right idea of what I spoke; for their language does not abound in variety of words, because their wants and passions are fewer than among us. But it is impossible to express his noble resentment at our savage treatment of the Houyhnhnm race; particularly after I had explained the manner and use of castrating horses among us, to hinder them from propagating their kind and to render them more servile. He said, if it were possible there could be any country where Yahoos alone were endued with reason, they certainly must be the governing animal, because reason in time will always prevail against brutal strength. But, considering the frame of our bodies, and especially of mine, he thought no creature of equal bulk was so ill-contrived for employing that reason in the common offices of life; whereupon he desired to know whether those among whom I lived resembled me or the Yahoos of his country? I assured him that I was as well shaped as most of my age; but the younger, and the females, were much more soft and tender, and the skins of the latter generally as white as milk. He said I differed indeed from other Yahoos, being much more cleanly, and not altogether so deformed; but, in point of real advantage, he thought I differed for the worse: that my nails were of no use either to my fore or hinder feet; as to my forefeet, he could not properly call them by that name, for he never observed me to walk upon them; that they were too soft to bear the ground; that I generally went with them uncovered; neither was the covering I sometimes wore on them of the same shape, or so strong as that on my feet behind; that I could not walk with any security, for if either of my hinder feet slipped, I must inevitably fail. He then began to find fault with other parts of my body: the flatness of my face; the prominence of my nose; mine eyes placed directly in front, so that I could not look on either side without turning my head; that I was not able to feed myself without lifting one of my forefeet to my mouth, and therefore nature had placed those joints to answer that necessity. He knew not what could be the use of those several clefts and divisions in my feet behind; that these were too soft to bear the hardness and sharpness of stones without a

covering made from the skin of some other brute; that my whole body wanted a fence against heat and cold, which I was forced to put on and off every day, with tediousness and trouble; and lastly, that he observed every animal in this country naturally to abhor the Yahoos, whom the weaker avoided and the stronger drove from them. So that, supposing us to have the gift of reason, he could not see how it were possible to cure that natural antipathy which every creature discovered against us; nor, consequently, how we could tame and render them serviceable. However, he would (as he said) debate the matter no farther, because he was more desirous to know my own story, the country where I was born, and the several actions and events of my life before I came hither.

I assured him how extremely desirous I was that he should be satisfied on every point; but I doubted much whether it would be possible for me to explain myself on several subjects, whereof his honour could have no conception; because I saw nothing in his country to which I could resemble them; that, however, I would do my best, and strive to express myself by similitudes, humbly desiring his assistance when I wanted proper words; which he was pleased to promise me.

I said, my birth was of honest parents, in an island called England, which was remote from his country as many days' journey as the strongest of his honour's servants could travel in the annual course of the sun; that I was bred a surgeon, whose trade it is to cure wounds and hurts in the body gotten by accident or violence; that my country was governed by a female man, whom we called queen; that I left it to get riches, whereby I might maintain myself and family when I should return; that in my last voyage I was commander of the ship, and had about fifty Yahoos under me, many of which died at sea, and I was forced to supply them by others picked out from several nations; that our ship was twice in danger of being sunk, the first time by a great storm, and the second by striking against a rock. Here my master interposed by asking me how I could persuade strangers out of different countries to venture with me after the losses I had sustained and the hazards I had run? I said, they were fellows of desperate fortunes, forced to fly from the places of their birth on account of their poverty or their crimes. Some were undone by lawsuits; others spent all they had in drinking, whoring, and gaming; others fled for treason; many for murder, theft, poisoning, robbery, perjury, forgery, coining false money, for committing rapes or sodomy; for flying from their colours[1] or deserting to the enemy; and most of them had broken prison; none of these durst return to their native countries, for fear of being hanged or of starving in a jail; and therefore they were under the necessity of seeking a livelihood in other places.

During this discourse, my master was pleased to interrupt me several times. I had made use of many circumlocutions in describing to him the nature of the several crimes for which most of our crew had been forced to fly their country. This labour took up several days' conversation before he was able to comprehend me. He was wholly at a loss to know what could be the use or necessity of practising those vices. To clear up which, I endeavoured to give some ideas of the desire of power and riches; of the terrible effects of lust, intemperance, malice, and envy. All this I was forced to define and describe by putting of cases[2] and making of suppositions. After which, like one whose imagination was struck with something never seen or heard of before, he would lift up his eyes with amazement and indignation. Power, government, war, law, punishment, and a thousand other things had no terms wherein that language could express them, which made the difficulty almost insuperable to give my master any conception of what I meant. But, being of an excellent understanding, much improved by contemplation and converse, he at last arrived at a competent knowledge of what human nature, in our parts of the world, is capable to perform, and desired I would give him some particular account of that land which we call Europe, but especially of my own country.

CHAPTER 5

(*The author, at his master's command, informs him of the state of England. The causes of war among the princes of Europe. The author begins to explain the English Constitution.*)

The reader may please to observe that the following extract of many conversations I had with my master contains a summary of the most material points, which were discoursed at several times for above two years; his honour often desiring fuller satisfaction as I farther improved in the Houyhnhnm tongue. I laid before him, as well as I could, the whole state of Europe; I discoursed of trade and manufactures, of arts and sciences; and the answers I gave to all the questions he made, as they arose upon several subjects, were a fund of conversation not to be exhausted. But I shall here only set down the substance of what passed between us concerning my own country, reducing it in order as well as I can, without any regard to time or other circumstances, while I strictly adhere to truth. My only concern is that I shall hardly be able to do justice to my master's arguments and expressions, which must needs suffer by my want of capacity, as well as by a translation into our barbarous English.

In obedience, therefore, to his honour's commands, I related to him the Revolution under the Prince of Orange; the long war with France entered into by the said prince and renewed by his successor, the present Queen, wherein the greatest powers of Christendom were engaged, and which still continued.[3] I computed, at his request, that about a million of Yahoos might have been killed in the whole progress of it, and perhaps a hundred or more cities taken, and five times as many ships burnt or sunk.

He asked me, what were the usual causes or motives that made one country go to war with another? I answered, they were innumerable; but I should only mention a few of the chief. Sometimes the ambition of princes, who never think they have land or people enough to govern; sometimes the corruption of ministers, who engage their master in a war in order to stifle or divert the clamour of the subjects against their evil administration. Difference in opinions has cost many millions of lives: for instance, whether flesh be bread, or bread be flesh; whether the juice of a certain berry be blood or wine; whether whistling be a vice or a virtue;

---

[1] *flying from their colours*   Deserting from their regiments.

[2] *putting of cases*   Presenting the circumstances and grounds upon which a claim rests (legal terminology).

[3] *the Revolution ... still continued*   Gulliver describes the Glorious Revolution of 1688, in which the Catholic King James II was deposed and the Protestant William of Orange crowned King, and the war between France and the Protestant allies that continued until the Peace of Utrecht, 1713.

whether it be better to kiss a post, or throw it into the fire; what is the best colour for a coat, whether black, white, red, or gray; and whether it should be long or short, narrow or wide, dirty or clean;[1] with many more. Neither are any wars so furious and bloody, or of so long a continuance, as those occasioned by difference in opinion, especially if it be in things indifferent.[2]

Sometimes the quarrel between two princes is to decide which of them shall dispossess a third of his dominions, where neither of them pretend to any right. Sometimes one prince quarrels with another for fear the other should quarrel with him. Sometimes a war is entered upon because the enemy is too strong; and sometimes because he is too weak. Sometimes our neighbours want the things which we have, or have the things which we want, and we both fight, till they take ours or give us theirs. It is a very justifiable cause of a war to invade a country after the people have been wasted by famine, destroyed by pestilence, or embroiled by factions among themselves. It is justifiable to enter into war against our nearest ally when one of his towns lies convenient for us, or a territory of land that would render our dominions round and complete. If a prince sends forces into a nation where the people are poor and ignorant, he may lawfully put half of them to death, and make slaves of the rest, in order to civilize and reduce[3] them from their barbarous way of living. It is a very kingly, honourable, and frequent practice, when one prince desires the assistance of another to secure him against an invasion, that the assistant, when he has driven out the invader, should seize on the dominions himself and kill, imprison, or banish the prince he came to relieve. Alliance by blood or marriage, is a frequent cause of war between princes; and the nearer the kindred is, the greater their disposition to quarrel. Poor nations are hungry, and rich nations are proud; and pride and hunger will ever be at variance. For these reasons, the trade of a soldier is held the most honourable of all others, because a soldier is a Yahoo hired to kill, in cold blood, as many of his own species, who have never offended him, as possibly he can.

There is likewise a kind of beggarly princes in Europe, not able to make war by themselves, who hire out their troops to richer nations for so much a day to each man; of which they keep three-fourths to themselves, and it is the best part of their maintenance; such are those in many northern parts of Europe.[4]

"What you have told me," said my master, "upon the subject of war, does indeed discover most admirably the effects of that reason you pretend to; however, it is happy that the shame is greater than the danger; and that nature has left you utterly incapable of doing much mischief. For, your mouths lying flat with your faces, you can hardly bite each other to any purpose, unless by consent. Then as to the claws upon your feet before and behind, they are so short and tender that one of our Yahoos would drive a dozen of yours before him. And therefore, in recounting the numbers of those who have been killed in battle, I cannot but think you have said the thing which is not."

I could not forbear shaking my head and smiling a little at his ignorance. And being no stranger to the art of war, I gave him a description of cannons, culverins,[5] muskets, carabines,[6] pistols, bullets, powder, swords, bayonets, battles, sieges, retreats, attacks, undermines, countermines,[7] bombardments, sea fights, ships sunk with a thousand men, twenty thousand killed on each side, dying groans, limbs flying in the air, smoke, noise, confusion, trampling to death under horses' feet, flight, pursuit, victory, fields strewed with carcasses left for food to dogs and wolves and birds of prey, plundering, stripping, ravishing, burning, and destroying. And to set forth the valour of my own dear countrymen, I assured him that I had seen them blow up a hundred enemies at once in a siege, and as many in a ship, and beheld the dead bodies drop down in pieces from the clouds, to the great diversion of all the spectators.

I was going on to more particulars when my master

---

[1] *whether flesh … or clean* These differences in opinion, all of which occur between different denominations of Christians, are over transubstantiation, the place of music in church ("whistling"), worship of the crucifix and other icons, and the proper style of vestments.

[2] *indifferent* Of no consequence, unimportant.

[3] *reduce* Reform, convert.

[4] *beggarly princes … Europe* George I, as Elector of Hanover, hired German mercenaries to defend his kingdom.

[5] *culverins* Large cannons.

[6] *carabines* Short firearms.

[7] *undermines* Mines placed underneath fortress walls; *countermines* Mines or excavations made by the defenders of a fortress to intercept the undermines.

commanded me silence. He said, whoever understood the nature of Yahoos might easily believe it possible for so vile an animal to be capable of every action I had named, if their strength and cunning equalled their malice. But, as my discourse had increased his abhorrence of the whole species, so he found it gave him a disturbance in his mind to which he was wholly a stranger before. He thought his ears, being used to such abominable words, might, by degrees, admit them with less detestation. That, although he hated the Yahoos of this country, yet he no more blamed them for their odious qualities than he did a gnnayh (a bird of prey) for its cruelty, or a sharp stone for cutting his hoof. But when a creature pretending to reason could be capable of such enormities, he dreaded lest the corruption of that faculty might be worse than brutality itself. He seemed therefore confident that, instead of reason, we were only possessed of some quality fitted to increase our natural vices; as the reflection from a troubled stream returns the image of an ill-shapen body not only larger, but more distorted.

He added that he had heard too much upon the subject of war, both in this and some former discourses. There was another point which a little perplexed him at present. I had informed him that some of our crew left their country on account of being ruined by law; that I had already explained the meaning of the word, but he was at a loss how it should come to pass that the law, which was intended for every man's preservation, should be any man's ruin. Therefore he desired to be further satisfied what I meant by law, and the dispensers thereof, according to the present practice in my own country, because he thought nature and reason were sufficient guides for a reasonable animal, as we pretended to be, in showing us what he ought to do, and what to avoid.

I assured his honour that the law was a science in which I had not much conversed, further than by employing advocates, in vain, upon some injustices that had been done me; however, I would give him all the satisfaction I was able.

I said there was a society of men among us, bred up from their youth in the art of proving, by words multiplied for the purpose, that white is black, and black is white, according as they are paid. To this society all the rest of the people are slaves.

For example, if my neighbour has a mind to my cow, he has a lawyer to prove that he ought to have my cow from me. I must then hire another to defend my right, it being against all rules of law that any man should be allowed to speak for himself. Now, in this case, I, who am the right owner, lie under two great disadvantages. First, my lawyer, being practised almost from his cradle in defending falsehood, is quite out of his element when he would be an advocate for justice, which is an unnatural office he always attempts with great awkwardness, if not with ill-will. The second disadvantage is that my lawyer must proceed with great caution, or else he will be reprimanded by the judges, and abhorred by his brethren, as one that would lessen the practice of the law. And therefore I have but two methods to preserve my cow. The first is to gain over my adversary's lawyer with a double fee, who will then betray his client by insinuating that he hath justice on his side. The second way is for my lawyer to make my cause appear as unjust as he can, by allowing the cow to belong to my adversary; and this, if it be skillfully done, will certainly bespeak[1] the favour of the bench.

Now, your honour is to know that these judges are persons appointed to decide all controversies of property, as well as for the trial of criminals, and picked out from the most dexterous lawyers who are grown old or lazy; and, having been biased all their lives against truth and equity, lie under such a fatal necessity of favouring fraud, perjury, and oppression, that I have known some of them refuse a large bribe from the side where justice lay, rather than injure the faculty[2] by doing anything unbecoming their nature or their office.

It is a maxim among these lawyers that whatever has been done before may legally be done again; and therefore they take special care to record all the decisions formerly made against common justice and the general reason of mankind. These, under the name of precedents, they produce as authorities to justify the most iniquitous opinions; and the judges never fail of directing accordingly.

In pleading, they studiously avoid entering into the merits of the cause; but are loud, violent, and tedious in dwelling upon all circumstances which are not to the purpose. For instance, in the case already mentioned, they never desire to know what claim or title my adver-

---

[1] *bespeak* Engage; gain.
[2] *faculty* Profession.

sary has to my cow; but whether the said cow were red or black; her horns long or short; whether the field I graze her in be round or square; whether she was milked at home or abroad; what diseases she is subject to, and the like. After which they consult precedents, adjourn the cause from time to time, and in ten, twenty, or thirty years come to an issue.[1]

It is likewise to be observed that this society has a peculiar cant and jargon of their own, that no other mortal can understand, and wherein all their laws are written, which they take special care to multiply; whereby they have wholly confounded the very essence of truth and falsehood, of right and wrong; so that it will take thirty years to decide whether the field left me by my ancestors for six generations belongs to me or to a stranger three hundred miles off.

In the trial of persons accused for crimes against the state, the method is much more short and commendable: the judge first sends to sound the disposition of those in power; after which he can easily hang or save a criminal, strictly preserving all due forms of law.

Here my master, interposing, said it was a pity that creatures endowed with such prodigious abilities of mind as these lawyers, by the description I gave of them, must certainly be, were not rather encouraged to be instructors of others in wisdom and knowledge. In answer to which I assured his honour that in all points out of their own trade they were usually the most ignorant and stupid generation among us, the most despicable in common conversation, avowed enemies to all knowledge and learning, and equally disposed to pervert the general reason of mankind in every other subject of discourse as in that of their own profession.

CHAPTER 6

(A continuation of the state of England under Queen Anne. The character of a first minister in the courts of Europe.)

My master was yet wholly at a loss to understand what motives could incite this race of lawyers to perplex, disquiet, and weary themselves by engaging in a confederacy of injustice, merely for the sake of injuring their fellow animals; neither could he comprehend

what I meant in saying they did it for hire. Whereupon I was at much pains to describe to him the use of money, the materials it was made of, and the value of the metals; that when a Yahoo had got a great store of this precious substance, he was able to purchase whatever he had a mind to: the finest clothing, the noblest houses, great tracts of land, the most costly meats and drinks, and have his choice of the most beautiful females. Therefore since money alone was able to perform all these feats, our Yahoos thought they could never have enough of it to spend or to save, as they found themselves inclined from their natural bent either to profusion or avarice. That the rich man enjoyed the fruit of the poor man's labour, and the latter were a thousand to one in proportion to the former. That the bulk of our people were forced to live miserably by labouring every day for small wages, to make a few live plentifully. I enlarged myself much on these and many other particulars to the same purpose; but his honour was still to seek,[2] for he went upon a supposition that all animals had a title to their share in the productions of the earth, and especially those who presided over the rest. Therefore he desired I would let him know what these costly meats were, and how any of us happened to want[3] them. Whereupon I enumerated as many sorts as came into my head, with the various methods of dressing them, which could not be done without sending vessels by sea to every part of the world, as well for liquors to drink as for sauces and innumerable other conveniences. I assured him that this whole globe of earth must be at least three times gone round before one of our better female Yahoos could get her breakfast, or a cup to put it in. He said, "That must needs be a miserable country which cannot furnish food for its own inhabitants." But what he chiefly wondered at was how such vast tracts of ground as I described should be wholly without fresh water, and the people put to the necessity of sending over the sea for drink. I replied that England (the dear place of my nativity) was computed to produce three times the quantity of food more than its inhabitants are able to consume, as well as liquors extracted from grain, or pressed out of the fruit of certain trees, which made excellent drink, and the same proportion in every other convenience of life. But, in

---

1   *to an issue* To a judgment.

2   *still to seek* Still unable to comprehend.

3   *want* Lack.

order to feed the luxury and intemperance of the males and the vanity of the females, we sent away the greatest part of our necessary things to other countries, from whence, in return, we brought the materials of diseases, folly, and vice, to spend among ourselves. Hence it follows of necessity that vast numbers of our people are compelled to seek their livelihood by begging, robbing, stealing, cheating, pimping, forswearing,[1] flattering, suborning,[2] forging, gaming, lying, fawning, hectoring, voting, scribbling, stargazing, poisoning, whoring, canting,[3] libelling, freethinking,[4] and the like occupations; every one of which terms I was at much pains to make him understand.

That wine was not imported among us from foreign countries to supply the want of water or other drinks, but because it was a sort of liquid which made us merry by putting us out of our senses; diverted all melancholy thoughts, begat wild extravagant imaginations in the brain, raised our hopes and banished our fears, suspended every office of reason for a time, and deprived us of the use of our limbs, until we fell into a profound sleep; although it must be confessed that we always awoke sick and dispirited; and that the use of this liquor filled us with diseases which made our lives uncomfortable and short.

But beside all this, the bulk of our people supported themselves by furnishing the necessities or conveniences of life to the rich and to each other. For instance, when I am at home and dressed as I ought to be, I carry on my body the workmanship of a hundred tradesmen; the building and furniture of my house employ as many more, and five times the number to adorn my wife.

I was going on to tell him of another sort of people, who get their livelihood by attending the sick; having upon some occasions informed his honour that many of my crew had died of diseases. But here it was with the utmost difficulty that I brought him to apprehend what I meant. He could easily conceive that a Houyhnhnm grew weak and heavy a few days before his death, or by some accident might hurt a limb; but that nature, who works all things to perfection, should suffer any pains to

breed in our bodies, he thought impossible, and desired to know the reason of so unaccountable an evil. I told him we fed on a thousand things which operated contrary to each other; that we ate when we were not hungry and drank without the provocation of thirst; that we sat whole nights drinking strong liquors without eating a bit, which disposed us to sloth, inflamed our bodies, and precipitated or prevented digestion; that prostitute female Yahoos acquired a certain malady which bred rottenness in the bones of those who fell into their embraces; that this and many other diseases were propagated from father to son, so that great numbers came into the world with complicated maladies upon them; that it would be endless to give him a catalogue of all diseases incident to human bodies, for they would not be fewer than five or six hundred, spread over every limb and joint—in short, every part, external and intestine, having diseases appropriated to itself. To remedy which, there was a sort of people bred up among us in the profession, or pretence, of curing the sick. And because I had some skill in the faculty, I would, in gratitude to his honour, let him know the whole mystery and method by which they proceed.

Their fundamental is that all diseases arise from repletion; from whence they conclude that a great evacuation of the body is necessary, either through the natural passage or upwards at the mouth. Their next business is from herbs, minerals, gums, oils, shells, salts, juices, sea-weed, excrements, barks of trees, serpents, toads, frogs, spiders, dead men's flesh and bones, birds, beasts, and fishes, to form a composition for smell and taste the most abominable, nauseous, and detestable they can possibly contrive, which the stomach immediately rejects with loathing, and this they call a vomit. Or else from the same storehouse, with some other poisonous additions, they command us to take in at the orifice above or below (just as the physician then happens to be disposed) a medicine equally annoying and disgustful to the bowels; which, relaxing the belly, drives down all before it; and this they call a purge, or a clyster. For nature (as the physicians allege) having intended the superior anterior orifice only for the intromission of solids and liquids, and the inferior posterior for ejection, these artists ingeniously considering that in all diseases nature is forced out of her seat; therefore, to replace her in it, the body must be treated in a manner directly

---

[1]   *forswearing* Committing perjury.

[2]   *suborning* Bribing.

[3]   *canting* Speaking in professional or technical language; using jargon.

[4]   *freethinking* Rejecting any religious belief or authority.

contrary, by interchanging the use of each orifice: forcing solids and liquids in at the anus, and making evacuations at the mouth.

But, besides real diseases, we are subject to many that are only imaginary, for which the physicians have invented imaginary cures; these have their several names, and so have the drugs that are proper for them; and with these our female Yahoos are always infested.

One great excellency in this tribe is their skill at prognostics, wherein they seldom fail; their predictions in real diseases, when they rise to any degree of malignity, generally portending death (which is always in their power when recovery is not); and therefore, upon any unexpected signs of amendment after they have pronounced their sentence, rather than be accused as false prophets, they know how to approve[1] their sagacity to the world by a seasonable dose.

They are likewise of special use to husbands and wives who are grown weary of their mates; to eldest sons, to great ministers of state, and often to princes.

I had formerly, upon occasion, discoursed with my master upon the nature of government in general, and particularly of our own excellent constitution, deservedly the wonder and envy of the whole world. But having here accidentally mentioned a minister of state, he commanded me, some time after, to inform him what species of Yahoo I particularly meant by that appellation.

I told him that a first or chief minister of state, who was the person I intended to describe, was the creature wholly exempt from joy and grief, love and hatred, pity and anger; at least, makes use of no other passions but a violent desire of wealth, power, and titles; that he applies his words to all uses except to the indication of his mind; that he never tells a truth but with an intent that you should take it for a lie; nor a lie but with a design that you should take it for a truth; that those he speaks worst of behind their backs are in the surest way of preferment; and whenever he begins to praise you to others, or to yourself, you are from that day forlorn. The worst mark you can receive is a promise, especially when it is confirmed with an oath; after which every wise man retires and gives over all hopes.

There are three methods by which a man may rise to be chief minister. The first is by knowing how, with prudence, to dispose of a wife, a daughter, or a sister; the second, by betraying or undermining his predecessor; and the third is by a furious zeal, in public assemblies, against the corruptions of the court. But a wise prince would rather choose to employ those who practise the last of these methods, because such zealots prove always the most obsequious and subservient to the will and passions of their master. That these ministers, having all employments at their disposal, preserve themselves in power by bribing the majority of a senate or great council; and at last, by an expedient called an Act of Indemnity[2] (whereof I described the nature to him), they secure themselves from after reckonings and retire from the public, laden with the spoils of the nation.

The palace of a chief minister is a seminary to breed up others in his own trade; the pages, lackeys, and porters, by imitating their master, become ministers of state in their several districts, and learn to excel in the three principal ingredients, of insolence, lying, and bribery. Accordingly, they have a subaltern court paid to them by persons of the best rank; and sometimes, by the force of dexterity and impudence, arrive, through several gradations, to be successors to their lord.

He is usually governed by a decayed wench, or favourite footman, who are the tunnels through which all graces are conveyed, and may properly be called, in the last resort, the governors of the kingdom.

One day my master, having heard me mention the nobility of my country, was pleased to make me a compliment which I could not pretend to deserve: that he was sure I must have been born of some noble family, because I far exceeded in shape, colour, and cleanliness, all the Yahoos of his nation, although I seemed to fail in strength and agility, which must be imputed to my different way of living from those other brutes; and besides I was not only endowed with the faculty of speech, but likewise with some rudiments of reason, to a degree that, with all his acquaintance, I passed for a prodigy.

He made me observe that among the Houyhnhnms, the white, the sorrel, and the iron gray were not so exactly shaped as the bay, the dapple gray, and the black; nor born with equal talents of mind, or a capacity to

---

[1] *approve* Demonstrate.

[2] *Act of Indemnity* Act that protects ministers from being prosecuted for illegal or unconstitutional activities undertaken, presumably with good intent, while in office.

improve them; and therefore continued always in the condition of servants, without ever aspiring to match out of[1] their own race, which in that country would be reckoned monstrous and unnatural.

I made his honour my most humble acknowledgments for the good opinion he was pleased to conceive of me, but assured him at the same time that my birth was of the lower sort, having been born of plain, honest parents, who were just able to give me a tolerable education; that nobility, among us, was altogether a different thing from the idea he had of it; that our young noblemen are bred from their childhood in idleness and luxury; that, as soon as years will permit, they consume their vigour, and contract odious diseases among lewd females; and when their fortunes are almost ruined, they marry some woman of mean birth, disagreeable person, and unsound constitution (merely for the sake of money), whom they hate and despise. That the productions of such marriages are generally scrofulous,[2] rickety, or deformed children; by which means the family seldom continues above three generations, unless the wife takes care to provide a healthy father among her neighbours or domestics, in order to improve and continue the breed. That a weak, diseased body, a meagre countenance and sallow complexion, are the true marks of noble blood; and a healthy robust appearance is so disgraceful in a man of quality that the world concludes his real father to have been a groom or a coachman. The imperfections of his mind run parallel with those of his body, being a composition of spleen,[3] dullness, ignorance, caprice, sensuality, and pride.

Without the consent of this illustrious body, no law can be enacted, repealed, or altered; and these nobles have likewise the decision of all our possessions, without appeal.

CHAPTER 7

(*The author's great love of his native country. His master's observations upon the constitution and administration of England, as described by the author, with parallel cases and comparisons. His master's observations upon human nature.*)

---

[1] *match out of* Choose a mate from outside of.

[2] *scrofulous* Infected with scrofula, a disease characterized by the inflammation and degeneration of the lymph nodes.

[3] *spleen* Melancholia, ill-humor, irritability.

The reader may be disposed to wonder how I could prevail on myself to give so free a representation of my own species among a race of mortals who are already too apt to conceive the vilest opinion of humankind, from that entire congruity between me and their Yahoos. But I must freely confess that the many virtues of those excellent quadrupeds, placed in opposite view to human corruptions, had so far opened my eyes and enlarged my understanding that I began to view the actions and passions of man in a very different light, and to think the honour of my own kind not worth managing;[4] which, besides, it was impossible for me to do before a person of so acute a judgment as my master, who daily convinced me of a thousand faults in myself, whereof I had not the least perception before, and which, with us, would never be numbered even among human infirmities. I had likewise learned, from his example, an utter detestation of all falsehood or disguise; and truth appeared so amiable to me that I determined upon sacrificing every thing to it.

Let me deal so candidly with the reader as to confess that there was yet a much stronger motive for the freedom I took in my representation of things. I had not yet been a year in this country before I contracted such a love and veneration for the inhabitants that I entered on a firm resolution never to return to humankind, but to pass the rest of my life among these admirable Houyhnhnms in the contemplation and practice of every virtue, where I could have no example or incitement to vice. But it was decreed by fortune, my perpetual enemy, that so great a felicity should not fall to my share. However, it is now some comfort to reflect that in what I said of my countrymen, I extenuated their faults as much as I durst before so strict an examiner; and upon every article gave as favourable a turn as the matter would bear. For, indeed, who is there alive that will not be swayed by his bias and partiality to the place of his birth?

I have related the substance of several conversations I had with my master during the greatest part of the time I had the honour to be in his service; but have indeed, for brevity sake, omitted much more than is here set down.

When I had answered all his questions, and his curiosity seemed to be fully satisfied, he sent for me one

---

[4] *managing* Looking after.

morning early, and commanded me to sit down at some distance (an honour which he had never before conferred upon me). He said he had been very seriously considering my whole story, as far as it related both to myself and my country; that he looked upon us as a sort of animals, to whose share, by what accident he could not conjecture, some small pittance of reason had fallen, whereof we made no other use than by its assistance to aggravate our natural corruptions and to acquire new ones, which nature had not given us. That we disarmed ourselves of the few abilities she had bestowed; had been very successful in multiplying our original wants, and seemed to spend our whole lives in vain endeavours to supply them by our own inventions. That, as to myself, it was manifest I had neither the strength nor agility of a common Yahoo; that I walked infirmly on my hinder feet; had found out a contrivance to make my claws of no use or defence, and to remove the hair from my chin, which was intended as a shelter from the sun and the weather; lastly, that I could neither run with speed nor climb trees like my brethren (as he called them), the Yahoos in his country.

That our institutions of government and law were plainly owing to our gross defects in reason and, by consequence, in virtue, because reason alone is sufficient to govern a rational creature; which was, therefore, a character we had no pretence to challenge, even from the account I had given of my own people; although he manifestly perceived that, in order to favour them, I had concealed many particulars, and often *said the thing which was not*.

He was the more confirmed in this opinion because he observed that, as I agreed in every feature of my body with other Yahoos, except where it was to my real disadvantage in point of strength, speed, and activity, the shortness of my claws, and some other particulars where nature had no part; so from the representation I had given him of our lives, our manners, and our actions, he found as near a resemblance in the disposition of our minds. He said the Yahoos were known to hate one another more than they did any different species of animals; and the reason usually assigned was the odiousness of their own shapes, which all could see in the rest, but not in themselves. He had therefore begun to think it not unwise in us to cover our bodies, and by that invention conceal many of our deformities from each other, which would else be hardly supportable. But he now found he had been mistaken, and that the dissensions of those brutes in his country were owing to the same cause with ours, as I had described them. For if (said he) you throw among five Yahoos as much food as would be sufficient for fifty, they will, instead of eating peaceably, fall together by the ears, each single one impatient to have all to itself; and therefore a servant was usually employed to stand by while they were feeding abroad, and those kept at home were tied at a distance from each other. That if a cow died of age or accident before a Houyhnhnm could secure it for his own Yahoos, those in the neighbourhood would come in herds to seize it, and then would ensue such a battle as I had described, with terrible wounds made by their claws on both sides, although they seldom were able to kill one another, for want of such convenient instruments of death as we had invented. At other times the like battles have been fought between the Yahoos of several neighbourhoods without any visible cause; those of one district watching all opportunities to surprise the next before they are prepared. But if they find their project has miscarried, they return home and, for want of enemies, engage in what I call a civil war among themselves.

That in some fields of his country there are certain shining stones of several colours, whereof the Yahoos are violently fond; and when part of these stones is fixed in the earth, as it sometimes happens, they will dig with their claws for whole days to get them out, and then carry them away and hide them by heaps in their kennels; but still looking round with great caution, for fear their comrades should find out their treasure. My master said he could never discover the reason of this unnatural appetite, or how these stones could be of any use to a Yahoo; but now he believed it might proceed from the same principle of avarice which I had ascribed to mankind. That he had once, by way of experiment, privately removed a heap of these stones from the place where one of his Yahoos had buried it; whereupon the sordid animal, missing his treasure, by his loud lamenting brought the whole herd to the place, there miserably howled, then fell to biting and tearing the rest; began to pine away, would neither eat, nor sleep, nor work till he ordered a servant privately to convey the stones into the same hole and hide them as before; which, when his

Yahoo had found, he presently recovered his spirits and good humour, but took good care to remove them to a better hiding place, and has ever since been a very serviceable brute.

My master further assured me, which I also observed myself, that in the fields where the shining stones abound, the fiercest and most frequent battles are fought, occasioned by perpetual inroads of the neighbouring Yahoos.

He said it was common, when two Yahoos discovered such a stone in a field, and were contending which of them should be the proprietor, a third would take the advantage, and carry it away from them both; which my master would needs contend to have some kind of resemblance with our suits at law; wherein I thought it for our credit not to undeceive him; since the decision he mentioned was much more equitable than many decrees among us, because the plaintiff and defendant there lost nothing beside the stone they contended for: whereas our courts of equity would never have dismissed the cause, while either of them had any thing left.

My master, continuing his discourse, said there was nothing that rendered the Yahoos more odious than their undistinguishing appetite to devour every thing that came in their way, whether herbs, roots, berries, the corrupted flesh of animals, or all mingled together; and it was peculiar in their temper that they were fonder of what they could get by rapine or stealth at a greater distance, than much better food provided for them at home. If their prey held out, they would eat till they were ready to burst; after which nature had pointed out to them a certain root that gave them a general evacuation.

There was also another kind of root, very juicy, but somewhat rare and difficult to be found, which the Yahoos sought for with much eagerness, and would suck it with great delight; it produced in them the same effects that wine has upon us. It would make them sometimes hug, and sometimes tear one another; they would howl, and grin, and chatter, and reel, and tumble, and then fall asleep in the mud.

I did indeed observe that the Yahoos were the only animals in this country subject to any diseases; which, however, were much fewer than horses have among us, and contracted not by any ill-treatment they meet with, but by the nastiness and greediness of that sordid brute.

Neither has their language any more than a general appellation for those maladies, which is borrowed from the name of the beast, and called *hnea-yahoo*, or Yahoo's evil; and the cure prescribed is a mixture of their own dung and urine, forcibly put down the Yahoo's throat. This I have since often known to have been taken with success, and do here freely recommend it to my countrymen for the public good, as an admirable specific against all diseases produced by repletion.

As to learning, government, arts, manufactures, and the like, my master confessed he could find little or no resemblance between the Yahoos of that country and those in ours; for he only meant to observe what parity there was in our natures. He had heard, indeed, some curious Houyhnhnms observe that in most herds there was a sort of ruling Yahoo (as among us there is generally some leading or principal stag in a park), who was always more deformed in body, and mischievous in disposition, than any of the rest; that this leader had usually a favourite as like himself as he could get, whose employment was to lick his master's feet and posteriors and drive the female Yahoos to his kennel; for which he was now and then rewarded with a piece of ass's flesh. This favourite is hated by the whole herd, and therefore, to protect himself, keeps always near the person of his leader. He usually continues in office till a worse can be found; but the very moment he is discarded, his successor, at the head of all the Yahoos in that district, young and old, male and female, come in a body, and discharge their excrements upon him from head to foot. But how far this might be applicable to our courts and favourites, and ministers of state, my master said I could best determine.

I durst make no return to this malicious insinuation, which debased human understanding below the sagacity of a common hound, who has judgment enough to distinguish and follow the cry of the ablest dog in the pack, without being ever mistaken.

My master told me there were some qualities remarkable in the Yahoos which he had not observed me to mention, or at least very slightly, in the accounts I had given of humankind. He said those animals, like other brutes, had their females in common; but in this they differed, that the she-Yahoo would admit the males while she was pregnant; and that the hes would quarrel and fight with the females as fiercely as with each other.

Both which practices were such degrees of infamous brutality as no other sensitive creature ever arrived at.

Another thing he wondered at in the Yahoos was their strange disposition to nastiness and dirt; whereas there appears to be a natural love of cleanliness in all other animals. As to the two former accusations, I was glad to let them pass without any reply, because I had not a word to offer upon them in defence of my species, which otherwise I certainly had done from my own inclinations. But I could have easily vindicated human-kind from the imputation of singularity upon the last article, if there had been any swine in that country (as unluckily for me there were not), which, although it may be a sweeter quadruped than a Yahoo, cannot, I humbly conceive, in justice pretend to more cleanliness; and so his honour himself must have owned, if he had seen their filthy way of feeding and their custom of wallowing and sleeping in the mud.

My master likewise mentioned another quality which his servants had discovered in several Yahoos, and to him was wholly unaccountable. He said a fancy would sometimes take a Yahoo to retire into a corner, to lie down, and howl, and groan, and spurn away all that came near him, although he were young and fat, wanted neither food nor water, nor did the servant imagine what could possibly ail him. And the only remedy they found was to set him to hard work, after which he would infallibly come to himself. To this I was silent out of partiality to my own kind; yet here I could plainly discover the true seeds of spleen, which only seizes on the lazy, the luxurious, and the rich; who, if they were forced to undergo the same regimen, I would undertake for the cure.

His honour had further observed that a female Yahoo would often stand behind a bank or a bush to gaze on the young males passing by, and then appear, and hide, using many antic gestures and grimaces, at which time it was observed that she had a most offensive smell; and when any of the males advanced, would slowly retire, looking often back, and, with a counterfeit show of fear, run off into some convenient place where she knew the male would follow her.

At other times, if a female stranger came among them, three or four of her own sex would get about her, and stare and chatter, and grin, and smell her all over, and then turn off with gestures that seemed to express

contempt and disdain.

Perhaps my master might refine a little in these speculations, which he had drawn from what he ob-served himself, or had been told him by others; however, I could not reflect without some amazement, and much sorrow, that the rudiments of lewdness, coquetry, censure, and scandal should have place by instinct in womankind.

I expected every moment that my master would accuse the Yahoos of those unnatural appetites in both sexes, so common among us. But nature, it seems, has not been so expert a schoolmistress; and these politer pleasures are entirely the productions of art and reason on our side of the globe.

CHAPTER 8

(*The author relates several particulars of the Yahoos. The great virtues of the Houyhnhnms. The education and exercise of their youth. Their general assembly.*)

As I ought to have understood human nature much better than I supposed it possible for my master to do, so it was easy to apply the character he gave of the Yahoos to myself and my countrymen; and I believed I could yet make further discoveries from my own obser-vation. I therefore often begged his honour to let me go among the herds of Yahoos in the neighbourhood; to which he always very graciously consented, being perfectly convinced that the hatred I bore these brutes would never suffer me to be corrupted by them; and his honour ordered one of his servants, a strong sorrel nag, very honest and good-natured, to be my guard; without whose protection I durst not undertake such adventures. For I have already told the reader how much I was pestered by these odious animals upon my first arrival; and I afterwards failed very narrowly three or four times of falling into their clutches when I happened to stray at any distance without my hanger. And I have reason to believe they had some imagination that I was of their own species, which I often assisted myself by stripping up my sleeves and showing my naked arms and breasts in their sight, when my protector was with me. At which times they would approach as near as they durst, and imitate my actions after the manner of monkeys, but ever with great signs of hatred; as a tame jackdaw[1] with cap and stockings is always persecuted by the wild ones when he happens to be got among them.

They are prodigiously nimble from their infancy. However, I once caught a young male of three years old and endeavoured, by all marks of tenderness, to make it quiet; but the little imp fell a-squalling, and scratching, and biting with such violence that I was forced to let it go; and it was high time, for a whole troop of old ones came about us at the noise; but, finding the cub was safe (for away it ran), and my sorrel nag being by, they durst not venture near us. I observed the young animal's flesh to smell very rank, and the stink was somewhat between a weasel and a fox, but much more disagreeable. I forgot another circumstance (and perhaps I might have the reader's pardon if it were wholly omitted), that while I held the odious vermin in my hands, it voided its filthy excrements of a yellow liquid substance all over my clothes; but by good fortune there was a small brook hard by, where I washed myself as clean as I could; although I durst not come into my master's presence until I were sufficiently aired.

By what I could discover, the Yahoos appear to be the most unteachable of all animals, their capacity never reaching higher than to draw or carry burdens. Yet I am of opinion, this defect arises chiefly from a perverse, restive[2] disposition; for they are cunning, malicious, treacherous, and revengeful. They are strong and hardy, but of a cowardly spirit, and, by consequence, insolent, abject, and cruel. It is observed that the red-haired of both sexes are more libidinous and mischievous than the rest, whom yet they much exceed in strength and activity.

The Houyhnhnms keep the Yahoos for present use in huts not far from the house; but the rest are sent abroad to certain fields, where they dig up roots, eat several kinds of herbs, and search about for carrion, or sometimes catch weasels and *luhimuhs* (a sort of wild rat), which they greedily devour. Nature has taught them to dig deep holes with their nails on the side of a rising ground, wherein they lie by themselves; only the kennels of the females are larger, sufficient to hold two or three cubs.

They swim from their infancy like frogs, and are able to continue long under water, where they often take fish, which the females carry home to their young. And, upon this occasion, I hope the reader will pardon my relating an odd adventure.

Being one day abroad with my protector the sorrel nag, and the weather exceeding hot, I entreated him to let me bathe in a river that was near. He consented, and I immediately stripped myself stark naked and went down softly into the stream. It happened that a young female Yahoo, standing behind a bank, saw the whole proceeding, and, inflamed by desire (as the nag and I conjectured), came running with all speed and leaped into the water within five yards of the place where I bathed. I was never in my life so terribly frightened. The nag was grazing at some distance, not suspecting any harm. She embraced me after a most fulsome manner. I roared as loud as I could, and the nag came galloping towards me, whereupon she quitted her grasp with the utmost reluctancy, and leaped upon the opposite bank, where she stood gazing and howling all the time I was putting on my clothes.

This was a matter of diversion to my master and his family, as well as of mortification to myself. For now I could no longer deny that I was a real Yahoo in every limb and feature, since the females had a natural propensity to me as one of their own species. Neither was the hair of this brute of a red colour (which might have been some excuse for an appetite a little irregular), but black as a sloe,[3] and her countenance did not make an appearance altogether so hideous as the rest of her kind; for I think she could not be above eleven years old.

Having lived three years in this country, the reader, I suppose, will expect that I should, like other travellers, give him some account of the manners and customs of its inhabitants, which it was indeed my principal study to learn.

As these noble *Houyhnhnms* are endowed by nature with a general disposition to all virtues, and have no conceptions or ideas of what is evil in a rational creature, so their grand maxim is to cultivate reason, and to be wholly governed by it. Neither is reason among them a point problematical—as with us, where men can argue with plausibility on both sides of the question—but

---

[1] *jackdaw* Small crow that is easily tamed and trained to imitate speech.

[2] *restive* Obstinate.

[3] *sloe* Small, sour, wild plum.

strikes you with immediate conviction; as it must needs do, where it is not mingled, obscured, or discoloured by passion and interest. I remember it was with extreme difficulty that I could bring my master to understand the meaning of the word "opinion," or how a point could be disputable; because reason taught us to affirm or deny only where we are certain; and beyond our knowledge we cannot do either. So that controversies, wranglings, disputes, and positiveness in false or dubious propositions are evils unknown among the Houyhn-hnms. In the like manner, when I used to explain to him our several systems of natural philosophy,[1] he would laugh that a creature pretending to reason should value itself upon the knowledge of other people's conjectures, and in things where that knowledge, if it were certain, could be of no use. Wherein he agreed entirely with the sentiments of Socrates, as Plato delivers them,[2] which I mention as the highest honour I can do that prince of philosophers. I have often since reflected what destruction such doctrine would make in the libraries of Europe, and how many paths of fame would be then shut up in the learned world.

Friendship and benevolence are the two principal virtues among the Houyhnhnms; and these not confined to particular objects, but universal to the whole race; for a stranger from the remotest part is equally treated with the nearest neighbour, and wherever he goes, looks upon himself as at home. They preserve decency and civility in the highest degrees, but are altogether igno-rant of ceremony. They have no fondness for their colts or foals, but the care they take in educating them proceeds entirely from the dictates of reason. And I observed my master to show the same affection to his neighbour's issue that he had for his own. They will have it that nature teaches them to love the whole species, and it is reason only that makes a distinction of persons, where there is a superior degree of virtue.

When the matron Houyhnhnms have produced one of each sex, they no longer accompany with[3] their consorts, except they lose one of their issue by some casualty, which very seldom happens; but in such a case they meet again; or when the like accident befalls a person whose wife is past bearing, some other couple bestow on him one of their own colts, and then go together a second time, until the mother is pregnant. This caution is necessary to prevent the country from being overburdened with numbers. But the race of inferior Houyhnhnms, bred up to be servants, is not so strictly limited upon this article: these are allowed to produce three of each sex, to be domestics in the noble families.

In their marriages they are exactly careful to choose such colours as will not make any disagreeable mixture in the breed. Strength is chiefly valued in the male, and comeliness in the female; not upon the account of love, but to preserve the race from degenerating; for where a female happens to excel in strength, a consort is chosen with regard to comeliness. Courtship, love, presents, jointures,[4] settlements, have no place in their thoughts, or terms whereby to express them in their language. The young couple meet and are joined merely because it is the determination of their parents and friends; it is what they see done everyday, and they look upon it as one of the necessary actions of a reasonable being. But the violation of marriage, or any other unchastity, was never heard of; and the married pair pass their lives with the same friendship and mutual benevolence that they bear to all others of the same species who come in their way, without jealousy, fondness, quarrelling, or discontent.

In educating the youth of both sexes their method is admirable, and highly deserves our imitation. These are not suffered to taste a grain of oats, except upon certain days, till eighteen years old; nor milk but very rarely; and in summer they graze two hours in the morning, and as many in the evening, which their parents likewise observe; but the servants are not allowed above half that time, and a great part of their grass is brought home, which they eat at the most convenient hours, when they can be best spared from work.

Temperance, industry, exercise, and cleanliness are the lessons equally enjoined to the young ones of both sexes; and my master thought it monstrous in us to give the females a different kind of education from the

---

[1]   *natural philosophy*   Science.

[2]   *sentiments of … them*   Socrates believed that only ethics, or human nature, was worth studying, because in studying the physical world we cannot know anything for certain, but can only form opinions and conjectures.

[3]   *accompany with*   Have sexual intercourse with.

[4]   *jointures*   Portions of estates reserved for the wife's sole ownership after her husband's death. A husband could not legally spend his wife's jointure without first obtaining her permission.

males, except in some articles of domestic management; whereby, as he truly observed, one half of our natives were good for nothing but bringing children into the world; and to trust the care of our children to such useless animals, he said was yet a greater instance of brutality.

But the Houyhnhnms train up their youth to strength, speed, and hardiness by exercising them in running races up and down steep hills and over hard stony grounds; and when they are all in a sweat, they are ordered to leap over head and ears into a pond or river. Four times a year the youth of a certain district meet to show their proficiency in running and leaping, and other feats of strength and agility; where the victor is rewarded with a song in his or her praise. On this festival, the servants drive a herd of Yahoos into the field, laden with hay, and oats, and milk, for a repast to the Houyhnhnms; after which these brutes are immediately driven back again, for fear of being noisome to the assembly.

Every fourth year, at the vernal equinox, there is a representative council of the whole nation, which meets in a plain about twenty miles from our house, and continues about five or six days. Here they inquire into the state and condition of the several districts; whether they abound or be deficient in hay, or oats, or cows, or Yahoos; and wherever there is any want (which is but seldom) it is immediately supplied by unanimous consent and contribution. Here likewise the regulation of children is settled: as, for instance, if a Houyhnhnm has two males, he changes one of them with another that has two females; and when a child has been lost by any casualty, where the mother is past breeding, it is determined what family in the district shall breed another to supply the loss.

CHAPTER 9

(A grand debate at the general assembly of the Houyhnhnms, and how it was determined. The learning of the Houyhnhnms. Their buildings. Their manner of burials. The defectiveness of their language.)

One of these grand assemblies was held in my time, about three months before my departure, whither my master went as the representative of our district. In this council was resumed their old debate, and indeed the only debate that ever happened in their country; whereof my master, after his return, gave me a very particular account.

The question to be debated was whether the Yahoos should be exterminated from the face of the earth. One of the members for the affirmative offered several arguments of great strength and weight, alleging that, as the Yahoos were the most filthy, noisome, and deformed animals which nature ever produced, so they were the most restive and indocible,[1] mischievous and malicious; they would privately suck the teats of the Houyhnhnms' cows, kill and devour their cats, trample down their oats and grass, if they were not continually watched, and commit a thousand other extravagancies. He took notice of a general tradition that Yahoos had not been always in their country, but that many ages ago two of these brutes appeared together upon a mountain; whether produced by the heat of the sun upon corrupted mud and slime, or from the ooze and froth of the sea, was never known; that these Yahoos engendered, and their brood in a short time grew so numerous as to overrun and infest the whole nation. That the Houyhnhnms, to get rid of this evil, made a general hunting, and at last enclosed the whole herd; and, destroying the older, every Houyhnhnm kept two young ones in a kennel, and brought them to such a degree of tameness as an animal so savage by nature can be capable of acquiring, using them for draught and carriage. That there seemed to be much truth in this tradition, and that those creatures could not be *yinhniamshy* (or aborigines of the land), because of the violent hatred the Houyhnhnms, as well as all other animals, bore them, which, although their evil disposition sufficiently deserved, could never have arrived at so high a degree if they had been aborigines, or else they would have long since been rooted out. That the inhabitants, taking a fancy to use the service of the Yahoos, had very imprudently neglected to cultivate the breed of asses, which are a comely animal, easily kept, more tame and orderly, without any offensive smell, strong enough for labour, although they yield to the other in agility of body; and, if their braying be no agreeable sound, it is far preferable to the horrible howlings of the Yahoos.

Several others declared their sentiments to the same

---

[1] *indocible* Incapable of being taught.

purpose, when my master proposed an expedient to the assembly, whereof he had indeed borrowed the hint from me. He approved of the tradition mentioned by the honourable member who spoke before, and affirmed that the two Yahoos said to be seen first among them had been driven thither over the sea; that, coming to land and being forsaken by their companions, they retired to the mountains and, degenerating by degrees, became in process of time much more savage than those of their own species in the country whence these two originals came. The reason of this assertion was that he had now in his possession a certain wonderful Yahoo (meaning myself) which most of them had heard of, and many of them had seen. He then related to them how he first found me; that my body was all covered with an artificial composure of the skins and hairs of other animals; that I spoke in a language of my own, and had thoroughly learned theirs; that I had related to him the accidents which brought me thither; that when he saw me without my covering, I was an exact Yahoo in every part, only of a whiter colour, less hairy, and with shorter claws. He added how I had endeavoured to persuade him that in my own and other countries the Yahoos acted as the governing, rational animal, and held the Houyhnhnms in servitude; that he observed in me all the qualities of a Yahoo, only a little more civilized by some tincture of reason, which, however, was in a degree as far inferior to the Houyhnhnm race as the Yahoos of their country were to me; that, among other things, I mentioned a custom we had of castrating Houyhnhnms when they were young, in order to render them tame; that the operation was easy and safe; that it was no shame to learn wisdom from brutes, as industry is taught by the ant, and building by the swallow (for so I translate the word *lyhannh*, although it be a much larger fowl). That this invention might be practised upon the younger Yahoos here, which, besides rendering them tractable and fitter for use, would in an age put an end to the whole species without destroying life. That in the mean time the Houyhnhnms should be exhorted to cultivate the breed of asses, which, as they are in all respects more valuable brutes, so they have this advantage, to be fit for service at five years old, which the others are not till twelve.

This was all my master thought fit to tell me at that time of what passed in the grand council. But he was pleased to conceal one particular, which related personally to myself, whereof I soon felt the unhappy effect, as the reader will know in its proper place, and whence I date all the succeeding misfortunes of my life.

The Houyhnhnms have no letters, and consequently their knowledge is all traditional. But there happening few events of any moment among a people so well united, naturally disposed to every virtue, wholly governed by reason, and cut off from all commerce with other nations, the historical part is easily preserved without burdening their memories. I have already observed that they are subject to no diseases, and therefore can have no need of physicians. However, they have excellent medicines, composed of herbs, to cure accidental bruises and cuts in the pastern or frog of the foot by sharp stones, as well as other maims and hurts in the several parts of the body.

They calculate the year by the revolution of the sun and moon, but use no subdivisions into weeks. They are well enough acquainted with the motions of those two luminaries, and understand the nature of eclipses; and this is the utmost progress of their astronomy.

In poetry they must be allowed to excel all other mortals; wherein the justness of their similes and the minuteness, as well as exactness, of their descriptions are indeed inimitable. Their verses abound very much in both of these, and usually contain either some exalted notions of friendship and benevolence or the praises of those who were victors in races and other bodily exercises. Their buildings, although very rude and simple, are not inconvenient, but well contrived to defend them from all injuries of cold and heat. They have a kind of tree which at forty years old loosens in the root and falls with the first storm; it grows very straight and, being pointed like stakes with a sharp stone (for the Houyhnhnms know not the use of iron), they stick them erect in the ground, about ten inches asunder, and then weave in oat straw, or sometimes wattles, betwixt them. The roof is made after the same manner, and so are the doors.

The Houyhnhnms use the hollow part between the pastern and the hoof of their forefeet as we do our hands, and this with greater dexterity than I could at first imagine. I have seen a white mare of our family thread a needle (which I lent her on purpose) with that joint. They milk their cows, reap their oats, and do all

the work which requires hands in the same manner. They have a kind of hard flints, which, by grinding against other stones, they form into instruments that serve instead of wedges, axes, and hammers. With tools made of these flints, they likewise cut their hay and reap their oats, which there grow naturally in several fields. The Yahoos draw home the sheaves in carriages, and the servants tread them in certain covered huts to get out the grain, which is kept in stores. They make a rude kind of earthen and wooden vessels, and bake the former in the sun.

If they can avoid casualties, they die only of old age, and are buried in the obscurest places that can be found, their friends and relations expressing neither joy nor grief at their departure; nor does the dying person discover the least regret that he is leaving the world, any more than if he were upon returning home from a visit to one of his neighbours. I remember my master having once made an appointment with a friend and his family to come to his house upon some affair of importance; on the day fixed, the mistress and her two children came very late; she made two excuses, first for her husband, who, as she said, happened that very morning to *lhnuwnh*. The word is strongly expressive in their language, but not easily rendered into English; it signifies, *to retire to his first Mother*. Her excuse for not coming sooner was that, her husband dying late in the morning, she was a good while consulting her servants about a convenient place where his body should be laid; and I observed she behaved herself at our house as cheerfully as the rest. She died about three months after.

They live generally to seventy or seventy-five years, very seldom to fourscore. Some weeks before their death they feel a gradual decay, but without pain. During this time they are much visited by their friends because they cannot go abroad with their usual ease and satisfaction. However, about ten days before their death, which they seldom fail in computing, they return the visits that have been made them by those who are nearest in the neighbourhood, being carried in a convenient sledge drawn by Yahoos; which vehicle they use, not only upon this occasion, but when they grow old, upon long journeys, or when they are lamed by any accident. And therefore, when the dying Houyhnhnms return those visits, they take a solemn leave of their friends, as if they were going to some remote part of the country where they designed to pass the rest of their lives.

I know not whether it may be worth observing that the Houyhnhnms have no word in their language to express any thing that is evil, except what they borrow from the deformities or ill qualities of the Yahoos. Thus they denote the folly of a servant, an omission of a child, a stone that cuts their feet, a continuance of foul or unseasonable weather, and the like, by adding to each the epithet of Yahoo. For instance, *hhnm Yahoo, whnaholm Yahoo, ynlhmndwihlma Yahoo,* and an ill-contrived house, *ynholmhnmrohlnw* Yahoo.

I could with great pleasure enlarge further upon the manners and virtues of this excellent people; but, intending in a short time to publish a volume by itself, expressly upon that subject, I refer the reader thither; and, in the meantime, proceed to relate my own sad catastrophe.

CHAPTER 10

(The author's economy[1] and happy life among the Houyhnhnms. His great improvement in virtue by conversing with them. Their conversations. The author has notice given him by his master that he must depart from the country. He falls into a swoon for grief, but submits. He contrives and finishes a canoe by the help of a fellow-servant, and puts to sea at a venture.)

I had settled my little economy to my own heart's content. My master had ordered a room to be made for me after their manner, about six yards from the house, the sides and floors of which I plastered with clay and covered with rush mats of my own contriving. I had beaten hemp, which there grows wild, and made of it a sort of ticking;[2] this I filled with the feathers of several birds I had taken with springes made of Yahoos' hairs, and were excellent food. I had worked two chairs with my knife, the sorrel nag helping me in the grosser[3] and more laborious part. When my clothes were worn to rags, I made myself others with the skins of rabbits, and of a certain beautiful animal about the same size, called *nnuhnoh*, the skin of which is covered with a fine down.

---

[1] *economy* Means of managing a household.

[2] *ticking* Strong material used to make mattress or pillow coverings.

[3] *grosser* Larger; heavier.

Of these I also made very tolerable stockings. I soled my shoes with wood, which I cut from a tree and fitted to the upper leather; and when this was worn out, I supplied it with the skins of Yahoos dried in the sun. I often got honey out of hollow trees, which I mingled with water, or ate with my bread. No man could more verify the truth of these two maxims, that *Nature is very easily satisfied*, and that *Necessity is the mother of invention*. I enjoyed perfect health of body and tranquillity of mind; I did not feel the treachery or inconstancy of a friend, nor the injuries of a secret or open enemy. I had no occasion of bribing, flattering, or pimping to procure the favour of any great man, or of his minion; I wanted no fence against fraud or oppression; here was neither physician to destroy my body, nor lawyer to ruin my fortune; no informer to watch my words and actions or forge accusations against me for hire; here were no gibers, censurers, backbiters, pickpockets, highwaymen, housebreakers, attorneys, bawds, buffoons, gamesters, politicians, wits, splenetics, tedious talkers, controvertists, ravishers, murderers, robbers, virtuosos;[1] no leaders or followers of party and faction; no encouragers to vice by seducement or examples; no dungeon, axes, gibbets, whipping-posts, or pillories; no cheating shopkeepers or mechanics; no pride, vanity, or affectation; no fops, bullies, drunkards, strolling whores, or poxes; no ranting, lewd, expensive wives; no stupid, proud pedants; no importunate, overbearing, quarrelsome, noisy, roaring, empty, conceited, swearing companions; no scoundrels raised from the dust upon the merit of their vices, or nobility thrown into it on account of their virtues; no lords, fiddlers, judges, or dancing masters.[2]

I had the favour of being admitted to several Houyhnhnms who came to visit or dine with my master; where his honour graciously suffered me to wait in the room and listen to their discourse. Both he and his company would often descend to ask me questions and receive my answers. I had also sometimes the honour of attending my master in his visits to others. I never presumed to speak, except in answer to a question; and then I did it with inward regret, because it was a loss of so much time for improving myself; but I was infi-

nitely delighted with the station of an humble auditor in such conversations, where nothing passed but what was useful, expressed in the fewest and most significant words; where, as I have already said, the greatest decency was observed, without the least degree of ceremony; where no person spoke without being pleased himself, and pleasing his companions; where there was no interruption, tediousness, heat, or difference of sentiments. They have a notion that when people are met together, a short silence does much improve conversation. This I found to be true; for during those little intermissions of talk, new ideas would arise in their minds, which very much enlivened the discourse. Their subjects are generally on friendship and benevolence; on order and economy; sometimes upon the visible operations of nature, or ancient traditions; upon the bounds and limits of virtue; upon the unerring rules of reason, or upon some determinations to be taken at the next great assembly; and often upon the various excellences of poetry. I may add, without vanity, that my presence often gave them sufficient matter for discourse because it afforded my master an occasion of letting his friends into the history of me and my country, upon which they were all pleased to descant in a manner not very advantageous to humankind; and for that reason I shall not repeat what they said; only I may be allowed to observe that his honour, to my great admiration, appeared to understand the nature of Yahoos much better than myself. He went through all our vices and follies, and discovered many which I had never mentioned to him, by only supposing what qualities a Yahoo of their country, with a small proportion of reason, might be capable of exerting; and concluded, with too much probability, how vile, as well as miserable, such a creature must be.

I freely confess that all the little knowledge I have of any value was acquired by the lectures I received from my master, and from hearing the discourses of him and his friends; to which I should be prouder to listen than to dictate to the greatest and wisest assembly in Europe. I admired the strength, comeliness, and speed of the inhabitants; and such a constellation of virtues in such amiable persons produced in me the highest veneration. At first, indeed, I did not feel that natural awe which the Yahoos and all other animals bear toward them; but it grew upon me by degrees, much sooner than I imag-

---

[1] *virtuosos* Those who have special interest in or knowledge of particular aspects of the arts or sciences.

[2] *dancing masters* Those who taught the art of dancing, a skill essential for social advancement.

ined, and was mingled with a respectful love and gratitude, that they would condescend to distinguish me from the rest of my species.

When I thought of my family, my friends, my countrymen, or the human race in general, I considered them as they really were, Yahoos in shape and disposition, perhaps a little more civilized, and qualified with the gift of speech; but making no other use of reason than to improve and multiply those vices whereof their brethren in this country had only the share that nature allotted them. When I happened to behold the reflection of my own form in a lake or fountain, I turned away my face in horror and detestation of myself, and could better endure the sight of a common Yahoo than of my own person. By conversing with the Houyhnhnms, and looking upon them with delight, I fell to imitate their gait and gesture, which is now grown into a habit; and my friends often tell me in a blunt way that I trot like a horse; which, however, I take for a great compliment. Neither shall I disown that in speaking I am apt to fall into the voice and manner of the Houyhnhnms, and hear myself ridiculed on that account without the least mortification.

In the midst of all this happiness, and when I looked upon myself to be fully settled for life, my master sent for me one morning a little earlier than his usual hour. I observed by his countenance that he was in some perplexity, and at a loss how to begin what he had to speak. After a short silence, he told me, he did not know how I would take what he was going to say; that, in the last general assembly, when the affair of the Yahoos was entered upon, the representatives had taken offence at his keeping a Yahoo (meaning myself) in his family, more like a Houyhnhnm than a brute animal. That he was known frequently to converse with me, as if he could receive some advantage or pleasure in my company; that such a practice was not agreeable to reason or nature, or a thing ever heard of before among them. The assembly did therefore exhort him either to employ me like the rest of my species, or command me to swim back to the place whence I came. That the first of these expedients was utterly rejected by all the Houyhnhnms who had ever seen me at his house or their own; for they alleged that because I had some rudiments of reason, added to the natural pravity[1] of those animals, it was to

be feared I might be able to seduce them into the woody and mountainous parts of the country, and bring them in troops by night to destroy the Houyhnhnms' cattle, as being naturally of the ravenous kind, and averse from labour.

My master added that he was daily pressed by the Houyhnhnms of the neighbourhood to have the assembly's exhortation executed, which he could not put off much longer. He doubted it would be impossible for me to swim to another country; and therefore wished I would contrive some sort of vehicle resembling those I had described to him, that might carry me on the sea; in which work I should have the assistance of his own servants, as well as those of his neighbours. He concluded that, for his own part, he could have been content to keep me in his service as long as I lived, because he found I had cured myself of some bad habits and dispositions by endeavouring, as far as my inferior nature was capable, to imitate the Houyhnhnms.

I should here observe to the reader that a decree of the general assembly in this country is expressed by the word *hnhloayn*, which signifies an exhortation, as near as I can render it; for they have no conception how a rational creature can be compelled, but only advised or exhorted, because no person can disobey reason without giving up his claim to be a rational creature.

I was struck with the utmost grief and despair at my master's discourse; and, being unable to support the agonies I was under, I fell into a swoon at his feet. When I came to myself, he told me that he concluded I had been dead (for these people are subject to no such imbecilities of nature). I answered in a faint voice that death would have been too great a happiness; that although I could not blame the assembly's exhortation or the urgency of his friends, yet, in my weak and corrupt judgment, I thought it might consist with reason to have been less rigorous. That I could not swim a league, and probably the nearest land to theirs might be distant above a hundred; that many materials, necessary for making a small vessel to carry me off, were wholly wanting in this country; which, however, I would attempt in obedience and gratitude to his honour, although I concluded the thing to be impossible, and therefore looked on myself as already devoted[2] to destruction. That the certain prospect of an unnatural

---

[1] *pravity* Depravity.

[2] *devoted* Doomed.

death was the least of my evils; for, supposing I should escape with life by some strange adventure, how could I think with temper[1] of passing my days among Yahoos, and relapsing into my old corruptions, for want of examples to lead and keep me within the paths of virtue. That I knew too well upon what solid reasons all the determinations of the wise Houyhnhnms were founded, not to be shaken by arguments of mine, a miserable Yahoo; and therefore, after presenting him with my humble thanks for the offer of his servants' assistance in making a vessel, and desiring a reasonable time for so difficult a work, I told him I would endeavour to preserve a wretched being; and, if ever I returned to England, was not without hopes of being useful to my own species by celebrating the praises of the renowned Houyhnhnms, and proposing their virtues to the imitation of mankind.

My master in a few words made me a very gracious reply, allowed me the space of two months to finish my boat, and ordered the sorrel nag, my fellow servant (for so at this distance I may presume to call him), to follow my instruction, because I told my master that his help would be sufficient, and I knew he had a tenderness for me.

In his company my first business was to go to that part of the coast where my rebellious crew had ordered me to be set on shore. I got upon a height, and, looking on every side into the sea, fancied I saw a small island toward the northeast. I took out my pocket glass, and could then clearly distinguish it above five leagues off, as I computed; but it appeared to the sorrel nag to be only a blue cloud; for, as he had no conception of any country beside his own, so he could not be as expert in distinguishing remote objects at sea, as we who so much converse in that element.

After I had discovered this island, I considered no further; but resolved it should, if possible, be the first place of my banishment, leaving the consequence to fortune.

I returned home and, consulting with the sorrel nag, we went into a copse at some distance, where I with my knife, and he with a sharp flint fastened very artificially, after their manner, to a wooden handle, cut down several oak wattles about the thickness of a walking staff, and some larger pieces. But I shall not trouble the reader with a particular description of my own mechanics; let it suffice to say that in six weeks time, with the help of the sorrel nag, who performed the parts that required most labour, I finished a sort of Indian canoe, but much larger, covering it with the skins of Yahoos, well stitched together with hempen threads of my own making. My sail was likewise composed of the skins of the same animal; but I made use of the youngest I could get, the older being too tough and thick; and I likewise provided myself with four paddles. I laid in a stock of boiled flesh of rabbits and fowls, and took with me two vessels, one filled with milk and the other with water.

I tried my canoe in a large pond near my master's house, and then corrected in it what was amiss, stopping all the chinks with Yahoos' tallow till I found it staunch[2] and able to bear me and my freight. And, when it was as complete as I could possibly make it, I had it drawn on a carriage very gently by Yahoos, to the seaside, under the conduct of the sorrel nag and another servant.

When all was ready, and the day came for my departure, I took leave of my master and lady, and the whole family, my eyes flowing with tears and my heart quite sunk with grief. But his honour, out of curiosity, and perhaps (if I may speak without vanity) partly out of kindness, was determined to see me in my canoe, and got several of his neighbouring friends to accompany him. I was forced to wait above an hour for the tide, and then, observing the wind very fortunately bearing toward the island to which I intended to steer my course, I took a second leave of my master; but as I was going to prostrate myself to kiss his hoof, he did me the honour to raise it gently to my mouth. I am not ignorant how much I have been censured for mentioning this last particular. Detractors are pleased to think it improbable that so illustrious a person should descend to give so great a mark of distinction to a creature so inferior as I. Neither have I forgotten how apt some travellers are to boast of extraordinary favours they have received. But, if these censurers were better acquainted with the noble and courteous disposition of the Houyhnhnms, they would soon change their opinion.

I paid my respects to the rest of the Houyhnhnms in his honour's company; then, getting into my canoe, I pushed off from shore.

---

[1] *temper* Composure.

[2] *staunch* Watertight.

CHAPTER II

(*The author's dangerous voyage. He arrives at New Holland, hoping to settle there. Is wounded with an arrow by one of the natives. Is seized and carried by force into a Portuguese ship. The great civilities of the Captain. The author arrives at England.*)

I began this desperate voyage on February 15, 1714–15,[1] at nine o'clock in the morning. The wind was very favourable; however, I made use at first only of my paddles; but considering I should soon be weary, and that the wind might chop about,[2] I ventured to set up my little sail; and thus, with the help of the tide, I went at the rate of a league and a half an hour, as near as I could guess. My master and his friends continued on the shore till I was almost out of sight; and I often heard the sorrel nag (who always loved me) crying out, *Hnuy illa nyha, majah Yahoo* ("Take care of thyself, gentle Yahoo").

My design was, if possible, to discover some small island uninhabited, yet sufficient by my labour to furnish me with the necessaries of life, which I would have thought a greater happiness than to be first minister in the politest court of Europe, so horrible was the idea I conceived of returning to live in the society and under the government of Yahoos. For in such a solitude as I desired, I could at least enjoy my own thoughts, and reflect with delight on the virtues of those inimitable Houyhnhnms, without any opportunity of degenerating into the vices and corruptions of my own species.

The reader may remember what I related when my crew conspired against me and confined me to my cabin: how I continued there several weeks without knowing what course we took; and when I was put ashore in the longboat, how the sailors told me with oaths, whether true or false, that they knew not in what part of the world we were. However, I did then believe us to be about 10 degrees southward of the Cape of Good Hope, or about 45 degrees southern latitude, as I gathered from some general words I overheard among them, being, I supposed, to the southeast in their intended voyage to Madagascar. And although this were little better than conjecture, yet I resolved to steer my course eastward, hoping to reach the southwest coast of New Holland,[3] and perhaps some such island as I desired lying westward of it. The wind was full west, and by six in the evening I computed I had gone eastward at least eighteen leagues when I spied a very small island about half a league off, which I soon reached. It was nothing but a rock with one creek, naturally arched by the force of tempests. Here I put in my canoe, and, climbing a part of the rock, I could plainly discover land to the east, extending from south to north. I lay all night in my canoe, and, repeating my voyage early in the morning, I arrived in seven hours to the southeast point of New Holland. This confirmed me in the opinion I have long entertained that the maps and charts place this country at least three degrees more to the east than it really is; which thought I communicated many years ago to my worthy friend, Mr. Herman Moll,[4] and gave him my reasons for it, although he has rather chosen to follow other authors.

I saw no inhabitants in the place where I landed, and, being unarmed, I was afraid of venturing far into the country. I found some shellfish on the shore and ate them raw, not daring to kindle a fire for fear of being discovered by the natives. I continued three days feeding on oysters and limpets,[5] to save my own provisions; and I fortunately found a brook of excellent water, which gave me great relief.

On the fourth day, venturing out early a little too far, I saw twenty or thirty natives upon a height, not above five hundred yards from me. They were stark naked men, women, and children round a fire, as I could discover by the smoke. One of them spied me and gave notice to the rest; five of them advanced toward me, leaving the women and children at the fire. I made what haste I could to the shore, and, getting into my canoe, shoved off. The savages, observing me retreat, ran after me; and, before I could get far enough into the sea,

---

[1] *1714–15*   Before the Gregorian calendar was adopted in 1752, the new year officially began on March 25. However, since many people also considered the new year to begin on January 1, the dates between January 1 and March 24, inclusive, were written according to both systems. Thus Gulliver leaves on February 15, 1715, according to our calendar.

[2] *chop about*   Suddenly change direction.

[3] *New Holland*   Australia.

[4] *Mr. Herman Moll*   Dutch cartographer (1678–1732) who prepared the maps for the early editions of *Gulliver's Travels*.

[5] *limpets*   Mollusks.

discharged an arrow which wounded me deeply on the inside of my left knee. (I shall carry the mark to my grave.) I apprehended the arrow might be poisoned, and, paddling out of the reach of their darts (being a calm day), I made a shift to suck the wound and dress it as well as I could.

I was at a loss what to do, for I durst not return to the same landing place, but stood to[1] the north, and was forced to paddle; for the wind, though very gentle, was against me, blowing northwest. As I was looking about for a secure landing-place, I saw a sail to the north-northeast, which appearing every minute more visible, I was in some doubt whether I should wait for them or no; but at last my detestation of the Yahoo race prevailed; and, turning my canoe, I sailed and paddled together to the south, and got into the same creek whence I set out in the morning, choosing rather to trust myself among these barbarians than live with European Yahoos. I drew up my canoe as close as I could to the shore, and hid myself behind a stone by the little brook, which, as I have already said, was excellent water.

The ship came within half a league of this creek, and sent her longboat with vessels to take in fresh water (for the place, it seems, was very well known), but I did not observe it till the boat was almost on shore, and it was too late to seek another hiding-place. The seamen at their landing observed my canoe and, rummaging it all over, easily conjectured that the owner could not be far off. Four of them, well armed, searched every cranny and lurking-hole till at last they found me flat on my face behind the stone. They gazed awhile in admiration at my strange uncouth dress; my coat made of skins, my wooden-soled shoes, and my furred stockings; from whence, however, they concluded I was not a native of the place, who all go naked. One of the seamen in Portuguese bid me rise, and asked who I was. I understood that language very well and, getting upon my feet, said I was a poor Yahoo banished from the Houyhnhnms, and desired they would please to let me depart. They admired to hear me answer them in their own tongue, and saw by my complexion I must be a European; but were at a loss to know what I meant by Yahoos and Houyhnhnms, and at the same time fell a laughing at my strange tone in speaking, which resem-

bled the neighing of a horse. I trembled all the while betwixt fear and hatred. I again desired leave to depart, and was gently moving to my canoe; but they laid hold of me, desiring to know, what country I was of? whence I came? with many other questions. I told them I was born in England, from whence I came about five years ago, and then their country and ours were at peace. I therefore hoped they would not treat me as an enemy, since I meant them no harm, but was a poor Yahoo seeking some desolate place where to pass the remainder of his unfortunate life.

When they began to talk, I thought I never heard or saw any thing more unnatural; for it appeared to me as monstrous as if a dog or a cow should speak in England, or a Yahoo in Houyhnhnmland. The honest Portuguese were equally amazed at my strange dress and the odd manner of delivering my words, which, however, they understood very well. They spoke to me with great humanity, and said they were sure the Captain would carry me *gratis*[2] to Lisbon, from whence I might return to my own country; that two of the seamen would go back to the ship to inform the Captain of what they had seen, and receive his orders; in the meantime, unless I would give my solemn oath not to fly, they would secure me by force. I thought it best to comply with their proposal. They were very curious to know my story, but I gave them very little satisfaction, and they all conjectured that my misfortunes had impaired my reason. In two hours the boat, which went laden with vessels of water, returned with the Captain's command to fetch me on board. I fell on my knees to preserve my liberty; but all was in vain, and the men, having tied me with cords, heaved me into the boat, from whence I was taken into the ship, and from thence into the Captain's cabin.

His name was Pedro de Mendez; he was a very courteous and generous person. He entreated me to give some account of myself, and desired to know what I would eat or drink; said I should be used as well as himself, and spoke so many obliging things that I wondered to find such civilities from a Yahoo. However, I remained silent and sullen; I was ready to faint at the very smell of him and his men. At last I desired something to eat out of my own canoe; but he ordered me a chicken and some excellent wine, and then directed that

---

[1] *stood to* Steered towards.

[2] *gratis* Latin: free of charge.

I should be put to bed in a very clean cabin. I would not undress myself, but lay on the bedclothes, and in half an hour stole out, when I thought the crew was at dinner; and, getting to the side of the ship, was going to leap into the sea and swim for my life, rather than continue among Yahoos. But one of the seamen prevented me, and, having informed the Captain, I was chained to my cabin.

After dinner Don Pedro came to me and desired to know my reason for so desperate an attempt; assured me he only meant to do me all the service he was able; and spoke so very movingly that at last I descended to treat him like an animal which had some little portion of reason. I gave him a very short relation of my voyage, of the conspiracy against me by my own men, of the country where they set me on shore, and of my five years residence there. All which he looked upon as if it were a dream or a vision; whereat I took great offence; for I had quite forgot the faculty of lying, so peculiar to Yahoos in all countries where they preside, and consequently their disposition of suspecting truth in others of their own species. I asked him whether it were the custom in his country to *say the thing that was not*? I assured him I had almost forgot what he meant by falsehood, and if I had lived a thousand years in Houyhnhnmland, I should never have heard a lie from the meanest servant. That I was altogether indifferent whether he believed me or not; but, however, in return for his favours, I would give so much allowance to the corruption of his nature as to answer any objection he would please to make, and then he might easily discover the truth.

The Captain, a wise man, after many endeavours to catch me tripping in some part of my story, at last began to have a better opinion of my veracity. But he added that since I professed so inviolable an attachment to truth, I must give him my word and honour to bear him company in this voyage without attempting anything against my life; or else he would continue me a prisoner till we arrived at Lisbon. I gave him the promise he required; but at the same time protested that I would suffer the greatest hardships rather than return to live among Yahoos.

Our voyage passed without any considerable accident. In gratitude to the Captain, I sometimes sat with him at his earnest request, and strove to conceal my antipathy against humankind, although it often broke out; which he suffered to pass without observation. But the greatest part of the day I confined myself to my cabin, to avoid seeing any of the crew. The Captain had often entreated me to strip myself of my savage dress, and offered to lend me the best suit of clothes he had. This I would not be prevailed on to accept, abhorring to cover myself with anything that had been on the back of a Yahoo. I only desired he would lend me two clean shirts, which, having been washed since he wore them, I believed would not so much defile me. These I changed every second day, and washed them myself.

We arrived at Lisbon, Nov. 5, 1715. At our landing, the Captain forced me to cover myself with his cloak to prevent the rabble from crowding about me. I was conveyed to his own house; and at my earnest request he led me up to the highest room backwards.[1] I conjured[2] him to conceal from all persons what I had told him of the Houyhnhnms, because the least hint of such a story would not only draw numbers of people to see me, but probably put me in danger of being imprisoned, or burnt by the Inquisition. The Captain persuaded me to accept a suit of clothes newly made; but I would not suffer the tailor to take my measure; however, Don Pedro being almost of my size, they fitted me well enough. He accoutred me with other necessaries, all new, which I aired for twenty-four hours before I would use them.

The Captain had no wife, nor above three servants, none of which were suffered to attend at meals; and his whole deportment was so obliging, added to very good human understanding, that I really began to tolerate his company. He gained so far upon me that I ventured to look out of the back window. By degrees I was brought into another room, from whence I peeped into the street, but drew my head back in a fright. In a week's time he seduced me down to the door. I found my terror gradually lessened, but my hatred and contempt seemed to increase. I was at last bold enough to walk the street in his company, but kept my nose well stopped with rue,[3] or sometimes with tobacco.

In ten days, Don Pedro, to whom I had given some account of my domestic affairs, put it upon me as a matter of honour and conscience that I ought to return

---

[1]   *backwards*   At the rear of the house.

[2]   *conjured*   Entreated.

[3]   *rue*   Strong-smelling leaves of the rue, a shrub.

to my native country, and live at home with my wife and children. He told me there was an English ship in the port just ready to sail, and he would furnish me with all things necessary. It would be tedious to repeat his arguments and my contradictions. He said it was altogether impossible to find such a solitary island as I desired to live in; but I might command in my own house, and pass my time in a manner as recluse as I pleased.

I complied at last, finding I could not do better. I left Lisbon the 24th day of November, in an English merchantman, but who was the master I never inquired. Don Pedro accompanied me to the ship and lent me twenty pounds. He took kind leave of me, and embraced me at parting, which I bore as well as I could. During this last voyage I had no commerce with the master or any of his men; but, pretending I was sick, kept close in my cabin. On the fifth of December, 1715, we cast anchor in the Downs, about nine in the morning, and at three in the afternoon I got safe to my house at Redriff.

My wife and family received me with great surprise and joy, because they concluded me certainly dead; but I must freely confess the sight of them filled me only with hatred, disgust, and contempt, and the more by reflecting on the near alliance I had to them. For although, since my unfortunate exile from the Houyhnhnm country, I had compelled myself to tolerate the sight of Yahoos, and to converse with Don Pedro de Mendez, yet my memory and imagination were perpetually filled with the virtues and ideas of those exalted Houyhnhnms. And when I began to consider that by copulating with one of the Yahoo species I had become a parent of more, it struck me with the utmost shame, confusion, and horror.

As soon as I entered the house, my wife took me in her arms and kissed me; at which, having not been used to the touch of that odious animal for so many years, I fell into a swoon for almost an hour. At the time I am writing, it is five years since my last return to England. During the first year, I could not endure my wife or children in my presence; the very smell of them was intolerable, much less could I suffer them to eat in the same room. To this hour they dare not presume to touch my bread or drink out of the same cup, neither was I ever able to let one of them take me by the hand. The first money I laid out was to buy two young stone-horses,[1] which I keep in a good stable; and next to them, the groom is my greatest favourite, for I feel my spirits revived by the smell he contracts in the stable. My horses understand me tolerably well; I converse with them at least four hours every day. They are strangers to bridle or saddle; they live in great amity with me and friendship to each other.

CHAPTER 12

(*The author's veracity. His design in publishing this work. His censure of those travellers who swerve from the truth. The author clears himself from any sinister ends in writing. An objection answered. The method of planting colonies. His native country commended. The right of the Crown to those countries described by the author is justified. The difficulty of conquering them. The author takes his last leave of the reader; proposes his manner of living for the future; gives good advice, and concludes.*)

Thus, gentle reader, I have given thee a faithful history of my travels for sixteen years and above seven months; wherein I have not been so studious of ornament as of truth. I could perhaps, like others, have astonished thee with strange improbable tales; but I rather chose to relate plain matter of fact, in the simplest manner and style, because my principal design was to inform, and not to amuse thee.

It is easy for us who travel into remote countries, which are seldom visited by Englishmen or other Europeans, to form descriptions of wonderful animals both at sea and land. Whereas a traveller's chief aim should be to make men wiser and better, and to improve their minds by the bad, as well as good, example of what they deliver concerning foreign places.

I could heartily wish a law was enacted that every traveller, before he were permitted to publish his voyages, should be obliged to make oath before the Lord High Chancellor that all he intended to print was absolutely true to the best of his knowledge; for then the world would no longer be deceived, as it usually is, while some writers, to make their works pass the better upon the public, impose the grossest falsities on the unwary reader. I have perused several books of travels

---

[1] *stone-horses* Stallions.

with great delight in my younger days; but having since gone over most parts of the globe, and been able to contradict many fabulous accounts from my own observation, it has given me a great disgust against this part of reading, and some indignation to see the credulity of mankind so impudently abused. Therefore, since my acquaintance were pleased to think my poor endeavours might not be unacceptable to my country, I imposed on myself, as a maxim never to be swerved from, that I would strictly adhere to truth; neither indeed can I be ever under the least temptation to vary from it while I retain in my mind the lectures and example of my noble master and the other illustrious Houyhnhnms of whom I had so long the honour to be an humble hearer.

—*Nec si miserum Fortuna Sinonem*
Finxit, vanum etiam, mendacemque improba finget.[1]

I know very well how little reputation is to be got by writings which require neither genius nor learning, nor indeed any other talent except a good memory or an exact journal. I know likewise that writers of travels, like dictionary-makers, are sunk into oblivion by the weight and bulk of those who come last, and therefore lie uppermost. And it is highly probable that such travellers who shall hereafter visit the countries described in this work of mine, may, by detecting my errors (if there be any) and adding many new discoveries of their own, jostle me out of vogue and stand in my place, making the world forget that ever I was an author. This indeed would be too great a mortification if I wrote for fame; but, as my sole intention was the public good, I cannot be altogether disappointed. For who can read of the virtues I have mentioned in the glorious Houyhnhnms without being ashamed of his own vices, when he considers himself as the reasoning, governing animal of his country? I shall say nothing of those remote nations where Yahoos preside; among which the least corrupted are the Brobdingnagians, whose wise maxims in morality and government it would be our happiness to observe. But I forbear descanting further, and rather leave the judicious reader to his own remarks and application.

I am not a little pleased that this work of mine can possibly meet with no censurers; for what objections can be made against a writer who relates only plain facts that happened in such distant countries where we have not the least interest with respect either to trade or negotiations? I have carefully avoided every fault with which common writers of travels are often too justly charged. Besides, I meddle not the least with any party, but write without passion, prejudice, or ill-will against any man, or number of men, whatsoever. I write for the noblest end, to inform and instruct mankind, over whom I may, without breach of modesty, pretend to some superiority, from the advantages I received by conversing so long among the most accomplished Houyhnhnms. I write without any view to profit or praise. I never suffer a word to pass that may look like reflection,[2] or possibly give the least offence, even to those who are most ready to take it. So that I hope I may with justice pronounce myself an author perfectly blameless; against whom the tribes of answerers, considerers, observers, reflectors, detectors, remarkers will never be able to find matter for exercising their talents.

I confess it was whispered to me that I was bound in duty, as a subject of England, to have given in a memorial[3] to a secretary of state at my first coming over, because whatever lands are discovered by a subject belong to the Crown. But I doubt whether our conquests in the countries I treat of would be as easy as those of Ferdinando Cortez over the naked Americans. The Lilliputians, I think, are hardly worth the charge of a fleet and army to reduce them; and I question whether it might be prudent or safe to attempt the Brobdingnagians; or whether an English army would be much at their ease with the Flying Island[4] over their heads. The Houyhnhnms indeed appear not to be so well prepared for war, a science to which they are perfect strangers, and especially against missive weapons. However, supposing myself to be a minister of state, I could never give my advice for invading them. Their prudence, unanimity, unacquaintedness with fear, and their love of their country would amply supply all defects in the

---

[1] *Nec ... finget* Latin: Nor, if cruel Fortune has made Sinon miserable, will she also make him false and a liar. See Virgil's *Aeneid*, 2.79–80. Sinon spoke these words to the Trojans when convincing them to accept the Greeks' gift of a wooden horse.

[2] *reflection* Imputation, accusation.

[3] *memorial* Record of events that is submitted to the government.

[4] *Flying Island* Reference to Part 3 of Gulliver's Travels, "A Voyage to Laputa," which is included on the website component of the anthology.

military art. Imagine twenty thousand of them breaking into the midst of an European army, confounding the ranks, overturning the carriages, battering the warriors' faces into mummy[1] by terrible yerks[2] from their hinder hoofs; for they would well deserve the character given to Augustus, *Recalcitrat undique tutus.*[3] But, instead of proposals for conquering that magnanimous nation, I rather wish they were in a capacity or disposition to send a sufficient number of their inhabitants for civilizing Europe, by teaching us the first principles of honour, justice, truth, temperance, public spirit, fortitude, chastity, friendship, benevolence, and fidelity. The names of all which virtues are still retained among us in most languages, and are to be met with in modern, as well as ancient authors; which I am able to assert from my own small reading.

But I had another reason which made me less forward[4] to enlarge His Majesty's dominions by my discoveries. To say the truth, I had conceived a few scruples with relation to the distributive justice of princes upon those occasions. For instance, a crew of pirates are driven by a storm they know not whither; at length a boy discovers land from the topmast; they go on shore to rob and plunder; they see a harmless people, are entertained with kindness; they give the country a new name; they take formal possession of it for their king; they set up a rotten plank or a stone for a memorial; they murder two or three dozen of the natives, bring away a couple more by force for a sample; return home, and get their pardon. Here commences a new dominion acquired with a title by divine right. Ships are sent with the first opportunity; the natives driven out or destroyed; their princes tortured to discover their gold; a free license given to all acts of inhumanity and lust, the earth reeking with the blood of its inhabitants. And this execrable crew of butchers, employed in so pious an expedition, is a modern colony, sent to convert and civilize an idolatrous and barbarous people!

But this description, I confess, does by no means affect the British nation, who may be an example to the whole world for their wisdom, care, and justice in planting colonies; their liberal endowments for the advancement of religion and learning; their choice of devout and able pastors to propagate Christianity; their caution in stocking their provinces with people of sober lives and conversations from this the mother kingdom; their strict regard to the distribution of justice, in supplying the civil administration through all their colonies with officers of the greatest abilities, utter strangers to corruption; and, to crown all, by sending the most vigilant and virtuous governors, who have no other views than the happiness of the people over whom they preside, and the honour of the king their master.

But, as those countries which I have described do not appear to have any desire of being conquered and enslaved, murdered or driven out by colonies, nor abound either in gold, silver, sugar, or tobacco, I did humbly conceive they were by no means proper objects of our zeal, our valour, or our interest. However, if those whom it more concerns think fit to be of another opinion, I am ready to depose, when I shall be lawfully called, that no European did ever visit those countries before me. I mean, if the inhabitants ought to be believed, unless a dispute may arise concerning the two Yahoos said to have been seen many years ago upon a mountain in Houyhnhnmland.

But, as to the formality of taking possession in my sovereign's name, it never came once into my thoughts; and if it had, yet, as my affairs then stood, I should perhaps in point of prudence and self-preservation have put it off to a better opportunity.

Having thus answered the only objection that can ever be raised against me as a traveller, I here take a final leave of all my courteous readers, and return to enjoy my own speculations in my little garden at Redriff; to apply those excellent lessons of virtue which I learned among the Houyhnhnms; to instruct the Yahoos of my own family as far as I shall find them docible animals; to behold my figure often in a glass, and thus, if possible, habituate myself by time to tolerate the sight of a human creature; to lament the brutality to Houyhnhnms in my own country, but always treat their persons with respect, for the sake of my noble master, his family, his friends, and the whole Houyhnhnm race, whom these of ours have the honour to resemble in all their lineaments, however their intellectuals[5] came to degenerate.

---

[1] *mummy* Pulp.

[2] *yerks* Blows.

[3] *Recalcitrat undique tutus* Latin: He kicks backwards, protected on all sides.

[4] *forward* Eager.

[5] *intellectuals* Intellects.

I began last week to permit my wife to sit at dinner with me, at the farthest end of a long table, and to answer (but with the utmost brevity) the few questions I asked her. Yet, the smell of a Yahoo continuing very offensive, I always keep my nose well stopped with rue, lavender, or tobacco leaves. And, although it be hard for a man late in life to remove old habits, I am not altogether out of hopes in some time to suffer a neighbour Yahoo in my company without the apprehensions I am yet under of his teeth or his claws.

My reconcilement to the Yahoo kind in general might not be so difficult if they would be content with those vices and follies only which nature has entitled them to. I am not in the least provoked at the sight of a lawyer, a pickpocket, a colonel, a fool, a lord, a gamester, a politician, a whoremonger, a physician, an evidence,[1] a suborner, an attorney, a traitor, or the like; this is all according to the due course of things. But when I behold a lump of deformity and diseases, both in body and mind, smitten with pride, it immediately breaks all the measures of my patience; neither shall I be ever able to comprehend how such an animal, and such a vice, could tally together. The wise and virtuous Houyhnhnms, who abound in all excellences that can adorn a rational creature, have no name for this vice in their language, which has no terms to express anything that is evil, except those whereby they describe the detestable qualities of their Yahoos, among which they were not able to distinguish this of pride, for want of thoroughly understanding human nature as it shows itself in other countries where that animal presides. But I, who had more experience, could plainly observe some rudiments of it among the wild Yahoos.

But the Houyhnhnms, who live under the government of reason, are no more proud of the good qualities they possess than I should be for not wanting a leg or an arm; which no man in his wits would boast of, although he must be miserable without them. I dwell the longer upon this subject from the desire I have to make the society of an English Yahoo by any means not insupportable; and therefore I here entreat those who have any tincture of this absurd vice, that they will not presume to come in my sight.

—1726

A Modest Proposal

For Preventing the Children of Poor People in Ireland from Being a Burden to Their Parents or the Country, and for Making Them Beneficial to the Public

It is a melancholy object to those who walk through this great town,[2] or travel in the country, when they see the streets, the roads, and cabin doors crowded with beggars of the female sex, followed by three, four, or six children, all in rags and importuning every passenger[3] for an alms. These mothers, instead of being able to work for their honest livelihood, are forced to employ all their time in strolling[4] to beg sustenance for their helpless infants, who, as they grow up, either turn thieves for want of work, or leave their dear native country to fight for the Pretender in Spain, or sell themselves to the Barbados.[5]

I think it is agreed by all parties that this prodigious number of children in the arms, or on the backs, or at the heels of their mothers, and frequently of their fathers, is, in the present deplorable state of the kingdom, a very great additional grievance; and therefore, whoever could find out a fair, cheap, and easy method of making these children sound and useful members of the commonwealth would deserve so well of the public as to have his statue set up for a preserver of the nation.

But my intention is very far from being confined to provide only for the children of professed beggars; it is of a much greater extent, and shall take in the whole number of infants at a certain age who are born of parents in effect as little able to support them as those who demand our charity in the streets.

As to my own part, having turned my thoughts for many years upon this important subject and maturely

---

[1] *evidence*   Witness.

[2] *this great town*   I.e., Dublin.

[3] *passenger*   Passerby.

[4] *strolling*   Wandering, roving.

[5] *the Pretender*   James Francis Edward Stuart, son of James II who was deposed from the throne in the Glorious Revolution due to his overt Catholicism. Catholic Ireland was loyal to Stuart, and the Irish were often recruited by France and Spain to fight against England; *Barbados*   Because of the extreme poverty in Ireland, many Irish people emigrated to the West Indies, selling their labor to sugar plantations in advance to pay for the voyage.

weighed the several schemes of other projectors,[1] I have always found them grossly mistaken in their computation. 'Tis true, a child just dropped from its dam may be supported by her milk for a solar year with little other nourishment, at most not above the value of two shillings, which the mother may certainly get, or the value in scraps, by her lawful occupation of begging; and it is exactly at one year old that I propose to provide for them in such a manner as, instead of being a charge upon their parents or the parish, or wanting food and raiment for the rest of their lives, they shall on the contrary contribute to the feeding, and partly to the clothing, of many thousands.

There is likewise another great advantage in my scheme, that it will prevent those abortions, and that horrid practice of women murdering their bastard children, alas, too frequent among us, sacrificing the poor innocent babes, I doubt,[2] more to avoid the expense than the shame, which would move tears and pity in the most savage and inhuman breast.

The number of souls in this kingdom being usually reckoned one million and a half, of these I calculate there may be about two hundred thousand couple whose wives are breeders, from which number I subtract thirty thousand couples who are able to maintain children, although I apprehend there cannot be as many under the present distresses of the kingdom; but this being granted, there will remain one hundred and seventy thousand breeders.

I again subtract fifty thousand for those women who miscarry, or whose children die by accident or disease within the year. There only remain one hundred and twenty thousand children of poor parents annually born. The question therefore is how this number shall be reared and provided for, which, as I have already said, under the present situation of affairs is utterly impossible by all the methods hitherto proposed. For we can neither employ them in handicraft or agriculture; we neither build houses (I mean in the country) nor cultivate land.[3] They can very seldom pick up a liveli-

hood by stealing till they arrive at six years old, except where they are of towardly parts,[4] although I confess they learn the rudiments much earlier, during which time they can however be properly looked upon only as probationers, as I have been informed by a principal gentleman in the county of Cavan, who protested to me that he never knew above one or two instances under the age of six, even in a part of the kingdom so renowned for the quickest proficiency in that art.

I am assured by our merchants that a boy or a girl before twelve years old is no saleable commodity; and even when they come to this age, they will not yield above three pounds, or three pounds and half a crown at most, on the Exchange,[5] which cannot turn to account[6] either to the parents or the kingdom, the charge of nutriment and rags having been at least four times that value.

I shall now therefore humbly propose my own thoughts, which I hope will not be liable to the least objection.

I have been assured by a very knowing American[7] of my acquaintance in London that a young healthy child well nursed is at a year old a most delicious, nourishing, and wholesome food, whether stewed, roasted, baked, or boiled; and I make no doubt that it will equally serve in a fricassee or a ragout.[8]

I do therefore humbly offer it to public consideration that of the hundred and twenty thousand children already computed, twenty thousand may be reserved for breed, whereof only one fourth part to be males, which is more than we allow to sheep, black cattle, or swine, and my reason is that these children are seldom the fruits of marriage, a circumstance not much regarded by our savages; therefore, one male will be sufficient to serve four females. That the remaining hundred thousand may at a year old be offered in sale to the persons of quality and fortune through the kingdom, always advising the mother to let them suck plentifully of the last month, so as to render them plump and fat for a good table. A child will make two dishes at an entertain-

---

[1] *projectors*   Those who design or propose experiments or projects.

[2] *doubt*   Think.

[3] *neither build ... land*   The British placed numerous restrictions on the Irish agricultural industry, retaining the majority of land for the grazing of sheep. The vast estates of British absentee landlords further contributed to Ireland's poverty.

[4] *towardly parts*   Promising; exceptionally able.

[5] *on the Exchange*   At the market.

[6] *turn to account*   Result in profit.

[7] *American*   I.e., Native American.

[8] *fricassee or a ragout*   Stews.

ment for friends, and when the family dines alone, the fore or hind quarter will make a reasonable dish, and seasoned with a little pepper or salt will be very good boiled on the fourth day, especially in winter.

I have reckoned upon a medium that a child just born will weigh twelve pounds, and in a solar year if tolerably nursed increase to twenty-eight pounds.

I grant this food will be somewhat dear,[1] and therefore very proper for landlords, who, as they have already devoured most of the parents, seem to have the best title to the children.

Infants' flesh will be in season throughout the year, but more plentiful in March, and a little before and after. For we are told by a grave author,[2] an eminent French physician, that, fish being a prolific diet,[3] there are more children born in Roman Catholic countries about nine months after Lent than at any other season; therefore, reckoning a year after Lent, the markets will be more glutted than usual because the number of popish infants is at least three to one in this kingdom, and therefore it will have one other collateral advantage by lessening the number of papists among us.

I have already computed the charge of nursing a beggar's child (in which list I reckon all cottagers,[4] labourers, and four fifths of the farmers) to be about two shillings per annum, rags included, and I believe no gentleman would repine to give ten shillings for the carcass of a good fat child, which, as I have said, will make four dishes of excellent nutritive meat when he hath only some particular friend or his own family to dine with him. Thus the Esquire[5] will learn to be a good landlord and grow popular among his tenants; the mother will have eight shillings net profit and be fit for work till she produces another child.

Those who are more thrifty (as I must confess the times require) may flay the carcass, the skin of which, artificially[6] dressed, will make admirable gloves for ladies and summer boots for fine gentlemen.

As to our city of Dublin, shambles[7] may be appointed for this purpose in the most convenient parts of it, and butchers we may be assured will not be wanting, although I rather recommend buying the children alive and dressing them hot from the knife, as we do roasting pigs.

A very worthy person, a true lover of his country, and whose virtues I highly esteem, was lately pleased, in discoursing on this matter, to offer a refinement upon my scheme. He said that, many gentlemen of this kingdom having of late destroyed their deer, he conceived that the want of venison might be well supplied by the bodies of young lads and maidens, not exceeding fourteen years of age nor under twelve, so great a number of both sexes in every county being now ready to starve for want of work and service; and these to be disposed of by their parents if alive, or otherwise by their nearest relations. But with due deference to so excellent a friend and so deserving a patriot, I cannot be altogether in his sentiments; for as to the males, my American acquaintance assured me from frequent experience that their flesh was generally tough and lean, like that of our schoolboys, by continual exercise, and their taste disagreeable, and to fatten them would not answer the charge. Then as to the females, it would, I think with humble submission, be a loss to the public because they soon would become breeders themselves. And besides, it is not improbable that some scrupulous people might be apt to censure such a practice (although indeed very unjustly) as a little bordering upon cruelty, which, I confess, hath always been with me the strongest objection against any project, however well intended.

But in order to justify my friend, he confessed that this expedient was put into his head by the famous Psalmanazar,[8] a native of the island of Formosa, who came from thence to London above twenty years ago, and in conversation told my friend that in his country, when any young person happened to be put to death the executioner sold the carcass to persons of quality as a

---

1 *dear* Expensive.

2 *grave author* Sixteenth-century satirist François Rabelais. See his *Gargantua and Pantagruel.*

3 *prolific diet* Causing increased fertility.

4 *cottagers* Country dwellers.

5 *Esquire* Knight's assistant.

6 *artificially* Artfully, skillfully.

7 *shambles* Slaughterhouses.

8 *Psalmanazar* George Psalmanazar (1679?–1763), a French adventurer who pretended to be a Formosan and published an account of Formosan customs, *Historical and Geographical Description of Formosa* (1704), which was later exposed as fraudulent. The story Swift recounts here is found in the second edition of Psalmanazar's work.

prime dainty, and that in his time the body of a plump girl of fifteen, who was crucified for an attempt to poison the emperor, was sold to his Imperial Majesty's Prime Minister of State and other great Mandarins of the court, in joints from the gibbet,[1] at four hundred crowns. Neither indeed can I deny that if the same use were made of several plump young girls in this town who, without one single groat[2] to their fortunes, cannot stir abroad without a chair,[3] and appear at the playhouse and assemblies in foreign fineries which they never will pay for, the kingdom would not be the worse.

Some persons of a desponding spirit are in great concern about that vast number of poor people who are aged, diseased, or maimed, and I have been desired to employ my thoughts what course may be taken to ease the nation of so grievous an encumbrance. But I am not in the least pain upon that matter because it is very well known that they are every day dying and rotting by cold and famine, and filth and vermin, as fast as can be reasonably expected. And as to the younger labourers, they are now in almost as hopeful a condition. They cannot get work, and consequently pine away for want of nourishment to a degree that if at any time they are accidentally hired to common labour, they have not strength to perform it; and thus the country and themselves are happily delivered from the evils to come.

I have too long digressed, and therefore shall return to my subject. I think the advantages by the proposal which I have made are obvious and many, as well as of the highest importance.

For first, as I have already observed, it would greatly lessen the number of papists, with whom we are yearly overrun, being the principal breeders of the nation as well as our most dangerous enemies, and who stay at home on purpose with a design to deliver the kingdom to the Pretender, hoping to take their advantage by the absence of so many good Protestants, who have chosen rather to leave their country than stay at home and pay tithes against their conscience to an Episcopal curate.

Secondly, the poorer tenants will have something valuable of their own, which by law may be made liable to distress[4] and help to pay their landlord's rent, their corn and cattle being already seized, and money a thing unknown.

Thirdly, whereas the maintenance of an hundred thousand children from two years old and upwards cannot be computed at less than ten shillings apiece per annum, the nation's stock will be thereby increased fifty thousand pounds per annum, besides the profit of a new dish introduced to the tables of all gentlemen of fortune in the kingdom who have any refinement in taste, and the money will circulate among ourselves, the goods being entirely of our own growth and manufacture.

Fourthly, the constant breeders, besides the gain of eight shillings sterling per annum by the sale of their children, will be rid of the charge of maintaining them after the first year.

Fifthly, this food would likewise bring great customs to taverns, where the vintners will certainly be so prudent as to procure the best receipts[5] for dressing it to perfection, and consequently have their houses frequented by all the fine gentlemen who justly value themselves upon their knowledge in good eating. And a skilful cook who understands how to oblige his guests will contrive to make it as expensive as they please.

Sixthly, this would be a great inducement to marriage, which all wise nations have either encouraged by rewards or enforced by laws and penalties. It would increase the care and tenderness of mothers toward their children, when they were sure of a settlement for life to the poor babes, provided in some sort by the public, to their annual profit instead of expense. We should soon see an honest emulation[6] among the married women, which of them could bring the fattest child to market. Men would become as fond of their wives during the time of their pregnancy as they are now of their mares in foal, their cows in calf, or sows when they are ready to farrow, nor offer to beat or kick them (as it is too frequent a practice) for fear of a miscarriage.

Many other advantages might be enumerated: for instance, the addition of some thousand carcasses in our exportation of barreled beef; the propagation of swine's flesh and improvement in the art of making good

---

[1] *gibbet* Gallows.

[2] *groat* Silver coin equal in value to four pence. It was removed from circulation in 1662, and thereafter "a groat" was used metaphorically to signify any very small sum.

[3] *chair* Sedan chair, which seated one person and was carried on poles by two men.

[4] *distress* Seizure of property for the payment of debt.

[5] *receipts* Recipes.

[6] *emulation* Rivalry.

bacon, so much wanted among us by the great destruction of pigs, too frequent at our tables, which are no way comparable in taste or magnificence to a well-grown, fat yearling child, which, roasted whole, will make a considerable figure at a Lord Mayor's feast or any other public entertainment. But this and many others I omit, being studious of brevity.

Supposing that one thousand families in this city would be constant customers for infants' flesh, besides others who might have it at merry-meetings, particularly weddings and christenings, I compute that Dublin would take off annually about twenty thousand carcasses, and the rest of the kingdom (where probably they will be sold somewhat cheaper) the remaining eighty thousand.

I can think of no one objection that will possibly be raised against this proposal, unless it should be urged that the number of people will be thereby much lessened in the kingdom. This I freely own, and it was indeed one principal design in offering it to the world. I desire the reader will observe that I calculate my remedy for this one individual kingdom of Ireland, and for no other that ever was, is, or, I think, ever can be upon earth. Therefore let no man talk to me of other expedients:[1] of taxing our absentees at five shillings a pound; of using neither clothes nor household furniture, except what is of our own growth and manufacture; of utterly rejecting the materials and instruments that promote foreign luxury; of curing the expensiveness of pride, vanity, idleness, and gaming[2] in our women; of introducing a vein of parsimony, prudence, and temperance; of learning to love our country, wherein we differ even from Laplanders and the inhabitants of Topinamboo;[3] of quitting our animosities and factions, nor act any longer like the Jews, who were murdering one another at the very moment their city was taken;[4] of

being a little cautious not to sell our country and consciences for nothing; of teaching landlords to have at least one degree of mercy toward their tenants; lastly, of putting a spirit of honesty, industry, and skill into our shopkeepers, who, if a resolution could now be taken to buy only our native goods, would immediately unite to cheat and exact upon us in the price, the measure, and the goodness, nor could ever yet be brought to make one fair proposal of just dealing, though often in earnest invited to it.

Therefore I repeat, let no man talk to me of these and the like expedients till he hath at least some glimpse of hope that there will ever be some hearty and sincere attempt to put them in practice.

But as to myself, having been wearied out for many years with offering vain, idle, visionary thoughts, and at length utterly despairing of success, I fortunately fell upon this proposal, which, as it is wholly new, so it hath something solid and real, of no expense and little trouble, full in our own power, and whereby we can incur no danger in disobliging England. For this kind of commodity will not bear exportation, the flesh being of too tender a consistence to admit a long continuance in salt, although perhaps I could name a country[5] which would be glad to eat up our whole nation without it.

After all, I am not so violently bent upon my own opinion as to reject any offer, proposed by wise men, which shall be found equally innocent, cheap, easy, and effectual. But before something of that kind shall be advanced in contradiction to my scheme, and offering a better, I desire the author or authors will be pleased maturely to consider two points.

First, as things now stand, how they will be able to find food and raiment for one hundred thousand useless mouths and backs.

And secondly, there being a round million of creatures in human figure throughout this kingdom whose whole subsistence, put into a common stock, would leave them in debt two million of pounds sterling, adding those who are beggars by profession to the bulk of farmers, cottagers, and labourers with their wives and children, who are beggars in effect.

I desire those politicians who dislike my overture, and may perhaps be so bold to attempt an answer, that they will first ask the parents of these mortals whether

---

[1] *other expedients* All of which Swift had already proposed in earnest attempts to remedy Ireland's poverty. See, for example, his *Proposal for the Universal Use of Irish Manufactures*. In early editions the following proposals were italicized to show the suspension of Swift's ironic tone.

[2] *gaming* Gambling.

[3] *Topinamboo* District in Brazil.

[4] *Jews ... was taken* According to the history of Flavius Joseph, Roman Emperor Titus's invasion and capture of Jerusalem in 70 BCE was aided by the fact that factional fighting had divided the city.

[5] *a country* I.e., England.

they would not at this day think it a great happiness to have been sold for food at a year old in the manner I prescribe, and thereby have avoided such a perpetual scene of misfortunes as they have since gone through by the oppression of landlords, the impossibility of paying rent without money or trade, the want of common sustenance, with neither house nor clothes to cover them from the inclemencies of the weather, and the most inevitable prospect of entailing[1] the like or greater miseries upon their breed forever.

I profess in the sincerity of my heart that I have not the least personal interest in endeavoring to promote this necessary work, having no other motive than the public good of my country by advancing our trade, providing for infants, relieving the poor, and giving some pleasure to the rich. I have no children by which I can propose to get a single penny, the youngest being nine years old, and my wife past childbearing.
—1729

In Context

Sermons and Tracts: Backgrounds to *A Modest Proposal*

Before adopting a bitingly satirical approach toward the oppression of Ireland in "A Modest Proposal," Swift wrote several sermons and tracts on the subject; two of these are excerpted below.

from Jonathan Swift, "Causes of the Wretched Condition of Ireland" (1726)

It is a very melancholy reflection, that such a country as ours, which is capable of producing all things necessary, and most things convenient for life, sufficient for the support of four times the number of its inhabitants, should yet lie under the heaviest load of misery and want, our streets crowded with beggars, so many of our lower sort of tradesmen, labourers, and artificers, not able to find clothes and food for their families.

I think it may therefore be of some use to lay before you the chief causes of this wretched condition we are in, and then it will be easier to assign what remedies are in our power towards removing, at least, some part of these evils.

For it is ever to be lamented, that we lie under many disadvantages, not by our own faults, which are peculiar to ourselves, and which no other nation under heaven hath any reason to complain of.

I shall, therefore, first mention some causes of our miseries, which I doubt are not to be remedied, until God shall put it in the hearts of those who are the stronger, to allow us the common rights and privileges of brethren, fellow subjects, and even of mankind.

The first cause of our misery is the intolerable hardships we lie under in every branch of our trade, by which we are become as *hewers of wood, and drawers of water*[2] to our rigorous neighbours.

The second cause of our miserable state is the folly, the vanity, and ingratitude of those vast numbers, who think themselves too good to live in the country which gave them birth, and still gives them bread, and rather choose to pass their days, and consume their wealth, and draw out the very vitals of their mother kingdom, among those who heartily despise them.

---

[1] *entailing* Bestowing, conferring.

[2] *hewers ... water* Those who perform menial tasks (from Joshua 9.21).

These I have but lightly touched on, because I fear they are not to be redressed, and, besides, I am very sensible how ready some people are to take offence at the honest truth; and, for that reason, I shall omit several other grievances, under which we are long likely to groan.

I shall therefore go on to relate some other causes of this nation's poverty, by which, if they continue much longer, it must infallibly sink to utter ruin.

The first is that monstrous pride and vanity in both sexes, especially the weaker sex, who, in the midst of poverty, are suffered to run into all kind of expense and extravagance in dress, and particularly priding themselves to wear nothing but what cometh from abroad, disdaining the growth or manufacture of their own country, in those articles where they can be better served at home with half the expense; and this is grown to such a height, that they will carry the whole yearly rent of a good estate at once on their body. And, as there is in that sex a spirit of envy, by which they cannot endure to see others in a better habit than themselves, so those, whose fortunes can hardly support their families in the necessaries of life, will needs vie with the richest and greatest amongst us, to the ruin of themselves and their posterity.

Neither are the men less guilty of this pernicious folly, who, in imitation of a gaudiness and foppery of dress, introduced of late years into our neighbouring kingdom, (as fools are apt to imitate only the defects of their betters) cannot find materials in their own country worthy to adorn their bodies of clay, while their minds are naked of every valuable quality.

Thus our tradesmen and shopkeepers, who deal in home-goods, are left in a starving condition, and only those encouraged who ruin the kingdom by importing among us foreign vanities.

Another cause of our low condition is our great luxury, the chief support of which is the materials of it brought to the nation in exchange for the few valuable things left us, whereby so many thousand families want the very necessaries of life.

Thirdly, in most parts of this kingdom the natives are from their infancy so given up to idleness and sloth, that they often choose to beg or steal, rather than support themselves with their own labour; they marry without the least view or thought of being able to make any provision for their families; and whereas, in all industrious nations, children are looked on as a help to their parents, with us, for want of being early trained to work, they are an intolerable burthen at home, and a grievous charge upon the public, as appeareth from the vast number of ragged and naked children in town and country, led about by strolling women, trained up in ignorance and all manner of vice.

Lastly, a great cause of this nation's misery, is that Egyptian bondage of cruel, oppressing, covetous landlords, expecting that all who live under them should *make bricks without straw*,[1] who grieve and envy when they see a tenant of their own in a whole coat, or able to afford one comfortable meal in a month, by which the spirits of the people are broken, and made for slavery; the farmers and cottagers, almost through the whole kingdom, being to all intents and purposes as real beggars, as any of those to whom we give our charity in the streets. And these cruel landlords are every day unpeopling their kingdom, by forbidding their miserable tenants to till the earth, against common reason and justice, and contrary to the practice and prudence of all other nations, by which numberless families have been forced either to leave the kingdom, or stroll about, and increase the number of our thieves and beggars.

---

[1] *Egyptian bondage … bricks without straw*   From Exodus 5.5–7, recalling the burdens laid upon the Israelites by the Pharaoh of Egypt.

from Jonathan Swift, *A Short View of the State of Ireland* (1727)

I am assured that it hath, for some time, been practised as a method of making men's court, when they are asked about the rate of lands, the abilities of tenants, the state of trade and manufacture in this kingdom, and how their rents are paid, to answer that in their neighbourhood, all things are in a flourishing condition, the rent and purchase of land every day increasing. And if a gentleman happens to be a little more sincere in his representations, besides being looked on as not well affected, he is sure to have a dozen contradictors at his elbow. I think it is no manner of secret why these questions are so *cordially* asked, or so *obligingly* answered.

But since, with regard to the affairs of this kingdom, I have been using all endeavours to subdue my indignation, to which, indeed, I am not provoked by any personal interest, being not the owner of one spot of ground in the whole island; I shall only enumerate by rules generally known, and never contradicted, what are the true causes of any countries flourishing and growing rich, and then examine what effects arise from those causes in the kingdom of Ireland.

The first cause of a kingdom's thriving, is the fruitfulness of the soil, to produce the necessaries and conveniences of life, not only sufficient for the inhabitants, but for exportation into other countries.

The second, is the industry of the people, in working up all their native commodities, to the last degree of manufacture.

The third, is the conveniency of safe ports and havens, to carry out their own goods, as much manufactured, and bring in those of others, as little manufactured, as the nature of mutual commerce will allow.

The fourth is, that the natives should, as much as possible, export and import their goods in vessels of their own timber, made in their own country.

The fifth, is the privilege of a free trade in all foreign countries which will permit them, except to those who are in war with their own prince or state.

The sixth, is, by being governed only by laws made with their own consent, for otherwise they are not a free people. And therefore, all appeals for justice, or applications for favour or preferment, to another country, are so many grievous impoverishments.

The seventh is, by improvement of land, encouragement of agriculture, and thereby increasing the number of their people, without which, any country, however blessed by nature, must continue poor.

The eighth, is the residence of the prince, or chief administrator of the civil power.

The ninth, is the concourse of foreigners for education, curiosity, or pleasure, or as to a general mart of trade.

The tenth, is by disposing all offices of honour, profit, or trust, only to the natives, or at least with very few exceptions, where strangers have long inhabited the country, and are supposed to understand, and regard the interest of it as their own.

The eleventh, is when the rents of lands, and profits of employments, are spent in the country which produced them, and not in another, the former of which will certainly happen, where the love of our native country prevails.

The twelfth, is by the public revenues being all spent and employed at home, except on the occasions of a foreign war.

The thirteenth is, where the people are not obliged, unless they find it for their own interest or conveniency, to receive any monies, except of their own coinage by a public mint, after the manner of all civilized nations.

The fourteenth, is a disposition of the people of a country to wear their own manufactures, and import as few incitements to luxury, either in clothes, furniture, food, or drink, as they possibly can live conveniently without.

There are many other causes of a nation's thriving, which I cannot at present recollect, but without advantage from at least some of these, after turning my thoughts a long time, I am not able to discover from whence our wealth proceeds, and therefore would gladly be better informed. In the meantime, I will here examine what share falls to Ireland of these causes, or of the effects and consequences.

It is not my intention to complain, but barely to relate facts; and the matter is not of small importance. For it is allowed, that a man who lives in a solitary house, far from help, is not wise in endeavouring to acquire, in the neighbourhood, the reputation of being rich, because those who come for gold, will go off with pewter and brass, rather than return empty. And in the common practice of the world, those who possess most wealth, make the least parade, which they leave to others, who have nothing else to bear them out, in showing their faces on the exchange.

As to the first cause of a nation's riches, being the fertility of the soil, as well as temperature of climate, we have no reason to complain, for, although the quantity of unprofitable land in this kingdom, reckoning bog, and rock, and barren mountain, be double in proportion to what it is in England; yet the native productions which both kingdoms deal in, are very near on equality in point of goodness, and might, with same encouragement, be as well manufactured. I except mines and minerals, in some of which, however, we are only defective in point of skill and industry.

In the second, which is the industry of the people, our misfortune is not altogether owing to our own fault, but to a million of discouragements.

The conveniency of ports and havens, which nature hath bestowed so liberally on this kingdom, is of no more use to us, than a beautiful prospect to a man shut up in a dungeon.

As to shipping of its own, Ireland is so utterly unprovided, that of all the excellent timber cut down within these fifty or sixty years, it can hardly be said, that the nation hath received the benefit of one valuable house to dwell in, or one ship to trade with.

Ireland is the only kingdom I ever heard or read of, either in ancient or modern story, which was denied the liberty of exporting their native commodities and manufactures, wherever they pleased, except to countries at war with their own prince or state. Yet this privilege, by the superiority of mere power, is refused us, in the most momentous parts of commerce, besides an act of navigation, to which we never consented, pinned down upon us, and rigorously executed, and a thousand other unexampled circumstances, as grievous, as they are invidious to mention. To go on to the rest.

It is too well known, that we are forced to obey some laws we never consented to, which is a condition I must not call by its true uncontroverted name, for fear of Lord Chief Justice Whitshed's[1] ghost, with his *Libertas & natale Solum*,[2] written as a motto on his coach, as it stood at the door of the court, while he was perjuring himself to betray both. Thus, we are in the condition of patients, who have physic[3] sent them by doctors at a distance, strangers to their constitution and the nature of their disease. And thus, we are forced to pay five hundred percent, to decide our properties, in all which, we have likewise the honour to be distinguished from the whole race of mankind.

As to improvement of land, those few who attempt that, or planting, through covetousness, or want of skill, generally leave things worse than they were, neither succeeding in trees nor hedges, and by running into the fancy of grazing, after the manner of the Scythians,[4] are every day depopulating the country.

---

[1] *Lord Chief Justice Whitshed* William Whitshed (1671–1727), outspoken judge (who died the year this tract was written) at the trial of the printer of Swift's *Drapier's Letters*, a pamphlet urging the Irish to wear only clothing manufactured in Ireland. Whitshed urged the grand jury to indict the printer, but the members refused to do so.

[2] *Libertas & natale Solum* Latin: Liberty and my native country.

[3] *physic* Medicine.

[4] *Scythians* Ancient nomadic people of Eurasia whose principal trade was grain.

We are so far from having a king to reside among us, that even the viceroy[1] is generally absent four-fifths of his time in the government.

No strangers from other countries make this a part of their travels, where they can expect to see nothing but scenes of misery and desolation.

Those who have the misfortune to be born here, have the least title to any considerable employment, to which they are seldom preferred, but upon a political consideration.

One third part of the rents of Ireland is spent in England, which, with the profit of employments, pensions, appeals, journeys of pleasure or health, education at the Inns of Court,[2] and both universities, remittances at pleasure, the pay of all superior officers in the army, and other incidents, will amount to a full half of the income of the whole kingdom, all clear profit to England.

We are denied the liberty of coining gold, silver, or even copper. In the Isle of Man,[3] they coin their own silver; every petty prince, vassal to the emperor, can coin what money he pleaseth. And in this, as in most of the articles already mentioned, we are an exception to all other states or monarchies that were ever known in the world.

As to the last, or fourteenth article, we take special care to act diametrically contrary to it in the whole course of our lives. Both sexes, but especially the women, despise and abhor to wear any of their own manufactures, even those which are better made than in other countries, particularly a sort of silk plaid, through which the workmen are forced to run a sort of gold thread that it may pass for Indian. Even ale and potatoes are imported from England, as well as corn. And our foreign trade is little more than importation of French wine, for which I am told we pay ready money.

Now, if all this be true, upon which I could easily enlarge, I would be glad to know by what secret method it is, that we grow a rich and flourishing people, without *Liberty, Trade, Manufactures, Inhabitants, Money,* or the *Privilege of Coining,* without *Industry, Labour,* or *Improvement of Lands,* and with more than half the rent and profits of the whole kingdom annually exported, for which we receive not a single farthing.

---

[1] *viceroy* Governor.

[2] *Inns of Court* Buildings in London where people are educated in the law and admitted to the bar.

[3] *Isle of Man* Island off the shore of Great Britain in the Irish Sea.

ALEXANDER POPE
1688 – 1744

Alexander Pope may have been speaking generally when he wrote, "The life of a wit is a warfare upon earth," but the statement is particularly applicable to his own life. In the highly competitive literary society of the time, one's rivals were quick to exploit any perceived weaknesses —personal or literary—and Pope was an easy target in many respects. As a result of tuberculosis of the bone (Pott's disease) contracted in his youth, Pope's spine was severely curved, and he only grew to four foot six. He was a Catholic, and as such was denied most of the privileges of British citizenship, including the right to vote and the right to inherit land. Pope was also a Tory, which, in the politically charged climate of Robert Walpole's Whig government, resulted in further persecution. Pope's rivals interpreted his Catholicism as evidence of treasonous Jacobism, his Tory sympathies as proof of disloyalty to his King and Parliament, and his disabled body as a sign of a malignant and twisted soul. Given this hostile environment it is surprising that Pope did not abandon his literary ambitions altogether. Instead, using the worst qualities of his society to his advantage, Pope built a reputation for himself as a satirist of civil follies and a champion of truth and moral virtue. Declaring that

"the proper study of mankind is man," he based his enormously successful literary career on social commentary, and on the documentation of contemporary experience.

Pope was born in London in 1688, the same year that a new Act of Parliament prohibited Catholics from living within ten miles of that city. Pope was privately educated (his religion also prevented him from attending schools); he read widely in his father's library and designed for himself an apprenticeship of translation and imitation of classical poets.

From the start Pope aspired to poetic greatness. His first independent publication, *An Essay on Criticism* (1711), sought to compress and comment upon all previous critical work concerning poetry. It was an unusual kind of production—an essay, written in verse, on the criticism of verse—that took the essays of Horace as its model. This ambitious and densely woven poem brought him his first personal attack: poet and dramatist John Dennis, finding himself cited as an example of a bad critic, issued a reply calling Pope a "hunch-backed toad." But the poem also brought Pope to the attention of prominent literary figures, including Richard Steele and Joseph Addison, whose influential "little senate" of Whig writers held court at the coffee house Buttons.

Political differences soon severed this new connection, however, and Pope later discovered that Addison was behind a plot to discredit his scholarship. Luckily he had developed other, more lasting friendships. Several of these were with fellow Catholics, such as Henry St. John (Lord Bolingbroke), Francis Atterbury (Bishop of Rochester, later imprisoned by Walpole as a Jacobite leader), Martha Blount (to whom Pope addressed his *Epistle to a Lady*, 1735), and John Caryll. Caryll's cousin Lord Petre became the subject of one of the most famous courtship scandals of the century when he snipped a lock of hair from the head of Arabella Fermor. She and her family took offense, and the situation had escalated into a feud when Caryll asked Pope to intervene by "laughing them together again" with a poem. The result, *The Rape of the Lock*, uses the inversion of the mock-heroic form to do justice to both the weight and the triviality of the event. The first published version (1712) succeeded in its objective of restoring good humor to the families, and the later release of the extended, five-canto poem (1714) charmed wider audiences with its imaginative play.

Pope's more famous group of friends were his fellow members of the Scriblerus Club, formed in 1714 by Pope, Jonathan Swift, John Gay, Dr. John Arbuthnot, Robert Harley (Lord Oxford), Thomas Parnell, and Lord Bolingbroke. The members focused upon an invented learned fool, Martinus Scriblerus, to whose work they attributed all that was tedious, narrow-minded, and pedantic in contemporary scholarship. The origins of Swift's *Gulliver's Travels* (1726), Pope's *The Dunciad* (1728), Gay's *The Beggar's Opera* (1728)—generally seen as the greatest satires of their age—may all be traced to the Club.

In 1714 Pope began using his refined translation skills to produce a verse translation of Homer's *Iliad* (1715–20); paid for by subscription and released in volumes, the translation made him enough money to acquire an estate in Twickenham. This estate provided a lifelong haven from the turmoil of the London literary and political scenes, and a removed position from which to write. With both his reputation as a poet and his financial well-being secured, Pope turned to higher philosophical and political writing—he also now began his work as a damaging satirist.

The Dunciad (1728–43) was Pope's most biting and direct satiric attack on his enemies. Structured as an ironic epic of praise to hack writers, it presented the most ludicrous and low quality writing of his contemporaries and some of his own early work, as a praiseworthy example of ideal literature. The piece starred Lewis Theobald—the scholar who had argued that Pope's edition of Shakespeare was erratic and unreliable—as King of the Dunces (crowned by the Goddess Dullness). Pope expanded and altered *The Dunciad* over time, keeping pace with the changing literary scene he attacked. *The New Dunciad* saw a new poet laureate, Colley Cibber, replace Theobald as anti-hero.

Often, Pope's most brilliant and humorous satiric passages are those that take incontrovertible facts about his subjects and pervert them to form desperately damaging pictures—as he does in his portrayal of Lord Hervey in the "Epistle to Arbuthnot," for example. The ferocity of these attacks, however, leads many readers to question what could possibly have warranted such animosity—particularly considering that attacks on some, such as Lady Mary Wortley Montagu, were pursued through an entire sequence of his greatest satires, published over the span of several years. The majority of his satires, however, convey an impression of pettiness, mediocrity, and dullness as forces capable of destroying culture. To Pope, low, vulgar, sensational art was not merely bad in an aesthetic sense; it was also immoral and could corrupt society if allowed to spread unchecked.

In contrast to his satire, Pope intended his *Essay on Man* (1733–34), he told Swift, to be "a book to make mankind look upon his life with comfort and pleasure, and put morality into good humour." An ambitious essay in verse, the poem analyzes aspects of human nature, and discusses humanity's place in the universe. Its first three epistles (there were four in total) were published anonymously to avoid the censure of his enemies, whose numbers had substantially increased since *The Dunciad* first appeared.

The *Essay on Man* was followed by Pope's *Imitations of Horace* (1733–40) and his *Moral Essays, or Epistles to Several Persons* (1731–35), many of which are also written in the Horatian mode. Bolingbroke had pointed out how well the Roman poet's lightly satirical style suited Pope's own purposes, and the poems written in this manner have been generally regarded as among the most finely crafted and carefully controlled of Pope's career. The "Epistle to Dr. Arbuthnot" (1735), perhaps his most famous, replies to all those who had attacked his "Person, Morals, and Family," defends his use of satire, and gives a controlled, carefully shaped account of his literary development.

By the time of his death in 1744, Pope had proven himself a master of a wide range of modes—among them pastoral, lyric, and mock-heroic. The diversity of Pope's poetic success is particularly remarkable given that almost all his poetry was composed in heroic couplets. Within this regular form of rhyming pairs of iambic pentameter lines, Pope was able to vary the mood and tone of his work enormously, and to convey the richness of the society he saw around him. Pope died at his villa in Twickenham, surrounded by numerous friends.

⌘ ⌘ ⌘

from *An Essay on Criticism*

An Essay on Criticism established Pope as a leading poet of his day. Samuel Johnson, in his biography of Pope, declared that even if Pope "had written nothing else," *An Essay on Criticism* "would have placed him among the first critics and the first poets, as it exhibits every mode of excellence that can embellish or dignify didactic composition." The poem reflects the range of Pope's reading, including all the well-known English, French, and Latin poets, as well as many Greek poets in the original. Pope's discursive essay in verse is in the tradition of Horace's *Ars Poetica* (*The Art of Poetry*) and French poet Nicolas Boileau's *Art Poétique* (1674). Like these poems, the *Essay on Criticism* uses simple and conversational language. It draws together a range of historical and intellectual knowledge, but does not aim for novelty; instead, it attempts to express generally accepted doctrines in a pleasing style, setting out precepts in language that exemplifies the precepts themselves. Covering topics from divinity to freedom of the press to everyday follies, the poem is characterized by its lively style, by its wide range of comic expression, and by its use of maxim and epigram. Many phrases in the poem have become proverbial—notable among them, line 625, "For fools rush in where angels fear to tread," and line 525, "To err is human, to forgive, divine."

An Essay on Criticism consists of three parts. The first describes an Edenic, golden era of art and criticism exemplified by Homer and other classical writers, considered to be especially well placed to observe Nature directly and reflect it in their art. The subject of the poem's second part is the decay and disorder Pope observes in the criticism of his day, which he attributes very largely to the divisive, egotistic nature of critics. The third part sets out a means of reformation through virtue, and a restoration of the ideals set out in Part 1. Although Pope's goals are generally conciliatory, and he

attempts to accommodate seemingly conflicting artistic values and views, there were nonetheless several people who took offense to parts of the poem. Many of Pope's fellow Catholics objected to his critical representation of their Church, and Pope's mocking allusions to dramatist John Dennis (1658–1734) sparked a public feud between the two that would last through both of their careers—the first of many such literary feuds Pope's writing would instigate.

An Essay on Criticism

PART I

'Tis hard to say, if greater want of skill
   Appear in writing or in judging ill;
But of the two less dang'rous is th'offense
To tire our patience than mislead our sense.
Some few in that, but numbers err in this,   5
Ten censure wrong for one who writes amiss;
A fool might once himself alone expose,
Now one in verse makes many more in prose.
   'Tis with our judgments as our watches, none
Go just alike, yet each believes his own.   10
In poets as true genius is but rare,
True taste as seldom is the critic's share;
Both must alike from Heav'n derive their light,
These born to judge, as well as those to write.
Let such teach others who themselves excel,   15
And censure freely who have written well.
Authors are partial to their wit, 'tis true,
But are not critics to their judgment too?
   Yet if we look more closely, we shall find
Most have the seeds of judgment in their mind: 20
Nature affords at least a glimm'ring light;
The lines, though touched but faintly, are drawn right.
But as the slightest sketch, if justly traced,
Is by ill colouring but the more disgraced,

25 So by false learning is good sense defaced:
Some are bewildered in the maze of schools,
And some made coxcombs Nature meant but fools.
In search of wit these lose their common sense,
And then turn critics in their own defence:
30 Each burns alike, who can, or cannot write,
Or° with a rival's, or an eunuch's spite.   *Either*
All fools have still an itching to deride,
And fain would be upon the laughing side.
If Maevius¹ scribble in Apollo's² spite,
35 There are who judge still worse than he can write.

Some have at first for wits, then poets passed,
Turned critics next, and proved plain fools at last.
Some neither can for wits nor critics pass,
As heavy mules are neither horse nor ass.
40 Those half-learned witlings, num'rous in our isle,
As half-formed insects on the banks of Nile;
Unfinished things, one knows not what to call,
Their generation's so equivocal:
To tell° 'em would a hundred tongues require,   *count*
45 Or one vain wit's, that might a hundred tire.

But you who seek to give and merit fame,
And justly bear a critic's noble name,
Be sure yourself and your own reach to know,
How far your genius, taste, and learning go;
50 Launch not beyond your depth, but be discreet,
And mark that point where sense and dullness meet.
Nature to all things fixed the limits fit,
And wisely curbed proud man's pretending° wit.   *aspiring*
As on the land while here the ocean gains,
55 In other parts it leaves wide sandy plains;
Thus in the soul while memory prevails,
The solid pow'r of understanding fails;
Where beams of warm imagination play,
The memory's soft figures melt away.
60 One science only will one genius fit,
So vast is art,° so narrow human wit: *scholarship*
Not only bounded to peculiar arts,
But oft in those confined to single parts.
Like kings we lose the conquests gained before,
65 By vain ambition still° to make them more;   *always*

Each might his sev'ral province well command,
Would all but stoop to what they understand.
First follow Nature, and your judgment frame
By her just standard, which is still the same;
70 Unerring Nature, still divinely bright,
One clear, unchanged, and universal light,
Life, force, and beauty must to all impart.
At once the source, and end, and test of art.
Art from that fund each just supply provides,
75 Works without show, and without pomp presides.
In some fair body thus th'informing° soul   *animating*
With spirits feeds, with vigour fills the whole,
Each motion guides, and every nerve sustains;
Itself unseen, but in th'effects remains.
80 Some, to whom Heav'n in wit has been profuse,
Want as much more to turn it to its use;
For wit and judgment often are at strife,
Though meant each other's aid, like man and wife.
'Tis more to guide than spur the Muse's steed,
85 Restrain his fury than provoke his speed;
The wingèd courser,³ like a gen'rous° horse,   *thoroughbred*
Shows most true mettle° when you check his   *character*
          course.

Those rules of old discovered, not devised,
Are Nature still, but Nature methodized;
90 Nature, like liberty, is but restrained
By the same laws which first herself ordained.

              .   .   .   .   .

You then whose judgment the right course would
          steer,
Know well each ancient's proper character;
120 His fable,° subject, scope° in every page;   *story, plot / purpose*
Religion, country, genius of his age:
Without all these at once before your eyes,
Cavil you may, but never criticize.
Be Homer's⁴ works your study and delight,
125 Read them by day, and meditate by night;
Thence form your judgment, thence your maxims
          bring,
And trace the Muses upward to their spring.
Still with itself compared, his text peruse;

---

¹ *Maevius* Notorious critic of the Augustan age who attacked, among others, Virgil (70–19 BCE) and Horace (65–8 BCE).

² *Apollo* In classical mythology, the god of poetry and the arts, among other things.

³ *courser* I.e., Pegasus, a winged horse of classical mythology associated with Muses and poetic inspiration.

⁴ *Homer* Ancient Greek epic poet (c. 8th century BCE).

And let your comment be the Mantuan Muse.

130　　　When first young Maro[1] in his boundless mind
A work t' outlast immortal Rome designed,
Perhaps he seemed above the critic's law,
And but from Nature's fountains scorned to draw;
But when t'examine every part he came,
135　Nature and Homer were, he found, the same.
Convinced, amazed, he checks the bold design,
And rules as strict his laboured work confine
As if the Stagirite[2] o'erlooked each line.
Learn hence for ancient rules a just esteem;
140　To copy Nature is to copy them.

　　　Some beauties yet no precepts can declare,
For there's a happiness as well as care.
Music resembles poetry, in each
Are nameless graces which no methods teach,
145　And which a master-hand alone can reach.
If, where the rules not far enough extend
(Since rules were made but to promote their end)
Some lucky license answers to the full
Th'intent proposed, that license is a rule.

·　　·　　·　　·　　·　　·

　　　Still green with bays each ancient altar stands
Above the reach of sacrilegious hands,
Secure from flames, from envy's fiercer rage,
Destructive war, and all-involving age.
185　See, from each clime the learned their incense bring!
Here in all tongues consenting° paeans[3] ring!　*in harmony*
In praise so just let every voice be joined,
And fill the gen'ral chorus of mankind.
Hail, bards triumphant! born in happier days,
190　Immortal heirs of universal praise!
Whose honours with increase of ages grow,
As streams roll down, enlarging as they flow;
Nations unborn your mighty names shall sound,
And worlds applaud that must not yet be found!
195　Oh, may some spark of your celestial fire,

The last, the meanest of your sons inspire
(That on weak wings, from far, pursues your flights,
Glows while he reads, but trembles as he writes)
To teach vain wits a science little known,
200　T'admire superior sense, and doubt their own!

PART 2

Of all the causes which conspire to blind
Man's erring judgment, and misguide the mind
What the weak head with strongest bias rules,
Is pride, the never-failing vice of fools.
205　Whatever Nature has in worth denied,
She gives in large recruits° of needful pride;　*supplies*
For as in bodies, thus in souls, we find
What wants in blood and spirits, swelled with wind:
Pride, where wit fails, steps in to our defence,
210　And fills up all the mighty void of sense.
If once right reason drives that cloud away,
Truth breaks upon us with resistless day.
Trust not yourself: but your defects to know,
Make use of every friend—and every foe.
215　　　A little learning is a dang'rous thing;
Drink deep, or taste not the Pierian[4] spring.
There shallow draughts intoxicate the brain,
And drinking largely sobers us again.

·　　·　　·　　·　　·　　·

　　　Whoever thinks a faultless piece to see,
Thinks what ne'er was, nor is, nor e'er shall be.
255　In every work regard the writer's end,
Since none can compass more than they intend;
And if the means be just, the conduct true,
Applause, in spite of trivial faults, is due.
As men of breeding, sometimes men of wit,
260　T'avoid great errors must the less commit,
Neglect the rules each verbal° critic lays,　*pedantic, petty*
For not to know some trifles is a praise.
Most critics, fond of some subservient art,
Still make the whole depend upon a part:
265　They talk of principles, but notions prize,
And all to one loved folly sacrifice.

---

[1]　*Mantuan Muse … Maro*　I.e., Virgil, classical Roman poet, who
was born near Mantua; also known as "Maro."

[2]　*Stagirite*　I.e., Aristotle (384–322 BCE), ancient Greek philosopher who was born in Stagira. He was the author of the *Poetics*,
which was (incorrectly) supposed to have established strict rules for
tragedies, governing place and time as well as action.

[3]　*paeans*　Triumphal or grateful songs.

---

[4]　*Pierian*　Sacred spring to the Muses.

Once on a time La Mancha's knight,[1] they say,
A certain bard encount'ring on the way,
Discoursed in terms as just, with looks as sage,
70   As e'er could Dennis,[2] of the Grecian stage;
Concluding all were desp'rate sots and fools
Who durst depart from Aristotle's rules.[3]
Our author, happy in a judge so nice,
Produced his play, and begged the knight's advice;
75   Made him observe the subject and the plot,
The manners, passions, unities; what not?
All which, exact to rule, were brought about,
Were but a combat in the lists left out.
"What! leave the combat out?" exclaims the knight.
80   "Yes, or we must renounce the Stagirite."
"Not so, by Heav'n!" he answers in a rage,
"Knights, squires, and steeds must enter on the stage."
"So vast a throng the stage can ne'er contain."
"Then build a new, or act it in a plain."
85   Thus critics of less judgment than caprice,
Curious,° not knowing, not exact,   *particular*
    but nice,°   *fastidious*
Form short ideas, and offend in arts
(As most in manners) by a love to parts.
        Some to conceit alone their taste confine,
90   And glitt'ring thoughts struck out at every line;
Pleased with a work where nothing's just or fit,
One glaring chaos and wild heap of wit.
Poets like painters, thus unskilled to trace
The naked nature and the living grace,
95   With gold and jewels cover every part,
And hide with ornaments their want of art.
True wit is Nature to advantage dressed,
What oft was thought, but ne'er so well expressed;
Something, whose truth convinced at sight we find,
100   That gives us back the image of our mind.
As shades more sweetly recommend the light,
So modest plainness sets off sprightly wit;
For works may have more wit than does 'em good,
As bodies perish through excess of blood.

305   Others for language all their care express,
And value books, as women men, for dress.
Their praise is still—"the style is excellent";
The sense they humbly take upon content.
Words are like leaves; and where they most abound,
310   Much fruit of sense beneath is rarely found.
False eloquence, like the prismatic glass,
Its gaudy colours spreads on every place;
The face of Nature we no more survey,
All glares alike, without distinction gay.
315   But true expression, like th'unchanging sun,
Clears and improves whate'er it shines upon;
It gilds all objects, but it alters none.
Expression is the dress of thought, and still
Appears more decent as more suitable.
320   A vile conceit in pompous words expressed
Is like a clown° in regal purple dressed   *peasant, rustic*
For diff'rent styles with diff'rent subjects sort,
As several garbs with country, town, and court.
Some by old words to fame have made pretence,
325   Ancients in phrase, mere moderns in their sense:
Such laboured nothings, in so strange a style,
Amaze th' unlearn'd, and make the learned smile;
Unlucky as Fungoso[4] in the play,
These sparks with awkward vanity display
330   What the fine gentleman wore yesterday;
And but so mimic ancient wits at best,
As apes our grandsires in their doublets dressed.
In words as fashions the same rule will hold,
Alike fantastic if too new or old:
335   Be not the first by whom the new are tried,
Nor yet the last to lay the old aside.
        But most by numbers° judge a poet's song,   *versification*
And smooth or rough, with them, is right or wrong.
In the bright Muse though thousand charms conspire,
340   Her voice is all these tuneful fools admire,
Who haunt Parnassus but to please their ear,
Not mend their minds; as some to church repair,
Not for the doctrine, but the music there.
These equal syllables alone require,
345   Though oft the ear the open vowels tire,
While expletives their feeble aid do join,
And ten low words oft creep in one dull line:

---

[1] *La Mancha's knight* I.e., the eponymous hero of Miguel de Cervantes's *Don Quixote* (1605–15).

[2] *Dennis* John Dennis (1658–1734), neo-classical literary critic with whom Pope feuded.

[3] *Aristotle's rules* I.e., the dramatic unities of time, place, and action.

[4] *Fungoso* Character from Ben Jonson's *Every Man out of his Humour* (1518).

While they ring round the same unvaried chimes,
With sure returns of still expected rhymes:
350 Where'er you find "the cooling western breeze,"
In the next line, it "whispers through the trees";
If crystal streams "with pleasing murmurs creep,"
The reader's threatened (not in vain) with "sleep";
Then, at the last and only couplet fraught
355 With some unmeaning thing they call a thought,
A needless Alexandrine[1] ends the song
That, like a wounded snake, drags its slow length along.
Leave such to tune their own dull rhymes, and know
What's roundly smooth or languishingly slow;
360 And praise the easy vigour of a line
Where Denham's strength and Waller's sweetness join.[2]
True ease in writing comes from art, not chance,
As those move easiest who have learned to dance.
'Tis not enough no harshness gives offence,
365 The sound must seem an echo to the sense:
Soft is the strain when Zephyr° gently blows,   *the west wind*
And the smooth stream in smoother numbers flows;
But when loud surges lash the sounding shore,
The hoarse, rough verse should like the torrent roar.
370 When Ajax[3] strives some rock's vast weight to throw,
The line too labours, and the words move slow;
Not so when swift Camilla[4] scours the plain,
Flies o'er th'unbending corn, and skims along the
      main.°   *sea*
Hear how Timotheus'[5] varied lays surprise,
375 And bid alternate passions fall and rise!
While, at each change, the son of Libyan Jove[6]
Now burns with glory, and then melts with love;
Now his fierce eyes with sparkling fury glow,

Now sighs steal out, and tears begin to flow:
380 Persians and Greeks like° turns of   *similar*
      nature° found,   *feelings*
And the world's victor stood subdued by sound!
The pow'r of music all our hearts allow,
And what Timotheus was, is Dryden[7] now.
      Avoid extremes, and shun the fault of such
385 Who still are pleased too little or too much.
At every trifle scorn to take offence,
That always shows great pride, or little sense;
Those heads, as stomachs, are not sure the best,
Which nauseate all, and nothing can digest.
390 Yet let not each gay turn thy rapture move,
For fools admire,° but men of sense approve: *marvel at*
As things seem large which we through mists descry,
Dullness is ever apt to magnify.

Some ne'er advance a judgment of their own,
But catch the spreading notion of the town;
410 They reason and conclude by precedent,
And own stale nonsense which they ne'er invent.
Some judge of authors names, not works, and then
Nor praise nor blame the writings, but the men.
Of all this servile herd, the worst is he
415 That in proud dullness joins with quality.°   *people of rank*
A constant critic at the great man's board,
To fetch and carry nonsense for my Lord.
What woeful stuff this madrigal[8] would be,
In some starved hackney[9] sonneteer, or me?
420 But let a lord once own the happy lines,
How the wit brightens! how the style refines!
Before his sacred name flies every fault,
And each exalted stanza teems with thought!
      The vulgar thus through imitation err;
425 As oft the learn'd by being singular;
So much they scorn the crowd, that if the throng
By chance go right, they purposely go wrong:
So schismatics the plain believers quit,
And are but damned for having too much wit.

---

1 *Alexandrine* Line of poetry with twelve syllables (as has line 357).

2 *Denham's strength ... join* Sir John Denham (1614/15–69), poet and courtier; Edmund Waller (1608–87), poet and politician. Both poets were known for their smooth, easy style.

3 *Ajax* The "greater Ajax" of Homer's *Illiad*, who is proverbially strong.

4 *Camilla* In classical mythology, a warrior virgin; she appears in Book 7 of Virgil's *Aeneid*.

5 *Timotheus* Greek poet and musician (4th century BCE) who played for Alexander the Great (356–323 BCE).

6 *Libyan Jove* I.e., Alexander the Great (356–323 BCE), Macedonian military leader; when he visited the oracle of Zeus Ammon ("Libyan Jove"), he was proclaimed son of the god.

7 *Dryden* John Dryden (1631–1700), leading poet, playwright, and critic of the Restoration.

8 *madrigal* Short lyric, especially one set to music.

9 *hackney* Doing or ready to do work for hire.

30 Some praise at morning what they blame at night;
   But always think the last opinion right.
   A muse by these is like a mistress used,
   This hour she's idolized, the next abused;
   While their weak heads, like towns unfortified,
35 'Twixt sense and nonsense daily change their side.
   Ask them the cause; they're wiser still, they say;
   And still° tomorrow's wiser than today.   *always*
   We think our fathers fools, so wise we grow;
   Our wiser sons, no doubt, will think us so.

               .   .   .   .

 0 Of old, those met rewards who could excel,
   And such were praised who but endeavoured well.
   Though triumphs were to gen'rals only due,
   Crowns were reserved to grace the soldiers too.
   Now, they who reach Parnassus' lofty crown,
 5 Employ their pains to spurn° some others down;   *kick*
   And while self-love each jealous writer rules,
   Contending wits become the sport of fools;
   But still the worst with most regret commend,
   For each ill author is as bad a friend.
 0 To what base ends, and by what abject ways,
   Are mortals urged through sacred lust of praise!
   Ah ne'er so dire a thirst of glory boast,
   Nor in the critic let the man be lost.
   Good-nature and good-sense must ever join;
 5 To err is human, to forgive, divine,
       But if in noble minds some dregs remain
   Not yet purged off, of spleen° and sour disdain;   *spite*
   Discharge that rage on more provoking crimes,
   Nor fear a dearth in these flagitious° times.   *extremely wicked*
 0 No pardon vile obscenity should find,
   Though wit and art conspire to move your mind;
   But dullness with obscenity must prove
   As shameful sure as impotence in love.

               .   .   .   .

PART 3

 0 Learn then what morals critics ought to show,
   For 'tis but half a judge's task, to know.
   'Tis not enough, taste, judgment, learning, join;
   In all you speak, let truth and
       candour° shine: *openness of mind*
   That not alone what to your sense is due
 5 All may allow; but seek your friendship too.

Be silent always when you doubt your sense;
And speak, though sure, with seeming diffidence:
Some positive, persisting fops we know,
Who, if once wrong, will needs be always so;
570 But you, with pleasure own your errors past,
And make each day a critic° on the last.   *critique*
    'Tis not enough, your counsel still be true;
Blunt truths more mischief than nice falsehoods do;
Men must be taught as if you taught them not,
575 And things unknown proposed as things forgot.
Without good breeding, truth is disapproved;
That only makes superior sense belov'd.

               .   .   .   .

The bookful blockhead, ignorantly read,
With loads of learned lumber in his head,
With his own tongue still edifies his ears,
615 And always list'ning to himself appears.
All books he reads, and all he reads assails,
From Dryden's *Fables* down to Durfey's *Tales*.[1]
With him, most authors steal their works, or buy;
Garth[2] did not write his own *Dispensary*.
620 Name a new play, and he's the poet's friend,
Nay showed his faults—but when would poets mend?
No place so sacred from such fops is barred,
Nor is Paul's church more safe than Paul's church yard:[3]
Nay, fly to altars; there they'll talk you dead:
625 For fools rush in where angels fear to tread.
Distrustful sense with modest caution speaks,
It still looks home, and short excursions makes;
But rattling nonsense in full volleys breaks,
And never shocked,° and never turned aside,   *stopped*
630 Bursts out, resistless, with a thund'ring tide.
    But where's the man, who counsel can bestow,
Still pleased to teach, and yet not proud to know?

---

[1] *Dryden's Fables ... Durfey's Tales* John Dryden's *Fables, Ancient and Modern* (1700) and Thomas D'Urfey's *Tales Tragical and Comical* (1704). D'Urfey's *Tales* is a poor imitation of Dryden's *Fables*.

[2] *Garth* Samuel Garth's *Dispensary* (1699) was closely modeled on Nicolas Boileau's *Le Lutrin* (1674); Garth's critics accused him of plagiarism.

[3] *Paul's church ... Paul's church yard* The former was used as a place for business meetings, and the latter was close to the booksellers' quarter.

Unbiased, or° by favour, or by spite: *either*
Not dully prepossessed, nor blindly right;
635   Though learn'd, well-bred; and though well-bred,
            sincere;
Modestly bold, and humanly severe:
Who to a friend his faults can freely show,
And gladly praise the merit of a foe?
Blest with a taste exact, yet unconfined;
640   A knowledge both of books and human kind;
Gen'rous° converse;° a soul exempt   *well-bred | conversation*
            from pride;
And love to praise, with reason on his side?
        Such once were critics; such the happy few,
Athens and Rome in better ages knew.

—1711

The Rape of the Lock:
An Heroi-Comical Poem in Five Cantos

To Mrs. Arabella Fermor[1]

Madam,

It will be in vain to deny that I have some regard for this piece, since I dedicate it to you. Yet you may bear me witness, it was intended only to divert a few young ladies, who have good sense and good humour enough, to laugh not only at their sex's little unguarded follies, but at their own. But, as it was communicated with the air of a secret, it soon found its way into the world. An imperfect copy having been offered to a bookseller,[2] you had the good nature for my sake to consent to the publication of one more correct; this I was forced to before I had executed half my design, for the machinery was entirely wanting to complete it.

The machinery, Madam, is a term invented by the critics to signify that part which the deities, angels, or demons are made to act in a poem; for the ancient poets are in one respect like many modern ladies: let an action be never so trivial in itself, they always make it appear of the utmost importance. These machines I determined to raise on a very new and odd foundation, the Rosicrucian[3] doctrine of spirits.

I know how disagreeable it is to make use of hard words before a lady, but 'tis so much the concern of a poet to have his works understood, and particularly by your sex, that you must give me leave to explain two or three difficult terms.

The Rosicrucians are a people I must bring you acquainted with. The best account I know of them is in a French book called *Le Comte de Gabalis*,[4] which both in its title and size is so like a novel that many of the fair sex have read it for one by mistake. According to these gentlemen, the four elements are inhabited by spirits, which they call Sylphs, Gnomes, Nymphs, and Salamanders.[5] The Gnomes, or demons of earth, delight in mischief, but the Sylphs, whose habitation is in the air, are the best-conditioned creatures imaginable. For they say any mortals may enjoy the most intimate familiarities with these gentle spirits, upon a condition very easy to all true adepts, an inviolate preservation of chastity.

As to the following cantos, all the passages of them are as fabulous[6] as the vision at the beginning, or the transformation at the end (except the loss of your hair, which I always mention with reverence). The human persons are as fictitious as the airy ones, and the character of Belinda, as it is now managed, resembles you in nothing but in beauty.

If this poem had as many graces as there are in your person, or in your mind, yet I could never hope it should pass through the world half so uncensured as you have done. But let its fortune be what it will, mine is happy enough, to have given me this occasion of

---

1   *Mrs. Arabella Fermor* Arabella Fermor was the daughter of a prominent Catholic family. She was celebrated for her beauty. Lord Robert Petre snipped off a lock of her hair, occasioning Pope's poem. Mrs. was a title of respect for married or unmarried women.

2   *bookseller* Publisher.

3   *Rosicrucian* Religious sect, originating in Germany, which existed in the seventeenth and eighteenth centuries. Its members were devoted to the study of arcane philosophy and mystical doctrines.

4   *Le Comte de Gabalais* Written by Abbé de Monfaucon de Villars and published in 1670, this was a lighthearted exploration of Rosicrucian philosophy. It was printed in duodecimo (about five by eight inches), a common size for novels and other inexpensive books.

5   *Salamanders* Salamanders were believed to be able to withstand, and live in, fire,

6   *fabulous* Mythical, fictional.

assuring you that I am, with the truest esteem,
 Madam,

  Your most obedient humble servant.

           A. POPE

Canto I. Illustration from the 1714 edition. The other four illustrations from this edition are reproduced below.

CANTO 1

What dire offence from amorous causes springs,
 What mighty contests rise from trivial things,
I sing—This verse to Caryll, Muse! is due;
This, even Belinda may vouchsafe to view:
5 Slight is the subject, but not so the praise,
If she inspire, and he approve my lays.°   *verses*
 Say what strange motive, Goddess! could compel
A well-bred lord to assault a gentle belle?
Oh say what stranger cause, yet unexplored,° *undiscovered*
10 Could make a gentle belle reject a lord?
In tasks so bold can little men engage,
And in soft bosoms dwells such mighty rage?
 Sol° through white curtains shot a timorous ray, *sun*
And oped those eyes that must eclipse the day;
15 Now lapdogs give themselves the rousing shake,
And sleepless lovers, just at twelve, awake:
Thrice rung the bell, the slipper knocked the ground,[1]
And the pressed watch[2] returned a silver sound.
Belinda still her downy pillow pressed,
20 Her guardian Sylph prolonged the balmy rest.
'Twas he had summoned to her silent bed
The morning dream[3] that hovered o'er her head.
A youth more glittering than a birthnight beau[4]
(That even in slumber caused her cheek to glow)
25 Seemed to her ear his winning lips to lay,
And thus in whispers said, or seemed to say:
 "Fairest of mortals, thou distinguished care
Of thousand bright inhabitants of air!
If e'er one vision touched thy infant thought,
30 Of all the nurse and all the priest have taught,
Of airy elves by moonlight shadows seen,
The silver token, and the circled green,[5]

---

[1] *slipper ... ground* She bangs her slipper on the floor to summon the maid.

[2] *pressed watch* "Repeater" watches would chime the time, to the nearest quarter hour, when the stem was pressed.

[3] *morning dream* Morning dreams were believed to be particularly portentous.

[4] *birthnight beau* On the birthday of the sovereign, members of the court dressed in their most lavish attire.

[5] *silver token* Fairies were said to skim the cream from the top of jugs of milk left overnight, leaving a silver coin in its place; *circled green* Rings in the grass that were said to be produced by dancing fairies.

Or virgins visited by angel powers,
With golden crowns and wreaths of heavenly flowers,
35 Hear and believe! thy own importance know,
Nor bound thy narrow views to things below.
Some secret truths, from learned pride concealed,
To maids alone and children are revealed.
What though no credit doubting wits may give?
40 The fair and innocent shall still believe.
Know then, unnumbered spirits round thee fly,
The light militia of the lower sky;
These, though unseen, are ever on the wing,
Hang o'er the box, and hover round the Ring.[1]
45 Think what an equipage° thou hast in air,   *retinue with vehicles*
And view with scorn two pages and a chair.°   *sedan chair*
As now your own, our beings were of old,
And once enclosed in woman's beauteous mold;
Thence, by a soft transition, we repair
50 From earthly vehicles to these of air.
Think not, when woman's transient breath is fled,
That all her vanities at once are dead:
Succeeding vanities she still regards,
And though she plays no more, o'erlooks the cards.
55 Her joy in gilded chariots, when alive,
And love of ombre,[2] after death survive.
For when the fair in all their pride expire,
To their first elements[3] their souls retire:
The sprites[4] of fiery termagants[5] in flame
60 Mount up, and take a Salamander's name.
Soft yielding minds to water glide away,
And sip, with Nymphs, their elemental tea.
The graver prude sinks downward to a Gnome,
In search of mischief still on earth to roam.
65 The light coquettes in Sylphs aloft repair,
And sport and flutter in the fields of air.
        "Know further yet, whoever fair and chaste

Rejects mankind, is by some Sylph embraced:
For spirits, freed from mortal laws, with ease
70 Assume what sexes and what shapes they please.[6]
What guards the purity of melting maids
In courtly balls, and midnight masquerades,
Safe from the treacherous friend, the daring spark,°   *suitor*
The glance by day, the whisper in the dark,
75 When kind occasion prompts their warm desires,
When music softens, and when dancing fires?
'Tis but their Sylph, the wise celestials know,
Though *honour* is the word with men below.
        "Some nymphs° there are, too conscious   *maidens*
            of their face,
80 For life predestined to the Gnomes' embrace.
These swell their prospects and exalt their pride
When offers are disdained, and love denied.
Then gay ideas° crowd the vacant brain,   *images*
While peers° and dukes, and all their sweeping train,   *nobles*
85 And garters, stars, and coronets[7] appear,
And in soft sounds, 'your Grace' salutes their ear.
'Tis these that early taint the female soul,
Instruct the eyes of young coquettes to roll,
Teach infant cheeks a bidden blush to know,
90 And little hearts to flutter at a beau.
        "Oft, when the world imagine women stray,
The Sylphs through mystic mazes guide their way,
Through all the giddy circle they pursue,
And old impertinence expel by new.
95 What tender maid but must a victim fall
To one man's treat,° but for another's ball?   *feast*
When Florio speaks, what virgin could withstand,
If gentle Damon did not squeeze her hand?
With varying vanities, from every part,
100 They shift the moving toyshop[8] of their heart;
Where wigs with wigs, with sword-knots[9] sword-knots
            strive,

---

1. *box* Private compartment in a theater; *the Ring* Circular drive that divides Hyde Park from Kensington Gardens.

2. *ombre* A popular card game.

3. *first elements* All things on earth had been thought to be made from the four elements (earth, air, fire, and water), and one of these four elements had been thought to be predominant in the temperament of each person.

4. *sprites* Spirits.

5. *termagants* Quarrelsome, turbulent, or hot-tempered women.

---

6. *spirits … please* Cf. Milton's *Paradise Lost*, 1.423–424, "For spirits when they please / Can either sex assume, or both." This is one of many allusions to Milton's epic poem.

7. *garters, stars, and coronets* Emblems of noble ranks.

8. *toyshop* Store that sold not only toys but various trinkets, accessories, and ornaments.

9. *sword-knots* Fashionable men of society wore ribbons knotted around the hilts of their swords. They also wore wigs.

Beaux banish beaux, and coaches coaches drive.
This erring mortals levity may call,
Oh blind to truth! the sylphs contrive it all.
105   "Of these am I, who thy protection claim,
A watchful sprite, and Ariel is my name.
Late, as I ranged the crystal wilds of air,
In the clear mirror of thy ruling star
I saw, alas! some dread event impend,
110 Ere to the main° this morning sun descend;   *sea*
But Heaven reveals not what, or how, or where:
Warned by thy Sylph, oh pious maid beware!
This to disclose is all thy guardian can:
Beware of all, but most beware of man!"
115   He said; when Shock,[1] who thought she slept too long,
Leaped up, and waked his mistress with his tongue.
'Twas then, Belinda, if report say true,
Thy eyes first opened on a billet-doux;°   *love letter*
Wounds, charms, and ardors were no sooner read,
120 But all the vision vanished from thy head.
   And now, unveiled, the toilet° stands   *dressing table*
      displayed,
Each silver vase in mystic order laid.
First, robed in white, the nymph intent adores,
With head uncovered, the cosmetic powers.
125 A heavenly image in the glass appears,
To that she bends, to that her eyes she rears.°   *lifts*
The inferior priestess,[2] at her altar's side,
Trembling begins the sacred rites of pride.
Unnumbered treasures ope at once, and here
130 The various offerings of the world appear;
From each she nicely culls with curious toil,
And decks the goddess with the glittering spoil.
This casket India's glowing gems unlocks,
And all Arabia breathes from yonder box.
135 The tortoise here and elephant unite,
Transformed to combs, the speckled and the white.
Here files of pins extend their shining rows,
Puffs, powders, patches,[3] Bibles, billet-doux.
Now awful° beauty puts on all its arms;   *awe-inspiring*

---

1 *Shock* Belinda's lapdog, named after a popular breed of long-haired, Icelandic toy poodle called the "shough," or "shock."

2 *inferior priestess* Betty, Belinda's maid.

3 *patches* Artificial beauty marks made of silk or plaster cut into various shapes and placed on the face, either for decoration or to hide an imperfection.

140 The fair each moment rises in her charms,
Repairs her smiles, awakens every grace,
And calls forth all the wonders of her face;
Sees by degrees a purer blush arise,
And keener lightnings quicken in her eyes.[4]
145 The busy Sylphs surround their darling care,
These set the head, and those divide the hair,
Some fold the sleeve, whilst others plait the gown;
And Betty's praised for labours not her own.

CANTO 2

Not with more glories, in the ethereal plain,
The sun first rises o'er the purpled main,
Than issuing forth, the rival of his beams

---

4 *keener ... eyes* As a result of drops of belladonna, or deadly nightshade, which enlarges the pupils.

Launched on the bosom of the silver Thames.[1]
5 Fair nymphs and well-dressed youths around her shone,
But every eye was fixed on her alone.
On her white breast a sparkling cross she wore,
Which Jews might kiss, and infidels adore.
Her lively looks a sprightly mind disclose,
10 Quick as her eyes, and as unfixed as those:
Favours to none, to all she smiles extends;
Oft she rejects, but never once offends.
Bright as the sun, her eyes the gazers strike,
And, like the sun, they shine on all alike.
15 Yet graceful ease, and sweetness void of pride,
Might hide her faults, if belles had faults to hide:
If to her share some female errors fall,
Look on her face, and you'll forget 'em all.
　　　This nymph, to the destruction of mankind,
20 Nourished two locks, which graceful hung behind
In equal curls, and well conspired to deck
With shining ringlets the smooth ivory neck.
Love in these labyrinths his slaves detains,
And mighty hearts are held in slender chains;
25 With hairy springes° we the birds betray;　　　*snares*
Slight lines of hair surprise the finny prey;
Fair tresses man's imperial race ensnare,
And beauty draws us with a single hair.
　　　The adventurous Baron the bright locks admired;
30 He saw, he wished, and to the prize aspired.
Resolved to win, he meditates the way,
By force to ravish, or by fraud betray;
For when success a lover's toil attends,
Few ask if fraud or force attained his ends.
35 　　　For this, ere Phoebus[2] rose, he had implored
Propitious Heaven, and every power adored,°　　　*worshiped*
But chiefly Love—to Love an altar built,
Of twelve vast French romances, neatly gilt.
There lay three garters, half a pair of gloves,
40 And all the trophies of his former loves.
With tender billet-doux he lights the pyre,
And breathes three amorous sighs to raise the fire.
Then prostrate falls, and begs with ardent eyes
Soon to obtain, and long possess the prize:

45 The powers gave ear, and granted half his prayer;
The rest the winds dispersed in empty air.
　　　But now secure the painted vessel glides,
The sunbeams trembling on the floating tides,
While melting music steals upon the sky,
50 And softened sounds along the waters die.
Smooth flow the waves, the zephyrs gently play,
Belinda smiled, and all the world was gay.
All but the Sylph—with careful thoughts oppressed,
The impending woe sat heavy on his breast.
55 He summons strait his denizens of air;
The lucid squadrons round the sails repair:
Soft o'er the shrouds[3] aerial whispers breathe
That seemed but zephyrs° to the train beneath.　　*mild breezes*
Some to the sun their insect-wings unfold,
60 Waft on the breeze, or sink in clouds of gold.
Transparent forms, too fine for mortal sight,
Their fluid bodies half dissolved in light,
Loose to the wind their airy garments flew,
Thin glittering textures of the filmy dew,
65 Dipped in the richest tincture of the skies,
Where light disports in ever-mingling dyes,
While every beam new transient colours flings,
Colours that change whene'er they wave their wings.
Amid the circle, on the gilded mast,
70 Superior by the head, was Ariel placed;
His purple pinions° opening to the sun,　　　*wings*
He raised his azure wand, and thus begun:
　　　"Ye Sylphs and Sylphids, to your chief give ear!
Fays, Fairies, Genii, Elves, and Demons, hear!
75 Ye know the spheres and various tasks assigned,
By laws eternal, to the aerial kind.
Some in the fields of purest ether[4] play,
And bask and whiten in the blaze of day.
Some guide the course of wandering orbs on high,
80 Or roll the planets through the boundless sky.
Some, less refined, beneath the moon's pale light
Pursue the stars that shoot athwart the night,
Or suck the mists in grosser[5] air below,
Or dip their pinions in the painted bow,
85 Or brew fierce tempests on the wintry main,

---

1 *Launched … Thames* Belinda voyages upstream to Hampton
Court for the day. By taking a boat she avoids the crowds and filth
in the streets.
2 *Phoebus* One of the names of Apollo, god of the sun.

3 *shrouds* Ropes that brace the mast of the ship.
4 *ether* Clear regions above the moon.
5 *grosser* Material, as opposed to ethereal, realms.

Or o'er the glebe[1] distill the kindly rain.
Others on earth o'er human race preside,
Watch all their ways, and all their actions guide:
Of these the chief the care of nations own,
90 And guard with arms divine the British Throne.

"Our humbler province is to tend the fair,
Not a less pleasing, though less glorious care:
To save the powder from too rude a gale,
Nor let the imprisoned essences° exhale;   *perfumes*
95 To draw fresh colours from the vernal flowers;
To steal from rainbows ere they drop in showers
A brighter wash;[2] to curl their waving hairs,
Assist their blushes, and inspire their airs;
Nay, oft in dreams invention we bestow,
To change a flounce, or add a furbelo.°   *pleated trim*

"This day, black omens threat the brightest fair
That e'er deserved a watchful spirit's care;
Some dire disaster, or by force or slight,
But what, or where, the Fates have wrapped in night.
Whether the nymph shall break Diana's law,[3]
Or some frail China jar receive a flaw,
Or stain her honour, or her new brocade,
Forget her prayers, or miss a masquerade,
Or lose her heart, or necklace, at a ball;
Or whether Heaven has doomed that Shock must fall.
Haste then, ye spirits! To your charge repair:
The fluttering fan be Zephyretta's care;
The drops° to thee, Brillante, we consign;   *diamond earrings*
And, Momentilla, let the watch be thine;
Do thou, Crispissa,[4] tend her favorite lock;
Ariel himself shall be the guard of Shock.

"To fifty chosen Sylphs, of special note,
We trust the important charge, the petticoat:
Oft have we known that sevenfold fence[5] to fail,
20 Though stiff with hoops, and armed with ribs of whale.
Form a strong line about the silver bound,
And guard the wide circumference around.

"Whatever spirit, careless of his charge,
His post neglects, or leaves the fair at large,
125 Shall feel sharp vengeance soon o'ertake his sins,
Be stopped in vials, or transfixed with pins,
Or plunged in lakes of bitter washes lie,
Or wedged whole ages in a bodkin's[6] eye;
Gums and pomatums° shall his flight restrain,   *hair ointments*
130 While clogged he beats his silken wings in vain,
Or alum styptics[7] with contracting power
Shrink his thin essence like a riveled° flower.   *shriveled*
Or, as Ixion[8] fixed, the wretch shall feel
The giddy motion of the whirling mill,
135 In fumes of burning chocolate shall glow,
And tremble at the sea that froths below!"

He spoke; the spirits from the sails descend;
Some, orb in orb, around the nymph extend;
Some thread the mazy° ringlets of her hair;   *maze-like*
140 Some hang upon the pendants of her ear.
With beating hearts the dire event they wait,
Anxious, and trembling for the birth of fate.

CANTO 3

Close by those meads forever crowned with flowers,
Where Thames with pride surveys his rising towers,
There stands a structure of majestic frame,[9]
Which from the neighboring Hampton takes its name.
5 Here Britain's statesmen oft the fall foredoom
Of foreign tyrants, and of nymphs at home;
Here thou, great Anna! whom three realms obey,
Dost sometimes counsel take—and sometimes tea.

Hither the heroes and the nymphs resort,
10 To taste awhile the pleasures of a court;
In various talk the instructive hours they passed,
Who gave the ball, or paid the visit last;

---

[1] *glebe* Fields.

[2] *wash* Liquid cosmetic.

[3] *break Diana's law* Lose her virginity (Diana was the Roman goddess of chastity).

[4] *Crispissa* From *crispere*, the Latin verb meaning "to curl."

[5] *sevenfold fence* Allusion to Achilles's "sevenfold shield" in *The Iliad*.

[6] *bodkin* Blunt needle with both a large and a small eye, used to draw ribbon through a hem.

[7] *alum styptics* Astringent substances applied to cuts to contract tissue and stop bleeding.

[8] *Ixion* Zeus punished Ixion, who had attempted to seduce Hera, by tying him to a continuously revolving wheel in Hades. Here the wheel would be that of a machine that beats hot chocolate to a froth.

[9] *structure … majestic frame* Hampton Court, largest of Queen Anne's residences, located about 12 miles up the Thames from London.

And swells her breast with conquests yet to come.
Straight the three bands prepare in arms to join,
30 Each band the number of the sacred nine.[3]
Soon as she spreads her hand, the aerial guard
Descend, and sit on each important card:
First Ariel perched upon a Matadore,[4]
Then each according to the rank they bore;
35 For Sylphs, yet mindful of their ancient race,
Are, as when women, wondrous fond of place.° *social status*
    Behold, four Kings in majesty revered,
With hoary whiskers and a forky beard;
And four fair Queens whose hands sustain a flower,
40 The expressive emblem of their softer power;
Four Knaves in garbs succinct,[5] a trusty band,
Caps on their heads, and halberds[6] in their hand;
And parti-coloured troops, a shining train,
Draw forth to combat on the velvet plain.
45   The skilful nymph reviews her force with care;
"Let Spades be trumps!" she said, and trumps they were.
    Now move to war her sable Matadores,
In show like leaders of the swarthy Moors.
Spadillio first, unconquerable lord!
50 Led off two captive trumps, and swept the board.
As many more Manillio forced to yield,
And marched a victor from the verdant field.
Him Basto followed, but, his fate more hard,
Gained but one trump and one plebeian card.
55 With his broad sabre next, a chief in years,
The hoary Majesty of Spades appears,
Puts forth one manly leg, to sight revealed,
The rest his many-coloured robe concealed.
The rebel Knave, who dares his prince engage,
60 Proves the just victim of his royal rage.

One speaks the glory of the British Queen,
And one describes a charming Indian screen;
15 A third interprets motions, looks, and eyes;
At every word a reputation dies.
Snuff, or the fan, supply each pause of chat,
With singing, laughing, ogling, and all that.
    Meanwhile, declining from the noon of day,
20 The sun obliquely shoots his burning ray;
The hungry judges soon the sentence sign,
And wretches hang that jurymen may dine;
The merchant from the Exchange[1] returns in peace,
And the long labours of the toilette cease.
25 Belinda now, whom thirst of fame invites,
Burns to encounter two adventurous knights
At ombre,[2] singly to decide their doom,

---

[1] *the Exchange* The Royal Exchange, located in the commercial center of London, was the principal market where merchants traded and where bankers and brokers met to do business.

[2] *ombre* In the game of ombre that Belinda plays against the two men, Pope conveys an accurate sense of the game, the rules of which are similar to those of bridge. Each of the three players receives 9 cards from the 40 that are used (8s, 9s, and 10s are discarded).

Belinda, as the challenger, or "ombre" (from the Spanish *hombre*, "man"), names the trumps. To win, she must make more tricks than either of the other two. For a complete description of the game, see Geoffrey Tillotson's Twickenham edition of Pope's poems, volume 2.

[3] *sacred nine* Muses.

[4] *Matadore* Matadores are the three highest cards of the game. When spades are trump, as they are here, the highest card is the ace of spades ("Spadillio"), followed by the two of spades ("Manillio"), and then the ace of clubs ("Basto").

[5] *succinct* Brief, short. The knaves are wearing short tunics.

[6] *halberds* Weapons that combined the spear and battle axe.

Even mighty Pam,[1] that kings and queens o'erthrew,
And mowed down armies in the fights of Loo,
Sad chance of war! now, destitute of aid,
Falls undistinguished by the victor Spade!
5   Thus far both armies to Belinda yield;
Now to the Baron fate inclines the field.
His warlike Amazon[2] her host invades,
The imperial consort of the crown of Spades.
The Club's black tyrant first her victim died,
10 Spite of his haughty mien° and barbarous pride.   *look*
What boots the regal circle on his head,
His giant limbs in state unwieldy spread?
That long behind he trails his pompous robe,
And of all monarchs only grasps the globe?
15   The Baron now his Diamonds pours apace;
The embroidered King, who shows but half his face,
And his refulgent Queen, with powers combined,
Of broken troops an easy conquest find.
Clubs, Diamonds, Hearts, in wild disorder seen,
20 With throngs promiscuous strew the level green.
Thus when dispersed a routed army runs,
Of Asia's troops, and Afric's sable sons,
With like confusion different nations fly,
Of various habit, and of various dye,
25 The pierced battalions disunited fall
In heaps on heaps; one fate o'erwhelms them all.
      The Knave of Diamonds tries his wily arts,
And wins (oh, shameful chance!) the Queen of Hearts.
At this, the blood the virgin's cheek forsook,
30 A livid paleness spreads o'er all her look;
She sees, and trembles at the approaching ill,
Just in the jaws of ruin, and Codille.[3]
And now (as oft in some distempered state)
On one nice trick depends the general fate.
35 An Ace of Hearts steps forth: the King unseen
Lurked in her hand, and mourned his captive Queen.
He springs to vengeance with an eager pace,
And falls like thunder on the prostrate Ace.
The nymph, exulting, fills with shouts the sky;
40 The walls, the woods, and long canals reply.

      O thoughtless mortals! ever blind to fate,
Too soon dejected, and too soon elate!
Sudden these honours shall be snatched away,
And cursed forever this victorious day.
105   For lo! the board with cups and spoons is crowned,
The berries crackle, and the mill turns round.[4]
On shining altars of Japan[5] they raise
The silver lamp; the fiery spirits blaze.
From silver spouts the grateful liquors glide,
110 While China's earth[6] receives the smoking tide.
At once they gratify their scent and taste,
And frequent cups prolong the rich repast.
Straight hover round the fair her airy band;
Some, as she sipped, the fuming liquor fanned,
115 Some o'er her lap their careful plumes displayed,
Trembling, and conscious of the rich brocade.
Coffee (which makes the politician wise,
And see through all things with his half-shut eyes)
Sent up in vapours to the Baron's brain
120 New stratagems, the radiant lock to gain.
Ah, cease, rash youth! desist ere 'tis too late,
Fear the just gods, and think of Scylla's[7] fate!
Changed to a bird, and sent to flit in air,
She dearly pays for Nisus' injured hair!
125   But when to mischief mortals bend their will,
How soon they find fit instruments of ill!
Just then, Clarissa drew with tempting grace
A two-edged weapon° from her shining case;   *pair of scissors*
So ladies in romance assist their knight,
130 Present the spear, and arm him for the fight.
He takes the gift with reverence, and extends
The little engine° on his fingers' ends;   *instrument*
This just behind Belinda's neck he spread,
As o'er the fragrant steams she bends her head.
135 Swift to the lock a thousand sprites repair,
A thousand wings, by turns, blow back the hair,

---

1 *Pam* The jack (knave) of clubs, the highest card in Loo, another popular card game.

2 *Amazon* Female warrior; here, the Queen of Spades.

3 *Codille* The defeat of the ombre.

---

4 *berries … round* The coffee beans ("berries") are roasted and then ground.

5 *altars of Japan* I.e., lacquered, or "japanned" tables, highly decorated and varnished tables. The style originated in Japan.

6 *China's earth* China cups.

7 *Scylla* According to Ovid's *Metamorphoses*, Scylla was turned into a seabird by her father, King Nisus, after she cut off his purple lock of hair (on which the kingdom's safety depended) to please her lover, Minos, who was besieging the city.

And thrice they twitched the diamond in her ear;
Thrice she looked back, and thrice the foe drew near.
Just in that instant, anxious Ariel sought
140 The close recesses of the virgin's thought;
As on the nosegay in her breast reclined,
He watched the ideas rising in her mind.
Sudden he viewed, in spite of all her art,
An earthly lover lurking at her heart.
145 Amazed, confused, he found his power expired,
Resigned to fate, and with a sigh retired.
        The Peer now spreads the glittering forfex°   scissors
            wide,
To enclose the lock; now joins it, to divide.
Even then, before the fatal engine closed,
150 A wretched Sylph too fondly interposed;
Fate urged the sheers, and cut the Sylph in twain
(But airy substance soon unites again).
The meeting points the sacred hair dissever
From the fair head, forever and forever!
155   Then flashed the living lightning from her eyes,
And screams of horror rend the affrighted skies.
Not louder shrieks to pitying heaven are cast,
When husbands or when lapdogs breathe their last,
Or when rich china vessels, fallen from high,
160 In glittering dust and painted fragments lie!
        "Let wreaths of triumph now my temples twine,"
The victor cried, "the glorious prize is mine!
While fish in streams, or birds delight in air,
Or in a coach and six the British fair,
165 As long as *Atalantis*[1] shall be read,
Or the small pillow grace a lady's bed,
While visits shall be paid on solemn days,
When numerous wax-lights in bright order blaze,
While nymphs take treats, or assignations give,
170 So long my honour, name, and praise shall live!
        "What time would spare, from steel receives its date,
And monuments, like men, submit to fate!
Steel could the labour of the Gods destroy,
And strike to dust the imperial towers of Troy;
175 Steel could the works of mortal pride confound,
And hew triumphal arches to the ground.

---
[1] *Atalantis* Delarivier Manley's *New Atalantis* was an enormously creative rendering of the latest political scandals and social intrigues, which she recreated as fiction.

What wonder then, fair nymph! thy hairs should feel
The conquering force of unresisted steel?"

CANTO 4

But anxious cares the pensive nymph oppressed,
And secret passions laboured in her breast.
Not youthful kings in battle seized alive,
Not scornful virgins who their charms survive,
5 Not ardent lovers robbed of all their bliss,
Not ancient ladies when refused a kiss,
Not tyrants fierce that unrepenting die,
Not Cynthia when her manteau's pinned awry,
Ever felt such rage, resentment, and despair,
10 As thou, sad virgin! for thy ravished hair.
        For, that sad moment when the sylphs withdrew,
And Ariel weeping from Belinda flew,
Umbriel, a dusky, melancholy sprite
As ever sullied the fair face of light,
15 Down to the central earth, his proper scene,

Repaired to search the gloomy Cave of Spleen.[1]
    Swift on his sooty pinions flits the Gnome,
And in a vapour reached the dismal dome.
No cheerful breeze this sullen region knows,
50 The dreaded east[2] is all the wind that blows.
Here, in a grotto, sheltered close from air,
And screened in shades from day's detested glare,
She sighs forever on her pensive bed,
Pain at her side, and megrim° at her head.   *migraine*
55 Two handmaids wait the throne: alike in place,
But differing far in figure and in face.
Here stood Ill-Nature like an ancient maid,
Her wrinkled form in black and white arrayed;
With store of prayers for mornings, nights, and noons
60 Her hand is filled; her bosom with lampoons.
    There Affectation, with a sickly mien,°   *appearance*
Shows in her cheek the roses of eighteen,
Practised to lisp, and hang the head aside,
Faints into airs, and languishes with pride;
65 On the rich quilt sinks with becoming woe,
Wrapped in a gown, for sickness and for show.
The fair ones feel such maladies as these,
When each new nightdress gives a new disease.
    A constant vapour o'er the palace flies,
70 Strange phantoms rising as the mists arise;
Dreadful as hermit's dreams in haunted shades,
Or bright as visions of expiring maids.
Now glaring fiends and snakes on rolling spires,°   *coils*
Pale spectres, gaping tombs, and purple fires;
75 Now lakes of liquid gold, Elysian scenes,
And crystal domes, and angels in machines.[3]
    Unnumbered throngs on every side are seen
Of bodies changed to various forms by spleen.
Here living teapots stand, one arm held out,
80 One bent; the handle this, and that the spout.
A pipkin° there like Homer's tripod[4] walks;   *small earthen pot*

Here sighs a jar, and there a goose pye[5] talks;
Men prove with child, as powerful fancy works,
And maids turned bottles call aloud for corks.
55 Safe passed the Gnome through this fantastic band,
A branch of healing spleenwort[6] in his hand.
Then thus addressed the power: "Hail, wayward Queen!
Who rule the sex to fifty from fifteen,
Parent of vapors and of female wit,
60 Who give the hysteric or poetic fit,
On various tempers act by various ways,
Make some take physic,° others scribble plays;   *medicine*
Who cause the proud their visits to delay,
And send the godly in a pet,[7] to pray.
65 A nymph there is that all thy power disdains,
And thousands more in equal mirth maintains.
But oh! if e'er thy Gnome could spoil a grace,
Or raise a pimple on a beauteous face,
Like citron-waters[8] matrons' cheeks inflame,
70 Or change complexions at a losing game;
If e'er with airy horns[9] I planted heads,
Or rumpled petticoats, or tumbled beds,
Or caused suspicion when no soul was rude,
Or discomposed the headdress of a prude,
75 Or e'er to costive lapdog gave disease,
Which not the tears of brightest eyes could ease—
Hear me, and touch Belinda with chagrin;
That single act gives half the world the spleen."
    The Goddess with a discontented air
80 Seems to reject him, though she grants his prayer.
A wondrous bag with both her hands she binds,
Like that where once Ulysses held the winds;[10]
There she collects the force of female lungs:

---

1 *Cave of Spleen* The spleen was thought to be the seat of melancholy or morose feelings, and "spleen" became a term used to cover any number of complaints including headaches, depression, irritability, hallucinations, or hypochondria.

2 *dreaded east* An east wind was thought to bring on attacks of spleen (also called "the vapors").

3 *machines* Conveyances, vehicles.

4 *Homer's tripod* In Homer's *Iliad* (Book 18), Vulcan makes three-legged stools that move by themselves.

5 [Pope's note] Alludes to a real fact, a Lady of distinction imagin'd herself in this condition.

6 *spleenwort* Herb said to cure ailments of the spleen. Here it is reminiscent of the golden bough that Aeneas carries for protection on his journey to the underworld (*Aeneid*, Book 6).

7 *pet* Fit of ill-humor.

8 *citron-waters* Lemon-flavored brandy-based liquor.

9 *horns* Sign of a cuckold. The horns here are "airy" because the wife's infidelity is only imagined by her jealous husband.

10 *Ulysses ... winds* In Homer's *Odyssey*, Aeolus, keeper of the winds, gives him a bag filled with all the winds that, if they blew, would hinder his journey home.

Sighs, sobs, and passions, and the war of tongues.
85 A vial next she fills with fainting fears,
Soft sorrows, melting griefs, and flowing tears.
The Gnome rejoicing bears her gifts away,
Spreads his black wings, and slowly mounts to day.
        Sunk in Thalestris'[1] arms the nymph he found,
90 Her eyes dejected and her hair unbound.
Full o'er their heads the swelling bag he rent,
And all the Furies issued at the vent.
Belinda burns with more than mortal ire,
And fierce Thalestris fans the rising fire.
95 "O wretched maid!" she spread her hands, and cried
(While Hampton's echoes, "Wretched maid!" replied),
"Was it for this you took such constant care
The bodkin, comb, and essence to prepare?
For this your locks in paper durance[2] bound,
100 For this with torturing irons wreathed around?
For this with fillets strained your tender head,
And bravely bore the double loads of lead?
Gods! shall the ravisher display your hair,
While the fops envy, and the ladies stare!
105 Honour forbid! at whose unrivaled shrine
Ease, pleasure, virtue, all, our sex resign.
Methinks already I your tears survey,
Already hear the horrid things they say,
Already see you a degraded toast,[3]
110 And all your honour in a whisper lost!
How shall I, then, your helpless fame defend?
'Twill then be infamy to seem your friend!
And shall this prize, the inestimable prize,
Exposed through crystal to the gazing eyes,
115 And heightened by the diamond's circling rays,
On that rapacious hand forever blaze?[4]
Sooner shall grass in Hyde Park Circus[5] grow,
And wits take lodgings in the sound of Bow;[6]
Sooner let earth, air, sea, to chaos fall,
120 Men, monkeys, lapdogs, parrots, perish all!"
        She said; then raging to Sir Plume repairs,
And bids her beau demand the precious hairs
(Sir Plume, of amber snuffbox justly vain,
And the nice conduct of a clouded° cane).   *marbled*
125 With earnest eyes and round unthinking face,
He first the snuffbox opened, then the case,
And thus broke out—"My Lord, why, what the devil?
Z—ds!° damn the lock! 'fore Gad, you must   *zounds*
        be civil!
Plague on't! 'tis past a jest—nay prithee, pox!
130 Give her the hair"—he spoke, and rapped his box.
        "It grieves me much," replied the Peer again,
"Who speaks so well should ever speak in vain.
But by this lock, this sacred lock I swear
(Which never more shall join its parted hair;
135 Which never more its honours shall renew,
Clipped from the lovely head where late it grew)
That while my nostrils draw the vital air,
This hand, which won it, shall forever wear."
He spoke, and, speaking, in proud triumph spread
140 The long-contended honours of her head.
        But Umbriel, hateful Gnome! forbears not so;
He breaks the vial whence the sorrows flow.
Then see! the nymph in beauteous grief appears,
Her eyes half languishing, half drowned in tears;
145 On her heaved bosom hung her drooping head,
Which with a sigh she raised, and thus she said:
        "Forever cursed be this detested day,
Which snatched my best, my favorite curl away!
Happy! ah ten times happy had I been,
150 If Hampton Court these eyes had never seen!
Yet am not I the first mistaken maid
By love of courts to numerous ills betrayed.
Oh, had I rather unadmired remained
In some lone isle, or distant northern land;
155 Where the gilt chariot never marks the way,
Where none learn ombre, none e'er taste bohea![7]
There kept my charms concealed from mortal eye,
Like roses that in deserts bloom and die.

---

[1] *Thalestris* Queen of the Amazons; here, suggesting a fierce, pugnacious woman.

[2] *paper durance* Curling papers, which were fastened to the hair with strips of hot lead. The head was then encircled by a fillet, or thin crown.

[3] *toast* Woman whose health is drunk. Since toasting a woman implied familiarity with her, it was detrimental to a lady's reputation if it was done too frequently, or by too many men.

[4] *Exposed ... blaze* I.e., the Baron will set the hair in a ring.

[5] *Hyde Park Circus* Another name for the Ring road in Hyde Park.

[6] *in the sound of Bow* Within the sound of the church bells of St. Mary-le-Bow in Cheapside, an unfashionable part of town.

[7] *bohea* Expensive Chinese black tea.

What moved my mind with youthful lords to roam?
50   Oh, had I stayed and said my prayers at home!
'Twas this the morning omens seemed to tell;
Thrice from my trembling hand the patch box fell;
The tottering china shook without a wind,
Nay, Poll[1] sat mute, and Shock was most unkind!
55   A Sylph too warned me of the threats of fate,
In mystic visions, now believed too late!
See the poor remnants of these slighted hairs!
My hands shall rend what even thy rapine spares.
These, in two sable ringlets taught to break,
60   Once gave new beauties to the snowy neck.
The sister lock now sits uncouth, alone,
And in its fellow's fate foresees its own;
Uncurled it hangs, the fatal shears demands,
And tempts once more thy sacrilegious hands.
65   Oh, hadst thou, cruel! been content to seize
Hairs less in sight, or any hairs but these!"

CANTO 5

She said; the pitying audience melt in tears,
But Fate and Jove[2] had stopped the Baron's ears.
In vain Thalestris with reproach assails,
For who can move when fair Belinda fails?
5   Not half so fixed the Trojan could remain,
While Anna begged and Dido raged in vain.[3]
Then grave Clarissa[4] graceful waved her fan;
Silence ensued, and thus the nymph began:
    "Say, why are beauties praised and honoured most,
10   The wise man's passion, and the vain man's toast?
Why decked with all that land and sea afford,
Why angels called, and angel-like adored?
Why round our coaches crowd the white-gloved beaux,
Why bows the side box from its inmost rows?

15   How vain are all these glories, all our pains,
Unless good sense preserve what beauty gains;
That men may say, when we the front box grace,
'Behold the first in virtue, as in face!'
Oh! if to dance all night, and dress all day,
20   Charmed the smallpox, or chased old age away,
Who would not scorn what housewife's cares produce,
Or who would learn one earthly thing of use?
To patch, nay ogle, might become a saint,
Nor could it sure be such a sin to paint.
25   But since, alas! frail beauty must decay,
Curled or uncurled, since locks will turn to grey;
Since painted, or not painted, all shall fade,
And she who scorns a man must die a maid;
What then remains but well our power to use,
30   And keep good humour still, whate'er we lose?
And trust me, dear! good humour can prevail,
When airs and flights and screams and scolding fail.
Beauties in vain their pretty eyes may roll;
Charms strike the sight, but merit wins the soul."

---

1   *Poll* Belinda's parrot.

2   *Jove* King of the gods (Roman).

3   *the Trojan ... vain* Commanded by the gods, Aeneas left his
distraught lover, Dido, to found the city of Rome. Dido's sister
Anna begged him to return, but he refused.

4   [Pope's note] A new character introduced in the subsequent
editions to open more clearly the moral of the poem, in a parody of
the speech of Sarpedon to Glaucus in Homer. [Cf. *Iliad* 12, in which
Sarpedon reflects on glory and urges Glaucus to join the attack on
Troy.]

35　　　So spoke the dame, but no applause ensued;[1]
　　Belinda frowned, Thalestris called her prude.
　　"To arms, to arms!" the fierce virago[2] cries,
　　And swift as lightning to the combat flies.
　　All side in parties, and begin the attack;
40　Fans clap, silks rustle, and tough whalebones crack;
　　Heroes' and heroines' shouts confusedly rise,
　　And base and treble voices strike the skies.
　　No common weapons in their hands are found;
　　Like Gods they fight, nor dread a mortal wound.
45　　　So when bold Homer makes the Gods engage,
　　And heavenly breasts with human passions rage;
　　'Gainst Pallas, Mars; Latona, Hermes[3] arms;
　　And all Olympus rings with loud alarms.
　　Jove's thunder roars, heaven trembles all around;
50　Blue Neptune storms, the bellowing deeps resound;
　　Earth shakes her nodding towers, the ground gives way,
　　And the pale ghosts start at the flash of day!
　　　　Triumphant Umbriel on a sconce's[4] height
　　Clapped his glad wings, and sat to view the fight.
55　Propped on their bodkin spears, the sprites survey
　　The growing combat, or assist the fray.
　　　　While through the press enraged Thalestris flies,
　　And scatters deaths around from both her eyes,
　　A beau and witling° perished in the throng—　inferior wit
60　One died in metaphor, and one in song.
　　"O cruel nymph! a living death I bear,"
　　Cried Dapperwit, and sunk beside his chair.
　　A mournful glance Sir Fopling upwards cast,
　　"Those eyes are made so killing"—was his last.
65　Thus on Maeander's flowery margin lies
　　The expiring swan, and as he sings he dies.[5]
　　　　When bold Sir Plume had drawn Clarissa down,

Chloe stepped in, and killed him with a frown;
　　She smiled to see the doughty° hero slain,　　valiant
70　But at her smile the beau revived again.
　　　　Now Jove suspends his golden scales[6] in air,
　　Weighs the men's wits against the lady's hair;
　　The doubtful beam long nods from side to side;
　　At length the wits mount up, the hairs subside.
75　　　See, fierce Belinda on the Baron flies
　　With more than usual lightning in her eyes;
　　Nor feared the chief the unequal fight to try,
　　Who sought no more than on his foe to die.[7]
　　But this bold lord, with manly strength endued,
80　She with one finger and a thumb subdued:
　　Just where the breath of life his nostrils drew,
　　A charge of snuff the wily virgin threw;
　　The Gnomes direct, to every atom just,
　　The pungent grains of titillating dust.
85　Sudden, with starting tears each eye o'erflows,
　　And the high dome re-echoes to his nose.
　　　　"Now meet thy fate," incensed Belinda cried,
　　And drew a deadly bodkin[8] from her side.
　　(The same, his ancient personage to deck,
90　Her great-great-grandsire wore about his neck
　　In three seal rings;[9] which after, melted down,
　　Formed a vast buckle for his widow's gown.
　　Her infant grandame's whistle next it grew,
　　The bells she jingled, and the whistle blew;
95　Then in a bodkin graced her mother's hairs,
　　Which long she wore, and now Belinda wears.)
　　　　"Boast not my fall," he cried, "insulting foe!
　　Thou by some other shalt be laid as low.
　　Nor think to die dejects my lofty mind;
100　All that I dread is leaving you behind!
　　Rather than so, ah let me still survive,
　　And burn in Cupid's flames—but burn alive."
　　　　"Restore the lock!" she cries, and all around,
　　"Restore the lock!" the vaulted roofs rebound.
105　Not fierce Othello in so loud a strain

1　[Pope's note] It is a verse frequently repeated in Homer after any speech, "So spoke ——, and all the heroes applauded."

2　*virago* Female warrior.

3　*Pallas* Athena, goddess of wisdom; *Mars* God of war; *Latona* Mother of Apollo and Diana; goddess of light; *Hermes* Amongst other attributions, god of deceit.

4　*sconce* Wall bracket for holding a candle; also a small fort or earthwork.

5　*Maeander ... dies* River in Phrygia (present-day Turkey). Swans were said to sing before their deaths.

6　*golden scales* Used by the god to weigh the fates of mortals, particularly in battle.

7　*to die* Metaphorically, to experience an orgasm.

8　*bodkin* Here, a sharp hairpin. (A bodkin was formerly also a name for a dagger.)

9　*seal rings* Rings used to imprint the wax that seals an envelope.

Roared for the handkerchief that caused his pain.[1]
But see how oft ambitious aims are crossed,
And chiefs contend 'till all the prize is lost!
The lock, obtained with guilt and kept with pain,
In every place is sought, but sought in vain;
With such a prize no mortal must be blessed,
So Heaven decrees! with Heaven who can contest?

    Some thought it mounted to the lunar sphere,
Since all things lost on earth are treasured there.
There heroes' wits are kept in ponderous vases,
And beaux' in snuffboxes and tweezer cases.
There broken vows and deathbed alms are found,
And lovers' hearts with ends of ribbon bound;
The courtier's promises, and sick man's prayers,
The smiles of harlots, and the tears of heirs,
Cages for gnats, and chains to yoke a flea,
Dried butterflies, and tomes of casuistry.[2]

    But trust the Muse—she saw it upward rise,
Though marked by none but quick poetic eyes
(So Rome's great founder[3] to the heavens withdrew,
To Proculus alone confessed in view);
A sudden star, it shot through liquid° air,   *transparent*
And drew behind a radiant trail of hair.
Not Berenice's[4] locks first rose so bright,
The heavens bespangling with disheveled light.
The Sylphs behold it kindling as it flies,
And, pleased, pursue its progress through the skies.

    This the beau monde shall from the Mall[5] survey,
And hail with music its propitious ray.
This the blessed lover shall for Venus take,

And send up vows from Rosamonda's Lake.[6]
This Partridge[7] soon shall view in cloudless skies
When next he looks through Galileo's eyes;[8]
And hence the egregious wizard shall foredoom
140   The fate of Louis, and the fall of Rome.

    Then cease, bright nymph! to mourn thy ravished hair,
Which adds new glory to the shining sphere!
Not all the tresses that fair head can boast
Shall draw such envy as the lock you lost.
145 For, after all the murders of your eye,
When, after millions slain, yourself shall die;
When those fair suns shall set, as set they must,
And all those tresses shall be laid in dust;
This lock the Muse shall consecrate to fame,
150 And 'midst the stars inscribe Belinda's name!
  —1717 (original, two-canto version published 1712)

Elegy to the Memory of an Unfortunate Lady

What beckoning ghost, along the moonlight shade
    Invites my step, and points to yonder glade?
'Tis she!—but why that bleeding bosom gored,
Why dimly gleams the visionary sword?
5 Oh ever beauteous, ever friendly! tell,
Is it in heaven a crime to love too well?
To bear too tender, or too firm a heart,
To act a lover's or a Roman's part?[9]
Is there no bright reversion[10] in the sky
10 For those who greatly think, or bravely die?

    Why bade ye else, ye powers, her soul aspire
Above the vulgar flight of low desire?
Ambition first sprung from your blest abodes,
The glorious fault of angels and of gods;

---

[1] *fierce Othello ... pain* See Shakespeare's *Othello* 3.4.

[2] *casuistry* The application of general rules of ethics or morality to specific matters of conscience (often through minutely detailed, yet ultimately false or evasive reasoning).

[3] *Rome's great founder* Romulus, who was apparently transported from earth in a storm cloud, never to be seen again except by Proculus, who claimed Romulus came to him in a vision from heaven.

[4] *Berenice* Berenice dedicated a lock of her hair to Aphrodite to ensure her husband's safe return from war. She placed the lock in Aphrodite's temple, but it disappeared the next day, and was reputed to have ascended to the heavens, where it became a new constellation.

[5] *the Mall* Walk in St. James's Park.

[6] *Rosamonda's Lake* Pond in St. James's Park that is associated with unhappy lovers. (According to legend, Rosamond was Henry II's mistress and was murdered by his queen.)

[7] [Pope's note] John Partridge was a ridiculous star-gazer who, in his almanacs every year, never failed to predict the downfall of the Pope, and the King of France, then at war with the English.

[8] *Galileo's eyes* Telescope.

[9] *act a ... Roman's part* Commit suicide.

[10] *reversion* Inheritance.

15 Thence to their images on earth it flows,
And in the breasts of kings and heroes glows!
Most souls, 'tis true, but peep out once an age,
Dull sullen prisoners in the body's cage;
Dim lights of life that burn a length of years,
20 Useless, unseen, as lamps in sepulchres;
Like eastern kings a lazy state they keep,
And close confined to their own palace sleep.
    From these perhaps (ere nature bade her die)
Fate snatched her early to the pitying sky.
25 As into air the purer spirits flow,
And separate from their kindred dregs below,[1]
So flew the soul to its congenial place,
Nor left one virtue to redeem her race.
    But thou, false guardian of a charge too good,
30 Thou, mean deserter of thy brother's blood!
See on these ruby lips the trembling breath,
These cheeks, now fading at the blast of death.
Cold is that breast which warmed the world before,
And those love-darting eyes must roll no more.
35 Thus, if eternal justice rules the ball,[2]
Thus shall your wives, and thus your children fall.
On all the line a sudden vengeance waits,
And frequent hearses shall besiege your gates;
There passengers° shall stand, and pointing say   passers-by
40 (While the long funerals[3] blacken all the way),
"Lo, these were they whose souls the Furies[4] steeled,
And cursed with hearts unknowing how to yield."
Thus unlamented pass the proud away—
The gaze of fools, and pageant of a day!
45 So perish all whose breast ne'er learned to glow
For others' good, or melt at others' woe.
    What can atone (oh ever-injured shade!)
Thy fate unpitied, and thy rites unpaid?

No friend's complaint, no kind domestic tear
50 Pleased thy pale ghost, or graced thy mournful bier.
By foreign hands thy dying eyes were closed;
By foreign hands thy decent limbs composed;
By foreign hands thy humble grave adorned;
By strangers honoured, and by strangers mourned!
55 What though[5] no friends in sable weeds appear,
Grieve for an hour, perhaps, then mourn a year,
And bear about the mockery of woe
To midnight dances, and the public show?
What though no weeping loves° thy ashes grace,   cupids
60 Nor polished marble emulate thy face?
What though no sacred earth allow thee room,
Nor hallowed dirge be muttered o'er thy tomb?[6]
Yet shall thy grave with rising flowers be dressed,
And the green turf lie lightly[7] on thy breast;
65 There shall the morn her earliest tears bestow,
There the first roses of the year shall blow;°   bloom
While angels with their silver wings o'ershade
The ground, now sacred by thy relics° made.   remains
    So peaceful rests, without a stone, a name,
70 What once had beauty, titles, wealth, and fame;
How loved, how honoured once, avails thee not,
To whom related, or by whom begot;
A heap of dust alone remains of thee,
'Tis all thou art, and all the proud shall be!
75   Poets themselves must fall, like those they sung,
Deaf the praised ear, and mute the tuneful tongue.
Even he whose soul now melts in mournful lays
Shall shortly want the generous tear he pays;
Then from his closing eyes thy form shall part,
80 And the last pang shall tear thee from his heart;
Life's idle business at one gasp be o'er,
The muse forgot, and thou beloved no more!
—1717

---

1. *into air … below*   This image of the separation of purer parts from "dregs" is taken from chemistry.

2. *the ball*   Earth, often shown as an orb in the hands of a personified Justice.

3. *funerals*   Funeral processions.

4. *Furies*   Erinyes or Eumenides, the three vengeful goddesses of Greek mythology who pursue and punish those who break natural laws (for example, by killing a family member or committing suicide).

---

5. *What though*   What does it matter if.

6. *What though … tomb*   Those who committed suicide could not be buried in consecrated ground.

7. *turf lie lightly*   From a popular Roman epitaph, "May the earth lie lightly on you" (*Sit tibi terra levis*).

Eloisa To Abelard [1]

THE ARGUMENT

Abelard and Eloisa flourished in the twelfth century; they were two of the most distinguished persons of their age in learning and beauty, but for nothing more famous than for their unfortunate passion. After a long course of calamities, they retired each to a several[2] convent, and consecrated the remainder of their days to religion. It was many years after this separation that a letter of Abelard's to a friend, which contained the history of his misfortunes, fell into the hands of Eloisa. This awakening all her tenderness occasioned those celebrated letters (out of which the following is partly extracted) which give so lively a picture of the struggles of grace and nature, virtue and passion.

In these deep solitudes and awful cells,
Where heavenly-pensive contemplation dwells,
And ever-musing melancholy reigns;
What means this tumult in a vestal's[3] veins?
5 Why rove my thoughts beyond this last retreat?
Why feels my heart its long-forgotten heat?
Yet, yet I love!—From Abelard it[4] came,
And Eloisa yet must kiss the name.
    Dear fatal[5] name! rest ever unrevealed,
10 Nor pass these lips in holy silence sealed.
Hide it, my heart, within that close disguise,

Where, mixed with God's, his loved idea° lies.   *mental image*
O write it not, my hand—the name appears
Already written—wash it out, my tears!
15 In vain lost Eloisa weeps and prays,
Her heart still dictates, and her hand obeys.
    Relentless walls! whose darksome round contains
Repentant sighs, and voluntary pains:
Ye rugged rocks! which holy knees have worn;
20 Ye grots and caverns shagged with horrid° thorn!   *bristling*
Shrines! where their vigils pale-eyed virgins keep,
And pitying saints, whose statues learn to weep![6]
Though cold like you, unmoved, and silent grown,
I have not yet forgot myself to stone.
25 All is not Heaven's while Abelard has part,
Still rebel nature holds out half my heart;
Nor prayers nor fasts its stubborn pulse restrain,
Nor tears, for ages taught to flow in vain.
    Soon as thy letters trembling I unclose,
30 That well-known name awakens all my woes.
Oh name forever sad! forever dear!
Still breathed in sighs, still ushered with a tear.
I tremble too, where'er my own I find,
Some dire misfortune follows close behind.
35 Line after line my gushing eyes o'erflow,
Led through a sad variety of woe:
Now warm in love, now withering in thy bloom,
Lost in a convent's solitary gloom!
There stern religion quenched th' unwilling flame,
40 There died the best of passions, love and fame.[7]
    Yet write, oh write me all, that I may join
Griefs to thy griefs, and echo sighs to thine.
Nor foes nor fortune take this power away;
And is my Abelard less kind than they?
45 Tears still are mine, and those I need not spare,
Love but demands what else were shed in prayer;
No happier task these faded eyes pursue,
To read and weep is all they now can do.
    Then share thy pain, allow that sad relief;
50 Ah, more than share it! Give me all thy grief.
Heaven first taught letters for some wretch's aid,
Some banished lover, or some captive maid;

---

1   *Eloisa To Abelard*   Peter or Pierre Abelard was a French philosopher and theologian who, in 1117, at the age of 38, fell in love with his 17-year-old pupil, Héloise. They became lovers and she gave birth to his child, and the two were secretly married. Héloise's uncle, enraged at Abelard's actions, hired a gang of thugs to attack and castrate him. The two lovers separated, Héloise entering a convent and Abelard a monastery. Both devoted their lives to God and went on to successful careers in the church. Several years later the two exchanged a series of letters in Latin, which were published in 1616. A romanticized French version appeared in 1687, and in 1713 this was translated into English. It was upon the English translation that Pope based his poem.

2   *several*   Separate.

3   *vestal*   In ancient Rome, vestal virgins were those devoted to the service of Vesta, goddess of the hearth, and to the maintenance of her sacred fire. "Vestal" later became synonymous with "virgin" or "nun."

4   *it*   The letter.

5   *fatal*   Name that has determined Eloisa's destiny, or fate.

---

6   *learn to weep*   Stone statues placed in damp places collect condensation, which then runs down their surfaces.

7   *fame*   Good reputation. Abelard's disgrace had ruined his good name and his professional ambitions.

They live, they speak, they breathe what love inspires,
Warm from the soul, and faithful to its fires,
55   The virgin's wish without her fears impart,
Excuse[1] the blush, and pour out all the heart,
Speed the soft intercourse from soul to soul,
And waft a sigh from Indus to the Pole.

Thou know'st how guiltless first I met thy flame,
60   When love approached me under friendship's name;
My fancy formed thee of angelic kind,
Some emanation of th' all-beauteous Mind.[2]
Those smiling eyes, attempering° every ray,   *soothing*
Shone sweetly lambent° with celestial day: *radiant*
65   Guiltless I gazed; heaven listened while you sung;
And truths divine came mended from that tongue.[3]
From lips like those what precept failed to move?
Too soon they taught me 'twas no sin to love.
Back through the paths of pleasing sense I ran,
70   Nor wished an angel whom I loved a man.
Dim and remote the joys of saints I see,
Nor envy them that heaven I lose for thee.

How oft, when pressed to marriage, have I said,
Curse on all laws but those which love has made!
75   Love, free as air, at sight of human ties
Spreads his light wings, and in a moment flies.
Let wealth, let honour, wait the wedded dame,
August her deed, and sacred be her fame;
Before true passion all those views remove,°   *disappear*
80   Fame, wealth, and honour! what are you to love?
The jealous god,[4] when we profane his fires,
Those restless passions in revenge inspires,
And bids them make mistaken mortals groan,
Who seek in love for aught but love alone.
85   Should at my feet the world's great master[5] fall,
Himself, his throne, his world, I'd scorn 'em all:
Not Caesar's empress would I deign to prove;°   *become*
No, make me mistress to the man I love;
If there be yet another name, more free,
90   More fond than mistress, make me that to thee!
Oh happy state! when souls each other draw,

When love is liberty, and nature, law:
All then is full, possessing, and possessed,
No craving void left aching in the breast:
95   Even thought meets thought ere from the lips it part,
And each warm wish springs mutual from the heart.
This sure is bliss (if bliss on earth there be)
And once the lot of Abelard and me.

Alas how changed! What sudden horrors rise!
100   A naked lover bound and bleeding lies!
Where, where was Eloise? Her voice, her hand,
Her poniard,° had opposed the dire command.   *dagger*
Barbarian, stay! that bloody stroke restrain;
The crime was common,° common be the pain.[6]   *shared*
105   I can no more; by shame, by rage suppressed,
Let tears and burning blushes speak the rest.

Canst thou forget that sad, that solemn day,
When victims at yon altar's foot we lay?
Canst thou forget what tears that moment fell,
110   When, warm in youth, I bade the world farewell?
As with cold lips I kissed the sacred veil,
The shrines all trembled, and the lamps grew pale:
Heaven scarce believed the conquest it surveyed,
And saints with wonder heard the vows I made.
115   Yet then, to those dread altars as I drew,
Not on the Cross my eyes were fixed, but you;
Not grace, or zeal, love only was my call,
And if I lose thy love, I lose my all.
Come! with thy looks, thy words, relieve my woe;
120   Those still at least are left thee to bestow.
Still on that breast enamoured let me lie,
Still drink delicious poison from thy eye,
Pant on thy lip, and to thy heart be pressed;
Give all thou canst—and let me dream the rest.
125   Ah no! instruct me other joys to prize,
With other beauties charm my partial eyes,
Full in my view set all the bright abode,
And make my soul quit Abelard for God.

Ah think at least thy flock deserves thy care,
130   Plants of thy hand, and children of thy prayer.
From the false world in early youth they fled,
By thee to mountains, wilds, and deserts led.

---

1   *Excuse*   Remove the need for.

2   *all-beauteous Mind*   God.

3   [Pope's note]   He was her preceptor in philosophy and divinity.

4   *jealous god*   Cupid.

5   *world's greatest master*   Most likely a reference to Alexander the Great.

6   *pain*   Punishment.

You raised these hallowed walls;[1] the desert smiled,
And paradise was opened in the wild.
35 No weeping orphan saw his father's stores
Our shrines irradiate,° or emblaze the floors;   *adorn*
No silver saints, by dying misers given,
Here bribed the rage of ill-requited heaven:
But such plain roofs as piety could raise,
40 And only vocal with the Maker's praise.
In these lone walls (their day's eternal bound)
These moss-grown domes with spiry turrets crowned,
Where awful arches make a noon-day night,
And the dim windows shed a solemn light,
45 Thy eyes diffused a reconciling ray,
And gleams of glory brightened all the day.
But now no face divine contentment wears,
'Tis all blank sadness, or continual tears.
See how the force of others' prayers I try
50 (Oh pious fraud of amorous charity!),
But why should I on others' prayers depend?
Come thou, my father, brother, husband, friend!
Ah let thy handmaid, sister, daughter move,
And, all those tender names in one, thy love!
55 The darksome pines that o'er yon rocks reclined
Wave high, and murmur to the hollow wind,
The wandering streams that shine between the hills,
The grots that echo to the tinkling rills,
The dying gales that pant upon the trees,
60 The lakes that quiver to the curling breeze;
No more these scenes my meditation aid,
Or lull to rest the visionary[2] maid.
But o'er the twilight groves and dusky caves,
Long-sounding isles° and intermingled graves,   *aisles*
65 Black Melancholy sits, and round her throws
A death-like silence, and a dread repose:
Her gloomy presence saddens all the scene,
Shades every flower, and darkens every green,
Deepens the murmur of the falling floods,
70 And breathes a browner horror on the woods.
    Yet here for ever, ever must I stay;
Sad proof how well a lover can obey!

Death, only death, can break the lasting chain;
And here even then, shall my cold dust remain,
175 Here all its frailties, all its flames resign,
And wait 'till 'tis no sin to mix with thine.
    Ah wretch! believed the spouse of God in vain,
Confessed within the slave of love and man.
Assist me heaven! But whence arose that prayer?
180 Sprung it from piety, or from despair?
Even here, where frozen chastity retires,
Love finds an altar for forbidden fires.
I ought to grieve, but cannot what I ought;
I mourn the lover, not lament the fault;
185 I view my crime, but kindle at the view,
Repent old pleasures, and solicit new;
Now turned to heaven, I weep my past offence,
Now think of thee, and curse my innocence.
Of all affliction taught a lover yet,
190 'Tis sure the hardest science[3] to forget!
How shall I lose the sin, yet keep the sense,[4]
And love th' offender, yet detest th' offence?
How the dear object from the crime remove,
Or how distinguish penitence from love?
195 Unequal[5] task! a passion to resign,
For hearts so touched, so pierced, so lost as mine.
Ere such a soul regains its peaceful state,
How often must it love, how often hate!
How often hope, despair, resent, regret,
200 Conceal, disdain—do all things but forget.
But let heaven seize it, all at once 'tis fired,
Not touched, but rapt; not wakened, but inspired!
Oh come! Oh teach me nature to subdue,
Renounce my love, my life, my self—and you.
205 Fill my fond heart with God alone, for He
Alone can rival, can succeed to thee.
    How happy is the blameless vestal's lot!
The world forgetting, by the world forgot.
Eternal sunshine of the spotless mind!
210 Each prayer accepted, and each wish resigned;
Labour and rest, that equal periods keep;
"Obedient slumbers that can wake and weep;"[6]

---

1 *You ... walls* When Abelard became abbot of St. Gildas-de-Rhuys, he gave Paraclete, the hermitage where he had originally established his monastic school, to Héloïse. She and her religious community had recently been evicted from their property. It was shortly after this that the two began their correspondence.

2 *visionary* Dreamy.

3 *science* Kind of knowledge.

4 *sense* Meaning both "sensation" and "faculty of perception."

5 *Unequal* Excessive.

6 *Obedient ... weep* From Richard Crashaw's *Description of a Religious House* (1648).

Desires composed, affections ever even;
Tears that delight, and sighs that waft to heaven.
215 Grace shines around her with serenest beams,
And whispering angels prompt her golden dreams.
For her th' unfading rose of Eden blooms,
And wings of seraphs shed divine perfumes;
For her the Spouse° prepares the bridal ring;[1]   *Christ*
220 For her white virgins hymenaeals° sing;   *wedding hymns*
To sounds of heavenly harps she dies away,
And melts in visions of eternal day.
      Far other dreams my erring soul employ,
Far other raptures, of unholy joy:
225 When at the close of each sad, sorrowing day,
Fancy restores what vengeance snatched away,
Then conscience sleeps, and leaving nature free,
All my loose soul unbounded springs to thee.
O curst, dear horrors of all-conscious° night!   *all-knowing*
230 How glowing guilt exalts° the keen delight!   *heightens, intensifies*
Provoking daemons all restraint remove,
And stir within me every source of love.
I hear thee, view thee, gaze o'er all thy charms,
And round thy phantom glue my clasping arms.
235 I wake—no more I hear, no more I view,
The phantom flies me, as unkind as you.
I call aloud; it hears not what I say;
I stretch my empty arms; it glides away.
To dream once more I close my willing eyes;
240 Ye soft illusions, dear deceits, arise!
Alas, no more!—methinks we wandering go
Through dreary wastes, and weep each other's woe,
Where round some mouldering tower pale ivy creeps,
And low-browed rocks hang nodding o'er the deeps.
245 Sudden you mount! You beckon from the skies;
Clouds interpose, waves roar, and winds arise.
I shriek, start up, the same sad prospect find,
And wake to all the griefs I left behind.
      For thee the fates, severely kind, ordain
250 A cool suspense from pleasure and from pain;
Thy life a long, dead calm of fixed repose;
No pulse that riots, and no blood that glows.
Still as the sea, ere winds were taught to blow,
Or moving spirit bade the waters flow;
255 Soft as the slumbers of a saint forgiven,

And mild as opening gleams of promised heaven.
      Come, Abelard! for what hast thou to dread?
The torch of Venus burns not for the dead.
Nature stands checked; religion disapproves;
260 Even thou art cold—yet Eloisa loves.
Ah hopeless, lasting flames! like those that burn
To light the dead, and warm th' unfruitful urn.[2]
      What scenes appear where'er I turn my view,
The dear ideas, where I fly, pursue,
265 Rise in the grove, before the altar rise,
Stain all my soul, and wanton in my eyes!
I waste the matin lamp[3] in sighs for thee,
Thy image steals between my God and me,
Thy voice I seem in every hymn to hear,
270 With every bead[4] I drop too soft a tear.
When from the censer clouds of fragrance roll,[5]
And swelling organs lift the rising soul,
One thought of thee puts all the pomp to flight,
Priests, tapers, temples, swim before my sight:
275 In seas of flame my plunging soul is drowned,
While altars blaze, and angels tremble round.
      While prostrate here in humble grief I lie,
Kind,° virtuous drops just gathering in my eye,   *natural*
While praying, trembling, in the dust I roll,
280 And dawning grace is opening on my soul:
Come, if thou darest, all charming as thou art!
Oppose thyself to heaven; dispute° my heart;   *contend for*
Come, with one glance of those deluding eyes
Blot out each bright idea of the skies;
285 Take back that grace, those sorrows, and those tears,
Take back my fruitless penitence and prayers,
Snatch me, just mounting, from the blest abode,
Assist the fiends and tear me from my God!
      No, fly me, fly me! far as pole from pole;
290 Rise Alps between us, and whole oceans roll!
Ah come not, write not, think not once of me,
Nor share one pang of all I felt for thee.
Thy oaths I quit,° thy memory resign;   *release you from*
Forget, renounce me, hate whate'er was mine.

---

1 *bridal ring* Certain orders of nuns wear a wedding ring to symbolize their marriage to Christ.

2 *like those … urn* The ancient Romans kept lamps perpetually burning in their tombs.

3 *matin lamp* Light used for the dawn service.

4 *bead* I.e., rosary bead.

5 *censer … fragrance roll* Incense was burned and its smoke diffused by the swinging of a container called a censer.

Fair eyes, and tempting looks (which yet I view!)
Long loved, adored ideas! all adieu!
O grace serene! oh virtue heavenly fair!
Divine oblivion of low-thoughted care!
Fresh blooming hope, gay daughter of the sky!
And faith, our early immortality![1]
Enter, each mild, each amicable guest!
Receive, and wrap me in eternal rest!

See in her cell sad Eloisa spread,
Propped on some tomb, a neighbour of the dead!
In each low wind methinks a spirit calls,
And more than echoes talk along the walls.
Here, as I watched the dying lamps around,
From yonder shrine I heard a hollow sound.
"Come, sister, come! (it said, or seemed to say)
Thy place is here, sad sister, come away!
Once like thyself, I trembled, wept, and prayed,
Love's victim then, though now a sainted maid:
But all is calm in this eternal sleep;
Here grief forgets to groan, and love to weep,
Even superstition loses every fear:
For God, not man, absolves our frailties here."

I come, I come! Prepare your roseate bowers,
Celestial palms, and ever-blooming flowers.
Thither, where sinners may have rest, I go,
Where flames refined in breasts seraphic glow.
Thou, Abelard, the last sad office[2] pay,
And smooth my passage to the realms of day;
See my lips tremble, and my eyeballs roll,
Suck my last breath, and catch my flying soul![3]
Ah no—in sacred vestments may'st thou stand,
The hallowed taper trembling in thy hand,
Present the Cross before my lifted eye,
Teach me at once, and learn of° me to die.   *from*
Ah then, thy once-loved Eloisa see!
It will be then no crime to gaze on me.
See from my cheek the transient roses fly!
See the last sparkle languish in my eye!
Till every motion, pulse, and breath, be o'er;
And even my Abelard be loved no more.

O death all-eloquent! you only prove
What dust we doat on, when 'tis man we love.
Then too, when fate shall thy fair frame destroy,
(That cause of all my guilt, and all my joy)
In trance ecstatic may thy pangs be drowned,
Bright clouds descend, and angels watch thee round,
From opening skies may streaming glories shine,
And saints embrace thee with a love like mine.

May one kind grave unite each hapless name,[4]
And graft my love immortal on thy fame!
Then, ages hence, when all my woes are o'er,
When this rebellious heart shall beat no more;
If ever chance two wandering lovers brings
To Paraclete's white walls and silver springs,
O'er the pale marble shall they join their heads,
And drink the falling tears each other sheds;
Then sadly say, with mutual pity moved,
"Oh may we never love as these have loved!"
From the full choir when loud Hosannas[5] rise,
And swell the pomp of dreadful sacrifice,[6]
Amid that scene, if some relenting eye
Glance on the stone where our cold relics lie,
Devotion's self shall steal a thought from heaven,
One human tear shall drop, and be forgiven.
And sure if fate some future bard shall join
In sad similitude of griefs to mine,
Condemned whole years in absence to deplore,°   *mourn*
And image charms he must behold no more;
Such if there be, who loves so long, so well,
Let him our sad, our tender story tell;[7]
The well-sung woes will sooth my pensive ghost;
He best can paint 'em, who shall feel 'em most.
—1717

---

[1] *faith ... immortality* I.e., faith in an afterlife provides the first experience of immortality.

[2] *last sad office* Last rites.

[3] *Suck ... soul* It was commonly believed that at the time of death the soul left the body through the mouth.

---

[4] [Pope's note] Abelard and Eloisa were interred in the same grave, or in monuments adjoining, in the monastery of the Paraclete. He died in the year 1142, she in 1163.

[5] *Hosannas* Exclamations of praise.

[6] *dreadful sacrifice* Term for the celebration of the Eucharist (mass), in which Christ's sacrifice is reenacted.

[7] *future bard ... tell* Pope is referring to himself. Though these lines are not confession or autobiographical fact, he probably hints at his feelings for Lady Mary Wortley Montagu, who was in Turkey with her husband at the time. This was well before Pope's fascination with her had turned to enmity.

from *An Essay on Man*

THE DESIGN

Having proposed to write some pieces on Human Life and Manners, such as, to use my Lord Bacon's expression, "come home to men's business and bosoms," I thought it more satisfactory to begin with considering Man in the abstract, his nature and his state: since to prove any moral duty, to enforce any moral precept, or to examine the perfection or imperfection of any creature whatsoever, it is necessary first to know what condition and relation it is placed in, and what is the proper end and purpose of its being.

The science of Human Nature is, like all other sciences, reduced to a few clear points: there are not many certain truths in this world. It is therefore in the anatomy of the mind, as in that of the body; more good will accrue to mankind by attending to the large, open, and perceptible parts, than by studying too much such finer nerves and vessels, the conformations and uses of which will for ever escape our observation. The disputes are all upon these last; and, I will venture to say, they have less sharpened the wits than the hearts of men against each other, and have diminished the practice more than advanced the theory of morality. If I could flatter myself that this Essay has any merit, it is in steering betwixt the extremes of doctrines seemingly opposite, in passing over terms utterly unintelligible and in forming a temperate, yet not inconsistent, and a short, yet not imperfect, system of ethics.

This I might have done in prose; but I chose verse, and even rhyme, for two reasons. The one will appear obvious; that principles, maxims, or precepts, so written, both strike the reader more strongly at first, and are more easily retained by him afterwards: the other may seem odd, but it is true: I found I could express them more shortly this way than in prose itself; and nothing is more certain than that much of the force as well as grace of arguments or instructions depends on their conciseness. I was unable to treat this part of my subject more in detail without becoming dry and tedious; or more poetically without sacrificing perspicuity to ornament, without wandering from the precision, or breaking the chain of reasoning. If any man can unite all these without diminution of any of them, I freely confess he will compass a thing above my capacity.

What is now published is only to be considered as a general Map of Man, marking out no more than the greater parts, their extent, their limits, and their connection, but leaving the particular to be more fully delineated in the charts which are to follow; consequently these epistles in their progress (if I have health and leisure to make any progress) will be less dry, and more susceptible of poetical ornament. I am here only opening the fountains, and clearing the passage: to deduce the rivers, to follow them in their course, and to observe their effects, may be a task more agreeable.

EPISTLE I

Awake, my St. John![1] leave all meaner things
To low ambition, and the pride of kings.
Let us (since life can little more supply
Than just to look about us and to die)
5 Expatiate[2] free o'er all this scene of man;
A mighty maze! but not without a plan;
A wild, where weeds and flowers promiscuous shoot,
Or garden, tempting with forbidden fruit.
Together let us beat[3] this ample field,
10 Try what the open, what the covert[4] yield;
The latent tracts, the giddy heights, explore
Of all who blindly creep, or sightless soar;
Eye Nature's walks, shoot Folly as it flies,

---

[1] *St. John* Henry St. John, Lord Bolingbroke, to whom Pope addressed all four epistles of the *Essay on Man*. Bolingbroke served as Secretary of State under the Tory administration of 1710–14, but fled to France in order to avoid being charged with treason when George I ascended the throne. He was pardoned in 1723 and returned to England, where he involved himself in the opposition to Robert Walpole's Whig government and continued his philosophical writing.

[2] *Expatiate* Meaning both to speak at length and to wander.

[3] *beat* Hunting term, meaning to flush game out from fields.

[4] *covert* Thick brush that could provide shelter to game.

And catch the Manners living as they rise;
Laugh where we must, be candid° where we can,   *generous*
But vindicate the ways of God to man.

Say first, of God above or man below,
What can we reason, but from what we know?
Of man, what see we but his station here,
From which to reason, or to which refer?
Through worlds unnumbered though the God be known,
'Tis ours to trace him only in our own.
He, who through vast immensity can pierce,
See worlds on worlds compose one universe,
Observe how system° into system runs,   *solar system*
What other planets circle other suns,
What varied being peoples every star,
May tell why Heaven has made us as we are.
But of this frame the bearings, and the ties,
The strong connections, nice dependencies,
Gradations just, has thy pervading soul
Looked through? or can a part contain the whole?

Is the great chain—that draws all to agree
And, drawn, supports°—upheld by God, or thee?   *sustains*

Presumptuous man! the reason wouldst thou find
Why formed so weak, so little, and so blind!
First, if thou canst, the harder reason guess,
Why formed no weaker, blinder, and no less!
Ask of thy mother earth why oaks are made
Taller or stronger than the weeds they shade?
Or ask of yonder argent fields above°   *night sky*
Why Jove's satellites[1] are less than Jove?

Of systems possible, if 'tis confessed
That wisdom infinite must form the best,
Where all must full, or not coherent, be,[2]
And all that rises, rise in due degree;
Then, in the scale of reasoning life, 'tis plain
There must be, somewhere, such a rank[3] as man,
And all the question (wrangle e'er so long)
Is only this, if God has placed him wrong?

Respecting man, whatever wrong we call,
May, must be right, as relative to all.
In human works, though laboured on with pain,
A thousand movements scarce one purpose gain;
In God's, one single can its end produce,
Yet serves to second too some other use.
So man, who here seems principal alone,
Perhaps acts second to some sphere unknown,
Touches some wheel, or verges to some goal;
'Tis but a part we see, and not a whole.

When the proud steed shall know why man restrains
His fiery course, or drives him o'er the plains;
When the dull ox, why now he breaks the clod,
Is now a victim, and now Egypt's god:[4]
Then shall man's pride and dullness comprehend
His actions', passions', being's use and end;
Why doing, suffering, checked, impelled; and why
This hour a slave, the next a deity.

Then say not man's imperfect, Heaven in fault;
Say rather, man's as perfect as he ought;
His knowledge measured to his state and place,
His time a moment, and a point his space.
If to be perfect in a certain sphere,
What matter soon or late, or here or there?
The blest today is as completely so
As who began a thousand years ago.

Heaven from all creatures hides the book of Fate,
All but the page prescribed, their present state;
From brutes what men, from men what spirits know,
Or who could suffer being here below?
The lamb thy riot° dooms to bleed today,   *extravagance*
Had he thy reason, would he skip and play?
Pleased to the last, he crops the flowery food,
And licks the hand just raised to shed his blood.
Oh, blindness to the future! kindly given,
That each may fill the circle marked by Heaven;
Who sees with equal eye, as God of all,
A hero perish or a sparrow fall,
Atoms or systems into ruin hurled,

---

[1] *Jove's satellites* Jupiter's moons. The last "e" in "satellites" is here pronounced, making this a four-syllable word. (Pope uses the Latin pronunciation.)

[2] *Where . . . be* The Great Chain of Being cannot contain any gaps; each level must be filled.

[3] *such a rank* I.e., one made up of rational animals.

[4] *Egypt's god* The Egyptians worshiped Apis, the sacred bull of Memphis, as a god.

90 And now a bubble burst, and now a world.
    Hope humbly then; with trembling pinions°   *wings*
      soar;
Wait the great teacher, Death, and God adore!
What future bliss, he gives not thee to know,
But gives that hope to be thy blessing now.
95 Hope springs eternal in the human breast:
Man never is, but always to be blest:
The soul, uneasy and confined from home,[1]
Rests and expatiates° in a life to come.   *roams*
Lo! the poor Indian, whose untutored mind
100 Sees God in clouds, or hears him in the wind;
His soul proud science never taught to stray
Far as the solar walk, or Milky Way;
Yet simple Nature to his hope has given,
Behind the cloud-topped hill, an humbler heaven;
105 Some safer world in depth of woods embraced,
Some happier island in the watery waste,
Where slaves once more their native land behold,
No fiends torment, no Christians thirst for gold!
To be, contents his natural desire,
110 He asks no angel's wing, no seraph's fire;
But thinks, admitted to that equal° sky,   *egalitarian*
His faithful dog shall bear him company.

    Go, wiser thou! and in thy scale of sense
Weigh thy opinion against Providence;
115 Call imperfection what thou fancy'st such,
Say, here he gives too little, there too much;
Destroy all creatures for thy sport or gust,°   *taste*
Yet cry, if man's unhappy, God's unjust;
If man alone engross not Heaven's high care,
120 Alone made perfect here, immortal there:
Snatch from his hand the balance[2] and the rod,
Rejudge his justice, be the God of God!
    In pride, in reasoning pride, our error lies;
All quit their sphere and rush into the skies.
125 Pride still is aiming at the blest abodes,
Men would be angels, angels would be gods.
Aspiring to be gods, if angels fell,
Aspiring to be angels, men rebel;

And who but wishes to invert the laws
130 Of order, sins against the Eternal Cause.

    Ask for what end the heavenly bodies shine;
Earth for whose use? Pride answers, "'Tis for mine.
For me kind Nature wakes her genial° power,   *generative*
Suckles each herb, and spreads out every flower;
135 Annual, for me the grape, the rose renew
The juice nectareous, and the balmy dew;
For me the mine a thousand treasures brings;
For me health gushes from a thousand springs;
Seas roll to waft me, suns to light me rise;
140 My footstool earth, my canopy[3] the skies."
    But errs not Nature from this gracious end,
From burning suns when livid deaths descend,[4]
When earthquakes swallow, or when tempests sweep
Towns to one grave, whole nations to the deep?
145 "No," 'tis replied, "the first Almighty cause
Acts not by partial, but by general laws;
The exceptions few; some change since all began,
And what created perfect?"—Why then man?
If the great end be human happiness,
150 Then Nature deviates; and can man do less?
As much that end a constant course requires
Of showers and sunshine, as of man's desires;
As much eternal springs and cloudless skies
As men forever temperate, calm, and wise.
155 If plagues or earthquakes break not Heaven's design,
Why then a Borgia or a Catiline?[5]
Who knows but he whose hand the lightning forms,
Who heaves old ocean, and who wings the storms,
Pours fierce ambition in a Caesar's mind,
160 Or turns young Ammon[6] loose to scourge mankind?
From pride, from pride our very reasoning springs;
Account for moral as for natural things:

---

[1] *from home* I.e., away from its heavenly home.

[2] *balance* Scales of justice.

[3] *canopy* Covering suspended above a throne.

[4] *From … descend* Incidences of pestilence and fever increased during the hottest months.

[5] *Borgia* The Borgias were a Renaissance Italian family notorious for the cruelty of their crimes; *Cataline* Lucius Sergius Cataline, the greedy Roman conspirator who was publicly denounced by Cicero for plotting against the republic.

[6] *Ammon* Alexander the Great.

Why charge we Heaven in those, in these[1] acquit?
In both, to reason right is to submit.
55   Better for us, perhaps it might appear,
Were there[2] all harmony, all virtue here;
That never air or ocean felt the wind;
That never passion discomposed the mind:
But ALL subsists by elemental strife,
70 And passions are the elements of life.
The general order, since the whole began,
Is kept in Nature, and is kept in man.

     What would this man? Now upward will he soar,
And, little less than angel, would be more;
75 Now looking downwards, just as grieved appears
To want the strength of bulls, the fur of bears.
Made for his use all creatures if he call,
Say what their use, had he the powers of all?
Nature to these, without profusion kind,
80 The proper organs, proper powers assigned;
Each seeming want compensated of course,[3]
Here with degrees of swiftness, there of force;[4]
All in exact proportion to the state;
Nothing to add, and nothing to abate.
5 Each beast, each insect, happy in its own;
Is Heaven unkind to man, and man alone?
Shall he alone, whom rational we call,
Be pleased with nothing, if not blest with all?
     The bliss of man (could pride that blessing find)
0 Is not to act or think beyond mankind;
No powers of body or of soul to share,
But what his nature and his state can bear.
Why has not man a microscopic eye?
For this plain reason, man is not a fly.
5 Say what the use, were finer optics given,
To inspect a mite, not comprehend the heaven?
Or touch, if tremblingly alive all o'er,
To smart and agonize at every pore?

Or quick effluvia[5] darting through the brain,
200 Die of a rose in aromatic pain?
If nature thundered in his opening ears,
And stunned him with the music of the spheres,[6]
How would he wish that Heaven had left him still
The whispering zephyr,° and the purling rill?   *breeze*
205 Who finds not Providence all good and wise,
Alike in what it gives, and what denies?

     Far as creation's ample range extends,
The scale of sensual, mental powers ascends:
Mark how it mounts to man's imperial race
210 From the green myriads in the peopled grass:
What modes of sight betwixt each wide extreme,
The mole's dim curtain, and the lynx's beam:[7]
Of smell, the headlong lioness between,
And hound sagacious on the tainted[8] green:
215 Of hearing, from the life that fills the flood
To that which warbles through the vernal wood:
The spider's touch, how exquisitely fine!
Feels at each thread, and lives along the line:
In the nice° bee, what sense so subtly true   *precise*
220 From poisonous herbs extracts the healing dew:[9]
How instinct varies in the groveling swine
Compared, half-reasoning elephant, with thine:
'Twixt that and reason, what a nice barrier;
Forever separate, yet forever near!
225 Remembrance and reflection how allied;
What thin partitions sense from thought divide:
And middle natures, how they long to join,
Yet never pass the insuperable line!
Without this just gradation, could they be
230 Subjected these to those, or all to thee?
The powers of all subdued by thee alone,
Is not thy reason all these powers in one?

---

[1]   *in those* The former; *in these* The latter.

[2]   *there* I.e., in the natural realm (whereas "here" indicates the moral realm of man).

[3]   *of course* Naturally; as a matter of course.

[4]   *Here ... force* [Pope's note] It is a certain axiom in the anatomy of creatures, that in proportion as they are formed for strength, their swiftness is lessened; or as they are formed for swiftness, their strength is lessened.

---

[5]   *effluvia* Sensory perceptions were thought to result from "effluvia," minuscule particles which bombarded the pores in streams.

[6]   *music of the spheres* Music believed to be made by the planets which only angels could hear.

[7]   *mole's ... beam* A popular theory of the time held that sight depended upon beams of light emitted from the eye.

[8]   *sagacious* Possessing an acute sense of smell; *tainted* I.e., with the scent of the hunted animal.

[9]   *healing dew* Honey, which was often used for medicinal purposes.

See, through this air, this ocean, and this earth,
All matter quick,[1] and bursting into birth.
235 Above, how high progressive life may go!
Around, how wide! how deep extend below!
Vast Chain of Being, which from God began,
Natures ethereal, human, angel, man,
Beast, bird, fish, insect, what no eye can see,
240 No glass[2] can reach! from infinite to thee,
From thee to nothing!—On superior powers
Were we to press, inferior might on ours:
Or in the full creation leave a void,
Where, one step broken, the great scale's destroyed:
245 From Nature's chain whatever link you strike,
Tenth or ten thousandth, breaks the chain alike.
      And if each system in gradation roll,
Alike essential to the amazing whole,
The least confusion but in one, not all
250 That system only, but the whole, must fall.
Let earth unbalanced from her orbit fly,
Planets and suns run lawless through the sky;
Let ruling angels from their spheres be hurled,
Being on being wrecked, and world on world,
255 Heaven's whole foundations to their centre nod,
And Nature tremble to the throne of God:
All this dread order break—for whom? for thee?
Vile worm!—oh, madness, pride, impiety!

      What if the foot, ordained the dust to tread,
260 Or hand to toil, aspired to be the head?
What if the head, the eye, or ear repined
To serve mere engines° to the ruling mind?   *instruments*
Just as absurd for any part to claim
To be another, in this general frame:
265 Just as absurd to mourn the tasks or pains
The great directing Mind of All ordains.
      All are but parts of one stupendous whole,
Whose body Nature is, and God the soul;
That, changed through all, and yet in all the same,
270 Great in the earth, as in the ethereal frame,
Warms in the sun, refreshes in the breeze,
Glows in the stars, and blossoms in the trees;
Lives through all life, extends through all extent,

Spreads undivided, operates unspent,
275 Breathes in our soul, informs our mortal part,
As full, as perfect in a hair as heart;
As full, as perfect in vile man that mourns,
As the rapt seraph that adores and burns;[3]
To him no high, no low, no great, no small;
280 He fills, he bounds, connects, and equals° all.   *makes equal*

      Cease then, nor ORDER imperfection name;
Our proper bliss depends on what we blame.
Know thy own point: this kind, this due degree
Of blindness, weakness, Heaven bestows on thee.
285 Submit—in this, or any other sphere,
Secure to be as blest as thou canst bear:
Safe in the hand of one disposing power,
Or in the natal, or the mortal hour.[4]
All Nature is but art unknown to thee;
290 All chance, direction which thou canst not see;
All discord, harmony not understood;
All partial evil, universal good:
And, spite of pride, in erring reason's spite,
One truth is clear: Whatever IS, is RIGHT.

EPISTLE 2

Know then thyself, presume not God to scan;°   *judge*
   The proper study of mankind is man.
Placed on this isthmus of a middle state,
A being darkly wise, and rudely great:
5 With too much knowledge for the skeptic side,
With too much weakness for the Stoic's pride,
He hangs between; in doubt to act or rest,
In doubt to deem himself a God or beast,
In doubt his mind or body to prefer,
10 Born but to die, and reasoning but to err;
Alike in ignorance, his reason such,
Whether he thinks too little, or too much:
Chaos of thought and passion, all confused;
Still by himself abused, or disabused;
15 Created half to rise, and half to fall;

---

1 *quick* Stirring with life.

2 *glass* Telescope or microscope.

3 *burns* With holy love. Seraphs, the highest of the nine orders of angels, were generally depicted in flame. Their name comes from the root of a Greek word meaning "to burn."

4 *mortal hour* Hour of death.

Great lord of all things, yet a prey to all;
Sole judge of truth, in endless error hurled:
The glory, jest, and riddle of the world!
    Go, wonderous creature! Mount where science guides;
Go, measure earth, weigh air, and state the tides;
Instruct the planets in what orbs to run,
Correct old time, and regulate the sun;
Go, soar with Plato to the empyreal sphere,[1]
To the first good, first perfect, and first fair;
Or tread the mazy° round his followers trod,   *labyrinthine*
And quitting sense[2] call imitating God;
As Eastern priests in giddy circles run,[3]
And turn their heads to imitate the sun.
Go teach eternal wisdom how to rule—
Then drop into thyself, and be a fool!
    Superior beings, when of late they saw
A mortal man unfold all Nature's law,
Admired such wisdom in an earthly shape,
And showed a Newton[4] as we show an ape.
    Could he, whose rules the rapid comet bind,
Describe or fix one movement of his mind?
Who saw its fires here rise, and there descend,
Explain his own beginning, or his end?
Alas, what wonder! Man's superior part
Unchecked may rise, and climb from art to art,
But when his own great work is but begun,
What reason weaves, by passion is undone.
    Trace science, then, with modesty thy guide;
First strip off all her equipage of pride,
Deduct what is but vanity, or dress,
Or learning's luxury, or idleness,
Or tricks to show the stretch of human brain,
Mere curious pleasure, or ingenious pain;
Expunge the whole, or lop th' excrescent parts
Of all, our vices have created arts.

Then see how little the remaining sum,
Which served the past, and must the times to come!

    Two principles in human nature reign:
Self-love, to urge, and reason, to restrain;
Nor this a good, nor that a bad we call,
Each works its end, to move or govern all;
And to their proper operation still
Ascribe all good; to their improper, ill.
    Self-love, the spring of motion, acts° the soul;   *activates*
Reason's comparing balance rules the whole.
Man, but for that, no action could attend,
And, but for this, were active to no end:
Fixed like a plant on his peculiar° spot,   *particular*
To draw nutrition, propagate, and rot;
Or, meteor-like, flame lawless through the void,
Destroying others, by himself destroyed.
    Most strength the moving principle requires;
Active its task, it prompts, impels, inspires.
Sedate and quiet the comparing lies,
Formed but to check, deliberate, and advise.
Self-love still stronger, as its objects nigh;
Reason's at distance, and in prospect lie.
That sees immediate good by present sense;
Reason, the future and the consequence.
Thicker than arguments, temptations throng,
At best more watchful this, but that more strong.
The action of the stronger to suspend
Reason still use, to reason still attend:
Attention, habit and experience gains,
Each strengthens reason, and self-love restrains.
    Let subtle schoolmen[5] teach these friends to fight,
More studious to divide than to unite,
And grace and virtue, sense and reason split,
With all the rash dexterity of wit:
Wits, just like fools, at war about a name,
Have full as oft no meaning, or the same.
Self-love and reason to one end aspire,
Pain their aversion, pleasure their desire;
But greedy that its object would devour,
This, taste the honey, and not wound the flow'r:

---

[1] *empyreal sphere* Highest heavens.

[2] *quitting sense* Leaving the body, as in a trance, with a pun on abandoning good sense.

[3] *priests ... run* Reference to dervishes, Muslim friars of various orders, some of which are known for their fantastic practices, such as whirling (hence the term "whirling dervish").

[4] *Newton* Physicist and mathematician Sir Isaac Newton (1642-1727).

[5] *schoolmen* Experts in formal logic and theology, particularly as taught in universities.

Pleasure, or wrong or rightly understood,
Our greatest evil or our greatest good.

    Modes of self-love the passions we may call;
'Tis real good, or seeming, moves them all;
95 But since not every good we can divide,°   *share*
And reason bids us for our own provide,
Passions, though selfish, if their means be fair,
List° under reason, and deserve her care;   *enlist*
Those, that imparted,[1] court a nobler aim,
100 Exalt their kind, and take some virtue's name.
    In lazy apathy let Stoics boast
Their virtue fixed; 'tis fixed as in a frost—
Contracted all, retiring to the breast;
But strength of mind is exercise, not rest:
105 The rising tempest puts in act the soul,
Parts it may ravage, but preserves the whole.
On life's vast ocean diversely we sail,
Reason the card,° but passion is the gale; *mariner's chart*
Nor God alone in the still calm we find,
110 He mounts the storm, and walks upon the wind.
    Passions, like elements, though born to fight,
Yet mixed and softened, in his° work unite:[2]   *God's*
These 'tis enough to temper and employ;
But what composes man, can man destroy?
115 Suffice that reason keep to Nature's road,
Subject, compound them, follow her and God.
Love, Hope, and Joy, fair pleasure's smiling train,
Hate, Fear, and Grief, the family of pain;
These, mixed with art, and to due bounds confined,
120 Make and maintain the balance of the mind—
The lights and shades, whose well accorded strife
Gives all the strength and colour of our life.
    Pleasures are ever in our hands or eyes,
And when in act they cease, in prospect rise;
125 Present to grasp, and future still to find,

The whole employ of body and of mind.
All spread their charms, but charm not all alike;
On different senses different objects strike;
Hence different passions more or less inflame,
130 As strong or weak, the organs of the frame;[3]
And hence one master passion in the breast,
Like Aaron's serpent,[4] swallows up the rest.
    As man, perhaps, the moment of his breath,
Receives the lurking principle of death;
135 The young disease, that must subdue at length,
Grows with his growth, and strengthens with his strength:[5]
So, cast and mingled with his very frame,
The mind's disease, its ruling passion, came;
Each vital humour, which should feed the whole,
140 Soon flows to this in body and in soul.
Whatever warms the heart or fills the head,
As the mind opens, and its functions spread,
Imagination plies her dangerous art,
And pours it all upon the peccant[6] part.
145   Nature its mother, habit is its nurse;
Wit, spirit, faculties but make it worse;
Reason itself but gives it edge and power,
As Heaven's blest beam turns vinegar more sour.
We, wretched subjects though to lawful sway
150 In this weak queen,[7] some favorite still obey.
Ah! if she lend not arms, as well as rules,
What can she more than tell us we are fools?
Teach us to mourn our nature, not to mend,
A sharp accuser, but a helpless° friend!   *unhelpful*
155 Or from a judge turn pleader, to persuade
The choice we make, or justify it made;
Proud of an easy conquest all along,
She but removes weak passions for the strong:

---

1. *Those, that imparted* I.e., the passions, when imbued with reason.

2. *Passions ... unite* The four elements of the universe (earth, air, fire, and water) had been traditionally believed to correspond to four humors (melancholy, blood, choler, and phlegm), of which, in different proportions, all human constitutions were thought to be formed. By the eighteenth century these notions were no longer taken as literal truth, but they retained their currency as metaphors.

3. *Hence ... frame* Different passions were thought to reside in and dominate different organs of the body.

4. *Aaron's serpent* Exodus 7.10–12 relates the story of Aaron, who cast down his rod before the Pharaoh and turned it into a snake. The Egyptian magicians did the same, but Aaron's serpent devoured theirs.

5. *As man ... strength* It was believed that the origin of some diseases was communicated to the foetus in the womb.

6. *peccant* Diseased.

7. *weak queen* Reason.

So, when small humors gather to a gout,[1]
50   The doctor fancies he has driven them out.
        Yes, Nature's road must ever be preferred;
Reason is here no guide, but still a guard:
'Tis hers to rectify, not overthrow,
And treat this passion more as friend than foe.
55   A mightier power the strong direction sends,
And several men impels to several ends;
Like varying winds, by other passions tossed,[2]
This drives them constant to a certain coast.
Let power or knowledge, gold or glory, please,
70   Or (oft more strong than all) the love of ease;
Through life 'tis followed, even at life's expense;
The merchant's toil, the sage's indolence,
The monk's humility, the hero's pride,
All, all alike, find reason on their side.
75   The eternal art,[3] educing good from ill,
Grafts on this passion our best principle.
'Tis thus the mercury of man is fixed:
Strong grows the virtue with his nature mixed;
The dross° cements what else were too refined,   *impurity*
80   And in one interest body acts with mind.
        As fruits ungrateful° to the planter's care   *unresponsive*
On savage stocks inserted learn to bear,[4]
The surest virtues thus from passions shoot,
Wild nature's vigor working at the root.
85   What crops of wit and honesty appear
From spleen, from obstinacy, hate, or fear!
See anger zeal and fortitude supply;
Even avarice, prudence; sloth, philosophy;
Lust, through some certain strainers well refined,
90   Is gentle love, and charms all womankind;
Envy, to which the ignoble mind's a slave,
Is emulation in the learned or brave;

Nor virtue, male or female, can we name,
But what will grow on pride, or grow on shame.
195   Thus Nature gives us (let it check our pride)
The virtue nearest to our vice allied;
Reason the bias turns to good from ill,
And Nero reigns a Titus,[5] if he will.
The fiery soul abhorred in Catiline,
200 In Decius charms, in Curtius[6] is divine.
The same ambition can destroy or save,
And make a patriot as it makes a knave.

        This light and darkness, in our chaos joined,
What shall divide? The God within the mind.[7]
205   Extremes in nature equal ends produce,
In man they join to some mysterious use;
Though each by turns the other's bound invade,
As, in some well-wrought picture, light and shade,
And oft so mix, the difference is too nice°   *subtle*
210 Where ends the virtue, or begins the vice.
        Fools! who from hence into the notion fall
That vice or virtue there is none at all.
If white and black blend, soften, and unite
A thousand ways, is there no black or white?
215 Ask your own heart, and nothing is so plain;
'Tis to mistake them costs the time and pain.

        Vice is a monster of so frightful mien,
As, to be hated, needs but to be seen;
Yet seen too oft, familiar with her face,
220 We first endure, then pity, then embrace;
But where the extreme of vice, was ne'er agreed.

---

[1] *gout* Thought to result from the body's attempt to rid itself of a redundancy of humors.

[2] *A mightier … tossed* I.e., God (the "mightier power") ensures that there are people of various temperaments and inclinations to carry out the assorted tasks necessary to the world's work.

[3] *eternal art* Providence.

[4] *fruits … bear* Grafts inserted in the stem of a wild plant.

[5] *Nero* Emperor of Rome who ordered his mother and sister murdered, and whose notorious cruelty and debauchery caused several revolts among his people, eventually leading him to commit suicide; *Titus* Celebrated as one of the most benevolent Roman emperors, he did much to alleviate the suffering and increase the happiness of his people. He is perhaps best known for the construction of the Roman Colosseum.

[6] *Decius* Roman consul who died defending his army against the Goths; *Curtius* According to Livy, in 445 BCE lightning struck near the Roman Forum, creating a large chasm. After an oracle claimed that the hole could be closed by Rome's most precious possession, Marcus Curtius jumped into it, wearing full armor and riding a fine horse. The chasm closed immediately.

[7] *This light … mind* Cf. Genesis 1.4.

Ask, "Where's the North?" At York, 'tis on the Tweed;[1]
In Scotland, at the Orcades;° and there,   *Orkney Islands*
At Greenland, Zembla,[2] or the Lord knows where:
225 No creature owns° it in the first degree,   *admits to*
But thinks his neighbour farther gone than he—
Even those who dwell beneath its very zone,
Or° never feel the rage, or° never own.   *either / or*
What happier natures shrink at with affright,
230 The hard[3] inhabitant contends is right.

    Virtuous and vicious every man must be,
Few in the extreme, but all in the degree;
The rogue and fool by fits is fair and wise,
And even the best, by fits, what they despise.
235 'Tis but by parts we follow good or ill,
For, vice or virtue, self directs it still;
Each individual seeks a several° goal,   *separate*
But Heaven's great view is one, and that the whole
That counter-works each folly and caprice;
240 That disappoints the effect of every vice
That happy frailties to all ranks applied—
Shame to the virgin, to the matron pride,
Fear to the statesman, rashness to the chief,
To kings presumption, and to crowds belief—
245 That virtue's ends from vanity can raise,
Which seeks no interest, no reward but praise;
And build on wants, and on defects of mind,
The joy, the peace, the glory of mankind.
    Heaven forming each on other to depend,
250 A master, or a servant, or a friend,
Bids each on other for assistance call,
'Till one man's weakness grows the strength of all.
Wants, frailties, passions closer still ally
The common interest, or endear the tie.
255 To these we owe true friendship, love sincere,
Each home-felt joy that life inherits here;
Yet from the same we learn, in its decline,
Those joys, those loves, those interests to resign:

Taught half by reason, half by mere decay,
260 To welcome death, and calmly pass away.
    Whate'er the passion, knowledge, fame, or pelf,°   *wealth*
Not one will change his neighbor with himself.
The learned is happy nature to explore,
The fool is happy that he knows no more;
265 The rich is happy in the plenty given,
The poor contents him with the care of heaven.
See the blind beggar dance, the cripple sing,
The sot° a hero, lunatic a king;   *drunkard*
The starving chemist° in his golden views   *alchemist*
270 Supremely blest, the poet in his muse.
    See some strange comfort every state attend,
And pride bestowed on all, a common friend.
See some fit passion every age supply;
Hope travels through, nor quits us when we die.
275   Behold the child, by Nature's kindly law
Pleased with a rattle, tickled with a straw;
Some livelier plaything gives his youth delight,
A little louder, but as empty quite:
Scarves, garters,[4] gold amuse his riper stage,
280 And beads[5] and prayer-books are the toys of age:
Pleased with this bauble still, as that before,
'Till tired he sleeps, and life's poor play is o'er!
    Meanwhile, opinion gilds with varying rays
Those painted clouds that beautify our days;
285 Each want of happiness by hope supplied,
And each vacuity of sense by pride.
These build as fast as knowledge can destroy;
In folly's cup still laughs the bubble, joy;
One prospect lost, another still we gain,
290 And not a vanity is given in vain.
Even mean self-love becomes, by force divine,
The scale to measure others' wants by thine.
See! and confess, one comfort still must rise;
'Tis this: though man's a fool, yet GOD IS WISE.
—1733

---

[1] *Tweed* River in southern Scotland.

[2] *Zembla* Novaya Zemlya, an archipelago off the Arctic coast of Russia.

[3] *hard* Hardened (i.e., to vice, as an inhabitant of the Arctic climate would be to the cold).

[4] *Scarves* Worn by Doctors of Divinity; *garters* Badges of the Knights of the Garter.

[5] *beads* Rosaries.

An Epistle from Mr. Pope to Dr. Arbuthnot[1]

Neque sermonibus vulgi dederis te, nee in Praemiis humanis
spem posueris rerum tuarum: suis te oportet illecebris ipsa
Virtus trahat ad verum decus. Quid de te alii loquantur,
ipsi videant, sed loquentur tamen.[2]

TULLY [*De Re Publica*, Lib. VI, cap. XXIII].

ADVERTISEMENT

This paper is a sort of bill of complaint, begun many
years since, and drawn up by snatches, as the several
occasions offered. I had no thoughts of publishing it till
it pleased some persons of rank and fortune (the authors
of *Verses to the Imitator of Horace*, and of an *Epistle to a
Doctor of Divinity from a Nobleman at Hampton Court*)[3]
to attack, in a very extraordinary manner, not only my
writings (of which, being public, the public judge) but
my person, morals, and family, whereof, to those who
know me not, a truer information may be requisite.
Being divided between the necessity to say something of
myself, and my own laziness to undertake so awkward a
task, I thought it the shortest way to put the last hand to
this epistle. If it have anything pleasing, it will be that
by which I am most desirous to please, the truth and the
sentiment; and if anything offensive, it will be only to
those I am least sorry to offend, the vicious or the
ungenerous.

Many will know their own pictures in it, there being
not a circumstance but what is true; but I have for the
most part spared their names, and they may escape
being laughed at if they please.

I would have some of them know, it was owing to
the request of the learned and candid friend to whom it
is inscribed that I make not as free use of theirs as they
have done of mine. However, I shall have this advantage
and honour on my side, that whereas, by their proceeding, any abuse may be directed at any man, no injury
can possibly be done by mine, since a nameless character
can never be found out but by its truth and likeness.

Shut, shut the door, good John![4] (fatigued I said)
Tie up the knocker, say I'm sick, I'm dead.
The Dog Star[5] rages! nay 'tis past a doubt,
All Bedlam, or Parnassus,[6] is let out:
Fire in each eye, and papers in each hand,   5
They rave, recite, and madden round the land.
      What walls can guard me, or what shades can hide?
They pierce my thickets, through my grot[7] they glide,
By land, by water, they renew the charge,
They stop the chariot, and they board the barge.[8]   10
No place is sacred, not the church is free,
Even Sunday shines no Sabbath day to me:
Then from the Mint[9] walks forth the man of rhyme,
Happy! to catch me just at dinner time.
      Is there a parson, much bemused in beer,[10]   15
A maudlin poetess, a rhyming peer,°   *member of the nobility*

---

[1] *Dr. Arbuthnot*   Formerly Queen Anne's physician, Arbuthnot was
a close friend of Swift and a fellow member of the Scriblerus Club.
Pope was spurred to complete this poem, which he had worked on
intermittently for several years, when he learned that Arbuthnot was
terminally ill. The poem, completed seven weeks before Arbuthnot's
death, was, Pope declared, "the best memorial I can leave, both of
my friendship to you, and to my character."

[2] *Neque.... tamen*   Latin: "You will neither give yourself to the
gossip of the vulgar, nor place your hope in the rewards of men for
the success of your affairs. Virtue herself, by her own allure, should
lead you to true honor. What others may say of you, regard as their
concern, for they will say it nevertheless." From *De Re Publica* 6.23,
by Marcus Tullius Cicero ("Tully").

[3] *authors ... Court*   Lady Mary Wortley Montagu and John, Lord
Hervey, respectively.

[4] *John*   John Serle, Pope's gardener and servant.

[5] *Dog Star*   Sirius, the brightest star in the constellation Canis
Major. In late summer Sirius sets with the sun, and it is therefore
associated with maddening heat. Late summer was also when poetry
recitals were held in ancient Rome.

[6] *Bedlam*   The Hospital of St. Mary's of Bethlehem, a London
hospital for the insane; *Parnassus*   Mountain in Greece that,
according to myth, was sacred to Apollo and the Muses, and was
therefore seen as the home of artistic inspiration.

[7] *my grot*   On Pope's property in Twickenham an underground
passage connected his house with his garden, which lay on the
opposite side of the road. He decorated this passage and turned it
into a beautiful grotto that functioned as a subterranean retreat.

[8] *board the barge*   Twickenham was on the Thames, enabling Pope
to travel to London by barge.

[9] *the Mint*   Area in London that was a sanctuary for debtors—they
could not be arrested while within its boundaries. Debtors could not
be arrested anywhere on Sundays.

[10] *parson ... beer*   Probably a reference to Poet Laureate Laurence
Eusden (the words "bemused in" play on his name), who was a
parson and notorious for his heavy drinking.

A clerk, foredoomed his father's soul to cross,
Who pens a stanza when he should engross?[1]
Is there who, locked from ink and paper, scrawls
20   With desperate charcoal round his darkened walls?
All fly to Twit'nam° and, in humble strain,   *Twickenham*
Apply to me to keep them mad or vain.
Arthur,[2] whose giddy son neglects the laws,
Imputes to me and my damned works the cause;
25   Poor Cornus[3] sees his frantic wife elope,
And curses wit, and poetry, and Pope.

　　Friend to my life (which did not you prolong,
The world had wanted many an idle song)
What drop or nostrum° can this plague remove?   *remedy*
30   Or which must end me, a fool's wrath or love?
A dire dilemma! Either way I'm sped,°   *dispatched, destroyed*
If foes, they write, if friends, they read me dead.
Seized and tied down to judge, how wretched I!
Who can't be silent, and who will not lie;
35   To laugh were want of goodness and of grace,
And to be grave exceeds all power of face.
I sit with sad civility, I read
With honest anguish and an aching head,
And drop at last, but in unwilling ears,
40   This saving counsel, "Keep your piece nine years."[4]

　　"Nine years!" cries he, who, high in Drury Lane,[5]
Lulled by soft zephyrs° through the broken pane,   *breezes*
Rhymes ere he wakes, and prints before term[6] ends,
Obliged by hunger and request of friends:
45   "The piece you think is incorrect: why, take it;
I'm all submission; what you'd have it, make it."

　　Three things another's modest wishes bound,
My friendship, and a prologue, and ten pound.

Pitholeon[7] sends to me: "You know his Grace.
50   I want a patron; ask him for a place."°   *job*
Pitholeon libeled me—"but here's a letter
Informs you, sir, 'twas when he knew no better.
Dare you refuse him? Curll[8] invites to dine;
He'll write a *Journal*, or he'll turn divine."[9]

55   　　Bless me! a packet.—"'Tis a stranger sues,
A virgin tragedy, an orphan muse."
If I dislike it, "Furies, death, and rage!"
If I approve, "Commend it to the stage."
There (thank my stars) my whole commission ends;
60   The players and I are, luckily, no friends.
Fired that the house° reject him, "'Sdeath,   *playhouse*
　　I'll print it
And shame the fools—your interest, sir, with Lintot."[10]
Lintot, dull rogue, will think your price too much.
"Not, sir, if you revise it, and retouch."
65   All my demurs but double his attacks;
At last he whispers, "Do, and we go snacks."°   *shares*
Glad of a quarrel, straight I clap the door,
Sir, let me see your works and you no more.

　　'Tis sung, when Midas' ears[11] began to spring
70   (Midas, a sacred person and a king),
His very minister, who spied them first,
(Some say his queen) was forced to speak, or burst.
And is not mine, my friend, a sorer case,

---

[7] [Pope's note] The name taken from a foolish poet at Rhodes, who pretended much to Greek. [This was a reference to Leonard Welsted, mentioned again on line 375, with whom Pope had quarreled.]

[8] *Curll* Edmund Curll, an unethical publisher who was notorious for publishing pirated, forged, and falsely ascribed works. He was one of Pope's primary adversaries and a frequent object of his attacks.

[9] *write ... divine* I.e., he will attack Pope in an article in the *London Journal* or will write a theological treatise.

[10] *Lintot* Bernard Lintot, the publisher who had issued Pope's early work, including his edition of Homer, but with whom Pope had since quarreled. Lintot, with Curll, figures in Pope's satire *The Dunciad.*

[11] *Midas' ears* King Midas of Lydia was given ass's ears by the god Apollo when he claimed to prefer Pan's rustic flute playing to the refined melodies of Apollo's lyre. Depending upon the version of the story, the secret of Midas's ears (which he hid under a turban) was first discovered by either the king's wife or his barber. The discoverer of the secret, unable to sleep, whispered the story either into a hole in the earth or a bed of reeds. Here Pope's references to the queen, minister, and king are allusions to Queen Caroline, first minister Robert Walpole, and King George II.

---

[1] *engross* Write in legal form; write out legal documents.

[2] *Arthur* Arthur Moore, a business man and Member of Parliament whose son, James Moore Smythe, was a writer, and one Pope scorned. Pope later accused him of stealing lines from his *Epistle To a Lady* for use in a play.

[3] *Cornus* From *cornu*, the Latin word for "horn," which was the emblem of the cuckold.

[4] *Keep ... years* I.e., before publishing it. This advice is taken from Horace's *Ars Poetica*, line 388.

[5] *high in Drury Lane* In a garret on Drury Lane, a street known for its theater but also for its squalid living quarters, which were home to many prostitutes and criminals.

[6] *term* Period during which the law courts were in session. The publishing seasons coincided with these legal terms.

When every coxcomb° perks them in my face?   *fool*

5   "Good friend, forbear! You deal in dangerous things;
I'd never name queens, ministers, or kings.
Keep close to ears, and those let asses prick;
'Tis nothing"—Nothing? if they bite and kick?
Out with it, *Dunciad*! Let the secret pass,
10 That secret to each fool, that he's an ass:
The truth once told (and wherefore should we lie?)
The Queen of Midas slept, and so may I.

You think this cruel? Take it for a rule,
No creature smarts so little as a fool.
15 Let peals of laughter, Codrus,[1] round thee break,
Thou unconcerned canst hear the mighty crack.
Pit, box, and gallery[2] in convulsions hurled,
Thou stand'st unshook amidst a bursting world.
Who shames a scribbler? Break one cobweb through,
20 He spins the slight, self-pleasing thread anew:
Destroy his fib or sophistry, in vain;
The creature's at his dirty work again;
Throned in the centre of his thin designs,
Proud of a vast extent of flimsy lines.
25 Whom have I hurt? Has poet yet, or peer,
Lost the arched eyebrow or Parnassian sneer?
And has not Colley[3] still his lord and whore?
His butchers Henley? his freemasons Moore?[4]
Does not one table Bavius[5] still admit?
30 Still to one bishop Philips[6] seem a wit?
Still Sappho[7]—"Hold! for God's sake—you'll offend.
No names—be calm—learn prudence of a friend:
I too could write, and I am twice as tall,

But foes like these!"—One flatterer's worse than all;
105 Of all mad creatures, if the learn'd are right,
It is the slaver kills, and not the bite.
A fool quite angry is quite innocent;
Alas! 'tis ten times worse when they repent.

One dedicates in high heroic prose,
110 And ridicules beyond a hundred foes;
One from all Grub Street[8] will my fame defend,
And, more abusive, calls himself my friend.
This prints my letters,[9] that expects a bribe,
And others roar aloud, "Subscribe, subscribe."[10]
115   There are, who to my person pay their court:
I cough like Horace, and though lean, am short;
Ammon's great son[11] one shoulder had too high,
Such Ovid's nose,[12] and "Sir! you have an eye—"
Go on, obliging creatures, make me see
120 All that disgraced my betters, met in me.
Say for my comfort, languishing in bed,
"Just so immortal Maro° held his head";   *Virgil*
And when I die, be sure you let me know
Great Homer died three thousand years ago.

125   Why did I write? What sin to me unknown
Dipped me in ink, my parents', or my own?
As yet a child, nor yet a fool to fame,
I lisped in numbers,° for the numbers came.   *meter*
I left no calling for this idle trade,
130 No duty broke, no father disobeyed.
The muse but served to ease some friend, not wife,
To help me through this long disease, my life,
To second, Arbuthnot! thy art and care,
And teach the being you preserved, to bear.°   *endure*

135   But why then publish? Granville the polite,
And knowing Walsh, would tell me I could write;
Well-natured Garth inflamed with early praise,

---

[1] *Codrus*   Fictional poet ridiculed by both Virgil and Juvenal.

[2] *Pit, box, and gallery*   Sections of the theater.

[3] *Colley*   Colley Cibber, Poet Laureate, who figured as King of the Dunces in the new edition of Pope's *Dunciad*.

[4] *Henley*   John Henley was an independent preacher who gave sensational orations on a variety of matters, both theological and mundane, for which he charged a shilling for admission. His oratory was set up in one of London's primary meat markets, and in 1729 he had given a sermon that claimed to trace the religious history and use of the butcher's calling; *Moore*   James Moore Smythe, who was a freemason.

[5] *Bavius*   Poet who attacked Virgil and Horace.

[6] *Philips*   Ambrose Philips, a rival poet who served as secretary to Hugh Boulter, Archbishop of Armagh.

[7] *Sappho*   Famous lyric poet of ancient Greece; also, Pope's poetic nickname for Lady Montagu.

[8] *Grub Street*   Collective term for literary hack writers, taken from the street in London of that name, where many such writers lived.

[9] *prints my letters*   Curll published an unauthorized version of Pope's letters in 1726.

[10] *subscribe*   Books were sometimes printed by subscription.

[11] *Ammon's great son*   Alexander the Great.

[12] *Ovid's nose*   Ovid's family name was Naso (from the Latin *nasus*, meaning "nose").

And Congreve loved, and Swift endured my lays;°   *verses*
The courtly Talbot, Somers, Sheffield read,
140 Even mitred Rochester would nod the head,
And St. John's self (great Dryden's friends before)
With open arms received one poet more.[1]
Happy my studies, when by these approved!
Happier their author, when by these beloved!
145 From these the world will judge of men and books,
Not from the Burnets, Oldmixons, and Cookes.[2]

     Soft were my numbers; who could take offence
While pure description held the place of sense?
Like gentle Fanny's[3] was my flowery theme,
150 A painted mistress, or a purling stream.
Yet then did Gildon[4] draw his venal quill;
I wished the man a dinner, and sat still.
Yet then did Dennis[5] rave in furious fret;
I never answered, I was not in debt.
155 If want provoked, or madness made them print,
I waged no war with Bedlam or the Mint.

     Did some more sober critic come abroad?
If wrong, I smiled; if right, I kissed the rod.[6]
Pains, reading, study are their just pretence,
160 And all they want is spirit, taste, and sense.
Commas and points they set exactly right,

And 'twere a sin to rob them of their mite.[7]
Yet ne'er one sprig of laurel[8] graced these
    ribalds,°   *abusive rascals*
From slashing Bentley down to piddling Tibbalds.[9]
165 Each wight[10] who reads not, and but scans and spells,
Each word-catcher that lives on syllables,
Even such small critics some regard may claim,
Preserved in Milton's or in Shakespeare's name.
Pretty! in amber to observe the forms
170 Of hairs, or straws, or dirt, or grubs, or worms;
The things, we know, are neither rich nor rare,
But wonder how the devil they got there?

     Were others angry? I excused them too;
Well might they rage; I gave them but their due.
175 A man's true merit 'tis not hard to find,
But each man's secret standard in his mind.
That casting weight[11] pride adds to emptiness,
This, who can gratify? for who can guess?
The bard[12] whom pilfered pastorals renown,
180 Who turns a Persian tale for half a crown,[13]
Just writes to make his barrenness appear,
And strains from hard-bound brains eight lines a year:
He who, still wanting though he lives on theft,
Steals much, spends little, yet has nothing left;
185 And he who now to sense, now nonsense leaning,
Means not, but blunders round about a meaning;
And he whose fustian's[14] so sublimely bad,

---

[1] *Granville … more*   This list of men—intended to establish Pope as a preeminent poet and Dryden's successor—names friends and supporters of Dryden who had also encouraged the young Pope. George Granville, William Walsh, and Sir Samuel Garth were all poets of note; William Congreve was a playwright; Charles Talbot, Duke of Shrewsbury; Lord Somers; and John Sheffield, Duke of Buckingham, were all statesmen and patrons. Francis Atterbury, Bishop of Rochester, and Henry St. John, Lord Bolingbroke, were both close friends of Pope.

[2] *Burnets, Oldmixons, and Cookes*   Three writers who had attacked Pope in print. In his note Pope calls them "authors of secret and scandalous history."

[3] *Fanny*   Lord Fanny was one of Pope's nicknames for John, Lord Hervey, a favorite of the Queen and a known bisexual whose effeminate manner and appearance were frequently commented upon.

[4] *Gildon*   Charles Gildon, a critic and writer who had occasionally condemned Pope's writing, at the instigation (Pope believed) of Joseph Addison, one of Pope's rivals; it is for this reason that Pope accuses Gildon of having a corrupt, or mercenary, pen.

[5] *Dennis*   John Dennis, another critic who had attacked Pope, though only after Pope had mocked him in his *Essay on Criticism.*

[6] *kissed the rod*   Accepted the criticism.

[7] *mite*   Very small or insignificant amount of money.

[8] *laurel*   Wreaths of laurel (sacred to Apollo) were used to crown celebrated poets in ancient Greece and Rome.

[9] *Bentley*   Richard Bentley, a great classical scholar who, however, earned ridicule for his edition of Milton's *Paradise Lost*, in which he arbitrarily placed in square brackets numerous passages that he felt were not up to Milton's standard, claiming they must have been slipped in by an amanuensis, without the blind poet's knowledge; *Tibbalds* Lewis Theobald, a scholar who used his expertise in Elizabethan literature to expose errors in Pope's edition of Shakespeare.

[10] *wight*   Human being (usually a contemptuous or belittling term).

[11] *casting weight*   Weight that tips the scale one way or the other; deciding factor.

[12] *bard*   Ambrose Philips, part of whose *Fifth Pastoral* Pope claimed was plagiarized from the work of an Italian poet. Philips had also published *Persian Tales*, a book of translated stories.

[13] *half a crown*   The fee usually charged by a prostitute.

[14] *fustian*   Inflated, lofty, and pompous language.

It is not poetry, but prose run mad:
All these, my modest satire bade translate,
And owned that nine such poets made a Tate.[1]
How did they fume, and stamp, and roar, and chafe!
And swear, not Addison himself was safe.

    Peace to all such! But were there one[2] whose fires
True genius kindles, and fair fame inspires,
Blessed with each talent and each art to please,
And born to write, converse, and live with ease:
Should such a man, too fond to rule alone,
Bear, like the Turk,[3] no brother near the throne;
View him with scornful, yet with jealous eyes,
And hate for arts that caused himself to rise;
Damn with faint praise, assent with civil leer,
And, without sneering, teach the rest to sneer;
Willing to wound, and yet afraid to strike,
Just hint a fault, and hesitate dislike;
Alike reserved to blame or to commend,
A timorous foe, and a suspicious friend;
Dreading even fools; by flatterers besieged,
And so obliging that he ne'er obliged;
Like Cato, give his little senate laws,[4]
And sit attentive to his own applause;
While wits and templars[5] every sentence raise,
And wonder with a foolish face of praise.

Who but must laugh, if such a man there be?
Who would not weep, if Atticus were he!

215   What though my name stood rubric°   *written in red*
      on the walls?
Or plastered posts, with claps,° in capitals?[6]   *placards*
Or smoking forth,[7] a hundred hawkers'° load, *street vendors'*
On wings of winds came flying all abroad?
I sought no homage from the race that write;
220 I kept, like Asian monarchs, from their sight:
Poems I heeded (now berhymed so long)
No more than thou, great George! a birthday song.[8]
I ne'er with wits or witlings passed my days
To spread about the itch of verse and praise;
225 Nor like a puppy daggled° through the town *traipsed, taken*
To fetch and carry sing-song up and down;
Nor at rehearsals sweat, and mouthed, and cried,
With handkerchief and orange[9] at my side;
But sick of fops, and poetry, and prate,
230 To Bufo left the whole Castilian[10] state.
    Proud as Apollo on his forked hill,
Sat full-blown Bufo, puffed by every quill;
Fed with soft dedication all day long,
Horace and he went hand in hand in song.
235 His library (where busts of poets dead,
And a true Pindar, stood without a head)[11]
Received of wits an undistinguished race,
Who first his judgment asked, and then a place:
Much they extolled his pictures, much his seat,° *estate*
240 And flattered every day, and some days eat;°   *ate*
Till grown more frugal in his riper days,
He paid some bards with port, and some with praise;

---

[1] *nine ... Tate* Nahum Tate, poet and dramatist, was poet laureate from 1692 to 1715. He was best known for his rewriting of Shakespeare's *King Lear*, in which he provided a happy ending. Pope is here playing on the expression "It takes nine tailors to make a man."

[2] *one* Joseph Addison, whose writing and wit Pope admired, but with whom Pope had quarreled after he discovered Addison had been behind a plot to discredit his edition of Homer's *Iliad*. His satirical nickname for Addison here, as elsewhere, is Atticus, after the Roman philosopher of that name, who was a friend of Cicero and a man renowned for his wisdom, generosity, and love of truth.

[3] *like the Turk* It was a popular stereotype at the time that Turkish monarchs would murder any kinsmen, particularly brothers, who could become rivals to the throne.

[4] *Cato ... laws* Addison had written an immensely popular tragedy about Cato, the virtuous Roman senator who chose to commit suicide rather than submit to Caesar's tyrannical authority, for which Pope had composed the prologue. This line, which satirically echoes one from that prologue, mocks the "little senate" of fellow Whig writers over whom Addison ruled during regular meetings at Button's Coffee House.

[5] *templars* Law students or young lawyers, some of whom had literary aspirations.

---

[6] *What though ... capitals* Allusions to publishers' methods of advertising new books.

[7] *smoking forth* I.e., hot off the press.

[8] *great George ... song* Each year the Poet Laureate was required to compose a birthday ode for the monarch.

[9] *orange* Oranges were commonly sold in theaters.

[10] *Bufo* Latin for "toad"; Bufo is the name given to a certain type of vain, tasteless, and self-absorbed patron; *Castilian* Castalia was the spring on Mount Parnassus that was sacred to Apollo and the Muses. It ran between the two peaks of the mountain (the "forked hill" of line 231), one of which was sacred to Apollo, the other to Bacchus.

[11] *busts ... head* Pope is mocking those who displayed headless busts and claim them to belong to statues of great poets.

To some a dry rehearsal[1] was assigned,
And others (harder still) he paid in kind.[2]
245 Dryden alone (what wonder?) came not nigh,
Dryden alone escaped this judging eye:
But still the great have kindness in reserve;
He helped to bury whom he helped to starve.[3]
        May some choice patron bless each gray goose quill!
250 May every Bavius have his Bufo still!
So when a statesman wants a day's defence,
Or envy holds a whole week's war with sense,
Or simple pride for flattery makes demands,
May dunce by dunce be whistled off my hands!
255 Blessed be the great! for those they take away,
And those they left me——for they left me Gay;[4]
Left me to see neglected genius bloom,
Neglected die, and tell it on his tomb;
Of all thy blameless life the sole return
260 My verse, and Queensberry weeping o'er thy urn!
Oh let me live my own, and die so too!
("To live and die is all I have to do");[5]
Maintain a poet's dignity and ease,
And see what friends, and read what books I please;
265 Above a patron, though I condescend
Sometimes to call a minister my friend.
I was not born for courts or great affairs;
I pay my debts, believe, and say my prayers,
Can sleep without a poem in my head,
270 Nor know if Dennis be alive or dead.
        Why am I asked what next shall see the light?
Heavens! was I born for nothing but to write?
Has life no joys for me? or (to be grave)
Have I no friend to serve, no soul to save?
275 "I found him close with Swift"——"Indeed? No doubt"

(Cries prating Balbus[6]) "something will come out."
'Tis all in vain, deny it as I will.
"No, such a genius never can lie still,"
And then for mine obligingly mistakes
280 The first lampoon Sir Will or Bubo[7] makes.
Poor guiltless I! and can I choose but smile,
When every coxcomb knows me by my style?
        Cursed be the verse, how well soe'er it flow,
That tends to make one worthy man my foe,
285 Give virtue scandal, innocence a fear,
Or from the soft-eyed virgin steal a tear!
But he who hurts a harmless neighbour's peace,
Insults fal'n worth, or beauty in distress,
Who loves a lie, lame slander helps about,
290 Who writes a libel, or who copies out:
That fop whose pride affects a patron's name,
Yet absent, wounds an author's honest fame;
Who can your merit selfishly approve,
And show the sense of it without the love;
295 Who has the vanity to call you friend,
Yet wants the honour, injured, to defend;
Who tells whate'er you think, whate'er you say,
And, if he lie not, must at least betray:
Who to the Dean and silver bell can swear,
300 And sees at Cannons what was never there:[8]
Who reads but with a lust to misapply,
Make satire a lampoon, and fiction lie.
A lash like mine no honest man shall dread,
But all such babbling blockheads in his stead.
305   Let Sporus[9] tremble——"What? that thing of silk,
Sporus, that mere white curd of ass's milk?
Satire or sense, alas! can Sporus feel?

---

[1] *dry rehearsal* Recitation of poetry that was not rewarded with alcohol.

[2] *paid in kind* I.e., Bufo paid them by reciting his own poetry.

[3] [Pope's note] Mr. Dryden, after having lived in exigencies, had a magnificent funeral bestowed upon him by the contributions of several persons of quality.

[4] *Gay* John Gay, a close friend of Pope, Swift, and Addison and a fellow member of the Scriblerus Club. Though Gay was the author of several popular works, including *The Beggar's Opera*, he failed to win patronage until, toward the end of his life, he was taken under the protection of the Duke and Duchess of Queensberry.

[5] *To live ... do* Line 94 of John Denham's *Of Prudence*.

[6] *Balbus* Latin: stammering.

[7] *Sir Will or Bubo* Sir William Yonge, a minor poet and political pawn of Walpole, and Bubb Dodington, a wealthy, extravagant, and corrupt politician who made a show of being a patron of the arts.

[8] *Who ... there* In Pope's *Epistle to Burlington*, his description of Timon's villa was mistaken (perhaps intentionally) for a satire of Cannons, the estate of the Duke of Chandos. The description of Timon's villa, unlike the real Cannons, had a chapel with a silver bell and a Dean.

[9] *Sporus* Sporus was a boy whom Roman Emperor Nero favored. He had him castrated and then married him in a large, public ceremony. Here Sporus is meant to represent Lord Hervey, a favorite of the Queen and a man whose effeminate manners and appearance were frequently commented upon.

Who breaks a butterfly upon a wheel?"[1]
Yet let me flap this bug with gilded wings,
This painted[2] child of dirt, that stinks and stings;
Whose buzz the witty and the fair annoys,
Yet wit ne'er tastes, and beauty ne'er enjoys;
So well-bred spaniels civilly delight
In mumbling of the game they dare not bite.
Eternal smiles his emptiness betray,
As shallow streams run dimpling all the way.
Whether in florid impotence he speaks,
And, as the prompter[3] breathes, the puppet squeaks;
Or at the ear of Eve,[4] familiar toad,
Half froth, half venom, spits himself abroad,
In puns, or politics, or tales, or lies,
Or spite, or smut, or rhymes, or blasphemies.
His wit all seesaw between that and this,
Now high, now low, now master up, now miss,
And he himself one vile antithesis.
Amphibious thing! that acting either part,
The trifling head or the corrupted heart,
Fop at the toilet,° flatterer at the board,[5]   *dressing table*
Now trips a lady, and now struts a lord.
Eve's tempter thus the rabbins° have expressed,   *rabbis*
A cherub's face, a reptile all the rest;
Beauty that shocks you, parts that none will trust,
Wit that can creep, and pride that licks the dust.
        Not fortune's worshipper, nor fashion's fool,
Not lucre's madman, nor ambition's tool,
Not proud, nor servile, be one poet's praise
That, if he pleased, he pleased by manly ways:
That flattery, even to kings, he held a shame,
And thought a lie in verse or prose the same:
That not in fancy's maze he wandered long,
But stooped[6] to truth, and moralized his song:
That not for fame, but virtue's better end,
He stood° the furious foe, the timid friend,   *withstood*
The damning critic, half-approving wit,

345 The coxcomb hit, or fearing to be hit;
Laughed at the loss of friends he never had,
The dull, the proud, the wicked, and the mad;
The distant threats of vengeance on his head,
The blow unfelt, the tear he never shed;
350 The tale revived, the lie so oft o'erthrown,
The imputed trash, and dullness not his own;
The morals blackened when the writings 'scape,
The libeled person, and the pictured shape;[7]
Abuse on all he loved, or loved him, spread,
355 A friend in exile, or a father dead;
The whisper that to greatness still too near,
Perhaps yet vibrates on his Sovereign's ear—
Welcome for thee, fair virtue! all the past:
For thee, fair virtue! welcome even the last!
360   "But why insult the poor, affront the great?"
A knave's a knave, to me, in every state;
Alike my scorn, if he succeed or fail,
Sporus at court, or Japhet[8] in a jail,
A hireling scribbler, or a hireling peer,
365 Knight of the Post corrupt, or of the Shire,[9]
If on a pillory, or near a throne,
He gain his prince's ear, or lose his own.
        Yet soft by nature, more a dupe than wit,
Sappho can tell you how this man was bit:[10]
370 This dreaded satirist Dennis will confess
Foe to his pride, but friend to his distress:[11]
So humble, he has knocked at Tibbald's door,
Has drunk with Cibber, nay has rhymed for Moore.
Full ten years slandered, did he once reply?

---

[1] *wheel* I.e., of torture.

[2] *painted* Lord Hervey was known to wear makeup.

[3] *the prompter* Walpole.

[4] *Eve* Queen Caroline. Cf. Milton's *Paradise Lost*, 4.799, in which the devil is described in this position.

[5] *board* Dining table.

[6] *stooped* Swooped, as a falcon does when it catches sight of its prey.

[7] *the pictured shape* Some caricatures of Pope showed him as a hunchbacked ape.

[8] *Japhet* Japhet Crook, a notorious forger who obtained several thousand pounds and two estates through forged deeds and wills before he was discovered, whereupon he was placed in the pillory, his ears were cut off, and he was locked in prison.

[9] *Knight ... Shire* A Knight of the Post made a living by giving false evidence; a Knight of the Shire represented his county in Parliament.

[10] *bit* Deceived.

[11] *Dennis ... distress* Near the end of his life Dennis fell into debt. In addition to publicly supporting Dennis's works, Pope helped to organize a benefit performance in his honor and contributed a prologue to the play that was performed.

375 Three thousand suns went down on Welsted's lie.[1]
To please a mistress one aspersed his life;
He lashed him not, but let her be his wife.
Let Budgell charge low Grub Street on his quill,
And write whate'er he pleased, except his will;[2]
380 Let the two Curlls of town and court[3] abuse
His father, mother, body, soul, and muse.
Yet why? that father held it for a rule
It was a sin to call our neighbour fool;
That harmless mother thought no wife a whore—
385 Hear this, and spare his family, James More!
Unspotted names, and memorable long,
If there be force in virtue, or in song.
    Of gentle blood (part shed in honour's cause,
While yet in Britain honour had applause)
390 Each parent sprung—"What fortune, pray?"—Their own,
And better got than Bestia's[4] from the throne.
Born to no pride, inheriting no strife,
Nor marrying discord in a noble wife,
Stranger to civil and religious rage,
395 The good man walked innoxious° through   doing no harm
        his age.
No courts he saw, no suits would ever try,
Nor dared an oath,[5] nor hazarded a lie.

Unlearned, he knew no schoolman's subtle art,
No language but the language of the heart.
400 By nature honest, by experience wise,
Healthy by temperance and by exercise;
His life, though long, to sickness passed unknown;
His death was instant, and without a groan.
Oh grant me thus to live, and thus to die!
405 Who sprung from kings shall know less joy than I.
    O friend! may each domestic bliss be thine!
Be no unpleasing melancholy mine:
Me, let the tender office long engage
To rock the cradle of reposing age,
410 With lenient° arts extend a mother's breath,   soothing
Make languor smile, and smooth the bed of death,
Explore the thought, explain the asking eye,
And keep a while one parent from the sky!
On cares like these if length of days attend,
415 May Heaven, to bless those days, preserve my friend,
Preserve him social, cheerful, and serene,
And just as rich as when he served a Queen!
Whether that blessing be denied, or given,
Thus far was right—the rest belongs to Heaven.
—1735 (WRITTEN 1731–34)

---

[1] *Welsted's lie* Leonard Welsted, who, according to Pope, claimed Pope had "occasioned a lady's death." Welsted was also one of those who maintained that Pope's *Epistle to Burlington* satirized the Duke of Chandos.

[2] *Budgell ... will* An article in the *Grub Street Journal* accused Eustace Budgell of forging the will of Matthew Tindal. Budgell believed (wrongly) that Pope had written the article.

[3] *two Curlls ... court* The Curll of the court is Lord Hervey; the other is Edmund Curll, the publisher.

[4] *Bestia* Corrupt Roman politician of the second century BCE. Here the name is probably meant to signify the Duke of Marlborough, who became rich by winning the favor of Queen Anne.

[5] *dared an oath* Pope's father refused both to renounce his Catholicism and to take oaths against the Pope. As a result, he was denied many of the rights of citizenship, including the rights to vote, attend schools, and inherit property.

Lady Mary Wortley Montagu
1689 – 1762

In keeping with expectations for women of her station, Lady Mary Wortley Montagu never published under her own name, but was nonetheless one of the most celebrated and admired female writers of her age. She is known today mainly for her letters, but wrote in a variety of genres, including poetry, fiction, and essays. Twentieth-century feminist literary critics have recovered and explored Montagu's writings on female sexual desire, gender relations, and her feminist critique of marriage. Unconventional, erudite, and independent, she referred to herself as "a sister of the quill."

Montagu was born Mary Pierrepont in London in 1689; her father, the Whig Evelyn Pierrepont, became an earl when she was one year old. At three years of age she lost her mother (born Lady Mary Fielding), whom she later imagined to have been a model of female forbearance at the hands of a libertine husband. The eldest of four children, in her youth Mary was surrounded by some of the leading figures of the London literary scene, including Joseph Addison, Richard Steele, and William Congreve. She also formed close friendships in her teenage years with a circle of upper- and middle-class literary women. As was standard for a young woman of her social and economic position, she was trained by a governess in the conventional accomplishments of a lady's curriculum, but Montagu's intellectual ambitions were broader. She duly embarked on a secret, self-directed education in Latin in her father's study; everyone around her assumed she was locked away reading novels. In 1712 she eloped with Edward Wortley Montagu, a Whig Member of Parliament, against the wishes of her father, who had intended her for another suitor to whom she objected. The couple had two children. In late 1715 Montagu barely survived a serious bout of smallpox. The disease had killed her only brother a few years earlier, and it left her severely scarred. Less than a year after her recovery she left for Constantinople with her husband, who had been appointed British Ambassador to Turkey.

Montagu's most memorable writing grew out of her experiences in what was then the Ottoman Empire. Fascinated by the cultures of Islamic Europe, Turkey, and the Mediterranean, she was an observant and sensitive traveler, and her letters home—to her sister, to Alexander Pope, and others—show the range of her curiosity, and include descriptions and insights into everyday life, religious issues, and literary matters. At Sofia in Bulgaria she visited the famed women's public baths, which she describes with a frankness and admiration unusual for a western visitor. Upon her return to England she edited and compiled what she called her *Embassy Letters* for publication after her death.

Montagu's sojourn in Turkey had a lasting impact not only in the world of letters but also in the field of public health. Having narrowly escaped death by smallpox herself, Montagu had her five-year-old son inoculated against the disease at Constantinople. Later, in 1721, the first inoculation in England was performed on her three-year-old daughter, and Montagu became a strong advocate of a procedure that was treated with great prejudice and suspicion by the English medical establishment. She was heavily criticized for promoting the practice, and she published "A Plain Account of

Inoculating the Smallpox" (1722), in which she castigates the medical profession for its blind self-interest, pseudonymously in a newspaper.

Montagu's "Six Town Eclogues," written in 1715 and 1716, have been widely admired. The poems (some of which were attributed to Pope and Gay) are biting, satirical, and studded with references to actual persons and their intrigues. Each of this series of six poems is written not in a rustic voice (as is traditional in the eclogue) but in that of a member or members of London "society." Among Montagu's many epistolary poems, the "Epistle from Mrs. Yonge to her Husband" is the complaint of a divorced wife whose philandering husband profits financially from the dissolution of the marriage.

Other significant writings include her essay #573 of Addison and Steele's *Spectator* (she was the only female contributor, and remained anonymous), and her own political periodical, *The Nonsense of Common-Sense* (1737–38). Montagu's learning, outspokenness and refusal to conform to the conventions of "female" behavior made her an easy target in a male-dominated literary scene. Beginning in 1728, Alexander Pope, her former correspondent, admirer, and occasional collaborator, launched a smear campaign against Montagu, the exact reasons for which remain unclear. Montagu responded to these attacks by ridiculing Pope's appearance, intellectual abilities, and writing. Their quarrel, all of it carried on in print, lasted on his side until after she left England.

In the 1730s the Montagus' marriage began to fail. In 1736 Montagu fell in love with the much younger bisexual Italian writer Francesco Algarotti, and launched an ardent epistolary relationship with him that lasted for five years. In 1739 she left London to reside in Italy, secretly intending to live with Algarotti. In Venice she conducted a salon, a regular social gathering of Venetian nobility, intelligentsia, and visiting luminaries. For the last twenty-five years of her life she lived mainly in Italy, but conducted various travels in Europe, including a kind of Grand Tour (traditionally a rite reserved for upper-class young men) in the early 1740s.

Near the end of her life Montagu returned to England. Back in London she received many visits by people who regarded her as a kind of living legend, a well-traveled woman of letters who had never refrained from asserting her own voice, nor from conducting herself according to her own rules. Her later prose writings, chiefly letters and fiction, are at last beginning to receive critical attention. She died of breast cancer in London in 1762 and was buried in Grosvenor Chapel in Hanover Square.

⌘ ⌘ ⌘

Saturday
The Small Pox[1]

Flavia

The wretched Flavia on her couch reclined,
   Thus breathed the anguish of a wounded mind.
A glass reversed in her right hand she bore,
For now she shunned the face she sought before.
5   How am I changed! Alas, how am I grown
A frightful spectre, to myself unknown!
Where's my complexion, where the radiant bloom

That promised happiness for years to come?
Then, with what pleasure I this face surveyed!
10 To look once more, my visits oft delayed!
Charmed with the view, a fresher red would rise,
And a new life shot sparkling from my eyes.
Ah, faithless glass, my wonted° bloom   *accustomed*
   restore!
Alas, I rave! That bloom is now no more!
15 The greatest good the gods on men bestow,
Even youth itself to me is useless now.
There was a time (Oh, that I could forget!)
When opera tickets poured before my feet,

---

[1] *Saturday ... Pox*   From *Six Town Eclogues*.

And at the Ring,[1] where brightest beauties shine,
The earliest cherries of the park were mine.
Witness, oh Lilly![2] And thou, Motteux,[3] tell
How much Japan[4] these eyes have made you sell!
With what contempt you saw me oft despise
The humble offer of the raffled prize.
For at each raffle still the prize I bore,
With scorn rejected, or with triumph wore.
Now beauty's fled, and presents are no more.

    For me, the patriot has the house[5] forsook,
And left debates to catch a passing look;
For me, the soldier has soft verses writ;
For me, the beau has aimed to be a wit;
For me, the wit to nonsense was betrayed;
The gamester° has for me his dun delayed   *gambler*
And overseen the card I would have paid.[6]
The bold and haughty, by success made vain,
Awed by my eyes has trembled to complain.
The bashful squire, touched with a wish unknown,
Has dared to speak with spirit not his own.
Fired by one wish, all did alike adore;
Now beauty's fled, and lovers are no more.

    As round the room I turn my weeping eyes,
New unaffected scenes of sorrow rise.
Far from my sight that killing picture bear,
The face disfigure, or the canvas tear!
That picture, which with pride I used to show,
The lost resemblance but upbraids me now.

And thou, my toilette, where I oft have sate,
While hours unheeded passed in deep debate
How curls should fall, or where a patch[7] to place,
If blue or scarlet best became my face,
Now on some happier nymph° thy aid bestow.   *maiden*
On fairer heads, ye useless jewels, glow!
No borrowed lustre can my charms restore;
Beauty is fled, and dress[8] is now no more.

    Ye meaner beauties, I permit you, shine;
Go triumph in the hearts that once were mine.
But 'midst your triumphs, with confusion know
'Tis to my ruin all your charms ye owe.
Would pitying heaven restore my wonted mien,[9]
You still might move unthought of and unseen —
But oh, how vain, how wretched is the boast
Of beauty faded and of Empire lost!
What now is left but weeping to deplore
My beauty fled and Empire now no more!

    Ye cruel chemists, what withheld your aid?
Could no pomatums[10] save a trembling maid?
How false and triffling is that art you boast;
No art can give me back my beauty lost!
In tears surrounded by my friends I lay,
Masked o're and trembling at the light of day.
Mirmillo[11] came, my fortune to deplore
(A golden headed cane, well carried, he bore);
Cordials, he cried, my spirits must restore—
Beauty is fled, and spirit is no more!
Galen the Grave, officious Squirt,[12] was there
With fruitless grief and unavailing care;

---

[1] *the Ring* West Carriage Drive, a circular drive that divides Hyde Park from Kensington Gardens. The most fashionable members of society would drive around the Ring, displaying themselves in their coaches.

[2] *Lilly* Charles Lillie, a celebrated perfumer and seller of snuff who owned a shop in the Strand. Lillie was also a printer of *The Tatler* and *The Spectator*.

[3] *Motteux* Peter Anthony Motteux, who described himself in a letter to the *Spectator* No. 288 as "an author turned dealer." Motteux was a former playwright and translator who went into business, establishing an East India warehouse in London, from which he sold tea, fabrics, china, fans, and other Indian and Chinese goods.

[4] *Japan* Word used loosely to refer to several common products of Japan at the time, including Japanese porcelain and silk.

[5] *house* House of Parliament.

[6] *gamester ... paid* Rather than immediately demanding the money due to him (his dun), the gambler was underwriting Flavia's next bet.

[7] *patch* Piece of silk or plaster, cut in various ornamental shapes (stars, half-moons, etc.), and put on the face either to hide a scar or imperfection, or simply as decoration.

[8] *dress* Act of adorning oneself.

[9] *mien* Expression or appearance of the face.

[10] *pomatums* Pomades, scented ointments for the skin.

[11] *Mirmillo* Sir Hans Sloane, a distinguished physician and the president of the Royal Society from 1727 to 1741.

[12] *Galen the Grave* Galen was John Gay's nickname for Dr. John Woodward, a natural historian, geologist, and physician whose work *The State of Physic and of Diseases* (1718) condemned the popular treatment of smallpox; *Squirt* Character in Samuel Garth's famous poem *The Dispensary* (1699), often referred to as "officious Squirt."

Machaon[1] too, the great Machaon, known
By his red cloak and his superior frown.
"And why," he cried, "this grief and this despair?
80 You shall again be well, again be fair,
Believe my oath" (with that an oath he swore)
False was his oath! My beauty is no more.

      Cease, hapless maid; no more thy tale pursue,
Forsake mankind and bid the world adieu.
85 Monarchs and beauties rule with equal sway;
All strive to serve, and glory to obey.
Alike unpitied when deposed they grow,
Men mock the idol of their former vow.

      Adieu, ye parks in some obscure recess,
90 Where gentle streams will weep at my distress,
Where no false friend will in my grief take part,
And mourn my ruin with a joyful heart.
There let me live in some deserted place,
There hide in shades this lost, inglorious face.
95 Ye operas, circles, I no more must view!
My toilette, patches, all the world, adieu!
—1716

The Reasons that Induced Dr. S. to Write a Poem called The Lady's Dressing Room[2]

The Doctor in a clean starched band,°   *clerical collar*
      His golden snuff box in his hand,
With care his diamond ring displays
And artful shows its various rays,
5 While grave he stalks down——Street,
His dearest Betty——to meet.
      Long had he waited for this hour,
Nor gained admittance to the bower,
Had joked and punned, and swore and writ,
10 Tried all his gallantry and wit,
Had told her oft what part he bore
In Oxford's schemes in days of yore,
But bawdy,° politics, nor satire   *lewd talk*

Could move this dull hard-hearted creature.
15 Jenny, her maid, could taste° a rhyme   *appreciate*
And, grieved to see him lose his time,
Had kindly whispered in his ear,
"For twice two pound you enter here;
My lady vows without that sum
20 It is in vain you write or come."
      The destined offering now he brought
And, in a paradise of thought,
With a low bow approached the dame,
Who smiling heard him preach his flame.
25 His gold she takes (such proofs as these
Convince most unbelieving shes)
And in her trunk rose up to lock it
(Too wise to trust it in her pocket)
And then, returned with blushing grace,
30 Expects the doctor's warm embrace.
      But now this is the proper place
Where morals stare me in the face,
And for the sake of fine expression
I'm forced to make a small digression.
35 Alas, for wretched humankind,
With learning mad, with wisdom blind!
The ox thinks he's for saddle fit
(As long ago friend Horace writ[3])
And men their talents still mistaking,
40 The stutterer fancies his is speaking.
With admiration oft we see
Hard features heightened by toupee,
The beau affects the politician,
Wit is the citizen's[4] ambition,
45 Poor Pope philosophy displays on
With so much rhyme and little reason,
And though he argues ne'er so long
That all is right, his head is wrong.[5]
      None strive to know their proper merit
50 But strain for wisdom, beauty, spirit,
And lose the praise that is their due
While they've th' impossible in view.

---

[1] *Machaon* Hero of *The Dispensary*; here Garth, Lady Mary's family doctor.

[2] *The Reasons ... Room* This poem is a response to Jonathan Swift's "The Lady's Dressing Room" (1732). Its original title was "The Dean's Provocation for Writing the Lady's Dressing Room."

[3] *ox ... Horace writ* Horace, *Epistles* 1.14.43: "The ox desires the saddle."

[4] *citizen* As distinguished from a member of the gentry or nobility; a tradesman.

[5] *That all ... wrong* Cf. Pope's *Essay on Man* (1733), which concludes, "One truth is clear, 'Whatever *is*, is right.'"

So have I seen the injudicious heir
To add one window the whole house impair.
5   Instinct the hound does better teach,
Who never undertook to preach;
The frighted hare from dogs does run
But not attempts to bear a gun.
Here many noble thoughts occur
0 But I prolixity abhor,
And will pursue th' instructive tale
To show the wise in some things fail.
     The reverend lover with surprise
Peeps in her bubbies,° and her eyes,   breasts
5 And kisses both, and tries—and tries.
The evening in this hellish play,
Beside his guineas thrown away,
Provoked the priest to that degree
He swore, "The fault is not in me.
0 Your damned close stool[1] so near my nose,
Your dirty smock, and stinking toes
Would make a Hercules as tame
As any beau that you can name."
     The nymph grown furious roared, "By God!
5 The blame lies all in sixty odd,"[2]
And scornful pointing to the door
Cried, "Fumbler, see my face no more."
"With all my heart I'll go away,
But nothing done, I'll nothing pay.
0 Give back the money." "How," cried she,
"Would you palm such a cheat on me!
For poor four pound to roar and bellow—
Why sure you want some new Prunella?"[3]
"I'll be revenged, you saucy quean"°   whore
5 (Replies the disappointed Dean),
"I'll so describe your dressing room
The very Irish shall not come."
She answered short, "I'm glad you'll write.
You'll furnish paper when I shite."
—1734

---

[1] *close stool*   Chamber pot enclosed in a stool or box.

[2] *in sixty odd*   I.e., in his old age.

[3] *Prunella*   Name commonly ascribed at the time to a prostitute or promiscuous woman; also, a type of cloth used to make clergymen's robes.

The Lover: A Ballad

At length, by so much importunity pressed,
Take, (Molly[4]), at once, the inside of my breast;
This stupid indifference so often you blame
Is not owing to nature, to fear, or to shame;
5 I am not as cold as a Virgin in lead,
Nor is Sunday's sermon so strong in my head;
I know but too well how time flies along,
That we live but few years and yet fewer are young.

But I hate to be cheated, and never will buy
10 Long years of repentance for moments of joy.
Oh, was there a man (but where shall I find
Good sense and good nature so equally joined?)
Would value his pleasure, contribute to mine,
Not meanly would boast, nor lewdly design,
15 Not over severe, yet not stupidly vain,
For I would have the power though not give the pain;

No pedant yet learnèd, not rakehelly[5] gay
Or laughing because he has nothing to say,
To all my whole sex obliging and free,
20 Yet never be fond of any but me;
In public preserve the decorums are just,
And show in his eyes he is true to his trust,
Then rarely approach, and respectfully bow,
Yet not fulsomely pert, nor yet foppishly low.

25 But when the long hours of public are past
And we meet with champagne and a chicken at last,
May every fond pleasure that hour endear,
Be banished afar both discretion and fear,
Forgetting or scorning the airs of the crowd
30 He may cease to be formal, and I to be proud,
Till lost in the joy we confess that we live,
And he may be rude, and yet I may forgive.

And that my delight may be solidly fixed,
Let the friend and the lover be handsomely mixed,
35 In whose tender bosom my soul might confide,

---

[4] *Molly*   Maria Skerrett, a friend of Montagu's and the mistress of Prime Minister Robert Walpole.

[5] *rakehelly*   In the manner of a rascal or scoundrel.

Whose kindness can sooth me, whose counsel could guide.
From such a dear lover as here I describe
No danger should fright me, no millions should bribe;
But till this astonishing creature I know,
40 As I long have lived chaste, I will keep myself so.

I never will share with the wanton coquette,
Or be caught by a vain affectation of wit.
The toasters[1] and songsters may try all their art
But never shall enter the pass of my heart.
45 I loathe the lewd rake,[2] the dressed fopling° despise;   *fool*
Before such pursuers the nice° virgin flies;   *fastidious*
And as Ovid has sweetly in parables told
We harden like trees, and like rivers are cold.[3]
—1747

Epistle from Mrs. Y[onge][4] to Her Husband

Think not this paper comes with vain pretense
To move your pity, or to mourn th' offense.
Too well I know that hard obdurate heart;
No softening mercy there will take my part,
5 Nor can a woman's arguments prevail,
When even your patron's wise example fails.[5]
But this last privilege I still retain;
Th' oppressed and injured always may complain.
Too, too severely laws of honor bind
10 The weak submissive sex of womankind.
If sighs have gained or force compelled our hand,

Deceived by art, or urged by stern command,
Whatever motive binds the fatal tie,
The judging world expects our constancy.
15 Just heaven! (for sure in heaven does justice reign,
Though tricks below that sacred name profane)
To you appealing I submit my cause,
Nor fear a judgment from impartial laws.
All bargains but conditional are made;
20 The purchase void, the creditor unpaid;
Defrauded servants are from service free;
A wounded slave regains his liberty.
For wives ill used no remedy remains,
To daily racks condemned, and to eternal chains.
25 From whence is this unjust distinction grown?
Are we not formed with passions like your own?
Nature with equal fire our souls endued,
Our minds as haughty, and as warm our blood;
O'er the wide world your pleasures you pursue,
30 The change is justified by something new;
But we must sigh in silence—and be true.
Our sex's weakness you expose and blame
(Of every prating[6] fop the common theme),
Yet from this weakness you suppose is due
35 Sublimer virtue than your Cato[7] knew.
Had heaven designed us trials so severe,
It would have formed our tempers then to bear.
And I have borne (oh, what have I not borne!)
The pang of jealousy, the insults of scorn.
40 Wearied at length, I from your sight remove,
And place my future hopes in secret love.
In the gay bloom of glowing youth retired,
I quit the woman's joy to be admired,
With that small pension your hard heart allows,
45 Renounce your fortune, and release your vows.
To custom (though unjust) so much is due;
I hide my frailty from the public view.
My conscience clear, yet sensible of shame,
My life I hazard, to preserve my fame.[8]
50 And I prefer this low inglorious state
To vile dependence on the thing I hate—

[1] *toasters* Those who propose toasts; i.e., admirers of women.

[2] *rake* Seducer of women.

[3] *as Ovid ... cold* In Ovid's *Metamorphosis*, the virgin Daphne is turned into a laurel tree to escape the advances of the god Apollo, while Arethusa prefers being transformed into a fountain to surrendering to the pursuits of the god Alpheus.

[4] *Mrs. Y[onge]* After Mrs. Yonge and her husband, infamous libertine William Yonge, were separated, she began an affair with another man. Though Mr. Yonge had had numerous affairs throughout their marriage, he successfully sued his wife's lover for damages and then filed for divorce. In a public, well-attended trial, Mr. Yonge was granted not only his divorce but also the majority of his ex-wife's fortune.

[5] *When ... fails* Prime Minister Robert Walpole also engaged in extra-marital affairs, but, unlike Yonge, he endured it when his wife did the same.

[6] *prating* Chattering, talking too much.

[7] *Cato* Roman politician Marcus Porcius Cato, an opponent of Caesar's who, after Caesar's victory, committed suicide rather than submit to his tyrannical authority.

[8] *fame* Good name or character.

But you pursue me to this last retreat.
Dragged into light, my tender crime is shown
And every circumstance of fondness known.
Beneath the shelter of the law you stand,
And urge my ruin with a cruel hand,
While to my fault thus rigidly severe,
Tamely submissive to the man you fear.[1]

This wretched outcast, this abandoned wife,
Has yet this joy to sweeten shameful life:
By your mean conduct, infamously loose,
You are at once my accuser and excuse.
Let me be damned by the censorious prude
(Stupidly dull, or spiritually lewd),
My hapless case will surely pity find
From every just and reasonable mind.
When to the final sentence I submit,
The lips condemn me, but their souls acquit.

No more my husband, to your pleasures go,

70 The sweets of your recovered freedom know.
Go: court the brittle friendship of the great,
Smile at his board,° or at his levee[2] wait;   *dining table*
And when dismissed, to madam's toilet[3] fly,
More than her chambermaids or glasses,° lie,   *mirrors*
75 Tell her how young she looks, how heavenly fair,
Admire the lilies and the roses there.
Your high ambition may be gratified,
Some cousin of her own be made your bride,
And you the father of a glorious race
80 Endowed with Ch—l's strength and Low—r's face.[4]
—1977 (written 1724)

---

[1] *the man you fear*   Sir Robert Walpole.

[2] *levee*   Assembly or reception of visitors.

[3] *toilet*   Dressing room, where it was fashionable for women of distinction to receive visitors as they were finishing their toilet.

[4] *Endowed ... face*   References to General Charles Churchill, who was thought to have had an affair with Lady Walpole, and Anthony Lowther, a well-known ladies' man.

ELIZA HAYWOOD
1693 – 1756

One of the most prolific writers of the eighteenth century is also one of the most elusive. Little is known of Eliza Haywood's private life, yet she produced more than 80 titles and wrote some of the most popular works of the first half of the century. Her fame began in 1719 when she published *Love in Excess; or, the Fatal Inquiry*, an amorous tale of adventure that became one of the best selling books of the early eighteenth century.

Born in London as Eliza Fowler, probably but not certainly in 1693, Haywood left London and married by 1714, when she began a theater apprenticeship in Dublin under the name Eliza Haywood. We know that she had two children (precisely when is unknown), and that her marriage had ended by 1717 when she returned to England and toured with various theater companies. One of her few letters suggests that she began writing to support herself and her children.

Love in Excess began a writing career that progressed at an astonishing pace: Haywood averaged five titles a year in the 1720s and produced two collected editions by 1725. From 1721 until 1724 she had a romantic relationship with the poet Richard Savage, and from 1724 probably until her death she lived with William Hatchett, a minor playwright and actor. Little else is known of her domestic life. Her first biographer, David Erskine Baker, claimed in 1764 that she deliberately obscured her history: "from a supposition of some improper liberties being taken with her character after death, by the intermixture of truth and falsehood with her history, she laid a solemn injunction on a person who was well acquainted with all the particulars of it, not to communicate to any one the least circumstance relating to her."

Although the details of Haywood's personal life remain vague, her public persona was well known. Her dozens of amorous fictions published in the 1720s and 1730s found a wide audience; she was dubbed the "Great arbitress of passion" by one contemporary poet, and "Mrs. Novel" by Henry Fielding (in his 1730 play *The Author's Farce*). *Fantomina* is representative of this early fiction. First published in her 1725 collection *Secret Histories, Novels, and Poems*, it explores male inconstancy, female agency, and sexual adventure, as well as the social repercussions of such adventure.

In the 1730s the pace of Haywood's fiction writing slowed as she returned to the theater. From 1729 to 1737 she wrote or co-wrote several plays and acted in at least six. Collaborating with William Hatchett, she produced the successful *Opera of Operas* in 1733, a musical adaptation of Fielding's *Tragedy of Tragedies*. During this period she also anonymously published *The Adventures of Eovaii, Princess of Ivajeo* (1736), a satire of English politics and—in particular—of Sir Robert Walpole, Prime Minister from 1721 to 1742. In subsequent years she translated works from French, wrote a 1741 parody of *Pamela*, became a publisher herself, continued to act in the theater, and in 1749 wrote a controversial political pamphlet that led to her arrest (though not her prosecution).

In the last fifteen years of her life, Haywood's writing became more domestic, moral, and didactic. Novels such as *The History of Miss Betsy Thoughtless* (1751) and *The History of Jemmy and Jenny Jessamy* (1753) endeavor not only to entertain readers but also to instruct them in such matters as courtship and marriage. She also published the first periodical written for women, *The Female*

Spectator, which appeared in 24 installments from April 1744 to May 1746 and touched on philosophical, political, and scientific, as well as literary, matters. In 1756 she began a new periodical entitled *The Young Lady*, but she announced in an early issue that she was too ill to continue with the journal. She died shortly thereafter, on 25 February 1756.

It was typical of the time that, however widely a woman writer might be read, she would also be criticized for having made writing her profession. In *The Dunciad* (1728) for example, Alexander Pope satirized those he considered to be hack writers, and castigated Haywood in particular. But other contemporaries acknowledged her talent, and present-day critics are increasingly recognizing her important contribution to the development of the novel. Haywood was one of the earliest novelists to explore inner states and feelings. Her reputation may well continue to grow: scholars continue to attribute newly-found titles to this prolific pioneer of the novel.

Fantomina

Eliza Haywood was first famous as an author of amatory fiction, her work raising the popularity of an already popular genre; *Fantomina: or, Love in a Maze* (1725) was one of her many novels of this kind. Although amatory fictions were read by both genders, such works were considered to be books by and for women, focusing on what was thought to be the female reader's greatest interest: sexual and romantic love. In their real lives, the women readers of books like *Fantomina* were disadvantaged by the sexual mores of the time. Celibacy before marriage was the rule—but it was a rule not enforced for men, while a woman discovered to have broken it faced disgrace. Social success (and financial stability) also required that an unmarried woman attract a husband without appearing improperly forward—and without attracting socially dangerous sexual advances. Amatory fictions offered imaginary escape from these confining expectations, but they also illustrated the dangers facing women who transgressed; the stories were presented as means of moral instruction. Whatever delight a reader might take in accounts of scandalous sexuality would be tempered by the story line. Unhappy consequences were inevitably imposed on women characters who acted upon their desires.

While its engagement with romance and sexuality certainly places *Fantomina* in the genre of amatory fiction, the work toys with the expectations of its eighteenth-century readers. Many amatory fictions—including some of Haywood's own—follow a formula in which an innocent woman becomes the passive victim of a deceitful, experienced man. In this formula, the seducer, having captured the woman's virtue, quickly tires of and abandons her; she weeps and protests, but is helpless to prevent him. In *Fantomina*, the unnamed heroine takes an atypically active role in orchestrating her own seduction, and her use of careful deception and disguise complicates the usual pattern of innocence betrayed.

An eighteenth-century audience may also have found *Fantomina* shockingly unclear in the moral attitude it displays toward its characters. The unnamed heroine's unwanted pregnancy and banishment to a French monastery may look like onerous consequences to present-day readers, but the heroine gets off lightly by the standards of the genre; usually, such amatory fictions ended with the heroine's repentance, death, or abject misery, with explicit didactic commentary from the narrator to emphasize the moral point. Some eighteenth-century readers may well have interpreted *Fantomina*'s ending as a just punishment for the heroine. But others might have entertained the thought that banishment to a convent would not necessarily mean an end to the sexual life of a literary character; nuns are a common subject in pornographic writing of the period, and in a number of amatory works of the period, lovers escape from convents.

It is worth noting that the heroine of *Fantomina* is only able to escape the social consequences of her actions for as long as she does because she has financial and personal freedom almost unheard-of for a real woman in the 1720s. The first three disguises she adopts—a well-off woman raped by a suitor and abandoned to a likely fate of prostitution, a maid exploited by her employer, and a widow at risk of poverty because inheritance laws do not protect her rights—provide a somewhat more realistic vision of women's circumstances in the period.

Haywood called *Fantomina* a "Masquerade Novel," and its central theme of disguise reflects the early eighteenth century's preoccupation with masks. Beginning in the late seventeenth century, women often wore masks to the theater; soon after, they began to wear them with elaborate costumes to masquerade balls, which reached a height of popularity in the 1720s. The concealed identity that masks represented offered women a respite from social conventions, allowing them to act relatively freely without fear for their reputations. For men, masked women possessed the allure of mystery; as William Wycherley dryly observed, "a woman masked, like a covered dish, gives a man curiosity and appetite." Perhaps not surprisingly, masquerades were an object of moral condemnation and quickly became associated with unsavory sexuality; at the time Haywood was writing *Fantomina*, the mask was widely considered a symbol of prostitution.

⌘ ⌘ ⌘

Fantomina: or, Love in a Maze

In love the victors from the vanquished fly.
They fly that wound, and they pursue that die.[1]

WALLER.

A young lady of distinguished birth, beauty, wit, and spirit happened to be in a box[2] one night at the playhouse, where, though there were a great number of celebrated toasts,[3] she perceived several gentlemen extremely pleased themselves with entertaining a woman who sat in a corner of the pit and, by her air and manner of receiving them, might easily be known to be one of those who come there for no other purpose than to create acquaintance with as many as seem desirous of it. She could not help testifying her contempt of men who, regardless either of the play or circle,[4] threw away their time in such a manner to some ladies that sat by her. But they, either less surprised by being more accustomed to such sights than she—who had been bred for the most part in the country—or not of a disposition to consider anything very deeply, took but little notice of it. She still thought of it, however, and the longer she reflected on it,

the greater was her wonder that men, some of whom she knew were accounted to have wit, should have tastes so very depraved. This excited a curiosity in her to know in what manner these creatures were addressed. She was young, a stranger to the world and, consequently, to the dangers of it, and, having nobody in town at that time to whom she was obliged to be accountable for her actions, did in everything as her inclinations or humours[5] rendered most agreeable to her. Therefore she thought it not in the least a fault to put in practice a little whim which came immediately into her head, to dress herself as near as she could in the fashion of those women who make sale of their favours and set herself in the way of being accosted as such a one, having at that time no other aim than the gratification of an innocent curiosity. She no sooner designed this frolic than she put it in execution and, muffling her hoods over her face, went the next night into the gallery-box[6] and, practicing as much as she had observed at that distance the behaviour of that woman, was not long before she found her disguise had answered the ends she wore it for. A crowd of purchasers of all degrees and capacities were in a moment gathered about her, each endeavouring to out-bid the other in offering her a price for her embraces. She listened to them all and was not a little diverted in her mind at the disappointment she should give to so many, each of which

---

[1] *"In love … die"* Edmund Waller, "To A.H., of the Different Successes of Their Loves" (1645), ll. 27–28.

[2] *box* Private compartment at a theater.

[3] *celebrated toasts* Beautiful women (toasted with drinks by men).

[4] *circle* I.e., dress circle; the lower gallery, with the most expensive seats.

[5] *humours* Temperaments.

[6] *gallery-box* Box in the higher and less expensive gallery.

thought himself secure of gaining her. She was told by them all that she was the most lovely woman in the world, and some cried, "Gad, she is mighty like my fine Lady Such-a-one"—naming her own name. She was naturally vain and received no small pleasure in hearing herself praised, though in the person of another and a supposed prostitute, but she dispatched as soon as she could all that had hitherto attacked her when she saw the accomplished Beauplaisir was making his way through the crowd as fast as he was able, to reach the bench she sat on. She had often seen him in the drawing room;[1] had talked with him (but then her quality and reputed virtue kept him from using her with that freedom she now expected he would do); and had discovered something in him which had made her often think she should not be displeased if he would abate some part of his reserve. Now was the time to have her wishes answered. He looked in her face and fancied, as many others had done, that she very much resembled that lady whom she really was, but the vast disparity there appeared between their characters prevented him from entertaining even the most distant thought that they could be the same. He addressed her at first with the usual salutations of her pretended profession, as, "Are you engaged, Madam? Will you permit me to wait on you home after the play? By Heaven, you are a fine girl! How long have you used this house?" and such like questions. But, perceiving she had a turn of wit and a genteel manner in her raillery[2] beyond what is frequently to be found among those wretches who are for the most part gentlewomen but by necessity, few of them having had an education suitable to what they affect to appear, he changed the form of his conversation and showed her it was not because he understood no better that he had made use of expressions so little polite. In fine,[3] they were infinitely charmed with each other. He was transported[4] to find so much beauty and wit in a woman who he doubted not but on very easy terms he might enjoy, and she found a vast deal of pleasure in conversing with him in this free and unrestrained manner. They passed their time all the play with an equal

satisfaction, but when it was over, she found herself involved in a difficulty which before never entered into her head, but which she knew not well how to get over. The passion he professed for her was not of that humble nature which can be content with distant adorations. He resolved not to part from her without the gratifications of those desires she had inspired and, presuming on the liberties which her supposed function allowed of, told her she must either go with him to some convenient house of his procuring or permit him to wait on her to her own lodgings. Never had she been in such a dilemma. Three or four times did she open her mouth to confess her real quality,[5] but the influence of her ill stars prevented it by putting an excuse into her head which did the business as well, and at the same time did not take from her the power of seeing and entertaining him a second time with the same freedom she had done this. She told him she was under obligations to a man who maintained her and whom she durst not disappoint, having promised to meet him that night at a house hard by.[6] This story, so like what those ladies sometimes tell, was not at all suspected by Beauplaisir. And, assuring her he would be far from doing her a prejudice, he desired that in return for the pain he should suffer in being deprived of her company that night, that she would order her affairs so as not to render him unhappy the next. She gave a solemn promise to be in the same box on the morrow evening, and they took leave of each other—he to the tavern to drown the remembrance of his disappointment, she in a hackney-chair[7] hurried home to indulge contemplation on the frolic she had taken, designing nothing less on her first reflections than to keep the promise she had made him, and hugging herself with joy that she had the good luck to come off undiscovered.

But these cogitations[8] were but of a short continuance; they vanished with the hurry of her spirits and were succeeded by others vastly different and ruinous. All the charms of Beauplaisir came fresh into her mind; she languished, she almost died for another opportunity of conversing with him, and not all the admonitions of

---

1   *drawing room*   Court assembly.

2   *raillery*   Banter.

3   *In fine*   In short.

4   *transported*   Enraptured.

5   *quality*   High social status.

6   *hard by*   Near by.

7   *hackney-chair*   One-seated vehicle for hire, carried on poles.

8   *cogitations*   Thoughts.

her discretion were effectual to oblige her to deny laying hold of that which offered itself the next night. She depended on the strength of her virtue to bear her safe through trials more dangerous than she apprehended this to be, and never having been addressed by him as Lady, was resolved to receive his devoirs as a town-mistress,[1] imagining a world of satisfaction to herself in engaging him in the character of such a one, and in observing the surprise he would be in to find himself refused by a woman who he supposed granted her favours without exception. Strange and unaccountable were the whimsies she was possessed of, wild and incoherent her desires, unfixed and undetermined her resolutions, but in that of seeing Beauplaisir in the manner she had lately done. As for her proceedings with him, or how a second time to escape him without discovering who she was, she could neither assure herself, nor whether or not in the last extremity she would do so. Bent, however, on meeting him, whatever should be the consequence, she went out some hours before the time of going to the playhouse and took lodgings in a house not very far from it, intending that, if he should insist on passing some part of the night with her, to carry him there, thinking she might with more security to her honour entertain him at a place where she was mistress than at any of his own choosing.

The appointed hour being arrived, she had the satisfaction to find his love in his assiduity.[2] He was there before her, and nothing could be more tender than the manner in which he accosted her. But from the first moment she came in to that of the play being done, he continued to assure her no consideration should prevail with him to part from her again, as she had done the night before, and she rejoiced to think she had taken that precaution of providing herself with a lodging to which she thought she might invite him without running any risk, either of her virtue or reputation. Having told him she would admit of his accompanying her home, he seemed perfectly satisfied and, leading her to the place, which was not above twenty houses distant,

would have ordered a collation[3] to be brought after them. But she would not permit it, telling him she was not one of those who suffered themselves to be treated at their own lodgings, and as soon she was come in, sent a servant belonging to the house to provide a very hand-some supper and wine, and everything was served to table in a manner which showed the director neither wanted[4] money, nor was ignorant how it should be laid out.

This proceeding, though it did not take from him the opinion that she was what she appeared to be, yet it gave him thoughts of her which he had not before. He believed her a mistress, but believed her to be one of a superior rank, and began to imagine the possession of her would be much more expensive than at first he had expected. But, not being of a humour to grudge any-thing for his pleasures, he gave himself no farther trouble than what were occasioned by fears of not having money enough to reach her price about him.

Supper being over, which was intermixed with a vast deal of amorous conversation, he began to explain himself more than he had done, and both by his words and behaviour let her know he would not be denied that happiness. the freedoms she allowed had made him hope. It was in vain she would have retracted the encouragement she had given; in vain she endeavoured to delay till the next meeting the fulfilling of his wishes. She had now gone too far to retreat. He was bold; he was resolute; she, fearful, confused, altogether unpre-pared to resist in such encounters, and rendered more so by the extreme liking she had to him. Shocked, how-ever, at the apprehension of really losing her honour, she struggled all she could, and was just going to reveal the whole secret of her name and quality when the thoughts of the liberty he had taken with her, and those he still continued to prosecute, prevented her with representing the danger of being exposed and the whole affair made a theme for public ridicule. Thus much, indeed, she told him: that she was a virgin and had assumed this manner of behaviour only to engage him. But that he little regarded, or if he had, would have been far from oblig-ing him to desist. Nay, in the present burning eagerness of desire, 'tis probable that had he been acquainted both

---

[1]   *receive ... town-mistress*   To receive his addresses as a prostitute would.

[2]   *in his assiduity*   In devoted attendance.

[3]   *collation*   Light meal.

[4]   *wanted*   Lacked.

with who and what she really was, the knowledge of her birth would not have influenced him with respect sufficient to have curbed the wild exuberance of his luxurious[1] wishes, or made him in that longing—that impatient moment—change the form of his addresses. In fine, she was undone, and he gained a victory so highly rapturous that, had he known over whom, scarce could he have triumphed more. Her tears, however, and the distraction she appeared in after the ruinous ecstasy was past, as it heightened his wonder, so it abated his satisfaction. He could not imagine for what reason a woman who, if she intended not to be a mistress, had counterfeited the part of one and taken so much pains to engage him, should lament a consequence which she could not but expect—and, till the last test, seemed inclinable to grant—and was both surprised and troubled at the mystery. He omitted nothing that he thought might make her easy and, still retaining an opinion that the hope of interest[2] had been the chief motive which had led her to act in the manner she had done (and believing that she might know so little of him as to suppose, now she had nothing left to give he might not make that recompence she expected for her favours), to put her out of that pain, he pulled out of his pocket a purse of gold, entreating her to accept of that as an earnest of what he intended to do for her, assuring her with ten thousand protestations that he would spare nothing which his whole estate could purchase to procure her content and happiness. This treatment made her quite forget the part she had assumed and, throwing it from her with an air of disdain, "Is this a reward," said she, "for condescensions such as I have yielded to? Can all the wealth you are possessed of make a reparation for my loss of honour? Oh no, I am undone beyond the power of heaven itself to help me!" She uttered many more such exclamations, which the amazed Beauplaisir heard without being able to reply to, till, by degrees sinking from that rage of temper, her eyes resumed their softening glances and, guessing at the consternation he was in, "No, my dear Beauplaisir," added she, "your love alone can compensate for the shame you have involved me in. Be you sincere and

constant, and I hereafter shall, perhaps, be satisfied with my fate and forgive myself the folly that betrayed me to you."

Beauplaisir thought he could not have a better opportunity than these words gave him of enquiring who she was and wherefore she had feigned herself to be of a profession which he was now convinced she was not. And after he had made her a thousand vows of an affection as inviolable and ardent[3] as she could wish to find in him, entreated she would inform him by what means his happiness had been brought about, and also to whom he was indebted for the bliss he had enjoyed. Some remains of yet unextinguished modesty and sense of shame made her blush exceedingly at this demand. But, recollecting herself in a little time, she told him so much of the truth as to what related to the frolic she had taken of satisfying her curiosity in what manner mistresses of the sort she appeared to be were treated by those who addressed them, but forbore discovering her true name and quality for the reasons she had done before—resolving, if he boasted of this affair he should not have it in his power to touch her character. She therefore said she was the daughter of a country gentleman who was come to town to buy clothes and that she was called Fantomina. He had no reason to distrust the truth of this story and was therefore satisfied with it, but did not doubt by the beginning of her conduct but that in the end she would be in reality the thing she so artfully had counterfeited, and had good nature enough to pity the misfortunes he imagined would be her lot. But to tell her so or offer his advice in that point was not his business, at least as yet.

They parted not till towards morning, and she obliged him to a willing vow of visiting her the next day at three in the afternoon. It was too late for her to go home that night; therefore, she contented herself with lying there. In the morning she sent for the woman of the house to come up to her and, easily perceiving by her manner that she was a woman who might be influenced by gifts, made her a present of a couple of broad pieces[4] and desired her that if the gentleman who had been there the night before should ask any questions

---

[1] *luxurious* Concerned with extravagant pleasures.

[2] *interest* Profit.

[3] *ardent* Passionate.

[4] *broad pieces* Coins worth twenty shillings each, a substantial sum for a prostitute but not for a gentlewoman.

concerning her, that he should be told she was lately come out of the country, had lodged there about a fortnight,[1] and that her name was Fantomina. "I shall," also added she, "lie but seldom here, nor, indeed, ever come but in those times when I expect to meet him. I would therefore have you order it so that he may think I am but just gone out if he should happen by any accident to call when I am not here, for I would not for the world have him imagine I do not constantly lodge here." The landlady assured her she would do everything as she desired and gave her to understand she wanted not the gift of secrecy.

Everything being ordered at this home for the security of her reputation, she repaired to the other, where she easily excused to an unsuspecting aunt, with whom she boarded, her having been abroad all night, saying she went with a gentleman and his lady in a barge to a little country seat[2] of theirs up the river, all of them designing to return the same evening, but that one of the bargemen happening to be taken ill on the sudden, and no other waterman to be got that night, they were obliged to tarry till morning. Thus did this lady's wit and vivacity assist her in all but where it was most needful. She had discernment to foresee and avoid all those ills which might attend the loss of her reputation, but was wholly blind to those of the ruin of her virtue, and, having managed her affairs so as to secure the one, grew perfectly easy with the remembrance she had forfeited the other. The more she reflected on the merits of Beauplaisir, the more she excused herself for what she had done. And the prospect of that continued bliss she expected to share with him took from her all remorse for having engaged in an affair which promised her so much satisfaction, and in which she found not the least danger of misfortune. "If he is really," said she, to herself, "the faithful, the constant lover he has sworn to be, how charming will be our amour? And if he should be false, grow satiated like other men, I shall but, at the worst, have the private vexation of knowing I have lost him—the intrigue being a secret, my disgrace will be so too. I shall hear no whispers as I pass, 'She is forsaken.' The odious word *forsaken* will never wound my ears, nor

will my wrongs excite either the mirth or pity of the talking world. It will not be even in the power of my undoer himself to triumph over me. And while he laughs at and perhaps despises the fond, the yielding Fantomina, he will revere and esteem the virtuous, the reserved Lady." In this manner did she applaud her own conduct and exult with the imagination that she had more prudence than all her sex beside. And it must be confessed indeed that she preserved an oeconomy[3] in the management of this intrigue beyond what almost any woman but herself ever did: in the first place, by making no person in the world a confidante in it, and in the next, in concealing from Beauplaisir himself the knowledge who she was. For though she met him three or four days in a week at that lodging she had taken for that purpose, yet as much as he employed her time and thoughts, she was never missed from any assembly she had been accustomed to frequent. The business of her love has engrossed her till six in the evening, and before seven she has been dressed in a different habit[4] and in another place. Slippers and a nightgown[5] loosely flowing has been the garb in which he has left the languishing Fantomina; laced and adorned with all the blaze of jewels has he, in less than an hour after, beheld at the royal chapel, the palace gardens, drawing room, opera, or play, the haughty, awe-inspiring lady. A thousand times has he stood amazed at the prodigious likeness between his little mistress and this court beauty, but was still as far from imagining they were the same as he was the first hour he had accosted her in the playhouse, though it is not impossible but that her resemblance to this celebrated lady might keep his inclination alive something longer than otherwise they would have been, and that it was to the thoughts of this as he supposed unenjoyed charmer she owed in great measure the vigour of his latter caresses.

But he varied not so much from his sex as to be able to prolong desire to any great length after possession. The rifled charms of Fantomina soon lost their poignancy[6] and grew tasteless and insipid. And when, the

---

[1]   *fortnight* Two weeks.

[2]   *seat* Residence.

[3]   *oeconomy* Frugal and judicious conduct; discretion.

[4]   *habit* Outfit.

[5]   *nightgown* Evening dress.

[6]   *poignancy* I.e., intensity.

season of the year inviting the company to the Bath,[1] she offered to accompany him, he made an excuse to go without her. She easily perceived his coldness and the reason why he pretended her going would be inconvenient, and endured as much from the discovery as any of her sex could do. She dissembled it, however, before him, and took her leave of him with the show of no other concern than his absence occasioned. But this she did to take from him all suspicion of her following him, as she intended and had already laid a scheme for. From her first finding out that he designed to leave her behind, she plainly saw it was for no other reason than that being tired of her conversation, he was willing to be at liberty to pursue new conquests and, wisely considering that complaints,[2] tears, swoonings, and all the extravagancies which women make use of in such cases have little prevailance over a heart inclined to rove, and only serve to render those who practice them more contemptible by robbing them of that beauty which alone can bring back the fugitive lover, she resolved to take another course. And, remembering the height of transport[3] she enjoyed when the agreeable Beauplaisir kneeled at her feet, imploring her first favours, she longed to prove[4] the same again. Not but a woman of her beauty and accomplishments might have beheld a thousand in that condition Beauplaisir had been, but with her sex's modesty she had not also thrown off another virtue equally valuable, though generally unfortunate: constancy. She loved Beauplaisir. It was only he whose solicitations could give her pleasure and, had she seen the whole species despairing, dying for her sake, it might, perhaps, have been a satisfaction to her pride, but none to her more tender inclination. Her design was once more to engage him. To hear him sigh, to see him languish, to feel the strenuous pressures of his eager arms, to be compelled, to be sweetly forced to what she wished with equal ardour was what she wanted and what she had formed a stratagem[5] to obtain, in

which she promised herself success.

She no sooner heard he had left the town than, making a pretence to her aunt that she was going to visit a relation in the country, she went towards Bath, attended but by two servants who she found reasons to quarrel with on the road and discharged. Clothing herself in a habit she had brought with her, she forsook the coach and went into a wagon, in which equipage she arrived at Bath. The dress she was in was a round-eared cap, a short red petticoat, and a little jacket of grey stuff.[6] All the rest of her accoutrements were answerable to these, and, joined with a broad country dialect, a rude[7] unpolished air (which she, having been bred in these parts, knew very well how to imitate), with her hair and eyebrows blacked, made it impossible for her to be known or taken for any other than what she seemed. Thus disguised did she offer herself to service in the house where Beauplaisir lodged, having made it her business to find out immediately where he was. Notwithstanding this metamorphosis she was still extremely pretty, and the mistress of the house, happening at that time to want a maid, was very glad of the opportunity of taking her. She was presently received into the family and had a post in it such as she would have chosen had she been left at her liberty: that of making the gentlemen's beds, getting them their breakfasts, and waiting on them in their chambers. Fortune in this exploit was extremely on her side. There were no others of the male sex in the house than an old gentleman who had lost the use of his limbs with the rheumatism and had come thither for the benefit of the waters,[8] and her beloved Beauplaisir, so that she was in no apprehensions of any amorous violence but where she wished to find it. Nor were her designs disappointed. He was fired with the first sight of her, and though he did not presently take any farther notice of her than giving her two or three hearty kisses, yet she, who now understood that language but too well, easily saw they were the prelude to more substantial joys. Coming the next morning to bring his chocolate as he had ordered, he caught her by

---

[1] *Bath* Resort town where people of fashion summered; it was known for its medicinal waters and its social opportunities.

[2] *complaints* Sorrowful utterances.

[3] *height of transport* Ecstasy.

[4] *prove* Experience.

[5] *stratagem* Scheme.

[6] *The dress ... grey stuff* Garments associated with the country; *stuff* Fashionable wool fabric.

[7] *rude* Simple.

[8] *benefit of the waters* Hot springs of Bath.

the pretty leg—which the shortness of her petticoat did not in the least oppose—then, pulling her gently to him, asked her how long she had been at service, how many sweethearts she had, if she had ever been in love, and many other such questions befitting one of the degree she appeared to be, all which she answered with such seeming innocence as more inflamed the amorous heart of him who talked to her. He compelled her to sit in his lap and, gazing on her blushing beauties, which, if possible, received addition from her plain and rural dress, he soon lost the power of containing himself. His wild desires burst out in all his words and actions. He called her "little angel," "cherubim"; swore he must enjoy her though death were to be the consequence; devoured her lips, her breasts with greedy kisses; held to his burning bosom her half-yielding, half-reluctant body; nor suffered her to get loose till he had ravaged all and glutted each rapacious sense with the sweet beauties of the pretty Celia—for that was the name she bore in this second expedition. Generous as liberality itself to all who gave him joy this way, he gave her a handsome sum of gold, which she durst not now refuse for fear of creating some mistrust and losing the heart she so lately had regained. Therefore, taking it with an humble curtsy and a well counterfeited show of surprise and joy, she cried, "O law, Sir! What must I do for all this?" He laughed at her simplicity and, kissing her again, though less fervently than he had done before, bade her not be out of the way when he came home at night. She promised she would not, and very obediently kept her word.

His stay at Bath exceeded not a month, but in that time his supposed country lass had persecuted him so much with her fondness that, in spite of the eagerness with which he first enjoyed her, he was at last grown more weary of her than he had been of Fantomina; which, she perceiving, would not be troublesome but, quitting her service, remained privately in the town till she heard he was on his return, and in that time provided herself of another disguise to carry on a third plot, which her inventing brain had furnished her with, once more to renew his twice-decayed ardours. The dress she had ordered to be made was such as widows wear in their first mourning, which, together with the most afflicted and penitential countenance that ever was seen, was no small alteration to her who used to seem all

gaiety. To add to this, her hair, which she was accustomed to wear very loose, both when Fantomina and Celia, was now tied back so strait,[1] and her pinners[2] coming so very forward, that there was none of it to be seen. In fine, her habit and her air[3] were so much changed that she was not more difficult to be known in the rude country girl than she was now in the sorrowful widow.

She knew that Beauplaisir came alone in his chariot[4] to Bath, and in the time of her being servant in the house where he lodged, heard nothing of any body that was to accompany him to London, and hoped he would return in the same manner he had gone. She therefore hired horses and a man to attend her to an inn about ten miles on this side Bath, where, having discharged them, she waited till the chariot should come by, which when it did, and she saw that he was alone in it, she called to him that drove it to stop a moment and, going to the door, saluted the master with these words:

The Distress'd and Wretched, Sir, (*said she,*) never fail to excite Compassion in a generous Mind; and I hope I am not deceiv'd in my Opinion that yours is such:—You have the Appearance of a Gentleman, and cannot, when you hear my Story, refuse that Assistance which is in your Power to give to an unhappy Woman, who without it, may be render'd the most miserable of all created Beings.

IT would not be very easy to represent the Surprise, so odd an Address created in the Mind of him to whom it was made.—She had not the Appearance of one who wanted Charity; and what other Favour she requir'd he cou'd not conceive: But telling her, she might command any Thing in his Power, gave her Encouragement to declare herself in this Manner: You may judge, (*resumed she,*) by the melancholy Garb I am in, that I have lately lost all that ought to be valuable to Womankind; but it is impossible for you to guess the Greatness of my Misfortune, unless you had known my Husband, who

original spelling

---

1 *strait* Tightly drawn.

2 *pinners* Cap, or the hanging flaps thereof, worn by women of high social standing.

3 *her habit and her air* Her dress and appearance.

4 *chariot* Lightweight four-wheeled carriage with seats in the back only.

was Master of every Perfection to endear him to a Wife's Affections.—But, notwithstanding, I look on myself as the most unhappy of my Sex in out-living him, I must so far obey the Dictates of my Discretion, as to take care of the little Fortune he left behind him, which being in the Hands of a Brother of his in *London*, will be all carry'd off to *Holland*, where he is going to settle; if I reach not the Town before he leaves it, I am undone for ever.—To which End I left *Bristol*, the Place where we liv'd, hoping to get a Place in the Stage at *Bath*, but they were all taken up before I came; and being, by a Hurt I got in a Fall, render'd incapable of travelling any long Journey on Horseback, I have no Way to go to *London*, and must be inevitably ruin'd in the Loss of all I have on Earth, without you have good Nature enough to admit me to take Part of your Chariot.

Here the feigned widow ended her sorrowful tale, which had been several times interrupted by a parenthesis of sighs and groans, and Beauplaisir, with a complaisant and tender air, assured her of his readiness to serve her in things of much greater consequence than what she desired of him, and told her it would be an impossibility of denying a place in his chariot to a lady who he could not behold without yielding one in his heart. She answered the compliments he made her but with tears, which seemed to stream in such abundance from her eyes that she could not keep her handkerchief from her face one moment. Being come into the chariot, Beauplaisir said a thousand handsome things to persuade her from giving way to so violent a grief, which, he told her, would not only be destructive to her beauty, but likewise her health. But all his endeavours for consolement appeared ineffectual, and he began to think he should have but a dull journey in the company of one who seemed so obstinately devoted to the memory of her dead husband that there was no getting a word from her on any other theme. But, bethinking himself of the celebrated story of the Ephesian matron,[1] it came into his head to make trial whether she who seemed equally

susceptible of sorrow might not also be so too of love. And, having began a discourse on almost every other topic, and finding her still incapable of answering, he resolved to put it to the proof if this would have no more effect to rouse her sleeping spirits. With a gay air, therefore, though accompanied with the greatest modesty and respect, he turned the conversation, as though without design, on that joy-giving passion, and soon discovered that was indeed the subject she was best pleased to be entertained with. For, on his giving her a hint to begin upon, never any tongue run more voluble[2] than hers on the prodigious power it had to influence the souls of those possessed of it to actions even the most distant from their intentions, principles, or humours. From that she passed to a description of the happiness of mutual affection, the unspeakable ecstasy of those who meet with equal ardency, and represented it in colours so lively, and disclosed by the gestures (with which her words were accompanied) and the accent of her voice so true a feeling of what she said that Beauplaisir, without being as stupid as he was really the contrary, could not avoid perceiving there were seeds of fire not yet extinguished in this fair widow's soul, which wanted but the kindling breath of tender sighs to light into a blaze. He now thought himself as fortunate as some moments before he had the reverse, and doubted not but that before they parted he should find a way to dry the tears of this lovely mourner to the satisfaction of them both. He did not, however, offer, as he had done to Fantomina and Celia, to urge his passion directly to her, but by a thousand little softening artifices, which he well knew how to use, gave her leave to guess he was enamoured. When they came to the inn where they were to lie, he declared himself somewhat more freely and, perceiving she did not resent it past forgiveness, grew more encroaching still. He now took the liberty of kissing away her tears and catching the sighs as they issued from her lips; telling her if grief was infectious, he was resolved to have his share; protesting he would gladly exchange passions with her and be content to bear her load of sorrow, if she would as willingly ease the burden of his love. She said little in answer to the

---

[1] *celebrated story ... matron*   The story originates in Petronius (d. 65 CE; see *Satyricon*, "Eumolpus," 111–12) and was adapted in 1659 by Sir Walter Charlton. In it, a woman famous for her chastity has sex with a soldier whom she encounters while mourning by the tomb of her recently deceased husband.

[2] *voluble*   Fluently.

strenuous pressures with which at last he ventured to enfold her, but not thinking it decent for the character she had assumed to yield so suddenly, and unable to deny both his and her own inclinations, she counterfeited a fainting and fell motionless upon his breast. He had no great notion that she was in a real fit, and the room they supped in happening to have a bed in it, he took her in his arms and laid her on it, believing that whatever her distemper was, that was the most proper place to convey her to. He laid himself down by her and endeavoured to bring her to herself, and she was too grateful to her kind physician at her returning sense to remove from the posture he had put her in, without his leave.

It may perhaps seem strange that Beauplaisir should in such near intimacies continue still deceived. I know there are men who will swear it is an impossibility, and that no disguise could hinder them from knowing a woman they had once enjoyed. In answer to these scruples, I can only say that besides the alteration which the change of dress made in her, she was so admirably skilled in the art of feigning that she had the power of putting on almost what face she pleased, and knew so exactly how to form her behaviour to the character she represented that all the comedians at both playhouses[1] are infinitely short of her performances. She could vary her very glances, tune her voice to accents the most different imaginable from those in which she spoke when she appeared herself. These aids from nature, joined to the wiles of art and the distance between the places where the imagined Fantomina and Celia were, might very well prevent his having any thought that they were the same, or that the fair widow was either of them. It never so much as entered his head, and, though he did fancy he observed in the face of the latter, features which were not altogether unknown to him, yet he could not recollect when or where he had known them. And, being told by her that from her birth she had never removed from Bristol, a place where he never was, he rejected the belief of having seen her and supposed his mind had been deluded by an idea of some other whom she might have a resemblance of.

They passed the time of their journey in as much happiness as the most luxurious gratification of wild desires could make them, and when they came to the end of it, parted not without a mutual promise of seeing each other often. He told her to what place she should direct a letter to him, and she assured him she would send to let him know where to come to her as soon as she was fixed in lodgings.

She kept her promise and, charmed with the continuance of his eager fondness,[2] went not home but into private lodgings, whence she wrote to him to visit her the first opportunity and enquire for the widow Bloomer. She had no sooner dispatched this billet than she repaired to the house where she had lodged as Fantomina, charging the people if Beauplaisir should come there, not to let him know she had been out of town. From thence she wrote to him, in a different hand, a long letter of complaint that he had been so cruel in not sending one letter to her all the time he had been absent, entreated to see him, and concluded with subscribing herself his unalterably affectionate Fantomina. She received in one day answers to both these. The first contained these lines:

To the charming Mrs. Bloomer

It would be impossible, my angel, for me to express the thousandth part of that infinity of transport the sight of your dear letter gave me. Never was woman formed to charm like you. Never did any look like you, write like you, bless like you; nor did ever man adore as I do. Since yesterday we parted, I have seemed a body without a soul, and had you not by this inspiring billet[3] gave me new life, I know not what by tomorrow I should have been. I will be with you this evening about five. O' tis an age till then! But the cursed formalities of duty oblige me to dine with my Lord, who never rises from table till that hour. Therefore, adieu till then, sweet lovely mistress of the soul and all the faculties of

Your most faithful,

BEAUPLAISIR.

The other was in this manner:

To the lovely FANTOMINA

---

1   *comedians at both playhouses*   Actors in the comedies staged by the licensed theaters at Drury Lane and Covent Garden, London.

2   *eager fondness*   Infatuation.
3   *billet*   Note.

If you were half so sensible as you ought of your own power of charming, you would be assured that to be unfaithful or unkind to you would be among the things that are in their very natures impossibilities. It was my misfortune, not my fault, that you were not persecuted every post with a declaration of my unchanging passion. But I had unluckily forgot the name of the woman at whose house you are, and knew not how to form a direction that it might come safe to your hands. And indeed, the reflection how you might misconstrue my silence brought me to town some weeks sooner than I intended. If you knew how I have languished to renew those blessings I am permitted to enjoy in your society, you would rather pity than condemn

Your ever faithful,

BEAUPLAISIR.

P.S. *I fear I cannot see you till tomorrow; some business has unluckily fallen out that will engross my hours till then. Once more, my dear, adieu.*

"Traitor!" cried she as soon as she had read them. "'Tis thus our silly, fond, believing sex are served when they put faith in man. So had I been deceived and cheated, had I like the rest believed, and sat down mourning in absence, and vainly waiting recovered tendernesses. How do some women," continued she, "make their life a hell, burning in fruitless expectations and dreaming out their days in hopes and fears, then wake at last to all the horror of despair? But I have outwitted even the most subtle of the deceiving kind, and while he thinks to fool me, he is himself the only beguiled person."

She made herself, most certainly, extremely happy in the reflection on the success of her stratagems and, while the knowledge of his inconstancy and levity of nature kept her from having that real tenderness for him she would else have had, she found the means of gratifying the inclination she had for his agreeable person in as full a manner as she could wish. She had all the sweets of love, but as yet had tasted none of the gall,[1] and was in a state of contentment which might be envied by the more delicate.

When the expected hour arrived, she found that her lover had lost no part of the fervency[2] with which he had parted from her. But when the next day she received him as Fantomina, she perceived a prodigious difference, which led her again into reflections on the unaccountableness of men's fancies, who still prefer the last conquest only because it is the last. Here was an evident proof of it, for there could not be a difference in merit because they were the same person, but the widow Bloomer was a more new acquaintance than Fantomina, and therefore esteemed more valuable. This, indeed, must be said of Beauplaisir, that he had a greater share of good nature than most of his sex, who, for the most part, when they are weary of an intrigue, break it entirely off without any regard to the despair of the abandoned nymph.[3] Though he retained no more than a bare pity and complaisance for Fantomina, yet, believing she loved him to an excess, he would not entirely forsake her, though the continuance of his visits was now become rather a penance than a pleasure.

The widow Bloomer triumphed some time longer over the heart of this inconstant, but at length her sway was at an end, and she sunk in this character to the same degree of tastelessness[4] as she had done before in that of Fantomina and Celia. She presently perceived it, but bore it as she had always done, it being but what she expected. She had prepared herself for it and had another project in embryo which she soon ripened into action. She did not, indeed, complete it altogether so suddenly as she had done the others, by reason there must be persons employed in it, and the aversion she had to any confidantes in her affairs, and the caution with which she had hitherto acted, and which she was still determined to continue, made it very difficult for her to find a way without breaking through that resolution to compass what she wished. She got over the difficulty at last, however, by proceeding in a manner if possible more extraordinary than all her former behaviour. Muffling herself up in her hood one day, she went into the park about the hour when there are a great

---

[1] *gall* Bitterness.

[2] *fervency* Passion.

[3] *nymph* Young woman.

[4] *tastelessness* Dullness.

many necessitous[1] gentlemen who think themselves above doing what they call "little things for a maintenance" walking in the Mall[2] to take a chameleon treat and fill their stomachs with air instead of meat.[3] Two of those, who by their physiognomy[4] she thought most proper for her purpose, she beckoned to come to her and, taking them into a walk more remote from company, began to communicate the business she had with them in these words: "I am sensible, Gentlemen," said she, "that, through the blindness of fortune and partiality of the world, merit frequently goes unrewarded, and that those of the best pretensions[5] meet with the least encouragement. I ask your pardon," continued she, perceiving they seemed surprised, "if I am mistaken in the notion that you two may, perhaps, be of the number of those who have reason to complain of the injustice of fate. But if you are such as I take you for, I have a proposal to make you which may be of some little advantage to you." Neither of them made any immediate answer, but appeared buried in consideration for some moments. At length, "We should, doubtless, Madam," said one of them, "willingly come into any measures to oblige you, provided they are such as may bring us into no danger, either as to our persons or reputations." "That which I require of you," resumed she, "has nothing in it criminal. All that I desire is secrecy in what you are entrusted, and to disguise yourselves in such a manner as you cannot be known if hereafter seen by the person on whom you are to impose. In fine, the business is only an innocent frolic, but if blazed abroad,[6] might be taken for too great a freedom in me. Therefore, if you resolve to assist me, here are five pieces to drink my health and assure you that I have not discoursed you on an affair I design not to proceed in. And when it is accomplished fifty more lie ready for your acceptance." These words and, above all, the money, which was a sum which 'tis probable

they had not seen of a long time, made them immediately assent to all she desired and press for the beginning of their employment. But things were not yet ripe for execution, and she told them that the next day they should be let into the secret, charging them to meet her in the same place at an hour she appointed. 'Tis hard to say which of these parties went away best pleased—they, that fortune had sent them so unexpected a windfall, or she, that she had found persons who appeared so well qualified to serve her.

Indefatigable in the pursuit of whatsoever her humour was bent upon, she had no sooner left her new-engaged emissaries than she went in search of a house for the completing her project. She pitched on one very large and magnificently furnished, which she hired by the week, giving them the money beforehand to prevent any inquiries. The next day she repaired to the park, where she met the punctual 'squires of low degree, and, ordering them to follow her to the house she had taken, told them they must condescend to appear like servants, and gave each of them a very rich livery.[7] Then, writing a letter to Beauplaisir in a character vastly different from either of those she had made use of as Fantomina or the fair widow Bloomer, ordered one of them to deliver it into his own hands, to bring back an answer, and to be careful that he sifted out nothing of the truth. "I do not fear," said she, "that you should discover to him who I am, because that is a secret of which you yourselves are ignorant, but I would have you be so careful in your replies that he may not think the concealment springs from any other reasons than your great integrity to your trust. Seem, therefore, to know my whole affairs, and let your refusing to make him partaker in the secret appear to be only the effect of your zeal for my interest and reputation." Promises of entire fidelity on the one side and reward on the other being passed, the messenger made what haste he could to the house of Beauplaisir and, being there told where he might find him, performed exactly the injunction that had been given him. But never astonishment exceeding that which Beauplaisir felt at the reading this billet, in which he found these lines:

To the all-conquering Beauplaisir

---

[1] *necessitous* In need of money, indigent.

[2] *the Mall* Fashionable pedestrian concourse in St. James's Park, London.

[3] *to take ... meat* The chameleon was believed to live on air.

[4] *physiognomy* Facial appearance.

[5] *pretensions* Claims (here, to merit).

[6] *blazed abroad* Made widely known.

[7] *livery* Uniform.

I imagine not that 'tis a new thing to you to be told you are the greatest charm in nature to our sex. I shall, therefore, not to fill up my letter with any impertinent praises on your wit or person, only tell you that I am infinite in love with both and, if you have a heart not too deeply engaged, should think myself the happiest of my sex in being capable of inspiring it with some tenderness. There is but one thing in my power to refuse you, which is the knowledge of my name, which, believing the sight of my face will render no secret, you must not take it ill that I conceal from you. The bearer of this is a person I can trust. Send by him your answer, but endeavour not to dive into the meaning of this mystery, which will be impossible for you to unravel and at the same time very much disoblige me. But, that you may be in no apprehensions of being imposed on by a woman unworthy of your regard, I will venture to assure you the first and greatest men in the kingdom would think themselves blessed to have that influence over me you have, though unknown to yourself, acquired. But I need not go about to raise your curiosity by giving you any idea of what my person is. If you think fit to be satisfied, resolve to visit me tomorrow about three in the afternoon, and, though my face is hid, you shall not want sufficient demonstration that she who takes these unusual measures to commence a friendship with you is neither old nor deformed. Till then I am,

> Yours,

> INCOGNITA.

He had scarce come to the conclusion before he asked the person who brought it from what place he came, the name of the lady he served, if she were a wife or widow, and several other questions directly opposite to the directions of the letter. But silence would have availed him as much as did all those testimonies of curiosity. No *Italian bravo*[1] employed in a business of the like nature performed his office with more artifice,[2] and the impatient enquirer was convinced that nothing but doing as he was desired could give him any light into the character of the woman who declared so violent a passion for him. And, little fearing any consequence which could ensue from such an encounter, he resolved to rest satisfied till he was informed of everything from herself, not imagining this Incognita varied so much from the generality of her sex as to be able to refuse the knowledge of anything to the man she loved with that transcendency of passion she professed, and which his many successes with the ladies gave him encouragement enough to believe. He therefore took pen and paper, and answered her letter in terms tender enough for a man who had never seen the person to whom he wrote. The words were as follows:

To the obliging and witty Incognita

Though to tell me I am happy enough to be liked by a woman such as by your manner of writing I imagine you to be is an honour which I can never sufficiently acknowledge, yet I know not how I am able to content myself with admiring the wonders of your wit alone. I am certain a soul like yours must shine in your eyes with a vivacity which must bless all they look on. I shall, however, endeavour to restrain myself in those bounds you are pleased to set me, till by the knowledge of my inviolable fidelity I may be thought worthy of gazing on that heaven I am now but to enjoy in contemplation. You need not doubt my glad compliance with your obliging summons. There is a charm in your lines which gives too sweet an idea of their lovely author to be resisted. I am all impatient for the blissful moment which is to throw me at your feet and give me an opportunity of convincing you that I am,

> Your everlasting slave,

> BEAUPLAISIR.

Nothing could be more pleased than she to whom it was directed at the receipt of this letter. But when she was told how inquisitive he had been concerning her character and circumstances, she could not forbear laughing heartily to think of the tricks she had played him and applauding her own strength of genius and force of resolution, which by such unthought-of ways could triumph over her lover's inconstancy and render that very temper which to other women is the greatest curse a means to make herself more blessed. "Had he been faithful to me," said she to herself, "either as Fantomina, or Celia, or the widow Bloomer, the most violent passion, if it does not change its object, in time will wither. Possession naturally abates the vigour of

---

1   *Italian bravo*   Hired soldier; here, a spy.

2   *artifice*   Cunning.

desire, and I should have had at best but a cold, insipid, husband-like lover in my arms. But by these arts of passing on him as a new mistress whenever the ardour (which alone makes love a blessing) begins to diminish for the former one, I have him always raving, wild, impatient, longing, dying. O that all neglected wives and fond abandoned nymphs would take this method! Men would be caught in their own snare and have no cause to scorn our easy, weeping, wailing sex!" Thus did she pride herself, as if secure she never should have any reason to repent the present gaiety of her humour. The hour drawing near in which he was to come, she dressed herself in as magnificent a manner as if she were to be that night at a ball at court, endeavouring to repair the want of those beauties which the vizard[1] should conceal by setting forth the others with the greatest care and exactness. Her fine shape and air and neck appeared to great advantage, and by that which was to be seen of her one might believe the rest to be perfectly agreeable. Beauplaisir was prodigiously charmed, as well with her appearance as with the manner she entertained him. But, though he was wild with impatience for the sight of a face which belonged to so exquisite a body, yet he would not immediately press for it, believing before he left her he should easily obtain that satisfaction. A noble collation being over, he began to sue for[2] the performance of her promise of granting everything he could ask, excepting the sight of her face and knowledge of her name. It would have been a ridiculous piece of affectation in her to have seemed coy in complying with what she herself had been the first in desiring. She yielded without even a show of reluctance. And if there be any true felicity in an amour such as theirs, both here enjoyed it to the full. But not in the height of all their mutual raptures could he prevail on her to satisfy his curiosity with the sight of her face. She told him that she hoped he knew so much of her as might serve to convince him she was not unworthy of his tenderest regard, and if he could not content himself with that which she was willing to reveal, and which was the conditions of their meeting, dear as he was to her she would rather part with him forever than consent to

gratify an inquisitiveness which, in her opinion, had no business with his love. It was in vain that he endeavoured to make her sensible of her mistake and that this restraint was the greatest enemy imaginable to the happiness of them both. She was not to be persuaded, and he was obliged to desist his solicitations, though determined in his mind to compass what he so ardently desired before he left the house. He then turned the discourse wholly on the violence of the passion he had for her, and expressed the greatest discontent in the world at the apprehensions of being separated; swore he could dwell forever in her arms, and with such an undeniable earnestness pressed to be permitted to tarry with her the whole night that had she been less charmed with his renewed eagerness of desire, she scarce would have had the power of refusing him. But in granting this request she was not without a thought that he had another reason for making it besides the extremity of his passion, and had it immediately in her head how to disappoint him.

The hours of repose being arrived, he begged she would retire to her chamber, to which she consented but obliged him to go to bed first, which he did not much oppose because he supposed she would not lie in her mask and doubted not but the morning's dawn would bring the wished discovery. The two imagined servants ushered him to his new lodging, where he lay some moments in all the perplexity imaginable at the oddness of this adventure. But she suffered not these cogitations to be of any long continuance. She came, but came in the dark, which, being no more than he expected by the former part of her proceedings, he said nothing of. But as much satisfaction as he found in her embraces, nothing ever longed for the approach of day with more impatience than he did. At last it came, but how great was his disappointment when, by the noises he heard in the street—the hurry of the coaches and the cries of penny-merchants[3]—he was convinced it was night nowhere but with him? He was still in the same darkness as before, for she had taken care to blind the windows in such a manner that not the least chink was left to let in day. He complained of her behaviour in terms that she would not have been able to resist yielding to if she had not been certain it would have been the

---

[1]   *vizard*   Mask worn at a masquerade ball.

[2]   *to sue for*   Beg for, ask for.

[3]   *penny-merchants*   Street merchants selling cheap goods.

ruin of her passion. She therefore answered him only as she had done before and, getting out of the bed from him, flew out of the room with too much swiftness for him to have overtaken her if he had attempted it. The moment she left him, the two attendants entered the chamber and, plucking down the implements which had screened him from the knowledge of that which he so much desired to find out, restored his eyes once more to day. They attended to assist him in dressing, brought him tea, and by their obsequiousness let him see there was but one thing which the mistress of them would not gladly oblige him in. He was so much out of humour, however, at the disappointment of his curiosity that he resolved never to make a second visit. Finding her in an outer room, he made no scruple of expressing the sense he had of the little trust she reposed in him, and at last plainly told her he could not submit to receive obligations from a lady who thought him uncapable of keeping a secret which she made no difficulty of letting her servants into. He resented; he once more entreated; he said all that man could do to prevail on her to unfold the mystery. But all his adjurations[1] were fruitless, and he went out of the house determined never to re-enter it till she should pay the price of his company with the discovery of her face and circumstances. She suffered him to go with this resolution and doubted not but he would recede from it when he reflected on the happy moments they had passed together. But if he did not, she comforted herself with the design of forming some other stratagem with which to impose on him a fourth time.

She kept the house and her gentlemen-equipage for about a fortnight, in which time she continued to write to him as Fantomina and the widow Bloomer, and received the visits he sometimes made to each. But his behaviour to both was grown so cold that she began to grow as weary of receiving his now insipid caresses as he was of offering them. She was beginning to think in what manner she should drop these two characters when the sudden arrival of her mother, who had been some time in a foreign country, obliged her to put an immediate stop to the course of her whimsical adventures. That lady, who was severely virtuous, did not approve of many things she had been told of the conduct of her daughter. And though it was not in the power of any person in the world to inform her of the truth of what she had been guilty of, yet she heard enough to make her keep her afterwards in a restraint little agreeable to her humour and the liberties to which she had been accustomed.

But this confinement was not the greatest part of the trouble of this now afflicted lady. She found the consequences of her amorous follies would be, without almost a miracle, impossible to be concealed: she was with child. And though she would easily have found means to have screened even this from the knowledge of the world had she been at liberty to have acted with the same unquestionable authority over herself as she did before the coming of her mother, yet now all her invention was at a loss for a stratagem to impose on a woman of her penetration.[2] By eating little, lacing prodigious strait, and the advantage of a great hoop-petticoat, however, her bigness was not taken notice of, and perhaps she would not have been suspected till the time of her going into the country, where her mother designed to send her and from whence she intended to make her escape to some place where she might be delivered with secrecy, if the time of it had not happened much sooner than she expected. A ball being at court, the good old lady was willing she should partake of the diversion of it as a farewell to the town. It was there she was seized with those pangs which none in her condition are exempt from. She could not conceal the sudden rack[3] which all at once invaded her, or, had her tongue been mute, her wildly rolling eyes, the distortion of her features, and the convulsions which shook her whole frame in spite of her would have revealed she laboured under some terrible shock of nature. Everybody was surprised; everybody was concerned; but few guessed at the occasion. Her mother grieved beyond expression, doubted not but she was struck with the hand of death, and ordered her to be carried home in a chair while herself followed in another. A physician was immediately sent for, but he, presently perceiving what was her distemper, called the old lady aside and told her

---

[1] *adjurations* Entreaties.

[2] *penetration* Discernment; mental acuteness.

[3] *rack* Pain.

it was not a doctor of his sex but one of her own her daughter stood in need of. Never was astonishment and horror greater than that which seized the soul of this afflicted parent at these words. She could not for a time believe the truth of what she heard, but he insisting on it and conjuring her to send for a midwife, she was at length convinced of it. All the pity and tenderness she had been for some moment before possessed of now vanished and were succeeded by an adequate shame and indignation. She flew to the bed where her daughter was lying and, telling her what she had been informed of and which she was now far from doubting, commanded her to reveal the name of the person whose insinuations had drawn her to this dishonour. It was a great while before she could be brought to confess anything, and much longer before she could be prevailed on to name the man whom she so fatally had loved. But the rack of nature growing more fierce, and the enraged old lady protesting no help should be afforded her while she persisted in her obstinacy, she, with great difficulty and hesitation in her speech, at last pronounced the name of Beauplaisir. She had no sooner satisfied her weeping mother than that sorrowful lady sent messengers at the same time for a midwife and for that gentleman who had occasioned the other's being wanted. He happened by accident to be at home and immediately obeyed the summons, though prodigiously surprised what business a lady so much a stranger to him could have to impart. But how much greater was his amazement when, taking him into her closet, she there acquainted him with her daughter's misfortune, of the discovery she had made, and how far he was concerned in it? All the idea one can form of wild astonishment was mean to what he felt. He assured her that the young lady her daughter was a person whom he had never more than at a distance admired, that he had indeed spoke to her in public company, but that he never had a thought which tended to her dishonour. His denials, if possible, added to the indignation she was before inflamed with. She had no longer patience and, carrying him into the chamber where she was just delivered of a fine girl, cried out, "I will not be imposed on. The truth by one of you shall be revealed." Beauplaisir, being brought to the bedside, was beginning to address himself to the lady in it to beg she would clear the mistake her mother was involved in,

when she, covering herself with the clothes and ready to die a second time with the inward agitations of her soul, shrieked out, "Oh, I am undone! I cannot live and bear this shame!" But the old lady, believing that now or never was the time to dive into the bottom of this mystery, forcing her to rear her head, told her she should not hope to escape the scrutiny of a parent she had dishonoured in such a manner and, pointing to Beauplaisir, "Is this the gentleman," said she, "to whom you owe your ruin? Or have you deceived me by a fictitious tale?"

"Oh no!" resumed the trembling creature, "He is indeed the innocent cause of my undoing. Promise me your pardon," continued she, "and I will relate the means." Here she ceased, expecting what she would reply, which, on hearing Beauplaisir cry out, "What mean you, Madam? I your undoing, who never harboured the least design on you in my life?" she did in these words: "Though the injury you have done your family," said she, "is of a nature which cannot justly hope forgiveness, yet be assured, I shall much sooner excuse you when satisfied of the truth than while I am kept in a suspense if possible as vexatious as the crime[1] itself is to me." Encouraged by this, she related the whole truth. And 'tis difficult to determine if Beauplaisir or the lady were most surprised at what they heard—he, that he should have been blinded so often by her artifices, or she, that so young a creature should have the skill to make use of them. Both sat for some time in a profound reverie, till at length she broke it first in these words: "Pardon, Sir," said she, "the trouble I have given you. I must confess it was with a design to oblige you to repair the supposed injury you had done this unfortunate girl by marrying her, but now I know not what to say. The blame is wholly hers, and I have nothing to request further of you than that you will not divulge the distracted folly she has been guilty of." He answered her in terms perfectly polite, but made no offer of that which perhaps she expected, though could not, now informed of her daughter's proceedings, demand. He assured her, however, that if she would commit the new-born lady to his care, he would discharge it faithfully. But neither of them would consent to that, and he took his leave, full of cogitations more confused than ever he

---

[1] *crime* Morally odious act.

had known in his whole life. He continued to visit there to enquire after her health every day, but the old lady perceiving there was nothing likely to ensue from these civilities but perhaps a renewing of the crime, she entreated him to refrain, and as soon as her daughter was in a condition, sent her to a monastery in France, the abbess of which had been her particular friend. And thus ended an intrigue which, considering the time it lasted, was as full of variety as any, perhaps, that many ages has produced.

—1725

IN CONTEXT

The Eighteenth-Century Sexual Imagination

from *A Present for a Servant-Maid* (1743)

> Eliza Haywood wrote extensively on romantic and sexual themes not only in her fiction and drama but also in a variety of nonfictional prose contexts. Among the most interesting of these works is *A Present for a Servant-Maid*, which was published anonymously in 1743. It went through several editions and was widely imitated. The work presents advice for young female servants and devotes a considerable amount of attention to the difficulties they are likely to face at the hands of the gentlemen in the households in which they work.

Dear Girls,

I think there cannot be a greater service done to the commonwealth (of which you are a numerous body) than to lay down some general rules for your behaviour, which, if observed, will make your condition as happy to yourselves as it is necessary to others. Nothing can be more melancholy than to hear continual complaints for faults which a very little reflection would render it almost as easy for you to avoid as to commit; most of the mistakes laid to your charge proceeding at first only from a certain indolence and inactivity of the mind, but, if not rectified in time, become habitual and difficult to be thrown off.

As the first step therefore towards being happy in service, you should never enter into a place[1] but with a view of *staying in it*; to which end I think it highly necessary that (as no mistress worth serving will take you without a character[2]) you should also make some enquiry into the place before you suffer yourself to be hired. There are some houses which appear well by *day*, that it would be little safe for a modest maid to sleep in at *night*: I do not mean those coffeehouses, bagnios, &c. which some parts of the town, particularly Covent Garden,[3] abounds with; for in those the very aspect of the persons who keep them are sufficient to show what manner of trade they follow. But houses which have no public show of business, are richly furnished, and where the mistress has an air of the strictest modesty, and perhaps affects a double purity of behaviour, yet under such roofs, and under the sanction of such women as I have described, are too frequently acted such scenes of debauchery as would startle even the owners of some common brothels. Great regard is therefore to be had to the character of the persons who recommend you, and the manner in which you heard of the place; for

---

[1] *place* Position (of employment).

[2] *character* I.e., a letter of character reference.

[3] *Covent Garden* Where many brothels were located.

those sort of people have commonly their emissaries at inns, watching the coming in of the wagons, and, if they find any pretty girls who come to town to go to service, presently hire them in the name of some person of condition, and by this means the innocent young creature, while she thanks God for her good fortune in being so immediately provided for, is ensnared into the service of the Devil. Here temptations of all kinds are offered her; she is not treated as a servant but a guest; her country habit is immediately stripped off, and a gay modish one put on in the stead; and then the designed victim, willing or unwilling, is exposed to sale to the first lewd supporter of her mistress's grandeur that comes to the house. If she refuses the shameful business for which she was hired, and prefers the preservation of her virtue to all the promises can be made her, which way can she escape? She is immediately confined, close watched, threatened, and at last forced to compliance. Then, by a continued prostitution withered in her bloom, she becomes despised, no longer affords any advantage to the wretch who betrayed her, and is turned out to infamy and beggary, perhaps too with the most loathsome of all diseases, which ends her miserable days in an hospital or workhouse, in case she can be admitted, though some have not had even that favour, but found their deathbed on a dunghill.

... This town at present abounds with such variety of allurements that a young heart cannot be too much upon its guard. It is those expensive ones, I mean, which drain your purse as well as waste your time: such as plays, the Wells,[1] and gardens, and other public shows and entertainments; places which it becomes nobody to be seen often at, and more especially young women in your station. All things that are invented merely for the gratification of luxury, and are of no other service than temporary delight, ought to be shunned by those who have their bread to get. Nor is it any excuse for you that a friend gives you tickets and it costs you nothing; it costs you at least what is more precious than money—your time; not only what you pass in seeing the entertainments, but what the idea and memory of them will take up. They are a kind of delicious poison to the mind, which pleasingly intoxicates and destroys all relish for any thing beside. If you could content yourselves with one sight and no more of any, or even all, these shows, or could you answer that they would engross your thoughts no longer than while you were spectators, the curiosity might be excusable. But it rarely happens that you have this command over yourselves; the music, the dances, the gay clothes and scenes make too strong an impression on the senses not to leave such traces behind as are entirely inconsistent either with good housewifery or the duties of your place. Avoid, therefore, such dangerous amusements....

Temptations from your Master: Being so much under his command, and obliged to attend him at any hour and at any place he is pleased to call you will lay you under difficulties to avoid his importunities, which it must be confessed are not easy to surmount; yet a steady resolution will enable you; and as a vigorous resistance is less to be expected in your station, your persevering may, perhaps, in time oblige him to desist and acknowledge you have more reason than himself: it is a duty, however, owing to yourself to endeavour it.

Behaviour to him, if a single man: If he happens to be a single man, and is consequently under less restraint, be as careful as you can, opportunities will not be wanting to prosecute his aim; and, as you cannot avoid hearing what he says, must humbly, and in the most modest terms you can, remonstrate to him the sin and shame he would involve you in; and omit nothing to make him sensible how cruel it is to go about to betray a person whom it is his duty to protect. Add that nothing shall ever prevail on you to forfeit your virtue; and take care that all your looks and gestures correspond with what you say: let no wanton smile or light coquette air give him room to suspect you are not so much displeased

---

[1]   *the Wells* Several locations of popular springs, such as Epsom Wells and Lambeth Wells, also offered other entertainments, such as gambling or concerts, in addition to their spas.

with the inclination he has for you as you would seem; for if he once imagines you deny but for the sake of form, it will the more inflame him, and render him more pressing than ever. Let your answers, therefore, be delivered with the greatest sedateness. Show that you are truly sorry, and more ashamed than vain that he finds anything in you to like....

If a married man: Greater caution is still to be observed if he is a married man. As soon as he gives you the least intimation of his design, either by word or action, you ought to keep as much as possible out of his way in order to prevent his declaring himself more plainly; and if, in spite of all your care, he find an opportunity of telling you his mind, you must remonstrate the wrong he would do his wife, and how much he demeans both himself and her by making such an offer to his own servant. If this is ineffectual and he continues to persecute you still, watching you wherever you go, both abroad and at home, and is so troublesome in his importunities that you cannot do your business quietly and regularly, your only way then is to give warning; but be very careful not to let your mistress know the motive of it. That is a point too tender to be touched upon even in the most distant manner, much less plainly told. Such a discovery would not only give her an infinite uneasiness (for in such cases the innocent suffer for the crimes of the guilty), but turn the inclination your master had for you into the extremest hatred. He may endeavour to clear himself by throwing the odium on you, for those who are unjust in one thing will be so in others; and you cannot expect that he who does not scruple to wrong his wife, and indeed his own soul, will make any to take away your reputation, when he imagines his own will be secured by it. He may pretend you threw yourself in his way when he was in liquor, or that, having taken notice of some indecencies in your carriage, and suspecting you were a loose creature, he had only talked a little idly to you as a trial how you would behave; and that it was because he did not persist as you expected, and offer you money, that you had made the discovery—partly out of malice, and partly to give yourself an air of virtue. But though he should not be altogether so unjust and cruel, nor allege any thing of this kind against you, it would be a thing which you never ought to forgive yourself for, if by any imprudent hint you gave occasion for a breach of that amity and confidence which is the greatest blessing of the married state, and when once dissolved, continual jarring and mutual discontent are the unfailing consequence.

from *Venus in the Cloister; or, The Nun in Her Smock* (1725)

At the end of *Fantomina* Haywood refers to the heroine being sent "to a monastery in France." For eighteenth-century readers, such a reference would almost certainly have carried with it connotations of debauchery; sexual activities in French nunneries were a frequent topic in the erotic fiction of the period. One of the best-known examples is *Vénus Dans Le Cloitre, Ou La Religieuse En Chemise,* a French pornographic novel originally printed in 1683 and translated into English as *Venus In The Cloister* in 1725. The following excerpt is related by Angelica, a 20-year-old nun; she is discussing the activities of Eugenia, another woman in the same nunnery.

Angel. I'll tell thee: I thought I saw one of the workmen enter her cell, and, tripping softly along the dormitory, I made up to her door, which having a large chink between the boards, I saw what I tell you. The first thing I beheld was Eugenia all naked with Frederick sitting by her, holding in his hand—which extremely surprised me, imagining to myself that she could never enjoy the excess of pleasure I afterwards found she did.

Said I to myself, "Lord! what pain must poor Eugenia undergo? How is it possible he should not tear her to pieces?" These were my thoughts, but I suppose he treated her very gently on account of her youth, for she was but bare fifteen. While I was thus busied in my thoughts, I heard Frederick say, "Eugenia, my dear, turn upon your back;" which after she had done, he got up and put his—into her—for my part I was quite frightened when I heard her cry out as if she were in excessive pain. This gave me, as thou may'st well imagine, a great deal of uneasiness, for I did not dare to come in for fear of surprising of them, which might have had perhaps but very ill consequences. However, a moment after I saw her move her legs and embrace her lover with both her arms after such an extraordinary manner as sufficiently expressed the utmost satisfaction.

Frederick was no less pleased with this encounter. "Ha!" said he, "what pleasure does thou give me!" In short, after endeavouring to exceed each other in the amorous combat, they softly sighed, and then for some small space reposed as in an ecstasy. And to show thee what love Eugenia had for her lover, I must tell thee that, notwithstanding this pleasing trance, she could not help now and then giving him many a kiss, nay, I think she kissed him all over, and spoke to him the kindest things in the world, which sufficiently convinced me what excess of joy she then received. This raised a desire in me to taste the same love potion, and indeed I even grew distracted with strong unknown longings and desires. I could not help thinking of it all night, and slept not a moment till the morning, and, by a lucky accident, fortune, who favoured my desires, gave me some consolation.

Print Culture, Stage Culture

CONTEXTS

With the Restoration of the monarchy in 1660 came the reopening of the theater, in whatever buildings could be found, and Charles II's issue of licences for two playhouses and companies. The major innovations were the proscenium arch (though much action still took place on an apron stage in front of the curtain), movable scenery, and women instead of boys playing the female roles. The new stage scenery took the form of painted flats trundled on and off in grooves in the stage, so that successive scenes—say, in the park, in the street, and indoors—would each be visually represented instead of entirely imagined by the audience. Theater managers sought increasingly ornate, complex scenery to accompany their productions. This was especially so for tragedy, which was often set in exotic locations and extreme circumstances, unlike comedy, which represented the life and society known by experience to the spectators. Updated versions of old plays were popular, and writers assumed a free hand in reshaping the originals. One of the era's most popular productions was Poet Laureate Nahum Tate's version of Shakespeare's *King Lear*, which held the stage for 150 years after its first performance in 1681, after the original had twice been revived unsuccessfully. The excerpt of Tate's *Lear* reprinted here gives a sense of the ways in which Tate changed the original text. While in the parallel scene in Shakespeare's *Lear*, Cordelia is executed after she and Lear are captured, and Lear then dies of grief, here both characters live and see their kingdom restored. Tate also removed the role of the Fool from the play entirely and undercut the character of Cordelia by having her fall in love with Edgar at the opening of the action, so that she has less to lose in defying her father, and acts largely in the interests of her future husband. Tate's *Lear* affirms that, even in the face of enormous adversity, "truth and virtue shall succeed at last." When Cordelia says, "Then there are gods, and virtue is their care," she is asserting precisely the kind of belief that is at least temporarily shaken by Shakespeare's play.

Restoration audiences liked to see good triumph in their tragedies and rightful government restored. In comedy they liked to see the love-lives of the young and fashionable, with a central couple bringing their courtship to a successful conclusion (often overcoming the opposition of their elders to do so). Heroines had to be chaste, but were independent-minded and outspoken; now that they were played by women, there was more mileage for the playwright in disguising them in men's clothes or giving them narrow escapes from rape. Heroes were generally anything but chaste, and sowed their wild oats in plenty before declaring their love to the heroine. To non-theater-goers these comedies were widely seen as licentious and morally suspect, holding up the antics of a small, privileged, and decadent class for admiration. This same class dominated the audiences of Restoration the-ater—groups of men, and women escorted by men attended, and Colley Cibber (actor, dramatist, theater manager, and later Poet Laureate) notes below, some women wore masks to the theater so that their reaction to bawdy or irreligious language or to overtly sexual scenes could not be observed.

Many middle-class people disapproved of the theater as a playground for the dissipated and irreligious upper classes. Of these, some wanted reform, and others wanted outright suppression. One of the most vociferous objectors to the theater was Jeremy Collier (1650–1726), a clergyman whose pamphlet *A Short View of the Immorality and Profaneness of the English Stage*, excerpted here, attacks writers such as William Congreve, William Wycherley, and John Dryden for their characters' sexual freedom and profane dialogue, and for bringing women and especially clergymen into disrespect. While Collier's *Short View* sparked many replies (particularly from those, such as Congreve, whom he had singled out) and much heated debate, he continued to voice his opinions in a series of pamphlets in the next decade: *A Defense of the Short View* (1698), *A Second Defense of the Short View* (1700), *A Dissuasive from the Playhouse* (1703), and *A Further Vindication of the Short View* (1707).

The excerpt below from a *Spectator* article by Joseph Addison describes the rise in England of what became another form of theater popular among the upper classes, the opera. This new genre, imported from Italy, received mixed reactions in eighteenth-century England. Many were delighted by the music, the star system among the singers, and the elaborate and expensive settings, but others could not understand the appeal of a libretto written in a language incomprehensible to its audience.

During the 1730s the theater became an important vehicle for political satire. John Gay and Henry Fielding set out to attack the government through stage works that proved highly popular. Robert Walpole's government responded to this challenge with the Licensing Act of 1737, the legal language of which is excerpted here. This decreed that all plays were subject to censorship by the office of the Lord Chamberlain, which had to pre-approve anything that would be acted. The act also re-stated the monopoly of the two licensed (or "patent") theaters, Drury Lane and Covent Garden. Both before and after the Act some venues circumvented this decree with illegitimate performances of burlettas, or by adding music to plays and charging admission for the music, rather than for the play. But for the moment the Licensing Act tightened up enforcement, through inspectors who would patrol London to ensure the law was not being broken. Although the Patent Act that limited theater numbers was dropped in 1843, the Lord Chamberlain retained the function of censoring plays until 1968, and movies are still licensed for public showing in most jurisdictions.

While the Licensing Act made life harder for playwrights, the Statute of Anne (1710) was designed to clarify the position of the industry of printing and bookselling (as "publishing" was then generally called). This statute, considered to be the first piece of copyright legislation, both established the "sole right and liberty" of booksellers and printers to sell the new works they had issued, and appeared to place a clear limit (in most cases, 14 years) on that right. In practice (as discussed in the general introduction to this period), it was not until the decision of the House of Lords in *Donaldson v. Beckett* in 1774, that the 14-year limit became a reality. Samuel Johnson's comments on the latter, recorded in Boswell's *Life of Samuel Johnson*, suggest some of its subsequent effects on the book trade.

The next two excerpts given below are responses to the proliferation of other forms of printed material in the late seventeenth and eighteenth centuries. In *Tatler* number 224 Joseph Addison comments on the growth of the advertising industry, while Samuel Johnson, in an article from his *Idler*, gives a disparaging view of the standards of reporting in England's weekly papers (of which, in 1760, there were over 150).

During this period women began to make up a significant percentage of the nation's numerous writers. Clara Reeve's *The Progress of Romance* (1785) was the first literary history of what we now call the novel. The excerpt chosen contains her discussion of three of the most notorious women writers of previous generations: Aphra Behn, Delarivier Manley, and Eliza Haywood. Since the time of their writing (especially that of Behn), fiction, like the stage, had acquired different conventions and become more frequently didactic. The excerpt chosen from Reeve reflects the way comment on women's writing tended to slide into comment on their lives, but her championship of Behn is remarkable given that by this date Behn was generally regarded as disreputable and her work corrupting.

James Lackington, a self-educated bookseller known for his commitment to selling books at the cheapest possible prices, estimated in 1792 that the reading public had quadrupled in the previous twenty years. In this excerpt from his *Memoirs*, he celebrates the increase in reading among women and "the lower classes of the community," and applauds booksellers (that is, publishers) as advancers of knowledge.

As the final passage in this section demonstrates, the eighteenth century's political climate was highly charged. The press in Britain had greater freedom than it did in absolute monarchies like that of France, or religious governments like that of colonial Massachusetts, but any work considered offensive or politically dangerous could be censored under the law of Seditious Libel. Daniel Defoe, Delarivier Manley, and Thomas Paine were among those charged with libel during the period; publishers, however, generally took the brunt of the blame for the production of such works, as is evident in the excerpt below of the trial of Paine's publisher, Thomas Williams.

⌘ ⌘ ⌘

from Nahum Tate, *The History of King Lear* (1681)

from ACT 5

(*Scene, a prison.*)

… (*Kent brought in.*)

LEAR.   Who are you?
My eyes are none o' th' best, I'll tell you straight;
Oh Albany! Well, sir, we are your captives,
And you are come to see death pass upon us.
5   Why this delay? Or is 't your Highness' pleasure
To give us first the torture? Say ye so?
Why here's old Kent and I, as tough a pair
As e'er bore tyrant's stroke—but my Cordelia,
My poor Cordelia here, O pity!
10   ALBANY.   Take off their chains. Though injured Majesty,
The Wheel of Fortune now has made her circle,
And blessings yet stand 'twixt thy grave and thee.
LEAR.   Com'st though, inhuman Lord, to sooth us back
To a fool's paradise of hope, to make
15   Our doom more wretched? Go to,[1] we are too well
Acquainted with misfortune to be gulled°   *deceived*
With lying hope; no, we will hope no more.
ALBANY.   I have a tale t'unfold so full of wonder
As cannot meet an easy faith;
20   But by that Royal injured head 'tis true.
KENT.   What would your Highness?
ALBANY.   Know the noble Edgar
Impeached Lord Edmund since the fight, of treason,
And dared him for the proof to fight combat,
25   In which the gods confirmed his charge by conquest;

I left ev'n now the traitor wounded mortally.
LEAR.   And whither ends this story?
ALBANY.   E'er they fought
Lord Edgar gave into my hands this paper,
30   A blacker scroll of treason, and of lust,
Than can be found in the records of Hell;
There, sacred sir, behold the characters
Of Goneril, the worst of daughters, but
More vicious wife.
35   CORDELIA.   Could there be yet addition to their guilt?
What will not they that wrong a father do?
ALBANY.   Since then my injuries, Lear, fall in with thine:
I have resolved the same redress for both.
KENT.   What says my Lord?
40   CORDELIA.   Speak, for me thought I heard
The charming voice of a descending god.
ALBANY.   The troops by Edmund raised, I have disbanded;
Those that remain are under my command.
What comfort may be brought to cheer your age
45   And heal your savage wrongs, shall be applied;
For to your Majesty we do resign
Your kingdom, save what part yourself conferred
On us in marriage.
KENT.   Hear you that, my liege?
50   CORDELIA.   Then there are gods, and virtue is their care.
LEAR.   Is't possible?
Let the spheres stop their course, the sun make halt,
The winds be hushed, the seas and fountains rest;
All nature pause, and listen to the change.
55   Where is my Kent, my Cajus?[2]
KENT.   Here, my liege.
LEAR.   Why, I have news that will recall thy youth;

---

[1]   *Go to*   Come on.

[2]   *Cajus*   I.e., Caius. Kent had assumed the name of Caius while he was disguised.

Ha! Didst thou hear't, or did th'inspiring gods
Whisper to me alone? Old Lear shall be
60   A king again.
    KENT.   The Prince, that like a god has power, has said it.
    LEAR.   Cordelia then shall be a queen, mark that:
    Cordelia shall be queen; winds catch the sound
    And bear it on your rosy wings to heaven.
65   Cordelia is a queen.

(*Re-enter Edgar with Gloucester.*)

ALBANY.   Look, Sir, where pious Edgar comes
    Leading his eye-less father: O my liege!
    His wondrous story will deserve your leisure:
    What he has done and suffered for your sake,
70   What for the fair Cordelia's.
    GLOUCESTER.   Where is my liege? Conduct me to his
        knees to hail
    His second birth of empire; my dear Edgar
    Has, with himself, revealed the King's blest restoration.
    LEAR.   My poor dark Gloucester
75   GLOUCESTER.   O let me kiss that once more sceptred
        hand!
    LEAR.   Hold, thou mistak'st the Majesty, kneel here;
    Cordelia has our pow'r, Cordelia's queen.
    Speak, is not that the noble suff'ring Edgar?
    GLOUCESTER.   My pious son, more dear than my lost
        eyes.
80   LEAR.   I wronged him too, but here's the fair amends.
    EDGAR.   Your leave, my liege, for an unwelcome
        message.
    Edmund (but that's a trifle) is expired;
    What more will touch you, your imperious daughters
    Goneril and haughty Regan, both are dead,
85   Each by the other poisoned at a banquet;
    This, dying, they confessed.
    CORDELIA.   O fatal period of ill-governed life!
    LEAR.   Ungrateful as they were, my heart feels yet
    A pang of nature for their wretched fall—
90   But, Edgar, I defer thy joys too long:
    Thou serv'dst distressed Cordelia; take her crowned:
    Th'imperial grace fresh blooming on her brow;
    Nay, Gloucester, thou hast here a father's right;
    Thy helping hand t'heap blessings on their head.

95   KENT.   Old Kent throws in his hearty wishes too.
    EDGAR.   The gods and you too largely recompence
    What I have done; the gift strikes merit dumb.
    CORDELIA.   Nor do I blush to own my self o'er-paid
    For all my suff'rings past.
100   GLOUCESTER.   Now, gentle gods, give Gloucester his
        discharge.
    LEAR.   No, Gloucester, thou hast business yet for life;
    Thou, Kent, and I, retired to some cool cell
    Will gently pass our short reserves of time
    In calm reflections on our fortunes past,
105   Cheered with relation of the prosperous reign
    Of this celestial pair; thus our remains
    Shall in an even course of thought be past,
    Enjoy the present hour, nor fear the last.
    EDGAR.   Our drooping country now erects her head,
110   Peace spreads her balmy wings, and plenty blooms.
    Divine Cordelia, all the gods can witness
    How much thy love to Empire I prefer!
    Thy bright example shall convince the world
    (Whatever storms of fortune are decreed)
115   That truth and virtue shall at last succeed.

(*Exeunt Omnes.*)[1]

from Colley Cibber, *An Apology for the Life of Mr. Colley Cibber* (1740)

… But while our authors took these extraordinary liberties with their wit, I remember the ladies were then observed to be decently afraid of venturing bare-faced to a new comedy, 'till they had been assured they might do it without the risk of an insult to their modesty—or, if their curiosity were too strong for their patience, they took care, at least, to save appearances, and rarely came upon the first days of acting but in masks (then daily worn, and admitted in the pit, the side boxes, and gallery), which custom, however, had so many ill consequences attending it, that it has been abolished these many years.[2]

---

[1]   *Exeunt Omnes*   Latin: Exit all.
[2]   *masks … years*   Masks came to denote prostitutes.

from Jeremy Collier, *A Short View of the Immorality and Profaneness of the English Stage* (1698)

INTRODUCTION

The business of plays is to recommend virtue and discountenance vice; to show the uncertainty of human greatness, the sudden turns of fate, and the unhappy conclusions of violence and injustice; 'tis to expose the singularities of pride and fancy, to make folly and falsehood contemptible, and to bring everything that is ill under infamy and neglect. This design has been oddly pursued by the English stage. Our poets write with a different view and are gone into another interest. 'Tis true, were their intentions fair, they might be serviceable to this purpose. They have in a great measure the springs of thought and inclination in their power. Show, music, action, and rhetoric are moving entertainments; and, rightly employed, would be very significant. But force and motion are things indifferent, and the use lies chiefly in the application. These advantages are now in the enemy's hand and under a very dangerous management. Like cannon seized, they are pointed the wrong way; and by the strength of the defense, the mischief is made the greater. That this complaint is not unreasonable I shall endeavor to prove by showing the misbehavior of the stage with respect to morality and religion. Their liberties in the following particulars are intolerable, *viz.*,[1] their smuttiness of expression; their swearing, profaneness, and lewd application of Scripture; their abuse of the clergy, their making their top characters libertines and giving them success in their debauchery. This charge, with some other irregularities, I shall make good against the stage and show both the novelty and scandal of the practice. And, first, I shall begin with the rankness and indecency of their language.…

from CHAPTER 1, THE IMMODESTY OF THE STAGE

… To argue the matter more at large.
Smuttiness is a fault in behavior as well as in religion. 'Tis a very coarse diversion, the entertainment of those who are generally least both in sense and station. The looser part of the mob have no true relish of decency and honor, and want education and thought to furnish out a genteel conversation. Barrenness of fancy makes them often take up with those scandalous liberties. A vicious imagination may blot a great deal of paper at this rate with ease enough. And 'tis possible convenience may sometimes invite to the expedient. The modern poets seem to use smut as the old ones did machines,[2] to relieve a fainting invention. When Pegasus[3] is jaded and would stand still, he is apt like other tits[4] to run into every puddle.

Obscenity in any company is a rustic, uncreditable talent, but among women 'tis particularly rude. Such talk would be very affrontive in conversation and not endured by any lady of reputation. Whence, then, comes it to pass that those liberties which disoblige so much in conversation should entertain upon the stage? Do women leave all the regards to decency and conscience behind them when they come to the playhouse? Or does the place transform their inclinations and turn their former aversions into pleasure? Or were their pretenses to sobriety elsewhere nothing but hypocrisy and grimace? Such suppositions as these are all satire and invective. They are rude imputations upon the whole sex. To treat the ladies with such stuff is no better than taking their money to abuse them. It supposes their imagination vicious and their memories ill-furnished, that they are practiced in the language of the stews[5] and pleased with the scenes of brutishness. When at the same time the customs of education and the laws of decency are so very cautious and reserved in regard to women—I say so very reserved—that 'tis almost a fault for them to understand they are ill-used. They can't discover their disgust without disadvantage, nor blush without disservice to their modesty. To appear with any skill in such cant looks as if they had fallen upon ill conversation or managed their curiosity amiss. In a word, he that treats the ladies with such discourse must conclude either that they like it or they do not. To

---

[1] *viz.*   Abbreviation of Latin word "videlicit," meaning "that is to say."

[2] *machines*   Moveable contrivances for the production of effects.

[3] *Pegasus*   Winged horse of the gods.

[4] *tits*   Small or low-grade horses; nags.

[5] *stews*   Brothels.

suppose the first is a gross reflection upon their virtue. And as for the latter case, it entertains them with their own aversion, which is ill-nature, and ill-manners enough in all conscience. And in this particular custom and conscience, the forms of breeding and the maxims of religion are on the same side. In other instances vice is often too fashionable. But here a man can't be a sinner without being a clown.[1]

In this respect the stage is faulty to a scandalous degree of nauseousness and aggravation. For:

The poets make women speak smuttily. Of this the places before-mentioned are sufficient evidence, and if there was occasion they might be multiplied to a much greater number. Indeed the comedies are seldom clear of these blemishes. And sometimes you have them in tragedy. ...

They represent their single ladies and persons of condition under these disorders of liberty. This makes the irregularity still more monstrous and a greater contradiction to Nature and probability. But rather than not be vicious, they will venture to spoil a character. ...

They have oftentimes not so much as the poor refuge of a double meaning to fly to. So that you are under a necessity either of taking ribaldry or nonsense. And when the sentence has two handles, the worst is generally turned to the audience. The matter is so contrived that the smut and scum of the thought now arises uppermost, and, like a picture drawn to sight, looks always upon the company.

And which is still more extraordinary, the prologues and epilogues are sometimes scandalous to the last degree. ... Now here, properly speaking, the actors quit the stage and remove from fiction into life. Here they converse with the boxes and pit and address directly to the audience. These preliminary and concluding parts are designed to justify the conduct of the play, and bespeak the favor of the company. Upon such occasions one would imagine, if ever, the ladies should be used with respect and the measures of decency observed. But here we have lewdness without shame or example. Here the poet exceeds himself. Here are such strains as would turn the stomach of an ordinary debauchee and be almost nauseous in the stews. And to make it the more agreeable, women are commonly picked out for this

service. Thus the poet courts the good opinion of the audience. This is the dessert he regales the ladies with at the close of the entertainment. It seems, he thinks, they have admirable palates! Nothing can be a greater breach of manners than such liberties as these. If a man would study to outrage quality and virtue, he could not do it more effectually. But:

Smut is still more insufferable with respect to religion. The heathen religion was in a great measure a mystery of iniquity. Lewdness was consecrated in the temples as well as practiced in the stews. Their deities were great examples of vice and worshipped with their own inclination. 'Tis no wonder therefore their poetry should be tinctured with their belief, and that the stage should borrow some of the liberties of their theology. This made Mercury's procuring and Jupiter's adultery the more passable in *Amphitryon*.[2] Upon this score, Gimnausium is less monstrous in praying the gods to send her store of gallants. And thus Chaerea defends his adventure by the precedent of Jupiter and Danae. But the Christian religion is quite of another complexion. Both its precepts and authorities are the highest discouragement to licentiousness. It forbids the remotest tendencies to evil, banishes the follies of conversation, and obliges us to sobriety of thought. That which might pass for raillery and entertainment in heathenism is detestable in Christianity. The restraint of the precept and the quality of the Deity and the expectations of futurity quite alter the case. ...

from CHAPTER 4, THE STAGE-POETS MAKE THEIR PRINCIPAL PERSONS VICIOUS AND REWARD THEM AT THE END OF THE PLAY

... Indeed, to make delight the main business of comedy is an unreasonable and dangerous principle, opens the way to all licentiousness, and confounds the distinction between mirth and madness. For if diversion is the chief end, it must be had at any price. No serviceable expedient must be refused, though never so scandalous. And thus the worst things are said, and the best abused; religion is insulted, and the most serious matters turned

---

[1] *clown* Oaf.

[2] *Amphitryon* Play by third-century BCE Roman comic playwright Plautus. Collier also refers here to plays by Roman comic playwright Terence (second century BCE).

into ridicule! As if the blind side of an audience ought to be caressed, and their folly and atheism entertained in the first place. Yes, if the palate is pleased, no matter though the body is poisoned! For can one die of an easier disease than diversion? But raillery apart, certainly mirth and laughing without respect to the cause are not such supreme satisfactions! A man has sometimes pleasure in losing his wits. Frenzy and possession will shake the lungs and brighten the face; and yet I suppose they are not much to be coveted. However, now we know the reason of the profaneness and obscenity of the stage, of their hellish cursing and swearing, and in short of their great industry to make God and goodness contemptible. 'Tis all to satisfy the company and make people laugh! A most admirable justification. What can be more engaging to an audience than to see a poet thus atheistically brave? To see him charge up to the cannon's mouth and defy the vengeance of Heaven to serve them? Besides, there may be somewhat of convenience in the case. To fetch diversion out of innocence is no such easy matter. There's no succeeding, it may be, in this method, without sweat and drudging. Clean wit, inoffensive humour, and handsome contrivance require time and thought. And who would be at this expense when the purchase is so cheap another way? 'Tis possible a poet may not always have sense enough by him for such an occasion. And since we are upon supposals, it may be the audience is not to be gained without straining a point and giving a loose to conscience. And when people are sick, are they not to be humoured? In fine, we must make them laugh, right or wrong, for delight is the chief end of comedy. Delight! He should have said debauchery. That's the English of the word and the consequence of the practice. But the original design of comedy was otherwise. And granting it was not so, what then? If the ends of things were naught,[1] they must be mended. Mischief is the chief end of malice, would it be then a blemish in ill nature to change temper and relent into goodness? The chief end of a madman, it may be, is to fire a house; must we not therefore bind him in his bed? To conclude. If delight without restraint or distinction, without conscience or shame, is the supreme law of comedy, 'twere well if we had less on't. Arbitrary pleasure

is more dangerous than arbitrary power. Nothing is more brutal than to be abandoned to appetite; and nothing more wretched than to serve in such a design.…

from Joseph Addison, *The Spectator* No. 18 (21 March 1711)

… Equitis quoque jam migravit ab aure voluptas
Omnis ad incertos oculos & gaudia vana.
—HORACE[2]

It is my design in this paper to deliver down to posterity a faithful account of the Italian opera, and of the gradual progress which it has made upon the English stage. For there is no question but our great grandchildren will be very curious to know the reason why their forefathers used to sit together like an audience of foreigners in their own country, and to hear whole plays acted before them in a tongue which they did not understand.

Arsinoe[3] was the first opera that gave us a taste of Italian music. The great success this opera met with produced some attempts of forming pieces upon Italian plans, which should give a more natural and reasonable entertainment than what can be met with in the elaborate trifles of that nation. This alarmed the poetasters and fiddlers of the town, who were used to deal in a more ordinary kind of ware; and therefore laid down an established rule, which is received as such to this day, *that nothing is capable of being well set to music, that is not nonsense.*

This maxim was no sooner received, but we immediately fell to translating the Italian operas; and as there was no great danger of hurting the sense of those extraordinary pieces, our authors would often make words of their own which were entirely foreign to the meaning of the passages they pretended to translate; their chief care being to make the numbers[4] of the English verse answer to those of the Italian, that both of

---

[1] *naught* I.e., wicked.

[2] *Equitis … Horace* Latin: "But now our nobles too are fops and vain, / Neglect the sense but love the Painted Scene." (Horace, Epistles 2.1. 87–88, translated by Creech.)

[3] *Arsinoe* *Arsinoe, Queen of Cyprus*, by Thomas Clayton (1705).

[4] *numbers* Metrical feet.

them might go to the same tune. Thus the famous song in *Camilla*,[1]

> Barbara si t'intendo, &c.
> Barbarous woman, yes, I know your meaning,

which expresses the resentments of an angry lover, was translated into that English lamentation

> Frail are a lover's hopes, &c.

And it was pleasant enough to see the most refined persons of the British nation dying away and languishing to notes that were filled with a spirit of rage and indignation. It happened also very frequently, where the sense was rightly translated, the necessary transposition of words which were drawn out of the phrase of one tongue into that of another made the music appear very absurd in one tongue, that was very natural in the other. I remember an Italian verse that ran thus word for word,

> And turned my rage into pity;

which the English for rhyme's sake translated,

> And into pity turned my rage.

By this means, the soft notes that were adapted to pity in the Italian fell upon the word *rage* in the English; and the angry sounds that were tuned to rage in the original, were made to express pity in the translation. It oftentimes happened, likewise, that the finest notes in the air fell upon the most insignificant words in the sentence. I have known the word *and* pursued through the whole gamut, have been entertained with many a melodious *the*, and have heard the most beautiful graces, quavers, and divisions bestowed upon *then*, *for*, and *from*; to the eternal honour of our English particles.[2]

The next step to our refinement was the introducing of Italian actors into our opera; who sung their parts in their own language, at the same time that our countrymen performed theirs in our native tongue. The king or

hero of the play generally spoke in Italian, and his slaves answered him in English; the lover frequently made his court, and gained the heart of his princess, in a language which she did not understand. One would have thought it very difficult to have carried on dialogues after this manner, without an interpreter between the persons that conversed together; but this was the state of the English stage for about three years.

At length the audience grew tired of understanding half the opera, and therefore, to ease themselves entirely of the fatigue of thinking, have so order'd it at present that the whole opera is performed in an unknown tongue. We no longer understand the language of our own stage; insomuch that I have often been afraid, when I have seen our Italian performers chattering in the vehemence of action, that they have been calling us names, and abusing us among themselves; but I hope, since we do put such an entire confidence in them, they will not talk against us before our faces, though they may do it with the same safety as if it were behind our backs. In the meantime I cannot forbear thinking how naturally an historian who writes two or three hundred years hence, and does not know the taste of his wise forefathers, will make the following reflection, *In the beginning of the eighteenth century the Italian tongue was so well understood in England that operas were acted on the public stage in that language.*

Once scarce knows how to be serious in the confutation of an absurdity that shows itself at the first sight. It does not want any great measure of sense to see the ridicule of this monstrous practice; but what makes it the more astonishing, it is not the taste of the rabble, but of persons of the greatest politeness, which has established it. . . .

from *The Licensing Act of 1737*

. . . And be it further enacted by the authority aforesaid that from and after the said twenty-fourth day of June, one thousand, seven hundred and thirty seven, no person shall for hire, gain, or reward act, perform, represent, or cause to be acted, performed, or represented any new interlude, tragedy, comedy opera, play, farce, or other part added to any old interlude, tragedy,

---

[1] *Camilla*   Italian opera first performed with an English libretto in 1706.

[2] *particles*   Prepositions; insignificant parts of speech.

comedy, opera, play, farce, or other entertainment of the stage, or any new prologue or epilogue unless a true copy be thereof be sent to the Lord Chamberlain of the King's household for the time being,[1] fourteen days at least before the acting, representing, or performing thereof, together with an account of the playhouse or other place where the same shall be and the time when the same is intended to be first acted, represented, or performed, signed by the master or manager, or one of the masters or managers of such playhouse or place, or company of actors therein.

4. And be it enacted by the authority aforesaid that from and after the said twenty-fourth day of June, one thousand, seven hundred and thirty seven, it shall and may be lawful to and for the said Lord Chamberlain for the time being, from time to time, and when and as often as he shall think fit, to prohibit the acting, performing or representing any interlude, tragedy, comedy, opera, play, farce or other entertainment of the stage, or any act, scene or part thereof, or any prologue or epilogue. And in case any person or persons shall for hire, gain or reward act, perform or represent, or cause to be acted, performed or represented, any interlude, tragedy, comedy, opera, play, farce or other entertainment of the stage, or any act, scene, or part thereof, or any prologue or epilogue, contrary to such prohibition as aforesaid; every person so offending shall for every such offence forfeit the sum of fifty pounds and every grant, licence, and authority (in any case there be any such) by or under which the said master or masters or manager or managers set up, formed, or continued such playhouse, or such company of actors, shall cease, determine and become absolutely void to all intents and purposes whatsoever.

5. Provided always that no person or persons shall be authorised by virtue of any letters patent from His Majesty, his heirs, successors or predecessors, or by the licence of the Lord Chamberlain of His Majesty's household for the time being, to act, represent, or perform for hire, gain, or reward, any interlude, tragedy, comedy, opera, play, farce, or other entertainment of the stage, or any part or parts therein, in any part of Great Britain, except in the City of Westminster and within

the liberties thereof, and in such places where His Majesty, his heirs or successors, shall in their royal persons reside, and during such residence only. …

from *The Statute of Anne* (1710)

An act for the encouragement of learning, by vesting the copies[2] of printed books in the authors or purchasers of such copies, during the times therein mentioned.

Whereas printers, booksellers, and other persons have of late frequently taken the liberty of printing, reprinting, and publishing, or causing to be printed, reprinted, and published, books and other writings, without the consent of the authors or proprietors of such books and writings, to their very great detriment, and too often to the ruin of them and their families: for preventing therefore such practices for the future, and for the encouragement of learned men to compose and write useful books, may it please Your Majesty that it may be enacted, and be it enacted by the Queen's most excellent Majesty, by and with the advice and consent of the Lords spiritual and temporal, and Commons in this present Parliament assembled, and by the authority of the same, that from and after the tenth day of April, one thousand seven hundred and ten, the author of any book or books already printed, who hath not transferred to any other the copy or copies of such book or books, share or shares thereof, or the bookseller or booksellers, printer or printers, or other person or persons, who hath or have purchased or acquired the copy or copies of any book or books, in order to print or reprint the same, shall have the sole right and liberty of printing such book and books for the term of one and twenty years, to commence from the said tenth day of April, and no longer; and that the author of any book or books already composed and not printed and published, or that shall hereafter be composed, and his assignee, or assigns, shall have the sole liberty of printing and reprinting such book and books for the term of fourteen years, to commence from the day of the first publishing the same, and no longer; and that if any other bookseller, printer,

---

[1] *for the time being* Currently holding office.

[2] *copies* Copyright.

or other person whatsoever, from and after the tenth day of April, one thousand seven hundred and ten, within the times granted and limited by this act, as aforesaid, shall print, reprint, or import, or cause to be printed, reprinted, or imported any such book or books, without the consent of the proprietor or proprietors thereof first had and obtained in writing, signed in the presence of two or more credible witnesses; or knowing the same to be so printed or reprinted, without the consent of the proprietors, shall sell, publish, or expose to sale, or cause to be sold, published, or exposed to sale, any such book or books, without such consent first had and obtained, as aforesaid, then such offender or offenders shall forfeit such book or books, and all and every sheet or sheets, being part of such book or books, to the proprietor or proprietors of the copy thereof, who shall forthwith damask[1] and make waste-paper of them. And further, that every such offender or offenders shall forfeit one penny for every sheet which shall be found in his, her, or their custody, either printed or printing, published or exposed to sale, contrary to the true intent and meaning of this act, the one moiety thereof to the Queen's most excellent Majesty, Her heirs and successors, and the other moiety thereof to any person or persons that shall sue for the same, to be recovered in any of Her Majesty's Courts of Record at Westminster, by action of debt, bill, plaint, or information, in which no wager of law, essoign,[2] privilege, or protection, or more than one imparlance,[3] shall be allowed.

And whereas many persons may through ignorance offend against this act, unless some provision be made whereby the property in every such book, as is intended by this act to be secured to the proprietor or proprietors thereof, may be ascertained, as likewise the consent of such proprietor or proprietors for the printing or reprinting of such book or books may from time to time be known; be it therefore further enacted by the authority aforesaid, that nothing in this act contained shall be construed to extend to subject any bookseller, printer, or other person whatsoever, to the forfeitures or penalties therein mentioned, for or by reason of the printing or reprinting of any book or books without such consent as aforesaid, unless the title to the copy of such book or books hereafter published shall, before such publication be entered in the register-book of the Company of Stationers, in such manner as hath been usual, which register-book shall at all times be kept at the hall of the said Company, and unless such consent of the proprietor or proprietors be in like manner entered, as aforesaid, for every of which several entries, six pence shall be paid, and no more; which said register-book may, at all reasonable and convenient times, be resorted to, and inspected by any bookseller, printer, or other person, for the purposes before mentioned, oned,[4] without any fee or reward; and the clerk of the said Company of Stationers, shall, when and as often as thereunto required, give a certificate under his hand of such entry or entries, and for every such certificate, may take a fee not exceeding six pence. . . .

Provided always, and it is hereby enacted, that nine copies of each book or books, upon the best paper, that from and after the said tenth day of April, one thousand seven hundred and ten, shall be printed and published, as aforesaid, or reprinted and published with additions, shall, by the printer and printers thereof, be delivered to the warehouse-keeper of the said Company of Stationers for the time being, at the Hall of the said Company, before such publication made, for the use of the Royal Library, the libraries of the Universities of Oxford and Cambridge, the libraries of the four universities in Scotland, the library of Sion College in London, and the library commonly called the library belonging to the Faculty of Advocates at Edinburgh respectively.[5] . . .

Provided nevertheless, that all actions, suits, bills, indictments, or informations for any offence that shall be committed against this act, shall be brought, sued, and commenced within three months next after such offence committed, or else the same shall be void and of none effect.

---

[1] *damask* Deface.

[2] *essoign* Excuse for non-appearance in court at an appointed time.

[3] *imparlance* Extension of time granted to allow the negotiation of an amicable settlement.

[4] *oned* Joined; united.

[5] *nine copies . . . respectively* This confirmed and extended to Scotland a law of 1662 which gave the copyright libraries or libraries of record their status. The Bodleian Library at Oxford already had such an agreement, negotiated in 1610. The Royal Library later became the nucleus of the British Library.

Provided always, that after the expiration of the said term of fourteen years, the sole right of printing or disposing of copies shall return to the authors thereof, if they are then living, for another term of fourteen years.

from James Boswell, *The Life of Samuel Johnson* (1791)

[20 July 1763]

Mr. Alexander Donaldson, bookseller of Edinburgh, had for some time opened a shop in London, and sold his cheap editions of the most popular English books, in defiance of the supposed common-law right of literary property. Johnson, though he concurred in the opinion which was afterwards sanctioned by a judgment of the House of Lords, that there was no such right,[1] was at this time very angry that the booksellers of London, for whom he uniformly professed much regard, should suffer from an invasion of what they had ever considered to be secure, and he was loud and violent against Mr. Donaldson. "He is a fellow who takes advantage of the law to injure his brethren; for, notwithstanding that the statute secures only fourteen years of exclusive right, it has always been understood by *the trade* that he who buys the copyright of a book from the author obtains a perpetual property;[2] and upon that belief, numberless bargains are made to transfer that property after the expiration of the statutory term. Now Donaldson, I say, takes advantage here, of people who have really an equitable title from usage; and if we consider how few of the books, of which they buy the property, succeed so well as to bring profit, we should be of opinion that the term of fourteen years is too short; it should be sixty years." DEMPSTER. "Donaldson, sir, is anxious for the encouragement of literature. He reduces the price of books, so that poor students may buy them." JOHNSON (laughing). "Well, sir, allowing that to be his motive, he is no better than Robin Hood, who robbed the rich in order to give to the poor."

It is remarkable that when the great question concerning literary property came to be ultimately tried before the supreme tribunal of this country, in consequence of the very spirited exertions of Mr. Donaldson, Dr. Johnson was zealous against a perpetuity; but he thought that the term of the exclusive right of authors should be considerably enlarged. He was then for granting a hundred years.[3]

Joseph Addison, *The Tatler* No. 224 (14 September 1710)

> *Materiam superabat Opus.*[4]
> — Ovid.

From my own apartment, September 13.

It is my custom, in a dearth of news, to entertain myself with those collections of advertisements that appear at the end of all our public prints.[5] These I consider as accounts of news from the little world, in the same manner that the foregoing parts of the paper are from the great. If in one we hear that a sovereign prince is fled from his capital city, in the other we hear of a tradesman who hath shut up his shop and run away. If in one we find the victory of a general, in the other we

---

[1] *in defiance ... no such right*   In the 1769 case of Millar *v.* Taylor, the court ruled that a common-law right of literary property still existed, despite the Statute of Anne's changes in statutory law. In other words, when the statutory rights granted by the Statute of Anne expired, common-law rights would remain in effect, thus preventing works from ever entering the public domain. *Donaldson v. Beckett*, in 1774, overturned Millar *v.* Taylor by deciding that the Statute of Anne, which granted the author possession of copyright for the period of 14 years, had completely exploded the previous protection of literary property under common law. In other words, if the copyright of the author, or the publisher who had purchased the copyright, had expired, he or she could not sue another bookseller, such as Donaldson, for reprinting.

[2] *he who buys ... property*   Reference to the custom of the time of perpetual copyright, according to which booksellers would buy and sell copyrights of books from earlier centuries—such as Shakespeare, Milton, John Dryden, and Aphra Behn—although they did not technically own these copyrights.

[3] *He was ... years*   The present-day duration of copyright in Britain and the United States is the life of the author plus seventy years, and in Canada it is the life of the author plus fifty years.

[4] *Materiam superbat Opus*   Latin: "The craftsmanship will surpass the material." From Ovid, *Metamorphoses* 2.5.

[5] *those collections ... prints*   Here Addison is referring to personal advertisements, though he goes on to discuss commercial advertising in the following paragraphs.

see the desertion of a private soldier. I must confess, I have a certain weakness in my temper that is often very much affected by these little domestic occurrences, and have frequently been caught with tears in my eyes over a melancholy advertisement. But to consider this subject in its most ridiculous lights, advertisements are of great use to the vulgar; first of all, as they are instruments of ambition. A man that is by no means big enough for the *Gazette*[1] may easily creep into the advertisements; by which means we often see an apothecary in the same paper of news with a plenipotentiary,[2] or a running-footman with an ambassador. An advertisement from Piccadilly goes down to posterity with an article from Madrid; and John Bartlett of Goodman's Fields is celebrated in the same paper with the Emperor of Germany. Thus the fable tells us that the wren mounted as high as the eagle by getting upon his back.

A second use which this sort of writings have been turned to of late years has been the management of controversy, insomuch that above half the advertisements one meets with now-a-days are purely polemical. The inventors of strops[3] for razors have written against one another this way for several years, and that with great bitterness; as the whole argument pro and con in the case of the morning-gowns is still carried on after the same manner. I need not mention the several proprietors of *Dr. Anderson's Pills*; nor take notice of the many satirical works of this nature so frequently published by Dr. Clark, who has had the confidence to advertise upon that learned knight, my very worthy friend, Sir William Read.[4] But I shall not interpose in their quarrel; Sir William can give him his own in advertisements that, in the judgment of the impartial, are as well penned as the Doctor's.

The third and last use of these writings is to inform the world where they may be furnished with almost every thing that is necessary for life. If a man has pains in his head, colics[5] in his bowels, or spots in his clothes, he may here meet with proper cures and remedies. If a man would recover a wife or a horse that is stolen or strayed; if he wants new sermons, electuaries,[6] ass's milk, or anything else, either for his body or his mind, this is the place to look for them in.

The great art in writing advertisements is the finding out a proper method to catch the reader's eye; without which, a good thing may pass over unobserved, or be lost among commissions of bankruptcy. Asterisks and hands[7] were formerly of great use for this purpose. Of late years, the *N.B.*[8] has been much in fashion; as also little cuts and figures,[9] the invention of which we must ascribe to the author of spring-trusses.[10] I must not here omit the blind Italian[11] character, which being scarce legible, always fixes and detains the eye, and gives the curious reader something like the satisfaction of prying into a secret.

But the great skill in an advertiser is chiefly seen in the style which he makes use of. He is to mention *the universal esteem, or general reputation,* of things that were never heard of. If he is a physician or astrologer, he must change his lodgings frequently, and (though he never saw anybody in them besides his own family) give public notice of it, *For the information of the nobility and gentry.* Since I am thus usefully employed in writing criticisms on the works of these diminutive authors, I must not pass over in silence an advertisement which has lately made its appearance, and is written altogether in a Ciceronian[12] manner. It was sent to me, with five shillings, to be inserted among my advertisements; but as it is a pattern of good writing in this way, I shall give it a place in the body of my paper.

---

[1] *Gazette* England's official newspaper, a record of military and political events, whose advertisements largely consisted of bankruptcy notices. The paper was, at the time, edited by Addison's friend and partner Richard Steele.

[2] *plenipotentiary* Envoy given absolute authority to act as he or she sees fit in a particular matter.

[3] *strops* Strips of leather for sharpening razors.

[4] *Sir William Read* Ophthalmologist to Queen Anne, who was knighted in 1705 for curing soldiers and sailors of blindness.

[5] *colics* I.e., pains.

[6] *electuaries* Medicinal pastes mixed with honey, preserve, or syrup.

[7] *hands* I.e., figures of hands drawn with their forefingers pointing.

[8] *N.B.* For *nota bene* (Latin: note well).

[9] *cuts and figures* I.e., illustrations and diagrams.

[10] *spring-trusses* Surgical appliances for applying pressure to a wound or hernia.

[11] *Italian* Italic.

[12] *Ciceronian* I.e., using inflated rhetoric. (Cicero was a celebrated Roman orator of the first century BCE.)

The highest compounded spirit of lavender, the most glorious (if the expression may be used) enlivening scent and flavour that can possibly be, which so raptures the spirits, delights the gust,[1] and gives such airs to the countenance, as are not to be imagined but by those that have tried it. The meanest sort of the thing is admired by most gentlemen and ladies; but this far more, as by far it exceeds it, to the gaining among all a more than common esteem. It is sold (in neat flint bottles fit for the pocket) only at the Golden Key in Warton's Court near Holborn Bars, for 3s. 6d.[2] with directions.

At the same time that I recommend the several flowers in which this spirit of lavender is wrapped up (if the expression may be used), I cannot excuse my fellow labourers for admitting into their papers several uncleanly advertisements, not at all proper to appear in the works of polite writers. Among these I must reckon the *Carminative Wind-expelling Pills*. If the Doctor had called them only his Carminative Pills, he had been as cleanly as one could have wished; but the second word entirely destroys the decency of the first. There are other absurdities of this nature so very gross that I dare not mention them; and shall therefore dismiss this subject with a public admonition to Michael Parrot, that he do not presume any more to mention a certain worm he knows of, which, by the way, has grown seven foot in my memory; for, if I am not much mistaken, it is the same that was but nine foot long about six months ago.

By the remarks I have here made, it plainly appears that a collection of advertisements is a kind of miscellany,[3] the writers of which, contrary to all authors, except men of quality,[4] give money to the booksellers who publish their copies. The genius of the bookseller is chiefly shown in his method of ranging and digesting these little tracts. The last paper I took up in my hands places them in the following order:

The True Spanish Blacking for Shoes, &c.

The Beautifying Cream for the Face, &c.

Pease and Plasters, &c.

Nectar and Ambrosia, &c.

Four Freehold Tenements of 15. l.[5] per Annum, &c.

The Present State of England, &c.[6]

Annotations upon the *Tatler*, &c.

A Commission of Bankrupt being awarded against B.L., Bookseller, *&c.*

---

from Samuel Johnson, *The Idler* No. 30 (11 November 1758)

… No species of literary men has lately been so much multiplied as the writers of news. Not many years ago the nation was content with one *Gazette*,[7] but now we have not only in the metropolis papers for every morning and every evening, but almost every large town has its weekly historian, who regularly circulates his periodical intelligence,[8] and fills the villages of his district with conjectures on the events of war, and with debates on the true interest of Europe.

To write news in its perfection requires such a combination of qualities that a man completely fitted for the task is not always to be found. In Sir Henry Wotton's[9] jocular definition, "An ambassador" is said to be "a man of virtue sent abroad to tell lies for the advantage of his country"; a news-writer is "a man without virtue, who writes lies at home for his own profit." To these compositions is required neither genius nor knowledge, neither industry nor sprightliness; but contempt of shame and indifference to truth are absolutely necessary. He who, by a long familiarity with infamy, has obtained these qualities, may confidently tell today what he intends to contradict tomorrow; he may affirm fearlessly what he knows that he shall be obliged to recant, and may write letters from Amsterdam or Dresden to himself.

---

[1] *gust* Sense of taste.

[2] *3s. 6d.* Three shillings and six pence.

[3] *miscellany* I.e., anthology.

[4] *men of quality* A dig at upper-class vanity authors.

[5] *l.* Pounds.

[6] *The Present State of England, &c.* An annual publication.

[7] *Gazette* England's official newspaper.

[8] *intelligence* Information.

[9] *Henry Wotton* Diplomat and writer (1568–1639).

In a time of war the nation is always of one mind, eager to hear something good of themselves and ill of the enemy. At this time the task of news-writers is easy; they have nothing to do but to tell that a battle is expected, and afterwards that a battle has been fought, in which we and our friends, whether conquering or conquered, did all, and our enemies did nothing.

Scarce anything awakens attention like a tale of cruelty. The writer of news never fails in the intermission of action to tell how the enemies murdered children and ravished virgins; and, if the scene of action be somewhat distant, scalps half the inhabitants of a province.

Among the calamities of war may be justly numbered the diminution of the love of truth, by the falsehoods which interest dictates and credulity encourages. A peace will equally leave the warrior and relater of wars destitute of employment; and I know not whether more is to be dreaded from streets filled with soldiers accustomed to plunder, or from garrets filled with scribblers accustomed to lie.

from Clara Reeve, *The Progress of Romance, through Times, Countries, Manners; with Remarks on the Good and Bad Effects of it, on them Respectively; in a Course of Evening Conversations* (1785)

EVENING 7

EUPHRASIA. ... Among our early novel-writers we must reckon Mrs. Behn. There are strong marks of genius in all this lady's works, but unhappily, there are some parts of them very improper to be read by, or recommended to, virtuous minds, and especially to youth. She wrote in an age, and to a court of licentious manners, and perhaps we ought to ascribe to these causes the loose turn of her stories. Let us do justice to her merits, and cast the veil of compassion over her faults. She died in the year 1689, and lies buried in the cloisters of Westminster Abbey. The inscription will show how high she stood in estimation at that time.

HORTENSIUS. Are you not partial to the sex of this genius, when you excuse in her what you would not to a man?

EUPHRASIA. Perhaps I may, and you must excuse me if I am so, especially as this lady had many fine and amiable qualities, besides her genius for writing.

SOPHRONIA. Pray let her rest in peace—you were speaking of the inscription on her monument, I do not remember it.

EUPHRASIA.   It is as follows:

> Mrs. APHRA BEHN, 1689.
> Here lies a proof that wit can never be
> Defence enough against mortality.

Let me add that Mrs. Behn will not be forgotten so long as the tragedy of *Oroonoko*[1] is acted; it was from her story of that illustrious African that Mr. Southern wrote that play, and the most affecting parts of it are taken almost literally from her.

HORTENSIUS. Peace be to her manes![2]   I shall not disturb her, or her works.

EUPHRASIA. I shall not recommend them to your perusal, Hortensius.

The next female writer of this class is Mrs. Manley,[3] whose works are still more exceptionable than Mrs. Behn's, and as much inferior to them in point of merit. She hoarded up all the public and private scandal within her reach, and poured it forth, in a work too well known in the last age, though almost forgotten in the present; a work that partakes of the style of the romance, and the novel. I forbear the name, and further observations on it, as Mrs. Manley's works are sinking gradually into oblivion. I am sorry to say they were once in fashion, which obliges me to mention them, otherwise I had rather be spared the pain of disgracing an author of my own sex.

SOPHRONIA. It must be confessed that these books of the last age were of worse tendency than any of those of the present.

---

[1] *tragedy of Oroonoko* Thomas Southern's stage adaptation of Aphra Behn's *Oroonoko*, first performed in 1695, was tremendously popular in the eighteenth century.

[2] *manes* Spirit.

[3] *Manley* Delarivier Manley, author of several *romans à clef* (which described and sometimes exaggerated the vices of actual people, mostly those in power, who appeared under fictitious names), including *The New Atalantis* (1709), for which she was arrested, and which is referred to here.

EUPHRASIA. My dear friend, there were bad books at all times, for those who sought for them. Let us pass them over in silence.

HORTENSIUS.   No, not yet. Let me help your memory to one more lady-author of the same class—Mrs. Haywood. She has the same claim upon you as those you have last mentioned.

EUPHRASIA. I had intended to have mentioned Mrs. Haywood, though in a different way, but I find you will not suffer any part of her character to escape you.

HORTENSIUS. Why should she be spared any more than the others?

EUPHRASIA. Because she repented of her faults, and employed the latter part of her life in expiating the offences of the former. There is reason to believe that the examples of the two ladies we have spoken of seduced Mrs. Haywood into the same track; she certainly wrote some amorous novels in her youth,[1] and also two books of the same kind as Mrs. Manley's capital work, all of which I hope are forgotten.

HORTENSIUS. I fear they will not be so fortunate; they will be known to posterity by the infamous immortality conferred upon them by Pope in his *Dunciad*.[2]

EUPHRASIA. Mr. Pope was severe in his castigations, but let us be just to merit of every kind. Mrs. Haywood had the singular good fortune to recover a lost reputation, and the yet greater honour to atone for her errors. She devoted the remainder of her life and labours to the service of virtue. Mrs. Haywood was one of the most voluminous female writers that ever England produced, none of her latter works are destitute of merit, though they do not rise to the highest pitch of excellence. *Betsy Thoughtless*[3] is reckoned her best novel; but those works

by which she is most likely to be known to posterity, are the *Female Spectator*, and the *Invisible Spy*.[4] This lady died so lately as the year 1758.

SOPHRONIA. I have heard it often said that Mr. Pope was too severe in his treatment of this lady; it was supposed that she had given some private offence, which he resented publicly as was too much his way.

HORTENSIUS. That is very likely, for he was not of a forgiving disposition. If I have been too severe also, you ladies must forgive me in behalf of your sex.

EUPHRASIA. Truth is sometimes severe. Mrs. Haywood's wit and ingenuity were never denied. I would be the last to vindicate her faults, but the first to celebrate her return to virtue, and her atonement for them.

SOPHRONIA. May her first writings be forgotten, and the last survive to do her honour!

---

from James Lackington, *Memoirs of the Forty-Five First Years of the Life of James Lackington, Bookseller* (1792)

I cannot help observing that the sale of books in general has increased prodigiously within the last twenty years. According to the best estimation I have been able to make, I suppose that more than four times the number of books are sold now than were sold twenty years since. The poorer sort of farmers, and even the poor country people in general, who before that period spent their winter evenings in relating stories of witches, ghosts, hobgoblins, &c, now shorten the winter nights by hearing their sons and daughters read tales, romances, &c; and on entering their houses, you may see *Tom Jones, Roderick Random*,[5] and other entertaining books, stuck up on their bacon racks, &c. If John goes to town with a load of hay, he is charged to be sure not to forget to bring home "Peregrine Pickle's Adven-

---

[1] *amorous novels … youth* Of the of list of Haywood's amorous "novels," the best known today may be *Love in Excess* (1719) and *Fantomina* (1725).

[2] *Pope in his Dunciad* Alexander's Pope's mock epic attack on Grub-Street writers, *The Dunciad*, features Eliza Haywood, with "two babes of love close clinging to her waist," as the prize in a pissing contest between rival booksellers Edmund Curll and William Chetwood.

[3] *Betsy Thoughtless* Haywood's *The History of Miss Betsy Thoughtless* (1751) was probably her best known work. In this didactic work, the heroine learns to behave better before being rewarded by true love. The morality evident in the novel probably does not represent repentance on the part of the author, but a successful shift to keep

with what the market then, a generation after her earliest works, demanded.

[4] *Female … Spy* Haywood's *The Female Spectator*, a highly successful periodical that she began in 1744, and *The Invisible Spy* (1755), a political tale.

[5] *Tom … Random* I.e., *The History of Tom Jones* (1749), by Henry Fielding, and *The Adventures of Roderick Random* (1748), by Tobias Smollett.

tures";[1] and when Dolly is sent to market to sell her eggs, she is commissioned to purchase "The History of Pamela Andrews."[2] In short, all ranks and degrees now read. But the most rapid increase of the sale of books has been since the termination of the late war.[3]

A number of book-clubs are also formed in every part of England, where each member subscribes a certain sum quarterly to purchase books; in some of these clubs the books, after they have been read by all the subscribers, are sold among them to the highest bidders, and the money produced by such sale is expended in fresh purchases, by which prudent and judicious mode each member has it in his power to become possessed of the work of any particular author he may judge deserving a superior degree of attention; and the members at large enjoy the advantage of a continual succession of different publications, instead of being restricted to a repeated perusal of the same authors; which must have been the case with many, if so rational a plan had not been adopted.

I have been informed that when circulating libraries were first opened, the booksellers were much alarmed, and their rapid increase added to their fears, and led them to think that the sale of books would be much diminished by such libraries. But experience has proved that the sale of books, so far from being diminished by them, has been greatly promoted, as from those repositories many thousand families have been cheaply supplied with books, by which the taste for reading has become much more general, and thousands of books are purchased every year by such as have first borrowed them at those libraries, and after reading, approving of them, become purchasers.

Circulating libraries have also greatly contributed towards the amusement and cultivation of the other sex; by far the greatest part of ladies have now a taste for books.

"——Learning, once the man's exclusive pride,

Seems verging fast towards the female side."[4]

It is true that I do not, with Miss Mary Wollstonecraft, "earnestly wish to see the distinction of sex confounded in society," not even with her exception, "unless where love animates the behaviour."[5] And yet I differ widely from those gentlemen who would prevent the ladies from acquiring a taste for books; and as yet I have never seen any solid reason advanced why ladies should not polish their understandings, and render themselves fit companions for men of sense. And I have often thought that one great reason why some gentlemen spend all their leisure hours abroad,[6] is, for want of rational companions at home; for, if a gentleman happens to marry a fine lady, as justly painted by Miss Wollstonecraft, or the square elbow family drudge, as drawn to the life by the same hand, I must confess that I see no great inducement that he has to desire the company of his wife, as she scarce can be called a rational companion, or one fit to be entrusted with the education of her children; and even Rousseau is obliged to acknowledge that it "is a melancholy thing for a father of a family, who is fond of home, to be obliged to be always wrapped up in himself, and to have nobody about him to whom he can impart his sentiments."[7] Lord Lyttleton advises well in the two following lines:

"Do you, my fair, endeavour to possess
An elegance of mind, as well as dress."[8]

---

[1] *Peregrine Pickle's Adventures* Tobias Smollett's *The Adventures of Peregrine Pickle* (1751).

[2] *The History ... Andrews* Samuel Richardson's *Pamela, or Virtue Rewarded* (1740).

[3] *the late war* The American Revolution.

[4] *Learning ... side* From William Cowper's *The Progress of Error* (1782), lines 429–30.

[5] *earnestly wish ... behavior* From Mary Wollstonecraft's *A Vindication of the Rights of Woman* (1792), Chapter 4.

[6] *abroad* I.e., out of the house.

[7] *Rousseau ... sentiments* Lackington is reflecting received wisdom when he supposes that the justification for educating women is not their own benefit but that of men. Here he quotes a passage from French philosopher Jean-Jacques Rousseau's *Émile* (1762) that Wollstonecraft also cites to support her argument that educated men would be happiest with compatible companions. Rousseau generally believed that women's education should be limited in order to maintain their innocence.

[8] *Do you ... dress* From *Advice to a Lady* (1733), lines 27–28, by First Baron Lord Lyttleton, a patron of literature.

I cannot help thinking that the reason why some of the eastern nations treat the ladies with such contempt, and look upon them in such a degrading point of view, is owing to their marrying them when mere children, both as to age and understanding, which last being entirely neglected, they seldom are capable of rational conversation, and of course are neglected and despised. But this is not the case with English ladies;[1] they now in general read, not only novels, although many of that class are excellent productions, and tend to polish both the heart and head; but they also read the best books in the English language, and many read the best works in various languages; and there are some thousands of ladies who come to my shop that know as well what books to choose, and are as well acquainted with works of taste and genius as any gentlemen in the kingdom, notwithstanding the sneer against novel-readers, &c.

The Sunday-schools are spreading very fast in most parts of England, which will accelerate the diffusion of knowledge among the lower classes of the community and in a very few years exceedingly increase the sale of books. Here permit me earnestly to call on every honest bookseller (I trust my call will not be in vain) as well as on every friend to the extension of knowledge, to unite (as *you* I am confident will) in a hearty Amen.

from Thomas Erskine, *Speech as Prosecution in the Seditious-Libel Trial of Thomas Williams for Publishing* Age of Reason, *by Thomas Paine* (1797)

A free and unlicensed press, in the just and legal sense of the expression, has led to all the blessings both of religion and government, which Great Britain or any part of the world at this moment enjoys, and it is calculated to advance mankind to still higher degrees of civilization and happiness. But this freedom, like every other, must be limited to be enjoyed, and like every human advantage, may be defeated by its abuse. An intellectual book, however erroneous, addressed to the intellectual world upon so profound and complicated a subject, can never work the mischief which this Indictment is calculated to repress. Such works will only incite the minds of men enlightened by study, to a closer investigation of a subject well worthy of their deepest and continued contemplation. The powers of the mind are given for human improvement in the progress of human existence. The changes produced by such reciprocations of lights and intelligences are certain in their progressions, and make their way imperceptibly, by the final and irresistible power of truth. But this book has no such object, and no such capacity: it presents no arguments to the wise and enlightened. On the contrary, it treats the faith and opinions of the wisest with the most shocking contempt, and stirs up men, without the advantages of learning, or sober thinking, to a total disbelief of every thing hitherto held sacred; and consequently to a rejection of all the laws and ordinances of the state, which stand only upon the assumption of their truth.

---

[1] *But this ... ladies* Here Lackington reflects another common line of thinking—that Asian and Middle-Eastern nations were inferior because of their supposedly inferior treatment of women.

JAMES THOMSON
1700 – 1748

Author of *The Seasons*, an innovative nature poem which became the eighteenth century's most popular work of poetry, James Thomson also published other poems and six plays. A member of a literary circle consisting of English and Scottish writers, many of whom played an active part in the opposition politics of the day, Thomson is perhaps now most often remembered for writing the words of what has become Britain's unofficial anthem, "Rule Britannia." This originated as a song in *Alfred, A Masque* (1740), which Thomson wrote with David Mallet to celebrate the birth of the Prince of Wales's first child, Princess Augusta. It is *The Seasons*, however, that secured his place as a leading poet of the early eighteenth century, as an influence on the Romantic poets of the late eighteenth and early nineteenth centuries, and as a major figure in Scottish literary tradition.

The son of a Presbyterian minister, James Thomson was born on 11 September 1700 and lived in Southdean in the south of Scotland until 1715. His early education included instruction in the Shorter Catechism and the Bible from his father, traditional Border songs and ballads from his mother, and the classics at Jedburgh Grammar School—all influences which surface in his work. After his father's death in 1716, Thomson's family moved to Edinburgh where James studied at the University of Edinburgh. Although Thomson completed the requisite four years, he did not take his degree. Planning to become a minister, he subsequently entered Divinity Hall in 1719 to begin a six-year course of study; that, too, he abandoned just before completion, moving to London in 1725.

Once in London, Thomson turned his attention more seriously to writing—*Winter* appeared in April 1726, and was an immediate publishing sensation. Thomson followed it with *Summer* (1727) and *Spring* (1728); "Autumn" first appeared as part of the collected *The Seasons* in 1730. In form *The Seasons* is a georgic, a poem about agricultural labor, the countryside, and the wealth produced there. The genre takes its name from Virgil's *Georgics*, written in Latin in the first century BCE and designed both as a farming manual for army veterans (who were issued with land as part of their retirement package) and also as a celebration of the natural riches produced by the land. This offered Thomson the opportunity to write on man's experience of Nature. Thomson returned repeatedly to *The Seasons*, publishing new editions in 1744 and again in 1746, each time increasing the poem's political and scientific content; the final version is substantially larger than that published in 1730.

During the years he was writing *The Seasons*, Thomson also worked as a tutor, initially to the son of a Scottish peer, Lord Binning. By May 1726 he was employed as a private tutor at a school run by hymn-writer and educator Isaac Watts, having already published *Winter* in April 1726; he remained at the school until November 1730, by which time he had published one play, *Sophonisba* (1730), a tribute to Newton entitled *A Poem Sacred to the Memory of Sir Isaac Newton* (1727), and the remaining three seasons: *Summer* (1727), *Spring* (1728), and "Autumn" as part of the collected *Seasons* (1730).

In November 1730, Thomson accompanied the son of his patron, Lord Charles Talbot, on a grand tour of France and Italy that lasted over a year. His Continental experiences spawned another ambitious, albeit less-successful poem, *Liberty*, the five books of which follow the goddess of Liberty throughout the history of the civilized world (1735–36).

By 1735, Thomson had moved to Richmond, just outside of London, where he eventually met and fell in love with fellow-Scotswoman Elizabeth Young, sister-in-law of a neighbor. Thomson courted her for three years, and was devastated by her final refusal in 1745; some have suggested that the strength of his feelings over this relationship lent force to the writing of his most romantic and successful play, *Tancred and Sigismunda* (1745). Thomson's final poem, *The Castle of Indolence* (1748), written in Spenserian stanzas, was the product of fifteen years' labor. It explores the seductive qualities of idleness, and many critics have found ambivalence in its ultimate celebration of the regenerating force of hard work. The poet was acknowledged to be intimately familiar with the subject-matter of the poem; he was as well known for his indolence and his love of food and drink as he was for his generosity and good humor.

Thomson did not live to see his last play, *Coriolanus* (1746), performed on stage in 1749, for he died of a fever weeks before his forty-eighth birthday on 27 August 1748. In 1762 his friends and admirers, including George III, memorialized him by erecting a monument in Westminster Abbey's Poets' Corner, funded by the proceeds of a posthumous edition of his collected *Works* (1762).

⌘ ⌘ ⌘

Winter [1]

See! Winter comes, to rule the varied year,
Sullen, and sad; with all his rising train,°   *group of attendants*
Vapours, and clouds, and storms: Be these my theme,
These, that exalt the soul to solemn thought,
5 And heavenly musing. Welcome kindred glooms!
Wished, wint'ry, horrors, hail! With frequent foot,
Pleased, have I, in my cheerful morn of life,[2]
When, nursed by careless solitude, I lived,
And sung of Nature with unceasing joy,
10 Pleased, have I wandered through your rough domains;
Trod the pure, virgin snows, my self as pure:
Heard the winds roar, and the big torrent burst:
Or seen the deep, fermenting tempest brewed,
In the red, evening sky. Thus passed the time,
15 Till, through the opening chambers of the south,[3]
Looked out the joyous Spring, looked out, and smiled.

Thee too, inspirer of the toiling swain![4]
Fair Autumn, yellow robed! I'll sing of thee,
Of thy last, tempered days, and sunny calms;
20 When all the golden hours are on the wing,
Attending thy retreat, and round thy wain,°   *wagon*
Slow-rolling, onward to the southern sky.

Behold! the well-poised hornet, hovering, hangs,
With quivering pinions,° in the genial blaze;   *wings*
25 Flies off, in airy circles: then returns,
And hums, and dances to the beating ray.
Nor shall the man, that, musing, walks alone,
And, heedless, strays within his radiant lists,°   *enclosed spaces*
Go unchastised away. Sometimes, a fleece
30 Of clouds, wide-scattering, with a lucid° veil,   *bright, clear*
Soft, shadow o'er th' unruffled face of heaven;
And, through their dewy sluices,[5] shed the sun,
With tempered influence down. Then is the time
For those, whom Wisdom and whom Nature charm,
35 To steal themselves from the degenerate crowd,
And soar above this little scene of things:
To tread low-thoughted Vice beneath their feet:

---

1 *Winter* Published in 1726, this is the first version of *Winter* and the first of the *Seasons* poems to appear.

2 *morn of life* Youth.

3 *chambers of the south* Reference to the southern sky in Job 9.9: "Which maketh Arcturus, Orion, and Pleiades, and the chambers of the south."

4 *swain* Country laborer, often a shepherd.

5 *sluices* Structures designed to regulate water.

To lay their passions in a gentle calm,
And woo lone Quiet, in her silent walks.

40   Now, solitary, and in pensive guise,
Oft let me wander o'er the russet mead,°   *meadow*
Or through the pining grove; where scarce is heard
One dying strain to cheer the woodman's toil:
Sad Philomel,[1] perchance, pours forth her plaint,° *lamentation*
45 Far, through the withering copse.°   *small wood*
      Meanwhile, the leaves
That, late, the forest clad with lively green,
Nipped by the drizzly night, and sallow-hued,
Fall, wavering, through the air; or shower amain,° *at full speed*
Urged by the breeze, that sobs amid the boughs.
50 Then list'ning hares forsake the rustling woods,
And, starting at the frequent noise, escape
To the rough stubble, and the rushy fen.°   *marsh*
Then woodcocks, o'er the fluctuating main,[2]
That glimmers to the glimpses of the moon,
55 Stretch their long voyage to the woodland glade:
Where, wheeling with uncertain flight, they mock
The nimble fowler's° aim. Now Nature droops; *bird hunter's*
Languish the living herbs with pale decay:
And all the various family of flowers
60 Their sunny robes resign. The falling fruits,
Through the still night, forsake the parent-bough,
That, in the first grey glances of the dawn,
Looks wild, and wonders at the wintry waste.°   *desolate land*

      The year, yet pleasing, but declining fast,
65 Soft, o'er the secret soul, in gentle gales,
A philosophic melancholy breathes,
And bears the swelling thought aloft to heaven.
Then forming fancy rouses to conceive,
What never mingled with the vulgar's° dream: *uneducated*
70 Then wake the tender pang, the pitying tear,
The sigh for suffering worth, the wish preferred° *put forward*
For humankind, the joy to see them blessed,
And all the social offspring of the heart!

Oh! bear me then to high, embowering[3] shades;
75 To twilight groves, and visionary vales;
To weeping grottos,° and to hoary[4] caves;
Where angel-forms are seen, and voices heard,
Sighed in low whispers, that abstract the soul,
From outward sense, far into worlds remote.

80   Now, when the western sun withdraws the day,
And humid evening, gliding o'er the sky,
In her chill progress checks the straggling beams,
And robs them of their gathered, vapoury prey,
Where marshes stagnate, and where rivers wind,
85 Cluster the rolling fogs, and swim along
The dusky-mantled lawn:° then slow descend,   *open land*
Once more to mingle with their wat'ry friends.
The vivid stars shine out, in radiant files;
And boundless ether[5] glows; till the fair moon
90 Shows her broad visage, in the crimsoned east;
Now, stooping, seems to kiss the passing cloud;
Now, o'er the pure cerulean,° rides sublime.   *sky-blue*
Wide the pale deluge floats, with silver waves,
O'er the skied[6] mountain, to the low-laid vale;
95 From the white rocks, with dim reflection, gleams,
And faintly glitters through the waving shades.

      All night, abundant dews, unnoted, fall,
And, at return of morning, silver o'er
The face of Mother Earth; from every branch
100 Depending,° tremble the translucent gems,   *dangling*
And, quivering, seem to fall away, yet cling,
And sparkle in the sun, whose rising eye,
With fogs bedimmed, portends a beauteous day.

      Now, giddy Youth, whom headlong passions fire,
105 Rouse the wild game, and stain the guiltless grove,
With violence, and death; yet call it sport,
To scatter ruin through the realms of love,

---

[1] *Philomel* Nightingale. The daughter of the King of Athens, Philomela was transformed into a nightingale after being pursued and raped by her brother-in-law, Tereus, King of Thrace.

[2] *main* Wide expanse.

[3] *embowering* Enclosed in trees.

[4] *hoary* White or grey with mold.

[5] *ether* Upper regions of space; the substance that comprises all the space beyond the moon.

[6] *skied* Appearing to reach the sky.

And peace, that thinks no ill: But these, the Muse,[1]
Whose charity, unlimited, extends
As wide as Nature works, disdains to sing,
Returning to her nobler theme in view—

    For, see! where Winter comes, himself,
      confessed,°   *revealed*
Striding the gloomy blast. First rains obscure
Drive through the mingling skies, with tempest foul;
Beat on the mountain's brow, and shake the woods,
That, sounding, wave below. The dreary plain
Lies overwhelmed, and lost. The bellying clouds
Combine, and deepening into night, shut up
The day's fair face. The wanderers of heaven,[2]
Each to his home, retire; save those that love
To take their pastime in the troubled air,
And, skimming, flutter round the dimply flood.
The cattle, from th' untasted fields, return,
And ask, with meaning low,° their   *moo*
    wonted° stalls;   *customary*
Or ruminate[3] in the contiguous° shade: *neighboring*
Thither, the household, feathery people crowd,
The crested cock, with all his female train,
Pensive, and wet. Meanwhile, the cottage swain
Hangs o'er th' enlivening blaze, and, taleful,° there *talkative*
Recounts his simple frolic: much he talks,
And much he laughs, nor wrecks the storm that blows
Without, and rattles on his humble roof.

    At last, the muddy deluge pours along,
Resistless, roaring; dreadful down it comes
From the chapt° mountain, and the mossy wild,   *fissured*
Tumbling through rocks abrupt, and sounding far:
Then o'er the sanded valley, floating, spreads,
Calm, sluggish, silent; till again constrained,
Betwixt two meeting hills, it bursts a way,
Where rocks and woods o'erhang the turbid° stream. *muddy*
There gathering triple force, rapid, and deep,
It boils, and wheels, and foams, and thunders through.

Nature! great parent! whose directing hand
Rolls round the seasons of the changeful year,
How mighty! how majestic are thy works!
With what a pleasing dread they swell the soul,
That sees, astonished! and, astonished, sings!
You too, ye Winds! that now begin to blow,
With boisterous sweep, I raise my voice to you.
Where are your stores,° ye viewless beings! say! *possessions*
Where your aerial magazines° reserved   *warehouses*
Against the day of tempest perilous?
In what untraveled country of the air,
Hushed in still silence, sleep you, when 'tis calm?

    Late, in the lowering[4] sky, red, fiery streaks
Begin to flush about; the reeling clouds
Stagger with dizzy aim, as doubting yet
Which master to obey: while rising, slow,
Sad, in the leaden-coloured east, the moon
Wears a bleak circle round her sullied orb.
Then issues forth the storm, with loud control,
And the thin fabric of the pillared air
O'erturns, at once. Prone, on th' uncertain main,
Descends th' ethereal force, and plows its waves,
With dreadful rift: from the mid-deep appears,
Surge after surge, the rising, wat'ry war.
Whitening, the angry billows roll immense,
And roar their terrors through the shuddering soul
Of feeble Man, amidst their fury caught,
And dashed upon his fate: Then, o'er the cliff,
Where dwells the sea-mew,° unconfined, they fly, *seagull*
And, hurrying, swallow up the sterile shore.

    The mountain growls; and all its sturdy sons
Stoop to the bottom of the rocks they shade:
Lone, on its midnight-side, and all aghast,
The dark, wayfaring stranger, breathless, toils,
And climbs against the blast—
Low waves the rooted forest, vexed,° and sheds *disturbed*
What of its leafy honours yet remains.
Thus, struggling through the dissipated grove,
The whirling tempest raves along the plain;
And, on the cottage thatched or lordly dome° *mansion*
Keen-fastening, shakes 'em to the solid base.

---

[1] *Muse* The Muses were nine daughters of Zeus and Mnemosyne, each of whom presided over and provided inspiration for an aspect of learning or the arts.

[2] *wanderers of heaven* Wild birds.

[3] *ruminate* Meaning both "chew the cud" and "meditate."

[4] *lowering* Dark and threatening.

Sleep, frighted, flies; the hollow chimney howls,
185   The windows rattle, and the hinges creak.

Then too, they say, through all the burdened air
Long groans are heard, shrill sounds, and distant sighs,
That, murmured by the demon of the night,
Warn the devoted wretch of woe, and death!
190   Wild uproar lords it wide: the clouds commixed,
With stars, swift-gliding, sweep along the sky.
All nature reels. But hark! the Almighty speaks:
Instant, the chidden° storm begins to pant,   rebuked
And dies, at once, into a noiseless calm.

195   As yet, 'tis midnight's reign; the weary clouds,
Slow-meeting, mingle into solid gloom:
Now, while the drowsy world lies lost in sleep,
Let me associate with the low-browed Night,
And Contemplation, her sedate compeer;°   companion
200   Let me shake off th' intrusive cares of day,
And lay the meddling senses all aside.

And now, ye lying vanities of life!
You ever-tempting, ever-cheating train!
Where are you now? and what is your amount?°   significance
205   Vexation, disappointment, and remorse.
Sad, sickening thought! and yet, deluded Man,
A scene of wild, disjointed visions past,
And broken slumbers, rises, still resolved,
With new-flushed hopes, to run your giddy round.

210   Father of light, and life! Thou Good Supreme!
O! teach me what is good! teach me thy self!
Save me from folly, vanity and vice,
From every low pursuit! and feed my soul,
With knowledge, conscious peace, and virtue pure,
215   Sacred, substantial, never-fading bliss!

Lo! from the livid east, or piercing north,
Thick clouds ascend, in whose capacious womb
A vapoury deluge lies, to snow congealed:
Heavy, they roll their fleecy world along;
220   And the sky saddens with th' impending storm.
Through the hushed air, the whitening shower descends,
At first, thin-wavering; till, at last, the flakes
Fall broad, and wide, and fast, dimming the day

With a continual flow. See! sudden, hoared,
225   The woods beneath the stainless burden bow,
Blackening, along the mazy° stream it melts;   winding
Earth's universal face, deep-hid, and chill,
Is all one dazzling waste. The labourer-ox
Stands covered o'er with snow, and then demands
230   The fruit of all his toil. The fowls of heaven,
Tamed by the cruel season, crowd around
The winnowing[1] store, and claim the little boon,°   favor
That Providence allows. The foodless wilds
Pour forth their brown inhabitants; the hare,
235   Though timorous° of heart, and hard beset   fearful
By death in various forms—dark snares, and dogs,
And more unpitying men—the garden seeks,
Urged on by fearless want. The bleating kind°   sheep
Eye the bleak heavens, and next, the glistening Earth,
240   With looks of dumb despair; then sad, dispersed,
Dig for the withered herb, through heaps of snow.

Now, shepherds, to your helpless charge be kind;
Baffle° the raging year, and fill their pens   defeat
With food, at will: lodge them below the blast,
245   And watch them strict; for from the bellowing east,
In this dire season, oft the whirlwind's wing
Sweeps up the burden of whole wintry plains
In one fierce blast, and o'er th' unhappy flocks,
Lodged in the hollow of two neighbouring hills,
250   The billowy tempest whelms;° till, upwards urged,   buries
The valley to a shining mountain swells,
That curls its wreaths amid the freezing sky.

Now, all amid the rigours of the year,
In the wild depth of Winter, while without
255   The ceaseless winds blow keen, be my retreat
A rural, sheltered, solitary scene;
Where ruddy fire and beaming tapers° join   candles
To chase the cheerless gloom: there let me sit,
And hold high converse with the mighty dead,
260   Sages of ancient time, as gods revered,
As gods beneficent, who blest mankind
With arts, and arms, and humanized a world,
Roused at th' inspiring thought—I throw aside

---

[1]   *winnowing*   Exposed to the wind so that the chaff is separated from the heavier grain.

The long-lived volume,[1] and, deep-musing, hail

55 The sacred shades, that, slowly-rising, pass

Before my wondering eyes—First, Socrates,[2]

Truth's early champion, martyr for his God:

Solon,[3] the next, who built his commonweal,°   *commonwealth*

On equity's firm base: Lycurgus,[4] then,

70 Severely good, and him of rugged Rome,

Numa,[5] who softened her° rapacious° sons.   *Rome's | greedy*

Cimon[6] sweet-souled, and Aristides[7] just.

Unconquered Cato,[8] virtuous in extreme;

With that attempered° hero,[9] mild, and firm,   *well-balanced*

75 Who wept the brother, while the tyrant bled.

Scipio,[10] the humane warrior, gently brave,

Fair learning's friend, who early sought the shade,

To dwell, with innocence and truth, retired.

And, equal to the best, the Theban,[11] he

280 Who, single, raised his country into fame.

Thousands behind, the boast of Greece and Rome,

Whom virtue owns, the tribute of a verse

Demand, but who can count the stars of heaven?

Who sing their influence on this lower world?

285 But see who yonder comes! nor comes alone,

With sober state, and of majestic mien,°   *bearing*

The Sister-Muses in his train—'tis he!

Maro![12] the best of poets, and of men!

Great Homer[13] too appears, of daring wing!

290 Parent of song! and, equal, by this side,

The British Muse,[14] joined hand in hand, they walk,

Darkling,° nor miss their way to fame's ascent.   *in the dark*

Society divine! Immortal minds!

Still visit thus my nights, for you reserved,

295 And mount my soaring soul to deeds like yours.

Silence! thou lonely power! the door be thine:

See, on the hallowed hour, that none intrude,

Save Lycidas,[15] the friend with sense refined,

Learning digested well, exalted faith,

300 Unstudied wit, and humour ever gay.

---

[1] *long-lived volume* *Parallel Lives*, a collection of paired biographies of prominent Greeks and Romans by Plutarch, Greek biographer (c. 46–120 CE).

[2] *Socrates* Greek philosopher (469–399 BCE) who considered the knowledge of one's self as the highest good; he was forced to drink poisonous hemlock after being convicted of corrupting Athens' youth and perpetuating religious heresies.

[3] *Solon* Athenian statesman (c. 639–c. 559 BCE) whose humane legal reforms contributed to the end of serfdom in Attica and established the democratic basis of the Athenian state.

[4] *Lycurgus* Although it is unclear whether he actually existed, Lycurgus is traditionally held to be the founder of the Spartan constitution.

[5] *Numa* Numa Pompilius (7th century BCE), second king of Rome after Romulus, believed to be responsible for the Roman ceremonial laws and religious rites that encouraged peace in the city.

[6] *Cimon* Athenian general and statesman (c. 510–449 BCE), remembered for both his military success against the Persians and his powerful influence in government.

[7] *Aristides* Athenian general and statesman (d. c. 468 BCE), known as Aristides the Just, who contributed significantly to Cimon's military success against the Persians.

[8] *Cato* Marcus Porcius Cato (95–46 BCE), Roman statesman known for his incorruptibility and honesty, who opposed Julius Caesar and was subsequently exiled; Cato marched six days across the African desert to join his allies in Utica after which he realized the futility of his campaign; he chose suicide rather than surrender to Caesar.

[9] *attempered hero* Timoleon, Greek statesman and military leader (d. c. 337 BCE) who successfully fought against the tyrants of Syracuse, where he subsequently set up a democratic government; when Timoleon's brother, Timophanes, attempted to declare himself the absolute ruler of their city, Corinth, Timoleon assisted in his brother's assassination, weeping all the while.

[10] *Scipio* Publius Cornelius Scipio Africanus (236–183 BCE), Roman general who conquered Spain and Carthage and defeated Hannibal in the Punic Wars.

[11] *the Theban* Possibly Pelopidas (d. 364 BCE), Theban general who rescued Thebes from Sparta in 379 BCE, or Epaminondas (c. 420–362 BCE), famous Greek military tactician under whom Pelopidas served.

[12] *Maro* Publius Virgilius Maro, or Virgil, Roman poet (70–19 BCE), author of *The Aeneid*, an epic detailing the life of Aeneas, mythical father of the Roman people, who embodied the Roman virtues, and *The Georgics*, poems recounting the joy of rural and farming life.

[13] *Homer* Greek poet (c. 700 BCE), putative author of *The Iliad*, an account of the Greeks' war with the Trojans, and *The Odyssey*, which tells the story of Odysseus's journey home after the war's end; Homer was believed to have been blind.

[14] *British Muse* John Milton (1608–74), English poet famous for such works as *Paradise Lost*, *Comus*, and *Paradise Regained*.

[15] *Lycidas* In his pastoral elegy *Lycidas* (1638), Milton laments the drowning death of his school fellow, Edward King; Thomson may be referring to his friend David Mallet, with whom he wrote the masque *Alfred* (1740).

Clear frost succeeds, and through the blue serene,
For sight too fine, the ethereal nitre[1] flies,
To bake the glebe,° and bind the slippery flood.   soil
This of the wintry season is the prime;
305 Pure are the days, and lustrous are the nights,
Brightened with starry worlds, till then unseen.
Meanwhile, the Orient, darkly red, breathes forth
An icy gale, that, in its mid career,
Arrests the bickering° stream. The nightly sky   noisy
310 And all her glowing constellations pour
Their rigid influence down: it freezes on
Till Morn, late-rising, o'er the drooping world
Lifts her pale eye, unjoyous: then appears
The various labour of the silent night,
315 The pendant icicle, the frost-work fair,
Where thousand figures rise, the crusted snow,
Though white, made whiter, by the fining° north.   refining
On blithesome° frolics bent, the youthful swains,   sprightly
While every work of man is laid at rest,
320 Rush o'er the wat'ry plains, and, shuddering, view
The fearful deeps below: or with the gun,
And faithful spaniel, range the ravaged fields,
And, adding to the ruins of the year,
Distress the feathery, or the footed game.

325   But hark! the nightly winds, with hollow voice,
Blow, blustering, from the south—the frost subdued,
Gradual, resolves into a weeping thaw.
Spotted, the mountains shine: loose sleet descends,
And floods the country round: the rivers swell,
330 Impatient for the day. Those sullen seas,
That wash th' ungenial° pole, will rest no more   inhospitable
Beneath the shackles of the mighty north;
But, rousing all their waves, resistless heave,
And hark! the length'ning roar, continuous, runs
335 Athwart° the rifted main; at once it bursts,   side to side
And piles a thousand mountains to the clouds!
Ill fares the bark,° the wretches' last resort,   boat
That, lost amid the floating fragments, moors
Beneath the shelter of an icy isle;
340 While night o'erwhelms the sea, and horror looks
More horrible. Can human hearts endure
Th' assembled mischiefs that besiege them round:

Unlist'ning hunger, fainting weariness,
The roar of winds, and waves, the crush of ice,
345 Now ceasing, now renewed with louder rage,
And bellowing round the main: nations remote,
Shook from their midnight-slumbers, deem they hear
Portentous thunder in the troubled sky.
More to embroil the deep, Leviathan[2]
350 And his unwieldy train, in horrid sport,
Tempest the loosened brine; while, through the gloom,
Far from the dire, inhospitable shore,
The lion's rage, the wolf's sad howl is heard,
And all the fell° society of night.   cruel
355 Yet Providence, that ever-waking eye,
Looks down, with pity, on the fruitless toil
Of mortals, lost to hope, and lights° them   causes to arrive
    safe   safe
Through all this dreary labyrinth of fate.

    'Tis done! dread Winter has subdued the year,
360 And reigns, tremendous, o'er the desert plains!
How dead the vegetable kingdom lies!
How dumb the tuneful! Horror wide extends
His solitary empire. Now, fond Man!
Behold thy pictured life: pass some few years,
365 Thy flow'ring Spring, thy short-lived Summer's strength,
Thy sober Autumn, fading into age,
And pale, concluding, Winter shuts thy scene,
And shrouds thee in the grave—where now, are fled
Those dreams of greatness? those unsolid hopes
370 Of happiness? those longings after fame?
Those restless cares? those busy, bustling days?
Those nights of secret guilt? those veering thoughts,
Flutt'ring 'twixt good and ill, that shared thy life?
All, now, are vanished! Virtue, sole, survives,
375 Immortal, mankind's never-failing friend,
His guide to happiness on high—and see!
'Tis come, the glorious morn! the second birth
Of Heaven, and Earth! Awakening Nature hears
Th' Almighty trumpet's voice, and starts to life,
380 Renewed, unfading. Now, th' eternal scheme,
That dark perplexity, that mystic maze,
Which sight could never trace, nor heart conceive,
To reason's eye, refined, clears up apace.°   speedily
Angels and men, astonished, pause—and dread

---

[1] *ethereal nitre* Substance believed to exist in air or plants and to
cause various phenomena.

[2] *Leviathan* Monster of the deep mentioned in Job 41.

5   To travel through the depths of Providence,
    Untried, unbounded. Ye vain learned! see,
    And, prostrate in the dust, adore that power,
    And goodness, oft arraigned.° See now   *accused of a fault*   10
        the cause,
    Why conscious worth, oppressed, in secret long
0   Mourned, unregarded: why the good man's share
    In life was gall, and bitterness of soul:
    Why the lone widow, and her orphans, pined,
    In starving solitude; while luxury,
    In palaces, lay prompting her low thought
5   To form unreal wants: why heaven-born faith,
    And charity, prime grace! wore the red marks
    Of persecution's scourge:° why licensed pain,   *whip*
    That cruel spoiler, that embosomed° foe,   *embraced*
    Embittered all our bliss. Ye good distressed!
0   Ye noble few! that, here, unbending, stand
    Beneath life's pressures—yet a little while,
    And all your woes are past. Time swiftly fleets,
    And wished eternity, approaching, brings
    Life undecaying, love without allay,
5   Pure flowing joy, and happiness sincere.
    —1726

Rule, Britannia [1]

5   When Britain first, at Heaven's command,
        Arose from out the azure main;°   *sea*
    This was the charter of the land,
        And guardian angels sung this strain:
5   "Rule, Britannia, rule the waves;
                Britons never will be slaves."

The nations not so blessed as thee
    Must, in their turns, to tyrants fall:
While thou shalt flourish great and free,
    The dread and envy of them all.   10
            "Rule," etc.

Still more majestic shalt thou rise,
    More dreadful, from each foreign stroke:
As the loud blast that tears the skies
15   Serves but to root thy native oak.
            "Rule," etc.

Thee haughty tyrants ne'er shall tame:
    All their attempts to bend thee down
Will but arouse thy generous flame,
20   But work their woe, and thy renown.
            "Rule," etc.

To thee belongs the rural reign;
    Thy cities shall with commerce shine:
All thine shall be the subject main,
25   And every shore it circles thine.
            "Rule," etc.

The Muses, still° with freedom found,   *always*
    Shall to thy happy coast repair:
Blessed isle! with matchless beauty crowned,
30   And manly hearts to guard the fair.
            "Rule, Britannia, rule the waves;
                Britons never will be slaves."
    —1740

---

[1] *Rule, Britannia* From Thomson's masque *Alfred* (1740), first
performed for the Prince and Princess of Wales. This song became so
popular that it has come to be considered the unofficial national
anthem of Britain ("Britannia" was the original name given to England
and Wales by the Romans).

Samuel Johnson
1709 – 1784

Samuel Johnson, the legendary eighteenth-century figure, has been referred to as a "great talker," "great moralist," "great man of letters," "great Cham of literature," and even, "a great man who looked like an idiot." One nineteenth-century British scholar declared that the reputation of Johnson's genius was such that he had come to embody for the English "all that we admire in ourselves." Johnson's rise from poverty and obscurity, his quick wit and forceful personality, his dedication to practical common sense and morality, his insatiable pursuit of knowledge, and his use of that knowledge for the cultural advancement of the English have all played a part in making him one of the most celebrated literary figures in British history.

The first three decades of Johnson's life gave little indication that he would one day claim such greatness. He was a premature, unhealthy infant who was not expected to survive childhood. He contracted scrofula soon after birth, the result of which was deep facial scarring, deafness in one ear, and blindness in one eye. As he grew older he suffered from a variety of nervous tics that caused him to twitch and mutter a good deal; until he began speaking, which he did with extraordinary eloquence, people often assumed him to be suffering from some mental disability. He was also prone to depression and was plagued by a series of anxieties, the most pervasive of which was an overwhelming fear of madness. This was strongest, according to James Boswell, "*at the very time* when he was giving proofs of a more than ordinary soundness of judgment and vigour."

Johnson excelled in school, however, and supplemented his education with voracious reading at home. His father was a bookseller, and Johnson chose his books indiscriminately from the available stacks. He arrived at Oxford one of the most qualified students the university had seen; nevertheless, his parents' meager funds did not allow him to stay through his second year. After a brief teaching post, a failed attempt to start a school, and several years of paralyzing depression, Johnson and his wife Tetty (whom he had married in 1735), moved to London.

In London Johnson joined the hundreds of others who earned their living by anonymous hack writing. As his poem *London* (1738) attests, "Slow rises worth, by poverty depressed." Johnson's career was helped along by his writing for *Gentleman's Magazine*, one of the most successful of London's journals. He also gained valuable employment compiling an annotated catalogue of the library of Edward Harley, Lord Oxford, for its purchaser, Thomas Osborne—a job that helped him to become a scholar who, as Adam Smith later claimed, "knew more books than any man alive."

In 1749, Johnson, who was becoming known for his extraordinary erudition, was hired by a group of London booksellers to compile the first comprehensive English dictionary. *The Dictionary of the English Language* (1755)—the first edition of which required nine years and the help of six assistants to complete—set the standard for all future dictionaries in the sheer volume of words it defined (40,000 in total), the various shades of meaning it distinguished, the logic and clarity of those definitions, and the hundreds of thousands of literary quotations (many of which Johnson wrote out from memory) that served as examples. Though Johnson's whimsical definition of lexicographer reads "a writer of dictionaries, a harmless drudge," many of the decisions he made in forming his dictionary became central tenets of modern lexicography. In particular, his choice to make the dictionary descriptive (a catalogue of all known words and their various uses) rather than prescriptive (a selective list to instruct in the proper use of the language and eliminate "low" or "vulgar" words) decisively shaped the role that dictionaries would play in the future development of the language.

During these years, "Dictionary Johnson" composed essays as a nightly diversion from the "drudgery" of lexicography. Over 200 of the moral, critical, and intellectual explorations he compiled were published in a periodical he produced twice weekly (frequently dashing off articles at the very last minute, with the printer's messenger waiting by his side), called *The Rambler* (1750–52). The practical wisdom and stark clarity of these essays won favor with readers, as did Johnson's careful study and description of human nature, his ability to apply reason to experience, and his celebrations of moral strength and virtue. He later resumed his essay writing with the lighter and more humorous weekly periodical *The Idler* (1758–60). *Rasselas, Prince of Abyssinia* (1759) broadened Johnson's reputation as a moralist. This work of fiction—part novel, part moral parable—tells the story of various characters who leave their idyllic home to embark on a fruitless search for one "choice of life" that will bring them endless happiness. The wit and compassion evident in this tale of the insatiability of the human mind made it Johnson's most enduringly popular work, and led Boswell to claim that he was not satisfied unless he reread it at least once a year.

In the latter half of the eighteenth century Johnson at last attained professional and financial security. For his dictionary work Oxford awarded him an honorary Master's degree in 1755 (followed in 1765 by a Doctorate of Law from Trinity College and in 1775 by a Doctorate of Civil Law, also from Oxford), and George III granted him an annual pension of £300. In 1765, after eight years of toil, he completed his edition of Shakespeare, which, with its preface, became an influential contribution to Shakespeare scholarship.

For a time after the death of his wife in 1752, Johnson led a rather solitary existence. Within a few years, however, he had met aspiring writer James Boswell and brewer Henry Thrale and his wife, Hester Thrale (later Piozzi), and had begun to travel for the first time in his life—with the Thrales to France and Wales and with Boswell to Scotland and the Hebrides. By now renowned for his powers of conversation, Johnson eventually found himself at the center of a large circle of leading men (which included painter Sir Joshua Reynolds, politician Edmund Burke, writer Oliver Goldsmith, and actor David Garrick), whose weekly discussions were motivated largely by a desire to hear Johnson talk.

Johnson's last major project was his *Lives of the English Poets* (1779–81). Asked by a group of publishers to write brief introductions to a small edition of English poets, Johnson so enjoyed the project that his pieces expanded beyond mere prefaces into comprehensive critical and historical texts. The publishers, recognizing that these 52 biographies and literary commentaries were powerful works of scholarship in their own right, released them as an independent text. The *Lives* demonstrates Johnson's belief in "the dignity and usefulness of biography" not merely as a source of historical information about a particular figure, but also as a revealing means of documenting human passions and desires with universal significance. He insisted that his biographies give detailed and truthful accounts of his subjects' vices as well as their virtues. For Johnson, it was the minute particularities of the subject that held the essence of each life. Johnson's theories of biography also had an impact on the deeply personal, intimately detailed biographies of him that his friends—most notably Boswell, but also Hester Thrale Piozzi—released after his death.

A few years before his death in 1784 Johnson observed, as he told Boswell, that "there is hardly a day in which there is not something about me in the papers." Historical research has confirmed the accuracy of this remark—Johnson's travel plans, various ailments, and movements about town were constantly reported. If there was no news to record, anecdotes were recycled or even invented. The force of Johnson's personality had captured the attention of the public, and the man who had once professed himself a "retired and uncourtly scholar" had become an integral part of the daily life of a nation. Johnson suffered a stroke in 1783 from which he never fully recovered; he died on 13 December 1784 and was buried in Westminster Abbey a week later.

⌘ ⌘ ⌘

The Vanity of Human Wishes

THE TENTH SATIRE OF JUVENAL IMITATED[1]

Let Observation, with extensive view,
Survey mankind, from China to Peru;
Remark each anxious toil, each eager strife,
And watch the busy scenes of crowded life;
5   Then say how hope and fear, desire and hate,
O'erspread with snares the clouded maze of fate,
Where wav'ring man, betrayed by vent'rous pride,
To tread the dreary paths without a guide,
As treach'rous phantoms in the mist delude,
10 Shuns fancied ills, or chases airy° good;   imaginary
How rarely reason guides the stubborn choice,
Rules the bold hand, or prompts the suppliant voice;
How nations sink, by darling schemes oppressed,
When vengeance listens to the fool's request.
15 Fate wings with every wish th'afflictive dart,
Each gift of nature, and each grace of art,
With fatal heat impetuous courage glows,
With fatal sweetness elocution flows,
Impeachment stops the speaker's pow'rful breath,
20 And restless fire precipitates on death.
But scarce observed, the knowing and the bold
Fall in the gen'ral massacre of gold;
Wide-wasting pest! that rages unconfined,
And crowds with crimes the records of mankind;
25 For gold his sword the hireling ruffian draws,
For gold the hireling judge distorts the laws;
Wealth heaped on wealth, nor truth nor safety buys,
The dangers gather as the treasures rise.
Let hist'ry tell where rival kings command,
30 And dubious title shakes the madded land,
When statutes glean the refuse of the sword,
How much more safe the vassal than the lord;
Low skulks the hind° beneath the rage of pow'r,   farm-worker
And leaves the wealthy traitor in the Tow'r,[2]
35 Untouched his cottage, and his slumbers sound,
Though confiscation's vultures hover round.
The needy traveler, secure and gay,
Walks the wild heath, and sings his toil away.
Does envy seize thee? crush th'upbraiding joy,
40 Increase his riches and his peace destroy;
Now fears in dire vicissitude invade,
The rustling brake° alarms, and quiv'ring shade,   thicket
Nor light nor darkness bring his pain relief,
One shows the plunder, and one hides the thief.
45 Yet still one gen'ral cry the skies assails,
And gain and grandeur load the tainted gales;
Few know the toiling statesman's fear or care,
Th' insidious rival and the gaping heir.
Once more, Democritus,[3] arise on earth,
50 With cheerful wisdom and instructive mirth,
See motley[4] life in modern trappings dressed,
And feed with varied fools th'eternal jest:
Thou who couldst laugh where want enchained caprice,
Toil crushed conceit, and man was of a piece;
55 Where wealth unloved without a mourner died,
And scarce a sycophant was fed by pride;
Where ne'er was known the form of mock debate,
Or seen a new-made mayor's unwieldy state;
Where change of fav'rites made no change of laws,

---

1   *The Vanity … Imitated*   In his imitation of Juvenal's satire of human ambition and failure, Johnson replaces the ancient Roman examples with modern ones and adds a background of Christian theology.

2   *Tow'r*   The Tower of London, where those accused of treason were imprisoned.

3   *Democritus*   Philosopher of ancient Greece who is occasionally called "the laughing philosopher" because of his response to the follies of humanity.

4   *motley*   Multicolored (a reference to the brightly-colored clothing worn by jesters and fools).

60 And senates heard before they judged a cause;
How wouldst thou shake at Britain's modish tribe,
Dart the quick taunt, and edge the piercing gibe?
Attentive truth and nature to descry,°   *perceive*
And pierce each scene with philosophic eye.
65 To thee were solemn toys or empty show,
The robes of pleasure and the veils of woe:
All aid the farce, and all thy mirth maintain,
Whose joys are causeless, or whose griefs are vain.
Such was the scorn that filled the sage's mind,
70 Renewed at ev'ry glance on humankind;
How just that scorn ere yet thy voice declare,
Search every state, and canvass° every prayer.   *scrutinize*
Unnumbered suppliants crowd Preferment's gate,
Athirst for wealth, and burning to be great;
75 Delusive Fortune hears th'incessant call,
They mount, they shine, evaporate, and fall.
On every stage the foes of peace attend,
Hate dogs their flight, and insult mocks their end.
Love ends with hope, the sinking statesman's door
80 Pours in the morning worshiper[1] no more;
For growing names the weekly scribbler lies,
To growing wealth the dedicator flies,
From ev'ry room descends the painted face,
That hung the bright Palladium[2] of the place,
85 And smoked in kitchens, or in auctions sold,
To better features yields the frame of gold;
For now no more we trace in ev'ry line
Heroic worth, benevolence divine:
The form distorted justifies the fall,
90 And detestation rids th'indignant wall.
But will not Britain hear the last appeal,
Sign her foes' doom, or guard her fav'rites' zeal?
Through Freedom's sons no more remonstrance rings,
Degrading nobles and controlling kings;
95 Our supple tribes repress their patriot throats,
And ask no questions but the price of votes;
With weekly libels and septennial ale,[3]
Their wish is full to riot and to rail.

In full-blown dignity, see Wolsey[4] stand,
100 Law in his voice, and fortune in his hand:
To him the church, the realm, their pow'rs consign,
Through him the rays of regal bounty shine,
Turned by his nod the stream of honor flows,
His smile alone security bestows:
105 Still to new heights his restless wishes tow'r,
Claim leads to claim, and pow'r advances pow'r;
Till conquest unresisted ceased to please,
And rights submitted, left him none to seize.
At length his sov'reign frowns—the train of state
110 Mark the keen glance, and watch the sign to hate.
Where'er he turns he meets a stranger's eye,
His suppliants scorn him, and his followers fly;
At once is lost the pride of awful state,
The golden canopy, the glitt'ring plate,
115 The regal palace, the luxurious board,
The liv'ried army, and the menial lord.
With age, with cares, with maladies oppressed,
He seeks the refuge of monastic rest.
Grief aids disease, remembered folly stings,
120 And his last sighs reproach the faith of kings.
Speak thou, whose thoughts at humble peace repine,
Shall Wolsey's wealth, with Wolsey's end be thine?
Or liv'st thou now, with safer pride content,
The wisest justice on the banks of Trent?[5]
125 For why did Wolsey near the steeps° of fate,   *precipices*
On weak foundations raise th'enormous weight?
Why but to sink beneath misfortune's blow,
With louder ruin to the gulfs below?
What gave great Villiers to th'assassin's knife,
130 And fixed disease on Harley's[6] closing life?
What murdered Wentworth, and what exiled Hyde,[7]
By kings protected, and to kings allied?

---

[1] *morning worshiper* Men of state would receive visitors and suppliants at morning receptions, or levees.

[2] *Palladium* Statue of Pallas Athena that was worshiped in Troy and which protected the city.

[3] *septennial ale* Those running for Parliament would give away free ale at the elections (usually held every seven years).

[4] *Wolsey* Lord Chancellor to Henry VIII until imprisoned for failing to obtain the King's divorce from Catherine of Aragon.

[5] *Trent* River that flows northeasterly through the center of England.

[6] *Villiers* George Villiers, first duke of Buckingham and a favorite of King James I. He was stabbed to death by an army officer in 1628; *Harley* Robert Harley, first earl of Oxford and powerful politician and statesman (1661–1724).

[7] *Wentworth* First earl of Stafford and advisor to Charles I who was executed in 1641 at the beginning of the civil war; *Hyde* First earl of Clarendon who was Lord Chancellor to Charles II but was impeached in 1667 and forced to flee to France.

What but their wish indulged in courts to shine,
And pow'r too great to keep, or to resign?
135 When first the college rolls receive his name,
The young enthusiast quits his ease for fame;
Through all his veins the fever of renown
Burns from the strong contagion of the gown;[1]
O'er Bodley's dome[2] his future labors spread,
140 And Bacon's[3] mansion trembles o'er his head.
Are these thy views? proceed, illustrious youth,
And virtue guard thee to the throne of Truth!
Yet should thy soul indulge the gen'rous heat,
Till captive Science yields her last retreat;
145 Should Reason guide thee with her brightest ray,
And pour on misty Doubt resistless day;
Should no false Kindness lure to loose delight,
Nor Praise relax, nor Difficulty fright;
Should tempting Novelty thy cell refrain,°   avoid
150 And Sloth effuse her opiate fumes in vain;
Should Beauty blunt on fops her fatal dart,
Nor claim the triumph of a lettered heart;
Should no disease thy torpid veins invade,
Nor Melancholy's phantoms haunt thy shade;°   spirit
155 Yet hope not life from grief or danger free,
Nor think the doom of man reversed for thee:
Deign on the passing world to turn thine eyes,
And pause awhile from letters, to be wise;
There mark what ills the scholar's life assail,
160 Toil, envy, want, the patron, and the jail.
See nations slowly wise, and meanly just,
To buried merit raise the tardy bust.
If dreams yet flatter, once again attend,
Hear Lydiat's life, and Galileo's end.[4]
165 Nor deem, when learning her last prize bestows,
The glitt'ring eminence exempt from foes;
See when the vulgar 'scape, despised or awed,

Rebellion's vengeful talons seize on Laud.[5]
From meaner minds, though smaller fines content,
170 The plundered palace or sequestered rent;
Marked out by dangerous parts° he meets the shock, talents
And fatal Learning leads him to the block:
Around his tomb let Art and Genius weep,
But hear his death, ye blockheads, hear and sleep.
175 The festal blazes, the triumphal show,
The ravished standard, and the captive foe,
The senate's thanks, the gazette's pompous tale,
With force resistless o'er the brave prevail.
Such bribes the rapid Greek[6] o'er Asia whirled,
180 For such the steady Romans shook the world;
For such in distant lands the Britons shine,
And stain with blood the Danube or the Rhine;
This pow'r has praise, that virtue scarce can warm,
Till fame supplies the universal charm.
185 Yet Reason frowns on War's unequal game,
Where wasted nations raise a single name,
And mortgaged states their grandsires' wreaths[7] regret,
From age to age in everlasting debt;
Wreaths which at last the dear-bought right convey
190 To rust on medals, or on stones decay.
On what foundation stands the warrior's pride,
How just his hopes let Swedish Charles[8] decide;
A frame of adamant, a soul of fire,
No dangers fright him, and no labors tire;
195 O'er love, o'er fear, extends his wide domain,
Unconquered lord of pleasure and of pain;
No joys to him pacific scepters yield,
War sounds the trump, he rushes to the field;
Behold surrounding kings their pow'r combine,
200 And one capitulate, and one resign;[9]
Peace courts his hand, but spreads her charms in vain;
"Think nothing gained," he cries, "till nought remain,

---

[1] *gown* Scholarly robe.

[2] *Bodley's dome* Bodleian Library at Oxford University.

[3] [Johnson's note] There is a tradition that the study of Friar Bacon, built on an arch over the bridge, will fall when a man greater than Bacon shall pass under it. [Roger Bacon was a noted medieval philosopher, and the bridge referred to is Folly Bridge, at Oxford, which was demolished in 1779.]

[4] *Lydiat's life* The mathematician Lydiat lived a life of poverty and was imprisoned for debt; *Galileo's end* Galileo died condemned of heresy as a result of his philosophical claims.

[5] *Laud* William Laud, archbishop of Canterbury during the reign of Charles I, executed for treason in 1645.

[6] *the rapid Greek* Alexander the Great.

[7] *wreaths* I.e., victory.

[8] *Swedish Charles* Charles XII of Sweden (1682–1718), a power-hungry king who, when he was defeated by the Russians, attempted to form an alliance with the Turks. Upon his return to Sweden he invaded Norway and was killed in battle.

[9] *And one ... resign* Frederick IV of Demark yielded to Charles, and Augustus II of Poland was deposed.

On Moscow's walls till Gothic[1] standards fly,
And all be mine beneath the polar sky."
5 The march begins in military state,
And nations on his eye suspended wait;
Stern Famine guards the solitary coast,
And Winter barricades the realms of Frost;
He comes, not want and cold his course delay—
10 Hide, blushing Glory, hide Pultowa's[2] day:
The vanquished hero leaves his broken bands,
And shows his miseries in distant lands;
Condemned a needy supplicant to wait,
While ladies interpose, and slaves debate.
15 But did not Chance at length her error mend?
Did no subverted empire mark his end?
Did rival monarchs give the fatal wound?
Or hostile millions press him to the ground?
His fall was destined to a barren strand,
20 A petty fortress, and a dubious hand;[3]
He left the name, at which the world grew pale,
To point a moral, or adorn a tale.
All times their scenes of pompous woes afford,
From Persia's tyrant to Bavaria's lord.[4]
25 In gay hostility, and barb'rous pride,
With half mankind embattled at his side,
Great Xerxes comes to seize the certain prey,
And starves exhausted regions in his way;
Attendant Flattery counts his myriads o'er,
30 Till counted myriads soothe his pride no more;
Fresh praise is tried till madness fires his mind,
The waves he lashes, and enchains the wind;
New pow'rs are claimed, new pow'rs are still bestowed,
Till rude resistance lops the spreading god;
35 The daring Greeks deride the martial show,
And heap their valleys with the gaudy foe;
Th'insulted sea with humbler thoughts he gains,

A single skiff to speed his flight remains;
Th'encumbered oar scarce leaves the dreaded coast
240 Through purple billows and a floating host.
The bold Bavarian, in a luckless hour,
Tries the dread summits of Cesarean power,
With unexpected legions bursts away,
And sees defenseless realms receive his sway;
245 Short sway! fair Austria spreads her mournful charms,
The queen, the beauty, sets the world in arms;
From hill to hill the beacon's rousing blaze
Spreads wide the hope of plunder and of praise;
The fierce Croatian, and the wild Hussar,[5]
250 And all the sons of ravage crowd the war;
The baffled prince in honor's flattering bloom
Of hasty greatness finds the fatal doom,
His foes' derision, and his subjects' blame,
And steals to death from anguish and from shame.
255 Enlarge my life with multitude of days,
In health, in sickness, thus the suppliant prays;
Hides from himself his state, and shuns to know,
That life protracted is protracted woe.
Time hovers o'er, impatient to destroy,
260 And shuts up all the passages of joy:
In vain their gifts the bounteous seasons pour,
The fruit autumnal, and the vernal flow'r,
With listless eyes the dotard views the store,
He views, and wonders that they please no more;
265 Now pall the tasteless meats, and joyless wines,
And Luxury° with sighs her slave resigns.   *pleasure*
Approach, ye minstrels, try the soothing strain,
Diffuse the tuneful lenitives° of pain: *palliatives*
No sounds alas would touch th'impervious ear,
270 Though dancing mountains witnessed Orpheus[6] near;
Nor lute nor lyre his feeble pow'rs attend,
Nor sweeter music of a virtuous friend,
But everlasting dictates crowd his tongue,
Perversely grave, or positively wrong.
275 The still returning tale, and ling'ring jest,
Perplex the fawning niece and pampered guest,
While growing hopes scarce awe the gathering sneer,

---

[1] *Gothic* Here, Swedish.

[2] *Pultowa* Location of Peter the Great's defeat of Charles in 1709.

[3] *dubious hand* It was believed the Charles was shot in battle by one of his own men.

[4] *Persia's tyrant ... Bavaria's lord* References to Xerxes and Charles Albert. Xerxes was the Persian king who invaded Greece using a bridge of ships to cross the Hellespont. After a storm broke up the bridge, he ordered his men to whip the wind and waves with chains. Charles Albert, Elector of Bavaria, was defeated by Maria Theresa of Austria in the War of the Austrian Succession (1740–48).

---

[5] *Hussar* Hungarian light cavalry.

[6] *Orpheus* Musician of Greek mythology who was able to make mountains move with his music.

And scarce a legacy can bribe to hear;
The watchful guests still hint the last offense,
280 The daughter's petulance, the son's expense,
Improve° his heady rage with treach'rous skill,   *increase*
And mold his passions till they make his will.
Unnumbered maladies his joints invade,
Lay siege to life and press the dire blockade;
285 But unextinguished Avarice still remains,
And dreaded losses aggravate his pains;
He turns, with anxious heart and crippled hands,
His bonds of debt, and mortgages of lands;
Or views his coffers with suspicious eyes,
290 Unlocks his gold, and counts it till he dies.
But grant, the virtues of a temp'rate prime
Bless with an age exempt from scorn or crime;
An age that melts with unperceived decay,
And glides in modest innocence away;
295 Whose peaceful day Benevolence endears,
Whose night congratulating Conscience cheers;
The gen'ral favorite as the gen'ral friend:
Such age there is, and who shall wish its end?
Yet ev'n on this her load Misfortune flings,
300 To press the weary minutes' flagging wings:
New sorrow rises as the day returns,
A sister sickens, or a daughter mourns.
Now kindred Merit fills the sable bier,
Now lacerated Friendship claims a tear.
305 Year chases year, decay pursues decay,
Still drops some joy from with'ring life away;
New forms arise, and different views engage,
Superfluous lags the vet'ran[1] on the stage,
Till pitying Nature signs the last release,
310 And bids afflicted worth retire to peace.
But few there are whom hours like these await,
Who set unclouded in the gulfs of fate.
From Lydia's monarch[2] should the search descend,
By Solon cautioned to regard his end,
315 In life's last scene what prodigies surprise,
Fears of the brave, and follies of the wise?

From Marlborough's[3] eyes the streams of dotage flow,
And Swift[4] expires a driveler and a show.
The teeming° mother, anxious for her
    race,°   *pregnant / offspring*
320 Begs for each birth the fortune of a face:
Yet Vane could tell what ills from beauty spring;
And Sedley[5] cursed the form that pleased a king.
Ye nymphs of rosy lips and radiant eyes,
Whom Pleasure keeps too busy to be wise,
325 Whom Joys with soft varieties invite,
By day the frolic, and the dance by night,
Who frown with vanity, who smile with art,
And ask the latest fashion of the heart,
What care, what rules your heedless charms shall save,
330 Each nymph your rival, and each youth your slave?
Against your fame with fondness hate combines,
The rival batters, and the lover mines.
With distant voice neglected Virtue calls,
Less heard and less, the faint remonstrance falls;
335 Tired with contempt, she quits the slipp'ry reign,
And Pride and Prudence take her seat in vain.
In crowd at once, where none the pass defend,
The harmless Freedom, and the private Friend.
The guardians yield, by force superior plied;
340 By Interest,° Prudence; and by Flattery, Pride.   *self-interest*
Now beauty falls betrayed, despised, distressed,
And hissing Infamy proclaims the rest.
Where then shall Hope and Fear their objects find?
Must dull Suspense corrupt the stagnant mind?
345 Must helpless man, in ignorance sedate,
Roll darkling[6] down the torrent of his fate?
Must no dislike alarm, no wishes rise,
No cries attempt the mercies of the skies?
Inquirer, cease, petitions yet remain,
350 Which Heav'n may hear, nor deem religion vain.

---

[1] *vet'ran* Of life, rather than of war.

[2] *Lydia's monarch* Croesus, the wealthy sixth-century BCE king of Lydia who was cautioned by the Athenian philosopher Solon that no man should count himself happy until he reached the end of his life. Later, Croesus was overthrown by King Cyrus of Persia.

[3] *Marlborough* John Churchill, first duke of Marlborough, was a great general during the War of Spanish Succession, but he was debilitated by two strokes before his death in 1722.

[4] *Swift* Poet Jonathan Swift became senile before his death, and it is believed that following his demise his servants were bribed to put him on display and allow souvenir hunters to take hairs from his head.

[5] *Vane … Sedley* Anne Vane and Catherine Sedley were the mistresses of Frederick, prince of Wales, and James II respectively.

[6] *darkling* In the dark.

Still raise for good the supplicating voice,
But leave to Heav'n the measure and the choice,
Safe in his power, whose eyes discern afar
The secret ambush of a specious prayer.
5 Implore his aid, in his decisions rest,
Secure whate'er he gives, he gives the best.
Yet when the sense of sacred presence fires,
And strong devotion to the skies aspires,
Pour forth thy fervors for a healthful mind,
10 Obedient passions, and a will resigned;
For love, which scarce collective° man can fill;   *as a whole*
For patience sov'reign o'er transmuted ill;
For faith, that panting for a happier seat,
Counts death kind Nature's signal of retreat:
15 These goods for man the laws of Heav'n ordain,
These goods he grants, who grants the power to gain;
With these celestial wisdom calms the mind,
And makes the happiness she does not find.
—1749

On the Death of Dr. Robert Levett[1]

Condemned to Hope's delusive mine,
    As on we toil from day to day,
By sudden blasts, or slow decline,
    Our social comforts drop away.

5 Well tried through many a varying year,
    See Levett to the grave descend;
Officious,° innocent, sincere,   *kind*
    Of every friendliness name the friend.

Yet still he fills affection's eye,
10   Obscurely° wise, and coarsely kind;   *quietly*
Nor, lettered° arrogance, deny   *scholarly*
    Thy praise to merit unrefined.

When fainting nature called for aid,
    And hovering Death prepared the blow,
15 His vigorous remedy displayed
    The power of art without the show.

In misery's darkest caverns known,
    His useful care was ever nigh,
Where hopeless Anguish poured his groan,
20   And lonely want retired to die.

No summons mocked by chill delay,
    No petty gain disdained by pride,
The modest wants of every day
    The toil of every day supplied.

25 His virtues walked their narrow round,
    Nor made a pause, nor left a void;
And sure th' Eternal Master found
    The single talent well employed.[2]

The busy day, the peaceful night,
30   Unfelt, uncounted, glided by;
His frame was firm, his powers were bright,
    Though now his eightieth year was nigh.

Then with no throbbing fiery pain,
    No cold gradations of decay,
35 Death broke at once the vital chain,
    And freed his soul the nearest way.
—1783

The Rambler No. 4
[ON FICTION]
Saturday, 31 March 1750

Simul et jucunda et idonea dicere vitae.
            —Horace, *Ars Poetica*, line 334
And join both profit and delight in one.
                                — Creech

The works of fiction with which the present generation seems more particularly delighted are such as
exhibit life in its true state, diversified only by accidents
that daily happen in the world, and influenced by
passions and qualities which are really to be found in
conversing with mankind.

    This kind of writing may be termed not improperly
the comedy of romance, and is to be conducted nearly

---

[1] *Dr. Robert Levett* Medical practitioner who worked among
London's poor. In later life he resided with Johnson, and died in
1782 at the age of 76.

[2] *single ... employed* Cf. the parable of the talents (Matthew 25.14–30).

by the rules of comic poetry. Its province is to bring about natural events by easy means, and to keep up curiosity without the help of wonder: it is therefore precluded from the machines[1] and expedients of the heroic romance, and can neither employ giants to snatch away a lady from the nuptial rites, nor knights to bring her back from captivity; it can neither bewilder its personages in deserts, nor lodge them in imaginary castles.

I remember a remark made by Scaliger upon Pontanus,[2] that all his writings are filled with the same images; and that if you take from him his lilies and his roses, his satyrs and his dryads, he will have nothing left that can be called poetry. In like manner, almost all the fictions of the last age will vanish if you deprive them of a hermit and a wood, a battle and a shipwreck.

Why this wild strain of imagination found reception so long in polite and learned ages, it is not easy to conceive; but we cannot wonder that, while readers could be procured, the authors were willing to continue it: for when a man had by practice gained some fluency of language, he had no further care than to retire to his closet,[3] let loose his invention, and heat his mind with incredibilities; a book was thus produced without fear of criticism, without the toil of study, without knowledge of nature, or acquaintance with life.

The task of our present writers is very different; it requires, together with that learning which is to be gained from books, that experience which can never be attained by solitary diligence, but must arise from general converse and accurate observation of the living world. Their performances have, as Horace expresses it, *plus oneris quantum veniae minus*, little indulgence, and therefore more difficulty.[4] They are engaged in portraits of which everyone knows the original, and can detect any deviation from exactness of resemblance. Other writings are safe, except from the malice of learning, but these are in danger from every common reader; as the slipper ill executed was censured by a shoemaker who

happened to stop in his way at the Venus of Apelles.[5] But the fear of not being approved as just copiers of human manners is not the most important concern that an author of this sort ought to have before him. These books are written chiefly to the young, the ignorant, and the idle, to whom they serve as lectures of conduct and introductions into life. They are the entertainment of minds unfurnished with ideas, and therefore easily susceptible of impressions; not fixed by principles, and therefore easily following the current of fancy; not informed by experience, and consequently open to every false suggestion and partial account.

That the highest degree of reverence should be paid to youth, and that nothing indecent should be suffered to approach their eyes or ears, are precepts extorted by sense and virtue from an ancient writer,[6] by no means eminent for chastity of thought. The same kind, though not the same degree, of caution, is required in everything which is laid before them, to secure them from unjust prejudices, perverse opinions, and incongruous combinations of images.

In the romances formerly written, every transaction and sentiment was so remote from all that passes among men that the reader was in very little danger of making any applications to himself; the virtues and crimes were equally beyond his sphere of activity; and he amused himself with heroes and with traitors, deliverers and persecutors, as with beings of another species, whose actions were regulated upon motives of their own, and who had neither faults nor excellencies in common with himself.

But when an adventurer is leveled with the rest of the world, and acts in such scenes of the universal drama, as may be the lot of any other man, young spectators fix their eyes upon him with closer attention, and hope by observing his behavior and success to regulate their own practices, when they shall be engaged in the like part.

For this reason these familiar histories may perhaps be made of greater use than the solemnities of professed

---

[1] *machines*   Unnatural agents or devices that advance the plot.

[2] *Scaliger upon Pontanus*   In his *Poetics* (1561), influential Renaissance humanist Julius Caesar Scaliger criticizes the Latin poetry of Italian poet Giovanni Pontano (1426–1503).

[3] *closet*   Private study.

[4] *Horace ... difficulty*   From *Epistles* 2.1.170.

[5] *slipper ... Apelles*   The fourth-century Greek painter Apelles was praised for the verisimilitude of his works. This story of a shoemaker finding fault with Venus's slipper (prompting Apelles to correct the painting) comes from the *Natural History* of Pliny the Elder.

[6] *an ancient writer*   Roman satirist Juvenal, in his *Satires*, 14.1–58.

morality, and convey the knowledge of vice and virtue with more efficacy than axioms and definitions. But if the power of example is so great as to take possession of the memory by a kind of violence, and produce effects almost without the intervention of the will, care ought to be taken that, when the choice is unrestrained, the best examples only should be exhibited; and that which is likely to operate so strongly should not be mischievous or uncertain in its effects.

The chief advantage which these fictions have over real life is that their authors are at liberty, though not to invent, yet to select objects, and to cull from the mass of mankind those individuals upon which the attention ought most to be employed; as a diamond, though it cannot be made, may be polished by art, and placed in such a situation as to display that lustre which before was buried among common stones.

It is justly considered as the greatest excellency of art to imitate nature; but it is necessary to distinguish those parts of nature which are most proper for imitation: greater care is still required in representing life, which is so often discolored by passion, or deformed by wickedness. If the world be promiscuously[1] described, I cannot see of what use it can be to read the account; or why it may not be as safe to turn the eye immediately upon mankind, as upon a mirror which shows all that presents itself without discrimination.

It is therefore not a sufficient vindication of a character that it is drawn as it appears, for many characters ought never to be drawn; nor of a narrative, that the train of events is agreeable to observation and experience, for that observation which is called knowledge of the world will be found much more frequently to make men cunning than good. The purpose of these writings is surely not only to show mankind, but to provide that they may be seen hereafter with less hazard; to teach the means of avoiding the snares which are laid by Treachery for Innocence, without infusing any wish for that superiority with which the betrayer flatters his vanity; to give the power of counteracting fraud, without the temptation to practice it; to initiate youth by mock encounters in the art of necessary defense, and to increase prudence without impairing virtue.

Many writers, for the sake of following nature, so mingle good and bad qualities in their principal personages, that they are both equally conspicuous; and as we accompany them through their adventures with delight, and are led by degrees to interest ourselves in their favor, we lose the abhorrence of their faults, because they do not hinder our pleasure, or, perhaps, regard them with some kindness for being united with so much merit.

There have been men indeed splendidly wicked, whose endowments threw a brightness on their crimes, and whom scarce any villainy made perfectly detestable, because they never could be wholly divested of their excellencies; but such have been in all ages the great corrupters of the world, and their resemblance ought no more to be preserved, than the art of murdering without pain.

Some have advanced, without due attention to the consequences of this notion, that certain virtues have their correspondent faults, and therefore that to exhibit either apart is to deviate from probability. Thus men are observed by Swift to be "grateful in the same degree as they are resentful."[2] This principle, with others of the same kind, supposes man to act from a brute impulse, and pursue a certain degree of inclination, without any choice of the object; for otherwise, though it should be allowed that gratitude and resentment arise from the same constitution of the passions, it follows not that they will be equally indulged when reason is consulted; yet unless that consequence be admitted, this sagacious maxim becomes an empty sound, without any relation to practice or to life.

Nor is it evident that even the first motions[3] to these effects are always in the same proportion. For pride, which produces quickness of resentment, will obstruct gratitude by unwillingness to admit that inferiority which obligation implies; and it is very unlikely that he who cannot think he receives a favor will acknowledge or repay it.

It is of the utmost importance to mankind that positions of this tendency should be laid open and confuted; for while men consider good and evil as springing from the same root, they will spare the one for the sake of the other and, in judging, if not of others at

---

[1] *Promiscuously* Indiscriminately.

[2] *Swift ... resentful* This comment was made by Pope in the *Miscellanies* he wrote with Swift.

[3] *motions* Impulses.

least of themselves, will be apt to estimate their virtues by their vices. To this fatal error all those will contribute who confound the colors of right and wrong, and, instead of helping to settle their boundaries, mix them with so much art that no common mind is able to disunite them.

In narratives where historical veracity has no place, I cannot discover why there should not be exhibited the most perfect idea of virtue; of virtue not angelical, nor above probability, for what we cannot credit we shall never imitate, but the highest and purest that humanity can reach, which, exercized in such trials as the various revolutions of things shall bring upon it, may, by conquering some calamities, and enduring others, teach us what we may hope, and what we can perform. Vice, for vice is necessary to be shown, should always disgust; nor should the graces of gaiety, or the dignity of courage, be so united with it as to reconcile it to the mind. Wherever it appears, it should raise hatred by the malignity of its practices, and contempt by the meanness of its stratagems; for while it is supported by either parts or spirit, it will be seldom heartily abhorred. The Roman tyrant[1] was content to be hated, if he was but feared; and there are thousands of the readers of romances willing to be thought wicked, if they may be allowed to be wits. It is therefore to be steadily inculcated that virtue is the highest proof of understanding, and the only solid basis of greatness; and that vice is the natural consequence of narrow thoughts, that it begins in mistake, and ends in ignominy.

The Rambler No. 60
[ON BIOGRAPHY]
Saturday, 13 October 1750

Quid sit pulchrum, quid turpe, quid utile, quid non,
Plenius et melius Chrysippo et Crantore dicit.
—Horace, *Epistles*, 1.2.3–4

Whose works the beautiful and base contain;
Of vice and virtue more instructive rules,
Than all the sober sages of the schools.

—Francis

All joy or sorrow for the happiness or calamities of others is produced by an act of the imagination that realizes the event however fictitious, or approximates it[2] however remote, by placing us, for a time, in the condition of him whose fortune we contemplate; so that we feel, while the deception lasts, whatever motions would be excited by the same good or evil happening to ourselves.

Our passions are therefore more strongly moved, in proportion as we can more readily adopt the pains or pleasures proposed to our minds, by recognizing them as once our own, or considering them as naturally incident to our state of life. It is not easy for the most artful writer to give us an interest in happiness or misery which we think ourselves never likely to feel, and with which we have never yet been made acquainted. Histories of the downfall of kingdoms and revolutions of empires are read with great tranquility; the imperial tragedy pleases common auditors only by its pomp of ornament and grandeur of ideas; and the man whose faculties have been engrossed by business, and whose heart never fluttered but at the rise or fall of stocks, wonders how the attention can be seized, or the affections agitated, by a tale of love.

Those parallel circumstances and kindred images to which we readily conform our minds are, above all other writings, to be found in narratives of the lives of particular persons; and therefore no species of writing seems more worthy of cultivation than biography, since none can be more delightful or more useful, none can more certainly enchain the heart by irresistible interest, or more widely diffuse instruction to every diversity of condition.

The general and rapid narratives of history, which involve a thousand fortunes in the business of a day and complicate innumerable incidents in one great transaction, afford few lessons applicable to private life, which derives its comforts and its wretchedness from the right or wrong management of things which nothing but their frequency makes considerable, *Parva, si non fiant quotidie,*[3] says Pliny, and which can have no place in

---

[1] *The Roman tyrant* Caligula (12–43 CE), as reported by the Roman historian Suetonis in his *Lives of the Caesars.*

[2] *approximates it* Brings it near.

[3] *Parva … quotidie* Latin: "Small matters, if they did not occur every day" (Pliny the Younger, *Epistles* 3.1).

those relations[1] which never descend below the consultation of senates, the motions of armies, and the schemes of conspirators.

I have often thought that there has rarely passed a life of which a judicious and faithful narrative would not be useful. For, not only every man has, in the mighty mass of the world, great numbers in the same condition with himself, to whom his mistakes and miscarriages, escapes and expedients, would be of immediate and apparent use; but there is such an uniformity in the state of man, considered apart from adventitious and separable decorations and disguises, that there is scarce any possibility of good or ill, but is common to humankind. A great part of the time of those who are placed at the greatest distance by fortune, or by temper, must unavoidably pass in the same manner; and though, when the claims of nature are satisfied, caprice, and vanity, and accident begin to produce discriminations and peculiarities, yet the eye is not very heedful or quick which cannot discover the same causes still terminating their influence in the same effects, though sometimes accelerated, sometimes retarded, or perplexed by multiplied combinations. We are all prompted by the same motives, all deceived by the same fallacies, all animated by hope, obstructed by danger, entangled by desire, and seduced by pleasure.

It is frequently objected to relations of particular lives that they are not distinguished by any striking or wonderful vicissitudes. The scholar who passed his life among his books, the merchant who conducted only his own affairs, the priest whose sphere of action was not extended beyond that of his duty, are considered as no proper objects of public regard, however they might have excelled in their several stations, whatever might have been their learning, integrity, and piety. But this notion arises from false measures of excellence and dignity and must be eradicated by considering that, in the esteem of uncorrupted reason, what is of most use is of most value.

It is, indeed, not improper to take honest advantages of prejudice, and to gain attention by a celebrated name; but the business of the biographer is often to pass slightly over those performances and incidents which produce vulgar greatness, to lead the thoughts into domestic privacies and display the minute details of daily life, where exterior appendages are cast aside and men excel each other only by prudence and by virtue. The account of Thuanus[2] is, with great propriety, said by its author to have been written that it might lay open to posterity the private and familiar character of that man, *cuius ingenium et candorem ex ipsius scriptis sunt olim semper miraturi*,[3] whose candor and genius will to the end of time be by his writings preserved in admiration.

There are many invisible circumstances which, whether we read as inquirers after natural or moral knowledge, whether we intend to enlarge our science[4] or increase our virtue, are more important than public occurrences. Thus Sallust,[5] the great master of nature, has not forgot, in his account of Catiline, to remark that "his walk was now quick, and again slow," as an indication of a mind revolving something with violent commotion. Thus the story of Melancthon[6] affords a striking lecture on the value of time by informing us that when he made an appointment, he expected not only the hour, but the minute to be fixed, that the day might not run out in the idleness of suspense; and all the plans and enterprises of De Witt[7] are now of less importance to the world than that part of his personal character which represents him as "careful of his health, and negligent of his life."

But biography has often been allotted to writers who seem very little acquainted with the nature of their task, or very negligent about the performance. They rarely afford any other account than might be collected from public papers, but imagine themselves writing a life when they exhibit a chronological series of actions or

[2] *The account of Thuanus* Nicolas Rigout's commentary on French historian Jacques-Auguste de Thou's *History of His Own Time* (1604–20).

[3] *cuius … miratori* Johnson translates the Latin in the words that follow.

[4] *science* Knowledge.

[5] *Sallust* First century BCE Roman historian who wrote a history of Roman politician Catiline's conspiracy against the Republic.

[6] *Melancthon* Protestant theologian (1497–1560), a biography of whom was written by Joachim Camerarius.

[7] *De Witt* Famous Dutch statesman (1625–72). The quotation following is from Sir William Temple's "Essay upon the Cure of the Gout" (1680).

[1] *relations* Narratives.

preferments; and so little regard the manners or behavior of their heroes that more knowledge may be gained of a man's real character by a short conversation with one of his servants than from a formal and studied narrative, begun with his pedigree and ended with his funeral.

If now and then they condescend to inform the world of particular facts, they are not always so happy as to select the most important. I know not well what advantage posterity can receive from the only circumstance by which Tickell[1] has distinguished Addison from the rest of mankind, the irregularity of his pulse: nor can I think myself overpaid for the time spent in reading the life of Malherb,[2] by being enabled to relate, after the learned biographer, that Malherb had two predominant opinions: one, that the looseness of a single woman might destroy all her boast of ancient descent; the other, that the French beggars made use very improperly and barbarously of the phrase "noble gentleman," because either word included the sense of both.

There are, indeed, some natural reasons why these narratives are often written by such as were not likely to give much instruction or delight, and why most accounts of particular persons are barren and useless. If a life be delayed till interest and envy are at an end, we may hope for impartiality, but must expect little intelligence; for the incidents which give excellence to biography are of a volatile and evanescent kind, such as soon escape the memory and are rarely transmitted by tradition. We know how few can portray a living acquaintance, except by his most prominent and observable particularities and the grosser features of his mind; and it may be easily imagined how much of this little knowledge may be lost in imparting it, and how soon a succession of copies will lose all resemblance of the original.

If the biographer writes from personal knowledge, and makes haste to gratify the public curiosity, there is danger lest his interest, his fear, his gratitude, or his tenderness overpower his fidelity and tempt him to conceal, if not to invent. There are many who think it an act of piety to hide the faults or failings of their friends, even when they can no longer suffer by their detection; we therefore see whole ranks of characters adorned with uniform panegyric, and not to be known from one another, but by extrinsic and casual circumstances. "Let me remember," says Hale, "when I find myself inclined to pity a criminal, that there is likewise a pity due to the country."[3] If we owe regard to the memory of the dead, there is yet more respect to be paid to knowledge, to virtue, and to truth.

The Rambler No. 155
[ON BECOMING ACQUAINTED WITH OUR REAL CHARACTERS]
Tuesday, 10 September 1751

Steriles transmisimus annos,
Haec aevi mihi prima dies, haec limina vitae.
—Statins, *Silvae*, 4.2.12-13

Our barren years are past;
Be this of life the first, of sloth the last.

—Elphinston

No weakness of the human mind has more frequently incurred animadversion than the negligence with which men overlook their own faults, however flagrant, and the easiness with which they pardon them, however frequently repeated.

It seems generally believed that, as the eye cannot see itself, the mind has no faculties by which it can contemplate its own state, and that therefore we have not means of becoming acquainted with our real characters; an opinion which, like innumerable other postulates, an enquirer finds himself inclined to admit upon very little evidence because it affords a ready solution of many difficulties. It will explain why the greatest abilities frequently fail to promote the happiness of those who possess them; why those who can distinguish with the utmost nicety the boundaries of vice and virtue suffer them to be confounded in their own conduct; why the active and vigilant resign their affairs implicitly to the

---

[1] *Tickell* Thomas Tickell's life of the essayist Joseph Addison was published in 1721.

[2] *Malherb* François de Malherbe (1555–1628), French poet whose biography was written by his friend the Marquis de Racan and published in 1651.

[3] *Let ... country* From *Life and Death of Sir Matthew Hale* (1682), by Gilbert Burnet.

management of others; and why the cautious and fearful make hourly approaches towards ruin, without one sigh of solicitude or struggle for escape.

When a position teems thus with commodious consequences, who can without regret confess it to be false? Yet it is certain that declaimers have indulged a disposition to describe the dominion of the passions as extended beyond the limits that nature assigned. Self-love is often rather arrogant than blind; it does not hide our faults from ourselves, but persuades us that they escape the notice of others, and disposes us to resent censures lest we should confess them to be just. We are secretly conscious of defects and vices which we hope to conceal from the public eye, and please ourselves with innumerable impostures by which, in reality, nobody is deceived.

In proof of the dimness of our internal sight, or the general inability of man to determine rightly concerning his own character, it is common to urge the success of the most absurd and incredible flattery, and the resentment always raised by advice, however soft, benevolent, and reasonable. But flattery, if its operation be nearly examined, will be found to owe its acceptance not to our ignorance but knowledge of our failures, and to delight us rather as it consoles our wants than displays our possessions. He that shall solicit the favour of his patron by praising him for qualities which he can find in himself will be defeated by the more daring panegyrist who enriches him with adscititious[1] excellence. Just praise is only a debt, but flattery is a present. The acknowledgement of those virtues on which conscience congratulates us is a tribute that we can at any time exact with confidence, but the celebration of those which we only feign, or desire without any vigorous endeavours to attain them, is received as a confession of sovereignty over regions never conquered, as a favourable decision of disputable claims, and is more welcome as it is more gratuitous.

Advice is offensive, not because it lays us open to unexpected regret, or convicts us of any fault which had escaped our notice, but because it shows us that we are known to others as well as to ourselves; and the officious monitor is persecuted with hatred, not because his accusation is false, but because he assumes that superiority which we are not willing to grant him, and has dared to detect what we desired to conceal.

For this reason advice is commonly ineffectual. If those who follow the call of their desires without enquiry whither they are going had deviated ignorantly from the paths of wisdom and were rushing upon dangers unforeseen, they would readily listen to information that recalls them from their errors, and catch the first alarm by which destruction or infamy is denounced. Few that wander in the wrong way mistake it for the right; they only find it more smooth and flowery, and indulge their own choice rather than approve it: therefore few are persuaded to quit it by admonition or reproof, since it impresses no new conviction, nor confers any powers of action or resistance. He that is gravely informed how soon profusion will annihilate his fortune hears with little advantage what he knew before, and catches at the next occasion of expence, because advice has no force to suppress his vanity. He that is told how certainly intemperance will hurry him to the grave runs with his usual speed to a new course of luxury, because his reason is not invigorated, nor his appetite weakened.

The mischief of flattery is not that it persuades any man that he is what he is not, but that it suppresses the influence of honest ambition by raising an opinion that honour may be gained without the toil of merit; and the benefit of advice arises commonly, not from any new light imparted to the mind, but from the discovery which it affords of the public suffrages. He that could withstand conscience is frighted at infamy, and shame prevails when reason was defeated.

As we all know our own faults, and know them commonly with many aggravations which human perspicacity cannot discover, there is, perhaps, no man, however hardened by impudence or dissipated by levity, sheltered by hypocrisy, or blasted by disgrace, who does not intend some time to review his conduct, and to regulate the remainder of his life by the laws of virtue. New temptations indeed attack him, new invitations are offered by pleasure and interest, and the hour of reformation is always delayed; every delay gives vice another opportunity of fortifying itself by habit; and the change

---

[1] *adscititious* In his *Dictionary*, Johnson defines this as, "taken in to complete something else, though originally extrinsic; supplemental; additional."

of manners, though sincerely intended and rationally planned, is referred to the time when some craving passion shall be fully gratified, or some powerful allurement cease its importunity.

Thus procrastination is accumulated on procrastination, and one impediment succeeds another, till age shatters our resolution, or death intercepts the project of amendment. Such is often the end of salutary purposes, after they have long delighted the imagination and appeased that disquiet which every mind feels from known misconduct, when the attention is not diverted by business or by pleasure.

Nothing surely can be more unworthy of a reasonable nature than to continue in a state so opposite to real happiness as that all the peace of solitude and felicity of meditation must arise from resolutions of forsaking it. Yet the world will often afford examples of men who pass months and years in a continual war with their own convictions, and are daily dragged by habit or betrayed by passion into practices which they closed and opened their eyes with purposes to avoid; purposes which, though settled on conviction, the first impulse of momentary desire totally overthrows.

The influence of custom is indeed such that to conquer it will require the utmost efforts of fortitude and virtue, nor can I think any man more worthy of veneration and renown than those who have burst the shackles of habitual vice. This victory, however, has different degrees of glory as of difficulty; it is more heroic as the objects of guilty gratification are more familiar, and the recurrence of solicitation more frequent. He that, from experience of the folly of ambition, resigns his offices, may set himself free at once from temptation to squander his life in courts, because he cannot regain his former station. He who is enslaved by an amorous passion may quit his tyrant in disgust, and absence will without the help of reason overcome by degrees the desire of returning. But those appetites to which every place affords their proper object, and which require no preparatory measures or gradual advances, are more tenaciously adhesive; the wish is so near the enjoyment that compliance often precedes consideration, and before the powers of reason can be summoned, the time for employing them is past.

Indolence is therefore one of the vices from which those whom it once infects are seldom reformed. Every other species of luxury operates upon some appetite that is quickly satiated, and requires some concurrence of art or accident which every place will not supply; but the desire of ease acts equally at all hours, and the longer it is indulged is the more increased. To do nothing is in every man's power; we can never want an opportunity of omitting duties. The lapse to indolence is soft and imperceptible because it is only a mere cessation of activity; but the return to diligence is difficult because it implies a change from rest to motion, from privation to reality.

Facilis descensus Averni:
Noctes atque dies patet atri janua Ditis:
Sed revocare gradum, superasque evadere ad auras,
Hoc opus, hic labor est.

—Aeneid, 6.126–29

The gates of Hell are open night and day;
Smooth the descent, and easy is the way:
But, to return, and view the cheerful skies;
In this, the task and mighty labour lies.

—Dryden

Of this vice, as of all others, every man who indulges it is conscious; we all know our own state, if we could be induced to consider it; and it might perhaps be useful to the conquest of all these ensnarers of the mind if at certain stated days life was reviewed. Many things necessary are omitted because we vainly imagine that they may be always performed, and what cannot be done without pain will for ever be delayed if the time of doing it be left unsettled. No corruption is great but by long negligence, which can scarcely prevail in a mind regularly and frequently awakened by periodical remorse. He that thus breaks his life into parts will find in himself a desire to distinguish every stage of his existence by some improvement, and delight himself with the approach of the day of recollection, as of the time which is to begin a new series of virtue and felicity.

The Idler No. 31
[ON IDLENESS]
Saturday, 18 November 1758

Many moralists have remarked that pride has, of all human vices, the widest dominion, appears in the greatest multiplicity of forms, and lies hid under the greatest variety of disguises; of disguises, which, like the moon's "veil of brightness," are both its "luster and its shade,"[1] and betray it to others, though they hide it from ourselves.

It is not my intention to degrade pride from this pre-eminence of mischief, yet I know not whether idleness may not maintain a very doubtful and obstinate competition.

There are some that profess idleness in its full dignity, who call themselves the Idle, as Busiris in the play "calls himself the Proud";[2] who boast that they do nothing, and thank their stars that they have nothing to do; who sleep every night till they can sleep no longer, and rise only that exercise may enable them to sleep again; who prolong the reign of darkness by double curtains, and never see the sun but to "tell him how they hate his beams";[3] whose whole labor is to vary the postures of indulgence, and whose day differs from their night but as a couch or chair differs from a bed.

These are the true and open votaries of idleness, for whom she weaves the garlands of poppies, and into whose cup she pours the waters of oblivion; who exist in a state of unruffled stupidity,[4] forgetting and forgotten; who have long ceased to live, and at whose death the survivors can only say that they have ceased to breathe.

But idleness predominates in many lives where it is not suspected, for being a vice which terminates in itself, it may be enjoyed without injury to others, and is therefore not watched like fraud, which endangers property, or like pride, which naturally seeks its gratifications in another's inferiority. Idleness is a silent and peaceful quality that neither raises envy by ostentation, nor hatred by opposition; and therefore nobody is busy to censure or detect it.

As pride sometimes is hid under humility, idleness is often covered by turbulence and hurry. He that neglects his known duty and real employment, naturally endeavors to crowd his mind with something that may bar out the remembrance of his own folly, and does any thing but what he ought to do with eager diligence, that he may keep himself in his own favor.

Some are always in a state of preparation, occupied in previous measures, forming plans, accumulating materials, and providing for the main affair. These are certainly under the secret power of idleness. Nothing is to be expected from the workman whose tools are forever to be sought. I was once told by a great master that no man ever excelled in painting who was eminently curious[5] about pencils[6] and colors.

There are others to whom idleness dictates another expedient, by which life may be passed unprofitably away without the tediousness of many vacant hours. The art is to fill the day with petty business, to have always something in hand which may raise curiosity, but not solicitude; and keep the mind in a state of action, but not of labor.

This art has for many years been practiced by my old friend Sober,[7] with wonderful success. Sober is a man of strong desires and quick imagination, so exactly balanced by the love of ease that they can seldom stimulate him to any difficult undertaking; they have, however, so much power that they will not suffer him to lie quite at rest, and though they do not make him sufficiently useful to others, they make him at least weary of himself.

Mr. Sober's chief pleasure is conversation; there is no end of his talk or his attention; to speak or to hear is equally pleasing; for he still fancies that he is teaching or learning something, and is free for the time from his own reproaches.

---

[1] *veil ... shade* From Samuel Butler's *Hudibras* (1663–78), 2.1.907–78.

[2] *Busiris ... Proud* From the play *Busiris* (1719), 1.1.13, by Edward Young.

[3] *tell ... beams* Satan in Milton's *Paradise Lost*, 4.37.

[4] *stupidity* Stupor.

[5] *curious* Fastidious.

[6] *pencils* Paintbrushes.

[7] *old friend Sober* Many of Johnson's friends believed the description of Sober was meant to be autobiographical.

But there is one time at night when he must go home, that his friends may sleep; and another time in the morning, when all the world agrees to shut out interruption. These are the moments of which poor Sober trembles at the thought. But the misery of these tiresome intervals he has many means of alleviating. He has persuaded himself that the manual arts are undeservedly overlooked; he has observed in many trades the effects of close thought and just ratiocination. From speculation he proceeded to practice, and supplied himself with the tools of a carpenter, with which he mended his coal-box very successfully, and which he still continues to employ, as he finds occasion.

He has attempted at other times the crafts of the shoemaker, tinman, plumber, and potter; in all these arts he has failed, and resolves to qualify himself for them by better information. But his daily amusement is chemistry. He has a small furnace, which he employs in distillation, and which has long been the solace of his life. He draws oils and waters, and essences and spirits, which he knows to be of no use; sits and counts the drops as they come from his retort, and forgets that, while a drop is falling, a moment flies away.

Poor Sober! I have often teased him with reproof, and he has often promised reformation; for no man is so much open to conviction as the idler, but there is none on whom it operates so little. What will be the effect of this paper I know not; perhaps he will read it and laugh, and light the fire in his furnace; but my hope is that he will quit his trifles and betake himself to rational and useful diligence.

The Idler No. 49
[WILL MARVEL]
Saturday, 24 March 1759

I supped three nights ago with my friend Will Marvel. His affairs obliged him lately to take a journey into Devonshire, from which he has just returned. He knows me to be a very patient hearer, and was glad of my company, as it gave him an opportunity of disburthening himself by a minute relation of the casualties of his expedition.

Will is not one of those who go out and return with nothing to tell. He has a story of his travels, which will strike a homebred citizen with horror, and has in ten days suffered so often the extremes of terror and joy that he is in doubt whether he shall ever again expose either his body or mind to such danger and fatigue.

When he left London the morning was bright, and a fair day was promised. But Will is born to struggle with difficulties. That happened to him which has sometimes, perhaps, happened to others. Before he had gone more than ten miles it began to rain. What course was to be taken! His soul disdained to turn back. He did what the king of Prussia might have done, he flapped his hat, buttoned up his cape, and went forwards, fortifying his mind by the stoical consolation that whatever is violent will be short.

His constancy was not long tried; at the distance of about half a mile he saw an inn, which he entered wet and weary, and found civil treatment and proper refreshment. After a respite of about two hours he looked abroad and, seeing the sky clear, called for his horse and passed the first stage without any other memorable accident.

Will considered that labour must be relieved by pleasure, and that the strength which great undertakings require must be maintained by copious nutriment; he therefore ordered himself an elegant supper, drank two bottles of claret, and passed the beginning of the night in sound sleep; but, waking before light, was forewarned of the troubles of the next day by a shower beating against his windows with such violence as to threaten the dissolution of nature. When he arose he found what he expected, that the country was under water. He joined himself, however, to a company that was travelling the same way, and came safely to the place of dinner, though every step of his horse dashed the mud into the air.

In the afternoon, having parted from his company, he set forward alone, and passed many collections of water of which it was impossible to guess the depth, and which he now cannot review without some censure of his own rashness; but what a man undertakes he must perform, and Marvel hates a coward at his heart.

Few that lie warm in their beds think what others undergo who have perhaps been as tenderly educated, and have as acute sensations as themselves. My friend was now to lodge the second night almost fifty miles from home, in a house which he never had seen before, among people to whom he was totally a stranger, not knowing whether the next man he should meet would prove good or bad; but seeing an inn of a good appearance, he rode resolutely into the yard, and knowing that respect is often paid in proportion as it is claimed, delivered his injunction to the hostler with spirit and, entering the house, called vigorously about him.

On the third day up rose the sun and Mr. Marvel. His troubles and his dangers were now such as he wishes no other man ever to encounter. The ways were less frequented, and the country more thinly inhabited. He rode many a lonely hour through mire and water, and met not a single soul for two miles together with whom he could exchange a word. He cannot deny that, looking round upon the dreary region and seeing nothing but bleak fields and naked trees, hills obscured by fogs, and flats covered with inundations, he did for some time suffer melancholy to prevail upon him, and wished himself again safe at home. One comfort he had, which was to consider that none of his friends were in the same distress, for whom, if they had been with him, he should have suffered more than for himself; he could not forbear sometimes to consider how happily the Idler is settled in an easier condition, who, surrounded like him with terrors, could have done nothing but lie down and die.

Amidst these reflections he came to a town and found a dinner, which disposed him to more cheerful sentiments: but the joys of life are short, and its miseries are long; he mounted and travelled fifteen miles more through dirt and desolation.

At last the sun set, and all the horrors of darkness came upon him. He then repented the weak indulgence by which he had gratified himself at noon with too long an interval of rest: yet he went forward along a path which he could no longer see, sometimes rushing suddenly into water, and sometimes encumbered with stiff clay, ignorant whither he was going, and uncertain whether his next step might not be the last.

In this dismal gloom of nocturnal peregrination his horse unexpectedly stood still. Marvel had heard many relations of the instinct of horses, and was in doubt what danger might be at hand. Sometimes he fancied that he

was on the bank of a river still and deep, and sometimes that a dead body lay across the track. He sat still awhile to recollect his thoughts; and as he was about to alight and explore the darkness, out stepped a man with a lantern, and opened the turnpike.[1] He hired a guide to the town, arrived in safety, and slept in quiet.

The rest of his journey was nothing but danger. He climbed and descended precipices on which vulgar mortals tremble to look; he passed marshes like the "Serbonian bog, where armies whole have sunk";[2] he forded rivers where the current roared like the eagre of the Severn;[3] or ventured himself on bridges that trembled under him, from which he looked down on foaming whirlpools, or dreadful abysses; he wandered over houseless heaths, amidst all the rage of the elements, with the snow driving in his face and the tempest howling in his ears.

Such are the colours in which Marvel paints his adventures. He has accustomed himself to sounding words and hyperbolical images till he has lost the power of true description. In a road through which the heaviest carriages pass without difficulty, and the post-boy every day and night goes and returns, he meets with hardships like those which are endured in Siberian deserts, and misses nothing of romantic danger but a giant and a dragon. When his dreadful story is told in proper terms, it is only that the way was dirty in winter, and that he experienced the common vicissitudes of rain and sunshine.

The Idler No. 81
[ON NATIVE AMERICANS]
Saturday, 3 November 1759

As the English army was passing towards Quebec[4] along a soft savanna between a mountain and a lake, one of the petty chiefs of the inland regions stood

---

[1] *turnpike* Bar across the road to stop travelers and collect tolls.

[2] *Serbonian ... sunk* · From Milton's *Paradise Lost*.

[3] *eagre* Tidal wave; *Severn* The longest river in England, flowing through Wales and England into the Bristol channel.

[4] *As ... Quebec* The English defeated the French in Quebec in October of 1759.

upon a rock surrounded by his clan, and from behind the shelter of the bushes contemplated the art and regularity of European war. It was evening, the tents were pitched, he observed the security with which the troops rested in the night, and the order with which the march was renewed in the morning. He continued to pursue them with his eye till they could be seen no longer, and then stood for some time silent and pensive.

Then turning to his followers,[1] "My children," said he, "I have often heard from men hoary with long life, that there was a time when our ancestors were absolute lords of the woods, the meadows, and the lakes, wherever the eye can reach or the foot can pass. They fished and hunted, feasted and danced, and when they were weary lay down under the first thicket, without danger and without fear. They changed their habitations as the seasons required, convenience prompted, or curiosity allured them, and sometimes gathered the fruits of the mountain, and sometimes sported in canoes along the coast.

"Many years and ages are supposed to have been thus passed in plenty and security; when at last a new race of men entered our country from the great ocean. They enclosed themselves in habitations of stone, which our ancestors could neither enter by violence, nor destroy by fire. They issued from those fastnesses, sometimes covered like the armadillo with shells, from which the lance rebounded on the striker, and sometimes carried by mighty beasts which had never been seen in our vales or forests, of such strength and swiftness that flight and opposition were vain alike. Those invaders ranged over the continent, slaughtering in their rage those that resisted, and those that submitted, in their mirth. Of those that remained, some were buried in caverns and condemned to dig metals for their masters; some were employed in tilling the ground, of which foreign tyrants devour the produce; and when the sword and the mines have destroyed the natives, they supply their place by human beings of another colour, brought from some distant country to perish here under toil and torture.

"Some there are who boast their humanity, and content themselves to seize our chases[2] and fisheries, who drive us from every track of ground where fertility and pleasantness invite them to settle, and make no war upon us except when we intrude upon our own lands.

"Others pretend to have purchased a right of residence and tyranny; but surely the insolence of such bargains is more offensive than the avowed and open dominion of force. What reward can induce the possessor of a country to admit a stranger more powerful than himself? Fraud or terror must operate in such contracts; either they promised protection which they never have afforded, or instruction which they never imparted. We hoped to be secured by their favour from some other evil, or to learn the arts of Europe, by which we might be able to secure ourselves. Their power they have never exerted in our defence, and their arts they have studiously concealed from us. Their treaties are only to deceive, and their traffic only to defraud us. They have a written law among them, of which they boast as derived from Him who made the earth and sea, and by which they profess to believe that man will be made happy when life shall forsake him. Why is not this law communicated to us? It is concealed because it is violated. For how can they preach it to an Indian nation when I am told that one of its first precepts forbids them to do to others what they would not that others should do to them.

"But the time perhaps is now approaching when the pride of usurpation shall be crushed, and the cruelties of invasion shall be revenged. The sons of rapacity have now drawn their swords upon each other and referred their claims to the decision of war; let us look unconcerned upon the slaughter, and remember that the death of every European delivers the country from a tyrant and a robber; for what is the claim of either nation but the claim of the vulture to the leveret,[3] of the tiger to the fawn? Let them then continue to dispute their title to regions which they cannot people, to purchase by danger and blood the empty dignity of dominion over mountains which they will never climb, and rivers which they will never pass. Let us endeavour, in the

---

[1] *Then … followers* The basis for this speech may have been one given by the chief of the Micmac that had been printed in *London Magazine* the previous year.

[2] *chases* Hunting grounds.

[3] *leveret* Young hare (under a year old).

meantime, to learn their discipline, and to forge their weapons; and when they shall be weakened with mutual slaughter, let us rush down upon them, force their remains to take shelter in their ships, and reign once more in our native country."

from *A Dictionary of the English Language*

from THE PREFACE

It is the fate of those who toil at the lower employments of life to be rather driven by the fear of evil than attracted by the prospect of good; to be exposed to censure without hope of praise; to be disgraced by miscarriage, or punished for neglect, where success would have been without applause, and diligence without reward.

Among these unhappy mortals is the writer of dictionaries, whom mankind have considered not as the pupil, but the slave, of science, the pioneer of literature, doomed only to remove rubbish and clear obstructions from the paths through which learning and genius press forward to conquest and glory, without bestowing a smile on the humble drudge that facilitates their progress. Every other author may aspire to praise: the lexicographer can only hope to escape reproach—and even this negative recompense has been yet granted to very few.

I have, notwithstanding this discouragement, attempted a dictionary of the English language, which, while it was employed in the cultivation of every species of literature, has itself been hitherto neglected, suffered to spread, under the direction of chance, into wild exuberance, resigned to the tyranny of time and fashion, and exposed to the corruptions of ignorance and caprices of innovation.

When I took the first survey of my undertaking, I found our speech copious without order, and energetic without rules: wherever I turned my view, there was perplexity to be disentangled and confusion to be regulated; choice was to be made out of boundless variety, without any established principle of selection; adulterations were to be detected, without a settled test of purity; and modes of expression to be rejected or received, without the suffrages of any writers of classical reputation or acknowledged authority.

Having therefore no assistance but from general grammar, I applied myself to the perusal of our writers; and, noting whatever might be of use to ascertain or illustrate any word or phrase, accumulated in time the materials of a dictionary, which, by degrees, I reduced to method, establishing to myself, in the progress of the work, such rules as experience and analogy suggested to me—experience, which practice and observation were continually increasing, and analogy, which, though in some words obscure, was evident in others.

In adjusting the orthography, which has been to this time unsettled and fortuitous, I found it necessary to distinguish those irregularities that are inherent in our tongue, and perhaps coeval with it, from others which the ignorance or negligence of later writers has produced. Every language has its anomalies which, though inconvenient and in themselves once unnecessary, must be tolerated among the imperfections of human things, and which require only to be registered that they may not be increased, and ascertained that they may not be confounded. But every language has likewise its improprieties and absurdities which it is the duty of the lexicographer to correct or proscribe.

… When we see men grow old and die at a certain time one after another, from century to century, we laugh at the elixir that promises to prolong life to a thousand years; and with equal justice may the lexicographer be derided, who, being able to produce no example of a nation that has preserved their words and phrases from mutability, shall imagine that his dictionary can embalm his language and secure it from corruption and decay, that it is in his power to change sublunary nature, and clear the world at once from folly, vanity, and affectation.

With this hope, however, academies have been instituted to guard the avenues of their languages, to retain fugitives, and repulse intruders. But their vigilance and activity have hitherto been vain: sounds are too volatile and subtle for legal restraints; to enchain syllables, and to lash the wind, are equally the undertakings of pride, unwilling to measure its desires by its strength. The French language has visibly changed under the inspection of the academy;[1] the style of Amelot's translation of Father Paul is observed by Le Courayer to be *un peu passé*;[2] and no Italian will maintain that the diction of any modern writer is not perceptibly different from that of Boccace, Machiavel, or Caro.[3]

Total and sudden transformations of a language seldom happen: conquests and migrations are now very rare. But there are other causes of change which, though slow in their operation and invisible in their progress, are perhaps as much superior to human resistance as the revolutions of the sky or intumescence of the tide. Commerce, however necessary, however lucrative, as it depraves the manners, corrupts the language; they that have frequent intercourse with strangers, to whom they endeavour to accommodate themselves, must in time learn a mingled dialect, like the jargon which serves the traffickers on the Mediterranean and Indian coasts. This will not always be confined to the exchange, the warehouse, or the port, but will be communicated by degrees to other ranks of the people, and be at last incorporated with the current speech.

There are likewise internal causes equally forcible. The language most likely to continue long without alteration would be that of a nation raised a little, and but a little, above barbarity, secluded from strangers, and totally employed in procuring the conveniences of life, either without books or, like some of the Mahometan countries, with very few: men thus busied and unlearned, having only such words as common use requires, would perhaps long continue to express the same notions by the same signs. But no such constancy can be expected in a people polished by arts, and classed by subordination, where one part of the community is sustained and accommodated by the labour of the other. Those who have much leisure to think will always be enlarging the stock of ideas, and every increase of knowledge, whether real or fancied, will produce new words or combinations of words. When the mind is unchained from necessity, it will range after convenience; when it is left at large in the fields of speculation, it will shift opinions; as any custom is disused, the words that expressed it must perish with it; as any opinion grows popular, it will innovate speech in the same proportion as it alters practice.

As, by the cultivation of various sciences, a language is amplified, it will be more furnished with words deflected from their original sense: the geometrician will talk of a courtier's *zenith*, or the *eccentric* virtue of a wild hero,[4] and the physician of *sanguine* expectations and *phlegmatic* delays.[5] Copiousness of speech will give opportunities to capricious choice, by which some words will be preferred and others degraded; vicissitudes of fashion will enforce the use of new, or extend the signification of known, terms. The tropes[6] of poetry will make hourly encroachments, and the metaphorical will become the current sense; pronunciation will be varied by levity or ignorance, and the pen must at length comply with the tongue; illiterate writers will at one time or other, by public infatuation, rise into renown, who, not knowing the original import of words, will use them with colloquial licentiousness, confound distinction, and forget propriety. As politeness increases some expressions will be considered as too gross and vulgar for the delicate, others as too formal and ceremonious for the gay and airy: new phrases are therefore adopted which must, for the same reasons, be in time dismissed.

---

[1] *The French ... academy* The Académie française, founded in 1635, was commissioned to purify and preserve the French language. The Académie published its dictionary in 1634.

[2] *style ... passé* Father Paul Sarpi was the author of the *History of the Council of Trent*, published in Italian in 1619. In 1739 Father Pierre François Le Courayer produced a new French translation of this work, replacing the 1683 translation by Amelot de la Houssaye, which Le Courayer referred to as "a bit outdated."

[3] *Boccace* Giovanni Boccaccio, the fourteenth-century author of the *Decameron*; *Machiavel* Fifteenth-century political philosopher Niccolò Machiavelli; *Caro* Annibale Caro, a fifteenth-century writer of pastoral romance.

[4] *the geometrician ... hero* "Zenith" and "eccentric" were formerly used solely as geometrical or astronomical terms, meaning "the point of the heavens directly above" and "not concentric (with another circle), or "not perfectly circular," respectively.

[5] *physician ... delays* "Sanguine" and "phlegmatic" were physicians' terms describing the predominance in the body of blood or phlegm, respectively. These terms were later used to describe the temperaments associated with these two humors: those who are sanguine are said to be hopeful and courageous, while those who are phlegmatic are sluggish and apathetic.

[6] *tropes* Figures of speech in which words are used in senses other than those that are accepted or standard.

Swift, in his petty treatise on the English language,[1] allows that new words must sometimes be introduced but proposes that none should be suffered to become obsolete. But what makes a word obsolete, more than general agreement to forbear it? and how shall it be continued, when it conveys an offensive idea, or recalled again to the mouths of mankind, when it has once become unfamiliar by disuse, and unpleasing by unfamiliarity?

There is another cause of alteration more prevalent than any other, which yet in the present state of the world cannot be obviated. A mixture of two languages will produce a third distinct from both, and they will always be mixed where the chief part of education, and the most conspicuous accomplishment, is skill in ancient or in foreign tongues. He that has long cultivated another language will find its words and combinations crowd upon his memory, and haste or negligence, refinement or affectation, will obtrude borrowed terms and exotic expressions.

[SELECTED ENTRIES]

Asthma. A frequent, difficult, and short respiration, joined with a hissing sound and a cough, especially in the night-time, and when the body is in a prone posture; because then the contents of the lower belly bear so against the diaphragm, as to lessen the capacity of the breast, whereby the lungs have less room to move. Quincy.

Bat. An animal having the body of a mouse and the wings of a bird; not with feathers, but with a sort of skin which is extended. It lays no eggs, but brings forth its young alive, and suckles them. It never grows tame, feeds upon flies, insects, and fatty substances, such as candles, oil, and cheese; and appears only in the summer evenings, when the weather is fine. Calmet.

Booby. (A word of no certain etymology. Henshaw thinks it a corruption of *bull-beef* [2] ridiculously; Skinner imagines it to be derived from *bobo*, foolish, Span.

Junius finds *bowbard* to be an old Scottish word for a *coward*, a *contemptible fellow*; from which he naturally deduces *booby*; but the original of *bowbard* is not known.) A dull, heavy, stupid fellow; a lubber.

Comedy. A dramatic representation of the lighter faults of mankind.

Epic. Narrative; comprising narrations, not acted, but rehearsed. It is usually supposed to be heroic, or to contain one great action achieved by a hero.

Lexicographer. A writer of dictionaries; a harmless drudge, that busies himself in tracing the original, and detailing the signification of words.

Novel. A small tale, generally of love.

Nowadays. (This word, though common and used by the best writers, is perhaps barbarous.) In the present age.

Oats. A grain, which in England is generally given to horses, but in Scotland supports the people.

To partialize. To make partial. A word, perhaps, peculiar to Shakespeare, and not unworthy of general use.
> Such neighbour-nearness to our sacred blood
> Should nothing privilege him, nor *partialize*
> Th'unstooping firmness of my upright soul.
>   Shakespeare.

Pastoral. A poem in which any action or passion is represented by its effects upon a country life; or according to the common practice in which speakers take upon them the character of shepherds; an idyll; a bucolic.

Patriot. One whose ruling passion is the love of his country. It is sometimes used for a factious disturber of the government.

Patron. One who countenances, supports, or protects. Commonly a wretch who supports with insolence, and is paid with flattery.

---

[1] *Swift ... language* Jonathan Swift's *A Proposal for Correcting, Improving, and Ascertaining the English Tongue* (1712); *petty* Small.

[2] *bull-beef* Literally, the flesh of bulls; also a term of abuse.

Precarious. Dependent; uncertain, because depending on the will of another; held by courtesy; changeable or alienable at the pleasure of another. No word is more unskilfully used than this with its derivatives. It is used for *uncertain* in all its senses; but it only means uncertain, as dependent on others: thus there are authors who mention the *precariousness* of an *account,* of the *weather,* of a *die.*

Rapport. Relation; reference; proportion. A word introduced by the innovator, Temple,[1] but not copied by others.

Reputeless. Disreputable; disgraceful. A word not inelegant, but out of use.
> Opinion, that did help me to the crown,
> Had left me in reputeless banishment,
> A fellow of no mark nor livelihood.
> > Shakespeare *Henry IV.*

Romance. A military fable of the middle ages; a tale of wild adventures in war and love.

Romantic. (1) Resembling the tales of romances; wild.
(2) Improbable; false.
(3) Fanciful; full of wild scenery.

Sonnet. A short poem consisting of fourteen lines, of which the rhymes are adjusted by a particular rule. It is not very suitable to the English language, and has not been used by any man of eminence since Milton.

Sonnetteer. A small poet, in contempt.

Stockjobber. A low wretch who gets money by buying and selling shares in the funds.

Tory. One who adheres to the ancient constitution of the state, and the apostolical hierarchy of the church of England, opposed to a whig.

Vastidity. Wideness; immensity. A barbarous word.

---
[1] *Temple* Sir William Temple, seventeenth-century English diplomat and author, perhaps best known for his essay *Of Ancient and Modern Learning* (1690).

> Perpetual durance,
> Through all the world's *vastidity.*   Shakespeare.

Vaulty.   Arched; concave. A bad word.
> I will kiss thy detestable bones,
> And put my eye-balls in thy *vaulty* brows,
> And ring these fingers with thy houshold worms.
> > Shakespeare.

Whig. The name of a faction.
—1755

from The Preface to *The Works of William Shakespeare*

Nothing can please many, and please long, but just representations of general nature. Particular manners can be known to few, and therefore few only can judge how nearly they are copied. The irregular combinations of fanciful invention may delight a while, by that novelty of which the common satiety of life sends us all in quest; but the pleasures of sudden wonder are soon exhausted, and the mind can only repose on the stability of truth.

Shakespeare is, above all writers, at least above all modern writers, the poet of nature, the poet that holds up to his readers a faithful mirror of manners and of life. His characters are not modified by the customs of particular places, unpracticed by the rest of the world; by the peculiarities of studies or professions, which can operate but upon small numbers; or by the accidents of transient fashions or temporary opinions: they are the genuine progeny of common humanity, such as the world will always supply, and observation will always find. His persons act and speak by the influence of those general passions and principles by which all minds are agitated, and the whole system of life is continued in motion. In the writings of other poets a character is too often an individual; in those of Shakespeare it is commonly a species.

It is from this wide extension of design that so much instruction is derived. It is this which fills the plays of Shakespeare with practical axioms and domestic wisdom. It was said of Euripides[1] that every verse was a precept, and it may be said of Shakespeare that from his Works may be collected a system of civil and economical[2] prudence. Yet his real power is not shown in the splendour of particular passages, but by the progress of his fable,[3] and the tenor of his dialogue; and he that tries to recommend him by select quotations will succeed like the pedant in *Hierocles*,[4] who, when he offered his house to sale, carried a brick in his pocket as a specimen.

It will not easily be imagined how much Shakespeare excels in accommodating his sentiments to real life, but by comparing him with other authors. It was observed of the ancient schools of declamation that the more diligently they were frequented, the more was the student disqualified for the world, because he found nothing there which he should ever meet in any other place. The same remark may be applied to every stage but that of Shakespeare. The theatre, when it is under any other direction, is peopled by such characters as were never seen conversing in a language which was never heard, upon topics which will never arise in the commerce of mankind. But the dialogue of this author is often so evidently determined by the incident which produces it, and is pursued with so much ease and simplicity, that it seems scarcely to claim the merit of fiction, but to have been gleaned by diligent selection out of common conversation, and common occurrences. Upon every other stage the universal agent is love, by whose power all good and evil is distributed, and every action quickened or retarded. To bring a lover, a lady, and a rival into the fable; to entangle them in contradictory obligations, perplex them with oppositions of interest, and harass them with violence of desires inconsistent with each other; to make them meet in rapture and part in agony; to fill their mouths with hyperbolical joy and outrageous sorrow; to distress them as nothing human ever was distressed; to deliver them as nothing human ever was delivered, is the business of a modern dramatist. For this, probability is violated, life is misrepresented, and language is depraved.[5] But love is only one of many passions, and as it has no great influence upon the sum of life, it has little operation in the dramas of a poet, who caught his ideas from the living world, and exhibited only what he saw before him. He knew that any other passion, as it was regular or exorbitant, was a cause of happiness or calamity.

Characters thus ample and general were not easily discriminated and preserved, yet perhaps no poet ever kept his personages more distinct from each other. I will not say with Pope[6] that every speech may be assigned to the proper speaker, because many speeches there are which have nothing characteristical; but perhaps, though some may be equally adapted to every person, it will be difficult to find any that can be properly transferred from the present possessor to another claimant. The choice is right, when there is reason for choice.

Other dramatists can only gain attention by hyperbolical or aggravated characters, by fabulous and unexampled excellence or depravity, as the writers of barbarous romances invigorated the reader by a giant and a dwarf; and he that should form his expectations of human affairs from the play, or from the tale, would be equally deceived. Shakespeare has no heroes; his scenes are occupied only by men, who act and speak as the reader thinks that he should himself have spoken or acted on the same occasion. Even where the agency is supernatural, the dialogue is level with life. Other writers disguise the most natural passions and most frequent incidents; so that he who contemplates them in the book will not know them in the world: Shakespeare approximates[7] the remote, and familiarizes the wonderful; the event which he represents will not happen, but if it were possible, its effects would probably be such as he has assigned; and it may be said that he has not only shown human nature as it acts in real exigencies, but as it would be found in trials to which it cannot be exposed.

---

[1] *Euripides*   Greek tragic poet of the fifth century BCE. The opinion is that of Cicero, stated in his *Letters to his Friends*, 16.8.

[2] *economical*   Johnson defines this in his *Dictionary* as "pertaining to the regulation of a household."

[3] *fable*   Defined by Johnson as "the series or contexture of events which constitute a poem epic or dramatic."

[4] *Hierocles*   Alexandrian philosopher of the fifth century CE.

---

[5] *depraved*   Debased.

[6] *Pope*   Alexander Pope, in the preface to his edition of Shakespeare's plays (1725).

[7] *approximates*   Brings near.

This therefore is the praise of Shakespeare, that his drama is the mirror of life; that he who has mazed[1] his imagination in following the phantoms which other writers raise up before him, may here be cured of his delirious ecstasies by reading human sentiment in human language; by scenes from which a hermit may estimate the transactions of the world, and a confessor[2] predict the progress of the passions.

His adherence to general nature has exposed him to the censure of critics, who form their judgements upon narrower principles. Dennis and Rymer[3] think his Romans not sufficiently Roman; and Voltaire[4] censures his kings as not completely royal. Dennis is offended that Menenius, a senator of Rome, should play the buffoon; and Voltaire perhaps thinks decency violated when the Danish usurper is represented as a drunkard.[5] But Shakespeare always makes nature predominate over accident; and if he preserves the essential character, is not very careful of distinctions superinduced and adventitious. His story requires Romans or kings, but he thinks only on men. He knew that Rome, like every other city, had men of all dispositions; and, wanting a buffoon, he went into the senate-house for that which the senate-house would certainly have afforded him. He was inclined to show a usurper and a murderer not only odious but despicable; he therefore added drunkenness to his other qualities, knowing that kings love wine like other men, and that wine exerts its natural power upon kings. These are the petty cavils of petty minds; a poet overlooks the casual distinction of country and condition, as a painter, satisfied with the figure, neglects the drapery.

The censure which he has incurred by mixing comic and tragic scenes, as it extends to all his works, deserves more consideration. Let the fact be first stated, and then examined.

Shakespeare's plays are not in the rigorous and critical sense either tragedies or comedies, but compositions of a distinct kind; exhibiting the real state of sublunary nature, which partakes of good and evil, joy and sorrow, mingled with endless variety of proportion and innumerable modes of combination; and expressing the course of the world, in which the loss of one is the gain of another; in which, at the same time, the reveller is hasting to his wine, and the mourner burying his friend; in which the malignity of one is sometimes defeated by the frolic of another; and many mischiefs and many benefits are done and hindered without design.

Out of this chaos of mingled purposes and casualties[6] the ancient poets, according to the laws which custom had prescribed, selected some the crimes of men, and some their absurdities; some the momentous vicissitudes of life, and some the lighter occurrences; some the terrors of distress, and some the gaieties of prosperity. Thus rose the two modes of imitation, known by the names of *tragedy* and *comedy*, compositions intended to promote different ends by contrary means, and considered as so little allied, that I do not recollect among the Greeks or Romans a single writer who attempted both.

Shakespeare has united the powers of exciting laughter and sorrow not only in one mind but in one composition. Almost all his plays are divided between serious and ludicrous characters, and, in the successive evolutions of the design, sometimes produce seriousness and sorrow, and sometimes levity and laughter.

That this is a practice contrary to the rules of criticism[7] will be readily allowed, but there is always an appeal open from criticism to nature. The end of writing is to instruct; the end of poetry is to instruct by pleasing.[8] That the mingled drama may convey all the instruction of tragedy or comedy cannot be denied,

---

[1] *mazed* Bewildered.

[2] *confessor* I.e., a priest.

[3] *Dennis* John Dennis, playwright and literary critic, author of *An Essay on the Genius and Writing of Shakespeare* (1712), and Thomas Rymer, historian and drama critic, author of *A Short View of Tragedy* (1693).

[4] *Voltaire* French philosopher; this criticism of Shakespeare occurs in his *Appeal to All the Nations of Europe* (1761).

[5] *Dennis is ... drunkard* References to Menenius of *Coriolanus*, who describes himself as a buffoon in 2.1, and to King Claudius in *Hamlet*.

[6] *casualties* Chance occurrences.

[7] *rules of criticism* Set forth by Horace and Sir Philip Sidney, among others.

[8] *The end ... pleasing* An idea that originated from Horace's *Art of Poetry*: "The poet's aim is either to profit or to please, or to blend in one the delightful and the useful."

because it includes both in its alternations of exhibition, and approaches nearer than either to the appearance of life by showing how great machinations and slender designs may promote or obviate one another, and the high and the low co-operate in the general system by unavoidable concatenation.[1]

It is objected that by this change of scenes the passions are interrupted in their progression, and that the principal event, being not advanced by a due gradation of preparatory incidents, wants at last the power to move, which constitutes the perfection of dramatic poetry. This reasoning is so specious, that it is received as true even by those who in daily experience feel it to be false. The interchanges of mingled scenes seldom fail to produce the intended vicissitudes of passion. Fiction cannot move so much, but that the attention may be easily transferred; and though it must be allowed that pleasing melancholy be sometimes interrupted by unwelcome levity, yet let it be considered likewise, that melancholy is often not pleasing, and that the disturbance of one man may be the relief of another; that different auditors have different habitudes; and that, upon the whole, all pleasure consists in variety.

The players, who in their edition divided our author's works into comedies, histories, and tragedies, seem not to have distinguished the three kinds, by any very exact or definite ideas.

An action which ended happily to the principal persons, however serious or distressful through its intermediate incidents, in their opinion constituted a comedy. This idea of a comedy continued long amongst us, and plays were written, which, by changing the catastrophe, were tragedies today and comedies tomorrow.

Tragedy was not in those times a poem of more general dignity or elevation than comedy; it required only a calamitous conclusion, with which the common criticism of that age was satisfied, whatever lighter pleasure it afforded in its progress.

History was a series of actions, with no other than chronological succession, independent on each other, and without any tendency to introduce or regulate the conclusion. It is not always very nicely distinguished from tragedy. There is not much nearer approach to

unity of action in the tragedy of *Antony and Cleopatra*, than in the history *of Richard the Second*. But a history might be continued through many plays; as it had no plan, it had no limits.

Through all these denominations of the drama, Shakespeare's mode of composition is the same; an interchange of seriousness and merriment, by which the mind is softened at one time, and exhilarated at another. But whatever be his purpose, whether to gladden or depress, or to conduct the story, without vehemence or emotion, through tracts of easy and familiar dialogue, he never fails to attain his purpose; as he commands us, we laugh or mourn, or sit silent with quiet expectation, in tranquillity without indifference.

When Shakespeare's plan is understood, most of the criticisms of Rymer and Voltaire vanish away. The play of *Hamlet* is opened, without impropriety, by two sentinels; Iago bellows at Brabantio's window, without injury to the scheme of the play, though in terms which a modern audience would not easily endure; the character of Polonius is seasonable and useful; and the grave-diggers themselves may be heard with applause.[2]

Shakespeare engaged in the dramatic poetry with the world open before him; the rules of the ancients were yet known to few; the public judgement was unformed; he had no example of such fame as might force him upon imitation, nor critics of such authority as might restrain his extravagance. He therefore indulged his natural disposition, and his disposition, as Rymer has remarked, led him to comedy. In tragedy he often writes with great appearance of toil and study, what is written at last with little felicity; but in his comic scenes, he seems to produce, without labour, what no labour can improve. In tragedy he is always struggling after some occasion to be comic, but in comedy he seems to repose, or to luxuriate, as in a mode of thinking congenial to his nature. In his tragic scenes there is always something wanting, but his comedy often surpasses expectation or desire. His comedy pleases by the thoughts and the language, and his tragedy for the greater part by incident and action. His tragedy seems to be skill, his comedy to be instinct.

---

[1] *concatenation* Linkage, union.

[2] *Iago … applause* Iago is a character in *Othello*. Polonius and the gravediggers are characters in *Hamlet*.

The force of his comic scenes has suffered little diminution from the changes made by a century and a half, in manners or in words. As his personages act upon principles arising from genuine passion, very little modified by particular forms, their pleasures and vexations are communicable to all times and to all places; they are natural, and therefore durable; the adventitious peculiarities of personal habits are only superficial dyes, bright and pleasing for a little while, yet soon fading to a dim tinct, without any remains of former lustre; but the discriminations of true passion are the colours of nature; they pervade the whole mass, and can only perish with the body that exhibits them. The accidental compositions of heterogeneous modes are dissolved by the chance which combined them; but the uniform simplicity of primitive qualities neither admits increase, nor suffers decay. The sand heaped by one flood is scattered by another, but the rock always continues in its place. The stream of time, which is continually washing the dissoluble fabrics of other poets, passes without injury by the adamant of Shakespeare.

If there be, what I believe there is, in every nation a style which never becomes obsolete, a certain mode of phraseology so consonant and congenial to the analogy[1] and principles of its respective language as to remain settled and unaltered; this style is probably to be sought in the common intercourse of life, among those who speak only to be understood, without ambition of elegance. The polite are always catching modish innovations, and the learned depart from established forms of speech in hope of finding or making better; those who wish for distinction forsake the vulgar,[2] when the vulgar is right; but there is a conversation above grossness and below refinement where propriety resides, and where this poet seems to have gathered his comic dialogue. He is therefore more agreeable to the ears of the present age than any other author equally remote, and among his other excellencies deserves to be studied as one of the original masters of our language.

These observations are to be considered not as unexceptionably constant, but as containing general and predominant truth. Shakespeare's familiar dialogue is affirmed to be smooth and clear, yet not wholly without ruggedness or difficulty; as a country may be eminently fruitful, though it has spots unfit for cultivation. His characters are praised as natural though their sentiments are sometimes forced and their actions improbable, as the earth upon the whole is spherical though its surface is varied with protuberances and cavities.

Shakespeare with his excellencies has likewise faults, and faults sufficient to obscure and overwhelm any other merit. I shall show them in the proportion in which they appear to me, without envious malignity or superstitious veneration. No question can be more innocently discussed than a dead poet's pretensions to renown; and little regard is due to that bigotry which sets candour higher than truth.

His first defect is that to which may be imputed most of the evil in books or in men. He sacrifices virtue to convenience, and is so much more careful to please than to instruct that he seems to write without any moral purpose. From his writings indeed a system of social duty may be selected, for he that thinks reasonably must think morally; but his precepts and axioms drop casually from him; he makes no just distribution of good or evil, nor is always careful to show in the virtuous a disapprobation of the wicked; he carries his persons indifferently through right and wrong, and at the close dismisses them without further care, and leaves their examples to operate by chance. This fault the barbarity of his age cannot extenuate; for it is always a writer's duty to make the world better, and justice is a virtue independent on time or place.

The plots are often so loosely formed that a very slight consideration may improve them, and so carelessly pursued, that he seems not always fully to comprehend his own design. He omits opportunities of instructing or delighting which the train of his story seems to force upon him, and apparently rejects those exhibitions which would be more affecting for the sake of those which are more easy.

It may be observed that in many of his plays the latter part is evidently neglected. When he found himself near the end of his work, and in view of his reward, he shortened the labour to snatch the profit. He therefore remits his efforts where he should most

---

[1] *analogy* Formative processes.

[2] *vulgar* Common.

vigorously exert them, and his catastrophe[1] is improbably produced or imperfectly represented.

He had no regard to distinction of time or place, but gives to one age or nation, without scruple, the customs, institutions, and opinions of another, at the expense not only of likelihood, but of possibility. These faults Pope has endeavoured, with more zeal than judgement, to transfer to his imagined interpolators.[2] We need not wonder to find Hector quoting Aristotle when we see the loves of Theseus and Hippolyta combined with the Gothic mythology of fairies.[3] Shakespeare, indeed, was not the only violator of chronology, for in the same age Sidney,[4] who wanted not the advantages of learning, has, in his *Arcadia,* confounded the pastoral with the feudal times, the days of innocence, quiet, and security, with those of turbulence, violence, and adventure.

In his comic scenes he is seldom very successful when he engages his characters in reciprocations of smartness and contests of sarcasm; their jests are commonly gross and their pleasantry licentious; neither his gentlemen nor his ladies have much delicacy, nor are sufficiently distinguished from his clowns[5] by any appearance of refined manners. Whether he represented the real conversation of his time is not easy to determine; the reign of Elizabeth is commonly supposed to have been a time of stateliness, formality, and reserve; yet perhaps the relaxations of that severity were not very elegant. There must, however, have been always some modes of gaiety preferable to others, and a writer ought to choose the best.

In tragedy his performance seems constantly to be worse, as his labour is more. The effusions of passion which exigence forces out are for the most part striking and energetic; but whenever he solicits his invention, or strains his faculties, the offspring of his throes is tumour,

meanness,[6] tediousness, and obscurity.

In narration he affects a disproportionate pomp of diction and a wearisome train of circumlocution, and tells the incident imperfectly in many words which might have been more plainly delivered in few. Narration in dramatic poetry is naturally tedious, as it is unanimated and inactive and obstructs the progress of the action; it should therefore always be rapid and enlivened by frequent interruption. Shakespeare found it an encumbrance and, instead of lightening it by brevity, endeavoured to recommend it by dignity and splendour.

His declamations or set speeches are commonly cold and weak, for his power was the power of nature; when he endeavoured, like other tragic writers, to catch opportunities of amplification and, instead of inquiring what the occasion demanded, to show how much his stores of knowledge could supply, he seldom escapes without the pity or resentment of his reader. ...

The objection arising from the impossibility of passing the first hour at Alexandria and the next at Rome supposes that when the play opens the spectator really imagines himself at Alexandria and believes that his walk to the theatre has been a voyage to Egypt, and that he lives in the days of Antony and Cleopatra. Surely he that imagines this may imagine more. He that can take the stage at one time for the palace of the Ptolemies may take it in half an hour for the promontory of Actium. Delusion, if delusion be admitted, has no certain limitation; if the spectator can be once persuaded that his old acquaintance are Alexander and Caesar, that a room illuminated with candles is the plain of Pharsalia or the bank of Granicus,[7] he is in a state of elevation above the reach of reason, or of truth, and from the heights of empyrean poetry may despise the circumscriptions of terrestrial nature. There is no reason why a mind thus wandering in ecstasy should count the clock, or why an hour should not be a century in that calenture[8] of the brains that can make the stage a field.

The truth is that the spectators are always in their senses and know, from the first act to the last, that the

---

[1] *catastrophe* Conclusion.

[2] *his imagined interpolators* I.e., those who published his plays. In his preface, Pope claimed that many of the faults in Shakespeare's plays were introduced by publishers, not by the writer himself.

[3] *We need ... fairies* Hector quotes Aristotle in *Troilus and Cressida*, 2.2.166–6; in *A Midsummer Night's Dream*, the characters of Theseus and Hippolyta parallel those of Oberon and Titania, the King and Queen of the fairies.

[4] *Sidney* Sir Philip Sidney, English poet and courtier.

[5] *clowns* Yokels.

[6] *tumour* Turgidity of language or style; *meanness* Baseness.

[7] *plain of ... Granicus* Locations of the victories of Julius Caesar and Alexander the Great, respectively.

[8] *calenture* Fever.

stage is only a stage and that the players are only players. They came to hear a certain number of lines recited with just gesture and elegant modulation. The lines relate to some action, and an action must be in some place; but the different actions that complete a story may be in places very remote from each other; and where is the absurdity of allowing that space to represent first Athens and then Sicily which was always known to be neither Sicily nor Athens, but a modern theatre?

By supposition, as place is introduced time may be extended; the time required by the fable elapses for the most part between the acts; for, of so much of the action as is represented, the real and poetical duration is the same. If in the first act preparations for war against Mithridates are represented to be made in Rome, the event of the war may without absurdity be represented, in the castastrophe, as happening in Pontus; we know that there is neither war nor preparation for war; we know that we are neither in Rome nor Pontus; that neither Mithridates nor Lucullus[1] are before us. The drama exhibits successive imitations of successive actions, and why may not the second imitation represent an action that happened years after the first if it be so connected with it that nothing but time can be supposed to intervene? Time is, of all modes of existence, most obsequious to the imagination; a lapse of years is as easily conceived as a passage of hours. In contemplation we easily contract the time of real actions, and therefore willingly permit it to be contracted when we only see their imitation.

It will be asked how the drama moves if it is not credited. It is credited with all the credit due to a drama. It is credited, whenever it moves, as a just picture of a real original, as representing to the auditor what he would himself feel if he were to do or suffer what is there feigned to be suffered or to be done. The reflection that strikes the heart is not that the evils before us are real evils, but that they are evils to which we ourselves may be exposed. If there be any fallacy, it is not that we fancy the players, but that we fancy ourselves unhappy for a moment; but we rather lament the possibility than suppose the presence of misery, as a

mother weeps over her babe when she remembers that death may take it from her. The delight of tragedy proceeds from our consciousness of fiction; if we thought murders and treasons real, they would please no more.

Imitations produce pain or pleasure not because they are mistaken for realities, but because they bring realities to mind. When the imagination is recreated[2] by a painted landscape, the trees are not supposed capable to give us shade, or the fountains coolness; but we consider how we should be pleased with such fountains playing beside us and such woods waving over us. We are agitated in reading the history of *Henry the Fifth*, yet no man takes his book for the field of Agincourt.[3] A dramatic exhibition is a book recited with concomitants that increase or diminish its effect. Familiar[4] comedy is often more powerful in the theatre than on the page; imperial tragedy is always less. The humour of Petruchio may be heightened by grimace; but what voice or what gesture can hope to add dignity or force to the soliloquy of Cato?[5]

A play read affects the mind like a play acted. It is therefore evident that the action is not supposed to be real, and it follows that between the acts a longer or shorter time may be allowed to pass, and that no more account of space or duration is to be taken by the auditor of a drama than by the reader of a narrative, before whom may pass in an hour the life of a hero or the revolutions of an empire.

Whether Shakespeare knew the unities and rejected them by design, or deviated from them by happy ignorance, it is, I think, impossible to decide and useless to inquire. We may reasonably suppose that when he rose to notice he did not want[6] the counsels and admonitions of scholars and critics, and that he at last deliberately persisted in a practice which he might have begun by chance. As nothing is essential to the fable but unity of action, and as the unities of time and place arise evidently from false assumptions, and, by circumscrib-

---

[1] *Mithridates ... Lucullus* King of Pontus and his Roman opponent, both of whom are characters in the tragedy *Mithridates* (1678) by Nathaniel Lee.

[2] *recreated* Enlivened.

[3] *field of Agincourt* Site of Henry V's 1415 defeat of French troops, depicted in Act 4 of Shakespeare's *Henry V.*

[4] *Familiar* Domestic.

[5] *Petruchio* Protagonist of *The Taming of the Shrew*; *Cato* Protagonist of Joseph Addison's *Cato* (1713), who contemplates suicide in a famous soliloquy (5.1).

[6] *want* Lack.

ing the extent of the drama, lessen its variety, I cannot think it much to be lamented that they were not known by him, or not observed; nor, if such another poet could arise, should I very vehemently reproach him that his first act passed at Venice, and his next in Cyprus.[1] Such violations of rules merely positive[2] become the comprehensive genius of Shakespeare, and such censures are suitable to the minute and slender criticism of Voltaire:

> *Non usque adeo permiscuit imis*
> *Longus summa dies, ut non, si voce Metelli*
> *Serventur leges, malint a Caesare tolli.*[3]

Yet when I speak thus slightly of dramatic rules, I cannot but recollect how much wit and learning may be produced against me; before such authorities I am afraid to stand, not that I think the present question one of those that are to be decided by mere authority, but because it is to be suspected that these precepts have not been so easily received but for better reasons than I have yet been able to find. The result of my inquiries, in which it would be ludicrous to boast of impartiality, is that the unities of time and place are not essential to a just drama, that though they may sometimes conduce to pleasure, they are always to be sacrificed to the nobler beauties of variety and instruction; and that a play, written with nice observation of critical rules, is to be contemplated as an elaborate curiosity, as the product of superfluous and ostentatious art, by which is shown rather what is possible than what is necessary.

He that, without diminution of any other excellence, shall preserve all the unities unbroken deserves the like applause with the architect who shall display all the orders[4] of architecture in a citadel without any deduction from its strength; but the principal beauty of a citadel is to exclude the enemy, and the greatest graces of a play are to copy nature and instruct life.

—1765

---

[1] *first act … Cyprus* As in the first two acts of *Othello*.

[2] *positive* Proceeding from custom and arbitrarily instituted.

[3] *Non … tolli* Latin: "The course of time does not bring such confusion that the laws would not rather be trampled upon by a Caesar than saved by a Metellus." From Lucan's *Pharsalia* (3.138-40), an epic poem of the Roman civil wars. Metellus was a minor Roman politician.

[4] *all the orders* I.e., Doric, Ionic, and Corinthian.

from *Lives of the English Poets*

from JOHN MILTON

I am now to examine *Paradise Lost*, a poem which, considered with respect to design, may claim the first place, and with respect to performance the second,[5] among the productions of the human mind.

By the general consent of critics the first praise of genius is due to the writer of an epic poem, as it requires an assemblage of all the powers which are singly sufficient for other compositions. Poetry is the art of uniting pleasure with truth, by calling imagination to the help of reason. Epic poetry undertakes to teach the most important truths by the most pleasing precepts, and therefore relates some great event in the most affecting manner. History must supply the writer with the rudiments of narration, which he must improve and exalt by a nobler art, must animate by dramatic energy, and diversify by retrospection and anticipation; morality must teach him the exact bounds and different shades of vice and virtue; from policy and the practice of life he has to learn the discriminations of character and the tendency of the passions, either single or combined; and physiology must supply him with illustrations and images. To put these materials to poetical use is required an imagination capable of painting nature and realizing fiction. Nor is he yet a poet till he has attained the whole extension of his language, distinguished all the delicacies of phrase, and all the colours of words, and learned to adjust their different sounds to all the varieties of metrical modulation.

Bossu[6] is of opinion that the poet's first work is to find a *moral*, which his fable is afterwards to illustrate and establish. This seems to have been the process only of Milton: the moral of other poems is incidental and consequent; in Milton's only it is essential and intrinsic. His purpose was the most useful and the most arduous: "to vindicate the ways of God to man";[7] to show the

---

[5] *second* With Homer's *Iliad* presumably ranked first.

[6] *Bossu* French abbot René le Bossu. The opinion referred to is expressed in his *Treatise on the Epic Poem* (1675).

[7] *to vindicate … man* A misquote of *Paradise Lost* 1.26, "justify the ways of God to men." Alexander Pope's *Essay on Man*, however, hoped to "vindicate the ways of God to man" (1.16).

reasonableness of religion, and the necessity of obedience to the Divine Law.

To convey this moral there must be a *fable*, a narration artfully constructed so as to excite curiosity and surprise expectation. In this part of his work Milton must be confessed to have equalled every other poet. He has involved in his account of the Fall of Man the events which preceded, and those that were to follow it: he has interwoven the whole system of theology with such propriety that every part appears to be necessary, and scarcely any recital is wished shorter for the sake of quickening the progress of the main action.

The subject of an epic poem is naturally an event of great importance. That of Milton is not the destruction of a city, the conduct of a colony, or the foundation of an empire. His subject is the fate of worlds, the revolutions of heaven and of earth; rebellion against the Supreme King raised by the highest order of created beings; the overthrow of their host and the punishment of their crime; the creation of a new race of reasonable creatures; their original happiness and innocence, their forfeiture of immortality, and their restoration to hope and peace.

Great events can be hastened or retarded only by persons of elevated dignity. Before the greatness displayed in Milton's poem all other greatness shrinks away. The weakest of his agents are the highest and noblest of human beings, the original parents of mankind; with whose actions the elements consented, on whose rectitude or deviation of will depended the state of terrestrial nature and the condition of all the future inhabitants of the globe. Of the other agents in the poem the chief are such as it is irreverence to name on slight occasions. The rest were lower powers;

> of which the least could wield
> Those elements, and arm him with the force
> Of all their regions;[1]

powers which only the control of Omnipotence restrains from laying creation waste and filling the vast expanse of space with ruin and confusion. To display the motives and actions of beings thus superior, so far as human reason can examine them or human imagination repre-

sent them, is the task which this mighty poet has undertaken and performed.

In the examination of epic poems much speculation is commonly employed upon the *characters*. The characters in the *Paradise Lost* which admit of examination are those of angels and of man; of angels good and evil, of man in his innocent and sinful state.

Among the angels the virtue of Raphael is mild and placid, of easy condescension and free communication; that of Michael is regal and lofty, and, as may seem, attentive to the dignity of his own nature. Abdiel and Gabriel appear occasionally and act as every incident requires; the solitary fidelity of Abdiel is very amiably painted.

Of the evil angels the characters are more diversified. To Satan, as Addison observes, such sentiments are given as suit "the most exalted and most depraved being."[2] Milton has been censured by Clarke[3] for the impiety which sometimes breaks from Satan's mouth. For there are thoughts, as he justly remarks, which no observation of character can justify, because no good man would willingly permit them to pass, however transiently, through his own mind. To make Satan speak as a rebel, without any such expressions as might taint the reader's imagination, was indeed one of the great difficulties in Milton's undertaking, and I cannot but think that he has extricated himself with great happiness. There is in Satan's speeches little that can give pain to a pious ear. The language of rebellion cannot be the same with that of obedience. The malignity of Satan foams in haughtiness and obstinacy; but his expressions are commonly general, and no otherwise offensive than as they are wicked.

The other chiefs of the celestial rebellion are very judiciously discriminated in the first and second books; and the ferocious character of Moloch appears, both in the battle and the council, with exact consistency.

To Adam and to Eve are given during their innocence such sentiments as innocence can generate and utter. Their love is pure benevolence and mutual veneration; their repasts are without luxury and their diligence without toil. Their addresses to their Maker

---

1 *of which ... regions* *Paradise Lost* 6.221–23.

2 *the most ... being* From essay no. 303 in *The Spectator*.

3 *Clarke* John Clarke, who criticizes Milton in his *Essay upon Study* (1731).

have little more than the voice of admiration and gratitude. Fruition left them nothing to ask, and Innocence left them nothing to fear.

But with guilt enter distrust and discord, mutual accusation, and stubborn self-defence; they regard each other with alienated minds and dread their Creator as the avenger of their transgression. At last they seek shelter in his mercy, soften to repentance, and melt in supplication. Both before and after the Fall the superiority of Adam is diligently sustained.

Of the *probable* and the *marvellous*, two parts of a vulgar[1] epic poem which immerge[2] the critic in deep consideration, the *Paradise Lost* requires little to be said. It contains the history of a miracle, of Creation and Redemption; it displays the power and the mercy of the Supreme Being: the probable therefore is marvellous, and the marvellous is probable. The substance of the narrative is truth; and as truth allows no choice, it is, like necessity, superior to rule. To the accidental or adventitious parts, as to every thing human, some slight exceptions may be made. But the main fabric is immovably supported. ...

In Milton every line breathes sanctity of thought and purity of manners, except when the train of the narration requires the introduction of the rebellious spirits; and even they are compelled to acknowledge their subjection to God in such a manner as excites reverence and confirms piety.

Of human beings there are but two; but those two are the parents of mankind, venerable before their fall for dignity and innocence, and amiable after it for repentance and submission. In their first state their affection is tender without weakness and their pity sublime without presumption. When they have sinned they show how discord begins in mutual frailty, and how it ought to cease in mutual forbearance; how confidence of the divine favour is forfeited by sin, and how hope of pardon may be obtained by penitence and prayer. A state of innocence we can only conceive, if indeed in our present misery it be possible to conceive it; but the sentiments and worship proper to a fallen and offending being we have all to learn, as we have all to practise.

The poet, whatever be done, is always great. Our progenitors in their first state conversed with angels; even when folly and sin had degraded them they had not in their humiliation "the port of mean suitors;"[3] and they rise again to reverential regard when we find that their prayers were heard.

As human passions did not enter the world before the Fall, there is in the *Paradise Lost* little opportunity for the pathetic; but what little there is has not been lost. That passion which is peculiar to rational nature, the anguish arising from the consciousness of transgression and the horrors attending the sense of the Divine Displeasure, are very justly described and forcibly impressed. But the passions are moved only on one occasion; sublimity is the general and prevailing quality of this poem—sublimity variously modified, sometimes descriptive, sometimes argumentative.[4] ...

Milton would not have excelled in dramatic writing; he knew human nature only in the gross, and had never studied the shades of character, nor the combinations of concurring or the perplexity of contending passions. He had read much and knew what books could teach; but had mingled little in the world, and was deficient in the knowledge which experience must confer.

Through all his greater works there prevails an uniform peculiarity of *diction,* a mode and cast of expression which bears little resemblance to that of any former writer, and which is so far removed from common use that an unlearned reader when he first opens his book finds himself surprised by a new language.

This novelty has been, by those who can find nothing wrong in Milton, imputed to his laborious endeavours after words suitable to the grandeur of his ideas. "Our language," says Addison, "sunk under him."[5] But the truth is that, both in prose and verse, he had formed his style by a perverse and pedantic principle. He was desirous to use English words with a foreign

---

[1] *vulgar* Common, familiar.

[2] *immerge* Immerse.

[3] *the port ... suitors* From *Paradise Lost* 11.8–9.

[4] *argumentative* I.e., contributing to the argument, or theme, of the poem.

[5] *Our ... him* From *Spectator* no. 297.

idiom. This in all his prose is discovered and condemned, for there judgement operates freely, neither softened by the beauty nor awed by the dignity of his thoughts; but such is the power of his poetry that his call is obeyed without resistance, the reader feels himself in captivity to a higher and a nobler mind, and criticism sinks in admiration.

Milton's style was not modified by his subject: what is shown with greater extent in *Paradise Lost* may be found in *Comus*.[1] One source of his peculiarity was his familiarity with the Tuscan poets: the disposition of his words is, I think, frequently Italian; perhaps sometimes combined with other tongues. Of him, at last, may be said what Jonson says of Spenser, that "he wrote no language,"[2] but has formed what Butler calls "a Babylonish dialect,"[3] in itself harsh and barbarous, but made by exalted genius and extensive learning the vehicle of so much instruction and so much pleasure that, like other lovers, we find grace in its deformity.

Whatever be the faults of his diction he cannot want the praise of copiousness and variety; he was master of his language in its full extent, and has selected the melodious words with such diligence that from his book alone the art of English poetry might be learned.

After his diction something must be said of his versification. "The measure," he says, "is the English heroic verse without rhyme."[4] Of this mode he had many examples among the Italians, and some in his own country. The Earl of Surrey[5] is said to have translated one of Virgil's books without rhyme, and besides our tragedies a few short poems had appeared in blank verse; particularly one tending to reconcile the nation to Raleigh's wild attempt upon Guiana,[6] and probably written by Raleigh himself. These petty performances cannot be supposed to have much influenced Milton, who more probably took his hint from Trisino's *Italia Liberata*;[7] and, finding blank verse easier than rhyme, was desirous of persuading himself that it is better.

"Rhyme," he says, and says truly, "is no necessary adjunct of true poetry."[8] But perhaps of poetry as a mental operation metre or music is no necessary adjunct; it is however by the music of metre that poetry has been discriminated in all languages, and in languages melodiously constructed with a due proportion of long and short syllables metre is sufficient. But one language cannot communicate its rules to another; where metre is scanty and imperfect some help is necessary. The music of the English heroic line strikes the ear so faintly that it is easily lost, unless all the syllables of every line cooperate together; this cooperation can be only obtained by the preservation of every verse unmingled with another as a distinct system of sounds, and this distinctness is obtained and preserved by the artifice of rhyme. The variety of pauses, so much boasted by the lovers of blank verse, changes the measures of an English poet to the periods of a declaimer; and there are only a few skilful and happy readers of Milton who enable their audience to perceive where the lines end or begin. "Blank verse," said an ingenious critic,[9] "seems to be verse only to the eye."

Poetry may subsist without rhyme, but English poetry will not often please; nor can rhyme ever be safely spared but where the subject is able to support itself. Blank verse makes some approach to that which is called the "lapidary style,"[10] has neither the easiness of prose nor the melody of numbers, and therefore tires by long continuance. Of the Italian writers without rhyme, whom Milton alleges as precedents, not one is popular; what reason could urge in its defence has been confuted by the ear.

But, whatever be the advantage of rhyme, I cannot prevail on myself to wish that Milton had been a rhymer, for I cannot wish his work to be other than it is;

---

[1] *Comus* Masque by Milton.

[2] *Jonson ... language* Poet Ben Jonson in his *Timber, or Discoveries* (1640), no. 116.

[3] *Butler ... dialect* Seventeenth-century poet Samuel Butler, in his satire *Hudibras* (1663), 1.1.93.

[4] *The measure ... rhyme* From Milton's preface to *Paradise Lost*.

[5] *Earl of Surrey* Henry Howard (1517–47), who completed blank-verse translations of books 2 and 4 of Virgil's *Aeneid*.

[6] *Raleigh's ... Guiana* Sir Walter Raleigh had, in 1595, led a search in Venezuela for the fabled Eldorado. The poem referred to is "Of Guiana, an Epic Song" (1596), actually by George Chapman.

[7] *Trisino's Italia Liberata* The epic poem *Italy Delivered from the Goths* (1547–48) by Giovanni Giorgio.

[8] *Rhyme ... poetry* From the preface to *Paradise Lost*.

[9] *ingenious critic* In his *Life of Johnson* 4.43, Boswell says this statement was made by art critic William Locke (1732–1810).

[10] *lapidary style* Style characteristic of monument inscriptions.

yet like other heroes he is to be admired rather than imitated. He that thinks himself capable of astonishing may write blank verse, but those that hope only to please must condescend to rhyme.

The highest praise of genius is original invention. Milton cannot be said to have contrived the structure of an epic poem, and therefore owes reverence to that vigour and amplitude of mind to which all generations must be indebted for the art of poetical narration, for the texture of the fable, the variation of incidents, the interposition of dialogue, and all the stratagems that surprise and enchain attention. But of all the borrowers from Homer, Milton is perhaps the least indebted. He was naturally a thinker for himself, confident of his own abilities and disdainful of help or hindrance; he did not refuse admission to the thoughts or images of his predecessors, but he did not seek them. From his contemporaries he neither courted nor received support; there is in his writings nothing by which the pride of other authors might be gratified or favour gained, no exchange of praise nor solicitation of support. His great works were performed under discountenance and in blindness, but difficulties vanished at his touch; he was born for whatever is arduous; and his work is not the greatest of heroic poems, only because it is not the first.
—1779

from ALEXANDER POPE

The person of Pope is well known not to have been formed by the nicest model. He has, in his account of the "Little Club,"[1] compare himself to a spider, and by another is described as protuberant behind and before. He is said to have been beautiful in his infancy; but he was of a constitution originally feeble and weak, and, as bodies of a tender frame are easily distorted, his deformity was probably in part the effect of his application. His stature was so low that to bring him to a level with common tables it was necessary to raise his seat. But his face was not displeasing, and his eyes were animated and vivid.

By natural deformity or accidental distortion his vital functions were so much disordered that his life was a "long disease."[2] His most frequent assailant was the headache, which he used to relieve by inhaling the steam of coffee, which he very frequently required.

Most of what can be told concerning his petty peculiarities was communicated by a female domestic of the Earl of Oxford, who knew him perhaps after the middle of life. He was then so weak as to stand in perpetual need of female attendance; extremely sensible of cold, so that he wore a kind of fur doublet under a shirt of very coarse warm linen with fine sleeves. When he rose he was invested in a bodice made of stiff canvas, being scarce able to hold himself erect till they were laced, and he then put on a flannel waistcoat. One side was contracted. His legs were so slender that he enlarged their bulk with three pair of stockings, which were drawn on and off by the maid; for he was not able to dress or undress himself, and neither went to bed nor rose without help. His weakness made it very difficult for him to be clean.

His hair had fallen almost all away, and he used to dine sometimes with Lord Oxford, privately, in a velvet cap. His dress of ceremony was black, with a tie-wig and a little sword ...

His declaration that his care for his works ceased at their publication was not strictly true. His parental attention never abandoned them; what he found amiss in the first edition, he silently corrected in those that followed. He appears to have revised the *Iliad* and freed it from some of its imperfections, and the *Essay on Criticism* received many improvements after its first appearance. It will seldom be found that he altered without adding clearness, elegance, or vigour. Pope had perhaps the judgement of Dryden; but Dryden certainly wanted the diligence of Pope.

In acquired knowledge the superiority must be allowed to Dryden, whose education was more scholastic[3] and who before he became an author had been allowed more time for study, with better means of information. His mind has a larger range, and he collects his images and illustrations from a more extensive circumference of science. Dryden knew more of

---

[1] *his account ... Club* Pope's account appears in *Guardian* no. 92.

[2] *long disease* From Pope's "Epistle to Dr. Arbuthnot," line 132: "This long disease, my life."

[3] *scholastic* Systematic; also, pertaining to formal logic.

man in his general nature, and Pope in his local manners. The notions of Dryden were formed by comprehensive speculation, and those of Pope by minute attention. There is more dignity in the knowledge of Dryden, and more certainty in that of Pope.

Poetry was not the sole praise of either, for both excelled likewise in prose; but Pope did not borrow his prose from his predecessor. The style of Dryden is capricious and varied, that of Pope is cautious and uniform; Dryden obeys the motions of his own mind, Pope constrains his mind to his own rules of composition. Dryden is sometimes vehement and rapid; Pope is always smooth, uniform, and gentle. Dryden's page is a natural field, rising into inequalities, and diversified by the varied exuberance of abundant vegetation; Pope's is a velvet lawn, shaven by the scythe, and levelled by the roller.

Of genius, that power which constitutes a poet; that quality without which judgement is cold and knowledge is inert; that energy which collects, combines, amplifies, and animates—the superiority must, with some hesitation, be allowed to Dryden. It is not to be inferred that of this poetical vigour Pope had only a little, because Dryden had more, for every other writer since Milton must give place to Pope; and even of Dryden it must be said that if he has brighter paragraphs, he has not better poems. Dryden's performances were always hasty, either excited by some external occasion, or extorted by domestic necessity; he composed without consideration, and published without correction. What his mind could supply at call, or gather in one excursion, was all that he sought, and all that he gave. The dilatory caution of Pope enabled him to condense his sentiments, to multiply his images, and to accumulate all that study might produce, or chance might supply. If the flights of Dryden therefore are higher, Pope continues longer on the wing. If of Dryden's fire the blaze is brighter, of Pope's the heat is more regular and constant. Dryden often surpasses expectation, and Pope never falls below it. Dryden is read with frequent astonishment, and Pope with perpetual delight....

Of *The Dunciad* the hint is confessedly taken from Dryden's *MacFlecknoe*, but the plan is so enlarged and diversified as justly to claim the praise of an original, and affords perhaps the best specimen that has yet appeared of personal satire ludicrously pompous.

That the design was moral, whatever the author might tell either his readers or himself, I am not convinced. The first motive was the desire of revenging the contempt with which Theobald had treated his *Shakespeare*,[1] and regaining the honour which he had lost, by crushing his opponent. Theobald was not of bulk enough to fill a poem, and therefore it was necessary to find other enemies with other names, at whose expense he might divert the public.

In this design there was petulance and malignity enough; but I cannot think it very criminal. An author places himself uncalled before the tribunal of criticism, and solicits fame at the hazard of disgrace. Dullness or deformity are not culpable in themselves, but may be very justly reproached when they pretend to the honour of wit or the influence of beauty. If bad writers were to pass without reprehension what should restrain them? *Impune diem consumpserit ingens "Telephus"*;[2] and upon bad writers only will censure have much effect. The satire which brought Theobald and Moore into contempt dropped impotent from Bentley like the javelin of Priam.[3]

All truth is valuable, and satirical criticism may be considered as useful when it rectifies error and improves judgement: he that refines the public taste is a public benefactor.

The beauties of this poem are well known; its chief fault is the grossness of its images. Pope and Swift had an unnatural delight in ideas physically impure, such as every other tongue utters with unwillingness, and of

---

[1] *Theobald* ... *Shakespeare* Pope made Lewis Theobald, a Shakespeare scholar who had pointed out several errors in Pope's edition of Shakespeare, the hero of his biting satire *The Dunciad*.

[2] *impune* ... *Telephus* Latin: "Shall an interminable *Telephus* consume an entire day with impunity?" (Juvenal's *Satires* 1.4–5). *Telephus* was a fifth century BCE play by the Greek dramatist Euripides.

[3] *Moore* James Moore Smythe, who Pope claimed had stolen lines from his *Epistle To a Lady* for use in a play; *Bentley* Richard Bentley, a classical scholar who in 1732 produced a controversial edition of Milton's *Paradise Lost*. Pope satirizes him in both *The Dunciad* and "An Epistle to Dr. Arbuthnot"; *Priam* King of Troy at the time of the Trojan War. He attempted to kill Neoptolemus, son of Achilles, but his feeble attempt was in vain, and he was then slain by Neoptolemus.

which every ear shrinks from the mention.

But even this fault, offensive as it is, may be forgiven for the excellence of other passages, such as the formation and dissolution of Moore, the account of the Traveller, the misfortune of the Florist, and the crowded thoughts and stately numbers which dignify the concluding paragraph.

The alterations which have been made in *The Dunciad*, not always for the better, require that it should be published, as in the last collection,[1] with all its variations.

The *Essay on Man* was a work of great labour and long consideration, but certainly not the happiest of Pope's performances. The subject is perhaps not very proper for poetry, and the poet was not sufficiently master of his subject; metaphysical morality was to him a new study, he was proud of his acquisitions, and, supposing himself master of great secrets, was in haste to teach what he had not learned. Thus he tells us, in the first Epistle, that from the nature of the Supreme Being may be deduced an order of beings such as mankind, because Infinite Excellence can do only what is best. He finds out that these beings must be "somewhere," and that "all the question is whether man be in a wrong place."[2] Surely if, according to the poet's Leibnitzian reasoning,[3] we may infer that man ought to be only because he is, we may allow that his place is the right place, because he has it. Supreme Wisdom is not less infallible in disposing than in creating. But what is meant by "somewhere" and "place" and "wrong place" it had been vain to ask Pope, who probably had never asked himself.

Having exalted himself into the chair of wisdom he tells us much that every man knows, and much that he does not know himself; that we see but little, and that the order of the universe is beyond our comprehension, an opinion not very uncommon; and that there is a chain of subordinate beings "from infinite to nothing," of which himself and his readers are equally ignorant.

But he gives us one comfort which, without his help, he supposes unattainable, in the position "that though we are fools, yet God is wise."

This *Essay* affords an egregious instance of the predominance of genius, the dazzling splendour of imagery, and the seductive powers of eloquence. Never were penury of knowledge and vulgarity of sentiment so happily disguised. The reader feels his mind full, though he learns nothing; and when he meets it in its new array no longer knows the talk of his mother and his nurse. When these wonder-working sounds sink into sense and the doctrine of the *Essay*, disrobed of its ornaments, is left to the powers of its naked excellence, what shall we discover? That we are, in comparison with our Creator, very weak and ignorant; that we do not uphold the chain of existence; and that we could not make one another with more skill than we are made. We may learn yet more: that the arts of human life were copied from the instinctive operations of other animals; that if the world be made for man, it may be said that man was made for geese. To these profound principles of natural knowledge are added some moral instructions equally new: that self-interest well understood will produce social concord; that men are mutual gainers by mutual benefits; that evil is sometimes balanced by good; that human advantages are unstable and fallacious, of uncertain duration and doubtful effect; that our true honour is not to have a great part, but to act it well; that virtue only is our own; and that happiness is always in our power.

Surely a man of no very comprehensive search may venture to say that he has heard all this before, but it was never till now recommended by such a blaze of embellishment or such sweetness of melody. The vigorous contraction of some thoughts, the luxuriant amplification of others, the incidental illustrations, and sometimes the dignity, sometimes the softness of the verses, enchain philosophy, suspend criticism, and oppress judgement by overpowering pleasure.

This is true of many paragraphs; yet if I had undertaken to exemplify Pope's felicity of composition before a rigid critic I should not select the *Essay on Man*, for it contains more lines unsuccessfully laboured, more harshness of diction, more thoughts imperfectly expressed, more levity without elegance, and more heavi-

---

[1] *last collection*   Published by Warburton in 1751.

[2] *somewhere ... place*   From *Essay on Man* 1.47–50.

[3] *Leibnitzian reasoning*   Reasoning of the sort used by German philosopher and mathematician Gottfried Wilhelm Leibnitz, who is known for his belief that this is necessarily "the best of all possible worlds."

ness without strength, than will easily be found in all his other works.

—1781

Letters

To Mrs. Thrale[1]
London, 10 July 1780

Dear Madam

If Mr. Thrale eats but half his usual quantity, he can hardly eat too much.[2] It were better however to have some rule, and some security. Last week I saw flesh but twice, and I think fish once, the rest was pease.[3]

You are afraid, you say, lest I extenuate[4] myself too fast, and are an enemy to violence: but did you never hear nor read, dear Madam, that every man has his genius, and that the great rule by which all excellence is attained, and all success procured, is to follow genius; and have you not observed in all our conversations that my genius is always in extremes; that I am very noisy, or very silent; very gloomy, or very merry; very sour, or very kind? And would you have me cross my genius, when it leads me sometimes to voracity and sometimes to abstinence? You know that the oracle[5] said follow your genius. When we get together again (but when, alas, will that be?) you can manage me, and spare me the solicitude of managing myself.

Poor Miss Owen[6] called on me on Saturday, with that fond and tender application which is natural to misery, when it looks to everybody for that help which nobody can give. I was melted; and soothed and counselled her as well as I could, and am to visit her tomorrow.

She gave a very honourable account of my dear Queeney and says of my master[7] that she thinks his manner and temper more altered than his looks, but of this alteration she could give no particular account; and all that she could say ended in this, that he is now sleepy in the morning. I do not wonder at the scantiness of her narration, she is too busy within to turn her eyes abroad.

I am glad that Pepys[8] is come, but hope that resolute temperance will make him unnecessary. I doubt he can do no good to poor Mr. Scrase.[9]

I stay at home to work, and yet do not work diligently; nor can tell when I shall have done, nor perhaps does anybody but myself wish me to have done; for what can they hope I shall do better? yet I wish the work was over, and I was at liberty. And what would I do if I was at liberty? Would I go to see Mrs. Aston and Mrs. Porter,[10] and see the old places, and sigh to find that my old friends are gone? Would I recall plans of life which I never brought into practice, and hopes of excellence which I once presumed, and never have attained? Would I compare what I now am with what I once expected to have been? Is it reasonable to wish for suggestions of shame, and opportunities of sorrow?

If you please, Madam, we will have an end of this, and contrive some other wishes. I wish I had you in an evening, and I wish I had you in a morning; and I wish I could have a little talk, and see a little frolic. For all this I must stay, but life will not stay.

I will end my letter and go to Blackmore's Life, when I have told you that

I am, &c,

SAM. JOHNSON.

---

1. *To Mrs. Thrale* Hester Thrale, close friend of Johnson.

2. *If … much* Thrale's husband, Henry, had recently suffered numerous strokes, and his health was continually deteriorating. Nevertheless, he continued to eat what both his doctors believed was an unhealthy amount of food.

3. *pease* Mashed peas.

4. *extenuate* Spread or make slim. Johnson was then working on his *Lives of the Poets*.

5. *the oracle* Persius, Roman satirical poet of the first century CE.

6. *Miss Owen* Distant cousin and close childhood friend of Mrs. Thrale.

7. *Queeney* The Thrales's eldest child; *my master* I.e., Henry Thrale.

8. *Pepys* One of the physicians who treated Mr. Thrale.

9. *Mr. Scrase* Friend of the Thrales.

10. *Mrs. Aston and Mrs. Porter* Johnson's friend and his stepdaughter, respectively. The former lived at Lichfield and the second at Stow Hill.

To Mrs. Thrale
Bolt Court, Fleet Street,
19 June 1783

Dear Madam

I am sitting down in no cheerful solitude to write a narrative which would once have affected you with tenderness and sorrow, but which you will perhaps pass over now with the careless glance of frigid indifference. For this diminution of regard, however, I know not whether I ought to blame you, who may have reasons which I cannot know, and I do not blame myself, who have for a great part of human life done you what good I could, and have never done you evil.

I had been disordered in the usual way, and had been relieved by the usual methods, by opium and cathartics, but had rather lessened my dose of opium.

On Monday the 16th I sat for my picture, and walked a considerable way with little inconvenience. In the afternoon and evening I felt myself light and easy, and began to plan schemes of life. Thus I went to bed, and in a short time waked and sat up, as has been long my custom, when I felt a confusion and indistinctness in my head, which lasted I suppose about half a minute; I was alarmed, and prayed God that however he might afflict my body, he would spare my understanding. This prayer, that I might try the integrity of my faculties, I made in Latin verse. The lines were not very good, but I knew them not to be very good: I made them easily, and concluded myself to be unimpaired in my faculties. Soon after I perceived that I had suffered a paralytic stroke, and that my speech was taken from me. I had no pain, and so little dejection in this dreadful state, that I wondered at my own apathy, and considered that perhaps death itself when it should come would excite less horror than seems now to attend it.

In order to rouse the vocal organs I took two drams. Wine has been celebrated for the production of eloquence. I put myself into violent motion, and I think repeated it; but all was vain. I then went to bed, and, strange as it may seem, I think, slept. When I saw light, it was time to contrive what I should do. Though God stopped my speech he left me my hand, I enjoyed a mercy which was not granted to my dear friend Law-

rence,[1] who now perhaps overlooks me as I am writing, and rejoices that I have what he wanted. My first note was necessarily to my servant, who came in talking, and could not immediately comprehend why he should read what I put into his hands.

I then wrote a card to Mr Allen,[2] that I might have a discreet friend at hand to act as occasion should require. In penning this note I had some difficulty; my hand, I knew not how nor why, made wrong letters. I then wrote to Dr. Taylor to come to me, and bring Dr. Heberden, and I sent to Dr. Brocklesby, who is my neighbour. My physicians are very friendly and very disinterested, and give me great hopes, but you may imagine my situation. I have so far recovered my vocal powers as to repeat the Lord's Prayer with no very imperfect articulation. My memory, I hope, yet remains as it was; but such an attack produces solicitude for the safety of every faculty.

How this will be received by you I know not. I hope you will sympathize with me; but perhaps My mistress gracious, mild, and good, Cries! Is he dumb? 'Tis time he shou'd.[3]

But can this be possible? I hope it cannot. I hope that what, when I could speak, I spoke of you, and to you, will be in a sober and serious hour remembered by you; and surely it cannot be remembered but with some degree of kindness. I have loved you with virtuous affection; I have honoured you with sincere esteem. Let not all our endearments be forgotten, but let me have in this great distress your pity and your prayers. You see I yet turn to you with my complaints as a settled and unalienable friend; do not, do not drive me from you, for I have not deserved either neglect or hatred.

To the girls, who do not write often, for Susy has written only once, and Miss Thrale owes me a letter,[4] I

---

[1] *Lawrence* Dr. Thomas Lawrence, who had been Johnson's' physician for several years, and who had died earlier that month.

[2] *Mr Allen* Johnson's landlord and neighbor.

[3] *My … should* Paraphrase of lines 181–82 of Jonathan Swift's *Verses on the Death of Dr. Swift*: "The Queen, so gracious, mild and good, / Cries, 'Is he gone? 'tis time he should.'"

[4] *the girls … letter* Johnson had been made guardian of the Thrales' children after Henry Thrale's death. Here he mentions two of the daughters, Susanna Arabella and Queeney, the eldest (who is therefore referred to as "Miss Thrale").

earnestly recommend, as their guardian and friend, that they remember their Creator in the days of their youth.

I suppose you may wish to know how my disease is treated by the physicians. They put a blister upon my back, and two from my ear to my throat, one on a side. The blister on the back has done little, and those on the throat have not risen. I bullied and bounced (it sticks to our last sand)[1] and compelled the apothecary to make his salve according to the *Edinburgh Dispensatory*,[2] that it might adhere better. I have two on now of my own prescription. They likewise give me salt of hartshorn,[3] which I take with no great confidence, but am satisfied that what can be done is done for me.

O God! give me comfort and confidence in Thee: forgive my sins; and if it be Thy good pleasure, relieve my diseases for Jesus Christ's sake. Amen.

I am almost ashamed of this querulous letter, but now it is written, let it go.

I am, &c.,
SAM. JOHNSON.

To Mrs. Thrale

2 July 1784

Madam

If I interpret your letter right, you are ignominiously married;[4] if it is yet undone, let us once more talk together. If you have abandoned your children and your religion, God forgive your wickedness; if you have forfeited your fame[5] and your country, may your folly do no further mischief. If the last act is yet to do, I who have loved you, esteemed you, reverenced you, and served you, I who long thought you the first of humankind, entreat that, before your fate is irrevocable, I may once more see you. I was, I once was,

Madam, most truly yours,

SAM. JOHNSON

I will come down, if you permit it.

To Mrs. Thrale

London, 8 July 1784[6]

Dear Madam

What you have done, however I may lament it, I have no pretence to resent, as it has not been injurious to me: I therefore breathe out one sigh more of tenderness, perhaps useless, but at least sincere.

I wish that God may grant you every blessing, that you may be happy in this world for its short continuance, and eternally happy in a better state; and whatever I can contribute to your happiness I am very ready to repay for that kindness which soothed twenty years of a life radically wretched.

Do not think slightly of the advice which I now presume to offer. Prevail upon Mr. Piozzi to settle in England. You may live here with more dignity than in Italy, and with more security. Your rank will be higher, and your fortune more under your own eye. I desire not to detail all my reasons, but every argument of prudence and interest is for England, and only some phantoms of imagination seduce you to Italy.

I am afraid however that my counsel is vain, yet I have eased my heart by giving it.

When Queen Mary[7] took the resolution of sheltering herself in England, the Archbishop of St. Andrew's, attempting to dissuade her, attended on her journey and, when they came to the irremeable[8] stream that separated the two kingdoms, walked by her side into the water, in the middle of which he seized her bridle, and, with earnestness proportioned to her danger and his own affection, pressed her to return. The Queen went

---

[1] *it … sand* Reference to Alexander Pope's *Epistles to Several Persons* 1.225, in which he says that a person's ruling passion continues until the end of his life.

[2] *Dispensatory* Book describing the preparation of medicines.

[3] *salts of hartshorn* Smelling salts.

[4] *If … married* Mrs. Thrale had written to Johnson to inform him that she intended to marry Gabriel Piozzi, an Italian musician. Because Piozzi was Roman Catholic and, as a result of his profession, was seen as her social inferior, and because Hester Thrale was a mature woman not needing or seeking financial support, the marriage was a scandalous one, and it resulted in strained relations between Hester Thrale Piozzi and her family and friends.

[5] *fame* Good reputation or character.

[6] *London … 1784* Johnson's former letter to Hester Thrale had brought him a severe and dignified letter of reproof.

[7] *Queen Mary* Mary, Queen of Scots, who sought refuge in England from the rebellion in Scotland. In England she was imprisoned and executed for conspiracy against Queen Elizabeth.

[8] *irremeable* Through which there is no return.

forward.—If the parallel reaches thus far, may it go no further. The tears stand in my eyes.

I am going into Derbyshire, and hope to be followed by your good wishes, for I am, with great affection,

Your, &c,

SAM. JOHNSON

Any letters that come for me hither will be sent me.

THOMAS GRAY

1716 – 1771

One of the most celebrated poems in the English language, Gray's "Elegy Written in a Country Churchyard" was written by a man who shunned celebrity and considered himself more a scholar than a poet. Thomas Gray published only a small body of work, but found a wide readership and excited considerable commentary. In the decades immediately following his death, writers such as Johnson, Wordsworth, and Coleridge recognized Gray's importance, and his work continues to be acknowledged as pivotal in the literature of the eighteenth century.

Gray was the fifth of twelve children born to Philip Gray, a scrivener, and Dorothy Antrobus, a milliner. His childhood was not a happy one; none of his siblings survived past infancy, and his mentally unstable father abused his mother. With his mother financing his education, Gray went to Eton in 1725 and spent some of the happiest years of his life in companionship with Horace Walpole (son of the prime minister, Sir Robert Walpole), Richard West, and Thomas Ashton. Interested in reading, poetry and Latin studies (at which Gray became very proficient), the boys formed a "quadruple alliance," in allusion to the 1718 European treaty of that name. After Eton, Gray, Walpole, and Ashton entered the University of Cambridge, while West went to the University of Oxford, but Gray cared for neither the society nor the studies at Cambridge, and he left without a degree in 1738. In 1739, Walpole invited him on an extended tour of the continent. They visited France, Switzerland, and Italy, but then in 1741 they quarrelled, parted, and subsequently remained estranged for several years. Gray returned to Cambridge and corresponded frequently with Richard West, whose health was poor and whose death in 1742 stunned Gray, inspiring not only his "Sonnet on the Death of Mr. Richard West" but elements of his other elegiac poetry as well.

In November 1745, Walpole and Gray were finally reconciled, an event that was central to Gray's literary career, as Walpole would become instrumental in publishing Gray's poetry. Three poems, "Ode on a Distant Prospect of Eton College," "Ode on the Spring" and "Ode on the Death of a Favourite Cat, Drowned in a Tub of Gold Fishes" (written about a cat of Walpole's), appeared anonymously in the 1748 *Miscellany* of Robert Dodsley, the leading London publisher. Gray had also for several years been working on the "Elegy," and in 1750 he sent the finished poem to Walpole, who circulated it in manuscript. This circulation soon forced Gray to publish the poem. He received word of an impending unauthorized version, so he released the poem himself on 15 February 1751, published on its own under the title *An Elegy Wrote in a Country Church Yard*.

Drawing on traditions that included landscape poetry, the funeral elegy, and graveyard poetry, the "Elegy" drew immediate and widespread praise from both critics and readers. It went through 12 editions by 1763, appeared in several periodicals, was imitated, parodied, and translated into numerous languages, and became arguably the most quoted poem in the English language. The reasons for its popularity were—and still are—as intriguing a subject as the poem itself. Besides simply being an excellently written piece, the poem represents the age: its style embodies neoclassical restraint while its themes echo the sentiments of sensibility, the movement in the mid-century towards the expression of "universal feelings." Samuel Johnson highlighted this characteristic of the poem when he concluded, "I rejoice to concur with the common reader... The Church-yard abounds with images which find a mirrour in every mind, and with sentiments to which every bosom returns an echo."

After the success of the *Elegy*, Dodsley published Gray's first collected edition of poems with illustrations by Richard Bentley (1753), and Gray turned to writing more elaborate poetry. In 1757, he was offered the Poet Laureateship, which he declined, and he published two Pindaric odes, "The Progress of Poesy" and "The Bard"—complex, allusive poems that puzzled many readers (and were parodied in two odes to "Oblivion" and "Obscurity"). In later years he studied more and wrote less, took walking tours, and, in 1768, accepted a professorship of modern history at Cambridge. He never married, and his most passionate relationships were with men. In 1769 he met and became devoted to a young Swiss nobleman, Charles Victor de Bonstetten. Gray planned to visit de Bonstetten in Switzerland, but he was taken suddenly ill before he could make the trip; he died in July 1771.

Gray is in many ways a study in contrasts. He is a transitional figure, poised between classicism and romanticism, and his poetry expresses universal themes that are often accompanied by a technically complex style. Because he read widely, he amassed a vast amount of knowledge that makes many of his poems highly allusive. His notebooks record volumes of material from such varied studies as Norse literature, botany, entomology, music, painting, and architecture. Despite his scholarship, he took only one degree (a baccalaureate in civil law, a subject he disliked), never delivered a lecture, and—for such a well-known poet—wrote very little. In temperament, he described himself as melancholic and others described him as socially withdrawn. His letters, however, reveal a superior intellect, a lively wit, and an understanding of his own literary challenges. In sending Walpole the "Elegy," Gray told him to "look upon it in the light of a thing with an end to it; a merit that most of my writings have wanted and are like to want."

⌘ ⌘ ⌘

Elegy Written in a Country Churchyard

The curfew tolls the knell[1] of parting day,
　The lowing herd wind slowly o'er the lea,[2]
The plowman homeward plods his weary way,
And leaves the world to darkness and to me.

Now fades the glimmering landscape on the sight,
And all the air a solemn stillness holds,

Save where the beetle wheels his droning flight,
And drowsy tinklings lull the distant folds;

Save that from yonder ivy-mantled tower
10　The moping owl does to the moon complain
Of such as, wand'ring near her secret bower,
Molest her ancient solitary reign.

Beneath those rugged elms, that yew-tree's shade,
Where heaves the turf in many a mouldering heap,
15　Each in his narrow cell for ever laid,
The rude° forefathers of the hamlet sleep.   *unlearned*

The breezy call of incense-breathing morn,
The swallow twittering from the straw-built shed,
The cock's shrill clarion or the echoing horn,
20　No more shall rouse them from their lowly bed.

---

[1] *curfew* From the French for "cover your fire," a medieval regulation that decreed that at an appointed hour (indicated by the ringing of a bell) all fires had to be covered and houses shut up for the night. The practice of ringing a bell at a certain hour of the evening (usually eight o'clock) persists in many towns; *knell* Sound made by a bell, especially one struck after a death.

[2] *lea* Meadow or area of grassland.

For them no more the blazing hearth shall burn,
Or busy housewife ply her evening care:
No children run to lisp their sire's return,
Or climb his knees the envied kiss to share.

25 Oft did the harvest to their sickle yield,
Their furrow oft the stubborn glebe° has broke;   *soil*
How jocund° did they drive their team afield!   *merrily*
How bowed the woods beneath their sturdy stroke!

Let not Ambition mock their useful toil,
30 Their homely joys, and destiny obscure;
Nor Grandeur hear, with a disdainful smile,
The short and simple annals of the poor.

The boast of heraldry, the pomp of power,
And all that beauty, all that wealth e'er gave,
35 Awaits alike th' inevitable hour.
The paths of glory lead but to the grave.

Nor you, ye Proud, impute to these the fault,
If Mem'ry o'er their tomb no trophies raise,
Where through the long-drawn aisle and fretted[1] vault
40 The pealing anthem swells the note of praise.

Can storied urn or animated bust
Back to its mansion call the fleeting breath?
Can Honour's voice provoke the silent dust,
Or Flattery soothe the dull cold ear of Death?

45 Perhaps in this neglected spot is laid
Some heart once pregnant with celestial fire;
Hands that the rod of empire might have swayed,
Or waked to ecstasy the living lyre.

But Knowledge to their eyes her ample page
50 Rich with the spoils of time did ne'er unroll;
Chill Penury repressed their noble rage,[2]
And froze the genial current of the soul.

Full many a gem of purest ray serene
The dark unfathomed caves of ocean bear:

55 Full many a flower is born to blush unseen
And waste its sweetness on the desert air.

Some village-Hampden[3] that with dauntless breast
The little tyrant of his fields withstood;
Some mute inglorious Milton[4] here may rest,
60 Some Cromwell[5] guiltless of his country's blood.

Th' applause of listening senates to command,
The threats of pain and ruin to despise,
To scatter plenty o'er a smiling land,
And read their hist'ry in a nation's eyes,

65 Their lot forbade: nor circumscribed alone
Their growing virtues, but their crimes confined;
Forbade to wade through slaughter to a throne,
And shut the gates of mercy on mankind,

The struggling pangs of conscious truth to hide,
70 To quench the blushes of ingenuous shame,
Or heap the shrine of Luxury and Pride
With incense kindled at the Muse's flame.[6]

---

[1] *fretted*   Carved with decorative patterns.

[2] *rage*   Ardor, enthusiasm.

[3] *Hampden*   John Hampden (1594–1643), member of Parliament who defied Charles I and died early in the ensuing civil war.

[4] *Milton*   John Milton (1608–74), English poet, dramatist.

[5] *Cromwell*   Oliver Cromwell (1599–1658), Commander-in-Chief and then Lord Protector of England during the republican or commonwealth period (1649–60).

[6] *With … flame*   After this line, the earliest extant draft of the poem contains four stanzas that appear to be an earlier ending to the poem:

The thoughtless World to Majesty may bow
Exalt the brave, and idolize Success
But more to Innocence their Safety owe
Than Power and Genius e'er conspired to bless

And thou, who mindful of the unhonour'd Dead
Dost in these Notes their artless Tale relate
By Night and lonely Contemplation led
To linger in the gloomy Walks of Fate

Hark how the sacred Calm, that broods around
Bids ev'ry fierce tumultuous Passion cease
In still small Accents whisp'ring from the Ground
A grateful Earnest of eternal Peace

No more with Reason and thyself at strife;
Give anxious Cares and endless Wishes room
But thro' the cool sequester'd Vale of Life
Pursue the silent Tenor of thy Doom.

Far from the madding crowd's ignoble strife,
Their sober wishes never learned to stray;
75 Along the cool sequestered vale of life
They kept the noiseless tenor of their way.

Yet ev'n these bones from insult to protect
Some frail memorial still erected nigh,
With uncouth rhymes and shapeless sculpture decked,
80 Implores the passing tribute of a sigh.

Their name, their years, spelt by th' unlettered muse,
The place of fame and elegy supply:
And many a holy text around she strews,
That teach the rustic moralist to die.

85 For who to dumb Forgetfulness a prey,
This pleasing anxious being e'er resigned,
Left the warm precincts of the cheerful day,
Nor cast one longing ling'ring look behind?

On some fond breast the parting soul relies,
90 Some pious drops the closing eye requires;
Ev'n from the tomb the voice of nature cries,
Ev'n in our ashes live their wonted fires.

For thee who, mindful of th' unhonoured dead,
Dost in these lines their artless tale relate;
95 If chance, by lonely Contemplation led,
Some kindred spirit shall inquire thy fate,

Haply some hoary-headed swain may say,
"Oft have we seen him at the peep of dawn
Brushing with hasty steps the dews away
00 To meet the sun upon the upland lawn.

"There at the foot of yonder nodding beech
That wreathes its old fantastic roots so high,

His listless length at noontide would he stretch,
And pore upon the brook that babbles by.

105 "Hard by yon wood, now smiling as in scorn,
Mutt'ring his wayward fancies he would rove,
Now drooping, woeful wan, like one forlorn,
Or crazed with care, or crossed in hopeless love.

"One morn I missed him on the customed hill,
110 Along the heath and near his favourite tree;
Another came; nor yet beside the rill,
Nor up the lawn, nor at the wood was he;

"The next with dirges due in sad array
Slow through the church-way path we saw him borne.
115 Approach and read (for thou can'st read) the lay,
Graved on the stone beneath yon aged thorn."

THE EPITAPH

Here rests his head upon the lap of earth
A youth to fortune and to fame unknown.
Fair Science° frowned not on his humble birth,   learning
120 *And Melancholy marked him for her own.*

Large was his bounty and his soul sincere,
Heaven did a recompense as largely send:
He gave to Misery all he had, a tear,
He gained from Heaven ('twas all he wished) a friend.

125 *No farther seek his merits to disclose,*
Or draw his frailties from their dread abode,
(There they alike in trembling hope repose)
The bosom of his Father and his God.
—1751

Christopher Smart

1722 – 1771

Christopher Smart produced several works of highly original poetry in the late 1750s and early 1760s. He also spent five of those years in a lunatic asylum, and much of the critical attention paid to Smart has centered on debates over the nature of his madness and the extent of its effect on his work. Whatever Smart's state, however, the poems themselves—particularly *Jubilate Agno* and *A Song to David*—have generally been recognized as boldly experimental and extremely influential. They have served as models for a variety of modern writers, including Anne Sexton, Alan Ginsberg, Edith Sitwell, Benjamin Britten, and Eli Mandel.

The son of a steward, Smart was born on 11 April 1722 at Shipbourne, Kent. He was educated at Cambridge, where he distinguished himself for his heavy drinking and inability to manage money (his friends once had to bail him out of debtors' prison), as well as for his academic excellence and prize-winning poetry.

Smart gave up a potential career at Cambridge to seek fame as a poet in London. There he made a living as a hack writer, contributing occasional pieces to various journals. He and the publisher John Newbery (whose step-daughter, Anna Maria Carnan, Smart married in 1753) started the journal *The Midwife: or the Old Woman's Magazine*, in which Smart wrote miscellaneous jokes, puns, and satirical pieces as the vastly popular Mary Midnight.

In 1756 Smart began to be overwhelmed by irrepressibly strong religious convictions. He would fall upon his knees and pray whenever the urge came upon him—in St. James's Park, in the Mall, in the streets—and oblige his friends to join him, often dragging them away from their dinners or out of their beds to do so. In 1757 Smart's family placed him in the London madhouse St. Luke's Hospital, where he was pronounced incurable. He was confined for most of the following six years.

Smart's most productive period occurred following his release in 1763. He completed many of the poems he had begun while confined, including his renowned *A Song to David* (1763), generally judged to be his greatest poem, and *Translations of the Psalms of David* (1765). Smart also translated the complete works of Horace into verse (a translation that remains highly regarded today). Tainted by his reputation as a madman, however, he was rarely taken seriously as a poet. In 1770 his debts caught up with him, and he was imprisoned in the King's Bench Prison. There he wrote his final poems, *Hymns for the Amusement of Children*, and remained until his death in 1771.

The surviving fragments of Smart's poem *Jubilate Agno* (*Rejoice in the Lamb*) were not printed until 1939, and these survived only because friends of the poet William Cowper had kept the manuscript, hoping to use it to better understand Cowper's own mental illness. Smart wrote *Jubilate Agno*, his ecstatic celebration of the omnipresence of the Divine Being, a few lines a day over a period of four years (1759–63) of confinement in the madhouse. As something of a journal of praise, it provides insight into his daily activities there. But in its experiments in poetic techniques it also moves toward an entirely new form of poetry. Like *A Song to David*, *Jubilate Agno* rejects the influences of Milton, Dryden, and Pope that had been evident in Smart's earlier poetry. Instead, with its alternating sections of lines beginning with "Let" and "For," it appears to draw on traditional Hebrew poetry, and resembles response readings such as those found in the Psalter, the Litany, and other texts in the *Book of Common Prayer*.

Although the story of Smart's life of confinement and death in prison is an unhappy one, his poetry is infused with an irrepressible sense of joy. In the most famous section of *Jubilate Agno*, "My Cat Jeoffry," Smart lovingly praises his cat, his sole companion in confinement. With witty wordplay and obscure scholarly references, Smart celebrates Jeoffry both as a source of comfort and love and as one of God's creatures, proof of his divine plan.

⌘ ⌘ ⌘

from *Jubilate Agno*
[MY CAT JEOFFRY]

For I will consider my Cat Jeoffry.
For he is the servant of the Living God duly and
    daily serving him.
For at the first glance of the glory of God in the East[1]
    he worships in his way.
For is this done by wreathing his body seven times
    round with elegant quickness.
For then he leaps up to catch the musk, which is the
    blessing of God upon his prayer.
For he rolls upon prank[2] to work it in.
For having done duty and received blessing he begins
    to consider himself.
For this he performs in ten degrees.
For first he looks upon his forepaws to see if they are
    clean.
For secondly he kicks up behind to clear away there.
For thirdly he works it upon stretch with the forepaws
    extended.
For fourthly he sharpens his paws by wood.
For fifthly he washes himself.
For Sixthly he rolls upon wash.
For Seventhly he fleas himself, that he may not be
    interrupted upon the beat.
For Eighthly he rubs himself against a post.
For Ninthly he looks up for his instructions.
For Tenthly he goes in quest of food.

For having considered God and himself he will
    consider his neighbor.
20 For if he meets another cat he will kiss her in kindness.
For when he takes his prey he plays with it to give it
    a chance.
For one mouse in seven escapes by his dallying.
For when his day's work is done his business more
    properly begins.
For he keeps the Lord's watch in the night against the
    adversary.
25 For he counteracts the powers of darkness by his
    electrical skin[3] & glaring eyes.
For he counteracts the Devil, who is death, by
    brisking about[4] the life.
For in his morning orisons he loves the sun and the
    sun loves him.
For he is of the tribe of Tiger.
For the Cherub Cat is a term of the Angel Tiger.[5]
30 For he has the subtlety and hissing of a serpent, which
    in goodness he suppresses.
For he will not do destruction if he is well fed, neither
    will he spit without provocation.
For he purrs in thankfulness, when God tells him he's
    a good Cat.
For he is an instrument for the children to learn
    benevolence upon.

---

1 *glory … East* Sunrise.

2 *upon prank* For a frolic; for a trick.

---

3 *electrical skin* An article in *The Gentleman's Magazine* 24 (1754) stated that cats have a natural electricity greater than that of any other animal.

4 *brisking about* Moving about briskly.

5 *Cherub … Tiger* Smart is referring to the fact that a cherub is a small angel, as a cat is a small tiger.

For every house is incomplete without him & a
blessing is lacking in the spirit.

35 For the Lord commanded Moses concerning the cats at
the departure of the Children of Israel from Egypt.[1]

For every family had one cat at least in the bag.

For the English Cats are the best in Europe.

For he is the cleanest in the use of his forepaws of any
quadruped.

For the dexterity of his defence is an instance of the
love of God to him exceedingly.

40 For he is the quickest to his mark of any creature.

For he is tenacious of his point.

For he is a mixture of gravity and waggery.[2]

For he knows that God is his Saviour.

For there is nothing sweeter than his peace when at rest.

45 For there is nothing brisker than his life when in
motion.

For he is of the Lord's poor and so indeed is he called
by benevolence perpetually—Poor Jeoffry! poor
Jeoffry! the rat has bit thy throat.

For I bless the name of the Lord Jesus that Jeoffry is
better.

For the divine spirit comes about his body to
sustain it in compleat° cat.   *complete*

For his tongue is exceeding pure so that it has
in purity what it wants in music.

50 For he is docile and can learn certain things.

For he can set up with gravity, which is patience upon
approbation.

For he can fetch and carry, which is patience in
employment.

For he can jump over a stick, which is patience upon
proof positive.

For he can spraggle° upon waggle[3] at the word
of command.   *sprawl*

55 For he can jump from an eminence into his
master's bosom.

For he can catch the cork and toss it again.

For he is hated by the hypocrite and miser.

For the former is afraid of detection.

For the latter refuses the charge.

60 For he camels his back to bear the first notion of
business.

For he is good to think on, if a man would express
himself neatly.

For he made a great figure in Egypt for his signal
services.

For he killed the Ichneumon-rat[4] very pernicious by
land.

For his ears are so acute that they sting again.[5]

65 For from this proceeds the passing quickness of his
attention.

For by stroking of him I have found out electricity.

For I perceived God's light about him both wax and
fire.

For the Electrical fire is the spiritual substance, which
God sends from heaven to sustain the bodies both
of man and beast.

For God has blessed him in the variety of his
movements.

70 For, though he cannot fly, he is an excellent clamberer.

For his motions upon the face of the earth are more
than any other quadruped.

For he can tread to all the measures upon the music.

For he can swim for life.

For he can creep.

—1939 (WRITTEN 1759–63)

---

[1] *Lord … Egypt* The Lord commanded the children of Israel to
take their flocks and herds with them upon departure (Exodus
13.32).

[2] *waggery* Mischievous jocularity.

[3] *upon waggle* While wiggling about.

---

[4] *Ichneumon-rat* Mongoose-like carnivorous mammal domesticated and revered by the ancient Egyptians for its ability to find and
destroy the eggs of crocodiles and other dangerous reptiles.

[5] *again* In response.

Transatlantic Currents
Contexts

B ritish and New World literatures have tended for centuries to be studied and taught in isolation from each other. Recently, however, both scholarship and pedagogy have begun to focus more frequently on the connections between Britain, Africa, and the Americas. There are of course necessary cultural distinctions to be made between, for instance, a tropical plantation, a barely established North American frontier settlement, and the fully developed urban bustle of London—but there are also connections to be acknowledged, as the flow of economic goods, people, and ideas across the sea in multiple directions influenced the development of literature in English on all shores of the Atlantic.

The slave trade was essential to the continued interchange; British merchants had become heavily engaged in the trade halfway through the seventeenth century, and their involvement continued to grow past the end of the eighteenth century. The trade operated in a loosely triangular form: ships transported manufactured goods from Europe to Africa to exchange for slaves; the slaves were brought to the Caribbean, where they were forced to engage in the production of luxury commodities such as sugar and tobacco; these products were then brought back to Europe for sale. The British colonies in North America also purchased slaves from Africa and traded with the Caribbean, exporting wood and food and importing luxury goods. Demand for slaves prompted the transportation of vast numbers of people: in the eighteenth century alone, about 6,500,000 slaves were traded, of whom an estimated 2,500,000 were shipped by British traders. This exchange created extraordinary economic growth for Britain and its colonies. And, in the latter half of the eighteenth century, the traffic of goods and people spawned intellectual and literary connections as authors, political campaigners, and theologians expressed their moral outrage over Britain's role in the slave trade and the treatment of slaves in British colonies.[1] As a result of growing opposition, the British slave trade would be outlawed in 1807, and all slaves in Britain and its colonies would be legally freed in 1834. (Anti-slavery laws were passed slightly earlier in Upper and Lower Canada and in some northern American states, with other states gradually following suit until official nationwide emancipation was achieved in 1865.)

While Africans were brought to the Americas by force, others came freely from England, Scotland, and Ireland. In rural areas, high rents and failing industry, combined with the promise of relatively cheap land and well-paid employment in the Americas, encouraged those who could afford the cost of travel to leave their homes behind—bringing to North America their families, their cultural influence, and their agricultural skills. Migrants from urban centers were more likely to travel individually; most of these were tradespeople or unskilled young men with few prospects at home. Although the English language and a blend of English, Scottish, and Irish culture dominated in the colonies, there were also regions with high concentrations of German, Dutch, and other settlers from continental Europe.

With settlement came conflict, both old and new. From the late seventeenth century to the 1760s, France and Britain engaged in a series of four wars, and their North American possessions fought each

---

[1] See the Contexts section "The Abolition of Slavery" (available in the online component of volume 3 of *The Broadview Anthology of British Literature*) for more material on the British anti-slavery movement.

other whenever the colonial powers did. England's self-image was deeply invested in the outcomes of its overseas battles; a mythology grew up around the death of General Wolfe, for example, in the wake of his defeat of French forces at Quebec, a moment which came to be seen as emblematic of the empire's glory. Pre-existing European conflicts blended with the conflicts of the New World. Colonists attempted to displace native people from useful land but also wanted to take advantage of the trade opportunities and military strength that alliances with tribes could afford.[1] The intercolonial wars of this period in North America are often called the French and Indian Wars, a somewhat misleading name, given that Native people participated on both sides. Greater numbers allied with the French in the hope of preventing further British expansion, but their hopes were disappointed when the French, in negotiating peace with Britain in 1763, ceded these tribes' territories without consulting them. Throughout the eighteenth century relations between colonists and Native people continued to be strained; while treaties were sometimes negotiated and alliances sometimes honored, that was far from the norm. Tribes often defended themselves with violence—both alongside their colonial allies and independently during times of peace between the colonies.

As the eighteenth century progressed and the Thirteen Colonies became more self-sufficient economically, they began as well to develop a more distinct sense of political identity. In the last half of the century, when the British government imposed a series of taxes and other legislation on the colonists without consulting local government in the Colonies, American dissenters responded with a cry of "no taxation without representation." Their argument was that, as Englishmen, they had a right to participate in the decisions of the British Parliament. This disagreement also created turmoil on the opposite side of the Atlantic, with the British pressed to define their political identity as an imperial power. In England, those defending the authority of the crown outnumbered those advocating concessions to the Colonies; although the British were forced to repeal the Stamp Act (the most controversial piece of legislation), they passed the Declaratory Act, a statement of their right to make law for the Colonies unilaterally. Opposition in the Colonies intensified, the British government passed increasingly invasive legislation, and the hostilities escalated into armed conflict; the Revolutionary War, which began in 1775, ended officially with American independence in 1783.

This did not, of course, end North America's relationship with Great Britain. The colonies of British North America (the eastern part of present-day Canada) still belonged to the empire, which continued to expand its territory to the west. And even the newly-formed United States of America remained far more closely tied to Britain, both economically and culturally, than to any other nation.

⌘ ⌘ ⌘

---

[1] See Samuel Johnson's imagining of a native perspective on colonization in *The Idler* No. 81 elsewhere in this anthology.

Slavery

from Richard Ligon, *A True & Exact History of the Island of Barbados* (1657)

In 1647, Richard Ligon found himself without money or opportunity in England and traveled to Barbados in the hope that his fortunes would change. They did not; a fever prompted his return to England in 1650, and he was thrown into debtors' prison shortly after his arrival home. His descriptions of life in Barbados shed valuable light on the early development of slavery in Britain's colonies—and on the development of the racist ideology that supported the institution.

The island is divided into three sorts of men, *viz.*[1] masters, servants, and slaves. The slaves and their posterity, being subject to their masters forever, are kept and preserved with greater care than the servants, who are theirs but for five years,[2] according to the law of the island. . . .

It has been accounted a strange thing that the negroes, being more than double the numbers of the Christians that are there—and they accounted a bloody people, where they think they have power or advantages, and the more bloody by how much they are more fearful than others—that these should not commit some horrid massacre upon the Christians, thereby to enfranchise[3] themselves, and become masters of the island. But there are three reasons that take away this wonder; the one is, they are not suffered to touch or handle any weapons; the other, that they are held in such awe and slavery as they are fearful to appear in any daring act; and seeing the mustering of our men and hearing their gunshot (that which nothing is more terrible to them), their spirits are subjugated to so low a condition as they dare not look up to any bold attempt. Besides these, there is a third reason, which stops all designs of that

kind, and that is, they are fetched from several parts of Africa, who speak several languages, and by that means one of them understands not another: for some of them are fetched from Guinny and Binny, some from Cutchew, some from Angola, and some from the River of Gambra.[4] And in some of these places where petty kingdoms are, they sell their subjects and such as they take in battle, whom they make slaves; and some mean men sell their servants, their children, and sometimes their wives; and think all good traffic[5] for such commodities as our merchants send them.

When they are brought to us, the planters buy them out of the ship, where they find them stark naked, and therefore cannot be deceived in any outward infirmity. They choose them as they do horses in a market; the strongest, youthfulest, and most beautiful yield the greatest prices. Thirty pound sterling is a price for the best man negro; and twenty-five, twenty-six, or twenty-seven pound for a woman; the children are at easier rates. And we buy them so as the sexes may be equal; for, if they have more men than women, the men who are unmarried will come to their masters and complain that they cannot live without wives, and desire him,[6] they may have wives. And he tells them that the next ship that comes, he will buy them wives, which satisfies them for the present; and so they expect the good time: which the master performing with them, the bravest fellow is to choose first, and so in order, as they are in place; and every one of them knows his better, and gives him the precedence, as cows do one another in passing through a narrow gate; for the most of them are as near beasts as may be, setting their souls aside. Religion they know none; yet most of them acknowledge a God, as appears by their motion and gestures: for, if one of them do another wrong, and he cannot revenge himself, he looks up to heaven for vengeance and holds up both his hands, as if the power must come from thence, that must do him right. Chaste they are as any people under the sun; for, when the men and women are together naked, they never cast their eyes towards the parts that

---

[1] *viz.*   Abbreviation of the Latin *videlicet*, meaning "namely."

[2] *the servants . . . five years*   At this time, it was a common practice for people to contract themselves as indentured servants, legally committing to a set number of years of unpaid labor, in exchange for passage to the Americas.

[3] *enfranchise*   Free.

[4] *Guinny . . . Gambra*   Places ranging along much of Africa's west coast, including Guinea, Benin, the Gambia River, and Cacheu (in present day Guinea-Bissau).

[5] *good traffic*   Reasonable trade.

[6] *desire him*   I.e., request of him that.

ought to be covered; and those amongst us that have breeches and petticoats, I never saw so much as a kiss, or embrace, or a wanton glance with their eyes between them. Jealous they are of their wives, and hold it for a great injury and scorn if another man make the least courtship to his wife....

[While I was using a compass] this negro Sambo comes to me, and seeing the needle wag, desired to know the reason of its stirring, and whether it were alive: I told him no, but it stood upon a point, and for a while it would stir, but by and by stand still, which he observed and found it to be true. The next question was why it stood one way and would not remove to any other point. I told him that it would stand no way but north and south, and upon that showed him the four cardinal points of the compass, east, west, north, south, which he presently learnt by heart and promised me never to forget it. His last question was why it would stand north. I gave this reason, because of the huge rocks of lodestone that were in the north part of the world, which had a quality to draw iron to it; and this needle, being of iron touched with a loadstone, it would always stand that way.

This point of philosophy was a little too hard for him, and so he stood in a strange muse;[1] which to put him out of, I bade him reach his axe and put it near to the compass, and remove it about; and, as he did so, the needle turned with it, which put him in the greatest admiration that ever I saw a man, and so quite gave over his questions, and desired me[2] that he might be made a Christian; for he thought to be a Christian was to be endued with all those knowledges he wanted.

I promised to do my best endeavour; and when I came home, spoke to the master of the plantation, and told him that poor Sambo desired much to be a Christian. But his answer was that the people of that island were governed by the laws of England, and by those laws we could not make a Christian a slave. I told him my request was far different from that, for I desired him to make a slave a Christian. His answer was that it was true, there was a great difference in that; but, being once

a Christian, he could no more account him a slave, and so lose the hold they had of them as slaves by making them Christians; and by that means should open such a gap as all the planters in the island would curse him. So I was struck mute, and poor Sambo kept out of the Church; as ingenious, as honest, and as good a natured poor soul, as ever wore black, or ate green....

Though there be a mark set upon these people which will hardly ever be wiped off, as of their cruelties when they have advantages, and of their fearfulness and falseness; yet no rule so general but hath his[3] exception: for I believe, and I have strong motives to cause me to be of that persuasion, that there are as honest, faithful, and conscionable people amongst them as amongst those of Europe or any other part of the world....

from John Woolman, "Considerations on the Keeping of Negroes" (1754)

> One of the first prominent Quakers to publicly oppose slavery, John Woolman was influential in increasing anti-slavery sentiment among Quakers, who came to play a significant role in the abolition movement. Born in New Jersey, he traveled to preach in the colonies and eventually in England. He abstained from using sugar, dyed clothing, and other products of slave labor.

"Forasmuch as ye did it to the least of these my brethren, ye did it unto me."

—Matthew 25.40

As many times there are different motives to the same action, and one does that from a generous heart which another does for selfish ends; the like may be said in this case.

There are various circumstances among those that keep negroes, and different ways by which they fall under their care; and I doubt not, there are many well disposed persons amongst them who desire rather to manage wisely and justly in this difficult matter, than to make gain of it.

---

[1] *muse* Act of reflection or musing.

[2] *desired me* Requested of me.

[3] *his* Its.

But the general disadvantage which these poor negroes lie under in an enlightened Christian country having often filled me with real sadness, I now think it my duty, through Divine aid, to offer some thoughts thereon to the consideration of others.

When we remember that all nations are of one blood, (Gen. 3.20)[1] that in this world we are but so-journers, that we are subject to the like afflictions and infirmities of body, the like disorders and frailties in mind, the like temptations, the same death, and the same judgment, and that the all-wise Being is Judge and Lord over us all, it seems to raise an idea of general brotherhood, and a disposition easy to be touched with a feeling of each other's afflictions; but when we forget those things, and look chiefly at our outward circum-stances, in this and some ages past, constantly retaining in our minds the distinction between us and them, with respect to our knowledge and improvement in things Divine, natural and artificial, our breasts being apt to be filled with fond notions of superiority, there is danger of erring in our conduct toward them.

We allow them to be of the same species with ourselves; odds is, we are in a higher station, and enjoy greater favour than they. And when it is thus that our heavenly Father endoweth some of his children with distinguished gifts, they are intended for good ends; but if those thus gifted are thereby lifted up above their brethren, not considering themselves as debtors to the weak, nor behaving themselves as faithful stewards, none who judge impartially can suppose them free from ingratitude.

When a people dwell under the liberal distribution of favours from heaven, it behooves them carefully to inspect their ways, and consider the purposes for which those favours are bestowed, lest, through forgetfulness of God and misusing his gifts, they incur his heavy displea-sure, whose judgments are just and equal, who exalteth and humbleth to the dust, as he seeth meet....

To prevent such an error, let us calmly consider their circumstance; and the better to do it, make their case ours. Suppose then that our ancestors and we had been exposed to constant servitude, in the more servile and inferior employments of life; that we had been destitute of the help of reading and good company; that amongst ourselves we had had but few wise and pious instructors; that the religious amongst our superiors seldom took notice of us; that while others in ease had plentifully heaped up the fruit of our labour, we had received barely enough to relieve nature; and being wholly at the command of others, had generally been treated as a contemptible, ignorant part of mankind; should we, in that case, be less abject than they now are? Again, if oppression be so hard to bear that a wise man is made mad by it, Eccl. 7.7,[2] then a series of oppressions, altering the behaviour and manners of a people is what may reasonably be expected.

When our property is taken contrary to our mind, by means appearing to us unjust, it is only through Divine influence, and the enlargement of heart from thence proceeding, that we can love our reputed oppres-sors. If the negroes fall short in this, an uneasy, if not a disconsolate disposition will be awakened, and remain like seeds in their minds, producing sloth and other habits which appear odious to us; and with which, had they been free men, they would not perhaps have been chargeable. These and other circumstances, rightly considered, will lessen the too great disparity which some make between us and them.

Integrity of heart has appeared in some of them; so that if we continue in the word of Christ, and our conduct towards them be seasoned with his love, we may hope to see the good effect of it. This, in a good degree, is the case with some into whose hands they have fallen; but that too many treat them otherwise, not seeming conscious of any neglect, is, alas! too evident.

When self-love presides in our minds, our opinions are biased in our own favour; and in this condition, being concerned with a people so situated that they have no voice to plead their own cause, there is danger of using ourselves to an undisturbed partiality, until, by long custom, the mind becomes reconciled with it, and the judgment itself infected. ...

"[Christ] hath laid down the best criterion by which mankind ought to judge of their own conduct, and others judge for them of theirs, one towards another,

---

[1] *Gen. 3.20* "And Adam called his wife's name Eve, because she was the mother of all living."

[2] *Eccl. 7.7* "Surely oppression maketh a wise man mad; and a gift destroyeth the heart."

viz.[1] 'Whatsoever ye would that men should do unto you, do ye even so to them.'[2] I take it that all men by nature are equally entitled to the equity of this rule, and under the indispensable obligations of it. One man ought not to look upon another man or society of men as so far beneath him that he should not put himself in their place, in all his actions towards them, and bring all to this test, *viz.* How should I approve of this conduct, were I in their circumstance, and they in mine?"[3]...

It may be objected that there is the cost of purchase, and risk of their lives to them who possess [slaves], and therefore it is needful that they make the best use of their time. In a practice just and reasonable, such objections may have weight; but if the work be wrong from the beginning, there is little or no force in them. If I purchase a man who has never forfeited his liberty, the natural right of freedom is in him; and shall I keep him and his posterity in servitude and ignorance? "How should I approve of this conduct, were I in his circumstances, and he in mine?"...

If we, by the operation of the Spirit of Christ, become heirs with him in the kingdom of his Father and are redeemed from the alluring counterfeit joys of this world, and the joy of Christ remain in us; to suppose that one in this happy condition can, for the sake of earthly riches, not only deprive his fellow-creatures of the sweetness of freedom, which, rightly used, is one of the greatest temporal blessings, but therewith neglect using proper means for their acquaintance with the Holy Scriptures and the advantage of true religion, seems at least a contradiction to reason....

To conclude, it is a great truth most certain that a life guided by wisdom from above, agreeably with justice, equity and mercy, is throughout consistent and amiable, and truly beneficial to society; the serenity and calmness of mind in it affords an unparalleled comfort in this life, and the end of it is blessed.

And it is no less true that they who in the midst of high favours remain ungrateful, and under all the advantages that a Christian can desire are selfish, earthly and sensual, do miss the true fountain of happiness and wander in a maze of dark anxiety, where all their treasures are insufficient to quiet their minds: hence, from an insatiable craving, they neglect doing good with what they have acquired, and too often add oppression to vanity, that they may compass[4] more.

Hannah More, "Slavery: A Poem" (1788)

Hannah More was already a very successful playwright when she became involved with England's circle of prominent abolitionist campaigners. Composed at the request of the Society for the Abolition of the Slave Trade in support of a parliamentary debate on the subject, "Slavery: A Poem" was widely circulated by anti-slavery committees.

If heaven has into being deigned to call
Thy light, O LIBERTY! to shine on all;
Bright intellectual sun! why does thy ray
To earth distribute only partial day?
5   Since no resisting cause from spirit flows
Thy penetrating essence to oppose;
No obstacles by nature's hand imprest,
Thy subtle and ethereal beams arrest;
Nor motion's laws can speed thy active course,
10   Nor strong repulsion's pow'rs obstruct thy force;
Since there is no convexity in MIND,[5]
Why are thy genial beams to parts confined?
While the chill North with thy bright ray is blest,
Why should fell darkness half the South invest?
15   Was it decreed, fair freedom! at thy birth,
That thou should'st ne'er irradiate°   *cast light on*
   all the earth?
While Britain basks in thy full blaze of light,
Why lies sad Afric quenched in total night?
  Thee only, sober Goddess! I attest,
20   In smiles chastised, and decent graces drest.
Not that unlicensed monster of the crowd,
Whose roar terrific bursts in peals so loud,

---

[1] *viz.* Abbreviation of the Latin *videlicet*, meaning "namely," or "that is to say."

[2] *Whatsoever ye ... to them* See Matthew 7.12.

[3] *[Christ] hath ... I in mine?* From Quaker writer Alexander Arscott's treatise *Some Considerations Relating to the Present State of the Christian Religion, Part Third* (1734).

[4] *compass* Attain.

[5] *Since there ... in MIND* Since the realm of thought is not curved like the earth.

Deaf'ning the ear of peace: fierce faction's tool;
Of rash sedition born, and mad misrule;
Whose stubborn mouth, rejecting reason's rein,
No strength can govern, and no skill restrain;
Whose magic cries the frantic vulgar draw
To spurn at order, and to outrage law;
To tread on grave authority and pow'r,
And shake the work of ages in an hour:
Convulsed° her voice, and pestilent her breath,   *Agitated*
She raves of mercy, while she deals out death:
Each blast is fate; she darts from either hand
Red conflagration° o'er th'astonished land;   *inferno*
Clamouring for peace, she rends the air with noise,
And to reform a part, the whole destroys.

   O, plaintive Southerne!¹ whose impassioned strain
So oft has waked my languid Muse in vain!
Now, when congenial° themes her cares engage,   *similar*
She burns to emulate thy glowing page;
Her failing efforts mock her fond° desires,   *foolish*
She shares thy feelings, not partakes thy fires.
Strange pow'r of song! the strain that warms the heart
Seems the same inspiration to impart;
Touched by the kindling energy alone,
We think the flame which melts us is our own;
Deceived, for genius we mistake delight,
Charmed as we read, we fancy we can write.

   Though not to me, sweet bard, thy pow'rs belong
Fair Truth, a hallowed guide! inspires my song.
Here Art would weave her gayest flow'rs in vain,
For Truth the bright invention would disdain.
For no fictitious ills these numbers flow,
But living anguish, and substantial woe;
No individual griefs my bosom melt,
For millions feel what Oronoko felt:
Fired by no single wrongs, the countless host
I mourn, by rapine° dragged from Afric's coast.   *plunder*

   Perish th'illiberal thought which would debase
The native genius of the sable° race!   *dark*
Perish the proud philosophy, which sought
To rob them of the pow'rs of equal thought!
Does then th'immortal principle within

Change with the casual colour of a skin?
65 Does matter govern spirit? or is mind
Degraded by the form to which 'tis joined?
   No: they have heads to think, and hearts to feel,
And souls to act, with firm, though erring, zeal;
For they have keen affections, kind desires,
70 Love strong as death, and active patriot fires;
All the rude energy, the fervid flame,
Of high-souled passion, and ingenuous shame:
Strong, but luxuriant virtues boldly shoot
From the wild vigour of a savage root.

75   Nor weak their sense of honour's proud control,
For pride is virtue in a pagan soul;
A sense of worth, a conscience of desert,°   *deserving praise*
A high, unbroken haughtiness of heart:
That self-same stuff which erst° proud   *once*
   empires swayed,
80 Of which the conquerors of the world were made.
Capricious fate of man! that very pride
In Afric scourged, in Rome was deified.

   No muse, O Quashi!² shall thy deeds relate,
No statue snatch thee from oblivious fate!
85 For thou wast born where never gentle Muse
On valour's grave the flow'rs of genius strews;
And thou wast born where no recording page
Plucks the fair deed from time's devouring rage.
Had fortune placed thee on some happier coast,
90 Where polished souls heroic virtue boast,
To thee, who sought'st a voluntary grave,
Th'uninjured honours of thy name to save,

---

¹ [More's note] Author of the tragedy of Oronoko. [Aphra Behn wrote the original *Oroonoko* (1688), about an African prince who became a British slave, but Thomas Southerne's stage adaptation (1695) was better known.]

² [More's note] It is a point of honour among negroes of high spirit to die rather than to suffer their glossy skin to bear the mark of the whip. Qua-shi had somehow offended his master, a young planter with whom he had been bred up in the endearing intimacy of a play-fellow. His services had been faithful; his attachment affectionate. The master resolved to punish him, and pursued him for that purpose. In trying to escape Qua-shi stumbled and fell; the master fell upon him; they wrestled long with doubtful victory; at length Qua-shi got uppermost, and, being firmly seated on his master's breast, he secured his legs with one hand, and with the other drew a sharp knife; then said, "Master, I have been bred up with you from a child; I have loved you as myself: in return, you have condemned me to a punishment of which I must ever have borne the marks: thus only can I avoid them"; so saying, he drew the knife with all his strength across his own throat, and fell down dead, without a groan, on his master's body. [More cites the source of this story as James Ramsay's *Essay on the Treatment and Conversion of African Slaves in the British Sugar Colonies* (1784).]

Whose generous arm thy barbarous master spared,
Altars had smoked, and temples had been reared.
95   Whene'er to Afric's shores I turn my eyes,
Horrors of deepest, deadliest guilt arise;
I see, by more than fancy's mirror shown,
The burning village, and the blazing town:
See the dire victim torn from social life,
100   The shrieking babe, the agonizing wife!
She, wretch forlorn! is dragged by hostile hands,
To distant tyrants sold, in distant lands!
Transmitted miseries, and successive chains,
The sole sad heritage her child obtains!
105   Ev'n this last wretched boon their foes deny,
To weep together, or together die.
By felon hands, by one relentless stroke,
See the fond links of feeling nature broke!
The fibres twisting round a parent's heart,
110   Torn from their grasp, and bleeding as they part.
      Hold, murderers, hold! not aggravate distress;
Respect the passions you yourselves possess;
Ev'n you, of ruffian heart, and ruthless hand,
Love your own offspring, love your native land.
115   Ah! leave them holy Freedom's cheering smile,
The heav'n-taught fondness for the parent soil;
Revere affections mingled with our frame,
In every nature, every clime the same;
In all, these feelings equal sway maintain;
120   In all the love of HOME and FREEDOM reign:
And Tempe's vale, and parched Angola's[1] sand,
One equal fondness of their sons command.
Th'unconquered savage laughs at pain and toil,
Basking in freedom's beams which gild his native soil.
125   Does thirst of empire, does desire of fame,
(For these are specious crimes) our rage inflame?
No: sordid lust of gold their fate controls,
The basest appetite of basest souls;
Gold, better gained, by what their ripening sky,
130   Their fertile fields, their arts[2] and mines supply.
      What wrongs, what injuries does oppression plead
To smooth the horror of th'unnatural deed?

What strange offence, what aggravated sin?
They stand convicted—of a darker skin!
135   Barbarians, hold! th'opprobious°   *disgraceful*
      commerce spare,
Respect his sacred image which they bear:[3]
Though dark and savage, ignorant and blind,
They claim the common privilege of kind;
Let Malice strip them of each other plea,[4]
140   They still are men, and men should still be free.
Insulted Reason loaths th'inverted trade—[5]
Dire change! the agent is the purchase made!
Perplexed, the baffled Muse involves° the tale;   *confuses*
Nature confounded, well may language fail!
145   The outraged Goddess with abhorrent eyes
Sees MAN the traffic, SOULS the merchandise!
      Plead not, in reason's palpable abuse,
Their sense of feeling callous and obtuse:[6]
From heads to hearts lies nature's plain appeal,
150   Though few can reason, all mankind can feel.
Though wit may boast a livelier dread of shame,
A loftier sense of wrong refinement claim;
Though polished manners may fresh wants invent,
And nice° distinctions nicer souls torment;   *fine*
155   Though these on finer spirits heavier fall,
Yet natural evils are the same to all.
Though wounds there are which reason's force may heal,
There needs no logic sure to make us feel.
The nerve, howe'er untutored, can sustain
160   A sharp, unutterable sense of pain;
As exquisitely fashioned in a slave,
As where unequal fate a sceptre[7] gave.
Sense is as keen where Congo's[8] sons preside,
As where proud Tiber[9] rolls his classic tide.
165   Rhetoric or verse may point the feeling line,

---

[3]   *Respect ... bear*   I.e., respect the fact that they are made in God's image.

[4]   *each other plea*   Every other argument.

[5]   *th'inverted trade*   The opposite trade; the use of white slaves by black people.

[6]   [More's note]   Nothing is more frequent than this cruel and stupid argument, that they do not feel the miseries inflicted on them as Europeans would do.

[7]   *sceptre*   Ornamental rod that is a symbol of royal authority.

[8]   *Congo*   River in Central Africa.

[9]   *Tiber*   River in Italy that passes through Rome.

---

[1]   *Tempe's vale*   River valley in Greece; *Angola*   Portuguese colony in sub-Saharan Africa.

[2]   [More's note]   Besides many valuable productions of the soil, cloths and carpets of exquisite manufacture are brought from the coast of Guinea.

They do not whet° sensation, but define. *sharpen*
Did ever slave less feel the galling° chain, *chafing*
When Zeno[1] proved there was no ill in pain?
Their miseries philosophic quirks deride,
70 Slaves groan in pangs disowned by Stoic pride.
    When the fierce Sun darts vertical his beams,
And thirst and hunger mix their wild extremes;
When the sharp iron[2] wounds his inmost soul,
And his strained eyes in burning anguish roll;
75 Will the parched negro find, ere he expire,
No pain in hunger, and no heat in fire?
    For him, when fate his tortured frame destroys,
What hope of present fame, or future joys?
For this, have heroes shortened nature's date;
80 For that, have martyrs gladly met their fate;
But him, forlorn, no hero's pride sustains,
No martyr's blissful visions soothe his pains;
Sullen, he mingles with his kindred dust,
For he has learned to dread the Christian's trust;
85 To him what mercy can that pow'r display,
Whose servants murder, and whose sons betray?
Savage! thy venial° error I deplore, *excusable*
They are not Christians who infest thy shore.
    O thou sad spirit, whose preposterous yoke
90 The great deliverer death, at length, has broke!
Released from misery, and escaped from care,
Go meet that mercy man denied thee here.
In thy dark home, sure refuge of th'opressed,
The wicked vex not, and the weary rest.
95 And, if some notions, vague and undefined,
Of future terrors have assailed thy mind;
If such thy masters have presumed to teach,
As terrors only they are prone to preach;
(For should they paint eternal mercy's reign,
00 Where were th'oppressor's rod, the captive's chain?)
If, then, thy troubled soul has learned to dread
The dark unknown thy trembling footsteps tread;
On HIM, who made thee what thou art, depend;

HE, who withholds the means, accepts the end.
205 Not thine the reckoning dire of LIGHT abused,
KNOWLEDGE disgraced, and LIBERTY misused;
On thee no awful judge incensed shall sit
For parts perverted, and dishonoured wit.
Where ignorance will be found the surest plea,
210 How many learn'd and wise shall envy thee!
    And thou, WHITE SAVAGE! whether lust of gold,
Or lust of conquest, rule thee uncontrolled!
Hero, or robber!—by whatever name
Thou plead thy impious claim to wealth or fame;
215 Whether inferior mischiefs be thy boast,
A petty tyrant rifling Gambia's coast:
Or bolder carnage track thy crimson way,
Kings dispossessed, and provinces thy prey;
Panting to tame wide earth's remotest bound;
220 All Cortez[3] murdered, all Columbus found;
O'er plundered realms to reign, detested Lord,
Make millions wretched, and thyself abhorred;——
In reason's eye, in wisdom's fair account,
Your sum of glory boasts a like amount;
225 The means may differ, but the end's the same;
Conquest is pillage with a nobler name.
Who makes the sum of human blessings less,
Or sinks the stock of general happiness,
No solid fame shall grace, no true renown,
230 His life shall blazon,° or his memory crown. *adorn*
    Had those advent'rous spirits who explore
Through ocean's trackless wastes, the far-sought shore;
Whether of wealth insatiate,° or of pow'r, *endlessly greedy*
Conquerors who waste, or ruffians who devour:
235 Had these possessed, O COOK![4] thy gentle mind,
Thy love of arts, thy love of humankind;
Had these pursued thy mild and liberal plan,
DISCOVERERS had not been a curse to man!
Then, blessed philanthropy! thy social hands
240 Had linked dissevered° worlds in brothers' *divided*
    bands;
Careless, if colour, or if clime° divide; *climate*

---

[1] *Zeno* Zeno of Citum (334 BCE–262 BCE), founder of Stoicism, a philosophy asserting that a wise person can be happy under any circumstances.

[2] [More's note] This is not said figuratively. The writer of these lines has seen a complete set of chains, fitted to every separate limb of these unhappy, innocent men; together with instruments for wrenching open the jaws, contrived with such cruelty as would shock the humanity of an inquisitor.

---

[3] *Cortez* Hérnan Cortés (1485–1547), a Spanish Conquistador whose expedition to Mexico resulted in the fall of the Aztec Empire.

[4] *COOK* Captain James Cook (1728–79), British explorer and cartographer who mapped many places that were previously unknown to or uncharted by Europeans. Although his discoveries prompted further colonization, Cook himself was friendly and sympathetic toward the indigenous peoples of all the places he visited.

Then, loved, and loving, man had lived, and died.
    The purest wreaths which hang on glory's shrine,
For empires founded, peaceful PENN![1] are thine;
245 No blood-stained laurels[2] crowned thy virtuous toil,
No slaughtered natives drenched thy fair-earned soil.
Still thy meek spirit in thy flock[3] survives,
Consistent still, *their* doctrines rule their lives;
Thy followers only have effaced the shame
250 Inscribed by SLAVERY on the Christian name.
    Shall Britain, where the soul of freedom reigns,
Forge chains for others she herself disdains?
Forbid it, Heaven! O let the nations know
The liberty she loves she will bestow;
255 Not to herself the glorious gift confined,
She spreads the blessing wide as humankind;
And, scorning narrow views of time and place,
Bids all be free in earth's extended space.
    What page of human annals can record
260 A deed so bright as human rights restored?
O may that god-like deed, that shining page,
Redeem OUR fame, and consecrate OUR age!
    And see, the cherub° Mercy from above,   *angel*
Descending softly, quits the sphere of love!
265 On feeling hearts she sheds celestial dew,
And breathes her spirit o'er th'enlightened few;
From soul to soul the spreading influence steals,
Till every breast the soft contagion feels.
She bears, exulting, to the burning shore
270 The loveliest office angel ever bore;
To vindicate the pow'r in Heaven adored,
To still the clank of chains, and sheathe the sword;
To cheer the mourner, and with soothing hands
From bursting hearts unbind th'oppressor's bands;
275 To raise the lustre of the Christian name,
And clear the foulest blot° that dims its fame.   *stain*
    As the mild Spirit hovers o'er the coast,
A fresher hue the withered landscapes boast;
Her healing smiles the ruined scenes repair,

---

[1] *PENN* William Penn (1644–1718), an influential Quaker and the founder of Pennsylvania, attempted to live peacefully with the Lenape, its aboriginal inhabitants.

[2] *laurels* Victories; accomplishments. Crowns made of leaves of the bay laurel were awarded in ancient Greece as a symbol of victory or poetic achievement.

[3] [More's note] The Quakers have emancipated all their slaves throughout America.

280 And blasted Nature wears a joyous air.
She spreads her blest commission from above,
Stamped with the sacred characters of love;
She tears the banner stained with blood and tears,
And, LIBERTY! thy shining standard rears!
285 As the bright ensign's° glory she displays,   *flag's*
See pale OPPRESSION faints beneath the blaze!
The giant dies! no more his frown appalls,
The chain untouched, drops off; the fetter° falls.   *shackle*
Astonished echo tells the vocal shore,
290 Opression's fall'n, and slavery is no more!
The dusky myriads° crowd the sultry[4] plain,   *multitudes*
And hail that mercy long invoked in vain.
Victorious pow'r! she bursts their two-fold bands,
And FAITH and FREEDOM spring from Mercy's
    hands.

Ann Yearsley, "A Poem on the Inhumanity of the Slave-Trade" (1788)

Ann Yearsley, a laboring-class milkwoman, was saved from near-destitution when Hannah More discovered her poetic abilities and became her patron. By the time Yearsley and More wrote their major abolitionist poems, both of which were published in the same year, the friendship had ended over disagreements as to how Yearsley's profits should be managed.

Bristol,[5] thine heart hath throbbed to glory.—Slaves,
E'en Christian slaves, have shook their chains, and
    gazed
With wonder and amazement on thee. Hence
Ye grov'ling souls, who think the term I give,
5 Of Christian slave, a paradox! to *you*
I do not turn, but leave you to conception
Narrow; with that be blest, nor dare to stretch
Your shackled souls along the course of Freedom.
    Yet, Bristol, list!° nor deem Lactilla's[6] soul   *listen*

---

[4] *sultry* Hot and humid, i.e., from hot work.

[5] *Bristol* A major port for marine trade and Yearsley's hometown; Bristol experienced great economic growth as a result of slavery.

[6] *Lactilla* Yearsley often refers to herself by this name, a reference to her work as a milkwoman.

Lessened by distance; snatch her rustic thought,
Her crude ideas, from their panting state,
And let them fly in wide expansion; lend
Thine energy, so little understood
By the rude million, and I'll dare the strain
Of Heav'n-born Liberty till Nature moves
Obedient to her voice. Alas! my friend,
Strong rapture dies within the soul, while Pow'r
Drags on his bleeding victims. Custom,[1] Law,
Ye blessings, and ye curses of mankind,
What evils do ye cause? We feel enslaved,
Yet move in your direction. Custom, thou
Wilt preach up filial piety; thy sons
Will groan, and stare with impudence at Heav'n,
As if they did abjure° the act, where Sin   renounce
Sits full on Inhumanity; the church
They fill with mouthing, vap'rous sighs and tears,
Which, like the guileful crocodile's,[2] oft fall,
Nor fall, but at the cost of human bliss.

Custom, thou hast undone us! led us far
From God-like probity,° from truth,   moral integrity
                and heaven.

But come, ye souls who feel for human woe,
Though dressed in savage guise! Approach, thou son,
Whose heart would shudder at a father's chains,
And melt o'er thy loved brother as he lies
Gasping in torment undeserved. Oh, sight
Horrid and insupportable! far worse
Than an immediate, an heroic death;
Yet to this sight I summon thee. Approach,
Thou slave of avarice, that canst see the maid
Weep o'er her inky sire! Spare me, thou God
Of all-indulgent Mercy, if I scorn
This gloomy wretch, and turn my tearful eye
To more enlightened beings. Yes, my tear
Shall hang on the green furze,[3] like pearly dew
Upon the blossom of the morn. My song
Shall teach sad Philomel[4] a louder note,

When Nature swells her woe. O'er suff'ring man
My soul with sorrow bends! Then come, ye few
Who feel a more than cold, material essence;
Here ye may vent your sighs, till the bleak North
Find its adherents aided.—Ah, no more!
The dingy youth comes on, sullen in chains;
He smiles on the rough sailor, who aloud
Strikes at the spacious heav'n, the earth, the sea,
In breath too blasphemous; yet not to him
Blasphemous, for he dreads not either:—lost
In dear internal imagery, the soul
Of Indian Luco[5] rises to his eyes,
Silent, not inexpressive: the strong beams
With eager wildness yet drink in the view
Of his too humble home, where he had left
His mourning father, and his Incilanda.

Curse on the toils spread by a Christian hand
To rob the Indian of his freedom! Curse
On him who from a bending parent steals
His dear support of age, his darling child;
Perhaps a son, or a more tender daughter,
Who might have closed his eyelids, as the spark
Of life gently retired. Oh, thou poor world!
Thou fleeting good to individuals! see
How much for thee they care, how wide they ope
Their helpless arms to clasp thee; vapour thou!
More swift than passing wind! thou leav'st them nought
Amid th'unreal scene, but a scant grave.

I know the crafty merchant will oppose
The plea of nature to my strain, and urge
His toils are for his children: the soft plea
Dissolves my soul—but when I sell a son,
Thou God of nature, let it be my own!

Behold that Christian! see what horrid joy
Lights up his moody features, while he grasps
The wished-for gold, purchase of human blood!
Away, thou seller of mankind! Bring on
Thy daughter to this market! bring thy wife!
Thine aged mother, though of little worth,
With all thy ruddy boys! Sell them, thou wretch,

---

[1] *Custom* Tradition; practices dictated by cultural habit.

[2] *crocodile* It was said that crocodiles cry as they devour their prey.

[3] *furze* Gorse, a prickly shrub.

[4] *Philomel* In Greek mythology, Philomela was raped by King Tereus and swore to tell the world of the injustice done to her. In some versions, the gods turned her into a nightingale (a bird known for its mournful song).

[5] *Indian Luco* Luco appears at times to be of African, and at others to be of Caribbean origin; such ambiguous portrayals of Africans and New World aboriginals were not uncommon in the eighteenth century.

And swell the price of Luco![1] Why that start?
Why gaze as thou wouldst fright me from my challenge
With look of anguish? Is it Nature strains
90 Thine heart-strings at the image? Yes, my charge
Is full against her, and she rends thy soul,
While I but strike upon thy pitiless ear,
Fearing her rights are violated.—Speak,
Astound the voice of Justice! bid thy tears
95 Melt the unpitying pow'r, while thus she claims
The pledges of thy love. Oh, throw thine arm
Around thy little ones, and loudly plead
Thou canst not sell thy children.—Yet, beware
Lest Luco's groan be heard; should that prevail,
100 Justice will scorn thee in her turn, and hold
Thine act against thy prayer. Why clasp, she cries,
That blooming youth? Is it because thou lov'st him?
Why Luco was belov'd: then wilt thou feel,
Thou selfish Christian, for thy private woe,
105 Yet cause such pangs to him that is a father?
Whence comes thy right to barter for thy fellows?
Where are thy statutes? Whose the iron pen
That gave thee precedent? Give me the seal
Of virtue, or religion, for thy trade,
110 And I will ne'er upbraid thee; but if force
Superior, hard brutality alone
Become thy boast, hence to some savage haunt,
Nor claim protection from my social laws.
        Luco is gone; his little brothers weep,
115 While his fond mother climbs the hoary° rock   *ancient*
Whose point o'er-hangs the main.° No Luco there,   *sea*
No sound, save the hoarse billows.° On she roves,   *waves*
With love, fear, hope, holding alternate rage
In her too anxious bosom. Dreary main!
120 Thy murmurs now are riot, while she stands
List'ning to ev'ry breeze, waiting the step
Of gentle Luco. Ah, return! return!
Too hapless mother, thy indulgent arms
Shall never clasp thy fettered Luco more.
125 See Incilanda! artless maid, my soul
Keeps pace with thee, and mourns. Now o'er the hill
She creeps, with timid foot, while Sol[2] embrowns
The bosom of the isle, to where she left

Her faithful lover: here the well-known cave,
130 By nature formed amid the rock, endears
The image of her Luco; here his pipe,
Formed of the polished cane,° neglected lies,   *plant stem*
No more to vibrate;° here the useless dart,   *produce sound*
The twanging bow, and the fierce panther's skin,
135 Salute the virgin's eye. But where is Luco?
He comes not down the steep, though he had vowed,
When the sun's beams at noon should sidelong gild
The cave's wide entrance, he would swift descend
To bless his Incilanda. Ten pale moons
140 Had glided by, since to his generous breast
He clasped the tender maid, and whispered love.
Oh, mutual sentiment! thou dang'rous bliss!
So exquisite, that Heav'n had been unjust
Had it bestowed less exquisite of ill;
145 When thou art held no more, thy pangs are deep,
Thy joys convulsive to the soul; yet all
Are meant to smooth th'uneven road of life.
        For Incilanda, Luco ranged the wild,
Holding her image to his panting heart;
150 For her he strained the bow, for her he stripped
The bird of beauteous plumage; happy hour,
When with these guiltless trophies he adorned
The brow of her he loved. Her gentle breast
With gratitude was filled, nor knew she aught
155 Of language strong enough to paint her soul,
Or ease the great emotion; whilst her eye
Pursued the gen'rous Luco to the field,
And glowed with rapture at his wished return.
        Ah, sweet suspense! betwixt the mingled cares
160 Of friendship, love, and gratitude, so mixed,
That ev'n the soul may cheat herself.—Down, down,
Intruding Memory! bid thy struggles cease,
At this soft scene of innate war. What sounds
Break on her ear? She, starting, whispers "Luco."
165 Be still, fond maid; list to the tardy step
Of leaden-footed woe. A father comes,
But not to seek his son, who from the deck
Had breathed a last adieu: no, he shuts out
The soft, fallacious gleam of hope, and turns
170 Within upon the mind: horrid and dark
Are his wild, unenlightened pow'rs: no ray
Of forced philosophy to calm his soul,
But all the anarchy of wounded nature.

---

[1] *swell the … of Luco* I.e., profit even more than you would have
by selling Luco alone.

[2] *Sol* In Roman mythology, the god of the sun.

Now he arraigns his country's gods, who sit,
In his bright fancy, far beyond the hills,
Unriveting the chains of slaves: his heart
Beats quick with stubborn fury, while he doubts
Their justice to his child. Weeping old man,
Hate not a Christian's God, whose record holds
Thine injured Luco's name. Frighted he starts,
Blasphemes the Deity, whose altars rise
Upon the Indian's helpless neck, and sinks,
Despising comfort, till by grief and age
His angry spirit is forced out. Oh, guide,
Ye angel-forms, this joyless shade to worlds
Where the poor Indian, with the sage, is proved
The work of a Creator. Pause not here,
Distracted maid! ah, leave the breathless form,
On whose cold cheek thy tears so swiftly fall,
Too unavailing! On this stone, she cries,
My Luco sat, and to the wand'ring stars
Pointed my eye, while from his gentle tongue
Fell old traditions of his country's woe.
Where now shall Incilanda seek him? Hence,
Defenceless mourner, ere the dreary night
Wrap thee in added horror. Oh, Despair,
How eagerly thou rend'st the heart! She pines
In anguish deep, and sullen: Luco's form
Pursues her, lives in restless thought, and chides
Soft consolation. Banished from his arms,
She seeks the cold embrace of death; her soul
Escapes in one sad sigh. Too hapless° maid!   *unfortunate*
Yet happier far than he thou lov'dst; his tear,
His sigh, his groan avail not, for they plead
Most weakly with a Christian. Sink, thou wretch,
Whose act shall on the cheek of Albion's° sons   *England's*
Throw Shame's red blush: thou, who hast
      frighted° far   *scared away*
Those simple wretches from thy God, and taught
Their erring minds to mourn his partial love,[1]
Profusely poured on thee, while they are left
Neglected to thy mercy. Thus deceived,
How doubly dark must be their road to death!
      Luco is borne around the neighb'ring isles,

Losing the knowledge of his native shore
Amid the pathless wave; destined to plant
The sweet luxuriant cane.° He strives to please,   *sugarcane*
Nor once complains, but greatly° smothers grief.   *nobly*
His hands are blistered, and his feet are worn,
Till ev'ry stroke dealt by his mattock[2] gives
Keen agony to life; while from his breast
The sigh arises, burdened with the name
Of Incilanda. Time inures the youth,
His limbs grow nervous, strained by willing toil;
And resignation, or a calm despair,
(Most useful either) lulls him to repose.
      A Christian renegade, that from his soul
Abjures the tenets of our schools, nor dreads
A future punishment, nor hopes for mercy,
Had fled from England, to avoid those laws
Which must have made his life a retribution
To violated justice, and had gained,
By fawning guile, the confidence (ill placed)
Of Luco's master. O'er the slave he stands
With knotted whip, lest fainting nature shun
The task too arduous, while his cruel soul,
Unnat'ral, ever feeds, with gross delight,
Upon his suff'rings. Many slaves there were,
But none who could suppress the sigh, and bend,
So quietly as Luco: long he bore
The stripes, that from his manly bosom drew
The sanguine° stream (too little prized);   *bloody*
      at length
Hope fled his soul, giving her struggles o'er,
And he resolved to die. The sun had reached
His zenith—pausing faintly, Luco stood,
Leaning upon his hoe, while mem'ry brought,
In piteous imag'ry, his aged father,
His poor fond mother, and his faithful maid:
The mental group in wildest motion set
Fruitless imagination; fury, grief,
Alternate shame, the sense of insult, all
Conspire to aid the inward storm; yet words
Were no relief, he stood in silent woe.
      Gorgon, remorseless Christian, saw the slave
Stand musing, 'mid the ranks, and, stealing soft
Behind the studious Luco, struck his cheek

---

1 [Yearsley's note] Indians have been often heard to say, in their
complaining moments, "God Almighty no love us well; he be good
to buckera [white people]; he bid buckera burn us; he no burn
buckera."

2 *mattock* Tool for digging.

With a too-heavy whip, that reached his eye,
Making it dark forever. Luco turned,
In strongest agony, and with his hoe
Struck the rude Christian on the forehead. Pride,
260 With hateful malice, seize on Gorgon's soul,
By nature fierce; while Luco sought the beach,
And plunged beneath the wave; but near him lay
A planter's barge, whose seamen grasped his hair
Dragging to life a wretch who wished to die.
265   Rumour now spreads the tale, while Gorgon's breath
Envenomed, aids her blast: imputed crimes
Oppose the plea of Luco, till he scorns
Even a just defence, and stands prepared.
The planters, conscious that to fear alone
270 They owe their cruel pow'r, resolve to blend
New torment with the pangs of death, and hold
Their victims high in dreadful view, to fright
The wretched number left. Luco is chained
To a huge tree, his fellow-slaves are ranged
275 To share the horrid sight; fuel is placed
In an increasing train, some paces back,
To kindle slowly, and approach the youth,
With more than native terror. See, it burns!
He gazes on the growing flame, and calls
280 For "water, water!" The small boon's denied.
E'en Christians throng each other, to behold
The different alterations of his face,
As the hot death approaches. (Oh, shame, shame
Upon the followers of Jesus! shame
285 On him that dares avow a God!) He writhes,
While down his breast glide the unpitied tears,
And in their sockets strain their scorched balls.
"Burn, burn me quick! I cannot die!" he cries:
"Bring fire more close!" The planters heed him not,
290 But still prolonging Luco's torture, threat°   *threaten*
Their trembling slaves around. His lips are dry,
His senses seem to quiver, ere they quit
His frame for ever, rallying strong, then driv'n
From the tremendous conflict. Sight no more
295 Is Luco's, his parched tongue is ever mute;
Yet in his soul his Incilanda stays,
Till both escape together. Turn, my muse,
From this sad scene; lead Bristol's milder soul
To where the solitary spirit roves,
300 Wrapt in the robe of innocence, to shades

Where pity breathing in the gale, dissolves
The mind, when fancy paints such real woe.
    Now speak, ye Christians (who for gain enslave
A soul like Luco's, tearing her[1] from joy
305 In life's short vale; and if there be a hell,
As ye believe, to that ye thrust her down,
A blind, involuntary victim), where
Is your true essence of religion? where
Your proofs of righteousness, when ye conceal
310 The knowledge of the deity from those
Who would adore him fervently? Your God
Ye rob of worshippers, his altars keep
Unhailed, while driving from the sacred font[2]
The eager slave, lest he should hope in Jesus.
315 Is this your piety? Are these your laws,
Whereby the glory of the Godhead spreads
O'er barb'rous climes? Ye hypocrites, disown
The Christian name, nor shame its cause: yet where
Shall souls like yours find welcome? Would the Turk,
320 Pagan, or wildest Arab, ope their arms
To gain such proselytes?° No; he that owns   *converts*
The name of Mussulman° would start, and shun   *Muslim*
Your worse than serpent touch; he frees his slave
Who turns to Mahomet.[3] The Spaniard[4] stands
325 Your brighter contrast; he condemns the youth
Forever to the mine; but ere the wretch
Sinks to the deep domain, the hand of faith
Bathes his faint temples in the sacred stream,
Bidding his spirit hope. Briton, dost thou
330 Act up to this? If so, bring on thy slaves
To Calv'ry's mount,[5] raise high their kindred souls
To him who died to save them: this alone
Will teach them calmly to obey thy rage,
And deem a life of misery but a day,
335 To long eternity. Ah, think how soon
Thine head shall on earth's dreary pillow lie,
With thy poor slaves, each silent, and unknown

---

1 *her* I.e., the soul.

2 *sacred font* Bowl of water for baptism.

3 [Yearsley's note] The Turk gives freedom to his slave on condition that he embraces Mahometism [Islam].

4 [Yearsley's note] The Spaniard, immediately on purchasing an Indian, gives him baptism.

5 *Calv'ry's mount* Mount Calvary is where Christ was crucified (See Luke 23.33).

To his once furious neighbour. Think how swift
The sands of time ebb out, for him and thee.
40 Why groans that Indian youth, in burning chains
Suspended o'er the beach? The lab'ring sun
Strikes from his full meridian° on the slave   *height*
Whose arms are blistered by the heated iron,
Which still corroding, seeks the bone. What crime
45 Merits so dire a death?[1] Another gasps
With strongest agony, while life declines
From recent amputation. Gracious God!
Why thus in mercy let thy whirlwinds sleep
O'er a vile race of Christians, who profane
50 Thy glorious attributes? Sweep them from earth,
Or check their cruel pow'r: the savage tribes
Are angels when compared to brutes like these.

    Advance, ye Christians, and oppose my strain:
Who dares condemn it? Prove from laws divine,
5 From deep philosophy, or social love,
That ye derive your privilege. I scorn
The cry of Av'rice, or the trade that drains
A fellow-creature's blood: bid Commerce plead
Her public good, her nation's many wants,
0 Her sons thrown idly on the beach, forbade
To seize the image of their God and sell it:[2]—
I'll hear her voice, and Virtue's hundred tongues
Shall sound against her. Hath our public good
Fell rapine° for its basis? Must our wants   *barbarous plunder*
5 Find their supply in murder? Shall the sons
Of Commerce shiv'ring stand, if not employed
Worse than the midnight robber? Curses fall

On the destructive system that shall need
Such base supports! Doth England need them? No;
370 Her laws, with prudence, hang the meagre thief
That from his neighbour steals a slender sum,
Though famine drove him on. O'er him the priest,
Beneath the fatal tree, laments the crime,
Approves the law, and bids him calmly die.
375 Say, doth this law, that dooms the thief, protect
The wretch who makes another's life his prey,
By hellish force to take it at his will?
Is this an English law, whose guidance fails
When crimes are swelled to magnitude so vast,
380 That Justice dare not scan them? Or does Law
Bid Justice an eternal distance keep
From England's great tribunal, when the slave
Calls loud on Justice only? Speak, ye few
Who fill Britannia's senate, and are deemed
385 The fathers of your country! Boast your laws,
Defend the honour of a land so fall'n,
That Fame from ev'ry battlement is flown,
And Heathens start, e'en at a Christian's name.

    Hail, social love! true soul of order, hail!
390 Thy softest emanations, pity, grief,
Lively emotion, sudden joy, and pangs,
Too deep for language, are thy own: then rise,
Thou gentle angel! spread thy silken wings
O'er drowsy man, breathe in his soul, and give
395 Her God-like pow'rs thy animating force,
To banish Inhumanity. Oh, loose
The fetters of his mind, enlarge his views,
Break down for him the bound° of avarice, lift   *limit*
His feeble faculties beyond a world
400 To which he soon must prove a stranger! Spread
Before his ravished eye the varied tints
Of future glory; bid them live to Fame,
Whose banners wave forever. Thus inspired,
All that is great, and good, and sweetly mild,
405 Shall fill his noble bosom. He shall melt,
Yea, by thy sympathy unseen, shall feel
Another's pang: for the lamenting maid
His heart shall heave a sigh; with the old slave
(Whose head is bent with sorrow) he shall cast
410 His eye back on the joys of youth, and say,
"Thou once couldst feel, as I do, love's pure bliss;
Parental fondness, and the dear returns

---

[1] [Yearsley's note] A Coromantin slave in Jamaica (who had frequently escaped to the mountains) was, a few years since, doomed to have his leg cut off. A young practitioner from England (after the surgeon of the estate had refused to be an executioner) undertook the operation, but after the removal of the limb, on the slave's exclaiming, "You buckera! God Almighty made dat leg; you cut it off! You put it on again?" was so shocked that the other surgeon was obliged to take up [close] the [blood] vessels, apply the dressings, &c. The Negro suffered without a groan, called for his pipe, and calmly smoked, till the absence of his attendant gave him an opportunity of tearing off his bandages, when he bled to death in an instant.
    Many will call this act of the Negro's stubbornness; under such circumstances, I dare give it a more glorious epithet, and that is *fortitude*. [Coromantins, from the Gold Coast, were often mentioned in anti-slavery writings as exemplars of defiant courage.]

[2] *Her sons … sell it* Commerce's complaint is that the slave traders will be unemployed if they are unable to sell people.

Of filial tenderness were thine, till torn
From the dissolving scene."——Oh, social love,
415 Thou universal good, thou that canst fill
The vacuum of immensity, and live
In endless void! thou that in motion first
Set'st the long lazy atoms,° by thy force   *particles*
Quickly assimilating, and restrained
420 By strong attraction; touch the soul of man;
Subdue him; make a fellow-creature's woe
His own by heart-felt sympathy, whilst wealth
Is made subservient to his soft disease.
    And when thou hast to high perfection wrought
425 This mighty work, say, "such is Bristol's soul."

Immigration to America

from William Moraley, *The Infortunate: The Voyage and Adventures of William Moraley, an Indentured Servant* (1743)

About half of the Europeans who came in search of
opportunity in the British colonies of North
America were indentured servants, people who sold
their freedom and their labor for a term of years in
exchange for the cost of travel to the New World.
One of these was William Moraley, who chose to
immigrate after his father's death left him impoverished. Although his decision to write an
autobiography was atypical of someone of his class,
Moraley—an individual without extensive family
ties, not wholly destitute but without promising
employment—was in other ways typical of the
migrants who left England's urban centers in the
eighteenth century. It was also a common experience
(and became even more so in the nineteenth
century) for migrants to America to return to Britain
after a few years, sometimes with their fortunes
made but frequently in disappointment. Still others,
even more unfortunate than Moraley, never
managed to save enough for passage home.

… [N]ot caring what became of me, it entered my
head to leave England and sell myself for a term of years
into the American plantations. Accordingly I repaired to
the Royal Exchange, to inform myself, by the printed
advertisements fixed against the walls, of the ships
bound to America; where musing by myself, a man
accosted me in the following manner. "Sir," said he, "I
have for some time observed you, and fancy your
condition of life is altered for the worse, and guess you
have been in better circumstances; but if you will take
my advice, I'll make it my business to find out some way
which may be of service to you. Perhaps you may
imagine I have a design to inveigle[1] you, but I assure
you I have none; and if you will accept a mug of beer, I
will impart what I have to propose to you." The man
appearing sincere, I gave ear to him.

    I was dressed at that time in a very odd manner. I
had on a red rug coat[2] with black lining, black buttons
and button holes, and black lace upon the pockets and
facing; an old worn out tie wig,[3] which had not been
combed out for above a fortnight;[4] an unshaven beard;
a torn shirt that had not been washed for above a
month; bad shoes; and stockings all full of holes.

    After he had shaved me, he proposed to me an
American voyage, and said there was a ship at Limehouse dock that would sail for Pennsylvania in three or
four days. "Sir," said I, "a person like me, oppressed by
Dame Fortune, need not care where he goes. All places
are alike to me; and I am very willing to accept of your
offer, if I could have some view of bettering my
condition of life, though I might have expected a better
fate than to be forced to leave my native country. But
adverse fortune is become familiar to me, by a series of
misfortunes; so had rather leave a place where I have no
prospect of advancing myself, than to continue here
where I have no friends to relieve me. Besides, in a
distant place, not being known, no person can reflect on
me for any ill management, which oftentimes discour-
ages one's friends from supporting one, knowing the ill
use that is made of their support."

    "Sir," says the person, "I'm entirely of your way of
thinking, and believe you will better yourself by
following my advice. I will recommend you to the
captain, who is bound for Philadelphia, in Pennsylvania,

---

[1] *inveigle* Deceitfully persuade.

[2] *rug coat* Coat made of coarse wool.

[3] *tie wig* Wig tied in the back with ribbon.

[4] *fortnight* Two weeks.

a country producing everything necessary for the support of life; and when your time is expired, you will be free to live in any of the Provinces of America."

Then he asked me, if I was bred to any business. I told him watchmaking was my occupation. He said he was afraid I would not do for any other business, that being of little service to the Americans; the useful trades being bricklayers, shoemakers, barbers, carpenters, joiners, smiths, weavers, bakers, tanners, and husband-men[1] more useful than all the rest. They bind themselves for four years; but if I would consent to bind myself for five, he said he would undertake to get me admitted. Those men brokers have generally for their pains three half crowns, given them by the masters of those vessels which they are employed for.

After we had drank two pints of beer, he paid the reckoning.[2] I absolutely agreed to go, and to that intent we went before Sir Robert Bailis, Lord Mayor, where I was sworn as not being a married person or an apprentice by indenture. He paid for my oath one shilling, a perquisite of[3] his clerk. From thence we went to London Bridge, to a stationer's shop, and there an Indenture of Servitude was drawn, which I signed. After this we took boat at Billingsgate, steered our course for Limehouse, where we arrived about eleven o'clock in the forenoon. The ship was named the *Bonetta*, of about 200 tons. ...

I observed several of my brother adventurers seemed very dejected, from whence I guessed they repented of their rashness. Soon after, dinner was brought on the table, which consisted of stewed mutton chops. I was very glad I had an opportunity of trying the temper of my tusks,[4] for I had not eaten meat for four days. I ate very heartily and washed down the mutton with about two quarts of small beer.[5] I began to think myself happy, being in a way to eat; and on this account became insensible of the condition I had brought myself to. In the afternoon, the master and mate being absent, I ventured into the cabin and, peeping into a chest, discovered a large quantity of raisins, of which I made

free with about two pound, and pocketed them for my own use. Besides, the small beer stood upon deck and was free of us at all times, so that laying all reflections aside, I comforted myself with the hopes of living well all the voyage, but was soon made sensible to the contrary when we set out to sea.

[On the voyage]

...[W]e were stinted in our allowance, being joined together in messes: five to each mess. Three biscuits were given to each man for the day, and a small piece of salt beef no bigger than a penny chop of mutton. Some days we had stockfish,[6] when every man was obliged to beat his share with a maul[7] to make it tender, with a little stinking butter for sauce.

Every morning and evening a captain called every one of us to the cabin door, where we received a thimble full of bad brandy. We were obliged to turn out every four hours, with the sailors, to watch; which was to prevent our falling sick by herding under deck.

In our voyage we observed little worth taking notice of till we were in latitude 33, when the sun was intensely hot, which so parched our bodies, having but a scanty allowance of water, not above three quarts to each mess. We attempted to drink the salt water, but it increased our thirst. Sometimes, but rarely, it rained, when we set our hats upon deck to catch the water; but it sliding down the sails gave it the taste of tar. ...

[In Pennsylvania]

My master employed me in his business: I continued satisfied with him for sometime; but being desirous to settle at Philadelphia during the rest of my servitude, I declared to him, I would stay no longer and desired him to dispose of me to some other master. ... This demand made him cross to me, and I attempted an escape, but was taken and put into prison; but was soon released, with a promise to satisfy my demand. About a fortnight after, we went to the Mayor of Philadelphia—his name was Griffith, a man of exact justice, though an Irishman —who reconciled us; so I returned back to Burlington,

---

[1] *husbandmen* Farmers.

[2] *reckoning* Cost.

[3] *perquisite of* Gratuity for.

[4] *temper of my tusks* I.e., condition of my teeth.

[5] *small beer* Thin beer containing little alcohol.

[6] *stockfish* Air dried, unsalted fish.

[7] *maul* Hammer.

and continued with him three years, he forgiving me the other two: I was ever after perfectly pleased with my master's behaviour to me, which was generous. ...

The condition of bought servants is very hard, notwithstanding their indentures are made in England, wherein it is expressly stipulated that they shall have at their arrival all the necessaries specified in those indentures to be given them by their future masters, such as clothes, meat, and drink. Yet upon complaint made to a magistrate against the master for nonperformance, the master is generally heard before the servant, and it is ten to one if he does not get his licks for his pains, as I have experienced upon the like occasion, to my cost.

If they endeavour to escape, which is next to impossible, there being a reward for taking up any person who travels without a pass, which is extended all over the British Colonies, their masters immediately issue out a reward for the apprehending them, from thirty shillings to five pound, as they think proper, and this generally brings them back again. Printed and written advertisements are also set up against the trees and public places in the town, besides those in the newspapers. Notwithstanding these difficulties, they are perpetually running away, but seldom escape, for a hot pursuit being made brings them back, when a justice settles the expenses, and the servant is obliged to serve a longer time. ...

At last ... the time of my servitude expired, and I became free. 'Tis impossible to express the satisfaction I found at being released from the precarious humour and dependence of my master. He accoutered[1] me in an indifferent manner, and gave me my discharge to find out a new way of living. I then went to Philadelphia and served one Edmund Lewis, a brisk young clock-maker; but he being unsettled, and of a roving temper (like master, like man!), I left him, and lived with Mr. Graham, a watch-maker, newly arrived, and nephew to the famous Mr. Graham in Fleet Street.[2] With him I continued ten weeks at ten shillings per week wages, and my board found me;[3] but he designing to settle at Antigua,[4] I left him.

Then I roamed about like a Roving Tartar[5] for the convenience of grazing, and for three weeks had no abiding place. In the nights I was forced to skulk about the extremity of the town, where I lay in a hayloft. ...

But this life not being likely to last long, ... I set my wits to work how to get home. But not presently hearing of a ship bound for England, I was reduced to such extremity that I looked like a picture of bad luck, and so thin that you might have seen my ribs through my skin, and I was greatly afraid of a consumption.[6] However, having some acquaintance in the country, I went about cleaning clocks and watches, and followed the occupation of a tinker; but not being well versed in that trade, where I mended one hole I was sure to make another. ...

I now began to be heartily tired with these ramblings, and endeavoured to make friends with masters of ships in order to get my passage. One morning, as I was forging a horseshoe, a grave Quaker, one Thomas Wetheril of Workington in Cumberland, told me he found the business I followed would do little for me, and advised me to return home, where he heard I had considerable relations. He said he had recommended me to Capt. Peel, whose ship then lay at the key and would sail in about five weeks.

I, who had before resolved to embrace the first opportunity that offered, readily entered into his measures, immediately left the horse shoe unfinished and went to the ship.

from Lady Lucan, "On the Present State of Ireland" (1768)

The British were highly alarmed by the numbers of migrants leaving Ireland in the late seventeenth and eighteenth centuries. The causes of emigration were apparent to English poet Margaret Bingham, Count-

---

1   *accoutered*   Equipped.

2   *famous ... Fleet Street*   George Graham (1675–1751), accomplished London clock-maker and inventor.

3   *my board found me*   My food and lodging provided to me.

4   *Antigua*   Island in the Caribbean.

5   *Roving Tartar*   Desert nomad.

6   *consumption*   Lung infection.

ess of Lucan, who observed firsthand the widespread poverty that weighed on the nation. While a series of climate-induced famines exacerbated the suffering of the poor, political mismanagement by the English government was a much larger problem. Legislation prevented the advancement of Ireland's industry while allowing England to exploit its resources, and absentee landlords living in England charged unreasonable rents to their poor tenants, drawing large amounts of money out of the Irish economy. The poorest Irish people were generally not, however, the ones to migrate; most of those who could afford to leave were the relatively well-off Scotch-Irish, who exerted strong cultural influence in colonial America, especially in the Appalachian region. The Irish poor would emigrate in vast numbers later on, prompted by the Great Famine of the nineteenth century.

See! with what pale and mournful look appears,
England! Thy faithful sister drowned in tears.
Thus wronged Hibernia° sues to Britain's throne: *Ireland*
Where is thy justice, where thy wisdom flown?
5 In me a suff'ring, loyal, people see,
Harassed and torn, by wanton tyranny.
Hear this, ye great, as from the feast ye rise,
Which every plundered element supplies!
Hear when fatigued, not nourished, ye have dined,
10 The food of thousands to its roots confined![1]
Eternal fasts that know no taste of bread;
Nor where who sows the corn, by corn is fed.

---

[1] [Lucan's note] The situation of these miserable people in the province that I am most acquainted with is truly lamentable. The lower class never eat meat or bread, not even on Christmas Day (when the poor of all other countries make a feast), but are confined to potatoes for food, and to water for their drink. A working man, who labours from six o'clock in the morning to six in the evening, has nothing to support him but roots and water; four pence is the price of a day labourer in Connaught; in other parts I believe it is something more, but a very trifle. Let his majesty ask those who have had the curiosity to visit the interior parts of the country; let him ask one of the lords of his bed-chamber, who lately made a tour through Ireland, and he will find that I do not exaggerate.—As to their cottages, such is their wretched poverty, that it is a known fact, the cottager frequently pulls it down to exempt himself from paying the hearth tax, which is two shillings only, but which he is absolutely unable to pay; and he and his family remain exposed to all the inclemencies of the open air, until the time of collecting this cruel tax is passed....

Throughout the year, no feast e'er crowns his
board,°   *table*
Four pence a day, ah! what can that afford?
15 So poor their country where they strive to live,
No ampler pay can starving farmers give.
Did you not blast us with a jealous eye,
Our industry and arts with yours would vie.
Nature's best face in our soft clime is shown,
20 And commerce here would gladly fix her throne.
E'en might that commerce far as India roam,
No Irish soul would chain that wealth at home.
Fools that ye are, to you that wealth would roll,
And, lodestone° like, you would attract the   *magnet*
whole.
25 But you are swayed by narrow policy,
And in a friend a hated rival see.
Our journals show with how profuse a hand
Hibernan senates give, on your demand;
Freely they give, nor aught from you require,
30 But justice, only justice they desire.
Your gratitude unlike our bounty flows;
Our idleness this truth too plainly shows;
One trade alone, your jealousy affords,[2]
(To paint such mighty folly, grant me words!)
35 One trade alone, is to this people given,
Though blessed with every requisite by Heaven.
And when for taxes, pensions, loud you cry,
Like fools you stop the means of your supply.
To English marts alone our wool must speed,[3]
40 And sinks or swells its value as they bid.
What free born souls will such oppression bear?

---

[2] [Lucan's note] The linen is the only trade carried on to any extent in Ireland, and this is unjustly cramped by English policy and acts of parliament....

[3] [Lucan's note] Ireland is not suffered to export any sort of woollen goods, even to those foreign markets where the English woollen manufactures are not sent. There are a variety of woollen and mixed goods which they are inclined to make in Ireland, ... which England does not run into, and which would be a most advantageous trade to Ireland. The French have beat out the English in several foreign markets, particularly in the Levant and Turkey, by making these goods; and they make them, shame to the English Parliament and ministry! with Irish smuggled wool. As to the inland woollen trade of Ireland, it is encumbered with every disadvantage, and receives every check that can be laid upon it; it is controlled and taxed so that a pair of knit woollen stockings, the labour of old age! cannot be exposed to sale without first paying a duty....

We sell to France, prevent us if you dare.
Thus laws too strict are ever useless made,
And enemies and rivals get your trade.
45 For us in vain our flocks their fleeces bear;
A sad reward for all the shepherd's care.
To card[1] or spin, the careful housewife fears,
She trembling draws the fleece, and spins with tears.
Early and late her weary hours are spent,
50 And much she toils to pay the landlord's rent.
But when to public sale her work she'd send,
A cruel seizure does her labours end.
Oh! Charlotte,[2] lend a while thy sacred ear,
While I recount the griefs thy subjects bear....
55 Oh! deign to tell our tale, we ask no more.
Thus shall our pious king our suff'rings hear,
And modest truth attain a monarch's ear.
Bred in a faith, they guard their souls sincere.[3]
For right or wrong, that faith to them is dear:
60 'Tis what their fathers and forefathers taught,
For which they suffered or for which they fought;
No wonder then, though wrapped in error's night,
They breed their sons in what they think is right,
Various religions, still they deem the same;
65 'Tis virtue always diff'ring but in name.
Our gavel laws,[4] few converts can create,
The persecuted soul grows obstinate.
A land of liberty can this be called,
Where by such tyrant laws we are enthralled?

70 That snatch the weapon from the father's hand,
His home exposing to the ruffian band?
Ah! wretched parents, little you foresee
Of gavel laws, the sad calamity;
Laws still accursed by the good and wise,
75 That teach the son his father to despise;
Most cruel laws, that can such acts approve,
Ah! sad return of our paternal love,
That from all ties of brotherhood deters,
And him, that's first a hypocrite prefers....
80 Ireland awake! Raise up thy drooping head,
Look to these laws, their consequences dread!...
Since toleration is Britania's pride,
Why, by such cruel laws, is Ireland tied?
Beware ye senators, look round in time,
85 Rebellion is not fixed to any clime;
For 'twould be strange, a most unnat'ral thing,
That he who hates his sire should love his king.
In trade, religion, every way oppressed,
You'll find, too late, such wrongs must be redressed.
90 Those riches in America you've lost,[5]
May soon again be found on Ireland's coast:
Open our ports at once with generous minds,
Let commerce be as free as waves and winds;
Seize quick the time, for now, consider well,
95 Whole quarters of the world at once rebel.

[1] *card* Prepare wool for spinning, i.e., by combing, parting, and straightening it with an iron-toothed comb called a card.

[2] *Charlotte* Queen Charlotte (1744–1818) of the United Kingdom.

[3] *Bred in ... souls sincere* Lucan's footnote explains that the majority of Ireland's inhabitants were Roman Catholics, and that as such their rights were heavily restricted by the penal laws; for instance, Catholics could not purchase property or hold public office. Although Lucan was not alone in citing the penal laws as a major cause of increasing Irish emigration, the extent to which the laws actually had that effect is now contested. Some of the Irish emigrants in the eighteenth century were Catholics, but most were Scotch-Irish Presbyterians, who were also affected by some, but not all, of the penal laws.

[4] *gavel laws* Part of the penal laws drawn from the Celtic tradition of Gavelkind, in which, upon the death of a father, his estate was shared equally among his sons. The gavel laws forced Catholics to undertake this practice—unless the eldest son converted to Protestantism, in which case he would inherit everything.

from Commissioners of the Customs in Scotland, *Report of the Examination of the Emigrants from the Counties of Caithness and Sutherland on Board the Ship Bachelor of Leith Bound to Wilmington in North Carolina* (1774)

British policymakers were equally concerned about the levels of emigration from Ireland and from Scotland; it was widely believed that before long the rural areas of both countries would be emptied of able laborers. Causes of emigration from Scotland were for the most part similar to those in Ireland: economic instability, unreasonably high rents, and

[5] *Those riches ... you've lost* Although the American Revolutionary War would not begin for a few more years, in 1768 opposition to British rule of the colonies was growing increasingly violent and pronounced.

the anticipation of greater opportunity in North America. Anxiety surrounding emigration prompted the gathering of reports such as the one excerpted below, in which emigrants explain their reasons for leaving Scotland behind.

John Catanach, aged fifty years, by trade a farmer, married, hath 4 children from 19 to 7 years old; resided last at Chabster in the parish of Rae in the county of Caithness, upon the estate of Mr. Alexander Nicolson, minister at Thurso; intends to go to Wilmington, North Carolina; left his own country because crops failed, bread became dear, the rents of his possession were raised from two to five pounds sterling; besides his pasture or common grounds were taken up by placing new tenants thereon, especially the grounds adjacent to his farm, which were the only grounds on which his cattle pastured. That this method of parking and placing tenants on the pasture grounds rendered his farm useless; his cattle died for want of grass, and his corn farm was unfit to support his family after paying the extravagant tack duty.[1] That beside the rise of rents and scarcity of bread, the landlord exacted arbitrary and oppressive services, such as obliging the declarant to labour up his ground, cast, win, lead and stack his peats;[2] mow, win and lead his hay, and cut his corn and lead it in the yard, which took up about 30 or 40 days of his servants and horses each year, without the least acknowledgment for it, and without victuals,[3] save the men that mowed the hay, who got their dinner only. That he was induced to emigrate by advices received from his friends in America; that provisions are extremely plenty and cheap, and the price of labour very high, so that people who are temperate and laborious have every chance of bettering their circumstances. Adds that the price of bread in the country he hath left is greatly enhanced by distilling,[4] that being for so long a time so scarce and dear,[5] and the price of cattle at the same time reduced full one half while the rents of lands have been raised nearly in the same proportion, all the smaller farms must inevitably be ruined.

James Duncan, aged twenty-seven years, by trade a farmer, married, hath two children, one five years the other 9 months old. Resided last at Mondle in the parish of Farr in the shire of Sutherland, upon the estate of Sutherland, intends to go to Wilmington in North Carolina; left his own country because crops failed him for several years, and among the last years of his labouring he scarce reaped any crop; bread became dear and the price of cattle so much reduced that one cow's price could only buy a boll of meal.[6] That the people on the estate of Sutherland were often supplied with meal from Caithness, but the farmers there had of late stopped the sale of their meal, because it rendered them a much greater profit by distilling. That he could find no employment at home whereby he could support his family. That he has very promising prospects by the advices from his friends in Carolina, as they have bettered their circumstances greatly since they went there by their labours. Lands being cheap and good provisions plenty, and the price of labour very encouraging.

William Sutherland aged twenty-four, married, left an only child at home. Resided last in the parish of Latheron and county of Caithness, upon the estate of John Sutherland of Forse. Goes to Carolina because he lost his cattle in 1772, and for a farm of 40/ rent, was obliged to perform with his family and his horses so many and so arbitrary services to his landlord at all times of the year, but especially in seed time and harvest, that he could not, in two years he possessed it, raise as much corn and[7] serve his family for six months. That, his little stock daily decreasing, he was encouraged to go to Carolina by the assurances of the fertility of the land, which yields three crops a year, by which means provisions are extremely cheap, wheat being sold at 3 shillings a boll, potatoes at 1 shilling, so that one man's labour will maintain a family of twenty persons. He has no money, therefore proposes to employ himself as a day labourer; his wife can spin and sew, and he has heard of many going out in the same way who are now substantial

---

1 *tack duty* Lease payment.

2 *labour up his ground* I.e., work his land; *cast* Cut; *win* Dry; *lead* Carry; *peats* Squares of bog soil used as fuel.

3 *victuals* Food.

4 *the price … distilling* I.e., the price of bread has increased because people are using their grain for alcohol instead.

5 *dear* Expensive.

6 *boll* Six bushels of ground grain, equivalent to about 360 pounds of wheat; *meal* The ground part of grain that is edible.

7 *as much corn and* Enough corn to.

farmers. At any rate he comforts himself in the hopes that he cannot be any worse than he has been at home.

Gilbert Stuart, *The Skater* (1782). Born in Rhode Island, Stuart traveled to England to launch his artistic career. He was apprenticed to another transatlantic artist, Benjamin West, until acclaim for this work, *The Skater*, established him as a popular success. The subject is Scottish politician William Grant, and the work was painted in London (Westminster Abbey is visible in the background). Stuart later returned to the United States, where he painted many important figures of early American politics; his 1796 portrait of George Washington is now reproduced on the American dollar bill.

from Benjamin Franklin, *Information to Those Who Would Remove to America* (1782)

Many persons in Europe, having directly or by letters expressed to the writer of this, who is well acquainted with North America, their desire of transporting and establishing themselves in that country, but who appear to have formed, through ignorance, mistaken ideas and expectations of what is to be obtained there; he thinks it may be useful, and prevent inconvenient, expensive, and fruitless removals and voyages of improper persons, if he gives some clearer and truer notions of that part of the world than appear to have hitherto prevailed.

He finds it is imagined by numbers that the inhabitants of North America are rich, capable of rewarding and disposed to reward all sorts of ingenuity; that they are at the same time ignorant of all the sciences, and, consequently, that strangers, possessing talents in the *belles-lettres*,[1] fine arts, &c., must be highly esteemed, and so well paid as to become easily rich themselves; that there are also abundance of profitable offices to be disposed of, which the natives are not qualified to fill; and that, having few persons of family[2] among them, strangers of birth must be greatly respected, and of course easily obtain the best of those offices, which will make all their fortunes; that the governments too, to encourage emigrations from Europe, not only pay the expense of personal transportation, but give lands *gratis*[3] to strangers, with negroes to work for them, utensils of husbandry,[4] and stocks of cattle. These are all wild imaginations; and those who go to America with expectations founded upon them will surely find themselves disappointed.

The truth is that though there are in that country few people so miserable as the poor of Europe, there are also very few that in Europe would be called rich; it is rather a general happy mediocrity[5] that prevails. There are few great proprietors of the soil, and few tenants;

---

[1] *belles-lettres* Literary writing.

[2] *persons of family* People born into a high social class.

[3] *gratis* Latin: free.

[4] *husbandry* Farming.

[5] *mediocrity* Averageness.

most people cultivate their own lands or follow some handicraft or merchandise; very few rich enough to live idly upon their rents or incomes, or to pay the high prices given in Europe for paintings, statues, architecture, and the other works of art that are more curious than useful. Hence the natural geniuses that have arisen in America with such talents have uniformly quitted that country for Europe, where they can be more suitably rewarded. It is true that letters and mathematical knowledge are in esteem there, but they are at the same time more common than is apprehended; there being already existing nine colleges or universities, *viz*.[1] four in New England, and one in each of the provinces of New York, New Jersey, Pennsylvania, Maryland, and Virginia, all furnished with learned professors; besides a number of smaller academies; these educate many of their youth in the languages, and those sciences that qualify men for the professions of divinity, law, or physic.[2] Strangers indeed are by no means excluded from exercising those professions; and the quick increase of inhabitants everywhere gives them a chance of employ, which they have in common with the natives. Of civil offices or employments, there are few; no superfluous ones, as in Europe; and it is a rule established in some of the states that no office should be so profitable as to make it desirable. The 36th article of the constitution of Pennsylvania runs expressly in these words: "As every freeman, to preserve his independence (if he has not a sufficient estate), ought to have some profession, calling, trade, or farm, whereby he may honestly subsist, there can be no necessity for, nor use in, establishing offices of profit; the usual effects of which are dependence and servility, unbecoming freemen, in the possessors and expectants; faction, contention, corruption, and disorder among the people. Wherefore, whenever an office, through increase of fees or otherwise, becomes so profitable as to occasion many to apply for it, the profits ought to be lessened by the legislature."

These ideas prevailing more or less in all the United States, it cannot be worth any man's while, who has a means of living at home, to expatriate himself in hopes of obtaining a profitable civil office in America; and as to military offices, they are at an end with the war, the armies being disbanded. Much less is it advisable for a person to go thither who has no other quality to recommend him but his birth. In Europe it has indeed its value; but it is a commodity that cannot be carried to a worse market than that of America, where people do not inquire concerning a stranger, *What is he?* but, *What can he do?* If he has any useful art, he is welcome; and if he exercises it, and behaves well, he will be respected by all that know him; but a mere man of quality who, on that account, wants to live upon the public by some office or salary will be despised and disregarded. The husbandman is in honor there, and even the mechanic, because their employments are useful. The people have a saying that God Almighty is himself a mechanic, the greatest in the universe; and he is respected and admired more for the variety, ingenuity, and utility of his handiworks than for the antiquity of his family. They are pleased with the observation of a negro, and frequently mention it, that *Boccarorra* (meaning the white men) *make de black man workee, make de horse workee, make de ox workee, make ebery ting workee; only de hog. He, de hog, no workee; he eat, he drink, he walk about, he go to sleep when he please, he libb like a gentleman.* According to these opinions of the Americans, one of them would think himself more obliged to a genealogist who could prove for him that his ancestors and relations for ten generations had been ploughmen, smiths, carpenters, turners, weavers, tanners, or even shoemakers, and consequently that they were useful members of society; than if he could only prove that they were gentlemen, doing nothing of value, but living idly on the labour of others, mere *fruges consumere nati*,[3] and otherwise good for nothing, till by their death their estates, like the carcass of the negro's gentleman-hog, come to be cut up.

With regard to encouragements for strangers from government, they are really only what are derived from good laws and liberty. Strangers are welcome because

---

1   *viz.*   Abbreviation of the Latin *videlicet*, meaning "namely" or "that is to say."

2   *physic*   Medical practice.

3   *fruges consumere nati*   Latin: born to consume the fruits (of the earth).

there is room enough for them all, and therefore the old inhabitants are not jealous of them; the laws protect them sufficiently so that they have no need of the patronage of great men; and everyone will enjoy securely the profits of his industry. But if he does not bring a fortune with him, he must work and be industrious to live. One or two years' residence gives him all the rights of a citizen; but the government does not at present, whatever it may have done in former times, hire people to become settlers by paying their passages, giving land, negroes, utensils, stock, or any other kind of emolument[1] whatsoever. In short, America is the land of labour, and by no means what the English call *Lubberland*,[2] and the French *Pays de Cocagne*,[3] where the streets are said to be paved with half-peck[4] loaves, the houses tiled with pancakes, and where the fowls fly about ready roasted, crying, *Come eat me!*

Who then are the kind of persons to whom an emigration to America may be advantageous? And what are the advantages they may reasonably expect?

Land being cheap in that country, from the vast forests still void of inhabitants, and not likely to be occupied in an age to come, insomuch that the propriety of an hundred acres of fertile soil full of wood may be obtained near the frontiers, in many places, for eight or ten guineas,[5] hearty young labouring men who understand the husbandry of corn and cattle, which is nearly the same in that country as in Europe, may easily establish themselves there. A little money saved of the good wages they receive there, while they work for others, enables them to buy the land and begin their plantation, in which they are assisted by the goodwill of their neighbours, and some credit. Multitudes of poor people from England, Ireland, Scotland, and Germany have by this means in a few years become wealthy farmers, who, in their own countries, where all the lands are fully occupied and the wages of labour low, could never have emerged from the poor condition wherein they were born.

From the salubrity[6] of the air, the healthiness of the climate, the plenty of good provisions, and the encouragement to early marriages by the certainty of subsistence in cultivating the earth, the increase of inhabitants by natural generation is very rapid in America, and becomes still more so by the accession of strangers; hence there is a continual demand for more artisans of all the necessary and useful kinds, to supply those cultivators of the earth with houses, and with furniture and utensils of the grosser sorts, which cannot so well be brought from Europe. Tolerably good workmen in any of those mechanic arts are sure to find employ, and to be well paid for their work, there being no restraints preventing strangers from exercising any art they understand, nor any permission necessary. If they are poor, they begin first as servants or journeymen; and if they are sober, industrious, and frugal, they soon become masters, establish themselves in business, marry, raise families, and become respectable citizens. ....

---

[1] *emolument* Payment or benefit.

[2] *Lubberland* The 1685 ballad "Invitation to Lubberland" describes a place of laziness and vice where the streets are "paved with pudding-pies" and the roofs tiled with pancakes.

[3] *Pays de Cocagne* French: Land of Plenty.

[4] *half-peck* I.e., large.

[5] *guineas* In the late 1700s, an average American wage-earner would be paid one guinea in about two weeks.

[6] *salubrity* Health-promoting quality.

from J. Hector St. John de Crèvecoeur, *Letters from an American Farmer* (1782)

Michel-Guillaume-Jean de Crèvecoeur was born in France into a family of minor nobility. He immigrated to New France and, after the English victory in the Seven Years' War, anglicized his name to J. Hector St. John de Crèvecoeur and became a citizen of New York. He first published *Letters from an American Farmer* in England, but it was read throughout Europe and Ameria, and its success prompted several editions and translations. Works of a similar tone, idealizing life in the colonies (and often written with a view to encouraging immigration) remained popular through to the late nineteenth century—though accounts that presented a less rosy view of the immigrant experience also gained wide currency.

I wish I could be acquainted with the feelings and thoughts which must agitate the heart and present themselves to the mind of an enlightened Englishman when he first lands on this continent. He must greatly rejoice that he lived at a time to see this fair country discovered and settled; he must necessarily feel a share of national pride when he views the chain of settlements which embellishes these extended shores. When he says to himself, this is the work of my countrymen, who, when convulsed by factions, afflicted by a variety of miseries and wants, restless and impatient, took refuge here. They brought along with them their national genius,[1] to which they principally owe what liberty they enjoy and what substance they possess. Here he sees the industry of his native country displayed in a new manner, and traces in their works the embryos of all the arts, sciences, and ingenuity which flourish in Europe. Here he beholds fair cities, substantial villages, extensive fields, an immense country filled with decent houses, good roads, orchards, meadows, and bridges, where an hundred years ago all was wild, woody and uncultivated! What a train of pleasing ideas this fair spectacle must suggest; it is a prospect which must inspire a good citizen with the most heartfelt pleasure. The difficulty consists in the manner of viewing so extensive a scene.

He is arrived on a new continent; a modern society offers itself to his contemplation, different from what he had hitherto seen. It is not composed, as in Europe, of great lords who possess everything and of a herd of people who have nothing. Here are no aristocratical families, no courts, no kings, no bishops, no ecclesiastical dominion, no invisible power giving to a few a very visible one; no great manufacturers employing thousands, no great refinements of luxury. The rich and the poor are not so far removed from each other as they are in Europe. Some few towns excepted, we are all tillers of the earth, from Nova Scotia to West Florida. We are a people of cultivators, scattered over an immense territory communicating with each other by means of good roads and navigable rivers, united by the silken bands of mild government, all respecting the laws, without dreading their power, because they are equitable. We are all animated with the spirit of an industry which is unfettered and unrestrained, because each person works for himself. If he travels through our rural districts he views not the hostile castle and the haughty mansion, contrasted with the clay-built hut and miserable cabin, where cattle and men help to keep each other warm, and dwell in meanness, smoke, and indigence.[2] A pleasing uniformity of decent competence appears throughout our habitations. The meanest of our log-houses is a dry and comfortable habitation. Lawyer or merchant are the fairest titles our towns afford; that of a farmer is the only appellation of the rural inhabitants of our country. It must take some time ere he can reconcile himself to our dictionary, which is but short in words of dignity and names of honour. There, on a Sunday, he sees a congregation of respectable farmers and their wives, all clad in neat homespun,[3] well mounted, or riding in their own humble wagons. There is not among them an esquire, saving the unlettered magistrate.[4] There he sees a parson as simple as his flock, a farmer who does not riot[5] on the labour of others. We have no princes, for whom we toil, starve, and bleed: we are the most perfect society now

---

[1] *genius* Particular spirit.

[2] *indigence* Destitution.

[3] *homespun* Clothing made from yarn spun at home.

[4] *esquire* Member of the gentry; *magistrate* Local court judge, usually a member of the gentry.

[5] *riot* Make merry; live indulgently.

existing in the world. Here man is free as he ought to be; nor is this pleasing equality so transitory as many others are. Many ages will not see the shores of our great lakes replenished with inland nations, nor the unknown bounds of North America entirely peopled. Who can tell how far it extends? Who can tell the millions of men whom it will feed and contain? for no European foot has as yet travelled half the extent of this mighty continent! The next wish of this traveller will be to know whence came all these people? they are mixture of English, Scotch, Irish, French, Dutch, Germans, and Swedes. From this promiscuous[1] breed, that race now called Americans have arisen. The eastern provinces must indeed be excepted, as being the unmixed descendants of Englishmen. ...

In this great American asylum, the poor of Europe have by some means met together, and in consequence of various causes; to what purpose should they ask one another what countrymen they are? Alas, two thirds of them had no country. Can a wretch who wanders about, who works and starves, whose life is a continual scene of sore affliction or pinching penury;[2] can that man call England or any other kingdom his country? A country that had no bread for him, whose fields procured him no harvest; who met with nothing but the frowns of the rich, the severity of the laws, with jails and punishments; who owned not a single foot of the extensive surface of this planet? No! urged by a variety of motives, here they came. Everything has tended to regenerate them; new laws, a new mode of living, a new social system; here they are become men: in Europe they were as so many useless plants, wanting vegetative mould[3] and refreshing showers; they withered, and were mowed down by want, hunger, and war; but now by the power of transplantation, like all other plants they have taken root and flourished! Formerly they were not numbered in any civil lists of their country, except in those of the poor; here they rank as citizens. By what invisible power has this surprising metamorphosis been performed? By that of the laws and that of their industry. The laws, the indulgent laws, protect them as they arrive, stamping on

them the symbol of adoption; they receive ample rewards for their labours; these accumulated rewards procure them lands; those lands confer on them the title of freemen, and to that title every benefit is affixed which men can possibly require. This is the great operation daily performed by our laws. From whence proceed these laws? From our government. Whence the government? It is derived from the original genius and strong desire of the people ratified and confirmed by the crown. This is the great chain which links us all, this is the picture which every province exhibits, Nova Scotia excepted. ...

What attachment can a poor European emigrant have for a country where he had nothing? The knowledge of the language, the love of a few kindred as poor as himself, were the only cords that tied him; his country is now that which gives him land, bread, protection, and consequence: *Ubi panis ibi patria*,[4] is the motto of all emigrants. What then is the American, this new man? He is either an European, or the descendant of an European, hence that strange mixture of blood, which you will find in no other country. I could point out to you a family whose grandfather was an Englishman, whose wife was Dutch, whose son married a French woman, and whose present four sons have now four wives of different nations. *He* is an American, who leaving behind him all his ancient prejudices and manners, receives new ones from the new mode of life he has embraced, the new government he obeys, and the new rank he holds.

He becomes an American by being received in the broad lap of our great *Alma Mater*.[5] Here individuals of all nations are melted into a new race of men, whose labours and posterity will one day cause great changes in the world. Americans are the western pilgrims, who are carrying along with them that great mass of arts, sciences, vigour, and industry which began long since in the east; they will finish the great circle. The Americans were once scattered all over Europe; here they are incorporated into one of the finest systems of population which has ever appeared, and which will hereafter become distinct by the power of the different climates

---

[1] *promiscuous* Varied.

[2] *pinching penury* I.e., penny-pinching destitution.

[3] *wanting ... mould* I.e., lacking fertilization.

[4] *Ubi panis ibi patria* Latin: Where there is bread, there is my homeland.

[5] *Alma Mater* Latin: Bountiful Mother.

they inhabit. The American ought therefore to love this country much better than that wherein either he or his forefathers were born. Here the rewards of his industry follow with equal steps the progress of his labour; his labour is founded on the basis of nature, SELF-INTEREST; can it want a stronger allurement? Wives and children, who before in vain demanded of him a morsel of bread, now, fat and frolicsome, gladly help their father to clear those fields whence exuberant crops are to arise to feed and to clothe them all; without any part being claimed, either by a despotic prince, a rich abbot, or a mighty lord. Here, religion demands but little of him; a small voluntary salary to the minister, and gratitude to God; can he refuse these? The American is a new man, who acts upon new principles; he must therefore entertain new ideas, and form new opinions. From involuntary idleness, servile dependence, penury, and useless labour, he has passed to toils of a very different nature, rewarded by ample subsistence.—This is an American.

from Anonymous, *Look Before You Leap* (1796)

Through the eighteenth and into the nineteenth century, persuasive writers strove to counter the excessive optimism of works promoting immigration to America. While their negative assessments were often based on fact, such was not always the case. Selfless honesty was generally not their primary motivation; concerned that Britain was losing its skilled laborers to the enticing possibilities of the New World, these writers tended to overstate the dangers and difficulties of immigrant life. Some even lied outright; the following is from the introduction to a supposedly "genuine collection of letters" from immigrant tradespeople. A contemporary review suspiciously remarked that the letters contained contradictory facts, as well as attempts at literary flair and philosophical contemplation "not such as those who use the chisel, the trowel, and the brush are likely to make in letters to their wives or friends."

from THE PREFACE

In America, the condition of society is extremely different from what it is in England, and those persons who have enjoyed the social pleasures and mixed intercourse of the metropolis, and of other great towns in this country, will find themselves very uncomfortable and dissatisfied when experiencing a different scene on the Western continent.

Such persons as have built their expectations on finding affluence and ease will meet with a familiar disappointment. What prospect is there of such extraordinary happiness in a country not matured and enriched by commerce, in a new discovered land, occupied in the interior by inhospitable savages and ravaged on the exterior by a late unmerciful war.

Let me now proceed to ask every artisan, mechanic, &c. who may peruse the succeeding letters what particular advantage he finds in them to engage his attention? What superiority of gratification over that enjoyed by persons of the same condition with himself in his own country? Has he found out that the Americans will press down to the shore, and receive him with open arms on his first landing, and vie with each other who shall be most profuse in rendering him offices of kindness and humanity? Does he find that easy complacency and friendly attention, which the canting crimp[1] has taught him to believe is the prominent characteristic of the Virginians? Has he met with the so much boasted encouragement and protection which was to raise him to the most astonishing degrees of preferment?

Does he hear from these experimental adventurers enrapturing accounts of an hospitable country, the fruits of whose luxurious soil are extensively distributed amongst its inhabitants to supply their wants and increase their comforts?

Does he hear of a wholesome climate congenial to the health and longevity of an Englishman, or of an unsettled and inauspicious atmosphere, the fatal effects of which so frequently destroy the most athletic and robust?

Does he find a mechanic can obtain a greater surplus from his earnings, when he has placed the expenses of his board, lodgings, washing, wearing apparel, and other incidents against the receipt of his income?

---

[1] *canting crimp* I.e., recruiter who lies to trick his victims into immigrating.

In fine,[1] does he remark any grateful sensations, any pleasing retrospect experienced by those persons who have quitted this country?

Where is the comfort they enjoy? What is the enchanting prospect before them? If he finds none of these blessings, friendships, gratifications, and prospects, for Heaven's sake! why, wretched as it is, quit his native country and plunge himself precipitately into another, infinitely more unlikely to procure him lasting enjoyment.

It has been well remarked that those who attempt and expect perfect happiness in this world are pursuing the ideal phantom of a sanguine[2] imagination. This may be well applied to the vain expectations raised in the minds of such credulous persons as seek superior comfort and felicity on the continent of America. They are pursuing that which it is not in the power of the country to bestow, and will most certainly be left the disappointed dupes of their own chimerical ideas.

The publisher is well aware of the obloquy[3] that will be cast upon this publication by the innumerable host of American kidnappers, and he well knows it will be their studied task and serious endeavour to controvert his assertions and to prove them fallacious. ... He knows they will confidently ask, If America be the place you have represented, what is the reason that, out of so many thousands who cross the Atlantic, so very few return? To this he as confidently answers. Many unfortunate speculators who have emigrated to America dare not return. The majority of those needy adventurers that have gone the same road cannot return; and many of those who have possessed the means have, alas! been snatched to that bourne from which no traveller returns.[4] The majority of those who have escaped the devouring jaws of death, and have had it in their power, *have* returned, injured in their finances and disappointed in their prospects, cursing the authors of their misery and their own credulity in becoming the passive dupes of such abominable duplicity.

General Wolfe and the Fall of Quebec

from "Anecdotes Relating to the Battle of Quebec" (March 1760)

The year after General Wolfe's much-celebrated capture of Quebec City, the capital of New France, the following retelling of events from a British soldier's perspective was printed in *The British Magazine*.

On the evening that preceded the battle, two French deserters were carried on board one of our men of war,[5] which lay near the north shore, commanded by Capt. Smith; and gave him intelligence that the garrison of Quebec expected that night to receive a convoy of provisions to be sent down the river in boats by Mons. de Bougainville,[6] who commanded a detached body above the town to watch the motions of General Wolfe. From this body to near the place where our troops landed, sentries were posted along shore, to challenge the boats and vessels as they should pass and give the alarm occasionally.[7] One of our captains embarked in the first boat, which was followed by the rest in a string, hugging the north shore. Being questioned by the first sentry, and understanding French perfectly well, answered to the *Qui vit*,[8] which is the challenging word, *la France*; then he asked *a quel regiment*, to what regiment; and the captain replying softly, *de la Reine*, which he knew was one of those under Bougainville, the sentry cried *passe*; and allowed all the boats to pass without further question, in full belief that they were the expected convoy. In the same manner the other sentries were deceived; though one, more wary than the rest, came running down to the shore, and called, *pourquoy est que vous ne parlez plus haut?* Why don't you speak with an audible voice? The English captain, whose presence of mind cannot be sufficiently admired, answered without hesitation, *Tai toi, soutre ou nous serons attrappeés*. "Hush, fool! or we shall be discovered

---

[1] *In fine* I.e., in conclusion.

[2] *sanguine* Optimistic.

[3] *obloquy* Public reproach.

[4] *bourne* Boundary; *been snatched … traveller returns* I.e., died.

---

[5] *men of war* Sailing ships armed with cannons.

[6] *Mons. de Bougainville* Louis Antoine de Bougainville (1729–1811), French admiral, who commanded an elite troop in the defense of Quebec City.

[7] *occasionally* I.e., at appropriate times.

[8] *Qui vit* French: Who lives?

and taken." Thus satisfied, the Frenchman retired, and our troops landed a little farther down without opposition. The first boat was piloted by a midshipman, who mistaking the landing-place in the dark, ordered the men to row past it; but the same captain who had acted so discreetly before insisted upon his being mistaken, and commanded the rowers to put ashore at the destined place, which he knew from having been formerly posted with his company on the opposite side of the river. This was another providential escape; for had the boats overshot the landing-place, confusion would have ensued, and in all probability the opportunity would have been lost.

The two French deserters, on board of Capt. Smith, perceiving our boats gliding down the river in the dark, began to shout and make a noise, declaring they were part of the convoy; and the captain, who was not acquainted with the intended attack, believing their information, had already given orders to point his guns at our own troops, when General Wolfe, in person, rowing alongside of him, prevented the discharge; which not only might have been fatal to our soldiers, but would have infallibly frustrated the design.

The common path that slanted up the hill from the landing-place was rendered impassable by ditches, which the enemy had dug across in several parts, and a kind of entrenchment near the top, defended by a piquet-guard.[1] Mr. Wolfe, having formed the men as they landed, divided them into detachments and ordered them to ascend the hill on both sides of the path. Though it was extremely steep and dangerous, the men scrambled up with surprising alacrity and expedition; the summit was first gained by the detachment under the command of the captain aforementioned. The French piquets threw in a straggling fire, which did little or no execution; then they retired with precipitation,[2] and the rest of our army assembled without further trouble....

Advanced parties from both sides piqueered[3] for some hours, and a great many of our officers and soldiers were wounded by a body of burghers[4] from Quebec, selected as good marksmen, who lay concealed in a field of corn opposite to our right. It was from these skulkers that General Wolfe received both his wounds, as he gave directions in the front of the line. The fatal ball took place just as the enemy were advancing to the charge; being unable to stand, he leaned upon the shoulder of a lieutenant, who sat down for that purpose. The French, after a very ineffectual fire, gave way immediately; upon which the lieutenant exclaimed, "They run!" "Who run?" cried the gallant Wolfe with great eagerness. "The enemy," replied the other. "What!" said the general, "do the rascals run already? Then I die happy." So saying, the glorious youth expired.

The action began about nine in the morning and was over in a few minutes, so that the courage of the English army was altogether disappointed; and such was the spirit of the soldiers, that they were mortified because they had not a better opportunity of showing their discipline and valour. All the officers agree that a finer body of troops was never seen.

from Horace Walpole, *Memoirs of the Last Ten Years of the Reign of King George II* (1822)

Horace Walpole (1717–97) was a Member of Parliament, but is much better remembered for his influence on gothic literature and architecture. His posthumously published *Memoirs of the Reign of George II* includes an account of the fall of Quebec that differs in several respects from that in *The British Magazine*.

... [A] desponding letter [was] received from General Wolfe before Quebec,[5] on the 14th of October. He had found the enterprise infinitely more difficult than he

---

[1] *piquet-guard* Soldiers guarding the hilltop; the initial English landing party intended to defeat this guard to clear the way for the rest of the army.

[2] *precipitation* Sudden haste.

[3] *piqueered* Skirmished.

[4] *burghers* Townspeople.

[5] *before Quebec* Before the Battle of Quebec, also known as the Battle of the Plains of Abraham.

had conceived, the country strong from every circumstance of situation: the French had a superior army, had called in every Canadian capable of bearing arms; twenty-two ship-loads of provisions had escaped Admiral Durell[1] and got into the town; Amherst[2] was not come up; and, above all, Montcalm,[3] the French general, had shown that he understood the natural strength of the country, had posted himself in the most advantageous situation, and was not to be drawn from it by any stratagem which Wolfe, assisted by the steady cooperation of our fleet, could put in practice. Wolfe himself was languishing with the stone[4] and a complication of disorders, which fatigue and disappointment had brought upon him. Townshend[5] and other officers had crossed him in his plans, but he had not yielded. Himself had been one of the warmest censurers of the miscarried expedition to Rochfort;[6] and he had received this high command upon the assurance that no dangers or difficulties should discourage him. His army wasted before his eyes by sickness; the season advanced fast which must put an end to his attempts; he had no choice remaining but in variety of difficulties. In the most artful terms that could be framed he left the nation uncertain whether he meant to prepare an excuse for desisting, or to claim the melancholy merit of having sacrificed himself without a prospect of success.

Three days after, an express arrived that Quebec was taken—a conquest heightened by the preceding gloom and despair. The rapidity with which our arms had prevailed in every quarter of the globe made us presume that Canada could not fail of being added to our acquisitions; and however arduously won, it would have sunk in value if the transient cloud that overcast the dawn of this glory had not made it burst forth with redoubled lustre. The incidents of dramatic fiction could not be conducted with more address to lead an audience from despondency to sudden exaltation, than accident prepared to excite the passions of a whole people. They despaired—they triumphed—and they wept—for Wolfe had fallen in the hour of victory! Joy, grief, curiosity, astonishment, were painted in every countenance: the more they enquired, the higher their admiration rose. Not an incident but was heroic and affecting!

Wolfe, between persuasion of the impracticability, unwillingness to leave any attempt untried that could be proposed, and worn out with anxiety of mind and body, had determined to make one last effort above the town. He embarked his forces at one in the morning, and passed the French sentinels in silence that were posed along the shore. The current carried them beyond the destined spot. They found themselves at the foot of a precipice, esteemed so impracticable that only a slight guard of one hundred and fifty men defended it. Had there been a path, the night was too dark to discover it. The troops, whom nothing could discourage, for these difficulties could not, pulled themselves and one another up by stumps and boughs of trees. The guard, hearing a rustling, fired down the precipice at random, as our men did up into the air; but terrified by the strangeness of the attempt, the French piquet[7] fled....

Daybreak discovered our forces in possession of the eminence.[8] Montcalm could not credit it when reported to him, but it was too late to doubt when nothing but a battle could save the town. Even then he held our attempt so desperate that, being shown the position of the English, he said, "*Oui, je les vois où ils ne doivent pas être.*"[9] Forced to quit his entrenchments, he said, "*S'il faut donc combattre, je vais le ecraser.*"[10] He prepared for engagement after lining the bushes with detachments of Indians. Our men, according to orders, reserved their

---

1. *twenty-two … Admiral Durell* Vice-Admiral Philip Durell (1707–66) had arrived too late to intercept the expected delivery of supplies from France.

2. *Amherst* Lord Jeffery Amherst (1717–97), military commander-in-chief in North America, had planned to join Wolfe but was delayed establishing a military foothold on Lake Champlain.

3. *Montcalm* Louis-Joseph de Montcalm-Gazon (1712–59), commander of the French forces in North America.

4. *the stone* Kidney stones.

5. *Townshend* George Townshend (1724–1807), later a Field Marshal and Marquess, would take command of the British forces after Wolfe's death. He thought Wolfe incompetent and disapproved of his decisions.

6. *Rochfort* Wolfe had participated in a 1757 attack on Rochefort, France, in which, despite initial success, the commander chose to withdraw.

7. *piquet* Guarding force.

8. *eminence* High ground.

9. *Oui … être* French: Yes, I see them where they should not be.

10. *S'il faut … ecraser* French: If we must fight, I will crush them.

fire with a patience and tranquility equal to the resolution they had exerted in clambering the precipice—but when they gave it, it took place with such terrible slaughter of the enemy that half an hour decided the day. The French fled precipitately,[1] and Montcalm, endeavouring to rally them, was killed on the spot....

The fall of Wolfe was noble indeed. He received a wound in the head, but covered it from his soldiers with his handkerchief. A second ball struck him in the belly; that too he dissembled.[2] A third hitting him in the breast, he sunk under the anguish and was carried behind the ranks. Yet, fast as life ebbed out, his whole anxiety centred on the fortune of the day. He begged to be borne nearer to the action, but his sight being dimmed by the approach of death, he entreated to be told what they who supported him saw: he was answered that the enemy gave ground. He eagerly repeated the question, heard the enemy was totally routed, cried "I am satisfied"—and expired.

Colonists and Native People

William Wordsworth, "Complaint of a Forsaken Indian Woman" (1798)

> In this poem (first published in *Lyrical Ballads*) Wordsworth addresses a subject that was common in poetry of the late eighteenth century: the image of the dying Indian.

When a Northern Indian, from sickness, is unable to continue his journey with his companions, he is left behind, covered over with deer-skins, and is supplied with water, food, and fuel if the situation of the place will afford it. He is informed of the track which his companions intend to pursue, and if he is unable to follow or overtake them, he perishes alone in the desert; unless he should have the good fortune to fall in with some other tribes of Indians. It is unnecessary to add that the females are equally, or still more, exposed to the same fate. See that very interesting work Hearne's *Journey from Hudson's Bay to the Northern Ocean.*[3] When the northern lights, as the same writer informs us, vary their position in the air, they make a rustling and a crackling noise. This circumstance is alluded to in the first stanza of the following poem.

Before I see another day,
Oh let my body die away!
In sleep I heard the northern gleams;
The stars they were among my dreams;
5 In sleep I did behold the skies,
I saw the crackling flashes drive;
And yet they are upon my eyes,
And yet I am alive.
Before I see another day,
10 Oh let my body die away!

My fire is dead: it knew no pain;
Yet is it dead, and I remain.
All stiff with ice the ashes lie;
And they are dead, and I will die.
15 When I was well, I wished to live,
For clothes, for warmth, for food, and fire;
But they to me no joy can give,
No pleasure now, and no desire.
Then here contented will I lie;
20 Alone I cannot fear to die.

Alas! you might have dragged me on
Another day, a single one!
Too soon despair o'er me prevailed;
Too soon my heartless spirit failed;
25 When you were gone my limbs were stronger;
And Oh how grievously I rue,
That, afterwards, a little longer,
My friends, I did not follow you!
For strong and without pain I lay,
30 My friends, when you were gone away.
My child! they gave thee to another,
A woman who was not thy mother.
When from my arms my babe they took,
On me how strangely did he look!

---

[1] *precipitately* Hastily.

[2] *dissembled* Disguised.

[3] *Hearne's ... Ocean* Explorer Samuel Hearne (1745–92) documented his experiences in *A Journey from Prince of Wales's Fort in Hudson's Bay to the Northern Ocean*, published posthumously in 1795.

35 Through his whole body something ran,
A most strange something did I see;
—As if he strove to be a man,
That he might pull the sledge for me.
And then he stretched his arms, how wild!
40 Oh mercy! like a little child.

My little joy! my little pride!
In two days more I must have died.

Then do not weep and grieve for me;
I feel I must have died with thee.
45 Oh wind, that o'er my head art flying,
The way my friends their course did bend,
I should not feel the pain of dying,
Could I with thee a message send.
Too soon, my friends, you went away;
50 For I had many things to say.

Benjamin West, *William Penn's Treaty with the Indians when he founded the Province of Pennsylvania in North America* (1771). Born in Pennsylvania, West was living in England when he painted this and the other large history paintings for which he is best known. The subject is William Penn, Quaker philosopher and founder of Pennsylvania, who was renowned for his unusually good relationship with the Lenape Indians of the region. Unlike other early settlers, who saw no need to compensate native people for their land, Penn negotiated an exchange with the Lenape, trading goods for signed documents ceding land to the colonists. Historians quite rightly point out that Penn and his settlers displaced the Lenape and forced them to conform to the needs of the colony; nevertheless, the relationship between the Pennsylvanians and the Lenape was remarkably peaceful for the period and was seen as representative of ideal Indian-settler relations. (See the color insert in this volume for another example of Benjamin West's work.)

I'll follow you across the snow,
You travel heavily and slow:
In spite of all my weary pain,
I'll look upon your tents again.
My fire is dead, and snowy white
The water which beside it stood;
The wolf has come to me tonight,
And he has stolen away my food.
Forever left alone am I,
Then wherefore should I fear to die?

My journey will be shortly run,
I shall not see another sun,

I cannot lift my limbs to know
If they have any life or no.
My poor forsaken child! if I
For once could have thee close to me,
With happy heart I then would die,
And my last thoughts would happy be.
I feel my body die away,
I shall not see another day.

from Susannah Johnson, *The Captive American, or A Narrative of the Suffering of Mrs. Johnson During Four Years Captivity with the Indians and French* (1797)

> The Seven Years' War was a global conflict involving France, Austria, and other allies fighting against Britain, Prussia, and their allies, both in Europe and through their colonial possessions in North and South America, Africa, India, and the Philippines. Susannah Johnson was living in present-day Charlestown, New Hampshire, during the early escalation of the North American conflict that would become part of this war. She and her family were captured by a raiding party of Abenaki Indians, who were allied with the French, having been largely forced out of New Hampshire by English colonization. The Abenaki held her captive for a few months before selling her to French settlers; when she was

finally released, more than three years had passed since her capture. Years later, Johnson dictated her story to a local lawyer, and it became one of the most widely read works in the popular genre of Indian captivity narratives.

from the INTRODUCTION

During ... the Cape Breton War,[1] the town of No. 4[2] could hardly be said to be inhabited; some adventurers had made a beginning, but few were considered as belonging to the town. Captain Stevens, whose valour is recorded as an instance of consummate generalship, part of the time kept the fort, which afforded a shelter to the enterprising settlers in times of imminent danger. But even his vigilance did not save the town from numerous scenes of carnage. At the commencement of the peace in 1749, the enterprising spirit of New England rose superior to the dangers of the forest, and they began to venture innovation. The Indians, still thirsty for plunder and rapine,[3] and regardless of the peace which their masters, the French, had concluded, kept up a flying warfare and committed several outrages upon lives and property; this kept the increasing inhabitants in a state of alarm for three or four years; most of the time they performed their daily work without molestation, but retreated to the fort at each returning night.

Our country has so long been exposed to the Indian wars that recitals of exploits and sufferings, of escapes and deliverances, have become both numerous and trite. The air of novelty will not be attempted in the following pages; simple facts, unadorned, are what the reader must expect; pity for my sufferings, and admiration at my safe return, is all that my history can excite. ...

---

[1] *Cape Breton War*   More commonly known as King George's War, the North American component of the War of the Austrian Succession, one of several conflicts between the major powers of Europe that spread to their colonies.

[2] *No. 4*   Present day Charlestown, New Hampshire.

[3] *rapine*   Pillage.

from CHAPTER 1

Everyone "was tremblingly alive" with fear. The Indians were reported to be on their march for our destruction, and our distance from sources of information gave full latitude for exaggerations of news before it reached our ears. The fears of the night were horrible beyond description, and even the light of day was far from dispelling painful anxiety. While looking from the windows of my log house, and seeing my neighbours tread cautiously by each hedge and hillock, lest some secreted savage might start forth to take their scalp, my fears would baffle description. Alarms grew greater and greater, till our apprehensions were too strongly confirmed by the news of the capture of Mr. Malony's family, on Merrimack River: this reached us about the 20th of August. Imagination now saw and heard a thousand Indians; and I never went round my own house without first looking with trembling caution by each corner, to see if a tomahawk was not raised for my destruction....

On the evening of the 29th of August our house was visited by a party of neighbours who spent the time very cheerfully with watermelons and flip[1] till midnight; they all then retired in high spirits, except a spruce young spark, who tarried to keep company with my sister. We then went to bed with feelings well tuned for sleep, and rested with fine composure till midway between daybreak and sunrise, when we were roused by neighbour Labarree's knocking at the door, who had shouldered his ax to do a day's work for my husband. Mr. Johnson slipped on his jacket and trousers, and stepped to the door to let him in. But by opening the door he opened a scene—terrible to describe!—Indians! Indians! were the first words I heard; he sprang to his guns, but Labarree, heedless of danger, instead of closing the door to keep them out, began to rally our hired men upstairs for not rising earlier. But in an instant a crowd of savages, fixed horribly for war, rushed furiously in. I screamed, and begged my friends to ask for quarters.[2] By this time they were all over the house, some upstairs, some hauling my sister out of bed; another had hold of me, and one was approaching Mr. Johnson, who stood in the middle of the floor to deliver himself up; but the Indian supposing that he would make resistance, and be more than his match, went to the door and brought three of his comrades, and the four bound him. I was led to the door, fainting and trembling; there stood my friend Labarree bound; Ebenezer Farnsworth, whom they found up in his chamber, they were putting in the same situation; and, to complete the shocking scene, my three little children were driven naked to the place where I stood. On viewing myself, I found that I too was naked. An Indian had purloined three gowns who, on seeing my situation, gave me the whole. I asked another for a petticoat, but he refused it. After what little plunder their hurry would allow them to get was confusedly bundled up, we were ordered to march. After going about twenty roods,[3] we fell behind a rising ground, where we halted to pack the things in a better manner; while there, a savage went back, as we supposed, to fire the buildings. Farnsworth proposed to my husband to go back with him, to get a quantity of pork from the cellar to help us on the journey; but Mr. Johnson prudently replied that by that means the Indians might find the rum, and in a fit of intoxication kill us all....

We all arrived safe on the other side of the river about four o'clock in the afternoon; a fire was kindled, and some of the stolen kettles were hung over it and filled with porridge. The savages took delight in viewing their spoil, which amounted to forty or fifty pounds in value. They then, with a truly savage yell, gave their war whoop and bade defiance to danger. As we tarried an hour in this place, I had time to reflect on our miserable situation. Captives, in the power of unmerciful savages, without provision and almost without clothes, in a wilderness where we must sojourn as long as the children of Israel did, for aught we knew; and, what added to our distress, not one of our savage masters could understand a word of English....

The fifth day's journey was an unvaried scene of fatigue. The Indians sent out two or three hunting parties, who returned without game. As we had in the morning consumed the last morsel of our meal, everyone now began to be seriously alarmed, and hunger, with all its horrors, looked us earnestly in the face. At night, we found the waters that run into Lake Champlain, which was over the height of land; before dark we

---

[1] *flip* Hot alcoholic beverage.

[2] *quarters* Mercy.

[3] *twenty roods* Almost 14 miles.

halted, and the Indians, by help of their punck,[1] which they carried in horns, made a fire. They soon adopted a plan to relieve their hunger: the horse was shot, and his flesh was in a few minutes broiling on embers, and they, with native gluttony, satiated their craving appetites. To use the term politeness in the management of this repast may be thought a burlesque, yet their offering the prisoners the best parts of the horse certainly bordered on civility; an epicure could not have catered nicer slices, nor, in that situation, served them up with more neatness. Appetite is said to be the best sauce, yet our abundance of it did not render savoury this novel steak. My children, however, ate too much, which made them very unwell for a number of days. Broth was made for me and my child,[2] which was rendered almost a luxury by the seasoning of roots. After supper, countenances began to brighten; those who had relished the meal exhibited new strength, and those who had only snuffed its effluvia[3] confessed themselves regaled. The evening was employed in drying and smoking what remained for future use. The night was a scene of distressing fears to me, and my extreme weakness had affected my mind to such a degree that every difficulty appeared doubly terrible. By the assistance of Scoggin,[4] I had been brought so far, yet so great was my debility, that every hour I was taken off and laid on the ground, to keep me from expiring. But now, alas! this conveyance was no more. To walk it was impossible. Inevitable death in the midst of woods one hundred miles wide appeared to be my only portion.

from CHAPTER 3

In the morning of the sixth day, the Indians exerted themselves to prepare one of their greatest dainties. The marrow bones of old Scoggin were pounded for a soup, and every root, both sweet and bitter, that the woods afforded was thrown in to give it a flavour. Each one partook of as much as his feelings would allow. The war whoop then resounded, with an infernal yell, and we

began to fix for a march. My fate was unknown till my master brought some bark and tied my petticoats as high as he supposed would be convenient for walking, and ordered me to "munch."[5] With scarce strength to stand alone, I went on half a mile with my little son and three Indians. The rest were advanced. My power to move then failed, the world grew dark, and I dropped down. I had sight enough to see an Indian lift his hatchet over my head, while my son screamed, "Ma'am do go, for they will kill you!" As I fainted, my last thought was that I should presently be in a world of spirits. When I awoke, my master was talking angrily with the savage who had threatened my life. By his gestures, I could learn that he charged him with not acting the honourable part of a warrior, by an attempt to destroy the prize of a brother. A whoop was given for the halt. My master helped me to the rest of the company, where a council was held, the result of which was that my husband should walk by my side and help me along. . . .

from CHAPTER 4

Whenever the warriors return from an excursion against an enemy, their return to the tribe or village must be designated by warlike ceremonial; the captives or spoil which may happen to crown their valour must be conducted in triumphant form and decorated to every possible advantage. For this end, we must now submit to painting; their vermilion,[6] with which they were ever supplied, was mixed with bear's grease, and every cheek, chin, and forehead must have a dash. We then rowed on within a mile of the town, where we stopped at a French house to dine; the prisoners were served with soup meagre[7] and bread. After dinner, two savages proceeded to the village to carry the glad tidings of our arrival. The whole atmosphere soon resounded from every quarter, with whoops, yells, shrieks, and screams. St. Francis, from the noise that came from it, might be supposed the centre of Pandemonium.[8] Our masters were not backward, they made every response they possibly could. The whole time were sailing from the French house, the

---

[1] *punck* Tinder.

[2] *my child* Johnson was in a late stage of pregnancy when she was taken, and her baby was born during the journey.

[3] *effluvia* Unpleasant smell.

[4] *Scoggin* Name of the horse.

[5] *munch* March, pronounced with an accent.

[6] *vermilion* Bright red pigment.

[7] *soup meagre* Green vegetable soup.

[8] *Pandemonium* Capital of Hell in Milton's *Paradise Lost*.

noise was direful to be heard. Two hours before sunset, we came to the landing at the village. No sooner had we landed than the yelling in the town was redoubled, and a cloud of savages of all sizes and sexes soon appeared running towards us; when they reached the boats, they formed themselves into a long parade, leaving a small space through which we must pass. Each Indian took his prisoner by the hand, and after ordering him to sing the war-song, began to march through the gauntlet. We expected a severe beating before we got through, but were agreeably disappointed when we found that each Indian only gave us a tap on the shoulder. We were led directly into the houses, each taking his prisoner to his own wigwam.... My new home was not the most agreeable; a large wigwam without a floor, with a fire in the centre, and only a few water vessels and dishes to eat from made of birch bark, and tools for cookery, made clumsily of wood, for furniture,[1] will not be thought a pleasing residence for one accustomed to civilized life.

from CHAPTER 5

Hasty pudding was presently brought forward for supper. A spacious bowl of wood, well filled, was placed in a central spot, and each one drew near with a wooden spoon. As the Indians never use seats, nor have any in their wigwams, my awkwardness in taking my position was a matter of no small amusement to my new companions. The squaws first fall upon their knees and then sit back upon their heels. This was a posture that I could not imitate. To sit in any other was thought by them indelicate and unpolite. But I advanced to my pudding with the best grace I could, not, however, escaping some of their funny remarks. When the hour for sleep came on (for it would be improper to call it bedtime, where beds were not) I was pointed to a platform, raised half a yard, where, upon a board covered with a blanket, I was to pass the night. The Indians threw themselves down in various parts of the building in a manner that more resembled cows in a shed than human beings in a house....

It was now the 15th day of October. Forty-five days had passed since my captivity, and no prospect but what was darkened with clouds of misfortune. The uneasiness

occasioned by indolence[2] was in some measure relieved by the privilege of making shirts for my brother.[3] At night and morn, I was allowed to milk the cows. The rest of the time I strolled gloomily about, looking sometimes into an unsociable wigwam, at others sauntering into the bushes, and walking on the banks of brooks. Once I went to a French house three miles distant to visit some friends of my brother's family, where I was entertained politely a week. At another time I went with a party to fish, accompanied by a number of squaws. My weakness obliged me to rest often, which gave my companions a poor opinion of me; but they showed no other resentment than calling me "no good squaw," which was the only reproach my sister ever gave when I displeased her. All the French inhabitants I formed an acquaintance with treated me with that civility which distinguishes the nation; once in particular, being almost distracted with an aching tooth, I was carried to a French physician across the river for relief. They prevailed on the Indians to let me visit them a day or two, during which time their marked attention and generosity claim my warmest gratitude. At parting, they expressed their earnest wishes to have me visit them again.

St. Francis contained about thirty wigwams, which were thrown disorderly into a clump. There was a church, in which mass was held every night and morning, and every Sunday; the hearers were summoned by a bell; and attendance was pretty general. Ceremonies were performed by a French friar, who lived in the midst of them for the salvation of their souls. He appeared to be in that place what the legislative branch is in civil governments, and the grand sachem the executive. The inhabitants lived in perfect harmony, holding most of their property in common. They were prone to indolence when at home, and not remarkable for neatness. They were extremely modest and apparently averse to airs of courtship. Necessity was the only thing that called them to action; this induced them to plant their corn and to undergo the fatigues of hunting. Perhaps I am wrong in calling necessity the only motive; revenge, which prompts them to war, has great power.

---

[1] *furniture* Equipment.

[2] *indolence* Idleness.

[3] *my brother* The Abenaki family holding Johnson captive has adopted her.

I had a numerous retinue of relations, which I visited daily; but my brother's house being one of the most decent in the village, I fared full as well at home. Among my connections was a little brother Sabaties, who brought the cows for me, and took particular notice of my child. He was a sprightly little fellow, and often amused me with feats performed with his bow and arrow. ...

In justice to the Indians, I ought to remark that they never treated me with cruelty to a wanton degree: few people have survived a situation like mine, and few have fallen into the savages disposed to more lenity and patience. Modesty has ever been a characteristic of every savage tribe, a truth which the whole of my family will join to corroborate to the extent of their knowledge. As they are aptly called the children of nature, those who have profited by refinement and education ought to abate part of the prejudice which prompts them to look with an eye of censure on this untutored race. Can it be said of civilized conquerors that they in the main are willing to share with their prisoners the last ration of food when famine stares them in the face? Do they ever adopt an enemy and salute him by the tender name of brother? And I am justified in doubting whether, if I had fallen into the hands of French soldiery, so much assiduity[1] would have been shown to preserve my life.

American Independence

from Edmund Burke, "Speech on Conciliation with the Colonies" (22 March 1775)

One English writer and politician very largely sympathetic to the cause of the American colonies in the 1770s was the Irish-born British politician Edmund Burke—later to become a prominent opponent of the French Revolution. Burke's approach took the continuity of history and circumstance into account at least as much as it did abstract principles. As these excerpts from an influential 1775 speech indicate, Burke saw the cause of the American colonies as emerging naturally from their

English traditions; in contrast, he saw the French Revolution as a violent rupture with the past.[2]

... I have in my hand two accounts: one a comparative state of the export trade of England to its colonies, as it stood in the year 1704, and as it stood in the year 1772; the other a state of the export trade of this country to its colonies alone, as it stood in 1772, compared with the whole trade of England to all parts of the world (the colonies included) in the year 1704. ...

The export trade to the colonies consists of three great branches: the African—which, terminating almost wholly in the colonies, must be put to the account of their commerce—the West Indian, and the North American. All these are so interwoven that the attempt to separate them would tear to pieces the contexture of the whole, and, if not entirely destroy, would very much depreciate the value of all the parts. I therefore consider these three denominations to be, what in effect they are, one trade.

The trade to the colonies, taken on the export side, at the beginning of this century, that is, in the year 1704, stood thus:—

Exports to North America and the West Indies.	£483,265
To Africa.	£86,665
	£569,930

In the year 1772, which I take as a middle year between the highest and lowest of those lately laid on your table, the account was as follows:—

To North America and the West Indies.	£4,791,734
To Africa.	£866,398
To which, if you add the export trade from Scotland, which had in 1704 no existence.	£364,000
	£6,022,132

From five hundred and odd thousand, it has grown to six millions. It has increased no less than twelvefold. ... But this is not all. Examine my second account. See how the export trade to the colonies alone in 1772

---

[1] *assiduity* Concerted attention.

[2] *French revolution ... the past* For Burke's and other opinions on the French Revolution, see "Contexts: The French Revolution and the Napoleonic Era" (in the online component of this anthology, volume 4).

stood in the other point of view; that is, as compared to the whole trade of England in 1704:—

The whole export trade of England, including that to the colonies, in 1704.	£6,509,000
Export to the colonies alone, in 1772.	£6,024,000
Difference.	£485,000

The trade with America alone is now within less than £500,000 of being equal to what this great commercial nation, England, carried on at the beginning of this century with the whole world! …

America, gentlemen say, is a noble object. It is an object well worth fighting for. Certainly it is, if fighting a people be the best way of gaining them. Gentlemen in this respect will be led to their choice of means by their complexions[1] and their habits. Those who understand the military art will of course have some predilection for it. Those who wield the thunder of the state may have more confidence in the efficacy of arms. But I confess, possibly for want of this knowledge, my opinion is much more in favour of prudent management than of force; considering force not as an odious, but a feeble instrument for preserving a people so numerous, so active, so growing, so spirited as this, in a profitable and subordinate connection with us.

First, Sir, permit me to observe that the use of force alone is but temporary. It may subdue for a moment, but it does not remove the necessity of subduing again; and a nation is not governed which is perpetually to be conquered.

My next objection is its uncertainty. Terror is not always the effect of force, and an armament is not a victory. If you do not succeed, you are without resource; for, conciliation failing, force remains; but, force failing, no further hope of reconciliation is left. Power and authority are sometimes bought by kindness; but they can never be begged as alms by an impoverished and defeated violence.

A further objection to force is that you impair the object by your very endeavors to preserve it. The thing you fought for is not the thing which you recover; but depreciated, sunk, wasted, and consumed in the contest. Nothing less will content me than whole America. I do not choose to consume its strength along with our own, because in all parts it is the British strength that I consume. I do not choose to be caught by a foreign enemy at the end of this exhausting conflict, and still less in the midst of it. I may escape; but I can make no insurance against such an event. Let me add, that I do not choose wholly to break the American spirit, because it is the spirit that has made the country.

Lastly, we have no sort of experience in favour of force as an instrument in the rule of our colonies. Their growth and their utility has been owing to methods altogether different. Our ancient indulgence has been said to be pursued to a fault. It may be so. But we know, if feeling is evidence, that our fault was more tolerable than our attempt to mend it; and our sin far more salutary[2] than our penitence.

These, Sir, are my reasons for not entertaining that high opinion of untried force by which many gentlemen, for whose sentiments in other particulars I have great respect, seem to be so greatly captivated. But there is still behind a third consideration concerning this object which serves to determine my opinion on the sort of policy which ought to be pursued in the management of America, even more than its population and its commerce—I mean its temper and character.

In this character of the Americans, a love of freedom is the predominating feature which marks and distinguishes the whole; and as an ardent is always a jealous affection, your colonies become suspicious, restive, and untractable[3] whenever they see the least attempt to wrest from them by force, or shuffle from them by chicane,[4] what they think the only advantage worth living for. This fierce spirit of liberty is stronger in the English colonies probably than in any other people of the earth, and this from a great variety of powerful causes; which, to understand the true temper of their minds and the direction which this spirit takes, it will not be amiss to lay open somewhat more largely.

First, the people of the colonies are descendants of Englishmen. England, Sir, is a nation which still, I hope, respects, and formerly adored, her freedom. The colonists

---

[1] *complexions* Personal attitudes.

[2] *salutary* Beneficial.

[3] *untractable* Difficult to manage.

[4] *chicane* Deceit.

emigrated from you when this part of your character was most predominant, and they took this bias and direction the moment they parted from your hands. They are therefore not only devoted to liberty, but to liberty according to English ideas and on English principles. Abstract liberty, like other mere abstractions, is not to be found. Liberty inheres in some sensible object; and every nation has formed to itself some favorite point, which by way of eminence becomes the criterion of their happiness. It happened, you know, Sir, that the great contests for freedom in this country were from the earliest times chiefly upon the question of taxing. … The colonies draw from [England], as with their life-blood, these ideas and principles. Their love of liberty, as with you, fixed and attached on this specific point of taxing. Liberty might be safe, or might be endangered, in twenty other particulars, without their being much pleased or alarmed. Here they felt its pulse; and as they found that beat, they thought themselves sick or sound. I do not say whether they were right or wrong in applying your general arguments to their own case. It is not easy, indeed, to make a monopoly of theorems and corollaries.[1] The fact is that they did thus apply those general arguments; and your mode of governing them, whether through lenity or indolence,[2] through wisdom or mistake, confirmed them in the imagination that they, as well as you, had an interest in these common principles.

…

The Americans will have no interest contrary to the grandeur and glory of England when they are not oppressed by the weight of it; and they will rather be inclined to respect the acts of a superintending legislature when they see them the acts of that power which is itself the security, not the rival, of their secondary importance. In this assurance my mind most perfectly acquiesces, and I confess I feel not the least alarm from the discontents which are to arise from putting people at their ease, nor do I apprehend the destruction of this empire from giving, by an act of free grace and indulgence, to two millions of my fellow-citizens some share of those rights upon which I have always been taught to value myself. …

from Benjamin Franklin,[3] *The Autobiography of Benjamin Franklin* (1793)

> Benjamin Franklin was a remarkable polymath—in addition to playing a major political role in the American Revolution, he was also a successful book printer, author, inventor, and scientist, among other things. Instrumental in the foundation of the United States, he was also influential in Europe; he acted as a negotiator with the British government and as a diplomat to France, where he was hugely popular. In the following excerpt from his *Autobiography*, he describes a journey to England at the beginning of the Revolution; fighting had just begun when his ship left the American coast.

The Assembly finally, finding the proprietaries[4] obstinately persisted in manacling their deputies with instructions inconsistent not only with the privileges of the people, but with the service of the Crown, resolved to petition the king against them, and appointed me their agent to go over to England, to present and support the petition. …

In the morning it was found by the soundings, &c., that we were near our port, but a thick fog hid the land from our sight. About nine o'clock the fog began to rise, and seemed to be lifted up from the water like the curtain at a play-house, discovering underneath the town of Falmouth, the vessels in its harbor, and the fields that surrounded it. A most pleasing spectacle to those who had been so long without any other prospects than the uniform view of a vacant ocean! And it gave us the more pleasure as we were now free from the anxieties which the state of war occasioned.

I set out immediately, with my son, for London, and we only stopped a little by the way to view Stonehenge on Salisbury Plain, and Lord Pembroke's house and gardens, with his very curious antiquities at Wilton.[5]

---

[1] *theorems and corollaries* Established propositions and what can be reasoned from them.

[2] *indolence* Laziness.

[3] *from Benjamin Franklin* Further selections from Franklin are available in the website component of this anthology.

[4] *the proprietaries* The Penn family, which had been granted governing rights to Pennsylvania by royal charter.

[5] *Lord Pembroke … Wilton* Wilton, the seat of the Earls of Pembroke, was (and is) renowned as a beautiful country estate.

We arrived in London the 27th of July, 1775. As soon as I was settled in a lodging Mr. Charles had provided for me, I went to visit Dr. Fothergill, to whom I was strongly recommended, and whose counsel respecting my proceedings I was advised to obtain. He was against an immediate complaint to government, and thought the proprietaries should first be personally applied to, who might possibly be induced by the interposition and persuasion of some private friends to accommodate matters amicably. I then waited on my old friend and correspondent Mr. Peter Collinson, who told me that John Hanbury, the great Virginia merchant, had requested to be informed when I should arrive, that he might carry me to Lord Granville's, who was then President of the Council, and wished to see me as soon as possible. I agreed to go with him the next morning. Accordingly Mr. Hanbury called for me and took me in his carriage to that nobleman's, who received me with great civility; and after some questions respecting the present state of affairs in America and discourse thereupon, he said to me: "You Americans have wrong ideas of the nature of your constitution; you contend that the king's instructions to his governors are not laws, and think yourselves at liberty to regard or disregard them at your own discretion. But those instructions are not like the pocket instructions given to a minister going abroad, for regulating his conduct in some trifling point of ceremony. They are first drawn up by judges learned in the laws; they are then considered, debated, and perhaps amended in Council, after which they are signed by the king. They are then, so far as relates to you, the law of the land, for THE KING IS THE LEGISLATOR OF THE COLONIES." I told his lordship this was new doctrine to me. I had always understood from our charters that our laws were to be made by our Assemblies, to be presented indeed to the king for his royal assent, but that being once given the king could not repeal or alter them. And as the Assemblies could not make permanent laws without his assent, so neither could he make a law for them without theirs. He assured me I was totally mistaken. I did not think so, however. And his lordship's conversation having a little

alarmed me as to what might be the sentiments of the Court concerning us, I wrote it down as soon as I returned to my lodgings. I recollected that about 20 years before, a clause in a bill brought into Parliament by the ministry had proposed to make the king's instructions laws in the colonies, but the clause was thrown out by the Commons, for which we adored them as our friends and friends of liberty, till by their conduct towards us in 1765 it seemed that they had refused that point of sovereignty to the king only that they might reserve it for themselves.

from Richard Price, *Observations on the Nature of Civil Liberty, the Principles of Government, and the Justice and Policy of the War with America* (1776)

> British preacher and writer Richard Price never left the British Isles, but his ideas influenced the political relationship between England and America on both sides. His pamphlets in support of the American Revolution were at the center of the English debate surrounding policy toward the Thirteen Colonies, and the first, excerpted below, played a role in encouraging the Americans to declare their independence.

from PART 2

Though clearly decided in my own judgment on this subject, I am inclined to make great allowances for the different judgments of others. We have been so used to speak of the colonies as *our* colonies, and to think of them as in a state of subordination to us, and as holding their existence in America only for our use, that it is no wonder the prejudices of many are alarmed when they find a different doctrine maintained. The meanest[1] person among us is disposed to look upon himself as having a body of subjects in America, and to be offended at the denial of his right to make laws for them, though perhaps he does not know what colour they are of, or what language they talk. Such are the natural prejudices of this country. But the time is coming, I hope, when the unreasonableness of them will be seen, and more just sentiments prevail. ...

---

[1] *meanest* Most inferior; of lowest social status.

from SECTION 1, *Of the Justice of the War with America*

The enquiry whether the war with the colonies is a just war will be best determined by stating the power over them, which it is the end of the war to maintain; and this cannot be better done than in the words of an act of parliament, made on purpose to define it. That act, it is well known, declares, "That this kingdom has power, and of right ought to have power to make laws and statutes to bind the colonies, and people of America, in all cases whatever."[1] Dreadful power indeed! I defy anyone to express slavery in stronger language. It is the same with[2] declaring "that we have a right to do with them what we please."…

But, probably, most persons will be for using milder language; and for saying no more than that the united legislatures of England and Scotland have of right power to tax the colonies, and a supremacy of legislature over America. But this comes to the same. If it means anything, it means that the property and the legislations of the colonies are subject to the absolute discretion of Great Britain, and ought of right to be so. The nature of the thing admits of no limitation. The colonies can never be admitted to be judges how far the authority over them in these cases shall extend. This would be to destroy it entirely. If any part of their property is subject to our discretion, the whole must be so. If we have a right to interfere at all in their internal legislations, we have a right to interfere as far as we think proper. It is self-evident that this leaves them nothing they can call their own.…

Much has been said of "the superiority of the British state." But what gives us our superiority? Is it our wealth? This never confers real dignity. On the contrary its effect is always to debase, intoxicate, and corrupt. Is it the number of our people? The colonies will soon be equal to us in number. Is it our knowledge and virtue? They are probably equally knowing and more virtuous. There are names among them that will not stoop to any names among the philosophers and politicians of this island.…

---

[1] *That this … whatever* Paraphrased passage from the Declaratory Act (1766), which stated that the British government "had, hath, and of right ought to have, full power and authority to make laws and statutes of sufficient force and validity to bind the colonies and people of America, subjects of the crown of Great Britain, in all cases whatsoever."

[2] *same with* Same as.

from SECTION 3, *Of the Policy of the War with America*

[W]hat deserves particular consideration here is that this [war] is a contest from which no advantages can possibly be derived. Not a revenue, for the provinces of America, when desolated, will afford no revenue, or, if they should, the expense of subduing them and keeping them in subjection will much exceed that revenue. Not any of the advantages of trade, for it is a folly, next to insanity, to think trade can be promoted by impoverishing our customers and fixing in their minds an everlasting abhorrence of us. It remains, therefore, that this war can have no other object than the extension of power. Miserable reflection! To sheath our swords in the bowels of our brethren and spread misery and ruin among a happy people for no other end than to oblige them to acknowledge our supremacy. How horrid! This is the cursed ambition that led a Caesar and an Alexander,[3] and many other mad conquerors, to attack peaceful communities and to lay waste the earth.

But a worse principle than even this influences some among us. Pride and the love of dominion are principles hateful enough, but blind resentment and the desire of revenge are infernal principles. And these, I am afraid, have no small share at present in guiding our public conduct. One cannot help indeed being astonished at the virulence with which some speak on the present occasion against the Colonies. For what have they done? Have they crossed the ocean and invaded us? Have they attempted to take from us the fruits of our labour and to overturn that form of government which we hold so sacred? This cannot be pretended. On the contrary, this is what we have done to them. We have transported ourselves to their peaceful retreats and employed our fleets and armies to stop up their ports, to destroy their commerce, to seize their effects, and to burn their towns. Would we but let them alone and suffer them to enjoy in security their property and governments, instead of disturbing us they would thank and bless us. And yet it is we who imagine ourselves ill-used. The truth is, we expected to find them a cowardly rabble who would lie quietly at our feet, and

---

[3] *Caesar* Julius Caesar, first-century BCE Roman general and statesman who helped form the Roman Empire and led the first Roman invasion of Britain; *Alexander* Alexander the Great, a fourth-century BCE Macedonian king who excelled as a military commander and who formed one of the largest ancient empires.

they have disappointed us. They have risen in their own defence and repelled force by force. They deny the plenitude of our power over them and insist upon being treated as free communities. It is this that has provoked us and kindled our governors into rage....

Thomas Jefferson, "A Declaration by the Representatives of the United States of America, in General Congress Assembled"[1] (1776)

> The American Revolutionary War had already begun when the Second Continental Congress, an assembly of delegates from the Thirteen Colonies, gathered to perform the functions of government, orchestrating the conduct of the war and the confederation of the colonies as a nation independent from the British Empire. Needing to provide an official explanation for the decision to sever allegiances to Great Britain, Congress appointed a committee of five people—including Thomas Jefferson, Benjamin Franklin, and John Adams—to draft a Declaration of Independence enumerating the American grievances against the Crown and the ideological justifications for rejecting British rule. The draft was edited by Congress and then immediately printed and distributed throughout the colonies; one copy was sent to England.
>
> The following text is the first complete draft of the Declaration, written by Thomas Jefferson and incorporating changes by other members of the drafting committee; it differs in a few major and many minor respects from the version that Congress eventually adopted. These changes highlight some of the tensions in America over the ideological content of the Declaration; for example, Congress altered Jefferson's expressions of disappointment in the British Empire and completely removed a paragraph relating to slavery. The most significant differences between the draft and final versions are indicated below in footnotes.

When in the course of human events it becomes necessary for a people to advance from that subordination in which they have hitherto remained,[2] and to assume among the powers of the earth the equal and independent station to which the laws of nature and of nature's God entitle them, a decent respect to the opinions of mankind requires that they should declare the causes which impel them to the change.

We hold these truths to be self-evident; that all men are created equal and independent; that from that equal creation they derive rights inherent and inalienable, among which are the preservation of life, and liberty, and the pursuit of happiness;[3] that to secure these ends, governments are instituted among men, deriving their just powers from the consent of the governed; that whenever any form of government shall become destructive of these ends, it is the right of the people to alter or to abolish it, and to institute new government, laying its foundation on such principles and organizing its power in such form as to them shall seem most likely to effect their safety and happiness. Prudence indeed will dictate that governments long established should not be changed for light and transient causes: and accordingly all experience hath shown that mankind are more disposed to suffer while evils are sufferable, than to right themselves by abolishing the forms to which they are accustomed. But when a long train of abuses and usurpations, begun at a distinguished period, and pursuing invariably the same object, evinces a design to reduce them to absolute despotism, it is their right, it is their duty, to throw off such government and to provide new guards for future security. Such has been the patient sufferance of the colonies; and such is now the necessity which constrains them to expunge their former systems of government. The history of his present majesty[4] is a history of unremitting injuries and usurpations, among which no one fact stands single or solitary

---

1   *A Declaration ... Congress Assembled*   The final version is titled "The unanimous Declaration of the thirteen united States of America."

2   *to advance ... hitherto remained*   The final version reads "to dissolve the political bands which have connected them with another."

3   *created equal ... of happiness*   The final version reads "created equal, that they are endowed by their Creator with certain unalienable rights, that among these are life, liberty, and the pursuit of happiness."

4   *his present majesty*   The final version reads "the present King of Great Britain."

to contradict the uniform tenor of the rest,[1] all of which have in direct object the establishment of an absolute tyranny over these states. To prove this, let facts be submitted to a candid world, for the truth of which we pledge a faith yet unsullied by falsehood.[2]

He has refused his assent to laws the most wholesome and necessary for the public good.

He has forbidden his governors to pass laws of immediate and pressing importance, unless suspended in their operation till his assent should be obtained; and when so suspended, he has neglected utterly to attend to them.

He has refused to pass other laws for the accommodation of large districts of people unless those people would relinquish the right of representation in the legislature, a right inestimable to them and formidable to tyrants only:[3]

He has dissolved Representative Houses repeatedly and continually, for opposing with manly firmness his invasions on the rights of the people:

He has refused for a long time after such dissolutions to cause others to be elected, whereby the legislative powers, incapable of annihilation, have returned to the people at large for their exercise,[4] the state remaining in the meantime exposed to all the dangers of invasion from without and convulsions within:

He has endeavoured to prevent the population of these states; for that purpose obstructing the laws for naturalization for foreigners; refusing to pass others to encourage their migrations hither; and raising the conditions of new appropriations of lands:[5]

He has suffered the administration of justice totally to cease in some of these colonies,[6] refusing his assent to laws for establishing judiciary powers:

He has made our judges dependent on his will alone for the tenure of their offices and amount of their salaries:

He has erected a multitude of new offices by a self-assumed power,[7] and sent hither swarms of officers to harass our people and eat out their substance:

He has kept among us in times of peace standing armies and ships of war:[8]

He has affected to render the military independent of and superior to the civil power:[9]

He has combined with others to subject us to a jurisdiction foreign to our constitutions and unacknowledged by our laws; giving his assent to their pretended acts of legislation:

For quartering large bodies of armed troops among us;

For protecting them by a mock-trial from punishment for any murders which they should commit on the inhabitants of these states;

For cutting off our trade with all parts of the world;

For imposing taxes on us without our consent;

For depriving us of the benefits of trial by jury;

---

[1] *among which ... the rest* These words are removed from the final version.

[2] *for the truth ... by falsehood* These words are removed from the final version.

[3] *He has refused ... tyrants only* In 1774, the elected government of the province of Quebec was replaced with an appointed one, and the new government refused to pass important laws until the people of Quebec stopped agitating for a return to the representative system. Similar changes were made to the government of Massachusetts; *tyrants only* In the final version, here is added the following complaint: "He has called together legislative bodies at places unusual, uncomfortable, and distant from the depository of their public records, for the sole purpose of fatiguing them into compliance with his measures." As retribution for the Boston Tea Party, the governor of Massachusetts forced its assembly to move to Salem, but kept the public records in Boston.

[4] *the legislative ... their exercise* I.e., because the people's right to good laws cannot be extinguished, but the government is prevented from exercising it on their behalf, the people are justified in undertaking government for themselves.

[5] *raising the conditions ... of lands* I.e., making it more difficult for new immigrants to obtain frontier land, thus discouraging immigration.

[6] *suffered the ... these colonies* The final version reads "obstructed the administration of justice, by."

[7] *by a self-assumed power* These words are removed from the final version.

[8] *and ships of war* The final version reads "without the consent of our legislatures."

[9] *He has affected ... civil power* By an order of the King, the power of the military commander-in-chief for the colonies superseded the power of all civil government in America.

For transporting us beyond seas to be tried for pretended offenses;[1]

For taking away our charters,[2] and altering fundamentally the forms of our governments;

For suspending our own legislatures and declaring themselves invested with power to legislate for us in all cases whatsoever:

He has abdicated government here, withdrawing his governors, and declaring us out of his allegiance and protection:[3]

He has plundered our seas, ravaged our coasts, burnt our towns and destroyed the lives of our people:

He is at this time transporting large armies of foreign mercenaries[4] to complete the works of death, desolation and tyranny, already begun with circumstances of cruelty and perfidy unworthy the head[5] of a civilized nation:

He has endeavoured to bring on the inhabitants of our frontiers the merciless Indian savages, whose known rule of warfare is an undistinguished destruction of all ages, sexes, and conditions of existence:

He has incited treasonable insurrections in our fellow-citizens, with the allurements of forfeiture and confiscation of our property:[6]

He has waged cruel war against human nature itself, violating its most sacred rights of life and liberty in the persons of a distant people who never offended him, captivating and carrying them into slavery in another hemisphere, or to incur miserable death in their transportation thither. This piratical warfare, the opprobrium of infidel powers, is the warfare of the CHRISTIAN king of Great Britain. Determined to keep open a market where MEN should be bought and sold, he has prostituted his negative for suppressing every legislative attempt to prohibit or to restrain this execrable commerce:[7] and that this assemblage of horrors might want no fact of distinguished dye,[8] he is now exciting those very people to rise in arms among us,[9] and to purchase that liberty of which he has deprived them by murdering the people upon whom he also obtruded them: thus paying off former crimes committed against the liberties of one people with crimes which he urges them to commit against the lives of another.[10]

In every stage of these oppressions we have petitioned for redress in the most humble terms; our repeated petitions have been answered by repeated injury. A prince whose character is thus marked by every act which may define a tyrant is unfit to be the ruler of a people who mean to be free.[11] Future ages will scarce believe that the hardiness of one man adventured, within the short compass of twelve years only, on so many acts of tyranny without a mask, over a people

---

[1] *For transporting … pretended offenses*   A 1774 Massachusetts bill entitled the magistrate to send accused criminals to England to be tried; of course, before the trial occurred, it could not be determined whether a transported prisoner was innocent or guilty; *pretended offenses*   Here, the following complaint is added in the final version: "For abolishing the free system of English laws in a neighbouring province, establishing therein an arbitrary government, and enlarging its boundaries so as to render it at once an example and fit instrument for introducing the same absolute rule into these colonies." The 1774 changes to the government of Quebec were seen as a means to appease the powerful Catholics there, in order to ensure the province's military allegiance in case of an American rebellion.

[2] *our charters*   In the final version, here is added "abolishing our most valuable laws."

[3] *withdrawing his … and protection*   The final version reads "by declaring us out of his protection and waging war against us."

[4] *foreign mercenaries*   The British hired many thousands of German soldiers to help fight the American rebels.

[5] *unworthy the head*   The final version reads "scarcely paralleled in the most barbarous ages, and totally unworthy the head."

[6] *He has endeavoured … our property*   The final version reads: "He has constrained our fellow citizens taken captive on the high seas to bear arms against their country, to become the executioners

of their friends and brethren, or to fall themselves by their hands.

"He has excited domestic insurrections among us, and has endeavoured to bring on the inhabitants of our frontiers the merciless Indian savages, whose known rule of warfare is an undistinguished destruction of all ages, sexes and conditions."

[7] *prostituted his … execrable commerce*   The king had vetoed resolutions against the slave trade—primarily at the insistence of slave-owners in the southern colonies.

[8] *want no … distinguished dye*   I.e., lack no equally reprehensible element.

[9] *he is now … among us*   The British government offered freedom to slaves who escaped their rebel masters and joined the war on the British side.

[10] *He has waged … of another*   This paragraph does not appear in the final version.

[11] *a people … be free*   The final version reads: "a free people."

fostered and fixed in principles of liberty.[1]

Nor have we been wanting in attentions to our British brethren. We have warned them from time to time of attempts by their legislature to extend a jurisdiction over these our states.[2] We have reminded them of the circumstances of our emigration and settlement here, no one of which could warrant so strange a pretension:[3] that these were effected at the expense of our own blood and treasure, unassisted by the wealth or the strength of Great Britain: that in constituting indeed our several forms of government, we had adopted one common king, thereby laying a foundation for perpetual league and amity with them: but that submission to their parliament was no part of our constitution, nor ever in idea, if history may be credited: and[4] we appealed to their native justice and magnanimity, as well as to the ties of our common kindred to disavow these usurpations which were likely to[5] interrupt our correspondence and connection. They too have been deaf to the voice of justice and of consanguinity,[6] and when occasions have been given them, by the regular course of their laws, of removing from their councils the disturbers of our harmony, they have by their free election re-established them in power. At this very time too they are permitting their chief magistrate to send over not only soldiers of our common blood, but Scotch and foreign mercenaries to invade and deluge us in blood. These facts have given the last stab to agonizing affection, and manly spirit bids us to renounce forever these unfeeling brethren. We must endeavour to forget our former love for them, and to hold them as we hold the rest of mankind, enemies in war, in peace friends. We might have been a free and a great people together; but a communication of grandeur and of freedom it seems is below their dignity. Be it so, since they will have it; the road to happiness and to glory is open to us too; we will climb it apart from them, and acquiesce in the necessity which denounces our eternal separation![7]

We therefore the representatives of the United States of America in General Congress assembled[8] do, in the name and by authority of the good people of these states, reject and renounce all allegiance and subjection to the kings of Great Britain and all others who may hereafter claim by, through, or under them; we utterly dissolve and break off all political connection which may have heretofore subsisted between us and the people or parliament of Great Britain; and finally we do assert and declare these colonies to be free and independent states,[9] and that as free and independent states they shall hereafter[10] have full power to levy war, conclude peace, contract alliances, establish commerce, and to do all other acts and things which independent states may of right do. And for the support of this declaration[11] we mutually pledge to each other our lives, our fortunes, and our sacred honour.

---

[1] *Future ages ... of liberty*   This sentence does not appear in the final version.

[2] *a jurisdiction ... our states*   The final version reads: "an unwarrantable jurisdiction over us."

[3] *so strange a pretension*   I.e., the notion that the people of the Thirteen Colonies were subject to the English Parliament as opposed to their own.

[4] *no one of which ... credited: and*   These words do not appear in the final version.

[5] *were likely to*   The final version reads: "would inevitably."

[6] *consanguinity*   Commonality of blood.

[7] *and when occasions ... eternal separation*   The final version reads: "We must, therefore, acquiesce in the necessity which denounces our separation, and hold them, as we hold the rest of mankind, enemies in war, in peace friends."

[8] *assembled*   In the final version, here is added "appealing to the supreme judge of the world for the rectitude of our intentions."

[9] *of these states ... independent states*   The final version reads: "of these colonies, solemnly publish and declare that these united colonies are, and of right ought to be, free and independent states; that they are absolved from all allegiance to the British Crown, and that all political connection between them and the state of Great Britain is and ought to be totally dissolved."

[10] *shall hereafter*   These words do not appear in the final version.

[11] *declaration*   In the final version, here is added "with a firm reliance on the protection of divine Providence."

from Thomas Paine, *The American Crisis* (1777)

Born in England, Thomas Paine immigrated to the Thirteen Colonies in 1774 and became a citizen of Pennsylvania just in time for the beginning of the Revolutionary War. His bestselling pamphlets *Common Sense* and *The American Crisis* were hugely important in exciting public opinion in support of the war. He later returned to England, where he wrote *Rights of Man* in support of the French Revolution.[1]

NUMBER 1

These are the times that try men's souls. The summer soldier and the sunshine patriot will, in this crisis, shrink from the service of his country, but he that stands it now deserves the love and thanks of man and woman. Tyranny, like hell, is not easily conquered; yet we have this consolation with us, that the harder the conflict, the more glorious the triumph. What we obtain too cheap, we esteem too lightly; 'tis dearness only that gives everything its value. Heaven knows how to set a proper price upon its goods; and it would be strange indeed, if so celestial an article as freedom should not be highly rated. Britain, with an army to enforce her tyranny, has declared, that she has a right (not only to tax) but "to bind us in all cases whatsoever,"[2] and if being bound in that manner is not slavery, then is there not such a thing as slavery upon earth. Even the expression is impious, for so unlimited a power can belong only to GOD.

Whether the independence of the Continent was declared too soon, or delayed too long, I will not now enter into as an argument; my own simple opinion is that had it been eight months earlier, it would have been much better. We did not make a proper use of last winter, neither could we, while we were in a dependent state. However, the fault, if it were one, was all our own; we have none to blame but ourselves. But no great deal is lost yet; all that Howe[3] has been doing for this month past is rather a ravage than a conquest, which the spirit of the Jersies[4] a year ago would have quickly repulsed, and which time and a little resolution will soon recover.

I have as little superstition in me as any man living, but my secret opinion has ever been, and still is, that GOD almighty will not give up a people to military destruction, or leave them unsupported to perish, who had so earnestly and so repeatedly sought to avoid the calamities of war by every decent method which wisdom

could invent. Neither have I so much of the infidel in me as to suppose that He has relinquished the government of the world, and given us up to the care of devils; and as I do not, I cannot see on what grounds the king of Britain can look up to Heaven for help against us: a common murderer, a highwayman, or a housebreaker, has as good a pretence as he.

---

[1] *Rights of … Revolution* See Paine's *Rights of Man*, excerpted in the online component of this anthology, volume 4.

[2] *to bind … whatsoever* Reference to a statement made in the Declaratory Act (1766): "[the British government] had, hath, and of right ought to have, full power and authority to make laws and statutes of sufficient force and validity to bind the colonies and people of America, subjects of the crown of Great Britain, in all cases whatsoever."

[3] *Howe* Sir William Howe (1729–1814), commander of the British forces during the War of Independence.

[4] *Jersies* Colonies of East and West Jersey; Paine is referring to Washington's successful surprise attack on Christmas Day of the previous year.

John Singleton Copley, *The Death of Major Peirson, 6 January 1781* (1783). France provided unofficial assistance to the Americans from the beginning of the Revolutionary War, but by the end of the war it was openly fighting against the English, as were Spain and the Dutch Republic. Battles related to the Revolutionary War occurred in India, the West Indies, and even in Europe; this painting depicts the results of a battle on the island of Jersey, a British possession off the coast of France. The governor of Jersey surrendered after an attack by the French, but British major Francis Peirson refused to accept the surrender and organized the defeat of the French forces. He died early in the battle and never learned of his success, but this painting depicts him dying at the moment of victory. The artist, John Singleton Copley, was born in New England and painted portraits there before immigrating to England, where he painted this and other historical works. (See the color insert in this volume for another important example.)

from Richard Price, *Observations on the Importance of the American Revolution* (1785)

OF THE IMPORTANCE OF THE REVOLUTION WHICH HAS ESTABLISHED THE INDEPENDENCE OF THE UNITED STATES

Having, from pure conviction, taken a warm part in favour of the British colonies (now the United States of America) during the late war and been exposed, in consequence of this, to much abuse and some danger, it must be supposed that I have been waiting for the issue[1] with anxiety. I am thankful that my anxiety is removed and that I have been spared to be a witness to that very issue of the war which has been all along the object of my wishes. With heartfelt satisfaction I see the revolution in favour of universal liberty which has taken place in America, a revolution which opens a new prospect in human affairs and begins a new era in the history of mankind, a revolution by which Britons themselves will be the greatest gainers, if wise enough to improve properly the check that has been given to the despotism of their ministers, and to catch the flame of virtuous liberty which has saved their American brethren.

The late war, in its commencement and progress, did great good by disseminating just sentiments of the rights of mankind and the nature of legitimate government, by exciting a spirit of resistance to tyranny which has emancipated one European country and is likely to emancipate others, and by occasioning the establishment in America of forms of government more equitable and more liberal than any that the world has yet known. But, in its termination, the war has done still greater good by preserving the new governments from that destruction in which they must have been involved, had Britain conquered, by providing, in a sequestrated continent possessed of many singular advantages, a place of refuge for oppressed men in every region of the world, and by laying the foundation there of an empire which may be the seat of liberty, science and virtue, and from whence there is reason to hope these sacred blessings will spread till they become universal and the time arrives when kings and priests shall have no more power to oppress, and that ignominious slavery which has hitherto debased the world exterminated. I therefore think I see the hand of providence in the late war working for the general good.

Reason, as well as tradition and revelation, lead us to expect that a more improved and happy state of human affairs will take place before the consummation of all things.[2] The world has hitherto been gradually improving. Light and knowledge have been gaining ground, and human life at present, compared with what it once was, is much the same that a youth approaching to manhood is compared with an infant....

OF THE NEGRO TRADE AND SLAVERY

The negro trade cannot be censured in language too severe. It is a traffic which, as it has been hitherto carried on, is shocking to humanity, cruel, wicked, and diabolical. I am happy to find that the United States are entering into measures for discountenancing[3] it and for abolishing the odious slavery which it has introduced. Till they have done this, it will not appear they deserve the liberty for which they have been contending. For it is self-evident that if there are any men whom they have a right to hold in slavery, there may be others who have had a right to hold them in slavery. I am sensible, however, that this is a work which they cannot accomplish at once. The emancipation of the negroes must, I suppose, be left in some measure to be the effect of time and of manners. But nothing can excuse the United States if it is not done with as much speed, and at the same time with as much effect, as their particular circumstances and situation will allow. I rejoice that on this occasion I can recommend to them the example of my own country. In Britain, a negro becomes a freeman the moment he sets his foot on British ground.[4]

---

[2] *consummation of all things*   End of the world as foretold in the Bible.

[3] *discountenancing*   Discouraging.

[4] *In Britain ... British ground*   Reference to a 1772 court ruling (Somersett's Case) that effectively outlawed the keeping of slaves in England. English people, however, continued to own slaves in other parts of the British Empire.

---

[1] *issue*   I.e., the resolution of the conflict.

William Cowper
1731 — 1800

William Cowper (pronounced Cooper) had an enormous readership during his generation, even though he spent most of his life in seclusion in the countryside, where he wrote the poems and letters for which he is best remembered. The inspiration for his best-known work came from his friend Lady Austen. When Cowper complained to her that he had nothing to write about, she suggested that he compose a poem in blank verse about his sofa. "The Sofa" did indeed become Book I of *The Task* (1785), engendering an extended work that is almost epic in its breadth of subject matter and style (while its domestic focus and absence of narrative are the very reverse of epic). *The Task* comprises six books, beginning with a playful narrative about the evolution of furniture, written in mock-heroic, Miltonic style. It moves on to myriad other

subjects, including a meditation on the immorality of slavery (a subject about which the author felt passionately) and an extended celebration of domestic and rural life. Cowper is at his finest when meditating upon the significance of commonplace items and the details of lush, pastoral scenes, using unadorned language that has sometimes been said to foreshadow the style of the later Romantics. Indeed, Samuel Taylor Coleridge called Cowper "the best modern poet." In addition to *The Task*, he remains known for his varied range of short poems, for his comic narrative "The Diverting History of John Gilpin," and for the astonishing contrasts between his outwardly ordinary life and his inner despair.

Cowper was born in Berkampstead, Hertfordshire, to the Reverend John Cowper and Ann Donne, whose family claimed a kinship with the poet John Donne. She died when Cowper was only six, and he believed that his later problems with depression stemmed partly from this premature loss. Cowper's early difficulties were aggravated by the relentless bullying he suffered at the hands of his schoolmates in school. He eventually studied law, a profession ill-suited to him and which he never practiced. When a relative tried to help him procure a position as Clerk of the Journals in the House of Lords, Cowper was thrown into terror at the prospect of the interview he would be required to attend. This caused his first suicide attempt, upon which he was incarcerated in an asylum. During this period Cowper wrote "Lines Written During a Period of Insanity," which describes his growing fear of the wrath of God for the "sin" he had committed against the Holy Ghost: "Him [Satan] the vindictive rod of angry justice / Sent quick and howling to the centre headlong; / I, fed with judgement, in a fleshly tomb, am / Buried above ground." Although Cowper would eventually find some respite from his despair upon his conversion to Evangelicalism, when he lost his first ecstatic religious feelings he was convinced he was damned, and his despondency returned, increased.

In 1765 Cowper moved to the home of Reverend Morley and Mary Unwin in Huntingdon. After Morley Unwin died two years later, Cowper moved with Mary and her children to Olney; he lived with her for the rest of his life. He wrote two famous paeans to Mary—"My Mary" and "To Mary Unwin"; she in turn devotedly nursed him through his depressions and encouraged his literary work. In Olney he came under the influence of John Newton, a fiery Evangelical preacher and ex-slave trader, who helped stoke his religious angst. During the period in which Cowper was still under Newton's sway, the two co-authored the hauntingly beautiful *Olney Hymns* (written in 1771–72 and published in 1779), which include Newton's "Amazing Grace" and Cowper's "Oh for a closer walk with God" and "God moves in a mysterious way."

Although he spent his years in Olney and later in Weston Underwood in isolation, Cowper became one of the most celebrated poets of his time. His 1782 volume *Poems by William Cowper, of the Inner Temple, Esq.*, which included eight satires, was received with great enthusiasm, ironically enough, for its "cheerfulness of spirit." 1785 saw publication of *The Task*, Cowper's *tour de force*, again with a very favorable response (including, it was said, from the Royal Family). His later works include a translation of Homer's *The Iliad* (1791).

Upon leaving Olney, Cowper continued to write long and evocative letters to friends; these letters have since become famous for their descriptive beauty and the simplicity of their language. Mary Unwin's prolonged illness and her death in 1796 again pushed Cowper to the limits of his sanity, and he spent the remainder of his life as an invalid, dying in 1800. Before he died, though, he wrote "The Castaway," a powerful poem that likens his own situation, in which he expected his soul to perish in damnation, to that of a sailor swept overboard who can see his "floating home" but knows that it is powerless to stop for him and that he will drown. The poem speaks to its author's sense of being cast out from the community of the saved; it has remained one of his best-known works.

⌘ ⌘ ⌘

Light Shining Out of Darkness

God moves in a mysterious way,
His wonders to perform;
He plants his footsteps in the sea,
And rides upon the storm.

5   Deep in unfathomable mines
Of never failing skill;
He treasures up his bright designs,
And works his Sovereign Will.

Ye fearful Saints fresh courage take,
10 The clouds ye so much dread
Are big with Mercy, and shall break
In blessings on your head.

Judge not the Lord by feeble sense,
But trust him for his Grace;
15 Behind a frowning Providence,
He hides a smiling face.

His purposes will ripen fast,
Unfolding every hour;

The bud may have a bitter taste,
20 But *wait*, to *smell the flower*.

Blind unbelief is sure to err,
And scan his work in vain;
God is his own Interpreter,
And he will make it plain.
—1772

from *The Task*

ADVERTISEMENT

The history of the following production is briefly this. A lady, fond of blank verse, demanded a poem of that kind from the author, and gave him the sofa for a subject. He obeyed; and having much leisure, connected another subject with it; and pursuing the train of thought which his situation and turn of mind led him, brought forth at length, instead of the trifle which he at first intended, a serious affair—a Volume.

In the poem, on the subject of education he would be very sorry to stand suspected of having aimed his censure at any particular school. His objections are such as naturally apply themselves to schools in general. If there were not, as for the most part there is, wilful neglect in those who manage them, and an omission even of such discipline as they are susceptible of, the objects are yet too numerous for minute attention; and the aching hearts of ten thousand parents mourning under the bitterest disappointments, attest the truth of the allegation. His quarrel therefore is with the mischief at large, and not with any particular instance of it.

from Book I: The Sofa

I sing the sofa. I, who lately sang
Truth, Hope, and Charity,[1] and touch'd with awe
The solemn chords, and with a trembling hand,
Escap'd with pain from that advent'rous flight,
5   Now seek repose upon an humbler theme;
The theme though humble, yet august and proud
Th' occasion—for the Fair[2] commands the song.
    Time was, when clothing sumptuous or for use,
Save their own painted skins, our sires had none.
10   As yet black breeches were not; satin smooth,
Or velvet soft, or plush with shaggy pile:
The hardy chief upon the rugged rock
Wash'd by the sea, or on the grav'ly bank
Thrown up by wintry torrents roaring loud,
15   Fearless of wrong, repos'd his weary strength.
Those barb'rous ages past, succeeded next
The birth-day of invention; weak at first,
Dull in design, and clumsy to perform.
Joint-stools were then created; on three legs
20   Upborn they stood. Three legs upholding firm
A massy slab, in fashion square or round.
On such a stool immortal Alfred[3] sat,
And sway'd the sceptre of his infant realms:
And such in ancient halls and mansions drear
25   May still be seen; but perforated sore,
And drill'd in holes, the solid oak is found,
By worms voracious eating through and through.
    At length a generation more refin'd

---

[1] *Truth, Hope, and Charity* Cowper wrote a series of satires, three of which were named *Truth*, *Hope*, and *Charity*.

[2] *the Fair* A woman, or women. Here, one woman, she who asked for the poem (see "Advertised").

[3] *Alfred* King Alfred the Great of England (849–899).

30   Improv'd the simple plan; made three legs four,
Gave them a twisted form vermicular,°   *wormlike*
And o'er the seat, with plenteous wadding stuff'd,
Induc'd a splendid cover, green and blue,
Yellow and red, of tap'stry richly wrought,
And woven close, or needle-work sublime.
35   There might ye see the peony spread wide,
The full-blown rose, the shepherd and his lass,
Lap-dog and lambkin with black staring eyes,
And parrots with twin cherries in their beak.
    Now came the cane from India, smooth and bright
40   With Nature's varnish; sever'd into stripes
That interlac'd each other, these supplied
Of texture firm a lattice-work, that brac'd
The new machine, and it became a chair.
But restless was the chair; the back erect
45   Distress'd the weary loins, that felt no ease;
The slipp'ry seat betray'd the sliding part
That press'd it, and the feet hung dangling down,
Anxious in vain to find the distant floor.
These for the rich: the rest, whom fate had plac'd
50   In modest mediocrity, content
With base materials, sat on well-tann'd hides,
Obdurate and unyielding, glassy smooth,
With here and there a tuft of crimson yarn,
Or scarlet crewel,° in the cushion fixt;   *embroidery yarn*
55   If cushion might be call'd, what harder seem'd
Than the firm oak of which the frame was form'd.
No want of timber then was felt or fear'd
In Albion's° happy isle. The lumber stood   *England's*
Pond'rous and fixt by its own massy weight.
60   But elbows still were wanting; these, some say,
An alderman of Cripplegate contriv'd:
And some ascribe th' invention to a priest
Burly and big, and studious of his ease.
But, rude at first, and not with easy slope
65   Receding wide, they press'd against the ribs,
And bruis'd the side; and, elevated high,
Taught the rais'd shoulders to invade the ears.
Long time elaps'd or e'er our rugged sires
Complain'd, though incommodiously pent in,
70   And ill at ease behind. The ladies first
'Gan murmur, as became the softer sex.
Ingenious fancy, never better pleas'd
Than when employ'd t' accommodate the fair,

Heard the sweet moan with pity, and devis'd
75 The soft settee; one elbow at each end,
And in the midst an elbow it receiv'd,
United yet divided, twain at once.
So sit two kings of Brentford[1] on one throne;
And so two citizens who take the air,
80 Close pack'd, and smiling, in a chaise and one.
But relaxation of the languid frame,
By soft recumbency of outstretch'd limbs,
Was bliss reserv'd for happier days. So slow
The growth of what is excellent; so hard
85 T' attain perfection in this nether world.
Thus first necessity invented stools,
Convenience next suggested elbow-chairs,
And luxury th' accomplish'd Sofa last.
        The nurse sleeps sweetly, hir'd to watch the sick,
90 Whom snoring she disturbs. As sweetly he,
Who quits the coach-box at the midnight hour
To sleep within the carriage more secure,
His legs depending at the open door.
Sweet sleep enjoys the curate in his desk,
95 The tedious rector drawling o'er his head;
And sweet the clerk below. But neither sleep
Of lazy nurse, who snores the sick man dead,
Nor his who quits the box at midnight hour
To slumber in the carriage more secure,
100 Nor sleep enjoy'd by curate in his desk,
Nor yet the dozings of the clerk, are sweet,
Compar'd with the repose the SOFA yields.
        Oh may I live exempted (while I live
Guiltless of pamper'd appetite obscene)
105 From pangs arthritic, that infest the toe
Of libertine excess. The SOFA suits
The gouty limb, 'tis true; but gouty limb,
Though on a SOFA, may I never feel:
For I have lov'd the rural walk through lanes
110 Of grassy swarth, close cropped by nibbling sheep,
And skirted thick with intertexture firm
Of thorny boughs; have lov'd the rural walk
O'er hills, through valleys, and by rivers' brink,
E'er since a truant boy I pass'd my bounds
115 T' enjoy a ramble on the banks of Thames;
And still remember, nor without regret

Of hours that sorrow since has much endear'd,
How oft, my slice of pocket store consum'd,
Still hung'ring, pennyless and far from home,
120 I fed on scarlet hips and stony haws,[2]
Or blushing crabs, or berries, that emboss
The bramble, black as jet, or sloes[3] austere.
Hard fare! but such as boyish appetite
Disdains not; nor the palate, undeprav'd
125 By culinary arts, unsav'ry deems.
No SOFA then awaited my return;
Nor SOFA then I needed. Youth repairs
His wasted spirits quickly, by long toil
Incurring short fatigue; and, though our years
130 As life declines speed rapidly away,
And not a year but pilfers as he goes
Some youthful grace that age would gladly keep;
A tooth or auburn lock, and by degrees
Their length and colour from the locks they spare;
135 Th' elastic spring of an unwearied foot
That mounts the stile with ease, or leaps the fence,
That play of lungs, inhaling and again
Respiring freely the fresh air, that makes
Swift pace or steep ascent no toil to me,
140 Mine have not pilfer'd yet; nor yet impair'd
My relish of fair prospect; scenes that sooth'd
Or charm'd me young, no longer young, I find
Still soothing and of pow'r to charm me still.
And witness, dear companion of my walks,
145 Whose arm this twentieth winter I perceive
Fast lock'd in mine, with pleasure such as love,
Confirm'd by long experience of thy worth
And well-tried virtues, could alone inspire—
Witness a joy that thou hast doubled long.
150 Thou know'st my praise of nature most sincere,
And that my raptures are not conjur'd up
To serve occasions of poetic pomp,
But genuine, and art partner of them all.
How oft upon yon eminence our pace
155 Has slacken'd to a pause, and we have born
The ruffling wind, scarce conscious that it blew,
While admiration, feeding at the eye,
And still unsated, dwelt upon the scene.

---

1 *two kings of Brentford* From George Villiers, Duke of Buckingham's satiric play *The Rehearsal* (1671).

2 *scarlet hips and stony haws* Rosehips and hawthorn fruit.

3 *sloes* Dark plumlike fruit of the blackthorn.

Thence with what pleasure have we just discern'd
The distant plough slow moving, and beside
His lab'ring team, that swerv'd not from the track,
The sturdy swain diminish'd to a boy!
Here Ouse,[1] slow winding through a level plain
Of spacious meads with cattle sprinkled o'er,
Conducts the eye along its sinuous course
Delighted. There, fast rooted in their bank,
Stand, never overlook'd, our fav'rite elms,
That screen the herdsman's solitary hut;
While far beyond, and overthwart° the stream   opposite
That, as with molten glass, inlays the vale,
The sloping land recedes into the clouds;
Displaying on its varied side the grace
Of hedge-row beauties numberless, square tow'r,
Tall spire, from which the sound of cheerful bells
Just undulates upon the list'ning ear,
Groves, heaths, and smoking villages, remote.
Scenes must be beautiful, which, daily view'd,
Please daily, and whose novelty survives
Long knowledge and the scrutiny of years.
Praise justly due to those that I describe.

    Nor rural sights alone, but rural sounds,
Exhilarate the spirit, and restore
The tone of languid Nature. Mighty winds,
That sweep the skirt of some far-spreading wood
Of ancient growth, make music not unlike
The dash of ocean on his winding shore,
And lull the spirit while they fill the mind;
Unnumber'd branches waving in the blast,
And all their leaves fast flutt'ring, all at once.
Nor less composure waits upon the roar
Of distant floods, or on the softer voice
Of neighb'ring fountain, or of rills that slip
Through the cleft rock, and, chiming as they fall
Upon loose pebbles, lose themselves at length
In matted grass, that with a livelier green
Betrays the secret of their silent course.
Nature inanimate employs sweet sounds,
But animated nature sweeter still,
To sooth and satisfy the human ear.
Ten thousand warblers cheer the day, and one
The live-long night: nor these alone, whose notes
Nice finger'd art must emulate in vain,

But cawing rooks, and kites[2] that swim sublime
In still repeated circles, screaming loud,
205 The jay, the pie, and ev'n the boding owl
That hails the rising moon, have charms for me.
Sounds inharmonious in themselves and harsh,
Yet heard in scenes where peace for ever reigns,
And only there, please highly for their sake....

from Book 6: THE WINTER WALK AT NOON

... The night was winter in his roughest mood;
The morning sharp and clear. But now at noon
Upon the southern side of the slant hills,
And where the woods fence off the northern blast,
5 The season smiles, resigning all its rage,
And has the warmth of May. The vault° is blue   sky
Without a cloud, and white without a speck
The dazzling splendour of the scene below.
Again the harmony comes o'er the vale;
10 And through the trees I view th' embattled tow'r
Whence all the music. I again perceive
The soothing influence of the wafted strains,
And settle in soft musings as I tread
The walk, still verdant, under oaks and elms,
15 Whose outspread branches overarch the glade.
The roof, though moveable through all its length
As the wind sways it, has yet well suffic'd,
And, intercepting in their silent fall
The frequent flakes, has kept a path for me.
20 No noise is here, or none that hinders thought.
The redbreast warbles still, but is content
With slender notes, and more than half suppress'd:
Pleas'd with his solitude, and flitting light
From spray to spray, where'er he rests he shakes
25 From many a twig the pendent drops of ice,
That tinkle in the wither'd leaves below.
Stillness, accompanied with sounds so soft,
Charms more than silence. Meditation here
May think down hours to moments. Here the heart
30 May give an useful lesson to the head,
And learning wiser grow without his books.
Knowledge and wisdom, far from being one,
Have oft-times no connection. Knowledge dwells
In heads replete with thoughts of other men;

---

[1] *Ouse* River in England.

[2] *rooks* Crow-like birds; *kites* Hawks.

35 Wisdom in minds attentive to their own.
   Knowledge, a rude unprofitable mass,
   The mere materials with which wisdom builds,
   Till smooth'd and squar'd and fitted to its place,
   Does but encumber whom it seems t' enrich.
40 Knowledge is proud that he has learn'd so much;
   Wisdom is humble that he knows no more.
   Books are not seldom talismans and spells,
   By which the magic art of shrewder wits
   Holds an unthinking multitude enthrall'd.
45 Some to the fascination of a name
   Surrender judgment, hood-wink'd. Some the style
   Infatuates, and through labyrinths and wilds
   Of error leads them by a tune entranc'd.
   While sloth seduces more, too weak to bear
50 The insupportable fatigue of thought,
   And swallowing, therefore, without pause or choice,
   The total grist° unsifted, husks and all.   grain
   But trees, and rivulets whose rapid course
   Defies the check of winter, haunts of deer,
55 And sheep-walks populous with bleating lambs,
   And lanes in which the primrose ere her time
   Peeps through the moss that clothes the hawthorn root,
   Deceive no student. Wisdom there, and truth,
   Not shy, as in the world, and to be won
60 By slow solicitation, seize at once
   The roving thought, and fix it on themselves.
        What prodigies can pow'r divine perform
   More grand than it produces year by year,
   And all in sight of inattentive man?
65 Familiar with th' effect we slight the cause,
   And, in the constancy of nature's course,
   The regular return of genial months,
   And renovation of a faded world,
   See nought to wonder at. Should God again,
70 As once in Gibeon,[1] interrupt the race
   Of the undeviating and punctual sun,
   How would the world admire! but speaks it less
   An agency divine, to make him know
   His moment when to sink and when to rise,
75 Age after age, than to arrest his course?
   All we behold is miracle; but, seen

So duly, all is miracle in vain.
Where now the vital energy that mov'd,
While summer was, the pure and subtle lymph[2]
80 Through th' imperceptible meand'ring veins
Of leaf and flow'r? It sleeps; and th' icy touch
Of unprolific winter has impress'd
A cold stagnation on th' intestine° tide.   confined
But let the months go round, a few short months,
85 And all shall be restor'd. These naked shoots,
Barren as lances, among which the wind
Makes wintry music, sighing as it goes,
Shall put their graceful foliage on again,
And, more aspiring, and with ampler spread,
90 Shall boast new charms, and more than they have lost.
Then, each in its peculiar honours clad,
Shall publish, even to the distant eye,
Its family and tribe. Laburnum, rich
In streaming gold; syringa, iv'ry pure;
95 The scentless and the scented rose; this red
And of an humbler growth, the other tall,
And throwing up into the darkest gloom
Of neighb'ring cypress, or more sable yew,
Her silver globes, light as the foamy surf
100 That the wind severs from the broken wave;
The lilac, various in array, now white,
Now sanguine, and her beauteous head now set
With purple spikes pyramidal, as if,
Studious of ornament, yet unresolv'd
105 Which hue she most approv'd, she chose them all;
Copious of flow'rs the woodbine, pale and wan,
But well compensating her sickly looks
With never-cloying odours, early and late;
Hypericum, all bloom, so thick a swarm
110 Of flow'rs, like flies clothing her slender rods,
That scarce a leaf appears; mezerion, too,
Though leafless, well attir'd, and thick beset
With blushing wreaths, investing ev'ry spray;
Althaea with the purple eye; the broom,
115 Yellow and bright, as bullion unalloy'd,

---

[1] *Gibeon* Ancient city north of Jerusalem, now el-Jib. From Joshua 10.13: "And the sun stood still [over Gibeon], and the moon stayed, until the people had avenged themselves upon their enemies."

[2] *lymph* In the second half of the eighteenth century, British physicians such as William Hunter and William Hewson, in studying the circulation and properties of human blood, noted the way in which the lymphatic system has connections with blood vessels, and concluded that the lymphatic system plays a key part in the absorption of nutrients.

Her blossoms and, luxuriant above all,
The jasmine, throwing wide her elegant sweets,
The deep dark green of whose unvarnish'd leaf
Makes more conspicuous, and illumines more
The bright profusion of her scatter'd stars.—
These have been, and these shall be in their day;
And all this uniform, uncolour'd scene,
Shall be dismantled of its fleecy load,
And flush into variety again.
From dearth to plenty, and from death to life,
Is Nature's progress when she lectures man
In heav'nly truth; evincing, as she makes
The grand transition, that there lives and works
A soul in all things, and that soul is God.
The beauties of the wilderness are his,
That make so gay the solitary place
Where no eye sees them. And the fairer forms
That cultivation glories in, are his.
He sets the bright procession on its way,
And marshals all the order of the year;
He marks the bounds which winter may not pass,
And blunts his pointed fury; in its case,
Russet and rude, folds up the tender germ,
Uninjur'd, with inimitable art;
And, ere one flow'ry season fades and dies,
Designs the blooming wonders of the next.
     Some say that, in the origin of things,
When all creation started into birth,
The infant elements receiv'd a law,
From which they swerve not since. That under force
Of that controlling ordinance they move,
And need not his immediate hand, who first
Prescrib'd their course, to regulate it now.
Thus dream they, and contrive to save a God
Th' incumbrance of his own concerns, and spare
The great Artificer of all that moves
The stress of a continual act, the pain
Of unremitted vigilance and care,
As too laborious and severe a task.
So man, the moth, is not afraid, it seems,
To span omnipotence, and measure might
That knows no measure, by the scanty rule
And standard of his own, that is today,
And is not ere tomorrow's sun go down!
But how should matter occupy a charge

Dull as it is, and satisfy a law
So vast in its demands, unless impell'd
To ceaseless service by a ceaseless force,
And under pressure of some conscious cause?
The Lord of all, himself through all diffus'd,
Sustains, and is the life of all that lives.
Nature is but a name for an effect,
Whose cause is God. He feeds the secret fire
By which the mighty process is maintain'd,
Who sleeps not, is not weary; in whose sight
Slow circling ages are as transient days;
Whose work is without labour; whose designs
No flaw deforms, no difficulty thwarts;
And whose beneficence no charge exhausts.
Him blind antiquity profan'd, not serv'd,
With self-taught rites, and under various names,
Female and male, Pomona, Pales, Pan,
And Flora, and Vertumnus;[1] peopling earth
With tutelary° goddesses and gods   *protective*
That were not; and commending, as they would,
To each some province, garden, field, or grove.
But all are under one. One spirit—His
Who wore the platted° thorns with bleeding brows—   *braided*
Rules universal nature. Not a flow'r
But shows some touch, in freckle, streak, or stain,
Of his unrivall'd pencil. He inspires
Their balmy odours, and imparts their hues,
And bathes their eyes with nectar, and includes,
In grains as countless as the sea-side sands,
The forms with which he sprinkles all the earth.
Happy who walks with him! whom what he finds
Of flavour or of scent in fruit or flow'r,
Or what he views of beautiful or grand
In nature, from the broad majestic oak
To the green blade that twinkles in the sun,
Prompts with remembrance of a present God!
His presence, who made all so fair, perceiv'd,
Makes all still fairer. As with him no scene
Is dreary, so with him all seasons please.
Though winter had been none, had man been true,
And earth be punish'd for its tenant's sake,
Yet not in vengeance; as this smiling sky,

---

1   *Pomona*   Roman goddess of fruit trees; *Pales*   Roman goddess of
shepherds, flocks, and cattle; *Pan*   Greek god of shepherds and
flocks; *Flora*   Roman goddess of blossoming spring flowers;
Vertumnus   Roman god of fruit trees, gardens, and seasons.

So soon succeeding such an angry night,
   And these dissolving snows, and this clear stream
205 Recov'ring fast its liquid music, prove....
—1785

The Castaway[1]

Obscurest night involved the sky,
   The Atlantic billows roared,
When such a destined wretch as I,
   Washed headlong from on board,
5 Of friends, of hope, of all bereft,
His floating home forever left.

No braver chief could Albion° boast   *England*
   Than he with whom he went,
Nor ever ship left Albion's coast,
10   With warmer wishes sent.
He loved them both, but both in vain,
Nor him beheld, nor her again.

Not long beneath the whelming brine,
   Expert to swim, he lay;
15 Nor soon he felt his strength decline,
   Or courage die away;
But waged with death a lasting strife,
Supported by despair of life.

He shouted; nor his friends had failed
20   To check the vessel's course,
But so the furious blast prevailed,
   That, pitiless perforce,
They left their outcast mate behind,
And scudded still before the wind.

25 Some succor yet they could afford;
   And, such as storms allow,
The cask, the coop,° the floated cord,°   *basket / rope*
   Delayed not to bestow.
But he (they knew) nor ship, nor shore,
30 Whate'er they gave, should visit more.

Nor, cruel as it seemed, could he
   Their haste himself condemn,
Aware that flight, in such a sea,
   Alone could rescue them;
35 Yet bitter felt it still to die
Deserted, and his friends so nigh.

He long survives, who lives an hour
   In ocean, self-upheld;
And so long he, with unspent power,
40   His destiny repelled;
And ever, as the minutes flew,
Entreated help, or cried, "Adieu!"

At length, his transient respite past,
   His comrades, who before
45 Had heard his voice in every blast,
   Could catch the sound no more.
For then, by toil subdued, he drank
The stifling wave, and then he sank.

No poet wept him; but the page
50   Of narrative sincere,
That tells his name, his worth, his age,
   Is wet with Anson's tear.
And tears by bards or heroes shed
Alike immortalize the dead.

55 I therefore purpose not, or dream,
   Descanting on his fate,
To give the melancholy theme
   A more enduring date:
But misery still delights to trace
60 Its semblance in another's case.

No voice divine the storm allayed,[2]
   No light propitious shone,
When, snatched from all effectual aid,
   We perished, each alone;
65 But I beneath a rougher sea,
And whelmed in deeper gulfs than he.
—1803

---

[1] *The Castaway* Based upon an occurrence documented in Lord George Anson's *Voyage Round the World* (1748), in which a sailor on Anson's ship was tossed overboard in a fierce storm and could not be rescued.

[2] *No voice ... allayed* See Matthew 8.26.

OLAUDAH EQUIANO OR GUSTAVUS VASSA

1745 – 1797

Olaudah Equiano's *The Interesting Life of Olaudah Equiano* was the first slave narrative written in English, and he is viewed by many as the originator of the genre. As such, his work is seen as the beginning of black literary tradition. His narrative became a central document for the abolitionist movement, showing readers the horrors of slavery while also demonstrating the eloquence of a native-born African who had been educated in the Western tradition, and displaying to the devout that black people were as capable of spiritual enlightenment as were whites.

Until recently Equiano's account of his early years was generally taken at face value; it was accepted that he had been born into the Ibo nation; that he had been kidnaped at the age of eleven and enslaved for some time in Africa; and that he was eventually brought across the Atlantic as a slave. In an important 1999 article and then in his 2005 biography of Equiano, historian Vincent Carretta challenged his account, citing two newly-discovered documents indicating that Equiano had been born not in Africa, but in Carolina. The issue may never be entirely resolved, but Carretta's arguments are now widely accepted. It is significant, however, that neither Carretta nor other scholars have challenged the authenticity of the information Equiano provides about life in Africa, the passage across the Atlantic, and so on; if Equiano himself was indeed born an American slave, he would have obtained such information directly from his fellow slaves. At issue, then, is not the fundamental reality of the account Equiano provides, but only whether the early part of his narrative represents a first-hand account or an act of creative imagination based on first-hand research.

Equiano's account of his life following his purchase by the British naval captain Michael Henry Pascal is not in dispute. As a slave to Pascal (who renamed him "Gustavus Vassa") Equiano began his career as a seaman. For the next ten or eleven years, Equiano traveled widely to the Mediterranean, Europe, and the Americas, and was engaged in several battles during the Seven Years' War (1756–63). Despite his years of service, Pascal sold Equiano for £40 to the Quaker Robert King, from whom Equiano was eventually able to buy his freedom in 1766.

After securing his freedom, Equiano settled in England. While slavery was still permitted in England's overseas colonies, it was frowned on at home, and there was a relatively large black population (10,000–20,000). Because he had most often been enslaved to British men, and because he had been baptized into the Anglican Church in 1759, Equiano considered himself "almost an Englishman." He had been taught to read and write while still a slave and he now used these skills to highlight the position of slaves and to petition for the abolition of slavery. He worked with several prominent abolitionists, including Granville Sharpe and William Wilberforce. When his narrative was published in 1789 it was widely read, and it became influential in furthering the abolitionists' cause. Equiano married in 1792 and had two daughters before he died in 1797.

⌘⌘⌘

from *The Interesting Narrative of the Life of
Olaudah Equiano, or Gustavus Vassa, the
African. Written by Himself*

CHAPTER 1

The author's account of his country, and their manners and
customs—Administration of justice—Embrenche— Marriage
ceremony, and public entertainments—Mode of living—
Dress—Manufactures Buildings—Commerce—Agriculture
—War and religion—Superstition of the natives—Funeral
ceremonies of the priests or magicians—Curious mode of
discovering poison—Some hints concerning the origin of the
author's countrymen, with the opinions of different writers on
that subject.

I believe it is difficult for those who publish their own
memoirs to escape the imputation of vanity; nor is
this the only disadvantage under which they labour: it is
also their misfortune that what is uncommon is rarely,
if ever, believed, and what is obvious we are apt to turn
from with disgust, and to charge the writer with impertinence. People generally think those memoirs only
worthy to be read or remembered which abound in
great or striking events, those, in short, which in a high
degree excite either admiration or pity: all others they
consign to contempt and oblivion. It is therefore, I
confess, not a little hazardous in a private and obscure
individual, and a stranger too, thus to solicit the indulgent attention of the public; especially when I own I
offer here the history of neither a saint, a hero, nor a
tyrant. I believe there are few events in my life which
have not happened to many: it is true the incidents of it
are numerous; and, did I consider myself an European,
I might say my sufferings were great: but when I compare my lot with that of most of my countrymen, I
regard myself as a particular favourite of Heaven, and
acknowledge the mercies of Providence in every occurrence of my life. If then the following narrative does not
appear sufficiently interesting to engage general attention, let my motive be some excuse for its publication.
I am not so foolishly vain as to expect from it either

immortality or literary reputation. If it affords any
satisfaction to my numerous friends, at whose request it
has been written, or in the smallest degree promotes the
interests of humanity, the ends for which it was undertaken will be fully attained, and every wish of my heart
gratified. Let it therefore be remembered that, in
wishing to avoid censure, I do not aspire to praise.

That part of Africa, known by the name of Guinea,
to which the trade for slaves is carried on, extends along
the coast above 3400 miles, from the Senegal to Angola,
and includes a variety of kingdoms. Of these the most
considerable is the kingdom of Benin,[1] both as to extent
and wealth, the richness and cultivation of the soil, the
power of its king, and the number and warlike disposition of the inhabitants. It is situated nearly under the
line,[2] and extends along the coast about 170 miles, but
runs back into the interior part of Africa to a distance
hitherto I believe unexplored by any traveller; and seems
only terminated at length by the empire of Abyssinia,
near 1500 miles from its beginning. This kingdom is
divided into many provinces or districts: in one of the
most remote and fertile of which, called Eboe, I was
born, in the year 1745, in a charming fruitful vale
named Essaka. The distance of this province from the
capital of Benin and the sea coast must be very considerable; for I had never heard of white men or Europeans,
nor of the sea. And our subjection to the king of Benin
was little more than nominal, for every transaction of
the government, as far as my slender observation extended, was conducted by the chiefs or elders of the
place. The manners and government of a people who
have little commerce with other countries are generally
very simple, and the history of what passes in one family
or village may serve as a specimen of a nation. My father
was one of those elders or chiefs I have spoken of, and
was styled Embrenche; a term, as I remember, importing the highest distinction, and signifying in our language a *mark* of grandeur. This mark is conferred on the
person entitled to it by cutting the skin across at the top
of the forehead, and drawing it down to the eyebrows;
and while it is in this situation applying a warm hand,

---

[1] *kingdom of Benin* This kingdom extended over part of present-
day Nigeria as well as present-day Benin.

[2] *under the line* South of the equator.

and rubbing it until it shrinks up into a thick weal[1] across the lower part of the forehead. Most of the judges and senators were thus marked; my father had long borne it. I had seen it conferred on one of my brothers, and I was also *destined* to receive it by my parents. Those Embrenche, or chief men, decided disputes and punished crimes, for which purpose they always assembled together. The proceedings were generally short, and in most cases the law of retaliation prevailed. I remember a man was brought before my father and the other judges for kidnapping a boy; and, although he was the son of a chief or senator, he was condemned to make recompense by a man or woman slave. Adultery, however, was sometimes punished with slavery or death, a punishment which I believe is inflicted on it throughout most of the nations of Africa, so sacred among them is the honour of the marriage bed, and so jealous are they of the fidelity of their wives. Of this I recollect an instance: a woman was convicted before the judges of adultery, and delivered over, as the custom was, to her husband to be punished. Accordingly he determined to put her to death; but it being found, just before her execution, that she had an infant at her breast; and no woman being prevailed on to perform the part of a nurse, she was spared on account of the child. The men, however, do not preserve the same constancy to their wives which they expect from them; for they indulge in a plurality, though seldom in more than two. Their mode of marriage is thus: both parties are usually betrothed when young by their parents (though I have known the males to betroth themselves). On this occasion a feast is prepared, and the bride and bridegroom stand up in the midst of all their friends, who are assembled for the purpose, while he declares she is thenceforth to be looked upon as his wife, and that no other person is to pay any addresses to her. This is also immediately proclaimed in the vicinity, on which the bride retires from the assembly. Some time after she is brought home to her husband, and then another feast is made, to which the relations of both parties are invited. Her parents then deliver her to the bridegroom, accompanied with a number of blessings, and at the same time they tie round her waist a cotton string of the thickness of a goose-quill, which none but married women are permitted to wear: she is now considered as completely his wife; and at this time the dowry is given to the new married pair, which generally consists of portions of land, slaves, and cattle, household goods, and implements of husbandry. These are offered by the friends of both parties; besides which the parents of the bridegroom present gifts to those of the bride, whose property she is looked upon before marriage; but after it she is esteemed the sole property of her husband. The ceremony being now ended, the festival begins, which is celebrated with bonfires, and loud acclamations of joy, accompanied with music and dancing.

We are almost a nation of dancers, musicians, and poets. Thus every great event, such as a triumphant return from battle or other cause of public rejoicing, is celebrated in public dances, which are accompanied with songs and music suited to the occasion. The assembly is separated into four divisions which dance either apart or in succession, and each with a character peculiar to itself. The first division contains the married men, who in their dances frequently exhibit feats of arms, and the representation of a battle. To these succeed the married women, who dance in the second division. The young men occupy the third; and the maidens the fourth. Each represents some interesting scene of real life, such as a great achievement, domestic employment, a pathetic story, or some rural sport; and as the subject is generally founded on some recent event, it is therefore ever new. This gives our dances a spirit and variety which I have scarcely seen elsewhere.[2] We have many musical instruments, particularly drums of different kinds, a piece of music which resembles a guitar, and another much like a stickado.[3] These last are chiefly used by betrothed virgins, who play on them on all grand festivals.

As our manners are simple, our luxuries are few. The dress of both sexes is nearly the same. It generally consists of a long piece of calico, or muslin, wrapped loosely round the body, somewhat in the form of a highland plaid. This is usually dyed blue, which is our

---

[1] *weal* Mark; welt.

[2] [Equiano's note] When I was in Smyrna I have frequently seen the Greeks dance after this manner.

[3] *stickado* Musical instrument similar to a xylophone.

favourite colour. It is extracted from a berry, and is brighter and richer than any I have seen in Europe. Besides this, our women of distinction wear golden ornaments; which they dispose with some profusion on their arms and legs. When our women are not employed with the men in tillage, their usual occupation is spinning and weaving cotton, which they afterwards dye and make it into garments. They also manufacture earthen vessels, of which we have many kinds. Among the rest tobacco pipes, made after the same fashion, and used in the same manner, as those in Turkey.[1]

Our manner of living is entirely plain; for as yet the natives are unacquainted with those refinements in cookery which debauch the taste: bullocks, goats, and poultry supply the greatest part of their food. These constitute likewise the principal wealth of the country, and the chief articles of its commerce. The flesh is usually stewed in a pan; to make it savoury we sometimes use also pepper and other spices, and we have salt made of wood ashes. Our vegetables are mostly plantains, eadas, yams, beans, and Indian corn.[2] The head of the family usually eats alone; his wives and slaves have also their separate tables. Before we taste food we always wash our hands: indeed our cleanliness on all occasions is extreme; but on this it is an indispensable ceremony. After washing, libation is made by pouring out a small portion of the drink in a certain place, for the spirits of departed relations, which the natives suppose to preside over their conduct and guard them from evil. They are totally unacquainted with strong or spirituous liquours, and their principal beverage is palm wine. This is gotten from a tree of that name by tapping it at the top and fastening a large gourd to it; and sometimes one tree will yield three or four gallons in a night. When just drawn it is of a most delicious sweetness; but in a few days it acquires a tartish and more spirituous flavour, though I never saw any one intoxicated by it. The same tree also produces nuts and oil. Our principal luxury is in perfumes; one sort of these is an odoriferous wood of delicious fragrance; the other a kind of earth, a small portion of which thrown into the fire diffuses a most powerful odour.[3] We beat this wood into powder, and mix it with palm oil; with which both men and women perfume themselves.

In our buildings we study convenience rather than ornament. Each master of a family has a large square piece of ground, surrounded with a moat or fence, or enclosed with a wall made of red earth tempered, which, when dry, is as hard as brick. Within this are his houses to accommodate his family and slaves, which, if numerous, frequently present the appearance of a village. In the middle stands the principal building, appropriated to the sole use of the master and consisting of two apartments, in one of which he sits in the day with his family; the other is left apart for the reception of his friends. He has besides these a distinct apartment in which he sleeps, together with his male children. On each side are the apartments of his wives, who have also their separate day and night houses. The habitations of the slaves and their families are distributed throughout the rest of the enclosure. These houses never exceed one story in height; they are always built of wood, or stakes driven into the ground, crossed with wattles and neatly plastered within and without. The roof is thatched with reeds. Our dayhouses are left open at the sides; but those in which we sleep are always covered and plastered in the inside with a composition mixed with cow-dung, to keep off the different insects which annoy us during the night. The walls and floors also of these are generally covered with mats. Our beds consist of a platform, raised three or four feet from the ground, on which are laid skins and different parts of a spongy tree called plantain. Our covering is calico or muslin, the same as our dress. The usual seats are a few logs of wood, but we have benches, which are generally perfumed, to accommodate strangers. These compose the greater part of our household furniture. Houses so constructed and furnished require but little skill to erect them. Every man is a sufficient architect for the purpose. The whole neighbourhood afford their unanimous assistance in building them and in return receive, and expect, no other recompense than a feast.

---

[1] [Equiano's note]   The bowl is earthen, curiously figured, to which a long reed is fixed as a tube. This tube is sometimes so long as to be borne by one, and frequently out of grandeur by two boys.

[2] *Indian corn*   Maize; corn.

[3] [Equiano's note]   When I was in Smyrna I saw the same kind of earth, and brought some of it with me to England; it resembles musk in strength, but is more delicious in scent, and is not unlike the smell of a rose.

As we live in a country where nature is prodigal of her favours, our wants are few and easily supplied; of course, we have few manufactures. They consist for the most part of calicoes, earthen ware, ornaments, and instruments of war and husbandry. But these make no part of our commerce, the principal articles of which, as I have observed, are provisions. In such a state money is of little use; however, we have some small pieces of coin, if I may call them such. They are made something like an anchor, but I do not remember either their value or denomination. We have also markets, at which I have been frequently with my mother. These are sometimes visited by stout mahogany-coloured men from the south west of us: we call them Oye-Eboe, which term signifies "red men living at a distance." They generally bring us firearms, gunpowder, hats, beads, and dried fish. The last we esteemed a great rarity, as our waters were only brooks and springs. These articles they barter with us for odoriferous woods and earth, and our salt of wood ashes. They always carry slaves through our land; but the strictest account is exacted of their manner of procuring them before they are suffered to pass. Sometimes indeed we sold slaves to them, but they were only prisoners of war, or such among us as had been convicted of kidnapping, or adultery, and some other crimes which we esteemed heinous. This practice of kidnapping induces me to think that, notwithstanding all our strictness, their principal business among us was to trepan[1] our people. I remember too they carried great sacks along with them, which not long after I had an opportunity of fatally seeing applied to that infamous purpose.

Our land is uncommonly rich and fruitful, and produces all kinds of vegetables in great abundance. We have plenty of Indian corn, and vast quantities of cotton and tobacco. Our pineapples grow without culture; they are about the size of the largest sugar-loaf,[2] and finely flavoured. We have also spices of different kinds, particularly pepper, and a variety of delicious fruits which I have never seen in Europe, together with gums of various kinds, and honey in abundance. All our industry is exerted to improve those blessings of nature. Agriculture is our chief employment, and everyone,

even the children and women, are engaged in it. Thus we are all habituated to labour from our earliest years. Everyone contributes something to the common stock, and as we are unacquainted with idleness, we have no beggars. The benefits of such a mode of living are obvious. The West India planters prefer the slaves of Benin or Eboe to those of any other part of Guinea, for their hardiness, intelligence, integrity, and zeal. Those benefits are felt by us in the general healthiness of the people, and in their vigour and activity; I might have added too in their comeliness.[3] Deformity is indeed unknown amongst us—I mean that of shape. Numbers of the natives of Eboe now in London might be brought in support of this assertion: for, in regard to complexion, ideas of beauty are wholly relative. I remember while in Africa to have seen three negro children who were tawny, and another quite white, who were universally regarded by myself and the natives in general, as far as related to their complexions, as deformed. Our women too were in my eyes at least uncommonly graceful, alert, and modest to a degree of bashfulness; nor do I remember to have ever heard of an instance of incontinence[4] amongst them before marriage. They are also remarkably cheerful. Indeed cheerfulness and affability are two of the leading characteristics of our nation.

Our tillage is exercised in a large plain or common some hours' walk from our dwellings, and all the neighbours resort thither in a body. They use no beasts of husbandry, and their only instruments are hoes, axes, shovels, and beaks, or pointed iron to dig with. Sometimes we are visited by locusts, which come in large clouds, so as to darken the air, and destroy our harvest. This however happens rarely, but when it does, a famine is produced by it. I remember an instance or two wherein this happened. This common is often the theatre of war; and therefore when our people go out to till their land, they not only go in a body, but generally take their arms with them for fear of a surprise; and when they apprehend an invasion they guard the avenue to their dwellings by driving sticks into the ground, which are so sharp at one end as to pierce the foot, and are generally dipped in poison. From what I can recol-

---

[1] *trepan* Trick.

[2] *sugar-loaf* A variety of pineapple popular in England at the time.

[3] *comeliness* Pleasing appearance; beauty of form.

[4] *incontinence* Unchastity.

lect of these battles, they appear to have been irruptions[1] of one little state or district on the other, to obtain prisoners or booty. Perhaps they were incited to this by those traders who brought the European goods I mentioned amongst us. Such a mode of obtaining slaves in Africa is common, and I believe more are procured this way, and by kidnapping, than any other.[2] When a trader wants slaves, he applies to a chief for them, and tempts him with his wares. It is not extraordinary if on this occasion he yields to the temptation with as little firmness and accepts the price of his fellow creatures' liberty with as little reluctance as the enlightened merchant. Accordingly he falls on his neighbours, and a desperate battle ensues. If he prevails and takes prisoners, he gratifies his avarice by selling them; but, if his party be vanquished, and he falls into the hands of the enemy, he is put to death: for, as he has been known to foment[3] their quarrels, it is thought dangerous to let him survive, and no ransom can save him, though all other prisoners may be redeemed. We have firearms, bows and arrows, broad two-edged swords and javelins; we have shields also which cover a man from head to foot. All are taught the use of these weapons; even our women are warriors, and march boldly out to fight along with the men. Our whole district is a kind of militia: on a certain signal given, such as the firing of a gun at night, they all rise in arms and rush upon their enemy. It is perhaps something remarkable that when our people march to the field a red flag or banner is borne before them. I was once a witness to a battle in our common. We had been all at work in it one day as usual when our people were suddenly attacked. I climbed a tree at some distance, from which I beheld the fight. There were many women as well as men on both sides; among others my mother was there, and armed with a broad sword. After fighting for a considerable time with great fury, and after many had been killed, our people obtained the victory and took their enemy's chief prisoner. He was carried off in great triumph, and, though he offered a large ransom for his life, he was put to death. A virgin of note among our enemies had been slain in the battle, and her arm was exposed in our market-place, where our trophies were always exhibited. The spoils were divided according to the merit of the warriors. Those prisoners which were not sold or redeemed we kept as slaves: but how different was their condition from that of the slaves in the West Indies! With us they do no more work than other members of the community, even their masters; their food, clothing, and lodging were nearly the same as theirs (except that they were not permitted to eat with those who were free-born), and there was scarce any other difference between them than a superior degree of importance which the head of a family possesses in our state, and that authority which, as such, he exercises over every part of his household. Some of these slaves have even slaves under them as their own property and for their own use.

As to religion, the natives believe that there is one Creator of all things, and that he lives in the sun and is girded round with a belt; that he may never eat or drink; but, according to some, he smokes a pipe, which is our own favourite luxury. They believe he governs events, especially our deaths or captivity; but, as for the doctrine of eternity, I do not remember to have ever heard of it: some however believe in the transmigration of souls in a certain degree. Those spirits which are not transmigrated, such as our dear friends or relations, they believe always attend them and guard them from the bad spirits or their foes. For this reason they always before eating, as I have observed, put some small portion of the meat, and pour some of their drink, on the ground for them; and they often make oblations of the blood of beasts or fowls at their graves. I was very fond of my mother, and almost constantly with her. When she went to make these oblations at her mother's tomb, which was a kind of small solitary thatched house, I sometimes attended her. There she made her libations and spent most of the night in cries and lamentations. I have been often extremely terrified on these occasions. The loneliness of the place, the darkness of the night, and the ceremony of libation, naturally awful and gloomy, were heightened by my mother's lamentations; and these, concurring with the cries of doleful birds by which these places were frequented, gave an inexpressible terror to the scene.

[1] *irruptions* Invasions.
[2] [Equiano's note] See Benezet's "Account of Africa" throughout.
[3] *foment* Stir up.

We compute the year from the day on which the sun crosses the line, and on its setting that evening there is a general shout throughout the land—at least, I can speak from my own knowledge, throughout our vicinity. The people at the same time make a great noise with rattles, not unlike the basket rattles used by children here, though much larger, and hold up their hands to heaven for a blessing. It is then the greatest offerings are made, and those children whom our wise men foretell will be fortunate are then presented to different people. I remember many used to come to see me, and I was carried about to others for that purpose. They have many offerings, particularly at full moons, generally two at harvest before the fruits are taken out of the ground; and when any young animals are killed, sometimes they offer up part of them as a sacrifice. These offerings, when made by one of the heads of a family, serve for the whole. I remember we often had them at my father's and my uncle's, and their families have been present. Some of our offerings are eaten with bitter herbs. We had a saying among us to any one of a cross temper, that "if they were to be eaten, they should be eaten with bitter herbs."

We practised circumcision like the Jews, and made offerings and feasts on that occasion in the same manner as they did. Like them also, our children were named from some event, some circumstance or fancied foreboding, at the time of their birth. I was named *Olaudah*, which, in our language, signifies "vicissitude" or "fortunate," also, one favoured, and having a loud voice and well spoken. I remember we never polluted the name of the object of our adoration; on the contrary, it was always mentioned with the greatest reverence; and we were totally unacquainted with swearing, and all those terms of abuse and reproach which find their way so readily and copiously into the languages of more civilized people. The only expressions of that kind I remember were "May you rot," or "May you swell," or "May a beast take you."

I have before remarked that the natives of this part of Africa are extremely cleanly. This necessary habit of decency was with us a part of religion, and therefore we had many purifications and washings; indeed almost as many and used on the same occasions, if my recollection does not fail me, as the Jews. Those that touched the dead at any time were obliged to wash and purify themselves before they could enter a dwelling-house. Every woman too, at certain times, was forbidden to come into a dwelling-house, or touch any person or any thing we ate. I was so fond of my mother I could not keep from her or avoid touching her at some of those periods, in consequence of which I was obliged to be kept out with her, in a little house made for that purpose, till offering was made, and then we were purified.

Though we had no places of public worship, we had priests and magicians, or wise men. I do not remember whether they had different offices, or whether they were united in the same persons, but they were held in great reverence by the people. They calculated our time and foretold events, as their name imported, for we called them Ah-affoe-way-cah, which signifies "calculators" or "yearly men," our year being called Ah-affoe. They wore their beards, and when they died they were succeeded by their sons. Most of their implements and things of value were interred along with them. Pipes and tobacco were also put into the grave with the corpse, which was always perfumed and ornamented, and animals were offered in sacrifice to them. None accompanied their funerals but those of the same profession or tribe. These buried them after sunset, and always returned from the grave by a different way from that which they went.

These magicians were also our doctors or physicians. They practised bleeding by cupping, and were very successful in healing wounds and expelling poisons. They had likewise some extraordinary method of discovering jealousy, theft, and poisoning; the success of which no doubt they derived from their unbounded influence over the credulity and superstition of the people. I do not remember what those methods were, except that as to poisoning: I recollect an instance or two, which I hope it will not be deemed impertinent here to insert, as it may serve as a kind of specimen of the rest, and is still used by the negroes in the West Indies. A virgin had been poisoned, but it was not known by whom. The doctors ordered the corpse to be taken up by some persons and carried to the grave. As soon as the bearers had raised it on their shoulders, they seemed seized with some sudden impulse, and ran to and fro unable to stop themselves. At last, after having passed through a number of thorns and prickly bushes unhurt, the corpse fell from them close to a house, and defaced it in the fall; and, the owner being taken up, he immediately confessed the poisoning.[1]

The natives are extremely cautious about poison. When they buy any eatable the seller kisses it all round before the buyer, to show him it is not poisoned; and the same is done when any meat or drink is presented, particularly to a stranger. We have serpents of different kinds, some of which are esteemed ominous when they appear in our houses, and these we never molest. I remember two of those ominous snakes, each of which was as thick as the calf of a man's leg, and in colour resembling a dolphin in the water, crept at different times into my mother's night-house, where I always lay with her, and coiled themselves into folds, and each time they crowed like a cock. I was desired by some of our wise men to touch these, that I might be interested in the good omens, which I did, for they were quite harmless and would tamely suffer themselves to be handled; and then they were put into a large open earthen pan and set on one side of the highway. Some of our snakes, however, were poisonous: one of them crossed the road one day when I was standing on it, and passed between my feet without offering to touch me, to the great surprise of many who saw it; and these incidents were accounted by the wise men, and therefore by my mother and the rest of the people, as remarkable omens in my favour.

Such is the imperfect sketch my memory has furnished me with of the manners and customs of a people among whom I first drew my breath. And here I cannot forbear suggesting what has long struck me very forcibly, namely, the strong analogy which even by this sketch, imperfect as it is, appears to prevail in the manners and customs of my countrymen and those of the Jews before they reached the Land of Promise, and particularly the patriarchs while they were yet in that pastoral state which is described in Genesis—an analogy which alone would induce me to think that the one people had sprung from the other. Indeed this is the opinion of Dr. Gill,[2] who, in his commentary on Genesis, very ably deduces the pedigree of the Africans from Afer and Afra, the descendants of Abraham by Keturah, his wife and concubine (for both these titles are applied to her). It is also conformable to the sentiments of Dr. John Clarke, formerly Dean of Sarum, in his *Truth of the Christian Religion*:[3] both these authors concur in ascribing to us this original. The reasonings of these gentlemen are still further confirmed by the scripture chronology; and if any further corroboration were required, this resemblance in so many respects is a strong evidence in support of the opinion. Like the Israelites in their primitive state, our government was conducted by our chiefs or judges, our wise men and elders; and the head of a family with us enjoyed a similar authority over his household with that which is ascribed to Abraham and the other patriarchs. The law of retaliation obtained almost universally with us as with them; and even their religion appeared to have shed upon us a ray of its glory, though broken and spent in its passage, or eclipsed by the cloud with which time, tradition, and ignorance might have enveloped it; for we had our circumcision (a rule I believe peculiar to that people); we had also our sacrifices and burnt-offerings, our washings and purifications, on the same occasions as they had.

As to the difference of colour between the Eboan Africans and the modern Jews, I shall not presume to account for it. It is a subject which has engaged the pens

[1] [Equiano's note] An instance of this kind happened at Montserrat in the West Indies in the year 1763. I then belonged to the Charming Sally, Capt. Doran. The chief mate, Mr. Mansfield, and some of the crew, being one day on shore, were present at the burying of a poisoned negro girl. Though they had often heard of the circumstance of the running in such cases, and had even seen it, they imagined it to be a trick of the corpse-bearers. The mate therefore desired two of the sailors to take up the coffin and carry it to the grave. The sailors, who were all of the same opinion, readily obeyed; but they had scarcely raised it to their shoulders before they began to run furiously about, quite unable to direct themselves, till at last, without intention, they came to the hut of him who had poisoned the girl. The coffin then immediately fell from their shoulders against the hut, and damaged part of the wall. The owner of the hut was taken into custody on this, and confessed the poisoning. I give this story as it was related by the mate and crew on their return to the ship. The credit which is due to it I leave with the reader.

[2] *Dr. Gill* John Gill (1697–1771), the Baptist author of *An Exposition of the Old Testament, in which Are Recorded the Original of Mankind, of the Several Nations of the World, and of the Jewish Nation in Particular....* (1788).

[3] *Dr. John ... Religion* John Clarke (1682–1757) published a translation of a seventeenth-century religious work by Hugo Grotius, *The Truth of the Christian Religion* (1627), in 1786.

of men of both genius and learning, and is far above my strength. The most able and Reverend Mr. T. Clarkson, however, in his much admired *Essay on the Slavery and Commerce of the Human Species*, has ascertained the cause in a manner that at once solves every objection on that account and, on my mind at least, has produced the fullest conviction. I shall therefore refer to that performance for the theory, contenting myself with extracting a fact as related by Dr. Mitchel.[1] "The Spaniards, who have inhabited America, under the torrid zone, for any time, are become as dark coloured as our native Indians of Virginia; of which *I myself have been a witness*." There is also another instance of a Portuguese settlement at Mitomba, a river in Sierra Leona, where the inhabitants are bred from a mixture of the first Portuguese discoverers with the natives, and are now become, in their complexion, and in the wooly quality of their hair, perfect negroes, retaining however a smattering of the Portuguese language.

These instances, and a great many more which might be adduced, while they show how the complexions of the same persons vary in different climates, it is hoped may tend also to remove the prejudice that some conceive against the natives of Africa on account of their colour. Surely the minds of the Spaniards did not change with their complexions! Are there not causes enough to which the apparent inferiority of an African may be ascribed, without limiting the goodness of God, and supposing he forbore to stamp understanding on certainly his own image, because "carved in ebony"? Might it not naturally be ascribed to their situation?

When they come among Europeans, they are ignorant of their language, religion, manners, and customs. Are any pains taken to teach them these? Are they treated as men? Does not slavery itself depress the mind, and extinguish all its fire and every noble sentiment? But, above all, what advantages do not a refined people possess over those who are rude and uncultivated. Let the polished and haughty European recollect that his ancestors were once, like the Africans, uncivilized, and even barbarous. Did Nature make *them* inferior to their sons? And should *they too* have been made slaves? Every rational mind answers, No. Let such

reflections as these melt the pride of their superiority into sympathy for the wants and miseries of their sable brethren, and compel them to acknowledge that understanding is not confined to feature or colour. If, when they look round the world, they feel exultation, let it be tempered with benevolence to others, and gratitude to God, "who hath made of one blood all nations of men for to dwell on all the face of the earth;[2] and whose wisdom is not our wisdom, neither are our ways his ways."

CHAPTER 2

The author's birth and parentage—His being kidnapped with his sister—Their separation—Surprise at meeting again—Are finally separated—Account of the different places and incidents the author met with till his arrival on the coast—The effect the sight of a slave ship had on him —He sails for the West Indies—Horrors of a slave ship—Arrives at Barbadoes, where the cargo is sold and dispersed.

I hope the reader will not think I have trespassed on his patience in introducing myself to him with some account of the manners and customs of my country.[3] They had been implanted in me with great care, and made an impression on my mind which time could not erase, and which all the adversity and variety of fortune I have since experienced served only to rivet and record; for, whether the love of one's country be real or imaginary, or a lesson of reason, or an instinct of nature, I still look back with pleasure on the first scenes of my life, though that pleasure has been for the most part mingled with sorrow.

I have already acquainted the reader with the time and place of my birth. My father, besides many slaves, had a numerous family, of which seven lived to grow up, including myself and a sister, who was the only daughter. As I was the youngest of the sons, I became, of course, the greatest favourite with my mother, and was always with her; and she used to take particular pains to form my mind. I was trained up from my earliest years in the art of war; my daily exercise was

---

[1] [Equiano's note] Philos. Trans. No. 476, Sect. 4, cited by Mr. Clarkson, p. 205.

[2] [Equiano's note] Acts, c. 17 v. 26.

[3] *my country* Equiano says he was born in Essaka, a country located in the interior of present-day Nigeria.

shooting and throwing javelins, and my mother adorned me with emblems after the manner of our greatest warriors. In this way I grew up till I was turned the age of eleven, when an end was put to my happiness in the following manner. Generally, when the grown people in the neighbourhood were gone far in the fields to labour, the children assembled together in some of the neighbours' premises to play; and commonly some of us used to get up a tree to look out for any assailant or kidnapper that might come upon us; for they sometimes took those opportunities of our parents' absence to attack and carry off as many as they could seize. One day, as I was watching at the top of a tree in our yard, I saw one of those people come into the yard of our next neighbour but one, to kidnap, there being many stout young people in it. Immediately on this I gave the alarm of the rogue, and he was surrounded by the stoutest of them, who entangled him with cords, so that he could not escape till some of the grown people came and secured him. But alas! ere long it was my fate to be thus attacked, and to be carried off, when none of the grown people were nigh. One day, when all our people were gone out to their works as usual, and only I and my dear sister were left to mind the house, two men and a woman got over our walls and in a moment seized us both, and, without giving us time to cry out or make resistance, they stopped our mouths and ran off with us into the nearest wood. Here they tied our hands and continued to carry us as far as they could, till night came on, when we reached a small house where the robbers halted for refreshment and spent the night. We were then unbound, but were unable to take any food; and, being quite overpowered by fatigue and grief, our only relief was some sleep, which allayed our misfortune for a short time.

The next morning we left the house and continued travelling all the day. For a long time we had kept the woods, but at last we came into a road, which I believed I knew. I had now some hopes of being delivered, for we had advanced but a little way before I discovered some people at a distance, on which I began to cry out for their assistance. But my cries had no other effect than to make them tie me faster and stop my mouth, and then they put me into a large sack. They also stopped my sister's mouth and tied her hands, and in this manner we proceeded till we were out of the sight of these people. When we went to rest the following night they offered us some victuals, but we refused it, and the only comfort we had was in being in one another's arms all that night, and bathing each other with our tears. But alas! we were soon deprived of even the small comfort of weeping together. The next day proved a day of greater sorrow than I had yet experienced, for my sister and I were then separated while we lay clasped in each other's arms. It was in vain that we besought them not to part us; she was torn from me and immediately carried away, while I was left in a state of distraction not to be described. I cried and grieved continually, and for several days I did not eat anything but what they forced into my mouth.

At length, after many days travelling, during which I had often changed masters, I got into the hands of a chieftain in a very pleasant country. This man had two wives and some children, and they all used me extremely well, and did all they could to comfort me—particularly the first wife, who was something like my mother. Although I was a great many days' journey from my father's house, yet these people spoke exactly the same language with us. This first master of mine, as I may call him, was a smith,[1] and my principal employment was working his bellows, which were the same kind as I had seen in my vicinity. They were in some respects not unlike the stoves here in gentlemen's kitchens, and were covered over with leather; and in the middle of that leather a stick was fixed, and a person stood up and worked it in the same manner as is done to pump water out of a cask with a hand pump. I believe it was gold he worked, for it was of a lovely bright yellow colour, and was worn by the women on their wrists and ankles.

I was there I suppose about a month, and they at last used to trust me some little distance from the house. This liberty I used in embracing every opportunity to inquire the way to my own home; and I also sometimes, for the same purpose, went with the maidens in the cool of the evenings to bring pitchers of water from the springs for the use of the house. I had also remarked where the sun rose in the morning and set in the evening as I had travelled along, and I had observed that my father's house was towards the rising of the sun. I therefore determined to seize the first opportunity of

---

[1] *smith*   One who works with metals.

making my escape, and to shape my course for that quarter; for I was quite oppressed and weighed down by grief after my mother and friends; and my love of liberty, ever great, was strengthened by the mortifying circumstance of not daring to eat with the free-born children, although I was mostly their companion.

While I was projecting my escape, one day an unlucky event happened which quite disconcerted my plan and put an end to my hopes. I used to be sometimes employed in assisting an elderly woman slave to cook and take care of the poultry, and one morning while I was feeding some chickens, I happened to toss a small pebble at one of them, which hit it on the middle and directly killed it. The old slave, having soon after missed the chicken, inquired after it; and on my relating the accident (for I told her the truth, because my mother would never suffer me to tell a lie), she flew into a violent passion, threatened that I should suffer for it, and, my master being out, she immediately went and told her mistress what I had done. This alarmed me very much, and I expected an instant flogging, which to me was uncommonly dreadful, for I had seldom been beaten at home. I therefore resolved to fly, and accordingly I ran into a thicket that was hard by and hid myself in the bushes. Soon afterwards my mistress and the slave returned, and, not seeing me, they searched all the house; but, not finding me, and I not making answer when they called to me, they thought I had run away, and the whole neighbourhood was raised in the pursuit of me. In that part of the country (as in ours) the houses and villages were skirted with woods, or shrubberies, and the bushes were so thick that a man could readily conceal himself in them so as to elude the strictest search. The neighbours continued the whole day looking for me, and several times many of them came within a few yards of the place where I lay hid. I then gave myself up for lost entirely and expected every moment, when I heard a rustling among the trees, to be found out and punished by my master. But they never discovered me, though they were often so near that I even heard their conjectures as they were looking about for me; and I now learned from them that any attempt to return home would be hopeless. Most of them supposed I had fled towards home, but the distance was so great, and the way so intricate, that they thought I

could never reach it, and that I should be lost in the woods. When I heard this I was seized with a violent panic and abandoned myself to despair. Night too began to approach, and aggravated all my fears. I had before entertained hopes of getting home, and I had determined when it should be dark to make the attempt; but I was now convinced it was fruitless, and I began to consider that, if possibly I could escape all other animals, I could not those of the human kind, and that, not knowing the way, I must perish in the woods. Thus was I like the hunted deer:

Ev'ry leaf and ev'ry whisp ring breath
Conveyed a foe, and ev'ry foe a death.[1]

I heard frequent rustlings among the leaves, and, being pretty sure they were snakes, I expected every instant to be stung by them. This increased my anguish, and the horror of my situation became now quite insupportable. I at length quitted the thicket, very faint and hungry, for I had not eaten or drank anything all the day, and crept to my master's kitchen, from whence I set out at first, and which was an open shed, and laid myself down in the ashes with an anxious wish for death to relieve me from all my pains. I was scarcely awake in the morning when the old woman slave, who was the first up, came to light the fire and saw me in the fireplace. She was very much surprised to see me, and could scarcely believe her own eyes. She now promised to intercede for me, and went for her master, who soon after came and, having slightly reprimanded me, ordered me to be taken care of and not to be ill-treated.

Soon after this my master's only daughter, and child by his first wife, sickened and died, which affected him so much that for some time he was almost frantic, and really would have killed himself, had he not been watched and prevented. However, in a small time afterwards he recovered, and I was again sold. I was now carried to the left of the sun's rising, through many different countries and a number of large woods. The people I was sold to used to carry me very often, when I was tired, either on their shoulders or on their backs. I saw many convenient, well

---

[1] *Ev'ry ... death* Cf. lines 287–88 of John Denham's "Cooper's Hill": "Now every leaf, and every moving breath / Presents a foe, and every foe a death."

built sheds along the roads, at proper distances to accommodate the merchants and travellers, who lay in those buildings along with their wives, who often accompany them; and they always go well armed.

From the time I left my own nation, I always found somebody that understood me, till I came to the sea coast. The languages of different nations did not totally differ, nor were they so copious as those of the Europeans, particularly the English. They were therefore easily learned, and while I was journeying thus through Africa I acquired two or three different tongues. In this manner I had been travelling for a considerable time when one evening, to my great surprise, whom should I see brought to the house where I was but my dear sister! As soon as she saw me she gave a loud shriek and ran into my arms. I was quite overpowered: neither of us could speak, but for a considerable time clung to each other in mutual embraces, unable to do any thing but weep. Our meeting affected all who saw us; and indeed I must acknowledge, in honour of those sable destroyers of human rights, that I never met with any ill treatment, or saw any offered to their slaves, except tying them when necessary, to keep them from running away. When these people knew we were brother and sister they indulged us together, and the man to whom I supposed we belonged lay with us, he in the middle, while she and I held one another by the hands across his breast all night; and thus for a while we forgot our misfortunes in the joy of being together. But even this small comfort was soon to have an end, for scarcely had the fatal morning appeared when she was again torn from me forever! I was now more miserable, if possible, than before. The small relief which her presence gave me from pain was gone, and the wretchedness of my situation was redoubled by my anxiety after her fate and my apprehensions lest her sufferings should be greater than mine, when I could not be with her to alleviate them. Yes, thou dear partner of all my childish sports! thou sharer of my joys and sorrows! happy should I have ever esteemed myself to encounter every misery for you, and to procure your freedom by the sacrifice of my own. Though you were early forced from my arms, your image has been always riveted in my heart, from which neither time nor fortune have been able to remove it; so that, while the thoughts of your sufferings have damped my prosperity, they have mingled with adversity and increased its bitterness. To that Heaven which protects the weak from the strong, I commit the care of your innocence and virtues, if they have not already received their full reward, and if your youth and delicacy have not long since fallen victims to the violence of the African trader, the pestilential stench of a Guinea ship,[1] the seasoning in the European colonies, or the lash and lust of a brutal and unrelenting overseer.

I did not long remain after my sister. I was again sold and carried through a number of places, till, after travelling a considerable time, I came to a town called Tinmah, in the most beautiful country I had yet seen in Africa. It was extremely rich, and there were many rivulets which flowed through it and supplied a large pond in the centre of the town, where the people washed. Here I first saw and tasted cocoa-nuts, which I thought superior to any nuts I had ever tasted before; and the trees, which were loaded, were also interspersed amongst the houses, which had commodious shades adjoining and were in the same manner as ours, the insides being neatly plastered and whitewashed. Here I also saw and tasted for the first time sugar cane. Their money consisted of little white shells the size of the fingernail. I was sold here for one hundred and seventy-two of them by a merchant who lived, and brought me, there. I had been about two or three days at his house when a wealthy widow, a neighbour of his, came there one evening and brought with her an only son, a young gentleman about my own age and size. Here they saw me; and, having taken a fancy to me, I was bought of the merchant and went home with them. Her house and premises were situated close to one of those rivulets I have mentioned, and were the finest I ever saw in Africa: they were very extensive, and she had a number of slaves to attend her. The next day I was washed and perfumed, and when mealtime came I was led into the presence of my mistress, and ate and drank before her with her son. This filled me with astonishment, and I could scarce help expressing my surprise that the young gentleman should suffer me, who was bound, to eat with him, who was free; and not only so, but that he would not at any time either eat or drink till I had taken first, because I was the eldest (which was agreeable to our custom). In-

---

[1] *Guinea ship* Slave ship from Guinea.

deed, everything here, and all their treatment of me, made me forget that I was a slave. The language of these people resembled ours so nearly that we understood each other perfectly. They had also the very same customs as we. There were likewise slaves daily to attend us, while my young master and I with other boys sported with our darts and bows and arrows, as I had been used to do at home. In this resemblance to my former happy state I passed about two months; and I now began to think I was to be adopted into the family, and was beginning to be reconciled to my situation and to forget by degrees my misfortunes, when all at once the delusion vanished; for, without the least previous knowledge, one morning early, while my dear master and companion was still asleep, I was wakened out of my reverie to fresh sorrow, and hurried away even amongst the uncircumcised.[1]

Thus at the very moment I dreamed of the greatest happiness I found myself most miserable, and it seemed as if fortune wished to give me this taste of joy only to render the reverse more poignant. The change I now experienced was as painful as it was sudden and unexpected. It was a change indeed from a state of bliss to a scene which is inexpressible by me, as it discovered to me an element I had never before beheld, and till then had no idea of, and wherein such instances of hardship and cruelty continually occurred, as I can never reflect on but with horror.

All the nations and people I had hitherto passed through resembled our own in their manners, customs, and language, but I came at length to a country, the inhabitants of which differed from us in all those particulars. I was very much struck with this difference, especially when I came among a people who did not circumcise, and ate without washing their hands. They cooked also in iron pots, and had European cutlasses and cross bows, which were unknown to us, and fought with their fists amongst themselves. Their women were not so modest as ours, for they ate and drank and slept with their men. But, above all, I was amazed to see no sacrifices or offerings among them. In some of those places the people ornamented themselves with scars, and likewise filed their teeth very sharp. They wanted

sometimes to ornament me in the same manner, but I would not suffer them, hoping that I might sometime be among a people who did not thus disfigure themselves, as I thought they did. At last I came to the banks of a large river which was covered with canoes, in which the people appeared to live with their household utensils and provisions of all kinds. I was beyond measure astonished at this, as I had never before seen any water larger than a pond or a rivulet, and my surprise was mingled with no small fear when I was put into one of these canoes and we began to paddle and move along the river. We continued going on thus till night; and when we came to land and made fires on the banks, each family by themselves, some dragged their canoes on shore, others stayed and cooked in theirs and laid in them all night. Those on the land had mats, of which they made tents, some in the shape of little houses. In these we slept, and after the morning meal we embarked again and proceeded as before. I was often very much astonished to see some of the women, as well as the men, jump into the water, dive to the bottom, come up again, and swim about.

Thus I continued to travel, sometimes by land, sometimes by water, through different countries and various nations, till, at the end of six or seven months after I had been kidnapped, I arrived at the seacoast. It would be tedious and uninteresting to relate all the incidents which befell me during this journey, and which I have not yet forgotten; of the various hands I passed through, and the manners and customs of all the different people among whom I lived. I shall therefore only observe that in all the places where I was the soil was exceedingly rich; the pumpkins, eadas,[2] plantains, yams, etc., etc., were in great abundance, and of incredible size. There were also vast quantities of different gums, though not used for any purpose, and everywhere a great deal of tobacco. The cotton even grew quite wild, and there was plenty of redwood. I saw no mechanics[3] whatever in all the way, except such as I have mentioned. The chief employment in all these countries was agriculture, and both the males and females, as with us, were brought up to it, and trained in the arts of war.

---

[1] *uncircumcised* I.e., heathens, foreigners.

[2] *eadas* Clearly a fruit or vegetable, but what sort is uncertain.

[3] *mechanics* Artisans.

The first object which saluted my eyes when I arrived on the coast was the sea, and a slave ship, which was then riding at anchor and waiting for its cargo. These filled me with astonishment, which was soon converted into terror when I was carried on board. I was immediately handled and tossed up, to see if I were sound, by some of the crew; and I was now persuaded that I had gotten into a world of bad spirits, and that they were going to kill me. Their complexions, too, differing so much from ours, their long hair, and the language they spoke (which was very different from any I had ever heard) united to confirm me in this belief. Indeed, such were the horrors of my views and fears at the moment that, if ten thousand worlds had been my own, I would have freely parted with them all to have exchanged my condition with that of the meanest slave in my own country. When I looked round the ship, too, and saw a large furnace or copper boiling, and a multitude of black people of every description chained together, every one of their countenances expressing dejection and sorrow, I no longer doubted of my fate; and, quite overpowered with horror and anguish, I fell motionless on the deck and fainted. When I recovered a little I found some black people about me who I believed were some of those who brought me on board and had been receiving their pay; they talked to me in order to cheer me, but all in vain. I asked them if we were not to be eaten by those white men with horrible looks, red faces, and loose hair. They told me I was not, and one of the crew brought me a small portion of spirituous liquor in a wine glass; but, being afraid of him, I would not take it out of his hand. One of the blacks therefore took it from him and gave it to me, and I took a little down my palate, which, instead of reviving me as they thought it would, threw me into the greatest consternation at the strange feeling it produced, having never tasted any such liquor before.

Soon after this the blacks who brought me on board went off, and left me abandoned to despair. I now saw myself deprived of all chance of returning to my native country, or even the least glimpse of hope of gaining the shore, which I now considered as friendly; and I even wished for my former slavery in preference to my present situation, which was filled with horrors of every kind, still heightened by my ignorance of what I was to undergo. I was not long suffered to indulge my grief; I was soon put down under the decks, and there I received such a salutation in my nostrils as I had never experienced in my life; so that, with the loathsomeness of the stench and crying together, I became so sick and low that I was not able to eat, nor had I the least desire to taste anything. I now wished for the last friend, death, to relieve me; but soon, to my grief, two of the white men offered me eatables; and, on my refusing to eat, one of them held me fast by the hands and laid me across, I think, the windlass,[1] and tied my feet while the other flogged me severely. I had never experienced anything of this kind before; and although, not being used to the water, I naturally feared that element the first time I saw it, yet nevertheless, could I have got over the nettings, I would have jumped over the side. But I could not, and besides, the crew used to watch us very closely who were not chained down to the decks, lest we should leap into the water, and I have seen some of these poor African prisoners most severely cut for attempting to do so, and hourly whipped for not eating. This indeed was often the case with myself.

In a little time after, amongst the poor chained men I found some of my own nation, which in a small degree gave ease to my mind. I inquired of these what was to be done with us; they gave me to understand we were to be carried to these white people's country to work for them. I then was a little revived and thought, if it were no worse than working, my situation was not so desperate. But still I feared I should be put to death; the white people looked and acted, as I thought, in so savage a manner—for I had never seen among any people such instances of brutal cruelty, and this not only shown towards us blacks, but also to some of the whites themselves. One white man in particular I saw, when we were permitted to be on deck, flogged so unmercifully with a large rope near the foremast that he died in consequence of it, and they tossed him over the side as they would have done a brute.[2] This made me fear these people the more, and I expected nothing less than to be treated in the same manner. I could not help expressing my fears and apprehensions to some of my countrymen.

---

[1] *windlass* On board ship, a mechanical contrivance used for winding ropes or chains.

[2] *brute* Non-human animal.

I asked them if these people had no country, but lived in this hollow place (the ship). They told me they did not, but came from a distant one. "Then," said I, "how comes it in all our country we never heard of them?" They told me because they lived so very far off. I then asked, where were their women? had they any like themselves? I was told they had. "And why," said I, "do we not see them?" They answered, because they were left behind. I asked how the vessel could go. They told me they could not tell, but that there were cloths put upon the masts by the help of the ropes I saw, and then the vessel went on; and the white men had some spell or magic they put in the water when they liked in order to stop the vessel. I was exceedingly amazed at this account, and really thought they were spirits. I therefore wished much to be from amongst them, for I expected they would sacrifice me. But my wishes were vain, for we were so quartered that it was impossible for any of us to make our escape.

While we stayed on the coast I was mostly on deck, and one day, to my great astonishment, I saw one of these vessels coming in with the sails up. As soon as the whites saw it, they gave a great shout, at which we were amazed; and the more so as the vessel appeared larger by approaching nearer. At last she came to an anchor in my sight, and when the anchor was let go I and my countrymen who saw it were lost in astonishment to observe the vessel stop, and were now convinced it was done by magic. Soon after this the other ship got her boats out, and they came on board of us, and the people of both ships seemed very glad to see each other. Several of the strangers also shook hands with us black people and made motions with their hands, signifying, I suppose, we were to go to their country; but we did not understand them. At last, when the ship we were in had got in all her cargo, they made ready with many fearful noises, and we were all put under deck, so that we could not see how they managed the vessel. But this disappointment was the least of my sorrow. The stench of the hold while we were on the coast was so intolerably loathsome that it was dangerous to remain there for any time, and some of us had been permitted to stay on the deck for the fresh air, but now that the whole ship's cargo were confined together, it became absolutely pestilential. The closeness of the place and the heat of the climate, added

to the number in the ship, which was so crowded that each had scarcely room to turn himself, almost suffocated us. This produced copious perspirations, so that the air soon became unfit for respiration from a variety of loathsome smells, and brought on a sickness among the slaves, of which many died, thus falling victims to the improvident avarice, as I may call it, of their purchasers. This wretched situation was again aggravated by the galling[1] of the chains, now become insupportable, and the filth of the necessary tubs, into which the children often fell, and were almost suffocated. The shrieks of the women and the groans of the dying rendered the whole a scene of horror almost inconceivable. Happily perhaps for myself, I was soon reduced so low here that it was thought necessary to keep me almost always on deck; and from my extreme youth I was not put in fetters. In this situation I expected every hour to share the fate of my companions, some of whom were almost daily brought upon deck at the point of death, which I began to hope would soon put an end to my miseries. Often did I think many of the inhabitants of the deep much more happy than myself. I envied them the freedom they enjoyed, and as often wished I could change my condition for theirs. Every circumstance I met with served only to render my state more painful and heighten my apprehensions and my opinion of the cruelty of the whites. One day they had taken a number of fishes; and when they had killed and satisfied themselves with as many as they thought fit, to our astonishment who were on the deck, rather than give any of them to us to eat as we expected, they tossed the remaining fish into the sea again, although we begged and prayed for some as well as we could, but in vain; and some of my countrymen, being pressed by hunger, took an opportunity, when they thought no one saw them, of trying to get a little privately; but they were discovered, and the attempt procured them some very severe floggings.

One day, when we had a smooth sea and moderate wind, two of my wearied countrymen who were chained together (I was near them at the time), preferring death to such a life of misery, somehow made through the nettings and jumped into the sea. Immediately another quite dejected fellow, who, on account of his illness, was

---

[1] *galling* Chafing.

suffered to be out of irons, also followed their example; and I believe many more would very soon have done the same if they had not been prevented by the ship's crew, who were instantly alarmed. Those of us that were the most active were in a moment put down under the deck, and there was such a noise and confusion amongst the people of the ship as I never heard before, to stop her and get the boat out to go after the slaves. However, two of the wretches were drowned; but they got the other, and afterwards flogged him unmercifully for thus attempting to prefer death to slavery.

In this manner we continued to undergo more hardships than I can now relate, hardships which are inseparable from this accursed trade. Many a time we were near suffocation from the want of fresh air, which we were often without for whole days together. This, and the stench of the necessary tubs, carried off many. During our passage I first saw flying fishes, which surprised me very much: they used frequently to fly across the ship, and many of them fell on the deck. I also now first saw the use of the quadrant;[1] I had often with astonishment seen the mariners make observations with it, and I could not think what it meant. They at last took notice of my surprise, and one of them, willing to increase it, as well as to gratify my curiosity, made me one day look through it. The clouds appeared to me to be land, which disappeared as they passed along. This heightened my wonder, and I was now more persuaded than ever that I was in another world, and that everything about me was magic.

At last we came in sight of the island of Barbados, at which the whites on board gave a great shout and made many signs of joy to us. We did not know what to think of this, but as the vessel drew nearer we plainly saw the harbour and other ships of different kinds and sizes, and we soon anchored amongst them off Bridgetown. Many merchants and planters now came on board, though it was in the evening. They put us in separate parcels and examined us attentively. They also made us jump, and pointed to the land, signifying we were to go there. We thought by this we should be eaten by these ugly men, as they appeared to us; and, when soon after we were all put down under the deck again, there was much dread and trembling among us, and nothing but bitter cries to

be heard all the night from these apprehensions, insomuch that at last the white people got some old slaves from the land to pacify us. They told us we were not to be eaten, but to work, and were soon to go on land, where we should see many of our country people. This report eased us much; and sure enough, soon after we were landed, there came to us Africans of all languages. We were conducted immediately to the merchant's yard, where we were all pent up together like so many sheep in a fold, without regard to sex or age. As every object was new to me, everything I saw filled me with surprise. What struck me first was that the houses were built with stories, and in every other respect different from those in Africa. But I was still more astonished on seeing people on horseback. I did not know what this could mean, and indeed I thought these people were full of nothing but magical arts. While I was in this astonishment, one of my fellow prisoners spoke to a countryman of his about the horses, who said they were the same kind they had in their country. I understood them, though they were from a distant part of Africa, and I thought it odd I had not seen any horses there; but afterwards, when I came to converse with different Africans, I found they had many horses amongst them, and much larger than those I then saw.

We were not many days in the merchant's custody before we were sold after their usual manner, which is this: on a signal given (as the beat of a drum), the buyers rush at once into the yard where the slaves are confined, and make choice of that parcel they like best. The noise and clamour with which this is attended, and the eagerness visible in the countenances of the buyers, serve not a little to increase the apprehensions of the terrified Africans, who may well be supposed to consider them as the ministers of that destruction to which they think themselves devoted. In this manner, without scruple, are relations and friends separated, most of them never to see each other again. I remember in the vessel in which I was brought over, in the men's apartment there were several brothers who, in the sale, were sold in different lots; and it was very moving on this occasion to see and hear their cries at parting. O ye nominal Christians![2] Might not an African ask you, "Learned you this from your God, who says unto you, 'Do unto all men as you

---

[1]   *quadrant* Instrument used for taking altitudes.

[2]   *nominal Christians* I.e., Christians in name only.

would men should do unto you'? Is it not enough that we are torn from our country and friends to toil for your luxury and lust of gain? Must every tender feeling be likewise sacrificed to your avarice? Are the dearest friends and relations, now rendered more dear by their separation from their kindred, still to be parted from each other, and thus prevented from cheering the gloom of slavery with the small comfort of being together and mingling their sufferings and sorrows? Why are parents to lose their children, brothers their sisters, or husbands their wives?" Surely this is a new refinement in cruelty, which, while it has no advantage to atone for it, thus aggravates distress and adds fresh horrors even to the wretchedness of slavery.

—1789

In Context

Reactions to Olaudah Equiano's Work

Reactions to the publication of Equiano's *Interesting Narrative* varied widely. At one extreme *The Oracle* and *The Star* attempted to discredit the work by asserting that Equiano had been born and bred in Santa Cruz in the West Indies rather than in Africa. (The writer of the piece in *The Oracle* went on to cast slurs against abolitionist William Wilberforce as well, falsely asserting that Wilberforce himself had an interest in a slave-owning plantation.) Excerpts from some of the reactions to Equiano's work in other journals are reproduced below; the comments in *The Analytical Review* may be of particular interest in that they were written by Mary Wollstonecraft.

from *The Analytic Review*, May 1789

The life of an African, written by himself, is certainly a curiosity, as it has been a favourite philosophic[1] whim to degrade the numerous nations, on whom the sun-beams more directly dart, below the common level of humanity, and hastily to conclude that nature, by making them inferior to the rest of the human race, designed to stamp them with a mark of slavery. How they were shaded down, from the fresh colour of northern rustics, to the sable hue seen on the African sands, is not our task to inquire, nor do we intend to draw a parallel between the abilities of a negro and European mechanic;[2] we shall only observe, that if these volumes do not exhibit extraordinary intellectual powers, sufficient to wipe off the stigma, yet the activity and ingenuity, which conspicuously appear in the character of Gustavus, place him on a par with the general mass of men, who fill the subordinate stations in a more civilized society than that which he was thrown into at his birth.

from *The Gentleman's Magazine*, June 1789

Among other contrivances (and perhaps one of the most innocent) to interest the national humanity in favour of the Negro slaves, one of them here writes his own history, as formerly another of them published his correspondence. These memoirs, written in a very unequal style, place the writer on a

---

[1] *philosophic* Scientific.

[2] *mechanic* Manual laborer.

par with the general mass of men in the subordinate stations of civilized society, and prove that there is no general rule without an exception.

from *The Monthly Review*, June 1789

We entertain no doubt of the general authenticity of this very intelligent African's story; though it is not improbable that some English writer has assisted him in the compilement, or, at least, the correction of his book; for it is sufficiently well-written. The *Narrative* wears an honest face; and we have conceived a good opinion of the man, from the artless manner in which he has detailed the variety of adventures and vicissitudes which have fallen to his lot. His publication appears very seasonable, at a time when negro-slavery is the subject of public investigation; and it seems calculated to increase the odium that has been excited against the West-India planters, on account of the cruelties that some are said to have exercised on their slaves, many instances of which are here detailed.

from *The General Magazine and Impartial Review*, July 1789

This is "a round unvarnished tale"[1] of the chequered adventures of an African, who early in life, was torn from his native country, by those savage dealers in a traffic disgraceful to humanity, and which has fixed a stain on the legislature of Britain. The *Narrative* appears to be written with much truth and simplicity. The author's account of the manners of the natives of his own province (Ebo) is interesting and pleasing; and the reader, unless perchance he is either a West-India planter, or Liverpool merchant, will find his humanity often severely wounded by the shameless barbarity practised towards the author's hapless countrymen in all our colonies; if he feel as he ought, the oppressed and the oppressors will equally excite his pity and indignation. That so unjust, so iniquitous a commerce may be abolished is our ardent wish; and we heartily join in our author's prayer, "That the God of Heaven may inspire the hearts of our Representatives in Parliament, with peculiar benevolence on that important day when so interesting a question is to be discussed; when thousands, in consequence of their determination, are to look for happiness or misery!"

---

[1] *a round unvarnished tale*   Cf. William Shakespeare, *Othello* 1.3.89.

READING POETRY

WHAT IS A POEM?

Most of us know what a poem is when we see one. Still, even poets find it difficult to define a poem, or poetry. In a lecture on "The Name and Nature of Poetry" (1933), the English poet A.E. Housman stated that he could "no more define poetry than a terrier can define a rat"; however, he added, "we both recognize the object by the symptoms which it provokes in us." Housman knew he was in the presence of poetry if he experienced a shiver down the spine, or "a constriction of the throat and a precipitation of water to the eyes." Implicit in Housman's response is a recognition that we have to go beyond mere formal characteristics—stanzas, rhymes, rhythms—if we want to know what poetry is, or why it differs from prose. Poetry both represents and *creates* emotions in a highly condensed way. Therefore, any definition of the genre needs to consider, as much as possible, the impact of poetry on us as readers or listeners.

Worth consideration too is the role of the listener or reader not only as passive recipient of a poem, but also as an active participant in its performance. Poetry is among other things the locus for a communicative exchange. A section below deals with the sub-genre of performance poetry, but in a very real sense all poetry is subject to performance. Poems are to be read aloud as well as on the page, and both in sensing meaning and in expressing sound the reader plays a vital role in bringing a poem to life, no matter how long dead its author may be; as W.H. Auden wrote memorably of his fellow poet W.B. Yeats, "the words of a dead man / Are modified in the guts of the living."

For some readers, poetry is, in William Wordsworth's phrase, "the breath and finer spirit of all knowledge" ("Preface" to the *Lyrical Ballads*). They look to poetry for insights into the nature of human experience, and expect elevated thought in carefully-wrought language. In contrast, other readers distrust poetry that seems moralistic or didactic. "We hate poetry that has a palpable design upon us," wrote John Keats to his friend J.H. Reynolds; rather, poetry should be "great & unobtrusive, a thing which enters into one's soul, and does not startle it or amaze it with itself but with its subject." The American poet Archibald MacLeish took Keats's idea a step further: in his poem "Ars Poetica" he suggested that "A poem should not mean / But be." MacLeish was not suggesting that a poem should lack meaning, but rather that meaning should inhere in the poem's expressive and sensuous qualities, not in some explicit statement or versified idea.

Whatever we look for in a poem, the infinitude of forms, styles, and subjects that make up the body of literature we call "poetry" is, in the end, impossible to capture in a definition that would satisfy all readers. All we can do, perhaps, is to agree that a poem is a discourse that is characterized by a heightened attention to language, form, and rhythm, by an expressiveness that works through figurative rather than literal modes, and by a capacity to stimulate our imagination and arouse our feelings.

THE LANGUAGE OF POETRY

To speak of "the language of poetry" implies that poets make use of a vocabulary that is somehow different from the language of everyday life. In fact, all language has the capacity to be "poetic," if by poetry we understand a use of language to which some special importance is attached. The ritualistic utterances of religious ceremonies sometimes have this force; so do the skipping rhymes of children in the schoolyard. We can distinguish such uses of language from the kind of writing we find in, say, a computer user's manual: the author of the manual can describe a given function in a variety of ways, whereas the magic of the skipping rhyme can be invoked only by getting the right words in the right order. So with the poet: he or she chooses particular words in a particular order; the *way* the poet speaks is as important to our understanding as what is said. This doesn't mean that an instruction manual couldn't have poetic qualities—indeed, modern poets have created "found" poems from even less likely materials—but it does mean that in poetry there is an intimate relation amongst language, form, and meaning, and that the writer deliberately structures and manipulates language to achieve very particular ends.

THE BEST WORDS IN THE BEST ORDER

Wordsworth provides us with a useful example of the way that poetry can invest quite ordinary words with a high emotional charge:

> No motion has she now, no force,
> She neither hears nor sees;
> Rolled round in earth's diurnal course
> With rocks, and stones, and trees.

To paraphrase the content of this stanza from "A Slumber Did My Spirit Seal," "she" is dead and buried. But the language and structures used here give this prosaic idea great impact. For example, the regular iambic meter of the two last lines conveys something of the inexorable motion of the earth and of Lucy embedded in it; the monosyllabic last line is a grim reminder of her oneness with objects in nature; the repeated negatives in the first two lines drive home the irreparable destructiveness of death; the alliteration in the third and fourth lines gives a tangible suggestion of roundness, circularity, repetition in terms of the earth's shape and motion, suggesting a cycle in which death is perhaps followed by renewal. Even the unusual word "diurnal" (which would not have seemed so unusual to Wordsworth's readers) seems "right" in this context; it lends more weight to the notion of the earth's perpetual movement than its mundane synonym "daily" (which, besides, would not scan here). It is difficult to imagine a change of any kind to these lines; they exemplify another attempted definition of poetry, this time by Wordsworth's friend Samuel Taylor Coleridge: "the best words in the best order" (*Table Talk*, 1827).

POETIC DICTION AND THE ELEVATED STYLE

Wordsworth's diction in the "Lucy" poem cited above is a model of clarity; he has chosen language that, in its simplicity and bluntness, conveys the strength of the speaker's feelings far more strongly than an elaborate description of grief in more conventionally "poetic" language might have done. Wordsworth, disturbed by what he felt was a deadness and artificiality in the poetry of his day, sought to "choose incidents and situations from common life" and to describe them in "a selection of language really used by men" ("Preface" to *Lyrical Ballads*). His plan might seem an implicit reproach of the "raised" style, the elevated diction of epic poetry we associate with John Milton's *Paradise Lost*:

> Anon out of the earth a fabric huge
> Rose like an exhalation, with the sound
> Of dulcet symphonies and voices sweet,

> Built like a temple, where pilasters round
> Were set, and Doric pillars overlaid
> With golden architrave; nor did there want
> Cornice or frieze, with bossy sculptures graven;
> The roof was fretted gold.
>
> (*Paradise Lost* I.710–17)

At first glance this passage, with its Latinate vocabulary and convoluted syntax, might seem guilty of inflated language and pretentiousness. However, Milton's description of the devils' palace in Hell deliberately seeks to distance us from its subject in order to emphasize the scale and sublimity of the spectacle, far removed from ordinary human experience. In other words, language and style in *Paradise Lost* are well adapted to suit a particular purpose, just as they are in "A Slumber Did My Spirit Seal," though on a wholly different scale. Wordsworth criticized the poetry of his day, not because of its elevation, but because the raised style was too often out of touch with its subject; in his view, the words did not bear any significant relation to the "truths" they were attempting to depict.

"PLAIN" LANGUAGE IN POETRY

Since Wordsworth's time, writers have been conscious of a need to narrow the apparent gap between "poetic" language and the language of everyday life. In much of the poetry of the past century, especially free verse, we can observe a growing approximation to speech—even to conversation—in the diction and rhythms of poetry. This may have something to do with the changed role of the poet, who today has discarded the mantle of teacher or prophet that was assumed by poets of earlier times, and who is ready to admit all fields of experience and endeavor as appropriate for poetry. The modern poet looks squarely at life, and can often find a provoking beauty in even the meanest of objects.

We should not assume, however, that a greater concern with the "ordinary," with simplicity, naturalness, and clarity, means a reduction in complexity or suggestiveness. A piece such as Stevie Smith's "Mother, Among the Dustbins," for all the casual and playful domesticity of some of its lines, skilfully evokes a range of emotions and sense impressions defying simple paraphrase.

IMAGERY, SYMBOLISM, AND FIGURES OF SPEECH

The language of poetry is grounded in the objects and phenomena that create sensory impressions. Sometimes the poet renders these impressions quite literally, in a series of *images* that seek to recreate a scene in the reader's mind:

> Only a man harrowing clods
> In a slow silent walk
> With an old horse that stumbles and nods
> Half asleep as they stalk.
>
> Only thin smoke without flame
> From the heaps of couch-grass;
> Yet this will go onward the same
> Though Dynasties pass.

Yonder a maid and her wight
Come whispering by:
War's annals will cloud into night
Ere their story die.

(Thomas Hardy, "In Time of 'The Breaking of Nations'")

Here, the objects of everyday life are re-created with sensory details designed to evoke in us the sensations or responses felt by the speaker viewing the scene. At the same time, the writer invests the objects with such significance that the poem's meaning extends beyond the literal to the symbolic: that is, the images come to stand for something much larger than the objects they represent. Hardy's poem moves from the presentation of stark images of rural life to a sense of their timelessness. By the last stanza we see the ploughman, the burning grass, and the maid and her companion as symbols of recurring human actions and motives that defy the struggles and conflicts of history.

IMAGISM

The juxtaposition of clear, forceful images is associated particularly with the Imagist movement that flourished at the beginning of the twentieth century. Its chief representatives (in their early work) were the American poets H.D. and Ezra Pound, who defined an image as "that which represents an intellectual and emotional complex in an instant of time." Pound's two-line poem "In a Station of the Metro" provides a good example of the Imagists' goal of representing emotions or impressions through the use of concentrated images:

The apparition of these faces in the crowd,
Petals on a wet, black bough.

As in a Japanese *haiku,* a form that strongly influenced the Imagists, the poem uses sharp, clear, concrete details to evoke both a sensory impression and the emotion or the atmosphere of the scene. Though the Imagist movement itself lasted only a short time (from about 1912 to 1917), it had a far-reaching influence on modern poets such as T.S. Eliot, and William Carlos Williams.

FIGURES OF SPEECH

Imagery often works together with figurative expression to extend and deepen the meaning or impact of a poem. "Figurative" language means language that is metaphorical, not literal or referential. Through "figures of speech" such as metaphor and simile, metonymy, synecdoche, and personification, the writer may alter the ordinary, denotative meanings of words in order to convey greater force and vividness to ideas or impressions, often by showing likenesses between unlike things.

With *simile,* the poet makes an explicit comparison between the subject (called the *tenor*) and another object or idea (known as the *vehicle*), using "as" or "like":

It is a beauteous evening, calm and free,
The holy time is quiet as a Nun
Breathless with adoration. …

In this opening to a sonnet, Wordsworth uses a visual image of a nun in devout prayer to convey in concrete terms the less tangible idea of evening as a "holy time." The comparison also introduces an emotional dimension, conveying something of the feeling that the scene induces in the poet. The simile can thus illuminate and expand meaning in a compact way. The poet may also extend the simile to elaborate at length on any points of likeness.

In *metaphor*, the comparison between tenor and vehicle is implied: connectives such as "like" are omitted, and a kind of identity is created between the subject and the term with which it is being compared. Thus in John Donne's "The Good-Morrow," a lover asserts the endless joy that he and his beloved find in each other:

> My face in thine eye, thine in mine appears,
> And true plain hearts do in the faces rest;
> Where can we find two better hemispheres,
> Without sharp north, without declining west?

Here the lovers are transformed into "hemispheres," each of them a half of the world not subject to the usual natural phenomena of wintry cold ("sharp north") or the coming of night ("declining west"). Thus, they form a perfect world in balance, in which the normal processes of decay or decline have been arrested. Donne renders the abstract idea of a love that defies change in pictorial and physical terms, making it more real and accessible to us. The images here are all the more arresting for the degree of concentration involved; it is not merely the absence of "like" or "as" that gives the metaphor such direct power, but the fusion of distinct images and emotions into a new idea.

Personification is the figure of speech in which the writer endows abstract ideas, inanimate objects, or animals with human characteristics. In other words, it is a type of implied metaphorical comparison in which aspects of a non-human subject are compared to the feelings, appearance, or actions of a human being. In the second stanza of his ode "To Autumn," Keats personifies the concept of autumnal harvesting in the form of a woman, "sitting careless on a granary floor, / Thy hair soft-lifted by the winnowing wind." Personification may also help to create a mood, as when Thomas Gray attributes human feelings to a hooting owl in "Elegy Written in a Country Church-Yard"; using such words as "moping" and "complain," Gray invests the bird's cries with the quality of human melancholy:

> … from yonder ivy-mantled tow'r
> The moping owl does to the moon complain
> Of such, as wand'ring near her secret bow'r,
> Molest her ancient solitary reign.

In his book *Modern Painters* (1856), the English critic John Ruskin criticized such attribution of human feelings to objects in nature. Calling this device the "pathetic fallacy," he objected to what he saw as an irrational distortion of reality, producing "a falseness in all our impressions of external things." Modern criticism, with a distrust of any notions of an objective "reality," tends to use Ruskin's term as a neutral label simply to describe instances of extended personification of natural objects.

Apostrophe, which is closely related to personification, has the speaker directly addressing a non-human object or idea as if it were a sentient human listener. Blake's "The Sick Rose," Shelley's "Ode to the West Wind" and his ode "To a Sky-Lark" all employ apostrophe, personifying the object addressed. Keats's "Ode on a Grecian Urn" begins by apostrophizing the urn ("Thou still unravish'd bride of quietness"), then addresses it in a series of questions and reflections through which the speaker attempts to unravel the urn's mysteries.

Apostrophe also appeals to or addresses a person who is absent or dead. W. H. Auden's lament "In Memory of W. B. Yeats" apostrophizes both the earth in which Yeats is to be buried ("Earth, receive an honoured guest") and the dead poet himself ("Follow, poet, follow right / To the bottom of the night …"). Religious prayers offer an illustration of the usefulness of apostrophe, since they are direct appeals from an earth-bound supplicant to an invisible god. The suggestion of strong emotion associated with such appeals is a common feature of apostrophe in poetry also, especially poetry with a religious theme, like Donne's "Holy Sonnets" (e.g., "Batter My Heart, Three-Personed God").

Metonymy and *synecdoche* are two closely related figures of speech that further illustrate the power of metaphorical language to convey meaning more intensely and vividly than is possible with prosaic statement. *Metonymy* (from the Greek, meaning "change of name") involves referring to an object or concept by substituting the name of another object or concept with which it is usually associated: for example, we might speak of "the Crown" when we mean the monarch, or describe the U.S. executive branch as "the White House." When the writer uses only part of something to signify the whole, or an individual to represent a class, we have an instance of *synecdoche*. T. S. Eliot provides an example in "The Love Song of J. Alfred Prufrock" when a crab is described as "a pair of ragged claws." Similarly, synecdoche is present in Milton's contemptous term "blind mouths" to describe the "corrupted clergy" he attacks in "Lycidas."

Dylan Thomas employs both metonymy and synecdoche in his poem "The Hand That Signed the Paper":

> The hand that signed the paper felled a city;
> Five sovereign fingers taxed the breath,
> Doubled the globe of dead and halved a country;
> These five kings did a king to death.
>
> The mighty hand leads to a sloping shoulder,
> The finger joints are cramped with chalk;
> A goose's quill has put an end to murder
> That put an end to talk.
>
> The hand that signed the treaty bred a fever,
> And famine grew, and locusts came;
> Great is the hand that holds dominion over
> Man by a scribbled name.
>
> The five kings count the dead but do not soften
> The crusted wound nor stroke the brow;
> A hand rules pity as a hand rules heaven;
> Hands have no tears to flow.

The "hand" of the poem is evidently a synecdoche for a great king who enters into treaties with friends and foes to wage wars, conquer kingdoms, and extend his personal power—all at the expense of his suffering subjects. The "goose quill" of the second stanza is a metonymy, standing for the pen used to sign the treaty or the death warrant that brings the war to an end.

Thomas's poem is an excellent example of the power of figurative language, which, by its vividness and concentrated force, can add layers of meaning to a poem, make abstract ideas concrete, and intensify the poem's emotional impact.

THE POEM AS PERFORMANCE: WRITER AND PERSON

Poetry is always dramatic. Sometimes the drama is explicit, as in Robert Browning's monologues, in which we hear the voice of a participant in a dialogue; in "My Last Duchess" we are present as the Duke reflects on the portrait of his late wife for the benefit of a visitor who has come to negotiate on behalf of the woman who is to become the Duke's next wife. Or we listen with amusement and pity as the dying Bishop addresses his venal and unsympathetic sons and tries to bargain with them for a fine burial ("The Bishop Orders His Tomb at St. Praxed's"). In such poems, the notion of a speaking voice is paramount: the speaker is a personage in a play, and the poem a means of conveying plot and character.

Sometimes the drama is less apparent, and takes the form of a plea, or a compliment, or an argument addressed to a silent listener. In Donne's "The Flea" we can infer from the poem the situation that has called it forth: a lover's advances are being rejected by his beloved, and his poem is an argument intended to overcome her reluctance by means of wit and logic. We can see a similar example in Marvell's "To His Coy Mistress": here the very shape of the poem, its three-paragraph structure, corresponds to the stages of the speaker's argument as he presents an apparently irrefutable line of reasoning. Much love poetry has this kind of background as its inspiration; the yearnings or lamentations of the lover are part of an imagined scene, not merely versified reflections about an abstraction called "love."

Meditative or reflective poetry can be dramatic too. Donne's "Holy Sonnets" are pleas from a tormented soul struggling to find its god; Tennyson's "In Memoriam" follows the agonized workings of a mind tracing a path from grief and anger to acceptance and renewed hope.

We should never assume that the speaker, the "I" of the poem, is simply a voice for the writer's own views. The speaker in W. H. Auden's "To an Unknown Citizen," presenting a summary of the dead citizen's life, appears to be an official spokesperson for the society which the citizen served ("Our report on his union"; "Our researchers ..." etc.). The speaker's words are laudatory, yet we perceive immediately that Auden's own views of this society are anything but approving. The speaker seems satisfied with the highly regimented nature of his society, one in which every aspect of the individual's life is under scrutiny and subject to correction. The only things necessary to the happiness of the "Modern Man," it seems, are "A phonograph, a radio, a car, and a frigidaire." The tone here is subtly ironic, an irony created by the gap between the imagined speaker's perception and the real feelings of the writer.

PERFORMANCE POETRY

Poetry began as an oral art, passed on in the form of chants, myths, ballads, and legends recited to an audience of listeners rather than readers. Even today, the dramatic qualities of a poem may extend beyond written text. "Performance poets" combine poetry and stagecraft in presenting their work to live audiences. Dramatic uses of voice, rhythm, body movement, music, and sometimes other visual effects make the "text" of the poem multi-dimensional. For example, Edith Sitwell's poem-sequence *Façade* (1922) was originally set to music: Sitwell read from behind a screen, while a live orchestra played. This performance was designed to enhance the verbal and rhythmic qualities of her poetry:

Beneath the flat and paper sky
The sun, a demon's eye
Glowed through the air, that mask of glass;
All wand'ring sounds that pass

Seemed out of tune, as if the light
Were fiddle-strings pulled tight.
The market-square with spire and bell
Clanged out the hour in Hell.
    (from *Façade*)

By performing their poetry, writers can also convey cultural values and traditions. The cultural aspect of performance is central to Black poetry, which originates in a highly oral tradition of folklore and storytelling. From its roots in Africa, this oral tradition has been manifested in the songs and stories of slaves, in spirituals, in the jazz rhythms of the Twenties and the Thirties and in the rebelliousness of reggae and of rap. Even when it remains "on the page," much Black poetry written in the oral tradition has a compelling rhythmic quality. The lines below from Linton Kwesi Johnson's "Mi Revalueshanary Fren," for example, blur the line between spoken poetry and song. Johnson often performs his "dub poetry" against reggae or hip-hop musical backings.

yes, people powa jus a showa evry howa
an evrybady claim dem democratic
but some a wolf an some a sheep
an dat is problematic

The chorus of Johnson's poems, with its constant repetitions, digs deeply into the roots of African song and chant. Its performance qualities become clearer when the poem is read aloud:

Husak
e ad to go
Honnicka
e ad to go
Chowcheskhu
e ad to go
Just like apartied
will av to go

To perform a poem is one way to see and hear poetry as multi-dimensional, cultural, historical, and often also political. Performance is also another way to discover how poetic "meaning" can be constructed in the dynamic relation between speaker and listener.

TONE: THE SPEAKER'S ATTITUDE

In understanding poetry, it is helpful to imagine a poem as having a "voice." The voice may be close to the poet's own, or that of an imagined character, a *persona* adopted by the poet. The tone of the voice will reveal the speaker's attitude to the subject, thus helping to shape our understanding and response. In speech we can indicate our feelings by raising or lowering our voices, and we can accompany words with physical actions. In writing, we must try to convey the tonal inflections of the speaking voice through devices of language and rhythm, through imagery and figures of speech, and through allusions and contrasts.

THE IRONIC TONE

Housman's poem "Terence, This Is Stupid Stuff" offers a useful example of ways in which manipulating tone can reinforce meaning. When Housman, presenting himself in the poem as "Terence," imagines himself to be criticized for writing gloomy poems, his response to his critics takes the form of an ironic alternative: perhaps they should stick to drinking ale:

> Oh, many a peer of England brews
> Livelier liquor than the Muse,
> And malt does more than Milton can
> To justify God's ways to man.

The tone here is one of heavy scorn. The speaker is impatient with those who refuse to look at the realities of life and death, and who prefer to take refuge in simple-minded pleasure. The ludicrous comparisons, first between the brewers who have been made peers of England and the classical Muse of poetry, then between malt and Milton, create a sense of disproportion and ironic tension; the explicit allusion to *Paradise Lost* ("To justify God's ways to man") helps to drive home the poet's bitter recognition that his auditors are part of that fallen world depicted by Milton, yet unable or unwilling to acknowledge their harsh condition. The three couplets that follow offer a series of contrasts: in each case, the first line sets up a pleasant expectation and the second dashes it with a blunt reminder of reality:

> Ale, man, ale's the stuff to drink
> For fellows whom it hurts to think:
> Look into the pewter pot
> To see the world as the world's not.
> And faith, 'tis pleasant till 'tis past:
> The mischief is that 'twill not last.

These are all jabs at the "sterling lads" who would prefer to lie in "lovely muck" and not think about the way the world is. Housman's sardonic advice is all the more pointed for its sharp and ironic tone.

POETIC FORMS

In poetry, language is intimately related to form, which is the structuring of words within identifiable patterns. In prose we speak of phrases, sentences, and paragraphs; in poetry, we identify structures by lines, stanzas, or complete forms such as the sonnet or the ode (though poetry in complete or blank verse has paragraphs of variable length, not formal stanzas: see below).

Rightly handled, the form enhances expression and meaning, just as a frame can define and enhance a painting or photograph. Unlike the photo frame, however, form in poetry is an integral part of the whole work. At one end of the scale, the term "form" may describe the *epic,* the lengthy narrative governed by such conventions as division into books, a lofty style, and the interplay between human and supernatural characters. At the other end lies the *epigram*, a witty and pointed saying whose distinguishing characteristic is its brevity, as in Alexander Pope's famous couplet,

> I am his Highness' dog at Kew;
> Pray tell me sir, whose dog are you?

Between the epic and the epigram lie many other poetic forms, such as the sonnet, the ballad, or the ode. "Form" may also describe stanzaic patterns like *couplets* and *quatrains*.

"FIXED FORM" POEMS

The best-known poetic form is probably the sonnet, the fourteen-line poem inherited from Italy (the word itself is from the Italian *sonetto*, little song or sound). Within those fourteen lines, whether the poet chooses the "Petrarchan" rhyme scheme or the "English" form (see below in the section on "Rhyme"), the challenge is to develop an idea or situation that must find its statement and its resolution within the strict confines of the sonnet frame. Typically, there is an initial idea, description, or statement of feeling, followed by a "turn" in the thought that takes the reader by surprise, or that casts the situation in an unexpected light. Thus in Sonnet 130, "My Mistress' Eyes Are Nothing Like the Sun," William Shakespeare spends the first three quatrains apparently disparaging his lover in a series of unfavorable comparisons—"If snow be white, why then her breasts are dun"—but in the closing couplet his point becomes clear:

> And yet, by heaven, I think my love as rare
> As any she belied with false compare.

In other words, the speaker's disparaging comparisons have really been parodies of sentimental clichés which falsify reality; his mistress has no need of the exaggerations or distortions of conventional love poetry.

Other foreign forms borrowed and adapted by English-language poets include the *ghazal* and the *pantoum*. The *ghazal*, strongly associated with classical Urdu literature, originated in Persia and Arabia and was brought to the Indian subcontinent in the twelfth century. It consists of a series of couplets held together by a refrain, a simple rhyme scheme (a/a, b/a, c/a, d/a...), and a common rhythm, but only loosely related in theme or subject. Some English-language practitioners of the form have captured the epigrammatic quality of the ghazal, but most do not adhere to the strict pattern of the classical form.

The *pantoum*, based on a Malaysian form, was imported into English poetry via the work of nineteenth-century French poets. Typically it presents a series of quatrains rhyming *abab*, linked by a pattern of repetition in which the second and fourth lines of a quatrain become the first and third lines of the stanza that follows. In the poem's final stanza, the pattern is reversed: the second line repeats the third line of the first stanza, and the last line repeats the poem's opening line, thus creating the effect of a loop.

Similar to the pantoum in the circularity of its structure is the *villanelle*, originally a French form, with five *tercets* and a concluding *quatrain* held together by only two rhymes (aba, aba, aba, aba, aba, abaa) and by a refrain that repeats the first line at lines 6, 12, and 18, while the third line of the first tercet reappears as lines 9, 15, and 19. With its interlocking rhymes and elaborate repetitions, the villanelle can create a variety of tonal effects, ranging from lighthearted parody to the sonorous and earnest exhortation of Dylan Thomas's "Do Not Go Gentle Into That Good Night."

STANZAIC FORMS

Recurring formal groupings of lines within a poem are usually described as "stanzas." Both the recurring and the formal aspects of stanzaic forms are important; it is a common misconception to think that any group of lines in a poem, if it is set off by line spaces, constitutes a stanza. If such a group of lines is not patterned as one of a recurring group sharing similar formal characteristics, however, then it may be more appropriate to refer to such irregular groupings in the way we do for prose—as paragraphs. A ballad is typically divided into stanzas; a prose poem or a poem written in free verse, on the other hand, will rarely be divided into stanzas.

A stanza may be identified by the number of lines and the patterns of rhyme repeated in each grouping. One of the simpler traditional forms is the *ballad stanza*, with its alternating four and three-foot lines and its *abcb* rhyme scheme. Drawing on this form's association with medieval ballads and legends, Keats produces the eerie mystery of "La Belle Dame Sans Merci":

> I saw pale kings and princes too,
> Pale warriors, death-pale were they all;
> They cried—"La Belle Dame sans Merci
> Hath thee in thrall!"

Such imitations are a form of literary allusion; Keats uses a traditional stanza form to remind us of poems like "Sir Patrick Spens" or "Barbara Allen" to dramatize the painful thralldom of love by placing it within a well-known tradition of ballad narratives with similar forms and themes.

The four-line stanza, or *quatrain*, may be used for a variety of effects: from the elegiac solemnity of Gray's "Elegy Written in a Country Churchyard" to the apparent lightness and simplicity of some of Emily Dickinson's poems. Tennyson used a rhyming quatrain to such good effect in *In Memoriam* that the form he employed (four lines of iambic tetrameter rhyming *abba*) is known as the "In Memoriam stanza."

Other commonly used forms of stanza include the *rhyming couplet, terza rima, ottava rima, rhyme royal*, and the *Spenserian stanza*. Each of these is a rhetorical unit within a longer whole, rather like a paragraph within an essay. The poet's choice among such forms is dictated, at least in part, by the effects that each may produce. Thus the *rhyming couplet* often expresses a complete statement within two lines, creating a sense of density of thought, of coherence and closure; it is particularly effective where the writer wishes to set up contrasts, or to achieve the witty compactness of epigram:

> Of all mad creatures, if the learn'd are right,
> It is the slaver kills, and not the bite.
> A fool quite angry is quite innocent:
> Alas! 'tis ten times worse when they repent.

> (from Pope, "Epistle to Dr. Arbuthnot")

Ottava rima, as its Italian name implies, is an eight-line stanza, with the rhyme scheme *abababcc*. Like the sonnet, it is long enough to allow the development of a single thought in some detail and complexity, with a concluding couplet that may extend the central idea or cast it in a wholly unexpected light. W.B. Yeats uses this stanza form in "Sailing to Byzantium" and "Among Schoolchildren." Though much used by Renaissance poets, it is particularly associated with George Gordon, Lord Byron's *Don Juan*, in which the poet exploits to the full its potential for devastating irony and bathos. It is long enough to allow the development of a single thought in some detail and complexity; the concluding couplet can then, sonnet-like, turn that thought upon its head, or cast it in a wholly unexpected light:

> Sagest of women, even of widows, she
>   Resolved that Juan should be quite a paragon,
> And worthy of the noblest pedigree
>   (His sire was of Castile, his dam from Aragon).
> Then for accomplishments of chivalry,
>   In case our lord the king should go to war again,
> He learned the arts of riding, fencing, gunnery,
> And how to scale a fortress—or a nunnery.
>
>   (*Don Juan* I.38)

FREE VERSE

Not all writers want the order and symmetry—some might say the restraints and limitations—of traditional forms, and many have turned to *free verse* as a means of liberating their thoughts and feelings. Deriving its name from the French "vers libre" made popular by the French Symbolistes at the end of the nineteenth century, free verse is characterized by irregularity of metre, line length, and rhyme. This does not mean that it is without pattern; rather, it tends to follow more closely than other forms the unforced rhythms and accents of natural speech, making calculated use of spacing, line breaks, and "cadences," the rhythmic units that govern phrasing in speech.

Free verse is not a modern invention. Milton was an early practitioner, as was Blake; however, it was the great modern writers of free verse—first Walt Whitman, then Pound, Eliot, and William Carlos Williams (interestingly, all Americans, at least originally)—who gave this form a fluidity and flexibility that could free the imagination to deal with any kind of feeling or experience. Perhaps because it depends so much more than traditional forms upon the individual intuitions of the poet, it is the form of poetic structure most commonly found today. The best practitioners recognize that free verse, like any other kind of poetry, demands clarity, precision, and a close connection between technique and meaning.

PROSE POETRY

At the furthest extreme from traditional forms lies poetry written in prose. Contradictory as this label may seem, the two have much in common. Prose has at its disposal all the figurative devices available to poetry, such as metaphor, personification, or apostrophe; it may use structuring devices such as verbal repetition or parallel syntactical structures; it can draw on the same tonal range, from pathos to irony. The difference is that prose poetry accomplishes its ends in sentences and paragraphs, rather than lines or stanzas. First given prominence by the French poet Charles Baudelaire (*Petits Poèmes en prose*, 1862), the form is much used to present fragments of heightened sensation, conveyed through vivid or impressionistic description. It draws upon such prosaic forms as journal entries, lists, even footnotes. Prose poetry should be distinguished from "poetic prose," which may be found in a variety of settings (from the King James Bible to the fiction of Jeanette Winterson); the distinction—which not all critics would accept—appears to lie in the writer's intention.

Christan Bok's *Eunoia* is an interesting example of the ways in which a writer of prose poetry may try to balance the demands of each medium. *Eunoia* is an avowedly experimental work in which each chapter is restricted to the use of a single vowel. The text is governed by a series of rules described by the author in an afterword; they include a requirement that all chapters "must allude to the art of writing. All sentences must accent internal rhyme through the use of syntactical parallelism. The text must exhaust the lexicon for each vowel, citing at least 98% of the available repertoire...." Having imposed such constraints upon the language and form of the work, Bok then sets himself the task of showing that "even under such improbable conditions of duress, language can still express an uncanny, if not sublime, thought." The result is a surrealistic narrative that blends poetic and linguistic devices to almost hypnotic effect.

THE POEM AS A MATERIAL OBJECT

Both free verse and prose poetry pay attention in different ways to the poem as a living thing on the printed page. But the way in which poetry is presented in material form is an important part of the existence of almost any form of poetry. In the six volumes of this anthology the material form of the poem is highlighted by the inclusion of a number of facsimile reproductions of poems of other eras in their earliest extant material form.

RHYTHM AND SCANSION

When we read poetry, we often become aware of a pattern of rhythm within a line or set of lines. The formal analysis of that rhythmic pattern, or "metre," is called *scansion*. The verb "to scan" may carry different meanings, depending upon the context: if the *critic* "scans" a line, he or she is attempting to determine the metrical pattern in which it is cast; if the *line* "scans," we are making the observation that the line conforms to particular metrical rules. Whatever the context, the process of scansion is based on the premise that a line of verse is built on a pattern of stresses, a recurring set of more or less regular beats established by the alternation of light and heavy accents in syllables and words. The rhythmic pattern so distinguished in a given poem is said to be the "metre" of that poem. If we find it impossible to identify any specific metrical pattern, the poem is probably an example of free verse.

QUANTITATIVE, SYLLABIC, AND ACCENTUAL-SYLLABIC VERSE

Although we owe much of our terminology for analyzing or describing poetry to the Greeks and Romans, the foundation of our metrical system is quite different from theirs. They measured a line of verse by the duration of sound ("quantity") in each syllable, and by the combination of short and long syllables. Such poetry is known as *quantitative* verse.

Unlike Greek or Latin, English is a heavily accented language. Thus poetry of the Anglo-Saxon period, such as *Beowulf*, was *accentual:* that is, the lines were based on a fixed number of accents, or stresses, regardless of the number of syllables in the line:

Oft Scyld Scefing   sceapena þreatum
   monegum maegþum   meodosetla ofteah.

Few modern poets have written in the accentual tradition. A notable exception was Gerard Manley Hopkins, who based his line on a pattern of strong stresses that he called "sprung rhythm." Hopkins experimented with rhythms and stresses that approximate the accentual quality of natural speech; the result is a line that is emphatic, abrupt, even harsh in its forcefulness:

I caught this morning morning's minion, kingdom of daylight's dauphin, dapple-dawn-drawn
   Falcon, in his riding

> Of the rolling level underneath him steady air ....
>
> (from "The Windhover")

Under the influence of French poetry, following the Norman invasion of the eleventh century, English writers were introduced to *syllabic* prosody: that is, poetry in which the number of syllables is the determining factor in the length of any line, regardless of the number of stresses or their placement. A few modern writers have successfully produced syllabic poetry.

However, the accentual patterns of English, in speech as well as in poetry, were too strongly ingrained to disappear. Instead, the native accentual practice combined with the imported syllabic conventions to produce the *accentual-syllabic* line, in which the writer works with combinations of stressed and unstressed syllables in lines of equal syllabic length. Geoffrey Chaucer was the first great writer to employ the accentual-syllabic line in English poetry:

> Ther was also a Nonne, a Prioresse,
> That of hir smiling was ful simple and coy.
> Hir gretteste ooth was but by sainté Loy,
> And she was clepéd Madame Eglantine.
>
> (from *The Canterbury Tales*)

The fundamental pattern here is the ten-syllable line (although the convention of sounding the final "e" at the end of a line in Middle English verse sometimes produces eleven syllables). Each line contains five stressed syllables, each of which alternates with one or two unstressed syllables. This was to become the predominant metre of poetry in English until the general adoption of free verse in the twentieth century.

IDENTIFYING POETIC METER

Conventionally, meter is established by dividing a line into roughly equal parts, based on the rise and fall of the rhythmic beats. Each of these divisions, conventionally marked by a bar, is known as a "foot," and within the foot there will be a combination of stressed and unstressed syllables, indicated by the prosodic symbols / (stressed) and x (unstressed).

> I know | that I | shall meet | my fate
> Somewhere | among | the clouds | above ...
>
> (from Yeats, "An Irish Airman Foresees His Death")

To describe the meter used in a poem, we must first determine what kind of foot predominates, and then count the number of feet in each line. To describe the resultant meter we use terminology borrowed from classical prosody. In identifying the meter of English verse we commonly apply the following labels:

iambic (x /): a foot with one weak stress followed by one strong stress

> ("Look home | ward, Ang | el, now, | and melt | with ruth")

trochaic (/ x): strong followed by weak

> ("Ty | ger! Ty | ger! bur | ning bright")

anapaestic (x x /): two weak stresses, followed by a strong

("I have passed | with a nod | of the head")

dactylic (/ x x): strong stress followed by two weak

("Hickory | dickory | dock")

spondaic (/ /): two strong stresses

("If hate | killed men,| Brother | Lawrence,
  God's blood,| would not | mine kill | you?")

We also use classical terms to describe the number of feet in a line. Thus, a line with one foot is *monometer*; with two feet, *dimeter*; three feet, *trimeter*; four feet, *tetrameter*; five feet, *pentameter*; and six feet, *hexameter*.

Scansion of the two lines from Yeats's "Irish Airman" quoted above shows that the predominant foot is iambic (x /), that there are four feet to each line, and that the poem is therefore written in *iambic tetrameters*. The first foot of the second line, however, may be read as a trochee ("Somewhere"); the variation upon the iambic norm here is an example of *substitution*, a means whereby the writer may avoid the monotony that would result from adhering too closely to a set rhythm. We very quickly build up an expectation about the dominant meter of a poem; the poet will sometimes disturb that expectation by changing the beat, and so through substitution create a pleasurable tension in our awareness.

The prevailing meter in English poetry is iambic, since the natural rhythm of spoken English is predominantly iambic. Nonetheless, poets may employ other rhythms where it suits their purpose. Thus W.H. Auden can create a solemn tone by the use of a trochaic meter(/ x):

Earth, receive an honoured guest;
William Yeats is laid to rest:
Let the Irish vessel lie
Emptied of its poetry.

The same meter may be much less funereal, as in Ben Jonson's song "*To Celia*":

Come, my Celia, let us prove,
While we may, the sports of love.
Time will not be ours forever;
He, at length, our good will sever.

The sense of greater pace in this last example derives in part from the more staccato phrasing, and also from the greater use of monosyllabic words. A more obviously lilting, dancing effect is obtained from anapaestic rhythm (x x /):

I sprang to the stirrup, and Joris, and he;
I galloped, Dirck galloped, we galloped all three.
"Good speed!" cried the watch, as the gatebolts undrew;
"Speed!" echoed the wall to us galloping through.
        (from *Browning*, "How They Brought the Good News from Ghent to Aix")

Coleridge wittily captured the varying effects of different meters in "Metrical Feet: Lesson for a Boy," which the poet wrote for his sons, and in which he marked the stresses himself:

> Trochee trips from long to short;
> From long to long in solemn sort
> Slow Spondee stalks; strong foot! yet ill able
> Ever to come up with Dactyl trisyllable.
> Iambics march from short to long:—
> With a leap and a bound the swift Anapaests throng....

A meter which often deals with serious themes is unrhymed iambic pentameter, also known as *blank verse*. This is the meter of Shakespeare's plays, notably his great tragedies; it is the meter, too, of Milton's *Paradise Lost*, to which it lends a desired sonority and magnificence; and of Wordsworth's "Lines Composed a Few Miles above Tintern Abbey," where the flexibility of the meter allows the writer to move by turns from description, to narration, to philosophical reflection.

RHYME, CONSONANCE, ASSONANCE, AND ALLITERATION

Perhaps the most obvious sign of poetic form is rhyme: that is, the repetition of syllables with the same or similar sounds. If the rhyme words are placed at the end of the line, they are known as *end-rhymes*. The opening stanza of Housman's "To an Athlete Dying Young" has two pairs of end-rhymes:

> The time you won your town the *race*
> We chaired you through the market-*place*;
> Man and boy stood cheering *by*,
> And home we brought you shoulder-*high*.

Words rhyming within a line are *internal rhymes*, as in the first and third lines of this stanza from Coleridge's "The Rime of the Ancient Mariner":

> The fair breeze *blew*, the white foam *flew*
> The furrow followed free;
> We were the *first* that ever *burst*
> Into that silent sea.

When, as is usually the case, the rhyme occurs in a stressed syllable, it is known as a *masculine rhyme*; if the rhyming word ends in an unstressed syllable, it is referred to as *feminine*. The difference is apparent in the opening stanzas of Alfred Tennyson's poem "The Lady of Shalott," where the first stanza establishes the basic iambic meter with strong stresses on the rhyming words:

> On either side the river *lie*
> Long fields of barley and of *rye*,
> That clothe the wold and meet the *sky*;
> And through the field the road runs *by*
> To many-towered Camelot ...

In the second stanza Tennyson changes to trochaic lines, ending in unstressed syllables and feminine rhymes:

> Willows whiten, aspens *quiver*,
> Little breezes dusk and *shiver*
> Through the wave that runs *forever*
> By the island in the *river*
> Flowing down to Camelot.

Not only does Tennyson avoid monotony here by his shift to feminine rhymes, he also darkens the mood by using words that imply a contrast with the bright warmth of day—"quiver," "dusk," "shiver"—in preparation for the introduction of the "silent isle" that embowers the Lady.

NEAR RHYMES

Most of the rhymes in "The Lady of Shalott" are exact, or "*perfect*" rhymes. However, in the second of the stanzas just quoted, it is evident that "forever" at the end of the third line is not a "perfect" rhyme; rather, it is an instance of "*near*" or "*slant*" rhyme. Such "*imperfect*" rhymes are quite deliberate; indeed, two stanzas later we find the rhyming sequence "early," "barley," "cheerly," and "clearly," followed by the rhymes "weary," "airy," and "fairy." As with the introduction of feminine rhymes, such divergences from one dominant pattern prevent monotony and avoid a too-mechanical sing-song effect.

More importantly, near-rhymes have an oddly unsettling effect, perhaps because they both raise and frustrate our expectation of a perfect rhyme. Their use certainly gives added emphasis to the words at the end of these chilling lines from Wilfred Owen's "*Strange Meeting*":

> For by my glee might many men have laughed,
> And of my weeping something had been left,
> Which must die now. I mean the truth untold,
> The pity of war, the pity war distilled.
> Now men will go content with what we spoiled,
> Or, discontent, boil bloody, and be spilled.

CONSONANCE AND ASSONANCE

In Owen's poem, the near-rhymes "laughed / left" and "spoiled / spilled" are good examples of *consonance*, which pairs words with similar consonants but different intervening vowels. Other examples from Owen's poem include "groined / groaned," "hall / Hell," "years / yours," and "mystery / mastery."

Related to consonance as a linking device is *assonance*, the echoing of similar vowel sounds in the stressed syllables of words with differing consonants (lane/hail, penitent/reticence). A device favored particularly by descriptive poets, it appears often in the work of the English Romantics, especially Shelley and Keats, and their great Victorian successor Tennyson, all of whom had a good ear for the musical quality of language. In the following passage, Tennyson makes effective use of repeated "o" and "ow" sounds to suggest the soft moaning of the wind as it spreads the seed of the lotos plant:

> The Lotos blooms below the barren peak,
> The Lotos blows by every winding creek;

> All day the wind breathes low with mellower tone;
> Through every hollow cave and alley lone
> Round and round the spicy downs the yellow Lotos dust is blown.
>
> (from "The Lotos-Eaters")

ALLITERATION

Alliteration connects words which have the same initial consonant. Like consonance and rhyme, alliteration adds emphasis, throwing individual words into strong relief, and lending force to rhythm. This is especially evident in the work of Gerard Manley Hopkins, where alliteration works in conjunction with the heavy stresses of *sprung rhythm*:

> Brute beauty and valour and act, oh, air, pride, plume, here
> Buckle! AND the fire that breaks from thee then, a billion
> Times told lovelier, more dangerous, O my chevalier!
>
> (from "The Windhover")

Like assonance, alliteration is useful in descriptive poetry, reinforcing an impression or mood through repeated sounds:

> Thou on whose stream, 'mid the steep sky's commotion,
> Loose clouds like Earth's decaying leaves are shed,
> Shook from the tangled boughs of Heaven and Ocean ....
>
> (from Percy Shelley, "Ode to the West Wind")

The repetition of "s" and "sh" sounds conveys the rushing sound of a wind that drives everything before it. This effect is also an example of *onomatopoeia*, a figure of speech in which the sound of the words seems to echo the sense.

RHYME AND POETIC STRUCTURE

Rhyme may play a central role in the structure of a poem. This is particularly apparent in the *sonnet* form, where the expression of the thought is heavily influenced by the poet's choice of rhyme-scheme. The "English" or "Shakespearean" sonnet has three quatrains rhyming *abab*, *cdcd*, *efef*, and concludes with a rhyming couplet, *gg*. This pattern lends itself well to the statement and restatement of an idea, as we find, for example, in Shakespeare's sonnet "That time of year thou mayst in me behold." Each of the quatrains presents an image of decline or decay—a tree in winter, the coming of night, a dying fire; the closing couplet then relates these images to the thought of an impending separation and attendant feelings of loss.

The organization of the "Italian" or "Petrarchan" sonnet, by contrast, hinges on a rhyme scheme that creates two parts, an eight-line section (the *octave*) typically rhyming *abbaabba*, and a concluding six-line section (the *sestet*) rhyming *cdecde* or some other variation. In the octave, the writer describes a thought or feeling; in the sestet, the writer may elaborate upon that thought, or may introduce a sudden "turn" or change of direction. A good example of the Italian form is Donne's "Batter My Heart, Three-Personed God."

The rhyming pattern established at the beginning of a poem is usually followed throughout; thus the opening sets up an expectation in the reader, which the poet may sometimes play on by means of an unexpected or surprising rhyme. This is especially evident in comic verse, where peculiar or unexpected rhymes can contribute a great deal to the comic effect:

> I shoot the Hippopotamus
> with bullets made of platinum,
>   Because if I use leaden ones
> his hide is sure to flatten 'em.
>
>   (Hilaire Belloc, "The Hippopotamus")

Finally, one of the most obvious yet important aspects of rhyme is its sound. It acts as a kind of musical punctuation, lending verse an added resonance and beauty. And as anyone who has ever had to learn poetry by heart will testify, the sound of rhyme is a powerful aid to memorization and recall, from helping a child to learn numbers—

> One, two,
> Buckle my shoe,
> Three, four,
> Knock at the door—

—to selling toothpaste through an advertising jingle in which the use of rhyme drives home the identity of a product:

> You'll wonder where the yellow went,
> When you brush your teeth with Pepsodent.

OTHER FORMS WITH INTERLOCKING RHYMES

Other forms besides the sonnet depend upon rhyme for their structural integrity. These include the *rondeau*, a poem of thirteen lines in three stanzas, with two half lines acting as a refrain, and having only two rhymes. The linking effect of rhyme is also essential to the three-line stanza called *terza rima*, the form chosen by Shelley for his "Ode to the West Wind," where the rhyme scheme (*aba, bcb, cdc* etc.) gives a strong sense of forward movement. But a poet need not be limited to particular forms to use interlocking rhyme schemes.

THE POET'S TASK

The poet's task, in Sir Philip Sidney's view, is to move us to virtue and well-doing by coming to us with

words set in delightful proportion, either accompanied with, or prepared for, the well-enchanting skill of music; and with a tale forsooth he cometh unto you, with a tale which holdeth children from play, and old men from the chimney corner; and pretending no more, doth intend the winning of the mind from wickedness to virtue: even as the child is often brought to take most wholesome things by hiding them in such other as have a pleasant taste.

(*The Defence of Poesy,* 1593)

Modern poets have been less preoccupied with the didactic or moral force of poetry, its capacity to win the mind to virtue; nonetheless, like their Renaissance counterparts, they view poetry as a means to understanding, a point of light in an otherwise dark universe. To Robert Frost, a poem "begins in delight and ends in wisdom":

It begins in delight, it inclines to the impulse, it assumes direction with the first line laid down, it runs a course of lucky events, and ends in a clarification of life—not necessarily a great clarification, such as sects and cults are founded on, but in a momentary stay against confusion.

("The Figure a Poem Makes," *Collected Poems,* 1939)

Rhyme and metre are important tools at the poet's disposal, and can be valuable aids in developing thought as well as in creating rhythmic or musical effects. However, the technical skills needed to turn a good line or create metrical complexities should not be confused with the ability to write good poetry. Sidney wryly observes in his *Defence of Poesy* that "there have been many excellent poets that never versified, and now swarm many versifiers that need never answer to the name of poets. ...it is not rhyming and versing that maketh a poet, no more than a long gown maketh an advocate." Technical virtuosity may arouse our admiration, but something else is needed to bring that "constriction of the throat and ... precipitation of water to the eyes" that A.E. Housman speaks about. What that "something" is will always elude definition, and is perhaps best left for readers and listeners to determine for themselves through their own encounters with poetry.

Maps

THE WORLD
(SOME PRE-1500 POINTS OF REFERENCE)

THE BRITISH ISLES c. 1500

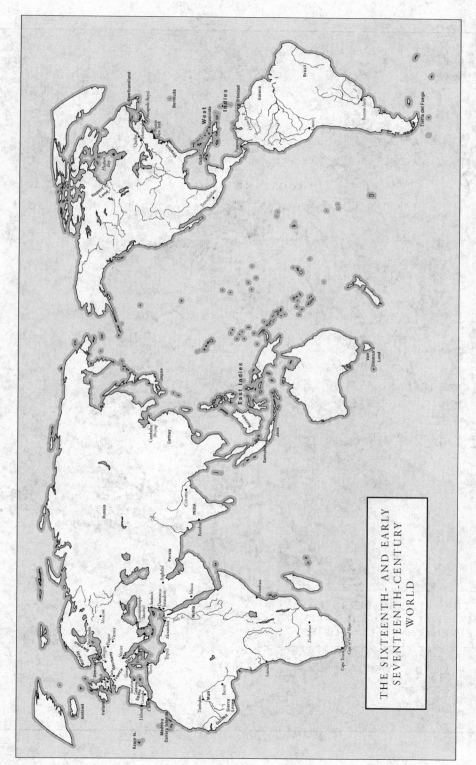

THE SIXTEENTH- AND EARLY
SEVENTEENTH-CENTURY
WORLD

THE BRITISH ISLES IN THE
SIXTEENTH AND THE EARLY
SEVENTEENTH CENTURIES

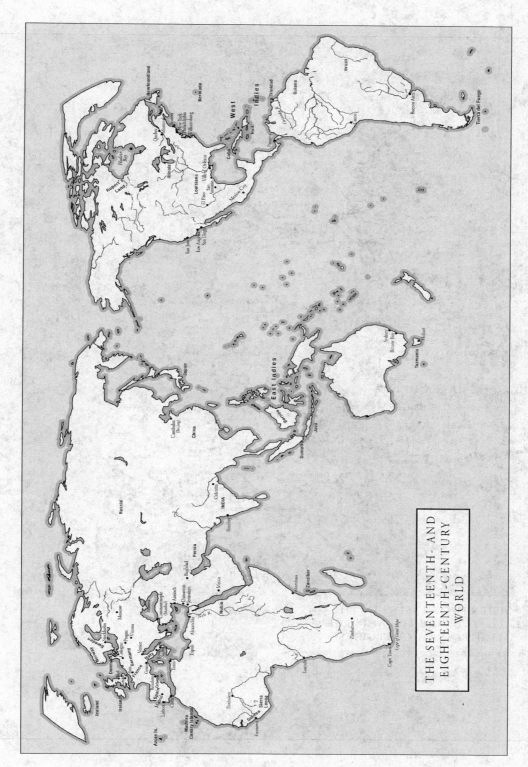

THE SEVENTEENTH- AND
EIGHTEENTH-CENTURY
WORLD

THE BRITISH ISLES IN THE
LATE SEVENTEENTH AND THE
EIGHTEENTH CENTURIES

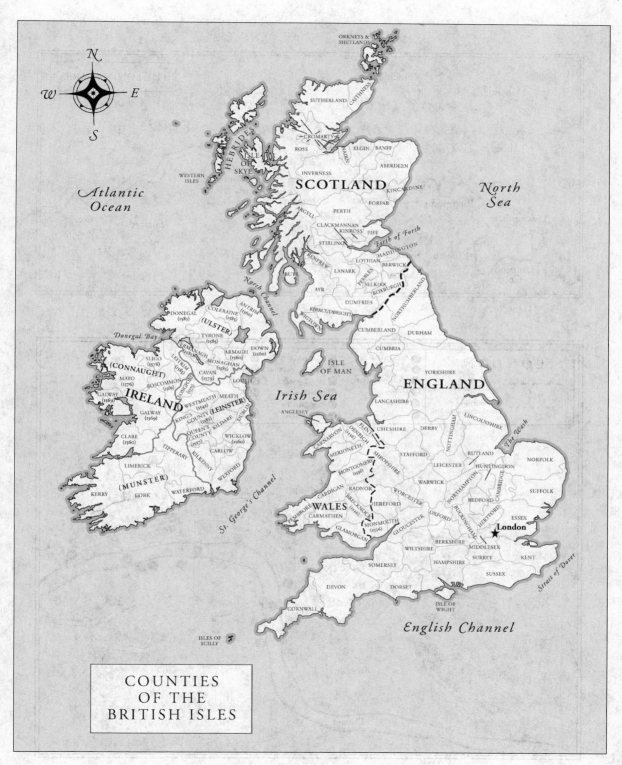

COUNTIES
OF THE
BRITISH ISLES

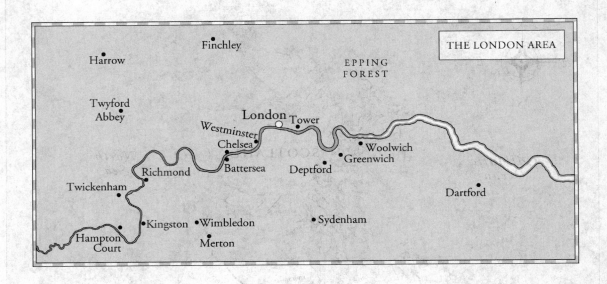

THE LONDON AREA

Finchley

Harrow

EPPING
FOREST

Twyford
Abbey

London   Tower
Westminster
Chelsea

Woolwich
Greenwich

Richmond   Battersea   Deptford

Twickenham

Dartford

Kingston   Wimbledon

Hampton
Court   Merton   Sydenham

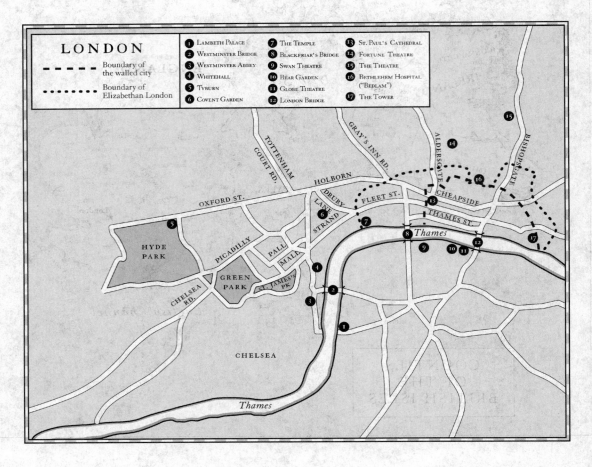

LONDON

- - - Boundary of
the walled city

···· Boundary of
Elizabethan London

1 LAMBETH PALACE
2 WESTMINSTER BRIDGE
3 WESTMINSTER ABBEY
4 WHITEHALL
5 TYBURN
6 COVENT GARDEN
7 THE TEMPLE
8 BLACKFRIAR'S BRIDGE
9 SWAN THEATRE
10 BEAR GARDEN
11 GLOBE THEATRE
12 LONDON BRIDGE
13 ST. PAUL'S CATHEDRAL
14 FORTUNE THEATRE
15 THE THEATRE
16 BETHLEHEM HOSPITAL
("BEDLAM")
17 THE TOWER

TOTTENHAM
COURT RD.

GRAY'S INN RD.

HOLBORN

ALDERSGATE

BISHOPSGATE

OXFORD ST.

DRURY
LANE

FLEET ST.   CHEAPSIDE

13

STRAND   THAMES ST.

HYDE
PARK

5

Thames

PICADILLY

PALL
MALL

GREEN
PARK

CHELSEA
RD.

ST. JAMES'S
PK.

CHELSEA

Thames

Monarchs and Prime Ministers of Great Britain

MONARCHS

HOUSE OF WESSEX

Egbert (Ecgberht)	829–39
Æthelwulf	839–58
Æthelbald	858–60
Æthelbert	860–66
Æthelred I	866–71
Alfred the Great	871–99
Edward the Elder	899–924
Athelstan	924–40
Edmund I	940–46
Edred (Eadred)	946–55
Edwy (Eadwig)	955–59
Edgar	959–75
Edward the Martyr	975–78
Æthelred II (the Unready)	978–1016
Edmund II (Ironside)	1016

DANISH LINE

Canute (Cnut)	1016–35
Harold I (Harefoot)	1035–40
Hardecanute	1040–42

WESSEX LINE, RESTORED

Edward the Confessor	1042–66
Harold II	1066

NORMAN LINE

William I (the Conqueror)	1066–87
William II (Rufus)	1087–1100
Henry I (Beauclerc)	1100–35
Stephen	1135–54

Harold II

William I

MONARCHS

**PLANTAGENET,
ANGEVIN LINE**

Henry II	1154–89
Richard I (Coeur de Lion)	1189–99
John (Lackland)	1199–1216
Henry III	1216–72
Edward I (Longshanks)	1272–1307
Edward II	1307–27
Edward III	1327–77
Richard II	1377–99

Henry VIII

**PLANTAGENET,
LANCASTRIAN LINE**

Henry IV	1399–1413
Henry V	1413–22
Henry VI	1422–61

**PLANTAGENET,
YORKIST LINE**

Edward IV	1461–83
Edward V	1483
Richard III	1483–85

HOUSE OF TUDOR

Henry VII	1485–1509
Henry VIII	1509–47
Edward VI	1547–53
Mary I	1553–58
Elizabeth I	1558–1603

Mary I

HOUSE OF STUART

James I	1603–25
Charles I	1625–49
(The Commonwealth)	1649–60
Oliver Cromwell	1649–58
Richard Cromwell	1658–59

MONARCHS

HOUSE OF STUART, RESTORED

Charles II	1660–85
James II	1685–88

HOUSE OF ORANGE AND STUART

William III and Mary II	1689–94
William III	1694–1702

HOUSE OF STUART

Anne	1702–14

HOUSE OF BRUNSWICK, HANOVER LINE

George I	1714–27
George II	1727–60
George III	1760–1820

George, Prince of Wales, Prince Regent

PRIME MINISTERS

George III

Sir Robert Walpole (Whig)	1721–42
Earl of Wilmington (Whig)	1742–43
Henry Pelham (Whig)	1743–54
Duke of Newcastle (Whig)	1754–56
Duke of Devonshire (Whig)	1756–57
Duke of Newcastle (Whig)	1757–62
Earl of Bute (Tory)	1762–63
George Grenville (Whig)	1763–65
Marquess of Rockingham (Whig)	1765–66
William Pitt the Elder (Earl of Chatham) (Whig)	1766–68
Duke of Grafton (Whig)	1768–70
Frederick North (Lord North) (Tory)	1770–82
Marquess of Rockingham (Whig)	1782
Earl of Shelburne (Whig)	1782–83
Duke of Portland	1783
William Pitt the Younger (Tory)	1783–1801
Henry Addington (Tory)	1801–04
William Pitt the Younger (Tory)	1804–06
William Wyndham Grenville (Baron Grenville) (Whig)	1806–07

MONARCHS

George, Prince of Wales, Prince Regent	1811–20
George IV	1820–30
William IV	1830–37
Victoria	1837–1901

Victoria

HOUSE OF SAXE-COBURG-GOTHA

Edward VII	1901–10

HOUSE OF WINDSOR

George V	1910–36

PRIME MINISTERS

Duke of Portland (Whig)	1807–09
Spencer Perceval (Tory)	1809–12
Earl of Liverpool (Tory)	1812–27
George Canning (Tory)	1827
Viscount Goderich (Tory)	1827–28
Duke of Wellington (Tory)	1828–30
Earl Grey (Whig)	1830–34
Viscount Melbourne (Whig)	1834
Sir Robert Peel (Tory)	1834–35
Viscount Melbourne (Whig)	1835–41
Sir Robert Peel (Tory)	1841–46
Lord John Russell (later Earl) (Liberal)	1846–52
Earl of Derby (Con.)	1852
Earl of Aberdeen (Tory)	1852–55
Viscount Palmerston (Lib.)	1855–58
Earl of Derby (Con.)	1858–59
Viscount Palmerston (Lib.)	1859–65
Earl Russell (Liberal)	1865–66
Earl of Derby (Con.)	1866–68
Benjamin Disraeli (Con.)	1868
William Gladstone (Lib.)	1868–74
Benjamin Disraeli (Con.)	1874–80
William Gladstone (Lib.)	1880–85
Marquess of Salisbury (Con.)	1885–86
William Gladstone (Lib.)	1886
Marquess of Salisbury (Con.)	1886–92
William Gladstone (Lib.)	1892–94
Earl of Rosebery (Lib.)	1894–95
Marquess of Salisbury (Con.)	1895–1902
Arthur Balfour (Con.)	1902–05
Sir Henry Campbell-Bannerman (Lib.)	1905–08
Herbert Asquith (Lib.)	1908–15
Herbert Asquith (Lib.)	1915–16

MONARCHS		PRIME MINISTERS	
		Andrew Bonar Law (Con.)	1922–23
		Stanley Baldwin (Con.)	1923–24
		James Ramsay MacDonald (Labour)	1924
		Stanley Baldwin (Con.)	1924–29
		James Ramsay MacDonald (Labour)	1929–31
		James Ramsay MacDonald (Labour)	1931–35
		Stanley Baldwin (Con.)	1935–37
Edward VIII	1936	Neville Chamberlain (Con.)	1937–40
George VI	1936–52	Winston Churchill (Con.)	1940–45
		Winston Churchill (Con.)	1945
		Clement Attlee (Labour)	1945–51
		Sir Winston Churchill (Con.)	1951–55
Elizabeth II	1952–	Sir Anthony Eden (Con.)	1955–57
		Harold Macmillan (Con.)	1957–63
		Sir Alex Douglas-Home (Con.)	1963–64
		Harold Wilson (Labour)	1964–70
		Edward Heath (Con.)	1970–74
		Harold Wilson (Labour)	1974–76
		James Callaghan (Labour)	1976–79
		Margaret Thatcher (Con.)	1979–90
		John Major (Con.)	1990–97
		Tony Blair (Labour)	1997–2007
		Gordon Brown (Labour)	2007–10
		David Cameron (Con.)	2010–

Winston Churchill

Glossary of Terms

Accent: the natural emphasis (stress) speakers place on a syllable.

Accentual Verse: poetry in which a line is measured only by the number of accents or stresses, not by the number of syllables.

Accentual-Syllabic Verse: the most common metrical system in traditional English verse, in which a line is measured by the number of syllables and by the pattern of accented (stressed) and unaccented (unstressed) syllables.

Aesthetes: members of a late nineteenth-century movement that valued "art for art's sake"—for its purely aesthetic qualities, as opposed to valuing art for the moral content it may convey, for the intellectual stimulation it may provide, or for a range of other qualities.

Alexandrine: a line of verse that is 12 syllables long. In English verse, the alexandrine is always an iambic hexameter: that is, it has six iambic feet. The most-often quoted example is the second line in a couplet from Alexander Pope's "Essay on Criticism" (1711): "A needless Alexandrine ends the song / That, like a wounded snake, drags its slow length along." See also *Spenserian stanza*.

Allegory: a narrative with both a literal meaning and secondary, often symbolic meaning or meanings. Allegory frequently employs personification to give concrete embodiment to abstract concepts or entities, such as feelings or personal qualities. It may also present one set of characters or events in the guise of another, using implied parallels for the purposes of satire or political comment, as in John Dryden's poem "Absalom and Achitophel."

Alliteration: the grouping of words with the same initial consonant (e.g., "break, blow, burn, and make me new"). The repetition of sound acts as a connector. See also *assonance* and *consonance*.

Alliterative Verse: poetry that employs alliteration of stressed syllables in each line as its chief structural principle.

Allusion: a reference, often indirect or unidentified, to a person, thing, or event. A reference in one literary work to another literary work, whether to its content or its form, also constitutes an allusion.

Ambiguity: an "opening" of language created by the writer to allow for multiple meanings or differing interpretations. In literature, ambiguity may be deliberately employed by the writer to enrich meaning; this differs from any unintentional, unwanted, ambiguity in non-literary prose.

Amphibrach: a metrical foot with three syllables, the second of which is stressed: x / x (e.g., sensation).

Analogy: a broad term that refers to our processes of noting similarities among things or events. Specific forms of analogy in poetry include *simile* and *metaphor* (see below).

Anapaest: a metrical foot containing two unstressed syllables followed by one stressed syllable: xx /
(e.g., underneath, intervene).

Anglican Church / Church of England: formed after Henry VIII's break with Rome in the 1530s,
the Church of England had acquired a permanently Protestant cast by the 1570s. There has remained
considerable variation within the Church, however, with distinctions often drawn among High
Church, Broad Church, and Latitudinarian. At one extreme High Church Anglicans (some of whom
prefer to be known as "Anglo-Catholics") prefer relatively elaborate church rituals not dissimilar in
form to those of the Roman Catholic Church and place considerable emphasis on church hierarchy,
while in the other direction Latitudinarians prefer relatively informal religious services and tend far
more towards egalitarianism.

Antistrophe: from Greek drama, the chorus's countermovement or reply to an initial movement
(strophe). See *ode* below.

Apostrophe: a figure of speech (a trope; see figures of speech below) in which a writer directly
addresses an object—or a dead or absent person—as if the imagined audience were actually listening.

Archetype: in literature and mythology, a recurring idea, symbol, motif, character, or place. To some
scholars and psychologists, an archetype represents universal human thought-patterns or experiences.

Assonance: the repetition of identical or similar vowel sounds in stressed syllables in which the
surrounding consonants are different: for example, "shame" and "fate"; "gale" and "cage"; or the long
"i" sounds in "Beside the pumice isle..."

Aubade: a lyric poem that greets or laments the arrival of dawn.

Ballad: a folk song, or a poem originally recited to an audience, which tells a dramatic story based
on legend or history.

Ballad Stanza: a quatrain with alternating four-stress and three-stress lines, rhyming *abcb*. A variant
is "common measure," in which the alternating lines are strictly iambic, and rhyme *abab*.

Ballade: a fixed form most commonly characterized by only three rhymes, with an 8-line stanza
rhyming *ababbcbc* and an envoy rhyming *bcbc*. Both Chaucer and Dante Gabriel Rossetti ("Ballad
of the Dead Ladies") adopted this form.

Baroque: powerful and heavily ornamented in style. "Baroque" is a term from the history of visual
art and of music that is sometimes also used to describe certain literary styles, such as that of Richard
Crashaw.

Bathos: an anticlimactic effect brought about by a writer's descent from an elevated subject or tone
to the ordinary or trivial.

Benedictine Rule: set of instructions for monastic communities, composed by Saint Benedict of
Nursia (died c. 457).

Blank Verse: unrhymed lines written in iambic pentameter, a form introduced to English verse by Henry Howard, Earl of Surrey, in his translation of parts of Virgil's *Aeneid* in 1547.

Bombast: inappropriately inflated or grandiose language.

Broadside: individual sheet of paper printed on only one side. From the sixteenth through to the eighteenth centuries broadsides of a variety of different sorts (e.g., ballads, political tracts, short satires) were sold on the streets.

Broken Rhyme: in which a multi-syllable word is split at the end of a line and continued onto the next, to allow an end-rhyme with the split syllable.

Burlesque: satire of a particularly exaggerated sort, particularly that which ridicules its subject by emphasising its vulgar or ridiculous aspects.

Caesura: a pause or break in a line of verse occurring where a phrase, clause, or sentence ends, and indicated in scansion by the mark II. If it occurs in the middle of the line, it is known as a "medial" caesura.

Canon: in literature, those works that are commonly accepted as possessing authority or importance. In practice, "canonical" texts or authors are those that are discussed most frequently by scholars and taught most frequently in university courses.

Canto: a sub-section of a long (usually epic) poem.

Canzone: a short song or poem, with stanzas of equal length and an envoy.

Carpe Diem: Latin (from Horace) meaning "seize the day." The idea of enjoying the moment is a common one in Renaissance love poetry. See, for example, Marvell's "To His Coy Mistress."

Catalexis: the omission of unstressed syllables from a line of verse (such a line is referred to as "catalectic"). In iambic verse it is usually the first syllable of the line that is omitted; in trochaic, the last. For example, in the first stanza of Housman's "To an Athlete Dying Young" the third line is catalectic: i.e., it has dropped the first, unstressed syllable called for by the poem's iambic tetrameter form: "The time you won your town the race / We chaired you through the market-place; / Man and boy stood cheering by, / And home we brought you shoulder-high."

Catharsis: the arousal through the performance of a dramatic tragedy of "emotions of pity and fear" to a point where "purgation" or "purification" occurs and the feelings are released or transformed. The concept was developed by Aristotle in his *Poetics* from an ancient Greek medical concept, and adapted by him into an aesthetic principle.

Chiasmus: a figure of speech (a scheme) that reverses word order in successive parallel clauses. If the word order is A-B-C in the first clause, it becomes C-B-A in the second: for example, Donne's line "She is all states, and all princes, I" ("The Sun Rising") incorporates this reversal (though with an ellipsis).

Classical: originating in or relating to ancient Greek or Roman culture. As commonly conceived, *classical* implies a strong sense of formal order. The term *neoclassical* is often used with reference to literature of the Restoration and eighteenth century that was strongly influenced by ancient Greek and Roman models.

Closet Drama: a play (typically in verse) written for private performance. The term came into use in the first half of the nineteenth century.

Colored Narrative: alternative term for *free indirect discourse*.

Comedy: as a literary term, used originally to denote that class of ancient Greek drama in which the action ends happily. More broadly the term has been used to describe a wide variety of literary forms of a more or less light-hearted character.

Commedia dell'arte: largely improvised comic performances conducted by masked performers and involving considerable physical activity. The genre of *commedia dell'arte* originated in Italy in the sixteenth century; it was influential throughout Europe for more than two centuries thereafter.

Commonwealth: from the fifteenth century, a term roughly equivalent to the modern "state," but tending to emphasize the commonality of interests among all citizens. In the seventeenth century Britain was named a commonwealth under Oliver Cromwell. In the twentieth century, the term came to be applied to associations of many nations; the British Commonwealth became the successor to the British Empire.

Conceit: an unusually elaborate metaphor or simile that extends beyond its original tenor and vehicle, sometimes becoming a "master" analogy for the entire poem (see, for example, Donne's "The Flea," and Robert Frost's sonnet "She is as in a field a silken tent"). Ingenious or fanciful images and comparisons were especially popular with the metaphysical poets of the seventeenth century, giving rise to the term "metaphysical conceit."

Concrete Poetry: an experimental form, most popular during the 1950s and 60s, in which the printed type itself forms a visual image of the poem's key words or ideas. See also *pattern poetry, assonance*.

Connotation: the implied, often unspoken meaning(s) of a given word, as distinct from its denotation, or literal meaning. Connotations may have highly emotional undertones and are usually culturally specific.

Conservative Party: See *Political Parties*.

Consonance: the pairing of words with similar initial and ending consonants, but with different vowel sounds (live/love, wander/wonder). See also *alliteration*.

Convention: aesthetic approach, technique, or practice accepted as characteristic and appropriate for a particular form. It is a convention of certain sorts of plays, for example, that the characters speak in blank verse, of other sorts of plays that characters speak in rhymed couplets, and of still other sorts of dramatic performances that characters frequently break into song to express their feelings.

Couplet: a pair of rhyming lines, usually in the same meter. If they form a complete unit of thought and are grammatically complete, the lines are known as a closed couplet. See also *heroic couplet* below.

Dactyl: a metrical foot containing one strong stress followed by two weak stresses: / xx (e.g., muttering, helplessly). A minor form known as "double dactyls" makes use of this meter for humorous purposes, e.g., "Jiggery pokery" or "Higgledy Piggledy."

Denotation: See *connotation* above.

Devolution: process through which a degree of political power was transferred in the late twentieth and early twenty-first centuries from the British government to assemblies in Scotland and in Wales.

Dialogue: words spoken by characters to one another. (When a character is addressing him or her self or the audience directly, the words spoken are referred to as a *monologue*.)

Diction: word choice. Whether the diction of a literary work (or of a literary character) is colloquial, conversational, formal, or of some other type contributes significantly to the tone of the text as well as to characterization.

Didacticism: aesthetic approach emphasizing moral instruction.

Dimeter: a poetic line containing two metrical feet.

Dirge: a song or poem that mourns someone's death. See also *elegy* and *lament* below.

Disestablishmentarianism: movement opposing an official state-supported religion, in particular the Church of England in that role.

Dissonance: harsh, unmusical sounds or rhythms which poets may use deliberately to achieve certain effects.

Dramatic Irony: this form of irony occurs when the audience's reception of a speech by a character on the stage is affected by the possession by the audience of information not available to the character.

Dramatic Monologue: a lyric poem that takes the form of an utterance by a single person addressing a silent listener. The speaker may be an historical personage (as in some of Robert Browning's dramatic monologues), a figure drawn from myth or legend (as in some of Tennyson's), or an entirely imagined figure, as in Webster's "A Castaway."

Dub Poetry: a form of protest poetry originating in Jamaica, with its roots in dance rhythms, especially reggae, and often accompanied in performance by drums and music. See also *rap* and *hip-hop*.

Duple Foot: A duple foot of poetry has two syllables. The possible duple forms are iamb (in which the stress is on the second of the two syllables), trochee (in which the stress is on the first of the two syllables), spondee (in which both are stressed equally), and pyrrhic (in which both syllables are unstressed).

Eclogue: now generally used simply as an alternative name for a pastoral poem. In classical times and in the early modern period, however, an *eclogue* (or *idyll*) was a specific type of pastoral poem—a dialogue or dramatic monologue involving rustic characters. (The other main sub-genre of the pastoral was the *georgic*.)

Elegiac Stanza: a quatrain of iambic pentameters rhyming *abab*, often used in poems meditating on death or sorrow. The best-known example is Thomas Gray's "Elegy Written in a Country Churchyard."

Elegy: a poem which formally mourns the death of a particular person (e.g., Tennyson's "In Memoriam") or in which the poet meditates on other serious subjects (e.g., Gray's "Elegy"). See also *dirge*.

Elision: omitting or suppressing a letter or an unstressed syllable at the beginning or end of a word, so that a line of verse may conform to a given metrical scheme. For example, the three syllables at the beginning of Shakespeare's sonnet 129 are reduced to two by the omission of the first vowel: "Th' expense of spirit in a waste of shame." See also *syncope*.

Ellipsis: the omission of a word or words necessary for the complete grammatical construction of a sentence, but not necessary for our understanding of the sentence.

End-Rhyme: See *rhyme*.

End-stopped: a line of poetry is said to be end-stopped when the end of the line coincides with a natural pause in the syntax, such as the conclusion of a sentence; e.g., in this couplet from Pope's "Essay on Criticism," both lines are end-stopped: "A little learning is a dangerous thing; / Drink deep, or taste not the Pierian spring." Compare this with *enjambement*.

Enjambement: the "running-on" of the sense from one line of poetry to the next, with no pause created by punctuation or syntax. (The more commonly found alternative is referred to as an *end-stopped line*.)

Envoy (Envoi): a stanza or half-stanza that forms the conclusion of certain French poetic forms, such as the *sestina* or the *ballade*. It often sums up or comments upon what has gone before.

Epic: a lengthy narrative poem, often divided into books and sub-divided into cantos. It generally celebrates heroic deeds or events, and the style tends to be lofty and grand. Examples in English include Spenser's *The Faerie Queene* and Milton's *Paradise Lost*.

Epic Simile: an elaborate simile, developed at such length that the vehicle of the comparison momentarily displaces the primary subject with which it is being compared.

Epigram: a very short poem, sometimes in closed couplet form, characterized by pointed wit.

Epigraph: a quotation placed at the beginning of a discourse to indicate or foreshadow the theme.

Epiphany: a moment at which matters of significance are suddenly illuminated for a literary character (or for the reader), typically triggered by something small and seemingly of little import. The term first came into wide currency in connection with the fiction of James Joyce.

Episodic Plot: plot comprising a variety of episodes that are only loosely connected by threads of story material (as opposed to plots that present one or more continually unfolding narratives where successive episodes build one on another).

Epithalamion: a poem celebrating a wedding. The best-known example in English is probably Edmund Spenser's "Epithalamion" (1595).

Eulogy: text expressing praise, especially for a distinguished person recently deceased.

Euphemism: mode of expression through which aspects of reality considered to be vulgar, crudely physical, or unpleasant are referred to indirectly rather than named explicitly. A variety of euphemisms exist for the processes of urination and defecation; *passed away* is often used as a euphemism for *died*. (The word *euphemism* has the same root as *Euphuism* (see below), but has taken on a different meaning.)

Euphony: pleasant, musical sounds or rhythms—the opposite of dissonance.

Euphuism: In the late sixteenth century John Lyly published a prose romance, *Euphues*, which employed a style that featured long sentences filled with balanced phrases and clauses, many of them adding little to the content. This highly mannered style was popular in the court of Elizabeth I for a few years following the publication of Lyly's famous work, and the style became known as *Euphuism*.

European Union: (EU) Group of nations formed in 1993 as the successor to the European Economic Community (Common Market). Britain first applied for membership in the latter in 1961; at first its efforts to join were blocked by the French government, but in 1973 Prime Minister Edward Heath successfully negotiated Britain's entry into the group. Britain has resisted some moves towards full integration with the European community, in particular retaining its own currency when other European nations adopted the Euro on 1 January 2002.

Exchequer: In earlier eras, the central royal financial office, responsible for receiving and keeping track of crown revenues. In later eras, part of the bureaucracy equivalent to the Ministry of Finance in Canada or the Treasury in the United States (the modern post of Chancellor of the Exchequer is equivalent to the American post of Secretary of the Treasury, the Canadian post of Minister of Finance or the Australian post of Treasurer).

Exposition: the setting out of material in an ordered form, either in speech or in writing. In a play those parts of the action that do not occur on stage but are rather recounted by the characters are frequently described as being presented in exposition. Similarly, when the background narrative is filled in near the beginning of a novel, such material is often described as having been presented in exposition. Somewhat confusingly, however, the term "expository prose" is usually used with reference not to fiction but to the setting forth of arguments or descriptions in the context of essays or other works of prose non-fiction.

Eye-Rhyme: See *rhyme* below.

Feminine Ending: the ending of a line of poetry on an "extra," and, especially, on an unstressed syllable. See, for example, the first line of Keat's "Ode on a Grecian Urn": "A thing of beauty is a joy forever," a line of iambic pentameter in which the final foot is an amphibrach rather than an iamb.

Feminine Rhyme: See *rhyme* below.

Figures of Speech: deliberate, highly concentrated uses of language to achieve particular purposes or effects on an audience. There are two kinds of figures: schemes and tropes. Schemes involve changes in word-sound and word-order, such as *alliteration* and *chiasmus*. Tropes play on our understandings of words to extend, alter, or transform meaning, as in *metaphor* and *personification*.

First-Person Narrative: narrative recounted using *I* and *me*. See also *narrative perspective*.

Fixed Forms: the term applied to a number of poetic forms and stanzaic patterns, many derived from French models, such as *ballade, rondeau, sestina, triolet,* and *villanelle*. Other "fixed forms" include the *sonnet, rhyme royal, haiku,* and *ottava rima*.

Folio: largest of several sizes of book page commonly used in the first few centuries after the introduction of the printing press. A folio size results from sheets of paper of at least 14 inches by 20 inches being folded in half (a folio page size will thus be at least 7 inches by 10 inches). When the same sheet is folded twice a quarto is produced, and when it is folded 3 times an octavo.

Foot: a unit of a line of verse which contains a particular combination of stressed and unstressed syllables. Dividing a line into metrical feet (*iambs, trochees,* etc.), then counting the number of feet per line, is part of *scansion*. See also *meter*.

Franklin: in the late medieval period, a landholder of free status, but ranking below the gentry.

Free Indirect Discourse: in prose fiction, commentary in which a seemingly objective and omniscient narrative voice assumes the point of view of one or more characters. When we hear through the third person narrative voice of Jane Austen's *Pride and Prejudice*, for example, that Mr. Darcy "was the proudest, most disagreeable man in the world, and every body hoped that he would never come there again," the narrative voice has assumed the point of view of "every body" in the community; we as readers are not meant to take it that Mr. Darcy is indeed the most disagreeable man in the world. Similarly, in the following passage from the same novel, we are likely to take it to read it as being the view of the character Charlotte that marriage is "the only honourable provision for well-educated young women of small fortune," not to take it to be an objective statement of perceived truth on the part of the novel's third person narrative voice:

> [Charlotte's] reflections were in general satisfactory. Mr. Collins to be sure was neither sensible nor agreeable; his society was irksome, and his attachment to her must be imaginary. But still he would be her husband. Without thinking highly either of men or of matrimony, marriage had always been her object; it was the only honourable provision for well-educated young women of small fortune, and however uncertain of giving happiness, must be their pleasantest preservative from want.

The term free indirect discourse may also be applied to situations in which it may not be entirely clear if the thoughts expressed emanate from the character, the narrator, or some combination of the two. (In the above-quoted passage expressing Charlotte's thoughts, indeed, some might argue that the statement concerning marriage should be taken as the expression of a belief that the narrative voice shares, at least in part.)

Free Verse: poetry that does not follow any regular meter, line length, or rhyming scheme. In many respects, though, free verse follows the complex natural "rules" and rhythmic patterns (or cadences) of speech.

Gaelic: Celtic language, variants of which are spoken in Ireland and Scotland.

Genre: a particular literary form. The concept of genre may be used with different levels of generality. At the most general, poetry, drama, and prose fiction are distinguished as separate genres. At a lower level of generality various sub-genres are frequently distinguished, such as (within drama) comedy and tragedy, or, at a still lower level of generality, Elizabethan domestic tragedy, Edwardian drawing-room comedy, and so on.

Georgic: (from Virgil's *Georgics*) a poem that celebrates the natural wealth of the countryside and advises how to cultivate and live in harmony with it. Pope's *Windsor Forest* and James Thomson's *Seasons* are classed as georgics. They were often said to make up, with eclogues, the two alliterative forms of pastoral poetry.

Ghazal: derived from Persian and Indian precedents, the ghazal presents a series of thoughts in closed couplets joined by a simple rhyme-scheme such as: *ab bb cb eb fb*, etc.

Gothic: in architecture and the visual arts, a term used to describe styles prevalent from the twelfth to the fourteenth centuries, but in literature a term used to describe work with a sinister or grotesque tone that seeks to evoke a sense of terror on the part of the reader or audience. Gothic literature originated as a genre in the eighteenth century with works such as Horace Walpole's *The Castle of Otranto*. To some extent the notion of the medieval itself then carried with it associations of the dark and the grotesque, but from the beginning an element of intentional exaggeration (sometimes verging on self-parody) attached itself to the genre. The Gothic trend of youth culture that began in the late twentieth century is less clearly associated with the medieval, but shares with the various varieties of Gothic literature (from Walpole in the eighteenth century, to Bram Stoker in the early twentieth, to Stephen King and Anne Rice in the late twentieth) a fondness for the sensational and the grotesque, as well as a propensity to self-parody.

Guilds: non-clerical associations that arose in the late Anglo-Saxon period, devoted both to social purposes (such as the organization of feasts for the members) and to piety. In the later medieval period guilds developed strong associations with particular occupations.

Haiku: a Japanese form, using three unrhymed lines of five, seven, and five syllables. Conventionally, it uses precise, concentrated images to suggest states of feeling.

Heptameter: a line containing seven metrical feet.

Heroic Couplet: a pair of rhymed iambic pentameters, so called because the form was much used in seventeenth and eighteenth-century poems and plays on heroic subjects.

Hexameter: a line containing six metrical feet.

Home Rule: movement dedicated to making Ireland politically independent from Britain.

Horatian Ode: inspired by the work of the Roman poet Horace, an ode that is usually calm and meditative in tone, and homostrophic (i.e., having regular stanzas) in form. Keats's odes are English examples.

House of Commons: elected legislative body, in Britain currently consisting of six hundred and fifty-nine members of Parliament. See also *Parliament*.

House of Lords: the "Upper House" of the British Houses of Parliament. Since the nineteenth century the House of Lords has been far less powerful than the elected House of Commons. The House of Lords is currently made up of both hereditary peers (Lords whose title is passed on from generation to generation) and life peers. As a result of legislation enacted by the Labour government of Tony Blair, the role of hereditary peers in Parliament is being phased out.

Humors: The four humors were believed in until the sixteenth and seventeenth centuries to be elements in the makeup of all humans; a person's temperament was thought to be determined by the way in which the humors were combined. When the *choleric* humor was dominant, the person would tend towards anger; when the *sanguine* humor was dominant, towards pleasant affability; when the *phlegmatic* humor was dominant, towards a cool and calm attitude and/or a lack of feeling or enthusiasm; and when the *melancholic* humor was dominant, towards withdrawal and melancholy.

Hymn: a song whose theme is usually religious, in praise of divinity. Literary hymns may praise more secular subjects.

Hyperbole: a *figure of speech* (a trope) that deliberately exaggerates or inflates meaning to achieve particular effects, such as the irony in A.E. Housman's claim (from "Terence, this is stupid stuff") that "malt does more than Milton can / To justify God's ways to man."

Iamb: the most common metrical foot in English verse, containing one unstressed syllable followed by a stressed syllable: x / (e.g., between, achieve).

Idyll: traditionally, a short pastoral poem that idealizes country life, conveying impressions of innocence and happiness.

Image: the recreation in words of objects perceived by the senses, sometimes thought of as "pictures," although other senses besides sight are involved. Besides this literal application, the term also refers more generally to the descriptive effects of figurative language, especially in *metaphor* and *simile*.

Imagism: a poetic movement that was popular mainly in the second decade of the twentieth century. The goal of Imagist poets (such as H.D. and Ezra Pound in their early work) was to represent emotions or impressions through highly concentrated imagery.

1640 GLOSSARY OF TERMS

Incantation: a chant or recitation of words that are believed to have magical power. A poem can achieve an "incantatory" effect through a compelling rhyme scheme and other repetitive patterns.

In Memoriam Stanza: a four-line stanza in iambic tetrameter, rhyming *abba*: the type of stanza used by Tennyson in *In Memoriam*.

Interlocking Rhyme: See *rhyme*.

Internal Rhyme: See *rhyme*.

Irony: a subtle form of humor in which a statement is understood to convey a quite different (and often entirely opposite) meaning. A writer achieves this by carefully making sure that the statement occurs in a context which undermines or twists the statement's "literal" meaning. *Hyperbole* and *litotes* are often used for ironic effect. *Sarcasm* is a particularly strong or crude form of irony (usually spoken), in which the meaning is conveyed largely by the tone of voice adopted; something said sarcastically is meant clearly to imply its opposite.

Labour Party: See *Political Parties*.

Lament: a poem which expresses profound regret or grief either because of a death, or because of the loss of a former, happier state.

Language Poetry: a movement that defies the usual lyric and narrative conventions of poetry, and that challenges the structures and codes of everyday language. Often seen as both politically and aesthetically subversive, its roots lie in the works of modernist writers like Ezra Pound and Gertrude Stein.

Liberal Party: See *Political Parties*.

Litotes: a *figure of speech* (a trope) in which a writer deliberately uses understatement to highlight the importance of an argument, or to convey an ironic attitude.

Liturgical Drama: drama based on and/or incorporating text from the liturgy—the text recited during religious services.

Lollard: member of the group of radical Christians that took its inspiration from the ideas of John Wyclif (c. 1330–84). The Lollards, in many ways precursors of the Protestant Reformation, advocated making the Bible available to all, and dedication to the principles of evangelical poverty in imitation of Christ.

Luddites: protestors against the mechanization of industry on the grounds that it was leading to the loss of employment and to an increase in poverty. In the years 1811 to 1816 there were several Luddite protests in which machines were destroyed.

Lyric: a poem, usually short, expressing an individual speaker's feelings or private thoughts. Originally a song performed with accompaniment on a lyre, the lyric poem is often noted for musicality of rhyme and rhythm. The lyric genre includes a variety of forms, including the *sonnet*, the *ode*, the *elegy*, the *madrigal*, the *aubade*, the *dramatic monologue*, and the *hymn*.

Madrigal: a lyric poem, usually short and focusing on pastoral or romantic themes. A madrigal is often set to music.

Masculine Ending: a metrical line ending on a stressed syllable. *Masculine Rhyme*: see *rhyme*.

Masque: an entertainment typically combining music and dance, with a limited script, extravagant costumes and sets, and often incorporating spectacular special effects. Masques, which were performed before court audiences in the early seventeenth century, often focused on royal themes and frequently drew on classical mythology.

Mass: Within Christianity, a church service that includes the sacrament of the Eucharist (Holy Communion), in which bread and wine are consumed which are believed by those of many Christian denominations to have been transubstantiated into the body and blood of Christ. Anglicans (Episcopalians) are more likely to believe the bread and wine merely symbolizes the body and blood.

Melodrama: originally a term used to describe nineteenth-century-plays featuring sensational story lines and a crude separation of characters into moral categories, with the pure and virtuous pitted against evil villains. Early melodramas employed background music throughout the action of the play as a means of heightening the emotional response of the audience. By extension, certain sorts of prose fictions or poems are often described as having melodramatic elements.

Metaphor: a *figure of speech* (in this case, a trope) in which a comparison is made or identity is asserted between two unrelated things or actions without the use of "like" or "as." The primary subject is known as the *tenor*; to illuminate its nature, the writer links it to wholly different images, ideas, or actions referred to as the *vehicle*. Unlike a *simile*, which is a direct comparison of two things, a metaphor "fuses" the separate qualities of two things, creating a new idea. For example, Shakespeare's "Let slip the dogs of war" is a metaphorical statement. The tenor, or primary subject, is "war"; the vehicle of the metaphor is the image of hunting dogs released from their leash. The line fuses the idea of war with the qualities of ravening bloodlust associated with hunting dogs.

Metaphysical Poets: a group of seventeenth-century English poets, notably Donne, Cowley, Marvell, and Herbert, who employed unusual difficult imagery and *conceits* (see above) in order to develop intellectual and religious themes. The term was first applied to these writers to mark as far-fetched their use of philosophical and scientific ideas in a poetic context.

Meter: the pattern of stresses, syllables, and pauses that constitutes the regular rhythm of a line of verse. The meter of a poem written in the English accentual-syllabic tradition is determined by identifying the stressed and unstressed syllables in a line of verse, and grouping them into recurring units known as feet. See *accent*, *accentual-syllabic*, *caesura*, *elision*, and *scansion*. For some of the better known meters, see *iamb*, *trochee*, *dactyl*, *anapaest*, and *spondee*. See also *monometer*, *dimeter*, *trimeter*, *tetrameter*, *pentameter*, and *hexameter*.

Methodist: Protestant denomination formed in the eighteenth century as part of the religious movement led by John and Charles Wesley. Originally a movement within the Church of England, Methodism entailed enthusiastic evangelism, a strong emphasis on free will, and a strict regimen of Christian living.

Metonymy: a *figure of speech* (a trope), meaning "change of name," in which a writer refers to an object or idea by substituting the name of another object or idea closely associated with it: for example, the substitution of "crown" for monarchy, "the press" for journalism, or "the pen" for writing. *Synecdoche* (see below) is a kind of metonymy.

Mock-heroic: a style applying the elevated diction and vocabulary of epic poetry to low or ridiculous subjects. An example is Alexander Pope's "The Rape of the Lock."

Monologue: words spoken by a character to him or herself or to an audience directly.

Monometer: a line containing one metrical foot.

Mood: This can describe the writer's attitude, implied or expressed, towards the subject (see *tone* below); or it may refer to the atmosphere that a writer creates in a passage of description or narration.

Motif: an idea, image, action, or plot element that recurs throughout a literary work, creating new levels of meaning and strengthening structural coherence. The term is taken from music, where it describes recurring melodies or themes. See also *theme*.

Narrative Perspective: in fiction, the point of view from which the story is narrated. A first-person narrative is recounted using *I* and *me*, whereas a third person narrative is recounted using *he, she, they*, and so on. When a narrative is written in the third person and the narrative voice evidently "knows" all that is being done and thought, the story is typically described as being recounted by an "omniscient narrator."

Neoclassical: adapted from or substantially influenced by the cultures of ancient Greece and Rome. The term *neoclassical* is often used to describe the ideals of Restoration and eighteenth-century writers and artists who looked to ancient Greek and Roman civilization for models.

Nobility: privileged class, the members of which are distinguished by the holding of titles. Dukes, Marquesses, Earls, Viscounts, and Barons (in that order of precedence) are all holders of hereditary titles—that is to say, in the British patrilineal tradition, titles passed on from generation to generation to the eldest son. The title of Baronet, also hereditary, was added to this list by James I. Holders of non-hereditary titles include Knights and Dames.

Nonconformist: general term used to describe one who does subscribe to the Church of England.

Nonsense Verse: light, humorous poetry which contradicts logic, plays with the absurd, and invents words for amusing effects. Lewis Carroll is one of the best-known practitioners of nonsense verse.

Octave: also known as "octet," the first eight lines in an Italian/Petrarchan sonnet, rhyming *abbaabba*. See also *sestet* and *sonnet*.

Octosyllabic: a line of poetry with eight syllables, as in iambic tetrameter.

Ode: originally a classical poetic form, used by the Greeks and Romans to convey serious themes. English poetry has evolved three main forms of ode: the Pindaric (imitative of the odes of the Greek poet Pindar); the Horatian (modeled on the work of the Roman writer Horace); and the irregular ode.

The Pindaric ode was an irregular stanza in English, has a tripartite structure of "strophe," "antistrophe," and "epode" (meaning turn, counterturn, and stand), modeled on the songs and movements of the Chorus in Greek drama. The Horatian ode is more personal, reflective, and literary, and employs a pattern of repeated stanzas. The irregular ode, as its name implies, avoids a recurrent stanza pattern, and is sometimes irregular in line length also (see, for example, Wordsworth's "Ode: Intimations of Immortality").

Onomatopoeia: a *figure of speech* (a scheme) in which a word "imitates" a sound, or in which the sound of a word seems to reflect its meaning.

Ottava Rima: an 8-line stanza, usually in iambic pentameter, with the rhyme scheme *ababababcc*. For an example, see Byron's *Don Juan*, or Yeats's "Sailing to Byzantium."

Oxymoron: a *figure of speech* (a trope) in which two words whose meanings seem contradictory are placed together, a paradox: for example, the phrase "darkness visible," from Milton's *Paradise Lost*.

Paean: a triumphant, celebratory song, often associated with a military victory.

Pale: in the medieval period, term for a protective zone around a fortress. As of the year 1500 three of these had been set up to guard frontiers of territory controlled by England—surrounding Calais in France, Berwick-upon-Tweed on the Scottish frontier, and Dublin in Ireland. The Dublin Pale was the largest of the three, and the term remained in use for a longer period there.

Pantoum: a poem in linked quatrains that rhyme *abab*. The second and fourth lines of one stanza are repeated as the first and third lines of the stanza that follows. In the final stanza the pattern is reversed: the second line repeats the third line of the first stanza, the fourth and final line repeats the first line of the first stanza.

Parliament: in Britain, the legislative body, comprising both the House of Commons and the House of Lords. Since the eighteenth century, the most powerful figure in the British government has been the Prime Minister rather than the monarch, the House of Commons has been the dominant body in Parliament, and members of the House of Commons have been organized in political parties. Since the mid-nineteenth century the effective executive in the British Parliamentary system has been the Cabinet, each member of which is typically in charge of a department of government. Unlike the American system, the British Parliamentary system (sometimes called the "Westminster system," after the location of the Houses of Parliament) brings together the executive and legislative functions of government, with the Prime Minister leading the government party in the House of Commons as well as directing the cabinet. By convention it is understood that the House of Lords will not contravene the wishes of the House of Commons in any fundamental way, though the "Upper House," as it is often referred to, may sometimes modify or reject legislation.

Parody: a close, usually mocking imitation of a particular literary work, or of the well-known style of a particular author, in order to expose or magnify weaknesses. Parody is a form of satire—that is, humor that may ridicule and scorn its object.

Pastiche: a discourse which borrows or imitates other writers' characters, forms, style, or ideas. Unlike a parody, a pastiche is usually intended as a compliment to the original writer.

Pastoral: in general, pertaining to country life; in prose, drama, and poetry, a stylized type of writing that idealizes the lives and innocence of country people, particularly shepherds and shepherdesses. Also see *eclogue, georgic, idyll,* above.

Pastoral Elegy: a poem in which the poet uses the pastoral style to lament the death of a friend, usually represented as a shepherd. Milton's "Lycidas" provides a good example of the form, including its use of such conventions as an invocation of the muse and a procession of mourners.

Pathetic Fallacy: a form of personification in which inanimate objects are given human emotions: for example, rain clouds "weeping." The word "fallacy" in this connection is intended to suggest the distortion of reality or the false emotion that may result from an exaggerated use of personification.

Pathos: the emotional quality of a discourse; or the ability of a discourse to appeal to our emotions. It is usually applied to the mood conveyed by images of pain, suffering, or loss that arouse feelings of pity or sorrow in the reader.

Pattern Poetry: a predecessor of modern concrete poetry, in which the shape of the poem on the page is intended to suggest or imitate an aspect of the poem's subject. George Herbert's "Easter Wings" is an example of pattern poetry.

Penny Dreadful: Victorian term for a cheap and poorly produced work of short fiction, usually of a sensational nature.

Pentameter: a line of verse containing five metrical feet.

Performance Poetry: poetry composed primarily for oral performance, often very theatrical in nature. See also *dub poetry* and *rap.*

Persona: the assumed identity or "speaking voice" that a writer projects in a discourse. The term "persona" literally means "mask." Even when a writer speaks in the first person, we should be aware that the attitudes or opinions we hear may not necessarily be those of the writer in real life.

Personification: a *figure of speech* (a trope), also known as "prosopopoeia," in which a writer refers to inanimate objects, ideas, or animals as if they were human, or creates a human figure to represent an abstract entity such as Philosophy or Peace.

Petrarchan Sonnet: the earliest form of the sonnet, also known as the Italian sonnet, with an 8-line octave and a 6-line sestet. The Petrarchan sonnet traditionally focuses on love and descriptions of physical beauty.

Phoneme: a linguistic term denoting the smallest unit of sound that it is possible to distinguish. The words *fun* and *phone* each have three phonemes, though one has three letters and one has five. (Each makes up a single syllable.)

Pindaric: See *ode.*

Plot: the organization of story materials within a literary work. The order in which story material is presented (especially causes and consequences); the inclusion of elements that allow or encourage the reader or audience to form expectations as to what is likely to happen; the decision to present some story material through exposition rather than in more extended form as part of the main action of the narrative—all these are matters of plotting.

Political Parties: The party names "Whig" and "Tory" began to be used in the late seventeenth century; before that time members of the House of Commons acted individually or through shifting and very informal factions. At first the Whigs and Tories had little formal organization either, but by the mid-eighteenth century parties had acknowledged leaders, and the leader of the party with the largest number of members in the House of Commons had begun to be recognized as the Prime Minister. The Tories evolved into the modern Conservative Party, and the Whigs into the Liberal Party. In the late nineteenth century the Labour Party was formed in an effort to provide better representation in Parliament for the working class, and since the 1920s Labour and the Conservatives have alternated as the party of government, with the Liberals reduced to third-party status. (Since 1988, when the Liberals merged with a breakaway faction from Labour known as the Social Democrats, this third party has been named the Liberal Democrats.)

Pre-Raphaelites: originally a group of Victorian artists and writers, formed in 1848. Their goal was to revive what they considered the simpler, fresher, more natural art that existed before Raphael (1483-1520). The poet Dante Gabriel Rossetti was one of the founders of the group.

Presbyterian: term applied to a group of Protestants (primarily English and Scottish) who advocated replacing the traditional hierarchical church in which bishops and archbishops governed lower level members of the clergy with a system in which all presbyters (or ministers) would be equal. The Presbyterians, originally led by John Knox, were strongly influenced by the ideas of John Calvin.

Prose Poem: a poetic discourse that uses prose formats (e.g., it may use margins and paragraphs rather than line breaks or stanzas) yet is written with the kind of attention to language, rhythm and cadence that characterizes verse.

Prosody: the study and analysis of meter, rhythm, rhyme, stanzaic pattern, and other devices of versification.

Protagonist: the central character in a literary work.

Prothalamion: a wedding song; a term coined by the poet Edmund Spenser, adapted from "epithalamion" (see above).

Public School: See *schools* below.

Pun: a play on words, in which a word with two or more distinct meanings, or two words with similar sounds, may create humorous ambiguities. Also known as *paranomasia*.

Puritan: term, originally applied only in a derogatory fashion but later widely accepted as descriptive, referring to those in England who favored religious reforms that went beyond those instituted as part of the Protestant Reformation, or, more generally, who were more forceful and uncompromising in pressing for religious purity both within the Church and in society as a whole.

Pyrrhic: a metrical foot containing two weak stresses: xx.

Quadrivium: group of four academic subjects (arithmetic, astronomy, geometry, and music) that made up part of the university coursework in the Middle Ages. There were studied after the more basic subjects of the *Trivium*.

Quantitative Meter: a metrical system used by Greek and Roman poets, in which a line of verse was measured by the "quantity," or length of sound of each syllable. A foot was measured in terms of syllables classed as long or short.

Quantity: duration of syllables in poetry. The line "There is a Garden in her face" (the first line from the poem of the same name by Thomas Campion) is characterized by the short quantities of the syllables. The last line of Thomas Hardy's "During Wind and Rain" has the same number of syllables as the line by Campion, but the quantities of the syllables are much longer—in other words, the line take much longer to say: "Down their carved names the rain drop ploughs."

Quatrain: a four-line stanza, usually rhymed.

Quintet: a five-line stanza. Sometimes given as *quintain*.

Rap: originally coined to describe informal conversation, "rap" now usually describes a style of performance poetry in which a poet will chant rhymed verse, sometimes improvised and usually with musical accompaniment that has a heavy beat.

Realism: as a literary term, the presentation through literature of material closely resembling real life. As notions both of what constitutes "real life" and of how it may be most faithfully represented in literature have varied widely, "realism" has taken a variety of meanings. The term *naturalistic* has sometimes been used a synonym for *realistic*; *naturalism* originated in the nineteenth century as a term denoting a form of realism focusing in particular on grim, unpleasant, or ugly aspects of the real.

Refrain: one or more words or lines repeated at regular points throughout a poem, often at the end of each stanza or group of stanzas. Sometimes a whole stanza may be repeated to create a refrain, like the chorus in a song.

Reggae: a style of heavily-rhythmic music from the West Indies with lyrics that are colloquial in language and often anti-establishment in content and flavor. First popularized in the 1960s and 1970s, reggae has had a lasting influence on performance poetry, rap, and dub.

Rhetoric: in classical Greece and Rome, the art of persuasion and public speaking. From the Middle Ages onwards, the study of rhetoric gave greater attention to style, particularly figures of speech. Today in poetics, the term rhetoric may encompass not only figures of speech, but also the persuasive effects of forms, sounds and word choices.

Rhyme: the repetition of identical or similar sounds, usually in pairs and generally at the ends of metrical lines.

End-rhyme: a rhyming word or syllable at the end of a line.

Eye Rhyme: rhyming that pairs words whose spellings are alike but whose pronunciations are different: for example, though/slough.

Feminine Rhyme: a two-syllable (also known as "double") rhyme. The first syllable is stressed and the second unstressed: for example, hasty/tasty. See also *triple rhyme* below.

Interlocking Rhyme: the repetition of rhymes from one stanza to the next, creating links that add to the poem's continuity and coherence. Examples may be found in Shelley's use of *terza rima* in "Ode to the West Wind" and in Dylan Thomas's villanelle "Do Not Go Gentle Into That Good Night."

Internal Rhyme: the placement of rhyming words within lines so that at least two words in a line rhyme with each other.

Masculine Rhyme: a correspondence of sound between the final stressed syllables at the end of two or more lines, as in grieve/leave, arr-ive/sur-vive.

Slant Rhyme: an imperfect or partial rhyme (also known as "near" or "half" rhyme) in which the final consonants of stressed syllables match but the vowel sounds do not. E.g., spoiled / spilled, taint / stint.

Triple Rhyme: a three-syllable rhyme in which the first syllable of each rhyme-word is stressed and the other two unstressed (e.g., lottery / coterie).

True Rhyme: a rhyme in which everything but the initial consonant matches perfectly in sound and spelling.

Rhyme Royal: a stanza of seven iambic pentameters, with a rhyme-scheme of *ababbcc*. This is also known as the Chaucerian stanza, as Chaucer was the first English poet to use this form. See also *septet*.

Rhythm: in speech, the arrangement of stressed and unstressed syllables creates units of sound. In song or verse, these units usually form a regular rhythmic pattern, a kind of beat, described in prosody as *meter*.

Romanticism: a major social and cultural movement, originating in Europe, that shaped much of Western artistic thought in the late eighteenth and nineteenth centuries. Opposing the ideal of controlled, rational order of the Enlightenment, Romanticism emphasizes the importance of spontaneous self-expression, emotion, and personal experience in producing art. In Romanticism, the "natural" is privileged over the conventional or the artificial.

Rondeau: a fifteen-line poem, generally octosyllabic, with only two rhymes throughout its three stanzas, and an unrhymed refrain at the end of the ninth and fifteenth lines, repeating part of the opening line.

Sarcasm: See *irony*.

Satire: literary work designed to make fun of or seriously criticize its subject. According to many literary theories of the Renaissance and neoclassical periods, the ridicule through satire of a certain sort of behavior may function for the reader or audience as a corrective of such behavior.

Scansion: the formal analysis of patterns of rhythm and rhyme in poetry. Each line of verse will have a certain number of fairly regular "beats" consisting of alternating stressed and unstressed syllables. To "scan" a poem is to count the beats in each line, to mark stressed and unstressed syllables and indicate their combination into "feet," to note pauses, and to identify rhyme schemes with letters of the alphabet.

Scheme: See *figures of speech*.

Schools: In the sixteenth and seventeenth centuries the different forms of school in England included Cathedral schools (often founded with a view to the education of members of the choir); grammar schools (often founded by towns or by guilds, and teaching a much broader curriculum than the modern sense of "grammar" might suggest, private schools, operated by private individuals out of private residences; and public schools, which (like the private schools and the grammar schools) operated independent of any church authority, but unlike the grammar schools and private schools were organized as independent charities, and often offered free education. Over the centuries certain of these public schools, while remaining not-for-profit institutions, began to accept fee-paying students and to adopt standards that made them more and more exclusive. In the eighteenth and nineteenth century attendance at such prestigious public boarding schools as Eton, Westminster, and Winchester had become almost exclusively the preserve of the upper classes; by the nineteenth century such "public" schools were the equivalent of private schools in North America. Though a few girls attended some early grammar schools, the greater part of this educational system was for boys only. Though a number of individuals of earlier periods were concerned to increase the number of private schools for girls, the movement to create a parallel girls' system of public schools and grammar schools dates from the later nineteenth century.

Septet: a stanza containing seven lines.

Serf: in the medieval period, a person of unfree status, typically engaged in working the land.

Sestet: a six-line stanza that forms the second grouping of lines in an Italian / Petrarchan sonnet, following the octave. See *sonnet* and *sestina*.

Sestina: an elaborate unrhymed poem with six 6-line stanzas and a 3-line envoy.

Shire: originally a multiple estate; since the late medieval period a larger territory forming an administrative unit—also referred to as a county.

Simile: a *figure of speech* (a trope) which makes an explicit comparison between a particular object and another object or idea that is similar in some (often unexpected) way. A simile always uses "like" or "as" to signal the connection. Compare with *metaphor* above.

Sonnet: a highly structured lyric poem, which normally has fourteen lines of iambic pentameter. We can distinguish four major variations of the sonnet.

   Italian/Petrarchan: named for the 14th-century Italian poet Petrarch, has an octave rhyming *abbaabba*, and a sestet rhyming *cdecde*, or *cdcdcd* (other arrangements are possible here). Usually, a turn in argument takes place between octave and sestet.

Miltonic: developed by Milton and similar to the Petrarchan in rhyme scheme, but eliminating the turn after the octave, thus giving greater unity to the poem's structure of thought.

Shakespearean: often called the English sonnet, this form has three quatrains and a couplet. The quatrains rhyme internally but do not interlock: *abab cdcd efef gg*. The turn may occur after the second quatrain, but is usually revealed in the final couplet. Shakespeare's sonnets are the best-known examples of this form.

Spenserian: after Edmund Spenser, who developed the form in his sonnet cycle *Amoretti*. This sonnet form has three quatrains linked through interlocking rhyme, and a separately rhyming couplet: *abab bcbc cdcd ee*.

Speaker: in the late medieval period, a member of the Commons in Parliament who spoke on behalf of that entire group. (The Commons first elected a Speaker in 1376.) In later eras the role of Speaker became one of chairing debates in the House of Commons and arbitrating disputes over matters of procedure.

Spenserian Stanza: a nine-line stanza, with eight iambic pentameters and a concluding alexandrine, rhyming *ababbcbcc*.

Spondee: a metrical foot containing two strong stressed syllables: // (e.g., blind mouths).

Sprung Rhythm: a modern variation of accentual verse, created by the English poet Gerard Manley Hopkins, in which rhythms are determined largely by the number of strong stresses in a line, without regard to the number of unstressed syllables. Hopkins felt that sprung rhythm more closely approximated the natural rhythms of speech than did conventional poetry.

Stanza: any lines of verse that are grouped together in a poem and separated from other similarly-structured groups by a space. In metrical poetry, stanzas share metrical and rhyming patterns; however, stanzas may also be formed on the basis of thought, as in irregular odes. Conventional stanza forms include the *tercet*, the *quatrain*, *rhyme royal*, the *Spenserian stanza*, the *ballad stanza*, and *ottava rima*.

Stream of Consciousness: narrative technique that attempts to convey in prose fiction a sense of the progression of the full range of thoughts and sensations occurring within a character's mind. Twentieth-century pioneers in the use of the stream of consciousness technique include Dorothy Richardson, Virginia Woolf, and James Joyce.

Stress: See *accent*.

Strophe: the first stanza in a Pindaric ode. This is followed by an *antistrophe* (see above), which presents the same metrical pattern and rhyme scheme, and finally by an *epode*, differing in meter from the preceding stanzas. Upon completion of this "triad," the entire sequence can recur. *Strophe* may also describe a stanza or other subdivision in other kinds of poem.

Sublime: a concept, most popular in eighteenth-century England, of the qualities of grandeur, power, and awe that may be inherent in or produced by undomesticated nature or great art. The sublime was thought of as higher and loftier than something that is merely beautiful.

Subplot: a line of story that is subordinate to the main storyline of a narrative. (Note that properly speaking a subplot is a category of story material, not of plot.)

Substitution: a deliberate change from the dominant pattern of stresses in a line of verse to create emphasis or variation. Thus the first line of Shakespeare's sonnet "'Shall I compare thee to a summer's day?' is decidedly iambic in meter ($x/x/x/x/x/$), whereas the second line substitutes a trochee ($/x$) in the opening foot: "Thou art more lovely and more temperate."

Subtext: implied or suggested meaning of a passage of text, or of an entire work.

Syllabic Verse: poetry in which the length of a line is measured solely by the number of syllables, regardless of accents or patterns of stress.

Syllable: vocal sound or group of sounds forming a unit of speech; a syllable may be formed with a single effort of articulation. Some syllables consist of a single phoneme (e.g., the word *I*, or the first syllable in the word *u*-ni-ty) but others may be made up of several phonemes (as with one-syllable words such as *lengths*, *splurged*, and *through*). By contrast, the much shorter words *ago*, *any*, and *open* each have two syllables.

Symbol: a word, image, or idea that represents something more, or other, than for what it at first appears to stand. Like metaphor, the symbol extends meaning; but while the tenor and vehicle of metaphor are bound in a specific relationship, a symbol may have a range of connotations. For example, the image of a rose may call forth associations of love, passion, transience, fragility, youth and beauty, among others. Depending upon the context, such an image could be interpreted in a variety of ways, as in Blake's lyric, "The Sick Rose." Though this power of symbolic representation characterizes all language, poetry most particularly endows the concrete imagery evoked through language with a larger meaning. Such meaning is implied rather than explicitly stated; indeed, much of the power of symbolic language lies in the reader's ability to make meaningful sense of it.

Syncope: in poetry, the dropping of a letter or syllable from the middle of a word, as in "trav'ler." Such a contraction allows a line to stay within a metrical scheme. See also *catalexis* and *elision*.

Synecdoche: a kind of *metonymy* in which a writer substitutes the name of a part of something to signify the whole: for example, "sail" for ship or "hand" for a member of the ship's crew.

Tercet: a group, or stanza, of three lines, often linked by an interlocking rhyme scheme as in *terza rima*. See also *triplet*.

Terza Rima: an arrangement of tercets interlocked by a rhyme scheme of *aba bcb cdc ded*, etc., and ending with a couplet that rhymes with the second-last line of the final tercet (for example, *efe, ff*). See, for example, Percy Shelley's "Ode to the West Wind."

Tetrameter: a line of poetry containing four metrical feet.

Theme: the governing idea of a discourse, conveyed through the development of the subject, and through the recurrence of certain words, sounds, or metrical patterns. See also *motif*.

Third-Person Narrative: See *narrative perspective*.

Tone: the writer's attitude toward a given subject or audience, as expressed though an authorial persona or "voice." Tone can be projected through particular choices of wording, imagery, figures of speech, and rhythmic devices. Compare *mood*.

Tories: See *Political Parties*.

Tragedy: in the traditional definition originating in discussions of ancient Greek drama, a serious narrative recounting the downfall of the protagonist. More loosely, the term has been applied to a wide variety of literary forms in which the tone is predominantly a dark one and the narrative does not end happily.

Transcendentalism: a philosophical movement that influenced such Victorian writers as Thomas Carlyle and Robert Browning. Also a mode of Romantic thought, Transcendentalism places the supernatural and the natural within one great Unity and believes that each individual person embodies aspects of the divine.

Trimeter: a line of poetry containing three metrical feet.

Triolet: a French form in which the first line appears three times in a poem of only eight lines. The first line is repeated at lines 4 and 7; the second line is repeated in line 8. The triolet has only two rhymes: *abaaabab*.

Triple Foot: poetic foot of three syllables. The possible varieties of triple foot are the anapest (in which two unstressed syllables are followed by a stressed syllable), the dactyl (in which a stressed syllable is followed by two unstressed lines), and the mollossus (in which all three syllables are stressed equally). English poetry tends to use duple rhythms far more frequently than triple rhythms.

Triplet: a group of three lines with the same end-rhyme, much used by eighteenth-century poets to vary or punctuate the flow of couplets. See also *tercet*.

Trivium: group of three academic subjects (dialectic, grammar, and rhetoric) that were part of the university curriculum in the Middle Ages. Their study precedes that of the more advanced subjects of the *quadrivium*.

Trochee: a metrical foot containing one strong stress followed by one weak stress: / x (heaven, lover).

Trope: any figure of speech that plays on our understandings of words to extend, alter, or transform "literal" meaning. Common tropes include *metaphor*, *simile*, *personification*, *hyperbole*, *metonymy*, *oxymoron*, *synecdoche*, and *irony*. See also *figures of speech*, above.

Turn (Italian "volta"): the point in a *sonnet* where the mood or argument changes. The turn may occur between the octave and sestet, i.e., after the eighth line, or in the final couplet, depending on the kind of sonnet.

Unities: Many literary theorists of the late sixteenth through late eighteenth centuries held that a play should ideally be presented as representing a single place, and confining the action to a single day and a single dominant event. They disapproved of plots involving gaps or long periods of time, shifts in place, or subplots. These concepts, which came to be referred to as the unities of space, time, and action, were based on a misreading of classical authorities (principally of Aristotle).

Vers de societé: French: literally, "verse about society." The term originated with poetry written by aristocrats and upper-middle-class poets that specifically disavows the ambition of creating "high art" while treating the concerns of their own group in verse forms that demonstrate a high degree of formal control (e.g., artful rhymes, surprising turns of diction).

Vers libre (French):   See *free verse* above.

Verse: a general term for works of poetry, usually referring to poems that incorporate some kind of metrical structure. The term may also describe a line of poetry, though more frequently it is applied to a stanza.

Villanelle: a poem usually consisting of 19 lines, with five 3-line stanzas (tercets) rhyming *aba*, and a concluding quatrain rhyming *abaa*. The first and third lines of the first tercet are repeated at fixed intervals throughout the rest of the poem. See, for example, Dylan Thomas's "Do Not Go Gentle Into That Good Night."

Whigs: See *Political Parties*.

Workhouse: public institution in which the poor were provided with a minimal level of sustenance and with lodging in exchange for work performed. Early workhouses were typically administered by individual parishes. In 1834 a unified system covering all of England and Wales was put into effect.

Zeugma: a *figure of speech* (trope) in which one word links or "yokes" two others in the same sentence, often to comic or ironic effect. For example, a verb may govern two objects, as in Pope's line "Or stain her honour, or her new brocade."

PERMISSIONS ACKNOWLEDGMENTS

"If this, our life, be less than but a day," and "When you are very old, by candle's flame": from LYRICS OF THE FRENCH RENAISSANCE: MAROT, DU BELLAY, RONSARD translated by Norman R. Shapiro, © Yale University Press, 2002. Reproduced with permission of the publisher.

Marlowe, Christopher. *The Tragical History of Dr. Faustus*, edited by Michael Keefer. Reproduced with permission of the editor.

"When in my weeping I inquire of Love": from WOMEN POETS OF THE ITALIAN RENAISSANCE: COURTLY LADIES AND COURTESANS, Edited by Laura Anna Stortoni. Translated by Laura Anna Stortoni and Mary Prentice Lillie (New York: Italica Press, 1997). Copyright 1997 by Laura Anna Stortoni. Used by permission of Italica Press.

Piozzi, Hester Lynch Salusbury Thrale. Reprinted by permission of the publisher from THE THRALES OF STREATHAM PARK, edited by Mary Hyde, pp.85–86, 105–07, 149–152, 163, 165–67, 175, Cambridge, Mass.: Harvard University Press, Copyright © 1976, 1977 by Mary Hyde.

ILLUSTRATION CREDITS

Page 230: Reproduced by permission of the Huntington Library. Page 235: Reproduced by permission of the Huntington Library. Page 252/53: Reproduced by permission of the Huntington Library. Page 286: Reproduced by permission of the Huntington Library. Page 299: Reproduced by permission of the Huntington Library. Page 320/21: Reproduced by permission of the Huntington Library. Page 333/34: Reproduced by permission of the Huntington Library. Page 417: Reproduced by permission of the Huntington Library. Page 531: Reproduced by permission of the National Portrait Gallery, London. Page 532: Reproduced by permission of the National Portrait Gallery, London. Page 541: Reproduced by permission of the National Portrait Gallery, London. Page 654: Reproduced by permission of the National Portrait Gallery, London. Page 724: Reproduced by permission of the National Portrait Gallery, London. Page 725: Reproduced by permission of the National Portrait Gallery, London. Page 851: Reproduced by kind permission of Viscount De L'Isle from his private collection at Penshurst Place. Page 861: Reproduced by permission of the National Portrait Gallery, London. Colour insert: Reproduced by permission of The Royal Collection © 2005 Her Majesty Queen Elizabeth II. Page 1020: Reproduced by permission of the TATE Gallery © Tate, London 2005. Page 1039: Reproduced by permission of the National Portrait Gallery, London. Page 1172: Reproduced by permission of the National Portrait Gallery, London. Page 1103: Reproduced by permission of the National Portrait Gallery, London. Page 1143: Reproduced by permission of the National Portrait Gallery, London. Page 1247: Reproduced by permission of the National Portrait Gallery, London. Page 1378: Reproduced by permission of the National Portrait Gallery, London. Page 1468: Reproduced by permission of the National Portrait Gallery, London. Page 1516: Reproduced by permission of the National Portrait Gallery, London. Page 1520: Reproduced by permission of the National Portrait Gallery, London.

Information on all translations used is provided in footnotes at the beginning of selections. Copyright permission to reproduce material translated or edited for this anthology and material reproduced or adapted here that originally appeared in other books published by Broadview Press may be sought from Broadview.

The publisher has endeavored to contact rights holders of all copyright material and would appreciate receiving any information as to errors or omissions.

Index of First Lines

INDEX OF AUTHORS AND TITLES